DELUXE ILLUSTRATED ATLAS OF THE WORLD

DELUXE ILLUSTRATED ATLAS OF THE WORLD

RAND McNALLY

CHICAGO • NEW YORK • SAN FRANCISCO

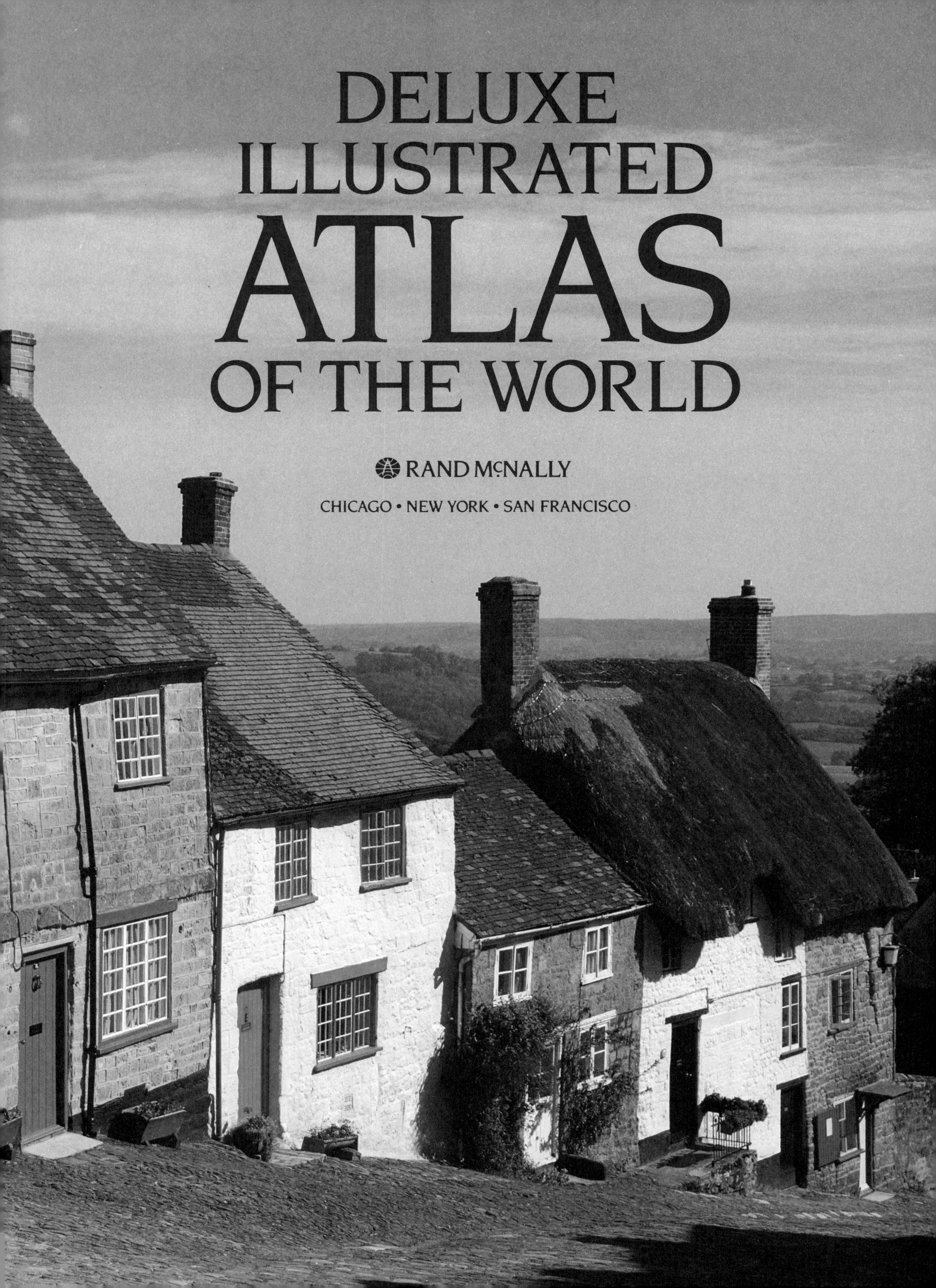

CONTENTS

Our Planet Earth Section

Part 1

THE EARTH AND THE UNIVERSE

2–3 The Making of the Universe
4–5 Earth in the Solar System
6–7 Earth as a Planet
8–9 Man Looks at the Earth

Part 2

MAKING AND SHAPING THE EARTH

10–11 Earth's Structure
12–13 Earth's Moving Crust
14–15 Folds, Faults and Mountain Chains
16–17 Rock Formation and History
18–19 Earth's Minerals
20–21 Earthquakes and Volcanoes
22–23 The Oceans
24–25 Landscape-makers: Water
26–27 Landscape-makers: Ice and Snow
28–29 Landscape-makers: The Seas
30–31 Landscape-makers: Wind and Weathering
32–33 Landscape-makers: Man

Part 3

THE EMERGENCE OF LIFE

34–35 The Source of Life
36–37 The Structure of Life
38–39 Earliest Life Forms
40–41 The Age of Reptiles
42–43 The Age of Mammals
44–45 Spread of Life
46–47 Spread of Man

Part 4

THE DIVERSITY OF LIFE

48–49 Earth's Natural Regions
50–51 Climate and Weather
52–53 Resources and Energy
54–55 Population Growth
56–57 Human Settlement
58–59 Trade and Transport
60–61 Polar Regions
62–63 Tundra and Taiga
64–65 Temperate Forests
66–67 Man and the Temperate Forests
68–69 Mediterranean Regions
70–71 Temperate Grasslands
72–73 Man and the Temperate Grasslands
74–75 Deserts
76–77 Man and the Deserts
78–79 Savannas
80–81 Man and the Savannas
82–83 Tropical Rainforests
84–85 Man and the Tropical Rainforests
86–87 Monsoon Regions
88–89 Mountain Regions
90–91 Freshwater Environments
92–93 Man and the Freshwater Environments
94–95 Seawater Environments
96–97 Man and the Seawater Environments

Part 5

UNDERSTANDING MAPS

98–99 Mapping, Old and New
100–101 The Language of Maps
102–103 How to Use Maps

104–111 Acknowledgments and Index

DELUXE
ILLUSTRATED ATLAS OF THE WORLD

ISBN: 528-83379-0

Library of Congress
Catalog Card Number: 89-40420

Printed in the United States of America by
Rand McNally & Company

Jacket photo by David Muench
Title page photo by Ric Ergenbright

International Map Section

PAGE		MAP NUMBER
114–115	Legend	
116–117	Index maps	
118–125	World Maps	1–4
126–155	Europe	5–20
156–173	Asia	21–29
174–189	Africa	30–37
190–213	North America	38–51
214–223	South America	52–56
224–237	Australia and Oceania	57–65
238–240	Antarctic and Arctic	66–67

Maps of the United States and Canada

PAGE	
241	Legend
242–243	United States
244	Alabama
245	Alaska
246	Arizona
247	Arkansas
248	California
249	Colorado
250	Connecticut
251	Delaware
252	Florida
253	Georgia
254	Hawaii
255	Idaho
256	Illinois
257	Indiana
258	Iowa
259	Kansas
260	Kentucky
261	Louisiana
262	Maine
263	Maryland
264	Massachusetts
265	Michigan
266	Minnesota
267	Mississippi
268	Missouri
269	Montana
270	Nebraska
271	Nevada
272	New Hampshire
273	New Jersey
274	New Mexico
275	New York
276	North Carolina
277	North Dakota
278	Ohio
279	Oklahoma
280	Oregon
281	Pennsylvania
282	Rhode Island
283	South Carolina
284	South Dakota
285	Tennessee
286	Texas
287	Utah
288	Vermont
289	Virginia
290	Washington
291	West Virginia
292	Wisconsin
293	Wyoming
294–295	Canada
296	Alberta
297	British Columbia
298	Manitoba
299	Maritime Provinces
300	Newfoundland
301	Ontario
302	Quebec
303	Saskatchewan
304	United States and Canada Information Table

Geographical Information & International Map Index

A · 1– A · 24	Geographical Information
A · 25– A · 144	International Map Index

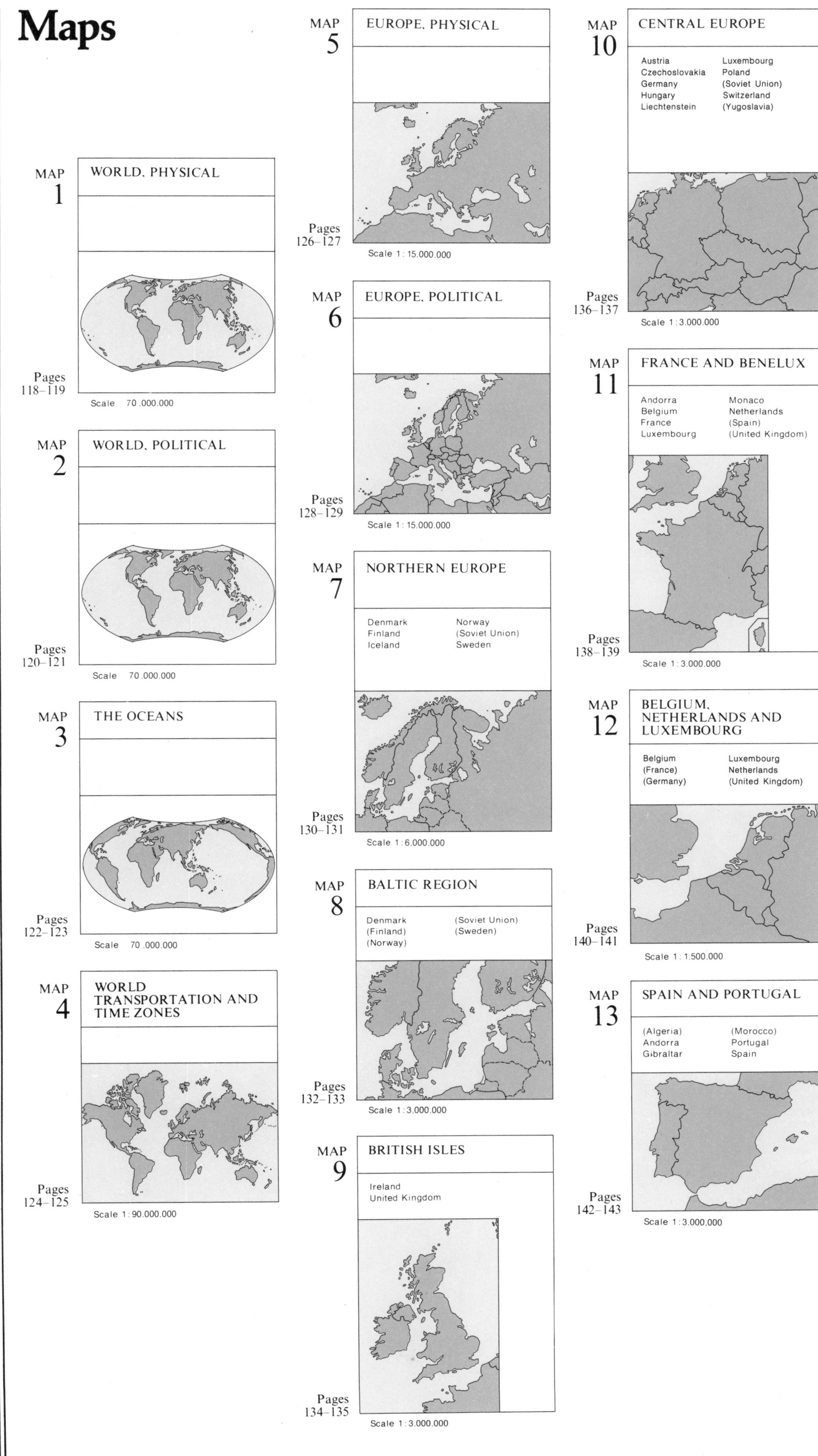

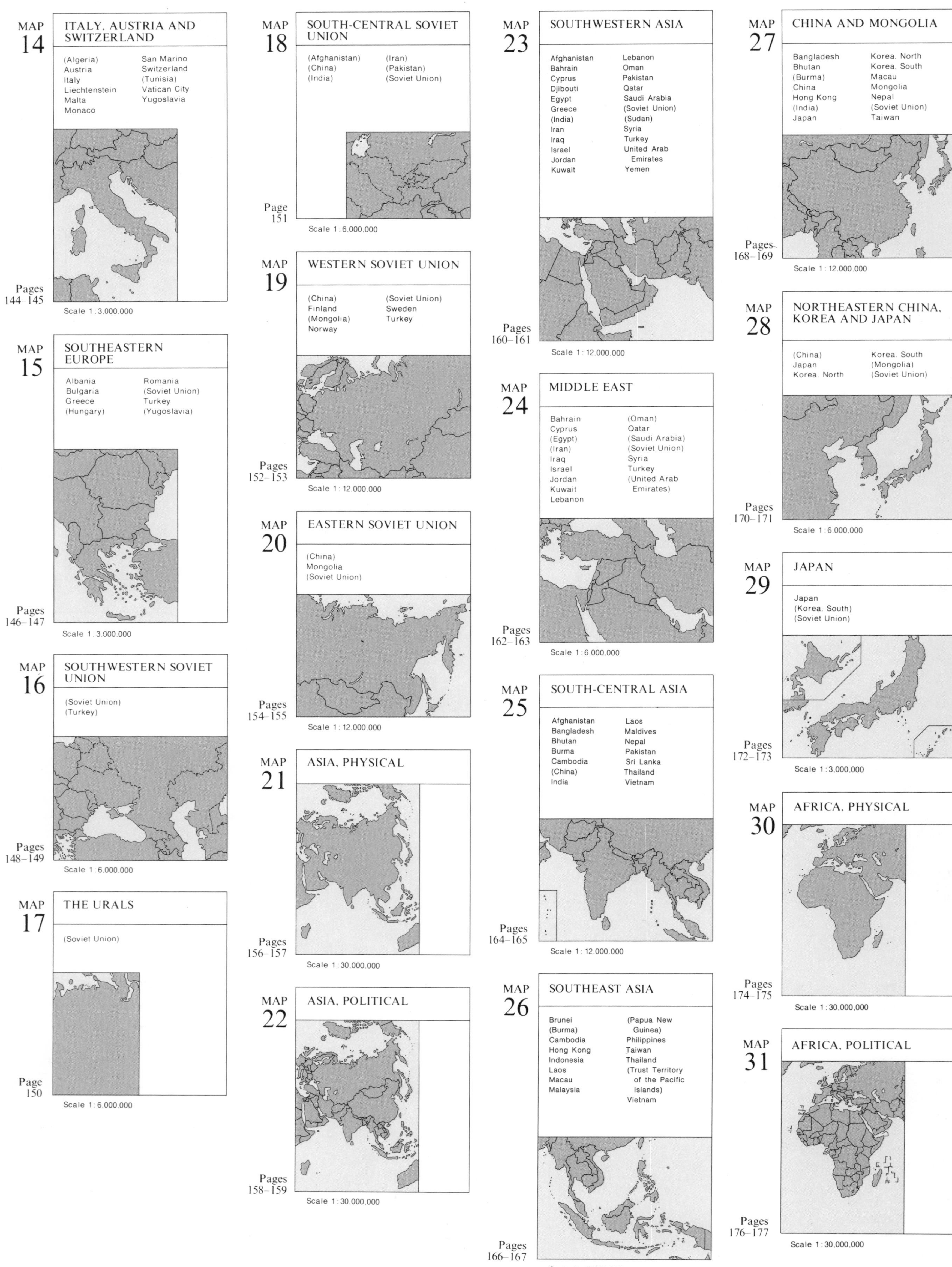

MAP 14 — ITALY, AUSTRIA AND SWITZERLAND
(Algeria), Austria, Italy, Liechtenstein, Malta, Monaco, San Marino, Switzerland, (Tunisia), Vatican City, Yugoslavia
Pages 144–145
Scale 1:3.000.000

MAP 15 — SOUTHEASTERN EUROPE
Albania, Bulgaria, Greece, (Hungary), Romania, (Soviet Union), Turkey, (Yugoslavia)
Pages 146–147
Scale 1:3.000.000

MAP 16 — SOUTHWESTERN SOVIET UNION
(Soviet Union), (Turkey)
Pages 148–149
Scale 1:6.000.000

MAP 17 — THE URALS
(Soviet Union)
Page 150
Scale 1:6.000.000

MAP 18 — SOUTH-CENTRAL SOVIET UNION
(Afghanistan), (China), (India), (Iran), (Pakistan), (Soviet Union)
Page 151
Scale 1:6.000.000

MAP 19 — WESTERN SOVIET UNION
(China), Finland, (Mongolia), Norway, (Soviet Union), Sweden, Turkey
Pages 152–153
Scale 1:12.000.000

MAP 20 — EASTERN SOVIET UNION
(China), Mongolia, (Soviet Union)
Pages 154–155
Scale 1:12.000.000

MAP 21 — ASIA, PHYSICAL
Pages 156–157
Scale 1:30.000.000

MAP 22 — ASIA, POLITICAL
Pages 158–159
Scale 1:30.000.000

MAP 23 — SOUTHWESTERN ASIA
Afghanistan, Bahrain, Cyprus, Djibouti, Egypt, Greece, (India), Iran, Iraq, Israel, Jordan, Kuwait, Lebanon, Oman, Pakistan, Qatar, Saudi Arabia, (Soviet Union), (Sudan), Syria, Turkey, United Arab Emirates, Yemen
Pages 160–161
Scale 1:12.000.000

MAP 24 — MIDDLE EAST
Bahrain, Cyprus, (Egypt), (Iran), Iraq, Israel, Jordan, Kuwait, Lebanon, (Oman), Qatar, (Saudi Arabia), (Soviet Union), Syria, Turkey, (United Arab Emirates)
Pages 162–163
Scale 1:6.000.000

MAP 25 — SOUTH-CENTRAL ASIA
Afghanistan, Bangladesh, Bhutan, Burma, Cambodia, (China), India, Laos, Maldives, Nepal, Pakistan, Sri Lanka, Thailand, Vietnam
Pages 164–165
Scale 1:12.000.000

MAP 26 — SOUTHEAST ASIA
Brunei, (Burma), Cambodia, Hong Kong, Indonesia, Laos, Macau, Malaysia, (Papua New Guinea), Philippines, Taiwan, Thailand, (Trust Territory of the Pacific Islands), Vietnam
Pages 166–167
Scale 1:12.000.000

MAP 27 — CHINA AND MONGOLIA
Bangladesh, Bhutan, (Burma), China, Hong Kong, (India), Japan, Korea, North, Korea, South, Macau, Mongolia, Nepal, (Soviet Union), Taiwan
Pages 168–169
Scale 1:12.000.000

MAP 28 — NORTHEASTERN CHINA, KOREA AND JAPAN
(China), Japan, Korea, North, Korea, South, (Mongolia), (Soviet Union)
Pages 170–171
Scale 1:6.000.000

MAP 29 — JAPAN
Japan, (Korea, South), (Soviet Union)
Pages 172–173
Scale 1:3,000.000

MAP 30 — AFRICA, PHYSICAL
Pages 174–175
Scale 1:30,000.000

MAP 31 — AFRICA, POLITICAL
Pages 176–177
Scale 1:30.000.000

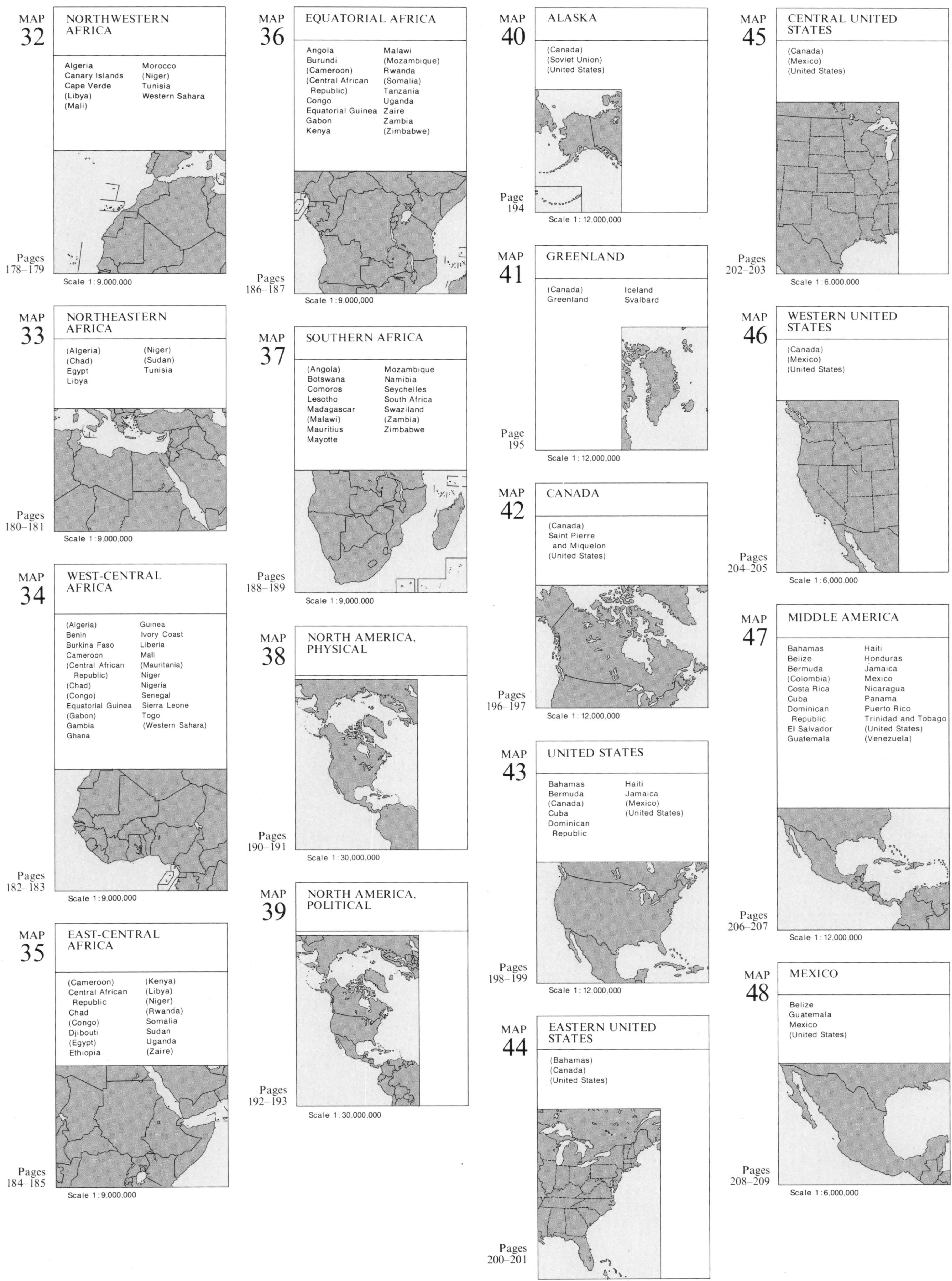
MAP 32
NORTHWESTERN AFRICA
Algeria
Canary Islands
Cape Verde
(Libya)
(Mali)
Morocco
(Niger)
Tunisia
Western Sahara
Pages 178–179
Scale 1:9,000,000
MAP 33
NORTHEASTERN AFRICA
(Algeria)
(Chad)
Egypt
Libya
(Niger)
(Sudan)
Tunisia
Pages 180–181
Scale 1:9,000,000
MAP 34
WEST-CENTRAL AFRICA
(Algeria)
Benin
Burkina Faso
Cameroon
(Central African Republic)
(Chad)
(Congo)
Equatorial Guinea
(Gabon)
Gambia
Ghana
Guinea
Ivory Coast
Liberia
Mali
(Mauritania)
Niger
Nigeria
Senegal
Sierra Leone
Togo
(Western Sahara)
Pages 182–183
Scale 1:9,000,000
MAP 35
EAST-CENTRAL AFRICA
(Cameroon)
Central African Republic
Chad
(Congo)
Djibouti
(Egypt)
Ethiopia
(Kenya)
(Libya)
(Niger)
(Rwanda)
Somalia
Sudan
Uganda
(Zaire)
Pages 184–185
Scale 1:9,000,000
MAP 36
EQUATORIAL AFRICA
Angola
Burundi
(Cameroon)
(Central African Republic)
Congo
Equatorial Guinea
Gabon
Kenya
Malawi
(Mozambique)
Rwanda
(Somalia)
Tanzania
Uganda
Zaire
Zambia
(Zimbabwe)
Pages 186–187
Scale 1:9,000,000
MAP 37
SOUTHERN AFRICA
(Angola)
Botswana
Comoros
Lesotho
Madagascar
(Malawi)
Mauritius
Mayotte
Mozambique
Namibia
Seychelles
South Africa
Swaziland
(Zambia)
Zimbabwe
Pages 188–189
Scale 1:9,000,000
MAP 38
NORTH AMERICA, PHYSICAL
Pages 190–191
Scale 1:30,000,000
MAP 39
NORTH AMERICA, POLITICAL
Pages 192–193
Scale 1:30,000,000
MAP 40
ALASKA
(Canada)
(Soviet Union)
(United States)
Page 194
Scale 1:12,000,000
MAP 41
GREENLAND
(Canada)
Greenland
Iceland
Svalbard
Page 195
Scale 1:12,000,000
MAP 42
CANADA
(Canada)
Saint Pierre and Miquelon
(United States)
Pages 196–197
Scale 1:12,000,000
MAP 43
UNITED STATES
Bahamas
Bermuda
(Canada)
Cuba
Dominican Republic
Haiti
Jamaica
(Mexico)
(United States)
Pages 198–199
Scale 1:12,000,000
MAP 44
EASTERN UNITED STATES
(Bahamas)
(Canada)
(United States)
Pages 200–201
Scale 1:6,000,000
MAP 45
CENTRAL UNITED STATES
(Canada)
(Mexico)
(United States)
Pages 202–203
Scale 1:6,000,000
MAP 46
WESTERN UNITED STATES
(Canada)
(Mexico)
(United States)
Pages 204–205
Scale 1:6,000,000
MAP 47
MIDDLE AMERICA
Bahamas
Belize
Bermuda
(Colombia)
Costa Rica
Cuba
Dominican Republic
El Salvador
Guatemala
Haiti
Honduras
Jamaica
Mexico
Nicaragua
Panama
Puerto Rico
Trinidad and Tobago
(United States)
(Venezuela)
Pages 206–207
Scale 1:12,000,000
MAP 48
MEXICO
Belize
Guatemala
Mexico
(United States)
Pages 208–209
Scale 1:6,000,000

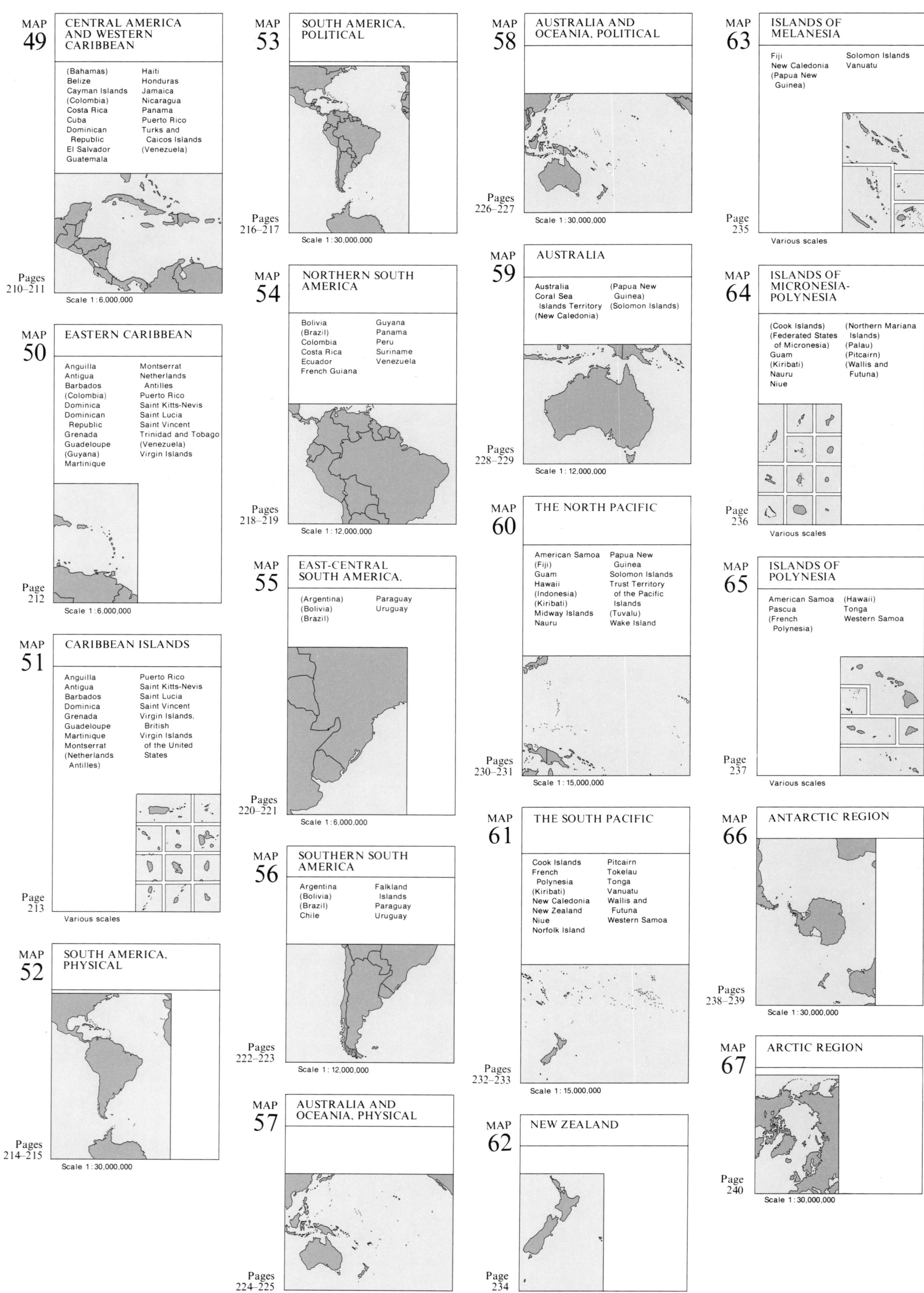

MAP 49 — CENTRAL AMERICA AND WESTERN CARIBBEAN
(Bahamas), Belize, Cayman Islands, (Colombia), Costa Rica, Cuba, Dominican Republic, El Salvador, Guatemala, Haiti, Honduras, Jamaica, Nicaragua, Panama, Puerto Rico, Turks and Caicos Islands, (Venezuela)
Pages 210–211
Scale 1:6,000,000

MAP 50 — EASTERN CARIBBEAN
Anguilla, Antigua, Barbados, (Colombia), Dominica, Dominican Republic, Grenada, Guadeloupe, (Guyana), Martinique, Montserrat, Netherlands Antilles, Puerto Rico, Saint Kitts-Nevis, Saint Lucia, Saint Vincent, Trinidad and Tobago, (Venezuela), Virgin Islands
Page 212
Scale 1:6,000,000

MAP 51 — CARIBBEAN ISLANDS
Anguilla, Antigua, Barbados, Dominica, Grenada, Guadeloupe, Martinique, Montserrat, (Netherlands Antilles), Puerto Rico, Saint Kitts-Nevis, Saint Lucia, Saint Vincent, Virgin Islands, British, Virgin Islands of the United States
Page 213
Various scales

MAP 52 — SOUTH AMERICA, PHYSICAL
Pages 214–215
Scale 1:30,000,000

MAP 53 — SOUTH AMERICA, POLITICAL
Pages 216–217
Scale 1:30,000,000

MAP 54 — NORTHERN SOUTH AMERICA
Bolivia, (Brazil), Colombia, Costa Rica, Ecuador, French Guiana, Guyana, Panama, Peru, Suriname, Venezuela
Pages 218–219
Scale 1:12,000,000

MAP 55 — EAST-CENTRAL SOUTH AMERICA,
(Argentina), (Bolivia), (Brazil), Paraguay, Uruguay
Pages 220–221
Scale 1:6,000,000

MAP 56 — SOUTHERN SOUTH AMERICA
Argentina, (Bolivia), (Brazil), Chile, Falkland Islands, Paraguay, Uruguay
Pages 222–223
Scale 1:12,000,000

MAP 57 — AUSTRALIA AND OCEANIA, PHYSICAL
Pages 224–225
Scale 1:30,000,000

MAP 58 — AUSTRALIA AND OCEANIA, POLITICAL
Pages 226–227
Scale 1:30,000,000

MAP 59 — AUSTRALIA
Australia, Coral Sea Islands Territory, (New Caledonia), (Papua New Guinea), (Solomon Islands)
Pages 228–229
Scale 1:12,000,000

MAP 60 — THE NORTH PACIFIC
American Samoa, (Fiji), Guam, Hawaii, (Indonesia), (Kiribati), Midway Islands, Nauru, Papua New Guinea, Solomon Islands, Trust Territory of the Pacific Islands, (Tuvalu), Wake Island
Pages 230–231
Scale 1:15,000,000

MAP 61 — THE SOUTH PACIFIC
Cook Islands, French Polynesia, (Kiribati), New Caledonia, New Zealand, Niue, Norfolk Island, Pitcairn, Tokelau, Tonga, Vanuatu, Wallis and Futuna, Western Samoa
Pages 232–233
Scale 1:15,000,000

MAP 62 — NEW ZEALAND
Page 234
Scale 1:6,000,000

MAP 63 — ISLANDS OF MELANESIA
Fiji, New Caledonia, (Papua New Guinea), Solomon Islands, Vanuatu
Page 235
Various scales

MAP 64 — ISLANDS OF MICRONESIA-POLYNESIA
(Cook Islands), (Federated States of Micronesia), Guam, (Kiribati), Nauru, Niue, (Northern Mariana Islands), (Palau), (Pitcairn), (Wallis and Futuna)
Page 236
Various scales

MAP 65 — ISLANDS OF POLYNESIA
American Samoa, Pascua, (French Polynesia), (Hawaii), Tonga, Western Samoa
Page 237
Various scales

MAP 66 — ANTARCTIC REGION
Pages 238–239
Scale 1:30,000,000

MAP 67 — ARCTIC REGION
Page 240
Scale 1:30,000,000

Our Planet Earth Section

Part 1

THE EARTH AND THE UNIVERSE

How the universe began · Earth's place in the Solar System
How the Earth became fit for life
Man looks at Earth from outer space

CREATION AND DESTRUCTION

Violent activity pervades our universe and has done so ever since the primordial fireball of creation. Evidence of violence comes from radio telescopes scanning the farthest reaches: entire galaxies may be exploding, torn apart by gravitational forces of unimaginable power. Some very large stars may burst apart in supernovas, spraying interstellar space with cosmic debris. From this violence new stars and new planets are constantly being formed throughout the universe.

The Big Bang theory (left) of the origin of the universe envisages all matter originating from one point in time and space—a point of infinite density. In the intensely hot Big Bang all the material that goes to make up the planets, stars and galaxies that we see now began to expand outward in all directions. This expansion has been likened to someone blowing up a balloon on which spots have been painted. As the air fills and expands the balloon, the spots get farther away from each other. Likewise, clusters of galaxies that formed from the original superdense matter began, and continue, to move away from neighboring clusters. The Big Bang generated enormous temperatures and the remnants of the event still linger throughout space. A leftover, background radiation provides a uniform and measurable temperature of 3°C. It is generally believed that the universe will continue to expand into complete nothingness.

Stars vary enormously in size, temperature and luminosity. The largest, so-called red giants like Antares (1)—the biggest yet known—or Aldebaran (2), are nearing the end of their lives: diminishing nuclear "fuel" causes their thinning envelopes to expand. Rigel (3) is many times brighter than our Sun (4)—a middle-aged star—but both are so-called main-sequence stars. Epsilon Eridani (5) is rather like the Sun. Wolf 359 (6) is a red dwarf.

Our Solar System was formed from a collapsing cloud of gas and dust (A). Collapse made the center hotter and denser (B) until nuclear reactions started. Heat blew matter from the heart of the now flattened, spinning disc (C). Heavier materials condensed closest to the young Sun, now a hot star, eventually forming the inner ring of planets; the lighter ones accumulated farther out, making up the atmosphere and composition of the giant outer planets (D).

The Making of the Universe

Most astronomers believe that the universe began in a great explosion of matter and energy – the "Big Bang" – about 15,000 million years ago. This event was implied by Einstein's theory of general relativity, as well as by more recent astronomical observations and calculations. But the clinching evidence came in 1965, when two American radio astronomers discovered a faint, uniform, background radiation which permeated all space. This they identified as the remnants of the primordial Big Bang.

Billions of galaxies exist outside our own Milky Way, each thousands of light-years across and filled with millions of stars. Found in clusters, they are either elliptical or spiral in form. The clusters recede from each other following the space-time geometry, as established by Hubble in 1929, proving that the universe is expanding.

The "exploding" galaxy M82 may be an example of the violence of our universe. Clouds of hydrogen gas, equivalent in mass to 5,000,000 suns, have been ejected from the nucleus at 160 km (100 miles) per second. Black holes may cause the explosions, when gravity sucks in all matter, so that even light cannot escape.

Our own cluster of galaxies (below), the Local Group (A), consists of about 30 members, weakly linked by the force of gravity. Earth lies in the second-largest galaxy, the Milky Way (B)—here shown edge-on and at an angle—which is a spiral galaxy of about 100,000 million stars. Its rotating "arms" are great masses of clouds, dust and stars that sweep around a dense nucleus. In the course of this new stars are regularly created from dust and gas. Our Sun (S) lies 33,000 light-years from the nucleus and takes 225 million years to complete an orbit. The Andromeda Galaxy (C), known to astronomers as M31, is the largest of our Local Group. It too is a spiral, and lies about two million light-years away. Roughly 130,000 light-years in diameter, it appears as a flattened disc, and indicates how our galaxy would look if viewed from outside. Two smaller elliptical galaxies, M32 and NGC 205, can also be seen.

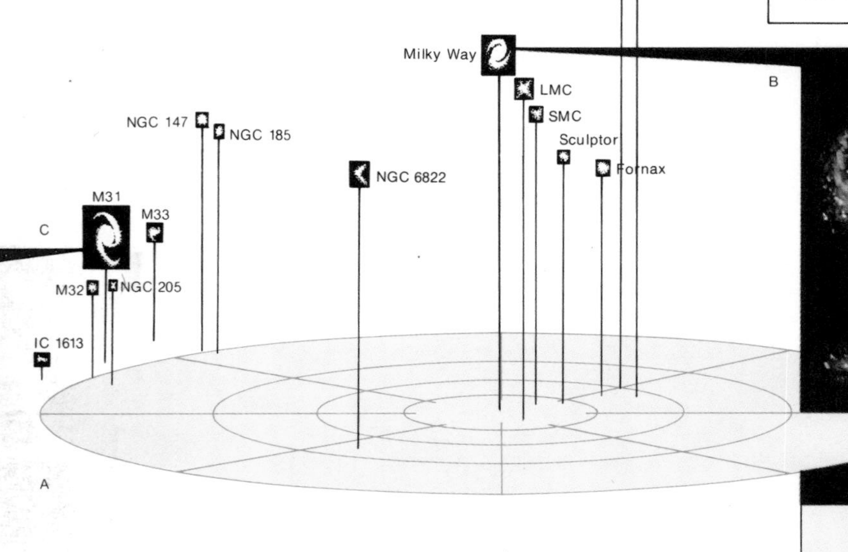

The generally accepted explanation for the so-called "cosmic microwave" background, detected by American astronomers Arno Penzias and Robert Wilson, is indeed that it is the echo of the Big Bang itself, the radio noise left over from the fireball of creation. In recognition of their discovery, Penzias and Wilson shared a Nobel Prize in 1978.

The Big Bang has also been identified by astronomers in other ways. All the evidence shows that the universe is expanding, and its constituent parts—clusters of galaxies, each containing thousands of millions of stars like our Sun—are moving away from each other at great speeds. From this and other evidence scientists deduce that long ago the galaxies must have been closer together, in a superdense phase, and that at some time in the remote past all the material in the universe must have started spreading out from a single point. But this "single point" includes not only all three-dimensional matter and space but also the dimension of time, as envisioned in Einstein's revolutionary concept of space-time. Einstein's theory of relativity describes the phenomenon, not in terms of galaxies moving through space in the expansion, but as being carried apart by the expansion of space-time itself. Space-time may be imagined as a rubber sheet speckled with paint blobs (galaxies), which move apart as the rubber sheet expands.

Galaxies consist of star systems, dust clouds and gases formed from the hot material exploding outward from the original cosmic fireball. Our own Milky Way system, the band of light that stretches across the night sky, is typical of many galaxies, containing millions of stars slowly rotating around a central nucleus.

Exploding space

The original material of the universe was hydrogen, the simplest of all elements. Nuclear reactions that occurred during the superdense phase of the Big Bang converted about 20 percent of the original hydrogen into helium, the next simplest element. So the first stars were formed from a mixture of about 80 percent hydrogen and 20 percent helium. All other matter in the universe, including the atoms of heavier elements such as carbon and oxygen—which help to make up the human body or the pages of this book—has been processed in further nuclear reactions. The explosion of a star—a relatively rare event called a supernova—scatters material across space, briefly radiating more energy than a trillion suns and ejecting matter into the cosmic reservoir of interstellar space. This is then reused to form new stars and planets.

Thus, from the debris of such explosions new stars can form to repeat the creative cycle, and at each stage more of the heavy elements are produced. Today's heavenly bodies are very much the products of stellar violence in the universe, and indeed the universe itself is now seen to be an area of violent activity. During the past two decades the old idea of the universe as a place of quiet stability has been increasingly superseded by evidence of intense activity on all scales. Astronomers have identified what appear to be vast explosions involving whole galaxies, as well as those of individual stars.

Black holes

The evidence of just why these huge explosions occur is often hard to obtain, because the exploding galaxies may be so far away that light from them takes millions of years to reach telescopes on Earth. But it is becoming increasingly accepted by astronomers that such violent events may be associated with the presence of black holes at the centers of some galaxies.

These black holes are regions in which matter has become so concentrated that the force of gravity makes it impossible for anything—even light itself—to escape. As stars are pulled into super-massive black holes they are torn apart by gravitational forces, and their material forms into a swirling maelstrom from which huge explosions can occur. Collapse into black holes, accompanied by violent outbursts from the maelstrom, may be the ultimate fate of all matter in the universe. For our own Solar System, however, such a fate is far in the future: the Sun in its present form is believed to have enough "fuel" to keep it going for at least another 5,000 million years.

A star is born

The origins of the Earth and the Solar System are intimately connected with the structure of our own galaxy, the Milky Way. There are two main types of galaxies: flattened, disc-shaped spiral galaxies (like the Milky Way), and the more rounded elliptical galaxies, which range in form from near spheres to cigar shapes. The most important feature of a spiral galaxy is that it is rotating, a great mass of stars sweeping around a common center. In our galaxy the Sun, located some way out from the galaxy's center, takes about 225 million years to complete one circuit, called a cosmic year.

New stars are born out of the twisting arms of a spiral galaxy, with each arm marking a region of debris left over from previous stellar explosions. These arms are in fact clouds of dust and gas, including nitrogen and oxygen. As the spiral galaxy rotates over a period of millions of years, the twisting arms are squeezed by a high-density pressure wave as they pass through the cycle of the cosmic year. With two main spiral arms twining around a galaxy such as our own, large, diffuse clouds get squeezed twice during each orbit around the center of the galaxy.

Even if one orbit takes as long as hundreds of millions of years, a score or more squeezes have probably occurred since the Milky Way was first formed thousands of millions of years ago. At a critical point, such repeated squeezing increases the density of a gas cloud so much that it begins to collapse rapidly under the inward pull of its own gravity. A typical cloud of this kind contains enough material to make many stars. As it breaks up it collapses into smaller clouds—which are also collapsing—and these become stars in their own right.

Our own Solar System may have been formed in this way from such a collapsing gas cloud, which went on to evolve into the system of planets that we know today.

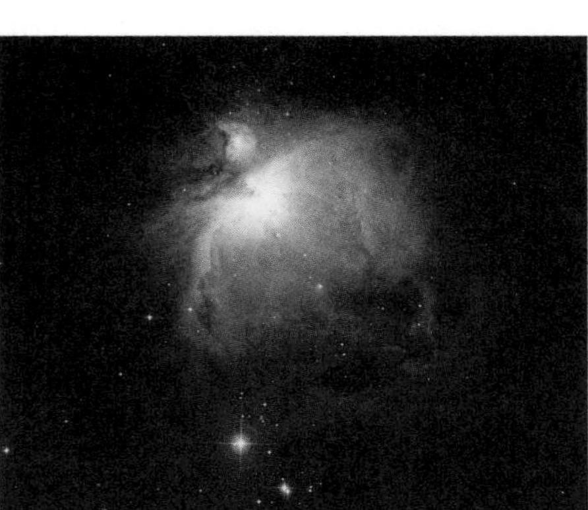

Stars are being born (left) in the Great Nebula of Orion, visible from Earth. The brilliant light comes from a cluster of very hot young stars, the Trapezium, surrounded by a glowing aura of hydrogen gas. Behind the visible nebula there is known to be a dense cloud where radio astronomers have detected emissions from interstellar molecules, and have identified high-density globules. These probably indicate that stars are starting to form.

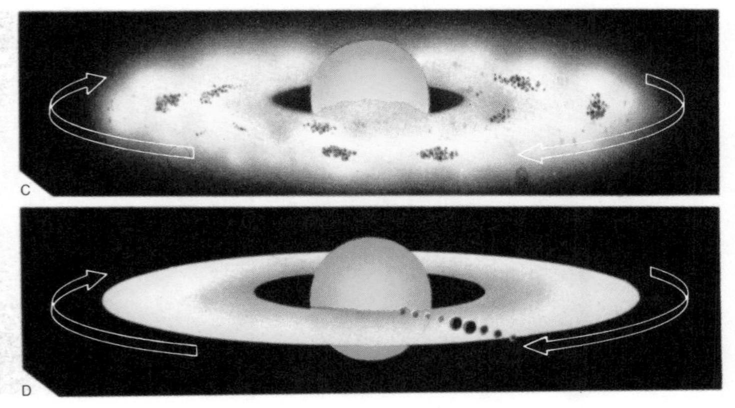

Earth in the Solar System

The Sun is an ordinary, medium-sized star located some two-thirds of the way from the center of our galaxy, the Milky Way. Yet it comprises more than 99 percent of the Solar System's total mass and provides all the light and heat that make life possible on Earth. This energy comes from nuclear reactions that take place in the Sun's hot, dense interior. The reactions convert hydrogen into helium, with the release of vast amounts of energy – the energy that keeps the Sun shining.

Nuclear reactions in the Sun's core maintain a temperature of some 15,000,000°C and this heat prevents the star from shrinking. The surface temperature is comparatively much lower —a mere 6,000°C. Thermonuclear energy-generating processes cause the Sun to "lose" mass from the center at the rate of four million tonnes of hydrogen every second. This mass is turned into energy (heat), and each gram of matter "burnt" produces the heat equivalent of 100 trillion electric fires. The Sun's total mass is so great, however, that it contains enough matter to continue radiating at its present rate for several thousand million years before it runs out of "fuel."

The Sun's retinue

The Solar System emerged from a collapsing gas cloud. In addition to the Sun there are at least nine planets, their satellites, thousands of minor planets (asteroids), comets and meteors. Most stars occur in pairs, triplets or in even more complicated systems, and the Sun is among a minority of stars in being alone except for its planetary companions. It does seem, however, that a single star with a planetary system offers the greatest potential for the development of life. When there are two or more stars in the same system, any planets are likely to have unstable orbits and to suffer from wide extremes of temperature.

The Solar System's structure is thought to be typical of a star that formed in isolation. As the hot young Sun threw material outward, inner planets (Mercury, Venus, Earth and Mars) were left as small rocky bodies, whereas outer planets (Jupiter, Saturn, Uranus and Neptune) kept their lighter gases and became huge "gas giants." Jupiter has two and a half times the mass of all the other planets put together. Pluto, a small object with a strange orbit, which sometimes carries it within the orbit of Neptune, is usually regarded as a ninth planet, but some astronomers consider it to be an escaped moon of Neptune or a large asteroid.

Planetary relations

Several planets are accompanied by smaller bodies called moons or satellites. Jupiter and Saturn have at least 17 and 22 respectively, whereas Earth has its solitary Moon. Sizes vary enormously, from Ganymede, one of Jupiter's large, so-called Galilean satellites, which has a diameter of 5,000 km (3,100 miles), to Mars' tiny Deimos, which is only 8 km (5 miles) across.

The Earth's Moon is at an average distance of 384,000 km (239,000 miles) and has a diameter of 3,476 km (2,160 miles). Its mass is $\frac{1}{81}$ of the Earth's. Although it is referred to as the Earth's satellite, the Moon is large for a secondary body. Some astronomers have suggested that the Earth/Moon system is a double planet. Certain theories of the origins of the Moon propose that it was formed from the solar nebula in the same way as the Earth was and very close to it. The Moon takes 27.3 days to orbit the Earth—exactly the same time that it takes to rotate once on its axis. As a result, it presents the same face to the Earth all the time.

Our planet's orbit around the Sun is not a perfect circle but an ellipse and so its distance from the Sun varies slightly. More importantly, the Earth is tilted, so that at different times of the year one pole or another "leans" toward the Sun. Without this tilt there would be no seasons. The angle of tilt is not constant: over tens of thousands of years the axis of the Earth "wobbles" like a slowly spinning top, so that the pattern of the seasons varies over the ages. These changes have been linked to recent ice ages, which seem to occur when the northern hemisphere has relatively cool summers.

Patterns of time

The Earth's movements on its axis and around the Sun give us our basic measurements of time—the day and the year—as well as setting the rhythm of the seasons and the ice ages. One rotation of the Earth on its axis—the time from one sunrise to the next—originally defined the day, and the time taken for one complete orbit around the Sun defined the year. Today, however, scientists define both the day and the year in terms of time units "counted" by precision instruments called atomic clocks.

A third basic rhythm is set not by the Sun but by the Moon, which runs through a cycle of phases $29\frac{1}{2}$ days long. This is the basis of the calendar month. But just as the modern calendar cannot cope with months $29\frac{1}{2}$ days long, so too it would have trouble with the precise year, which is, inconveniently, just less than $365\frac{1}{4}$ days long. This is the reason for leap years, by means of which an extra day is added to the month of February every fourth year.

Even this system does not keep the calendar exactly in step with the Sun. Accordingly, the leap year is left out in the years which complete centuries, such as 1900, but retained when they divide exactly by 400. The year 2000 will, therefore, be a leap year. With all these corrections, the average length of the calendar year is within 26 seconds of the year defined by the Earth's movements around the Sun. Thus the calendar will be one day out of step with the heavens in the year 4906.

Cosmic rubble

The other planets are too small and too far away to produce noticeable effects on the Earth, but the smallest members of the Sun's family, the asteroids, can affect us directly. Some of them have orbits that cross the orbit of the Earth around the Sun. From time to time they penetrate the Earth's atmosphere: small fragments burn up high in the atmosphere as meteors, whereas larger pieces may survive to strike the ground as meteorites. These in fact provide an echo of times gone by. All the planets, as the battered face of the Moon shows, suffered collisions from many smaller bodies in the course of their evolution from the collapsing pre-solar gas cloud.

Eclipses occur because the Moon, smaller than the Sun, is closer to Earth and looks just as big. This means that when all three are lined up the Moon can blot out the Sun, causing a solar eclipse. When the Earth passes through the main shadow cone, or umbra, the eclipse is total; in the area of partial shadow, or penumbra, a partial eclipse is seen. A similar effect is produced when Earth passes between the Moon and the Sun, causing a lunar eclipse. At most full moons, eclipses do not occur; the Moon passes either above or below the Earth's shadow, because the Moon's orbit is inclined at an angle of 5° to the orbit of the Earth.

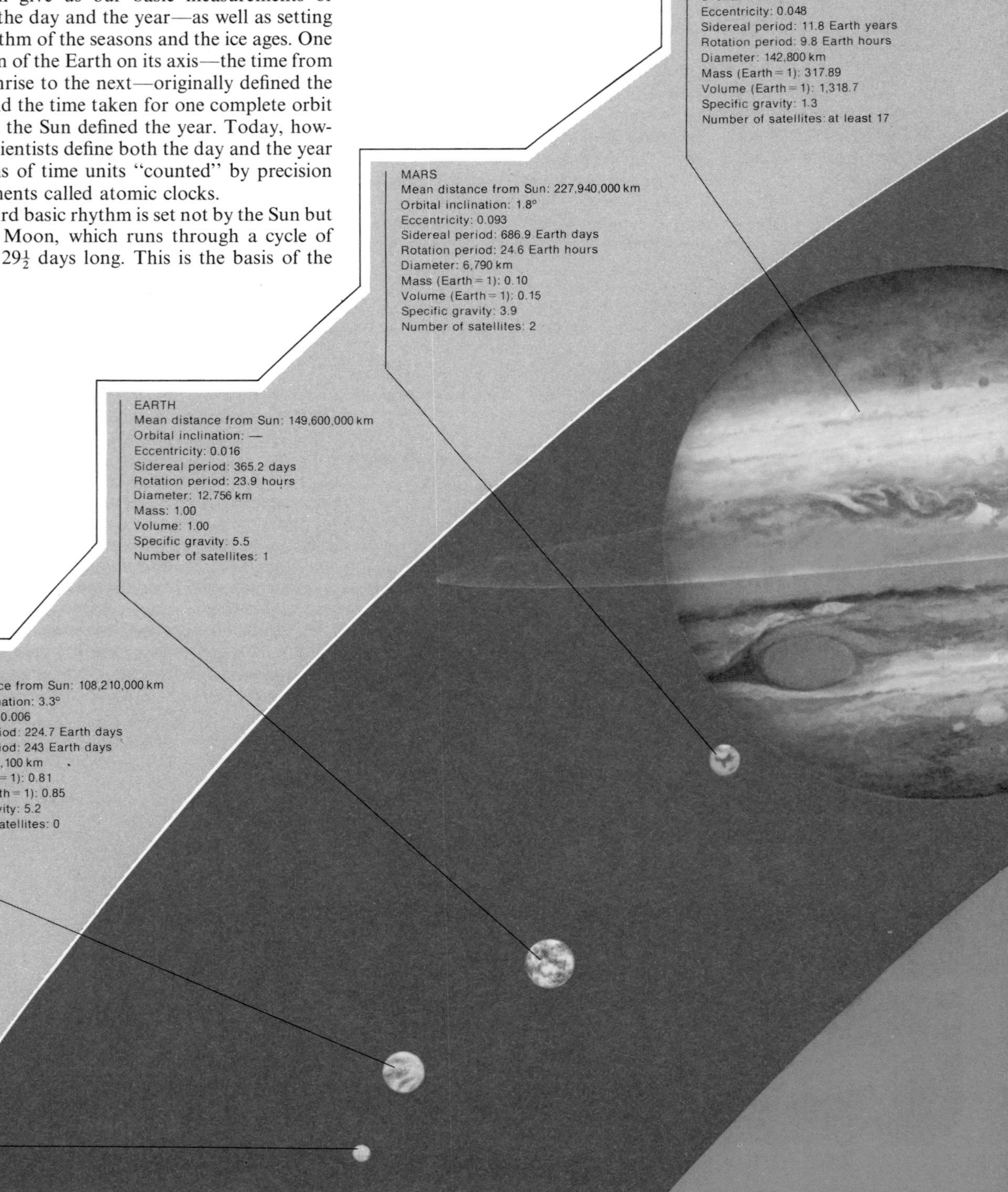

MEMBERS OF THE SOLAR SYSTEM

The Sun has nine planetary attendants. They are best compared in terms of orbital data (distance from the Sun, inclination of orbit to the Earth's orbit, and eccentricity, which means the departure of a planet's orbit from circularity); planetary periods (the time for a planet to go around the Sun—sidereal periods, and the time it takes for one axial revolution—the rotation period); and physical data (equatorial diameter, mass, volume and density or specific gravity—the weight of a substance compared with the weight of an equal volume of water).

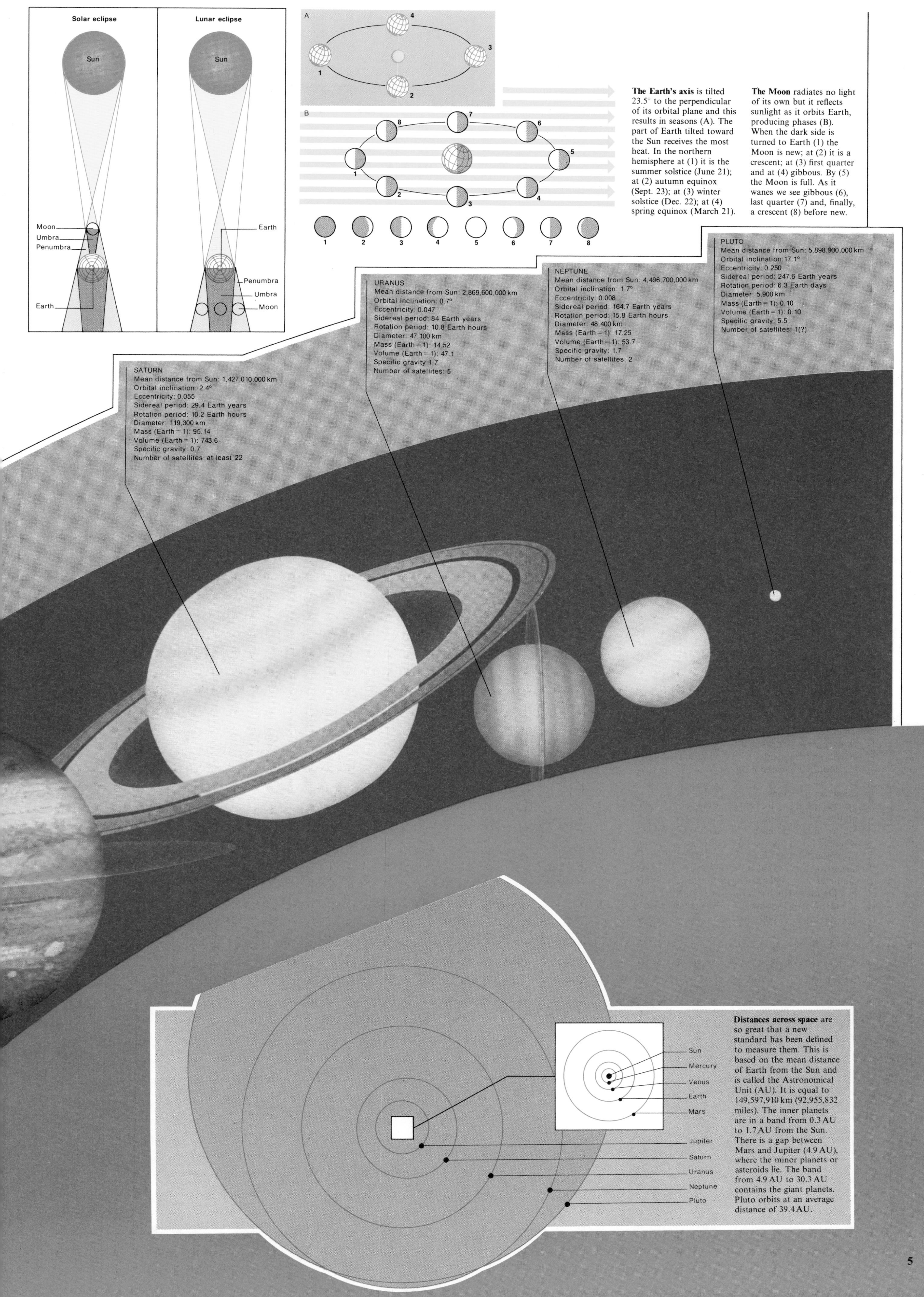

The Earth's axis is tilted 23.5° to the perpendicular of its orbital plane and this results in seasons (A). The part of Earth tilted toward the Sun receives the most heat. In the northern hemisphere at (1) it is the summer solstice (June 21); at (2) autumn equinox (Sept. 23); at (3) winter solstice (Dec. 22); at (4) spring equinox (March 21).

The Moon radiates no light of its own but it reflects sunlight as it orbits Earth, producing phases (B). When the dark side is turned to Earth (1) the Moon is new; at (2) it is a crescent; at (3) first quarter and at (4) gibbous. By (5) the Moon is full. As it wanes we see gibbous (6), last quarter (7) and, finally, a crescent (8) before new.

Distances across space are so great that a new standard has been defined to measure them. This is based on the mean distance of Earth from the Sun and is called the Astronomical Unit (AU). It is equal to 149,597,910 km (92,955,832 miles). The inner planets are in a band from 0.3 AU to 1.7 AU from the Sun. There is a gap between Mars and Jupiter (4.9 AU), where the minor planets or asteroids lie. The band from 4.9 AU to 30.3 AU contains the giant planets. Pluto orbits at an average distance of 39.4 AU.

Earth as a Planet

Viewed from space, the Earth appears to be an ordinary member of the group of inner planets orbiting the Sun. But the Earth is unique in the Solar System because it has an atmosphere that contains oxygen. It is the nature of this surrounding blanket of air that has allowed higher life forms to evolve on Earth and provides their life-support system. At the same time the atmosphere acts as a shield to protect living things from the damaging effects of radiation from the Sun.

Any traces of gas that may have clung to the newly formed Earth were soon swept away into space by the heat of the Sun before it attained a stable state powered by nuclear fusion. Farther out in the Solar System, the Sun's heat was never strong enough to blow these gases away into space, so that even today the giant planets retain atmospheres composed of these primordial gases—mostly methane and ammonia.

The evolution of air

Until the Sun "settled down," Earth was a hot, airless ball of rock. The atmosphere and oceans—like the atmospheres of Venus and Mars—were produced by the "outgassing" of material from the hot interior of the planet as the crust cooled. Volcanoes erupted constantly and produced millions of tonnes of ash and lava. They also probably yielded, as they do today, great quantities of gas, chiefly carbon dioxide, and water vapor. A little nitrogen and various sulphur compounds were also released. Other things being equal, we would expect rocky planets, like the young Earth, to have atmospheres rich in carbon dioxide and water vapor. Venus and Mars do indeed have carbon dioxide atmospheres today, but the Earth now has a nitrogen/oxygen atmosphere. This results from the fact that life evolved on Earth, converting the carbon dioxide to oxygen and storing carbon in organic remains such as coal. Some carbon dioxide was also dissolved in the oceans. The Earth's oxygen atmosphere is a clear sign of life; the carbon dioxide atmospheres of Venus and Mars suggest the absence of life. Why did the Earth begin to evolve in a different way from the other inner planets?

When the Sun stabilized, Earth, Venus and Mars started off down the same evolutionary road, and carbon dioxide and water vapor were the chief constituents of the original atmospheres. On Venus the temperature was hot enough for the water to remain in a gaseous form, and both the water vapor and carbon dioxide in the Venusian atmosphere trapped heat by means of the so-called "greenhouse effect." In this process, radiant energy from the Sun passes through the atmospheric gases and warms the ground. The warmed ground re-radiates heat energy, but at infrared wavelengths, with the result that carbon dioxide and water molecules absorb it and stop it escaping from the planet. Instead of acting like a window, the atmosphere acts like a mirror for outgoing energy. As a result, the surface of Venus became hotter still. Today the surface temperature has stabilized at more than 500°C.

Mars, farther out from the Sun than Earth, was never hot enough for the greenhouse effect to dominate. The red planet once had a much thicker atmosphere than it does today, but, being smaller than the Earth, its gravity is too weak to retain a thick atmosphere. As a result, the planet cooled into a frozen desert as atmospheric gases escaped into space. Mars then, in fact, suffered a climatic change. At one time—hundreds of millions of years ago—there must have been running water because traces of old riverbeds still scar the Martian surface. Today, however, Mars has a thin atmosphere of carbon dioxide and surface temperatures below zero.

Earth—the ideal home

On Earth conditions were just right. Water stayed as a liquid and formed the oceans, while some carbon dioxide from outgassing went into the atmosphere, and some dissolved in the oceans. The resulting modest greenhouse effect

The thermosphere extends from 80 km (50 miles) up to 400 km (250 miles). Within this zone temperatures rise steadily with height to as much as 1,650°C (3,000°F), but the air is so thin that temperature is not a meaningful concept. At this height the air is mostly composed of nitrogen molecules to a height of 200 km (125 miles), when oxygen molecules become the dominant constituent.

The mesosphere is between 50 and 80 km (30 and 50 miles) above ground level. The stratopause is its lower limit and the mesopause its upper. This zone of the atmosphere is mainly distinguished by its ever decreasing temperatures and, unlike the stratosphere, it does not absorb solar energy.

The stratosphere is the level above the troposphere and extends as far as 50 km (30 miles). The chemical composition of the air up to this height is nearly constant and, in terms of volume, it is composed of nitrogen (78%) and oxygen (20%). The rest is mostly argon and other trace elements. The percentage of carbon dioxide (0.003) is small but crucial because this gas absorbs heat. There is virtually no water vapor or dust in this region of the atmosphere, but it does include the ozone layer, which is strongest between 20 km (12 miles) and 40 km (24 miles) high.

The troposphere extends from ground level to a height of between 10 and 15 km (6 and 9 miles). This height varies with latitude and season of the year: it is greater at the Equator than at the poles. Most weather phenomena occur in this zone. Mixed with the gases of the troposphere is water vapor and millions of tiny dust particles, around which vapor condenses to form clouds. The upper limit of this zone is called the tropopause.

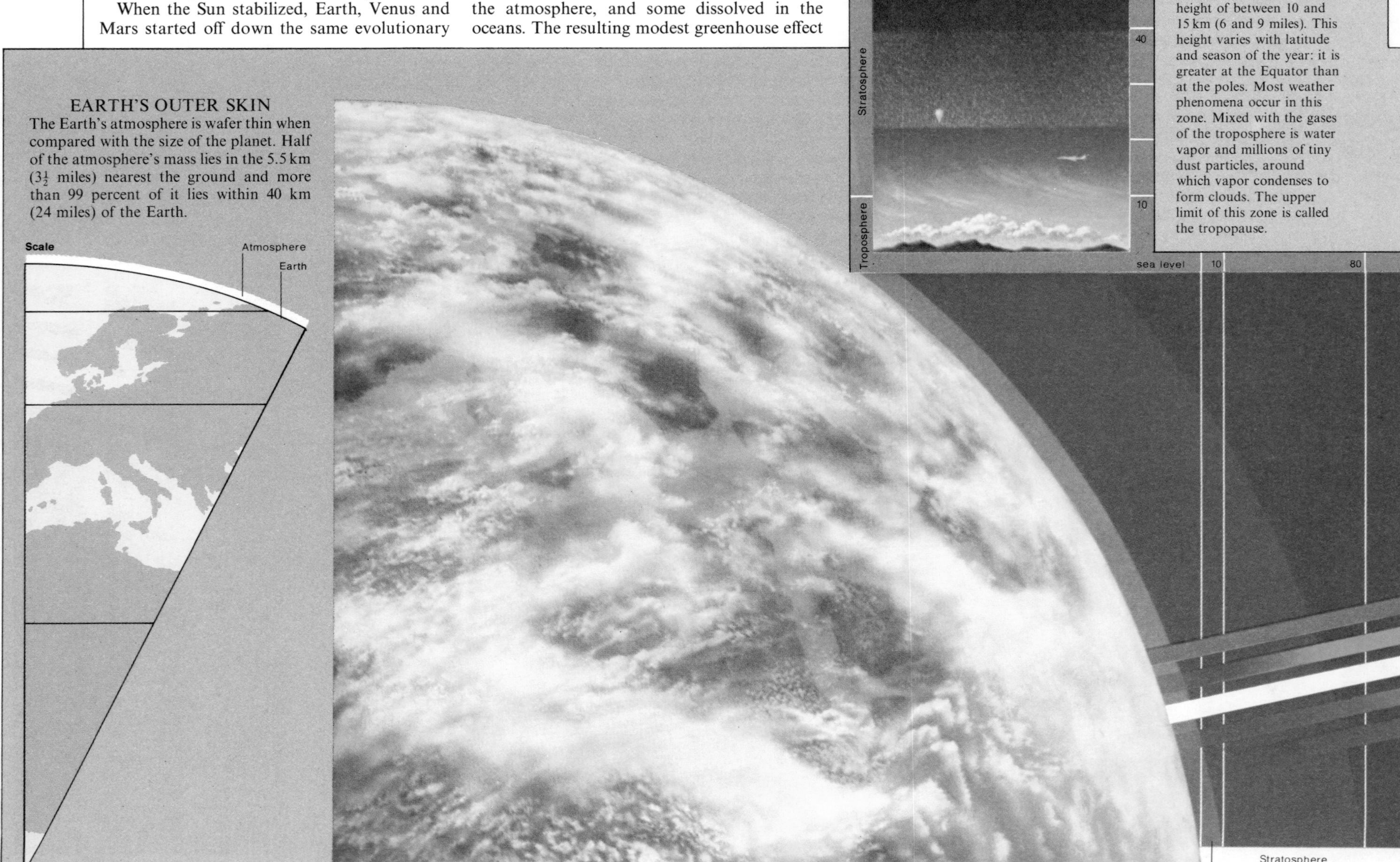

EARTH'S OUTER SKIN

The Earth's atmosphere is wafer thin when compared with the size of the planet. Half of the atmosphere's mass lies in the 5.5 km ($3\frac{1}{2}$ miles) nearest the ground and more than 99 percent of it lies within 40 km (24 miles) of the Earth.

Earth reduced by 90% in proportion to this scale

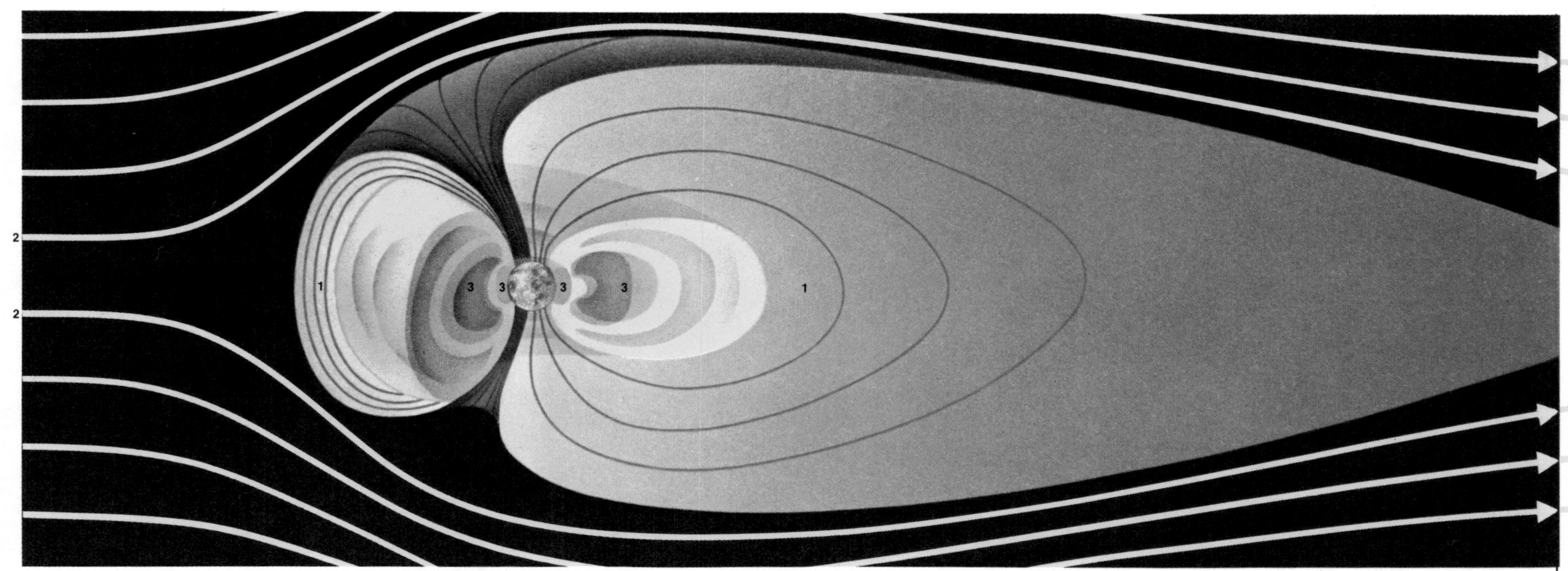

was compensated for by the formation of shiny white clouds of water droplets which reflected some of the Sun's radiation back into space. Our planet stabilized with an average temperature of 15°C. This proved ideal for the emergence of life, which evolved first in the seas and then moved onto land, converting carbon dioxide into oxygen as it did so.

In any view from space, planet Earth is dominated by water—in blue oceans and white clouds—and water is the key to life as we know it. Animal life—oxygen-breathing life—could only evolve after earlier forms of life had converted the atmosphere to an oxygen-rich state. The nature of the air today is a product of life as well as being vital to its existence.

An atmospheric layer cake

Starting at ground level, the first zone of the atmosphere is the troposphere, kept warm near the ground by the greenhouse effect but cooling to a chilly −60°C at an altitude of 15 km (9 miles). Above the troposphere is a warming layer, the stratosphere, in which energy from the Sun is absorbed and temperatures increase to reach 0°C at an altitude of 50 km (30 miles). The energy—in the form of ultraviolet radiation—is absorbed by molecules of ozone, a form of oxygen. Without the ozone layer in the atmosphere, ultraviolet rays would penetrate the ground and sterilize the land surface: without life, there would be no oxygen from which an ozone layer could form.

The Earth's magnetic field behaves as if there were a huge bar magnet placed inside the globe, with its magnetic axis tilted at a slight angle to the geographical north–south axis. The speed of rotation of the liquid core differs from that of the mantle, producing an effect like a dynamo (below). The region in which the magnetic field extends beyond the Earth is the magnetosphere (1). Streams of charged particles (2) from the Sun distort its shape into that of a teardrop. Zones of the magnetosphere include the Van Allen Belts (3), which are regions of intense radioactivity where magnetic particles are "trapped."

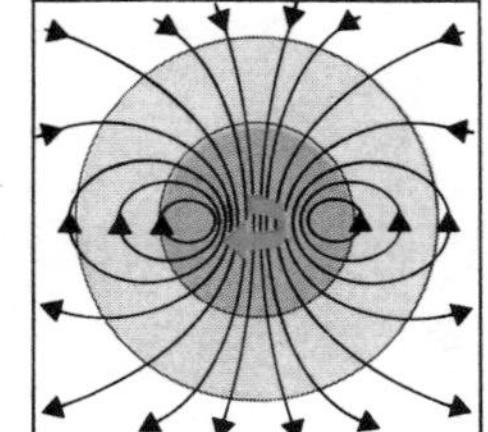

Above the stratosphere, another cooling layer, the mesosphere, extends up to 80 km (50 miles), at which point the temperature has fallen to about −100°C. Above this level the gases of the atmosphere are so thin that the standard concept of temperature is no real guide to their behavior, and from the mesosphere outwards the atmosphere is best described in terms of its electrical properties.

In the outer layers of the atmosphere, the Sun's energy is absorbed by individual atoms in such a way that it strips electrons off them, leaving behind positively charged ions, which give the region its name—the ionosphere. A few hundred kilometers above the Earth's surface, gravity is so feeble that electromagnetic forces begin to determine the behavior of the charged particles, which are shepherded along the lines of force in the Earth's magnetic field. Above 500 km (300 miles), the magnetic field is so dominant that yet another region, the magnetosphere, is distinguished. This is the true boundary between Earth and interplanetary space.

The magnetosphere has been likened to the hull of "spaceship Earth." Charged particles (the solar wind) streaming out from the Sun are deflected around Earth by the magnetosphere like water around a moving ship, while the region of the Earth's magnetic influence in space trails "downstream" away from the Sun like the wake of a ship. The Van Allen Belts, at altitudes of 3,000 and 15,000 km (1,850 and 9,300 miles) are regions of space high above the Equator where particles are trapped by the magnetic field. Particles spilling out of the belts spiral towards the polar regions of Earth, producing the spectacle of the auroras—the northern and southern lights. The Earth and Mercury are the only inner planets with magnetospheres such as this. The cause of the Earth's magnetism is almost certainly the planet's heavy molten core, which is composed of magnetic materials.

The Earth's atmosphere exhibits a great variety of characteristics on a vertical scale. As well as variations of temperature and the electrical properties of the air, there are differences in chemical composition—in the mixture of gases and water vapor—according to altitude. The Earth's gravitational pull means that air density and pressure decrease with altitude. Pressure of about 1,000 millibars at sea level falls to virtually nothing (10^{-42} millibars) by a height of 700 km (435 miles) above the Earth. All these factors, and their interrelationships, help to maintain the Earth's atmosphere as a protective outer covering or radiation shield and an essential life-support system.

The ionosphere is another name for the atmospheric layer beyond 80 km (50 miles). The region is best described in terms of the electrical properties of its constituents rather than by temperature. It is here that ionization occurs. Gamma and X-rays from the Sun are absorbed by atoms and molecules of nitrogen and oxygen and, as a result, each molecule or atom gives up one or more of its electrons, thus becoming a positively charged ion. These ions reflect radio waves and are used to bounce back radio waves transmitted from the surface of the Earth.

The exosphere is the layer above the thermosphere and it extends from 400 km (250 miles) up to about 700 km (435 miles), the point at which, it may be said, space begins. It is almost a complete vacuum because most of its atoms and molecules of oxygen escape the Earth's gravity.

The magnetosphere includes the exosphere, but it extends far beyond the atmosphere—to a distance of between 64,000 and 130,000 km (40,000 and 80,000 miles) above the Earth. It represents the Earth's external magnetic field and its outer limit is called the magnetopause.

The atmosphere protects the Earth from harmful solar radiation and also from bombardment by small particles from space. Most meteors (particles orbiting the Sun) burn up in the atmosphere, but meteorites (debris of minor planets) reach the ground. Of all incoming solar radiation, only visible light, radio waves and infrared rays reach the surface of Earth. X-rays are removed in the ionosphere, and ultraviolet and some infrared radiations are filtered out in the stratosphere. Studies of such radiations have, therefore, to be made from observatories in space.

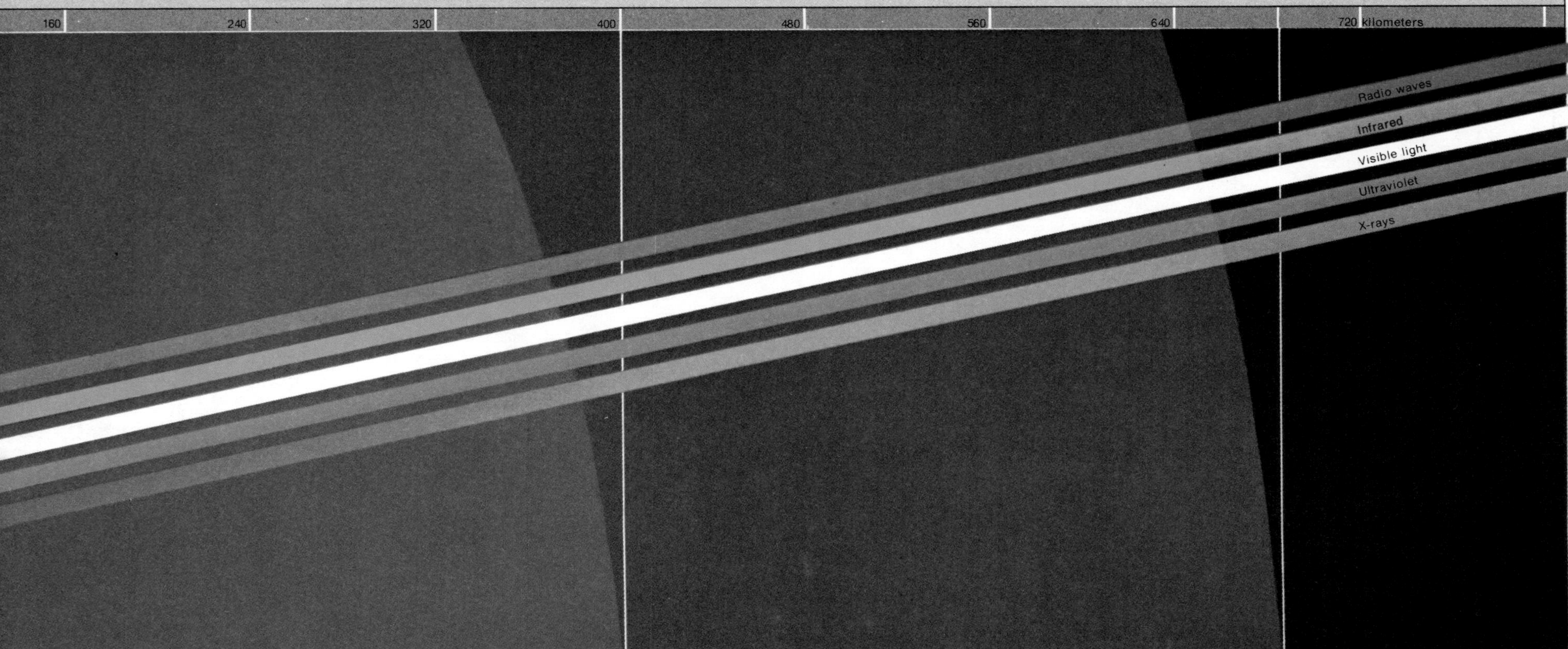

Man Looks at the Earth

Orbiting satellites keep a detailed watch on the Earth's land surface, oceans and atmosphere, feeding streams of data to meteorologists, geologists, oceanographers, farmers, fishermen and many others. Some information would be unobtainable by any other means. Surveys from orbit are quicker and less expensive than from aircraft, for example, because a satellite can scan a much larger area. And, surprisingly enough, certain features on the ground are easier to see from space.

Landsat (A) circles Earth 14 times every 24 hours at a height of 920 km (570 miles). Every 25 seconds it surveys 34,250 sq km (13,225 sq miles).

MAPPING AND MEASURING

Man has been looking at Earth from satellites since the beginning of the 1960s, and has firmly established the value of surveys from space to those engaged in a variety of earthly pursuits. Chief of these activities are resource management, ranging from monitoring the spread of deserts and river silting to locating likely mineral deposits; environmental protection, which includes observing delicate ecosystems and natural disasters; and a whole range of mapping and land-use planning.

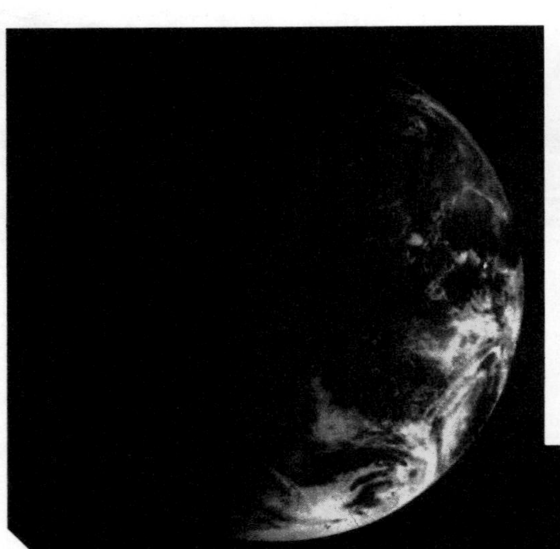

1

2

Satellites give us a greater overview of numerous aspects of life on Earth than any earthbound eye could see.

Of all the information gleaned from satellites, accurate weather forecasts are of particular social and economic value. The first weather satellite was Tiros 1 (Television and Infrared Observation Satellite), launched by the United States in 1960. By the time Tiros 10 ceased operations in 1967, the series had sent back more than half a million photographs, firmly establishing the value of satellite imagery.

Tiros was superseded by the ESSA (Environmental Science Services Administration) and the NOAA (National Oceanic and Atmospheric Administration) satellites. These orbited the Earth from pole to pole, and they covered the entire globe during the course of a day. Other weather satellites, such as the European Meteosat, are placed in geostationary orbit over the Equator, which means they stay in one place and continually monitor a single large region.

Watching the weather

In addition to photographing clouds, weather satellites monitor the extent of snow and ice cover, and they measure the temperature of the oceans and the composition of the atmosphere. Information about the overall heat balance of our planet gives clues to long-term climatic change, and includes the effects on climate of human activities such as the burning of fossil fuels and deforestation.

Infrared sensors allow pictures to be taken at night as well as during the day. The temperature of cloud tops, measured by infrared devices, is a guide to the height of the clouds. In a typical infrared image, high clouds appear white because they are the coldest, lower clouds and land areas appear gray, and oceans and lakes are black. Information on humidity in the atmosphere is provided by sensors tuned to wavelengths between 5.5 and 7 micrometers, at which water vapor strongly absorbs the radiation.

To "see" inside clouds, where infrared and visible light cannot penetrate, satellites use sensors tuned to short-wavelength radio waves (microwaves) around the 1.5 centimeter wavelength. These sensors can reveal whether or not clouds will give rise to heavy rainfall, snow or hail. Microwave sensors are also useful for locating ice floes in polar regions, making use of the different microwave reflections from land ice, sea ice and open water.

Satellites that send out such pictures are in relatively low orbits, at a height of about 1,000 km (620 miles), and they pass over each part of the Earth once every 12 hours. But to build up a global model of the Earth's weather and climate, meteorologists need continual information on wind speed and direction at various levels in the atmosphere, together with temperature and humidity profiles. This data is provided by geostationary satellites. Cloud photographs taken every half-hour give information on winds, and computers combine this with temperature and humidity soundings to give as complete a model as is possible of the Earth's atmosphere.

Increasing attention is also being paid to the Earth's surface, notably by means of a series of satellites called Landsat (originally ERTS or Earth Resource Technology Satellites), the first of which was launched by the United States in 1972. The third and current Landsat is in a similar pole-to-pole orbit as the weather satellites, but its cameras are more powerful and they make more detailed surveys of the Earth. Landsat rephotographs each part of the Earth's surface every 18 days.

How to map resources

The satellite has two sensor systems: a television camera, which takes pictures of the Earth using visible light; and a device called a multispectral scanner, which scans the Earth at several distinct wavelengths, including visible light and infrared. Data from the various channels of the multispectral scanner can be combined to produce so-called false-color images, in which each wavelength band is assigned a color (not necessarily its real one) to emphasize features of interest.

An important use of Landsat photographs is for making maps, particularly of large countries with remote areas that have never been adequately surveyed from the ground. Several countries, including Brazil, Canada and China, have set up ground stations to receive Landsat data directly. Features previously unknown or incorrectly mapped, including rivers, lakes and glaciers, show up readily on Landsat images. Urban mapping and hence planning are aided by satellite pictures that can distinguish areas of industry, housing and open parkland.

Landsat photographs have also proved invaluable for agricultural land-use planning. They are used for estimates of soil types and for determining land-use patterns. Areas of crop disease or dying vegetation are detectable by their different colors. Yields of certain crops such as wheat can now be accurately predicted from satellite imagery, so that at last it is becoming possible to keep track of the worldwide production of vital food crops. Fresh water, too, is one of our most valuable resources, and knowing its sources and seasonal variation is vital to irrigation projects.

Finally, the geologist and mineral prospector have benefited from remote sensing. Features such as fault lines and different types of sediments and rocks show up clearly on Landsat pictures. This allows geologists to select promising areas in which the prospector can look for mineral deposits.

Another way to study the Earth is by bouncing radar beams off it. Radar sensing indicates the nature of soil or rock on land and movement of water at sea, for example. This was not done by Landsat, but by equipment aboard the United States' Skylab and by a short-lived American satellite called Seasat. The Soviet Union has included Earth surveying in its Salyut program, and resource mapping is also a feature of the spacelab aboard the American space shuttle. All these activities help man to manage the limited resources on our planet and to preserve the environment.

3

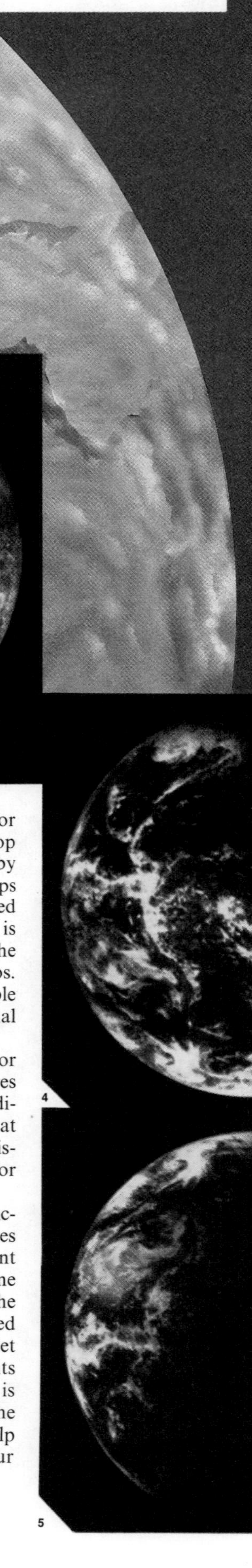

4

5

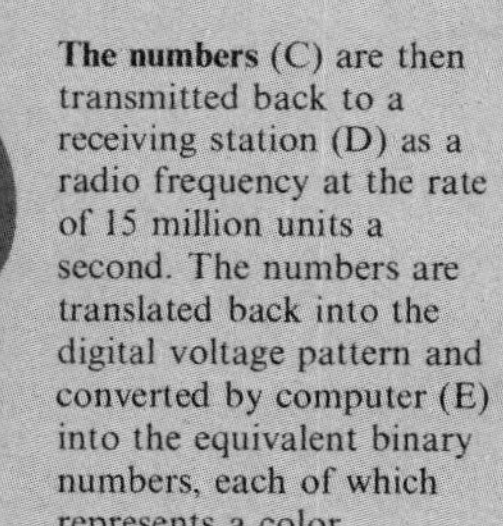

A multispectral scanner (B) has an oscillating mirror (1) that focuses visible and near infrared radiation on to a detector (2). This converts the intensity of the radiation into a voltage. An electronics unit (3) turns the voltage pattern into a series of digitized numbers that can be fed into a computer.

The numbers (C) are then transmitted back to a receiving station (D) as a radio frequency at the rate of 15 million units a second. The numbers are translated back into the digital voltage pattern and converted by computer (E) into the equivalent binary numbers, each of which represents a color.

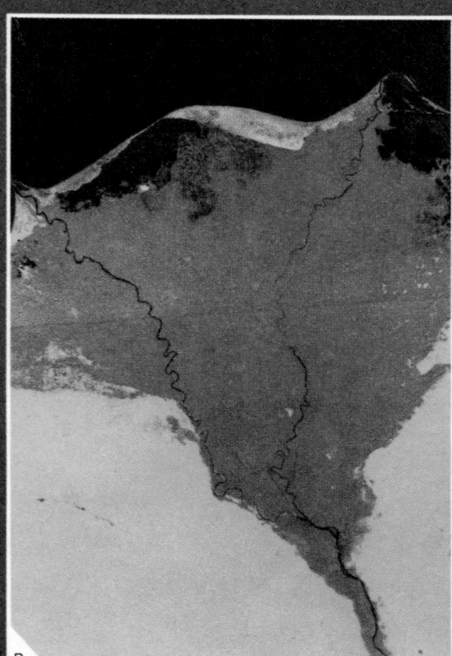

Observation of waterways and coastal areas (above) shows pollution and deposition of sediments. This is of importance to the fishing industry. Fish congregate in areas where upwelling brings nutrients to the surface, for example. The large yellow-orange halo around Akimiski Island in James Bay (A)—a southern extension of Hudson Bay in Canada—is fine sediment resulting from wave action on a silty shore. Seeing the sediment in this way helps to determine current patterns in the Bay. In a predominantly desert area, the Nile delta (B) stands out dramatically. The red is an intensively cultivated area: cotton is the main crop. The larger irrigation canals can be seen on the photograph. Thermal imagery, or heat capacity mapping, is used to identify rocks, to study the effects of urban "heat islands," to estimate soil moisture and snow melt, and to map shallow ground water. In this photograph of the northeast coast of North America (C) purple represents the coldest temperatures—in Lakes Erie and Ontario. The coldest parts of the Atlantic Ocean are deep blue, whereas warmer waters near the coast are light blue. Green is the warmer land, but also the Gulf Stream in the lower right part of the image. Brown, yellow and orange represent successively warmer land surface areas. Red is hot regions around cities and coal-mining regions found in eastern Pennsylvania (to the upper left of center in the picture); and, finally, gray and white are the very hottest areas—the urban heat islands of Baltimore, Philadelphia and New York City. Black areas in the upper left are cold clouds. The temperature range of the image is about 30°C (55°F).

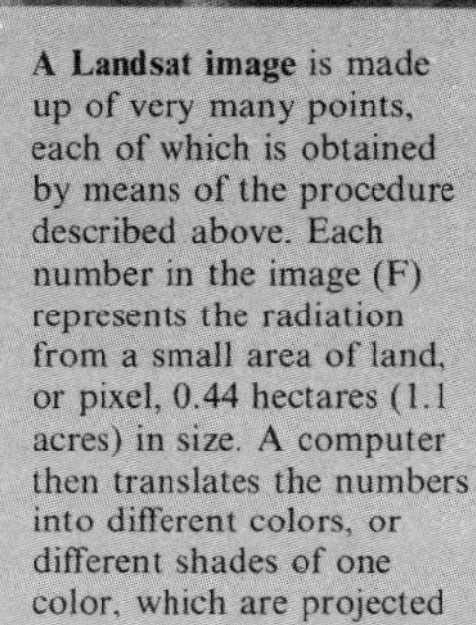

A Landsat image is made up of very many points, each of which is obtained by means of the procedure described above. Each number in the image (F) represents the radiation from a small area of land, or pixel, 0.44 hectares (1.1 acres) in size. A computer then translates the numbers into different colors, or different shades of one color, which are projected on to a TV screen (G) and the image is seen for the first time. Finally, photographs of this false-color image are produced (H). This picture, showing a forest fire in the Upper Peninsula, Michigan, is of use to those engaged in forest management. Other satellite data of use in forestry include types of trees, patterns of growth and the spread of disease.

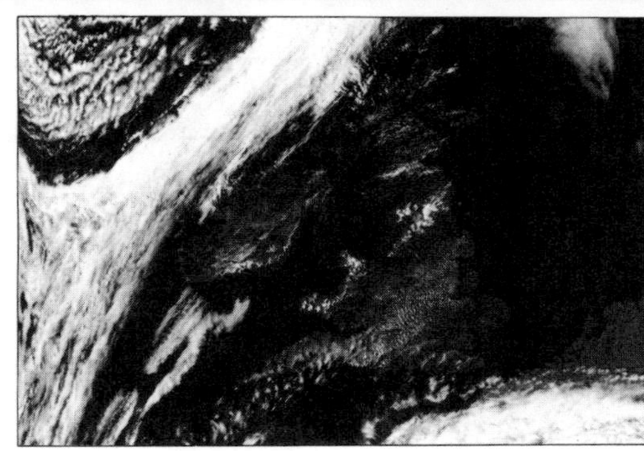

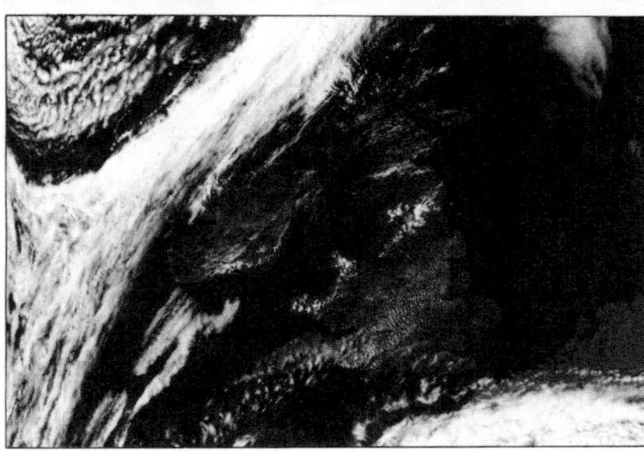

Weather satellite imagery can save lives and property by giving advance warning of bad weather conditions, as well as providing day-to-day forecasts. This Tiros image (left) shows a cold front moving west of Ireland with low-level wave clouds over southern and central England. There are low-pressure systems over northern France and to the northwest of Ireland.

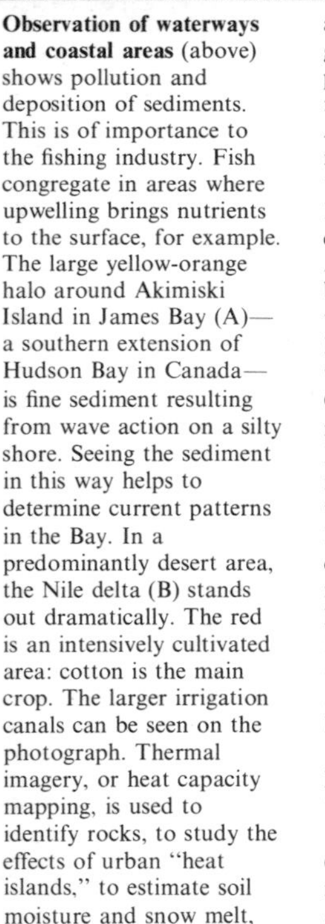

The Earth seen from space shows phases just like the Moon, Mercury and Venus do to us. These dramatic photographs were taken from a satellite moving at 35,885 km (22,300 miles) above South America at 7.30 am (1), 10.30 am (2), noon (3), 3.30 pm (4) and at 10.30 pm (5), and clearly show the Earth in phase.

LANDSAT AND THE FARMER

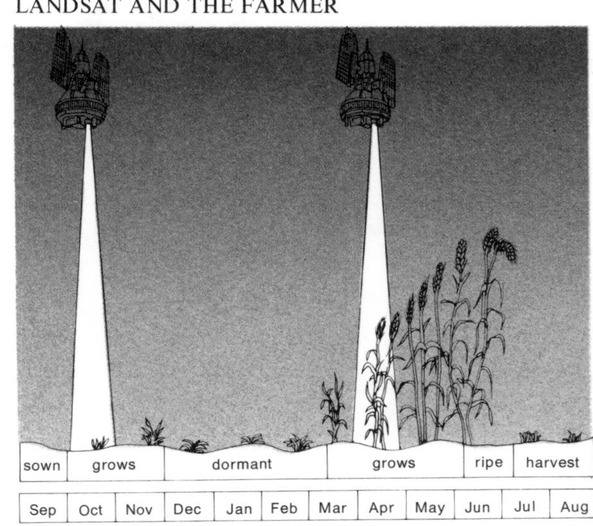

Agriculturists benefit from "multitemporal analysis" by satellites (left). This is the comparison of data from the same field recorded on two or more dates. It is also able to differentiate crops, which may have an identical appearance, or signature, on one day, but on another occasion exhibit different rates of growth. The pattern of growth is different for small grains than most other crops. A "biowindow" is the period of time in which vegetation is observed. These three biowindows (right) show the emergence and ripening (light blue to red to dark blue) of wheat in May, July and August.

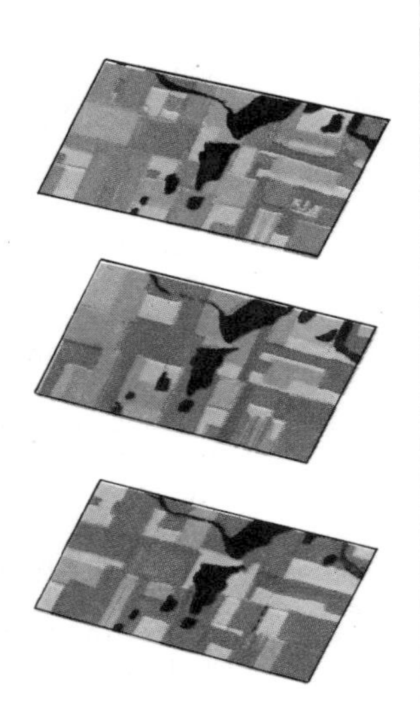

Part 2

MAKING AND SHAPING THE EARTH

The structure and substance of the Earth
Forces that move continents · Forces that fashion Earth's landscapes
How man has changed the face of the Earth

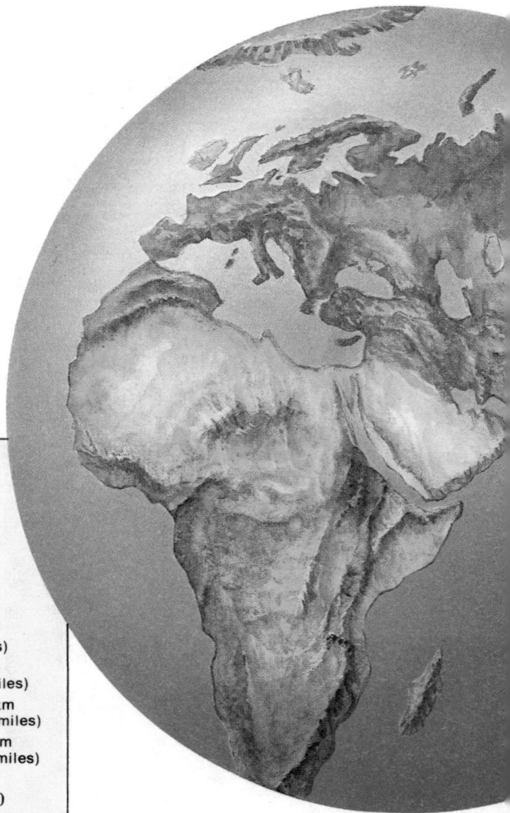

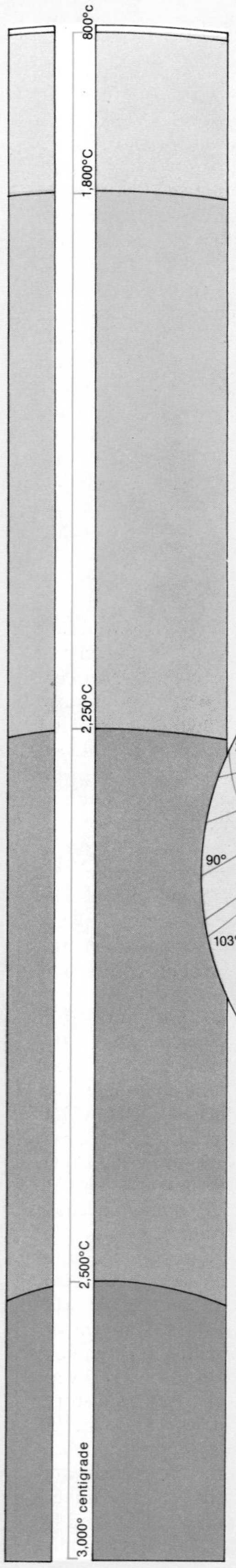

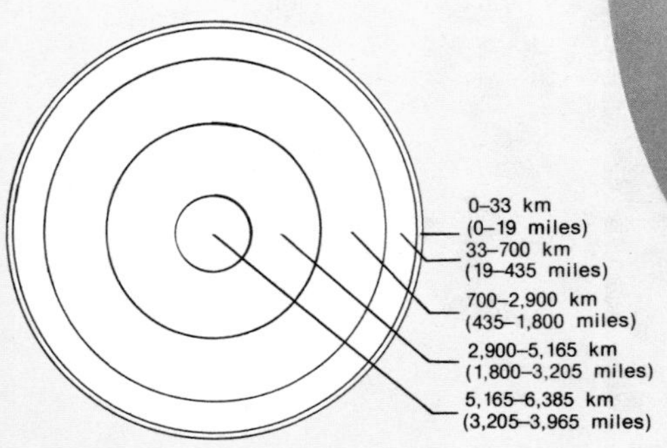

800°c
1,800°C
2,250°C
2,500°C
3,000° centigrade

Crust
Upper mantle
Lower mantle
Outer core
Core

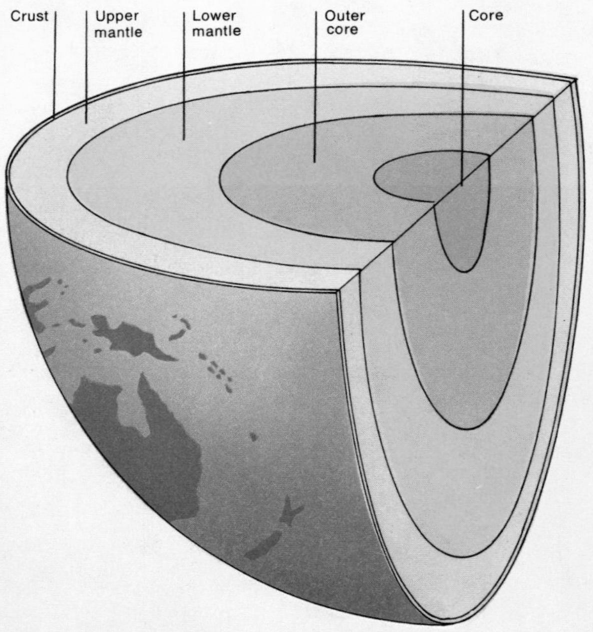

0–33 km (0–19 miles)
33–700 km (19–435 miles)
700–2,900 km (435–1,800 miles)
2,900–5,165 km (1,800–3,205 miles)
5,165–6,385 km (3,205–3,965 miles)

The internal structure of the Earth, in its simplest form, is composed of a crust, a mantle with an upper and lower layer, and a core, which has an inner region. Temperatures in the Earth increase with depth, as is observed in a deep mine shaft or bore-hole, but the prediction of temperatures within the Earth is made difficult by the fact that different rocks conduct heat at different rates: rock salt, for example, has 10 times the heat conductivity of coal. Also, estimates have to take into account the abundance of heat-generating atoms in a rock. Radioactive atoms are concentrated toward the Earth's surface so the planet has, in effect, a thermal blanket to keep it warm. The temperature at the center of the Earth is believed to be approximately 3,000°C (5,400°F).

A NEW GEOLOGY

A revolution in geological thinking during the first half of this century transformed man's ideas about the structure of the planet Earth. The science of palaeomagnetism, which studies the magnetic properties of rocks and the history of the Earth's magnetic field, and later the new science of marine geology, contributed greatly to the refinement of theories such as continental drift. Man has even looked beyond the Earth for knowledge of this planet's innermost depths.

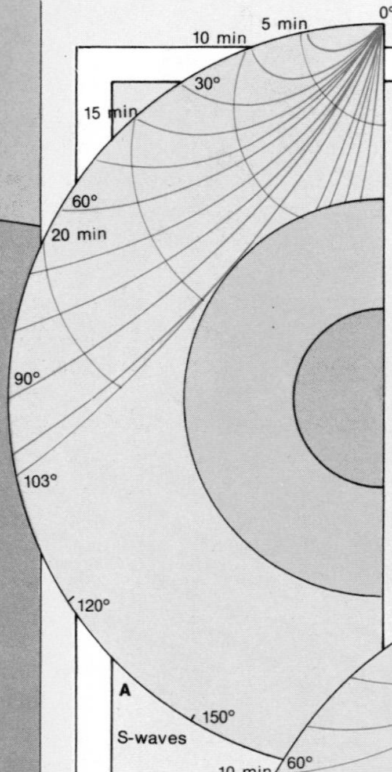

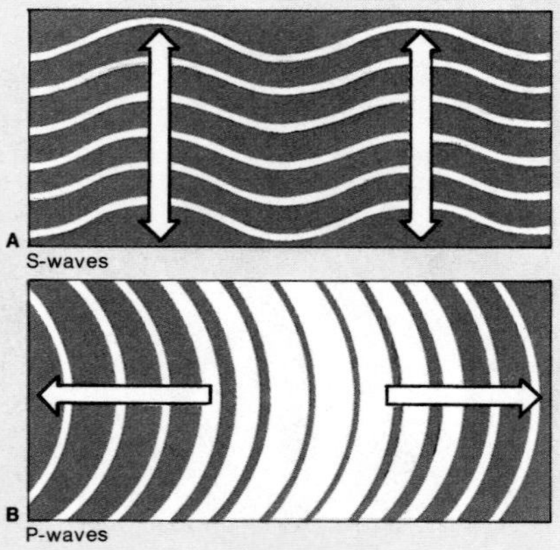

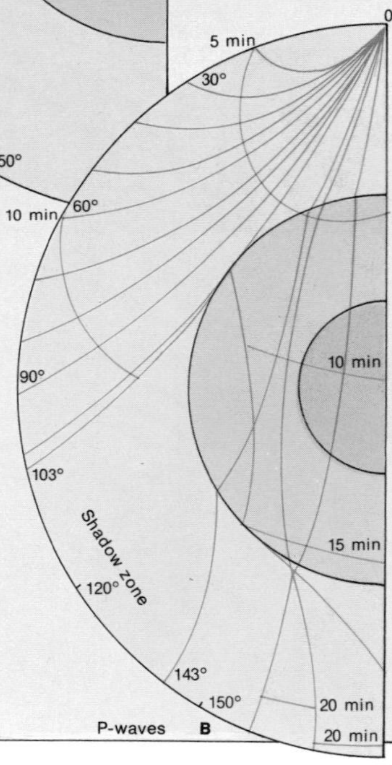

5 min
0°
10 min
30°
15 min
60°
20 min
90°
103°
120°
150°
A
S-waves

A
S-waves
B
P-waves

0°
5 min
30°
10 min
60°
10 min
90°
103°
Shadow zone
15 min
120°
143°
150°
20 min
20 min
P-waves
B

By plotting the pathways of shock waves propagated by an earthquake it is possible to construct a kind of X-ray picture of the Earth's interior. Seismic waves (blue lines) travel at different speeds through materials of different density. (Red lines represent distance traveled by waves during certain time intervals.) Secondary, shear or S-waves cause particles of rock to vibrate vertically. Primary, or P-waves are compressional and cause rock movement backwards and forwards. S-waves can only pass through solids (as can be seen in A) whereas P-waves pass through gases, liquids and solids (as seen in B). They increase in speed as they pass through the denser mantle and core. The region where no earthquake waves reach the surface is an earthquake shadow zone.

180°W
120°W
60°W
0°

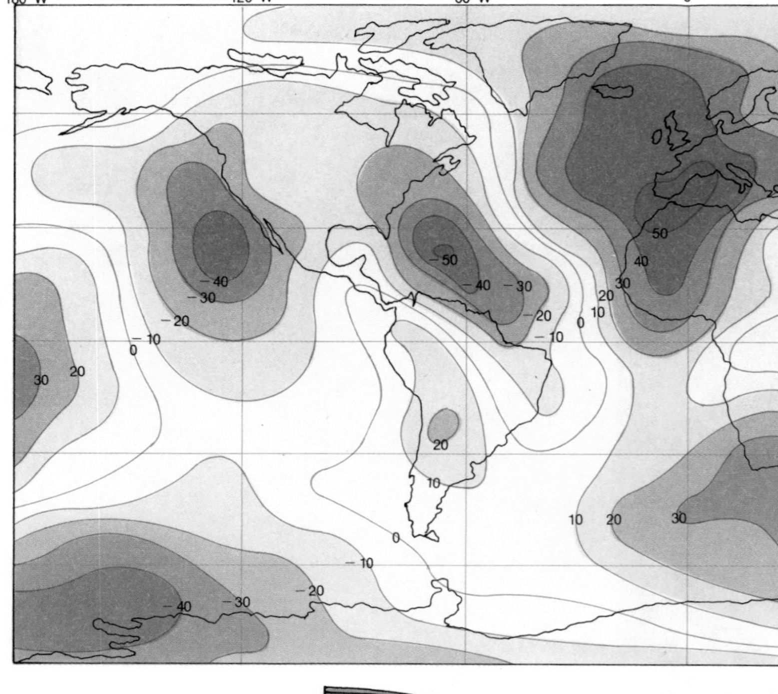

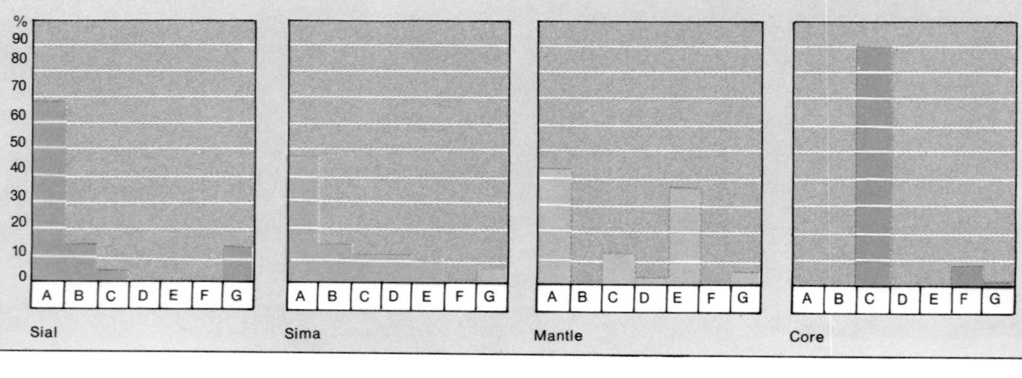

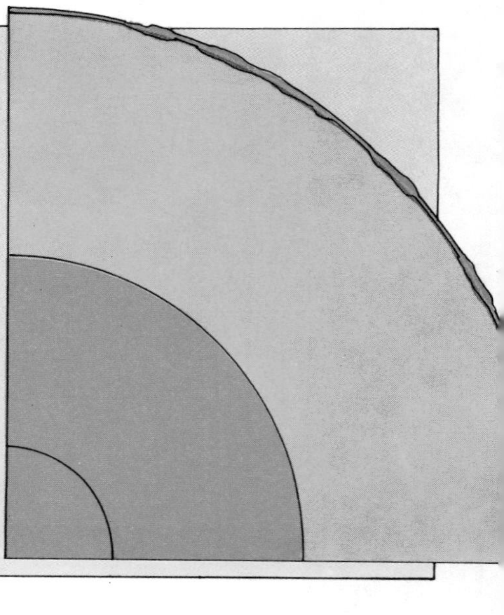

The chemical composition of the Earth varies from crust to core. The upper crust of continents (sial) is mainly granite, rich in aluminum and silicon, whereas oceanic crust (sima) is largely basalt, made of magnesium and silicon. The mantle is composed of rocks that are rich in magnesium and iron silicates, whereas the core, it is believed, is made of iron and nickel oxides.

%
A B C D E F G
Sial
Sima
Mantle
Core

A Silicon
B Aluminum
C Iron
D Calcium
E Magnesium
F Nickel
G Other

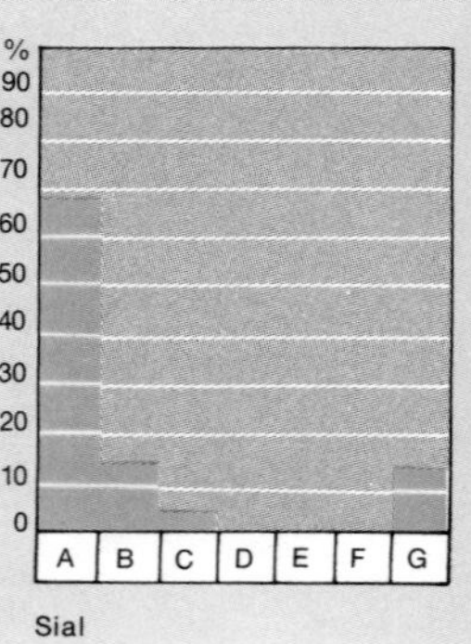

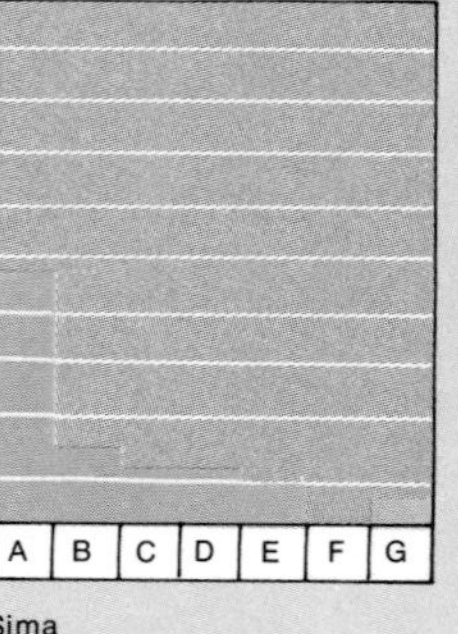

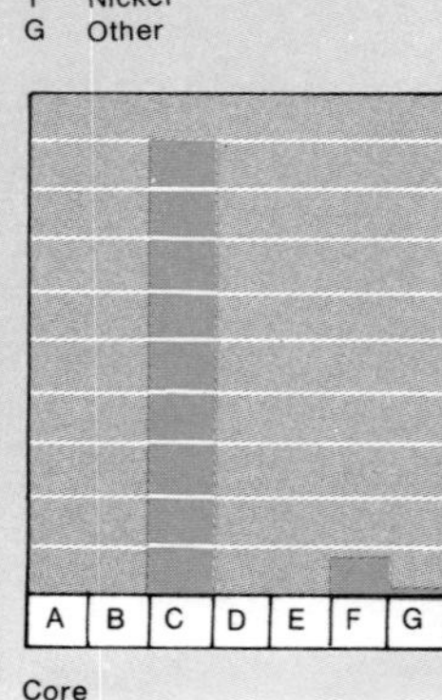

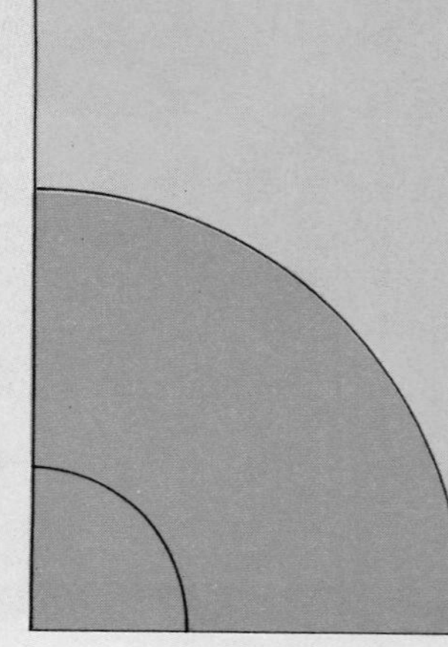

Earth's Structure

The Earth is made up of concentric shells of different kinds of material. Immediately beneath us is the crust; below that is the mantle; and at the center of the globe is the core. Knowledge of the internal structure of Earth is the key to an understanding of the substances of Earth and an appreciation of the forces at work, not only deep in the center of the planet but also affecting the formation of surface features and large-scale landscapes. The workings of all these elements are inextricably linked.

A 17th-century diagram of the Earth shows an internal structure of fire and subterranean rivers.

Our knowledge of the Earth is largely restricted to the outer crust. The deepest hole that man has drilled reaches only 10 km (6 miles)—less than 1/600th of the planet's radius—and so our knowledge about the rest of the Earth has had to come via indirect means: by the study of earthquake waves, and a comparison between rocks on Earth and those that make up meteorites—small fragments of asteroids and other minor planetary bodies that originated from similar materials to the Earth.

The Earth's crust

The outermost layer of the Earth is called the crust. The crust beneath the oceans is different from the material that makes up continental crust. Ocean crust is formed at mid-ocean ridges where melted rocks (magma) from the mantle rise up in great quantities and solidify to form a layer a few kilometers thick over the mantle. As this ocean crust spreads out from the ridge it becomes covered with deep-ocean sediments. The ocean crust was initially called "sima," a word made up from the first two letters of the characteristic elements—silicon and magnesium. Sima has a density of 2.9 gm/cc (1 gm/cc is the density of water).

Continental crust was named "sial"—from silicon and aluminum, the most abundant elements. Sial is lighter than sima with a density of 2.7 gm/cc. The continental crust is like a series of giant rafts, 17 to 70 km (9–43 miles) thick. As a result of numerous collisions and breakages, these continental rafts have been bulldozed into their present shape, but they have been forming for at least 4,000 million years. The oldest known rocks, in Greenland, are 3,750 million years old, which is only about 800 million years younger than the Earth itself. The complex history of the continents' evolution over this vast time span makes construction of an ideal cross section difficult, but the rocks of the lower two-thirds of the crust appear to be denser (2.9 gm/cc) than the upper levels.

The Moho, or Mohorovičić discontinuity, discovered in 1909, marks the base of the crust and the beginning of the mantle rocks, where the density increases from 2.9 to 3.3 gm/cc. The Moho is at an average depth of 10 km (6 miles) under the sea and 35 km (20 miles) below land.

The mantle

Our knowledge of the mantle comes from mantle rocks that are sometimes brought to the surface. These are even more enriched in magnesium oxides than the sima, with lesser amounts of iron and calcium oxides. The uppermost mantle to a depth of between 60 and 100 km (40–60 miles), together with the overlying crust, forms the rigid lithosphere, which is divided into plates. Below this is a pasty layer, or asthenosphere, extending to a depth of 700 km (435 miles). The upper mantle is separated from the lower mantle by another discontinuity where the density of the rock increases from 3.3 to 4.3 gm/cc.

Scientists now believe that the mantle is the planetary motor force behind the movements of the continents. By studying in detail the chemistry of the volcanic rocks that have come directly from the mantle, they have gathered much information about this mantle motor. The rocks that come up along oceanic ridges and form new oceanic crust reveal by their chemical composition that they have formed from mantle that has undergone previous melting. By contrast, islands such as Hawaii and Iceland have formed from mantle material that, for the most part, has never been melted before. One explanation for these chemical observations is that, while the top 700 km (435 miles) of the mantle region is moving in accordance with movement of the plates, the mantle beneath it is moving independently and sending occasional rivers of unaltered material through the surface to form islands like volcanic Hawaii.

The core

Structurally, the most important boundary in the Earth lies at a depth of 2,900 km (1,800 miles) below the surface, where the rock density almost doubles from about 5.5 to 9.9 gm/cc. This is known as the Gutenberg discontinuity and was discovered in 1914. Below this level the material must have the properties of a liquid since certain earthquake waves cannot penetrate it. Scientists infer from the composition of meteorites, some of which are composed of iron and nickel, that this deep core material is composed largely of iron, with some nickel and perhaps lighter elements such as silicon. The processes involved in the formation of a planet have been compared to the separation of the metals (the core) from the slag (the mantle and crust) in a blast furnace.

The core has a radius of 3,485 km (2,165 miles) and makes up only one-sixth of the Earth's volume, yet it has one-third of its mass. In the middle of the liquid outer core there is an even denser ball with a radius of 1,220 km (760 miles)—two-thirds the size of the Moon—where, under intense pressure, the metals have solidified. The inner core is believed to be solid iron and nickel and is 20 percent denser (12–13 gm/cc) than the surrounding liquid.

Electric currents in the core are the only possible source of the Earth's magnetic field. This drifts and alters in a way which could arise only from some deeply buried fluid movement. At the top of the core, the pattern of the field moves about 100 m (330 ft) west each day. Every million years or so during the Earth's history, the north–south magnetic poles have switched so that compasses pointed south, not north.

The dynamo that generates magnetism and its strange variations is still not fully understood. Motion in the core may be powered by giant slabs of metal that crystallize out from the liquid and sink to join the inner core. Our knowledge of the Earth's structure has increased greatly over the last 50 years, but many intriguing questions remain to be answered.

The Earth is not a sphere but an ellipsoid (below) that is flattened at the poles, where the radius is 6,378 km (3,960 miles), and bulging at the Equator, where the radius is 6,536 km (4,060 miles). This results from the Earth's rapid rotation. But, rather than a perfect ellipsoid, the true shape is a "geoid"—the actual shape of sea level—which is lumpy, with variations away from ellipsoid of up to 80 m (260 ft) (left). This reflects major variations in density in Earth's outer layers.

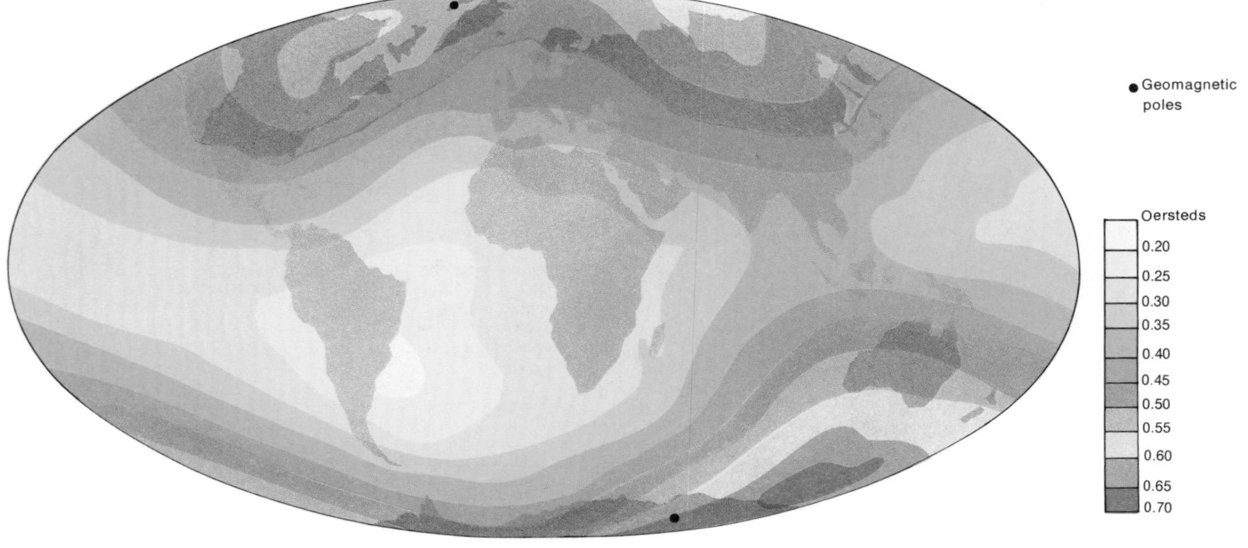

The Earth's magnetic field is strongest at the poles and weakest in equatorial regions. If the field were simply like a bar magnet inside the globe, lines of intensity would mirror lines of latitude; but the field is inclined at an angle of 11° to the Earth's axis. The geomagnetic poles are similarly inclined and they do not coincide with the geographic poles. In reality, the field is much more complex than that of a bar magnet. In addition, over long periods of time, the magnetic poles and the north–south orientation of the field change slowly. The strength of the Earth's magnetic field is measured in units called oersteds.

Earth's Moving Crust

The top layer of the Earth is known as the lithosphere and is composed of the crust and the uppermost mantle. It is divided into six major rigid plates and several smaller platelets that move relative to each other, driven by movements that lie deep in the Earth's liquid mantle. The plate boundaries correspond to the zones of earthquakes and the sites of active volcanoes. The concept of plate tectonics – that the Earth's crust is mobile despite being rigid – emerged in the 1960s and helped to confirm the early twentieth-century theory of continental drift proposed by Alfred Wegener.

THE DYNAMIC EARTH

As early as the 17th century, the English philosopher Francis Bacon noted that the coasts on either side of the Atlantic were similar and could be fitted together like pieces of a jigsaw puzzle. Three hundred years later Alfred Wegener proposed the theory of continental drift, but no one would believe the Earth's rigid crust could move. Today, geological evidence has provided the basis for the theory of plate tectonics, which demonstrates that the Earth's crust is slowly but continually moving.

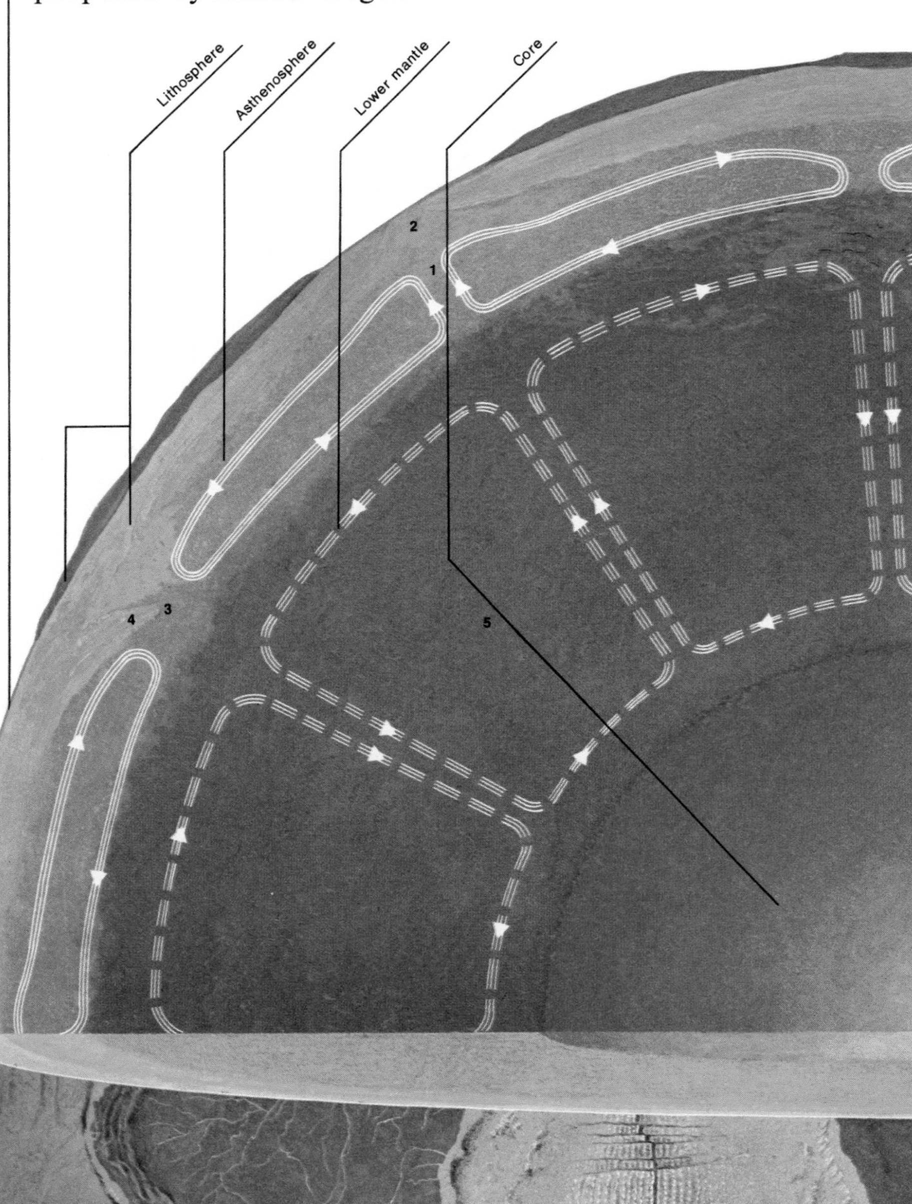

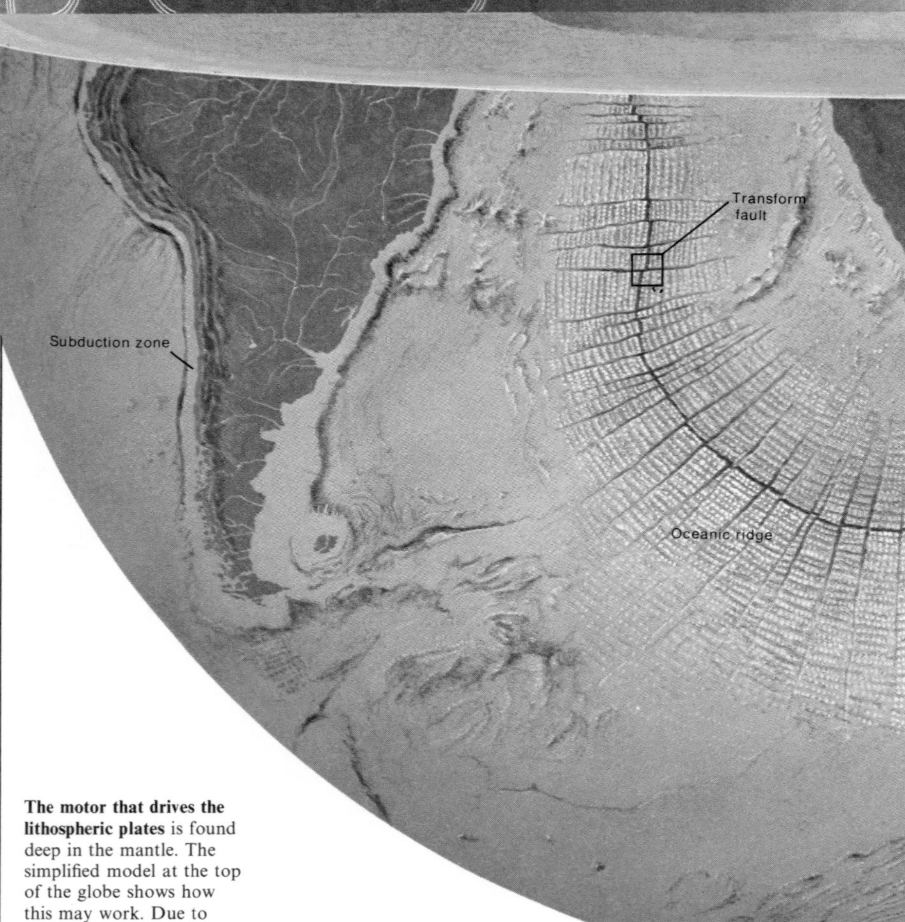

The motor that drives the lithospheric plates is found deep in the mantle. The simplified model at the top of the globe shows how this may work. Due to temperature differences in the mantle, slow convection currents circulate. Where two current cycles move upwards together and separate (1), the plates bulge and move apart along mid-ocean ridges (2). Where there is a downward moving current (3), the plates move together and sometimes one slips under the other to form a subduction zone (4). Another model proposes that the convection currents are found deep in the mantle (5). Only time and more research, however, will reveal the true mechanism of plate movement.

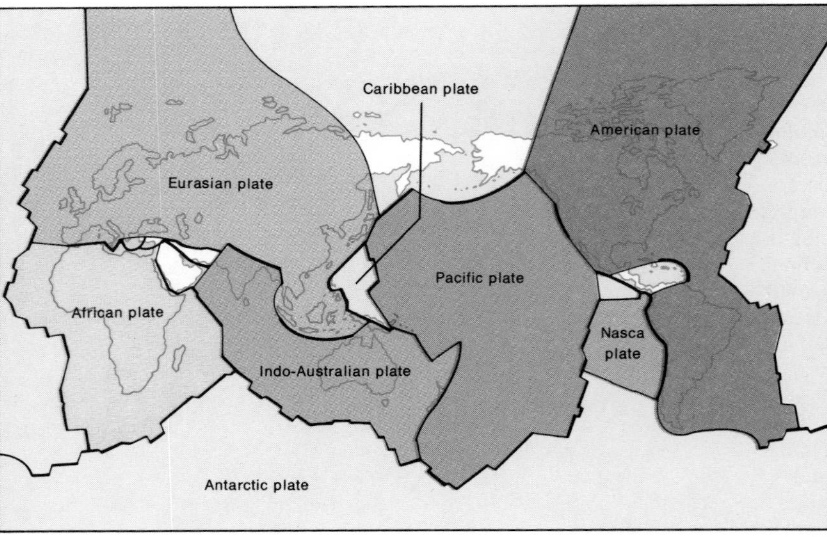

Earth's lithosphere—the rocky shell, or crust—is made up of six major plates and several smaller platelets, each separated from each other by ridges, subduction zones or transcurrent faults. The plates grow bigger by accretion along the mid-ocean ridges, are destroyed at subduction zones beneath the trenches, and slide beside each other along the transcurrent faults. The African and Antarctic plates have no trenches along their borders to destroy any of their crust, so they are growing bigger. This growth is compensated by the subduction zone that is developing to the north of the Tonga Islands and subduction zones in the Pacific. Conversely, the Pacific and Indo-Australian plates are shrinking. Along the plate boundaries magma wells up from the mantle to form volcanoes. Here, too, are the origins of earthquakes as the plates collide or slide slowly past each other.

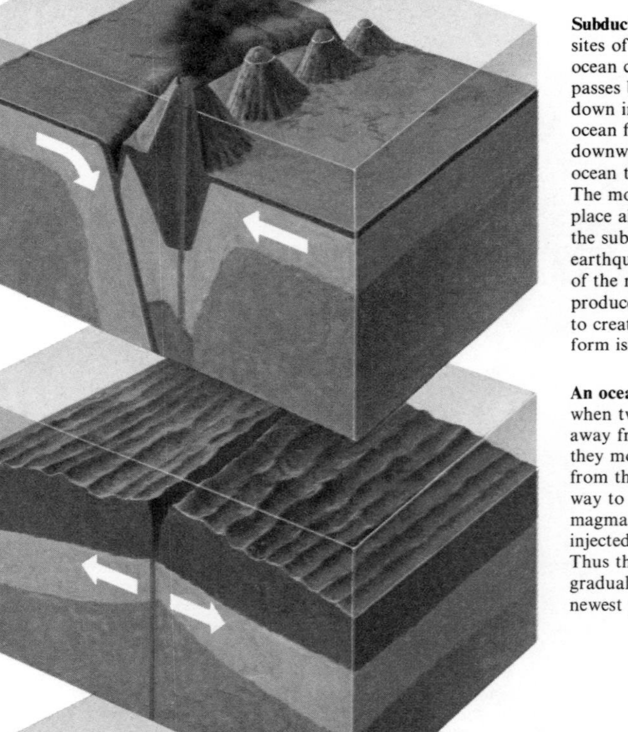

Subduction zones are the sites of destruction of the ocean crust. As one plate passes beneath another down into the mantle, the ocean floor is pulled downward and a deep ocean trench is formed. The movement taking place along the length of the subduction zone causes earthquakes, while melting of the rock at depth produces magma that rises to create the volcanoes that form island arcs.

An oceanic ridge is formed when two plates move away from each other. As they move, molten magma from the mantle forces its way to the surface. This magma cools and is in turn injected with new magma. Thus the oceanic ridge is gradually forming the newest part of Earth's crust.

Transform, or transcurrent, faults are found where two plates slide past each other. They may, for example, link two parts of a ridge (A, B). A study of the magnetic properties of the seabed may suggest a motion shown by the white arrows, but the true movements of the plates are shown by the red arrows. The transform fault is active only between points (2) and (3). Between points (1) and (2) and between (3) and (4) the scar of the fault is healed and the line of the fault is no longer a plate boundary.

The early evidence for continental drift was gathered by Alfred Wegener, a German meteorologist. He noticed that the coastlines on each side of the Atlantic Ocean could be made to fit together, and that much of the geological history of the flanking continents—shown by fossils, structures and past climates—also seemed to match. Wegener compared the two sides of the Atlantic with a sheet of torn newspaper and reasoned that if not just one line of print but 10 lines match then there is a good case for arguing that the two sides were once joined. Yet for 50 years continental drift was generally considered to be a fanciful dream.

Seafloor spreading

In the 1950s the first geological surveys of the oceans began, and a 60,000 km (37,200 mile) long chain of mountains was discovered running down the center of the Atlantic Ocean, all round the Antarctic, up to the Indian Ocean, into the Red Sea and up the Eastern Pacific Ocean into Alaska. Along the axis of this mid-ocean ridge system there was often a narrow, deep rift valley. In places this ridge was offset along sharp fractures in the ocean floor.

The breakthrough in developing the global plate tectonic theory came with the first large-scale survey of the ocean floor. Magnetometers, which were developed during World War II for tracking submarines, showed the ocean floor to be magnetically striped. The ocean floor reveals magnetic characteristics because the ocean crust basalts are full of tiny crystals of the magnetic mineral magnetite. As the basalt cooled, the magnetic field of these crystals aligned itself with the Earth's magnetic field. This would be insignificant if it were not for the fact that the magnetic pole of the Earth has switched from north to south at different times in the past. Half the magnetite compasses of the ocean floor point south rather than north.

In the middle 1960s, two Cambridge geophysicists, Drummond Matthews and Fred Vine, noticed that the pattern of stripes was symmetrical around the mid-ocean ridge. Such an extraordinary and unlikely symmetry could mean only one thing—any two matching stripes must originally have been formed together at the mid-ocean ridge and then moved away from each other as newer crust formed between them to create new stripes. It was soon calculated that the North Atlantic Ocean was growing wider by about 2 cm ($\frac{3}{4}$ in) a year. At last, drifting continents was accepted.

Consumption of the seafloor

Seafloor spreading soon became included in an even more sensational model—plate tectonics. If the oceans are growing wider, then either the whole planet is expanding or the spreading ocean floor is consumed elsewhere. In the late 1950s a global network of seismic stations had been set up to monitor nuclear explosions and earthquakes. For the first time the positions of all earthquakes could be accurately defined.

It was found that the zones of earthquake activity were predominantly narrow, following the mid-ocean ridges and extending along the rim of the Pacific, beneath the island arcs of the West Pacific and beneath the continental margins in the East Pacific as well as underlying the Alpine-Himalayan Mountain Belt. The seismic zones around the Pacific dipped away from the ocean and continued to depths as great as 700 km (430 miles). They intercepted the surface at the curious arc-shaped deep-ocean trenches. It had been known for 20 years that the pull of gravity over these trenches is strangely reduced, so to survive they must continually be dragged downwards. Here was the site of ocean-floor consumption—now known as a subduction zone. Subduction zones must be efficient at consuming ocean crust because no known ocean crust is older than 200 million years—less than five percent of Earth's lifetime.

The oceanic lithosphere (the Earth's rocky crust) is extraordinarily rigid. Even where the oceanic lithosphere becomes consumed within subduction zones it still maintains its rigidity. As it bends down into the Earth it tends to corrugate, forming very long folds. These corrugations give rise to the pattern of chains of deep-ocean trenches and chains of volcanic islands formed above the subduction zone.

As oceanic lithosphere grows older it cools, contracts and sinks. From the depth of the ocean floor it is possible to make an accurate estimate of the age of the crust beneath. Even the steepness of the subduction zone is a function of the age, and therefore the density, of the lithosphere. The oldest crust provides the strongest downward pull and hence the steepest angle of dip of the subduction zone.

As well as the spreading ridges (constructive margins) and the subduction zones (destructive margins) there is another kind of plate boundary (conservative margins), where the plates slip past one another along a major fault such as the San Andreas Fault of California.

The past positions of the continents

Continental drift is thus the result of the creation and destruction of oceanic lithosphere, but only the continents can record the oceanic plate motions taking place more than 200 million years ago. The discovery of ancient lines of subduction zone volcanoes can testify to the destruction of long-gone oceans. One particularly important technique for finding the positions of the continents is to study the magnetism of certain rocks, particularly lavas, that record the position of the north–south magnetic poles at the time when the rock cooled. If the rock "compass" points, for example, west, then the continent must have rotated by 90°. The vertical dip of the rock compass can reveal the approximate latitude of the rock at its formation (the dip increases from horizontal at the Equator to vertical at the magnetic poles).

As longitude is entirely arbitrary (defined on the position of Greenwich) one can only hope to gain the relative positions of the continents with regard to one another. The best additional information is provided by studies of fossils—if the remains of shallow-water marine organisms are very different they must have been separated by an ocean. The full impact of continental drift on the development of land animals and plants is only beginning to be realized.

THE DRIFTING CONTINENTS

It is now accepted that the continents have changed their positions during the past millions of years, and by studying the magnetism preserved in the rocks the configuration of the continents has been plotted for various geological times. The sequence of continental drifting, illustrated below, begins with one single landmass—the so-called supercontinent Pangaea—and the ancestral Pacific Ocean, called the Panthalassa Ocean. Pangaea first split into a northern landmass called Laurasia and a southern block called Gondwanaland, and subsequently into the continents we see today. The maps illustrate the positions of the continents in the past, where they are now and their predicted positions in 50 million years' time.

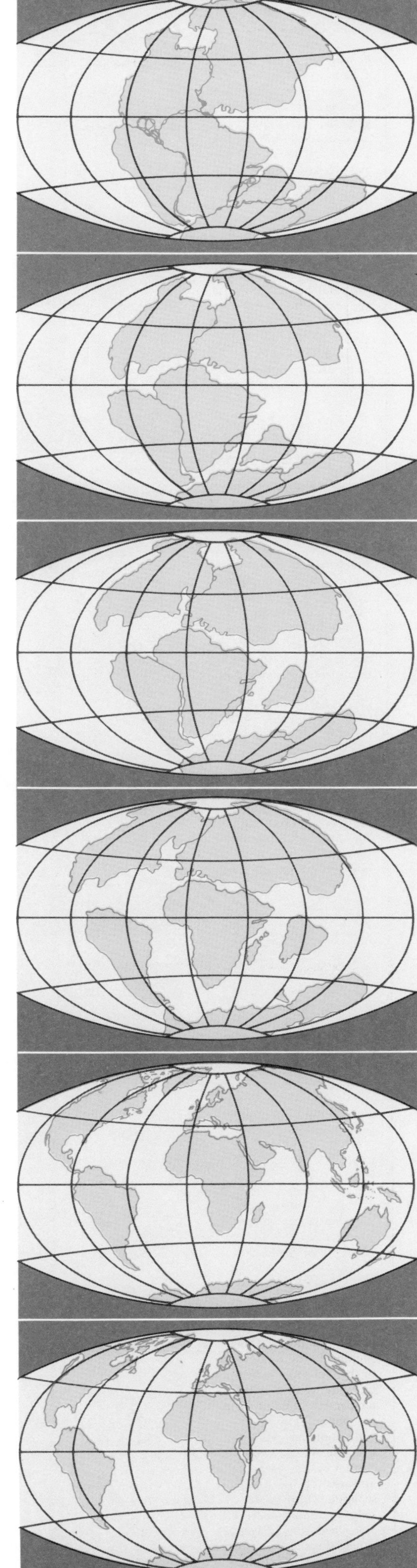

225 million years ago one large landmass, the supercontinent Pangaea, exists and Panthalassa forms the ancestral Pacific Ocean. The Tethys Sea separates Eurasia and Africa and forms an ancestor of the Mediterranean Sea.

180 million years ago Pangaea splits up, the northern block of continents, Laurasia, drifts northwards and the southern block, Gondwanaland, begins to break up. India separates and the South American–African block divides from Australia–Antarctica. New ocean floor is created between the continents.

135 million years ago the Indian plate continues its northward drift and Eurasia rotates to begin to close the eastern end of the Tethys Sea. The North Atlantic and the Indian Ocean have opened up and the South Atlantic is just beginning to form.

65 million years ago Madagascar has split from Africa and the Tethys Sea has closed, with the Mediterranean Sea opening behind it. The South Atlantic Ocean has opened up considerably, but Australia is still joined to the Antarctic and India is about to collide with Asia.

The present day: India has completed its northward migration and collided with Asia, Australia has set itself free from Antarctica, and North America has freed itself from Eurasia to leave Greenland between them. During the past 65 million years (a relatively short geological span of time) nearly half of the present-day ocean floor has been created.

50 million years in the future, Australia may continue its northward drift, part of East Africa will separate from the mainland, and California west of the San Andreas Fault will separate from North America and move northwards. The Pacific Ocean will become smaller, compensating for the increase in size of both the Atlantic and Indian oceans. The Mediterranean Sea will disappear as Africa moves to the north.

Magnetic surveys of the seabed helped build the plate tectonics theory. Research vessels equipped with magnetometers sailed back and forth over a mid-ocean ridge and recorded the varying magnetism of the seabed. The Earth's magnetic pole has switched from north to south at different times in the past, and this mapping revealed a striped magnetic pattern on the seabed. It was noticed that the stripes on either side of the ridge were symmetrical. The explanation was that the matching stripes must have formed together and moved apart as more crust was injected between them—a notion that was subsequently supported by dating of the seafloor.

3 2 1 0 1 3

Time in millions of years

Folds, Faults and Mountain Chains

The continents are great rafts of lighter rock that float in the mantle of the Earth. When drifting continents collide, great mountain chains are thrown up as the continental crust is forced to thicken to absorb the impact of the collision. The highest mountains are formed out of thick piles of sediment that are built up from the debris of erosion constantly washed off the land and deposited on the continental margins. Through the massive deformations of rock faults and folds these remains of old mountains become recycled, thus building new mountains from the remains of old ones.

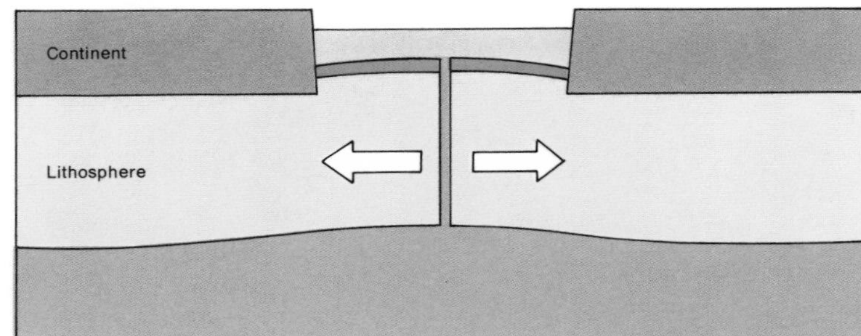

For the formation of mountain ranges such as the Appalachians or the Himalayas, or the Caledonian mountain chain of Norway, Scotland and Newfoundland, the pattern of development is very much the same. First, a widening ocean with passive margins is located between two continents.

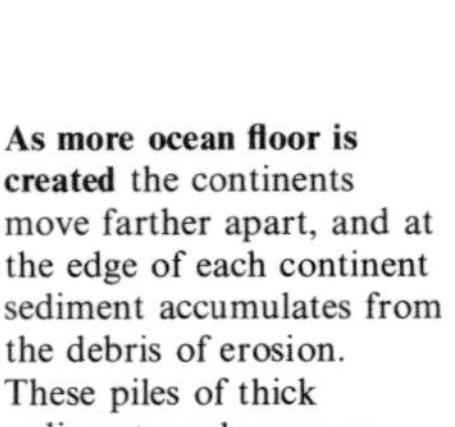

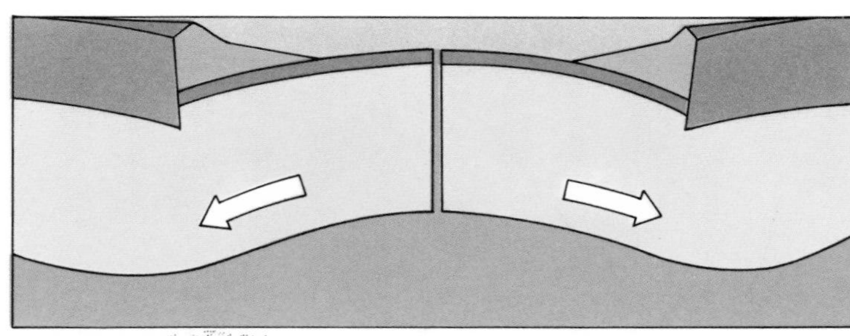

As more ocean floor is created the continents move farther apart, and at the edge of each continent sediment accumulates from the debris of erosion. These piles of thick sediment are known as sedimentary basins.

For the formation of the Appalachians, the ancestral Atlantic Ocean began to close, a subduction zone was formed at the ocean–continent boundary, and the oceanic lithosphere began to be absorbed into the mantle. Magma intruded to form granite "plutons" and volcanoes, and much of the sedimentary basin was metamorphosed.

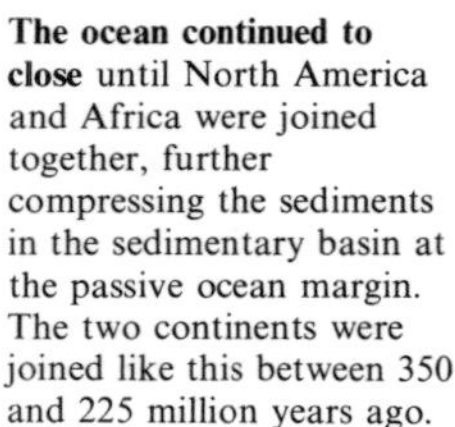

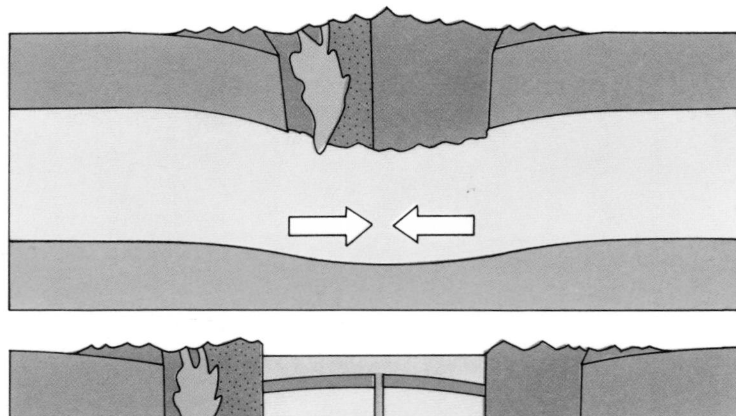

The ocean continued to close until North America and Africa were joined together, further compressing the sediments in the sedimentary basin at the passive ocean margin. The two continents were joined like this between 350 and 225 million years ago.

About 180 million years ago, after the original Appalachians had been worn down in size, the present Atlantic Ocean opened along a new break in the continental crust, offset from the line of the original mountains. As the continents split, so the crust became stretched along great curved faults.

Parts of the ancient Appalachian mountains have been eroded to sea level, leaving the Appalachians, that formed on the edge of the old continent, inland.

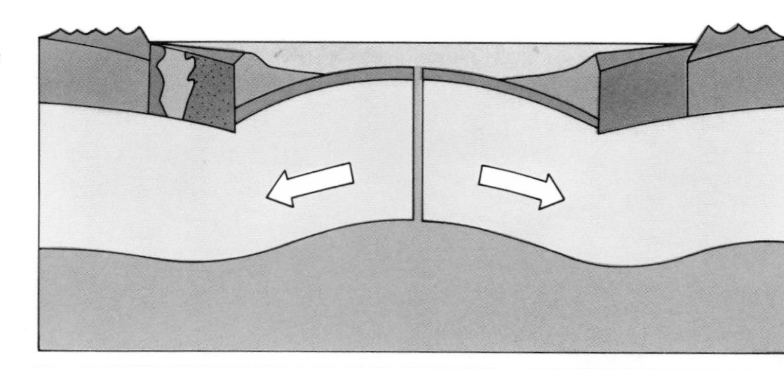

BIRTH AND DEATH OF A MOUNTAIN
Mountains are thrust upward by the pressure exerted by the moving plates of the Earth's crust, and are formed out of the sediments that have been eroded from the continental masses. Young mountains are lofty and much folded, but the agents of erosion and weathering soon begin to reduce their height, and over many millions of years the mountain range is eroded to sea level. This eroded material accumulates in the sea at the edge of the continents and becomes the building material for another phase of mountain building.

1

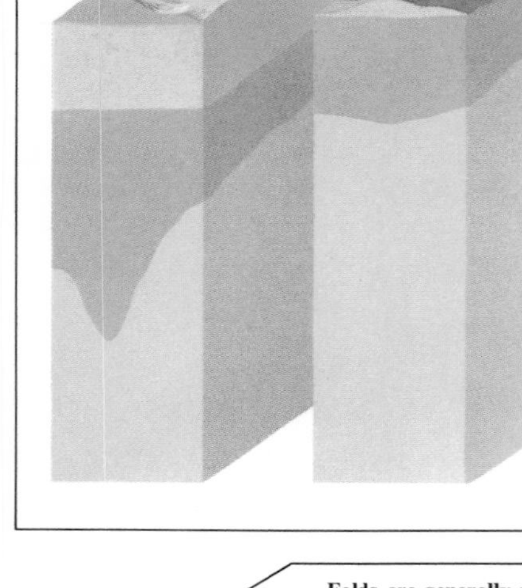

ISOSTASY
The continents float in the Earth's mantle, and because they are only slightly less dense (2.67 g/cc compared to 3.27 g/cc), 85% of their bulk lies below sea level. Thus the higher the mountain the deeper the mountain root. And as the crust can exist only to a maximum depth of about 70 km (43 miles) before it is liquefied in the mantle, mountains can never rise above a maximum of 10 km (6 miles) above sea level.

1 2 3 4 5

Folds are generally related to underlying faults. The commonest simple folds are monoclines, formed when a single fault exhibits underlying movement. With continued movement a simple symmetrical anticline (1) may fold unevenly to form an asymmetric anticline (2). More movement bends the strata further into a recumbent fold (3) and eventually the strata break to form an overthrust fold (4). Over a long period an overthrust fold may be pushed many kilometers from its original position to form a nappe (5). Faults are generally of three kinds: faults of tension known as normal faults, when one block drops down (6); faults of horizontal shear (7), known as strike-slip faults; and faults of compression (8), known as thrust faults.

The highest mountains are the product of continental collisions. As the rocks are squeezed, folded and faulted, the original continental crust becomes shortened and thickened. Although the overall extent and height of mountain chains is controlled by mountain building, the whole range can only be viewed from a spacecraft. For the earthbound mountain visitor the familiar shapes of peaks and valleys are those formed by mountain destruction (1). Snow at high altitudes consolidates to form ice that moves slowly downhill in the form of glaciers. To wear away a mountain range at an average of 5 km (3 miles) above sea level requires the removal of more than 20 km (12 miles) of rock, as the thick continental crust that floats in the underlying mantle rises to compensate for the loss of surface mass. Half-eroded mountains (2), such as the Appalachians, pictured above, may linger on for tens of millions of years until, like large regions of the Canadian interior, the mountains are all eroded away and only the hard crystalline surface rocks that were once buried 20 km (12 miles) underground remain (3).

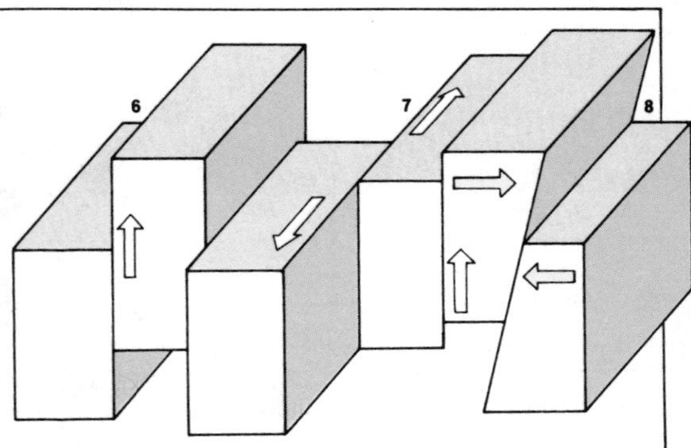

Continents float in the Earth's mantle like icebergs in the sea—more than four-fifths of their bulk lies beneath the surface. The continental crust is 28 km (17 miles) thick at sea level, and where mountains rise above this level there is a corresponding thickening in the crust beneath. The maximum thickness of crust is 70 km (43 miles), so mountains can only ever rise to a maximum height of approximately 10 km (6 miles) above sea level. This relation between upper and underlying crust is known as isostasy, or state of equal pressure.

As mountains become eroded, the process of isostatic rebound allows them to recover about 85 cm (34 in) for every 1 meter (40 in) removed. When, after about 100 million years, a major mountain range has been eroded down to sea level, the rocks exposed at the surface are those that were 15–25 km (9–15 miles) underground when the mountains were at their highest. Such rocks are coarsely crystalline, and make up the fabric of the old, tough continental crust.

Sedimentary basins

As early as the nineteenth century it was noticed that the biggest mountains formed where there had previously been the thickest pile of sediments. According to the principle of isostasy, a thick pile of sediments can form only where the Earth's crust is thin and sinking. The Aegean Sea in the eastern Mediterranean, for example, is at present being pulled apart, and therefore becoming thinner. Over the next few million years, as the Aegean crust sinks, a thick pile of sediments—a sedimentary basin—will accumulate. Most sedimentary basins are at present shallow seas, and form the continental shelves. The depth of water over these shelf seas has been determined by the erosion that accompanied the lowest sea levels of the past 100 million years—about 140 m (460 ft) below the present sea level.

Mountain building

When continents collide, it is the regions of stretched crust that are the first to absorb some of the impact. Such a former sedimentary basin is being turned into the Zagros Mountains of southwestern Iran as Arabia advances northeastward into Asia. The individual blocks of continental crust appear to be sliding back along curved faults, and the sediments that have built up over the thinned crust are now being forced into folds.

Early in the life of such a sedimentary basin sea water may become cut off from the ocean and evaporate to form extensive deposits of salt. Such salt deposits reduce friction and allow the folded pile of sediments overlying the continental blocks to become disconnected and to slide up to 100 km (62 miles) away from the collision zone. In the Zagros Mountains this process has only just begun, but in older mountain ranges, such as the Canadian Rockies or the European Alps, the formation of nappes—disconnected sediment piles forced ahead of the main compression zone—has been widespread.

As mountain ranges often form out of the sedimentary basins along the boundaries between a continent and the ocean, new mountains tend to add on to the fringes of the continents. In North America, for example, the oldest remnants of ranges that make up large tracts of the Canadian shield are found in the center of the continent, while the process of mountain building is continuing in the west. Other continents show a more complex pattern of mountain ranges through subsequent phases of splitting and amalgamation, and the Himalayas and the Urals have formed where smaller continents have come together to make up the continent of Asia.

The boundary between the continent and the ocean along the western coast of the Atlantic Ocean is not a plate boundary and is therefore termed passive, in contrast to active boundaries such as the eastern coast of the Pacific Ocean, where the ocean plate is moving down into the mantle at a subduction zone beneath the Andean mountain chain. The highest Andean mountains are tall volcanoes of andesite (formed from magmas pouring off the underlying subduction zone). The bulk of the mountain range consists of enormous underground batholiths, in which the magma has solidified before being able to erupt, and compressed and uplifted sedimentary basins formed along the continental margin.

The crustal region immediately beyond the volcanoes that form above subduction zones, however, is very often in tension and in the process of being pulled apart. This appears to be caused by mantle material being dragged down with the oceanic lithosphere. Small ocean basins, such as the Sea of Japan, may open up under such conditions.

Folds and faults

When movement of the Earth's crust has taken place along a planar fracture through sedimentary rocks, it can be easily identified by the breaks in the layers, and such planes of movement are known as faults. Folds form where rock layers bend rather than break. Generally, faults form when rocks are brittle, and folds are found when rocks are plastic.

Sediments close to the surface are often so soft that they behave plastically, as do rocks at depths greater than 15–20 km (9–12 miles), where the continental crust is of sufficiently high temperature and pressure for slow rock flow to take place. Thus most continental faults are found between these levels. All major folds found in soft sediments apparently have a fault of some kind beneath them, and it is the failure of the fault to pass right through to the surface that creates the fold.

Folds are often extremely complicated and some geologists have tended to describe them in extraordinary detail, but in fact they are little more than brush strokes in the overall picture. Pre-existing faults beneath the folds tend to determine the folds' orientation. Once a continental fault has formed, it provides a plane of weakness wherever the continental crust is subject to stress. Many faults around the Mediterranean Sea came into existence during a period of tension, and these are now being reactivated and produce the large earthquakes associated with the continuing collision of Africa with Europe.

At the end of all the complications and intricacies of continental collision, the final phase of mountain building—that involving uplift—remains perhaps the least understood. In the last two million years, for example, while man has been increasingly active on Earth, 2,500,000 sq km (almost 1,000,000 sq miles) of Tibet has risen 4,000 m (2 miles). But the origin of such gigantic and rapid movement lies within the Earth's mantle.

Rock Formation and History

All the rocks on Earth are interrelated through the rock cycle – a never-ending chain of processes that forms and modifies rocks and minerals on the Earth's surface, in its crust and in the mantle. These events are powered both by energy from the Sun and the heat of the Earth itself, and the processes include the forces of nature – from wind and water to the movements of the continents. This geological cycle of creation and destruction is one of the most distinctive features of our planet. Each feature of geological activity, each agent of landscape-making is but a stage of the continuing rock cycle.

CONSTANT CHANGE

The processes of formation and destruction of the three basic rock types—igneous, sedimentary and metamorphic—are linked in an interminable cycle of change. Igneous rocks are thrown up from inside the Earth, are eroded and eventually laid down as sediments. As accumulated sediments sink into the Earth, they are changed by heat and pressure—metamorphosed—before surfacing again in the processes of mountain building.

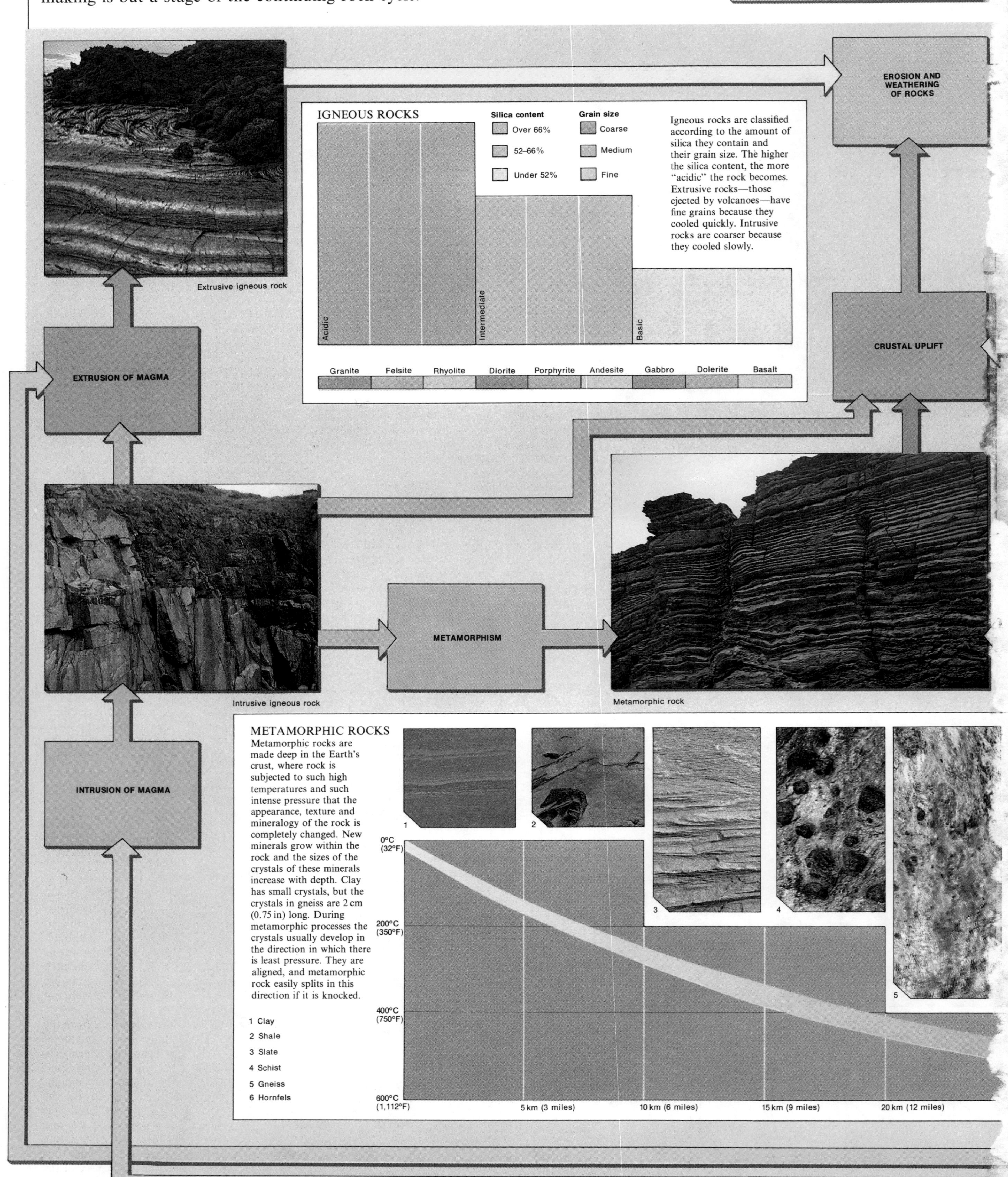

Igneous rocks are classified according to the amount of silica they contain and their grain size. The higher the silica content, the more "acidic" the rock becomes. Extrusive rocks—those ejected by volcanoes—have fine grains because they cooled quickly. Intrusive rocks are coarser because they cooled slowly.

METAMORPHIC ROCKS

Metamorphic rocks are made deep in the Earth's crust, where rock is subjected to such high temperatures and such intense pressure that the appearance, texture and mineralogy of the rock is completely changed. New minerals grow within the rock and the sizes of the crystals of these minerals increase with depth. Clay has small crystals, but the crystals in gneiss are 2 cm (0.75 in) long. During metamorphic processes the crystals usually develop in the direction in which there is least pressure. They are aligned, and metamorphic rock easily splits in this direction if it is knocked.

1 Clay
2 Shale
3 Slate
4 Schist
5 Gneiss
6 Hornfels

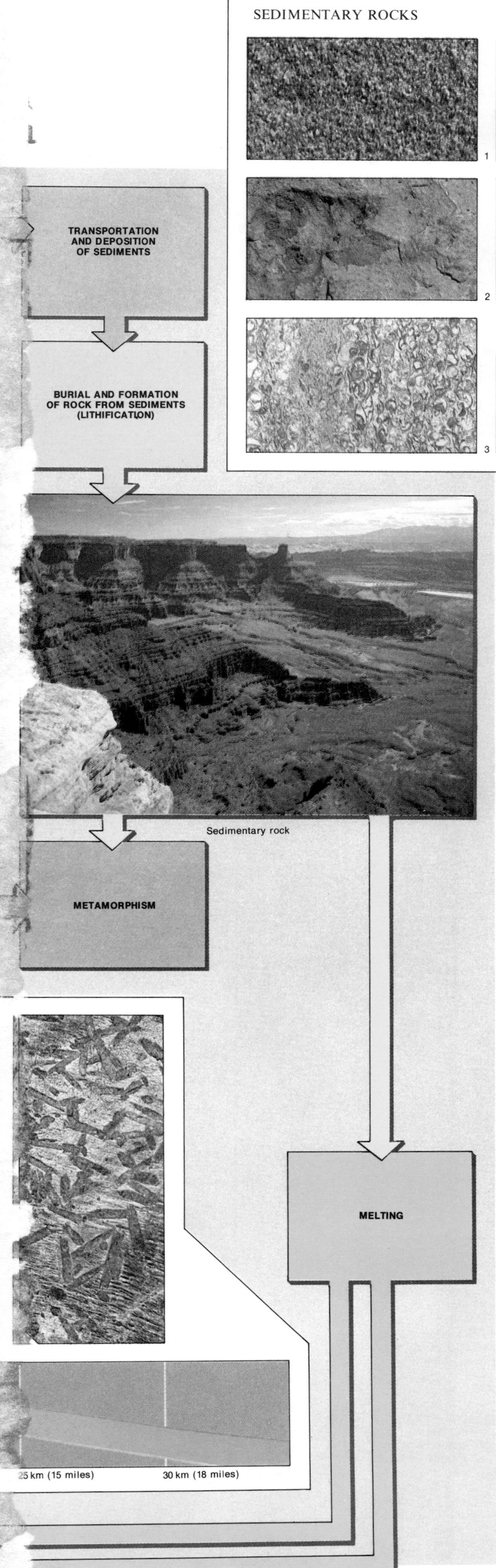

SEDIMENTARY ROCKS

Sediments can be turned into rock by means of three main processes. Cementation is the term used when water percolates between grains of sand. As it does so, any iron oxide, silica or calcium carbonate that were in solution are deposited in thin layers around the grains, thus cementing them into a hard sandstone (1). As more sediment is laid down, the increasing weight of the sediments on top exerts pressure on the underlying layers. Water is squeezed out and a dense rock is formed (2) by the process of compaction. This is the way clay becomes mudstone. Finally, during mountain-building processes forces are exerted on rock minerals that cause them to recrystallize into a solid mass of rock (3) that has no spaces between its mineral constituents.

All the rocks on Earth are formed at one stage or another in what is known as the rock cycle. All high ground on the continents suffers erosion; the eroded material is transported and deposited on lower ground; in time, these sediments may be elevated by mountain-building processes and so, in turn, become eroded. If, between their formation and destruction, sediments pass deep into the Earth's crust, they may be transformed by heat or pressure into metamorphic rock; or, at even greater depths, they may melt to form yet another kind of rock—igneous rock.

Materials at the bottom of a thick pile of sediments may be heated enough to melt. If this material then cools and solidifies underground, it is called plutonic rock. Sometimes, however, it escapes to the surface by means of a short cut—a volcano—to become part of the rock cycle. On the other hand, some sediments are lost off the edge of the continents on to the deep ocean floor, and they disappear into the mantle of the Earth by means of the downward movements of the oceanic crust. A measure of the difference between the input and the output of the continental rock cycle is a measure of how fast the continental crust is increasing or decreasing. Scientists believe it is increasing—at a rate of between 0.1 and 1.0 cu km a year.

Types of rock

The range of rock types found on the continents has been classified under three headings: sedimentary, igneous and metamorphic. Sedimentary rocks include all those formed at low temperatures on the Earth's surface; igneous rocks have all solidified from molten rock, or magma; and metamorphic rocks are sedimentary or igneous rocks that have changed their nature under conditions of high temperature and pressure.

There is a certain amount of difficulty in defining the boundaries between the different types. Ash formed from solidified magma falling out of the air after a volcanic eruption is igneous, but what if it should move downhill in a mudslide? If a metamorphic rock is deeply buried it may start to melt and form a "migmatite," which is part liquid and part solid. Is this igneous? And where does the boundary lie between a deeply buried sediment and a metamorphic rock? Coal seams that have been thoroughly metamorphosed from their original peat deposits are found as layers in unaltered sandstones. This classification does, however, provide a useful preliminary guide to understanding the nature of different types of rock.

Rock types are defined by studying their texture, the way they were formed, and their composition. There are interesting textural similarities between evaporites—salt deposits formed as an inland sea dries up—and some plutonic igneous rocks. Both have crystallized directly from a liquid. There are similarities between sandstones and plutonic "cumulates," which form at the base of enormous magma reservoirs where strong magma currents deposit thick layers of crystals. So rock types must be defined in terms of more than just texture.

Rock formation

The simplest sedimentary rocks are those made up of whole fragments of eroded material. "Scree" deposits that accumulate at the base of a cliff or a steep valley side from angular rock fragments that have broken off the rock face above can make a sedimentary "breccia." A rock made from rounded stream pebbles is a "conglomerate." Further erosion reduces the rock into three components: dissolved ions (atoms with an electrical charge) such as those of calcium or magnesium; mineral grains (sand) that cannot be broken down chemically, such as quartz; and a variety of minerals containing sheet-like layers of silicate and alumina (silicon and aluminum oxides)—the minerals that are often the main constituents of clays.

A river carrying these minerals first deposits the sand, and then the clay, while the dissolved ions pass out into the sea, where some are absorbed by living organisms and used to construct protective shells and rigid skeletons. When the creatures die, the shells and bones again become part of the rock cycle, building up great thicknesses of limestone.

Igneous rocks are chemically far more complex than are sedimentary rocks, but are texturally simpler. The slower the magma cools, the larger are the crystals that form within it. If it cools too quickly it may not crystallize at all, forming instead a super-cooled liquid, or glass. A plutonic igneous rock—one cooled deep underground—is coarse grained; a volcanic rock is fine grained. A rock can, however, have both large and small crystals, testifying to a more complex history.

The most striking feature of Earth magmas is their uniformity. With few exceptions, they are all rich in silica. The greater the silica content, the higher their viscosity (resistance to flowing). Those rich in silica tend to solidify underground. The complex chemistry of magmas comes from the melting of the variety of minerals making up the mantle.

The chemistry of metamorphic rocks is like that of their igneous or sedimentary starting materials. As these become more deeply buried and heated, the constituent minerals grow larger. A mudstone metamorphoses to a slate, then to a schist and finally a gneiss. The "slatiness" or "schistosity" of these rocks is provided by micas and other sheet-shaped mineral grains. Such minerals require abundant alumina to form. If this is not present in the starting rock, it will be metamorphosed into more granular material.

A record in the rocks

Rocks contain an unwritten history of the Earth. Sedimentary rocks hold information about climates of the past and fossil relics of organisms that lived when the sediments were laid down. Igneous rocks record periods of crustal activity that relate to the movements of the continents; and metamorphic rocks indicate periods of uplift that exposed previously buried rock. From such information it is possible to construct a geological time scale. Although fossils are a useful means of correlating one pile of sediment with another, good fossils go back only 600 million years. Earlier organisms are believed to have been soft bodied and were not easily fossilized.

The only complete time scale comes from the radioactive "clocks" in many igneous and metamorphic rocks. Certain forms of natural elements, or isotopes, are unstable and emit energy. By measuring the amount of "daughter" atoms that have been formed by the radioactive decay of a larger "parent" atom, it is possible to determine the age of a rock and events in the history of its formation. The dating of rocks from radioactive decay has thus enabled a true time scale for the history of the Earth to be constructed.

Earth's Minerals

Minerals are the basic ingredients of the Earth, from crust to core. They make up not only the ores on which man has based much of his technology, and the gemstones which he values for their beauty or rarity, but also the components of rocks, pebbles and sands. Two million years ago minerals – in the form of stones – provided early man with his first tools. Today, man's use of minerals, such as uranium for nuclear power or silicon for microcomputers, is revolutionizing our lives.

SUBSTANCES OF THE EARTH
Minerals are made up of chemical elements, arranged according to various crystal structures. Man's chief interest in minerals has been as precious stones and, increasingly, as a resource in the form of useful metal ores. But of the 2,500 minerals so far identified, the majority are rock-forming substances—the material components of the Earth. Relatively infrequent geological processes over vast time spans are responsible for concentrating minerals dispersed through rocks into richer deposits, and it is these economically important ores that have provided man with his supply of workable mineral resources through the ages.

Minerals, and the metals derived from them, have always had an inherent fascination for man, as well as providing the basis for his technology. Gold in particular, which was worked in Egypt as early as 5000 BC, still retains its mysterious attraction. Because of its chemical inactivity it is imperishable, immutable and nontarnishing, and has served as the basis of world trade for almost 2,000 years. Copper has been smelted since the early part of the third millennium BC, to be replaced eventually by harder alloys. Arsenical bronze, for instance, bridged the gap between the Copper and Bronze ages (bronze is an alloy of copper and tin). More complex technology was needed for the working of iron, which began *c.* 1100 BC, whereas brass (an alloy of copper and zinc) did not appear until Roman times.

Although the steel-making process had its roots in antiquity, it was not until the nineteenth century that new techniques changed man's attitude to minerals. Before the modern age of plastics, the capacity to produce steel was the hallmark of industrial development, and together with coal it formed the linchpin of western industrial progress. Today minerals have come to assume their greatest importance as exploitable—but nonrenewable—resources.

Components of the Earth

The terms "mineral," "rock" and "stone" are often used interchangeably, but in fact all rocks are made up of minerals, which are natural and usually inorganic substances with a particular chemical makeup and crystal structure.

Certain stones have properties that satisfy basic human needs for beauty and color. Some possess a flashing sparkle, others have special optical characteristics such as refraction and dispersion ("fire"), or contain inclusions that give rise to phenomena like the "asterism" found in opals and sapphires. About 100 such minerals are classified as gemstones and valued for their beauty, durability or rarity.

Most minerals occur as either pure (ore) deposits or mixed with other minerals in rocks—an economically important difference. Their exploitation has been vastly extended in recent decades through our greater understanding of the mineral-forming processes that take place in the Earth's crust. All mineral ores result from a separation process in which a mineral-rich solution separates into its various components according to the temperature, pressure and composition of the original mixture. Precipitation is the simplest kind of separation, as when calcium salts separate from circulating groundwater to yield stalactites and stalagmites in caves, in the form of calcite crystals.

Mineral formation

Most deposits of metallic ores originate in the intense physicochemical activity that takes place at the boundaries between the Earth's huge crustal plates. Very high concentrations of minerals occur in association with warm solutions coming from springs in the seabed, notably along the spreading zones in the southeastern Pacific Ocean, the Red Sea, the African Rift Valley and the Gulf of Aden. This process also occurs in shallow-water volcanic areas, as near the Mediterranean island of Thira and the submarine volcano of Bahu Wuhu, Indonesia. Cold seawater penetrates the crust and leaches out minerals from the basalts of these "hot spots," returning to the surface of the seabed as hot springs. The minerals then precipitate in the cold, oxygen-rich seawater.

Mineral separation may also occur when part of the deep-seated magma forces its way into the upper layers of the Earth's crust and begins to cool. The great plugs of magma that form the rock kimberlite, in which diamonds are found, must have come from a depth of at least 100 km (62 miles). If the magma reaches the surface through fissures as extrusive rocks, the pattern of minerals in the surrounding rocks is also changed by a process called contact metamorphism, with various bands or zones of minerals occurring at various distances from the contact boundary.

As rocks become weathered, mineral concentrations that resist weathering may be left. Alternatively, all the weathered materials may be transported by running water, becoming concentrated as they are sorted out according to their different densities. Gold is the best-known example of this alluvial type of mineral deposit—known as a placer deposit. If the minerals are washed into the sea, they may be distributed over deltas or over the seafloor, but when this happens the concentrations of minerals are usually very low.

Mineral energy

Fossil fuels such as coal and petroleum are major mineral sources of energy. But with the twentieth-century discovery of nuclear fission, uranium also became an important energy resource. The richest deposits occur, as with other minerals, as veins deposited in fractures by hot-water movements. These deposits, consisting of a uranium oxide called pitchblende, were the first to be mined, for example at Joachimstal (Czechoslovakia), Great Bear Lake (Canada) and Katanga (Zaire). Weathered products of such rocks, redeposited as sandstones, also contain uranium, as in Wyoming (USA) and in the Niger basin. In many respects uranium is similar to silver: both occur with similar geological abundance, their ores are enriched about 2,000 times during processing, and the metals are recovered by using chemicals to dissolve the metal selectively and then by "stripping" the metal from the solution.

MINERALS FROM THE OCEAN
Ocean sediments that originally came from land contain organic matter that absorbs the oxygen in the sediments. As a result, solutions of minerals such as manganese and iron are released, seeping upwards through the debris. When they come in contact with the oxygen in seawater they are precipitated, condensing into so-called "manganese" nodules in amounts that may eventually prove to be a valuable source of mineral wealth. Metallic elements also accumulate very slowly from the seawater itself.

METAL-RICH BRINES
Scientists have recently discovered deep hollows on the floor of the Red Sea and other similar enclosed basins connected with rift valleys. These prevent normal circulation of water and form undersea pools of hot, high-density brines. The brines contain sulphur and other minerals in very high concentrations, and overlie sediments rich in metals such as zinc, copper, lead, silver and gold. Hot springs in fissures below the pools escape into them, carrying up solutions of the metallic minerals which combine with sulphur to create a concentrated broth rich in metals.

METALS FROM THE INTERIOR
Rift zones on the bed of the Pacific Ocean, where the Earth's crustal plates are slowly separating, provide sensational visual evidence of metallic ores in the actual process of creation. Seawater percolates through the fractured surface to the molten rock below, where it leaches out the soluble metallic components, erupting in superheated hydrothermal springs to form geysers of mineral-rich water. Oxygen in the cold water of the seafloor causes the minerals to condense out, precipitating in plumes of dark powder. Continental drift, collision and sedimentation over millions of years will eventually incorporate these deposits into the landmasses.

Uranium, chromium and many other minerals are widely distributed through the Earth's crust, but they are valuable as a resource only if the technology exists to extract them economically. In mineral development, the high-grade ores are worked out first, followed by the poorer deposits if demand remains or increases. With uranium, the low-grade deposits contain far more of the total quantity of the mineral, but these are worth exploiting because of uranium's importance and because the technology exists. Chromium, on the other hand, is currently extracted only from high-grade ores. Large deposits of low-grade ores do exist, but technology for exploiting them economically has not yet been developed.

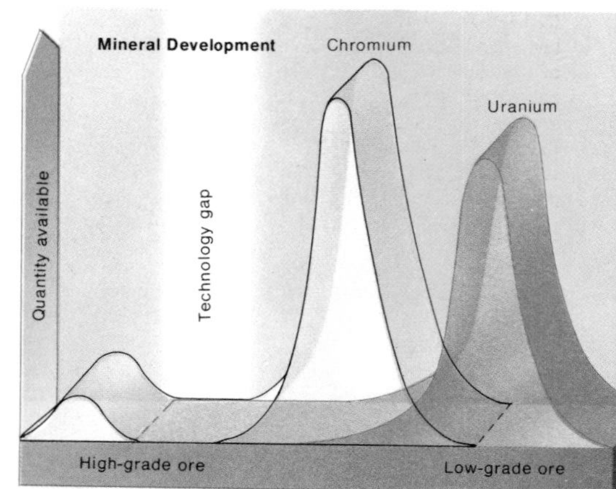

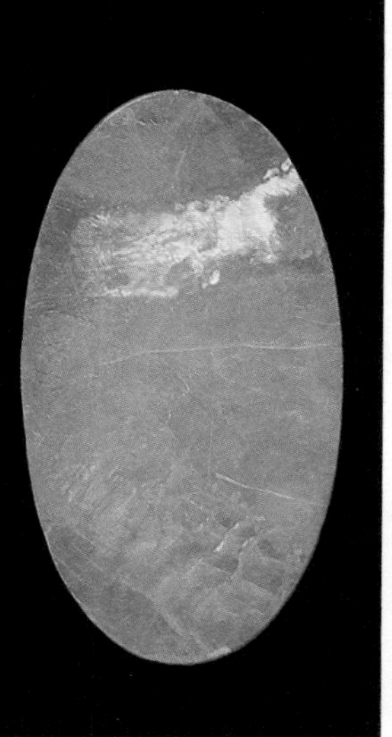

Opal (above), a silica mineral, often contains impurities which give it a range of colors. These flash and change according to the angle of vision, a result of the interference of light along minute internal cracks in the stone.

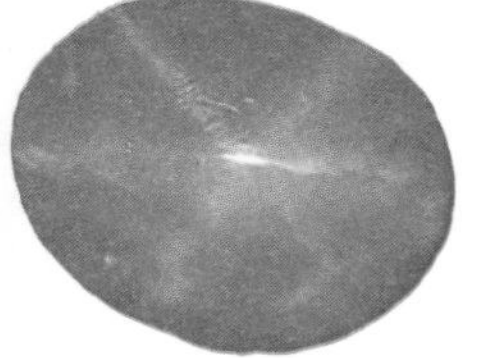

Sapphire gemstone (left), a form of the dull gray mineral carborundum (below), owes its color to inclusions of titanium and iron. If cut with a rounded top it gives a starry effect known as asterism.

MINERALS IN THE SERVICE OF MAN

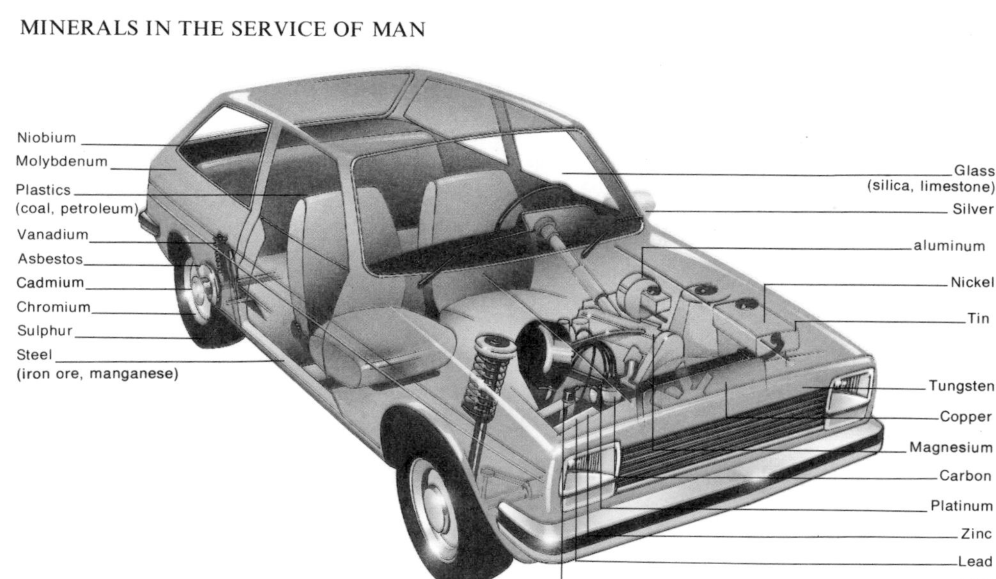

The modern automobile makes use of a whole alphabet of minerals in its composition, from aluminum to zinc. The importance of plastics, made from petroleum and coal, is constantly increasing, but the need for specialist metals is as great as ever. Cadmium, for example, is used in electroplating; carbon goes into making electrodes and graphite seals; transistors and electric contact points require platinum; sulphur is present in vulcanizing rubber and lubricants; lamp filaments contain tungsten. Of basic metals, iron and steel still account for almost three-quarters of the total quantity of the metals used; lead for 1.19 percent and copper for only 0.94 percent. But the amount of useful metal is often a small fraction of the rock that has to be mined and processed. A copper ore, for instance, only yields about 0.7 percent of metal, so to equip a single car's radiator with copper well over one and a half tonnes of rock will have to be excavated, of which 99.3 percent will simply be discarded.

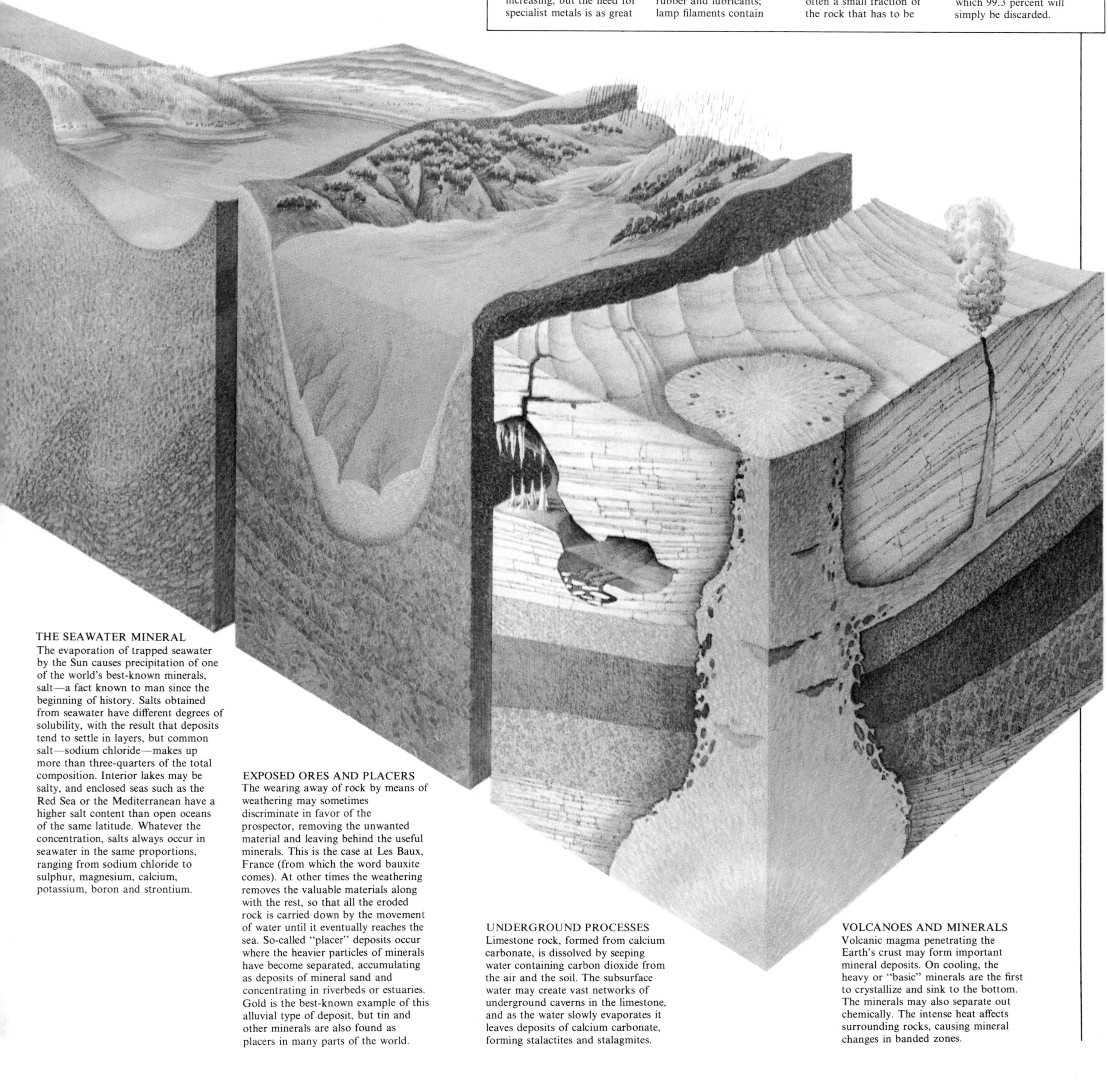

THE SEAWATER MINERAL

The evaporation of trapped seawater by the Sun causes precipitation of one of the world's best-known minerals, salt—a fact known to man since the beginning of history. Salts obtained from seawater have different degrees of solubility, with the result that deposits tend to settle in layers, but common salt—sodium chloride—makes up more than three-quarters of the total composition. Interior lakes may be salty, and enclosed seas such as the Red Sea or the Mediterranean have a higher salt content than open oceans of the same latitude. Whatever the concentration, salts always occur in seawater in the same proportions, ranging from sodium chloride to sulphur, magnesium, calcium, potassium, boron and strontium.

EXPOSED ORES AND PLACERS

The wearing away of rock by means of weathering may sometimes discriminate in favor of the prospector, removing the unwanted material and leaving behind the useful minerals. This is the case at Les Baux, France (from which the word bauxite comes). At other times the weathering removes the valuable materials along with the rest, so that all the eroded rock is carried down by the movement of water until it eventually reaches the sea. So-called "placer" deposits occur where the heavier particles of minerals have become separated, accumulating as deposits of mineral sand and concentrating in riverbeds or estuaries. Gold is the best-known example of this alluvial type of deposit, but tin and other minerals are also found as placers in many parts of the world.

UNDERGROUND PROCESSES

Limestone rock, formed from calcium carbonate, is dissolved by seeping water containing carbon dioxide from the air and the soil. The subsurface water may create vast networks of underground caverns in the limestone, and as the water slowly evaporates it leaves deposits of calcium carbonate, forming stalactites and stalagmites.

VOLCANOES AND MINERALS

Volcanic magma penetrating the Earth's crust may form important mineral deposits. On cooling, the heavy or "basic" minerals are the first to crystallize and sink to the bottom. The minerals may also separate out chemically. The intense heat affects surrounding rocks, causing mineral changes in banded zones.

Earthquakes and Volcanoes

Earthquakes and volcanic eruptions challenge man's faith in the stability of the world, but these violent releases of energy testify to our planet's ever-dynamic activity. Earthquakes are caused when the rigid crust is driven past or over itself by underlying movements that extend deep into the Earth's mantle. Stress builds up until it exceeds the strength of the rocks, when there follows a sudden movement. Volcanoes occur where molten rock, or magma, from the mantle forces its way to the surface through lines of weakness in the crust, often at the lithospheric plate boundaries.

Earthquakes occur when slabs of the Earth's crust move in relation to each other. The focus of the earthquake is the point where movement occurs (1), and the epicenter is the point on the surface directly above it (2). Blue lines represent zones of surface damage as measured on the Modified Mercalli scale.

MODIFIED MERCALLI SCALE

I Earthquake not felt, except by a few.

II Felt on upper floors by few at rest. Swinging of suspended objects.

III Quite noticeable indoors, especially on upper floors. Standing cars may sway.

IV Felt indoors. Dishes and windows rattle, standing cars rock. Like a heavy truck hitting a building.

V Felt by nearly all, many wakened. Fragile objects broken, plaster cracked, trees and poles disturbed.

VI Felt by all, many run outdoors. Slight damage, heavy furniture moved, some fallen plaster.

VII People run outdoors. Average homes slightly damaged, substandard ones badly damaged. Noticed by car drivers.

VIII Well-built structures slightly damaged, others badly damaged. Chimneys and monuments collapse. Car drivers disturbed.

IX Well-designed buildings badly damaged, substantial ones greatly damaged, shifted off foundations. Conspicuous ground cracks open up.

X Well-built wood-structures destroyed, masonry structures destroyed. Rails bent, ground cracked, landslides. Rivers overflow.

XI Few masonry structures left standing. Bridges and underground pipes destroyed. Broad cracks in ground. Earth slumps.

XII Damage total. Ground waves seem like sea waves. Line of sight disturbed, objects thrown into the air.

The Earth's crust generally breaks along pre-existing planes of weakness, or faults. Such breakages give rise to an "explosive" release of stress that is familiar to surface dwellers as the vibrations of an earthquake.

Not all earthquakes, however, take place along pre-existing faults, otherwise no new faults would be generated. Many recent large earthquakes have been located immediately north of the Tonga Islands because a giant rent is developing through previously unbroken ocean crust. The crust to the south is being swallowed down into the mantle and that to the north continues at the surface to be subducted farther to the west. Once a fault has formed, however, it remains a plane of weakness even though the two sides tend to become partly resealed, so that when movement does occur there is a considerable release of energy.

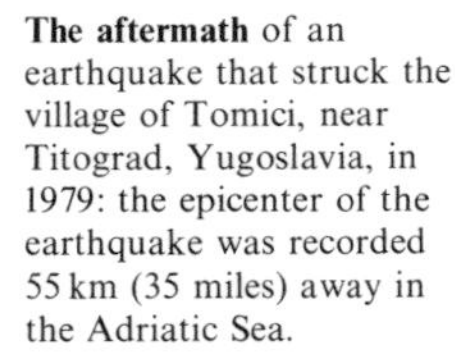

The aftermath of an earthquake that struck the village of Tomici, near Titograd, Yugoslavia, in 1979: the epicenter of the earthquake was recorded 55 km (35 miles) away in the Adriatic Sea.

Measuring earthquakes

Earthquakes are quantified in two ways. The actual energy release (magnitude) at the source of the earthquake (the focus) is measured on the Richter scale, a log scale where every unit of increase represents approximately 24 times the energy release. A magnitude 7 earthquake is roughly equivalent to the explosion of a one megaton nuclear bomb (one million tonnes of TNT). The strongest earthquake recorded this century was a magnitude 8.5 event in Alaska in 1964. Earthquakes as they are perceived are measured on the Modified Mercalli scale by their impact in terms of the amount of surface destruction. A medium-size earthquake under a town, such as that beneath Tangshan, China, in 1976 which killed more than a quarter of a million people, might record higher on the Mercalli scale than the Alaska event, which affected a large but sparsely populated region.

The magnitude of the earthquake depends on the frictional resistance that has to be overcome before movement can take place. This total frictional resistance, therefore, increases with the area of the fault plane. So the bigger the fault plane that moves, the bigger the earthquake. The largest earthquakes occur on wide fault planes that dip at a very shallow angle and can pass through a great deal of relatively shallow crust that will not deform plastically.

Earthquakes are unlikely to occur where rocks are plastic and can flow to accommodate the buildup of stress. Some faults, such as the San Andreas Fault in the western United States, pass from brittle rocks into a plastic zone at depths of only a few kilometers. Therefore, the next San Francisco earthquake cannot be as great as the 1964 Alaskan one, although this may be of little comfort to the potential victims. Along some sections of the San Andreas Fault the plastic zone comes directly to the surface, and motion occurs without large earthquakes.

Earthquake prediction is still in its infancy, although it is recognized that a number of phenomena may occur before a major earthquake—the ground may swell, the electrical conductivity of groundwater may change, and the water height of wells may rapidly alter.

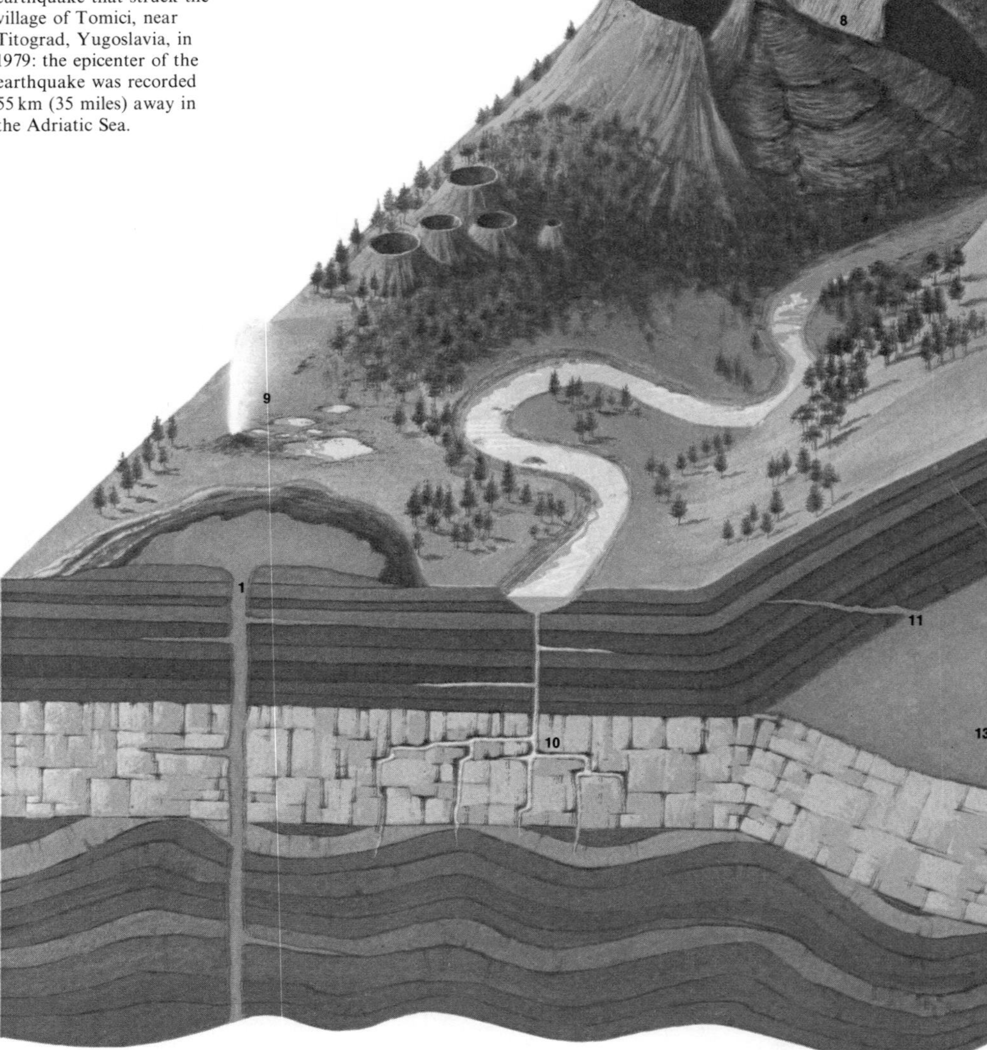

How volcanoes are formed

Volcanoes, although spectacular, are safer than earthquakes. While an average of 20,000 people are killed each year in earthquakes, only about 400 are killed by volcanoes; and many of the victims die from starvation due to crop failure after heavy ash falls.

Volcanoes are formed when molten rock (magma) escapes through the Earth's crust to the Earth's surface. Most of this magma forms within the upper mantle between 30 and 100 km (20–60 miles) underground. The temperature increases with depth between 20° and 50°C per km (35°–90°F per 3,250 ft) from the crust to the mantle, but even so the rocks are normally not hot enough to melt.

Basaltic magmas, found along mid-ocean spreading ridges and oceanic islands, are formed when hot, deep mantle rises and, on reduction of pressure, begins to melt. Such "basic" magmas generally have low silica and water content, a high temperature and flow easily—often, as in Hawaii, "quietly erupting" to form volcanoes with very gentle gradients known as shield volcanoes. Silica-rich magma forms under continental crust. Ocean crust sucks up water after it has formed at the oceanic spreading ridges and much of this water later becomes taken with the crust down a subduction zone, where it helps to lower the melting point of both mantle and ocean-crust rocks.

By the time these magmas reach the surface they are cooler and have a higher water content than basalts. These "intermediate" or andesite magmas are also more viscous (less willing to flow) because they contain more silica. The eruptions are more explosive as the water and other gases dissolve out of the magma as it approaches the surface, and the lava remains close to the volcanic vent, building up the archetypal steep-sided conical stratified volcano, such as Mount Fujiyama in Japan. Sometimes the conical form may be destroyed in catastrophic eruptions, as has happened at Mount St Helens in the United States.

The most violent of all eruptions are found where magmas from the mantle have penetrated and melted a great thickness of continental rocks, so as to create highly viscous silica- and water-rich "acid" magmas. As such magmas approach the surface they may turn into a red-hot froth that blasts out from fissures to cover enormous areas in a volcanic material known as ignimbrite. The most extensive eruption known to have occurred in the past 2,000 years was probably on Mount Taupo, on North Island, New Zealand. In AD 150 it discharged some

10 cu km ($2\frac{1}{2}$ cu miles) of ignimbrite in about 15 minutes—spreading across the landscape at more than 100 m (330 ft) per second.

Other more explosive eruptions, such as that of Krakatoa in 1883, or Santorini more than 3,000 years ago, can result in the collapse of the volcano into the underlying magma chamber after it has become partly emptied during an eruption to create a caldera. Many of the largest explosions are caused by the mixing of water with magma—at Krakatoa the cataclysm probably resulted from seawater breaking into the magma and flashing straight to steam, thereby allowing more seawater to enter until the chain reaction could set off more energy than the most powerful nuclear bomb.

Predicting at least the approximate time of an eruption is relatively easy. Small earthquakes indicate that a new batch of magma is rising toward the surface. Many volcanoes also swell prior to an eruption and release gases that indicate the arrival of new magma.

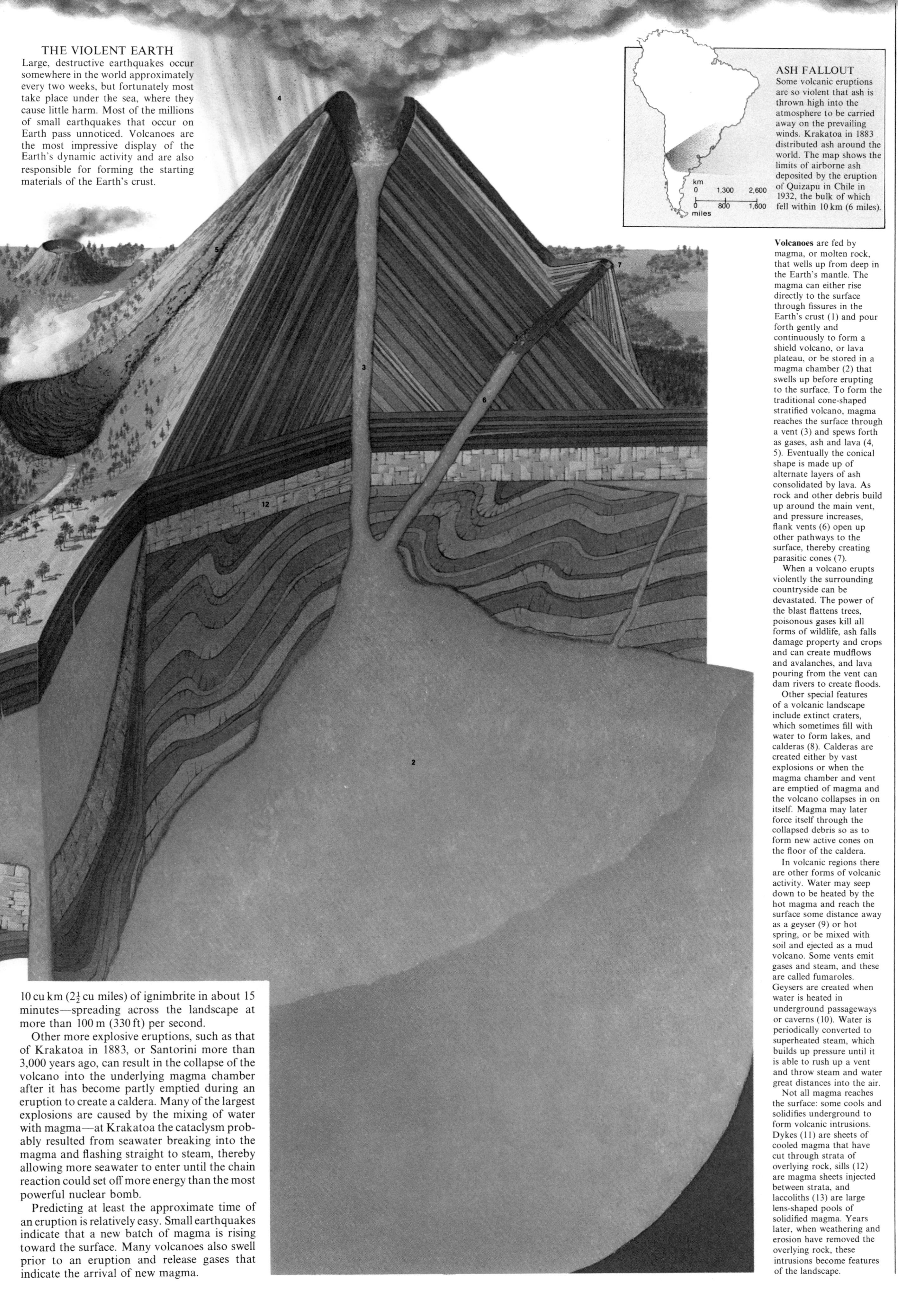

THE VIOLENT EARTH
Large, destructive earthquakes occur somewhere in the world approximately every two weeks, but fortunately most take place under the sea, where they cause little harm. Most of the millions of small earthquakes that occur on Earth pass unnoticed. Volcanoes are the most impressive display of the Earth's dynamic activity and are also responsible for forming the starting materials of the Earth's crust.

ASH FALLOUT
Some volcanic eruptions are so violent that ash is thrown high into the atmosphere to be carried away on the prevailing winds. Krakatoa in 1883 distributed ash around the world. The map shows the limits of airborne ash deposited by the eruption of Quizapu in Chile in 1932, the bulk of which fell within 10 km (6 miles).

Volcanoes are fed by magma, or molten rock, that wells up from deep in the Earth's mantle. The magma can either rise directly to the surface through fissures in the Earth's crust (1) and pour forth gently and continuously to form a shield volcano, or lava plateau, or be stored in a magma chamber (2) that swells up before erupting to the surface. To form the traditional cone-shaped stratified volcano, magma reaches the surface through a vent (3) and spews forth as gases, ash and lava (4, 5). Eventually the conical shape is made up of alternate layers of ash consolidated by lava. As rock and other debris build up around the main vent, and pressure increases, flank vents (6) open up other pathways to the surface, thereby creating parasitic cones (7).

When a volcano erupts violently the surrounding countryside can be devastated. The power of the blast flattens trees, poisonous gases kill all forms of wildlife, ash falls damage property and crops and can create mudflows and avalanches, and lava pouring from the vent can dam rivers to create floods.

Other special features of a volcanic landscape include extinct craters, which sometimes fill with water to form lakes, and calderas (8). Calderas are created either by vast explosions or when the magma chamber and vent are emptied of magma and the volcano collapses in on itself. Magma may later force itself through the collapsed debris so as to form new active cones on the floor of the caldera.

In volcanic regions there are other forms of volcanic activity. Water may seep down to be heated by the hot magma and reach the surface some distance away as a geyser (9) or hot spring, or be mixed with soil and ejected as a mud volcano. Some vents emit gases and steam, and these are called fumaroles. Geysers are created when water is heated in underground passageways or caverns (10). Water is periodically converted to superheated steam, which builds up pressure until it is able to rush up a vent and throw steam and water great distances into the air.

Not all magma reaches the surface: some cools and solidifies underground to form volcanic intrusions. Dykes (11) are sheets of cooled magma that have cut through strata of overlying rock, sills (12) are magma sheets injected between strata, and laccoliths (13) are large lens-shaped pools of solidified magma. Years later, when weathering and erosion have removed the overlying rock, these intrusions become features of the landscape.

The Oceans

Earth is the water planet. Of all the planets of the solar system only the Earth has abundant liquid water, and 97 percent of this surface water is found in the seas and oceans. The water of the oceans appears to be passive and unchanging, whereas the rain and rivers seem active, but this is far from true. In reality the oceans are a turmoil of giant sluggish rivers – far larger than any of the land rivers – and of circulating surface currents that are driven by the prevailing winds.

No topographic map of the Earth can be drawn unless there is some kind of base line from which to measure depths and heights. This base line has always been taken as the level of the sea, yet the sea is perpetually changing level. One can choose some kind of average to call "sea level," but even today different countries have defined that base line in different ways. The currents found within the sea itself can also give the water surface a slope—the calm Sargasso Sea off the northern coast of South America is, for example, about 1.5 m (5 ft) higher than the water to the west adjacent to the Gulf Stream.

Waves

The changes in the level of the sea, at its surface, provide the most familiar image of motion within the waters. Various changes take place over many different time periods, but the most rapid are those that we call waves.

Waves are produced by the wind moving over the water and catching on the surface. They can move at between 15 and 100 km/hr (10–60 mph) and wave crests may be separated by up to 300 m (1,000 ft) in the open ocean. In general, the greater the wavelength, the faster the wave's speed and the farther the distance traveled by the wave. Waves that have traveled a long way from the winds that created them are known as swell. Without the wind continually pushing them they become symmetrical and smooth. Wind waves produce spilling breakers more like the rapids of a mountain torrent, whereas swell produces giant plunging breakers.

A combination of strong winds and low atmospheric pressure associated with storms can cause yet another kind of wave, known as a storm surge. A storm surge is formed by the water being driven ahead of the wind, and rising as the atmospheric pressure weighing down on the water decreases. Where storms drive water into funnel-shaped coasts, the water can rise more than 10 m (33 ft) above normal sea level, flooding large areas of low-lying land at the head of the bay. Venice, the Netherlands and Bangladesh have been particularly subject to destructive storm surges. Other catastrophic changes in sea level have their origins in the seabed. These are tsunamis (Japanese for "high-water in the harbor") and are generally triggered by underwater earthquakes that suddenly raise or lower large areas of the seafloor.

Tides

As the Earth orbits around the Sun the water in the oceans experiences a changing pull of gravity from both the Moon and the Sun. The Sun is overhead once a day, and because the Moon is itself orbiting the Earth, it is overhead once every 24 hours 50 minutes. The pull of gravity from the Sun is less than half that from the Moon, and so it is the Moon that sets the rhythm of the water movements we call tides. The variation in gravitational pull from the Moon is extremely small, however, and even if the whole of the Earth were covered with deep water a tide of only about 30 cm (12 in) would be produced, rushing around the world keeping pace with the circling Moon. Yet the tides in shallow coastal regions are often very much higher than this—for example, up to 18 m (60 ft) in the Bay of Fundy, Canada. The seas and bays with the highest tides are located where the whole mass of water is resonating—rebounding backwards and forwards like water in a bath, as the smaller tides in the outlying oceans push it twice each day.

The Bay of Fundy experiences a particularly high tidal range because it happens to have a resonant frequency—a range of movement—very close to the 12½-hour frequency between tides. Large enclosed seas such as the Mediterranean have very small tides because there is no outside push from an ocean to set them resonating. In contrast, where water movement associated with the tides passes through a narrow channel it can produce tidal currents of up to 30 km/hr (19 mph), such as the famous maelstrom of northern Norway.

After these relatively short-lived disturbances the sea returns to its normal, or at least to its average, level again. When the total volume of free water at the Earth's surface alters, or when the shapes of the ocean basins vary, the sea level itself may start to wander.

How does the volume of water vary? It can be buried in rocks—but the steam clouds above volcanoes return such water so it is normally recycled rather than lost. Some vapor can be broken down through radiation in the upper atmosphere and the hydrogen lost to outer space, but this is relatively insignificant. Or it can be frozen and stacked up on land in the form of ice—this is significant as we are still living in an ice age. The lowest ice-age sea levels produced beaches at about 130 m (430 ft) below present sea level, and the low-lying coastal regions of that period have now become flooded to form the continental shelves.

The salt content of the oceans

Average ocean water contains about 35 parts per 1,000 of salts which include 14 elements in concentrations greater than 1 part per million—the most abundant being sodium and chlorine. Where there is considerable surface evaporation, for example in enclosed seas such as the Dead Sea, the salt concentration builds up and the water becomes denser. Where the sea-surface is turning to ice the salt also becomes concentrated in the water.

The coldest, saltiest ocean water comes from the Antarctic. As it is also the densest it hugs the ocean bottom as it flows northwards, reaching as far as the latitudes of Spain. A similar current from the Arctic is slightly lighter and therefore rides above it—but traveling southwards, as far as the southern Atlantic. A second slightly lighter body of Antarctic water rides above the Arctic water—again traveling northwards. Where these water movements meet each other they rise up, bringing to the surface oxygenated water that can support a profusion of life in oceans that have been compared to a desert because of their lack of biological activity. Unlikely as it seems, it is the icy, stormy, polar waters that provide the lungs of the oceans.

Depth in meters

0 1 2 3 4 5 6 7 8

1 Sun Earth Moon Neap tide

2 Sun Moon Earth Spring tide

3 Sun Moon Earth Neap tide

4 Sun Moon Earth Spring tide

Both the Sun and the Moon exert gravitational pull on the water in the oceans, but the pull of the Sun is less than half that of the Moon. It is the Moon, therefore, that sets the rhythm of the tides. Because the Moon orbits the Earth every 24 hours and 50 minutes, the time of high or low tide advances approximately an hour each day. When the Moon is in its first and last quarters (1, 3) it forms a right angle with the Earth and the Sun and the gravitational fields are opposed, thus causing only a small difference between high and low tide. These are called neap tides. When the Sun, Moon and Earth lie in a straight line (2, 4), at the full and the new Moon, then the high tides become higher and the low tides lower. These are the spring tides. The graph illustrates tidal range over a period of a month.

Depth in meters

0 / 1,000 / 2,000 / 3,000 / 4,000 / 5,000 / 6,000 / 7,000 / 8,000

1 Continent
2 Continental shelf
3 Continental slope
4 Continental rise
5 Submarine canyon
6 Abyssal plain
7 Abyssal hills
8 Mid-ocean ridge
9 Oceanic trench
10 Island arc
11 Continental sea

THE CHANGING OCEANS

Nearly two-thirds of the Earth's surface is covered by the seas and oceans and this great expanse of water is continually in movement. The most familiar movements are waves formed by the wind and the rising and falling tides that respond to the position of the Moon. But even greater movements take place. Currents driven by prevailing winds form whirlpools an ocean in width, and below the surface flow great rivers of colder water. Sea level is also rising as ice melts from the polar caps.

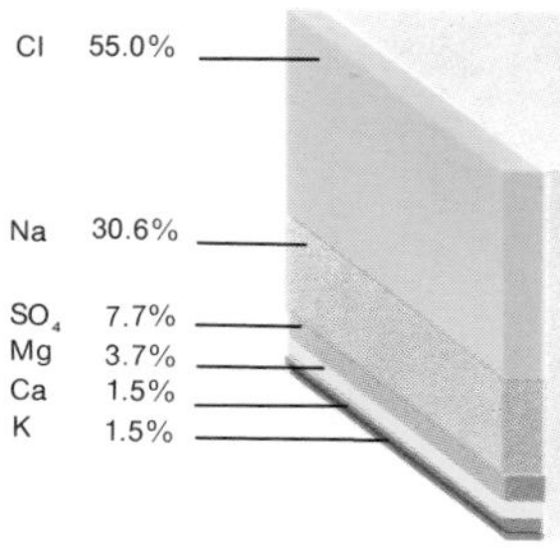

Cl 55.0%
Na 30.6%
SO_4 7.7%
Mg 3.7%
Ca 1.5%
K 1.5%

Seawater is about 96% pure water and the rest is made up of dissolved salts. Many elements are present in minute quantities, but only chlorine (Cl), sodium (Na), sulphate (SO_4), magnesium (Mg), calcium (Ca) and potassium (K) appear in concentrations of more than 1% of the total dissolved salts.

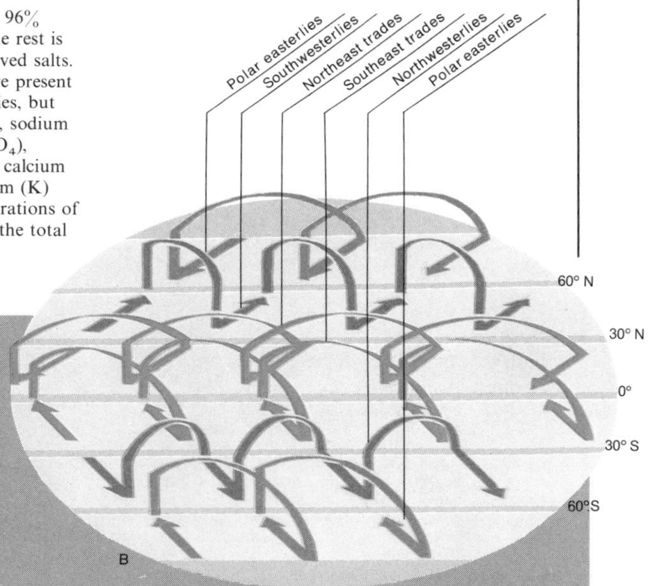

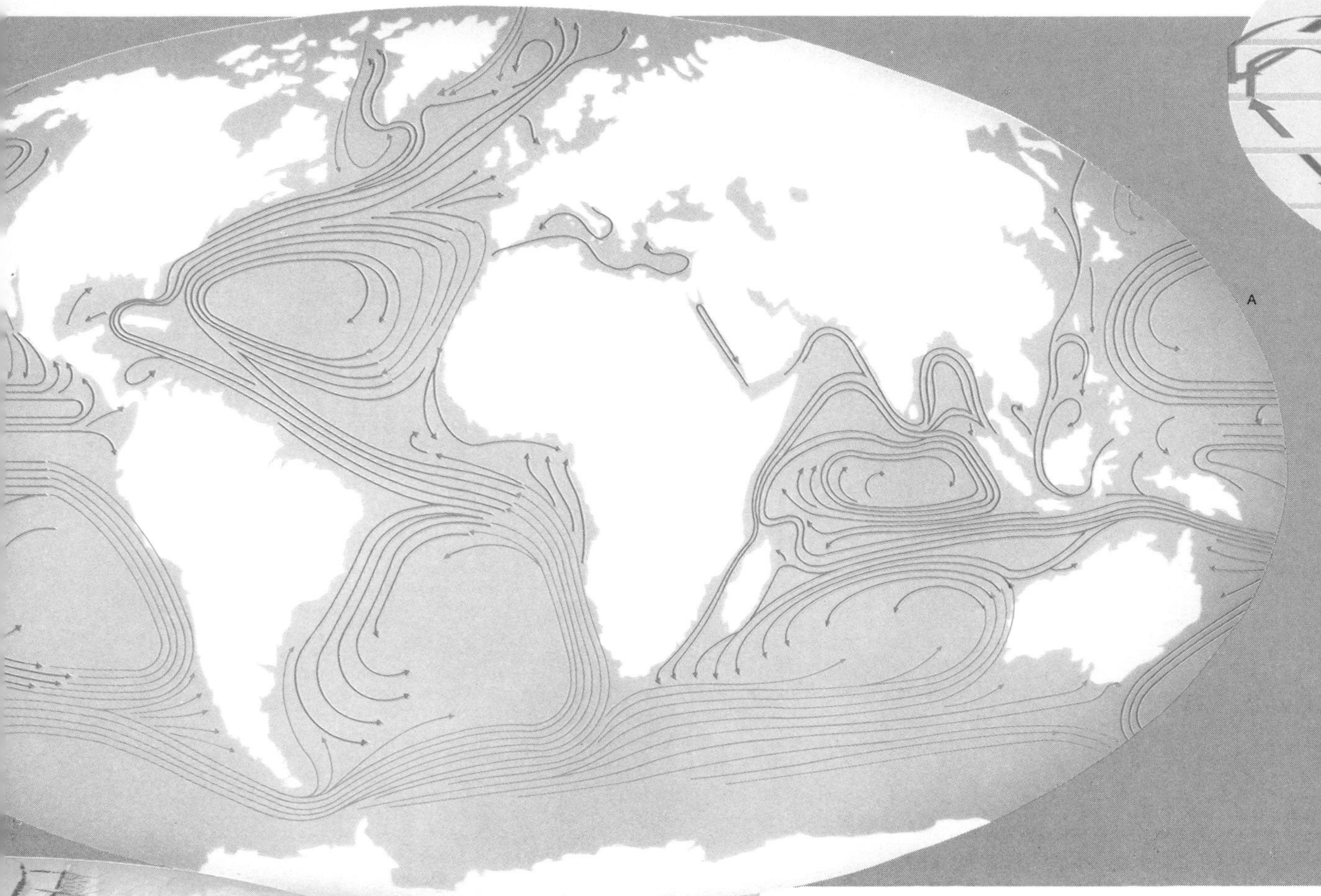

Polar easterlies
Southwesterlies
Northeast trades
Southeast trades
Northwesterlies
Polar easterlies
60° N
30° N
0°
30° S
60° S
B
A

The surface currents of the world's oceans (A) are driven by the prevailing winds (B). The winds and the spinning motion of the Earth drive the currents into gyres—massive whirlpools the width of an ocean. These gyres draw warm water away from the Equator and pull cold polar waters towards it. The centers of gyres are characterized by areas of high pressure, around which winds circulate. Because the Earth is spinning, gyres formed in the northern hemisphere rotate in a clockwise direction, whereas those of the southern hemisphere turn anticlockwise. In all, there are five major gyres, made up of the 38 major named currents. The formation of warm (red) and cold (blue) surface currents is not difficult to understand, given the regions from which they flow. However, even in temperate and subtropical regions, the warm waters of the oceans' surfaces have a permanent layer of cold water beneath them. This cold layer has been formed in the polar regions, where, as the ocean waters have been chilled, they have sunk and then spread out into all the other major ocean basins of the world. The warm subtropical and temperate waters float like an oil slick, from 10 m to 550 m (33–1,900 ft) thick, on top of this cold layer. There is very little mixing between the two layers because the warm water is lighter than the cold water.

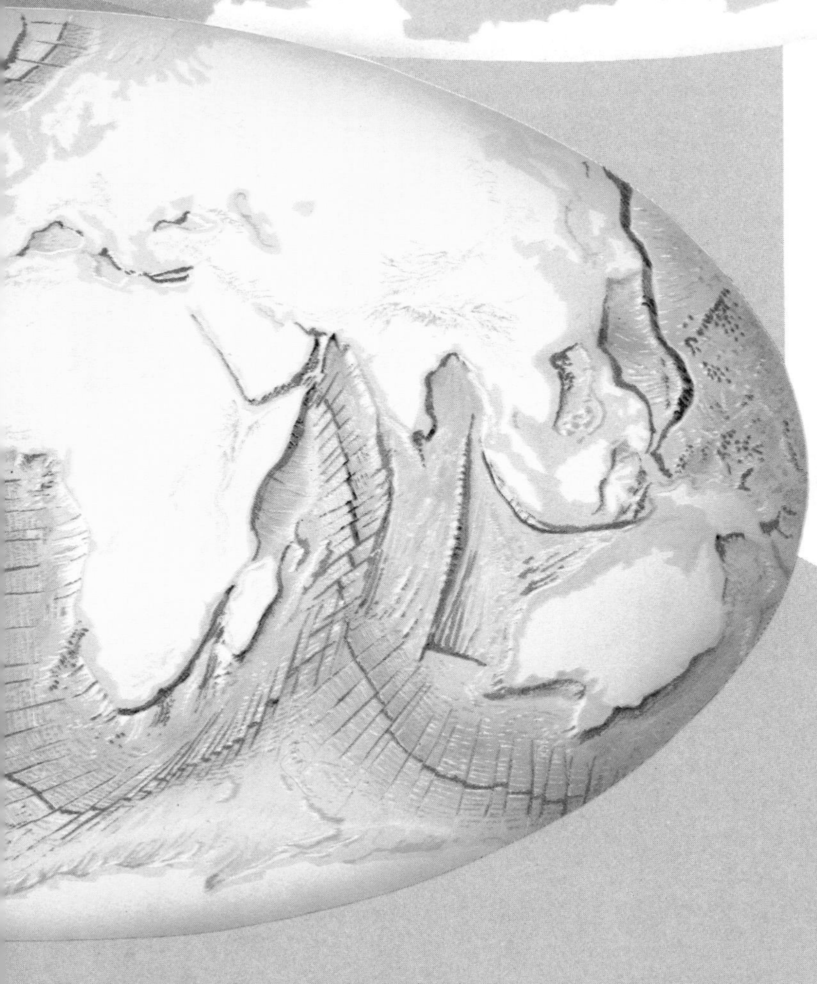

Much of the Earth's water is locked up as ice and stacked on the land. As the ice melts the sea level rises. Only 20,000 years ago the sea level was a full 100 m (330 ft) lower than it is today, and the continental shelves were dry land. About 10,000 years ago the sea level was rising as fast as 3 cm (1 in) each year. Today the melting ice is causing the sea level to rise about 1 mm (0.04 in) each year: only a small increment, but if all the ice melted, the sea level would rise by about 60 m (197 ft) and would flood many of the world's major cities.

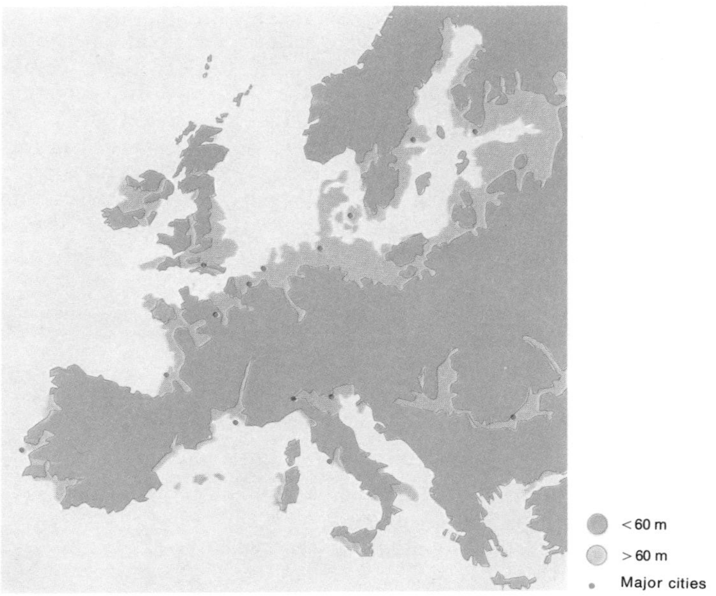

<60 m
>60 m
Major cities

The seabed, more uniform than the land surface, also contains a landscape of underwater features that resemble the plains, valleys and mountains of the continents. Off the edge of continents lie the flat, shallow continental shelves, which are bounded by the steeper incline of the continental slope, which meets the true ocean floor at the continental rise. Here deep submarine canyons may be found. These seem to be in a process of continual erosion from turbidity currents. River water pouring into major estuaries and carrying sediment can also scour out the slope—especially during periods of low sea level. The abyssal plain is rarely interrupted by volcanic hills and mountains. The largest chains are at the mid-ocean ridge, where two crustal plates are moving apart and new ocean floor is being created. At some ocean margins deep trough-shaped valleys or trenches are the sites of ocean floor consumption at a subduction zone. The volcanic island arcs that form behind it sometimes isolate a continental sea.

TSUNAMIS

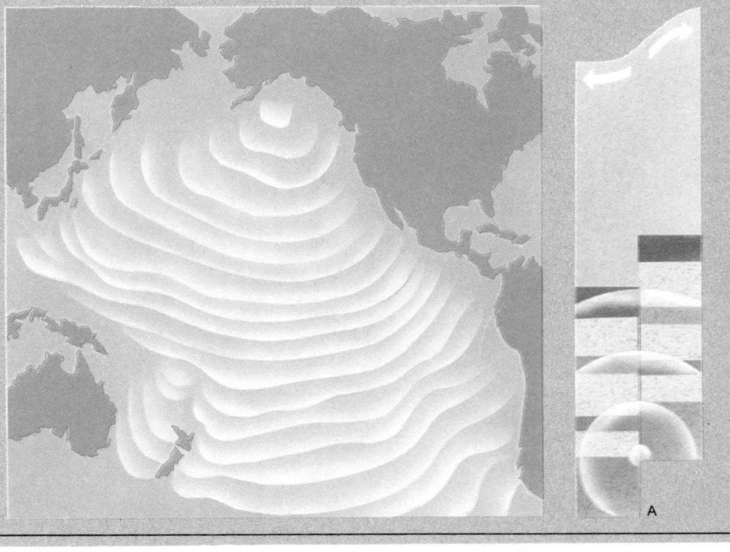

Tsunamis are generated by massive underwater earthquakes (A) and are common around the Pacific. They can travel at more than 700 km/hr (435 mph) and individual waves may occur at intervals of 15 minutes, or 200 km (125 miles). Low-lying atolls of the Pacific have extremely steep sides underwater, and are generally unharmed, but the gently shelving islands such as Hawaii slow down the tsunami and build it into a giant wave 30 m (100 ft) or more in height. This map plots the hourly position of a tsunami that originated south of Alaska.

A

Landscape-makers: Water

Of all the natural agents of erosion at work on the Earth's surface, water is probably the most powerful. Many of the finer details of the landscape, from the contouring of hills and valleys to the broad spread of plains, are the work of water. In recent years we have come to understand more fully the subtle factors at work in a river, for example, as it deepens mountain gorges or builds up sedimentary layers in its approach to the sea. The full force of a waterfall, the instability of a meandering stream, the multiple layering of river terraces – all are features of this most versatile landscape-maker.

Ninety-seven percent of the world's water is in the oceans, another two percent is locked up in the ice caps of Greenland and Antarctica, which leaves one percent only on the surface of Earth, under the ground and in the air. The importance of this one percent is, however, inestimable: most life forms could not exist without it, and yet at the same time many are threatened by it, in the form of flood and storm.

The Sun's energy "powers" the evaporation of water from the oceans. Water vapor then circulates in the atmosphere and is precipitated as rain or snow over land, from which it eventually drains back to the oceans. This is the vast, never-ending water cycle. Water in the air that falls as, for example, rain is replaced on average every 12 days. The total water supply remains constant and is believed to be exactly the same as it was 3,000 million years ago.

From raindrops to rivers

Rain falling on to the surface of the land has a great deal of energy: large drops may hit the ground with a terminal velocity of about 35 km/hr (20 mph). If the rain falls on bare soil, it splashes upwards, breaking off and transporting tiny fragments of soil, which come to rest downhill. Vegetation-covered soil breaks the impact and some of the rain may evaporate without ever reaching the ground.

Soil is rather like a sponge. If the holes or pores are very small, rain finds it difficult to penetrate and water runs over the surface of the soil. If the pores are large, rain infiltrates, filling up the pore spaces. Soils that are thin, have low infiltration rates, or already have a lot of water in them, are very susceptible to overland flow. The water may then concentrate into a channel called a gully, and this can have a dramatic effect upon the landscape. The creation of gullies, together with the splash effect, leads to soil erosion. The problem is particularly severe in semiarid regions, where rainfall is sporadic but intense, vegetation is sparse and overgrazing is common. In extreme cases, badlands are formed and by this time recuperation of the land is impossible or is prohibitively expensive.

Where the infiltration rate is high, water percolates through the soil and eventually into the bedrock. There are two well-defined regions, the saturated and the unsaturated. The upper limit of the saturated zone is the water table. Beneath this, water moves at a rate of a few meters a day, but in rocks such as limestone it can move much more quickly along cracks and joints. In most rock types there are some soluble components which are removed as water continually flows through. In limestone regions, the dissolution of calcium salts results in spectacular cave formations.

Groundwater often provides a vital source for domestic consumption. In porous materials, especially chalk, water is stored in large quantities. Such strata are called aquifers and in some areas, notably North Africa, it is believed that water being pumped up now resulted from rainfall when the climate was wetter tens of thousands of years ago.

Water from a number of sources—from overland flow, soil seepage and springs draining aquifers—produces the flow in rivers. Groundwater appears days or even weeks after a heavy rainfall, but overland flow reaches the channel in hours, producing the sudden peak in flow that may cause flooding and occasionally great damage farther downstream. Flood waves usually rise quickly in mountain areas and the wave moves downstream as the river collects more and more water from its tributaries. Eventually, although the volume continues to increase downstream, the flood wave becomes broader and flatter, so it moves more slowly and causes less damage. The most serious floods occur after intense rainfall on already saturated soils where upland rivers issue on to plains.

Rivers at work

The work of a river from its source to its mouth involves three processes, the first of which is erosion. This includes corrasion, or abrasion—the grinding of rocks and stones against the river's banks and bed—which produces both

A RIVER SYSTEM

Rivers form by the accumulation of runoff water, groundwater and from springs and small streams. Few rivers reach the sea without gaining tributaries, thus forming a river system. Highland regions at source are called catchment areas and the total area drained by a river system is the drainage basin.

The course of a river from source to mouth includes distinctive stages and land forms. All rivers flow from high ground to lower ground. Many rise in an upland area where precipitation is heavy. The upper course is where vertical erosion is dominant and the resulting valley is narrow, deep and V-shaped. A gorge is formed if this downcutting is particularly rapid. If the river has a winding course, the valley walls project to produce interlocking spurs. In the middle course erosion is lateral rather than vertical and the valley takes a more open V-shape. The river may start to meander and bluffs are formed as interlocking spurs are eroded. In the lower course the river deposits much material as it meanders across an almost flat flood plain. The bed is sometimes higher than the plain and the river has raised banks, or levées, formed from material deposited when the river is in flood. Ox-bow lakes are common, as is a delta where the slow-flowing river enters the sea.

The hydrological cycle involves a vast transfer of water from sea to air to land, and back to sea again. Water evaporates from the world's oceans and is carried by maritime air masses towards land, where it condenses and is precipitated in the form of rain or snow. This water then evaporates from the ground surface; drains off the surface into lakes, rivers or seas; seeps as groundwater into rivers, lakes or seas; or is taken in by vegetation from the soil and then transpired.

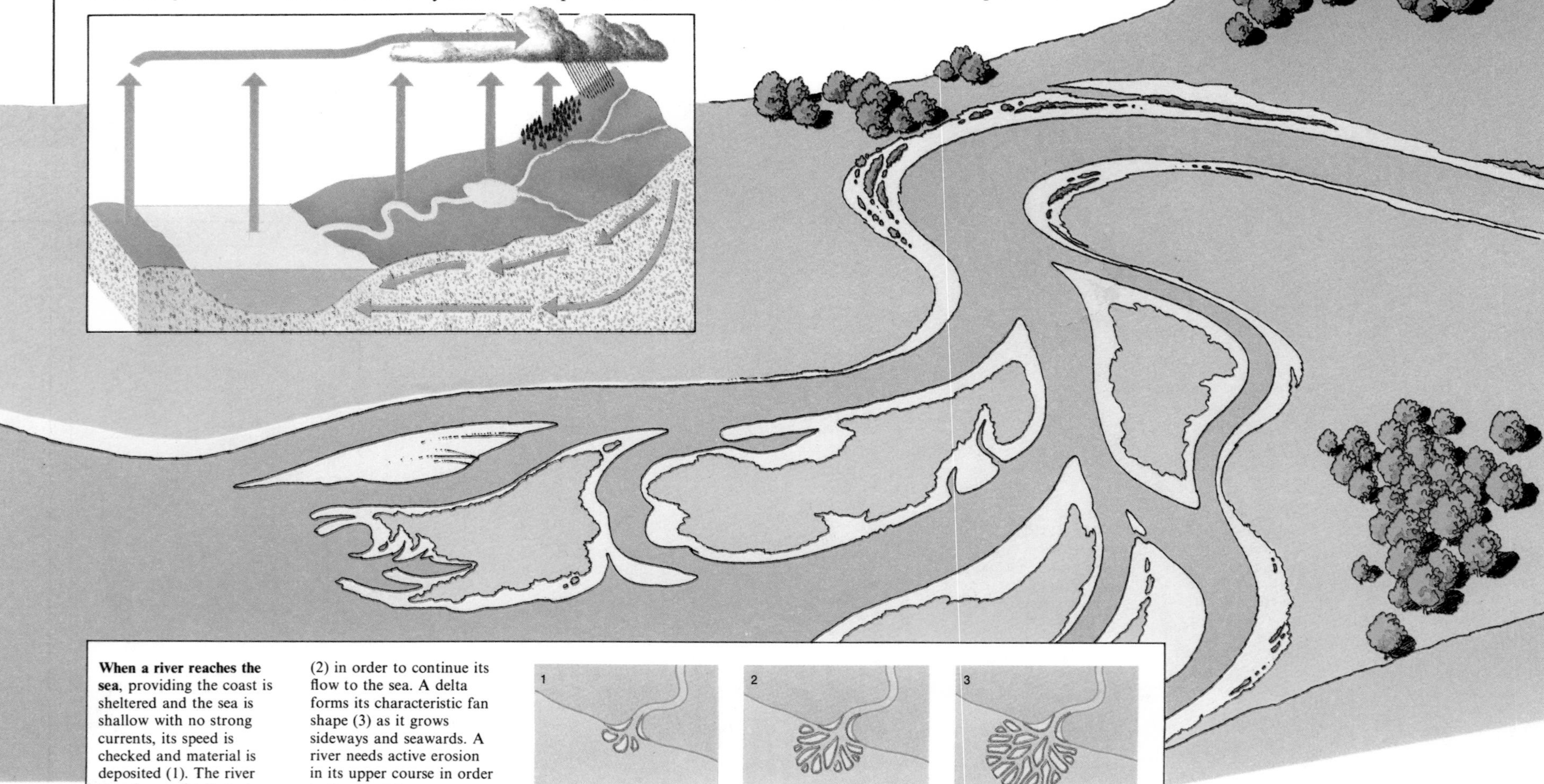

When a river reaches the sea, providing the coast is sheltered and the sea is shallow with no strong currents, its speed is checked and material is deposited (1). The river then forms distributaries (2) in order to continue its flow to the sea. A delta forms its characteristic fan shape (3) as it grows sideways and seawards. A river needs active erosion in its upper course in order to form a delta.

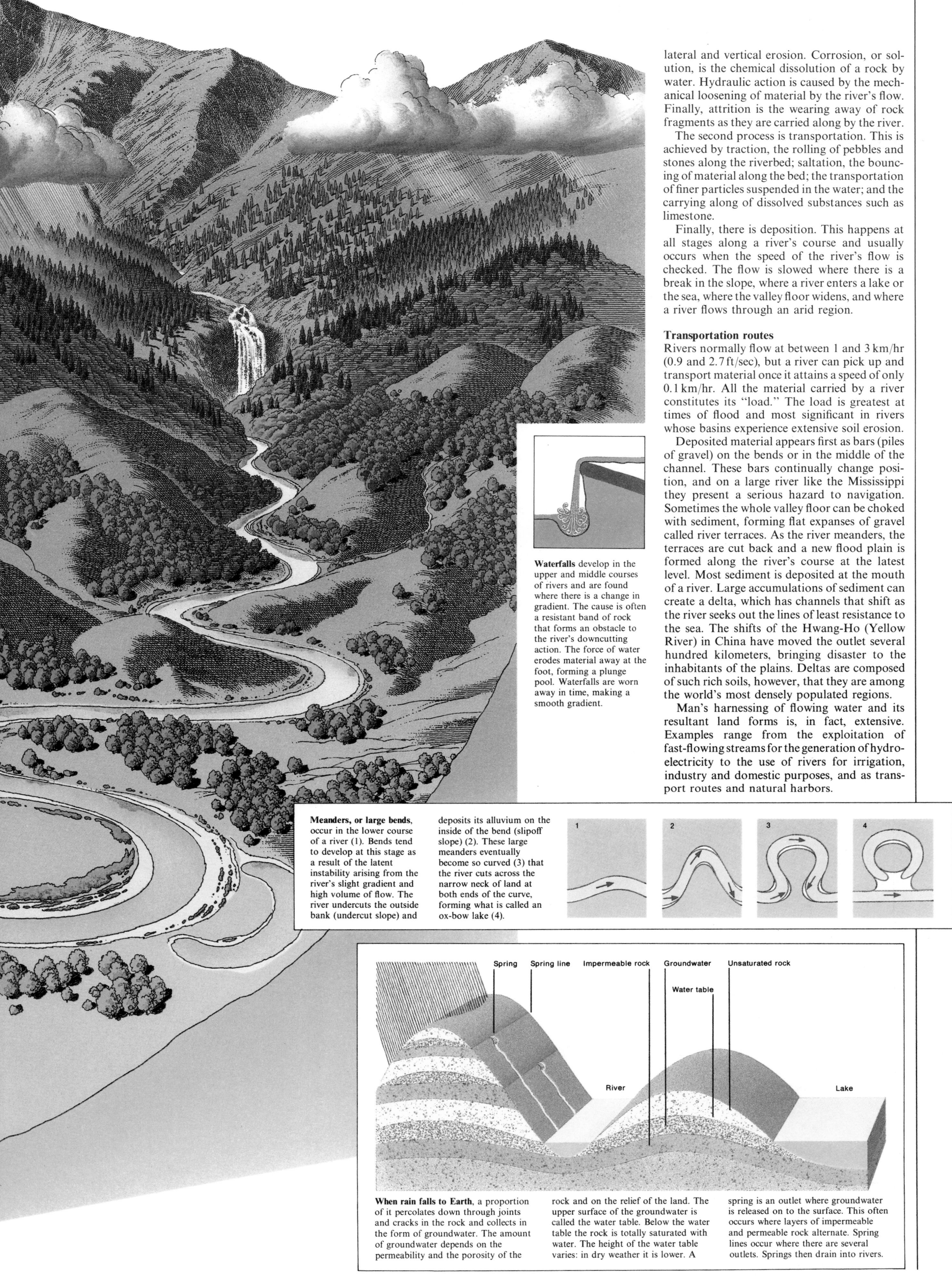

lateral and vertical erosion. Corrosion, or solution, is the chemical dissolution of a rock by water. Hydraulic action is caused by the mechanical loosening of material by the river's flow. Finally, attrition is the wearing away of rock fragments as they are carried along by the river.

The second process is transportation. This is achieved by traction, the rolling of pebbles and stones along the riverbed; saltation, the bouncing of material along the bed; the transportation of finer particles suspended in the water; and the carrying along of dissolved substances such as limestone.

Finally, there is deposition. This happens at all stages along a river's course and usually occurs when the speed of the river's flow is checked. The flow is slowed where there is a break in the slope, where a river enters a lake or the sea, where the valley floor widens, and where a river flows through an arid region.

Transportation routes

Rivers normally flow at between 1 and 3 km/hr (0.9 and 2.7 ft/sec), but a river can pick up and transport material once it attains a speed of only 0.1 km/hr. All the material carried by a river constitutes its "load." The load is greatest at times of flood and most significant in rivers whose basins experience extensive soil erosion.

Deposited material appears first as bars (piles of gravel) on the bends or in the middle of the channel. These bars continually change position, and on a large river like the Mississippi they present a serious hazard to navigation. Sometimes the whole valley floor can be choked with sediment, forming flat expanses of gravel called river terraces. As the river meanders, the terraces are cut back and a new flood plain is formed along the river's course at the latest level. Most sediment is deposited at the mouth of a river. Large accumulations of sediment can create a delta, which has channels that shift as the river seeks out the lines of least resistance to the sea. The shifts of the Hwang-Ho (Yellow River) in China have moved the outlet several hundred kilometers, bringing disaster to the inhabitants of the plains. Deltas are composed of such rich soils, however, that they are among the world's most densely populated regions.

Man's harnessing of flowing water and its resultant land forms is, in fact, extensive. Examples range from the exploitation of fast-flowing streams for the generation of hydroelectricity to the use of rivers for irrigation, industry and domestic purposes, and as transport routes and natural harbors.

Waterfalls develop in the upper and middle courses of rivers and are found where there is a change in gradient. The cause is often a resistant band of rock that forms an obstacle to the river's downcutting action. The force of water erodes material away at the foot, forming a plunge pool. Waterfalls are worn away in time, making a smooth gradient.

Meanders, or large bends, occur in the lower course of a river (1). Bends tend to develop at this stage as a result of the latent instability arising from the river's slight gradient and high volume of flow. The river undercuts the outside bank (undercut slope) and deposits its alluvium on the inside of the bend (slipoff slope) (2). These large meanders eventually become so curved (3) that the river cuts across the narrow neck of land at both ends of the curve, forming what is called an ox-bow lake (4).

When rain falls to Earth, a proportion of it percolates down through joints and cracks in the rock and collects in the form of groundwater. The amount of groundwater depends on the permeability and the porosity of the rock and on the relief of the land. The upper surface of the groundwater is called the water table. Below the water table the rock is totally saturated with water. The height of the water table varies: in dry weather it is lower. A spring is an outlet where groundwater is released on to the surface. This often occurs where layers of impermeable and permeable rock alternate. Spring lines occur where there are several outlets. Springs then drain into rivers.

Landscape-makers: Ice and Snow

A series of glacial periods has punctuated the Earth's history for the last two million years. During the last glacial, the ice covered an area nearly three times larger than that covered by ice sheets and glaciers today. Its remnants are still found in the ice caps of the world: most present-day glacial ice is in Antarctica and Greenland in two great ice sheets which together contain about 97 percent of all the Earth's ice. The rest is in glaciers in Iceland, the Alps and other high mountain chains.

During the Earth's major glacial periods, ice sheets almost as big as that of present-day Antarctica spread over the northern part of North America, reaching as far south as the Ohio River, and over northern Europe as far south as southern England, the Netherlands and southern Poland. Today glacial activity is more restricted, but the mechanisms by which it carves dramatic features of the Earth's landscape remain the same.

Types of glacier

There are six main types of ice mass: cirque glaciers, which occupy basin-shaped depressions in mountain areas; valley glaciers; piedmont glaciers, in which the ice spreads in a lobe over a lowland; floating ice tongues and ice shelves; mountain ice caps; and ice sheets. Climate and relief are responsible for these differences, but glaciers can also be classified according to their internal temperatures.

Cold glaciers are those in which the ice temperature is below freezing point and they are frozen to the rock beneath. This condition, which hinders the movement of glaciers, exists in many parts of Antarctica and Greenland, where air temperatures are low, as well as at high altitudes in some lower-latitude mountain regions. Temperate glaciers, on the other hand, show internal temperatures at or close to the melting point of ice. Unlike cold glaciers, they are not frozen to the rock beneath and can therefore slide over it. Ice melts on the surface of the glacier when the weather is warm, and underneath the glacier as it is warmed by geothermal heat from inside the Earth. Streams collecting meltwater may flow over, through or under the ice and emerge at the ice edge. In other glaciers, cold ice may overlie temperate ice.

Glaciers are formed from snow that, as it accumulates year after year, becomes compacted, turning first into "névé" or "firn" and eventually, after several years or even decades, into glacial ice. This process of accumulation is offset by ablation, through which ice is lost by melting, evaporation or, in glaciers that end in the sea or in lakes, by calving. If accumulation exceeds ablation, the glacier increases in size; conversely, if ablation is higher, the glacier shrinks and eventually disappears.

Glaciers move because of the force of gravity. The fastest-moving glaciers, for example those of coastal Greenland which descend steeply from areas of great accumulation, move at speeds of more than 20 m (65 ft) a day. A few meters a day is more common, however. Some glaciers move exceptionally quickly in surges, which usually last for a few weeks; rates of more than 100 m (330 ft) a day have been recorded. At the other extreme, some glaciers or parts of glaciers—the central zones of ice sheets and ice caps for example—are virtually motionless. When the ice in a glacier is subject to pressure or tension—as it flows down a valley, for example—it behaves rather like a plastic substance and changes its shape to fit the contours of the valley. Part or all of the movement of a glacier is accomplished by means of this internal deformation. In temperate glaciers, or glaciers whose lower layers are temperate, there is also basal sliding. Movement of a glacier produces cracks or crevasses in areas where stress exceeds the strength of the ice.

The work of glaciers

Glaciers and ice sheets can profoundly modify the landscape by both erosion and deposition. Measured rates of erosion of bedrock may be as much as several millimeters a year. Rock surfaces are scratched, or striated, and worn down by the constant grinding action (abrasion) of rock fragments embedded in the base of the ice. The extreme pressure of thick glacial ice on a basal boulder has been known to rupture solid bedrock beneath it.

The products of bedrock erosion range from fine clays and silts produced by abrasion, to large boulders picked up and transported by the ice. Some rocks have been carried hundreds of kilometers, from southern Scandinavia to

A U-shaped valley, such as Langdale (below) in the English Lake District, is a clear indication of a glaciated past. The floor is quite flat and the valley sides rise steeply from it.

A crevasse (below left) is created by stress within a glacier. Internally, the ice is rather like plastic but its surface is rigid and brittle. This causes tension and cracking on the surface.

This erratic (below right) is made of Silurian grit, yet it sits on a limestone perch. Ice left Yorkshire 20,000 years ago, since when the limestone surface has been lowered by solution.

Before the onset of glaciation a mountain region is often sculpted largely by the work of rivers and the processes of weathering. The hills are rounded and the valleys are V-shaped (1). During a period of glacial activity, valleys become filled with snow and eventually glaciers and, after thousands of years, the region shows a typically glaciated landscape (2). When the ice has finally disappeared there remains a glacial trough (3) with hanging valleys, truncated spurs, waterfalls and all the landforms associated with deposition of material.

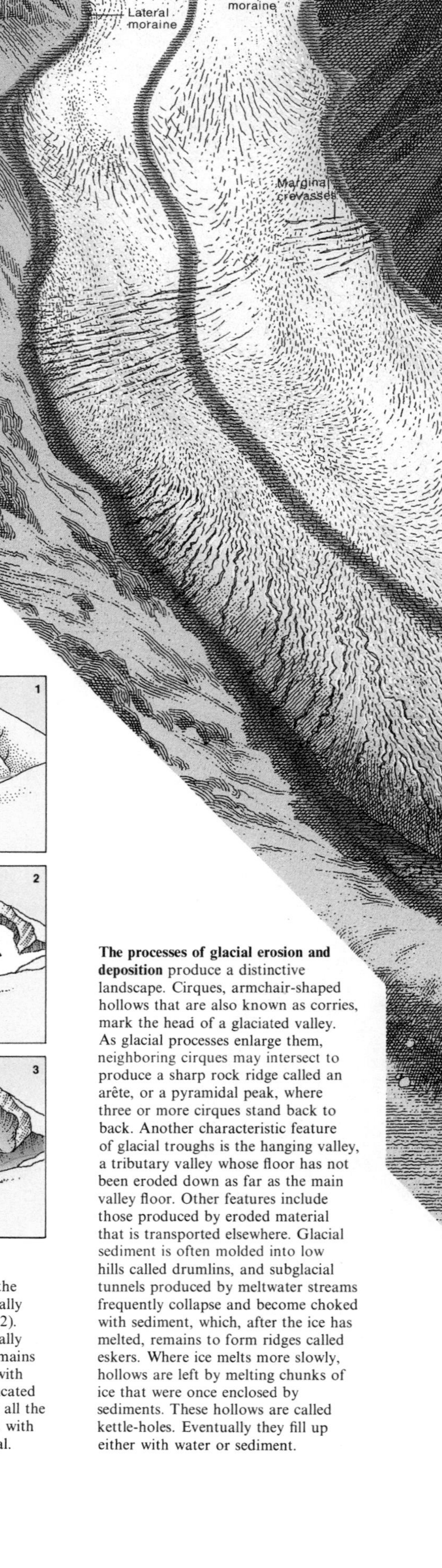

The processes of glacial erosion and deposition produce a distinctive landscape. Cirques, armchair-shaped hollows that are also known as corries, mark the head of a glaciated valley. As glacial processes enlarge them, neighboring cirques may intersect to produce a sharp rock ridge called an arête, or a pyramidal peak, where three or more cirques stand back to back. Another characteristic feature of glacial troughs is the hanging valley, a tributary valley whose floor has not been eroded down as far as the main valley floor. Other features include those produced by eroded material that is transported elsewhere. Glacial sediment is often molded into low hills called drumlins, and subglacial tunnels produced by meltwater streams frequently collapse and become choked with sediment, which, after the ice has melted, remains to form ridges called eskers. Where ice melts more slowly, hollows are left by melting chunks of ice that were once enclosed by sediments. These hollows are called kettle-holes. Eventually they fill up either with water or sediment.

THE SNOW LINE

Glaciation is still evident today in regions that are above the snow line—the lowest limit of perpetual snow cover. The height of the snow line varies with latitude: from about 5,200 m (17,000 ft) at the Equator, to 2,700 m (9,000 ft) in the Alps, to 1,200 m (4,000 ft) in Scandinavia and sea level nearer the north and south polar regions.

A glaciated valley exhibits a distinctive shape and profile. A cross section shows a U-shape, while longitudinally the valley floor is marked by a series of rocky steps and basins. The zone of accumulation is characterized by a cirque, in which snow collects to produce a firn field. A bergschrund is a type of crevasse that opens up near the top of the firn field where the head of the glacier is pulled away from the cirque walls. A rock step is where the gradient becomes much steeper. The speed of the ice flow is accelerated and consequent tension within the ice creates a number of deep crevasses called an ice fall. The zone of ablation has large accumulations of various kinds of rock debris.

Glacial erosion of rock surfaces is typified by a roche moutonnée, a resistant rock hummock that lies in the path of the ice. The upstream side is smooth as a result of abrasion by rock debris that is frozen into the base of the glacier. This debris scratches and scrapes rock, producing striations. The downstream side is rough as a result of ice plucking. Meltwater removes the small blocks of rock.

A great variety of material arrives at the terminus or snout of a glacier—ranging from large blocks of rock and boulders to very finely ground rock "flour." All the material is dropped in a haphazard way as the ice melts. The mixture of clay and boulders is termed glacial till. If the ice margin remains stationary, till accumulates to form a terminal moraine. If the snout recedes continuously, no ridge forms.

eastern England, for example, and such far-traveled rocks are termed erratics. The finer sediments, compacted at the base of the glacier by the weight of the overlying ice, form till or boulder clay.

The surface of a glacier is often strewn with rock debris, which either rests on the ice or is within the glacier and revealed as the ice melts. Lateral moraines consist of rock debris that has accumulated along the sides of the glacier as a result of rockfall from, and erosion of, the valley sides. Where two glaciers join, the inner lateral moraines merge to form a medial moraine. In the ablation zone, the surface of the glacier becomes increasingly laden with debris "melting out" so that the ice may become completely buried. At the end of the glacier all rock debris is dumped, forming a terminal moraine.

Meltwater streams pouring out from glaciers or flowing in tunnels beneath them can be powerful agents of erosion and can transport large quantities of sediment. Bedrock surfaces become potholed and carved by channels that are eroded with great speed. As the streams emerge from the edge of the ice, they carry with them and deposit vast quantities of sand and gravel which form flood plains (outwash plains). Alternatively, meltwater streams may deposit sediment between the edge of the glacier and valley side, leaving a "kame terrace" when the ice finally melts. Meltwater streams feeding glacial lakes that are dammed by a glacier or moraine, for example, construct deltas of sand and gravel and lay down finer sediments (varved clays) on the lake floor.

Snow processes

Snow plays a smaller part than glacial ice in landform sculpture. Its most important role is in avalanches, which, in mountain regions, regularly bring down thousands of tonnes of rock debris. The mixture of snow, rock and other debris forms avalanche boulder tongues on the flat ground where the avalanche comes to rest and the snow melts. Gullies (avalanche chutes) on mountain slopes are swept clean of loose debris several times a year and they are gradually enlarged. Snow patches that remain stationary on more gentle slopes or in hollows encourage rock weathering under and around them. Such a process, termed nivation, may lead to deepening and enlargement of hollows and further snow accumulation. This is one way in which new glaciers are formed.

Landscape-makers: The Seas

The coastline is both the birthplace and the graveyard of the land. Over tens of thousands of years, geological uplift of a continent, or a fall in sea level, may create an emerging fringe of new land, whereas a period of submergence drowns the coasts and floods the adjacent river valleys, destroying land but producing some of the most attractive coastal landscapes. More rapid are the changes brought about by the sea itself. Erosion of coastal rocks or beaches can cut back the coastline at a rate of several meters a year, whereas other coastlines are built up at a comparable rate from marine sediments.

Changing coastlines are apparent on a human time scale. In temperate latitudes, beaches tend to be combed down and narrowed by winter waves, only to be restored during the calmer weather of summer. They may be lost one week and replenished the next, demonstrating an invaluable ability to recover from the wounds of all but the most devastating storms. Cliffs are generally much less dynamic, particularly if composed of resistant rock, but any loss that they suffer is permanent because there is no process that is capable of rebuilding them.

Coasts vary greatly around the world. Tropical areas often have wide beaches made up of fine material which in many cases forms broad mangrove swamps that collect sediment and build up the coast. In more exposed tropical zones coral reefs are common, either fringing the shore or (particularly where the sea level is rising) separated from the shore by a lagoon to give a barrier reef. Continued submergence of a small island surrounded by such a reef may produce an atoll. In contrast, Arctic beaches are narrow and coarse, and may be icebound for up to 10 months each year. Recession of soft rock cliffs results more from melting of ice in the ground than from wave erosion.

Waves at work

Across great expanses of open ocean energy is transferred from the wind to the sea surface to produce waves, thus fueling the machine that ultimately creates the coast. Originating as waves with heights of up to 20 or even 30 m (65–100 ft), they lose part of their energy quite rapidly as they travel, and once they have been reduced in height to the lower but more widely spaced ocean swell, they continue to travel across enormous distances.

The coasts of western Europe receive waves produced almost 10,000 km (6,200 miles) away off Cape Horn, and swell reaching California has sometimes crossed more than 11,000 km

Cliffs are attacked by waves at the zone that lies between high tide (HT) and low tide (LT). The rate of erosion depends on the strength and jointing pattern of the rock and the angle at which the strata are presented to the sea. Erosion begins when water and rocks are hurled at the cliff and new fragments are broken off. The pressure of the water also compresses air in joints and cracks to shatter the rock face. As the base of the cliff is attacked, a notch (1) may be cut, and as this is made deeper the cliff above collapses. Eventually a wave-cut platform (2) is created, the top of which is exposed at low tide. The debris from the cliff is carried along the coast or deposited offshore (3). The shallow seabed now slows down incoming waves: they attack the cliff (4), but their energy is reduced. In calm water, for example at the head of a bay (5), wave energy is diffused and light material such as sand is deposited as beaches.

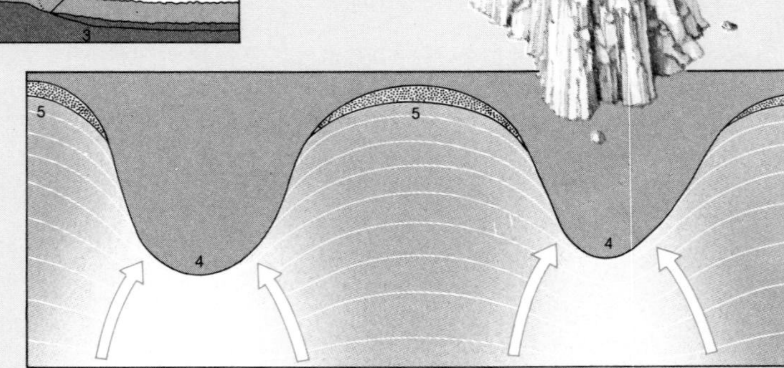

Light material such as mud, sand and shingle is carried by the sea. Waves tend to push the particles obliquely up a beach (right), but the backwash moves the material down again at right-angles to the shore. Thus the materials move in a zigzag fashion along the beach (1). This is known as longshore drift. When the load-carrying capacity of the waves is reduced for any reason, the material is deposited and forms a variety of features. The largest beaches (2) are found in the calmest waters such as in bays or at river mouths, with the finest grains sorted out nearest to the sea and larger pebbles stranded higher up. Spits (3) and bars (4) are sand ridges deposited across a bay or river mouth. When one end of the ridge is attached to the land it is called a spit. Spits are very often shaped like a hook as waves are refracted around the tip of land. Bars are formed where sand is deposited in shallow water offshore across the entrances to bays and run parallel to the coastline. Dunes, pictured above, are formed when sand on the beach is driven inland by onshore winds. Very often they isolate flooded land behind them to form coastal features such as salt marshes and mud flats.

THE SEA COAST

The coastline is continually changing, whether day by day as the tides sift and sort the sand and shingle on the beaches, or over tens of thousands of years as the erosive power of waves carves out headlands and bays. And over millions of years the coastline is subjected to major changes of sea level, whether it is the land uplifting or sinking, or the sea itself rising or receding. Today, interference by man can damage the coast. Dam building and river-channel engineering drastically reduce the amount of sediment reaching the coast; and sea walls built to protect the coast and groynes constructed to retard sand removal both pose a long-term threat to adjacent coasts, which become starved of the sediment that previously supplied their beaches.

When a headland has been created (below), wave erosion continues on both sides and a cave (1) may be formed. After many years of wave action the cave will break through to the other side and an arch (2) may be created.

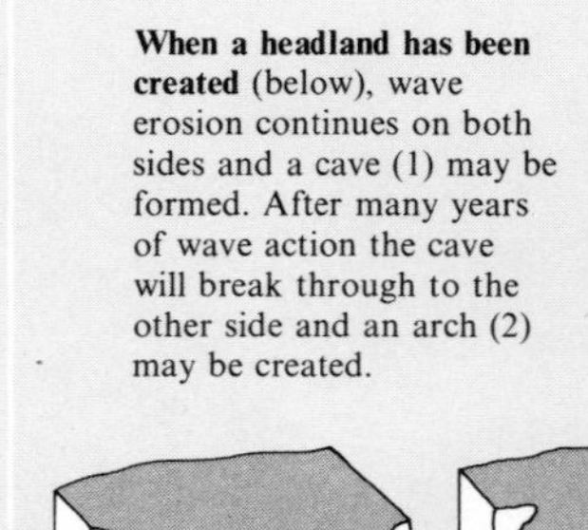

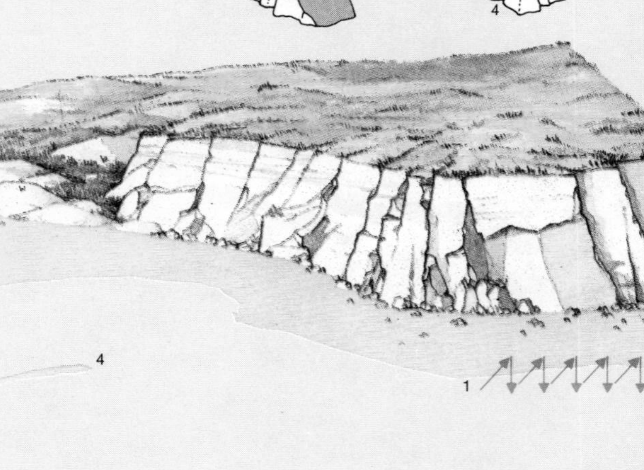

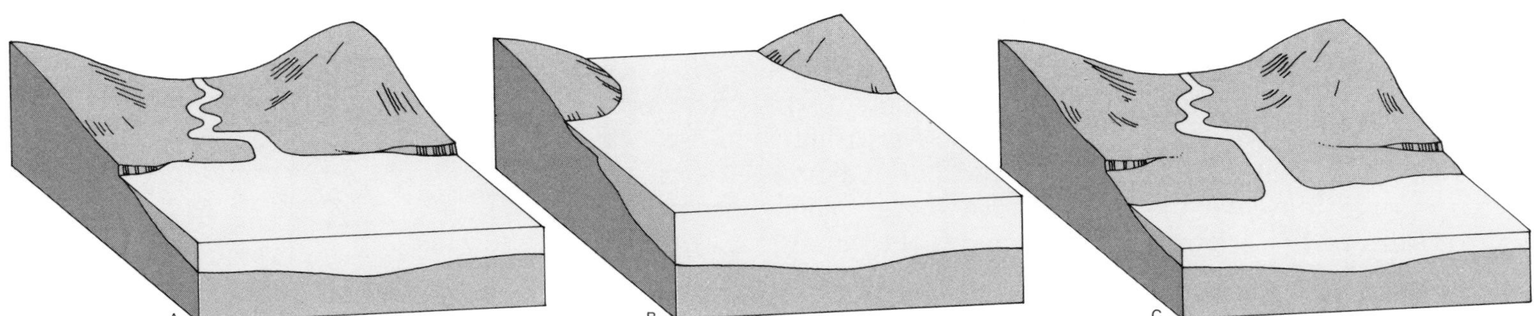

There are two major kinds of coastline—coastlines of submergence and coastlines of emergence. They are created by either a sinking or an uplift of the land, or by a change in sea level. A coastline with wave-cut cliffs and a river valley (A), for example, that experiences a rise in sea level will produce a new coastline (B) with a drowned estuary, coastal uplands isolated as islands, and a submerged coastal plain. The same coastline subjected to a drop in sea level (C) results in an extended river, abandoned cliffs far inland, and a raised beach that forms a new coastal plain.

(6,800 miles) of the Pacific from the storm belt south of New Zealand. The waves thus act as a giant conveyor for the energy that is finally used up in a few seconds of intense activity. Few other natural systems gather their energy so widely and then concentrate it so effectively.

A ball floating on the sea surface shows that, although a passing wave form moves forward, the water (and ball) follow a near-circular path and end up almost where they started. Beneath the surface the water follows similar orbits, but the amount of movement becomes progressively less with depth, until it dies out altogether. The greater the wavelength (the distance between crests) the greater is the depth of disturbance.

Long-swell waves approaching a gentle shore start disturbing the seabed far from the coast and these waves slow up, pack closer together and increase in height until they become unstable, thus producing the spilling white surf that carries much sediment to build up wide sandy beaches. Shorter local storm waves disturb the water to less depth, and thus reach much closer inshore before they interact with the seabed. Such waves do not therefore break until they plunge directly down on to the beach, leading to severe erosion, which results in the production of steep pebble beaches.

Waves slow up in shallow water, and so an undulating seabed causes their crests to bend and change their direction of approach. As a result, waves converge toward headlands (where their erosional attack is concentrated), but they diverge as they enter bays, spreading out their energy and encouraging the deposition of the sediment they carry across the seabed close inshore. The high-energy waves at the headlands remove any rock fragments that become detached and transport them to the beaches that form at the bayheads.

Erosional coasts

Much of the local variability of coastal scenery results from differing rates of erosion on different types of rock. Bays are cut back rapidly into soft rocks such as clay, sand or gravel. Headlands are evidence that the sea takes longer to remove higher areas of harder rock such as granite or limestone. Despite the enormous power of storm waves, erosion of resistant rocks is slow and relies on any weakness that the sea can exploit.

Joints, faults and bedding planes are etched out by the water and by rock fragments hurled against them by breaking waves. Air compressed into such crevices by water pressure widens and deepens them into cracks and then into caves. In this way a solid cliff face can be eroded to form the great variety of features.

Resistant rocks can form steep, simple cliffs of great height—more than 600 m (2,000 ft) in some places—and the sea may have to undercut them to produce collapse and retreat. Cliffs of weaker rocks rarely reach 100 m (330 ft) in height and are more rapidly eroded by atmospheric processes, by running water and by landslips. There the role of the sea is largely confined to removing the rock debris from the foot of the cliff. Soft rock cliffs are gently sloping but complex in form.

Coasts of deposition

Although waves bend as they approach the shore, they rarely become completely parallel to the coastline. Wave crests drive sediment obliquely toward the beach, whereas the troughs carry it back directly offshore down the beach slope. In this way, sand and pebbles are transported in a zigzag motion, called longshore drift, away from the areas where they are produced. One such source of material is cliff erosion, but on average about 95 percent of the material moving on to beaches was originally carried to the coast by rivers.

Beaches are built up wherever longshore drift is impeded (for example, by a headland) or where wave and current energy is reduced (as at the head of a bay). An abundant supply of sediment may build a sandbar across the mouth of a bay or in shallow water offshore. Where the coast changes direction, longshore drift may continue in its original direction and build a spit out from the land. Depositional features may become strengthened by vegetation. Plants may take root and bind together newly deposited sediments, but they constitute relatively delicate coasts that are vulnerable to erosion if for any reason they are not continually supplied with fresh deposits of sediment.

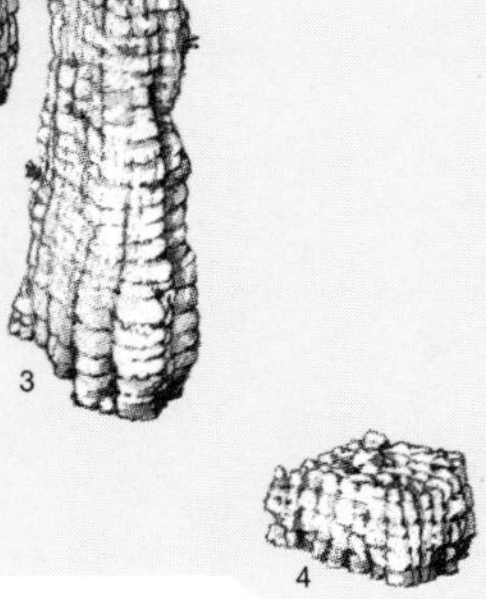

2
3
4

Further wave erosion (above) causes the roof of the arch to collapse, leaving an isolated column of rock called a stack (3). Another cave, and then an arch, may be formed behind the stack, which itself may be eroded to a short stump (4).

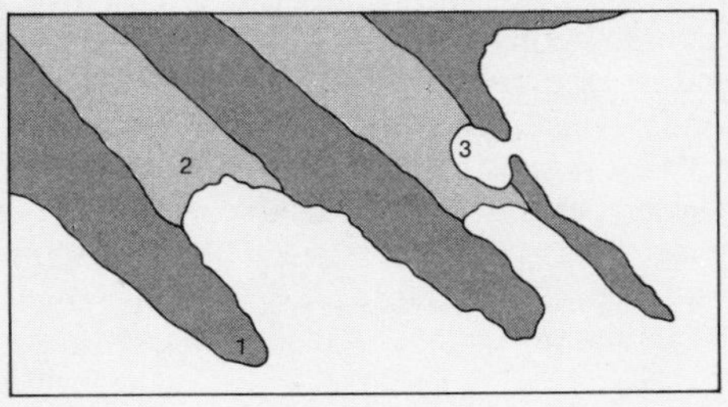

Headlands alternating with bays are found where bands of strong (1) and weak (2) rocks meet the coast at an angle and there is a varied resistance to erosion. The bays are first carved out of the softer rock, leaving the waves to attack the headlands of hard rock. If, in contrast, the strata lie parallel to the coast, then the hard rock has few irregular indentations except where the sea has broken through to the soft rock behind and has scoured out a cove (3).

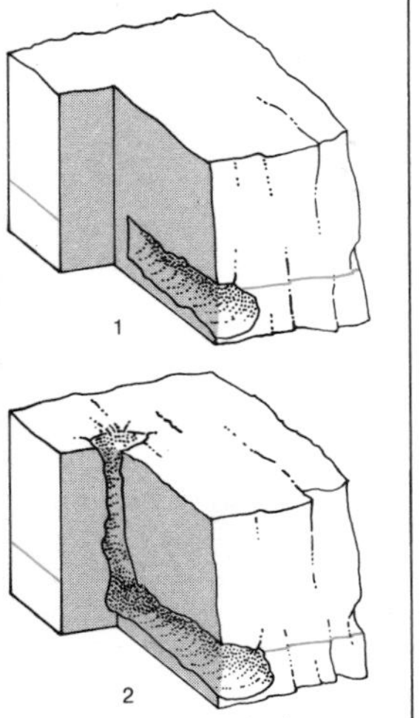

1
2
3

1
2

Gloups are formed when waves first erode a cave, then extend it backward as a long shaft running into the cliff (1). If the roof collapses at one point, a blowhole, or gloup (2), is formed. If the whole roof collapses, a deep cleft called a geo is created.

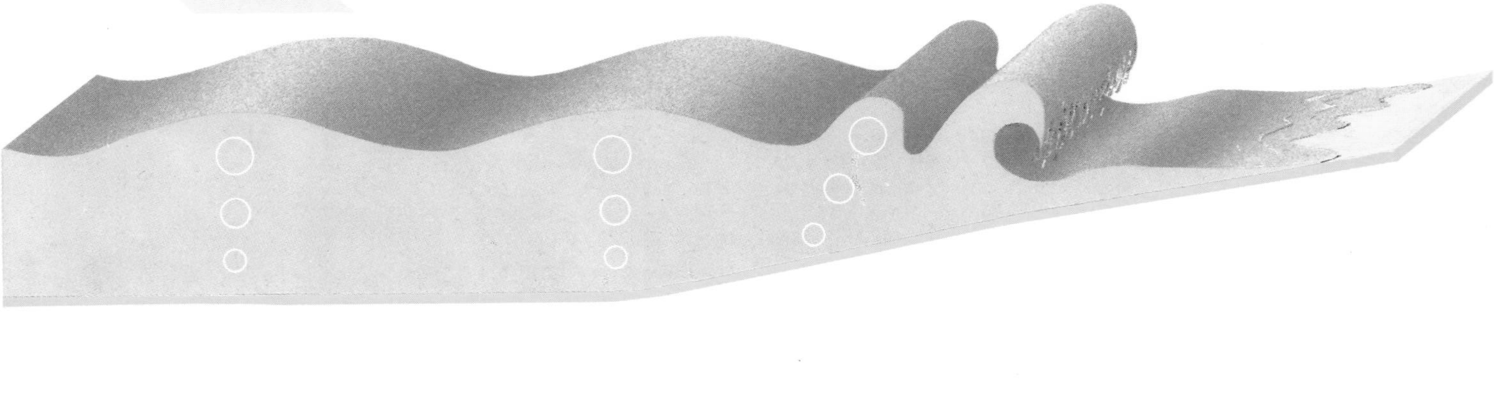

Waves are generated by wind on the surface of the sea. It is the shape of the wave that travels forward—the individual water particles move in near-circular orbits. Disturbance diminishes with depth to about half a wavelength. Waves break when they strike a sloping shore, and the wave height is about the same as the depth of the water.

Landscape-makers: Wind and Weathering

Winds are part of the global circulation of air and they can affect landforms wherever surface material is loose and unprotected by vegetation. The effects of a strong wind are a familiar sight—whether in the dust clouds that rise from a plowed field after a dry spell, or in the sand swept along the beach on a windy day. Weathering is the disintegration and decomposition of rocks through their exposure to the atmosphere. It includes the changes that destroy the original structure of rocks, and few on the Earth's surface have not been weathered at one time or another in the history of our evolving landscape.

Sand dunes cover only 20 percent of the world's deserts, and tend to be concentrated in a small number of sand seas, or ergs, such as the Erg Bourharet in Algeria (above).

Active and fixed dunes in Africa and western Asia

Fixed sand dunes

Active sand dunes

Most sand seas today are being actively molded by winds. The landscape has long been shaped by wind, and some dune fields produced in dry climates in the distant past may be "fossilized" now by soils and vegetation cover. Desertification often occurs where this vegetation is disturbed by man.

Direction of wind

Longitudinal, or seif, dunes (below) are long, narrow ridges that lie parallel to the direction of prevailing winds. Surface heating and wind flow produce vertical spiraling motions of air.

Many rocks are formed deep in the Earth, where they are in equilibrium with the forces that created them. If they become exposed at the surface, they are in disequilibrium with atmospheric forces. This brings about the changes—adjustments to atmospheric and organic agents—that we call weathering. Products of weathering are moved by agents of erosion, one of which is the wind. Where the surface is protected, for example by vegetation, the wind has little effect, but where strong winds attack loose surface material that is unprotected, erosion, abrasion and deposition may occur, producing characteristic landforms.

How wind shapes the surface

Strong winds occur in many places, but nowhere are they more effective in forming the surface of the land than in deserts, where their work is largely unhindered by vegetation. There the wind can pick up material and then, charged with sand particles, blast away at the ground, carrying away the debris and depositing it. Many notorious desert winds are associated with sand movement and dust storms—the harmattan of West Africa and the sirocco of the Middle East, for example.

Wind erosion occurs where winds charged with sand attack soils or rock. Dry soils may be broken up and the resulting debris, which includes soil nutrients, is carried away as dust. This poses a serious problem, especially when arid and semiarid lands experience drought. Wind erosion involving the lifting and blowing away of loose material from the ground surface is called deflation.

Erosion by sand and rock fragments carried by winds is called abrasion. In this way winds erode individual surface pebbles into distinctive shapes known as ventifacts. They can also mold larger rock masses into aerodynamic shapes known as yardangs—features that often look rather like upturned rowing boats. Some of these features are so large that they have been identified only since satellite photographs have become available. Finally, winds erode by attrition, which involves the mutual wearing down of particles as they are carried along.

Winds can transport material in three different ways. They can lift loose, sand-sized particles into the air and carry them downwind along trajectories that resemble those of ballistic missiles: the particles rise steeply and descend along gentle flight paths. This produces a bouncing movement known as saltation in a layer extending approximately 1 m (3 ft) above the

EROSION AND WEATHERING

Winds result from the differential heating of regions of the globe. They act indirectly as agents of erosion through water or waves, but they also directly affect the surface of the Earth, molding landforms either by erosion or deposition. The nature of weathering processes and the rate at which they operate depend upon climate, the properties of the rock and the conditions of the biosphere. Both wind erosion and the various weathering processes are significant landscape-makers.

Direction of wind

in 2 1 — cm 5 4 3 2 1

Grain path

Rebound

Sand cloud

Surface creep

Loose sand surface

Sand particles move in a series of long jumps—a process called saltation. Particles describe a curved path (above), the height and length of which depends upon the mass of the grain, the wind velocity and the number of other particles moving around. Saltation only occurs in a layer extending up to approximately 1 m (3 ft) above the ground surface. Sand grains moving in this way are also responsible for the abraded base of features such as pedestal rocks (right). These landforms are weathered first—for example by the crystallization of salts—and are then eroded by the sand-laden winds.

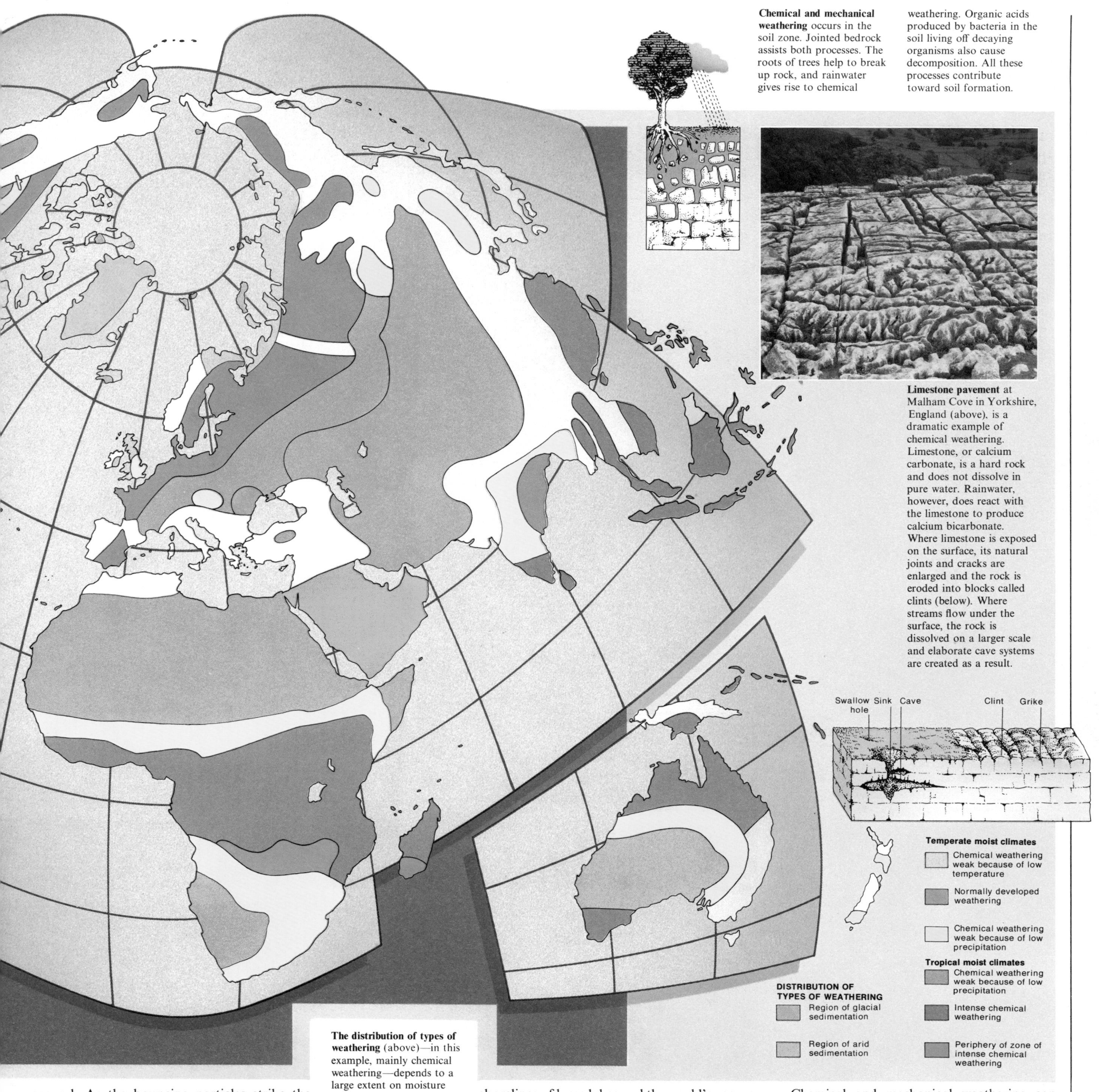

Chemical and mechanical weathering occurs in the soil zone. Jointed bedrock assists both processes. The roots of trees help to break up rock, and rainwater gives rise to chemical weathering. Organic acids produced by bacteria in the soil living off decaying organisms also cause decomposition. All these processes contribute toward soil formation.

Limestone pavement at Malham Cove in Yorkshire, England (above), is a dramatic example of chemical weathering. Limestone, or calcium carbonate, is a hard rock and does not dissolve in pure water. Rainwater, however, does react with the limestone to produce calcium bicarbonate. Where limestone is exposed on the surface, its natural joints and cracks are enlarged and the rock is eroded into blocks called clints (below). Where streams flow under the surface, the rock is dissolved on a larger scale and elaborate cave systems are created as a result.

The distribution of types of weathering (above)—in this example, mainly chemical weathering—depends to a large extent on moisture and temperature. When classifying regions with different rates of chemical weathering in terms of climatic zones, many areas of the world can be placed into one of two principal categories: tropical moist climates and temperate moist climates. The white areas on the map are mountain ranges or regions of tectonic activity where there is no appreciable weathering mantle.

ground. As the bouncing particles strike the surface, they push other particles along the ground (creep or drift). Fine particles that are disturbed by saltation rise up into the airflow and are carried away as dust (suspension).

The materials eroded and transported by winds must eventually come to rest in features of deposition. The most extensive of which are sand dunes. Sand seas at first sight appear to be random and complex, rather like a choppy ocean, but their features generally fall into three size groups: small ripples, which have a wavelength of up to 3 m (10 ft) and a height of 20 cm (8 in); dunes, with a wavelength of 20–300 m (65–1,000 ft) and a height of up to 30 m (68 ft); and sand mountains or "draa," which have a wavelength of 1–3 km (0.6–1.5 miles) and rise to a height of up to 200 m (650 ft). Within each size group various forms can be explained in terms of the nature of the sand and the kinds of winds that blow over it. Where winds blow consistently from one direction, long linear dunes form parallel or transverse to the wind direction. Where sand supply is limited, horned "barchan" dunes may form. If winds blow from several directions during a year, then star-shaped dunes and other complex patterns appear. Sand dunes are also common along the shorelines of large lakes and the world's oceans, where onshore winds can pile quite extensive areas of loose drifting sand.

Agents of weathering

Weathering takes two forms: mechanical weathering breaks up rock without altering its mineral constituents, whereas chemical weathering changes in some way the nature of mineral crystals. One agent of mechanical weathering is temperature change. It used to be thought that rocks disintegrated as a result of a huge daily range of temperature (thermal weathering). Despite travelers' tales of rocks splitting in the desert night with cracks like pistol shots, there is little evidence to support this view. In the presence of water, however, alternate heating and cooling of rocks does result in fracture. Frost is also an effective rock breaker. The freezing of water and expansion of ice in the cracks and pores of rocks create disruptive pressures; alternate freezing and thawing eventually causes pieces of rock to break off in angular fragments. Finally, the roots of plants and trees grow into the joints of rock and widen them, thus loosening the structure of the rock. Animals burrowing through the soil can have a similar effect on rocks.

Chemical and mechanical weathering can work hand in hand. In arid regions, for example, the crystallization of salts results in the weathering of rock. As water evaporates from the rock surface, salt crystals grow (from minerals dissolved in the water) in small openings in the rock. In time these crystals bring to bear enough pressure to break off rock fragments from the parent block.

Chemical weathering is most effective in humid tropical climates, however, and it usually involves the decomposition of rocks as a result of their exposure to air and rainwater, which contains dissolved chemicals. Carbon dioxide from the air, for example, becomes dissolved in rainwater, making it into weak carbonic acid. This reacts with minerals such as calcite, which is found in many rocks. Similarly, rocks can be oxidized by oxygen in the air. This happens to rocks that contain iron, for example, if they are exposed on the surface: a reddish iron oxide is produced which causes the rocks to crumble.

Over many thousands, even millions, of years, the processes of mechanical and chemical weathering have affected many of the rocks on the Earth's surface. When rocks are weakened in such a way, they then fall prey to the agents of erosion—water, ice, winds and waves.

Landscape-makers: Man

Man has done much to reshape the face of the planet since his first appearance on Earth more than two million years ago. Early man did little to harm the environment but, with the rise of agriculture, the landscape began to change. An increasing population and the growth of urban settlements gradually created greater demands for agricultural land and living space. But industrialization during the last 200 years has had the biggest impact. Man's search for and exploitation of the Earth's resources has to a large extent transformed the natural landscape and at the same time created totally artificial man-made environments.

MAN THE GEOLOGICAL AGENT

In 1864 a conservationist named George Perkins Marsh introduced the thesis that "man in fact made the Earth" rather than the converse. The idea of man as a geological agent was further developed in the 1920s. Man modifies the landscape in many ways; sometimes he transforms the Earth completely—he even creates land where no land was before.

Man's major impact on the landscape has been through forest clearance. He made the first attack on natural forests about 8,000 years ago in Neolithic times in northern and western Europe, as revealed by the changing composition of tree pollen deposited in bogs. After Roman times, especially in the Mediterranean region, there was another spate of forest clearance, so that by the Middle Ages little original forest survived in the Old World. As population and emigration increased, it was the turn of trees in the New World and Africa to fall before the axe and plow. Man's present voracious appetite for timber and its products could, if unchecked, clear most of the Earth's great forests by the end of this century.

Forest clearance not only changes the appearance of the landscape but can alter the balance of nature within a region. The hydrological cycle may be affected, and soil erosion may be increased, which in turn chokes rivers with sediment and leads to the silting up of harbors and estuaries. The coastal area of Valencia in Spain, for example, has widened by nearly 4 km (2.5 miles) since Roman times, much of which can be accounted for by forest clearance, and subsequent soil erosion and the deposition of the material by rivers as they near the sea. Reafforestation of an area can reduce soil erosion and the threat of flooding. Landscape management can reduce wind speeds: for example, shelter belts in the Russian steppes have been planted over distances of more than 100 km (62 miles).

Water management

The second great impact of man has been on the waterways of the world. The most spectacular changes are caused by the construction of dams to make vast new lakes. Such projects have frequently had effects far beyond those originally anticipated. The Aswan High Dam on the River Nile was completed in 1970, creating Lake Nasser and making possible the irrigation of an additional 550,000 hectares (1,358,000 acres) in upper Egypt. But some would argue that the dam holds back silt from the rivers and stores it in the lake, a fact that has seriously reduced the rate of silting in the Nile delta. This has resulted in increased salinity and some loss of fertility of the soil, as well as changes to the delta's coastline. The storage of silt in Lake Nasser has caused increased erosion of the riverbed downstream and the undermining of the foundations of bridges and barrages.

Other man-made changes to rivers include straightening and canalization, usually for

Massive power plants (left) symbolize man's modifications to the landscape in modern, industrialized society. Demand for energy and mineral resources has led to the creation of huge holes in the ground like this borax mine (below left) in the Mojave desert in California. The open pit is 100 m (330 ft) deep, 1,460 m (4,800 ft) long and 915 m (3,000 ft) wide. In opening up resource areas in Brazil, the Trans-Amazonian highway has disturbed the forest (below).

Hong Kong's bustling waterfront (below) captures the true essence of urban man. If space is in short supply, he expands his world vertically and maximizes his use of every square meter. Central business districts in the world's major cities reflect this concern with space.

flood protection, but also to prevent the channel from shifting. As long ago as the third millennium BC, during the reign of Emperor Yao, a hydraulic engineer was apparently appointed to control the wandering course of the Hwang-Ho (Yellow River), and the system he devised survived for at least 1,500 years. Even so, over the centuries, the river has changed course radically, and today measures are still being taken to control the fine sediment that the river carries and the flooding caused by its deposition. The Missouri River in the United States is estimated to erode material from an area of about 3,680 hectares (9,000 acres) annually over a length of 1,220 km (758 miles). It is little wonder that engineers attempt to control rivers by means of realignment or try to "train" a river's flow by using concrete stays.

New land from old

The continuing pressure of population on food resources and the need to create new agricultural land illustrate still further the impact of man as a landscape shaper. As part of irrigation projects land is often leveled and new waterways are created in the form of canals. Pakistan has one of the most extensive man-made irrigation systems in the world. It controls almost completely the flow of the Indus, Sutlej and Punjab rivers through some 640 km (400 miles) of linking canals.

A huge demand for rice in many parts of southeastern Asia has led to farmers terracing steep slopes on many mountainous islands. In the Netherlands, about one-third of the entire cultivated area of the country is land that has been reclaimed from the sea. In the future more grandiose schemes are likely. Any large-scale expansion of agricultural land in the Soviet Union will be mainly dependent on water supply. There have been plans since the 1930s to divert northward-flowing rivers to irrigated areas in the south and west. This idea, and it is believed that it might become a reality by the turn of the century, could have serious implications for the waters of the Arctic Ocean. If the amount of fresh water flowing into the ocean is reduced, salinity will increase, thus affecting the melting of ice floes and, consequently, sea level.

Man has also made his mark along the coastlines, from small-scale measures, such as the construction of groynes—wooden piles that reduce the amount of sand that is transported along the beach by wave action—to large-scale man-made harbors.

Modern man, the urban dweller of the machine age, has brought great changes to the face of the landscape. The need for materials for the construction of the urban fabric has led to the creation of huge quarries, in which building stone and road-building materials are extracted from the ground. Demand for energy and minerals leads to extensive modification of the landscape, especially where mineral deposits are near the surface and can be extracted by open-cast mining. The largest holes on Earth (excluding ocean basins) are those that result from the extraction of fuel (coal) and minerals.

The side effects of mining can be detrimental to the environment. Land may subside and despoliation of the landscape by slag heaps, for example, is considerable. Escaping coal dust can suffocate vegetation in a mining area, and gases given off during some mining operations can also damage plant and animal life.

Reclamation of spoiled areas is obligatory in many countries. Old open-cast workings are often filled with water to be used for recreational facilities, and slag heaps are treated and planted with vegetation: research has produced certain strains of plants that will grow even in the most acidic soils.

The true impact of man

During the last hundred years or so man has become much more aware of his role as an agent of landscape creation and destruction. The significance of man the landscape-maker, in comparison with slow, natural changes, is the speed with which he effects transformation, the sheer amount of energy which he can apply to a relatively small area, and the selectiveness and determination with which he applies that energy. Man's increased impact has not been a smooth and continuous process: it has occurred at different rates in different places and at different times. While it can be argued that some landscapes have been constructed which themselves conserve and often beautify the natural environment, man's active role has primarily been destructive: he has transformed the Earth's surface, perhaps irreversibly.

THE DUTCH POLDERS

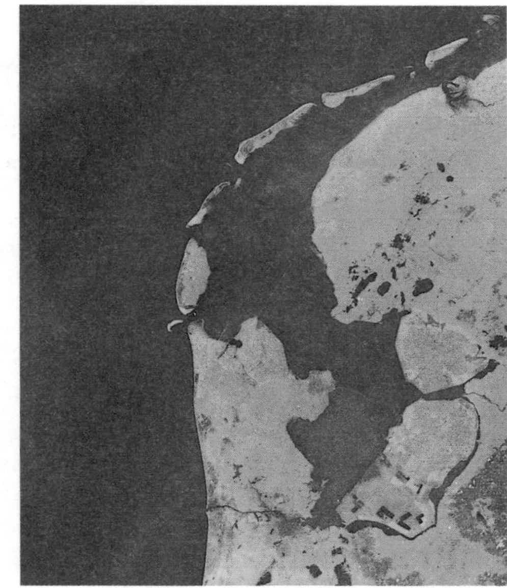

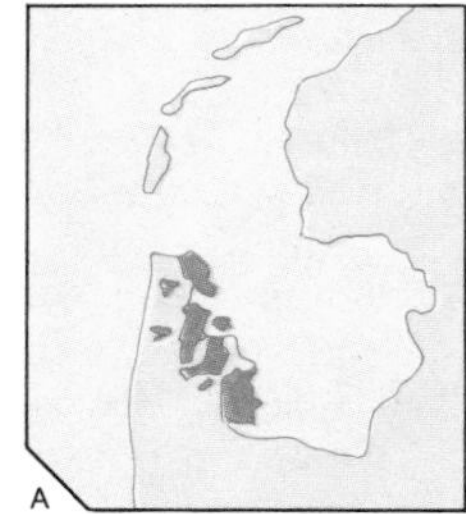

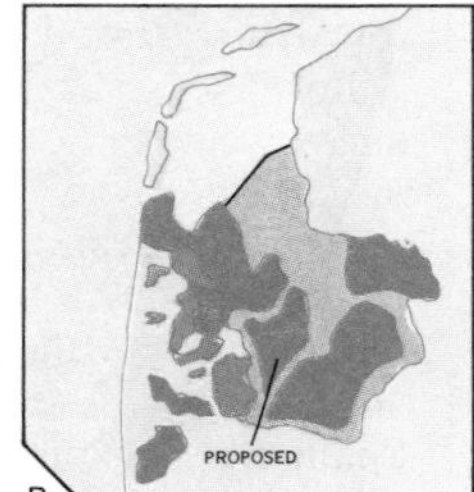

Reclamation of the Dutch polders from the North Sea is an example of man creating land. Many centuries ago a large part of what is now the western Netherlands was beneath the sea. From the 15th to the 17th centuries (A) dykes were constructed to enclose land and protect it against inundation from the sea, and enable it to be farmed. Later, windmills were used to drain away sea water. Further reclamation in the 19th and 20th centuries (B) has brought the total area to 165,000 hectares (408,000 acres). In 1932 a 40 km (25 mile) dam was completed, enclosing the Zuider Zee—which is now a freshwater lake that was renamed the IJsselmeer—and reducing Holland's vulnerable coastline by 320 km (200 miles). To create a polder, a dyke is built and the water pumped out. Reeds are grown to help dry out the soil. After a few years drains are put in to remove water remaining. Newly created polders (light blue) show up well on this satellite image (top).

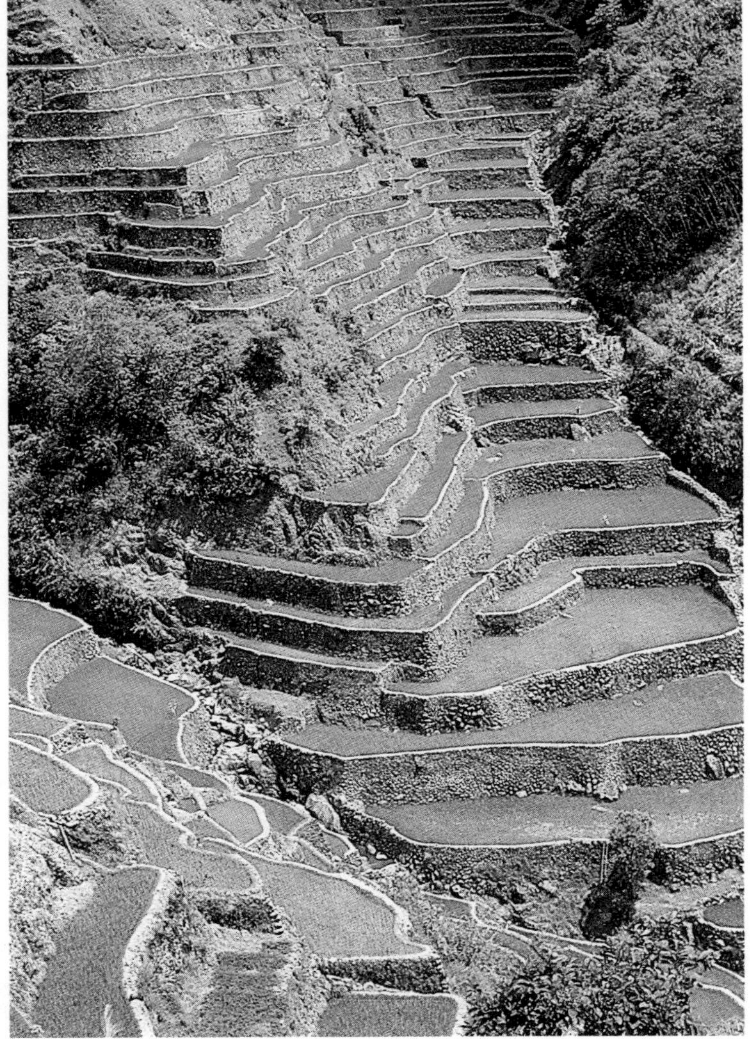

Man-made environments have become increasingly complex and large scale. Highway construction—this vast interchange (left) is in Chicago—is typical of the extensive use of land for modern transport systems alone. The acreage of land use classified as urban continues to increase. Man's endeavors to make still more land available for his many purposes have extended to cultivating previously inhospitable desert lands (above). More than half the land in Israel is naturally unproductive because of its aridity. By means of elaborate water carriage and storage schemes and scientifically researched irrigation projects, the desert has been totally transformed from a barren wasteland into intensively cultivated fields. Output from agriculture can also be increased by terracing. In densely populated areas, or mountainous regions, as in Luzon in the Philippines (right), man's skillful landscaping has completely reshaped the topography.

Part 3

THE EMERGENCE OF LIFE

How life on Earth began and developed
How life has evolved and spread over the planet
How man came to inherit the Earth

THE STAGES OF LIFE

Simple organic molecules, the precursors of life, could certainly have evolved in Earth's primitive atmosphere. Energy from the Sun, volcanoes and electric storms had the power to combine the basic chemicals into the amino acids and other molecules that are the constituents of living matter, forming droplets of "pre-life" in pools and on shorelines. Concentrations of droplets collected around some minerals, coagulating in a "soup" of long-chain polymers—proteins and nucleic acids which together form the living cell. Thus far have scientists re-created life's origins, but the combining of proteins and nucleic acids into a living unit remains to be achieved.

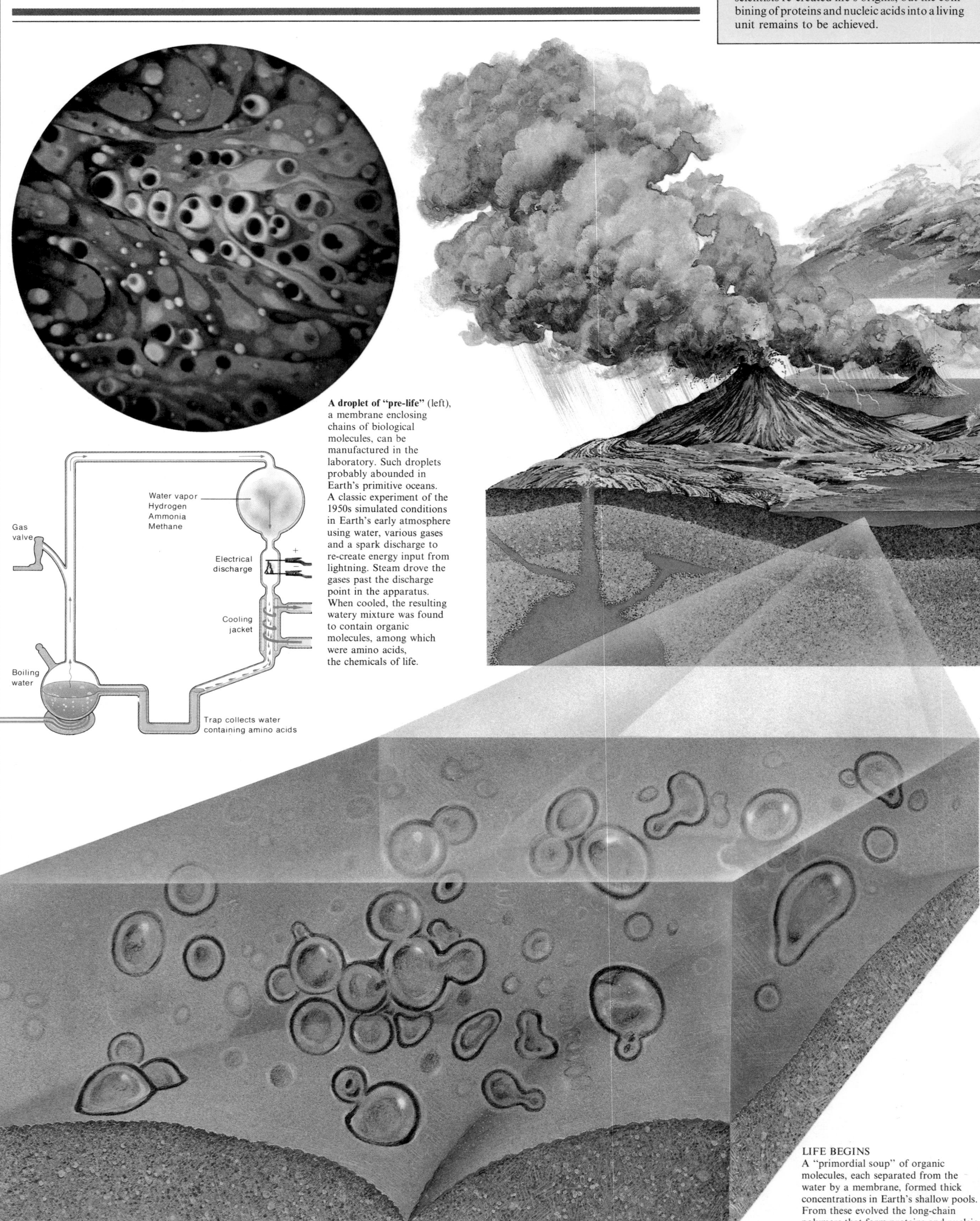

A droplet of "pre-life" (left), a membrane enclosing chains of biological molecules, can be manufactured in the laboratory. Such droplets probably abounded in Earth's primitive oceans. A classic experiment of the 1950s simulated conditions in Earth's early atmosphere using water, various gases and a spark discharge to re-create energy input from lightning. Steam drove the gases past the discharge point in the apparatus. When cooled, the resulting watery mixture was found to contain organic molecules, among which were amino acids, the chemicals of life.

LIFE BEGINS
A "primordial soup" of organic molecules, each separated from the water by a membrane, formed thick concentrations in Earth's shallow pools. From these evolved the long-chain polymers that form proteins and nucleic acids in every living cell.

The Source of Life

Life may have come to Earth from outer space – some meteorites contain life-like organic molecules – but the basic constituents of life, the biochemical structures called proteins and nucleic acids, could just as well have formed on Earth itself. By simulating possible primitive conditions on Earth, and applying a likely energy source, American scientists of the 1950s manufactured, from inorganic substances, the amino acids that form the subunits of all living things.

THE RADIANT SUN
A dense atmosphere of water vapor and various gases—but not oxygen—formed round the cooling planet Earth after its creation 4,600 million years ago. Oxygen in the atmosphere would have prevented the evolution of life from nonliving organic matter by blocking the Sun's ultraviolet radiation (which may have provided energy for the forming of organic compounds), and free oxygen would also have destroyed such compounds as they began to accumulate.

THE PRIMITIVE ATMOSPHERE
Volcanic eruptions drove water vapor and gases into the atmosphere of the young Earth; lightning and other discharges of atmospheric electricity accompanied the torrential rain; dissolved minerals collected in the pools. These were some of the preconditions for life on Earth, whereby mixtures of organic compounds in water may have combined to form more complex units essential for life.

Water played a key part in the creation of life on Earth. At first the temperature of the newly formed planet was far too high for water to exist in a liquid state. Instead, it formed a dense atmosphere of steam, which, as the Earth cooled, condensed into droplets of rain that poured down for perhaps thousands of years. This torrential, thundery rain eroded the land and dissolved the minerals, which collected in pools on the surface.

Earth's original atmosphere was also very different from today's. Most importantly, it contained no free oxygen, the gas which makes air-breathing life possible; the primitive atmosphere was composed of carbon monoxide, carbon dioxide, hydrogen and nitrogen. But the absence of oxygen created two conditions that are essential if life is to evolve. First, without oxygen the atmosphere could have no layer of ozone (an oxygen compound), which now acts as a barrier to most of the Sun's high-energy radiation (mainly ultraviolet light). Second, the absence of free oxygen meant that any complex chemicals that might be formed would not immediately break down again. Thus the molecules of life could form.

The chemistry of life

Life may be distinguished from nonlife in three ways: living organisms are able to increase the complexity of their parts through synthetic, self-building reactions; they obtain and use energy by breaking down chemical compounds; and they can make new copies of themselves.

It is the combined properties of the chemicals of life that make them so special, not just the chemicals themselves. Experiments in the last few decades have given us a very good idea of how life could have arisen from the simple, nonliving chemicals which compose it. In the early 1950s, Harold Urey and Stanley Miller simulated the atmosphere of a primitive world by filling a flask with water, ammonia, methane and hydrogen. They supplied it with energy in the form of heat and an electric spark—to simulate lightning—and the experiment was left to run for a week.

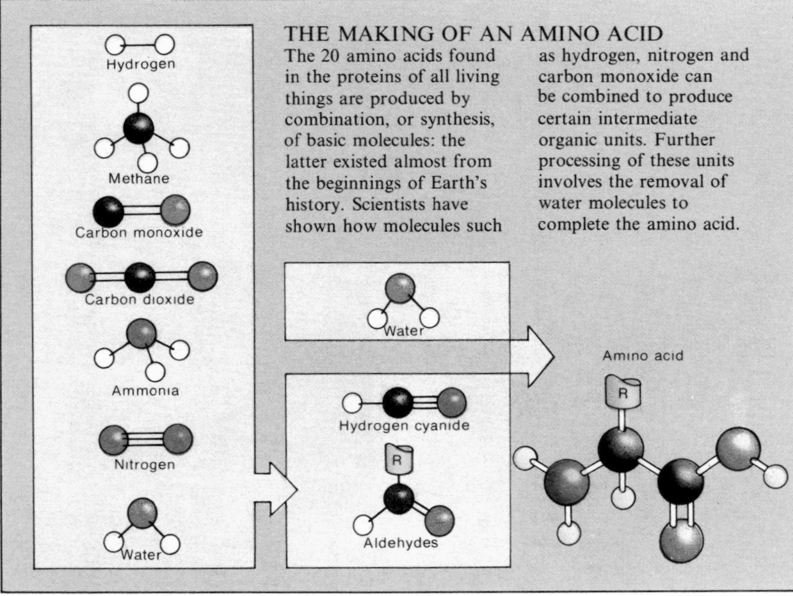

THE MAKING OF AN AMINO ACID
The 20 amino acids found in the proteins of all living things are produced by combination, or synthesis, of basic molecules: the latter existed almost from the beginnings of Earth's history. Scientists have shown how molecules such as hydrogen, nitrogen and carbon monoxide can be combined to produce certain intermediate organic units. Further processing of these units involves the removal of water molecules to complete the amino acid.

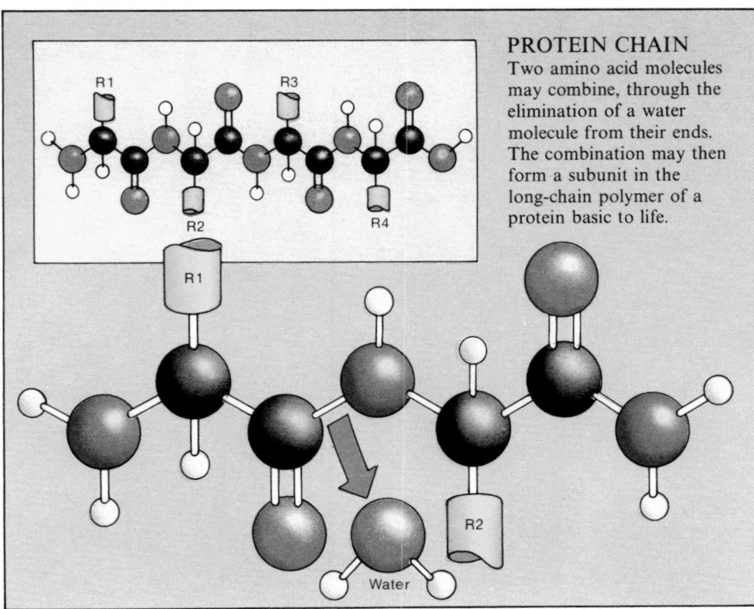

PROTEIN CHAIN
Two amino acid molecules may combine, through the elimination of a water molecule from their ends. The combination may then form a subunit in the long-chain polymer of a protein basic to life.

Analyzing the mixture formed, they found it contained many chemicals that are associated with living things, particularly nitrogen compounds called amino acids—the really important chemicals of life. Further experiments brought together other gas mixtures, including the one that is now thought to have covered the young Earth, and these gave similar results, as long as there was no free oxygen present. The resulting mixture of organic compounds in water came to be known as the "primordial soup," and it is from this "soup" that life may have emerged.

Miller and Urey had shown that the basic substances of life can be derived from a primitive atmosphere. But there are still large gaps in our understanding of how these substances became more organized and self-regulating: in other words, how they became alive. More complex molecular structures somehow developed through the linking up of the basic units to form long, chain-like sequences of larger units, called polymers. But how this happened is still not fully understood.

The two most important classes of biological molecules are proteins and nucleic acids, both of which are polymers. Proteins are the building materials of living matter, the chief components of muscles, skin and hair. They also form enzymes—the chemicals that control biochemical reaction in living cells. Nucleic acids—DNA (deoxyribonucleic acid) and RNA (ribonucleic acid)—are so called because they are found in the central nuclei of cells. They are the cell's genetic material, the raw stuff of heredity. They act as the memories and the messengers of life, storing information in units called genes, and releasing that information to the cells when it is needed. Nucleic acids can reproduce themselves and, without this ability, life would not exist or continue.

The basic units that link together to form proteins are amino acids, and all proteins in living organisms are made up of just 20 different amino acids. In chemical terms, a protein molecule is a polymer consisting of a long chain of amino acid units joined together in a particular sequence, and the code to this sequence is held by DNA.

How living chemicals joined

Experiments with simulated primordial conditions have produced many amino acids other than the 20 commonly found in proteins. All amino acids (and other types of chemicals) tend to "stick" onto the surface of clay, but those 20 found in proteins stick particularly well to clays rich in the metal nickel. This suggests that the first proteins may have been formed in pools or on the fringes of seas, where the primordial soup was in contact with nickel-rich clays. There heat from the Sun or a volcano could have combined the amino acids to form a primitive protein.

The four classes of chemicals that form the basic components of nucleic acids have also, like the amino acids, been "cooked up" in a primordial soup, and they too will stick to clay to form long-chain polymers. And, just as nickel-rich clays are best at absorbing the amino acid constituents of protein, so clays rich in zinc absorb the building blocks of nucleic acids. This suggests that such clays could have been the birthplace of genes, which are the "messengers" of inheritance.

However, the coupling of proteins and nucleic acids, which together form the living cell, has yet to be explained, and it is improbable that proteins or nucleic acids alone could have provided the basis for life.

The Russian biochemist I. A. Oparin has shown that, in water, solutions of polymers (such as proteins) have a tendency to form droplets surrounded by an outer membrane very like that which encloses living cells. As these droplets grow by absorbing more polymers, some split in two when they become too large for stability. If such a droplet had protein enzymes to harness energy and make more polymers, and if it had nucleic acids with instructions for making those proteins, and if each new droplet received a complete copy of the nucleic acid instructions, the droplet would be alive—it would be a living cell.

The Structure of Life

All life forms stem from a single cell, and every cell contains in its nucleus instructions for the re-creation of the organism of which it forms a part. These are encoded in chromosomes, which contain the miraculous molecular substance of DNA, sectioned into units of heredity called genes. The genetic code determines in detail the physical characteristics of an individual creature, so that variations in DNA cause variations in the individual. Scientists believe that it is the interaction of the individual variation with the environment that ultimately leads to the evolution of the similar, interbreeding groups of creatures that are known as species.

THE HIDDEN SECRET
Dramatic discoveries in recent decades have revolutionized biology, the primary life science. Scientists can now trace parts of the genetic blueprint that lays down the pattern for every form of life, linking the large-scale unfolding of species that we know as evolution with the ultramicroscopic activity of the molecules within the nucleus of every cell. This may be the secret behind the rich diversity of life on Earth.

Deoxyribonucleic acid (DNA) consists of a "backbone" of alternating sugar and phosphate molecules, and to each sugar is attached one of four nitrogenous bases (adenine, guanine, thymine and cytostine, or A, G, T, C). A single gene might contain 2,000 of these bases, and in the body cell of a human being the 46 chromosomes (thread-like bodies of DNA and protein) run to 3,000 million bases. The sequence of these bases stores the information for making amino acids into proteins, just as the sequence of letters in this sentence stores the information for making a particular verbal structure. But the DNA alphabet has only four letters (A, G, T, C).

The thread of life

DNA is a double molecule, resembling a twisted ladder, its two main strands twining around each other to form the famous double helix. The strands are linked by pairs of bases—A and T, or G and C—whose shape is such that each pair fits together neatly, like pieces of a jigsaw, to form the rungs of the DNA ladder. As a result, the information on the strands can be duplicated by "unzipping" the double helix and making new strands by using the old ones as templates. DNA stores, duplicates and passes on the information that makes life alive.

Cells multiply by splitting in two, and each newly made cell thus gets instructions for its existence by the mechanism of heredity, the gene. But heredity is a word more often applied to the passing on of DNA from an organism to its offspring. In sexual reproduction the offspring gets some of the DNA (usually half) from one parent, and the rest from the other, ending up with a unique mix all of its own.

The laws of heredity

Man has long known that characteristics can be passed on from one generation to the next, for he has been selectively breeding crops and animals for thousands of years. However, it was not until the mid-nineteenth century that an obscure Austrian monk, Gregor Mendel (1822–84), discovered the laws that govern inheritance, and his work was ignored until the beginning of the twentieth century, when more powerful microscopes made possible the direct observation of the cell.

Mendel experimented with pea plants because they had easily recognizable traits, and because, although normally self-fertilizing, they could be cross-fertilized with pollen from a different plant. Mendel made many crosses between different pure-bred plants and found that in the offspring, or hybrids, some characters always prevailed over others: red flowers over white, tall plants over short, and so on. He called the prevailing characters dominant, and the nonprevailing characters recessive. He then let the first-generation hybrids self-fertilize, and found not only that the recessive traits reappeared in the hybrids' offspring, but also that they reappeared in a constant proportion of three dominant to one recessive; the second generation contained three times as many red-flowered peas as white-flowered peas.

To explain his results, Mendel proposed that each plant had two hereditary "factors"—today called alleles—for each character, and that the dominant factor suppressed the recessive factor. If a plant inherited both a dominant and a recessive factor, the dominant one would prevail. Only if both factors were recessive would the recessive character be apparent. Mendel found many other pairs of traits where one form was dominant and the other recessive. He established that permutations arising from the crossing of the two first-generation hybrids allows the dominant gene to be present in three out of four crosses in the second generation; but in the fourth cross, only the two recessive alleles of the genes are present. So there is always a three-to-one ratio of dominant to recessive.

Theories of evolution

Mendel's work was of course unknown to his contemporaries, Charles Darwin and Alfred Russel Wallace, who even then were providing solutions to the major mystery of biology—the way that species evolve, change and develop over time. Evolution was not a new idea in Darwin's day. In 1809 the French naturalist Jean-Baptiste Lamarck had proposed a theory of the inheritance of acquired characteristics, suggesting that new habits learned by an organism in response to environmental change may become physically incorporated in the animal's descendants. For instance, the fact that the ancestral giraffe had to stretch its neck to reach food might give its offspring long necks to enable them to reach food more easily. Less satisfactory than the "natural selection" theory of Darwin and Wallace (who independently reached the same conclusion), Lamarckism founders on the fact that there is no genetic mechanism enabling acquired characters to pass on in this way.

Darwin's theory of natural selection has three key elements: all individuals vary, and some variations are passed on to the next generation; the gap between the potential and the actual number of offspring reproduced by organisms is very wide and implies that not all will survive; organisms best adapted to the environment will survive, their offspring will have been selected, and the favorable variation will spread through the population, perhaps eventually changing it.

Genetic variation, the mainspring of natural selection, is reflected in variations of DNA, the material substance of heredity. Changes in the order of DNA's nitrogenous bases—called mutations—produce changes in the proteins which are usually, but not always, harmful. More important than these is the effect of genes recombining in sexually reproduced offspring.

Sexual reproduction provides the offspring with two sets of DNA, one from each parent. The processes that give rise to a half-set of chromosomes in a sperm or egg shuffle and recombine the genes on each chromosome to provide new combinations. Then, when sperm and egg fuse together at fertilization, the half-sets come together and even more combinations are produced. The world's enormous diversity of life can be explained in terms of a struggle that favors certain genetic combinations.

Genes

Protein (myoglobin)
Amino acids

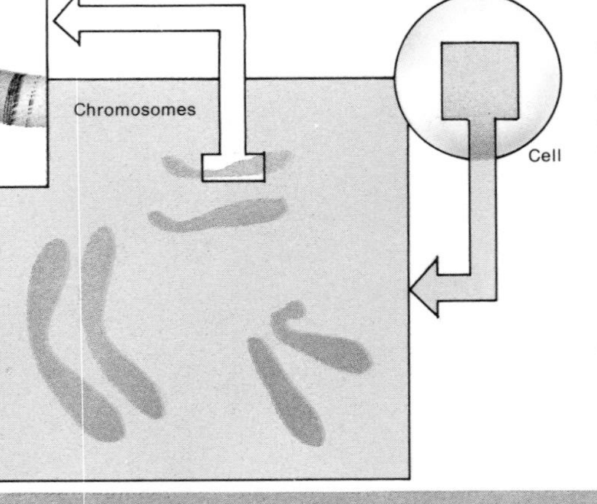

The cell is the basic unit of all life, and every cell contains in its nucleus the thread-like structures, called chromosomes, that control heredity. Each species has its own number of chromosomes, and the number is always the same for that species. Chromosomes are sectioned into genes, units of heredity made of DNA molecules. DNA acts like a code, specifying the order and number of amino acids that make up proteins—the organic compounds characteristic of all life.

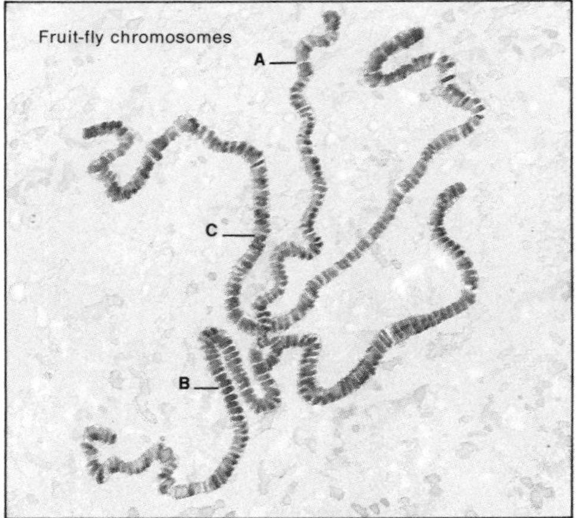

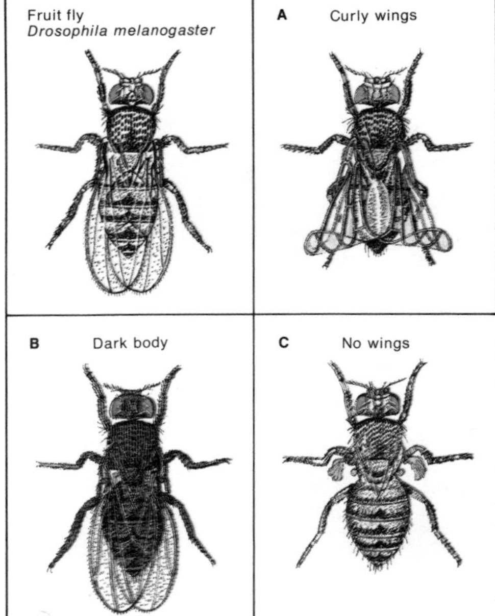

Chromosomes (below left) of the fruit fly, much magnified, show bands of DNA arranged in sections that correspond exactly with specific genes, the chemical units of heredity. The proof of this correspondence came when the American geneticist Hermann Muller introduced the use of ionizing radiation to damage the fruit flies' chromosomes at ultramicroscopic points, causing precise point mutations in offspring of parents whose DNA had been damaged at the places indicated. Random mutations may occur in any organism, and not only as a result of radiation. A gradual accumulation of minor mutations may lead to evolutionary change.

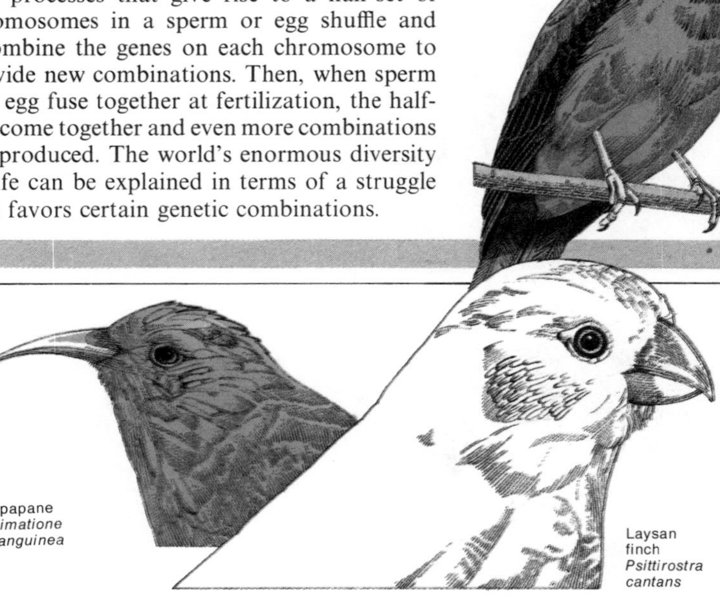

Some human traits, such as eye color, are inherited as single factors (below). In such cases one gene is dominant over the other, recessive, gene, and the gene giving a brown eye color is always dominant over that which gives a blue eye color. The chromosomes carrying eye-color genes (A) pair (B) and duplicate (C, D) before dividing twice (E, F) in the process known as meiosis, or reduction division. This ensures that the offspring gets half the chromosomes from the male and half from the female parent, so each new cell gets both genes when sperm and egg unite. But because brown-eye genes are dominant over blue, all offspring have brown eyes, with the blue-eye gene hidden. But if two brown-eyed parents carry recessive blue-eye genes, half the male sperm cells have blue-eye genes, and the female eggs carry a gene for either blue or brown eyes. So the two recessive genes have a one-in-four chance of being combined to produce a blue-eyed child, no brown-eye genes being present.

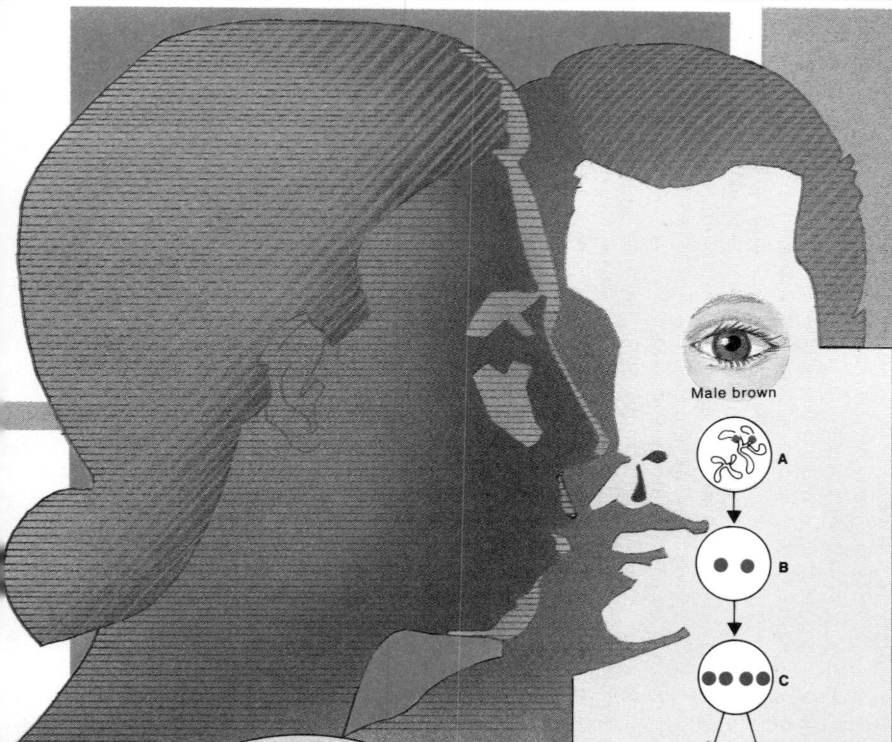

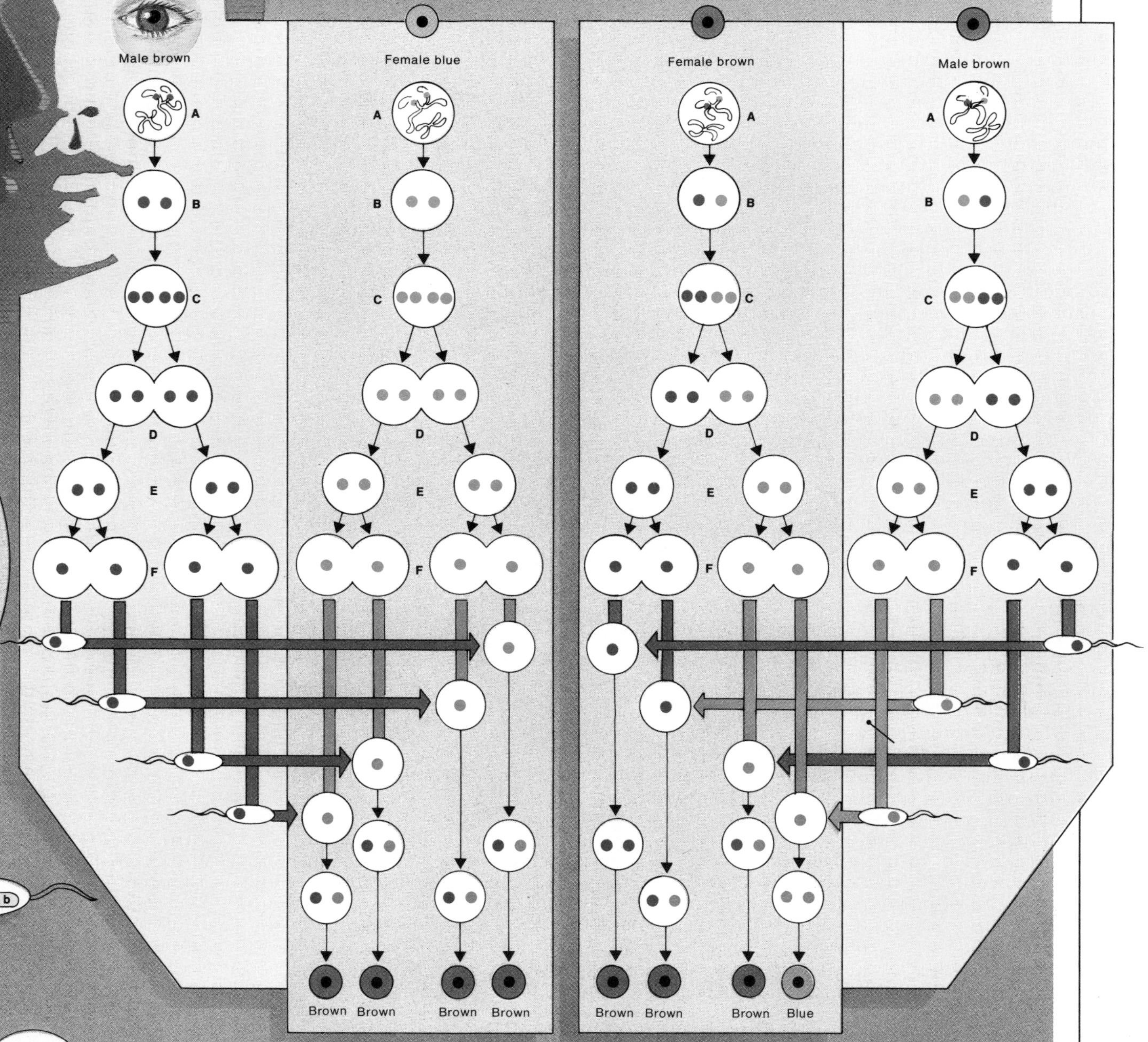

Male brown | Female blue | Female brown | Male brown

Brown Brown Brown Brown | Brown Brown Brown Blue

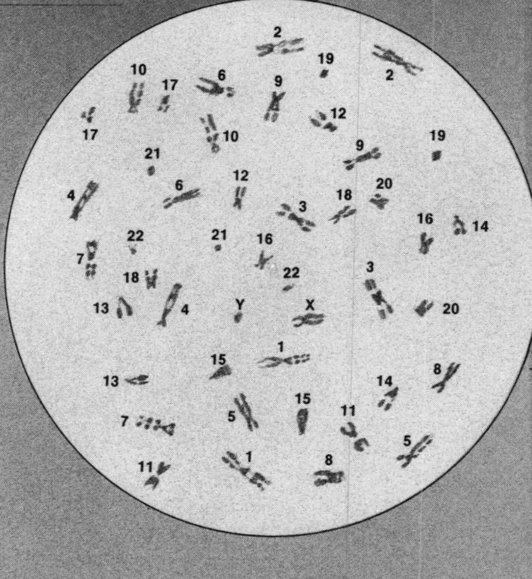

A human body cell (above) contains 46 chromosomes—22 matching pairs and the chromosomes (X, Y) which determine sex. Males have X and Y, females X and X. In sexual reproduction (right) traits carried by the male sperm and the female egg combine in the zygote, the fertilized egg from which new life starts. All growth is the result of repeated cell division, or mitosis, where the nucleus forms paired chromosomes that duplicate themselves; the cell splits, and the chromosomes re-form in the nucleus of the new cells. Sex cells are produced by reduction division, or meiosis, with each cell taking only one from each pair of chromosomes, which exchange corresponding segments in the process called recombination. The genes are thus reshuffled at each generation, so that new combinations of gene traits are available for selection each time meiosis takes place. The result is genetic diversity, with many possibilities for the species to adapt to a changing environment.

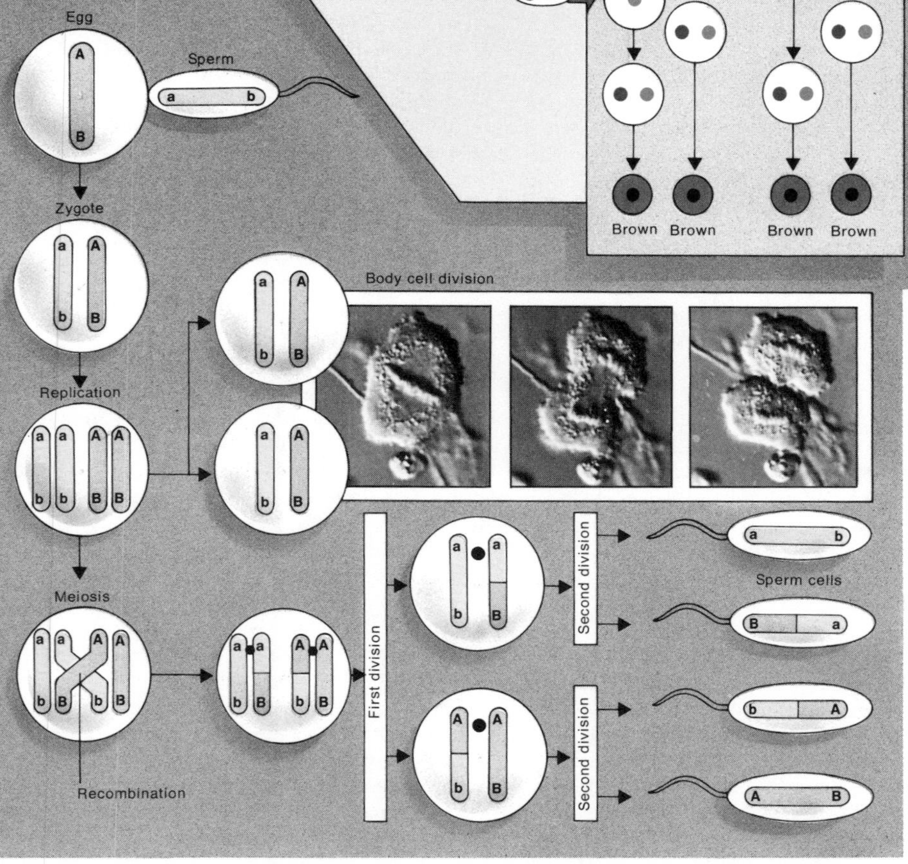

Egg | Sperm | Zygote | Replication | Body cell division | Meiosis | Recombination | First division | Second division | Sperm cells

A diversity of forms (left) has stemmed from a single ancestor of the Hawaiian honeycreeper, which now numbers 14 species. These have adapted in their mid-Pacific isolation to fill niches usually taken by other birds, ranging from the nectar-feeding iiwi to the Laysan finch with its thick beak for cracking seeds, and the short-billed apapane, which includes insects in its diet. But the honeycreepers' success in divergence may have led to overspecialization, with at least eight species now extinct. The Australian marsupial mouse and the Indian spiny mouse (right) look very similar, due to the fact that they fill similar ecological niches, but they belong to groups evolving separately for almost 100 million years.

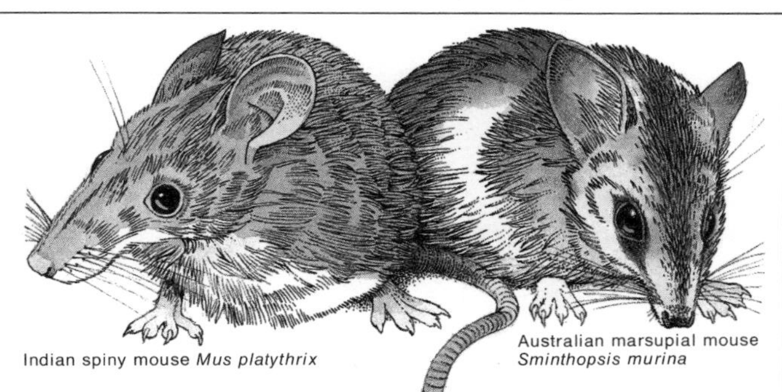
Indian spiny mouse *Mus platythrix*

Australian marsupial mouse *Sminthopsis murina*

VARIANT FORMS

Dark forms of many insects, such as the peppered moth *Biston betularia*, have developed widely in industrial areas of the world since the industrial age. The dark variant, resulting from a single genetic mutation, escapes the eye of predators against the black, lichen-free bark of soot-darkened trees (top), whereas the typical pale form is very conspicuous. In rural, unpolluted areas where tree trunks are light and lichen covered (bottom) the well-concealed pale form is much commoner. *Biston*'s rapid evolutionary response is remarkable: in 1849 only one dark example was recorded at Manchester, England, but by 1900 98% of the moths caught in the area were of the dark type. A similar change occurred in other industrial areas, during the period when the most coal was being burned and the population was most rapidly expanding. But with today's clean-air laws the number of pale moths in these areas is once again on the increase.

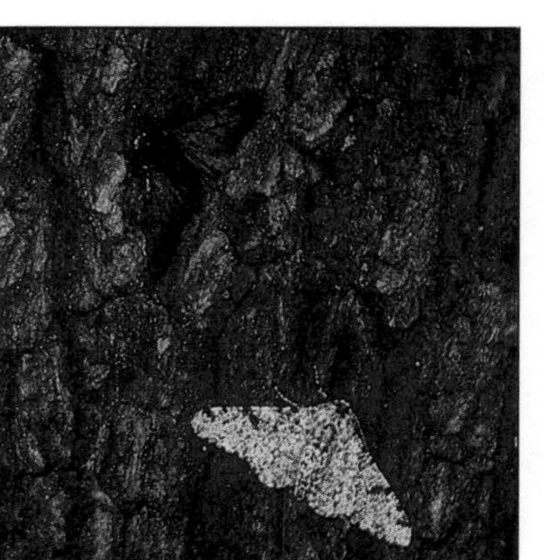

Earliest Life Forms

Earth's original atmosphere lacked oxygen, without which there could be no survival for air-breathing creatures. This vital gas was supplied by life itself, in the form of microscopic organisms that flourished in the atmosphere of the time and emitted oxygen as "waste." In this way a breathable atmosphere built up; increasingly complex life forms were able to develop in the seas; early plants and insects gained a foothold on the shores; and, finally, larger animals could survive on land.

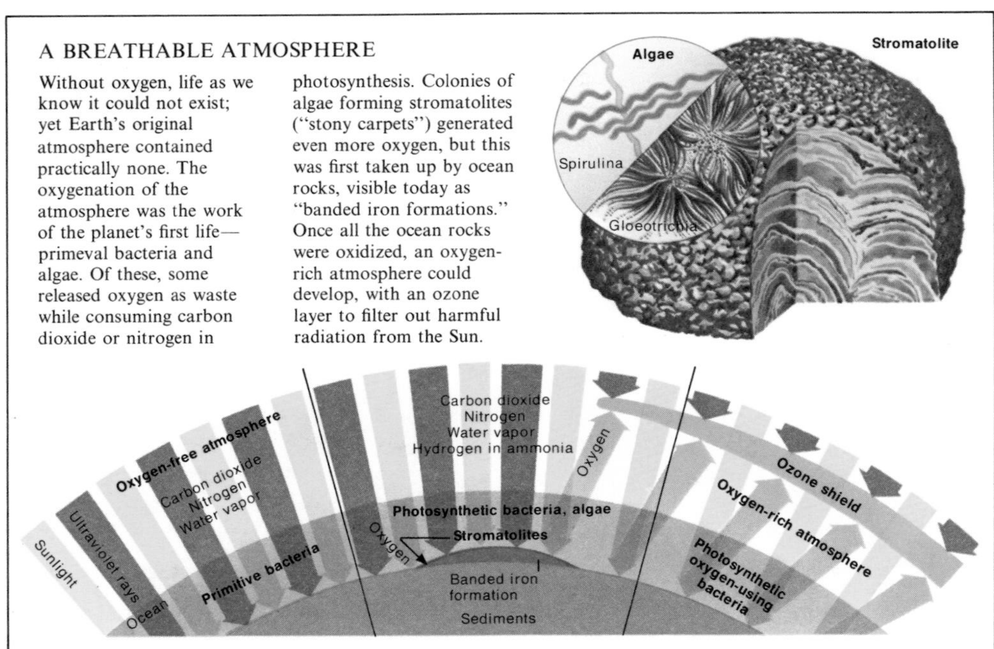

A BREATHABLE ATMOSPHERE

Without oxygen, life as we know it could not exist; yet Earth's original atmosphere contained practically none. The oxygenation of the atmosphere was the work of the planet's first life—primeval bacteria and algae. Of these, some released oxygen as waste while consuming carbon dioxide or nitrogen in photosynthesis. Colonies of algae forming stromatolites ("stony carpets") generated even more oxygen, but this was first taken up by ocean rocks, visible today as "banded iron formations." Once all the ocean rocks were oxidized, an oxygen-rich atmosphere could develop, with an ozone layer to filter out harmful radiation from the Sun.

Scientists have identified bacteria-like microfossils in the rocks that were formed more than 3,500 million years ago. Some of these organisms appear to have been capable of photosynthesis—the process of utilizing sunlight, water and carbon dioxide for "food," with release of oxygen as the vitally important by-product. As a result, surplus oxygen very gradually accumulated in the Earth's atmosphere, forming an upper-atmosphere shield of ozone (which kept out damaging ultraviolet radiation from the Sun) and providing an oxygen-rich atmosphere in which breathing life could develop.

At least five types of microfossil have been found in ancient sediments of Western Australia, aged about 3,560 million years, and these provide the earliest evidence of life so far discovered. Other early proof of life comes from the so-called "stromatolites," some of which may date back as far as 3,400 million years. These curious columns, growing in warm, shallow waters, are formed of blue-green algae which have entrapped chalky sediments, bacteria and other microfossils. Their study is made easier by the fact that similar structures have developed at later geological times, and some are even being formed at the present day.

Living below the surface of the water and not initially reliant on oxygen for life, such bacteria and algae were shielded from the Sun's ultraviolet rays as they imperceptibly altered the Earth's atmosphere. For hundreds of millions of years life of this kind persisted, with few obvious developments or changes.

Breathing life

About 1,800 million years ago, the effects of these microscopic photosynthesizers became dramatically apparent in the "rusting" of the ocean sediments, when the red color of the rocks being formed at that time indicates that there was enough free oxygen on Earth to bring about the process known as oxidation. Once the ocean rocks capable of absorbing oxygen had done so, forming the red "banded iron formations" known to geologists, oxygen could enter the atmosphere in ever greater quantities.

It has been estimated that a breathable atmosphere existed on Earth about 1,700 million years ago, and aerobic (oxygen-using) organisms first became abundant not very long afterwards. These organisms were single celled, and it may have been almost 1,000 million years before multicellular animals evolved. The fossilized remains of animals alive 800 million years ago have been found in many parts of the world, but it is not yet known whether multicellular animals had a long history before these earliest known forms, or whether they had developed and radiated rapidly from a creature capable of feeding as well as photosynthesizing.

One of the earliest collections of animals of this type was discovered in the Ediacara Sandstones of the Flinders Range in Australia, where some 650 million years ago the rocks once formed part of an ancient beach. Here a spectacular collection of soft-bodied animals, similar to today's coelenterates (such as jellyfish) and worms, was washed ashore and preserved in silt from the nearby shallow sea. Comparable, mainly floating forms have been found in other parts of the world in rocks dating from between 650 and 580 million years ago.

The first vertebrates

One of the most important changes in animal life seems to have occurred about 580 million years ago. At that date many creatures evolved hard, protective shells, which also acted as areas of muscle attachment and as support for their bodies—in other words, as external skeletons. Hard shells were more easily preserved as fossils than the soft bodies of earlier animals, so rich collections have been recovered from rocks of the Cambrian Period, beginning 580 million years ago, as well as from later strata.

The first fish-like animals—the earliest true vertebrates—are found in rocks of the Ordovician Period, from about 500 million years ago, and these were in many ways very similar to the lampreys and hagfishes of today. But unlike them, these ancient creatures were heavily armored with external bone. They must have been poor swimmers, living mainly on the seabed and filtering edible particles from the sediments, which they sucked into their jawless mouths. From them arose true fishes, with backbones, jaws and teeth, and they came to replace the less efficient earlier forms.

During the Devonian Period, about 400 million years ago, the fishes diversified greatly, adapting to fit all kinds of aquatic environments. Some grew to a huge size, such as *Dunkleosteus*, which achieved a length of up to 9 m (29 ft 7 in), although it belonged to a group of fishes that retained heavy armor. Some of these curious creatures probably used their stilt-like pectoral fins to hitch themselves across the beds of the pools in which they lived.

From water to land

The fishes that teemed in the seas and fresh waters of the Devonian world found their way into difficult environments such as swamps and oasis pools, where there was a danger of drying out in the warmer weather. Many of these fishes had rudimentary lungs, and one group developed powerful jointed fins.

Such marginal habitats were not ideal for fishes, but they were nevertheless rich in species, and it is from them that the first land vertebrates developed. When the water dried up they survived, for their strong fins held them up so that they did not flop over helplessly.

They found themselves in a new, dry world, but one which was already inhabited, at least round the water's edges, with plants related to modern liverworts, mosses and club mosses. There were also numerous invertebrate animals such as millipedes, spiders and wingless insects. These plants and animals provided shelter and food, so that the environment was not wholly hostile to larger animals.

The first steps on land probably took the form of strong flexions of the body—desperate swimming movements which swung the fins forward, pegging the animal's position in the drying mud. But in a very short time geologically, animals had evolved in which the rays of the lobe fins had vanished, leaving stubby legs with which the animals—no longer fishes but amphibians—could haul themselves over land. But they still had to return to water to breed and lay eggs.

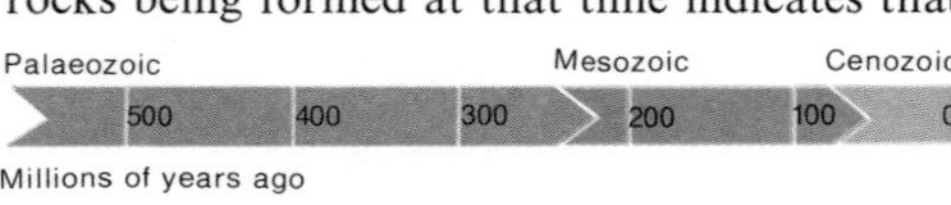

A timescale of life on Earth emerges from the record of fossils embedded in rock strata. Major breaks in faunas (animal assemblages) separate eras coinciding roughly with periods of intense mountain-building activity. These eras are broken down into geological periods, which are separated by lesser faunal breaks and which are generally named from the area where rocks of that age were first discovered. The geological eras and periods do not imply particular rock types.

THE FIRST SHELLED CREATURES
These evolved (right) in the seas when conditions allowed soft-bodied life to form protective casings. In the fossil record of 550 million years ago, soft and shelled forms are found. The trilobites (1, 2, 3)—a now extinct order of woodlouse-like animals—dominated the scene, but other early arthropods (4) included a possible insect ancestor (5), and there may even have been an ancestor to fish (6). Sponges (7), crinoids (8), early moluscs (9), bristleworms (10) and lampshells (11) were plentiful, but other creatures (12) are bewilderingly strange.

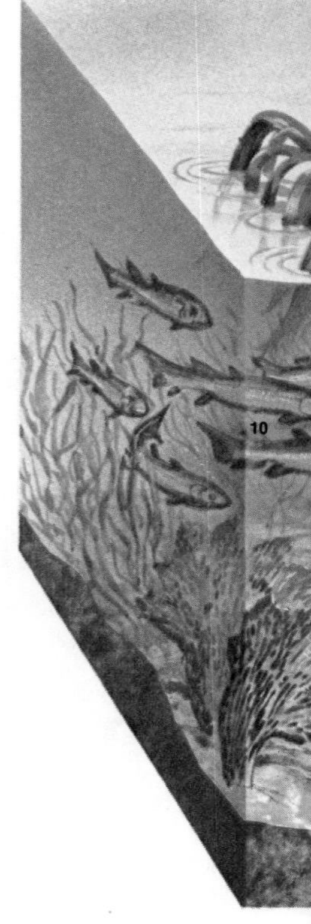

THE FIRST AMPHIBIANS
Amphibians (1) emerged some 345 million years ago (right), inhabiting swampy environments with luxuriant vegetation—club mosses and ferns (2, 3) that made up the early coal forests. Lungfish (4) were well adapted to life in oxygen-poor waters, but the move to land was probably made by related fish with a passage linking nostrils to throat—*Eusthenopteron* (5). Land offered food (6, 7, 8) and suitably damp conditions for a possibly stranded aquatic animal.

The Solar System forms
5,000 million years
Earth forms
4,000
Oldest micro-fossils
Oxygen-creating bacteria
Stromatolites, blue-green algae
3,000
Ozone shield forms
Oxygen in atmosphere
2,000
Breathable atmosphere
Many oxygen-using animals
Sexual repro-duction
1,000
900
Multi-cellular life
800
700
Soft-bodied animals
600
Shelled/skeletal animals
CAMBRIAN
550
First fishes
ORDOVICIAN

LIFE ON SEA AND LAND

For more than half the Earth's existence, its atmosphere has been hostile to air-breathing life. Then, about 1,600 million years ago, the photosynthesizing action of minute organisms built up enough free oxygen in the atmosphere for more complex oxygen-dependent forms to develop. The first multicellular life led to the soft-bodied animals of the pre-Cambrian time—worms, jellyfish and sea pens. About 580 million years ago many animals developed hard parts, including shells. Over 1,200 new marine species date from this period, and the evolutionary explosion came to fill the Earth's seas with fishes. Some of these had powerful jointed fins and rudimentary lungs, and lived in swamps where primitive plants and insects had already made the move to land. As the pools dwindled the stranded animals could survive by breathing air.

THE AGE OF JELLYFISH
Jellyfish (left) and other soft-bodied animals flourished in the pre-Cambrian seas, more than 600 million years ago. The forms of one group, imprinted on sand, have been preserved as fossils in the Australian Ediacara Sandstones. They include varieties similar to modern jellyfish (1, 2); worm-like crawlers (3); sea pens (4) very like modern types; segmented worms (5); "three-legged" creatures like no known animal (6); and sand casts of burrowing worms (7).

LIVING FOSSILS
Some life forms that emerged 570 million years ago have survived virtually unchanged to the present day. These "living fossils" include *Lingula* (left), today found in warm, brackish coastal waters, poor in oxygen and unsuited to most life, off the Pacific and Indian oceans. *Neopilina* (below), a primitive marine mollusc first found alive in 1952, has features unlike other molluscs but suggesting much closer affinities with the annelids (worms) and arthropods (insects, crabs, etc.).

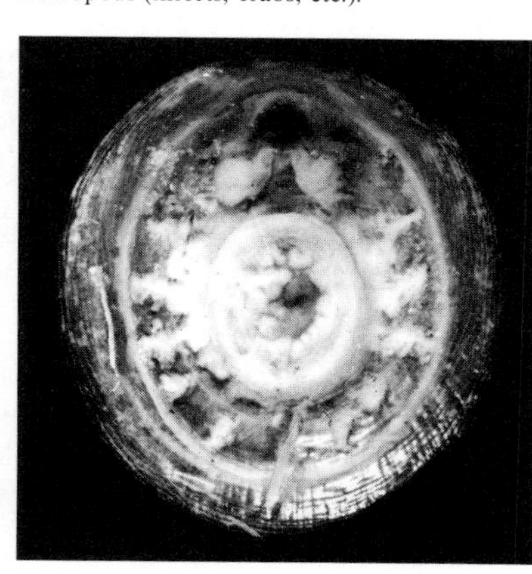

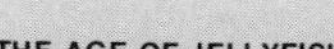

THE AGE OF JELLYFISH
1 Jellyfish (*Ediacaria*)
2 Jellyfish (*Medusina*)
3 Flatworm (*Dickinsonia costata*)
4 Sea pens (*Rangea, Charnia*)
5 Segmented worms (*Spriggina floundersi*)
6 Unknown animal (*Tribrachidium*)
7 Burrowing worm (fossil casts)
8 Sponges and algae (hypothetical)

THE FIRST SHELLED CREATURES
1 Trilobites (*Waptia*)
2 Trilobites (*Marella splendens*)
3 Trilobite (*Olenoides serratus*)
4 Primitive arthropod (*Perspicaris dictynna*)
5 Primitive arthropod (*Aysheaia pedunculata*)
6 Ancestral lancelet fish (*Branchiostoma*)
7 Sponge (*Vauxia*)
8 Crinoids (*Echmatocrinus*)
9 Mollusc (*Wiwaxia*)
10 Bristleworm (*Nereis*)
11 Brachiopod (*Lingulella*)
12 Unknown animal (*Hallucigenia sparsa*)

THE AGE OF FISHES
1 Primitive plant (*Nematophyton*)
2 Psilophite plant (*Asteroxylon*)
3 Psilophite plant (*Rhynia*)
4 Primitive insect (*Rhyniella*)
5 Placoderm fish (*Bothriolepis*)
6 Placoderm fish (*Phyllolepis*)
7 Placoderm fish (*Dunkleosteus*)
8 Early shark (*Cladoselache*)
9 Lungfish (*Dipterus*)
10 Lobe-fin fish (*Osteolepis*)
11 Crustacean (*Montecaris*)

THE FIRST AMPHIBIANS
1 Amphibian (*Ichthyostega*)
2 Club moss (*Cyclostigma*)
3 Fern (*Pseudosporochnus*)
4 Lungfish (*Scaumenacia*)
5 Rhipidistian fish (*Eusthenopteron*)
6 Millipede (*Acantherpestes ornatus*)
7 Early scorpion (*Palaeophonus*)
8 Spider-like creature (*Palaeocharinoides*)
9 Small plant (*Sciadophyton*)

THE AGE OF FISHES
Fishes (left) filled the brackish Devonian waters, about 350 million years ago, while primitive plants and insects had pioneered the land. Giant weeds (1) grew above muddy waters, and vascular plants (2, 3) colonized the shores, sheltering early insects (4). Primitive fishes (5, 6, 7) remained, but ray-finned types (8)—ancestors of modern fish—were dominant. However, it was from the lobe-finned fishes (9, 10) that the first land vertebrates emerged.

Diversification of fishes | 450 | SILURIAN | First land plants | 400 | DEVONIAN | First insects | First amphibians

The Age of Reptiles

When the Carboniferous Period began, the world was already populated with animals and plants of many kinds. The oceans were full of fishes, invertebrates and aquatic plants. The land, meanwhile, was producing dramatic new species: giant mosses and ferns, spiders and insects and, most important of all, the rapidly evolving amphibians. These creatures were taking the first evolutionary steps on a path that would lead to some of the most remarkable creatures ever to live – the dinosaurs.

The broad, low-lying, swampy plains of the late Carboniferous provided ideal conditions for the world's early plants. They spread and diversified, and some of them grew to enormous size. Giant club mosses, huge horsetails and luxuriant tree ferns took on the proportions of modern-day trees and formed the world's first forests. These new forests were full of animal life: primitive spiders and scorpions hunting their prey, giant dragonflies hovering over the marshy waters and other insects scavenging or hunting on the mossy forest floor or in the branches of the "trees." In the huge coal-forest swamps, the most advanced of all animals, the amphibians, were rapidly evolving. Some of these would ultimately return to life in the water. But others were developing stronger legs and were becoming better able to cope with an existence on dry land.

It was from this second group that the reptiles evolved—the first animals to be equipped with waterproof skins. Unlike their amphibian ancestors, they could stay out of the water indefinitely without losing their body fluids through their skins. They were no longer tied to the water's edge and the pattern of life was revolutionized. The world was soon inhabited by the first wave of land vertebrates—reptiles, which then rapidly diversified.

Included among these first reptiles were creatures known as sailbacks. They had a row of long, bony spines that supported a great fin running down from the back of their heads to the base of their tails. This whole apparatus functioned as a heat-exchange organ: the fin absorbed heat from the atmosphere in the early, cooler parts of the day, when the animal was cold, and blushed off warmth later, when it became overheated. Unlike the cold-blooded reptiles, sailbacked reptiles could, to a certain extent, regulate their body temperatures.

Mammal-like reptiles

It was only about 50 million years later, however, that animals skeletally identical to mammals were found throughout the world. Almost certainly these creatures had a degree of warm-bloodedness. But they were all rather small—the biggest was no larger than a domestic cat—and this may account for their decline. They were destined to be overshadowed for many millions of years by the dinosaurs.

The late Triassic Period, about 200 million years ago, is marked by a sudden decline in the

THE RULING REPTILES
Seymouria and other advanced amphibians evolved to form the first reptiles, such as *Scutosaurus*. From these a multitude of adaptations evolved. Some herbivores, such as *Corythosaurus*, developed 2,000 or more teeth, to help them consume tough, fibrous food plants. Another herbivorous group attained enormous size—*Brachiosaurus* weighed as much as 80 tonnes—and this may have been an adaptation to regulate body temperature (large objects lose and gain heat more slowly than small objects). Another adaptation, but one that developed mainly in the carnivores, was that of offensive weaponry: *Deinonychus* had a huge sickle-shaped claw on each hind foot and the later *Tyrannosaurus* combined a massive body with a jagged mouthful of 60 teeth. Armor plating was a defensive adaptation, produced by herbivores such as *Triceratops*, whereas speed of movement was developed both by some herbivores and by small carnivores such as *Struthiomimus*.

Corythosaurus

Seymouria

Scutosaurus

Deinonychus

THE MAMMAL LINE
Sailbacks such as *Dimetrodon* mark the beginning of mammal history. These reptiles had developed the first method of regulating body temperature—each was equipped with a large fin on its back which acted as a heat-exchange organ, a living solar panel. From these strange creatures, para-mammals such as *Lystrosaurus* evolved, animals with many mammal-like features. Some of the later members of this group, such as *Thrinaxodon*, probably even had fur on their bodies. Then, about 200 million years ago, the first true warm-blooded mammals, such as *Morganucodon*, developed. But by this time the group as a whole was declining in response to reptilian competition. Mammals would have to wait 140 million years before becoming successful again.

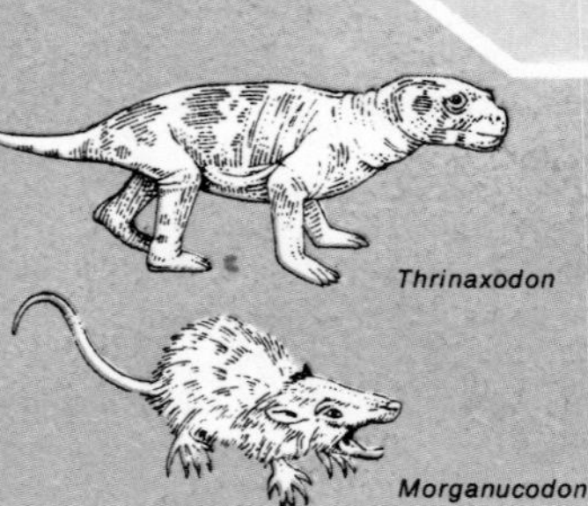

COAL FORMATION
Coal consists of carbon from plant remains and most of it was formed in the swamp-forests from which reptiles emerged. First, peat formed from rotted vegetation. Sea levels rose, ocean covered the peat bogs and marine sediments were laid down. The resulting pressure converted peat to coal. The cycle recurred and the deepest coal seams were compressed and hardened.

Coal-forming forest swamp
Peat layer
Lignite seam
Bituminous seam
Anthracite seam

Palaeozoic | Mesozoic | Cenozoic
500 | 400 | 300 | 200 | 100 | 0
Millions of years ago

Three geological eras mark the evolution of life on Earth. It was the Mesozoic era, beginning 230 million years ago, that spanned the age of reptiles. Until then, throughout the Palaeozoic era, life had been slowly evolving from the primitive organisms that appeared 400 million years earlier.

By the Mesozoic, the earliest reptiles had developed. Among their descendants were dinosaurs and early representatives of the mammalian line. Mammals, however, would have to wait another 165 million years, until the Cenozoic, before they achieved dominance.

Cycadale

Gingko biloba

The plant communities underwent as many developments in the course of the Mesozoic era as did the reptiles. The end of the Palaeozoic saw changes in climate—the Permian Period was much drier than the Carboniferous. Giant horsetails, ferns and club mosses that had formed the world's first forests gave way to other types of plant: early conifers and their relatives (the gymnosperms) came to the fore. These new species, such as the Cycadales, had evolved a new, improved method of reproduction—using seeds not spores. By Jurassic times, the climate had changed again and the moist conditions supported dense forests of ferns and of conifers. The final major Mesozoic development took place in Cretaceous times, when the flowering plants evolved.

CARBONIFEROUS | 300 | Earliest reptiles | PERMIAN | Early conifers | 250 | First radiation of reptiles | TRIASSIC | First mammals | Secon

EVOLUTION AND ADAPTATION

Once their amphibian ancestors had crawled from the swamps, reptiles rapidly evolved and developed a remarkable range of adaptations: they took to the air, invaded the seas and held dominion over the land. By early Jurassic times, they had firmly established their claim to the title Ruling Reptiles. Another group of early reptile descendants led to the mammals, and although these were long overshadowed by the dinosaurs, they were destined to rise to dominance.

mammal-like reptiles and by the extraordinary evolutionary radiation of the so-called Archosaurs ("ruling reptiles"). These began to fill every available ecological niche. They evolved into carnivores, herbivores and omnivores. They included the Crocodilians, which adapted to a life in the water; the flying pterosaurs, which were the first vertebrates to fly, and, most important of all, the dinosaurs, whose evolutionary reign over the land was to endure for the next 140 million years.

Dinosaurs adapted well to life on the land. They developed "fully erect" limbs (not unlike those of the later higher mammals) rather than the splayed legs found in most other reptiles. The new position of their limbs, which gave them the necessary mobility on dry land, was also accompanied by a general increase in size. But the dinosaurs were not the only land reptiles of the time; many other forms, including tortoises, snakes and lizards, were also carving their niches during the Mesozoic era.

Similarly, the pterosaurs did not remain the only creatures of the sky. By 170 million years ago, birds in the form of claw-winged *Archaeopteryx* had evolved, and these were to prove a serious challenge to the primitive winged reptiles which had poor flying abilities.

Aquatic reptiles

Just as the land and the air were rapidly inhabited by newly evolving forms, so the water produced many new developments. Several of the Mesozoic reptiles began to adapt to aquatic life in ways often parallel to present-day mammals: the long-necked, fish-eating plesiosaurs led a life much like that of seals; the larger pliosaurs had a streamlined shape similar to that of certain whales; some mollusc-eating placodonts could be likened to the walrus; and the elegant icthyosaurs were in many ways like dolphins. Large invertebrates were also found in the seas. The most dramatic of these were the ammonites—shelled relatives of the octopus—some of which grew to more than 2 m (6 ft) in size. Among fishes a new type emerged, the Teleosts, and these were destined to become the dominant fishes of the modern world.

Wholesale extinction

At the end of the Cretaceous Period, the reptiles were flourishing. Then suddenly, 65 million years ago, a catastrophe occurred. Virtually every species, including all the large animals, were wiped out. Throughout the Mesozoic, a series of dinosaurs and other reptiles had been evolving and slowly becoming extinct, but they were always replaced by other species. This wholesale extinction was unprecedented.

The cause of the catastrophe is unknown, but since the nature of the Earth itself was unchanged, it seems likely that some outside phenomenon was responsible. One theory suggests that a large meteorite collided with the Earth, throwing enough dust into the atmosphere to blot out the sun for several years—long enough to kill almost all the green plants on land and in the sea. If this was the case, only small animals that fed on carrion, decaying vegetation, seeds or nuts could hope to survive. Whatever the cause, the reign of the reptiles was at an end, leaving the small, adaptable mammals and birds to recolonize the virtually empty planet during the Cenozoic era.

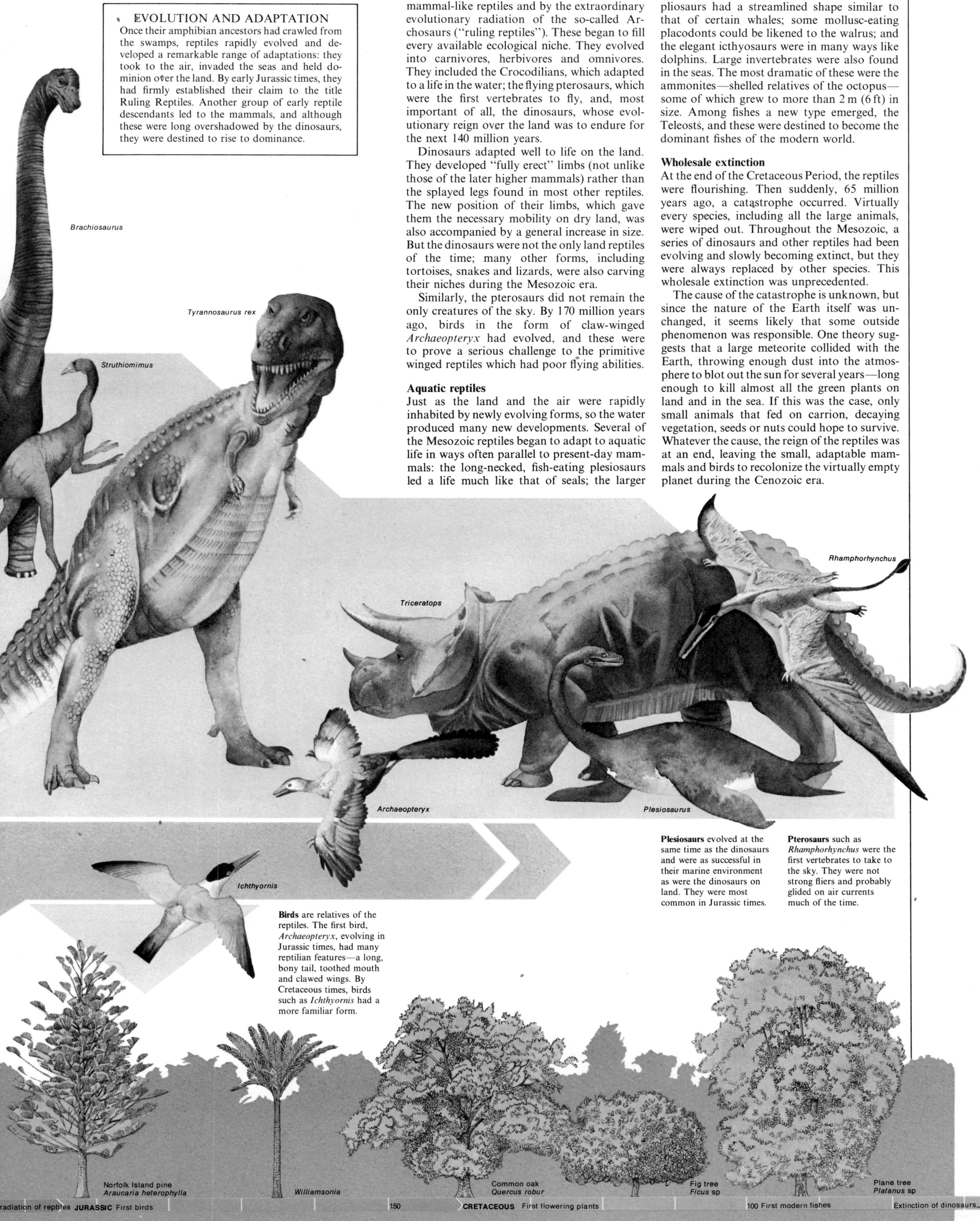

Plesiosaurs evolved at the same time as the dinosaurs and were as successful in their marine environment as were the dinosaurs on land. They were most common in Jurassic times.

Pterosaurs such as *Rhamphorhynchus* were the first vertebrates to take to the sky. They were not strong fliers and probably glided on air currents much of the time.

Birds are relatives of the reptiles. The first bird, *Archaeopteryx*, evolving in Jurassic times, had many reptilian features—a long, bony tail, toothed mouth and clawed wings. By Cretaceous times, birds such as *Ichthyornis* had a more familiar form.

The Age of Mammals

After the time of the great dying, 65 million years ago, reptiles never regained the importance they had achieved during the Mesozoic era. A new era, the Cenozoic, had begun. On the continental landmasses, mammals and birds, newly released from 160 million years of reptilian domination, began to occupy their niches in the rich, empty habitats. They flourished and diversified, and the cold-blooded reptiles became second-class citizens in a world of warm-blooded animals.

While reptiles still dominated the world, during the late Mesozoic, a new group of mammals had arisen. These were the first creatures on Earth to give birth to fully formed, live young. Until this time, the most advanced of the mammals had been marsupials whose young were still virtually embryos at birth and had to develop in the mother's pouch, or marsupium. The new mammals had evolved a more sophisticated system—the mother retained the fetus safely inside her body until it was fully formed, nourishing it during this time through a special organ, the placenta, developed during pregnancy. These mammals, the placentals, were destined to become the major mammalian group.

Although all the Mesozoic placentals were small, they had already evolved into a number of different forms that existed alongside the dinosaurs. Besides the insectivores, which were the ancestral type, they included early representatives of the Primates (precursors of modern monkeys and apes), the Carnivores, and the now extinct Condylarthrans (primitive hoofed mammals). When suddenly, 65 million years ago, there was no longer competition from the large land reptiles, these early groups rapidly evolved and extravagant forms developed.

But just as the first reptiles had passed through an early evolution, largely to be replaced by a second evolutionary wave, so the first large mammals were, in many cases, superseded by other, more successful lines. In the earliest part of the Cenozoic era, the different groups of placentals, although not closely related, all tended to be heavy limbed and heavy tailed and to walk on the whole length of their feet (as do modern bears) or on thick, stubby toes. These ungainly, thickset mammals soon died out. Some became extinct because their descendants, more efficiently adapted to their environment, overtook and replaced them. Others, such as the powerful taeniodonts and the large rodent-like tillodonts, seem to have been evolutionary blind alleys.

Spectacular developments

It was the Oligocene Period, 36 million years ago, that saw the end of most of these early essays in mammalian gigantism, but, in many parts of the world, they were replaced by others just as spectacular. In South America, the giant sloths and glyptodonts (massive relatives of the armadillos) survived until comparatively recently. The ground sloths, at least, were contemporaries of the first men on the continent.

As each group of early mammals evolved, during the early and middle part of the Cenozoic era, many of their developments closely reflected changes taking place in their environment. The first horse-like creature, for example, was *Hyracotherium*, also called *Eohippus* or "dawn horse." It lived 54 million years ago and was a small, multi-toed creature, well adapted to its densely forested habitat. The teeth of its descendants gradually changed in size and complexity, but it was not until the Miocene Period, nearly 20 million years later, that any radical alterations took place. This was the time when grasses (the Gramineae), until then a rare family of plants, came to the fore. The world's plains suddenly became clothed in a food plant very suitable for the attention of grazing creatures such as the early horses.

Animals of the grasslands

Horses and many other animals moved from the forests to make use of this new and abundant food supply. Once on the plains, different adaptations for survival were required: high-crowned teeth to deal with tough grasses; limbs enabling the animal to run tirelessly without extra, unwanted weight from supporting side toes (which were lost); large eyes capable of seeing for long distances and placed far back on the head for detecting predators approaching from any direction (as a result of which, however, the ability to judge distances ahead had to be sacrificed). Thus, the modern horses are plains-dwelling animals, perfectly adapted to their present way of life.

Mammals reached the climax of diversity during the Pliocene Period, 10 million years ago. But in the following period, the Pleistocene, ice sheets swept down from the polar regions and from the high mountains of the north, bringing massive and sudden changes to the ecology of virtually every region in the world. This dramatic disturbance to the environment brought extinction to an enormous number of species.

The survivors consisted mainly of the smaller species. Unfortunately for many of them, however, they included *Homo sapiens*. Man rose to success at the end of the Pleistocene and has, in the last 10,000 years, taken dominion over virtually every part of the world. During this time, he has proved far more destructive to other animal species than any natural force has ever been. More than 5,000 years ago, the giant sloths may have been a dying species, but there is no doubt that early human hunters hurried on their extinction. Since then, the list of species eliminated by man has grown ever longer. Today the human race is causing the extinction of both animals and plants at a rate comparable to that of 65 million years ago, when some dramatic natural catastrophe swept the dinosaurs from the face of the world. Unless man, the super-efficient species, can curb his numbers and his destructive activities, a new age of dying may soon be upon the world.

By early Cenozoic times, many forms had evolved from the insectivorous mammals of the Mesozoic Period. *Miacis*, *Hyaenodon* and *Oxyaena* were flesh eaters. Plant-eating mammals, such as Taeniodonts, *Arsinoitherium* and *Phenacodus* (one of the first hoofed mammals), had also evolved, while other early forms, such as *Andrewsarchus*, were omnivorous. The early Primates, however, remained insect eaters for millions of years.

EARLY STAGES

Miacis

Andrewsarchus

Arsinc

Hyaenodon

The Carnivores diversified into two major types—the cats and their kin (Aeluroidea), and the dogs and their relatives (Arctoidea). During the Oligocene Period, about 36 million years ago, Aeluroidea gave rise not only to early relatives of modern cats, such as sabre-toothed *Hoplophoneus*, but also to two other families, the civets and the hyenas. At the same time, Arctoidea also diversified and produced the dogs, weasels, bears and racoons. It was a complex group, with many forms that were later to become extinct—the massive bear-dogs, such as *Daphoenus*, for example, which lived during the Miocene Period. Cats and dogs evolved to exploit different habitats. The cats adapted to life in forests, and learned to hide and then stalk and ambush their prey. Dogs evolved as plains animals, and used pack-hunting techniques to catch fleet-footed, grassland animals.

Perissodactyls and Artiodactyls were two important groups that evolved from the primitive hoofed mammals; Perissodactyls had an odd number of toes on each foot, Artiodactyls had an even number. These two groups suffered very different fortunes. Artiodactyls are still at the height of their success; the early stock produced the modern pig, camel, deer, giraffe, hippopotamus, antelope, sheep, goat and cow. Perissodactyls, however, are in decline and the only survivors are the horse, rhinoceros and tapir. But they were once important and many, now-extinct, kinds such as *Moropus* and *Brontotherium* existed alongside more familiar types such as *Hyracotherium*. Few remained after the Pliocene Period, however. This was when the Artiodactyls came to the fore. They, too, had had casualties—the pig-like *Archaeotherium* was by then extinct—but many other Artiodactyls, such as the early giraffe, *Palaeotragus*, were evolving. Most important, however, was small *Archaeomeryx*, for it had developed the key to Artiodactyl success—it was a ruminant and this enabled it to make the best possible use of the world's new grasslands.

Diatryma

Euryapteryx

CENOZOIC BIRDS

Giant flightless birds came to the fore more than once during the Cenozoic era. *Diatryma*, a massive, flesh-eating bird, ruled the North American grasslands in early Cenozoic times, while mammals were still small, fairly primitive and easily dominated. *Euryapteryx* and its relatives (the moas) evolved in New Zealand, where, because there were no mammals, they filled an empty ecological niche.

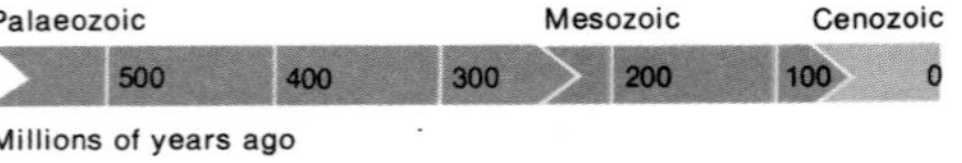

Three geological eras mark the slow evolution of life on Earth. The Palaeozoic era, 570 million years ago, saw the appearance of the first primitive life forms. By the end of the era, 340 million years later, the reptiles had evolved and the following Mesozoic era was the age of reptilian domination. This reign over the land ended 65 million years ago as the Cenozoic era began. Then mammals came to the fore and the age of mammalian dominance of the world had dawned.

EARLY GRASSES

Grasses first appeared in the densely forested lands of 60 million years ago. Probably similar to the sedges (right) found in wet woodland areas today, they offered an attractive meal to many mammals. But it was not until the Miocene Period, when a change in climate reduced forest cover, that grasses became widespread. Then many forest creatures migrated to grassland areas.

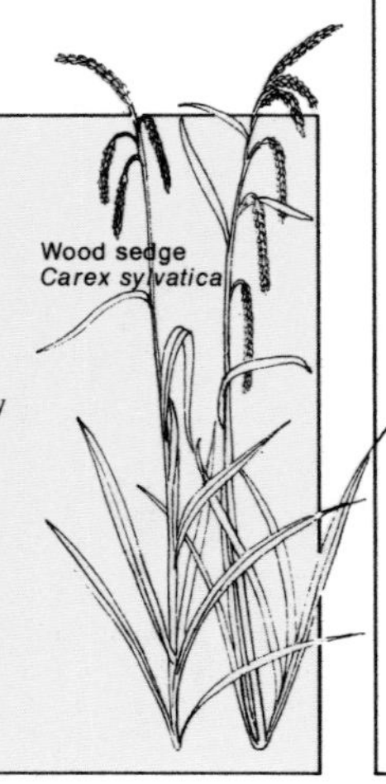

THE MARSUPIALS

Thylacosmilus and mouse-like *Argyrolagus* were two of the many forms of marsupial mammal that evolved in Cenozoic times in South America. Almost everywhere else, the marsupials, unable to compete with their more efficient placental cousins, met with an early extinction. But in two remote regions—South America (then separate from North America) and Australia—there was no competition from placentals, and there the marsupials flourished.

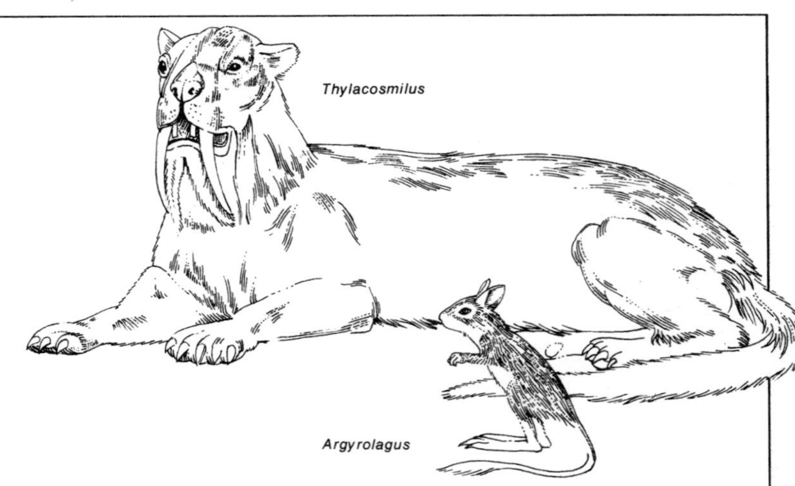

TERTIARY First radiation of mammals and birds — Forest horses — Second radiation of mammals

Palaeocene 60 **Eocene** 50 40 **Oligocene**

THE SPREAD OF MAMMALS

Before the death of the dinosaurs, mammals were quietly evolving and diversifying. But as soon as the reign of the reptiles ended, this gentle pace of development changed to a bewilderingly rapid proliferation throughout the world. New species and complete new orders appeared one after another. Old orders rapidly adapted or, overtaken by newer, more efficient groups, died out.

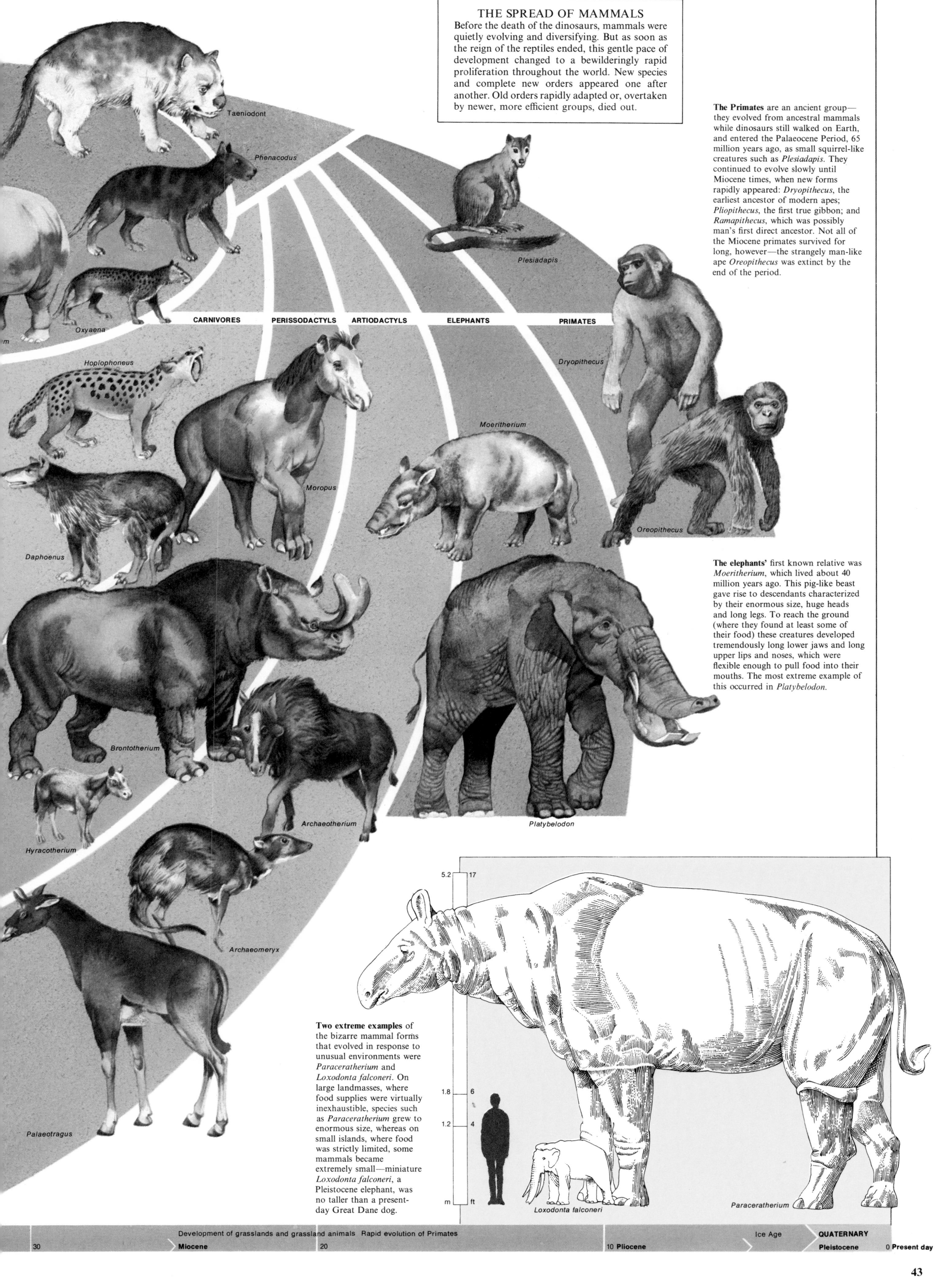

The Primates are an ancient group—they evolved from ancestral mammals while dinosaurs still walked on Earth, and entered the Palaeocene Period, 65 million years ago, as small squirrel-like creatures such as *Plesiadapis*. They continued to evolve slowly until Miocene times, when new forms rapidly appeared: *Dryopithecus*, the earliest ancestor of modern apes; *Pliopithecus*, the first true gibbon; and *Ramapithecus*, which was possibly man's first direct ancestor. Not all of the Miocene primates survived for long, however—the strangely man-like ape *Oreopithecus* was extinct by the end of the period.

The elephants' first known relative was *Moeritherium*, which lived about 40 million years ago. This pig-like beast gave rise to descendants characterized by their enormous size, huge heads and long legs. To reach the ground (where they found at least some of their food) these creatures developed tremendously long lower jaws and long upper lips and noses, which were flexible enough to pull food into their mouths. The most extreme example of this occurred in *Platybelodon.*

Two extreme examples of the bizarre mammal forms that evolved in response to unusual environments were *Paraceratherium* and *Loxodonta falconeri*. On large landmasses, where food supplies were virtually inexhaustible, species such as *Paraceratherium* grew to enormous size, whereas on small islands, where food was strictly limited, some mammals became extremely small—miniature *Loxodonta falconeri*, a Pleistocene elephant, was no taller than a present-day Great Dane dog.

Spread of Life

Different parts of the Earth have their own characteristic groups of animals, and this pattern of distribution caused nineteenth-century zoologists to divide the world into zoogeographical regions. Charles Darwin suggested how these assemblages of animals may have come about by the process of evolution. But we now know that movements of the Earth's land surfaces are also responsible for the present-day distribution of many of the world's animal species and groups.

The evolution of a major group of animals, such as the reptiles or the mammals, tends to follow a set pattern in five stages. First the original ancestral group spreads out, with each subgroup adapting to its environment. This process, called adaptive radiation, results in a variety of different kinds of animals, each suited to life in a particular niche or habitat—determined largely by food supply and environmental conditions. The different kinds then move into all of the areas they can reach in which the environment is right, producing the second stage of widespread distribution.

Competition for food or living space, or changes in climate may then cause some forms to decline and disappear from parts of the range, resulting in a third stage of discontinuous distribution. Any further reduction leads to isolated relict populations—the fourth stage—in which the animal exists only in one or two limited areas. The final stage is extinction.

In all distribution patterns, however, there is not only an ecological element but also a historical one, with past events determining where animals are and where they are not. There are thus two basic types of distribution: continuous, where the area is not interrupted by an insurmountable barrier (such as a mountain range), and discontinuous, where the area of distribution is subdivided and there is no way that members of one group can interchange with members of another.

One of these factors—the earliest and most important—is the (continuing) movement of the Earth's tectonic plates. This caused the supercontinent Pangaea to break up, probably in the Triassic Period (225–180 million years ago), and the continental masses to drift apart to their present positions. New oceans developed, separating the Americas from the Euro-African block and splitting both from Antarctica. Madagascar and Australia became islands, India moved north from Africa to join the Asian block, and mountain ranges such as the Alps, Andes, Rockies and Himalayas were thrown up. As a result, animal types that had already evolved on Pangaea or its fragments before they had significantly separated (i.e. all the major invertebrate groups and most of the earlier vertebrates) can be expected to exist on all the present-day continents.

Bridging the continents

Independently of these activities, ice ages occurred from time to time, resulting in the vast accumulations of ice at the poles and a consequent general lowering of the sea level by as much as 100 m (330 ft). This temporarily exposed the previously submerged continental shelves, providing additional land for colonization, and new corridors that linked existing areas, such as the land bridge that appeared between Alaska and Siberia.

Groups that had evolved after the breakup of Pangaea, e.g. the hare, squirrel and dog families, made use of land bridges as the climate allowed, and came to occupy more than one continent. Flying animals—birds and bats—also made intercontinental crossings and established themselves on both sides of oceans, although a surprising number of these have remained very restricted in distribution. But most animals have to stay where they are because of special dietary or environmental requirements, or because they are "trapped" on islands, such as Madagascar and Australia, and cannot get off. These areas have the most distinctive faunas in the world.

Barriers and corridors

The extent to which an expanding group can spread from its original area depends on whether there are barriers, such as mountain ranges, deserts or seas, or corridors that link major areas in which the animals can live. Different animals have different environmental requirements, and so a topographical feature that is a barrier for one may be a corridor for another.

The dispersal of many animals is achieved by "hopping" from lake to lake across a continent, or from island to island across a sea. Some, such as insects, are good at this, whereas others, such as land mammals, are bad. Thus a considerable range of weevils (Curculionidae) are found on islands from New Caledonia to the Marquesas, some 6,500 km (4,000 miles) across the southern Pacific Ocean, whereas the marsupials of the region are concentrated in Australia, Papua New Guinea and a few adjacent islands, with only one genus reaching the Celebes and none crossing Wallace's Line into Borneo.

An example of colonization by "hopping" is seen on the volcanic island of Krakatoa near Java, which exploded in 1883 destroying all life. Within 25 years there were 263 species of animals on the island. Most were insects, but there were three species of land snails, two species of reptiles and 16 of birds. In another 22 years, 46 species of vertebrates had arrived, including two species of rats.

The effect of man

Animal distribution cannot be considered merely as a natural phenomenon, because it has been greatly and increasingly modified by man's impact on the environment. Agricultural practice has made large sections of the land area unsuitable for many of the animals that originally lived there, notably through the clearing of forests and the draining of marshes.

Man has also introduced animals, either deliberately or accidentally, to regions where they were not endemic. The rabbit in Australia and the deer in New Zealand were both deliberately introduced, but rats, cockroaches and many other animals have been accidentally transported throughout the world on ships and aircraft. The enormous growth in human population has driven many animals from their natural homes and into more remote environments, such as mountains. Indeed, in the past century human interference has altered the pattern of animal distribution more drastically than any topographic or climatic change.

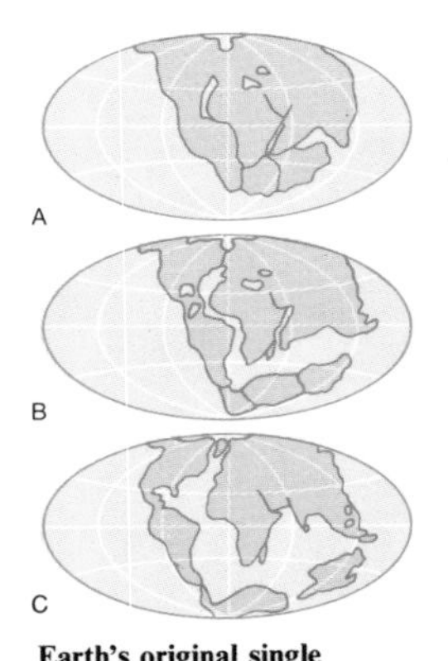

Earth's original single landmass, Pangaea (A), probably began to break up more than 200 million years ago. Species that had already evolved diversified on the Noah's Arks of the drifting supercontinents (B), called Laurasia and Gondwanaland. As the process continued (C), related animals flourished in the separated continents of the southern hemisphere.

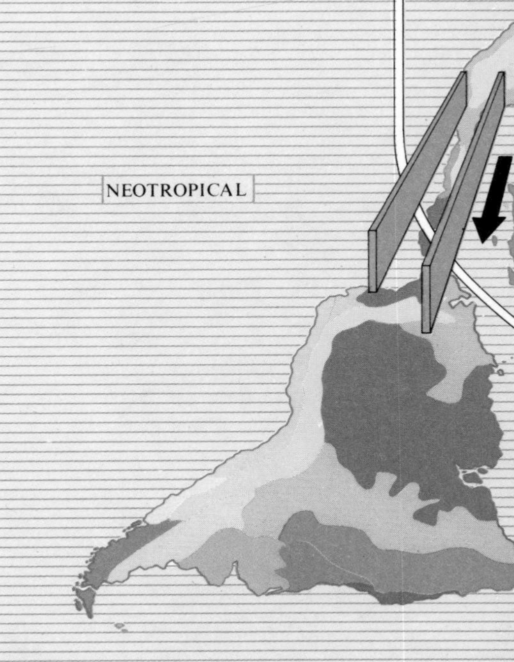

PATTERNS OF ANIMALS

Over the ages the shape of the Earth has changed. Whole continents have moved; mountains and deserts have grown; land bridges between continents have opened and closed. These events, together with food supply, climate and other animals, account for the present natural pattern of life in the six zoogeographical regions, each containing a unique mix of animals. But man's activities have drastically affected this natural distribution in all parts of the world.

NEARCTIC

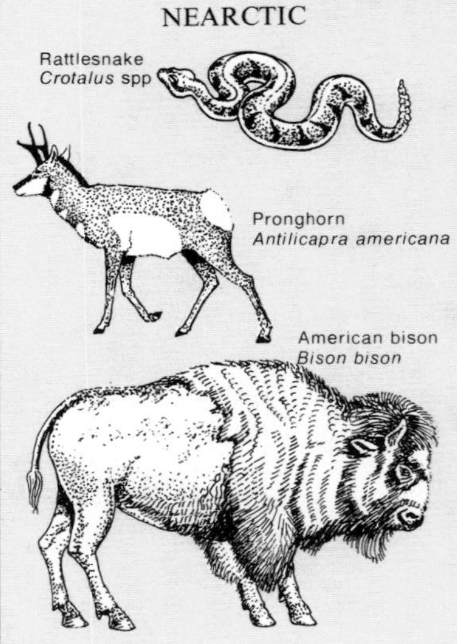

The Nearctic or "New North" region covers all of North America, from the highlands of Mexico in the south to Greenland and the Aleutian Islands in the north. Its climate and vegetation resemble that of the Palearctic region, and many of its mammals crossed over from the Palearctic via the Bering land bridge, which linked Siberia and Alaska when the sea level was lower. Animals unique to the Nearctic group include the pronghorn, an antelope-like mammal that inhabits the grasslands and plains of western and central America, and the bison, another large mammal that inhabits the prairies. Several species of rattlesnake also belong to the Nearctic group, although they are not exclusive to this region.

NEOTROPICAL

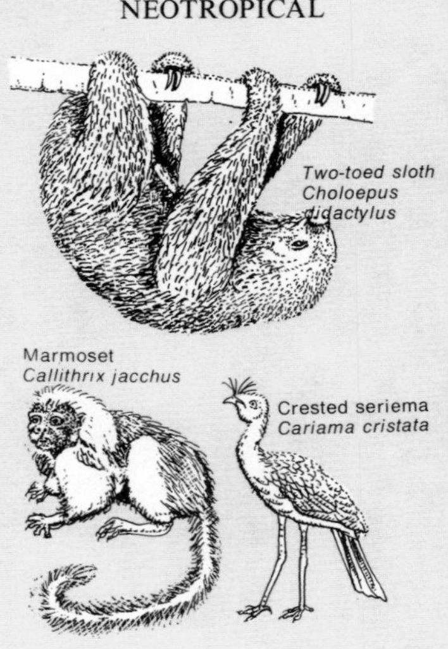

The Neotropical or "New Tropical" region consists of South America, the West Indies and most of Mexico. The climate and vegetation are mostly tropical—only the southern tip is in the temperate zone—and it is linked to the Nearctic by the Central American corridor. The Neotropical region has more distinctive families than any other. These include, among mammals, the sloth, which inhabits the tropical forests and has adapted to an upside-down existence. Among birds, the long-legged crested seriema is also unique to the region. Neotropical monkeys, such as the marmoset, have lateral-facing nostrils, which distinguish them from their downward-nosed relatives found in the Old World.

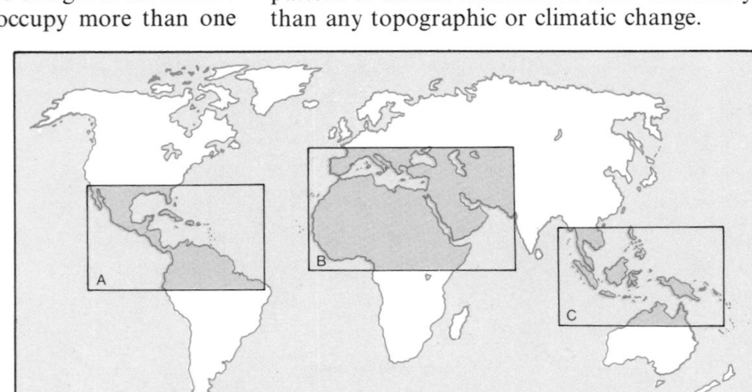

Land routes around the world have altered with the ages, sometimes allowing invaders to penetrate new lands, or closing to form natural sanctuaries for less efficient animals. The Central American isthmus (A) opened South America to placental mammals from the north. The Sahara desert closed most of Africa (B) to Eurasian species. Asia and Australia (C) share "island hoppers" in the transitional zones, but sea barriers have kept the regions separate.

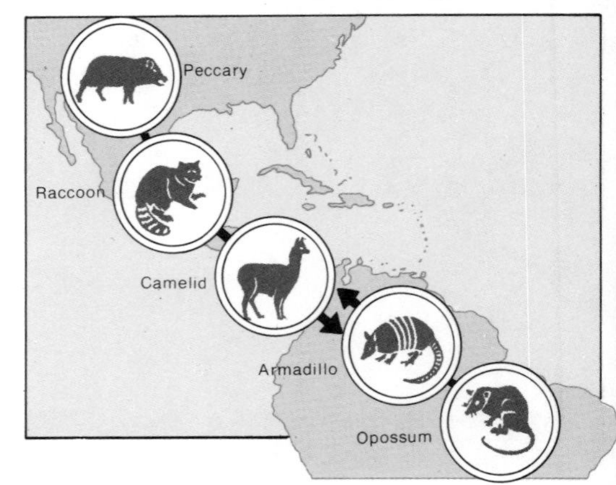

A land bridge between the Americas emerged about three million years ago, breaking the long isolation of the south. The primitive pouched mammals which had developed there were now threatened by more advanced mammals from the north, and many extinctions followed. Northern invaders included peccaries, raccoons and a llama-like camelid. But members of the armadillo and opossum families were successful in making their way to the northern region.

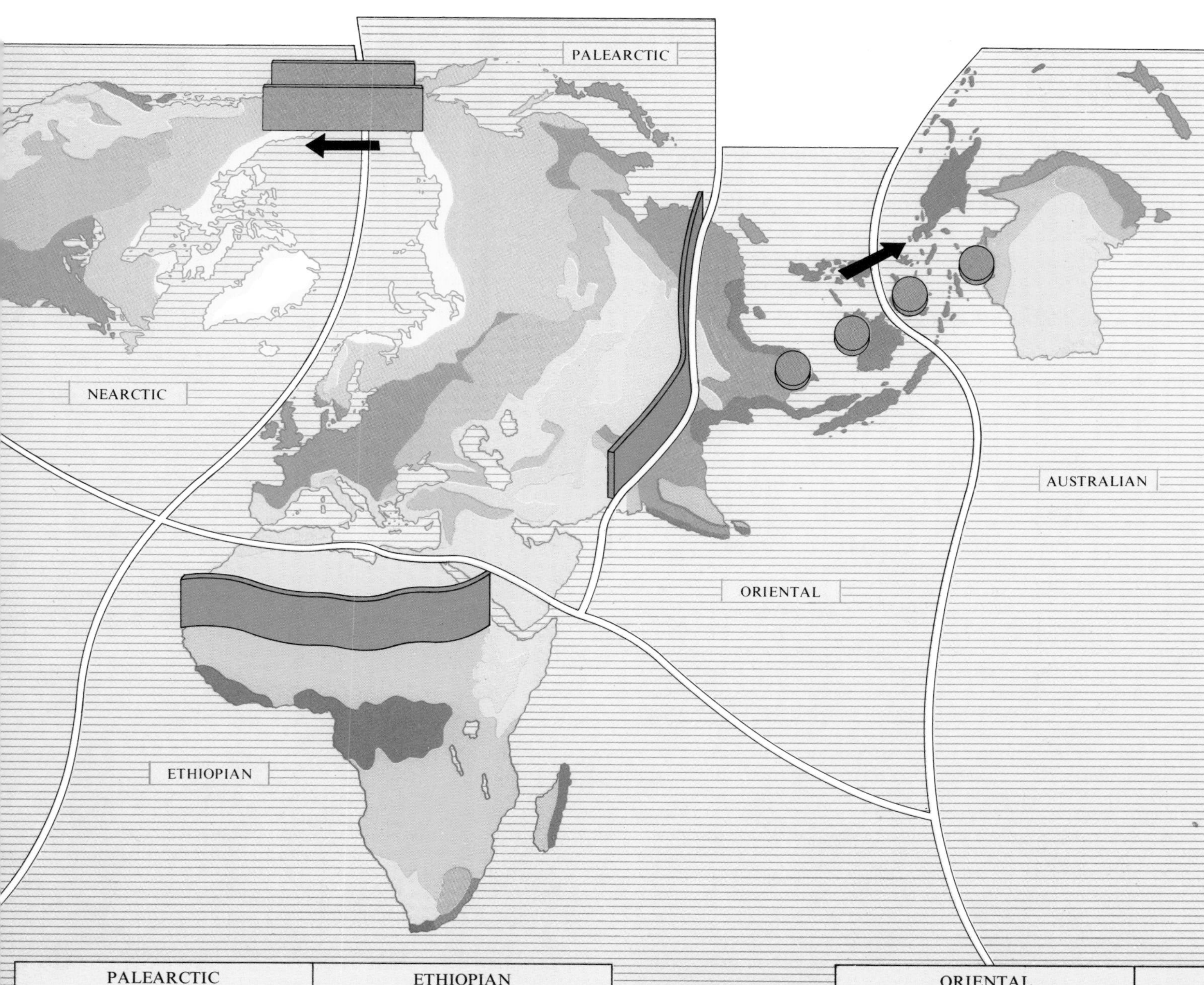

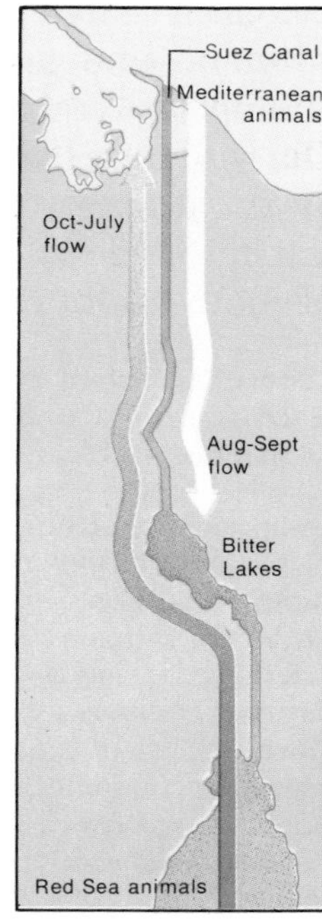

The man-made filter of the Suez Canal, cut in 1869, is an animal corridor between the Mediterranean and Red Sea. But movement is mainly from the latter, for the channel passes through the hot, salty Bitter Lakes, favoring animals adapted to these conditions, and the current flows northwards for 10 months of the year. However, not all the 130 invading species are likely to survive Mediterranean conditions.

PALEARCTIC

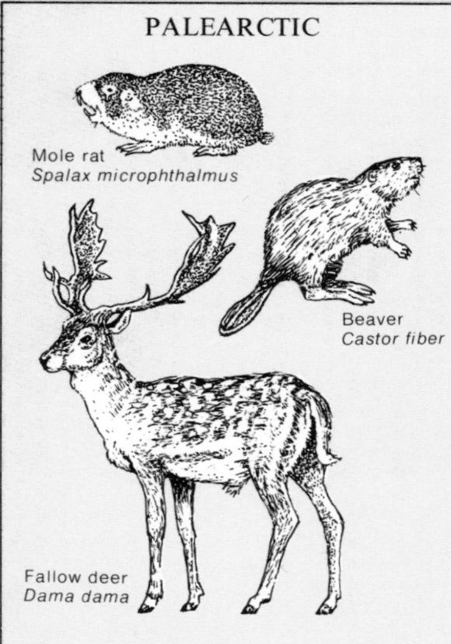

The Palearctic or "Old North" region covers the entire northerly part of the Old World, with seas to the north, east and west. To the south, the Sahara desert and the Himalaya mountains form barriers that separate the Palearctic from the Ethiopian and Oriental regions, although these regions are all part of the same landmass. One of the few species of mammals unique to the Palearctic is the Mediterranean mole rat, a thick-furred rodent. Another Palearctic rodent, the beaver, is shared with the Nearctic region. Fallow deer occur throughout Europe. They have been introduced by man into many other parts of the world, but their origin is almost certainly Mediterranean.

ETHIOPIAN

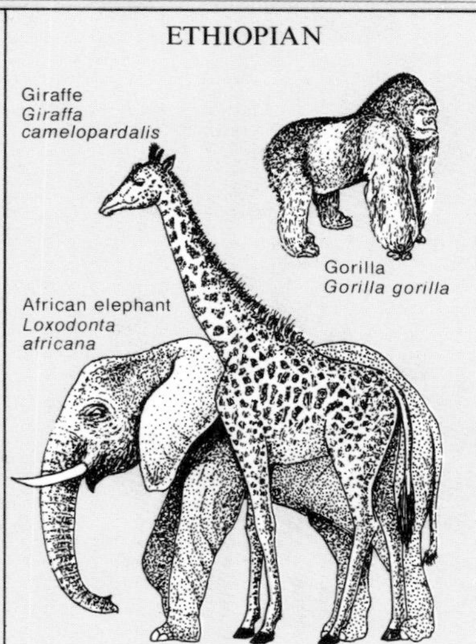

The Ethiopian region includes southern Arabia as well as all Africa south of the Sahara. It resembles in many ways the Neotropical region and is almost as rich in unique families. Its fauna also has much in common with the Oriental region. Unique mammals include the giraffe, at 5.5 m (18 ft) the tallest of living land animals, which inhabits the savanna. The region also supports two of the world's four great apes, the gorilla and the chimpanzee, which are found in the forests of western and central Africa. (The other great apes, the orangutan and the gibbon, are Oriental.) The African elephant is distinguished from its Indian relative by its greater size and by its huge ears and massive tusks.

Polar
Tundra
Taiga
Mountain
Temperate forest
Temperate grassland
Mediterranean
Savanna
Tropical rainforest
Monsoon
Desert
Barrier
Corridor
Stepping stone
Prevailing movement

ORIENTAL

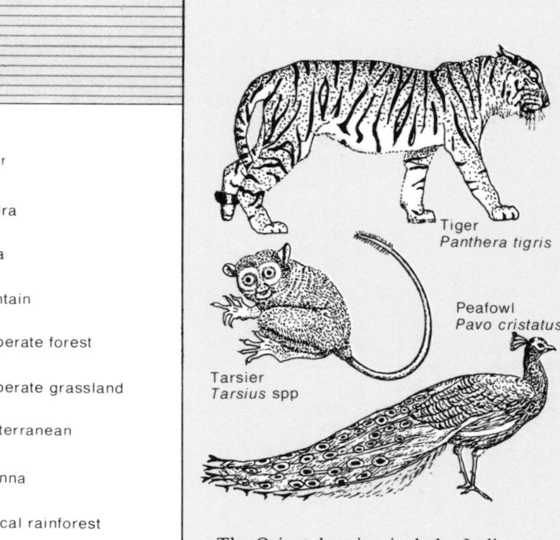

The Oriental region includes India, southern China, southeastern Asia and part of Malaysia. It is bounded to the north by the Himalayas and on either side by ocean, and is separated from the Australian region by a line known as Wallace's Line. It shares a quarter of its mammal families with Africa, but has more primates than any other region. The tarsier, a small relative of the monkey, is unique to southeastern Asia and represents an important early stage of primate evolution. The tiger was once widespread, but its natural habitats are steadily diminishing and the tiger itself is in danger of extinction by man. The peacock is one of the region's many brilliantly colored birds.

AUSTRALIAN

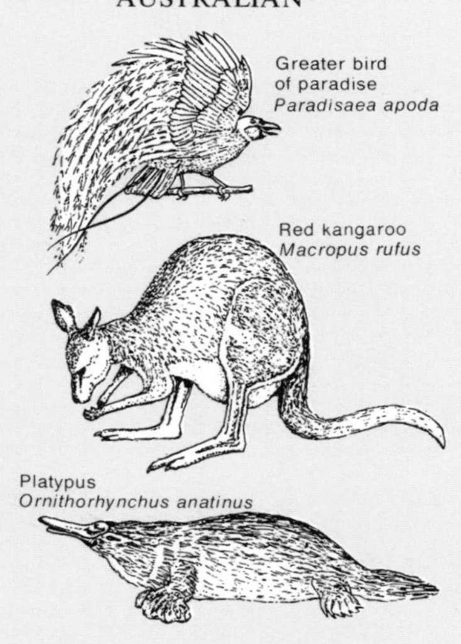

The Australian region is unique in having no land connection with any other region. Its native fauna has developed in isolation from the rest of the world for at least 50 million years. Most of the mammals are marsupial—animals such as the kangaroo that carry their young in a pouch. Even more of a biological curiosity than the marsupials is the duckbilled platypus, a monotreme or egg-laying mammal. It lives along the banks of streams in Australia and Tasmania, and lays small, leathery eggs like those of snakes and turtles, but it is a true mammal and nurses its young with milk. Some 13 bird families are unique to the region, including the magnificent bird of paradise.

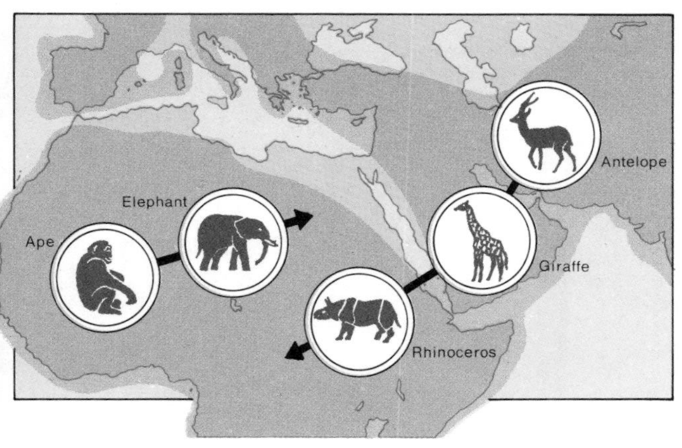

A desert barrier gradually began to form in northern Africa about nine million years ago, replacing the forest corridor between the Ethiopian and Palearctic regions. During the change, many animals typical of the African plains moved in from the north, including ancestors of today's antelopes, giraffes and rhinoceroses. But African animals also moved up north: early elephants and, much later, apes, which may have been precursors of modern man.

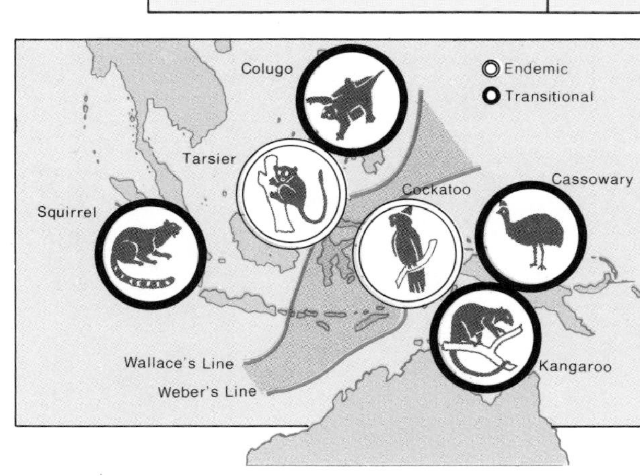

The transitional area of "Wallacea" contains animals from both the Oriental and Australian regions, bounded by Wallace's and Weber's Lines, but few have crossed to the other region. Some Oriental mammals, such as tarsiers, are found in Wallacea, but the gliding colugo and varieties of squirrel are not. The Australian cockatoo has reached the transition area, but the flightless cassowary and the tree kangaroo have not.

Spread of Man

Modern Man, *Homo sapiens sapiens*, has proved a highly successful animal since his emergence some 50,000 years ago: today more than 4,000 million members of this subspecies of the *Homo* (Man) group occupy the Earth, living in even the most inhospitable regions. But the fossil record shows that man's lineage goes back millions of years, with different stages of development leading to a greater control of the environment, and with climate itself helping man's ultimate domination of Earth.

Man's lineage may go back at least 14 million years to a small woodland creature known as *Ramapithecus* (Rama's ape). Since the first discoveries of *Ramapithecus* in the Indian subcontinent, its fossils have come to light in many parts of the world, including China, eastern Europe, Turkey and eastern Africa. Fossil remains show that it survived for several million years until, about eight million years ago, there is a tantalizing gap in the fossil record. Then, about four and a half million years later (according to recent discoveries in eastern Africa), we have solid evidence of an upright hominid—a member of man's zoological family. This is "Lucy," a fossil skeleton found in 1973 by Donald Johanson and Tom Gray, and subsequently classified with many other finds as *Australopithecus afarensis.*

This may be man's ancestral "rootstock," but a little later there existed two kinds of "ape-man" (*Australopithecus*), and our own direct ancestor Handy Man (*Homo habilis*). Datable volcanic ash found with the fossils provides a time scale and indicates that, about two million years ago, ape-man and "true" man lived side by side in the lush grassland that then covered the eastern African plains.

One and a half million years ago, according to the fossil evidence, there was again only one hominid species. The varieties of australopithecines had died out, and Handy Man (*Homo habilis*) had apparently evolved into Upright Man (*Homo erectus*). Remains of Upright Man have been found in many regions of the world, from various parts of Africa and Europe to China and Indonesia, although not in the Americas. But there is reason to believe that it was in Africa, well over one million years ago, that he evolved from his ancestor, and began a very gradual expansion out of the continent.

Upright Man had about one million years to spread across the Old World, adapting as he did so to local conditions, just as people of today are adapted in their various ways. He was a nomadic hunter gatherer, socially organized in groups. His skills included the use of fire and cooking, as well as the making of quite large structures out of wood. Recent discoveries suggest that, during the million years of his existence, *Homo erectus* gradually evolved into the next stage of man – *Homo sapiens.*

The next step is revealed most clearly in fossils from more than 100,000 to less than 50,000 years ago. Called Neanderthal Man in Europe, Solo Man in Indonesia, and Rhodesian Man in southern Africa, these types of human being were all descendants of *Homo erectus.*

Variable in brain size, but with prominent eyebrow ridges and receding jaws, they may have been dead ends on the evolutionary road; or some may have led to, or been incorporated in, Modern Man (*Homo sapiens sapiens*).

THE AFRICAN CRADLE
Handy Man (*Homo habilis*), who shared the East African grasslands two million years ago with a related "ape-man" species, was a slender and agile creature with a human way of walking and a capacity for conceptual thought, as evidenced in systematic making of tools. Handy Man collected stones, often from far away, and reshaped them into purpose-made tools, using other stones. Fossil remains suggest that these earliest humans were efficient hunters as well as scavengers of larger predators' kills, and that they brought food to campsites, probably sharing it among the whole group, rather than eating it on the spot. Such specifically human characteristics as the sharing of food may have helped our ancestors to survive their more primitive hominid relations.

MAN THE FIRE-BRINGER
Upright Man (*Homo erectus*) emerged about 1.5 million years ago, evolving from his predecessor, Handy Man. For one million years these people developed and adapted, spreading over most of the Old World and following a nomadic hunter-gatherer life-style, assisted by a more sophisticated tool technology. The cooler climates of northern Asia and Europe may have encouraged their most impressive innovation—the use of fire for warmth, cooking and hunting game—and also their ability to construct quite elaborate shelters. It seems likely that they possessed language; and traces of ocher lumps at a campsite perhaps 400,000 years old suggest the possibility of ritual adornment or some kind of body painting.

THE HUMANIZING OF MAN
Modern man's predecessor, although called Wise Man (*Homo sapiens*), was long regarded as more brutish than human. But widespread finds have now changed this image, as can be seen in an old and an updated reconstruction of the same Neanderthal skull (right). Many scientists believe that these people showed a human concern for each other, burying their dead with ceremonial reverence, and looking after disabled members of the group. In their Neanderthal form they inhabited Europe and the Middle East from about 100,000 to 40,000 years ago, and were perhaps adapted to ice-age conditions. *Homo sapiens* counterparts of Neanderthal Man also occur in Africa and southeastern Asia.

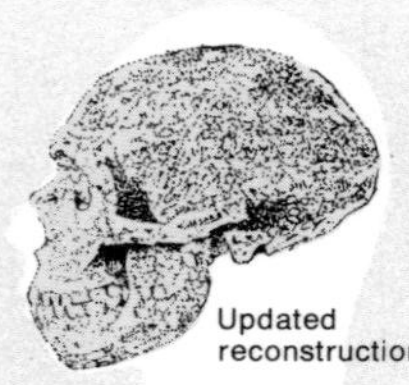
Updated reconstruction

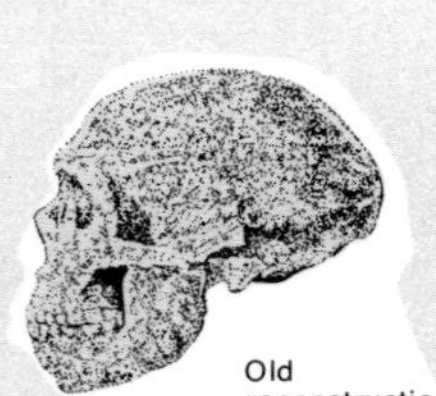
Old reconstruction

The burial of a Neanderthal man took place 60,000 years ago at Shanidar in the Iraq highlands. Fossil traces suggest that the body was laid on a bed of branches, and that flowers were brought to the grave and placed deliberately around the body. The flowers included many varieties still known locally for their medicinal properties. Ritual burials occur at many Neanderthal sites, from the Pyrenees to Soviet Asia, and indicate a sensitivity that contradicts Neanderthal Man's traditional image.

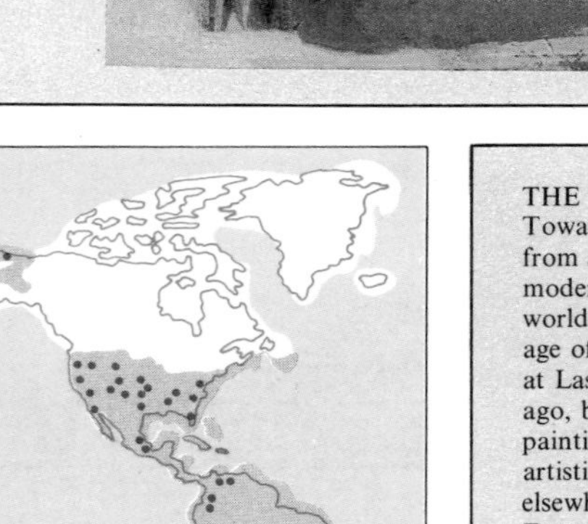

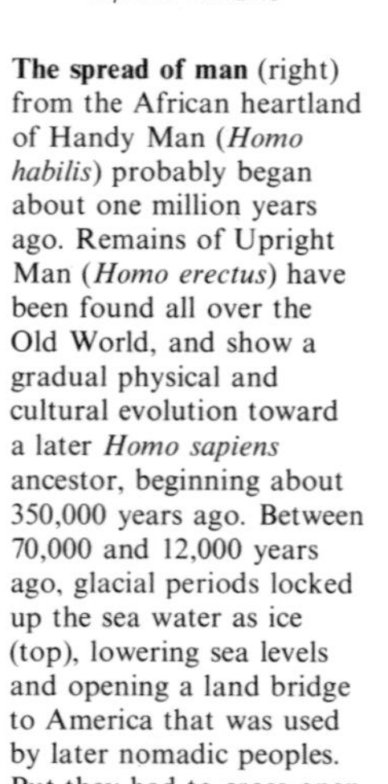

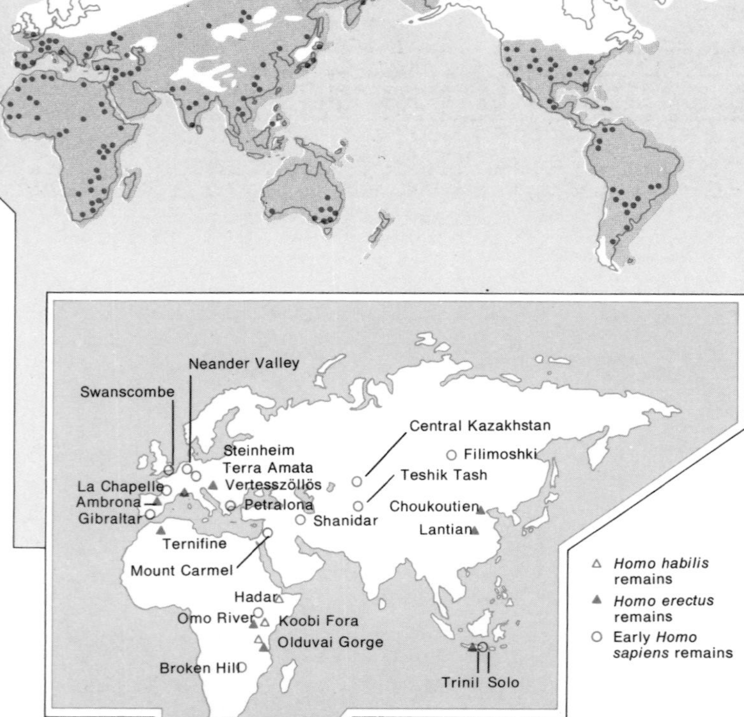

The spread of man (right) from the African heartland of Handy Man (*Homo habilis*) probably began about one million years ago. Remains of Upright Man (*Homo erectus*) have been found all over the Old World, and show a gradual physical and cultural evolution toward a later *Homo sapiens* ancestor, beginning about 350,000 years ago. Between 70,000 and 12,000 years ago, glacial periods locked up the sea water as ice (top), lowering sea levels and opening a land bridge to America that was used by later nomadic peoples. But they had to cross open sea to reach Australia.

THE AGE OF ART
Toward the end of the last Ice Age, from about 35,000 years ago, truly modern humans began to depict their world in wonderfully vivid terms. The age of art may have reached its peak at Lascaux, France, some 15,000 years ago, but less well-preserved cave paintings from Africa show that the artistic impulse was equally present elsewhere. Called Cro-Magnon Man in Europe, these people spread to all parts of the world, crossing to the Americas by way of the Bering land bridge (when ice locked up the water of the straits), and even venturing over the seas to Australia. Physically these people were just like present-day humans. They led a nomadic, hunter-gathering life, living in large, organized groups, hunting such animals as mammoths, reindeer, bison and horses, and using a technology, as well as an artistry, far in advance of anything previously developed.

Fossils almost four million years old, found since 1973, may mark the ancestral "rootstock" of humanity, but the earliest form of true man is thought to be *Homo habilis*, who shared his African habitat with "ape-man" relatives some two million years ago. His successor, *Homo erectus*, spread over Asia and Europe, evolving gradually into modern man's predecessors, creatures whose large brow ridges belie many typically human characteristics. These were replaced by Modern Man.

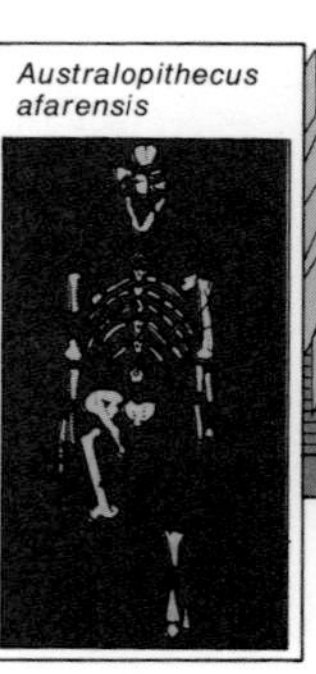

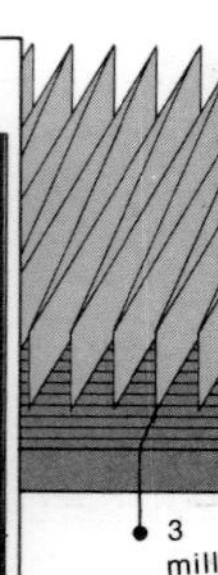

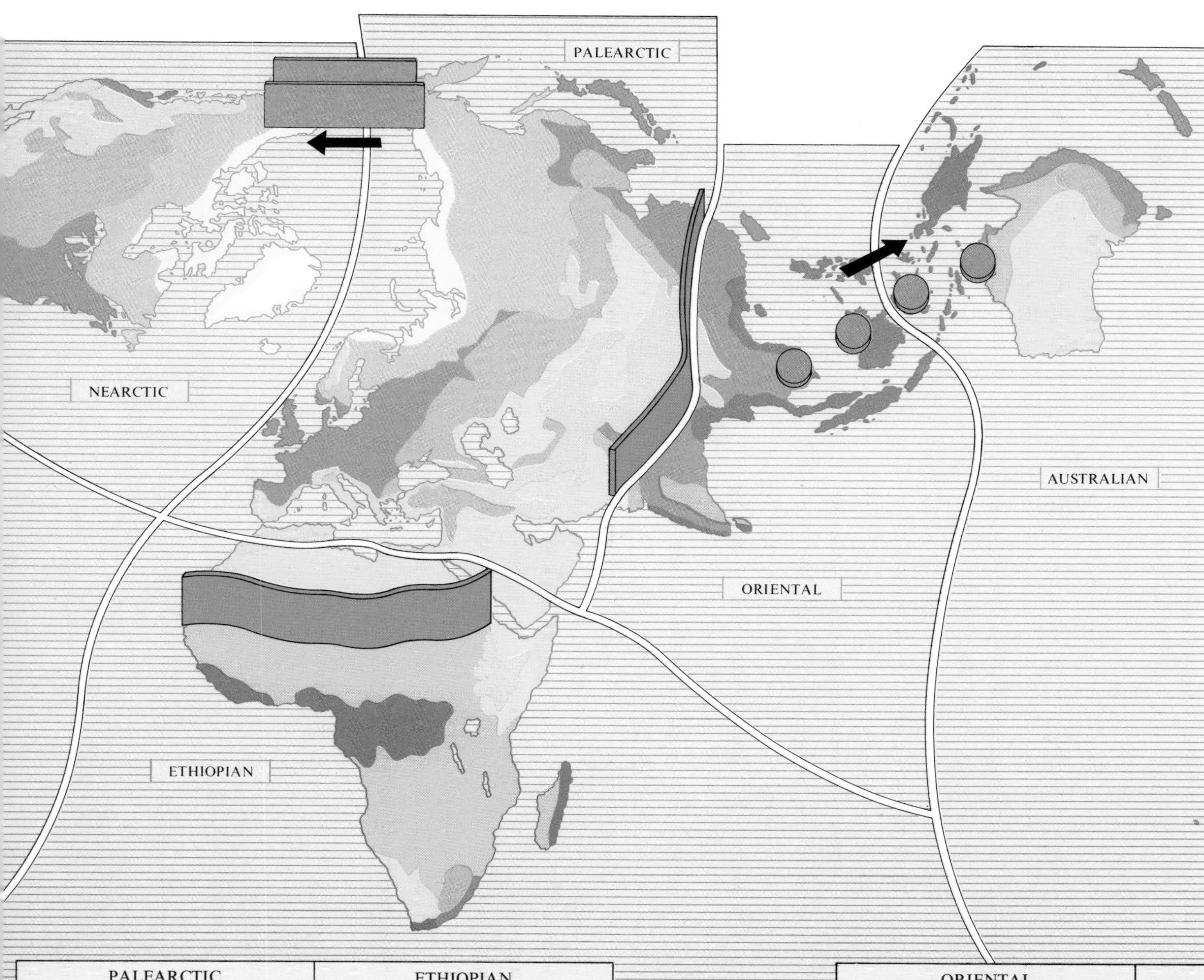

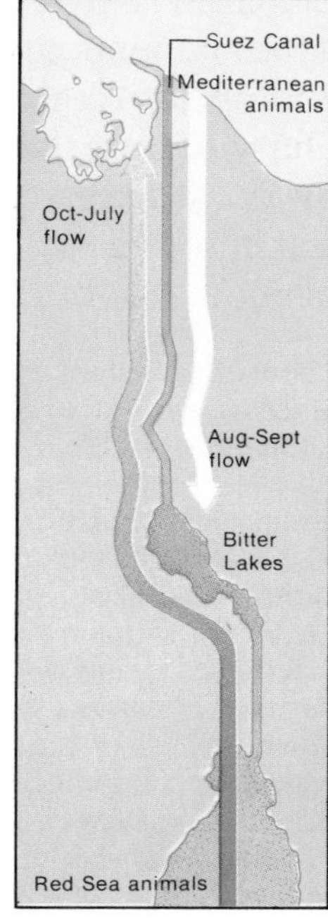

The man-made filter of the Suez Canal, cut in 1869, is an animal corridor between the Mediterranean and Red Sea. But movement is mainly from the latter, for the channel passes through the hot, salty Bitter Lakes, favoring animals adapted to these conditions, and the current flows northwards for 10 months of the year. However, not all the 130 invading species are likely to survive Mediterranean conditions.

PALEARCTIC

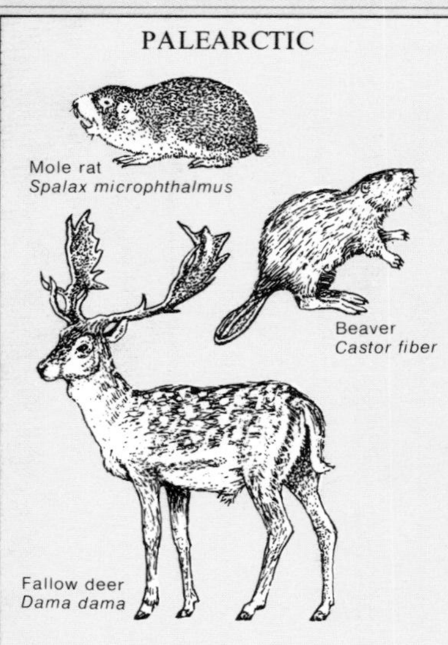

The Palearctic or "Old North" region covers the entire northerly part of the Old World, with seas to the north, east and west. To the south, the Sahara desert and the Himalaya mountains form barriers that separate the Palearctic from the Ethiopian and Oriental regions, although these regions are all part of the same landmass. One of the few species of mammals unique to the Palearctic is the Mediterranean mole rat, a thick-furred rodent. Another Palearctic rodent, the beaver, is shared with the Nearctic region. Fallow deer occur throughout Europe. They have been introduced by man into many other parts of the world, but their origin is almost certainly Mediterranean.

ETHIOPIAN

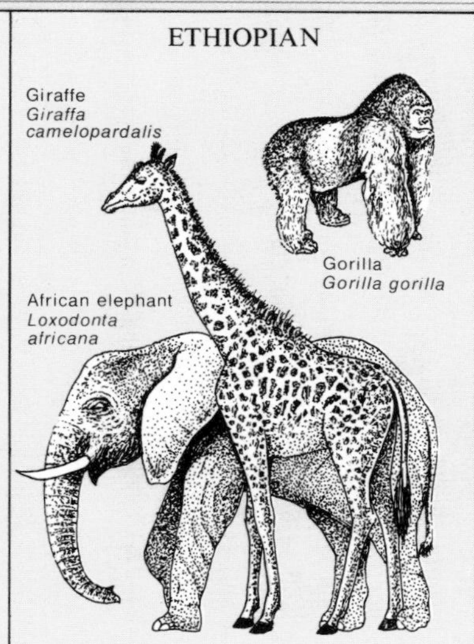

The Ethiopian region includes southern Arabia as well as all Africa south of the Sahara. It resembles in many ways the Neotropical region and is almost as rich in unique families. Its fauna also has much in common with the Oriental region. Unique mammals include the giraffe, at 5.5 m (18 ft) the tallest of living land animals, which inhabits the savanna. The region also supports two of the world's four great apes, the gorilla and the chimpanzee, which are found in the forests of western and central Africa. (The other great apes, the orangutan and the gibbon, are Oriental.) The African elephant is distinguished from its Indian relative by its greater size and by its huge ears and massive tusks.

- Polar
- Tundra
- Taiga
- Mountain
- Temperate forest
- Temperate grassland
- Mediterranean
- Savanna
- Tropical rainforest
- Monsoon
- Desert
- Barrier
- Corridor
- Stepping stone
- Prevailing movement

ORIENTAL

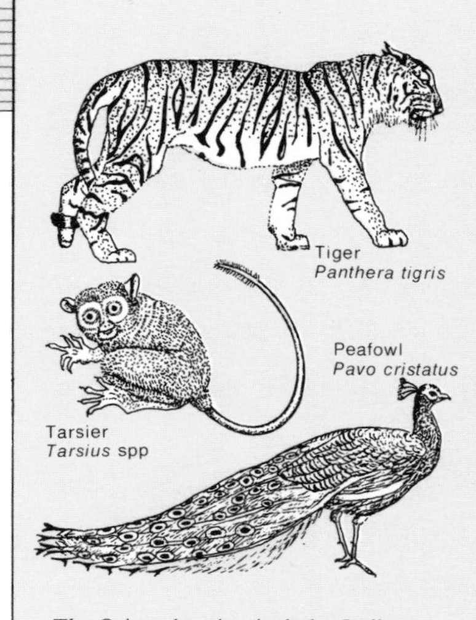

The Oriental region includes India, southern China, southeastern Asia and part of Malaysia. It is bounded to the north by the Himalayas and on either side by ocean, and is separated from the Australian region by a line known as Wallace's Line. It shares a quarter of its mammal families with Africa, but has more primates than any other region. The tarsier, a small relative of the monkey, is unique to southeastern Asia and represents an important early stage of primate evolution. The tiger was once widespread, but its natural habitats are steadily diminishing and the tiger itself is in danger of extinction by man. The peacock is one of the region's many brilliantly colored birds.

AUSTRALIAN

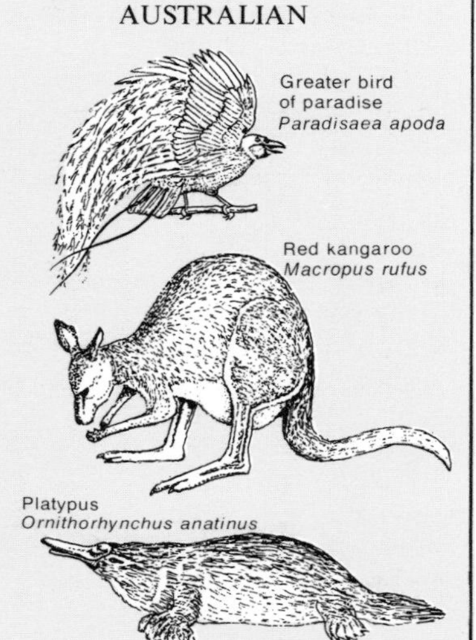

The Australian region is unique in having no land connection with any other region. Its native fauna has developed in isolation from the rest of the world for at least 50 million years. Most of the mammals are marsupial—animals such as the kangaroo that carry their young in a pouch. Even more of a biological curiosity than the marsupials is the duckbilled platypus, a monotreme or egg-laying mammal. It lives along the banks of streams in Australia and Tasmania, and lays small, leathery eggs like those of snakes and turtles, but it is a true mammal and nurses its young with milk. Some 13 bird families are unique to the region, including the magnificent bird of paradise.

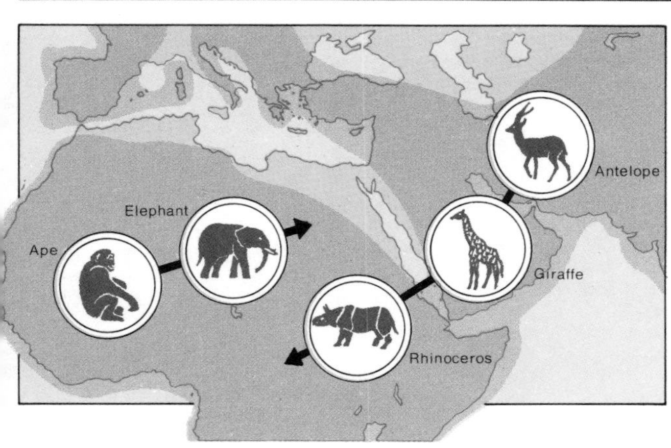

A desert barrier gradually began to form in northern Africa about nine million years ago, replacing the forest corridor between the Ethiopian and Palearctic regions. During the change, many animals typical of the African plains moved in from the north, including ancestors of today's antelopes, giraffes and rhinoceroses. But African animals also moved up north: early elephants and, much later, apes, which may have been precursors of modern man.

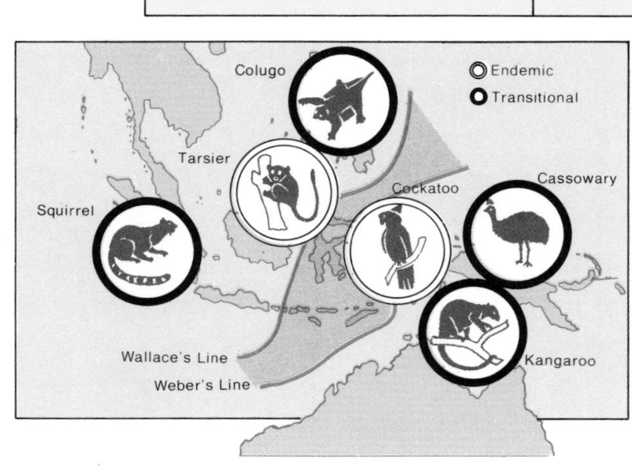

The transitional area of "Wallacea" contains animals from both the Oriental and Australian regions, bounded by Wallace's and Weber's Lines, but few have crossed to the other region. Some Oriental mammals, such as tarsiers, are found in Wallacea, but the gliding colugo and varieties of squirrel are not. The Australian cockatoo has reached the transition area, but the flightless cassowary and the tree kangaroo have not.

Spread of Man

Modern Man, *Homo sapiens sapiens*, has proved a highly successful animal since his emergence some 50,000 years ago: today more than 4,000 million members of this subspecies of the *Homo* (Man) group occupy the Earth, living in even the most inhospitable regions. But the fossil record shows that man's lineage goes back millions of years, with different stages of development leading to a greater control of the environment, and with climate itself helping man's ultimate domination of Earth.

Man's lineage may go back at least 14 million years to a small woodland creature known as *Ramapithecus* (Rama's ape). Since the first discoveries of *Ramapithecus* in the Indian subcontinent, its fossils have come to light in many parts of the world, including China, eastern Europe, Turkey and eastern Africa. Fossil remains show that it survived for several million years until, about eight million years ago, there is a tantalizing gap in the fossil record. Then, about four and a half million years later (according to recent discoveries in eastern Africa), we have solid evidence of an upright hominid—a member of man's zoological family. This is "Lucy," a fossil skeleton found in 1973 by Donald Johanson and Tom Gray, and subsequently classified with many other finds as *Australopithecus afarensis.*

This may be man's ancestral "rootstock," but a little later there existed two kinds of "ape-man" (*Australopithecus*), and our own direct ancestor Handy Man (*Homo habilis*). Datable volcanic ash found with the fossils provides a time scale and indicates that, about two million years ago, ape-man and "true" man lived side by side in the lush grassland that then covered the eastern African plains.

One and a half million years ago, according to the fossil evidence, there was again only one hominid species. The varieties of australopithecines had died out, and Handy Man (*Homo habilis*) had apparently evolved into Upright Man (*Homo erectus*). Remains of Upright Man have been found in many regions of the world, from various parts of Africa and Europe to China and Indonesia, although not in the Americas. But there is reason to believe that it was in Africa, well over one million years ago, that he evolved from his ancestor, and began a very gradual expansion out of the continent.

Upright Man had about one million years to spread across the Old World, adapting as he did so to local conditions, just as people of today are adapted in their various ways. He was a nomadic hunter gatherer, socially organized in groups. His skills included the use of fire and cooking, as well as the making of quite large structures out of wood. Recent discoveries suggest that, during the million years of his existence, *Homo erectus* gradually evolved into the next stage of man – *Homo sapiens.*

The next step is revealed most clearly in fossils from more than 100,000 to less than 50,000 years ago. Called Neanderthal Man in Europe, Solo Man in Indonesia, and Rhodesian Man in southern Africa, these types of human being were all descendants of *Homo erectus.*

Variable in brain size, but with prominent eyebrow ridges and receding jaws, they may have been dead ends on the evolutionary road; or some may have led to, or been incorporated in, Modern Man (*Homo sapiens sapiens*).

THE AFRICAN CRADLE
Handy Man (*Homo habilis*), who shared the East African grasslands two million years ago with a related "ape-man" species, was a slender and agile creature with a human way of walking and a capacity for conceptual thought, as evidenced in systematic making of tools. Handy Man collected stones, often from far away, and reshaped them into purpose-made tools, using other stones. Fossil remains suggest that these earliest humans were efficient hunters as well as scavengers of larger predators' kills, and that they brought food to campsites, probably sharing it among the whole group, rather than eating it on the spot. Such specifically human characteristics as the sharing of food may have helped our ancestors to survive their more primitive hominid relations.

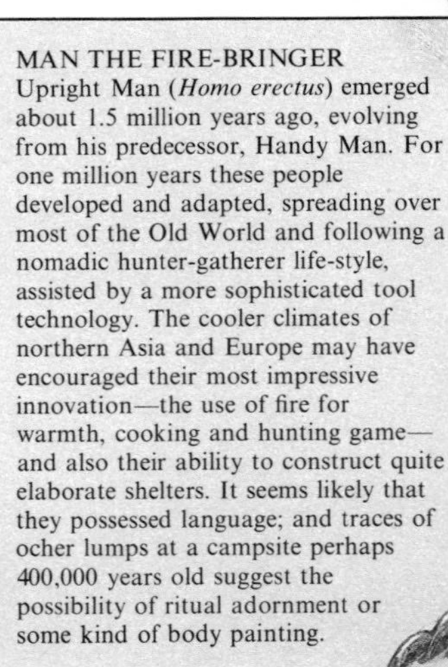

MAN THE FIRE-BRINGER
Upright Man (*Homo erectus*) emerged about 1.5 million years ago, evolving from his predecessor, Handy Man. For one million years these people developed and adapted, spreading over most of the Old World and following a nomadic hunter-gatherer life-style, assisted by a more sophisticated tool technology. The cooler climates of northern Asia and Europe may have encouraged their most impressive innovation—the use of fire for warmth, cooking and hunting game—and also their ability to construct quite elaborate shelters. It seems likely that they possessed language; and traces of ocher lumps at a campsite perhaps 400,000 years old suggest the possibility of ritual adornment or some kind of body painting.

THE HUMANIZING OF MAN
Modern man's predecessor, although called Wise Man (*Homo sapiens*), was long regarded as more brutish than human. But widespread finds have now changed this image, as can be seen in an old and an updated reconstruction of the same Neanderthal skull (right). Many scientists believe that these people showed a human concern for each other, burying their dead with ceremonial reverence, and looking after disabled members of the group. In their Neanderthal form they inhabited Europe and the Middle East from about 100,000 to 40,000 years ago, and were perhaps adapted to ice-age conditions. *Homo sapiens* counterparts of Neanderthal Man also occur in Africa and southeastern Asia.

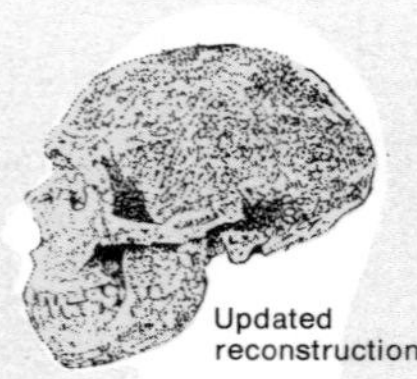

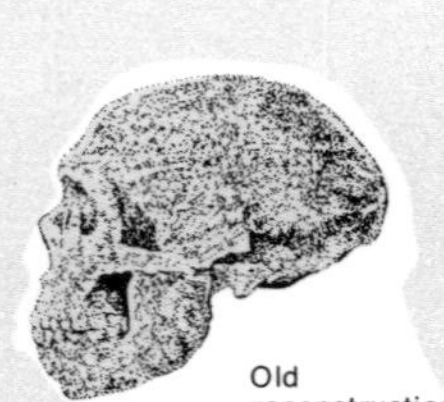

The burial of a Neanderthal man took place 60,000 years ago at Shanidar in the Iraq highlands. Fossil traces suggest that the body was laid on a bed of branches, and that flowers were brought to the grave and placed deliberately around the body. The flowers included many varieties still known locally for their medicinal properties. Ritual burials occur at many Neanderthal sites, from the Pyrenees to Soviet Asia, and indicate a sensitivity that contradicts Neanderthal Man's traditional image.

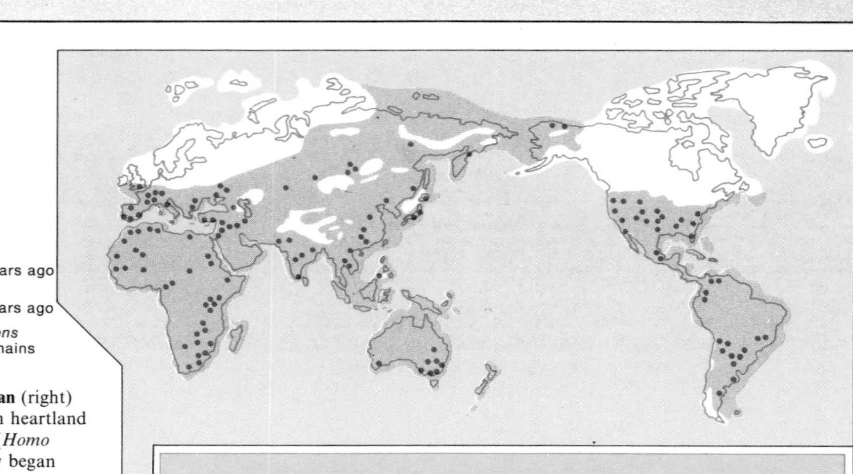

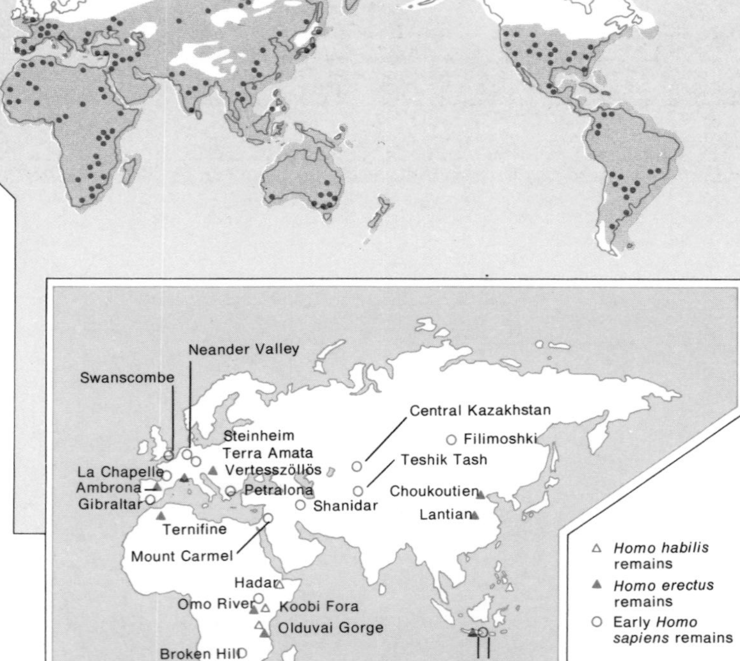

The spread of man (right) from the African heartland of Handy Man (*Homo habilis*) probably began about one million years ago. Remains of Upright Man (*Homo erectus*) have been found all over the Old World, and show a gradual physical and cultural evolution toward a later *Homo sapiens* ancestor, beginning about 350,000 years ago. Between 70,000 and 12,000 years ago, glacial periods locked up the sea water as ice (top), lowering sea levels and opening a land bridge to America that was used by later nomadic peoples. But they had to cross open sea to reach Australia.

THE AGE OF ART
Toward the end of the last Ice Age, from about 35,000 years ago, truly modern humans began to depict their world in wonderfully vivid terms. The age of art may have reached its peak at Lascaux, France, some 15,000 years ago, but less well-preserved cave paintings from Africa show that the artistic impulse was equally present elsewhere. Called Cro-Magnon Man in Europe, these people spread to all parts of the world, crossing to the Americas by way of the Bering land bridge (when ice locked up the water of the straits), and even venturing over the seas to Australia. Physically these people were just like present-day humans. They led a nomadic, hunter-gathering life, living in large, organized groups, hunting such animals as mammoths, reindeer, bison and horses, and using a technology, as well as an artistry, far in advance of anything previously developed.

Fossils almost four million years old, found since 1973, may mark the ancestral "rootstock" of humanity, but the earliest form of true man is thought to be *Homo habilis*, who shared his African habitat with "ape-man" relatives some two million years ago. His successor, *Homo erectus*, spread over Asia and Europe, evolving gradually into modern man's predecessors, creatures whose large brow ridges belie many typically human characteristics. These were replaced by Modern Man.

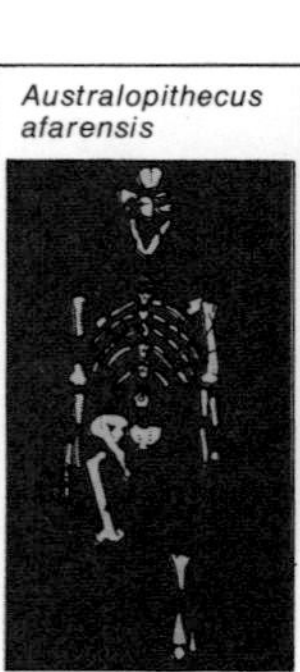

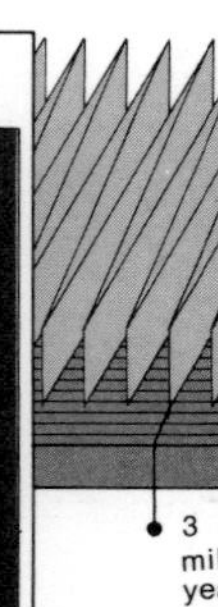

UNFOLDING HUMANITY

Two million years ago, bands of small, upstanding, large-brained, tool-using creatures roamed the African plains. These were our progenitors, Handy Man (*Homo habilis*). A million years later, a more evolved human type spread over the Old World, building shelters and using fire against the cold. This so-called Upright Man (*Homo erectus*) gradually evolved into our modern ancestors, who reached into every part of the world.

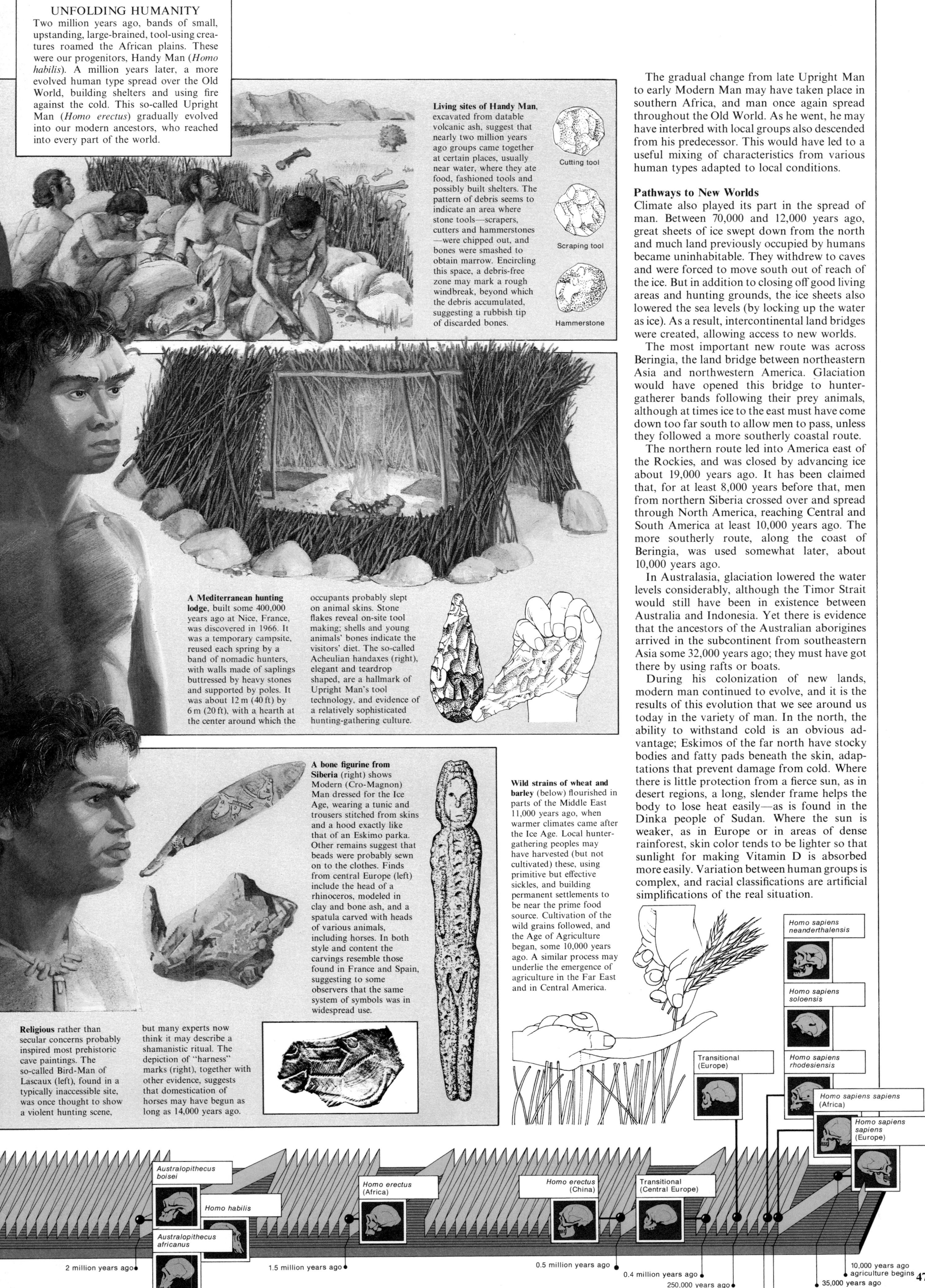

Living sites of Handy Man, excavated from datable volcanic ash, suggest that nearly two million years ago groups came together at certain places, usually near water, where they ate food, fashioned tools and possibly built shelters. The pattern of debris seems to indicate an area where stone tools—scrapers, cutters and hammerstones—were chipped out, and bones were smashed to obtain marrow. Encircling this space, a debris-free zone may mark a rough windbreak, beyond which the debris accumulated, suggesting a rubbish tip of discarded bones.

A Mediterranean hunting lodge, built some 400,000 years ago at Nice, France, was discovered in 1966. It was a temporary campsite, reused each spring by a band of nomadic hunters, with walls made of saplings buttressed by heavy stones and supported by poles. It was about 12 m (40 ft) by 6 m (20 ft), with a hearth at the center around which the occupants probably slept on animal skins. Stone flakes reveal on-site tool making; shells and young animals' bones indicate the visitors' diet. The so-called Acheulian handaxes (right), elegant and teardrop shaped, are a hallmark of Upright Man's tool technology, and evidence of a relatively sophisticated hunting-gathering culture.

A bone figurine from Siberia (right) shows Modern (Cro-Magnon) Man dressed for the Ice Age, wearing a tunic and trousers stitched from skins and a hood exactly like that of an Eskimo parka. Other remains suggest that beads were probably sewn on to the clothes. Finds from central Europe (left) include the head of a rhinoceros, modeled in clay and bone ash, and a spatula carved with heads of various animals, including horses. In both style and content the carvings resemble those found in France and Spain, suggesting to some observers that the same system of symbols was in widespread use.

Religious rather than secular concerns probably inspired most prehistoric cave paintings. The so-called Bird-Man of Lascaux (left), found in a typically inaccessible site, was once thought to show a violent hunting scene, but many experts now think it may describe a shamanistic ritual. The depiction of "harness" marks (right), together with other evidence, suggests that domestication of horses may have begun as long as 14,000 years ago.

Wild strains of wheat and barley (below) flourished in parts of the Middle East 11,000 years ago, when warmer climates came after the Ice Age. Local hunter-gathering peoples may have harvested (but not cultivated) these, using primitive but effective sickles, and building permanent settlements to be near the prime food source. Cultivation of the wild grains followed, and the Age of Agriculture began, some 10,000 years ago. A similar process may underlie the emergence of agriculture in the Far East and in Central America.

The gradual change from late Upright Man to early Modern Man may have taken place in southern Africa, and man once again spread throughout the Old World. As he went, he may have interbred with local groups also descended from his predecessor. This would have led to a useful mixing of characteristics from various human types adapted to local conditions.

Pathways to New Worlds

Climate also played its part in the spread of man. Between 70,000 and 12,000 years ago, great sheets of ice swept down from the north and much land previously occupied by humans became uninhabitable. They withdrew to caves and were forced to move south out of reach of the ice. But in addition to closing off good living areas and hunting grounds, the ice sheets also lowered the sea levels (by locking up the water as ice). As a result, intercontinental land bridges were created, allowing access to new worlds.

The most important new route was across Beringia, the land bridge between northeastern Asia and northwestern America. Glaciation would have opened this bridge to hunter-gatherer bands following their prey animals, although at times ice to the east must have come down too far south to allow men to pass, unless they followed a more southerly coastal route.

The northern route led into America east of the Rockies, and was closed by advancing ice about 19,000 years ago. It has been claimed that, for at least 8,000 years before that, men from northern Siberia crossed over and spread through North America, reaching Central and South America at least 10,000 years ago. The more southerly route, along the coast of Beringia, was used somewhat later, about 10,000 years ago.

In Australasia, glaciation lowered the water levels considerably, although the Timor Strait would still have been in existence between Australia and Indonesia. Yet there is evidence that the ancestors of the Australian aborigines arrived in the subcontinent from southeastern Asia some 32,000 years ago; they must have got there by using rafts or boats.

During his colonization of new lands, modern man continued to evolve, and it is the results of this evolution that we see around us today in the variety of man. In the north, the ability to withstand cold is an obvious advantage; Eskimos of the far north have stocky bodies and fatty pads beneath the skin, adaptations that prevent damage from cold. Where there is little protection from a fierce sun, as in desert regions, a long, slender frame helps the body to lose heat easily—as is found in the Dinka people of Sudan. Where the sun is weaker, as in Europe or in areas of dense rainforest, skin color tends to be lighter so that sunlight for making Vitamin D is absorbed more easily. Variation between human groups is complex, and racial classifications are artificial simplifications of the real situation.

Part 4

THE DIVERSITY OF LIFE

Earth's habitats from the Poles to the Equator
Plants and animals of the Earth's natural regions
Man the preserver and man the destroyer

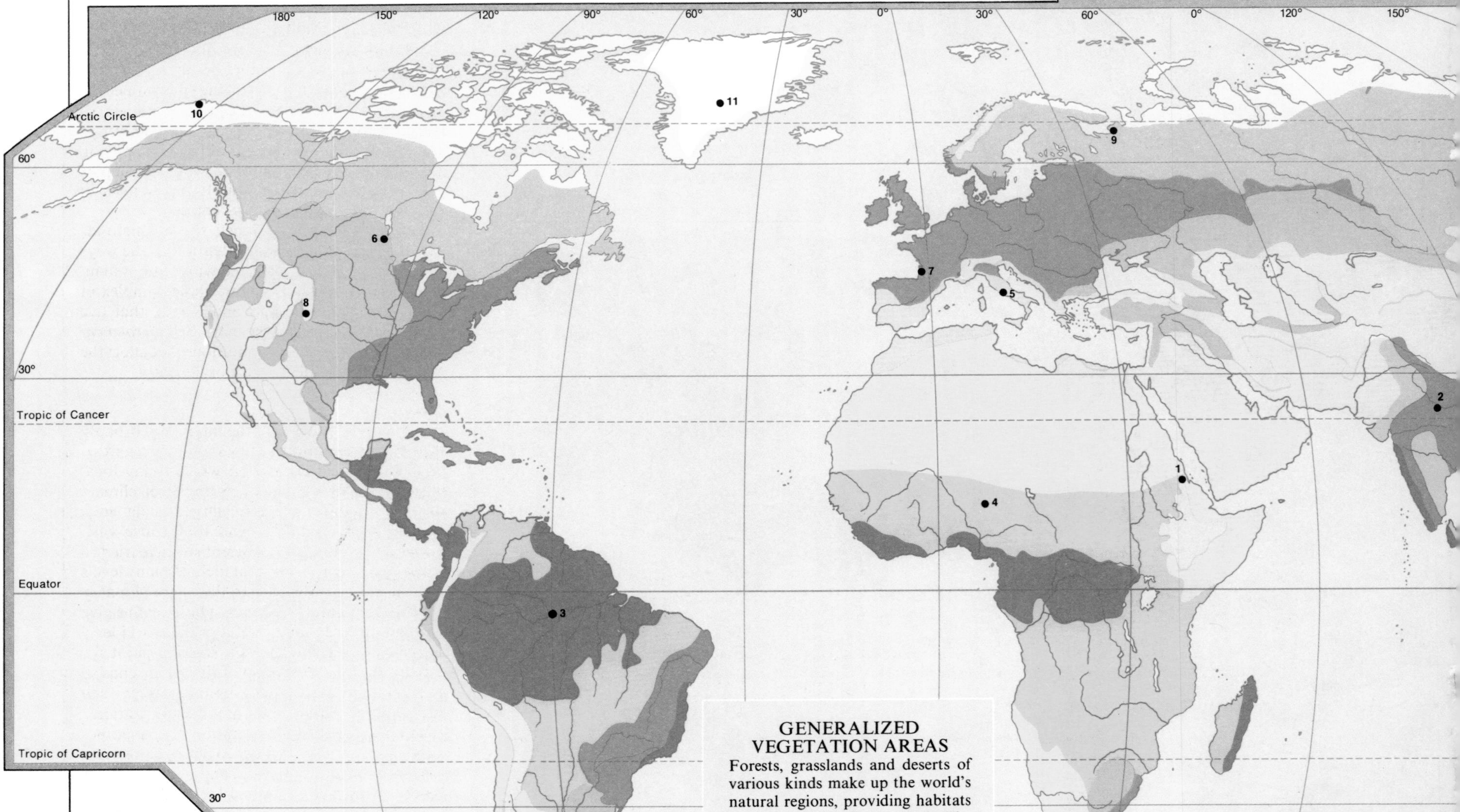

WEATHER STATIONS

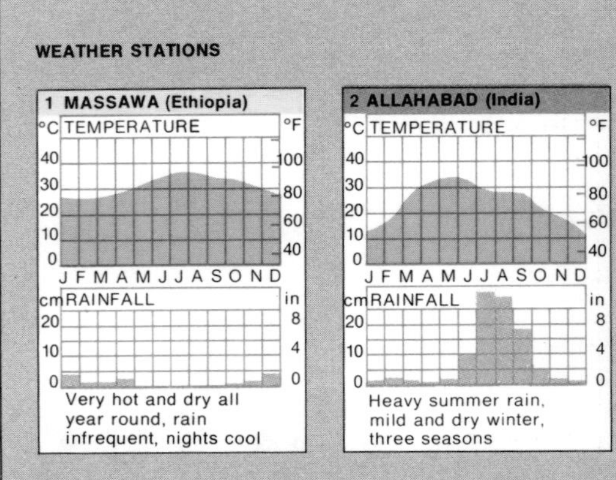

GENERALIZED VEGETATION AREAS

Forests, grasslands and deserts of various kinds make up the world's natural regions, providing habitats for particular kinds of animals. The total community—the biome—is a product of climate, vegetation, animals, soils—and man himself.

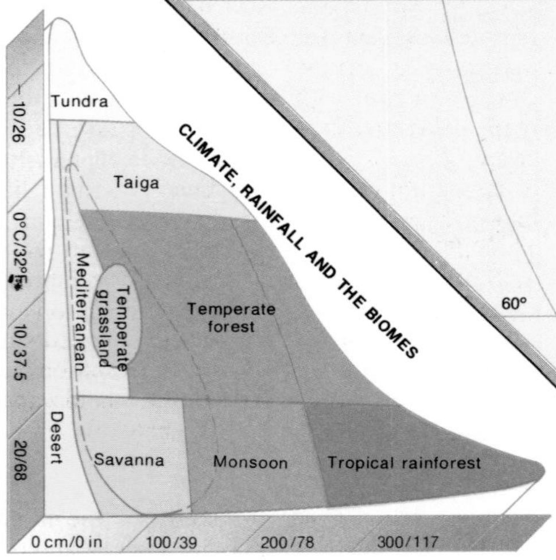

The Natural Regions: Desert; Monsoon; Tropical rainforest; Savanna; Mediterranean; Temperate grassland; Temperate forest; Mountain; Taiga; Tundra; Polar

Arctic Circle · Tropic of Cancer · Equator · Tropic of Capricorn · Antarctic Circle

CLIMATE, RAINFALL AND THE BIOMES

Tundra · Taiga · Temperate grassland · Temperate forest · Mediterranean · Desert · Savanna · Monsoon · Tropical rainforest

Temperature and rainfall (above) govern the world's zones of plant and animal life. Dryness prevents tree growth both in icy tundra and in hot deserts. Wetter conditions cause savannas and grasslands to yield to forest biomes, tropical or temperate (the dotted line indicates zones within which variations occur).

A broad correlation (below) between soil types, climate and vegetation areas shows the interconnections that define the biomes. The soil of the biome is related to climatic conditions and is also modified by plant and animal activity, but soil types are not necessarily confined to any one particular biome.

SOIL AND THE BIOMES

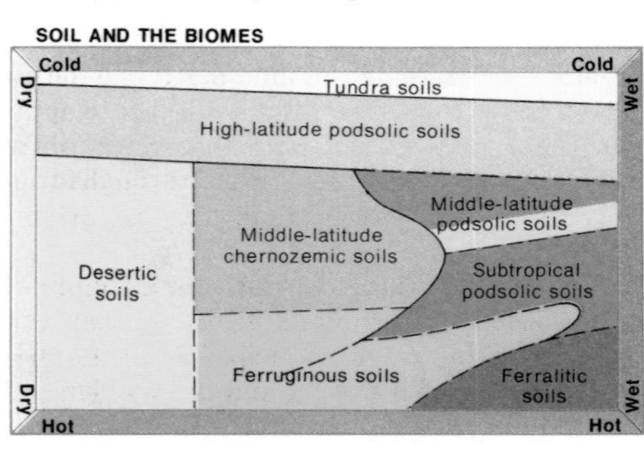

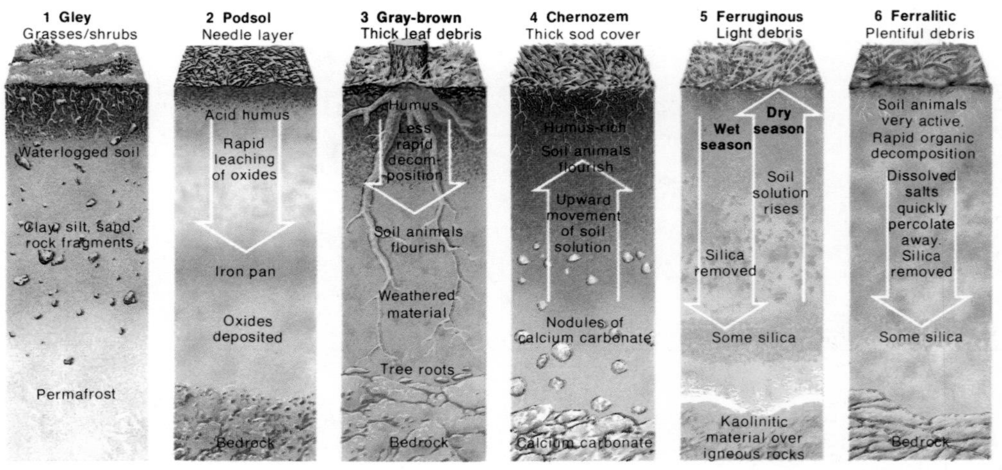

1 Gley — Grasses/shrubs: Waterlogged soil; Clay, silt, sand, rock fragments; Permafrost

2 Podsol — Needle layer: Acid humus; Rapid leaching of oxides; Iron pan; Oxides deposited; Bedrock

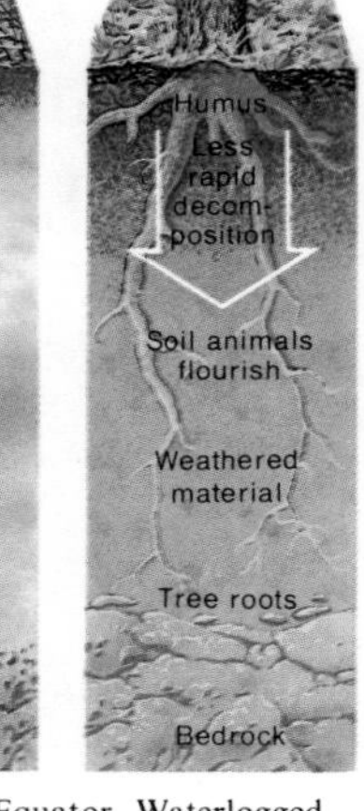

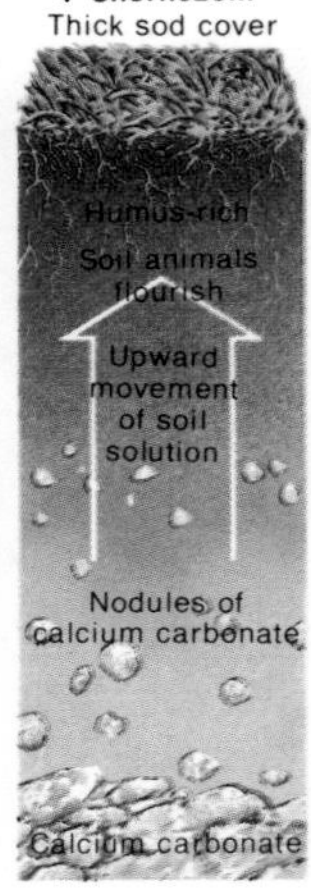

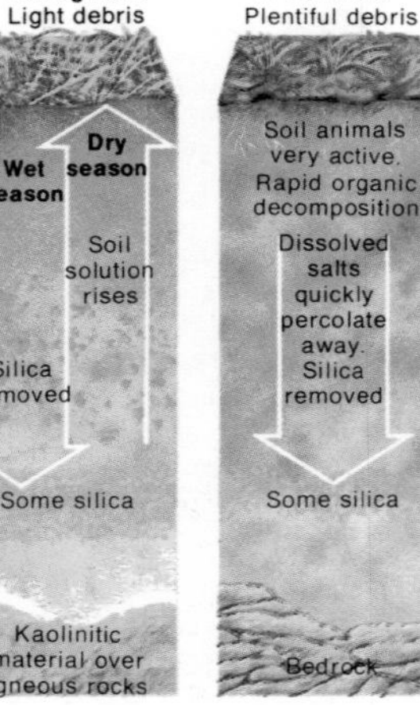

Soil profiles (above) from surface to bedrock reflect the influence of climate and vegetation on the rock. Depths vary from 1 m in the tundra to 30–40 m at the Equator. Waterlogged gley (1) may form above tundra permafrost. Podsol (2) is typical of taiga forests, where spring snow-melt is heavily leached through a needle layer, sometimes forming an iron "pan." Gray-brown forest soil (3) has rich, organic humus, as has chernozem (4), the typical temperate grassland soil. Ferruginous soils (5) occur in dry-season tropical climates (monsoon, savanna), and ferralitic soils (6) where there is constant rainfall.

ECOSYSTEM DYNAMICS

An ecosystem consists of a group of organisms and its physical environment. A marshland ecosystem from North America (right) shows the dynamic interactions between plant and animal communities and their habitats, which include climate, soil and water. The energy and food in the system initially derive from the Sun—the main energy source for living things, notably plants. Plants are food for herbivores, on land and in water; herbivores are food for carnivores; decomposers (bacteria and fungi) nourish plants, breaking down dead bodies into compounds.

Earth's Natural Regions

Geographers have long looked for ways of classifying conditions such as climate, soil and vegetation to describe the general similarities and differences from area to area throughout the world. By identifying distinctive patterns of climate and vegetation they have provided a convenient global division into natural regions or biomes. And recent developments in ecology – the study of plants and animals in relation to their environments – have given such divisions a greater depth.

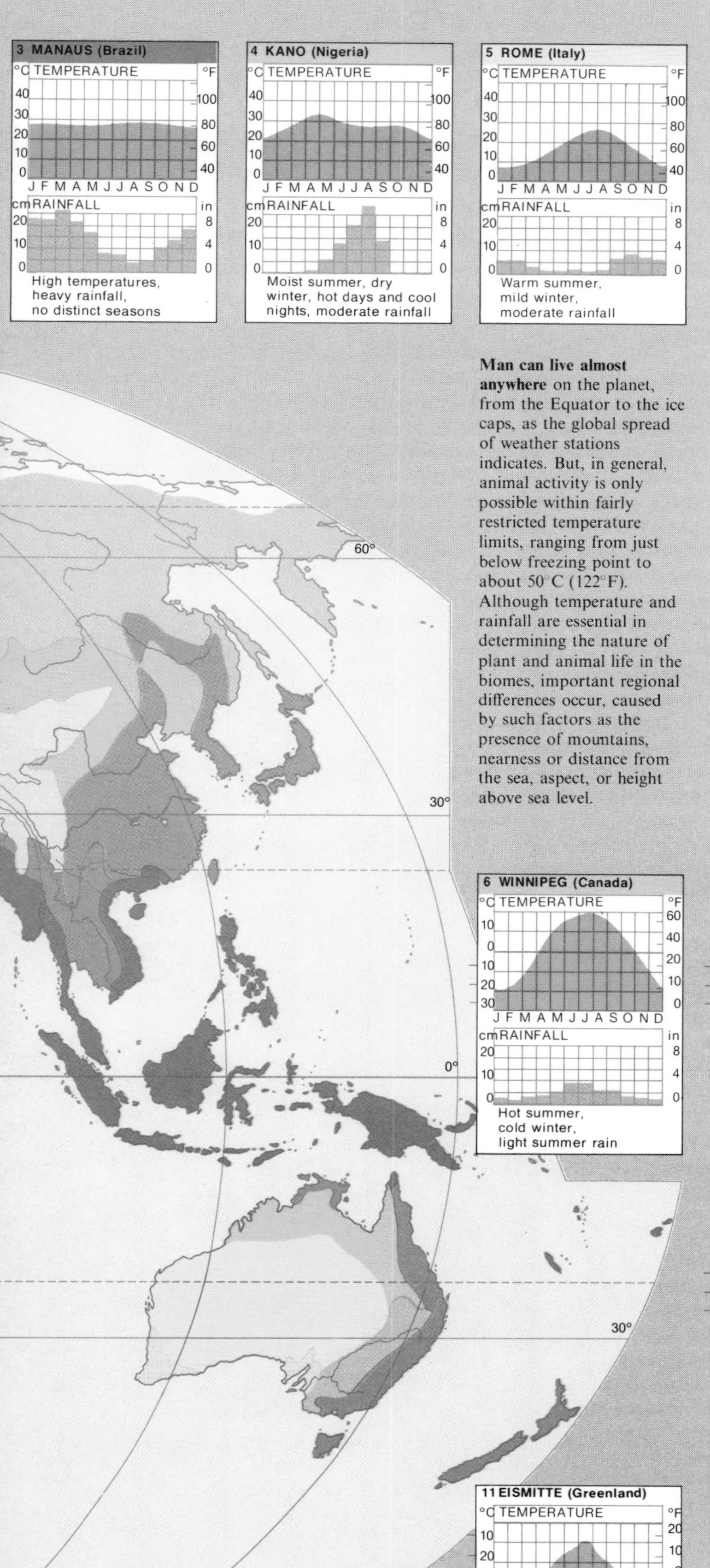

Man can live almost anywhere on the planet, from the Equator to the ice caps, as the global spread of weather stations indicates. But, in general, animal activity is only possible within fairly restricted temperature limits, ranging from just below freezing point to about 50°C (122°F). Although temperature and rainfall are essential in determining the nature of plant and animal life in the biomes, important regional differences occur, caused by such factors as the presence of mountains, nearness or distance from the sea, aspect, or height above sea level.

7 BORDEAUX (France) — TEMPERATURE / RAINFALL — Warm summer, mild winter, four distinct seasons

8 PIKE'S PEAK (USA) — TEMPERATURE / RAINFALL — 4,300 m (14,111 ft) Temperature decreases with increasing altitude

9 ARKHANGELSK (USSR) — TEMPERATURE / RAINFALL — Short summer, long and cold winter, light summer rain

10 BARROW (Alaska) — TEMPERATURE / RAINFALL — Brief summer, very long and cold winter, very light rainfall

Divisions according to climate were first suggested by the Greek philosopher Aristotle, and his ideas were still in use until about 100 years ago. Aristotle posited a number of climatic zones—called torrid, temperate and frigid—defined by latitude. But with time it became increasingly apparent that the complex distribution of atmospheric pressure, winds, rainfall and temperature could not be related to such a simple frame. Nineteenth-century scientists divided the world into 35 climatic provinces. Then in 1900 the German meteorologist Wladimir Köppen produced a more sophisticated climatic classification based on temperature and moisture conditions related to the needs of plants. At about the same time other scientists studied the distribution of vegetation types throughout the world. These studies together provided the basis for much of the later work on climatic regions.

An important step forward was made in 1904 by the British geographer A. J. Herbertson. He argued that subdivision of physical environments should take into account the distribution of the various phenomena as they related to each other. He conceived the idea of *natural regions*, each with "a certain unity of configuration (relief), climate and vegetation." His final classification contained four groups or regions: Polar Types, Cool Temperate Types, Warm Temperate Types and Tropical Hot Lands. Herbertson's scheme, controversial at first, was later much used for teaching geography.

Ecology

Meanwhile the study of environmental problems had been advanced by the idea of *ecology*, the relationship of living things between each other and their surroundings. The term was first used in 1868 by Ernst Haeckel, the German biologist, but it was not until the end of the nineteenth century that scientists really began to study life forms in relation to their habitat. In addition to the central ideas of interdependence between the members of plant and animal communities and between the community and the physical environment, there now came the suggestion that communities develop in a sequence that leads to a "climax"—a final step of equilibrium or balance. Their climax stage depends on conditions of climate or soil.

Later the British botanist A. G. Tansley, a leading exponent of ecological thinking, introduced the term *ecosystem* to describe a group of living organisms and its effective environment. Tansley's definition of 1935 referred to the whole system, including "not only the organism complex, but also the whole complex of physical factors forming what we call the environment of the biome." The idea became very influential and has been used in the social sciences as well as in the natural ones. But it is difficult to apply in practice, partly because of the highly complex and often diverse interactions that take place in different parts of the ecosystem.

Ecologists have developed special methods and have given particular attention to the ways in which energy is transferred within the system. The term *biome* refers to the whole complex of organisms, both animals and plants, that live together naturally as a society. By *environment* is meant all the external conditions that affect the life and development of an organism.

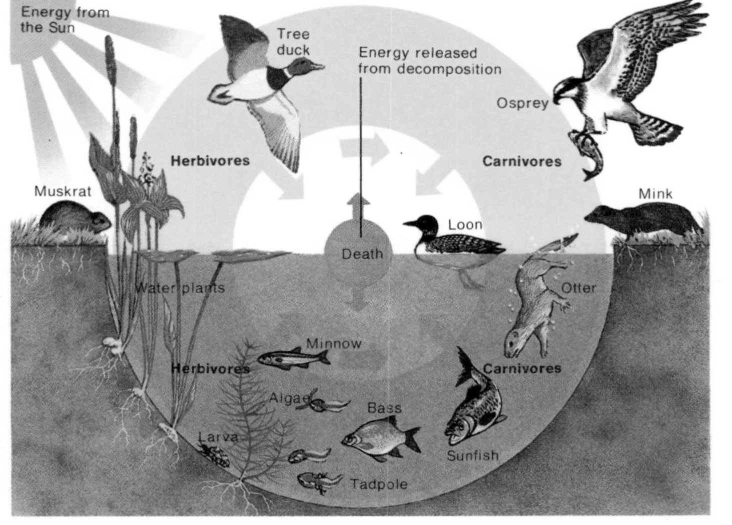

Biomes

The biomes shown on the map are broadly drawn generalizations. They should be regarded as idealized regions, within which many local variations may exist—for example, of climate or soil conditions. On a larger scale such features as mountain ranges may cause variations at a regional level. Scientists have tried to work out "hierarchies" that include many levels or orders of scale leading to the major climatic-vegetation realms or biomes. These realms give a broad picture that is useful at the world level of scale, and which forms a starting point for further analysis. Any map of the biomes has to have lines to indicate the boundaries of each region, but these too are generalizations. Although climate and vegetation do sometimes change abruptly from place to place, more often there are transitional zones, and the boundaries on the maps give the broad locations of these.

Herbertson's concept of natural regions attempted also to take account of the influence of man as an important factor in the environment. But he was not totally successful in including man in his analysis, no doubt because of the complexity of the problems involved and because of the immense influence that man has had upon the natural vegetation of the world. The cutting of forests, the drainage and reclamation of land, the introduction, use and spread of cultivated plants, the domestication of animals, the development of sophisticated systems of agriculture and many other actions all create, over large areas of the biomes, landscapes that are more man-made than natural.

Resource systems

An idea that clarifies the study of the interrelations of societies and environments, and the ways in which these change with the passage of time, is that of the *resource system*. This is a model of a population of human beings and their social and economic characteristics, including their technical skills and resources, together with those aspects of the natural environment that affect them and which they influence. The model includes the sequences by which natural materials are obtained, transformed and used. It tries to show how societies are organized according to their natural resources, the effects of that use, and the ways in which natural conditions limit or expand the life and work of the society. But it is easier to apply such a model to societies that have direct relations with natural conditions, through farming, fishing or forestry, than to great urban–industrial complexes.

The sections that follow present a picture of the diversity of habitats from ice caps to equatorial forests, the principal ways man has modified the environment and the problems of maintaining healthy resource systems.

Climate and Weather

The pattern of world climates depends largely on great circulations of air in the atmosphere. These movements of air are driven by energy from the Sun, and they transfer surplus heat from the tropics to the polar regions. Over a long period of time – such as months, seasons or years – they create the climate. Over a short period – day by day, or week by week – they form the weather. Together, climate and weather are among the most significant natural components of the world's diverse environments.

The world's tropical zones receive more heat from the Sun than they re-emit into space, and so their land and sea surfaces become warm. The polar regions, on the other hand, emit more radiation than they receive, and so they become cold. Warm air is less dense than cold air, and this means that atmospheric pressure becomes low at the Equator and high at the poles. As a result, a circulation of air—both vertical and horizontal—is set up. But because of the Earth's rotation and the distribution of land and sea there is not a simple air circulation pattern in each hemisphere; winds are deflected to the right in the northern hemisphere and to the left in the southern hemisphere, a phenomenon known as the Coriolis effect.

A climatic patchwork

When warm air rises it expands and cools and the water vapor it is carrying condenses to form clouds. For this reason heavy, showery rain is frequent in the belt of rising air near the Equator. In the subtropical zones (where the air is sinking), clouds evaporate and the weather is fine. Air moves out of the subtropical high-pressure belts in the lower atmosphere. Some of it flows towards the poles and meets colder air, flowing out of the polar high-pressure region, in a narrow zone called the polar front. This convergence of air is concentrated around low-pressure systems known as depressions.

The pattern of climates does not remain constant throughout the year because of seasonal changes in the amount of radiation from the Sun—the "fuel" of the atmospheric engine. In June, when the northern hemisphere is tilted towards the Sun, the radiation is at a maximum at latitude 23°N and all the climatic belts shift northwards. In December it is summer in the southern hemisphere and all the belts move southwards.

Climate is also affected by the distribution of land and sea across the globe. The temperature of the land changes more quickly than that of

TYPES OF WEATHER

There is a constant flow of air between the world's polar and tropical regions, and this has a prime effect on the weather in other regions. In the high and middle latitudes cold and warm fronts succeed each other, and along coasts sea fogs often form. In temperate and tropical regions thunderstorms are frequent, and the tropics are characterized by the turbulent storms known as hurricanes in the Caribbean area and typhoons in the Pacific.

POLAR WEATHER

Weather in high latitudes is marked by consistently low temperatures—on the ice caps temperatures are nearly always below freezing. At the poles the sun never rises for six months of the year and for the remaining six months it never sets. Even in summer it stays low on the horizon and its rays are so slanted that they bring very little warmth. On the tundra the temperature rises above freezing for a few months in summer, but severe frosts are likely to occur at any time. As well as being bitterly cold, polar weather is predominantly dry. The lower the temperature the less moisture the air can contain. Clouds, when they form, are high, thin sheets of cirrostratus. Composed of ice crystals, they often produce a halo effect around the sun. Snow, when it falls, is usually dry and powdery.

DEPRESSIONS

Low-pressure weather systems, or depressions, form when polar and subtropical air masses converge. Cloud and rain usually occur at the boundary, or front, of the different air masses. Seen in cross section, a fully developed depression shows both warm (A) and cold (B) fronts. As the wave of warm air rises over the cold, its moisture condenses into the "layered" clouds that usually precede a warm front. Behind the warm front, cold air forces under the warm air, producing the wedge-shaped cold front.

FOG

Fogs form as a result of the condensation of water vapor in the air; they may occur when warm, moist air is cooled by its passage over a cold surface. Off the coast of California, for example, air near the surface of the sea is cooled by the cold California current and sea fog is frequent. The air at higher levels is still warm and acts like a lid over the fog, and mountains prevent the fog from dispersing in an easterly direction. Fumes and smoke are trapped by this temperature inversion, creating the notorious Los Angeles smog.

THUNDERSTORMS

These develop when air is unstable to a great height. Particularly violent storms occur when cold, dry air masses meet warm, moist air, causing the latter to rise rapidly. As the warm air surges upwards it cools and its moisture condenses into cumulonimbus, or thunder, clouds. Flat cloud tops mark the level where stable air occurs again. Quickly moving raindrops and hail in the clouds become electrically charged and cause lightning, and the explosion of heated air along the path of the flash creates the sound wave that is heard as thunder.

HURRICANES

These are tropical storms on a vast scale that build up over warm oceans. Their core is an area of low pressure around which large quantities of warm, moist air are carried to the high atmosphere at great speed. The Earth's rotation is responsible for the huge swirling movement: in the northern hemisphere the movement is anticlockwise, in the southern hemisphere it is clockwise. Towering bands of clouds produce torrential rain. The central region, or "eye," of a hurricane, however, has light winds, clear skies and no rainfall.

THE WORLD'S CLIMATIC REGIONS

Climate is the characteristic weather of a region over a long period of time. It is often described in terms of average monthly and yearly temperatures and rainfall. These in turn depend largely on latitude, which determines whether a region is basically hot or cold and whether it has pronounced seasonal changes. Climate is also influenced by prevailing winds, by ocean currents and by geographical features such as the distribution of land and water. Highland climates are influenced by altitude and are always cooler than those of nearby lowland regions. Tropical climates are always warm. Near the Equator rain falls for most of the year, but towards the subtropics the wet and dry seasons are more marked. Temperate climates reflect the conflict between warm and cold air masses. They range from the Mediterranean type with hot, dry summers and mild, moist winters to the cooler, wetter climates of higher latitudes. The subarctic is mainly cold and humid; polar climates are always cold and mainly dry.

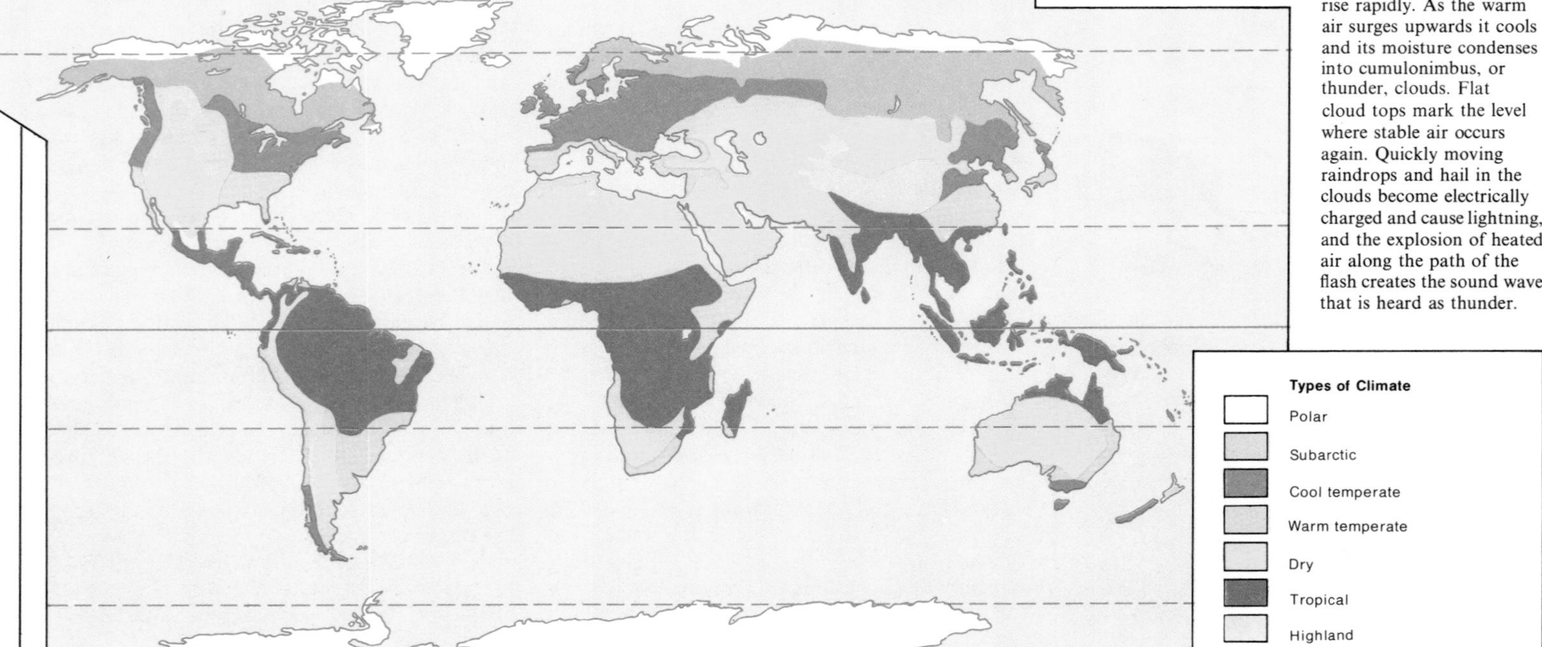

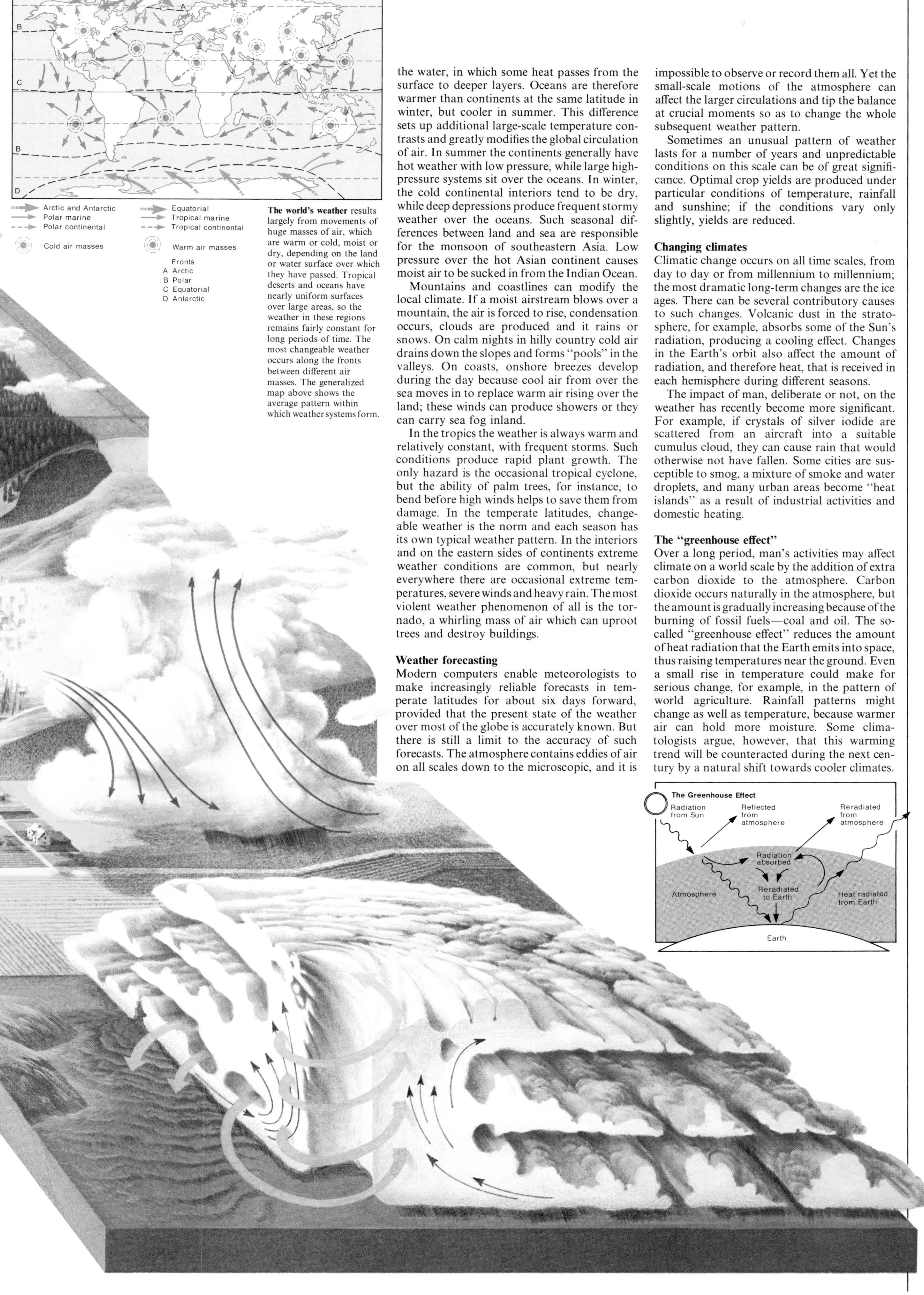

The world's weather results largely from movements of huge masses of air, which are warm or cold, moist or dry, depending on the land or water surface over which they have passed. Tropical deserts and oceans have nearly uniform surfaces over large areas, so the weather in these regions remains fairly constant for long periods of time. The most changeable weather occurs along the fronts between different air masses. The generalized map above shows the average pattern within which weather systems form.

the water, in which some heat passes from the surface to deeper layers. Oceans are therefore warmer than continents at the same latitude in winter, but cooler in summer. This difference sets up additional large-scale temperature contrasts and greatly modifies the global circulation of air. In summer the continents generally have hot weather with low pressure, while large high-pressure systems sit over the oceans. In winter, the cold continental interiors tend to be dry, while deep depressions produce frequent stormy weather over the oceans. Such seasonal differences between land and sea are responsible for the monsoon of southeastern Asia. Low pressure over the hot Asian continent causes moist air to be sucked in from the Indian Ocean.

Mountains and coastlines can modify the local climate. If a moist airstream blows over a mountain, the air is forced to rise, condensation occurs, clouds are produced and it rains or snows. On calm nights in hilly country cold air drains down the slopes and forms "pools" in the valleys. On coasts, onshore breezes develop during the day because cool air from over the sea moves in to replace warm air rising over the land; these winds can produce showers or they can carry sea fog inland.

In the tropics the weather is always warm and relatively constant, with frequent storms. Such conditions produce rapid plant growth. The only hazard is the occasional tropical cyclone, but the ability of palm trees, for instance, to bend before high winds helps to save them from damage. In the temperate latitudes, changeable weather is the norm and each season has its own typical weather pattern. In the interiors and on the eastern sides of continents extreme weather conditions are common, but nearly everywhere there are occasional extreme temperatures, severe winds and heavy rain. The most violent weather phenomenon of all is the tornado, a whirling mass of air which can uproot trees and destroy buildings.

Weather forecasting

Modern computers enable meteorologists to make increasingly reliable forecasts in temperate latitudes for about six days forward, provided that the present state of the weather over most of the globe is accurately known. But there is still a limit to the accuracy of such forecasts. The atmosphere contains eddies of air on all scales down to the microscopic, and it is impossible to observe or record them all. Yet the small-scale motions of the atmosphere can affect the larger circulations and tip the balance at crucial moments so as to change the whole subsequent weather pattern.

Sometimes an unusual pattern of weather lasts for a number of years and unpredictable conditions on this scale can be of great significance. Optimal crop yields are produced under particular conditions of temperature, rainfall and sunshine; if the conditions vary only slightly, yields are reduced.

Changing climates

Climatic change occurs on all time scales, from day to day or from millennium to millennium; the most dramatic long-term changes are the ice ages. There can be several contributory causes to such changes. Volcanic dust in the stratosphere, for example, absorbs some of the Sun's radiation, producing a cooling effect. Changes in the Earth's orbit also affect the amount of radiation, and therefore heat, that is received in each hemisphere during different seasons.

The impact of man, deliberate or not, on the weather has recently become more significant. For example, if crystals of silver iodide are scattered from an aircraft into a suitable cumulus cloud, they can cause rain that would otherwise not have fallen. Some cities are susceptible to smog, a mixture of smoke and water droplets, and many urban areas become "heat islands" as a result of industrial activities and domestic heating.

The "greenhouse effect"

Over a long period, man's activities may affect climate on a world scale by the addition of extra carbon dioxide to the atmosphere. Carbon dioxide occurs naturally in the atmosphere, but the amount is gradually increasing because of the burning of fossil fuels—coal and oil. The so-called "greenhouse effect" reduces the amount of heat radiation that the Earth emits into space, thus raising temperatures near the ground. Even a small rise in temperature could make for serious change, for example, in the pattern of world agriculture. Rainfall patterns might change as well as temperature, because warmer air can hold more moisture. Some climatologists argue, however, that this warming trend will be counteracted during the next century by a natural shift towards cooler climates.

Resources and Energy

Resources, it has been said, comprise mankind's varying needs from generation to generation and are valued because of the uses societies can make of them. They represent human appraisals and are the products of man's ingenuity and experience. While natural resources remain vitally important in themselves, they must always be regarded as the rewards of human skill in locating, extracting and exploiting them. The development of resources depends on many factors, including the existence of a demand, adequate transport facilities, the availability of capital and the accessibility, quality and quantity of the resource itself.

A dictionary defines the term "resource" as "a means of aid or support," implying anything that lends support to life or activity. Man has always assessed nature with an eye to his own needs, and it is these varying needs that endow resources with their usefulness. Fossil fuels such as oil have lain long in the Earth, but it was not until about 1900 that the large-scale needs fostered by the rising demands of motor vehicles led to the development of new techniques for locating and extracting this raw material. Today oil has also become precious in the manufacture of a wide variety of industrial products, which themselves are resources that are much used by other industries.

The nature of resources

Resources can be most usefully classified in two groups: "renewable" and "nonrenewable." The latter is composed of materials found at or near the Earth's surface, which are sometimes known as "physical" resources. They include such essential minerals as uranium, iron, copper, nickel, bauxite, gold, silver, lead, mercury and tungsten. Oil, coal and natural gas are the principal nonrenewable fuel and energy resources, but after they have been used for producing heat or power their utility is lost and part of the geological capital of 325 million years of history is gone for ever. Some minerals such as iron and its product, steel, can be recycled and renewed, however. "Renewable" resources are basically biological, being the food and other vegetable matter which life needs to sustain human needs. Provided soil quality is maintained, their productivity may even be increased as better strains of plants and breeds of animals are developed.

Work has long been in progress to improve renewable resources, and has moved forward to manufacturing vegetable-flavored protein (VFP) from soybeans as a meat substitute and to viable experiments to extract protein from leaves. In Brazil, many cars have been converted to run successfully on alcohol extracted from sugar. One renewable resource—the tree—can be closely related to other resources: some conservationists are alarmed at the overuse of firewood as a source of fuel and energy in the semiarid areas of Africa. This may be an important factor in increasing the tendency for the deserts to spread in that continent, and in such a situation there is a new realization of the concept of closely managing resources such as soil, timber and fisheries. This is partly because we have a clearer understanding of the ecology of vegetation and the important interdependence of climate, soil, plants and animal life. Much, however, remains to be done.

The politics of nonrenewable resources

Today we are naturally troubled about the availability of natural resources. Oil is a prime cause for concern. Although many believe that production will grow until the mid-2020s and that new oil reserves will be discovered, oil's scarcity, based on a growing rate of demand and increasingly wasteful use, is now widely accepted. Because, like many resources, it is unevenly distributed, those countries with large and accessible supplies—such as the members of OPEC—have used their political power on a number of occasions to raise oil's price, with adverse effects on the economies of most importers. Ironically, these substantial price rises have had the effect of stimulating exploration and development in many new areas; there are already signs of increased production in China.

Other nonrenewable resources are also distributed unevenly, but have not been mined on any scale comparable with their availability; vast reserves of coal in the USSR and China have not been worked on any scale resembling their known extent.

New energy sources

As resources such as oil become less available and more expensive, the renewable resources of power such as water, wind, waves and solar energy, all of which are currently under study or development, will receive new injections of capital. Attention will also have to be paid to more widespread nuclear energy production. Energy has been called "the ultimate resource," and it is imperative that we make wise provisions for its future availability.

Future resources

It has been calculated that within four years of the launch of Sputnik I, more than 3,000 products resulting from space research were put into commercial production. These included new alloys, ceramics, plastics, fabrics and chemical compounds. Satellite developments have meant that land use can now be measured quickly and potential mineral sources closely identified. A satellite capable of converting solar power to electricity and contributing to the Earth's energy deficit has been widely discussed, while the Moon and planets have been mooted as future possible sources of minerals.

Conclusions

Resources are, in the main, the products of man's skill, ingenuity and expertise, and their widespread use, as in the case of timber and iron for shipbuilding, became apparent only as man's needs for them became clear. Our forebears were once concerned about the availability of flint, seaweed, charcoal and natural rubber; countries even went to war over supplies of spices. Today our requirements are slightly different—we no longer depend only on local sites for resources, and improved transport facilities and appropriate technologies have lowered the costs of obtaining materials for manufacture.

Nevertheless, the principles remain the same. A continual search for new resources capable of exploitation and wide application must be maintained, together with a close regard for the value of the renewable resources such as animal and vegetable products required to support man in his search for new resources. Perhaps the most vital consideration is the need for wise policies of conservation relating to the proven reserves of nonrenewable resources still in the ground, and the careful future use of such valuable deposits known or thought to exist.

The world's extraction of its resources highlights the inequality of their distribution. Each resource shown on the map is attributed to the three countries with the largest production percentages of that commodity. So, in 1976, the three leading bauxite producers were Australia (26.69%), Jamaica (14.19%) and Rep. of Guinea (13.9%). Usually, the larger and more wealthy a state the greater its monopoly of resources—although the tiny Pacific island of New Caledonia produces more than 14% of the world's nickel. China is reputed to mine 75% of the world's tungsten and to be increasing its oil supply rapidly. Energy consumption figures are for the year 1976, since when there have been some outstanding changes to patterns of availability, perhaps most noticeably in Britain's new-found oil and gas surplus. Bahrain and Tobago, too small to be shown on this map, also have surpluses of energy production.

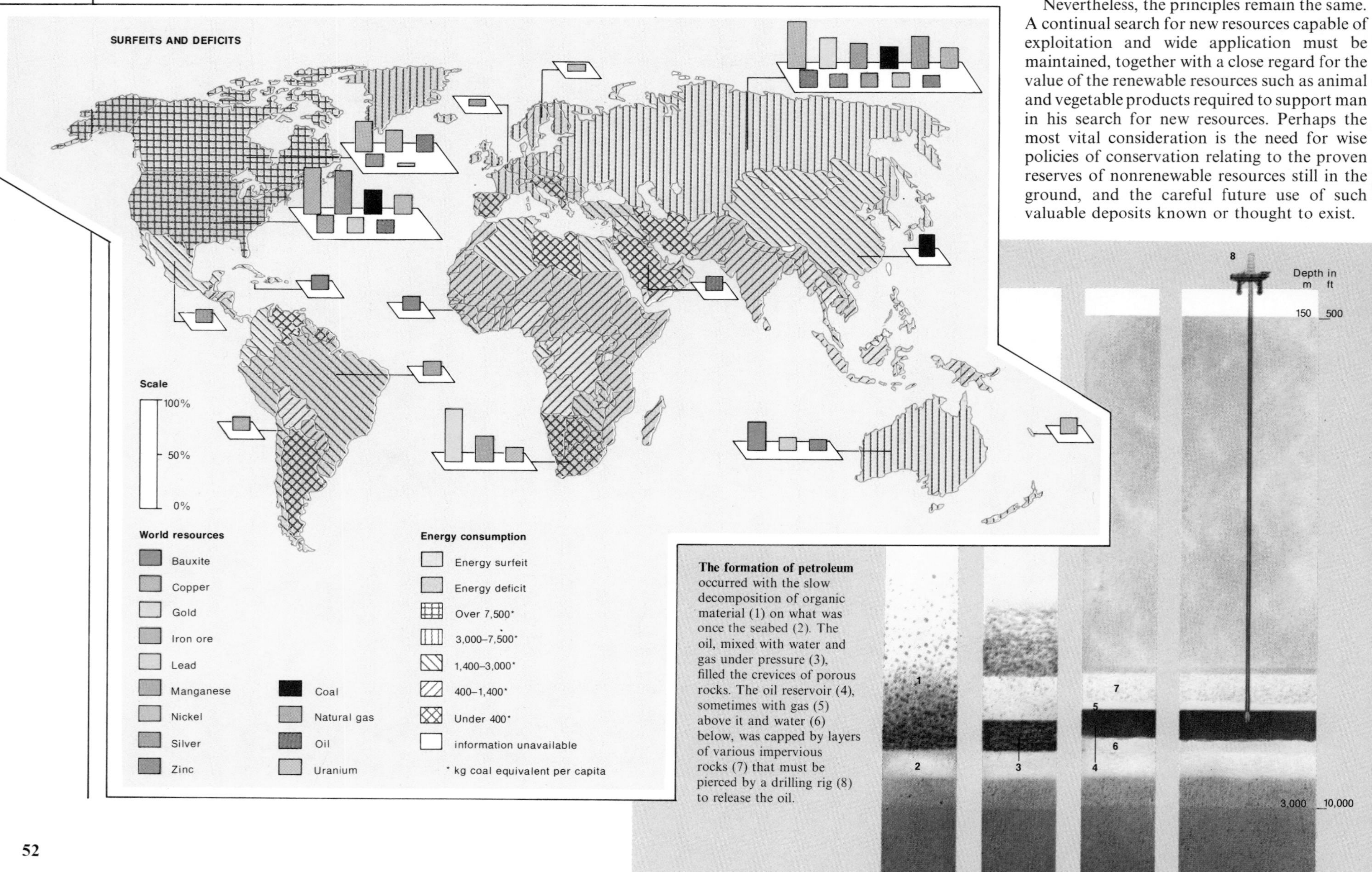

The formation of petroleum occurred with the slow decomposition of organic material (1) on what was once the seabed (2). The oil, mixed with water and gas under pressure (3), filled the crevices of porous rocks. The oil reservoir (4), sometimes with gas (5) above it and water (6) below, was capped by layers of various impervious rocks (7) that must be pierced by a drilling rig (8) to release the oil.

MAN'S ENDURING INGENUITY

A continuing search for new energy supplies has led man to explore potential oil sources in the offshore waters of the main continental landmasses. A firmly anchored production platform exemplifies the many new sites from which oil is being extracted, in an attempt to reduce reliance on the monopoly of reserves held by powerful organizations such as OPEC.

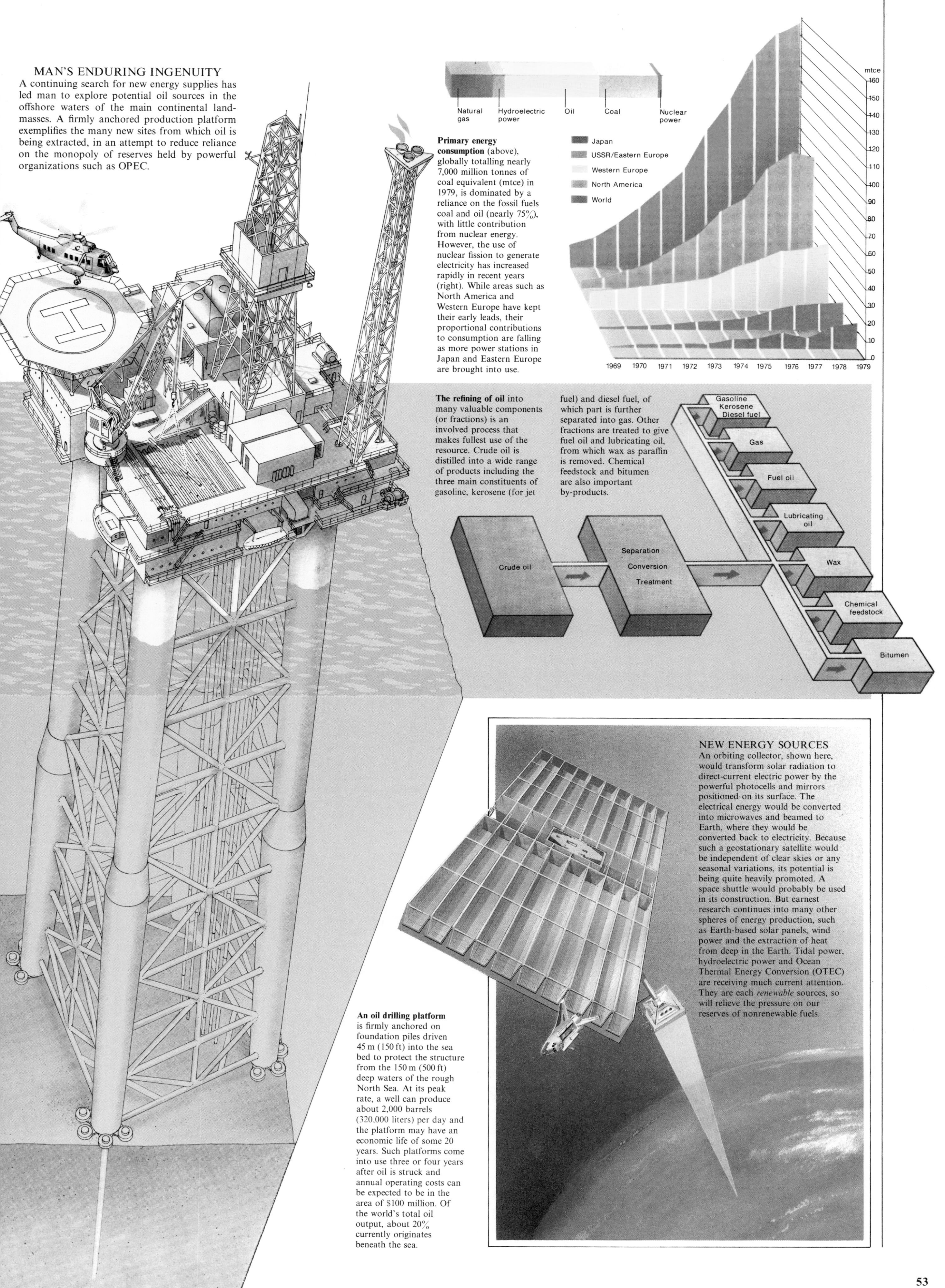

Primary energy consumption (above), globally totalling nearly 7,000 million tonnes of coal equivalent (mtce) in 1979, is dominated by a reliance on the fossil fuels coal and oil (nearly 75%), with little contribution from nuclear energy. However, the use of nuclear fission to generate electricity has increased rapidly in recent years (right). While areas such as North America and Western Europe have kept their early leads, their proportional contributions to consumption are falling as more power stations in Japan and Eastern Europe are brought into use.

The refining of oil into many valuable components (or fractions) is an involved process that makes fullest use of the resource. Crude oil is distilled into a wide range of products including the three main constituents of gasoline, kerosene (for jet fuel) and diesel fuel, of which part is further separated into gas. Other fractions are treated to give fuel oil and lubricating oil, from which wax as paraffin is removed. Chemical feedstock and bitumen are also important by-products.

NEW ENERGY SOURCES

An orbiting collector, shown here, would transform solar radiation to direct-current electric power by the powerful photocells and mirrors positioned on its surface. The electrical energy would be converted into microwaves and beamed to Earth, where they would be converted back to electricity. Because such a geostationary satellite would be independent of clear skies or any seasonal variations, its potential is being quite heavily promoted. A space shuttle would probably be used in its construction. But earnest research continues into many other spheres of energy production, such as Earth-based solar panels, wind power and the extraction of heat from deep in the Earth. Tidal power, hydroelectric power and Ocean Thermal Energy Conversion (OTEC) are receiving much current attention. They are each *renewable* sources, so will relieve the pressure on our reserves of nonrenewable fuels.

An oil drilling platform is firmly anchored on foundation piles driven 45 m (150 ft) into the sea bed to protect the structure from the 150 m (500 ft) deep waters of the rough North Sea. At its peak rate, a well can produce about 2,000 barrels (320,000 liters) per day and the platform may have an economic life of some 20 years. Such platforms come into use three or four years after oil is struck and annual operating costs can be expected to be in the area of $100 million. Of the world's total oil output, about 20% currently originates beneath the sea.

Population Growth

Every minute of every day, more than 250 children are born into the world. The Earth's population now stands at about 4,300 million and is continuing to grow extremely rapidly. The problems associated with such growth are enormous – already, about two-thirds of the world's people are underfed, according to United Nations' recommended standards of nutrition. And an even greater number live in very poor housing conditions, have inadequate access to medical facilities, receive little or no education and, at present, have no hope of improving their lot. As yet, there are no simple or immediate solutions.

World population (millions)

6,000
5,000
4,000
3,000
2,000
1,000

1970 1980 1990 2000
Year

World population
Projected world population

If the world's population continues to grow at its present rate, by the year 2000 there could be more than 6,400 million people on Earth (above). Such growth rates are only a recent phenomenon—for most of mankind's existence on Earth the numbers grew slowly (right). Then in the late 18th century, scientific and industrial developments and the discovery of new food sources (the prairies of the New World) raised living standards. Death rates declined and populations grew rapidly.

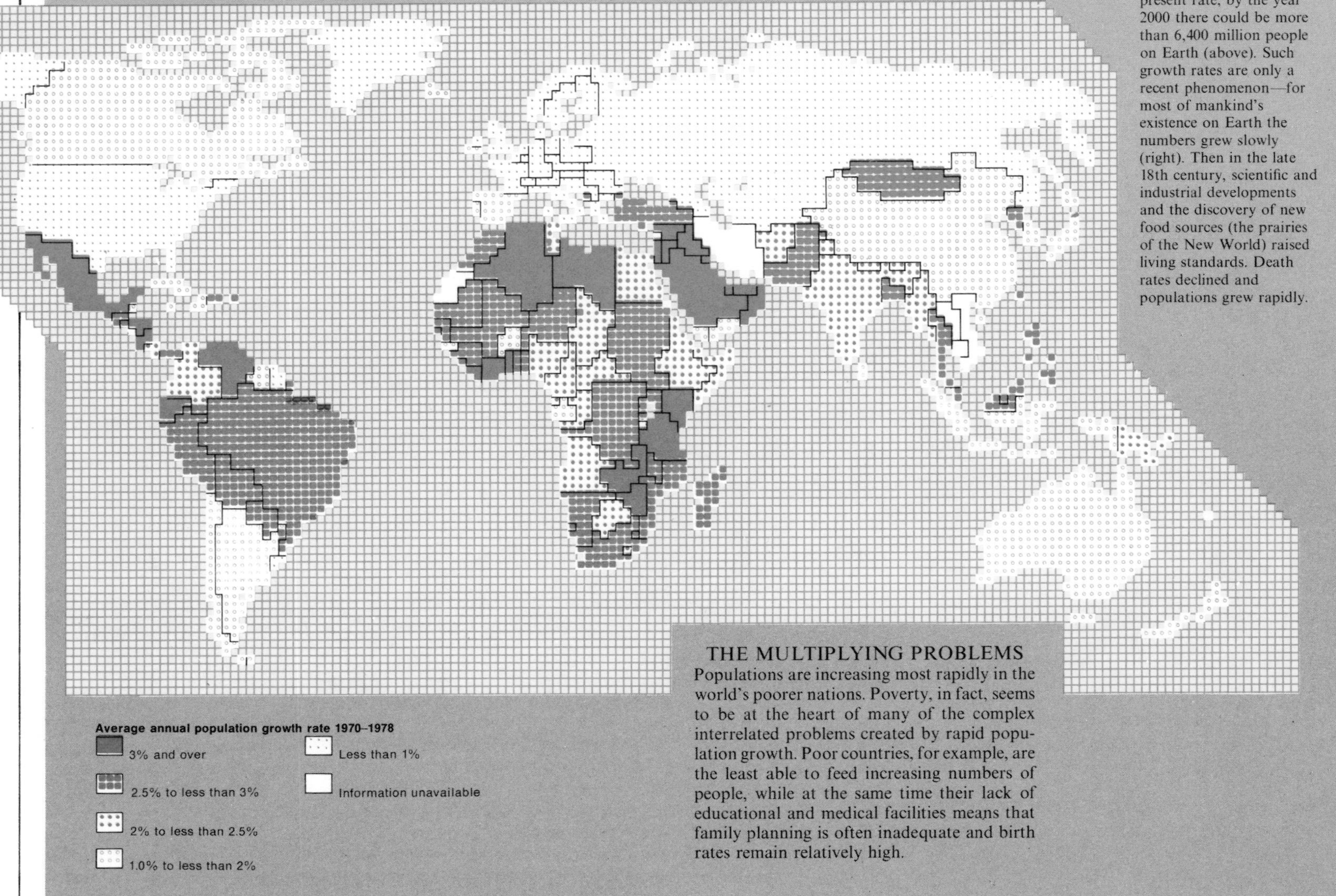

THE MULTIPLYING PROBLEMS

Populations are increasing most rapidly in the world's poorer nations. Poverty, in fact, seems to be at the heart of many of the complex interrelated problems created by rapid population growth. Poor countries, for example, are the least able to feed increasing numbers of people, while at the same time their lack of educational and medical facilities means that family planning is often inadequate and birth rates remain relatively high.

In 1830, there were only about 1,000 million people on Earth. By 1930, this figure had doubled. And by 1975, it had doubled again. If the present rate of increase continues, it will have doubled again by the year 2020.

This may not happen—it is extremely difficult to predict how world population will behave. What is certain is that it will continue to increase and, moreover, that this increase will not be evenly distributed. Since more than 50 percent of the human race lives in Asia, it is inevitable that the largest population increases will take place there. In fact, by the year 2000, the population of Asia may well have grown from about 2,000 million to more than 3,600 million. Substantial increases, of 400 million or more, will probably also occur in Africa, and Latin America is growing equally quickly.

In more prosperous North America and Europe, however, population growth seems to be stabilizing as women have fewer children and families become smaller—several countries, such as West Germany, now record a zero population growth rate. The poorer countries, the so-called Third World, are therefore gaining, and will probably continue to gain, an increasing share of the world's people. In 1930, about 64 percent of the human race lived in the poor countries of Asia, Africa and Latin America. By 1980, this proportion had increased to more than 75 percent. Population growth in these regions is creating enormous problems. It is estimated that there are now more than 800 million people living in absolute poverty in the developing world, and these numbers can but increase as populations swell.

An obvious solution is to reduce birth rates, but this cannot be achieved quickly. In much of Africa and Asia, a very high proportion of the population is made up of young people who are, or soon will be, of childbearing age. Population increases are therefore inevitable. This will probably change as family planning becomes more widespread and women have fewer children, but such relief lies in the future and is likely to affect the poorest countries last. The most pressing problem for the growing numbers of impoverished people today is that of hunger.

Food – the fundamental problem

In theory, no food supply problem should exist—already enough food is produced in the world to feed a population of 5,500 million people. In fact, however, two-thirds of this food is consumed by the rich industrialized nations, and supplies are not reaching many of those in need. The developed nations dominate world food markets because developing nations, and people within those nations, are too poor to buy food, and are themselves unable to produce sufficient quantities to feed their growing populations. The answer to undernutrition and malnutrition lies largely in raising the incomes of poor peoples and improving distribution of supplies of food.

At a local level, food produced or imported by developing countries must reach those in need at a price they can afford. One way of doing this is to encourage the rural poor to produce their own food. Small-scale, intensively farmed plots often prove to be the most efficient form of agriculture in areas where labor is plentiful. At present, many of the rural poor are either without land, or hold plots on extremely unfavorable terms of tenancy. By providing land, appropriate technology (small-scale, inexpensive farming equipment such as windpumps to draw water for irrigation), financial aid and information and education, small farmers could be helped to farm their land as effectively and efficiently as possible.

At a national level, too, developing countries must become more self-sufficient in food. This has already been achieved in some countries. India, although at one time heavily dependent upon imports of one of its staple foodstuffs—rice—has now increased production on such a scale that imports are no longer necessary. Unfortunately, for many developing countries this is not the case. Zaire, for example, was once an exporter of food. Today the country can no longer produce enough to keep pace with the demands of its own expanding population. At a world level, food production must be maintained as well, for unless production is kept high, prices are unstable and at times of bad harvests the poorer nations cannot afford to import essential supplies.

Food alone, however, is not enough to solve

Millions
6,000
5,000
4,000
3,000
2,000
1,000
0

10,000 9000 8000 7000 6000 5000 4000 3000 1000BC 0 AD1000 2000

FEEDING THE WORLD

How are the growing numbers of people on Earth to be fed when millions are already undernourished? In the short term, the food problem could be solved by improving distribution of supplies that are already available. But the world can also be made to produce more food. Fertilizers and pest control can make land more productive and genetic engineering could produce higher-yielding and more nutritious crops.

The world will have to produce more food than it does today (below) if future populations are to be fed. At present, large areas of the Earth's land surface cannot be farmed—they are either too cold, dry, marshy, mountainous or forested. Cultivatable areas could be extended, given the necessary investment.

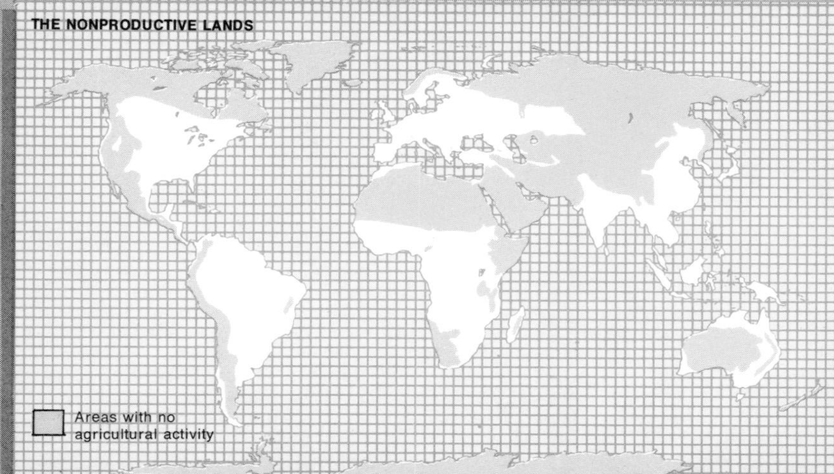

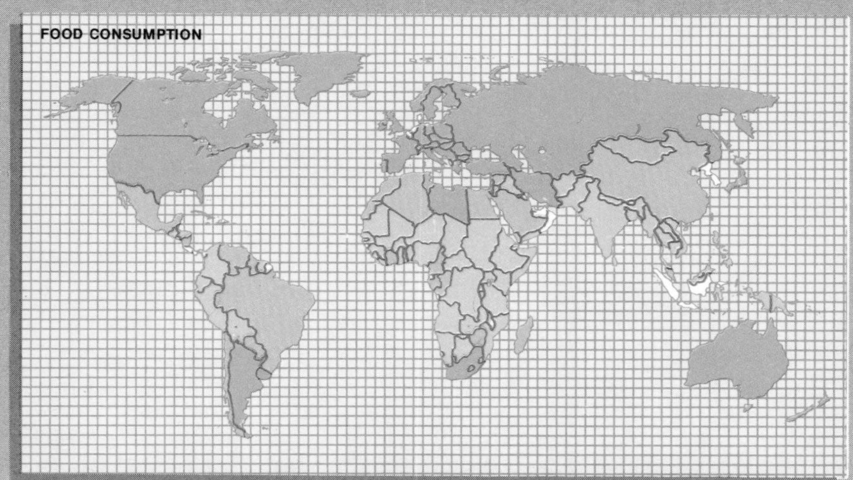

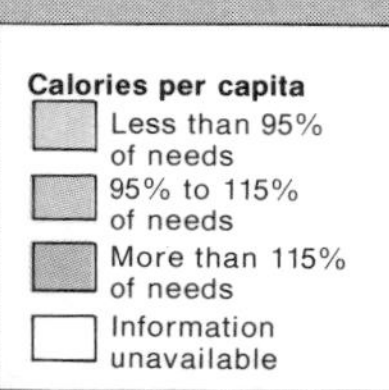

Malnutrition is widespread throughout the developing nations of Africa, Asia and South America. The problem is made worse by the fact that populations in these countries are growing more rapidly than anywhere else in the world.

THE HEALTH OF NATIONS

Many developing nations are severely short of medical and welfare facilities for their growing populations. Yet these are the very countries with high incidences of disease—mainly because of malnutrition, lack of clean water supplies, and inadequate and overcrowded housing. Furthermore, without health services family planning facilities are not widely available, and expanding populations continue to strain existing resources.

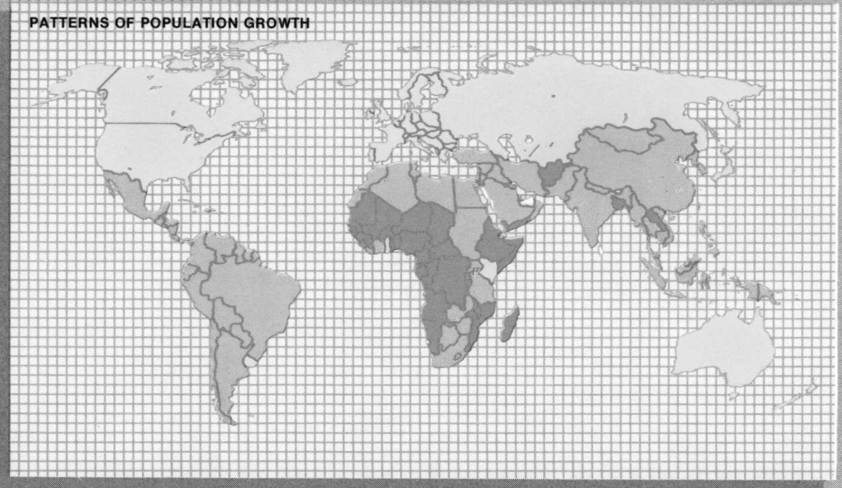

As a country's health facilities improve, its mortality rates decline. Birth rates, however, do not immediately fall (above). Thus, ironically, an improvement in facilities at first exacerbates the problem of rapid growth in population. A country with a declining death rate and a high birth rate gains an increasing percentage of young people who are, or will be, of child-bearing age. Population pyramids (right) plot the percentage balance between age and youth in a nation.

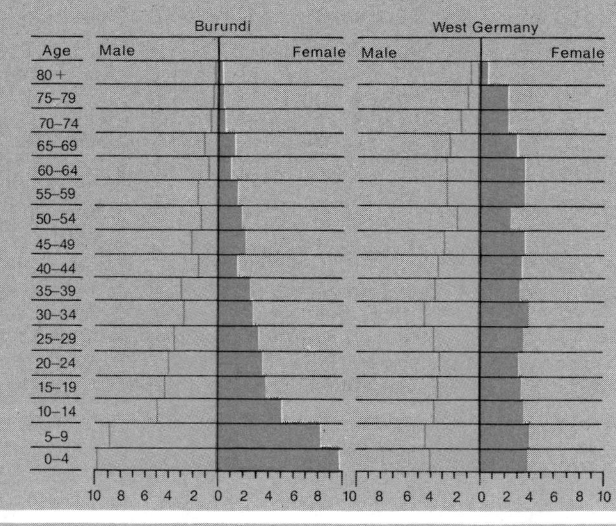

the problems created by population growth. Broadly based economic development, such as in manufacturing and industry, is essential if developing countries are to have the income and other resources to enable them to cope with their evergrowing numbers of people.

Economic growth

To achieve economic development, certain obstacles must be overcome. First, the Third World needs energy supplies at a price it can afford, for, with the exception of Nigeria and the now-rich Middle East, most developing regions are woefully short of the energy resources needed to fuel growth. Second, for sustained economic development a skilled labor force is required, as are educational facilities to provide the necessary skills from within the nations themselves. Third, investment is required to enable developing nations to exploit the resources they do have—minerals, for example. And this investment must be on terms that are as beneficial to the developing nations as they are to powerful multinational organizations that frequently fund such projects. Finally, and most important, more enlightened social and political outlooks are needed within many countries if their growing populations of impoverished people are to benefit from any economic development and consequent increase in national wealth.

It has been said that wealth is the best method of contraception and, judging by the history of population growth in the rich industrialized nations, this seems to be the case. If it is, economic development of the Third World may well alleviate many of the problems created by population growth.

INCOME

When the income level of a population is raised sufficiently, it seems that birth rates ultimately decline. This has been the pattern that has emerged in the Western world. If this is the case, then economic development of the Third World countries could eventually help to stabilize world population growth, as well as provide nations with the means to cope. It could also help provide for their growing numbers.

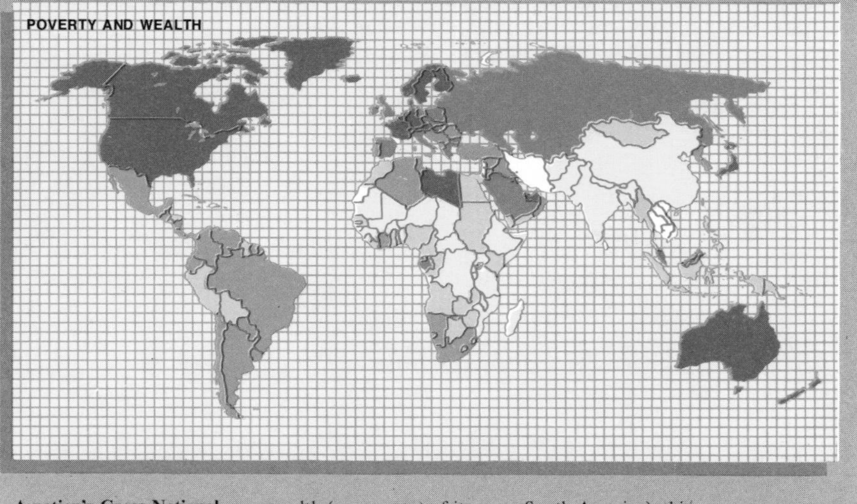

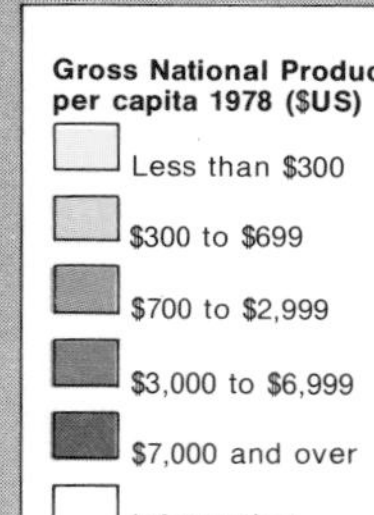

A nation's Gross National Product (GNP), when divided by the number of its population, gives some indication of the relative wealth (or poverty) of its people. But because national wealth is not evenly distributed in many countries (particularly in South America), this figure can conceal the extreme poverty of very large numbers of a nation's people.

EDUCATIONAL RESOURCES

Education is essential if the people of the developing world are to be equipped to improve their lot. Basic education on health and hygiene could dramatically reduce the incidence of disease; education about birth control would help lower birth rates; agricultural advice could help the rural poor to produce more food. Finally, general schooling is required to provide skilled labor.

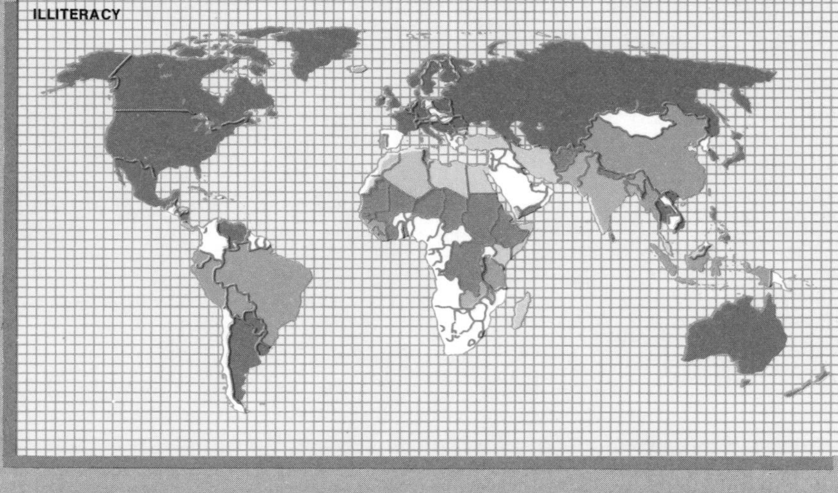

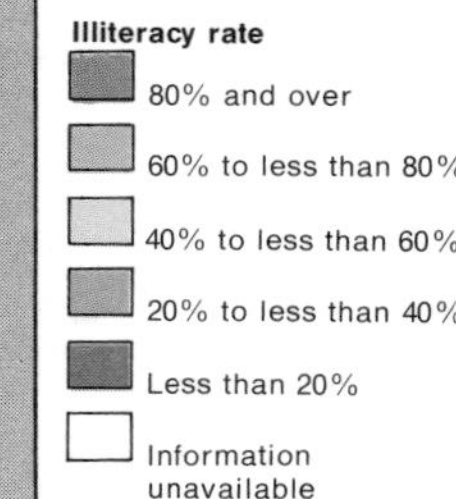

Literacy rates are in fact improving in developing countries and national expenditure on schools is growing more quickly than is population. Two major problems are, first, the social traditions that severely restrict the number of girls attending school and, second, the reluctance of many rural poor to send to school children who provide valuable manual labor on the land.

Human Settlement

Man is naturally a gregarious animal. As an agriculturist he first settled in small communities, but it was not long before the emergence of towns and cities. Now nearly half the world's people live in these larger settlements, and by the year 2000, for the first time in history, more people will live in cities than in the countryside. Cities have grown up for various reasons, and are unevenly distributed across the world; but it is in the developing countries that the most rapid rates of urban growth are today taking place.

City life has a long and varied history going back to the early population centers of the Tigris–Euphrates, Indus and Nile valleys. Administrative and political needs led to the development of capital cities. Some, like London and Paris, evolved on conveniently located river crossings; others, such as Canberra, Islamabad and Brasilia, have locations that were deliberately planned.

Types of towns and cities

Market towns were established to exchange produce and, as trade expanded, hierarchies of service centers became established. These ranged from small "central places" that supplied rural areas with simple goods and services from elsewhere, to large cities that provided highly specialized services. Through such centrally placed systems, rural areas became connected with major industrialized areas. Mining towns such as Johannesburg, South Africa, and Broken Hill, Australia, sprang up as man began to exploit the Earth's mineral resources, their locations determined by the presence of rich ore deposits. Fishing ports and settlements dependent on forestry fall into the same group.

Increasing specialization, exemplified by the Black Country, England, and the Ruhr, West Germany, was a feature of European industrial development in the eighteenth and nineteenth centuries, and was based on the availability of capital investment and the presence of sources of fuel and power, especially water and steam power. Such industrialized cities relied on newly developed forms of transport to bring in new materials and to carry away manufactured products. Chicago is a good example of the relationship between the development of rail and water routes and the growth of a city as a market, agricultural processing and manufacturing center. As transport developed, further specialized centers concentrated on locomotive, ship or aircraft construction.

Uneven settlement patterns

Across the world, density and distribution of population are uneven. The land surface of the Earth as a whole has a density of 28 people per sq km (73 per sq mile) although Manhattan, for example, has 26,000 per sq km (63,340 per sq mile) and Australia has only 1.5 per sq km (4 per sq mile). In Brazil, towns and cities are mostly sited in the rich southeast, in contrast to a sparseness of settlement in its interior. Contrasts also occur between Mediterranean North Africa and the deserted Sahara to the south; or Canada of the St. Lawrence and the Canadian Shield to the north. Here the causes are not hard to find: extremes of climate, terrain and vegetation form effective barriers to settlement. Geographers estimate that two-thirds of the world's population lives within 500 km (310 miles) of the sea.

Any true consideration of human settlements must, however, be placed within the context of the economic, political and social systems in which they have evolved. Physical considerations alone cannot fully explain the urban concentrations of Western Europe, Japan or the northeastern USA, or the comparative absence of cities elsewhere. Only 5 percent of Malawi's and 4.7 percent of New Guinea's populations live in towns; in Belgium the percentage is 87, in Australia 86, in the UK 78 and in the USA 73.5. The figure for Norway is only 42 percent. Urbanization is a varied phenomenon and cities grow for many reasons.

The attractions of the city

Cities have always acted as magnets to poor or unemployed rural populations, and migrations from the countryside have assisted high rates of city growth. Very large cities—Tokyo, New York and Los Angeles—are still found in the northern world, but many cities with far faster growth rates are sited in the Third World, especially in Asia. There the total number of inhabitants living in towns and cities is still much lower than in Europe, but centers such as Shanghai, Karachi, Bandung, New Delhi, Seoul, Jakarta and Manila are among the world's most rapidly expanding urban centers. Perhaps as many as a third of these city dwellers in Asia, Africa and Latin America put up with makeshift housing in shanty towns that present enormous problems of health, sanitation, education and unemployment: city growth in the developing world is a daunting prospect.

People on the move

In the past, one solution to population pressure on the land could be found in the migrations which occurred on a large scale from Asia into Europe, from Europe to the Americas and Australasia, and from China into southeastern Asia. But as claims are being made on almost every habitable area of the Earth, mass migrations have largely declined in importance. Many nations restrict movement to or from their countries. Australia has strict immigration quotas; Vietnam and the USSR restrict emigration for largely ideological reasons. Large movements of labor still take place, however, from the poorer regions of the Mediterranean to the industrial cities of France and Germany. Migrant workers from neighboring countries in Africa also play an essential part in the mining economy of South Africa.

New trends in urbanization

In many industrialized countries, a strong process of decentralization is leading to reductions in the populations of cities and corresponding increases in those of the suburbs and beyond. In 1951 the geographer Jean Gottman showed how groups of city regions tend to form chains of functionally linked cities, to which he gave the term "megalopolis." His prime example was Megalopolis, USA, stretching from north of Boston to south of Washington DC. Similar settlements occur in the Tokyo–Yokohama–Osaka area of Japan and the Ruhr megalopolis of northwestern Europe. Ultimately, equally drastic and large-scale patterns are likely to emerge in the already overcrowded human settlements of the Third World.

THE DISTRIBUTION OF POPULATION

Human settlement is highly uneven because it is related to many social and topographical factors. At first, man was tied to the sites of his crops and the grazing land of his cattle; life in nonrural centers only became a typical feature of population development as specialized services came into demand and towns and cities arose to support these needs. But during the 20th century there has been a vast increase in urban populations, particularly in Third World countries.

Oil and gas deposits
Iron ore railroads
Farming
Towns
Hydroelectric projects
Iron ore railroads
Current oil and gas pipelines

Ciudad Guayana
Ciudad Bolivar
VENEZUELA
GUYANA

Expanding settlements (above) and new lines of communication are being developed in the poorly populated eastern lowlands of Venezuela in order fully to exploit the resources being discovered there. Huge deposits of iron ore and large supplies of oil and gas have been located, and Ciudad Bolivar and Ciudad Guayana have become steel-making and service centers. To feed the people of these new settlements, agriculture has been greatly expanded.

Boston
New York City
Philadelphia
Baltimore
Washington DC
Richmond

Immigration to the United States (below) from Europe was partly responsible for the growth of the vast Washington–Boston urban mass known as "Megalopolis." Since World War II, more immigrants have come from Puerto Rico and Mexico.

Immigrants in 000s: 0, 1,000, 2,000, 3,000, 4,000, 5,000, 6,000, 7,000, 8,000, 9,000 (estimated)
Year: 1840, 1860, 1880, 1900, 1920, 1940, 1960, 1980

Migrating refugees, the world total of which increases on average by 2,000–3,000 every day, can affect settlement patterns. The Ugandan children (below) fled to the northern province of Karamoja in the wake of the 1979 war with Tanzania and the resultant famine that occurred in much of Uganda.

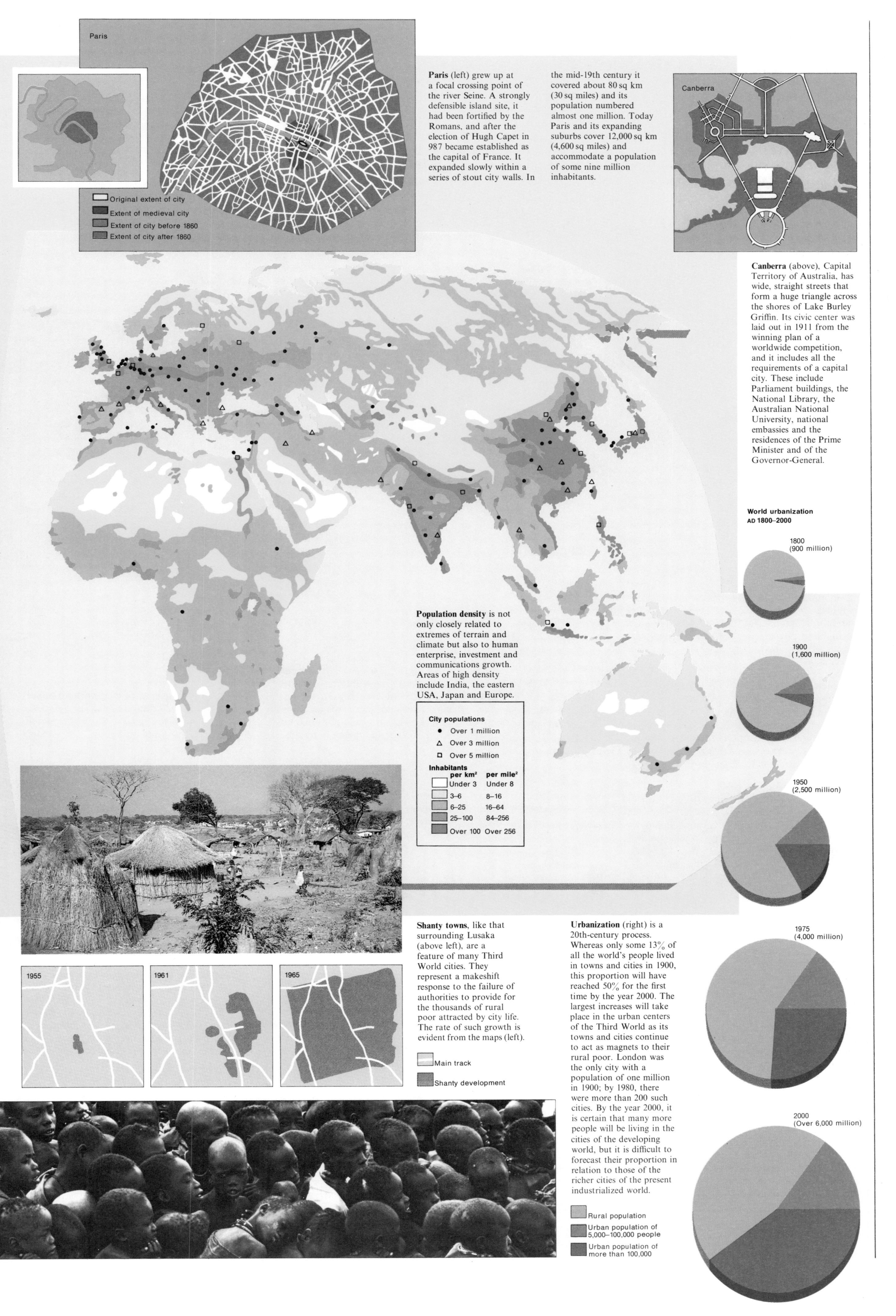

Paris (left) grew up at a focal crossing point of the river Seine. A strongly defensible island site, it had been fortified by the Romans, and after the election of Hugh Capet in 987 became established as the capital of France. It expanded slowly within a series of stout city walls. In the mid-19th century it covered about 80 sq km (30 sq miles) and its population numbered almost one million. Today Paris and its expanding suburbs cover 12,000 sq km (4,600 sq miles) and accommodate a population of some nine million inhabitants.

Canberra (above), Capital Territory of Australia, has wide, straight streets that form a huge triangle across the shores of Lake Burley Griffin. Its civic center was laid out in 1911 from the winning plan of a worldwide competition, and it includes all the requirements of a capital city. These include Parliament buildings, the National Library, the Australian National University, national embassies and the residences of the Prime Minister and of the Governor-General.

Population density is not only closely related to extremes of terrain and climate but also to human enterprise, investment and communications growth. Areas of high density include India, the eastern USA, Japan and Europe.

Shanty towns, like that surrounding Lusaka (above left), are a feature of many Third World cities. They represent a makeshift response to the failure of authorities to provide for the thousands of rural poor attracted by city life. The rate of such growth is evident from the maps (left).

Urbanization (right) is a 20th-century process. Whereas only some 13% of all the world's people lived in towns and cities in 1900, this proportion will have reached 50% for the first time by the year 2000. The largest increases will take place in the urban centers of the Third World as its towns and cities continue to act as magnets to their rural poor. London was the only city with a population of one million in 1900; by 1980, there were more than 200 such cities. By the year 2000, it is certain that many more people will be living in the cities of the developing world, but it is difficult to forecast their proportion in relation to those of the richer cities of the present industrialized world.

Trade and Transport

It is a commonplace that we live in a "shrinking" world. During the last century the development of communications has been so rapid that man appears almost to have conquered the challenge of distance; but such a concept depends on the kind of area to be covered and the cost of transporting goods in relation to their value, bulk and perishability. People, goods and services become accessible by trade. Transport makes trade possible: trade's demands lead to improvements in transport.

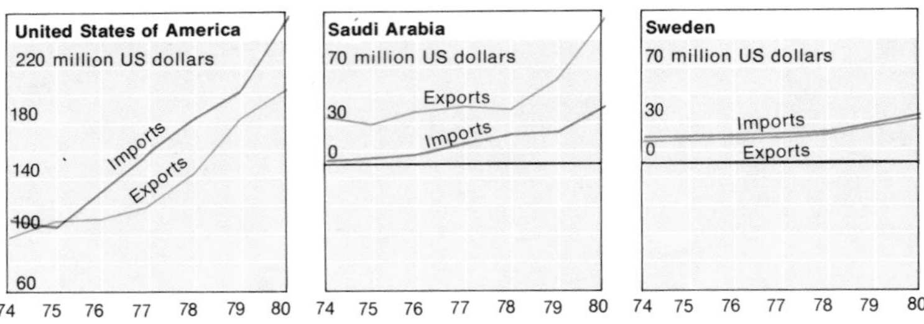

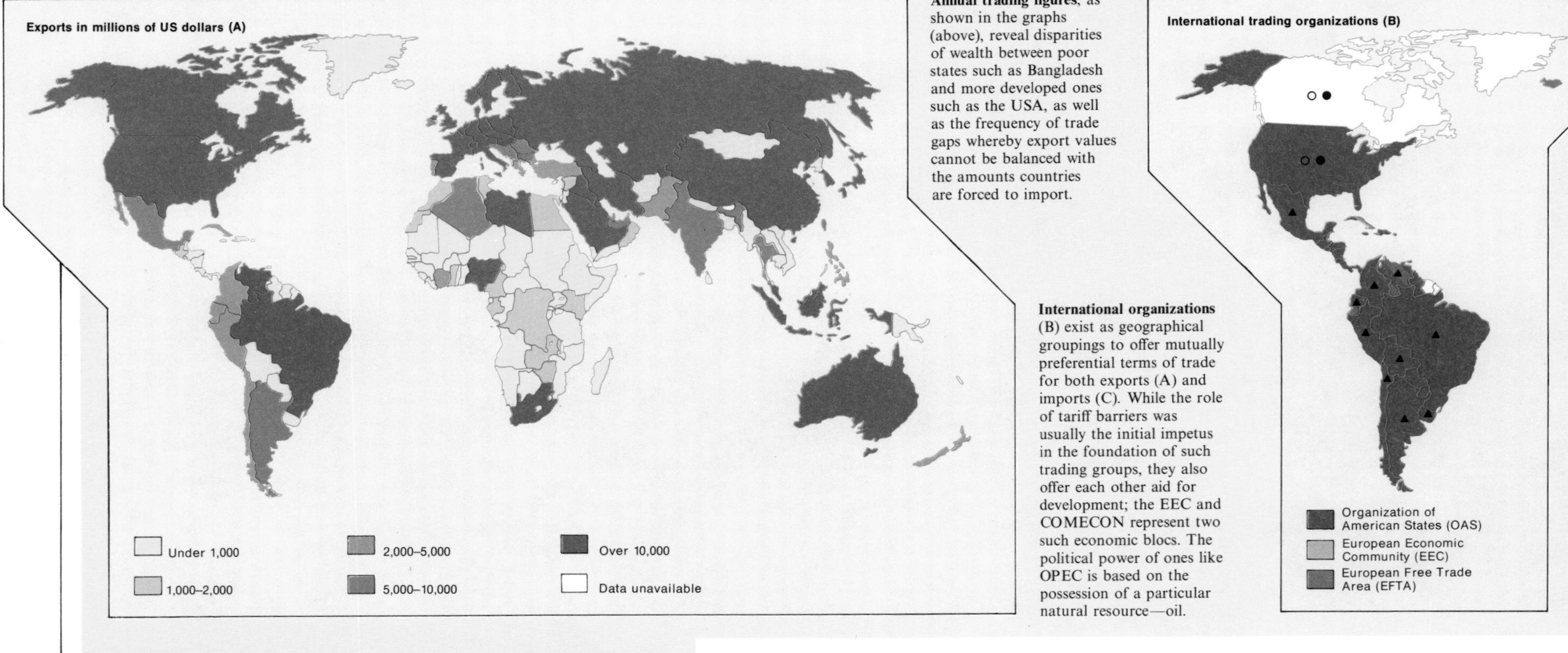

Annual trading figures, as shown in the graphs (above), reveal disparities of wealth between poor states such as Bangladesh and more developed ones such as the USA, as well as the frequency of trade gaps whereby export values cannot be balanced with the amounts countries are forced to import.

International organizations (B) exist as geographical groupings to offer mutually preferential terms of trade for both exports (A) and imports (C). While the role of tariff barriers was usually the initial impetus in the foundation of such trading groups, they also offer each other aid for development; the EEC and COMECON represent two such economic blocs. The political power of ones like OPEC is based on the possession of a particular natural resource—oil.

Japanese export of electronic products (1979)

29.7% Audio parts
24.2% Radios
23.6% Stereos etc
12.7% TVs
9.8% Video recorders

Electronic products comprise only one-sixth of Japanese exports (left); their high export value and reputation for quality make their sales abroad vital to Japan's economy. Trading links (below) with industrialized countries are very well established; now Japan is mounting new export drives to sell its products to much less traditional markets.

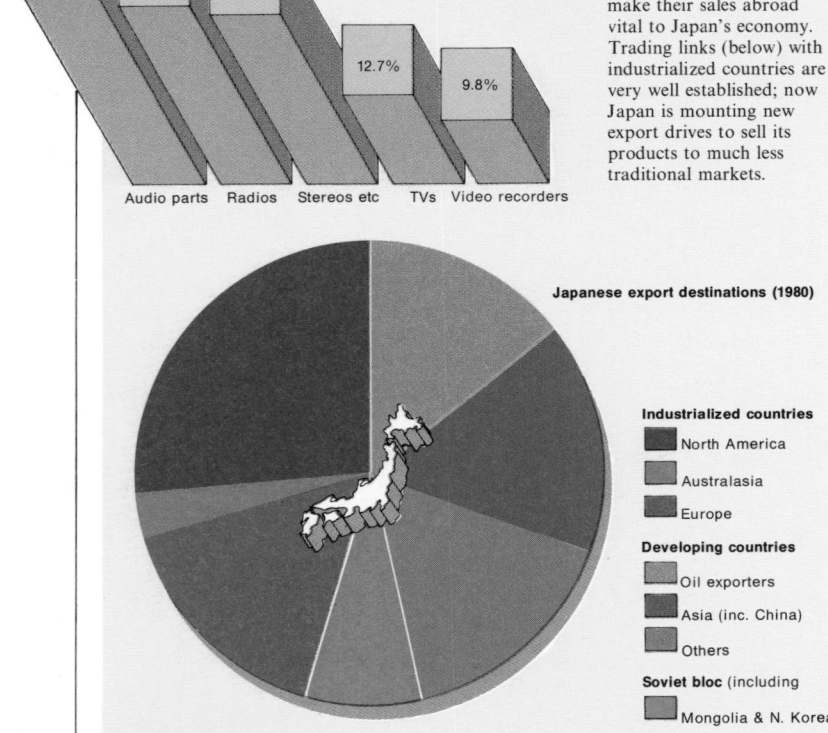

Japanese export destinations (1980)

Industrialized countries
North America
Australasia
Europe
Developing countries
Oil exporters
Asia (inc. China)
Others
Soviet bloc (including Mongolia & N. Korea)

It is only a little more than two centuries since navigators completed the mapping of the world's major landmasses and much less since the mapping of the continental interiors was completed—even today some gaps still remain. Canals like the Suez (1869) and Panama (1915) reduced the extent of long sea voyages—the Suez Canal shortened the distance from northwestern Europe to India by 15,000 km (9,300 miles)—so that in transport terms, the various parts of the world became more accessible, especially as steamships and motor vessels replaced sailing ships, and time distances were reduced still further by the airplane.

Locational advantages

Inland waterways, roads and railroads opened up new areas for mining or specialized agriculture, and created opportunities for the manufacture of goods and for the distribution of the finished products. The contrast, however, between locations such as London, Tokyo or Chicago (which are accessible to all forms of transport) and parts of South America where modern transport hardly penetrates, has become much more marked over the years. New transport developments tend to connect major centers first of all, and thus increase their already high locational status.

Such developments must nevertheless be seen in the light of the demand for communications and trade between different points, the nature of the goods being carried and the actual cost of transport. Transport improvements have allowed different parts of the world to share ideas and products; ironically, they have also made such places more dissimilar, since each area of the Earth has had the chance to specialize in the services it can provide most efficiently.

Specialization of area

Before the widespread development of canals and railroads, road transport was expensive and towns and villages tended to be more self-sufficient. Railroads played a vital role in reducing transport costs in relation to distance and in providing an opportunity for different areas to specialize. After the emergence of railroad networks in North America, specialized areas of agricultural production quickly developed because they were well adjusted to the climatic conditions needed for growing maize (corn), cotton, fruit and fresh vegetables for the new urban markets. In the southern hemisphere, steamships and the introduction of refrigeration enabled meat, butter and cheese to be kept fresh on their journeys to the north.

This concept of specialization of area is basic to world trading patterns, since regions tend to concentrate on commodities and services that they can exchange for other specialized goods and products from other regional or world markets. Countries and areas do best when they concentrate on products for which they have comparative cost advantages in terms of the presence of natural resources, the availability of the skills to develop them, and a demand for the products. Enterprise in adapting natural conditions for the production of goods at competitive price levels is also important. Settlers in New

Man's expanding world

Technological change in transport has resulted in important reductions in the cost of trade. A man trading on foot might travel half the area a draft horse could cover in a 12-hour day, but it was the acceptance of steam after *The Rocket* (1829) that made trade more reliable and greatly expanded the potential for international commerce. Modern jet airliners can easily fly thousands of kilometers in half a day, and while they are being used more and more for freight, most bulk freight is still carried by train or by specialized cargo vessel. The graph below plots changing transport technology.

0 120 240 360 480 600 720 840 960 1,080 1,200 1,320 1,440 1,560
Kilometers traveled in 12 hours

THE WEALTH OF NATIONS

Economists measure a country's richness in terms of Gross National Product (GNP), the value of the goods and services available for consumption and for adding to its wealth. The difference in value between its exported and imported goods is often an important aspect of a nation's economy, and effective systems to transport such goods must play a major role in overseas trade. The 1980 Brandt Report highlighted the huge gap between the income of the rich world and the poverty of many developing states, but solutions to such problems of inequality will be difficult to obtain.

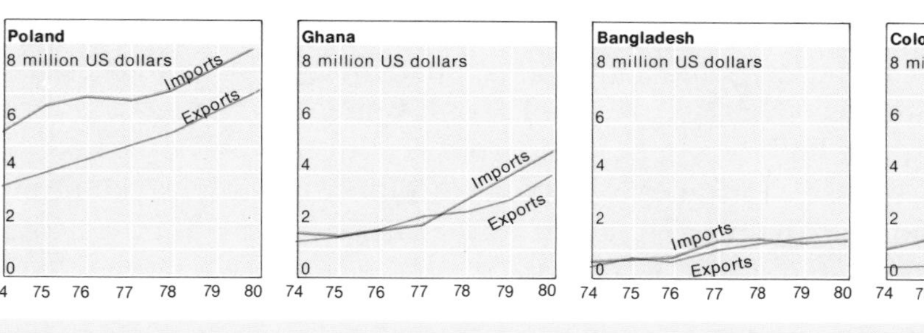
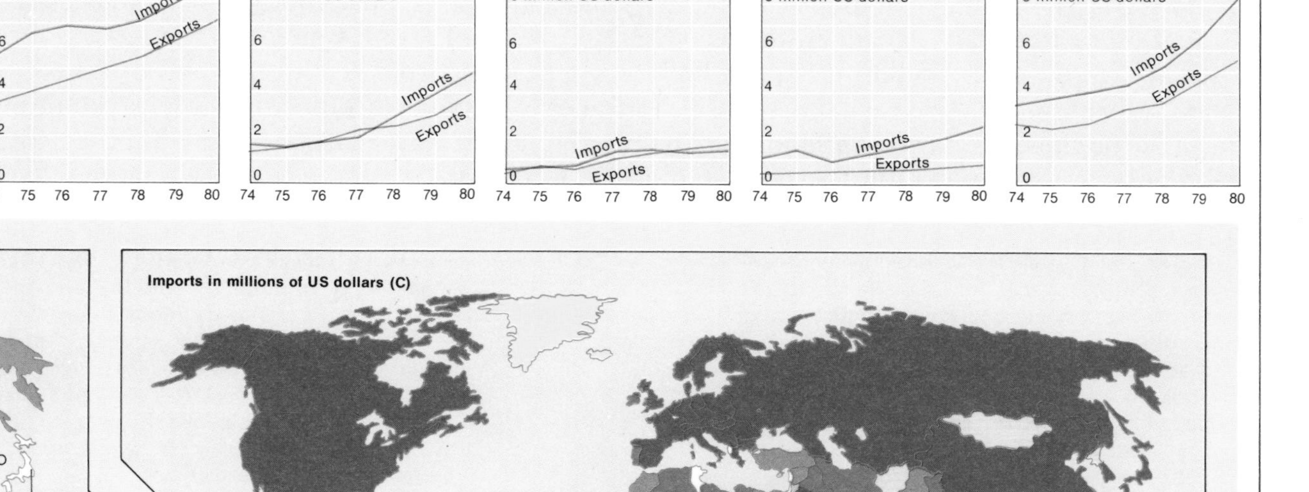

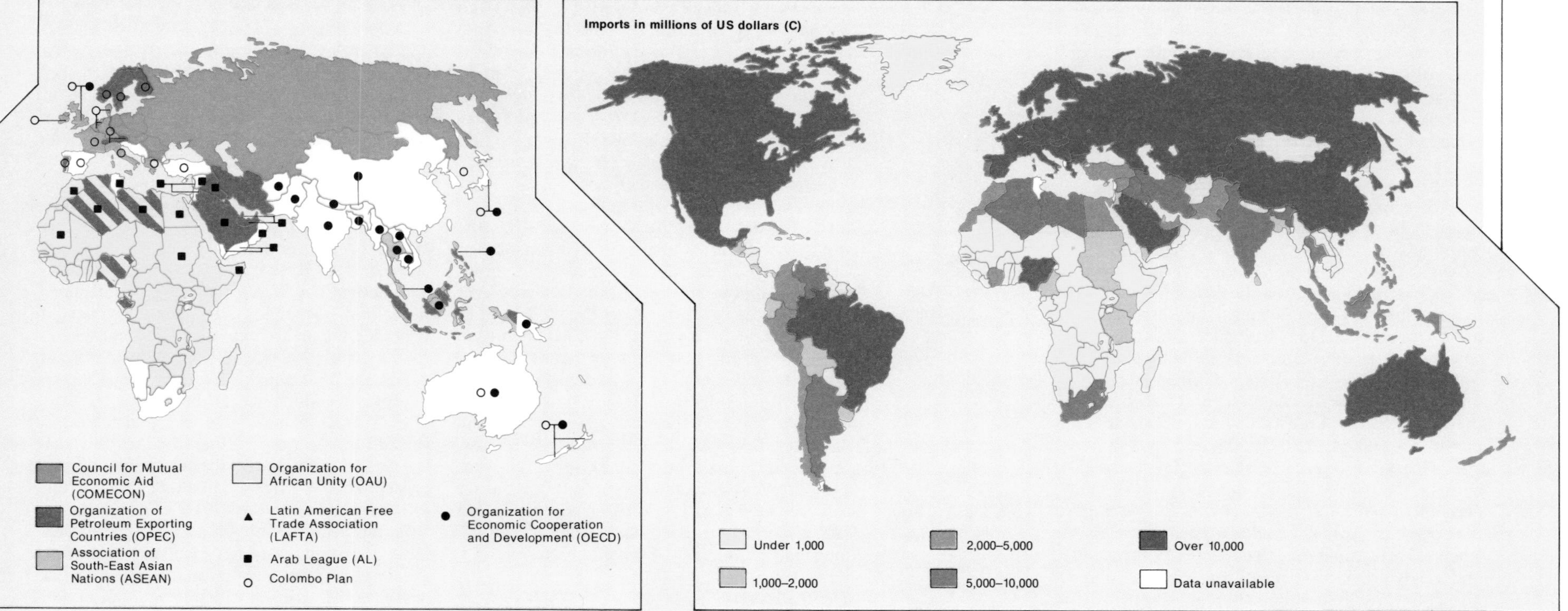

Zealand, for example, had little hesitation in clearing the prevailing tussock grass to create a new pastoral environment for their large-scale production of sheep and dairy products.

In the real world, however, there are many impediments to the operation of a free market system, and it is unwise for states like New Zealand to assume that they will always dominate Commonwealth dairy trade.

Impediments to free markets

Countries erect protectionist tariff barriers to assist their home industries and/or to obtain extra revenue. Import or export quotas may be imposed, and trade agreements with other countries give special preference to certain commodities. Problems arise from the exchange of currencies and their fluctuations in value. Tariff barriers may be erected for political, welfare or defense reasons. Sometimes special measures may be adopted to encourage the internal production of certain goods rather than obtaining them more cheaply from abroad, and such methods may be economically important to a new country that has always relied on the export of raw materials for its income but now wishes domestically to manufacture previously imported goods.

Political ties are vital to the groupings of certain countries. For reasons of international politics, countries such as those of the Soviet bloc trade with each other rather than with the outside world; and historical links, as between the UK and the Commonwealth, France and her ex-colonies, and Spain and Portugal with Latin America, are also influential. The European Economic Community (EEC) is composed of countries that have formed a strong bloc among the developed countries.

Rich man, poor man

The developed countries of "the North" have more than 80 percent of the world's manufacturing income but only a quarter of its population, whereas the poorer peoples of "the South" number 3,000 million and receive only a fifth of world income. Attempts have been made to obtain a better economic balance. The 1948 General Agreement on Tariffs and Trade (GATT) and the United Nations Conference on Trade and Development (UNCTAD) provided mechanisms for multinational trade negotiations, and the World Bank and the International Monetary Fund (IMF) together with the 1960 International Development Association (IDA) have all provided easier loans for less developed states.

The widening gap between rich and poor countries has led to understandable demands for a new international order calling for basic changes in the structure of world production, aid and trade, and the transfer of resources. The 1980 Independent Commission on International Development Issues (The Brandt Commission) advocated just such a transfer to the Third World. But during a major world recession there seems little sign of any international political will strong enough to take action on the scale needed to solve the problems that contrasts in wealth and poverty involve.

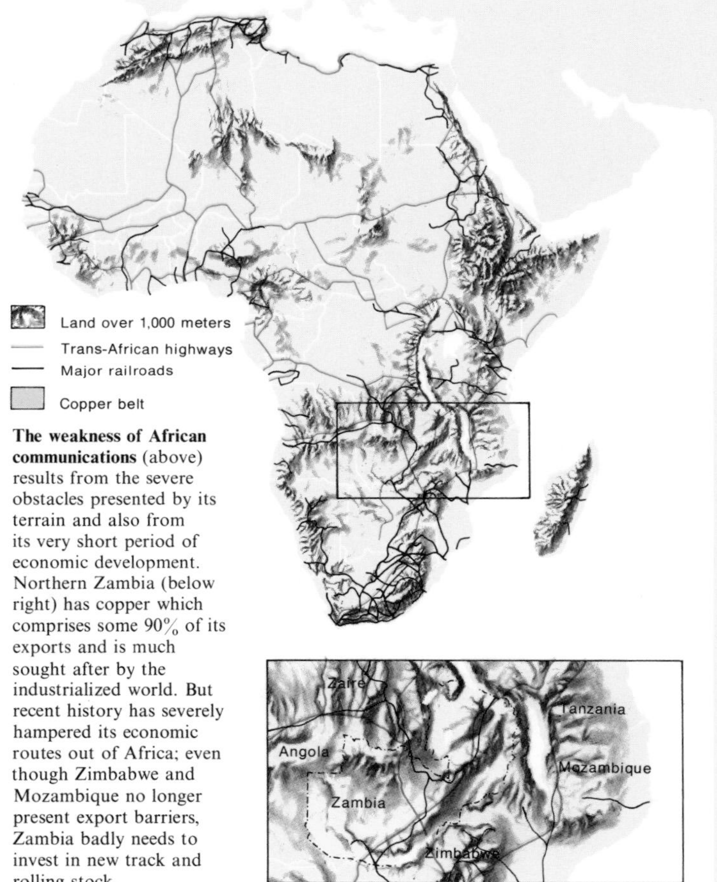

The weakness of African communications (above) results from the severe obstacles presented by its terrain and also from its very short period of economic development. Northern Zambia (below right) has copper which comprises some 90% of its exports and is much sought after by the industrialized world. But recent history has severely hampered its economic routes out of Africa; even though Zimbabwe and Mozambique no longer present export barriers, Zambia badly needs to invest in new track and rolling stock.

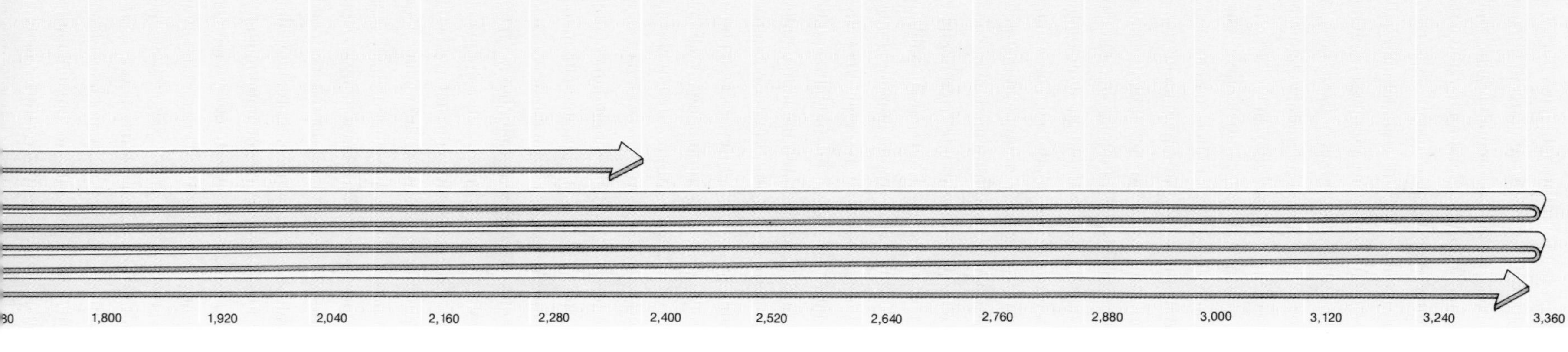

Polar Regions

Sunless in winter, and capped with permanent land ice and shifting sea ice, the world's polar regions present an image of intense and everlasting cold. But permanent ice caps have been the exception rather than the rule in the 4,600 million years of Earth's history. The most recent intensification of the present ice age (which began at least two million years ago) reached its maximum about 20,000 years ago and still continues to fluctuate. Polar conditions preclude all but the toughest life forms on land, but the plankton-rich waters attract many animals, and man is beginning to exploit the polar regions' potential.

There have been about a dozen ice ages since the world began. During the intervening periods there was still a zonal pattern of world temperatures, with hot equatorial regions and cooler poles. But the ice caps, which are both chilling and self-sustaining, were absent altogether—the poles being cold temperate rather than ice-bound. The shiny ice surfaces of today's poles reflect more than 90 percent of the solar radiation which reaches them from the low-angled summer sun, while in winter the sun never rises at all. Thus the regions are now permanently ice capped.

Antarctica, the great southern polar continent, lies under an ice mantle 14 million sq km (5.4 million sq miles) in area, and sometimes more than 4,000 m (13,000 ft) thick. Many of its neighboring islands also carry permanent ice. In the Arctic, the three islands of Greenland lie under a pall of ice of subcontinental size, more than 1.8 million sq km (700,000 sq miles) in area and up to 3,000 m (9,800 ft) thick.

The ice cover of polar seas varies. The central core of the Arctic Ocean carries a mass of permanent pack ice, slowly circulating within the polar basin, which is added to each winter by a belt of ice forming over the open sea. Currents and winds break this up to form pack ice that also circulates, gradually melting in summer or drifting south. Antarctica too is surrounded by fast ice, which breaks up in spring to form a broad belt of persistent pack ice. Circulating slowly about the continent, the pack ice forms huge gyres spreading far to the north, dotted with tabular bergs that have broken away from the continental ice sheet.

The frozen land

In the present glacial phase, the ice caps reached their farthest spread about 20,000 years ago, and then began the retreat which brought them, some 10,000 to 12,000 years ago, to their current position and size. Since then the climate of the polar regions has been both warmer and colder than it is at the present time.

The coldness of the poles is caused by the tilt of the Earth's axis, which prevents sunlight from reaching them at all in the winter. Even in summer, little heat is received from the sun because of the low angle at which its rays reach the surface; much even of this is reflected away by the ice.

Arctic spring
Arctic summer
Arctic winter
Arctic autumn

The fluctuating nature of the polar climates creates very difficult conditions for plants and animals. Very little will grow on the terrestrial ice caps, but water scarcity rather than cold is the most important factor inhibiting plant growth: the small patches of lichens, algae and mosses that occur on rock faces and nunataks (points of rock jutting above the land ice) are usually in the path of a snowmelt runnel. Vegetation patches sometimes contain tiny populations of insects and mites, which may be active for only a few days each year when the sun warms them from a state of dormancy.

However, these tiny scattered plant communities appear all over Antarctica wherever rock surfaces break through the ice cap, and have been seen less than 300 km (190 miles) from the South Pole, and on peaks 2,000 m (6,600 ft) above sea level. Insects and mites occur within 600 km (380 miles) of the Pole itself. In specially favored positions on the Antarctic Peninsula and the offshore islands, carpets of moss and grasses may be seen. Conditions around the northern terrestrial ice cap are similar, with aridity, strong winds and cold discouraging all but the hardiest plants and the smallest, toughest animal colonies.

The frozen seas

The marine ice caps, by contrast, are relatively lively places, especially during summer, when days are long and the sea ice is patchy. Waterlanes between floes are often rich in microscopic algae and the minute zooplanktonic animals that feed on them. These animals in turn attract fish, sea birds and seals in their thousands, as well as whales—including the largest baleen species. Some of the richest patches of sea are close to islands where strong currents stir the water and bring nutrients to the surface, and these attract semipermanent populations of seals and birds. The birds breed on the island cliffs and feed in the sheltered waters among the ice; the seals may breed on the ice itself, producing their pups on a floating nursery where food is close at hand.

Different species of seals are found on inshore and offshore ice environments. In the Arctic, bearded and ringed seals, which produce their young in spring as the inshore ice begins to break up, are often preyed upon by floe-riding polar bears; Eskimos too prize both species for their meat, blubber and skins. Farther out on the offshore pack ice live hooded and harp seals, where their pups are safe from all but the shipborne commercial hunters. In the Antarctic, Weddell seals are the inshore species, whereas crabeater and Ross seals prefer the distant pack ice. Crabeaters, which feed largely on planktonic krill (once thought to be crab larvae), are probably the most numerous of all seal species, with a population estimated at 10 to 15 million.

Sea ice in the north provides a precarious platform on which coastal human populations of the Arctic, such as Eskimos, can extend their winter hunting range. When the land is snowbound and animals are scarce, the sea may still provide food for hunters skilled in fishing, and in stalking seals to their breathing holes.

Nonindigenous inhabitants of the ice caps have greatly increased in recent years, following the discovery and exploitation of oil in the north, as well as other valuable minerals in both the regions. Scientists and technicians today occupy bases and weather stations which in some cases, such as the Amundsen-Scott at the South Pole, are several decades old and have to be maintained by means of aircraft.

EARTH'S FROZEN LIMITS

The permanent ice around Earth's poles covers whole oceans, as well as landmasses of immense size. These ice sheets fluctuate, and on land may be thousands of meters thick, sometimes covering all but the highest mountains, and allowing hardly any life. In the circumpolar seas, however, conditions encourage a very rich growth of plankton, and this supports a plentiful and varied range of wildlife. Man, too, is active in the Arctic, where there are indigenous populations. But in the far south the presence of man is confined to scientists and their support groups. The Antarctic Treaty of 1959 has reserved the continent for nonpolitical scientific use.

THE FAR SOUTH

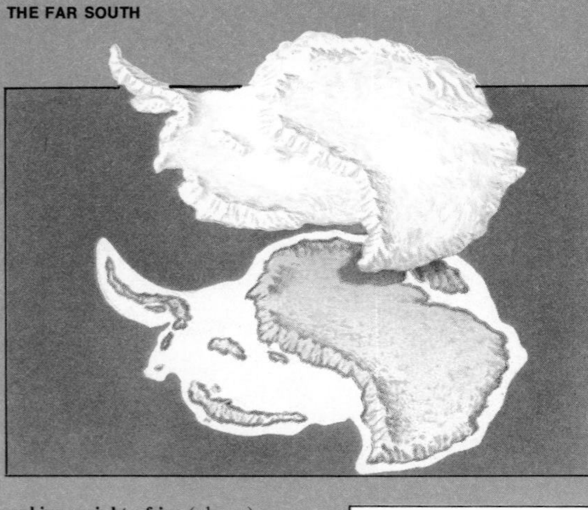

A crushing weight of ice (above) permanently covers the continent and seas of Antarctica, forcing much of the land below sea level. The Antarctic convergence (right), the line at which northern and southern water masses meet, marks a sharp change in temperature and marine life. Especially in areas of upwelling, nutrients make these waters rich in plankton. This feeds a multitude of shrimp-like krill that provide food for a huge number of other animals—fish, penguins, flying birds, seals and whales. The Antarctic landmass allows little natural life, but since the 1959 Antarctic Treaty it has proved to be an area of international scientific cooperation.

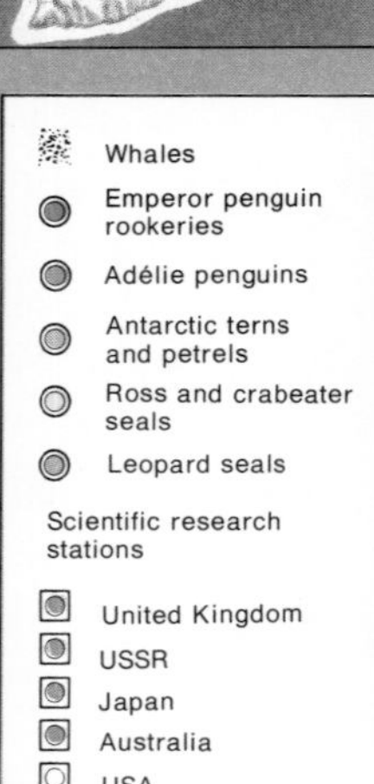

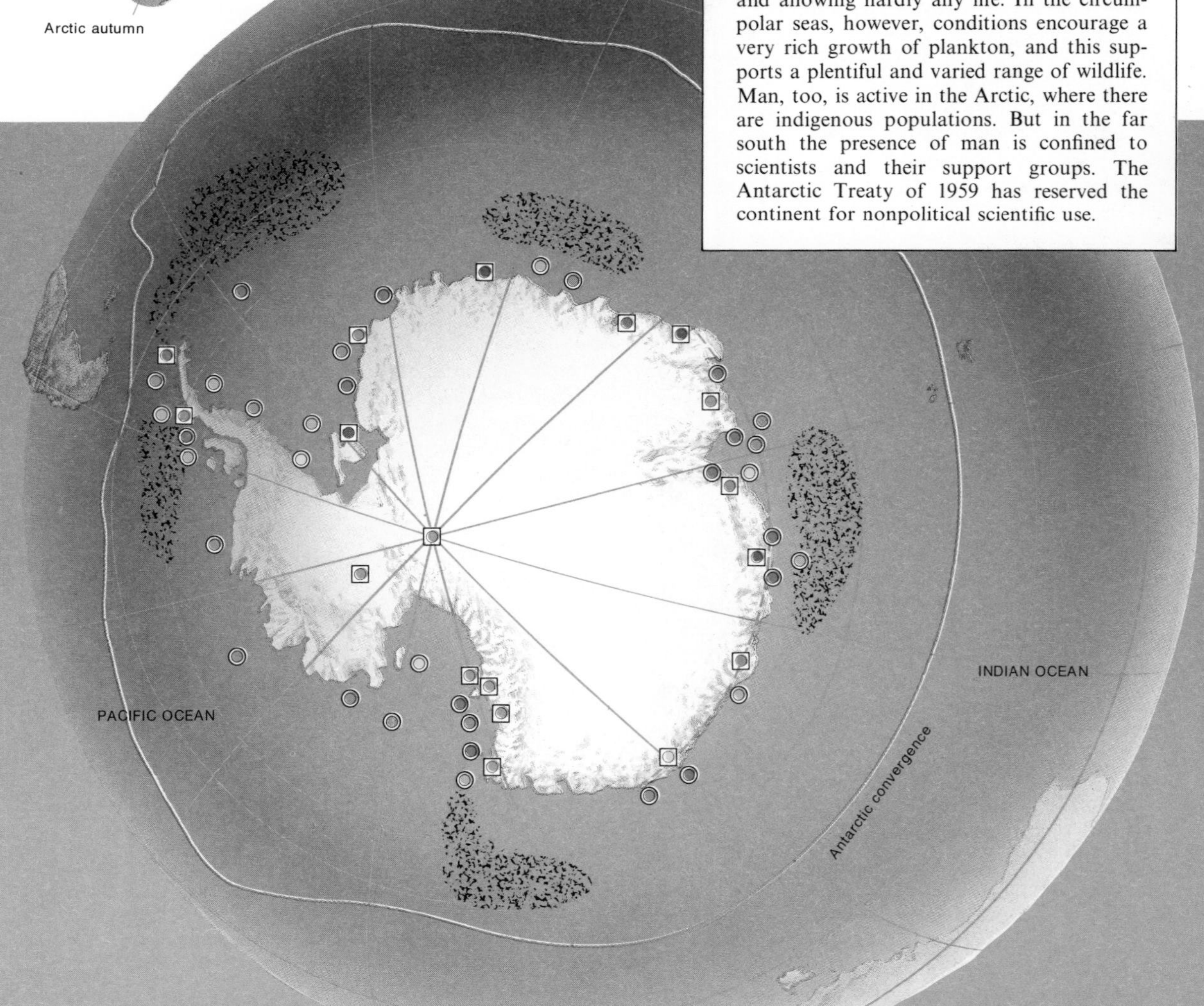

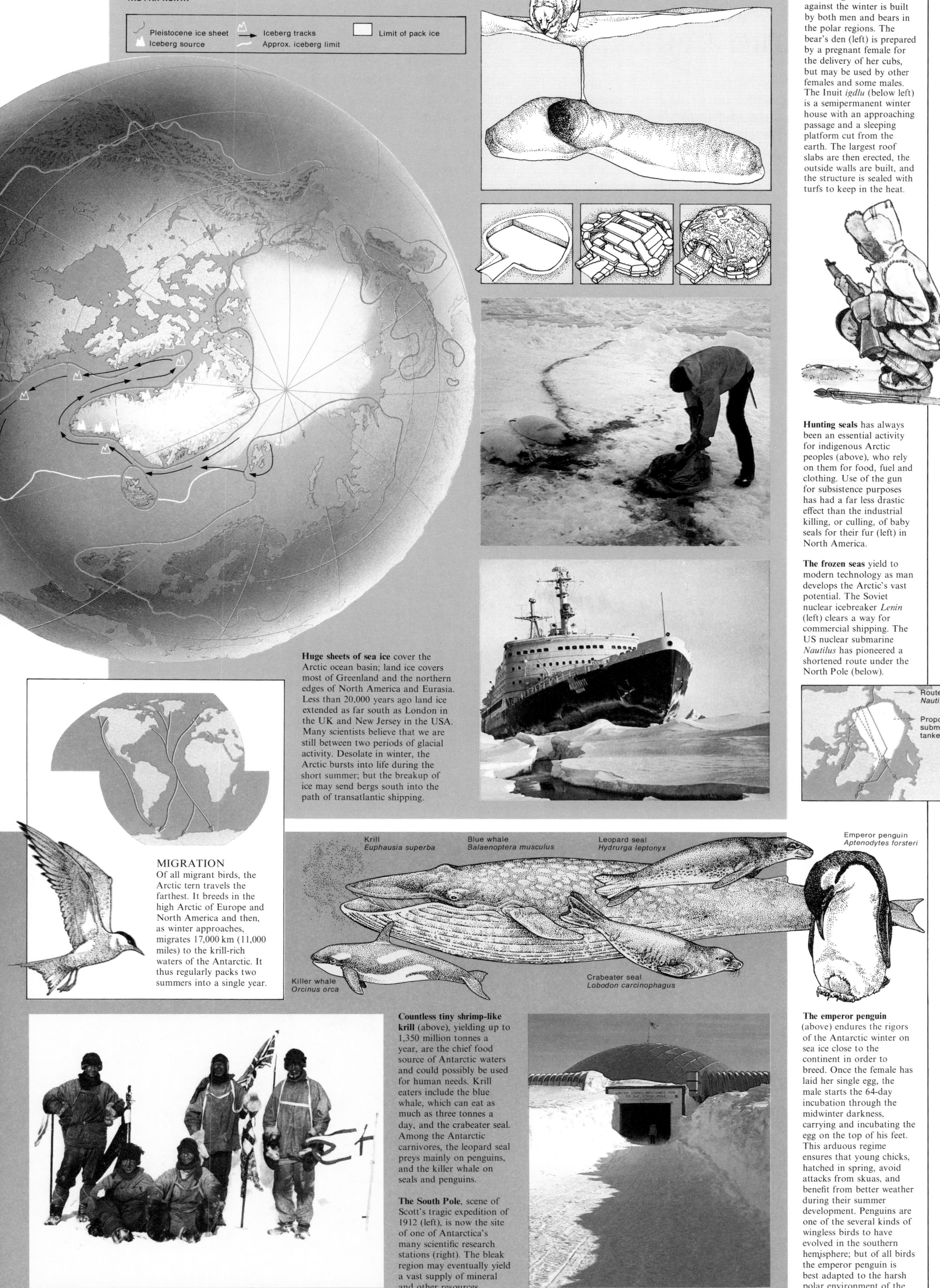

An underground shelter against the winter is built by both men and bears in the polar regions. The bear's den (left) is prepared by a pregnant female for the delivery of her cubs, but may be used by other females and some males. The Inuit *igdlu* (below left) is a semipermanent winter house with an approaching passage and a sleeping platform cut from the earth. The largest roof slabs are then erected, the outside walls are built, and the structure is sealed with turfs to keep in the heat.

Hunting seals has always been an essential activity for indigenous Arctic peoples (above), who rely on them for food, fuel and clothing. Use of the gun for subsistence purposes has had a far less drastic effect than the industrial killing, or culling, of baby seals for their fur (left) in North America.

The frozen seas yield to modern technology as man develops the Arctic's vast potential. The Soviet nuclear icebreaker *Lenin* (left) clears a way for commercial shipping. The US nuclear submarine *Nautilus* has pioneered a shortened route under the North Pole (below).

Huge sheets of sea ice cover the Arctic ocean basin; land ice covers most of Greenland and the northern edges of North America and Eurasia. Less than 20,000 years ago land ice extended as far south as London in the UK and New Jersey in the USA. Many scientists believe that we are still between two periods of glacial activity. Desolate in winter, the Arctic bursts into life during the short summer; but the breakup of ice may send bergs south into the path of transatlantic shipping.

MIGRATION

Of all migrant birds, the Arctic tern travels the farthest. It breeds in the high Arctic of Europe and North America and then, as winter approaches, migrates 17,000 km (11,000 miles) to the krill-rich waters of the Antarctic. It thus regularly packs two summers into a single year.

Countless tiny shrimp-like krill (above), yielding up to 1,350 million tonnes a year, are the chief food source of Antarctic waters and could possibly be used for human needs. Krill eaters include the blue whale, which can eat as much as three tonnes a day, and the crabeater seal. Among the Antarctic carnivores, the leopard seal preys mainly on penguins, and the killer whale on seals and penguins.

The South Pole, scene of Scott's tragic expedition of 1912 (left), is now the site of one of Antarctica's many scientific research stations (right). The bleak region may eventually yield a vast supply of mineral and other resources.

The emperor penguin (above) endures the rigors of the Antarctic winter on sea ice close to the continent in order to breed. Once the female has laid her single egg, the male starts the 64-day incubation through the midwinter darkness, carrying and incubating the egg on the top of his feet. This arduous regime ensures that young chicks, hatched in spring, avoid attacks from skuas, and benefit from better weather during their summer development. Penguins are one of the several kinds of wingless birds to have evolved in the southern hemisphere; but of all birds the emperor penguin is best adapted to the harsh polar environment of the Antarctic region.

Tundra and Taiga

Tundra is land that has been exposed for only about 8,000 years, since the retreat of the ice caps, and only relatively recently occupied by plants. In consequence, few plants and animals have yet had time to adapt to the virtually soilless and treeless environment. The less rigorous conditions of neighboring taiga forest allow a longer growing season and a somewhat wider range of species. The delicately balanced ecology of both areas is being increasingly threatened, however, by the activities of man.

"Tundra," from a Lapp word meaning "rolling, treeless plain," defines the narrow band of open, low ground that surrounds the Arctic Ocean. It lies north of the line beyond which the temperature of the warmest month usually fails to reach 10°C (50°F). North of this trees do not generally grow well, so the line forms a natural frontier between tundra and the broad band of coniferous forest that circles the northern hemisphere to its south between about 60°N and 48°N. This forest, forming the world's largest and most uninterrupted area of vegetation, is usually referred to by its Russian name of "taiga."

Cheerless landscapes

The tundra presents a desolate and restrictive environment for most of the year: in winter there are several months of semidarkness. While there is considerable variation in the climates of places at the same latitude, temperatures average only −5°C (23°F) and are well below freezing for many months of the year. Frost-free days are restricted to a few weeks in midsummer and even then, although days are warmer, the sun is never high in the sky. Nearly all tundra has been free from ice for only a few thousand years. As a result, it either has no soil at all or has developed only a thin covering of sandy, muddy or peaty soil, successfully colonized by only a few types of plants.

Trimmed by such grazing animals as hares, musk oxen and reindeer or caribou, and by strong winds carrying abrasive rock dust and ice particles, typical tundra vegetation forms a low, patchy mat a few centimeters deep. Much of it grows on permafrost — ground that thaws superficially in summer but remains perennially frozen beneath the surface. Here drainage is poor, shallow ponds are frequent and the scanty soils tend to be waterlogged and acidic. Nevertheless, a small number of grasses, sedges, mosses and marsh plants may grow well and the summer tundra in flower can be an impressive sight. Knee-high forests of dwarf birch, willow and alder grow in valleys sheltered from the strong and biting wind.

The taiga also is a dark and monotonous habitat. Again, while there is a good deal of variation in climatic conditions, on average the region has somewhat milder summers than the tundra with mean average temperatures of 2–6°C (34–42°F), less wind and a slightly longer growing season. The taiga is mostly older than the tundra, and its soils have had longer to mature. They support a small number of tree species, with coniferous spruce, pine, fir and larch predominating. Short-season broadleaves such as willows, alders, birches and poplars tend to occur on the better soils of river valleys and the edges of forest lakes.

Animals of the far north

The number of animal species supported throughout the year by tundra and taiga is also comparatively small, with interdependent populations that may fluctuate wildly from season to season. In winter both tundra and taiga are silent, although far from deserted. Mice, voles and lemmings remain active, living in tunnels under the snow, which keeps them well insulated from the wind and subzero temperatures. Above the snow Arctic hares forage; they tend to gather in snow-free areas where food can still be found. Arctic foxes are mainly tundra animals and the musk oxen, too, winter on high, exposed tundra where their dense, shaggy coats protect them from the worst

Tundra
Taiga

The circumpolar north that surrounds the permanently frozen ice cap is dominated by tundra—open plain that remains snowfree for only several months in the summer—and taiga, the vast coniferous forest stretching right round the northern hemisphere. The Siberian taiga, for example, is one-third larger than the entire United States.

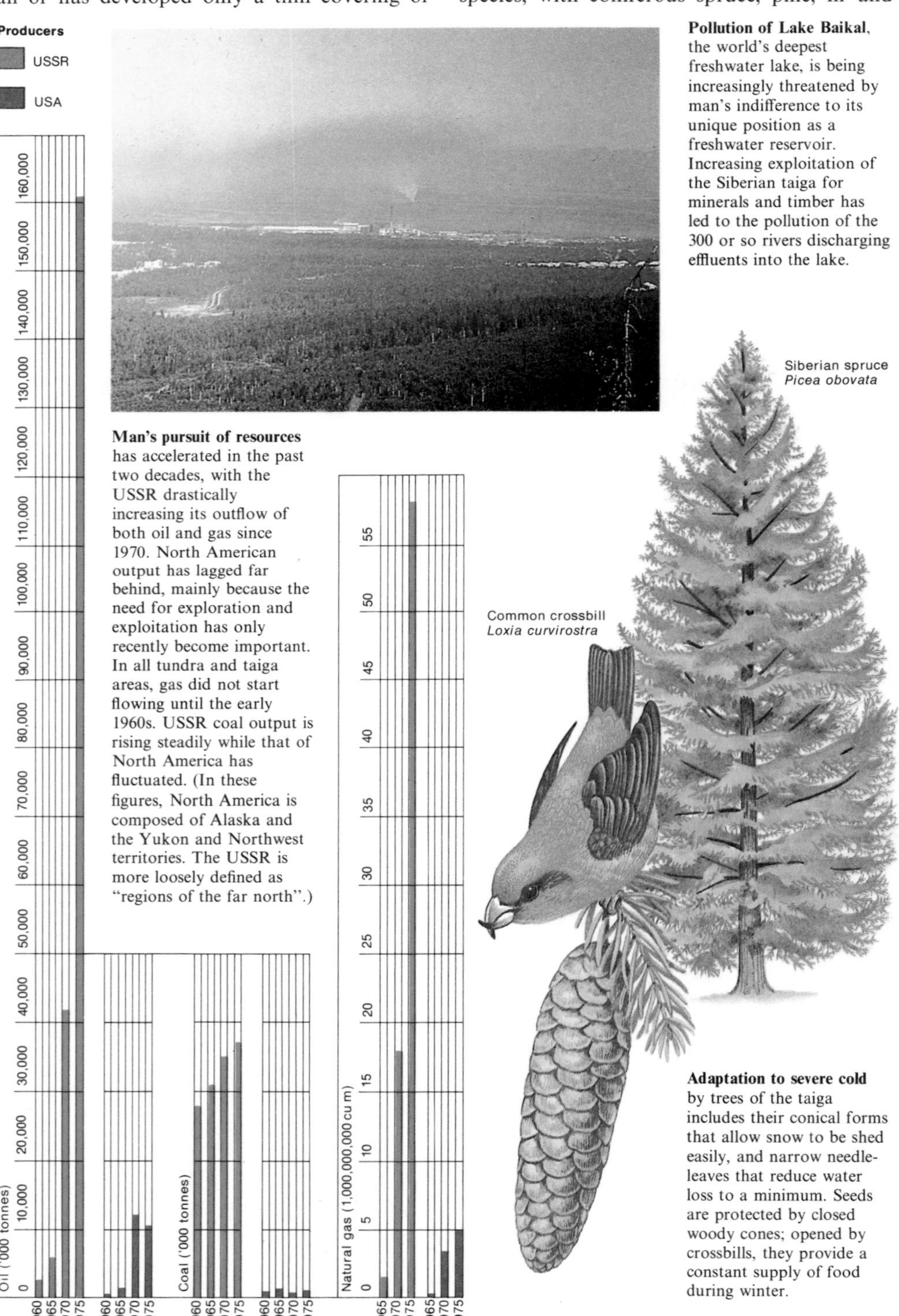

Pollution of Lake Baikal, the world's deepest freshwater lake, is being increasingly threatened by man's indifference to its unique position as a freshwater reservoir. Increasing exploitation of the Siberian taiga for minerals and timber has led to the pollution of the 300 or so rivers discharging effluents into the lake.

Man's pursuit of resources has accelerated in the past two decades, with the USSR drastically increasing its outflow of both oil and gas since 1970. North American output has lagged far behind, mainly because the need for exploration and exploitation has only recently become important. In all tundra and taiga areas, gas did not start flowing until the early 1960s. USSR coal output is rising steadily while that of North America has fluctuated. (In these figures, North America is composed of Alaska and the Yukon and Northwest territories. The USSR is more loosely defined as "regions of the far north".)

Adaptation to severe cold by trees of the taiga includes their conical forms that allow snow to be shed easily, and narrow needle-leaves that reduce water loss to a minimum. Seeds are protected by closed woody cones; opened by crossbills, they provide a constant supply of food during winter.

Movement in these regions takes many directions. The capercaillie spends all winter in the taiga, where it thrives on the abundant conifer needles, buds and shoots. Some move southward into deciduous woods during the summer months. The Arctic skua breeds on the tundra but moves to the warmer oceans in winter, while the tundra movements of the all-scavenging raven and the snowy owl are governed by those of their prey. The raven picks clean the carcasses left by other predators; the snowy owl feeds on small rodents such as mice and lemmings, as does the Arctic fox. Lemmings remain static and inconspicuous in normal years but some populations expand rapidly every third or fourth year, leading to mass local migration in every direction, possibly caused by an abundance of vegetation that encourages more frequent breeding.

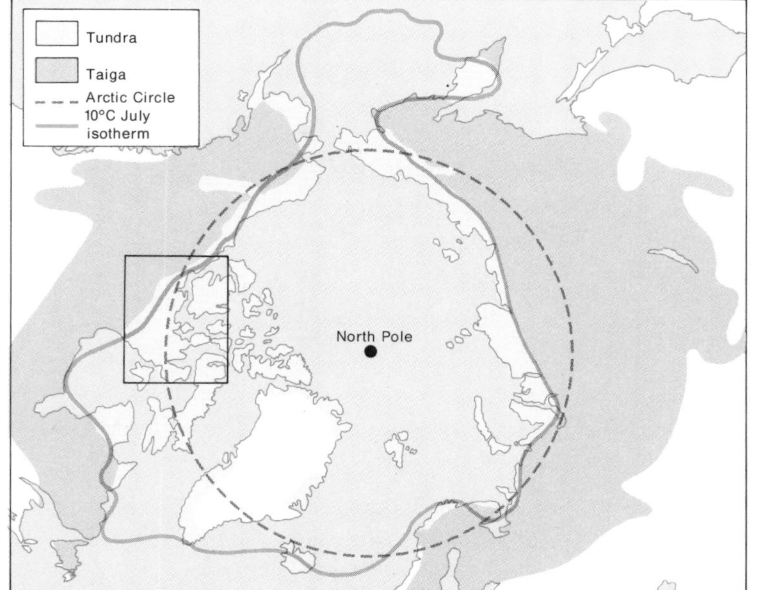

The rough boundary between the tundra and taiga—the tree line—approximates to the 10°C July isotherm, the climatic point north of which trees fail to grow successfully. Seasonal caribou migration in the Canadian barren grounds (boxed) is shown in the main diagram (below). Such migration is also undertaken by reindeer in northern Eurasia.

The summer tundra—seen here in Swedish Lapland—provides a wide cover of low plants including "reindeer mosses" and other lichens. Grazing reindeer return minerals to the soil. Shallow ponds form as the frozen ground above the permafrost thaws for a few months in summer. Mountains stay partly snow covered in the warmest weather and are a prominent physical feature of the tundra.

weather. Bears, badgers, beavers and squirrels are common taiga mammals. Elk and reindeer (in North America, moose and caribou) winter in the shelter of the taiga; wolves are mostly woodland animals in winter, following their prey to the open tundra in spring. Red foxes, coyotes, mink and wolverines also move to the tundra in summer.

Snow buntings, ptarmigans and snowy owls live on the tundra throughout the coldest months and are fully adapted to life there. Crossbills and capercaillies are among taiga residents, equipped to live on its abundant conifer buds, seeds and needles. Enormous populations of migrant birds, especially water birds and waders, fly north to both tundra and taiga with the spring thaw. Waxwings, bramblings, siskins and redpolls leave their temperate latitudes to feed on the lush and fast-growing vegetation and the profusion of insects that appear as soon as the snows begin to melt.

Man in the northlands

These circumpolar regions act as a strategic buffer between the USA and the USSR. Situated between the world's greatest centers of population, they are now crisscrossed with air routes. A total population of about nine million people currently inhabits the tundra and taiga. Numbers have been increased by the immigration of technicians and administrators during the last few decades; oil prospecting and mining, forest exploitation and other activities of these newcomers is altering the seminomadic lives of the million or so aboriginal peoples such as the Khanty (Ostyaks) and Nentsy (Samoyeds) of the USSR, the Samer (Lapps) of Scandinavia and the Soviet Union, and the Inuit (formerly Eskimos) of North America. New roads, exploitation of minerals and forests, and pipeline construction have disrupted the migration of their reindeer (caribou) and their land has been appropriated for hydroelectric schemes.

In the taiga, the Soviets are constructing railroads and towns and extracting huge amounts of timber; they have prospected widely and successfully for gold, nickel, iron, tin, mica, diamonds and tungsten, and have discovered vast reserves of oil and natural gas in western Siberia. Alaskan oil, discovered in 1968, now flows across the state at 54–62°C (130–145°F), and to protect the permafrost from this heat the pipeline has had to be elevated for half its 1,300 km (800 mile) length. The pipe's route to the ice-free port of Valdez has interfered with the migration of caribou; hunting and other pressures have led to a drop in their population from three million to some 200,000 in about 30 years. Only official protection has saved the musk ox from a similar fate. These bleak areas are so vast and inhospitable that living space there will never be threatened. However, if only on a local scale, their ecologies are under increasing pressure from man.

Many Norwegian Lapps (or Samer) derive their income from reindeer, which they domesticated many centuries ago to provide meat, milk and skins. Now they follow them through the seasons along well-worn and familiar routes. Such nomadic life styles are becoming rarer as Samer settle down.

MOVEMENT THROUGH THE SEASONS

Life on tundra and taiga is dominated by the mark of the seasons. In this diagrammatic representation of the north–south migration of the American caribou, each block represents the same area of terrain through the 12 months of the year. From February to April, the caribou move north in a steady file from the forest, emerging to eat the newly exposed lichen and moving to grounds where calving takes place in late May and early June. In the summer months they disperse freely before returning south in smaller groups on a broader front in late July and August. Rutting and mating take place in October/early November before the caribou regain the shelter of the taiga.

Calving
Calving
July
August
September
October
Rutting and mating
66½°N Arctic Circle
62°N Approximate tree line
November
December

Musk ox *Ovibos moschatus*

Brent goose *Branta bernicla*

Rock ptarmigan *Lagopus mutus*

Arctic hare *Lepus arcticus*

Wolf *Canis lupus*

Wolverine *Gulo gulo*

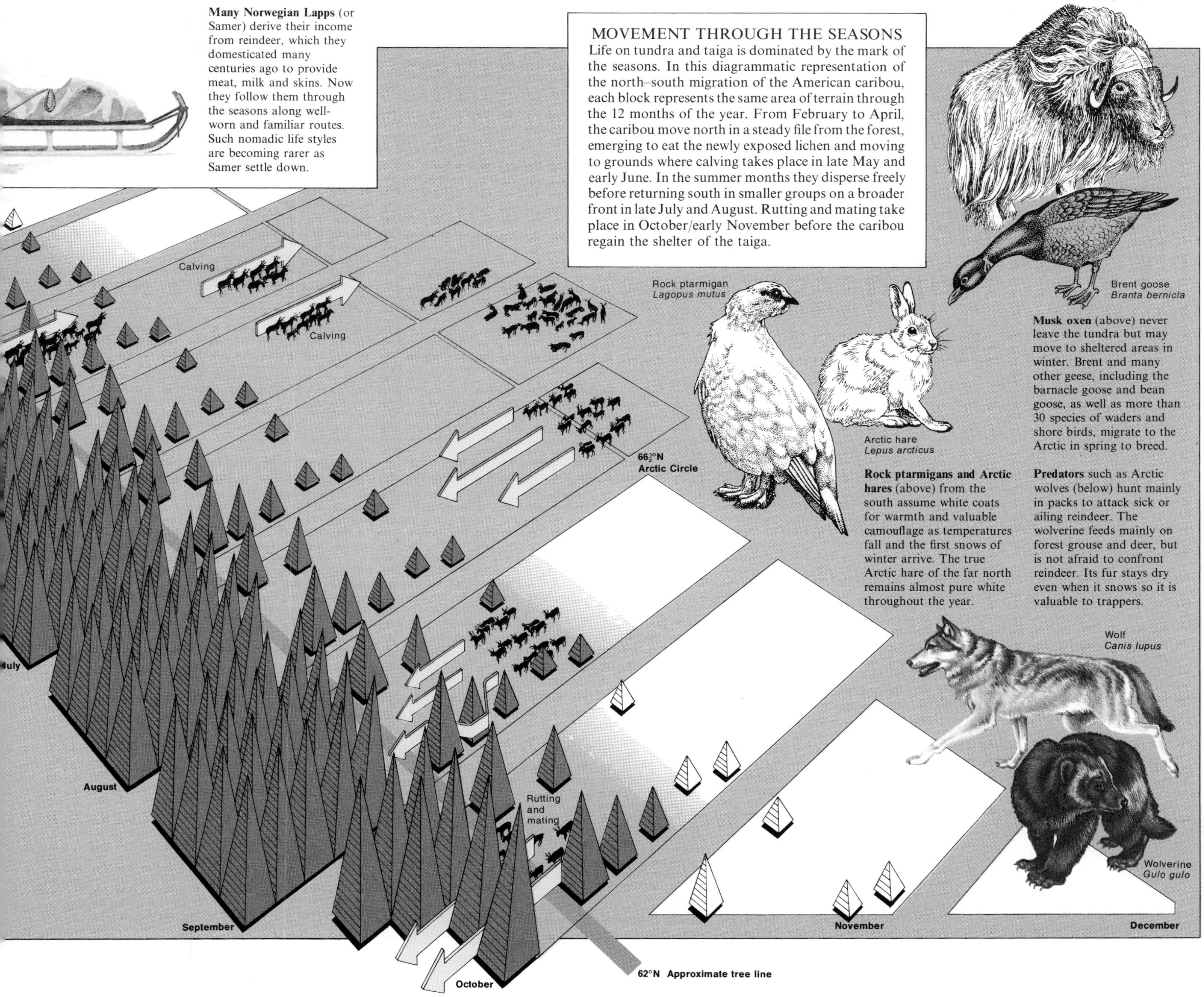

Musk oxen (above) never leave the tundra but may move to sheltered areas in winter. Brent and many other geese, including the barnacle goose and bean goose, as well as more than 30 species of waders and shore birds, migrate to the Arctic in spring to breed.

Rock ptarmigans and Arctic hares (above) from the south assume white coats for warmth and valuable camouflage as temperatures fall and the first snows of winter arrive. The true Arctic hare of the far north remains almost pure white throughout the year.

Predators such as Arctic wolves (below) hunt mainly in packs to attack sick or ailing reindeer. The wolverine feeds mainly on forest grouse and deer, but is not afraid to confront reindeer. Its fur stays dry even when it snows so it is valuable to trappers.

Temperate Forests

At one time, dense, primeval forests blanketed large areas of North America, Europe and eastern Asia. Almost all of the trees that flourished in these temperate regions were deciduous – they shed their leaves in autumn, stood bare branched through winter and produced new foliage every spring. Little of this forest now exists. The few remaining pockets, however, still provide habitats for a large range of shade-loving plants: lichens and fungi, tree-hugging mosses, scrambling creepers and shrubs. And this vegetation in turn provides sanctuary for a surprisingly wide variety of forest creatures.

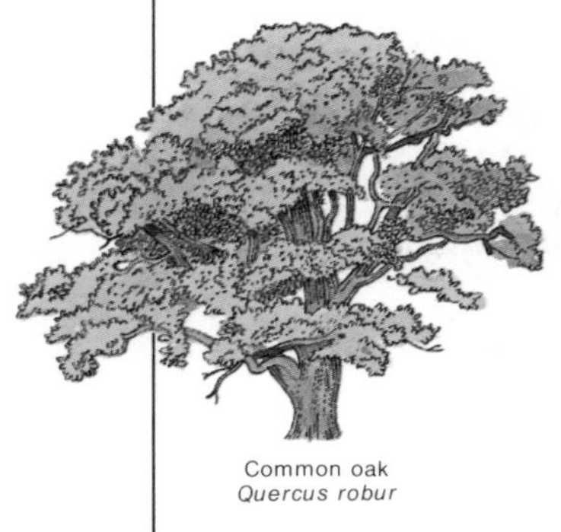

Common oak
Quercus robur

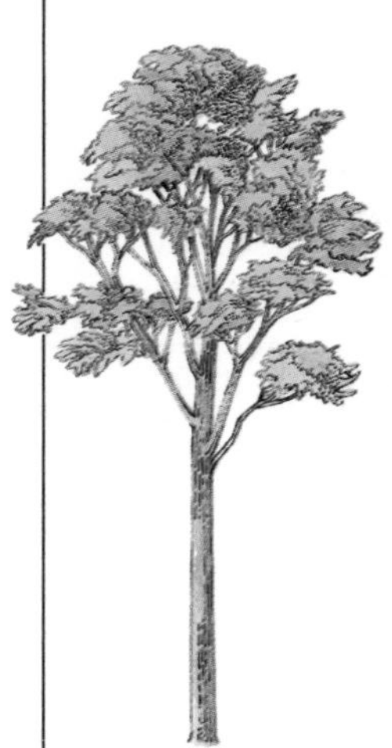

Silver beech
Nothofagus menziesii

Deciduous trees such as the oak (top) make up the temperate forests in cooler temperate regions. In milder, wetter climates, where the seasons are less distinct, evergreens such as southern beech (above) are typical temperate species.

The greater part of the temperate forest zone lies in the northern hemisphere, where winter soil temperatures reduce the ability of plants to absorb water. Hence the trees tend to shed their leaves, which use up moisture through evaporation. In the southern hemisphere, however, the temperate latitudes encourage a type of rainforest in such areas as southern Chile, Tasmania, New Zealand and parts of southeastern Australia. Here the climate is maritime, often with high rainfall and frequent fogs, and evergreen rather than deciduous types of trees grow. Temperate rainforests also occur in the northern hemisphere, in China and in northwestern and northeastern North America.

Deciduous forest consists of a mixture of trees, sometimes with one variety predominant. In central Europe, beech is the leading—and sometimes the only—tree species, whereas oaks mixed with other species made up the forest farther west and east. In North America, beech and maple were once extensive.

The climate in temperate forest zones varies sharply according to seasons—summers tend to be warm, winters moderately cold, and rainfall fairly regular. In fact, the seasonal rhythm is a central feature of temperate forests, and it affects the entire ecosystem—the whole community of plants and animals found there. Soils are generally of the fertile "brown earth" type: the leaf litter of deciduous forests in particular breaks down easily, and is quickly worked into the soil by burrowing animals such as earthworms. In wetter or rockier regions, the soil is more "podsolic"—bleached, sandy and less fertile than the true brown earths.

After the ice

Two million years ago, a series of ice sheets began to extend into the temperate latitudes. In Europe, species moving south before the advancing cold were cut off from the warmer climates by the east–west run of mountains. As a result, many varieties of plants and animals were killed off. Species were reduced still further in islands such as Britain, where the newly formed barriers of the English Channel, Irish Sea and North Sea made recolonization even more difficult after the ice had retreated.

Eastern Asia was one of the few areas in the world that escaped the extreme climatic changes of the ice ages and therefore its temperate forests, unlike those of Europe, still contain an enormous variety of tree species. North America also fared better than Europe, for although glaciers at one time extended deep into the continent, the north–south direction of the mountain ranges allowed relatively easy migration of trees southwards as the climate worsened. Hence most species survived and were able to reoccupy their former territories when the ice retreated. As a result, some 40 species of deciduous trees occur in the North American forests, and contribute to the spectacular display of color during the autumn, notably in the eastern USA. But a combination of climatic change and, more recently and importantly, of intense human activity, has meant that the remnants of temperate forest seen today differ greatly from the original forest in both composition and form. Only in remote regions such as the southern Appalachian Mountains do substantial areas of the original forest survive. Elsewhere, regrowth has occurred, but much of this is essentially scrub woodland.

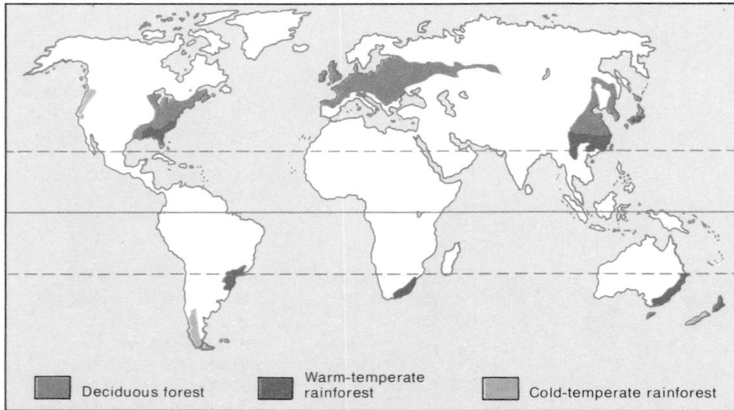

Natural distribution: in the northern hemisphere's temperate zone deciduous forests occur in the cooler areas—in eastern USA, northeastern China, Korea, the northern parts of Japan's Honshu island and western Europe. These forests only give way to evergreens in the warmer and wetter parts of the zone. In the southern hemisphere, the climate is generally rather milder throughout the temperate zone and so there are virtually no deciduous forests. Evergreen forests, however, can be found in southeastern South Africa, Chile, New Zealand, Australia and Tasmania.

The forest structure

Mature temperate deciduous forest is made up of distinct horizontal layers, particularly where the dominant tree is the oak, which allows enough light for a rich shrub layer to grow beneath it. The largest trees, such as oak, maple or ash, may be 25–50 m (80–160 ft) tall, and beneath them grows a prominent layer of smaller trees such as hazel, hornbeam or yew. Lower down again, a varied ground cover of perennial herbs, ferns, lichens and mosses flourishes in the comparative dampness of the forest floor. Because the trees are bare of leaves in winter, many of the plants growing on the forest floor take advantage of the warmth and light of spring to flower early in the year before the main trees come into full leaf and prevent the sun from reaching them. Various woody climbers, such as ivy and honeysuckle, are also present, growing over the trees and shrubs.

Much of the food supply in temperate forests is locked up in the trees themselves, but the annual fall of leaves in the deciduous forests produces a soil rich in nourishment. This supports a vast quantity of life, ranging in size from earthworms and insects to microscopic bacteria of the soil. The death of individual trees and branches also releases the food supply back to the earth. In shady, damp locations, insects, fungi, bacteria and other decomposing agents break down the leaves and other plant and animal debris more quickly, returning them to the soil as food for new plants.

Creatures of the forest

Temperate forests once contained many varieties of animal life, including several species of large animals. Herbivores such as wild oxen, wood bison, elk and moose ate grass and leaves; scavengers such as wild pigs rooted in the forest floor; predators such as wolves preyed on the other animals. Most of these have now been hunted to extinction by man or are extremely rare. Smaller animals still survive in comparatively large numbers, and include squirrels, chipmunks and raccoons, hedgehogs, wood mice, badgers and foxes.

The bird life of temperate forests is very diverse. Some species are insect eaters, exploring the bark and crevices for insects and grubs. Others, such as the wood pigeon, concentrate on seeds. Yet others, like the tawny owl, are predators. Complex interactions between predators and prey have developed at all levels of the forest, from the high canopy to the rotting ground litter, with each group evolving more efficient techniques of capture or escape in a kind of evolutionary race for survival.

The invertebrate insect life is also extremely varied and numerous, and forms a key component of the ecosystem. Oaks are particularly rich in insect life, and more than 100 species of moths feed on their leaves.

The plant and animal life of the temperate forest is remarkably rich and plentiful. And yet it is only a fraction of what once existed. Ever since man has occupied these regions he has found them so suited to his needs that he has long since cleared most of the original tree cover, replaced it with "civilization" and, in the process, destroyed innumerable species of forest wildlife.

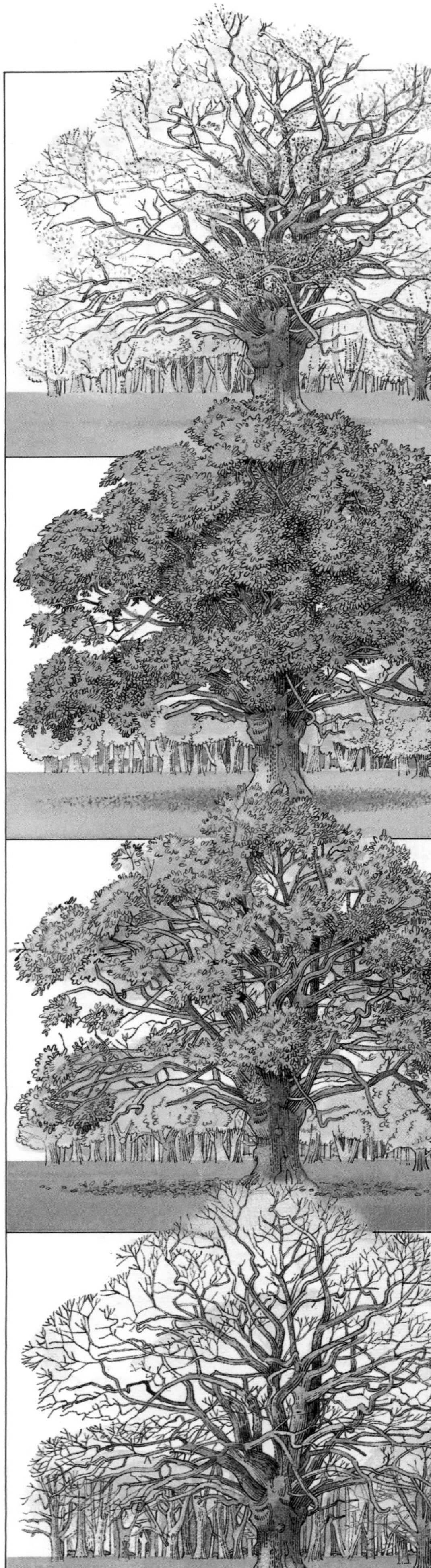

THE SEASONAL CYCLE

It is the cycle of the four seasons that gives the temperate deciduous forest its distinctive character. All animals and plants have adapted their ways of life to cope with the seasonal changes in heat, light, moisture and food. The yearly shedding and regrowth of the forest's leaves is one of the most striking and important of adaptations to the seasonal cycle and one that affects all other life in the forest. In summer the leafy canopy of the trees blocks out the sunlight from the forest floor and creates unsuitable conditions for many other plants to flourish. When the leaves fall they form a layer over the soil and provide winter protection for the plant roots and hibernating animals beneath the ground. Finally, once the dead leaves have been broken down, they give fertility to the soil and provide food for future generations of plants.

SPRING
Between February and April, the low spring sun climbs steadily higher in the sky and, streaming through the still leafless branches of the trees, falls more directly on the forest floor, warming the soil and melting the last frosts. As soon as the days become warmer the sluggish sap in the trees begins to flow more quickly, carrying nutrients to the branches, where leaf buds start to form.

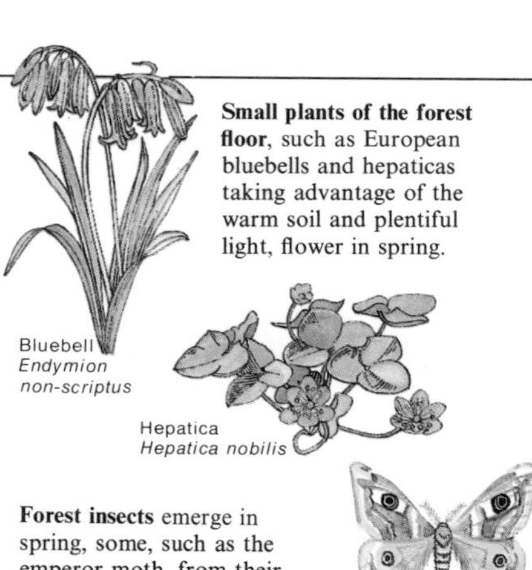

Bluebell *Endymion non-scriptus*

Small plants of the forest floor, such as European bluebells and hepaticas taking advantage of the warm soil and plentiful light, flower in spring.

Hepatica *Hepatica nobilis*

Forest insects emerge in spring, some, such as the emperor moth, from their winter cocoons, some from hibernation and some newly hatched from eggs.

Small emperor moth *Saturnia pavonia*

European blackbird *Turdus merula*

Birds building nests in early spring make use of the forest's winter litter—broken twigs, dead leaves and dried grasses all serve as construction materials.

White-tailed deer *Odocoileus virginianus*

Woodchuck *Marmota monax*

Western European hedgehog *Erinaceus europaeus*

New plant growth and the increase in insects provide food for such animals as the North American woodchuck and the European hedgehog that wake thin and hungry from months of hibernation. Deer and other non-hibernating animals are also weak and thin—indeed many may have died during the harsh weather. The spring birth of young, however, soon restores their numbers.

SUMMER
By early summer the leaves of the trees are fully grown. They form a dense canopy, blocking out the sun and cooling the soil of the forest floor. Most of the small ground plants have long since finished flowering, but their leaves remain green and they continue actively storing food in their roots ready for their rapid spring growth.

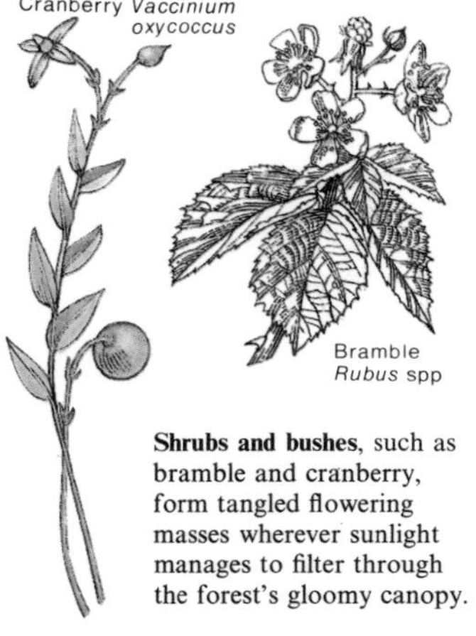

Cranberry *Vaccinium oxycoccus*

Bramble *Rubus spp*

Shrubs and bushes, such as bramble and cranberry, form tangled flowering masses wherever sunlight manages to filter through the forest's gloomy canopy.

Hordes of insects inhabit the forest in summer, living off the vast supply of food plants. The European stag beetle feeds on the sap of chestnut and oak trees.

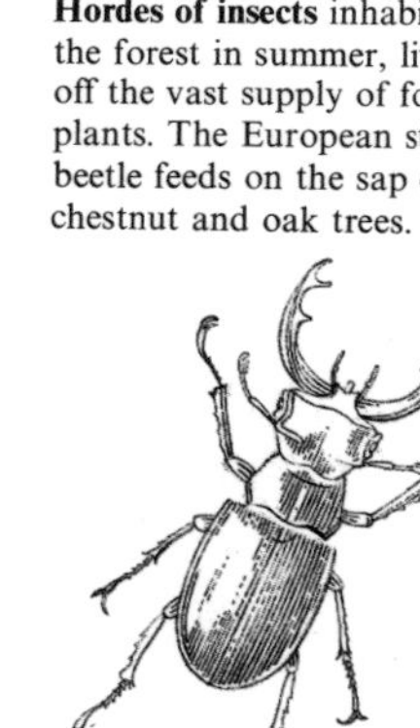

Stag beetle *Lucanus cervus*

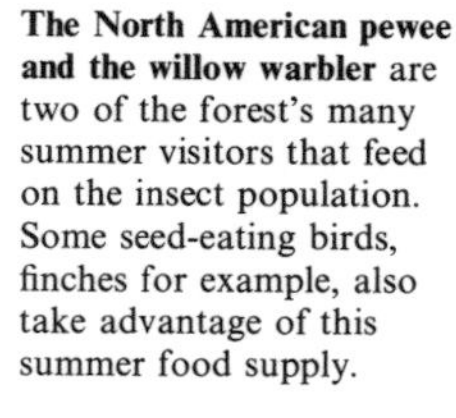

Willow warbler *Phylloscopus trochilus*

The North American pewee and the willow warbler are two of the forest's many summer visitors that feed on the insect population. Some seed-eating birds, finches for example, also take advantage of this summer food supply.

Eastern wood pewee *Contopus virens*

Hazel mouse *Muscardinus avellanarius*

The hazel mouse protects its young by raising them in a summer nest, which it builds in a tree: almost every creature in the forest is viewed as a source of food by some other animal and the young litters are particularly at risk.

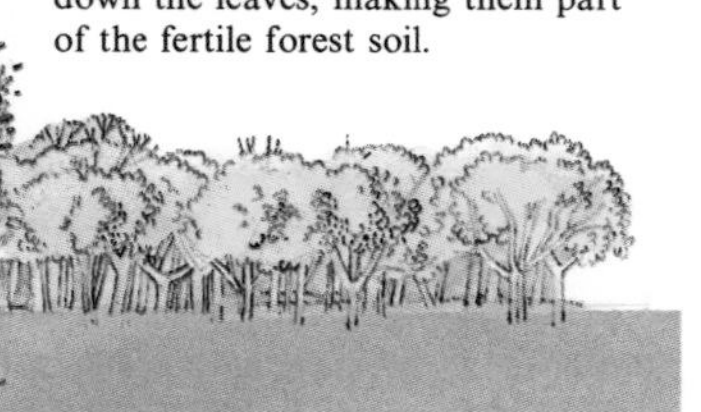

AUTUMN
As the autumn days grow shorter and cooler the forest foliage begins to turn color; the trees are responding to the drop in temperature and are cutting off the food supply to their leaves, which lose their green color and fall to the ground, forming a thick carpet on the forest's floor. Rain, frost, insects, earthworms and fungi then break down the leaves, making them part of the fertile forest soil.

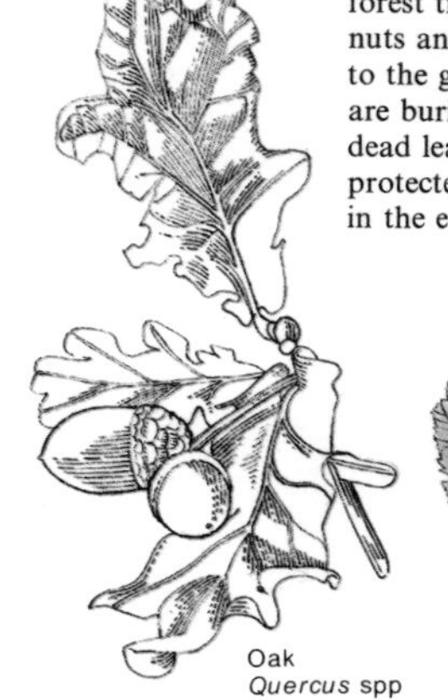

Oak *Quercus spp*

Ripe fruits and seeds of the forest trees—acorns, beech nuts and hazel nuts—drop to the ground, where a few are buried in the layers of dead leaves and remain protected until they sprout in the early spring.

Common hazel *Corylus avellana*

Acorn woodpecker *Melanerpes formicivorus*

Preparing for winter, the acorn woodpecker stores seeds in holes that it drills in tree trunks. Chipmunks hide supplies of nuts in their winter nests.

Eastern chipmunk *Tamias striatus*

American black bear *Ursus americanus*

The black bear of North America, like other winter hibernators, consumes vast quantities of food during autumn to build up its winter stores of food in the form of body fat.

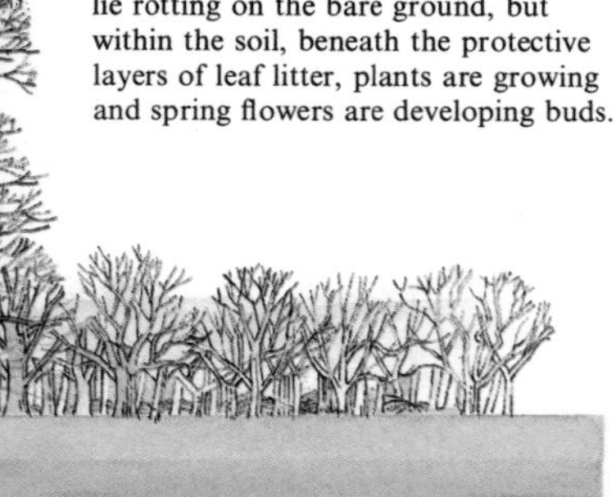

WINTER
By winter, only evergreen shrubs and a few small hardy plants remain green. Many of the plants of the forest floor lose their green leaves during the first deep frost. The leaves of the trees still lie rotting on the bare ground, but within the soil, beneath the protective layers of leaf litter, plants are growing and spring flowers are developing buds.

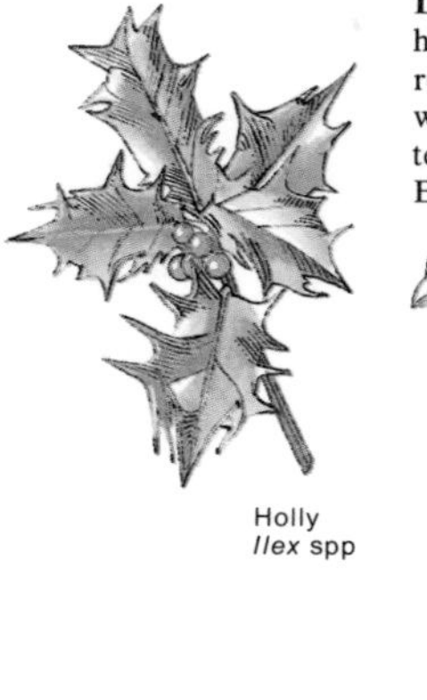

Holly *Ilex spp*

Late-fruiting plants, such as holly, mistletoe and dog rose, provide food for winter residents of the temperate forest such as the European hawfinch.

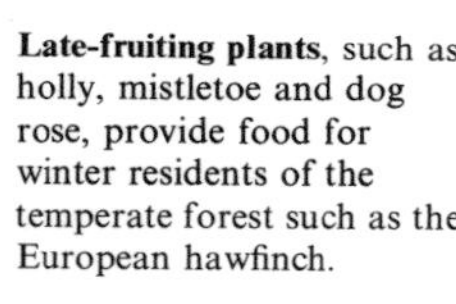

Hawfinch *Coccothraustes coccothraustes*

European woodcock *Scolopax rusticola*

North American screech owl *Otus asio*

Owls and foxes remain fairly active in winter, regularly leaving their nests or lairs to catch small animals or birds that are also in search of food.

Woodcocks are insect-eaters. They can survive winter by prizing insects from the soil with their long beaks, providing that the ground is not too deeply frozen.

European badger *Meles meles*

Red fox *Vulpes vulpes*

European badgers, like racoons, opossums, bears and skunks, are "shallow" hibernators. On mild winter days they wake and go to search for food.

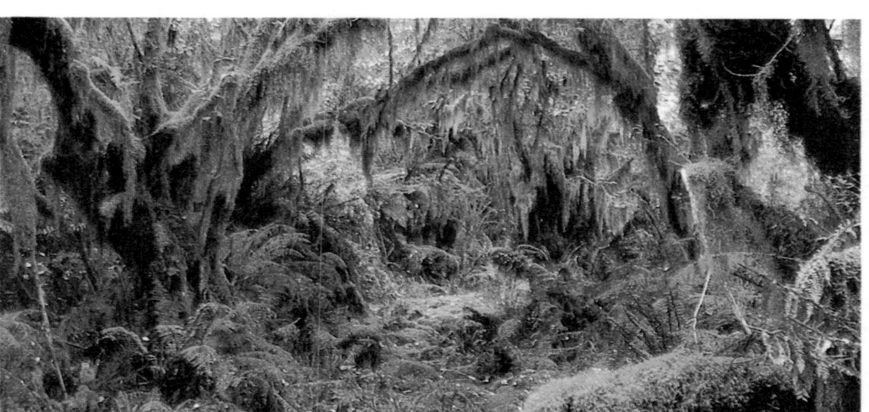

THE EVERGREEN TEMPERATE RAINFORESTS

There are two main kinds of temperate rainforest, the warm temperate, such as can still be found on North Island, New Zealand (left), and the cold temperate, such as that of the Chilean coast. Both of these kinds of forest have one major feature in common: they have enough water for even the most moisture-greedy plants, such as mosses and ferns, to grow throughout the year. The animal life of the forest is also affected by the abundance of rain, so that snails, slugs, frogs and other water-loving creatures flourish. Most temperate rainforest is of the warm-temperate kind, normally found on the edges of subtropical regions, and the vegetation, with palms, lianas, bamboos, as well as ferns and mosses, is similar to, although less rich than, the tropical rainforest's vegetation. The cold-temperate rainforests grow in cooler regions but their coastal position means that the climate is milder and wetter than inland (where deciduous trees dominate). Their vegetation is less lush and less varied than the warm-temperate forests, but mosses and ferns grow in abundance. Broad-leaved evergreens, such as New Zealand's southern beech, are the most common trees of these forests, although on the northwestern coast of North America Douglas firs and other conifers outnumber the broad-leaved evergreen species.

Man and the Temperate Forests

Temperate forests have suffered enormously at the hands of man. For the great civilizations of China, Europe and, later, North America the forests not only yielded cropland for expanding populations but also contributed materials and fuel for early technologies. More recently the demands of industry have reduced the forests still further. But today, scientists believe that this depleted resource could again play an important role in providing energy, food and materials for future generations.

PREHISTORIC FORESTS
Hunter gatherers made clearings in the forest when they cut brushwood for building shelters and for fuel (1): human impact on the temperate forest was small. But 7,000 years ago in Europe, 6,000 years ago in eastern Asia and 1,000 years ago in eastern North America, the first farming communities of the temperate forest (2) began to clear larger pockets of forest to provide land for crops and timber for houses and tools.

PERMANENT SETTLEMENT
The Bronze Age and, later, the Iron Age laid the foundations of Chinese and Western civilizations. The forest shrank as permanent settlements grew (3) and, with the use of metals and improved technology, agricultural land was extended (4). But the forest was recognized as an important resource and areas were protected. Management techniques were introduced that, especially in medieval Europe, changed dense forest to coppice woods (5).

EARLY INDUSTRIAL TIMES
Sources of cropland and timber had been discovered in the New World, but in the Far East and Europe forests were drastically reduced. Virtually no Chinese forest remained, and in Europe nations began importing timber to serve growing industrial needs (6). To help solve shortages, plantations were established on country estates (7), which were often landscaped into parkland and planted with introduced species of trees (8).

The aurochs, or wild ox, was one of the many forest animals that provided food for early hunter gatherers. Once man began to farm the land, he domesticated some of these animals—the wild boar, the aurochs and the wild turkey.

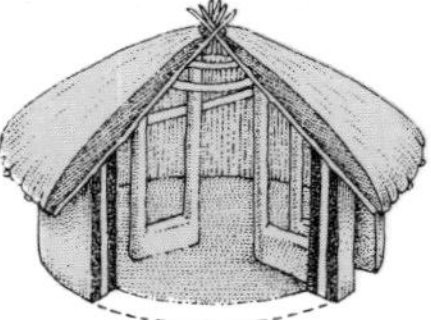

The dwellings of the late Neolithic Chinese were relatively sophisticated, reflecting an increasingly settled way of life that was soon to alter the landscape as forests were felled to provide building materials and land to plant crops.

The fortified villages and the farms of the Eastern Woodland Indians were set in semipermanent clearings cut in the North American forest. Before European settlement, however, human populations were small and deforestation was negligible.

Grain harvesting is depicted in a Chinese tomb image. By the 1st century AD, China contained nearly 60 million people, and agriculture, along with stock raising and metal mining, was drastically depleting the tree cover.

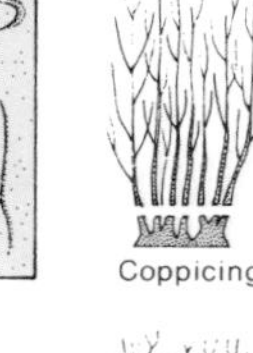

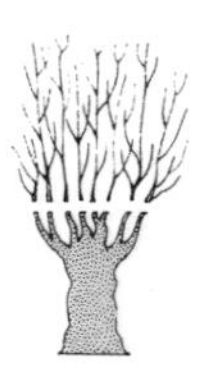

Coppicing and pollarding allowed continual cropping of forests. Branches were cut from trees, the bases of which were left to regrow shoots. This technique reduced the density of tree cover, encouraging a richer growth of ground plants.

Production of charcoal (below), which was a basic raw material for smelting in early industrial times, was responsible for much deforestation of the land.

Human interference with the forests goes back deep into prehistory. There is evidence that fire was used to stampede hunted animals in southern Europe as long as 400,000 years ago. Human populations, while they remained small, had only a slight effect on the vast stretches of primeval forest. Even so, hunting practices and the use of fire to clear land reduced some of the forests of Europe and Asia even before the invention of agriculture. In the New World, too, Eastern Woodland Indians had already affected the North American forests, and early Maori hunters had burned much of the tree cover of New Zealand by the time Europeans arrived.

Nevertheless it was the development of agriculture in Neolithic (New Stone Age) times that had the first really destructive effect on the temperate forests. Clearings were made for crops and the felled trees provided fuel and building material for the new communities. Large forest animals suffered as well, some (such as deer) being hunted for food and others (such as wolves) because they threatened grazing animals. But it was the population increase resulting from the new, settled way of life that caused the extension of man-made cropland deep into former forests.

With man's development of metals, more forests were destroyed: wood and charcoal were used for smelting and the new iron tools made tree clearance easier and more thorough. Firing of forests was also a familiar military ploy, used by such warriors as the Romans.

Medieval woodlands

By medieval times, large tracts of forest had been cleared in Europe and in the Far East, although in the former area there remained extensive royal hunting forest reserves. Local woodlands were carefully managed to serve the needs of the community; the techniques used included pollarding and coppicing.

Pollarding involved the cropping of main branches at a certain height above ground. In coppicing, the "coppice with standards" method was used to harvest the smaller species, such as hazel and hornbeam, whereas the standards (such as oaks) were cut on a longer rotation of 100 years or so. Alternatively, the oak itself could be part of the coppice crop, its stems being cut near ground level so that shoots arose from the stump, to be cut 10 to 20 years later. For local communities, industries and cities, forests provided a variety of materials for building, tanning and fencing, as well as dyestuffs, charcoal and domestic fuel.

The growth of the iron and shipbuilding industries in the sixteenth century devastated so much woodland and forest that in many regions good timber became scarce and had to be imported from considerable distances. The pressure on woodland continued until the production of coke and cheap coal brought some relaxation, but by the early twentieth century the coppice system had broken down and management of Europe's woodlands had largely been abandoned. In Europe the poor state of the deciduous forests was further worsened by two world wars. Many countries have since set up organizations with the specific task of building reserves of timber. Economic pressures, however, have led to the planting mainly of quick-growing conifers, rather than typical trees of the temperate deciduous forest.

New World forests

The migrants who settled in the New World were the descendants of the people who had largely destroyed the forests of Europe. Confronted by the temperate deciduous forests of eastern North America, they virtually continued where they had left off. Tracts were cleared to create arable and range land and to provide the massive amounts of timber needed for the colonization, industrialization and urbanization of North America. With the opening of the prairie lands for agriculture, however,

Disturbance to the natural vegetation has occurred throughout the temperate forest zone. Exploitation of this biome's greatest resource, its agricultural potential, has been one of the major causes of deforestation. The only forests that have escaped major disturbance are in remote areas, too rocky or too steep for cultivation. Today, intensive farming is still a major economic activity of the temperate forest regions. But farmland is not the only important resource to have disturbed the forests. Mining for key minerals such as copper, iron and coal, all of which made possible the development of Western and Chinese civilization, has also contributed to destruction of the forest cover. For centuries the forests provided man with food, fuel and materials, but, ironically, it has been the removal of the forest that has enabled man to exploit the most important of these regions' resources.

THE CHANGING LANDSCAPE

Mankind has been occupying the temperate forest regions for many thousands of years, at first with little effect on the natural forest ecology. But during the last 2,000 years human activity has destroyed the original tree cover at an accelerating pace. As populations increased and economies developed—at different rates in the three major regions—forests disappeared to be replaced by farms, cities, industries and communications networks. Today, scarcely any of the original forest cover remains.

THE 19TH CENTURY
The Industrial Revolution developed in Europe and the New World, large towns and cities sprang up (9), pushing back the woodlands and forests still farther. This process was aided by the spreading network of railroads (10). Coke, iron and other minerals were replacing timber products as raw materials for growing industries (11), but demands were still made on the forests to provide, for example, railway sleepers and mine pit props.

FORESTS TODAY
The 20th century has seen an increasing trend towards urbanization in areas that were once temperate forest. Housing complexes (12) and new factory sites (13) cover large areas, while roadbuilding (14), industrial agriculture (15) and open-cast mining (16) destroy remaining woodland. Leisure areas (17) and nature reserves protect some woods, but plantations of exotic conifers (18) do not always provide suitable wildlife habitats.

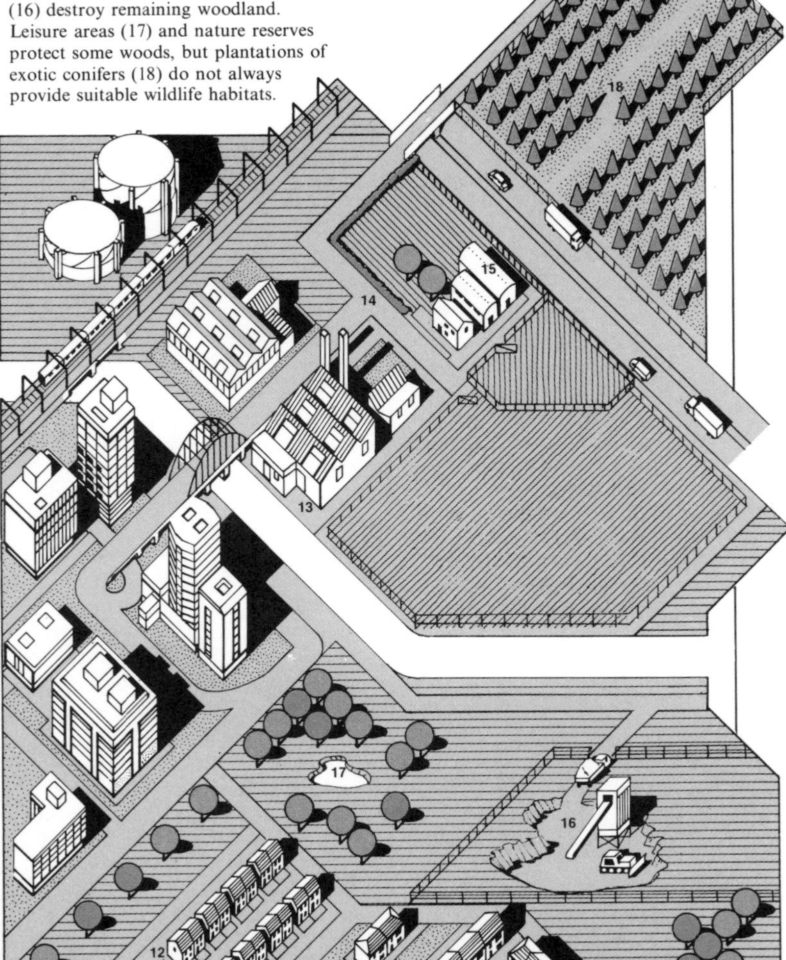

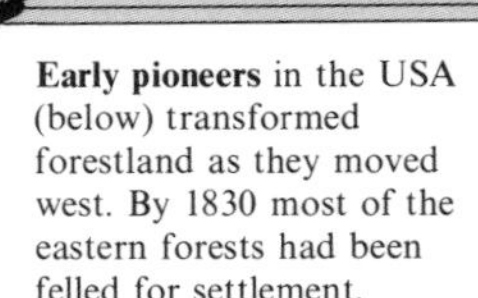

Early pioneers in the USA (below) transformed forestland as they moved west. By 1830 most of the eastern forests had been felled for settlement.

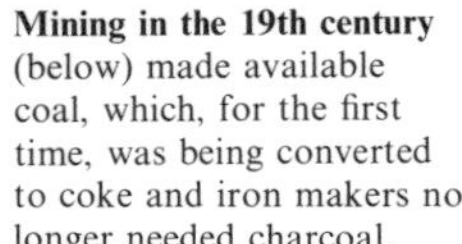

Mining in the 19th century (below) made available coal, which, for the first time, was being converted to coke and iron makers no longer needed charcoal.

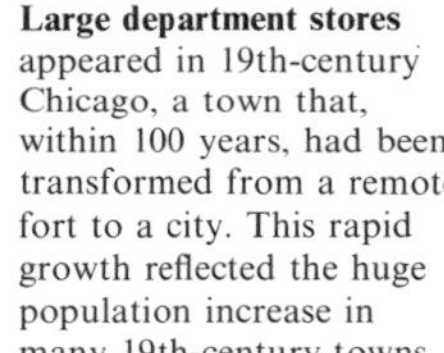

Large department stores appeared in 19th-century Chicago, a town that, within 100 years, had been transformed from a remote fort to a city. This rapid growth reflected the huge population increase in many 19th-century towns.

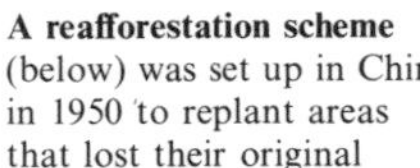

A reafforestation scheme (below) was set up in China in 1950 to replant areas that lost their original forest cover many centuries ago. Similar projects are under way in many other temperate forest regions.

The European wood bison has escaped extinction because one herd of the animals has lived, for centuries, in a royal hunting reserve. Today, wildlife parks throughout temperate regions protect endangered forest species.

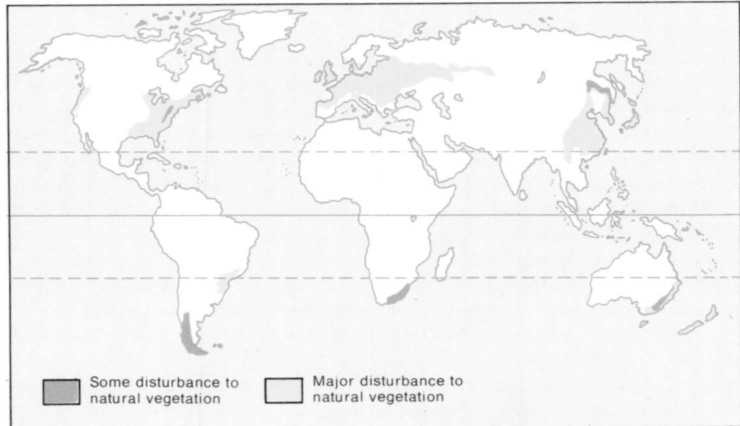

the pressures shifted, some of the east coast deciduous forest grew up again, and it is possible that parts of the eastern USA may have nearly as much forest cover now as when the settlers first arrived. Nevertheless, other areas of forestland have been destroyed in recent decades by strip mining and the creation of a vast road and rail network. In the southern hemisphere, especially in the last 200 years, the temperate rainforests of Australia and New Zealand have been subjected to much the same pattern of events, although on a smaller and somewhat less devastating scale.

Conservation

Today the general need to preserve and extend the woodlands is clearly recognized, but great uncertainty exists about their future. The demand for hardwoods for veneers, quality papermaking and furniture still exceeds supply. Oak is still the preferred material for some types of boat building and, especially in Europe, for joinery work. But one of the major difficulties with forestry as a land use is forecasting future trends within the industry, largely as a result of the long-term nature of the crop—hardwood trees planted today will not yield their timber until well into the next century. Government tax policies can be all important in deciding whether the majority of woodlands are, or will continue to be, sound economic investments.

Temperate forests and woodlands still exist in sizeable quantities in central Europe and the USA, but many of today's plots, particularly in western Europe, are far too small for efficient conservation of plant and animal life, and are isolated from other woods. As a result, successful breeding and exchange of genetic material is very difficult, especially when modern agriculture is rapidly destroying the linking corridors of hedgerows. The use of woodlands for recreation is also presenting considerable problems. Controlling agencies have been formed to cope with leisure demands, and a start has been made in the multiple use of forests for recreation, conservation and timber felling, but progress still needs to be made in harmonizing these potentially conflicting interests. Meanwhile, natural expanses of woodland and forest are still being lost to agricultural and urban expansion and to plantations of nonnative conifers.

Temperate forests are a biologically efficient form of land use. In terms of biomass—the amount of living material (animal and plant) in any one area—they could still play an important role in the provision of food, materials and even renewable energy. Thus on scientific, economic and aesthetic grounds a strong case can be made for immediate conservation measures.

Mediterranean Regions

Forests of evergreen trees once covered much of the Mediterranean regions. They flourished in spite of the hot, rainless summer months – as the original plant life, they had evolved to survive such harsh conditions. Man, however, has proved to be a greater threat than the climate. He introduced domestic animals and cleared the land to grow crops; the natural vegetation was burned, browsed and plowed into nonexistence. Man's activities left behind tracts of impoverished soil which rapidly became scrubland. Today, scrub is the most typical vegetation in all the Mediterranean climate zones throughout the world.

CONVERGENCE
Isolated from each other by enormous areas of land and ocean, regions with a Mediterranean type of climate rarely have any plant species in common. But, by a process known as "convergent evolution," the plant communities in each of these areas have produced remarkably similar responses to their similar environments. This can be seen in the conifer communities, the broad-leaved evergreen trees, and in the various hardy shrubs and ground plants typical of each of the regions.

California's Monterey pine and other Mediterranean conifers—South African podocarps and Chile pines, for example—have needle-shaped leaves that prevent rapid loss of water from such trees during drought.

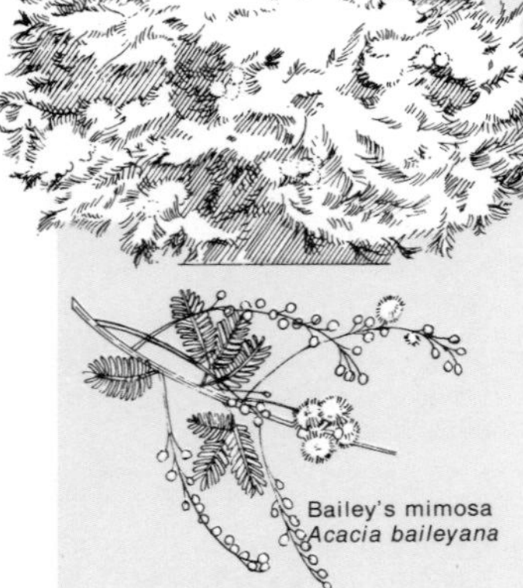

Nonconiferous evergreens such as Australia's acacias and eucalypts, Chile's *quillajas* and California's evergreen oaks are typical Mediterranean trees. Their leathery leaves limit summer moisture loss.

Shrubs and ground plants show various adaptations to drought. South African proteas and Europe's laurel have thick evergreen leaves. Narrow leaves and water-storing roots are other common adaptations.

Long, hot, dry summers and warm, moist winters form the seasonal rhythm of the "Mediterranean" year. This climatic pattern can be found in small areas of nearly every continent in the world, typically on the western side of landmasses and in the mild, temperate latitudes. North America's "Mediterranean" is in California, South America's occurs in Chile and Africa's lies at the southern tip of Cape Province. Australia has two small "Mediterranean" areas, one on the southern coast and one on the western. Europe's Mediterranean region, which has given its name to this climate, covers much of the southern part of the continent and extends into northern Africa.

Wherever Mediterranean conditions prevail, the native plant life has adapted to survive the scanty annual rainfall and the long summer droughts. Some species have developed deep root systems that can tap low summer water tables, and many of the ground plants—such as bulbs and aromatic herbs—grow vigorously only in early summer while rain still moistens the soil. But it is the broad-leaved evergreens with their drought-resistant leaves that are the most typical of the Mediterranean areas.

This natural pattern of vegetation has been drastically altered by man. In southern Europe in particular, almost all the original evergreen forests have long since been destroyed and thickets of fast-growing, tough scrub plants have grown up in their place. This scrub, which once probably covered only small areas, is now so widespread that it is considered the most typically Mediterranean of all kinds of vegetation. It is the *maquis* of France, the *macchia* of Italy and the *mattoral* of Spain. A similar type of vegetation (although containing different species) can also be found in South Africa's fynbos, in California's chapparal, and in Australia's tracts of natural mallee scrub.

Classical land use
Southern Europe, with its long history of human settlement, farming and pastoralism, is the most altered of all the Mediterranean regions. Over the centuries vast tracts of original vegetation have been removed, either by farmers (for crop growing) or by grazing animals. And, particularly on the steep slopes and rocky outcrops, this has resulted in extensive deterioration and erosion of the soil. Agriculture generally has less serious effects upon the vegetation than has animal grazing. Mankind has learned, over many hundreds of years, which are the most suitable crops for the various soils, terrain and climatic conditions of the region. The Mediterranean "triad" of wheat on the lowlands and olives and vines on the hills has been a successful combination since Classical times.

Pastoral plundering of the land, however, has more serious consequences. The virtually omnivorous goat is particularly damaging and can strip a whole forest of its foliage, bark, shrubs, ground plants and grass. After such an assault the vegetation rarely returns to its former condition; normally, a scrubby growth of kermes oak and shrubs springs up to form a typical maquis-type vegetation.

The rise and fall of each great Mediterranean civilization has seen forests destroyed in one area after another. The Greek colonization of southern Italy was provoked by deforestation and soil erosion in Attica. The Romans extended clearance north to the Po valley and into eastern Tunisia. From the seventh century onwards, Muslims made great inroads into the forests of North Africa as well as southern and eastern Spain; and in the north of Spain and southern France, medieval monks cleared forested valleys. During the seventeenth and eighteenth centuries large areas of Provence and Italy were cleared to plant vines and this process continued in the 1800s, when the great wine-producing areas of Languedoc and Algeria were established. During this time the iron industries of Spain and northern Italy, with their growing need for charcoal, were adding to the destruction. Recent reafforestation efforts have been puny compared to past degradation.

Protected species
But throughout this history of forest removal some tree species have been protected. These have been the natural tree crops that have, at times, supported complete peasant economies. The chestnut forests of Corsica, for example, sustained a large rural population until this century; the chestnuts provided flour for bread and fodder for pigs. In Portugal and Sardinia the cork-oak forests are still important today.

It is the olive, however, symbol of peace and of New Testament landscapes, that is the Mediterranean's most characteristic tree crop. Of all the Mediterranean plants, it is the most perfectly adapted to its environment, with its deep roots to search out scarce water and its hard, shiny leaves to conserve what it finds. In fact, the summer drought is essential to olive growers for it encourages the build-up of oil in the fruit. Paradoxically, however, the olive—like the vine, the fig and many other "Mediterranean" crops—did not originate in the Mediterranean but was introduced from Asia Minor.

In spite of massive destruction of the natural landscape, mankind has learned many valuable lessons during his occupation of this region. Ideas that were to become important in laying the foundations of sound land management policy were developed in the Mediterranean area. Hillside terracing, irrigation, crop rotation and manuring were all, from necessity, practiced from early times. The flourishing agricultural industries of the world's other Mediterranean regions—the wine industry of California, the vast soft-fruit plantations of Australia and the citrus industry of South Africa—all owe a considerable debt to the generations of farmers who learned to exploit the red soils of the Mediterranean basin.

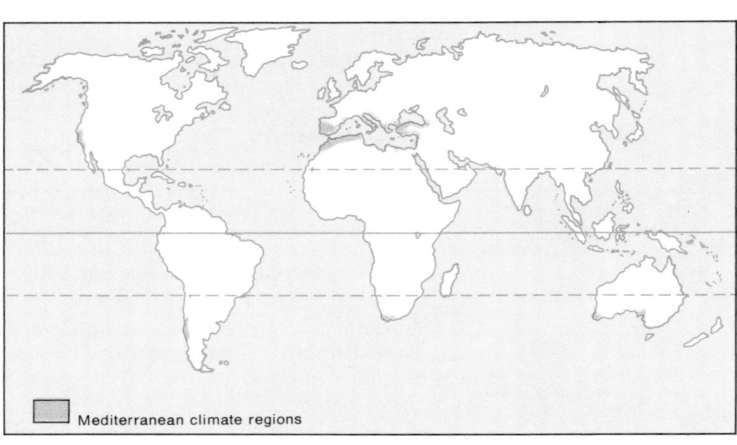

The Mediterranean regions occur between the latitudes 30° and 40°, on the western and southwestern sides of the continents. These areas are affected in summer by the high-pressure systems of nearby desert regions, and in winter by wet, low-pressure systems brought in from the oceans and over the land by the prevailing Westerlies. This distinct seasonal shifting of major influences on the climate produces the hot, waterless summers and warm, moist, sometimes stormy winters typical of the Mediterranean climate.

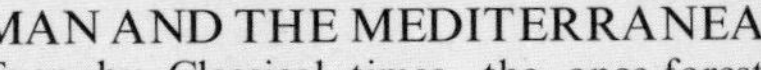

MAN AND THE MEDITERRANEAN
Even by Classical times, the once-forested lands fringing the Mediterranean Sea were suffering from massive deforestation and soil erosion. In the 5th century BC, Plato described the bare, dry hills of Attica, recently stripped of their woodlands. "What now remains," he wrote, "is like the skeleton of a sick man, all the fat and soft earth having been wasted away." By the end of the Classical period, irreparable damage had been done. At the same time, however, mankind was gradually learning through the mistakes he had already made. Suitable patterns of land use, better farming practices and improved land management techniques were slowly being adopted and were enabling man to make better use of the much-altered Mediterranean landscape.

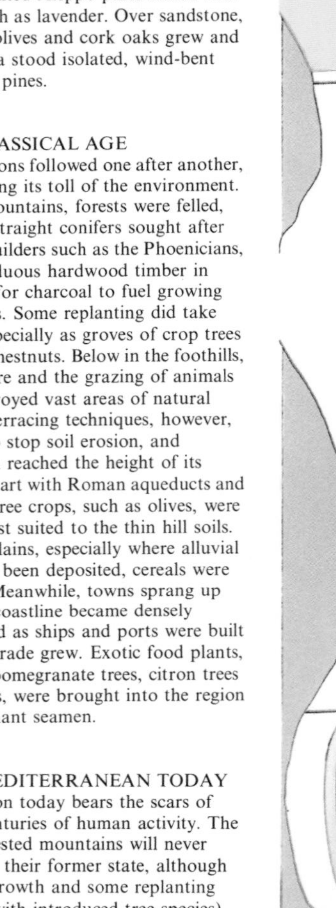

THE ORIGINAL LANDSCAPE
The landscape, unaltered by man, held a rich variety of vegetation. On high mountains, conifers such as black pine and cedar grew. On the lower slopes, these gave way to warmth-tolerant deciduous trees such as Turkey oak. In the foothills and valleys, forests of holm oaks, strawberry trees and other broad-leaved evergreens flourished. Limestone outcrops, common in the area, supported a poorer vegetation. Here, stunted Aleppo pines mixed with herbs such as lavender. Over sandstone, scrubby olives and cork oaks grew and by the sea stood isolated, wind-bent maritime pines.

THE CLASSICAL AGE
Civilizations followed one after another, each taking its toll of the environment. In the mountains, forests were felled, the tall, straight conifers sought after by shipbuilders such as the Phoenicians, and deciduous hardwood timber in demand for charcoal to fuel growing industries. Some replanting did take place, especially as groves of crop trees such as chestnuts. Below in the foothills, agriculture and the grazing of animals had destroyed vast areas of natural forest. Terracing techniques, however, helped to stop soil erosion, and irrigation reached the height of its Classical art with Roman aqueducts and canals. Tree crops, such as olives, were found best suited to the thin hill soils. On the plains, especially where alluvial soils had been deposited, cereals were grown. Meanwhile, towns sprang up and the coastline became densely populated as ships and ports were built and sea trade grew. Exotic food plants, such as pomegranate trees, citron trees and vines, were brought into the region by merchant seamen.

THE MEDITERRANEAN TODAY
The region today bears the scars of many centuries of human activity. The once-forested mountains will never return to their former state, although some regrowth and some replanting (mostly with introduced tree species) has occurred. As in Classical times, hillsides are terraced and planted with vines and fruit trees. But with modern irrigation and fertilizing, land is less readily exhausted and abandoned now. On the plains, native shrubs, such as lavender, are commercially cultivated and grain is widely grown, particularly durum wheat used for making pasta. Cork oaks are planted, especially over dry sandstone areas, but indigenous vegetation has not suffered by this—scrubby woodland is more widespread than ever and can be found throughout the landscape. Perhaps the single most important part of the Mediterranean basin today is the coastline, for this has produced the region's major modern industry—tourism.

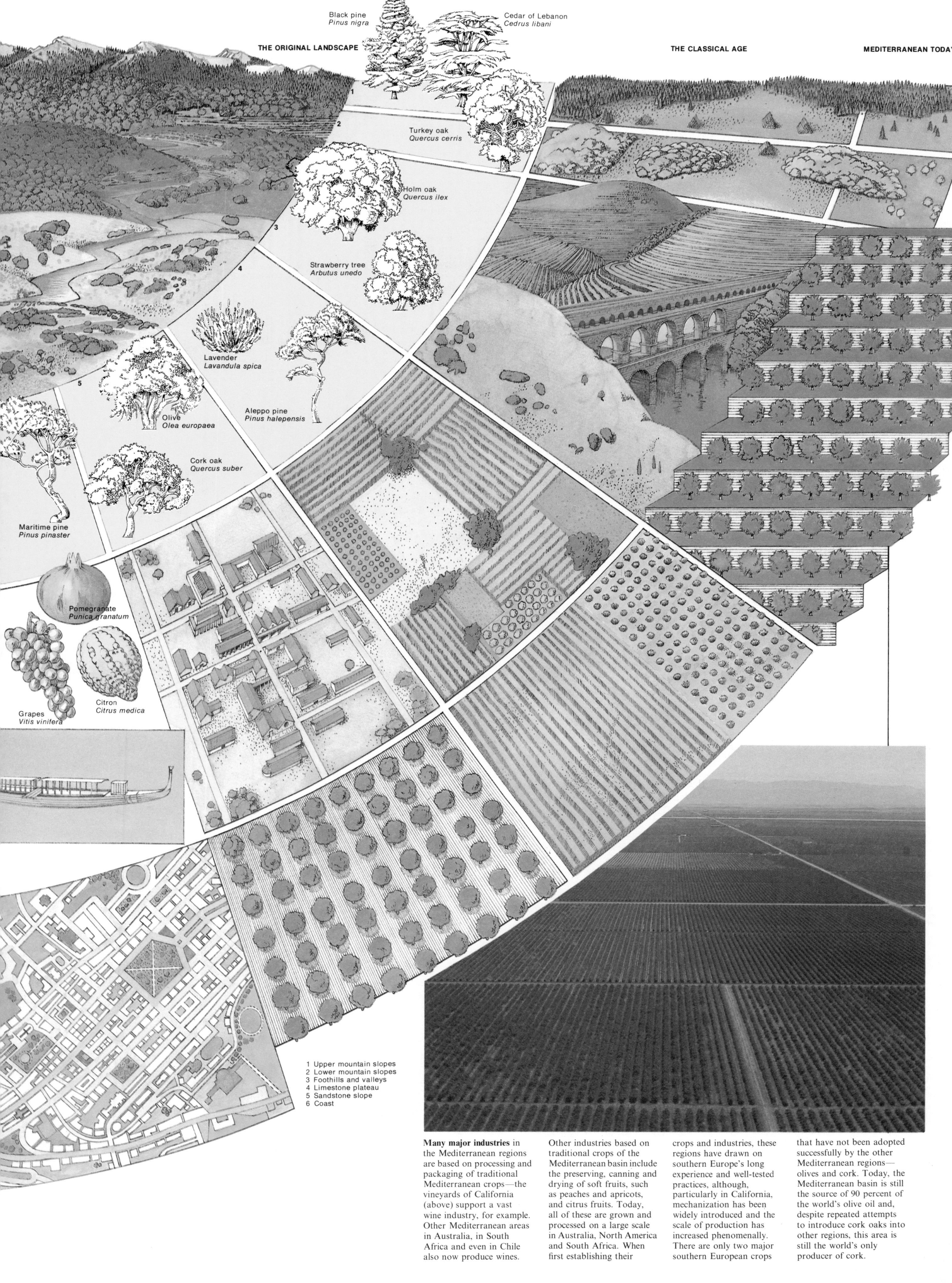

Many major industries in the Mediterranean regions are based on processing and packaging of traditional Mediterranean crops—the vineyards of California (above) support a vast wine industry, for example. Other Mediterranean areas in Australia, in South Africa and even in Chile also now produce wines. Other industries based on traditional crops of the Mediterranean basin include the preserving, canning and drying of soft fruits, such as peaches and apricots, and citrus fruits. Today, all of these are grown and processed on a large scale in Australia, North America and South Africa. When first establishing their crops and industries, these regions have drawn on southern Europe's long experience and well-tested practices, although, particularly in California, mechanization has been widely introduced and the scale of production has increased phenomenally. There are only two major southern European crops that have not been adopted successfully by the other Mediterranean regions—olives and cork. Today, the Mediterranean basin is still the source of 90 percent of the world's olive oil and, despite repeated attempts to introduce cork oaks into other regions, this area is still the world's only producer of cork.

Temperate Grasslands

Compared with other flowering plants, grasses are newcomers to the Earth. They appeared only 60 million years ago, but since then they have proved to be an extremely successful family of plants. Today, the grasses dominate large areas of the world's natural vegetation and play a vital part in the intricate balance of plant and animal life in these regions. In spite of the inroads made by man, vast stretches of original grassland still cover the interiors of the North American and Eurasian landmasses.

The prairies of North America and the steppes of Eurasia extend far into the interiors of the northern continents. These are the best known and the most extensive of the world's temperate grasslands. The southern hemisphere, however, has examples in the veld of South Africa and the pampas of South America. Extensive grasslands also occur in southern Australia, although these are sometimes described as semiarid scrub because of the high average temperatures and the prolonged droughts in the region.

Temperate grasslands probably developed wherever the rainfall was too low to support forest and too high to result in semiarid regions, conditions found typically in the interiors of large continents. Continental interiors tend to be somewhat drier than coastal regions, but they are also characterized by extreme changes in temperature from one season to the next. In the North American grasslands, for example, winter temperatures may fall well below freezing whereas summer temperatures of 38°C (100°F) are not unusual. And these sharp fluctuations in seasonal temperature greatly influence how much of the rainfall is made available to plants. In summer particularly, when most of the rain falls, high temperatures, strong winds and lack of protective tree cover cause much of the moisture to evaporate before it can be absorbed into the soil.

Climatic conditions are not the only factor responsible for the distribution and form of the temperate grasslands. There are many pointers that indicate the importance of fire in determining their continuing existence and their extent. Natural fires, caused by lightning and fueled by the dry summer grasses, have always been a feature of these regions, but more recently, man-made fires have been crucial in fixing the boundary between forest and grassland.

Trees and shrubs frequently invade the margins of grasslands, but whenever there is a fire few of them survive. Grasses, however, have certain characteristics that enable them to withstand the potentially destructive impact of fire. The growing point of grasses is at the base of the leaves, close to the ground, and so destruction of the leaves above this point does not interrupt growth—in fact it may stimulate it. These same characteristics also serve to protect grasses from destruction by grazing animals. The large animals of these lands, such as the North American bison and the Eurasian horse, are able to crop the grasses without permanently damaging their food supply.

Grazers and predators

Large migrating herbivores with a strong herd instinct characterize one of the major types of temperate grassland animal. In the North American grasslands the bison (which may have numbered 60 million before being virtually exterminated by settlers) and the antelope-like pronghorn were the major examples of large herbivores. In Eurasia large herds of saiga antelopes, wild horses and asses at one time roamed the steppes, although they too have suffered from human activities, as has South America's largest grassland herd animal, the pampas deer. As these herds of grazing animals have been reduced, so have the carnivorous animals of the grasslands that preyed upon them. At one time, however, these predators played an important part in protecting the grasslands by continually keeping the numbers of grazing herd animals in check.

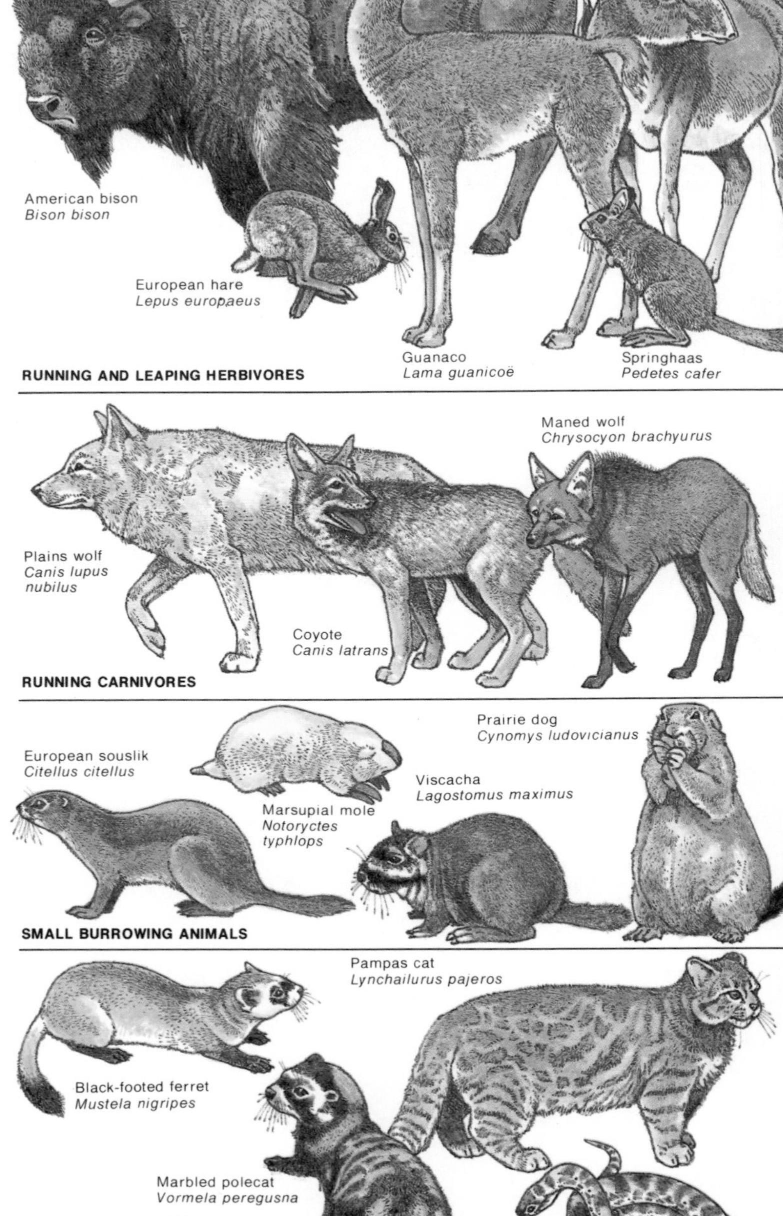

Russian tarragon
Artemisia dracunculoides

The dominant native species of grass varies from area to area. In the undisturbed prairies, for example, tall bluestem and Indian grass grow in the east and in wet central lowlands and mix with switch grass in drier parts. Farther west and on high land in the east, little bluestem and also western wheatgrass grow. June grass grows in the north, and buffalo grass and blue grama grow farthest west.

Many flowering herbs grow in the grasslands and have developed resistance to summer droughts: Russian tarragon has narrow leaves to help prevent moisture evaporation; rhizomes and bulbs, such as Eurasia's iris and anemone, store water in their specialized "root" systems.

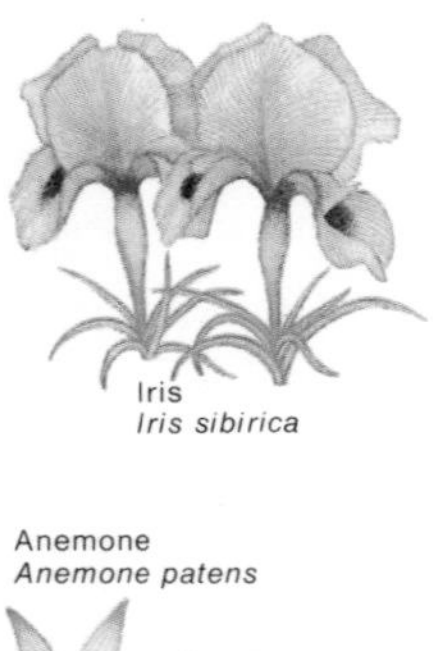

Iris
Iris sibirica

Anemone
Anemone patens

Blue grama grass
Bouteloua gracilis

Little bluestem
Andropogon scoparius

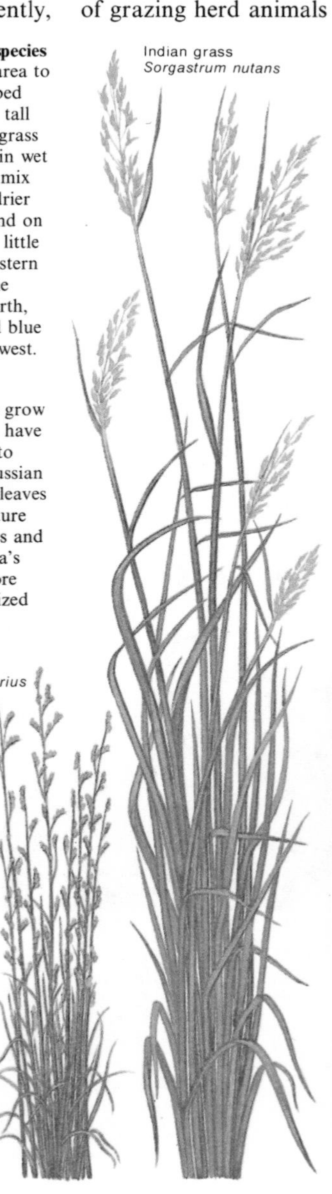

Indian grass
Sorgastrum nutans

The natural distribution of the temperate grasslands is dictated mainly by rainfall: most occur in continental interiors where there is too little rain for forest but enough to prevent desert from forming. Between these limits the large range in rainfall allows three main types of grassland: tall grass in wetter areas, mid-grass, and short grass in drier parts. The largest grasslands exist in North America, Eurasia, South America, in Australia's Murray–Darling river basin and on the South African plateau.

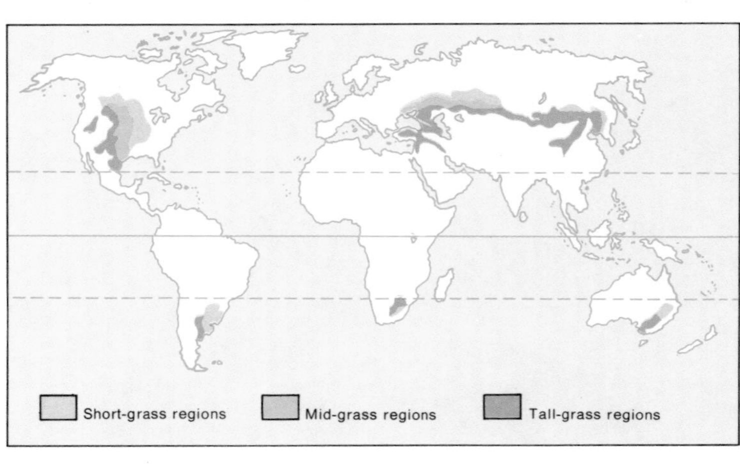

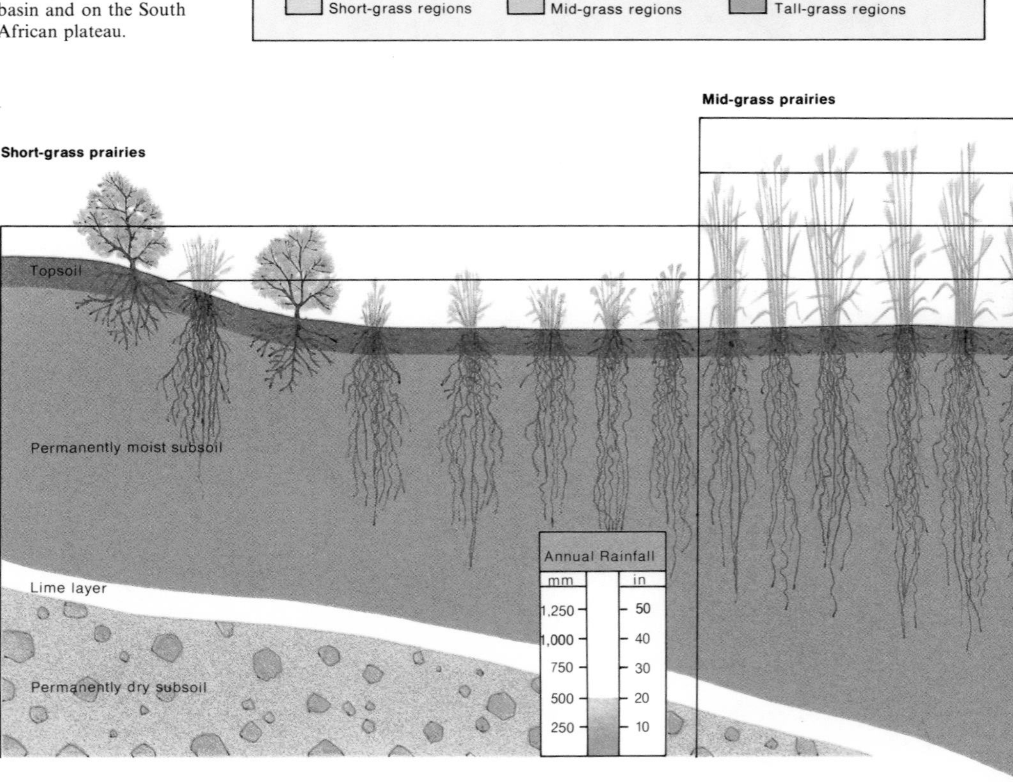

GRASSLAND ADAPTATION

Animals of these regions have had to adapt to a difficult environment: vast, treeless expanses of grass offer little protection from harsh weather or predators. Different animals have found various answers to the problem and a clearly defined pattern of these adaptations can be traced throughout the grasslands.

Running and leaping herbivores survive because of their ability to move faster than a pursuer. The larger animals such as the Eurasian saiga, North America's bison and pronghorn and the guanaco of South America are runners. The leaping herbivores are usually smaller creatures that escape danger by bounding away to bolt-holes. They include the European hare and the African springhaas.

Running carnivores follow, and prey on, running and leaping herbivores. These animals, such as the coyote and the now extinct plains wolf of North America, and South America's maned wolf, also depend on speed—to enable them to catch their prey.

Small burrowing animals hide from predators by digging under the ground. Some, such as Australia's marsupial mole, spend most of their lives below ground. Others, such as the European souslik, South America's viscacha and North America's prairie dog, live and sleep under the ground but come to the surface to find food.

Small carnivores concentrate on the burrowers as their main source of food. They either, like the pampas cat, rely on surprise attack of their prey, or, like Eurasia's marbled polecat and the grasslands' many kinds of snake, depend on their long, lithe shape to follow creatures into their burrows.

Two distinctive types of grassland bird can be distinguished: the sky birds, which spend long periods of time on the wing, and the ground birds.

Birds of the sky include songbirds such as the skylark which, having no perch from which to proclaim its territory, sings in the sky, and birds of prey such as Eurasia's tawny eagle and North America's red-tailed hawk and prairie falcon, which ride the thermals scanning the ground for their prey.

Ground birds rarely take to the wing, although none has actually lost the ability to fly when necessary. They include birds such as the New World sage grouse and burrowing owl (which lives below ground in abandoned prairie dog burrows), the black grouse of Eurasia and songbirds such as North America's meadowlark.

Insects and other invertebrates have developed many different survival techniques. Some use camouflage: the praying mantis resembles a leaf bud and the tumble bug is the color of the dark grassland soil. Grasshoppers are miniature leaping herbivores and earthworms are small-scale versions of the grassland burrowers.

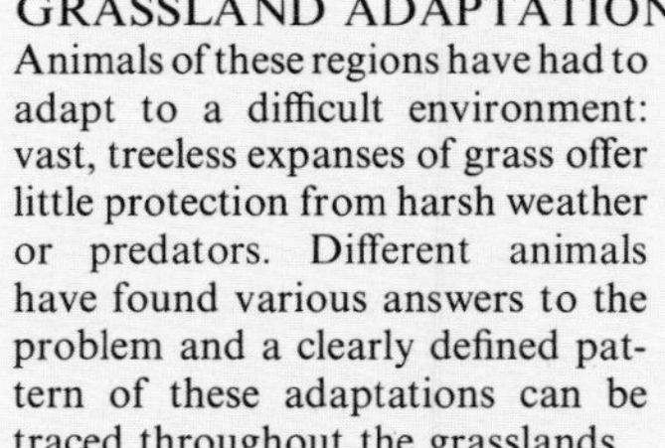

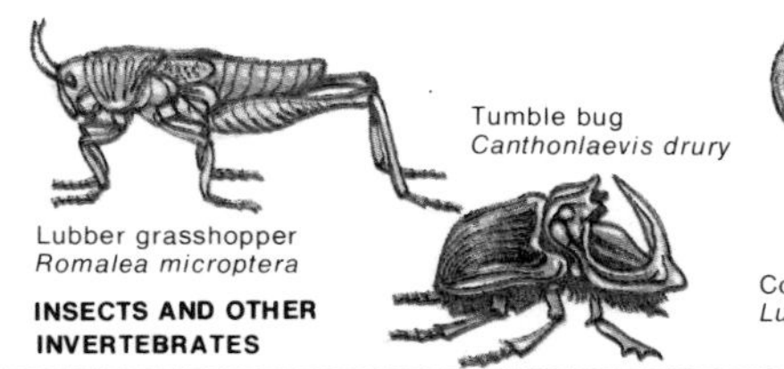

Another major type of animal found in the temperate grasslands, and one that is better adapted to survive man's activities, is the small, burrowing animal, for example the prairie dog and the gopher of North America, the viscacha of South America and the little ground squirrel known as the souslik in Eurasia.

Unlike the large herd animals, these creatures tend not to migrate. Many of them live together in complex, permanent, underground communities. The colonial "townships" of the prairie dog, for example, may house more than one million individuals, which each year excavate vast quantities of the grassland soil. This has considerable effect upon the structure of the soil. By bringing up earth from lower layers to the surface, these animals are responsible for changing the mineral content of certain areas of topsoil. This then encourages isolated pockets of different plant species to flourish.

A third group of grassland animals, consisting of insects and other invertebrates such as earthworms, has an even more important effect upon the soil. They live in or on the soil and play a vital role in maintaining grassland fertility. These creatures may be herbivores, carnivores or primary (first stage) decomposers (which break down such material as dead grass and animal remains). These three types of activity allow a complete range of organic matter to be processed and incorporated into the earth, where it is further broken down by the second-stage decomposers, the countless millions of soil bacteria. In this way nutrients continuously flow back to the earth and restore its fertility.

Fertile black earths

The topsoil of temperate grassland regions, therefore, contains large amounts of organic material, which is produced every year and is quickly incorporated into the soil. The low and intermittent rainfall and the protective cover of grasses mean that the topsoil undergoes little chemical leaching, a process in which minerals are removed and carried down to lower layers by rainfall percolating through the earth. The soils are thus dark in color, generally fertile and of the "black earth" type ("chernozem" in Russian) which is, at least at first, capable of producing high yields of crops.

The most suitable and most widely grown crops are, predictably, the cultivated grasses, and it is these grasses that provide more food for mankind (either directly as grain or indirectly as animal fodder) than any other source. The temperate grassland biome is therefore an important agricultural resource. Undisturbed natural grasslands, however, are also valuable resources. They need to be preserved both for the information that they can provide about how complex communities of wildlife function efficiently, and because, as a rich source of genetic material, they hold many of the answers to the major agricultural problems that probably lie ahead for the human race.

A typical cross section, based on the North American prairies, shows temperate grasslands in relation to rainfall. Annual rainfall determines the depth of the permanently moist subsoil, which in turn dictates the length to which grass roots can grow. Tall grasses have deep root systems and need a considerable depth of moist subsoil. As the rainfall decreases, they gradually give way to shorter grass species. Short grasses require less water and their shallower roots are well suited to drier regions. On dry margins, desert plants start to dominate, and on the wet margins, trees appear.

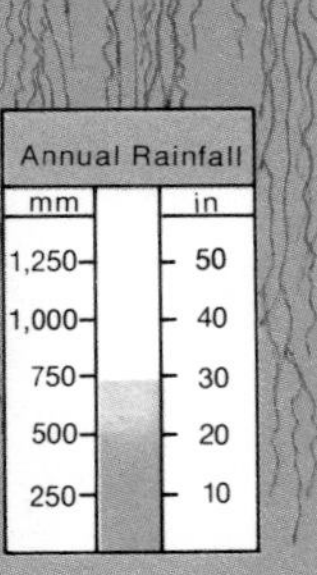

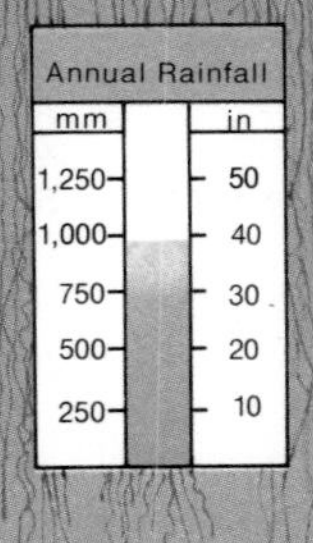

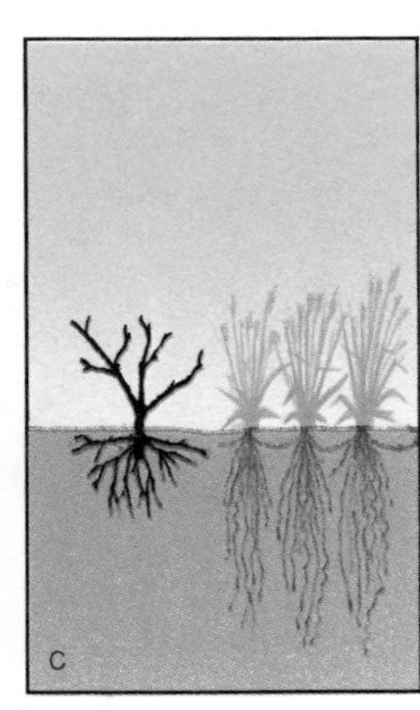

Fire plays a major part in fixing and maintaining the natural boundaries of the temperate grasslands, where tree saplings and shrubs are continually attempting to invade (A). Man-made fires are recent phenomena, natural fires have always occurred. In summer, low-pressure systems build up in continental interiors, causing violent electrical storms. The dry sward of summer grass is easily ignited by lightning and fire is quickly spread by wind. Shrubs and saplings are killed or badly damaged by fire, but grasses, with their growing points close to the soil, remain unharmed (B). They may even benefit from this "pruning" and grow more quickly. Some species grow new buds from their underground shoots. Removal of the main shoot may encourage growth of "tillers" (shoots growing out sideways), which then increase the spread of the grasses as they begin to invade the area left vacant by the dead, or slowly recuperating, shrubs (C).

Man and the Temperate Grasslands

The vast areas of temperate grassland lay virtually empty until the end of the eighteenth century. Over the next 125 years they were occupied by millions of people, most of them migrants from overcrowded Europe. By 1914, the grasslands had become the granaries and the stockyards of the world. Today, they are still the most important food-producing regions on Earth and their riches, properly distributed, are the world's first reserve against the possibility of a hungry future for the human race.

The great nineteenth-century migration to the grasslands proved of immense significance to the human race. It meant that, within a single century, the area of productive land available was suddenly enlarged by thousands of millions of hectares. In all of mankind's history, such a thing had never happened before.

But before the grasslands could be occupied a number of major problems had to be solved. First, in order to reach these regions it was almost always necessary to travel deep into the continental interiors, and there were few navigable rivers and no mechanized forms of transportation for early pioneers. Second, with virtually no indigenous population, newcomers had to learn by their mistakes how best to exploit the new and unfamiliar environment. Third, even if settlers succeeded in using the land, they still had to find markets for their produce.

A number of technological developments, however, that took place in the nineteenth century provided the right combination of circumstances for the opening up of the grasslands. The Industrial Revolution in Europe produced the steamship and the railway locomotive, which created both a means of travel to and from these distant parts and an internal transport system for moving produce to ports and markets. It also produced the kind of machinery needed to plow and farm the great new open spaces; it made it possible for one family to cultivate an area 50 times as large as that which most farmers had known in Europe. Industrialization also threw thousands of Europeans out of work, and therefore provided a large supply of eager migrants. And it crowded further thousands into cities, thus creating vast markets for the settlers' produce.

It was the coming together of these various circumstances that acted as the catalyst and converted, for example, the Russian penetration of the Eurasian steppes in the late eighteenth

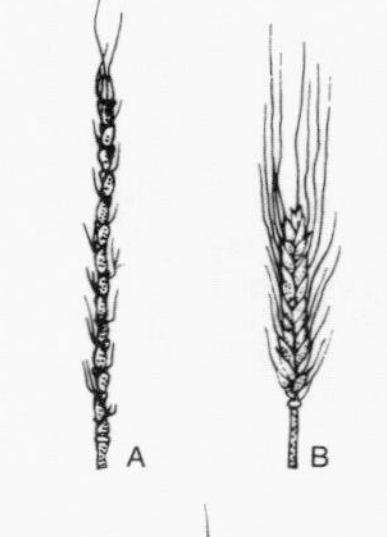

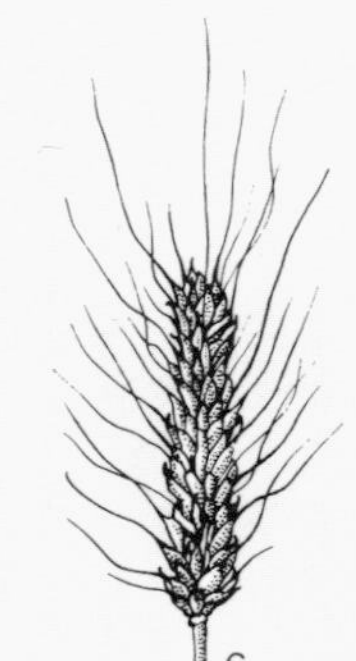

THE CRADLE OF AGRICULTURE

Stands of wild einkorn (A), emmer wheat (B) and wild barleys can be seen today in the grassy foothills that flank the Taurus and the Zagros mountains, and the uplands of northern Israel. It was in this region 10,000 years ago that the world's earliest farmers gathered seeds from these species and sowed the first crops. Wild einkorn is probably the oldest of all wheats and the parent of every modern variety—including the most important and most widely grown kind of grain in the world today, common bread wheat (C).

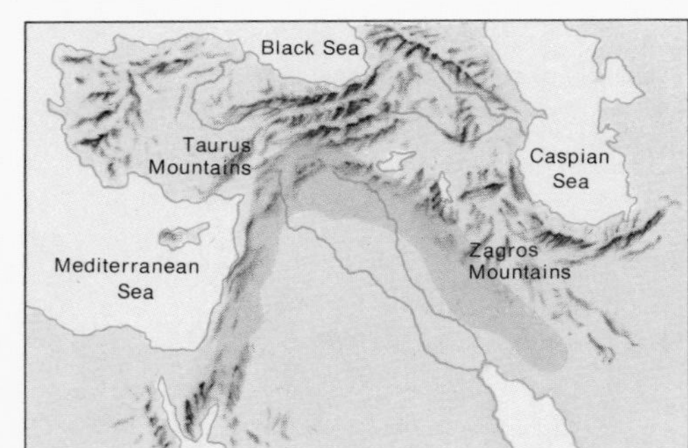

GRASSLAND EXPLOITATION

Today, temperate grasslands provide mankind with a superabundance of food. But the vast potential of these regions was not exploited until the mid-19th century, when mass migration by Europeans, combined with new technology, allowed full-scale development and settlement.

BEFORE EUROPEAN SETTLEMENT The grasslands were sparsely populated. Most of the indigenous tribespeoples were nomadic hunters and gatherers. They wandered widely over the regions, making temporary camps (1) as they followed the movement of their quarry—the plentiful herds of grazing animals (2). These peoples made little impact on the natural grasslands.

GRASSLAND SETTLERS Early pioneers relied on animal-drawn transport (3), primitive farm tools (4) and unpredictable free-range livestock grazing (5). During the 19th century, farming became more productive: better equipment cultivated larger areas (6); barbed wire made stock raising efficient (7); railways and the telegraph improved communication (8).

Tehuelche Indians (above) adopted horses for hunting from early Spanish settlers to the pampas. In South Africa and North America, too, the introduced horse became a valued asset for grassland hunters. For people of the Eurasian steppes, for example the Mongols (right), native horses have always been culturally important.

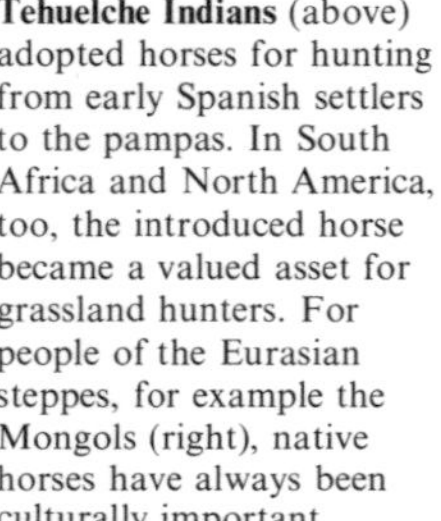

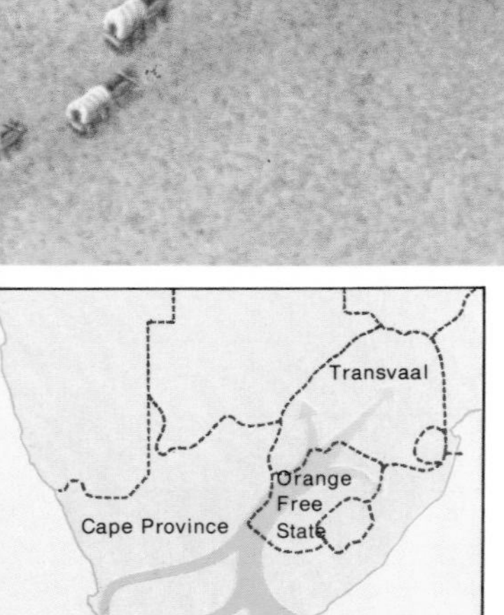

The South African veld was first settled by Europeans after 1836 (left). Dutch farmers (Boers), rejecting British rule of the Cape Colony, trekked north in search of new land. Moving into the Transvaal they discovered rich grassland, recently emptied of its original inhabitants, who had fled to escape the aggressive attentions of neighboring Zulus.

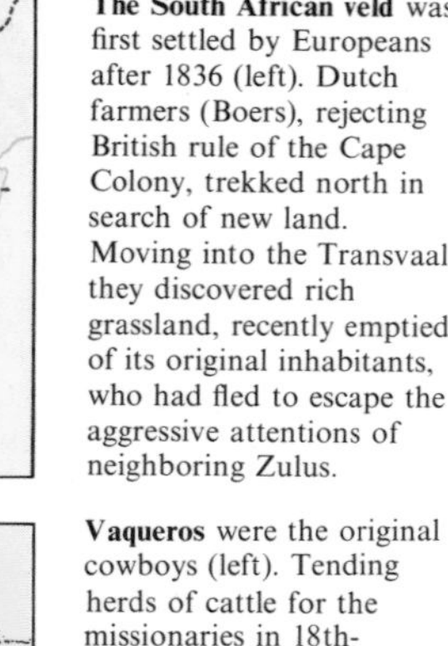

Vaqueros were the original cowboys (left). Tending herds of cattle for the missionaries in 18th-century California, they developed techniques and traditions that served hundreds of later cowboys working the prairie ranges. In other grassland regions, as free-range stock raising became important, similar "cowboy" professions evolved—the Australian stockman and the gaucho of South America.

century into the explosive movement of hundreds of thousands of settlers a few years later. In the USA, too, by the year 1850, settlement had reached and then rapidly crossed the Mississippi. In the Argentine, genuine colonization of the pampas had begun, in South Africa, the Boers had reached the high veld, and in Australia pioneer settlers were moving outwards from the various areas of coastal settlement into the scrub grasslands of the interior.

Farmers or ranchers?

The fundamental question posed for these settlers was whether their newly found land should be used for crops or for livestock. Most grasslands have a dry edge and a wet edge, and it was therefore sensible to use the drier parts for stock raising and the wetter parts for cultivation. But the question was complicated by the fact that most of the newcomers were cultivators, and also that the line dividing dry from wet was vague—worse, it shifted from year to year.

Early attempts to define the dividing line tended to be ignored by the settlers themselves, and they pushed the limit of cultivation into areas where plowing the soil led to its destruction. Several generations of farmers had to learn this bitter lesson, and they learned only slowly: the worst disasters on the American grasslands occurred in the 1930s and created the infamous Dust Bowl region in the dry grasslands of the Midwest. Similarly, the Soviet Virgin Lands Program for growing cereal crops on the dry steppes was established in 1954 and is still experiencing difficulties.

Special methods are required both for farming and for ranching the grasslands successfully. Farming has to take account of the open, treeless surface, the scanty and variable rainfall and the comparatively shallow topsoil. To minimize the risk of soil erosion, farmers plant windbreaks, plow fields along the contour, and protect the soil with a covering of the previous year's stubble and by planting cover crops in rotation with cereals. Ranchers, too, have learned to live with variable rainfall. They build stock ponds, irrigate areas of fodder crops to be used as a reserve in dry years and avoid overstocking and consequent overgrazing, which destroys the quality of the grass.

Food for the world

Today, the world's principal trading supplies of cereals and meat flow from these lands, over the networks of railway which link the grasslands to mill towns, slaughter yards and ports of shipment such as Adelaide in Australia, Buenos Aires in Argentina and Montreal in Canada. Without these links to large towns, the grasslands would be of little value, for even today their populations are sparse and the local markets are relatively insignificant.

Throughout most of the world, however, the human population continues to soar and it remains to be seen whether the grasslands can continue to supply these growing numbers with food. Undoubtedly, the output of cereals and meat can be increased, although at considerable cost in fertilizers, new crop strains, more irrigation and more machines. On the other hand, the problem at present is not mainly one of production, nor will it be in the near future. The land can produce more, but there is no point in doing so unless the yields can be made available where they are most needed.

The world's hungry people live in other regions, many of them in countries that are unable to afford imported food supplies, particularly during those years when prices are high. The major importers of temperate grassland produce are the rich industrialized nations, such as those of western Europe. Furthermore, much of the grain imported by these countries is not consumed by humans but used to feed stalled, beef-producing cattle—a highly inefficient way of using these supplies. Consequently, unless producer nations and wealthy importing nations can create a system for produce to reach those in need of it, extra output from the grasslands will be irrelevant.

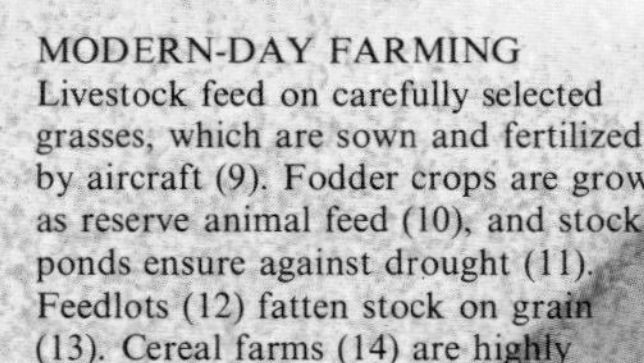

MODERN-DAY FARMING
Livestock feed on carefully selected grasses, which are sown and fertilized by aircraft (9). Fodder crops are grown as reserve animal feed (10), and stock ponds ensure against drought (11). Feedlots (12) fatten stock on grain (13). Cereal farms (14) are highly mechanized, and road and rail serve even the remotest regions (15).

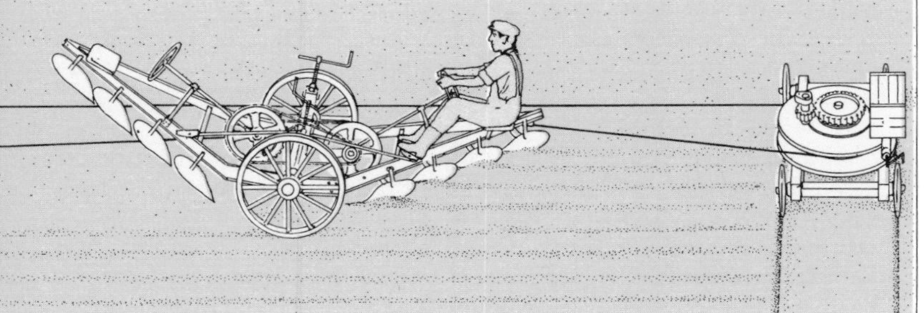

The steam-driven plow (below) went through many developments to reduce its unwieldiness and heaviness. The version produced in 1858 used a traction engine and pulley wheel system. The plow was drawn back and forth between these by a power-driven cable. This design was, however, superseded by the steam tractor, which, although unsuited to small European fields, was ideal for drawing multifurrow plows across the grasslands.

Sand-smothered farms in the heart of the Dust Bowl were rapidly abandoned during the 1930s and 40s (above). This was one costly lesson that man had to learn in the process of developing the grasslands. Traditionally grazing land, the western part of the prairies was first plowed this century. Years of drought arrived, crops died and the desert encroached.

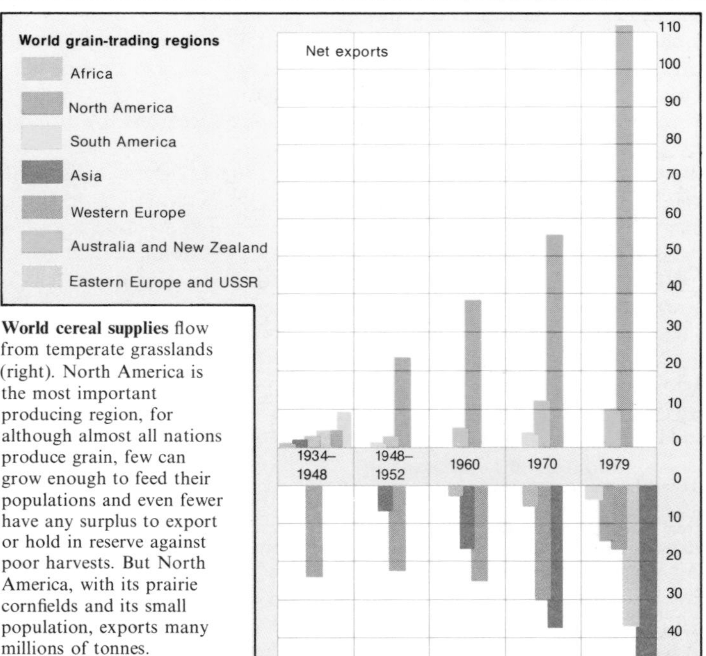

World cereal supplies flow from temperate grasslands (right). North America is the most important producing region, for although almost all nations produce grain, few can grow enough to feed their populations and even fewer have any surplus to export or hold in reserve against poor harvests. But North America, with its prairie cornfields and its small population, exports many millions of tonnes.

Deserts

Much of the Earth's land surface is so short of water that it is defined as desert. Not all deserts are hot, sandy wastelands; some are cold, some are rocky, but all lack moisture for most of the year. Even so, a surprising variety of plants and animals have adapted to these hostile environments. Plants have developed ingenious ways of surviving long periods of drought, and many desert animals shelter during the intense heat of the day, emerging only at night to feed.

LIFE IN THE DESERT

The overriding need to obtain and conserve water dictates the pattern of desert life. Many plants close their pores during the day and most daytime creatures limit their activity to early morning and late afternoon. At night the temperature drops sharply and dew provides welcome moisture. Some plants bloom at night, and the desert is alive with insects, night-hunting birds, reptiles and small mammals.

DESERTS BY DAY

Many birds are at home in the desert. The lanner falcon of Africa and Asia gets all the moisture it needs from its diet of small birds and rodents. Sandgrouse live in the open deserts of Eurasia and North Africa; mainly seed eaters, they must make long flights each day to find water. Roadrunners, in American deserts, hunt insects, lizards and small rattlesnakes.

Lanner falcon *Falco biarmicus*

Pallas's sandgrouse *Syrrhaptes paradoxus*

Roadrunner *Geococcyx californianus*

Large mammals are nomadic and obtain most of the moisture they need from plants. Camels can go for long periods without food or water because their humped back stores fat which can be drawn on when food is scarce, and water stored in their body tissues prevents dehydration. Addax antelopes survive entirely on plants. They roam remote parts of the Sahara, their broad hooves enabling them to travel easily over soft sand. Gazelles rely on speed. Small and fleet footed, they are able to disperse quickly over great distances to find food and water.

Arabian camel *Camelus dromedarius*

Asian camel *Camelus bactrianus*

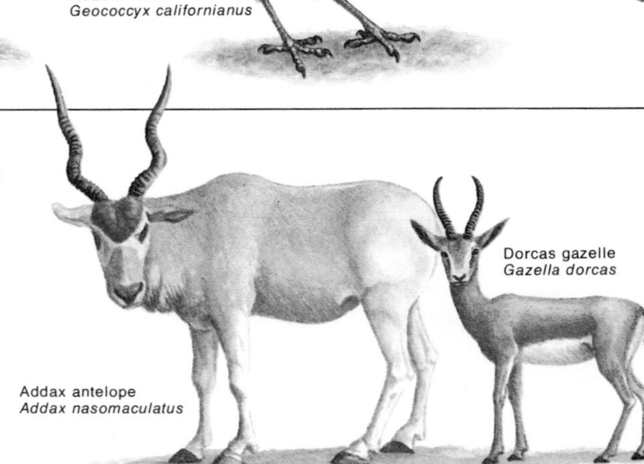

Insects and reptiles are well adapted to desert life. Desert locusts, when overpopulation threatens their food supply, change from a solitary to a swarming migratory form. Harvester ants store seeds against times of drought; desert tortoises withstand drought by becoming torpid. Lizards are cold blooded and need the sun to warm them, but must shelter from the intense heat of midday. The thorny devil, a small Australian ant-eating lizard, is protected from potential predators by its prickly scales.

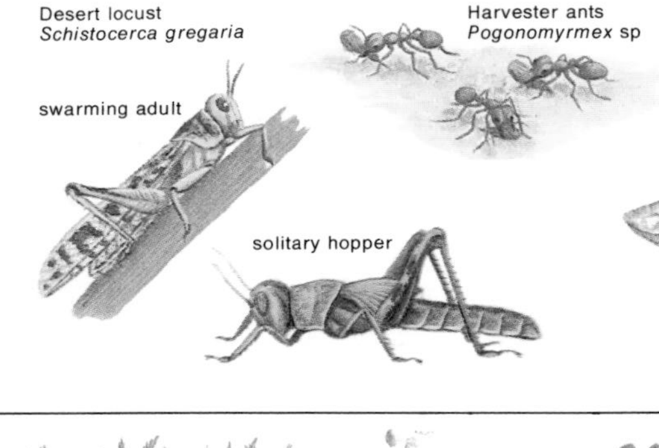

Desert tortoise *Gopherus polyphemus*

Gridiron-tailed lizard *Callisaurus draconoides*

Thorny devil *Moloch horridus*

Desert plants have evolved various ways of coping successfully with drought. The ocotillo of southwestern America sheds its leaves, reducing its need for water. Euphorbias, and cacti such as the prickly pear, store water in their stems. Blue kleinia, a South African succulent, has a waxy coating that limits water loss. Agaves mature very slowly, building up reserves of food and water in their leaves before they flower. Esparto, a needlegrass, is typical of many desert grasses.

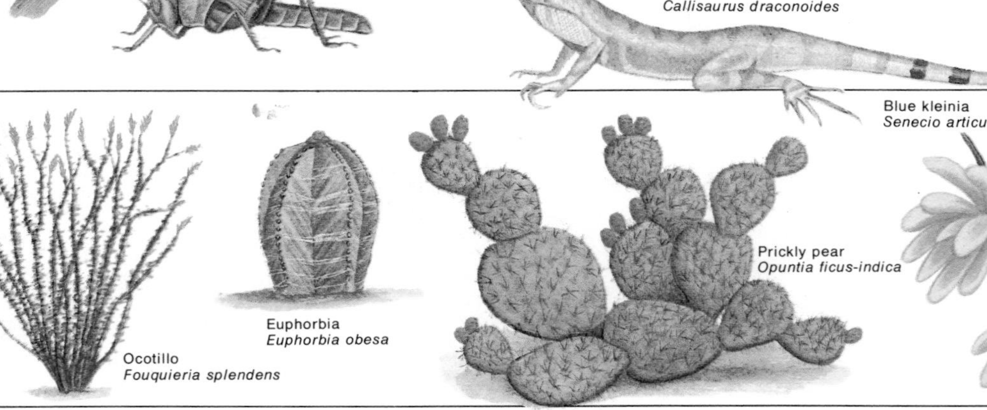

Agave *Agave americana*

Deserts occur where rainfall is low and infrequent and where any moisture quickly evaporates or disappears instantly into the parched ground. In the driest deserts, rainfall rarely exceeds 100 mm (4 in) a year, and is so unreliable that some places may have no rain for 10 years or more. These are deserts in the truest sense of the word: harsh wildernesses that are almost totally without life. Regions with less than 255 mm (10 in) of rain a year are generally classified as arid and those with less than 380 mm (15 in) as semiarid.

Hot deserts have very high daytime temperatures in summer, although they drop sharply at night, and the winters are relatively mild. In the so-called cold deserts the summers are hot but the winters are so cold that temperatures may fall as low as −30°C (−22°F).

Desert climates and landscapes

In the subtropical latitudes, swept by hot, drying winds, high-pressure weather systems prevent rain clouds from forming. In these regions, rain comes only from local storms or follows low-pressure weather systems (often seasonal) when they move in across the desert. Large areas of central Asia have become desert because they are so far from the sea that clouds have shed all their rain before they reach them. Other deserts occur because mountains cut them off from moisture-bearing winds. The Andes, for example, shelter the drylands of Argentina, and a high sierra stops rain from reaching the Mojave and Great Basin deserts of North America. Rain is also rare on the western sides of continents where cold ocean currents flow from the polar regions towards the Equator.

Desert climates vary not only from place to place but also with time. Over short periods rainfall is much less predictable than it is in temperate regions and droughts are frequent. Some droughts, such as those that occur along the southern fringe of the Sahara, are so severe that it may seem that the climate has changed permanently. But most droughts are short-lived and are followed by years of normal (although sparse) rainfall. Over longer periods of time, however, desert climates do change. Prehistoric cave drawings in the Saharan highlands, for example, show that elephants, rhinoceroses and even hippopotamuses—animals that are at home in wetter climates—lived in these now dry, barren uplands in a more moist period between 7,000 and 4,000 years ago.

Desert landscapes also vary enormously. They are as contrasted as the Colorado canyon country of the United States and the sandy wastes of the Middle East, but most include one or more of several basic features: steep, rocky mountain slopes, broad plains, basin floors dominated by dry lake beds or sand seas, and canyon-like valleys. In low-lying areas, evaporation sometimes leaves a glistening residue of salt. Where there is soil, it is often sandy or consists of little more than fragmented rock, and because plant life is usually sparse there is little or no humus to enrich the ground.

Where water is life

Plant growth depends on water, and desert plants are usually widely spaced to reduce competition for what little moisture is available. Many plants rely on short, sharp rainstorms; others make use of dew and grow in locations, such as crevices in rocks, where water can accumulate. Some complete their life cycle in a single wet season, producing seeds that lie dormant during the following drought and germinate only when enough moisture is available for them to grow. These are the ephemerals that carpet the desert with a brief but brilliant display of flowers shortly after rain has fallen.

Most desert plants, however, are able to tolerate or resist drought. These are the xerophytes ("dry plants") and phreatophytes ("deep-water plants"). Xerophytic trees and shrubs have a wide-spreading network of shallow roots that take in water from a large area of ground. Many xerophytes also limit the amount of water

Adaptations to desert life: kangaroo rats, jerboas and gerbils (A) make prodigious leaps with their long back legs to escape predators, and some desert lizards (B) run at high speed on their hind legs when pursued, using their tail for balance. Spadefoot toads have scoop-like hind feet with which they dig burrows to avoid the intense heat of day. Skinks use flattened toes fringed with scales to "swim" through the sand. Fan-toed geckos have toes that spread into fans at the tips, enabling them to walk easily on sand dunes, and the Namib palmate gecko has webbed feet that support it on loose sand.

The saguaro dominates the desert landscapes of Mexico and southern America. Immensely slow growing, it can take 200 years to reach its full height, and more than four-fifths of its weight may be water stored in its stem to be used in times of drought. To minimize water loss, it opens its pores only at night to absorb carbon dioxide and to help radiate heat accumulated by day.

Five great arid regions are bordered by semi-arid steppe and scrub. Cold deserts—the Gobi in central Asia, the Great Basin in North America and the Patagonian Desert in South America—lie in the higher latitudes. Cold ocean currents also affect climate, causing fogs to form over coastal deserts in southwest Africa, South America and Baja California, Mexico.

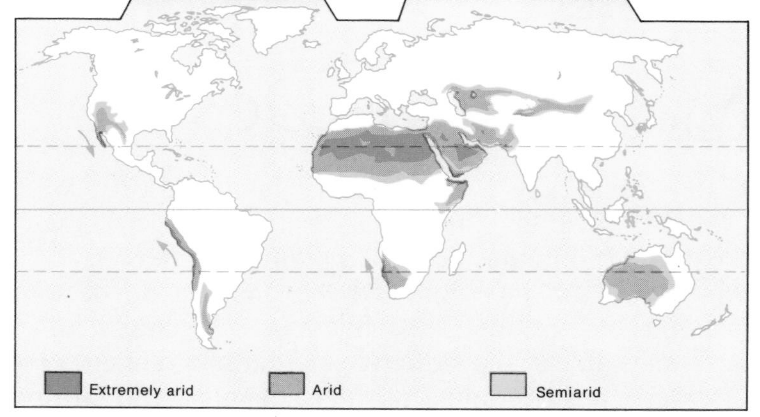

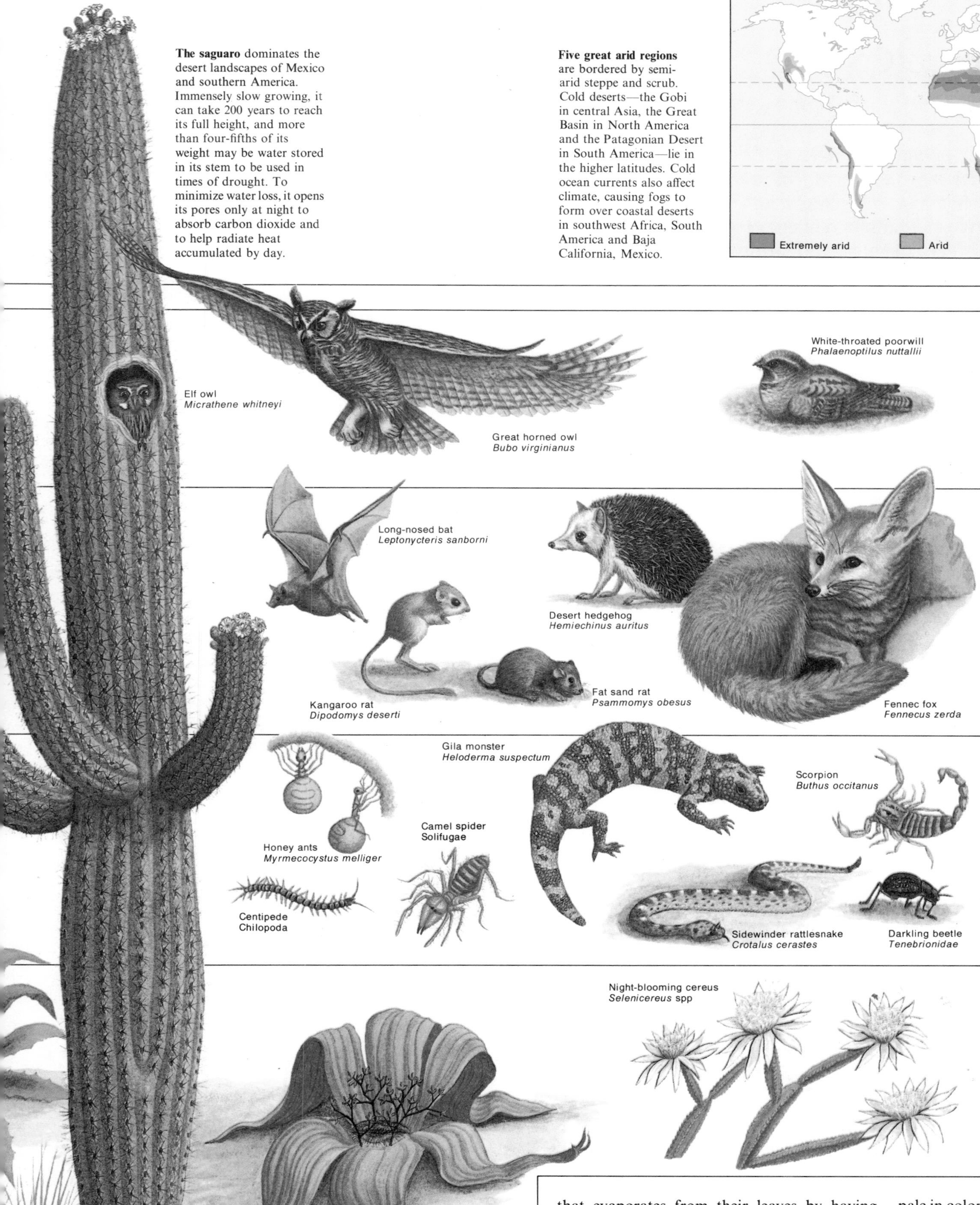

DESERTS BY NIGHT

Elf owl
Micrathene whitneyi

Great horned owl
Bubo virginianus

White-throated poorwill
Phalaenoptilus nuttallii

Owls and nightjars hunt under cover of darkness. Elf owls shelter by day, emerging at dusk to catch insects, and great horned owls often come into the desert at night to hunt. The poorwill, a small desert nightjar, is known to American Indians as "the sleeper." An insect eater, it sometimes survives the rigors of winter, when food is scarce, by hibernating.

Long-nosed bat
Leptonycteris sanborni

Kangaroo rat
Dipodomys deserti

Desert hedgehog
Hemiechinus auritus

Fat sand rat
Psammomys obesus

Fennec fox
Fennecus zerda

Most small animals are active at night. Nectar-eating bats visit plants that blossom at night, pollinating the flowers while they feed. American kangaroo rats obtain water from a dry diet of seeds and conserve moisture by producing very concentrated urine. The sand rat of North Africa feeds on salty succulents and excretes great quantities of extremely salty urine. Hedgehogs are mainly insect eaters; the long ears of desert species help to disperse body heat. The Saharan fennec, the smallest type of desert fox, hunts lizards, rodents and locusts.

Honey ants
Myrmecocystus melliger

Centipede
Chilopoda

Camel spider
Solifugae

Gila monster
Heloderma suspectum

Scorpion
Buthus occitanus

Sidewinder rattlesnake
Crotalus cerastes

Darkling beetle
Tenebrionidae

Among insects and other invertebrates the hunt for food intensifies at night. Honey ants gather nectar; centipedes and camel spiders hunt insects. The gila monster, a poisonous American lizard, eats centipedes, eggs and sometimes other lizards, and uses its tail to store fat. The sidewinder, a small rattlesnake, is active mainly at night, leaving its distinctive parallel tracks in the sand. Scorpions emerge from their burrows to stalk insects and spiders, and darkling beetles feed on dry, decomposing vegetation.

Night-blooming cereus
Selenicereus spp

Welwitschia
Welwitschia mirabilis

Saguaro cactus
Cereus giganteus

Some desert plants are nocturnal, in the sense that they bloom only at night or make use of the dew that forms when the temperature falls. The welwitschia, unique to the Namib Desert in southwest Africa, has broad, sprawling leaves on which moisture condenses at night. The night-blooming cereus of the American deserts flowers for a single night in summer. Like other nocturnal plants, its flowers are luminously pale and strongly scented to attract pollinating night insects.

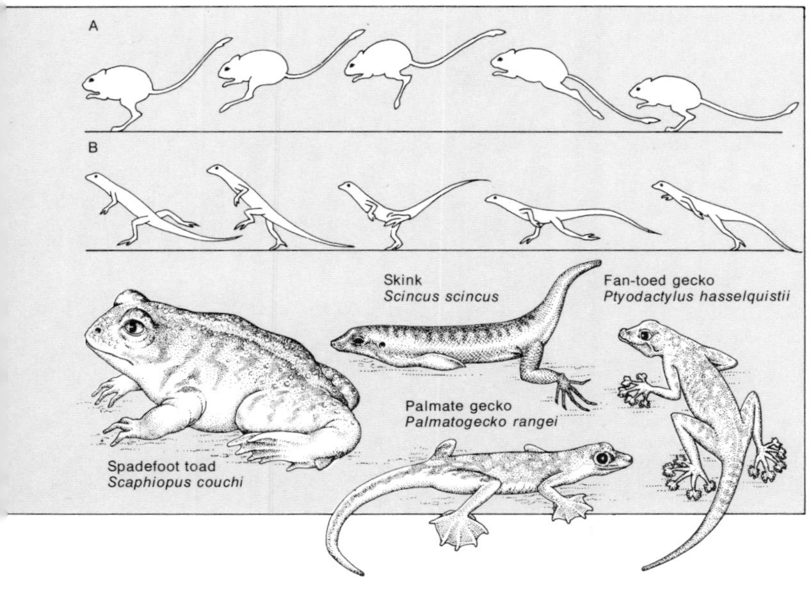

that evaporates from their leaves by having small leaves, or by shedding them in the dry season. Some produce a protective covering of hairs or a coating of wax to prevent loss of moisture and to help to withstand heat.

Succulent plants, such as cacti and euphorbias, store water in their thick stems. Their leaves are usually reduced to spines, and their round or cylindrical shape also helps to reduce water loss. Spines have the added advantage in the desert of discouraging foraging animals.

The drought-resisting phreatophytes—date palms, mesquite and cottonwood trees, for example—have a similar variety of adaptations to dry conditions, but their most typical feature is a long tap root that draws water from great depths. Many plants can also tolerate the presence of salt in the soil. These are the halophytes ("salt plants") such as saltbush and other small shrubs that grow in and around salt pans.

The struggle to survive

Animals, too, need to obtain and conserve water at all costs and to be able to adjust to extremes of temperature. Most are small enough to shelter under stones or in burrows during the intense heat of day; others survive adverse conditions by becoming dormant or by migrating. For most desert creatures it is also an advantage to be inconspicuous, and many are pale in color so that they are hard to see against their light background of sand or stones.

Many animals, especially those that are active by day, show adaptations that are strikingly similar to those of desert plants. Frogs and toads are activated by rain, emerging from dormancy to feed and mate in temporary pools and then quickly burying themselves until the next rain falls. Mammals have hairy coats that reduce water loss and also help to keep their body temperature at a tolerable level. Most desert insects have a waxy coating that serves much the same purpose.

Some geckos and other lizards store food, in the form of fat, in their tails, and camels store fat in their humped backs to sustain them when food is scarce. Honey ants force-feed nectar to some members of the colony, creating living "honey pots" for the rest of the community to feed from in times of drought. Many creatures are able to survive on the moisture contained in their food, and rarely need to drink. Most desert dwellers also have extremely efficient kidneys that produce very concentrated urine, so that little or no moisture is lost in the process.

Man enjoys no such advantages. Nevertheless, he still seeks to live in deserts, as he has for thousands of years, and the pressures he exerts on the environment may well have irrevocably changed much of the world's desert landscapes.

A

B

Skink
Scincus scincus

Fan-toed gecko
Ptyodactylus hasselquistii

Palmate gecko
Palmatogecko rangei

Spadefoot toad
Scaphiopus couchi

Man and the Deserts

Water is the key to man's survival in deserts: where water has been available, great civilizations have flourished, and man's dream of making the desert bloom has become a reality. More recently, discoveries of great mineral wealth have spurred the opening up of some of Earth's most inhospitable regions. But while man's ingenuity has made many deserts both habitable and productive, the human tendency to increase the extent of deserts has become a problem of international proportions.

Given water, much is possible, and not surprisingly man has tended to settle where water is most readily available: along the courses of rivers (such as the Nile) that rise outside the desert, and around oases fed by springs or by wells that tap groundwater supplies. But desert rainfall is so unreliable that often runoff and spring flow are uncertain in quantity and timing. Much groundwater is either also unreliable or it is fossil water that has accumulated in the geological past and is not being replenished by today's rainfall. Thus in areas such as southern Libya and some of the oasis settlements of the Arabian Gulf, and in America's arid west, groundwater is a nonrenewable resource that is being rapidly depleted.

Making water go farther

Man has also used great ingenuity to secure water supplies and to transport them to where they are needed. Runoff from flash floods that follow rare desert storms may be collected in channels and distributed to crops in nearby fields, and terracing slopes to trap runoff is a traditional way of obtaining the maximum benefit from limited rainfall. Reservoirs, ranging from the small night tanks of the southern Atacama desert in Chile to the massive artificial lakes along the Colorado river in the United States, store seasonally or perennially unreliable runoff. Also, surface runoff may be increased by reducing the permeability of runoff surfaces, a solution engineered by the Nabataeans in the Negev desert more than 2,000 years ago and being reemployed by the Israelis today.

The transport of water is a fundamental desert activity. Open canals are typical, usually carrying water to irrigated fields—a practice used throughout the fertile crescent of Mesopotamia more than 8,000 years ago and still widespread today. A striking alternative are the ancient qanats, which limit the evaporation of water while it is in transit. Qanats are still found in the Middle East, although today pipelines are increasingly used.

Ultimately the conversion of salt water to fresh water may ensure plentiful supplies for many desert regions. The process is expensive, but large-scale desalination has already become a reality in some affluent communities such as oil-rich Saudi Arabia and Kuwait. Increasing emphasis is also being placed on more efficient use of existing freshwater supplies: in Egypt and Israel, waste water from towns is being purified and recycled for use in agriculture.

Cultivating the desert

The successful control of water has enabled large areas of otherwise arid and semiarid land to be made productive. The Egyptian civilization along the Nile depended, and still depends, on the management of seasonal floodwaters. In North America, the large-scale, long-distance piping of water has made central

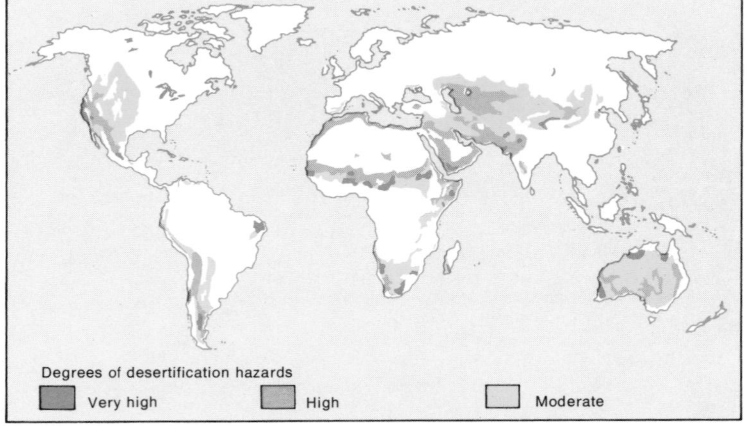

Desertification—the advance of desert areas across the Earth—now affects more than 30 million sq km (12 million sq miles) and deserts are continuing to expand at an alarming rate. In recent years, on the southern edge of the Sahara alone, as much as 650,000 sq km (250,900 sq miles) of land that was once productive have been lost, and in places there is little left to show where the Sahara ends and the Sahel–Sudan region begins. Intense and often inappropriate human pressures are major causes, frequently aggravated by drought: overcultivating vulnerable land, chopping down trees for fuelwood and grazing too many livestock, especially on the margins of arid lands.

THE SHIFTING SANDS

Recent decades have seen unprecedented changes in the world's deserts. Increasing pressure on the environment, especially from pastoralists and farmers, has caused extensive damage and a rapid expansion of barren land. In many desert regions, nomadism has long been the only way in which man could survive, except in oases. Today, even these traditional ways of life are changing as the exploitation of oil and other mineral resources, and the introduction of new agricultural techniques, are drawing many of the deserts into a spectacular new age of development.

The traditional pastoral response to limited water supplies and forage in desert regions is nomadic livestock herding, still practiced by the Tuareg of the northern Sahara (right) and by tribal groupings in Mongolia (left). The nomadic way of life has, however, become severely restricted in recent years. Long-distance migrations are often incompatible with the requirements of the modern state, and the poor rewards no longer match the incentives to settle in towns and cities.

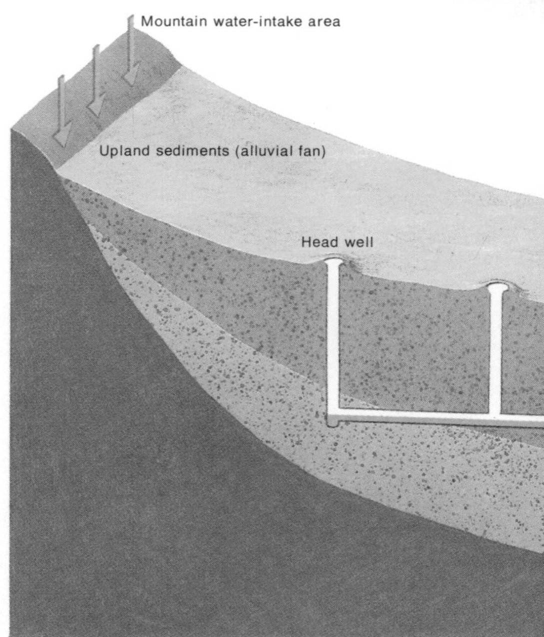

Oases have provided welcome refuges in deserts since ancient times. Secure water supplies from wells or springs make settled life possible in the midst of the most arid landscapes. Many oases are intensively cultivated with three tiers of vegetation: tall date palms shade orchards of citrus fruits, apricots, peaches, pomegranates and figs, and both palms and orchard trees shade the ground crops of vegetables and cereals. Irrigation channels distribute water to the desert soils, which are frequently rich in plant foods although they lack humus. Windbreaks help to protect cultivated land from erosion and from migrating dunes, although many oases are losing the battle with encroaching sands and the oasis people are leaving to find work in the oil fields.

California the most productive agricultural region in the world. But while irrigation can bring enormous benefits, it can also create problems. Too much water causes waterlogging of the land, and where water evaporates in the dry desert air, concentrations of dissolved salts build up in the soil.

Farming without irrigation is possible only where rainfall, although meager, is sufficient to sustain crops with a short growing season. Soil moisture is conserved by using dry surface mulches, by fallowing and crop rotation, by planting seeds sparsely and by controlling weeds. Geneticists are also producing new varieties of cereal crops that can survive for weeks without water. Dry farming, however, is precarious. Especially at times of drought it can cause serious problems of soil erosion, chiefly by the action of wind.

Man the desert maker

The extension of dry farming into unsuitable regions, and waterlogging and the accumulation of salts in irrigated areas, are major causes of desertification—the spread of deserts into formerly habitable land. Other major causes are the overgrazing of livestock on land with too little forage and the removal of trees and shrubs for firewood by communities that have no alternative fuel supply. A sequence of drier than normal years does the rest.

Many scientists believe that desertification can be reversed, provided the pressures on the land are reduced sufficiently to allow vegetation to recover. But desertification affects such huge areas, often crossing national frontiers, that broad-scale, international cooperation is needed to coordinate reductions in population and livestock pressures and to improve understanding of drought.

In some countries the battle against desertification has already begun. In China, extensive planting of drought-tolerant trees has created windbreaks to control sand movement and to protect farmland. In Algeria, a broad belt of trees has been planted to keep the Sahara at bay, and in Iran, advancing dunes have been halted by spraying them with petroleum residue: when the spray dries it forms a mulch that retains moisture and allows vegetation to grow, and much desert land has been reclaimed.

The deserts' riches

The exploitation of resources has also led to an "opening up" of many deserts. The rushes for precious metals in Arizona, Australia and South Africa started man's development of these regions in the nineteenth century. Some minerals, such as the evaporite deposits of Searles Basin in California and the nitrates of the Atacama desert in Chile, are actually products of the arid environment.

A resource that deserts also possess in abundance is solar power, and in many hot, dry regions the heat of the sun is used to evaporate mineral-rich solutions of salts, as well as being harnessed as a source of energy. Sunshine and the dry, clear air are also drawing ever-increasing numbers of tourists to the "sun cities" of the western United States and to Saharan oases, which were, until recently, only remote desert outposts.

No resource, however, has created as much attention or wealth as has oil. Oil has transformed the fortunes of several desert nations and provided an economic boom that has led to rapid industrialization and spectacular urban growth. The benefits of such growth in terms of affluence are substantial. The problems—the weakening of traditional desert societies, the submerging of traditional cities in the concrete labyrinths of modern complexes, and the precariousness of prosperity that is based on finite resources—are also clear.

Mineral wealth provides a powerful incentive for man's development of arid lands, and today the flow of oil rather than water is often a measure of a desert nation's prosperity. In some of the world's most desolate regions, flares signal the presence of modern "oases" where fossil fuels are being extracted—products, like the fossil waters that are sometimes trapped in the same sedimentary rocks, of the desert's geological past. Uranium, another mineral "fuel," also often lies beneath desert sands. Arid environments may also provide a rich harvest of other minerals: potash, phosphates and nitrates, valuable sources of commercial fertilizers; gypsum, manganese and salt; and borax, source of the element boron, used in nuclear reactors.

A "plastic" revolution has helped transform much of Israel's desert hinterland into productive farmland. Plastic cloches, plastic mulches and greenhouses trap moisture and reduce evaporation, and water trickled through thin plastic tubes irrigates the plants' roots with a minimum of wastage. Such innovative agricultural techniques enable Israel to produce most of its own food requirements, and fruit and vegetables grown in the relatively mild desert winters are also exported to Europe, where they command high prices.

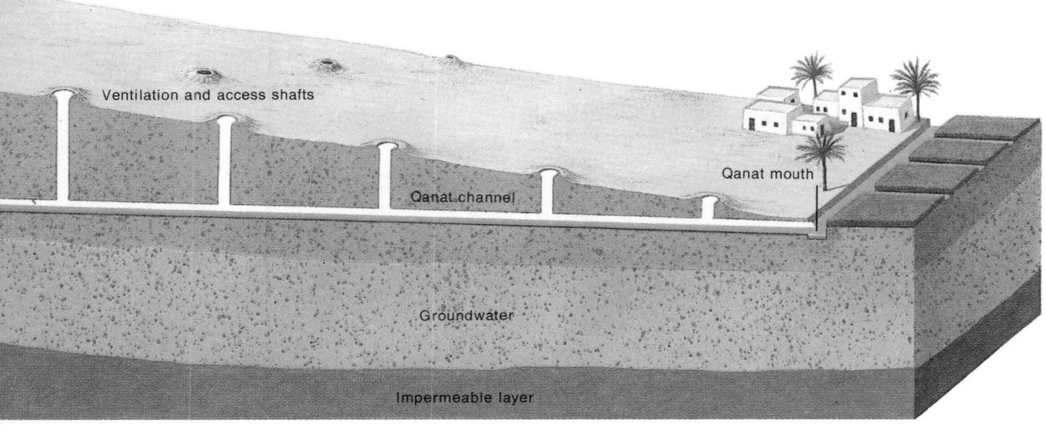

One of the most ingenious ways man has devised of bringing water to desert regions is by the ancient underground system known as the qanat. Invented by the Persians in the first millennium BC, qanats tap groundwater in upland sediments and carry it by gravity to the surface on lower land. The head well is dug first, sometimes to a depth of 100 m (330 ft), until water is reached. A line of shafts is then sunk to provide ventilation and to give access to the channel being tunneled below. Work begins at the mouth end, and a typical channel is 10–20 km (6–12 miles) long when completed, depending on the depth of the head well and the slope of the land. Its slight gradient ensures that water flows freely but gently down to ground level. Surface canals then divert the water to where it is needed. Thousands of such qanats are still in use, their routes marked by mounds of excavated debris.

Many desert plants have a bright future when they are grown on a commercial scale. Oil from the bean-like seeds of the jojoba plant, native to America's arid southwest, is remarkably similar to oil from sperm whales and has a multitude of uses, particularly as a high-grade industrial lubricant. Other promising plants are the latex-yielding guayule shrub of American and Mexican deserts, and a variety of dandelion from central Asia, both of which are being cultivated as a source of rubber.

Savannas

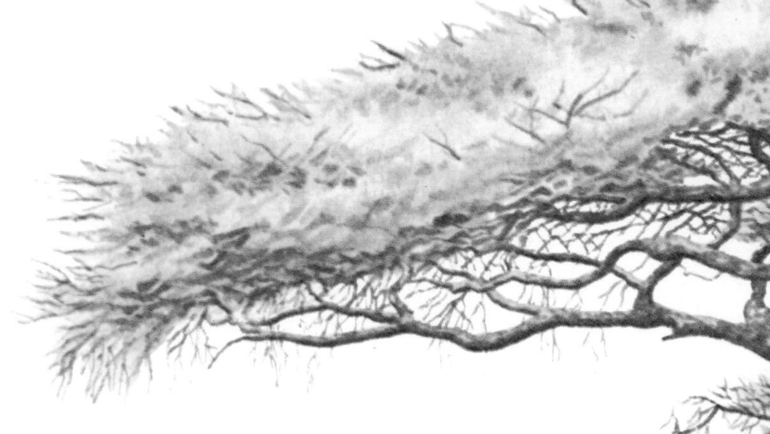

Between the tropical rainforest and desert regions lie large stretches of savanna, which are characterized by seasonal rainfall and long periods of drought. Those nearest to the forests usually take the form of open woodland, whereas those nearest to the deserts consist of widely scattered thorn scrub or tufts of grass. Unlike temperate grasslands, where the summers are hot but the winters are cold, savanna regions are always warm and in the wet season rain falls in heavy tropical downpours.

The most extensive areas of savanna are in Africa, north and south of the rainforest, and in South America, where the two main regions are the *llanos* of Venezuela, north of the Amazon rainforest, and the *campos* of Brazil in the south. Smaller areas of savanna also occur in Australia, India and southeastern Asia.

Savannas range from thickly wooded grasslands to almost treeless plains. Some are the result of man's destruction of the forest, and most are maintained in their present state by the high incidence of fire, both natural and man-made. The grasses tend to be taller and coarser than their temperate counterparts and they grow in tufts rather than as a uniform ground cover. In areas of high rainfall some grasses grow up to 4.5 m (15 ft) tall. Trees and bushes are usually widely spaced so that they do not compete with each other for water in the dry season. Humid, or moist, savannas experience 3 to 5 dry months a year, dry savannas 6 to 7 months, and thornbush savannas 8 to 10 months. Rainfall also varies widely, from more than 1,200 mm (47 in) a year in humid savannas to as little as 200 mm (8 in) where the savanna merges into desert.

Types of savannas

Humid woodland savanna presents an abrupt contrast to the rainforest. Trees tend to be scattered and some are so low growing that they are dwarfed by the tall grass that springs up during the summer rains. In the dry season the grass fuels fierce fires, which destroy all except thick-barked, large-leaved deciduous trees. Consequently, the proportion of fire-resistant trees and shrubs is large, and the grass quickly regenerates with the coming of the next rains.

In Africa this type of savanna is known as Guinea savanna north of the rainforest and as miombo savanna south of the rainforest. In South America it is known as *campo cerrado*, from the Portuguese words meaning field (*campo*) and dense. (*Campos sujos* are *campos* in which stretches of open grassland predominate and *campos limpos* are grasslands from which trees are entirely absent.) The *llanos*, or plains, of northern South America are grasslands interspersed with forests and swamps.

North of the Guinea savanna in Africa lies a belt known as Sudan savanna. The annual rainfall is in the range 500 to 1,000 mm (20–40 in) and the dry season lasts from October to April. This is typical dry savanna. Tall grasses between 1 and 1.5 m (3–5 ft) form an almost continuous ground cover and acacias and other thorny trees dot the landscape, together with branching dôm palms and massive water-storing baobab trees. Because of the interrupted tree cover the old name given to many savannas of this type was orchard steppe, and this description gives a good idea of the countryside. Like the humid woodland savannas it is maintained by regular burning of the grass in the dry season, and there is a delicate balance and interaction between climate, soil, vegetation, animals and fire. On the desert margins the grasses grow in short tufts and the scattered acacias are seldom more than 3 m (10 ft) tall. The scrub and grasses are too widely dispersed for fires to spread, and this type of savanna is modified not by fire but by aridity and blistering heat.

Thorn-scrub and thorn-forest savannas frequently form transitional zones between tropical forests and grasslands. The *caatinga*, or "light forest," of northeastern Brazil is a typical thorn-forest savanna. Long, hot, dry seasons alternate with erratic downpours of rain, and the rate of evaporation is high. Drought-resisting trees and thorny shrubs mix with bromeliads, cacti and palm trees.

Abundance of life

No other environment supports animals so spectacular in size and so immense in numbers as do the African savannas. In spite of the concentration of animal life, however, competition for food is not severe. Each species has its own preferences and feeds from different levels of the vegetation. Giraffes and elephants can easily reach the upper branches of trees, antelopes feed on bushes at different heights from the ground, zebras and impalas eat the grasses and warthogs root for the underground parts of plants. With the onset of the dry season, massed herds assemble for the great migrations that are a major part of savanna life, moving to areas where rain has recently fallen and new grass is plentiful.

Following the grazing animals are the large predators: the lions, leopards and cheetahs. Wild dogs hunt in packs, and the scavengers—jackals, hyenas and vultures—move in to dispose of the remains of the kill.

The savannas of South America and Australia are much poorer in animal species. The only mammal of any size on the South American savanna is the elusive, nocturnal maned wolf, which eats almost anything from small animals to wild fruit. On the Australian savanna the largest inhabitant is the kangaroo, and the prime predator—apart from man—is the dingo, or native dog.

Many of the resident savanna birds are ground-living species such as the ostrich in Africa and its counterparts, the rhea in South America and the emu in Australia. The warm African climate attracts large numbers of visiting birds, which migrate each year across the Sahara to escape from the severe winter of the northern hemisphere.

For many thousands of years man has lived in harmony with the savanna. Within the last century, however, and in recent decades in particular, the savanna has come under increasing pressure. Inevitably, there is competition between the needs of the environment and those of the human population, and the future of the savanna is very much in the balance.

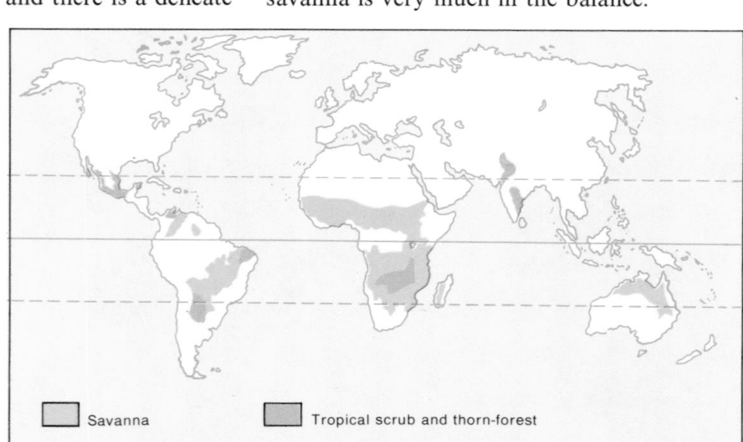

On each side of the Equator are broad tracts of tropical grassland known as savannas. In these regions there are distinct wet and dry seasons and temperatures are high all the year round, seldom falling below 21°C (70°F). Rain falls mainly in the hottest months, whereas the cooler months are generally dry. Thorn-scrub and thorn-forest savannas occur where the rainfall is more erratic; they have relatively little grass cover, and trees and bushes can tolerate long periods of drought.

THE AFRICAN SAVANNA

More than a third of Africa is savanna, the vast parklike plains and gently rolling foothills providing the setting for a supreme wildlife spectacle. Vegetation is the basis of the immense wealth of animal life. It supports the large herds of grazing animals, and they return nutrients to the grassland in their droppings. The plant eaters, in turn, provide food for the hunters and for the scavengers that play an indispensable role by keeping the savanna free from carrion. Most of the plant-eating animals are agile and swift-footed, which enables them to escape from their enemies, and live in herds, which also provides some protection in the open habitat. Many of the animals, both predators and prey, are camouflaged: stripes or spots, at a distance, help to break up their outline; dappled markings merge with the pattern of sunlight and shade in the undergrowth; and tawny colors make them difficult to see against a background of dry grass.

THE PLANT EATERS
Most plant eaters have adapted to feeding at a particular level of the vegetation. Giraffes browse on acacia tips that other animals cannot reach and elephants use their trunks to tear down succulent branches and leaves, although both feed on low-growing vegetation when it is easily available. Elephants will also uproot trees to gather leaves that are otherwise out of reach. The black rhinoceros plucks low-growing twigs and leaves by grasping them with its upper lip (the white rhinoceros has a broad, square mouth for grazing on grass). Eland often use their horns to collect twigs by twisting and breaking them. Zebra, wildebeest, topi and gazelle all graze on the same grasses, but at different stages of the plants' growth.

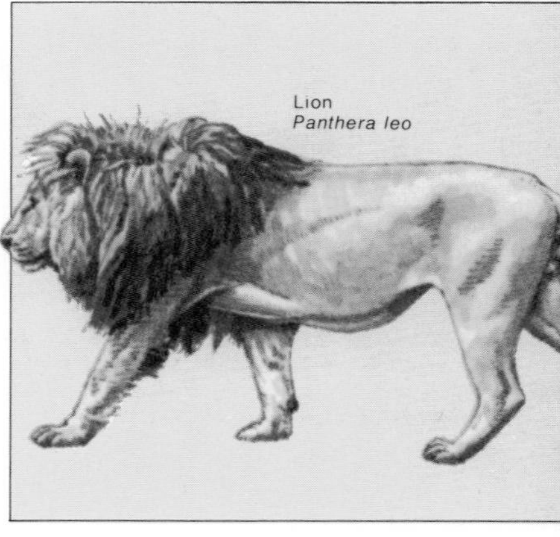

HUNTERS OF THE PLAINS
The plant eaters provide rich hunting for the carnivores. Lions kill the largest prey and hunt in family groups; the lioness usually makes the kill but the male is the first to eat. The leopard is a solitary hunter. It lies in ambush or stalks its prey, mainly at night, in brush country where it has ground cover. Cheetahs are the swiftest of all the hunters. They usually hunt in pairs in open grassland, stalking their prey and then charging in a lightning-fast sprint. Hunting dogs travel in well-organized packs. They exhaust their quarry by chasing it to a standstill and attacking as a team. Whereas lions, leopards and cheetahs usually kill by leaping for the neck or throat, packs of hunting dogs characteristically attack from the rear.

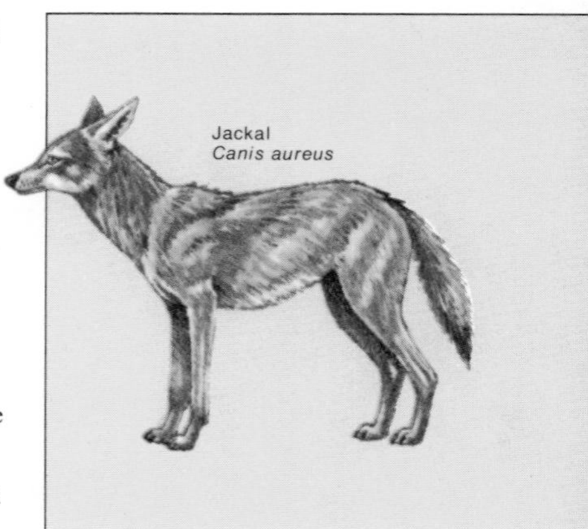

THE SCAVENGERS
When the hunters have eaten, the scavengers move in. Jackals, small and quick, make darting runs to snatch titbits while packs of hyenas use their powerful bone-crushing jaws to demolish the bulk of the carcass. Hyenas are the most voracious of the carnivores, often driving the primary predator from its kill. Vultures are frequently the first to see a kill as they circle high in the sky, but must await their turn to feed on the skin and scraps because their descent attracts the more aggressive scavengers. Carrion beetles, carrion flies and the larvae of the horn-boring moth dispose of what is left. Most of the large scavengers, particularly the hyenas, also do their own hunting, singling out prey that is small, weak or sickly.

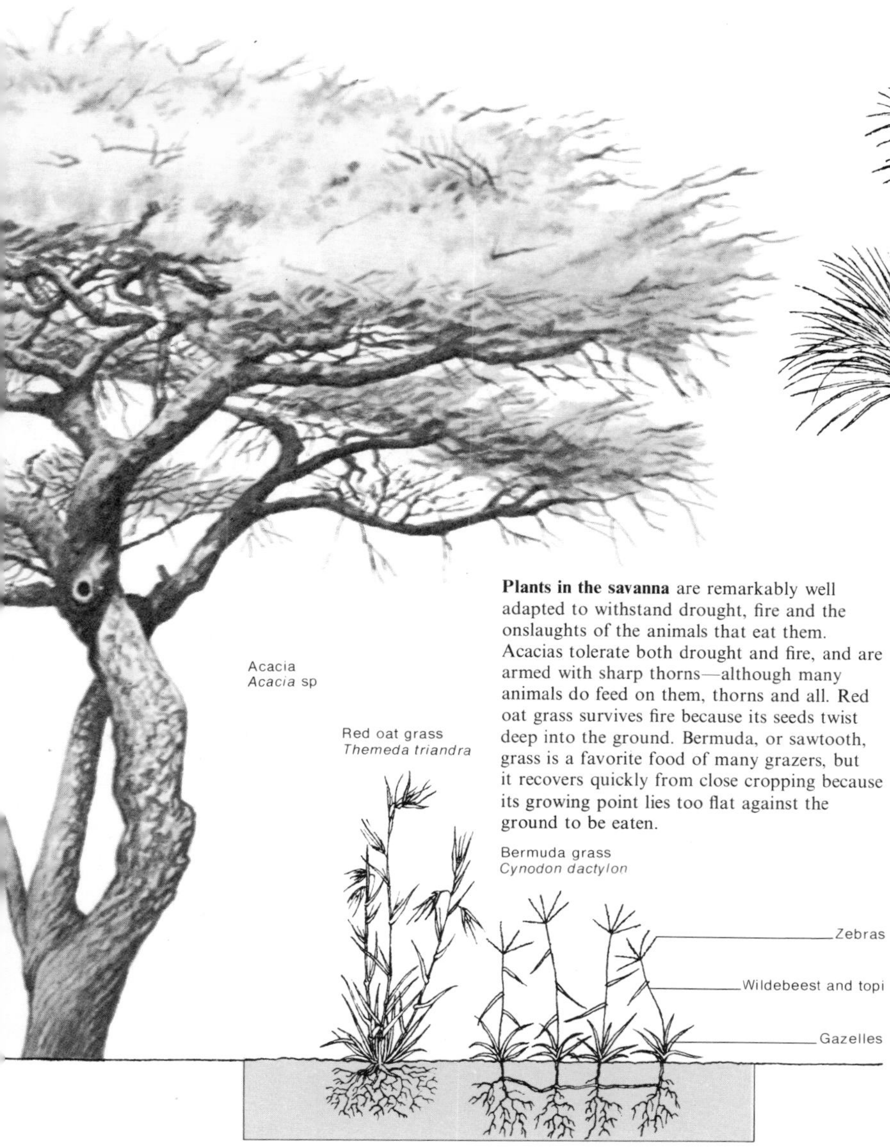

Acacia
Acacia sp
Red oat grass
Themeda triandra
Bermuda grass
Cynodon dactylon
Zebras
Wildebeest and topi
Gazelles

Plants in the savanna are remarkably well adapted to withstand drought, fire and the onslaughts of the animals that eat them. Acacias tolerate both drought and fire, and are armed with sharp thorns—although many animals do feed on them, thorns and all. Red oat grass survives fire because its seeds twist deep into the ground. Bermuda, or sawtooth, grass is a favorite food of many grazers, but it recovers quickly from close cropping because its growing point lies too flat against the ground to be eaten.

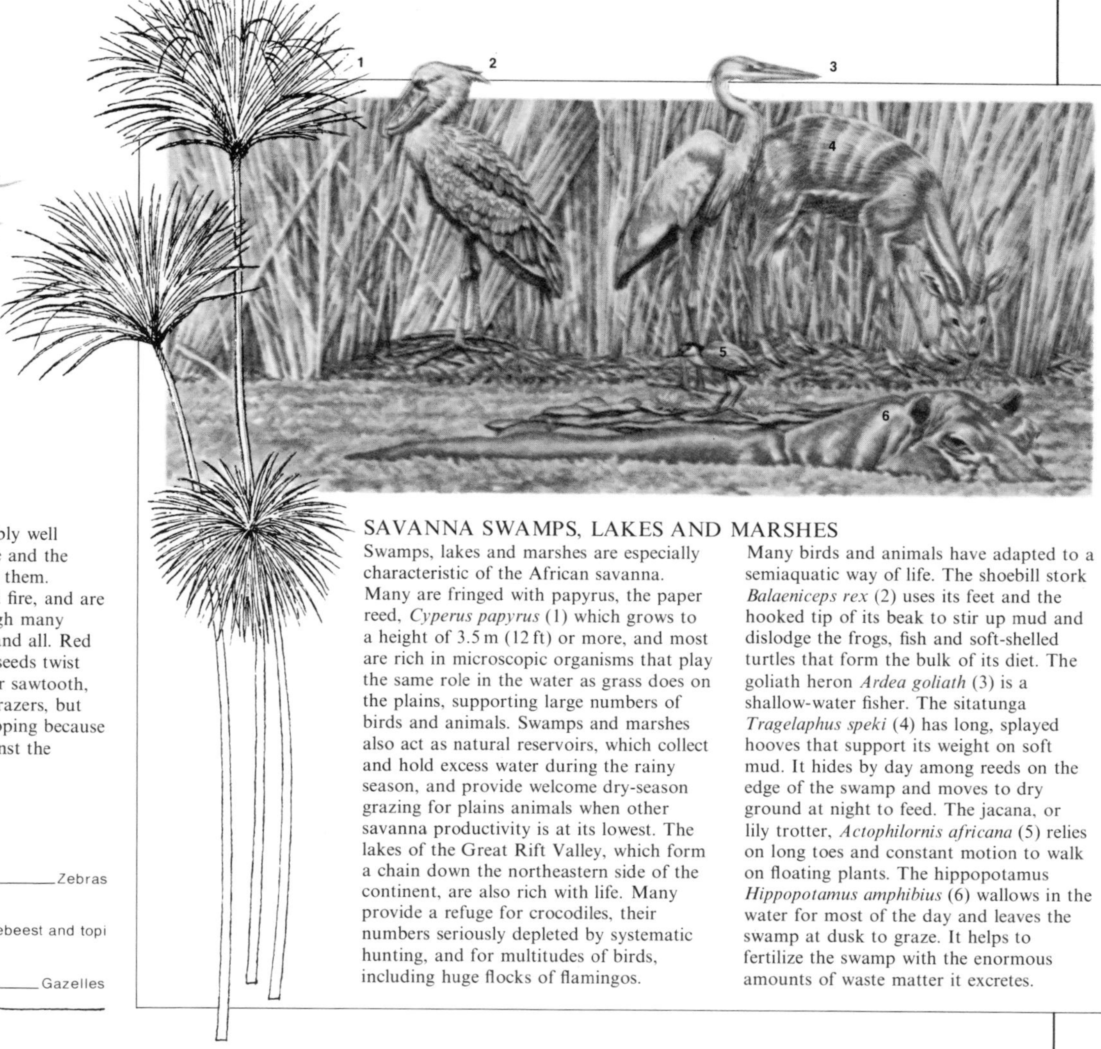

1
2
3
4
5
6

SAVANNA SWAMPS, LAKES AND MARSHES

Swamps, lakes and marshes are especially characteristic of the African savanna. Many are fringed with papyrus, the paper reed, *Cyperus papyrus* (1) which grows to a height of 3.5 m (12 ft) or more, and most are rich in microscopic organisms that play the same role in the water as grass does on the plains, supporting large numbers of birds and animals. Swamps and marshes also act as natural reservoirs, which collect and hold excess water during the rainy season, and provide welcome dry-season grazing for plains animals when other savanna productivity is at its lowest. The lakes of the Great Rift Valley, which form a chain down the northeastern side of the continent, are also rich with life. Many provide a refuge for crocodiles, their numbers seriously depleted by systematic hunting, and for multitudes of birds, including huge flocks of flamingos.

Many birds and animals have adapted to a semiaquatic way of life. The shoebill stork *Balaeniceps rex* (2) uses its feet and the hooked tip of its beak to stir up mud and dislodge the frogs, fish and soft-shelled turtles that form the bulk of its diet. The goliath heron *Ardea goliath* (3) is a shallow-water fisher. The sitatunga *Tragelaphus speki* (4) has long, splayed hooves that support its weight on soft mud. It hides by day among reeds on the edge of the swamp and moves to dry ground at night to feed. The jacana, or lily trotter, *Actophilornis africana* (5) relies on long toes and constant motion to walk on floating plants. The hippopotamus *Hippopotamus amphibius* (6) wallows in the water for most of the day and leaves the swamp at dusk to graze. It helps to fertilize the swamp with the enormous amounts of waste matter it excretes.

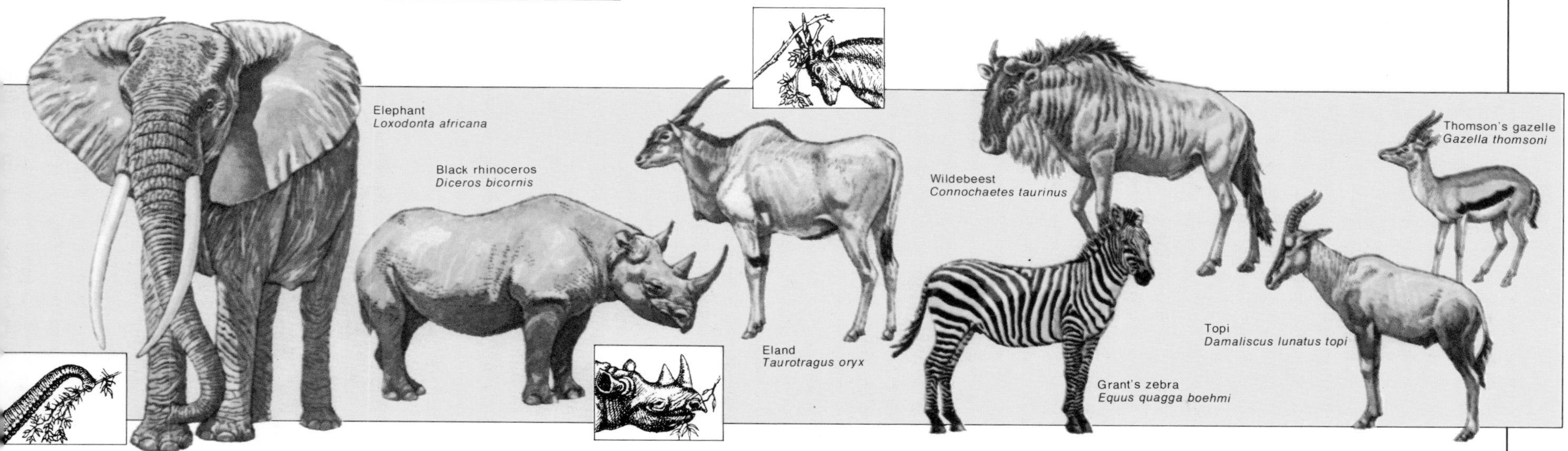

Elephant
Loxodonta africana
Black rhinoceros
Diceros bicornis
Eland
Taurotragus oryx
Wildebeest
Connochaetes taurinus
Grant's zebra
Equus quagga boehmi
Topi
Damaliscus lunatus topi
Thomson's gazelle
Gazella thomsoni

Cheetah
Acinonyx jubatus
Leopard
Panthera pardus
Cape hunting dog
Lycaon pictus

White-backed vulture
Pseudogyps africanus
Carrion beetle
Carrion fly
Spotted hyena
Crocuta crocuta
Horn-boring
moth larva

Ostrich
Struthio camelus
Secretary bird
Sagittarius serpentarius

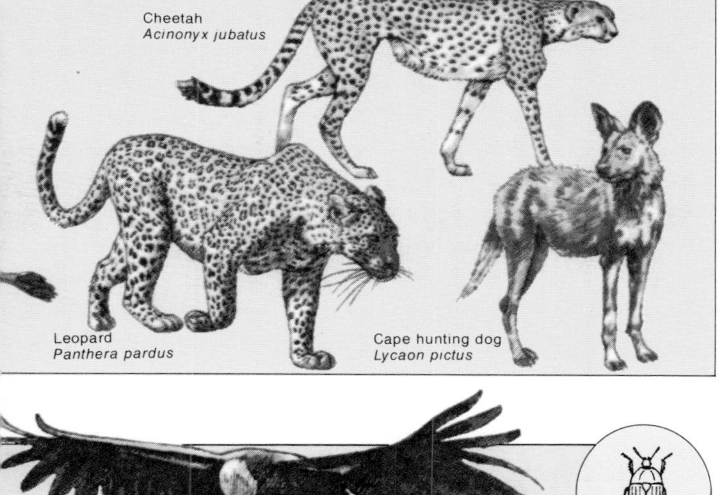

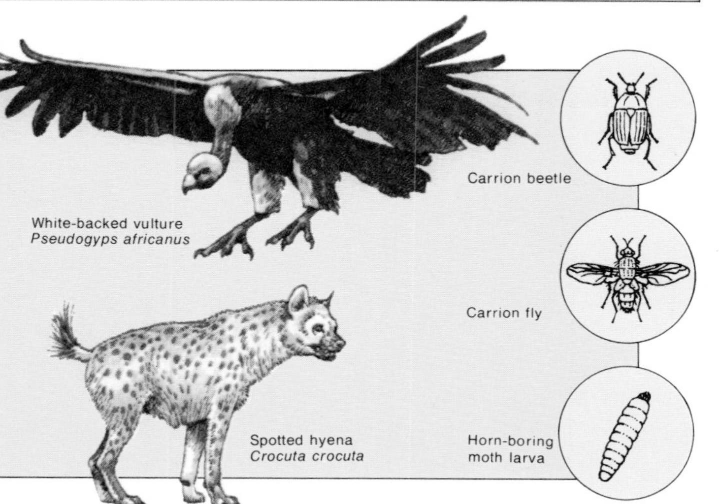

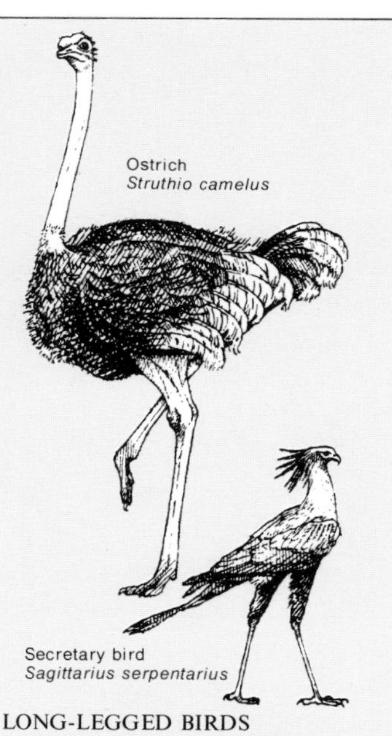

LONG-LEGGED BIRDS

The ostrich, up to 2.4 m (8 ft) tall, can see for great distances across the plains and can outrun most of its enemies. Its territory is often shared with grazing animals, such as wildebeest, which take advantage of the ostrich's keen sight to alert them to danger. The secretary bird (so-called because of its quill-like crest) strides through the grass hunting small mammals, insects and snakes; it kills snakes by battering them with its powerful, long-clawed feet.

Large termite mounds are a distinctive feature of many savanna landscapes. The mounds, or termitaria, are made of soil excavated by the termites and bound with their saliva. Thick walls help to keep the interior at a constant temperature, and some species of termite cultivate fungus "gardens" as a source of food. The royal chamber deep inside the mound is occupied by the colony's queen, grossly distended with eggs, and her consort. Predators include the aardwolf and the aardvark. The aardwolf is related to the hyena but is smaller and has weak jaws; it digs the termites out of their mound and scoops them up with its long sticky tongue. The aardvark, distantly related to the elephant, uses its powerful hoof-like claws to break into termite nests.

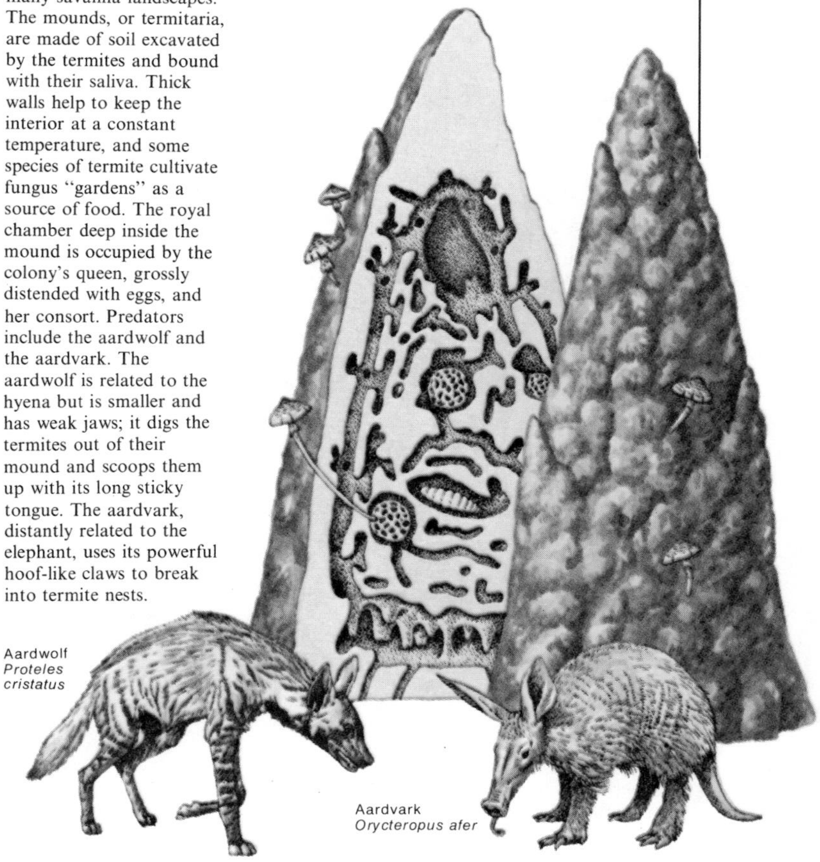

Aardwolf
Proteles cristatus
Aardvark
Orycteropus afer

Man and the Savannas

In their natural state, savannas are among the most strikingly productive of all Earth's regions. Before the coming of man they supported a wealth of animal life that has seldom been surpassed. As yet they are relatively undeveloped, but many of them lie in areas where the pressures of population growth are becoming increasingly acute. Wisely used, they offer great hope for the future, both as cattle lands and for the cultivation of food crops. But without proper management savannas can rapidly turn into wasteland, and man will be the poorer for the loss of such a great natural resource.

Throughout much of the savannas the climate is semiarid and the soils tend to be poor: stripped of their plant cover, they bake hard and crack during the long months of hot sunshine, and during the wet season they often become waterlogged or are washed away by the rains. Man's indiscriminate use of fire, unwise agricultural methods and the unrestricted grazing of domestic animals have already led to much soil loss, and erosion is widespread in tropical Africa, Asia, South America and Australia.

Systematic burning has long been practiced by the people of the savannas. Large areas are burned each year to clear land for agriculture or to remove dead grass and encourage a fresh growth to feed livestock. The resulting ash provides much-needed nutrients for crops, and the grasses rapidly produce new green shoots that provide a rich pasture for domestic herds. But although the short-term effects may be beneficial, repeated burning is harmful to the vegetation, the animals and the soil.

Trees are always more or less damaged by fire. Their trunks become twisted and gnarled, fresh shoots are killed and young trees are prevented from growing. Constant burning can destroy some species altogether, and when they disappear so too does the wildlife that depends on them for food and shelter.

Grasses, on the other hand, may be encouraged by burning, and the lush new growth that springs up when the first rains break the long dry season provides welcome nourishment for domestic herds and game animals alike. But whereas game animals move freely over the range, cropping grasses at various stages of growth, cattle tend to feed on grass only in the neighborhood of wells and other sources of drinking water. They may trample the soil and continue to graze the same area until the grass is completely suppressed.

The hazards of large projects
Cultivation in marginal areas that are unsuited to intensive agriculture also contributes to the impoverishment of the savanna. The Sahel and Sudan savannas on the fringes of the Sahara are particularly vulnerable to large-scale development projects that fail to take account of local climate and soil. Mechanized agriculture in fragile areas bordering the desert may well lead to soil erosion and dustbowl conditions, and large-scale irrigation schemes often result in waterlogging and an accumulation of salts in the soil. Cultivation in the savannas requires understanding and care. Many smaller schemes are safer—and usually more productive—than a few large ones, but not all planners yet realize that agricultural methods that are effective in temperate regions seldom come up to expectations in tropical climates.

Man first inhabited the savannas, as he did many other regions of the world, as a hunter and gatherer. He took from the land only what he needed from day to day, and although he used fire as a hunting tool, his impact was little more than that of any other savanna inhabitant. In East Africa, groups of nomadic Hadza (left) still hunt game and collect roots, fruit and the honey of wild bees, building grass huts as temporary shelters.

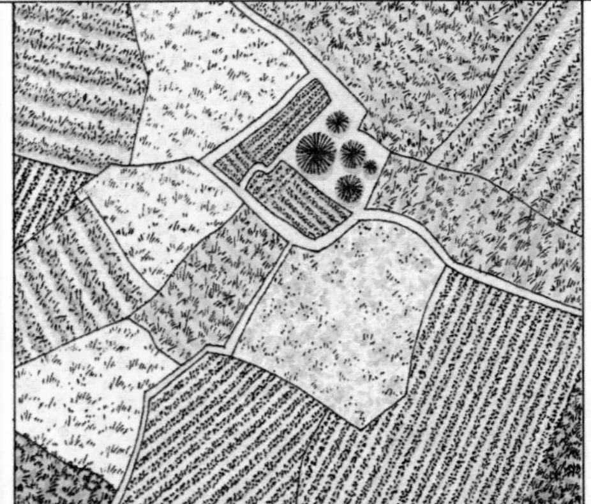

Small farms are scattered over much of the savannas. Plots close to houses are farmed continuously; beyond them lie the main fields, where periods of cultivation are usually followed by periods of fallow. Maize, millet and peanuts are the main food crops, and early and late crops are sometimes sown on the same plot to extend the growing season. Most of the work is done by hand, and any surplus to a family's needs is sold.

THE VULNERABLE WILDERNESS

Nowhere has man's impact on the tropical grasslands been felt more keenly than in Africa, although much of what is happening in Africa is happening also in savannas elsewhere. The majority of the people still live on the land, where the determining factor is the length and severity of the annual dry season. In the moister savannas the people are primarily cultivators, while in savannas that are too dry to sustain agriculture the main occupation is raising livestock. Most of the savannas are as yet sparsely settled, but competition is inevitably growing between man and wildlife, particularly in Africa, for the remaining tracts of relatively untouched wilderness.

The development of mineral resources and industries has led to an increasing movement of people—mainly young adults—from rural areas to towns and mining centers, attracted by opportunities for work—often at the expense of agriculture, since the heavy work of farming is left to the women, old people and children. Mining enterprises such as those in the Zambian Copper Belt (above), may recruit large labor forces from the surrounding countryside. Mining also dramatically alters the landscape, especially where the bedrock containing the ore reaches the surface and is quarried in huge terraces. The need for electricity to power mining and other industries leads, in turn, to the development of hydroelectric schemes, many of which entail resettling people whose villages are flooded by the creation of large artificial lakes.

Large areas of savanna have been set aside in East and Central Africa, and to a lesser extent in South America and Australia, as national parks and reserves where the landscape is kept intact and animals can be studied in their natural habitats. In Africa, observation platforms are frequently built close to waterholes where animals congregate to drink, and wardens use light aircraft to patrol the vast areas involved. Camel units are also used to patrol near-desert regions where much of the wildlife flourishes. Animals, such as elephants, whose numbers can grow out of control in the protected environment of the reserves are culled by licensed hunters to prevent the vegetation being destroyed. Culling maintains the health of the community as a whole and is also an economic source of meat in many countries where the people are short of protein foods.

Similarly, the introduction of European breeds of cattle into the savannas has not been an unqualified success. Not only are these breeds more susceptible to tropical pests and diseases than are the local varieties, but they are also adversely affected by the hot climate and their productivity is greatly reduced. In Africa and Brazil, native breeds are replacing more recent importations, and their productivity is being enhanced by selective breeding. In Australia, where most of the cattle are of British stock, tropical zebu, or humped cattle, are being introduced into the herds.

In the future, much more of the savanna may be developed as ranch lands, because the temperate grasslands will become less able to support enough animals to satisfy the world demand for meat. The *llanos* of Venezuela, the *campos* of Brazil and the tropical grasslands of Argentina and Australia already carry large herds of beef cattle. Throughout the savannas, however, ranching is still hampered by lack of water, poor natural pasture and remoteness from markets. In Africa, where herding is mainly nomadic, the sinking of wells by government organizations is changing the traditional ways of life, and cattle raising on a commercial scale is likely to become increasingly important. In Africa, too, the conservation and controlled cropping of game animals could become one of the most productive—and constructive—forms of land use.

Game as a resource

The value of game animals as a source of food is considerable. Buffaloes, for example, and kangaroos in Australia, can thrive on natural grasses that will not even maintain the weight of domestic stock, and they show greater gains in weight than African and European cattle on most forms of vegetation, while several species of antelopes can survive on a water ration that is wholly inadequate for cattle.

In recent years attention has been directed toward the economics of controlled cropping of wild game, and of ranching animals such as eland, which can be kept as if they were domesticated stock and can convert poor pasture into excellent meat. Game animals are also more resistant than cattle to the tsetse fly, which infests large areas of Africa and transmits the disease trypanosomiasis (known as nagana in cattle and as sleeping sickness in man).

But for the most part game animals are still considered to be a nuisance by man, and it is perhaps fortunate that by denying much of the savanna to domestic animals—and to man—the tsetse fly has preserved these regions from exploitation at the expense of the game. Many countries have also set aside large tracts of savanna as national parks and game reserves, where the natural environment is preserved and the wildlife can thrive.

Safeguarding the savanna

At a time when the pressure of the expanding human population calls for the development of areas hitherto uninhabited or only sparsely populated, it may seem paradoxical to maintain that the development of national parks and nature reserves is essential to the welfare of mankind. The aim of game conservation, however, is not simply to preserve rare or unusual animals for the enjoyment of posterity, or even for their scientific interest. It is to ensure that the land is put to its most economic and efficient use. The next few decades will show whether the savannas of the world will be developed into major sources of food and revenue for the countries that own them, or whether they will be misused and degraded into desert.

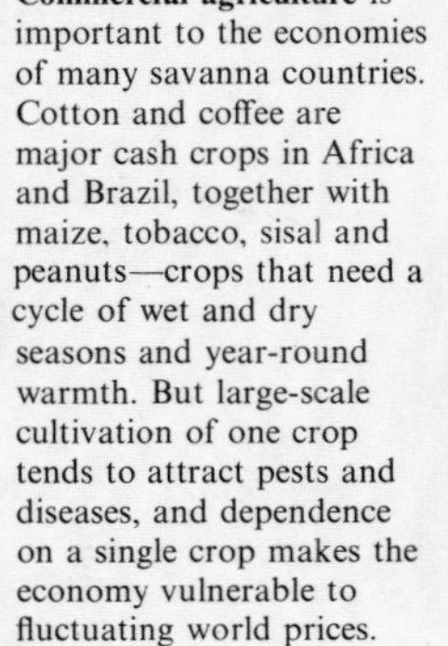

Commercial agriculture is important to the economies of many savanna countries. Cotton and coffee are major cash crops in Africa and Brazil, together with maize, tobacco, sisal and peanuts—crops that need a cycle of wet and dry seasons and year-round warmth. But large-scale cultivation of one crop tends to attract pests and diseases, and dependence on a single crop makes the economy vulnerable to fluctuating world prices.

Cattle rearing takes the place of cultivation in areas that are too dry to be cropped successfully. In Africa, people such as the Masai are nomadic herders, moving their cattle long distances in search of pasture. Wealth is counted in terms of the numbers rather than the quality of the cattle they own, but improved management of their herds and better control of animal diseases are now making their cattle much more productive.

SAVANNA FIRES

Fires have been sweeping the savannas for thousands of years. Hunters set fires to flush game from cover, farmers use fire to clear land for crops, and cattle owners burn off parched, unpalatable grasses to make way for a fresh new growth for their stock. At the end of the dry season, when fires are particularly fierce, large areas of savanna lie under a thin haze of smoke.

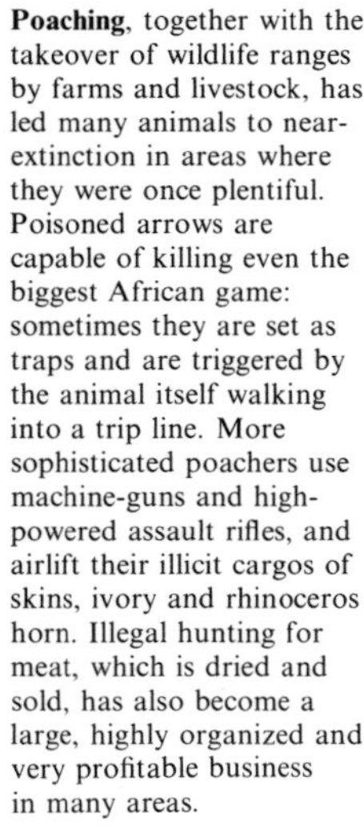

Poaching, together with the takeover of wildlife ranges by farms and livestock, has led many animals to near-extinction in areas where they were once plentiful. Poisoned arrows are capable of killing even the biggest African game: sometimes they are set as traps and are triggered by the animal itself walking into a trip line. More sophisticated poachers use machine-guns and high-powered assault rifles, and airlift their illicit cargos of skins, ivory and rhinoceros horn. Illegal hunting for meat, which is dried and sold, has also become a large, highly organized and very profitable business in many areas.

Game animals also provide the spectacular displays that attract tourists and make tourism an important source of income for many developing nations. Today, most tourists pursue game with cameras instead of guns. The hunting that led to the wholesale slaughter of wildlife in previous years is banned, and so is the traffic in trophies, although even in the sanctuary provided by parks and reserves animals still fall prey to poachers.

Animals are frequently transferred from areas where they are at risk to safer areas such as game parks and reserves. In Kenya, helicopters came to the rescue of a herd of rare antelopes when their range was threatened by a proposed irrigation scheme and moved them to Tsavo National Park. Animals are also moved to introduce new blood to small, isolated herds or to restock areas from which they have been lost.

Tropical Rainforests

Crested tree swift
Hemiprocne longipennis

Crowned eagle
Stephanoaetus coronatus

Tropical rainforests, extremely rich in both plant and animal life, consist of a series of layered or stratified habitats. These range from the dark and humid forest floor through a layer of shrubs to the emerging tops of the scattered giant trees towering above the dense main canopy of the forest. Each layer of vegetation is a miniature life zone containing a wide selection of animal species. These can be divided into a number of ecological groups according to their various ways of life, and many have evolved special adaptations to enable them to make maximum use of the plentiful food supply surrounding them.

Tropical rainforests occur only in the regions close to the Equator; they have a heavy rainfall and a uniformly hot and moist climate. There are slightly more of these forests in the northern half of the world than in the southern half and they occur at altitudes of up to 1,500 m (5,000 ft). Temperatures are normally between 24°C and 30°C (77°–86°F) and rarely fall below 21°C (70°F) or rise above 32°C (90°F). The skies are often cloudy and the rain falls more or less evenly throughout the year. Rainfall is usually more than 2,000 mm (78 in) a year and is never less than 1,500 mm (59 in). A distinctive feature of this tropical, humid climate is that the average daily temperature range is much greater than the range between the hottest and coolest months.

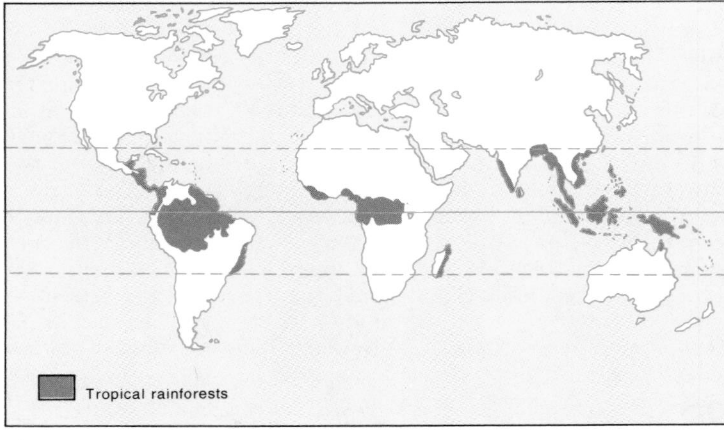

Tropical rainforests are located in the hot and wet equatorial lands of Latin America, West Africa, Madagascar and Asia. These areas have consistently high temperatures throughout the year and receive high rainfall from the moist and unstable winds blowing in from the oceans.

A stratified habitat

There are usually three to five overlapping layers in the mature tropical rainforest. The tallest trees (called "emergents") rise above a closed, dense canopy formed by the crowns of less tall trees, which nevertheless can reach more than 40 m (130 ft) tall. Below this canopy is a third or middle layer of trees—the understory; their crowns do not meet but they still form a dense layer of growth about 5–20 m (16–65 ft) tall. The fourth layer consists of woody shrubs of varying heights between 1–5 m (3–16 ft). The bottom layer comprises decomposers (fungi) that rarely reach 50 cm (20 in) in height.

Although the trees are so tall, few of them have really thick trunks. Nearly all are evergreens, shedding their dark, leathery leaves and growing new ones continuously. Many of the larger species grow buttresses—thin, triangular slabs of hardwood that spread out from the bases of their trunks. These support the trees, so removing the need for a heavy outlay of energy and resources on deep root systems. Hanging lianas (vines), thin and strong as rope, vanish like cables into the mass of foliage. They are especially abundant on riverbanks, where the canopy of trees is thinner; their leaves and flowers appear only among the treetops.

Epiphytes—plants that grow on other plants but do not take their nourishment from them—festoon the trunks and branches of trees, and up to 80 may grow on a single tree. They include many kinds of orchid and bromeliad. Their aerial roots make use of a humus substitute derived from the remains of other plants, often brought together by ants. The bases of their leaves may be broad and bowl shaped and collect and hold water; they also provide homes for a variety of insects and reptiles.

Rainforest soils are not as fertile as might be supposed by the luxuriance of their vegetation. On the contrary, the silicates and compounds necessary for plant growth are leached away by the rain to leave red or yellow soils of poor quality. This process, known as laterization, is widespread in the humid tropics. Humus is rapidly broken down by bacteria, fungi and termites, while earthworms, which in more temperate regions normally contribute to the mixing of humus with mineral particles, are usually absent.

In rainforests there are often up to 25 different tree species on a single hectare of land (60 species to the acre). Most temperate forests have only a fifth of this number, with nothing like the abundance of plants that grow in the tropics. This incredible variety supports—directly or indirectly—a corresponding variety of animal species which has an abundant food supply because the forest never ceases to be productive. This is why most mammals do not move far; they stay where their food grows.

Life in the canopy

The dense leaves and branches of the canopy provide the most food and so support the greatest number of species. Macaws and toucans (from the American tropics) and parrots and trogons (which live in forests throughout the tropics) eat the fruit growing in the

The hummingbird numbers about 300 species, most of which are confined to the forests of South America. It is renowned for its ability to hover while gathering nectar, a feat achieved by the almost 180° rotations of its wings, which beat rapidly more than 80 times per second.

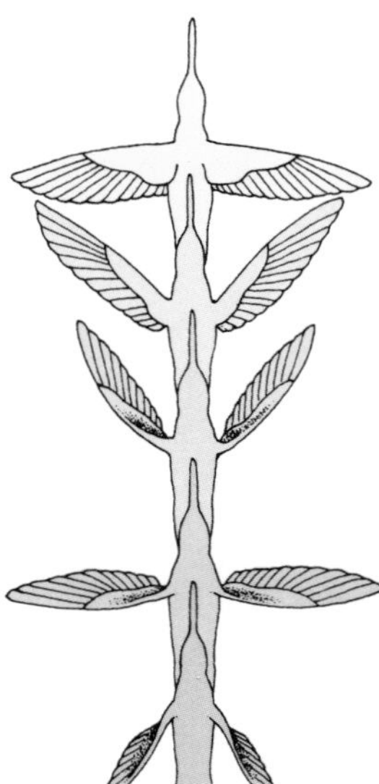

THE LAYERS OF THE FOREST

Stratification—the existence of distinct layers of forest vegetation—is especially pronounced in the tropics, where there are usually five main storys. These can overlap greatly and may vary in height from area to area. The large differences between the layers present many varied habitats and ecological niches for a very wide range of animals.

CANOPY LAYER
This dense story exerts a powerful influence on the levels below since its trees, which grow between 20 m (65 ft) and 40 m (130 ft) tall, form such a thick layer of vegetation that they cut off sunlight from the forest below. The canopy is noted for the diversity of its fauna. Many birds and animals are adapted to running along branches to get the flowers, fruits or nuts that form their diets. The pointed tips of canopy leaves encourage rapid drainage.

MIDDLE LAYER
This understory comprises trees from 5 m (16 ft) to 20 m (65 ft) tall whose long, narrow crowns do not become quite so dense as those of the canopy. There is very often no clear distinction, however, between this level and the canopy. Middle-layer trees are strong enough to bear large animals such as leopards that spend part of their lives on the ground. Epiphytes are plentiful in this layer.

Leopard
Panthera pardus

SHRUB LAYER
The vegetation of this level is sparse in comparison with that above it and consists of treelets and woody shrubs that rarely reach 5 m (16 ft). These grow up in any available space between the abundant boles of large trees. Life in this story exists equally well at ground level.

Four-striped squirrel
Funisciurus lemniscatus

Oriental civet
Viverra tangalunga

Tree pangolin
Manis tricuspis

GROUND LAYER
Shade-tolerant herbs, ferns and tree seedlings represent the only flora at ground level; there is no grass there. Light is less than one percent of full daylight so that many mammals are well camouflaged in the gloom, whereas others have compact bodies to facilitate movement through the undergrowth. Ants and termites are well adapted to the high humidity and darkness of the forest floor. Fungi and a host of invertebrates quickly break down the litter of rotting leaves, fruit and fallen branches to provide vital nutrients for the fast-growing trees of the tropical rainforest.

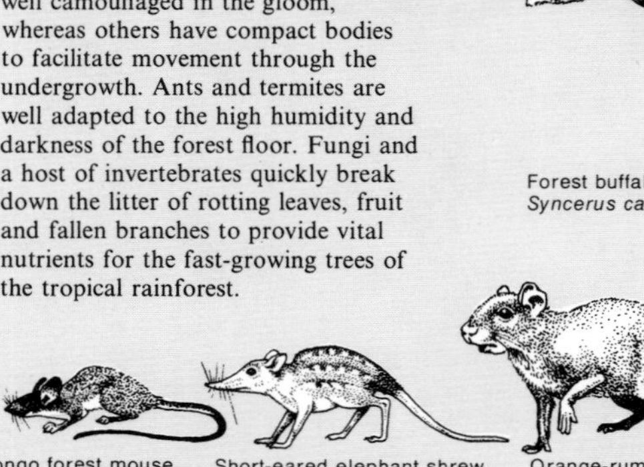

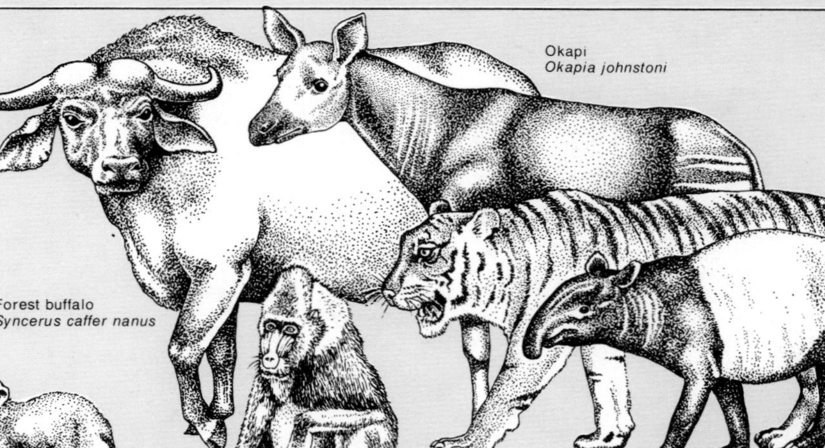

Moth orchid
Phalaenopsis sanderana

Flowering plants of the forest include epiphytes such as bromeliads and orchids like the species of *Phalaenopsis* illustrated here. Epiphytes grow on other plants such as trees where they can receive sunlight and are nourished by humus in the bark. Many epiphytic orchids have swellings in their roots or at the bases of their leaves where water can be stored. Seventy species of *Phalaenopsis* grow in southeast Asian forests and *P. sanderana*, one of the most beautiful, was first discovered in the Philippines in 1882.

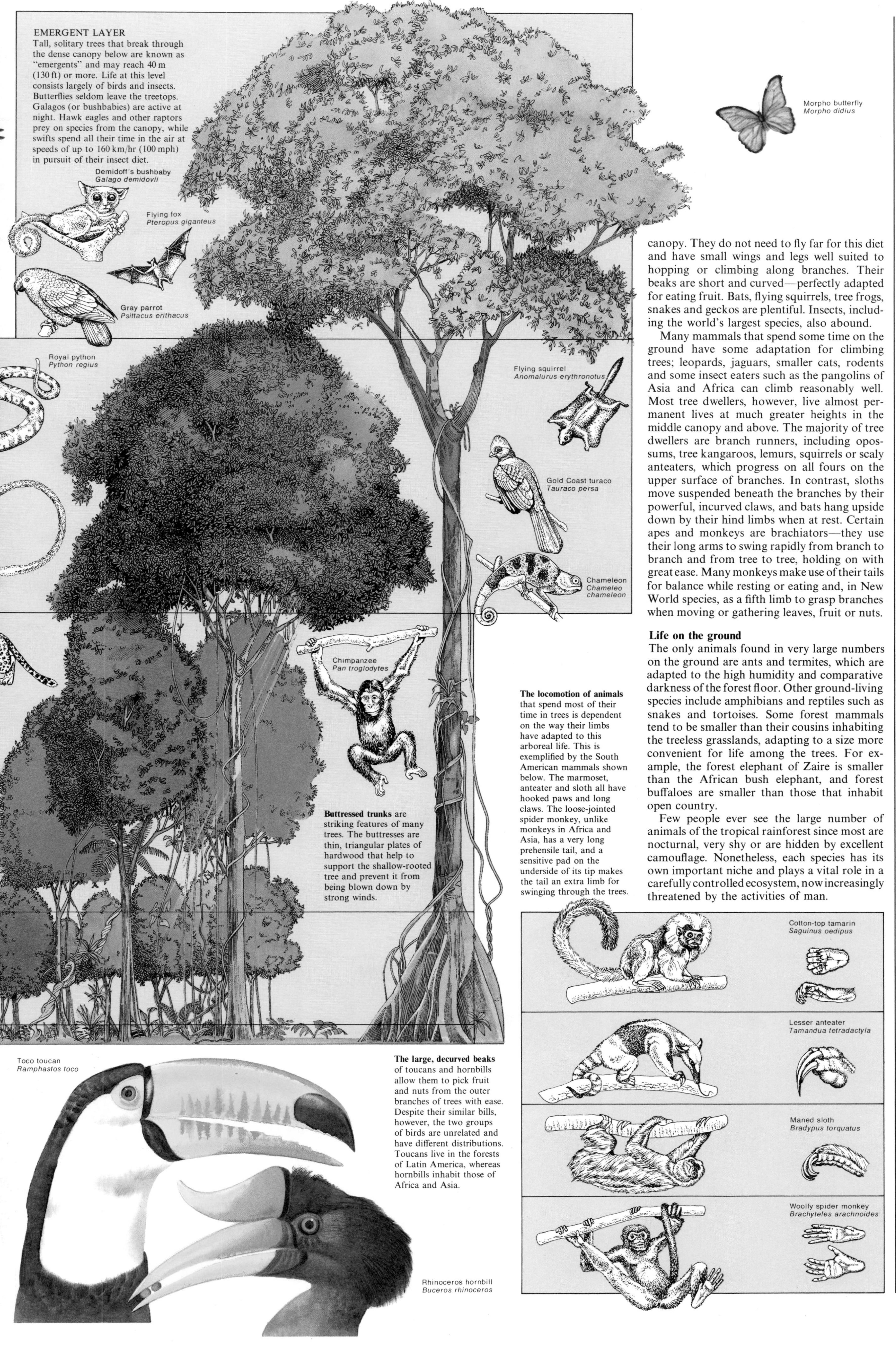

EMERGENT LAYER
Tall, solitary trees that break through the dense canopy below are known as "emergents" and may reach 40 m (130 ft) or more. Life at this level consists largely of birds and insects. Butterflies seldom leave the treetops. Galagos (or bushbabies) are active at night. Hawk eagles and other raptors prey on species from the canopy, while swifts spend all their time in the air at speeds of up to 160 km/hr (100 mph) in pursuit of their insect diet.

Buttressed trunks are striking features of many trees. The buttresses are thin, triangular plates of hardwood that help to support the shallow-rooted tree and prevent it from being blown down by strong winds.

The locomotion of animals that spend most of their time in trees is dependent on the way their limbs have adapted to this arboreal life. This is exemplified by the South American mammals shown below. The marmoset, anteater and sloth all have hooked paws and long claws. The loose-jointed spider monkey, unlike monkeys in Africa and Asia, has a very long prehensile tail, and a sensitive pad on the underside of its tip makes the tail an extra limb for swinging through the trees.

The large, decurved beaks of toucans and hornbills allow them to pick fruit and nuts from the outer branches of trees with ease. Despite their similar bills, however, the two groups of birds are unrelated and have different distributions. Toucans live in the forests of Latin America, whereas hornbills inhabit those of Africa and Asia.

canopy. They do not need to fly far for this diet and have small wings and legs well suited to hopping or climbing along branches. Their beaks are short and curved—perfectly adapted for eating fruit. Bats, flying squirrels, tree frogs, snakes and geckos are plentiful. Insects, including the world's largest species, also abound.

Many mammals that spend some time on the ground have some adaptation for climbing trees; leopards, jaguars, smaller cats, rodents and some insect eaters such as the pangolins of Asia and Africa can climb reasonably well. Most tree dwellers, however, live almost permanent lives at much greater heights in the middle canopy and above. The majority of tree dwellers are branch runners, including opossums, tree kangaroos, lemurs, squirrels or scaly anteaters, which progress on all fours on the upper surface of branches. In contrast, sloths move suspended beneath the branches by their powerful, incurved claws, and bats hang upside down by their hind limbs when at rest. Certain apes and monkeys are brachiators—they use their long arms to swing rapidly from branch to branch and from tree to tree, holding on with great ease. Many monkeys make use of their tails for balance while resting or eating and, in New World species, as a fifth limb to grasp branches when moving or gathering leaves, fruit or nuts.

Life on the ground

The only animals found in very large numbers on the ground are ants and termites, which are adapted to the high humidity and comparative darkness of the forest floor. Other ground-living species include amphibians and reptiles such as snakes and tortoises. Some forest mammals tend to be smaller than their cousins inhabiting the treeless grasslands, adapting to a size more convenient for life among the trees. For example, the forest elephant of Zaire is smaller than the African bush elephant, and forest buffaloes are smaller than those that inhabit open country.

Few people ever see the large number of animals of the tropical rainforest since most are nocturnal, very shy or are hidden by excellent camouflage. Nonetheless, each species has its own important niche and plays a vital role in a carefully controlled ecosystem, now increasingly threatened by the activities of man.

Man and the Tropical Rainforests

Every three seconds a portion of original rainforest the size of a football field disappears as man fells the trees and extends his cultivation. Although tropical conditions allow rapid regrowth of secondary forest, the loss of primary forest is destroying thousands of plant and animal species that will never again be seen on Earth. Even by conservative estimates, it is likely that all the world's primary tropical forest will have disappeared within 85 years unless the trend is reversed.

The activities of man have only recently begun to threaten the tropical rainforest. Since prehistoric times, forests have offered shelter to people who, lacking any knowledge of agriculture, have existed as hunters and gatherers. They used only stone and wooden weapons such as bows and arrows to kill their animal prey, and collected berries, fruit and honey from their surroundings. Their influence on the forest environment was minimal and today a few races such as African pygmies and the Punans of Borneo still live in such a simple state of balance with nature. The Punans, for example, have no permanent homes, but use leaves and branches to construct temporary shelters that are used for only a few weeks before being abandoned. The pygmies build similar homes.

Shifting agriculture
Most forest dwellers, however, live in more permanent settlements and grow most of their food in forest clearings they have made. Such people are expert at chopping down trees in order to set fire to them, and this "slash-and-burn" farming results in small areas littered with charred logs and stumps whose ashes enrich the ground. Crops such as wild tapioca (cassava or manioc) are widely grown, but after a year or two the soil loses the little fertility it once had so that a new tract of forest has to be cleared and burned. Such shifting agriculture provides food for more than 200 million inhabitants of the Third World. As a farming system it has been used throughout the world for more than 2,000 years. When there were few farmers per kilometer the land was allowed to lie fallow for at least 10 years so that the soil could recover. Today, however, population pressures are so great that fallow periods have been drastically reduced and a swift repetition of slash-and-burn degrades and removes nutrients from the soil.

Effects on world climate
Tropical forest floors seldom have deep layers of humus so that, once trees are removed, the shallow topsoil is exposed and soon becomes eroded. In turn, this reduces the capacity of the ground to retain moisture, and without this sponge-like effect runoff can become very erratic and lead to floods, such as those that frequently occur in India and Bangladesh. Estuary sedimentation is often greatly increased

A DIMINISHING RESOURCE
This idealized tract of rainforest includes many of the activities of man that are daily endangering the survival of the forest. Shifting "slash-and-burn" cultivation and excessive logging present the greatest threats. Antidotes such as reafforestation have so far made very little headway.

Living in harmony with the forest are small groups of hunter gatherers who mainly live on a flesh diet, killing their prey with bows and arrows. Nuts and berries supplement this diet, and leaves gathered from the immediate jungle cover their temporary dome-shaped shelters. These are abandoned as an area becomes exhausted and the tribe moves on. Twenty or so pygmies need about 500 sq km (200 sq miles) to support themselves.

Selective logging by gangs of men seeking out the straightest and most valuable hardwood species has been the most common form of tree extraction, even though 75 percent of the canopy might have to be destroyed to remove just a few important trees. Today heavy axes are being replaced by power saws that have no difficulty in cutting down the large buttresses that were once left behind.

Plantation forestry has made increasing inroads into the forests over the decades. The commercial advantage of products that can be cropped several times during the hardwoods' maturation period is becoming increasingly apparent to farmers in the regions. Many rubber plantations in southeastern Asia consist of small holdings that have tended to encroach upon the forest, and intercropping now takes place between the long-established trees.

Shifting cultivation converts thousands of square kilometers of primary forest to substandard cultivation every year. Forest is cleared by slash-and-burn, the resulting fertile clearing is cropped with staples such as manioc, and then left to degrade to secondary forest once the ash-strewn ground has lost its poor fertility. Inevitably, the ground becomes permanently degraded. One encouraging antidote to the futility of such shifting agriculture is the recent strategy of agroforestry (as used by countries such as Nigeria and Thailand), which encourages the planting of fast-growing trees at the same time as the farmer's normal crops. Such intercropping offers considerable financial incentives to the small itinerant farmer.

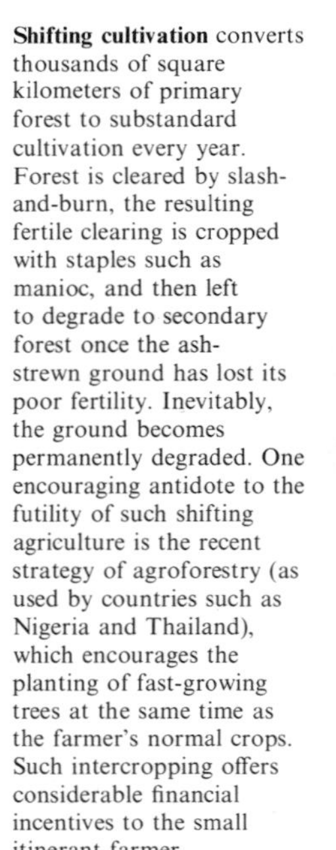

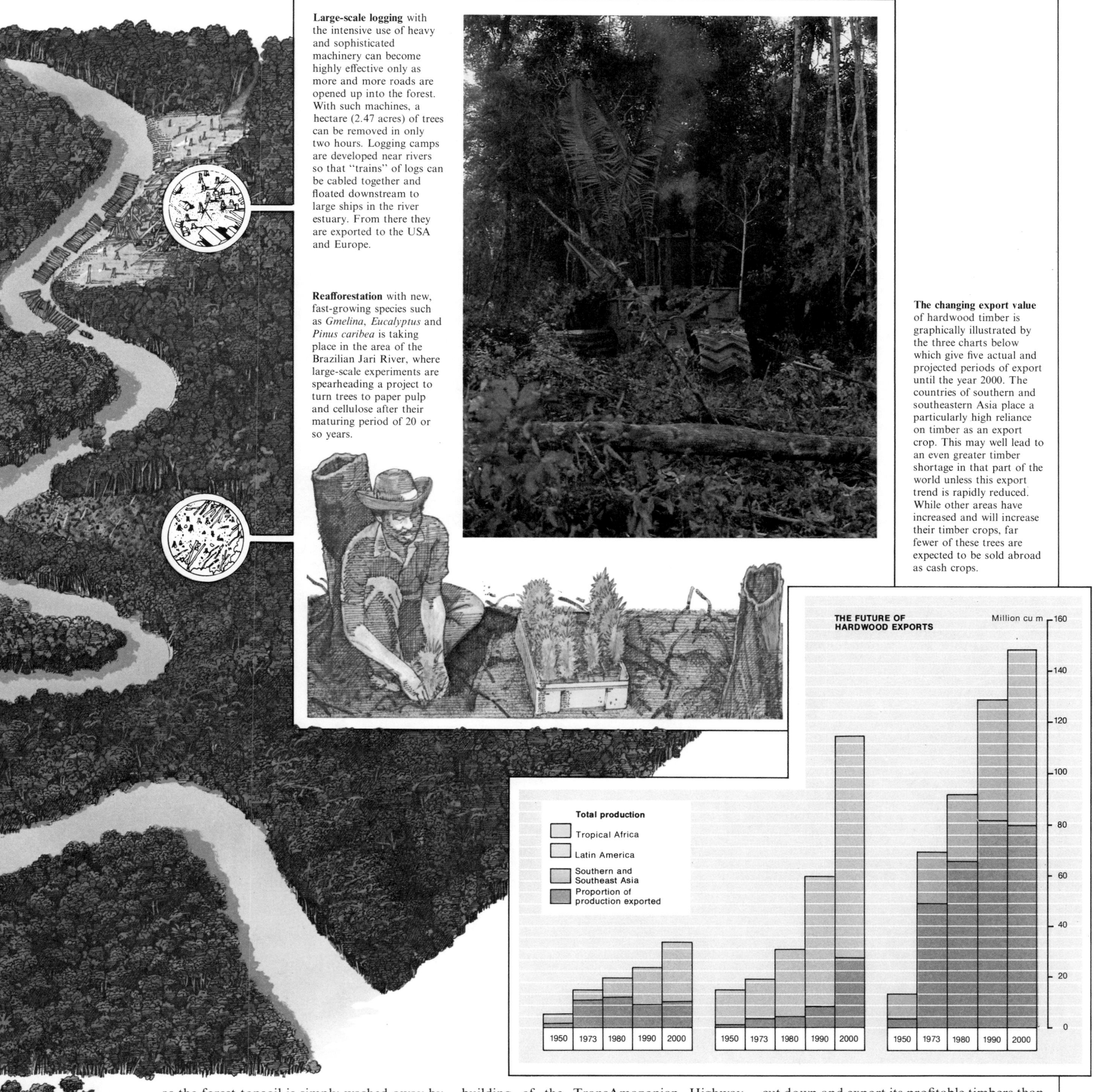

Large-scale logging with the intensive use of heavy and sophisticated machinery can become highly effective only as more and more roads are opened up into the forest. With such machines, a hectare (2.47 acres) of trees can be removed in only two hours. Logging camps are developed near rivers so that "trains" of logs can be cabled together and floated downstream to large ships in the river estuary. From there they are exported to the USA and Europe.

Reafforestation with new, fast-growing species such as *Gmelina*, *Eucalyptus* and *Pinus caribea* is taking place in the area of the Brazilian Jari River, where large-scale experiments are spearheading a project to turn trees to paper pulp and cellulose after their maturing period of 20 or so years.

The changing export value of hardwood timber is graphically illustrated by the three charts below which give five actual and projected periods of export until the year 2000. The countries of southern and southeastern Asia place a particularly high reliance on timber as an export crop. This may well lead to an even greater timber shortage in that part of the world unless this export trend is rapidly reduced. While other areas have increased and will increase their timber crops, far fewer of these trees are expected to be sold abroad as cash crops.

as the forest topsoil is simply washed away by torrential rain. In parts of Asia, deforestation has caused changes in water flow that have interfered with the production of new high-yield rice crops.

Tropical forests contain an enormous store of carbon, and some authorities believe that its release into the air (as carbon dioxide) when the forest is burned down may be as great in volume as that released by the rest of the world's fossil fuels. The higher proportion of carbon dioxide in the atmosphere may lead to an increase in global temperatures, especially at the poles. Trees also release oxygen into the air through photosynthesis, and some scientists have estimated that half of the world's oxygen is derived from this source. Others estimate that half of the rainfall of the Amazon basin is generated by the forest itself, so that any great reduction in tree cover would turn Amazonia into a much drier region.

Threats to Amazonia

Much attention has been paid to the situation of Amazonia, covering as it does some 6.5 million sq km ($2\frac{1}{2}$ million sq miles). In an attempt to give better access to timber and mineral reserves, the Brazilian government's building of the TransAmazonian Highway (3,000 km or 1,860 miles long) has opened the way to deforestation, and settlers have been encouraged to make small holdings on the cleared forest beside the road. Between 1966 and 1978, the government calculated that farmers and big business interests had turned 80,000 sq km (31,000 sq miles) of forest into grazing land for 6 million cattle intended for hamburgers. However, like the wholesale extraction of timber, this has proved to be of doubtful economic value. Because costs rise steeply as less accessible areas are tapped, expenses tend to eliminate logging profits.

Threats in Africa

Even greater threats to tropical forest land have come from less cautious and realistic governments, such as that of Ivory Coast. There neither shifting agriculture nor excessive logging for valuable export sales appear to be under any sort of control. Accordingly, between 1966 and 1974, the area of forest declined from 156,000 sq km (60,000 sq miles) to 54,000 sq km (20,000 sq miles), much of the latter being secondary forest that can never be returned to its original status. Like many other developing countries, Ivory Coast has been more keen to cut down and export its profitable timbers than to think about protecting its invaluable forest environment. Inevitably, forest farmers move into cleared areas and often establish plantation cash crops such as coffee, cocoa and rubber, while the establishment of national parks to curtail depletion has often had very little profitable effect. The Malaysian rainforest is also disappearing rapidly, through widescale logging and open-cast mining for bauxite (aluminum ore).

A large proportion of the world's rainforest occurs in tropical countries faced with severe problems of population control. It is therefore inevitable that the pressures on such forests will be great. Human interference does more than merely destroy the primary forest, to be replaced in time by secondary growth; more importantly, the wholesale removal of trees also drastically reduces the vast genetic reservoir contained in the number of plant and animal species the forests harbor. This in itself is a sound ecological argument for preserving forests and for reversing current trends towards monoculture in the tropics. All the warnings about forest depletion appear to be clear, yet there seems little hope that man will heed them until it is too late.

Monsoon Regions

The word monsoon often conjures up the image of torrential rain and steaming tropical jungles. Yet such a view is misleading, for very great contrasts occur in the regions of the tropical world with a monsoon climate. What distinguishes monsoon regions is not so much the amount of rainfall or the permanently high temperatures, but the dramatic contrast between seasons, with an extended dry season as an essential feature. And in fact the word monsoon derives from the Arabic word for season.

THE SEASON OF RAIN

Life in the monsoon regions balances on the expectation of seasonal heavy rain. In much of India, for instance, 85 percent of the annual rainfall occurs during the limited monsoon periods, and humans as well as plants and animals depend on it wholly. About half the world's people live in these regions, in communities whose rhythm of life necessarily reflects the rains' seasonal nature.

This contrast between wet and dry seasons reflects the reversals of winds over sea and land, which in the northern hemisphere blow from the northeast in the dry winter season, and from the southwest in the wet summer periods.

The monsoon regions occur most widely in southern, southeastern and eastern Asia to the south of latitude 25°N, and in western and central Africa north of the Equator, but there are also smaller regions with a characteristically monsoon climate in eastern Africa, northern Australia and central America. Despite the similar overall climatic pattern, however, the monsoon regions are otherwise very diverse.

Before human settlement the original vegetation of the monsoon regions reflected the dominance of an extended dry season followed by a period of violent rainfall. Typical forest cover was provided by the sal (*Shorea robusta*) deciduous forest, which adjusts to extended periods of moisture deficiency by shedding its leaves. However, within the monsoon region rainfall varies from 200 mm (8 in) a year to more than 20,000 mm (800 in), and the rainy periods may vary between three and nine months.

The range of vegetation found in the monsoon regions reflects this diversity. Where tropical rainforest alters to monsoon forest, as in eastern Java, there is a sharp fall in the total number of plant and animal species, and species adapted to endure seasonal drought begin to be seen. At the other extreme of rainfall the forest thins and shades into semidesert vegetation in India's northwest. But if there is a "type" of monsoon vegetation it is tropical deciduous forest, with sal as the dominant species.

As well as contrasts in climate, the monsoon regions also exhibit pronounced changes in temperature and vegetation as a result of variations in altitude. The Western Ghats of India and the foothills of the Himalayas in Assam both rise to more than 2,500 m (8,200 ft). Temperatures decrease sharply at such altitudes with corresponding changes in vegetation. In southern India on the Nilgiri Hills a wet temperate forest is characteristic, with an intermingling of temperate and tropical species. Magnolias, planes and elms all grow there.

Many parts of the world experience "monsoon" winds, blowing from sea to land in summer, and from land to sea in winter; but typical monsoon vegetation is most clearly seen in the regions of southeastern Asia and the Indian subcontinent. In climatic terms, however, the monsoon circulation of seasonal wind reversals, with wetter summers and dry winters, also affects considerable areas of Africa, South America and northern Australia.

Annual rainfall more than 500 mm (20 in), with wet and dry seasons

Agriculture in monsoon regions

Despite its extensive area there is no part of the monsoon world that is untouched by man and by man's activities. In southern Asia, agricultural activity can be traced back at least 5,000 years, and there have been agricultural settlements throughout the monsoon regions for at least 1,500 years. Man's activity and the grazing of domesticated animals have interfered with, and progressively modified, the natural vegetation. The range of species indicates that, in the whole of the monsoon biome, there is now virtually no primary forest left. The pace of man's interference has speeded up considerably over the last 100 years. As a result, less than 10 percent of the land in southern Asia is now forested, and other parts of the monsoon regions are similarly losing their forest cover.

Many of today's farming methods incorporate traditional cultivation practices, but there have also been very significant changes in recent decades. Traditional agriculture in the monsoon regions has been developed to take into account the seasonal nature of its rainfall pattern and the total rainfall received. The fundamental role of water throughout the region and the absence of low temperatures have placed great importance on either cultivating crops that can tolerate the seasonal rainfall pattern, or on providing irrigation.

Through most of southern Asia, overwhelmingly the most populous of the monsoon regions, the most important single crop is rice, which covers about one-third of the total cultivated area. Rice needs a great deal of water and for this reason is grown mainly in areas of high irrigation, such as the delta lands of the southern and eastern coasts of India, and in areas where rainfall is more than 1,500 mm (59 in) a year. Its cultivation creates a very distinctive landscape as a result of the fact that rice must spend much of its growing period with a few centimeters of water over the soil.

Rice cultivation gives the monsoon regions their characteristic pattern of paddy fields, but other cereal crops such as wheat, the millets and sorghum are also very important. These can tolerate far drier conditions than can rice and occur in areas such as central India or upland Thailand, where uncertain and less abundant rainfall puts a premium on drought tolerance.

Even with traditional crops, man has often interfered extensively with the environment in order to increase yields and attempt to guarantee successful cropping. Traditional irrigation schemes range from diverting rivers at times of flood, in order to lead water to dry land, to digging wells and building small reservoirs. But recent technological developments have brought a new dimension to agricultural activity in the monsoon regions. Large-scale dam and irrigation canal schemes have become important in Africa as well as in monsoon Asia. The introduction and speed of electric or diesel "pumpsets" have transformed well irrigation in regions with extensive groundwater. The reliable water supply that irrigation can give has brought in its train the opportunity for farmers to adopt a wide range of new farming practices. Chemical fertilizers and new strains of seed have made possible great increases in the productivity of the land in many parts of the monsoon regions, but their use is generally restricted to areas of reliable water supply.

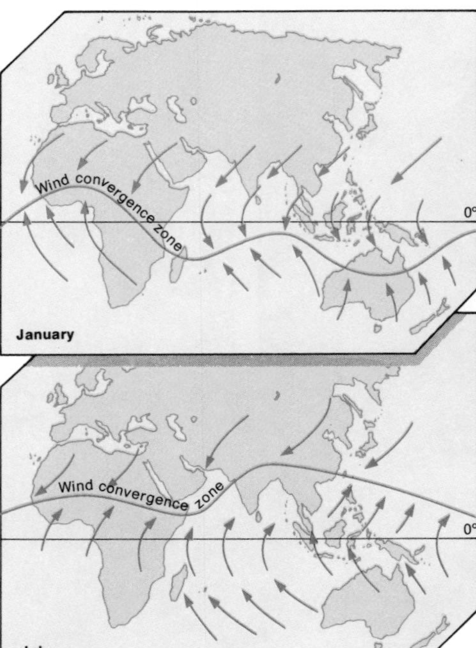

Heat differences in the atmosphere cause the seasonal wind reversals (left) characteristic of monsoon circulation. In January the northern hemisphere is tilted away from the sun, and cold, dry winds blow from the central Asian landmass toward the Equator. Here they change direction (an effect of the Earth's rotation), converge with other winds, and drop their rain. In July the situation is reversed when the heated Asian landmass attracts a flow of cooler air from the equatorial oceans, which moves northward with the sun. The moist air condenses on reaching land, and the monsoon rains descend.

Subsistence cultivation over thousands of years has been by far the most important element in the transformation of the landscape and vegetation of the monsoon world, but the introduction of plantation cultivation during the last centuries has also had a major effect. Tea plantations, for instance, have led to the almost total replacement of natural vegetation in the hills of southern India and Sri Lanka.

Populations in all the countries of the monsoon regions are rapidly increasing, and demands for economic development are constantly growing, placing increasing pressures on the environment, pressures which to date have seemed almost irresistible.

DISAPPEARING ANIMALS

The dwindling wildlife of southeastern Asia includes species that may be regarded locally as pests—a fact that makes their protection difficult outside game reserves. Animals such as the tiger and the wild pig are doubly threatened as human cultivation spreads into the natural habitat: their hunting and foraging grounds are reduced, and their destruction of crops or livestock provides villagers with an obvious incentive for killing them in order to protect their own livelihoods.

SELF-SUFFICIENCY IN CHINA

Local materials are turned into saleable products at a ratan factory in southern China. This factory is not owned by the state but by the village-sized brigade responsible for the manufacturing. The brigade functions as a smaller economic unit within the Ting Chow people's commune of 20 to 30 villages, but is encouraged to act independently, owning what it creates. The commune takes care of such matters as waterways—it contains 82 km (51 miles) of canals.

UPLAND AREAS
Year-round warmth, seasonal rain, and population pressure have led to the development of even comparatively inaccessible upland areas of the monsoon règions. Terracing, an age-old practice, provides subsistence for local populations and crops for local markets; irrigation dams and tea plantations reflect development on an industrial scale. Tea grows on well-drained hillsides where the climate allows the plant to survive frequent leaf removal. The younger the leaf the better the tea, in general, but local variation is wide.

FERTILE FORESTLANDS
Human demands for agricultural land, fuel and building materials have virtually destroyed all the natural monsoon forest cover. But although clearance has left some areas bare, the climate allows luxuriant regrowth elsewhere. Teak, sal and bamboo all provide useful materials, both locally and for export. The extraction and transport of the timber to riverbanks is often carried out more effectively by elephants, responding sensitively to the *mahout*'s directions, than by machines. Bamboo, most widely used today for paper making, may even be erected as scaffolding for skyscrapers.

THE CROWDED COASTS
Rice is such a staple diet of monsoon peoples, from eastern India to middle China, that in many Asian languages it is synonymous with the word for food. Originally a swamp grass, it grows best in lower river and delta regions with a large and dependable water supply, where young shoots can be transplanted to flooded fields for maximum growth. The climate may allow three crops to be grown in one year, with plowing, transplanting and reaping all taking place at the same time. Groves of coconuts often merge with rice fields, and both contribute to the agricultural village economy that still characterizes most of the region. On the coastline of southeastern Asia, mangroves trap the thick silt of the rivers in their tangled roots, reclaiming land from the sea. Industries such as tin mining bring in valuable foreign exchange, but the drift from villages to towns and the rapidly growing populations often raise more problems than they solve.

Mountain Regions

A quarter of Earth's land surface lies at heights of 1,000 m (3,300 ft) or more above sea level. But the highland regions are thinly populated by man, who is, generally speaking, a lowland dweller (most major population centers are less than 100 m (330 ft) above sea level). Some formerly lowland animals have fled from man to the harsh refuge of the mountains, joining with specially adapted plants and wildlife, but today man himself is finding the highland regions increasingly useful and desirable.

The world's highest mountain peaks rise to almost 9.6 km (6 miles) above sea level, but these heights are small compared to the total diameter of the Earth. The rough surface of an orange would have mountains higher than the Himalayas if scaled up to world size. But mountain environments, although they vary enormously from system to system, all tend to demand remarkable endurance and adaptability from the plants and animals that inhabit them.

Altitude rather than geological variation determines conditions of life on mountains. The temperature falls by 2°C with every 300 m (3.4°F every 1,000 ft)—hence the snowcapped beauty of the heights—and life forms must be adapted to increasingly harsh conditions as height increases. As a result, zones of different life occur at different levels, from tropical forests (at the base of low-latitude mountains) to arctic-type life in the zone of ice and snow at the summit. The latitude of the mountain affects the heights to which these zones extend: trees occur at 2,300 m (7,500 ft) in the southern Alps, whereas farther north, in central Sweden, trees cannot survive above 1,000 m (3,300 ft).

Life at the top

The specially adapted plant and animal life of the mountains occurs above the tree line, for here the variations in living conditions reach their greatest extremes. A plant that has found a foothold on a bare rock face may have to endure intense heat, even where the average temperature is low, when the summer sun blazing through the clear air warms the slabs to tropical temperatures. But when that part of the mountain falls into shadow, the temperature decreases very rapidly, often assisted by the high winds that blow almost constantly throughout the year in many mountain areas.

Soil necessary for plant life develops with the breakdown of the rock through the agency of water, frost and ice. Lichens, whose acids may aid in this destruction, can survive at very high levels, and as they die may add some humus to the newly forming soil. This may first accumulate in sheltered places where plants requiring high humidity, such as mosses and filmy ferns, are found. Flowering plants follow where a greater depth of soil has formed, although some grow in cracks between rocks.

Flowering plants of the mountains all tend to be small (to avoid harsh, drying winds), deep rooted (to anchor the plant firmly), and abundantly flowering (to benefit from the short growing season). Many unrelated species have independently developed a similar cushion form. This enables them to shed excess rainwater easily and to retain heat better in a tight tangle of stems and leaves, where the temperature may be more than 10°C (18°F) higher than that of the outside air. Insects sheltering there are well placed to perform the vital task of pollination. But pollinating insects are relatively rare at high altitudes, and some mountain plants are wind pollinated. The brilliant color of many others may be to increase their attractiveness for the insects. Nearly all upland plants are very slow-growing perennials, and many are evergreen, with leaves that exploit all available light.

Some large animals, such as the ibex or the Rocky Mountain goat, are adapted to spend their lives among the rocks and slopes. These stocky creatures, with hooves that act rather like suction cups, produce their summer young in the security of the heights, although in winter they descend to the shelter of the upper forests. Among smaller mammals, most of which are rodents, some dig burrows in which they hibernate through the winter. Others have very thick insulating coats, and may stay awake through the coldest weather in burrows under the snow.

Refugees from the lowlands

Some mountain animals, particularly carnivorous mammals and birds, have been driven by human persecution into remote mountain fastnesses. Many birds of prey, which could otherwise survive well in lowland areas, have their last strongholds among the mountains. They survive by feeding on small rodents, many of which are extremely wary. Some upland birds feed on insects or on seeds, but their number is comparatively small. The Alpine chough is one of the most interesting of mountain birds, for it has learned to find food among the scraps provided by climbers and skiers, whom it often follows to very high altitudes.

Insects and other small invertebrates, like their Arctic counterparts, may take several years to mature. Some are wingless, and many tend to fly low in order not to be blown away from their home range. Jumping spiders have been seen at heights of 6,700 m (22,000 ft) on the slopes of Mount Everest, where they exist on small flies and springtails, but even above this level springtails and glacier "fleas" occur where there are no plants, apparently surviving on wind-blown insects and pollen grains.

Man and the mountains

The remote beauty of the mountains has led many peoples to identify them as the abode of the gods, but man himself prefers to live in the more convenient lowlands. The rarefied atmosphere of the heights makes physical work difficult, although some mountain-dwelling peoples have developed adaptations of the blood system to enable them to carry scarce oxygen more efficiently. The short growing season prevents cultivation of all but the hardiest cereal crops, and most uplanders rely on their livestock—cattle, sheep, llamas or yaks—for their existence. The animals are often driven to high pasture during the summer, descending to the valleys in the winter.

Modern, urbanized man finds the beauty and freshness of mountains increasingly attractive. Climbers have invaded most of the world's mountain regions, and in winter hosts of skiers flock to the resorts. Many important wildlife sanctuaries and national parks, particularly in the United States, are in mountain areas.

Lowland populations often rely on the pure mountain streams for both water and energy. Whole upland valleys are sometimes flooded to store water for distant conurbations. And the forceful flow of the water as it descends from the snow-fed heights is frequently harnessed to produce electricity for entire regions hundreds of kilometers away. The clear mountain air also offers the best conditions for astronomical observation, and most observatories today are built in dry, cloudless mountain areas.

LIFE ON THE HEIGHTS

Mountain climates become colder the higher one goes. This change in conditions creates distinctive horizontal zones of plant and animal life, although the pattern may vary according to the latitude and aspect of a mountain. Some life forms manage to eke out a precarious existence even on the roof of the world. Lower down, the brief growing season encourages a short burst of plant and animal activity above the timber line, conspicuous for the brightly colored summer flowers. Man mainly inhabits the lower slopes and valleys. He exploits mountain resources but rarely lives on the inhospitable heights.

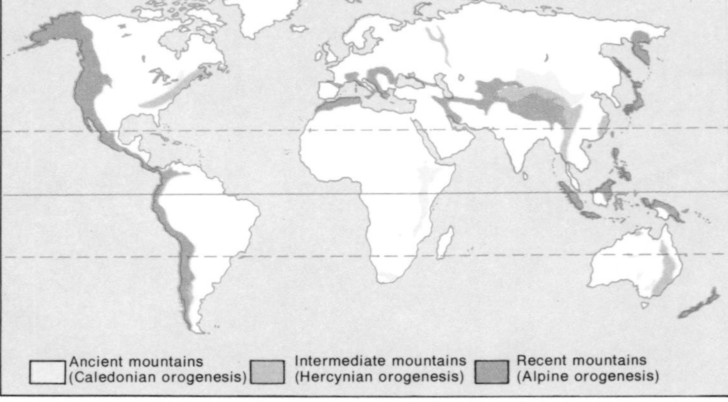

Activity in Earth's crust has produced mountains in every continent (left). Some thrust up sharply, while older mountains have been eroded to rounded shapes. The Scottish Highlands were made by mountain-building forces 400 million years ago (170 million years before the Appalachians and the Urals). The Rockies are 70 million years old and the Alps 15 million years old.

Many peoples have believed that the gods have their abodes in the high places of the world. Tibet (above), one of the highest and most mountainous of all countries, has a large number of religious sites. Modern man also finds the clear, dry air suitable for the study of heavenly bodies: most modern observatories, such as Kitt Peak, USA (right), are built on mountain sites far from cities.

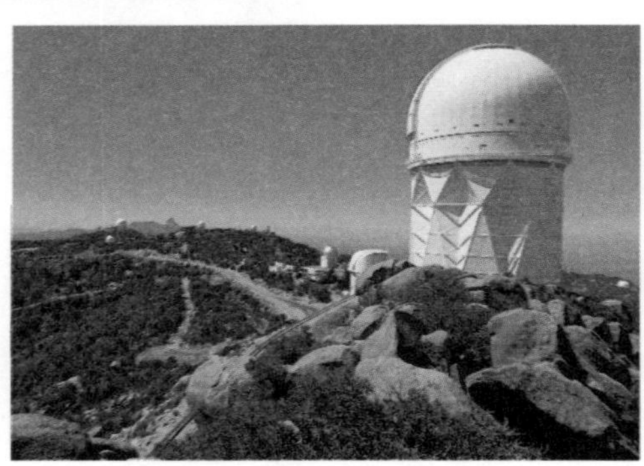

MOUNTAIN ADAPTATIONS

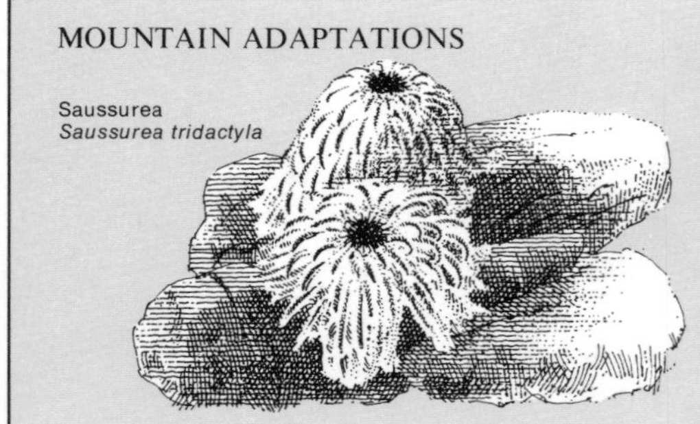

Ingenious adaptations to harsh mountain conditions have been evolved by many plants, most of which have tiny cells with thick sap that does not freeze easily. Saussurea masks itself with white hair to reduce evaporation from the leaf surface. Alpine soldanellas are active even under snow, pushing up their flowers before the thaw.

SNOWBOUND PEAKS
Perpetual snow, violent winds and atmospheric dryness impose harsh conditions on life in the high Himalayas. But wind-blown organic debris from the plains does support some life forms—springtails, flies and jumping spiders—where the air is too dry to allow even lichens to survive. Lower down, a cushion plant may take root in a rock-base niche, but there is little other vegetation. Among birds, the Alpine chough is a scavenger that has followed Everest expeditions to heights of 7,900 m (26,000 ft).

MOUNTAIN MEADOWS
Between the snow line and the zone of coniferous trees, the Himalayan slopes exhibit a glorious variety of flowering plants during summer. Small and slow growing, these often have bright flowers which attract pollinating insects such as fly-like *Diptera*. The pika and other small, thick-furred rodents are the most common animals, although larger creatures, such as blue (bharal) sheep and yaks, also find summer pasturage at these heights. Snow leopards tend to inhabit the coniferous forests, but they travel up to higher parts to prey on the grazing herds. Few people live within the zone, but some Sherpas take their yak herds as high as 4,600 m (15,000 ft) for summer grazing, and even grow crops of potatoes at this height. Their permanent villages, however, are on the lower alpine slopes.

FORESTED SLOPES
Isolated birches mark the tree line—the transition from meadow to coniferous and rhododendron forest. In the upper parts of the forest, trees are dwarfed by cold and lack of moisture, and are twisted and bent from the wind. These low and tangled masses provide shelter for animals such as the Asian black bear and the red panda. Below the conifers lies a zone of broad-leaved evergreens, and in the foothills these in turn give way to tropical monsoon forests of sal trees (*Shorea robusta*) and thickets of bamboo. The raucous flocks of hill mynahs represent just one of the many kinds of birds found in this zone, which has the widest range of wildlife of all the kinds of mountain vegetation. Unfortunately, many species are in danger of extinction, for here man has settled, cut down forests and terraced hillsides to grow crops.

Animals and humans adapt to mountain conditions in many ways. The Rocky Mountain goat (left) has evolved a fleecy undercoat and hooves with concave pads to grip on any surface. Comparison of the blood counts (right) of a lowlander (A) and an Andean (B) shows how the latter has a higher total content and more red cells.

The golden eagle *Aquila chrysaetos* (left) epitomizes the grandeur of the heights. Although it lives and nests in remote regions, it could equally well find its food in the lowlands were it not for human competition. An eagle's territory may cover 130 sq km (50 sq miles): it preys on small mammals and even (it is believed) on young deer and lambs. It mates for life and returns each year to the same nest.

Freshwater Environments

Broad, muddy rivers, fast-running streams, miniature ponds and deep, ancient lakes all provide their own distinctive environments for populations of animals and colonies of aquatic plants. And in spite of the fact that these, the world's freshwater systems, contain only a minute proportion of the Earth's total supplies of water, the remarkable variety and richness of the wildlife they support make them among the most valuable and significant of all the world's natural habitats.

Fresh water is never really pure for, like sea water, and indeed like all other natural waters, it contains various dissolved minerals. Fresh water differs from seawater only in the relatively low concentrations of the minerals it contains. But these mineral traces are extremely important; they provide essential nutrients without which freshwater plants could not exist. And without plant life, there would be virtually no animal life either.

Not all parts of every freshwater system are rich in both plants and animals. Large, deep lakes are very similar to oceans—no light can penetrate their gloomy depths, and few plants can live in these conditions. The surface waters, on the other hand, where light is plentiful, teem with microscopic floating plants, mainly single-celled algae such as desmids and diatoms. The edges of lakes provide a different set of conditions again, for here the water is shallow and light can penetrate right through it. Plants can take root in the silt on the bottom, grow up through the water and thrust their leaves out into the light and air. Edges of lakes and, for the same reasons, the waters of small ponds are usually full of such plant life, which in turn supports many freshwater animals.

Running waters

Just as the still waters of lakes and ponds offer a variety of habitats, so the running waters of rivers support many different forms of life, each adapted to the particular conditions of its environment. In the upper reaches, where rivers are scarcely more than upland streams, water is fast flowing and clear of silt. Few plants, except close-clinging mosses, can gain a hold on the bare stony bottom and most of the fish are well muscled and strong bodied to enable them to withstand the constant tug of the current. As a river swells to form a mature lowland water course, however, it becomes slower moving and the water is warmer and richer in nutrients. Plants grow readily in these lower reaches and provide a supply of food for aquatic animals.

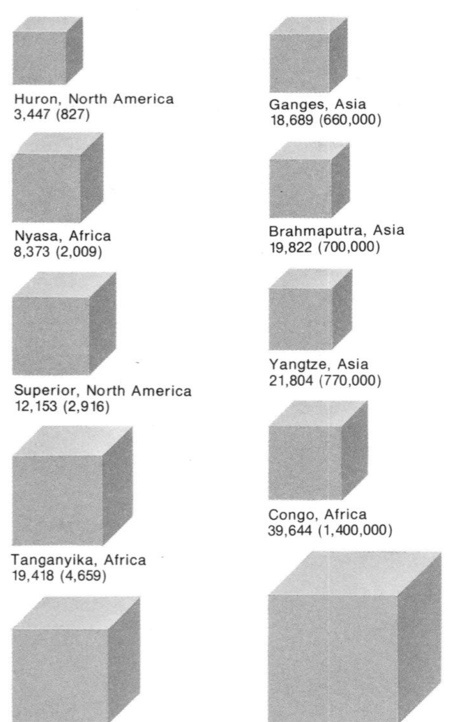

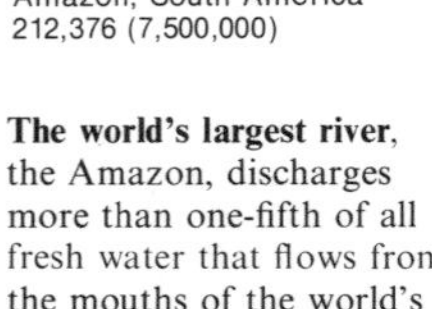

The five largest lakes in the world hold more than 53% of all fresh water that flows over the land. The rest of the world's lakes account for another 45%.

The world's largest river, the Amazon, discharges more than one-fifth of all fresh water that flows from the mouths of the world's rivers into the oceans.

With such a wide range of conditions, freshwater environments support an enormous variety of animal life—insects, fishes, amphibians, reptiles, mammals and birds. In some ways insects are the most important of all these creatures: freshwater systems contain more insects and other invertebrates, representing a greater variety of species, than any other kind of animal. Furthermore, these, the smallest representatives of the freshwater animal world, provide one of the most important links in the complex freshwater food chain.

Insects may be the most numerous, but fishes are probably the most familiar of all freshwater creatures, and they certainly show some of the greatest varieties of adaptations to the many different habitats. Their sizes vary from the tiny, 14 mm ($\frac{1}{2}$ in) of the virtually transparent dwarf goby fish found in small streams and lakes in the Philippines to the 4 m (14 ft) of the arapaima found in deep rivers in tropical South America. Their feeding habits vary from those of the ferocious carnivorous piranha of South America to those of the North American paddle fish which, although more than three times the size of the largest piranha, feed solely on microscopic organisms which they filter from the water with their specially adapted throats.

The breeding habits of freshwater fish also vary widely, from the carefully maternal instincts of the African mouthbreeding cichlids—these retain the developing eggs safely in their mouths until the offspring hatch—to the rather more common ejection of eggs into the water, where their fertilization and survival is simply left to chance. Other adaptations include the ability to breathe air (as does the African lungfish), to leap waterfalls (a common practice among migrating salmon) and to emit an electric shock of up to 600 volts (an adaptation of the South American electric eel).

Creatures of the water's edge

Of all the other major groups of animals, amphibians (such as frogs and toads) are probably the most reliant on freshwater systems. Because their skins must not dry out and they have to lay their eggs in water, few amphibians can venture far from the water's edge. And because they cannot tolerate the salt in seawater (it causes them to lose their body fluids through their skins) they are totally dependent upon fresh water for their existence. Reptiles, rather less typical of freshwater environments, range in size from miniature North American terrapins to the giant crocodiles that live along the banks of the Nile. Freshwater mammals, on the other hand, with the considerable exception of the hippopotamus, all tend to be rather small creatures such as otters, beavers, coypus, aquatic moles and water shrews.

Birds are another important group of freshwater creatures. Although few birds are truly aquatic an enormous number of species live in or near freshwater systems and take advantage of the various food supplies: the plants and fish within the waters; the bankside vegetation and small animal life; and the many forms of freshwater insects. Marshes and swamps, for example, provide some of the richest bird habitats in the world.

Also numbered among the species dependent on Earth's freshwater systems is man. And although strictly a nonaquatic, land-living animal, man uses more fresh water than any other creature. His needs seem to be inexhaustible as he harnesses, channels, diverts and often pollutes freshwater systems throughout the world. Unfortunately, the vast requirements of the human race are not always compatible with the rather more humble needs of all other species that depend upon fresh water.

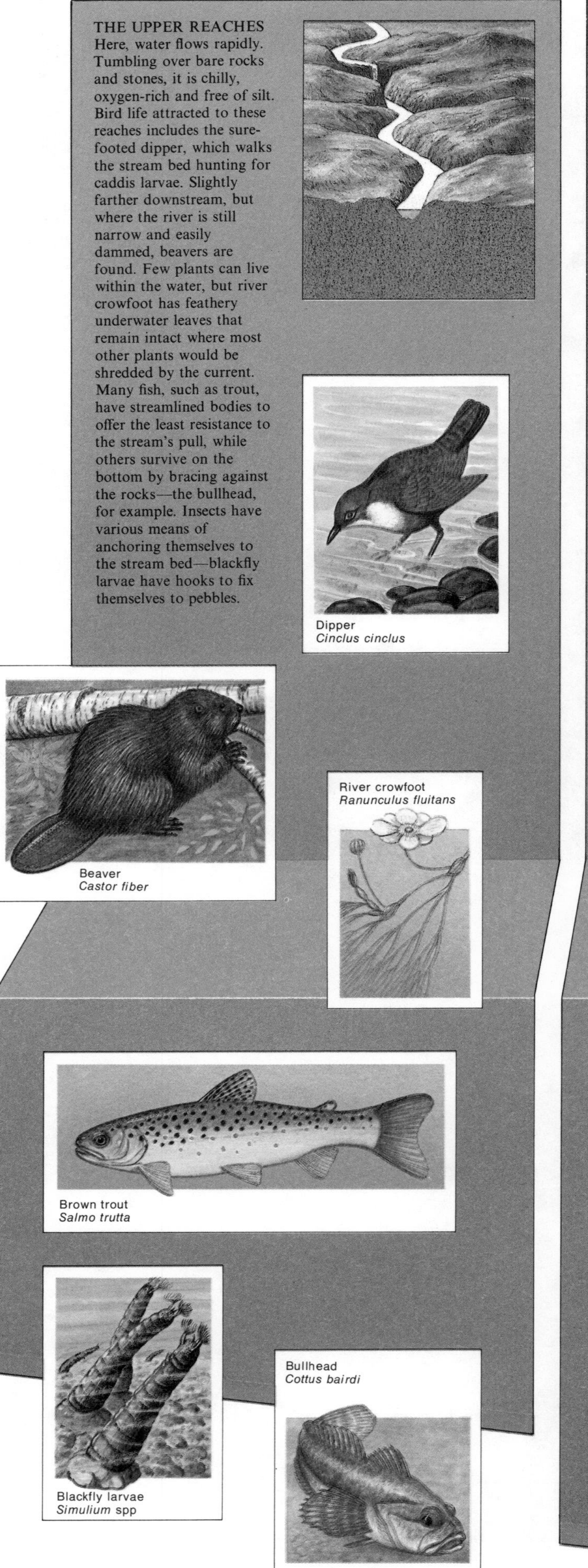

THE UPPER REACHES
Here, water flows rapidly. Tumbling over bare rocks and stones, it is chilly, oxygen-rich and free of silt. Bird life attracted to these reaches includes the sure-footed dipper, which walks the stream bed hunting for caddis larvae. Slightly farther downstream, but where the river is still narrow and easily dammed, beavers are found. Few plants can live within the water, but river crowfoot has feathery underwater leaves that remain intact where most other plants would be shredded by the current. Many fish, such as trout, have streamlined bodies to offer the least resistance to the stream's pull, while others survive on the bottom by bracing against the rocks—the bullhead, for example. Insects have various means of anchoring themselves to the stream bed—blackfly larvae have hooks to fix themselves to pebbles.

Dipper *Cinclus cinclus*

Beaver *Castor fiber*

River crowfoot *Ranunculus fluitans*

Brown trout *Salmo trutta*

Blackfly larvae *Simulium* spp

Bullhead *Cottus bairdi*

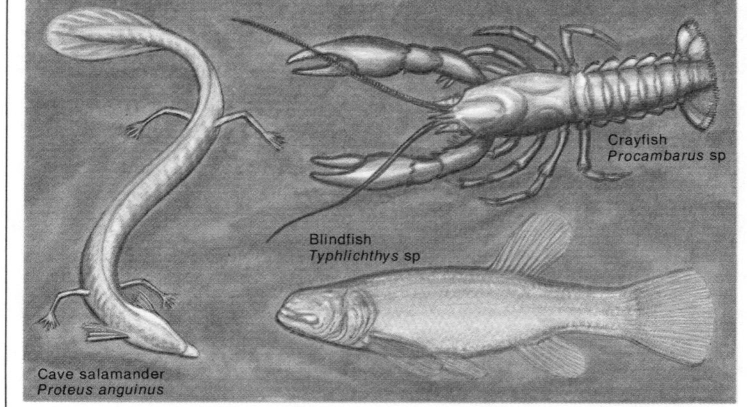

Crayfish *Procambarus* sp

Blindfish *Typhlichthys* sp

Cave salamander *Proteus anguinus*

THE LIFE OF A RIVER

As a river makes its way from its upland source to the sea, it gradually changes its character. And at every stage in its progress, the animals and plants that inhabit the riverbanks and the waters reflect these changes by their adaptations to their environments. Most distinctive and dramatic are those adaptations produced in the wildlife of the upper and lower river reaches.

THE LOWER REACHES

The slowly flowing river and its muddy banks are rich in animals and plants. Many birds live along the water's edge; spoonbills wade in the shallows, filtering food from the water with their beaks. The banks, fringed with reedmaces and other plants, provide habitats for many reptiles, such as the American painted turtle, and mammals, such as the platypus. Plants also grow on the water—they range from large waterlilies to tiny algae that are food for river fishes: Africa's upside-down-feeding catfish, for example. In these waters, mammals as well as fish are to be found—Amazonian manatees live entirely aquatic lives. The plentiful river plants, such as curled pondweed, provide food for water snails and other herbivores, and cover for predators such as pike. Crustacea and insects living in the silt of the river-bed are food for bottom-feeding fish such as the strange-looking North American paddle fish.

African spoonbill
Platalea alba

Southern painted turtle
Chrysemys picta dorsalis

LAKES: CHANGE AND EVOLUTION

No two lakes are alike: each is virtually a self-contained world for its population of aquatic animals and plants. Furthermore, no individual lake remains the same for long: in every lake, slow, inexorable changes in conditions are gradually but constantly changing the balance of species inhabiting the lake bed, the bankside and the water.

Changing conditions may be caused by one of several processes. Accumulating sediments, one of the most common of these processes, may eliminate a lake altogether. The water becomes shallower as sediments thicken (1) and these sediments are then added to and consolidated by water plants taking root. Ultimately, land plants (2) invade the area.

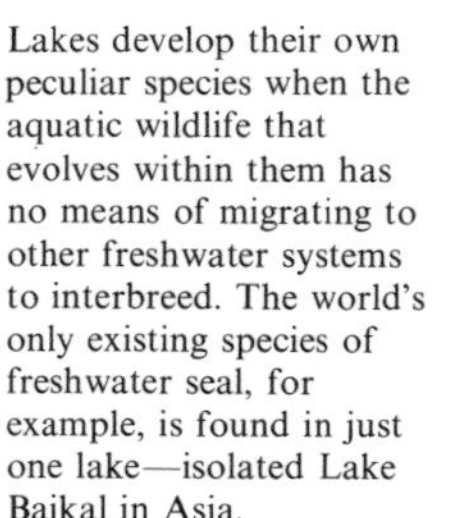

Lakes develop their own peculiar species when the aquatic wildlife that evolves within them has no means of migrating to other freshwater systems to interbreed. The world's only existing species of freshwater seal, for example, is found in just one lake—isolated Lake Baikal in Asia.

Baikal seal
Phoca sibirica

Reedmace
Typha sp

Platypus
Ornithorhynchus anatinus

Waterlily
Nymphaea sp

African catfish
Synodontis batensoda

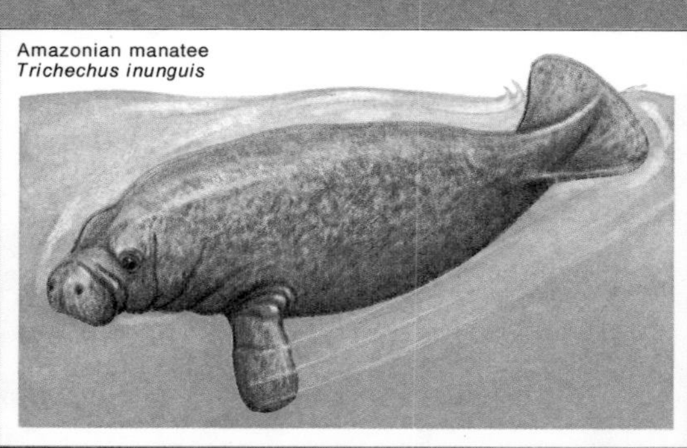

Amazonian manatee
Trichechus inunguis

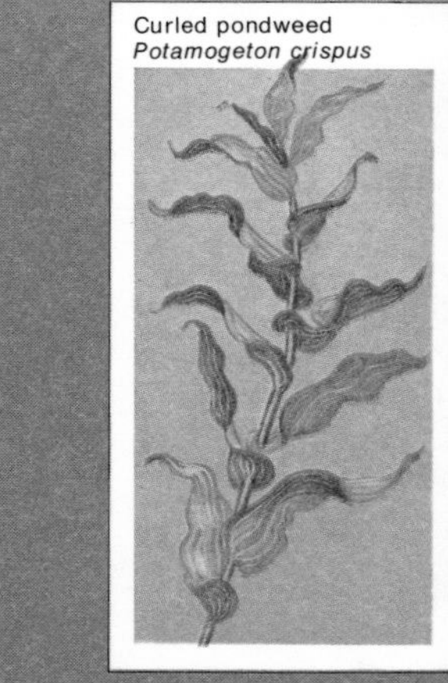

Curled pondweed
Potamogeton crispus

White ramshorn snail
Planorbis albus

Pike
Esox lucius

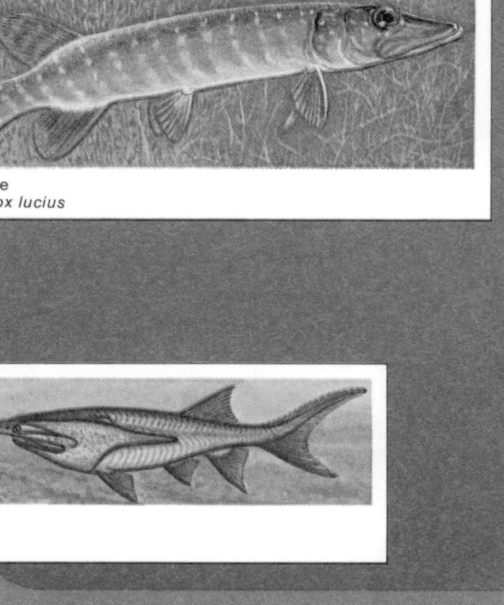

Paddle fish
Polydon spathula

DARK WATERS

Underground rivers that flow through many of the world's cave systems support surprising numbers of creatures that have adapted to the permanent darkness. Many of these, such as the American cave crayfish, have lost the coloration of their surface-living kin. Some, such as Kentucky blind fishes, no longer possess eyes. Some salamanders are sighted and black when born, but become blind and colorless by adulthood.

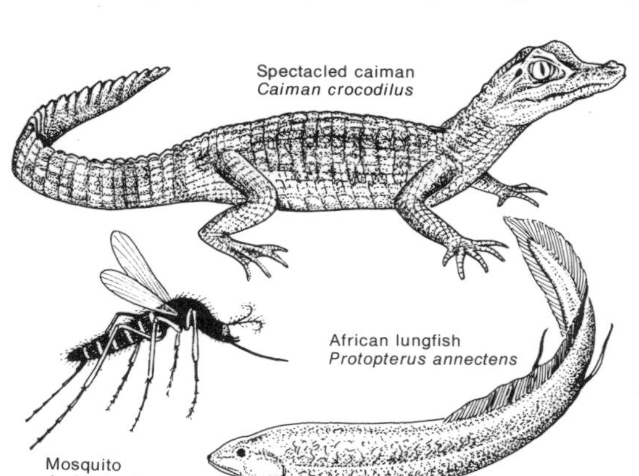

Spectacled caiman
Caiman crocodilus

African lungfish
Protopterus annectens

Mosquito
Aedes impiger

WETLANDS

Marshes and swamps are the richest of freshwater habitats. Wading birds, such as Asia's painted stork *Ibis leucocephalus* (above), are particularly common. Reptiles include caimans, which lay their eggs in swamps' warm, rotting vegetation. Of the many insects, mosquitoes are probably the most numerous, and of the many fishes, African lungfish are perhaps best adapted to life in wetlands. They survive drought, when marshes dry up, by their ability to breathe air.

Man and the Freshwater Environments

From earliest times, man has been finding new uses for and making new demands upon the world's freshwater resources. Today, the whole of modern society depends upon a vast supply to serve its agricultural, industrial, domestic and other needs. To meet the ever-growing demand for water, man has performed remarkable engineering feats: altering the courses of rivers, creating and destroying lakes, drowning valleys and tapping water sources that lie deep within the Earth.

THE VERSATILE RESOURCE

Every day, more than seven trillion liters (12 trillion pints) of water are removed from the world's freshwater systems. Almost all of this water is then directed to one of four destinations—some is destined for industry, a certain amount is piped to towns and cities for use in public services and in homes, some is fed to agricultural regions, and the rest is stored in reservoirs for future use.

INDUSTRY 19.5%

DOMESTIC 4.4%

AGRICULTURE 73.8%

RESERVOIRS 2.3%

Water is essential to human life. Simply to remain alive, an active adult living in a temperate climate needs a liquid intake of about two liters ($3\frac{1}{2}$ pints) every day. In warmer climates, the body's fluid requirements are even greater. Consequently, man has always been tied to reliable sources of drinking water—rivers, springs, lakes and ponds—and the availability of these, until very recently, has dictated the routes of all his wanderings and determined the sites of all his settlements.

From the time of the earliest human settlements, however, man has looked upon freshwater systems not simply as a source of drinking water but also as an increasingly useful resource for a multitude of other purposes. Today, water enters into virtually every aspect of modern life, and enormous quantities are used in agriculture, in industry, in the home, in the production of energy, for transport and for recreation.

Man obtains fresh water by trapping it as it passes through one of the stages in the hydrological cycle—the never-ending circulation of Earth's waters from the ocean, to the atmosphere, to land. This cycle can be traced from the point at which water evaporates from the sea. The water vapor is blown across the land and falls as rain, hail or snow. Some then evaporates, but the rest completes the cycle by flowing over the land or through the soil or rocks back to the sea. It is at this point in its journey that man obtains his water supplies—from lakes (1), boreholes and wells (2) and dammed rivers (3). These supplies are then either used locally, or are transported by pipe or canal (4) to reservoirs (5) where they are stored ready for distribution.

Movement of water in the hydrological cycle

Water-bearing rock

The farmer's resource

Of all the major activities that rely on fresh water, agriculture is by far the world's largest consumer. In much of Europe and North America, rainfall is usually plentiful and lack of sufficient water for crops is rarely a problem. But in other parts of the world the climate simply does not produce enough rainfall and water shortages are a perennial problem. There, irrigation is not just a sophisticated technique to improve the yields and increase the varieties of crops grown; it is, and always has been, an essential element of agriculture.

Methods of irrigation range from small-scale devices—such as miniature windpumps—used in many developing countries simply to lift water from rivers for bankside crops, to vast dams, reservoirs and canal systems such as the Indus River project in Pakistan, which irrigates 10 million hectares (25 million acres) of land.

Traditional irrigation techniques usually involve using open channels or furrows for conducting water to fields. But one of the major problems with these, particularly in hot climates, is that much of the water evaporates and is lost before it can be used. Several new techniques, such as sprinklers and drip-feed systems, have recently been developed, however, to help make more efficient use of available supplies.

Although the most severe water deficiencies are experienced in the dry subtropical and tropical regions of the world, the temperate regions of North America and Europe, in spite of their relatively wet climates, do suffer shortages. Large towns and cities rarely have enough locally available rainfall or river flow to satisfy both domestic demand and the insatiable needs of industry. In the developed nations, industry consumes more water than any other activity.

Industrial demands

Fresh water is not only an integral part of almost every manufacturing process, it has other important industrial uses. As a source of power, it has been used since the early days of civilization—water wheels were one of man's first industrial inventions. Today, these simple devices are rarely seen in industrial societies, but water power is more important than ever before. Giant dams allow enormous volumes of water to be controlled and the power harnessed to drive turbines and generate electricity.

Freshwater systems have also, for centuries, provided industry with an important means of transporting its goods, and canal systems are still an essential part of industrial infrastructure in many countries of the world: the Europa Canal, when completed, will link three of Europe's major rivers, the Rhine, Main and Danube, and so form a continuous waterway running east–west across the breadth of Europe. Already, the finished sections of the canal are carrying oil, chemicals, fertilizers, coal, coke and building materials to and from some of Europe's major industrial regions.

Many of Europe's waterways date back to the great canal-building days of the Industrial Revolution. Although a few of these are still used for commerce, many are today considered too narrow to transport economical quantities of goods. Some, however, are now finding a role to play in one of the world's fastest-growing new industries—the leisure market. Today, canals provide a wide range of aquatic activities for holiday makers, tourists and sportsmen.

Recreation and sport

Freshwater systems throughout the world, in fact, are rapidly being recognized and developed as major recreational resources. Lakes and reservoirs are stocked with fish for anglers, silted waterways are dredged to provide sailing and swimming facilities, and old quarries and open-cast workings are landscaped and flooded to provide entirely new freshwater systems purely for leisure pursuits. The projects not only help to rejuvenate previously misused land, they also provide significant incomes to otherwise underdeveloped areas, especially highland regions that are too remote to attract other industries, and are unsuitable for farming.

Unfortunately, however, few of the world's freshwater systems can continue indefinitely to absorb the ever-growing demands that are being made upon them. Overuse of water resources is already a problem and has led to the pollution and destruction of many water systems—in some places overtapping has lowered water tables so drastically that rivers and lakes have been permanently destroyed. Although steps have been taken to protect certain waterways, legislation to guard against misuse and overuse is costly, time consuming and, inevitably, comes up against vested interests. Nevertheless, stringent conservation measures are becoming increasingly necessary if society is to maintain one of its most precious resources.

RESERVOIRS

About 70 trillion liters (15 trillion gallons) of fresh water are held in storage during any one year. Reservoirs ensure a continuous supply of water in spite of the inevitable seasonal fluctuations in demand and in the natural supply from rivers and rainfall. And where reservoirs are formed by damming rivers, there are additional benefits—the vast quantities of water held can be controlled and the power used to generate electricity. The Kariba Dam in Zimbabwe (right) has the potential for producing 8,500 million kilowatt hours of electrical power every year.

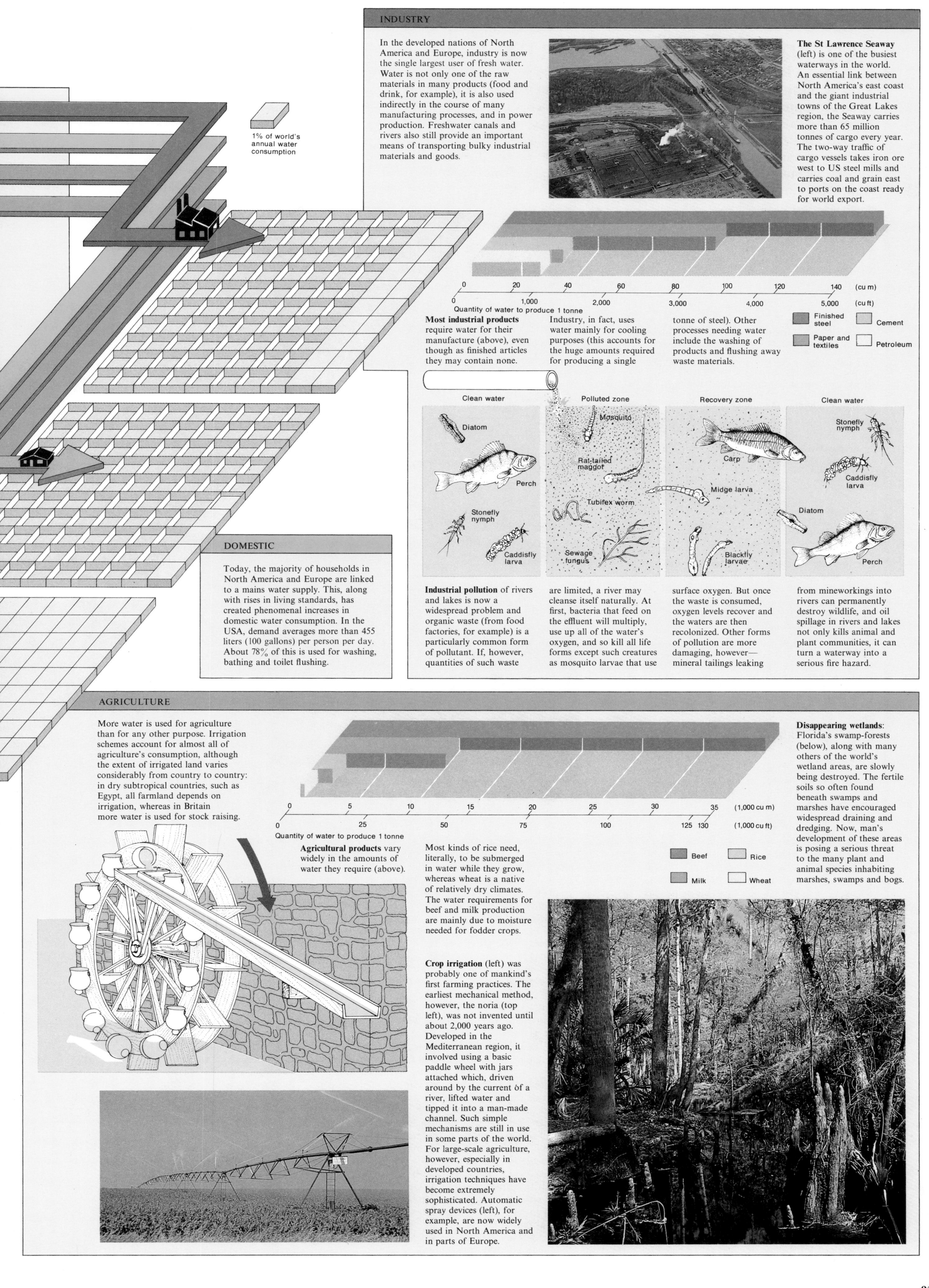

INDUSTRY

In the developed nations of North America and Europe, industry is now the single largest user of fresh water. Water is not only one of the raw materials in many products (food and drink, for example), it is also used indirectly in the course of many manufacturing processes, and in power production. Freshwater canals and rivers also still provide an important means of transporting bulky industrial materials and goods.

The St Lawrence Seaway (left) is one of the busiest waterways in the world. An essential link between North America's east coast and the giant industrial towns of the Great Lakes region, the Seaway carries more than 65 million tonnes of cargo every year. The two-way traffic of cargo vessels takes iron ore west to US steel mills and carries coal and grain east to ports on the coast ready for world export.

Most industrial products require water for their manufacture (above), even though as finished articles they may contain none. Industry, in fact, uses water mainly for cooling purposes (this accounts for the huge amounts required for producing a single tonne of steel). Other processes needing water include the washing of products and flushing away waste materials.

Industrial pollution of rivers and lakes is now a widespread problem and organic waste (from food factories, for example) is a particularly common form of pollutant. If, however, quantities of such waste are limited, a river may cleanse itself naturally. At first, bacteria that feed on the effluent will multiply, use up all of the water's oxygen, and so kill all life forms except such creatures as mosquito larvae that use surface oxygen. But once the waste is consumed, oxygen levels recover and the waters are then recolonized. Other forms of pollution are more damaging, however—mineral tailings leaking from mineworkings into rivers can permanently destroy wildlife, and oil spillage in rivers and lakes not only kills animal and plant communities, it can turn a waterway into a serious fire hazard.

DOMESTIC

Today, the majority of households in North America and Europe are linked to a mains water supply. This, along with rises in living standards, has created phenomenal increases in domestic water consumption. In the USA, demand averages more than 455 liters (100 gallons) per person per day. About 78% of this is used for washing, bathing and toilet flushing.

AGRICULTURE

More water is used for agriculture than for any other purpose. Irrigation schemes account for almost all of agriculture's consumption, although the extent of irrigated land varies considerably from country to country: in dry subtropical countries, such as Egypt, all farmland depends on irrigation, whereas in Britain more water is used for stock raising.

Agricultural products vary widely in the amounts of water they require (above). Most kinds of rice need, literally, to be submerged in water while they grow, whereas wheat is a native of relatively dry climates. The water requirements for beef and milk production are mainly due to moisture needed for fodder crops.

Crop irrigation (left) was probably one of mankind's first farming practices. The earliest mechanical method, however, the noria (top left), was not invented until about 2,000 years ago. Developed in the Mediterranean region, it involved using a basic paddle wheel with jars attached which, driven around by the current of a river, lifted water and tipped it into a man-made channel. Such simple mechanisms are still in use in some parts of the world. For large-scale agriculture, however, especially in developed countries, irrigation techniques have become extremely sophisticated. Automatic spray devices (left), for example, are now widely used in North America and in parts of Europe.

Disappearing wetlands: Florida's swamp-forests (below), along with many others of the world's wetland areas, are slowly being destroyed. The fertile soils so often found beneath swamps and marshes have encouraged widespread draining and dredging. Now, man's development of these areas is posing a serious threat to the many plant and animal species inhabiting marshes, swamps and bogs.

Seawater Environments

The oceans form by far the largest of the world's habitable environments, covering almost three-quarters of the Earth's surface at an average depth of more than 3,500 m (11,500 ft). Little more than a century ago, scientists believed that the deep sea's low temperatures, perpetual darkness and immense pressures made life in these regions completely untenable. But we now know that animals live at all depths in the ocean, even at the bottom of trenches more than 11,000 m (36,000 ft) deep.

THE PATTERN OF MARINE LIFE
The distribution of life in the seas is like an inverted pyramid whose broad base is formed by billions of minute single-celled plants—the phytoplankton. Plants need sunlight and nutrient salts, so phytoplankton occurs only in the upper, sunlit layers and where salts are present. Elsewhere, the distribution of marine life thins out rapidly.

Shore life belongs to both land and sea, and thus has to cope with a wide range of conditions. Seaweeds get all their food from the sea and are quite unlike land plants. Many animals take refuge below the surface: tellin shell molluscs sift food particles through special "lips"; lugworms swallow sand, digesting any organic matter; cockles take in food and eject waste through two siphons. Some birds have bills adapted for opening bivalve molluscs.

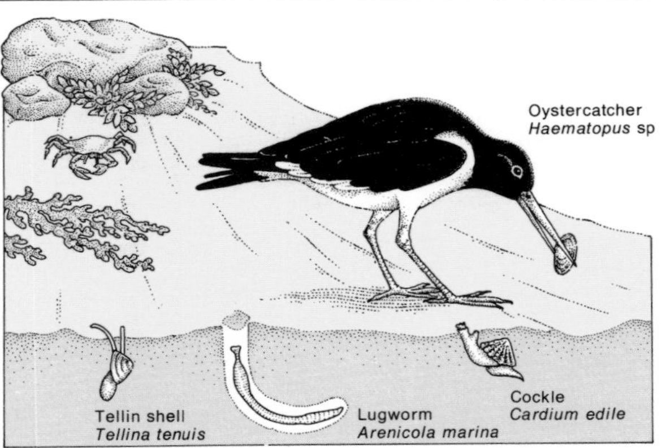

Marine plant life consists largely of diatoms—minute single-celled specks, each enclosed in a lidded box of silicon. Dinoflagellates, classed as plants but able to swim, dominate warmer waters. Both are food for copepods, the flea-sized grazers whose total weight, in the North Sea alone, is some seven million tonnes.

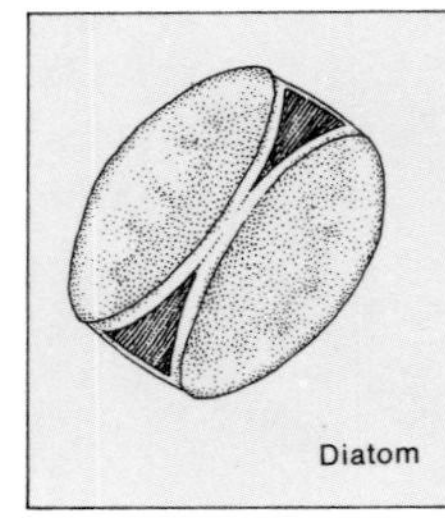

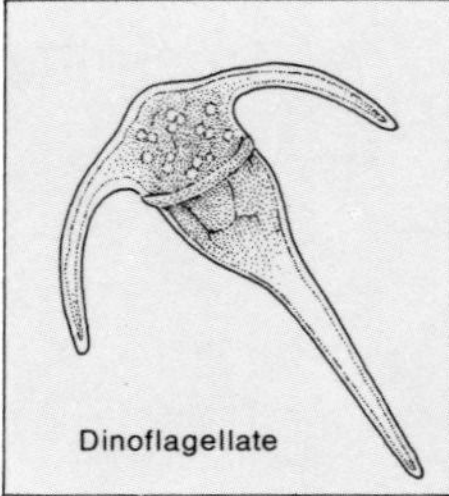

A coral atoll, forming in warm shallow water round an extinct volcano, makes up a living aquarium for thousands of tropical marine life forms. Countless billions of tiny polyps, each secreting a hard, calcareous skeleton, form the first layer of the reef, but die as the volcano gradually sinks. Their skeletons provide a base for further layers of corals, which enclose the sinking island to create a shallow, salt water lagoon. Different coral species in the same reef provide homes for a great variety of life.

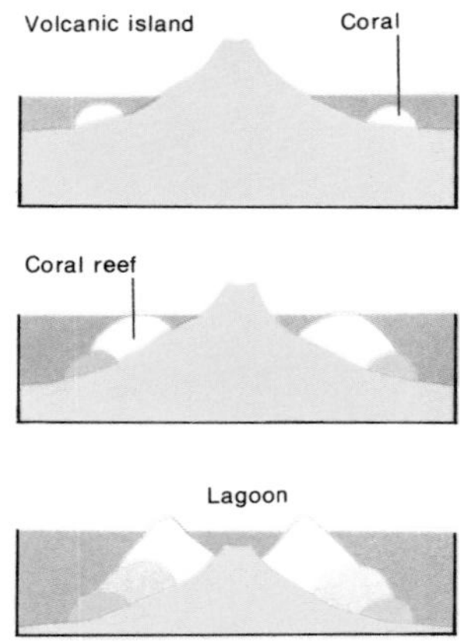

Life is by no means evenly distributed throughout the oceans, either vertically or horizontally. The great majority of marine creatures are concentrated in the upper few hundred meters, for the biological organization of life in the seas, as on land, depends on photosynthesis (the process by which plants use the Sun's energy to combine carbon dioxide and water to produce more complex compounds). This near-surface layer is the euphotic ("well-lighted") zone.

Some of the Sun's rays are reflected from the surface of the sea, and those that penetrate are scattered and absorbed as they pass through the water, so that even in the clearest oceanic water there is insufficient light to support photosynthesis at depths greater than about 100 m (330 ft). In turbid inshore regions, where the water is less clear, this near-surface layer may be reduced to a very few meters. So the large seaweeds that anchor themselves to the seabed are restricted to the small areas of the sea where the water is sufficiently shallow to allow them to photosynthesize. Of much greater importance over most of the oceans are the tiny floating plants of the phytoplankton, which live suspended in the sunlit surface layers.

Pastures of the sea

Phytoplankton, like all plant life, requires not only sunlight for survival but also adequate supplies of nutrient salts and chemical trace elements. River waters carry down considerable quantities of dissolved mineral salts and other matter, so that high levels of phytoplankton production may occur locally around major estuaries. But a far more important source of nutrient supply to the euphotic zone is the recycling of salts that have sunk into the deeper layers, locked up in the bodies of plants and animals or in their fecal pellets.

In those areas of the oceans that overlie the continental shelves (about six percent of the total), the depth is nowhere more than about 200 m (650 ft), and the nutrient-rich bottom water is fairly readily brought back to the surface by currents and the stirring effect of storms. This stirring can reach much greater depths in near-polar latitudes, where the "water column" is not layered by temperature but remains more or less uniformly cold from top to bottom. In the Antarctic, cold (and therefore heavy) surface water sinks and is replaced by nutrient-rich water that may surface from depths of 1,000 m (3,300 ft).

In subtropical and tropical regions of the open ocean, where the warm surface layer is only a few tens of meters deep, the temperature falls rapidly with depth. There is little exchange between deep and shallow layers, and the euphotic zone receives an adequate supply of nutrient salts only in certain areas. These occur between westward-flowing and eastward-flowing currents in each of the major oceans. The Earth's rotation causes these currents to diverge so as to create an upwelling of nutrient-rich water along their common boundaries. Finally, in restricted coastal regions of the tropics and subtropics the local climatic conditions cause an offshore movement of surface water, which is again replaced by upwelling nutrient-rich deep water. The central oceanic regions, including the deep blue subtropical waters, are in effect the deserts of the sea.

Sea grazers and carnivores

The abundance of animals in the oceans closely follows that of the plants. But very few of the larger marine animals can feed directly on the phytoplankton because the individual plants are so small—often only a fraction of a millimeter across. Instead, the phytoplankton supports an amazingly diverse community of planktonic animals, which also spend their lives in mid-water and are swept along by the ocean currents. This community, the zooplankton, includes many different protozoans (single-celled animals), crustaceans, worms and molluscs, and also the juvenile stages of fishes and of many invertebrate animals that live as adults on the seabed. Most members of the zooplankton are very small and many of them graze on the phytoplankton. But some planktonic animals, particularly among the jellyfish and salps, may be a meter or more across and are voracious carnivores feeding on their planktonic neighbors. In turn, the zooplankton provides food for many of the active swimmers such as the fishes and baleen whales, while at the top of the food chain are larger carnivores including

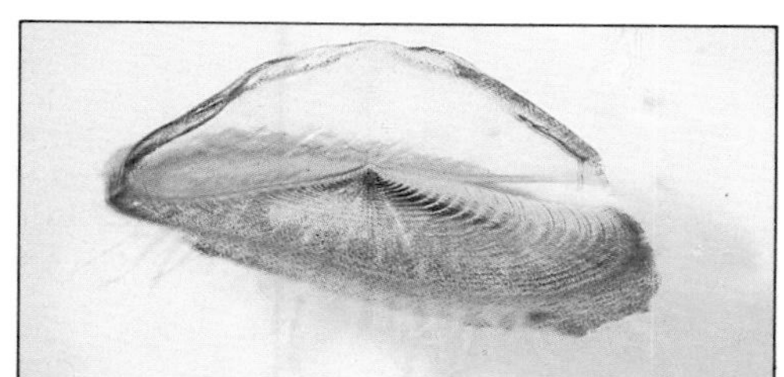

The by-the-wind sailor, *Velella*, is a so-called colonial animal, consisting of a whole collection of animals that function as a single individual. The gas-filled float of its body carries a vertical sail to catch the wind, and below dangle a group of modified polyps specialized for particular roles such as deterrence, reproduction, feeding and digesting.

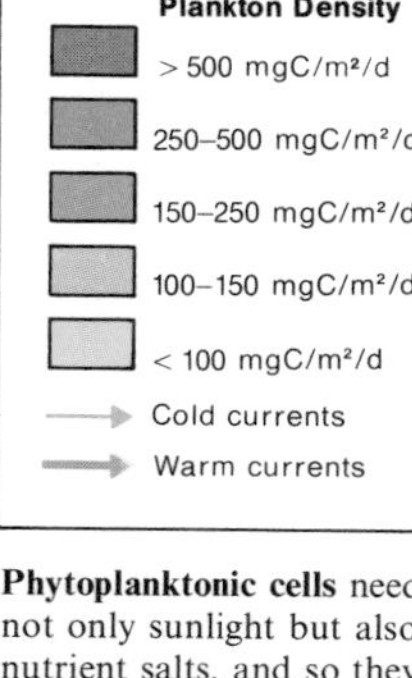

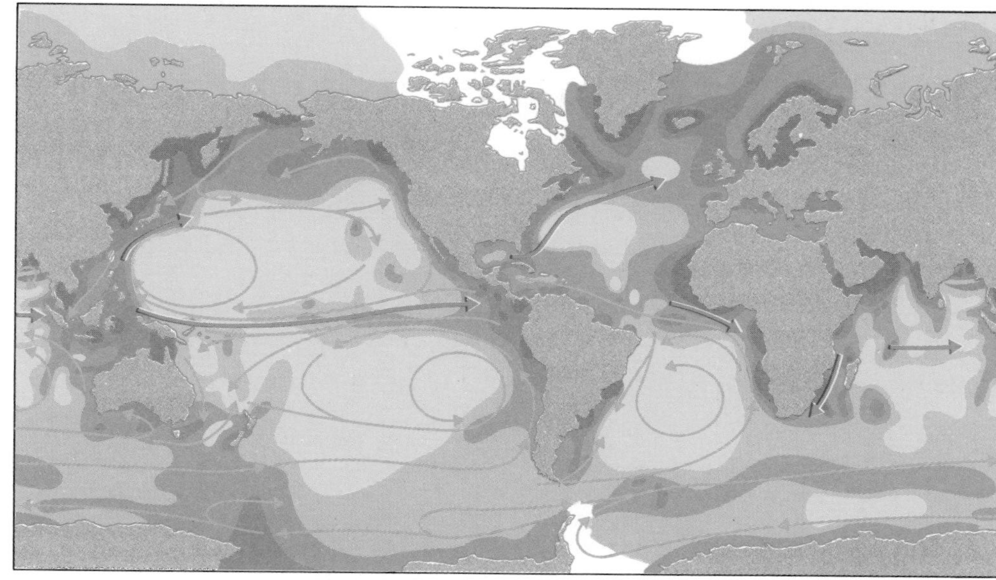

Phytoplanktonic cells need not only sunlight but also nutrient salts, and so they are restricted to areas where these are available: coastal regions, high latitudes (particularly the Antarctic), narrow tongues extending across the tropical regions of the main ocean basins, and a number of subtropical upwelling regions.

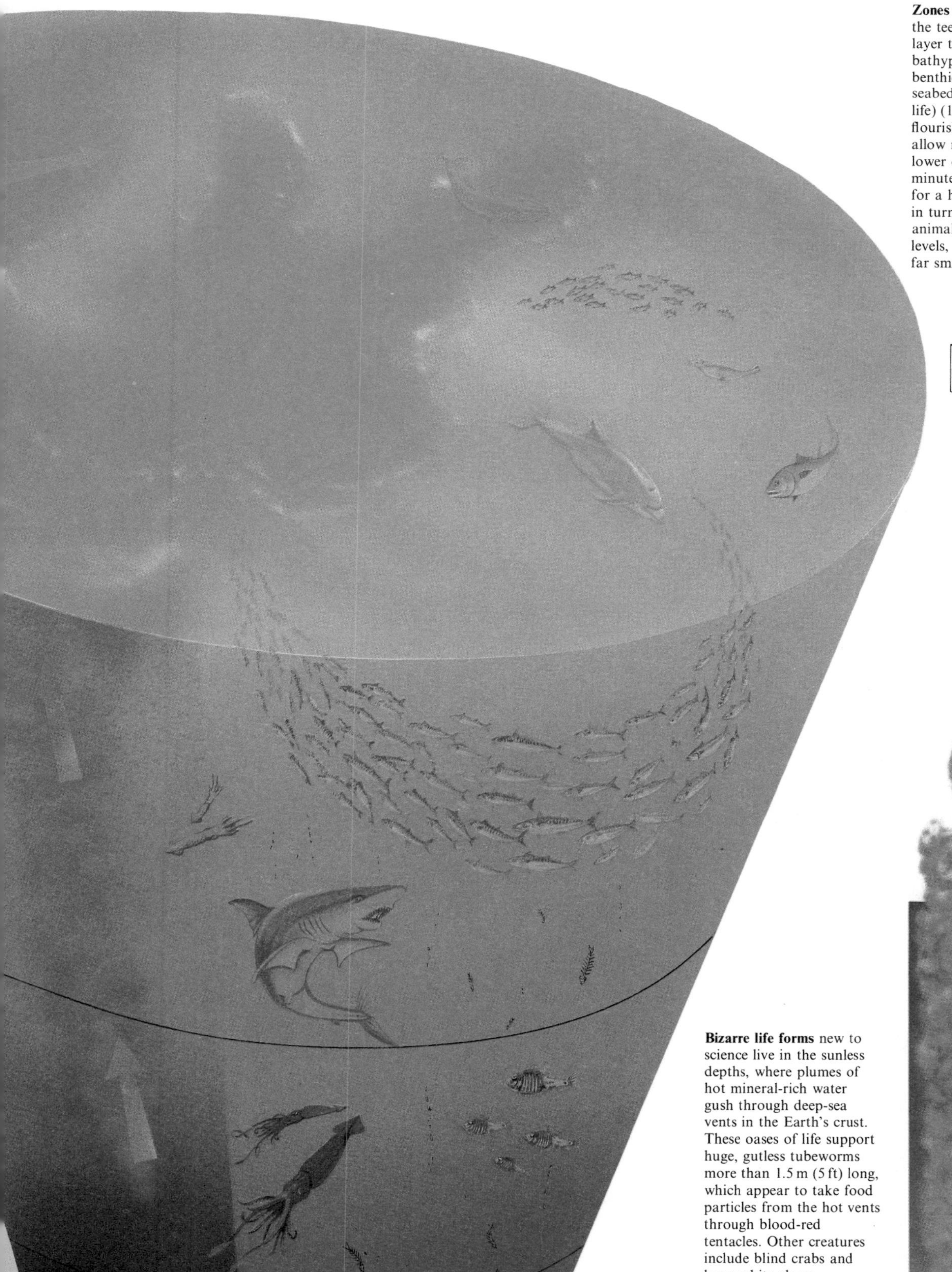

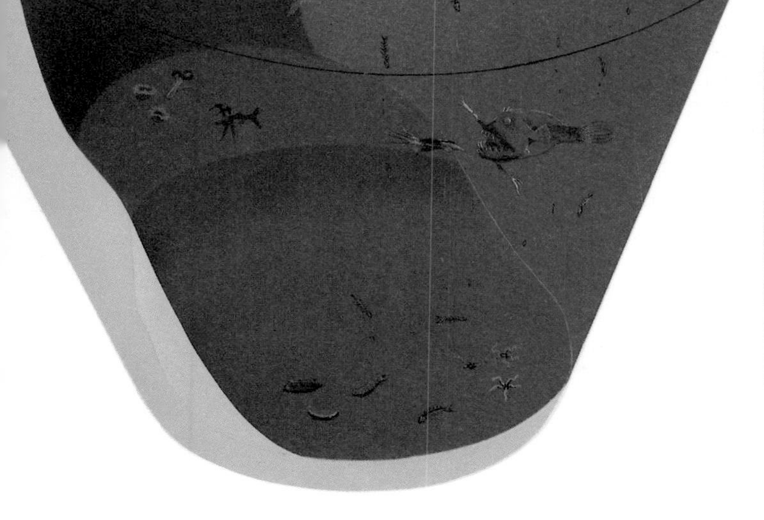

Zones of life (below) extend from the teeming euphotic ("well-lighted") layer to the sparsely populated bathypelagic ("deep-sea") depths, while benthic ("bottom") life occurs at all seabed levels. Phytoplankton (plant life) (1) dictates the pattern of the rest, flourishing where surface conditions allow nutrient salts to well up from lower depths. Herbivores such as minute zooplankton (2) provide food for a host of surface-layer life, which in turn feeds larger predators. Dead animals and fecal pellets fall to lower levels, where they sustain life, but in far smaller quantity.

1 Phytoplankton
2 Zooplankton
3 Blue whale *Balaenoptera musculus*
4 Herring *Clupea harengus*
5 Gray seal *Halichoerus grypus*
6 Bluefin tuna *Thunnus thynnus*
7 Bottlenosed dolphin *Tursiops truncatus*
8 Mackerel *Scomber scomber*
9 Common squid *Loligo* spp
10 White shark *Carcharadon carcharias*
11 Hatchet fish *Argyropelecus hemigymnus*
12 Giant squid *Architeuthis* spp
13 Sea anemone *Cerianthus orientalis*
14 Tripod fish *Benthosaurus grallator*
15 Scarlet shrimp *Notostomus longirostris*
16 Angler fish *Linophryne bicornis*
17 Brittle star *Ophiothrix fragilis*
18 Sea cucumber class Holothuroidea

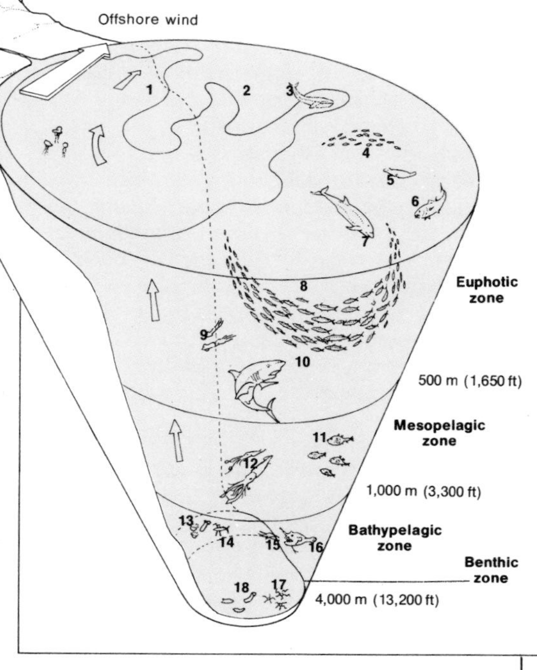

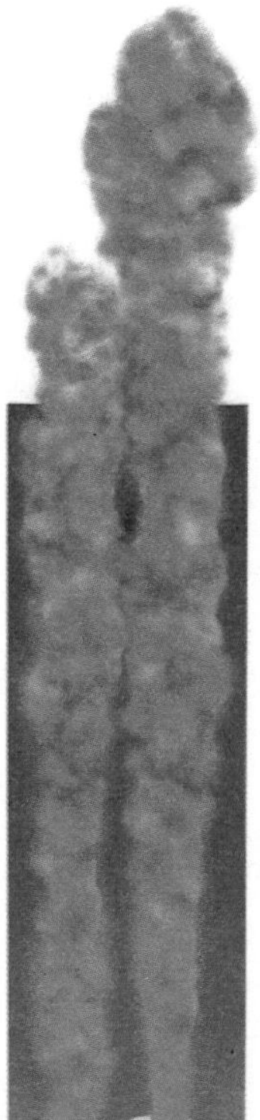

Bizarre life forms new to science live in the sunless depths, where plumes of hot mineral-rich water gush through deep-sea vents in the Earth's crust. These oases of life support huge, gutless tubeworms more than 1.5 m (5 ft) long, which appear to take food particles from the hot vents through blood-red tentacles. Other creatures include blind crabs and large white clams.

sharks, tuna-like fishes and toothed whales.

Beneath the euphotic zone, of course, there can be no herbivores at all, although some animals that spend the daylight hours in the deeper layers move upwards at night to feed in the plankton-rich surface waters. All of the permanent members of the deep-living communities are dependent for food upon material that sinks or is carried downwards from the euphotic zone. Many of them feed on dead animal remains and fecal material as it sinks through the water column or after it reaches the seabed. These detritus eaters in turn support the predatory carnivores that feed upon the detritivores or upon each other.

In shallow areas the food material that reaches the bottom supports complex communities, notably the rich and varied groups of invertebrates and fishes associated with coral reefs. In the deep sea, however, where the euphotic zone is separated from the seabed by several kilometers of water, much of the sinking material is recycled within the water column and relatively little reaches the bottom. Life on the deep-sea floor therefore becomes more and more sparse with increasing depth, but in recent years scientists have discovered that this community includes a surprising number of fishes, some many meters in length. So far man's knowledge of these deep-sea communities is relatively meager, but with our increasing use of the deep oceans we may need to know much more about the life in this environment.

Man and the Seawater Environments

For thousands of years man has used the oceans as a source of food and other materials, and as a repository for wastes. But only in the last 100 years have technological advances and fast-growing human populations had a significant effect, to a point where overfishing and pollution are becoming a cause for concern. Harvesting of krill and seaweeds may ease the pressure on traditional seafoods, but legal restrictions on dumping of wastes or on overfishing are notoriously hard to enforce.

Until about the middle of the nineteenth century the seas had always seemed to be a boundless source of food and of income for fishermen who were brave enough to face the elements with their relatively small sailing ships and primitive gear. But once fishing vessels began to be fitted with steam engines in the 1880s they became relatively independent of the weather, while improvements in the fishing gear itself, such as steam-powered winches in trawling and harpoon guns in whaling, made the whole business of fishing much more efficient.

At first these advances resulted in enormous increases in catches, but in many fisheries this was rapidly followed by a distressing fall in the catch per unit of effort—that is, it was becoming more and more difficult in successive years to catch the same amount of fish as before. In most fisheries the initial response to this situation was to increase the size and number of fishing vessels and to search for new fishing grounds. But as the fishing pressure on the stocks increased, with smaller fish being captured, often before they were able to reproduce, the catch per unit of effort frequently continued to fall.

In many cases attempts were made to counter the effects of overfishing by introducing regulations to control the mesh size of the nets, so allowing the small fish to escape; by establishing closed seasons or quotas of fish which might legitimately be taken from a particular fishing ground in any one year; or even, as in the case of the British herring fishery in the late 1970s, by imposing a complete ban on fishing. Moral questions also sometimes intervene, as in whaling operations, which, many conservationists believe, have driven some species close to extinction despite attempts to rationalize the fisheries.

Fisheries in decline

The North Sea trawl fishery, the first to be affected by the new technology in the nineteenth century, has been declining in terms of catch per unit of effort since the early decades of this century. Dramatic but short-lived improvements after the "closed seasons" of the two world wars proved that fishing pressure had a serious effect on stocks, but by the 1970s many North Sea fishing ports had become almost deserted. This decline put pressure on more distant fishing grounds used by European fishermen, and recent decades have been marked by a series of fishing disputes, with nations fighting for the continued existence of their fisheries despite clear evidence that there are not enough catchable fish to satisfy everyone.

A similar story of declining catches during the present century could be told of many of the old-established fisheries around the world, but at the same time the demand for fish in a protein-hungry world has increased. To satisfy this demand the total annual world catch increased by about seven percent from the end of World War II until the early 1970s, by this time reaching a figure of around 60–70 million tonnes. But this increase was achieved only by exploiting previously unfished stocks or new geographical areas. Such an increase cannot go on indefinitely, for we are rapidly running out of "new" areas and some of the new fisheries have already shown the same symptoms of overfishing as the older ones—and sometimes even more dramatically.

New foods from the sea

The indications are that the present total catch is close to the maximum that can be obtained from relatively conventional fisheries even with careful management, and that, to increase the total, or even to sustain it, we must look to completely new sources such as krill, the shrimp-like food of the whalebone whales. Estimates of the sustainable annual catch of krill in the Antarctic range from about 50 to 500 million tonnes, that is up to about seven times as much as the current total from all other fisheries put together. Of course, the use of such an enormous quantity of small crustaceans would present considerable problems. Part of it might be converted into a protein-rich paste for human consumption, but much would be used indirectly as a feed for farm animals.

Many larger seaweeds are already cropped in several parts of the world, particularly in Japan, and are used not only for human food but also for animal food and in many industrial processes. About one million tonnes of seaweed are taken each year, but because seaweeds grow naturally only in relatively shallow areas of the oceans this figure could probably not be significantly increased using natural populations. However, seaweeds can be grown artificially on frames floating over deep water. Experiments suggest that, by enriching the surface layers through artificial upwelling of nutrient-rich deep water, each square kilometer of such a floating seaweed farm could produce enough food to feed 1,000–2,000 people, and enough energy and other products to satisfy the needs of a further 1,000. With an estimated 260 million sq km (100 million sq miles) of "arable" surface, the seas might thus support up to 10 times the present world population.

Polluted waters

Of course, the present century has seen an increase not only in what man takes out of the sea but also in the harmful substances that he throws into it. Not only oil but many other substances are dumped into the seas accidentally or intentionally, usually either in the discharged effluent from industrial plant or as a result of agricultural chemicals being leached into rivers and thence into the ocean. In many cases the amounts are very small compared with the amounts present in the oceans as a whole; the problem is that they are usually released, and accumulate, in restricted inshore areas near which we live and from which we obtain most of our sea-caught food.

Since the 1930s there have been both national and international attempts to control pollution by legislation, and since 1958 a series of United Nations conferences has sought agreement on many aspects of international maritime law, including pollution. Despite many prophecies of imminent doom, it does not seem that marine pollution yet poses any general threat to humanity. Nevertheless, with ever-increasing industrialization and the production of more and more toxic materials, including radioactive wastes, it is essential that we monitor the effects of man's activities on the ocean.

THE MARINE RESOURCES
Modern technology has enabled man to expand his age-old exploitation of the seas to the limit in some areas, and a need for the careful management of our marine resource is imperative. But in some fields, such as energy and the extraction of fresh water, the seas may yield inexhaustible riches.

The ocean is home to the Bajau (above), the "sea gypsies" of southeastern Asia, who inhabit a tract of sea and islands stretching more than 6,500 km (4,000 miles). Each group has its own clan pattern, blazoned on the sails of their *praus*. The Bajau may live on the open sea in clusters of boats, or in stilt-house villages built over estuaries.

The deep-sea drilling ship *Glomar Challenger* (above) plays an important role in surveying and prospecting the oceans. It can drill in water depths of 7,000 m (23,000 ft) and obtain core samples 1,200 m (4,000 ft) below the ocean bed. The ship is positioned over the drill hole through signals from a sonar beacon to hydrophones in the hull.

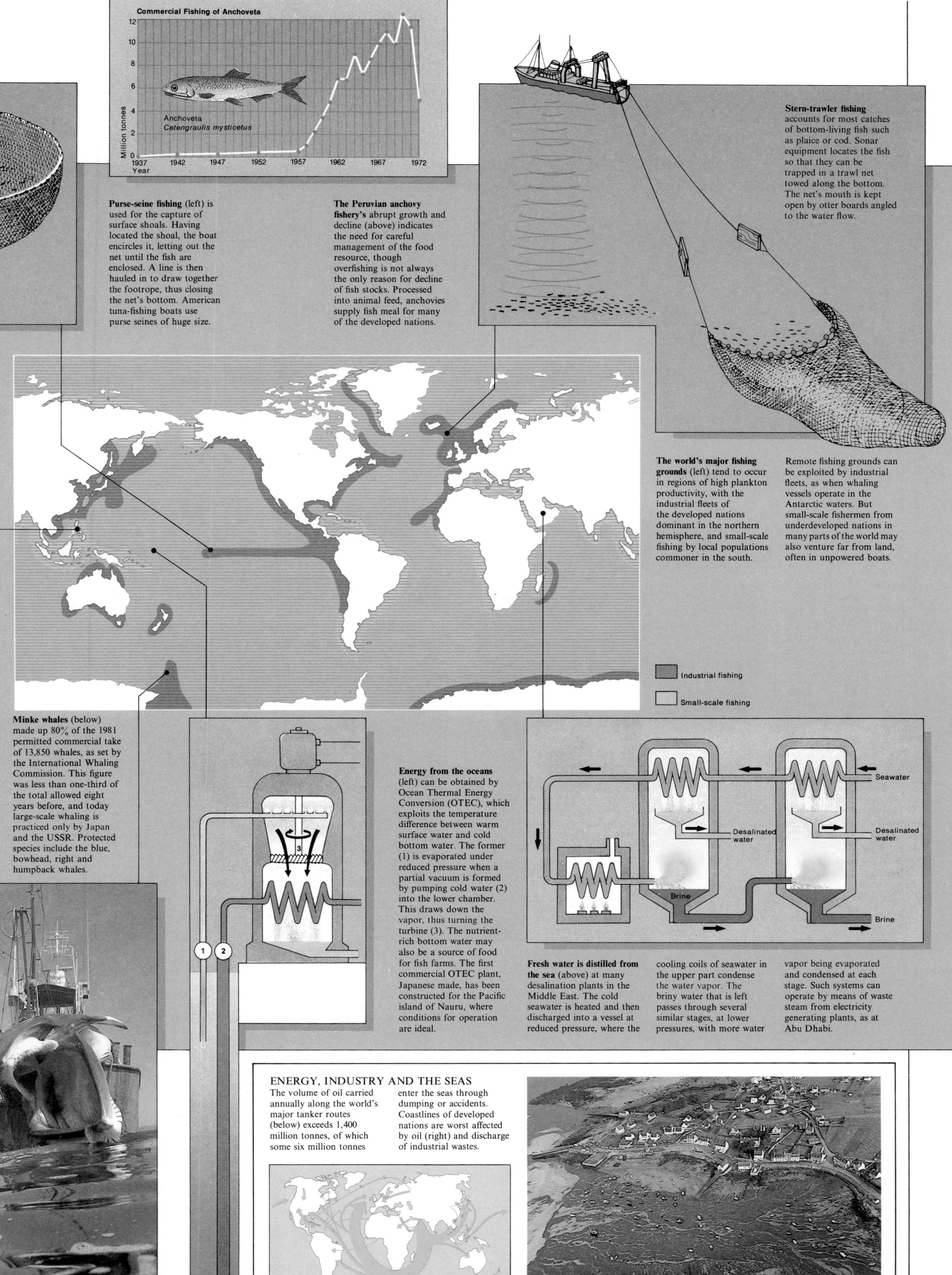

Purse-seine fishing (left) is used for the capture of surface shoals. Having located the shoal, the boat encircles it, letting out the net until the fish are enclosed. A line is then hauled in to draw together the footrope, thus closing the net's bottom. American tuna-fishing boats use purse seines of huge size.

The Peruvian anchovy fishery's abrupt growth and decline (above) indicates the need for careful management of the food resource, though overfishing is not always the only reason for decline of fish stocks. Processed into animal feed, anchovies supply fish meal for many of the developed nations.

Stern-trawler fishing accounts for most catches of bottom-living fish such as plaice or cod. Sonar equipment locates the fish so that they can be trapped in a trawl net towed along the bottom. The net's mouth is kept open by otter boards angled to the water flow.

The world's major fishing grounds (left) tend to occur in regions of high plankton productivity, with the industrial fleets of the developed nations dominant in the northern hemisphere, and small-scale fishing by local populations commoner in the south.

Remote fishing grounds can be exploited by industrial fleets, as when whaling vessels operate in the Antarctic waters. But small-scale fishermen from underdeveloped nations in many parts of the world may also venture far from land, often in unpowered boats.

Minke whales (below) made up 80% of the 1981 permitted commercial take of 13,850 whales, as set by the International Whaling Commission. This figure was less than one-third of the total allowed eight years before, and today large-scale whaling is practiced only by Japan and the USSR. Protected species include the blue, bowhead, right and humpback whales.

Energy from the oceans (left) can be obtained by Ocean Thermal Energy Conversion (OTEC), which exploits the temperature difference between warm surface water and cold bottom water. The former (1) is evaporated under reduced pressure when a partial vacuum is formed by pumping cold water (2) into the lower chamber. This draws down the vapor, thus turning the turbine (3). The nutrient-rich bottom water may also be a source of food for fish farms. The first commercial OTEC plant, Japanese made, has been constructed for the Pacific island of Nauru, where conditions for operation are ideal.

Fresh water is distilled from the sea (above) at many desalination plants in the Middle East. The cold seawater is heated and then discharged into a vessel at reduced pressure, where the cooling coils of seawater in the upper part condense the water vapor. The briny water that is left passes through several similar stages, at lower pressures, with more water vapor being evaporated and condensed at each stage. Such systems can operate by means of waste steam from electricity generating plants, as at Abu Dhabi.

ENERGY, INDUSTRY AND THE SEAS

The volume of oil carried annually along the world's major tanker routes (below) exceeds 1,400 million tonnes, of which some six million tonnes enter the seas through dumping or accidents. Coastlines of developed nations are worst affected by oil (right) and discharge of industrial wastes.

Part 5

UNDERSTANDING MAPS

What maps are and how they are made
New horizons and latest developments in maps and mapmaking
How to read the language of maps

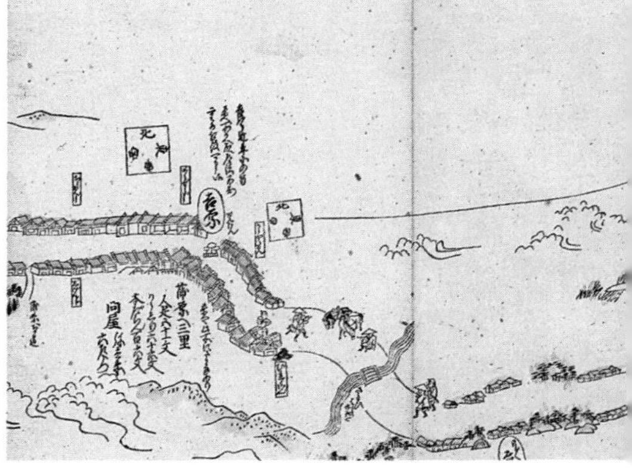

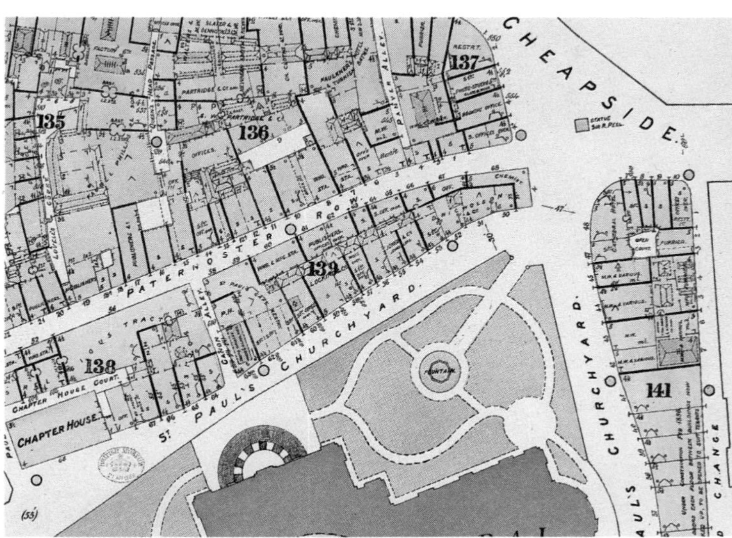

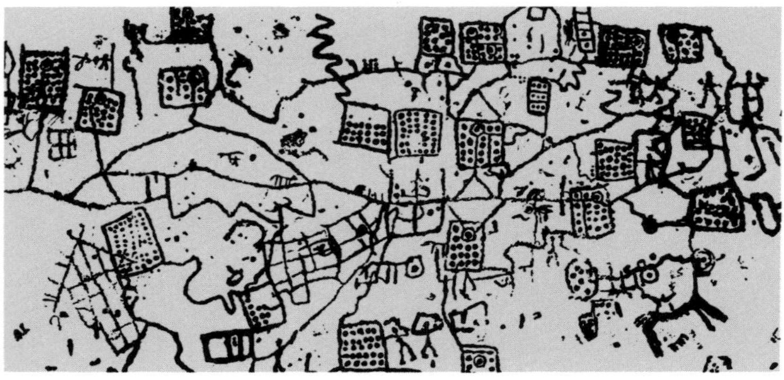

Maps defining territory and ownership are almost as old as the human territorial instinct itself. The rock-carving maps of the Val Camonica, Italy (above), dating from the second and first millennia BC, show stippled square fields, paths, river lines, houses, and even humans and animals. It is uncertain whether their purpose was legal, but the need to establish ownership is a basic function of many maps, as seen in a detail from Goad's 19th-century insurance map of London (left), where every occupation is recorded.

Elegant road maps with pictorial and geographical features have been produced by many different cultures. The woodcut map of the Tōkaidō (detail above), the great Japanese highway, 555 km (345 miles) long, between Edo (Tokyo) and Kyoto, was drawn as a panorama by the famous artist Moronobu in 1690. Its pictorial details do not prevent it being an accurate representation of the road's track. A Mexican map of the Tepetlaoztoc valley (right) drawn in 1583 marks roads with footprints between parallel lines, and hill ranges with wavy lines. Symbols in panels represent place-names.

America first appears as a separate continent (below) in an inset to Martin Waldseemüller's world map of 1507, with the two hemispheres facing each other. Presiding over the Old World is Claudius Ptolemy, the 2nd-century geographer whose remarkably scientific maps, copied and recopied over a thousand years, were revised and emended by Waldseemüller to show some of the results of Portuguese exploration. His New World counterpart is the Italian Amerigo Vespucci, one of the early explorers of the continent, after whom it was named. This is the first map to show the Pacific (not yet named) as an ocean between America and Asia. The west coast of South America, still to be explored by Europeans, seems to be inspired guesswork. The island between the landmasses is Cipango (Japan) known from Marco Polo.

The earliest surviving Chinese globe (above) was made in 1623 by two Jesuit missionaries, probably for the emperor of China. The long legend in Chinese expresses terms and ideas derived from early Chinese cosmology. It describes the Earth as "floating in the Heavens like the yolk of an egg . . . with all objects having mass tending toward its center"—one of the first known references to gravity.

1 2

High-altitude photography (left) allows accurate updating of topographic maps (right), while data gathering by satellites (above) expands the range. Landsat satellites carry electronic remote-sensing equipment that detects the energy emitted by surface materials and translates it into images. Healthy plants may show as bright red, sparse vegetation as pink, barren lands as light gray, and urban areas as green or dark gray. The folded shape of the Appalachians (1) is clearly seen; the Canada–US border (2) is revealed by land-use patterns; silt from the Mississippi (3) builds up the delta. Sudan irrigation (4) shows up as brilliant red.

Mapping, Old and New

Mapmaking must have its origins in the earliest ages of human history, since people of preliterate as well as literate cultures possess an innate skill in map drawing. This innate capacity is further indicated by the ease with which almost anyone can sketch in the sand or on paper simple directions for showing the way. But maps may also define territory and express man's idea of the world in graphic representation. Today, modern technology has vastly extended the scope of cartography.

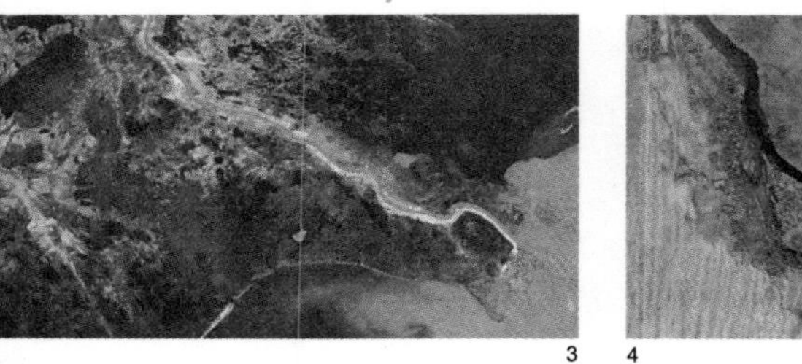

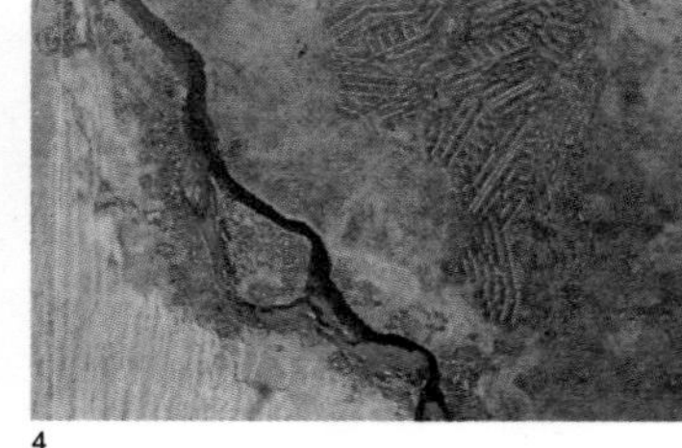

3 4

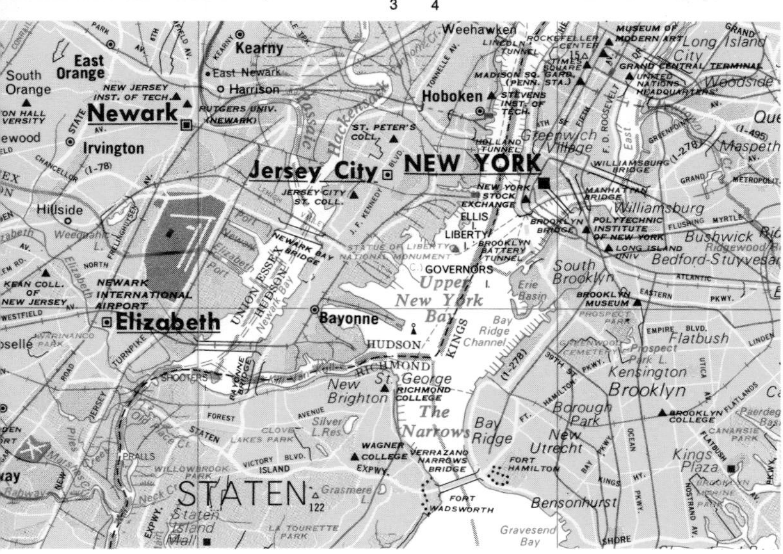

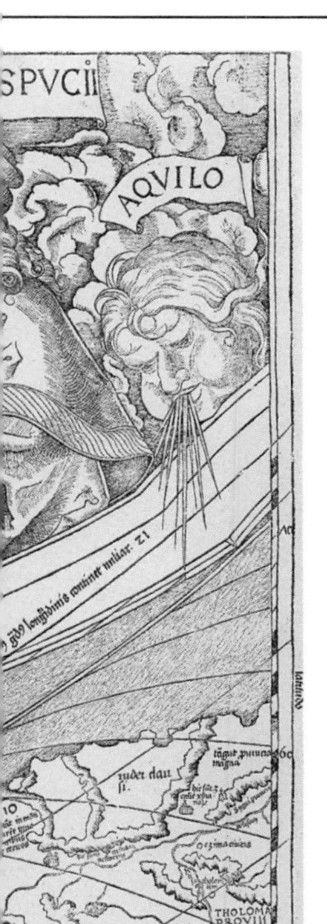

Space technology helps cartographers to map even interior details of the planet: its geology and mineral wealth. A photo (below) taken from Gemini 12 at an altitude of 272 km (168 miles) forms the basis of a geologic sketch map of SW Asia (below right), showing the oil-rich area around the region between the Persian Gulf and the Gulf of Oman. The symbol S on the map indicates salt plugs; diamonds show fold trends; double-headed arrows anticlines.

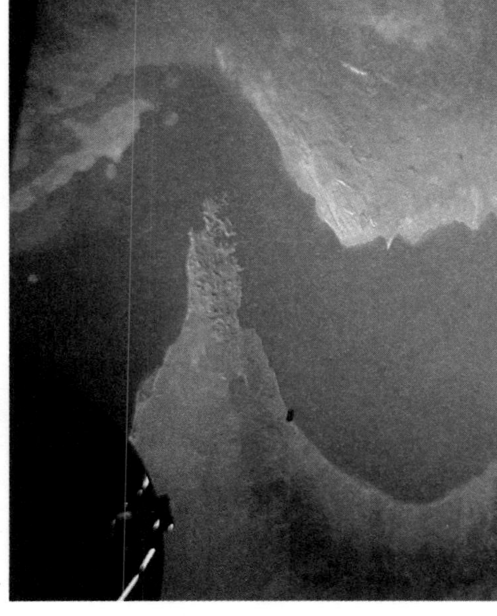

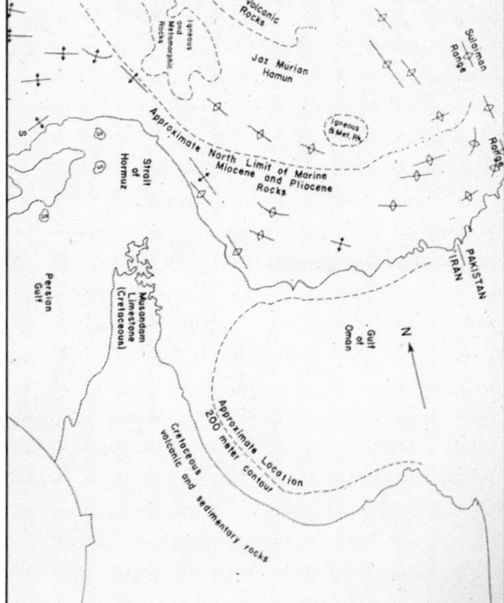

Many non-European cultures developed ingenious route-map techniques: the North American Indians, for example, made sketch maps of routes on birch bark. These were diagrammatic maps in which directions and distances were not accurate but relationships were true, as in New York Subway or London Underground maps. The people of the Marshall Islands in the western Pacific made route maps over the seas, depicting the direction of the main seasonal wave swells in relation to the islands.

Although maps of routes are the simplest type of map in concept, they developed complex forms as cartography progressed. A road map of the whole Roman Empire, drawn about AD 280, survives today in a thirteenth-century copy known as the Peutinger Table. Hernando Cortes, the Spanish conqueror, made his way across Mexico in the 1520s with the help of pre-conquest Mexican maps painted on cloth. These showed roads with double lines or colored bands marked with footprints. Another type of map is the strip map depicting a single road along its entire length. Pictorial maps of the Tōkaidō highway from Edo to Kyoto in Japan, made from a survey of 1651, were popular in the Edo period of Japanese history.

Nautical charts evolved as a special type of direction-finding map to meet the needs of seamen. Those of the late Middle Ages came to be known as "portolan" charts, from the word "portolani," or sailing directions. They showed the sea and adjacent coasts superimposed on a network of radiating compass lines.

Territorial maps

Another basic type of map derives from man's sense of territorial possession. The earliest example of a "cadastral" plan (a map showing land parcels and property boundaries) appears to be that preserved as rock carvings at Bedolina in Val Camonica in northern Italy. However, in the ancient civilizations of Mesopotamia and Egypt, land surveying had become an established profession by 2000 BC. An idea of what Egyptian surveyors' plans of 1000 BC were like can be seen from the "Fields of the Dead" representing the Egyptians' idea of life after death. These show plots of land surrounded by water and intersected by canals. The Romans used cadastral surveys to determine land ownership and assess tax liability.

Another form of map showing territorial demarcations is the map of administrative units. The Chinese in the thirteenth century AD were making official district maps to help in the organization of grain supplies and the collection of taxes. Many of their gazetteers (*fang chih*), written in the form of local geographies and histories from the eleventh century onward, were illustrated with maps. Political maps showing the boundaries of states were increasingly significant in European cartography from the sixteenth century onward.

A third major class of map is the general or topographical map expressing man's perception of the world, its regions and its place in the universe. A Babylonian world map of the seventh century BC is drawn on a clay tablet and shows the Earth as a circular disc surrounded by the Earthly Ocean. With the ancient Greeks, geography developed on scientific principles. The treatise on mapmaking by Claudius Ptolemy (AD 87–150), later known as the *Geographia*, was the most famous cartographic text of the period. It influenced the Arabic geographers of the Middle Ages, notably Muhammad Ibn Muhammad, Al-Idrisi (1099–1164), and with the revival of Ptolemy in fifteenth-century Europe became one of the major works of the Renaissance. Published, with engraved maps, at Bologna in 1477, the *Geographia* ranks as the first printed atlas in the western world. The invention of techniques of engraving in wood and copper facilitated a wide diffusion of geographical knowledge through the map-publishing trade. The first atlas made up of modern maps to a uniform design was Abraham Ortelius's *Theatrum Orbis Terrarum* published at Antwerp in 1570. From 1492, when Martin Behaim made his "Erdapfel" at Nürnberg, globes also became popular, and globemakers vied with each other to make larger and more elaborate ones to keep pace with the growth of knowledge about the world.

Over the last two hundred years cartography has made rapid and remarkable advances. Observatories built in Paris in 1671 and at Greenwich in 1675 enabled the location of places to be established more exactly with the use of astronomical tables. Improvements in surveying instruments facilitated more accurate and rapid land survey. France was the pioneer in establishing (from 1679 onward) a national survey on a geometrical basis of triangulation. By the end of the eighteenth century national surveys on small and medium scales had been begun by most European countries. In the United States the Geological Survey was set up in 1879 to undertake the topographical and geological mapping of the country.

Mapping today

Since World War II cartographic techniques have undergone a revolution. The use of air survey and photogrammetry has made it possible to map most of the Earth's surface. Electronic distance measurement by laser or light beams in surveying, and digital computers in mapping, are among the most recent advances in methods. Mosaics or air photography are used to produce orthophoto maps which can supplement or substitute for the conventional topographic map. Artificial satellites and manned space craft make it possible to provide a world-wide framework of geodetic networks.

Earth Resource Technology Satellites (ERTS) imagery has made it possible to map mountain ranges in Africa and features on the surface of Antarctica that were hitherto unknown. The imagery is made available by means of remote-sensing instruments, carried by the satellites, that are sensitive to invisible portions of the electromagnetic spectrum—longer and shorter wavelengths than can be sensed by the human eye. Remote-sensing instruments usually work in the infrared bands. They can also pick up the energy emitted by all types of surface material—rocks, soils, vegetation, water and man-made structures—and produce photographs or images from it.

The Language of Maps

Mapmakers for more than 4,000 years have tried to find the best way to represent the shape and features of the three-dimensional Earth on two-dimensional paper, parchment and cloth. The measurement of distance and direction is a basic requirement for accurate surveys, but until about 1800 theoretical understanding of the method was well in advance of the technical equipment available. Today the use of lasers and light beams sometimes takes the place of direct measurement on the ground.

A reference system must be used to show distance and direction correctly in the construction of maps. The simplest type is the rectangular or square grid. The Chinese mapmaker Pei Xin made a map with a grid in about AD 270, and this system remained in continuous use in China until modern times. The Roman system of centuriation, a form of division of public lands on a square or rectangular basis, was also a "coordinate" system starting from a point of origin at the intersection of two perpendicular axes. Roman surveyors' maps, dating from the first century AD, are the earliest known European maps based on a grid system.

Latitude and longitude

Makers of small-scale regional maps and of world maps in early times also had to take account of the fact that the Earth is a sphere. The Greeks derived from the Babylonians the idea of dividing a circle into 360 degrees. In the second century BC the Greek geographer Eratosthenes (*c.* 276–194 BC) was the first to calculate the circumference of the globe and was reported to have made a world map based on the concept of the Earth's sphericity. From this the Greeks went on to develop the system of spherical coordinates which remains in use today. The poles at each end of the Earth's axis provide reference points for the Earth in its rotation in relation to the celestial sphere. Parallel circles around the Earth are degrees of latitude and express the idea of distance north or south of the Equator. Lines of longitude running north and south through the poles express east–west distances. One meridian is chosen as the meridian of origin, known as the prime meridian.

Whereas latitude from early times could be observed from the height of the Sun or (in the northern hemisphere) from the position of the Pole Star at night, accurate observations of longitude were not possible until the middle of the eighteenth century, when the chronometer was invented and more accurate astronomical tables were provided. In 1884 most countries agreed, at an international conference in Washington DC, to adopt the prime meridian through the Royal Greenwich Observatory in England and to calculate longitude to 180 degrees east and west of Greenwich.

Projection and distortion

The mathematical system by which the spherical surface of the Earth is transferred to the plane surface of a map is called a map projection. The Greek geographer Ptolemy gave instructions in his geographical treatise of AD 150 for the construction of two projections. When the *Geographia* was revised in Europe in the fifteenth century, and navigators began sailing across the oceans, mapmakers devised new projections more appropriate to the expanding geographical knowledge of the world. The Dutch geographer Gerard Mercator invented the projection named after him, applying it to his world chart of 1569. This cylindrical projection, in which all points are at true compass courses from each other, was of great benefit to navigators and is still one of the most commonly used projections. Another advance was made when Johann Heinrich Lambert of Alsace (1728–1777) invented the azimuthal equal-area projection, in which the sizes of all areas are represented on the projection in correct proportion to one another, and the conformal projection, in which at any point on the map the scale is constant in all directions.

Since all projections involve deformation of the geometry of the globe, the cartographer has to choose the one that best suits the purpose of his map. "Conformal" or "orthomorphic" projections, in which angular relations (or shape) are preserved, are widely used for the construction of topographical maps. "Equivalent" or "equal-area" projections retain relative sizes and are particularly useful for general reference maps displaying economic, historical, political and other geographical phenomena.

Since the mid-fifteenth century, European mapmakers have generally arranged their maps with north at the top of the sheet. Earlier maps, however, were not standardized in this way. The circular world maps of the Middle Ages were orientated with east at the top, because this was where the terrestrial paradise was traditionally sited. Indeed, the word "orientation" originally meant the arrangement of something so as to face east.

Map scale

Scale is another basic property of a map. The scale of a map is the ratio of the distance on the map to the actual distance represented. Whereas the Babylonians, Egyptians, Greeks and Romans drew surveys to scale, in medieval Europe mapmakers used customary methods of estimating. The earliest known local map since Roman times which is drawn to scale (it displays a scale bar) is a plan of Vienna, 1422.

Projection, grid, orientation and scale form the framework of a map. The language of maps in concept and content is much more complex. To represent the surface of the Earth on a map, the cartographer must select and generalize from a vast quantity of material, using symbols and conventional signs as codes.

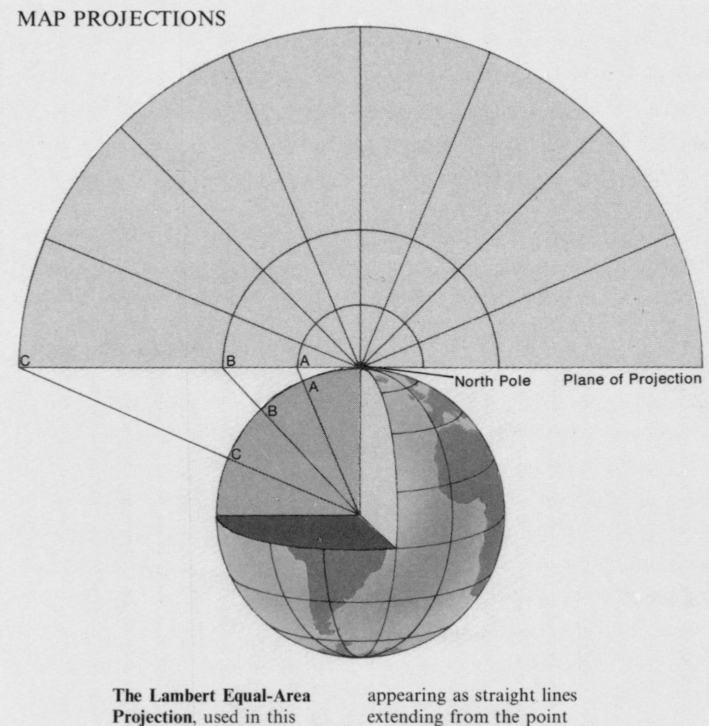

The Lambert Equal-Area Projection, used in this atlas, may be visualized as a flat plane placed at a tangent to the globe, with the lines of longitude appearing as straight lines extending from the point of tangency, the North Pole (above). Deformation increases away from this point (below).

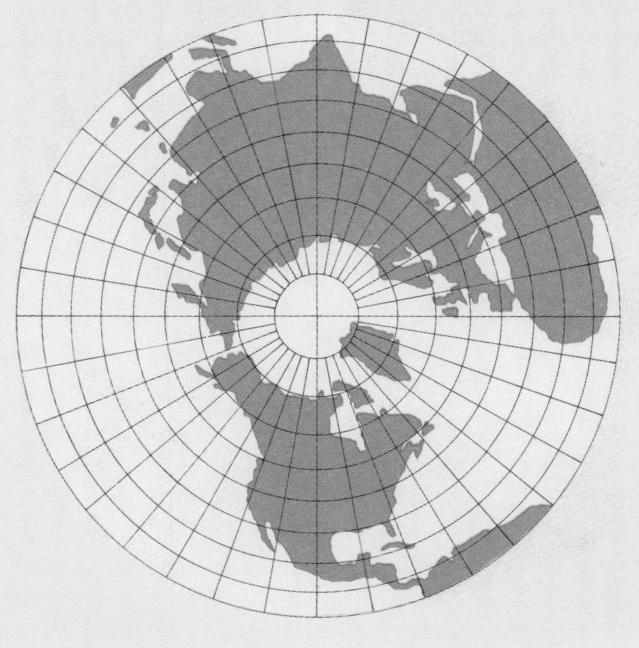

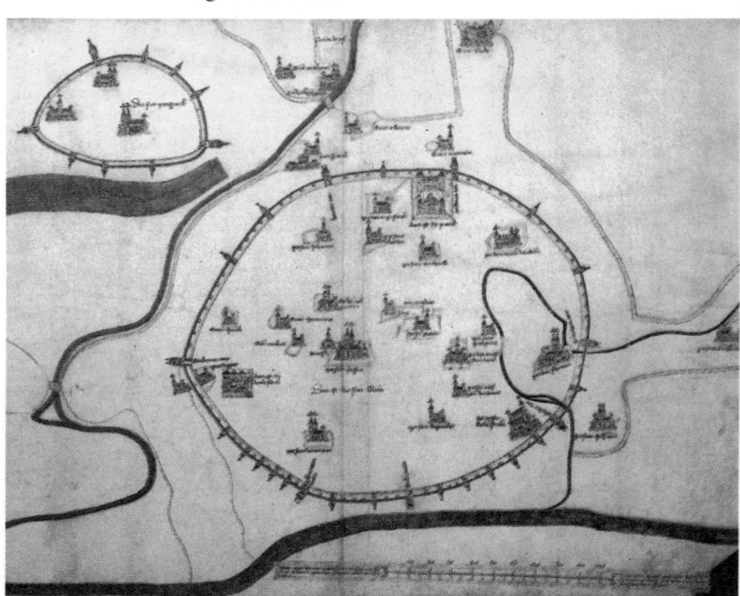

Map scales express the relationship between a distance measured on the map and the true distance on the ground. A plan of Vienna (left), originally made in 1422, is drawn in the bird's-eye-view style typical of early medieval town plans. But the scale bar at its foot shows that it has been explicitly drawn to scale, indicating that the concept of a uniform scale had been grasped in medieval Europe.

Direction and distance are concepts used in the relative location of two or more points (below). These concepts are organized according to a general frame of reference, with direction following the grid system of coordinates. Thus places shown in (A) can be precisely located in terms of longitude and of latitude (B), with the degrees further subdivided into one-sixtieths of minutes.

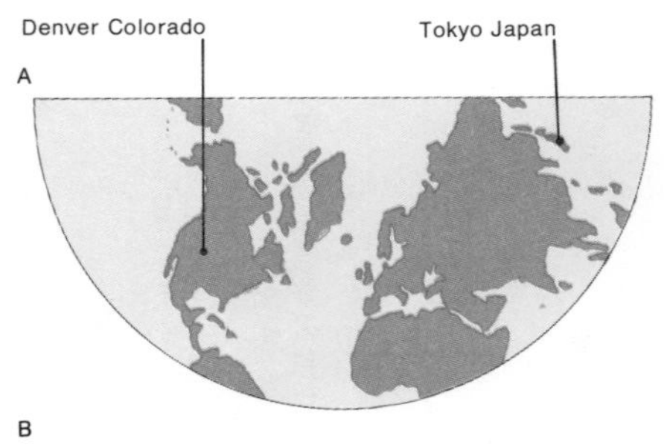

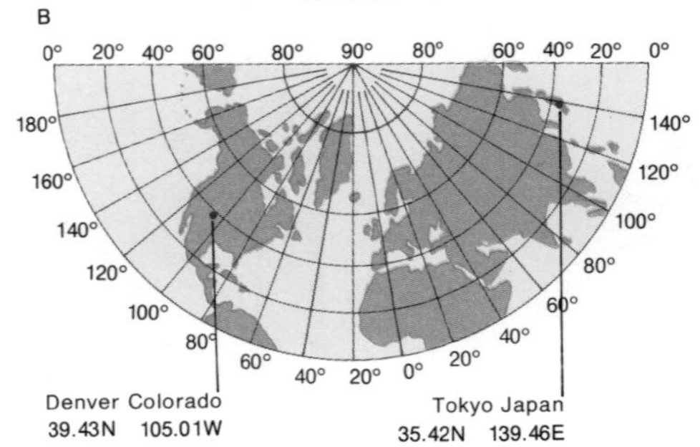

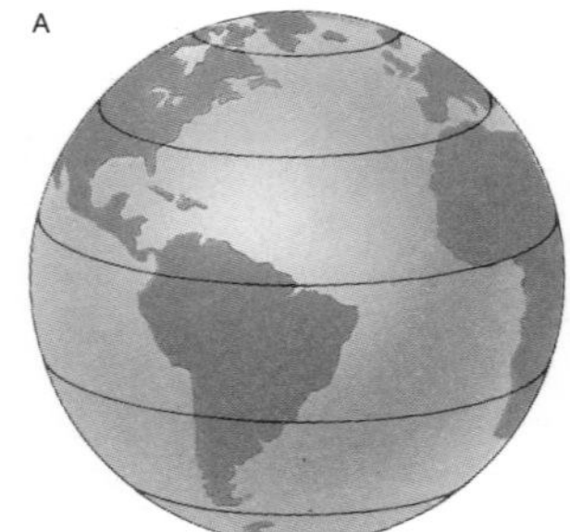

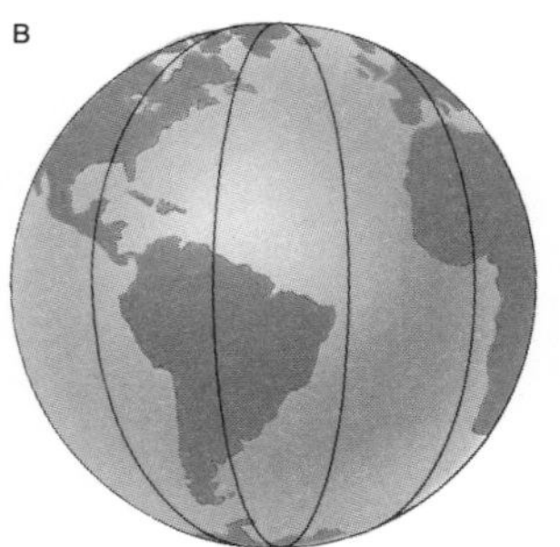

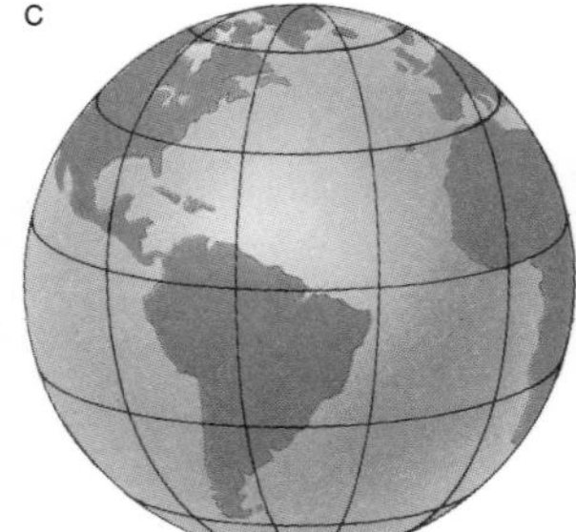

Superimposed on the globe (left), lines of latitude (A) and longitude (B) allow every place to be exactly located in terms of a coordinate system (C). The parallels of latitude measure distance from 0° to 90° north and south of the Equator. The meridians of longitude measure distance from 0° to 180° east and west of a "prime meridian" at Greenwich.

The Hammer Projection (far right), developed from the Lambert Projection of one hemisphere (right), is designed to show the whole world in a single view, and is used in this atlas in a version modified by Wagner and known as the Hammer-Wagner Projection. The Earth appears as an ellipse because the lines of longitude are plotted at twice their horizontal distance from the center line, and numbered at twice their previous values. The central meridian is half the length of the Equator.

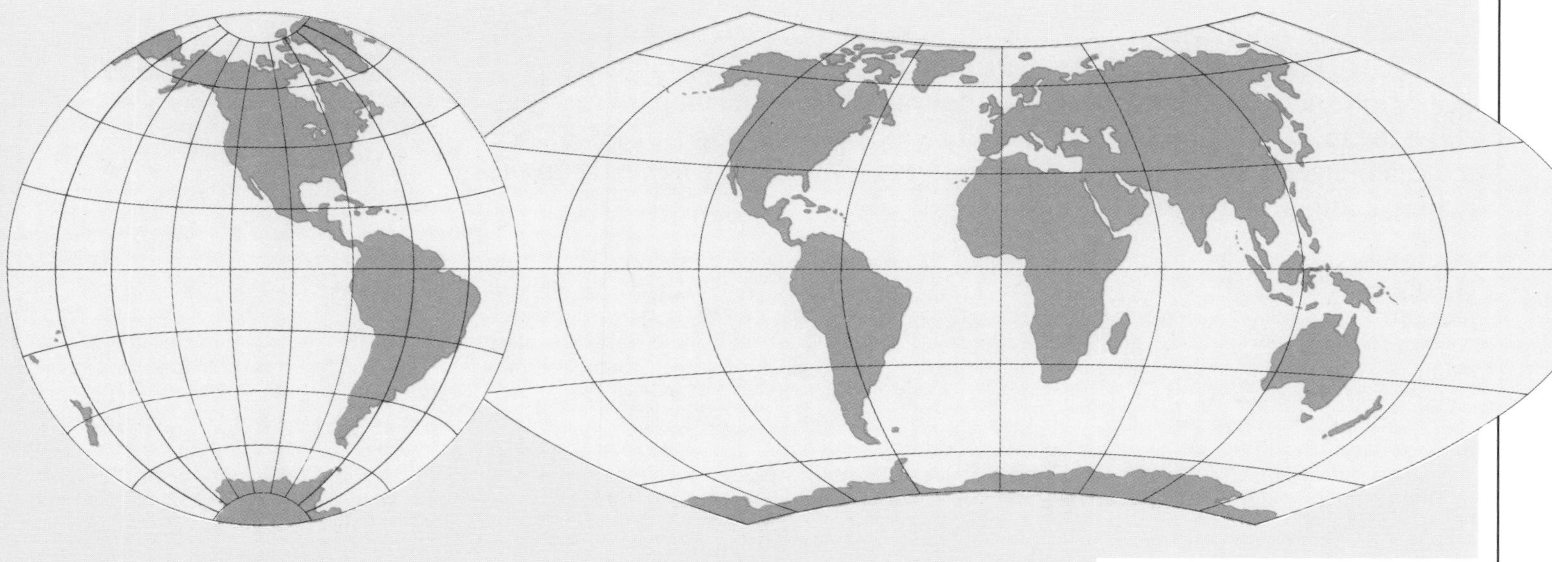

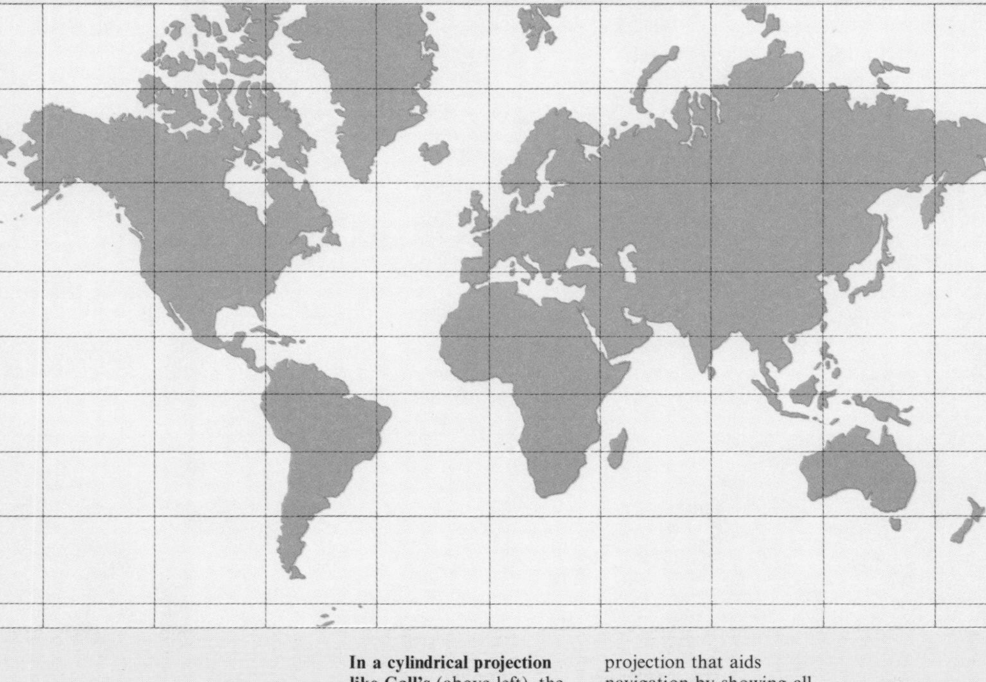

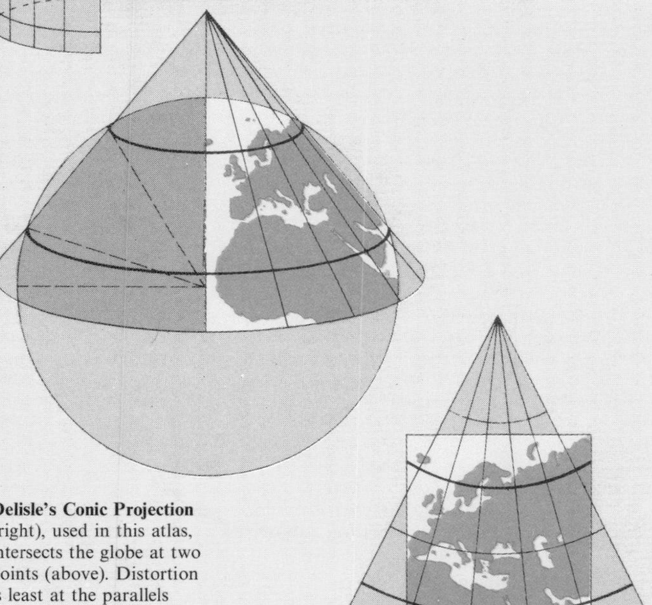

In a cylindrical projection like Gall's (above left), the sphere is "unwrapped" on to a cylinder, making a complete transformation to a flat surface. Mercator's Projection (above), devised in 1569, is a cylindrical projection that aids navigation by showing all compass directions as straight lines. A projection (below), based on Peters', distorts shape to show land surface area ratios, emphasizing the Third World.

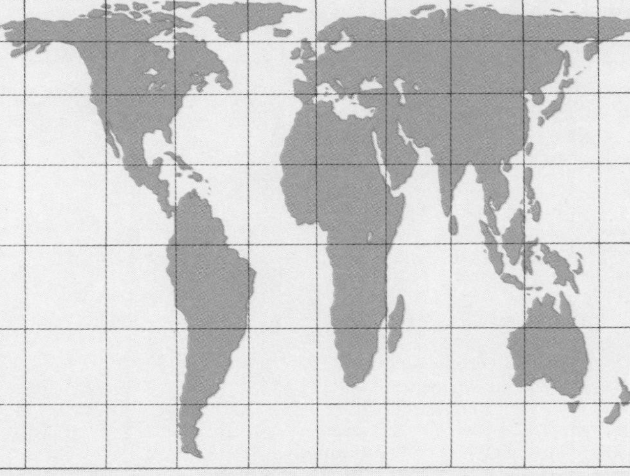

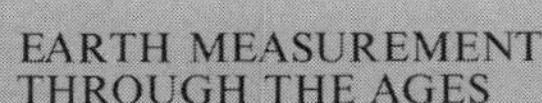

Delisle's Conic Projection (right), used in this atlas, intersects the globe at two points (above). Distortion is least at the parallels where the cone "touches" the globe, increasing with distance from them. Thus it is good for mid-latitudes.

Photogrammetric plotting instruments (above) are now used in the preparation of large-scale accurate topographic maps. These are sophisticated machines that provide very precise measurements, plotting the map data in orthogonal projection.

The theodolite (above), a basic surveying instrument dating back to the 16th century, can measure angles and directions horizontally and vertically. A swivel telescope with cross-hairs inside it permits accurate alignment, and it may be used in the field.

EARTH MEASUREMENT THROUGH THE AGES

Surveying—the technique of making accurate measurements of the Earth's surface—is as old as civilization and has been an essential element in mankind's development of his environment. The need to establish land boundaries arose at least 3,500 years ago in the fertile valleys of the Nile, Tigris and Euphrates rivers. Man's urge to explore and to describe the world also led to the development of instruments determining position, distance and direction. The astrolabe, sometimes called the world's oldest scientific instrument, may date to the 3rd century BC. Today's techniques make increasing use of computers.

An Egyptian wall painting (left) from the middle of the second millennium BC shows what appears to be the measurement of a grain field by means of a rope with knots at regular intervals on its length.

The astrolabe (right), used in classical times to observe the positions of celestial bodies, became a navigational instrument in the Middle Ages, when it was developed to permit establishment of latitude.

How to Use Maps

Today maps play a role more important than ever before in increasing our knowledge of the Earth, its regions and peoples. How maps communicate knowledge is now a subject of scientific study. The process comprises the collection and mapping of the data and the reading of the map. In this final stage the map user is all important. Through him the map is transformed into an image in the mind, and the effectiveness of the map depends on the reader being able to understand it.

The cartographer's map has to convey an objective picture of reality. To compile the map the cartographer selects and generalizes information, taking into account the purpose of his map. If he is making a topographical reference map, he has to reduce the three-dimensional landforms of the Earth on to the flat surface of the map. He adds cultural detail such as towns, roads and railroads, and features not apparent to the eye, such as administrative boundaries. On the topographical base map he adds appropriate place-names, using typefaces which reflect their class and significance. All this requires the classification of phenomena, with emphasis to direct the reader's attention.

Themes and symbolization

The cartographer who seeks not merely to represent visible features but to convey geographical ideas about specific phenomena uses the techniques of thematic cartography, where the emphasis is on one or two elements, or themes. Maps today provide one of the most effective means of communicating many kinds of data and ideas relating to the world and its peoples. Their extensive use makes them an important force in education, planning, recreation and in many other human affairs.

The map is designed in code, with symbols to represent features, and a legend, or key, to explain them. There are three types of symbol: point, line and area. Point symbols usually denote places, which may be distinguished into classes by the shape, color and size of the symbol. Line symbols express connections, such as roads or traffic flow, and they may also define and distinguish areas. Area symbols in which variations of color are often combined with patterns of lines or dots are used to depict spatial phenomena, such as types of soil, vegetation and density of population.

How much detail can be shown on a map will depend on its scale, which controls the process of generalization. Scale expresses the relationship of the distance on the map to the distance on the Earth, with the distance on the map always given as the unit 1. It is denoted in various ways: as a representative fraction such as 1:1,000,000; as a written statement; or by means of a graph or bar. Some map scales have become widely used and are generally familiar to map users. The scale 1:25,000 is ideal for walkers and relief can be shown in detail. That of 1:50,000 is a typical medium scale for national surveys. The publication of an international map of the world on a scale of one to one million (1:1,000,000) has been in progress since 1909. On this scale 1 mm represents 1 km on the ground. The regional maps of countries in this atlas are drawn on scales of 1:6,000,000, 1:3,000,000 and 1:1,500,000; those of the continents are at 1:30,000,000 and 1:15,000,000. The Map Section index maps show the arrangement.

Terrain depiction

Since the early days of map making in ancient Chinese and classical Greek and Roman civilizations, map makers have been concerned to show the configuration of the land. For many centuries they symbolized mountains and hills by pictorial features often looking like caterpillars or sugar loaves. As topographical mapping developed in Europe from the seventeenth century onward, new techniques were devised to improve the visual impression of the features and to depict them accurately in terms of height and location. The system of hachuring (shading with fine parallel or crossed lines), first used in 1674, gives a good idea of relief but not of height. The use of contours, which became general from the nineteenth century onward, is more exact in representing actual elevation, but for many regions, especially those of irregular relief, the appearance of the land is lost.

The addition of hypsometric tints (tints between contours which show elevation) helps clarify the elevation. Applying shadows to the form of the land through the process called hill shading or relief shading creates a visual impression of the configuration of the land surface. Hypsometric tints combined with hill shading gives both elevation information and surface form of the area being depicted, leading to an almost three-dimensional effect.

Maps are classed (right) as either general (A) or thematic (B,C). The purpose of a general reference map is to provide locational information, showing how the positions of various geographical phenomena relate to each other. Thematic maps concentrate on a particular type of information, or theme, such as the distribution of people (B) or rainfall (C), and are generally based on statistical data.

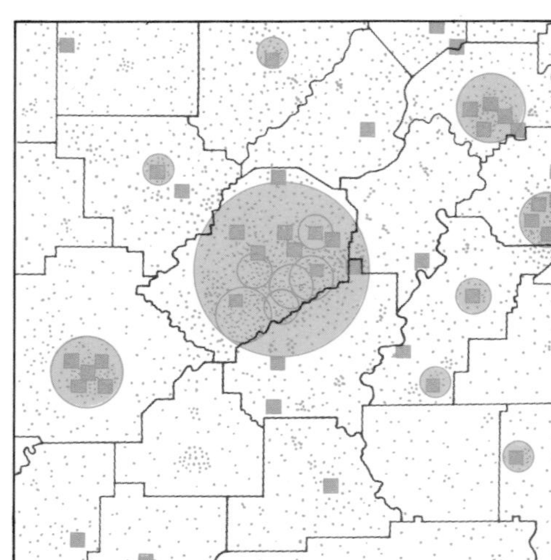

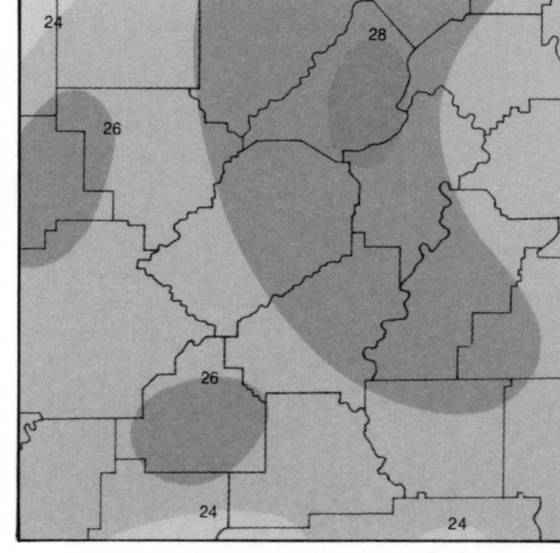

Scale 1:12,000,000

The ratio between a map's dimensions and those of the physical world is defined by the map scale (left and below), with the map distance always given as the unit 1. The larger the reduction, the smaller the scale, so that a scale of 1:6,000,000—1 mm (.04 in) to 6 km (3.74 miles)—is twice that of 1:12,000,000 (.04 in to 7.5 miles). The size of the scale reflects the amount of detail that needs to be shown. The projections are the Lambert Azimuthal Equal-Area (left) and Delisle Conic Equidistant (below).

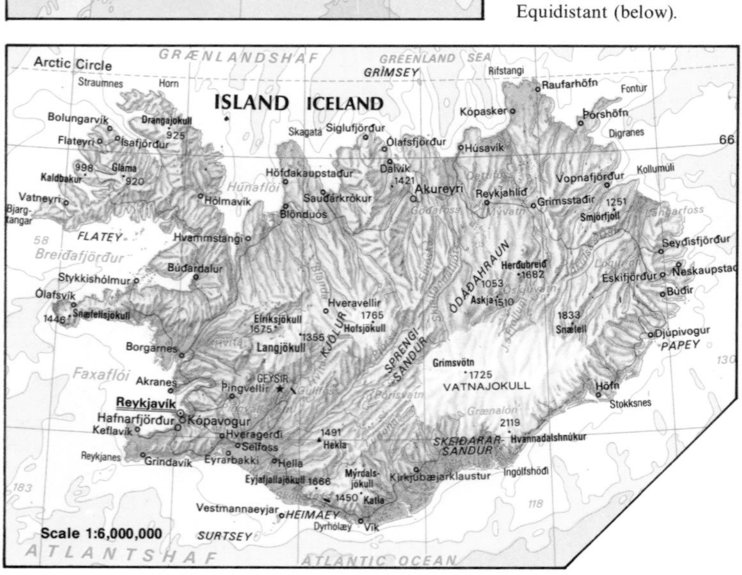

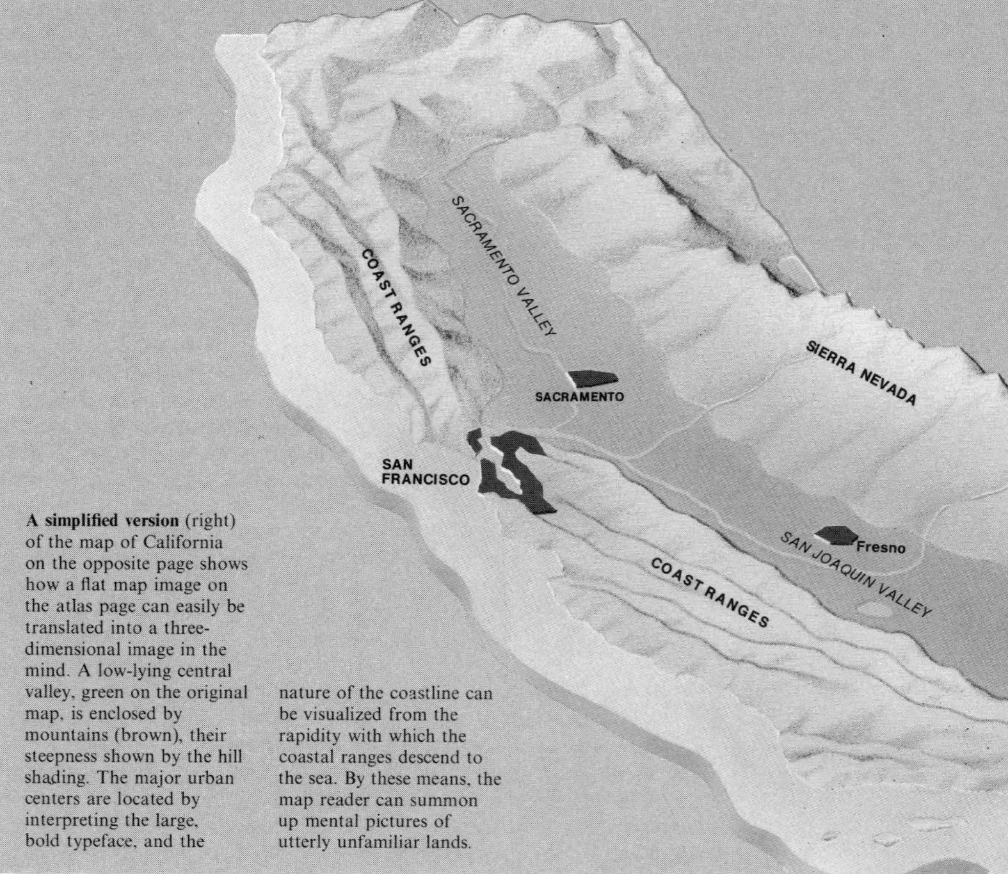

A simplified version (right) of the map of California on the opposite page shows how a flat map image on the atlas page can easily be translated into a three-dimensional image in the mind. A low-lying central valley, green on the original map, is enclosed by mountains (brown), their steepness shown by the hill shading. The major urban centers are located by interpreting the large, bold typeface, and the nature of the coastline can be visualized from the rapidity with which the coastal ranges descend to the sea. By these means, the map reader can summon up mental pictures of utterly unfamiliar lands.

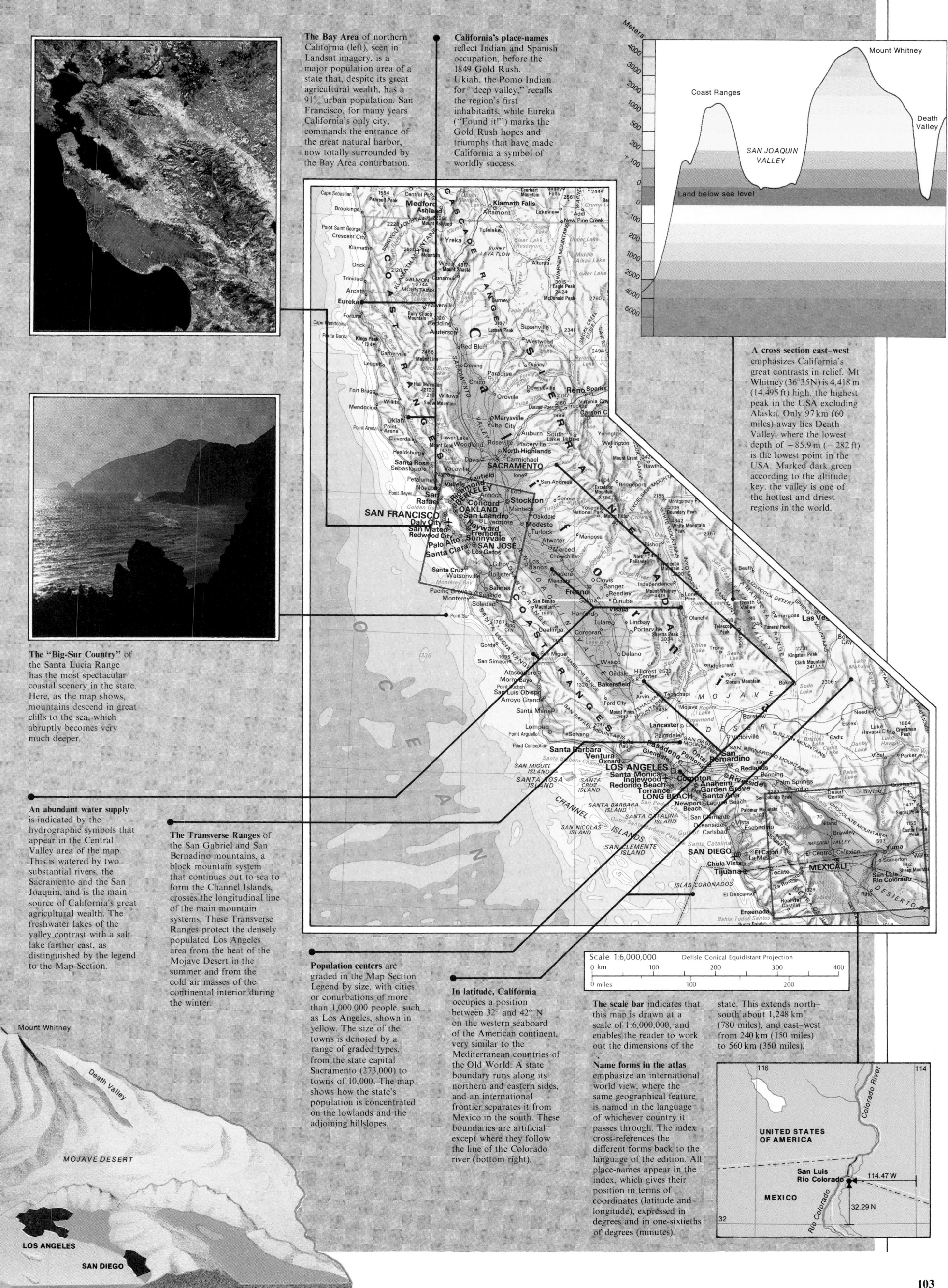

The Bay Area of northern California (left), seen in Landsat imagery, is a major population area of a state that, despite its great agricultural wealth, has a 91% urban population. San Francisco, for many years California's only city, commands the entrance of the great natural harbor, now totally surrounded by the Bay Area conurbation.

California's place-names reflect Indian and Spanish occupation, before the 1849 Gold Rush. Ukiah, the Pomo Indian for "deep valley," recalls the region's first inhabitants, while Eureka ("Found it!") marks the Gold Rush hopes and triumphs that have made California a symbol of worldly success.

A cross section east–west emphasizes California's great contrasts in relief. Mt Whitney (36°35N) is 4,418 m (14,495 ft) high, the highest peak in the USA excluding Alaska. Only 97 km (60 miles) away lies Death Valley, where the lowest depth of −85.9 m (−282 ft) is the lowest point in the USA. Marked dark green according to the altitude key, the valley is one of the hottest and driest regions in the world.

The "Big-Sur Country" of the Santa Lucia Range has the most spectacular coastal scenery in the state. Here, as the map shows, mountains descend in great cliffs to the sea, which abruptly becomes very much deeper.

An abundant water supply is indicated by the hydrographic symbols that appear in the Central Valley area of the map. This is watered by two substantial rivers, the Sacramento and the San Joaquin, and is the main source of California's great agricultural wealth. The freshwater lakes of the valley contrast with a salt lake farther east, as distinguished by the legend to the Map Section.

The Transverse Ranges of the San Gabriel and San Bernardino mountains, a block mountain system that continues out to sea to form the Channel Islands, crosses the longitudinal line of the main mountain systems. These Transverse Ranges protect the densely populated Los Angeles area from the heat of the Mojave Desert in the summer and from the cold air masses of the continental interior during the winter.

Population centers are graded in the Map Section Legend by size, with cities or conurbations of more than 1,000,000 people, such as Los Angeles, shown in yellow. The size of the towns is denoted by a range of graded types, from the state capital Sacramento (273,000) to towns of 10,000. The map shows how the state's population is concentrated on the lowlands and the adjoining hillslopes.

In latitude, California occupies a position between 32° and 42° N on the western seaboard of the American continent, very similar to the Mediterranean countries of the Old World. A state boundary runs along its northern and eastern sides, and an international frontier separates it from Mexico in the south. These boundaries are artificial except where they follow the line of the Colorado river (bottom right).

The scale bar indicates that this map is drawn at a scale of 1:6,000,000, and enables the reader to work out the dimensions of the state. This extends north–south about 1,248 km (780 miles), and east–west from 240 km (150 miles) to 560 km (350 miles).

Name forms in the atlas emphasize an international world view, where the same geographical feature is named in the language of whichever country it passes through. The index cross-references the different forms back to the language of the edition. All place-names appear in the index, which gives their position in terms of coordinates (latitude and longitude), expressed in degrees and in one-sixtieths of degrees (minutes).

ACKNOWLEDGMENTS

Senior Executive Art Editor
Michael McGuinness

Executive Editor
James Hughes

Coordinating Editor
Dian Taylor

Editors
Lesley Ellis
Judy Garlick
Ken Hewis

Art Editor
Mike Brown

Designers
Sue Rawkins
Lisa Tai

Picture Researcher
Flavia Howard

Researchers
Nicholas Law
Nigel Morrison
Alicia Smith

Editorial Assistant
Barbara Gish

Proofreader
Kathie Gill

Indexers
Hilary and Richard Bird

Production Controller
Barry Baker

Typesetting by Servis Filmsetting Limited, Manchester, England

Reproduction by Gilchrist Brothers Limited, Leeds, England

CONTRIBUTORS AND CONSULTANTS

GENERAL CONSULTANT
Professor Michael Wise, CBE, MC, BA, PhD, D.Univ, Professor of Geography, London School of Economics and Political Science

EDITORIAL CONSULTANT
John Clark

Frances Atkinson, BSc

British Museum (Natural History), Botany Library

Robert W. Bradnock, MA, PhD, Lecturer in Geography with special reference to South Asia at the School of Oriental and African Studies, University of London

Michael J. Bradshaw, MA, Principal Lecturer in Geography, College of St Mark and St John, Plymouth

Dr J. M. Chapman, BSc, ARCS, PhD, MIBiol, Lecturer in Biology, Queen Elizabeth College, University of London

Dr Jeremy Cherfas, Departmental Demonstrator in Zoology, Oxford University

Dr M. J. Clark, Senior Lecturer in Geomorphology, Geography Department, Southampton University

J. L. Cloudsley-Thompson, MA, PhD(Cantab), DSc(Lond), Hon DSc(Khartoum), Professor of Zoology, Birkbeck College, University of London

Professor R. U. Cooke, Department of Geography, University College, London

Professor Clifford Embleton, MA, PhD, Department of Geography, King's College, University of London

Dr John Gribbin, Physics Consultant to *New Scientist* magazine

Dr John M. Hellawell, BSc, PhD, FIBiol, MIWES, Principal, Environmental Aspects, Severn Trent Water Authority, Birmingham

Dr Garry E. Hunt, BSc, PhD, DSc, FRAS, FRMetS, FIMA, MBCS, Head of Atmospheric Physics, Imperial College, London

David K. C. Jones, Lecturer in Geography, London School of Economics and Political Science

Dr Russell King, Department of Geography, University of Leicester

Dr D. McNally, Assistant Director, University of London Observatory

Meteorological Office, Berkshire

Dr Robert Muir Wood, PhD

Dr B. O'Connor, Department of Geography, University of London

J. H. Paterson, MA, Professor of Geography in the University of Leicester

Dr Nigel Pears, Department of Geography, University of Leicester

Joyce Pope, BA

Dr A. L. Rice, Institute of Oceanographic Sciences, Wormley, Surrey

Ian Ridpath, science writer and broadcaster

Royal Geographical Society

Helen Scoging, BSc, Department of Geography, London School of Economics and Political Science

Bernard Stonehouse, DPhil, MA, BSc, Chairman, Post-Graduate School of Environmental Science, University of Bradford

Dr Christopher B. Stringer, PhD, Senior Scientific Officer, Palaeontology Department, British Museum (Natural History)

J. B. Thornes, Professor of Physical Geography and Head of Department, Bedford College, University of London

UN Information Office and Library

Professor J. E. Webb, DSc, *Emeritus*, Department of Zoology, Westfield College, University of London

Peter B. Wright, BSc, MPhil

UNDERSTANDING MAPS
Helen Wallis, MA, DPhil, FSA, The Map Librarian, British Library

A great many other individuals, organizations, and institutions have given invaluable advice and assistance during the preparation of this Our Planet Earth Section and the publishers wish to extend their thanks to them all.

ILLUSTRATION CREDITS

Maps in the Our Planet Earth Section by Creative Cartography Limited unless otherwise specified. Map of the world's climatic regions, page 50, adapted from *An Introduction to Climate* 4th edition by Trewartha/*Elements of Geography* by G. T. Trewartha, A. H. Robinson and E. H. Hammond © McGraw-Hill Book Co., N.Y., 1967. Used with permission of McGraw-Hill Book Co. Map diagram page 101 (bottom) courtesy Doctor Arno Peters.

2–3 *Exploding universe* Product Support (Graphics); *others* Quill. **4–5** Bob Chapman. **6–7** Bob Chapman. **8–9** Mick Saunders; *Landsat diagrams* Gary Marsh; *biowindows* Chris Forsey. **10–11** Mick Saunders. **12–13** Bob Chapman. **14–15** *Diagrams* Chris Forsey; *mountain sequence* Donald Myall. **16–17** Colin Salmon. **18–19** Peter Morter; *graph* Mick Saunders; *car* Peter Owen. **20–21** Bob Chapman; *diagram* Chris Forsey; *map* Colin Salmon. **22–23** Chris Forsey (*including maps*). **24–25** Brian Delf. **26–27** Brian Delf. **28–29** Dave Etchell/John Ridyard. **30–31** Creative Cartography Ltd. **32–33** Mick Saunders. **34–35** Chris Forsey; *experiment* Gary Hincks; *others* Mick Saunders. **36–37** Chris Forsey; *fruit flies, birds and mice* Donald Myall. **38–39** Chris Forsey; *time scale* Mick Saunders; *stromatolite and diagram* Garry Hincks. **40–41** Donald Myall; *time scale* Mick Saunders. **42–43** Donald Myall; *time scale* Mick Saunders. **44–45** Creative Cartography Ltd. **46–47** Donald Myall; *diagram* Kai Choi; *skulls* Jim Robins. **48–49** Creative Cartography Ltd. **50–51** Peter Morter; *diagram* Marilyn Clark. **52–53** Kai Choi. **54–55** Creative Cartography Ltd. **56–57** Creative Cartography Ltd. **58–59** Creative Cartography Ltd. **60–61** Creative Cartography Ltd; *illustrations* Jim Robins. **62–63** *Migration diagram and graph* Kai Choi; *illustrations* Coral Mula. **64–65** Donald Myall. **66–67** *Landscape diagram* Bill le Fever; *illustrations* Russell Barnett. **68–69** Donald Myall. **70–71** Jim Robins; *plants, bottom left* Andrew Macdonald. **72–73** Rory Kee; *bottom left* Russell Barnett; *plow* Kai Choi; *grains and graph* Creative Cartography Ltd. **74–75** Bob Bampton/The Garden Studio; *animal adaptations* Russell Barnett. **76–77** Donald Myall; *qanat* Bob Chapman. **78–79** David Ashby. **80–81** David Ashby. **82–83** Coral Mula; *trees, orchid, toucan and hornbill* Donald Myall. **84–85** Jim Robins. **86–87** Creative Cartography Ltd. **88–89** Brian Delf; *blood counts diagram* Colin Salmon. **90–91** Bob Chapman; *animals and plants* Rod Sutterby. **92–93** Kai Choi; *hydrological cycle* Bob Chapman. **94–95** Andy Farmer; *shore and plant life* Russell Barnett; *coral atoll* Colin Salmon. **96–97** Creative Cartography Ltd. **98–99** *Topographic maps* Rand McNally; *sketch map* Space Frontiers Ltd. **100–101** *Diagrams* Creative Cartography Ltd. **102–103** *Maps* Istituto Geografico De Agostini; Rand McNally; *diagrams* Creative Cartography Ltd.

INDEX

PICTURE CREDITS

Credits read from top to bottom and from left to right on each page. Images that extend over two pages are credited to the left-hand page only.

2 US Naval Observatory; California Institute of Technology and Carnegie Institution of Washington. **3** Both pictures from Royal Observatory, Edinburgh. **8** All pictures from NASA. **9** All pictures from NASA except top and top right, courtesy of Garry Hunt, Laboratory of Planetary Atmospheres, University College, London. **14–15** Maurice and Sally Landre/Colorific! **16–17** All pictures courtesy of Dr Basil Booth, Geoscience Features. **18** Institute of Geological Sciences. **19** Paul Brierley; Institute of Geological Sciences. **20** Camera Press, London. **26** Barnaby's Picture Library; Barnaby's Picture Library; Institute of Geological Sciences. **28** Dr Alan Beaumont. **30** Tom Sheppard/Robert Harding Picture Library; Professor Ronald Cooke. **31** Institute of Geological Sciences. **32** Stuart Windsor; Sefton Photo Library, Manchester; Rio Tinto Zinc; Douglas Botting; Aspect Picture Library. **33** NASA; Mireille Vautier; Explorer/Vision International. **34** Paul Brierley. **37** Paediatric Research Unit, Guy's Hospital Medical School; Dr Laurence Cook, Zoology Department, University of Manchester. **39** Both pictures from British Museum (Natural History). **46** Colophoto Hans Hinz. **47** Dr P. G. Bahn, School of Archaeology and Oriental Studies, University of Liverpool/Musée des Antiquités Nationales, St. Germain-en-Laye. **56** UNICEF (Photo no. 8675 by H. Dalrymple). **57** Dr A. M. O'Connor, Department of Geography, University College, London. **61** International Fund for Animal Welfare; K. Kunov/Novosti Press Agency; Popperfoto; Charles Swithinbank. **62** Alan Robson. **63** Gösta Hakansson/Frank Lane Agency. **65** G. R. Roberts. **67** Anglo-Chinese Educational Trust; Aerofilms. **69** Ted Streshinsky. **72** Engraving from *At Home with the Patagonians.* **73** The Mansell Collection. **76** J. Bitsch/Zefa; Penny Tweedie/Colorific! **77** Alan Hutchison Library; Bill Holden/Zefa. **80** Syndication International; Gerald Cubitt/Bruce Coleman Ltd; Bruce Coleman Ltd. **81** Alan Hutchison Library; R. and M. Borland/Bruce Coleman Ltd; M. P. Kahl/Bruce Coleman Ltd; Jan and Des Bartlett/Bruce Coleman Ltd. **84** J. von Puttkamer/Alan Hutchison Library. **85** Marion Morrison. **86–87** Richard and Sally Greenhill. **88** Alan Hutchison Library; The Association of Universities for Research in Astronomy, Inc. **89** Gunter Ziesler/Bruce Coleman Ltd. **91** Mike Price/Bruce Coleman Ltd. **92** Ian Murphy. **93** Paolo Koch/Vision International; J. Allan Cash; M. Timothy O'Keefe/Bruce Coleman Ltd. **94** Heather Angel. **95** Institute of Oceanographic Sciences. **96** Fritz Prenzel/Bruce Coleman Ltd; Gordon Williamson/Bruce Coleman Ltd. **97** Martin Rogers/Susan Griggs Agency. **98** British Library; British Museum; Centro Camuno di Studi Preistorici; British Library; NASA; NASA; Rand McNally; British Museum; British Museum. **99** British Museum; NASA; NASA; Rand McNally; Space Frontiers Ltd; Paul G. Lowman/NASA Goddard SFC/Space Frontiers Ltd. **100** Historisches Museum, Vienna. **101** Hunting Surveys Ltd; Michael Holford/Science Museum, London; Michael Holford; Michael Holford/Science Museum, London. **103** Space Frontiers Ltd; F. Damm/Zefa.

Page numbers in *italic* refer to the illustrations and their captions.

A

aardvark, *79*
aardwolf, *79*
aborigines, 47
Abu Dhabi, *97*
Acacia, 78; *78–9*; *A. baileyana, 68*
Acantherpestes ornatus, 39
Acinonyx jubatus, 79
Actophilornis africana, 79
Addax nasomaculatus, 74
Adelaide, 73
Aden, Gulf of, 18
Adriatic Sea, *20*
Aedes impiger, 91
Aegean Sea, 15
Aeluroidea, *42*
Africa: aquifers, 24; cities, 56; climate, 68; continental drift, 15, 44; *12–13*; deforestation, 32; deserts, 30; *30, 75*; early man, 46–7; *46*; energy sources, 52; mapping, 99; monsoon regions, 86; *86*; mountain building, *14*; population growth, 54; *55*; savannas, 78, 80, 81; *78–81*; spread of mammals to, *44*; transport, *59*; tropical rainforests, 83, 84–5; *82–3, 85*
African Rift Valley, 18
Agave americana, 74
agouti, orange-rumped, *82*
agriculture, 44, 58–9; and climate, 51; grasslands, 72–3; *72–3*; improvements, *55*; irrigation, 25, 32, 33, 68, 76–7, 80, 86, 92; *76–7, 93*; land reclamation, 33; *33*; Mediterranean regions, 68; *68–9*; monsoon regions, 86; *87*; prehistoric, *47*; satellite monitoring, 8; *9*; savannas, 80–1; *80–1*; and temperate forests, 66–7; *66–7*; Third World, 54; tropical rainforests, 84; *84*; use of water, 92; *92–3*
Ailurus fulgens, 89
air pressure, 7
air surveys, maps, 99
aircraft, *58*
Akimiski Island, *9*
Al-Idrisi, 99
Alaska, 13, 20, 44, 63; *44, 62*
Alauda arvensis, 71
Aldebaran, *2*
aldehydes, *35*
alder, 62
Aleutian Islands, *44*
algae, 38, 60, 90; *38–9*
Algeria, 68, 77; *30*
Allahabad, *48*
alluvial deposits, 18; *19*
Alopex lagopus, 62
Alpine-Himalayan Mountain Belt, 13
Alpine soldanella, *88*
Alps, 15, 26, 44, 88; *27, 88*
alumina, 17
aluminum, *10*
aluminum oxide, 17
Amazon river, *90*
Amazonia, 85; *32*
Ambrona, *46*
amino acids, 35, 36; *34–5*
ammonia, 6; *35*
ammonites, 41
amphibians, 38, 40, 83, 90; *38–40*
Amundsen-Scott base, 60
anchovy, *97*
Andes, 15, 44, 74
andesite, 15, 20; *16*
Andrewsarchus, 42
Andromeda Galaxy (M31), *3*
Andropogon scoparius, 70
Anemone patens, 70
angler fish, *95*
animals, *see* mammals
annelids, *39*
Anomalurus erythronotus, 83
Antarctic Treaty (1959), *60*
Antarctica: glaciers, 26; ice, 24, 26, 60; krill, 60, 96; *60–1*; mapping, 99; ocean, 94; *95*; ocean currents, 22; plate tectonics, 13, 44; *12–13;* whaling, *97*
Antares, *2*
anteater, lesser, *83*; scaly, 83
antelope, 81; *42, 45, 81*; Addax, *74*
anticlines, *14, 99*
Antilicapra americana, 44
ants, 82, 83; harvester, *74*; honey, 75; *75*
apapane, *36–7*
apes, 83; *45*
Appalachian Mountains, 64; *14–15, 88, 98*
Aptenodytes forsteri, 61
aquifers, 24
Aquila chrysaetos, 89; *A. rapax, 71*
Arabia, 15; *45*
Arabs, 99
arapaima, 90
Araucaria heterophylla, 41
Arbutus unedo, 69
Archaeomeryx, 42–3
Archaeopteryx, 41; *41*
Archaeotherium, 42–3
Architeuthis spp., *95*
Archosaurs, 41
Arctic, 22, 28, 60; *60–1*
Arctic Ocean, 33, 60, 62; *61*
Arctoidea, *42*
Ardea goliath, 79
Arenicola marina, 94
arêtes, *26*
Argentina, 73, 74, 81; *60*
argon, *6*
Argyrolagus, 42
Argyropelecus hemigymnus, 95
Aristotle, 49
Arizona, 77
Arkhangelsk, *49*
armadillos, 42; *44*
arsenical bronze, 18
Arsinoitherium, 42
art, prehistoric, *46*
Artemisia dracunculoides, 70
arthropods, *38–9*
Artiodactyls, *41–2*
ash fallout, volcanoes, *21*
ash trees, 64
Asia: climate, 51; continental drift, 15, 44; *13*; deserts, 74; early man, 47; *46*; monsoon regions, 86; *86–7*; mountain formation, 15; population growth, 54; *55*; satellite mapping, *99*; savanna, 78, 80; spread of animals to, *44–5*; temperate forests, 64, 66; *64, 66–7*; tropical rainforests, 85; *82–5*; urbanization, 56
Asia Minor, 68
Assam, 86
Association of South-East Asian Nations (ASEAN), *59*
asterism, 18; *19*
asteroids, 4, 11; *5*
Asteroxylon, 39
asthenosphere, 11
astrolabes, *101*
Astronomical Units (AU), *5*
astronomy, 3–5; *88*
Aswan High Dam, 32
Atacama desert, 76, 77
Atlantic Ocean: currents, 22; plate tectonics, 15; *13, 14*; satellite observations, *9*
atmosphere: and the climate, 50–1; and creation of life, 35; *35*; creation of oxygen in, 38; *38*; and destruction of rainforests, 85; Earth's, 6–7; *6–7*; hydrological cycle, 24; pressure, 7; structure, 7; *6–7*
atomic clocks, 4
Attica, 68; *68*
auroras, 7
auroch, *66*
Australia: and Antarctica, *60*; climate, 68; continental drift, 44; *13*; early man, 47; fossils, 38; *39*; grasslands, 70, 73; *70, 73*; marsupials, 44; *42, 45*; minerals, 77; monsoon regions, 86; population density, 56; *57*; rainforest, 64; savanna, 78, 80, 81; *80*; spread of animals to, *44*; temperate forests, 64, 67; *64*; wine, *69*
Australian zoogeographical region, *45*
Australopithecus afarensis, 46; *46*; *A. africanus, 47*; *A. boisei, 47*
autumn equinox, *5*
avalanches, 27
Aysheaia pedunculata, 39

B

Babylonians, 99, 100
Bacon, Francis, *12*
bacteria, 38, 64, 71, 82; *31, 38*
badgers, 63, 64; *65*
badlands, 24
Bahu Wuhu, 18
Baikal, Lake, *62, 90–1*
Bailey's mimosa, *68*
Baja California, *75*
Bajau, *96*
Balaeniceps rex, 79
Balaenoptera musculus, 61, 95
Baltimore, *9, 56*

bamboo, *65, 87*
Bandung, 56
Bangladesh, 22, 84
baobab tree, 78
Barrow, Alaska, *49*
basalt, 13, 18, 20; *16*
batholiths, 15
bats, 44, 83; long-nosed, *75*
Les Baux, *19*
bauxite, 52, 85; *19, 52*
beaches, 28, 29; *28*
bear-dogs, *42–3*
bears, 42, 63; *42*; Asiatic black, *89*; North American black, *65*; polar, 60; *61*
beaver, 63, 90; *45, 90*
Bedolina, 99
beech, 64; silver, *64*; southern, *65*
Behaim, Martin, *99*
Belgium, 56
Benthosaurus grallator, *95*
bergschrund, *27*
Bering land bridge, 47; *44*
Bermuda grass, *79*
bharal sheep, *89*
"Big Bang" theory, universe, 3; *2*
biomes, 49; *48–9*
birch, 62
bird of paradise, *45*
birds: deserts, *74–5*; evolution, 41, 42; *41*; flightless, *42*; freshwater environment, 90; *90–1*; migration, *61*; mountains, 88; *89*; natural selection, *36–7*; polar regions, 60; *60–1*; savanna, 78; *79*; spread of, 44; *45*; temperate forests, 64; *65*; temperate grasslands, *71*; tropical rainforests, 82–3; tundra and taiga, 63; *63–4*
birth control, 54, 55; *55*
bison, 70; *44, 70–1*; European wood, 64; *67*
Bison bison, *44, 70*
Biston betularia, *37*
Bitter Lakes, *45*
bitumen, *53*
Black Country, England, 56
black holes, 3; *3*
blackbird, *65*
blackfly, *90, 93*
blindfish, *90*
blue grama grass, *70*
blue-green algae, 38
blue kleinia, *74*
bluebells, *65*
bluefin, tuna, *95*
Boers, 73; *72*
borax, *32, 77*
Bordeaux, *49*
Borneo, 44, 84
boron, *19*
Bos grunniens, *89*
Boston, 56; *56*
Bothriolepsis, *39*
boulder clay, 27
Bouteloua gracilis, *70*
brachiopods, *39*
Brachiosaurus, *40–1*
Brachyteles arachnoides, *83*
Bradypus torquatus, *83*
Brahmaputra river, *90*
brambles, *65*
brambling, 63
Branchiostoma, *39*
Brandt Commission, 59; *59*
Branta bernicla, *63*
Brasilia, 56
brass, 18
Brazil, 8, 52, 56, 78, 81, 85; *32, 81, 85*
breccia, 17
brines, metal-rich, *18*
bristleworms, *38–9*
Britain, 26, 27, 56, 59, 64, 96; *9, 93*
brittle star, *95*
Broken Hill, 56
bromeliads, 78, 82; *82*
Brontotherium, *42–3*
bronze, 18
Bronze Age, 18; *66*
Bubo virginianus, *75*
Buceros rhinoceros, *83*
Buenos Aires, 73
buffalo, 81; forest, 83; *82*
buffalo grass, *70*
bullhead, *90*
bunting, snow, 63
Burley Griffin, Lake, *57*
Buteo jamaicensis, *71*
Buthus occitanus, *75*
by-the-wind sailor, *95*

C

cacti, 75, 78; *75*
caddisfly, *93*
cadastral plans, 99
cadmium, *19*
Caiman crocodilus, *91*
calcite, 18, 31
calcium, 17; *19, 23*
calcium carbonate, *17, 19*
calcium salts, 18, 24
calderas, 21; *21*
Caledonian mountains, *14*
calendar, 4
California, 13, 28–9, 68, 77; *13, 32, 50, 69, 72, 102–3*
California Current, *50*
Callisaurus draconoides, *74*
Callithrix jacchus, *44*
Cambrian Period, 38
camelids, *44*
camels, 75; *42, 74*
Camelus bactrianus, *74*; *C. dromedarius*, *74*
Canada: grasslands, 73; mountain building, 15; *15*; population density, 56; satellites, 8; *9, 98*; tides, 22; tundra, *63*; uranium deposits, 18; *see also* North America
canals, 32–3, 76, 92; *93*
Canberra, 56; *57*
Canis aureus, *78*; *C. latrans*, *70*; *C. lupus*, *63*; *C.l. nubilus*, *70*
Canthonlaevis drury, *71*
Cape Horn, 28
Cape Province, 68
capercaillie, 63; *62*
Capet, Hugh, King of France, *57*
carbon, *19*
carbon dioxide: in amino acids, *35*; in atmosphere, 6, 85; *6, 19*; "greenhouse effect," 6, 51; *51*
carbon monoxide, *35*
carbonic acid, 31
Carboniferous Period, 40; *40*
carborundum, *19*
Carcharadon carcharias, *95*
Cardium edile, *94*
Carex sylvatica, *42*
Cariama cristata, *44*
Caribbean, *50*
caribou, 62, 63; *62*
Carmel, Mount, *46*
carnivores, 41, 42, 70; *40–1, 42, 70–1*
carp, *93*
carrion beetle, *78–9*
carrion fly, *78–9*
cartography, 99–100, 102; *98–103*
cassowary, *45*
Castor fiber, *45, 90*
cat family, *42–3*
catfish, African, *91*
cattle, 81, 88; *42–3, 81*
caves, 18, 24; *19, 90–1*
cedar of Lebanon, *68–9*
Cedrus libani, *69*
Celebes, 44
cells, 35, 36; *36–7*
cementation, *17*
Cenozoic era, 41, 42; *42*
centipedes, *75*
Central America, 47, 86; *44*
Centrocercus urophasianus, *71*
Cereus giganteus, *75*
Cerianthus orientalis, *95*
Cetengraulis mysticetus, *97*
chalk, 24
Chameleo chameleon, *83*
chameleon, *83*
La Chapelle, *46*
charcoal, 66, 68; *66, 68*
Charnia, *39*
cheetah, 78; *78–9*
chemical weathering, 31; *31*
chernozem soils, 71; *48*
chestnut, 68; *68*
Chicago, 56, 58; *32–3, 67*
Chile, 64, 68, 76, 77; *21, 60, 64–5, 68–9*
Chilopoda, *75*
chimpanzee, *45, 83*
China, *45*; communes, *86*; deforestation, *66–7*; deserts, 77; early man, 46; earthquakes, 20; mapping, 8, 99, 100, 102; *98*; oil, 52; population movements, 56; rivers, 25, 33; temperate forests, 64; *64*
chipmunk, 64; eastern, *65*
chlorine, 22; *23*
Choloepus didactylus, *44*
chough, Alpine, 88; *89*
Choukoutien, *46*
chromium, *18, 19*
chromosomes, 36; *36–7*
chronometers, 100
Chrysemys picta dorsalis, *91*
cichlids, 90
Cinclus cinclus, *90*
cirques, 26; *26–7*
Citellus citellus, *70*
cities, 56; *32, 57, 67*
citron, *68–9*
Citrus medica, *69*
Ciudad Bolivar, *56*
Ciudad Guayana, *56*
civet, *42*; oriental, *82*
Cladoselache, *39*
clams, *95*
clay, 27, 29, 35; *16–17, 27*
cliffs, 28, 29; *28–9*
climate, 49–51; *48–51*; deserts, 74; *75*; grasslands, 70; *70–1*; Mediterranean, 68; *68*; monsoon, 86; *86–7*; mountains, 88; polar, 60; satellite monitoring, 8; *9*; savanna, 78, 80; *78*; and the spread of man, 47; taiga, 62; tropical rainforests, 82; *82*; tundra, 62
clouds, 8, 50; *50–1*
club mosses, 38, 40; *38–40*
Clupea harengus, *95*
coal, 6, 17, 18, 52, 66; *40, 52–3, 62, 67*
coal forests, 40; *38*
coastlines, 28–9, 33; *28–9, 33*
Coccothraustes coccothraustes, *65*
cockatoo, *45*
cockle, *94*
cockroaches, 44
cocoa, 85
coconuts, *87*
coelenterates, 38
coffee, 85; *81*
Colombia, *59*
Colombo Plan, *59*
Colorado, 74
Colorado river, 76; *103*
colugo, *45*
comets, 4
Commonwealth, 59
compaction, rock formation, *17*
compass navigation, 100; *101*
computers, mapping, 99; *101*
Condylarthrans, 42
conformal projections, 100
"conglomerate," rocks, 17
Congo river, *90*
conic projections, *101*
conifers, 62, 66; *40, 62, 65, 68*
Connochaetes taurinus, *79*
contact metamorphism, 18
continental drift, 12–13, 15, 18, 44; *12–13*
continental shelf, 15, 22, 44, 94; *23*
continental slope, *22–3*
continents, mountain formation, 15; *14–15*
Contopus virens, *65*
contours, maps, 102
convergent evolution, *68*
copepod, *94*
copper, 18, 52; *18–19, 52, 59*
Copper Age, 18
coppicing trees, 66; *66*
coral reefs, 28, 95; *94*
core, Earth's, 11; *10*
Coriolis effect, 50
corries, *26*
Corsica, 68
Cortes, Hernando, 99
Corvus corax, *62*
Corylus avellana, *65*
Corythosaurus, *40*
"cosmic microwave" radiation, 3
cosmic years, 3
cotton, *81*
cotton-top tamarin, *83*
cottonwood tree, 75
Cottus bairdi, *90*
Council for Mutual Economic Aid (COMECON), *58–9*
cowboys, *72*
coyote, 63; *70–1*
coypu, 90
crabs, *39, 95*
cranberry, *65*
crayfish, *90*
crested seriema, *44*
Cretaceous Period, 41; *40–1*
crevasses, *26–7*
crinoids, *38–9*
crocodiles, 90; *79, 91*
Crocodilians, 41
Crocuta crocuta, *79*
Cro-Magnon Man, *46–7*
crossbills, 63; *62*
Crotalus spp., *44*; *C. cerastes*, *75*
crowfoot, river, *90*
crust, Earth's, 11, 13; *10, 12–13*
crustaceans, 94; *39*
crystals, rocks, *16*
"cumulates," rocks, 17
Curculionidae, 44
currents, oceans, 22; *23*
cushion pink, *89*
Cycadales, *40*
cyclones, 51
Cyclostigma, *39*
Cynodon dactylon, *79*
Cynomys ludovicianus, *70*
Cyperus papyrus, *79*
Czechoslovakia, 18

D

Dama dama, *45*
Damaliscus lunatus topi, *79*
dandelion, *77*
Danube, river, 92
Daphoenus, *42–3*
darkling beetle, *75*
Darwin, Charles, 36, 44
Dasyprocta aguti, *82*
"dawn horse," 42
Dead Sea, 22
Death Valley, *103*
deciduous trees, 64; *64–5*
deer, 44, 66; *42, 45, 62–3*; pampas, 70; white-tailed, *65*
deforestation, 8, 32, 52, 66–7; *66–7*
Deimos, 4
Deinonychus, *40*
deltas, 25; *24*
Demidoff's bushbaby, *83*
Deomys ferrugineus, *82*
deoxyribonucleic acid, *see* DNA
depressions, weather, 50; *50*
desalination, 76
deserts, 30, 52, 74–7; *30, 74–7*
desmids, 90
Devonian Period, 38; *38–9*
diamonds, 18, 63
diatoms, 90; *93, 94*
Diatryma, *42*
Diceros bicornis, *79*
Dickinsonia costata, *39*
diesel fuel, *53*
Dimetrodon, *40*
dingo, 78

Dinka, 47
dinoflagellates, *94*
dinosaurs, 40–1; *40–1*
diorite, *16*
Dipodomys deserti, 75
dipper, *90*
Diptera sp., *89*
Dipterus, *39*
disease, *55*
DNA (deoxyribonucleic acid), 35, 36; *36*
dogs, 44; *42*; Cape hunting, *78–9*; wild, 78
dolerite, *16*
dolphin, bottlenosed, *95*
Dorcas gazelle, *74*
dragonflies, 40
Drosophila melanogaster, 36
drumlins, *26*
dry farming, 77
Dryopithecus, 43
Dunkleosteus, 38; *39*
dykes, volcanic, *21*

E

eagle, crowned, *82*; golden, *89*; hawk, *83*; tawny, *71*
Earth: crust, 13, 15; *12–13, 14*; latitude and longitude, 100; *100–1*; as a planet, 6–7; *6–7*; satellite observations, 8; *8–9*; in the Solar System, 4; *4–5*; structure of, 11; *10–11*
Earth Resource Technology Satellites (ERTS), 8, 99
earthquakes: causes, 20; *20*; plate tectonics, 12, 13, 15; *12*; and the structure of the Earth, 11; *10*; tsunamis, 22; *23*
earthworms, 64, 71, 82; *71*
Eastern Woodland Indians, 66; *66*
Echmatocrinus, 39
eclipses, *4*
ecology, 49
economic development, 55
ecosystems, 49; *48–9*
Ediacara Sandstones, 38; *39*
Edo, 99; *98*
education, *55*
Egypt, 18, 76, 99, 100; *93, 101*
Einstein, Albert, 3
Eismitte, *49*
eland, 81; *78–9*
electric eel, 90
elephants, 78; *43, 45, 78, 80, 87*; forest, 83
elk, 63, 64
elm, 86
emu, 78
Endymion non-scriptus, 65
energy: fossil fuels, 8, 18, 52; *53*; nuclear power, 18, 52; *53*; from the oceans, *53, 97*; sources, 52; *52–3*; in the Sun, 4; in the Third World, 55; water power, 25, 63, 88, 92; *53, 92*
England, *see* Britain
English Channel, 64
environment, 49
Environmental Science Services Administration (ESSA), 8
enzymes, 35
Eohippus, 42
epicenter, earthquakes, *20*
epiphytes, 82; *82*
Epsilon Eridani, *2*
Equal-Area Projection, 100
equivalent projections, 100
equinox, *5*
Equus quagga boehmi, 79
Eratosthenes, 100
Erg Bourharet, *30*
Erie, Lake, *9*
Erinaceus europaeus, 65
erosion, 17; by ice, 26–7; *26–7*; mountains, *15*; by the sea, 28–9; *28–9*; soil, 24, 32, 68, 73, 77, 80; *68*; by water, 24–5; *24–5*; by wind, 30–1; *30–1*
erratics, 27; *26*
eskers, *26*
Eskimos, 47, 60, 63; *47, 61*
Esox lucius, 91
esparto grass, *74*
Ethiopian zoogeographical region, *45*
Eucalyptus, 85
Euphasia superba, 61
Euphorbia obesa, 74
euphorbias, 75; *74*
Euphrates, river, 56; *101*
Eurasia, 70–1, 72–3; *13, 61, 70, 72*
Europa Canal, 92
Europe: coasts, 28; continental drift, 15, 44; early man, 46; *46*; energy, *53*; ice ages, 26; population, 54, 56; *57*; temperate forests, 64, 66, 67; *64, 66–7*; water, 92; *93*
European Economic Community (EEC), 59; *58*
European Free Trade Area (EFTA), *58*
Euryapteryx, 42
Eusthenopteron, 38–9
evaporites, 17
Everest, Mount, 88
evergreen trees, 64, 68, 82; *64–5, 68*
evolution, theory of, 36, 44
exosphere, *7*
extrusive rocks, 18; *16*
eyes, genetics, *37*

F

Falco biarmicus, 74; *F. mexicanus, 71*
fallow deer, *45*
faults: in the Earth's crust, 15; *14–15*; and earthquakes, 20; plate tectonics, 13; *12*
felsite, *16*
Fennecus zerda, 75
ferns, 40, 64, 88; *38–40, 65*
ferralitic soils, *48*
ferret, black-footed, *70*
ferruginous soils, *48*
fertilizers, 86; *68, 77*
Ficus sp., *41*
fig tree, 68; *41*
Filimoshki, *46*
finch, Laysan, *36–7*
fir, 62; Douglas, *65*
fire: savannas, 78, 80; *81*; temperate grasslands, 70; *71*
firn ice, 26; *27*
fish, 38, 41, 90, 94–5, 96; *39, 90–1, 94–5, 96–7*
fishing, 96; *9, 96–7*
flamingo, *79*
flatworms, *39*
flies, *89*
Flinders Range, 38
flood plains, 25, 27; *24–5*
floods, 22, 24, 33
Florida, *93*
flowering plants, *40*
flying fox, *83*
flying squirrels, 83
fog, *50–1*
folds, in the Earth's crust, 15; *14, 99*
food, 52, 54, 73; *55*
forests: deforestation, 8, 32, 52, 66–7; rainforests, 64, 82–5; *48, 65, 82–5*; satellite observations, 8; *9*; taiga, 62–3; *62–3*; temperate, 64, 66–7; *48, 64–7*
fossil fuels, 8, 18, 52; *53*
fossils, 17, 38, 46
Fourquieria splendens, 74
foxes, 63, 64; *65*; Arctic, 62; *62*; fennec, *75*
France, 9, 56, 59, 68, 99; *19, 46–7, 57, 60*
freshwater environments, 8, 32–3, 90, 92; *90–3*
frogs, 75, 90; *65*; pouched tree, *82*; tree, 83
frost, weathering, 31
fruit flies, *36*
fuels, *see* energy
Fujiyama, Mount, 20
fumaroles, *21*
Fundy, Bay of, 22
fungi, 64, 82
Funisciurus lemniscatus, 82

G

gabbro, *16*
galago, *83*
Galago demidovii, 83
galaxies, 3; *3*
game animals, 80, 81; *81*
gamma rays, *7*
Ganges river, *90*
Ganymede, 4
gas, natural, 52, 63; *52–3, 62*
gases, in the universe, 3, 4, 6; *2*
Gastrotheca ovifera, 82
Gazella dorcas, 74; *G. thomsonii, 79*
gazelle, *78*; Thomson's, *79*
gazetteers, 99
geckos, 75, 83; fan-toed, *74–5*; palmate, *74–5*
Gemini, 99
gemstones, 18; *19*
General Agreement of Tariffs and Trade (GATT), 59
genes, 35, 36; *37*
genetics, 35, 36; *36–7*
Geococcyx californianus, 74
geology: minerals, 18; *18–19*; mountains, 15; plate tectonics, 13; rock formation, 17; *16–17*; satellite monitoring, 8; *9, 99*
gerbil, *74–5*
Germany, West, 54, 56
geysers, 18; *21*
Ghana, *59*
gibbons, *43, 45*
Gibraltar, *46*
Gila monster, *75*
Gingko biloba, 40
Giraffa camelopardalis, 45, 78
giraffes, 78; *42, 45, 78*
glacial periods, *see* ice ages
glacial till, 27; *27*
glacial troughs, *26*
glaciers, 26–7; *15, 26–7*
glass, natural, 17
gley, *48*
globes, cartographical, 99; *98*
Gloeotrichia, *38*
Glomar Challenger, 96
gloups, *29*
glyptodonts, 42
Gmelina, 85
gneiss, 17; *16*
Goad, *98*
goats, 68; *42*; Rocky Mountain, 88; *89*
Gobi desert, *75*
goby fish, dwarf, 90
gold, 18, 52, 63; *18, 19, 52*
goliath heron, *79*
Gondwanaland, *13, 44*
goose, *63*; Brent, *63*
gopher, 71
gopher snake, *70*
Gopherus polyphemus, 74
gorges, *24*
Gorilla gorilla, 45
gorillas, *45*
Gottman, Jean, 56
Gracula religiosa, 89
Gramineae, 42
granite, 29; *10, 16*
grasses, 42, 62, 70–1; *42, 70–1* savannas, 78, 80; *79*
grasshoppers, *71*
grasslands, 42; *42, 48*; savannas, 78–81; *78–81*; temperate, 70–3; *70–3*
gravity, 98; deep-ocean trenches, 13; effects on Earth's atmosphere, 7; and the tides, 22; *22*
Gray, Tom, 46
gray-brown forest soils, *48*
Great Basin desert, 74; *75*
Great Bear lake, 18
Great Nebula of Orion, *3*
Great Rift Valley, *79*
Greece, ancient, 68, 99, 100, 102
"greenhouse effect," 6–7, 51
Greenland, 11, 24, 26, 60; *13, 44, 61*
Greenwich Observatory, 99, 100; *100*
grid system in mapping, 100; *100*
groundwater, 24, 76; *25, 76*
grouse, *63*; black *71*; sage, *71*
guanaco, *70–1*
guayule, *77*
Gulf Stream, 22; *9*
gullies, 24, 27
Gulo gulo, 63
Gutenberg discontinuity, 11
gymnosperms, *40*
gyres, 60; *23*

H

hachuring, maps, 102
Hadar, *46*
Hadza, *80*
Haeckel, Ernst, 49
Haematopus sp., *94*
hagfish, 38
Halichoerus grypus, 95
Hallucigenia sparsa, 39
halophytes, 75
Hammer-Wagner Projection, *101*
Handy Man, 46; *46–7*
hanging valleys, *26*
hares, 44; *70–1*; Arctic, 62; *63*
harmattan, 30
hatchet fish, *95*
Hawaii, 11, 20; *23*
Hawaiian honeycreeper, *37*
hawfinch, *65*
hazel, 64, 66; *65*
headlands, 29; *28–9*
heat capacity mapping, *9*
hedgehog, 64; *65*; desert, *75*
helium, 3
Heloderma suspectum, 75
Hemiechinus auritus, 75
Hemiprocne longipennis, 82
Hepatica nobilis, 65
hepaticas, *65*
Herbertson, A.J., 49
herbivores, 41, 70; *40–1, 70–1*
heredity, 36; *36–7*
herring, 96; *95*
hill mynah bird, *89*
hill shading, maps, 102
Himalayas, 15, 44, 86, 88; *14, 45*
Himatione sanguinea, 36
hippopotamus, 90; *42, 79*
Hippopotamus amphibius, 79
holly, *65*
Holothuroidea, *95*
Homo erectus, 46–7; *46–7*; *H. habilis*, 46; *46–7*; *H. sapiens*, 42, 46; *H.s. neanderthalensis 47*; *H.s. rhodesiensis*, 47; *H.s. sapiens, 47*; *H.s. soloensis, 47*
honeysuckle, 64
Hong Kong, *32–3*
Honshu, *64*
Hoplophoneus, 42–3
hornbeam, 64, 66
hornbill, rhinoceros, *83*
horn-boring moth, *78–9*
horses, 42, 70; *42–3, 72*
horsetails, 40; *40*
hot springs, *21*
Hubble, *3*
Hudson Bay, *9*
hummingbirds, *82*
Huron, Lake, *90*
hurricanes, *50–1*
Hwang-Ho, 25, 33
Hyaenodon, 42
hydroelectric power, 25, 63, 88, 92; *53, 92*
hydrogen, 3; *35*
hydrogen cyanide, *35*
hydrological cycle, 24, 32; *24, 92*
hydrothermal springs, *18*
Hydrurga leptonyx, 61
hyena, 78; *42–3, 78–9*
hypsometric tints, maps, 102
Hyracotherium, 42; *42–3*

I

ibex, 88
Ibis leucocephalus, *91*
ice, *23*; effects on landscape, 26–7; *26–7*; polar, 60; *60–1*; satellite monitoring, 8; sheets, 26; shelves, 26
ice ages, 4, 22, 26, 42, 44, 47, 51, 60, 64
ice falls, *27*
icebergs, 60; *61*
Iceland, 11, 26
Ichthyornis, *41*
Ichthyostega, *39*
icthyosaurs, 41
igneous rocks, 17; *16*
ignimbrite, 20–1
iiwi, *36–7*
IJsselmeer, *33*
Ilex spp., *65*
impala, 78
India, 44, 54. 78, 84, 86; *13*, *45*, *57*
Indian grass, *70*
Indian Ocean, 13, 51; *13*, *39*
Indians, North American, 66, 99; *66*, *103*
Indo-Australian plate, *12*
Indonesia, 18, 46
Indus river, 33, 56, 92
Industrial Revolution, 18, 56, 72, 92; *67*
industry, 66, 92; *66–7*, *93*
infrared radiation, 99; *7*
insectivores, 42; *42*
insects: in deserts, 75; *74–5*; evolution, 38, 40; *39*; freshwater environments, 90; genetics, *36–7*; mountain regions, 88; *89*; polar regions, 60; spread of, 44; temperate forest regions, 64; *65*; temperate grassland regions, 71; *71*; tropical rainforest, 83
International Development Association (IDA), 59
International Monetary Fund (IMF), 59
International Whaling Commission, *97*
intrusive rocks, *16*
Inuit, 63; *61*
invertebrates, 38, 41; *71*, *75*
ionosphere, 7; *7*
Iran, 15, 77
Iraq, *46*
Ireland, *9*
Iris sibirica, *70*
Irish Sea, 64
iron, 11, 18, 52, 63; *10*, *18–19*, *52*, *67*
Iron Age, *66*
iron industry, 66, 68
iron oxide, *17*
irrigation, 25, 32, 33, 68, 76–7, 80, 86, 92; *76–7*, *93*
Islamabad, 56
island arcs, *12*, *23*
isostasy, 15; *14*
isostatic rebound, 15
isotopes, 17
Israel, 76; *33*, *77*
Italy, 68, 99; *98*
Ivory Coast, 85
ivy, 64

J

jacana, *79*
jackal, 78; *78*
jaguar, 83
Jakarta, 56
Japan: and the Antarctic, *60*; energy sources, *53*, *97*; maps, 99; *98*; seaweed, 96; temperate forests, *64*; trade, *58*; urbanization, 56; *57*; volcanoes, 20; whaling, *97*
Japan, Sea of, 15
Jari river, *85*
Java, 44, 86
jellyfish, 38, 94; *39*
jerboa, *74–5*
Jesuits, *98*
Joachimstal, 18
Johannesburg, 56
Johanson, Donald, 46
jojoba, *77*
June grass, *70*
Jupiter, 4; *4–5*
Jurassic, *40–1*

K

kame terraces, 27
kangaroo, 78, 81; *45*; tree, 83
Kano, *49*
Karachi, 56
Karamoja, *56*
Kariba Dam, *92*
Katanga, 18
Kazakhstan, *46*
Kenya, *81*
kerosene, *53*
kettle-holes, *26–7*
Khanty, 63
kimberlite, 18
Kitt Peak, *88*
Koobi Fora, *46*
Köppen, Wladimir, 49
Krakatoa, 21, 44; *21*
krill, 60, 96; *60–1*
Kuwait, 76
Kyoto, 99; *98*

L

laccoliths, *20–1*
Lagopus mutus, *63*
Lagostomus maximus, *70*
Lake District (England), *26*
lakes, 32, 90, 92; *21*, *79*, *90–1*, *93*
Lama guanicoe, *70*
Lamarck, Jean-Baptiste, 36
Lambert Equal-Area Projection, *100–1*
Lambert, Johann Heinrich, 100; *100–1*
lampreys, 38
lampshells, *38*
lancelet fish, *39*
land reclamation, 33; *33*
land surveys, 99, 100; *101*
Landsat, 8; *8–9*, *98*, *103*
landscape: effects of ice and snow, 26–7; *26–7*; influence of the sea, 28–9; *28–9*; man's influence on, 32–3; *32–3*; water erosion, 24–5; *24–5*; weathering, 30–1; *30–1*; wind erosion, 30–1
Langdale, *26*
Languedoc, 68
langur, sacred, *82*
lanner falcon, *74*
Lantian, *46*
Lapland, *63*
Lapps, 63; *63*
larch, 62
Lascaux, *46*
lateral moraine, 27; *26*
Latin America, 54, 56, 59; *82–3*
Latin American Free Trade Association (LAFTA), *59*
latitude, 100; *100*
Laurasia, *13*, *44*
lava, 6, 13, 20–1; *21*
lava plateaus, *20–1*
Lavandula spica, *69*
lavender, *69*
lead, 52; *18–19*, *52*
leap years, 4
lemmings, 62; *62*
Lemmus lemmus, *62*
lemur, 83
Lenin (nuclear icebreaker), *61*
leopard, 78, 83; *78–9*, *82*; snow, *89*
Leptonycteris sanborni, *75*
Lepus arcticus, *63*; *L. europaeus*, *70*
lianas, 82; *65*
Libya, 76
lichen, 60, 64, 88; *63*
life: earliest forms, 38–9; *38–9*; evolution of, 4, 6, 7; origins of, 35; *34–5*; structure of, 36; *36–7*
light waves, *7*
lily-trotter, *79*
limestone, 17, 24, 25, 29; *19*, *26*, *31*, *68*
limestone pavements, *31*
Lingula, *39*
Lingulella, *39*
Linophryne bicornis, *95*
lions, 78; *78*
literacy, *55*
lithosphere, 11, 12, 13; *12*
little bluestem, *70*
liverworts, 38
"living fossils," *39*
lizards, 41, 75; *74–5*; gridiron-tailed, *74*
llamas, 88
lobe-fin fish, *39*
Lobodon carcinophagus, *61*
locusts, *74*
Loligo spp., *95*
London, 56, 58; *57*, *61*, *98*
longitude, 100; *100–1*
longshore drift, 29
Los Angeles, 56; *50*, *103*
Loxia curvirostra, *62*
Loxodonta africana, *45*, *79*; *L. falconeri*, *43*
Lucanus cervus, *65*
lugworm, *94*
Lumbricus terrestris, *71*
lunar eclipses, *4*
lungfish, 90; *38–9*, *91*
Lusaka, *57*
Luzon, *33*
Lycaon pictus, *79*
Lynchailurus pajeros, *70*
Lystrosaurus, *40*
Lyurus tetrix, *71*

M

M32 (galaxy), *3*
M82 (galaxy), *3*
macaw, 82–3
mackerel, *95*
Macropus rufus, *45*
Macroscelides proboscideus, *82*
Madagascar, 44; *13*, *82*
magma, 11, 15, 17, 20; *12*, *19*, *21*
magma plugs, 18
magnesium, 11, 17; *10*, *19*, *23*
magnetic field, Earth's, 7
magnetism, Earth's, 11, 13; *10–13*
magnetite, 13
magnetopause, *7*
magnetosphere, 7; *7*
magnolia, 86
Main, river, 92
Malawi, 56
Malaysia, 85; *45*
Malham Cove, *31*
malnutrition, 54; *55*
mammals: in deserts, 75; *74–5*; evolution, 40, 41, 42, 44; *40*; *42–3*; monsoon regions, *86*; mountain regions, 88; *89*; in oceans, 94; savanna, 78; *78–9*; spread of, 44; *44–5*; temperate forests, 64; *65*; temperate grasslands, 70–1; *70*; tropical rainforest, 83; *83–4*
man: chromosomes, *37*; and the deserts, 76–7; *76–7*; effect on environment, 32–3, 44, 49; *32–3*; evolution, 42; *43*; and freshwater environments, 92; *92–3*; influence on grasslands, 72–3; *72–3*; influence on landscape, 32–3; *32–3*; influence on savannas, 80–1; *80–1*; influence on temperate forests, 66–7; *66–7*; influence on weather, 51; and mountain regions, 88; and the oceans, 96; *96–7*; population distribution, 56–7; *56–7*; population growth, 54; *54–5*; spread of, 46–7; *46–7*; and tropical rainforests, 84–5; *84–5*
manatee, Amazonian, *91*
Manaus, *49*
mandrill, *82*
Mandrillus sphinx, *82*
manganese, *18*, *52*
manganese nodules, *18*
mangroves, 28; *87*
Manhattan, 56
Manila, 56
Manis tricuspis, *82*
Mantis religiosa, *71*
mantle, Earth's, 11, 12–13; *10*, *12*
Maoris, 66
map projections, 100; *100–1*
maps; making, 99–100; *98–101*; by satellite, 8, 99; *8*, *98–9*; using, 102; *102–3*
maples, 64
Marella splendens, *39*
market towns, 56
marmoset, *44*, *83*
Marmota monax, *65*
Marquesas Islands, 44
Mars, 4, 6; *4–5*
Marsh, George Perkins, *32*
Marshall Islands, 99
marshes, 90; *79*, *91*, *93*
marshlands, *48–9*
marsupial mole, *70–1*
marsupials, 42, 44; *42*, *44–5*
Masai, *81*
Massawa, *48*
Matthews, Drummond, 13
meadowlark, *71*
meanders, river, 25; *24–5*
mechanical weathering, 31; *31*
Meconopsis horridula, *89*
medial moraine, 27
Mediterranean regions, 68; *68–9*; continental faults, 15; deforestation, 32, 68; *68–9*; irrigation, 93; mineral deposits, 18; spread of animals, *45*
Mediterranean Sea: continental drift, *13*; population migration, 56; salt, *19*; spread of animals, *45*; tides, 22
Medusina, *39*
megalopolis, 56; *56*
Melanerpes formicivorus, *65*
Meles meles, *65*
Mendel, Gregor, 36
Mercator, Gerard, 100
Mercator projection, 100; *101*
mercury, 52
Mercury, 4, 7; *4*
mesopause, *6*
Mesopotamia, 76, 99
mesosphere, 7; *6*
Mesozoic era, 41, 42; *40*, *42*
mesquite, 75
metals, 18, 52; *18–19*, *52*
metamorphic rocks, 17; *16*
meteorites, 4, 11, 35, 41; *7*
meteors, 4; *7*
Meteosat, 8
methane, 6; *35*
Mexico, 99; *44*, *56*, *75*, *77*, *98*
Miacis, *42*
mica, 17, 63
mice, 62; *62*; Congo forest, *82*; hazel, *65*; Indian spiny, *37*; marsupial, *37*; wood, 64
Michigan, *9*
Micrathene whitneyi, *75*
microcomputers, 18
microfossils, 38
mid-ocean ridges, 11, 13, 20; *12*, *23*
Middle East, 30, 55, 74, 76; *46–7*, *97*
midges, *93*
migmatite, 17
migration, 56; *56*
Milky Way, 3; *3*
Miller, Stanley, 35
millipedes, 38; *39*
minerals, 18; *18–19*
mining, 33; *66–7*, *80*
mink, 63
Miocene Period, 42; *42–3*
Mississippi river, 25, 73; *98*
Missouri river, 33
mites, 60
moas, 42
Modified Mercalli scale, 20; *20*

Moeritherium, 43
Mohorovičić discontinuity, 11
Mojave desert, 74; *32, 103*
mole, aquatic, 90; marsupial, *70–1*
mole rats, *45*
molluscs, 94; *38–9*
Moloch horridus, 74
Mongolia, *76–7*
Mongols, *72*
monkeys, 83; woolly spider, *83*
monoclines, *14*
monsoon, 51, 86; *86–7*
Montecaris, 39
Montreal, 73
Moon, 4, 22; *4–5, 22*
moose, 63, 64
moraine, 27; *27*
Morganucodon, 40
Moronobu, *98*
Moropus, 42–3
Morpho butterfly, *83*
Morpho didius, 83
mosquitos, *91, 93*
mosses, 38, 60, 62, 64, 88; *65*
moths, 64; peppered, *37*; small emperor, *65*
motorcars, metals, 52; *19*
mountain regions, 88; *88–9*; avalanches, 27; and deserts, 74; formation, 15; *14–15*; ice caps, 26; and climate, 51
Mozambique, *59*
mud volcanoes, *21*
Muller, Hermann, *36*
Murray-Darling river, *70*
Mus platythrix, 37
Muscardinus avellanarius, 65
musk ox, 62–3; *63*
Muslims, 68
Mustela nigripes, 70
mutations, genetic, 36; *36*
Myrmecocystus melliger, 75

N

Nabataeans, 76
Namib Desert, *75*
nappes, 15; *14*
Nasser, Lake, 32
National Oceanic and Atmospheric Administration (NOAA), 8
natural selection, 36
Nauru, *97*
Nautilus, 61
navigation charts, 99, 100; *101*
Neander Valley, *46*
Neanderthal Man, 46; *46*
neap tides, *22*
Nearctic zoogeographical region, *44*
Negev Desert, 76
Nematophyton, 39
Nentsy, 63
Neolithic, 32, 66; *66*
Neopilina, 39
Neotropical zoogeographical region, *44*
Neptune, 4; *5*
Nereis, 39
Netherlands, 22, 26, 33; *33*
névé ice, 26
New Caledonia, 44
New Delhi, 56
New Guinea, 56
New Jersey, *61*
New York City, 56; *9, 56*
New Zealand, 20–1, 29, 44, 59, 64, 66, 67; *42, 60, 64–5*
Newfoundland, *14*
NGC 205 (galaxy), *3*
Nice, *47*
nickel, 11, 35, 52, 63; *10, 52*
Niger basin, 18
Nigeria, 55; *84*
night-blooming cereus, *75*
nightjar, *75*
Nile, river, 32, 56, 76, 90; *101*
Nile delta, 32; *9*
Nilgiri Hills, 86
nitrates, *77*
nitrogen, 6; *6, 35*
nivation, 27
nomads, *72, 76*
Norfolk Island pine, *41*
North Africa, 24, 56, 68
North America: climate, 68; *50*; continental drift, 44; *13*; deforestation, 32; *67*; deserts, 74; early man, 47; energy, *53*; fish, 90; flightless birds, *42*; temperate grasslands, 70–1, 72–3; *70, 72–3*; ice ages, 26; mapping, *98*; mountain building, 15; *14*; polar regions, *61*; population growth, 54; prairies, 70–1; *70*; satellite observations, *9*; temperate forests, 64, 66–7; *65–7*; transport, 58; tundra and taiga, 63; *62*; water resources, 92; *93*
North Sea, 64, 96; *53, 94*
northern lights, 7
Norway, 22, 56; *14, 63*
Nothofagus menziesii, 64
Notoryctes typhlops, 70
Notostomus longirostris, 95
nuclear energy, 18, 52; *53*
nuclear reactions, in the Sun, 4
nucleic acids, 35; *34*
Nyasa, Lake, *90*
Nyctea scandiaca, 62
Nymphaea spp., *91*

O

oaks, 64, 66, 67; *64–5*; common, *41*; cork, 68; *68–9*; holm, *68–9*; kermes, 68; Turkey, *68–9*
oases, 76; *76*
observatories, 99; *88*
Ocean Thermal Energy Conversion (OTEC), *53, 97*
oceans, 94–6; *94–7*; charts, 99, 100; *101*; currents, 22, 94; *23*; desalination plants, 76; in the hydrological cycle, 24; influence on climate, 50–1; influence on landscape, 28–9, *28–9*; mid-ocean ridges, 11, 13, 20; *12, 23*; mineral content of seawater, *23*; mineral deposits, 18; *18*; plate tectonics, 13; polar, 60; salt content, 22; *19*; seabed, 11; *23*; sedimentary deposits, 17; tides, 22; *22*; trenches, 13, 23; *23*; waves, 22, 28–9
Ochotona roylei, 89
ocotillo, *74*
Odocoileus virginianus, 65
Ohio river, 26
oil, 52, 60, 63, 77; *52–3, 62, 77, 97, 99*
okapi, *82*
Okapia johnstoni, 82
Olduvai Gorge, *46*
Olea europaea, 69
Olenoides serratus, 39
Oligocene Period, 42
olive, 68; *68–9*
Oman, Gulf of, *99*
omnivores, 41
Omo river, *46*
Ontario, Lake, *9*
opals, 18; *19*
Oparin, I.A., 35
Ophiothrix fragilis, 95
opossum, 83; *44*
Opuntia ficus-indica, 74
orangutan, *45, 82*
orchids, 82; *82*; moth, *82*
Orcinus orca, 60
Ordovician Period, 38
Oreamnos americanus, 89
Oreopithecus, 43
Organization for African Unity (OAU), *59*
Organization for Economic Cooperation and Development (OECD), *59*
Organization of American States (OAS), *58*
Organization of Petroleum Exporting Countries (OPEC), 52; *53, 58–9*
Oriental zoogeographical region, *45*
Orion, Great Nebula, *3*
Ornithorhynchus anatinus, 45, 91
Ortelius, Abraham, *Theatrum Orbis Terrarum*, 99
orthogonal projection, *101*
orthomorphic projection, 100
orthophoto maps, 99
Orycteropus afer, 79
Osaka, 56
Osteolepis, 39
ostrich, 78; *79*
Ostyaks, 63
Otus asio, 65
outwash plains, 27
overthrust folds, *14*
Ovibos moschatus, 63
owl, burrowing, *71*; elf, *75*; great horned, *75*; North American screech, *65*; snowy, 63; *62*; tawny, 64
ox, musk, *63*; wild, 64; *66*
oxbow lakes, *24–5*
Oxyaena, 42–3
oxygen: in atmosphere, 6, 7, 85; *6*; and creation of life, 35, 38; *35, 38*
oystercatcher, *94*
ozone layer, 7, 35, 38; *6, 38*

P

Pacific Ocean: charts, 99; *98*; "living fossils," *39*; mineral deposits, 18; *18*; ocean swell, 29; plate tectonics, 13, 15; *12–13*; spread of life across, 44; tsunamis, *23*; typhoons, *50*
pack ice, 60
paddlefish, 90; *91*
Pakistan, 33, 92
Palaeocene Period, *43*
Palaeocharinoides, 39
palaeomagnetism, *10*
Palaeophonus, 39
Palaeotragus, 42–3
Palaeozoic era, *40, 42*
Palearctic zoogeographical region, *44–5*
Pallas's sandgrouse, *74*
palm trees, 51, 78; *65*; date palm, *76*; dôm palm, 78
Palmatogecko rangei, 75
pampas cat, *70–1*
Pan troglodytes, 83
Panama Canal, 58
panda, red, *89*
Pangaea, 44; *13, 44*
pangolin, 83; *82*
Panthalassa Ocean, *13*
Panthera leo, 78; *P. pardus, 79, 82*; *P. tigris, 45, 86*; *P.t. tigris, 82*; *P. uncia, 89*
Papua New Guinea, 44
papyrus, *79*
Paraceratherium, 43
Paradisaea apoda, 45
paraffin, *53*
Paris, 56, 99; *57*
parrots, 82–3; gray, *83*
Parrya lanuginosa, 89
Parthenium argentatum, 77
Patagonian Desert, 75
Pavo cristatus, 45
peafowl, *45*
peccary, *44*
pedestal rocks, *30*
Pedetes cafer, 70
Pei Xin, 100
penguin, Emperor, *60–1*
Pennsylvania, *9*
Penzias, Arno, 3
perch, *93*
Perissodactyls, *42*
permafrost, 62; *48, 63*
Permian Period, *40*
Persian Gulf, *99*
Persians, *77*
Perspicaris dictynna, 39
Peru, *97*
Peters' projection, *101*
Petralona, *46*
petrels, *60*
petroleum, *see* oil
Peutinger Table, 99
pewee, Eastern wood, *65*
Phalaenopsis spp., *82*; *P. sanderana, 82*
Phalaenoptilus nuttalli, 75
Phenacodus, 42–3
Philadelphia, *9, 56*
Philippines, 90; *33, 59, 82*
Phoca sibirica, 91
phosphates, *77*
photogrammetry, 99; *101*
photosynthesis, 38, 85, 94; *38*
phreatophytes, 74, 75
Phyllolepis, 39
Phylloscopus trochilus, 65
phytoplankton, 94; *95*
Picea obovata, 62
piedmont glaciers, 26
pigs, 64; *42*; wild, *86*
pike, *91*
Pikes Peak, *49*
pine, 62; Aleppo, *68–9*; black, *68–9*; Chile, *68*; maritime, *68–9*; Monterey, *68*
Pinus caribea, 85; *P. halepensis, 69*; *P. nigra, 69*; *P. pinaster, 69*; *P. radiata, 68*
piranha, 90
pitchblende, 18
Pituophis melanoleucus, 70
place-names, *103*
placental mammals, 42
placer deposits, 18; *19*
placoderm fish, *39*
placodonts, 41
plane tree, 86; *41*
planets: atmospheres, 6–7; origins of, 3, 4; *2*; statistics, *4–5*
plankton, 60, 94–5; *60, 95, 97*
Planorbis albus, 91
plants, *see* vegetation
Platalea alba, 91
Platanus spp., *41*
plate tectonics, 15, 18, 44; *12–13*
platinum, *19*
Plato, *68*
Platybelodon, 43
platypus, *45, 91*
Pleistocene Period, 42
Plesiadapis, 43
plesiosaurs, 41; *41*
Plesiosaurus, 41
Pliocene Period, 42
Pliopithecus, 43
pliosaurs, 41
Pluto, 4; *5*
plutonic rock, 17
Po Valley, 68
poaching, *81*
podocarps, *68*
podsols, 64; *48*
Pogonomyrmex spp., *74*
Poland, 26; *59*
polar regions, 8, 22, 50, 60; *23, 50, 60–1*
polders, *33*
polecat, marbled, *70–1*
pollarding trees, 66; *66*
pollution, 92, 96; *9, 62, 93, 97*
Polo, Marco, *98*
Polydon spathula, 91
polymers, 35; *34–5*
polyps, *94–5*
pomegranate, *69*
pondweed, curled, *91*
Pongo pygmaeus, 82
poplars, 62
poppy, Himalayan blue, *89*
population distribution, 56–7; *56–7*
population growth, 54; *54–5*
porphyrite, *16*
portolan charts, 99
Portugal, 59, 68
Potamogeton crispus, 91
potash, *77*
potassium, *19, 23*
poverty, 54; *54–5*
prairie dog, 71; *70–1*
prairie falcon, *71*
prawn, scarlet, *95*
praying mantis, *71*
precious stones, 18

Presbytis entellus, *82*
prickly pear, *74*
Primates, 42; *42*, *43*
"primordial soup," 35; *34*
Primula rosea, *89*
Procambarus spp., *90*
pronghorn, 70; *44*, *71*
protea, giant, *68*
Protea cynaroides, *68*
proteins, 35, 52; *34–5*
Proteles cristatus, *79*
Proteus anguinus, *90*
Protopterus annectens, *91*
protozoans, 94
Provence, 68
Psammomys obesus, *75*
Pseudogyps africanus, *79*
Pseudois nayaur, *89*
Pseudosporochnus, *39*
psilophites, *39*
Psittacus erithacus, *83*
Psittirostra cantans, *36*
ptarmigan, 63; rock, *63*
Pteropus giganteus, *83*
pterosaurs, 41
Ptolemy, Claudius, *Geographia*, 99, 100; *98*
Ptyodactylus hasselquistii, *75*
Puerto Rico, *56*
Punans, 84
Punica granatum, *69*
Punjab river, 33
purse-seine fishing, *96–7*
pygmies, 84
pyramidal peaks, *26*
Pyrrhocorax graculus, *89*
python, royal, *82–3*
Python regius, *83*

Q

qanats, 76; *76–7*
quartz, 17
Quercus spp., *65*; *Q. cerris*, *69*; *Q. ilex*, *69*; *Q. robur*, *41*, *64*; *Q. suber*, *69*
quillajas, *68*
Quizapu, *21*

R

rabbits, 44
raccoons, 64; *42*, *44*
radar sensing, 8
radiation, infrared, 99; *7*; ultraviolet, 7, 35, 38
radio astronomy, 3
radio waves, *7*
radioactive "clocks," 17
railroads, 58, 72; *67*
rainfall, 24, 51, 70, 74, 82, 86; *24–5*, *48*, *50*, *64*, *68*, *70–1*
rainforests, 64, 82–3, 84–5; *65*, *82–3*, *84–5*
Ramapithecus, 46; *43*
Rangea, *39*
Rangifer tarandus, *62*
Ranunculus fluitans, *90*
rats, 44; fat sand, *75*; kangaroo, *74–5*
rat-tailed maggot, *93*
rattlesnakes, *44*
raven, *62*
recreation, 92
recumbent folds, *14*
red giants, stars, 2
red oat grass, *79*
Red Sea, 13, 18; *18–19*, *45*
red-tailed hawk, *71*
redpolls, 63
reedmace, *91*
reindeer, 62, 63; *63*
relativity, theory of, 3
relief shading, maps, 102
reptiles, 40–1, 44, 90; *40–1*
reservoirs, 76, 86, 92; *92*
resource systems, 49
resources, 52
Rhamphastos toco, *83*
Rhamphorhynchus, *41*
rhea, 78
Rhine, river, 92
rhinoceros, *42*, *45*, *78–9*
rhipidistian fish, *39*
Rhizophora mangle, *87*
Rhodesian Man, 46
rhododendron, *89*
Rhynia, *39*
Rhyniella, *39*
rhyolite, *16*
ribonucleic acid, *see* RNA
rice, 33, 85, 86; *87*, *93*
Richmond, Virginia, *56*
Richter scale, 20
rift valleys, 13; *18*
Rigel, *2*
river terraces, 25
rivers, 17, 24–5, 32–3, 90; *24–5*, *90–1*, *93*
RNA (ribonucleic acid), 35
road maps, *98*
roadrunner, *74*
roche moutonée, *27*
rock cycle, 17
rocks: dating, 17; earthquakes, 20; erosion by ice, 26–7; *26–7*; formation, 17; *16–17*; minerals, 18; *18–19*; weathering, 18, 30–1; *19*, *30–1*
Rocky Mountains, 15, 44; *88*
Romalea microptera, *71*
Roman Empire, 18, 66, 68, 99, 100, 102; *57*, *68*
Rome, *49*
Royle's pika, *89*
rubber, 85; *84*
"rubber" dandelion, *77*
Rubus sp., *65*
Ruhr, 56
ruminants, *42*

S

Sacramento, *103*
Sacramento river, *103*
Sagittarius serpentarius, *79*
Saguaro cactus, *75*
Saguinus oedipus, *83*
Sahara, 56, 74, 77, 78, 80; *44–5*, *76*
Sahel, 80; *76*
saiga, 70; *70–1*
Saiga tatarica, *70*
sailbacks, 40; *40*
St Helens, Mount, 20
St Lawrence river, 56
St Lawrence Seaway, *93*
sal, 86; *87*, *89*
salamander, cave, *90*
Salmo trutta, *90*
salmon, 90
salps, 94
salt, 22, 77
salt deposits, 15, 17; *19*, *99*
saltation, 30; *30*
saltbush, 75
Salticus scenicus, *89*
Salyut, 8
Samer, 63; *63*
Samoyeds, 63
San Andreas Fault, 13, 20; *13*
San Bernadino mountains, *103*
San Francisco, 20; *103*
San Gabriel mountains, *103*
San Joaquin river, *103*
sand, 17, 29, 30; *17*, *28*, *30*
sand dunes, 30–1; *30*
sandstone, 17, 18; *17*, *68*
Santa Lucia Range, *103*
Santorini, 21
sapphire, 18; *19*
Sardinia, 68
Sargasso Sea, 22
satellites, 8, 52; *8–9*, *53*; mapping, 99; *98–9*
Saturn, 4; *5*
Saturnia pavonia, *65*
Saudi Arabia, 76; *58*
Saussurea tridactyla, *88*
savannas, 78, 80–1; *48*, *78–81*
scale, maps, 100, 102; *100*, *102–3*
Scandinavia, 26, 63; *27*
Scaphiopus couchi, *75*
Scaumenacia, *39*
schist, 17; *16*
Schistocera gregaria, *74*
Sciadophyton, *39*
Scincus scincus, *74–5*
Scolopax rusticola, *65*
Scomber scomber, *95*
scorpions, 40; *39*, *75*
Scotland, *14*, *88*
Scott, Captain, *61*
Scottish Highlands, *88*
screes, 17
scrubland, 68
Scutosaurus, *40*
seas, *see* oceans
sea anemone, *95*
sea cucumber, *95*
sea level, 22, 33; *23*
sea pens, *39*
seals, 60; *61*; Baikal, *91*; crabeater, 60; *60–1*; gray, *95*; leopard, *60–1*; Ross, 60; *60*
Searles Basin, 77
Seasat, 8
seasons, 4; *5*
seawater environments, *see* oceans
seaweed, 94, 96; *94*
secretary bird, *79*
sedges, 62; *42*
sedimentary basins, 15; *14*
sedimentary rocks, 17
sediments: deposited by the sea, 29; folds, 15; glacial, 27; *26*; river deposits, 25, 32; *24–5*; rock formation, 17; *17*
Seine, river, *57*
Selenarctos thibetanus, *89*
Selenicereus spp., *75*
Senecio articulatus, *74*
Seoul, 56
sewage fungus, *93*
sexual reproduction, 36; *37*
Seymouria, *40*
shading, maps, 102
shale, *16*
Shanghai, 56
Shanidar, *46*
sharks, 95; *39*; white, *95*
sheep, 88; *42*; blue (bharal), *89*
shield volcanoes, 20; *21*
shipbuilding, *68*
shoebill stork, *79*
Shorea robusta, 86; *89*
shrew, short-eared elephant, *82*; tree, *82*; water, 90
sial, 11; *10*
Siberia, 44, 47, 63; *44*, *47*, *62*
sidewinder rattlesnake, *75*
Sierra Nevada, *102–3*
silica, 17, 20; *16–17*
silicates, 17
silicon, 11, 18; *10*
silicon oxide, 17
sills, *21*
Silurian grit, *26*
silver, 18, 52; *18*, *52*
sima, 11; *10*
Simmondsia californica, *77*
Simulium spp., *90*
sirocco, 30
siskin, 63
sitatunga, *79*
skink, *74–5*
skuas, *61*; Arctic, *62*
Skylab, 8
skylark, *71*
"slash-and-burn" agriculture, 84; *84*
slate, 17; *16*
sloths, 42, 83; *44*; maned, *83*
slugs, *65*
Sminthopsis murina, *37*
smog, 51; *50*
snails, *65*; white ramshorn, *91*
snakes, 41, 83
snow, 24, 26, 27; *24*
snow line, *27*
sodium, 22; *23*
sodium chloride, *see* salt
soil: erosion, 24, 30, 32, 68, 73, 77, 80; *68*; mountains, 88; savannas, 80; temperate forests, 64; temperate grasslands, 71; *70–1*; tropical rainforests, 82, 84–5; types, *48*
Solar System, 3, 4; *2*, *4–5*
solar wind, 7
Soldanella alpina, *88*
Solifugae, *75*
Solo Man, 46; *46*
solstice, *5*
Sorgastrum nutans, *70*
souslik, 71; *70*
South Africa, 56, 68, 70, 73, 77; *64*, *69*, *70*, *72*
South America: climate, 68; continental drift, 44; *13*; deserts, *75*; early mammals, 42; early man, 47; fish, 90; grasslands, 70–1; *70*, *72*; mapping, *98*; marsupials, *42*; population growth, *55*; savannas, 78, 80; *80*; spread of mammals to, *44*; transport, 58; tropical rainforests, *82–3*
South Pole, 60; *61*
southern lights, 7
soybeans, 52
space-time, Einstein's theory of, 3
Spain, 22, 32, 59, 68
Spalax microphthalmus, *45*
spectacled caiman, *91*
Speotyto cunicularia, *71*
spiders, 38, 40; *39*; camel, *75*; jumping, 88; *89*
spiral galaxies, 3
spirulina, *38*
sponges, *38–9*
spoonbill, *91*
Spriggina floundersi, *39*
spring equinox, *5*
spring tides, *22*
springhaas, *70–1*
springs, *25*
spruce, 62; Siberian, *62*
squid, *95*
squirrels, 44, 63, 64; *45*; flying, *83*; four-striped, *82*
Sri Lanka, 86
stag beetle, *65*
stalactites, 18; *19*
stalagmites, 18; *19*
stars, 3; *2–3*
steel, 18, 52; *19*, *93*
Steinheim, *46*
Stephanoaetus coronatus, *82*
Stercorarius parasiticus, *62*
Stipa tenacissima, *74*
stonefly, *93*
stork, painted, *91*
storm surges, 22
storms, 51; *50–1*
stratopause, *6*
stratosphere, 7; *6*
strawberry tree, *68–9*
streams, glacial, 26, 27
striations, 26; *27*
strike-slip faults, *14–15*
stromatolites, 38; *38*
strontium, *19*
Struthio camelus, *79*
Struthiomimus, *40–1*
Sturnella neglecta, *71*
subarctic climate, *50*
subduction zones, 13, 15, 20; *12*, *23*
subtropical zones, 50; *50*
Sudan, 47, 78, 80; *76*, *98*
Suez Canal, 58; *45*
sugarcane, 52
sulphate, *23*
sulphur, 6; *18–19*
summer solstice, *5*
Sun, 3; *2–3*; and creation of life, *35*; eclipses, *4*; effect on Earth's atmosphere, 7; energy, 4; evaporation of water from oceans, 24; gravitational pull on oceans, 22; *22*; influence on climate, 50; and the oceans, 94; radiation, *7*; solar power, 52, 77; *53*
Superior, Lake, *90*
supernovae, 3
surveying, 99, 100; *101*
Sus scrofa, *86*
Sutlej river, 33
swamps, 28, 90; *79*, *91*, *93*
Swanscombe, *46*
Sweden, 88; *58*, *63*
swift, crested tree, *82*

switchgrass, *70*
symbols, maps, 102; *103*
Syncerus caffer nanus, 82
Synodontis batensoda, 91
Syrrhaptes paradoxus, 74

T

taeniodonts, 42; *42–3*
taiga, 62–3; *48, 62–3*
Tamandua tetradactyla, 83
Tamias striatus, 65
Tanganyika, Lake, *90*
Tangshan, 20
Tansley, A.G., 49
Tanzania, *56*
tapioca, 84
tapir, *42*; Malayan, *82*
Tapirus indicus, 82
Taraxacum kok-saghyz, 77
tarragon, Russian, *70*
tarsier, *45*
Tarsius spp., *45*
Tasmania, 64; *45, 64*
Taupo, Mount, 20–1
Tauraco persa, 83
Taurotragus oryx, 79
tea, 86; *87*
Tehuelche Indians, *72*
Teleosts, 41
tellin shell, *94*
Tellina tenuis, 94
temperate forests, 64, 66–7; *64–7*
temperate grasslands, 70–3; *70–3*
temperate zones, *50*
Tenebrionidae, 75
Tepetlaoztoc, *98*
terminal moraine, 27; *27*
termites, 82, 83; *79*
tern, Antarctic, *60*; Arctic, *61*
Ternifine, *46*
Terra Amata, *46*
terraces, 33, 76; *33, 87*; river, 25
terrapins, 90
territorial maps, 99
Teshik Tash, *46*
Tethys Sea, *13*
Tetrao urogallus, 62
Thailand, 86; *84*
thematic cartography, 102; *102*
Themeda triandra, 79
theodolites, *101*
thermal imagery, *9*
thermosphere, *6–7*
Thira, 18
Third World, 59; energy, 55; urbanization, 56; *57*
thorny devil, *74*
three-dimensional maps, *102–3*
Thrinaxodon, 40
thrust faults, *14–15*
thunderstorms, *50–1*
Thunnus thynnus, 95
Thylacosmilus, 42
Tibet, 15; *88*
tidal power, 52; *53*
tides, 22; *22*
tiger, *45, 82, 86*
Tigris-Euphrates, 56; *101*
tillodonts, 42
time, 4; Einstein's theory of space-time, 3
Timor Strait, 47
tin, 18, 63; *19, 87*
Ting Chow, *86*
Tiros, 8; *9*
titanium, *19*
Titograd, *20*
toads, 75, 90; spadefoot, *74–5*
Toco toucan, *83*
Tokaido highway, 99; *98*
Tokyo, 56, 58
Tomici, *20*
Tonga Islands, 20; *12*
topi, *79*
topographical maps, 99, 100, 102; *101*
tornados, 51
tortoises, 41, 83; desert, *74*
toucan, 82–3; *83*
tourism, 77, 92; *68, 81*
towns and cities, *see* cities
trace elements, in the atmosphere, *6*
trade, 58–9; *58–9*
Tragelaphus speki, 79
Trans-Amazonian highway, *32*
transcurrent faults, *12*
transform faults, *12*
transport 56, 58–9, 72; *58–9*
Transvaal, *72*
Trapezium, *3*
tree ferns, 40
tree kangaroo, *45*
trees: as fuel, 52; savannas, 78, 80; *see also* forests
trenches, oceanic, 13, 23; *23*
Triassic Period, 40–1, 44
Tribrachidium, 39
Triceratops, 40–1
Trichechus inunguis, 91
trilobites, *38–9*
Trinil, *46*
tripod fish, *95*
trogons, 82–3
tropical rainforest, 82–5; *82–5*
tropical regions, 28, 50, 51; *50*
tropopause, *6*
troposphere, 7; *6*
trout, brown, *90*
trypanosomiasis, 81
Tsavo National Park, *81*
tsetse fly, 81
tsunamis, 22; *23*
Tuareg, *76*
tubeworms, *95*
tubifex worm, *93*
tumble bug, *71*
tundra, 62–3; *48, 50, 62–3*
tungsten, 52, 63; *19*
Tunisia, 68
Tupaia glis, 82
turaco, Gold Coast, *83*
Turdus merula, 65
Turkey, 46
Tursiops truncatus, 95
turtle, southern painted, *91*
Typha spp., *91*
Typhlichthys spp., *90*
typhoons, *50*
Tyrannosaurus, 40–1

U

Uganda, *56*
ultraviolet radiation, 7, 35, 38; *35*
United Nations, 54, 96
United Nations Conference on Trade and Development (UNCTAD), 59
United States of America: and Antarctica, *60*; deserts, 74; earthquake zones, 20; Geological Survey, 99; immigration, *56*; mountain regions, 88; population distribution, 56; *57*; prairies, 73; river management, 33; satellites, 8; temperate forests, *64*; trade, *58*; uranium deposits, 18; volcanoes, 20; water, 76–7; *93*; *see also* North America
universe: measurement of space, *5*; origins of, 2–3
Upright Man, 46–7; *46–7*
Urals, 15; *88*
uranium, 18, 52; *18, 52, 77*
Uranus, 4; *5*
urbanization, 56; *57*
Ursus americanus, 65
USSR: and Antarctica, *60*; coal, 52; emigration restrictions, 56; river management, 33; satellites, 8; steppes, 32, 72–3; trade, 59; tundra and taiga, 63; *62*; whaling, *97*

V

Vaccinium oxycoccus, 65
Val Camonica, 99; *98*
Valdez, 63
Valencia, 32
valley glaciers, 26
valleys: glaciated, *26–7*; hanging, *26*; river, *24*
Van Allen Belts, 7
varved clays, 27
Vauxia, 39
vegetation: deserts, 74–5; *74–5*; evolution, *40*; freshwater environments, 90; *90–1*; Mediterranean regions, 68; monsoon regions, 86; mountains, 88; *88–9*; polar regions, 60; savannas, *79*; satellite mapping, *98*; temperate grasslands, 70; *70–1*; tropical rainforests, 82; *82–3*; tundra, 62; zones, 49; *48–9*
Velella, 95
Venezuela, 78, 81; *56*
Venice, 22
Venus, 4, 6; *4*
vertebrates, 38, 40–1; *39*
Vertesszöllös, *46*
Vespucci, Amerigo, *98*
Vestiaria coccinea, 36
Vienna, 100; *100*
Vietnam, 56
Vine, Fred, 13
vines, grape 68; *68–9*
viscacha, 71; *70–1*
Vitis vinifera, 69
Viverra tangalunga, 82
volcanoes, 6; coral reefs, *94*; formation, 20–1; *21*; influence on climate, 51; intrusions, *21*; mineral deposits, 18; *19*; mountain formation, 15; plate tectonics, 12; *12*; and the primitive atmosphere, *35*; rock formation, 17; *16*
voles, 62
Vormela peregusna, 70
Vulpes vulpes, 65
vultures, 78; *78–9*

W

Wagner Projection, Hammer-, *101*
Waldseemüller, Martin, *98*
Wallace, Alfred Russel, 36
Wallace's Line, 44; *45*
Waptia, 39
warbler, willow, *65*
warthog, 78
Washington, 56; *56*
water: and the creation of life, 35; *35*; desalination, *97*; in deserts, 76; *76–7*; effects on landscape, 24–5; *24–5*; as key to life, 7; map symbols, *103*; water cycle, 24, 32; *24, 92*; water power, 25, 63, 88, 92; *53, 92*; water table, 24; *25*; *see also* freshwater environments; marshes; oceans; rivers; swamps
water vapor, in atmosphere, 22, 24; *6*
waterfalls, *25–6*
waterlily, *91*
waves, 22, 28–9; *23, 28–9*
waxwing, 63
weasels, *42*
weather, 50–1; *50–1*; forecasts, 8, 51; *9*
weathering, rocks, 18, 30–1; *19, 30–1*
Weber's Line, *45*
weevils, 44
Wegener, Alfred, 12, 13
Welwitschia mirabilis, 75
West Indies, *44*
Western Ghats, 86
western wheatgrass, *70*
whales, 60, 94–5; *60*; blue, *60–1, 95, 97*; killer, *60–1*; minke, *96–7*
whaling, 96; *96–7*
wheat, 73; *68–9, 73–4, 93*
white-throated poorwill, *75*
Whitney, Mount, *103*
wildebeest, *78*
Williamsonia, 41
willow, 62
Wilson, Robert, 3
winds: effects on landscape, 30–1; *30–1*; on oceans, 22
Winnipeg, *49*
winter solstice, *5*
Wiwaxia, 39
Wolf 359, *2*
wolverines, 63; *63*
wolves, 63, 64, 66; *63*; maned, 78; *70–1*; plains, *70–1*
wood-pigeon, 64
wood sedge, *42*
woodchuck, *65*
woodcock, *65*
woodpecker, acorn, *65*
World Bank, 59
worms, 38, 94; *39*
Wyoming, 18

X

X-rays, *7*
xerophytes, 74–5
Xin, Pei, 100

Y

yak, 88; *89*
Yangtze river, *90*
Yao, Emperor of China, 33
yardangs, 30
Yellow river, 25, 33
yew, 64
Yokohama, 56
Yorkshire, *26, 31*
Yugoslavia, *20*
Yukon, *62*

Z

Zagros Mountains, 15
Zaire, 18, 54, 83
Zambia, *59, 80*
zebra, 78; *78–9*; Grant's, *79*
zebu, 81
Zimbabwe, *59, 92*
zinc, 18, 35; *18, 52*
zooplankton, 60, 94
Zulus, *72*
Zuider Zee, *33*

INTERNATIONAL MAP SECTION CREDITS AND ACKNOWLEDGMENTS

Cartographic and Geographic Director
Giuseppe Motta

Geographic Research
G. Baselli
M. Colombo

Toponymy and Translation
C. Carpine
M. Colombo
H. R. Fischer
R. Nuñez de las Cuevas
Rand McNally Cartographic Research Staff
I. Straube

Computerized Data Organization
C. Bardesono
E. Ciano
G. Comoglio
E. Di Costanzo

Index
S. Osnaghi
T. Tomasini

Cartographic Editor
V. Castelli

Cartographic Compilation
G. Albera
L. Cairo
C. Camera
G. Conti
G. Fizzotti
G. Gambaro
M. Mochetti
O. Passarelli
M. Peretti
G. Rassiga
A. Saino
F. Valsecchi

Terrain Illustration
S. Andenna
E. Ferrari

Cartographic Production
F. Tosi
G. Capitini
A. Carnero

Filmsetting
S. Fiorini
P. L. Gatta
E. Geranio
G. Ghezzi
L. Lorena
R. Martelli
E. Morchio
M. Morganti
C. Pezzana
P. Uglietti
D. Varalli

Photographic Processing
G. Fracassina
G. Klaus
L. Mella

Coordination
S. Binda
L. Pasquali
G. Zanetta

The editors wish to thank the many organizations, institutions and individuals who have given their valuable help and advice during the preparation of this International Map Section. Special thanks are extended to the following:

Agenzia Novosti, Rome, Italy
D. Arnold, Acting Chief of Documentation and Terminology Section, United Nations, New York, USA
Australian Bureau of Statistics, Brisbane, Australia
J. Breu, United Nations Group of Experts on Geographical Names, Vienna, Austria
Bureau Hydrographique International, Monaco, Principality of Monaco
Canada Map Office, Ottawa, Canada
Cartactual, Budapest, Hungary
Census and Statistical Department, Tripoli, Libya
Central Bureau of Statistics, Accra, Ghana
Central Bureau of Statistics, Jerusalem, Israel
Central Bureau of Statistics, Ministry of Economic Planning and Development, Nairobi, Kenya
Central Department of Statistics, Riyadh, Saudi Arabia
Central Statistical Board of the USSR, Moscow, USSR
Central Statistical Office, London, UK
Centro de Informaçao e Documentaçao Estadistica, Rio de Janeiro, Brazil
Committee for the Reform of Chinese Written Language, Peking, China
Danmark Statistik, Copenhagen, Denmark
Defense Mapping Agency, Distribution Office for Latin America, Miami, USA
Defense Mapping Agency, Washington DC, USA
Department of National Development and Energy, Division of National Mapping, Belconnen ACT, Australia
Department of State Coordinator for Maps and Publications, Washington DC, USA
Department of State Map Division, Sofia, Bulgaria
Department of Statistics, Wellington, New Zealand
Direcçao Nacional de Estadística, Maputo, Mozambique
Dirección de Cartografía Naciónal, Caracas, Venezuela
Dirección de Estadística y Censo de la Repubblica de Panamá, Panama
Dirección General de Estadística, Mexico City, Mexico
Dirección General de Estadística y Censos, San Salvador, El Salvador
Direcţia Centrala de Statisticǎ, Bucharest, Romania
Directorate of National Mapping, Kuala Lumpur, Malaysia
Directorate of Overseas Surveys, London, UK
Elaborazione Dati e Disegno Automatico, Torino, Italy
Federal Office of Statistics, Lagos, Nigeria
Federal Office of Statistics, Prague, Czechoslovakia
Geographical Research Institute, Hungarian Academy of Sciences, Budapest, Hungary
Geological Map Service, New York, USA
G. Gomez de Silva, Chief Conference Services Section, United Nations Environment Programme, New York, USA
Government of the People's Republic of Bangladesh, Statistics Division, Ministry of Planning, Dacca, Bangladesh
High Commissioner for Trinidad and Tobago, London, UK
L. Iarotski, World Health Organization, Geneva, Switzerland Information Division, Valletta, Malta
Institut für Angewandte Geodäsie, Frankfurt, West Germany
Institut Géographique, Abidjan, Ivory Coast
Institut Géographique du Zaïre, Kinshasa, Zaïre
Institut Géographique National, Brussels, Belgium
Institut Géographique National, Paris, France
Institut Haïtien de Statistique, Port-au-Prince, Haiti
Institut National de Géodésie et Cartographie, Antananarivo, Madagascar
Institut National de la Statistique, Tunis, Tunisia
Institute of Geography, Polish Academy of Sciences, Warsaw, Poland
Instituto Geográfico Militar, Buenos Aires, Argentina
Instituto Nacional de Estadística, La Paz, Bolivia
Instituto Nacional de Estadística, Madrid, Spain
Istituto Centrale di Statistica, Rome, Italy
Istituto Geografico Militare, Florence, Italy
Istituto Idrografico della Marina, Genoa, Italy
Landesverwaltung des Fürstentums, Vaduz, Liechtenstein
Ministère des Affaires Economiques, Brussels, Belgium
Ministère des Ressources Naturelles, des Mines et des Carrières, Kigali, Rwanda
Ministère des Travaux Publics, des Transports et de l'Urbanisme, Ouagadougou, Upper Volta
Ministry of Finance, Department of Statistics and Research, Nicosia, Cyprus
Ministry of Lands, Housing and Urban Development, Surveys and Mapping Division, Dar es Salaam, Tanzania
Ministry of the Interior, Jerusalem, Israel
National Census and Statistics Office, Manila, Philippines
National Central Bureau of Statistics, Stockholm, Sweden
National Geographic Society, Washington DC, USA
National Institute of Polar Research, Tokyo, Japan
National Ocean Survey, Riverdale, Maryland, USA
National Statistical Institute, Lisbon, Portugal
National Statistical Office, Zomba, Malawi
National Statistical Service of Greece, Athens, Greece
J. Novotny, Prague, Czechoslovakia
Office Nationale de la Recherche Scientifique et Technique, Yaoundé, Cameroon
Officina Comercial del Gobierno de Colombia, Rome, Italy
Ordnance Survey of Ireland, Dublin, Ireland
Österreichisches Statistisches Zentralamt, Vienna, Austria
Państwowe Przedsiebiorstwo Wydawnictw Kartograficznych, Warsaw, Poland
Scott Polar Research Institute, University of Cambridge, Cambridge, UK
Secrétariat d'Etat au Plan, Algiers, Algeria
Servicio Geografico Militar, Montevideo, Uruguay
Z. Shiying, Research Institute of Surveying and Mapping, Peking, China
Statistisches Bundesamt, Wiesbaden, West Germany
Statistisk Sentralbyrå, Oslo, Norway
Survey and National Mapping Department, Kuala Lumpur, Malaysia
Ufficio Turismo e Informazioni della Turchia, Rome, Italy
United States Board on Geographic Names, Washington DC, USA
M. C. Wu, Chinese Translation Service, United Nations, New York, USA
Z. Youguang, Committee for the Reform of Chinese Written Language, Peking, China

The editors are also grateful for the assistance provided by the following embassies, consulates and official state representatives:

Angolan Embassy, Rome
Australian Embassy, Rome
Austrian Embassy, Rome
Embassy of Bangladesh, Rome
Embassy of Botswana, Brussels
Brazilian Embassy, Rome
British Embassy, Rome
Burmese Embassy, Rome
Embassy of Cameroon, Rome
Embassy of Cape Verde, Lisbon
Consulate of Chad, Rome
Chilean Embassy, Rome
Embassy of the People's Republic of China in Italy, Rome
Danish Embassy, Rome
Embassy of El Salvador, Rome
Ethiopian Embassy, Rome
Finnish Embassy, Rome
Embassy of the German Democratic Republic, Rome
Greek Embassy, Rome
Honduras Republic Embassy, Rome
Hungarian Embassy, Rome
Consulate General of Iceland, Rome
Embassy of India, Rome
Embassy of the Republic of Indonesia, Rome
Embassy of the Islamic Republic of Iran, Rome
Irish Embassy, Rome
Embassy of Israel, Rome
Japanese Embassy, Rome
Korean Embassy, Rome
Luxembourg Embassy, Rome
Embassy of Malta, Rome
Mexican Embassy, Rome
Moroccan Embassy, Rome
Netherlands Embassy, Rome
Embassy of New Zealand, Rome
Embassy of Niger, Rome
Embassy of Pakistan, Rome
Peruvian Embassy, Rome
Philippine Embassy, Rome
Romanian Embassy, Rome
Somali Embassy, Rome
South African Embassy, Rome
Spanish Embassy, Rome
Consulate General of Switzerland, Milan
Royal Thai Embassy, Rome
Consulate of Upper Volta, Rome
Uruguay Embassy, Rome
Embassy of the Socialist Republic of Vietnam in Italy, Rome
Permanent Mission of Yemen to United Nations Educational, Scientific and Cultural Organization, Paris

International Map Section

Hydrographic and Topographic Features
Symboles hydrographiques et morphologiques
Gewässer- und Geländeformen
Idrografia, Morfologia
Hidrografía y morfología

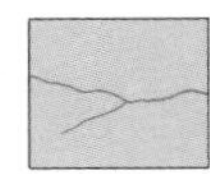

River, Stream
Cours d'eau permanent
Ständig wasserführender Fluß
Corso d'acqua perenne
Corriente de agua de régimen permanente

Lake
Lac d'eau douce
Süßwassersee
Lago d'acqua dolce
Lago de agua dulce

Rocks
Ecueils, Roches
Klippen, Felsriffe
Scogli, Rocce
Escollos, Rocas

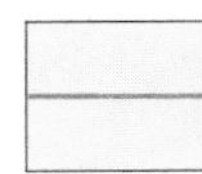

Summer Limit of Pack Ice
Limite du pack en été
Packeisgrenze im Sommer
Limite estivo del pack ghiacciato
Límite estival de banco de hielo

Intermittent Stream
Cours d'eau intermittent
Zeitweilig wasserführender Fluß
Corso d'acqua periodico
Corriente de agua intermitente

Intermittent Lake
Lac d'eau douce temporaire
Zeitweiliger Süßwassersee
Lago d'acqua dolce periodico
Lago de agua dulce intermitente

Reef, Atoll
Barrière, Atoll
Riff, Atoll
Barriera, Atollo
Barrera de arrecifes

Winter Limit of Pack Ice
Limite du pack en hiver
Packeisgrenze im Winter
Limite invernale del pack ghiacciato
Límite invernal de banco de hielo

Disappearing Stream
Perte de cours d'eau
Versickernder Fluß
Corso d'acqua che si inabissa
Corriente de agua que desaparece

Salt Lake
Lac d'eau salée
Salzsee
Lago d'acqua salata
Lago de agua salada

Mangrove
Mangrove
Mangrove
Mangrovie
Manglar

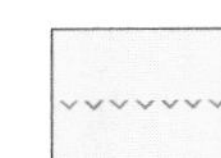

Limit of Icebergs
Limite des glaces flottantes
Treibeisgrenze
Limite dei ghiacci alla deriva
Límite de hielo a la deriva

Undefined or Fluctuating River Course
Cours d'eau incertain
Fluß mit veränderlichem Lauf
Fiume dal corso incerto
Corriente de agua incerta

Intermittent Salt Lake
Lac d'eau salée temporaire
Zeitweiliger Salzsee
Lago d'acqua salata periodico
Lago de agua salada intermitente

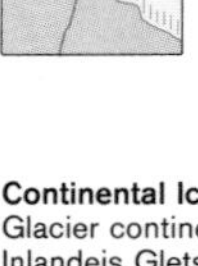

Continental Ice-cap
Glacier continental
Inlandeis. Gletscher
Ghiacciaio continentale
Glaciar continental

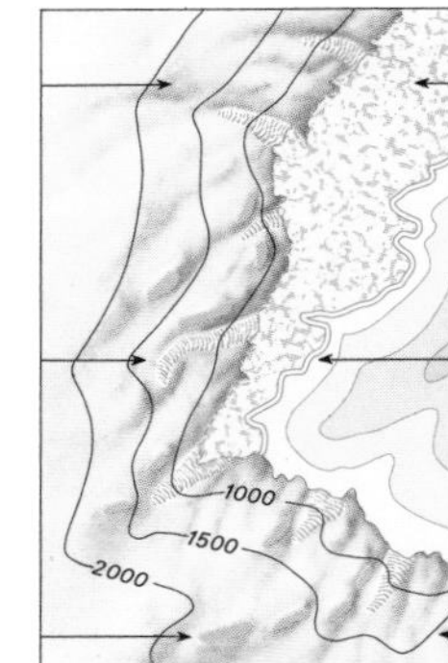

Ice Shelf
Banquise
Schelfeis oder Eisschelf
Banchisa polare (Ice-shelf)
Banquisa

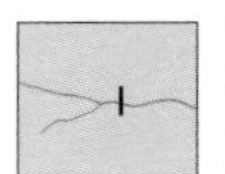

Waterfall, Rapids, Cataract
Chute, Rapide, Cataracte
Wasserfall, Stromschnelle, Katarakt
Cascata, Rapida, Cateratta
Cascada, Rapido, Catarata

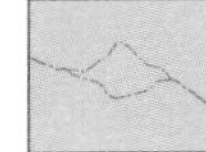

Dry Lake Bed
Lac asséché
Trockener Seeboden
Alveo di lago asciutto
Lecho de lago seco

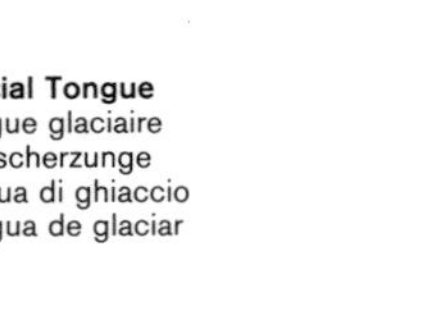

Glacial Tongue
Langue glaciaire
Gletscherzunge
Lingua di ghiaccio
Lengua de glaciar

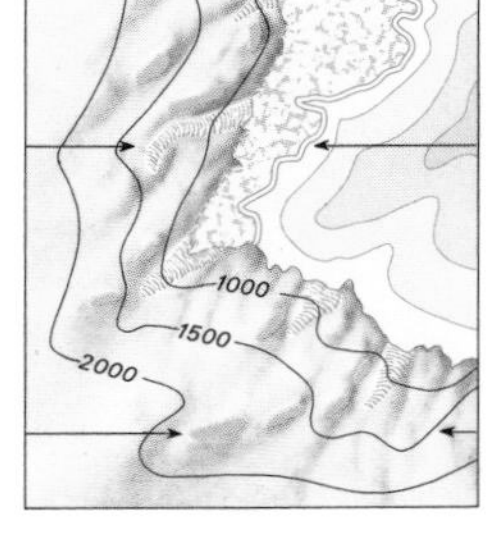

Limit of Ice Shelf
Limite de la banquise
Schelfeisgrenze
Limite della banchisa
Límite de la banquisa

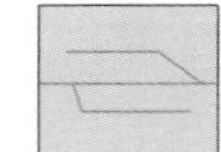

Canal
Canal
Kanal
Canale
Canal

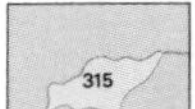

Lake Surface Elevation
Cote du lac au-dessus du niveau de la mer
Höhe des Seespiegels
Altitudine del lago
Elevación de lago sobre el nivel del mar

Rocky Areas (Antarctica)
Région de roches (Antarctique)
Eisfreie Gebiete, Gebirge (Antarktika)
Aree rocciose (Antartide)
Area rocosa (Antártida)

Contour Lines in Continental Ice
Courbes de niveau dans les régions glaciaires
Höhenlinien auf vergletschertem Gebiet
Curve altimetriche nelle aree ghiacciate
Curvas de nivel en aréas heladas

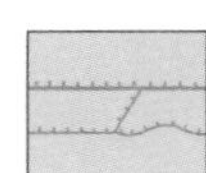

Navigable Canal
Canal navigable
Schiffbarer Kanal
Canale navigabile
Canal navegable

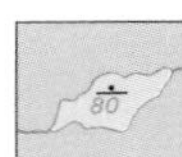

Lake Depth
Profondeur du lac
Seetiefe
Profondità del lago
Profundidad del lago

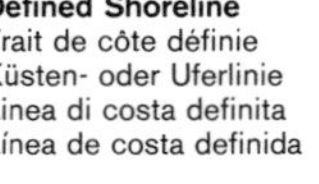

Defined Shoreline
Trait de côte définie
Küsten- oder Uferlinie
Linea di costa definita
Línea de costa definida

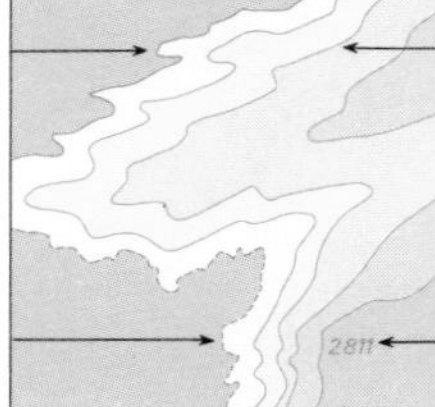

Bathymetric Contour
Courbe bathymétrique
Tiefenlinie
Curva batimetrica
Curva batimétrica

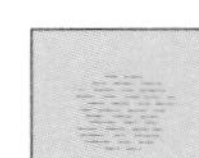

Swamp
Marais
Sumpf
Palude d'acqua dolce
Pantano

Sand Area
Région de sable, Désert
Sandgebiet, Sandwüste
Area sabbiosa, Deserto
Zona arenosa, desierto

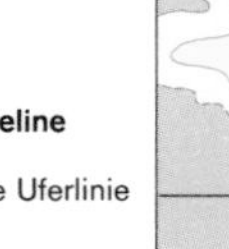

Undefined or Fluctuating Shoreline
Trait de côte indéfinie
Unbestimmte oder veränderliche Uferlinie
Linea di costa indefinita
Línea de costa indefinida

Depth of Water
Valeur de sonde
Tiefenzahl
Quota batimetrica
Cota batimétrica

Salt Marsh
Marais d'eau salée
Salzsumpf
Palude d'acqua salata
Pantano de agua salada

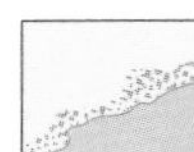

Sandbank, Sandbar
Banc de sable
Sandbank
Bassofondo sabbioso
Banco submarino de arena

Mountain Range
Chaîne de montagnes
Bergkette
Catena di monti
Cadena montañosa

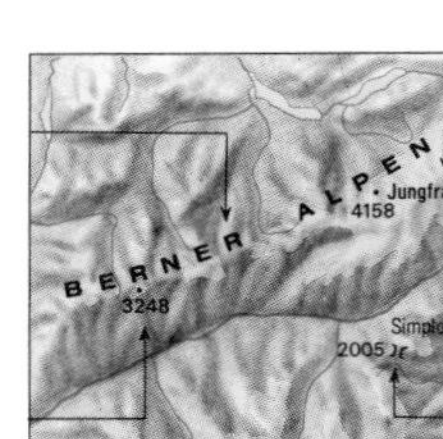

Mountain
Mont
Berg, Bergmassiv
Monte
Monte

Salt Pan
Marais salant
Salzpfanne
Salina
Salina

Port Facilities
Installations portuaires
Hafenanlagen
Impianti portuali
Instalaciones portuarias

Elevation
Cote, Altitude
Höhenzahl
Quota altimetrica
Cota altimétrica

Mountain Pass, Gap
Passage, Col, Port
Paß, Joch, Sattel
Passo, Colle, Valico
Paso, Collado, Puerto de montaña

Key to Elevation and Depth Tints
Hypsométrie, Bathymétrie
Höhenstufen, Tiefenstufen
Altimetria, Batimetria
Altimetría, Batimetría

Scales in Metric and English Measures
Échelle des teintes hypsométriques et bathymétriques
Farbskala der Höhen- und Tiefenstufen
Scala delle tinte Altimetriche e Batimetriche
Escala de tintas hypsométricas y batimétricas

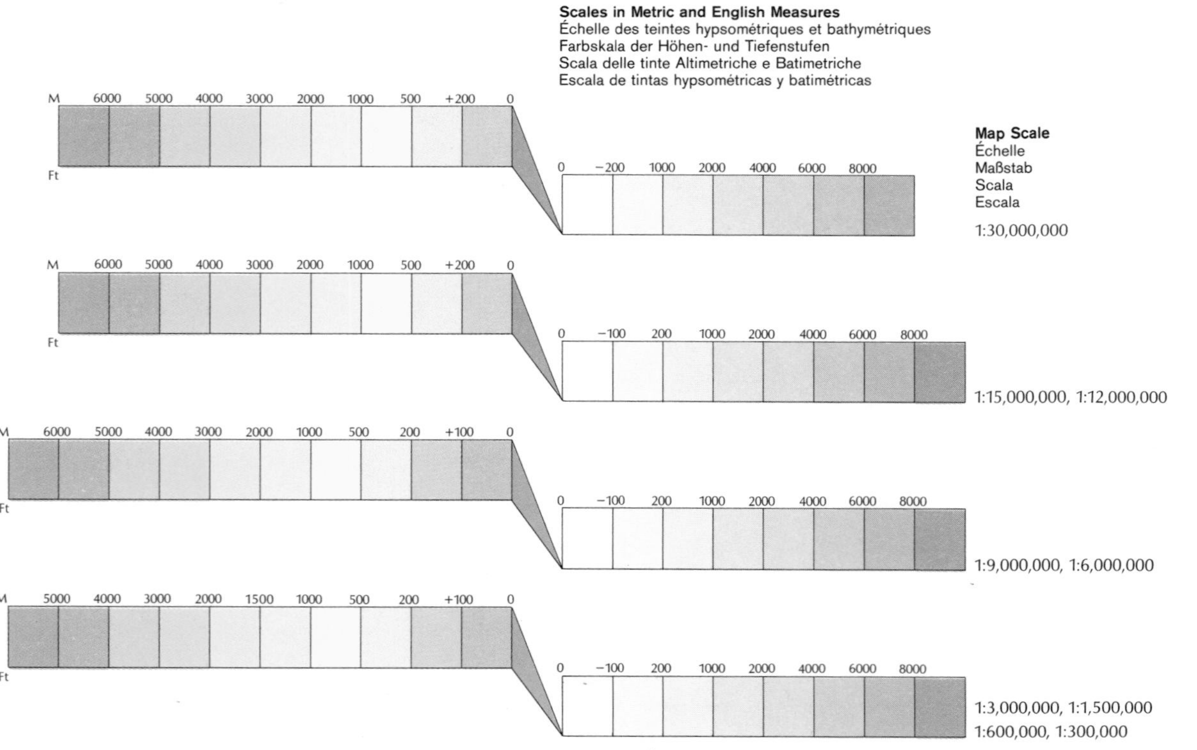

Map Scale
Échelle
Maßstab
Scala
Escala

1:30,000,000

1:15,000,000, 1:12,000,000

1:9,000,000, 1:6,000,000

1:3,000,000, 1:1,500,000
1:600,000, 1:300,000

−155

Land Elevation Below Sea Level
Dépression et cote au-dessous du niveau de la mer
Senke mit Tiefenzahl unter dem Meeresspiegel
Depressione e quota sotto il livello del mare
Depresión y elevación bajo el nivel del mar

Map Projections
Projections cartographiques
Kartennetzentwürfe
Proiezioni cartografiche
Proyecciones cartográficas

The projections appearing in this atlas have been plotted by computer

Les réseaux des projections ont été obtenus par élaboration automatique à partir de formules mathématiques

Die Kartennetze aller im Atlas vorkommenden Abbildungen wurden mit Hilfe der Datenverarbeitung (EDV) völlig neu errechnet

I disegni delle proiezioni presenti in quest'opera sono stati realizzati interamente ex-novo con l'uso del computer e del plotter a partire dalle formule matematiche

El reticulado de las proyecciones (redes geográficas) incluidas en esta obra han sido obtenidas por proceso automático a partir de las formulas matemáticas

The meanings of the symbols on the Legend pages are in English, French, German, Italian, and Spanish languages to permit the interpretation of the maps by a broad readership.

Boundaries, Capitals
Frontières, Soulignements / Confini, Sottolineature
Grenzen, Unterstreichungen / Límites, Subrayados

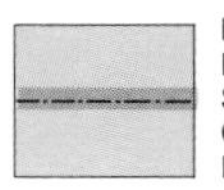

Defined International Boundary
Frontière internationale définie
Staatsgrenze
Confine di Stato definito
Límite de Nación definido

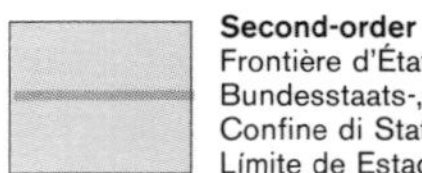

Second-order Political Boundary
Frontière d'État fédéré, Région
Bundesstaats-, Regionsgrenze
Confine di Stato federato, Regione
Límite de Estado federado, Región

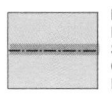

International Boundary (Continent Maps)
Frontière internationale (Continents)
Staatsgrenze (Erdteilkarten)
Confine di Stato (Carte dei Continenti)
Límite de Nación (Continentes)

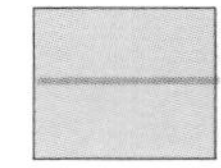

Third-order Political Boundary
Frontière de Province, Comté, Bezirk
Provinz-, Grafschafts-, Bezirksgrenze
Confine di Provincia, Contea, Bezirk
Límite de Provincia, Condado, Bezirk

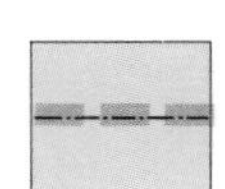

Undefined International Boundary
Frontière internationale indéfinie
Nicht genau festgelegte Staatsgrenze
Confine di Stato indefinito
Límite de Nación indefinido

Administrative District Boundary (U.S.S.R.)
Frontière de Circonscription
Kreisgrenze
Confine di Circondario
Límite de Circunscripción administrativa

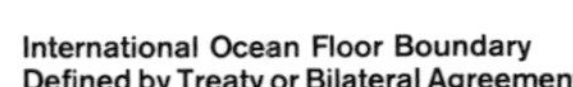

International Ocean Floor Boundary Defined by Treaty or Bilateral Agreement
Frontière d'état en mer définie par traités et conventions bilatéraux
Durch Verträge festgelegte Staatsgrenze im Meeresgebiet
Confine di Stato nel mare definito da trattati e convenzioni bilaterali
Límite de Nación en el Mar definido por los tratados bilaterales

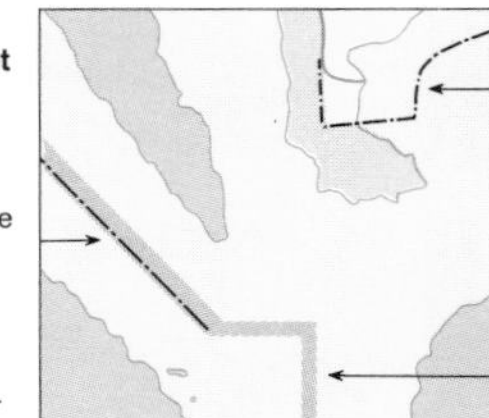

International Ocean Floor Boundary
Frontière d'état en mer
Staatsgrenze im Meeresgebiet
Confine di Stato nel mare
Límite de Nación en el mar

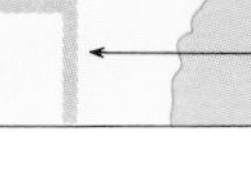

Undefined Ocean Floor Boundary
Frontière indéfinie d'état tracée en meer
Unbestimmte Staatsgrenze im Meeresgebiet
Confine di Stato indefinito nel mare
Límite indefinido de Nación en el mar

National Capital
Capitale d'État
Hauptstadt eines unabhängigen Staates
Capitale di Stato
Capital de Nación

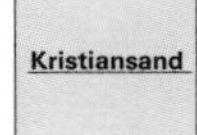

Third-order Capital
Capitale de Province, Comté, Bezirk
Provinz-, Grafschafts-, Bezirkshauptstadt
Capoluogo di Provincia, Contea, Bezirk
Capital de Provincia, Condado, Bezirk

RIGA

Dependency or Second-order Capital
Capitale d'État fédéré, Région
Bundesstaats-, Regionshauptstadt
Capitale di Stato federato, Regione
Capital de Estado federado, Región

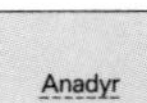

Administrative District Capital (U.S.S.R.)
Capitale de Circonscription
Kreishauptstadt
Capoluogo di Circondario
Capital de Circunscripción administrativa

Other Symbols
Symboles divers / Simboli vari
Sonstige Zeichen / Signos varios

International Airport
Aéroport international
Internationaler Flughafen
Aeroporto internazionale
Aeropuerto internacional

Church, Monastery, Abbey
Monastère, Église, Abbaye
Kloster, Kirche, Abtei
Monastero, Chiesa, Abbazia
Monasterio, Iglesia, Abadía

Lighthouse
Phare
Leuchtturm
Faro
Faro

Castle
Château
Burg, Schloß
Castello
Castillo

Dam
Barrage
Staudamm, Staumauer
Diga artificiale, Sbarramento
Presa

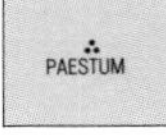

Ruin, Archeological Site
Ruine, Centre archéologique
Ruine, Archäologisches Zentrum
Rovina, Zona archeologica
Ruina, Zona arqueológica

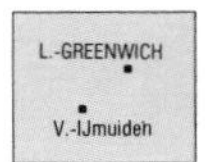

Section of a City
Faubourg
Stadt- oder Ortsteil
Sobborgo urbano
Suburbio

Monument, Historic Site, etc.
Monument
Denkmal
Monumento
Monumento

Bidon V

Uninhabited Locality, Hamlet
Ville inhabitée, Ferme, Hameau
Unbewohnte Stadt, Gehöft, Weiler
Città disabitata, Fattoria, Nucleo di case
Ciudad despoblada, Granja, Casar

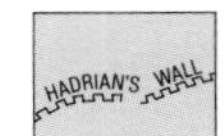

Wall
Muraille
Wall, Mauer
Vallo, Muraglia
Muralla

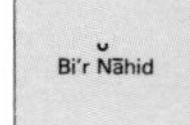

Periodically Inhabited Oasis
Oasis habitées périodiquement
Zeitweilig bewohnte Oase
Oasi periodicamente abitate
Oasis periodicamente habitados

Point of Interest
Curiosité
Sehenswürdigkeit
Curiositá
Curiosidad

Scientific Station
Base géophysique
Geophysikalische Beobachtungsstation
Base geofisica
Base geofísica

Cave
Grotte, Caverne
Höhle
Grotta, Caverna
Cueva, Gruta

Populated Places
Population / Popolazione
Bevölkerung / Población

Continent Maps
Cartes des Continents / Carte dei Continenti
Erdteilkarten / Mapas de Continentes

< 25 000
25 000-100 000
100 000-250 000
250 000-1 000 000
> 1 000 000

Regional Maps
Cartes à plus grande échelle / Carte di sviluppo
Karten größeren Maßstabs / Mapas a gran escala

< 10 000
10 000-25 000
25 000-100 000
100 000-250 000
250 000-1 000 000
> 1 000 000

Symbols represent population of inhabited localities
Les symboles représentent le nombre d'habitants des localités
Die Signaturen entsprechen der Einwohnerzahl des Ortes
I simboli sono relativi al valore demografico dei centri abitati
Los simbolos son proporcionales a la población del lugar

Town area symbol represents the shape of the urban area
Le petit plan de la ville reproduit la configuration de l'aire urbaine
Die Plansignatur stellt die Gestalt des Stadtgebietes dar
La piantina della città rappresenta la configurazione dell'area urbana
El pequeño plano de la ciudad representa la forma del area urbana

Transportation
Communications / Comunicazioni
Verkehrsnetz / Comunicaciones

Primary Railway
Chemin de fer principal
Hauptbahn
Ferrovia principale
Ferrocarril principal

Secondary Railway
Chemin de fer secondaire
Sonstige Bahn
Ferrovia secondaria
Ferrocarril secundario

Motorway, Expressway
Autoroute
Autobahn
Autostrada
Autopista

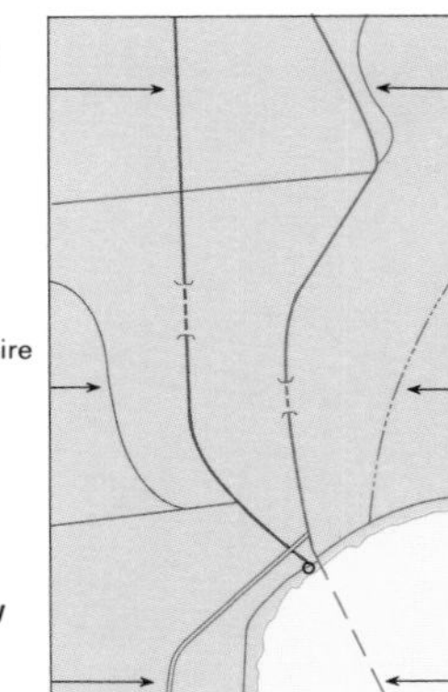

Road
Route de grande communication, Autres Routes
Fernverkehrsstraße, andere Straßen
Strada principale, Altre Strade
Carretera principal, Otras Carreteras

Trail, Caravan Route
Piste, Voie caravanière
Wüstenpiste, Karawanenweg
Pista nel deserto, Carovaniera
Pista en el desierto, Via de Carabanas

Ferry, Shipping Lane
Bac, Ligne maritime
Fähre, Schiffahrtslinie
Traghetto, Linea di navigazione
Transbordador (Ferry), Línea de navegación

Type Styles
Caractères utilisés pour la toponymie / Caratteri usati per la toponomastica
Zur Namenschreibung verwendete Schriftarten / Caracteres utilizados para la toponimia

ITALY
Hessen RIBE

Political Units
Etat, Dépendance, Division administrative
Staat, abhängiges Gebiet, Verwaltungsgliederung
Stato, Dipendenza, Divisione amministrativa
Nación, Dependencia, Division administrativa

Ankaratra Monte Bianco
Tsiafajavona Ngorongoro Crater
Nevado del Tolima Kings Peak

Small Mountain Range, Mountain, Peak
Petit massif, Mont, Cime
Bergmassiv, Berg, Gipfel
Piccolo gruppo montuoso, Monte, Vetta
Macizo pequeño, Monte, Cima

LABRADOR SEA
Gulf of Alaska Hudson Bay
Estrecho de Magallanes

Sea, Gulf, Bay, Strait
Mer, Golfe, Baie, Détroit
Meer, Golf, Bucht, Meeresstraße
Mare, Golfo, Baia, Stretto
Mar, Golfo, Bahía, Estrecho

SAXONY
THRACE SUSSEX

Historical or Cultural Region
Région historique ou culturelle
Historische oder Kulturlandschaft
Regione storico - culturale
Región histórica y cultural

Cabo de São Vicente Land's End
Mizen Head Point Conception
Col de la Perche Passo della Cisa

Cape, Point, Pass
Cap, Pointe, Passe
Kap, Landspitze, Paß
Capo, Punta, Passo
Cabo, Punta, Paso

West Mariana Basin
Galapagos Fracture Zone
Mid-Atlantic Ridge

Undersea Features
Formes du relief sous-marin
Formen des Meeresbodens
Forme del rilievo sottomarino
Formas del relieve submarino

PATAGONIA
BASSIN DE RENNES
PENÍNSULA DE YUCATÁN

Physical Region (plain, peninsula)
Région physique (plaine, péninsule)
Landschaft (Ebene, Halbinsel)
Regione fisica (pianura, penisola)
Región natural (llanura, península)

MAHÉ ALDABRA ISLANDS
CORSE CHANNEL ISLANDS
SULU ARCHIPELAGO

Island, Archipelago
Ile, Archipel
Insel, Archipel
Isola, Arcipelago
Isla, Archipiélago

Tarfaya
Tombouctou
Agadir
Nouakchott
BRAZZAVILLE
CASABLANCA

Size of type indicates relative importance of inhabited localities
La dimension des caractères indique l'importance d'une localité
Die Schriftgröße entspricht der Gesamtbedeutung des Ortes
La grandezza del carattere è proporzionale all'importanza della località
La dimensión de los caracteres de imprenta indica la importancia de la localidad

PYRENEES
CUMBRIAN MOUNTAINS
SIERRA DE GÁDOR LA SILA

Mountain Range
Chaîne de montagnes
Bergkette, Gebirge
Catena di monti
Cadena montañosa

Thames Po Victoria Falls
Lotagipi Swamp Göta kanal
Lago Maggiore

River, Waterfall, Cataract, Canal, Lake
Fleuve, Chute d'eau, Cataracte, Canal, Lac
Fluß, Wasserfall, Katarakt, Kanal, See
Fiume, Cascata, Cateratta, Canale, Lago
Río, Cascada, Catarata, Canal, Lago

INDEX MAPS

WORLD PHYSICAL AND POLITICAL MAPS

1/2 1:70,000,000

THE OCEANS

3 1:70,000,000

WORLD TRANSPORTATION AND TIME ZONES

4 1:90,000,000

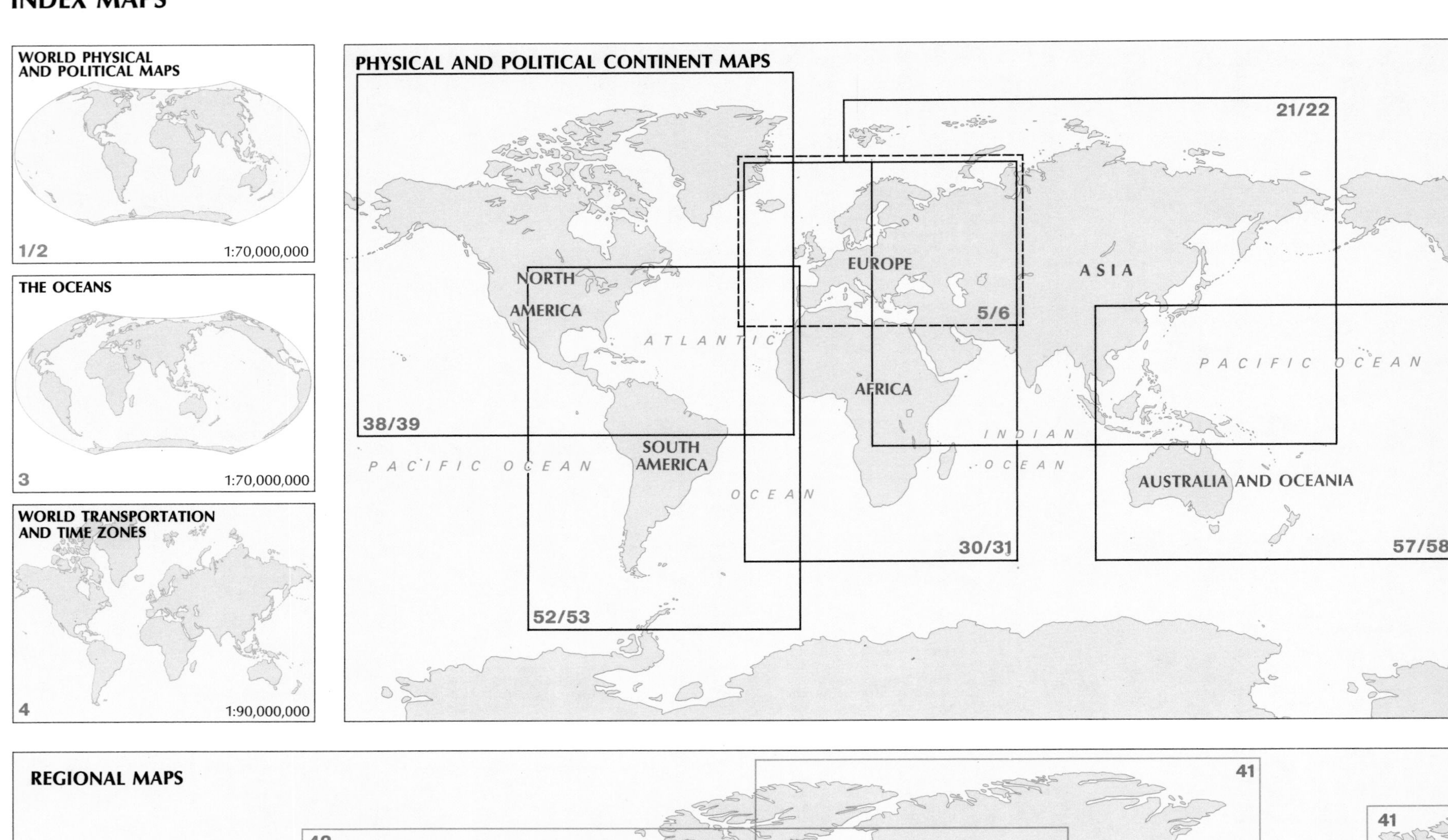

REGIONAL MAPS

41
42
Greenland
Thule
40
Alaska
Nome
Fairbanks
Anchorage
Inuvik
Yellowknife
Godthåb
ICELAND
Reykjavik
NORWAY
SWEDEN
FINLAND
Helsinki
Oslo
Stockholm
Juneau
Churchill
CANADA
Edmonton
Aleutian Islands
40
43
45 Regina
Winnipeg
Vancouver
Québec
44
Ottawa
Boston
New York
ATLANTIC
OCEAN
UNITED STATES
Denver
San Francisco
St. Louis
Washington
Los Angeles
Houston
New Orleans
46
Miami
BAHAMAS
Havana
CUBA
JAMAICA
HAITI
DOMINICAN REP.
Puerto Rico
51
Caribbean Islands
51
Mexico City
MEXICO
48
BELIZE
HONDURAS
GUATEMALA
EL SALVADOR
NICARAGUA
Managua
COSTA RICA
PANAMA
49
Caracas
TRINIDAD AND TOBAGO
VENEZUELA
GUYANA
SURINAME
French Guiana
50
54
Bogotá
COLOMBIA
Quito
ECUADOR
47
Galapagos Islands
54
PACIFIC OCEAN
Manaus
Belém
BRAZIL
PERU
Lima
Brasília
La Paz
BOLIVIA
Rio de Janeiro
PARAGUAY
Asunción
Easter Island
65
Santiago
Buenos Aires
URUGUAY
Montevideo
CHILE
ARGENTINA
55
56
ATLANTIC
OCEAN
IRELAND
Dublin
UNITED KINGDOM
London
DENMARK
Copenhagen
Berlin
POLAND
Warsaw
GERMANY
Paris
FRANCE
ITALY
Rome
GREECE
Athens
Madrid
Lisbon
SPAIN
PORTUGAL
Azores
Madeira Islands
Rabat
Algiers
Tunis
TUNISIA
MOROCCO
Tripoli
ALGERIA
Canary Islands
El Aaiún
LIBYA
Western Sahara
CAPE VERDE
MAURITANIA
Nouakchott
MALI
NIGER
CHAD
32
SENEGAL
Niamey
N'Djamena
GAMBIA
Bamako
BURKINA FASO
GUINEA-BISSAU
GUINEA
Conakry
SIERRA LEONE
Monrovia
LIBERIA
GHANA
Abidjan
Accra
NIGERIA
Lagos
IVORY COAST
TOGO
BENIN
CAMEROON
Yaoundé
34
EQUATORIAL GUINEA
SAO TOME AND PRINCIPE
Libreville
GABON
CONGO
ZAIRE
Brazzaville
Kinshasa
Luanda
ANGOLA
Windhoek
NAMIBIA
BOTSWANA
Gaborone
SOUTH AFRICA
Cape Town
41
Svalbard
19

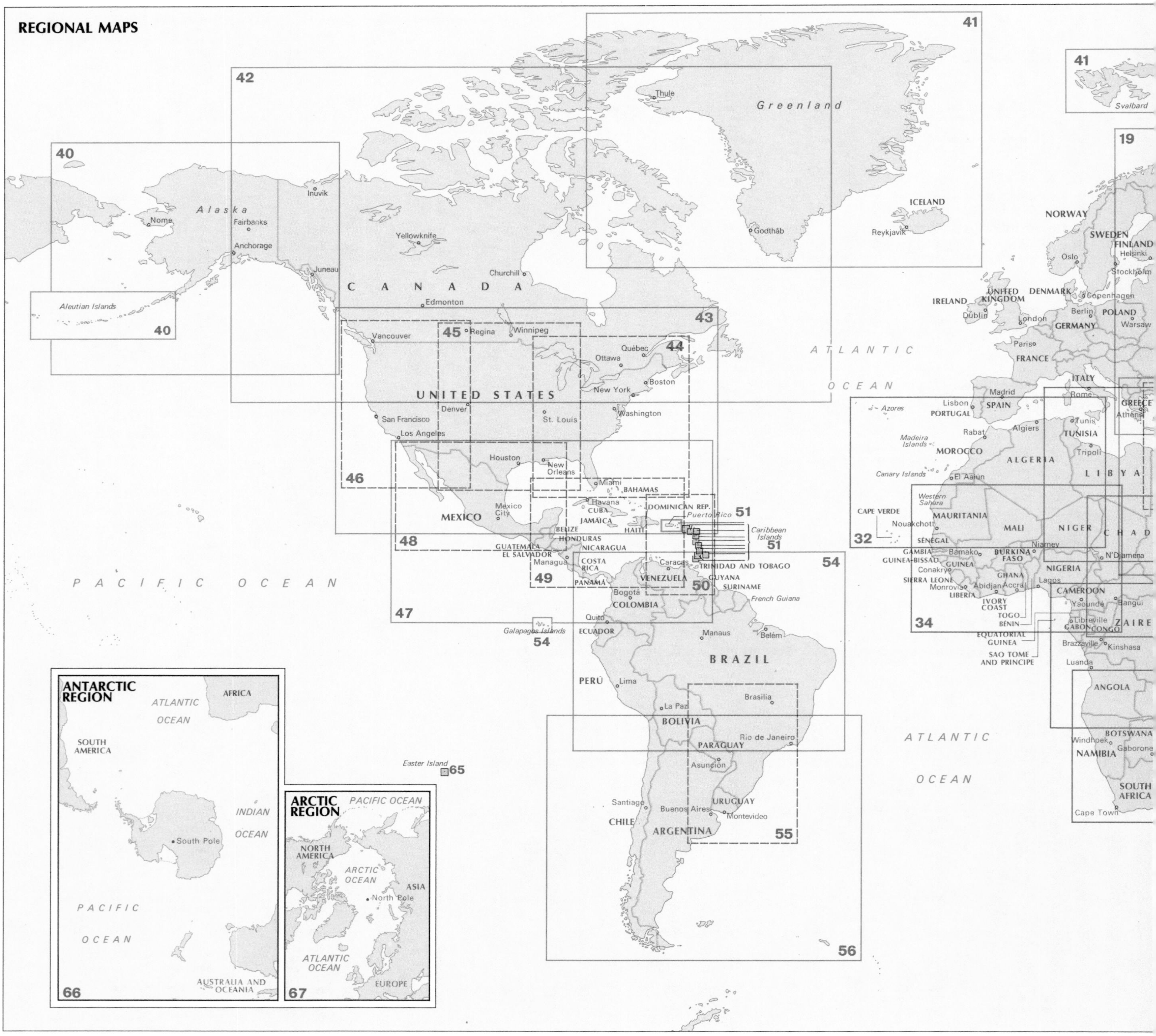

ANTARCTIC REGION

ATLANTIC OCEAN
AFRICA
SOUTH AMERICA
INDIAN OCEAN
South Pole
PACIFIC OCEAN
AUSTRALIA AND OCEANIA
66

ARCTIC REGION

PACIFIC OCEAN
NORTH AMERICA
ARCTIC OCEAN
ASIA
North Pole
ATLANTIC OCEAN
EUROPE
67

REGIONAL MAPS OF EUROPE

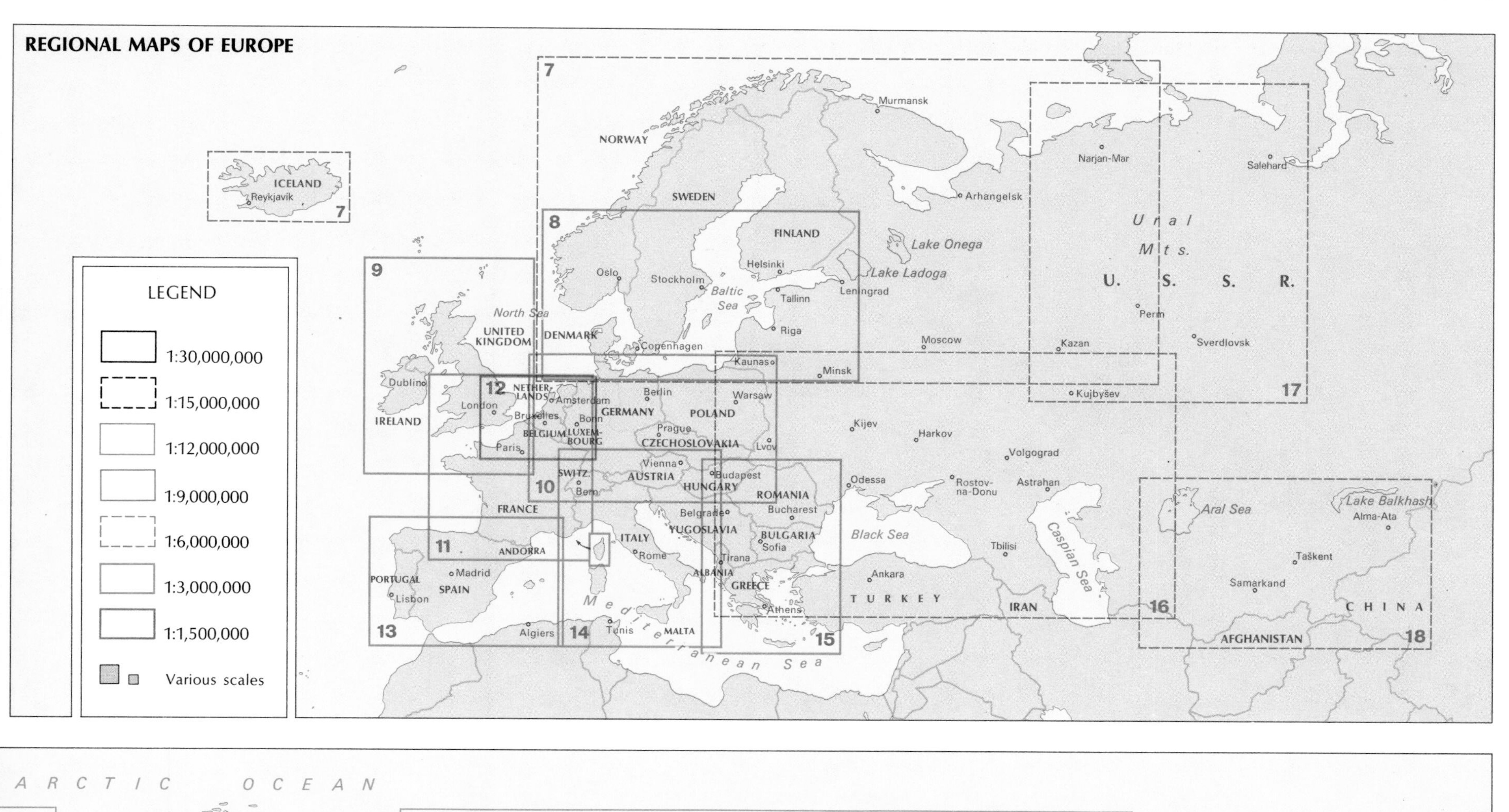

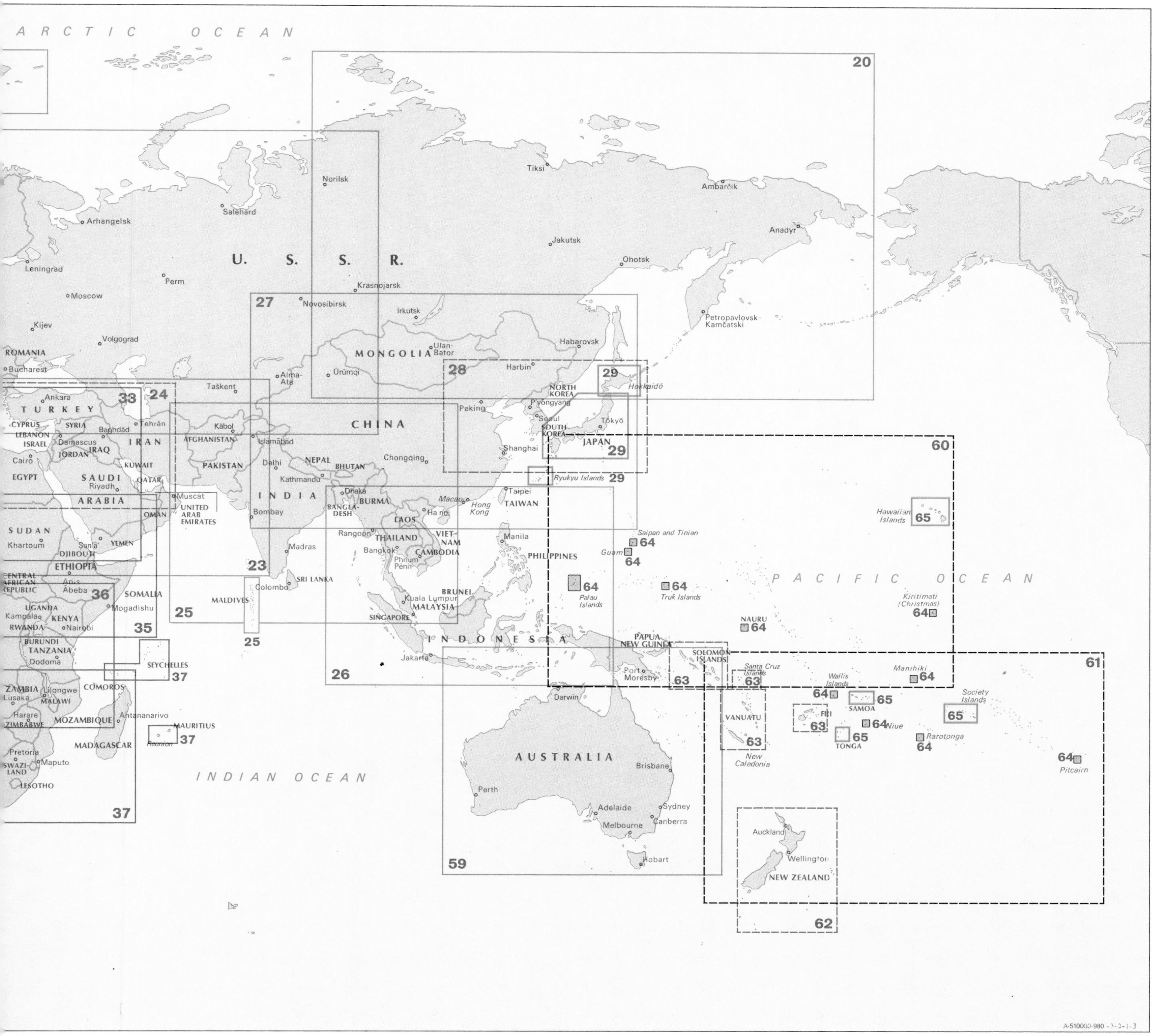

ARCTIC OCEAN

U. S. S. R.

Norilsk, Tiksi, Ambarčik, Salehard, Arhangelsk, Leningrad, Perm, Moscow, Jakutsk, Anadyr, Ohotsk, Krasnojarsk, Novosibirsk, Irkutsk, Petropavlovsk-Kamčatski, Kijev, Volgograd, Habarovsk, ROMANIA, Bucharest

MONGOLIA, Ulan-Bator, Alma-Ata, Ürümqi, Harbin, Taškent

Ankara, TURKEY, CYPRUS, SYRIA, LEBANON, ISRAEL, Damascus, Baghdad, Tehrān, IRAN, Cairo, JORDAN, IRAQ, KUWAIT, EGYPT, SAUDI ARABIA, Riyadh, QATAR, Muscat, UNITED ARAB EMIRATES, OMAN, SUDAN, Khartoum, Sana, YEMEN, DJIBOUTI, ETHIOPIA, CENTRAL AFRICAN REPUBLIC, Addis Abeba, SOMALIA, Mogadishu, UGANDA, Kampala, KENYA, RWANDA, Nairobi, BURUNDI, TANZANIA, Dodoma, SEYCHELLES, ZAMBIA, Lusaka, Lilongwe, MALAWI, COMOROS, Harare, ZIMBABWE, MOZAMBIQUE, Antananarivo, MAURITIUS, Réunion, MADAGASCAR, Pretoria, Maputo, SWAZILAND, LESOTHO

Kābol, AFGHANISTAN, Islāmābād, PAKISTAN, Delhi, NEPAL, BHUTAN, Kathmandu, INDIA, Bombay, Dhaka, BANGLADESH, BURMA, Madras, SRI LANKA, Colombo, MALDIVES

CHINA, Peking, NORTH KOREA, P'yongyang, Seoul, SOUTH KOREA, Hokkaidō, Tōkyō, JAPAN, Shanghai, Chongqing, Ryukyu Islands, Taipei, TAIWAN, Macau, Hong Kong, Ha-noi, LAOS, VIETNAM, Rangoon, THAILAND, Bangkok, CAMBODIA, Phnum Penh, Manila, PHILIPPINES, BRUNEI, Kuala Lumpur, MALAYSIA, SINGAPORE, INDONESIA, Jakarta

PACIFIC OCEAN, Hawaiian Islands, Saipan and Tinian, Guam, Palau Islands, Truk Islands, NAURU, Kiritimati (Christmas), PAPUA NEW GUINEA, Port Moresby, SOLOMON ISLANDS, Santa Cruz Islands, Manihiki, Wallis Islands, SAMOA, Society Islands, VANUATU, FIJI, Niue, TONGA, Rarotonga, New Caledonia, Pitcairn

Darwin, AUSTRALIA, Perth, Brisbane, Adelaide, Sydney, Canberra, Melbourne, Hobart, Auckland, Wellington, NEW ZEALAND

INDIAN OCEAN

20 23 24 25 26 27 28 29 33 35 36 37 59 60 61 62 63 64 65

A-510002-980

Map 1 **WORLD, PHYSICAL**

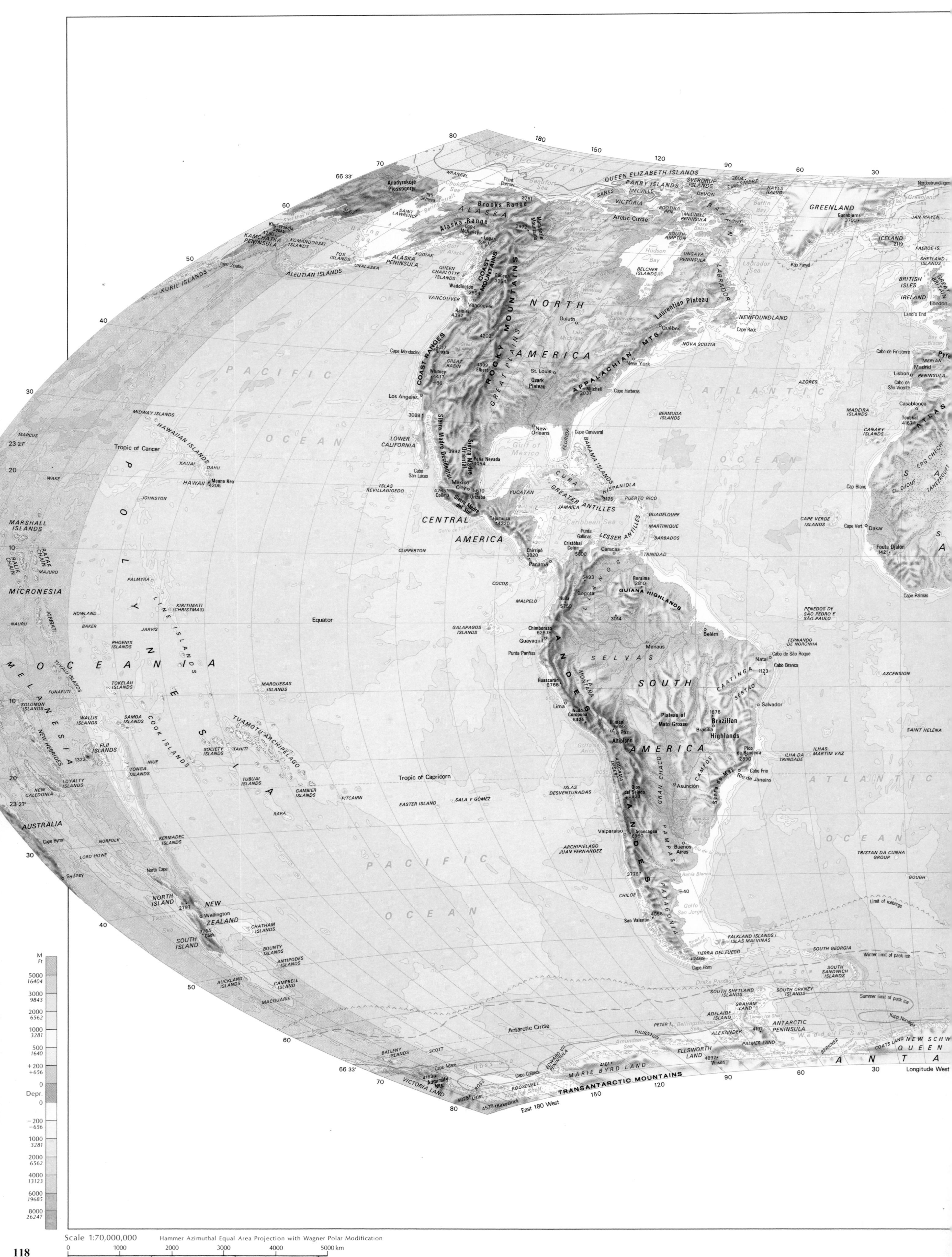

Scale 1:70,000,000 Hammer Azimuthal Equal Area Projection with Wagner Polar Modification

0 1000 2000 3000 4000 5000 km

0 1000 2000 3000 miles

ARCTIC OCEAN
SPITSBERGEN
FRANZ JOSEPH LAND
SEVERNAYA ZEMLYA
NEW SIBERIAN ISLANDS
WRANGEL
NOVAYA ZEMLYA
Barents Sea
Kara Sea
Laptev Sea
East Siberian Sea
Chukchi Sea
Bering Strait
YAMAL PENINSULA
Byrranga Mts.
North Cape
Norwegian Sea
LAPLAND
KOLA PENINSULA
SCANDINAVIA
FINLAND
KARELIA
Leningrad
Stockholm
Lindesnes
North Sea
Baltic Sea
Moscow
Berlin
Kiev
Vienna
Paris
Mont Blanc
ALPS
CARPATHIAN MTS.
UKRAINE
E U R O P E
CORSICA
Rome
SARDINIA
BALEARIC ISLANDS
SICILY
Algiers
Athens
Istanbul
BALKAN PENINSULA
ANATOLIA
TAURUS MTS.
CRETE
CYPRUS
Black Sea
CAUCASUS
Elbrus
Baku
Ararat
CASPIAN DEPRESSION
KIRGHIZ STEPPE
URAL MOUNTAINS
Narodnaja
WESTERN SIBERIAN PLAIN
Central Siberian Uplands
S I B E R I A
Verkhoyansk Mountains
Cherski Mts.
Arctic Circle
Pobeda
Suntar-Khayata
Stanovoy Upland
Stanovoy Range
Sayan Mts.
Irkutsk
Novosibirsk
Kazakh Hills
K A Z A K H S T A N
A L T A I
A S I A
Beluha
DZUNGARIAN BASIN
TIAN SHAN
Pobedy
TURKISTAN
KYZYLKUM
KARAKUMY
Kopetdag
Pamir
Kongur
K2
Hindu Kush
Karakoram
KASHMIR
TAKLA MAKAN
Altun Shan
Muztag
KUNLUN SHAN
Qilian Shan
Plateau of Tibet
Tanggula Shan
Nyainqêntanglha Shan
Gongga Shan
Everest
HIMALAYAS
Nanda Devi
Delhi
GREAT INDIAN DESERT
HINDUSTAN
Karachi
BALUCHISTAN
Tehran
Damavand
Elburz
Plateau of Iran
ZAGROS MTS.
MESOPOTAMIA
SYRIA
PALESTINE
Tripoli
Cairo
SINAI PEN.
AN NAFUD
Jabal Shammar
ARABIAN PENINSULA
NAJD
QATAR
Mecca
AR RUB' AL KHALI
OMAN
Ra's al Hadd
Gulf of Oman
Persian Gulf
Red Sea
Gulf of Aden
Aden
SOCOTRA
Cape Guardafui
Greater Khingan Range
MANCHURIA
Harbin
GOBI DESERT
Peking
Qin Ling
CHINA
Shanghai
Canton
Nan Ling
Wuyi Shan
TAIWAN
Sea of Japan
HOKKAIDO
HONSHU
Fuji
Tokyo
Seoul
SHIKOKU
KYUSHU
JAPAN
Yellow Sea
East China Sea
RYUKYU ISLANDS
IZU ISLANDS
SAKHALIN
Sikhote Alin
Sea of Okhotsk
KURIL ISLANDS
KAMCHATKA PENINSULA
Kljucevskaja Sopka
KOMANDORSKI ISLANDS
Bering Sea
ALASKA
ALASKA PENINSULA
SAINT LAWRENCE
FOX ISLANDS
UNALASKA
ALEUTIAN ISLANDS
PACIFIC OCEAN
MIDWAY ISLANDS
HAWAIIAN ISLANDS
KAUAI
OAHU
BONIN ISLANDS
DAITO ISLANDS
VOLCANO ISLANDS
MARCUS
Tropic of Cancer
PARECE VELA
WAKE
JOHNSTON
MARIANA ISLANDS
SAIPAN
GUAM
Philippine Sea
PHILIPPINE ISLANDS
LUZON
Manila
MINDORO
PANAY
NEGROS
MINDANAO
Apo
PALAWAN
HAINAN
PARACEL ISLANDS
Hanoi
TONKIN
INDOCHINA
ANNAM
Ngoc Linh
Ho Chi Minh
COCHIN CHINA
Ca Mau Point
Bangkok
Rangoon
BENGAL
Calcutta
Satpura Range
DECCAN
Eastern Ghats
Western Ghats
Bombay
Arabian Sea
Bay of Bengal
KUTCH
LAKSHADWEEP
Anai Mudi
Cape Comorin
SRI LANKA
Pidurutalagala
ANDAMAN ISLANDS
NICOBAR ISLANDS
MALDIVE ISLANDS
MALAY PENINSULA
SUMATRA
Kerinci
Singapore
NATUNA ISLANDS
BORNEO
Kinabalu
NANSHAN ISLAND
MENTAWAI ISLANDS
Equator
CELEBES
HALMAHERA
MOLUCCAS
CERAM
ARU
GREATER SUNDA ISLANDS
Jakarta
JAVA
Semeru
BALI
LESSER SUNDA ISLANDS
FLORES
SUMBAWA
SUMBA
TIMOR
Timor Sea
Arafura Sea
CHRISTMAS
COCOS ISLANDS
Puncak Jaya
NEW GUINEA
Victoria
BISMARCK ARCHIPELAGO
SOLOMON ISLANDS
PALAU ISLANDS
YAP ISLANDS
CAROLINE ISLANDS
TRUK ISLANDS
SENYAVIN ISLANDS
MARSHALL ISLANDS
RATAK CHAIN
RALIK CHAIN
MAJURO
MICRONESIA
MELANESIA
POLYNESIA
O C E A N I A
NAURU
KIRIBATI
HOWLAND
BAKER
PHOENIX ISLANDS
TUVALU ISLANDS
FUNAFUTI
TOKELAU ISLANDS
WALLIS ISLANDS
SAMOA ISLANDS
COOK ISLANDS
NIUE
FIJI ISLANDS
TONGA ISLANDS
NEW HEBRIDES
LOYALTY ISLANDS
NEW CALEDONIA
LOUISIADE ARCHIPELAGO
Coral Sea
Cape York
CAPE YORK PENINSULA
GREAT BARRIER REEF
ARNHEM LAND
Gulf of Carpentaria
KIMBERLEY PLATEAU
Barkly Tableland
GREAT SANDY DESERT
Macdonnell Ranges
North West Cape
GIBSON DESERT
AUSTRALIA
GREAT ARTESIAN BASIN
GREAT VICTORIA DESERT
GREAT DIVIDING RANGE
Cape Byron
Perth
Cape Naturaliste
Great Australian Bight
Sydney
Kosciusko
Melbourne
Bass Strait
TASMANIA
South East Cape
Tasman Sea
NORFOLK
LORD HOWE
KERMADEC ISLANDS
North Cape
NORTH ISLAND
Wellington
NEW ZEALAND
Cook
SOUTH ISLAND
CHATHAM ISLANDS
BOUNTY ISLANDS
ANTIPODES ISLANDS
AUCKLAND ISLANDS
CAMPBELL ISLAND
MACQUARIE
INDIAN OCEAN
SEYCHELLES ISLANDS
AMIRANTE ISLANDS
CHAGOS ARCHIPELAGO
DIEGO GARCIA
ALDABRA ISLANDS
ZANZIBAR
Cabo Delgado
COMORO ISLANDS
Cap d'Ambre
Massif du Tsaratanana
MADAGASCAR
Cap Sainte-Marie
Mozambique Channel
CARGADOS CARAJOS SHOALS
MAURITIUS
REUNION
MASCARENE ISLANDS
RODRIGUES
Tropic of Capricorn
ILE AMSTERDAM
ILE SAINT PAUL
PRINCE EDWARD ISLANDS
MARION
ILES CROZET
ILES KERGUELEN
HEARD
BOUVET
AFRICA
SAHARA
GRAND ERG
TRIPOLITANIA
CYRENAICA
LIBYAN DESERT
FEZZAN
Ahaggar
Tibesti
Emi Koussi
Adrar des Iforas
Aïr
TÉNÉRÉ
Ennedi
Darfur
Khartoum
NUBIAN DESERT
ARABIAN DESERT
Ras Dashan
Nabi Shu'ayb
Ethiopian Plateau
Addis Abeba
OGADEN
Massif des Bongo
AS SUDD
Jos Plateau
Adamaoua
Cameroon
Lagos
Gulf of Guinea
BIOKO
SÃO TOMÉ
Cap Lopez
CONGO BASIN
Ruwenzori
Kirinyaga
Nairobi
Kilimanjaro
RIFT VALLEY
Lake Victoria
Lake Tanganyika
Kinshasa
Mitumba Range
Serra Môco
NAMIB DESERT
KALAHARI DESERT
Maputo
Thabana Ntlenyana
Drakensberg
Cape Town
Cape of Good Hope
Kaap Agulhas
Antarctic Circle
RIISER-LARSEN PENINSULA
Cape Ann
ENDERBY LAND
MAC. ROBERTSON COAST
PRINCESS ELIZABETH LAND
American Highland
Cape Poinsett
Davis Sea
Dumont D'Urville Sea
ADÉLIE COAST
BALLENY ISLANDS
SCOTT
WILKES LAND
VICTORIA LAND
Admiralty Mountains
Cape Adare
Lister
Kirkpatrick
ROSS
Ross Sea
ROOSEVELT
EDWARD VII PENINSULA
TRANSANTARCTIC MTS.
MAUD LAND
ANTARCTICA
East of Greenwich
East 180 West
66 33'
23 27'
A-510000-780

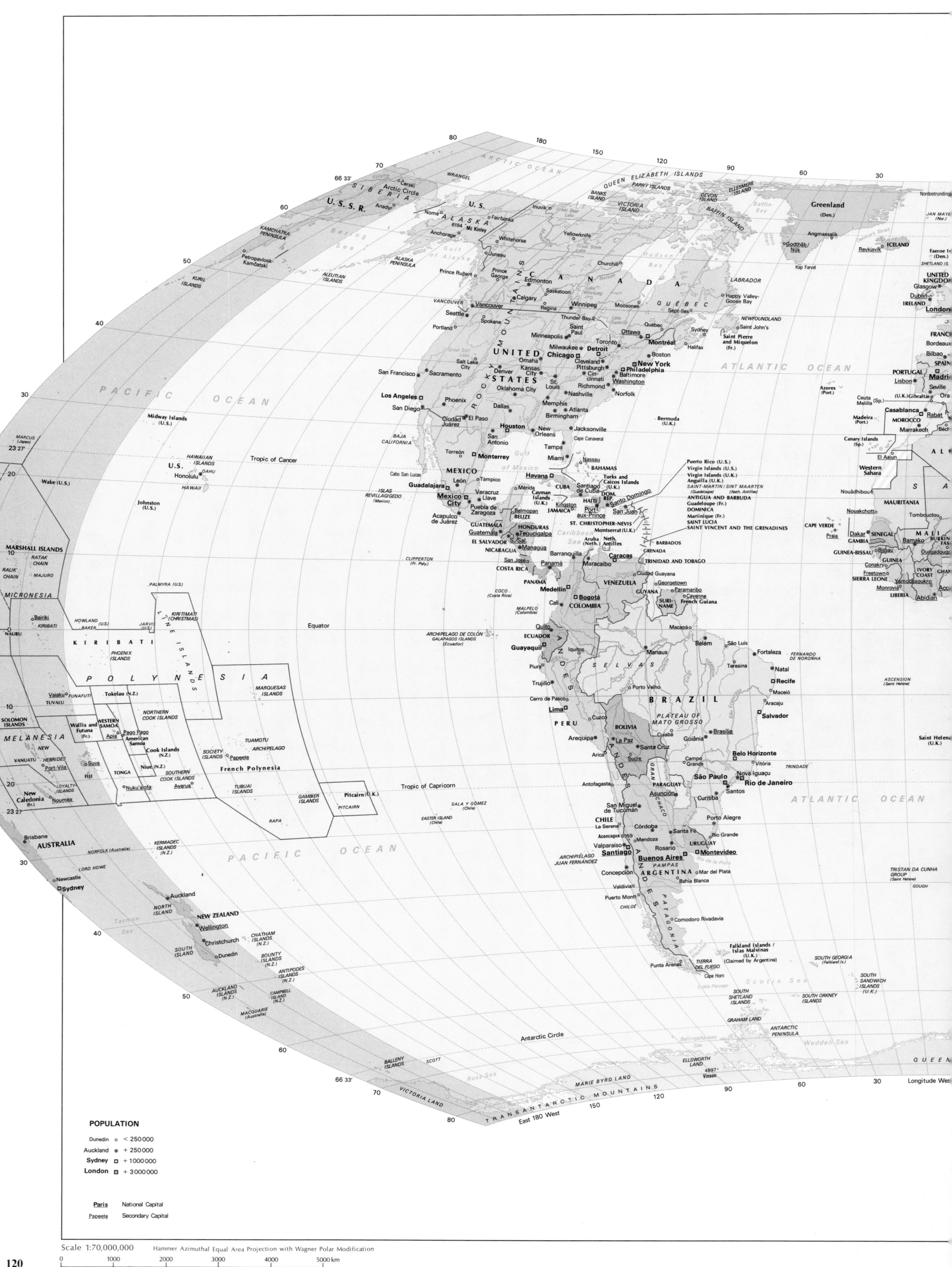
ARCTIC OCEAN
QUEEN ELIZABETH ISLANDS
U. S. S. R.
SIBERIA
Arctic Circle
Cerski
Anadyr
WRANGEL
Nome
ALASKA
Fairbanks
6194 Mc Kinley
Anchorage
Bering Sea
KAMCHATKA PENINSULA
Petropavlosk-Kamčatski
KURIL ISLANDS
ALEUTIAN ISLANDS
ALASKA PENINSULA
Gulf of Alaska
U. S.
Inuvik
Whitehorse
Juneau
Yellowknife
BANKS ISLAND
VICTORIA ISLAND
PARRY ISLANDS
DEVON ISLAND
ELLESMERE ISLAND
BAFFIN ISLAND
Baffin Bay
Greenland
(Den.)
Angmassalik
Godthåb/Nũk
Kap Farvel
ICELAND
Reykjavik
Faeroe Is. (Den.)
SHETLAND IS.
Nordostrundingen
JAN MAYEN (Nor.)
Hudson Bay
Churchill
Prince Rupert
Prince George
Edmonton
Saskatoon
Calgary
Regina
Winnipeg
CANADA
Moosonee
QUÉBEC
Sept-Iles
LABRADOR
Happy Valley-Goose Bay
NEWFOUNDLAND
Saint John's
Saint Pierre and Miquelon (Fr.)
VANCOUVER
Vancouver
Seattle
Spokane
Portland
Thunder Bay
Saint Paul
Minneapolis
Milwaukee
Detroit
Toronto
Ottawa
Québec
Montréal
Sydney
Halifax
Boston
New York
Philadelphia
Baltimore
Washington
Chicago
Cleveland
Pittsburgh
Cincinnati
Richmond
Norfolk
Omaha
Kansas City
Denver
St. Louis
Salt Lake City
San Francisco
Sacramento
Los Angeles
San Diego
Phoenix
Oklahoma City
Nashville
Memphis
Atlanta
Birmingham
Dallas
El Paso
Ciudad Juárez
Houston
San Antonio
New Orleans
Jacksonville
Cape Canaveral
Tampa
Miami
UNITED STATES
ROCKY MOUNTAINS
ATLANTIC OCEAN
PACIFIC OCEAN
Bermuda (U.K.)
Azores (Port.)
Midway Islands (U.S.)
MARCUS (Japan)
23 27′
Tropic of Cancer
HAWAIIAN ISLANDS
OAHU
Honolulu
HAWAII
U.S.
Wake (U.S.)
Johnston (U.S.)
BAJA CALIFORNIA
Torreón
Monterrey
Gulf of Mexico
MEXICO
Cabo San Lucas
León
Tampico
Guadalajara
Mérida
Veracruz Llave
Mexico City
Puebla de Zaragoza
Acapulco de Juárez
ISLAS REVILLAGIGEDO (Mexico)
Havana
CUBA
Cayman Islands (U.K.)
Nassau
BAHAMAS
Turks and Caicos Islands (U.K.)
Santiago de Cuba
DOM. REP.
Santo Domingo
HAITI
Port-au-Prince
Kingston
JAMAICA
San Juan
Belmopan
BELIZE
GUATEMALA
Guatemala
HONDURAS
Tegucigalpa
EL SALVADOR
San Salvador
NICARAGUA
Managua
San José
COSTA RICA
Panamá
PANAMA
ST. CHRISTOPHER-NEVIS
Montserrat (U.K.)
Aruba (Neth.)
Neth. Antilles
Caribbean Sea
Puerto Rico (U.S.)
Virgin Islands (U.S.)
Virgin Islands (U.K.)
Anguilla (U.K.)
SAINT-MARTIN / SINT MAARTEN (Guadeloupe) (Neth. Antilles)
ANTIGUA AND BARBUDA
Guadeloupe (Fr.)
DOMINICA
Martinique (Fr.)
SAINT LUCIA
SAINT VINCENT AND THE GRENADINES
BARBADOS
GRENADA
TRINIDAD AND TOBAGO
Barranquilla
Maracaibo
Caracas
VENEZUELA
Ciudad Guayana
Georgetown
GUYANA
Paramaribo
SURINAME
Cayenne
French Guiana
Medellín
Bogotá
Cali
COLOMBIA
CLIPPERTON (Fr. Poly.)
COCO (Costa Rica)
MALPELO (Colombia)
ARCHIPIÉLAGO DE COLÓN GALAPAGOS ISLANDS (Ecuador)
Equator
Quito
ECUADOR
Guayaquil
Iquitos
Piura
Trujillo
Cerro de Pasco
Lima
PERU
Cuzco
Arequipa
Macapá
Belém
São Luís
Fortaleza
FERNANDO DE NORONHA
Teresina
Manaus
Natal
Recife
Maceió
Aracaju
Salvador
SELVAS
Porto Velho
BRAZIL
PLATEAU OF MATO GROSSO
BOLIVIA
La Paz
Santa Cruz
Sucre
Cuiabá
Goiânia
Brasília
Belo Horizonte
Vitória
TRINIDADE
Campo Grande
São Paulo
Nova Iguaçu
Rio de Janeiro
Santos
Arica
Antofagasta
GRAN CHACO
PARAGUAY
Asunción
Curitiba
Porto Alegre
San Miguel de Tucumán
CHILE
La Serena
Aconcagua 6959
Córdoba
Santa Fe
Rio Grande
Mendoza
Valparaíso
Santiago
Rosario
URUGUAY
Buenos Aires
Montevideo
Rio de la Plata
PAMPAS
ARGENTINA
Mar del Plata
Bahía Blanca
Concepción
Valdivia
Puerto Montt
CHILOÉ
ARCHIPIÉLAGO JUAN FERNÁNDEZ
SALA Y GÓMEZ (Chile)
EASTER ISLAND (Chile)
PATAGONIA
ANDES
Comodoro Rivadavia
Falkland Islands / Islas Malvinas (U.K.) (Claimed by Argentina)
Punta Arenas
TIERRA DEL FUEGO
Cape Horn
Drake Passage
Scotia Sea
SOUTH GEORGIA (Falkland Is.)
SOUTH SANDWICH ISLANDS (U.K.)
SOUTH ORKNEY ISLANDS
SOUTH SHETLAND ISLANDS
GRAHAM LAND
ANTARCTIC PENINSULA
Weddell Sea
Bellingshausen Sea
Antarctic Circle
ELLSWORTH LAND
4897 Vinson
MARIE BYRD LAND
TRANSANTARCTIC MOUNTAINS
Ross Sea
SCOTT
BALLENY ISLANDS
VICTORIA LAND
East 180 West
Longitude West
ASCENSION (Saint Helena)
Saint Helena (U.K.)
TRISTAN DA CUNHA GROUP (Saint Helena)
GOUGH
ATLANTIC OCEAN
UNITED KINGDOM
Glasgow
Dublin
IRELAND
London
FRANCE
Bordeaux
Bilbao
SPAIN
PORTUGAL
Lisbon
Madrid
Seville
(U.K.) Gibraltar
Ceuta Melilla (Sp.)
Casablanca
Rabat
MOROCCO
Marrakech
Madeira (Port.)
Canary Islands (Sp.)
El Aaiún
Western Sahara
Nouâdhibou
MAURITANIA
Nouakchott
Tombouctou
CAPE VERDE
Praia
Dakar
SENEGAL
GAMBIA
Banjul
Bamako
MALI
GUINEA-BISSAU
Bissau
GUINEA
Conakry
Freetown
SIERRA LEONE
Monrovia
LIBERIA
IVORY COAST
Yamoussoukro
Abidjan
Ouagadougou
MARSHALL ISLANDS
RATAK CHAIN
RALIK CHAIN
MAJURO
MICRONESIA
PALMYRA (U.S.)
KIRITIMATI (CHRISTMAS)
LINE ISLANDS
JARVIS (U.S.)
HOWLAND (U.S.)
BAKER
Bairiki
KIRIBATI
NAURU
PHOENIX ISLANDS
POLYNESIA
MARQUESAS ISLANDS
Vaiaku
FUNAFUTI
TUVALU
Tokelau (N.Z.)
NORTHERN COOK ISLANDS
SOLOMON ISLANDS
Wallis and Futuna (Fr.)
WESTERN SAMOA
Apia
Pago Pago
American Samoa
MELANESIA
NEW HEBRIDES
VANUATU
Port-Vila
Suva
FIJI
TONGA
Cook Islands (N.Z.)
Niue (N.Z.)
SOUTHERN COOK ISLANDS
Avarua
Nuku'alofa
SOCIETY ISLANDS
Papeete
TUAMOTU ARCHIPELAGO
French Polynesia
TUBUAI ISLANDS
GAMBIER ISLANDS
Pitcairn (U.K.)
PITCAIRN
RAPA
Tropic of Capricorn
New Caledonia (Fr.)
LOYALTY ISLANDS
Nouméa
Brisbane
AUSTRALIA
NORFOLK (Australia)
KERMADEC ISLANDS (N.Z.)
LORD HOWE
Newcastle
Sydney
Auckland
NORTH ISLAND
NEW ZEALAND
Wellington
Christchurch
Dunedin
SOUTH ISLAND
Tasman Sea
CHATHAM ISLANDS (N.Z.)
BOUNTY ISLANDS (N.Z.)
ANTIPODES ISLANDS (N.Z.)
AUCKLAND ISLANDS (N.Z.)
CAMPBELL ISLAND (N.Z.)
MACQUARIE (Australia)
POPULATION
Dunedin ○ < 250000
Auckland ◉ + 250000
Sydney ▫ + 1000000
London ▣ + 3000000
Paris National Capital
Papeete Secondary Capital
Scale 1:70,000,000
Hammer Azimuthal Equal Area Projection with Wagner Polar Modification
0 1000 2000 3000 4000 5000 km
0 1000 2000 3000 miles

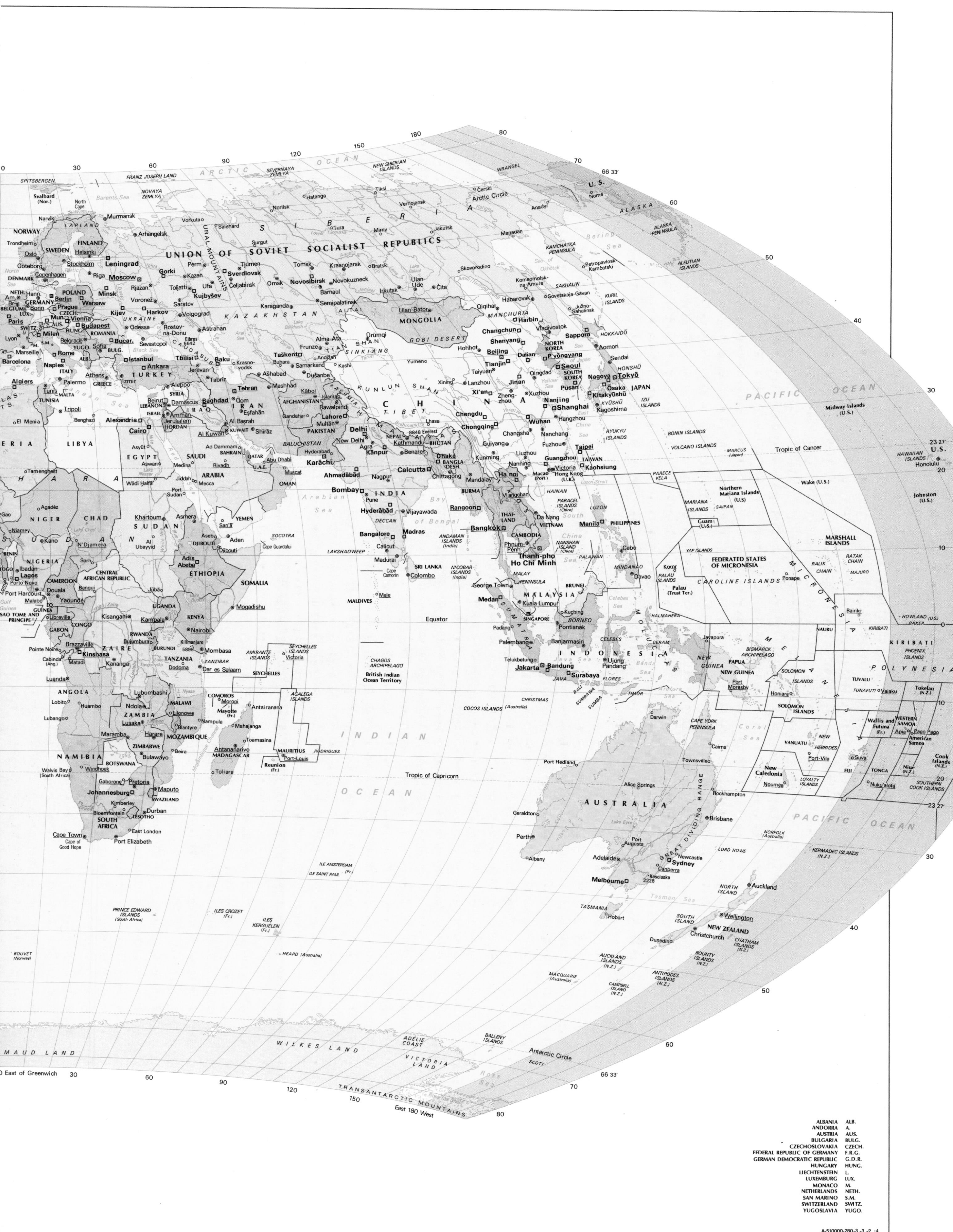
ARCTIC OCEAN
UNION OF SOVIET SOCIALIST REPUBLICS
SIBERIA
KAZAKHSTAN
UKRAINE
URAL MOUNTAINS
MONGOLIA
GOBI DESERT
CHINA
TIBET
MANCHURIA
JAPAN
NORTH KOREA
SOUTH KOREA
INDIA
PAKISTAN
AFGHANISTAN
IRAN
IRAQ
SYRIA
TURKEY
SAUDI ARABIA
EGYPT
LIBYA
SUDAN
CHAD
NIGER
NIGERIA
ETHIOPIA
SOMALIA
KENYA
ZAIRE
ANGOLA
ZAMBIA
NAMIBIA
BOTSWANA
SOUTH AFRICA
MOZAMBIQUE
MADAGASCAR
TANZANIA
INDIAN OCEAN
PACIFIC OCEAN
AUSTRALIA
NEW ZEALAND
INDONESIA
MALAYSIA
PHILIPPINES
PAPUA NEW GUINEA
FEDERATED STATES OF MICRONESIA
MARSHALL ISLANDS
KIRIBATI
POLYNESIA
MELANESIA
MICRONESIA
MAUD LAND
WILKES LAND
VICTORIA LAND
TRANSANTARCTIC MOUNTAINS
Arctic Circle
Tropic of Cancer
Equator
Tropic of Capricorn
Antarctic Circle
66 33'
23 27'
0 East of Greenwich
East 180 West
Moscow
Leningrad
Beijing
Shanghai
Tokyo
Seoul
Delhi
Bombay
Calcutta
Karāchi
Tehran
Baghdad
Cairo
Bangkok
Jakarta
Manila
Sydney
Melbourne
Wellington
Auckland
Cape Town
Johannesburg
Nairobi
Kinshasa
ALBANIA ALB.
ANDORRA A.
AUSTRIA AUS.
BULGARIA BULG.
CZECHOSLOVAKIA CZECH.
FEDERAL REPUBLIC OF GERMANY F.R.G.
GERMAN DEMOCRATIC REPUBLIC G.D.R.
HUNGARY HUNG.
LIECHTENSTEIN L.
LUXEMBURG LUX.
MONACO M.
NETHERLANDS NETH.
SAN MARINO S.M.
SWITZERLAND SWITZ.
YUGOSLAVIA YUGO.
A-510000-280-3 -3 -2 -4

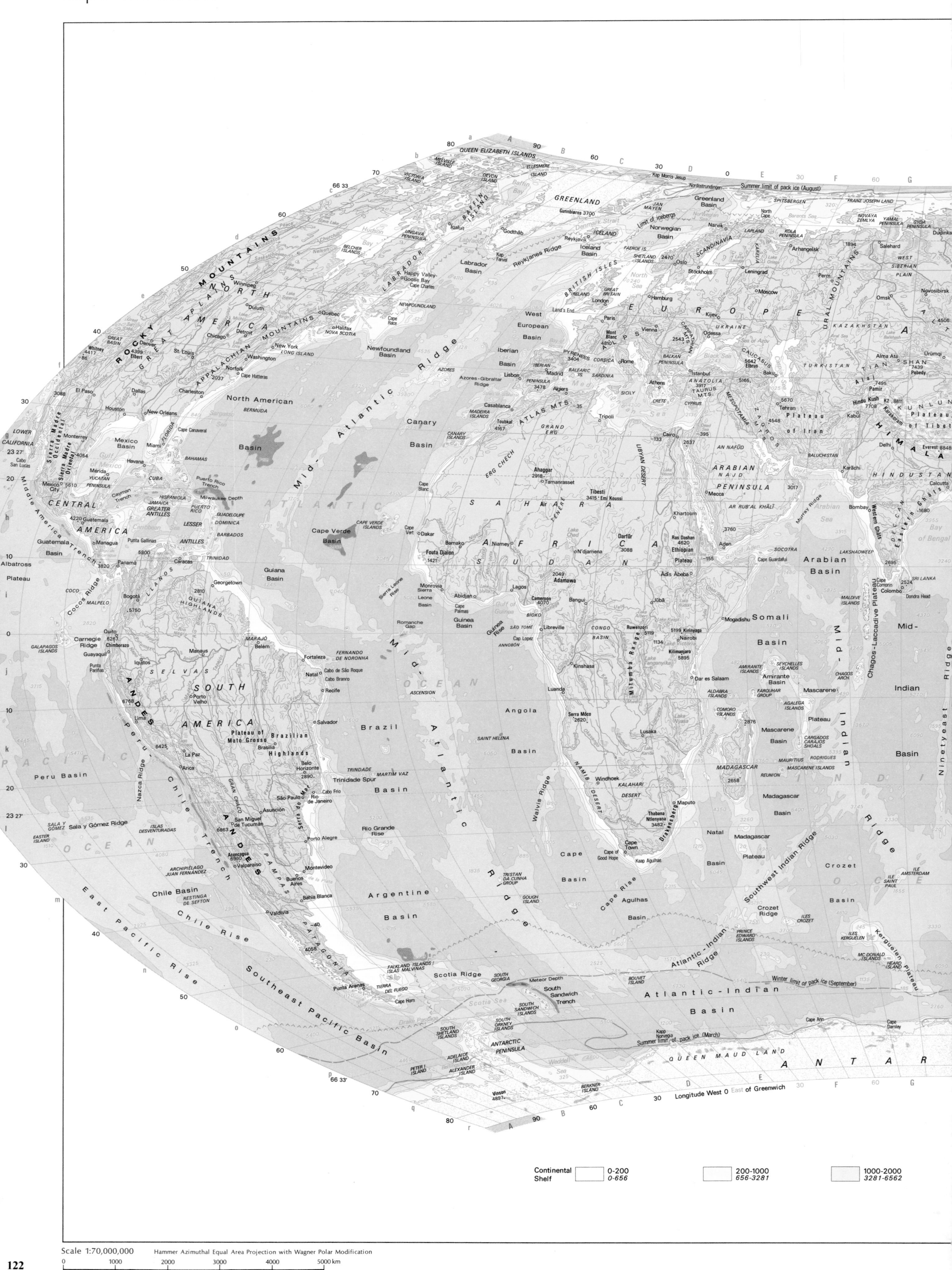

Scale 1:70,000,000 Hammer Azimuthal Equal Area Projection with Wagner Polar Modification

0 1000 2000 3000 4000 5000 km

0 1000 2000 3000 miles

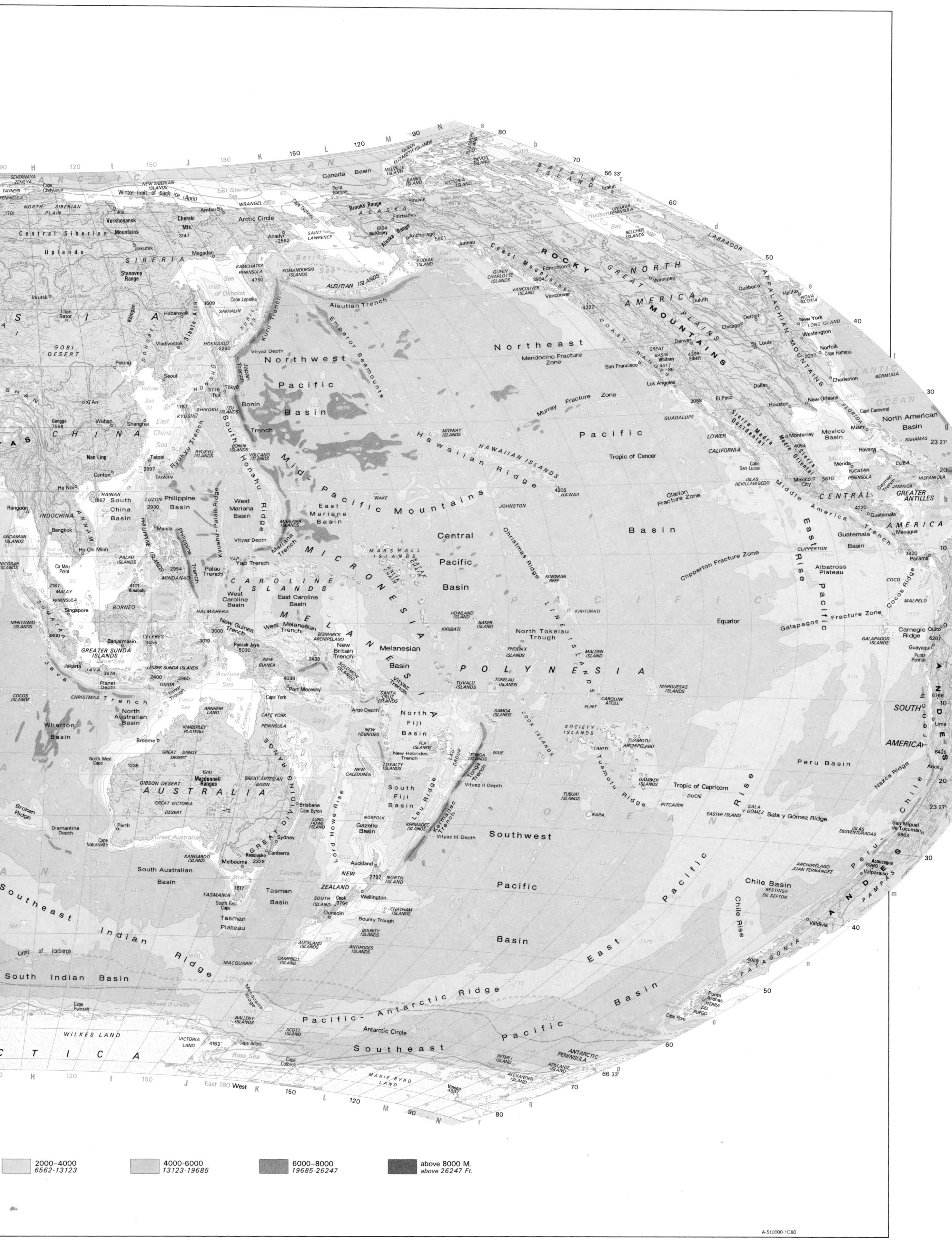

Canada Basin
Beaufort Sea
Winter limit of pack ice (April)
Arctic Circle
Central Siberian Uplands
SIBERIA
Brooks Range
ALASKA
Fairbanks
Anchorage
ALEUTIAN ISLANDS
Aleutian Trench
Emperor Seamounts
Kuril Trench
Japan Trench
Vityaz Depth
Northwest Pacific Basin
Bonin Trench
South Honshu Ridge
Ryukyu Trench
Philippine Trench
Philippine Basin
West Mariana Basin
Mariana Trench
East Mariana Basin
Mid-Pacific Mountains
HAWAIIAN ISLANDS
Hawaiian Ridge
Northeast Pacific Basin
Mendocino Fracture Zone
Murray Fracture Zone
Tropic of Cancer
Clarion Fracture Zone
Clipperton Fracture Zone
Central Pacific Basin
MICRONESIA
CAROLINE ISLANDS
West Caroline Basin
East Caroline Basin
MARSHALL ISLANDS
Christmas Ridge
LINE ISLANDS
North Tokelau Trough
MELANESIA
Melanesian Basin
West Melanesian Trench
New Guinea Trench
POLYNESIA
North Fiji Basin
South Fiji Basin
Lau Ridge
Tonga Trench
Kermadec Trench
Vityaz II Depth
Vityaz III Depth
Lord Howe Rise
Tasman Basin
Tasman Plateau
South Australian Basin
Southeast Indian Ridge
South Indian Basin
Limit of icebergs
Wharton Basin
North Australian Basin
Java Trench
Planet Depth
Timor Trough
AUSTRALIA
GREAT DIVIDING RANGE
NEW ZEALAND
Southwest Pacific Basin
Tuamotu Ridge
Tropic of Capricorn
Sala y Gómez Ridge
East Pacific Rise
Albatross Plateau
Equator
Galapagos Fracture Zone
Cocos Ridge
Carnegie Ridge
Peru Basin
Nazca Ridge
Peru-Chile Trench
Chile Basin
Chile Rise
Southeast Pacific Basin
Pacific-Antarctic Ridge
Antarctic Circle
ROCKY MOUNTAINS
NORTH AMERICA
GREAT PLAINS
APPALACHIAN MOUNTAINS
North American Basin
Mexico Basin
CENTRAL AMERICA
Middle America Trench
Guatemala Basin
SOUTH AMERICA
ANDES
PATAGONIA
ASIA
CHINA
GOBI DESERT
INDOCHINA
South China Basin
WILKES LAND
MARIE BYRD LAND
ANTARCTIC PENINSULA
2000–4000
6562-13123
4000-6000
13123-19685
6000–8000
19685-26247
above 8000 M.
above 26247 Ft.
A-510000-1C80

Map 4 **WORLD TRANSPORTATION AND TIME ZONES**

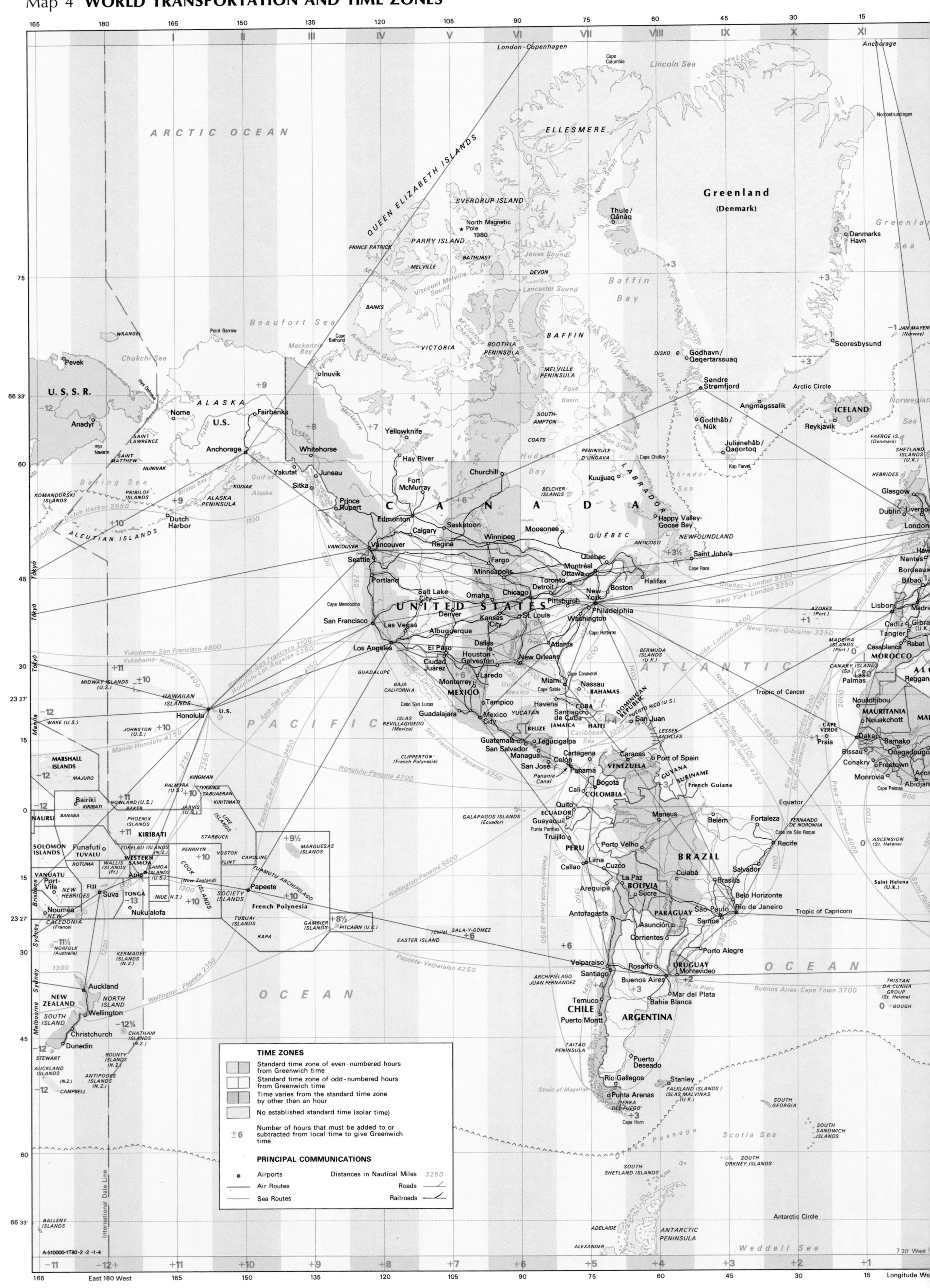

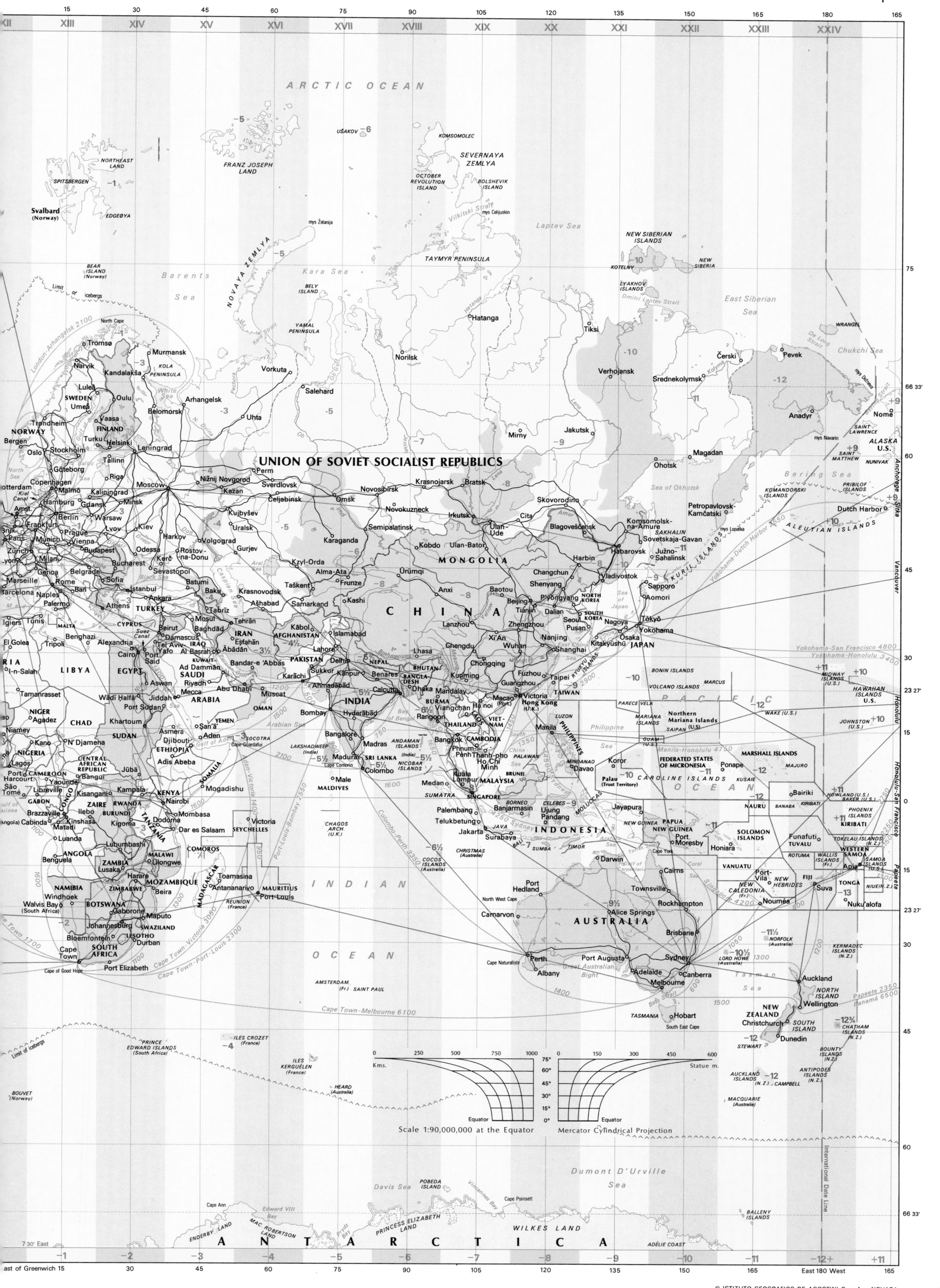
ARCTIC OCEAN
UNION OF SOVIET SOCIALIST REPUBLICS
MONGOLIA
CHINA
INDIA
INDONESIA
AUSTRALIA
INDIAN OCEAN
PACIFIC OCEAN
ANTARCTICA
JAPAN
Scale 1:90,000,000 at the Equator
Mercator Cylindrical Projection
International Date Line

Scale 1:15,000,000 Lambert Azimuthal Equal Area Projection

Longitude East 10 of Greenwich

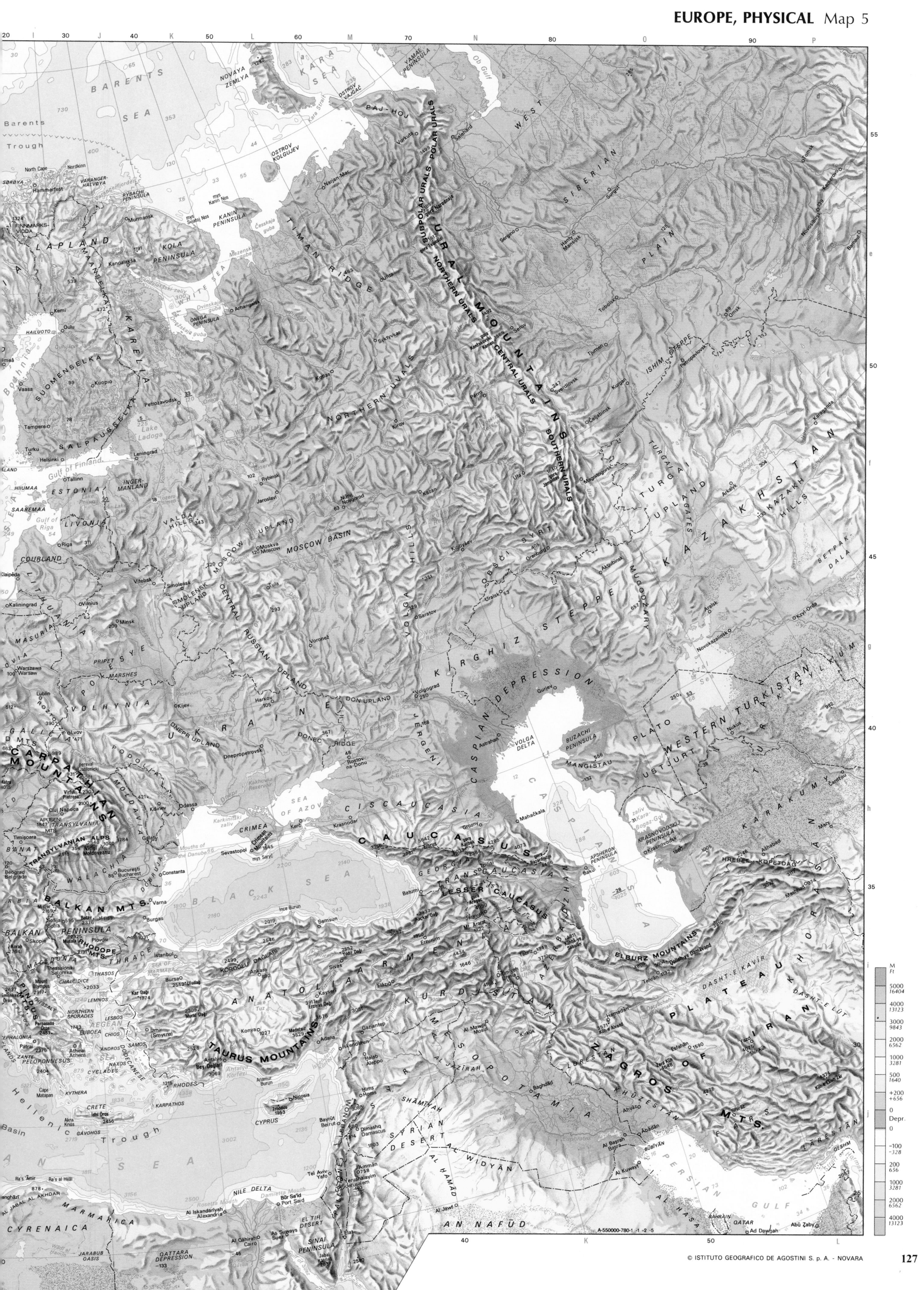
BARENTS SEA
Barents Trough
NOVAYA ZEMLYA
KARA SEA
YAMAL PENINSULA
OSTROV VAJGAČ
PAJ-HOJ
OSTROV KOLGUJEV
Ob Gulf
WEST SIBERIAN PLAIN
North Cape
Nordkinn
Hammerfest
VARANGER-HALVØYA
RYBACHI PENINSULA
Murmansk
KANIN PENINSULA
mys Kanin Nos
mys Svjatoj Nos
Česskaja guba
FINNMARKSVIDDA
LAPLAND
KOLA PENINSULA
Kandalakša
WHITE SEA
Mezenskaja guba
Dvinskaja guba
Onežskaja guba
ONEGA PENINSULA
Arhangelsk
TIMAN RIDGE
Narjan-Mar
Vorkuta
Salehard
POLAR URALS
SUBPOLAR URALS
NORTHERN URALS
CENTRAL URALS
SOUTHERN URALS
URAL MOUNTAINS
Surgut
Hanty-Mansijsk
Sergino
Tobolsk
Omsk
Tjumen
Serov
ISHIM STEPPE
Petropavlovsk
Novosibirsk
Barnaul
Kemi
Oulu
HAILUOTO
KARELIA
Gulf of Bothnia
SUOMENSELKÄ
Kuopio
Vaasa
Tampere
Turku
Helsinki
SALPAUSSELKÄ
Petrozavodsk
Lake Onega
Lake Ladoga
Leningrad
Syktyvkar
Kotlas
Uhta
NORTHERN UVALS
Kirov
Perm
Sverdlovsk
Čeljabinsk
Kurgan
Magnitogorsk
Ufa
Karaganda
Gulf of Finland
Tallinn
HIIUMAA
SAAREMAA
ESTONIA
INGERMANLAND
Rybinsk
Jaroslavl
Nižnij Novgorod
Kazan
TURGAI UPLAND
TURGAI GATES
KAZAKH HILLS
KAZAKHSTAN
Arkalyk
Gulf of Riga
LIVONIA
VALDAI HILLS
MOSCOW UPLAND
Moskva Moscow
MOSCOW BASIN
VOLGA HILLS
Kujbyšev
OBŠČIJ SYRT
Orenburg
Aktjubinsk
MUGODZARY
BETPAK-DALA
Riga
COURLAND
Klaipėda
Vitebsk
Smolensk
SMOLENSK UPLAND
CENTRAL RUSSIAN UPLAND
Tula
Uralsk
STEPPE
Aralsk
Kzyl-Orda
LITHUANIA
Kaliningrad
Vilnius
Minsk
Saratov
MASURIA
Voronež
Novokazalinsk
KIRGHIZ STEPPE
KYZYLKUM
Warszawa Warsaw
PRIPET MARSHES
POLESYE
CASPIAN DEPRESSION
Gurjev
Aral Sea
WESTERN TURKISTAN
Lublin
VOLHYNIA
Kijev
Harkov
UKRAINE
DON UPLAND
Volgograd
DNEPR UPLAND
DONEC RIDGE
JERGENI
Astrahan
VOLGA DELTA
BUZACHI PENINSULA
PLATO USTJURT
MANGISTAU
Nukus
GALICIA
Lvov
Dnepropetrovsk
Rostov-na-Donu
CARPATHIAN MOUNTAINS
PODOLIA
MOLDAVIA
CASPIAN SEA
SEA OF AZOV
CISCAUCASIA
Krasnodar
Kerč
Groznyj
Mahačkala
zaliv Kara-Bogaz-Gol
KRASNOVODSKIJ PENINSULA
Krasnovodsk
KARAKUMY
Čardžou
Mary
Ashabad
Cluj Napoca
APUSENI MTS.
TRANSYLVANIA
Odessa
Kišinev
Karkinitskij zaliv
CRIMEA
Crimean Mountains
CAUCASUS
gora Elbrus
gora Kazbek
gora Bazardjuzju
APSHERON PENINSULA
Baku
HREBET KOPETDAG
Timişoara
TRANSYLVANIAN ALPS
BANAT
Galaţi
Mouths of the Danube
Sevastopol
mys Saryč
Beograd Belgrade
WALACHIA
Bucureşti Bucharest
DOBRUJA
Constanta
GEORGIA
TRANSCAUCASIA
LESSER CAUCASUS
Batumi
BLACK SEA
Varna
BALKAN MTS.
Burgas
İnce Burun
Samsun
Sofija Sofia
BALKAN PENINSULA
Skopje
RHODOPE MTS.
THRACE
İstanbul
SEA OF MARMARA
Erzurum
Mt. Ararat
ARMENIAN
Tabriz
ELBURZ MOUNTAINS
Kolle-ye Damāvand
Tehrān
DASHT-E KAVĪR
DASHT-E LŪT
MACEDONIA
Thessaloniki Salonika
CHALCIDICE
THASOS
Mount Olympus
PINDUS MTS.
Bursa
Ankara
KÖROĞLU DAĞLARI
Sivas
Elāziğ
LEMNOS
NORTHERN SPORADES
LESBOS
EUBOEA
CHIOS
İzmir (Smyrna)
ANATOLIA
Kayseri
KURDISTAN
AZARBAYJAN
Hamadān
PLATEAU OF IRAN
Esfahān
Yazd
KEPHALONIA
Pátrai
PELOPONNESUS
ZANTE
Athinai Athens
ANDROS
SAMOS
DODECANESE
NAXOS
CYCLADES
Konya
TAURUS MOUNTAINS
Adana
Gaziantep
Mosul
Kirkuk
MESOPOTAMIA
ZAGROS MTS.
LORESTĀN
KHŪZESTĀN
Antalya
Bey Dağları
RHODES
Antalya Körfezi
Anamur Burun
Halab Aleppo
AL JAZĪRAH
Baghdād
Cape Matapan
KYTHERA
CRETE
KARPATHOS
Nicosia
CYPRUS
Hims Homs
SHĀMĪYAH
Ahvāz
Ābādān
FĀRS
LĀRESTĀN
Hellenic Trough
Basin
GAVDHOS
Akra Krios
Bayrūt Beirut
LEBANON
Dimashq Damascus
SYRIAN DESERT
AL WIDYĀN
Al Basrah Basra
BŪSHEHR
PERSIAN GULF
Al Kuwayt
Tel Aviv-Yafo
Yerushalayim Jerusalem
ʽAmmān
AL ḤAMĀD
Ra's al Hilāl
AL JABAL AL AKHDAR
NILE DELTA
Rosetta Mouth
Damietta Mouth
Bûr Sa'îd Port Said
Al Iskandarīyah Alexandria
MARMARICA
CYRENAICA
EL TIH DESERT
Al Jawf
AN NAFŪD
AL HASA
BAHRAIN
QATAR
Ad Dawḥah
Abū Ẓaby
Al Qāhirah Cairo
As Suways Suez
SINAI PENINSULA
JARABUB OASIS
QATTARA DEPRESSION
Jabal Katrînah
M Ft
5000 16404
4000 13123
3000 9843
2000 6562
1000 3281
500 1640
+200 +656
0 Depr.
0
-100 -328
200 656
1000 3281
2000 6562
4000 13123
A-550000-780-1 -1 -2 -5

Greenland (Den.)
KING CHRISTIAN IX LAND
KING FREDERIK VI COAST
Denmark Strait
Greenland Sea
JAN MAYEN (Norway)
BEAR ISLAND (Norway)
ICELAND
Arctic Circle
Norwegian Sea
Faeroe Islands (Den.)
SHETLAND ISLANDS
ORKNEY ISLANDS
HEBRIDES
ROCKALL
ATLANTIC OCEAN
NORWAY
SWEDEN
DENMARK
North Sea
IRELAND
UNITED KINGDOM
Celtic Sea
English Channel
NETHERLANDS
BELGIUM
LUXEMBOURG
GERMANY
POLAND
CZECHOSLOVAKIA
AUSTRIA
SWITZERLAND
LIECHTENSTEIN
HUNGARY
YUGOSLAVIA
ALBANIA
FRANCE
Bay of Biscay
SPAIN
PORTUGAL
ANDORRA
MONACO
SAN MARINO
VATICAN CITY
ITALY
CORSICA (Fr.)
SARDINIA
SICILY
MALTA
Ligurian Sea
Tyrrhenian Sea
Ionian Sea
Adriatic Sea
BALEARIC ISLANDS
MEDITERRANEAN SEA
Azores (Portugal)
Madeira (Portugal)
Canary Islands (Spain)
MOROCCO
ATLAS MOUNTAINS
ALGERIA
TUNISIA
LIBYA
TRIPOLITANIA
Western Sahara
GRAND ERG OCCIDENTAL
GRAND ERG ORIENTAL
Gulf of Sidra

Scale 1:15,000,000
Lambert Azimuthal Equal Area Projection
0 200 400 600 800 1000 km
0 250 500 miles
Longitude East 10 of Greenwich

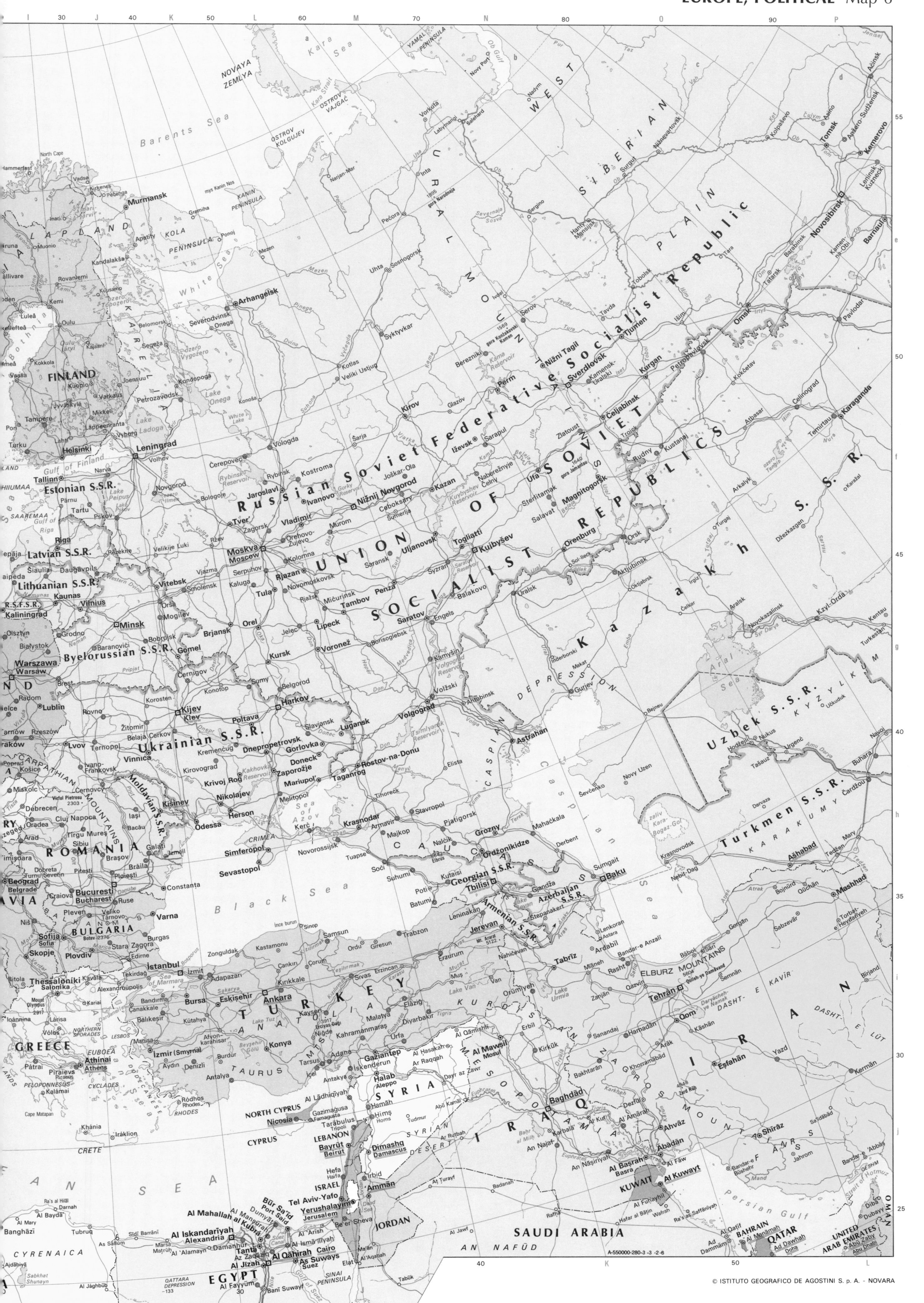

Barents Sea
Kara Sea
NOVAYA ZEMLYA
YAMAL PENINSULA
OSTROV KOLGUJEV
KANIN PENINSULA
KOLA PENINSULA
White Sea
LAPLAND
FINLAND
Helsinki
Tallinn
Estonian S.S.R.
Latvian S.S.R.
Riga
Lithuanian S.S.R.
Vilnius
Kaliningrad
Byelorussian S.S.R.
Minsk
Warszawa
Warsaw
Ukrainian S.S.R.
Kijev
Kiev
Moldavian S.S.R.
Kišinev
ROMANIA
Bucuresti
Bucharest
BULGARIA
Sofija
Sofia
GREECE
Athinai
Athens
TURKEY
Ankara
Istanbul
ANATOLIA
TAURUS
Murmansk
Arhangelsk
Leningrad
Moskva
Moscow
Russian Soviet Federative Socialist Republic
UNION OF SOVIET SOCIALIST REPUBLICS
WEST SIBERIAN PLAIN
URAL MOUNTAINS
Kazakh S.S.R.
Uzbek S.S.R.
Turkmen S.S.R.
Ašhabad
Georgian S.S.R.
Tbilisi
Armenian S.S.R.
Jerevan
Azerbaijan S.S.R.
Baku
Black Sea
Sea of Azov
CRIMEA
CAUCASUS
Caspian Sea
CASPIAN DEPRESSION
Aral Sea
KYZYLKUM
KARAKUMY
Volgograd
Kujbyšev
Gorki
Nižnij Novgorod
Kazan
Perm
Sverdlovsk
Čeljabinsk
Omsk
Novosibirsk
Tomsk
Kemerovo
Barnaul
Karaganda
Tjumen
Orenburg
Saratov
Rostov-na-Donu
Harkov
Odessa
Dnepropetrovsk
Doneck
Astrahan
SYRIA
Dimashq
Damascus
LEBANON
Bayrūt
Beirut
ISRAEL
Yerushalayim
Jerusalem
Tel Aviv-Yafo
JORDAN
Ammān
IRAQ
Baghdād
IRAN
Tehrān
ELBURZ MOUNTAINS
ZAGROS MOUNTAINS
DASHT-E KAVĪR
DASHT-E LŪT
KUWAIT
Al Kuwayt
BAHRAIN
Al Manāmah
QATAR
Ad Dawhah
Doha
UNITED ARAB EMIRATES
Abū Zaby
Abu Dhabi
SAUDI ARABIA
AN NAFŪD
Persian Gulf
Strait of Hormuz
EGYPT
Al Qāhirah
Cairo
Al Iskandarīyah
Alexandria
SINAI PENINSULA
NORTH CYPRUS
Nicosia
CYPRUS
CRETE
RHODES
CYCLADES
PELOPONNESUS
CYRENAICA
QATTARA DEPRESSION
Gulf of Finland
Gulf of Riga
SYRIAN DESERT
MESOPOTAMIA
KURDISTAN
A-550000-280-3 -3 -2-6

ÍSLAND ICELAND
Arctic Circle
GRÆNLANDSHAF
GREENLAND SEA
Reykjavík
Akureyri
VATNAJÖKULL
ATLANTSHAF
ATLANTIC OCEAN
Long. West 20 of Greenwich
NORGE
NORWAY
NORSKE HAVET
NORWEGIAN SEA
SVERIGE
SWEDEN
SUOMI/
FINLAND
DANMARK
DENMARK
DEUTSCHLAND
GERMANY
POLSKA
POLAND
Eesti NSV
Estonian SSR
Latvijas PSR
Latvian SSR
Lietuvos TSR
Lithuanian SSR
RSFSR
Belorusskaja SSR
Byelorussian SSR
NORDSJØEN
NORTH SEA
Norwegian Trench
Skagerrak
Kattegat
BALTIC SEA
Gulf of Bothnia
Gulf of Finland
Gulf of Riga
LAPLAND
FINNMARK
Oslo
Bergen
Trondheim
Stavanger
Kristiansand
Tromsø
Narvik
Bodø
Kiruna
Luleå
Umeå
Sundsvall
Gävle
Uppsala
STOCKHOLM
Göteborg
Malmö
Norrköping
Linköping
Jönköping
Visby
GOTLAND
ÖLAND
BORNHOLM (Danmark)
COPENHAGEN KØBENHAVN
Århus
Ålborg
Odense
HELSINKI/HELSINGFORS
Turku/Åbo
Tampere/Tammerfors
Oulu/Uleåborg
Rovaniemi
Vaasa/Vasa
ÅLAND
TALLINN
Tartu
RIGA
Liepāja
Klaipėda
Šiauliai
Daugavpils
KAUNAS
VILNIUS
MINSK
Pskov
KALININGRAD
GDAŃSK (DANZIG)
Gdynia
SZCZECIN STETTIN
BYDGOSZCZ
BERLIN
HAMBURG
BREMEN
HANNOVER
Lübeck
Kiel
Rostock
Scale 1:6,000,000
Delisle Conic Equidistant Projection
0 100 200 300 400 km
0 100 200 miles
West 0 East

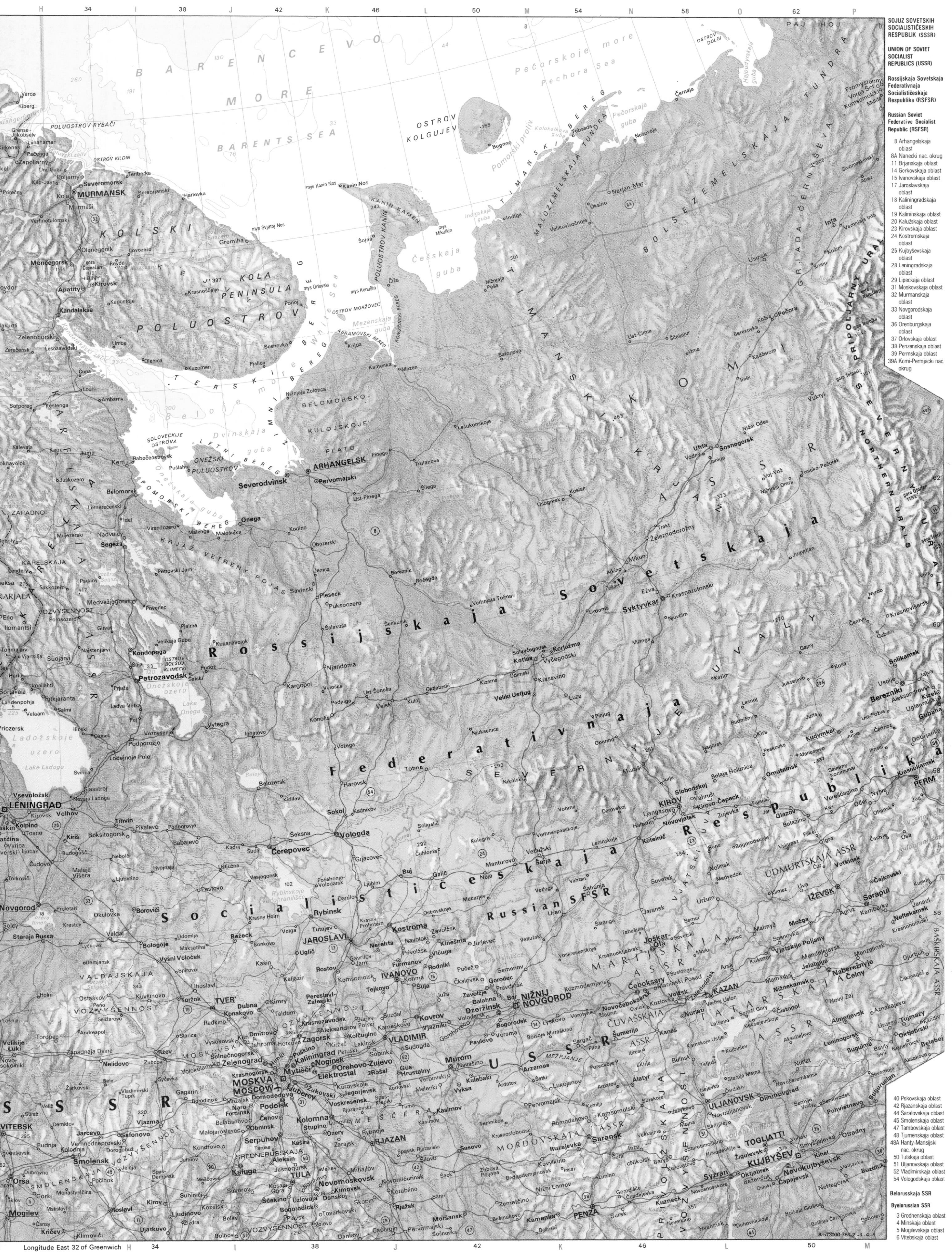

A-573000-780-2 -3-4-5

Scale 1:3,000,000 Delisle Conic Equidistant Projection

0 50 100 150 200 km

0 50 100 miles

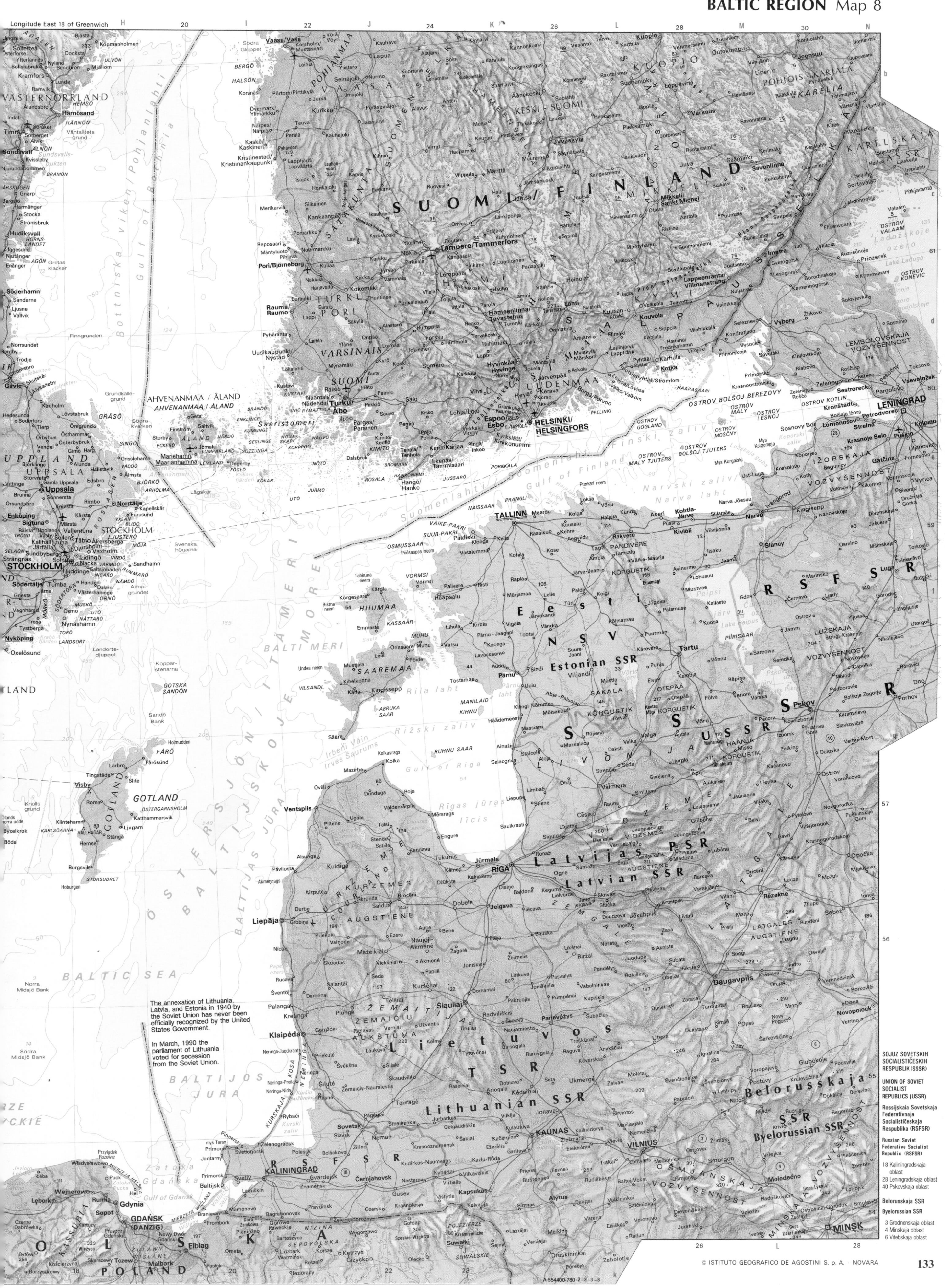
Longitude East 18 of Greenwich
SUOMI / FINLAND
Gulf of Bothnia
Gulf of Finland
Suomenlahti
Finski zaliv
Gulf of Riga
Rižski zaliv
Rīgas jūras līcis
BALTIC SEA
BALTI MERI
ÖSTERSJÖN / ITÄMERI
BALTIJSKOJE MORE
BALTIJAS JŪRA
BALTIJOS JŪRA
Eesti NSV
Estonian SSR
Latvijas PSR
Latvian SSR
Lietuvos TSR
Lithuanian SSR
Belorusskaja SSR
Byelorussian SSR
RSFSR
SSSR
USSR
POLSKA
POLAND
GOTLAND
AHVENANMAA / ÅLAND
STOCKHOLM
HELSINKI/ HELSINGFORS
TALLINN
RIGA
VILNIUS
KAUNAS
KALININGRAD
LENINGRAD
MINSK
GDAŃSK (DANZIG)
The annexation of Lithuania, Latvia, and Estonia in 1940 by the Soviet Union has never been officially recognized by the United States Government.
In March, 1990 the parliament of Lithuania voted for secession from the Soviet Union.
SOJUZ SOVETSKIH SOCIALISTIČESKIH RESPUBLIK (SSSR)
UNION OF SOVIET SOCIALIST REPUBLICS (USSR)
Rossijskaja Sovetskaja Federativnaja Socialističeskaja Respublika (RSFSR)
Russian Soviet Federative Socialist Republic (RSFSR)
18 Kaliningradskaja oblast
28 Leningradskaja oblast
40 Pskovskaja oblast
Belorusskaja SSR
Byelorussian SSR
3 Grodnenskaja oblast
4 Minskaja oblast
6 Vitebskaja oblast

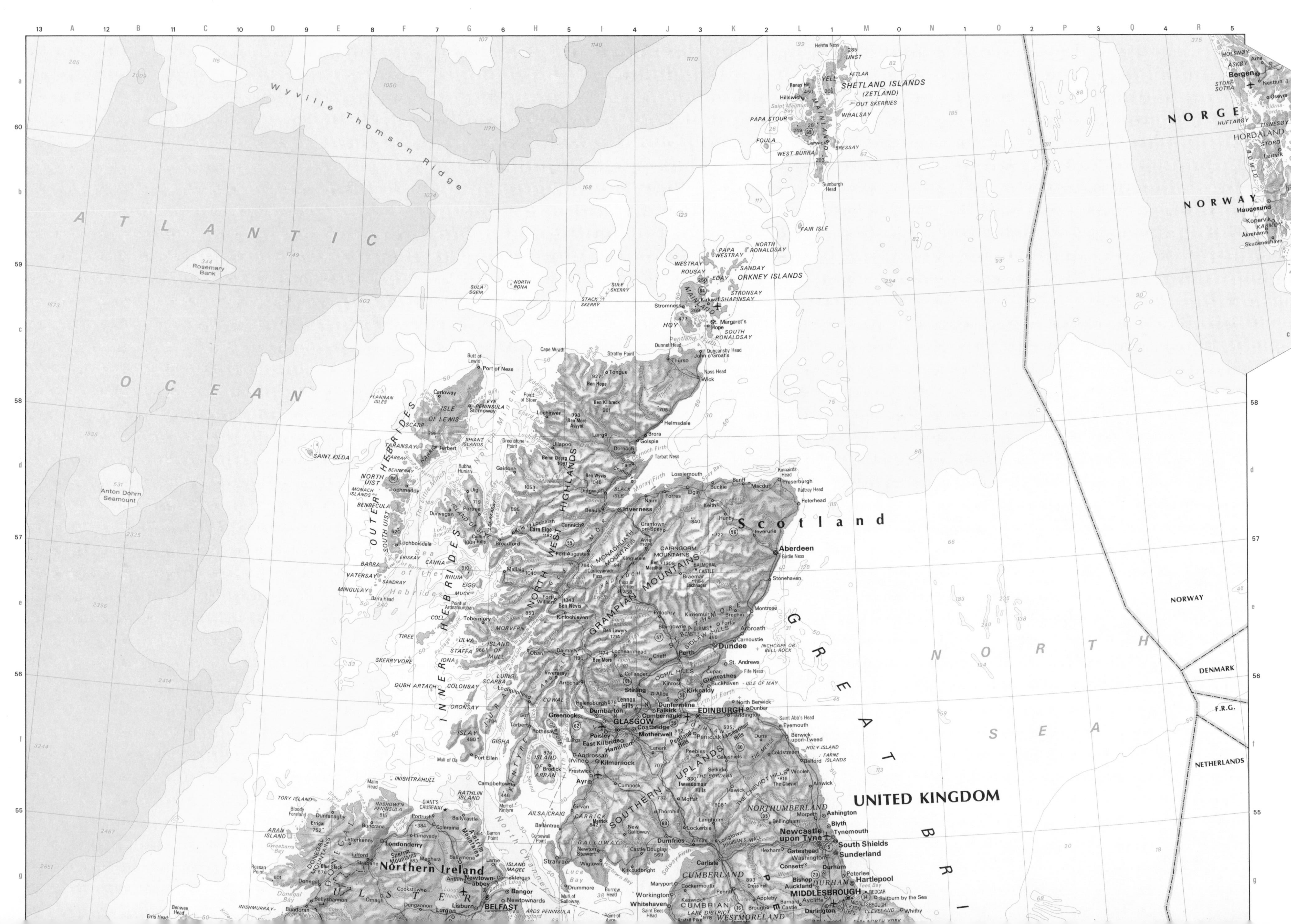
ATLANTIC OCEAN
Wyville Thomson Ridge
Rosemary Bank
Anton Dohrn Seamount
SAINT KILDA
SHETLAND ISLANDS (ZETLAND)
FAIR ISLE
ORKNEY ISLANDS
NORGE
NORWAY
Bergen
Haugesund
NORWAY
DENMARK
F.R.G.
NETHERLANDS
NORTH SEA
UNITED KINGDOM
GREAT BRITAIN
Scotland
Aberdeen
Inverness
Dundee
EDINBURGH
GLASGOW
CAIRNGORM MOUNTAINS
GRAMPIAN MOUNTAINS
NORTH WEST HIGHLANDS
SOUTHERN UPLANDS
OUTER HEBRIDES
INNER HEBRIDES
Newcastle upon Tyne
South Shields
Sunderland
Hartlepool
MIDDLESBROUGH
Carlisle
North Channel
Northern Ireland
BELFAST
Londonderry

UNITED KINGDOM OF GREAT BRITAIN AND NORTHERN IRELAND

England
1 Greater London

METROPOLITAN COUNTIES
2 Greater Manchester
3 Merseyside
4 South Yorkshire
5 Tyne and Wear
6 West Midlands
7 West Yorkshire

NON-METROPOLITAN COUNTIES
8 Avon
9 Bedfordshire
10 Berkshire
11 Buckinghamshire
12 Cambridgeshire
13 Cheshire
14 Cleveland
15 Cornwall/Isles of Scilly
16 Cumbria
17 Derbyshire
18 Devon
19 Dorset
20 Durham
21 East Sussex
22 Essex
23 Gloucestershire
24 Hampshire
25 Hereford & Worcester
26 Hertfordshire
27 Humberside
28 Isle of Wight
29 Kent
30 Lancashire
31 Leicestershire
32 Lincolnshire
33 Norfolk
34 Northamptonshire
35 Northumberland
36 North Yorkshire
37 Nottinghamshire
38 Oxfordshire
39 Salop
40 Somerset
41 Staffordshire
42 Suffolk
43 Surrey
44 Warwickshire
45 West Sussex
46 Wiltshire

Wales
COUNTIES
47 Clwyd
48 Dyfed
49 Gwent
50 Gwynedd
51 Mid Glamorgan
52 Powys
53 South Glamorgan
54 West Glamorgan

Scotland
REGIONS
55 Highland
56 Grampian
57 Tayside
58 Fife
59 Lothian
60 Borders
61 Central
62 Strathclyde
63 Dumfries and Galloway

ISLANDS AREA
64 Orkney
65 Shetland
66 Western Isles

(A) CROWN DEPENDENCY
(B) CROWN DEPENDENCY

Scale 1:3,000,000 Delisle Conic Equidistant Projection

0 50 100 150 200 km

0 50 100 miles

Longitude West 0 East of Greenwich

M	Ft
4000	13123
2000	6562
1000	3281
500	1640
200	656
0	
−100	−328
Depr.	
0	
+100	+328
200	656
500	1640
1000	3281

Map 10 CENTRAL EUROPE

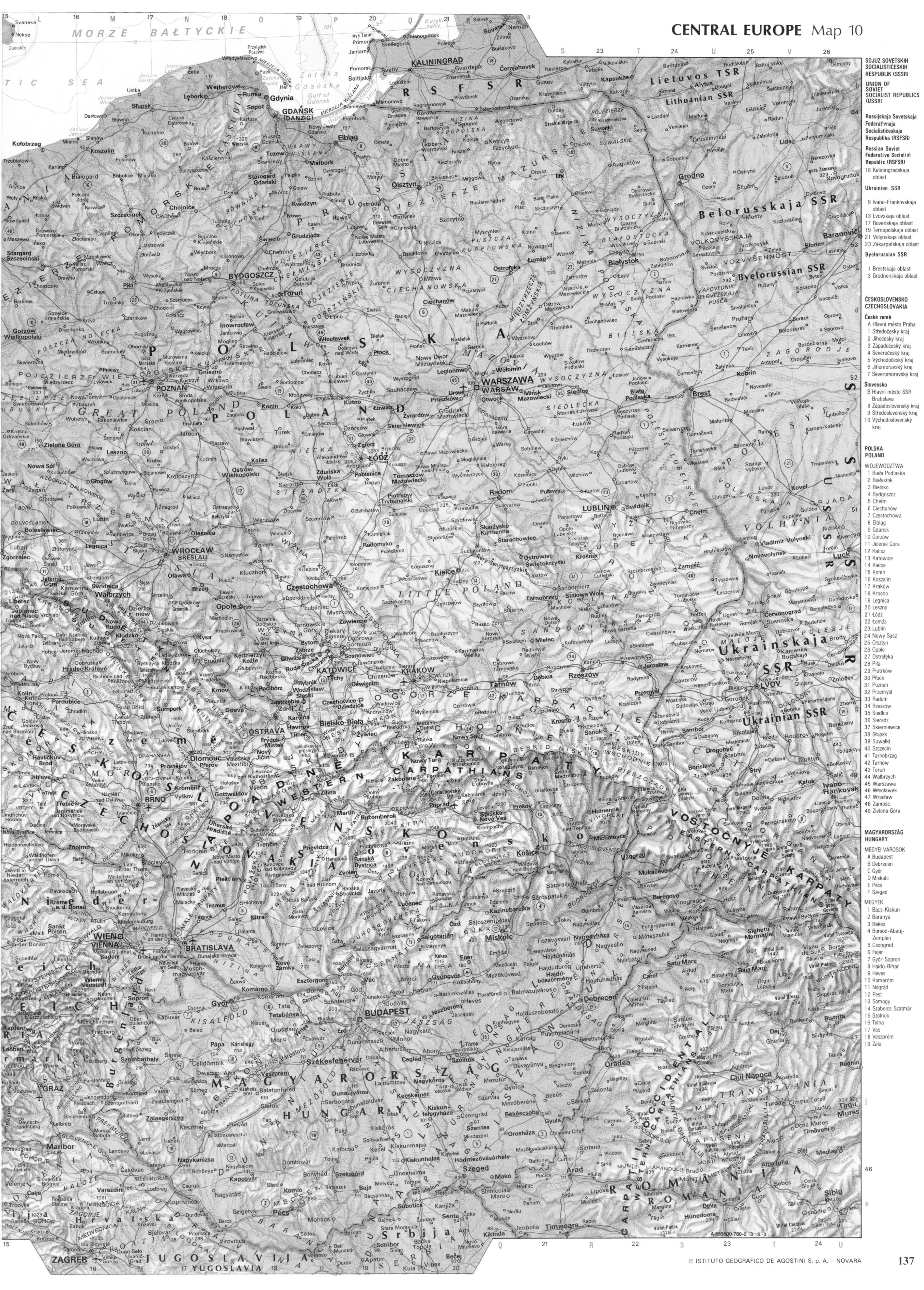
CENTRAL EUROPE Map 10
SOJUZ SOVETSKIH SOCIALISTIČESKIH RESPUBLIK (SSSR)
UNION OF SOVIET SOCIALIST REPUBLICS (USSR)
Rossijskaja Sovetskaja Federativnaja Socialističeskaja Respublika (RSFSR)
Russian Soviet Federative Socialist Republic (RSFSR)
18 Kaliningradskaja oblast
Ukrainian SSR
9 Ivano-Frankovskaja oblast
13 Lvovskaja oblast
17 Rovenskaja oblast
19 Ternopolskaja oblast
21 Volynskaja oblast
23 Zakarpatskaja oblast
Byelorussian SSR
1 Brestskaja oblast
3 Grodnenskaja oblast
ČESKOSLOVENSKO
CZECHOSLOVAKIA
České země
A Hlavni město Praha
1 Středočeský kraj
2 Jihočeský kraj
3 Západočeský kraj
4 Severočeský kraj
5 Východočeský kraj
6 Jihomoravský kraj
7 Severomoravský kraj
Slovensko
B Hlavni město SSR Bratislava
8 Západoslovenský kraj
9 Středoslovenský kraj
10 Východoslovenský kraj
POLSKA
POLAND
WOJEWÓDZTWA
1 Biała Podlaska
2 Białystok
3 Bielsko
4 Bydgoszcz
5 Chełm
6 Ciechanów
7 Częstochowa
8 Elbląg
9 Gdansk
10 Gorzów
11 Jelenia Góra
12 Kalisz
13 Katowice
14 Kielce
15 Konin
16 Koszalin
17 Kraków
18 Krosno
19 Legnica
20 Leszno
21 Łódź
22 Łomża
23 Lublin
24 Nowy Sącz
25 Olsztyn
26 Opole
27 Ostrołęka
28 Piła
29 Piotrków
30 Płock
31 Poznań
32 Przemyśl
33 Radom
34 Rzeszów
35 Siedlce
36 Sieradz
37 Skierniewice
38 Słupsk
39 Suwałki
40 Szczecin
41 Tarnobrzeg
42 Tarnów
43 Toruń
44 Wałbrzych
45 Warszawa
46 Włocławek
47 Wrocław
48 Zamość
49 Zielona Góra
MAGYARORSZÁG
HUNGARY
MEGYEI VÁROSOK
A Budapest
B Debrecen
C Győr
D Miskolc
E Pécs
F Szeged
MEGYÉK
1 Bács-Kiskun
2 Baranya
3 Békés
4 Borsod-Abaúj-Zemplén
5 Csongrád
6 Fejér
7 Győr-Sopron
8 Haidú-Bihar
9 Heves
10 Komaróm
11 Nógrád
12 Pest
13 Somogy
14 Szabolcs-Szatmár
15 Szolnok
16 Tolna
17 Vas
18 Veszprém
19 Zala
MORZE BAŁTYCKIE
KALININGRAD
R S F S R
Lietuvos TSR
Lithuanian SSR
Belorusskaja SSR
Byelorussian SSR
GDAŃSK (DANZIG)
BYDGOSZCZ
POZNAŃ
P O L S K A
POLAND
WARSZAWA
WARSAW
ŁÓDŹ
LUBLIN
Brest
Grodno
WROCŁAW
BRESLAU
KATOWICE
KRAKÓW
LITTLE POLAND
Ukrainskaja SSR
Ukrainian SSR
LVOV
KARPATY
CARPATHIANS
Č E S K O S L O V E N S K O
OSTRAVA
BRNO
BRATISLAVA
WIEN
VIENNA
Košice
M A G Y A R O R S Z Á G
HUNGARY
BUDAPEST
Debrecen
Szeged
Cluj Napoca
TRANSYLVANIA
R O M Â N I A
Timişoara
GRAZ
ZAGREB
J U G O S L A V I J A
YUGOSLAVIA
A-559500-780-2-3-3-3

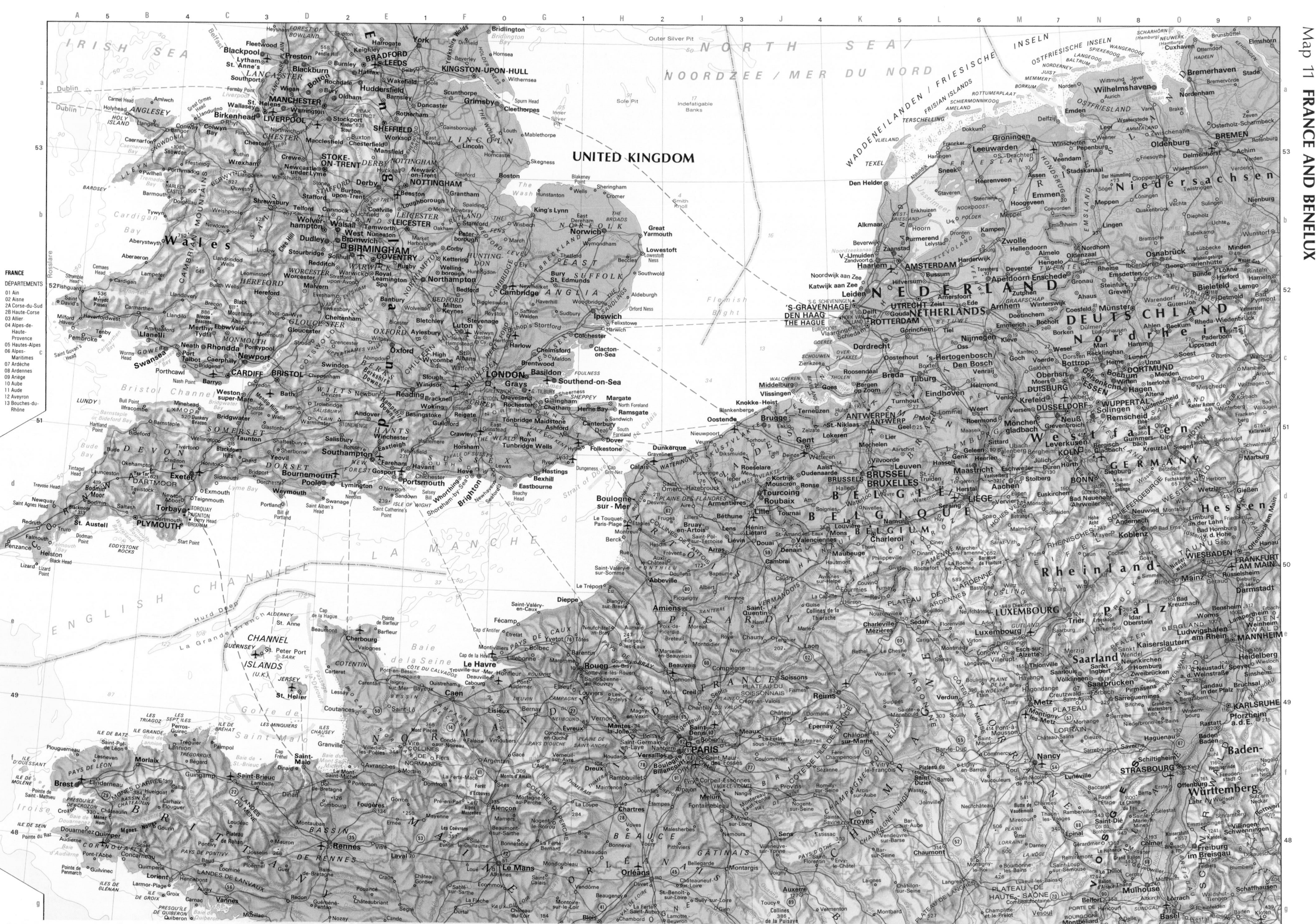
UNITED KINGDOM
NORTH SEA/
NOORDZEE / MER DU NORD
IRISH SEA
ENGLISH CHANNEL
LA MANCHE
CHANNEL ISLANDS (U.K.)
Wales
NEDERLAND
NETHERLANDS
DEUTSCHLAND
GERMANY
BELGIQUE
BELGIUM
LUXEMBOURG
LONDON
PARIS
AMSTERDAM
BRUSSEL
BRUXELLES
FRANCE
DÉPARTEMENTS
01 Ain
02 Aisne
2A Corse-du-Sud
2B Haute-Corse
03 Allier
04 Alpes-de-Haute-Provence
05 Hautes-Alpes
06 Alpes-Maritimes
07 Ardèche
08 Ardennes
09 Ariège
10 Aube
11 Aude
12 Aveyron
13 Bouches-du-Rhône

FRANCE
SUISSE
SWITZERLAND
ITALIA
ESPAÑA
SPAIN
OCÉAN ATLANTIQUE
ATLANTIC OCEAN
Golfe de Gascogne / Golfo de Vizcaya
Bay of Biscay
Golfe du Lion
MER MÉDITERRANÉE
MEDITERRANEAN SEA
Algerian Basin
MASSIF CENTRAL
PYRÉNÉES
ANDORRA
CORSE
CORSICA
PROVENCE
BORDEAUX
TOULOUSE
MARSEILLE
LYON
NANTES
TORINO
BARCELONA
ZARAGOZA
BILBAO
Scale 1:3,000,000
Delisle Conic Equidistant Projection
Longitude East 2 of Greenwich
© ISTITUTO GEOGRAFICO DE AGOSTINI S. p. A. - NOVARA

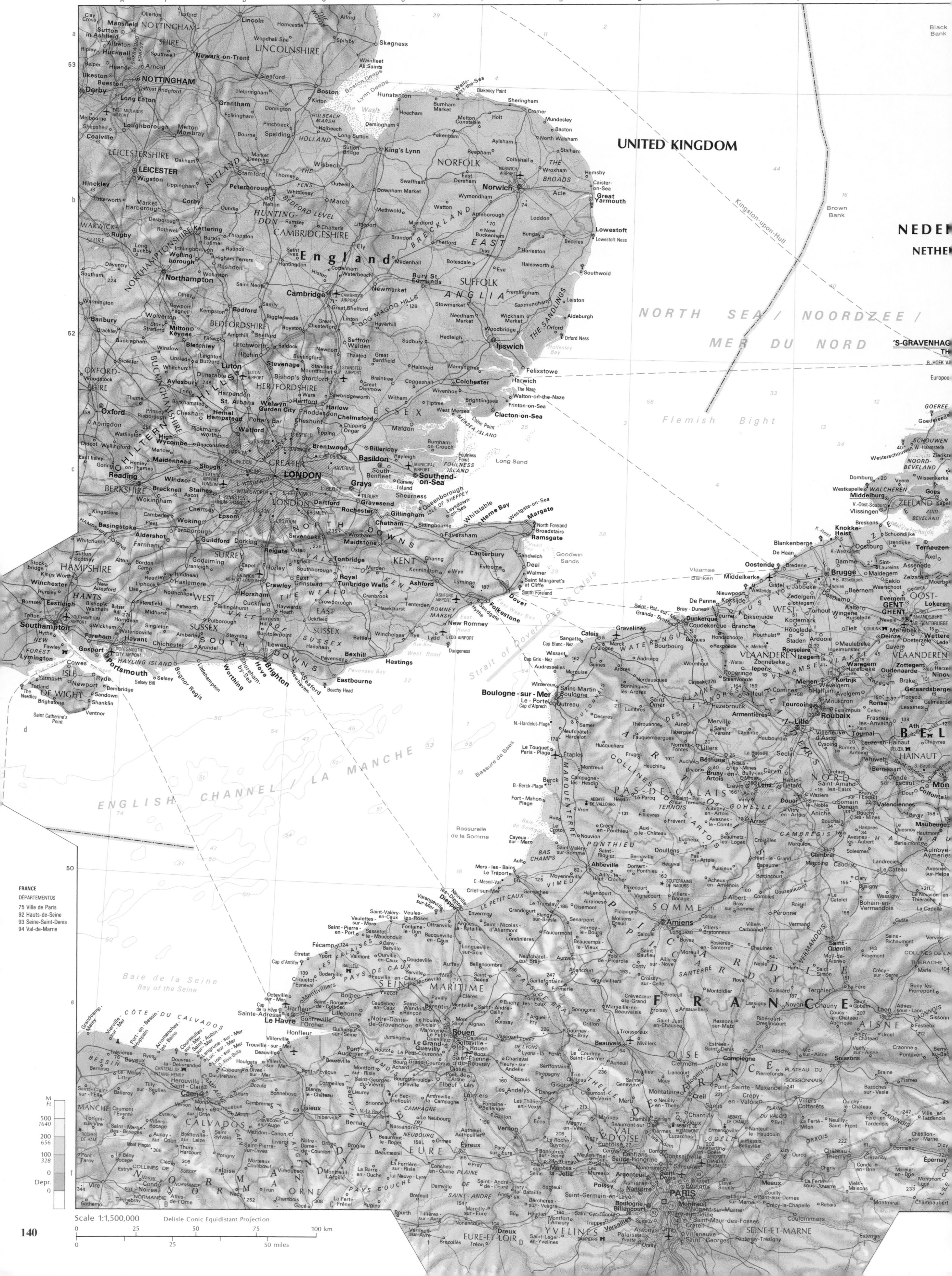

FRANCE
DÉPARTEMENTOS
75 Ville de Paris
92 Hauts-de-Seine
93 Seine-Saint-Denis
94 Val-de-Marne

M	Ft
500	1640
200	656
100	328
0	0
Depr.	

Scale 1:1,500,000 Delisle Conic Equidistant Projection

0 25 50 75 100 km

0 25 50 miles

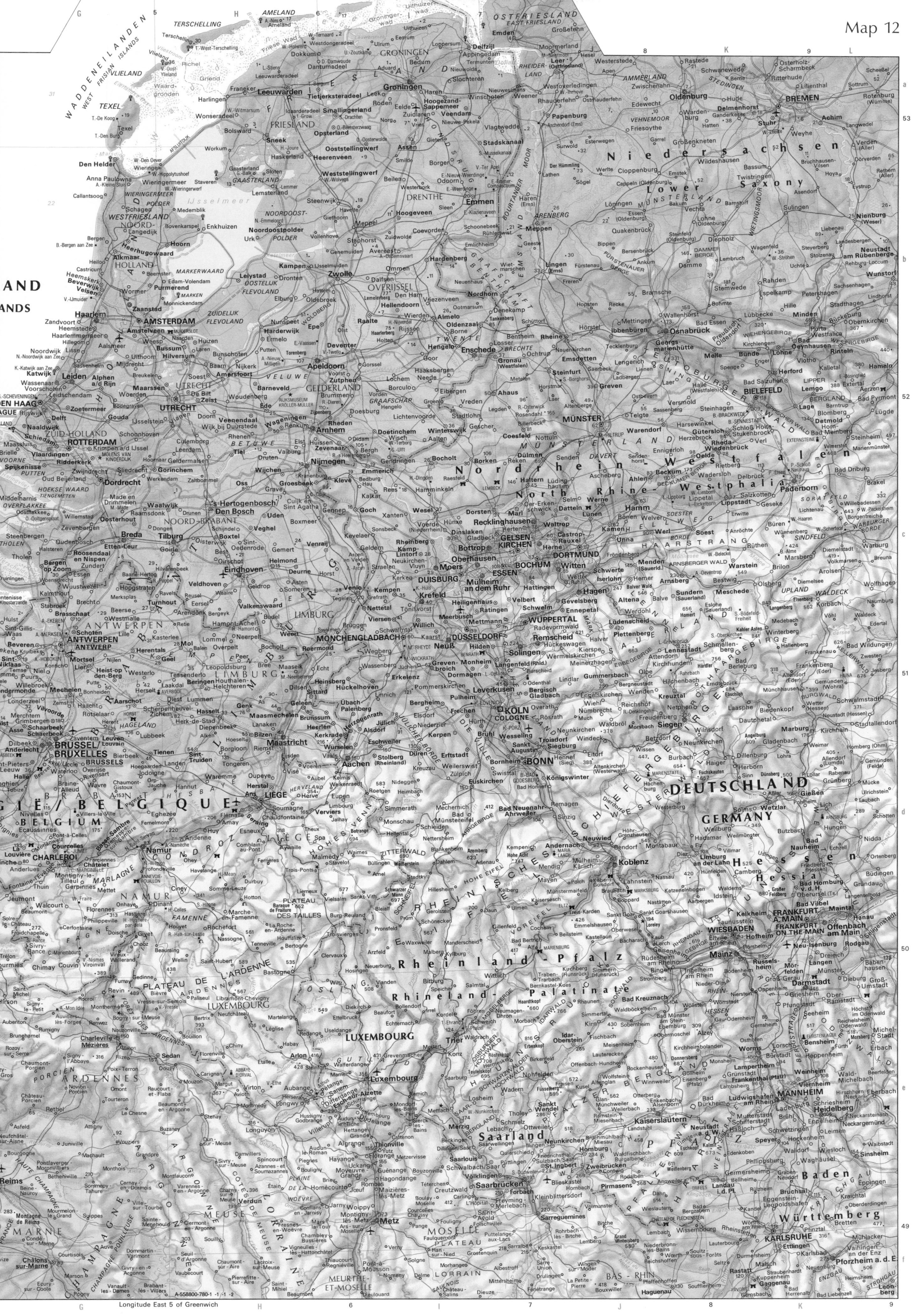

WADDENEILANDEN
WEST FRISIAN ISLANDS
OSTFRIESLAND
EAST FRIESLAND
FRIESLAND
GRONINGEN
DRENTHE
OVERIJSSEL
GELDERLAND
UTRECHT
NOORD-HOLLAND
ZUID-HOLLAND
NOORD-BRABANT
LIMBURG
ZEELAND
IJsselmeer
Niedersachsen
Lower Saxony
Nordrhein-Westfalen
North Rhine-Westphalia
DEUTSCHLAND
GERMANY
Hessen
Hessia
Rheinland-Pfalz
Rhineland-Palatinate
Saarland
Baden
Württemberg
LUXEMBOURG
BELGIË / BELGIQUE
BELGIUM
ARDENNES
LORRAINE
CHAMPAGNE
AMSTERDAM
ROTTERDAM
UTRECHT
BRUSSEL
BRUXELLES
BRUSSELS
ANTWERPEN
ANTWERP
LIÈGE
KÖLN
COLOGNE
BONN
DÜSSELDORF
DORTMUND
ESSEN
DUISBURG
FRANKFURT A. MAIN
FRANKFURT ON THE MAIN
MANNHEIM
KARLSRUHE
BREMEN
Longitude East 5 of Greenwich

Longitude West 5 of Greenwich
MAR CANTÁBRICO
RÍAS ALTAS
RÍAS BAJAS
COSTA VERDE
OCEANO ATLÁNTICO
ATLANTIC OCEAN
OCÉANO ATLÁNTICO
PORTUGAL
SPAIN
ESPAÑA
AL MAGHRIB
MOROCCO
CORDILLERA CANTÁBRICA
SUBMESETA NORTE
OLD CASTILE
NEW CASTILE
SUBMESETA SUR
SISTEMA CENTRAL
SIERRA MORENA
SISTEMA PENIBÉTICO
SIERRA NEVADA
EXTREMADURA
ALENTEJO
ALGARVE
LA MANCHA
COSTA DEL SOL
COSTA DE LA LUZ
Golfo de Cádiz
Estrecho de Gibraltar
Alborán Basin
MADRID
LISBOA
LISBON
PORTO
Sevilla
SEVILLE
Córdoba
Málaga
Granada
Cádiz
Salamanca
Valladolid
Zamora
León
Burgos
Toledo
Badajoz
Mérida
Cáceres
Huelva
Coimbra
Faro
Setúbal
Évora
Braga
Vigo
La Coruña
Santiago de Compostela
Oviedo
Gijón
Santander
Bilbao
Gibraltar (U.K.)
Ceuta (Sp.)
Tanger
Tétouan
Melilla (Sp.)
Scale 1:3,000,000
Delisle Conic Equidistant Projection
0 50 100 150 200 km
0 50 100 miles

FRANCE
LANGUEDOC
PROVENCE
PYRÉNÉES
ANDORRA
CATALUÑA
ARAGÓN
NAVARRA
VALENCIA
MURCIA
ALGERIA
AL JAZĀ'IR
ISLAS BALEARES
BALEARIC ISLANDS
MALLORCA
MAJORCA
MENORCA
MINORCA
IBIZA IVIZA
FORMENTERA
MEDITERRANEAN SEA
BAHR MEDITERRANEAN
Algerian Basin
Golfe du Lion
Gulf of Lion
Golfo de Valencia
COSTA BRAVA
COSTA DORADA
COSTA DEL AZAHAR
COSTA BLANCA
TOULOUSE
MARSEILLE
Montpellier
Perpignan
BARCELONA
VALENCIA
ZARAGOZA SARAGOSSA
Alicante
MURCIA
Cartagena
Almería
PALMA
AL JAZĀ'IR ALGIERS
ORAN
ATLAS TELLIEN
Genova
Ajaccio

Map 14 ITALY, AUSTRIA AND SWITZERLAND

SCHWEIZ / SUISSE / SVIZZERA / SVIZRA / SWITZERLAND
KANTONE / CANTONS / CANTONI / CHANTUNS
1 Zürich
2 Bern / Berne
3 Luzern
4 Uri
5 Schwyz
6 Unterwalden ob dem Wald
7 Unterwalden nid dem Wald
8 Glarus
9 Zug
10 Freiburg / Fribourg
11 Solothurn
12 Basel - Stadt
13 Basel - Landschaft
14 Schaffhausen
15 Appenzell Ausser - Rhoden
16 Appenzell Inner - Rhoden
17 Sankt Gallen
18 Graubünden / Grigioni / Grischun
19 Aargau
20 Thurgau
21 Ticino
22 Vaud
23 Wallis / Valais
24 Neuchâtel
25 Genève
26 Jura
Tyrrhenian Basin
MAR TIRRENO
TYRRHENIAN SEA
MAR DI SARDEGNA
ARCIPELAGO CAMPANO
IONIAN SEA
Golfo di Taranto
Gulf of Taranto
MAR MEDITERRANEO
Canale di Sicilia
Strait of Sicily
Canale di Malta
Malta Channel
ADRIATIC
SHQIPERIA ALBANIA
CORSICA
Sardegna
Sardinia
Sicilia
Sicily
Lazio
Molise
Campania
Puglia
Basilicata
Calabria
ROMA
CITTÀ DEL VATICANO
VATICAN CITY
NAPLES NAPOLI
PALERMO
MESSINA
CATANIA
BARI
Cagliari
Sassari
Taranto
Catanzaro
Reggio di Calabria
Siracusa
ISOLE EOLIE O LIPARI
ISOLE EGADI
ISOLE PONZIANE
PONTIC ISLANDS
ISOLE PELAGIE
PANTELLERIA
MALTA
TŪNIS
TUNISIA
AL JAZĀ'IR
ALGERIA
Annaba
Bizerte
Sūsah
Scale 1:3,000,000
Delisle Conic Equidistant Projection
Longitude East 11 of Greenwich
0 50 100 150 200 km
0 50 100 miles
© ISTITUTO GEOGRAFICO DE AGOSTINI S. p. A. - NOVARA

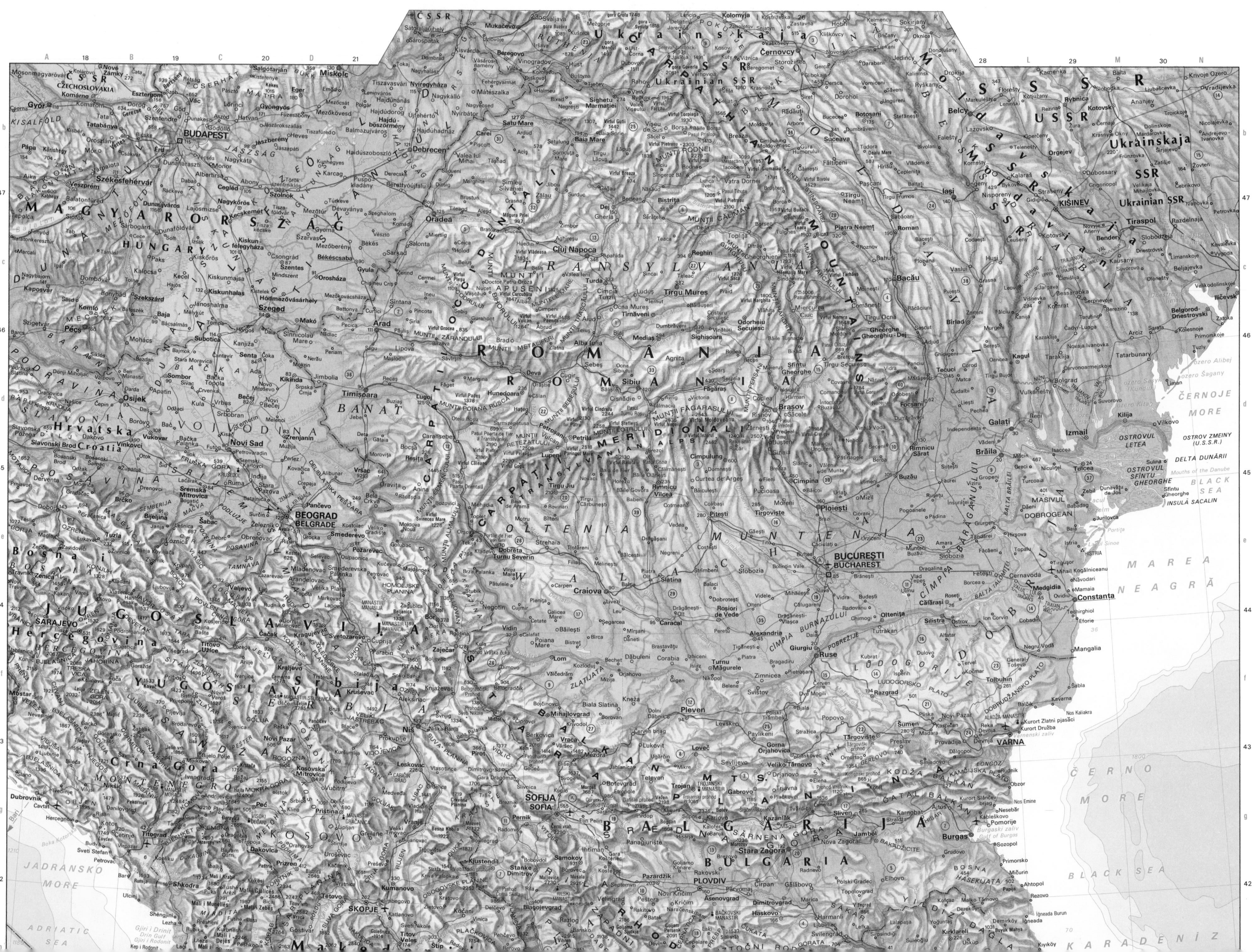
ROMÂNIA
ROMANIA
MAGYARORSZÁG
HUNGARY
BĂLGARIJA
BULGARIA
JUGOSLAVIJA
YUGOSLAVIA
BUCUREŞTI
BUCHAREST
BUDAPEST
BEOGRAD
BELGRADE
SOFIJA
SOFIA
SKOPJE
SARAJEVO
KIŠINEV
MAREA NEAGRĂ
ČERNOJE MORE
ČERNO MORE
BLACK SEA
JADRANSKO MORE
ADRIATIC SEA
ČSSR
CZECHOSLOVAKIA
Ukrainskaja SSR
Ukrainian SSR
Moldavskaja SSR
TRANSYLVANIA
CARPATHIAN MOUNTAINS
TRANSYLVANIAN ALPS
OLTENIA
MUNTENIA
BANAT
VOJVODINA
Crna Gora
Hrvatska
Croatia
Srbija
Bosna i Hercegovina
DELTA DUNĂRII
Mouths of the Danube
Constanţa
Varna
Burgas
Plovdiv
Ruse
Craiova
Cluj Napoca
Iaşi
Timişoara
Debrecen
Szeged
Novi Sad
Niš
Galaţi
Brăila
Braşov
Ploieşti
Sibiu
Oradea
Arad
Tiraspol
Izmail

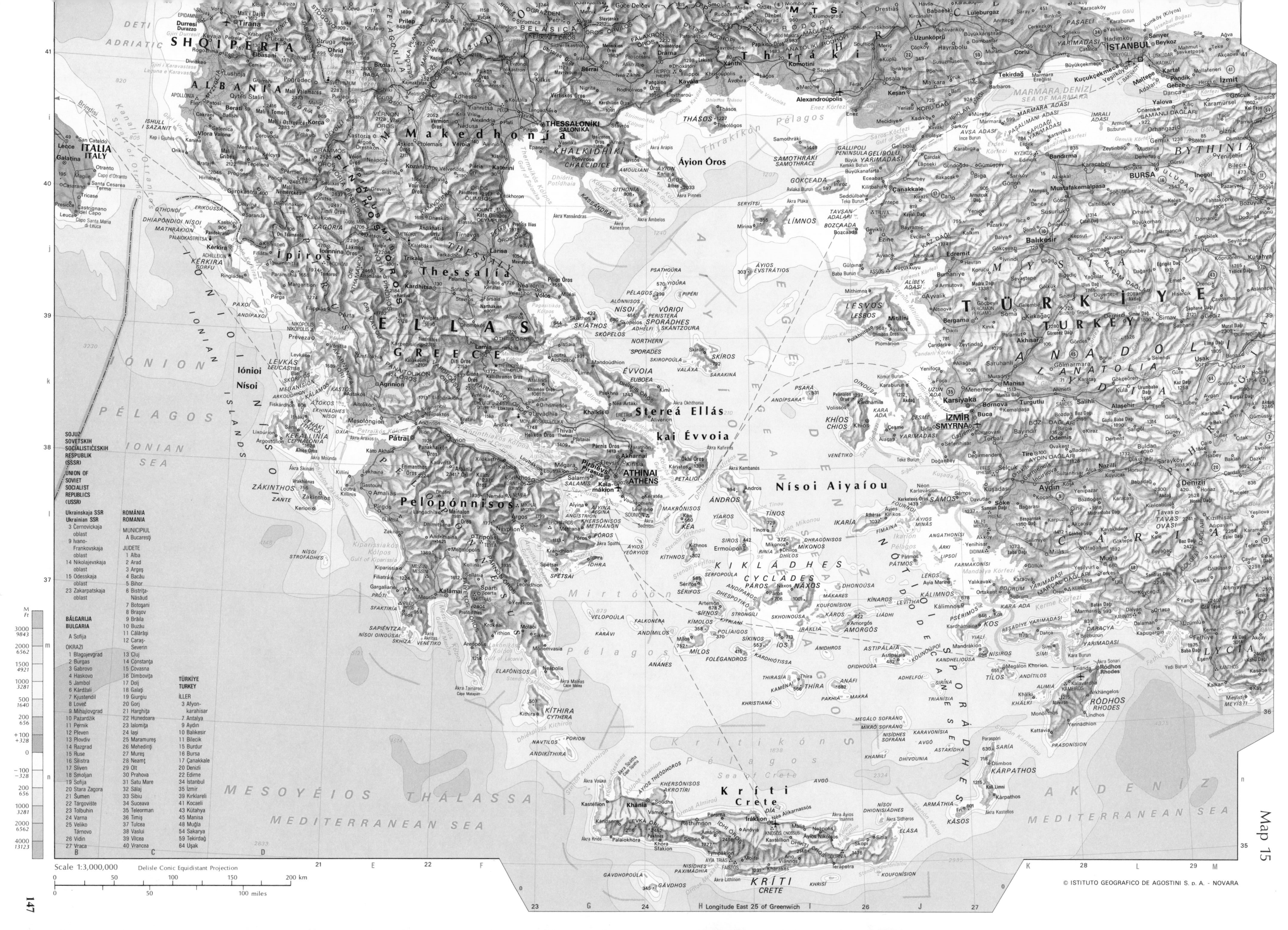

ELLÁS
GREECE
TÜRKIYE
TURKEY
ANADOLU
ANATOLIA
SHQIPËRIA
ALBANIA
ITALIA
ITALY
Makedhonía
Thessalía
Pelopónnisos
Stereá Ellás
kai Évvoia
Ípiros
Thráki
Kríti
Crete
Nísoi Aiyaíou
KIKLÁDHES
CYCLADES
NÓTIOI SPORÁDHES
DODECANESE
Iónioi Nísoi
IONIAN ISLANDS
IONIAN SEA
PÉLAGOS
AIYAÍON PÉLAGOS
AEGEAN SEA
MESOYÉIOS THÁLASSA
MEDITERRANEAN SEA
AKDENIZ
MARMARA DENIZI
SEA OF MARMARA
Mirtóön Pélagos
Kritikón Pélagos
Sea of Crete
Strait of Otranto
Áyion Óros
ATHÍNAI
ATHENS
THESSALONÍKI
SALONIKA
ISTANBUL
IZMIR
SMYRNA
BURSA
Pátrai
Lárisa
Iráklion
Khaniá
Ródhos
Rhodes
Tirana
Durrës
Brindisi
Lecce
Scale 1:3,000,000
Delisle Conic Equidistant Projection
H Longitude East 25 of Greenwich
© ISTITUTO GEOGRAFICO DE AGOSTINI S. p. A. - NOVARA

Map 16 SOUTHWESTERN SOVIET UNION

SOJUZ SOVETSKIH SOCIALISTIČESKIH RESPUBLIK (SSSR)
UNION OF SOVIET SOCIALIST REPUBLICS (USSR)
Rossijskaja Sovetskaja Federativnaja Socialističeskaja Respublika (RSFSR)
Russian Soviet Federative Socialist Republic (RSFSR)
3 Krasnodarski kraj
3A Adygejskaja avtonomnaja oblast
6 Stavropolski kraj
6A Karačajevo-Čerkesskaja avtonomnaja oblast
9 Astrahanskaja oblast
10 Belgorodskaja oblast
11 Brjanskaja oblast
12 Čeljabinskaja oblast
14 Gorkovskaja oblast
15 Ivanovskaja oblast
17 Jaroslavskaja oblast
18 Kaliningradskaja oblast
19 Kalininskaja oblast
20 Kalužskaja oblast
23 Kirovskaja oblast
24 Kostromskaja oblast
25 Kujbyševskaja oblast
26 Kurganskaja oblast
27 Kurskaja oblast
29 Lipeckaja oblast
31 Moskovskaja oblast
33 Novgorodskaja oblast
36 Orenburgskaja oblast
37 Orlovskaja oblast
38 Penzenskaja oblast
40 Pskovskaja oblast
41 Rostovskaja oblast
42 Rjazanskaja oblast
44 Saratovskaja oblast
45 Smolenskaja oblast
47 Tambovskaja oblast
50 Tulskaja oblast
51 Uljanovskaja oblast
52 Vladimirskaja oblast
53 Volgogradskaja oblast
55 Voronežskaja oblast
Ukrainskaja SSR
Ukrainian SSR
1 Čerkasskaja oblast
2 Černigovskaja oblast
3 Černovickaja oblast
4 Dnepropetrovskaja oblast
5 Doneckaja oblast
6 Harkovskaja oblast
7 Hersonskaja oblast
8 Hmelnickaja oblast
9 Ivano-Frankovskaja oblast
10 Kijevskaja oblast
11 Kirovogradskaja oblast
12 Krymskaja oblast
13 Lvovskaja oblast
14 Nikolajevskaja oblast
15 Odesskaja oblast
16 Poltavskaja oblast
17 Rovenskaja oblast
18 Sumskaja oblast
19 Ternopolskaja oblast
20 Vinnickaja oblast
21 Volynskaja oblast
22 Vorošilovgradskaja oblast
23 Zakarpatskaja oblast
24 Zaporožskaja oblast
25 Žitomirskaja oblast
Belorusskaja SSR
Byelorussian SSR
1 Brestskaja oblast
2 Gomelskaja oblast
3 Grodnenskaja oblast
4 Minskaja oblast
5 Mogilevskaja oblast
6 Vitebskaja oblast
Kazahskaja SSR
Kazakh SSR
1 Aktjubinskaja oblast
7 Gurjevskaja oblast
9 Kzyl-Ordinskaja oblast
11 Kustanajskaja oblast
12 Mangyšlakskaja oblast
18 Uralskaja oblast
Gruzinskaja SSR
Georgian SSR
1 Jugo-Osetinskaja avtonomnaja oblast
Azerbajdžanskaja SSR
Azerbaijan SSR
1 Nagorno-Karabahskaja avtonomnaja oblast
Turkmenskaja SSR
Turkmen SSR
1 Ašhabadskaja oblast
3 Krasnovodskaja oblast
5 Tašauzskaja oblast
Longitude East 42 of Greenwich

Map 17 THE URALS

SOJUZ SOVETSKIH SOCIALISTIČESKIH RESPUBLIK (SSSR)

UNION OF SOVIET SOCIALIST REPUBLICS

Rossijskaja Sovetskaja Federativnaja Socialističeskaja Respublika (RSFSR)

Russian Soviet Federated Socialist Republic

- 8 Arhangelskaja oblast
- 8A Nenecki nac. okrug
- 12 Čeljabinskaja oblast
- 14 Gorkovskaja oblast
- 23 Kirovskaja oblast
- 24 Kostromskaja oblast
- 25 Kujbiševskaja oblast
- 26 Kurganskaja oblast
- 35 Omskaja oblast
- 36 Orenburgskaja oblast
- 39 Permskaja oblast
- 39A Komi-Permjacki nac. okrug
- 44 Saratovskaja oblast
- 46 Sverdlovskaja oblast
- 48 Tjumenskaja oblast
- 48A Hanty-Mansijski nac. okrug
- 48B Jamalo-Nenecki nac. okrug
- 51 Uljanovskaja oblast
- 54 Vologodskaja oblast

Kazahskaja SSR

Kazakh SSR

- 3 Celinogradskaja oblast
- 10 Kokčetavskaja oblast
- 11 Kustanajskaja oblast
- 15 Severo-Kazahstanskaja oblast
- 17 Turgajskaja oblast

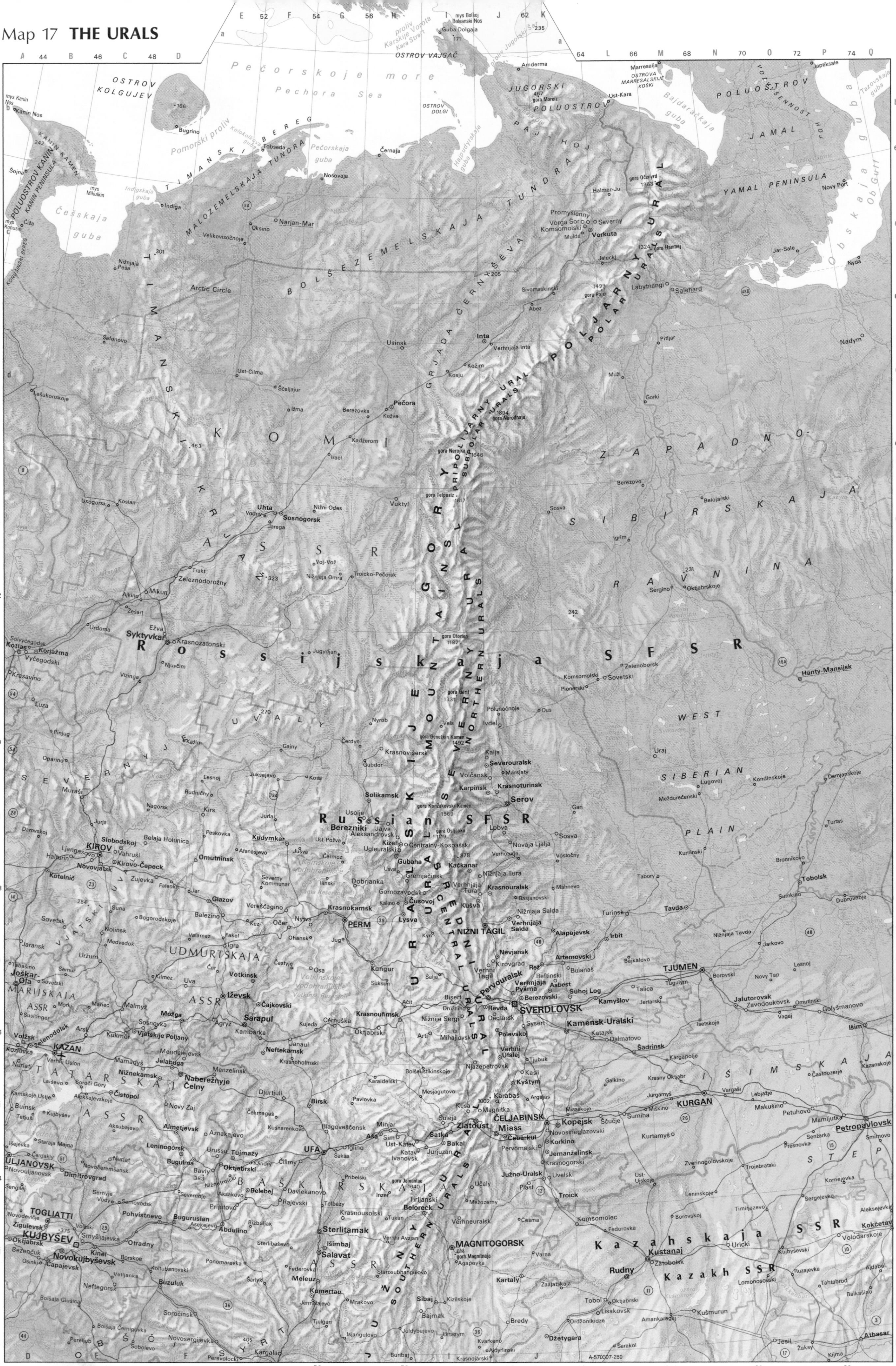

M / Ft: 1000 / 3281; 500 / 1640; 200 / 656; +100 / +328; 0; −100 / −328; 200 / 656

Scale 1:6,000,000 Delisle Conic Equidistant Projection

0 100 200 300 400 km

0 100 200 miles

Longitude East 60 of Greenwich

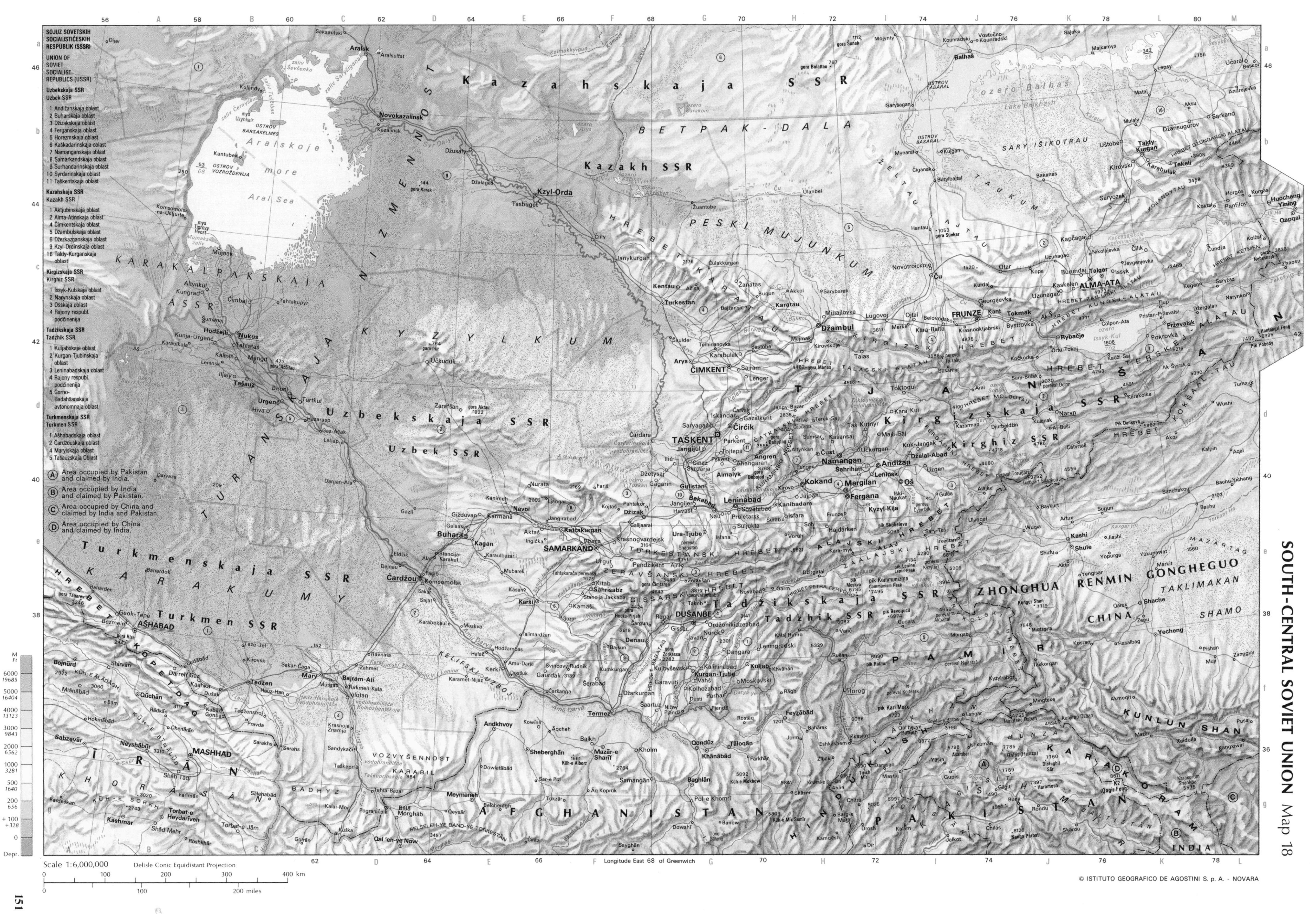
SOJUZ SOVETSKIH SOCIALISTIČESKIH RESPUBLIK (SSSR)
UNION OF SOVIET SOCIALIST REPUBLICS (USSR)
Uzbekskaja SSR
Uzbek SSR
1 Andižanskaja oblast
2 Buharskaja oblast
3 Džizakskaja oblast
4 Ferganskaja oblast
5 Horezmskaja oblast
6 Kaškadarinskaja oblast
7 Namanganskaja oblast
8 Samarkandskaja oblast
9 Surhandarinskaja oblast
10 Syrdarinskaja oblast
11 Taškentskaja oblast
Kazahskaja SSR
Kazakh SSR
1 Aktjubinskaja oblast
2 Alma-Atinskaja oblast
4 Čimkentskaja oblast
5 Džambulskaja oblast
6 Džezkazganskaja oblast
9 Kzyl-Ordinskaja oblast
16 Taldy-Kurganskaja oblast
Kirgizskaja SSR
Kirghiz SSR
1 Issyk-Kulskaja oblast
2 Narynskaja oblast
3 Ošskaja oblast
4 Rajony respubl. podčinenija
Tadžikskaja SSR
Tadzhik SSR
1 Kuljabskaja oblast
2 Kurgan-Tjubinskaja oblast
3 Leninabadskaja oblast
4 Rajony respubl. podčinenija
5 Gorno-Badahšanskaja avtonomnaja oblast
Turkmenskaja SSR
Turkmen SSR
1 Ašhabadskaja oblast
2 Čardžouskaja oblast
4 Maryjskaja oblast
5 Tašauzskaja Oblast
A Area occupied by Pakistan and claimed by India.
B Area occupied by India and claimed by Pakistan.
C Area occupied by China and claimed by India and Pakistan.
D Area occupied by China and claimed by India.
Kazahskaja SSR
Kazakh SSR
BETPAK-DALA
PESKI MUJUNKUM
KARAKALPAKSKAJA ASSR
KYZYLKUM
Uzbekskaja SSR
Uzbek SSR
Turkmenskaja SSR
Turkmen SSR
KARAKUMY
Aral'skoje more
Aral Sea
ozero Balhaš
Lake Balkhash
Kirgizskaja SSR
Kirghiz SSR
Tadžikskaja SSR
Tadzhik SSR
ZHONGHUA RENMIN GONGHEGUO
CHINA
TAKLIMAKAN SHAMO
PAMIR
ĀFGHĀNISTĀN
ĪRĀN
PAKISTAN
INDIA
TAŠKENT
DUŠANBE
FRUNZE
ALMA-ATA
AŠHABAD
SAMARKAND
MASHHAD
M Ft
6000 19685
5000 16404
4000 13123
3000 9843
2000 6562
1000 3281
500 1640
200 656
+ 100 +328
0
Depr.
Scale 1:6,000,000
Delisle Conic Equidistant Projection
Longitude East 68 of Greenwich
0 100 200 300 400 km
0 100 200 miles
© ISTITUTO GEOGRAFICO DE AGOSTINI S. p. A. - NOVARA

Map 19
SOJUZ SOVETSKIH SOCIALISTIČESKIH RESPUBLIK (SSSR)
UNION OF SOVIET SOCIALIST REPUBLICS (USSR)
Rossijskaja Sovetskaja Federativnaja Socialističeskaja Respublika (RSFSR)
Russian Soviet Federative Socialist Republic (RSFSR)
3 Krasnodarski kraj
3A Adygejskaja avt. oblast
6 Stavropolski kraj
6A Karačajevo-Čerkessakaja avt. oblast
8 Arhangelskaja oblast
8A Nenecki nac. okr.
9 Astrahanskaja oblast
10 Belgorodskaja oblast
11 Brjanskaja obl.
12 Čeljabinskaja obl.
14 Gorkovskaja obl.
15 Ivanovskaja obl.
17 Jaroslavskaja obl.
18 Kaliningradskaja oblast
19 Kalininskaja obl.
20 Kalužskaja obl.
23 Kirovskaja obl.
24 Kostromskaja obl.
25 Kujbyševskaja oblast
26 Kurganskaja obl.
27 Kurskaja obl.
28 Leningradskaja oblast
29 Lipeckaja obl.
31 Moskovskaja obl.
32 Murmanskaja obl.
33 Novgorodskaja oblast
35 Omskaja obl.
36 Orenburgskaja oblast
37 Orlovskaja obl.
38 Penzenskaja obl.
39 Permskaja obl.
39A Komi-Permjacki nac. okr.
40 Pskovskaja obl.
41 Rostovskaja obl.
42 Rjazanskaja obl.
44 Saratovskaja obl.
45 Smolenskaja obl.
46 Sverdlovskaja obl.
47 Tambovskaja obl.
48 Tjumenskaja obl.
48A Hanty-Mansijski nac. okr.
50 Tulskaja obl.
51 Uljanovskaja obl.
52 Vladimirskaja obl.
53 Volgogradskaja oblast
54 Vologodskaja obl.
55 Voronežskaja obl.
Ukrainskaja SSR
Ukrainian SSR
1 Čerkasskaja obl.
2 Černigovskaja obl.
3 Černovickaja obl.
4 Dnepropetrovskaja oblast
5 Doneckaja obl.
6 Harkovskaja obl.
7 Hersonskaja obl.
8 Hmelnickaja obl.
9 Ivano-Frankovskaja oblast
10 Kijevskaja obl.
NORGE
NORWAY
SVERIGE
SWEDEN
SUOMI
FINLAND
SCANDINAVIA
LAPLAND
BARENCEVO MORE
BARENTS SEA
NOVAJA ZEMLJA
NOVAYA ZEMLYA
MURMANSK
ARHANGELSK
LENINGRAD
HELSINKI
STOCKHOLM
OSLO
KØBENHAVN
TALLINN
RIGA
VILNIUS
MINSK
MOSKVA
MOSCOW
WARSZAWA
POLSKA
POLAND
KIJEV
Ukrainskaja SSR
Belorusskaja SSR
Byelorussian SSR
ROMÂNIA
BUCUREŞTI
BALGARIJA
ČERNOJE MORE
BLACK SEA
ISTANBUL
ANKARA
TÜRKIYE
TURKEY
KUZEY KIBRIS
NORTH CYPRUS
KIPROS
CYPRUS
MEDITERRANEAN SEA
SŪRĪYAH
SYRIA
LUBNĀN
LEBANON
BAYRŪT
DIMASHQ
YISRA'EL
ISRAEL
AL ʿIRĀQ
IRAQ
ĪRĀN
TBILISI
JEREVAN
BAKU
KASPIJSKOJE MORE
CASPIAN SEA
ASTRAHAN
VOLGOGRAD
ROSTOV-NA-DONU
HARKOV
ODESSA
NIŽNIJ NOVGOROD
KAZAN
KUJBYŠEV
SARATOV
ORENBURG
PERM
SVERDLOVSK
ČELJABINSK
UFA
MAGNITOGORSK
Kazakhskaja SSR
Turkmenskaja SSR
AŠHABAD
KARAKUMY
PLATO USTJURT
Aral'skoje more
Aral Sea
KARAKALPAKSKAJA ASSR
KOMI ASSR
Rossija
URAL
KARELIJA
KARELIAN ASSR
Scale 1:12,000,000
Delisle Conic Equidistant Projection
Longitude East 55 of Greenwich
0 200 400 600 800 km
0 200 400 miles

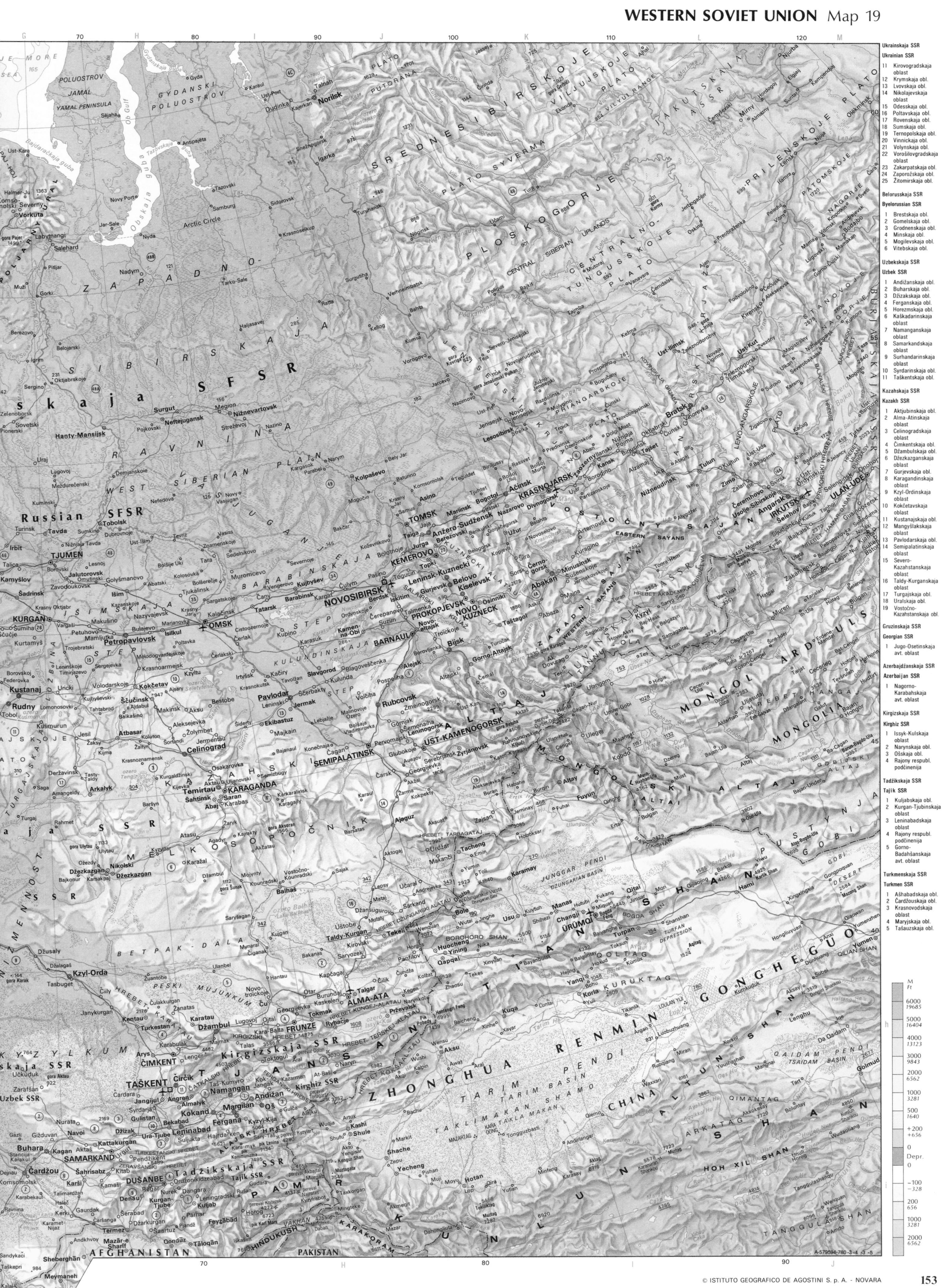

Ukrainskaja SSR
Ukrainian SSR
11 Kirovogradskaja oblast
12 Krymskaja obl.
13 Lvovskaja obl.
14 Nikolajevskaja oblast
15 Odesskaja obl.
16 Poltavskaja obl.
17 Rovenskaja obl.
18 Sumskaja obl.
19 Ternopolskaja obl.
20 Vinnickaja obl.
21 Volynskaja obl.
22 Vorošilovgradskaja oblast
23 Zakarpatskaja obl.
24 Zaporožskaja obl.
25 Žitomirskaja obl.
Belorusskaja SSR
Byelorussian SSR
1 Brestskaja obl.
2 Gomelskaja obl.
3 Grodnenskaja obl.
4 Minskaja obl.
5 Mogilevskaja obl.
6 Vitebskaja obl.
Uzbekskaja SSR
Uzbek SSR
1 Andižanskaja obl.
2 Buharskaja obl.
3 Džizakskaja obl.
4 Ferganskaja obl.
5 Horezmskaja obl.
6 Kaškadarinskaja oblast
7 Namanganskaja oblast
8 Samarkandskaja oblast
9 Surhandarinskaja oblast
10 Syrdarinskaja obl.
11 Taškentskaja obl.
Kazahskaja SSR
Kazakh SSR
1 Aktjubinskaja obl.
2 Alma-Atinskaja oblast
3 Celinogradskaja oblast
4 Čimkentskaja obl.
5 Džambulskaja obl.
6 Džezkazganskaja oblast
7 Gurjevskaja obl.
8 Karagandinskaja oblast
9 Kzyl-Ordinskaja oblast
10 Kokčetavskaja oblast
11 Kustanajskaja obl.
12 Mangyšlakskaja oblast
13 Pavlodarskaja obl.
14 Semipalatinskaja oblast
15 Severo-Kazahstanskaja oblast
16 Taldy-Kurganskaja oblast
17 Turgajskaja obl.
18 Uralskaja obl.
19 Vostočno-Kazahstanskaja obl.
Gruzinskaja SSR
Georgian SSR
1 Jugo-Osetinskaja avt. oblast
Azerbajdžanskaja SSR
Azerbaijan SSR
1 Nagorno-Karabahskaja avt. oblast
Kirgizskaja SSR
Kirghiz SSR
1 Issyk-Kulskaja oblast
2 Narynskaja obl.
3 Oššskaja obl.
4 Rajony respubl. podčinenija
Tadžikskaja SSR
Tajik SSR
1 Kuljabskaja obl.
2 Kurgan-Tjubinskaja oblast
3 Leninabadskaja oblast
4 Rajony respubl. podčinenija
5 Gorno-Badahšanskaja avt. oblast
Turkmenskaja SSR
Turkmen SSR
1 Ašhabadskaja obl.
2 Čardžouskaja obl.
3 Krasnovodskaja oblast
4 Maryjskaja obl.
5 Tašauzskaja obl.
M
Ft
6000
19685
5000
16404
4000
13123
3000
9843
2000
6562
1000
3281
500
1640
+200
+656
0
Depr.
0
−100
−328
200
656
1000
3281
2000
6562

Map 20

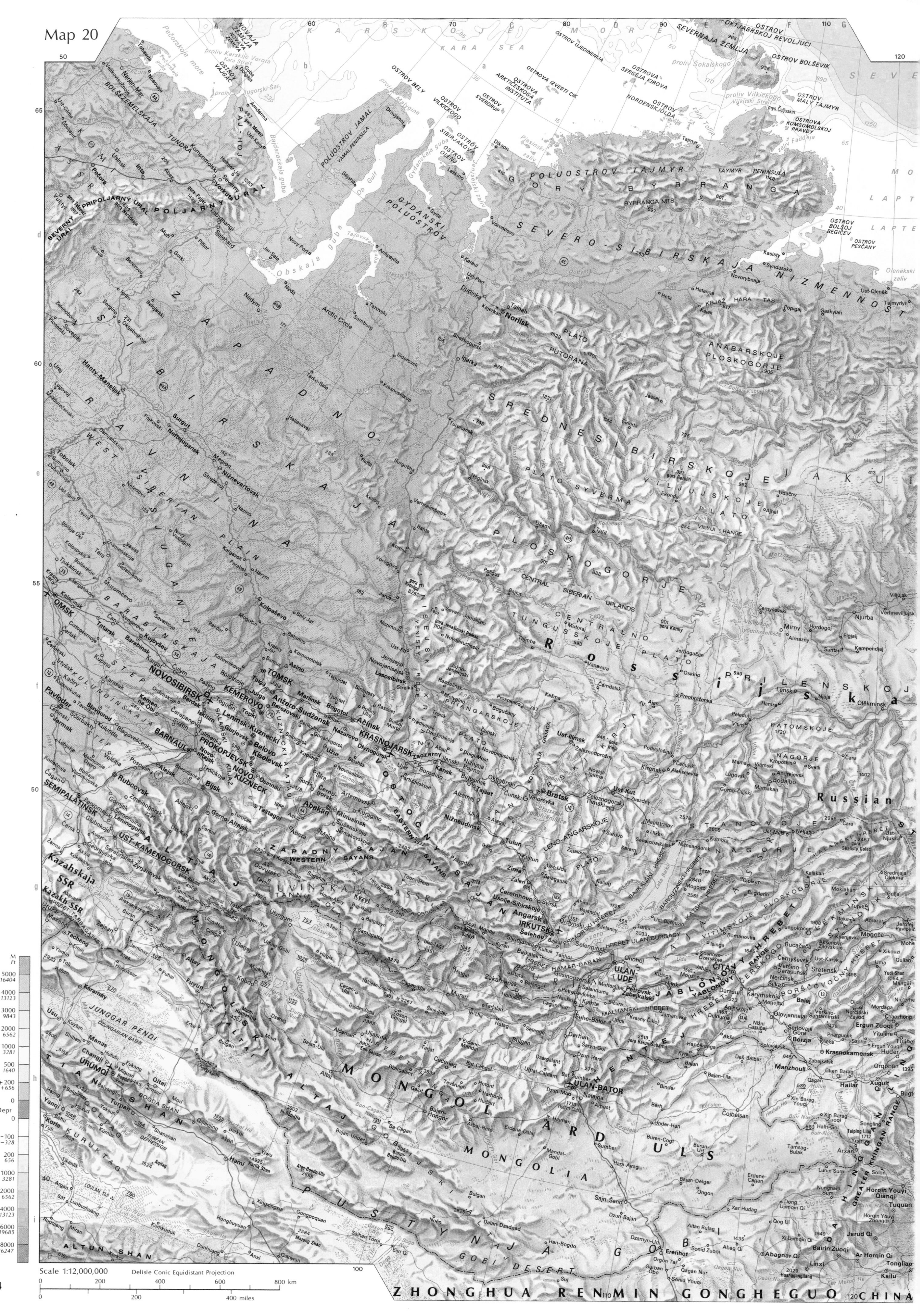
KARSKOJE MORE
KARA SEA
OSTROV OKTJABRSKOJ REVOLJUCI
SEVERNAJA ZEMLJA
OSTROV BOL'ŠEVIK
OSTROV BELY
POLUOSTROV JAMAL
YAMAL PENINSULA
GYDANSKI POLUOSTROV
POLUOSTROV TAJMYR
TAYMYR PENINSULA
GORY BYRRANGA
BYRRANGA MTS.
SEVERO-SIBIRSKAJA NIZMENNOST
ZAPADNO-SIBIRSKAJA RAVNINA
WEST SIBERIAN PLAIN
VASJUGAN'JE
BARABINSKAJA STEP
KULUNDINSKAJA STEP
PLATO PUTORANA
ANABARSKOJE PLOSKOGORJE
SREDNESIBIRSKOJE PLOSKOGORJE
CENTRAL SIBERIAN UPLANDS
PLATO SYVERMA
VILJUJSKOJE PLATO
VILYUI RANGE
CENTRAL'NO TUNGUSSKOJE PLATO
ROSSIJSKAJA
Russian
PRIANGARSKOJE PLATO
LENO-ANGARSKOJE PLATO
PRILENSKOJE PLATO
PATOMSKOJE NAGORJE
STANOVOJE NAGORJE
VOSTOČNY SAJAN
EASTERN SAYANS
ZAPADNY SAJAN
WESTERN SAYANS
ALTAJ
TUVINSKAJA ASSR
Kazahskaja SSR
Kazakh SSR
JABLONOVY HREBET
YABLONOVY RANGE
HENTEJ
MONGOL ARDULS
MONGOLIA
MONGOL'SKI ALTAJ
GOBI ALTAJ
GOBI DESERT
JUNGGAR PENDI
DZUNGARIAN BASIN
TIAN SHAN
BOGDA SHAN
TURPAN PENDI
TURFAN DEPRESSION
KURUKTAG
ALTUN SHAN
DA HINGGAN LING
GREATER KHINGAN RANGE
ZHONGHUA RENMIN GONGHEGUO
CHINA
NOVOSIBIRSK
OMSK
TOMSK
KEMEROVO
BARNAUL
PROKOPJEVSK
NOVOKUZNECK
KRASNOJARSK
IRKUTSK
ULAN-UDE
ULAN-BATOR
URUMQI
SEMIPALATINSK
UST-KAMENOGORSK
Norilsk
Bratsk
Vorkuta
Salehard
Surgut
Nižnevartovsk
Tobolsk
Abakan
Čita
Pavlodar
Kyzyl
Hami
Turpan
Hailar
Manzhouli
Erenhot
Scale 1:12,000,000
Delisle Conic Equidistant Projection
0 200 400 600 800 km
0 200 400 miles
M Ft
5000 16404
4000 13123
3000 9843
2000 6562
1000 3281
500 1640
+200 +656
0
Depr
0
-100 -328
200 656
1000 3281
2000 6562
4000 13123
6000 19685
8000 26247

SOJUZ SOVETSKIH SOCIALISTIČESKIH RESPUBLIK (SSSR)
UNION OF SOVIET SOCIALIST REPUBLICS (USSR)
Rossijskaja Sovetskaja Federativnaja Socialističeskaja Respublika (RSFSR)
Russian Soviet Federated Socialist Republic (RSFSR)
1 Altajski kraj
1A Gorno-Altajskaja avtonomnaja oblast
2 Habarovski kraj
2A Jevrejskaja avtonomnaja oblast
4 Krasnojarski kraj
4A Hakasskaja avtonomnaja oblast
4B Evenkijski nac. okrug
4C Tajmyrski (Dolgano-Nenecki) nac. okrug
5 Primorski krai
7 Amurskaja oblast
8A Nenecki nac. okrug
13 Čitinskaja oblast
13A Aginski Burjatski nac. okrug
16 Irkutskaja oblast
16A Ust-Ordynski Burjatski nac. okrug
21 Kamčatskaja oblast
21A Korjakski nac. okrug
22 Kemerovskaja oblast
30 Magadanskaja oblast
30A Čukotski nac. okrug
34 Novosibirskaja oblast
35 Omskaja oblast
43 Sahalinskaja oblast
48 Tjumenskaja oblast
48A Hanty-Mansijski nac. okrug
48B Jamalo-Nenecki nac. okrug
49 Tomskaja oblast
Kazahskaja SSR
Kazakh SSR
13 Pavlodarskaja oblast
14 Semipalatinskaja oblast
19 Vostočno-Kazahstanskaja oblast
NOVOSIBIRSKIJE OSTROVA
NEW SIBERIAN ISLANDS
OSTROV WRANGEL
ČUKOTSKOJE MORE
CHUKCHI SEA
VOSTOČNO-SIBIRSKOJE MORE
EAST SIBERIAN SEA
Alaska (U.S.)
ČUKOTSKI POLUOSTROV
CHUKCHI PENINSULA
ANADYRSKOJE PLOSKOGORJE
KORJAKSKOJE NAGORJE
KOLYMSKAJA NIZMENNOST
HREBET ČERSKOGO
VERHOJANSKI HREBET
Jakutsk
Magadan
POLUOSTROV KAMČATKA
KAMCHATKA PENINSULA
Petropavlovsk-Kamčatski
OHOTSKOJE MORE
SEA OF OKHOTSK
BERINGOVO MORE
BERING SEA
Aleutian Trench
KURILSKIJE OSTROVA
KURIL ISLANDS
Kuril Basin
Kuril Trench
OSTROV SAHALIN
SAKHALIN
Južno-Sahalinsk
HABAROVSK
Komsomolsk-na-Amure
Blagoveščensk
VLADIVOSTOK
Nahodka
HARBIN
CHANGCHUN
QIQIHAR
MANCHURIA
HOKKAIDO
SAPPORO
HAKODATE
NIPPON
JAPAN
JAPONSKOJE MORE
SEA OF JAPAN
TIHI OKEAN
PACIFIC OCEAN
Longitude East 150 of Greenwich

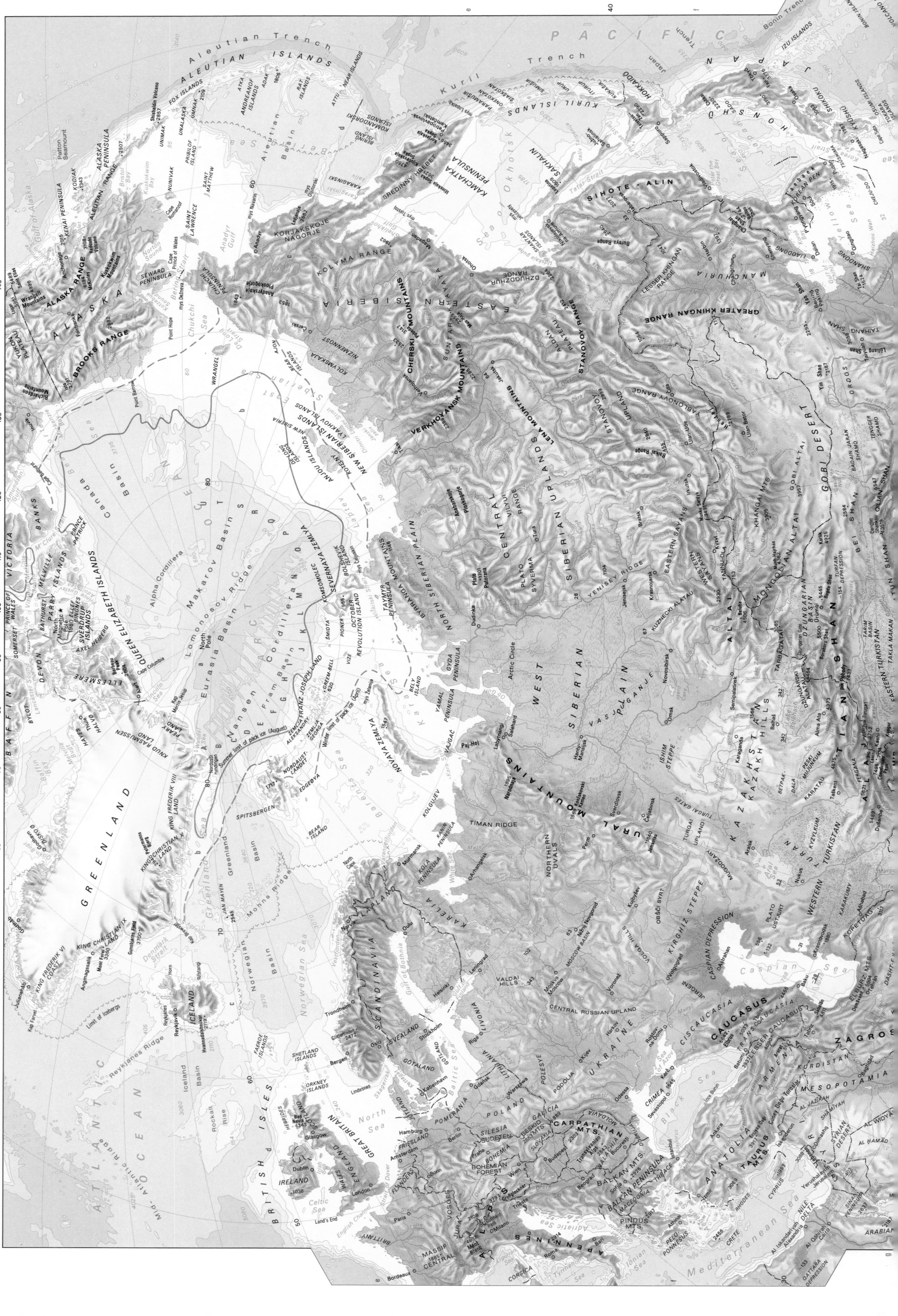

PACIFIC
ALEUTIAN ISLANDS
KAMCHATKA PENINSULA
KURIL ISLANDS
HOKKAIDO
HONSHU
SAKHALIN
SIHOTE-ALIN
KOLYMA RANGE
EASTERN SIBERIA
CHERSKI MOUNTAINS
VERKHOYANSK MOUNTAINS
STANOVOY RANGE
GREATER KHINGAN RANGE
MANCHURIA
GOBI DESERT
CENTRAL SIBERIAN UPLANDS
NORTH SIBERIAN PLAIN
WEST SIBERIAN PLAIN
URAL MOUNTAINS
KAZAKH HILLS
TIAN SHAN
ALTAI
ARCTIC OCEAN
GREENLAND
ICELAND
SCANDINAVIA
BRITISH ISLES
GREAT BRITAIN
IRELAND
CARPATHIAN MTS.
BALKAN PENINSULA
CAUCASUS
ANATOLIA
TAURUS MTS.
CASPIAN DEPRESSION
Caspian Sea
Black Sea
Mediterranean Sea
ZAGROS
ALASKA
BROOKS RANGE
ALASKA RANGE
QUEEN ELIZABETH ISLANDS
NOVAYA ZEMLYA
SEVERNAYA ZEMLYA
NEW SIBERIAN ISLANDS

INDIAN OCEAN
Arabian Sea
Bay of Bengal
Arabian Basin
Somali Basin
Mascarene Basin
Madagascar Basin
Mid-Indian Basin
Wharton Basin
North Australian Basin
Mid-Indian Ridge
Ninetyeast Ridge
Broken Ridge
Southwest Indian Ridge
Chagos-Laccadive Plateau
Mascarene Plateau
Madagascar Plateau
Java Trench
Murray Ridge
Nikitin Seamount
Equator
Tropic of Capricorn
ARABIAN PENINSULA
HINDUSTAN
INDIA
DECCAN
WESTERN GHATS
EASTERN GHATS
MALABAR COAST
COROMANDEL COAST
SRI LANKA (CEYLON)
HIMALAYA
KUNLUN SHAN
PLATEAU OF TIBET
HINDUKUSH
KARAKORAM
PLATEAU OF IRAN
ZAGROS MTS.
BALUCHISTAN
INDOCHINA
MALAY PENINSULA
SUMATRA
JAVA
KALIMANTAN (BORNEO)
CELEBES
GREATER SUNDA ISLANDS
LESSER SUNDA ISLANDS
PHILIPPINE ISLANDS
LUZON
MINDANAO
MOLUCCAS
NEW GUINEA
TIMOR
HAINAN
TAIWAN (FORMOSA)
RYUKYU ISLANDS
MALDIVE ISLANDS
LAKSHADWEEP
ANDAMAN ISLANDS
NICOBAR ISLANDS
CHAGOS ARCHIPELAGO
SEYCHELLES ISLANDS
AMIRANTE ISLANDS
MASCARENE ISLANDS
MADAGASCAR
COMORO ISLANDS
SOCOTRA
ETHIOPIAN PLATEAU
OGADEN
AUSTRALIA
GREAT SANDY DESERT
GIBSON DESERT
GREAT VICTORIA DESERT
NULLARBOR PLAIN
KIMBERLEY PLATEAU
Timor Sea
Red Sea
Persian Gulf
Gulf of Aden
Gulf of Oman
Gulf of Thailand
Gulf of Tonkin
Strait of Malacca
Java Sea
Celebes Sea
Philippine Basin
Kyushu-Palau Ridge
Scale 1:30,000,000
Lambert Azimuthal Equal Area Projection
Longitude East 80 of Greenwich
0 500 1000 1500 2000 km
0 500 1000 miles
M 6000 5000 4000 3000 2000 1000 500 +200 0 Depr. 0 -200 1000 2000 4000 6000 8000
Ft 19685 16404 13123 9843 6562 3281 1640 +656 0 -656 3281 6562 13123 19685 26247
A-515200-780-1 -1 -2 -5

PACIFIC OCEAN
ARCTIC OCEAN
ATLANTIC OCEAN
UNION OF SOVIET SOCIALIST REPUBLICS
CANADA
Alaska (U.S.)
Greenland (Den.)
ICELAND
NORWAY
SWEDEN
FINLAND
MONGOLIA
JAPAN
KAZAKHSTAN
TURKEY
IRAQ
UNITED KINGDOM
IRELAND
FRANCE
ITALY
GERMANY
POLAND
CZECHOSLOVAKIA
HUNGARY
ROMANIA
YUGOSLAVIA
BULGARIA
GREECE
ALBANIA
CYPRUS
SYRIA
JORDAN
ISRAEL
EGYPT
North Pole
CENTRAL SIBERIAN UPLANDS
WEST SIBERIAN PLAIN
VERKHOYANSK MOUNTAINS
CHERSKI MOUNTAINS
KAMCHATKA PENINSULA
ALEUTIAN ISLANDS
KURIL ISLANDS
SAKHALIN
NOVAYA ZEMLYA
SEVERNAYA ZEMLYA
NEW SIBERIAN ISLANDS
FRANZ JOSEPH LAND
TAYMYR PENINSULA
GOBI
Barents Sea
Kara Sea
Laptev Sea
East Siberian Sea
Chukchi Sea
Bering Sea
Sea of Okhotsk
Norwegian Sea
Greenland Sea
North Sea
Black Sea
Mediterranean Sea
Moskva
Leningrad
Novosibirsk
Sverdlovsk
Irkutsk
Vladivostok
Jakutsk
Murmansk
Oslo
Stockholm
Helsinki
London
Paris
Berlin
Warszawa
Praha
Wien
Budapest
Bucureşti
Sofija
Beograd
Roma
İstanbul
Ankara
Tbilisi
Baku
Tehrān
Baghdād
Dimashq
Al Qāhirah
Ulan-Bator
Tōkyō
Sapporo
Anchorage
Fairbanks
Reykjavík
Dublin
Edinburgh

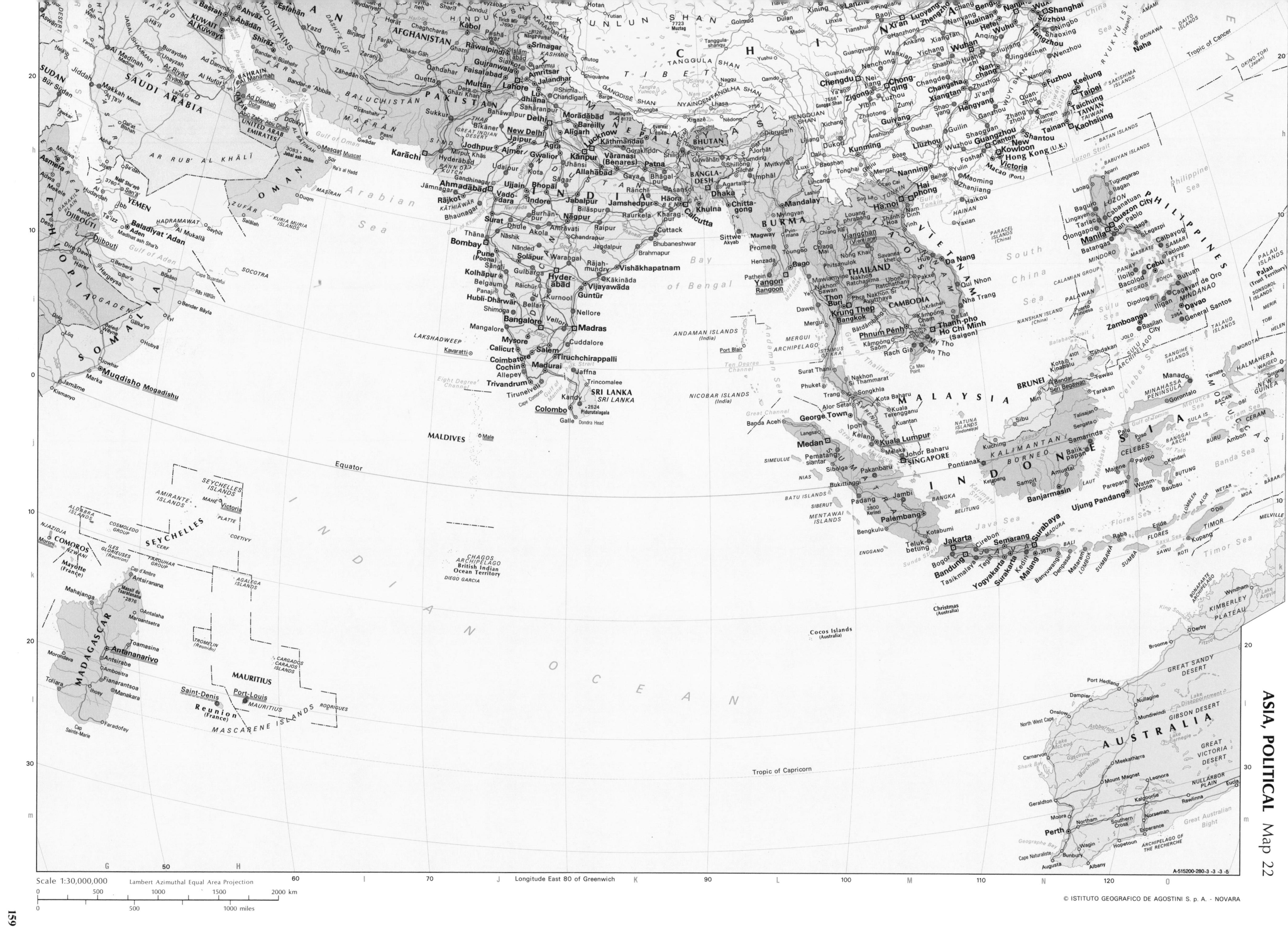
PHILIPPINES
Manila
INDIA
PAKISTAN
AFGHANISTAN
SAUDI ARABIA
YEMEN
OMAN
BURMA
THAILAND
VIETNAM
CAMBODIA
MALAYSIA
INDONESIA
AUSTRALIA
SRI LANKA
MALDIVES
MADAGASCAR
MAURITIUS
SEYCHELLES
BANGLADESH
BHUTAN
NEPAL
BRUNEI
SINGAPORE
Arabian Sea
Bay of Bengal
Andaman Sea
South China Sea
Equator
Tropic of Capricorn
Tropic of Cancer
Longitude East 80 of Greenwich
Scale 1:30,000,000
Lambert Azimuthal Equal Area Projection
0 500 1000 1500 2000 km
0 500 1000 miles
A-515200-280-3 -3 -5
© ISTITUTO GEOGRAFICO DE AGOSTINI S. p. A. - NOVARA

Scale 1:12,000,000 Delisle Conic Equidistant Projection

0 200 400 600 800 km

0 200 400 miles

AFGHANISTAN
VELĀYAT
1 Badakhshan
2 Bādghīsāt
3 Baghlān
4 Balkh
5 Bāmīān
6 Farāh
7 Fāryāb
8 Ghazni
9 Ghowr
10 Helmand
11 Herāt
12 Jowzjān
13 Kābol
14 Kāpīsā
15 Konarha
16 Laghmān
17 Lowgar
18 Nangarhār
19 Nīmrūz
20 Orūzgān
21 Paktīā
22 Parvān
23 Qandahar
24 Qondūz
25 Samangān
26 Takhār
27 Vardak
28 Zābol

ĪRĀN
OSTĀN
1 Āzarbāijān-e Gharbī
2 Āzarbāijān-e Sharqī
3 Bakhtarān
4 Boyer Ahmadī-e Kohkīlūyeh
5 Būshehr
6 Chahār Mahāl-e Bakhtīārī
7 Esfahān
8 Fārs
9 Gīlān
10 Hamadān
11 Hormozgān
12 Īlām
13 Kermān
14 Khorāsān
15 Khūzestān
16 Kordestān
17 Lorestān
18 Markazi
19 Māzandarān
20 Semnān
21 Sīstān-e Balūchestān
22 Yazd
23 Zanjān

KARADENİZ
BLACK SEA
KARADENİZ
TÜRKİYE
TURKEY
ANADOLU
KÖROĞLU DAĞLARI
TOROS DAĞLARI
TAURUS MTS.
GÜNEYDOĞU TOROSLAR
DOĞU KARADENİZ DAĞLARI
İSTANBUL
ANKARA
İZMİR
(SMYRNA)
BURSA
ESKİŞEHİR
KONYA
ADANA
Antalya
Trabzon
Samsun
Sivas
Kayseri
Diyarbakır
Erzurum
Batumi
ELLAS
GREECE
KIKLÁDHES
CYCLADES
NOTIOI SPORÁDHES
DODECANESE
RODHOS
RHODES
KRÍTI
CRETE
KUZEY KIBRIS
NORTH CYPRUS
North Cyprus unilaterally declared its independence November, 1983.
KÍPROS
CYPRUS
Lefkoşa
Nicosia
Levkosía
Lemesós / Limassol
AKDENİZ /
AL BAHR AL-MUTAWASSIṬ /
YAM KHATIKHON /
MEDITERRANEAN SEA
Area occupied by Israel
(A) Golan Heights area:
Occupied by Israel since 1967.
Unilaterally annexed by Israel, 1981.
(B) West Bank area:
Unilaterally annexed by Jordan, 1950.
Occupied by Israel since 1967.
Status to be determined.
(C) Gaza Strip:
Occupied by Israel since 1967.
Status to be determined.
SŪRĪYAH
SYRIA
DIMASHQ
DAMASCUS
HALAB
ALEPPO
Ḥimṣ
Homs
LUBNĀN
LEBANON
BEIRUT
BAYRŪT
YISRA'EL
ISRAEL
TEL AVIV-YAFO
YERUSHALAYIM
JERUSALEM
AL URDUN
JORDAN
'AMMĀN
BĀDIYAT ASH SHĀM
SYRIAN DESERT
AL ḤAMĀD
AL 'ARABĪYAH AS SAʻŪDĪYAH
AL ḤIJĀZ
AL MADĪNAH
Medina
MIṢR
EGYPT
AL QĀHIRAH
CAIRO
AL ISKANDARĪYAH
ALEXANDRIA
NILE DELTA
Būr Sa'īd
Port Said
As Suways
Suez
SĪNĀ'
SINAI PENINSULA
AL BAHR AL AHMAR
RED SEA
AS SAHRĀ' ASH SHARQĪYAH
AS SAHRĀ' AL GHARBĪYAH
WESTERN DESERT
MUNKHAFAD AL QAṬṬĀRAH
QATTARA DEPRESSION
ASWĀN
AL JAWF
AL AQABAH
AL ALBAYAN
AL URDUN
JORDAN
MUḤĀFAẒAT
1 Al Balqā'
2 Al Karak
3 Al Khalīl
4 Al Quds
5 'Ammān
6 Irbid
7 Ma'ān
8 Nābulus
West Bank: Occupied by Israel
YISRA'EL
ISRAEL
MEḤOZ
1 HaDarom
2 HaMerkaz
3 HaẒafon
4 Ḥefa
5 Tel Aviv
6 Yerushalayim
SŪRĪYAH
SYRIA
MINṬAQAT
14 Dimashq
MUḤAFAẒAT
1 Al Ḥasakah
2 Al Lādhiqiyah
3 Al Qunayṭirah
4 Ar Raqqah
5 As Suwaydā'
6 Dar'ā
7 Dayr Az Zawr
8 Dimashq
9 Ḥalab
10 Ḥamāh
11 Ḥimṣ
12 Idlib
13 Ṭarṭūs
Golan Heights: Occupied by Israel
M
Ft
5000
16404
4000
13123
3000
9843
2000
6562
1000
3281
500
1640
200
656
+100
+328
0
Depr.
0
−100
−328
200
656
1000
3281
2000
6562
4000
13123
Scale 1:6,000,000
Delisle Conic Equidistant Projection
0 100 200 300 400 km
0 100 200 miles
Longitude East 40 of Greenwich
A-569495-780-5 -4 -4 -5

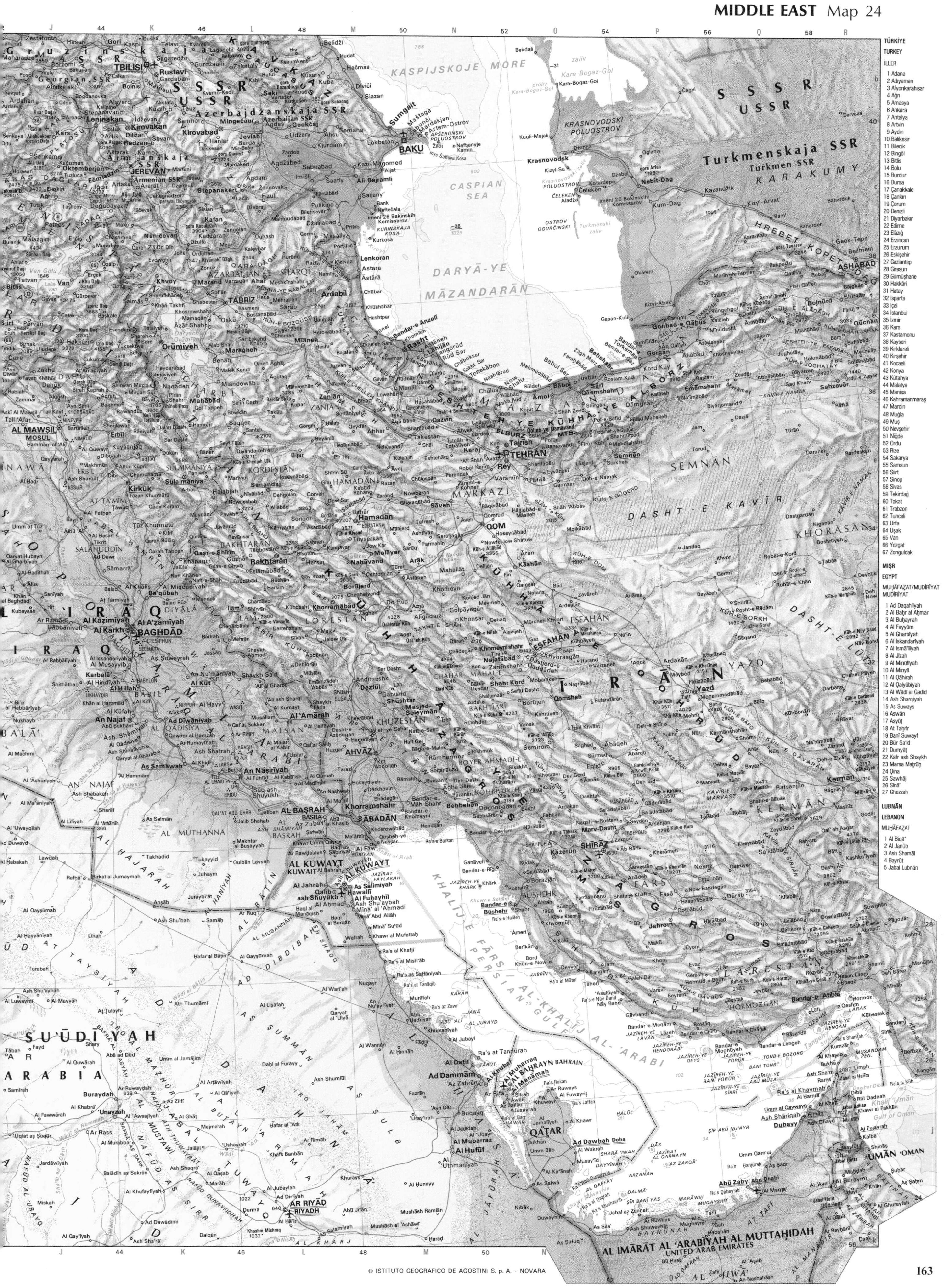
TÜRKİYE
TURKEY
İLLER
1 Adana
2 Adıyaman
3 Afyonkarahisar
4 Ağrı
5 Amasya
6 Ankara
7 Antalya
8 Artvin
9 Aydın
10 Balıkesir
11 Bilecik
12 Bingöl
13 Bitlis
14 Bolu
15 Burdur
16 Bursa
17 Çanakkale
18 Çankırı
19 Çorum
20 Denizli
21 Diyarbakır
22 Edirne
23 Elâzığ
24 Erzincan
25 Erzurum
26 Eskişehir
27 Gaziantep
28 Giresun
29 Gümüşhane
30 Hakkâri
31 Hatay
32 Isparta
33 İçel
34 İstanbul
35 İzmir
36 Kars
37 Kastamonu
38 Kayseri
39 Kırklareli
40 Kırşehir
41 Kocaeli
42 Konya
43 Kütahya
44 Malatya
45 Manisa
46 Kahramanmaraş
47 Mardin
48 Muğla
49 Muş
50 Nevşehir
51 Niğde
52 Ordu
53 Rize
54 Sakarya
55 Samsun
56 Siirt
57 Sinop
58 Sivas
59 Tekirdağ
60 Tokat
61 Trabzon
62 Tunceli
63 Urfa
64 Uşak
65 Van
66 Yozgat
67 Zonguldak
MIŞR
EGYPT
MUḨĀFAẒAT/MUDĪRĪYAT
MUDĪRĪYAT
1 Ad Daqahlīyah
2 Al Baḩr al Aḩmar
3 Al Buḩayrah
4 Al Fayyūm
5 Al Gharbīyah
6 Al Iskandarīyah
7 Al Ismā'īlīyah
8 Al Jīzah
9 Al Minūfīyah
10 Al Minyā
11 Al Qāhirah
12 Al Qalyūbīyah
13 Al Wādī al Gadīd
14 Ash Sharqiyah
15 As Suways
16 Aswān
17 Asyūţ
18 At Taḩrīr
19 Banī Suwayf
20 Būr Sa'īd
21 Dumyāţ
22 Kafr ash Shaykh
23 Marsa Maţrūḩ
24 Qina
25 Sawhāj
26 Sīnā'
27 Ghazzah
LUBNĀN
LEBANON
MUḨĀFAẒAT
1 Al Biqā'
2 Al Janūb
3 Ash Shamāl
4 Bayrūt
5 Jabal Lubnān
SSSR
USSR
Turkmenskaja SSR
Turkmen SSR
KARAKUMY
KASPIJSKOJE MORE
CASPIAN SEA
DARYĀ-YE MĀZANDARĀN
KRASNOVODSKI POLUOSTROV
TBILISI
BAKU
JEREVAN
Azerbajdžanskaja SSR
Azerbaijan SSR
Armjanskaja SSR
Armenian SSR
TEHRĀN
IRĀN
DASHT-E KAVĪR
SEMNĀN
KHORĀSĀN
ESFAHĀN
YAZD
KERMĀN
ELBURZ MTS.
ZAGROS
AL 'IRĀQ
IRAQ
BAGHDĀD
AL MAWSIL
MOSUL
AL BAŞRAH
AL KUWAYT
KUWAIT
AL BAḨRAYN BAHRAIN
QAṬAR
Ad Dawḩah Doha
AR RIYĀḌ
RIYADH
AS SUʻŪDĪYAH
SAUDI ARABIA
AL KHALĪJ AL-'ARABĪ
PERSIAN GULF
AL IMĀRĀT AL 'ARABĪYAH AL MUTTAḨIDAH
UNITED ARAB EMIRATES
'UMĀN OMAN
Abū Ẓaby Abu Dhabi
Dubayy
Ash Shāriqah
Ra's al Khaymah
Bandar-e 'Abbās
Shīrāz
Ahvāz
Ābādān
Qom
Hamadān
Bakhtarān
Tabrīz
Rasht
Mashhad

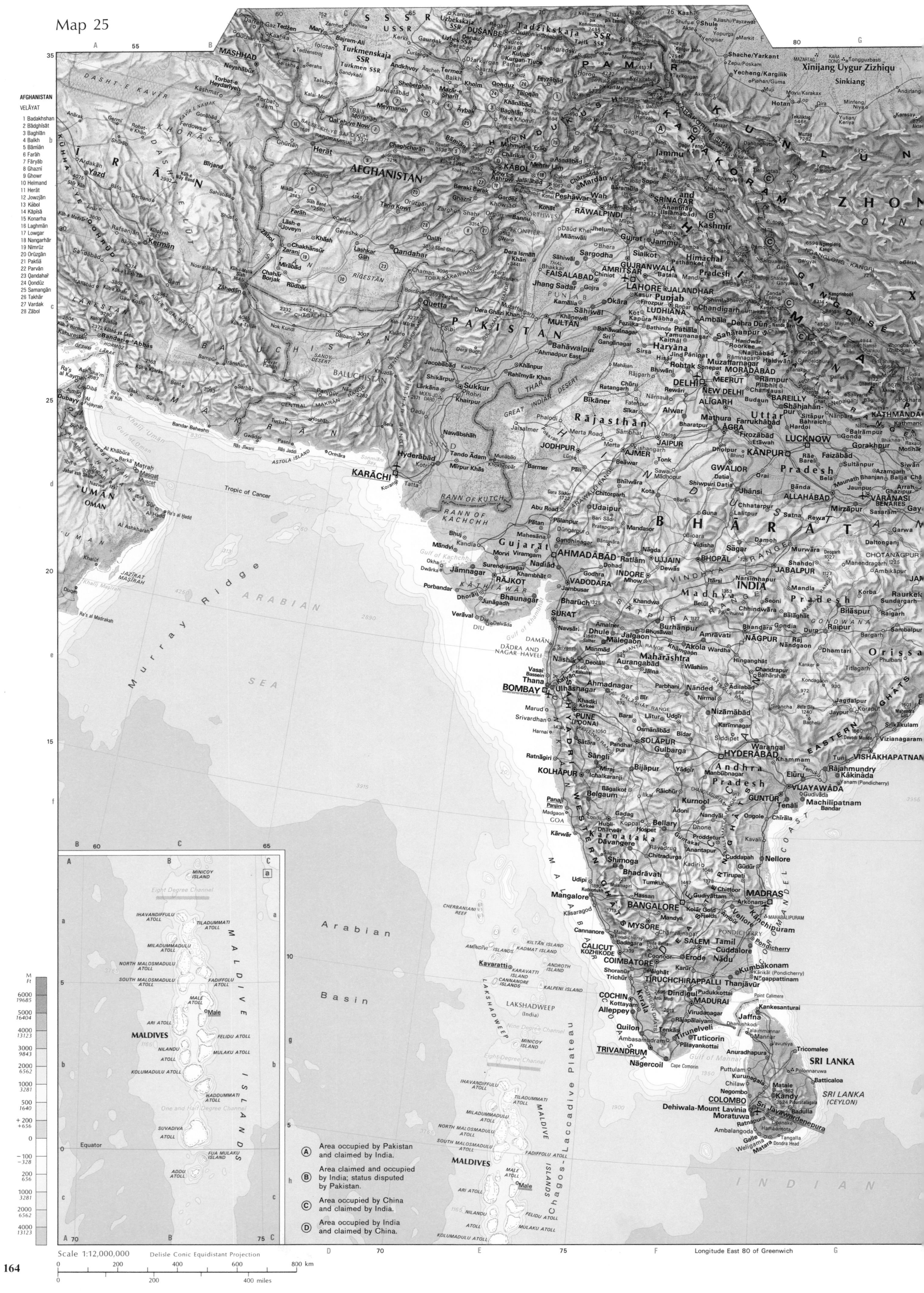

AFGHANISTAN
VELĀYAT
1 Badakhshān
2 Bādghīsāt
3 Baghlān
4 Balkh
5 Bāmīān
6 Farāh
7 Fāryāb
8 Ghaznī
9 Ghowr
10 Helmand
11 Herāt
12 Jowzjān
13 Kābol
14 Kāpīsā
15 Konarha
16 Laghmān
17 Lowgar
18 Nangarhār
19 Nimrūz
20 Orūzgān
21 Paktīā
22 Parvān
23 Qandahār
24 Qondūz
25 Samangān
26 Takhār
27 Vardak
28 Zābol
Ⓐ Area occupied by Pakistan and claimed by India.
Ⓑ Area claimed and occupied by India; status disputed by Pakistan.
Ⓒ Area occupied by China and claimed by India.
Ⓓ Area occupied by India and claimed by China.
M Ft
6000 19685
5000 16404
4000 13123
3000 9843
2000 6562
1000 3281
500 1640
+200 +656
0
−100 −328
200 656
1000 3281
2000 6562
4000 13123
Scale 1:12,000,000
Delisle Conic Equidistant Projection
0 200 400 600 800 km
0 200 400 miles
Longitude East 80 of Greenwich
AFGHANISTAN
PAKISTAN
INDIA
BHĀRAT
SRI LANKA
SRI LANKA (CEYLON)
MALDIVES
MALDIVE ISLANDS
LAKSHADWEEP (India)
Xinjiang Uygur Zizhiqu
Sinkiang
Turkmenskaja SSR
Turkmen SSR
Uzbekskaja SSR
Tadžikskaja SSR
Tajik SSR
ARABIAN SEA
Arabian Basin
Murray Ridge
Chagos-Laccadive Plateau
Tropic of Cancer
Equator
INDIAN
Gulf of Oman
Gulf of Kachchh
Gulf of Khambhāt
Gulf of Mannar
RANN OF KUTCH
RANN OF KACHCHH
GREAT INDIAN DESERT
THAR
DASHT-E KAVĪR
HINDU KUSH
PAMIR
KARAKORAM
KUNLUN
HIMALAYA
KARĀCHI
BOMBAY
DELHI
NEW DELHI
MADRAS
BANGALORE
HYDERĀBĀD
AHMADĀBĀD
LAHORE
KĀBOL
MASHHAD
LUCKNOW
KĀNPUR
JAIPUR
NĀGPUR
PUNE (POONA)
COLOMBO
KATHMANDU

CHINA
MYANMAR
BURMA
MUANG THAI
THAILAND
KAMPUCHEA
CAMBODIA
MALAYSIA
INDONESIA
BANGLADESH
VIET-NAM
BAY OF BENGAL
ANDAMAN AND NICOBAR (India)
ANDAMAN ISLANDS
NICOBAR ISLANDS
Andaman Basin
Gulf of Thailand
Gulf of Tonkin
SOUTH CHINA SEA
HAINAN DAO
PLATEAU OF TIBET
MALAY PENINSULA
SUMATERA
CHENGDU
CHONGQING
KUNMING
WUHAN
GUANGZHOU
HA NOI
HAI PHONG
YANGON
RANGOON
MANDALAY
KRUNG THEP BANGKOK
PHNUM PENH
THANH-PHO HO CHI MINH (SAIGON)
KUALA LUMPUR
SINGAPORE
MEDAN
CALCUTTA
DHAKA
CHITTAGONG
Sittwe (Akyab)
Port Blair
Vientiane
DA NANG
MACAU
Ocean

Scale 1:12,000,000 at the Equator   Mercator Cylindrical Projection

0 200 400 600 800 km

0 200 400 miles

PHILIPPINE SEA

Philippine Basin

West Mariana Basin

PACIFIC OCEAN

PILIPINAS

PHILIPPINES

TAIWAN

LUZON

MINDANAO

FEDERATED STATES OF MICRONESIA

CAROLINE ISLANDS

Palau

Belau

(Trust Territory)

West Caroline Basin

INDONESIA

SULAWESI

CELEBES

HALMAHERA

IRIAN JAYA

PAPUA NEW GUINEA

BANDA SEA

ARAFURA SEA

TIMOR SEA

AUSTRALIA

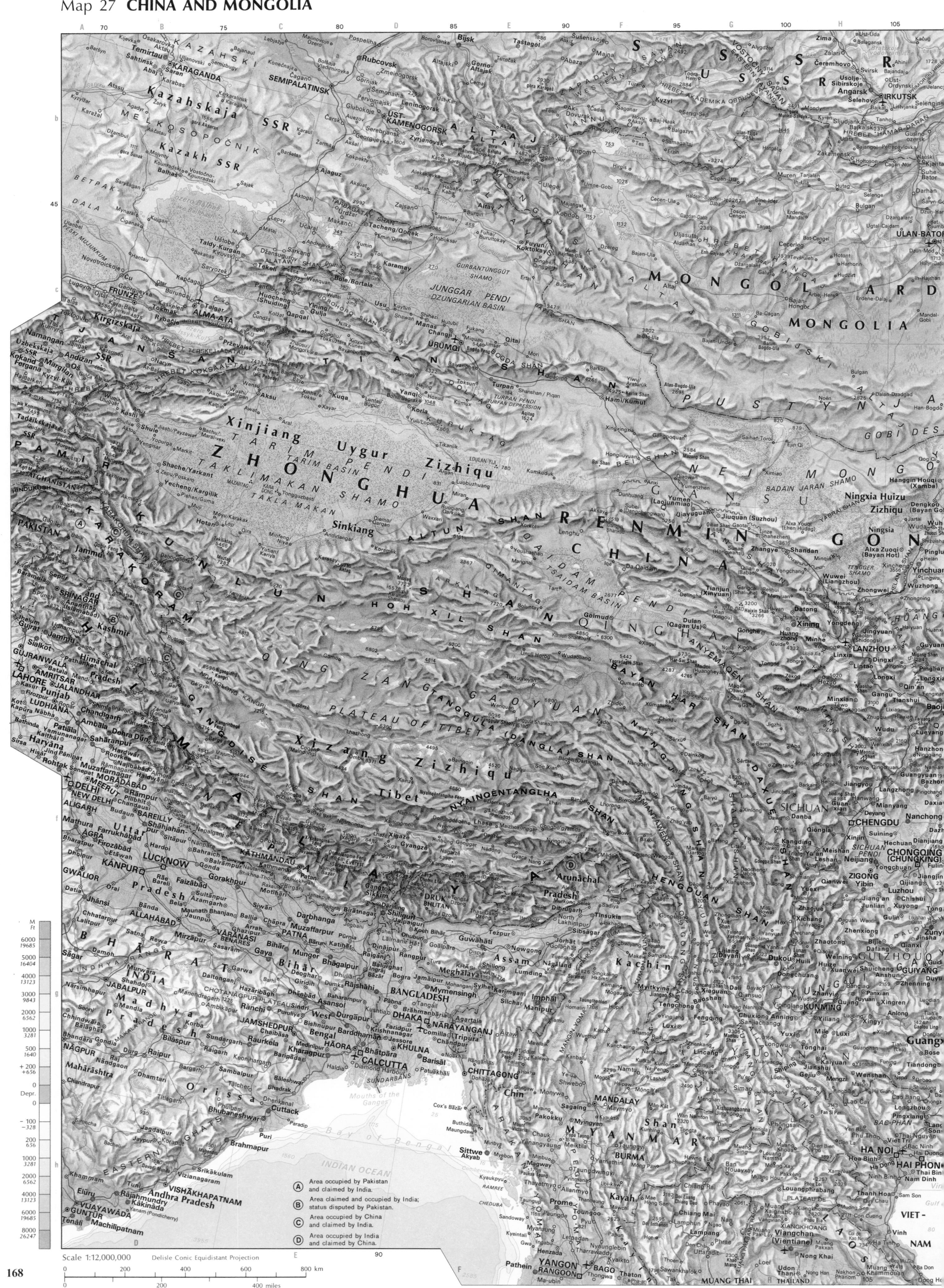
Kazahskaja SSR
Kazakh SSR
MELKOSOPOČNIK
BETPAK-DALA
Kirgizskaja SSR
Tadžikskaja SSR
Uzbekskaja SSR
PAMIR
AFGHANISTAN
PAKISTAN
S S S R
U S S R
MONGOL ARD
MONGOLIA
GOBĬ DES
ALTAJ
MONGOL ALTAJN NURUU
JUNGGAR PENDI
DZUNGARIAN BASIN
GURBANTÜNGGÜT SHAMO
TIAN SHAN
TARIM PENDI
TARIM BASIN
TAKLIMAKAN SHAMO
TAKLA MAKAN
Xinjiang Uygur Zizhiqu
Sinkiang
ZHONGHUA RENMIN GONGHEGUO
CHINA
NEI MONGOL
GANSU
Ningxia Huizu Zizhiqu
BADAIN JARAN SHAMO
TURPAN PENDI
TURFAN DEPRESSION
ALTUN SHAN
KUNLUN SHAN
KARAKORAM
QAIDAM PENDI
TSAIDAM BASIN
HOH XIL SHAN
QINGHAI
QING ZANG GAOYUAN
PLATEAU OF TIBET
TANGGULA (DANGLA) SHAN
Xizang Zizhiqu
Tibet
NYAINQENTANGLHA SHAN
NINGJING SHAN
GANGDISÊ SHAN
HIMALAYA
Arunāchal Pradesh
BAYAN HAR SHAN
DAXUE SHAN
HENGDUAN SHAN
SICHUAN PENDI
SICHUAN
YUNGUI
GUIZHOU
Kashmir
Himāchal Pradesh
Punjab
Haryāna
Uttar Pradesh
BHĀRAT
INDIA
Madhya Pradesh
Bihār
Bengal
Orissa
Andhra Pradesh
Mahārāshtra
Assam
Meghālaya
NEPAL
BHUTAN
DRUK
BANGLADESH
Kachin
Chin
Shan
MYANMAR
BURMA
MUANG THAI
THAILAND
LAOS
VIET-NAM
Bay of Bengal
INDIAN OCEAN
Mouths of the Ganges
SUNDARBANS
EASTERN GHATS
CHOTANAGPUR PLATEAU
ALMA-ATA
FRUNZE
KARAGANDA
SEMIPALATINSK
UST-KAMENOGORSK
IRKUTSK
ULAN-BATOR
ÜRÜMQI
LANZHOU
CHENGDU
CHONGQING (CHUNGKING)
KUNMING
GUIYANG
HA NOI
HAI PHONG
DELHI
NEW DELHI
LAHORE
KĀNPUR
LUCKNOW
PATNA
CALCUTTA
DHAKA
KATHMANDU
MANDALAY
YANGON
RANGOON
VISHĀKHAPATNAM
Area occupied by Pakistan and claimed by India.
Area claimed and occupied by India; status disputed by Pakistan.
Area occupied by China and claimed by India.
Area occupied by India and claimed by China.
M
Ft
6000 19685
5000 16404
4000 13123
3000 9843
2000 6562
1000 3281
500 1640
+200 +656
0
Depr.
0
-100 -328
200 656
1000 3281
2000 6562
4000 13123
6000 19685
8000 26247
Scale 1:12,000,000
Delisle Conic Equidistant Projection
0 200 400 600 800 km
0 200 400 miles

NIPPON
JAPAN
CHOSŎN M.I.K.
NORTH KOREA
TAEHAN-MIN'GUK
SOUTH KOREA
Japan Basin
SEA OF JAPAN
YELLOW SEA
EAST CHINA SEA
DONG HAI / HIGASHI-SHINA-KAI
HUANG HAI / HWANG-HAE
SOUTH CHINA SEA
NAN HAI
South China Basin
Philippine Basin
PHILIPPINE SEA
PACIFIC OCEAN
Tropic of Cancer
Shikoku Basin
Nankai Trough
Ryukyu Trench
RYUKYU ISLANDS
NANSEI-SHOTŌ
TAIWAN
PHILIPPINES
PILIPINAS
LUZON
HAINAN
Hong Kong (U.K.)
BEIJING PEKING
TIANJIN (TIENTSIN)
SHANGHAI
NANJING (NANKING)
WUHAN
HARBIN
SHENYANG
DALIAN
P'YŎNGYANG
SEOUL SŎUL
PUSAN
TŌKYŌ
YOKOHAMA
ŌSAKA
KYŌTO
NAGOYA
SAPPORO
VLADIVOSTOK
HABAROVSK
Russian SFSR
Rossijskaja SFSR
Nei Mongol Zizhiqu
Inner Mongolia
GOBI
HOKKAIDŌ
HONSHŪ
SHIKOKU
KYŪSHŪ
ZHONGHUA
RENMIN
GONGHEGUO
CHINA
1 Beijing Shi
2 Shanghai Shi
3 Tianjin Shi
Longitude East 120 of Greenwich
A-569700-780-1 -1 -2 -3

Map 28 NORTHEASTERN CHINA, KOREA AND JAPAN

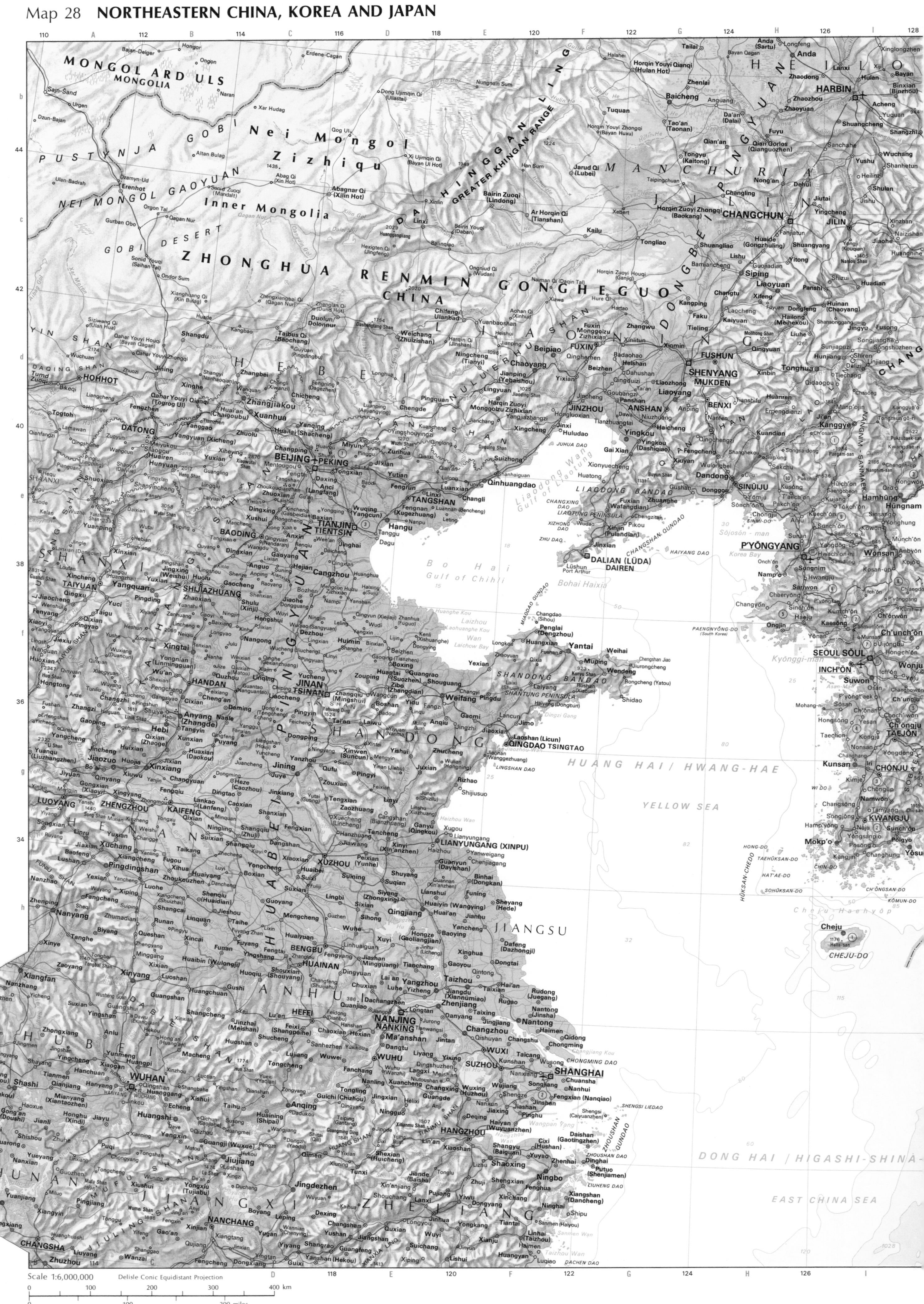

Scale 1:6,000,000 Delisle Conic Equidistant Projection

0 100 200 300 400 km

0 100 200 miles

NIPPON
JAPAN
CHOSŎN M.I.K.
NORTH KOREA
TAEHAN-MIN'GUK
SOUTH KOREA
U S S R
HOKKAIDŌ
HONSHŪ
SHIKOKU
KYŪSHŪ
JAPONSKOJE MORE/
TONG-HAE/NIPPON-KAI
SEA OF JAPAN
Japan Basin
Yamato Rise
OHOTSKOJE MORE/
HOK-KAI
SEA OF OHOTSK
TAIHEIYŌ
PACIFIC OCEAN
Japan Trench
Bonin Trench
Nankai Trench
Shikoku Basin
South Honshu Ridge
Izu-shotō
Oki Ridge
SAPPORO
HAKODATE
AOMORI
AKITA
SENDAI
NIIGATA
TŌKYŌ
YOKOHAMA
KAWASAKI
NAGOYA
KYŌTO
ŌSAKA
KŌBE
HIROSHIMA
KITAKYŪSHŪ
FUKUOKA
NAGASAKI
KUMAMOTO
KAGOSHIMA
PUSAN
VLADIVOSTOK
CH'ŎNGJIN
NIPPON
JAPAN
1 Hokkaidō Ken
2 Aomori Ken
3 Iwate Ken
4 Miyagi Ken
5 Akita Ken
6 Yamagata Ken
7 Fukushima Ken
8 Ibaraki Ken
9 Tochigi Ken
10 Gunma Ken
11 Saitama Ken
12 Chiba Ken
13 Tōkyō To
14 Kanagawa Ken
15 Niigata Ken
16 Toyama Ken
17 Ishikawa Ken
18 Fukui Ken
19 Yamanashi Ken
20 Nagano Ken
21 Gifu Ken
22 Shizuoka Ken
23 Aichi Ken
24 Mie Ken
25 Shiga Ken
26 Kyōto Fu
27 Ōsaka Fu
28 Hyōgo Ken
29 Nara Ken
30 Wakayama Ken
31 Tottori Ken
32 Shimane Ken
33 Okayama Ken
34 Hiroshima Ken
35 Yamaguchi Ken
36 Tokushima Ken
37 Kagawa Ken
38 Ehime Ken
39 Kōchi Ken
40 Fukuoka Ken
41 Saga Ken
42 Nagasaki Ken
43 Kumamoto Ken
44 Ōita Ken
45 Miyazaki Ken
46 Kagoshima Ken
CHOSŎN M.I.K.
NORTH KOREA
1 Chagang-Do
2 Ch'ŏngjin Si
3 Hamgyŏng-Namdo
4 Hamgyŏng-Pukto
5 Hwanghae-Namdo
6 Hwanghae-Pukto
7 Kaesŏng Si
8 Kangwŏn-Do
9 P'yŏngan-Namdo
10 P'yŏngan-Pukto
11 P'yŏngyang Si
12 Yanggang-Do
TAEHAN-MIN'GUK
SOUTH KOREA
1 Cheju-Do
2 Chŏlla-Namdo
3 Chŏlla-Pukto
4 Ch'ungch'ŏng-Namdo
5 Ch'ungch'ŏng-Pukto
6 Kangwŏn-Do
7 Kyŏnggi-Do
8 Kyŏngsang-Namdo
9 Kyŏngsang-Pukto
10 Pusan Si
11 Sŏul Si
ZHONGHUA RENMIN GONGHEGUO
CHINA
1 Beijing Shi
2 Shanghai Shi
3 Tianjin Shi
M
Ft
3000 9843
2000 6562
1000 3281
500 1640
200 656
+100 +328
0
−100 −328
200 656
1000 3281
2000 6562
4000 13123
6000 19685
8000 26247
Ⓐ Ostrov Kunašir, ostrov Iturup and Malaja Kurilskaja Grjada, occupied by the U.S.S.R. since 1945, are claimed by Japan pending a final peace treaty.
J Longitude East 130 of Greenwich

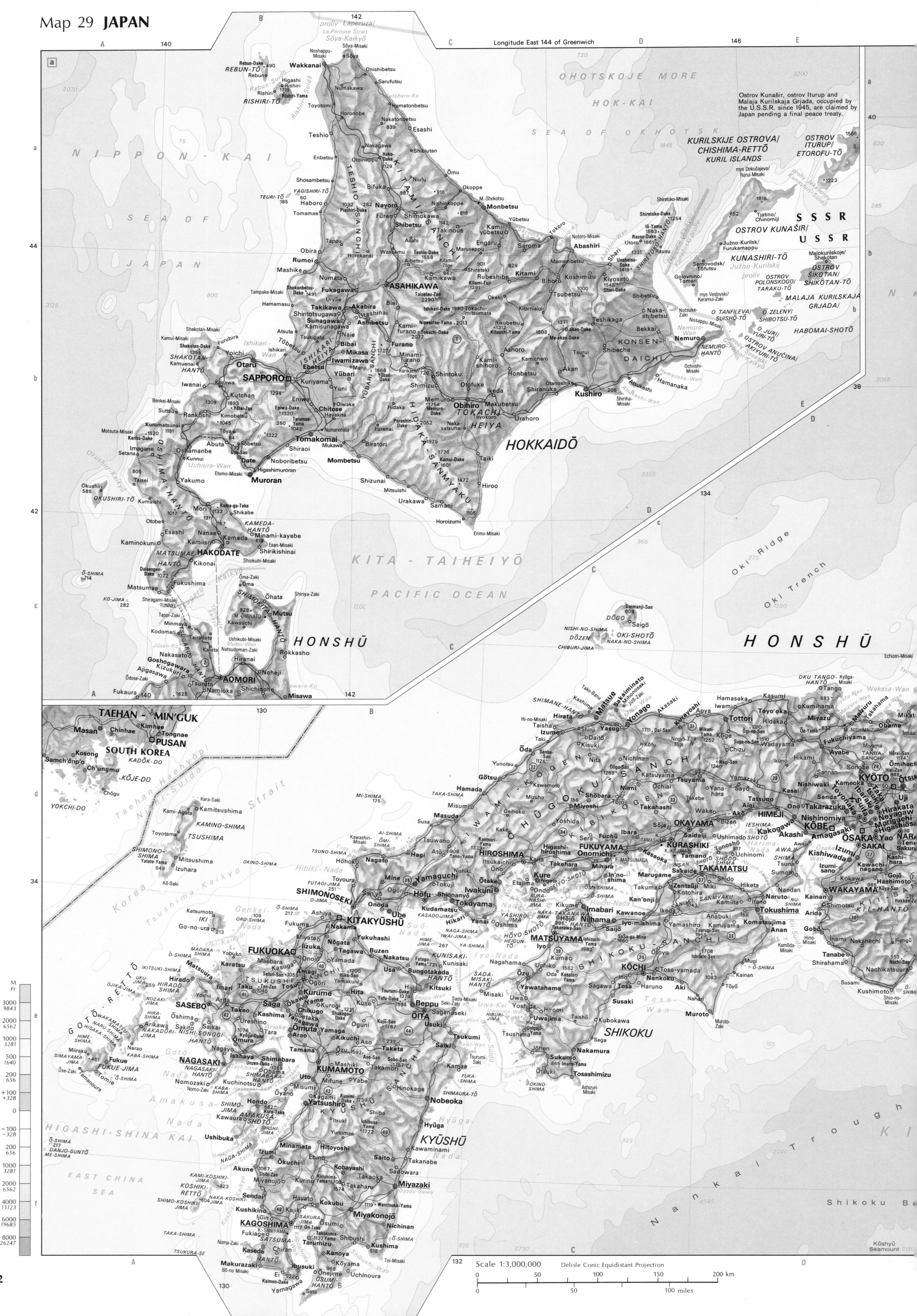
Longitude East 144 of Greenwich
Ostrov Kunašir, ostrov Iturup and Malaja Kurilskaja Grjada, occupied by Japan since 1945, are claimed by the U.S.S.R. pending a final peace treaty.
HOKKAIDŌ
HONSHŪ
SHIKOKU
KYŪSHŪ
SOUTH KOREA
PACIFIC OCEAN
SEA OF JAPAN
SEA OF OKHOTSK
EAST CHINA SEA
Scale 1:3,000,000
Delisle Conic Equidistant Projection

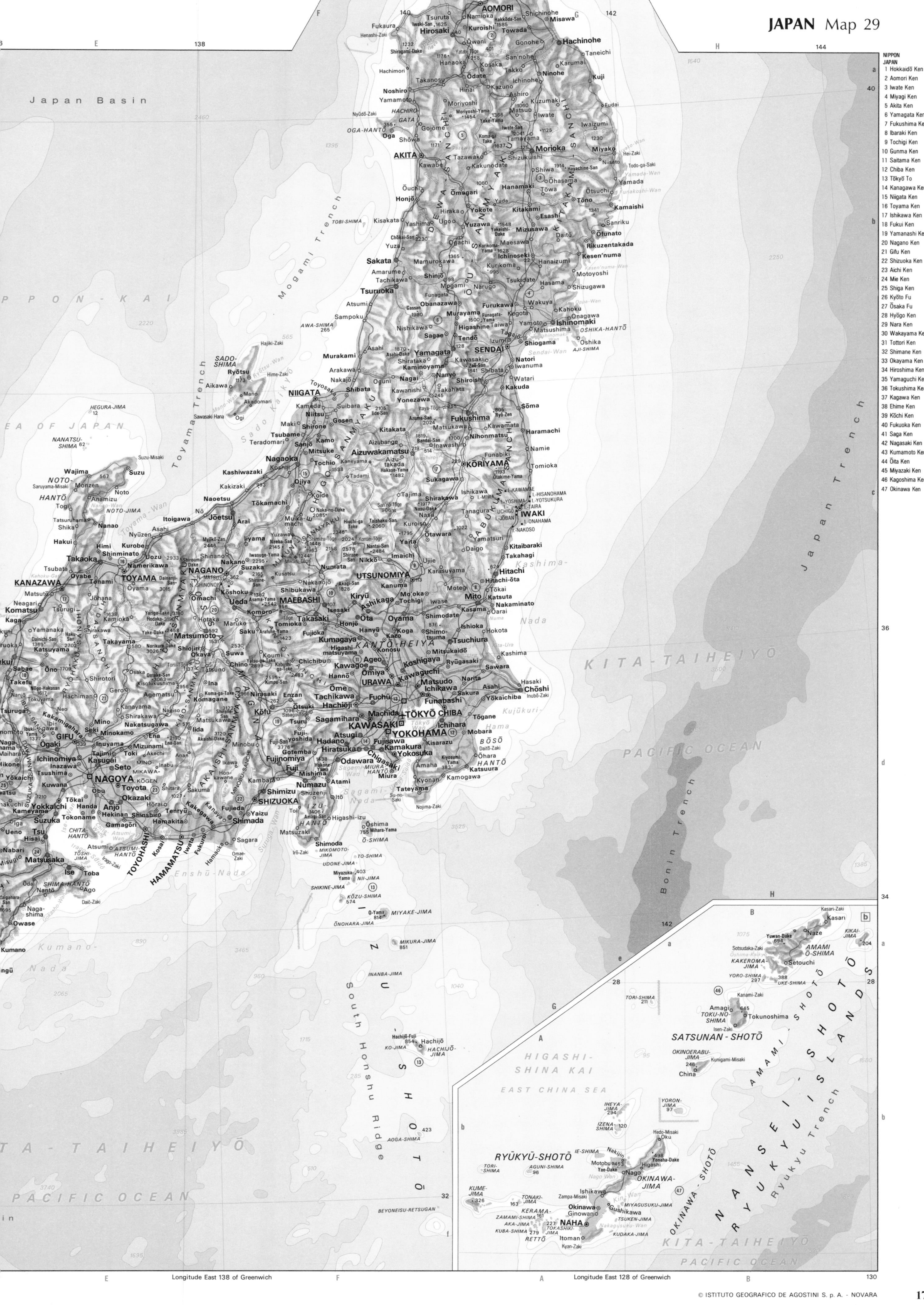
NIPPON
JAPAN
1 Hokkaidō Ken
2 Aomori Ken
3 Iwate Ken
4 Miyagi Ken
5 Akita Ken
6 Yamagata Ken
7 Fukushima Ken
8 Ibaraki Ken
9 Tochigi Ken
10 Gunma Ken
11 Saitama Ken
12 Chiba Ken
13 Tōkyō To
14 Kanagawa Ken
15 Niigata Ken
16 Toyama Ken
17 Ishikawa Ken
18 Fukui Ken
19 Yamanashi Ken
20 Nagano Ken
21 Gifu Ken
22 Shizuoka Ken
23 Aichi Ken
24 Mie Ken
25 Shiga Ken
26 Kyōto Fu
27 Ōsaka Fu
28 Hyōgo Ken
29 Nara Ken
30 Wakayama Ken
31 Tottori Ken
32 Shimane Ken
33 Okayama Ken
34 Hiroshima Ken
35 Yamaguchi Ken
36 Tokushima Ken
37 Kagawa Ken
38 Ehime Ken
39 Kōchi Ken
40 Fukuoka Ken
41 Saga Ken
42 Nagasaki Ken
43 Kumamoto Ken
44 Ōita Ken
45 Miyazaki Ken
46 Kagoshima Ken
47 Okinawa Ken
Japan Basin
NIPPON-KAI
SEA OF JAPAN
Mogami Trench
Toyama Trench
Sado Kaikyō
SADO-SHIMA
NOTO-HANTŌ
AOMORI
Hirosaki
Hachinohe
AKITA
Morioka
Miyako
Kamaishi
Sakata
Tsuruoka
Yamagata
SENDAI
Ishinomaki
NIIGATA
Nagaoka
Fukushima
KŌRIYAMA
Aizuwakamatsu
Iwaki
UTSUNOMIYA
MAEBASHI
Mito
Hitachi
NAGANO
TOYAMA
KANAZAWA
GIFU
NAGOYA
SHIZUOKA
Hamamatsu
Toyohashi
KAWASAKI
TŌKYŌ
CHIBA
YOKOHAMA
Chōshi
KANTŌ-HEIYA
BŌSŌ HANTŌ
IZU-HANTŌ
Enshū-Nada
Kumano-Nada
Kashima-Nada
KITA-TAIHEIYŌ
PACIFIC OCEAN
Japan Trench
Bonin Trench
IZU-SHOTŌ
South Honshu Ridge
Ōshima
MIYAKE-JIMA
HACHIJŌ-JIMA
AOGA-SHIMA
BEYONEISU-RETSUGAN
HIGASHI-SHINA KAI
EAST CHINA SEA
SATSUNAN-SHOTŌ
AMAMI-SHOTŌ
AMAMI Ō-SHIMA
TOKU-NO-SHIMA
OKINOERABU-JIMA
RYŪKYŪ-SHOTŌ
OKINAWA-JIMA
OKINAWA-SHOTŌ
NAHA
NANSEI-SHOTŌ
RYUKYU ISLANDS
Ryukyu Trench
KERAMA-RETTŌ
Longitude East 138 of Greenwich
Longitude East 128 of Greenwich

Gulf of Guinea
Equator
Guinea Basin
Guinea Rise
Mid-Atlantic Ridge
Romanche Gap
ASCENSION
859
OCEAN
Brazil Basin
SAINT HELENA
862
Angola Basin
ILHA DA TRINDADE
ILHAS MARTIM VAZ
Tropic of Capricorn
Walvis Ridge
Ewing Seamount
Valdivia Seamount
Vema Seamount
Wüst Seamount
Cape Basin
TRISTAN DA CUNHA
INACCESSIBLE
NIGHTINGALE
TRISTAN DA CUNHA GROUP
GOUGH
Discovery Tablemount
Cape Rise
Agulhas Basin
Agulhas Plateau
Argentine Basin
Meteor Seamount
Atlantic-Indian Ridge
BOUVET
932
Falkland Plateau
Scotia Ridge
SHAG ROCKS
SOUTH GEORGIA
East Scotia Basin
Scotia Sea
South Sandwich Trench
Meteor Depth
SOUTH SANDWICH ISLANDS
Atlantic-Indian Basin
Maud Seamount
CONGO BASIN
MONTS MITUMBA
SOUTHERN GUINEA
PLANALTO DO BIE
KALAHARI DESERT
NAMIB DESERT
HOE KAROO
GROOT KAROO
DRAKENSBERG
LEBOMBO MTS.
WILD COAST
Cape Town/Kaapstad
Cape of Good Hope
Kaap Agulhas
Port Elizabeth
Durban
Maputo
Pretoria
Gaborone
Windhoek
Lüderitz
Walvisbaai
Bulawayo
Harare
Lusaka
Lubumbashi
Luanda
Benguela
Kinshasa
Brazzaville
Libreville
Kampala
Nairobi
Mombasa
Dar es Salaam
Mogadishu
ZANZIBAR
PEMBA
MAFIA
BAJUN ISLANDS
PATTA ISLAND
JUBALAND
Somali Basin
SEYCHELLES ISLANDS
AMIRANTE ISLANDS
ALDABRA ISLANDS
COMORO ISLANDS
AGALEGA ISLANDS
Mascarene Plateau
Mascarene Basin
CARGADOS CARAJOS ISLANDS
MASCARENE ISLANDS
MAURITIUS
RÉUNION
RODRIGUES
Mid-Indian Ridge
MADAGASCAR
Antsiranana
Toliara
Mozambique Channel
BASSAS DA INDIA
EUROPA
Mozambique Plateau
Natal Basin
Madagascar Plateau
Madagascar Basin
INDIAN OCEAN
Southwest Indian Ridge
Crozet Basin
AMSTERDAM
911
SAINT PAUL
Crozet Ridge
PRINCE EDWARD ISLANDS
ILES CROZET
Ob Tablemount
Lena Tablemount
Limit of icebergs
Winter limit of pack ice (September)
ILES KERGUELEN
MC DONALD ISLANDS
HEARD ISLAND
Kerguelen Plateau
South Indian Basin
Scale 1:30,000,000
Lambert Azimuthal Equal Area Projection
0 500 1000 1500 2000 km
0 500 1000 miles
Longitude East 20 of Greenwich
M Ft
6000 19685
5000 16404
4000 13123
3000 9843
2000 6562
1000 3281
500 1640
+200 +656
0
Depr.
0
−200 −656
1000 3281
2000 6562
4000 13123
6000 19685
8000 26247
A-519394-780-1.-1.-1.-5

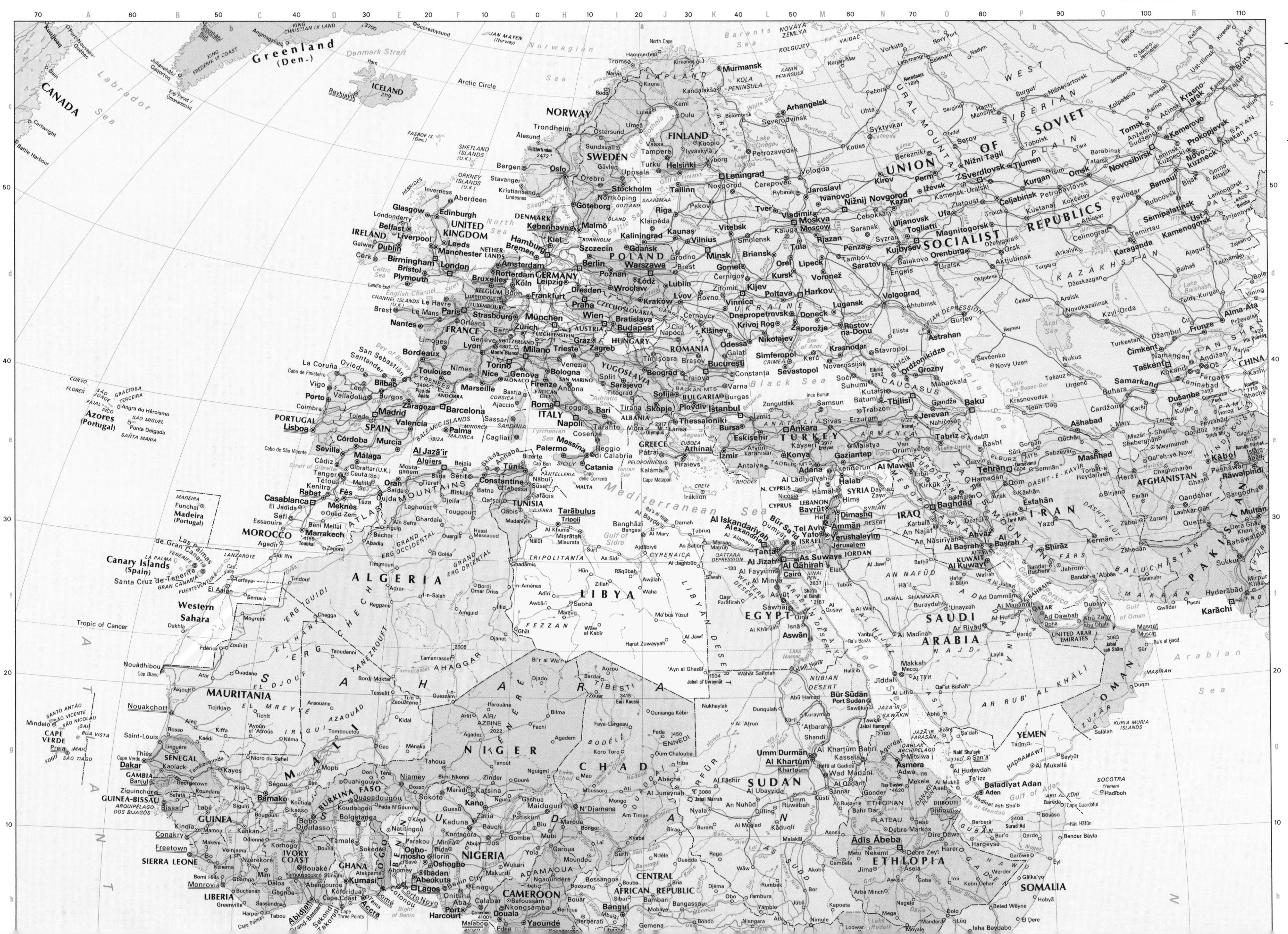
Greenland (Den.)
CANADA
ICELAND
NORWAY
SWEDEN
FINLAND
UNITED KINGDOM
IRELAND
FRANCE
SPAIN
PORTUGAL
ITALY
GERMANY
POLAND
ROMANIA
YUGOSLAVIA
GREECE
TURKEY
UNION OF SOVIET SOCIALIST REPUBLICS
IRAN
IRAQ
AFGHANISTAN
PAKISTAN
SAUDI ARABIA
YEMEN
OMAN
MOROCCO
ALGERIA
LIBYA
EGYPT
SUDAN
CHAD
NIGER
MALI
MAURITANIA
Western Sahara
SENEGAL
GUINEA
SIERRA LEONE
LIBERIA
IVORY COAST
GHANA
NIGERIA
CAMEROON
CENTRAL AFRICAN REPUBLIC
ETHIOPIA
SOMALIA
Mediterranean Sea
Black Sea
Tropic of Cancer
Arctic Circle

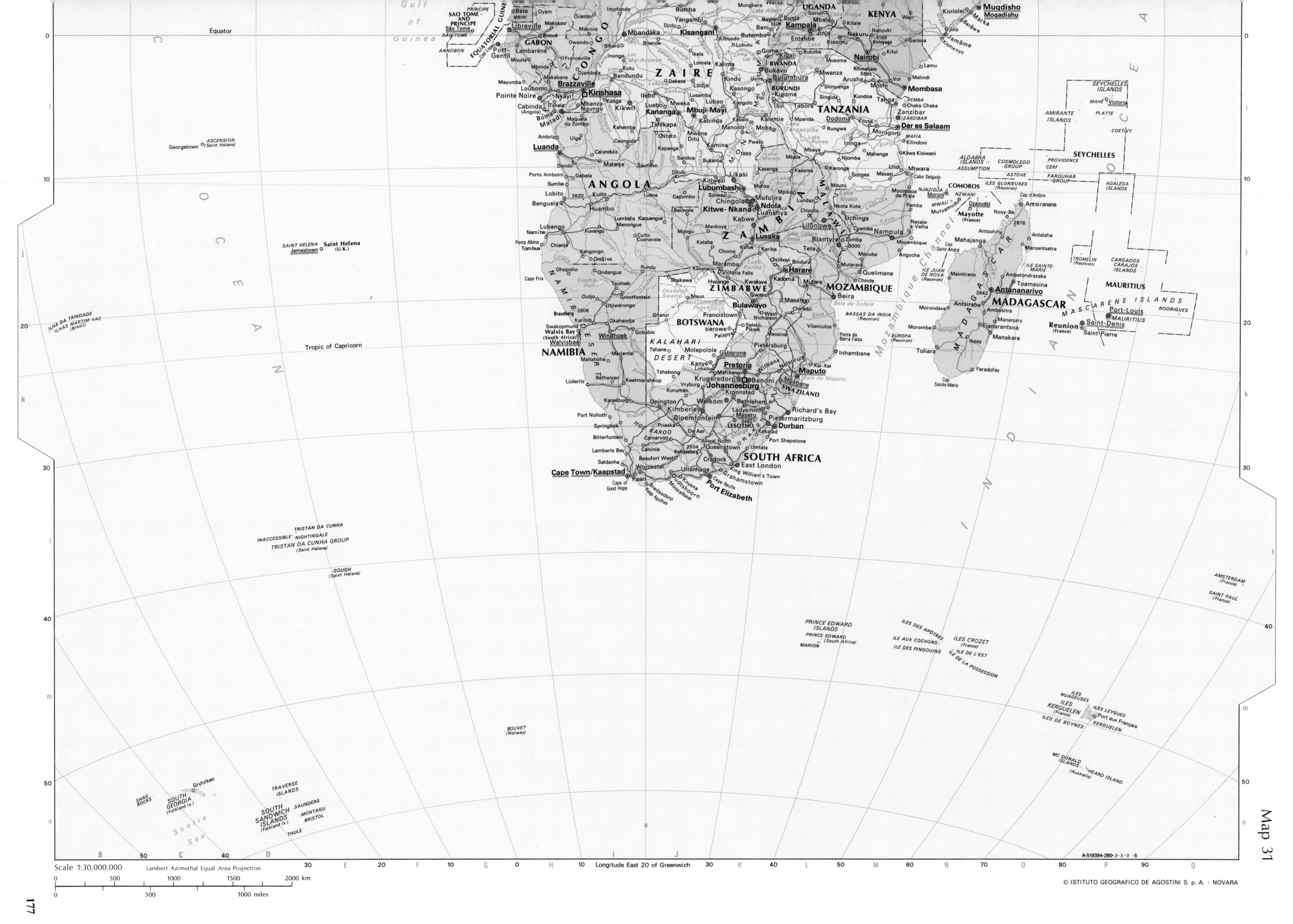
ZAIRE
CONGO
GABON
ANGOLA
NAMIBIA
BOTSWANA
ZIMBABWE
ZAMBIA
MALAWI
MOZAMBIQUE
MADAGASCAR
TANZANIA
KENYA
UGANDA
RWANDA
BURUNDI
SOUTH AFRICA
LESOTHO
SWAZILAND
SEYCHELLES
COMOROS
MAURITIUS
MASCARENE ISLANDS
Mozambique Channel
KALAHARI DESERT
NAMIB DESERT
Tropic of Capricorn
Equator
Gulf of Guinea
INDIAN OCEAN
Saint Helena (U.K.)
Georgetown ASCENSION (Saint Helena)
TRISTAN DA CUNHA GROUP (Saint Helena)
GOUGH (Saint Helena)
BOUVET (Norway)
PRINCE EDWARD ISLANDS
ILES CROZET (France)
ILES KERGUELEN (France)
HEARD ISLAND (Australia)
AMSTERDAM (France)
SAINT PAUL (France)
SOUTH GEORGIA (Falkland Is.)
SOUTH SANDWICH ISLANDS (Falkland Is.)
Reunion (France)
Cape Town/Kaapstad
Johannesburg
Pretoria
Durban
Port Elizabeth
Windhoek
Luanda
Kinshasa
Lusaka
Harare
Maputo
Antananarivo
Dar es Salaam
Nairobi
Mombasa
Scale 1:30,000,000
Lambert Azimuthal Equal Area Projection
Longitude East 20 of Greenwich
© ISTITUTO GEOGRAFICO DE AGOSTINI S. p. A. - NOVARA

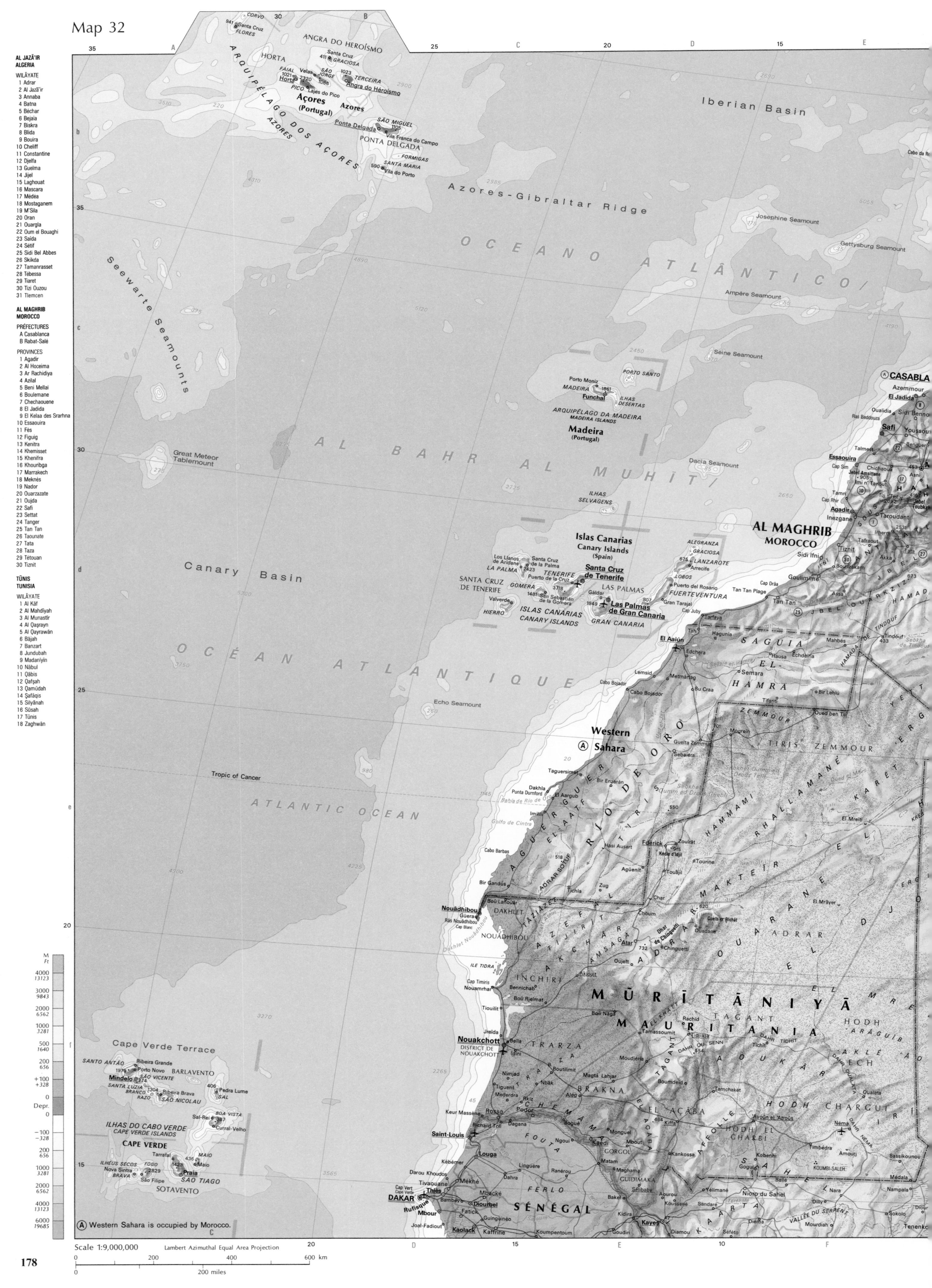
AL JAZĀ'IR
ALGERIA
WILĀYATE
1 Adrar
2 Al Jazā'ir
3 Annaba
4 Batna
5 Béchar
6 Bejaïa
7 Biskra
8 Blida
9 Bouira
10 Cheliff
11 Constantine
12 Djelfa
13 Guelma
14 Jijel
15 Laghouat
16 Mascara
17 Médéa
18 Mostaganem
19 M'Sila
20 Oran
21 Ouargla
22 Oum el Bouaghi
23 Saïda
24 Sétif
25 Sidi Bel Abbes
26 Skikda
27 Tamanrasset
28 Tebessa
29 Tiaret
30 Tizi Ouzou
31 Tlemcen
AL MAGHRIB
MOROCCO
PRÉFECTURES
A Casablanca
B Rabat-Salé
PROVINCES
1 Agadir
2 Al Hoceima
3 Ar Rachidiya
4 Azilal
5 Beni Mellal
6 Boulemane
7 Chechaouene
8 El Jadida
9 El Kelaa des Srarhna
10 Essaouira
11 Fès
12 Figuig
13 Kenitra
14 Khemisset
15 Khenifra
16 Khouribga
17 Marrakech
18 Meknès
19 Nador
20 Ouarzazate
21 Oujda
22 Safi
23 Settat
24 Tanger
25 Tan Tan
26 Taounate
27 Tata
28 Taza
29 Tétouan
30 Tiznit
TŪNIS
TUNISIA
WILĀYATE
1 Al Kāf
2 Al Mahdīyah
3 Al Munastīr
4 Al Qaşrayn
5 Al Qayrawān
6 Bājah
7 Banzart
8 Jundubah
9 Madanīyīn
10 Nābul
11 Qābis
12 Qafşah
13 Qamūdah
14 Şafāqis
15 Silyānah
16 Sūsah
17 Tūnis
18 Zaghwān
ARQUIPÉLAGO DOS AÇORES
Açores (Portugal)
Iberian Basin
Azores-Gibraltar Ridge
OCEANO ATLÂNTICO
Seewarte Seamounts
ARQUIPÉLAGO DA MADEIRA
MADEIRA ISLANDS
Madeira (Portugal)
AL BAHR AL MUHĪT
Great Meteor Tablemount
Islas Canarias
Canary Islands
(Spain)
Canary Basin
AL MAGHRIB
MOROCCO
OCÉAN ATLANTIQUE
Western Sahara
Tropic of Cancer
ATLANTIC OCEAN
MŪRĪTĀNIYĀ
MAURITANIA
Cape Verde Terrace
ILHAS DO CABO VERDE
CAPE VERDE ISLANDS
CAPE VERDE
SÉNÉGAL
Ⓐ Western Sahara is occupied by Morocco.
Scale 1:9,000,000
Lambert Azimuthal Equal Area Projection
0 200 400 600 km
0 200 miles

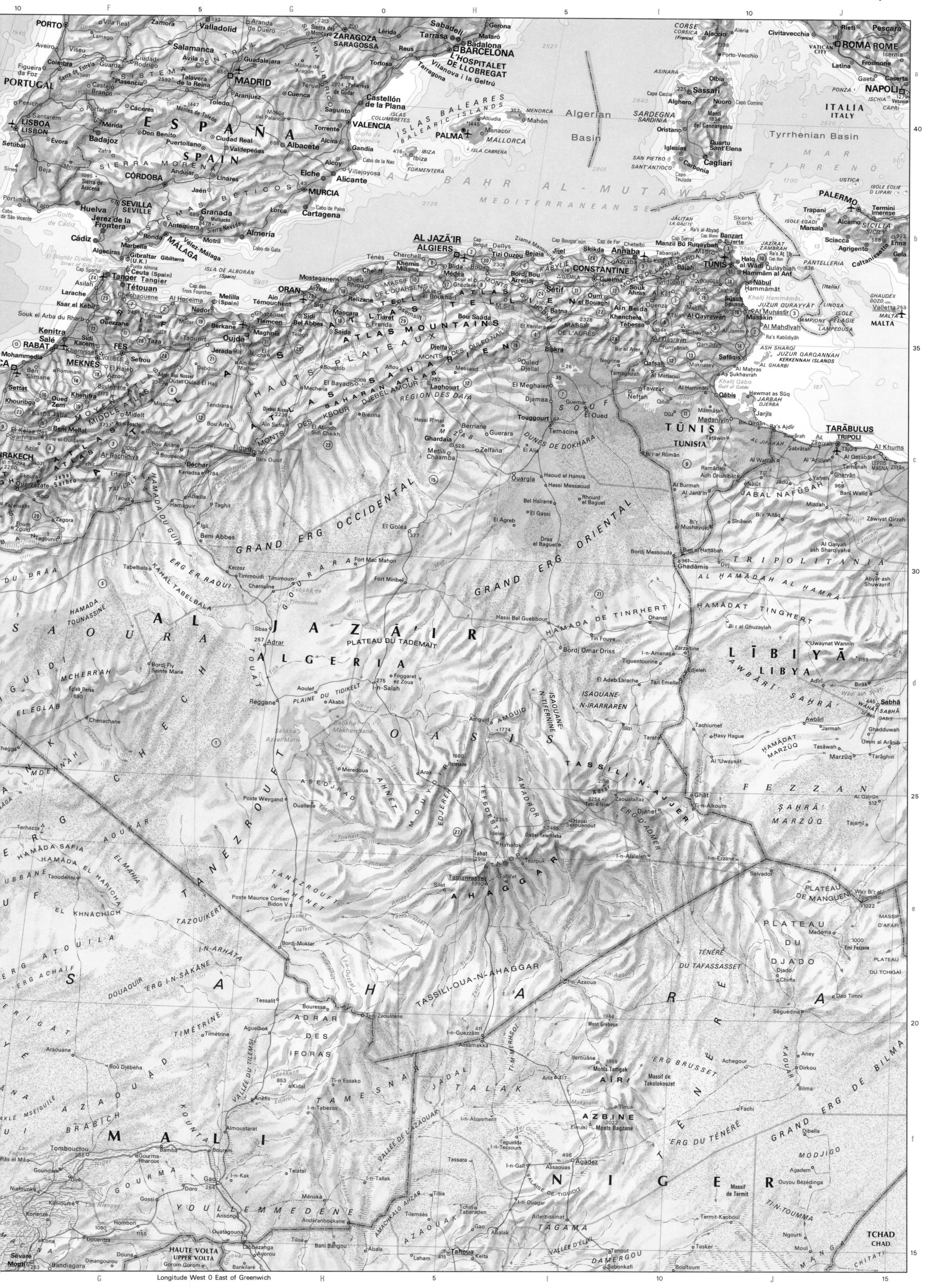
ESPAÑA
SPAIN
PORTUGAL
MADRID
LISBOA
LISBON
BARCELONA
VALENCIA
ISLAS BALEARES
BALEARIC ISLANDS
Algerian Basin
Tyrrhenian Basin
ITALIA
ITALY
ROMA ROME
NAPOLI
SARDEGNA
SARDINIA
MALTA
AL JAZĀ'IR
ALGIERS
ALGERIA
TŪNIS
TUNISIA
LĪBIYĀ
LIBYA
TARĀBULUS
TRIPOLI
RABAT
FÈS
MEKNÈS
ORAN
CONSTANTINE
ATLAS MOUNTAINS
GRAND ERG OCCIDENTAL
GRAND ERG ORIENTAL
PLATEAU DU TADEMAIT
AHAGGAR
TASSILI-N-AJJER
FEZZAN
S A H A R A
MALI
NIGER
TCHAD
CHAD
HAUTE VOLTA
UPPER VOLTA
Tombouctou
Agadez
Tamanrasset
Longitude West 0 East of Greenwich

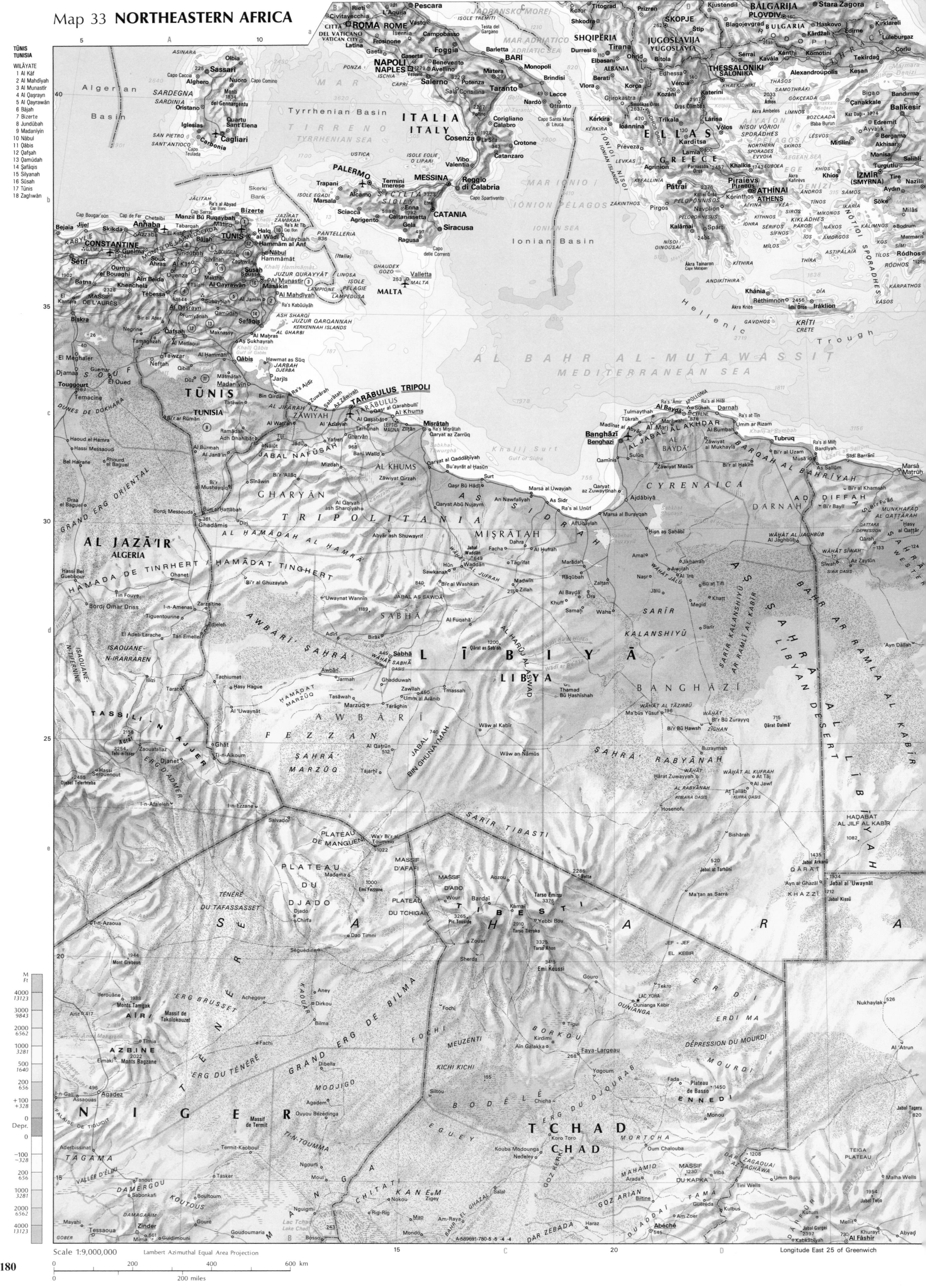

Map 33 NORTHEASTERN AFRICA
TŪNIS
TUNISIA
WILĀYATE
1 Al Kāf
2 Al Mahdīyah
3 Al Munastīr
4 Al Qaşrayn
5 Al Qayrawān
6 Bājah
7 Bizerte
8 Jundūbah
9 Madanīyīn
10 Nābul
11 Qābis
12 Qafşah
13 Qamūdah
14 Şafāqis
15 Silyanah
16 Sūsah
17 Tūnis
18 Zaghwān
Algerian Basin
SARDEGNA
SARDINIA
Cagliari
Tyrrhenian Basin
TIRRENO
TYRRHENIAN SEA
ITALIA
ITALY
ROMA ROME
NAPOLI NAPLES
PALERMO
MESSINA
SICILIA
SICILY
BARI
SHQIPËRIA
Tirana
JUGOSLAVIJA
YUGOSLAVIA
SKOPJE
BĂLGARIJA
THESSALONÍKI
SALONIKA
ELLAS
GREECE
ATHÍNAI
ATHENS
İZMİR
(SMYRNA)
MAR IONIO
IONIAN SEA
Ionian Basin
MALTA
Valletta
Hellenic Trough
KRÍTI
CRETE
AL BAHR AL-MUTAWASSIT
MEDITERRANEAN SEA
CONSTANTINE
Annaba
Bizerte
TŪNIS
Sūsah
Şafāqis
Qābis
TŪNIS
TUNISIA
ȚARĀBULUS TRIPOLI
Mişrātah
Banghāzī
Benghazi
Darnah
Tubruq
Khalīj Surt
Gulf of Sidra
CYRENAICA
TRIPOLITANIA
GHARYĀN
AL KHUMS
AS SIDRAH
MIŞRĀTAH
DARNAH
AL JAZĀ'IR
ALGERIA
GRAND ERG ORIENTAL
HAMADA DE TINRHERT / HAMĀDAT TINGHERT
AL ḨAMĀDAH AL ḨAMRĀ'
AWBĀRĪ
SABHĀ
Sabhā
LĪBIYĀ
LIBYA
FEZZAN
BANGHĀZĪ
SARĪR KALANSHIYŪ
AS SAHRĀ' AL LĪBĪYAH
LIBYAN DESERT
BAHR AR RAMLA AL KABĪR
SAHRĀ' RABYĀNAH
TASSILI-N-AJJER
ERG D'ADMER
SARĪR TIBASTI
PLATEAU DE MANGUENI
PLATEAU DU DJADO
TÉNÉRÉ DU TAFASSASSET
TIBESTI
Emi Koussi
SAHARA
ERG BRUSSET
AÏR
AZBINE
GRAND ERG DE BILMA
ERG DU TÉNÉRÉ
BORKOU
Faya-Largeau
ERDI MA
DÉPRESSION DU MOURDI
ENNEDI
BODÉLÉ
NIGER
TCHAD
CHAD
KANEM
Agadez
Zinder
Abéché
Lac Tchad
Lake Chad
M
Ft
4000 13123
3000 9843
2000 6562
1000 3281
500 1640
200 656
+100 +328
0
Depr.
0
-100 -328
200 656
1000 3281
2000 6562
4000 13123
Scale 1:9,000,000
Lambert Azimuthal Equal Area Projection
0 200 400 600 km
0 200 miles
Longitude East 25 of Greenwich

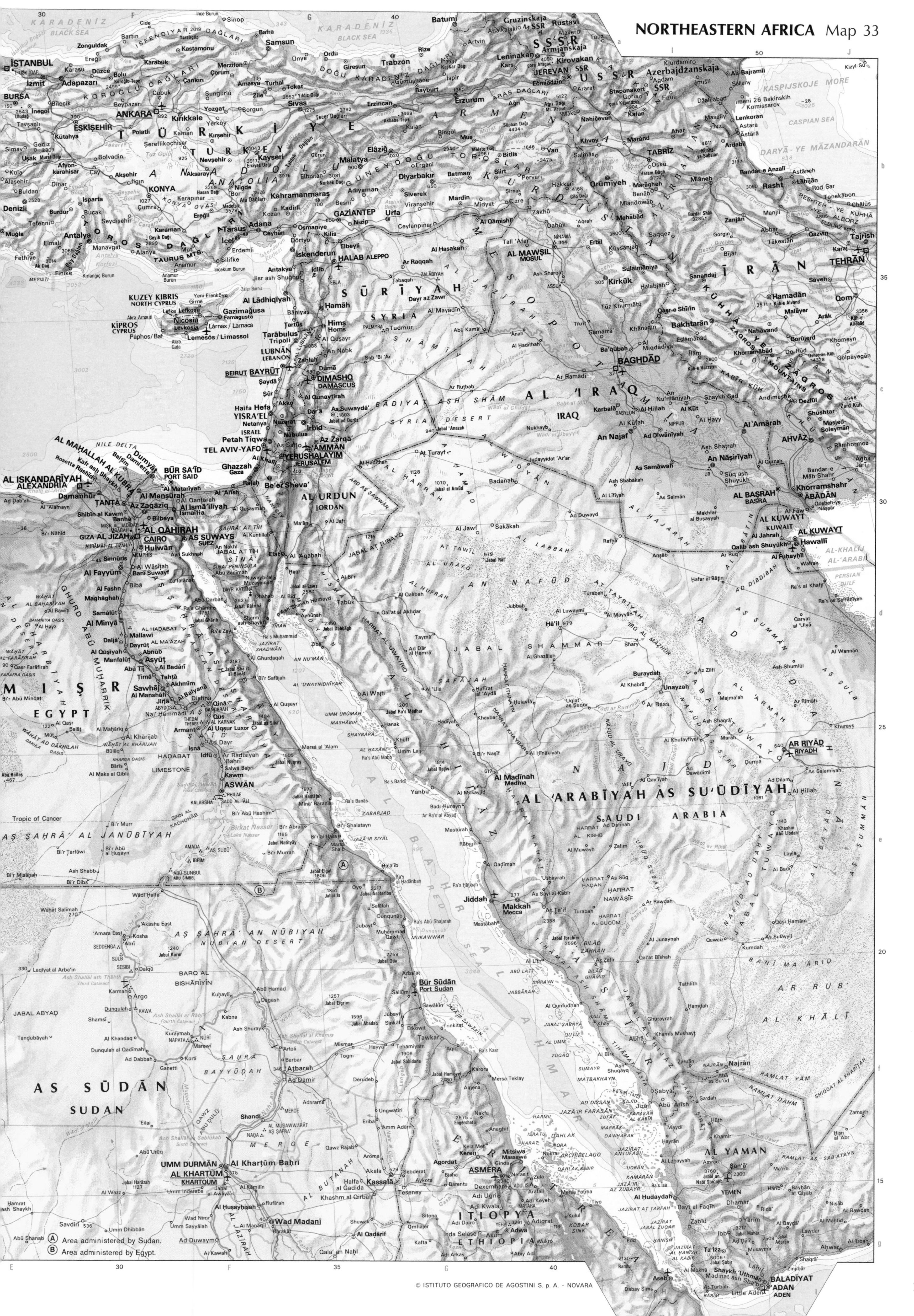
KARADENIZ
BLACK SEA
İSTANBUL
BURSA
ANKARA
TÜRKİYE
TURKEY
ANADOLU
ANATOLIA
KONYA
Adana
TOROS DAĞLARI
TAURUS MTS.
KUZEY KIBRIS
NORTH CYPRUS
KÍPROS
CYPRUS
Nicosia
Batumi
SSSR
USSR
Azerbajdžanskaja SSR
Armjanskaja SSR
JEREVAN
KASPIJSKOJE MORE
CASPIAN SEA
ARMENIA
KURDISTAN
TABRĪZ
TEHRĀN
ĪRĀN
ZAGROS MOUNTAINS
SŪRĪYAH
SYRIA
HALAB ALEPPO
Al Lādhiqīyah
Ḥimṣ
Ḥamāh
LUBNĀN
LEBANON
BEIRUT BAYRŪT
DIMASHQ
DAMASCUS
YISRA'EL
ISRAEL
TEL AVIV-YAFO
YERUSHALAYIM
JERUSALEM
'AMMĀN
AL URDUN
JORDAN
MESOPOTAMIA
AL MAWṢIL
MOSUL
BAGHDĀD
AL 'IRĀQ
IRAQ
BĀDIYAT ASH SHĀM
SYRIAN DESERT
AL BAṢRAH
BASRA
AL KUWAYT
KUWAIT
AL-KHALĪJ AL-'ARABĪ
PERSIAN GULF
AN NAFŪD
AL ISKANDARĪYAH
ALEXANDRIA
NILE DELTA
BŪR SA'ĪD
PORT SAID
AL QĀHIRAH
CAIRO
AS SUWAYS
SUEZ
SĪNĀ'
SINAI PENINSULA
MIṢR
EGYPT
Tropic of Cancer
ASWĀN
AŞ ŞAḤRĀ' AN NŪBIYAH
NUBIAN DESERT
AS SŪDĀN
SUDAN
UMM DURMĀN
AL KHARṬŪM
KHARTOUM
Būr Sūdān
Port Sudan
AL BAḤR AL AḤMAR
RED SEA
AL ḤIJĀZ
NAJD
AL 'ARABĪYAH AS SU'ŪDĪYAH
SAUDI ARABIA
AR RIYĀḌ
RIYADH
Al Madīnah
Medina
Makkah
Mecca
Jiddah
AR RUB' AL KHĀLĪ
AL YAMAN
YEMEN
Ṣan'ā'
BALADĪYAT ADAN
ADEN
ASMERA
ERITREA
ITIOPYA
ETHIOPIA
Area administered by Sudan.
Area administered by Egypt.

WEST-CENTRAL AFRICA

LIBERIA

COUNTIES
1 Bong
2 Cape Mount
3 Grand Bassa
4 Grand Gedeh
5 Lofa
6 Maryland
7 Montserrado
8 Nimba
9 Sinoe

**CÔTE D'IVOIRE
IVORY COAST**

DÉPARTEMENTS
1 Abengourou
2 Abidjan
3 Aboisso
4 Adzopé
5 Agboville
6 Biankouma
7 Bondoukou
8 Bongouanou
9 Bouaflé
10 Bouaké
11 Bouna
12 Boundiali
13 Dabakala
14 Daloa
15 Danané
16 Dimbokro
17 Divo
18 Ferkessédougou
19 Gagnoa
20 Guiglo
21 Issia
22 Katiola
23 Korhogo
24 Lakota
25 Man
26 Mankono
27 Odienné
28 Oumé
29 Sassandra
30 Séguéla
31 Soubré
32 Tengréla
33 Touba
34 Zuenoula

**HAUTE-VOLTA
UPPER VOLTA**

DÉPARTEMENTS
1 Centre
2 Centre-Est
3 Centre-Nord
4 Centre-Ouest
5 Est
6 Hauts-Bassins
7 Komoé
8 Nord
9 Sahel
10 Sud-Ouest
11 Volta Noire

TOGO

RÉGIONS
1 Centre
2 Kara
3 Maritime
4 Plateaux
5 Savanes

BÉNIN

PROVINCES
1 Atakora
2 Atlantique
3 Borgou
4 Mono
5 Ouémé
6 Zou

(A) Abuja is the future federal capital of Nigeria.
(B) The political subdivisions shown for Guinea represent statistical areas and are not recognized for administrative purposes.

Scale 1:9,000,000 Lambert Azimuthal Equal Area Projection

0 200 400 600 km
0 200 miles

Longitude West 5 of Greenwich

A-589495-280

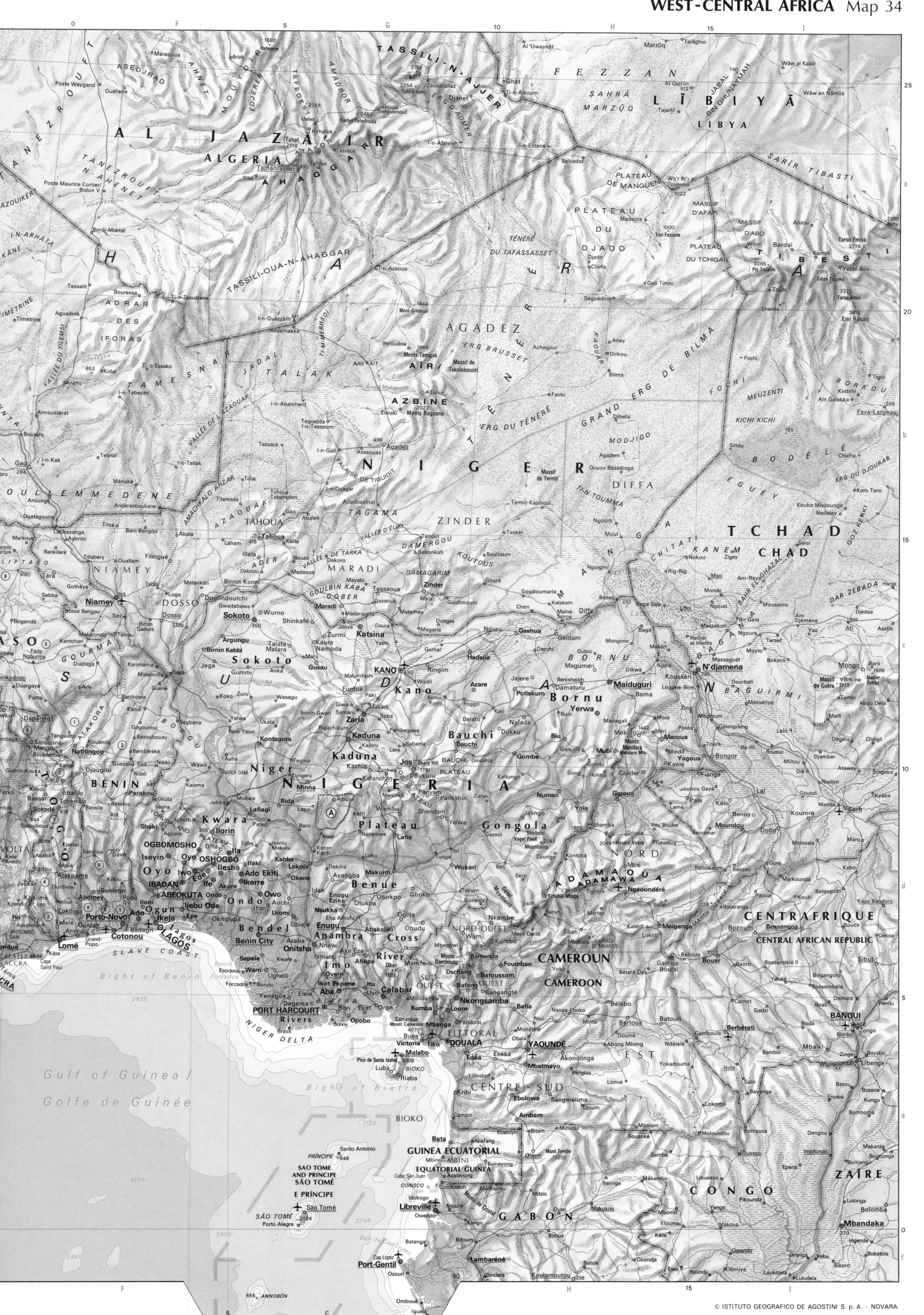
AL JAZĀ'IR
ALGERIA
LĪBIYĀ
LIBYA
FEZZAN
NIGER
TCHAD
CHAD
NIGERIA
CAMEROUN
CAMEROON
CENTRAFRIQUE
CENTRAL AFRICAN REPUBLIC
GUINEA ECUATORIAL
EQUATORIAL GUINEA
SAO TOME AND PRINCIPE
SÃO TOMÉ E PRÍNCIPE
GABON
CONGO
ZAÏRE
BÉNIN
TOGO
AHAGGAR
TASSILI-N-AJJER
TASSILI-OUA-N-AHAGGAR
AÏR
TIBESTI
BORKOU
BODÉLÉ
TÉNÉRÉ
GRAND ERG DE BILMA
ERG DU TÉNÉRÉ
PLATEAU DU DJADO
AGADEZ
ZINDER
MARADI
TAHOUA
NIAMEY
DOSSO
DIFFA
KANEM
BORNU
Sokoto
Kano
Kaduna
Bauchi
Plateau
Gongola
Kwara
Oyo
Ondo
Ogun
Lagos
Bendel
Anambra
Imo
Rivers
Cross River
Benue
Niger
Niamey
Sokoto
KANO
Zaria
Kaduna
Jos
Maiduguri
N'djamena
IBADAN
OGBOMOSHO
OSHOGBO
ABEOKUTA
LAGOS
Porto-Novo
Cotonou
Lomé
Benin City
Onitsha
Enugu
PORT HARCOURT
Calabar
DOUALA
YAOUNDÉ
Malabo
BIOKO
Bata
Libreville
Port-Gentil
São Tomé
BANGUI
Mbandaka
Sarh
Garoua
Ngaoundéré
NIGER DELTA
SLAVE COAST
Bight of Benin
Bight of Biafra
Gulf of Guinea
Golfe de Guinée
ANNOBÓN

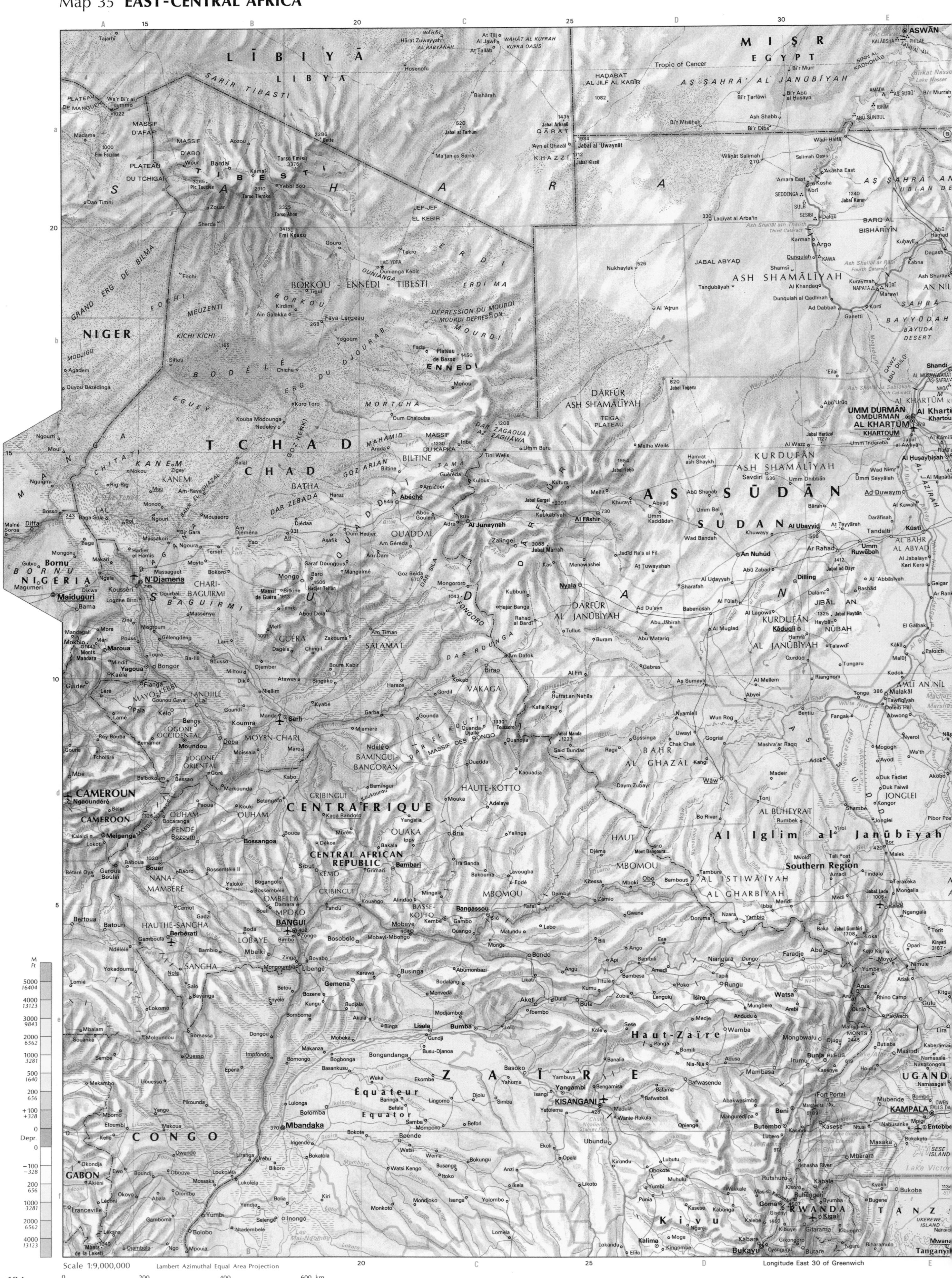
LĪBIYĀ
LIBYA
MIṢR
EGYPT
Tropic of Cancer
AṢ ṢAḤRĀ' AL JANŪBĪYAH
NIGER
TCHAD
CHAD
AS SŪDĀN
SUDAN
NIGERIA
CAMEROUN
CAMEROON
CENTRAFRIQUE
CENTRAL AFRICAN REPUBLIC
CONGO
GABON
ZAÏRE
RWANDA
UGANDA
TIBESTI
BORKOU - ENNEDI - TIBESTI
ENNEDI
BODÉLÉ
KANEM
BATHA
BILTINE
OUADDAÏ
GUÉRA
SALAMAT
CHARI-BAGUIRMI
MAYO-KEBBI
TANDJILÉ
LOGONE OCCIDENTAL
LOGONE ORIENTAL
MOYEN-CHARI
VAKAGA
BAMINGUI-BANGORAN
HAUTE-KOTTO
OUHAM
OUHAM-PENDÉ
OUAKA
NANA-MAMBÉRÉ
KEMO-GRIBINGUI
OMBELLA-MPOKO
BASSE-KOTTO
MBOMOU
HAUT-MBOMOU
LOBAYE
HAUTE-SANGHA
SANGHA
ASH SHAMĀLĪYAH
DĀRFŪR ASH SHAMĀLĪYAH
DĀRFŪR AL JANŪBĪYAH
KURDUFĀN ASH SHAMĀLĪYAH
KURDUFĀN AL JANŪBĪYAH
BAḤR AL GHAZĀL
AL BUḤEYRAT
JONGLEI
Al Iqlīm al Janūbīyah
Southern Region
AL ISTIWĀ'ĪYAH AL GHARBĪYAH
Haut-Zaïre
Équateur
Equator
Kivu
N'Djamena
Al Kharṭūm
KHARTOUM
Umm Durmān
OMDURMAN
Bangui
Kisangani
Mbandaka
Kampala
Aswān
Lake Victoria
Scale 1:9,000,000
Lambert Azimuthal Equal Area Projection
Longitude East 30 of Greenwich
0 200 400 600 km
0 200 miles

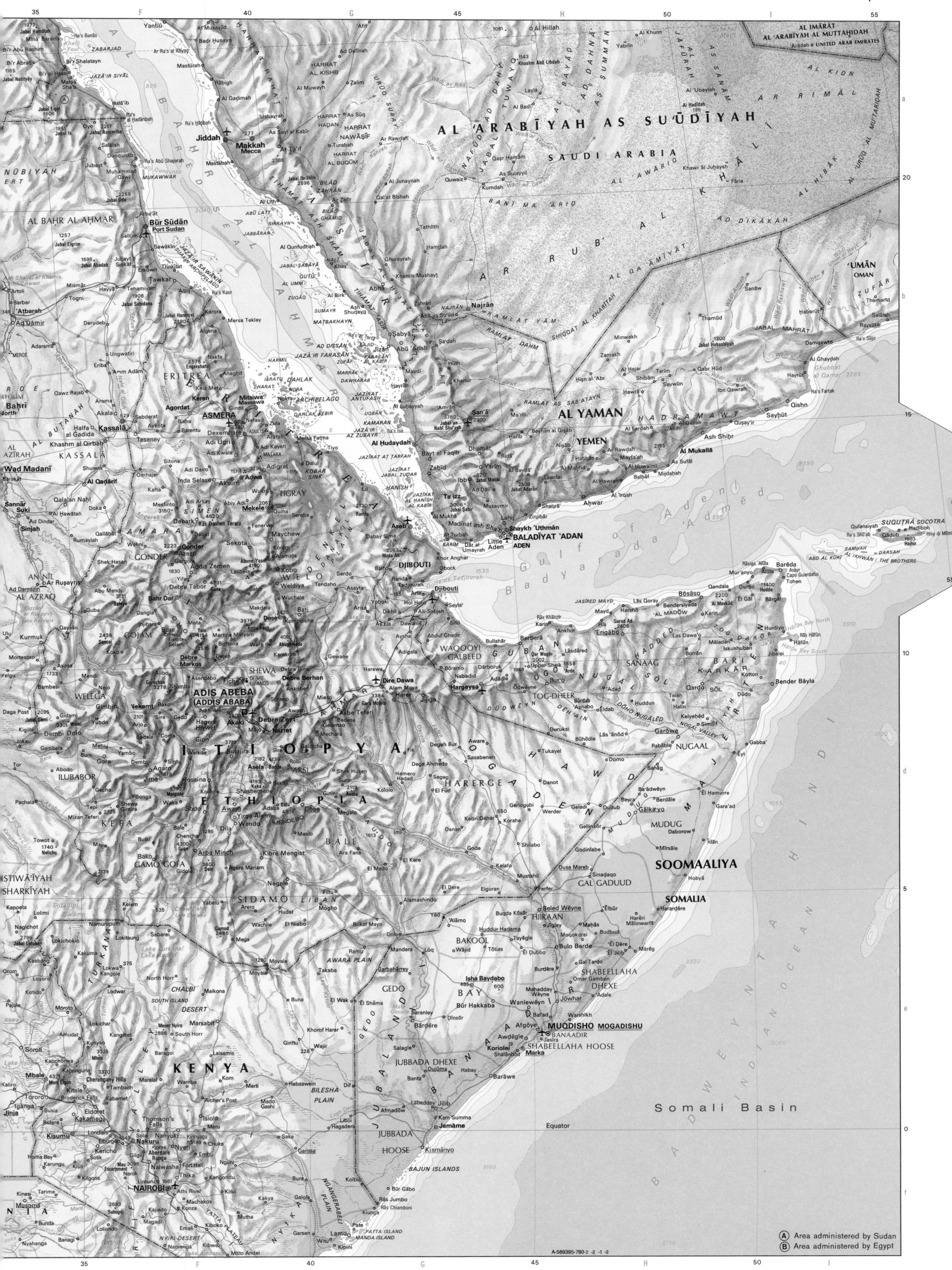

NIGERIA
CAMEROUN
CAMEROON
CENTRAFRIQUE
CENTRAL AFRICAN REPUBLIC
GUINEA ECUATORIAL
EQUATORIAL GUINEA
SÃO TOMÉ E PRINCIPE
GABON
CONGO
ZAÏRE
ANGOLA
Namibia
BOTSWANA
OCÉAN ATLANTIQUE
OCEANO ATLÂNTICO
ATLANTIC OCEAN
Angola Basin
Bight of Biafra
YAOUNDÉ
DOUALA
BANGUI
Libreville
BRAZZAVILLE
KINSHASA
LUANDA
Pointe Noire
Port-Gentil
Matadi
Mbandaka
KISANGANI
KANANGA
MBUJI-MAYI
Équateur
Bandundu
Kasai Occidental
Kasai Oriental
Bas-Zaïre
Shaba
BAROTSELAND
CAPRIVI ZIPFEL
CAPRIVI STRIP
OVAMBOLAND
SKELETON COAST
Scale 1:9,000,000
Lambert Azimuthal Equal Area Projection
0 200 400 600 km
0 200 miles

Al Iqlīm al Janūbīyah
Southern Region
AS SŪDĀN
SUDAN
ĪTIOPYA
ETHIOPIA
KENYA
UGANDA
SOOMAALIYA
SOMALIA
RWANDA
BURUNDI
TANZANIA
Tanganyika
Zanzibar
INDIAN OCEAN
ZAMBIA
MALAWI
ZIMBABWE
MOÇAMBIQUE
MOZAMBIQUE
MADAGASIKARA
MADAGASCAR
COMOROS / COMOROS
ARCHIPEL DES COMORES
SEYCHELLES
Canal de Moçambique
Mozambique Channel
MUQDISHO
MOGADISHU
NAIROBI
MOMBASA
KAMPALA
DAR ES SALAAM
LUSAKA
HARARE
LUBUMBASHI
Blantyre
Lilongwe
Nampula
ANTANANARIVO
Mahajanga
Mayotte (France)
Lake Victoria
Lake Tanganyika
Lake Turkana / Lake Rudolf
Longitude East 30 of Greenwich
A-589500-780-1 -1 -1 -2

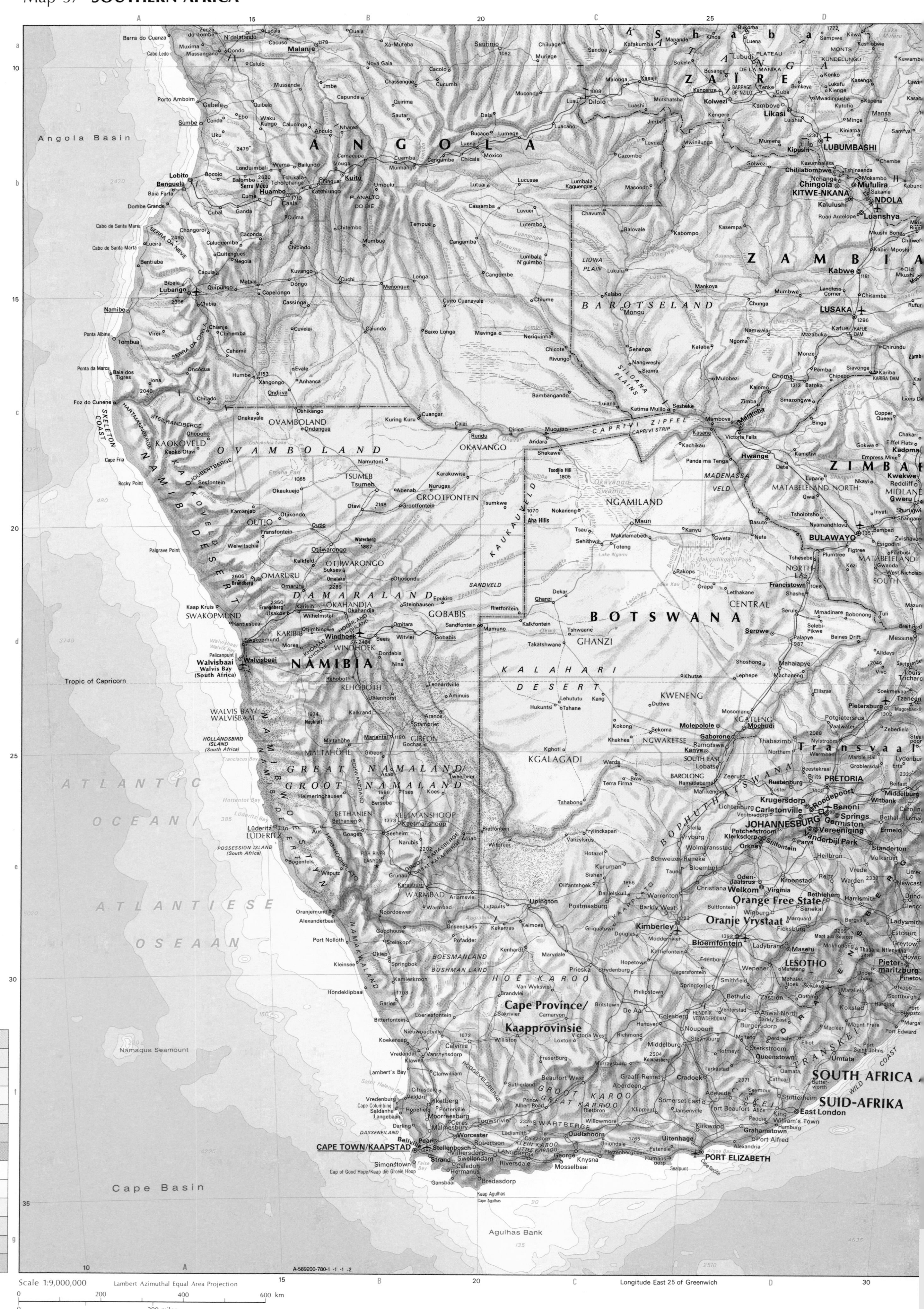
ANGOLA
ZAIRE
ZAMBIA
ZIMBABWE
NAMIBIA
BOTSWANA
SOUTH AFRICA
SUID-AFRIKA
LESOTHO
Angola Basin
ATLANTIC OCEAN
ATLANTIESE OSEAAN
Cape Basin
Agulhas Bank
Namaqua Seamount
Tropic of Capricorn
Walvis Bay (South Africa)
WALVIS BAY/ WALVISBAAI
HOLLANDSBIRD ISLAND (South Africa)
POSSESSION ISLAND (South Africa)
OVAMBOLAND
KAOKOVELD
DAMARALAND
GREAT NAMALAND/ GROOT NAMALAND
NAMIB DESERT
NAMIBWOESTYN
SKELETON COAST
CAPRIVI ZIPFEL
BAROTSELAND
NGAMILAND
KALAHARI DESERT
GHANZI
KGALAGADI
KWENENG
CENTRAL
BOPHUTHATSWANA
Transvaal
Orange Free State
Oranje Vrystaat
Cape Province/ Kaapprovinsie
HOE KAROO
GROOT KAROO
GREAT KAROO
TRANSKEI
Luanda
Malanje
Lobito
Benguela
Huambo
Kuito
Lubango
Namibe
Saurimo
Luena
Kolwezi
Likasi
LUBUMBASHI
Chingola
Mufulira
KITWE-NKANA
NDOLA
Luanshya
Kabwe
LUSAKA
Livingstone
Hwange
BULAWAYO
Gweru
Francistown
Serowe
Maun
Gaborone
Molepolole
Kanye
Mochudi
Lobatse
Tsumeb
Grootfontein
Otjiwarongo
Omaruru
Swakopmund
Walvisbaai
Windhoek
Rehoboth
Gobabis
Keetmanshoop
Lüderitz
Mariental
Oranjemund
Upington
Kimberley
Bloemfontein
PRETORIA
JOHANNESBURG
Pietersburg
Maseru
Pietermaritzburg
East London
PORT ELIZABETH
CAPE TOWN/KAAPSTAD
Stellenbosch
Worcester
Oudtshoorn
George
Mosselbaai
Uitenhage
Grahamstown
Cape of Good Hope/Kaap die Goeie Hoop
Kaap Agulhas
Cape Agulhas
Scale 1:9,000,000
Lambert Azimuthal Equal Area Projection
Longitude East 25 of Greenwich
0 200 400 600 km
0 200 miles
A-589200-780-1 -1 -1 -2

CAUCASUS
UKRAINE
CARPATHIAN MTS.
BOHEMIA
FLANDERS
English Channel
GREAT BRITAIN
ENGLAND
WALES
IRELAND
SCOTLAND
BRITISH ISLES
North Sea
JUTLAND
POMERANIA
LITHUANIA
Baltic Sea
SCANDINAVIA
LAPLAND
KARELIA
KOLA PENINSULA
NORTHERN UVALS
TIMAN RIDGE
URAL MOUNTAINS
WEST SIBERIAN PLAIN
Norwegian Sea
Norwegian Basin
SHETLAND ISLANDS
ORKNEY ISLANDS
FAEROE IS.
ICELAND
Reykjanes Ridge
Iceland Basin
Mid-Atlantic Ridge
West European Basin
AZORES
Newfoundland Basin
Labrador Basin
Limit of Icebergs
Denmark Strait
JAN MAYEN
BEAR ISLAND
SPITSBERGEN
Greenland Basin
Greenland Sea
Barents Sea
NOVAYA ZEMLYA
FRANZ JOSEPH LAND
Winter limit of pack ice (April)
Summer limit of pack ice (August)
Kara Sea
YAMAL PENINSULA
GYDA PENINSULA
SEVERNAYA ZEMLYA
TAYMYR PENINSULA
NORTH SIBERIAN PLAIN
CENTRAL SIBERIAN UPLANDS
Laptev Sea
NEW SIBERIAN ISLANDS
Nansen Cordillera
Fram Basin
Eurasia Basin
North Pole
Lomonosov Ridge
Makarov Basin
Alpha Cordillera
Canada Basin
Beaufort Sea
ARCTIC OCEAN
GREENLAND
KING CHRISTIAN IX LAND
KING FREDERICK VI COAST
KING CHRISTIAN X LAND
KING FREDERIK VIII LAND
KNUD RASMUSSEN LAND
Davis Strait
Baffin Bay
BAFFIN
ELLESMERE
DEVON
AXEL HEIBERG
SVERDRUP ISLANDS
North Magnetic Pole 1980
QUEEN ELIZABETH ISLANDS
PARRY ISLANDS
MELVILLE
PRINCE PATRICK
BANKS
VICTORIA
PRINCE OF WALES
SOMERSET
BOOTHIA PENINSULA
KING WILLIAM
Arctic Circle
Hudson Strait
Hudson Bay
Foxe Basin
SOUTHAMPTON
James Bay
BELCHER ISLANDS
UNGAVA PENINSULA
LABRADOR
LAURENTIAN PLATEAU
NEWFOUNDLAND
CAPE BRETON ISLAND
NOVA SCOTIA
PRINCE EDWARD ISLAND
ANTICOSTI
CLAY BELT
GREAT
ROCKY MOUNTAINS
MACKENZIE MOUNTAINS
Franklin Mountains
Richardson Mountains
BROOKS RANGE
ALASKA
ALASKA RANGE
YUKON PLATEAU
COAST MOUNTAINS
CASSIAR MOUNTAINS
ALEXANDER ARCHIPELAGO
QUEEN CHARLOTTE ISLANDS
VANCOUVER ISLAND
Gulf of Alaska
KENAI PENINSULA
KODIAK
ALASKA PENINSULA
ALEUTIAN ISLANDS
Aleutian Trench
Aleutian Basin
Bering Sea
Bering Strait
SEWARD PENINSULA
Norton Sound
Bristol Bay
SAINT LAWRENCE
SAINT MATTHEW
Chukchi Sea
CHUKCHI PENINSULA
WRANGEL
East Siberian Sea
BEAR ISLANDS
Anadyr Gulf
KOLYMSKAJA NIZMENNOST
CHERSKI MTS.
VERKHOYANSK MTS.
STANOVOY RANGE
DZHUGDZHUR RANGE
KORJAKSKOJE NAGORJE
KAMCHATKA PENINSULA
SREDINNY HREBET
KOMANDORSKI ISLANDS
Sea of Okhotsk
SAKHALIN
KURIL ISLANDS
Kuril Trench
HOKKAIDO
Sea of Japan
SIHOTE-ALIN
LESSER KHINGAN RANGE
Mendocino Fracture Zone
PACIFIC

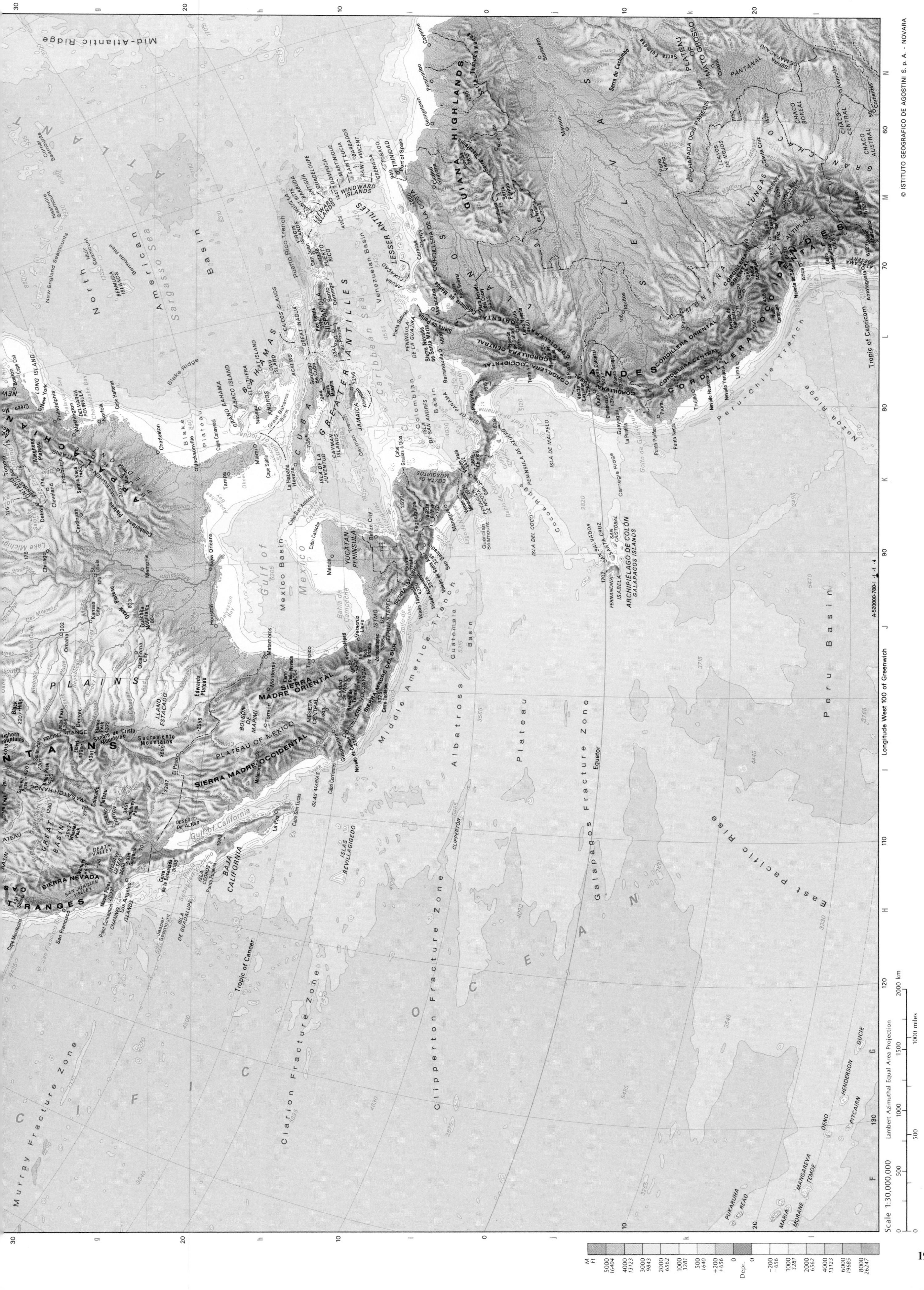

Longitude West 100 of Greenwich

Scale 1:30,000,000

Lambert Azimuthal Equal Area Projection

0 500 1000 1500 2000 km

0 500 1000 miles

M	Ft
5000	16404
4000	13123
3000	9843
2000	6562
1000	3281
500	1640
+200	+656
0	0
Depr.	
0	0
−200	−656
1000	3281
2000	6562
4000	13123
6000	19685
8000	26247

A-520000-780-1 -1 -1 -4

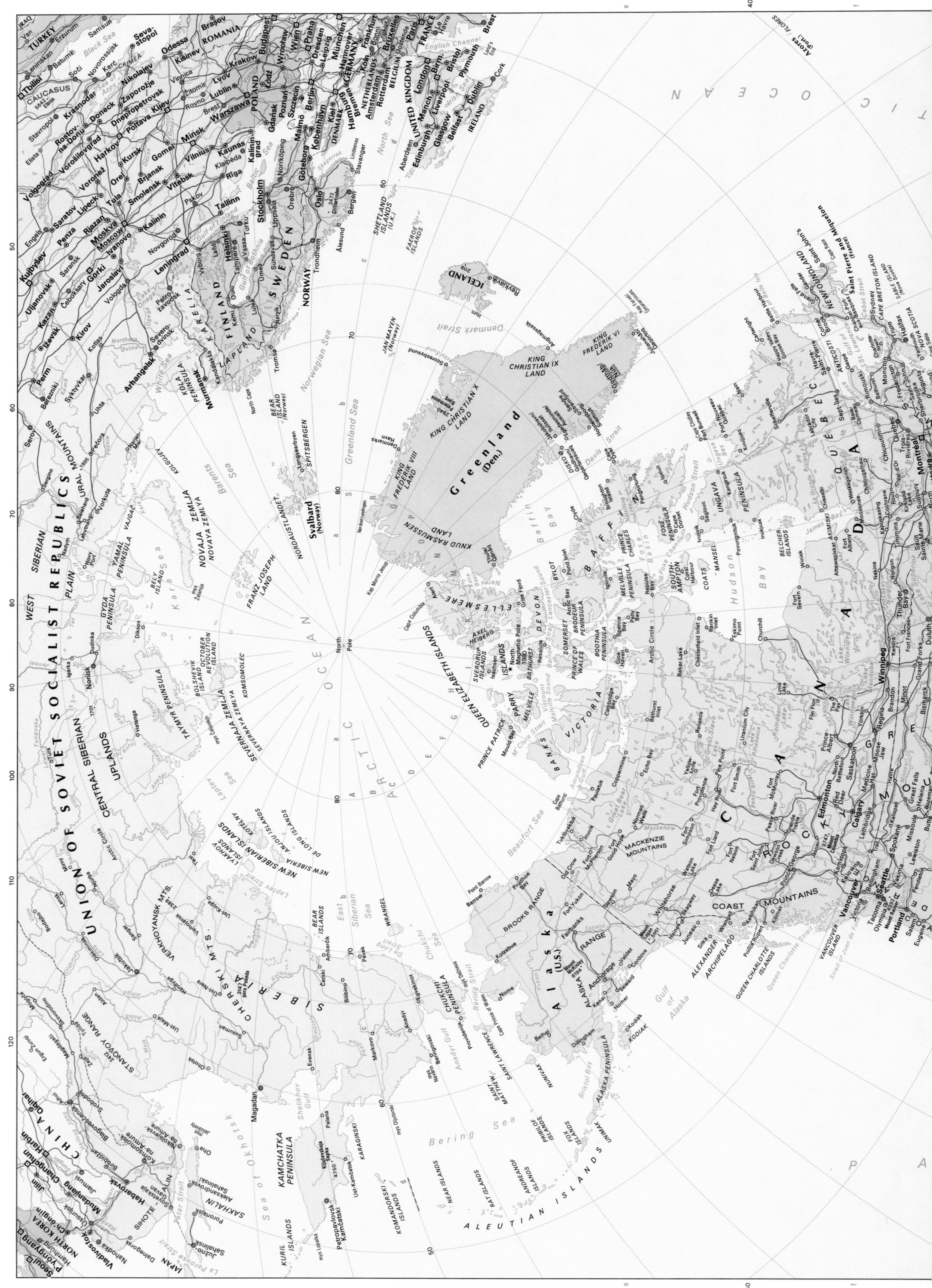
Greenland
(Den.)
Alaska
(U.S.)
UNION OF SOVIET SOCIALIST REPUBLICS
ICELAND
FINLAND
SWEDEN
NORWAY
UNITED KINGDOM
IRELAND
POLAND
FRANCE
Svalbard
(Norway)
BAFFIN
VICTORIA
QUEEN ELIZABETH ISLANDS
ALEUTIAN ISLANDS
Bering Sea
Hudson Bay
Baffin Bay
Beaufort Sea
North Pole

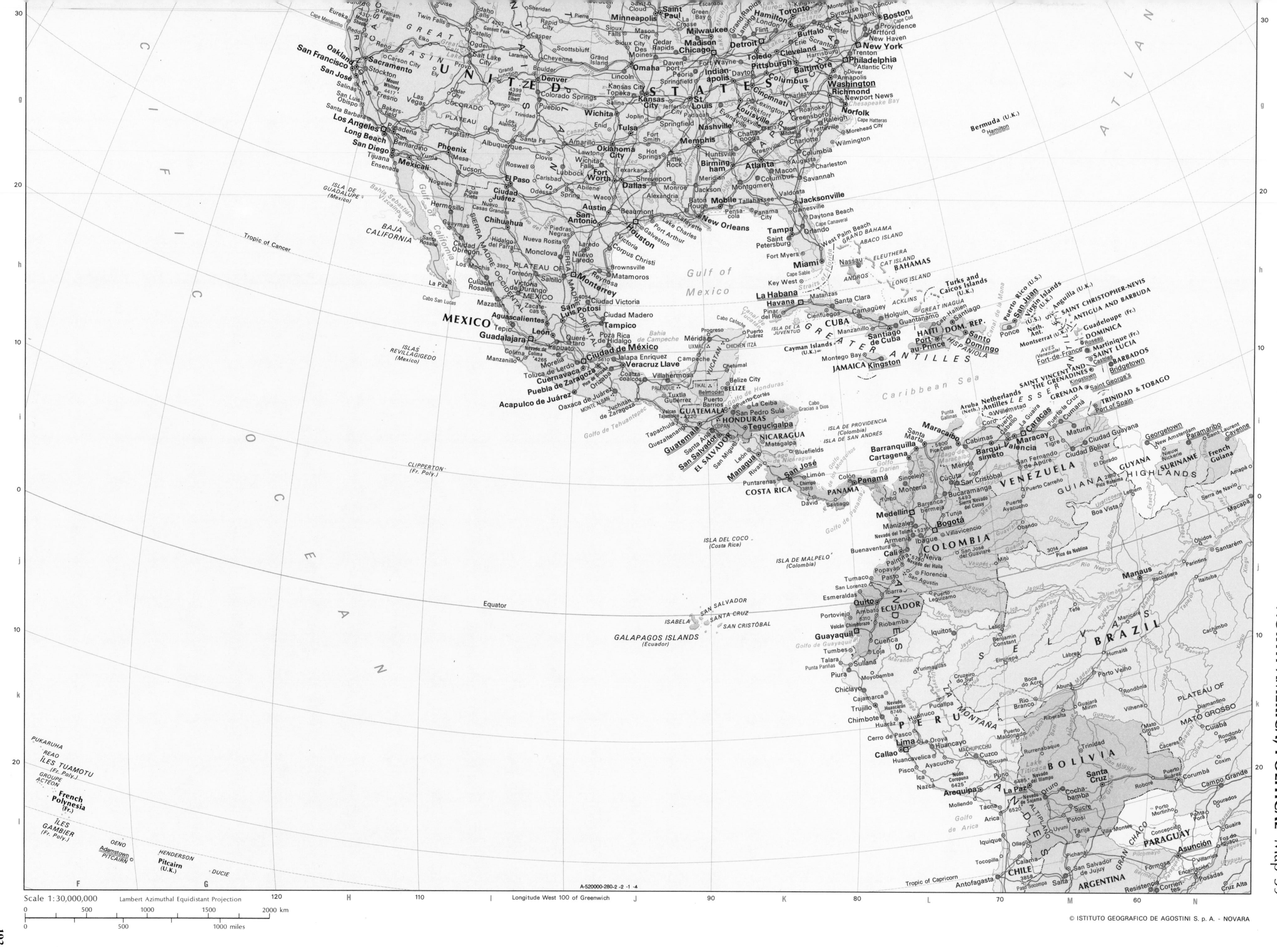
PACIFIC OCEAN
ATLANTIC
UNITED STATES
MEXICO
Gulf of Mexico
Caribbean Sea
GREATER ANTILLES
LESSER ANTILLES
CUBA
BAHAMAS
JAMAICA
HAITI
DOM. REP.
GUATEMALA
BELIZE
HONDURAS
EL SALVADOR
NICARAGUA
COSTA RICA
PANAMA
COLOMBIA
VENEZUELA
GUYANA
SURINAME
French Guiana
ECUADOR
PERU
BOLIVIA
BRAZIL
CHILE
ARGENTINA
PARAGUAY
GALAPAGOS ISLANDS (Ecuador)
Bermuda (U.K.)
French Polynesia (Fr.)
Pitcairn (U.K.)
Tropic of Cancer
Equator
Tropic of Capricorn
Longitude West 100 of Greenwich
Scale 1:30,000,000
Lambert Azimuthal Equidistant Projection
0 500 1000 1500 2000 km
0 500 1000 miles
A-520000-280-2 -2 -1 -4
© ISTITUTO GEOGRAFICO DE AGOSTINI S. p. A. - NOVARA

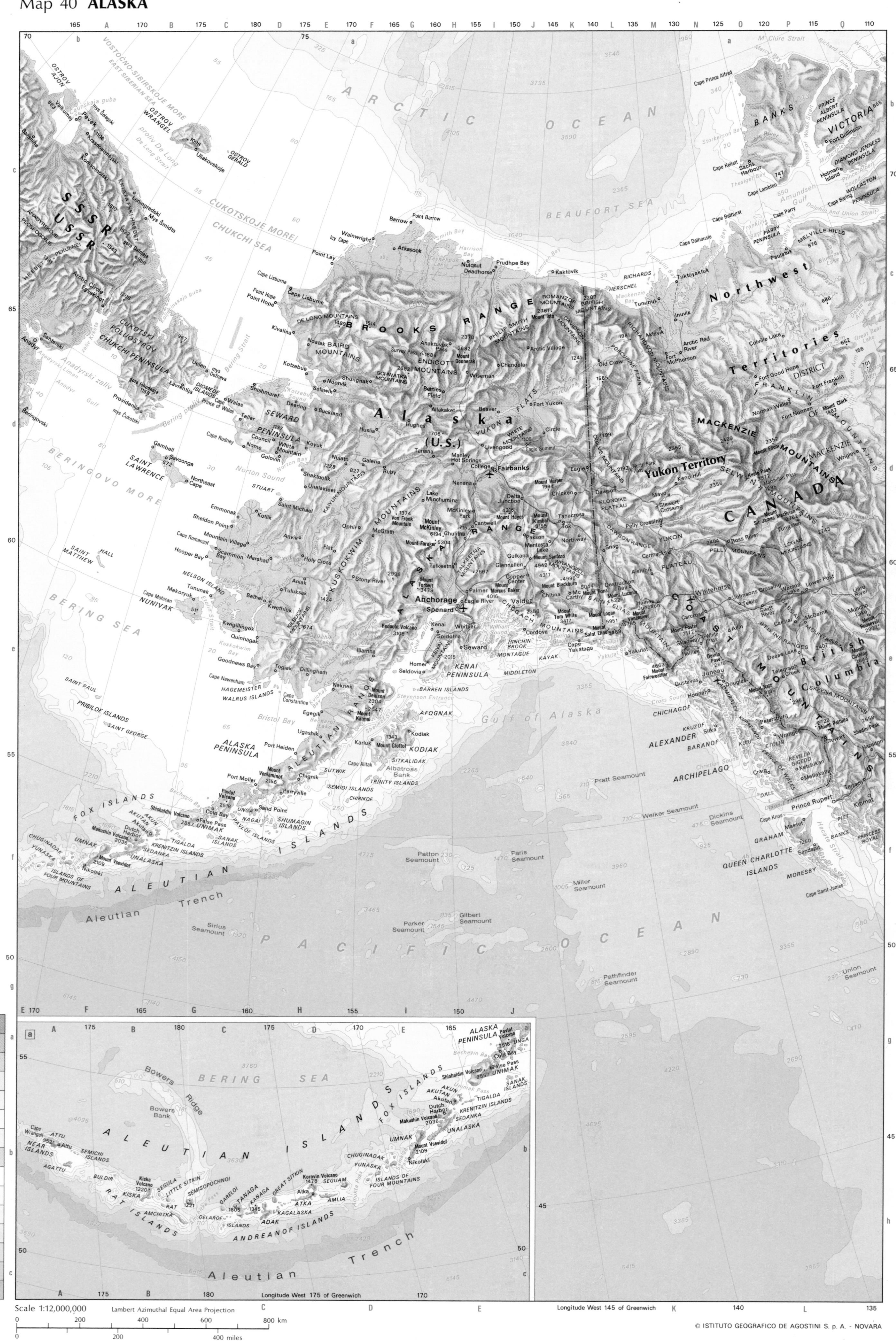

Scale 1:12,000,000 Lambert Azimuthal Equal Area Projection

0 200 400 600 800 km

0 200 400 miles

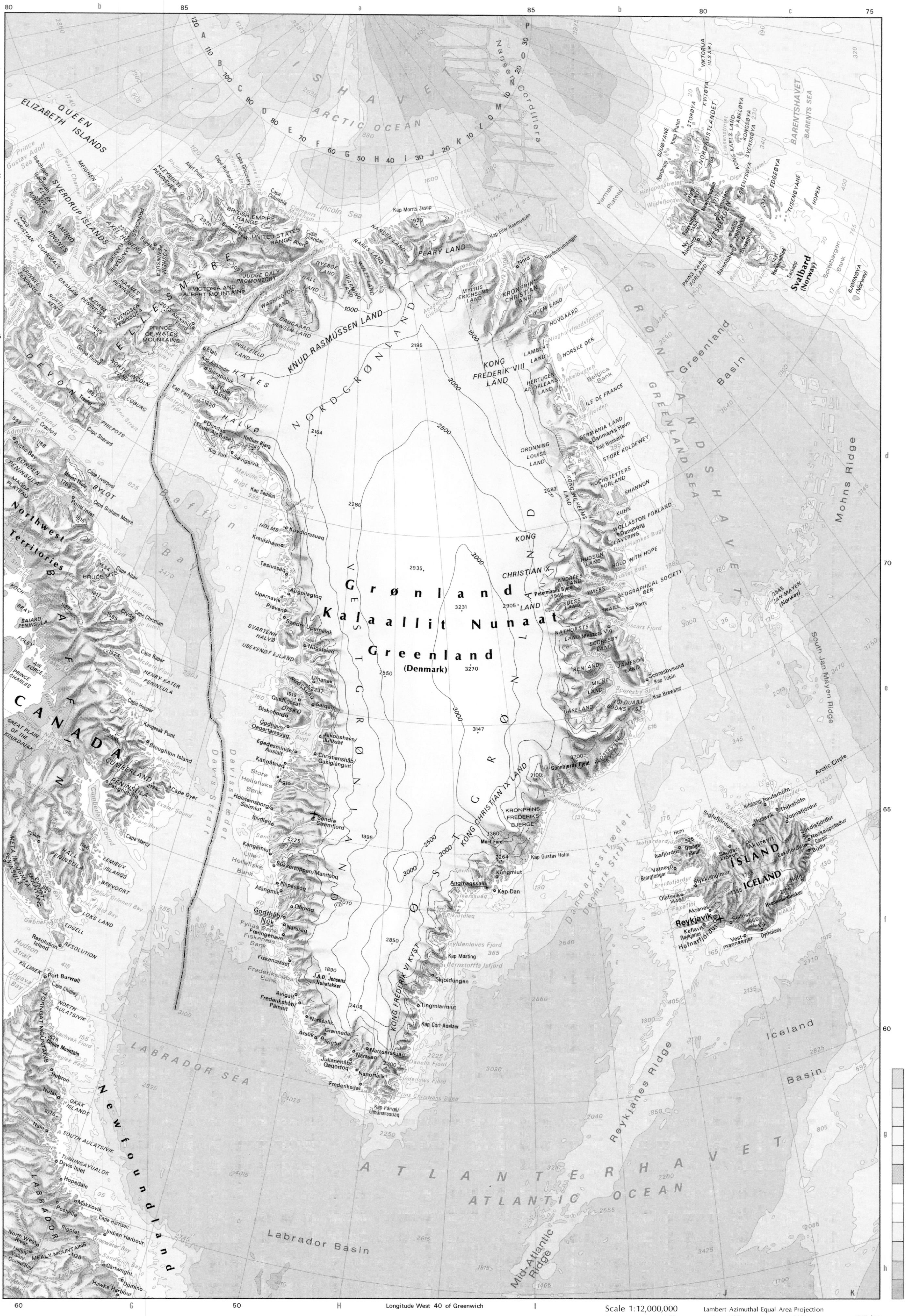

Grønland
Kalaallit Nunaat
Greenland
(Denmark)

ARCTIC OCEAN
ATLANTIC OCEAN
LABRADOR SEA
Baffin Bay
Davis Strait
Denmark Strait
GREENLAND SEA
CANADA
ISLAND / ICELAND
Svalbard (Norway)
Jan Mayen (Norway)

Longitude West 40 of Greenwich

Scale 1:12,000,000
Lambert Azimuthal Equal Area Projection
0 200 400 600 800 km
0 200 400 miles

M	Ft
3000	9843
2000	6562
1000	3281
500	1640
200	656
0	
100	328
200	656
1000	3281
2000	6562
4000	13123

ARCTIC OCEAN
Canada Basin
BEAUFORT SEA
QUEEN ELIZABETH ISLANDS
PARRY ISLANDS
BANKS
VICTORIA
PRINCE OF WALES
DISTRICT OF MACKENZIE
Northwest Territories
Yukon Territory
Alaska (U.S.)
BROOKS RANGE
ALASKA RANGE
MACKENZIE MOUNTAINS
COAST MOUNTAINS
ROCKY MOUNTAINS
GREAT PLAINS
British Columbia
Alberta
Saskatchewan
Manitoba
CANADA
UNITED STATES
Washington
Oregon
California
Idaho
Nevada
Montana
Wyoming
North Dakota
South Dakota
Gulf of Alaska
PACIFIC OCEAN
VANCOUVER ISLAND
QUEEN CHARLOTTE ISLANDS
ALEXANDER ARCHIPELAGO
Great Slave Lake
Great Bear Lake
Lake Athabasca
Anchorage
Fairbanks
Whitehorse
Yellowknife
Prince Rupert
Prince George
VANCOUVER
Victoria
EDMONTON
CALGARY
Saskatoon
Regina
WINNIPEG
SEATTLE
PORTLAND
Spokane
Boise
M Ft
5000 16404
4000 13123
3000 9843
2000 6562
1000 3281
500 1640
200 656
0
−100 −328
200 656
1000 3281
2000 6562
4000 13123
Scale 1:12,000,000
Lambert Azimuthal Equal Area Projection
0 200 400 600 800 km
0 200 400 miles
Longitude West 100 of Greenwich

British Columbia
Alberta
Saskatchewan
Manitoba
CANADA
Washington
Oregon
Idaho
Montana
North Dakota
South Dakota
Wyoming
Nebraska
Nevada
Utah
Colorado
Kansas
California
Arizona
New Mexico
Oklahoma
Texas
UNITED STATES
ROCKY MOUNTAINS
GREAT PLAINS
GREAT BASIN
COLORADO PLATEAU
SIERRA NEVADA
SIERRA MADRE OCCIDENTAL
SIERRA MADRE ORIENTAL
BAJA CALIFORNIA
Golfo de California
MÉXICO
PACIFIC OCEAN
OCÉANO PACÍFICO
Clarion Fracture Zone
Tropic of Cancer
SEATTLE
PORTLAND
SAN FRANCISCO
SACRAMENTO
OAKLAND
SAN JOSE
LOS ANGELES
SAN DIEGO
PHOENIX
Salt Lake City
DENVER
EL PASO
DALLAS
FORT WORTH
HOUSTON
SAN ANTONIO
AUSTIN
OKLAHOMA CITY
OMAHA
CALGARY
VANCOUVER
WINNIPEG
MONTERREY
CHIHUAHUA
GUADALAJARA
CIUDAD DE MÉXICO
MEXICO CITY
Scale 1:12,000,000
Lambert Azimuthal Equidistant Projection
Longitude West 100 of Greenwich
0 200 400 600 800 km
0 200 400 miles
M Ft
5000 16404
4000 13123
3000 9843
2000 6562
1000 3281
500 1640
200 656
0
Depr.
0
100 328
200 656
1000 3281
2000 6562
4000 13123
6000 19685
8000 26247

Ontario
Québec
New Brunswick
Prince Edward Island
Nova Scotia
Maine
Michigan
Wisconsin
Iowa
Illinois
Indiana
Ohio
Pennsylvania
New York
West Virginia
Virginia
Kentucky
Tennessee
North Carolina
South Carolina
Georgia
Alabama
Mississippi
Louisiana
Arkansas
Missouri
Florida
Delaware
ATLANTIC OCEAN
Sargasso Sea
Blake Plateau
Blake Ridge
Blake Basin
New England Seamounts
Kelvin Seamount
Georges Bank
Gulf of Mexico/Golfo de México
Mexico Basin
Bermuda (U.K.)
BAHAMAS
CUBA
JAMAICA
HAITI
REPÚBLICA DOMINICANA
DOMINICAN REPUBLIC
Cayman Islands (U.K.)
Turks and Caicos Islands (U.K.)
WEST INDIES
INDIAS OCCIDENTALES
GREATER ANTILLES
Yucatan Basin
Cayman Trench
PENÍNSULA DE YUCATÁN
YUCATAN PENINSULA
BELIZE
CHICAGO
DETROIT
TORONTO
MONTREAL
OTTAWA
QUEBEC
BOSTON
NEW YORK
PHILADELPHIA
BALTIMORE
WASHINGTON
PITTSBURGH
CLEVELAND
CINCINNATI
INDIANAPOLIS
COLUMBUS
MILWAUKEE
SAINT PAUL
ST. LOUIS
KANSAS CITY
LOUISVILLE
NASHVILLE
MEMPHIS
ATLANTA
BIRMINGHAM
NEW ORLEANS
MOBILE
JACKSONVILLE
TAMPA
MIAMI
RICHMOND
NORFOLK
LA HABANA
HAVANA
KINGSTON
PORT-AU-PRINCE
SANTO DOMINGO
SANTIAGO

CANADA
Québec
Ontario
New Brunswick
Nova Scotia
Maine
New Hampshire
Massachusetts
Connecticut
Rhode Island
New York
New Jersey
Pennsylvania
Delaware
Maryland
Virginia
West Virginia
Ohio
Michigan
Indiana
Illinois
Wisconsin
Kentucky
Iowa
Minnesota
Missouri
ATLANTIC
Georges Bank
Hudson Canyon
Gulf of Maine
MONTREAL
OTTAWA
TORONTO
BOSTON
NEW YORK
PHILADELPHIA
BALTIMORE
WASHINGTON
PITTSBURGH
CLEVELAND
DETROIT
CHICAGO
MILWAUKEE
INDIANAPOLIS
CINCINNATI
COLUMBUS
LOUISVILLE
ST. LOUIS
RICHMOND
BUFFALO
ROCHESTER
HAMILTON
Québec
Saint John
Fredericton
Portland
Bangor
Duluth
Superior
Thunder Bay
Sudbury
TOLEDO

Scale 1:16,000,000

Delisle Conic Equidistant Projection

Longitude West 78 of Greenwich

M	Ft
1000	3281
500	1640
200	656
+100	+328
0	0
−100	−328
200	656
1000	3281
2000	6562
4000	13123
6000	19685

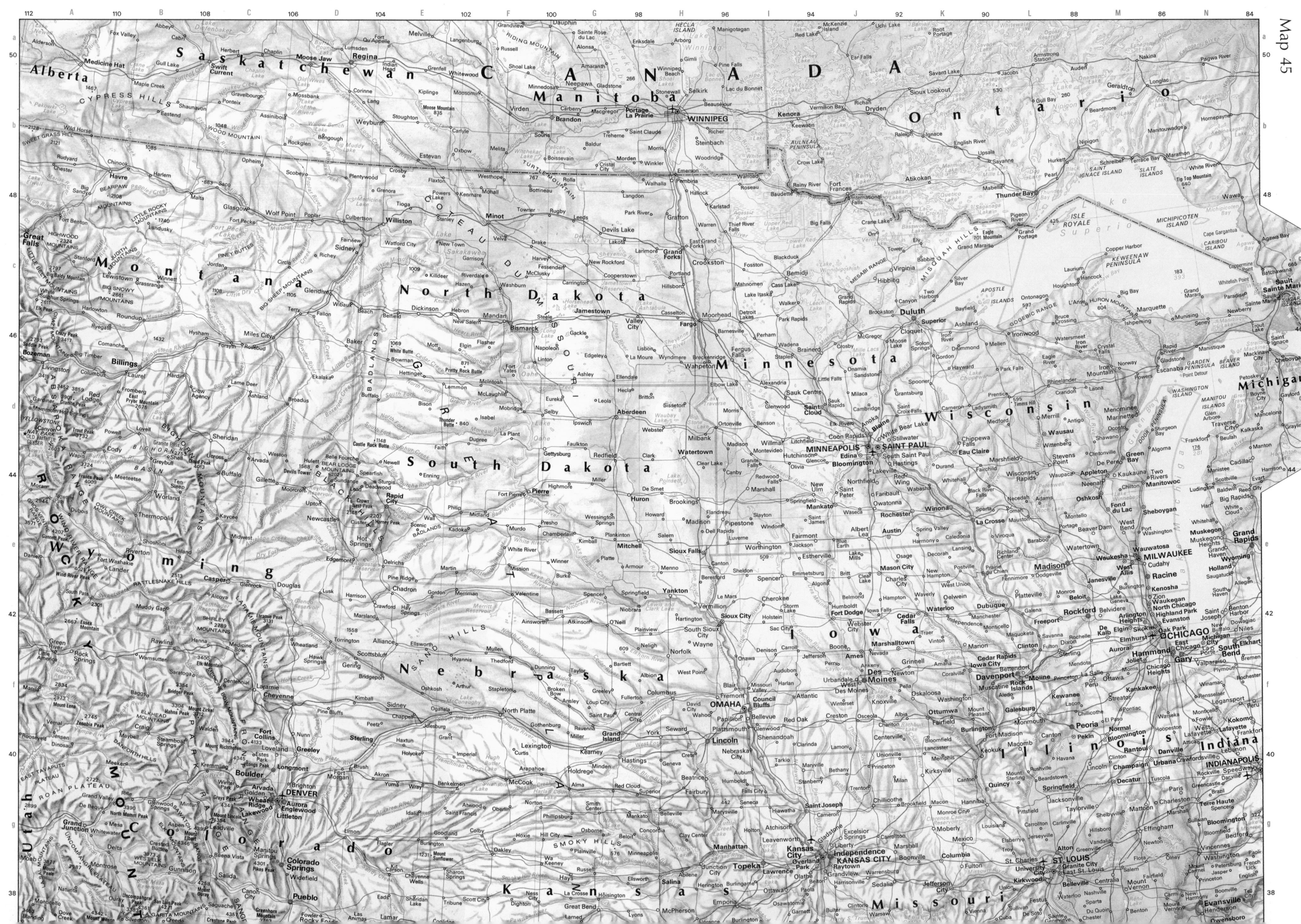
CANADA
Alberta
Saskatchewan
Manitoba
Ontario
Montana
North Dakota
South Dakota
Minnesota
Wisconsin
Michigan
Wyoming
Nebraska
Iowa
Illinois
Indiana
Colorado
Kansas
Missouri
Utah
ROCKY MOUNTAINS
Lake Superior
WINNIPEG
MINNEAPOLIS
SAINT PAUL
MILWAUKEE
CHICAGO
OMAHA
DENVER
KANSAS CITY
ST. LOUIS
INDIANAPOLIS

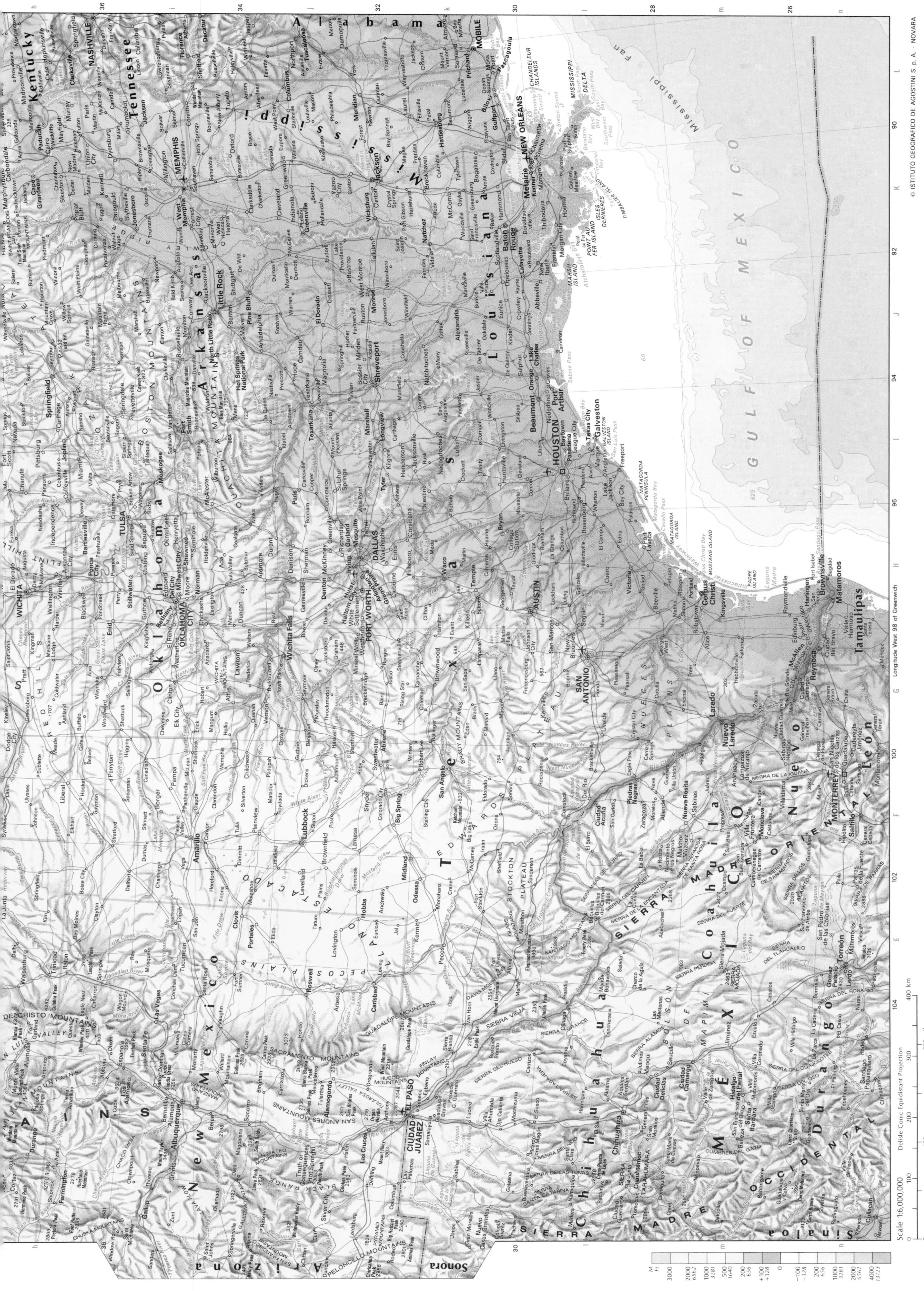

Scale 1:16,000,000

Delisle Conic Equidistant Projection

0 100 200 300 400 km

0 100 200 miles

Longitude West 98 of Greenwich

M	ft
3000	
2000	6562
1000	3281
500	1640
200	656
+100	+328
0	
−100	−328
200	656
1000	3281
2000	6562
4000	13123

C A N A D A
British Columbia
Alberta
Saskatchewan
North Dakota
South Dakota
Nebraska
Montana
Idaho
Wyoming
Washington
Oregon
Nevada
Utah
Colorado
P A C I F I
COAST MOUNTAINS
COLUMBIA MOUNTAINS
CASCADE RANGE
BIGHORN MOUNTAINS
SEATTLE
SPOKANE
PORTLAND
CALGARY
VANCOUVER
DENVER
SALT LAKE CITY

Longitude West 116 of Greenwich

Scale 1:6,000,000

Delisle Conic Equidistant Projection

0 100 200 300 400 km

0 100 200 miles

M	4000	3000	2000	1000	500	200	+100	0	Depr.	−100	200	1000	2000	4000	6000
Ft	13123	9843	6562	3281	1640	656	+328	0		−328	656	3281	6562	13123	19685

MÉXICO

ESTADOS

D.F. Distrito Federal
1 Aguascalientes
2 Baja California Norte
3 Baja California Sur
4 Campeche
5 Coahuila
6 Colima
7 Chiapas
8 Chihuahua
9 Durango
10 Guanajuato
11 Guerrero
12 Hidalgo
13 Jalisco
14 México
15 Michoacán
16 Morelos
17 Nayarit
18 Nuevo León
19 Oaxaca
20 Puebla
21 Querétaro
22 Quintana Roo
23 San Luis Potosi
24 Sinaloa
25 Sonora
26 Tabasco
27 Tamaulipas
28 Tlaxcala
29 Veracruz
30 Yucatán
31 Zacatecas

M	Ft
5000	16404
4000	13123
3000	9843
2000	6562
1000	3281
500	1640
+200	+656
0	
Depr.	
0	
−100	−328
200	656
1000	3281
2000	6562
4000	13123
6000	19685
8000	26247

Scale 1:12,000,000 Lambert Azimuthal Equal Area Projection

0 200 400 600 800 km

0 200 400 miles

Longitude West 90 of Greenwich

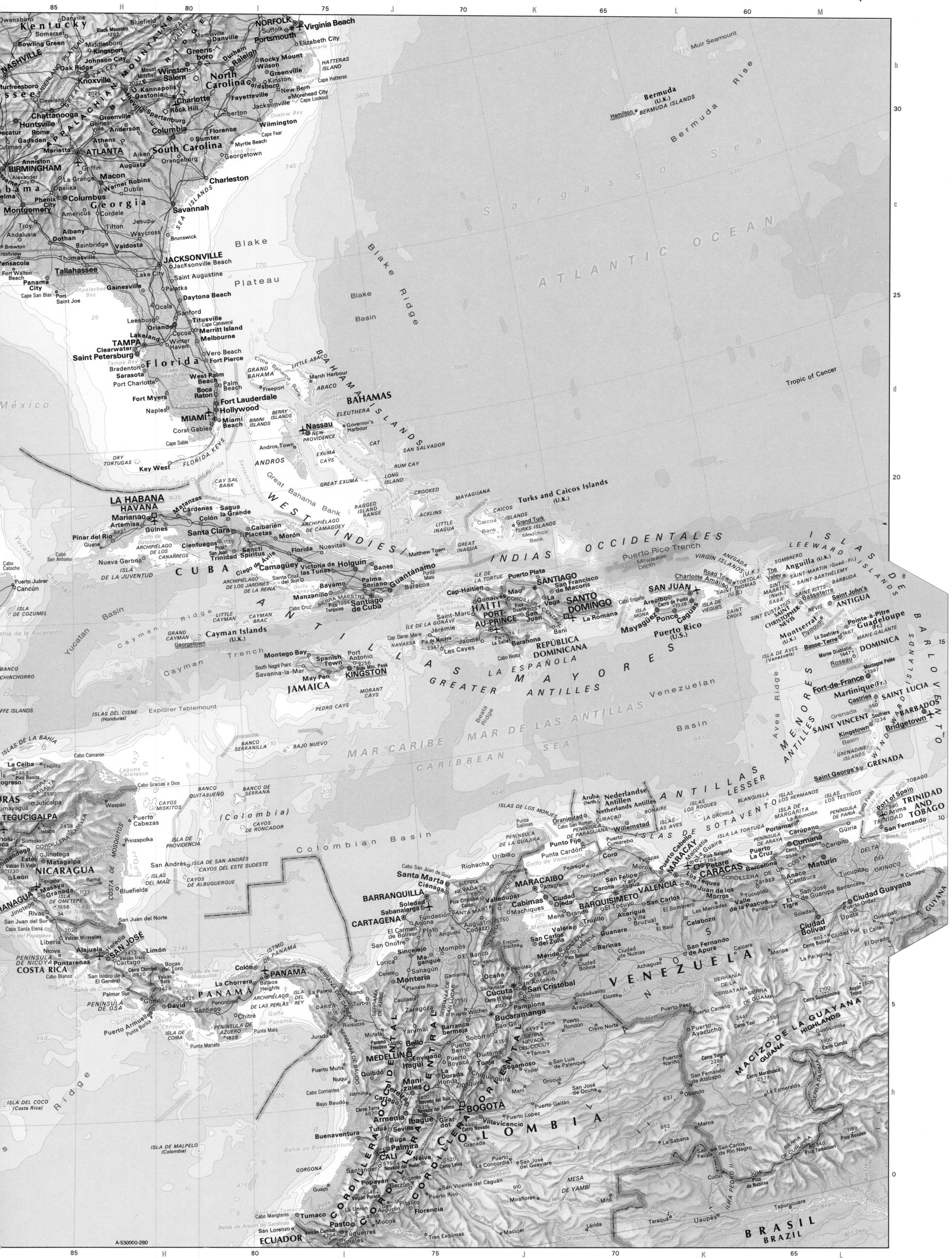

California
Arizona
New Mexico
UNITED S
Baja California Norte
Baja California Sur
Sonora
Chihuahua
Coahui
Durango
Zacatecas
Nayarit
Aguascalientes
Jalisco
Colima
Michoac
SAN DIEGO
Tijuana
MEXICALI
Yuma
Tucson
Nogales
EL PASO
CIUDAD JUÁREZ
Hermosillo
Guaymas
Ciudad Obregon
Los Mochis
Chihuahua
CULIACÁN ROSALES
Mazatlán
Victoria de Durango
Tepic
GUADALAJARA
La Paz
Golfo de California
SIERRA MADRE OCCIDENTAL
ALTIPLANICIE MEXICANA
PLATEAU OF MEXICO
BOLSÓN DE MAPIMI
ISLA CEDROS
ISLA TIBURÓN
ISLAS MARÍAS
ISLAS REVILLAGIGEDO (Mexico)
ISLA SOCORRO
ISLA CLARIÓN
ISLA SAN BENEDICTO
ISLA ROCA PARTIDA
Cedros Trench
Middle A
Tropic of Cancer
Rosa Seamount
Mathematicians Seamount
OCÉANO PACÍFICO
PACIFIC OCEAN
M / Ft
4000 13123
3000 9843
2000 6562
1000 3281
500 1640
200 656
+100 +328
0
Depr.
0
−100 −328
200 656
1000 3281
2000 6562
4000 13123
6000 19685
Scale 1:6,000,000
Delisle Conic Equidistant Projection
0 100 200 300 400 km
0 100 200 miles
Longitude West 104 of Greenwich

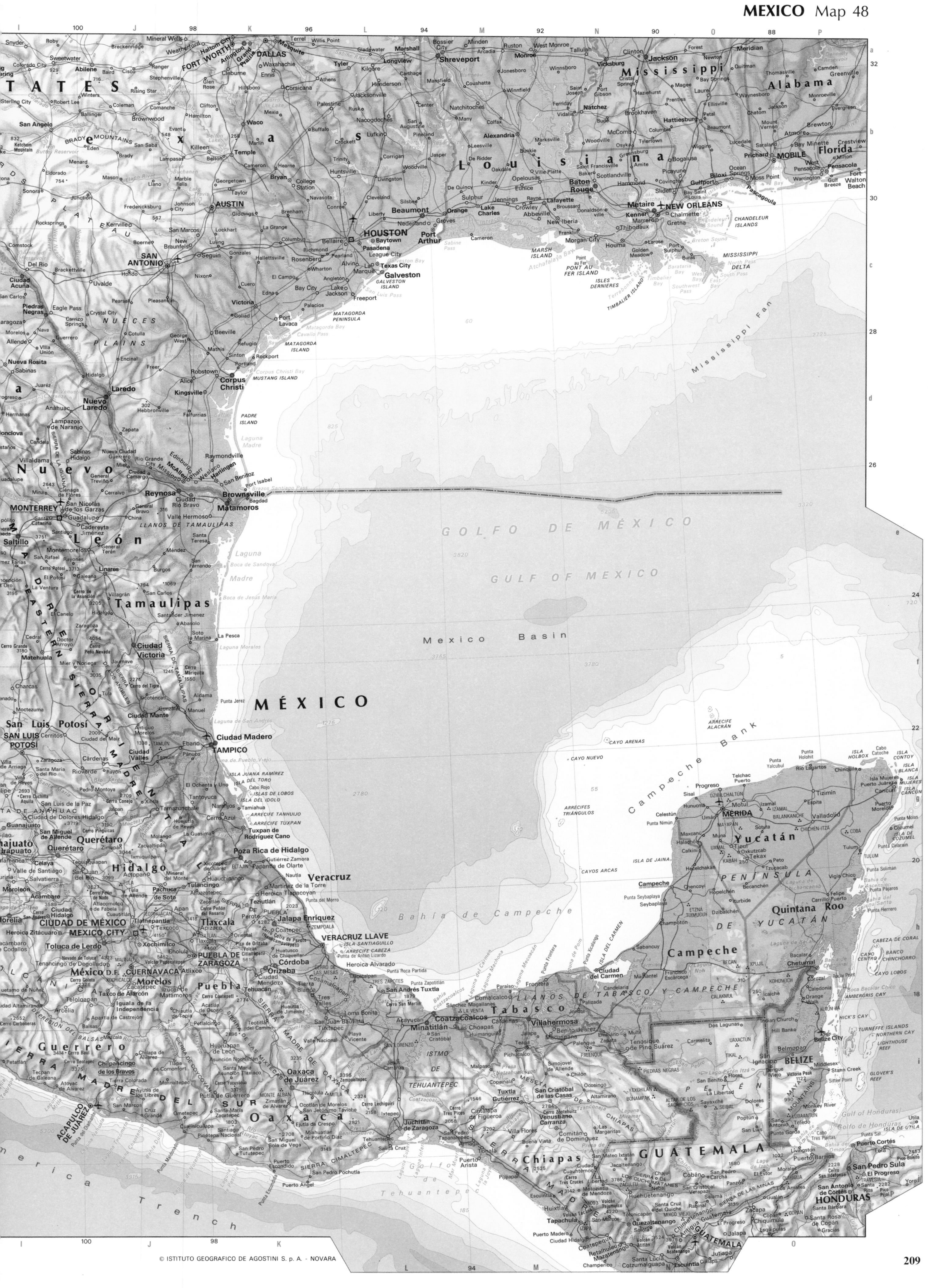

MÉXICO
GOLFO DE MÉXICO
GULF OF MEXICO
Mexico Basin
Bahía de Campeche
Campeche Bank
Mississippi Fan
Golfo de Tehuantepec
America Trench
Mississippi
Alabama
Louisiana
Florida
Texas
Nuevo León
Tamaulipas
San Luis Potosí
Querétaro
Hidalgo
Veracruz
Tlaxcala
Puebla
Morelos
Guerrero
Oaxaca
Tabasco
Chiapas
Campeche
Yucatán
Quintana Roo
PENÍNSULA DE YUCATÁN
GUATEMALA
BELIZE
HONDURAS
PETÉN
SIERRA MADRE ORIENTAL
SIERRA MADRE DEL SUR
SIERRA MADRE
ISTMO DE TEHUANTEPEC
LLANOS DE TABASCO Y CAMPECHE
LLANOS DE TAMAULIPAS
NUECES PLAINS
DALLAS
FORT WORTH
HOUSTON
AUSTIN
SAN ANTONIO
Shreveport
Jackson
Baton Rouge
NEW ORLEANS
MOBILE
Corpus Christi
Galveston
Laredo
Brownsville
Matamoros
MONTERREY
Saltillo
Ciudad Victoria
TAMPICO
Ciudad Madero
SAN LUIS POTOSÍ
Guanajuato
CIUDAD DE MÉXICO
MEXICO CITY
PUEBLA DE ZARAGOZA
CUERNAVACA
Toluca de Lerdo
Jalapa Enríquez
VERACRUZ LLAVE
Córdoba
Orizaba
Oaxaca de Juárez
ACAPULCO DE JUÁREZ
Chilpancingo de los Bravos
Coatzacoalcos
Minatitlán
Villahermosa
Tuxtla Gutiérrez
Tapachula
Ciudad del Carmen
Campeche
MÉRIDA
Progreso
Chetumal
Belize City
GUATEMALA
San Pedro Sula
Puerto Barrios

Map 49 CENTRAL AMERICA AND WESTERN CARIBBEAN

Scale 1:6,000,000 Delisle Conic Equidistant Projection

BAHAMAS
BAHAMA ISLANDS
Nassau
NEW PROVIDENCE
ELEUTHERA ISLANDS
CAT ISLAND
GREAT EXUMA ISLAND
LONG ISLAND
ATLANTIC OCEAN
Tropic of Cancer
Turks and Caicos Islands
(U.K.)
GREAT INAGUA ISLAND
Puerto Rico Trench
HAÏTI
PORT-AU-PRINCE
HISPANIOLA
SANTO DOMINGO
REPÚBLICA DOMINICANA
DOMINICAN REPUBLIC
Puerto Rico
(U.S.)
SAN JUAN
JAMAICA
Kingston
SANTIAGO DE CUBA
Camagüey
Holguín
ISLAS GREATER ANTILLES MAYORES
MAR DE LAS ANTILLAS
CARIBBEAN SEA
Colombian Basin
Venezuelan Basin
Nederlandse Antillen
Netherlands Antilles
ANTILLAS MENORES
LESSER ANTILLES
ISLAS DE SOTAVENTO
Dependencias Federales
Aruba
(Neth.)
CARACAS
MARACAIBO
BARRANQUILLA
CARTAGENA
VENEZUELA
COLOMBIA
Longitude West 74 of Greenwich
CUBA
PROVINCIAS
1 Camagüey
2 Ciego de Ávila
3 Cienfuegos
4 Ciudad de la Habana
5 Granma
6 Guantánamo
7 Holguín
8 La Habana
9 Las Tunas
10 Matanzas
11 Pinar del Río
12 Sancti Spíritus
13 Santiago de Cuba
14 Villaclara
BELIZE
DISTRICTS
1 Belize
2 Cayo
3 Corozal
4 Orange Walk
5 Stann Creek
6 Toledo
GUATEMALA
DEPARTAMENTOS
1 Alta Verapaz
2 Baja Verapaz
3 Chimaltenango
4 Chiquimula
5 El Progreso
6 Escuintla
7 Guatemala
8 Huehuetenango
9 Izabal
10 Jalapa
11 Jutiapa
12 Petén
13 Quezaltenango
14 Quiché
15 Retalhuleu
16 Sacatepéquez
17 San Marcos
18 Santa Rosa
19 Sololá
20 Suchitepéquez
21 Totonicapán
22 Zacapa
HONDURAS
DEPARTAMENTOS
1 Atlántida
2 Choluteca
3 Colón
4 Comayagua
5 Copán
6 Cortés
7 El Paraíso
8 Francisco Morazán
9 Gracias a Dios
10 Intibucá
11 Islas de la Bahía
12 La Paz
13 Lempira
14 Ocotepeque
15 Olancho
16 Santa Bárbara
17 Valle
18 Yoro
NICARAGUA
DEPARTAMENTOS
1 Boaco
2 Carazo
3 Chinandega
4 Chontales
5 Estelí
6 Granada
7 Jinotega
8 León
9 Madriz
10 Managua
11 Masaya
12 Matagalpa
13 Nueva Segovia
14 Río San Juan
15 Rivas
16 Zelaya
COSTA RICA
PROVINCIAS
1 Alajuela
2 Cartago
3 Guanacaste
4 Heredia
5 Limón
6 Puntarenas
7 San José
PANAMÁ
PROVINCIAS
1 Bocas del Toro
2 Chiriquí
3 Coclé
4 Colón
5 Darién
6 Herrera
7 Los Santos
8 Panamá
9 San Blas
10 Veraguas

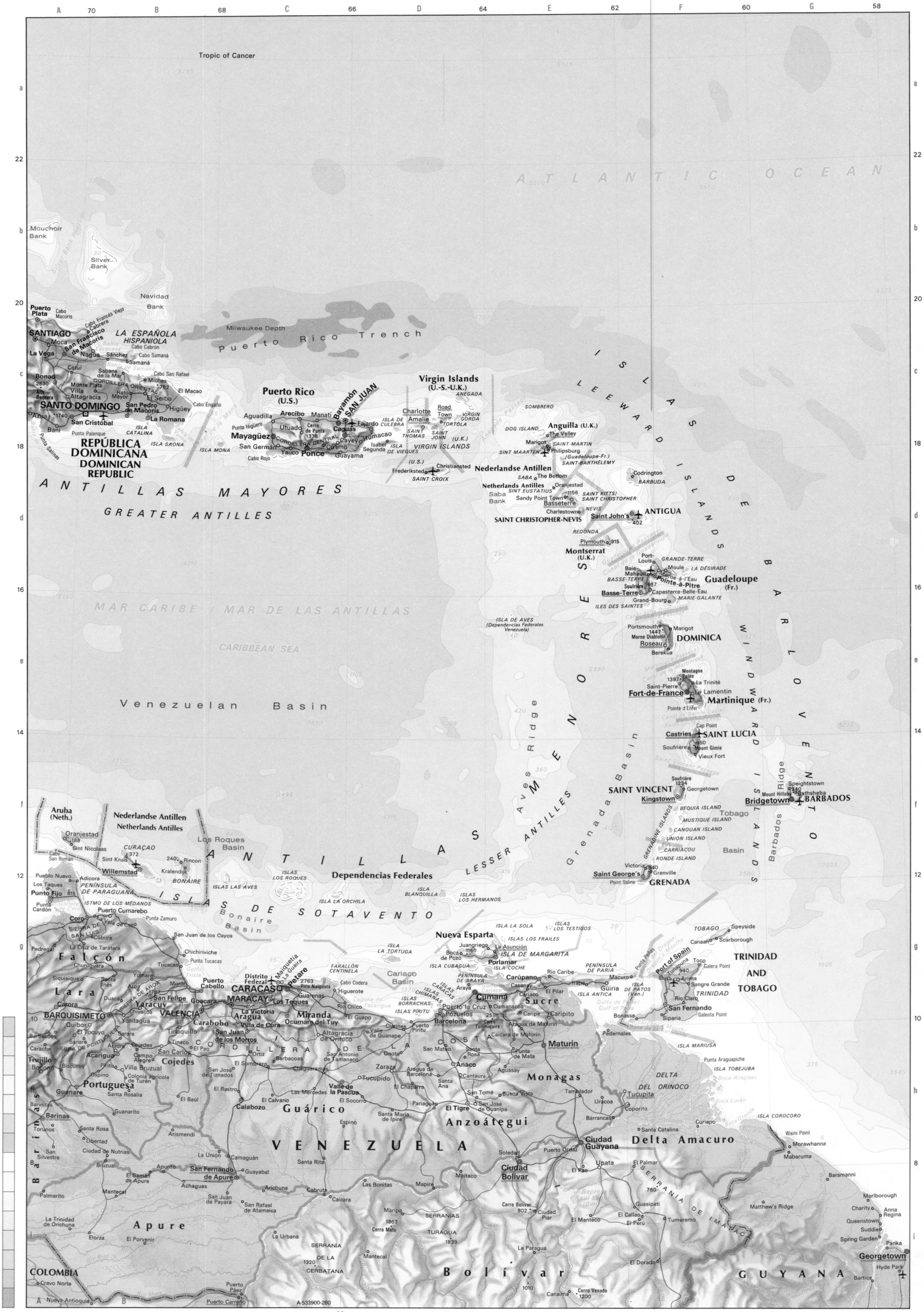

Scale 1:6,000,000 Delisle Conic Equidistant Projection

Longitude West 64 of Greenwich

0 100 200 300 400 km

0 100 200 miles

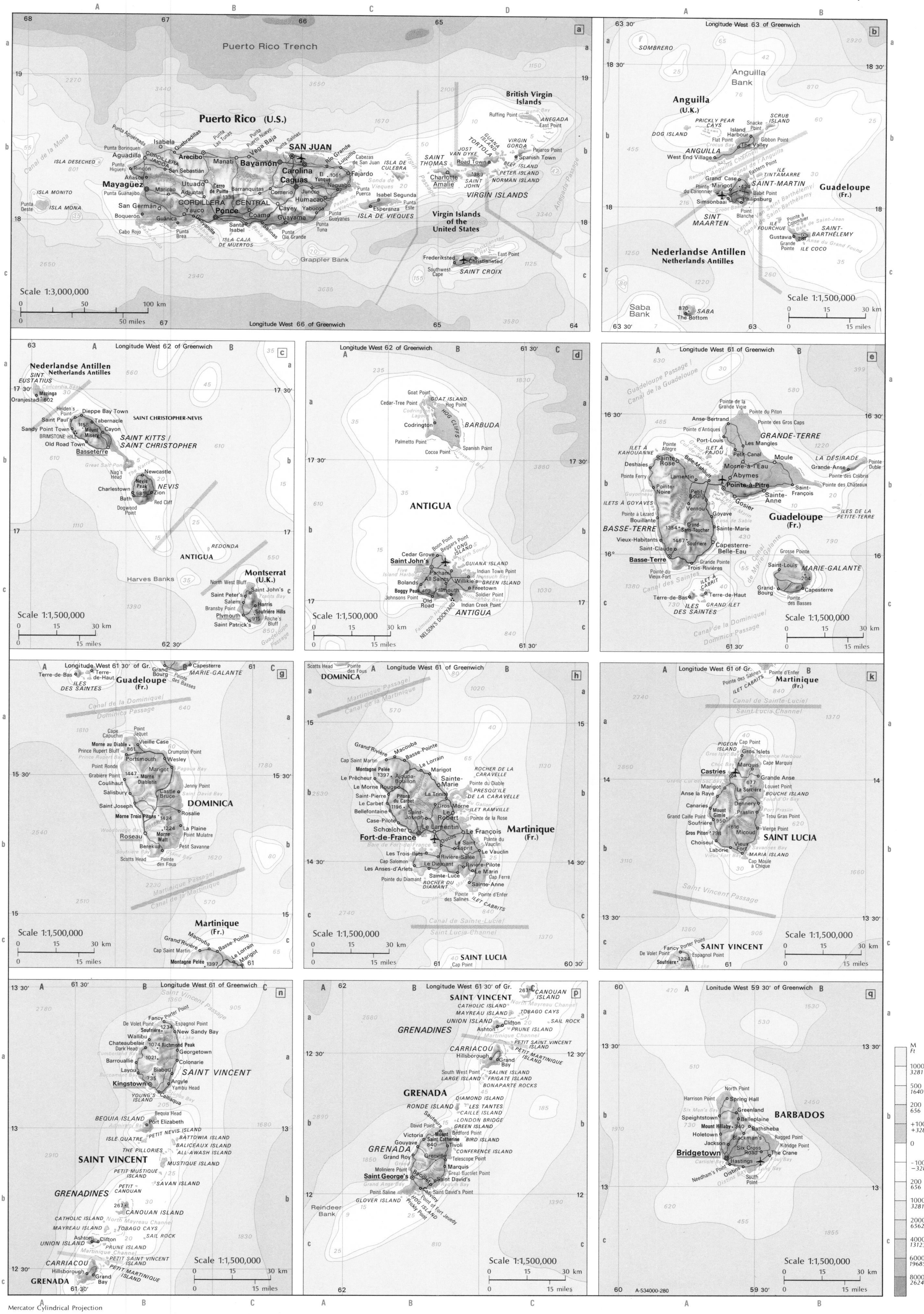
Puerto Rico (U.S.)
SAN JUAN
Mayagüez
Ponce
Bayamón
Carolina
Caguas
Puerto Rico Trench
British Virgin Islands
Virgin Islands of the United States
Anguilla (U.K.)
SAINT-MARTIN
SINT MAARTEN
Nederlandse Antillen
Netherlands Antilles
SAINT KITTS / SAINT CHRISTOPHER
NEVIS
Montserrat (U.K.)
BARBUDA
ANTIGUA
Guadeloupe (Fr.)
GRANDE-TERRE
BASSE-TERRE
MARIE-GALANTE
DOMINICA
Martinique (Fr.)
SAINT LUCIA
SAINT VINCENT
GRENADINES
GRENADA
BARBADOS
Bridgetown
Scale 1:3,000,000
Scale 1:1,500,000
Mercator Cylindrical Projection

SOUTH AMERICA, PHYSICAL

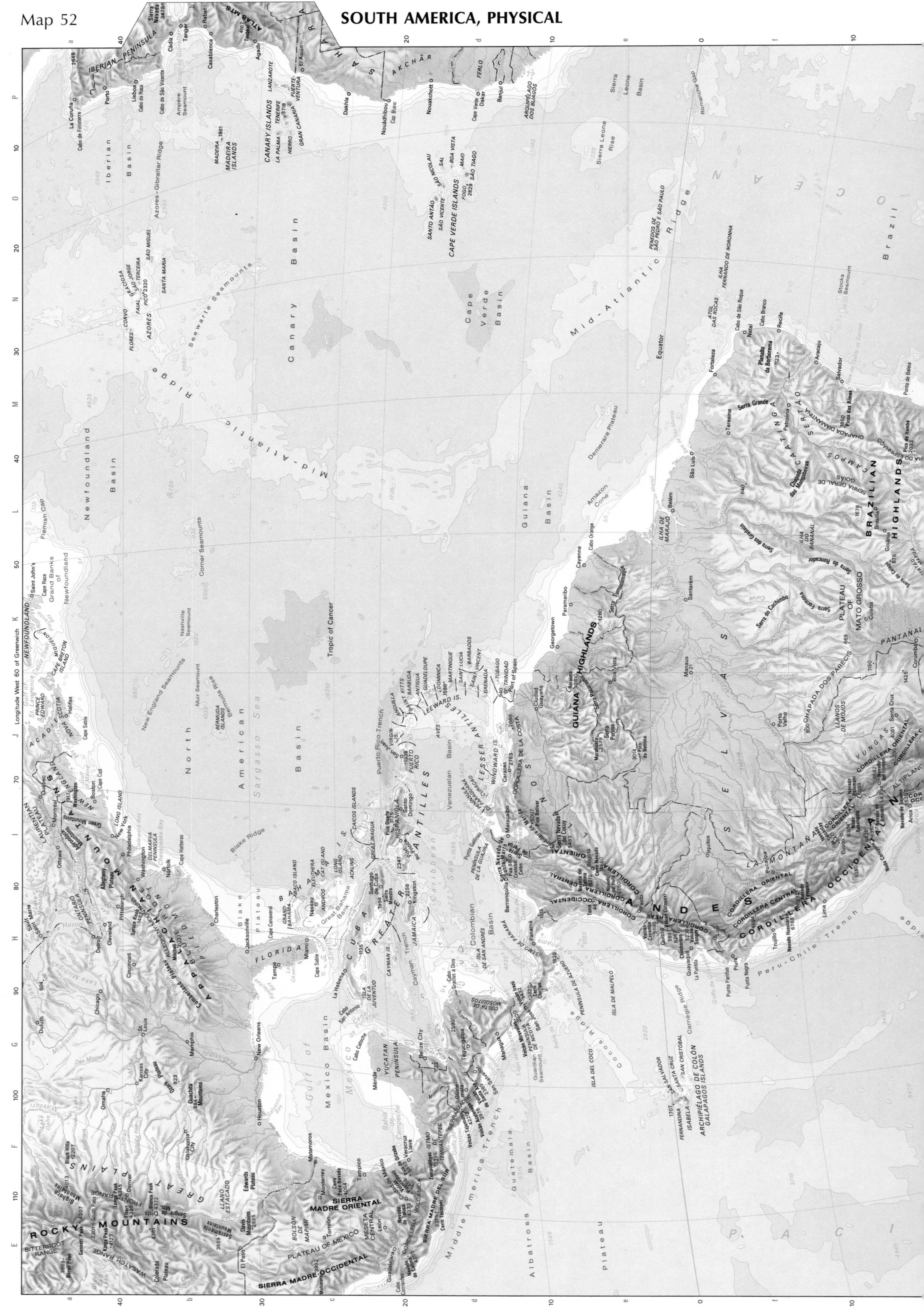

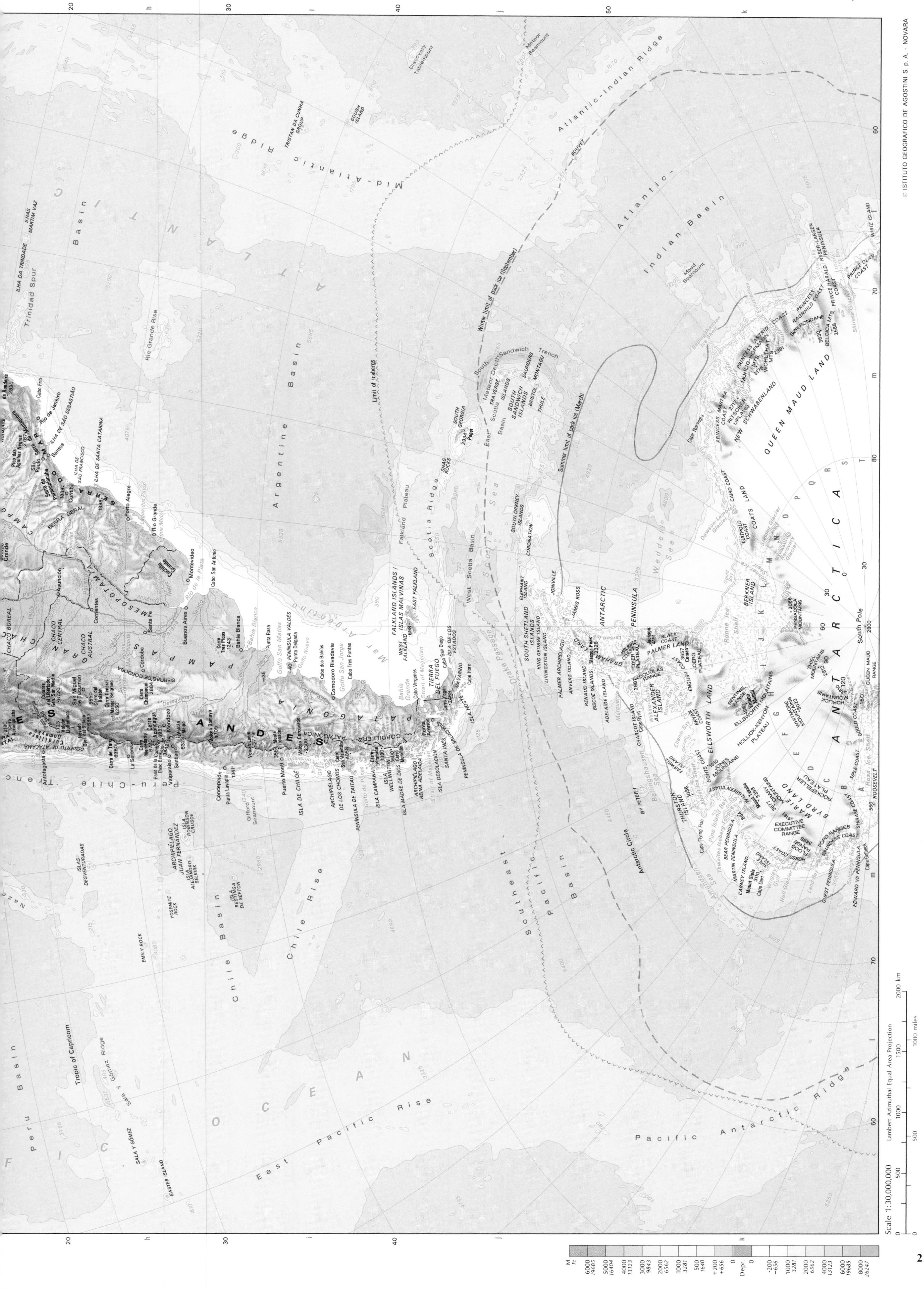

Scale 1:30,000,000

Lambert Azimuthal Equal Area Projection

0 500 1000 1500 2000 km

0 500 1000 miles

M	6000	5000	4000	3000	2000	1000	500	+200	0	Depr.	0	-200	1000	2000	4000	6000	8000
Ft	19685	16404	13123	9843	6562	3281	1640	+656	0		0	−656	3281	6562	13123	19685	26247

SOUTH AMERICA, POLITICAL

The Antarctic Region is not a political entity and its status is regulated by the Antarctic Treaty signed in Washington, D.C. in 1959. The treaty binds the states which signed the agreement to use the region solely for peaceful purposes and scientific research.

Scale 1:30,000,000
Lambert Azimuthal Equal Area Projection
0 500 1000 1500 2000 km
0 500 1000 miles

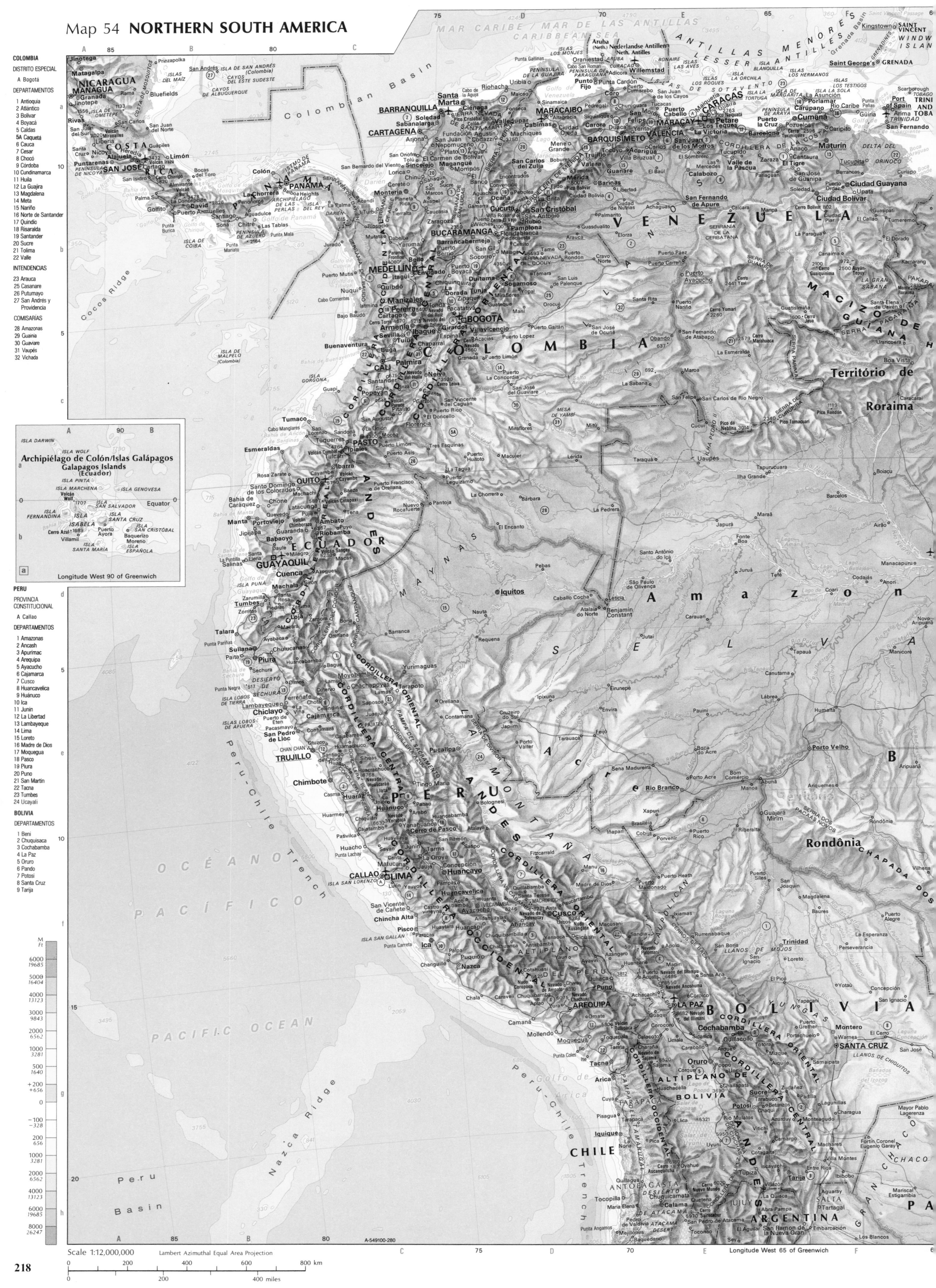

Map 54 NORTHERN SOUTH AMERICA
COLOMBIA
DISTRITO ESPECIAL
A Bogotá
DEPARTAMENTOS
1 Antioquia
2 Atlántico
3 Bolívar
4 Boyacá
5 Caldas
5A Caquetá
6 Cauca
7 Cesar
8 Chocó
9 Córdoba
10 Cundinamarca
11 Huila
12 La Guajira
13 Magdalena
14 Meta
15 Nariño
16 Norte de Santander
17 Quindío
18 Risaralda
19 Santander
20 Sucre
21 Tolima
22 Valle
INTENDENCIAS
23 Arauca
25 Casanare
26 Putumayo
27 San Andrés y Providencia
COMISARÍAS
28 Amazonas
29 Guainia
30 Guaviare
31 Vaupés
32 Vichada
Archipiélago de Colón/Islas Galápagos
Galapagos Islands
(Ecuador)
Longitude West 90 of Greenwich
PERU
PROVINCIA CONSTITUCIONAL
A Callao
DEPARTAMENTOS
1 Amazonas
2 Ancash
3 Apurímac
4 Arequipa
5 Ayacucho
6 Cajamarca
7 Cusco
8 Huancavelica
9 Huánuco
10 Ica
11 Junín
12 La Libertad
13 Lambayeque
14 Lima
15 Loreto
16 Madre de Dios
17 Moquegua
18 Pasco
19 Piura
20 Puno
21 San Martin
22 Tacna
23 Tumbes
24 Ucayali
BOLIVIA
DEPARTAMENTOS
1 Beni
2 Chuquisaca
3 Cochabamba
4 La Paz
5 Oruro
6 Pando
7 Potosí
8 Santa Cruz
9 Tarija
COLOMBIA
VENEZUELA
ECUADOR
PERU
BOLIVIA
CHILE
ARGENTINA
PACIFIC OCEAN
OCÉANO PACÍFICO
CARIBBEAN SEA
Scale 1:12,000,000
Lambert Azimuthal Equal Area Projection
Longitude West 65 of Greenwich

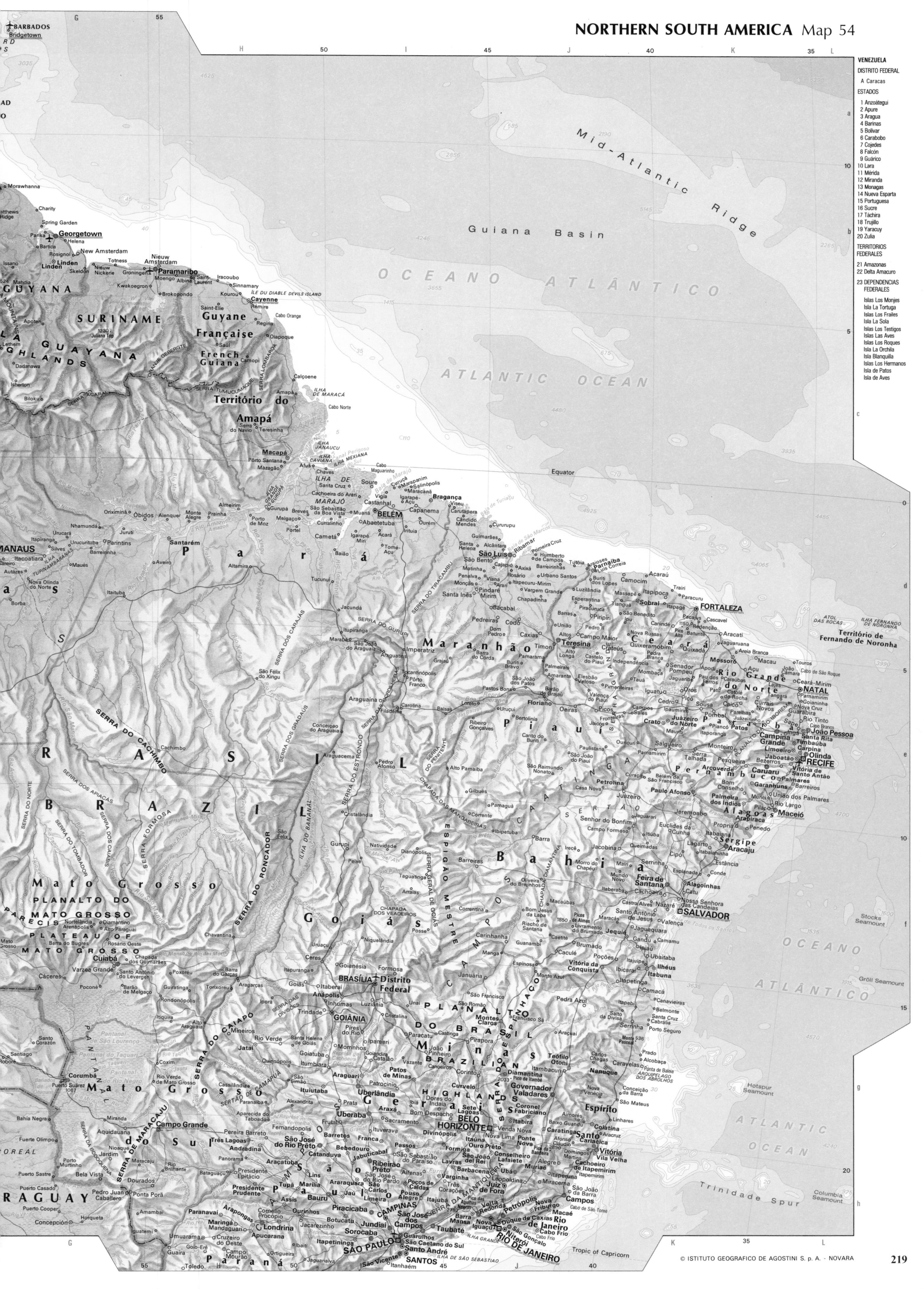
VENEZUELA
DISTRITO FEDERAL
A Caracas
ESTADOS
1 Anzoátegui
2 Apure
3 Aragua
4 Barinas
5 Bolívar
6 Carabobo
7 Cojedes
8 Falcón
9 Guárico
10 Lara
11 Mérida
12 Miranda
13 Monagas
14 Nueva Esparta
15 Portuguesa
16 Sucre
17 Táchira
18 Trujillo
19 Yaracuy
20 Zulia
TERRITORIOS FEDERALES
21 Amazonas
22 Delta Amacuro
23 DEPENDENCIAS FEDERALES
Islas Los Monjes
Isla La Tortuga
Islas Los Frailes
Isla La Sola
Islas Los Testigos
Islas Las Aves
Islas Los Roques
Isla La Orchila
Isla Blanquilla
Islas Los Hermanos
Isla de Patos
Isla de Aves
BARBADOS
Bridgetown
Mid-Atlantic Ridge
Guiana Basin
OCEANO ATLÂNTICO
ATLANTIC OCEAN
Equator
GUYANA
Georgetown
New Amsterdam
SURINAME
Paramaribo
Guyane Française
French Guiana
Cayenne
Território do Amapá
Macapá
ILHA DE MARAJÓ
BELÉM
Santarém
MANAUS
Pará
São Luís
Maranhão
Teresina
Ceará
FORTALEZA
Piauí
Rio Grande do Norte
NATAL
Paraíba
João Pessoa
Pernambuco
RECIFE
Olinda
Alagoas
Maceió
Sergipe
Aracaju
Bahia
SALVADOR
Território de Fernando de Noronha
ATOL DAS ROCAS
BRAZIL
Mato Grosso
PLANALTO DO MATO GROSSO
PLATEAU OF MATO GROSSO
Cuiabá
Goiás
GOIÂNIA
BRASÍLIA
Distrito Federal
Minas Gerais
BELO HORIZONTE
Espírito Santo
Vitória
Mato Grosso do Sul
Campo Grande
São Paulo
SÃO PAULO
SANTOS
Rio de Janeiro
RIO DE JANEIRO
Niterói
CAMPINAS
Paraná
PARAGUAY
Tropic of Capricorn
Trinidade Spur
SERRA DO RONCADOR
SERRA DO CACHIMBO
SERRA DOS CARAJÁS
CHAPADA DIAMANTINA
ESPIGÃO MESTRE
PLANALTO DO BRASIL
BRAZILIAN HIGHLANDS
CAATINGA
SERTÃO
PANTANAL

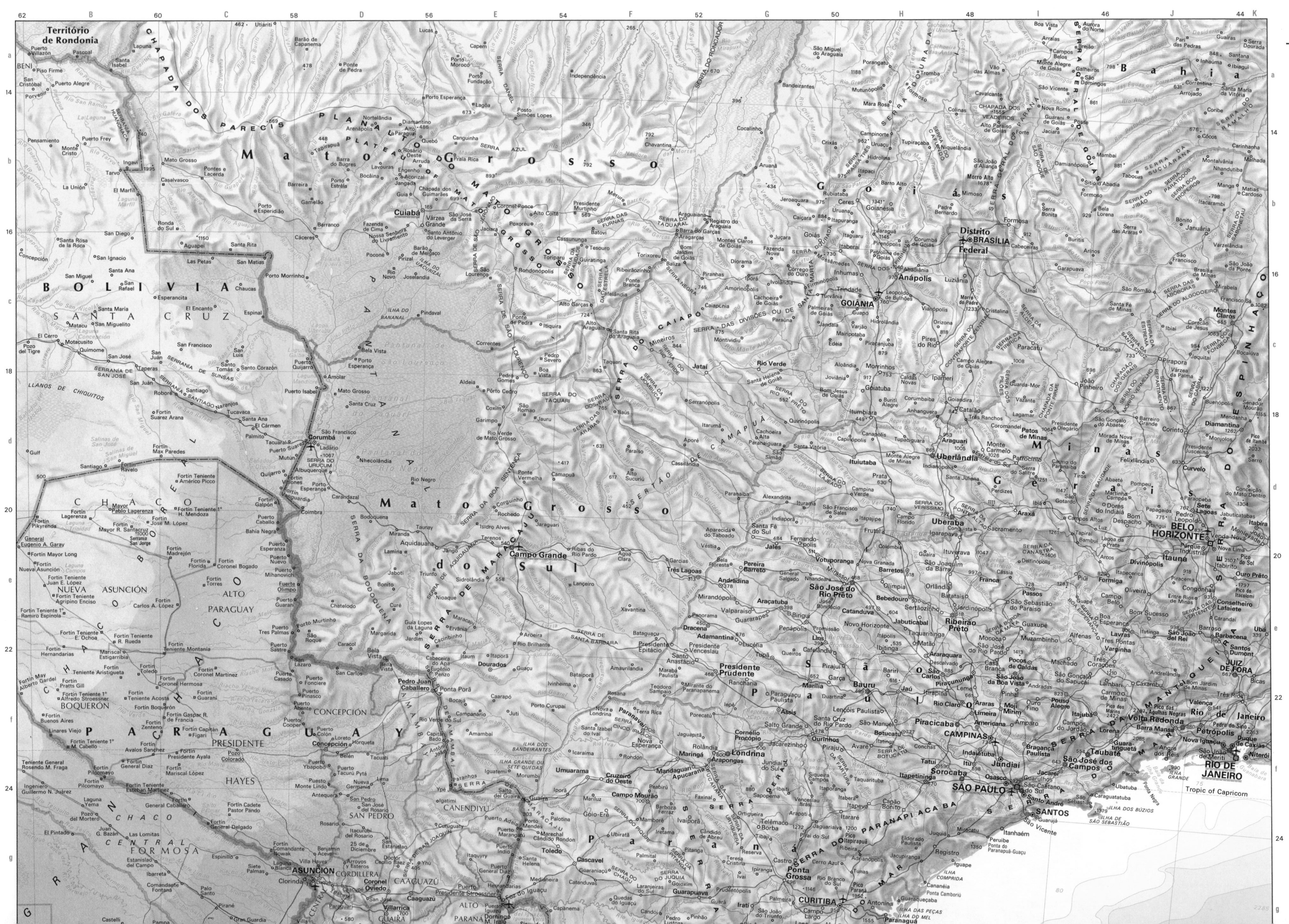
Território de Rondonia
BOLIVIA
SANTA CRUZ
CHAPADA DOS PARECIS
Mato Grosso
Mato Grosso do Sul
Goiás
Minas Gerais
Bahia
São Paulo
Paraná
PARAGUAY
PANTANAL
CHACO
BOQUERÓN
PRESIDENTE HAYES
CONCEPCIÓN
SAN PEDRO
ALTO PARAGUAY
NUEVA ASUNCIÓN
CORDILLERA
CAAGUAZÚ
CANENDIYU
GRAN CHACO
FORMOSA
Distrito Federal
BRASÍLIA
GOIÂNIA
Anápolis
BELO HORIZONTE
RIO DE JANEIRO
Niterói
Petrópolis
Volta Redonda
Juiz de Fora
SÃO PAULO
CAMPINAS
SANTOS
CURITIBA
Ponta Grossa
Londrina
Maringá
Uberlândia
Uberaba
Ribeirão Preto
Bauru
Presidente Prudente
Campo Grande
Cuiabá
Corumbá
Dourados
Pedro Juan Caballero
ASUNCIÓN
Concepción
Tropic of Capricorn
SERRA DA BODOQUENA
SERRA DO MAR

URUGUAY
DEPARTAMENTOS
1 Artigas
2 Canelones
3 Cerro Largo
4 Colonia
5 Durazno
6 Flores
7 Florida
8 Lavalleja
9 Maldonado
10 Montevideo
11 Paysandú
12 Río Negro
13 Rivera
14 Rocha
15 Salto
16 San José
17 Soriano
18 Tacuarembó
19 Treinta y Tres
Scale 1:6,000,000
Lambert Azimuthal Equal Area Projection
Longitude West 52 of Greenwich
© ISTITUTO GEOGRAFICO DE AGOSTINI S. p. A. - NOVARA
PORTO ALEGRE
MONTEVIDEO
BUENOS AIRES
LA PLATA
ROSARIO
SANTA FE
MAR DEL PLATA
Florianópolis
Pelotas
Rio Grande
Garnet Bank
ATLANTIC OCEAN
OCEANO ATLÂNTICO
MAR ARGENTINO

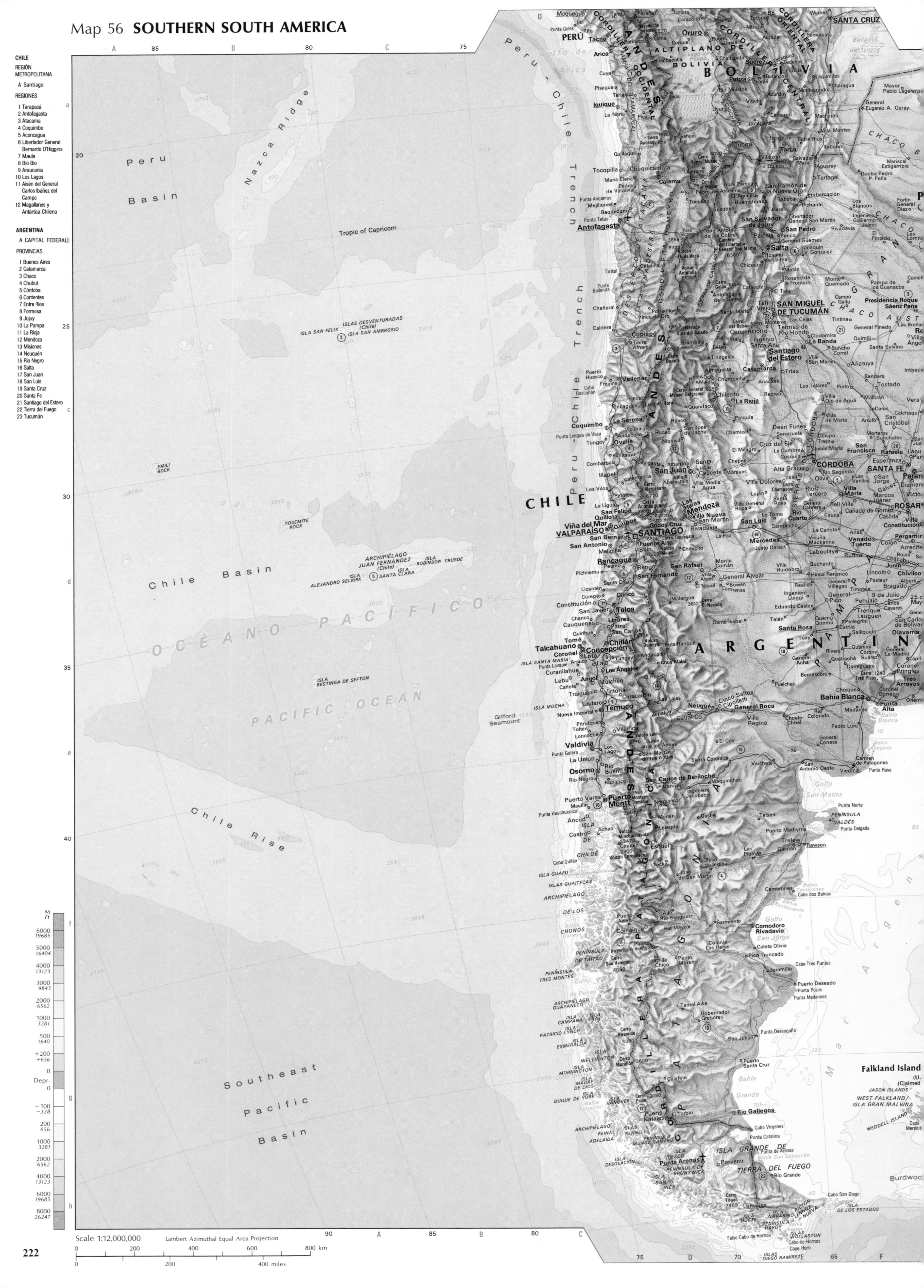
Map 56 SOUTHERN SOUTH AMERICA
CHILE
REGIÓN METROPOLITANA
A Santiago
REGIONES
1 Tarapacá
2 Antofagasta
3 Atacama
4 Coquimbo
5 Aconcagua
6 Libertador General Bernardo O'Higgins
7 Maule
8 Bío Bío
9 Araucanía
10 Los Lagos
11 Aisén del General Carlos Ibáñez del Campo
12 Magallanes y Antártica Chilena
ARGENTINA
A CAPITAL FEDERAL
PROVINCIAS
1 Buenos Aires
2 Catamarca
3 Chaco
4 Chubut
5 Córdoba
6 Corrientes
7 Entre Ríos
8 Formosa
9 Jujuy
10 La Pampa
11 La Rioja
12 Mendoza
13 Misiones
14 Neuquén
15 Río Negro
16 Salta
17 San Juan
18 San Luis
19 Santa Cruz
20 Santa Fe
21 Santiago del Estero
22 Tierra del Fuego
23 Tucumán
Peru Basin
Nazca Ridge
Peru - Chile Trench
Tropic of Capricorn
ISLAS DESVENTURADAS (Chile)
ISLA SAN FELIX
ISLA SAN AMBROSIO
EMILI ROCK
YOSEMITE ROCK
ARCHIPIÉLAGO JUAN FERNÁNDEZ (Chile)
ISLA ROBINSON CRUSOE
ISLA ALEJANDRO SELKIRK
ISLA SANTA CLARA
Chile Basin
OCÉANO PACÍFICO
PACIFIC OCEAN
ISLA RESTINGA DE SEFTON
Gifford Seamount
Chile Rise
Southeast Pacific Basin
CHILE
PERÚ
BOLIVIA
ARGENTINA
ANDES
ALTIPLANO
CORDILLERA OCCIDENTAL
CORDILLERA ORIENTAL
CORDILLERA CENTRAL
DESIERTO DE ATACAMA
PATAGONIA
SANTIAGO
Antofagasta
Iquique
Arica
Valparaíso
Viña del Mar
Concepción
Talcahuano
Temuco
Valdivia
Osorno
Puerto Montt
Punta Arenas
Mendoza
CÓRDOBA
SAN MIGUEL DE TUCUMÁN
Salta
SANTA FE
Bahía Blanca
Neuquén
Comodoro Rivadavia
Río Gallegos
ISLA GRANDE DE TIERRA DEL FUEGO
ISLA DE CHILOÉ
Falkland Islands
WEST FALKLAND / ISLA GRAN MALVINA
Scale 1:12,000,000
Lambert Azimuthal Equal Area Projection
0 200 400 600 800 km
0 200 400 miles

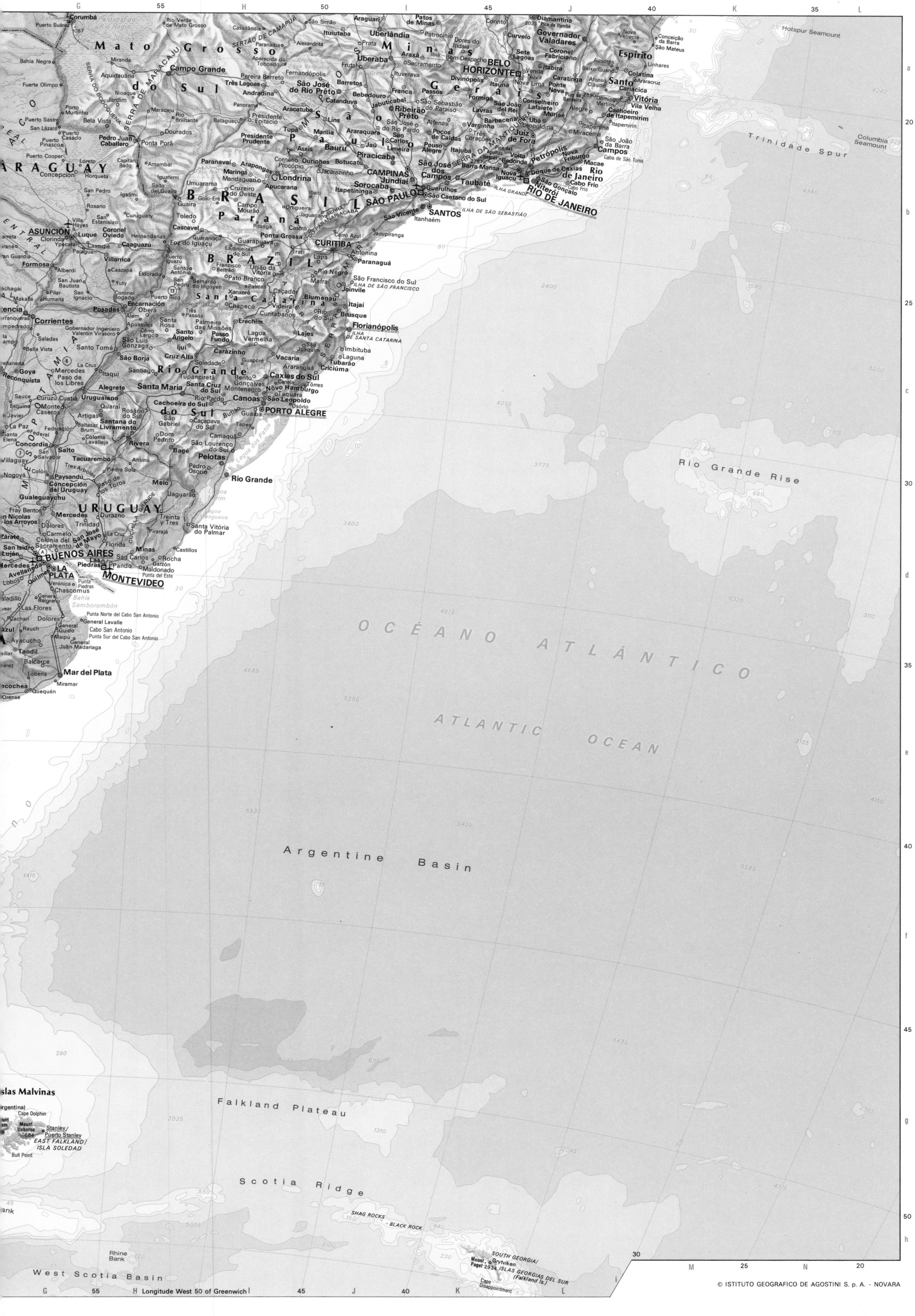

OCÉANO ATLÁNTICO
ATLANTIC OCEAN
Argentine Basin
Rio Grande Rise
Falkland Plateau
Scotia Ridge
West Scotia Basin
Trinidade Spur
Hotspur Seamount
Columbia Seamount
Rhine Bank
SHAG ROCKS
BLACK ROCK
SOUTH GEORGIA/ ISLAS GEORGIAS DEL SUR (Falkland Is.)
Grytviken
Cape Disappointment
Islas Malvinas
Cape Dolphin
Stanley/ Puerto Stanley
EAST FALKLAND/ ISLA SOLEDAD
Bull Point
BRASIL
BRAZIL
URUGUAY
PARAGUAY
Mato Grosso do Sul
Minas Gerais
São Paulo
Paraná
Santa Catarina
Rio Grande do Sul
Espírito Santo
BELO HORIZONTE
RIO DE JANEIRO
SÃO PAULO
CURITIBA
PORTO ALEGRE
BUENOS AIRES
MONTEVIDEO
LA PLATA
ASUNCIÓN
Campo Grande
Florianópolis
Vitória
Santos
Campinas
Londrina
Pelotas
Rio Grande
Mar del Plata
Corrientes
Posadas
Encarnación
Uberlândia
Uberaba
Ribeirão Prêto
Juiz de Fora
Niterói
Petrópolis
Joinville
Blumenau
Caxias do Sul
Santa Maria
Bahía Samborombón
Longitude West 50 of Greenwich

Map 57 AUSTRALIA AND OCEANIA, PHYSICAL

M	Ft
6000	19685
5000	16404
4000	13123
3000	9843
2000	6562
1000	3281
500	1640
+200	+656
0	
Depr.	
0	
−200	−656
1000	3281
2000	6562
4000	13123
6000	19685
8000	26247

Scale 1:30,000,000 Lambert Azimuthal Equal Area Projection

0 500 1000 1500 2000 km

0 500 1000 miles

Longitude East 170 of Greenwich

A-590000-780

Murray Fracture Zone
HAWAIIAN ISLANDS
Hawaiian Ridge
MIDWAY ISLANDS
Tropic of Cancer
Northeast
Pacific Basin
Clarion Fracture Zone
PACIFIC OCEAN
Clipperton Fracture Zone
Christmas Ridge
LINE ISLANDS
Equator
PHOENIX ISLANDS
POLYNESIA
TOKELAU ISLANDS
SAMOA ISLANDS
NORTHERN COOK ISLANDS
MARQUESAS ISLANDS
TUAMOTU ARCHIPELAGO
COOK ISLANDS
SOCIETY ISLANDS
LEEWARD ISLANDS
WINDWARD ISLANDS
TONGA ISLANDS
SOUTHERN COOK ISLANDS
Tropic of Capricorn
TUBUAI ISLANDS
Tuamotu Ridge
GAMBIER ISLANDS
KERMADEC ISLANDS
Kermadec Trench
Tonga Trench
East Pacific Rise
EASTER ISLAND
PACIFIC OCEAN
Southwest
Pacific
Basin
CHATHAM ISLANDS
LOWER CALIFORNIA
SIERRA MADRE OCCIDENTAL
PLATEAU OF MEXICO
Tahiti
Honolulu
HAWAII
Mauna Kea
Los Angeles
PITCAIRN
HENDERSON
DUCIE
OENO
CLIPPERTON
ISLAS REVILLAGIGEDO

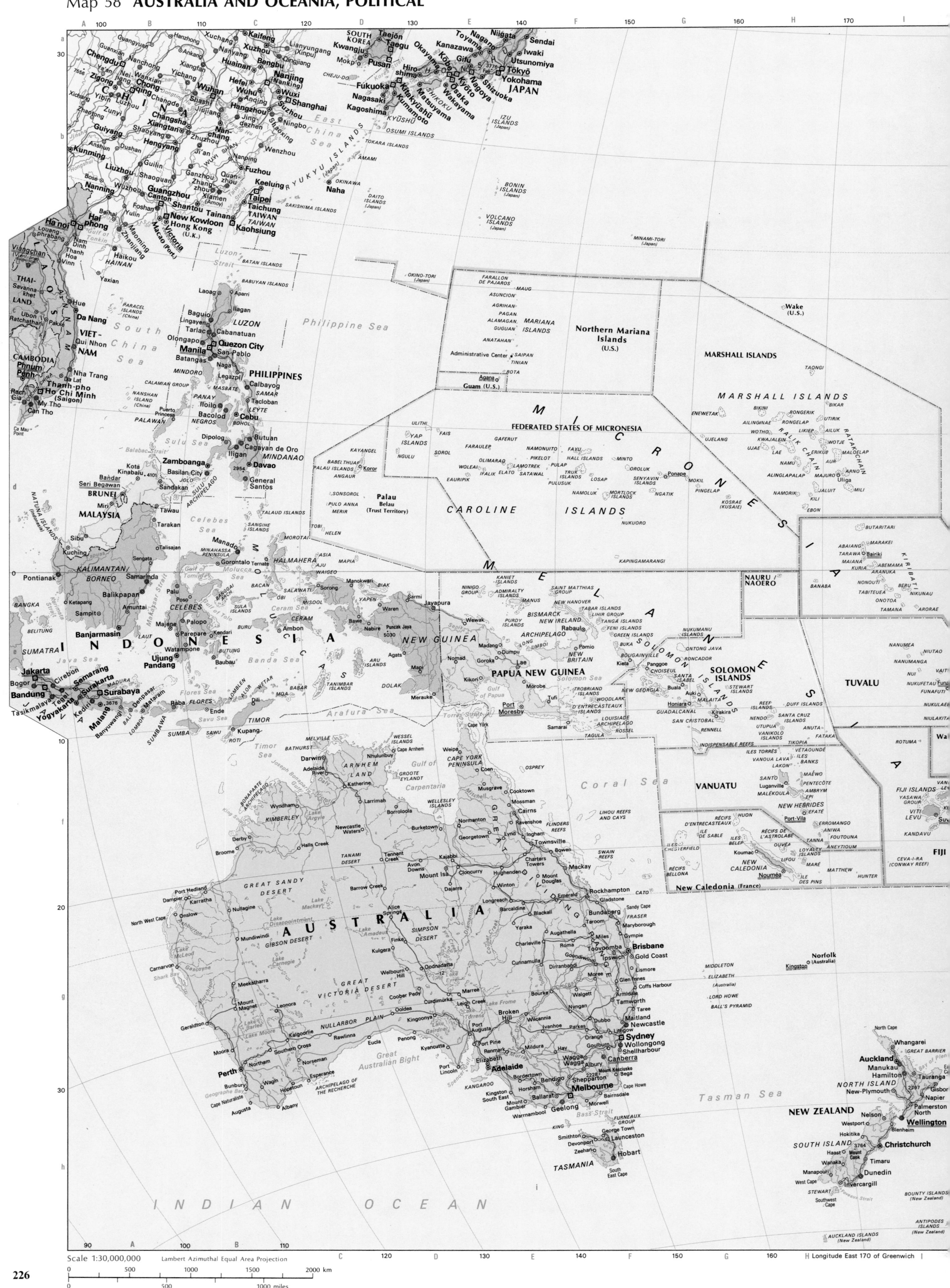

Scale 1:30,000,000 Lambert Azimuthal Equal Area Projection

0 500 1000 1500 2000 km

0 500 1000 miles

UNITED STATES
MEXICO
BAJA CALIFORNIA
Los Angeles
Long Beach
San Diego
Phoenix
Tucson
El Paso
Ciudad Juárez
Mexicali
Tijuana
Ensenada
Hermosillo
Chihuahua
Guaymas
Ciudad Obregón
Los Mochis
Culiacán Rosales
La Paz
Mazatlán
Torreón
Victoria de Durango
Monclova
ISLA DE GUADALUPE (Mexico)
ISLAS REVILLAGIGEDO (Mexico)
CLIPPERTON (French Polynesia)
Tropic of Cancer
Midway Islands (U.S.)
KURE
PEARL AND HERMES
LISIANSKI
LAYSAN
MARO
GARDNER PINNACLES
FRENCH FRIGATE SHOALS
NECKER
NIHOA
HAWAIIAN ISLANDS
Hawaii (U.S.)
NIIHAU
KAUAI
KAULA
OAHU
Honolulu
MOLOKAI
MAUI
LANAI
KAHOOLAWE
Hawi
Hilo
HAWAII
Johnston (U.S.)
PACIFIC OCEAN
KINGMAN (U.S.)
PALMYRA (U.S.)
TERAINA (WASHINGTON)
TABUAERAN (FANNING)
KIRITIMATI (CHRISTMAS)
LINE ISLANDS
JARVIS (U.S.)
HOWLAND (U.S.)
BAKER (U.S.)
Equator
WINSLOW
PHOENIX ISLANDS
KANTON
ENDERBURY
MCKEAN
BIRNIE
RAWAKI (PHOENIX)
NIKUMARORO (GARDNER)
ORONA (HULL)
MANRA (SYDNEY)
CARONDELET
KIRIBATI
MALDEN
STARBUCK
POLYNESIA
Tokelau (New Zealand)
ATAFU
NUKUNONU
TOKELAU ISLANDS
FAKAOFO
PENRHYN
CAROLINE
VOSTOK
FLINT
SWAINS
WESTERN SAMOA
SAMOA ISLANDS
SAVAI'I
Apia
UPOLU
Pago Pago
TUTUILA
MANUA ISLANDS
American Samoa (U.S.)
Wallis and Futuna (France)
Mata-Utu
WALLIS
UVEA
FUTUNA
ALOFI
HORN ISLANDS
RINGGOLD ISLES
NIUAFO'OU
TAFAHI
NIUATO PUTAPU
TONGA
FONUALEI
LAU GROUP
VAVA'U GROUP
HA'APAI GROUP
TONGA ISLANDS
VATOA
KOTU GROUP
ONO-I-LAU ISLANDS
NOMUKA GROUP
Nuku'alofa
TONGATAPU GROUP
ATA
MINERVA REEFS
ANTIOPE
Alofi
Niue (New Zealand)
BEVERIDGE
RAKAHANGA
MANIHIKI
PUKAPUKA
NASSAU
NORTHERN COOK ISLANDS
SUWARROW
Cook Islands (New Zealand)
PALMERSTON
AITUTAKI
MANUAE
TAKUTEA
MITIARO
ATIU
MAUKE
SOUTHERN COOK ISLANDS
RAROTONGA
Avarua
MANGAIA
EIAO
NUKU HIVA
UA HUKA
MARQUESAS ISLANDS
UA POU
HIVA OA
TAHUATA
FATU HIVA
TUAMOTU ARCHIPELAGO
RANGIROA
MANIHI
ILES DU ROI GEORGES
ILES DU DÉSAPPOINTEMENT
PUKAPUKA
MATAIVA
ILES PALLISER
APATAKI
ARATIKA
TAKUME
FANGATAU
MOTU ONE
LEEWARD ISLANDS
MAUPITI
MANUAE
BORA-BORA
HUAHINE
KAUKURA
FAKARAVA
FAKAHINA
MAUPIHAA
RAIATEA
TETIAROA
Papeete
MAKEMO
MOOREA
TAHITI
TAHANEA
MOTUTUNGA
MARUTEA
TATAKOTO
AMANU
SOCIETY ISLANDS
WINDWARD ISLANDS
RAVAHERE
HAO
PUKARUHA
VAHITAHI
REAO
MANUANGI
AHUNUI
HEREHERETUE
ILES DU DUC DE GLOUCESTER
TUREIA
GROUPE ACTÉON
MURUROA
MARUTEA
MARIA
RURUTU
French Polynesia
TEMATANGI
FAGATAUFA
MARIA
RIMATARA
TUBUAI
TUBUAI ISLANDS
RAEVAVAE
MORANE
MANGAREVA
TEMOE
GAMBIER ISLANDS
OENO
HENDERSON
DUCIE
PITCAIRN
Adamstown
Pitcairn (U.K.)
Tropic of Capricorn
RAPA
ILOTS DE BASS
RAOUL
MACAULEY
KERMADEC ISLANDS (New Zealand)
CURTIS
L'ESPERANCE ROCK
SALA Y GÓMEZ (Chile)
EASTER ISLAND (Chile)
ERNEST LEGOUVÉ
MARIA THERESA
CHATHAM ISLANDS (New Zealand)
CHATHAM
PITT
A-590000-280-2 -2 -2 -3

M / Ft
4000 / 13123
3000 / 9843
2000 / 6562
1000 / 3281
500 / 1640
+ 200 / +656
0
Depr.
0
− 100 / −328
200 / 656
1000 / 3281
2000 / 6562
4000 / 13123
6000 / 19685
8000 / 26247

Scale 1:12,000,000 Delisle Conic Equidistant Projection

0 200 400 600 800 km

0 200 400 miles

Longitude East

PAPUA NEW GUINEA
NEW GUINEA
PULAU IRIAN
Gulf of Papua
Port Moresby
Solomon Basin
New Britian Trench
NEW BRITAIN
BISMARCK ARCHIPELAGO
NEW IRELAND ISLAND
SOLOMON ISLANDS
BOUGAINVILLE ISLAND
SANTA ISABEL ISLAND
NEW GEORGIA ISLANDS
GUADALCANAL ISLAND
MALAITA ISLAND
SAN CRISTOBAL ISLAND
Honiara
LOUISIADE ARCHIPELAGO
D'ENTRECASTEAUX ISLANDS
Torres Strait
Thursday Island
CAPE YORK PENINSULA
Gulf of Carpentaria
WESSEL ISLANDS
GOVE PENINSULA
GROOTE EYLANDT
MORNINGTON ISLAND
WELLESLEY ISLANDS
BARKLY TABLELAND
CORAL SEA
Coral Sea Basin
Coral Sea Islands Territory
GREAT BARRIER REEF
GREAT DIVIDING RANGE
Cairns
Townsville
Mackay
Rockhampton
Mount Isa
Queensland
GREAT ARTESIAN BASIN
SIMPSON DESERT
Tropic of Capricorn
Nouvelle-Calédonie
New Caledonia
(France)
PACIFIC OCEAN
Kelso Bank
Kejpel Bank
Bundaberg
Maryborough
FRASER ISLAND
Toowoomba
Ipswich
BRISBANE
Gold Coast
STURT DESERT
DARLING DOWNS
GREY RANGE
New South Wales
Broken Hill
Dubbo
Tamworth
Armidale
Coffs Harbour
Port Macquarie
Newcastle
SYDNEY
Wollongong
Canberra
Australian Capital Territory
LORD HOWE ISLAND
(Australia)
BALL'S PYRAMID
MIDDLETON REEF
ELIZABETH REEF
ADELAIDE
Port Augusta
Whyalla
EYRE PENINSULA
KANGAROO ISLAND
Mildura
RIVERINA
Wagga Wagga
Albury
Victoria
Bendigo
Ballarat
MELBOURNE
Geelong
WILSONS PROMONTORY
Bass Strait
KING ISLAND
FURNEAUX GROUP
FLINDERS ISLAND
Tasmania
Launceston
Hobart
Tasman Basin
TASMAN SEA
140
155
160
165

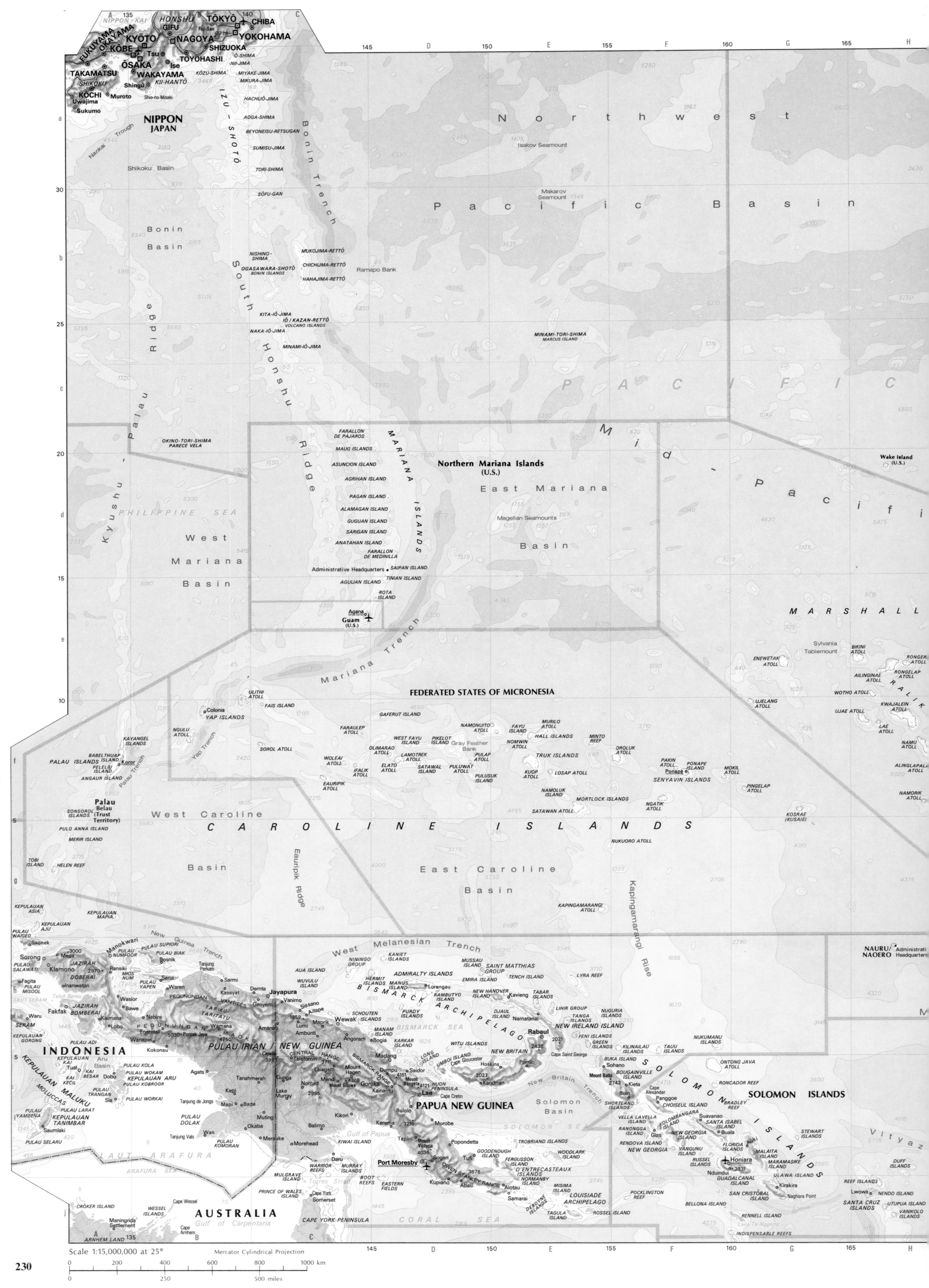
NIPPON-KAI
HONSHU
TŌKYŌ
CHIBA
YOKOHAMA
GIFU
FUKUYAMA
OKAYAMA
KYŌTO
NAGOYA
KŌBE
SHIZUOKA
Tsu
TOYOHASHI
ŌSAKA
Ise
TAKAMATSU
WAKAYAMA
SHIKOKU
Shingū
KII-HANTŌ
KŌCHI
Muroto
Uwajima
Sukumo
Shio-no-Misaki
Ō-SHIMA
NII-JIMA
KŌZU-SHIMA
MIYAKE-JIMA
MIKURA-JIMA
HACHIJŌ-JIMA
AOGA-SHIMA
BEYONEISU-RETSUGAN
SUMISU-JIMA
TORI-SHIMA
SŌFU-GAN
NIPPON
JAPAN
Nankai Trough
Shikoku Basin
IZU-SHOTŌ
Bonin Trench
Bonin Basin
South Honshu Ridge
NISHINO-SHIMA
OGASAWARA-SHOTŌ
BONIN ISLANDS
MUKOJIMA-RETTŌ
CHICHIJIMA-RETTŌ
HAHAJIMA-RETTŌ
Ramapo Bank
KITA-IŌ-JIMA
IŌ / KAZAN-RETTŌ
VOLCANO ISLANDS
NAKA-IŌ-JIMA
MINAMI-IŌ-JIMA
Northwest Pacific Basin
Isakov Seamount
Makarov Seamount
MINAMI-TORI-SHIMA
MARCUS ISLAND
PACIFIC
Mid-Pacific
Palau-Kyushu Ridge
OKINO-TORI-SHIMA
PARECE VELA
PHILIPPINE SEA
West Mariana Basin
West Mariana Ridge
FARALLON DE PAJAROS
MAUG ISLANDS
ASUNCION ISLAND
AGRIHAN ISLAND
PAGAN ISLAND
ALAMAGAN ISLAND
GUGUAN ISLAND
SARIGAN ISLAND
ANATAHAN ISLAND
FARALLON DE MEDINILLA
Administrative Headquarters
SAIPAN ISLAND
TINIAN ISLAND
AGUIJAN ISLAND
ROTA ISLAND
MARIANA ISLANDS
Northern Mariana Islands
(U.S.)
East Mariana Basin
Magellan Seamounts
Agana
Guam
(U.S.)
Mariana Trench
Wake Island
(U.S.)
MARSHALL
RALIK
Sylvania Tablemount
BIKINI ATOLL
RONGERIK ATOLL
RONGELAP ATOLL
ENEWETAK ATOLL
AILINGINAE ATOLL
WOTHO ATOLL
UJELANG ATOLL
UJAE ATOLL
KWAJALEIN ATOLL
LAE ATOLL
NAMU ATOLL
AILINGLAPALAP ATOLL
NAMORIK ATOLL
FEDERATED STATES OF MICRONESIA
ULITHI ATOLL
FAIS ISLAND
Colonia
YAP ISLANDS
NGULU ATOLL
Yap Trench
GAFERUT ISLAND
FARAULEP ATOLL
SOROL ATOLL
NAMONUITO ATOLL
FAYU ISLAND
MURILO ATOLL
HALL ISLANDS
MINTO REEF
WEST FAYU ISLAND
PIKELOT ISLAND
Gray Feather Bank
OLIMARAO ATOLL
NOMWIN ATOLL
OROLUK ATOLL
LAMOTREK ATOLL
PULAP ATOLL
TRUK ISLANDS
WOLEAI ATOLL
ELATO ATOLL
SATAWAL ISLAND
PULUWAT ATOLL
IFALIK ATOLL
PULUSUK ISLAND
KUOP ATOLL
LOSAP ATOLL
PAKIN ATOLL
PONAPE ISLAND
Ponape
MOKIL ATOLL
SENYAVIN ISLANDS
PINGELAP ATOLL
EAURIPIK ATOLL
NAMOLUK ISLAND
MORTLOCK ISLANDS
NGATIK ATOLL
SATAWAN ATOLL
KOSRAE (KUSAIE)
KAYANGEL ISLANDS
BABELTHUAP ISLAND
PALAU ISLANDS
Koror
PELELIU ISLAND
ANGAUR ISLAND
Palau Trench
Palau
Belau
(Trust Territory)
SONSOROL ISLANDS
PULO ANNA ISLAND
MERIR ISLAND
TOBI ISLAND
HELEN REEF
West Caroline Basin
CAROLINE ISLANDS
Eauripik Ridge
East Caroline Basin
NUKUORO ATOLL
Kapingamarangi Rise
KAPINGAMARANGI ATOLL
KEPULAUAN ASIA
KEPULAUAN MAPIA
KEPULAUAN AJU
PULAU WAIGEO
New Guinea Trench
West Melanesian Trench
NAURU
NAOERO
Administrative Headquarters
Manokwari
PULAU SUPIORI
PULAU NUMFOOR
PULAU BIAK
Bosnik
Saonek
Sorong
Mega
JAZIRAH DOBERAI
Klamono
Ransiki
PULAU SALAWATI
Tanjung Perkam
Sarmi
PULAU MISOOL
Fagita
Inanwatan
PULAU YAPEN
Serui
Teluk Cenderawasih
Demta
Jayapura
Kansyat
Genyem
Vanimo
Sissano
Aitape
Wewak
Wasior
PEGUNUNGAN VAN REES
Bawe
Teluk Berau
JAZIRAH BOMBERAI
Fakfak
Kaimana
Waru
Nabire
SERAM
Lobo
Enarotali
Wamena
Wanapiri
Puncak Jaya
KEPULAUAN GORONG
PULAU ADI
Kokonau
INDONESIA
PULAU IRIAN / NEW GUINEA
CENTRAL RANGE
Telefomin
Ambunti
Lumi
Maprik
Amanab
Angoram
Bogia
SCHOUTEN ISLANDS
AUA ISLAND
WUVULU ISLAND
NININGO GROUP
KANIET ISLANDS
HERMIT ISLANDS
MANUS ISLAND
Lorengau
ADMIRALTY ISLANDS
BISMARCK ARCHIPELAGO
MUSSAU ISLAND
SAINT MATTHIAS GROUP
EMIRA ISLAND
TENCH ISLAND
NEW HANOVER ISLAND
Kavieng
TABAR ISLANDS
LYRA REEF
RAMBUTYO ISLAND
DJAUL ISLAND
LIHIR GROUP
NUGURIA ISLANDS
TANGA ISLANDS
PURDY ISLANDS
Namatanai
NEW IRELAND ISLAND
BISMARCK SEA
MANAM ISLAND
KARKAR ISLAND
WITU ISLANDS
Rabaul
FENI ISLANDS
GREEN ISLANDS
KILINAILAU ISLANDS
TAUU ISLANDS
NUKUMANU ISLANDS
Madang
LONG ISLAND
UMBOI ISLAND
Cape Gloucester
NEW BRITAIN
Cape Saint George
Pomio
Hoskins
Kandrian
BUKA ISLAND
Sohano
ONTONG JAVA ATOLL
Mount Balbi
BOUGAINVILLE ISLAND
Kieta
SOLOMON ISLANDS
Aru Basin
KEPULAUAN KAI
Tual
PULAU KOLA
PULAU WOKAM
KEPULAUAN ARU
Dobo
PULAU KOBROOR
Agats
Tanahmerah
KAI BESAR
KAI KECIL
MALUKU
MOLUCCAS
KEPULAUAN
PULAU TRANGAN
PULAU WORKAI
PULAU LARAT
PULAU YAMDENA
KEPULAUAN TANIMBAR
Saumlaki
Laiagam
Mount Hagen
Mendi
Mount Giluwe
Goroka
Kainantu
Nomad
Lake Murray
BISMARCK RANGE
Dumpu
Saidor
Mount Bangeta
HUON PENINSULA
Lae
Cape Cretin
Vitiaz Strait
PAPUA NEW GUINEA
New Britain Trench
Solomon Basin
Tanjung de Jongs
Keni
Mapi
Bade
PULAU DOLAK
Muting
Okaba
Merauke
Tanjung Vals
Wan
PULAU KOMORAN
PULAU SELARU
Kikori
Kerema
Bulolo
Morobe
Balimo
Gulf of Papua
Tapini
Mount Victoria
Popondetta
Morehead
Daru
Port Moresby
Sogeri
Tufi
GOODENOUGH ISLAND
FERGUSSON ISLAND
TROBRIAND ISLANDS
WOODLARK ISLAND
D'ENTRECASTEAUX ISLANDS
NORMANBY ISLAND
OWEN STANLEY RANGE
Kupiano
Abau
Alotau
Samarai
MISIMA ISLAND
LOUISIADE ARCHIPELAGO
DEBOYNE ISLANDS
TAGULA ISLAND
ROSSEL ISLAND
SOLOMON SEA
WARRIOR REEFS
MURRAY ISLANDS
BOOT REEFS
EASTERN FIELDS
MULGRAVE ISLAND
Torres Strait
Cape York
PRINCE OF WALES ISLAND
Somerset
CAPE YORK PENINSULA
CORAL SEA
LAUT ARAFURA
ARAFURA SEA
CROKER ISLAND
WESSEL ISLANDS
Cape Wessel
AUSTRALIA
Gulf of Carpentaria
Maningrida Settlement
Cape Arnhem
ARNHEM LAND
SHORTLAND ISLANDS
Buin
Cape Alexander
CHOISEUL ISLAND
Panggoe
BRADLEY REEF
RONCADOR REEF
VELLA LAVELLA ISLAND
KOLOMBANGARA ISLAND
Suavanao
SANTA ISABEL ISLAND
Buala
RANONGGA ISLAND
Gizo
NEW GEORGIA ISLAND
NEW GEORGIA
RENDOVA ISLAND
VANGUNU ISLAND
RUSSELL ISLANDS
FLORIDA ISLANDS
Auki
MALAITA ISLAND
Honiara
Nduindui
GUADALCANAL ISLAND
MARAMASIKE ISLAND
ULAWA ISLAND
STEWART ISLANDS
Kirakira
SAN CRISTÓBAL ISLAND
Naghora Point
POCKLINGTON REEF
BELLONA ISLAND
RENNELL ISLAND
INDISPENSABLE REEFS
REEF ISLANDS
NENDO ISLAND
Lwowa
SANTA CRUZ ISLANDS
UTUPUA ISLAND
VANIKOLO ISLANDS
DUFF ISLANDS
Vityaz
Scale 1:15,000,000 at 25°
Mercator Cylindrical Projection
0 200 400 600 800 1000 km
0 250 500 miles

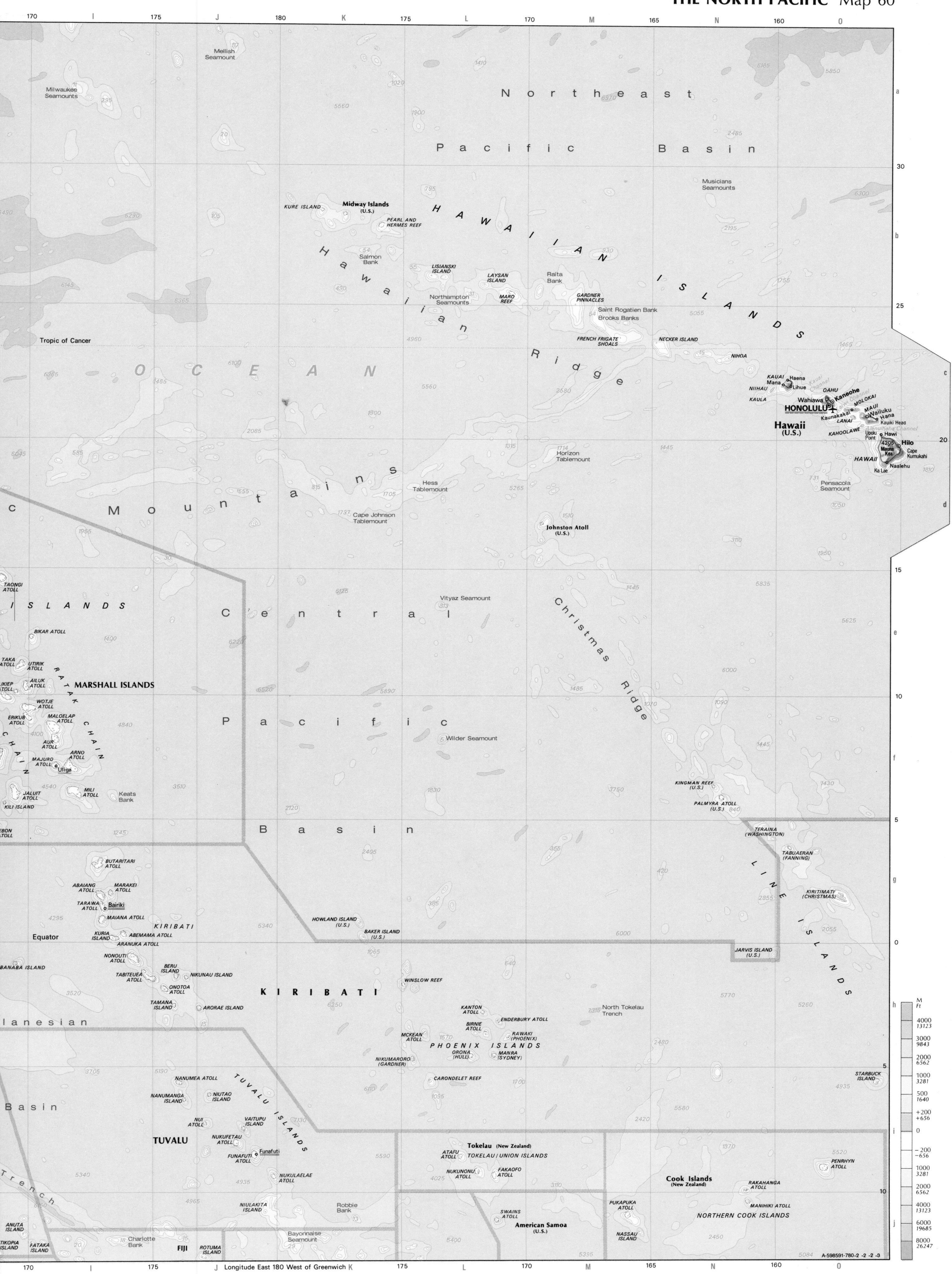
Northeast Pacific Basin
HAWAIIAN ISLANDS
Hawaiian Ridge
Midway Islands (U.S.)
KURE ISLAND
PEARL AND HERMES REEF
LISIANSKI ISLAND
LAYSAN ISLAND
MARO REEF
GARDNER PINNACLES
FRENCH FRIGATE SHOALS
NECKER ISLAND
NIHOA
KAUAI
NIIHAU
KAULA
OAHU
MOLOKAI
LANAI
MAUI
KAHOOLAWE
HAWAII
HONOLULU
Hilo
Hawaii (U.S.)
Johnston Atoll (U.S.)
Mid-Pacific Mountains
OCEAN
Central Pacific Basin
Christmas Ridge
Tropic of Cancer
Equator
MARSHALL ISLANDS
RATAK CHAIN
KIRIBATI
PHOENIX ISLANDS
LINE ISLANDS
TUVALU ISLANDS
TUVALU
Tokelau (New Zealand)
TOKELAU / UNION ISLANDS
American Samoa (U.S.)
Cook Islands (New Zealand)
NORTHERN COOK ISLANDS
FIJI
KINGMAN REEF (U.S.)
PALMYRA ATOLL (U.S.)
HOWLAND ISLAND (U.S.)
BAKER ISLAND (U.S.)
JARVIS ISLAND (U.S.)
Longitude East 180 West of Greenwich
A-598591-780-2 -2 -2 -3

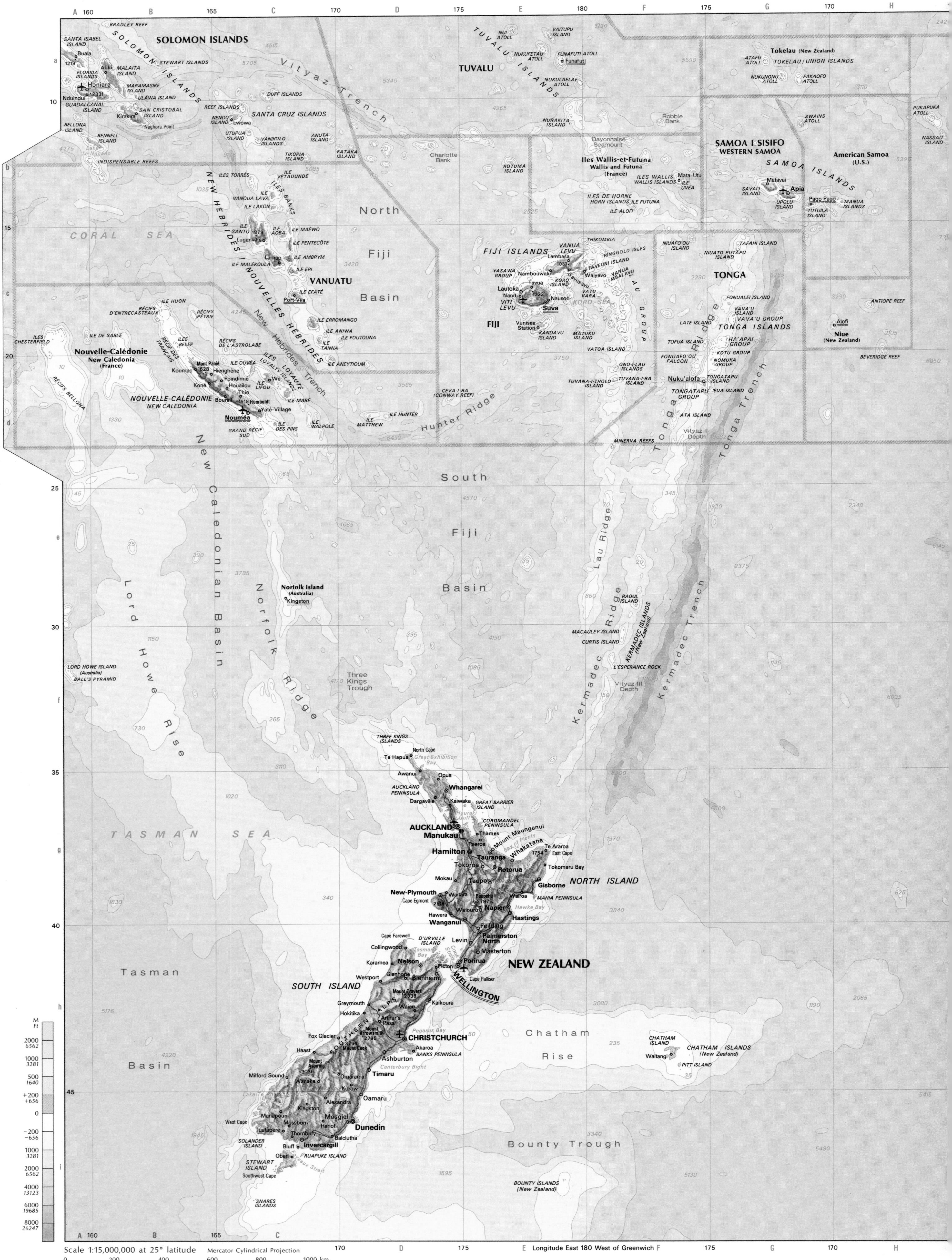

Scale 1:15,000,000 at 25° latitude Mercator Cylindrical Projection

Longitude East 180 West of Greenwich

0 200 400 600 800 1000 km

0 250 500 miles

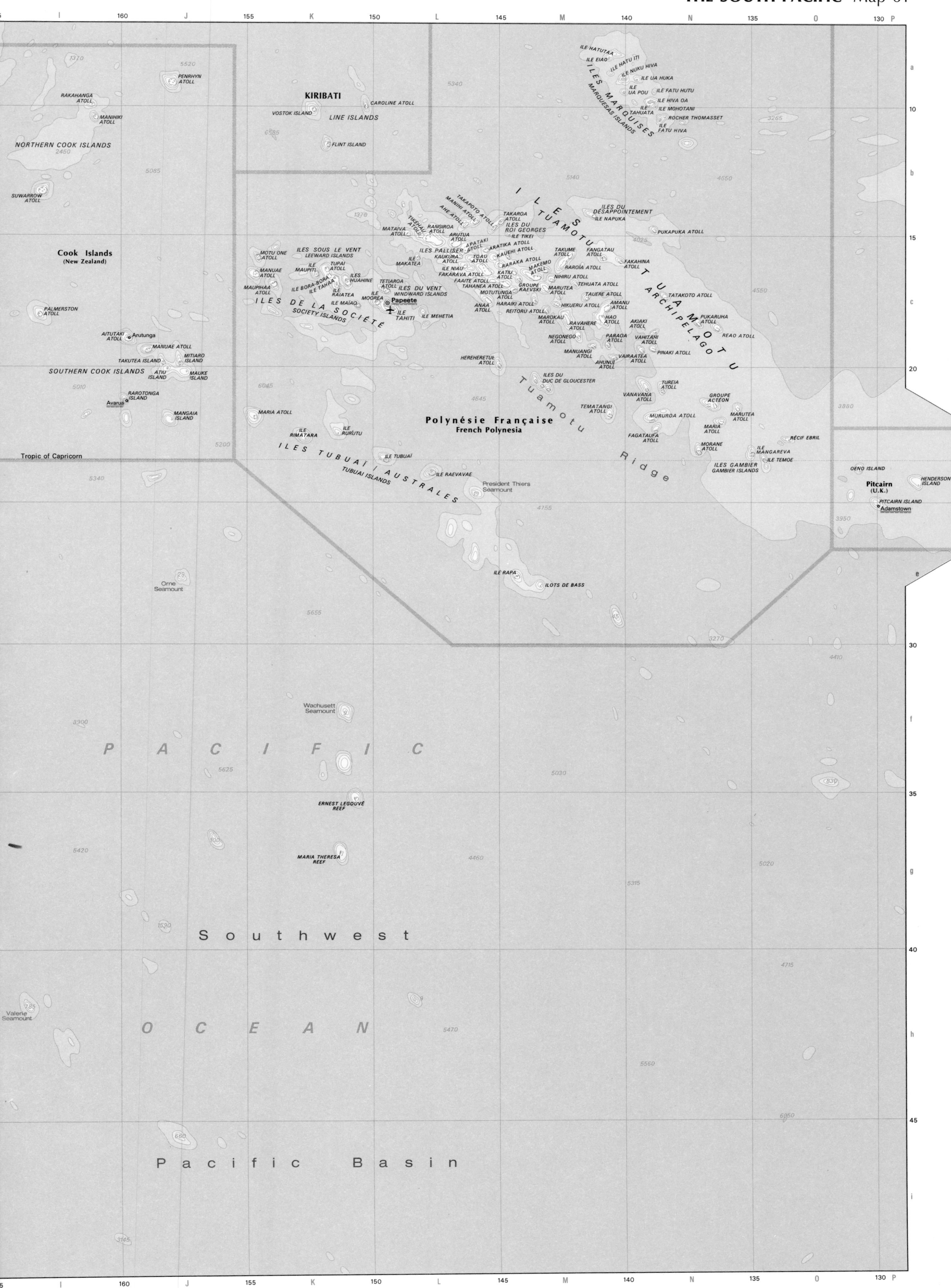
KIRIBATI
LINE ISLANDS
VOSTOK ISLAND
CAROLINE ATOLL
FLINT ISLAND
PENRHYN ATOLL
RAKAHANGA ATOLL
MANIHIKI ATOLL
NORTHERN COOK ISLANDS
SUWARROW ATOLL
Cook Islands
(New Zealand)
PALMERSTON ATOLL
AITUTAKI ATOLL
Arutunga
MANUAE ATOLL
TAKUTEA ISLAND
MITIARO ISLAND
SOUTHERN COOK ISLANDS
ATIU ISLAND
MAUKE ISLAND
RAROTONGA ISLAND
Avarua
MANGAIA ISLAND
Tropic of Capricorn
ILES MARQUISES
MARQUESAS ISLANDS
ILE HATUTAA
ILE EIAO
ILE HATU ITI
ILE NUKU HIVA
ILE UA HUKA
ILE UA POU
ILE FATU HUTU
ILE HIVA OA
ILE TAHUATA
ILE MOHOTANI
ROCHER THOMASSET
ILE FATU HIVA
ILES TUAMOTU
TUAMOTU ARCHIPELAGO
ILES DU DESAPPOINTEMENT
ILE NAPUKA
PUKAPUKA ATOLL
TAKAPOTO ATOLL
MANIHI ATOLL
AHE ATOLL
TIKEHAU ATOLL
RANGIROA ATOLL
MATAIVA ATOLL
TAKAROA ATOLL
ILES DU ROI GEORGES
ILE TIKEI
ARUTUA ATOLL
APATAKI ATOLL
ARATIKA ATOLL
KAUEHI ATOLL
ILES PALLISER
KAUKURA ATOLL
TOAU ATOLL
ILE MAKATEA
ILE NIAU
FAKARAVA ATOLL
FAAITE ATOLL
TAHANEA ATOLL
RARAKA ATOLL
MAKEMO ATOLL
KATIU ATOLL
TAKUME ATOLL
FANGATAU ATOLL
FAKAHINA ATOLL
RAROIA ATOLL
NIHIRU ATOLL
TEHUATA ATOLL
MOTUTUNGA ATOLL
GROUPE RAEVSKI
MARUTEA ATOLL
TAUERE ATOLL
TATAKOTO ATOLL
ANAA ATOLL
HARAIKI ATOLL
REITORU ATOLL
HIKUERU ATOLL
AMANU ATOLL
MAROKAU ATOLL
RAVAHERE ATOLL
HAO ATOLL
AKIAKI ATOLL
PUKARUHA ATOLL
REAO ATOLL
NEGONEGO ATOLL
PARAOA ATOLL
VAHITAHI ATOLL
MANUANGI ATOLL
VAIRAATEA ATOLL
AHUNUI ATOLL
PINAKI ATOLL
HEREHERETUE ATOLL
ILES DU DUC DE GLOUCESTER
TUREIA ATOLL
VANAVANA ATOLL
GROUPE ACTEON
TEMATANGI ATOLL
MURUROA ATOLL
MARUTEA ATOLL
MARIA ATOLL
FAGATAUFA ATOLL
RECIF EBRIL
MORANE ATOLL
ILE MANGAREVA
ILE TEMOE
ILES GAMBIER
GAMBIER ISLANDS
Tuamotu Ridge
MOTU ONE ATOLL
ILES SOUS LE VENT
LEEWARD ISLANDS
MANUAE ATOLL
ILE MAUPITI
TUPAI ATOLL
ILES HUAHINE
MAUPIHAA ATOLL
ILE BORA-BORA
ILE TAHAA
ILE RAIATEA
TETIAROA ATOLL
ILES DU VENT
WINDWARD ISLANDS
ILE MAIAO
ILE MOOREA
Papeete
ILE TAHITI
ILE MEHETIA
ILES DE LA SOCIÉTÉ
SOCIETY ISLANDS
Polynésie Française
French Polynesia
MARIA ATOLL
ILE RIMATARA
ILE RURUTU
ILE TUBUAÏ
ILE RAEVAVAE
ILES TUBUAÏ / AUSTRALES
TUBUAI ISLANDS
President Thiers Seamount
ILE RAPA
ILOTS DE BASS
OENO ISLAND
Pitcairn
(U.K.)
HENDERSON ISLAND
PITCAIRN ISLAND
Adamstown
Orne Seamount
Wachusett Seamount
ERNEST LEGOUVÉ REEF
MARIA THERESA REEF
Valerie Seamount
PACIFIC
Southwest
OCEAN
Pacific Basin

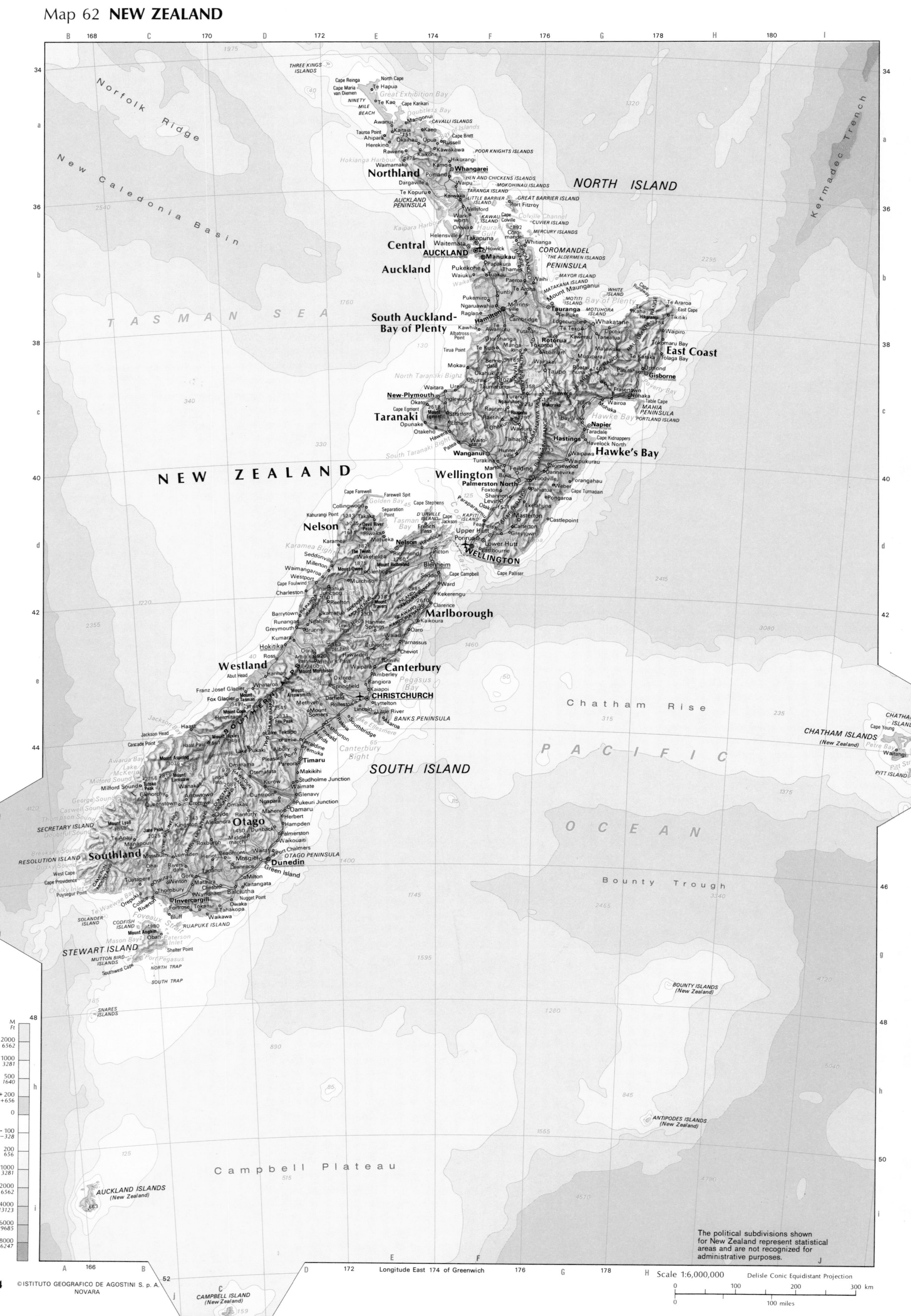
NORTH ISLAND
SOUTH ISLAND
NEW ZEALAND
TASMAN SEA
PACIFIC OCEAN
Norfolk Ridge
New Caledonia Basin
Kermadec Trench
Chatham Rise
Bounty Trough
Campbell Plateau
Northland
Central Auckland
AUCKLAND
South Auckland-Bay of Plenty
Taranaki
East Coast
Hawke's Bay
Wellington
WELLINGTON
Nelson
Marlborough
Westland
Canterbury
CHRISTCHURCH
Otago
Southland
Dunedin
Invercargill
STEWART ISLAND
CHATHAM ISLANDS (New Zealand)
BOUNTY ISLANDS (New Zealand)
ANTIPODES ISLANDS (New Zealand)
AUCKLAND ISLANDS (New Zealand)
CAMPBELL ISLAND (New Zealand)
SNARES ISLANDS
THREE KINGS ISLANDS
M Ft
2000 6562
1000 3281
500 1640
+200 +656
0
-100 -328
200 656
1000 3281
2000 6562
4000 13123
6000 19685
8000 26247
Longitude East 174 of Greenwich
Scale 1:6,000,000
Delisle Conic Equidistant Projection
0 100 200 300 km
0 100 miles
The political subdivisions shown for New Zealand represent statistical areas and are not recognized for administrative purposes.

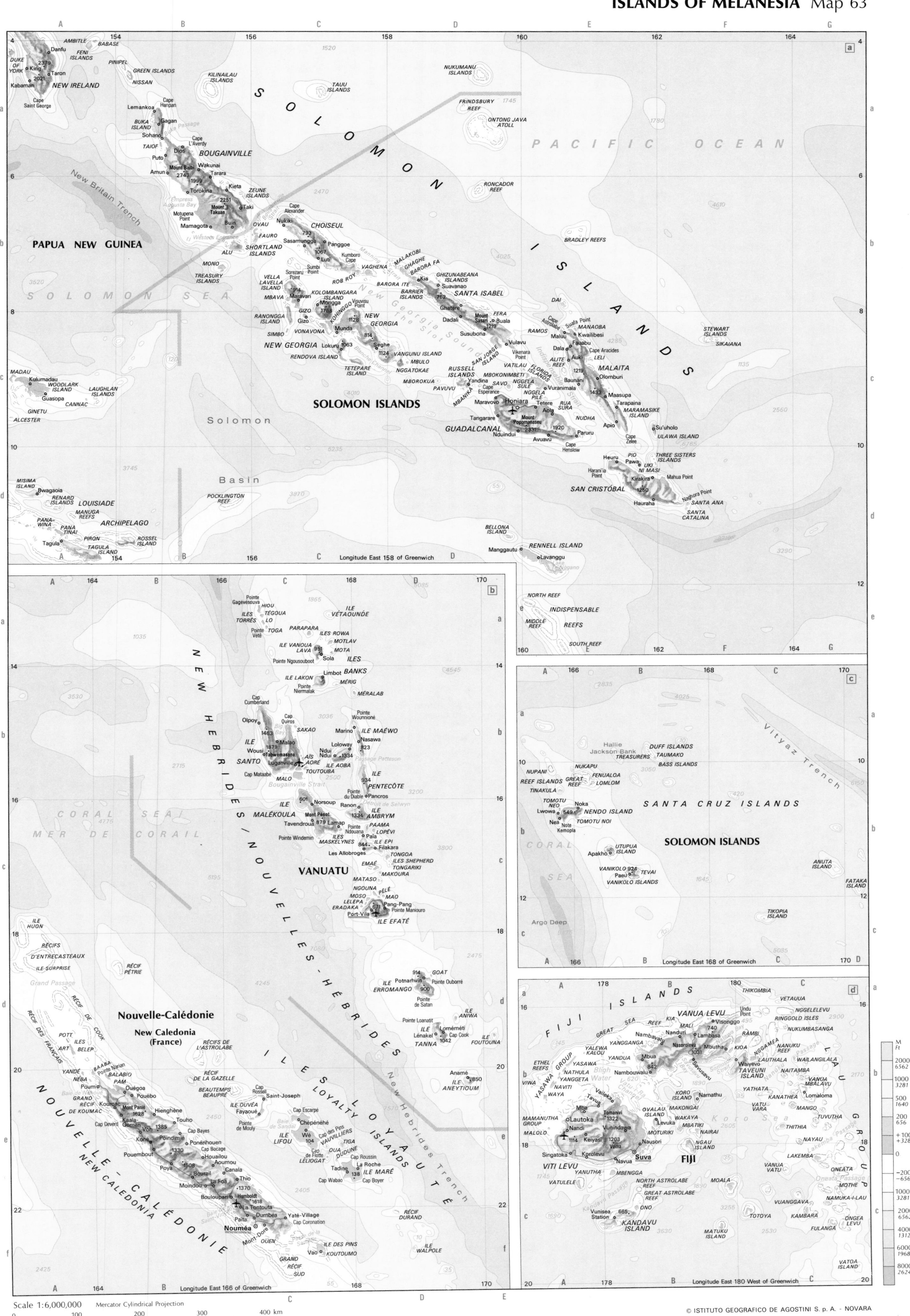
SOLOMON ISLANDS
PACIFIC OCEAN
PAPUA NEW GUINEA
SOLOMON SEA
Solomon Basin
New Britain Trench
NEW IRELAND
BOUGAINVILLE
BUKA ISLAND
CHOISEUL
SANTA ISABEL
NEW GEORGIA
MALAITA
GUADALCANAL
Honiara
SAN CRISTÓBAL
RENNELL ISLAND
BELLONA ISLAND
ONTONG JAVA ATOLL
LOUISIADE ARCHIPELAGO
ROSSEL ISLAND
Longitude East 158 of Greenwich
NEW HEBRIDES / NOUVELLES-HÉBRIDES
VANUATU
ILES BANKS
ILES TORRÈS
SANTO
ILE MAÉWO
PENTECÔTE
MALÉKOULA
AMBRYM
ILE EFATÉ
Port-Vila
ILE ERROMANGO
TANNA
ILE ANIWA
CORAL SEA
MER DE CORAIL
Nouvelle-Calédonie
New Caledonia (France)
NOUVELLE-CALÉDONIE
NEW CALEDONIA
Nouméa
ILES LOYAUTÉ
LOYALTY ISLANDS
ILE OUVÉA
LIFOU
ILE MARÉ
ILE DES PINS
New Hebrides Trench
Longitude East 166 of Greenwich
SANTA CRUZ ISLANDS
SOLOMON ISLANDS
DUFF ISLANDS
NENDO ISLAND
UTUPUA ISLAND
VANIKOLO ISLANDS
TIKOPIA ISLAND
ANUTA ISLAND
FATAKA ISLAND
Vityaz Trench
Longitude East 168 of Greenwich
FIJI ISLANDS
FIJI
VANUA LEVU
VITI LEVU
Suva
Lautoka
Nandi
TAVEUNI ISLAND
KANDAVU ISLAND
YASAWA GROUP
LAU GROUP
Koro Sea
Longitude East 180 West of Greenwich
Scale 1:6,000,000
Mercator Cylindrical Projection

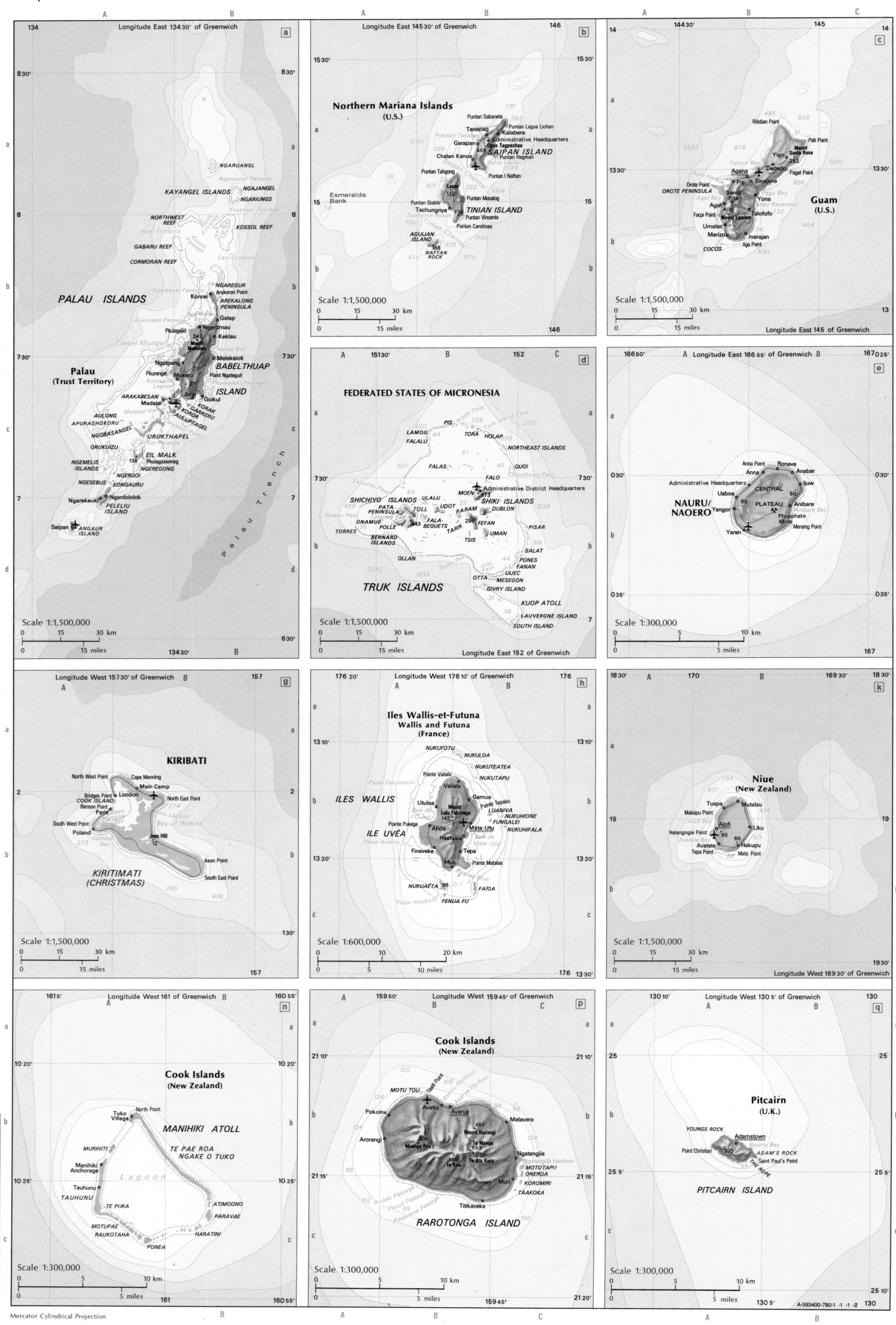
PALAU ISLANDS
Palau
(Trust Territory)
BABELTHUAP ISLAND
Palau Trench
Northern Mariana Islands
(U.S.)
SAIPAN ISLAND
TINIAN ISLAND
Guam
(U.S.)
FEDERATED STATES OF MICRONESIA
TRUK ISLANDS
NAURU/
NAOERO
KIRIBATI
KIRITIMATI
(CHRISTMAS)
Iles Wallis-et-Futuna
Wallis and Futuna
(France)
ILES WALLIS
ILE UVÉA
Niue
(New Zealand)
Cook Islands
(New Zealand)
MANIHIKI ATOLL
Cook Islands
(New Zealand)
RAROTONGA ISLAND
Pitcairn
(U.K.)
PITCAIRN ISLAND
Scale 1:1,500,000
Scale 1:300,000
Scale 1:600,000
Mercator Cylindrical Projection

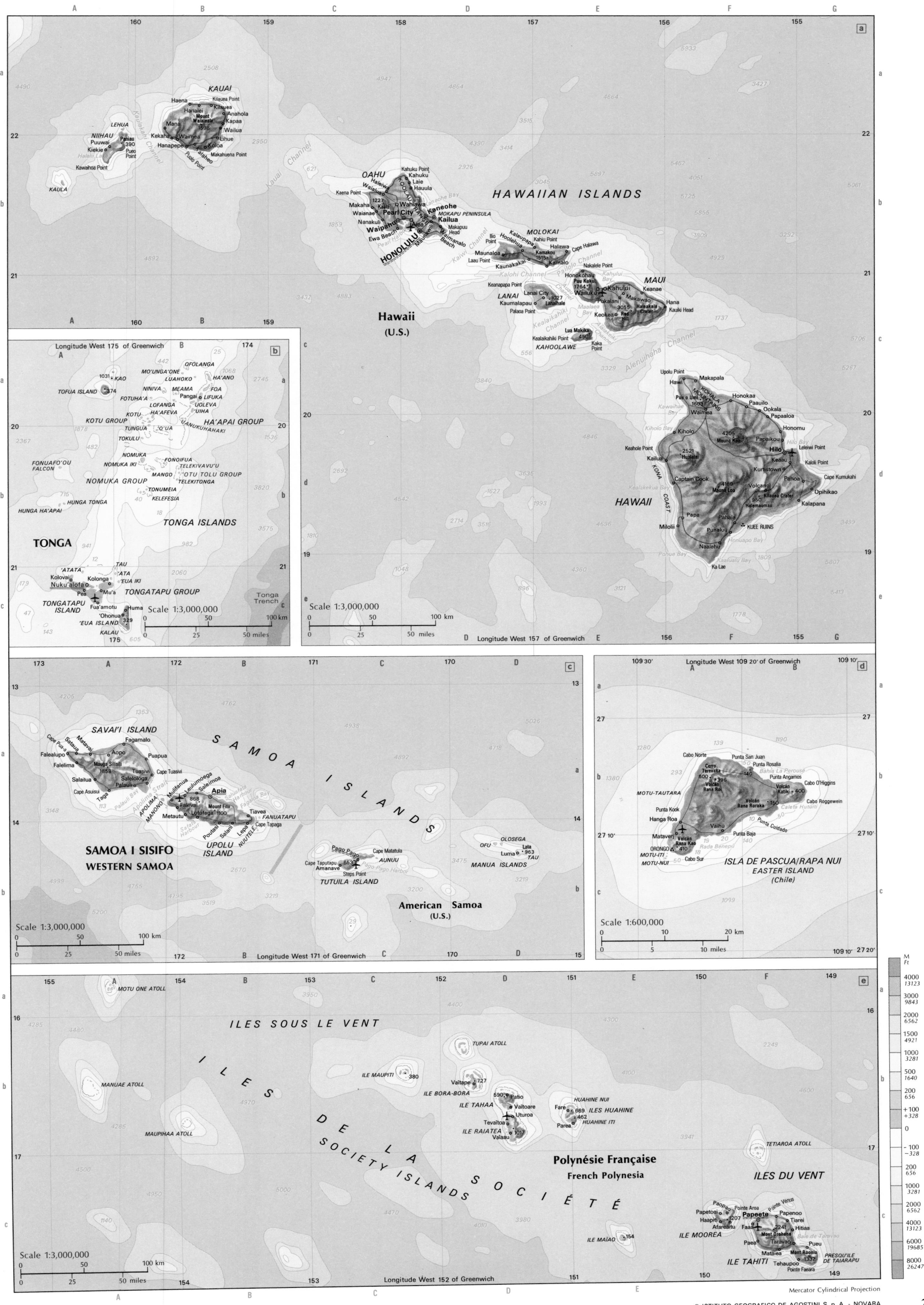
KAUAI
NIIHAU
LEHUA
KAULA
OAHU
HONOLULU
Pearl City
Kaneohe
Kailua
HAWAIIAN ISLANDS
MOLOKAI
LANAI
MAUI
KAHOOLAWE
Hawaii
(U.S.)
HAWAII
Hilo
Kailua
Scale 1:3,000,000
Longitude West 157 of Greenwich
Longitude West 175 of Greenwich
HA'APAI GROUP
NOMUKA GROUP
TONGA ISLANDS
TONGA
TONGATAPU GROUP
Nuku'alofa
TONGATAPU ISLAND
'EUA ISLAND
Tonga Trench
SAMOA ISLANDS
SAVAI'I ISLAND
UPOLU ISLAND
Apia
SAMOA I SISIFO
WESTERN SAMOA
TUTUILA ISLAND
MANUA ISLANDS
American Samoa
(U.S.)
Longitude West 171 of Greenwich
Longitude West 109 20' of Greenwich
Hanga Roa
ISLA DE PASCUA/RAPA NUI
EASTER ISLAND
(Chile)
Scale 1:600,000
ILES SOUS LE VENT
ILES DE LA SOCIÉTÉ
SOCIETY ISLANDS
Polynésie Française
French Polynesia
ILES DU VENT
ILE TAHITI
Papeete
ILE MOOREA
Longitude West 152 of Greenwich
Mercator Cylindrical Projection

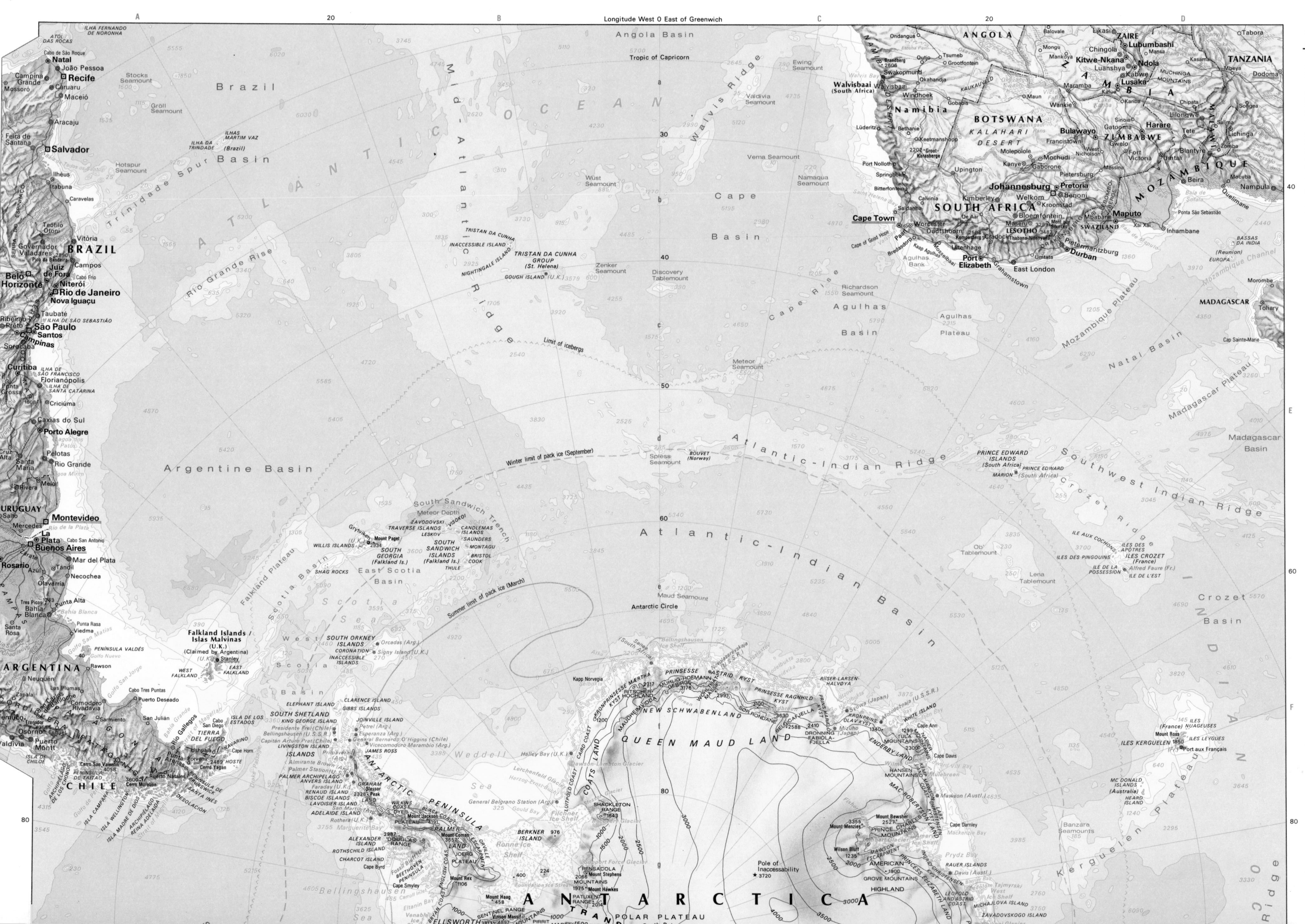
Longitude West 0 East of Greenwich
Angola Basin
Tropic of Capricorn
Antarctic Circle
ANGOLA
ZAMBIA
TANZANIA
MALAWI
MOZAMBIQUE
ZIMBABWE
BOTSWANA
Namibia
SOUTH AFRICA
LESOTHO
SWAZILAND
MADAGASCAR
Cape Town
Johannesburg
Pretoria
Durban
Maputo
BRAZIL
Rio de Janeiro
São Paulo
Salvador
Recife
Porto Alegre
URUGUAY
Montevideo
Buenos Aires
ARGENTINA
CHILE
Falkland Islands / Islas Malvinas
SOUTH GEORGIA
SOUTH SANDWICH ISLANDS
SOUTH ORKNEY ISLANDS
SOUTH SHETLAND ISLANDS
ANTARCTIC PENINSULA
ANTARCTICA
QUEEN MAUD LAND
NEW SCHWABENLAND
ENDERBY LAND
COATS LAND
Weddell Sea
Pole of Inaccessibility
POLAR PLATEAU
Brazil Basin
Cape Basin
Agulhas Basin
Argentine Basin
Atlantic-Indian Basin
Atlantic-Indian Ridge
Mid-Atlantic Ridge
Walvis Ridge
Rio Grande Rise
Scotia Sea
South Sandwich Trench
Madagascar Basin
Mozambique Plateau
Natal Basin
Southwest Indian Ridge
Crozet Basin
Kerguelen Plateau
Winter limit of pack ice (September)
Summer limit of pack ice (March)
Limit of icebergs

AUSTRALIA
NEW ZEALAND
PACIFIC OCEAN
Tasman Basin
Southwest Pacific Basin
Pacific - Antarctic Ridge
Southeast Indian Ridge
South Australian Basin
East Pacific Rise
Antarctic Circle
Winter limit of pack ice (September)
Limit of icebergs
WILKES LAND
Scale 1:30,000,000
Polar Azimuthal Projection
Longitude West 180 East of Greenwich
The Antarctic region is not a political entity and its status is regulated by the Antarctic Treaty signed in Washington, D.C. in 1959. The treaty binds the states which signed the agreement to use the region solely for peaceful purposes and scientific research.
© ISTITUTO GEOGRAFICO DE AGOSTINI S. p. A. - NOVARA

Scale 1:30,000,000 Polar Azimuthal Projection

Longitude West 0 East of Greenwich

UNITED STATES AND CANADA MAP SECTION

MAP LEGEND

CULTURAL FEATURES

Political Boundaries

International

Secondary (State)

County

Populated Places

Cities, towns, and villages

Symbol size represents population of the place

Chicago
Gary
Racine
Glenview
Edgewood

Type size represents relative importance of the place

Major Urban Areas
Area of continuous commercial, industrial, and residential development in and around a major city

- Community within a city
- Capital of major political unit
- Capital of U.S. state
- County Seat
- Military Installation

Transportation

Major Highway

Railroad

Tunnel

Miscellaneous

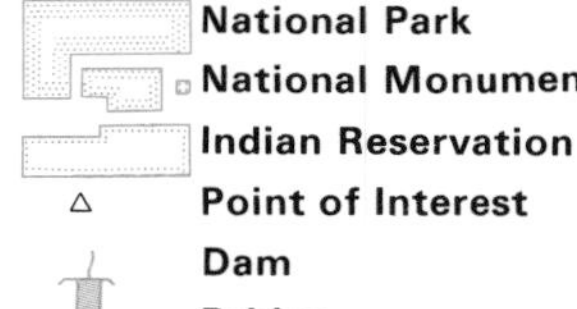

National Park

National Monument

Indian Reservation

Point of Interest

Dam

Bridge

Pier

LAND FEATURES

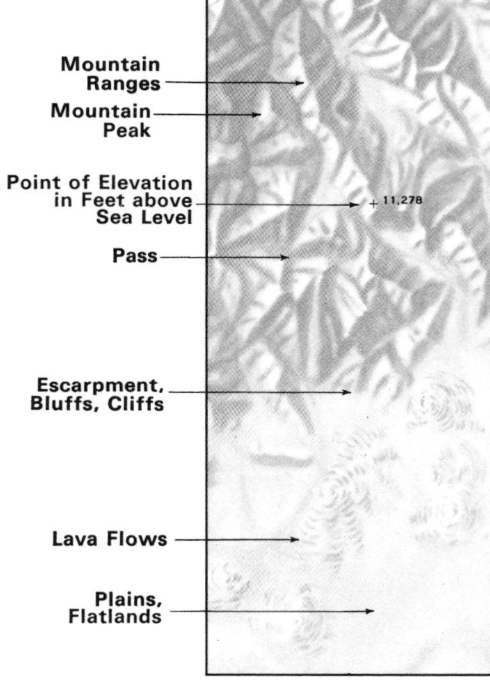

WATER FEATURES

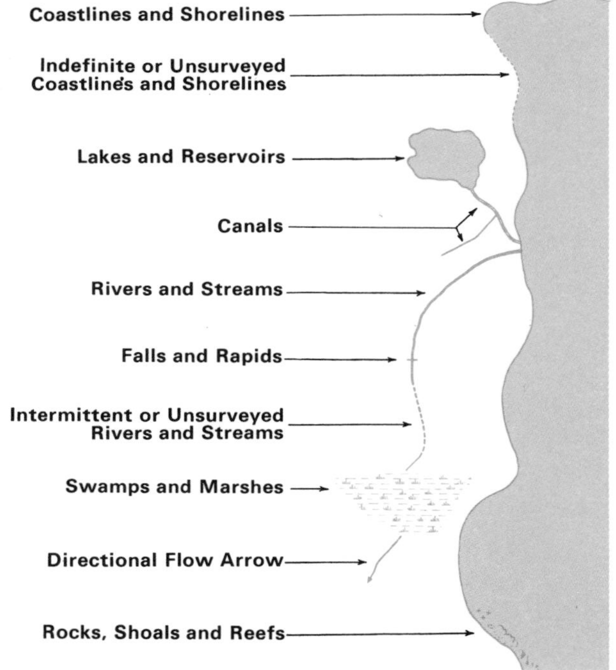

TYPE STYLES USED TO NAME FEATURES

Note: Size of type varies according to importance and available space. Letters for names of major features are spread across the extent of the feature.

Example	Feature
CANADA	Country, State, or Province
Naval Air Station	Military Installation
CROCKETT	County
UINTA DESERT	Major Terrain Features
MT. MORIAH	Individual Mountain
MESA VERDE SAN XAVIER	National Park or Monument, Indian Res.
NUNIVAK	Island or Coastal Feature
Ocean Lake River Canal	Hydrographic Features

A-520500-71
COSMO SERIES UNITED STATES
Copyright by
RAND McNALLY & COMPANY
Made in U. S. A.
Same Scale as Main Map
HAWAIIAN ISLANDS
ALEUTIAN ISLANDS
ALASKA
Statute Miles
Kilometers
WASHINGTON
OREGON
CALIFORNIA
NEVADA
IDAHO
MONTANA
WYOMING
UTAH
COLORADO
ARIZONA
NEW MEXICO
NORTH DAKOTA
SOUTH DAKOTA
NEBRASKA
KANSAS
OKLAHOMA
TEXAS
BRITISH COLUMBIA
ALBERTA
SASKATCHEWAN
MANITOBA
BAJA CALIFORNIA NORTE
SONORA
CHIHUAHUA
COAHUILA
NUEVO LEON
TAMAULIPAS
Pacific Ocean
Gulf of California
GREAT BASIN
Seattle
Portland
San Francisco
Los Angeles
San Diego
Salt Lake City
Denver
Phoenix
Las Vegas
El Paso
Dallas
Ft. Worth
San Antonio
Houston
Oklahoma City
Wichita
Omaha
Winnipeg
Calgary
Edmonton
Vancouver
Spokane
Boise
Helena
Cheyenne
Santa Fe
Albuquerque
Tucson
Bismarck
Pierre
Anchorage
Fairbanks
Juneau
Honolulu

Lambert Conformal Conic Projection
SCALE 1:12,000,000 1 Inch = 189 Statute Miles

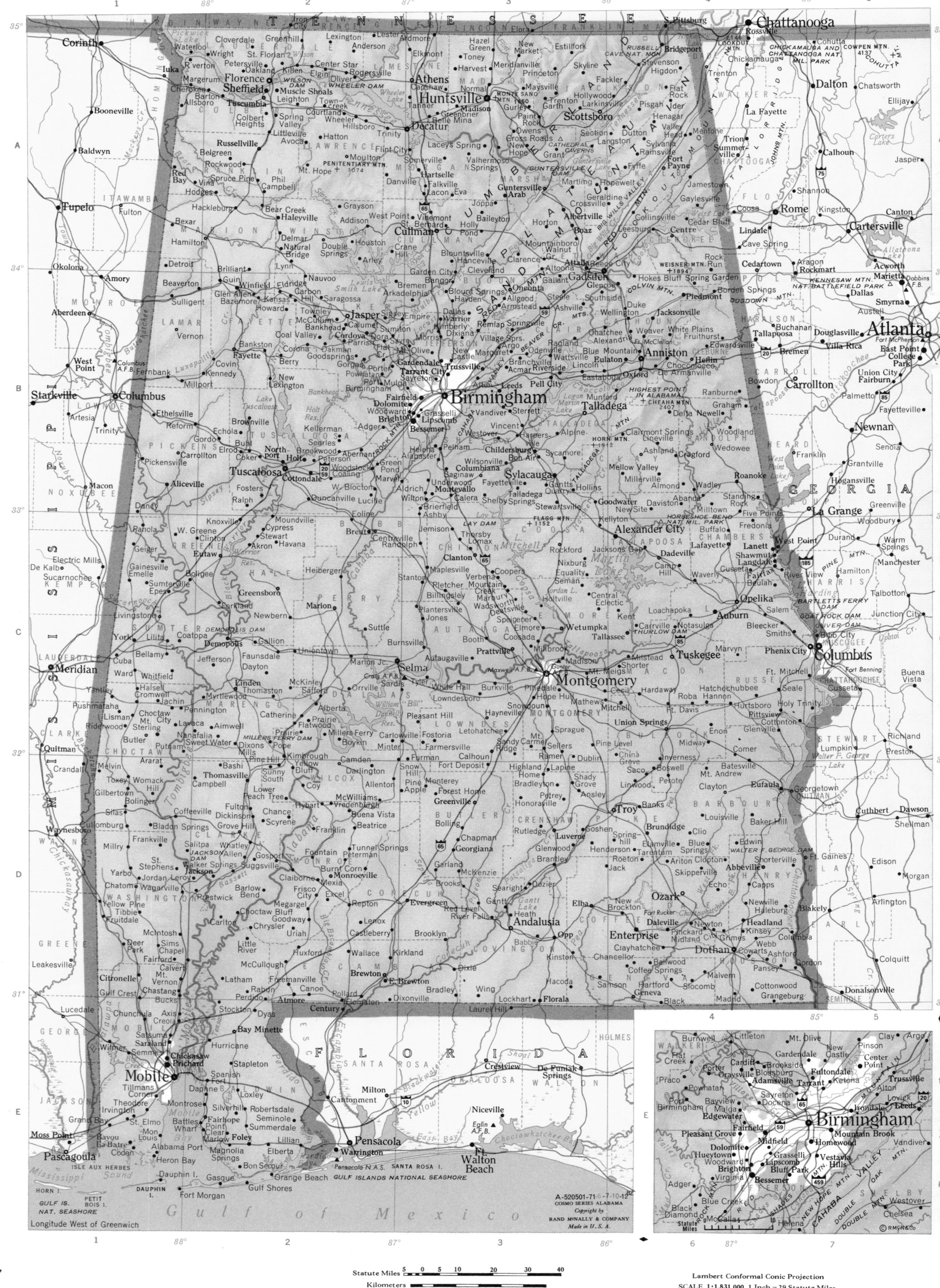

Cities and Towns

Albertville 12,039 **A3**
Alexander City 13,807 **C4**
Andalusia 10,415 **D3**
Anniston 29,523 **B4**
Arab 5,967 **A3**
Athens 14,558 **A3**
Atmore 8,789 **D2**
Auburn 28,471 **C4**
Bay Minette 7,455 **E2**
Bessemer 31,729 **B3**
Birmingham 286,799 **B3**
Bluff Park 12,000 **g7**
Boaz 7,151 **A3**
Brewton 6,680 **D2**
Center Point 23,317 **f7**
Childersburg 5,084 **B3**
Clanton 5,832 **C3**
Cullman 13,084 **A3**
Decatur 42,002 **A3**
Demopolis 7,678 **C2**
Dothan 48,750 **D4**
Enterprise 18,033 **D4**
Eufaula 12,097 **D4**
Fairfield 13,242 **B3**
Fayette 5,287 **B2**
Florence 37,029 **A2**
Fort Payne 11,485 **A4**
Gadsden 47,565 **A3**
Geneva 4,866 **D4**
Greenville 7,807 **D3**
Guntersville 7,041 **A3**
Haleyville 5,306 **A2**
Hamilton 5,093 **A2**
Hartselle 8,858 **A3**
Homewood 21,412 **g7**
Hueytown 13,478 **g6**
Huntsville 142,513 **A3**
Jackson 6,073 **D2**
Jacksonville 9,735 **B4**
Jasper 11,894 **B2**
Lanett 6,897 **C4**
Leeds 8,638 **B3**
Mobile 200,452 **E1**
Monroeville 5,674 **D2**
Montgomery 177,857 **C3**
Moundville 1,310 **C2**
Mountain Brook 19,718 **g7**
Muscle Shoals 8,911 **A2**
Northport 14,291 **B2**
Opelika 21,896 **C4**
Opp 7,204 **D3**
Ozark 13,188 **D4**
Pell City 6,616 **B3**
Phenix City 26,928 **C4**
Piedmont 5,544 **B4**
Prattville 18,647 **C3**
Prichard 39,541 **E1**
Roanoke 5,896 **B4**
Russellville 8,195 **A2**
Saraland 9,833 **E1**
Scottsboro 14,758 **A3**
Selma 26,684 **C2**
Sheffield 11,903 **A2**
Spanish Fort 3,415 **E2**
Sylacauga 12,708 **B3**
Talladega 19,128 **B3**
Tallassee 4,763 **C4**
Troy 12,945 **D4**
Tuscaloosa 75,211 **B2**
Tuscumbia 9,137 **A2**
Tuskegee 13,327 **C4**
Vestavia Hills 15,722 **g7**
Warrior 3,260 **B3**
Wetumpka 4,341 **C3**

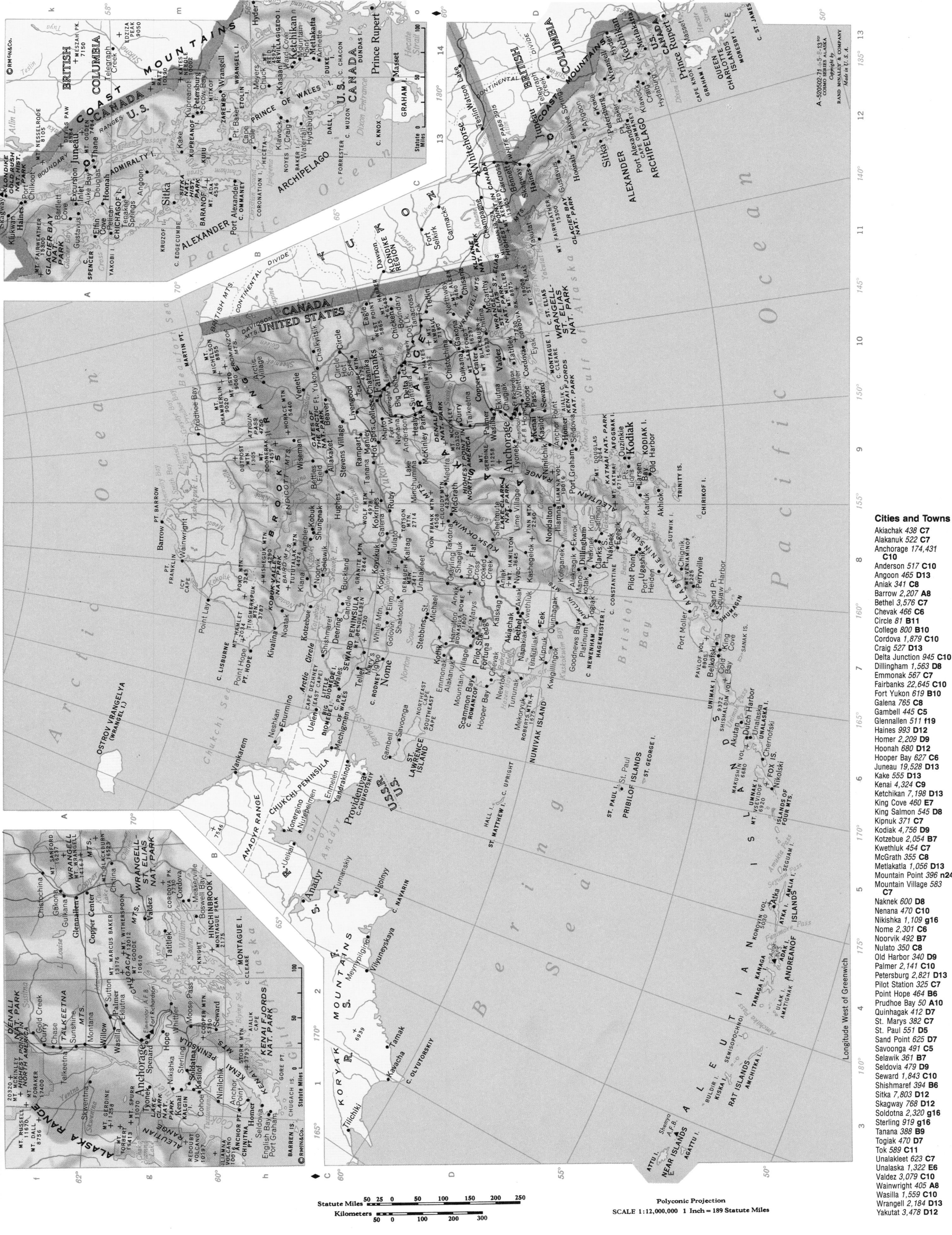

Cities and Towns

Akiachak *438* **C7**
Alakanuk *522* **C7**
Anchorage *174,431* **C10**
Anderson *517* **C10**
Angoon *465* **D13**
Aniak *341* **C8**
Barrow *2,207* **A8**
Bethel *3,576* **C7**
Chevak *466* **C6**
Circle *81* **B11**
College *800* **B10**
Cordova *1,879* **C10**
Craig *527* **D13**
Delta Junction *945* **C10**
Dillingham *1,563* **D8**
Emmonak *567* **C7**
Fairbanks *22,645* **C10**
Fort Yukon *619* **B10**
Galena *765* **C8**
Gambell *445* **C5**
Glennallen *511* **f19**
Haines *993* **D12**
Homer *2,209* **D9**
Hoonah *680* **D12**
Hooper Bay *627* **C6**
Juneau *19,528* **D13**
Kake *555* **D13**
Kenai *4,324* **C9**
Ketchikan *7,198* **D13**
King Cove *460* **E7**
King Salmon *545* **D8**
Kipnuk *371* **C7**
Kodiak *4,756* **D9**
Kotzebue *2,054* **B7**
Kwethluk *454* **C7**
McGrath *355* **C8**
Metlakatla *1,056* **D13**
Mountain Point *396* **n24**
Mountain Village *583* **C7**
Naknek *600* **D8**
Nenana *470* **C10**
Nikishka *1,109* **g16**
Nome *2,301* **C6**
Noorvik *492* **B7**
Nulato *350* **C8**
Old Harbor *340* **D9**
Palmer *2,141* **C10**
Petersburg *2,821* **D13**
Pilot Station *325* **C7**
Point Hope *464* **B6**
Prudhoe Bay *50* **A10**
Quinhagak *412* **D7**
St. Marys *382* **C7**
St. Paul *551* **D5**
Sand Point *625* **D7**
Savoonga *491* **C5**
Selawik *361* **B7**
Seldovia *479* **D9**
Seward *1,843* **C10**
Shishmaref *394* **B6**
Sitka *7,803* **D12**
Skagway *768* **D12**
Soldotna *2,320* **g16**
Sterling *919* **g16**
Tanana *388* **B9**
Togiak *470* **D7**
Tok *589* **C11**
Unalakleet *623* **C7**
Unalaska *1,322* **E6**
Valdez *3,079* **C10**
Wainwright *405* **A8**
Wasilla *1,559* **C10**
Wrangell *2,184* **D13**
Yakutat *3,478* **D12**

ARIZONA

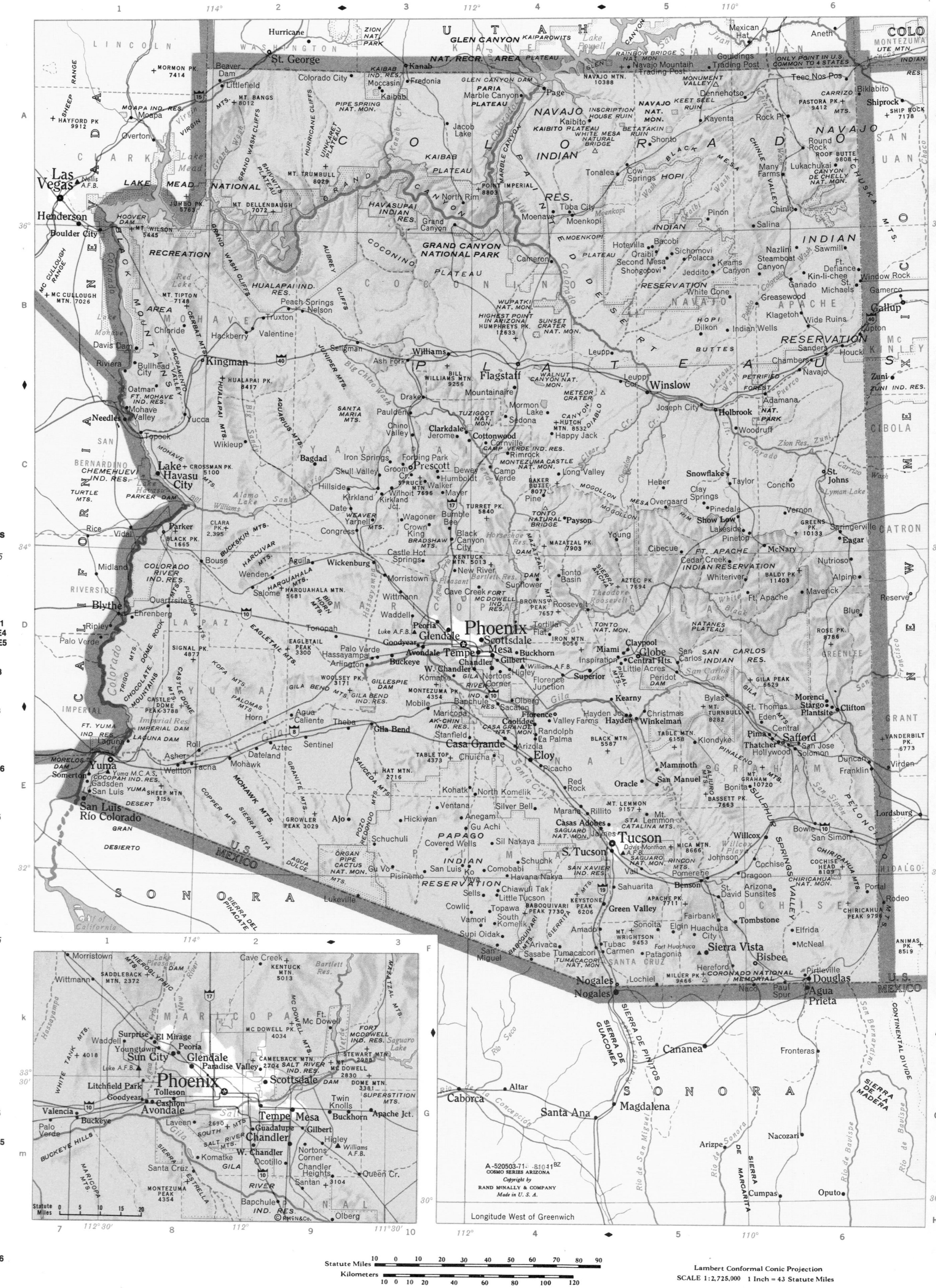

Cities and Towns

Ajo *5,189* **E3**
Apache Junction *9,935* **m9**
Avondale *8,168* **D3**
Bagdad *2,331* **C2**
Benson *4,190* **F5**
Bisbee *7,154* **F6**
Buckeye *3,434* **D3**
Bullhead City *5,000* **B1**
Casa Grande *14,971* **E4**
Casas Adobes *5,300* **E5**
Chandler *29,673* **D4**
Chinle *2,815* **A6**
Chino Valley *2,858* **C3**
Claypool *2,362* **D5**
Clifton *4,245* **D6**
Coolidge *6,851* **E4**
Cottonwood *4,550* **C3**
Douglas *13,058* **F6**
Eagar *2,791* **C6**
Eloy *6,240* **E4**
Flagstaff *34,743* **B4**
Florence *3,391* **D4**
Fort Defiance *3,431* **B6**
Gila Bend *1,585* **E3**
Gilbert *5,717* **D4**
Glendale *97,172* **D3**
Globe *6,886* **D5**
Green Valley *7,999* **F5**
Holbrook *5,785* **C5**
Kayenta *3,343* **A5**
Kearny *2,646* **D5**
Kingman *9,257* **B1**
Lake Havasu City *15,909* **C1**
Mammoth *1,906* **E5**
Mesa *152,453* **D4**
Miami *2,716* **D5**
Nogales *15,683* **F5**
Oracle *2,484* **E5**
Page *4,907* **A4**
Paradise Valley *11,085* **k9**
Parker *2,542* **C1**
Payson *5,068* **C4**
Peoria *12,307* **D3**
Phoenix *789,704* **D3**
Prescott *20,055* **C3**
Riviera *4,500* **B1**
Sacaton *1,951* **D4**
Safford *7,010* **E6**
St. Johns *3,368* **C6**
San Carlos *2,668* **D5**
San Luis *1,946* **E1**
San Manuel *5,443* **E5**
Scottsdale *88,622* **D4**
Sedona *5,368* **C4**
Sells *1,864* **F4**
Show Low *4,298* **C5**
Sierra Vista *24,937* **F5**
Snowflake *3,510* **C5**
Somerton *5,761* **E1**
South Tucson *6,554* **E5**
Sun City *40,505* **k8**
Superior *4,600* **D4**
Taylor *1,915* **C5**
Tempe *106,743* **D4**
Thatcher *3,374* **E6**
Tombstone *1,632* **F5**
Tuba City *5,041* **A4**
Tucson *330,537* **E5**
Wickenburg *3,535* **D3**
Willcox *3,243* **E6**
Williams *2,266* **B3**
Window Rock *2,230* **B6**
Winslow *7,921* **C5**
Yuma *42,481* **E1**

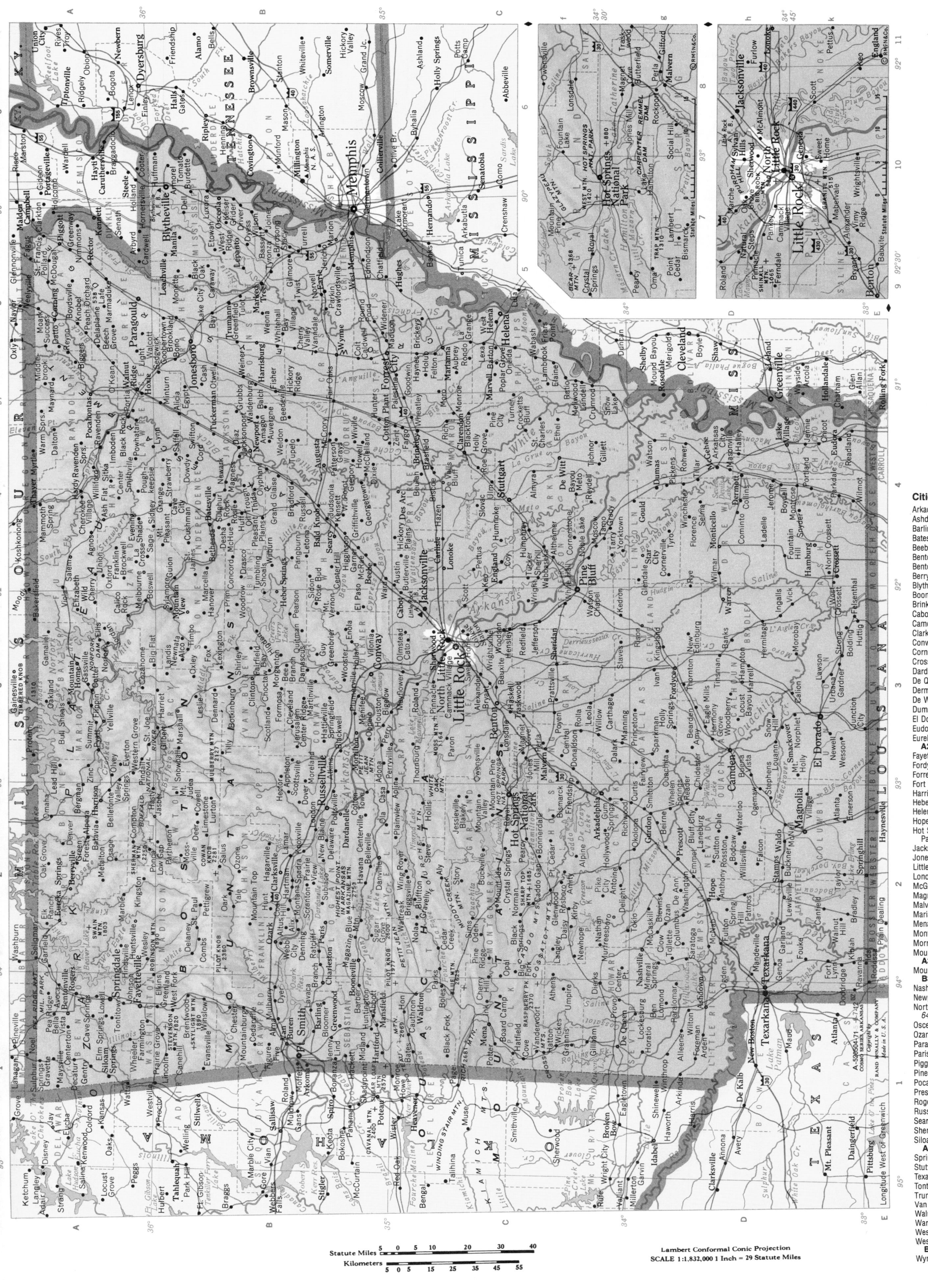

Cities and Towns

Arkadelphia *10,005* **C2**
Ashdown *4,218* **D1**
Barling *3,761* **B1**
Batesville *8,263* **B4**
Beebe *3,599* **B4**
Benton *17,717* **C3**
Bentonville *8,756* **A1**
Berryville *2,966* **A2**
Blytheville *23,844* **B6**
Booneville *3,718* **B2**
Brinkley *4,909* **C4**
Cabot *4,806* **C3**
Camden *15,356* **D3**
Clarksville *5,237* **B2**
Conway *20,375* **B3**
Corning *3,650* **A5**
Crossett *6,706* **D4**
Dardanelle *3,621* **B2**
De Queen *4,594* **C1**
Dermott *4,731* **D4**
De Witt *3,928* **C4**
Dumas *6,091* **D4**
El Dorado *25,270* **D3**
Eudora *3,840* **D4**
Eureka Springs *1,989* **A2**
Fayetteville *36,608* **A1**
Fordyce *5,175* **D3**
Forrest City *13,803* **B5**
Fort Smith *71,636* **B1**
Harrison *9,567* **A2**
Heber Springs *4,589* **B3**
Helena *9,598* **C5**
Hope *10,290* **D2**
Hot Springs National Park *35,781* **C2**
Jacksonville *27,589* **C3**
Jonesboro *31,530* **B5**
Little Rock *158,461* **C3**
Lonoke *4,128* **C4**
McGehee *5,671* **D4**
Magnolia *11,909* **D2**
Malvern *10,163* **C3**
Marianna *6,220* **C5**
Mena *5,154* **C1**
Monticello *8,259* **D4**
Morrilton *7,355* **B3**
Mountain Home *8,066* **A3**
Mountain View *2,147* **B3**
Nashville *4,554* **D2**
Newport *8,339* **B4**
North Little Rock *64,288* **C3**
Osceola *8,881* **B6**
Ozark *3,597* **B2**
Paragould *15,248* **A5**
Paris *3,991* **B2**
Piggott *3,762* **A5**
Pine Bluff *56,636* **C3**
Pocahontas *5,995* **A5**
Prescott *4,103* **D2**
Rogers *17,429* **A1**
Russellville *14,031* **B2**
Searcy *13,612* **B4**
Sherwood *10,406* **C3**
Siloam Springs *7,940* **A1**
Springdale *23,458* **A1**
Stuttgart *10,941* **C4**
Texarkana *21,459* **D1**
Tontitown *615* **A1**
Trumann *6,405* **B5**
Van Buren *12,020* **B1**
Walnut Ridge *4,152* **A5**
Warren *7,646* **D3**
West Helena *11,367* **C5**
West Memphis *28,138* **B5**
Wynne *7,805* **B5**

Cities and Towns

Anaheim *219,494* **F5**
Antioch *42,683* **h9**
Bakersfield *105,735* **E4**
Berkeley *103,328* **D2**
Beverly Hills *32,367* **m12**
Burbank *84,625* **E4**
Calexico *14,412* **F6**
Chico *26,603* **C3**
Chula Vista *83,927* **F5**
Concord *103,255* **h8**
Costa Mesa *82,562* **n13**
Davis *36,640* **C3**
East Los Angeles *110,017* **m12**
El Cajon *73,892* **F5**
El Centro *23,996* **F6**
Escondido *64,355* **F5**
Eureka *24,153* **B1**
Fairfield *58,099* **C2**
Fremont *131,945* **D2**
Fresno *217,289* **D4**
Fullerton *102,034* **n13**
Garden Grove *123,307* **n13**
Glendale *139,060* **m12**
Hayward *94,342* **h8**
Huntington Beach *170,505* **F4**
Indio *21,611* **F5**
Lancaster *48,027* **E4**
Lompoc *26,267* **E3**
Long Beach *361,334* **F4**
Los Angeles *2,966,850* **E4**
Marysville *9,898* **C3**
Menlo Park *26,369* **k8**
Merced *36,499* **D3**
Modesto *106,602* **D3**
Monterey *27,558* **D3**
Napa *50,879* **C2**
Newport Beach *62,556* **n13**
Oakland *339,337* **D2**
Oceanside *76,698* **F5**
Ontario *88,820* **E5**
Oxnard *108,195* **E4**
Palm Springs *32,366* **F5**
Palo Alto *55,225* **D2**
Pasadena *118,072* **E4**
Pomona *92,742* **E5**
Redding *41,995* **B2**
Redwood City *54,951* **D2**
Richmond *74,676* **D2**
Riverside *170,591* **F5**
Sacramento *275,741* **C3**
Salinas *80,479* **D3**
San Bernardino *118,794* **E5**
San Clemente *27,325* **F5**
San Diego *875,538* **F5**
San Francisco *678,974* **D2**
San Jose *629,546* **D3**
San Juan Capistrano *18,959* **F5**
San Luis Obispo *34,252* **E3**
Santa Ana *204,023* **F5**
Santa Barbara *74,414* **E4**
Santa Cruz *41,483* **D2**
Santa Maria *39,685* **E3**
Santa Monica *88,314* **m12**
Santa Rosa *83,320* **C2**
South Lake Tahoe *20,681* **C4**
Stockton *149,779* **D3**
Sunnyvale *106,618* **k8**
Torrance *129,881* **n12**
Tulare *22,526* **D4**
Turlock *26,287* **D3**
Vallejo *80,303* **C2**
Ventura *74,393* **E4**
Visalia *49,729* **D4**
Yuba City *18,736* **C3**

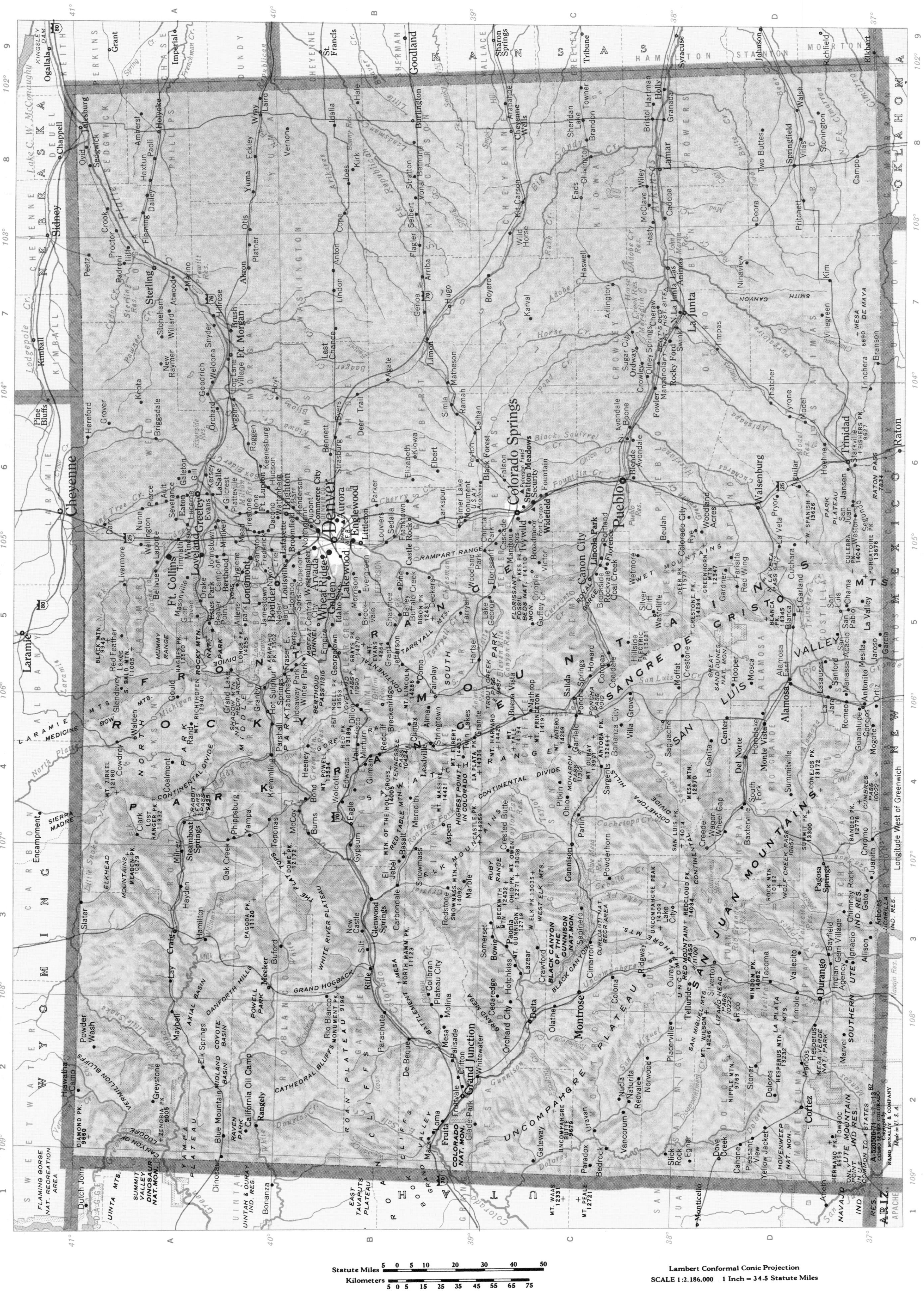

Statute Miles 5 0 5 10 20 30 40 50

Kilometers 5 0 5 15 25 35 45 55 65 75

Lambert Conformal Conic Projection

SCALE 1:2,186,000 1 Inch = 34.5 Statute Miles

Cities and Towns

Alamosa *6,830* **D5**
Arvada *84,576* **B5**
Aspen *3,678* **B4**
Aurora *158,588* **B6**
Black Forest *3,372* **C6**
Boulder *76,685* **A5**
Breckenridge *818* **B4**
Brighton *12,773* **B6**
Broomfield *20,730* **B5**
Burlington *3,107* **B8**
Canon City *13,037* **C5**
Castle Rock *3,921* **B6**
Central City *329* **B5**
Clifton *5,223* **B2**
Colorado Springs *214,821* **C6**
Commerce City *16,234* **B6**
Cortez *7,095* **D2**
Craig *8,133* **A3**
Delta *3,931* **C2**
Denver *492,365* **B6**
Durango *11,649* **D3**
Englewood *30,021* **B6**
Estes Park *2,703* **A5**
Evans *5,063* **A6**
Evergreen *6,376* **B5**
Fort Collins *65,092* **A5**
Fort Lupton *4,251* **A6**
Fort Morgan *8,768* **A7**
Fountain *8,324* **C6**
Glenwood Springs *4,637* **B3**
Golden *12,237* **B5**
Grand Junction *27,956* **B2**
Greeley *53,006* **A6**
Gunnison *5,785* **C4**
Holyoke *2,092* **A8**
Julesburg *1,528* **A8**
Lafayette *8,985* **B5**
La Junta *8,338* **D7**
Lakewood *113,808* **B5**
Lamar *7,713* **C8**
Las Animas *2,818* **C7**
Leadville *3,879* **B4**
Limon *1,805* **B7**
Littleton *28,631* **B6**
Longmont *42,942* **A5**
Louisville *5,593* **B5**
Loveland *30,244* **A5**
Meeker *2,356* **A3**
Monte Vista *3,902* **D4**
Montrose *8,722* **C3**
Northglenn *29,847* **B6**
Ouray *684* **C3**
Pagosa Springs *1,331* **D3**
Pueblo *101,686* **C6**
Rangely *2,113* **A2**
Rifle *3,215* **B3**
Rocky Ford *4,804* **C7**
Salida *4,870* **C5**
Security *11,000* **C6**
Springfield *1,657* **D8**
Steamboat Springs *5,098* **A4**
Sterling *11,385* **A7**
Stratton Meadows *6,223* **C6**
Telluride *1,047* **D3**
Trinidad *9,663* **D6**
USAF Academy *8,000* **C6**
Vail *2,261* **B4**
Walsenburg *3,945* **D6**
Westminster *50,211* **B5**
Wheat Ridge *30,293* **B5**
Widefield *7,500* **C6**
Windsor *4,277* **A6**
Wray *2,131* **A8**
Yuma *2,824* **A8**

CONNECTICUT

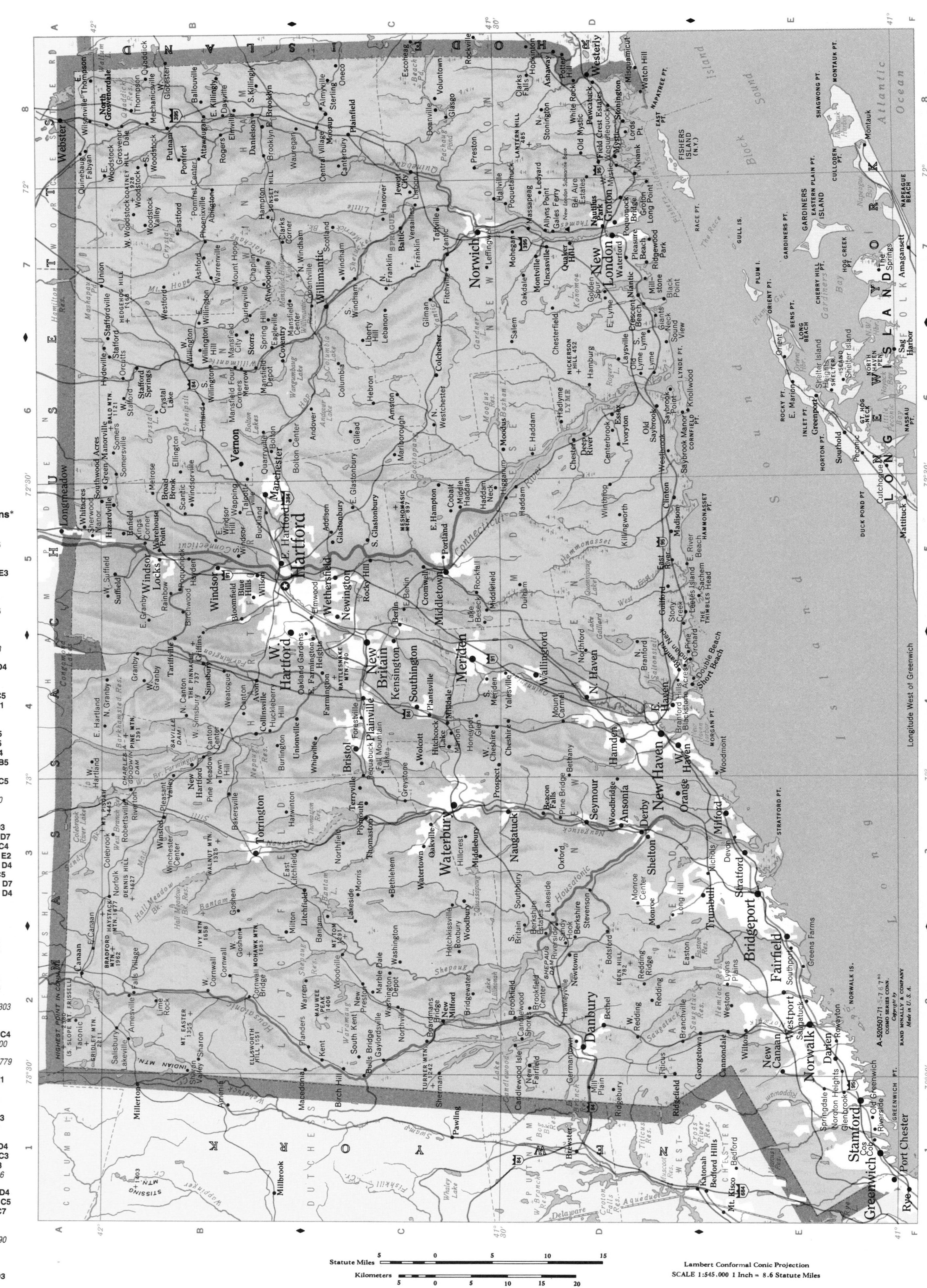

Cities and Towns*

Ansonia *19,039* **D3**
Bethel *8,755* **D2**
Bloomfield *7,400* **B5**
Blue Hills *6,600* **B5**
Branford *5,438* **D4**
Bridgeport *142,546* **E3**
Bristol *57,370* **C4**
Cheshire *5,722* **D4**
Clinton *11,195* **D5**
Cromwell *10,100* **C5**
Danbury *60,470* **D2**
Darien *18,892* **E2**
Derby *12,346* **D3**
East Hartford *52,563* **B5**
East Haven *25,028* **D4**
Enfield *8,151* **B5**
Fairfield *54,849* **E2**
Glastonbury *7,049* **C5**
Greenwich *59,578* **E1**
Groton *10,086* **D7**
Hamden *51,071* **D4**
Hartford *136,392* **B5**
Hazardville *5,436* **B5**
Kensington *7,502* **C4**
Manchester *49,761* **B5**
Meriden *57,118* **C4**
Middletown *39,040* **C5**
Milford *49,101* **E3**
Monroe Center *6,950* **D3**
Mystic *2,333* **D8**
Naugatuck *26,456* **D3**
Nautilus Park *6,500* **D7**
New Britain *73,840* **C4**
New Canaan *17,931* **E2**
New Haven *126,109* **D4**
Newington *28,841* **C5**
New London *28,842* **D7**
North Haven *22,080* **D4**
Norwalk *77,767* **E2**
Norwich *38,074* **C7**
Oakville *8,737* **C3**
Orange *13,237* **D3**
Plainville *16,401* **C4**
Plantsville *5,700* **C4**
Portland *8,383* **C5**
Putnam *6,855* **B8**
Ridgefield *6,066* **D2**
Seymour *13,434* **D3**
Shelton *31,314* **D3**
Sherwood Manor *6,303* **A5**
Simsbury *5,488* **B4**
Southington *17,400* **C4**
South Windsor *10,200* **B5**
Southwood Acres *9,779* **B5**
Stamford *102,453* **E1**
Storrs *11,394* **B7**
Stratford *50,541* **E3**
Terryville *5,234* **C3**
Torrington *30,987* **B3**
Trumbull *32,989* **E3**
Vernon *27,974* **B6**
Wallingford *37,274* **D4**
Waterbury *103,266* **C3**
Watertown *6,000* **C3**
West Hartford *61,306* **B4**
West Haven *53,184* **D4**
Wethersfield *26,013* **C5**
Willimantic *14,652* **C7**
Wilton *6,500* **E2**
Windsor *17,517* **B5**
Windsor Locks *12,190* **B5**
Winsted *8,092* **B3**
Wolcott *5,500* **C4**
Woodbridge *7,600* **D3**

*Populations are for localities, not incorporated towns.

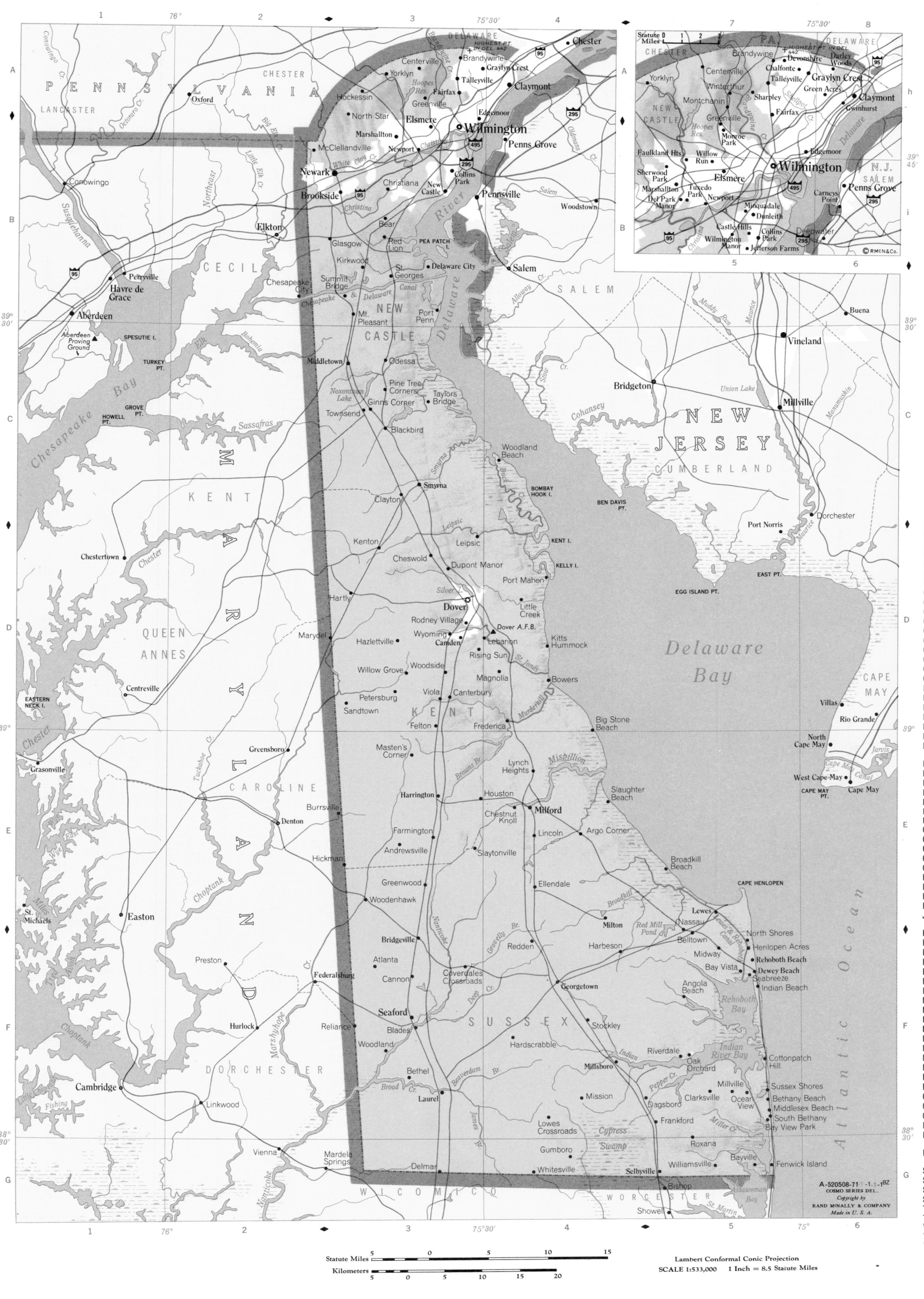

Cities and Towns

Bear *950* **B3**
Bethany Beach *330* **F5**
Blades *664* **F3**
Bridgeville *1,238* **F3**
Broadkill Beach *200* **E5**
Brookside *15,255* **B3**
Camden *1,757* **D3**
Canterbury *500* **D3**
Castle Hills *1,950* **I7**
Chalfonte *2,200* **h7**
Cheswold *269* **D3**
Christiana *500* **B3**
Clarksville *450* **F5**
Claymont *10,022* **A4**
Clayton *1,216* **C3**
Collins Park *2,850* **B3**
Dagsboro *344* **F5**
Delaware City *1,858* **B3**
Delmar *948* **G3**
Dewey Beach *1,500* **F5**
Dover *23,507* **D3**
Dunleith *2,700* **I7**
Dupont Manor *1,059* **D3**
Edgemoor *7,397* **A3**
Ellendale *361* **E4**
Elsmere *6,493* **B3**
Fairfax *2,850* **A3**
Felton *547* **D3**
Frankford *828* **F5**
Frederica *864* **D4**
Georgetown *1,710* **F4**
Graylyn Crest *5,000* **A3**
Greenwood *578* **E3**
Gumboro *200* **G4**
Gwinhurst *1,400* **h8**
Harbeson *250* **F4**
Harrington *2,405* **E3**
Hockessin *950* **A3**
Houston *357* **E3**
Jefferson Farms *2,400* **I7**
Kenton *243* **D3**
Kirkwood *400* **B3**
Laurel *3,052* **F3**
Leipsic *228* **D3**
Lewes *2,197* **E5**
Lincoln *500* **E4**
Little Creek *230* **D4**
Marshallton *3,950* **B3**
Middletown *2,946* **C3**
Midway *500* **F5**
Milford *5,366* **E4**
Millsboro *1,233* **F4**
Milton *1,359* **E4**
Minquadale *1,700* **I7**
Newark *25,247* **B2**
New Castle *4,907* **B3**
Newport *1,167* **B3**
Oak Orchard *250* **F5**
Ocean View *495* **F5**
Odessa *384* **C3**
Port Penn *300* **B3**
Rehoboth Beach *1,730* **F5**
Rodney Village *1,100* **D3**
St. Georges *500* **B3**
Seaford *5,256* **F3**
Selbyville *1,251* **G5**
Smyrna *4,750* **C3**
Talleyville *6,880* **A3**
Townsend *386* **C3**
Willow Run *1,950* **I7**
Wilmington *70,195* **B3**
Wilmington Manor *2,000* **I7**
Wyoming *960* **D3**
Yorklyn *600* **A3**

FLORIDA

Cities and Towns

Bartow *14,780* **E5**
Belle Glade *16,535* **F6**
Boca Raton *49,505* **F6**
Boynton Beach *35,624* **F6**
Bradenton *30,170* **E4**
Brandon *29,100* **E4**
Cape Canaveral *5,733* **D6**
Cape Coral *32,103* **F5**
Carol City *47,349* **s13**
Clearwater *85,528* **E4**
Cocoa *16,096* **D6**
Coral Gables *43,241* **G6**
Daytona Beach *54,176* **C5**
Deerfield Beach *39,193* **F6**
De Land *15,354* **C5**
Delray Beach *34,325* **F6**
Dunedin *30,203* **D4**
Fort Lauderdale *153,279* **F6**
Fort Myers *36,638* **F5**
Fort Pierce *33,802* **E6**
Fort Walton Beach *20,829* **u15**
Gainesville *81,371* **C4**
Hallandale *36,517* **G6**
Hialeah *145,254* **G6**
Hollywood *121,323* **F6**
Homestead *20,668* **G6**
Immokalee *11,038* **F5**
Jacksonville *540,920* **B5**
Kendall *51,000* **s13**
Key Largo *7,447* **G6**
Key West *24,382* **H5**
Kissimmee *15,487* **D5**
Lake City *9,257* **B4**
Lakeland *47,406* **D5**
Lake Worth *27,048* **F6**
Largo *58,977* **E4**
Leesburg *13,191* **D5**
Marathon *7,508* **H5**
Margate *35,900* **F6**
Melbourne *46,536* **D6**
Merritt Island *30,708* **D6**
Miami *346,865* **G6**
Miami Beach *96,298* **G6**
Miramar *32,813* **s13**
Naples *17,581* **F5**
New Smyrna Beach *13,557* **C6**
North Miami *36,553* **G6**
North Miami Beach *36,481* **s13**
Ocala *37,170* **C4**
Orlando *128,291* **D5**
Panama City *33,346* **u16**
Pembroke Pines *35,776* **r13**
Pensacola *57,619* **u14**
Pinellas Park *32,811* **E4**
Plantation *48,653* **r13**
Plant City *17,064* **D4**
Pompano Beach *52,618* **F6**
Port Charlotte *25,770* **F4**
Riviera Beach *26,489* **F6**
St. Augustine *11,985* **C5**
St. Petersburg *238,647* **E4**
Sanford *23,176* **D5**
Sarasota *48,868* **E4**
Sebring *8,736* **E5**
Tallahassee *81,548* **B2**
Tampa *271,523* **E4**
Tarpon Springs *13,251* **D4**
Titusville *31,910* **D6**
Venice *12,153* **E4**
Vero Beach *16,176* **E6**
West Palm Beach *63,305* **F6**
West Pensacola *24,571* **u14**
Winter Haven *21,119* **D5**

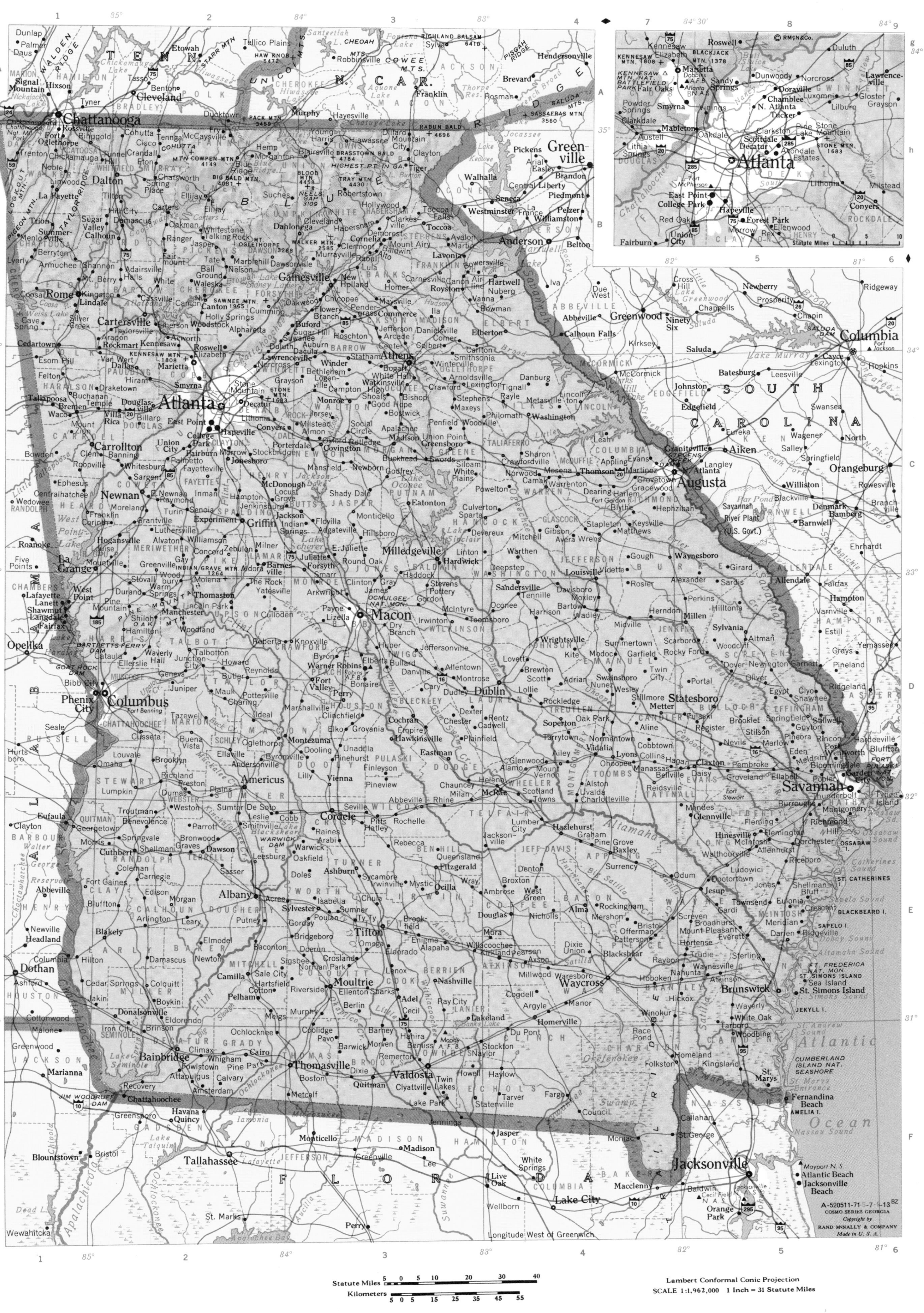

Cities and Towns

Adel *5,592* **E3**
Albany *74,550* **E2**
Americus *16,120* **D2**
Athens *42,549* **C3**
Atlanta *425,022* **C2**
Augusta *47,532* **C5**
Bainbridge *10,553* **F2**
Blakely *5,880* **E2**
Brunswick *17,605* **E5**
Buford *6,578* **B2**
Cairo *8,777* **F2**
Calhoun *5,563* **B2**
Camilla *5,414* **E2**
Carrollton *14,078* **C1**
Cartersville *9,247* **B2**
Cedartown *8,619* **B1**
Cochran *5,121* **D3**
College Park *24,632* **C2**
Columbus *169,441* **D2**
Cordele *11,184* **E3**
Covington *10,586* **C3**
Dalton *20,939* **B2**
Dawson *5,699* **E2**
Decatur *18,404* **C2**
Douglas *10,980* **E4**
Douglasville *7,641* **C2**
Dublin *16,083* **D4**
Eastman *5,330* **D3**
East Point *37,486* **C2**
Elberton *5,686* **B4**
Fitzgerald *10,187* **E3**
Forest Park *18,782* **h8**
Fort Oglethorpe *5,443* **B1**
Fort Valley *9,000* **D3**
Gainesville *15,280* **B3**
Griffin *20,728* **C2**
Hinesville *11,309* **E5**
Kennesaw *5,095* **B2**
La Fayette *6,517* **B1**
La Grange *24,204* **C1**
Lawrenceville *8,928* **C3**
Mableton *20,200* **h7**
Macon *116,896* **D3**
Marietta *30,829* **C2**
Martinez *16,472* **C4**
Milledgeville *12,176* **C3**
Monroe *8,854* **C3**
Moultrie *15,708* **E3**
Newnan *11,449* **C2**
North Atlanta *22,800* **h8**
Perry *9,453* **D3**
Quitman *5,188* **F3**
Rome *29,654* **B1**
Roswell *23,337* **B2**
St. Simons Island *6,566* **E5**
Sandersville *6,137* **D4**
Sandy Springs *20,300* **h8**
Savannah *141,390* **D5**
Smyrna *20,312* **C2**
Statesboro *14,866* **D5**
Stone Mountain *4,867* **C2**
Swainsboro *7,602* **D4**
Sylvester *5,860* **E3**
Thomaston *9,682* **D2**
Thomasville *18,463* **F3**
Thomson *7,001* **C4**
Tifton *13,749* **E3**
Toccoa *9,104* **B3**
Tucker *18,200* **h8**
Valdosta *37,596* **F3**
Vidalia *10,393* **D4**
Warner Robins *39,893* **D3**
Waycross *19,371* **E4**
Waynesboro *5,760* **C4**

HAWAII

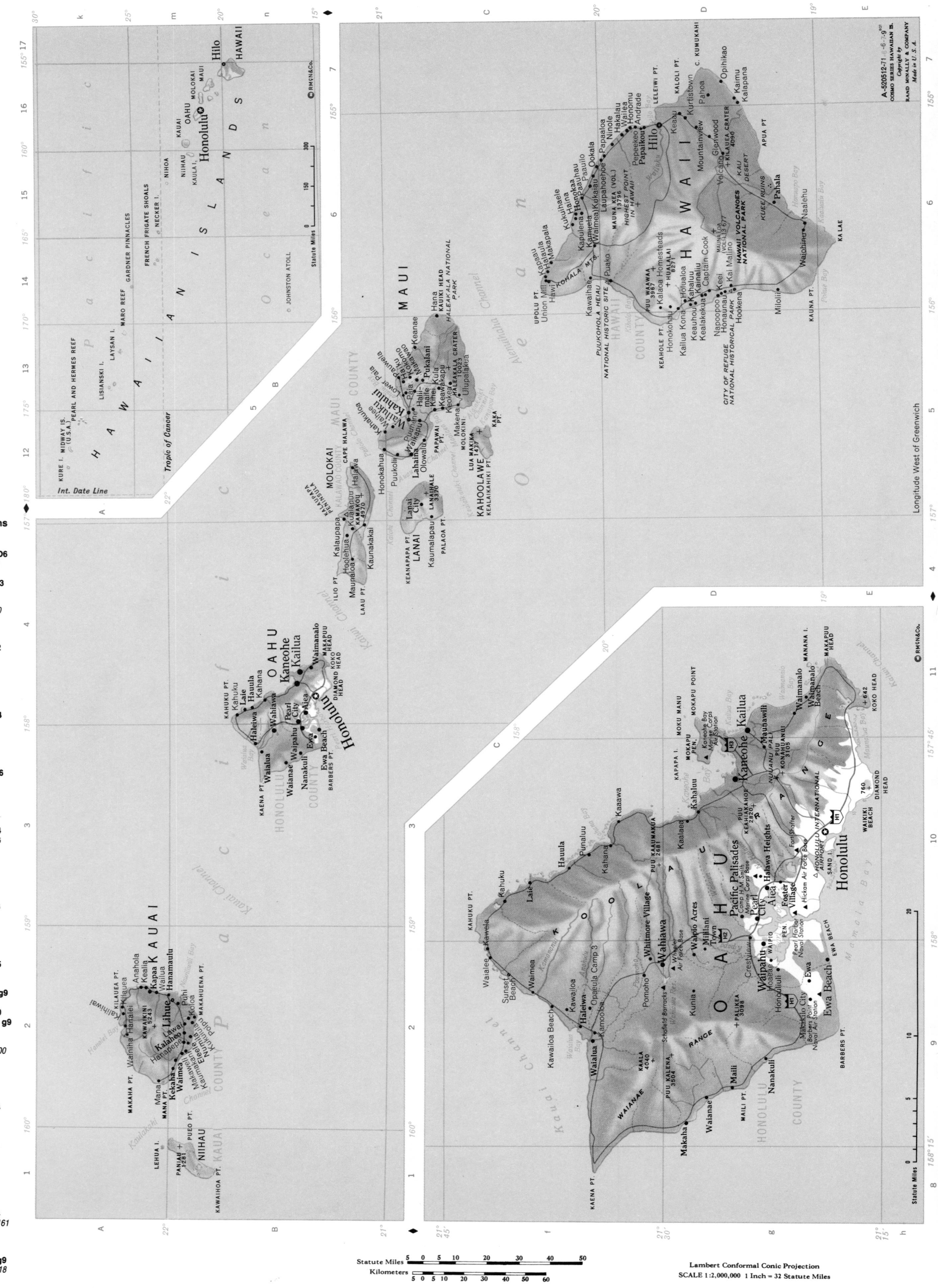

Cities and Towns

Aiea *15,200* **B4**
Anahola *915* **A2**
Captain Cook *2,008* **D6**
Crestview *1,000* **g10**
Ewa *2,637* **B3**
Ewa Beach *14,369* **B3**
Foster Village *3,700* **g10**
Halawa Heights *7,000* **g10**
Haleiwa *2,412* **B3**
Haliimaile *741* **C5**
Hanamaulu *3,227* **B2**
Hanapepe *1,417* **B2**
Hauula *2,997* **B4**
Hawi *795* **C6**
Hilo *35,269* **D6**
Holualoa *1,243* **D6**
Honokaa *1,936* **C6**
Honolulu *365,048* **B4**
Kaaawa *959* **f10**
Kahaluu *2,925* **g10**
Kahuku *935* **B4**
Kahului *12,978* **C5**
Kailua *35,812* **B4**
Kailua Kona *4,751* **D6**
Kalaheo *2,500* **B2**
Kamuela *1,179* **C6**
Kaneohe *29,919* **B4**
Kapaa *4,467* **A2**
Kaumakani *888* **B2**
Kaunakakai *2,231* **B4**
Kealakekua *1,033* **D6**
Kekaha *3,260* **B2**
Keokea *900* **C5**
Kihei *5,644* **C5**
Kilauea *895* **A2**
Koloa *1,457* **B2**
Kula *1,300* **C5**
Kurtistown *1,200* **D6**
Lahaina *6,095* **C5**
Laie *4,643* **B4**
Lanai City *2,092* **C5**
Lawai *950* **B2**
Lihue *4,000* **B2**
Lower Paia *1,500* **C5**
Maili *5,026* **g9**
Makaha *7,905* **g9**
Makakilo City *7,691* **g9**
Makawao *1,066* **C5**
Maunawili *2,200* **g10**
Mililani Town *20,351* **g9**
Naalehu *1,168* **D6**
Nanakuli *8,185* **B3**
Pacific Palisades *9,500* **g10**
Pahala *1,619* **D6**
Pahoa *923* **D7**
Paia *1,000* **C5**
Papaikou *1,567* **D6**
Pearl City *33,000* **B4**
Pepeekeo *1,800* **D6**
Puhi *991* **B2**
Pukalani *3,950* **C5**
Sunset Beach *800* **f9**
Volcano *900* **D6**
Wahiawa *16,911* **B3**
Waialua *4,051* **B3**
Waianae *5,000* **B3**
Wailua *1,587* **A2**
Wailuku *10,260* **C5**
Waimanalo *3,562* **B4**
Waimanalo Beach *4,161* **g11**
Waimea *1,569* **B2**
Waipahu *29,139* **B3**
Waipio Acres *4,091* **g9**
Whitmore Village *2,318* **f9**

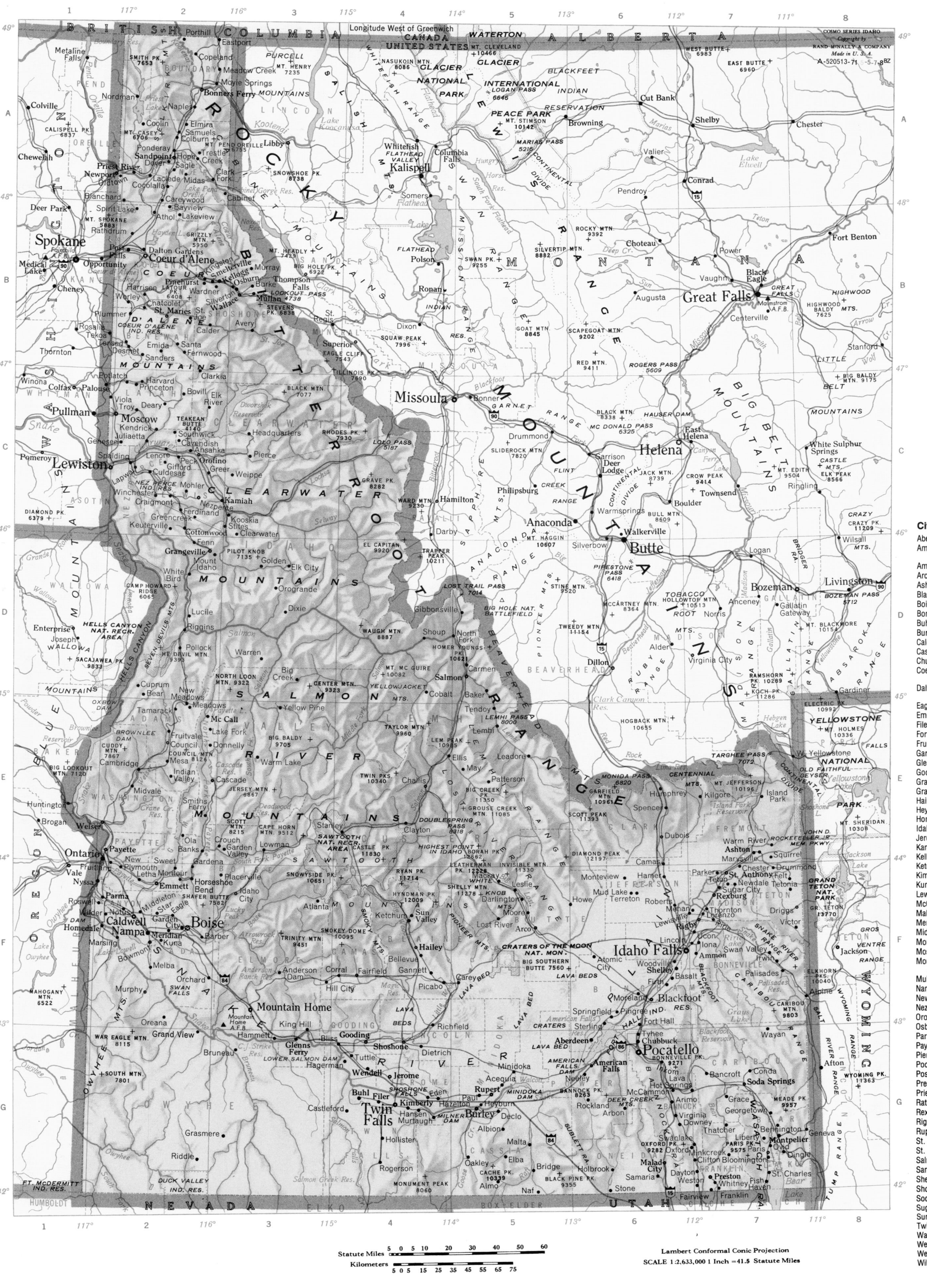

Cities and Towns

Aberdeen *1,528* **G6**
American Falls *3,626* **G6**
Ammon *4,669* **F7**
Arco *1,241* **F5**
Ashton *1,219* **E7**
Blackfoot *10,065* **F6**
Boise *102,160* **F2**
Bonners Ferry *1,906* **A2**
Buhl *3,629* **G4**
Burley *8,761* **G5**
Caldwell *17,699* **F2**
Cascade *945* **E2**
Chubbuck *7,052* **G6**
Coeur d'Alene *20,054* **B2**
Dalton Gardens *1,795* **B2**
Eagle *2,620* **F2**
Emmett *4,605* **F2**
Filer *1,645* **G4**
Fort Hall *900* **F6**
Fruitland *2,559* **F2**
Garden City *4,571* **F2**
Glenns Ferry *1,374* **G3**
Gooding *2,949* **G4**
Grace *1,216* **G7**
Grangeville *3,666* **D2**
Hailey *2,109* **F4**
Heyburn *2,889* **G5**
Homedale *2,078* **F2**
Idaho Falls *39,590* **F6**
Jerome *6,891* **G4**
Kamiah *1,478* **C2**
Kellogg *3,417* **B2**
Ketchum *2,200* **F4**
Kimberly *2,307* **G4**
Kuna *1,767* **F2**
Lewiston *27,986* **C1**
McCall *2,188* **E2**
Malad City *1,915* **G6**
Meridian *6,658* **F2**
Middleton *1,901* **F2**
Montpelier *3,107* **G7**
Moscow *16,513* **C2**
Mountain Home *7,540* **F3**
Mullan *1,269* **B3**
Nampa *25,112* **F2**
New Plymouth *1,186* **F2**
Nezperce *517* **C2**
Orofino *3,711* **C2**
Osburn *2,220* **B3**
Parma *1,820* **F2**
Payette *5,448* **E2**
Pierce *1,060* **C3**
Pocatello *46,340* **G6**
Post Falls *5,736* **B2**
Preston *3,759* **G7**
Priest River *1,639* **A2**
Rathdrum *1,369* **B2**
Rexburg *11,559* **F7**
Rigby *2,624* **F7**
Rupert *5,476* **G5**
St. Anthony *3,212* **F7**
St. Maries *2,794* **B2**
Salmon *3,308* **D5**
Sandpoint *4,460* **A2**
Shelley *3,300* **F6**
Shoshone *1,242* **G4**
Soda Springs *4,051* **G7**
Sugar City *1,022* **F7**
Sun Valley *545* **F4**
Twin Falls *26,209* **G4**
Wallace *1,736* **B3**
Weiser *4,771* **E2**
Wendell *1,974* **G4**
Wilder *1,260* **F2**

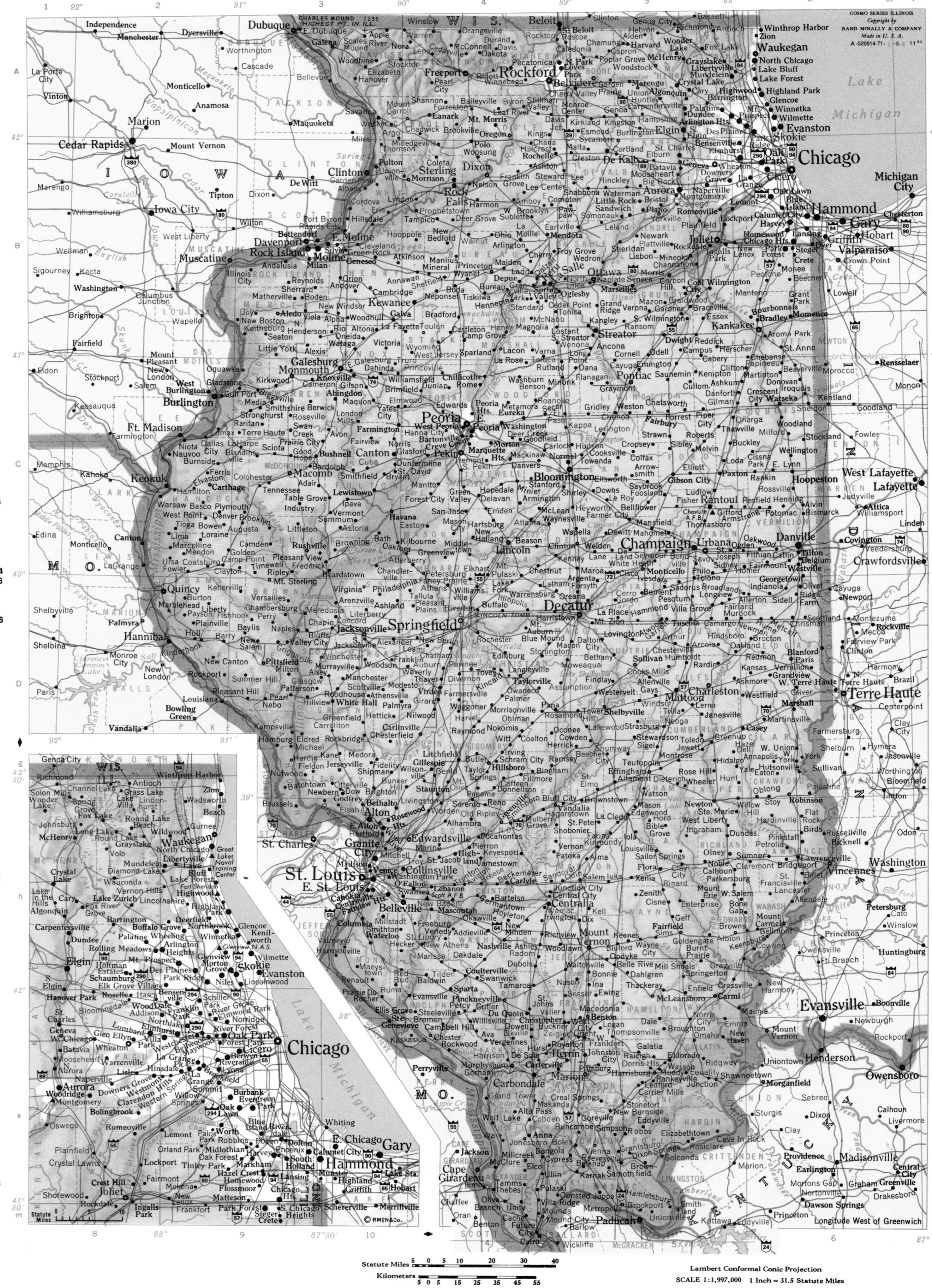

Cities and Towns

Alton *34,171* **E3**
Arlington Heights *66,116* **A5**
Aurora *81,293* **B5**
Belleville *41,580* **E4**
Berwyn *46,849* **k9**
Bloomington *44,189* **C4**
Bourbonnais *13,280* **B6**
Brookfield *19,395* **k9**
Cahokia *18,904* **E3**
Cairo *5,931* **F4**
Calumet City *39,697* **B6**
Canton *14,626* **C3**
Carbondale *26,414* **F4**
Centralia *15,126* **E4**
Champaign *58,133* **C5**
Charleston *19,355* **D5**
Chicago *3,005,072* **B6**
Cicero *61,232* **B6**
Danville *38,985* **C6**
Decatur *94,081* **D5**
De Kalb *33,099* **B5**
Des Plaines *53,568* **A6**
Dixon *15,701* **B4**
Downers Grove *42,572* **B5**
East St. Louis *55,200* **E3**
Elgin *63,981* **A5**
Elmhurst *44,276* **B6**
Evanston *73,706* **A6**
Freeport *26,266* **A4**
Galena *3,876* **A3**
Galesburg *35,305* **C3**
Granite City *36,815* **E3**
Gurnee *7,179* **h9**
Highland Park *30,611* **A6**
Jacksonville *20,284* **D3**
Joliet *77,956* **B5**
Kankakee *30,141* **B6**
Kewanee *14,508* **B4**
Lake Forest *15,245* **A6**
La Salle *10,347* **B4**
Lincoln *16,327* **C4**
Lombard *36,897* **k8**
Macomb *19,863* **C3**
Marion *14,031* **F5**
Mattoon *19,055* **D5**
Moline *46,278* **B3**
Monmouth *10,706* **C3**
Mount Prospect *52,634* **A6**
Mount Vernon *17,193* **E5**
Nauvoo *1,133* **C2**
Normal *35,672* **C5**
North Chicago *38,774* **A6**
Oak Lawn *60,590* **B6**
Oak Park *54,887* **B6**
Ottawa *18,166* **B5**
Pekin *33,967* **C4**
Peoria *124,160* **C4**
Peru *10,886* **B4**
Pontiac *11,227* **C5**
Quincy *42,554* **D2**
Rockford *139,712* **A4**
Rock Island *46,928* **B3**
Salem *7,813* **E5**
Schaumburg *53,305* **h8**
Skokie *60,278* **A6**
Springfield *100,054* **D4**
Sterling *16,281* **B4**
Streator *14,795* **B5**
Taylorville *11,386* **D4**
Urbana *35,978* **C5**
Vandalia *5,338* **E4**
Waukegan *67,653* **A6**
Wheaton *43,043* **B5**
Zion *17,861* **A6**

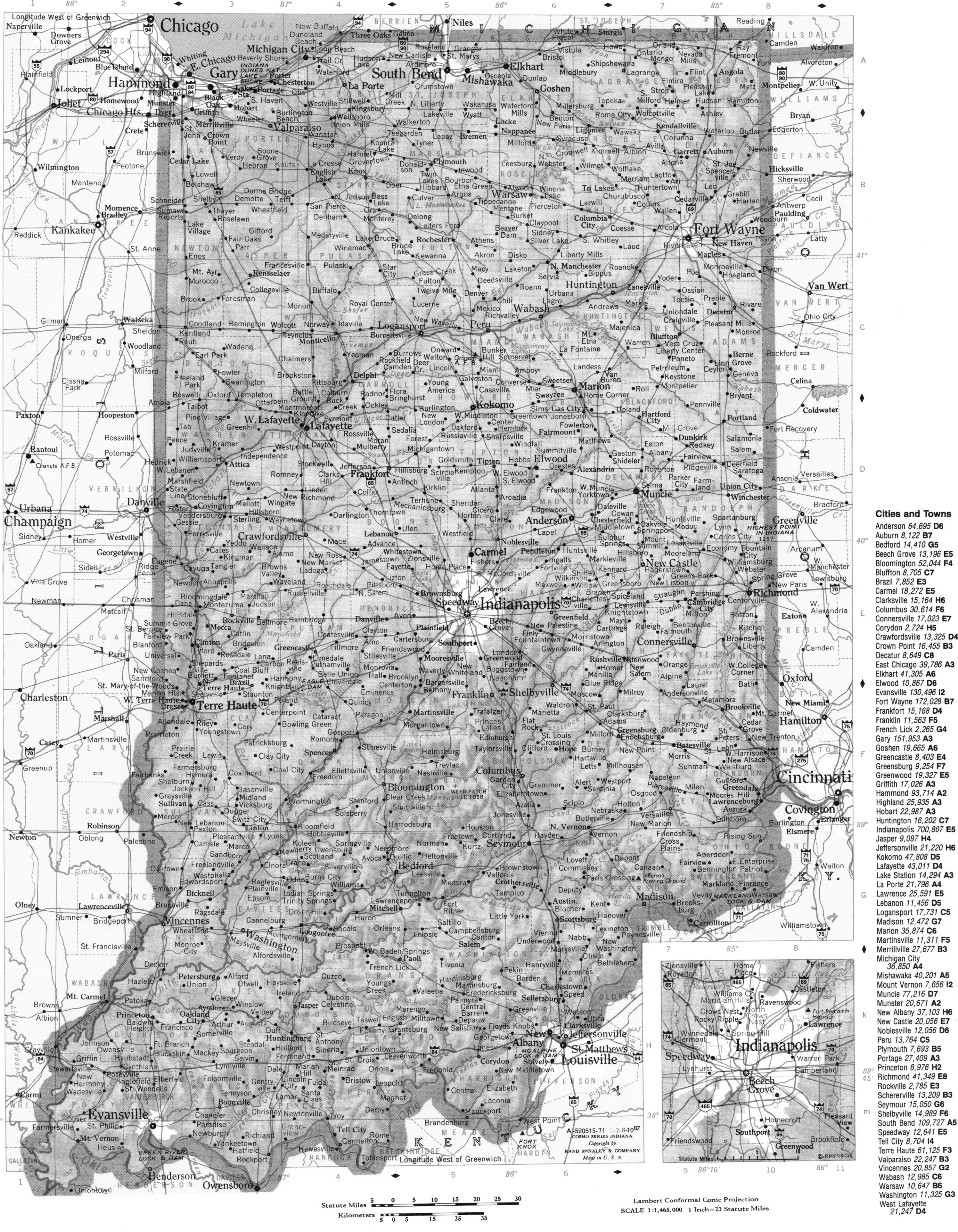

Cities and Towns

Anderson *64,695* **D6**
Auburn *8,122* **B7**
Bedford *14,410* **G5**
Beech Grove *13,196* **E5**
Bloomington *52,044* **F4**
Bluffton *8,705* **C7**
Brazil *7,852* **E3**
Carmel *18,272* **E5**
Clarksville *15,164* **H6**
Columbus *30,614* **F6**
Connersville *17,023* **E7**
Corydon *2,724* **H5**
Crawfordsville *13,325* **D4**
Crown Point *16,455* **B3**
Decatur *8,649* **C8**
East Chicago *39,786* **A3**
Elkhart *41,305* **A6**
Elwood *10,867* **D6**
Evansville *130,496* **I2**
Fort Wayne *172,028* **B7**
Frankfort *15,168* **D4**
Franklin *11,563* **F5**
French Lick *2,265* **G4**
Gary *151,953* **A3**
Goshen *19,665* **A6**
Greencastle *8,403* **E4**
Greensburg *9,254* **F7**
Greenwood *19,327* **E5**
Griffith *17,026* **A3**
Hammond *93,714* **A2**
Highland *25,935* **A3**
Hobart *22,987* **A3**
Huntington *16,202* **C7**
Indianapolis *700,807* **E5**
Jasper *9,097* **H4**
Jeffersonville *21,220* **H6**
Kokomo *47,808* **D5**
Lafayette *43,011* **D4**
Lake Station *14,294* **A3**
La Porte *21,796* **A4**
Lawrence *25,591* **E5**
Lebanon *11,456* **D5**
Logansport *17,731* **C5**
Madison *12,472* **G7**
Marion *35,874* **C6**
Martinsville *11,311* **F5**
Merrillville *27,677* **B3**
Michigan City *36,850* **A4**
Mishawaka *40,201* **A5**
Mount Vernon *7,656* **I2**
Muncie *77,216* **D7**
Munster *20,671* **A2**
New Albany *37,103* **H6**
New Castle *20,056* **E7**
Noblesville *12,056* **D6**
Peru *13,764* **C5**
Plymouth *7,693* **B5**
Portage *27,409* **A3**
Princeton *8,976* **H2**
Richmond *41,349* **E8**
Rockville *2,785* **E3**
Schererville *13,209* **B3**
Seymour *15,050* **G6**
Shelbyville *14,989* **F6**
South Bend *109,727* **A5**
Speedway *12,641* **E5**
Tell City *8,704* **I4**
Terre Haute *61,125* **F3**
Valparaiso *22,247* **B3**
Vincennes *20,857* **G2**
Wabash *12,985* **C6**
Warsaw *10,647* **B6**
Washington *11,325* **G3**
West Lafayette *21,247* **D4**

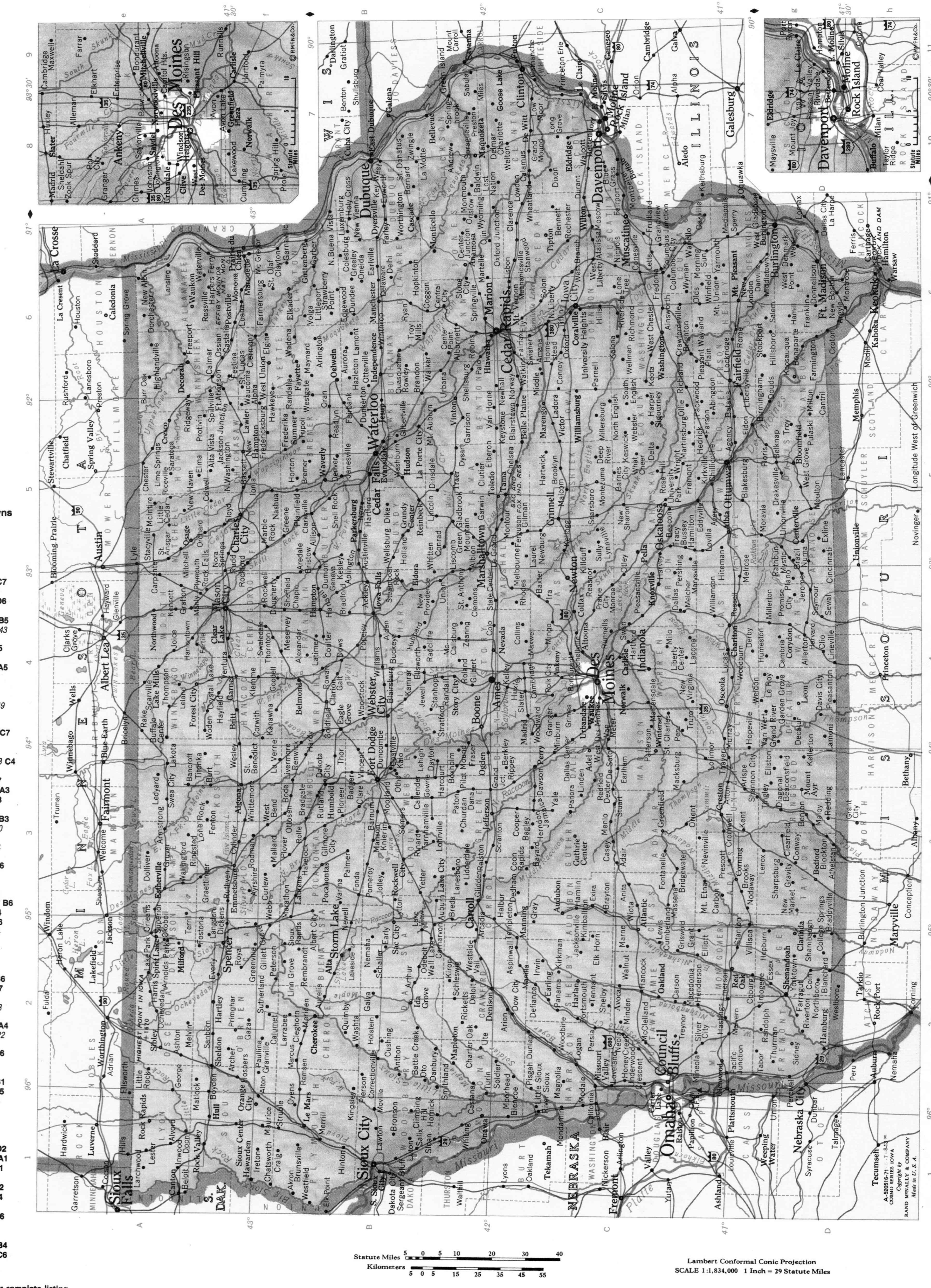

Cities and Towns

Algona 6,289 **A3**
Amana 600 **C6**
Ames 45,775 **B4**
Anamosa 4,958 **B6**
Ankeny 15,429 **C4**
Atlantic 7,789 **C2**
Bettendorf 27,381 **C7**
Boone 12,602 **B4**
Burlington 29,529 **D6**
Carroll 9,705 **B3**
Cedar Falls 36,322 **B5**
Cedar Rapids 110,243 **C6**
Centerville 6,558 **D5**
Chariton 4,987 **C4**
Charles City 8,778 **A5**
Cherokee 7,004 **B2**
Clarinda 5,458 **D2**
Clinton 32,828 **C7**
Council Bluffs 56,449 **C2**
Creston 8,429 **C3**
Davenport 103,264 **C7**
Decorah 7,991 **A6**
Denison 6,675 **B2**
Des Moines 191,003 **C4**
De Witt 4,512 **C7**
Dubuque 62,321 **B7**
Emmetsburg 4,621 **A3**
Estherville 7,518 **A3**
Fairfield 9,428 **C6**
Fort Dodge 29,423 **B3**
Fort Madison 13,520 **D6**
Glenwood 5,280 **C2**
Grinnell 8,868 **C5**
Guttenberg 2,428 **B6**
Hampton 4,630 **B4**
Harlan 5,357 **C2**
Humboldt 4,794 **B3**
Independence 6,392 **B6**
Indianola 10,843 **C4**
Iowa City 50,508 **C6**
Iowa Falls 6,174 **B4**
Jefferson 4,854 **B3**
Keokuk 13,536 **D6**
Knoxville 8,143 **C4**
Le Mars 8,276 **B1**
Manchester 4,942 **B6**
Maquoketa 6,313 **B7**
Marion 19,474 **B6**
Marshalltown 26,938 **B5**
Mason City 30,144 **A4**
Mount Pleasant 7,322 **D6**
Muscatine 23,467 **C6**
Newton 15,292 **C4**
Oelwein 7,564 **B6**
Orange City 4,588 **B1**
Oskaloosa 10,989 **C5**
Ottumwa 27,381 **C5**
Pella 8,349 **C5**
Perry 7,053 **C3**
Red Oak 6,810 **D2**
Sheldon 5,003 **A2**
Shenandoah 6,274 **D2**
Sioux Center 4,588 **A1**
Sioux City 82,003 **B1**
Spencer 11,726 **A2**
Storm Lake 8,814 **B2**
Urbandale 17,869 **C4**
Vinton 5,040 **B5**
Washington 6,584 **C6**
Waterloo 75,985 **B5**
Waverly 8,444 **B5**
Webster City 8,572 **B4**
West Branch 1,867 **C6**
West Des Moines 21,894 **C4**

See main index for complete listing.

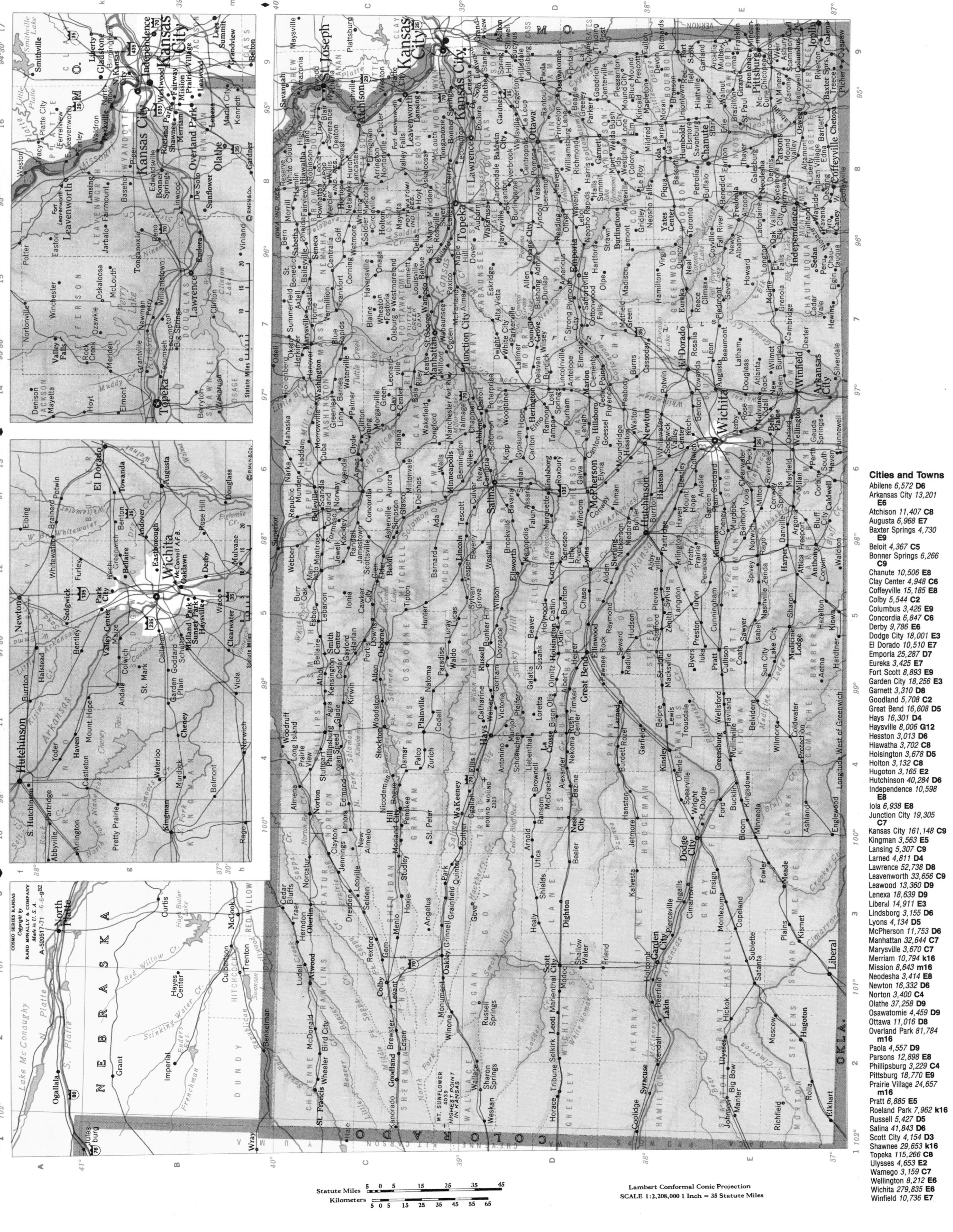

Cities and Towns

Abilene *6,572* **D6**
Arkansas City *13,201* **E6**
Atchison *11,407* **C8**
Augusta *6,968* **E7**
Baxter Springs *4,730* **E9**
Beloit *4,367* **C5**
Bonner Springs *6,266* **C9**
Chanute *10,506* **E8**
Clay Center *4,948* **C6**
Coffeyville *15,185* **E8**
Colby *5,544* **C2**
Columbus *3,426* **E9**
Concordia *6,847* **C6**
Derby *9,786* **E6**
Dodge City *18,001* **E3**
El Dorado *10,510* **E7**
Emporia *25,287* **D7**
Eureka *3,425* **E7**
Fort Scott *8,893* **E9**
Garden City *18,256* **E3**
Garnett *3,310* **D8**
Goodland *5,708* **C2**
Great Bend *16,608* **D5**
Hays *16,301* **D4**
Haysville *8,006* **G12**
Hesston *3,013* **D6**
Hiawatha *3,702* **C8**
Hoisington *3,678* **D5**
Holton *3,132* **C8**
Hugoton *3,165* **E2**
Hutchinson *40,284* **D6**
Independence *10,598* **E8**
Iola *6,938* **E8**
Junction City *19,305* **C7**
Kansas City *161,148* **C9**
Kingman *3,563* **E5**
Lansing *5,307* **C9**
Larned *4,811* **D4**
Lawrence *52,738* **D8**
Leavenworth *33,656* **C9**
Leawood *13,360* **D9**
Lenexa *18,639* **D9**
Liberal *14,911* **E3**
Lindsborg *3,155* **D6**
Lyons *4,134* **D5**
McPherson *11,753* **D6**
Manhattan *32,644* **C7**
Marysville *3,670* **C7**
Merriam *10,794* **k16**
Mission *8,643* **m16**
Neodesha *3,414* **E8**
Newton *16,332* **D6**
Norton *3,400* **C4**
Olathe *37,258* **D9**
Osawatomie *4,459* **D9**
Ottawa *11,016* **D8**
Overland Park *81,784* **m16**
Paola *4,557* **D9**
Parsons *12,898* **E8**
Phillipsburg *3,229* **C4**
Pittsburg *18,770* **E9**
Prairie Village *24,657* **m16**
Pratt *6,885* **E5**
Roeland Park *7,962* **k16**
Russell *5,427* **D5**
Salina *41,843* **D6**
Scott City *4,154* **D3**
Shawnee *29,653* **k16**
Topeka *115,266* **C8**
Ulysses *4,653* **E2**
Wamego *3,159* **C7**
Wellington *8,212* **E6**
Wichita *279,835* **E6**
Winfield *10,736* **E7**

KENTUCKY

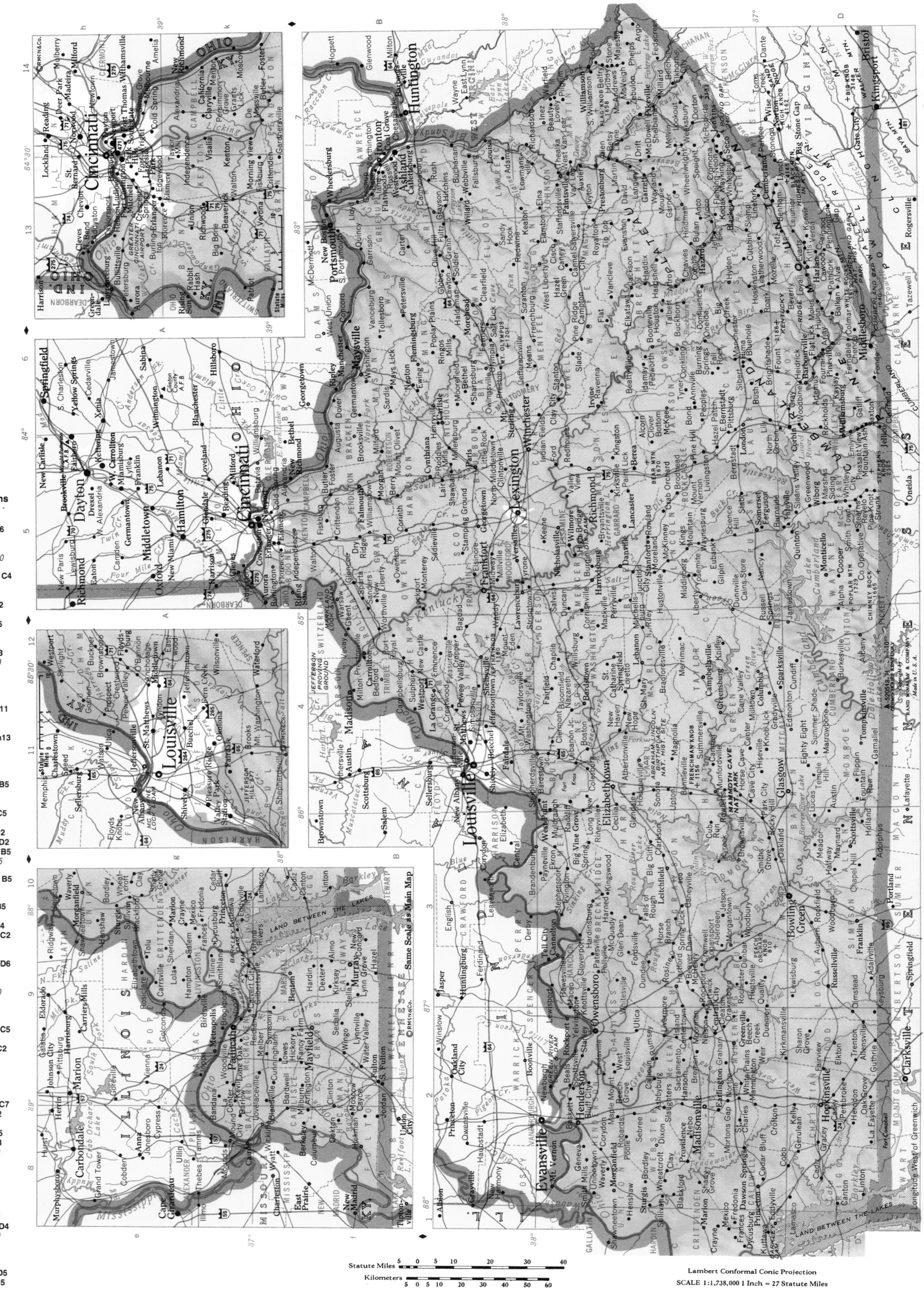

Cities and Towns

Alexandria 4,735 **B5**
Ashland 27,064 **B7**
Barbourville 3,333 **D6**
Bardstown 6,155 **C4**
Berea 8,226 **C5**
Bowling Green 40,450 **D3**
Campbellsville 8,715 **C4**
Carrollton 3,967 **B4**
Cave City 2,098 **C4**
Central City 5,214 **C2**
Corbin 8,075 **D5**
Covington 49,563 **A5**
Cynthiana 5,881 **B5**
Danville 12,942 **C5**
Edgewood 7,230 **h13**
Elizabethtown 15,380 **C4**
Elsmere 7,203 **B5**
Erlanger 14,433 **A5**
Fairdale 7,315 **B4**
Fern Creek 16,866 **g11**
Flatwoods 8,354 **B7**
Florence 15,586 **A5**
Fort Mitchell 7,297 **h13**
Fort Thomas 16,012 **h14**
Frankfort 25,973 **B5**
Franklin 7,738 **D3**
Georgetown 10,972 **B5**
Glasgow 12,958 **C4**
Greenville 4,631 **C2**
Harrodsburg 7,265 **C5**
Hazard 5,371 **C6**
Henderson 24,834 **C2**
Hopkinsville 27,318 **D2**
Independence 7,998 **B5**
Jeffersontown 15,795 **B4**
Lawrenceburg 5,167 **B5**
Lebanon 6,590 **C4**
Leitchfield 4,533 **C3**
Lexington 204,165 **B5**
London 4,002 **C5**
Louisville 298,840 **B4**
Madisonville 16,979 **C2**
Mayfield 10,705 **f9**
Maysville 7,983 **B6**
Middlesboro 12,251 **D6**
Monticello 5,677 **D5**
Morehead 7,789 **B6**
Mount Sterling 5,820 **B6**
Murray 14,248 **f9**
Newport 21,587 **A5**
Nicholasville 10,319 **C5**
Okolona 20,039 **g11**
Owensboro 54,450 **C2**
Paducah 29,315 **e9**
Paris 7,935 **B5**
Pikeville 4,756 **C7**
Pleasure Ridge Park 27,332 **g11**
Prestonsburg 4,011 **C7**
Providence 4,434 **C2**
Radcliff 14,519 **C4**
Richmond 21,705 **C5**
Russellville 7,520 **D3**
St. Matthews 13,519 **B4**
Scottsville 4,278 **D3**
Shelbyville 5,329 **B4**
Shepherdsville 4,454 **C4**
Shively 16,819 **B4**
Somerset 10,649 **C5**
Tompkinsville 4,366 **D4**
Valley Station 20,000 **g11**
Versailles 6,427 **B5**
Westwood 5,973 **B7**
Williamsburg 5,560 **D5**
Winchester 15,216 **C5**

See main index for complete listing.

Statute Miles 5 0 5 10 20 30 40

Kilometers 5 0 5 10 20 30 40 50 60

Lambert Conformal Conic Projection
SCALE 1:1,738,000 1 Inch = 27 Statute Miles

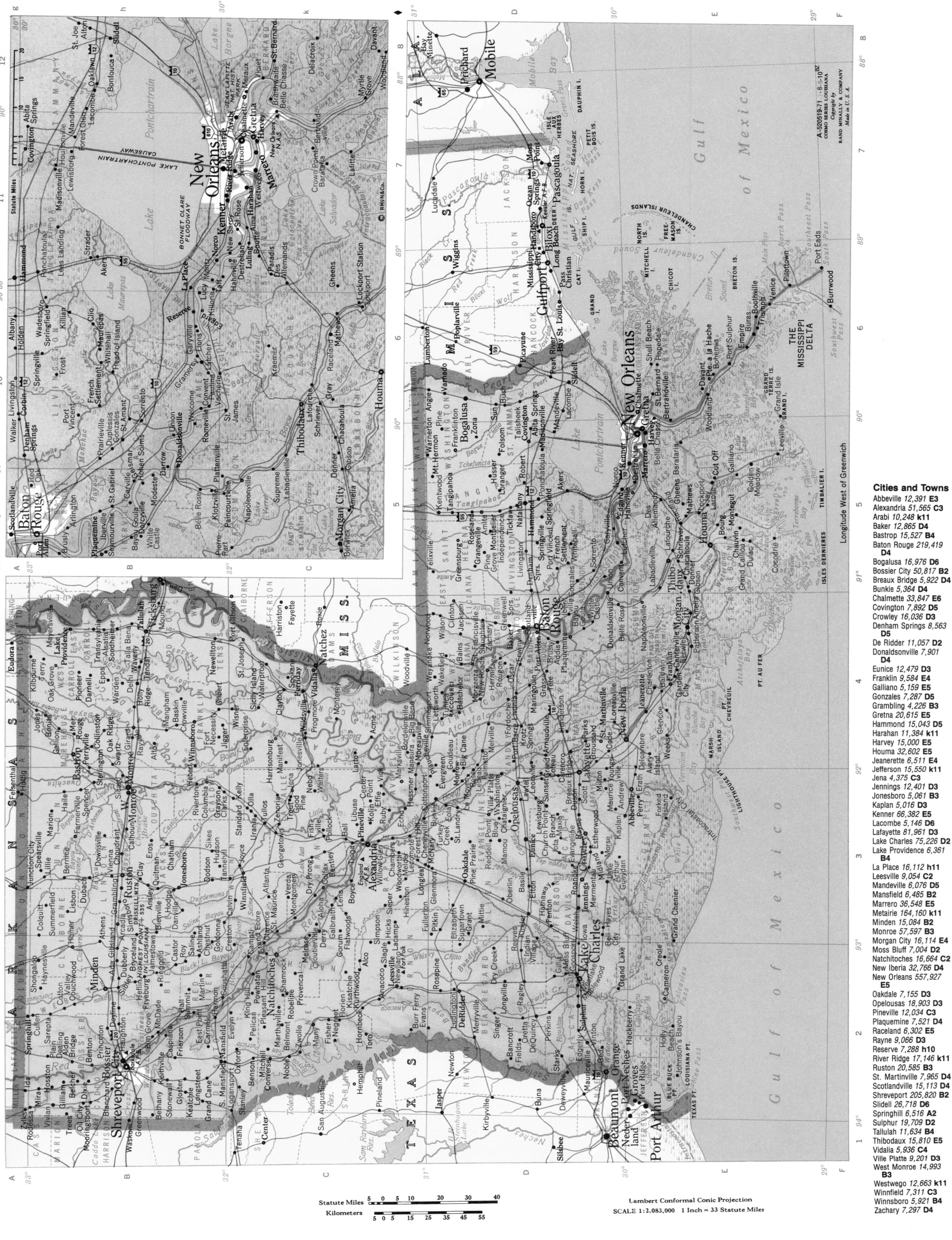

Cities and Towns

Abbeville *12,391* **E3**
Alexandria *51,565* **C3**
Arabi *10,248* **k11**
Baker *12,865* **D4**
Bastrop *15,527* **B4**
Baton Rouge *219,419* **D4**
Bogalusa *16,976* **D6**
Bossier City *50,817* **B2**
Breaux Bridge *5,922* **D4**
Bunkie *5,364* **D4**
Chalmette *33,847* **E6**
Covington *7,892* **D5**
Crowley *16,036* **D3**
Denham Springs *8,563* **D5**
De Ridder *11,057* **D2**
Donaldsonville *7,901* **D4**
Eunice *12,479* **D3**
Franklin *9,584* **E4**
Galliano *5,159* **E5**
Gonzales *7,287* **D5**
Grambling *4,226* **B3**
Gretna *20,615* **E5**
Hammond *15,043* **D5**
Harahan *11,384* **k11**
Harvey *15,000* **E5**
Houma *32,602* **E5**
Jeanerette *6,511* **E4**
Jefferson *15,550* **k11**
Jena *4,375* **C3**
Jennings *12,401* **D3**
Jonesboro *5,061* **B3**
Kaplan *5,016* **D3**
Kenner *66,382* **E5**
Lacombe *5,146* **D6**
Lafayette *81,961* **D3**
Lake Charles *75,226* **D2**
Lake Providence *6,361* **B4**
La Place *16,112* **h11**
Leesville *9,054* **C2**
Mandeville *6,076* **D5**
Mansfield *6,485* **B2**
Marrero *36,548* **E5**
Metairie *164,160* **k11**
Minden *15,084* **B2**
Monroe *57,597* **B3**
Morgan City *16,114* **E4**
Moss Bluff *7,004* **D2**
Natchitoches *16,664* **C2**
New Iberia *32,766* **D4**
New Orleans *557,927* **E5**
Oakdale *7,155* **D3**
Opelousas *18,903* **D3**
Pineville *12,034* **C3**
Plaquemine *7,521* **D4**
Raceland *6,302* **E5**
Rayne *9,066* **D3**
Reserve *7,288* **h10**
River Ridge *17,146* **k11**
Ruston *20,585* **B3**
St. Martinville *7,965* **D4**
Scotlandville *15,113* **D4**
Shreveport *205,820* **B2**
Slidell *26,718* **D6**
Springhill *6,516* **A2**
Sulphur *19,709* **D2**
Tallulah *11,634* **B4**
Thibodaux *15,810* **E5**
Vidalia *5,936* **C4**
Ville Platte *9,201* **D3**
West Monroe *14,993* **B3**
Westwego *12,663* **k11**
Winnfield *7,311* **C3**
Winnsboro *5,921* **B4**
Zachary *7,297* **D4**

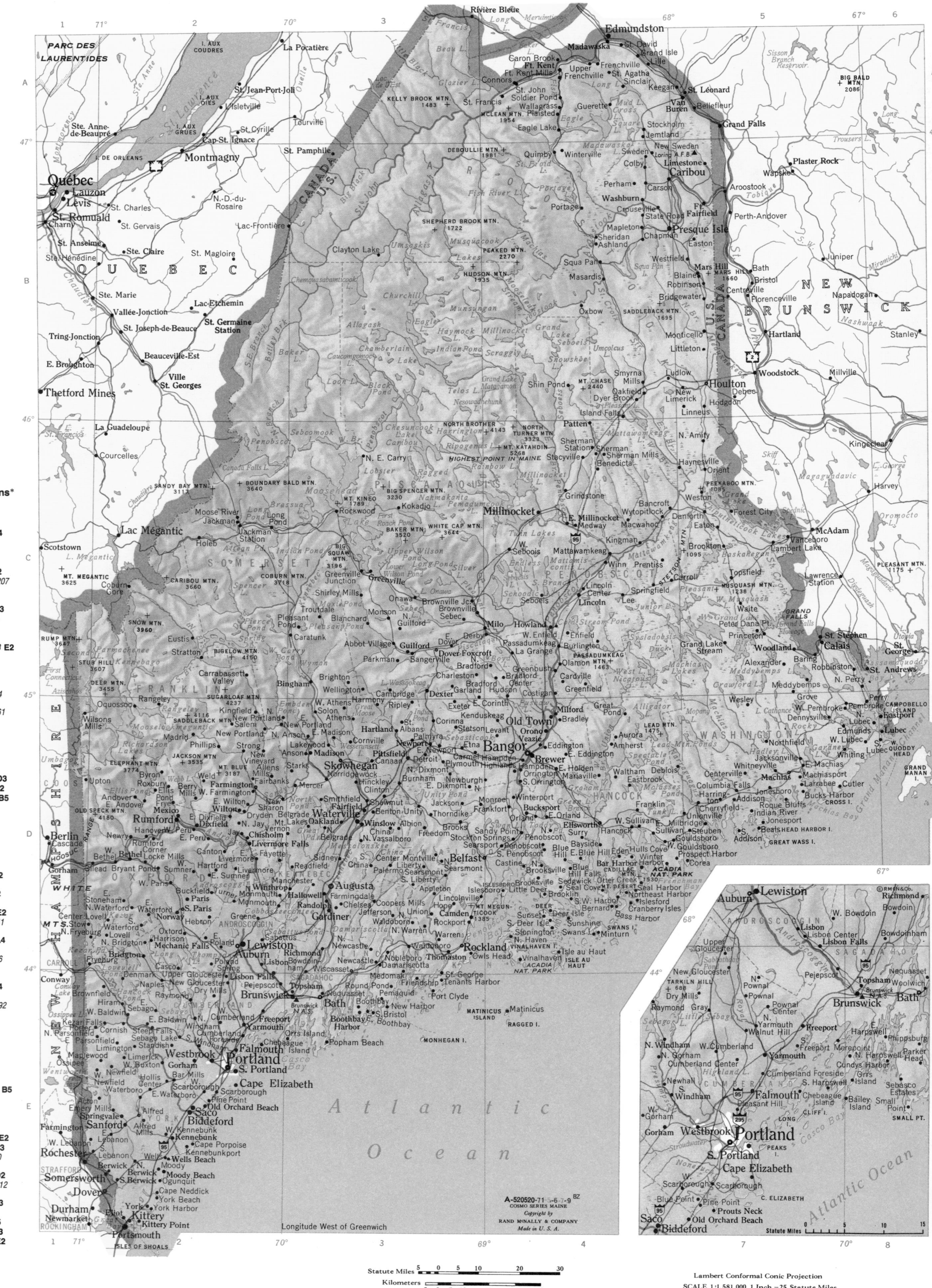

Cities and Towns*

Auburn *23,128* **D2**
Augusta *21,819* **D3**
Bangor *31,643* **D4**
Bar Harbor *2,685* **D4**
Bath *10,246* **E3**
Belfast *6,243* **D3**
Berwick *2,378* **E2**
Biddeford *19,638* **E2**
Boothbay Harbor *2,207* **E3**
Brewer *9,017* **D4**
Brunswick *10,990* **E3**
Bucksport *2,853* **D4**
Calais *4,262* **C5**
Camden *3,743* **D3**
Cape Elizabeth *7,838* **E2**
Caribou *9,916* **B5**
Cumberland Center *2,015* **g7**
Dexter *3,118* **C3**
Dover-Foxcroft *2,974* **C3**
East Millinocket *2,361* **C4**
Eastport *1,982* **D6**
Eliot *2,450* **E2**
Ellsworth *5,179* **D4**
Fairfield *3,169* **D3**
Falmouth *6,853* **E2**
Farmingdale *2,014* **D3**
Farmington *3,583* **D2**
Fort Fairfield *2,282* **B5**
Fort Kent *2,375* **A4**
Freeport *1,906* **E2**
Gardiner *6,485* **D3**
Gorham *4,052* **E2**
Hallowell *2,502* **D3**
Hampden *2,300* **D4**
Houlton *5,730* **B5**
Kennebunk *3,294* **E2**
Kittery *5,465* **E2**
Lewiston *40,481* **D2**
Lincoln *3,524* **C4**
Lisbon Falls *4,370* **E2**
Livermore Falls *2,441* **D2**
Madawaska *4,165* **A4**
Madison *2,788* **D3**
Mechanic Falls *2,616* **D2**
Mexico *3,207* **D2**
Millinocket *7,567* **C4**
Milo *2,255* **C4**
North Windham *5,492* **E2**
Norway *2,653* **D2**
Oakland *3,387* **D3**
Old Orchard Beach *6,291* **E2**
Orono *10,578* **D4**
Pittsfield *3,117* **D3**
Portland *61,572* **E2**
Presque Isle *11,172* **B5**
Rockland *7,919* **D3**
Rumford *6,256* **D2**
Saco *12,921* **E2**
Sanford *10,268* **E2**
Scarborough *2,280* **E2**
Skowhegan *6,517* **D3**
South Berwick *2,120* **E2**
South Paris *2,128* **D2**
South Portland *22,712* **E2**
Thomaston *2,348* **D3**
Topsham *4,657* **E3**
Van Buren *3,282* **A5**
Waterville *17,779* **D3**
Westbrook *14,976* **E2**
Wilton *2,262* **D2**
Winslow *5,903* **D3**
Winthrop *3,264* **D3**
Yarmouth *2,421* **E2**
York *3,130* **E2**

***Populations are for localities, not incorporated towns.**

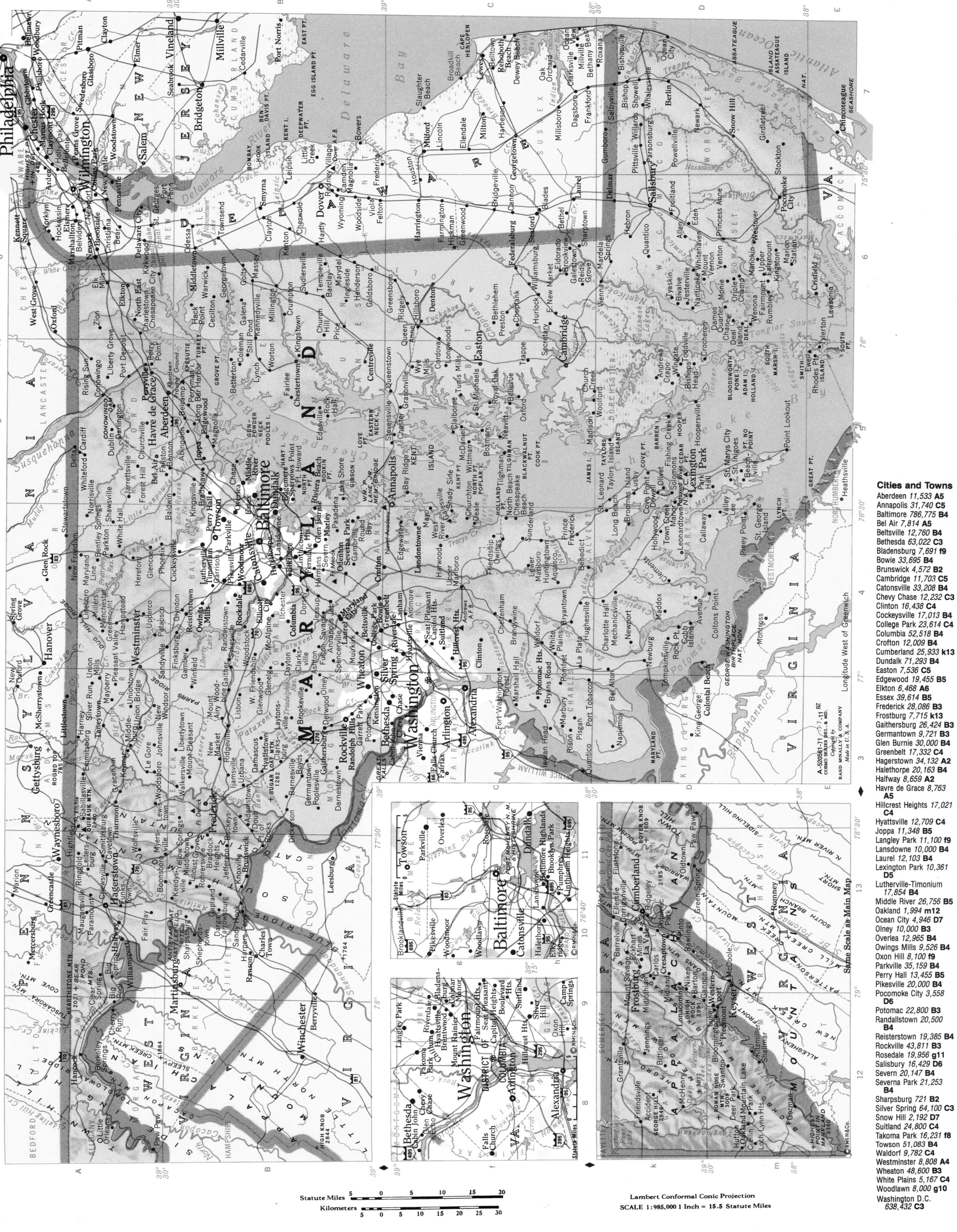

Cities and Towns

Aberdeen *11,533* **A5**
Annapolis *31,740* **C5**
Baltimore *786,775* **B4**
Bel Air *7,814* **A5**
Beltsville *12,760* **B4**
Bethesda *63,022* **C3**
Bladensburg *7,691* **f9**
Bowie *33,695* **B4**
Brunswick *4,572* **B2**
Cambridge *11,703* **C5**
Catonsville *33,208* **B4**
Chevy Chase *12,232* **C3**
Clinton *16,438* **C4**
Cockeysville *17,013* **B4**
College Park *23,614* **C4**
Columbia *52,518* **B4**
Crofton *12,009* **B4**
Cumberland *25,933* **k13**
Dundalk *71,293* **B4**
Easton *7,536* **C5**
Edgewood *19,455* **B5**
Elkton *6,468* **A6**
Essex *39,614* **B5**
Frederick *28,086* **B3**
Frostburg *7,715* **k13**
Gaithersburg *26,424* **B3**
Germantown *9,721* **B3**
Glen Burnie *30,000* **B4**
Greenbelt *17,332* **C4**
Hagerstown *34,132* **A2**
Halethorpe *20,163* **B4**
Halfway *8,659* **A2**
Havre de Grace *8,763* **A5**
Hillcrest Heights *17,021* **C4**
Hyattsville *12,709* **C4**
Joppa *11,348* **B5**
Langley Park *11,100* **f9**
Lansdowne *10,000* **B4**
Laurel *12,103* **B4**
Lexington Park *10,361* **D5**
Lutherville-Timonium *17,854* **B4**
Middle River *26,756* **B5**
Oakland *1,994* **m12**
Ocean City *4,946* **D7**
Olney *10,000* **B3**
Overlea *12,965* **B4**
Owings Mills *9,526* **B4**
Oxon Hill *8,100* **f9**
Parkville *35,159* **B4**
Perry Hall *13,455* **B5**
Pikesville *20,000* **B4**
Pocomoke City *3,558* **D6**
Potomac *22,800* **B3**
Randallstown *20,500* **B4**
Reisterstown *19,385* **B4**
Rockville *43,811* **B3**
Rosedale *19,956* **g11**
Salisbury *16,429* **D6**
Severn *20,147* **B4**
Severna Park *21,253* **B4**
Sharpsburg *721* **B2**
Silver Spring *64,100* **C3**
Snow Hill *2,192* **D7**
Suitland *24,800* **C4**
Takoma Park *16,231* **f8**
Towson *51,083* **B4**
Waldorf *9,782* **C4**
Westminster *8,808* **A4**
Wheaton *48,600* **B3**
White Plains *5,167* **C4**
Woodlawn *8,000* **g10**
Washington D.C. *638,432* **C3**

MASSACHUSETTS

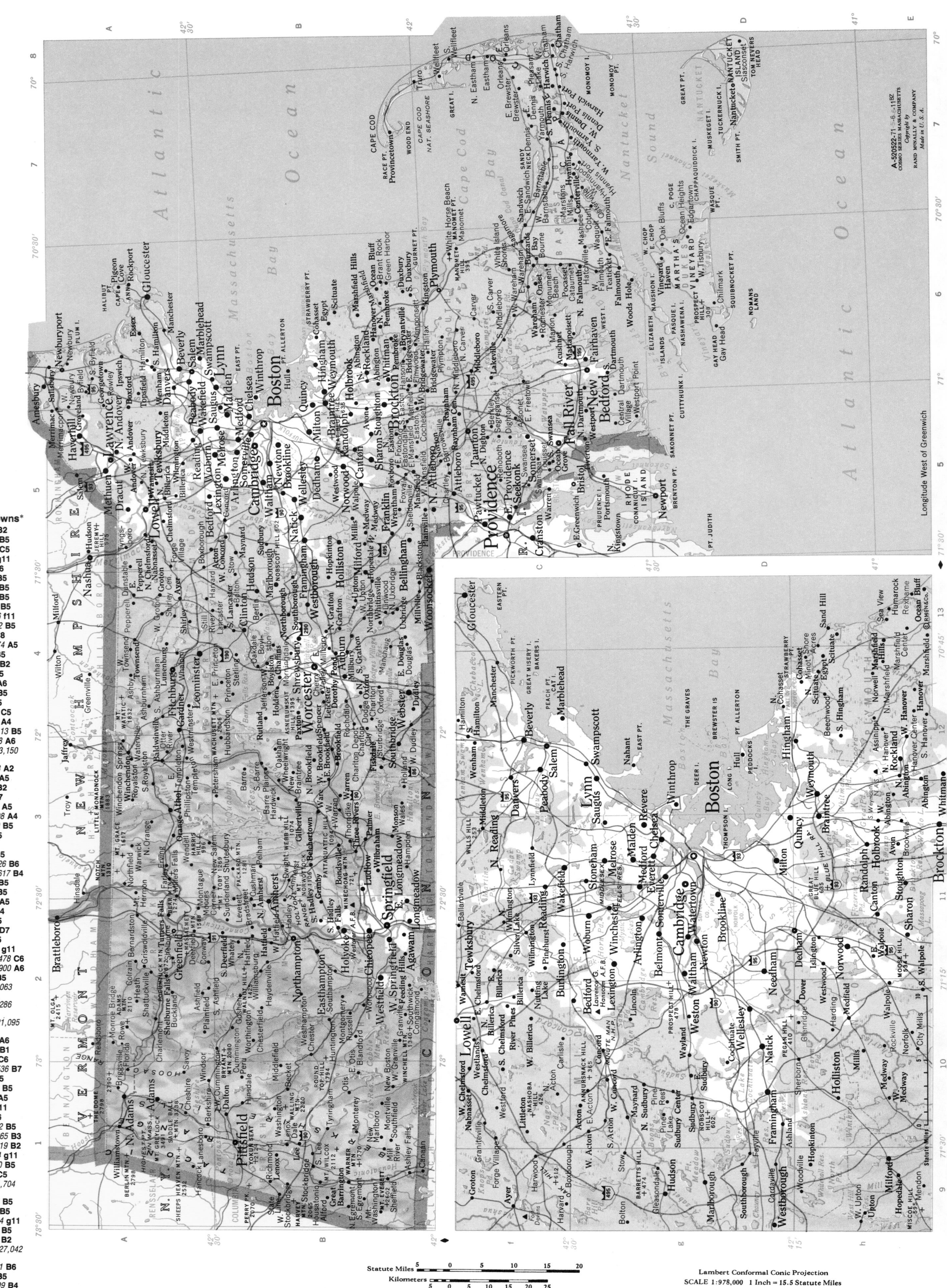

Cities and Towns*

Amherst 26,300 **B2**
Arlington 48,219 **B5**
Attleboro 34,196 **C5**
Belmont 26,100 **g11**
Beverly 37,655 **A6**
Boston 562,994 **B5**
Braintree 36,337 **B5**
Brockton 95,172 **B5**
Brookline 55,062 **B5**
Burlington 23,486 **f11**
Cambridge 95,322 **B5**
Chatham 1,922 **C8**
Chelmsford 31,174 **A5**
Chelsea 25,431 **B5**
Chicopee 55,112 **B2**
Concord 6,400 **B5**
Danvers 24,100 **A6**
Dedham 25,298 **B5**
Dracut 21,249 **A5**
Fall River 92,574 **C5**
Fitchburg 39,580 **A4**
Framingham 65,113 **B5**
Gloucester 27,768 **A6**
Great Barrington 3,150 **B1**
Greenfield 14,198 **A2**
Haverhill 46,865 **A5**
Holyoke 44,678 **B2**
Hyannis 8,000 **C7**
Lawrence 63,175 **A5**
Leominster 34,508 **A4**
Lexington 29,479 **B5**
Lowell 92,418 **A5**
Lynn 78,471 **B6**
Malden 53,386 **B5**
Marblehead 20,126 **B6**
Marlborough 30,617 **B4**
Medford 58,076 **B5**
Melrose 30,055 **B5**
Methuen 36,701 **A5**
Milford 23,390 **B4**
Milton 25,860 **B5**
Nantucket 3,229 **D7**
Natick 29,461 **B5**
Needham 27,901 **g11**
New Bedford 98,478 **C6**
Newburyport 15,900 **A6**
Newton 83,622 **B5**
North Adams 18,063 **A1**
Northampton 29,286 **B2**
North Attleboro 21,095 **C5**
Peabody 45,976 **A6**
Pittsfield 51,974 **B1**
Plymouth 7,232 **C6**
Provincetown 3,536 **B7**
Quincy 84,743 **B5**
Randolph 22,218 **B5**
Reading 22,678 **A5**
Revere 42,423 **g11**
Salem 38,220 **A6**
Somerville 77,372 **B5**
Southbridge 16,665 **B3**
Springfield 152,319 **B2**
Stoneham 21,424 **g11**
Stoughton 26,710 **B5**
Taunton 45,001 **C5**
Vineyard Haven 1,704 **D6**
Wakefield 24,895 **B5**
Waltham 58,200 **B5**
Watertown 34,384 **g11**
Wellesley 27,209 **B5**
Westfield 36,465 **B2**
West Springfield 27,042 **B2**
Weymouth 55,601 **B6**
Woburn 36,626 **B5**
Worcester 161,799 **B4**

*Populations are for localities, not incorporated towns.

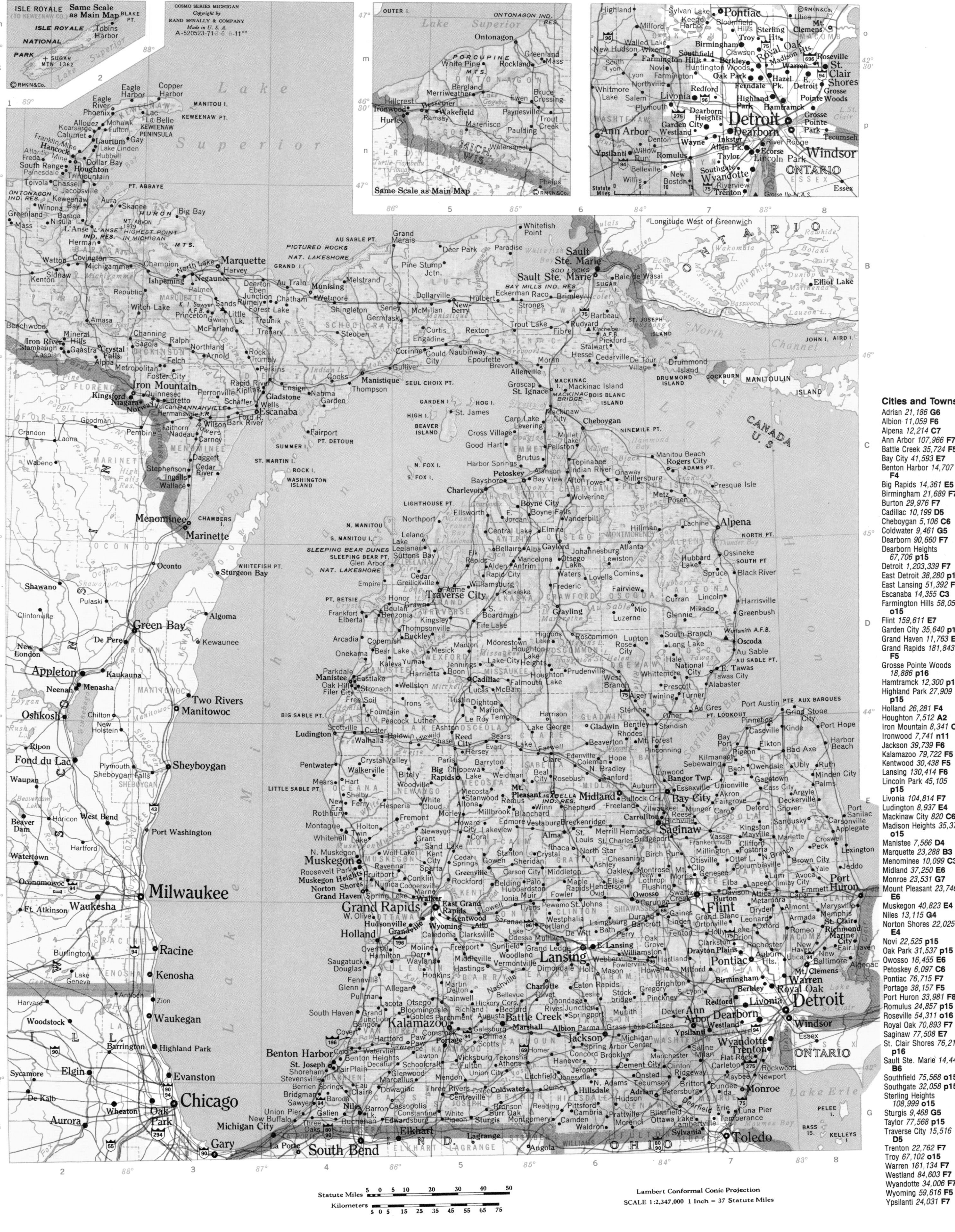

Cities and Towns

Adrian *21,186* **G6**
Albion *11,059* **F6**
Alpena *12,214* **C7**
Ann Arbor *107,966* **F7**
Battle Creek *35,724* **F5**
Bay City *41,593* **E7**
Benton Harbor *14,707* **F4**
Big Rapids *14,361* **E5**
Birmingham *21,689* **F7**
Burton *29,976* **F7**
Cadillac *10,199* **D5**
Cheboygan *5,106* **C6**
Coldwater *9,461* **G5**
Dearborn *90,660* **F7**
Dearborn Heights *67,706* **p15**
Detroit *1,203,339* **F7**
East Detroit *38,280* **p16**
East Lansing *51,392* **F6**
Escanaba *14,355* **C3**
Farmington Hills *58,056* **o15**
Flint *159,611* **E7**
Garden City *35,640* **p15**
Grand Haven *11,763* **E4**
Grand Rapids *181,843* **F5**
Grosse Pointe Woods *18,886* **p16**
Hamtramck *12,300* **p15**
Highland Park *27,909* **p15**
Holland *26,281* **F4**
Houghton *7,512* **A2**
Iron Mountain *8,341* **C2**
Ironwood *7,741* **n11**
Jackson *39,739* **F6**
Kalamazoo *79,722* **F5**
Kentwood *30,438* **F5**
Lansing *130,414* **F6**
Lincoln Park *45,105* **p15**
Livonia *104,814* **F7**
Ludington *8,937* **E4**
Mackinaw City *820* **C6**
Madison Heights *35,375* **o15**
Manistee *7,566* **D4**
Marquette *23,288* **B3**
Menominee *10,099* **C3**
Midland *37,250* **E6**
Monroe *23,531* **G7**
Mount Pleasant *23,746* **E6**
Muskegon *40,823* **E4**
Niles *13,115* **G4**
Norton Shores *22,025* **E4**
Novi *22,525* **p15**
Oak Park *31,537* **p15**
Owosso *16,455* **E6**
Petoskey *6,097* **C6**
Pontiac *76,715* **F7**
Portage *38,157* **F5**
Port Huron *33,981* **F8**
Romulus *24,857* **p15**
Roseville *54,311* **o16**
Royal Oak *70,893* **F7**
Saginaw *77,508* **E7**
St. Clair Shores *76,210* **p16**
Sault Ste. Marie *14,448* **B6**
Southfield *75,568* **o15**
Southgate *32,058* **p15**
Sterling Heights *108,999* **o15**
Sturgis *9,468* **G5**
Taylor *77,568* **p15**
Traverse City *15,516* **D5**
Trenton *22,762* **F7**
Troy *67,102* **o15**
Warren *161,134* **F7**
Westland *84,603* **F7**
Wyandotte *34,006* **F7**
Wyoming *59,616* **F5**
Ypsilanti *24,031* **F7**

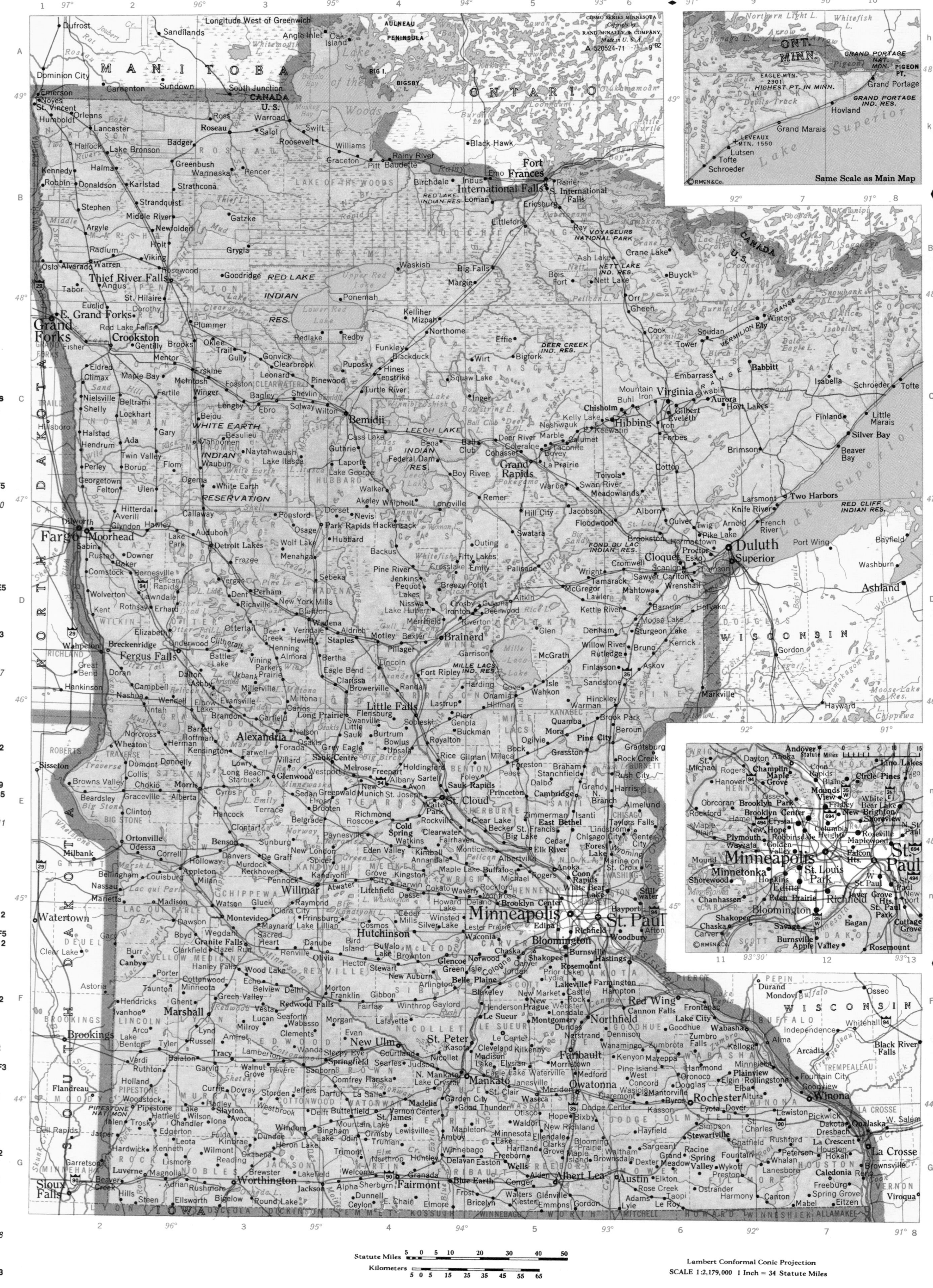

Cities and Towns

Albert Lea *19,200* **G5**
Alexandria *7,608* **E3**
Anoka *15,634* **E5**
Apple Valley *21,818* **n12**
Austin *23,020* **G6**
Bemidji *10,949* **C4**
Blaine *28,558* **m12**
Bloomington *81,831* **F5**
Brainerd *11,489* **D4**
Brooklyn Center *31,230* **E5**
Brooklyn Park *43,332* **m12**
Burnsville *35,674* **F5**
Chisholm *5,930* **C6**
Cloquet *11,142* **D6**
Columbia Heights *20,029* **m12**
Coon Rapids *35,826* **E5**
Cottage Grove *18,994* **n13**
Crookston *8,628* **C2**
Crystal *25,543* **m12**
Detroit Lakes *7,106* **D3**
Duluth *92,811* **D6**
Eagan *20,700* **n12**
East Bethel *6,626* **E5**
East Grand Forks *8,537* **C2**
Eden Prairie *16,263* **n12**
Edina *46,073* **F5**
Ely *4,820* **C7**
Fairmont *11,506* **G4**
Faribault *16,241* **F5**
Fergus Falls *12,519* **D2**
Fridley *30,228* **m12**
Golden Valley *22,775* **n12**
Grand Marais *1,289* **k9**
Grand Rapids *7,934* **C5**
Hibbing *21,193* **C6**
Hutchinson *9,244* **F4**
International Falls *5,611* **B5**
Inver Grove Heights *17,171* **n12**
Lakeville *14,790* **F5**
Litchfield *5,904* **E4**
Little Falls *7,250* **E4**
Mankato *28,651* **F5**
Maple Grove *20,525* **m12**
Maplewood *26,990* **n12**
Marshall *11,161* **F3**
Minneapolis *370,951* **F5**
Minnetonka *38,683* **n12**
Montevideo *5,845* **F3**
Moorhead *29,998* **D2**
Morris *5,367* **E3**
New Brighton *23,269* **m12**
New Hope *23,087* **m12**
New Ulm *13,755* **F4**
Northfield *12,562* **F5**
Owatonna *18,632* **F5**
Pipestone *4,887* **G2**
Plymouth *31,615* **m12**
Red Wing *13,736* **F6**
Redwood Falls *5,210* **F3**
Richfield *37,851* **F5**
Rochester *57,890* **F6**
Roseville *35,820* **m12**
St. Cloud *42,566* **E4**
St. Louis Park *42,931* **n12**
St. Paul *270,230* **F5**
St. Peter *9,056* **F5**
Shoreview *17,300* **m12**
South St. Paul *21,235* **n12**
Thief River Falls *9,105* **B2**
Virginia *11,056* **C6**
Waseca *8,219* **F5**
West St. Paul *18,527* **n12**
White Bear Lake *22,538* **E5**
Willmar *15,895* **E3**
Winona *25,075* **F7**
Worthington *10,243* **G3**

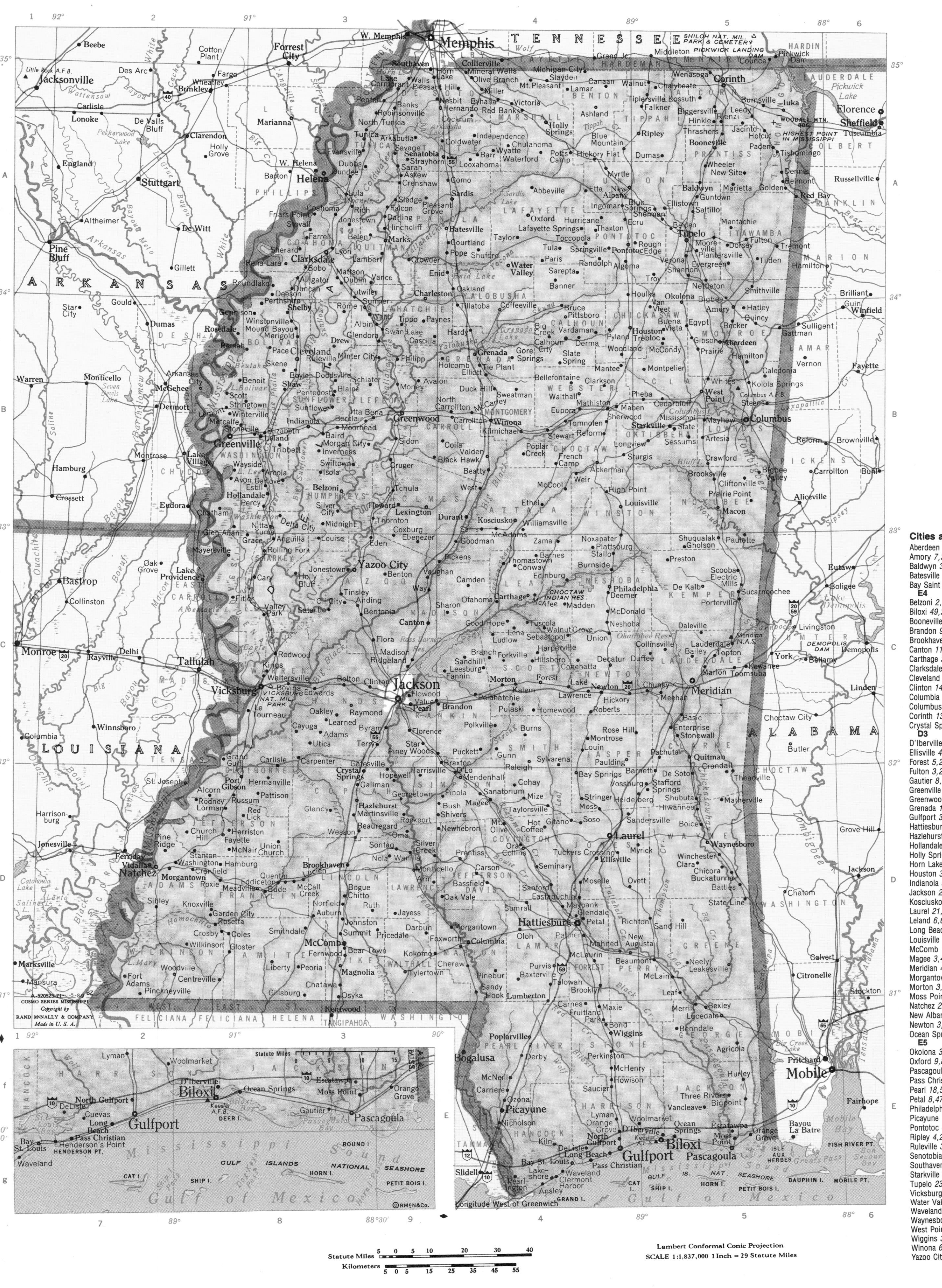

Cities and Towns

Aberdeen *7,184* **B5**
Amory *7,307* **B5**
Baldwyn *3,427* **A5**
Batesville *4,692* **A4**
Bay Saint Louis *7,891* **E4**
Belzoni *2,982* **B3**
Biloxi *49,311* **E5**
Booneville *6,199* **A5**
Brandon *9,626* **C4**
Brookhaven *10,800* **D3**
Canton *11,116* **C3**
Carthage *3,453* **C4**
Clarksdale *21,137* **A3**
Cleveland *14,524* **B3**
Clinton *14,660* **C3**
Columbia *7,733* **D4**
Columbus *27,383* **B5**
Corinth *13,839* **A5**
Crystal Springs *4,902* **D3**
D'Iberville *9,000* **E5**
Ellisville *4,652* **D4**
Forest *5,229* **C4**
Fulton *3,238* **A5**
Gautier *8,917* **f8**
Greenville *40,613* **B2**
Greenwood *20,115* **B3**
Grenada *12,641* **B4**
Gulfport *39,676* **E4**
Hattiesburg *40,829* **D4**
Hazlehurst *4,437* **D3**
Hollandale *4,336* **B3**
Holly Springs *7,285* **A4**
Horn Lake *4,326* **A3**
Houston *3,747* **B4**
Indianola *8,221* **B3**
Jackson *202,895* **C3**
Kosciusko *7,415* **B4**
Laurel *21,897* **D4**
Leland *6,667* **B3**
Long Beach *7,967* **g7**
Louisville *7,323* **B4**
McComb *12,331* **D3**
Magee *3,497* **D4**
Meridian *46,577* **C5**
Morgantown *3,445* **D2**
Morton *3,303* **C4**
Moss Point *18,998* **E5**
Natchez *22,015* **D2**
New Albany *7,072* **A4**
Newton *3,708* **C4**
Ocean Springs *14,504* **E5**
Okolona *3,409* **B5**
Oxford *9,882* **A4**
Pascagoula *29,318* **E5**
Pass Christian *5,014* **E4**
Pearl *18,580* **C3**
Petal *8,476* **D4**
Philadelphia *6,434* **C4**
Picayune *10,361* **E4**
Pontotoc *4,723* **A4**
Ripley *4,271* **A5**
Ruleville *3,332* **B3**
Senotobia *5,013* **A4**
Southaven *16,071* **A3**
Starkville *15,169* **B5**
Tupelo *23,905* **A5**
Vicksburg *25,434* **C3**
Water Valley *4,147* **A4**
Waveland *4,186* **E4**
Waynesboro *5,349* **D5**
West Point *8,811* **B5**
Wiggins *3,205* **E4**
Winona *6,177* **B4**
Yazoo City *12,092* **C3**

Cities and Towns

Arnold *19,141* **C7**
Aurora *6,437* **E4**
Ballwin *12,656* **f12**
Belton *12,708* **C3**
Berkeley *15,922* **f13**
Blue Springs *25,927* **h11**
Bolivar *5,919* **D4**
Boonville *6,959* **C5**
Branson *2,550* **E4**
Bridgeton *18,445* **C7**
Cape Girardeau *34,361* **D8**
Carthage *11,104* **D3**
Caruthersville *7,958* **E8**
Charleston *5,230* **E8**
Chillicothe *9,089* **B4**
Clayton *14,273* **f13**
Clinton *8,366* **C7**
Columbia *62,061* **C5**
Concord *20,896* **f13**
De Soto *5,993* **C7**
Dexter *7,043* **E8**
Eureka *3,862* **f12**
Excelsior Springs *10,424* **B3**
Farmington *8,270* **D7**
Ferguson *24,740* **C7**
Festus *7,574* **C7**
Florissant *55,372* **f13**
Fulton *11,046* **C6**
Gladstone *24,990* **h10**
Grandview *24,502* **C3**
Hannibal *18,811* **B6**
Independence *111,806* **B3**
Jackson *7,827* **D8**
Jefferson City *33,619* **C5**
Jennings *17,026* **f13**
Joplin *39,023* **D3**
Kansas City *448,159* **B3**
Kennett *10,145* **E7**
Kirksville *17,167* **A5**
Kirkwood *27,987* **f13**
Lebanon *9,507* **D5**
Lees Summit *28,741* **C3**
Liberty *16,251* **B3**
Malden *6,096* **E8**
Marshall *12,781* **B4**
Maryville *9,558* **A3**
Mehlville *22,900* **f13**
Mexico *12,276* **B6**
Moberly *13,418* **B5**
Monett *6,148* **E4**
Neosho *9,493* **E3**
Nevada *9,044* **D3**
Overland *19,620* **f13**
Perryville *7,343* **D8**
Poplar Bluff *17,139* **E7**
Raytown *31,759* **h11**
Richmond Heights *11,516* **f13**
Rolla *13,303* **D6**
St. Charles *37,379* **C7**
Ste. Genevieve *4,481* **D7**
St. Joseph *76,691* **B3**
St. Louis *453,085* **C7**
St. Peters *14,700* **C7**
Sappington *11,388* **f13**
Sedalia *20,927* **C4**
Sikeston *17,431* **E8**
Spanish Lake *20,632* **f13**
Springfield *133,116* **D4**
Sullivan *5,461* **C6**
Trenton *6,811* **A4**
University City *42,738* **C7**
Warrensburg *13,807* **C4**
Washington *9,251* **C6**
Webster Groves *23,097* **f13**
West Plains *7,741* **E6**

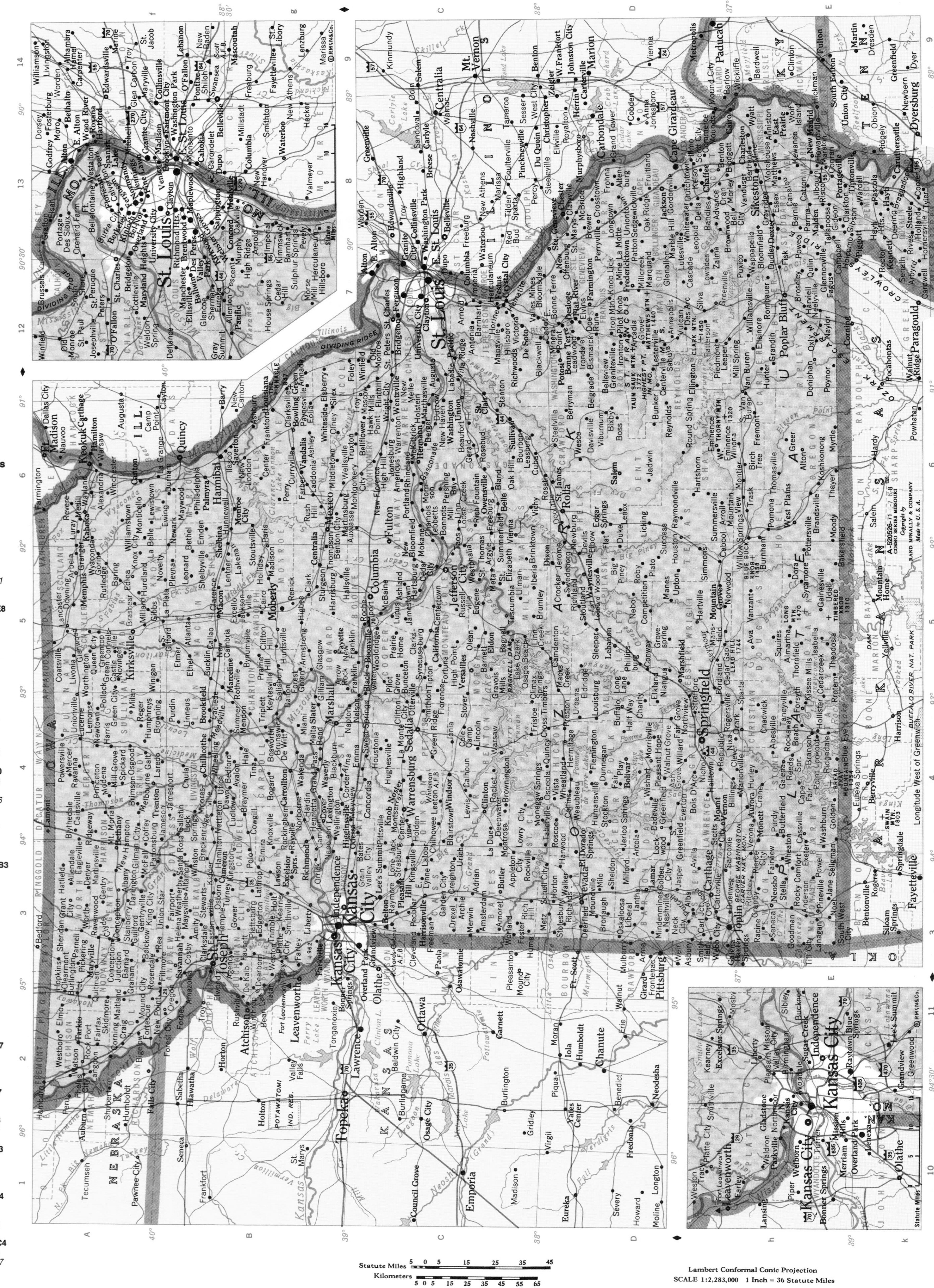

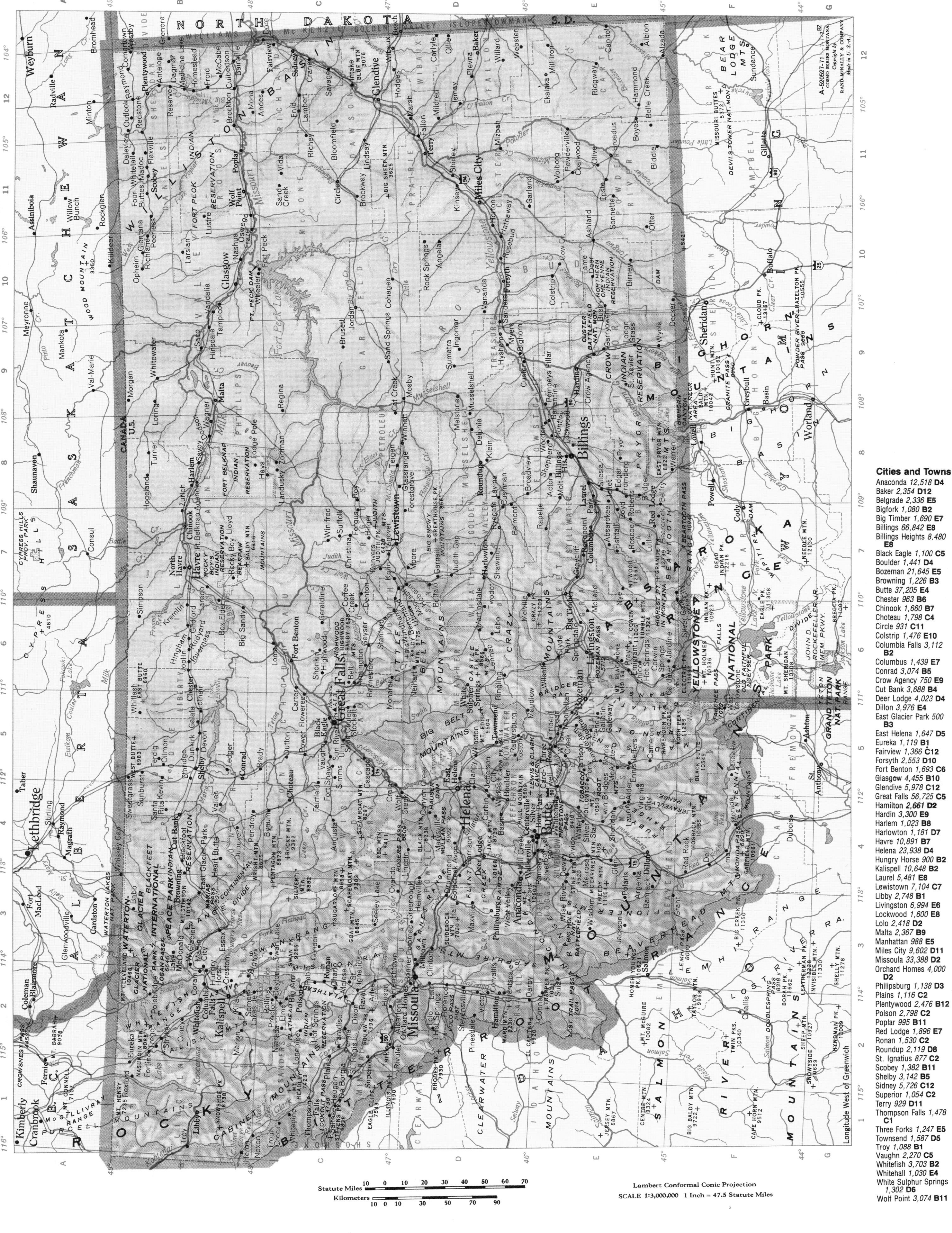

Cities and Towns

Anaconda *12,518* **D4**
Baker *2,354* **D12**
Belgrade *2,336* **E5**
Bigfork *1,080* **B2**
Big Timber *1,690* **E7**
Billings *66,842* **E8**
Billings Heights *8,480* **E8**
Black Eagle *1,100* **C5**
Boulder *1,441* **D4**
Bozeman *21,645* **E5**
Browning *1,226* **B3**
Butte *37,205* **E4**
Chester *963* **B6**
Chinook *1,660* **B7**
Choteau *1,798* **C4**
Circle *931* **C11**
Colstrip *1,476* **E10**
Columbia Falls *3,112* **B2**
Columbus *1,439* **E7**
Conrad *3,074* **B5**
Crow Agency *750* **E9**
Cut Bank *3,688* **B4**
Deer Lodge *4,023* **D4**
Dillon *3,976* **E4**
East Glacier Park *500* **B3**
East Helena *1,647* **D5**
Eureka *1,119* **B1**
Fairview *1,366* **C12**
Forsyth *2,553* **D10**
Fort Benton *1,693* **C6**
Glasgow *4,455* **B10**
Glendive *5,978* **C12**
Great Falls *56,725* **C5**
Hamilton *2,661* **D2**
Hardin *3,300* **E9**
Harlem *1,023* **B8**
Harlowton *1,181* **D7**
Havre *10,891* **B7**
Helena *23,938* **D4**
Hungry Horse *900* **B2**
Kalispell *10,648* **B2**
Laurel *5,481* **E8**
Lewistown *7,104* **C7**
Libby *2,748* **B1**
Livingston *6,994* **E6**
Lockwood *1,600* **E8**
Lolo *2,418* **D2**
Malta *2,367* **B9**
Manhattan *988* **E5**
Miles City *9,602* **D11**
Missoula *33,388* **D2**
Orchard Homes *4,000* **D2**
Philipsburg *1,138* **D3**
Plains *1,116* **C2**
Plentywood *2,476* **B12**
Polson *2,798* **C2**
Poplar *995* **B11**
Red Lodge *1,896* **E7**
Ronan *1,530* **C2**
Roundup *2,119* **D8**
St. Ignatius *877* **C2**
Scobey *1,382* **B11**
Shelby *3,142* **B5**
Sidney *5,726* **C12**
Superior *1,054* **C2**
Terry *929* **D11**
Thompson Falls *1,478* **C1**
Three Forks *1,247* **E5**
Townsend *1,587* **D5**
Troy *1,088* **B1**
Vaughn *2,270* **C5**
Whitefish *3,703* **B2**
Whitehall *1,030* **E4**
White Sulphur Springs *1,302* **D6**
Wolf Point *3,074* **B11**

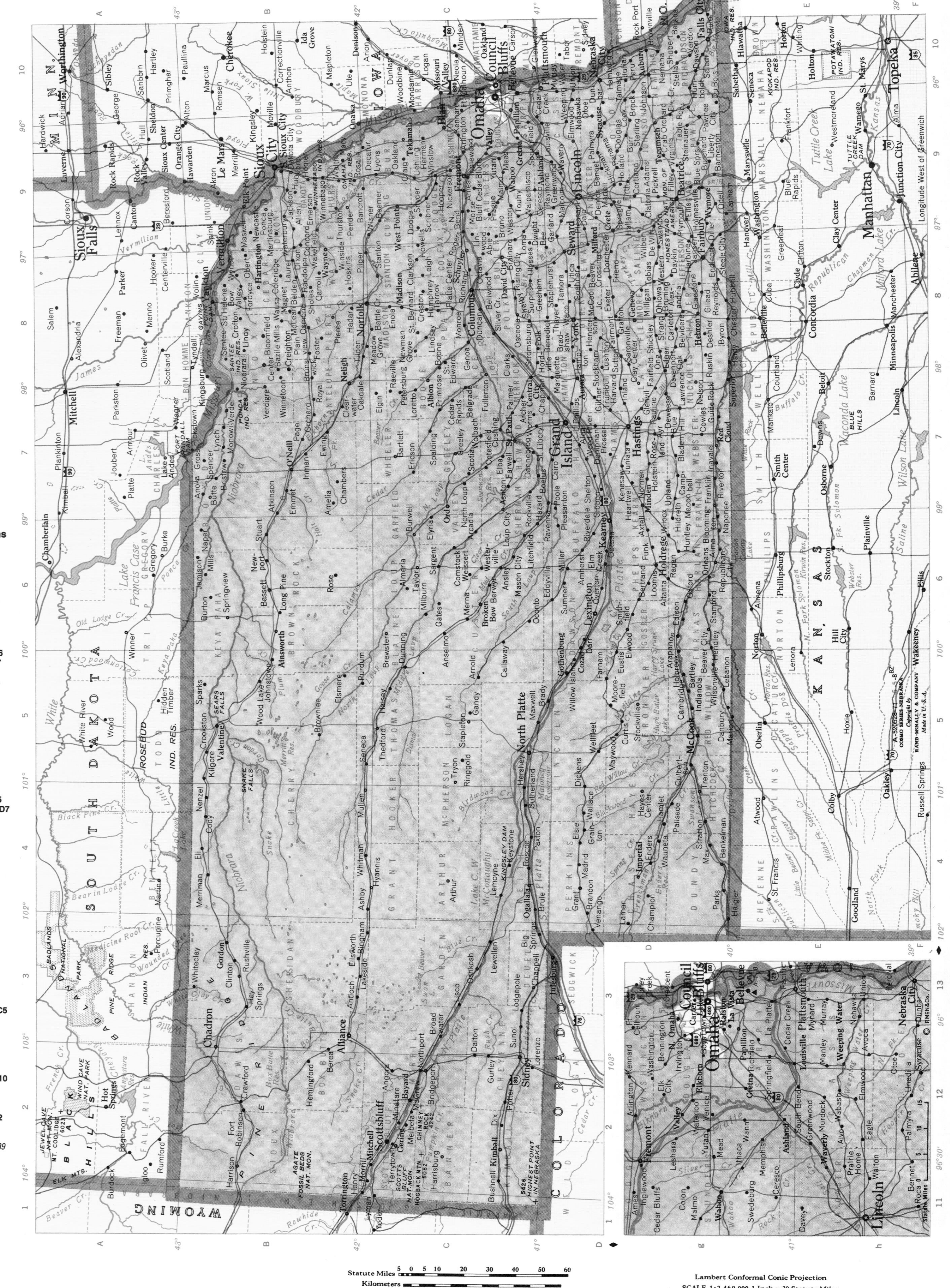

Cities and Towns

Ainsworth *2,256* **B6**
Albion *1,997* **C7**
Alliance *9,920* **B3**
Ashland *2,274* **C9**
Atkinson *1,521* **B7**
Auburn *3,482* **D10**
Aurora *3,717* **D7**
Beatrice *12,891* **D9**
Bellevue *21,813* **C10**
Blair *6,418* **C9**
Bridgeport *1,668* **C2**
Broken Bow *3,979* **C6**
Central City *3,083* **C7**
Chadron *5,933* **B3**
Columbus *17,328* **C8**
Cozad *4,453* **D6**
Crete *4,872* **D9**
David City *2,514* **C8**
Fairbury *4,885* **D8**
Falls City *5,374* **D10**
Fremont *23,979* **C9**
Fullerton *1,506* **C8**
Geneva *2,400* **D8**
Gering *7,760* **C2**
Gibbon *1,531* **D7**
Gordon *2,167* **B3**
Gothenburg *3,479* **D5**
Grand Island *33,180* **D7**
Gretna *1,609* **C9**
Hartington *1,730* **B8**
Hastings *23,045* **D7**
Hebron *1,906* **D8**
Holdrege *5,624* **D6**
Imperial *1,941* **D4**
Kearney *21,158* **D6**
Kimball *3,120* **C2**
La Vista *9,588* **g12**
Lexington *7,040* **D6**
Lincoln *171,932* **D9**
McCook *8,404* **D5**
Madison *1,950* **C8**
Milford *2,108* **D8**
Minden *2,939* **D7**
Mitchell *1,956* **C2**
Nebraska City *7,127* **D10**
Neligh *1,893* **B7**
Norfolk *19,449* **B8**
North Platte *24,509* **C5**
Ogallala *5,638* **C4**
Omaha *313,911* **C10**
O'Neill *4,049* **B7**
Ord *2,658* **C7**
Papillion *6,399* **C9**
Pierce *1,535* **B8**
Plattsmouth *6,295* **D10**
Ralston *5,143* **g12**
St. Paul *2,094* **C7**
Schuyler *4,151* **C8**
Scottsbluff *14,156* **C2**
Seward *5,713* **D8**
Sidney *6,010* **C3**
South Sioux City *9,339* **B9**
Stanton *1,603* **C8**
Superior *2,502* **D7**
Syracuse *1,638* **D9**
Tecumseh *1,926* **D9**
Tekamah *1,886* **C9**
Valentine *2,829* **B5**
Valley *1,716* **C9**
Wahoo *3,555* **C9**
Waverly *1,726* **D9**
Wayne *5,240* **B8**
West Point *3,609* **C9**
Wilber *1,624* **D9**
Wymore *1,841* **D9**
York *7,723* **D8**

Statute Miles 5 0 5 10 20 30 40 50 60
Kilometers 5 0 5 15 35 55 75 95

Lambert Conformal Conic Projection
SCALE 1:2,460,000 1 Inch = 39 Statute Miles

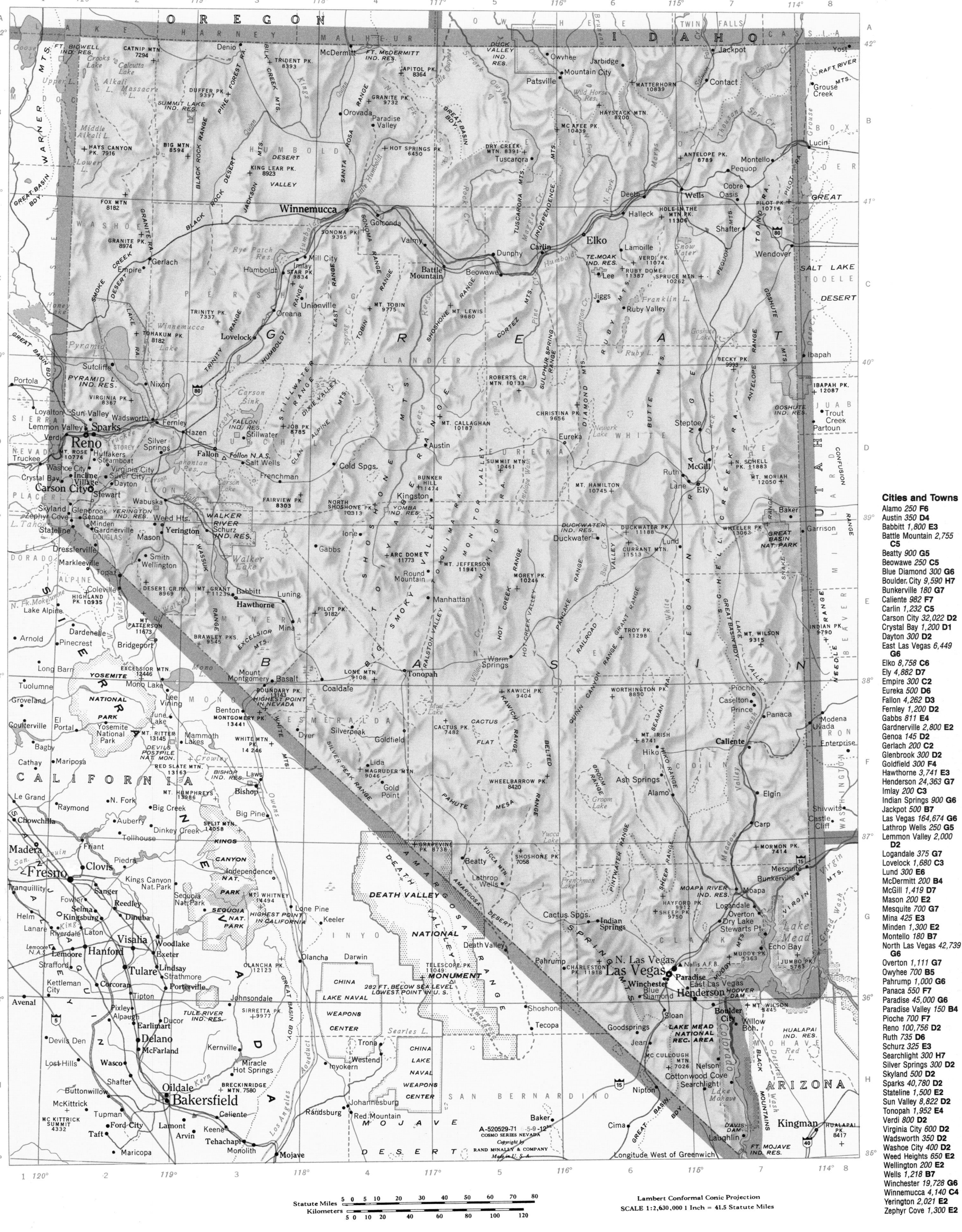

Cities and Towns

Alamo *250* **F6**
Austin *350* **D4**
Babbitt *1,800* **E3**
Battle Mountain *2,755* **C5**
Beatty *900* **G5**
Beowawe *250* **C5**
Blue Diamond *300* **G6**
Boulder City *9,590* **H7**
Bunkerville *180* **G7**
Caliente *982* **F7**
Carlin *1,232* **C5**
Carson City *32,022* **D2**
Crystal Bay *1,200* **D1**
Dayton *300* **D2**
East Las Vegas *6,449* **G6**
Elko *8,758* **C6**
Ely *4,882* **D7**
Empire *300* **C2**
Eureka *500* **D6**
Fallon *4,262* **D3**
Fernley *1,200* **D2**
Gabbs *811* **E4**
Gardnerville *2,800* **E2**
Genoa *145* **D2**
Gerlach *200* **C2**
Glenbrook *300* **D2**
Goldfield *300* **F4**
Hawthorne *3,741* **E3**
Henderson *24,363* **G7**
Imlay *200* **C3**
Indian Springs *900* **G6**
Jackpot *500* **B7**
Las Vegas *164,674* **G6**
Lathrop Wells *250* **G5**
Lemmon Valley *2,000* **D2**
Logandale *375* **G7**
Lovelock *1,680* **C3**
Lund *300* **E6**
McDermitt *200* **B4**
McGill *1,419* **D7**
Mason *200* **E2**
Mesquite *700* **G7**
Mina *425* **E3**
Minden *1,300* **E2**
Montello *180* **B7**
North Las Vegas *42,739* **G6**
Overton *1,111* **G7**
Owyhee *700* **B5**
Pahrump *1,000* **G6**
Panaca *550* **F7**
Paradise *45,000* **G6**
Paradise Valley *150* **B4**
Pioche *700* **F7**
Reno *100,756* **D2**
Ruth *735* **D6**
Schurz *325* **E3**
Searchlight *300* **H7**
Silver Springs *300* **D2**
Skyland *500* **D2**
Sparks *40,780* **D2**
Stateline *1,500* **E2**
Sun Valley *8,822* **D2**
Tonopah *1,952* **E4**
Verdi *800* **D2**
Virginia City *600* **D2**
Wadsworth *350* **D2**
Washoe City *400* **D2**
Weed Heights *650* **E2**
Wellington *200* **E2**
Wells *1,218* **B7**
Winchester *19,728* **G6**
Winnemucca *4,140* **C4**
Yerington *2,021* **E2**
Zephyr Cove *1,300* **E2**

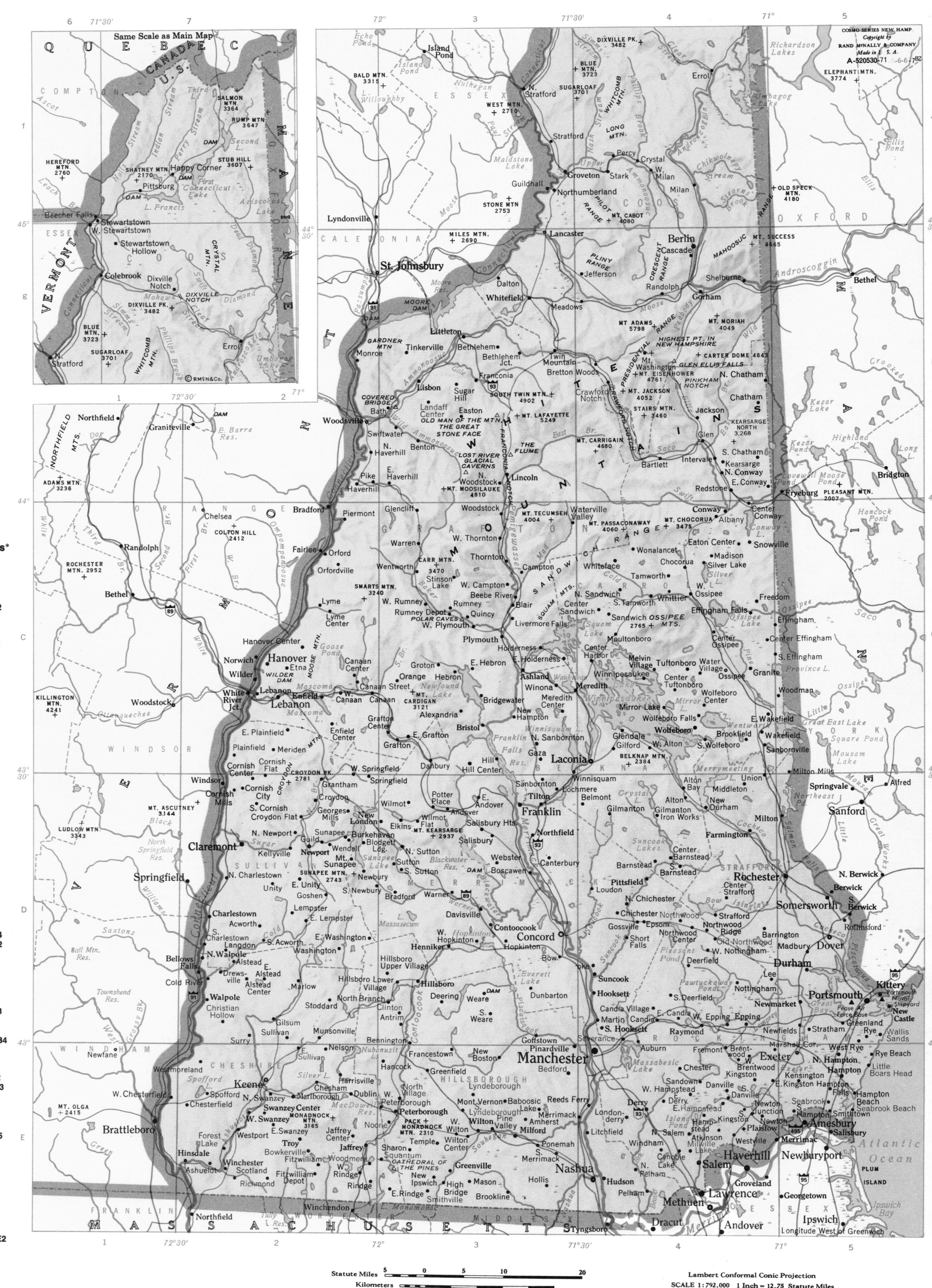

Cities and Towns*

Antrim *1,142* **D3**
Ashland *1,479* **C3**
Bedford *1,300* **E3**
Berlin *13,084* **B4**
Bristol *1,258* **C3**
Charlestown *1,294* **D2**
Claremont *14,557* **D2**
Colebrook *1,131* **g7**
Concord *30,400* **D3**
Contoocook *1,499* **D3**
Conway *1,781* **C4**
Derry *12,248* **E4**
Dover *22,377* **D5**
Durham *8,448* **D5**
Enfield *1,581* **C2**
Epping *1,384* **D4**
Exeter *8,947* **E5**
Farmington *3,284* **D4**
Franconia *600* **B3**
Franklin *7,901* **D3**
Goffstown *2,500* **D3**
Gorham *2,180* **B4**
Greenville *1,447* **E3**
Groveton *1,389* **A3**
Hampton *6,779* **E5**
Hanover *6,861* **C2**
Henniker *1,538* **D3**
Hillsboro *1,797* **D3**
Hinsdale *1,546* **E2**
Hooksett *1,868* **D4**
Hudson *6,248* **E4**
Jaffrey *2,684* **E2**
Keene *21,449* **E2**
Laconia *15,575* **C4**
Lancaster *2,134* **B3**
Lebanon *11,134* **C2**
Lincoln *950* **B3**
Lisbon *1,151* **B3**
Littleton *4,480* **B3**
Manchester *90,936* **E4**
Marlborough *1,231* **E2**
Meredith *1,202* **C3**
Merrimack *1,200* **E4**
Milford *6,289* **E3**
Milton *1,000* **D5**
Nashua *67,865* **E4**
New Castle *975* **D5**
New London *1,335* **D3**
Newmarket *3,749* **D5**
Newport *4,388* **D2**
North Conway *2,184* **B4**
Northfield *1,340* **D3**
North Hampton *1,000* **E5**
North Walpole *950* **D2**
Peterborough *2,100* **E3**
Pinardville *4,500* **E3**
Pittsfield *1,584* **D4**
Plaistow *1,800* **E4**
Plymouth *3,628* **C3**
Portsmouth *26,254* **D5**
Raymond *1,192* **D4**
Rochester *21,560* **D5**
Salem *11,500* **E4**
Somersworth *10,350* **D5**
South Hooksett *1,200* **D4**
Suncook *4,698* **D4**
Tilton *1,230* **D3**
Troy *1,318* **E2**
West Swanzey *1,022* **E2**
Whitefield *1,005* **B3**
Wilton *1,310* **E3**
Winchester *1,732* **E2**
Wolfeboro *2,000* **C4**
Woodsville *1,195* **B2**

*Populations are for localities, not incorporated towns.

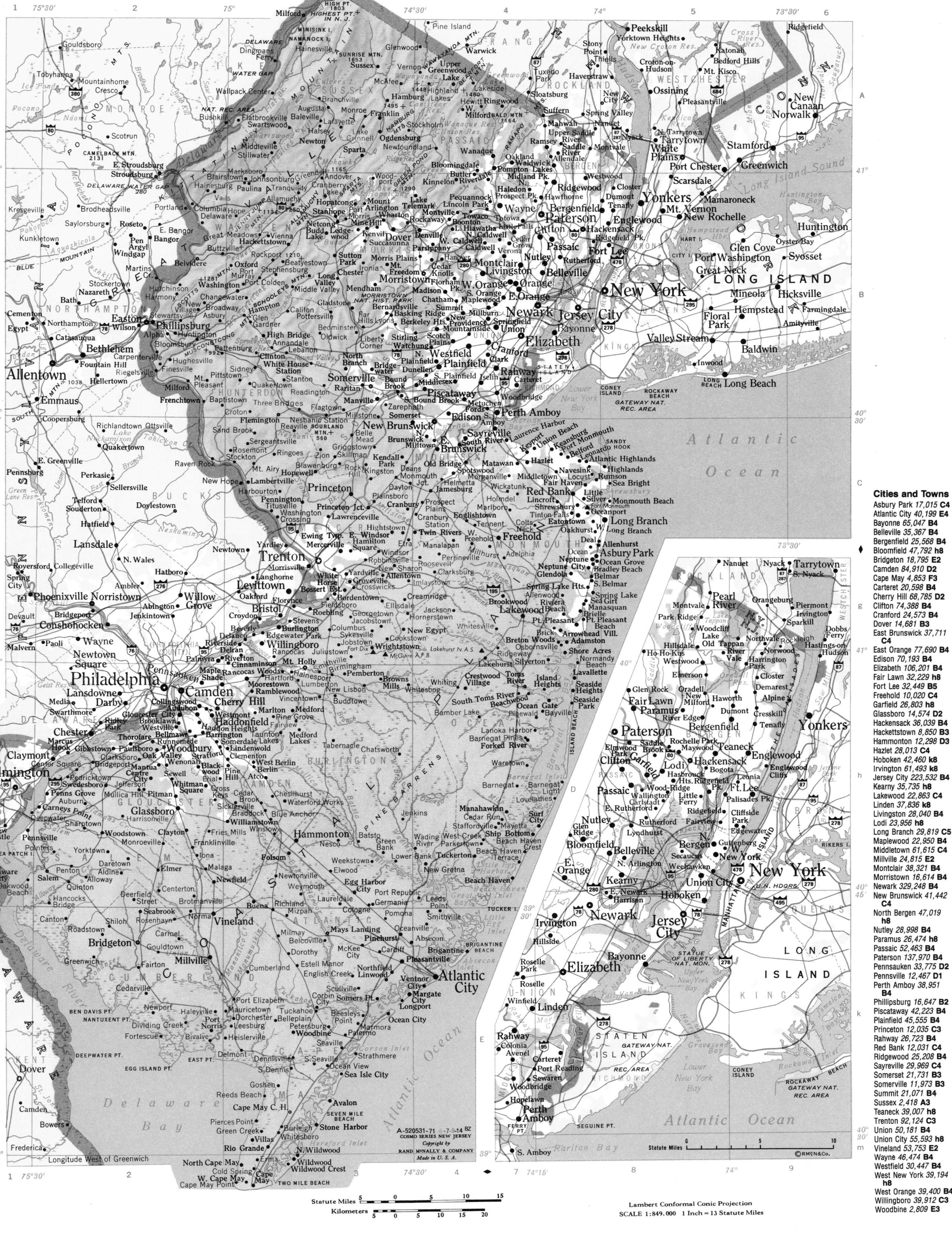

Cities and Towns

Asbury Park *17,015* **C4**
Atlantic City *40,199* **E4**
Bayonne *65,047* **B4**
Belleville *35,367* **B4**
Bergenfield *25,568* **B4**
Bloomfield *47,792* **h8**
Bridgeton *18,795* **E2**
Camden *84,910* **D2**
Cape May *4,853* **F3**
Carteret *20,598* **B4**
Cherry Hill *68,785* **D2**
Clifton *74,388* **B4**
Cranford *24,573* **B4**
Dover *14,681* **B3**
East Brunswick *37,711* **C4**
East Orange *77,690* **B4**
Edison *70,193* **B4**
Elizabeth *106,201* **B4**
Fair Lawn *32,229* **h8**
Fort Lee *32,449* **B5**
Freehold *10,020* **C4**
Garfield *26,803* **h8**
Glassboro *14,574* **D2**
Hackensack *36,039* **B4**
Hackettstown *8,850* **B3**
Hammonton *12,298* **D3**
Hazlet *28,013* **C4**
Hoboken *42,460* **k8**
Irvington *61,493* **k8**
Jersey City *223,532* **B4**
Kearny *35,735* **h8**
Lakewood *22,863* **C4**
Linden *37,836* **k8**
Livingston *28,040* **B4**
Lodi *23,956* **h8**
Long Branch *29,819* **C5**
Maplewood *22,950* **B4**
Middletown *61,615* **C4**
Millville *24,815* **E2**
Montclair *38,321* **B4**
Morristown *16,614* **B4**
Newark *329,248* **B4**
New Brunswick *41,442* **C4**
North Bergen *47,019* **h8**
Nutley *28,998* **B4**
Paramus *26,474* **h8**
Passaic *52,463* **B4**
Paterson *137,970* **B4**
Pennsauken *33,775* **D2**
Pennsville *12,467* **D1**
Perth Amboy *38,951* **B4**
Phillipsburg *16,647* **B2**
Piscataway *42,223* **B4**
Plainfield *45,555* **B4**
Princeton *12,035* **C3**
Rahway *26,723* **B4**
Red Bank *12,031* **C4**
Ridgewood *25,208* **B4**
Sayreville *29,969* **C4**
Somerset *21,731* **B3**
Somerville *11,973* **B3**
Summit *21,071* **B4**
Sussex *2,418* **A3**
Teaneck *39,007* **h8**
Trenton *92,124* **C3**
Union *50,181* **B4**
Union City *55,593* **h8**
Vineland *53,753* **E2**
Wayne *46,474* **B4**
Westfield *30,447* **B4**
West New York *39,194* **h8**
West Orange *39,400* **B4**
Willingboro *39,912* **C3**
Woodbine *2,809* **E3**

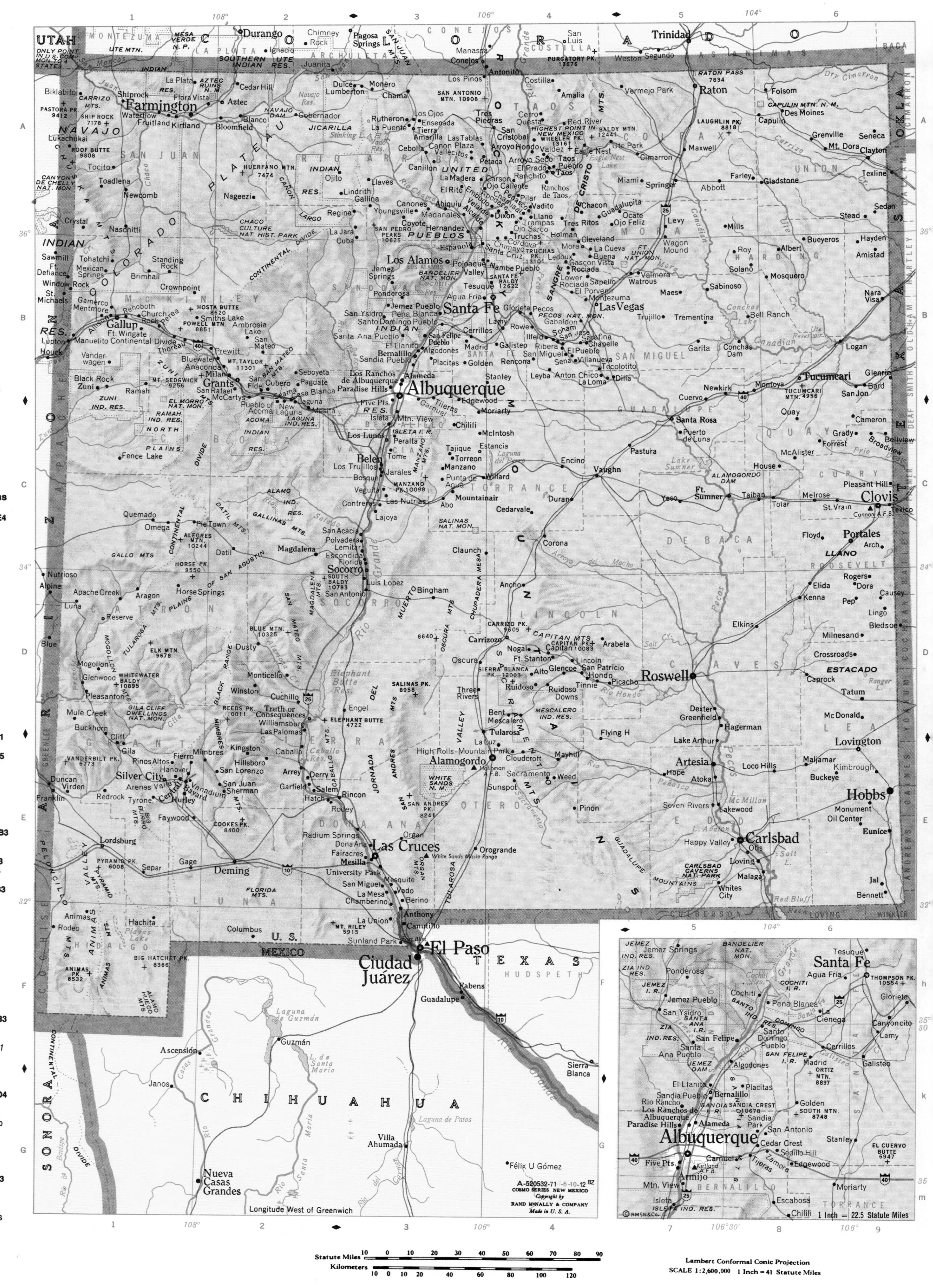

Cities and Towns

Alameda 7,800 **B3**
Alamagordo 24,024 **E4**
Albuquerque 331,767 **B3**
Anthony 3,285 **F3**
Armijo 18,900 **k7**
Artesia 10,385 **E5**
Aztec 5,512 **A2**
Bayard 3,036 **E1**
Belen 5,617 **C3**
Bernalillo 3,012 **B3**
Bloomfield 4,881 **A2**
Carlsbad 25,496 **E5**
Carizozo 1,222 **D4**
Central 1,968 **E1**
Chama 1,090 **A3**
Chimayo 1,993 **A4**
Clayton 2,968 **A6**
Clovis 31,194 **C6**
Crownpoint 1,134 **B1**
Deming 9,964 **E2**
Dulce 1,648 **A2**
Espanola 6,803 **B3**
Eunice 2,970 **E6**
Farmington 31,222 **A1**
Five Points 5,500 **B3**
Fort Sumner 1,421 **C5**
Gallup 18,167 **B1**
Grants 11,439 **B2**
Hatch 1,028 **E2**
Hobbs 29,153 **E6**
Hurley 1,616 **E1**
Isleta 1,246 **C3**
Jal 2,675 **E6**
Jemez Pueblo 1,503 **B3**
Kirtland 2,358 **A1**
La Luz 1,194 **D4**
Las Cruces 45,086 **E3**
Las Vegas 14,322 **B4**
Lordsburg 3,195 **E1**
Los Alamos 11,039 **B3**
Los Lunas 3,525 **C3**
Los Ranchos de Albuquerque 2,702 **B3**
Loving 1,355 **E5**
Lovington 9,727 **E6**
Magdalena 1,022 **C2**
Mescalero 1,259 **D4**
Mesilla 2,029 **E3**
Milan 3,747 **B2**
Moriarty 1,276 **C3**
Mountain View 1,900 **C3**
Paradise Hills 5,096 **B3**
Portales 9,940 **C6**
Questa 1,202 **A4**
Ranches of Taos 1,411 **A4**
Raton 8,225 **A5**
Roswell 39,676 **D5**
Ruidoso 4,260 **D4**
Ruidoso Downs 949 **D4**
Santa Fe 48,953 **B4**
Santa Rosa 2,469 **C5**
Santo Domingo Pueblo 2,082 **B3**
Shiprock 7,237 **A1**
Silver City 9,887 **E1**
Socorro 7,173 **C3**
Springer 1,657 **A5**
Sunland Park 3,377 **F3**
Taos 3,369 **A4**
Tesuque 1,014 **B4**
Thoreau 1,099 **B1**
Truth or Consequences 5,219 **D2**
Tucumcari 6,765 **B6**
Tularosa 2,536 **D3**
University Park 4,383 **E3**
Zuni 5,551 **B1**

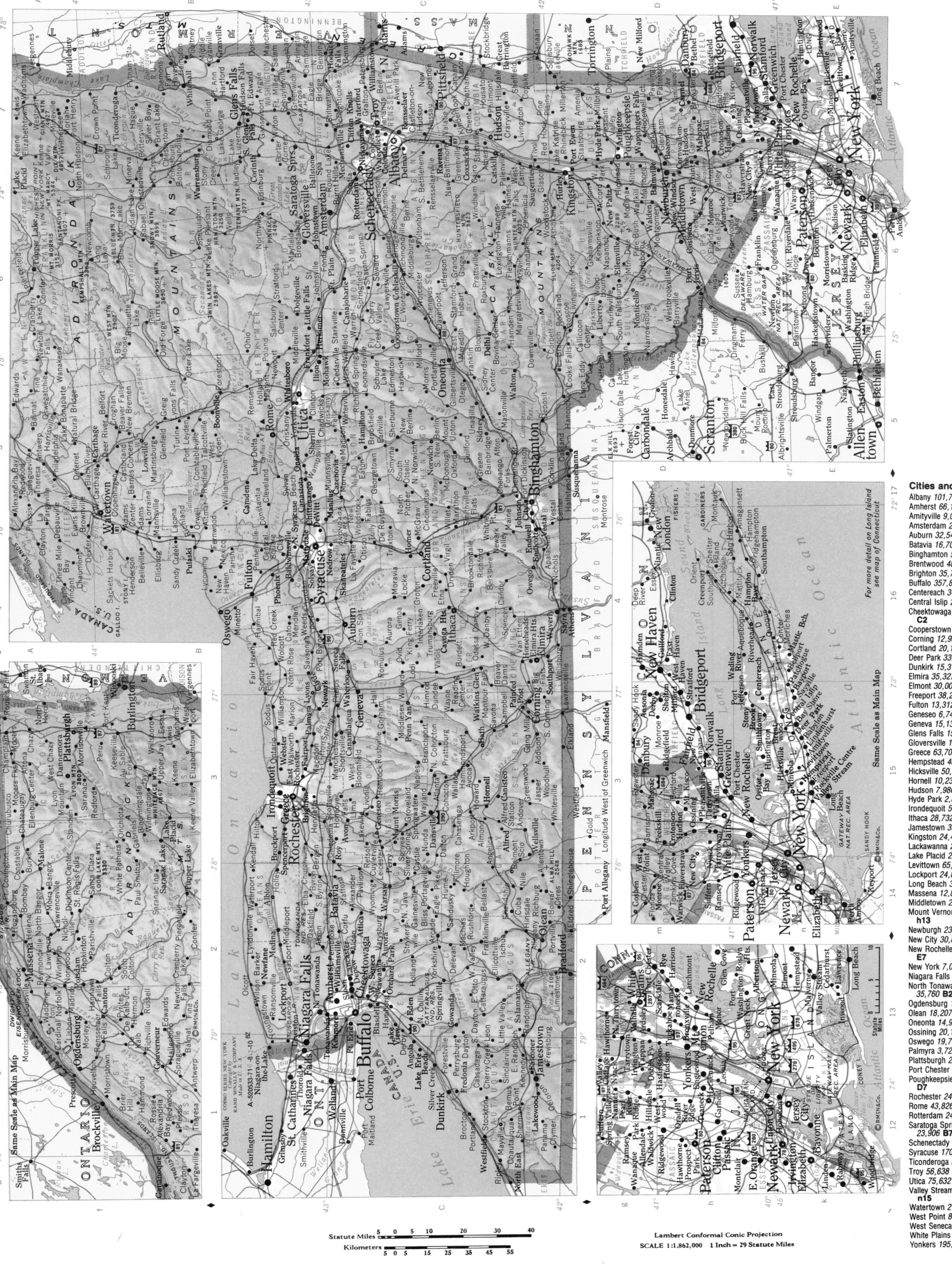

Cities and Towns

Albany *101,727* **C7**
Amherst *66,100* **C2**
Amityville *9,076* **E7**
Amsterdam *21,872* **C6**
Auburn *32,548* **C4**
Batavia *16,703* **C2**
Binghamton *55,860* **C5**
Brentwood *48,800* **E7**
Brighton *35,776* **B3**
Buffalo *357,870* **C2**
Centereach *34,600* **n15**
Central Islip *26,000* **n15**
Cheektowaga *100,400* **C2**
Cooperstown *2,342* **C6**
Corning *12,953* **C3**
Cortland *20,138* **C4**
Deer Park *33,400* **n15**
Dunkirk *15,310* **C1**
Elmira *35,327* **C4**
Elmont *30,000* **k13**
Freeport *38,272* **n15**
Fulton *13,312* **B4**
Geneseo *6,746* **C3**
Geneva *15,133* **C4**
Glens Falls *15,897* **B7**
Gloversville *17,836* **B6**
Greece *63,700* **B3**
Hempstead *40,404* **n15**
Hicksville *50,000* **E7**
Hornell *10,234* **C3**
Hudson *7,986* **C7**
Hyde Park *2,805* **D7**
Irondequoit *57,648* **B3**
Ithaca *28,732* **C4**
Jamestown *35,775* **C1**
Kingston *24,481* **D6**
Lackawanna *22,701* **C2**
Lake Placid *2,490* **A7**
Levittown *65,400* **E7**
Lockport *24,844* **B2**
Long Beach *34,073* **E7**
Massena *12,851* **f10**
Middletown *21,454* **D6**
Mount Vernon *66,713* **h13**
Newburgh *23,438* **D6**
New City *30,800* **D6**
New Rochelle *70,794* **E7**
New York *7,071,639* **E7**
Niagara Falls *71,384* **B1**
North Tonawanda *35,760* **B2**
Ogdensburg *12,375* **f9**
Olean *18,207* **C2**
Oneonta *14,933* **C5**
Ossining *20,196* **D7**
Oswego *19,793* **B4**
Palmyra *3,729* **B3**
Plattsburgh *21,057* **f11**
Port Chester *23,565* **E7**
Poughkeepsie *29,757* **D7**
Rochester *241,741* **B3**
Rome *43,826* **B5**
Rotterdam *24,800* **C6**
Saratoga Springs *23,906* **B7**
Schenectady *67,972* **C7**
Syracuse *170,105* **B4**
Ticonderoga *2,938* **B7**
Troy *56,638* **C7**
Utica *75,632* **B5**
Valley Stream *35,769* **n15**
Watertown *27,861* **B5**
West Point *8,000* **D7**
West Seneca *51,210* **C2**
White Plains *46,999* **D7**
Yonkers *195,351* **E7**

NORTH CAROLINA

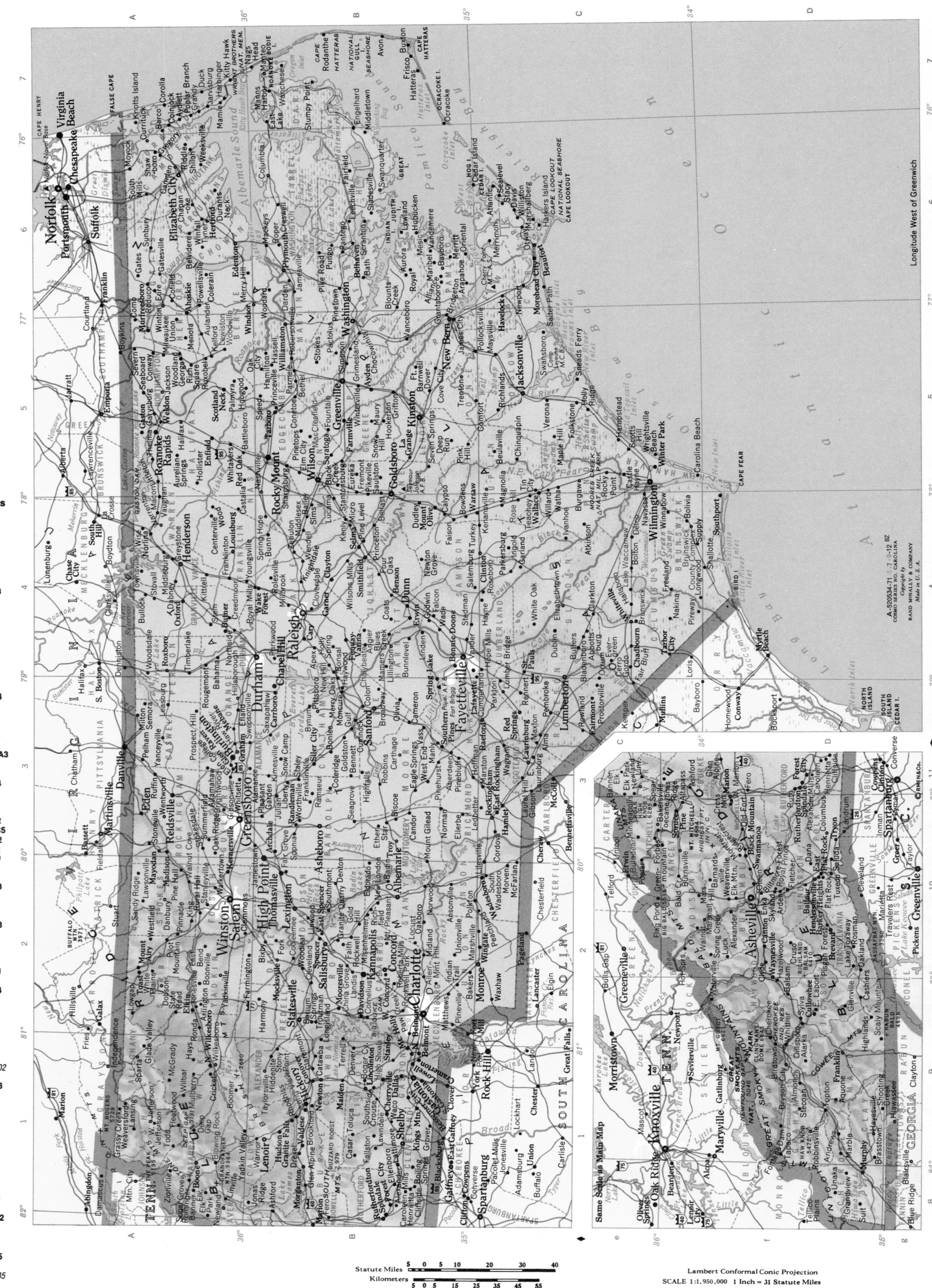

Cities and Towns

Albemarle *15,110* **B2**
Archdale *5,326* **B3**
Asheboro *15,252* **B3**
Asheville *53,583* **f10**
Boone *10,191* **A1**
Brevard *5,323* **f10**
Burlington *37,266* **A3**
Carrboro *7,336* **B3**
Chapel Hill *32,421* **B3**
Charlotte *314,447* **B2**
Clemmons *7,401* **A2**
Clinton *7,552* **C4**
Concord *16,942* **B2**
Dunn *8,962* **B4**
Durham *100,538* **B4**
Eden *15,672* **A3**
Edenton *5,357* **A6**
Elizabeth City *13,784* **A6**
Fayetteville *59,507* **B4**
Forest City *7,688* **B1**
Garner *10,073* **B4**
Gastonia *47,333* **B1**
Goldsboro *31,871* **B5**
Graham *8,674* **A3**
Greensboro *155,642* **A3**
Greenville *35,740* **B5**
Havelock *17,718* **C6**
Henderson *13,522* **A4**
Hendersonville *6,862* **f10**
Hickory *20,757* **B1**
High Point *63,808* **B2**
Jacksonville *18,237* **C5**
Kannapolis *34,564* **B2**
Kernersville *6,802* **A2**
Kings Mountain *9,080* **B1**
Kinston *25,234* **B5**
Laurinburg *11,480* **C3**
Lenoir *13,748* **B1**
Lexington *15,711* **B2**
Lincolnton *4,879* **B1**
Lumberton *18,241* **C3**
Monroe *12,639* **C2**
Mooresville *8,575* **B2**
Morehead City *4,359* **C6**
Morganton *13,763* **B1**
Mount Airy *6,862* **A2**
Mount Olive *4,876* **B4**
Nags Head *1,020* **B7**
New Bern *14,557* **B5**
Newton *7,624* **B1**
Oxford *7,603* **A4**
Plymouth *4,571* **B6**
Raleigh *150,255* **B4**
Reidsville *12,492* **A3**
Roanoke Rapids *14,702* **A5**
Rockingham *8,300* **C3**
Rocky Mount *41,283* **B5**
Roxboro *7,532* **A4**
Salisbury *22,677* **B2**
Sanford *14,773* **B3**
Selma *4,762* **B4**
Shelby *15,310* **B1**
Smithfield *7,288* **B4**
Southern Pines *8,620* **B3**
Statesville *18,622* **B2**
Swannanoa *5,586* **f10**
Tarboro *8,634* **B5**
Thomasville *14,144* **B2**
Washington *8,418* **B5**
Whiteville *5,565* **C4**
Williamston *6,159* **B5**
Wilmington *44,000* **C5**
Wilson *34,424* **B5**
Winston-Salem *131,885* **A2**

Statute Miles 5 0 5 10 20 30 40
Kilometers 5 0 5 15 25 35 45 55

Lambert Conformal Conic Projection
SCALE 1:1,950,000 1 Inch = 31 Statute Miles

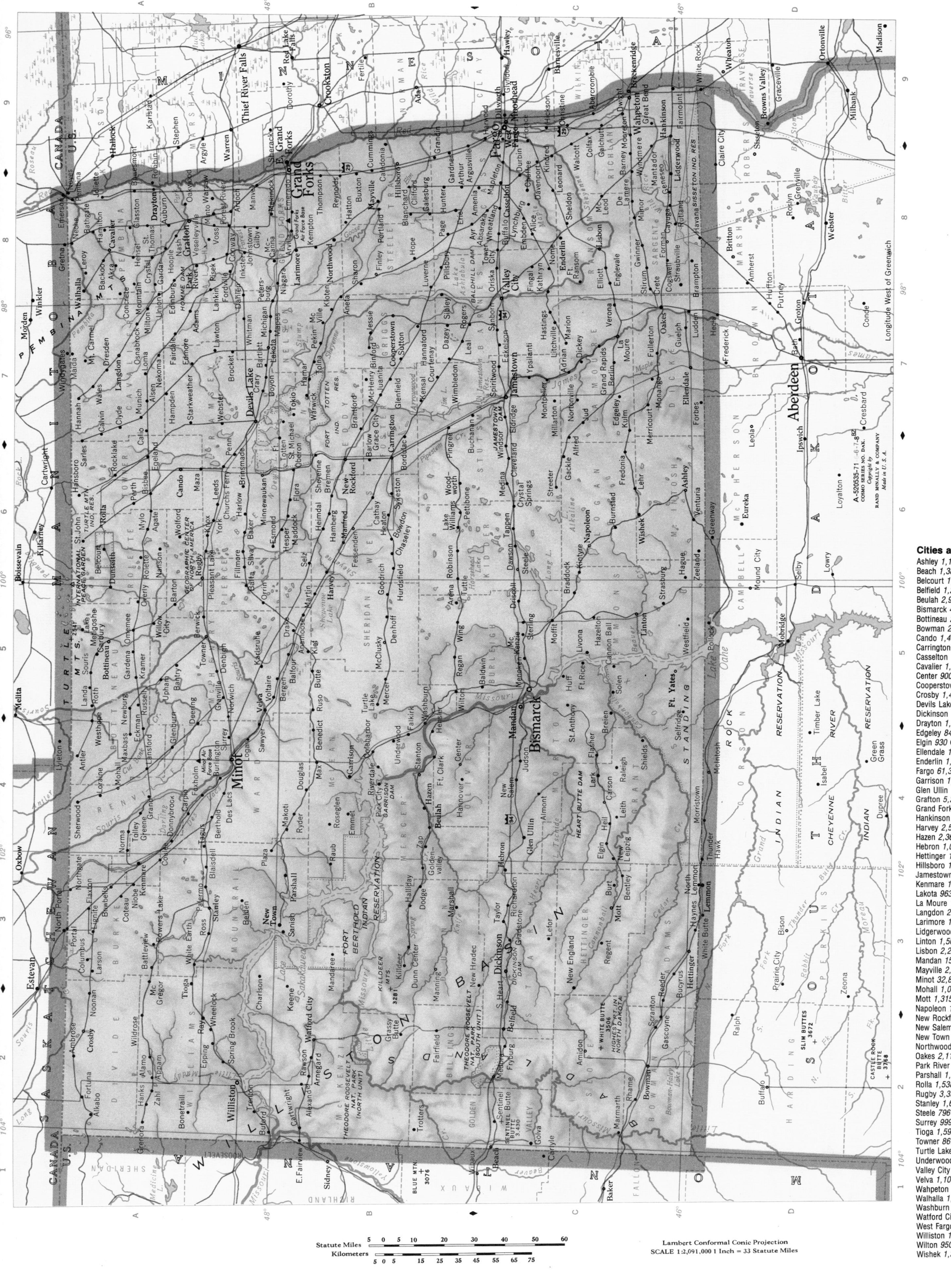

Cities and Towns

Ashley *1,192* **C6**
Beach *1,381* **C1**
Belcourt *1,803* **A6**
Belfield *1,274* **C2**
Beulah *2,908* **B4**
Bismarck *44,485* **C5**
Bottineau *2,829* **A5**
Bowman *2,071* **C2**
Cando *1,496* **A6**
Carrington *2,641* **B6**
Casselton *1,661* **C8**
Cavalier *1,505* **A8**
Center *900* **B4**
Cooperstown *1,308* **B7**
Crosby *1,469* **A2**
Devils Lake *7,442* **A7**
Dickinson *15,924* **C3**
Drayton *1,082* **A8**
Edgeley *843* **C7**
Elgin *930* **C4**
Ellendale *1,967* **C7**
Enderlin *1,151* **C8**
Fargo *61,383* **C9**
Garrison *1,830* **B4**
Glen Ullin *1,125* **C4**
Grafton *5,293* **A8**
Grand Forks *43,765* **B8**
Hankinson *1,158* **C9**
Harvey *2,527* **B6**
Hazen *2,365* **B4**
Hebron *1,078* **C3**
Hettinger *1,739* **D3**
Hillsboro *1,600* **B8**
Jamestown *16,280* **C7**
Kenmare *1,456* **A3**
Lakota *963* **A7**
La Moure *1,077* **C7**
Langdon *2,335* **A7**
Larimore *1,524* **B8**
Lidgerwood *971* **C8**
Linton *1,561* **C5**
Lisbon *2,283* **C8**
Mandan *15,513* **C5**
Mayville *2,255* **B8**
Minot *32,843* **A4**
Mohall *1,049* **A4**
Mott *1,315* **C3**
Napoleon *1,103* **C6**
New Rockford *1,791* **B6**
New Salem *1,081* **C4**
New Town *1,335* **B3**
Northwood *1,240* **B8**
Oakes *2,112* **C7**
Park River *1,844* **A8**
Parshall *1,059* **B3**
Rolla *1,538* **A6**
Rugby *3,335* **A6**
Stanley *1,631* **A3**
Steele *796* **C6**
Surrey *999* **A4**
Tioga *1,597* **A3**
Towner *867* **A5**
Turtle Lake *802* **B5**
Underwood *1,329* **B4**
Valley City *7,774* **C8**
Velva *1,101* **A5**
Wahpeton *9,064* **C9**
Walhalla *1,429* **A8**
Washburn *1,767* **B5**
Watford City *2,119* **B2**
West Fargo *10,099* **C9**
Williston *13,336* **A2**
Wilton *950* **B5**
Wishek *1,345* **C6**

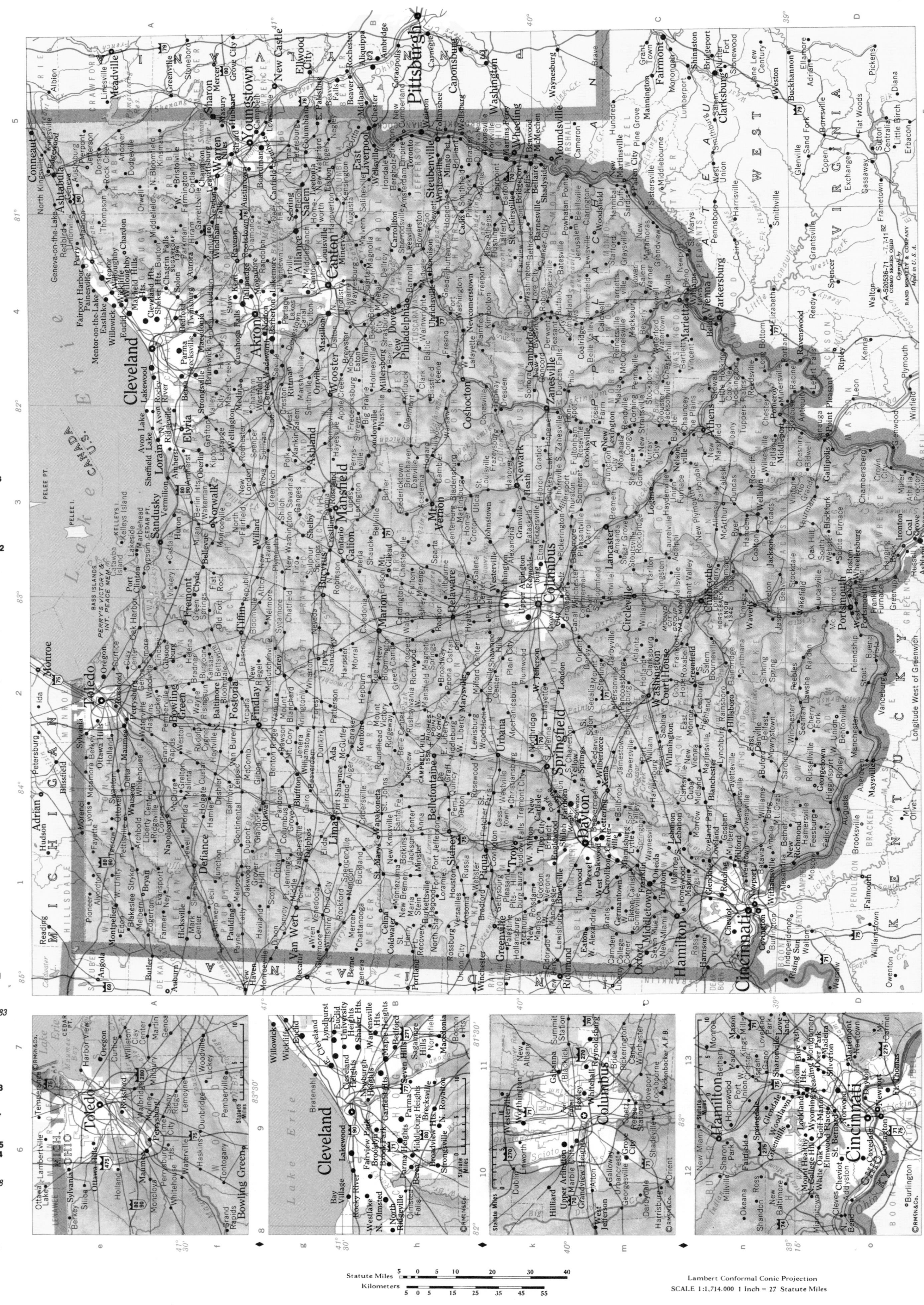

Cities and Towns

Akron *237,177* **A4**
Alliance *24,315* **B4**
Ashland *20,326* **B3**
Ashtabula *23,449* **A5**
Athens *19,743* **C3**
Barberton *29,751* **A4**
Bellefontaine *11,888* **B2**
Boardman *39,161* **A5**
Bowling Green *25,728* **A2**
Brunswick *28,104* **A4**
Bucyrus *13,433* **B3**
Cambridge *13,573* **B4**
Canton *93,077* **B4**
Chillicothe *23,420* **C3**
Cincinnati *385,457* **C1**
Circleville *11,700* **C3**
Cleveland *573,822* **A4**
Cleveland Heights *56,438* **A4**
Columbus *565,032* **C2**
Conneaut *13,835* **A5**
Coshocton *13,405* **B4**
Cuyahoga Falls *43,890* **A4**
Dayton *193,444* **C1**
Defiance *16,810* **A1**
Delaware *18,780* **B2**
East Cleveland *36,957* **g9**
East Liverpool *16,687* **B5**
Elyria *57,538* **A3**
Euclid *59,999* **A4**
Findlay *35,594* **A2**
Fostoria *15,743* **A2**
Fremont *17,834* **A2**
Greenville *12,999* **B1**
Hamilton *63,189* **C1**
Ironton *14,290* **D3**
Kettering *61,186* **C1**
Lakewood *61,963* **A4**
Lancaster *34,953* **C3**
Lima *47,381* **B1**
Lorain *75,416* **A3**
Mansfield *53,927* **B3**
Marietta *16,467* **C4**
Marion *37,040* **B2**
Massillon *30,557* **B4**
Medina *15,268* **A4**
Mentor *42,065* **A4**
Middletown *43,719* **C1**
Mount Vernon *14,323* **B3**
Newark *41,200* **B3**
New Philadelphia *16,883* **B4**
North Olmsted *36,486* **h9**
Norwalk *14,358* **A3**
Oxford *17,655* **C1**
Parma *92,548* **A4**
Piqua *20,480* **B1**
Portsmouth *25,943* **D3**
Salem *12,869* **B5**
Sandusky *31,360* **A3**
Shaker Heights *32,487* **A4**
Springfield *72,563* **C2**
Steubenville *26,400* **B5**
Strongsville *28,577* **A4**
Tiffin *19,549* **A2**
Toledo *354,635* **A2**
Upper Arlington *35,648* **B2**
Urbana *10,762* **B2**
Van Wert *11,035* **B1**
Warren *56,629* **A5**
Washington Court House *12,682* **C2**
Westerville *23,414* **B3**
Wooster *29,289* **B4**
Xenia *24,653* **C2**
Youngstown *115,436* **A5**
Zanesville *28,655* **C4**

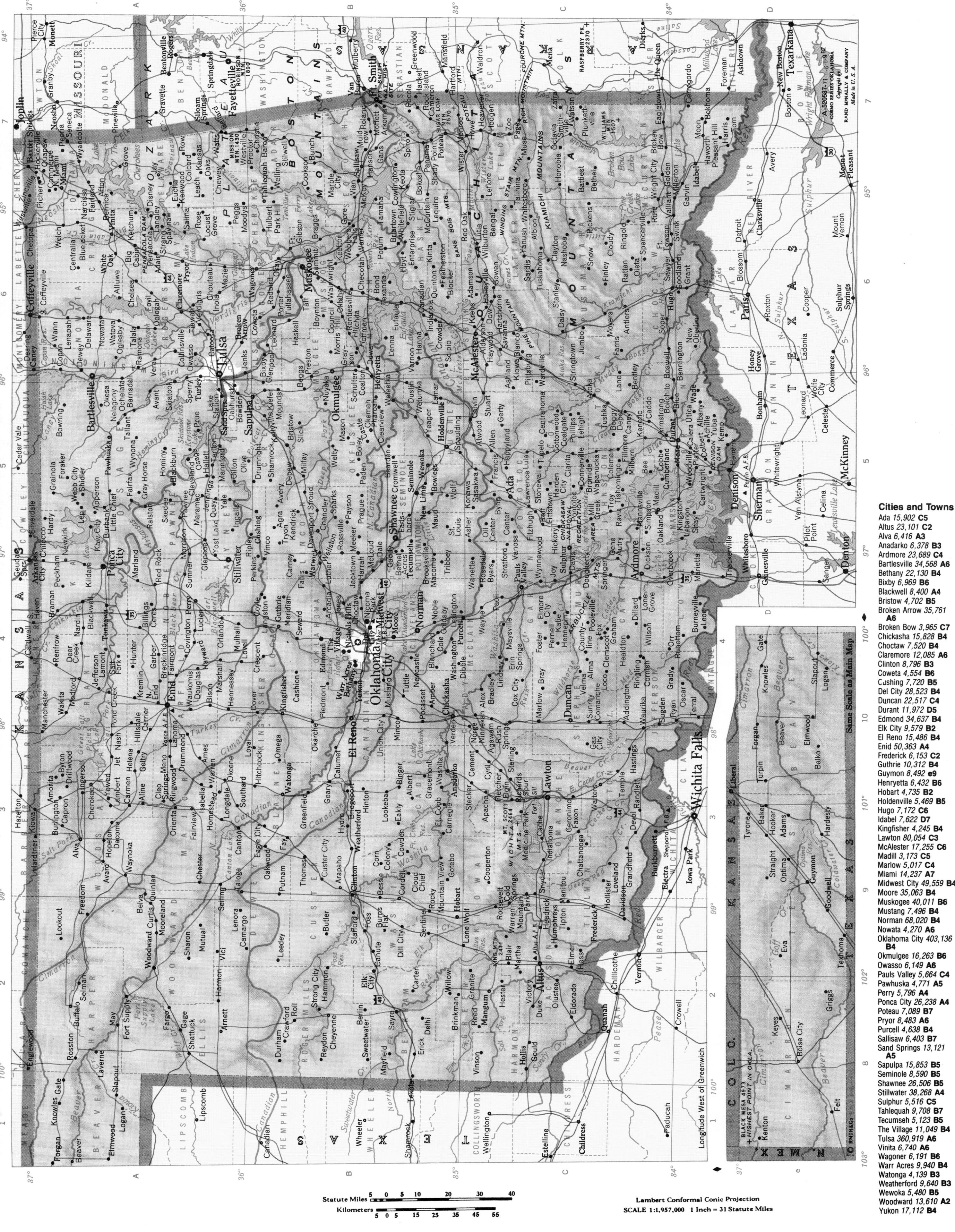

Cities and Towns

Ada *15,902* **C5**
Altus *23,101* **C2**
Alva *6,416* **A3**
Anadarko *6,378* **B3**
Ardmore *23,689* **C4**
Bartlesville *34,568* **A6**
Bethany *22,130* **B4**
Bixby *6,969* **B6**
Blackwell *8,400* **A4**
Bristow *4,702* **B5**
Broken Arrow *35,761* **A6**
Broken Bow *3,965* **C7**
Chickasha *15,828* **B4**
Choctaw *7,520* **B4**
Claremore *12,085* **A6**
Clinton *8,796* **B3**
Coweta *4,554* **B6**
Cushing *7,720* **B5**
Del City *28,523* **B4**
Duncan *22,517* **C4**
Durant *11,972* **D5**
Edmond *34,637* **B4**
Elk City *9,579* **B2**
El Reno *15,486* **B4**
Enid *50,363* **A4**
Frederick *6,153* **C2**
Guthrie *10,312* **B4**
Guymon *8,492* **e9**
Henryetta *6,432* **B6**
Hobart *4,735* **B2**
Holdenville *5,469* **B5**
Hugo *7,172* **C6**
Idabel *7,622* **D7**
Kingfisher *4,245* **B4**
Lawton *80,054* **C3**
McAlester *17,255* **C6**
Madill *3,173* **C5**
Marlow *5,017* **C4**
Miami *14,237* **A7**
Midwest City *49,559* **B4**
Moore *35,063* **B4**
Muskogee *40,011* **B6**
Mustang *7,496* **B4**
Norman *68,020* **B4**
Nowata *4,270* **A6**
Oklahoma City *403,136* **B4**
Okmulgee *16,263* **B6**
Owasso *6,149* **A6**
Pauls Valley *5,664* **C4**
Pawhuska *4,771* **A5**
Perry *5,796* **A4**
Ponca City *26,238* **A4**
Poteau *7,089* **B7**
Pryor *8,483* **A6**
Purcell *4,638* **B4**
Sallisaw *6,403* **B7**
Sand Springs *13,121* **A5**
Sapulpa *15,853* **B5**
Seminole *8,590* **B5**
Shawnee *26,506* **B5**
Stillwater *38,268* **A4**
Sulphur *5,516* **C5**
Tahlequah *9,708* **B7**
Tecumseh *5,123* **B5**
The Village *11,049* **B4**
Tulsa *360,919* **A6**
Vinita *6,740* **A6**
Wagoner *6,191* **B6**
Warr Acres *9,940* **B4**
Watonga *4,139* **B3**
Weatherford *9,640* **B3**
Wewoka *5,480* **B5**
Woodward *13,610* **A2**
Yukon *17,112* **B4**

OREGON

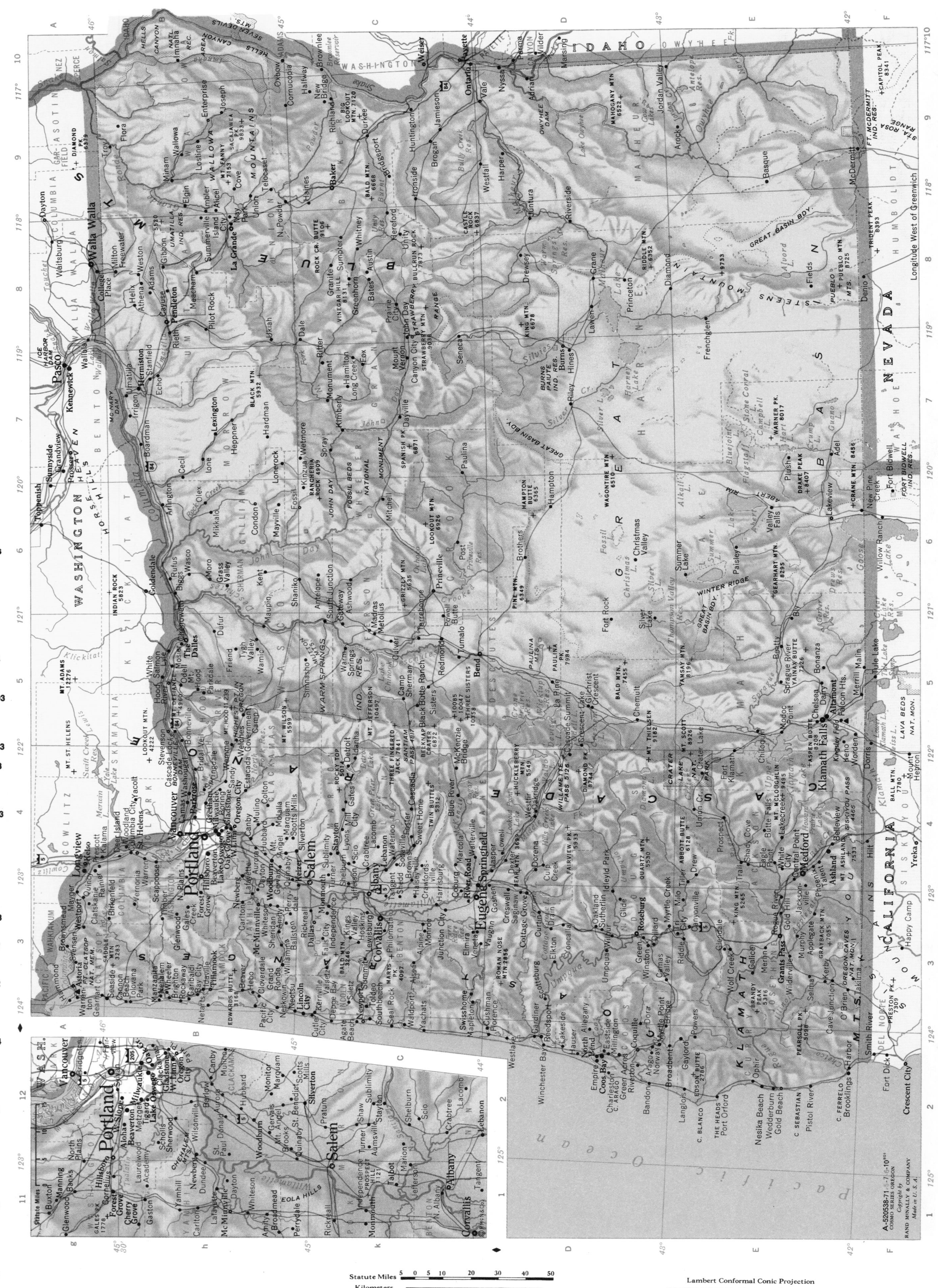

Statute Miles 5 0 5 10 20 30 40 50

Kilometers 5 0 5 15 25 35 45 55 65 75

Lambert Conformal Conic Projection

SCALE 1:2,329,000 1 Inch = 37 Statute Miles

Cities and Towns

Albany *26,678* **C3**
Aloha *10,000* **h12**
Altamont *19,805* **E5**
Ashland *14,943* **E4**
Astoria *9,998* **A3**
Baker *9,471* **C9**
Beaverton *30,582* **B4**
Bend *17,263* **C5**
Burns *3,579* **D7**
Canby *7,659* **B4**
Central Point *6,357* **E4**
Coos Bay *14,424* **D2**
Coquille *4,481* **D2**
Corvallis *40,960* **C3**
Cottage Grove *7,148* **D3**
Crater Lake *25* **E4**
Dallas *8,530* **C3**
Eugene *105,624* **C3**
Florence *4,411* **D2**
Forest Grove *11,499* **B3**
Gladstone *9,500* **B4**
Grants Pass *15,032* **E3**
Gresham *33,005* **B4**
Hermiston *9,408* **B7**
Hillsboro *27,664* **B4**
Hood River *4,329* **B5**
Independence *4,024* **C3**
John Day *2,012* **C8**
Keizer *18,592* **C3**
Klamath Falls *16,661* **E5**
La Grande *11,354* **B8**
Lake Oswego *22,527* **B4**
Lakeview *2,770* **E6**
Lebanon *10,413* **C4**
Lincoln City *5,469* **C3**
McMinnville *14,080* **B3**
Medford *39,603* **E4**
Metzger *5,544* **h12**
Milton-Freewater *5,086* **B8**
Milwaukie *17,931* **B4**
Monmouth *5,594* **C3**
Myrtle Creek *3,365* **D2**
Newberg *10,394* **B4**
Newport *7,519* **C2**
North Bend *9,779* **D2**
Oak Grove *11,640* **B4**
Ontario *8,814* **C10**
Oregon City *14,673* **B4**
Parkrose *21,103* **B4**
Pendleton *14,521* **B8**
Portland *366,383* **B4**
Prineville *5,276* **C6**
Redmond *6,452* **C5**
Reedsport *4,984* **D2**
River Road *10,370* **C3**
Roseburg *16,644* **D3**
St. Helens *7,064* **B4**
Salem *89,233* **C4**
Scappoose *3,213* **B4**
Seaside *5,193* **B3**
Silverton *5,168* **C4**
Springfield *41,621* **C4**
Stayton *4,396* **C4**
Sutherlin *4,560* **D3**
Sweet Home *6,921* **C4**
The Dalles *10,820* **B5**
Tigard *14,286* **h12**
Tillamook *3,981* **B3**
Tri City *3,439* **E3**
Umatilla *3,199* **B7**
West Linn *12,956* **B4**
West Slope *5,364* **g12**
White City *5,445* **E4**
Woodburn *11,196* **B4**

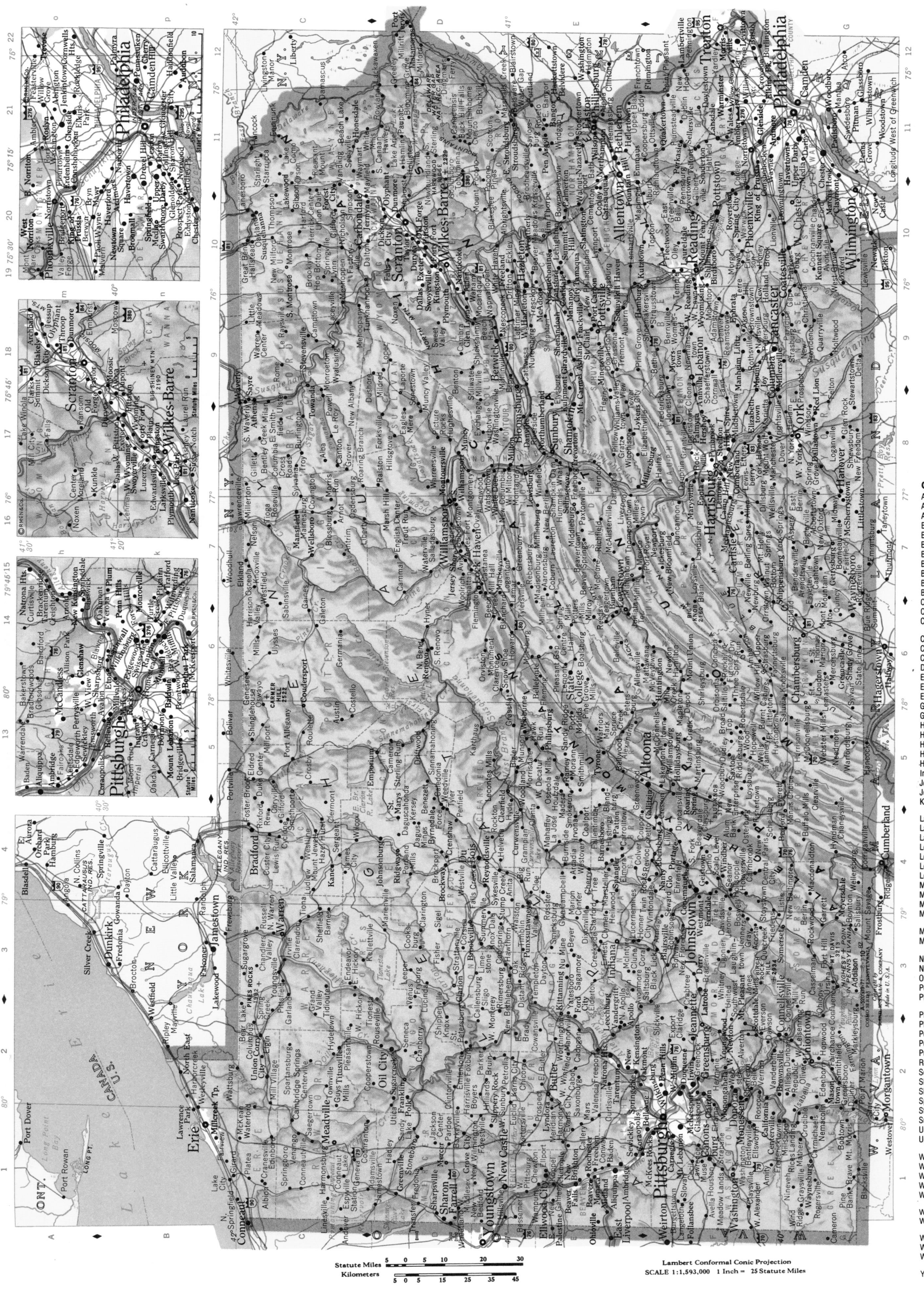

Cities and Towns

Aliquippa *17,094* **E1**
Allentown *103,758* **E11**
Altoona *57,078* **E5**
Beaver Falls *12,525* **E1**
Berwick *11,850* **D9**
Bethel Park *34,755* **k14**
Bethlehem *70,419* **E11**
Bloomsburg *11,717* **E9**
Bradford *11,211* **C4**
Broomall *23,642* **p20**
Butler *17,026* **E2**
Carbondale *11,255* **C10**
Carlisle *18,314* **F7**
Chambersburg *16,174* **G6**
Chester *45,794* **G11**
Coatesville *10,698* **G10**
Connellsville *10,319* **F2**
Du Bois *9,290* **D4**
Easton *26,027* **E11**
Ephrata *11,095* **F9**
Erie *119,123* **B1**
Gettysburg *7,194* **G7**
Greensburg *17,558* **F2**
Hanover *14,890* **G8**
Harrisburg *53,264* **F8**
Havertown *36,000* **G11**
Hazleton *27,318* **E10**
Hershey *9,000* **F8**
Indiana *16,051* **E3**
Jeannette *13,106* **F2**
Johnstown *35,496* **F4**
King of Prussia *18,200* **F11**
Lancaster *54,725* **F9**
Lansdale *16,526* **F11**
Latrobe *10,799* **F3**
Lebanon *25,711* **F9**
Levittown *78,600* **F12**
Lewistown *9,830* **E6**
Lock Haven *9,617* **D7**
McKeesport *31,012* **F2**
Meadville *15,544* **C1**
Middletown *10,122* **F8**
Millcreek Township *44,303* **B1**
Monroeville *30,977* **k14**
Mount Lebanon *34,414* **F1**
New Castle *33,621* **D1**
Norristown *34,684* **F11**
Oil City *13,881* **D2**
Penn Hills *57,632* **F2**
Philadelphia *1,688,210* **G11**
Pittsburgh *423,959* **F1**
Plum *25,390* **k14**
Pottstown *22,729* **F10**
Pottsville *18,195* **E9**
Punxsutawney *7,479* **E4**
Reading *78,686* **F10**
Scranton *88,117* **D10**
Shamokin *10,357* **E8**
Sharon *19,057* **D1**
Springfield *25,326* **p20**
State College *36,130* **E6**
Sunbury *12,292* **E8**
Uniontown *14,510* **G2**
Upper Darby *50,200* **G11**
Warminster *35,543* **F11**
Warren *12,146* **C3**
Washington *18,363* **F1**
Waynesboro *9,726* **G6**
West Chester *17,435* **G10**
West Mifflin *26,552* **F2**
Wilkes-Barre *51,551* **D10**
Wilkinsburg *23,669* **F2**
Williamsport *33,401* **D7**
Willow Grove *21,300* **F11**
York *44,619* **G8**

RHODE ISLAND

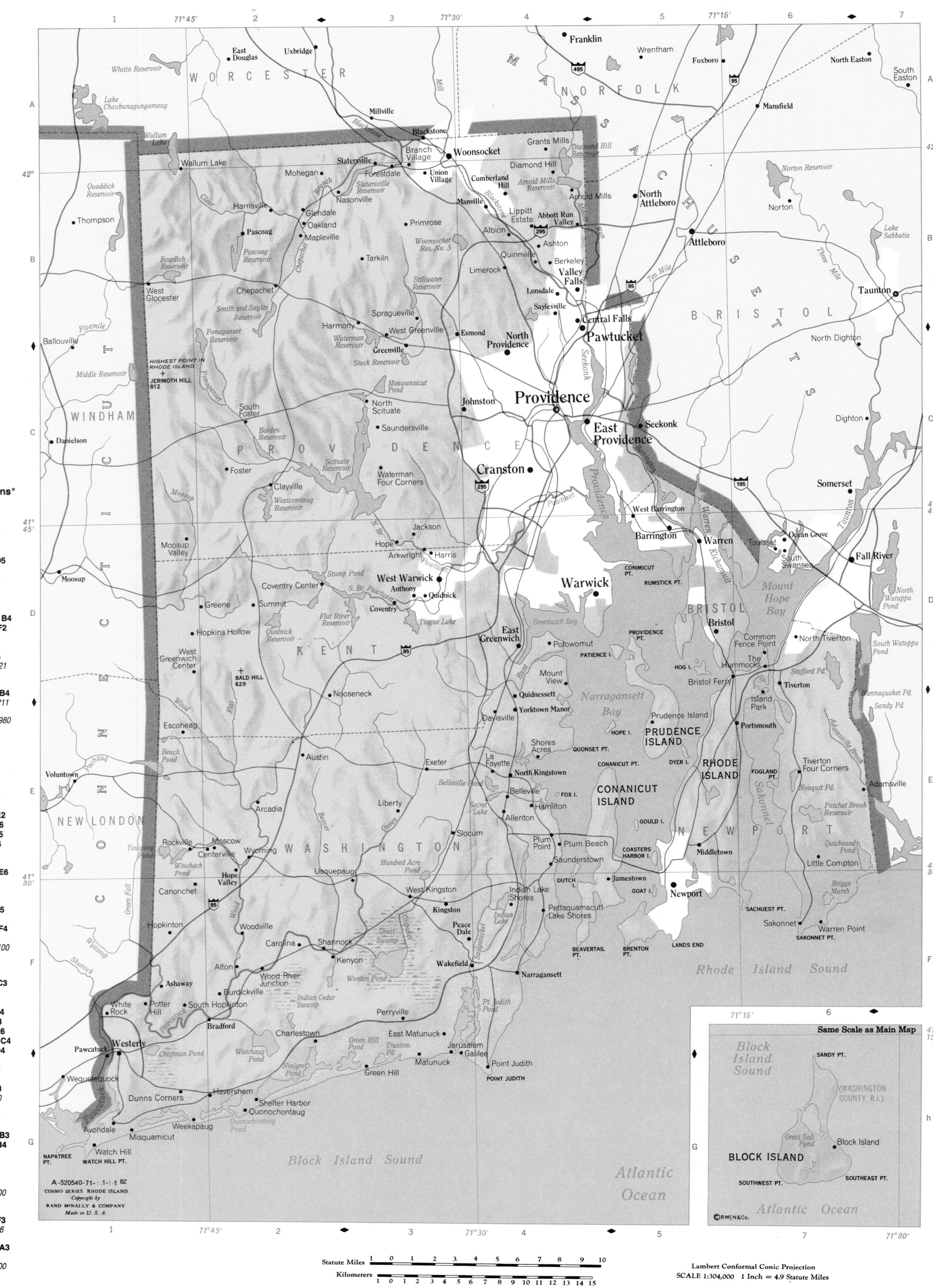

Cities and Towns*

Albion *1,200* **B4**
Allenton *600* **E4**
Anthony *4,500* **D3**
Arnold Mills *600* **B4**
Ashaway *1,747* **F1**
Ashton *875* **B4**
Barrington *16,174* **D5**
Berkeley *930* **B4**
Block Island *620* **h7**
Bradford *1,354* **F1**
Bristol *20,128* **D5**
Carolina *500* **F2**
Central Falls *16,995* **B4**
Charlestown *1,200* **F2**
Chepachet *900* **B2**
Coventry *8,000* **D3**
Cranston *71,992* **C4**
Cumberland Hill *5,421* **B4**
Davisville *550* **E4**
Diamond Hill *1,150* **B4**
East Greenwich *10,211* **D4**
East Providence *50,980* **C4**
Esmond *3,500* **B4**
Forestdale *450* **B3**
Glendale *600* **B2**
Greenville *7,576* **C3**
Harmony *800* **B3**
Harris *1,000* **D3**
Harrisville *1,224* **B2**
Hope *490* **D3**
Hope Valley *1,414* **E2**
Island Park *1,000* **E6**
Jamestown *4,040* **F5**
Johnston *24,907* **C4**
Kingston *5,419* **F3**
La Fayette *680* **E4**
Little Compton *300* **E6**
Lonsdale *4,100* **B4**
Manville *3,100* **B4**
Mapleville *900* **B2**
Middletown *3,350* **E5**
Mount View *560* **D4**
Narragansett *3,342* **F4**
Newport *29,259* **F5**
North Kingstown *3,100* **E4**
North Providence *29,188* **C4**
North Scituate *325* **C3**
Oakland *500* **B2**
Pascoag *3,807* **B2**
Pawtucket *71,204* **C4**
Peace Dale *3,100* **F3**
Portsmouth *4,300* **E6**
Providence *156,804* **C4**
Quidnessett *3,300* **D4**
Quidnick *2,300* **D3**
Saylesville *3,200* **B4**
Shannock *600* **D2**
Slatersville *2,000* **A3**
South Hopkinton *500* **F1**
Spragueville *430* **B3**
Tiverton *7,653* **D6**
Union Village *2,400* **B3**
Valley Falls *10,892* **B4**
Wakefield *3,400* **F3**
Warren *10,640* **D5**
Warwick *87,123* **D4**
Watch Hill *500* **G1**
West Barrington *3,700* **C5**
Westerly *14,093* **F1**
West Kingston *700* **F3**
West Warwick *27,026* **D3**
Woonsocket *45,914* **A3**
Wyoming *600* **E2**
Yorktown Manor *2,500* **E4**

*Populations are for localities, not incorporated towns.

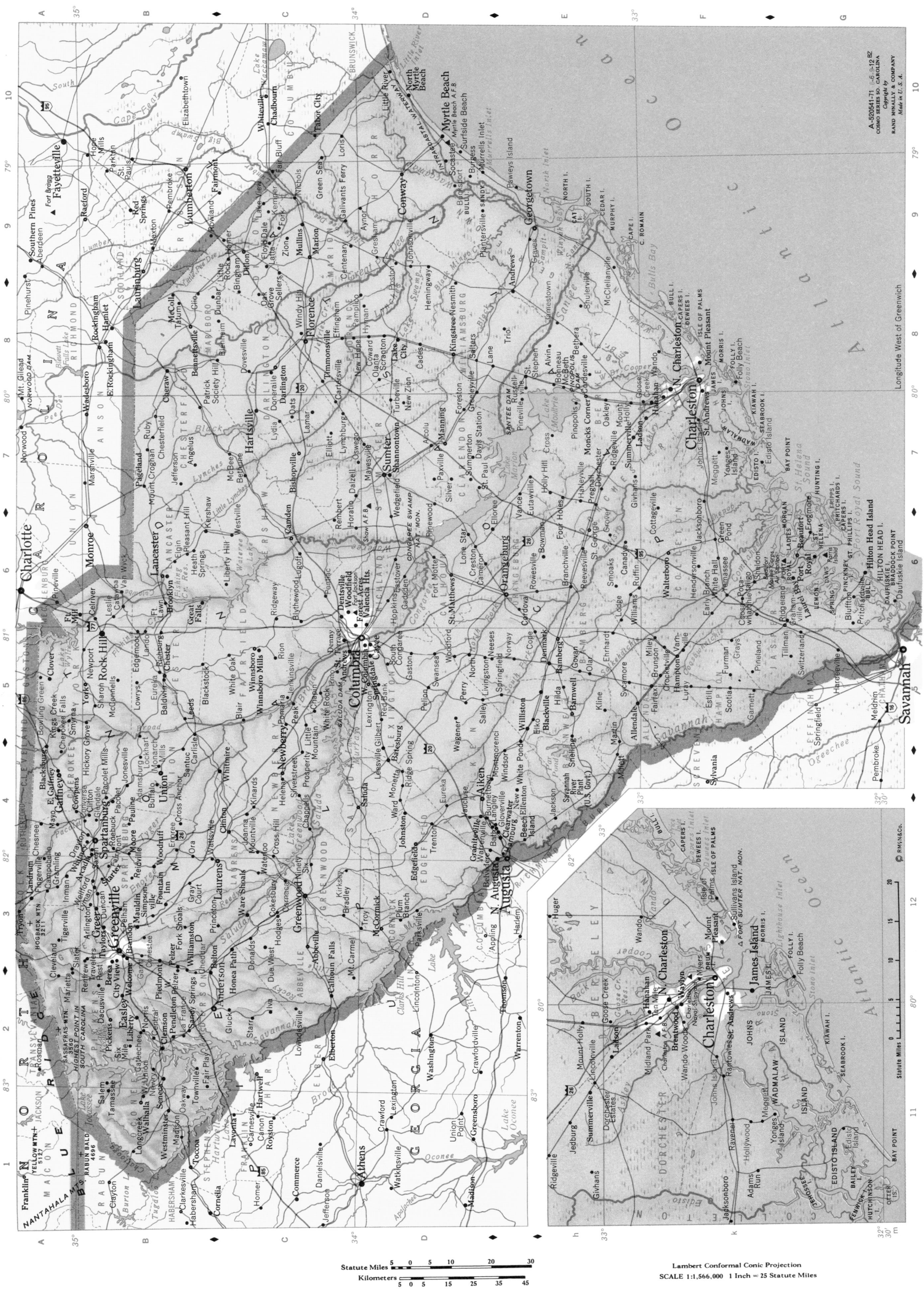

Cities and Towns

Abbeville *5,833* **C3**
Aiken *14,978* **D4**
Allendale *4,400* **E5**
Anderson *27,965* **B2**
Barnwell *5,572* **E5**
Batesburg *4,023* **D4**
Beaufort *8,634* **G6**
Belton *5,312* **B3**
Belvedere *6,859* **D4**
Bennettsville *8,774* **B8**
Berea *7,500* **B3**
Bishopville *3,429* **C7**
Camden *7,462* **C6**
Cayce *11,701* **D5**
Charleston *69,510* **F8**
Cheraw *5,654* **B8**
Chester *6,820* **B5**
Clemson *8,118* **B2**
Clinton *8,596* **C4**
Columbia *100,385* **C5**
Conway *10,240* **D9**
Cowpens *2,023* **A4**
Darlington *7,989* **C8**
Denmark *4,434* **E5**
Dillon *7,060* **C9**
Easley *14,264* **B2**
Florence *29,176* **C8**
Fort Mill *4,162* **A6**
Fountain Inn *4,226* **B3**
Gaffney *13,453* **A4**
Georgetown *10,144* **E9**
Goose Creek *17,811* **F7**
Greenville *58,242* **B3**
Greenwood *21,613* **C3**
Greer *10,525* **B3**
Hanahan *13,224* **F7**
Hartsville *7,631* **C7**
Hilton Head Island *11,344* **G6**
Honea Path *4,114* **C3**
James Island *24,124* **k12**
Kingstree *4,147* **D8**
Ladson *13,246* **F7**
Lake City *6,731* **D8**
Lancaster *9,703* **B6**
Laurel Bay *5,238* **G6**
Laurens *10,587* **C3**
Manning *4,746* **D7**
Marion *7,700* **C9**
Mauldin *8,143* **B3**
Moncks Corner *3,699* **E7**
Mount Pleasant *14,209* **F8**
Mullins *6,068* **C9**
Myrtle Beach *18,446* **D10**
Newberry *9,866* **C4**
North Augusta *13,593* **D4**
North Charleston *62,534* **F8**
North Myrtle Beach *3,960* **D10**
Orangeburg *14,933* **E6**
Rock Hill *35,344* **B5**
St. Andrews *9,908* **F7**
St. Andrews *20,245* **C5**
Seneca *7,436* **B2**
Shannontown *7,900* **D7**
Simpsonville *9,037* **B3**
Spartanburg *43,826* **B4**
Summerville *6,706* **E7**
Sumter *24,890* **D7**
Taylors *12,100* **B3**
Union *10,523* **B4**
Walhalla *3,977* **B1**
West Columbia *10,409* **D5**
Williamston *4,310* **B3**
Woodruff *5,171* **B3**
York *6,412* **B5**

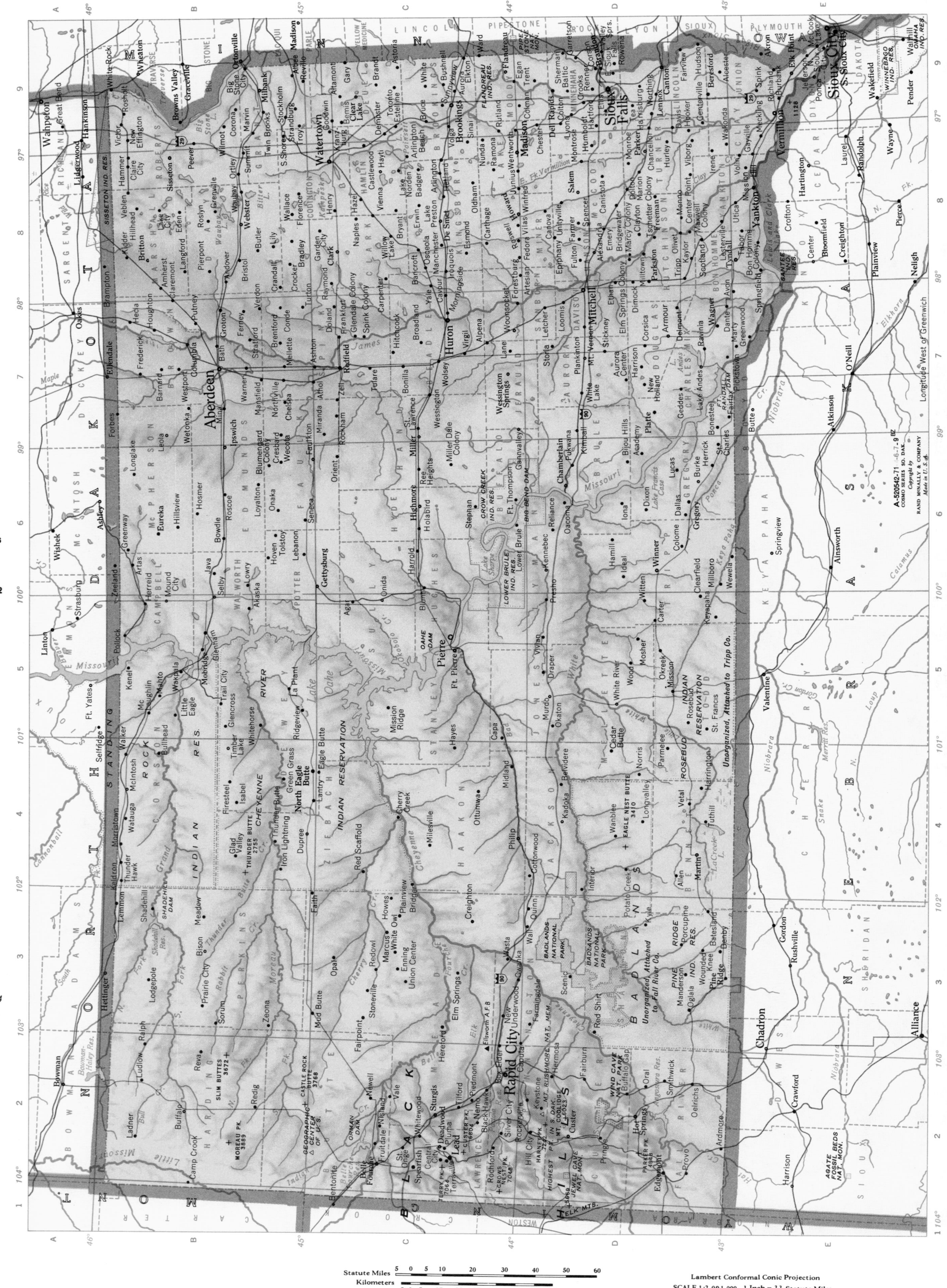

Cities and Towns

Aberdeen *25,851* **B7**
Alcester *885* **D9**
Arlington *991* **C8**
Armour *819* **D7**
Belle Fourche *4,692* **C2**
Beresford *1,865* **D9**
Black Hawk *1,608* **C2**
Box Elder *3,186* **C2**
Brandon *2,589* **D9**
Britton *1,590* **B8**
Brookings *14,951* **C9**
Burke *859* **D6**
Canton *2,886* **D9**
Centerville *892* **D9**
Chamberlain *2,258* **D6**
Clark *1,351* **C8**
Clear Lake *1,310* **C9**
Custer *1,830* **D2**
Deadwood *2,035* **C2**
De Smet *1,237* **C8**
Edgemont *1,468* **D2**
Elk Point *1,661* **E9**
Eureka *1,360* **B6**
Faulkton *981* **B6**
Flandreau *2,114* **C9**
Fort Pierre *1,789* **C5**
Freeman *1,462* **D8**
Garretson *963* **D9**
Gettysburg *1,623* **C6**
Gregory *1,503* **D6**
Groton *1,230* **B7**
Hartford *1,207* **D9**
Highmore *1,055* **C6**
Hot Springs *4,742* **D2**
Howard *1,169* **C8**
Huron *13,000* **C7**
Ipswich *1,153* **B6**
Lake Andes *1,029* **D7**
Lead *4,330* **C2**
Lemmon *1,871* **B3**
Lennox *1,827* **D9**
Martin *1,018* **D4**
Milbank *4,120* **B9**
Miller *1,931* **C7**
Mitchell *13,916* **D7**
Mobridge *4,174* **B5**
North Eagle Butte *1,354* **B4**
North Sioux City *1,992* **E9**
Parker *999* **D8**
Parkston *1,545* **D8**
Philip *1,088* **C4**
Pierre *11,973* **C5**
Pine Ridge *3,059* **D3**
Platte *1,334* **D7**
Rapid City *46,492* **C2**
Redfield *3,027* **C7**
Salem *1,486* **D8**
Scotland *1,022* **D8**
Selby *884* **B5**
Sioux Falls *81,343* **D9**
Sisseton *2,789* **B8**
Spearfish *5,251* **C2**
Springfield *1,377* **E8**
Sturgis *5,184* **C2**
Tyndall *1,253* **E8**
Vermillion *10,136* **E9**
Volga *1,221* **C9**
Wagner *1,453* **D7**
Wall *770* **D3**
Watertown *15,649* **C8**
Webster *2,417* **B8**
Wessington Springs *1,203* **C7**
Winner *3,472* **D6**
Yankton *12,011* **E8**

Statute Miles 5 0 5 10 20 30 40 50 60
Kilometers 5 0 5 15 25 35 45 55 65 75

Lambert Conformal Conic Projection
SCALE 1:2,091,000 1 Inch = 33 Statute Miles

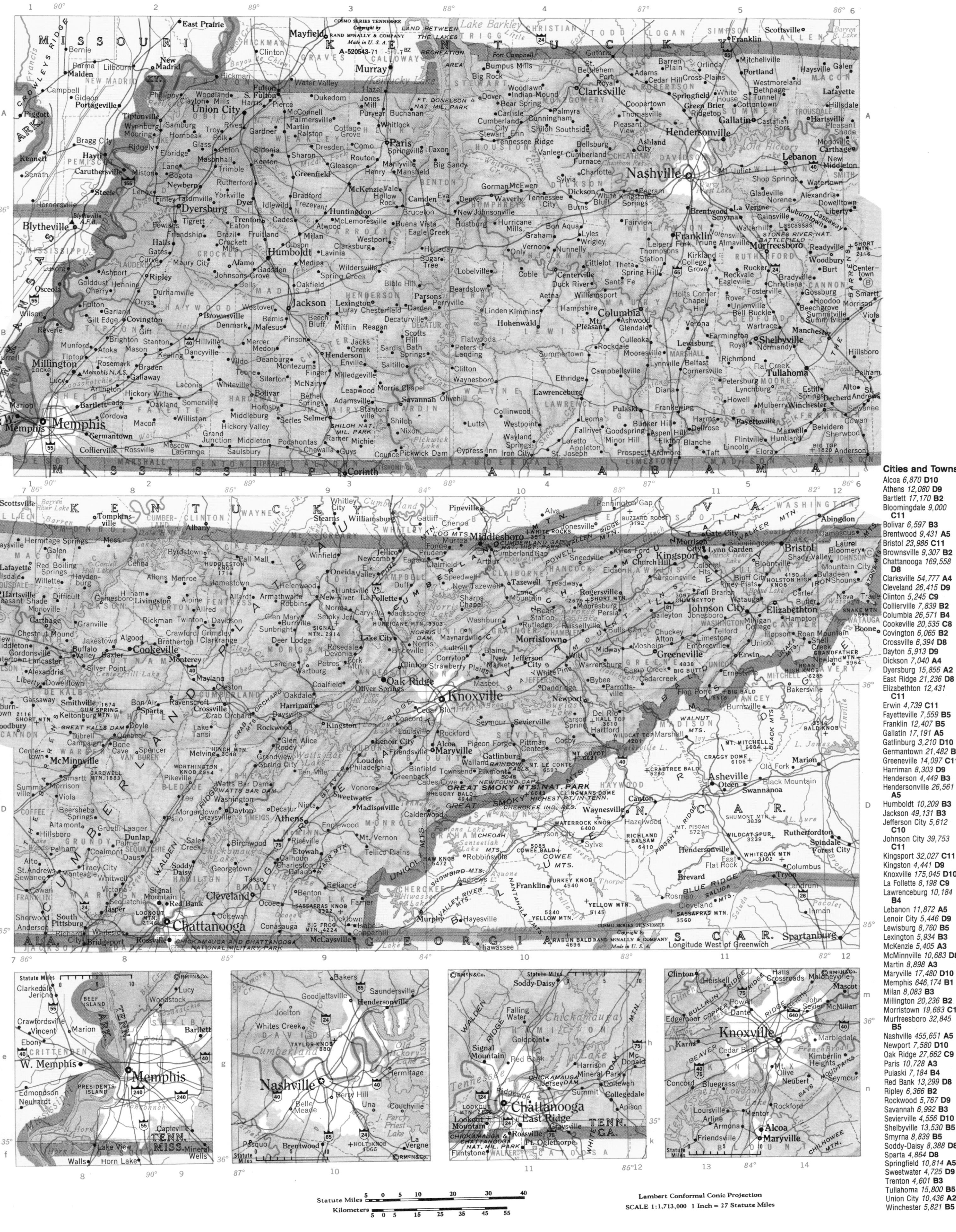

Cities and Towns

Alcoa *6,870* **D10**
Athens *12,080* **D9**
Bartlett *17,170* **B2**
Bloomingdale *9,000* **C11**
Bolivar *6,597* **B3**
Brentwood *9,431* **A5**
Bristol *23,986* **C11**
Brownsville *9,307* **B2**
Chattanooga *169,558* **D8**
Clarksville *54,777* **A4**
Cleveland *26,415* **D9**
Clinton *5,245* **C9**
Collierville *7,839* **B2**
Columbia *26,571* **B4**
Cookeville *20,535* **C8**
Covington *6,065* **B2**
Crossville *6,394* **D8**
Dayton *5,913* **D9**
Dickson *7,040* **A4**
Dyersburg *15,856* **A2**
East Ridge *21,236* **D8**
Elizabethton *12,431* **C11**
Erwin *4,739* **C11**
Fayetteville *7,559* **B5**
Franklin *12,407* **B5**
Gallatin *17,191* **A5**
Gatlinburg *3,210* **D10**
Germantown *21,482* **B2**
Greeneville *14,097* **C11**
Harriman *8,303* **D9**
Henderson *4,449* **B3**
Hendersonville *26,561* **A5**
Humboldt *10,209* **B3**
Jackson *49,131* **B3**
Jefferson City *5,612* **C10**
Johnson City *39,753* **C11**
Kingsport *32,027* **C11**
Kingston *4,441* **D9**
Knoxville *175,045* **D10**
La Follette *8,198* **C9**
Lawrenceburg *10,184* **B4**
Lebanon *11,872* **A5**
Lenoir City *5,446* **D9**
Lewisburg *8,760* **B5**
Lexington *5,934* **B3**
McKenzie *5,405* **A3**
McMinnville *10,683* **D8**
Martin *8,898* **A3**
Maryville *17,480* **D10**
Memphis *646,174* **B1**
Milan *8,083* **B3**
Millington *20,236* **B2**
Morristown *19,683* **C10**
Murfreesboro *32,845* **B5**
Nashville *455,651* **A5**
Newport *7,580* **D10**
Oak Ridge *27,662* **C9**
Paris *10,728* **A3**
Pulaski *7,184* **B4**
Red Bank *13,299* **D8**
Ripley *6,366* **B2**
Rockwood *5,767* **D9**
Savannah *6,992* **B3**
Sevierville *4,556* **D10**
Shelbyville *13,530* **B5**
Smyrna *8,839* **B5**
Soddy-Daisy *8,388* **D8**
Sparta *4,864* **D8**
Springfield *10,814* **A5**
Sweetwater *4,725* **D9**
Trenton *4,601* **B3**
Tullahoma *15,800* **B5**
Union City *10,436* **A2**
Winchester *5,821* **B5**

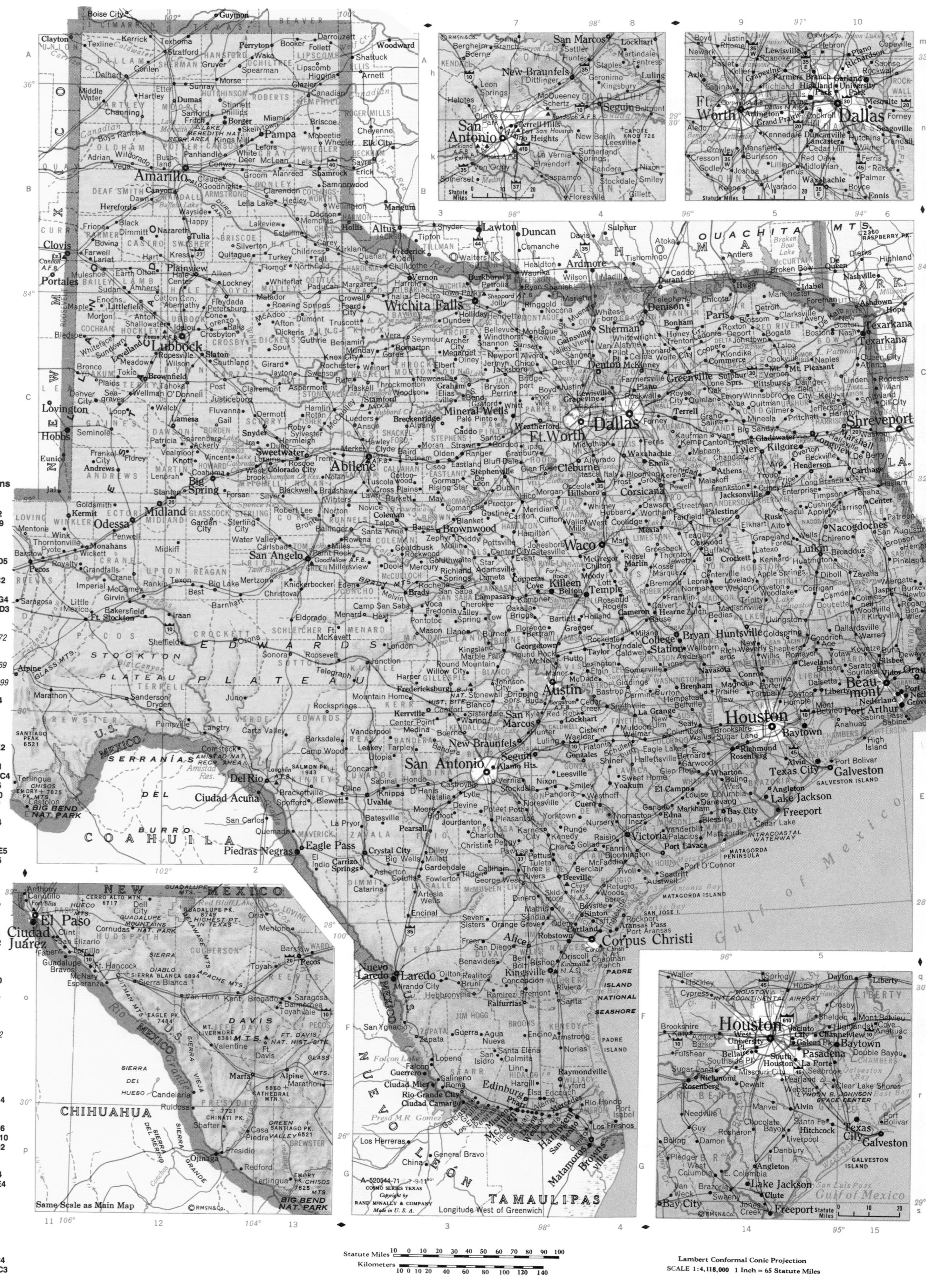

Cities and Towns

Abilene *98,315* **C3**
Alice *20,961* **F3**
Amarillo *149,230* **B2**
Arlington *160,113* **n9**
Austin *345,496* **D4**
Bay City *17,837* **E5**
Baytown *56,923* **E5**
Beaumont *118,102* **D5**
Beeville *14,574* **E4**
Big Spring *24,804* **C2**
Borger *15,837* **B2**
Brownsville *84,997* **G4**
Brownwood *19,396* **D3**
Bryan *44,337* **D4**
Cleburne *19,218* **C4**
College Station *37,272* **D4**
Conroe *18,034* **D5**
Copperas Cove *19,469* **D4**
Corpus Christi *231,999* **F4**
Corsicana *21,712* **C4**
Dallas *904,078* **C4**
Del Rio *30,034* **E2**
Denison *23,884* **C4**
Denton *48,063* **C4**
Eagle Pass *21,407* **E2**
Edinburg *24,075* **F3**
El Paso *425,259* **o11**
Fort Worth *385,164* **C4**
Galveston *61,902* **E5**
Garland *138,857* **n10**
Grand Prairie *71,462* **n10**
Greenville *22,161* **C4**
Harlingen *43,543* **F4**
Hereford *15,853* **B1**
Houston *1,595,138* **E5**
Huntsville *23,936* **D5**
Irving *109,943* **n10**
Kerrville *15,276* **D3**
Killeen *46,296* **D4**
Kingsville *28,808* **F4**
Lake Jackson *19,102* **E5**
Laredo *91,449* **F3**
Longview *62,762* **C5**
Lubbock *173,979* **C2**
Lufkin *28,562* **D5**
McAllen *66,281* **F3**
Marshall *24,921* **C5**
Mesquite *67,053* **n10**
Midland *70,525* **D1**
Mineral Wells *14,468* **C3**
Nacogdoches *27,149* **D5**
New Braunfels *22,402* **E3**
Odessa *90,027* **D1**
Orange *23,628* **D6**
Palestine *15,948* **D5**
Pampa *21,396* **B2**
Paris *25,498* **C5**
Pasadena *112,560* **r14**
Pecos *12,855* **D1**
Plainview *22,187* **B2**
Port Arthur *61,251* **E6**
Richardson *72,496* **n10**
San Angelo *73,240* **D2**
San Antonio *786,023* **E3**
San Benito *17,988* **F4**
San Marcos *23,420* **E4**
Sherman *30,413* **C4**
Temple *42,354* **D4**
Texarkana *31,271* **C5**
Texas City *41,403* **E5**
Uvalde *14,178* **E3**
Victoria *50,695* **E4**
Waco *101,261* **D4**
Waxahachie *14,264* **C4**
Wichita Falls *94,201* **C3**

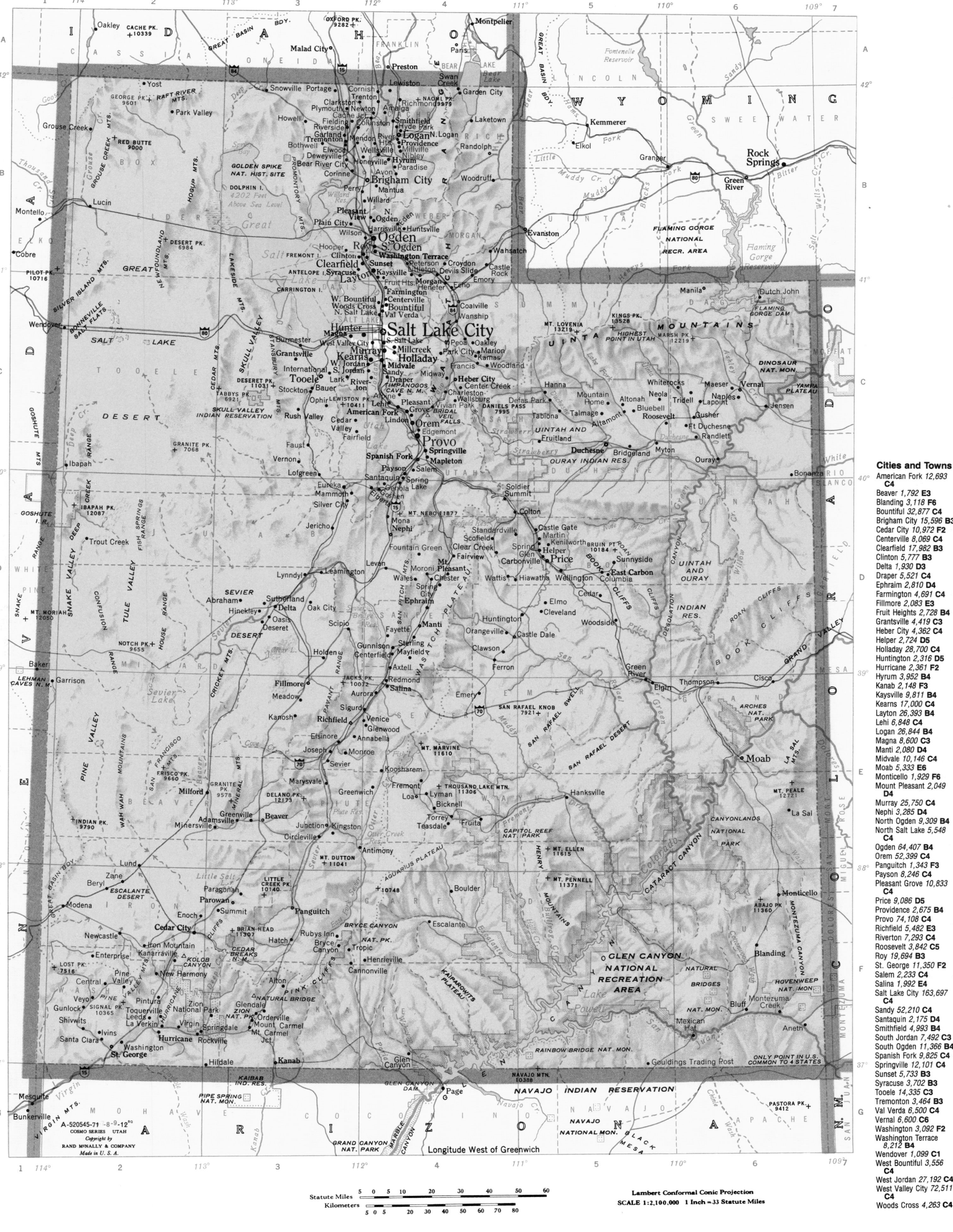

Cities and Towns

American Fork *12,693* **C4**
Beaver *1,792* **E3**
Blanding *3,118* **F6**
Bountiful *32,877* **C4**
Brigham City *15,596* **B3**
Cedar City *10,972* **F2**
Centerville *8,069* **C4**
Clearfield *17,982* **B3**
Clinton *5,777* **B3**
Delta *1,930* **D3**
Draper *5,521* **C4**
Ephraim *2,810* **D4**
Farmington *4,691* **C4**
Fillmore *2,083* **E3**
Fruit Heights *2,728* **B4**
Grantsville *4,419* **C3**
Heber City *4,362* **C4**
Helper *2,724* **D5**
Holladay *28,700* **C4**
Huntington *2,316* **D5**
Hurricane *2,361* **F2**
Hyrum *3,952* **B4**
Kanab *2,148* **F3**
Kaysville *9,811* **B4**
Kearns *17,000* **C4**
Layton *26,393* **B4**
Lehi *6,848* **C4**
Logan *26,844* **B4**
Magna *8,600* **C3**
Manti *2,080* **D4**
Midvale *10,146* **C4**
Moab *5,333* **E6**
Monticello *1,929* **F6**
Mount Pleasant *2,049* **D4**
Murray *25,750* **C4**
Nephi *3,285* **D4**
North Ogden *9,309* **B4**
North Salt Lake *5,548* **C4**
Ogden *64,407* **B4**
Orem *52,399* **C4**
Panguitch *1,343* **F3**
Payson *8,246* **C4**
Pleasant Grove *10,833* **C4**
Price *9,086* **D5**
Providence *2,675* **B4**
Provo *74,108* **C4**
Richfield *5,482* **E3**
Riverton *7,293* **C4**
Roosevelt *3,842* **C5**
Roy *19,694* **B3**
St. George *11,350* **F2**
Salem *2,233* **C4**
Salina *1,992* **E4**
Salt Lake City *163,697* **C4**
Sandy *52,210* **C4**
Santaquin *2,175* **D4**
Smithfield *4,993* **B4**
South Jordan *7,492* **C3**
South Ogden *11,366* **B4**
Spanish Fork *9,825* **C4**
Springville *12,101* **C4**
Sunset *5,733* **B3**
Syracuse *3,702* **B3**
Tooele *14,335* **C3**
Tremonton *3,464* **B3**
Val Verda *6,500* **C4**
Vernal *6,600* **C6**
Washington *3,092* **F2**
Washington Terrace *8,212* **B4**
Wendover *1,099* **C1**
West Bountiful *3,556* **C4**
West Jordan *27,192* **C4**
West Valley City *72,511* **C4**
Woods Cross *4,263* **C4**

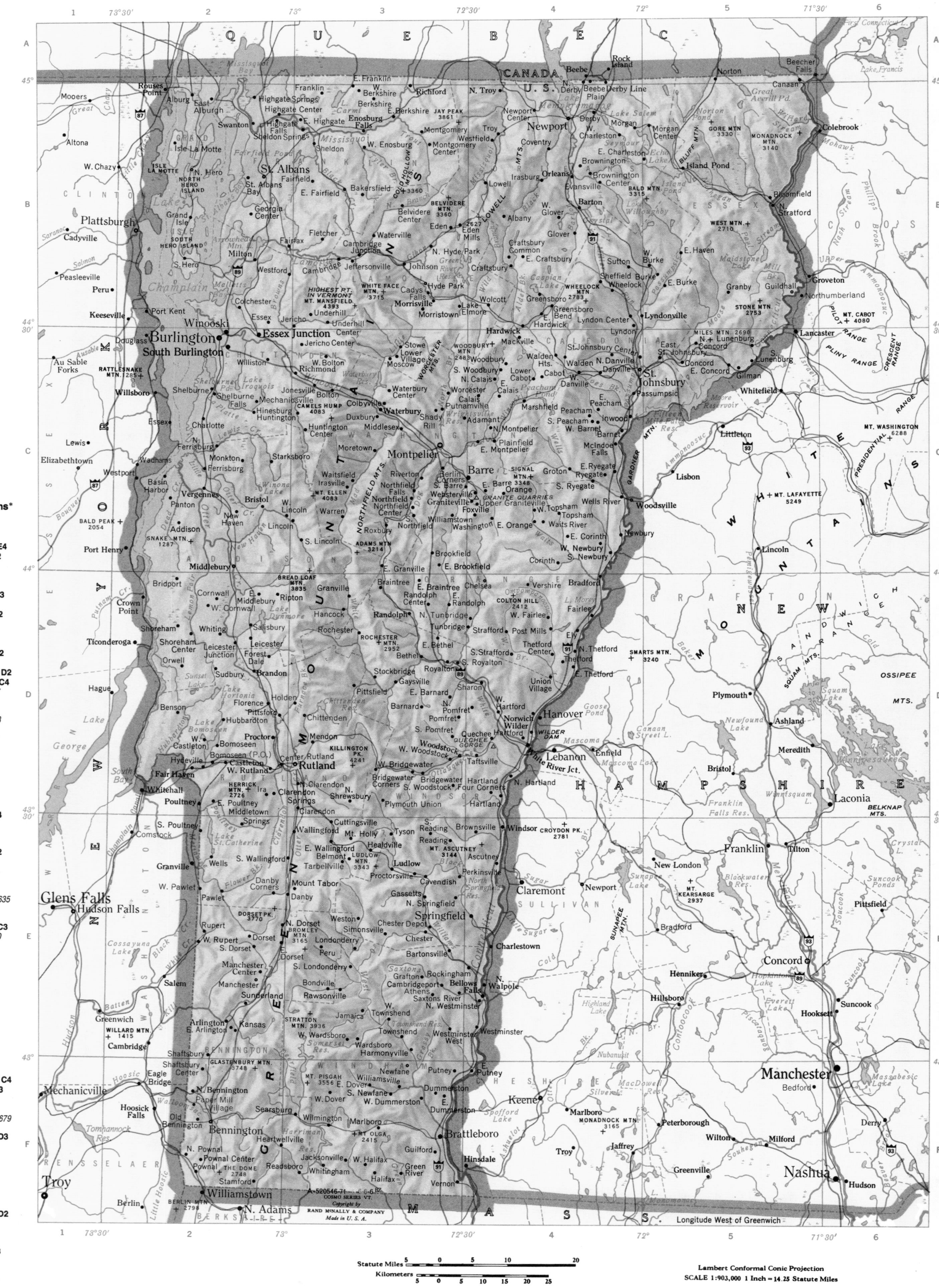

Cities and Towns*

Arlington 800 **E2**
Barre 9,824 **C4**
Barton 1,062 **B4**
Bellows Falls 3,456 **E4**
Bennington 8,600 **F2**
Bethel 900 **D3**
Bradford 831 **D4**
Brandon 1,720 **D2**
Brattleboro 11,886 **F3**
Bristol 1,793 **C2**
Burlington 37,712 **C2**
Castleton 600 **D2**
Derby 598 **B4**
Dorset 550 **E2**
East Arlington 600 **E2**
East Barre 900 **C4**
East Middlebury 550 **D2**
East Montpelier 600 **C4**
Enosburg Falls 1,207 **B3**
Essex 800 **B2**
Essex Junction 7,033 **C2**
Fair Haven 2,819 **D2**
Gilman 550 **C5**
Graniteville 600 **C4**
Hardwick 1,476 **B4**
Hartford 600 **D4**
Jericho 1,340 **B3**
Johnson 1,393 **B3**
Ludlow 1,352 **E3**
Lyndonville 1,401 **B4**
Manchester 563 **E2**
Manchester Center 1,060 **E2**
Middlebury 4,000 **C2**
Milton 1,411 **B2**
Montpelier 8,241 **C3**
Morrisville 2,074 **B3**
Newport 4,756 **B4**
North Bennington 1,635 **F2**
Northfield 2,033 **C3**
Northfield Falls 600 **C3**
North Springfield 750 **E3**
North Troy 717 **B4**
Norwich 1,000 **D4**
Orleans 983 **B4**
Pittsford 666 **D2**
Plainfield 599 **C4**
Poultney 1,554 **D2**
Proctor 1,998 **D2**
Putney 1,100 **F3**
Randolph 2,217 **D3**
Richford 1,471 **B3**
Richmond 865 **C3**
Rutland 18,436 **D3**
St. Albans 7,308 **B2**
St. Johnsbury 6,400 **C4**
Saxtons River 593 **E3**
Shaftsbury 700 **E2**
South Barre 900 **C3**
South Burlington 10,679 **C2**
South Royalton 700 **D3**
Springfield 5,632 **E4**
Stowe 531 **C3**
Swanton 2,520 **B2**
Vergennes 2,273 **C2**
Wallingford 800 **E3**
Waterbury 1,892 **C3**
Websterville 600 **C4**
West Rutland 2,351 **D2**
White River Junction 2,379 **D4**
Wilder 1,328 **D4**
Williamstown 650 **C3**
Wilmington 545 **F3**
Winooski 6,318 **C2**
Woodstock 1,178 **D3**

*Populations are for localities, not incorporated towns.

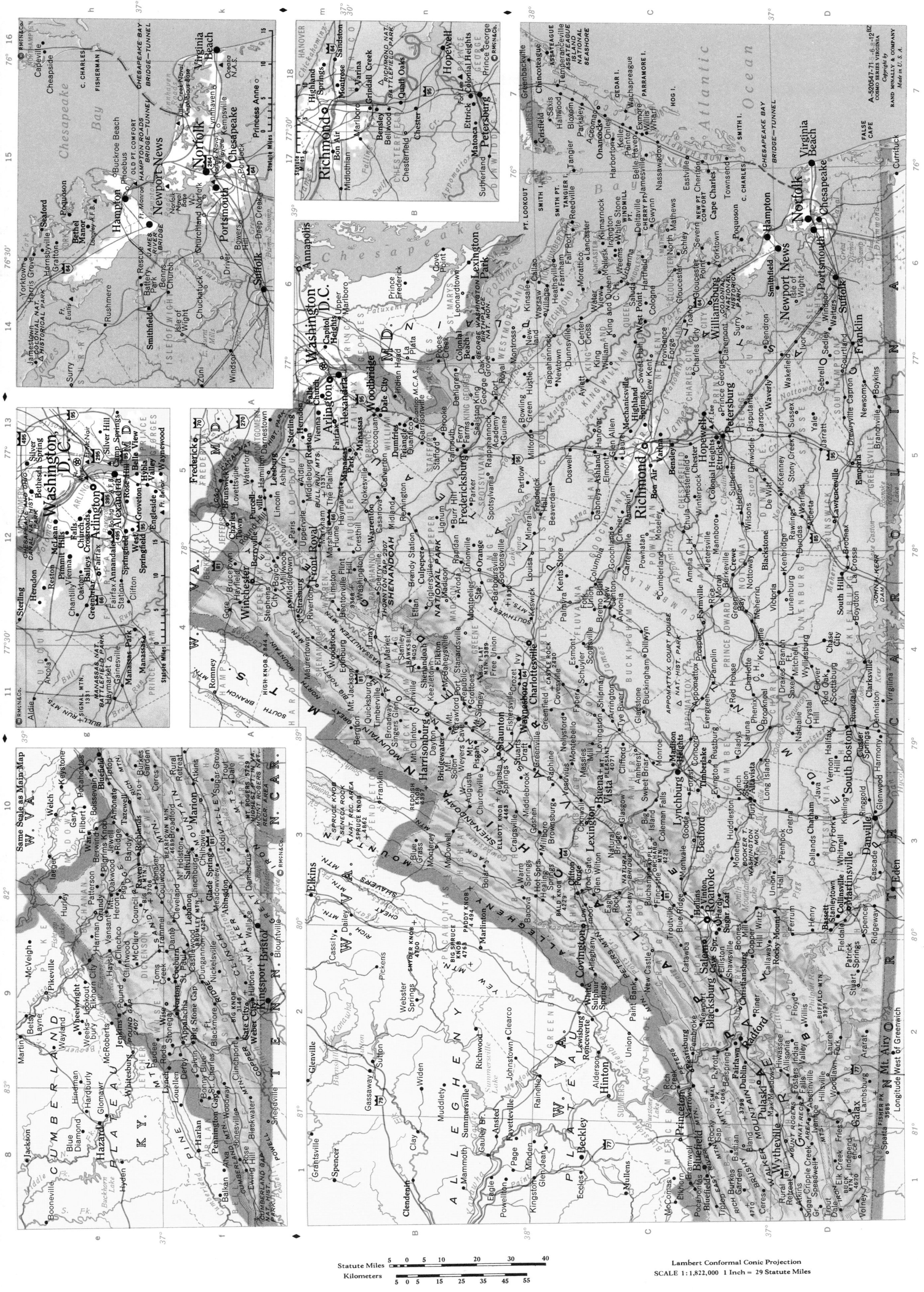

Cities and Towns

Alexandria 103,217 B5
Annandale 35,300 g12
Appomattox 1,345 C4
Arlington 152,700 B5
Bedford 5,991 C3
Big Stone Gap 4,748 f9
Blacksburg 30,638 C2
Bluefield 5,946 C1
Bon Air 13,000 C5
Bristol 19,042 f9
Buena Vista 6,717 C3
Charlottesville 39,916 B4
Chesapeake 114,486 D6
Chester 7,000 C5
Chincoteague 1,607 C7
Christiansburg 10,345 C2
Clifton Forge 5,046 C3
Collinsville 7,400 D3
Colonial Heights 16,509 C5
Covington 9,063 C3
Culpeper 6,621 B5
Dale City 23,000 B5
Danville 45,642 D3
Emporia 4,840 D5
Engleside 21,400 g12
Fairfax 19,390 B5
Farmville 6,067 C4
Franklin 7,308 D6
Fredericksburg 15,322 B5
Front Royal 11,126 B4
Galax 6,524 D2
Hampton 122,617 C6
Harrisonburg 19,671 B4
Herndon 11,449 B5
Highland Springs 7,500 C5
Hollins 11,000 C3
Hopewell 23,397 C5
Leesburg 8,357 A5
Lexington 7,292 C3
Lynchburg 66,743 C3
McLean 22,000 g12
Manassas 15,438 B5
Manassas Park 6,524 B5
Marion 7,029 f10
Martinsville 18,149 D3
Mechanicsville 9,000 C5
Newport News 144,903 D6
Norfolk 266,979 D6
Norton 4,757 f9
Petersburg 41,055 C5
Poquoson 8,726 C6
Portsmouth 104,577 D6
Pulaski 10,106 C2
Radford 13,225 C2
Reston 32,000 B5
Richlands 5,796 e10
Richmond 219,214 C5
Roanoke 100,220 C3
Salem 23,958 C2
Shenandoah 1,861 B4
South Boston 7,093 D4
Springfield 12,500 g12
Staunton 21,857 B3
Sterling 12,000 A5
Suffolk 47,621 D6
Tazewell 4,468 e10
Vienna 15,469 B5
Vinton 8,027 C3
Virginia Beach 262,199 D7
Waynesboro 15,329 B4
West Springfield 16,000 g12
Williamsburg 9,870 C6
Winchester 20,217 A4
Woodbridge 35,000 B5
Wytheville 7,135 D1
Yorktown 390 C6

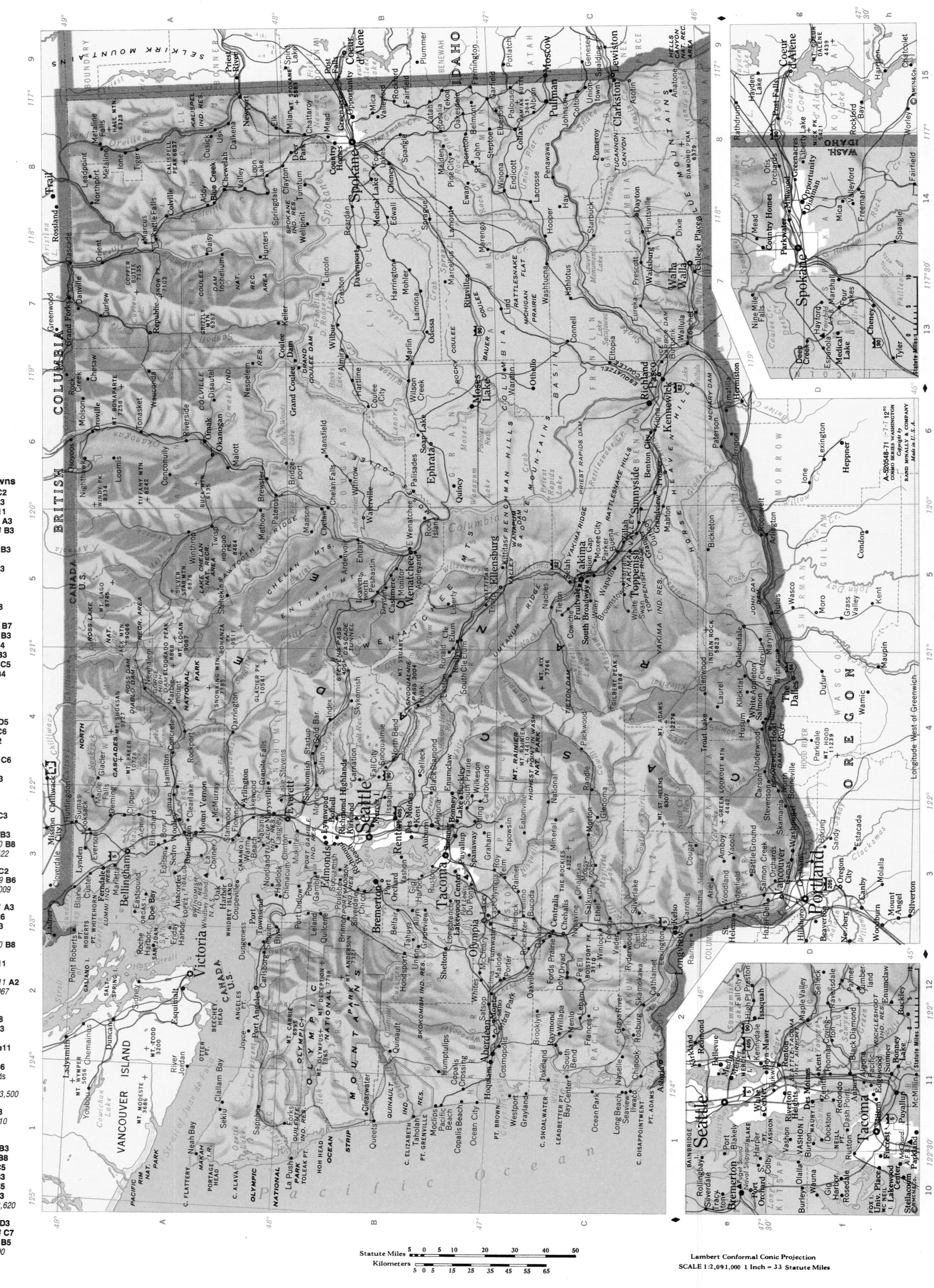

Cities and Towns

Aberdeen *18,739* **C2**
Anacortes *9,013* **A3**
Bellevue *73,903* **e11**
Bellingham *45,794* **A3**
Bonney Lake *5,328* **B3**
Bothell *7,943* **B3**
Bremerton *36,208* **B3**
Camas *5,681* **D3**
Centralia *11,555* **C3**
Chehalis *6,100* **C3**
Chelan *2,802* **B5**
Cheney *7,630* **B8**
Clarkston *6,903* **C8**
Colville *4,510* **A8**
Coulee Dam *1,412* **B7**
Des Moines *7,378* **B3**
Dishman *9,900* **g14**
Edmonds *27,679* **B3**
Ellensburg *11,752* **C5**
Enumclaw *5,427* **B4**
Ephrata *5,359* **B6**
Everett *54,413* **B3**
Ferndale *3,855* **A3**
Forks *3,060* **B1**
Goldendale *3,575* **D5**
Grandview *5,615* **C6**
Hoquiam *9,719* **C2**
Kelso *11,129* **C3**
Kennewick *34,397* **C6**
Kent *23,152* **B3**
Kirkland *18,779* **B3**
Lacey *13,940* **B3**
Lakewood Center *51,300* **B3**
Longview *31,052* **C3**
Lynden *4,022* **A3**
Lynnwood *22,641* **B3**
Medical Lake *3,600* **B8**
Mercer Island *21,522* **B3**
Montesano *3,247* **C2**
Moses Lake *10,629* **B6**
Mount Vernon *13,009* **A3**
Oak Harbor *12,271* **A3**
Okanogan *2,302* **A6**
Olympia *27,447* **B3**
Omak *4,007* **A6**
Opportunity *17,600* **B8**
Othello *4,454* **C6**
Parkland *22,300* **f11**
Pasco *18,425* **C6**
Port Angeles *17,311* **A2**
Port Townsend *6,067* **A3**
Prosser *3,896* **C6**
Pullman *23,579* **C8**
Puyallup *18,251* **B3**
Quincy *3,525* **B6**
Redmond *23,318* **e11**
Renton *30,612* **B3**
Richland *33,578* **C6**
Richmond Highlands *20,300* **B3**
Riverton Heights *33,500* **f11**
Seattle *493,846* **B3**
Sedro Woolley *6,110* **A3**
Shelton *7,629* **B2**
Snohomish *5,294* **B3**
Spokane *171,300* **B8**
Sunnyside *9,225* **C5**
Tacoma *158,501* **B3**
Toppenish *6,517* **C5**
Tumwater *6,705* **B3**
University Place *13,620* **f10**
Vancouver *42,834* **D3**
Walla Walla *25,618* **C7**
Wenatchee *17,257* **B5**
White Center *19,700* **e11**
Yakima *49,826* **C5**

Statute Miles 5 0 5 10 20 30 40 50
Kilometers 5 0 5 15 25 35 45 55 65

Lambert Conformal Conic Projection
SCALE 1:2,091,000 1 Inch = 33 Statute Miles

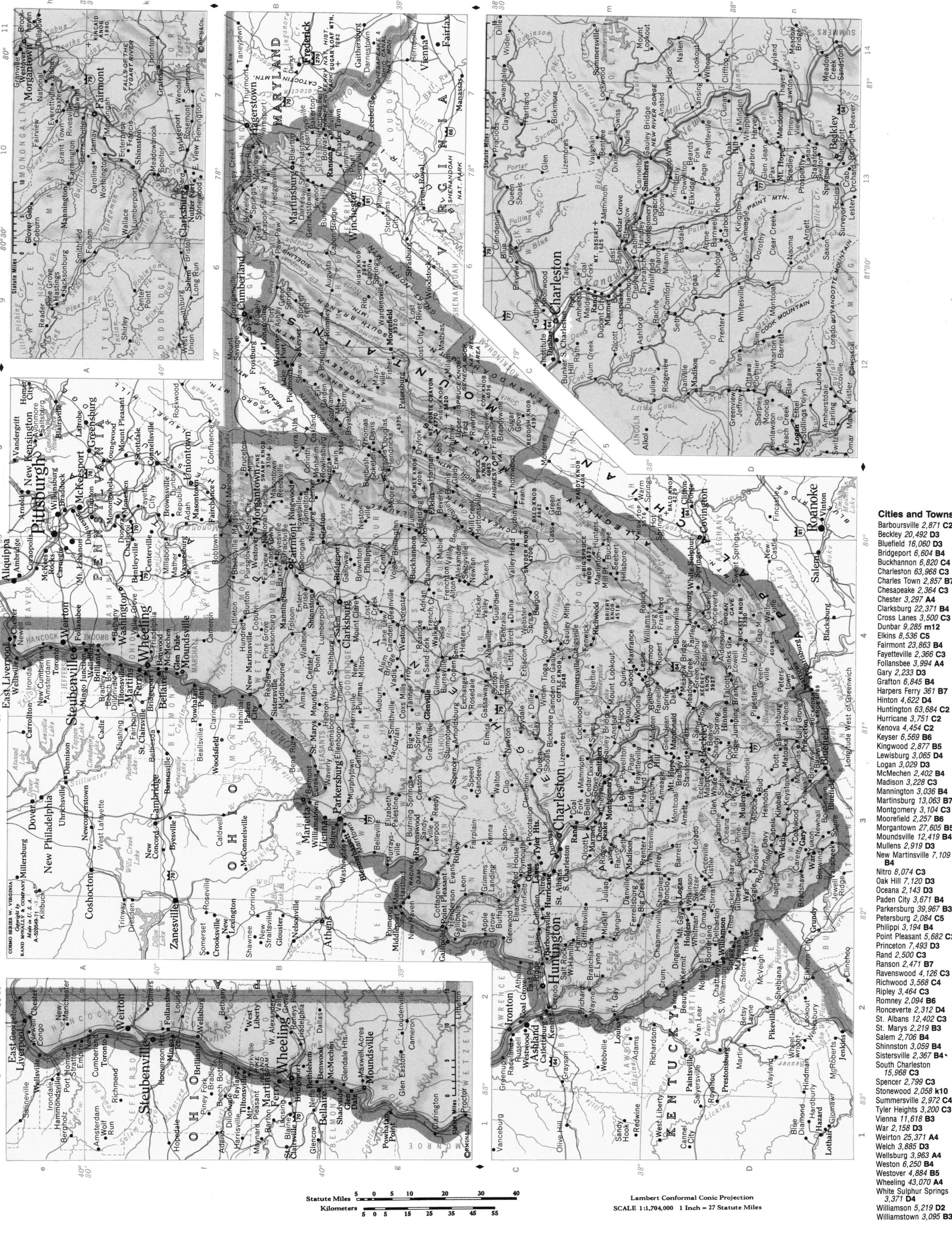

Cities and Towns

Barboursville *2,871* **C2**
Beckley *20,492* **D3**
Bluefield *16,060* **D3**
Bridgeport *6,604* **B4**
Buckhannon *6,820* **C4**
Charleston *63,968* **C3**
Charles Town *2,857* **B7**
Chesapeake *2,364* **C3**
Chester *3,297* **A4**
Clarksburg *22,371* **B4**
Cross Lanes *3,500* **C3**
Dunbar *9,285* **m12**
Elkins *8,536* **C5**
Fairmont *23,863* **B4**
Fayetteville *2,366* **C3**
Follansbee *3,994* **A4**
Gary *2,233* **D3**
Grafton *6,845* **B4**
Harpers Ferry *361* **B7**
Hinton *4,622* **D4**
Huntington *63,684* **C2**
Hurricane *3,751* **C2**
Kenova *4,454* **C2**
Keyser *6,569* **B6**
Kingwood *2,877* **B5**
Lewisburg *3,065* **D4**
Logan *3,029* **D3**
McMechen *2,402* **B4**
Madison *3,228* **C3**
Mannington *3,036* **B4**
Martinsburg *13,063* **B7**
Montgomery *3,104* **C3**
Moorefield *2,257* **B6**
Morgantown *27,605* **B5**
Moundsville *12,419* **B4**
Mullens *2,919* **D3**
New Martinsville *7,109* **B4**
Nitro *8,074* **C3**
Oak Hill *7,120* **D3**
Oceana *2,143* **D3**
Paden City *3,671* **B4**
Parkersburg *39,967* **B3**
Petersburg *2,084* **C5**
Philippi *3,194* **B4**
Point Pleasant *5,682* **C2**
Princeton *7,493* **D3**
Rand *2,500* **C3**
Ranson *2,471* **B7**
Ravenswood *4,126* **C3**
Richwood *3,568* **C4**
Ripley *3,464* **C3**
Romney *2,094* **B6**
Ronceverte *2,312* **D4**
St. Albans *12,402* **C3**
St. Marys *2,219* **B3**
Salem *2,706* **B4**
Shinnston *3,059* **B4**
Sistersville *2,367* **B4**
South Charleston *15,968* **C3**
Spencer *2,799* **C3**
Stonewood *2,058* **k10**
Summersville *2,972* **C4**
Tyler Heights *3,200* **C3**
Vienna *11,618* **B3**
War *2,158* **D3**
Weirton *25,371* **A4**
Welch *3,885* **D3**
Wellsburg *3,963* **A4**
Weston *6,250* **B4**
Westover *4,884* **B5**
Wheeling *43,070* **A4**
White Sulphur Springs *3,371* **D4**
Williamson *5,219* **D2**
Williamstown *3,095* **B3**

WISCONSIN

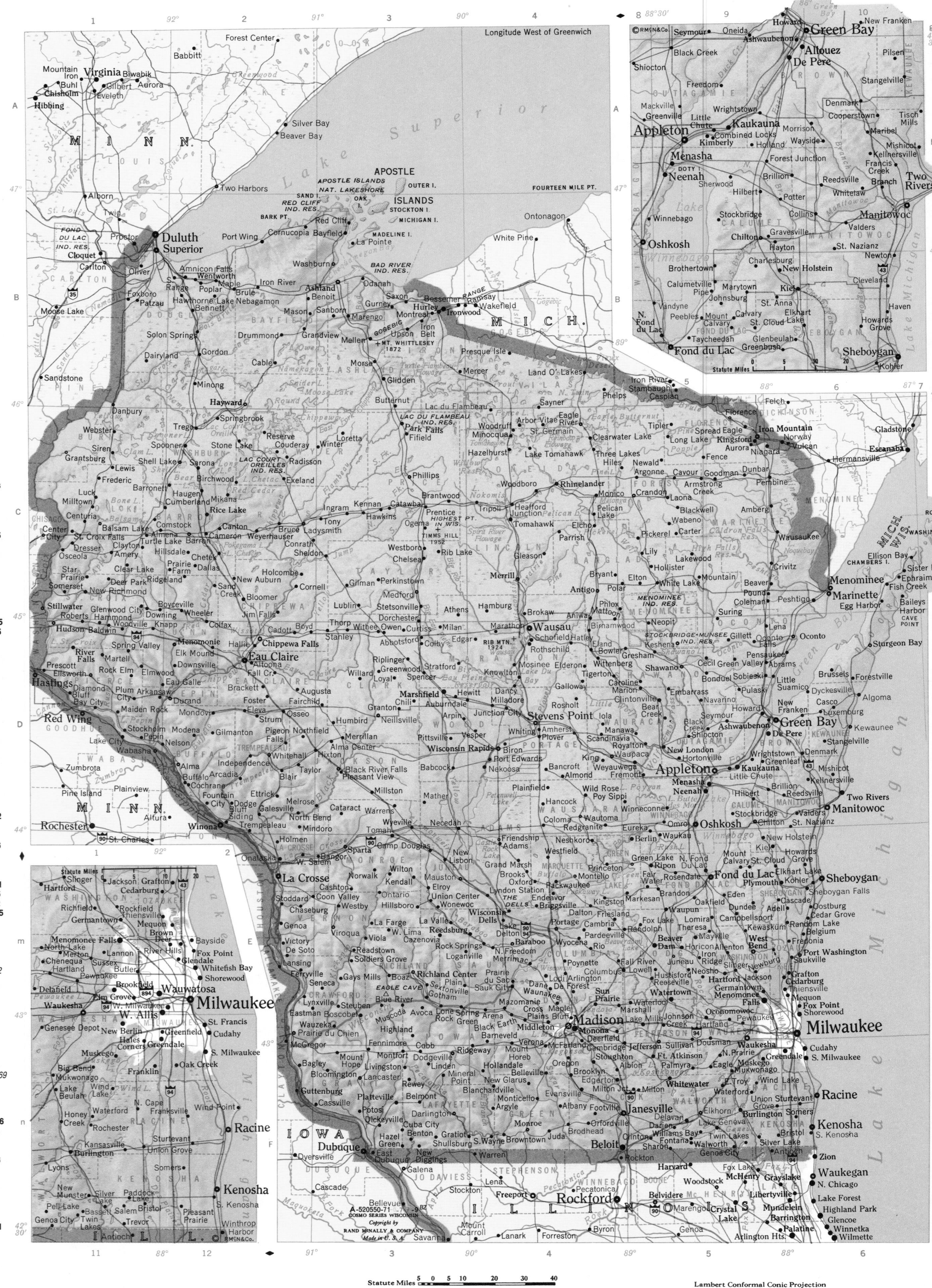

Cities and Towns

Antigo *8,653* **C4**
Appleton *58,913* **D5**
Ashland *9,115* **B3**
Baraboo *8,081* **E4**
Beaver Dam *14,149* **E5**
Beloit *35,207* **F4**
Brookfield *34,035* **m11**
Burlington *8,385* **F5**
Chippewa Falls *12,270* **D2**
Cudahy *19,547* **F6**
De Pere *14,892* **D5**
Eau Claire *51,509* **D2**
Fond du Lac *35,863* **E5**
Fort Atkinson *9,785* **F5**
Franklin *16,871* **n11**
Green Bay *87,899* **D6**
Greendale *16,928* **F5**
Greenfield *31,467* **n11**
Hayward *1,698* **B2**
Hudson *5,434* **D1**
Janesville *51,071* **F4**
Kaukauna *11,310* **D5**
Kenosha *77,685* **F6**
La Crosse *48,347* **E2**
Lake Geneva *5,612* **F5**
Madison *170,616* **E4**
Manitowoc *32,547* **D6**
Marinette *11,965* **C6**
Marshfield *18,290* **D3**
Menasha *14,728* **D5**
Menomonee Falls *27,845* **E5**
Menomonie *12,769* **D2**
Mequon *16,193* **E6**
Merrill *9,578* **C4**
Milwaukee *636,236* **E6**
Monroe *10,027* **F4**
Muskego *15,277* **F5**
Neenah *22,432* **D5**
New Berlin *30,529* **n11**
New London *6,210* **D5**
Oak Creek *16,932* **n12**
Oconomowoc *9,909* **E5**
Oconto *4,505* **D6**
Oshkosh *49,620* **D5**
Park Falls *3,192* **C3**
Platteville *9,580* **F3**
Portage *7,896* **E4**
Port Washington *8,612* **E6**
Prairie du Chien *5,859* **E2**
Racine *85,725* **F6**
Reedsburg *5,038* **E3**
Rhinelander *7,873* **C4**
Rice Lake *7,691* **C2**
River Falls *9,019* **D1**
Shawano *7,013* **D5**
Sheboygan *48,085* **E6**
South Milwaukee *21,069* **F6**
Stevens Point *22,970* **D4**
Stoughton *7,589* **F4**
Sturgeon Bay *8,847* **D6**
Sun Prairie *12,931* **E4**
Superior *29,571* **B1**
Tomah *7,204* **E3**
Two Rivers *13,354* **D6**
Watertown *18,113* **E5**
Waukesha *50,365* **E5**
Waupun *8,132* **E5**
Wausau *32,426* **D4**
Wauwatosa *51,308* **m11**
West Allis *63,982* **m11**
West Bend *21,484* **E5**
Whitefish Bay *14,930* **m12**
Whitewater *11,520* **F5**
Wisconsin Dells *2,521* **E4**
Wisconsin Rapids *17,995* **D4**

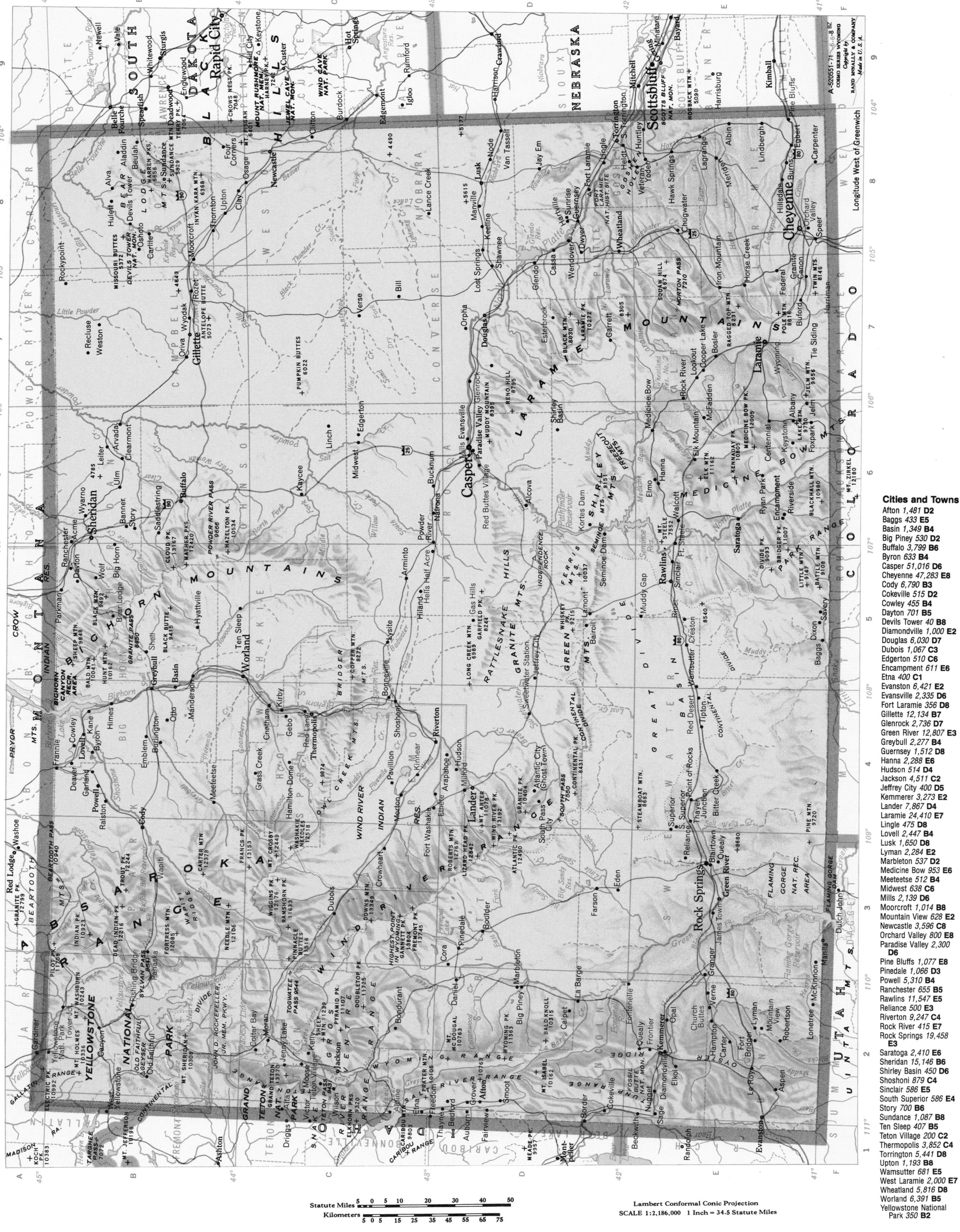

Lambert Conformal Conic Projection
SCALE 1:2,186,000 1 Inch = 34.5 Statute Miles

Statute Miles 5 0 5 10 20 30 40 50
Kilometers 5 0 5 15 25 35 45 55 65 75

Cities and Towns

Afton *1,481* **D2**
Baggs *433* **E5**
Basin *1,349* **B4**
Big Piney *530* **D2**
Buffalo *3,799* **B6**
Byron *633* **B4**
Casper *51,016* **D6**
Cheyenne *47,283* **E8**
Cody *6,790* **B3**
Cokeville *515* **D2**
Cowley *455* **B4**
Dayton *701* **B5**
Devils Tower *40* **B8**
Diamondville *1,000* **E2**
Douglas *6,030* **D7**
Dubois *1,067* **C3**
Edgerton *510* **C6**
Encampment *611* **E6**
Etna *400* **C1**
Evanston *6,421* **E2**
Evansville *2,335* **D6**
Fort Laramie *356* **D8**
Gillette *12,134* **B7**
Glenrock *2,736* **D7**
Green River *12,807* **E3**
Greybull *2,277* **B4**
Guernsey *1,512* **D8**
Hanna *2,288* **E6**
Hudson *514* **D4**
Jackson *4,511* **C2**
Jeffrey City *400* **D5**
Kemmerer *3,273* **E2**
Lander *7,867* **D4**
Laramie *24,410* **E7**
Lingle *475* **D8**
Lovell *2,447* **B4**
Lusk *1,650* **D8**
Lyman *2,284* **E2**
Marbleton *537* **D2**
Medicine Bow *953* **E6**
Meeteetse *512* **B4**
Midwest *638* **C6**
Mills *2,139* **D6**
Moorcroft *1,014* **B8**
Mountain View *628* **E2**
Newcastle *3,596* **C8**
Orchard Valley *800* **E8**
Paradise Valley *2,300* **D6**
Pine Bluffs *1,077* **E8**
Pinedale *1,066* **D3**
Powell *5,310* **B4**
Ranchester *655* **B5**
Rawlins *11,547* **E5**
Reliance *500* **E3**
Riverton *9,247* **C4**
Rock River *415* **E7**
Rock Springs *19,458* **E3**
Saratoga *2,410* **E6**
Sheridan *15,146* **B6**
Shirley Basin *450* **D6**
Shoshoni *879* **C4**
Sinclair *586* **E5**
South Superior *586* **E4**
Story *700* **B6**
Sundance *1,087* **B8**
Ten Sleep *407* **B5**
Teton Village *200* **C2**
Thermopolis *3,852* **C4**
Torrington *5,441* **D8**
Upton *1,193* **B8**
Wamsutter *681* **E5**
West Laramie *2,000* **E7**
Wheatland *5,816* **D8**
Worland *6,391* **B5**
Yellowstone National Park *350* **B2**

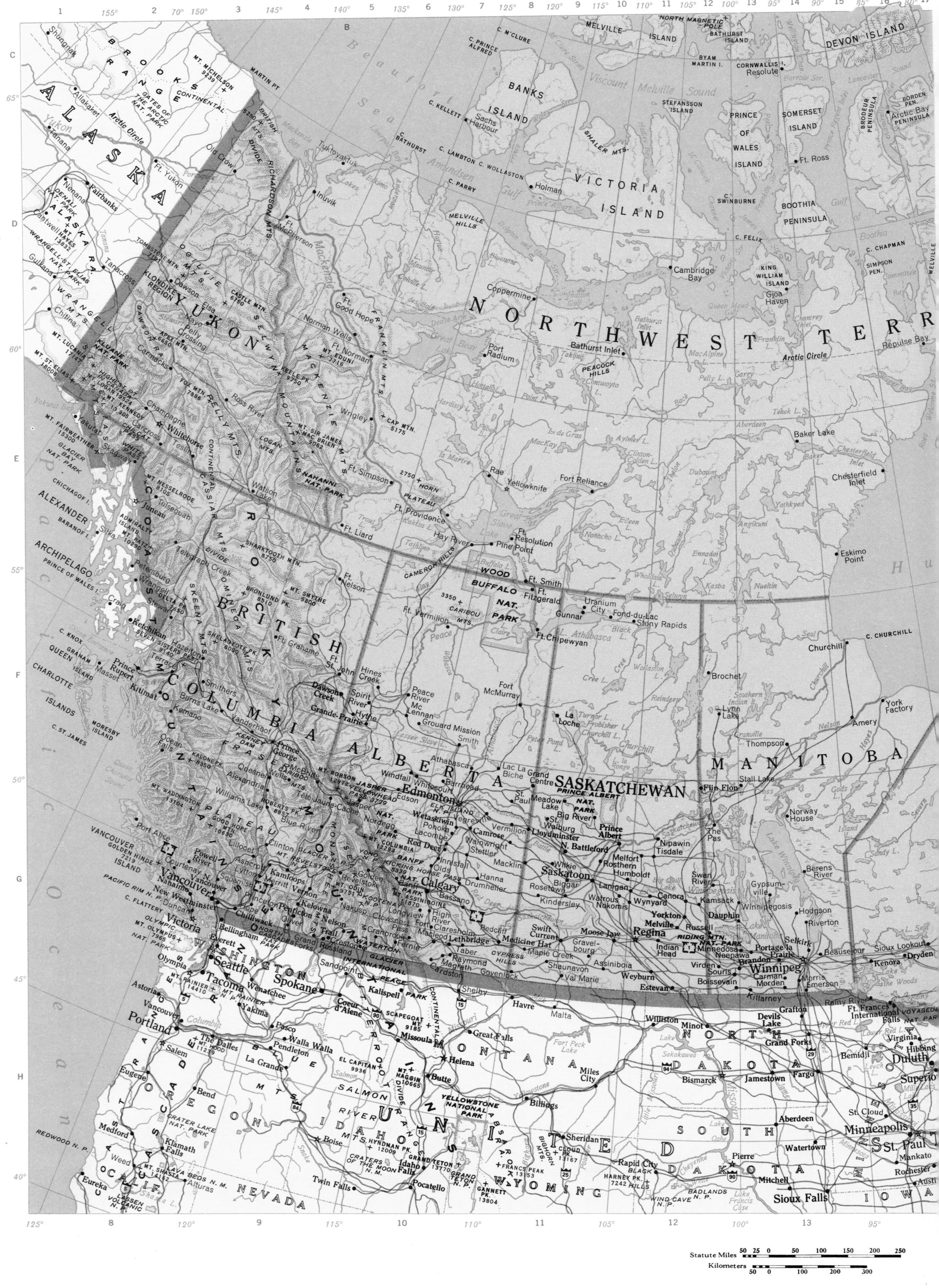
ALASKA
YUKON
NORTHWEST TERR
BRITISH COLUMBIA
ALBERTA
SASKATCHEWAN
MANITOBA
VICTORIA ISLAND
BANKS ISLAND
MELVILLE ISLAND
DEVON ISLAND
PRINCE OF WALES ISLAND
SOMERSET ISLAND
BOOTHIA PENINSULA
KING WILLIAM ISLAND
QUEEN CHARLOTTE ISLANDS
VANCOUVER ISLAND
ALEXANDER ARCHIPELAGO
BROOKS RANGE
MACKENZIE MOUNTAINS
SELWYN MTS.
ROCKY MTS.
COAST MTS.
WASHINGTON
OREGON
IDAHO
MONTANA
WYOMING
NORTH DAKOTA
SOUTH DAKOTA
NEVADA
CALIF.
IOWA
Beaufort Sea
Pacific Ocean
Arctic Circle
Fairbanks
Whitehorse
Dawson
Yellowknife
Edmonton
Calgary
Vancouver
Victoria
Seattle
Spokane
Tacoma
Portland
Regina
Saskatoon
Winnipeg
Churchill
Inuvik
Prince Rupert
Prince George
Kamloops
Lethbridge
Medicine Hat
Moose Jaw
Prince Albert
Red Deer
Helena
Missoula
Boise
Billings
Bismarck
Fargo
Duluth
Minneapolis
St. Paul
Sioux Falls
Pierre
Rapid City
Statute Miles 50 25 0 50 100 150 200 250
Kilometers 50 0 100 200 300

Lambert Conformal Conic Projection
SCALE 1:12,000,000 1 Inch = 189 Statute Miles

Northwest Territories

Cities and Towns

Alert **k9**
Arctic Bay *375* **B16**
Baker Lake *954* **D13**
Bathurst Inlet *20* **C11**
Cambridge Bay *815* **C12**
Chesterfield Inlet *249* **D14**
Coppermine *352* **C15**
Eskimo Point *1,022* **D14**
Eureka **m34**
Ft. Franklin *521* **C8**
Ft. Good Hope *463* **C7**
Ft. Laird *405* **D8**
Ft. McPherson *632* **C6**
Ft. Norman *286* **D7**
Ft. Providence *605* **D9**
Ft. Resolution *480* **D10**
Ft. Simpson *980* **D8**
Ft. Smith *2,298* **D10**
Gjoa Haven *523* **C13**
Hay River *2,863* **D9**
Inuvik *3,147* **C6**
Norman Wells *420* **C7**
Pine Point *1,861* **D10**
Rae *1,378* **D9**
Rankin Inlet *1,109* **D14**
Repulse Bay *352* **C15**
Snowdrift *253* **D10**
Spence Bay *431* **C14**
Yellowknife *9,483* **D10**

Yukon

Cities and Towns

Carmacks *256* **D5**
Carcross *216* **D6**
Dawson *697* **D5**
Destruction Bay *45* **D5**
Elas *336* **D5**
Faro *1,652* **D6**
Haines Junction *366* **D5**
Mayo *398* **D5**
Old Crow *243* **C5**
Pelly Crossing *182* **D5**
Ross River *294* **D6**
Teslin *310* **D6**
Watson Lake *748* **D7**
Whitehorse *14,814* **D6**

Alberta

Cities and Towns

Airdrie *8,414* **D3**
Athabasca *1,731* **B4**
Banff *4,208* **D3**
Barrhead *3,736* **B3**
Bonnyville *4,454* **B5**
Bow Island *1,491* **E5**
Brooks *9,421* **D5**
Calgary *592,743* **D3**
Camrose *12,570* **C4**
Canmore *3,484* **D3**
Cardston *3,267* **E4**
Coaldale *4,579* **E4**
Cochrane *3,544* **D3**
Cold Lake *2,110* **B5**
Coronation *1,309* **C5**
Crowsnest Pass *7,306* **E3**
Devon *3,885* **C4**
Didsbury *3,095* **D3**
Drayton Valley *5,042* **C3**
Drumheller *6,508* **D4**
Edmonton *532,246* **C4**
Edson *5,835* **C2**
Fairview *2,869* **A1**
Fort Chipewyan *944* **f8**
Fort Macleod *3,139* **E4**
Fort McMurray *31,000* **A5**
Fort Saskatchewan *12,169* **C4**
Gibbons *2,276* **C4**
Grand Centre *3,146* **B5**
Grande Cache *4,523* **C1**
Grande Prairie *24,263* **B1**
Grimshaw *2,316* **A2**
Hanna *2,806* **D5**
High Prairie *2,506* **B2**
High River *4,792* **D4**
Hinton *8,342* **C2**
Innisfail *5,247* **C4**
Jasper *3,269* **C1**
Lac La Biche *2,007* **B5**
La Crete *479* **f7**
Lake Louise *355* **D2**
Leduc *12,471* **C4**
Lethbridge *54,072* **E4**
Lloydminster *15,031* **C5**
Magrath *1,576* **E4**
Medicine Hat *40,380* **D5**
Morinville *4,657* **C4**
Nordegg *63* **C2**
Okotoks *3,847* **D4**
Olds *4,813* **D3**
Peace River *5,907* **A2**
Pincher Creek *3,757* **E4**
Ponoka *5,221* **C4**
Raymond *2,837* **E4**
Redcliff *3,876* **D5**
Red Deer *46,393* **C4**
Rocky Mountain House *4,698* **C3**
St. Albert *31,996* **C4**
St. Paul *4,884* **B5**
Sherwood Park *29,285* **C4**
Slave Lake *4,506* **B3**
Smith *216* **B3**
Spruce Grove *10,326* **C4**
Stettler *5,136* **C4**
Stony Plain *4,839* **C3**
Strathmore *2,986* **D4**
Swan Hills *2,497* **B3**
Sylvan Lake *3,779* **C3**
Taber *5,988* **E4**
Valleyview *2,061* **B2**
Vegreville *5,251* **C4**
Vermilion *3,766* **C5**
Vulcan *1,489* **D4**
Wainwright *4,266* **C5**
Westlock *4,424* **B4**
Wetaskiwin *9,597* **C4**
Whitecourt *5,585* **B3**

British Columbia

Cities and Towns

Abbotsford *12,745* **f13**
Armstrong *2,683* **D8**
Burnaby *136,494* **f13**
Burns Lake *1,777* **B5**
Campbell River *15,832* **D5**
Castlegar *6,902* **E9**
Chase *1,777* **D8**
Chetwynd *2,553* **B7**
Chilliwack *40,642* **f14**
Comax *6,607* **E5**
Courtenay *8,992* **E5**
Cranbrook *15,915* **E10**
Creston *4,190* **E9**
Cumberland *1,947* **E5**
Dawson Creek *11,373* **B7**
Duncan *4,228* **g12**
Enderby *1,816* **D8**
Esquimalt *15,870* **h12**
Fernie *5,444* **E10**
Fort Langley *2,326* **f13**
Fort Nelson *3,724* **m18**
Fort St. James *2,284* **B5**
Fort St. John *13,891* **A7**
Fraser Lake *1,543* **B5**
Fruitvale *1,904* **E9**
Gibsons *2,594* **E6**
Golden *3,476* **D9**
Grand Forks *3,486* **E8**
Houston *1,714* **B4**
Invermere *1,969* **D9**
Kamloops *64,048* **D7**
Kelowna *59,196* **E8**
Kimberley *7,375* **E9**
Kitimat *12,814* **B3**
Ladysmith *4,558* **g12**
Lake Cowichan *2,391* **g11**
Langley *15,124* **f13**
Lillooet *1,725* **D7**
Masset *1,569* **C1**
Merritt *6,110* **D7**
Mission *9,948* **f13**
Nanaimo *47,069* **f12**
Nelson *9,143* **E9**
New Westminster *38,55* **f13**
North Vancouver *33,952* **E6**
Oak Bay *16,990* **h12**
100 Mile House *1,925* **D7**
Osoyoos *2,738* **E8**
Parksville *5,216* **E5**
Penticton *23,181* **E8**
Port Alberni *19,892* **E5**
Port Alice *1,668* **D4**
Port Coquitlam *27,535* **f13**
Port Hardy *3,778* **D4**
Powell River *13,423* **E5**
Prince George *67,559* **C6**
Prince Rupert *16,197* **B2**
Qualicum Beach *2,844* **E5**
Quesnel *8,240* **C6**
Revelstoke *5,544* **D8**
Richmond *96,154* **f12**
Salmon Arm *1,946* **D8**
Sidney *7,946* **g12**
Smithers *4,570* **B4**
Squamish *1,590* **E6**
Summerland *7,473* **E8**
Terrace *10,914* **B3**
Trail *9,599* **E9**
Ucluelet *1,593* **E5**
Vancouver *414,281* **f12**
Vanderhoof *2,323* **C5**
Vernon *19,987* **D8**
Victoria *64,379* **h12**
Warfield *1,969* **E9**
White Rock *13,550* **f13**
Williams Lake *8,362* **C**

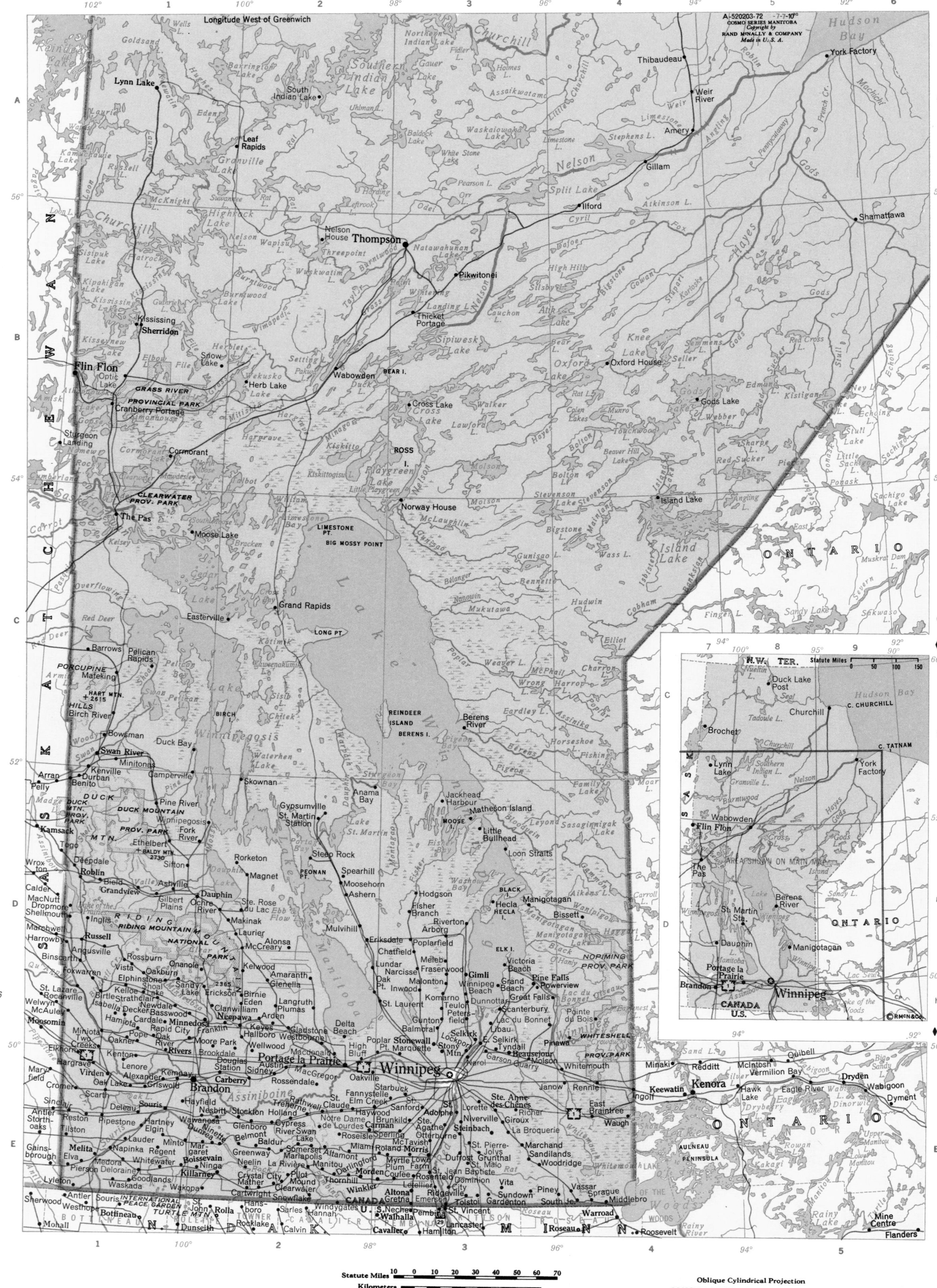

Manitoba

Cities and Towns

Altona *2,757* **E3**
Arborg *974* **D3**
Ashern *570* **D2**
Beausejour *2,462* **D3**
Berens River *238* **C3**
Birch River *597* **C1**
Birtle *887* **D1**
Boissevain *1,660* **E1**
Brandon *36,242* **E2**
Camperville *586* **D1**
Carberry *1,510* **E2**
Carman *2,408* **E2**
Churchill *1,304* **f9**
Cormorant *445* **B1**
Cranberry Portage *948* **B1**
Cross Lake *510* **B3**
Dauphin *8,971* **D1**
Deloraine *1,136* **E1**
Duck Bay *594* **C1**
Easterville *589* **C2**
Emerson *762* **E3**
Flin Flon *8,261* **B1**
Gilbert Plains *812* **D1**
Gillam *1,427* **A4**
Gladstone *964* **D2**
Glenboro *741* **E2**
Grand Rapids *567* **C2**
Grandview *1,013* **D1**
Hamiota *728* **D1**
Ilford *149* **A4**
Killarney *2,342* **E2**
Lac-du-Bonnet *985* **D3**
Lorette *1,092* **E3**
Lynn Lake *2,087* **A1**
MacGregor *795* **E2**
Manigotagan *216* **D3**
Manitou *861* **E2**
Melita *1,156* **E1**
Minnedosa *2,637* **D2**
Moose Lake *557* **C1**
Morden *4,579* **E2**
Morris *1,570* **E3**
Neepawa *3,425* **D2**
Niverville *1,329* **E3**
Norway House *441* **C3**
Pilot Mound *838* **E2**
Pine Falls *885* **D3**
Plum Coulee *592* **E3**
Portage-la-Prairie *13,086* **E2**
Rivers *1,107* **D1**
Roblin *1,953* **D1**
Rossburn *696* **D1**
Russell *1,660* **D1**
Ste. Anne-des-Chênes *1,338* **E3**
St. Laurent *1,114* **D3**
St. Pierre-Jolys *919* **E3**
Ste. Rose-du-Lac *1,090* **D2**
Selkirk *10,037* **D3**
Sherridon *138* **B1**
Shoal Lake *835* **D1**
Snow Lake *1,853* **B1**
Souris *1,731* **E1**
South Indian Lake *770* **A2**
Steinbach *6,676* **E3**
Stonewall *2,210* **D3**
Stony Mountain *1,313* **D3**
Swan River *3,782* **C1**
The Pas *6,390* **C1**
Thompson *14,288* **B3**
Virden *2,940* **E1**
Wabowden *655* **B2**
Winkler *5,046* **E3**
Winnipeg *564,473* **E3**
Winnipegosis *855* **D2**
York Factory **A5**

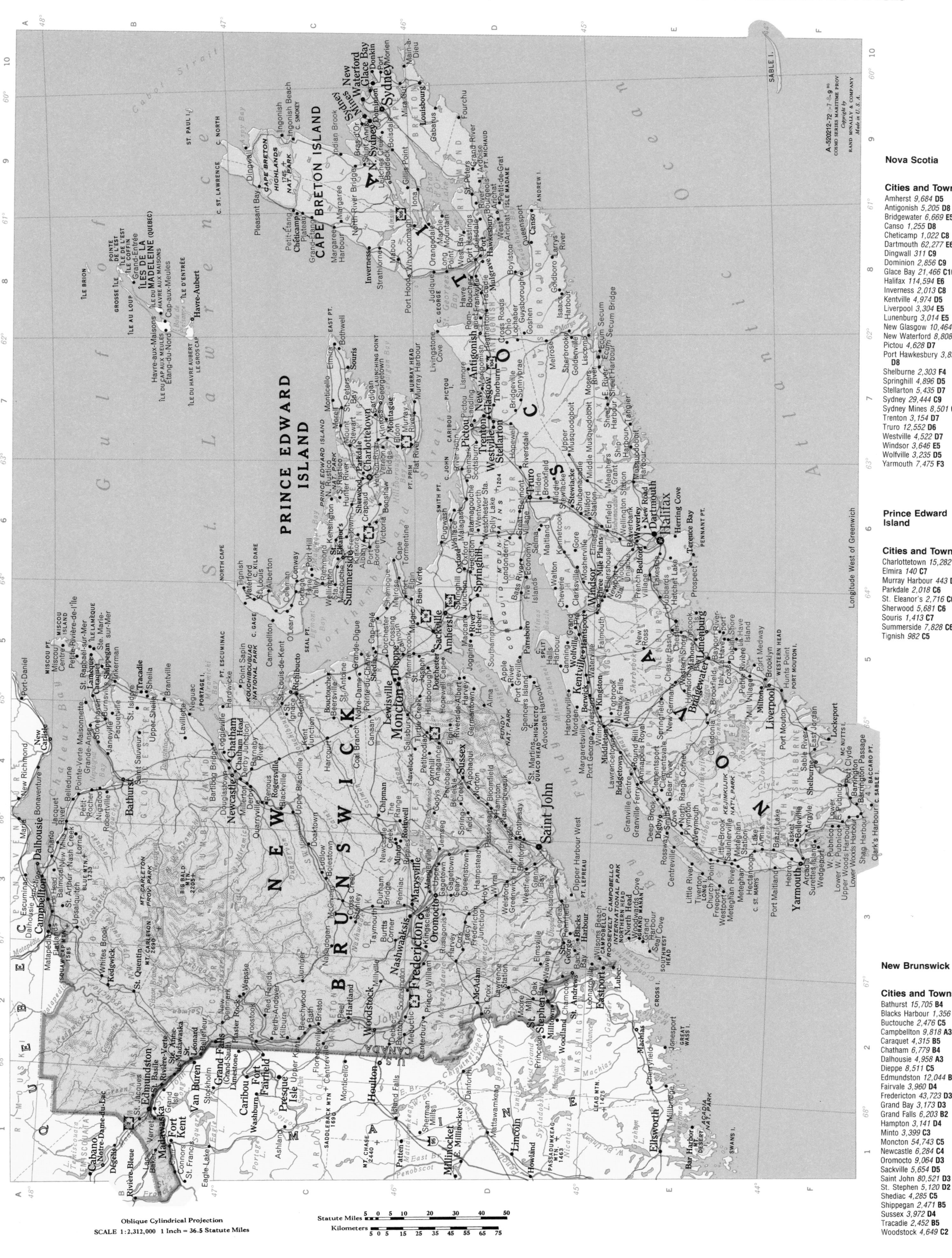

Nova Scotia

Cities and Towns

Amherst *9,684* **D5**
Antigonish *5,205* **D8**
Bridgewater *6,669* **E5**
Canso *1,255* **D8**
Cheticamp *1,022* **C8**
Dartmouth *62,277* **E6**
Dingwall *311* **C9**
Dominion *2,856* **C9**
Glace Bay *21,466* **C10**
Halifax *114,594* **E6**
Inverness *2,013* **C8**
Kentville *4,974* **D5**
Liverpool *3,304* **E5**
Lunenburg *3,014* **E5**
New Glasgow *10,464* **D7**
New Waterford *8,808* **C9**
Pictou *4,628* **D7**
Port Hawkesbury *3,850* **D8**
Shelburne *2,303* **F4**
Springhill *4,896* **D5**
Stellarton *5,435* **D7**
Sydney *29,444* **C9**
Sydney Mines *8,501* **C9**
Trenton *3,154* **D7**
Truro *12,552* **D6**
Westville *4,522* **D7**
Windsor *3,646* **E5**
Wolfville *3,235* **D5**
Yarmouth *7,475* **F3**

Prince Edward Island

Cities and Towns

Charlottetown *15,282* **C6**
Elmira *140* **C7**
Murray Harbour *443* **D7**
Parkdale *2,018* **C6**
St. Eleanor's *2,716* **C6**
Sherwood *5,681* **C6**
Souris *1,413* **C7**
Summerside *7,828* **C6**
Tignish *982* **C5**

New Brunswick

Cities and Towns

Bathurst *15,705* **B4**
Blacks Harbour *1,356* **D3**
Buctouche *2,476* **C5**
Campbellton *9,818* **A3**
Caraquet *4,315* **B5**
Chatham *6,779* **B4**
Dalhousie *4,958* **A3**
Dieppe *8,511* **C5**
Edmundston *12,044* **B1**
Fairvale *3,960* **D4**
Fredericton *43,723* **D3**
Grand Bay *3,173* **D3**
Grand Falls *6,203* **B2**
Hampton *3,141* **D4**
Minto *3,399* **C3**
Moncton *54,743* **C5**
Newcastle *6,284* **C4**
Oromocto *9,064* **D3**
Sackville *5,654* **D5**
Saint John *80,521* **D3**
St. Stephen *5,120* **D2**
Shediac *4,285* **C5**
Shippegan *2,471* **B5**
Sussex *3,972* **D4**
Tracadie *2,452* **B5**
Woodstock *4,649* **C2**

NEWFOUNDLAND

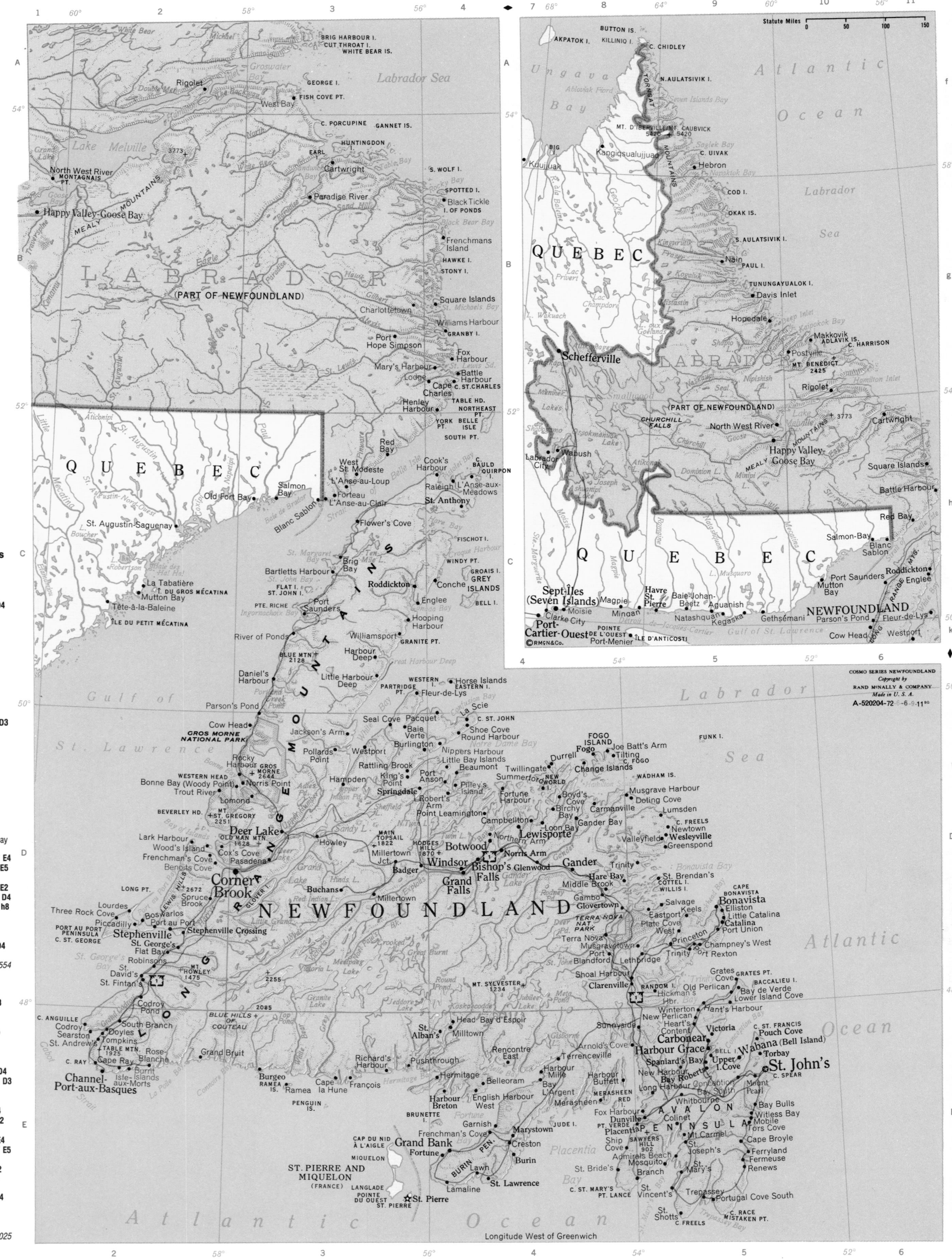

Newfoundland

Cities and Towns

Badger 1,090 D3
Baie Verte 2,491 D3
Bay Bulls 1,081 E5
Bay Roberts 4,512 E5
Bishop's Falls 4,395 D4
Bonavista 4,460 D5
Botwood 4,074 D4
Buchans 1,655 D3
Burgeo 2,504 E3
Burin 2,904 E4
Carbonear 5,335 E5
Cartwright 658 D4
Catalina 1,162 D5
Channel-Port-aux-Basques 5,988 E2
Clarenville 2,878 D4
Corner Brook 24,339 D3
Deer Lake 4,348 D3
Dunville 1,817 E5
Durrell 1,145 D4
Fogo 1,105 D4
Fortune 2,473 E4
Gambo 2,932 D4
Gander 10,404 D4
Glenwood 1,129 D4
Glovertown 2,165 D4
Grand Bank 3,901 E4
Grand Falls 8,765 D4
Happy Valley-Goose Bay 7,103 B1
Harbour Breton 2,464 E4
Harbour Grace 2,988 E5
Hare Bay 1,520 D4
Isle-aux-Morts 1,238 E2
Joe Batt's Arm 1,155 D4
Labrador City 11,538 h8
La Scie 1,422 D4
Lewisporte 3,963 D4
Marystown 6,299 E4
Middle Brook 1,083 D4
Milltown 1,376 E4
Musgrave Harbour 1,554 D5
Nain 938 g9
Norris Arm 1,216 D4
Norris Point 1,033 D3
Pasadena 2,685 D3
Placentia 2,204 E5
Pouch Cove 1,522 E5
Ramea 1,386 E3
Red Bay 316 C3
Rigolet 271 A2
Robert's Arm 1,005 D4
Rocky Harbour 1,273 D3
Roddickton 1,142 C3
St. Alban's 1,968 E4
St. Anthony 3,107 C4
St. George's 1,756 D2
St. John's 83,770 E5
St. Lawrence 2,012 E4
Spaniard's Bay 2,125 E5
Springdale 3,501 D3
Stephenville 8,876 D2
Stephenville Crossing 2,172 D2
Summerford 1,198 D4
Torbay 3,394 E5
Trepassey 1,473 E5
Twillingate 1,506 D4
Upper Island Cove 2,025 E5
Victoria 1,870 E5
Wabana (Bell Island) 4,254 E5
Wabush 3,155 h8
Wesleyville 1,225 D5
Windsor 5,747 D4

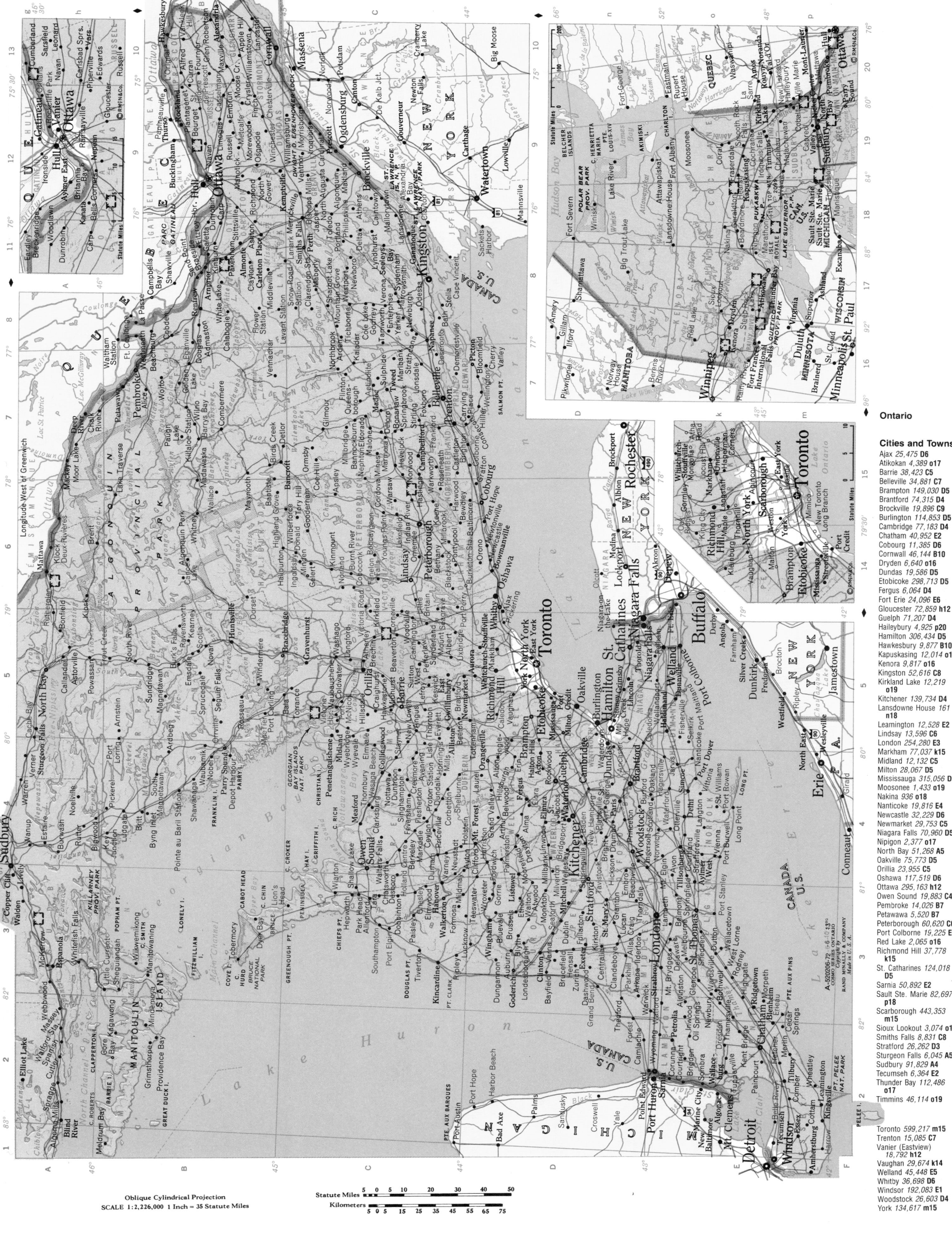

Ontario

Cities and Towns

Ajax *25,475* **D6**
Atikokan *4,389* **o17**
Barrie *38,423* **C5**
Belleville *34,881* **C7**
Brampton *149,030* **D5**
Brantford *74,315* **D4**
Brockville *19,896* **C9**
Burlington *114,853* **D5**
Cambridge *77,183* **D4**
Chatham *40,952* **E2**
Cobourg *11,385* **D6**
Cornwall *46,144* **B10**
Dryden *6,640* **o16**
Dundas *19,586* **D5**
Etobicoke *298,713* **D5**
Fergus *6,064* **D4**
Fort Erie *24,096* **E6**
Gloucester *72,859* **h12**
Guelph *71,207* **D4**
Haileybury *4,925* **p20**
Hamilton *306,434* **D5**
Hawkesbury *9,877* **B10**
Kapuskasing *12,014* **o19**
Kenora *9,817* **o16**
Kingston *52,616* **C8**
Kirkland Lake *12,219* **o19**
Kitchener *139,734* **D4**
Lansdowne House *161* **n18**
Leamington *12,528* **E2**
Lindsay *13,596* **C6**
London *254,280* **E3**
Markham *77,037* **k15**
Midland *12,132* **C5**
Milton *28,067* **D5**
Mississauga *315,056* **D5**
Moosonee *1,433* **o19**
Nakina *936* **o18**
Nanticoke *19,816* **E4**
Newcastle *32,229* **D6**
Newmarket *29,753* **C5**
Niagara Falls *70,960* **D5**
Nipigon *2,377* **o17**
North Bay *51,268* **A5**
Oakville *75,773* **D5**
Orillia *23,955* **C5**
Oshawa *117,519* **D6**
Ottawa *295,163* **h12**
Owen Sound *19,883* **C4**
Pembroke *14,026* **B7**
Petawawa *5,520* **B7**
Peterborough *60,620* **C6**
Port Colborne *19,225* **E5**
Red Lake *2,065* **o16**
Richmond Hill *37,778* **k15**
St. Catharines *124,018* **D5**
Sarnia *50,892* **E2**
Sault Ste. Marie *82,697* **p18**
Scarborough *443,353* **m15**
Sioux Lookout *3,074* **o17**
Smiths Falls *8,831* **C8**
Stratford *26,262* **D3**
Sturgeon Falls *6,045* **A5**
Sudbury *91,829* **A4**
Tecumseh *6,364* **E2**
Thunder Bay *112,486* **o17**
Timmins *46,114* **o19**
Toronto *599,217* **m15**
Trenton *15,085* **C7**
Vanier (Eastview) *18,792* **h12**
Vaughan *29,674* **k14**
Welland *45,448* **E5**
Whitby *36,698* **D6**
Windsor *192,083* **E1**
Woodstock *26,603* **D4**
York *134,617* **m15**

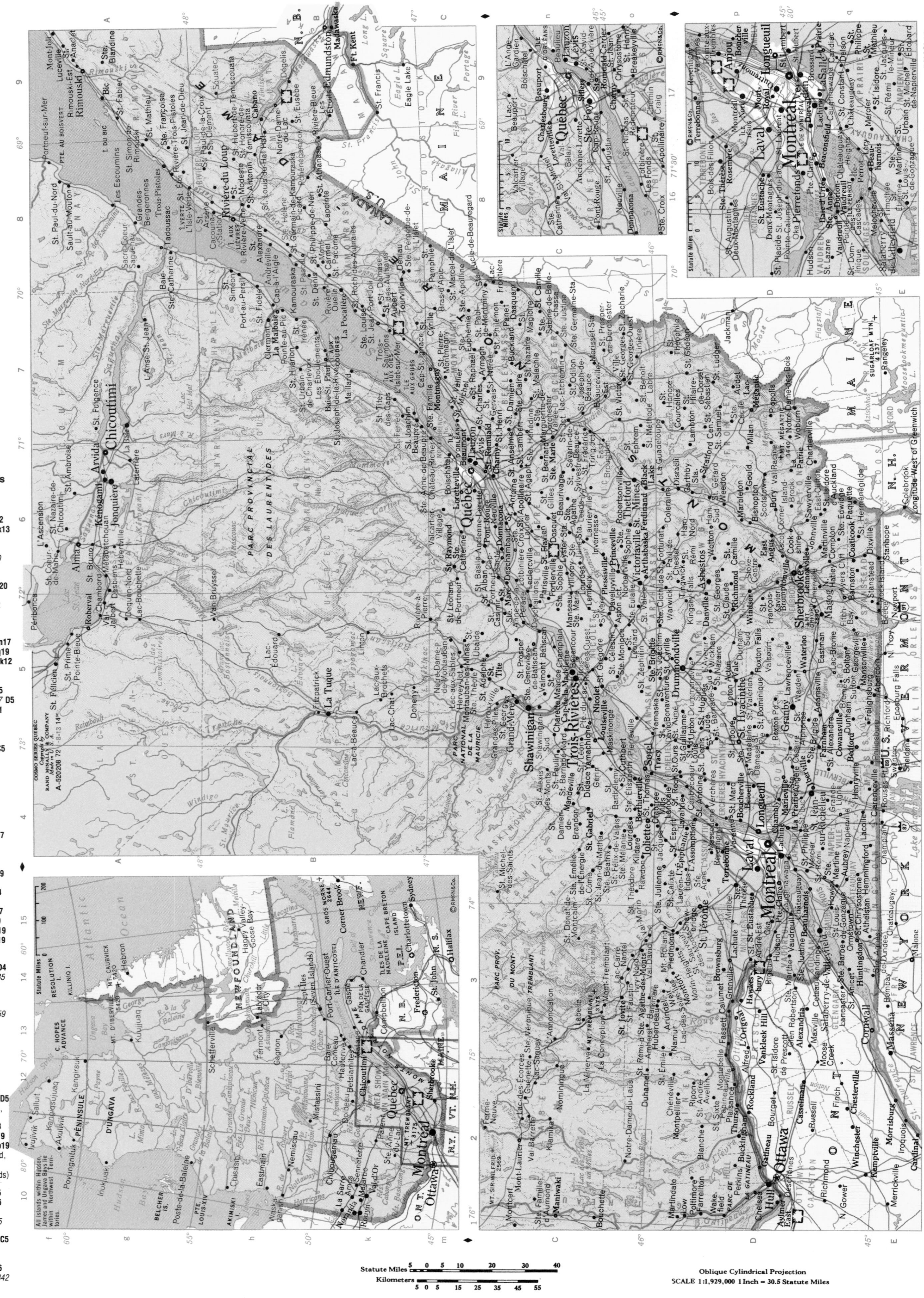

Quebec

Cities and Towns

Alma *26,322* **A6**
Anjou *37,346* **p19**
Asbestos *7,967* **D6**
Aylmer East *26,695* **D2**
Baie-Comeau *12,866* **k13**
Beauport *60,447* **n17**
Bécancour *10,247* **C5**
Bellin (Kangiqsuk) *270* **f12**
Beloeil *17,540* **D4**
Boucherville *29,704* **p20**
Brossard *52,232* **q20**
Buckingham *7,992* **D2**
Cap-de-la-Madeleine *32,626* **C5**
Chambly *12,190* **D4**
Charlesbourg *68,326* **n17**
Châteauguay *36,928* **q19**
Chibougamau *10,732* **k12**
Chicoutimi *60,064* **A6**
Coaticook *6,271* **D6**
Cowansville *12,240* **D5**
Drummondville *27,347* **D5**
Fort-George *2,222* **h11**
Gaspé *17,261* **k14**
Gatineau *74,988* **D2**
Granby *38,069* **D5**
Grand' Mère *15,442* **C5**
Hauterive *13,995* **k13**
Hull *56,225* **D2**
Iberville *8,587* **D4**
Joliette *16,987* **C4**
Jonquière *60,354* **A6**
La Baie *20,935* **A7**
Lachine *37,521* **q19**
Lachute *11,729* **D3**
Lac Mégantic *6,119* **D7**
LaSalle *76,299* **q19**
La Tuque *11,556* **B5**
Laval *268,335* **p19**
Longueuil *124,320* **p19**
Magog *13,604* **D5**
Mascouche *20,345* **D4**
Matane *13,612* **k13**
Montmagny *12,405* **C7**
Montréal *980,354* **q19**
Mont-Royal *19,247* **p19**
Pierrefonds *38,390* **q19**
Pointe-aux-Trembles *36,270* **p20**
Pointe-Claire *24,571* **D4**
Poste-de-la-Baleine *435* **g11**
Québec *166,474* **n17**
Rimouski *29,120* **A9**
Rivière-du-Loup *13,459* **B8**
Roberval *11,429* **A5**
Rouyn *17,224* **k11**
Ste. Anne-de-Beaupré *3,292* **B7**
St. Félicien *9,058* **A5**
Ste. Foy *68,883* **n17**
St. Georges *3,344* **C5**
St. Hyacinthe *38,246* **D5**
St. Jean-sur-Richelieu, *35,640* **D4**
St. Jérôme *25,123* **D3**
St. Laurent *65,900* **p19**
Ste. Thérese *18,750* **p19**
Salaberry-de-Valleyfield, *29,574* **q18**
Sept-Îles (Seven Islands) *29,262* **h13**
Shawinigan *23,011* **C5**
Sherbrooke *74,075* **D6**
Sorel *20,347* **C4**
Thetford Mines *19,965* **C6**
Trois-Rivières *50,466* **C5**
Val-d'Or *21,371* **k11**
Verdun *61,287* **q19**
Victoriaville *21,838* **C6**
Ville St. Georges *10,342* **C7**

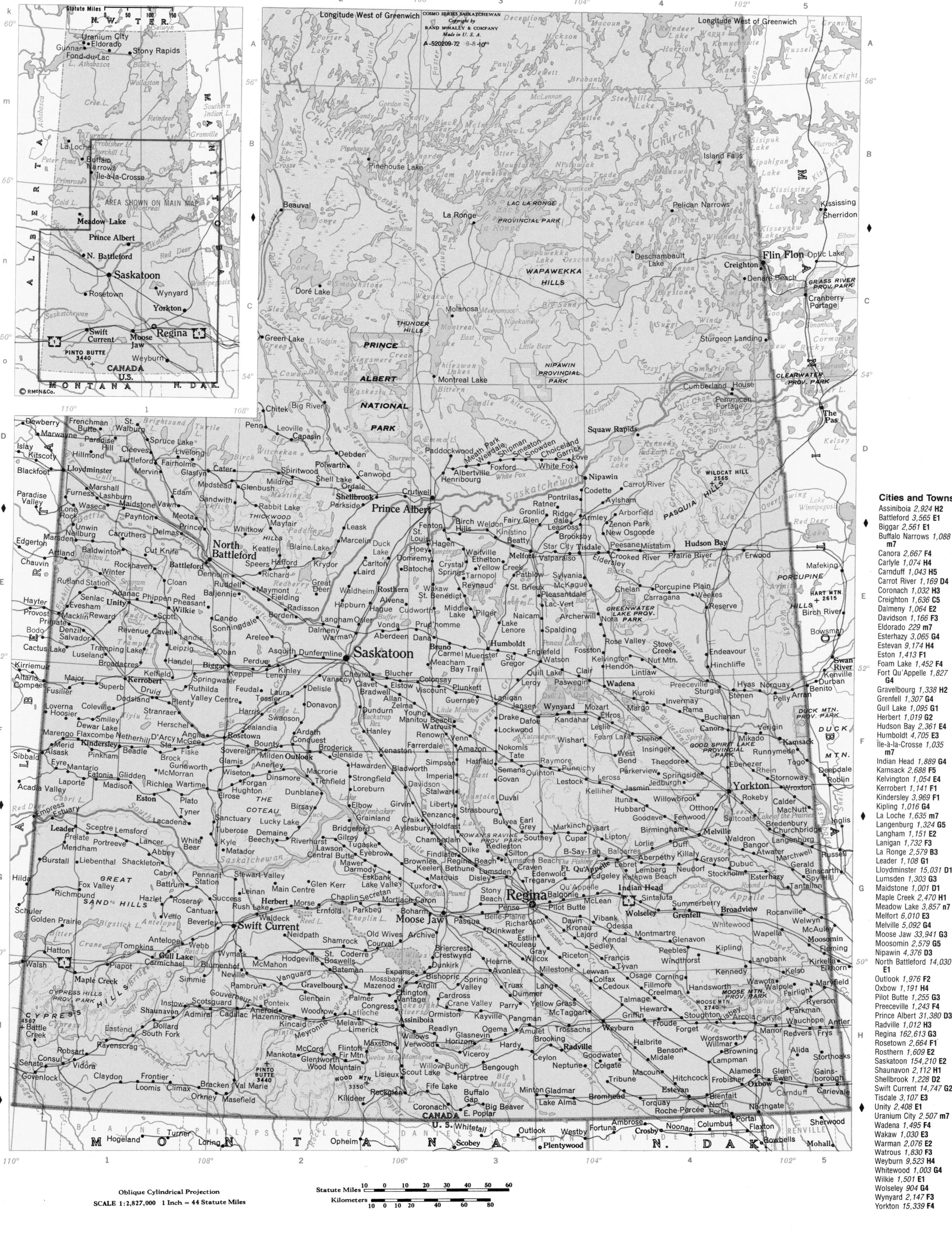
Longitude West of Greenwich
COSMO SERIES SASKATCHEWAN
Copyright by RAND McNALLY & COMPANY
Made in U. S. A.
A-520209-72
AREA SHOWN ON MAIN MAP
PRINCE ALBERT NATIONAL PARK
LAC LA RONGE PROVINCIAL PARK
NIPAWIN PROVINCIAL PARK
GREENWATER LAKE PROV. PARK
GOOD SPIRIT LAKE PROVINCIAL PARK
DUCK MTN. PROV. PARK
MOOSE MTN. PROV. PARK
CYPRESS HILLS PROV. PARK
ROWAN'S RAVINE PROV. PARK
GRASS RIVER PROV. PARK
CLEARWATER PROV. PARK
Oblique Cylindrical Projection
SCALE 1:2,827,000 1 Inch = 44 Statute Miles
Statute Miles
Kilometers
Cities and Towns
Assiniboia 2,924 H2
Battleford 3,565 E1
Biggar 2,561 E1
Buffalo Narrows 1,088 m7
Canora 2,667 F4
Carlyle 1,074 H4
Carnduff 1,043 H5
Carrot River 1,169 D4
Coronach 1,032 H3
Creighton 1,636 C5
Dalmeny 1,064 E2
Davidson 1,166 F3
Eldorado 229 m7
Esterhazy 3,065 G4
Estevan 9,174 H4
Eston 1,413 F1
Foam Lake 1,452 F4
Fort Qu'Appelle 1,827 G4
Gravelbourg 1,338 H2
Grenfell 1,307 G4
Gull Lake 1,095 G1
Herbert 1,019 G2
Hudson Bay 2,361 E4
Humboldt 4,705 E3
Île-à-la-Crosse 1,035 m7
Indian Head 1,889 G4
Kamsack 2,688 F5
Kelvington 1,054 E4
Kerrobert 1,141 F1
Kindersley 3,969 F1
Kipling 1,016 G4
La Loche 1,635 m7
Langenburg 1,324 G5
Langham 1,151 E2
Lanigan 1,732 F3
La Ronge 2,579 B3
Leader 1,108 G1
Lloydminster 15,031 D1
Lumsden 1,303 G3
Maidstone 1,001 D1
Maple Creek 2,470 H1
Meadow Lake 3,857 n7
Melfort 6,010 E3
Melville 5,092 G4
Moose Jaw 33,941 G3
Moosomin 2,579 G5
Nipawin 4,376 D3
North Battleford 14,030 E1
Outlook 1,976 F2
Oxbow 1,191 H4
Pilot Butte 1,255 G3
Preeceville 1,243 F4
Prince Albert 31,380 D3
Radville 1,012 H3
Regina 162,613 G3
Rosetown 2,664 F1
Rosthern 1,609 E2
Saskatoon 154,210 E2
Shaunavon 2,112 H1
Shellbrook 1,228 D2
Swift Current 14,747 G2
Tisdale 3,107 E3
Unity 2,408 E1
Uranium City 2,507 m7
Wadena 1,495 F4
Wakaw 1,030 E3
Warman 2,076 E2
Watrous 1,830 F3
Weyburn 9,523 H4
Whitewood 1,003 G4
Wilkie 1,501 E1
Wolseley 904 G4
Wynyard 2,147 F3
Yorkton 15,339 F4

United States and Canada Information Table

United States

STATE	CAPITAL	LARGEST CITY	ENTERED UNION AS STATE		GREATEST MEASUREMENT				HIGHEST POINT			OFFICIAL FLOWER
			Date of Entry	Rank of Entry	N-S km	N-S mi	E-W km	E-W mi	Location	Altitude m	Altitude ft	
Alabama	Montgomery	Birmingham	Dec. 14, 1819	22	531	*330*	322	*200*	Cheaha Mtn.	734	*2,407*	Camellia
Alaska	Juneau	Anchorage	Jan. 3, 1959	49	2,144	*1,332*	3,621	*2,250*	McKinley, Mt.	6,194	*20,320*	Forget-me-not
Arizona	Phoenix	Phoenix	Feb. 14, 1912	48	628	*390*	539	*335*	Humphreys Pk.	3,851	*12,633*	Saguaro Cactus Blossom
Arkansas	Little Rock	Little Rock	June 15, 1836	25	386	*240*	443	*275*	Magazine Mtn.	839	*2,753*	Apple Blossom
California	Sacramento	Los Angeles	Sept. 9, 1850	31	1,287	*800*	604	*375*	Whitney, Mt.	4,417	*14,491*	Golden Poppy
Colorado	Denver	Denver	Aug. 1, 1876	38	435	*270*	612	*380*	Elbert, Mt.	4,399	*14,433*	Rocky Mountain Columbine
Connecticut	Hartford	Bridgeport	Jan. 9, 1788	5	121	*75*	145	*90*	Frissell, Mt.	725	*2,380*	Mountain Laurel
Delaware	Dover	Wilmington	Dec. 7, 1787	1	153	*95*	56	*35*	In New Castle County	137	*448*	Peach Blossom
District of Columbia	Washington	Washington	January, 1791	. . .	24	*15*	24	*15*	Unnamed	125	*410*	American Beauty Rose
Florida	Tallahassee	Jacksonville	March 3, 1845	27	740	*460*	644	*400*	In Walton County	105	*345*	Orange Blossom
Georgia	Atlanta	Atlanta	Jan. 2, 1788	4	507	*315*	402	*250*	Brasstown Bald	1,458	*4,784*	Cherokee Rose
Hawaii	Honolulu	Honolulu	Aug. 21, 1959	50	1,070	*665*	2,575	*1,600*	Mauna Kea	4,205	*13,796*	Hibiscus
Idaho	Boise	Boise	July 3, 1890	43	772	*480*	491	*305*	Borah Pk.	3,859	*12,662*	Syringa
Illinois	Springfield	Chicago	Dec. 3, 1818	21	612	*380*	330	*205*	Charles Mound	376	*1,235*	Native Violet
Indiana	Indianapolis	Indianapolis	Dec. 11, 1816	19	426	*265*	257	*160*	In Wayne County	383	*1,257*	Peony
Iowa	Des Moines	Des Moines	Dec. 28, 1846	29	330	*205*	499	*310*	In Osceola County	509	*1,670*	Wild Rose
Kansas	Topeka	Wichita	Jan. 29, 1861	34	330	*205*	660	*410*	Sunflower, Mt.	1,231	*4,039*	Native Sunflower
Kentucky	Frankfort	Louisville	June 1, 1792	15	282	*175*	563	*350*	Black Mtn.	1,263	*4,145*	Goldenrod
Louisiana	Baton Rouge	New Orleans	April 30, 1812	18	443	*275*	483	*300*	Driskill Mtn.	163	*535*	Magnolia
Maine	Augusta	Portland	March 15, 1820	23	499	*310*	338	*210*	Katahdin, Mt.	1,606	*5,268*	White Pine Cone and Tassel
Maryland	Annapolis	Baltimore	April 28, 1788	7	193	*120*	322	*200*	Backbone Mtn.	1,024	*3,360*	Black-eyed Susan
Massachusetts	Boston	Boston	Feb. 6, 1788	6	177	*110*	306	*190*	Greylock, Mt	1,064	*3,491*	Mayflower
Michigan	Lansing	Detroit	Jan. 26, 1837	26	644	*400*	499	*310*	Arvon, Mt.	603	*1,979*	Apple Blossom
Minnesota	St. Paul	Minneapolis	May 11, 1858	32	644	*400*	563	*350*	Eagle Mtn.	701	*2,301*	Pink and White Lady's-slipper
Mississippi	Jackson	Jackson	Dec. 10, 1817	20	547	*340*	290	*180*	Woodall Mtn.	246	*806*	Magnolia
Missouri	Jefferson City	Kansas City	Aug. 10, 1821	24	451	*280*	483	*300*	Taum Sauk Mtn.	540	*1,772*	Hawthorn
Montana	Helena	Billings	Nov. 8, 1889	41	507	*315*	917	*570*	Granite Pk.	3,901	*12,799*	Bitterroot
Nebraska	Lincoln	Omaha	March 1, 1867	37	338	*210*	668	*415*	In Kimball County	1,654	*5,426*	Goldenrod
Nevada	Carson City	Las Vegas	Oct. 31, 1864	36	781	*485*	507	*315*	Boundary Pk.	4,005	*13,140*	Sagebrush
New Hampshire	Concord	Manchester	June 21, 1788	9	298	*185*	145	*90*	Washington, Mt.	1,917	*6,288*	Purple Lilac
New Jersey	Trenton	Newark	Dec. 18, 1787	3	267	*166*	113	*70*	High Point	550	*1,803*	Purple Violet
New Mexico	Santa Fe	Albuquerque	Jan. 6, 1912	47	628	*390*	563	*350*	Wheeler Pk.	4,011	*13,161*	Yucca
New York	Albany	New York	July 26, 1788	11	499	*310*	531	*330*	Marcy, Mt.	1,629	*5,344*	Rose
North Carolina	Raleigh	Charlotte	Nov. 21, 1789	12	322	*200*	837	*520*	Mitchell, Mt.	2,037	*6,684*	Dogwood
North Dakota	Bismarck	Fargo	Nov. 2, 1889	39	338	*210*	579	*360*	White Butte	1,069	*3,506*	Wild Prairie Rose
Ohio	Columbus	Columbus	March 1, 1803	17	370	*230*	330	*205*	Campbell Hill	472	*1,550*	Scarlet Carnation
Oklahoma	Oklahoma City	Oklahoma City	Nov. 16, 1907	46	338	*210*	740	*460*	Black Mesa	1,516	*4,973*	Mistletoe
Oregon	Salem	Portland	Feb. 14, 1859	33	467	*290*	604	*375*	Hood, Mt.	3,426	*11,239*	Oregon Grape
Pennsylvania	Harrisburg	Philadelphia	Dec. 12, 1787	2	290	*180*	499	*310*	Davis, Mt.	979	*3,213*	Mountain Laurel
Rhode Island	Providence	Providence	May 29, 1790	13	80	*50*	56	*35*	Jerimoth Hill	247	*812*	Violet
South Carolina	Columbia	Columbia	May 23, 1788	8	346	*215*	459	*285*	Sassafras Mtn.	1,085	*3,560*	Carolina Jessamine
South Dakota	Pierre	Sioux Falls	Nov. 2, 1889	40	386	*240*	579	*360*	Harney Pk.	2,207	*7,242*	Pasque Flower
Tennessee	Nashville	Memphis	June 1, 1796	16	193	*120*	692	*430*	Clingmans Dome	2,025	*6,643*	Iris
Texas	Austin	Houston	Dec. 29, 1845	28	1,143	*710*	1,223	*760*	Guadalupe Pk.	2,667	*8,749*	Bluebonnet
Utah	Salt Lake City	Salt Lake City	Jan. 4, 1896	45	555	*345*	443	*275*	Kings Pk.	4,123	*13,528*	Sego Lily
Vermont	Montpelier	Burlington	March 4, 1791	14	249	*155*	145	*90*	Mansfield, Mt.	1,339	*4,393*	Red Clover
Virginia	Richmond	Virginia Beach	June 25, 1788	10	330	*205*	684	*425*	Rogers, Mt.	1,746	*5,729*	Dogwood
Washington	Olympia	Seattle	Nov. 11, 1889	42	370	*230*	547	*340*	Rainier, Mt.	4,392	*14,410*	Western Rhododendron
West Virginia	Charleston	Charleston	June 20, 1863	35	322	*200*	362	*225*	Spruce Knob	1,482	*4,862*	Big Rhododendron
Wisconsin	Madison	Milwaukee	May 29, 1848	30	483	*300*	467	*290*	Timms Hill	595	*1,951*	Wood Violet
Wyoming	Cheyenne	Cheyenne	July 10, 1890	44	443	*275*	587	*365*	Gannett Pk.	4,207	*13,804*	Indian Paintbrush
UNITED STATES	Washington, D.C.	New York	. . .	. . .	. . .	. . .	. . .	. . .	McKinley, Mt.	6,194	*20,320*	. . .

Canada

PROVINCE	CAPITAL	LARGEST CITY	ENTERED CONFEDERATION		GREATEST MEASUREMENT				HIGHEST POINT			FLORAL EMBLEM
			Date of Entry	Rank of Entry	N-S km	N-S mi	E-W km	E-W mi	Location	Altitude m	Altitude ft	
Alberta	Edmonton	Edmonton	Sept. 1, 1905	8	1,207	*750*	644	*400*	Columbia, Mt.	3,747	*12,293*	Wild Rose
British Columbia	Victoria	Vancouver	July 20, 1871	6	1,263	*785*	1,022	*635*	Fairweather, Mt.	4,663	*15,300*	Dogwood
Manitoba	Winnipeg	Winnipeg	July 15, 1870	5	1,207	*750*	740	*460*	Baldy Mtn.	832	*2,730*	Pasque Flower
New Brunswick	Fredericton	St. John	July 1, 1867	1	378	*235*	314	*195*	Carleton, Mt.	820	*2,690*	Purple Violet
Newfoundland	St. John's	St. John's	March 31, 1949	10	1,545	*960*	1,022	*635*	Caubvick, Mt. (Mont d'Iberville)	1,652	*5,420*	Pitcher Plant
Northwest Territories	Yellowknife	Yellowknife	. . .	. . .	2,414	*1,500*	3,219	*2,000*	Unnamed	2,773	*9,098*	Mountain Avens
Nova Scotia	Halifax	Halifax	July 1, 1867	1	177	*110*	314	*195*	White Hill	532	*1,745*	Trailing Arbutus
Ontario	Toronto	Toronto	July 1, 1867	1	1,489	*925*	1,682	*1,045*	Ishpatina Ridge	693	*2,274*	White Trillium
Prince Edward Island	Charlottetown	Charlottetown	July 1, 1873	7	80	*50*	177	*110*	Unnamed	142	*466*	Lady's-slipper
Quebéc	Quebéc	Montréal	July 1, 1867	1	1,915	*1,190*	1,545	*960*	d'Iberville, Mont (Mt. Caubvick)	1,652	*5,420*	White Garden Lily
Saskatchewan	Regina	Saskatoon	Sep. 1, 1905	8	1,207	*750*	636	*395*	Unnamed	1,392	*4,567*	Prairie Lily
Yukon Territory	Whitehorse	Whitehorse	. . .	. . .	1,054	*655*	909	*565*	Logan, Mt.	5,951	*19,524*	Fireweed
CANADA	Ottawa	Toronto	. . .	. . .	. . .	. . .	. . .	. . .	Logan, Mt.	5,951	*19,524*	. . .

Geographical Information and International Map Index

A • 2–A • 7	WORLD INFORMATION TABLE
A • 8–A • 10	WORLD GEOGRAPHICAL TABLES
A • 11	MAJOR METROPOLITAN AREAS OF THE WORLD
A • 12–A • 15	POPULATIONS OF MAJOR CITIES
A • 16	TRANSLITERATION SYSTEMS
A • 17–A • 24	GEOGRAPHICAL GLOSSARY
A • 25–A • 144	INTERNATIONAL MAP INDEX

World Nations

This table gives the area, population, population density, form of government, capital and location of every country in the world.

Area figures include inland water.

The populations are estimates made by Rand McNally on the basis of official data, United Nations estimates and other available information.

Besides specifying the form of government for all political areas, the table classifies them into five groups according to their political status. Units labeled *A* are independent sovereign nations. Units labeled *B* are independent as regards internal affairs, but for purposes of foreign affairs they are under the protection of another country. Units labeled *C* are colonies, overseas territories, dependencies, etc. of other countries. Units labeled *D* are states, provinces or other major administrative subdivisions of important countries. Units in the table with no letter designations are regions, islands or other areas that do not constitute separate political units by themselves.

Map Plate numbers refer to the International Map section of the atlas.

Country, Division, or Region: English (Conventional)	Local Name	Area km²	Area sq mi	Population 1/1/89	Population Density per km²	Population Density per sq mi	Form of Government and Political Status	Capital	Continent and Map Plate
Afars and Issas, *see* Djibouti	...	...	...	...	...	...	...	...	...
† AFGHANISTAN	Afghānestān	652,225	*251,826*	14,655,000	22	*58*	Republic	*A* Kābol	Asia 23
Africa	...	30,300,000	*11,700,000*	642,100,000	21	*55*	...	...	Africa 30-31
Alabama	Alabama	133,913	*51,704*	4,125,000	31	*80*	State (U.S.)	*D* Montgomery	N. Amer 44
Alaska	Alaska	1,530,693	*591,004*	558,000	0.4	*0.9*	State (U.S.)	*D* Juneau	N. Amer 40
† ALBANIA	Shqiperia	28,748	*11,100*	3,181,000	111	*287*	Socialist republic	*A* Tirana	Europe 15
Alberta	Alberta	661,190	*255,287*	2,450,000	3.7	*9.6*	Province (Canada)	*D* Edmonton	N. Amer 42
† ALGERIA	Al Jazā'ir	2,381,741	*919,595*	24,215,000	10	*26*	Socialist republic	*A* Al Jazā'ir (Algiers)	Africa 32
American Samoa	American Samoa (English) / Amerika Samoa (Samoan)	199	*77*	40,000	201	*519*	Unincorporated territory (U.S.)	*C* Pago Pago	Oceania 65
Andaman and Nicobar Islands	Andaman and Nicobar Islands	8,293	*3,202*	... [1]	...	...	Territory (India)	*D* Port Blair	Asia 25
ANDORRA	Andorra	453	*175*	51,000	113	*291*	Coprincipality (Spanish and French protection)	*B* Andorra la Vella	Europe 13
† ANGOLA	Angola	1,246,700	*481,354*	8,385,000	6.7	*17*	Socialist republic	*A* Luanda	Africa 36
ANGUILLA	Anguilla	91	*35*	7,000	77	*200*	Dependent territory (U.K. protection)	*B* The Valley	N. Amer 51
Anhui	Anhui	140,000	*54,054*	53,970,000	386	*998*	Province (China)	*D* Hefei	Asia 28
Antarctica	...	14,000,000	*5,400,000*	... [1]	...	...	...	...	Antarctica 66
† ANTIGUA AND BARBUDA	Antigua	443	*171*	84,000	190	*491*	Parliamentary state	*A* St. John's	N. Amer 51
Arabian Peninsula	...	3,010,000	*1,112,000*	34,630,000	12	*31*	...	...	Asia 23
† ARGENTINA	Argentina	2,780,092	*1,073,400*	32,205,000	12	*30*	Republic	*A* Buenos Aires	S. Amer 56
Arizona	Arizona	295,264	*114,002*	3,558,000	12	*31*	State (U.S.)	*D* Phoenix	N. Amer 46
Arkansas	Arkansas	137,764	*53,191*	2,410,000	17	*45*	State (U.S.)	*D* Little Rock	N. Amer 45
Armenian S.S.R.	Armjanskaja S.S.R.	29,800	*11,506*	3,505,000	118	*305*	Soviet socialist republic (U.S.S.R.)	*D* Jerevan	Asia 16
ARUBA	Aruba	193	*75*	66,000	342	*880*	Self-governing territory (Netherlands protection)	*B* Oranjestad	N. Amer 49
Ascension	Ascension	88	*34*	1,800	20	*53*	Dependency (St. Helena)	*C* Georgetown	Africa 30-31
Asia	...	45,000,000	*17,400,000*	3,130,600,000	70	*180*	...	...	Asia 21-22
† AUSTRALIA	Australia	7,682,300	*2,966,155*	16,955,000	2.2	*5.7*	Federal parliamentary state	*A* Canberra	Oceania 59
Australian Capital Territory	Australian Capital Territory	2,400	*927*	281,000	117	*303*	Territory (Australia)	*D* Canberra	Oceania 59
† AUSTRIA	Österreich	83,855	*32,377*	7,584,000	90	*234*	Federal republic	*A* Wien (Vienna)	Europe 14
Azerbaijan S.S.R.	Azerbajdžanskaja S.S.R.	86,600	*33,436*	7,020,000	81	*210*	Soviet socialist republic (U.S.S.R.)	*D* Baku	Asia 16
Azores	Açores	2,247	*868*	260,000	116	*300*	Autonomous region (Portugal)	*D* Ponta Delgada	Europe 32
Baden-Wurttemberg	Baden-Württemberg	35,751	*13,804*	9,445,000	264	*684*	State (Fed. Rep. of Germany)	*D* Stuttgart	Europe 10
† BAHAMAS	Bahamas	13,939	*5,382*	243,000	17	*45*	Parliamentary state	*A* Nassau	N. Amer 47
† BAHRAIN	Al Baḩrayn	662	*256*	458,000	692	*1,789*	Monarchy	*A* Al Manāmah (Manama)	Asia 24
Balearic Islands	Islas Baleares	5,014	*1,936*	771,000	154	*398*	Province (Spain)	*D* Palma	Europe 13
Baltic Republics	...	174,000	*67,182*	7,995,000	46	*119*	...	...	Europe ...
† BANGLADESH	Bangladesh	143,998	*55,598*	111,390,000	774	*2,003*	Republic	*A* Dhaka	Asia 25
† BARBADOS	Barbados	430	*166*	255,000	593	*1,536*	Parliamentary state	*A* Bridgetown	N. Amer 51
Bavaria	Bayern	70,553	*27,241*	11,135,000	158	*409*	State (Fed. Rep. of Germany)	*D* München (Munich)	Europe 10
† BELGIUM	Belgique (French) / België (Flemish)	30,518	*11,783*	9,862,000	323	*837*	Constitutional monarchy	*A* Bruxelles (Brussels)	Europe 12
† BELIZE	Belize	22,963	*8,866*	184,000	8.0	*21*	Parliamentary state	*A* Belmopan	N. Amer 49
Benelux	...	74,889	*28,914*	25,045,000	334	*866*	...	...	Europe 12
† BENIN	Bénin	112,622	*43,484*	4,725,000	42	*109*	Socialist republic	*A* Porto-Novo and Cotonou	Africa 34
Berlin (West)	Berlin (West)	480	*185*	1,925,000	4,010	*10,405*	State (Fed. Rep. of Germany)	*D* Berlin (West)	Europe 10
Bermuda	Bermuda	54	*21*	56,000	1,037	*2,667*	Dependent territory (U.K.)	*C* Hamilton	N. Amer 47
† BHUTAN	Druk	46,500	*17,954*	1,519,000	33	*85*	Monarchy (Indian protection)	*B* Thimphu	Asia 25
Bioko	Bioko	2,034	*785*	83,000	41	*106*	Province of Equatorial Guinea	*D* Malabo	Africa 34
† BOLIVIA	Bolivia	1,098,581	*424,165*	7,184,000	6.5	*17*	Republic	*A* La Paz and Sucre	S. Amer 54
BOPHUTHATSWANA [2]	Bophuthatswana	40,509	*15,641*	2,202,000	54	*141*	National state (South African protection)	*B* Mmabatho	Africa 37
Borneo, Indonesian	Kalimantan	539,460	*208,287*	8,480,000	16	*41*	Part of Indonesia (4 provinces)	...	Asia 26
† BOTSWANA	Botswana	582,000	*224,711*	1,230,000	2.1	*5.5*	Republic	*A* Gaborone	Africa 37
† BRAZIL	Brasil	8,511,965	*3,286,488*	145,930,000	17	*44*	Federal republic	*A* Brasília	S. Amer 54-56
Bremen	Bremen	404	*156*	645,000	1,597	*4,135*	State (Fed. Rep. of Germany)	*D* Bremen	Europe 10
British Columbia	British Columbia (English) / Columbie-Britannique (French)	947,800	*365,948*	2,965,000	3.1	*8.1*	Province (Canada)	*D* Victoria	N. Amer 42
British Indian Ocean Territory	British Indian Ocean Territory	60	*23*	... [1]	...	...	Dependent territory (U.K.)	*C* ...	Africa 22
† BRUNEI	Brunei	5,765	*2,226*	247,000	43	*111*	Monarchy	*A* Bandar Seri Begawan	Asia 26
† BULGARIA	Balgarija	110,912	*42,823*	8,997,000	81	*210*	Socialist republic	*A* Sofija (Sofia)	Europe 15
† BURKINA FASO	Burkina Faso	274,200	*105,869*	8,596,000	31	*81*	Provisional military government	*A* Ouagadougou	Africa 34
† BURMA	Myanmar	676,577	*261,228*	41,860,000	62	*160*	Socialist republic	*A* Yangon (Rangoon)	Asia 25
† BURUNDI	Burundi	27,830	*10,745*	5,200,000	187	*484*	Provisional military government	*A* Bujumbura	Africa 36
† Byelorussian S.S.R.	Belorusskaja S.S.R.	207,600	*80,155*	10,215,000	49	*127*	Soviet socialist republic (U.S.S.R.)	*D* Minsk	Europe 16
California	California	411,041	*158,704*	28,630,000	70	*180*	State (U.S.)	*D* Sacramento	N. Amer 46
† CAMBODIA	Kâmpŭchéa	181,035	*69,898*	6,760,000	37	*97*	Socialist republic	*A* Phnum Pénh (Phnom Penh)	Asia 26
† CAMEROON	Cameroon (English) / Cameroun (French)	475,442	*183,569*	11,495,000	24	*63*	Republic	*A* Yaoundé	Africa 34
† CANADA	Canada	9,970,610	*3,849,674*	25,895,000	2.6	*6.7*	Federal parliamentary state	*A* Ottawa	N. Amer 42
Canary Islands	Islas Canarias	7,273	*2,808*	1,535,000	211	*547*	Part of Spain (2 provinces)	...	Africa 32
† CAPE VERDE	Cabo Verde	4,033	*1,557*	359,000	89	*231*	Republic	*A* Praia	Africa 32
Cayman Islands	Cayman Islands	259	*100*	25,000	97	*250*	Dependent territory (U.K.)	*C* Georgetown	N. Amer 49
Celebes	Sulawesi	189,216	*73,057*	12,405,000	66	*170*	Part of Indonesia (4 provinces)	...	Asia 26
† CENTRAL AFRICAN REPUBLIC	Centrafrique	622,984	*240,535*	3,089,000	5.0	*13*	Republic	*A* Bangui	Africa 35
Central America	...	520,000	*200,000*	28,195,000	54	*141*	...	...	N. Amer 49
Central Asia, Soviet	...	1,277,100	*493,090*	33,145,000	26	*67*	...	...	Asia 19
Ceylon, *see* Sri Lanka	...	...	...	...	...	...	...	...	...
† CHAD	Tchad	1,284,000	*495,755*	4,845,000	3.8	*9.8*	Republic	*A* N'Djamena	Africa 35

Country, Division, or Region English (Conventional)	Local Name	Area km²	Area sq mi	Population 1/1/89	Population Density per km²	Population Density per sq mi	Form of Government and Political Status	Capital	Continent	Map Plate
Channel Islands	...	194	*75*	137,000	706	*1,827*	...	...	Europe	9
† CHILE	Chile	756,626	*292,135*	12,925,000	17	*44*	Provisional military government	*A* Santiago	S. Amer	56
† CHINA (excl. Taiwan)	Zhongguo Renmin Gongheguo	9,631,600	*3,718,782*	1,094,700,000	114	*294*	Socialist republic	*A* Beijing (Peking)	Asia	27
China (Nationalist), *see* Taiwan	...	...	...	...	...	...	...	...	...	...
Christmas Island	Christmas Island	135	*52*	2,000	15	*38*	External territory (Australia)	*C* Flying Fish Cove	Oceania	26
CISKEI [2]	Ciskei	7,790	*3,008*	1,006,000	129	*334*	National state (South African protection)	*B* Bisho	Africa	37
Cocos (Keeling) Islands	Cocos (Keeling) Islands	14	*5.4*	600	43	*111*	Part of Australia	...	Oceania	22
† COLOMBIA	Colombia	1,141,748	*440,831*	30,465,000	27	*69*	Republic	*A* Bogotá	S. Amer	54
Colorado	Colorado	269,602	*104,094*	3,392,000	13	*33*	State (U.S.)	*D* Denver	N. Amer	45
† COMOROS (excl. Mayotte)	Al-Qumur (Arabic) / Comores (French)	2,171	*838*	436,000	201	*520*	Federal islamic republic	*A* Moroni	Africa	37
† CONGO	Congo	342,000	*132,047*	2,191,000	6.4	*17*	Socialist republic	*A* Brazzaville	Africa	36
Connecticut	Connecticut	12,999	*5,019*	3,233,000	249	*644*	State (U.S)	*D* Hartford	N. Amer	44
COOK ISLANDS	Cook Islands	236	*91*	17,000	72	*187*	Self-governing territory (New Zealand protection)	*B* Avarua	Oceania	61
Coral Sea Islands Territory	Coral Sea Islands Territory	2.6	*1.0*	[1]	...	...	External territory (Australia)	*C* ...	Oceania	59
Corsica	Corse	8,681	*3,352*	253,000	29	*75*	Part of France (2 departments)	*D* ...	Europe	11
† COSTA RICA	Costa Rica	51,100	*19,730*	2,990,000	59	*152*	Republic	*A* San José	N. Amer	49
† CUBA	Cuba	110,861	*42,804*	10,440,000	94	*244*	Socialist republic	*A* La Habana (Havana)	N. Amer	49
Curacao	Curaçao	444	*171*	167,000	376	*977*	Division of Netherlands Antilles (Neth.)	*D* Willemstad	N. Amer	49
† CYPRUS	Kipros (Greek) / Kıbrıs (Turkish)	5,896	*2,276*	573,000	97	*252*	Republic	*A* Nicosia (Levkosía)	Asia	24
CYPRUS, NORTH	Kuzey Kıbrıs	3,355	*1,295*	172,000	51	*133*	Republic	*A* Nicosia (Lefkoşa)	Asia	24
† CZECHOSLOVAKIA	Československo	127,905	*49,384*	15,605,000	122	*316*	Federal socialist republic	*A* Praha (Prague)	Europe	10
Delaware	Delaware	5,297	*2,045*	655,000	124	*320*	State (U.S.)	*D* Dover	N. Amer	44
† DENMARK	Danmark	43,092	*16,638*	5,135,000	119	*309*	Constitutional monarchy	*A* København (Copenhagen)	Europe	8
Denmark and Possessions	...	2,220,091	*857,182*	5,238,000	2.4	*6.1*	...	...	...	...
District of Columbia	District of Columbia	179	*69*	619,000	3,458	*8,971*	Federal district (U.S.)	*D* Washington	N. Amer	44
† DJIBOUTI	Djibouti	23,200	*8,958*	324,000	14	*36*	Republic	*A* Djibouti	Africa	35
† DOMINICA	Dominica	752	*290*	100,000	133	*345*	Republic	*A* Roseau	N. Amer	51
† DOMINICAN REPUBLIC	República Dominicana	48,442	*18,704*	7,069,000	146	*378*	Republic	*A* Santo Domingo	N. Amer	49
† ECUADOR	Ecuador	283,561	*109,484*	10,345,000	36	*94*	Republic	*A* Quito	S. Amer	54
† EGYPT	Mişr	1,001,450	*386,662*	52,490,000	52	*136*	Socialist republic	*A* Al Qāhirah (Cairo)	Africa	33
Ellis Islands, *see* Tuvalu	...	...	...	...	...	...	...	...	...	...
† EL SALVADOR	El Salvador	21,041	*8,124*	5,122,000	243	*630*	Republic	*A* San Salvador	N. Amer	49
England	England	130,439	*50,363*	47,510,000	364	*943*	Administrative division (U.K.)	*D* London	Europe	9
† EQUATORIAL GUINEA	Guinea Ecuatorial	28,051	*10,831*	438,000	16	*40*	Republic	*A* Malabo	Africa	36
Estonian S.S.R.	Eesti N.S.V.	45,100	*17,413*	1,585,000	35	*91*	Soviet socialist republic (U.S.S.R.)	*D* Tallinn	Europe	8
† ETHIOPIA	Itiopya	1,251,282	*483,123*	48,470,000	39	*100*	Socialist republic	*A* Ādīs Ābeba (Addis Ababa)	Africa	35
Eurasia	...	54,900,000	*21,200,000*	3,816,000,000	70	*180*	...	...	...	...
Europe	...	9,900,000	*3,800,000*	685,400,000	69	*180*	...	...	Europe	5-6
FAEROE ISLANDS	Føroyar	1,399	*540*	48,000	34	*89*	Self-governing territory (Danish protection)	*B* Thorshavn	Europe	6
Falkland Islands [3]	Falkland Islands (English) / Islas Malvinas (Spanish)	12,173	*4,700*	2,000	0.2	*0.4*	Dependent territory (U.K.)	*C* Stanley	S. Amer	56
† FIJI	Fiji (French) / Viti (Fijian)	18,333	*7,078*	749,000	41	*106*	Republic	*A* Suva	Oceania	63
† FINLAND	Suomi (Finnish) / Finland (Swedish)	338,145	*130,559*	4,949,000	15	*38*	Republic	*A* Helsinki (Helsingfors)	Europe	7
Florida	Florida	151,949	*58,668*	12,605,000	83	*215*	State (U.S.)	*D* Tallahassee	N. Amer	44
† FRANCE (excl. Overseas Departments)	France	547,026	*211,208*	55,970,000	102	*265*	Republic	*A* Paris	Europe	11
France and Possessions	...	667,359	*257,667*	57,780,000	87	*224*	...	... Paris	...	...
French Guiana	Guyane Française	91,000	*35,135*	93,000	1.0	*2.6*	Overseas department (France)	*C* Cayenne	S. Amer	54
French Polynesia	Polynésie Française	4,000	*1,544*	194,000	49	*126*	Overseas territory (France)	*C* Papeete	Oceania	61
French West Indies	...	2,880	*1,112*	678,000	235	*610*	...	...	N. Amer	50
Fujian	Fujian	123,000	*47,491*	28,355,000	231	*597*	Province (China)	*D* Fuzhou	Asia	27
† GABON	Gabon	267,667	*103,347*	1,056,000	3.9	*10*	Republic	*A* Libreville	Africa	36
Galapagos Islands	Archipiélago de Colón (Islas Galápagos)	7,964	*3,075*	10,000	1.3	*3.3*	Province (Ecuador)	*D* Baquerizo Moreno	S. Amer	54
† GAMBIA	Gambia	11,295	*4,361*	789,000	70	*181*	Republic	*A* Banjul	Africa	34
Gansu	Gansu	390,000	*150,580*	21,345,000	55	*142*	Province (China)	*D* Lanzhou	Asia	27
Georgia	Georgia	152,587	*58,914*	6,401,000	42	*109*	State (U.S.)	*D* Atlanta	N. Amer	44
Georgian S.S.R.	Gruzinskaja S.S.R.	69,700	*26,911*	5,330,000	76	*198*	Soviet socialist republic (U.S.S.R.)	*D* Tbilisi	Asia	16
† GERMAN DEMOCRATIC REPUBLIC (EAST GERMANY)	Deutsche Demokratische Republik	108,333	*41,828*	16,582,000	153	*396*	Socialist republic	*A* Berlin (Ost-) (East Berlin)	Europe	10
† GERMANY, FEDERAL REPUBLIC OF (WEST GERMANY)	Bundesrepublik Deutschland	248,707	*96,027*	61,380,000	247	*639*	Federal republic	*A* Bonn	Europe	10
Germany (entire)	...	357,040	*137,855*	77,960,000	218	*566*	...	...	Europe	10
† GHANA	Ghana	238,533	*92,098*	14,575,000	61	*158*	Provisional military government	*A* Accra	Africa	34
Gibraltar	Gibraltar	6.0	*2*	31,000	5,167	*13,478*	Dependent territory (U.K.)	*C* Gibraltar	Europe	13
Gilbert Islands, *see* Tuvalu	...	...	...	...	...	...	...	...	...	...
Great Britain, *see* United Kingdom	...	...	...	...	...	...	...	...	...	...
† GREECE	Ellas	131,944	*50,944*	10,030,000	76	*197*	Republic	*A* Athínai (Athens)	Europe	15
GREENLAND	Kalaallit Nunaat (Inuit) / Grønland (Danish)	2,175,600	*840,004*	55,000	0.1	*0.1*	Self-governing territory (Danish protection)	*B* Godthåb (Nūk)	N. Amer	41
† GRENADA	Grenada	344	*133*	95,000	276	*714*	Parliamentary state	*A* St. George's	N. Amer	51
Guadeloupe (incl. Dependencies)	Guadeloupe	1,780	*687*	340,000	191	*495*	Overseas department (France)	*C* Basse-Terre	N. Amer	51
Guam	Guam	541	*209*	137,000	253	*656*	Unincorporated territory (U.S.)	*C* Agana	Oceania	64
Guangdong	Guangdong	197,000	*76,062*	58,730,000	298	*772*	Province (China)	*D* Guangzhou (Canton)	Asia	27
† GUATEMALA	Guatemala	108,889	*42,042*	8,818,000	81	*210*	Republic	*A* Guatemala	N. Amer	49
Guernsey (incl. Dependencies)	Guernsey	78	*30*	56,000	718	*1,867*	Bailiwick (Channel Islands)	*C* St. Peter Port	Europe	9
† GUINEA	Guinée	245,857	*94,926*	6,999,000	28	*74*	Provisional military government	*A* Conakry	Africa	34
† GUINEA-BISSAU	Guiné-Bissau	36,125	*13,948*	962,000	27	*69*	Republic	*A* Bissau	Africa	34
Guizhou	Guizhou	174,000	*67,182*	30,980,000	178	*461*	Province (China)	*D* Guiyang	Asia	27
† GUYANA	Guyana	214,969	*83,000*	765,000	3.6	*9.2*	Republic	*A* Georgetown	S. Amer	54
Hainan	Hainan	34,000	*13,127*	6,520,000	192	*497*	Province (China)	*D* Haikou	Asia	27
† HAITI	Haïti	27,750	*10,714*	6,346,000	229	*592*	Provisional military government	*A* Port-au-Prince	N. Amer	49
Hamburg	Hamburg	755	*292*	1,555,000	2,060	*5,325*	State (Fed. Rep. of Germany)	*D* Hamburg	Europe	10
Hawaii	Hawaii	16,765	*6,473*	1,110,000	66	*171*	State (U.S.)	*D* Honolulu	N. Amer	60
Hebei	Hebei	203,000	*78,379*	58,020,000	286	*740*	Province (China)	*D* Shijiazhuang	Asia	28
Heilongjiang	Heilongjiang	460,000	*177,607*	34,810,000	76	*196*	Province (China)	*D* Harbin	Asia	27
Henan	Henan	167,000	*64,479*	80,900,000	484	*1,255*	Province (China)	*D* Zhengzhou	Asia	27
Hesse	Hessen	21,114	*8,152*	5,575,000	264	*684*	State (Fed. Rep. of Germany)	*D* Wiesbaden	Europe	10

Country, Division, or Region English (Conventional)	Local Name	Area km²	Area sq mi	Population 1/1/89	Population Density per km²	Population Density per sq mi	Form of Government and Political Status	Capital	Continent and Map Plate	
Hispaniola	La Española	76,192	*29,418*	13,415,000	176	*456*	. . . .		N. Amer . . .	49
Holland, *see* Netherlands	. . .	. . .	. . .	. . .	. . .	. . .	. . . .		. . . .	. . .
†HONDURAS	Honduras	112,088	*43,277*	5,047,000	45	*117*	Republic	*A* Tegucigalpa	N. Amer . . .	49
Hong Kong	Hong Kong (English) / Xianggang (Chinese)	1,068	*412*	5,731,000	5,366	*13,910*	Dependent territory (U.K.)	*C* Victoria (Hong Kong)	Asia	27
Hubei	Hubei	188,000	*72,587*	51,560,000	274	*710*	Province (China)	*D* Wuhan	Asia	27
Hunan	Hunan	211,000	*81,468*	58,790,000	279	*722*	Province (China)	*D* Changsha	Asia	27
†HUNGARY	Magyarország	93,033	*35,920*	10,580,000	114	*295*	Socialist republic	*A* Budapest	Europe . . .	10
†ICELAND	Ísland	103,000	*39,769*	248,000	2.4	*6.2*	Republic	*A* Reykjavík	Europe . . .	7
Idaho	Idaho	216,435	*83,566*	1,010,000	4.7	*12*	State (U.S.)	*D* Boise	N. Amer . . .	46
Illinois	Illinois	149,888	*57,872*	11,615,000	77	*201*	State (U.S.)	*D* Springfield	N. Amer . . .	45
†INDIA (incl. part of Jammu and Kashmir)	India (English) / Bhārat (Hindi)	3,203,975	*1,237,062*	825,000,000	257	*667*	Federal republic	*A* New Delhi	Asia	25
Indiana	Indiana	94,320	*36,417*	5,539,000	59	*152*	State (U.S.)	*D* Indianapolis	N. Amer . . .	44
†INDONESIA	Indonesia	1,919,443	*741,101*	185,860,000	97	*251*	Republic	*A* Jakarta	Asia	26
Inner Mongolia	Nei Mongol Gaoyuan	1,200,000	*463,323*	20,020,000	17	*43*	Autonomous region (China)	*D* Hohhot	Asia	27
Iowa	Iowa	145,752	*56,275*	2,818,000	19	*50*	State (U.S.)	*D* Des Moines	N. Amer . . .	45
†IRAN	Īrān	1,648,000	*636,296*	52,760,000	32	*83*	Islamic republic	*A* Tehrān	Asia	23
†IRAQ	Al ʿIrāq	438,317	*169,235*	17,900,000	41	*106*	Republic	*A* Baghdād	Asia	24
†IRELAND	Ireland (English) / Éire (Gaelic)	70,283	*27,136*	3,524,000	50	*130*	Republic	*A* Dublin (Baile Átha Cliath)	Europe . . .	9
ISLE OF MAN	Isle of Man	572	*221*	62,000	108	*281*	Self-governing territory (U.K. protection)	*B* Douglas	Europe . . .	9
†ISRAEL (excl. Occupied Areas)	Yisra'el (Hebrew) / Isrāʾīl (Arabic)	20,770	*8,019*	4,374,000	211	*545*	Republic	*A* Yerushalayim (Jerusalem)	Asia	24
Israeli Occupied Areas [4]	. . .	7,632	*2,947*	1,728,000	226	*586*	. . . .		Asia	24
†ITALY	Italia	301,268	*116,320*	57,500,000	191	*494*	Republic	*A* Roma (Rome)	Europe . . .	14
†IVORY COAST	Côte d'Ivoire	320,763	*123,847*	11,400,000	36	*92*	Republic	*A* Abidjan and Yamoussoukro [5]	Africa	34
†JAMAICA	Jamaica	10,991	*4,244*	2,470,000	225	*582*	Parliamentary state	*A* Kingston	N. Amer . . .	49
†JAPAN	Nippon	377,801	*145,870*	123,000,000	326	*843*	Constitutional monarchy	*A* Tōkyō	Asia	29
Java	Jawa	132,187	*51,038*	106,140,000	803	*2,080*	Part of Indonesia (5 provinces)		Asia	26
Jersey	Jersey	116	*45*	81,000	698	*1,800*	Bailiwick (Channel Islands)	*C* St. Helier	Europe . . .	9
Jiangsu	Jiangsu	102,000	*39,382*	65,240,000	640	*1,657*	Province (China)	*D* Nanjing (Nanking)	Asia	28
Jiangxi	Jiangxi	165,000	*63,707*	36,235,000	220	*569*	Province (China)	*D* Nanchang	Asia	27
Jilin	Jilin	187,000	*72,201*	24,195,000	129	*335*	Province (China)	*D* Changchun	Asia	27
Johnston Atoll	Johnston Atoll	1.3	*0.5*	300	231	*600*	Unincorporated territory (U.S.) . . .	*C* . . .	Oceania . . .	60
†JORDAN (excl. West Bank)	Al Urdun	91,000	*35,135*	2,904,000	32	*83*	Constitutional monarchy	*A* ʿAmmān	Asia	24
Kansas	Kansas	213,109	*82,282*	2,500,000	12	*30*	State (U.S.)	*D* Topeka	N. Amer . . .	45
Kashmir, Jammu and	Jammu and Kashmir	222,801	*86,024*	8,960,000	40	*104*	Disputed territory (India and Pakistan)	*D* . . .	Asia	25
Kazakh S.S.R.	Kazahskaja S.S.R.	2,717,300	*1,049,156*	16,680,000	6.1	*16*	Soviet socialist republic (U.S.S.R.)	*D* Alma-Ata	Asia	19
Kentucky	Kentucky	104,672	*40,414*	3,741,000	36	*93*	State (U.S.)	*D* Frankfort	N. Amer . . .	44
†KENYA	Kenya	582,646	*224,961*	25,825,000	44	*115*	Republic	*A* Nairobi	Africa	36
Kerguelen Islands	Iles Kerguélen	6,993	*2,700*	100	. . .	. . .	Part of French Southern and Antarctic Territories	*C* . . .	S. Amer . . .	30-31
Kirghiz S.S.R.	Kirgizskaja S.S.R.	198,500	*76,641*	4,330,000	22	*56*	Soviet socialist republic (U.S.S.R.)	*D* Frunze	Asia	18
KIRIBATI	Kiribati	726	*280*	69,000	95	*246*	Republic	*A* Bairiki	Oceania . . .	60
KOREA, NORTH	Chosŏn Minjujuŭi Inmin Konghwaguk	120,538	*46,540*	22,250,000	185	*478*	Socialist republic	*A* P'yŏngyang	Asia	28
KOREA, SOUTH	Taehan-min'guk	98,484	*38,025*	42,840,000	435	*1,127*	Republic	*A* Sŏul (Seoul)	Asia	28
Korea (entire)	. . .	219,022	*84,565*	65,090,000	297	*770*	. . . .		Asia	28
†KUWAIT	Al Kuwayt	17,818	*6,880*	2,002,000	112	*291*	Constitutional monarchy	*A* Al Kuwayt (Kuwait)	Asia	24
Kwangsi	Guangxi Zhuangzu Zizhiqu	237,000	*91,506*	40,285,000	170	*440*	Autonomous region (China)	*D* Nanning	Asia	27
Labrador	Labrador	292,218	*112,826*	31,000	0.1	*0.3*	Part of Newfoundland province (Canada)		N. Amer . . .	42
†LAOS	Lao	236,800	*91,429*	3,892,000	16	*43*	Socialist republic	*A* Viangchan (Vientiane)	Asia	26
Latin America	. . .	20,500,000	*8,000,000*	372,800,000	18	*47*	. . . .		N.A., S.A.	52-53
Latvian S.S.R.	Latvijas P.S.R.	63,700	*24,595*	2,695,000	42	*110*	Soviet socialist republic (U.S.S.R.)	*D* Rīga	Europe . . .	8
†LEBANON	Lubnān	10,400	*4,015*	3,351,000	322	*835*	Republic	*A* Bayrūt (Beirut)	Asia	24
†LESOTHO	Lesotho	30,355	*11,720*	1,689,000	56	*144*	Constitutional monarchy	*A* Maseru	Africa	37
Liaoning	Liaoning	151,000	*58,301*	38,645,000	256	*663*	Province (China)	*D* Shenyang (Mukden)	Asia	28
†LIBERIA	Liberia	99,067	*38,250*	2,553,000	26	*67*	Republic	*A* Monrovia	Africa	34
†LIBYA	Lībiyā	1,759,540	*679,362*	4,019,000	2.3	*5.9*	Socialist republic	*A* Ṭarābulus (Tripoli)	Africa	33
LIECHTENSTEIN	Liechtenstein	160	*62*	29,000	181	*468*	Constitutional monarchy	*A* Vaduz	Europe . . .	14
Lithuanian S.S.R. [6]	Lietuvos T.S.R.	65,200	*25,174*	3,715,000	57	*148*	Soviet socialist republic (U.S.S.R.)	*D* Vilnius	Europe . . .	8
Louisiana	Louisiana	123,672	*47,750*	4,517,000	37	*95*	State (U.S.)	*D* Baton Rouge	N. Amer . . .	45
Lower Saxony	Niedersachsen	47,438	*18,316*	7,195,000	152	*393*	State (Fed. Rep. of Germany) . . .	*D* Hannover	Europe . . .	10
†LUXEMBOURG	Luxembourg (French) / Lezebuurg (Luxembourgish)	2,586	*998*	368,000	142	*369*	Constitutional monarchy	*A* Luxembourg	Europe . . .	12
Macao	Macau	17	*6.6*	432,000	25,412	*65,455*	Chinese territory under Portuguese administration	*C* Macau	Asia	27
†MADAGASCAR	Madagasikara	587,041	*226,658*	11,250,000	19	*50*	Republic	*A* Antananarivo	Africa	37
Madeira	Madeira	794	*307*	277,000	349	*902*	Autonomous region (Portugal) . . .	*D* Funchal	Europe . . .	32
Maine	Maine	86,156	*33,265*	1,205,000	14	*36*	State (U.S.)	*D* Augusta	N. Amer . . .	44
†MALAWI	Malaŵi	118,484	*45,747*	8,440,000	71	*184*	Republic	*A* Lilongwe	Africa	36
Malaya	Semenanjung Malaysia	131,312	*50,700*	14,240,000	108	*281*	Part of Malaysia (11 states)	*D* . . .	Asia	26
†MALAYSIA	Malaysia	330,228	*127,502*	17,255,000	52	*135*	Federal constitutional monarchy	*A* Kuala Lumpur	Asia	26
†MALDIVES	Maldives	298	*115*	209,000	701	*1,817*	Republic	*A* Male	Asia	25
†MALI	Mali	1,240,000	*478,767*	9,039,000	7.3	*19*	Republic	*A* Bamako	Africa	34
†MALTA	Malta	316	*122*	370,000	1,171	*3,033*	Republic	*A* Valletta	Europe . . .	14
Manitoba	Manitoba	649,950	*250,947*	1,095,000	1.7	*4.4*	Province (Canada)	*D* Winnipeg	N. Amer . . .	42
Maritime Provinces	. . .	134,590	*51,965*	1,734,000	13	*33*	. . . .		N. Amer . . .	42
MARSHALL ISLANDS	Marshall Islands	181	*70*	40,000	221	*571*	Republic (U.S. protection)	*B* Uliga	Oceania . . .	60
Martinique	Martinique	1,100	*425*	338,000	307	*795*	Overseas department (France) . . .	*C* Fort-de-France	N. Amer . . .	51
Maryland	Maryland	27,094	*10,461*	4,605,000	170	*440*	State (U.S.)	*D* Annapolis	N. Amer . . .	44
Massachusetts	Massachusetts	21,461	*8,286*	5,880,000	274	*710*	State (U.S.)	*D* Boston	N. Amer . . .	44
†MAURITANIA	Mūrītāniyā (Arabic) / Mauritanie (French)	1,030,700	*397,956*	1,948,000	1.9	*4.9*	Provisional military government	*A* Nouakchott	Africa	32
†MAURITIUS (incl. Dependencies)	Mauritius	2,040	*788*	1,057,000	518	*1,341*	Parliamentary state	*A* Port-Louis	Africa	37
Mayotte [7]	Mayotte	373	*144*	79,000	212	*549*	Territorial collectivity (France) . . .	*C* Dzaoudzi and Mamoudzou [5]	Africa	37
†MEXICO	México	1,972,547	*761,605*	85,300,000	43	*112*	Federal republic	*A* Ciudad de México (Mexico City)	N. Amer . . .	48

Country, Division, or Region English (Conventional)	Local Name	Area km²	Area sq mi	Population 1/1/89	Population Density per km²	Population Density per sq mi	Form of Government and Political Status	Capital	Continent	Map Plate
Michigan	Michigan	251,506	*97,107*	9,186,000	37	*95*	State (U.S.)	*D* Lansing	N. Amer	44
MICRONESIA, FEDERATED STATES OF	Federated States of Micronesia	702	*271*	108,000	154	*399*	Republic (U.S. protection)	*B* Ponape	Oceania	60
Middle America	. . .	2,730,000	*1,050,000*	85,300,000	31	*81*	. . .	. . .	N. Amer	47
Midway Islands	Midway Islands	5.2	*2.0*	500	96	*250*	Unincorporated territory (U.S.)	*C* . . .	Oceania	60
Minnesota	Minnesota	224,329	*86,614*	4,283,000	19	*49*	State (U.S.)	*D* St. Paul	N. Amer	45
Mississippi	Mississippi	123,519	*47,691*	2,647,000	21	*56*	State (U.S.)	*D* Jackson	N. Amer	45
Missouri	Missouri	180,514	*69,697*	5,145,000	29	*74*	State (U.S.)	*D* Jefferson City	N. Amer	45
Moldavian S.S.R.	Moldavskaja S.S.R.	33,700	*13,012*	4,260,000	126	*327*	Soviet socialist republic (U.S.S.R.)	*D* Kišinev (Kishinev)	Europe	16
MONACO	Monaco	1.9	*0.7*	29,000	15,263	*41,429*	Constitutional monarchy	*A* Monaco	Europe	11
†MONGOLIA	Mongol Ard Uls	1,565,000	*604,250*	2,097,000	1.3	*3.5*	Socialist republic	*A* Ulan-Bator (Ulaanbaatar)	Asia	27
Montana	Montana	380,845	*147,045*	814,000	2.1	*5.5*	State (U.S.)	*D* Helena	N. Amer	46
Montserrat	Montserrat	103	*40*	12,000	117	*300*	Dependent territory (U.K.)	*C* Plymouth	N. Amer	51
†MOROCCO (excl. Western Sahara)	Al Maghrib	446,550	*172,414*	25,600,000	57	*148*	Consitutional monarchy	*A* Rabat	Africa	32
†MOZAMBIQUE	Moçambique	799,379	*308,642*	17,660,000	22	*57*	Socialist republic	*A* Maputo	Africa	37
NAMIBIA (excl. Walvis Bay)	Namibia	823,144	*317,818*	1,337,000	1.6	*4.2*	Republic	*A* Windhoek	Africa	37
NAURU	Nauru (English) / Naoero (Nauruan)	21	*8.1*	9,000	429	*1,111*	Republic	*A* Domaneab	Oceania	64
Navassa Island	Navassa Island	4.9	*1.9*	. . .(1)	. . .	. . .	Unincorporated territory (U.S.)	*C* . . .	N. Amer	49
Nebraska	Nebraska	200,336	*77,350*	1,599,000	8.0	*21*	State (U.S.)	*D* Lincoln	N. Amer	45
†NEPAL	Nepāl	147,181	*56,827*	18,415,000	125	*324*	Constitutional monarchy	*A* Kāṭhmāṇḍāū	Asia	25
†NETHERLANDS	Nederland	41,785	*16,133*	14,815,000	355	*918*	Constitutional monarchy	*A* Amsterdam and 's-Gravenhage (The Hague)	Europe	12
NETHERLANDS ANTILLES	Nederlandse Antillen	800	*309*	194,000	243	*628*	Self-governing territory (Netherlands protection)	*B* Willemstad	N. Amer	50
Nevada	Nevada	286,354	*110,562*	1,061,000	3.7	*9.6*	State (U.S.)	*D* Carson City	N. Amer	46
New Brunswick	New Brunswick (English) / Nouveau-Brusnwick (French)	73,440	*28,355*	718,000	9.8	*25*	Province (Canada)	*D* Fredericton	N. Amer	42
New Caledonia	Nouvelle-Calédonie	19,079	*7,366*	161,000	8.4	*22*	Overseas territory (France)	*C* Nouméa	Oceania	63
New England	New England	172,685	*66,674*	12,955,000	75	*194*	Part of U.S. (6 states)	. . .	N. Amer	43
Newfoundland	Newfoundland (English) / Terre-Neuve (French)	405,720	*156,649*	571,000	1.4	*3.6*	Province (Canada)	*D* St. John's	N. Amer	42
Newfoundland (island)	Newfoundland (English) / Terre-Neuve (French)	108,860	*42,031*	540,000	5.0	*13*	Part of Newfoundland province (Canada)	. . .	N. Amer	42
New Hampshire	New Hampshire	24,030	*9,278*	1,089,000	45	*117*	State (U.S.)	*D* Concord	N. Amer	44
New Hebrides, *see* Vanuatu	. . .	. . .	. . .	. . .	. . .	. . .	. . .	. . .	. . .	. . .
New Jersey	New Jersey	20,168	*7,787*	7,739,000	384	*994*	State (U.S.)	*D* Trenton	N. Amer	44
New Mexico	New Mexico	314,927	*121,594*	1,547,000	4.9	*13*	State (U.S.)	*D* Santa Fe	N. Amer	45
New South Wales	New South Wales	801,600	*309,500*	5,820,000	7.3	*19*	State (Australia)	*D* Sydney	Oceania	59
New York	New York	136,588	*52,737*	17,880,000	131	*339*	State (U.S.)	*D* Albany	N. Amer	44
†NEW ZEALAND	New Zealand	268,112	*103,519*	3,391,000	13	*33*	Parliamentary state	*A* Wellington	Oceania	62
†NICARAGUA	Nicaragua	130,000	*50,193*	3,689,000	28	*73*	Republic	*A* Managua	N. Amer	49
†NIGER	Niger	1,267,000	*489,191*	7,329,000	5.8	*15*	Provisional military government	*A* Niamey	Africa	34
†NIGERIA	Nigeria	923,768	*356,669*	113,580,000	123	*318*	Provisional military government	*A* Lagos and Abuja (5)	Africa	34
Ningsia	Ningxia Huizu Zizhiqu	66,000	*25,483*	4,270,000	65	*168*	Autonomous region (China)	*D* Yinchuan	Asia	27
NIUE	Niue	263	*102*	2,400	9.1	*24*	Self-governing territory (New Zealand protection)	*B* Alofi	Oceania	64
Norfolk Island	Norfolk Island	36	*14*	2,000	56	*143*	External territory (Australia)	*C* Kingston	Oceania	61
North America	. . .	24,400,000	*9,400,000*	420,100,000	17	*45*	. . .	. . .	N. Amer	38-39
North Borneo, *see* Sabah	. . .	. . .	. . .	. . .	. . .	. . .	. . .	. . .	. . .	. . .
North Carolina	North Carolina	136,412	*52,669*	6,532,000	48	*124*	State (U.S.)	*D* Raleigh	N. Amer	44
North Dakota	North Dakota	183,117	*70,702*	676,000	3.7	*9.6*	State (U.S.)	*D* Bismarck	N. Amer	45
Northern Ireland	Northern Ireland	14,122	*5,453*	1,575,000	112	*289*	Administrative division (U.K.)	*D* Belfast	Europe	9
NORTHERN MARIANA ISLANDS	Northern Mariana Islands	477	*184*	22,000	46	*120*	Commonwealth (U.S. protection)	*B* Saipan (island)	Oceania	60
Northern Territory	Northern Territory	1,346,200	*519,771*	168,000	0.1	*0.3*	Territory (Australia)	*D* Darwin	Oceania	59
North Rhine-Westphalia	Nordrhein-Westfalen	34,068	*13,154*	16,685,000	490	*1,268*	State (Fed. Rep. of Germany)	*D* Düsseldorf	Europe	10
Northwest Territories	Northwest Territories (English) / Territoires du Nord-Ouest (French)	3,426,320	*1,322,910*	56,000	. . .	. . .	Territory (Canada)	*D* Yellowknife	N. Amer	42
†NORWAY (incl. Svalbard and Jan Mayen)	Norge	386,975	*149,412*	4,221,000	11	*28*	Constitutional monarchy	*A* Oslo	Europe	7
Nova Scotia	Nova Scotia (English) / Nouvelle-Écosse (French)	55,490	*21,425*	886,000	16	*41*	Province (Canada)	*D* Halifax	N. Amer	42
Oceania (incl. Australia)	. . .	8,500,000	*3,300,000*	26,300,000	3.1	*8.0*	. . .	. . .	Oceania	57-58
Ohio	Ohio	115,995	*44,786*	10,780,000	93	*241*	State (U.S.)	*D* Columbus	N. Amer	44
Oklahoma	Oklahoma	181,188	*69,957*	3,327,000	18	*48*	State (U.S.)	*D* Oklahoma City	N. Amer	45
†OMAN	'Umān	212,457	*82,030*	1,284,000	6.0	*16*	Monarchy	*A* Masqaṭ (Muscat)	Asia	23
Ontario	Ontario	1,068,580	*412,581*	9,375,000	8.8	*23*	Province (Canada)	*D* Toronto	N. Amer	42
Oregon	Oregon	251,426	*97,076*	2,743,000	11	*28*	State (U.S.)	*D* Salem	N. Amer	46
Orkney Islands	Orkney Islands	976	*377*	19,000	19	*50*	Part of Scotland (U.K.)	*D* Kirkwall	Europe	9
PACIFIC ISLANDS, TRUST TERRITORY OF THE	Trust Territory of the Pacific Islands	508	*196*	15,000	30	*77*	United Nations trusteeship (U.S. administration)	*B* Saipan (island)	Oceania	60
†PAKISTAN (incl. part of Jammu and Kashmir)	Pākistān	879,902	*339,732*	108,990,000	124	*321*	Federal Islamic republic	*A* Islāmābād	Asia	25
PALAU	Palau (English) / Belau (Palauan)	508	*196*	15,000	30	*77*	Part of Trust Territory of the Pacific Islands	*B* Koror	Oceania	60
†PANAMA	Panamá	77,082	*29,762*	2,346,000	30	*79*	Republic	*A* Panamá	N. Amer	49
†PAPUA NEW GUINEA	Papua New Guinea	462,840	*178,704*	3,639,000	7.9	*20*	Parliamentary state	*A* Port Moresby	Oceania	60
†PARAGUAY	Paraguay	406,752	*157,048*	4,210,000	10	*27*	Republic	*A* Asunción	S. Amer	56
Peking	Beijing	16,800	*6,487*	10,070,000	599	*1,552*	Autonomous city (China)	*D* Beijing (Peking)	Asia	28
Pennsylvania	Pennsylvania	119,261	*46,047*	11,950,000	100	*260*	State (U.S.)	*D* Harrisburg	N. Amer	44
†PERU	Perú	1,285,216	*496,225*	21,535,000	17	*43*	Republic	*A* Lima	S. Amer	54
†PHILIPPINES	Pilipinas (Tagalog) / Philippines (English)	300,000	*115,831*	60,110,000	200	*519*	Republic	*A* Manila	Asia	26
Pitcairn (incl. Dependencies)	Pitcairn	49	*19*	70	1.4	*3.7*	Dependent territory (U.K.)	*C* Adamstown	Oceania	61
†POLAND	Polska	312,683	*120,728*	37,955,000	121	*314*	Socialist republic	*A* Warszawa (Warsaw)	Europe	10
†PORTUGAL	Portugal	91,985	*35,516*	10,445,000	114	*294*	Republic	*A* Lisboa (Lisbon)	Europe	13
Prairie Provinces	Prairie Provinces	1,963,470	*758,100*	4,575,000	2.3	*6.0*	Part of Canada (3 provinces)	. . .	N. Amer	42
Prince Edward Island	Prince Edward Island / Île-du Prince-Édouard (French)	5,660	*2,185*	130,000	23	*59*	Province (Canada)	*D* Charlottetown	N. Amer	42

Country, Division, or Region English (Conventional)	Local Name	Area km²	Area sq mi	Population 1/1/89	Population Density per km²	Population Density per sq mi	Form of Government and Political Status	Capital	Continent and Map Plate
PUERTO RICO	Puerto Rico	9,104	*3,515*	3,301,000	363	*939*	Commonwealth (U.S. protection)	*B* San Juan	N. Amer 51
†QATAR	Qaṭar	11,437	*4,416*	400,000	35	*91*	Monarchy	*A* Ad Dawḥah (Doha)	Asia 24
Qinghai	Qinghai	721,000	*278,380*	4,270,000	5.9	*15*	Province (China)	*D* Xining	Asia 27
Quebec	Québec	1,540,680	*594,860*	6,595,000	4.3	*11*	Province (Canada)	*D* Québec	N. Amer 42
Queensland	Queensland	1,727,200	*666,876*	2,849,000	1.6	*4.3*	State (Australia)	*D* Brisbane	Oceania 59
Reunion	Réunion	2,504	*967*	580,000	232	*600*	Overseas department (France)	*C* Saint-Denis	Africa 37
Rhineland-Palatinate	Rheinland-Pfalz	19,848	*7,663*	3,605,000	182	*470*	State (Fed. Rep. of Germany)	*D* Mainz	Europe 10
Rhode Island	Rhode Island	3,139	*1,212*	994,000	317	*820*	State (U.S.)	*D* Providence	N. Amer 44
Rhodesia, *see* Zimbabwe	. . .	. . .	. . .	. . .	. . .	. . .	. . .	. . .	. . .
Rodrigues	Rodrigues	104	*40*	35,000	337	*875*	Part of Mauritius	. . .	Africa 30-31
†ROMANIA	România	237,500	*91,699*	23,085,000	97	*252*	Socialist republic	*A* București (Bucharest)	Europe 15
Russian Soviet Federative Socialist Republic	Rossijskaja Sovetskaja Federativnaja Socialističeskaja Respublika	17,075,400	*6,592,849*	147,780,000	8.7	*22*	Soviet socialist republic (U.S.S.R.)	*D* Moskva (Moscow)	Eur.-Asia 19-20
Russian S.F.S.R. in Europe	Rossijskaja S.F.S.R.	3,955,818	*1,527,350*	107,940,000	27	*71*	. . .	. . .	Europe 19
†RWANDA	Rwanda	26,338	*10,169*	7,192,000	273	*707*	Republic	*A* Kigali	Africa 36
Saarland	Saar	2,569	*992*	1,035,000	403	*1,043*	State (Fed. Rep. of Germany)	*D* Saarbrücken	Europe 10
Sabah	Sabah	73,711	*28,460*	1,405,000	19	*49*	State (Malaysia)	*D* Kota Kinabalu	Asia 26
†ST. CHRISTOPHER-NEVIS	St. Christopher-Nevis	269	*104*	47,000	175	*452*	Parliamentary state	*A* Basseterre	N. Amer 51
St. Helena (incl. Dependencies)	St. Helena	419	*162*	7,800	19	*48*	Dependent territory (U.K.)	*C* Jamestown	Africa 31
†ST. LUCIA	St. Lucia	616	*238*	148,000	240	*622*	Parliamentary state	*A* Castries	N. Amer 51
St. Pierre and Miquelon	St.-Pierre et Miquelon	242	*93*	6,500	27	*70*	Overseas department (France)	*C* Saint-Pierre	N. Amer 42
†ST. VINCENT AND THE GRENADINES	St. Vincent	388	*150*	125,000	322	*833*	Parliamentary state	*A* Kingstown	N. Amer 51
SAN MARINO	San Marino	61	*24*	24,000	393	*1,000*	Republic	*A* San Marino	Europe 14
†SAO TOME AND PRINCIPE	São Tomé e Príncipe	964	*372*	119,000	123	*320*	Republic	*A* São Tomé	Africa 34
Sarawak	Sarawak	125,205	*48,342*	1,610,000	13	*33*	State (Malaysia)	*D* Kuching	Asia 26
Sardinia	Sardegna	24,090	*9,301*	1,665,000	69	*179*	Autonomous region (Italy)	*D* Cagliari	Europe 14
Saskatchewan	Saskatchewan	652,330	*251,866*	1,030,000	1.6	*4.1*	Province (Canada)	*D* Regina	N. Amer 42
†SAUDI ARABIA	Al 'Arabīyah as Su'ūdīyah	2,240,000	*864,869*	15,775,000	7.0	*18*	Monarchy	*A* Ar Riyāḍ (Riyadh)	Asia 23
Scandinavia	. . .	1,320,000	*510,000*	23,045,000	17	*45*	. . .	. . .	Europe 7
Schleswig-Holstein	Schleswig-Holstein	15,727	*6,072*	2,580,000	164	*425*	State (Fed. Rep. of Germany)	*D* Kiel	Europe 10
Scotland	Scotland	77,167	*29,794*	5,150,000	67	*173*	Administrative division (U.K.)	*D* Edinburgh	Europe 9
†SENEGAL	Sénégal	196,722	*75,955*	7,394,000	38	*97*	Republic	*A* Dakar	Africa 34
†SEYCHELLES	Seychelles	453	*175*	70,000	155	*400*	Republic	*A* Victoria	Africa 37
Shaanxi	Shaanxi	196,000	*75,676*	31,420,000	160	*415*	Province (China)	*D* Xi'an (Sian)	Asia 27
Shandong	Shandong	153,000	*59,074*	80,790,000	528	*1,368*	Province (China)	*D* Jinan	Asia 27
Shanghai	Shanghai	5,800	*2,239*	12,700,000	2,190	*5,672*	Autonomous city (China)	*D* Shanghai	Asia 28
Shanxi	Shanxi	157,000	*60,618*	27,475,000	175	*453*	Province (China)	*D* Taiyuan	Asia 27
Shetland Islands	Shetland Islands	1,433	*553*	24,000	17	*43*	Part of Scotland (U.K.)	*D* Lerwick	Europe 9
Sichuan	Sichuan	569,000	*219,692*	106,950,000	188	*487*	Province (China)	*D* Chengdu	Asia 27
Sicily	Sicilia	25,708	*9,926*	5,195,000	202	*523*	Autonomous region (Italy)	*D* Palermo	Europe 14
†SIERRA LEONE	Sierra Leone	72,325	*27,925*	4,015,000	56	*144*	Republic	*A* Freetown	Africa 34
†SINGAPORE	Singapore (English) / Singapura (Malay)	636	*236*	2,663,000	4,187	*11,284*	Republic	*A* Singapore	Asia 26
Sinkiang	Xingiang Uygur Zizhiqu	1,647,000	*635,910*	14,230,000	8.6	*22*	Autonomous region (China)	*D* Ürümqi	Asia 27
†SOLOMON ISLANDS	Solomon Islands	28,369	*10,953*	295,000	10	*27*	Parliamentary state	*A* Honiara	Oceania 63
†SOMALIA	Soomaaliya	637,657	*246,201*	8,118,000	13	*33*	Socialist republic	*A* Muqdisho (Mogadishu)	Africa 35
†SOUTH AFRICA (incl. Walvis Bay)	South Africa (English) / Suid-Afrika (Afrikaans)	1,123,226	*433,680*	35,480,000	32	*82*	Republic	*A* Pretoria, Cape Town, and Bloemfontein	Africa 37
South America	. . .	17,800,000	*6,900,000*	287,500,000	16	*42*	. . .	. . .	S. Amer 52-53
South Australia	South Australia	984,000	*379,925*	1,435,000	1.5	*3.8*	State (Australia)	*D* Adelaide	Oceania 59
South Carolina	South Carolina	80,590	*31,116*	3,494,000	43	*112*	State (U.S.)	*D* Columbia	N. Amer 44
South Dakota	South Dakota	199,740	*77,120*	713,000	3.6	*9.2*	State (U.S.)	*D* Pierre	N. Amer 45
South Georgia (incl. Dependencies)	South Georgia	3,755	*1,450*	. . .(1)	. . .	. . .	Dependent territory (U.K.)	*C* . . .	S. Amer 56
South West Africa, *see* Namibia	. . .	. . .	. . .	. . .	. . .	. . .	. . .	. . .	. . .
Soviet Union, *see* Union of Soviet Socialist Republics	. . .	. . .	. . .	. . .	. . .	. . .	. . .	. . .	. . .
†SPAIN	España	504,750	*194,885*	39,330,000	78	*202*	Constitutional monarchy	*A* Madrid	Europe 13
Spanish North Africa (8)	Plazas de Soberanía en el Norte de África	32	*12*	100,000	3,125	*8,333*	Five possessions (Spain)	*C* . . .	Africa 13
Spanish Sahara, *see* Western Sahara	. . .	. . .	. . .	. . .	. . .	. . .	. . .	. . .	. . .
†SRI LANKA	Sri Lanka	64,652	*24,962*	16,730,000	259	*670*	Socialist republic	*A* Colombo and Sri Jayawardenapura	Asia 25
†SUDAN	As Sūdān	2,505,813	*967,500*	24,255,000	9.7	*25*	Republic	*A* Al Kharṭūm (Khartoum)	Africa 35
Sumatra	Sumatera	473,606	*182,860*	36,140,000	76	*198*	Part of Indonesia (7 provinces)	. . .	Asia 26
†SURINAME	Suriname	163,820	*63,251*	398,000	2.4	*6.3*	Provisional military government	*A* Paramaribo	S. Amer 54
†SWAZILAND	Swaziland	17,364	*6,704*	727,000	42	*108*	Monarchy	*A* Mbabane and Lobamba (5)	Africa 37
†SWEDEN	Sverige	449,964	*173,732*	8,444,000	19	*49*	Constitutional monarchy	*A* Stockholm	Europe 7
SWITZERLAND	Schweiz (German) / Suisse (French) / Svizzera (Italian)	41,293	*15,943*	6,590,000	160	*413*	Federal republic	*A* Bern (Berne)	Europe 14
†SYRIA	Sūrīyah	185,180	*71,498*	11,530,000	62	*161*	Socialist republic	*A* Dimashq (Damascus)	Asia 24
TAIWAN	Taiwan	36,002	*13,900*	20,125,000	559	*1,448*	Republic	*A* Taipei	Asia 27
Tajik S.S.R.	Tadžikskaja S.S.R.	143,100	*55,251*	5,135,000	36	*93*	Soviet socialist republic (U.S.S.R.)	*D* Dušanbe (Dushanbe)	Asia 18
†TANZANIA	Tanzania	945,087	*364,900*	24,055,000	25	*66*	Republic	*A* Dar es Salaam and Dodoma (5)	Africa 36
Tasmania	Tasmania	67,800	*26,178*	452,000	6.7	*17*	State (Austl.)	*D* Hobart	Oceania 59
Tennessee	Tennessee	109,150	*42,143*	4,913,000	45	*117*	State (U.S.)	*D* Nashville	N. Amer 44
Texas	Texas	691,022	*266,805*	17,415,000	25	*65*	State (U.S.)	*D* Austin	N. Amer 45
†THAILAND	Muang Thai	513,115	*198,115*	55,375,000	108	*280*	Constitutional monarchy	*A* Krung Thep (Bangkok)	Asia 26
Tibet	Xizang Zizhiqu	1,222,000	*471,817*	2,080,000	1.7	*4.4*	Autonomous region (China)	*D* Lhasa	Asia 27
Tientsin	Tianjin	11,000	*4,247*	8,430,000	766	*1,985*	Autonomous city (China)	*D* Tianjin (Tientsin)	Asia 28
†TOGO	Togo	56,785	*21,925*	3,393,000	60	*155*	Republic	*A* Lomé	Africa 34
Tokelau	Tokelau	12	*4.6*	1,700	142	*370*	Island territory (New Zealand)	*C* . . .	Oceania 61
TONGA	Tonga	699	*270*	100,000	143	*370*	Constitutional monarchy	*A* Nuku'alofa	Oceania 61
Transcaucasia	. . .	186,100	*71,853*	15,855,000	85	*221*	. . .	. . .	Asia 16
TRANSKEI (2)	Transkei	42,000	*16,216*	3,900,000	93	*241*	National state (South African protection)	*B* Umtata	Africa 37
†TRINIDAD AND TOBAGO	Trinidad and Tobago	5,128	*1,980*	1,295,000	253	*654*	Republic	*A* Port of Spain	N. Amer 50
Tristan da Cunha	Tristan da Cunha	104	*40*	300	2.9	*7.5*	Dependency (St. Helena)	*C* Edinburgh	Africa 30-31

Country, Division, or Region English (Conventional)	Local Name	Area km²	Area sq mi	Population 1/1/89	Population Density per km²	Population Density per sq mi	Form of Government and Political Status	Capital	Continent and Map Plate
†TUNISIA	Tunisie (French) / Tūnis (Arabic)	163,610	63,170	7,876,000	48	125	Republic	A Tūnis	Africa 32
†TURKEY	Türkiye	779,452	300,948	51,970,000	67	173	Republic	A Ankara	Eur.-Asia 24
Turkey in Europe	. . .	23,764	9,175	5,025,000	211	548	. . .	. . .	Europe 24
Turkmen S.S.R.	Turkmenskaja S.S.R.	488,100	188,456	3,545,000	7.3	19	Soviet socialist republic (U.S.S.R.)	D Ašhabad	Asia 19
Turks and Caicos Islands	Turks and Caicos Islands	430	166	10,000	23	60	Dependent territory (U.K.)	C Grand Turk	N. Amer 49
TUVALU	Tuvalu	26	10	8,700	335	870	Parliamentary state	A Funafuti	Oceania 60
†UGANDA	Uganda	241,139	93,104	16,725,000	69	180	Republic	A Kampala	Africa 36
†Ukrainian S.S.R.	Ukrainskaja S.S.R.	603,700	233,090	51,620,000	86	221	Soviet socialist republic (U.S.S.R.)	D Kijev (Kiev)	Europe 16
†UNION OF SOVIET SOCIALIST REPUBLICS	Sojuz Sovetskich Socialističeskich Respublik	22,274,900	8,600,387	287,550,000	13	33	Federal socialist republic	A Moskva (Moscow)	Eur.-Asia 19-20
U.S.S.R. in Europe	. . .	4,974,818	1,920,789	182,030,000	37	95	. . .	. . .	Europe . . .
†UNITED ARAB EMIRATES	Al Imārāt al 'Arabīyah al Muttaḩidah	83,600	32,278	2,047,000	24	63	Federation of monarchs	A Abū Ẓaby (Abu Dhabi)	Asia 23
†UNITED KINGDOM	United Kingdom	242,496	93,629	57,090,000	235	610	Constitutional monarchy	A London	Europe 9
United Kingdom and Possessions	. . .	258,127	99,664	63,180,000	245	634	. . .	. . .	. . .
†UNITED STATES	United States	9,529,202	3,679,245	247,410,000	26	67	Federal republic	A Washington	N. Amer 43
United States and Possessions	. . .	9,541,271	3,683,905	251,180,000	26	68	. . .	. . .	. . .
Upper Volta, *see* Burkina Faso	. . .	. . .	. . .	. . .	. . .	. . .	. . .	. . .	. . .
†URUGUAY	Uruguay	175,016	67,574	3,184,000	18	47	Republic	A Montevideo	S. Amer 55
Utah	Utah	219,895	84,902	1,732,000	7.9	20	State (U.S.)	D Salt Lake City	N. Amer 46
Uzbek S.S.R.	Uzbekskaja S.S.R.	447,400	172,742	20,135,000	45	117	Soviet socialist republic (U.S.S.R.)	D Taškent (Tashkent)	Asia 19
†VANUATU	Vanuatu	12,189	4,706	155,000	13	33	Republic	A Port-Vila	Oceania 63
VATICAN CITY	Città del Vaticano	0.4	0.2	800	2,000	4,000	Ecclesiastical city-state	A Vatican City	Europe 14
VENDA [2]	Venda	6,875	2,654	556,000	81	209	National state (South African protection)	B Thohoyandou	Africa 37
†VENEZUELA	Venezuela	912,050	352,145	19,010,000	21	54	Federal republic	A Caracas	S. Amer 54
Vermont	Vermont	24,900	9,614	556,000	22	58	State (U.S.)	D Montpelier	N. Amer 44
Victoria	Victoria	227,600	87,877	4,325,000	19	49	State (Australia)	D Melbourne	Oceania 59
†VIETNAM	Viet Nam	329,556	127,242	66,030,000	200	519	Socialist republic	A Ha Noi	Asia 26
Virginia	Virginia	105,576	40,763	6,031,000	57	148	State (U.S.)	D Richmond	N. Amer 44
Virgin Islands of the United States	Virgin Islands of the United States	344	133	106,000	308	797	Unincorporated territory (U.S.)	C Charlotte Amalie	N. Amer 51
Virgin Islands, British	British Virgin Islands	153	59	13,000	85	220	Dependent territory (U.K.)	C Road Town	N. Amer 51
Wake Island	Wake Island	7.8	3.0	300	38	100	Unincorporated territory (U.S.)	C . . .	Oceania 60
Wales	Wales	20,768	8,019	2,855,000	137	356	Administrative Division (U.K.)	D Cardiff	Europe 9
Wallis and Futuna	Îles Wallis et Futuna	255	98	15,000	59	153	Overseas territory (France)	C Mata-Utu	Oceania 61
Washington	Washington	176,479	68,139	4,630,000	26	68	State (U.S.)	D Olympia	N. Amer 46
Western Australia	Western Australia	2,525,500	975,101	1,625,000	0.6	1.7	State (Australia)	D Perth	Oceania 59
Western Sahara	. . .	266,000	102,703	97,000	0.4	0.9	Occupied by Morocco	C El Aaiún	Africa 32
†WESTERN SAMOA	Western Samoa (English) / Samoa i Sisifo (Samoan)	2,842	1,097	180,000	63	164	Constitutional monarchy	A Apia	Oceania 65
West Indies	West Indies (English) / Indias Occidentales (Spanish)	235,000	91,000	33,130,000	141	364	. . .	. . .	N. Amer 47
West Virginia	West Virginia	62,771	24,236	1,886,000	30	78	State (U.S.)	D Charleston	N. Amer 44
Wisconsin	Wisconsin	171,491	66,213	4,828,000	28	73	State (U.S.)	D Madison	N. Amer 45
Wyoming	Wyoming	253,322	97,808	494,000	2.0	5.1	State (U.S.)	D Cheyenne	N. Amer 46
†YEMEN	Al Yaman	531,869	205,356	12,661,000	24	62	Islamic republic	A Şan'ā'	Asia 23
†YUGOSLAVIA	Jugoslavija	255,804	98,766	23,970,000	94	243	Federal socialist republic	A Beograd (Belgrade)	Europe 14-15
Yukon Territory	Yukon Territory	483,450	186,661	24,000	0.1	0.1	Territory (Canada)	D Whitehorse	N. Amer 42
Yunnan	Yunnan	436,000	168,341	35,580,000	82	211	Province (China)	D Kunming	Asia 27
†ZAIRE	Zaïre	2,345,409	905,568	33,795,000	14	37	Republic	A Kinshasa	Africa 36
†ZAMBIA	Zambia	752,614	290,586	7,682,000	10	26	Republic	A Lusaka	Africa 36
Zanzibar	Zanzibar	1,660	641	634,000	382	989	Part of Tanzania	. . . Zanzibar	Africa 36
Zhejiang	Zhejiang	102,000	39,382	42,255,000	414	1,073	Province (China)	D Hangzhou	Asia 27
†ZIMBABWE	Zimbabwe	390,759	150,873	9,003,000	23	60	Republic	A Harare	Africa 37
WORLD	. . .	149,900,000	57,900,000	5,192,000,000	35	90	. . .	. . .	1-2

† Member of the United Nations (1988).
. . . None, or not applicable.
[1] No permanent population.
[2] Bophuthatswana, Ciskei, Transkei, and Venda are not recognized by the United Nations.
[3] Claimed by Argentina.
[4] Includes West Bank, Golan Heights, and Gaza Strip.
[5] Future capital.
[6] On March 11, 1990 Lithuania unilaterally declared its independence from the Soviet Union.
[7] Claimed by Comoros.
[8] Comprises Ceuta, Melilla, and several small islands.

World Geographical Tables

The Earth: Land and Water

	Total Area		Area of Land			Area of Oceans and Seas		
	km²	*sq mi*	km²	*sq mi*	%	km²	*sq mi*	%
Earth	510,100,000	*197,000,000*	149,900,000	*57,900,000*	29.4	360,200,000	*139,100,000*	70.6
N. Hemisphere	255,050,000	*98,500,000*	106,429,000	*41,109,000*	41.6	148,762,600	*57,448,300*	58.4
S. Hemisphere	255,050,000	*98,500,000*	43,471,000	*16,791,000*	17.0	211,437,400	*81,651,700*	83.0

The Continents

Continent	Area km² *sq mi*	Population Estimate (1/1/89)	Population per km² *sq mi*	Mean Elevation m *ft*	Highest Elevation m/*ft*	Lowest Elevation m/*ft* (below sea level)	Highest Recorded Temperature °C/°*F*	Lowest Recorded Temperature °C/°*F*
Europe	9,900,000 *3,800,000*	685,400,000	69 *180*	300 *980*	gora Elbrus, U.S.S.R. 5,642/*18,510*	Caspian Sea, U.S.S.R.-Iran -28/*-92*	Sevilla, Spain 50°/*122°*	Ust-Ščugor, U.S.S.R. -55°/*-67°*
Asia	45,000,000 *17,400,000*	3,130,600,000	70 *180*	910 *3,000*	Everest, China-Nepal 8,848/*29,028*	Dead Sea, Israel-Jordan -403/*-1,322*	Tirat Zevi, Israel 54°/*129°*	Ojmjakon and Verkhoyansk, U.S.S.R. -68°/*-90°*
Africa	30,300,000 *11,700,000*	642,100,000	21 *55*	580 *1,900*	Kilimanjaro, Tanzania 5,895/*19,340*	Lac Assal, Djibouti -155/*-509*	Al 'Azīzīyah, Libya 58°/*136°*	Ifrane, Morocco -24°/*-11°*
North America	24,400,000 *9,400,000*	420,100,000	17 *45*	610 *2,000*	Mt. McKinley, U.S. 6,194/*20,320*	Death Valley, U.S. -86/*-282*	Death Valley, U.S. 57°/*134°*	Northice, Greenland -66°/*-87°*
South America	17,800,000 *6,900,000*	287,500,000	16 *42*	550 *1,800*	Cerro Aconcagua, Argentina 6,960/*22,835*	Salinas Chicas -42/*-138*	Rivadavia, Argentina 49°/*120°*	Sarmiento, Argentina -33°/*-27°*
Oceania, incl. Australia	8,500,000 *3,300,000*	26,300,000	3 *8*	....	Mt. Wilhelm, Papua New Guinea 4,509/*14,793*	Lake Eyre, Australia -12/*-39*	Cloncurry, Australia 53°/*128°*	Charlotte Pass, Australia -22°/*-8°*
Australia	7,682,300 *2,966,155*	16,955,000	2 *6*	300 *1,000*	Mt. Kosciusko, Australia 2,228/*7,310*	Lake Eyre, Austraila -12/*-39*	Cloncurry, Australia 53°/*128°*	Charlotte Pass, Australia -22°/*-8°*
Antarctica	14,000,000 *5,400,000*	....	... ...	1,830 *6,000*	Vinson Massif 4,897/*116,06*	sea level	Vanda Station 15°/*59°*	Vostok -89°/*-129°*
World	149,900,000 *57,900,000*	5,192,000,000	35 *90*	....	Everest, China-Nepal 8,848/*29,028*	Dead Sea, Israel-Jordan -403/*-1,322*	Al 'Azīzīyah, Libya 58°/*136°*	Vostok -89°/*-129°*

Principal Mountains

Mountain	Country	Height M	*Ft*
Europe			
Elbrus, gora	U.S.S.R.	5,642	*18,510*
Dyhtau, gora	U.S.S.R.	5,204	*17,073*
Blanc, Mont	△France-△Italy	4,807	*15,771*
Rosa, Monte	Italy-△Switzerland	4,634	*15,203*
Matterhorn	Italy-Switzerland	4,478	*14,692*
Grossglockner	△Austria	3,797	*12,457*
Teide, Pico de	△Spain (Canary Is.)	3,718	*12,198*
Aneto, Pico de	Spain	3,404	*11,168*
Etna	Italy	3,323	*10,902*
Zugspitze	Austria-△Germany, Fed. Rep. of	2,963	*9,721*
Ólimbos, Óros	△Greece	2,917	*9,570*
Corno Grande	Italy	2,912	*9,554*
Gerlachovský štít	△Czechoslovakia	2,663	*8,737*
Glittertind	△Norway	2,472	*8,110*
Kebnekaise	△Sweden	2,111	*6,926*
Narodnaja, gora	U.S.S.R.	1,895	*6,217*
Nevis, Ben	△United Kingdom	1,343	*4,406*
Asia			
Everest	△China-△Nepal	8,848	*29,028*
K2 (Qogir Feng)	China-△Pakistan	8,611	*28,250*
Kānchenjunga	△India-Nepal	8,598	*28,208*
Makālu	China-Nepal	8,481	*27,825*
Dhaulāgiri	Nepal	8,172	*26,810*
Annapurna	Nepal	8,078	*26,504*
Muztag	China	7,723	*25,338*
Tirich Mīr	Pakistan	7,690	*25,230*
Kommunizma, pik (Communism Peak)	△U.S.S.R.	7,495	*24,590*
Pobedy, pik	China-U.S.S.R.	7,439	*24,406*
Damāvand, Qolleh-ye	△Iran	5,604	*18,386*
Ağrı Dağı, Büyük (Mt. Ararat)	△Turkey	5,122	*16,804*
Jaya, Puncak	△Indonesia	5,030	*16,503*
Ključevskaja Sopka, vulkan	U.S.S.R.	4,750	*15,584*
Kinabalu, Gunong	△Malaysia	4,101	*13,455*
Yushan	△Taiwan	3,997	*13,114*
Fuji-San	△Japan	3,776	*12,388*
Nabī Shu'ayb, Jabal an	△Yemen	3,760	*12,336*
Apo, Mt.	△Philippines	2,954	*9,692*
Shaykh, Jabal ash- (Mt. Hermon)	Lebanon-△Syria	2,814	*9,232*
Mayon, Mt.	Philippines	2,462	*8,077*
Chili-san	△South Korea	1,915	*6,283*
Meron, Hare	△Israel	1,208	*3,963*
Africa			
Kilimanjaro	△Tanzania	5,895	*19,340*
Kirinyaga (Mt. Kenya)	△Kenya	5,199	*17,058*
Margherita	△Uganda-△Zaire	5,109	*16,762*
Ras Dashan Terara	△Ethiopia	4,620	*15,158*
Toubkal, Jebel	△Morocco	4,165	*13,665*
Cameroon, Mt.	△Cameroon	4,100	*13,451*
North America			
McKinley, Mt.	△United States	6,194	*20,320*
Logan, Mt.	△Canada	5,951	*19,524*
Orizaba, Pico de	△Mexico	5,610	*18,406*
Popocatépetl, Volcán	Mexico	5,452	*17,887*
Whitney, Mt.	United States	4,417	*14,491*
Elbert, Mt.	United States	4,399	*14,433*
Rainier, Mt.	United States	4,392	*14,410*
Shasta, Mt.	United States	4,317	*14,162*
Pikes Pk.	United States	4,301	*14,110*
Tajumulco, Volcán	△Guatemala	4,220	*13,845*
Mauna Kea	United States	4,205	*13,796*
Grand Teton	United States	4,197	*13,770*
Waddington, Mt.	Canada	3,994	*13,104*
Robson, Mt.	Canada	3,954	*12,972*
Chirripó, Cerro	△Costa Rica	3,819	*12,530*
Gunnbjørns Fjeld	△Greenland	3,700	*12,139*
Duarte, Pico	△Dominican Rep.	3,175	*10,417*
Mitchell, Mt.	United States	2,037	*6,684*
Marcy, Mt.	United States	1,629	*5,344*
South America			
Aconcagua, Cerro	△Argentina	6,960	*22,835*
Ojos del Salado, Nevado	Argentina-△Chile	6,863	*22,516*
Huascarán, Nevado	△Peru	6,746	*22,133*
Illimani, Nevado del	△Bolivia	6,682	*21,923*
Chimborazo, Volcán	△Ecuador	6,310	*20,702*
Cristóbal Colón, Pico	△Colombia	5,800	*19,029*
Neblina, Pico da	△Brazil-Venezuela	3,014	*9,888*
Oceania			
Wilhelm, Mt.	△Papua New Guinea	4,509	*14,793*
Cook, Mt.	△New Zealand	3,764	*12,349*
Kosciusko, Mt.	△Australia	2,228	*7,310*
Antarctica			
Vinson Massif	△Antarctica	4,897	*16,066*
Kirkpatrick, Mt.	Antarctica	4,528	*14,856*

△ Highest mountain in country.

Oceans, Seas, and Gulfs

Name	Area km²	Area *sq mi*	Greatest Depth m	Greatest Depth *ft*
Pacific Ocean	165,200,000	*63,800,000*	11,020	*36,155*
Atlantic Ocean	82,400,000	*31,800,000*	9,220	*30,249*
Indian Ocean	74,900,000	*28,900,000*	7,450	*24,442*
Arctic Ocean	14,000,000	*5,400,000*	5,450	*17,881*
Arabian Sea	3,864,000	*1,492,000*	5,800	*19,029*
South China Sea	3,447,000	*1,331,000*	5,560	*18,241*
Caribbean Sea	2,753,000	*1,063,000*	7,680	*25,197*
Mediterranean Sea	2,505,000	*967,000*	5,020	*16,470*
Bering Sea	2,269,000	*876,000*	4,096	*13,438*
Bengal, Bay of	2,173,000	*839,000*	5,258	*17,251*
Okhotsk, Sea of	1,603,000	*619,000*	3,372	*11,063*
Norwegian Sea	1,546,000	*597,000*	4,020	*13,189*
Mexico, Gulf of	1,544,000	*596,000*	4,380	*14,370*
East China Sea	1,248,000	*482,000*	4,424	*14,514*
Hudson Bay	1,230,000	*475,000*	259	*850*

Waterfalls

Waterfall	Country	River	Height m	Height *ft*
Angel	Venezuela	Churún	972	*3,189*
Tugela	South Africa	Tugela	948	*3,110*
Yosemite	United States	Yosemite Creek	739	*2,425*
Sutherland	New Zealand	Arthur	579	*1,900*
Gavarnie	France	Gave de Pau	421	*1,381*
Lofoi	Zaire	Lofoi	384	*1,260*
Krimml	Austria	Krimml	381	*1,250*
Takakkaw	Canada	Yoho	380	*1,248*
Staubbach	Switzerland	Staubbach	305	*1,001*
Mardalsfoss	Norway	. . .	297	*974*
Gersoppa	India	Sharavati	253	*830*
Kaieteur	Guyana	Potaro	247	*810*

Principal Rivers

River	Continent	Length km	Length *mi*
Nile	Africa	6,671	*4,145*
Amazon-Ucayali	South America	6,400	*4,000*
Yangtze (Chang Jiang)	Asia	6,300	*3,900*
Yellow (Huang He)	Asia	5,464	*3,395*
Ob-Irtyš	Asia	5,410	*3,362*
Río de la Plata-Paraná	South America	4,876	*3,030*
Congo (Zaïre)	Africa	4,700	*2,900*
Paraná	South America	4,500	*2,800*
Amur (Heilong Jiang)	Asia	4,416	*2,744*
Lena	Asia	4,400	*2,700*
Mekong	Asia	4,200	*2,600*
Niger	Africa	4,200	*2,600*
Jenisej	Asia	4,092	*2,543*
Mississippi	North America	3,779	*2,348*
Missouri	North America	3,726	*2,315*
Volga	Europe	3,531	*2,194*
São Francisco	South America	3,199	*1,988*
Rio Grande	North America	3,034	*1,885*
Indus	Asia	2,900	*1,800*
Danube	Europe	2,858	*1,776*
Yukon	North America	2,849	*1,770*
Brahmaputra	Asia	2,849	*1,770*
Salween (Thanlwin)	Asia	2,816	*1,750*
Zambezi	Africa	2,700	*1,700*
Tocantins	South America	2,639	*1,640*
Orinoco	South America	2,600	*1,600*
Paraguay	South America	2,591	*1,610*
Amudarja	Asia	2,540	*1,578*
Murray	Australia	2,520	*1,566*
Ganges	Asia	2,511	*1,560*
Euphrates	Asia	2,430	*1,510*
Ural	Asia	2,428	*1,509*
Arkansas	North America	2,348	*1,459*
Colorado	North America (U.S.-Mex.)	2,334	*1,450*
Syrdarja	Asia	2,205	*1,370*
Tarim	Asia	2,137	*1,328*
Orange	Africa	2,100	*1,300*
Negro	South America	2,100	*1,300*
Irrawaddy (Ayeyarwady)	Asia	2,100	*1,300*
Red	North America	2,044	*1,270*
Columbia	North America	2,000	*1,200*
Xingu	South America	1,979	*1,230*
Ucayali	South America	1,963	*1,220*
Saskatchewan-Bow	North America	1,939	*1,205*
Peace	North America	1,923	*1,195*
Tigris	Asia	1,899	*1,180*
Sungari	Asia	1,835	*1,140*
Pechora	Europe	1,809	*1,124*
Limpopo	Africa	1,800	*1,100*
Snake	North America	1,670	*1,038*

Principal Islands

Island	Area km²	Area *sq mi*	Highest Point Name	Highest Point m	Highest Point *ft*
Grønland (Greenland)	2,175,600	*840,000*	Gunnbjørns Fjeld	3,700	*12,139*
New Guinea	800,000	*309,000*	Puncak Jaya	5,030	*16,503*
Borneo	744,100	*287,300*	Gunong Kinabalu	4,101	*13,455*
Madagascar	587,000	*227,000*	Maromokotro	2,876	*9,436*
Baffin Island	507,451	*195,928*	Unnamed	2,591	*8,501*
Sumatera (Sumatra)	473,606	*182,860*	Gunung Kerinci	3,800	*12,467*
Honshū	230,966	*89,176*	Fuji-San	3,776	*12,388*
Great Britain	229,978	*88,795*	Ben Nevis	1,343	*4,406*
Victoria Island	217,291	*83,897*	Mt. Bumpus	655	*2,149*
Ellesmere Island	196,236	*75,767*	Barbeau Peak	2,604	*8,543*
Sulawesi (Celebes)	189,216	*73,057*	Bulu Rantekombola	3,455	*11,335*
South Island	149,883	*57,870*	Mt. Cook	3,764	*12,349*
Jawa (Java)	132,187	*51,038*	Gunung Semeru	3,676	*12,060*
Seram (Ceram)	118,625	*45,801*	Gunung Binaiya	3,019	*9,905*
North Island	114,669	*44,274*	Mt. Ruapehu	2,797	*9,177*
Cuba	110,800	*42,800*	Pico Turquino	1,994	*6,542*
Newfoundland	108,860	*42,031*	Unnamed	814	*2,670*
Luzon	104,688	*40,420*	Mt. Pulog	2,930	*9,613*
Ísland (Iceland)	103,000	*39,800*	Hvannadalshnúkur	2,119	*6,952*
Mindanao	94,630	*36,537*	Mt. Apo	2,954	*9,692*
Ireland	84,400	*32,600*	Carrauntoohil	1,038	*3,406*
Hokkaidō	83,515	*32,245*	Taisetsu-Zan	2,290	*7,513*
Novaja Zemlja (Novaya Zemlya)	82,600	*31,900*	Unnamed	1,547	*5,075*
Sahalin, ostrov (Sakhalin)	76,400	*29,500*	gora Lopatina	1,609	*5,279*
Hispaniola	76,000	*29,300*	Pico Duarte	3,175	*10,417*
Banks Island	70,028	*27,038*	Unnamed	747	*2,451*
Tasmania	67,800	*26,200*	Mt. Ossa	1,617	*5,305*
Sri Lanka	64,600	*24,900*	Pidurutalagala	2,524	*8,281*
Devon Island	55,247	*21,331*	Unnamed	1,887	*6,191*
Tierra del Fuego, Isla Grande de	48,200	*18,600*	Cerro Yogan	2,469	*8,100*

Major Lakes

Lake	Location	Area km²	Area *sq mi*	Depth m	Depth *ft*
Caspian Sea	Iran-U.S.S.R.	370,990	*143,240*	1,025	*3,363*
Superior, L.	Canada-U.S.	82,100	*31,700*	406	*1,332*
Victoria, L.	Africa	69,463	*26,820*	85	*279*
Aral'skoje more (Aral Sea)	U.S.S.R.	64,100	*24,700*	68	*223*
Huron, L.	Canada-U.S.	60,000	*23,000*	229	*750*
Michigan, L.	U.S.	57,800	*22,300*	282	*924*
Tanganyika. L.	Africa	31,986	*12,350*	1,463	*4,800*
Bajkal, ozero (L. Baikal)	U.S.S.R.	31,500	*12,200*	1,620	*5,315*
Great Bear Lake	Canada	31,326	*12,095*	413	*1,356*
Nyasa, L.	Africa	28,878	*11,150*	695	*2,280*
Great Slave Lake	Canada	28,568	*11,030*	614	*2,015*
Erie, L.	Canada-U.S.	25,667	*9,910*	62	*204*
Winnipeg, L.	Canada	24,387	*9,416*	28	*92*
Ontario, L.	Canada-U.S.	19,529	*7,540*	243	*798*
Balhaš, ozero (L. Balkhash)	U.S.S.R.	18,300	*7,100*	26	*85*
Chad, L.	Africa	16,300	*6,300*	7	*24*
Onežskoje ozero (L. Onega)	U.S.S.R.	9,720	*3,753*	127	*417*
Eyre, L.	Australia	9,500	*3,700*	1	*4*
Titicaca, Lago	Bolivia-Peru	8,300	*3,200*	302	*990*
Nicaragua, Lago de	Nicaragua	8,158	*3,150*	70	*230*
Mai-Ndombe, Lac	Zaire	8,000	*3,100*	11	*36*
Athabasca, L.	Canada	7,935	*3,064*	124	*407*
Reindeer Lake	Canada	6,650	*2,568*	219	*720*
Tônlé Sab, Bœng	Cambodia	6,500	*2,500*	12	*39*
Rudolf, L.	Ethiopia-Kenya	6,405	*2,473*	219	*720*
Torrens, L.	Australia	5,900	*2,300*	*	*
Albert, L.	Uganda-Zaire	5,594	*2,160*	51	*168*
Vänern	Sweden	5,584	*2,156*	99	*325*

* Intermittently dry lake

Drainage Basins

Name	Continent	Area km²	Area *sq mi*
Amazon	South America	6,151,000	*2,375,000*
Congo (Zaïre)	Africa	3,823,000	*1,476,000*
Mississippi-Missouri	North America	3,230,000	*1,247,000*
Río de la Plata-Paraná	South America	3,100,000	*1,197,000*
Ob'-Irtyš	Asia	2,989,000	*1,154,000*
Nile	Africa	2,802,000	*1,082,000*
Lena	Asia	2,489,000	*961,000*
Amur-Argun	Asia	2,051,000	*792,000*
Niger	Africa	1,891,000	*730,000*
Yangtze (Chang Jiang)	Asia	1,826,000	*705,000*
Mackenzie	North America	1,572,000	*607,000*
Volga	Europe	1,360,000	*525,000*
Zambezi	Africa	1,331,000	*514,000*
St. Lawrence	North America	1,303,000	*503,000*

World Geographical Tables

Historical Population of the World

AREA	1650	1750	1800	1850	1900	1914	1920	1939	1950	1989
Europe	*100,000,000*	*140,000,000*	*190,000,000*	265,000,000	400,000,000	470,000,000	453,000,000	526,000,000	530,000,000	685,400,000
Asia	*335,000,000*	*476,000,000*	*593,000,000*	*754,000,000*	*932,000,000*	*1,006,000,000*	*1,000,000,000*	*1,247,000,000*	*1,418,000,000*	3,130,600,000
Africa	*100,000,000*	*95,000,000*	*90,000,000*	*95,000,000*	*118,000,000*	*130,000,000*	*140,000,000*	170,000,000	199,000,000	642,100,000
North America	*5,000,000*	*5,000,000*	*13,000,000*	*39,000,000*	106,000,000	141,000,000	147,000,000	186,000,000	219,000,000	420,100,000
South America	*8,000,000*	*7,000,000*	*12,000,000*	*20,000,000*	38,000,000	55,000,000	61,000,000	90,000,000	111,000,000	287,500,000
Oceania, incl. Australia	*2,000,000*	*2,000,000*	*2,000,000*	*2,000,000*	6,000,000	8,000,000	9,000,000	11,000,000	13,000,000	26,300,000
Australia					4,000,000	5,000,000	6,000,000	7,000,000	8,000,000	16,955,000
World	*550,000,000*	*725,000,000*	*900,000,000*	*1,175,000,000*	*1,600,000,000*	*1,810,000,000*	*1,810,000,000*	*2,230,000,000*	*2,490,000,000*	5,192,000,000

Figures in italics represent very rough estimates.

Largest Countries: Population

Country	Population 1/1/89
1. China	1,094,700,000
2. India	825,000,000
3. U.S.S.R.	287,550,000
4. United States	247,410,000
5. Indonesia	185,860,000
6. Brazil	145,930,000
7. Japan	123,010,000
8. Nigeria	113,580,000
9. Bangladesh	111,390,000
10. Pakistan	108,990,000
11. Mexico	85,300,000
12. Vietnam	66,030,000
13. Germany, Fed. Rep.	61,380,000
14. Philippines	60,110,000
15. Italy	57,500,000
16. United Kingdom	57,090,000
17. France	55,970,000
18. Thailand	55,375,000
19. Iran	52,760,000
20. Egypt	52,490,000
21. Turkey	51,970,000
22. Ethiopia	48,470,000
23. South Korea	42,840,000
24. Burma	41,860,000
25. Spain	39,330,000
26. Poland	37,955,000
27. South Africa	35,480,000
28. Zaire	33,795,000
29. Argentina	32,205,000
30. Colombia	30,465,000
31. Canada	25,895,000
32. Kenya	25,825,000
33. Morocco	25,600,000
34. Sudan	24,255,000
35. Algeria	24,215,000
36. Tanzania	24,055,000
37. Yugoslavia	23,970,000
38. Romania	23,085,000
39. North Korea	22,250,000
40. Peru	21,535,000
41. Taiwan	20,125,000
42. Venezuela	19,010,000
43. Nepal	18,415,000
44. Iraq	17,900,000
45. Mozambique	17,660,000

Largest Countries: Area

Country	Area km²	*sq mi*
1. U.S.S.R.	22,274,900	*8,600,387*
2. Canada	9,970,610	*3,849,674*
3. China	9,631,600	*3,718,782*
4. United States	9,529,202	*3,679,245*
5. Brazil	8,511,965	*3,286,488*
6. Australia	7,682,300	*2,966,155*
7. India	3,203,975	*1,237,062*
8. Argentina	2,780,092	*1,073,400*
9. Sudan	2,505,813	*967,500*
10. Algeria	2,381,741	*919,595*
11. Zaire	2,345,409	*905,568*
12. Saudi Arabia	2,240,000	*864,869*
13. Greenland	2,175,600	*840,004*
14. Mexico	1,972,547	*761,605*
15. Indonesia	1,919,443	*741,101*
16. Libya	1,759,540	*679,362*
17. Iran	1,648,000	*636,296*
18. Mongolia	1,565,000	*604,250*
19. Peru	1,285,216	*496,225*
20. Chad	1,284,000	*495,755*
21. Niger	1,267,000	*489,191*
22. Ethiopia	1,251,282	*483,123*
23. Angola	1,246,700	*481,354*
24. Mali	1,240,000	*478,767*
25. Colombia	1,141,748	*440,831*
26. South Africa	1,123,226	*433,680*
27. Bolivia	1,098,581	*424,165*
28. Mauritania	1,030,700	*397,956*
29. Egypt	1,001,450	*386,662*
30. Tanzania	945,087	*364,900*
31. Nigeria	923,768	*356,669*
32. Venezuela	912,050	*352,145*
33. Pakistan	879,902	*339,732*
34. Mozambique	799,379	*308,642*
35. Turkey	779,452	*300,948*
36. Chile	756,626	*292,135*
37. Zambia	752,614	*290,586*
38. Burma	676,577	*261,228*
39. Afghanistan	652,225	*251,826*
40. Somalia	637,657	*246,201*
41. Central African Republic	622,984	*240,535*
42. Madagascar	587,041	*226,658*
43. Kenya	582,646	*224,961*
44. Botswana	582,000	*224,711*
45. France	547,026	*211,208*

Smallest Countries: Population

Country	Population 1/1/89
1. Vatican City	800
2. Niue	2,400
3. Anguilla	7,000
4. Tuvalu	8,700
5. Nauru	9,000
6. Palau	15,000
7. Cook Islands	17,000
8. Northern Mariana Is.	22,000
9. San Marino	24,000
10. Liechtenstein	29,000
Monaco	29,000
11. Marshall Islands	40,000
12. St. Christopher-Nevis	47,000
13. Faeroe Islands	48,000
14. Andorra	51,000
15. Greenland	55,000
16. Isle of Man	62,000
17. Aruba	66,000
18. Kiribati	69,000
19. Seychelles	70,000
20. Antigua	84,000
21. Grenada	95,000
22. Dominica	100,000
Tonga	100,000
23. Micronesia, Federated States of	108,000
24. Sao Tome and Principe	119,000
25. St. Vincent	125,000
26. St. Lucia	148,000
27. Vanuatu	155,000
28. Cyprus, North	172,000
29. Western Samoa	180,000
30. Belize	184,000
31. Netherlands Antilles	194,000
32. Maldives	209,000
33. Bahamas	243,000
34. Brunei	247,000
35. Iceland	248,000
36. Barbados	255,000
37. Solomon Islands	295,000
38. Djibouti	324,000
39. Cape Verde	359,000
40. Luxembourg	368,000
41. Malta	370,000
42. Suriname	398,000

Smallest Countries: Area

Country	Area km²	*sq mi*
1. Vatican City	0.4	*0.2*
2. Monaco	1.9	*0.7*
3. Nauru	21	*8.1*
4. Tuvalu	26	*10*
5. San Marino	61	*24*
6. Anguilla	91	*35*
7. Liechtenstein	160	*62*
8. Marshall Islands	181	*70*
9. Aruba	193	*75*
10. Cook Islands	236	*91*
11. Niue	263	*102*
12. St. Christopher-Nevis	269	*104*
13. Maldives	298	*115*
14. Malta	316	*122*
15. Grenada	344	*133*
16. St. Vincent	388	*150*
17. Barbados	430	*166*
18. Antigua	443	*171*
Andorra	453	*175*
19. Seychelles	453	*175*
20. Northern Mariana Is.	477	*184*
21. Palau	508	*196*
22. Isle of Man	572	*221*
23. St. Lucia	616	*238*
24. Singapore	636	*236*
25. Bahrain	662	*256*
26. Tonga	699	*270*
27. Micronesia, Federated States of	702	*271*
28. Kiribati	726	*280*
29. Dominica	752	*290*
30. Netherlands Antilles	800	*309*
31. Sao Tome and Principe	964	*372*
32. Faeroe Islands	1,399	*540*
33. Mauritius	2,040	*788*
34. Comoros	2,171	*838*
35. Luxembourg	2,586	*998*
36. Western Samoa	2,842	*1,097*
37. Cyprus, North	3,355	*1,295*
38. Cape Verde	4,033	*1,557*
39. Trinidad and Tobago	5,128	*1,980*
40. Brunei	5,765	*2,226*
41. Cyprus	5,896	*2,276*
42. Venda	6,875	*2,654*
43. Ciskei	7,790	*3,008*

Highest Population Densities

Country	Density per km²	*sq mi*
1. Monaco	15,263	*41,429*
2. Singapore	4,187	*11,284*
3. Vatican City	2,000	*4,000*
4. Malta	1,171	*3,033*
5. Bangladesh	774	*2,003*
6. Maldives	701	*1,817*
7. Bahrain	692	*1,789*
8. Barbados	593	*1,536*
9. Taiwan	559	*1,448*
10. Mauritius	518	*1,341*
11. South Korea	435	*1,127*
12. Nauru	429	*1,111*
13. San Marino	393	*1,000*
14. Puerto Rico	363	*939*
15. Netherlands	355	*918*
16. Aruba	342	*880*
17. Tuvalu	335	*870*
18. Japan	326	*843*
19. Belgium	323	*837*
20. Lebanon	322	*835*
21. St. Vincent	322	*833*
22. Grenada	276	*714*
23. Rwanda	273	*707*
24. Sri Lanka	259	*670*
25. India	257	*667*
26. Trinidad and Tobago	253	*654*
27. Germany, Fed. Rep. of	247	*639*
28. El Salvador	243	*630*
29. Netherlands Antilles	243	*628*
30. St. Lucia	240	*622*

Lowest Population Densities

Country	Density per km²	*sq mi*
1. Greenland	...	*0.1*
2. Mongolia	1.3	*3.5*
3. Mauritania	1.9	*4.9*
4. Botswana	2.1	*5.5*
5. Australia	2.2	*5.7*
6. Libya	2.3	*5.9*
7. Iceland	2.4	*6.2*
8. Suriname	2.4	*6.3*
9. Canada	2.6	*6.7*
10. Guyana	3.6	*9.2*
11. Chad	3.8	*9.8*
12. Gabon	3.9	*10*
13. Central African Republic	5.0	*13*
14. Niger	5.8	*15*
15. Oman	6.0	*16*
16. Congo	6.4	*17*
Bolivia	6.5	*17*
Angola	6.7	*17*
17. Saudi Arabia	7.0	*18*
18. Mali	7.3	*19*
19. Papua New Guinea	7.9	*20*
20. Belize	8.0	*21*
21. Niue	9.1	*24*
22. Sudan	9.7	*25*
23. Algeria	10	*26*
Zambia	10	*26*
24. Paraguay	10	*27*
Solomon Islands	10	*27*
25. Norway	11	*28*

... Less than 0.1

Major Metropolitan Areas of the World

This table lists the major metropolitan areas of the world according to their estimated population on January I, 1989. For convenience in reference, the areas are grouped by major region with the total for each region given. The number of areas by population classification is given in parentheses with each size group.

For ease of comparison, each metropolitan area has been defined by Rand McNally according to consistent rules. A metropolitan area includes a central city, neighboring communities linked to it by continuous built-up areas, and more distant communities if the bulk of their population is supported by commuters to the central city. Some metropolitan areas have more than one central city; in such cases each central city is listed.

SIZE	ANGLO-AMERICA	LATIN AMERICA	EUROPE	U.S.S.R.	WEST ASIA	EAST ASIA	AFRICA-OCEANIA
Over 15,000,000 (6)	New York	Ciudad de México (Mexico City) São Paulo				Ōsaka-Kōbe-Kyōto Sŏul (Seoul) Tōkyō-Yokohama	
10,000,000-15,000,000 (9)	Los Angeles	Buenos Aires Rio de Janeiro	London Paris	Moskva (Moscow)	Bombay Calcutta		Al Qāhirah (Cairo)
5,000,000-10,000,000 (18)	Chicago Philadelphia-Trenton-Wilmington San Francisco-Oakland-San Jose	Lima		Leningrad	Delhi-New Delhi İstanbul Karāchi Madras Tehrān	Beijing (Peking) Jakarta Krung Thep (Bangkok) Manila Shanghai Taipei Tianjin (Tientsin) Victoria (Hong Kong)	
3,000,000-5,000,000 (38)	Boston Dallas-Fort Worth Detroit-Windsor Houston Miami-Fort Lauderdale Toronto Washington	Belo Horizonte Bogotá Caracas Guadalajara Santiago	Athínai (Athens) Barcelona Berlin Essen-Dortmund-Duisburg (Ruhr Area) Madrid Milano (Milan) Roma (Rome)		Baghdād Bangalore Dhaka (Dacca) Hyderābād, India Lahore	Guangzhou (Canton) Nagoya Pusan Yangon (Rangoon) Shenyang (Mukden) Singapore Ho Chi Minh (Saigon) Wuhan	Al Iskandarīyah (Alexandria) Johannesburg Kinshasa Lagos Melbourne Sydney
2,000,000-3,000,000 (49)	Atlanta Baltimore Cleveland Minneapolis-St. Paul Montréal Phoenix Pittsburgh St. Louis San Diego-Tijuana Seattle-Tacoma	Fortaleza La Habana (Havana) Medellín Monterrey Porto Alegre Recife Salvador	Birmingham Bruxelles (Brussels) București (Bucharest) Budapest Hamburg Katowice-Bytom-Gliwice Lisboa (Lisbon) Manchester Napoli (Naples) Warszawa (Warsaw)	Baku Doneck-Makejevka Gorki Kijev (Kiev) Taškent	Ahmadābād Ankara Colombo Kānpur Pune (Poona)	Bandung Chongqing (Chungking) Harbin Kuala Lumpur Nanjing (Nanking) Sapporo-Otaru Surabaya Taegu Xi'an (Sian)	Cape Town Casablanca Al Jazā'ir (Algiers)
1,500,000-2,000,000 (57)	Cincinnati Denver	Brasília Cali Curitiba Guayaquil Montevideo San Juan Santo Domingo	Amsterdam Beograd (Belgrade) Frankfurt am Main Glasgow København (Copenhagen) Köln (Cologne) Leeds-Bradford Liverpool München (Munich) Stuttgart Torino (Turin) Wien (Vienna)	Char'kov (Kharkov) Dnepropetrovsk Kujbyšev (Kuybyshev) Minsk Novosibirsk Sverdlovsk	Al Kuwayt (Kuwait) 'Ammān Ar Riyāḍ (Riyadh) Bayrūt (Beirut) Chittagong Dimashq (Damascus) İzmir Jiddah Mashhad Nāgpur Tel Aviv-Yafo	Changchun (Hsinking) Chengdu (Chengtu) Dalian (Lüda) Fukuoka Ha Noi Hiroshima-Kure Jinan (Tsinan) Kaohsiung Kitakyūshū-Shimonoseki Medan P'yŏngyang Semarang Taiyuan	Abidjan Adis Abeba Al Kharṭūm-Umm Durmān (Khartoum-Omdurman) Dakar Dar es Salaam Durban
1,000,000-1,500,000 (105)	Buffalo-Niagara Falls-St. Catharines Columbus El Paso-Ciudad Juárez Hartford-New Britain Indianapolis Kansas City Milwaukee New Orleans Portland Riverside-San Bernardino Sacramento St. Petersburg-Clearwater San Antonio Vancouver	Barranquilla Belém Campinas Córdoba Goiânia Guatemala La Paz Maracaibo Puebla Quito Rosario Santos	Antwerpen (Antwerp) Dublin (Baile Átha Cliath) Düsseldorf Hannover Lille-Roubaix Łódź Lyon Mannheim Marseille Newcastle-Sunderland Nürnberg Porto Praha (Prague) Rotterdam Sofija (Sofia) Stockholm Valencia	Alma-Ata Čeljabinsk (Chelyabinsk) Jerevan Kazan Odessa Omsk Perm Rīga Rostov-na-Donu Saratov Tbilisi Ufa Volgograd	Asansol Coimbatore Eşfahān Faisalabad Halab (Aleppo) Indore Jaipur Kābol Lucknow Madurai Patna Rāwalpindi-Islāmābād Surat Tabrīz Vārānasi (Benares)	Anshan Baotou Changsha Fushun Guiyang (Kweiyang) Hangzhou (Hangchow) Jilin (Kirin) Kunming Kwangju Lanzhou (Lanchow) Nanchang Palembang Qingdao (Tsingtao) Qiqihar (Tsitsihar) Sendai Shijiazhuang Tangshan Ujung Pandang (Makasar) Ürümqi Zhengzhou (Chengchow)	Accra Adelaide Brisbane Douala Harare Ibadan Luanda Maputo Nairobi Perth Pretoria Rabat-Salé Ṭarābulus (Tripoli) Tūnis
Total by region (282)	38	36	48	26	43	61	30

Populations of Major Cities

The largest and most important of the world's major cities are listed in the following table. Also included are some smaller cities because of their regional significance.

Local official name forms have been used throughout the table. When a commonly used "conventional" name form exists, it has been featured within parentheses, following the official name. Each city name is followed by the English name of its country. Names in the United States, the United Kingdom, and Canada are further distinguished by the name of the state, region, or province in which they are located.

Many cities have population figures within parentheses following the country name. These are metropolitan populations, comprising the central city and its suburbs. When a city is within the metropolitan area of another city the name of the metropolitan central city is specified in parentheses preceded by a *. The symbol † identifies a political district population which includes some rural population. For these cities the estimated city population has been based upon the district figure.

The population of each city has been dated for ease of comparison. The date is followed by a letter designating: Census (C) or Official Estimate (E).

City and Country	Population	Date
Aachen, Fed. Rep. of Ger. (535,000)	239,170	87E
Ābādān, Iran	296,081	76C
Abidjan, Ivory Coast	1,500,000	83E
Abū Ẓaby (Abu Dhabi), United Arab Emirates	242,975	80C
Acapulco [de Juárez], Mexico	301,900	80C
Accra, Ghana (1,250,000)	859,640	84C
Adana, Turkey	777,550	85C
Ad Dawḥah (Doha), Qatar (310,000)	217,294	86E
Addis Ababa, see Ādīs Ābeba		
Adelaide, Australia (977,721)	14,157	86C
Aden, see Baladiyat ʿAdan		
Ādīs Ābeba (Addis Ababa), Ethiopia (1,500,000)	1,412,575	84C
Agana, Guam (44,000)	896	80C
Āgra, India (747,318)	694,190	81C
Aguascalientes, Mexico	293,152	80C
Ahmadābād, India (2,400,000)	2,059,725	81C
Ahvāz, Iran	471,000	82E
Akita, Japan	296,400	85C
Akron, Oh., U.S. (614,100)	237,177	80C
Albany, N.Y., U.S. (729,100)	101,727	80C
Al Baṣrah, Iraq	616,700	85E
Albuquerque, N.M., U.S. (453,200)	332,336	80C
Aleppo, see Halab		
Alexandria, see Al Iskandarīyah		
Algiers, see Al Jazā'ir		
Al Iskandarīyah (Alexandria), Egypt (3,350,000)	2,821,000	85E
Al Jazā'ir (Algiers), Algeria (2,300,000)	1,721,607	83E
Al Jīzah (Giza), Egypt (*Al Qāhirah)	1,608,400	85E
Al Kharṭūm (Khartoum), Sudan (1,450,000)	476,218	83C
Al Kuwayt (Kuwait), Kuwait (1,375,000)	44,335	85C
Allahābād, India (650,070)	616,050	81C
Alma-Ata, U.S.S.R. (1,170,000)	1,108,000	87E
Al Madīnah (Medina), Saudi Arabia	290,000	80E
Al Maḥallah al Kubrā, Egypt (375,000)	328,700	85E
Al Manāmah (Manama), Bahrain (224,643)	108,684	81C
Al Manṣurah, Egypt (375,000)	328,700	85E
Al Mawṣil (Mosul), Iraq	570,920	85E
Al Qāhirah (Cairo), Egypt (9,300,000)	6,205,000	85E
Amagasaki, Japan (*Ōsaka)	509,110	85C
ʿAmmān, Jordan (1,250,000)	833,500	86E
Amritsar, India	594,840	81C
Amsterdam, Netherlands (1,860,000)	679,140	86E
Anchorage, Ak., U.S. (184,300)	174,431	80C
Andorra la Vella, Andorra	14,928	82C
Ankara, Turkey (2,400,000)	2,235,035	85C
Annaba (Bône), Algeria (†348,322)	302,700	83E
Anshan, China	1,300,000	87E
Antananarivo, Madagascar	663,000	85E
Antwerpen (Antwerp), Belgium (1,100,000)	490,524	83E
Apia, Western Samoa	33,170	81C
Arequipa, Peru (446,942)	108,020	81C
Arkhangelsk, U.S.S.R.	416,000	87E
Arnhem, Netherlands (294,085)	127,960	86E
Ar Riyāḍ (Riyadh), Saudi Arabia	1,250,000	80E
Asansol, India (1,050,000)	183,370	81C
As Suways (Suez), Egypt	254,000	85E
Astrahan, U.S.S.R.	509,000	87E
Asunción, Paraguay (700,000)	455,517	82C
Athínai (Athens), Greece (3,027,331)	885,737	81C
Atlanta, Ga., U.S. (1,962,500)	425,022	80C
Auckland, New Zealand (850,000)	149,046	86C
Augsburg, Fed. Rep. of Ger. (405,000)	245,960	87E
Austin, Tx., U.S. (430,200)	345,890	80C
Baghdād, Iraq (4,000,000)	2,200,000	85E
Bakhtarān, Iran	532,000	82E
Baku, U.S.S.R. (2,005,000)	1,115,000	87E
Baladiyat ʿAdan (Aden), Yemen (318,000)	176,100	84E
Balikpapan, Indonesia (†279,852)	208,040	80C
Baltimore, Md., U.S. (1,960,400)	786,741	80C
Bamako, Mali	600,000	80E
Bandar Seri Begawan, Brunei	63,868	81C
Bandung, Indonesia (1,800,000)	1,461,407	80C
Bangalore, India (2,950,000)	2,476,355	81C
Banghāzī (Benghazi), Libya	367,600	81E
Bangkok, see Krung Thep		
Bangui, Cen. Afr. Rep.	473,800	84E
Banjul, Gambia (95,000)	44,536	83C
Barcelona, Spain (4,040,000)	1,694,064	86E
Barnaul, U.S.S.R. (655,000)	596,000	87E
Barquisimeto, Venezuela	497,630	81C
Barranquilla, Colombia	1,140,000	85C
Basel, Switzerland (575,000)	173,160	87E
Basse-Terre, Guadeloupe (26,000)	13,656	82C
Basseterre, St. Chris.-Nevis	14,725	80C
Baton Rouge, La., U.S. (434,400)	238,876	80C
Bayrūt (Beirut), Lebanon (1,675,000)	509,000	82
Beijing (Peking), China (6,450,000)	5,970,000	87E
Beirut, see Bayrūt		
Belém, Brazil (1,200,000)	1,116,578	85E
Belfast, N. Ire., U.K. (685,000)	318,600	84E
Belgrade, see Beograd		
Belize City, Belize	39,041	80C
Belmopan, Belize	2,907	80C
Belo Horizonte, Brazil (2,950,000)	2,114,429	85E
Benares, see Vārānasi		
Bengbu, China (†612,600)	403,900	86E
Benxi, China	840,000	87E
Beograd (Belgrade), Yugoslavia (1,400,000)	936,200	81C
Bergamo, Italy (340,000)	121,840	81C
Berlin, Ost- (East), Ger. Dem. Rep. (*Berlin, West)	1,236,248	87E
Berlin, West, Fed. Rep. of Ger. (3,825,000)	1,879,225	87E
Bern (Berne), Switzerland (298,800)	137,134	87E
Bhopāl, India	671,010	81C
Bielefeld, Fed. Rep. of Ger. (515,000)	299,360	87E
Bilbao, Spain (985,000)	378,221	86E
Billings, Mt., U.S. (96,100)	66,842	80C
Birmingham, Eng., U.K. (2,675,000)	1,013,995	81C
Birmingham, Al., U.S. (747,400)	286,799	80C
Bissau, Guinea-Bissau	109,486	79C
Blackpool, Eng., U.K. (280,000)	146,290	81C
Bloemfontein, South Africa (235,000)	104,380	85C
Bogor, India (560,000)	246,940	80C
Bogotá, Colombia (4,550,000)	4,260,000	85C
Boise, Id., U.S. (164,200)	102,160	80C
Bologna, Italy (530,000)	455,850	81C
Bombay, India (9,950,000)	8,243,405	81C
Bonn, Fed. Rep. of Ger. (570,000)	291,439	87E
Bordeaux, France (640,012)	208,150	82C
Boston, Ma., U.S. (3,971,700)	562,994	80C
Brasília, Brazil	1,567,709	85E
Bratislava, Czechoslovakia	417,100	86E
Braunschweig, Fed. Rep. of Ger. (330,000)	247,830	87E
Brazzaville, Congo	595,102	84C
Bremen, Fed. Rep. of Ger. (800,000)	521,976	87E
Brest, France (201,145)	156,060	82C
Bridgetown, Barbados (115,000)	7,466	80C
Brighton, Eng., U.K. (420,000)	134,580	81C
Brisbane, Australia (1,149,401)	705,755	86C
Bristol, Eng., U.K. (1,630,000)	413,860	81C
Bruxelles / Brussel (Brussels), Belgium (2,395,000)	137,738	83E
Bucaramanga, Colombia	550,000	85C
București (Bucharest), Romania (2,250,000)	1,989,823	86E
Budapest, Hungary (2,565,000)	2,104,700	88E
Buenos Aires, Argentina (10,750,000)	2,922,829	80C
Buffalo, N.Y., U.S. (1,483,000)	357,870	80C
Bujumbura, Burundi	229,980	83E
Bulawayo, Zimbabwe	413,810	82C
Burlington, Vt., U.S. (115,300)	37,712	80C
Bursa, Turkey	612,510	85C
Būr Saʿīd (Port Said), Egypt	374,000	85E
Cádiz, Spain (240,000)	160,839	84E
Cagliari, Italy (300,000)	232,780	81C
Cairo, see Al Qāhirah		
Calcutta, India (11,100,000)	3,305,006	81C
Calgary, Alta., Can. (671,326)	636,100	86C
Cali, Colombia (1,400,000)	1,350,565	85C
Calicut (Kozhikode), India (546,058)	394,440	81C
Callao, Peru (*Lima)	264,133	81C
Campinas, Brazil (1,125,000)	841,010	85E
Canberra, Australia (271,362)	247,194	86C
Cannes, France (295,525)	72,250	82C
Canton, see Guangzhou		
Cape Town, South Africa (1,790,000)	776,617	85C
Caracas, Venezuela (3,600,000)	3,041,000	81E
Cardiff, Wales, U.K. (625,000)	262,310	81C
Cartagena, Colombia	531,420	85C
Casablanca, Morocco (2,475,000)	2,139,204	82C
Castries, St. Lucia	50,798	84E
Catania, Italy (515,000)	378,520	81C
Cayenne, French Guiana	38,093	82C
Cebu, Philippines (600,000)	490,280	80C
Čeljabinsk (Chelyabinsk), U.S.S.R. (1,300,000)	1,119,000	87E
Chandīgarh, India (422,841)	373,780	81C
Changchun, China (†1,910,000)	1,740,000	87E
Changshu, China (†998,000)	281,300	86E
Changzhou, China	522,700	86E
Chao'an, China (†1,214,500)	265,400	86E
Charleston, W.V., U.S. (236,300)	63,968	80C
Charlotte, N.C., U.S. (479,200)	315,473	80C
Chattanooga, Tn., U.S. (359,200)	169,728	80C
Chengdu, China (†2,640,000)	1,810,000	87E
Chiba, Japan (*Tōkyō)	788,930	85C
Chicago, Il., U.S. (7,717,100)	3,005,072	80C
Chiclayo, Peru (279,527)	213,090	81C
Chihuahua, Mexico	385,600	80C

City and Country	Population	Date
Chittagong, Bangladesh (1,391,877)	980,000	81C
Ch'ŏngjin, N. Korea	490,000	81E
Chongqing (Chungking), China (†2,830,000)	2,450,000	87E
Chŏnju, S. Korea	426,470	85C
Christchurch, New Zealand (320,000)	168,200	86C
Chungking, see Chongqing		
Cincinnati, Oh., U.S. (1,480,100)	385,457	80C
Ciudad de México, Mexico (14,100,000)	8,831,079	80C
Ciudad Juárez, Mexico (*El Paso)	544,490	80C
Clermont-Ferrand, France (256,189)	147,360	82C
Cleveland, Oh., U.S. (2,218,400)	573,822	80C
Cochin, India (685,836)	513,240	81C
Coimbatore, India (965,000)	704,510	81C
Cologne, see Köln		
Colombo, Sri Lanka (2,050,000)	623,000	83E
Columbia, S.C., U.S. (375,900)	101,229	80C
Columbus, Oh., U.S. (963,600)	565,032	80C
Conakry, Guinea	705,280	83C
Concepción, Chile (535,000)	267,890	82C
Constanța, Romania	327,670	86E
Constantine, Algeria	448,570	83E
Córdoba, Argentina (1,070,000)	993,050	80C
Córdoba, Spain	291,370	84E
Cotonou, Benin	215,000	80E
Coventry, Eng., U.K. (645,000)	318,710	81C
Cúcuta, Colombia (440,000)	445,000	85C
Cuernavaca, Mexico	192,770	80C
Curitiba, Brazil (1,700,000)	1,279,205	85E
Cusco, Peru (184,550)	89,563	81C
Dakar, Senegal	1,428,084	85E
Dalian (Lüda), China	1,680,000	87E
Dallas, Tx., U.S. (2,727,300)	904,078	80C
Dandong, China	579,800	86E
Danzig, see Gdańsk		
Daqing, China (†850,000)	620,000	87E
Dar es Salaam, Tanzania	757,346	78C
Darmstadt, Fed. Rep. of Ger. (305,000)	133,570	87E
Datong, China (†1,020,000)	790,000	87E
Davao, Philippines (†610,375)	408,770	80C
Dayton, Oh., U.S. (768,200)	193,536	80C
Delhi, India (7,200,000)	4,884,234	81C
Denver, Co., U.S. (1,405,300)	492,365	80C
Des Moines, Ia., U.S. (320,400)	191,003	80C
Detroit, Mi., U.S. (4,691,900)	1,202,463	80C
Dhaka, Bangladesh (3,430,312)	2,365,695	81C
Dhānbād, India (825,000)	120,220	81C
Dimashq (Damascus), Syria (1,850,000)	1,259,000	86E
Djibouti, Djibouti	120,000	76E
Dnepropetrovsk, U.S.S.R. (1,600,000)	1,182,000	87E
Doneck, U.S.S.R. (2,220,000)	1,090,000	87E
Dongguan, China (†1,208,500)	254,900	86E
Dortmund, Fed. Rep. of Ger. (*Essen)	568,160	87E
Douala, Cameroon	853,000	85E
Dresden, Ger. Dem. Rep. (670,000)	519,810	87E
Dublin (Baile Átha Cliath), Ireland (1,140,000)	502,749	86C
Duisburg, Fed. Rep. of Ger. (*Essen)	514,620	87E
Durban, South Africa (1,550,000)	634,301	85C
Dušanbe, U.S.S.R.	582,000	87E
Düsseldorf, Fed. Rep. of Ger. (1,190,000)	560,572	87E
Ecatepec de Morelos, Mexico (*Ciudad de México)	741,820	80C
Edinburgh, Scot., U.K. (630,000)	408,822	81C
Edmonton, Alta., Can. (785,465)	573,980	86C
El Paso, Tx., U.S. (1,037,700)	425,259	80C
Enschede, Netherlands (288,000)	144,040	86E
Erbīl, Iraq	333,900	85E
Eṣfahān (Isfahan), Iran	927,000	82E
Essen, Fed. Rep. of Ger. (4,950,000)	615,421	87E
Faisalabad, Pakistan	1,104,209	81C
Fargo, N.D., U.S (108,800)	61,383	80C
Fès, Morocco (535,000)	448,820	82C
Firenze (Florence), Italy (650,000)	453,293	81C
Florianópolis, Brazil (365,000)	178,400	85E
Fortaleza, Brazil (1,825,000)	1,582,414	85E

City and Country	Population	Date
Fort-de-France, Martinique (116,017)	99,844	82C
Fort Worth, Tx., U.S. (*Dallas)	385,164	80C
Frankfurt am Main, Fed. Rep. of Ger. (1,855,000)	592,411	87E
Freetown, Sierra Leone (315,000)	276,600	74C
Frunze, U.S.S.R.	632,000	87E
Fukuoka, Japan (1,750,000)	1,160,440	85C
Funabashi, Japan (*Tōkyō)	506,960	85C
Funafuti, Tuvalu	2,191	79C
Fushun, China	1,270,000	87E
Fuxian, China (†960,700)	246,200	86E
Fuxin, China	690,000	87E
Fuzhou, China (†1,210,000)	890,000	87E
Gaborone, Botswana	95,163	86E
Gdańsk (Danzig), Poland (909,000)	468,400	87E
General Sarmiento, Argentina (*Buenos Aires)	502,920	80C
Genève (Geneva), Switzerland (460,000)	160,645	87E
Genova (Genoa), Italy (830,000)	760,300	81C
Gent (Ghent), Belgium (465,000)	236,540	83E
Georgetown, Cayman Islands	11,500	87E
Georgetown, Guyana (188,000)	78,500	83E
George Town (Pinang), Malaysia (495,000)	248,240	80C
Gifu, Japan	411,740	85C
Giza, see Al Jīzah		
Glasgow, Scot., U.K. (1,800,000)	754,586	81C
Godthåb (Nûk), Greenland	10,972	86E
Goiânia, Brazil (990,000)	923,330	85E
Gorki, U.S.S.R. (2,005,000)	1,425,000	87E
Göteborg, Sweden (710,894)	429,330	87E
Granada, Spain	280,590	86E
Graz, Austria (325,000)	243,160	81C
Grenoble, France (392,021)	156,640	82C
Guadalajara, Mexico (2,325,000)	1,626,152	80C
Guadalupe, Mexico (*Monterrey)	370,520	80C
Guangzhou (Canton), China (†3,360,000)	3,050,000	87E
Guarulhos, Brazil (*São Paulo)	571,700	86E
Guatemala, Guatemala (1,100,000)	754,243	81C
Guayaquil, Ecuador (1,255,000)	1,204,532	82C
Guilin, China (†457,500)	342,200	86E
Guiyang, China (†1,400,000)	1,010,000	87E
Gujranwala, Pakistan (658,753)	600,990	81C
Gwalior, India (555,862)	539,010	81C
Haicheng, China (†984,800)	210,700	86E
Haikou, China (†289,600)	209,200	86E
Hai Phong, Vietnam (†1,279,067)	385,210	79C
Halab (Aleppo), Syria (1,115,000)	1,060,002	83E
Halifax, N.S., Can. (295,990)	113,570	86C
Hamamatsu, Japan	514,110	85C
Hamburg, Fed. Rep. of Ger. (2,225,000)	1,571,267	87E
Hamilton, Bermuda (15,000)	1,676	85E
Hamilton, Ont., Can. (557,029)	306,720	86C
Handan, China (†1,010,000)	850,000	87E
Hannover, Fed. Rep. of Ger. (1,000,000)	505,718	87E
Ha Noi (Hanoi), Vietnam (1,500,000)	897,500	79C
Hāora (Howrah), India (*Calcutta)	744,420	81C
Harare, Zimbabwe (890,000)	656,011	82C
Harbin, China	2,670,000	87E
Harkov, U.S.S.R. (1,905,000)	1,587,000	87E
Hartford, Ct., U.S. (1,013,600)	136,392	80C
Havana, see La Habana		
Ḥefa (Haifa), Israel (435,000)	223,400	87E
Hefei, China (†900,000)	720,000	87E
Hegang, China	588,300	86E
Helsinki, Finland (900,000)	484,263	84E
Hibli, India	527,100	81C
Ḥims (Homs), Syria	346,870	81C
Hiroshima, Japan (1,575,000)	1,044,118	85C
Hohhot, China (†810,000)	650,000	87E
Hong Kong, see Victoria		
Honiara, Solomon Is.	30,499	86C
Honolulu, Ha., U.S. (762,600)	365,048	80C
Houston, Tx., U.S. (2,755,100)	1,595,138	80C
Huainan, China (†1,090,000)	690,000	87E
Hyderābād, India (2,750,000)	2,187,262	81C
Ibadan, Nigeria	1,144,000	87E
Ilorin, Nigeria	380,000	87E

City and Country	Population	Date
Inch'ŏn, S. Korea (*Seoul)	1,386,991	85C
Indianapolis, In., U.S. (1,072,500)	700,807	80C
Indore, India (850,000)	829,320	81C
Irkutsk, U.S.S.R.	609,000	87E
Isfahan, see Eṣfahān		
Islāmābād, Pakistan (*Rāwalpindi)	204,364	81C
İstanbul, Turkey (5,750,000)	5,475,982	85C
Iževsk, U.S.S.R.	631,000	87E
İzmir, Turkey (1,550,000)	1,489,772	85C
Jabalpur, India (757,303)	614,160	81C
Jackson, Ms., U.S. (306,900)	202,895	80C
Jacksonville, Fl., U.S. (635,900)	540,920	80C
Jaipur, India (1,025,000)	977,160	81C
Jakarta, Indonesia (8,600,000)	6,503,449	80C
Jamshedpur, India (669,580)	438,380	81C
Jaroslavl, U.S.S.R.	634,000	87E
Jerevan, U.S.S.R. (1,280,000)	1,168,000	87E
Jiaozuo, China (†509,900)	335,400	86E
Jīddah, Saudi Arabia	1,300,000	80E
Jinan, China	1,460,000	87E
Jinzhou, China (†790,000)	690,000	87E
Jixi, China (†820,000)	700,000	87E
João Pessoa, Brazil (550,000)	348,500	85E
Jodhpur, India	506,340	81C
Johannesburg, South Africa (3,650,000)	632,369	85C
Kābol, Afghanistan	972,836	81E
Kagoshima, Japan	530,500	80C
Kaifeng, China (†629,100)	458,800	86E
Kalinin, U.S.S.R.	447,000	87E
Kaliningrad, U.S.S.R.	394,000	87E
Kampala, Uganda	460,000	82E
Kano, Nigeria	538,300	87E
Kānpur, India (1,875,000)	1,481,789	81C
Kansas City, Mo., U.S. (1,272,400)	448,033	80C
Kaohsiung, Taiwan (1,785,000)	1,302,849	85E
Karāchi, Pakistan (5,300,000)	4,901,627	81C
Karaganda, U.S.S.R.	633,000	87E
Karl-Marx-Stadt, Ger. Dem. Rep. (450,000)	313,790	87E
Kāthmāṇḍāu, Nepal (320,000)	235,160	81C
Katowice, Poland (2,778,000)	367,300	87E
Kawasaki, Japan (*Tōkyō)	1,088,624	85C
Kayseri, Turkey	373,930	85C
Kazan, U.S.S.R. (1,120,000)	1,068,000	87E
Keelung (Chilung), Taiwan	351,520	85E
Kemerovo, U.S.S.R.	520,000	87E
Khartoum, see Al Kharṭūm		
Khulna, Bangladesh	648,350	81C
Kiel, Fed. Rep. of Ger. (335,000)	245,682	86E
Kigali, Rwanda	181,600	83E
Kijev (Kiev), U.S.S.R. (2,850,000)	2,544,000	87E
Kingston, Jamaica (770,000)	586,930	82C
Kingston-upon-Hull, Eng., U.K. (350,000)	322,140	81C
Kingstown, St. Vin. and the Gren. (27,948)	18,378	84E
Kinshasa, Zaire	3,000,000	86E
Kisangani (Stanleyville), Zaire	282,650	84C
Kišinev, U.S.S.R.	663,000	87E
Kitakyūshū, Japan (1,525,000)	1,056,402	85C
Kitchener, Ont., Can. (311,195)	150,600	86C
Kitwe-Nkana, Zambia (283,962)	207,500	80C
Knoxville, Tn., U.S. (490,000)	175,045	80C
Kōbe, Japan (*Ōsaka)	1,410,834	85C
København (Copenhagen), Denmark (1,685,000)	473,000	86E
Köln (Cologne), Fed. Rep. of Ger. (1,760,000)	914,336	87E
Kowloon, Hong Kong (*Victoria)	799,123	81C
Kraków, Poland (828,000)	744,000	87E
Krasnodar, U.S.S.R.	623,000	87E
Krasnojarsk, U.S.S.R.	899,000	87E
Krivoj Rog, U.S.S.R.	698,000	87E
Krung Thep (Bangkok), Thailand (6,450,000)	5,446,708	86E
Kuala Lumpur, Malaysia (1,475,000)	919,610	80C
Kujbyšev, U.S.S.R. (1,510,000)	1,280,000	87E
Kumamoto, Japan	555,710	85C
Kumasi, Ghana (600,000)	348,880	84C
Kunming, China (†1,520,000)	1,280,000	87E
Kuwait, see Al Kuwayt		
Kwangju, S. Korea (975,000)	905,890	85C
Kyōto, Japan (*Ōsaka)	1,479,218	85C
Lagos, Nigeria (3,800,000)	1,213,000	87E

Metropolitan area populations are shown in parentheses.
* City is located within the metropolitan area of another city; for example, Kyōto, Japan is located in the Ōsaka metropolitan area.
† Population of entire municipality or district, including rural area.

C Census
E Official estimate

City and Country	Population	Date
La Habana (Havana), Cuba (1,975,000)	1,914,466	81C
Lahore, Pakistan (3,025,000)	2,707,215	81C
Lansing, Mi., U.S. (352,600)	130,414	80C
Lanzhou, China (†1,390,000)	1,270,000	87E
La Paz, Bolivia	992,592	85E
La Plata, Argentina (*Buenos Aires)	477,170	80C
Las Palmas de Gran Canaria, Spain	372,270	86E
Las Vegas, Nv., U.S. (453,800)	164,674	80C
Lausanne, Switzerland (259,900)	124,200	87E
Leeds, Eng., U.K. (1,540,000)	445,242	81C
Le Havre, France (254,595)	199,380	82C
Leicester, Eng., U.K. (495,000)	324,390	81C
Leipzig, Ger. Dem. Rep. (700,000)	550,641	87E
Leningrad, U.S.S.R. (5,750,000)	4,393,000	87E
León, Mexico	593,000	80C
Leshan, China (†972,300)	307,300	86E
Lexington, Ky., U.S. (255,600)	204,165	80C
Libreville, Gabon	235,700	85E
Liège, Belgium (755,000)	207,496	83E
Lille, France (1,020,000)	168,424	82C
Lilongwe, Malawi	175,000	85E
Lima, Peru (4,608,010)	371,122	81C
Linyi, China (†1,365,000)	190,000	86E
Linz, Austria (355,000)	199,910	81C
Lisboa (Lisbon), Portugal (2,250,000)	807,167	81C
Little Rock, Ar., U.S. (382,000)	167,744	80C
Liuzhou, China	660,000	87E
Liverpool, Eng., U.K. (1,525,000)	538,809	81C
Ljubljana, Yugoslavia (†305,211)	205,600	81C
Łódź, Poland (1,061,000)	847,400	87E
Lomas de Zamora, Argentina (*Buenos Aires)	510,130	80C
Lomé, Togo	369,926	81C
London, Ont., Can. (342,302)	269,140	86C
London, Eng., U.K. (11,100,000)	6,851,400	81C
Los Angeles, Ca., U.S. (9,763,600)	2,968,579	80C
Louisville, Ky., U.S. (891,400)	298,694	80C
Luanda, Angola	1,200,000	82E
Lubumbashi, Zaire	543,260	84C
Lucknow, India (1,060,000)	895,721	81C
Ludhiāna, India	607,050	81C
Luoyang, China (1,060,000)	740,000	87E
Lusaka, Zambia	535,830	80C
Luxembourg, Luxembourg (133,000)	78,924	81C
Lvov, U.S.S.R.	767,000	87E
Lyon, France (1,275,000)	413,095	82C
Madison, Wi., U.S. (294,300)	170,616	80C
Madras, India (4,475,000)	3,276,622	81C
Madrid, Spain (4,650,000)	3,123,713	86E
Madurai, India (960,000)	820,890	81C
Magdeburg, Ger. Dem. Rep. (400,000)	288,970	87E
Magnitogorsk, U.S.S.R.	430,000	87E
Makkah (Mecca), Saudi Arabia	550,000	80E
Malabo, Equatorial Guinea	30,710	83C
Málaga, Spain	595,260	86E
Malang, Indonesia	511,780	80C
Male, Maldives	46,334	85E
Malmö, Sweden (445,000)	230,050	87E
Managua, Nicaragua	644,588	81E
Manama, see Al Manāmah		
Manaus, Brazil	809,910	85E
Manchester, Eng., U.K. (2,775,000)	437,612	81C
Manchester, N.H., U.S. (129,300)	90,936	80C
Mandalay, Burma	532,890	83C
Manila, Philippines (6,800,000)	1,630,485	80C
Manizales, Colombia	330,000	85C
Mannheim, Fed. Rep. of Ger. (1,400,000)	294,648	87E
Maputo, Mozambique	755,300	80C
Maracaibo, Venezuela	929,000	81E
Mar del Plata, Argentina	414,690	80C
Mariupol', U.S.S.R.	529,000	87E
Marrakech, Morocco (535,000)	439,720	82C
Marseille, France (1,225,000)	874,436	82C
Maseru, Lesotho	14,686	76C
Masqaṭ (Muscat), Oman	50,000	81E
Mbabane, Swaziland	53,000	84E
Mbuji-Mayi, Zaire	423,360	84C
Medan, Indonesia	1,208,678	80C
Medellín, Colombia	2,095,000	85C
Medina, see Al Madīndah		
Meknès, Morocco (375,000)	319,780	82C
Melbourne, Australia (2,832,893)	60,828	86C
Memphis, Tn., U.S. (852,900)	646,174	80C
Mendoza, Argentina (650,000)	119,080	80C
Mexicali, Mexico (365,000)	341,550	80C
Mexico City, see Ciudad de México		
Miami, Fl., U.S. (2,827,300)	346,865	80C
Middlesbrough (Teesside), Eng., U.K. (580,000)	158,510	81C
Milano (Milan), Italy (3,775,000)	1,634,638	81C
Milwaukee, Wi., U.S. (1,374,700)	636,297	80C
Minneapolis, Mn., U.S. (2,012,400)	370,951	80C
Minsk, U.S.S.R. (1,600,000)	1,543,000	87E
Mobile, Al., U.S. (361,900)	200,452	80C
Mombasa, Kenya	425,600	84E
Mönchengladbach, Fed. Rep. of Ger. (410,000)	255,080	87E
Monrovia, Liberia	425,000	84E
Monterrey, Mexico (2,015,000)	1,090,009	80C
Montevideo, Uruguay (1,550,000)	1,246,500	85C
Montgomery, Al., U.S. (225,000)	177,857	80C
Montréal, Que., Can. (2,921,357)	1,015,420	86C
Morón, Argentina (*Buenos Aires)	598,420	80C
Moroni, Comoros	20,112	80C
Moskva (Moscow), U.S.S.R. (12,900,000)	8,614,000	87E
Mudanjiang, China	630,000	87E
Multān, Pakistan (732,070)	696,310	81C
München (Munich), Fed. Rep. of Ger. (1,955,000)	1,274,716	87E
Münster, Fed. Rep. of Ger.	267,620	87E
Muqdisho (Mogadishu), Somalia	600,000	83E
Murcia, Spain (†305,221)	200,300	84E
Murmansk, U.S.S.R.	432,000	87E
Mysore, India (479,081)	441,750	81C
Naberežnyje Čelny (Brežnev), U.S.S.R.	480,000	87E
Nagasaki, Japan	449,380	85C
Nagoya, Japan (4,800,000)	2,116,381	85C
Nāgpur, India (1,302,066)	1,219,461	81C
Nairobi, Kenya	1,103,600	84E
Nanchang, China (†1,190,000)	1,030,000	87E
Nancy, France (306,982)	96,310	82C
Nanjing (Nanking), China	2,290,000	87E
Nanning, China (†960,000)	690,000	87E
Nantes, France (464,857)	240,530	82C
Napoli (Naples), Italy (2,765,000)	1,210,503	81C
Nashville, Tn., U.S. (633,900)	455,651	80C
Nassau, Bahamas	135,000	82E
Natal, Brazil	510,100	85E
N'Djamena, Chad	303,000	79E
Netzahualcóyotl, Mexico (*Ciudad de México)	1,341,230	80C
Newark, N.J., U.S. (*New York)	329,248	80C
Newcastle, Australia (405,089)	129,490	86C
Newcastle upon Tyne, Eng., U.K. (1,300,000)	199,064	81C
New Delhi, India (*Delhi)	273,036	81C
New Kowloon, Hong Kong (*Victoria)	1,651,064	81C
New Orleans, La., U.S. (1,185,000)	557,927	80C
Newport, Wales, U.K. (310,000)	115,890	81C
New York, N.Y., U.S. (16,800,900)	7,071,639	80C
Niamey, Niger	399,100	83C
Nice, France (449,496)	337,080	82C
Nicosia, Cyprus (185,000)	48,221	82E
Nikolajev, U.S.S.R.	501,000	87E
Ningbo, China (†1,030,000)	560,000	87E
Niterói, Brazil (*Rio de Janeiro)	441,680	85E
Norfolk, Va., U.S. (795,600)	266,979	80C
North York, Ont., Can. (*Toronto)	556,290	86C
Nottingham, Eng., U.K. (655,000)	273,300	81C
Nouakchott, Mauritania	285,000	87E
Nouméa, New Caledonia (83,000)	60,112	83C
Nova Iguaçu, Brazil (*Rio de Janeiro)	592,800	85E
Novokuzneck, U.S.S.R.	589,000	87E
Novosibirsk, U.S.S.R. (1,580,000)	1,423,000	87E
Nuku'alofa, Tonga	21,265	86C
Nürnberg, Fed. Rep. of Ger. (1,030,000)	467,392	87E
Odessa, U.S.S.R. (1,210,000)	1,141,000	87E
Ogbomosho, Nigeria	582,900	87E
Okayama, Japan	572,470	85C
Oklahoma City, Ok., U.S. (742,000)	403,484	80C
Omaha, Nb., U.S. (538,600)	322,133	80C
Omdurman, see Umm Durmān		
Omsk, U.S.S.R. (1,160,000)	1,134,000	87E
Oran, Algeria	663,500	83E
Orenburg, U.S.S.R.	537,000	87E
Orlando, Fl., U.S. (619,300)	128,291	80C
Orūmīyeh, Iran	263,000	82E
Ōsaka, Japan (16,450,000)	263,624	85C
Osasco, Brazil (*São Paulo)	591,560	85E
Oshogbo, Nigeria	380,800	87E
Oslo, Norway (720,000)	448,747	83E
Ostrava, Czechoslovakia (755,000)	327,790	86E
Ottawa, Ont., Can. (819,263)	300,763	86C
Ouagadougou, Burkina Faso	442,223	85C
Palembang, Indonesia	786,600	80C
Palermo, Italy	699,690	81C
Palma, Spain	311,197	84E
Panamá, Panama (625,000)	413,992	82E
Papeete, French Polynesia (80,000)	23,496	83C
Paramaribo, Suriname (192,810)	67,905	80C
Paris, France (9,775,000)	2,127,100	86E
Patna, India (1,025,000)	776,370	81C
Peking, see Beijing		
Penza, U.S.S.R.	540,000	87E
Perm, U.S.S.R. (1,145,000)	1,075,000	87E
Perth, Australia (994,472)	79,409	86C
Peshāwar, Pakistan (566,248)	506,890	81C
Philadelphia, Pa., U.S. (5,208,600)	1,688,210	80C
Phnum Pénh, Cambodia	700,000	86E
Phoenix, Az., U.S. (1,482,400)	790,044	80C
Pingxiang, China (†1,286,700)	368,700	86E
Pittsburgh, Pa., U.S. (2,218,800)	423,959	80C
Ploiești, Romania (300,000)	234,880	86E
Plovdiv, Bulgaria	349,140	86E
Pointe-à-Pitre, Guadeloupe (83,000)	25,310	82C
Port-au-Prince, Haiti (760,000)	684,284	82C
Port Elizabeth, South Africa (690,000)	272,840	85C
Port Harcourt, Nigeria	327,300	87E
Portland, Me., U.S. (193,800)	61,572	80C
Portland, Or., U.S. (1,227,200)	368,139	80C
Port-Louis, Mauritius (415,000)	138,272	86E
Port Moresby, Papua New Guinea	123,624	80C
Porto (Oporto), Portugal (1,225,000)	327,368	81C
Porto Alegre, Brazil (2,600,000)	1,272,121	85E
Port of Spain, Trinidad and Tobago (370,000)	55,800	80C
Porto-Novo, Benin	123,000	80E
Port Said, see Būr Sa'īd		
Portsmouth, Eng., U.K. (485,000)	174,210	81C
Port-Vila, Vanuatu (18,000)	13,067	86E
Poznań, Poland (672,000)	578,100	87E
Praha (Prague), Czechoslovakia (1,310,000)	1,193,513	86E
Praia, Cape Verde	37,480	80C
Pretoria, South Africa (960,000)	443,059	85C
Providence, R.I., U.S. (921,800)	156,804	80C
Puebla [de Zaragoza], Mexico (1,055,000)	835,750	80C
Pune, India (1,775,000)	1,203,351	81C
Pusan, S. Korea (3,550,000)	3,514,798	85C
P'yŏngyang, N. Korea (1,600,000)	1,283,000	80E
Qingdao, China	1,270,000	87E
Qiqihar, China (†1,300,000)	1,150,000	87E
Qom, Iran	424,000	82E
Québec, Que., Can. (603,267)	164,580	86C
Quetta, Pakistan (285,791)	244,840	81C
Quezon City, Philippines (*Manila)	1,165,865	80C
Quilmes, Argentina (*Buenos Aires)	446,580	80C
Quito, Ecuador (1,050,000)	890,355	82C
Rabat, Morocco (980,000)	518,616	82C
Rājkot, India	445,070	81C
Raleigh, N.C., U.S. (282,800)	150,255	80C
Rānchī, India (502,771)	489,620	81C
Rangoon, see Yangon		
Rāwalpindi, Pakistan (1,040,000)	457,091	81C
Recife, Brazil (2,625,000)	1,287,623	85E
Reno, Nv., U.S. (176,200)	100,756	80C
Reykjavík, Iceland (130,722)	88,745	84E
Ribeirão Prêto, Brazil	383,120	85E
Richmond, Va., U.S. (690,600)	219,214	80C
Rīga, U.S.S.R. (990,000)	900,000	87E

City and Country	Population	Date
Rio de Janeiro, Brazil (10,150,000)	5,603,388	85E
Riverside, Ca., U.S. (768,300)	170,591	80C
Riyadh, see Ar Riyāḍ		
Rjazan, U.S.S.R.	508,000	87E
Rochester, N.Y., U.S. (816,200)	241,741	80C
Roma (Rome), Italy (3,115,000)	2,830,569	81C
Rosario, Argentina (1,045,000)	938,120	80C
Rostov-na-Donu, U.S.S.R. (1,145,000)	1,004,000	87E
Rotterdam, Netherlands (1,110,000)	571,372	86E
Rouen, France (379,879)	101,945	82C
Rouseau, Dominica	9,348	84E
Sacramento, Ca., U.S. (866,400)	275,741	80C
Safāqis, Tunisia (310,000)	231,910	84C
Saigon, see Ho Chi Minh		
St. Catharines, Ont., Can. (343,258)	123,450	86C
St.-Étienne, France (317,228)	204,950	82C
St. George's, Grenada (25,000)	4,788	81C
St. John's, Antigua and Barbuda	24,359	77E
St. Louis, Mo., U.S. (2,203,000)	452,801	80C
St. Paul, Mn., U.S. (*Minneapolis)	270,230	80C
St. Petersburg, Fl., U.S. (852,300)	238,647	80C
Sakai, Japan (*Ōsaka)	818,270	85C
Salem, India (518,615)	361,390	81C
Salt Lake City, Ut., U.S. (682,400)	163,034	80C
Salvador, Brazil (2,050,000)	1,804,438	85E
Samarkand, U.S.S.R.	388,000	87E
Ṣan'ā', Yemen	277,818	81C
San Antonio, Tx., U.S. (968,200)	786,023	80C
San Diego, Ca., U.S. (2,098,500)	875,538	80C
San Francisco, Ca., U.S. (4,683,200)	678,974	80C
San José, Costa Rica (670,000)	241,464	84C
San Jose, Ca., U.S. (*San Francisco)	629,400	80C
San Juan, Puerto Rico (1,775,260)	424,600	80C
San Luis Potosí, Mexico (470,000)	362,370	80C
San Miguel de Tucumán, Argentina (525,000)	392,880	80C
San Salvador, El Salvador (920,000)	459,902	85E
San Sebastián, Spain (285,000)	180,040	86E
Santiago, Chile (4,025,000)	425,924	82C
Santo André, Brazil (São Paulo)	635,120	85E
Santo Domingo, Dominican Rep.	1,313,172	81C
Santos, Brazil (1,065,000)	460,100	85E
São Bernardo do Campo, Brazil (*São Paulo)	562,480	85E
São Luís, Brazil (600,000)	227,900	85E
São Paulo, Brazil (15,175,000)	10,063,110	85E
São Tomé, Sao Tome and Prin.	17,380	70C
Sapporo, Japan (1,900,000)	1,542,979	85C
Sarajevo, Yugoslavia (†448,500)	374,500	81C
Saratov, U.S.S.R. (1,170,000)	918,000	87E
Sargodha, Pakistan (291,362)	231,890	81C
Savannah, Ga., U.S. (212,800)	141,651	80C
Scarborough, Ont., Can. (*Toronto)	484,670	86C
Seattle, Wa., U.S. (2,077,100)	493,846	80C
Semarang, Indonesia	820,140	80C
Semipalatinsk, U.S.S.R.	330,000	87E
Sendai, Japan (1,175,000)	700,250	85C
Seoul, see Sŏul		
Sevilla (Seville), Spain (945,000)	668,350	86E
's-Gravenhage (The Hague), Netherlands (770,000)	443,961	86E
Shanghai, China (9,300,000)	7,100,000	87E
Shantou, China (†770,000)	550,000	87E
Sheffield, Eng., U.K. (710,000)	470,680	81C
Shenyang (Mukden), China (†4,290,000)	3,840,000	87E
Shīrāz, Iran	800,000	82E
Shubrā al Khaymah, Egypt (*Al Qāhirah)	515,500	85E
Sialkot, Pakistan (302,009)	258,140	81C
Singapore, Singapore (3,000,000)	2,631,000	88E
Sioux Falls, S.D., U.S. (92,200)	81,343	80C
Sofija (Sofia), Bulgaria (1,205,000)	1,119,152	86E
Solāpur, India (514,860)	511,100	81C
Sŏul (Seoul), S. Korea (14,100,000)	9,639,110	85C
Southampton, Eng., U.K. (415,000)	211,320	81C
Soweto, South Africa (*Johannesburg)	521,940	85C
Springfield, Il., U.S. (154,200)	100,054	80C
Springfield, Ma., U.S. (485,900)	152,319	80C
Srīnagar, India (606,002)	594,770	81C
Stalingrad, see Volgograd		
Stockholm, Sweden (1,449,972)	663,217	87E
Stoke-on-Trent, Eng., U.K. (440,000)	272,440	81C
Strasbourg, France (400,000)	248,710	82C
Stuttgart, Fed. Rep. of Ger. (1,925,000)	565,486	87E
Suez, see As Suways		
Suichang, China (†2,216,500)	363,500	86E
Suixian, China (†1,281,600)	187,700	86E
Surabaya, Indonesia	2,027,913	80C
Surakarta, Indonesia (575,000)	469,530	80C
Surat, India (913,806)	776,580	81C
Suva, Fiji (141,273)	69,665	86C
Suzhou, China	720,000	87E
Sverdlovsk, U.S.S.R. (1,575,000)	1,331,000	87E
Swansea, Wales, U.K. (275,000)	172,430	81C
Sydney, Australia (3,364,858)	86,311	86C
Syracuse, N.Y., U.S. (518,600)	170,105	80C
Szczecin, Poland (449,000)	395,000	87E
Tabrīz, Iran	852,000	82E
Tacoma, Wa., U.S. (*Seattle)	158,501	80C
Taegu, S. Korea	2,029,853	85C
Taejŏn, S. Korea	866,140	85C
Tai'an, China (†1,325,400)	215,900	86E
Taichung, Taiwan	674,930	85E
Tainan, Taiwan	639,880	85E
Taipei, Taiwan (5,725,000)	2,507,620	85E
Taiyuan, China (†1,930,000)	1,660,000	87E
Tallinn, U.S.S.R.	478,000	87E
Tampa, Fl., U.S. (594,500)	271,598	80C
Tampico, Mexico (435,000)	267,950	80C
Tanger (Tangier), Morocco (370,000)	266,340	82C
Tangshan, China (†1,410,000)	1,060,000	87E
Ţanţā, Egypt	364,700	85E
Ţarābulus (Tripoli), Libya	858,500	81E
Taškent (Tashkent), U.S.S.R. (2,370,000)	2,124,000	87E
Tbilisi, U.S.S.R. (1,380,000)	1,194,000	87E
Tegucigalpa, Honduras	597,500	85E
Tehrān, Iran (6,400,000)	5,734,199	82C
Tel Aviv-Yafo, Israel (1,670,000)	320,300	87E
Teresina, Brazil (525,000)	425,300	85E
Thanh Pho Ho Chi Minh (Saigon), Vietnam (3,100,000)	2,700,849	79C
The Hague, see 's-Gravenhage		
Thessaloníki, Greece (706,180)	406,410	81C
Thimphu, Bhutan	12,000	82E
Thunder Bay, Ont., Can. (122,217)	112,272	86C
Tianjin (Tientsin), China (†5,460,000)	4,880,000	87E
Tianshui, China (†953,200)	209,500	86E
Tijuana, Mexico (*San Diego)	429,500	80C
Tirana, Albania	210,800	84E
Tiruchchirāppalli, India (609,548)	362,040	81C
Tlalnepantla, Mexico (*Ciudad de México)	778,170	80C
Togliatti (Stavropol), U.S.S.R.	627,000	87E
Tōkyō, Japan (27,700,000)	8,354,615	85C
Tomsk, U.S.S.R.	489,000	87E
Torino (Turin), Italy (1,600,000)	1,103,520	81C
Toronto, Ont., Can. (3,427,168)	612,289	86C
Torreón, Mexico (575,000)	328,080	80C
Toulon, France (410,393)	179,420	82C
Toulouse, France (541,271)	347,990	82C
Tours, France (262,786)	132,209	82C
Tripoli, see Ţarābulus		
Trivandrum, India (520,125)	483,080	81C
Trujillo, Peru (354,301)	202,460	81C
Tsun Wan, Hong Kong (*Victoria)	599,010	81C
Tucson, Az., U.S. (495,600)	336,503	80C
Tula, U.S.S.R. (635,000)	538,000	87E
Tulsa, Ok., U.S. (742,000)	360,919	80C
Tūnis, Tunisia (1,225,000)	596,654	84C
Ufa, U.S.S.R. (1,110,000)	1,092,000	87E
Ujung Pandang (Makasar), Indonesia	708,460	80C
Ulan-Bator, Mongolia	488,200	85E
Ulsan, S. Korea	551,010	85C
Umm Durmān (Omdurman), Sudan (*Khartoum)	526,280	83C
Utrecht, Netherlands (511,195)	229,930	86E
Vadodara (Baroda), India (744,881)	734,470	81C
Vaduz, Liechtenstein	4,920	87E
Valencia, Spain (1,270,000)	738,575	86E
Valletta, Malta (215,000)	9,263	87E
Valparaíso, Chile (700,000)	265,350	82C
Vancouver, B.C., Can. (1,380,729)	431,147	86C
Vārānasi (Benares), India (925,000)	708,640	81C
Venezia (Venice), Italy (415,000)	332,770	81C
Veracruz [Llave], Mexico (385,000)	284,820	80C
Vereeniging, South Africa (525,000)	60,580	85C
Verona, Italy	261,208	81C
Viangchan (Vientiane), Laos	377,000	85C
Victoria, B.C., Can. (255,547)	66,300	86C
Victoria, Hong Kong (4,515,000)	1,183,621	81C
Victoria, Seychelles	23,000	74C
Vienna, see Wien		
Vientiane, see Viangchan		
Vilnius, U.S.S.R.	566,000	87E
Vishākhapatnam, India (603,530)	565,320	81C
Vitória, Brazil (735,000)	201,500	85E
Vladivostok, U.S.S.R.	615,000	87E
Volgograd (Stalingrad), U.S.S.R. (1,335,000)	988,000	87E
Volta Redonda, Brazil (375,000)	219,260	85E
Voronež, U.S.S.R.	872,000	87E
Vorošilovgrad, U.S.S.R.	509,000	87E
Warszawa (Warsaw), Poland (2,323,000)	1,664,700	87E
Washington, D.C., U.S. (3,221,400)	638,432	80C
Weifang, China (†1,042,200)	312,500	86E
Wellington, New Zealand (350,000)	137,495	86C
Wichita, Ks., U.S. (372,200)	279,835	80C
Wien (Vienna), Austria (1,875,000)	1,489,153	85E
Wiesbaden, Fed. Rep. of Ger. (795,000)	266,540	87E
Willemstad, Netherlands Antilles (130,000)	31,883	81C
Wilmington, De., U.S. (*Philadelphia)	70,195	80C
Windhoek, Namibia	120,000	84E
Windsor, Ont., Can. (253,988)	193,110	86C
Winnipeg, Man., Can. (625,304)	594,550	86C
Wrocław, Poland	640,000	87E
Wuhan, China	3,490,000	87E
Wuppertal, Fed. Rep. of Ger. (830,000)	374,217	87E
Wuxi, China	860,000	87E
Wuxing (Huzhou), China (†964,400)	208,500	86E
Xiamen, China (†546,400)	343,700	86E
Xi'an, China (†2,390,000)	2,050,000	87E
Xiaogan, China (†1,204,400)	125,500	86E
Xining, China	610,000	87E
Xuzhou, China	840,000	87E
Yancheng, China (†1,251,400)	258,400	86E
Yangon (Rangoon), Burma (2,800,000)	2,458,712	83C
Yaoundé, Cameroon	583,000	85E
Yerushalayim (Jerusalem), Israel (490,000)	468,900	87E
Yichun, China	830,000	87E
Yokohama, Japan (*Tōkyō)	2,992,926	85C
Yulin, China (†1,228,800)	115,600	86E
Zagreb, Yugoslavia	768,700	81C
Zanzibar, Tanzania	110,669	78C
Zaozhuang, China (†1,592,000)	292,200	86E
Zaporožje, U.S.S.R.	875,000	87E
Zaragoza (Saragossa), Spain	596,080	86E
Zhangjiakou, China (†626,500)	492,800	86E
Zhengzhou, China (†1,610,000)	1,170,000	87E
Zhongshan, China (†1,059,700)	238,700	86E
Zibo, China (†2,330,000)	830,000	87E
Zurich, Switzerland (860,000)	349,549	87E

Metropolitan area populations are shown in parentheses.
* City is located within the metropolitan area of another city; for example, Kyōto, Japan is located in the Ōsaka metropolitan area.
† Population of entire municipality or district, including rural area.

C Census
E Official estimate

Transliteration Systems

Toponymy: Criteria Used for the Writing of Names on the Maps

The language of geography is a language which defines geographic features in universally recognized terms. In creating this language, toponymy experts and cartographers have confronted complex problems in finding terms which are universally acceptable. So that the reader can fully understand the maps in this atlas, here is a brief explanation of how the toponyms (place-names for geographic features) have been written, particularly those relating to regions or countries where the Roman alphabet is not used. Among these are the Slavic-speaking nations such as the Soviet Union, Yugoslavia and Bulgaria; and China and Japan, which use ideographic characters. Of the European countries, Greece has its own alphabet, which is totally different from the Roman alphabet. Many of the Islamic countries use Arabic, with variations derived from local dialects.

There are two basic systems for Romanizing writing. The first is by phonetic transcription, using combinations of different alphabetical signs for each language when the phonetic sound in other languages should be maintained. For example, the Italian sound "sc" (which must be followed by an "e" or "i" to remain soft) in French is "ch," in English is "sh," and in German is "sch."

The second system is transliteration, in which the words, letters or characters of one language are represented or spelled in the letters or characters of another language.

Chinese, Japanese and Arabic Languages

Various Asian and African countries use non-Roman forms in their writing. For example, the Chinese and Japanese languages use ideographic characters instead of an alphabet, and these ideographic characters are transformed into the Roman alphabet through phonetic transcription. Until recently, one of the methods used for transforming Chinese was the Wade-Giles system, named for its English authors. Used in this atlas is the Pinyin system, which was approved by the Chinese government in 1958 and has been incorporated into the official maps of the People's Republic of China. The Pinyin system also has been adopted by the United States Board on Geographic Names and is used in official United Nations documents. The Pinyin names, however, often are accompanied by the Wade-Giles form, as the latter was widely known.

In Japan, ideographic characters are used, although the Roman alphabet is used in many Japanese scientific works. Japan uses two principal systems for standardizing names. They are the Kunreisiki, used by the government in official publications, and the Hepburn method. Adopted for this atlas is the Hepburn method, the system used in international English-language publications and by the United States Board on Geographic Names.

Romanization of the Arabic alphabet, which is used in many Islamic countries, is by transliteration. Since English and French are still used as an international language in many Arab countries, the name forms proposed by the major English and French sources have been taken into consideration. Generally, the systems proposed by the United States Board on Geographic Names and the Permanent Committee on Geographical Names have been used for most Asian countries and Arab-speaking countries.

Greek, Russian and Other Slavic Languages

Practically all written languages in Europe use the Roman alphabet. The differences in phonetics and grammar are shown by the use of diacritical marks and by groupings of consonants, vocals and syllables which give meaning to the various tones in the language. According to a centuries-old tradition, each written language maintains its formal characters, using the translated form rather than the phonetic transcription when a geographical term must be given in another language. This system, therefore, makes it more a translation than a transliteration.

In the Aegean area, Greek and the Greek alphabet are particularly significant because of historical links to the beginning of European civilization. The 1962 United States Board on Geographic Names and the Permanent Committee on Geographical Names systems, based on modern Greek pronunciation, have been used in transcribing toponyms from official sources for these maps. (The table that follows has an example indicating essential norms for Romanizing the modern Greek alphabet.)

A different situation arises in countries using the Cyrillic alphabet. Six principal Slavic languages using this alphabet are Russian, Byelorussian, Ukrainian, Bulgarian, Serbian, and Macedonian. The Cyrillic alphabet also is used by the non-Slavic people of the central Soviet Union. The nomenclature of these regions has been transliterated in accordance with the system proposed by the International Organization for Standardization, taking into consideration sounds and letters and uses of the diacritical marks normal in Slavic languages. The International Organization for Standardization method is accepted and used in bibliographical works and international documents. (The table which follows gives the relationship between the letters of the Cyrillic and Roman alphabets for the above six languages.) An exception to this transliteration is made by the Soviet Balkan republics of Estonia, Latvia and Lithuania. Here the name forms deriving from the national languages have been adopted, using the Roman alphabet.

Special Cases: Conventional Forms and Multilinguals

Cartographic nomenclature generally derives from the official nomenclature of the sovereign and nonsovereign countries, although a number of cases need an explanation.

In numerous situations, English conventional forms are used along with the local or conventional name in referring to a geographical entity used outside the official language area. For example, Vienna, Prague, Copenhagen and Moscow are English forms for Wien, Praha, København and Moskva, respectively. There have been cases, however, where the conventional or historical form commonly used in English cartography has been applied with the same meaning. Thus, Peking and Nanking are the English conventional forms for Beijing and Nanjing, while Tsinan, Tientsin and Mukden are the former conventional spellings or names for Jinan, Tianjin and Shenyang, respectively. Other examples are Saigon, the former name for Ho Chi Minh, Vietnam; and Bangkok, the name for Krung Thep, which is used in Thailand.

The lack of reliable data for countries, especially ex-colonies without a firm national cartographic tradition, has made it necessary to utilize mapping skills of former colonist nations such as France, the United Kingdom and Belgium. A lack of data has led to the adoption of French and British forms in many areas, as these two languages are widely used for official purposes.

Another special case is that of the multilingual areas. Many countries and areas officially recognize two or more written and spoken languages; therefore, all of the principal written forms appear on the maps. This is true, for example, of Belgium where the official languages are French and Dutch (e.g. Bruxelles/Brussel) and of Italian regions such as Valle d'Aosta and Alto Adige, where French, German and Italian are used (e.g. Aosta/Aoste) (Bolzano/Bozen).

In preparing this atlas, each of these special cases has been taken into full consideration within the limits of the scale, space and readability of the maps.

Transliteration of the Cyrillic Alphabet
(International System—ISO)

Cyrillic Letter	Roman Letter		Cyrillic Letter	Roman Letter	
А а	a		О о	o	
Б б	b		П п	p	
В в	v		Р р	r	
Г г	g		С с	s	
Д д	d		Т т	t	
Е е	e	initially, after a vowel or after the mute sign "Ъ", becomes "je"	У у	u	
			Ф ф	f	
			Х х	h	
Ё ё	ё		Ц ц	c	
Ж ж	ž		Ч ч	č	
З з	z		Ш ш	š	
И и	i		Щ щ	šč	
Й й	j	not written if preceded by "И" or "Ы"	Ъ ъ	—	not written
			Ы ы	y	
К к	k		Ь ь	—	not written
Л л	l		Э э	e	
М м	m		Ю ю	ju	
Н н	n		Я я	ja	

Transcription of Modern Greek
(U.S. B. G. N./P.C.G.N.)

Greek Letter (or combination)	Roman Letter (or combination)		Greek Letter (or combination)	Roman Letter (or combination)	
Α α	a		μπ	b	beginning a word
αι	ai			mb	within a word
αυ	av		Ν ν	n	
Β β	v		ντ	d	beginning a word
Γ γ	g			nd	within a word
γγ	ng		Ξ ξ	x	
γκ	g	beginning a word	Ο ο	o	
			οι	oi	
	ng	within a word	ου	ou	
			Π π	p	
Δ δ	d		Ρ ρ	r	
Ε ε	e		Σ σ	s	
ει	i		ς	s	ending a word
ευ	ev		Τ τ	t	
Ζ ζ	z		τζ	tz	
Η η	i		Υ υ	i	
ηυ	iv		υι	i	
Θ θ	th		Φ φ	f	
Ι ι	i		Χ χ	kh	
Κ κ	k		Ψ ψ	ps	
Λ λ	l		Ω ω	o	
Μ μ	m				

The "Geographical Glossary" lists the principal geographical terms used on the maps. All of these terms, including abbreviations, prefixes and suffixes, appear in the cartographic table as they appear on the maps. Terms are listed in accordance with the English alphabet, without consideration of diacritical marks on letters or of particular groups of letters.
Prefixes and suffixes relating to principal names or forming part of geographical toponyms are followed or preceded by a dash and the language to which they refer: e.g. Chi-/*Dan.* (Chi, a Danish prefix, means large); -bor/*Slvn.* (-bor, a Slovakian suffix, means city). Suffixes can also appear as words in themselves. In this case, the suffix and primary word are coupled together: e.g. Berg, -berg (Berg, which means mountain, can be used alone or as part of another word, such as Hapsberg).

Certain terms are followed or preceded by their abbreviation used on the maps. Both instances are listed: e.g. Fjord, Fj. and Fj., Fjord.
All geographical terms are identified by the language or languages to which each belongs. The language or languages in italics follows the term: e.g. Abbey/*Eng.*; -bad/*Nor., Dut., Swed., Germ.* Each term is translated into a corresponding English term or terms.
Below is a table identifying the abbreviations of various language names used on the maps. Note that certain abbreviations represent a group of languages, instead of one language: e.g. Ural. is the abbreviation for Uralic, a group word for Udmurt, Komi, and Nenets.
Alt. = Altaic (Turkmen, Tatar, Bashkir, Kazakh, Karalpak, Nogai, Kirghiz, Uzbek, Uigur, Altaic, Ýakut, Khakass)
Ban. = Bantu (KiSwahili, ChiLuba, Lingala, KiKongo)
Cauc. = Caucasian (Chechen, Ingush, Kalmuck, Georgian)
Iran. = Iranian (Baluchi, Tagus)
Mel. = Melanesian (Fijian, New Caledonian, Micronesian, Nauruan)
Mong. = Mongolian (Buryat, Khalka Mongol)
Poly. = Polynesian (Maori, Samoan, Tongan, Tahitian, Hawaiian)
Sah. = Saharan (Kanuri, Tubu)
Som. = Somalian (Somali, Galla)
Sud. = Sudanese (Peul, Ehoué, Mossi, Yoruba, Ibo)
Ural. = Uralic (Udmurt, Komi, Nenets).
Because of their technical application to geography, some geographical terms may not fully correspond with the meaning given for them in some dictionaries.

Abbreviations of Language Names

Abbreviations in English	English	Abbreviations in English	English	Abbreviations in English	English	Abbreviations in English	English	Abbreviations in English	English	Abbreviations in English	English
Afr.	Afrikaans	**Bulg.**	Bulgarian	**Fr.**	French	**Khm.**	Khmer	**Pers.**	Persian	**Som.**	Somalian
A.I.	American Indian	**Burm.**	Burmese	**Gae.**	Gaelic	**Kor.**	Korean	**Pol.**	Polish	**Sp.**	Spanish
Alb.	Albanian	**Cat.**	Catalan	**Georg.**	Georgian	**K.S.**	Khoi-San	**Poly.**	Polynesian	**Sud.**	Sudanese
Alt.	Altaic	**Cauc.**	Caucasian	**Germ.**	German	**Laot.**	Laotian	**Port.**	Portuguese	**Swa.**	Swahili
Amh.	Amharic	**Chin.**	Chinese	**Gr.**	Greek	**Lapp.**	Lappish	**Prov.**	Provençal	**Swed.**	Swedish
Ar.	Arabic	**Cz.**	Czech	**Hebr.**	Hebrew	**Latv.**	Latvian	**Rmsh.**	Romansh	**Tam.**	Tamil
Arm.	Armenian	**Dan.**	Danish	**Hin.**	Hindi	**Lith.**	Lithuanian	**Rom.**	Romanian	**Thai**	Thai
Az.	Azerbaidzhani	**Dut.**	Dutch	**Hung.**	Hungarian	**Mal.**	Malay	**Rus.**	Russian	**Tib.**	Tibetan
Ban.	Bantu	**Eng.**	English	**Icel.**	Icelandic	**Malag.**	Malagasy	**Sah.**	Saharan	**Tur.**	Turkish
Bas.	Basque	**Esk.**	Eskimo	**Indon.**	Indonesian	**Mel.**	Melanesian	**S.C.**	Serbo-Croatian	**Ural.**	Uralic
Beng.	Bengali	**Est.**	Estonian	**Ir.**	Irish	**Mong.**	Mongolian			**Urdu**	Urdu
Ber.	Berber	**Far.**	Faroese	**Iran.**	Iranian	**Nep.**	Nepalese	**Sin.**	Sinhalese	**Viet.**	Vietnamese
Br.	Breton	**Finn.**	Finnish	**It.**	Italian	**Nor.**	Norwegian	**Slvk.**	Slovak	**Wall.**	Walloon
		Fle.	Flemish	**Jap.**	Japanese	**Pash.**	Pashto	**Slvn.**	Slovene	**Wel.**	Welsh

Glossary of Geographical Terms

A

Local Form	English
A- / *Ban.*	people
A' / *Icel.*	river
Å / *Dan.; Nor.; Swed.*	stream
a., an / *Germ.*	on
Aa / *Germ.*	stream
Aache / *Germ.*	stream
Aaiún / *Ar.*	springs
Aan / *Dut.; Fle.*	on
Āb / *Pers.*	stream
Ābād / *Pers.*	city, town
Abad, -abad / *Pers.*	city, town
Ābār / *Ar.*	spring
Abbadia / *It.*	abbey
Abbaye / *Fr.*	abbey
Abbazia / *It.*	abbey
Abbi / *Amh.*	great
Abd / *Ar.*	servant
Abeba / *Amh.*	flower
Aber / *Br.; Wel.*	estuary
Abhang / *Germ.*	slope
Abū / *Ar.*	father, master
Abyad / *Ar.*	white
Abyaḍ / *Ar.*	white
Abyār / *Ar.*	well
Abyss / *Eng.*	ocean depth, deep
Ach / *Germ.*	stream
Achaïf / *Ar.*	dunes
Ache / *Germ.*	stream
Achter / *Afr.; Dut.; Fle.*	back
Acqua / *It.*	water
Açu / *A.I.*	great
Açude / *Port.*	reservoir, dam
Ada / *Tur.*	island
Adalar / *Tur.*	archipelago
Adası / *Tur.*	island
Addis / *Amh.*	new
Adi / *Amh.*	village
Adrar / *Ber.*	mount, mountains
Aéroport / *Fr.*	airport
Aeroporto / *It.; Port.*	airport
Aeropuerto / *Sp.*	airport
Af / *Som.*	mouth, gorge
Afsluitdijk / *Dut.*	dam
Agadir / *Ber.*	castle
Ağiz / *Tur.*	mouth
Agro / *Sp.; It.*	plain
Agua / *Sp.*	water
Aguja / *Sp.*	needle
Agulha / *Port.*	needle, promontory
Ahal / *Georg.*	new
Aḥmar / *Ar.*	red
Ahrāmāt / *Ar.*	pyramids
Ahzar / *Ber.*	wadi
Aigialós / *Gr.*	coast
Aigue / *Prov.*	water
Aiguille / *Fr.*	needle
Ain / *Ar.*	spring
Ait / *Ar.; Ber.*	sons
Aivi, -aivi / *Lapp.*	mountain
Ak / *Tur.*	white
'Aklé / *Ar.*	dunes
Akmeņs / *Latv.*	stone
Ákra / *Gr.*	point
Akti / *Gr.*	coast
Ala / *Malag.*	forest
Ala / *Finn.*	low, lower
Alan / *Tur.*	field
Alb / *Rom.*	white
Albo / *Sp.*	white
Albufera / *Sp.*	lagoon
Alcalá / *Sp.*	castle
Alcázar / *Sp.*	castle
Aldea / *Sp.*	village
Alföld / *Hung.*	lowland
Ali / *Amh.*	mountain
Alia / *Poly.*	stream
Alin / *Mong.*	range
Alm / *Germ.*	mountain pasture
Alor / *Mal.*	river
Alp / *Germ.*	mountain pasture
Alpe / *Germ.; Fr.; It.*	mountain pasture
Alps / *Eng.*	mountains
Alsó / *Hung.*	low, lower
Alt / *Germ.*	old
Altin / *Tur.*	lower
Altiplano / *Sp.*	plateau
Alto / *Sp.; It.; Port.*	high
Altopiano / *It.*	plateau
Älv / *Swed.*	river
Am / *Kor.*	mountain, peak
Amane / *Ber.*	water
Amba / *Amh.*	mountain
Ambato / *Malag.*	rock
An / *Gae.*	of
An, a. / *Germ.*	on
Ana / *Poly.*	grotto
Anatolikós / *Gr.*	eastern
Äng / *Swed.*	meadow
Angra / *Port.*	bay, anchorage
Ani- / *Malag.*	center
Áno / *Gr.*	upper
Ânou / *Ber.*	well
Anse / *Fr.*	inlet
Ant- / *Malag.*	center
Ao / *Chin.; Khm.; Thai*	gulf
'Âouâna / *Ar.*	well
Apă / *Rom.*	water
'Aqabat / *Ar.*	pass
Aqueduc / *Fr.*	aqueduct
Ar / *Mong.*	north
Ar / *Sin.; Tam.*	river
'Arâguîb / *Ar.*	hills
Arba / *Amh.*	mount
Arbore / *Rom.*	tree
Archipiélago / *Sp.*	archipelago
Arcipelago / *It.*	archipelago
Arḍ / *Ar.*	region
Ard- / *Gae.*	high
Areg / *Ar.*	dune
Areia / *Port.*	beach
Arena / *Sp.*	beach
Argent / *Fr.*	silver
Arhipelag / *Rus.*	archipelago
Arkhaíos / *Gr.*	old, antique
Arm / *Eng.; Germ.*	branch
Arquipélago / *Port.*	archipelago
Arr., Arroyo / *Sp.*	stream
Arrecife / *Sp.*	reef
Arroio / *Port.*	stream
Art / *Tur.*	pass, watershed
Aru / *Sin.; Tam.*	river
Ås / *Dan.; Nor.; Swed.*	hills
Asfar / *Ar.*	yellow
Asif / *Ber.*	river
Asky / *Alt.*	lower
Áspros / *Gr.*	white
Assa / *Ber.*	wadi
Atalaya / *Sp.*	frontier
Áth / *Gae.*	ford
Átha / *Gae.*	ford
Atol / *Port.*	atoll
Au / *Germ.*	meadow
Aue / *Germ.*	irrigated field
Aust / *Nor.*	east
Austur / *Icel.*	east
Ava / *Poly.*	canal
Aven / *Fr.*	doline, sink
Awa / *Poly.*	bay
Áyios / *Gr.*	saint
'Ayn / *Ar.*	spring, well
'Ayoún / *Ar.*	springs, wells
'Ayoûn / *Ar.*	spring
Aza / *Ber.*	wadi
Azraq / *Ar.*	light blue
Azul / *Port.; Sp.*	light blue
Azur / *Fr.*	light blue

B

Local Form	English
B., Bay / *Eng.*	bay
b., bei / *Germ.*	by
B., Bucht / *Germ.*	bay
Ba / *Sud.*	river
Ba- / *Ban.*	people
Ba / *Mel.*	hill, mountain
Baai / *Afr.*	bay
Bab / *Ar.*	gate
Bac / *Viet.*	north
Bach / *Germ.*	brook, torrent
Bacino / *It.*	reservoir
Back / *Eng.*	ridge
Back / *Swed.*	brook
Bäck / *Swed.*	brook
Backe / *Swed.*	hill
Bad, -bad / *Dan.; Germ.; Nor.; Swed.*	thermal springs
Baden, -baden / *Germ.*	thermal springs
Bādiyat / *Ar.*	desert
Badwēynta / *Som.*	ocean
Badyarada / *Som.*	gulf
Baeg / *Kor.*	white
Bæk / *Dan.*	brook
Bælt / *Dan.*	strait
Bagni / *It.*	thermal springs
Baharu / *Mal.*	new
Bahia / *Port.*	bay
Bahía / *Sp.*	bay
Bahir / *Ar.*	river, lake, sea
Bahnhof / *Germ.*	railway station
Bahr / *Ar.*	wadi
Baḥr / *Ar.*	river, lake, sea
Baḥrat / *Ar.*	lake
Bahri / *Ar.*	north, northern
Baḥrī / *Ar.*	north
Bahrīyah / *Ar.*	northern
Bai / *Chin.*	white
Băi / *Rom.*	thermal springs
Baia / *Port.*	bay
Baie / *Fr.*	bay
Baigne / *Fr.*	seaside resort
Baile / *Gae.*	city, town
Bain / *Fr.*	thermal springs
Bains / *Fr.*	thermal springs
Baixo / *Port.*	low, lower
Bajan / *Mong.*	rich
Bajo / *Sp.*	low
Bajrak / *Alb.*	tribe
Bakhtīyārī / *Pers.*	western
Bakki / *Icel.*	hill
Bālā / *Pers.*	high
Bald / *Eng.*	peak
Balka / *Rus.*	gorge
Balkan / *Bulg.; Tur.*	mountain range
Ballin / *Gae.*	mouth
Ballon / *Fr.*	dome
Bally / *Gae.*	city, town
Balta / *Rom.*	marsh
Báltos / *Gr.*	marsh
Ban / *Laot.*	village
Bana / *Jap.*	promontory
Baňa / *Slvk.*	mine
Bañados / *Sp.*	marsh
Banc / *Fr.*	bank
Banco / *It.; Sp.*	bank
Band / *Pers.*	dam, mountain range
Bandao / *Chin.*	peninsula
Bandar / *Ar.; Mal.; Pers.*	port, market
Bang / *Indon.; Mal.*	stream
Bangou / *Sah.*	well
Banhado / *Port.*	marsh
Bani / *Ar.*	sons
Banja / *Bulg.; S.C.; Slvn.*	thermal springs
Banjaran / *Mal.*	mountain range
Banka / *Rus.*	sandbank
Banke / *Dan.*	bank
Baño / *Sp.*	thermal springs
Banský / *Cz.*	upper
Bánya / *Hung.*	mine
Bar / *Gae.*	peak
Bar / *Eng.*	sandbar

Geographical Glossary

Local Form	English
Bar / Hin.	great
Bāra / Hin.	great
Bara / S.C.	pond
Barā / Urdu	great
Barajı / Tur.	dam
Barat / Indon.; Mal.	west, western
Barkas / Lith.	castle, city, town
Barlovento / Sp.	windward
Barq / Ar.	hill
Barra / Port.; Sp.	bar, bank
Barrage / Fr.	dam
Barragem / Port.	reservoir
Barranca / Sp.	gorge
Barranco / Port.; Sp.	gorge
Barre / Fr.	bar
Barun / Mong.	western
Bas / Fr.	low
-bas / Rus.	reservoir
Bassa / Port.	flat
Bassejn / Rus.	reservoir
Bassin / Fr.	basin
Bassure / Fr.	flat
Bassurelle / Fr.	flat
Bašta / S.C.	garden
Bataille / Fr.	battle
Batalha / Port.	battle
Batang / Indon.; Mal.	river
Batha / Sah.	stream
Baţīn / Ar.	depression
Bāţlāq / Pers.	marsh
Batu / Mal.	rock
Bayan / Mong.	rich
Bayır / Tur.	mountain, slope
Bayou / Fr.	branch, stream
Bayt / Ar.	house
Bazar / Pers.	market
Be / Malag.	great
Beau / Fr.	beautiful
Becken / Germ.	basin
Bed / Eng.	river bed
Beek / Dut.	creek
Be'er / Hebr.	spring
Bei / Chin.	north
Bei, b. / Germ.	by
Beida / Ar.	white
Beinn / Gae.	mount
Bel / Ar.	son
Bel / Bulg.	white
Bel / Tur.	pass
Beled / Ar.	village
Belen / Tur.	mount
Belet / Ar.	village
Beli / S.C.; Slvn.	white
Beli / Tur.	pass
Bellah / Sah.	well
Belogorje / Rus.	mountains
Belt / Dan.; Germ.	strait
Bely / Rus.	white
Bělý / Cz.	white
Ben / Ar.	son
Ben / Gae.	mount
Bender / Pers.	port, market
Bendi / Tur.	dam
Beni / Ar.	son
Beo / S.C.	white
Bereg / Rus.	bank
Berg, -berg / Afr.; Dut.; Fle.; Germ.; Nor.; Swed.	mount
Berge / Afr.	mountain
Bergen / Dut.; Fle.	dunes
Bergland / Germ.	upland
Bermejo / Sp.	red
Besar / Mal.	great
Betsu / Jap.	river
Betta / Tam.	mountain
Bhani / Hin.	community
Bharu / Mal.	new
Bheag / Gae.	little
Bīābān / Pers.	desert
Biały / Pol.	white
Bianco / It.	white
Bien / Viet.	lake
Bight / Eng.	bay
Bijeli / S.C.	white
Bill / Eng.	promontory
Bilo / S.C.	range
Bílý / Cz.	white
Binnen / Dut.; Fle.; Germ.	inner
Biqā' / Ar.	valley
Bir / Ar.	well
Bi'r / Ar.	well
Birkat / Ar.	pond
Bistrica / Bulg.; S.C.; Slvn.	stream
Bjarg / Icel.	rock
Bjerg / Dan.	mount
Bjeshkët / Alb.	mountain pasture
Blaauw / Afr.	blue
Blanc / Fr.	white
Blanco / Sp.	white
Blau / Germ.	blue
Bleu / Fr.	blue
Bluff / Eng.	cliff
Bo- / Ban.	people
Bo / Chin.	white
Bo / Swed.	habitation
Boca / Sp.	gap, mouth

Local Form	English
Bôca / Port.	gap, mouth
Bocage / Fr.	forest
Bocca / It.	gap, pass
Bocchetta / It.	gap, pass
Bodden / Germ.	bay, lagoon
Boden / Germ.	soil
Bœng / Khm.	lake, marsh
Bog / Eng.	marsh
Bogaz / Alt.; Az.; Tur.	strait
Boğazi / Tur.	strait
Bogdo / Mong.	high
Bogen / Nor.	bay
Bois / Fr.	forest
Boka / S.C.	channel
Boloto / Rus.	marsh
Bolšoj / Rus.	great
Bolsón / Sp.	basin
Bom / Port.	good
Bong / Kor.	peak
Bongo / Malag.	upland
Bor / Cz.; Rus.	coniferous forest
Bór / Pol.	forest
-bor / Slvn.	city, town
Bóras / Gr.	north
Börde / Germ.	fertile plain
Bordj / Ar.	fort
Bóreios / Gr.	northern
Borg, -borg / Dan.; Nor.; Swed.	castle
Borgo / It.	village
Born / Germ.	spring
Bory / Pol.	forest
Bosch / Dut.; Fle.	forest
Bosco / It.	wood
Bosque / Sp.	forest
Bosse / Fr.	hill
Botn / Nor.	bay
Bou / Ar.	father, master
Bouche / Fr.	mouth
Boula / Sud.	well
Bourg / Fr.	city, town
Bourne, - bourne / Eng.	frontier
Boven / Afr.	upper
Boz / Tur.	grey
Bozorg / Pers.	great
Brána / Cz.	gate
Braña / Sp.	mountain pasture
Branche / Fr.	branch
Branco / Port.	white
Braţul / Rom.	branch
Bravo / Sp.	wild
Brazo / Sp.	branch
Brdo / Cz.; S.C.	hill
Bre / Nor.	glacier
Bredning / Dan.	bay
Breg / Alb.; Bulg.; S.C.	hill, coast
Brjag / Bulg.	bank
Bro / Dan.; Nor.; Swed.	bridge
Brod / Bulg.; Cz.; Rus.; S.C.; Slvk.; Slvn.	ford
Bród / Pol.	ford
Bron / Afr.	spring
Bronn / Germ.	spring
Bru / Nor.	bridge
Bruch / Germ.	peat-bog
Bruchzone / Germ.	fracture zone
Bruck, -bruck / Germ.	bridge
Brücke / Germ.	bridge
Brug / Dut.; Fle.	bridge
Brugge / Dut.; Fle.	bridge
Bruk / Nor.	factory
Brunn / Swed.	spring
-brunn / Germ.	spring
Brunnen / Germ.	spring
Brygg / Swed.	bridge
Brzeg / Pol.	coast
Bū / Ar.	father, master
Bucht, B. / Germ.	bay
Bugt / Dan.	bay
Buḩayrat / Ar.	lake, lagoon
Bühel / Germ.	hill
Bühl / Germ.	hill
Buhta / Rus.	bay
Bukit / Mal.	mountain, peak
Bukt / Nor.; Swed.	bay
Buku / Indon.	hill, mountain
Bulag / Mong.; Tur.	spring
Bulak / Mong.; Tur.	spring
Būlāq / Tur.	spring
Bult / Afr.	hill
Bulu / Indon.	mountain
Bur / Som.	mount
Būr / Ar.	port
Burg, - burg / Afr.; Ar.; Dut.; Eng.; Germ.	castle
Burgh / Eng.	city, town
Burgo / Sp.	village
Burha / Hin.	old
Buri / Thai	city, town
Burj / Ar.	village
Burn / Eng.	stream
Burnu / Tur.	promontory
Burqat / Ar.	mount, marsh
Burun / Tur.	cape
Busen / Germ.	bay
Busu / Ban.	land
Būtat / Ar.	lake, pond
Butte / Eng.; Fr.	flat-topped hill

Local Form	English
Büyük / Tur.	great
By / Eng.	near
By, -by / Dan.; Nor.; Swed.	city, town
Bystrica / Cz.; Slvk.	stream
Bystrzyca / Pol.	stream

C

Local Form	English
C., Cap / Cat.; Fr.; Rom.	cape
C., Cape / Eng.	cape
C., Colle / It.	pass
Caatinga / A.I.	forest
Cabeça / Port.	peak
Cabeço / Port.	peak
Cabeza / Sp.	peak
Cabezo / Sp.	peak, mountain
Cabo / Port.; Sp.	cape
Cachoeira / Port.	waterfall, rapids
Cachopo / Port.	reef
Cadena / Sp.	range
Caer / Wel.	castle
Cagan / Cauc.; Mong.	white
Cairn / Gae.	hill
Čāj / Az.; Tur.	river
Cajdam / Mong.	salt marsh
Caka / Chin.	lake
Cala / Sp.; It.	inlet
Calar / Sp.	plateau
Caldas / Sp.; Port.	thermal springs
Caleta / Sp.	inlet
Camp / Cat.; Fr.; Eng.	field
Campagna / It.	plain
Campagne / Fr.	plain
Campo / Sp.; It.; Port.	field
Cañada / Sp.	gorge, ravine
Canale / It.	canal, channel
Caño / Sp.	branch
Cañón / Sp.	gorge
Canyon / Eng.	gorge
Cao / Viet.	mountain
Cap, C. / Cat.; Fr.; Rom.	cape
Car / Gae.	castle
Càrn / Gae.	peak
Carrera / Sp.	road
Carrick / Gae.	rock
Casale / It.	hamlet
Cascada / Sp.	waterfall
Cascata / It.	waterfall
Castel / It.	castle
Castell / Cat.	castle
Castello / It.	castle
Castelo / Port.	castle
Castillo / Sp.	castle
Castro / Sp.; It.	village
Catarata / Sp.	cataract
Catena / It.	mountain range
Catinga / Port.	degraded forest
Cauce / Sp.	river bed
Causse / Fr.	highland
Cava / It.	stone quarry
Çay / Tur.	river
Cay / Eng.	islet, island
Caye / Fr.	island
Cayo / Sp.	islet, island
Ceann / Gae.	promontory
Centralny / Rus.	middle
Čeren / Alb.	black
Černi / Bulg.	black
Černý / Cz.	black
Čërny / Rus.	black
Cerrillo / Sp.	hill
Cerrito / Sp.	hill
Cerro / Sp.; Port.	hill, mountain
Cêrro / Port.	hill, mountain
Červen / Bulg.	red
Červony / Rus.	red
Cetate / Rom.	city, town
Chaco / Sp.	scrubland
Chāh / Pers.	well
Chaïf / Ar.	dunes
Chaîne / Fr.	mountain range
Champ / Fr.	field
Chang / Chin.	highland
Chapada / Port.	highland
Chapadão / Port.	highland
Château / Fr.	castle
Châtel / Fr.	castle
Chāy / Tur.	river
Chedo / Kor.	archipelago
Chenal / Fr.	canal
Cheng / Chin.	city, town, wall
Cheon / Kor.	city, river
Chergui / Ar.	eastern
Cherry, -cherry / Hin.; Tam.	city, town
Chew / Amh.	salt mine, salt
Chhâk / Khm.	bay
Chhotla / Hin.	little
Chi- / Ban.	great
Chi / Chin.	marsh, lake
Chi / Kor.	lake, pond
Chi- / Swa.	land
Chiang / Thai	city, town
Chico / Sp.	little
Chine / Eng.	ridge
Ch'on / Kor.	station

Local Form	English
Ch'ŏn / Kor.	river
Chŏsuji / Kor.	reservoir
Chott / Ar.	salt marsh
Chu / Chin.; Viet.	mountain, hill
Chuŏr phnum / Khm.	mountain range
Chute / Fr.	waterfall
Chutes / Fr.	waterfalls
Cidade / Port.	city, town
Ciems / Latv.	village
Čierny / Slvk.	black
Cime / Fr.	peak
Cîmp / Rom.	field
Cîmpie / Rom.	plain
Cinco / Sp.; Port.	five
Citeli / Georg.	red
Città / It.	city, town
Ciudad / Sp.	city, town
Ckali / Georg.	water
Ckaro / Georg.	spring
Co / Chin.	lake
Col / Cat.; Fr.	pass
Colina / Port.; Sp.	hill
Coll / Cat.	hill
Collado / Sp.	pass
Colle, C. / It.	pass
Collina / It.	hill
Colline / Fr.	hill
Colonia / Sp.; It.	colony
Coma / Sp.	hill country
Comb / Eng.	basin
Comba / Sp.	basin
Combe / Fr.	basin
Comté / Fr.	county, shire
Con / Viet.	island
Conca / It.	depression
Condado / Sp.	county, shire
Cone / Eng.	volcanic cone
Cône / Fr.	volcanic cone
Contraforte / Port.	front range
Cordal / Sp.	crest
Cordilheira / Port.	mountain range
Cordillera / Sp.	mountain range
Coring / Chin.	lake
Corixa / A.I.	stream
Corno / It.	peak
Cornone / It.	peak
Corrente / It.; Port.	stream
Corriente / Sp.	stream
Costa / Sp.; It.; Port.	coast
Côte / Fr.	coast
Coteau / Fr.	height, slope
Coxilha / Port.	ridge
Craig / Gae.	rock
Cratère / Fr.	crater
Cresta / Sp.; It.	crest
Crêt / Fr.	crest
Crête / Fr.	crest
Crkva / S.C.	church
Crni / S.C.; Slvn.	black
Crven / S.C.	red
Csatorna / Hung.	canal
Cuchilla / Sp.	ridge
Cuenca / Sp.	basin
Cuesta / Sp.	escarpment
Cueva / Sp.	cave
Čuka / Bulg.; S.C.	peak
Çukur / Tur.	well
Cu Lao / Viet.	island
Cumbre / Sp.	peak
Cun / Chin.	village
Cura / A.I.	stone
Curr / Alb.	rock
Cy., City / Eng.	city, town
Czarny / Pol.	black

D

Local Form	English
Da / Chin.	great
Da / Viet.	mountain, peak
Daal / Dut.; Fle.	valley
Daba / Mong.	pass
Daba / Som.	hill
Daban / Chin.; Mong.	pass
Dae / Kor.	great
Dağ / Tur.	mountain
Dağ., Dağı / Tur.	mountain
Dāgh / Pers.; Tur.	mountain
Dağı, Dağ. / Tur.	mountain
Dağları / Tur.	mountain range
Dahar / Ar.	hill
Dahr / Ar.	plateau, escarpment
Dai / Chin.; Jap.	great
Daiet / Ar.	marsh
Dak / Viet.	stream
Dake / Jap.	mountain
Dakhla / Ar.	depression
Dakhlet / Ar.	depression, bay
Dal, -dal / Afr.; Dan.; Dut.; Fle.; Nor.; Swed.	valley
Dala / Alt.	steppe, plain
Dalaj / Mong.	lake, sea
Dalan / Mong.	wall
Dallol / Sud.	valley, torrent
Dalur / Icel.	valley
Damm / Germ.	dam
Dan / Kor.	point

Local Form	English
Danau / *Indon.*	lake
Danda / *Nep.*	mountains
Dao / *Chin.*	island, peninsula
Dao / *Viet.*	island
Dar / *Ar.*	house, region
Dar / *Swa.*	port
Dara / *Tur.*	torrent, valley
Darb / *Ar.*	track
Darja / *Alt.*	river, sea
Darya, Daryā / *Pers.*	river, sea
Daryācheh / *Pers.*	lake, sea
Daš / *Alt.; Az.*	rock
Dasht / *Pers.*	desert, plain
Dawḥat / *Ar.*	bay
Dayr / *Ar.*	convent
De / *Sp.; Fr.*	of
Deal / *Rom.*	hill
Dearg / *Gae.*	red
Debre / *Amh.*	hill, monastery
Dega / *Som.*	stone
Deh / *Pers.*	village
Dēḥ / *Som.*	stream
Deich / *Germ.*	dike
Dél / *Hung.*	south
Delft / *Dut.; Fle.*	deep
Delger / *Mong.*	wide, market
-den / *Eng.*	city, town
Deniz / *Tur.*	sea
Denizi / *Tur.*	sea
Dent / *Fr.*	peak
Deo / *Laot.; Viet.*	pass
Dépression / *Fr.*	depression
Depressione / *It.*	depression
Der / *Som.*	high
Dera / *Hin.; Urdu*	temple
Derbent / *Tur.*	gorge, pass
Dere / *Tur.*	river, valley
Désert / *Fr.*	desert
Desfiladero / *Sp.*	pass
Desh / *Hin.*	land, country
Desierto / *Sp.*	desert
Det / *Alb.*	sea
Détroit / *Fr.*	strait
Deux / *Fr.*	two
Dezh / *Pers.*	castle
Dhar / *Ar.*	heights, hills
Dhār / *Hin.; Urdu*	mountain
Dhitikós / *Gr.*	western
Dien / *Khm.; Viet.*	rice-field
Diep / *Dut.; Fle.*	deep, strait
Dijk, -dijk / *Dut.; Fle.*	dam
Ding / *Chin.*	mountain, peak
Dique / *Sp.*	dam
Di Sopra / *It.*	upper
Di Sotto / *It.*	lower
Distrito / *Sp.; Port.*	district
Diu / *Hin.*	island
Diz / *Pers.*	castle
Djebel / *Ar.*	mountain
Dji / *Ban.*	water
Djup / *Swed.*	deep
Do / *Kor.*	Island
Do / *S.C.*	valley
Dō / *Jap.*	island, administrative division
Dōho / *Som.*	valley
Doi / *Thai*	mountain, peak
Dol / *Bulg.; Cz.; Rus.; S.C.*	valley
Doł / *Pol.*	valley
Dolen / *Bulg.*	low
Dolgi / *Rus.*	long
Dolina / *Bulg.; Cz.; Pol.; Rus.; S.C.; Slvn.*	valley
Dolni / *Bulg.*	low
Dolni / *Pol.*	lower
Dolny / *Pol.*	lower
Domb / *Hung.*	hill
Dôme / *Fr.*	dome
Dong / *Chin.; Viet.*	east
Dong / *Kor.*	city, town
Dong / *Thai*	mountain
Dong / *Viet.*	marsh, plain
Donji / *S.C.*	low, lower
Dorf, -dorf / *Germ.*	village
Doroga / *Rus.*	road
Dorp, -dorp / *Afr.; Dut.; Fle.*	village
Dos / *Rom.*	ridge
Dos / *Sp.*	two
Douarn / *Br.*	land
Dougou / *Sud.*	settlement
Doukou / *Sud.*	settlement
Down / *Eng.*	hill
Drâa / *Ar.*	dunes, hills
Dracht / *Germ.*	sandbank
Draw / *Eng.*	ravine, valley
Drif / *Afr.*	ford
Drift / *Afr.*	ford
Droichead / *Gae.*	bridge
Droûs / *Ar.*	crest
Dry / *Pash.*	river
Dubh / *Gae.*	black
Dugi / *S.C.*	long
Dugu / *Sud.*	settlement
Dun / *Gae.*	castle
Duna / *Sp.; It.*	dune
Düne / *Germ.*	dune
Dungar / *Hin.*	mountain
Dūngar / *Hin.*	mountain
Duong / *Viet.*	stream
Durchbruch / *Germ.*	gorge
Ḍurg / *Hin.*	castle
-durga / *Hin.*	castle
Duży / *Pol.*	great
Dvor / *Cz.*	court
Dvorec / *Rus.*	castle
Dvůr / *Cz.*	castle
Dwór / *Pol.*	court
Džebel / *Bulg.*	mountain
Dzong / *Tib.*	fort, monastery

E

Local Form	English
Ea / *Thai*	river
Eau / *Fr.*	water
Ebe / *Ban.*	forest
Ebene / *Germ.*	plain
Eck / *Germ.*	point
Eclusa / *Sp.*	lock
Écluse / *Fr.*	lock
Écueil / *Fr.*	cliff
Edeien / *Ber.*	sand desert
Edjérir / *Ber.*	wadi
Egg / *Germ.; Nor.*	crest, point
Eglab / *Ar.*	hills
Ehi / *Sah.*	mountain
Eid / *Nor.*	isthmus
Eiland / *Afr.*	island
Eisen / *Germ.*	iron
Eisenerz / *Germ.*	iron ore
El / *Amh.*	well
Elv, -elv / *Nor.*	river
Embalse / *Sp.*	reservoir
Embouchure / *Fr.*	mouth
Emi / *Sah.*	mountain
En / *Fr.*	in
Ende / *Germ.*	end
Enneri / *Sah.*	stream
Ennis / *Gae.*	island
Enseada / *Port.*	Bay, inlet
Ensenada / *Sp.*	bay, inlet
Ér / *Hung.*	stream
Erdö / *Hung.*	forest
Erg / *Ar.*	sand desert
Erz / *Germ.*	ore
Espigão / *Port.*	plateau
Ēstān / *Pers.*	land
Este / *Sp.*	east
Estero / *Sp.*	estuary, marsh
Estrecho / *Sp.*	strait
Estreito / *Port.*	strait
Estuaire / *Fr.*	estuary
Estuário / *Port.*	estuary
Estuario / *Sp.; It.*	estuary
Észak / *Hung.*	north
Étang / *Fr.*	pond
Ewaso / *Ban.*	river
Ey / *Icel.*	island
Eyja / *Icel.*	island
Eyjar / *Icel.*	islands
Eylandt / *Dut.*	island
Ežeras / *Lith.*	lake
Ezers / *Latv.*	lake

F

Local Form	English
Fa / *Mel.*	stream
Falaise / *Fr.*	cliff
Fall, -fall / *Germ.; Eng.; Swed.*	waterfall
Falls / *Eng.*	waterfall
Falu / *Hung.*	village
-falva / *Hung.*	village
Fan / *Sah.*	village
Faraglione / *It.*	cliff
Farallón / *Sp.*	cliff
Faro / *Sp.; It.*	lighthouse
Farvand / *Dan.*	strait
Fehér / *Hung.*	white
Fehn / *Germ.*	peat fen, peat-bog
Fekete / *Hung.*	black
Feld / *Dan.; Germ.*	field
Fell / *Eng.*	upland moor
Fell / *Icel.*	mountain
Fels / *Germ.*	rock
Fen / *Eng.*	marsh, peat-bog
Feng / *Chin.*	mountain, peak
Feste / *Germ.*	fort
Festung / *Germ.*	fort
Fier / *Rom.*	iron
Firn / *Germ.*	snow-field
Firth / *Eng.*	estuary, fjord
Fiume / *It.*	river
Fjäll / *Swed.*	mountain
Fjärd / *Swed.*	fjord
Fjell / *Nor.*	mountain
Fjöll / *Icel.*	mountain
Fjord, Fj. / *Dan.; Nor.; Swed.*	fjord
Fjörður / *Icel.*	fjord, bay
Fleuve / *Fr.*	river
Fließ / *Germ.*	torrent
Fljót / *Icel.*	river
Flói / *Icel.*	bay, gulf
Floresta / *Sp.; Port.*	forest
Flow / *Eng.*	strait
Flughafen / *Germ.*	airport
Fluß / *Germ.*	river
Fo / *Mel.*	stream
Foa / *Mel.*	stream
Foa / *Poly.*	cove
Foce / *It.*	mouth
Föld / *Hung.*	plain
Fonn / *Nor.*	glacier
Fontaine / *Fr.*	fountain
Fonte / *It.; Port.*	spring
Fontein / *Afr.; Dut.*	spring
Foort / *Afr.; Dut.*	ford
Forca / *It.*	pass
Forcella / *It.*	defile
Ford / *Rus.*	fjord
Förde / *Germ.*	fjord, gulf
Foreland / *Eng.*	promontory
Foresta / *It.*	forest
Forêt / *Fr.*	forest
Fors / *Swed.*	rapids, waterfall
Forst / *Germ.; Dut.*	forest
Forte / *It.; Port.*	fort
Fortin / *Sp.*	fort
Fosa / *Sp.*	trench
Foss / *Icel.; Nor.*	rapids, waterfall
Fossé / *Fr.*	trench
Foum / *Ar.*	pass
Fourche / *Fr.*	pass
Foz / *Sp.; Port.*	mouth
Frei / *Germ.*	free
Fronteira / *Port.*	frontier
Frontera / *Sp.*	frontier
Frontón / *Sp.*	promontory
Fuente / *Sp.*	spring
Fuerte / *Sp.*	fort
Fuji / *Jap.*	mountain
Fūlat / *Ar.*	marsh
Furt / *Germ.*	ford
Fushë / *Alb.*	plain

G

Local Form	English
G., Gora / *Bulg.; Rus.; S.C.*	mountain, hill
G., Gunung / *Indon.*	mountain
Ga / *Jap.*	bay
Ga / *Mel.*	mountain, peak
Gabel / *Germ.*	pass
Gaissa / *Lapp.*	mountain
Gala / *Sin.; Tam.*	mountain
Gam / *Hin.; Urdu*	village
Gamle / *Nor.; Swed.*	old
Gana / *Sud.*	little
Gang / *Germ.*	passage
Gang / *Chin.*	port, bay
Gang / *Kor.*	stream, bay
Gang / *Tib.*	glacier
Ganga / *Hin.*	river
Ganj / *Hin.; Urdu*	market
-gaon / *Hin.*	city, town
Gaoyuan / *Chin.*	plateau
Gap / *Kor.*	point
Gar / *Hin.*	house
Gara / *Bulg.*	station
Gara / *Ar.*	hills, range
Gară / *Rom.*	station
Garaet / *Ar.*	marsh, intermittent lake
Garam / *Beng.; Hin.; Urdu*	village
-gard / *Pol.*	city, town
Gård, -gård / *Dan.; Nor.; Swed.*	farmhouse
Gardaneh / *Pers.*	pass
Gare / *Fr.*	railway station
Garet / *Ar.*	hill
Garh, -garh / *Hin.; Urdu*	castle
Garhi / *Hin.; Nep.; Urdu*	fort
Garten / *Germ.*	garden
Gat / *Dan.; Fle.; Dut.*	strait
Gata / *Jap.*	bay, lake
Gau, -gau / *Germ.*	district
Gäu, -gäu / *Germ.*	district
Gavan / *Rus.*	port
Gave / *Bas.*	torrent
Gawa / *Jap.*	river
Geb., Gebirge / *Germ.*	mountain range
Gebergte / *Afr.; Dut.*	mountain range
Gebirge, Geb. / *Germ.*	mountain range
Geç., Geçit / *Tur.*	pass
Geçidi / *Tur.*	pass
Geçit, Geç. / *Tur.*	pass
Geysir / *Icel.*	geyser
Ghar / *Hin.; Urdu*	house
Ghar / *Pash.*	mountain, mountain range
Gharbīyah / *Ar.*	western
Ghat / *Hin.; Nep.; Urdu*	pass
Ghubbat / *Ar.*	bay
Ghurd / *Ar.*	dune
Gi / *Kor.*	peninsula
Giang / *Viet.*	stream
Giri / *Hin.; Urdu*	mountain, hill
Girlo / *Rus.*	branch
Gjebel / *Ar.*	mountain
Gji / *Alb.*	bay
Glace / *Fr.*	ice
Glaciar / *Sp.*	glacier
Glacier / *Eng.; Fr.*	glacier
Glen / *Gae.*	valley
Gletscher / *Germ.*	glacier
Gobi / *Mong.*	desert
Godār / *Pers.*	ford
Gok / *Kor.*	river
Gök / *Tur.*	blue
Gol / *Cauc.; Mong.*	river
Göl / *Tur.*	lake
Gola / *It.*	gorge
Gold / *Germ.; Eng.*	gold
Golet / *S.C.*	mountain
Golf / *Germ.*	gulf
Golfe / *Fr.*	gulf
Golfete / *Sp.*	inlet
Golfo / *Sp.; It.; Port.*	gulf
Goljam / *Bulg.*	great
Gölü / *Tur.*	lake
Gong / *Tib.*	high
Gonggar / *Tib.*	mountain
Gongo / *Ban.*	mountain
Góra / *Pol.*	mountain
Gora, G. / *Bulg.; Rus.; S.C.*	mountain, hill
Gorica / *S.C.; Slvn.*	hill
Gorje / *S.C.*	mountain range
Gorlo / *Rus.*	gorge
Gorm / *Gae.*	blue
Gorni / *Bulg.; S.C.; Slvn.*	upper
Gornji / *S.C.; Slvn.*	upper
Górny / *Pol.*	high
Gorod / *Rus.*	city, town
Gorodok / *Rus.*	village
Gorski / *Bulg.*	upper
Gory / *Rus.*	mountains
-gou / *Chin.*	river
Goulbi / *Sud.*	river, lake
Goulbin / *Sud.*	wadi
Goulet / *Fr.*	gap
Gour / *Ar.*	hills, range
Gourou / *Sud.*	wadi
Goz / *Sah.*	dune
Graafschap / *Dut.*	county, shire
Graben / *Germ.*	ditch, canal
Gracht / *Dut.*	canal
Grad, -grad / *Bulg.; Rus.; S.C.; Slvn.*	city, town, castle
Gradac / *S.C.*	castle
Gradec / *Bulg.*	village
Gradec / *Slvn.*	castle
Græn / *Icel.*	green
Gran / *Sp.; It.*	great
Grande / *Sp.; It.; Port.*	great
Grao / *Cat.; Sp.*	gap
Grat / *Germ.*	crest
Grève / *Fr.*	beach
Grind / *Germ.*	peak
Grjada / *Rus.*	range
Gród, -gród / *Pol.*	castle, city, town
Grön / *Icel.*	green
Grond / *Afr.*	soil
Gronden / *Dut.; Fle.*	flat
Groot / *Afr.; Dut.; Fle.*	great
Groß / *Germ.*	great
Grotta / *It.*	grotto
Grotte / *Fr.; Germ.*	grotto
Grube / *Germ.*	mine
Grün / *Germ.*	green
Grunn / *Nor.*	ground
Gruppe / *Germ.*	mountain system
Gruppo / *It.*	mountain system
Gua / *Mal.*	cave
Guaçu / *A.I.*	great
Guan / *Chin.*	pass
Guazú / *A.I.*	great
Guba / *Rus.*	bay
Guchi / *Jap.*	strait
Guelb / *Ar.*	hill, mountain
Guelta / *Ar.*	well
Guic / *Br.*	village
Güney / *Tur.*	south, southern
Gunong / *Mal.*	mountain
Guntō / *Jap.*	archipelago
Gunung, G. / *Indon.*	mountain
Guo / *Chin.*	state, land
Gur / *Rom.*	mountain
Guri / *Jap.*	cliff
Gurud / *Ar.*	hills, dunes
Gyár / *Hung.*	factory

H

Local Form	English
Haag / *Dut.; Fle.*	hedge
-håb / *Dan.*	port
Haḍabat / *Ar.*	highland
Hadd / *Ar.*	point
Hadjer / *Ar.*	hill, mountain
Hae / *Kor.*	bay, sea
Haehyeop / *Kor.*	strait

Local Form	English
Haf / *Icel.*	sea
Ḩafar / *Ar.*	well
Hafen / *Germ.*	port
Haff / *Germ.*	lagoon
Hafīr / *Ar.*	spring, ditch
Hafnar / *Icel.*	port
Hāfūn / *Som.*	bay
Hage / *Dan.*	point
Hage / *Dut.; Fle.*	hedge
Hågna / *Swed.*	peak
Hai / *Chin.*	sea, lake, bay
Hain / *Germ.*	forest
Haixia / *Chin.*	strait
Ḩajar / *Ar.*	hill, mountain
Hajar / *Ar.*	hill country
Halbinsel / *Germ.*	peninsula
Halma / *Hung.*	hill
Halom / *Hung.*	hill
Halq / *Ar.*	gap
Hals / *Nor.*	peninsula
Halvø / *Dan.*	peninsula
Halvøy / *Nor.*	peninsula
Hama / *Jap.*	beach
Hamāda / *Ar.*	rocky desert
Ḩamādah / *Ar.*	plateau
Ḩamādat / *Ar.*	plateau
Hammam / *Ar.*	thermal springs
Ḩammām / *Ar.*	well
Hamn / *Nor.; Swed.*	port
Hamrā' / *Ar.*	red
Hāmūn / *Jap.*	salt lake
Hana / *Jap.*	cape
Hana / *Poly.*	bay
Hane / *Tur.*	house
Hang / *Kor.*	port
Hank / *Ar.*	escarpment, plateau
Hantō / *Jap.*	peninsula
Har / *Hebr.*	mountain
Hara / *Mong.*	black
Harar / *Swa.*	well
Ḩarrah / *Ar.*	lava field
Ḩarrat / *Ar.*	lava field
Hasi / *Ar.*	well
Ḩasi / *Ar.*	well
Hassi / *Ar.*	well
Ḩasy / *Ar.*	well
Haug / *Nor.*	hill
Haupt- / *Germ.*	principal
Haure / *Lapp.*	lake
Haus / *Germ.*	house
Hausen / *Germ.*	village
Haut / *Fr.*	high
Hauteur / *Fr.*	hill
Hauts Plateaux / *Fr.*	highlands
Hauz / *Pers.*	reservoir
Hav / *Dan.; Nor.; Swed.*	sea, gulf
Haven / *Eng.; Fle.; Dut.*	port
Havn / *Dan.; Nor.*	port
Havre / *Fr.*	port
Hawr / *Ar.*	lake, marsh
Ház / *Hung.*	house
-háza / *Hung.*	house
Hazm / *Ar.*	height, mountain range
He / *Chin.*	river
Head / *Eng.*	headland
Hed / *Dan.; Swed.*	heath
Hegy / *Hung.*	mountain
Hegység / *Hung.*	mountain
Hei / *Nor.*	heath
Heide / *Germ.*	heath
Heijde / *Dut.; Fle.*	heath
Heilig / *Germ.*	saint
Heim, -heim / *Germ.; Nor.*	house
Heiya / *Jap.*	plain
-hely / *Hung.*	locality
Hem / *Swed.*	home
Hen / *Br.*	old
Higashi / *Jap.*	east, eastern
Hima / *Hin.*	ice
Himal / *Nep.*	peak
Hisar / *Tur.*	castle
Ho / *Chin.*	reservoir, river
Ho / *Kor.*	river, reservoir
Hō / *Jap.*	mountain
Hoch / *Germ.*	high, upper
Hochland / *Germ.*	highland
Hochplato / *Afr.*	highland
Hodna / *Ar.*	highland
Hoek / *Dut.; Fle.*	cape
Hof / *Dut.; Germ.*	court
Höfn / *Icel.*	port
Høg / *Nor.*	peak
Hög / *Swed.*	mountain
Hogna / *Nor.*	peak
Höhe / *Germ.*	peak
Høj / *Dan.*	hill
Hoj / *Ural.*	mountain range
Hok / *Jap.*	north
Hoku / *Jap.*	north, northern
Holm / *Dan.; Nor.; Swed.*	island
Holz / *Germ.*	forest
Hon / *Viet.*	island, point
Hong / *Chin.; Viet.*	red
Hono / *Poly.*	bay, anchorage
Hoog / *Afr.; Dut.; Fle.*	high
Hook / *Eng.*	point
Hoorn / *Afr.; Dut.; Fle.*	cape, point
Hora / *Cz.; Slvk.*	point
Horn / *Eng.; Germ.; Icel.; Nor.; Swed.*	point
Horní / *Cz.*	high
Horný / *Slvk.*	upper
Horst / *Germ.*	mountain
Horvot / *Hebr.*	ruins
Hory / *Cz.; Slvk.*	mountain range
Hout / *Dut.; Fle.*	forest
Hovd, -hovd / *Dan.; Nor.*	cape
Ḩowz / *Pers.*	basin
Hrad / *Cz.; Slvk.*	castle, city, town
Hradiště / *Cz.*	citadel
Hřeben / *Cz.*	crest
Hrebet / *Rus.*	mountain range
Hu / *Rmsh.*	lake
Huang / *Chin.*	yellow
Hude / *Germ.*	pasture
Huerta / *Sp.*	market garden
Hügel / *Germ.*	hill
Hügelland / *Germ.*	hill country
Huis, -huis / *Afr.; Dut.; Fle.*	house
Huisie / *Afr.*	house
Huizen, -huizen / *Dut.*	houses
Huk / *Afr.; Dan.; Swed.*	cape
Hum / *S.C.*	hill
Hurst / *Eng.*	grove
Hus / *Dut.; Nor.; Swed.*	house
Huta / *Pol.; Slvk.*	hut
Hütte / *Germ.*	hut
Hver / *Icel.*	crater
Hvit / *Icel.*	white
Hvost / *Rus.*	spit

I

Local Form	English
I., Island / *Eng.*	island
Ierós / *Gr.*	holy
Igarapé / *A.I.*	river
Ighazer / *Ber.*	torrent
Ighil / *Ber.*	hill
Iguidi / *Ber.*	dunes
Ih / *Mong.*	great
Ike / *Jap.*	pond
Ile / *Fr.*	island
Ilha / *Port.*	island
Iller / *Tur.*	administrative division
Ilot / *Fr.*	islet
Imi / *Ar.*	spring
I-n / *Ber.*	well
Inch / *Gae.*	island
Inder / *Dan.; Nor.*	inner
Indre / *Nor.*	inner
Inferiore / *It.*	lower
Inish / *Gae.*	island
Insel / *Germ.*	island
Insulă / *Rom.*	island
Inver / *Gae.*	mouth
Irhazér / *Ber.*	wadi
Irmak / *Tur.*	river
'Irq / *Ar.*	dunes
Is / *Nor.*	glacier
Ís / *Icel.*	ice
Isblink / *Dan.*	glacier
Ishi / *Jap.*	rock
Iske / *Alt.*	old
Isla / *Sp.*	island
Iso / *Finn.*	great
Iso / *Jap.*	cliff
Isola / *It.*	island
Isthmós / *Gr.*	isthmus
Istmo / *Sp.; It.*	isthmus
Ita / *A.I.*	stone
Itä / *Finn.*	east
Itivdleq / *Esk.*	isthmus
Iwa / *Jap.*	rock, cliff
Iztočni / *Bulg.*	eastern
Izvor / *Bulg.; Rom.; S.C.; Slvn.*	spring

J

Local Form	English
J., Jazīrat / *Ar.*	island
J., Jiang / *Chin.*	river
Jabal / *Ar.*	mountain
Jaha / *Ural.*	river
Jam / *Ural.*	lake, river
Jama / *Rus.*	cave
Jan / *Alt.*	great
Janga / *Tur.*	north
Jangi / *Alt.; Iran.*	new
Janūbīyah / *Ar.*	southern
Jar / *Rus.*	bank
Järv / *Est.*	lake
Järve / *Finn.*	lake
Järvi / *Finn.*	lake
Jasirēd / *Som.*	island
Jaun / *Latv.*	new
Jaur / *Lapp.*	lake
Jaure / *Lapp.*	lake
Javr / *Lapp.*	lake
Javrre / *Lapp.*	lake
Jazā'ir / *Ar.*	islands
Jazīrat, J. / *Ar.*	island
Jazovir / *Bulg.*	reservoir
Jbel / *Ar.*	mountain
Jebel / *Ar.*	mountain
Jedid / *Ar.*	new
Jedo / *Kor.*	archipelago
Jezero / *S.C.; Slvn.*	lake
Jezioro / *Pol.*	lake
Jhil / *Hin.; Urdu*	lake
Jian / *Chin.*	mountain
Jiang, J. / *Chin.*	river
Jiao / *Chin.*	cape, cliff
Jibāl / *Ar.*	mountain
Jih / *Cz.*	south
Jima / *Jap.*	island
Jin / *Kor.*	cove
Jing / *Chin.*	spring
Jisr / *Ar.*	bridge
Joch / *Germ.*	pass
Jõgi / *Est.*	river
Jøkel / *Nor.*	glacier
Joki / *Finn.*	river
Jokka / *Lapp.*	river
Jökull / *Icel.*	glacier
Jord, -jord / *Nor.*	earth
Ju / *Ural.*	river
Judeţ / *Rom.*	district
Jugan / *Ural.*	river
Jura / *Lith.*	sea
Jūra / *Latv.*	sea
Jūras Līcis / *Latv.*	bay
Jūrmala / *Latv.*	beach
Jurt / *Cauc.*	village
Južni / *Bulg.; S.C.; Slvn.*	southern
Južny / *Rus.*	southern
Juzur / *Ar.*	islands

K

Local Form	English
Ka / *Poly.*	lake
Kaap / *Afr.*	cape
Kabīr / *Ar.*	great
Kae / *Kor.*	inlet
Kāf / *Ar.*	peak, mountain
Kafr / *Ar.*	village
Kaga / *Ban.*	hills, mountain range
Kahal / *Ar.*	plateau, escarpment
Kai / *Jap.*	sea
Kaikyō / *Jap.*	strait
Kaise / *Lapp.*	mountain
Kal / *Pers.*	stream
Kala / *Az.; Kor.*	fort
Kala / *Finn.*	river
Kala / *Hin.*	black
Kala / *Tur.*	castle
Kalaa / *Ar.*	castle
Kalaki / *Georg.*	city, town
Kale / *Tur.*	castle
Kali / *Hin.*	black
Kali / *Indon.; Mal.*	bay, river
Kallio / *Finn.*	rock
Kaln / *Latv.*	mountain
Kalós / *Gr.*	beautiful, good
Kamen / *Bulg.; Rus.; S.C.; Slvn.*	mountain, peak
Kámen / *Cz.*	rock
Kameň / *Slvk.*	rock
Kami / *Jap.*	upper
Kamień / *Pol.*	rock
Kamm / *Germ.*	crest
Kamp / *Germ.*	field
Kâmpóng / *Khm.*	village
Kámpos / *Gr.*	field
Kampung / *Indon.; Mal.*	village
Kan., Kanal / *Alb.; Dan.; Germ.; Nor.; Rus.; S.C.; Slvn.; Swed.; Tur.*	canal, channel
Kanaal / *Dut.; Fle.*	canal
Kanał / *Pol.*	canal
Kanal, Kan. / *Alb.; Dan.; Germ.; Nor.; Rus.; S.C.; Slvn.; Swed.; Tur.*	canal, channel
Kand, -kand / *Pers.; Tur.*	city, town
Kang / *Chin.; Kor.*	bay, river
Kangas / *Fle.*	heath
Kange / *Esk.*	east
Kangri / *Tib.*	snow-capped mountain
Kantara / *Ar.*	bridge
Kaôh / *Khm.*	island
Kap / *Dan.; Germ.*	cape
Kapija / *S.C.*	gate, gorge
Kapp / *Nor.*	cape
Kar / *Tib.*	white
Kar / *Ural.*	city, town
Kara / *Tur.*	black
Karang / *Indon.; Mal.*	sandbank, cliff
Kari / *Finn.*	cliff
Kariba / *Ban.*	gorge
Kariet / *Ar.*	village
Karki / *Finn.*	peninsula
Kastel / *Germ.*	castle
Kástron / *Gr.*	fort, city, town
Káto / *Gr.*	lower
Kaupstadur / *Icel.*	city, town
Kaupunki / *Finn.*	city, town
Kavīr / *Pers.*	salt desert
Kawa / *Jap.*	river
Kawm / *Ar.*	hill
Kebir / *Ar.*	great
Kedi / *Georg.*	mountain range
Kédia / *Ar.*	mountain, plateau
Kedim / *Ar.*	old
Kef / *Ar.*	mountain
Kefála / *Gr.*	mountain, peak
Kefar / *Hebr.*	village
Kei / *Jap.*	river
Kelet / *Hung.*	east
Ken / *Gae.*	cape
Kent / *Alt.; Iran.; Tur.*	city, town
Kenya / *Swa.*	fog
Kep / *Alb.*	cape
Kep., Kepulauan / *Mal.*	archipelago
Kepulauan, Kep. / *Mal.*	archipelago
Kereszt / *Hung.*	cross
Kerk / *Dut.; Fle.*	church
Keski / *Finn.*	middle
Kette / *Germ.*	mountain range
Keur / *Sud.*	village
Key / *Eng.*	coral island
Kha / *Tib.*	valley
Khal / *Hin.*	canal
Khalīj / *Ar.*	gulf
Khand / *Hin.*	district
Khao / *Thai*	hill, mountain
Kharābeh / *Pers.*	ruins
Khashm / *Ar.*	promontory
Khatt / *Ar.*	wadi
Khawr / *Ar.*	mouth, bay
Khazzān / *Ar.*	dam
Khemis / *Ar.*	fifth
Khersónisos / *Gr.*	peninsula
Khirbat / *Ar.*	ruins
Khlong / *Thai*	stream, mouth
Khokhok / *Thai*	isthmus
Khor / *Ar.*	mouth, bay
Khóra / *Gr.*	land
Khorion / *Gr.*	village
Khowr / *Pers.*	bay
Khrisós / *Gr.*	gold
Ki- / *Ban.*	little
Kibali / *Sud.*	river
Kil / *Gae.*	church
Kilde / *Dan.*	spring
Kilima / *Swa.*	mountain
Kill / *Gae.*	strait
Kilwa / *Ban.*	lake
Kin / *Gae.*	cape
Kinn / *Nor.*	cape, point
Kirche / *Germ.*	church
Kirk / *Eng.*	church
Kis / *Hung.*	little
Kisiwa / *Swa.*	island
Kita / *Jap.*	north, northern
Kızıl / *Tur.*	red
Klein / *Afr.; Dut.; Germ.*	little
Kliff / *Germ.*	cliff
Klint / *Dan.*	reef
Klip / *Afr.; Dut.*	rock, cliff
Klit / *Dan.*	dune
Kloof / *Afr.; Dut.*	gorge
Kloster / *Dan.; Germ.; Nor.; Swed.*	convent
Knob / *Eng.*	mountain
Knock / *Gae.*	mountain, hill
Ko / *Jap.*	bay, lake, little
Ko / *Sud.*	stream
Ko / *Thai*	island, point
Købing / *Dan.*	town
Kogel / *Germ.*	dome
Kōgen / *Jap.*	plateau
Koh / *Hin.; Pers.*	mountain, mountain range
Kol / *Alt.*	river, valley
Kol / *Alt.; Tur.*	lake
Koll / *Nor.*	peak
Kólpos / *Gr.*	gulf
Kong / *Dan.; Nor.; Swed.*	king
Kong / *Indon.; Mal.*	mountain
Kong / *Viet.*	mountain, hill
Konge / *Ban.*	river
König / *Germ.*	king
Koog / *Germ.*	polder
Kop / *Afr.*	hill
Kopec / *Cz.; Slvk.*	hill
Kopf / *Germ.*	peak
Köping / *Swed.*	town
Köprü / *Tur.*	bridge
Körfezi / *Tur.*	gulf
Korfi / *Gr.*	rock
Koro / *Mel.*	mountain, island
Koro / *Sud.*	old
Koru / *Tur.*	forest
Kosa / *Rus.*	spit
Koška / *Rus.*	cliff
Koski / *Finn.*	rapids
Kosui / *Jap.*	lake
Kot / *Urdu*	castle
Kota / *Mal.*	city, town
Kotal / *Pash.; Pers.*	pass
Kotar / *S.C.*	cultivated area
Kotlina / *Pol.*	basin

Local Form	English
Kotlovina / *Rus.*	basin, plain
Kou / *Chin.*	mouth, pass
Kourou / *Sud.*	well
Kowr / *Pers.*	river
Kowtal / *Pers.*	pass
Koy / *Tur.*	bay
Köy / *Tur.*	village
Kraal / *Afr.*	village
Kraina / *Pol.*	land
Kraj / *Rus.; S.C.*	land
Kraj / *Rus.*	administrative division
Krajina / *S.C.*	land
Krak / *Ar.*	hill, castle
Krans / *Afr.*	mountain
Kras / *S.C.; Slvn.*	karst landscape
Krasny / *Rus.*	red
Kreb / *Ar.*	hills, mountain range
Kriaž / *Ar.*	mountain range
Krš / *S.C.*	karst area, limestone area
Krung / *Thai*	city, town
Ksar / *Ar.*	castle
Ksour / *Ar.*	fortified village
Ku- / *Ban.*	river branch
Kuala / *Mal.*	river, mouth
Kubra / *Ar.*	bridge
Küçük / *Tur.*	little
Kuduk / *Tur.*	spring
Kūh / *Pers.*	mountain
Kūhhā / *Pers.*	mountain range
Kul / *Alt.; Iran.; Tur.*	lake
Kulam, -kulam / *Hin.; Tam.*	pond
Kulle / *Swed.*	hill
Kulm / *Germ.*	peak
Kultuk / *Rus.*	bay
Kum / *Tur.*	dunes, sand desert
Kuppe / *Germ.*	dome, seamount
Kurayb / *Ar.*	hill
Kurgan / *Alt.*	hill
Kurgan / *Tur.*	fort
Kuro / *Jap.*	black
Kurort / *Bulg.; Germ.; Rus.*	spa
Kust / *Dut.; Fle.*	coast
Kust- / *Swed.*	coast
Küste / *Germ.*	coast
Kút / *Hung.*	spring
Kuyu / *Tur.*	spring
Kvemo / *Georg.*	low, lower
Kwa / *Ban.*	village
Kylä / *Finn.*	village
Kyle / *Gae.*	strait, channel
Kyō / *Jap.*	strait
Kyrka / *Swed.*	church
Kyst / *Dan.; Nor.*	coast
Kyun / *Burm.*	island
Kyūryō / *Jap.*	hills, mountains
Kyzyl / *Tur.*	red
Kzyl / *Tur.*	red

L

Local Form	English
L., Lake, Lago / *Eng.; It.; Port.; Sp.*	lake
La / *Tib.*	pass
Laagte / *Afr.*	stream, valley
Labuan / *Indon.; Mal.*	bay, port
Lac / *Fr.*	lake
Lach / *Som.*	stream, wadi
Lacul / *Rom.*	lake
Lae / *Poly.*	cape, point
Laem / *Thai*	bay, port
Låg / *Nor.; Swed.*	low, lower
Lag / *Swed.*	stream, wadi
Läge / *Swed.*	beach
Lagh / *Som.*	stream, wadi
Lago, L. / *It.; Port.; Sp.*	lake
Lagoa / *Port.*	lagoon
Laguna / *Alb.; It.; Rus.; Sp.*	lagoon, lake
Lagune / *Fr.*	lagoon
Laht / *Est.*	bay
Lahti / *Finn.*	bay, gulf
Laks / *Finn.*	bay
Lalla / *Ar.*	saint
Lampi / *Finn.*	pond
Lande / *Fr.*	heath
Lang / *Afr.; Dut.; Germ.*	long
Lang / *Viet.*	village
Lao / *Chin.*	old
Lapa / *Poly.*	mountain range, peak
Largo / *Port.; Sp.*	basin
Las / *Pol.*	forest
Las, Lās / *Som.*	well
Laut / *Mal.*	sea
Law / *Gae.*	hill, mountain
Lázně / *Cz.*	thermal springs
Lednik / *Rus.*	glacier
Leite / *Germ.*	coast
Lekh / *Nep.*	mountain range
Les / *Bulg.; Cz.; Rus.; Slvk.*	forest
Leso / *Rus.*	forested
Levante / *It.; Sp.*	eastern
Levkós / *Gr.*	white
Levy / *Rus.*	left
Lha / *Tib.*	temple
Lhari / *Hin.; Nep.*	mountain
Lho / *Tib.*	south
Lido / *It.*	sandbar
Liedao / *Chin.*	archipelago
Liehtao / *Chin.*	archipelago
Liels / *Latv.*	great
Lilla / *Swed.*	little
Lille / *Dan.; Nor.*	little
Liman / *Alb.; Rus.; Tur.*	lagoon, bay
Liman / *Tur.*	bay, port
Limin / *Gr.*	port
Limni / *Gr.*	lake
Ling / *Chin.*	mountain range, peak
Linna / *Finn.*	castle
Liqen / *Alb.*	lake
Lithos / *Gr.*	stone
Litoral / *Port.; Sp.*	littoral
Litorale / *It.*	littoral
Llan / *Wel.*	church
Llano / *Sp.*	plain
Llanura / *Sp.*	plain
Lo- / *Ban.*	river
Loch / *Gae.*	lake, inlet
Loch / *Germ.*	grotto
Loka / *Slvn.*	forest
Loma / *Sp.*	hill
Long / *Indon.*	stream
Loo / *Dut.; Fle.*	clearing
Lough / *Gae.*	lake
Loutrá / *Gr.*	thermal springs
Ložbina / *Rus.*	depression
Lu- / *Ban.*	river
Lua / *Ban.*	river
Lua / *Mel.*	island, reef
Lua / *Poly.*	crater
Luang / *Thai*	yellow
Luch / *Germ.*	peat-bog
Lücke / *Germ.*	pass
Lug / *Rus.*	meadow
Luka / *S.C.; Slvn.*	port
Lule / *Lapp.*	east, eastern
Lum / *Alb.*	river
Lund / *Dan.; Swed.*	forest
Lung / *Rom.*	long
Lung / *Tib.*	valley
Luoto / *Finn.*	shoal
Lurg / *Pers.*	salt flat
Lut / *Pers.*	desert

M

Local Form	English
M., Monte / *It.; Port.; Sp.*	mountain
Ma / *Ar.*	water
Ma- / *Ban.*	people
Maa / *Est.; Finn.*	island, land
Ma'arrat / *Ar.*	height
Machi / *Jap.*	district
Macizo / *Sp.*	massif
Madhya / *Hin.*	central
Madīnah / *Ar.*	city, town
Madīq / *Ar.*	strait
Mado / *Swa.*	well
Madu / *Tam.*	pond
Mae / *Thai*	stream
Mae nam / *Thai*	stream, mouth
Magh / *Gae.*	plain
Mägi / *Est.*	mountain
Măgura / *Rom.*	height
Mahā / *Hin.*	great
Mahal / *Hin.; Urdu*	palace
Mai / *Amh.; Ban.*	stream
Majdan / *S.C.*	quarry
Mäki / *Finn.*	mountain, hill
Makrós / *Gr.*	long
Mala / *Hin.; Tam.*	mountain
Malai / *Hin.; Tam.*	mountain
Malal / *A.I.*	fence
Malhão / *Port.*	dome
Mali / *Alb.*	mountain
Mali / *S.C.; Slvn.*	little
Malki / *Bulg.*	little
Malla / *Tam.*	mountain
Maly / *Rus.*	little
Malý / *Cz.; Slvk.*	little
Mały / *Pol.*	little
Man / *Kor.*	bay
Manastir / *Bulg.; S.C.*	monastery
Manche / *Fr.*	channel
Mar / *It.; Port.; Sp.*	sea
Mar / *Tib.*	red
Mar / *Ural.*	city, town
Marais / *Fr.*	marsh
Marché / *Fr.*	market
Mare / *Fr.*	pond
Mare / *It.; Rom.*	sea
Mare / *Rom.*	great
Marea / *Rom.*	sea
Marécage / *Fr.*	marsh
Marios / *Lith.*	reservoir
Marisma / *Sp.*	marsh
Mark / *Dan.; Nor.; Swed.*	land
Markt / *Germ.*	market
Marsa / *Ar.*	anchorage, bay
Marsch / *Germ.*	marsh
Maru / *Jap.*	mountain
Mas / *Prov.*	farmhouse
Maşabb / *Ar.*	mouth
Mashra' / *Ar.*	landing, pier
Masivul / *Rom.*	massif
Massiv / *Germ.; Rus.*	massif
Mata / *Poly.*	point
Mata / *Port.; Sp.*	forest
Mata / *Som.*	waterfall
Mato / *Port.; Sp.*	forest
Matsu / *Jap.*	point
Mauna / *Poly.*	mountain
Mávros / *Gr.*	black
Mayo / *Sud.*	river
Maza / *Lith.*	little
Mazar / *Pers.; Tur.*	sanctuary
Mazs / *Latv.*	little
Me / *Khm.*	river
Me / *Mel.*	hill, mountain
Me / *Thai*	great
Medina / *Ar.*	city, town
Medjez / *Ar.*	ford
Meer / *Dut.; Fle.*	lake
Meer / *Germ.*	lake, sea
Megálos / *Gr.*	great
Mégas / *Gr.*	great
Megye / *Hung.*	district
Mélas / *Gr.*	black
Melkosopočnik / *Rus.*	hill country
Mellan / *Swed.*	central
Men / *Chin.*	gate, channel
Ménez / *Br.*	mountain
Menzel / *Ar.*	bivouac
Meos / *Indon.*	island
Mer / *Fr.*	sea
Mercato / *It.*	market
Merdja / *Ar.*	lagoon, marsh
Meri / *Est.; Finn.*	sea
Meridional / *Rom.; Sp.*	southern
Merin / *A.I.*	little
Merja / *Ar.*	lagoon, marsh
Mers / *Ar.*	port
Mersa / *Ar.*	port
Mesa / *Sp.*	mesa, tableland
Meseta / *Sp.*	plateau
Mésos / *Gr.*	central
Mesto / *Bulg.; S.C.; Slvk.; Slvn.*	city, town
Město / *Cz.*	city, town
Mestre / *Port.*	principal
Meydan / *Tur.*	square
Meẓad / *Hebr.*	castle
Mező / *Hung.*	field
Mgne., Montagne / *Fr.*	mountain
Mgnes., Montagnes / *Fr.*	mountains
Miao / *Chin.*	temple
Miasto / *Pol.*	city, town
Mic / *Rom.*	little
Middel / *Afr.; Dut.; Fle.*	middle
Midi / *Fr.*	noon, south
Między / *Pol.*	central
Miedzyrzecze / *Pol.*	interfluve
Mierzeja / *Pol.*	sand spit
Mifraz / *Hebr.*	bay, gulf
Miftah / *Ar.*	gorge
Mikrós / *Gr.*	little
Mina / *Port.; Sp.*	mine
Mīnā' / *Ar.*	port
Minami / *Jap.*	south, southern
Minamoto / *Jap.*	spring
Minato / *Jap.*	port
Mine / *Jap.*	peak
Mirim / *A.I.*	little
Misaki / *Jap.*	cape
Mittel- / *Germ.*	middle
Mo / *Chin.*	sand desert
Mo / *Nor.; Swed.*	heath
Moana / *Poly.*	lake
Mogila / *Bulg.; Rus.*	hill
Moku / *Poly.*	island
Mølle / *Dan.*	mill
Monasterio / *Sp.*	monastery
Mond / *Afr.; Dut.; Fle.*	mouth
Mong / *Burm.; Thai; Viet.*	city, town
Moni / *Gr.*	monastery
Mont / *Cat.; Fr.*	mountain
Montagna / *It.*	mountain
Montagne, Mgne. / *Fr.*	mountain
Montagnes, Mgnes. / *Fr.*	mountains
Montaña / *Sp.*	mountain
Monte, M. / *It.; Port.; Sp.*	mountain
Monts, Mts. / *Fr.*	mountains
Moos / *Germ.*	moor
Mór / *Gae.*	great
More / *Bulg.; Rus.; S.C.*	sea
More / *Gae.*	great
Mori / *Jap.*	mountain, forest
Morne / *Fr.*	mountain
Moron / *Mong.*	river
Morro / *Port.; Germ.*	hill, peak
Morrón / *Sp.*	mountain
Morze / *Pol.*	sea
Most / *Bulg.; Cz.; Pol.; Rus.; S.C.; Slvn.*	bridge
Moto / *Jap.*	spring
Motte / *Fr.*	hill
Motu / *Mel.; Poly.*	island, rock
Moutier / *Fr.*	monastery
Movilă / *Rom.*	hill
Moyen / *Fr.*	central
Mta / *Georg.*	mountain
Mts., Monts, Mountains / *Eng.; Fr.*	mountains
Muang / *Laot.; Thai*	city, town, land
Muara / *Indon.; Mal.*	mouth
Muela / *Sp.*	mountain
Mühle / *Germ.*	mill
Mui / *Mel.*	point
Mui / *Viet.*	point, cape
Muiden / *Dut.; Fle.*	mouth
Muir / *Gae.*	sea
Mukh / *Hin.*	mouth
Mull / *Gae.*	promontory
Münde / *Germ.*	mouth
Mündung / *Germ.*	mouth
Municipiul / *Rom.*	commune
Munkhafaḍ / *Ar.*	depression
Münster / *Germ.*	monastery
Munte / *Rom.*	mountain
Muntele / *Rom.*	mountain
Munţii / *Rom.*	mountain range
Muren / *Mong.*	river
Mushāsh / *Ar.*	spring
Muz / *Tur.*	ice
Muztagh / *Tur.*	snow-capped mountain
Mwambo / *Ban.*	rock, cliff
Myit / *Burm.*	stream
Mynydd / *Wel.*	mountain
Myo / *Burm.*	city, town
Mýri / *Icel.*	marsh
Mys / *Rus.*	cape

N

Local Form	English
Na / *Cz.; Pol.; Rus.; S.C.; Slvn.*	on
Nab / *Ar.*	spring
Nad / *Cz.; Pol.; Rus.*	on
Nada / *Jap.*	bay, sea
Nadi, -nadi / *Hin.; Urdu*	river
Næs / *Dan.*	point
Nafūd / *Ar.*	dunes
Nag / *Tib.*	black
Nagar, -nagar / *Hin.; Tib.*	city, town
Nagaram / *Hin.; Tam.*	city, town
Nagorje / *Rus.*	plateau, mountains
Nagy / *Hung.*	great
Nahr / *Ar.*	river
Naikai / *Jap.*	sea
Naka / *Jap.*	central
Nakhon / *Thai*	city, town
Nam / *Burm.; Laot.; Thai*	river
Nam / *Kor.*	south
Namakzar / *Pers.*	salt desert
Nan / *Chin.*	south
Narrows / *Eng.*	strait
Narssaq / *Esk.*	plain, valley
Näs / *Swed.*	cape
Nationalpark / *Swed.; Germ.*	national park
Nau / *Lith.*	new
Nauja / *Lith.*	new
Navolok / *Rus.*	cape, promontory
Ne / *Jap.*	cliff
Neder / *Fle.; Dut.*	low
Neem / *Est.*	cape
Negro / *Port.; Sp.*	black
Negru / *Rom.*	black
Nehir / *Tur.*	river
Nei / *Chin.*	inner
Nene, -nene / *Ban.*	great
Néos / *Gr.*	new
Nero / *It.*	black
Nes / *Icel.; Nor.*	cape
Ness / *Gae.*	promontory
Neu / *Germ.*	new
Neuf / *Fr.*	new
Nevado / *Sp.*	snow-capped mountain
Nez / *Fr.*	cape
Ngok / *Viet.*	mountain, peak
Ngolo / *Ber.*	great
Ni / *Kor.*	village
Niecka / *Pol.*	basin
Niemi / *Finn.*	peninsula
Nieuw / *Fle.; Dut.*	new
Nij / *Dut.*	new
Nīl / *Hin.*	blue
Nishi / *Jap.*	west
Niski / *Pol.*	lower
Nisko / *S.C.*	low
Nisoi / *Gr.*	islands
Nisos / *Gr.*	island
Nizina / *Pol.*	lowland
Nížina / *Cz.*	depression
Nízký / *Cz.*	low, lower

Local Form	English
Nizmennost / *Rus.*	lowland, depression
Nižni / *Rus.*	low, lower
Nižný / *Slvk.*	low, lower
No / *Mel.*	stream
Nock / *Gae.*	ridge
Noir / *Fr.*	black
Non / *Thai*	hill
Nong / *Thai*	lake, marsh
Noord / *Afr.; Fle.; Dut.*	north
Noordoost / *Afr.; Fle.; Dut.*	northeast
Nor / *Arm.*	new
Nord / *Fr.; It.; Germ.*	north
Nördlich / *Germ.*	northern
Nørdre / *Dan.; Nor.*	northern
Norra / *Swed.*	northern
Nørre / *Dan.*	northern
Norte / *Sp.*	north
Nos / *Bulg.; Rus.; S.C.; Slvn.*	cape
Nosy / *Malag.*	island
Nótios / *Gr.*	southern
Nou / *Rom.*	new
Novi / *Bulg.; S.C.; Slvn.*	new
Novo / *Port.*	new
Novy / *Rus.*	new
Nový / *Cz.; Slvk.*	new
Now / *Pers.*	new
Nowy / *Pol.*	new
Nudo / *Sp.*	mountain
Nuevo / *Sp.*	new
Nui / *Viet.*	mountain
Numa / *Jap.*	marsh, lake
Nummi / *Finn.*	heath
Nunatak / *Esk.*	peak
Nuovo / *It.*	new
Nur / *Chin.*	lake
Nusa / *Mal.*	island
Nut, -nut / *Nor.*	peak
Nuwara / *Sin.; Tam.*	city, town
Nuwe / *Afr.*	new
Nyanza / *Ban.*	water, river, lake
Nyasa / *Ban.*	lake
Nyeong / *Kor.*	pass
Nyika / *Ban.*	upland
Nyŏng / *Kor.*	mount, pass
Nyugat / *Hung.*	west

O

Local Form	English
Ō / *Jap.*	great
Ó / *Hung.*	old
Ö / *Swed.*	island
Ø, -ø / *Dan.; Nor.*	island
Öar / *Swed.*	islands
Ober / *Germ.*	upper
Oblast / *Rus.*	province
Obo / *Mong.*	mountain, hill
Occidental / *Fr.; Rom.; Sp.*	western
Océan / *Fr.*	ocean
Océano / *Sp.*	ocean
Oceano / *It.; Port.*	ocean
Ocnă / *Rom.*	salt mine
Odde / *Dan.; Nor.*	promontory
Oeste / *Port.; Sp.*	west
Oever / *Fle.; Dut.*	bank
Oewer / *Afr.*	bank
Oie / *Germ.*	islet
Ojos / *Sp.*	spring
Oka / *Jap.*	coast
Oke / *Sud.*	height
Okean / *Rus.*	ocean
Oki / *Jap.*	bay
Okrug / *Rus.*	district
Ola / *Alt.*	city, town
Omuramba / *K.S.*	stream
Onder / *Afr.*	under
Oni / *Malag.*	river
Oos / *Afr.*	east
Oost / *Fle.; Dut.*	east
Oostelijk / *Dut.*	eastern
Opatija / *Slvn.*	abbey
Or / *Fr.*	gold
Oraş / *Rom.*	city, town
Óri / *Gr.*	mountains
Oriental / *Fr.; Port.; Rom.; Sp.*	eastern
Orientale / *It.*	eastern
Orilla / *Sp.*	bank
Órmos / *Gr.*	bay
Óros / *Gr.*	mountain
Ország / *Hung.*	land
Ort / *Germ.*	cape
Orta / *Tur.*	central
Orto / *Alt.*	central
Oseaan / *Afr.*	ocean
Ōshima / *Jap.*	large island
Ost / *Dan.; Germ.*	east
Öst / *Swed.*	east
Ostān, -ostān / *Pers.*	province
Øster / *Dan.; Nor.*	east, eastern
Öster / *Swed.*	east, eastern
Östlich / *Germ.*	eastern
Ostrog / *Rus.*	castle
Ostrov / *Rus.*	island
Ostrovul / *Rom.*	island
Ostrów / *Pol.*	island
Ostrvo / *S.C.*	island
Otok / *S.C.; Slvn.*	island
Otrog / *Rus.*	front range (mountains)
Oua / *Mel.*	stream
Ouar / *Ar.*	rocky desert
Oud / *Fle.; Dut.*	old
Oued / *Ar.*	wadi
Ouest / *Fr.*	west
Ouled / *Ar.*	son
Oum / *Ar.*	mother
Ouro / *Port.*	gold
Outu / *Poly.*	cape
Ova / *Ban.*	people
Ova / *Tur.*	plain
Ovasi / *Tur.*	plain
Øver / *Nor.*	over
Över / *Swed.*	over
Övre / *Swed.*	over
Øy / *Dan.; Nor.*	island
oz., Ozero / *Rus.*	lake
Ozek / *Alt.*	hollow
Ozera / *Rus.*	lakes
Ozero, oz. / *Rus.*	lake

P

Local Form	English
P., Pulau / *Mal.; Indon.*	island
Pää / *Finn.*	principal
Pad / *Rus.*	valley
Padang / *Indon.*	plain
Padiş / *Rom.*	upland
Padół / *Pol.*	valley
Pădure / *Rom.*	forest
Pahorek / *Cz.*	hill
Pahorkatina / *Cz.*	plateau, hills
País / *Port.; Sp.*	land, country
Pak / *Thai*	mouth
Pala / *It.*	peak
Palaiós / *Gr.*	old
Palanka / *S.C.*	village
Pali / *Poly.*	cliff
-palli / *Hin.*	village
Pampa / *Sp.*	plain, prairie
Panda / *Swa.*	junction
Panev / *Cz.*	basin
Pantanal / *Sp.*	swamp
Pantano / *Sp.*	swamp, lake
Pao / *Mel.*	hill
Pará / *A.I.*	river
Paramera / *Sp.*	desert highland
Páramo / *Sp.*	moor
Paraná / *A.I.*	river
Parbat / *Hin.; Urdu*	mountain
Parc / *Fr.*	park
Parco / *It.*	park
Parco Nazionale / *It.*	national park
Pardo / *Port.*	grey
Parque / *Sp.*	park
Parque Nacional / *Sp.; Port.*	national park
Pas / *Fr.; Rom.*	pass, strait
Pasaje / *Sp.*	passage
Pasir / *Mal.*	sand, beach
Paso / *Sp.*	pass
Passágem / *Port.*	passage
Passe / *Fr.*	pass
Passo / *It.; Port.*	pass
Pasul / *Rom.*	pass
Patak / *Hung.*	stream
Patam, -patam / *Hin.*	city, town
Patnā / *Hin.*	city, town
Patnam, -patnam / *Hin.*	city, town
Pattinam, -pattinam / *Hin.*	city, town
Pays / *Fr.*	land, country
Pazar / *Tur.*	market
Pea / *Est.*	cape
Pech / *Cat.*	hill
Pedhiás / *Gr.*	plain
Pedra / *Port.*	rock, mountain
Peg., Pegunungan / *Mal.; Indon.*	mountain range
Pegunungan, Peg. / *Mal.; Indon.*	mountain range
Pélagos / *Gr.*	sea
Pele / *Poly.*	peak, hill
Pen / *Br.*	principal
Pen / *Br.; Gae.*	cape, mountain
Peña / *Sp.*	peak
Pendi / *Chin.*	basin
Pendiente / *Sp.*	slope
Penha / *Port.*	peak
Peninsula / *Port.; Sp.*	peninsula
Péninsule / *Fr.*	peninsula
Penisola / *It.*	peninsula
Peñon / *Sp.*	rock, island
Pente / *Fr.*	slope
Perekop / *Rus.*	channel
Pereval / *Rus.*	pass
Perevoz / *Rus.*	ford
Pertuis / *Fr.*	strait
Peščara / *S.C.*	sandy soil
Peski / *Rus.*	sand desert
Petit / *Fr.*	little
Pétra / *Gr.*	rock
Phanom / *Thai; Khm.*	mountain range, mountain
Phau / *Laot.*	mountain
Phnum / *Khm.*	hill, mountain
Phu / *Viet.*	mountain, hill
Phum / *Thai*	forest
Phumĭ / *Khm.*	village
Pi / *Chin.*	cape
Piana, Pianura / *It.*	plain
Piano / *It.*	plain
Piatră / *Rom.*	stone
Pic / *Cat.; Fr.*	peak
Picacho / *Sp.*	peak
Piccolo / *It.*	little
Pico / *Port.; Sp.*	peak
Piedra / *Sp.*	rock, cliff
Pietra / *It.*	stone
Pieve / *It.*	parish
Pik / *Rus.*	peak
Pils / *Latv.*	city, town
Pinar / *Sp.*	pine forest
Pingyuan / *Chin.*	plain
Pioda / *It.*	crest
Pirgos / *Gr.*	tower, peak
Pīsh / *Pers.*	anterior, before
Pitkä / *Finn.*	great
Piton / *Fr.*	mountain, peak
Piz / *Rmsh.*	peak
Pizzo / *It.*	peak
Pjasăci / *Bulg.*	beach
Plaat / *Fle.; Dut.*	sandbank
Plage / *Fr.*	beach
Plaine / *Fr.*	plain
Plan / *Fr.*	plain
Planalto / *Port.*	plateau
Planina / *Bulg.*	mountain
Plano / *Sp.*	plain
Plas / *Dut.; Fle.*	lake, marsh
Plato / *Bulg.; Rus.*	plateau
Platosu / *Tur.*	plateau
Platte / *Germ.*	plain, plateau
Plav / *S.C.*	blue
Plavnja / *Rus.*	marsh
Playa / *Sp.*	beach
Ploskogorje / *Rus.*	plateau
Plou / *Br.*	church
Po / *Kor.*	port
Po / *Chin.*	lake, white
P'o / *Kor.*	bay, lake
Poa / *Mel.*	hill
Poarta / *Rom.*	pass
Poartă / *Rom.*	gate
Pobla / *Cat.*	village
Pobrzeże / *Pol.*	littoral, coast
Poço / *Port.*	well
Poço / *Port.*	point
Pod / *Cz.; Pol.; Rus.; S.C.; Slvn.*	bridge
Podkamenny / *Rus.*	stony
Poggio / *It.*	hill
Pohja / *Finn.*	north, northern
Pohjois- / *Finn.*	north
Pojezierze / *Pol.*	lake region
Pol / *Pers.*	bridge
Pol, -pol / *Rus.*	city, town
Pola / *Port.; Sp.*	village
Polder / *Fle.; Dut.*	reclaimed land
Pole / *Pol.*	field
Pólis / *Gr.*	city, town
Poljana / *Bulg.; Rus.; S.C.; Slvn.*	field, terrace
Poljarny / *Rus.*	polar
Polje / *S.C.; Slvn.*	valley, field, basin
Poluostrov / *Rus.*	peninsula
Pomorije / *Bulg.*	littoral
Pomorze / *Pol.*	littoral
Ponente / *It.*	western
Pont / *Cat.; Fr.*	bridge
Ponta / *Port.*	point
Ponte / *It.; Port.*	bridge
Póntos / *Gr.*	sea
Poort / *Afr.; Fle.; Dut.*	pass
Pore, -pore / *Hin.; Urdu*	city, town
Porog / *Rus.*	rapids
Porte / *Fr.*	gate
Portile / *Rom.*	gorge
Portillo / *Sp.*	pass
Portița / *Rom.*	small gate
Porto / *It.*	port
Pôrto / *Port.*	port
Posht / *Pers.*	back, posterior
Potjo / *Indon.*	peak
Potok / *Bulg.; Cz.; Pol.; Rus.; S.C.; Slvn.*	stream
Póvoa / *Port.*	village
Pozo / *Sp.*	well
Pozzo / *It.*	well
Pradesh / *Hin.*	region, state
Prado / *Sp.*	meadow
Praia / *Port.*	beach
Prato / *It.*	meadow
Pré / *Fr.*	meadow
Prealpi / *It.*	prealps
Presa / *Sp.*	reservoir
Presqu'île / *Fr.*	peninsula
Prêto / *Port.*	black
Priehradni nádrž / *Cz.*	reservoir
Pripoljarny / *Rus.*	subpolar
Pristan / *Rus.*	port
Prohod / *Bulg.*	pass
Proliv / *Rus.*	strait
Promontoire / *Fr.*	promontory
Průchod / *Cz.*	pass
Przedgorze / *Pol.*	front range (mountains)
Przełęcz / *Pol.*	pass
Przemysł / *Pol.*	industry
Przylądek / *Pol.*	cape
Pua / *Mel.*	hill
Puebla / *Sp.*	village
Puente / *Sp.*	bridge
Puerto / *Sp.*	port, pass
Puig / *Cat.*	peak
Puits / *Fr.*	well
Pul / *Pash.*	bridge
Pulau, P. / *Mal.; Indon.*	island
Pulau Pulau / *Mal.*	islands
Pulo / *Mal.; Indon.*	island
Puna / *A.I.*	upland
Puncak / *Indon.*	mountain
Punjung / *Mal.; Indon.*	mountain
Punt / *Afr.*	point
Punta / *It.; Sp.*	point
Pur, -pur / *Hin.; Urdu*	city, town
-pura / *Hin.; Urdu*	city, town
Pura / *Indon.*	city, town, temple
Puri, -puri / *Hin.; Urdu*	city, town
Pus / *Alb.*	spring
Pušča / *Rus.*	forest
Pustynja / *Rus.*	desert
Puszcza / *Pol.*	heath
Puszta / *Hung.*	lowland
Put / *Afr.*	well
Put / *Rus.; S.C.*	road
Putra, -putra / *Hin.*	son
Puu / *Poly.*	mountain, volcano
Puy / *Fr.*	peak
Pwell / *Wel.*	pond
Pyeong / *Kor.*	plain
Pyhä / *Finn.*	saint

Q

Local Form	English
Qagan / *Mong.*	white
Qala / *Pash.*	fortified town
Qal'at / *Ar.*	castle
Qalb / *Ar.*	hill
Qalīb / *Ar.*	spring
Qalīq / *Ar.*	spring
Qanāt / *Ar.*	canal
Qantara / *Ar.*	bridge
Qaqortoq / *Esk.*	white
Qar / *Som.*	mountain
Qara / *Pers.*	black
Qarah / *Tur.*	black
Qārat / *Ar.*	height, mountain
Qāret / *Ar.*	village, hill
Qaryah / *Ar.*	village
Qaryat / *Ar.*	village
Qaşr / *Ar.*	castle
Qawz / *Ar.*	dunes
Qeqertarssuaq / *Esk.*	peninsula
Qezel / *Tur.*	red
Qi / *Chin.*	river
Qing / *Chin.*	blue, green
Qiryat / *Hebr.*	city, town
Qolleh / *Pers.*	mountain, peak
Qu / *Chin.*	river, canal
Quan dao / *Viet.*	islands
Quebracho / *Sp.*	stream
Quebrada / *Sp.*	gorge, stream
Quedas / *Port.*	waterfalls
Qulbān / *Ar.*	well
Qundao / *Chin.*	archipelago
Qūr / *Ar.*	height, hill
Qytet / *Alb.*	city, town
Qyteti / *Alb.*	city, town

R

Local Form	English
R., Rio, River / *Eng.; Sp.*	river
Rada / *It.; Sp.*	anchorage
Rade / *Fr.*	anchorage
Rags / *Latv.*	cape
Rahad / *Ar.*	lake, pond
Rajon / *Rus.*	district
Rak / *Fle.; Dut.*	strait
Rakai / *Poly.*	reef
Ramla / *Ar.*	sand
Rancho / *Port.; Sp.*	farm, ranch
Rand / *Afr.; Germ.*	escarpment
Range / *Eng.*	mountain range
Rann / *Urdu*	marsh
Rano / *Malag.*	water
Ranta / *Finn.*	bank, beach
Rapide / *Fr.*	rapids
Ras / *Amh.*	peak
Rās / *Ar.*	point, cape

Local Form	English
Ras, Râs / *Ar.*	promontory, peak
Rāsiga / *Som.*	promontory
Rass / *Ar.*	promontory, peak
Rassa / *Lapp.*	mountain
Ráth / *Gae.*	castle
Raunina / *Bulg.; Rus.*	plain
Raz / *Fr.*	strait
Razliv / *Rus.*	flood plain
Récif / *Fr.*	reef
Recife / *Port.*	reef
Reede / *Germ.; Dut.; Slvn.*	anchorage
Reek / *Afr.; Gae.*	mountain range
Reg / *Pash.*	dunes
Région / *Fr.*	region
Rei / *Port.*	king
Reka / *Bulg.; Rus.; S.C.; Slvn.*	river
Řeka / *Cz.*	river
Réma / *Gr.*	torrent
Renne / *Dan.; Nor.*	deep
Reprêsa / *Port.*	dam, reservoir
Represa / *Sp.*	dam, reservoir
República / *Port.; Sp.*	republic
République / *Fr.*	republic
Rés., Réservoir / *Fr.*	reservoir
Res., Reservoir / *Eng.*	reservoir
Réservoir, Rés. / *Fr.*	reservoir
Reshteh / *Pers.*	mountain range
Respublika / *Rus.*	republic
Restinga / *Port.*	cliff, sandbank
Retsugan / *Jap.*	reef
Rettō / *Jap.*	archipelago
Rev / *Dan.; Nor.; Swed.*	reef
Rey / *Sp.*	king
Ri / *Tib.*	mountain
Ria / *Sp.*	estuary
Riacho / *Port.*	stream
Rialto / *It.*	plateau
Rialto / *It.*	rise
Riba / *Port.*	bank
Ribeira / *Port.*	river
Ribeirão / *Port.*	stream
Ribeiro / *Port.*	stream
Ribera / *Sp.*	coast
Ribnik / *Slvn.*	pond
Rid / *Bulg.*	mountain range
Rif / *Icel.*	cliff
Riff / *Germ.*	reef
Rīg / *Pash.*	dunes
Rijeka / *S.C.*	river
Rimāl / *Ar.*	sand desert
Rincón / *Sp.*	peninsula between two rivers
Ring / *Tib.*	long
Rinne / *Germ.*	trench
Rio / *Port.*	river
Río, R. / *Sp.*	river
Rîu / *Rom.*	river
Riva / *It.*	bank
Rive / *Fr.*	bank
Rivera / *Sp.*	brook, stream
Rivier, -rivier / *Afr.; Dut.; Fle.*	river
Riviera / *It.*	coast
Rivière / *Fr.*	river
Roads / *Eng.*	anchorage
Roc / *Fr.*	rock
Roca / *Port.; Sp.*	rock
Rocca / *It.*	castle
Roche / *Fr.*	rock
Rocher / *Fr.*	rock
Rock / *Eng.*	rock
Rod / *Pash.*	river
Rode / *Germ.*	tilled soil
Rodnik / *Rus.*	spring
Rog / *Rus.; S.C.; Slvn.*	peak
Roi / *Fr.*	king
Rojo / *Sp.*	red
Roque / *Sp.*	rock
Rot / *Germ.*	red
Roto / *Poly.*	lake
Rouge / *Fr.*	red
Równina / *Pol.*	plain
Rt / *S.C.; Slvn.*	cape
Ru / *Tib.*	mountain
Ruck / *Germ.*	ridge
Rücken / *Germ.*	ridge
Rud / *Pers.*	river
Ruda / *Cz.; Slvk.*	mine
Ruda / *Pol.*	ore
Rūdbār / *Pers.*	river
Rudha / *Gae.*	point
Rudnik / *Rus.; S.C.; Slvn.*	mine
Rug / *Fle.; Dut.*	ridge
Ruggen / *Afr.*	ridge
Ruina / *Sp.*	ruins
Ruine / *Fr.; Dut.; Germ.*	ruins
Rujm / *Ar.*	hill
Run / *Eng.*	stream

S

Local Form	English
S., See / *Germ.*	lake, sea
Saar / *Est.*	island
Saari / *Finn.*	island
Sabbia / *It.*	sand
Sabkhat / *Ar.*	salt flat, salt marsh
Sable / *Fr.; Eng.*	beach
Sacca / *It.*	anchorage
Saco / *Port.*	bay
Sad / *Cz.; Slvk.*	park
Sad / *Pers.*	wall
Sadd / *Ar.; Pers.*	cataract, dam
Safid / *Pash.; Urdu; Hin.*	white
Şafrā' / *Ar.*	desert
Sāgar / *Hin.*	reservoir
Saguia / *Ar.*	irrigation canal
Sahara / *Ar.*	desert
Sahel / *Ar.*	plain, coast
Sahr / *Iran.*	city, town
Şaḩrā' / *Ar.*	desert
Said / *Ar.*	sweet
Saj / *Alt.*	stream, valley
Saki / *Jap.*	point
Sala / *Latv.; Lith.*	island
Saladillo / *Sp.*	salt desert
Salar / *Sp.*	salt lake
Sale / *Ural.*	village
Salina / *It.; Sp.*	salt flat, salt marsh
Saline / *Dut.; Fr.; Germ.*	salt flat, salt marsh
Salmi / *Finn.*	strait
Salseleh-ye Kūh / *Pers.*	mountain range
Salto / *Port.; Sp.*	waterfall, rapids
Salz / *Germ.*	salt
Samudera / *Indon.*	ocean
Samudra / *Hin.*	lake
Samut / *Thai*	sea
San / *Jap.; Kor.*	mountain
San / *It.; Sp.*	saint
Sanchi / *Jap.*	mountain range
Sand / *Dan.; Eng.; Nor.; Swed.; Germ.*	beach
Šand / *Mong.*	spring
Sandur / *Icel.*	sand
Sank / *Pers.*	rock
Sankt, St. / *Germ.; Swed.*	saint
Sanmaeg / *Kor.*	mountain range
Sanmyaku / *Jap.*	mountain range
Sansanné / *Sud.*	campsite
Santo / *It.; Port.; Sp.*	saint
Santuario / *It.*	sanctuary
São / *Port.*	saint
Sar / *Pers.*	cape; peak
Šar / *Rus.; Tur.*	strait
Saraf / *Ar.*	well
Sari / *Finn.*	island
Sarı / *Tur.*	yellow
Sarīr / *Ar.*	rocky desert
Sary / *Tur.*	yellow
Sasso / *It.*	stone
Sat / *Rom.*	village
Sattel / *Germ.*	pass
Saurum / *Latv.*	strait
Schleuse / *Germ.*	lock
Schloß / *Germ.*	castle
Schlucht / *Germ.*	gorge
Schnee / *Germ.*	snow
Schwarz / *Germ.*	black
Scoglio / *It.*	cliff
Se / *Jap.*	bank, shoal
Sebkha / *Ar.*	salt flat
Sebkhet / *Ar.*	salt flat
Sed / *Ar.*	dam
Seda / *Ural.*	mountain
See, S. / *Germ.*	lake, sea
Sefra / *Ar.*	yellow
Segara / *Indon.*	lagoon
Şehir / *Tur.*	city, town
Seki / *Jap.*	dam
Selat / *Mal.; Indon.*	strait
Selatan / *Indon.*	southern
Selkä / *Finn.*	ridge, lake
Sella / *It.*	pass
Selo / *Bulg.; Rus.; S.C.; Slvn.*	village
Selsela Kohe / *Pers.*	mountain range
Selva / *It.; Sp.*	forest
Semenanjung / *Mal.*	peninsula
Sen / *Jap.*	mountain
Seong / *Kor.*	castle
Sep / *Alt.*	canal
Serīr / *Ar.*	rocky desert
Serra / *Cat.; Port.*	mountain range
Serra / *It.*	mountain
Serrania / *Sp.*	mountain range
Sertão / *Port.*	steppe
Seto / *Jap.*	strait
Sett., Settentrionale / *It.*	northern
Settentrionale, Sett. / *It.*	northern
Seuil / *Fr.*	sill
Sev / *Arm.*	black
Sever / *Rus.*	north
Severny / *Rus.*	northern
Sfînt / *Rom.*	saint
Sfîntu / *Rom.*	saint
Sgeir / *Gae.*	cliff
Sha'b / *Ar.*	cliff
Shahr / *Pers.; Hin.*	city, town
Sha'īb / *Ar.*	stream
Shallāl / *Ar.*	cataract
Shām / *Ar.*	north; northern
Shamo / *Chin.*	sand desert
Shan / *Chin.*	mountain, mountain range
Shan / *Gae.*	old
Shand / *Mong.*	spring
Shankou / *Chin.*	pass
Shaqq / *Ar.*	wadi
Sharm / *Ar.*	bay
Sharqī / *Ar.*	east, eastern
Sharqīyah / *Ar.*	eastern
Shatt / *Ar.*	river, salt lake
Shatt / *Tur.*	stream
Shën / *Alb.*	saint
Sheng / *Chin.*	province
Shi / *Chin.*	city, town
Shibīn / *Ar.*	village
Shih / *Chin.*	rock
Shima / *Jap.*	island
Shimo / *Jap.*	lower
Shin / *Jap.*	new
Shō / *Jap.*	island
Shotō / *Jap.*	archipelago
Shū / *Jap.*	administrative division
Shui / *Chin.*	river
Shuiku / *Chin.*	reservoir
Shur / *Pers.*	salt
Sidhiros / *Gr.*	iron
Sidi / *Ar.*	master
Sieben / *Germ.*	seven
Sierra / *Sp.*	mountain range
Sikt / *Ural.*	village
Sillon / *Fr.*	furrow
Šine / *Mong.*	new
Sink / *Eng.*	depression
Sinn / *Ar.*	point
Sint / *Dut.; Fle.*	saint
Sirt / *Tur.*	mountain range
Sirtlar / *Tur.*	mountain range
Sistema / *It.; Sp.*	mountain system
Siyāh / *Pers.*	black
Sjø / *Nor.*	lake
Sjö / *Swed.*	lake, sea
Skag / *Icel.*	peninsula
Skala / *Bulg.; Rus.*	rock
Skála / *Slvk.*	rock
Skar / *Nor.*	pass
Skär / *Swed.*	cliff
Skeir / *Gae.*	cliff
Skerry / *Gae.*	cliff
Skog / *Nor.; Swed.*	forest
Skóg / *Icel.*	forest
Skov / *Dan.; Nor.*	forest
Slatina / *S.C.; Slvn.*	mineral water
Slätt / *Swed.*	plain
Slieve / *Gae.*	mountain
Slot / *Dut.; Fle.*	castle
Slott / *Nor.; Swed.*	castle
Slough / *Eng.*	creek, pond, marsh
Sluis / *Dut.; Fle.*	sluice
Små / *Swed.*	little
Sne / *Nor.*	snow
Sneeuw / *Afr.; Dut.*	snow
Snežny / *Rus.*	snowy
Snø / *Nor.*	snow
So / *Kor.*	little
Sø / *Dan.; Nor.*	lake; sea
So / *Ural.*	passage
Söder / *Swed.*	south
Södra / *Swed.*	southern
Solončak / *Rus.*	salt flat
Sommet / *Fr.*	peak
Son / *Viet.*	mountain
Sønder / *Dan.; Nor.*	southern
Søndre / *Dan.*	southern
Sone / *Jap.*	bank
Song / *Viet.*	river
Sopka / *Rus.*	volcano
Sopočnik / *Rus.*	mountain system
Soprana / *It.*	upper
Šor, Sor / *Alt.*	salt marsh
Sos / *Sp.*	upon
Sotavento / *Sp.*	leeward
Sotoviento / *Sp.*	leeward
Sottana / *It.*	lower
Souk / *Ar.*	market
Souq / *Ar.*	market
Sour / *Ar.*	rampart
Source / *Eng.; Fr.*	spring
Souto / *Port.*	forest
Spitze / *Germ.*	peak
Spruit / *Afr.*	current
Sreden / *Bulg.*	central
Sredni / *Rus.*	central
Średni / *Pol.*	central
Srednji / *S.C.; Slvn.*	central
St., Saint, Sankt / *Eng.; Fr.; Germ.; Swed.*	saint
Stadhur / *Icel.*	city, town
Stadt, -stadt / *Germ.*	city, town
Stag / *Eng.*	city, town
Stagno / *It.*	pond
-stan / *Hin.; Pers.; Urdu*	land
Star / *Bulg.*	old
Stari / *S.C.; Slvn.*	old
Stary / *Pol.; Rus.*	old
Starý / *Cz.; Slvk.*	old
Stat / *Afr.; Dan.; Fle.; Nor.; Dut.; Swed.*	city, town
Stathmós / *Gr.*	railway station
Stausee / *Germ.*	reservoir
Stavrós / *Gr.*	cross
Sted / *Dan.; Nor.*	place
Stedt / *Germ.*	place
Stein, -stein / *Nor.; Germ.*	stone
Sten / *Nor.; Swed.*	stone
Stena / *S.C.; Slvn.*	rock
Stěna / *Cz.*	mountain range
Stenón / *Gr.*	strait, pass
Step / *Rus.*	steppe
-sthān / *Hin.; Pers.; Urdu*	land
Stift / *Germ.*	foundation
Štít / *Cz.; Slvk.*	peak
Stock / *Germ.*	massif
Stok / *Pol.*	slope
Stor / *Dan.; Nor.; Swed.*	great
Store / *Dan.*	great
Stræde / *Dan.*	strait
Strana / *Rus.*	land
Strand / *Germ.; Nor.; Swed.; Afr.; Dan.*	beach
Straße / *Germ.*	street, road
Strath / *Gae.*	valley
Straum / *Nor.; Swed.*	stream
Střední / *Cz.*	central
Stredný / *Slvk.*	central
Strelka / *Rus.*	spit
Stret / *Nor.*	strait
Stretto / *It.*	strait
Strom / *Germ.*	stream
Strøm / *Nor.*	stream
Ström / *Swed.*	stream
Stroom / *Dut.*	stream
Su / *Jap.*	sandbank
Su / *Tur.*	river
Suando / *Finn.*	pond
Suid / *Afr.*	south
Suidō / *Jap.*	strait
Sul / *Port.*	south
Sund / *Dan.; Nor.; Swed.; Germ.*	strait
Sungai / *Mal.*	river
Sunn / *Nor.*	south
Sūq / *Ar.*	market
Sur / *Fr.*	on
Sur / *Sp.*	south
Surkh / *Pers.*	red
Suu / *Finn.*	mouth, river mouth
Suur / *Cat.*	great
Svart / *Nor.; Swed.*	black
Sveti / *S.C.; Slvn.*	saint
Swa / *Ban.*	great
Swart / *Afr.*	black
Święty / *Pol.*	saint
Syrt / *Alt.*	ridge
Szállás / *Hung.*	village
Szczyt / *Pol.*	peak
Szeg / *Hung.*	bend
Székes / *Hung.*	residence
Szent / *Hung.*	saint
Sziget / *Hung.*	river island

T

Local Form	English
Tadi / *Ban.*	rock, cliff
Tae / *Kor.*	great
Tafua / *Poly.*	mountain
Tag / *Alt.; Tur.*	mountain
Tahta / *Ar.*	lower
Tahti / *Ar.*	lower
Tai / *Chin.; Jap.*	great
Taipale / *Finn.*	isthmus
Tajga / *Rus.*	forest
Take / *Jap.*	mountain
Tal / *Germ.*	valley
Tala / *Mong.*	plain, steppe
Tala / *Ber.*	spring
Tall / *Ar.*	hill
Talsperre / *Germ.*	dam
Tam / *Viet.*	stream
Tamgout / *Ber.*	peak
Tan / *Chin.; Kor.*	sandbank
Tana / *Malag.*	city, town
Tanana / *Malag.*	city, town
Tandjung / *Mal.*	cape, point
Tanezrouft / *Ber.*	desert
Tang / *Tib.*	upland
Tangeh / *Pers.*	strait
Tanjong / *Mal.*	cape, point
Tanjung, Tg. / *Indon.*	cape, point
Tanout / *Ber.*	well
Tao / *Chin.*	island
Taourirt / *Ber.*	peak
Targ / *Pol.*	market
Tărg / *Bulg.*	market
Tarn / *Eng.*	glacial lake
Tarso / *Sah.*	crater
Taš / *Alt.*	stone

Geographical Glossary

Local Form	English
Tassili / *Ber.*	upland
Tau / *Tur.*	mountain
Taung / *Burm.*	mountain
Ṭawīl / *Ar.*	hill
Tégi / *Sah.*	hill
Teguidda / *Ber.*	well
Tehi / *Ber.*	pass, mountain
Teich / *Germ.*	pond
Tell / *Tur.*	hill
Telok / *Mal.*	bay, port
Teluk / *Mal.*	bay, port
Tempio / *It.*	temple
Ténéré / *Ber.*	rocky desert
Tengah / *Indon.; Mal.*	central
Tepe / *Tur.*	hill
Tepesi / *Tur.*	hill
Termas / *Sp.*	thermal springs
Terme / *It.*	thermal springs
Terra / *It.; Dut.*	land, earth
Terrazzo / *It.*	guyot, tablemount
Terre / *Fr.*	land, earth
Teso / *Cat.*	hill
Téssa / *Ber.*	wadi, depression
Testa / *It.*	point
Tête / *Fr.*	peak
Tetri / *Georg.*	white
Teu / *Poly.*	reef
Teze / *Alt.*	new
Tg., Tanjung / *Indon.*	cape, point
Thaba / *Ban.*	mountain
Thabana / *Ban.*	mountain
Thal / *Germ.*	valley
Thálassa / *Gr.*	sea
Thale / *Thai*	lagoon
Thamad / *Ar.*	well
Theós / *Gr.*	god
Thermes / *Fr.*	thermal springs
Thog / *Tib.*	high, upper
Tian / *Chin.*	field
Tiefe / *Germ.*	deep
Tierra / *Sp.*	land, earth
Timur / *Indon.; Mal.*	eastern
Tind / *Nor.*	mountain
Tinto / *Sp.*	black
Tirg / *Rom.*	market
Tis / *Amh.*	new
Tizgui / *Ber.*	forest
Tizi / *Ber.*	pass
Tjåkko / *Lapp.*	mountain
Tjärn / *Swed.*	tarn, glacial lake
Tji / *Mal.*	stream
To / *Kor.*	island
To / *Mel.*	stream
Tō / *Jap.*	island
Tó / *Hung.*	lake
To / *Ural.*	lake
Tobe / *Tur.*	hill
Tofua / *Poly.*	mountain
Tog / *Som.*	valley
Tōge / *Jap.*	pass
Tokoj / *Alt.*	forest
Tônle / *Khm.*	stream, lake
Tope / *Dut.*	peak
Toplice / *S.C.; Slvn.*	thermal springs
Topp / *Nor.*	peak
Tor / *Gae.*	rock
Tor / *Germ.*	gate
Torbat / *Pers.*	tomb
Törl / *Germ.*	pass
Torp / *Swed.*	hut
Torre / *Cat.; It.; Sp.; Port.*	tower
Torrente / *It.; Sp.*	torrent, stream
Tossa / *Cat.*	mountain, peak
Tota / *Sin.*	port
Tour / *Fr.*	tower
Traforo / *It.*	tunnel
Träsk / *Swed.*	lake
Trg / *S.C.*	market
Trog / *Germ.*	trough, trench
Trois / *Fr.*	three
Trung / *Viet.*	central
Tse / *Tib.*	peak, point
Tsi / *Chin.*	pond
Tskali / *Georg.*	river
Tsu / *Jap.*	bay
Tulūl / *Ar.*	hills
Tünel / *Pers.*	tunnel
Tunturi / *Lapp.*	mountain, tundra
Tur'ah / *Ar.*	irrigation canal
Turm / *Germ.*	tower
Turn / *Rom.*	tower
Turó / *Cat.*	dome
Tuz / *Tur.*	salt
Týn / *Cz.*	fortress
U	
U., Unter-, Upon / *Eng.; Germ.*	under, lower
Uaimh / *Gae.*	cave
Uchi / *Jap.*	bay
Udde / *Swed.*	cape
Údolní nádrž / *Cz.*	reservoir
Uebi / *Som.*	river
Új- / *Hung.*	new
Ujście / *Pol.*	mouth
Ujung / *Indon.*	point, cape
Ul / *Chin.; Mong.*	mountain, mountain range
Ula / *Mong.*	mountain range
Ulan / *Mong.*	red
Uls / *Mong.*	state
Umi / *Jap.*	bay
Umm / *Ar.*	mother, spring
Umne / *Mong.*	south
Under / *Mong.*	mountain, peak
Ungur / *Alt.*	cave
Unter-, U. / *Germ.*	under, lower
Upar / *Hin.*	river
'Uqlat / *Ar.*	well
Ūr / *Tam.*	city, town
Ura / *Jap.*	bay, coast
Ura / *Alt.*	depression
Urd / *Mong.*	south
Uru / *Tam.*	city, town
Ušće / *S.C.*	mouth
Uske / *Alt.*	upper
Ust / *Rus.*	mouth
Ústí / *Cz.*	mouth
Ustup / *Rus.*	terrace
Utan / *Indon.; Mal.*	forest
Utara / *Indon.*	north, northern
Uusi / *Finn.*	new
Uval / *Rus.*	height
Úval / *Cz.*	mountain
'Uwaynāt / *Ar.*	well
Uzboj / *Alt.*	river bed
Uzun / *Tur.*	long
Užūrekis / *Lith.*	gulf
V	
Va / *Alb.*	ford
Va / *Ural.*	water, river
Vaara / *Finn.*	mountain
Väärti / *Finn.*	bay
Vad / *Rom.*	ford
Vær / *Nor.*	port
Våg / *Nor.*	bay
Vähä / *Finn.*	little
Väike / *Est.*	little
Väin / *Est.*	strait
Val / *Fr.; It.*	valley
Val / *Rom.; Rus.*	wall
Valico / *It.*	pass
Vall / *Cat.*	valley
Vall / *Swed.*	pasture
Valle / *It.; Sp.*	valley
Vallée / *Fr.*	valley
Vallei / *Afr.*	valley
Vallo / *It.*	wall
Valta / *Finn.*	cape
Váltos / *Gr.*	marsh
Valul / *Rom.*	wall
Vann / *Dan.; Nor.*	water, lake
Vanua / *Mel.*	land
Vár / *Hung.*	fort
Vara / *Finn.*	mountain
Varoš / *S.C.*	city, town
Város / *Hung.*	city, town
Varre / *Lapp.*	mountain
Vary / *Cz.*	spring
Vas / *S.C.; Slvn.*	village
Vásár / *Hung.*	market
Väst / *Swed.*	west
Väster / *Swed.*	western
Vatn / *Icel.; Nor.*	lake
Vatten / *Swed.*	water, lake
Vatu / *Mel.; Poly.*	island, reef
Vdhr., Vodohranilišče / *Rus.*	reservoir
Vechiu / *Rom.*	old
Vecs / *Latv.*	old
Veen / *Dut.; Fle.*	moor
Vega / *Sp.*	irrigated crops
Veld / *Afr.; Dut.; Fle.*	field
Veli / *S.C.; Slvn.*	great
Velik / *Bulg.*	great
Veliki / *Rus.; S.C.; Slvn.*	great
Veliký / *Cz.*	great
Velký / *Cz.*	great
Vel'ky / *Slvk.*	great
Vella / *Cat.*	old
Ver / *Ural.*	forest
Verde / *It.; Sp.*	green
Verh / *Rus.*	peak
Verhni / *Rus.*	upper
Verk / *Swed.*	factory
Vermelho / *Port.*	red
Vert / *Fr.*	green
Ves / *Cz.*	village
Vesi / *Finn.*	water, lake
Vest / *Dan.; Nor.*	west
Vester / *Dan.; Nor.*	western
Vestur / *Icel.*	west
Vetta / *It.*	summit
Viaduc / *Fr.*	viaduct
Vidda / *Nor.*	upland
Vidde / *Nor.*	upland
Viejo / *Sp.*	old
Vier / *Germ.*	four
Viertel / *Germ.*	quarter
Vieux / *Fr.*	old
Vig / *Dan.*	bay
Vik / *Icel.; Nor.; Swed.*	gulf, bay
Vila / *Port.*	city, town
Villa / *Sp.*	city, town
Ville, -ville / *Eng.; Fr.*	city, town
Vinh / *Viet.*	bay
Virful / *Rom.*	peak, mountain
Virta / *Finn.*	river
Višni / *Rus.*	high
Visok / *S.C.*	high
Víz / *Hung.*	water
Víztároló / *Hung.*	reservoir
Vlakte / *Dut.; Fle.*	plain
Vlei / *Afr.*	pond
Vliet / *Dut.; Fle.*	river
Vloer / *Afr.*	depression
Voda / *Bulg.; Cz.; Rus.; S.C.; Slvn.*	water
Vodny put / *Rus.*	stream, canal
Vodohranilišče, vdhr. / *Rus.*	reservoir
Vodopad / *Rus.*	waterfall
Volcan / *Fr.*	volcano
Volcán / *Sp.*	volcano
Voll / *Nor.*	meadow
Vórios / *Gr.*	northern
Vorota / *Rus.*	gate
Vorrás / *Gr.*	north
Vostočny / *Rus.*	eastern
Vostok / *Rus.*	east
Vötn / *Icel.*	lake, water
Vož / *Ural.*	mouth
Vozvyšennost / *Rus.*	upland
Vpadina / *Rus.*	depression
Vrah / *Bulg.*	peak
Vrata / *Bulg.; S.C.; Slvn.*	pass
Vrch / *Cz.; Slvk.*	mountain
Vrch / *S.C.; Slvn.*	peak
Vrchní / *Cz.*	upper
Vrchovina / *Cz.*	upland
Vulcan / *Rom.; Rus.*	volcano
Vulcano / *It.*	volcano
Vulkan / *Germ.; Rus.*	volcano
Vuopio / *Lapp.*	bend
Vuori / *Finn.*	rock
Východný / *Cz.*	eastern
Vyšný / *Slvk.*	upper
Vysoki / *Rus.*	high
Vysoky / *Cz.; Slvk.*	high
Vyšši / *Cz.*	high
W	
W., Wādī / *Ar.*	wadi
Wa / *Ban.*	people
Wabe / *Amh.*	stream
Wad / *Ar.*	wadi
Wad / *Dut.*	tidal flat
Wādī, W. / *Ar.*	wadi
Wāḥāt / *Ar.*	oasis
Wai / *Mel.; Poly.*	stream
Wal / *Afr.*	wall
Wala / *Hin.*	mountain range
Wald / *Germ.*	forest
Wan / *Burm.*	village
Wan / *Chin.; Jap.*	bay
Wand / *Germ.*	bluff
War / *Som.*	pond
Wār / *Ar.*	desert
-waram / *Hin.; Tam.*	village
Wasser / *Germ.*	water
Wat / *Pol.*	wall
Wat / *Thai*	church
Waterval / *Afr.; Dut.*	waterfall
Watt / *Germ.*	tidal flat
Wāw / *Ar.*	oasis
Weald / *Eng.*	wooded country
Webi / *Som.*	stream
Weg / *Germ.*	way, road
Wei / *Chin.*	cape, point
Weide / *Germ.*	pasture
Weiler / *Germ.*	village
Weiß / *Germ.*	white
Weon / *Kor.*	field
Wer / *Som.*	pond
Werder / *Germ.*	river island
Werk / *Germ.*	factory
Wes / *Afr.*	west
Westlich / *Germ.*	western
Westr- / *Sca.*	western
Wēyn / *Som.*	great
Wēyne / *Som.*	great
Wick / *Eng.*	village
Wiek / *Germ.*	bay
Wielki / *Pol.*	great
Wieś / *Pol.*	village
Wijk / *Dut.; Fle.*	quarter, district
-willer / *Germ.*	village
Woda / *Pol.*	water
Woestyn / *Afr.*	desert
Wold / *Dut.; Fle.; Eng.*	forest
Wörth / *Germ.*	river island
Woud / *Dut.; Fle.*	forest
Wschodni / *Pol.*	eastern
Wysoczyzna / *Pol.*	upland
Wysoki / *Pol.*	upper
Wyspa / *Pol.*	island
Wyżyna / *Pol.*	highland
Wzgórze / *Pol.*	hill
X	
Xi / *Chin.*	west
Xia / *Chin.*	gorge, strait
Xian / *Chin.*	county, shire
Xiang / *Chin.*	village
Xiao / *Chin.*	little
Xin / *Chin.*	new
Xu / *Chin.*	island
Y	
Yam / *Hebr.*	lake, sea
Yama / *Jap.*	mountain
Yan / *Chin.*	mountain
Yang / *Chin.*	strait, ocean
Yani / *Tur.*	new
Yar / *Tur.*	gorge
Yarimada / *Tur.*	peninsula
Yazı / *Tur.*	plain
Yegge / *Sah.*	well
Yeni / *Tur.*	new
Yeon / *Kor.*	sea
Yeong / *Kor.*	mountain
Yeşil / *Tur.*	green
Ylä / *Finn.*	upper
Yli- / *Finn.*	upper
Yō / *Jap.*	ocean
Yobe / *Sud.*	great
Yŏm / *Kor.*	island
Yoma / *Burm.*	mountain range
Yŏn / *Kor.*	lake, pond
Yŏng / *Kor.*	mountain, peak
Ytter / *Nor.; Swed.*	outer
Yttre / *Swed.*	outer
Yu / *Chin.*	old
Yu / *Chin.*	island
Yu / *Jap.*	thermal spring
Yüan / *Chin.*	spring, river
Yunhe / *Chin.*	canal
Z	
Zāb / *Ar.*	river
Zachodni / *Pol.*	western
Zaki / *Jap.*	cape
Zalew / *Pol.*	gulf
Zaliv / *Bulg.; Rus.; S.C.; Slvn.*	gulf
Zaljev / *Slvn.*	bay
Zámek / *Cz.*	castle
Zan / *Jap.*	mountain
Zand / *Dut.; Fle.*	sand
Zandt / *Dut.; Fle.*	sand
Zangbo / *Chin.*	river
Zapad / *Rus.*	west
Zapaden / *Bulg.*	western
Zapadni / *S.C.; Slvn.*	western
Západní / *Cz.*	western
Zapadny / *Rus.*	western
Zapovednik / *Rus.*	reserve
Zatoka / *Pol.*	gulf
Zavod / *Rus.*	roadstead
Zāwiyat / *Ar.*	monastery
Zdrój / *Pol.*	thermal springs
Ze / *Jap.*	islet
Zee / *Dut.; Fle.*	sea
Zelëny / *Rus.*	green
Žem / *Lith.*	land, country
Země / *Cz.; Slvk.*	land, country
Zemlja / *Rus.*	land
Zen / *Jap.*	mountain
Zhan / *Chin.*	mountain
Zhen / *Chin.*	market
Zhong / *Chin.*	central
Zhou / *Chin.*	quarter, district
Zhuang / *Chin.*	village
Ziemia / *Pol.*	land
Zigos / *Gr.*	pass
Zipfel / *Germ.*	tip, point
Ziwa / *Swa.*	marsh
Zizhiqu / *Chin.*	autonomous region
Zlato / *Bulg.*	gold
Zuid / *Dut.; Fle.*	south
Zuidelijk / *Dut.*	southern
Żuława / *Pol.*	marsh
Zun / *Mong.*	east
Zwart / *Dut.*	black
Zwei / *Germ.*	two

International Map Index

All of the toponyms (place-names) which appear on the maps are listed in the International Map Index. Each entry includes the following: Place-name and, where applicable, other forms by which it is written or known; a symbol, where applicable, indicating what kind of feature it is; the number of the map on which it appears; and the map-reference letters and geographical coordinates indicating its location on the map.

Toponyms

Each toponym, or place-name, is written in full, with accents and diacritical marks. Since many countries have more than one official language, many of these forms are included on the maps. For example, many Belgian place-names are listed as follows: Bruxelles/Brussel; Antwerpen/Anvers, and vice versa, Brussel/Bruxelles; Anvers/Antwerpen. In Italy, certain regions have a special status—they are largely autonomous and officially bilingual. As a result, Index listings appear as follows: Aosta/Aoste; Alto Adige/Sud Tirol, and vice versa. One name, however, may be the only name on the map.

In China, the written forms of commonly used regional languages have been taken into account. These forms are enclosed in parenthesis following the official name: e.g. Xiangshan (Dancheng). However, when the regional is listed first, it is linked to the official name with an→: e.g. Dancheng→Xiangshan. The same style is used for former or historical name forms: e.g. Rhodesia→Zimbabwe and Zimbabwe (Rhodesia).

Place-names for major features (countries, major cities, and large physical features), where applicable, include the English conventional form identified by (EN) and linked in the local name or names with an = sign: e.g. Italia=Italy (EN), and vice versa, Italy (EN)=Italia. Former English names are linked in the Index to the conventional form by an→.

Symbols

The last component with the place-name is a symbol, where applicable, specifying the broad category of the feature named. A table preceding the Index lists all of the symbols used and their meanings; this information also appears as a footnote on each page of the Index. Place-names without symbols are cities and towns.

Alphabetization

Place-names are listed in English alphabetical order—26 letters, from A to Z—because of its international usage. Names including two or more words are listed alphabetically according to the first letter of the word: e.g. De Ruyter is listed under D; Le Havre is listed under L. Names with the prefix Mc are listed as if spelled Mac. The generic portion of a name (lake, sierra, mountain, etc.) is placed after the name: e.g. Lake Erie is listed as Erie, Lake; Sierra Morena is listed as Morena, Sierra. In Spanish, "ch" and "ll" groups and the letter "n" are included respectively under C, L, and N, without any distinction.

The same place-name sometimes is listed in the Index several times. It may because of the various translations of a name, or it may be that several places have the same name.

Various translations of a name appear as follows:

Danube (EN)=Dunav   Danube (EN)=Donau
Danube (EN)=Dunărea   Danube (EN)=Dunaj

Several places with the same name appear as follows; however, only in these cases is the location—abbreviated and enclosed in brackets—included. A table of these abbreviations precedes the Index.

Abbeville [U.S.]   Aberdeen [Scot.-U.K.]
Abbeville [Fr.]   Aberdeen [N.C.-U.S.]
Aberdeen [S. Afr.]

Map Number

Each map in the atlas is identified by a number. Where multiple maps are on one page, each map is additionally identified by a boxed letter in the upper-right-hand corner of the map. In the Index listing following the place-name and its variations in language and spelling, where applicable, is the number of the map on which it appears. If the map is one of several on a page, the Index listing includes the map number and letter.

Although a place-name may appear on one or more maps, it is indexed to only one map. Most places are indexed to the regional maps. However, if a place-name appears on either the physical or political continental maps, it is indexed to one of the two types of map. For example, a river or mountain would be indexed to a physical continental map; a city or state would be indexed to a political continental map.

Map-Reference Letters and Geographical Coordinates

The next elements in the Index listing are the map-reference letters and the geographical coordinates, respectively, locating the place on the map.

Map-reference letters consist of a capital and a lowercase letter. Capital letters are across the top and bottom of the maps; lowercase letters are down the sides. The map-reference letters assigned to each place-name refer to the location of the name within the area formed by grid lines connecting the geographical coordinates on either sides of the letters.

Geographical coordinates are the latitude (N for North, S for South) and longitude (E for East, W for West) expressed in degrees and minutes and based on the prime meridian, Greenwich.

Map-reference letters and coordinates for extensive geographical features, such as mountain ranges and countries, are given for the approximate central point of the area. Those for waterways, such as canals and rivers, are given for the mouth of the river, the point where it enters another river or where the feature reaches the map margin. On this page are sample maps showing points to which features are indexed according to map-reference letters and coordinates.

On most maps there is not enough space to place all of the names of administrative subdivisions. In these cases the location of the place is shown on the map by a circled letter or number and the place-name and circled letter or number are listed in the map margin. The map-reference numbers and coordinates for these places refer to the location of the circled letter or number on the map.

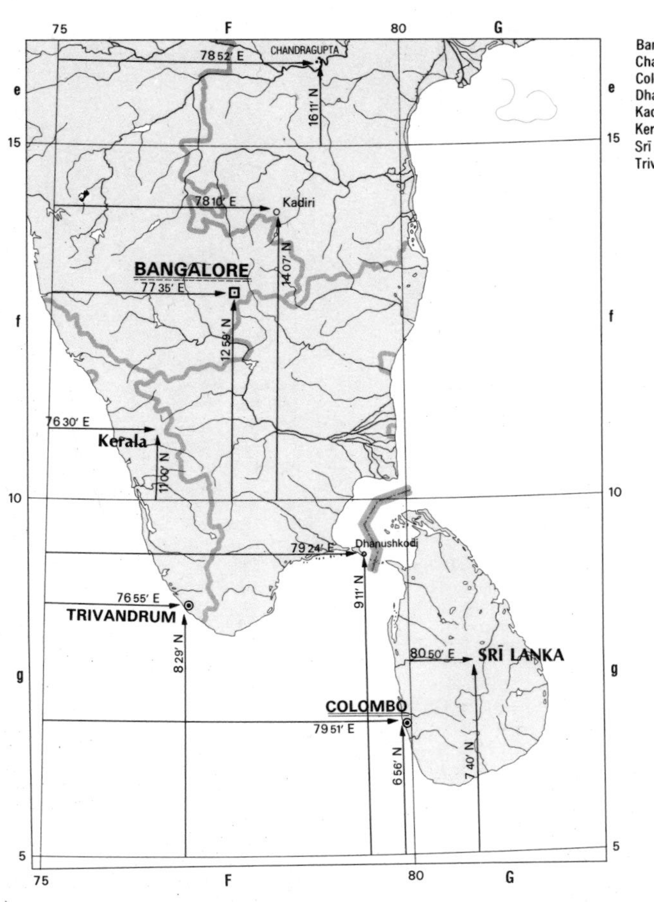

Bangalore	25	Ff	12°59'N	77°35'E
Chandragupta	35	Fe	16°11'N	78°52'E
Colombo	25	Fg	6°56'N	79°51'E
Dhanushkodi	25	Fg	9°11'N	79°24'E
Kadiri	25	Ff	14°07'N	78°10'E
Kerala	25	Ff	11°00'N	76°30'E
Srī Lanka	25	Gg	7°40'N	80°50'E
Trivandrum	25	Fg	8°29'N	76°55'E

Alaska	38	Dc	65°00'N	153°00'W
Alaska, Gulf of-	38	Ed	58°00'N	146°00'W
Alexander Archipelago	38	Fd	56°30'N	134°00'W
Barrow, Point-	38	Db	71°23'N	156°30'W
Bering Strait	38	Cc	65°30'N	169°00'W
Coast Mountains	38	Gd	55°00'N	129°00'W
Kodiak	38	Dd	57°30'N	153°30'W
Yukon	38	Cc	62°33'N	163°59'W

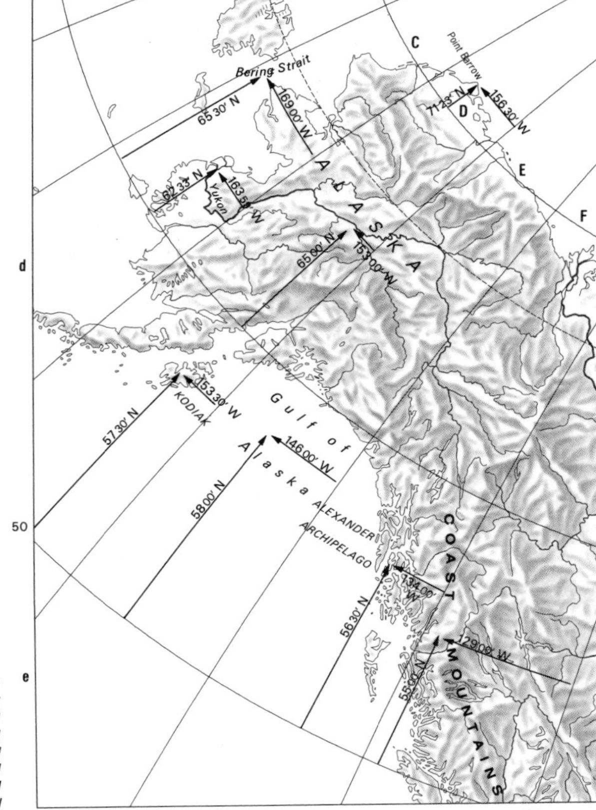

List of Abbreviations

Abz.-U.S.S.R. Azerbaijan S.S.R., U.S.S.R.
Afg. Afghanistan
Afr. Africa
Agl. Anguilla
Ak.-U.S. Alaska, U.S.
Al.-U.S. Alabama, U.S.
Alb. Albania
Alg. Algeria
Alta.-Can. Alberta, Canada
Am. Sam. American Samoa
And. Andorra
Ang. Angola
Ant. Antarctica
Ar.-U.S. Arkansas, U.S.
Arg. Argentina
Arm.-U.S.S.R. Armenian S.S.R., U.S.S.R.
Asia Asia
Atg. Antigua and Barbuda
Aus. Austria
Austl. Australia
Az.-U.S. Arizona, U.S.
Azr. Azores
Bah. Bahamas
Bar. Barbados
B.A.T. British Antarctic Territory
B.C.-Can. British Columbia, Canada
Bel. Belgium
Ben. Benin
Ber. Bermuda
Bhr. Bahrain
Bhu. Bhutan
Blz. Belize
Bnd. Burundi
Bngl. Bangladesh
Bol. Bolivia
Bots. Botswana
Braz. Brazil
Bru. Brunei
Bul. Bulgaria
Bur. Burma
Burkina Burkina Faso
B.V.I. British Virgin Islands
Bye.-U.S.S.R. Byelorussian S.S.R., U.S.S.R.
Ca.-U.S. California, U.S.
Cam. Cameroon
C. Amer. Central America
Can. Canada
Can. Is. Canary Islands
C.A.R. Central African Republic
Cay. Is Cayman Islands
Chad Chad
Chan. Is. Channel Islands
Chile Chile
China China
Co.-U.S. Colorado, U.S.
Cocos Is. Cocos Islands
Col. Colombia
Con. Congo
Cook Cook Islands
Cor. Sea Is. Coral Sea Islands
C.R. Costa Rica
Ct.-U.S. Connecticut, U.S.
Cuba Cuba
C.V. Cape Verde
Cyp. Cyprus
Czech. Czechoslovakia
D.C.-U.S. District of Columbia, U.S.
De.-U.S. Delaware, U.S.
Den. Denmark
Dji. Djibouti
Dom. Dominica
Dom. Rep. Dominican Republic
Ec. Ecuador
Eg. Egypt
El Sal. El Salvador
Eng.-U.K. England, U.K.
Eq. Gui. Equatorial Guinea
Est.-U.S.S.R. Estonian S.S.R., U.S.S.R.
Eth. Ethiopia
Eur. Europe
Falk. Is. Falkland Islands
Far. Is. Faeroe Islands
Fiji Fiji
Fin. Finland
Fl.-U.S. Florida, U.S.
Fr. France
Fr. Gui. French Guiana
Fr. Poly. French Polynesia
F.S.M. Federated States of Micronesia
Ga.-U.S. Georgia, U.S.
Gabon Gabon
Gam. Gambia
Geo.-U.S.S.R. Georgian S.S.R., U.S.S.R.
Ger. Germany
Ghana Ghana
Gib. Gibraltar
Grc. Greece
Gren. Grenada
Grld. Greenland
Guad. Guadeloupe
Guam Guam
Guat. Guatemala
Gui. Guinea
Gui. Bis. Guinea Bissau
Guy. Guyana
Haiti Haiti
Hi.-U.S. Hawaii, U.S.
H.K. Hong Kong
Hond. Honduras
Hun. Hungary
Ia.-U.S. Iowa, U.S.
I.C. Ivory Coast
Ice. Iceland
Id.-U.S. Idaho, U.S.
Il.-U.S. Illinois, U.S.
In.-U.S. Indiana, U.S.
India India
Indon. Indonesia
I. of M. Isle of Man
Iran Iran
Iraq Iraq
Ire. Ireland
Isr. Israel
It. Italy
Jam. Jamaica
Jap. Japan
Jor. Jordan
Kam. Cambodia
Kaz.-U.S.S.R. Kazakh S.S.R., U.S.S.R.
Kenya Kenya
Ker. Is. Kermadec Islands
Kir. Kiribati
Kirg.-U.S.S.R. Kirghiz S.S.R., U.S.S.R.
Ks.-U.S. Kansas, U.S.
Kuw. Kuwait
Ky.-U.S. Kentucky, U.S.
La.-U.S. Louisiana, U.S.
Laos Laos
Lat.-U.S.S.R. Latvian S.S.R., U.S.S.R.
Lbr. Liberia
Leb. Lebanon
Les. Lesotho
Lib. Libya
Liech. Liechtenstein
Lith.-U.S.S.R. Lithuanian S.S.R., U.S.S.R.
Lux. Luxembourg
Ma.-U.S. Massachusetts, U.S.
Mac. Macao
Mad. Madagascar
Mala. Malaysia
Mald. Maldives
Mali Mali
Malta Malta
Man.-Can. Manitoba, Canada
Mar. Is. Marshall Islands
Mart. Martinique
Maur. Mauritius
May. Mayotte
Mco. Monaco
Md.-U.S. Maryland, U.S.
Me.-U.S. Maine, U.S.
Mex. Mexico
Mi.-U.S. Michigan, U.S.
Mid. Is. Midway Islands
Mn.-U.S. Minnesota, U.S.
Mo.-U.S. Missouri, U.S.
Mold.-U.S.S.R. Moldavian S.S.R., U.S.S.R.
Mong. Mongolia
Mont. Montserrat
Mor. Morocco
Moz. Mozambique
Ms.-U.S. Mississippi, U.S.
Mt.-U.S. Montana, U.S.
Mtna. Mauritania
Mwi. Malawi
Nam. Namibia
N. Amer. North America
Nauru Nauru
N.B.-Can. New Brunswick, Canada
Nb.-U.S. Nebraska, U.S.
N.C.-U.S. North Carolina, U.S.
N. Cal. New Caledonia
N.D.-U.S. North Dakota, U.S.
Nep. Nepal
Neth. Netherlands
Neth. Ant. Netherlands Antilles
Newf.-Can. Newfoundland, Canada
N.H.-U.S. New Hampshire, U.S.
Nic. Nicaragua
Nig. Nigeria
Niger Niger
N. Ire.-U.K. Northern Ireland, U.K.
N.J.-U.S. New Jersey, U.S.
N. Kor. North Korea
N.M.-U.S. New Mexico, U.S.
N. M. Is. Northern Mariana Islands
Nor. Norway
Nor. I. Norfolk Island
N.S.-Canada Nova Scotia, Canada
Nv.-U.S. Nevada, U.S.
N.W.T.-Can. Northwest Territories, Canada
N.Y.-U.S. New York, U.S.
N.Z. New Zealand
Ocn. Oceania
Oh.-U.S. Ohio, U.S.
Ok.-U.S. Oklahoma, U.S.
Oman Oman
Ont.-Ont. Ontario, Canada
Or.-U.S. Oregon, U.S.
Pa.-U.S. Pennsylvania, U.S.
Pak. Pakistan
Pal. Palau
Pan. Panama
Pap. N. Gui. Papua New Guinea
Par. Paraguay
Pas. Pascua
P.E.I.-Can. Prince Edward Island, Canada
Peru Peru
Phil. Philippines
Pit. Pitcairn
Pol. Poland
Port. Portugal
P.R. Puerto Rico
Qatar Qatar
Que.-Can. Quebec, Canada
Reu. Reunion
R.I.-U.S. Rhode Island, U.S.
Rom. Romania
R.S.F.S.R.-U.S.S.R. Russian Soviet Federative Socialist Republic, U.S.S.R.
Rwn. Rwanda
S. Afr. South Africa
S. Amer. South America
Sao T.P. Sao Tome and Principe
Sask.-Can. Saskatchewan, Canada
Sau. Ar. Saudi Arabia
S.C.-U.S. South Carolina, U.S.
Scot.-U.K. Scotland, U.K.
S.D.-U.S. South Dakota, U.S.
Sen. Senegal
Sey. Seychelles
Sing. Singapore
S. Kor. South Korea
S.L. Sierra Leone
S. Lan. Sri Lanka
S.M. San Marino
S.N.A. Spanish North Africa
Sol. Is. Solomon Islands
Som. Somalia
Sp. Spain
St. C.N. Saint Christopher-Nevis
St. Hel. Saint Helena
St. Luc. Saint Lucia
St. P.M. Saint Pierre and Miquelon
St. Vin. Saint Vincent and the Grenadines
Sud. Sudan
Sur. Suriname
Sval. Svalbard
Swe. Sweden
Switz. Switzerland
Syr. Syria
Tad.-U.S.S.R. Tajik S.S.R., U.S.S.R.
Tai. Taiwan
Tan. Tanzania
T.C. Is. Turks and Caicos Islands
Thai. Thailand
Tn.-U.S. Tennessee, U.S.
Togo Togo
Ton. Tonga
Trin. Trinidad and Tobago
T.T.P.I. Trust Territory of the Pacific Islands
Tun. Tunisia
Tur. Turkey
Tur.-U.S.S.R. Turkmen S.S.R., U.S.S.R.
Tuv. Tuvalu
Tx.-U.S. Texas, U.S.
U.A.E. United Arab Emirates
Ug. Uganda
U.K. United Kingdom
Ukr.-U.S.S.R. Ukrainian S.S.R., U.S.S.R.
Ur. Uruguay
U.S. United States
U.S.S.R. Union of Soviet Socialist Republics
Ut.-U.S. Utah, U.S.
Uzb.-U.S.S.R. Uzbek S.S.R., U.S.S.R.
Va.-U.S. Virginia, U.S.
Van. Vanuatu
V.C. Vatican City
Ven. Venezuela
Viet. Vietnam
V.I.U.S. Virgin Islands of the U.S.
Vt.-U.S. Vermont, U.S.
Wa.-U.S. Washington, U.S.
Wake Wake Island
Wales-U.K. Wales, U.K.
W.F. Wallis and Futuna
Wi.-U.S. Wisconsin, U.S.
W. Sah. Western Sahara
W. Sam. Western Samoa
W.V.-U.S. West Virginia, U.S.
Wy.-U.S. Wyoming, U.S.
Yem. Yemen
Yugo. Yugoslavia
Yuk.-Can. Yukon, Canada
Zaire Zaire
Zam. Zambia
Zimb. Zimbabwe

List of Symbols

Plains and Associated Features
Plain, Basin, Lowland
Delta
Salt Flat

Valleys and Depressions
Valley, Gorge, Ravine, Canyon
Cave, Crater, Quarry
Karst Features
Depression
Polder, Reclaimed Marsh

Vegetational Features
Desert, Dunes
Forest, Woods
Heath, Steppe, Tundra, Moor
Oasis

Political/Administrative Units
1 Independent Nation
2 State, Canton, Region
3 Province, Department, County, Territory, District
4 Municipality
5 Colony, Dependency, Administered Territory

Geographical Regions
Continent
Physical Region
Historical or Cultural Region

Mountain Features
Mount, Mountain, Peak
Volcano
Hill
Mountains, Mountain Range
Hills, Escarpment
Plateau, Highland, Upland
Pass, Gap

Coastal Features
Cape, Point
Coast, Beach
Cliff
Peninsula, Promontory
Isthmus
Sandbank, Tombolo, Sandbar

Islands Rocks, Reefs
Island
Atoll
Rock, Reef
Islands, Archipelago
Rocks, Reefs
Coral Reef

Hydrographic Features
Well, Spring
Geyser, Fumarole
River, Stream, Brook
Waterfall, Rapids, Cataract
River Mouth, Estuary
Lake
Salt Lake
Intermittent Lake, Dry Lake Bed
Reservoir, Artificial Lake
Swamp, Marsh, Pond
Irrigation Canal, Navigable Canal, Ditch, Aqueduct

Ice Features
Glacier, Snowfield
Ice Shelf, Pack Ice

Marine Features
Ocean
Sea
Gulf, Bay
Strait, Fjord, Sea Channel
Lagoon, Anchorage

Submarine Features
Bank, Shoal
Seamount
Rise, Plateau, Tablemount
Seamount Chain, Ridge
Platform, Shelf
Basin, Depression
Escarpment, Slope, Sea Scarp
Fracture
Trench, Abyss, Valley, Canyon

Other Features
National Park, Nature Reserve
Scenic Area, Point of Interest
Recreation Site, Sports Arena
Cave, Cavern
Historic Site, Memorial, Mausoleum, Museum
Ruins
Wall, Walls, Tower, Castle, Fortress
Church, Abbey, Cathedral, Sanctuary
Temple, Synagogue, Mosque
Research or Scientific Station
Airport, Heliport
Port, Dock
Lighthouse
Mine
Tunnel
Dam, Bridge

A

Name	Page	Grid	Lat.	Long.
Å	7	Cc	67.53N	12.59 E
Aa [Eur.]	12	Ic	51.50N	6.25 E
Aa [Fr.]	11	Ic	51.01N	2.06 E
Aa [Fr.]	12	Dd	50.44N	2.18 E
Aa [Ger.]	12	Kb	52.07N	8.41 E
Aa [Ger.]	12	Jb	52.15N	7.18 E
Aachen	10	Cf	50.46N	6.06 E
Aalen	10	Gh	48.50N	10.06 E
A'ālī an Nīl [3]	35	Ed	9.15N	33.00 E
Aalsmeer	12	Gb	52.15N	4.45 E
Aalst/Alost	11	Kd	50.56N	4.02 E
Aalten	12	Ic	51.55N	6.35 E
Aalter	12	Fc	51.05N	3.27 E
Äänekoski	7	Fe	62.36N	25.44 E
Aa of Weerijs	12	Gc	51.35N	4.46 E
Aar	12	Kd	50.23N	8.00 E
Aarau	14	Cc	47.25N	8.02 E
Aarbergen	12	Kd	50.13N	8.03 E
Aare	14	Cc	47.37N	8.13 E
Aargau [2]	14	Cc	47.30N	8.10 E
Aarlen/Arlon	11	Le	49.41N	5.49 E
Aarschot	11	Kd	50.59N	4.50 E
Aat/Ath	11	Jd	50.38N	3.47 E
Aazanèn	13	Ii	35.06N	3.02W
Āb	24	Md	36.00N	48.05 E
Aba [Nig.]	31	Hh	5.07N	7.22 E
Aba [Zaire]	31	Hk	3.52N	30.14 E
Aba/Ngawa	27	He	32.55N	101.45 E
Abā ad Dūd	24	Ki	27.02N	44.04 E
Abā as Su'ūd	23	Ff	17.28N	44.06 E
Abacaxis, Rio-	54	Gd	3.54S	58.50W
Abaco Island	38	Lg	26.25N	77.10W
Abacou, Pointe l'-	49	Kd	18.03N	73.47W
Abadab. Jabal-	35	Fb	18.53N	35.59 E
Ābādān	22	Gf	30.10N	48.50 E
Ābādeh [Iran]	23	Hc	31.10N	52.37 E
Ābādeh [Iran]	24	Oh	29.08N	52.52 E
Abadiânia	55	Hc	16.06S	48.48W
Abadla	31	Ge	31.01N	2.43W
Abaeté	55	Jd	19.09S	45.27W
Abaeté, Rio-	55	Jd	18.02S	45.12W
Abaetetuba	54	Id	1.42S	48.54W
Abagnar Qi (Xilin Hot)	22	Ne	43.58N	116.08 E
Abag Qi (Xin Hot)	27	Jc	44.01N	114.59 E
Abai	55	Eh	26.01S	55.57W
Abaiang Atoll	57	Id	1.51N	172.58 E
Abaj	19	Hf	49.38N	72.50 E
Abaji	34	Gd	8.28N	6.57 E
Abajo Mountains	46	Kh	37.50N	109.25W
Abakaliki	34	Gd	6.20N	8.03 E
Abakan	20	Ef	53.43N	91.30 E
Abakan	22	Ld	53.43N	91.26 E
Abakwasimbo	36	Eb	0.36N	28.43 E
Abala [Con.]	36	Cc	1.21S	15.30 E
Abala [Niger]	34	Fc	14.56N	3.26 E
Abalak	34	Gb	15.27N	6.17 E
Aban	20	Ee	56.40N	96.10 E
Abancay	54	Df	13.35S	72.55W
Abancourt	12	De	49.42N	1.46 E
Abanga	36	Bb	0.13N	10.28 E
Abano Terme	14	Fe	45.21N	11.47 E
Ābār al Jidd	24	Hf	32.50N	39.50 E
Abarqū	23	Hc	31.08N	53.17 E
Abarqu, Kavīr-e-	24	Og	31.00N	53.50 E
Abashiri	27	Pc	44.01N	144.17 E
Abashiri-Gawa	29a	Db	43.56N	144.09 E
Abashiri-Ko	29a	Da	44.00N	144.10 E
Abashiri-Wan	29a	Da	44.00N	144.35 E
Abasolo	48	Je	24.04N	98.22W
Abatski	19	Hd	56.18N	70.28 E
Abau	60	Dj	10.11S	148.42 E
Abava	7	Eh	57.06N	21.54 E
Abay=Blue Nile (EN)	30	Kg	15.38N	32.31 E
Abaya, Lake-	30	Kh	6.20N	37.55 E
Abaza	20	Ef	52.39N	90.06 E
Abbadia San Salvatore	14	Fh	42.53N	11.41 E
Abbah Quşūr	14	Co	35.57N	8.50 E
Āb Bārīk	24	Oh	29.45N	52.37 E
'Abbāsābād	24	Qd	36.20N	56.25 E
Abbekås	8	Ei	55.24N	13.36 E
Abberton Reservoir	12	Cc	51.50N	0.55 E
Abbeville [Fr.]	11	Hd	50.06N	1.50 E
Abbeville [La.-U.S.]	45	Jl	29.58N	92.08W
Abbeville [S.C.-U.S.]	44	Fh	34.10N	82.23W
Abbey	46	Ka	50.43N	108.45W
Abbeyfeale/Mainistir na Féile	9	Di	52.24N	9.18W
Abbiategrasso	14	Ce	45.24N	8.54 E
Abbot, Mount-	59	Jd	20.03S	147.45 E
Abbot Ice Shelf	66	Pf	72.45S	96.00W
'Abd Al 'Azīz, Jabal-	24	Id	36.25N	40.20 E
'Abd al Kūrī	21	Hh	12.12N	52.13 E
Ābdānān	24	Lf	32.57N	47.26 E
Abdul Ghadir	35	Gc	10.42N	42.59 E
Abdulino	19	Fe	53.42N	53.38 E
Abe, Lake-	35	Gc	11.10N	41.45 E
Abéché	31	Jg	13.49N	20.49 E
Abeek	12	Hc	51.15N	6.00 E
Abe-Gawa	29	Fd	34.55N	138.22 E
Abeløya	41	Pc	79.00N	30.15 E
Abelvær	7	Cd	64.44N	11.11 E
Abemama Atoll	57	Id	0.21N	173.51 E
Abenab	37	Bc	19.12S	18.06 E
Abengourou [3]	34	Ed	6.35N	3.25W
Abengourou	31	Gh	6.44N	3.29W
Åbenrå	7	Bi	55.02N	9.26 E
Åbenrå Fjord	8	Ci	55.05N	9.35 E
Abeokuta	31	Hh	7.09N	3.21 E
Āb-e-Pany	23	If	37.06N	68.20 E
Aberayron	9	Ii	52.15N	4.15W
Aberdare Range	30	Ki	0.25S	36.38 E
Aberdeen [Id.-U.S.]	46	Ie	42.57N	112.50W
Aberdeen [Md.-U.S.]	44	If	39.30N	76.14W
Aberdeen [Ms.-U.S.]	45	Lj	33.49N	88.33W
Aberdeen [N.C.-U.S.]	44	Hh	35.08N	79.26W
Aberdeen [S.Afr.]	37	Cf	32.29S	24.03 E
Aberdeen [Scot.-U.K.]	6	Fd	57.10N	2.04W
Aberdeen [S.D.-U.S.]	39	Je	45.28N	98.29W
Aberdeen [Wa.-U.S.]	43	Cb	46.59N	123.50W
Aberdeen Lake	42	Hd	64.28N	99.00W
Abergavenny	9	Kj	51.50N	3.00W
Aberystwyth	9	Ii	52.25N	4.05W
Abetone	14	Ef	44.08N	10.40 E
Abez	19	Gb	66.32N	61.46 E
Abhā	22	Gh	18.13N	42.30 E
Abhainn an Chláir/Clare	9	Dh	53.20N	9.03W
Abhainn an Lagáin/Lagan	9	Hg	54.37N	5.53W
Abhainn na Bandan/Bandon	9	Ej	51.40N	8.30W
Abhainn na Deirge/Derg	9	Fg	54.40N	7.25W
Abhar	24	Md	36.02N	49.45 E
Abhar	23	Gb	36.09N	49.13 E
Abhazskaja ASSR [3]	19	Eg	43.00N	41.10 E
Abibe, Serrania de-	54	Cb	8.00N	76.30W
Abidjan	31	Gh	5.19N	4.02W
Abidjan [3]	34	Ed	5.30N	4.30W
Abilene [Ks.-U.S.]	45	Hg	38.55N	97.13W
Abilene [Tx.-U.S.]	39	Jf	32.27N	99.44W
Abingdon	9	Lj	51.41N	1.17W
Abinsk	16	Kg	44.52N	38.10 E
Abiquiu	45	Ch	36.12N	106.19W
Abiquiu Reservoir	45	Ch	36.18N	106.32W
Abisko	7	Eb	68.20N	18.51 E
Abitibi	42	Jf	51.04N	80.55W
Abitibi, Lake-	38	Le	48.42N	79.45W
Abiy Adi	35	Fc	13.37N	39.01 E
Abiyata, Lake-	35	Fd	7.38N	38.36 E
Abja-Paluoja	8	Kf	58.02N	25.14 E
Abnūb	33	Fd	27.16N	31.09 E
Åbo/Turku	6	Ic	60.27N	22.17 E
Abo, Massif d'-	35	Ba	21.41N	16.08 E
Abóboras, Serra das-	55	Jc	16.12S	44.35W
Abodo	35	Ed	7.50N	34.25 E
Aboisso [3]	34	Ed	5.28N	3.02W
Aboisso	34	Ed	5.28N	3.12W
Abomey	31	Hh	7.11N	1.59 E
Abong Mbang	34	He	3.59N	13.11 E
Abony	10	Pi	47.11N	20.00 E
Aborigen, Pik-	20	Jd	62.05N	149.10 E
Aborlar	26	Ge	9.26N	118.33 E
Aborrebierg	8	Ej	54.59N	12.32 E
Abou Deïa	35	Bc	11.27N	19.17 E
Abou Goulem	35	Cc	13.37N	21.38 E
Abovjan	16	Ni	40.14N	44.37 E
Abrād, Wādī-	23	Gf	15.51N	46.05 E
Abraham's Bay	49	Kb	22.21N	72.55W
Abramovski Bereg	7	Kc	66.25N	43.05 E
Abrántes	13	De	39.28N	8.12W
Abra Pampa	56	Gb	22.43S	65.42W
Abrego	49	Ki	8.04N	73.14W
Abreojos, Punta-	47	Bc	26.42N	113.35W
'Abrī	35	Ea	20.48N	30.20 E
Abrolhos, Arquipélago dos-	54	Kg	18.00S	38.40W
Abrud	15	Gc	46.16N	23.04 E
Abruka, Ostrov-/Abruka Saar	8	Jf	58.08N	22.25 E
Abruka Saar/Abruka, Ostrov-	8	Jf	58.08N	22.25 E
Abruzzi [2]	14	Hh	42.20N	13.45 E
Absaroka Range	43	Fc	44.45N	109.50W
Abtenau	14	Hc	47.33N	13.21 E
Abū, Ḩād, Wādī-	24	Ei	27.46N	33.30 E
Abū ad Duhūr	24	Ge	35.44N	37.02 E
Abū 'Alī	24	Mi	27.20N	49.33 E
Abū al Khaşīb	24	Lg	30.27N	47.59 E
Abū an Na'am	24	Hj	25.14N	38.49 E
Abū 'Arīsh	23	Ff	16.58N	42.50 E
Abū Ballaş	33	Ee	24.26N	27.39 E
Abū Daghmah	24	Hd	36.25N	38.15 E
Abū Darbah	33	Fd	28.29N	33.20 E
Abu Dhabi (EN)=Abū Z̧aby	22	Hg	24.28N	54.22 E
Abū Ḩadrīyah	24	Mi	27.20N	48.58 E
Abū Ḩamad	31	Kg	19.32N	33.19 E
Abū Ḩammād	24	Dg	30.32N	31.40 E
Abū Ḩarbah, Jabal-	24	Ei	27.17N	33.13 E
Abū Ḩashā'ifah, Khalīj-	24	Bg	31.16N	27.25 E
Abuja	31	Hh	9.10N	7.11 E
Abu Jābirah	35	Dc	11.04N	26.51 E
Abū Jifān	24	Lj	24.31N	47.43 E
Abū Kabīr	24	Dg	30.44N	31.40 E
Abū Kamāl	23	Fc	34.27N	40.55 E
Abukuma-Gawa	29	Gb	38.06N	140.52 E
Abukuma-Sanchi	29	Gc	37.20N	140.45 E
Abū Latt	33	Hf	19.58N	40.08 E
Abū Libdah, Khashm-	33	Ie	22.58N	46.13 E
Abū Maţāriq	35	Dc	10.58N	26.17 E
Abu Mendi	35	Fc	11.47N	35.42 E
Abumônbazi	36	Db	3.42N	22.10 E
Abū Muḩarrik, Ghurd-	33	Ed	27.00N	30.00 E
Abū Musā, Jazīreh-ye-	23	Id	25.52N	55.03 E
Abunā	53	Jf	9.42S	65.23W
Abuná, Rio-	52	Jf	9.41S	65.23W
Abune Yosef	35	Fc	12.09N	39.12 E
Abū Qīr	24	Dg	31.19N	30.04 E
Abū Qīr, Khalīj-	24	Dg	31.20N	30.15 E
Abū Qumayyis, Ra's-	24	Nj	24.34N	51.30 E
Abu Road	25	Ed	24.29N	72.47 E
Abū Sawmah, Ra's-	24	Ei	26.51N	33.59 E
Abū Shanab	35	Dc	13.57N	27.47 E
Abu Simbel (EN)=Abū Sumbul	33	Fe	22.22N	31.38 E
Abū Şukhayr	24	Kg	31.52N	44.27 E
Abū Sumbul=Abu Simbel (EN)	33	Fe	22.22N	31.38 E
Abuta	28	Pc	42.31N	140.46 E
Abut Head	62	De	43.06S	170.15 E
Abū Tij	33	Fd	27.02N	31.19 E
Abū Ţurţūr, Jabal-	24	Cj	25.20N	30.00 E
Abū'Urūq	35	Eb	15.54N	30.27 E
Abuyemeda	35	Fc	10.38N	39.43 E
Abū Zabad	35	Dc	12.21N	29.15 E
Abū Z̧aby=Abu Dhabi (EN)	22	Hg	24.28N	54.22 E
Abū Zanīmah	33	Fd	29.03N	33.06 E
Abwong	35	Ed	9.07N	32.12 E
Åby	8	Gf	58.40N	16.11 E
Abyaḑ	35	Dc	13.46N	26.28 E
Abyaḑ, Al Baḩr al-=White Nile (EN)	30	Kg	15.38N	32.31 E
Abyaḑ, Al Baḩr al-=White Nile (EN) [3]	35	Ec	12.40N	32.30 E
Abyaḑ, Ar Ra's al-	23	Ee	23.32N	38.32 E
Abyaḑ, Jabal-	35	Db	18.55N	28.40 E
Abyaḑ, Ra's al-=Blanc, Cape- (EN)	30	He	37.20N	9.50 E
Abyār Alī	24	Hj	24.25N	39.33 E
Abyār ash Shuwayrif	33	Bd	29.59N	14.16 E
Åbybro	7	Bh	57.09N	9.45 E
Abydos	33	Fd	26.11N	31.55 E
Abyei	35	Dd	9.36N	28.26 E
Ābyek	24	Nd	36.02N	50.31 E
Abymes	51e	Ab	16.16N	61.31W
Acacías	54	Dc	3.59N	73.47W
Academy Gletscher	41	Ib	81.45N	33.35W
Acadie	38	Me	46.00N	65.00W
Acaill/Achill	9	Dh	54.00N	10.00W
Acajutla	49	Cg	13.36N	89.50W
Acalayong	34	Ge	1.05N	9.40 E
Acámbaro	47	Dd	20.02N	100.44W
Acandí	54	Cb	8.31N	77.17W
Acaponeta	47	Cd	22.30N	105.22W
Acaponeta, Río-	48	Gf	22.20N	105.37W
Acapulco de Juárez	39	Jh	16.51N	99.55W
Acará	54	Id	1.57S	48.11W
Acarai, Serra-	54	Gc	1.50N	57.40W
Acaraú	54	Jd	2.53S	40.07W
Acaray, Río-	55	Eg	25.29S	54.42W
Acari, Rio- [Braz.]	54	Ge	5.18S	59.42W
Acari, Rio- [Braz.]	55	Jb	16.00S	45.03W
Acarigua	54	Eb	9.33N	69.12W
Acatenango, Volcán-	38	Jh	14.30N	91.40W
Acatlán de Osorio	48	Jh	18.12N	98.03W
Acayucan	47	Fe	17.57N	94.55W
Accéglio	14	Af	44.28N	7.00 E
Aččitau, Gora-	18	Cc	42.07N	60.31 E
Accomac	44	Jg	37.43N	75.40W
Accra	31	Gh	5.33N	0.13W
Acebal	55	Bk	33.14S	60.50W
Acebuches	48	Hc	28.15N	102.43W
Aceguá [Braz.]	55	Ej	31.52S	54.09W
Aceguá [Ur.]	55	Ej	31.52S	54.12W
Aceh [3]	26	Cf	4.10N	96.50 E
Acerenza	14	Jj	40.48N	15.56 E
Acerra	14	Ij	40.57N	14.22 E
Achacachi	54	Eg	16.03S	68.43W
Achaguas	54	Eb	7.46N	68.14W
Achaïf, 'Erg-	34	Ea	20.49N	4.34W
Achao	56	Ff	42.28S	73.30W
Achegour	34	Hb	19.03N	11.53 E
Acheng	27	Mb	45.32N	126.56 E
Acheux-en-Amiénois	12	Ed	50.04N	2.32 E
Achiet-le-Grand	12	Ed	50.08N	2.47 E
Achill/Acaill	9	Dh	54.00N	10.00W
Achilleion	15	Cj	39.34N	19.55 E
Achill Head/Ceann Acla	9	Ch	53.59N	10.13W
Achim	10	Fc	53.02N	9.01 E
Achim	35	Bb	15.53N	19.31 E
Achterwasser	10	Jb	54.00N	13.57 E
Acı Gölü	24	Cd	37.50N	29.54 E
Ačinsk	22	Ld	56.17N	90.30 E
Acıpayam	24	Cd	37.25N	29.22 E
Acireale	14	Jm	37.37N	15.10 E
Acîş	15	Fb	47.32N	22.47 E
Ačisaj	18	Gc	43.33N	68.53 E
Ačit	17	Hh	56.48N	57.54 E
Ačit-Nur	27	Fb	49.30N	90.30 E
Acklins	38	Lg	22.25N	74.00W
Acklins, The Bight of-	49	Jb	22.30N	74.15W
Acle	12	Db	52.38N	1.33 E
Acobamba	54	Df	12.48S	74.34W
Acolin	11	Jh	46.49N	3.23 E
Aconcagua [2]	56	Fd	32.15S	70.50W
Aconcagua, Cerro-	52	Ji	32.39S	70.00W
Açor, Serra de-	13	Ed	40.13N	7.48W
Açores=Azores (EN) [5]	31	Ee	38.30N	28.00W
Açores, Arquipélago dos-=Azores (EN)	30	Ee	38.30N	28.00W
Acorizal	55	Db	15.12S	56.22W
Acoyapa	49	Eh	11.58N	85.10W
Acquapendente	14	Fh	42.44N	11.52 E
Acquasanta Terme	14	Hh	42.46N	13.24 E
Acquasparta	14	Gh	42.41N	12.33 E
Acquaviva delle Fonti	14	Kj	40.54N	16.50 E
Acqui Terme	14	Cf	44.41N	8.28 E
Acraman, Lake-	59	Hf	32.05S	135.25 E
Acre [2]	54	Ee	9.00S	70.00W
Acre, Rio-	52	Jf	8.45S	67.22W
Acri	14	Kk	39.29N	16.23 E
Actéon, Groupe-	57	Ng	21.20S	136.30W
Actopan	48	Jg	20.16N	98.56W
Açu	54	Ke	5.34S	36.54W
Acuña	55	Di	29.55S	57.58W
Ada [Ghana]	34	Fd	5.47N	0.38 E
Ada [Ok.-U.S.]	43	He	34.46N	96.41W
Ada [Yugo.]	15	Dd	45.48N	20.08 E
Adaba	35	Fd	7.03N	39.31 E
'Adād	35	Hb	8.23N	46.48 E
'Adādle	35	Gd	9.45N	44.41 E
Adair, Bahia-	48	Cb	31.30N	113.50W
Adair, Cape -	42	Kb	71.31N	71.24W
Adaja	13	Hc	41.32N	4.52W
Adak	40a	Cb	51.45N	176.40W
Adalar	15	Mi	40.52N	29.07 E
'Adale	35	He	2.46N	46.20 E
Ådalen	8	Ga	63.20N	17.30 E
Adalselv	8	Dd	60.04N	10.11 E
Adam, Mount-	56	Hh	51.34S	60.04W
Adamantina	55	Ge	21.42S	51.04W
Adamaoua=Adamawa (EN)	30	Ih	7.00N	15.00 E
Adamawa (EN)=Adamaoua	30	Ih	7.00N	15.00 E
Adamello	14	Ed	46.09N	10.30 E
Adamovka	16	Ud	51.32N	59.59 E
Adams	45	Le	43.58N	89.49W
Adams, Mount-	43	Cb	46.12N	121.28W
Adams Lake	46	Fa	51.13N	119.33W
Adams River	42	Ff	50.54N	119.33W
Adam's Rock	64q	Ab	25.04S	130.05W
Adamstown	58	Ng	25.04S	130.05W
Adamuz	13	Hf	38.02N	4.31W
Adana	22	Ff	37.01N	35.18 E
Adapazarı	24	Db	40.46N	30.24 E
Adarama	35	Eb	17.05N	34.54 E
Adarān, Jabal-	33	Ig	13.46N	45.08 E
Adare, Cape-	66	Kf	71.17S	170.14 E
Adavale	59	Ie	25.55S	144.36 E
Adda [It.]	5	Gf	45.08N	9.53 E
Adda [Sud.]	35	Cd	9.51N	24.50 E
Aḑ Ḑab'ah	33	Ec	31.02N	28.26 E
Ad Dabbah	35	Eb	18.03N	30.57 E
Ad Dafīnah	33	He	23.18N	41.58 E
Aḑ Ḑafrah	24	Ok	23.25N	53.25 E
Ad Dahnā'	21	Gg	24.30N	48.10 E
Addala-Šuhgelmeer, Gora-	16	Oh	42.20N	46.15 E
Aḑ Ḑāli'	33	Hg	13.42N	44.44 E
Ad Damazin	35	Ec	11.49N	34.23 E
Ad 'Dāmir	35	Eb	17.35N	33.58 E
Ad Dammām	22	Hg	26.26N	50.07 E
Ad Dār al Ḩamrā'	23	Ed	27.19N	37.44 E
Ad Dawādimī	23	Fe	24.28N	44.18 E
Ad Dawḩah=Doha (EN)	22	Hg	25.17N	51.32 E
Ad Dawr	24	Je	34.27N	43.47 E
Ad Dayr	33	Fd	25.20N	32.35 E
Ad Dibdibah	24	Lh	28.00N	46.30 E
Aḑ Ḑiffah	33	Ec	30.30N	25.30 E
Ad Dikākah	35	Ib	19.25N	51.30 E
Ad Dilam	23	Ge	23.59N	47.10 E
Ad Dindar	35	Ec	13.20N	34.05 E
Ad Dir'īyah	24	Lj	24.48N	46.32 E
Ad Dissān	33	Hf	16.56N	41.41 E
Addis Zemen	35	Fc	12.05N	37.44 E
Ad Dīwānīya	23	Fc	31.59N	44.56 E
Addu Atoll	21	Jj	0.25S	73.10 E
Ad Du'ayn	35	Dc	11.26N	26.09 E
Ad Duwayd	24	Jg	30.13N	42.18 E
Ad Duwaym	35	Ec	14.00N	32.19 E
Adel [Ga.-U.S.]	44	Fj	31.18N	83.25W
Adel [Or.-U.S.]	46	Fe	42.11N	119.54W
Adelaide [Austl.]	58	Eh	34.56S	138.36 E
Adelaide [Bah.]	44	Im	25.00N	77.31W
Adelaide [S.Afr.]	37	Df	32.42S	26.20 E
Adelaide Island	66	Qe	67.15S	68.30W
Adelaide Peninsula	42	Hc	68.05N	97.50W
Adelaide River	58	Ef	13.15S	131.06 E
Adelaye	35	Cd	7.07N	22.49 E
Adelboden	14	Bd	46.30N	7.33 E
Adèle Island	59	Ec	15.30S	123.10 E
Adélie, Terre-	66	Ie	67.00S	139.00 E
Ademuz	13	Kd	40.04N	1.17W
Aden (EN)=Baladiyat 'Adan	22	Gh	12.46N	45.01 E
Aden, Gulf of-	30	Lg	12.00N	48.00 E
Aden, Gulf of- (EN)='Admēd, Badyarada-	30	Lg	12.00N	48.00 E
Adenau	12	Id	50.23N	6.56 E
Ader	30	Hg	14.10N	5.05 E
Aderbissinat	34	Gb	15.37N	7.52 E
Adhan, Jabal-	24	Qj	25.27N	56.13 E
Adh Dhahībāt	32	Jc	32.01N	10.42 E
Adh Dhayd	24	Pj	25.17N	55.53 E
Adhélfi	15	Gj	39.08N	23.59 E
Adhelfoi	15	Jm	36.25N	26.37 E
'Adhırīyāt, Jıbāl- al-	24	Gg	30.25N	36.48 E
Adi, Pulau-	26	Jg	4.18S	133.26 E
Adiaké	34	Ed	5.16N	3.17W
Adi Arkay	35	Fc	13.31N	38.00 E
Adícora	54	Ea	11.57N	69.48W
Adi Dairo	35	Fc	14.21N	38.12 E
Adigala	35	Gc	10.24N	42.18 E
Adige/Etsch	5	Hf	45.10N	12.20 E
Adigrat	35	Fc	14.16N	39.28 E
Adi Keyeh	35	Fc	14.48N	39.23 E
Adi Kwala	35	Fc	14.37N	38.51 E
Ādilābād	25	Fe	19.40N	78.32 E
Adīrī	31	If	27.30N	13.16 E
Adirondack Mountains	38	Le	44.00N	74.00W
Adis Abeba	31	Kh	9.01N	38.46 E
Adis Alem	35	Fd	9.03N	38.24 E
Adi Ugri	35	Fc	14.53N	38.49 E
Adiyaman	23	Eb	37.46N	38.17 E
Adjud	15	Kc	46.06N	27.10 E
Adjuntas	51a	Bb	18.09N	66.43W
'Admēd, Badyarada-=Aden, Gulf of- (EN)	30	Lg	12.00N	48.00 E
Admer, Erg d'-	32	Ie	24.12N	9.10 E
Admiralty	40	Me	57.50N	134.30W
Admiralty Bay	51n	Ba	13.00N	61.16W
Admiralty Gulf	59	Fb	14.20S	125.50 E
Admiralty Inlet	42	Ib	72.30N	86.00W
Admiralty Islands	57	Fe	2.10S	147.00 E
Admiralty Mountains	66	Kf	71.45S	168.30 E
Admont	14	Ic	47.34N	14.27 E
Ado	34	Fd	6.36N	2.56 E
Ado Ekiti	34	Gd	7.38N	5.13 E
Adok	35	Ed	8.11N	30.19 E
Adolfo Gonzales Chaves	55	Bn	38.02S	60.06W
Adolfo López Mateos, Presa-	48	Fe	25.05N	107.20W
Adonara, Pulau-	26	Hh	8.20S	123.10 E
Ādoni	25	Fe	15.38N	77.17 E
Adra	13	Ih	36.44N	3.01W
Adrano	14	Im	37.40N	14.50 E
Adrar	30	Ff	20.30N	13.30W
Adrar	31	Gf	27.54N	0.17W
Adrar	30	Hf	25.12N	8.10 E
Adrar [Alg.] [3]	32	Gd	27.00N	1.00W
Adrar [Mtna.] [3]	32	Ee	21.00N	11.00W
Adré	35	Cc	13.28N	22.12 E
Adria	14	Ge	45.03N	12.03 E
Adrian	44	Ee	41.54N	84.02W
Adrianópolis	55	Hg	24.41S	48.50W
Adriatic, Deti-=Adriatic Sea (EN)	5	Hg	43.00N	16.00 E
Adriatico, Mar-=Adriatic Sea (EN)	5	Hg	43.00N	16.00 E
Adriatic Sea (EN)=Adriatic, Deti-	5	Hg	43.00N	16.00 E
Adriatic Sea (EN)=Adriatico, Mar-	5	Hg	43.00N	16.00 E
Adriatic Sea (EN)=Jadransko More	5	Hg	43.00N	16.00 E
Aduard	12	Ia	53.15N	6.25 E
Adula	14	Dd	46.30N	9.05 E
Adulis	35	Fb	15.15N	39.37 E
Adur	12	Bd	50.49N	0.16W
Adusa	36	Eb	1.23N	28.01 E
Adventure Bank (EN)	14	Gm	37.20N	12.10 E
Adwa	31	Kg	14.10N	38.55 E
Adyča	21	Pc	68.13N	135.03 E
Adygalah	20	Jd	62.57N	146.25 E
Adygejskaja Avt. Oblast [3]	19	Eg	44.30N	40.05 E
Adžarskaja ASSR [3]	19	Eg	41.40N	42.10 E
Adzopé [3]	34	Ed	6.15N	3.45W
Adzopé	34	Ed	6.06N	3.52W
Adzva	17	Ic	66.36N	59.28 E
Aegean Sea (EN)=Aiyaíon Pélagos	5	Ih	39.00N	25.00 E
Aegean Sea (EN)=Ege Denizi	5	Ih	39.00N	25.00 E
Aegina (EN) = Aiyina	15	Gl	37.40N	23.30 E
Aegviidu	8	Ke	59.17N	25.37 E
Aeon Point	64g	Bb	1.46N	157.11W
Aerfort na Sionainne/Shannon	9	Ei	52.42N	8.57W
Ærø	8	Dj	54.55N	10.20 E
Ærøskøbing	8	Dj	54.53N	10.25 E
Aerzen	12	Lb	52.02N	9.16 E
Afafi, Massif d'-	34	Ha	22.15N	15.00 E
'Afak	24	Kf	32.04N	45.15 E
Afanasjevo	7	Mg	58.54N	53.16 E
Afareaitu	65e	Fc	17.33S	149.47W
Afars and Issas→Djibouti [1]	31	Lg	11.30N	43.00 E
Aff	11	Dg	47.43N	2.07W
Affollé	30	Fg	16.55N	10.25W
Affrica, Scoglio d'-	14	Eh	42.20N	10.05 E
Afghanistan [1]	22	If	33.00N	65.00 E
Afgōye	35	He	2.09N	45.07 E
'Afīf	23	Fe	23.55N	42.56 E
Afikpo	34	Gd	5.53N	7.55 E
Afipski	16	Kg	44.52N	38.50 E
Aflou	32	Hc	34.07N	2.06 E
Afmadōw	35	Ge	0.29N	42.06 E
Afognak	40	Ie	58.15N	152.30W
Afonso Cláudio	54	Jh	20.05S	41.08W
Afon Teifi	9	Ii	52.06N	4.43W
Afon Tywi	9	Ij	51.40N	4.15W
Afragola	14	Ij	40.55N	14.18 E
Afrērā, Lake-	35	Gc	13.20N	41.03 E
Africa	30	Jh	10.00N	22.00 E
African Islands	30	Mi	4.53S	43.24 E
Afşin	24	Gc	38.36N	36.55 E
Afsluitdijk	11	La	53.00N	5.15 E
Afton	46	Je	42.44N	110.56W
Afuá	54	Hd	0.10S	50.23W
'Afula	24	Ff	32.36N	35.17 E
Afyonkarahisar	22	Ff	38.45N	30.40 E
Agadem	31	Ig	16.50N	13.17 E
Agadez	31	Hg	16.58N	7.59 E
Agadez [2]	34	Hb	19.45N	10.15 E
Agadir	31	Ge	30.25N	9.37W
Agadir [3]	32	Fc	30.00N	9.00W
Agadyr	19	Hf	48.17N	72.53 E
Agalega Islands	30	Mj	10.24S	56.30 E
Agalta, Sierra de-	47	Ge	15.00N	85.53W
Agan	19	Hc	61.23N	74.35 E
Agana	58	Fc	13.28N	144.45 E
Agano-Gawa	28	Of	37.57N	139.07 E
Aga Point	64c	Bb	13.14N	144.43 E
Agapovka	17	Ij	53.18N	59.10 E
Agaro	35	Fd	7.53N	36.36 E
Agartala	22	Lg	23.49N	91.16 E
Agassiz Pool	45	Ib	48.20N	95.58W
Agat	64c	Bb	13.23N	144.39 E
Agat Bay	64c	Bb	13.24N	144.39 E
Agats	58	Ee	5.33S	138.08 E
Agattu	40a	Ab	52.25N	173.35 E
Agawa Bay	44	Eb	47.22N	84.33W
Agawa Bay	44	Eb	47.20N	84.42W
Agboville	34	Ed	5.56N	4.13W
Agboville [3]	34	Ed	6.00N	4.15W
Agdam	19	Eh	39.58N	46.57 E
Agdaš	16	Oi	40.38N	47.29 E
Agde	11	Jk	43.19N	3.28 E
Agde, Cap d'-	11	Jk	43.16N	3.30 E
Agder	8	Cf	58.25N	8.15 E
Agdz	32	Fc	30.27N	7.56W
Agdžabedi	16	Oi	40.03N	47.28 E
Agematsu	29	Ed	35.47N	137.41 E
Agen	11	Gj	44.12N	0.38 E
Ageo	29	Fd	35.58N	139.35 E
Agepsta, Gora-	16	Lh	43.32N	40.30 E
Ager	14	Hb	48.05N	13.51 E
Agere Mariam	35	Fd	5.39N	38.15 E
Agersø	8	Di	55.10N	11.10 E
Agger	12	Jd	50.48N	7.11 E
Āghā Jārī	23	Gc	30.42N	49.50 E
Aghireşu	15	Gc	46.53N	23.15 E
Agiabampo, Estero de-	48	Ed	26.15N	109.15W
Ağın	24	Hc	38.57N	38.43 E

Index Symbols

[1] Independent Nation
[2] State, Region
[3] District, County
[4] Municipality
[5] Colony, Dependency
Continent
Physical Region
Historical or Cultural Region
Mount, Mountain
Volcano
Hili
Mountains, Mountain Range
Hills, Escarpment
Plateau, Upland
Pass, Gap
Plain, Lowland
Delta
Salt Flat
Valley, Canyon
Crater, Cave
Karst Features
Depression
Polder
Desert, Dunes
Forest, Woods
Heath, Steppe
Oasis
Cape, Point
Coast, Beach
Cliff
Peninsula
Isthmus
Sandbank
Island
Atoll
Rock, Reef
Islands, Archipelago
Rocks, Reefs
Coral Reef
Well, Spring
Geyser
River, Stream
Waterfall Rapids
River Mouth, Estuary
Lake
Salt Lake
Intermittent Lake
Reservoir
Swamp, Pond
Canal
Glacier
Ice Shelf, Pack Ice
Ocean
Sea
Gulf, Bay
Strait, Fjord
Lagoon
Bank
Seamount
Tablemount
Ridge
Shelf
Basin
Escarpment, Sea Scarp
Fracture
Trench, Abyss
National Park, Reserve
Point of Interest
Recreation Site
Cave, Cavern
Historic Site
Ruins
Wall, Walls
Church, Abbey
Temple
Scientific Station
Airport
Port
Lighthouse
Mine
Tunnel
Dam, Bridge

Aginski Burjatskij Nacionalnyj Okrug 20 Gf 51.00N 114.30 E
Aginskoje 20 Gf 51.03N 114.33 E
Agnew 59 Ee 28.01S 120.30 E
Agnibilékrou 34 Ed 7.08N 3.12W
Agnita 15 Hd 45.58N 24.37 E
Agno 14 Fe 45.32N 11.21 E
Agnone 14 Ii 41.48N 14.22 E
Ago 29 Ed 34.19N 136.50 E
Agoare 34 Fd 8.30N 3.25 E
Agogna 14 Ce 45.04N 8.54 E
Agön 8 Gc 61.35N 17.25 E
Agordat 31 Kg 15.32N 37.53 E
Agordo 14 Gd 46.17N 12.02 E
Agout 11 Hk 43.47N 1.41 E
Āgra 22 Jg 27.11N 78.01 E
Agrahanski Poluostrov 16 Oh 43.45N 47.35 E
Agramunt 13 Nc 41.47N 1.06 E
Agreda 13 Kc 41.51N 1.56W
Ağrı 23 Fb 39.44N 43.03 E
Ağrı Dağı = Mount Ararat (EN) 21 Gf 39.40N 44.24 E
Agričaj 16 Oi 41.17N 46.43 E
Agrigento 6 Hh 37.19N 13.34 E
Agrihan Island 57 Fc 18.46N 145.40 E
Agrij 15 Gb 47.15N 23.16 E
Agrinion 15 Ek 38.38N 21.25 E
Agropoli 14 Ij 40.21N 14.59 E
Agro Pontino 14 Gi 41.25N 12.55 E
Agryz 7 Mh 56.31N 53.01 E
Agto 41 Ge 67.37N 53.49W
Agua Brava, Laguna- 48 Gf 22.10N 105.32W
Agua Caliente, Cerro- 47 Cc 26.27N 106.12W
Aguachica 54 Db 8.18N 73.38W
Agua Clara 55 Fe 20.27S 52.52W
Aguada de Pasajeros 49 Gb 22.23N 80.51W
Aguadez, Irhazer Oua-n- 34 Gb 17.28N 6.26 E
Aguadilla 49 Nd 18.26N 67.09W
Aguadulce 49 Gi 8.15N 80.33W
Agua Fria River 46 Ij 33.23N 112.21W
Agua Limpa, Rio- 55 Gb 14.58S 51.20W
Aguán, Rio- 49 Ef 15.57N 85.44W
Aguanaval, Rio- 48 Hf 25.28N 102.53W
Aguapei 55 Cc 16.12S 59.43W
Aguapei, Rio- 56 Jb 21.03S 51.47W
Aguapei, Rio- 55 Cb 15.53S 58.25W
Agua Prieta 39 If 31.18N 109.34W
Aguaray 56 Hb 22.16S 63.44W
Aguaray Guazú, Rio- [Par.] 55 Dg 24.05S 56.40W
Aguaray Guazú, Rio- [Par.] 55 Dg 24.47S 57.19W
Aguasay 50 Eh 9.25N 63.44W
Aguascalientes 39 Ig 21.53N 102.18W
Aguascalientes 47 Dd 22.00N 102.30W
Aguasvivas 13 Lc 41.20N 0.25W
Agua Verde, Rio- 55 Da 13.42S 56.43W
Agua Vermelha, Représa- 56 Ja 19.53S 50.17W
Agudo [Braz.] 55 Fi 29.38S 53.15W
Agudo [Sp.] 13 Hf 38.59N 4.52W
Agueda 13 Fc 41.02N 6.56W
Águeda 13 Dd 40.34N 8.27W
Aguelhok 34 Fb 19.28N 0.51 E
Agüenit 32 Ee 22.11N 13.08W
Aguerguer 30 Ff 23.09N 16.01W
Aguijan Island 57 Fc 14.51N 145.34 E
Aguilar de Campóo 13 Hb 42.48N 4.16W
Aguilar de la Frontera 13 Hg 37.31N 4.39W
Aguilas 13 Kg 37.24N 1.35W
Aguililla 48 Hh 18.44N 102.44W
Aguirre, Rio- 50 Fh 8.28N 61.02W
Aguja, Cabo de la- 54 Da 11.21N 73.59W
Agujereada, Punta- 51a Ab 18.31N 67.08W
Agul 20 Ee 55.40N 95.45 E
Agulhas, Cape-(EN) = Agulhas, Kaap- 30 Jl 34.50S 20.00 E
Agulhas, Kaap- = Agulhas, Cape-(EN) 30 Jl 34.50S 20.00 E
Agulhas Negras, Pico das- 52 Lh 22.23S 44.38W
Agulhas Plateau (EN) 30 Jm 40.00S 26.00 E
Agung, Gunung- 26 Gh 8.21S 115.30 E
Aguni-Shima 27 Mf 26.35N 127.15 E
Agupey, Rio- 55 Di 29.07S 56.36W
Agustin Codazzi 54 Da 10.02N 73.15W
Ağva 24 Cb 41.05N 29.50 E
Ahaggar 30 Hf 23.10N 5.50 E
Ahaggar, Tassili-oua-n- 30 Hf 20.30N 5.00 E
Aha Hills 37 Cc 19.45S 21.10 E
Ahalcihe 19 Eg 41.38N 42.59 E
Ahalkalaki 19 Eg 41.25N 43.29 E
Ahangaran 18 Gd 40.57N 69.37 E
Ahar 23 Gb 38.28N 47.04 E
Ahat 15 Mk 38.39N 29.47 E
Ahaus 10 Cd 52.04N 7.00 E
Ahe Atoll 57 Mf 14.30S 146.18W
Ahenet, Tanezrouft-n- 32 He 22.00N 1.00 E
Ahini 20 Ff 53.18N 105.01 E
Ahipara 62 Ea 35.10S 173.09 E
Ahja Jõgi 8 Lf 58.19N 27.15 E
Ahlat 24 Jc 38.45N 42.29 E
Ahlen 10 De 51.45N 7.55 E
Ahmadābād 22 Jg 23.02N 72.37 E
Aḥmadī 24 Qi 27.56N 56.42 E
Ahmadnagar 25 Ee 19.05N 74.44 E
Ahmadpur East 25 Ec 29.09N 71.16 E
Ahmar 30 Lh 9.23N 41.13 E
Aḥmar, Al Baḥr al- = Red Sea (EN) 30 Kf 25.00N 38.00 E
Ahmeta 16 Nh 42.02N 45.11 E
Ahmetli 15 Kk 38.31N 27.57 E
Ahnet 32 He 24.35N 3.15 E
Ahoa 64h Ab 13.17S 176.12W
Ahome 48 Ee 25.55N 109.11W
Ahon, Tarso- 35 Ba 20.23N 18.18 E
Ahr 10 Df 50.33N 7.17 E
Ahram 24 Nh 28.52N 51.16 E
Ahrāmāt al Jīzah 33 Fd 29.55N 31.05 E
Ahrensburg 10 Gc 53.41N 10.15 E
Ahrgebirge 12 Id 50.31N 6.54 E
Ahse 12 Jc 51.42N 7.51 E
Ahsu 16 Pi 40.35N 48.26 E
Ähtäri 7 Ee 62.02N 21.20 E
Ähtärinjärvi 8 Kb 62.40N 24.05 E
Ähtävänjoki 7 Fe 63.38N 22.48 E
Ahtopol 15 Kg 42.06N 27.57 E
Ahtuba 5 Kf 46.42N 48.00 E
Ahtubinsk 6 Kf 48.14N 46.14 E
Ahtyrka 19 De 50.19N 34.55 E
Ahuacapán 49 Cg 13.55N 89.51W
Ahuazotepec 48 Jg 20.03N 98.09W
Ahunui Atoll 57 Mf 19.35S 140.28W
Åhus 7 Di 55.55N 14.17 E
Ahvāz 22 Gf 31.19N 48.42 E
Ahvenanmaa/Åland 7 Ef 60.15N 20.00 E
Ahvenanmaa/Åland = Aland Islands (EN) 5 Hc 60.15N 20.00 E
Ahvenanmeri 8 Hd 60.00N 19.30 E
Aḥwar 23 Gg 13.31N 46.42 E
Aibag Gol 28 Ad 41.42N 110.24 E
Aibetsu 29a Cb 43.55N 142.33 E
Aichach 10 Hh 48.28N 11.08 E
Aichi Ken 28 Ng 35.00N 137.07 E
Aiea 65a Db 21.23N 157.56W
Aigle 14 Ad 46.20N 6.59 E
Aigoual, Mont- 11 Jj 44.07N 3.35 E
Aiguá 55 El 34.12S 54.45W
Aigues 11 Kj 44.07N 4.43 E
Aigues-Mortes 11 Kk 43.34N 4.11 E
Aiguilles 11 Mj 44.47N 6.52 E
Aiguillon 11 Gj 44.18N 0.21 E
Aigurande 11 Hh 46.26N 1.50 E
Ai He 28 Hd 40.13N 124.30 E
Aihui (Heihe) 22 Od 50.13N 127.26 E
Aikawa 29 Fb 38.02N 138.14 E
Aiken 43 Ke 33.34N 81.44W
Ailao Shan 27 Hg 23.15N 102.20 E
Aillette 12 Fe 49.35N 3.10 E
Ailinginae Atoll 57 Hc 11.08N 166.24 E
Aillte an Mhothair/Moher, Cliffs of- 9 Di 52.58N 9.27W
Ailly-le-Haut-Clocher 12 Dd 50.05N 1.59 E
Ailly-sur-Noye 12 Ee 49.45N 2.22 E
Ailsa Craig 9 Hf 55.16N 5.07W
Ailuk Atoll 57 Hc 10.20N 169.56 E
Aim 20 Ie 58.48N 134.12 E
Aimogasta 56 Gc 28.33S 66.49W
Aimorés 54 Jg 19.30S 41.04W
Ain 11 Lh 46.10N 5.20 E
Ain 11 Li 45.48N 5.10 E
Ainazi/Ajnazi 7 Fh 57.52N 24.25 E
Ain Beida 32 Ib 35.48N 7.24 E
Ain Beni Mathar 32 Gc 34.01N 2.01W
Ain Bessem 13 Ph 36.18N 3.40 E
Ain Boucif 13 Pi 35.53N 3.09 E
Ain Defla 13 Nh 36.16N 1.58 E
Ain el Berd 13 Li 35.21N 0.31W
Ain el Hammam 13 Qh 36.34N 4.19 E
Ain el Turck 13 Li 35.44N 0.46W
Ain Galakka 35 Bb 18.05N 18.31 E
Ainos Óros 15 Dk 38.07N 20.40 E
Ain Oulmene 13 Ri 35.55N 5.18 E
Ain Oussera 13 Oi 35.27N 2.54 E
Ain Sefra 31 Ge 32.45N 0.35W
Ainsworth 45 Ge 42.33N 99.52W
Ain Taghrout 13 Rh 36.08N 5.05 E
Ain Tedeles 13 Mh 36.00N 0.18 E
Ain Témouchent 32 Gb 35.18N 1.08W
Ain Tolba 13 Ki 35.15N 1.15W
Aioi 29 Dd 34.49N 134.28 E
Aiquile 54 Eg 18.10S 65.10W
Air/Azbine 30 Hg 18.00N 8.30 E
Airabu, Pulau- 26 Ef 2.46N 106.14 E
Airai 64a Bc 7.21N 134.34 E
Airaines 12 De 49.58N 1.57 E
Airão 54 Fd 1.56S 61.22W
Airbangis 26 Cf 0.12N 99.23 E
Airdrie 46 Ha 51.18N 114.02W
Aire 11 Id 50.38N 2.24 E
Aire [Eng.-U.K.] 9 Mh 53.44N 0.54W
Aire [Fr.] 11 Ke 49.19N 4.49 E
Aire, Canal d'- 11 Id 50.38N 2.25 E
Aire, Isla del- 13 Qe 39.47N 4.16 E
Aire-sur-l'Adour 11 Fk 43.42N 0.16W
Air Force 42 Kc 67.55N 74.05W
Airolo 14 Cd 46.33N 8.35 E
Ais 63b Cb 15.26S 167.15 E
Aisch 10 Hg 49.46N 11.01 E
Aisén del General Carlos Ibáñez del Campo 56 Fg 46.00S 73.00W
Aishihik 42 Dd 61.34N 137.30W
Ai-Shima 29 Bd 34.30N 131.18 E
Aisne 11 Je 49.30N 3.30 E
Aisne 11 Ie 49.26N 2.50 E
Aisne à la Marne, Canal de l'- 11 Je 49.24N 3.55 E
Aïssa, Djebel- 32 Gc 32.51N 0.30W
Aitana, Pico- 13 Lf 38.39N 0.16W
Aitape 60 Ch 3.08S 142.21 E
Aitolikón 15 Ek 38.26N 21.21 E
Aitutaki Atoll 57 Lf 18.52S 159.45W
Ait Youssef ou Ali 13 Ii 35.09N 3.55W
Aiud 15 Gc 46.18N 23.43 E
Aiviekste 7 Fh 56.36N 25.44 E
Aiviekste/Ajviekste 7 Fh 56.36N 25.44 E
Aiwokako Passage 64a Bb 7.39N 134.33 E
Aix, Ile d'- 11 Eh 46.01N 1.10W
Aix-en-Provence 11 Lk 43.32N 5.26 E
Aix-sur-Vienne 11 Hi 45.48N 1.08 E
Aix-les-Bains 11 Li 45.42N 5.55 E
Aiyaion Pélagos = Aegean Sea (EN) 5 Ih 39.00N 25.00 E
Aiyina 15 Gl 37.45N 23.26 E
Aiyina = Aegina (EN) 15 Gl 37.40N 23.30 E
Aiyinion 15 Fi 40.30N 22.33 E
Aiyion 15 Fk 38.15N 22.05 E
Aizawl 25 Id 23.44N 92.43 E
Aizenay 11 Eh 46.44N 1.37W
Aizpute/Ajzpute 7 Eh 56.45N 21.39 E
Aizubange 29 Fc 37.34N 139.49 E
Aizutakada 29 Fc 37.29N 139.48 E
Aizuwakamatsu 28 Of 37.30N 139.56 E
Ajā', Jabal- 24 Ii 27.30N 41.30 E
'Ajab Shīr 24 Kd 37.28N 45.54 E
Ajaccio 6 Gg 41.55N 8.44 E
Ajaccio, Golfe d'- 11a Ab 41.50N 8.41 E
Ajaguz 22 Ke 47.58N 80.27 E
Ajakli 20 Eb 70.13N 95.55 E
Ajan [R.S.F.S.R.] 20 Fe 59.38N 106.45 E
Ajan [R.S.F.S.R.] 20 Ie 56.27N 138.10 E
Ajanka 20 Ld 63.40N 167.30 E
Ajanta Range 25 Fd 20.30N 76.00 E
Ajat 17 Kj 52.54N 62.50 E
Ajax Peak 46 Id 45.20N 113.40W
Ajdābiyā 31 Je 30.46N 20.14 E
Ajdabul 19 Ge 52.42N 69.01 E
Ajdar 16 Ke 48.42N 39.13 E
Ajdar, Solončak- 18 Fd 40.50N 66.50 E
Ajdovščina 14 He 45.53N 13.53 E
Ajdyrlinski 17 Ij 52.03N 59.50 E
Ajhal 20 Gc 66.00N 111.32 E
Ajigasawa 28 Pd 40.47N 140.12 E
Aji-Shima 29 Gb 38.15N 141.30 E
Ajjer, Tassili-n- 30 Hf 25.30N 9.00 E
Ajka 10 Ni 47.06N 17.34 E
Ajke, Ozero- 16 Vd 50.55N 61.35 E
Ajkino 17 De 62.15N 49.56 E
'Ajlūn 24 Ff 32.20N 35.45 E
'Ajmah, Jabal al- 24 Fh 29.12N 34.02 E
'Ajmān 23 Id 25.25N 55.27 E
Ajmer 22 Jg 26.27N 74.38 E
Ajnaži/Ainaži 7 Fh 57.52N 24.25 E
Ajni 18 Ge 39.23N 68.36 E
Ajo 43 Ee 32.22N 112.52W
Ajo, Cabo de- 13 Ia 43.31N 3.35W
Ajon, Ostrov- 21 Sc 69.50N 168.40 E
Ajoupa-Bouillon 51h Ab 14.50N 61.08W
Ajsary 19 He 53.05N 71.00 E
Ajtos 15 Kg 42.42N 27.15 E
Aju, Kepulauan- 26 Jf 0.28N 131.03 E
'Ajūz, Jabal al- 24 Dj 25.49N 30.43 E
Ajviekste 7 Fh 56.36N 25.44 E
Ajviekste/Aiviekste 7 Fh 56.36N 25.44 E
Ajzpute/Aizpute 7 Eh 56.45N 21.39 E
Akaba 34 Fd 7.57N 1.03 E
Akabira 28 Qc 43.30N 142.04 E
Akabli 32 Hd 26.42N 1.22 E
Akademika Obručeva, Hrebet- 20 Ef 51.30N 96.45 E
Akadomari 29 Fc 37.54N 138.24 E
Aka-Gawa 29 Fb 38.54N 139.50 E
Akagi-San 29 Fc 36.33N 139.11 E
Akaishi-Dake 29 Fd 35.27N 138.09 E
Akaishi-Sanmyaku 29 Fd 35.25N 138.10 E
Akajaure 7 Dc 67.42N 17.30 E
Aka-Jima 29b Ab 26.14N 127.17 E
Akaki 35 Fd 8.51N 38.48 E
Akala 35 Fb 15.38N 36.12 E
Akan 29a Db 43.08N 144.07 E
Akan-Gawa 29a Db 43.00N 144.16 E
Akar 24 Dc 38.38N 31.06 E
Akarnaniká Óri 15 Dk 38.45N 21.00 E
Akaroa 61 Dh 43.48S 172.59 E
Akasaki 29 Cd 35.31N 133.38 E
'Akasha East 35 Ea 21.05N 30.43 E
Akashi 28 Mg 34.38N 134.59 E
Akbaba Tepe 24 Hc 39.32N 39.33 E
Akbajtal, Pereval- 19 Hh 38.31N 73.41 E
Akbou 13 Qh 36.28N 4.32 E
Akbulak 19 Fe 51.03N 55.37 E
Akbura 18 Id 40.34N 72.45 E
Akçaabat 24 Hb 40.59N 39.34 E
Akçadağ 24 Gc 38.21N 37.59 E
Akçakale 24 Hd 36.41N 38.56 E
Akçakara Dağı 24 Ic 38.40N 40.52 E
Akçakoca 24 Db 41.05N 31.09 E
Akçaova [Tur.] 15 Mh 41.03N 29.57 E
Akçaova [Tur.] 15 Ll 37.30N 28.02 E
Akčatau 19 Hf 47.59N 74.02 E
Akçay 15 Ll 37.50N 28.15 E
Akçay 15 Mm 36.36N 29.45 E
Akchār 30 Ff 20.20N 14.28W
Ak Dağ [Tur.] 24 Ib 40.35N 41.46 E
Ak Dağ [Tur.] 23 Cb 36.32N 29.34 E
Akdağ [Tur.] 24 Gd 37.53N 37.56 E
Akdağ [Tur.] 24 Fb 40.57N 35.55 E
Akdağ [Tur.] 24 Cc 39.15N 28.49 E
Akdağ [Tur.] 15 Ll 37.42N 28.56 E
Akdağ [Tur.] 15 Mk 38.18N 29.58 E
Akdağ [Tur.] 15 Jk 38.33N 26.30 E
Ak Dağlar 24 Gc 39.30N 36.00 E
Ak Dağları 24 Ic 38.48N 40.12 E
Akdağmadeni 24 Fc 39.40N 35.54 E
Akdeniz = Mediterranean Sea (EN) 5 Hh 35.00N 20.00 E
Ak-Dovurak 20 Ef 51.10N 90.40 E
Akechi 29 Ed 35.18N 137.22 E
Ake Eze 34 Gd 5.55N 7.40 E
Akera 16 Oj 39.09N 46.48 E
Åkersberga 8 He 59.29N 18.18 E
Akershus 7 Cf 60.00N 11.10 E
Aketi 31 Jh 2.44N 23.46 E
Akharnai 15 Gk 38.05N 23.44 E
Akhdar, al Jabal al- 21 Hg 23.30N 57.00 E
Akhḍar, Al Jabal al- 30 Je 32.30N 21.30 E
Akhḍar, Wādī al- 24 Gh 28.35N 36.35 E
Akhelóös 15 Ej 38.18N 21.10 E
Akhisar 23 Cb 38.55N 27.51 E
Akhmīm 33 Fd 26.34N 31.44 E
Akhtarīn 24 Gd 36.31N 37.20 E
Aki 29 Ce 33.30N 133.53 E
Akiaki Atoll 61 Nc 18.30S 139.12W
Akiéni 36 Bc 1.11S 13.53 E
Akimiski 38 Kd 53.00N 81.20W
Akimovka 16 If 46.42N 35.09 E
Aki-Nada 29 Cd 34.05N 132.40 E
Åkirkeby 8 Fi 55.04N 14.56 E
Akita 22 Qf 39.43N 140.07 E
Akita Ken 28 Pe 39.45N 140.20 E
Akjoujt 31 Fg 19.44N 14.22W
Akka 32 Fd 29.25N 8.15W
Akkanburluk 17 Mj 52.46N 66.35 E
'Akko 23 Ec 32.55N 35.05 E
Akkol 18 Hc 43.25N 70.47 E
Akköy 24 Bd 37.29N 27.15 E
Akkystau 19 Ff 47.17N 51.03 E
Aklavik 42 Dc 68.14N 135.02W
Aklé Mseiguilé 34 Eb 16.20N 4.45W
Akmené/Akmene 8 Jh 56.14N 22.43 E
Akmene/Akmené 8 Jh 56.14N 22.43 E
Akmenrags/Akmeņrags 8 Ih 56.54N 20.55 E
Akmeņrags/Akmenrags 8 Ih 56.54N 20.55 E
Akmeqit 27 Cd 37.05N 76.55 E
Akniste 8 Kh 56.10N 25.54 E
Akö 29 Dd 34.45N 134.23 E
Akobo 30 Kh 7.48N 33.03 E
Akobo 31 Kh 7.47N 33.01 E
Akola 22 Jg 20.44N 77.00 E
Akonolinga 34 He 3.46N 12.15 E
Akosombo Dam 34 Fd 6.16N 0.03 E
Akpatok 42 Kd 60.24N 68.05W
Akqi 27 Cc 40.50N 78.01 E
Ákra Ámbelos 15 Gj 39.56N 23.56 E
Ákra Kambanós 15 Hl 37.59N 24.45 E
Akranes 7a Ab 64.19N 22.06W
Ákra Spathí 15 Gl 37.27N 23.31 E
Åkrehamn 7 Ag 59.16N 5.11 E
Akritas, Ákra- = Akritas, Cape- (EN) 15 Em 36.43N 21.53 E
Akritas Cape- (EN) = Akritas, Ákra- 15 Em 36.43N 21.53 E
Akron [Co.-U.S.] 45 Ef 40.10N 103.13W
Akron [Oh.-U.S.] 43 Kc 41.04N 81.31W
Akrotiri 24 Ee 34.36N 32.57 E
Akša 20 Gf 50.17N 113.17 E
Aksaj 16 Oh 43.32N 46.55 E
Aksaj [Kaz.-U.S.S.R.] 19 Fe 51.13N 53.01 E
Aksaj [R.S.F.S.R.] 16 Kf 47.15N 39.52 E
Aksakal 15 Li 40.09N 28.07 E
Aksakovo 17 Gi 54.02N 54.09 E
Aksaray 23 Db 38.23N 34.03 E
Aksay 27 Fd 39.28N 94.15 E
Akşehir 23 Db 38.21N 31.25 E
Akşehir Gölü 24 Dc 38.30N 31.28 E
Akseki 24 Dd 37.02N 31.48 E
Aksenovo-Zilovskoje 20 Gf 53.00N 117.35 E
'Aks-e Rostam 24 Ph 28.23N 54.52 E
Aksoran, Gora 19 Hf 48.25N 75.30 E
Akstafa 16 Ni 41.13N 45.27 E
Akstafa 16 Ni 41.06N 45.28 E
Aksu [China] 22 Ke 41.09N 80.15 E
Aksu [Kaz.-U.S.S.R.] 19 He 52.28N 71.59 E
Aksu [Kaz.-U.S.S.R.] 18 Lb 45.34N 79.30 E
Aksu [Kaz.-U.S.S.R.] 19 Hf 46.20N 78.15 E
Aksu [Tur.] 15 Ll 37.56N 28.56 E
Aksu [Tur.] 24 Dd 36.51N 30.54 E
Aksuat 19 If 47.48N 82.50 E
Aksubajevo 7 Mi 54.52N 50.50 E
Aksu He 21 Ke 40.28N 80.52 E
Aksum 35 Fc 14.07N 38.44 E
Ak-Šyjrak 18 Ld 41.49N 78.44 E
Aktag 27 Dd 36.45N 84.40 E
Aktaš [R.S.F.S.R.] 20 Df 50.18N 87.44 E
Aktaš [Uzb.-U.S.S.R.] 19 Gh 39.55N 65.53 E
Aktau 19 He 50.16N 73.07 E
Aktau, Gora- 19 Gg 41.45N 64.30 E
Aktjubinsk 6 Le 50.17N 57.10 E
Aktjubinskaja Oblast 19 Ff 48.00N 58.00 E
Ak-Tjuz 18 Kc 42.50N 76.07 E
Akto 27 Cd 39.05N 76.02 E
Aktogaj 19 Hf 47.01N 79.40 E
Akula 36 Db 2.22N 20.11 E
Akun 40a Eb 54.12N 165.35W
Akune 28 Kh 32.01N 130.11 E
Akure 34 Gd 7.15N 5.12 E
Akureyri 6 Eb 65.40N 18.06W
Akuseki-Jima 28 Jj 29.28N 129.33 E
Akutan 40a Eb 54.10N 165.55W
Akutan 40a Eb 54.08N 165.46W
Akyab → Sittwe 22 Lg 20.09N 92.54 E
Akyazı 24 Db 40.41N 30.37 E
Akžajkyn, Ozero- 18 Fb 44.55N 67.45 E
Akzăl 19 If 49.13N 81.30 E
Ål 8 Cd 60.38N 8.34 E
Alà, Monti di- 14 Dj 40.35N 9.16 E
Alabama 38 Kf 31.08N 87.57W
Alabama 43 Je 32.50N 87.30W
Al'Abbāsīyah 35 Ec 12.10N 31.18 E
Alaca 24 Fb 40.10N 34.51 E
Alaçam Dağlari 15 Lj 39.20N 28.32 E
Alaçan 24 Fb 41.37N 35.37 E
Alaçati 15 Jk 38.16N 26.23 E
Aladağ 24 Jc 43.35N 39.20 E
Ala Dağ [Tur.] 24 Jb 40.11N 42.49 E
Ala Dağ [Tur.] 24 Ed 37.58N 32.04 E
Alādāgh, Kūh-e- 24 Qd 37.13N 57.30 E
Ala Dağları 24 Fd 37.55N 35.13 E
Aladža 16 Rj 39.21N 53.12 E
Aladža Manastir 15 Lf 43.17N 28.01 E
Alagir 16 Nh 43.01N 44.12 E
Alagna Valsesia 14 Be 45.51N 7.56 E
Alagnon 11 Ji 45.27N 3.19 E
Alagoas 54 Ke 9.30S 36.30W
Alagoinhas 53 Mg 12.07S 38.26W
Alagón 13 Kc 41.46N 1.07W
Alagón 13 Fe 39.44N 6.53W
Ala Gou 27 Ec 42.42N 89.12 E
Alahanpanjang 26 Dg 1.05S 100.47 E
Alahärmä 7 Fe 63.14N 22.51 E
Al Aḥmadī 24 Mh 29.05N 48.04 E
Alaid, Vulkan 20 Kf 50.50N 155.33 E
Alajärvi 7 Fe 63.00N 23.49 E
Alajku 19 Hg 40.18N 74.29 E
Alajski Hrebet 21 Jf 39.45N 72.30 E
Alajuela 49 Eh 10.30N 84.30W
Alajuela 47 Hf 10.01N 84.13W
Alajuela, Lago- 49 Hi 9.05N 79.24W
Alakol, Ozero- 21 Ke 46.05N 81.50 E
Alakurtti 7 Hc 66.59N 30.20 E
Alalakeiki Channel 65a Ec 20.35N 156.30W
Al 'Alamayn 31 Je 30.49N 28.57 E
Alalau, Rio- 54 Fd 0.30S 61.10W
Al 'Amādīyah 24 Jd 37.06N 43.29 E
Alamagan Island 57 Fc 17.36N 145.50 E
Al 'Amārah 23 Gc 31.50N 47.09 E
'Alam ar Rūm, Ra's- 24 Bg 31.22N 27.21 E
Alāmarvdasht 24 Oi 27.52N 52.34 E
Alamashindo 35 Ge 4.51N 42.04 E
Alamata 35 Fc 12.25N 39.37 E
Alameda 45 Ci 35.11N 106.37W
Alaminos 26 Gc 16.10N 119.59 E
Al 'Āmirīyah 24 Cg 31.01N 29.48 E
Alamito Creek 45 Dl 29.31N 104.17W
Alamitos, Sierra de los- 48 Hd 26.20N 102.15W
'Alāmo 35 Ge 4.23N 43.09 E
Alamo 46 Hh 37.22N 115.10W
Alamogordo 43 Fe 32.54N 105.57W
Alamos 47 Cc 27.01N 108.56W
Alamos, Sierra- 48 Gc 28.25N 105.00W
Alamosa 43 Fd 37.28N 105.52W
Al Anbār 24 If 34.00N 42.00 E
Åland/Ahvenanmaa 7 Ef 60.15N 20.00 E
Åland/Ahvenanmaa = Aland Islands (EN) 5 Hc 60.15N 20.00 E
Aland Islands (EN) = Ahvenanmaa/Åland 5 Hc 60.15N 20.00 E
Aland Islands (EN) = Åland/Ahvenanmaa 5 Hc 60.15N 20.00 E
Ålandsbro 8 Gb 62.40N 17.50 E
Ålandshav 8 Hd 60.00N 19.30 E
Alange 13 Ff 38.47N 6.15W
Alanje 49 Fi 8.24N 82.33W
Alanya 23 Db 36.33N 32.01 E
Alaotra, Lac- 37 Hc 17.30S 48.30 E
Alapaha River 44 Fj 30.26N 83.06W
Alapajevsk 19 Gd 57.52N 61.42 E
Alaplı 24 Db 41.08N 31.25 E
Al 'Aqabah = Aqaba (EN) 23 Dd 29.31N 35.00 E
Al 'Aqabah aş Şaghīrah 24 Ej 24.14N 32.53 E
Al 'Arabīyah As-Su'ūdīyah = Saudi Arabia (EN) 22 Gg 25.00N 45.00 E
Alarcón, Embalse de- 13 Je 39.45N 2.20W
Al 'Arīsh 33 Fc 31.08N 33.48 E
Al 'Armah 24 Lj 25.30N 46.30 E
Al Arṭāwīyah 24 Ki 26.30N 45.20 E
Alas, Selat- 26 Gh 8.40S 116.40 E
Al 'Aşab 24 Pk 23.20N 54.10 E
Alaşehir 24 Cc 38.21N 28.32 E
Al Ashkharah 23 Ie 21.47N 59.30 E
Al 'Āshūrīyah 24 Jg 31.02N 43.05 E
Alaska 40 Ic 65.00N 153.00W
Alaska 38 Dc 65.00N 153.00W
Alaska, Gulf of- 38 Ed 58.00N 146.00W
Alaska Peninsula 38 Dd 57.00N 158.00W
Alaska Range 38 Ec 62.30N 150.00W
Alassio 14 Cf 44.00N 8.10 E
Alastaro 8 Jd 60.57N 22.51 E
Alat 18 De 39.26N 63.48 E
Alataw Shan 27 Cb 45.00N 80.00 E
Alataw Shankou = Dzungarian Gate (EN) 21 Ke 45.25N 82.25 E
Al 'Athāmīn 24 Jg 30.35N 43.40 E
Alatri 14 Hi 41.43N 13.21 E
Al 'Aṭrun 31 Jg 18.11N 26.36 E
Alatyr 7 Li 54.52N 46.36 E
Alatyr 19 Ee 54.50N 46.36 E
Alava 13 Jb 42.50N 2.45W
Alava, Cape- 46 Cb 48.10N 124.43W
Alaverdi 19 Eg 41.08N 44.37 E
Alavijeh 24 Nf 33.03N 51.05 E
Alavo/Alavus 7 Fe 62.35N 23.37 E
Alavus/Alavo 7 Fe 62.35N 23.37 E
Al 'Awāliq 23 Gg 14.15N 46.30 E
Al 'Awāriq 35 Ha 20.25N 48.40 E
Al 'Awsajīyah 24 Ki 26.04N 44.08 E
'Ālayh 24 Ff 33.48N 35.36 E
Al 'Ayn [Sau.Ar.] 24 Hj 25.04N 38.06 E
Al 'Ayn [U.A.E.] 24 Pj 24.13N 55.45 E
Alayor 13 Qe 39.56N 4.08 E
Al 'Ayyāṭ 24 Dh 29.37N 31.15 E
Al A'ẓamīyah 24 Kf 33.23N 44.22 E
Alazani 16 Oi 41.03N 46.40 E
Alazeja 20 Kb 70.55N 153.40 E
Al 'Azīzīyah 33 Bc 32.32N 13.01 E
Alazores, Puerto de los- 13 Hg 37.05N 4.15W
Alb [Ger.] 12 Ke 49.04N 8.20 E
Alb [Ger.] 10 Ei 47.35N 8.08 E
Alba 15 Gc 46.08N 23.30 E
Alba 14 Cf 44.42N 8.02 E
Alba Adriatica 14 Hh 42.50N 13.56 E
Al Bāb 24 Gd 36.22N 37.31 E
Albac 15 Fc 46.27N 22.58 E
Albacete 6 Fh 38.59N 1.51W
Albacete 13 Kf 38.50N 2.00W
Al Badārī 33 Fd 26.59N 31.25 E
Alba de Tormes 13 Gd 40.49N 5.31W
Al Badi 33 Ie 22.02N 46.34 E
Al Bādī 24 Ie 35.56N 41.32 E
Ålbæk 8 Dg 57.36N 10.25 E
Ålbæk Bugt 8 Dg 57.35N 10.30 E
Al Bahrah 24 Lh 29.40N 47.52 E
Al Baḥr al Aḥmar 35 Fb 19.50N 35.30 E
Al Baḥrayn 21 Hg 26.00N 50.30 E

Index Symbols

Independent Nation
State, Region
District, County
Municipality
Colony, Dependency
Continent
Physical Region
Historical or Cultural Region
Mount, Mountain
Volcano
Hill
Mountains, Mountain Range
Hills, Escarpment
Plateau, Upland
Pass, Gap
Plain, Lowland
Delta
Salt Flat
Valley, Canyon
Crater, Cave
Karst Features
Depression
Polder
Desert, Dunes
Forest, Woods
Heath, Steppe
Oasis
Cape, Point
Coast, Beach
Cliff
Peninsula
Isthmus
Sandbank
Island
Atoll
Rock, Reef
Islands, Archipelago
Rocks, Reefs
Coral Reef
Well, Spring
Geyser
River, Stream
Waterfall Rapids
River Mouth, Estuary
Lake
Salt Lake
Intermittent Lake
Reservoir
Swamp, Pond
Canal
Glacier
Ice Shelf, Pack Ice
Ocean
Sea
Gulf, Bay
Strait, Fjord
Lagoon
Bank
Seamount
Tablemount
Ridge
Shelf
Basin
Escarpment, Sea Scarp
Fracture
Trench, Abyss
National Park, Reserve
Point of Interest
Recreation Site
Cave, Cavern
Historic Site
Ruins
Wall, Walls
Church, Abbey
Temple
Scientific Station
Airport
Port
Lighthouse
Mine
Tunnel
Dam, Bridge

Al Baḥrayn = Bahrain (EN) 22 Hg 26.00N 50.29 E
Albaida 13 Lf 38.51N 0.31W
Alba Iulia 15 Gc 46.04N 23.35 E
Albalate del Arzobispo 13 Lc 41.07N 0.31W
Al Balyanā 33 Fd 26.14N 32.00 E
Alban 11 Ik 43.54N 2.28 E
Albanel, Lac- 42 Kf 51.05N 73.05W
Albani, Colli- 14 Gi 41.45N 12.45 E
Albania (EN) = Shqipëria 6 Hg 41.00N 20.00 E
Albano, Lago- 14 Gi 41.45N 12.40 E
Albano Laziale 14 Gi 41.44N 12.39 E
Albany 38 Kd 52.17N 81.31W
Albany [Austl.] 58 Ch 35.02S 117.53 E
Albany [Ga.-U.S.] 43 Ke 31.35N 84.10W
Albany [Ky.-U.S.] 44 Eg 36.42N 85.08W
Albany [N.Y.-U.S.] 39 Le 42.39N 73.45W
Albany [Or.-U.S.] 43 Cc 44.38N 123.06W
Alba Posse 55 Eh 27.33S 54.42W
Albarche 13 He 39.58N 4.46W
Albardón 56 Gd 31.26S 68.32W
Albarracín 13 Kd 40.25N 1.26W
Albarracín, Sierra de- 13 Kd 40.30N 1.30W
Al Baṣalīyah Qiblī 24 Ej 25.06N 32.47 E
Al Baṣrah 24 Lg 30.30N 47.27 E
Al Baṣrah = Basra (EN) 22 Gf 30.30N 47.47 E
Al Baṭḥā' 24 Kg 31.07N 45.54 E
Al Bāṭin 24 Lh 29.00N 46.35 E
Al Bāṭinah 21 Hg 23.45N 57.20 E
Albatross Bank (EN) 40 Ie 56.10N 152.20W
Albatross Bay 59 Ib 12.45S 141.43 E
Albatross Plateau (EN) 3 Mi 10.00N 103.00W
Albatross Point 62 Fc 38.07S 174.40 E
Al Batrūn 24 Fe 34.15N 35.39 E
Al Bawīṭī 33 Ed 28.21N 28.52 E
Al Bayāḍ 21 Gg 22.00N 47.00 E
Al Bayḍā' 33 Dc 32.00N 21.30 E
Al Bayḍā' 33 Cd 28.21N 18.58 E
Al Bayḍā' 31 Je 32.46N 21.43 E
Al Bayḍā' 33 Ig 13.58N 45.35 E
Albegna 14 Fh 42.30N 11.11 E
Albemarle 44 Gh 35.21N 80.12W
Albemarle Sound 43 Ld 36.03N 76.12W
Albenga 14 Cf 44.03N 8.13 E
Alberdi 56 Ic 26.10S 58.09W
Albères, Chaîne des- 11 Il 42.28N 2.56 E
Albères, Montes-/Les Alberes 11 Il 42.28N 2.56 E
Albergaria-a-Velha 13 Dd 40.42N 8.29W
Alberique 13 Le 39.07N 0.31W
Alberobello 14 Lj 40.47N 17.16 E
Albert 11 Id 50.00N 2.39 E
Albert, Canal-/Albert Kanaal = Albert Canal (EN) 11 Ld 50.39N 5.37 E
Albert, Lake- [Afr.] 30 Kh 1.40N 31.00 E
Albert, Lake- [Or.-U.S.] 46 Ee 42.38N 120.13W
Albert, Lake- (EN) = Mobuto Sese Seko, Lac- 30 Kh 1.40N 31.00 E
Alberta 42 Gf 55.00N 115.00W
Albert Canal (EN) = Albert, Canal-/Albert Kanaal 11 Ld 50.39N 5.37 E
Albert Canal (EN) = Albert Kanaal/Albert, Canal- 11 Ld 50.39N 5.37 E
Albert Edward, Mount- 59 Ja 8.23S 147.27 E
Albert Edward Bay 42 Hc 69.35N 103.10W
Alberti 56 He 35.02S 60.16W
Albertirsa 10 Pi 47.15N 19.37 E
Albert Kanaal/Albert, Canal- = Albert Canal (EN) 11 Ld 50.39N 5.37 E
Albert Lea 43 Ic 43.39N 93.22W
Albert Nile 30 Kh 3.36N 32.02 E
Albertville [Al.-U.S.] 44 Dh 34.16N 86.12W
Albertville [Fr.] 11 Mi 45.41N 6.23 E
Albestroff 12 If 48.56N 6.51 E
Albi 11 Ik 43.56N 2.09 E
Albia 45 Jf 41.02N 92.48W
Al Bid' 24 Fh 28.28N 35.01 E
Albina 54 Hb 5.30N 54.03W
Albina, Ponta- 30 Ij 15.51S 11.44 E
Albino 14 De 45.46N 9.47 E
Albion [Mi.-U.S.] 44 Ed 42.15N 84.45W
Albion [Nb.-U.S.] 45 Hf 41.42N 98.00W
Albion [N.Y.-U.S.] 44 Hd 43.15N 78.12W
Al Biqā' 24 Ge 34.10N 36.10 E
Al Bi'r 23 Ed 28.51N 36.15 E
Al Bi'r al Jadīd 23 Ed 26.01N 38.29 E
Al Birk 23 Ff 18.13N 41.33 E
Albis 14 Cc 47.20N 8.30 E
Albo, Monte- 14 Dj 40.32N 9.35 E
Albocácer/Albocasser 13 Md 40.21N 0.02 E
Albocasser/Albocácer 13 Md 40.21N 0.02 E
Alborán, Isla de- 5 Fh 35.58N 3.02W
Alboran Basin (EN) 13 Ii 36.00N 4.00W
Ålborg 6 Gd 57.03N 9.56 E
Ålborg Bugt 7 Ch 56.45N 10.30 E
Alborz, Reshteh-ye Kūhhā-ye- = Elburz Mountains (EN) 21 Hf 36.00N 53.00 E
Albox 13 Jg 37.23N 2.08W
Albret, Pays d'- 11 Fj 44.10N 0.20W
Albū 'Alī 24 Je 34.49N 43.35 E
Albufeira 13 Dg 37.05N 8.15W
Albū Gharz, Sabkhat- 24 Ie 34.45N 41.15 E
Al Buḥeyrat 35 Dd 7.00N 29.30 E
Al Bumbah 33 Dc 32.13N 23.00 E
Albuñol 13 Ih 36.47N 3.12W
Albuquerque [Braz.] 55 Dd 19.23S 57.26W
Albuquerque [N.M.-U.S.] 39 If 35.05N 106.40W
Albuquerque, Cayos de- 47 Hf 12.10N 81.50W
Al Burayj 24 Ge 34.15N 36.46 E
Al Buraymī 23 Ie 24.15N 55.45 E
Al Burmah 32 Ic 31.45N 9.02 E
Alburquerque 13 Fe 39.13N 7.00W
Albury [Austl.] 58 Fh 36.05S 146.55 E
Albury [N.Z.] 62 Df 44.14S 170.53 E
Al Buṭanah 30 Kg 15.00N 35.00 E
Al Buṭayn 24 Kj 25.52N 45.50 E
Alby 8 Fb 62.30N 15.28 E
Alcácer do Sal 13 Df 38.22N 8.30W
Alcáçovar 13 Df 38.25N 8.13W
Alcalá de Chivert 13 Md 40.18N 0.14 E
Alcalá de Guadaira 13 Gg 37.20N 5.50W
Alcalá de Henares 13 Id 40.29N 3.22W
Alcalá del Júcar 13 Ke 39.12N 1.26W
Alcalá de los Gazules 13 Gh 36.28N 5.44W
Alcalá del Río 13 Gg 37.31N 5.59W
Alcalá la Real 13 Ig 37.28N 3.56W
Alcamo 14 Gm 37.59N 12.58 E
Alcanadre 13 Mc 41.37N 0.12 E
Alcañices 13 Fc 41.42N 6.21W
Alcañiz 13 Lc 41.03N 0.08W
Alcántara 13 Fe 39.43N 6.53W
Alcântara 54 Jd 2.24S 44.24W
Alcantara 14 Jm 37.49N 15.16 E
Alcántara, Embalse de- 13 Fe 39.45N 6.48W
Alcantarilla 13 Kg 37.58N 1.13W
Alcaraz 13 Jf 38.40N 2.29W
Alcaraz, Sierra de- 13 Jf 38.35N 2.25W
Alcaudete 13 Hg 37.36N 4.05W
Alcázar de San Juan 13 Ie 39.24N 3.12W
Alcester 63a Ac 9.33S 152.25 E
Alcira/Alzira 13 Le 39.09N 0.26W
Alcobaça [Braz.] 54 Kg 17.30S 39.13W
Alcobaça [Port.] 13 De 39.33N 8.59W
Alcobendas 13 Id 40.32N 3.38W
Alcoi/Alcoy 13 Lf 38.42N 0.28W
Alcolea del Pinar 13 Jc 41.02N 2.28W
Alcorta 55 Bk 33.32S 61.07W
Alcoutim 13 Eg 37.28N 7.28W
Alcova 46 Le 42.37N 106.36W
Alcoy/Alcoi 13 Lf 38.42N 0.28W
Alcubierre, Sierra de- 13 Lc 41.44N 0.29W
Alcudia 13 Pe 39.52N 3.07 E
Alcúdia, Badia d'-/Alcudia, Bahia de- 13 Pe 39.48N 3.13 E
Alcudia, Bahia de-/Alcúdia, Badia d'- 13 Pe 39.48N 3.13 E
Alcudia, Sierra de- 13 Hf 38.35N 4.35W
Aldabra Group 37b Ab 9.25S 46.22 E
Aldabra Islands 30 Li 9.25S 46.22 E
Aldama [Mex.] 48 Jf 22.55N 98.04W
Aldama [Mex.] 47 Cc 28.51N 105.54W
Aldan 22 Od 58.37N 125.24 E
Aldan [R.S.F.S.R.] 20 Hd 63.20N 129.25 E
Aldan [U.S.S.R.] 21 Oc 63.28N 129.35 E
Aldan Plateau (EN) = Aldanskoje Nagorje 21 Od 57.30N 127.30 E
Aldanskoje Nagorje = Aldan Plateau (EN) 21 Od 57.30N 127.30 E
Aldarhan 27 Gb 47.42N 96.36 E
Alde 12 Db 52.10N 1.32 E
Aldeburgh 9 Oi 52.09N 1.35 E
Aldeia 55 Ed 18.12S 55.10W
Aldeia, Serra da- 55 Ic 17.00S 46.50W
Alderney 9 Kl 49.43N 2.12W
Aldershot 12 Bc 51.15N 0.46W
Alderson 46 Ja 50.18N 111.26W
Aledo 45 Kf 41.12N 90.45W
Aleg 31 Fg 17.03N 13.53W
Alegranza 32 Ed 29.23N 13.30W
Alegre 54 Jh 20.46S 41.32W
Alegre, Rio- 55 Cb 15.14S 59.58W
Alegrete 56 Ic 29.46S 55.46W
Alej 20 Df 52.50N 83.25 E
Alejandra 55 Ci 29.54S 59.50W
Alejandro Selkirk, Isla- 52 Hi 33.45S 80.46W
Alejsk 20 Df 52.28N 82.45 E
Aleksandrija 16 He 48.40N 33.07 E
Aleksandrov 19 Dd 56.25N 38.42 E
Aleksandrov Gaj 19 Ee 50.08N 48.32 E
Aleksandrovka 16 He 48.59N 32.13 E
Aleksandrovsk 17 Hg 59.10N 57.35 E
Aleksandrovskoje 16 Mg 44.39N 43.00 E
Aleksandrovsk-Sahalinsk 22 Qd 50.54N 142.10 E
Aleksandrów Kujawski 10 Od 52.52N 18.42 E
Aleksandrów Łódzki 10 Pe 51.49N 19.19 E
Aleksandry, Zemlja- 21 Ga 80.45N 46.00 E
Aleksejevka [Kaz.-U.S.S.R.] 19 If 48.26N 85.40 E
Aleksejevka [Kaz.-U.S.S.R.] 19 He 51.58N 70.59 E
Aleksejevka [Kaz.-U.S.S.R.] 17 Nj 53.31N 69.28 E
Aleksejevka [R.S.F.S.R.] 19 De 50.39N 38.42 E
Aleksejevsk 20 Fe 57.50N 108.23 E
Aleksejevskoje 7 Mi 55.19N 50.03 E
Aleksin 16 Jb 54.31N 37.07 E
Aleksinac 15 Ef 43.32N 21.43 E
Alem 56 Ic 27.31S 55.15W
Ålem 7 Dh 56.57N 16.23 E
Alem Maya 35 Gd 9.27N 41.58 E
Ålen 8 Db 62.51N 11.17 E
Alençon 11 Gf 48.26N 0.05 E
Alenquer 54 Hd 1.56S 54.46W
Alenuihaha Channel 60 Oc 20.26N 156.00W
Alépé 34 Ed 5.30N 3.39W
Aleppo (EN) = Ḥalab 22 Ff 36.12N 37.10 E
Aléria 11a Ba 42.06N 9.31 E
Aléria, Plaine d'- 11a Ba 42.05N 9.30 E
Alert 39 Ma 82.30N 62.00W
Alert Bay 46 Ba 50.35N 126.55W
Alès 11 Kj 44.08N 4.05 E
Alešd 15 Fb 47.04N 22.25 E
Alessandria 14 Cf 44.54N 8.37 E
Ålestrup 8 Ch 56.42N 9.30 E
Ålesund 6 Gc 62.28N 6.09 E
Aleutian Basin (EN) 38 Ad 57.00N 177.00 E
Aleutian Islands 38 Bd 52.00N 176.00W
Aleutian Range 38 Dd 59.00N 155.00W
Aleutian Trench (EN) 3 Je 51.00N 179.00 E
Alexander, Cape- 60 Fi 6.35S 156.30 E
Alexander, Kap- 41 Ec 78.10N 72.45W
Alexander Archipelago 38 Fd 56.30N 134.00W
Alexanderbaai 37 Be 28.40S 16.30 E
Alexander City 43 Je 32.56N 85.57W
Alexander Island 66 Qe 71.00S 70.00W
Alexandra 61 Ci 45.15S 169.24 E
Alexandra Fiord 42 Ka 79.17N 75.00W
Alexandretta (EN) = İskenderun 22 Ff 36.37N 36.07 E
Alexandretta, Gulf of- (EN) = İskenderun Körfezi 23 Eb 36.30N 35.40 E
Alexándria 15 Fi 40.38N 22.27 E
Alexandria [Austl.] 59 Hc 19.05S 136.40 E
Alexandria [La.-U.S.] 39 Jf 31.18N 92.27W
Alexandria [Mn.-U.S.] 43 Hb 45.53N 95.22W
Alexandria [Rom.] 15 If 43.59N 25.20 E
Alexandria [S.Afr.] 37 Df 33.39S 26.24 E
Alexandria [Va.-U.S.] 44 If 38.49N 77.06W
Alexandria (EN) = Al Iskandarīyah [Eg.] 31 Je 31.12N 29.54 E
Alexandria Bay 44 Jc 44.20N 75.55W
Alexandrina, Lake- 59 Hg 35.25S 139.10 E
Alexandrita 54 Hg 19.42S 50.27W
Alexandroúpolis 6 Ig 40.51N 25.52 E
'Aleyak, Godār-e- 24 Qd 36.30N 57.45 E
Alf 10 Df 50.03N 7.07 E
Alfabia, Sierra de- 13 Oe 39.45N 2.48 E
Alfambra 13 Kd 40.21N 1.07W
Al Fardah 35 Hc 14.51N 48.26 E
Alfaro 13 Kb 42.11N 1.45W
Al Fāshir 31 Jg 13.38N 25.21 E
Al Fashn 33 Fd 28.49N 30.54 E
Alfatar 15 Kf 43.57N 27.17 E
Al Fathah 24 Je 35.04N 43.34 E
Al Fāw 23 Gd 29.58N 48.29 E
Al Fawwārah 24 Ji 26.03N 43.05 E
Al Fayyūm 31 Kf 29.19N 30.58 E
Alfbach 12 Jd 50.03N 7.08 E
Alfeld 10 Fe 51.59N 9.50 E
Alfenas 54 Ih 21.26S 45.57W
Al Fifi 35 Dc 10.03N 25.01 E
Alfiós 15 El 37.37N 21.27 E
Alföld 5 If 47.15N 20.25 E
Alfonsine 14 Gf 44.30N 12.03 E
Alford 12 Ca 53.15N 0.11 E
Ålfotbreen 8 Ac 61.45N 5.40 E
Alfreton 12 Aa 53.06N 1.23W
Alfta 7 Df 61.21N 16.05 E
Al Fuḥayḥīl 23 Gd 29.05N 48.08 E
Al Fuhūd 24 Lg 30.58N 46.43 E
Al Fujayrah 23 Id 25.06N 56.21 E
Al Fūlah 35 Dc 11.48N 28.24 E
Al Fuqahā' 33 Cd 27.50N 16.21 E
Al Furāt = Euphrates (EN) 21 Gf 31.00N 47.25 E
Al Fuwayriṭ 24 Ni 26.02N 51.22 E
Alga 19 Ff 49.55N 57.20 E
Algador 13 Ie 39.55N 3.53W
Al Gārah 24 Ih 29.52N 40.15 E
Algarås 8 Ff 58.48N 14.14 E
Ålgård 8 Af 58.46N 5.51 E
Algarrobo 49 Jh 10.12N 74.04W
Algarve 13 Dg 37.10N 8.15W
Algarve 5 Fh 37.10N 8.15W
Algeciras 6 Fh 36.08N 5.30W
Algeciras, Bahia de- 13 Gh 36.09N 5.25W
Algena 35 Fb 17.20N 38.34 E
Algeria (EN) = Al Jazā'ir 31 Hf 28.00N 3.00 E
Algerian Basin (EN) 5 Gh 39.00N 5.00 E
Al Gharaq as Sulṭānī 24 Dh 29.08N 30.42 E
Al Gharbī 32 Jc 34.40N 11.13 E
Al Ghāṭ 24 Ki 26.00N 45.03 E
Al Ghaydah 23 Hf 16.12N 52.15 E
Alghero 14 Cj 40.33N 8.19 E
Alghero, Rada d'- 14 Cj 40.35N 8.20 E
Älghult 8 Fg 57.01N 15.34 E
Al Ghurāb 24 Dj 25.20N 30.20 E
Al Ghurayfah 24 Qk 23.59N 56.29 E
Al Ghurdaqah 33 Fd 27.14N 33.50 E
Algiers (EN) = Al Jazā'ir 31 He 36.47N 3.03 E
Algiers (EN) = Al Jazā'ir 32 Hb 36.35N 3.00 E
Algoa Bay 30 Jl 33.50S 25.50 E
Algodoeiro, Serra do- 55 Jc 16.30S 44.45W
Algoma 45 Md 44.36N 87.27W
Algoma Uplands 44 Fb 47.00N 83.35W
Algona 45 Ie 43.04N 94.14W
Algonquin Park 44 Hc 45.27N 78.26W
Algrange 12 Ie 49.21N 6.03 E
Al Ḥabakah 24 Jh 29.51N 42.16 E
Al Ḥadd 23 Ie 22.29N 59.58 E
Al Ḥadīdah 35 Ia 21.31N 50.28 E
Al Ḥadīthah 23 Fc 34.07N 42.23 E
Al Ḥadīthah 24 Gg 31.28N 37.08 E
Al Ḥaḍr 24 Je 35.35N 42.44 E
Al Haffah 24 Ge 35.35N 36.02 E
Al Ḥajharah 23 Fc 30.25N 44.30 E
Al Ḥā'ir 24 Lj 24.23N 46.50 E
Al Ḥajar 35 Hb 16.08N 47.50 E
Al Hajar 23 Ie 23.15N 57.30 E
Al Halfāyah 24 Lg 31.49N 47.26 E
Alhama 13 Kb 42.11N 1.45W
Al Ḥamād 21 Ff 32.00N 39.30 E
Alhama de Granada 13 Ih 37.00N 3.59W
Alhama de Murcia 13 Kg 37.51N 1.25W
Alhamilla, Sierra- 13 Jh 36.58N 2.20W
Al Ḥammām 32 Ic 33.54N 9.48 E
Al Ḥammām [Eg.] 24 Cg 30.50N 29.23 E
Al Ḥammām [Iraq] 24 Kg 31.08N 44.04 E
Al Ḥamrā 24 Pj 25.42N 55.47 E
Al Ḥanīyah 24 Kh 29.10N 45.50 E
Al Ḥarrah 24 Ch 28.20N 29.07 E
Al Ḥarrah 24 Hg 31.00N 38.40 E
Al Harūj al Aswad 30 If 27.00N 17.10 E
Al Ḥasā 24 Fg 30.49N 35.59 E
Al Ḥasā' 21 Gg 26.35N 48.10 E
Al Ḥasakah 23 Fb 36.29N 40.45 E
Al Ḥasan 24 Je 34.39N 43.43 E
Al Ḥasānī 24 Gj 24.58N 37.05 E
Alhaurín el Grande 13 Hh 36.38N 4.41W
Al Ḥawāmidīyah 24 Dh 29.54N 31.15 E
Al Ḥawātah 35 Ec 13.25N 34.38 E
Al Ḥawjā' 24 Hh 28.59N 38.34 E
Al Ḥawrah 35 Hc 13.49N 47.35 E
Al Ḥayy 23 Gc 32.10N 46.03 E
Al Ḥayz 33 Ed 28.02N 28.39 E
Al Hibāk 23 He 20.20N 53.10 E
Al Ḥijāz 21 Fg 24.30N 38.30 E
Al Hillah 33 Ie 23.50N 46.51 E
Al Ḥillah 23 Fc 32.29N 44.25 E
Al Ḥinākīyah 23 Fe 24.51N 40.31 E
Al Hindīyah 24 Kf 32.32N 44.13 E
Al Ḥinnāh 24 Mi 26.56N 48.45 E
Al Hirmil 24 Ge 34.23N 36.23 E
Al Hoceima 32 Gb 35.15N 3.55W
Al Hoceima 32 Gb 35.00N 4.15W
Alhucemas, Peñón de- 13 Ii 35.13N 3.53W
Al Ḥudaydah 22 Gh 14.48N 42.57 E
Al Ḥufrah 33 Cd 29.30N 17.55 E
Al Ḥufrah 23 Ed 28.49N 38.15 E
Al Hufūf 22 Gg 25.22N 49.34 E
Al Hūj 24 Hh 29.00N 38.25 E
Al Ḥunayy 24 Mj 24.48N 48.45 E
Al Ḥuṣayḥiṣah 35 Ec 14.44N 33.18 E
Al Ḥuwaimī 23 Fg 13.58N 47.40 E
Al Ḥuwayyiṭ 24 Ij 25.36N 40.23 E
Al Ḥyyānīyah 24 Jh 28.42N 42.18 E
'Alīābād [Iran] 23 Id 28.37N 55.51 E
'Alīābād [Iran] 24 Le 35.04N 46.58 E
'Alīābād [Iran] 24 Nd 36.37N 51.33 E
Alīābād 24 Pd 36.56N 54.50 E
Alīābād, Kūh-e- 23 Hc 34.13N 50.46 E
Aliaga 13 Ld 40.40N 0.42W
Aliağa 24 Bc 38.48N 26.59 E
Aliákmon 15 Fi 40.30N 22.40 E
'Alī al Gharbī 24 Lf 32.27N 46.41 E
'Alī ash Sharqī 24 Lf 32.07N 46.44 E
Ali-Bajramly 19 Eh 39.55N 48.57 E
Alibej, Ozero- 15 Nd 45.50N 30.00 E
Alibey Adasi 15 Jj 39.20N 26.38 E
Alibo 35 Fd 9.53N 37.05 E
Alibori 34 Fc 11.56N 3.17 E
Alibunar 15 Dd 45.04N 20.58 E
Alicante 6 Fh 38.21N 0.29W
Alicante 13 Lf 38.30N 0.30W
Alicante, Golfo de- 13 Lf 38.20N 0.15W
Alice [S.Afr.] 37 Df 32.47S 26.50 E
Alice [Tx.-U.S.] 43 Hf 27.45N 98.04W
Alice, Punta- 14 Lk 39.12N 17.09 E
Alice Springs 58 Eg 23.42S 133.53 E
Aliceville 44 Ci 33.08N 88.09W
Alicudi 14 Il 38.30N 14.20 E
Alīgarh 22 Jg 28.02N 78.17 E
Alīgūdarz 24 Mf 33.24N 49.41 E
Alihe → Oroqen Zizhiqi 27 La 50.35N 123.42 E
Alijó 13 Ec 41.16N 7.28W
Alijos, Rocas- 47 Ad 24.57N 115.44W
'Alī Jūq, Kūh-e- 24 Ng 31.30N 51.45 E
Al Ikhwan 21 Hh 12.08N 53.10 E
Al Ikhwān 24 Fi 26.19N 34.52 E
Alima 30 Ii 1.36S 16.36 E
Al Imārāt al 'Arabīyah al Muttaḥidah = United Arab Emirates (EN) 22 Hg 24.00N 54.00 E
Alimiá 15 Km 36.16N 27.43 E
Alindao 35 Cd 5.02N 21.13 E
Alinglapalap Atoll 57 Hd 7.08N 168.16 E
Alingsås 7 Ch 57.56N 12.31 E
Aliquippa 44 Ge 40.38N 80.16W
Al 'Irāq = Iraq (EN) 22 Gf 33.00N 44.00 E
Al'Irq 33 Dd 29.01N 21.31 E
Al 'Irqah 23 Gg 13.40N 47.18 E
Ali-Sabjeh 35 Gc 11.08N 42.43 E
'Alī Shāh 'Avaz 24 Ne 35.39N 51.04 E
Al Iskandarīyah [Eg.] = Alexandria (EN) 31 Je 31.12N 29.54 E
Al Iskandarīyah [Iraq] 24 Kf 32.53N 44.21 E
Aliskerovo 20 Lc 67.52N 167.40 E
Al Ismā'īlīyah = Ismailia (EN) 33 Fc 30.35N 32.16 E
Al Istiwā'īyah al Gharbīyah 35 Dd 5.20N 28.30 E
Al Istiwā'īyah al Sharkīyah 35 Ed 5.20N 33.50 E
Alistráti 15 Gh 41.04N 23.58 E
Alitak, Cape- 40 Ie 56.51N 154.21W
Alite Reef 63a Ec 8.53S 160.38 E
Alitus/Alytus 19 Ce 54.25N 24.08 E
Alivérion 15 Hk 38.25N 24.02 E
Aliwal North 31 Jl 30.44S 26.40 E
Al Jabalayn 35 Ec 12.36N 32.48 E
Al Jadīdah [Eg.] 24 Cj 25.34N 28.51 E
Al Jadīdah [Sau.Ar.] 24 Mj 25.39N 49.32 E
Al Jafr 24 Gg 30.18N 36.13 E
Al Jāfūrah 35 Ia 23.25N 50.17 E
Al Jāfūrah 24 Nj 25.00N 50.15 E
Al Jaghbūb 31 Jf 29.45N 24.31 E
Al Jahrah 23 Gc 29.20N 47.40 E
Al Jalāmīd 23 Fc 31.17N 40.06 E
Al Jamalīyah 24 Nj 25.37N 51.05 E
Al Jamm 32 Jb 35.18N 10.43 E
Al Janā'in 32 Jc 31.44N 10.09 E
Aljat 16 Pj 39.58N 49.27 E
Al Jawf [Lib.] 31 Jf 24.12N 23.18 E
Al Jawf [Sau.Ar.] 22 Fg 29.50N 39.52 E
Al Jazā'ir = Algeria (EN) 31 Hf 28.00N 3.00 E
Al Jazā'ir = Algiers (EN) 32 Hb 36.35N 3.00 E
Al Jazā'ir = Algiers (EN) 31 He 36.47N 3.03 E
Al Jazā'ir-El Harrach 13 Ph 36.43N 3.08 E
Al Jazīrah 35 Ec 14.40N 33.30 E
Al Jazīrah [Asia] 21 Gf 35.10N 42.00 E
Al Jazīrah [Sud.] 30 Kg 14.25N 33.00 E
Aljezur 13 Dg 37.19N 8.48W
Aljibe 13 Gh 36.31N 5.37W
Al Jifārah 30 Ie 32.30N 11.45 E
Al Jiwā' 23 He 23.00N 54.00 E
Al Jīzah = Giza (EN) 31 Ke 30.01N 31.13 E
Al Jubayl 23 Gd 27.01N 49.40 E
Al Jubaylah 24 Lj 24.54N 46.27 E
Al Junaynah [Sau.Ar.] 33 He 20.17N 42.48 E
Al Junaynah [Sud.] 31 Jg 13.27N 22.27 E
Al Juraid 24 Mi 27.11N 49.52 E
Aljustrel 13 Dg 37.52N 8.10W
Alka 40a Db 52.15N 174.30W
Al Kaba'ish 24 Lg 30.58N 47.00 E
Al Kāf 32 Ib 36.00N 9.00 E
Al Kāf 32 Ib 36.11N 8.43 E
Alkali Lake 46 Ff 41.42N 119.50W
Al Kamāsin 23 Fe 20.25N 44.48 E
Al Kāmilīn 35 Eb 15.05N 33.11 E
Al Karak 24 Fg 31.11N 35.42 E
Al Karkh 24 Kf 33.20N 44.20 E
Al Karnak 33 Fd 25.43N 32.39 E
Al Kawah 35 Ec 13.44N 32.30 E
Al Kāẓimīyah 24 Kf 33.22N 44.20 E
Alken 12 Hd 50.52N 5.18 E
Al Khabrā' 23 Fd 26.04N 43.33 E
Al Khābūra 23 Ie 23.50N 57.18 E
Al-Khalīj al-'Arabi = Persian Gulf (EN) 21 Hg 27.00N 51.00 E
Al Khalīl 24 Fg 31.32N 35.06 E
Al Khālis 24 Kf 33.51N 44.32 E
Al Khandaq 35 Eb 18.36N 30.34 E
Al Khārijah 31 Kf 25.26N 30.33 E
Al Kharj 24 Lj 24.10N 47.30 E
Al Kharṭūm = Khartoum (EN) 35 Eb 15.50N 33.00 E
Al Kharṭūm = Khartoum (EN) 31 Kg 15.36N 32.32 E
Al Kharṭūm Baḥrī = Khartoum North (EN) 31 Kg 15.38N 32.33 E
Al Khaṣab 24 Qi 26.12N 56.15 E
Al Khaṭṭ 24 Qk 25.37N 56.01 E
Al Khawr 24 Nj 25.40N 51.30 E
Al Khidr 24 Kg 31.12N 45.33 E
Al Khubar 23 Hd 26.17N 50.12 E
Al Khufayfīyah 24 Ke 24.55N 44.42 E
Al Khums 33 Bc 31.20N 14.10 E
Al Khums 31 Ie 32.39N 14.16 E
Al Khunn 35 Ha 23.18N 49.15 E
Al Khuwayr 24 Ni 26.04N 51.05 E
Al Kidn 35 Ia 22.30N 54.00 E
Al Kilḥ Sharq 24 Ej 25.03N 32.52 E
Alkionidhon, Kólpos- 15 Fk 38.05N 23.00 E
Al Kir'ānah 24 Nj 25.00N 51.03 E
Alkmaar 11 Kb 52.37N 4.44 E
Al Kūfah 24 Kf 32.02N 44.24 E
Al Kumayt 24 Lf 32.02N 46.52 E
Al Kuntillah 33 Fc 30.00N 34.41 E
Al Kushḥ 24 Ei 26.14N 32.05 E
Al Kut 23 Gc 32.30N 45.49 E
Al Kuwayt = Kuwait (EN) 22 Gg 29.30N 47.45 E
Al Kuwayt = Kuwait (EN) 22 Gg 29.20N 47.59 E
Al Labbah 24 Ih 29.20N 41.30 E
Al Lādhiqīyah = Latakia (EN) 22 Ff 35.31N 35.07 E
Allagash River 44 Mb 47.05N 69.20W
Al Lagowa 35 Dc 11.24N 29.08 E
Allahābād 22 Kg 25.27N 81.51 E
Allah-Jun 20 Id 60.27N 134.57 E
Allah-Jun 20 Id 61.08N 137.59 E
Allahüekber DaGı 24 Jb 40.35N 42.32 E
Allakaket 40 Ic 66.34N 152.41W
Allanmyo 25 Je 19.22N 95.13 E
Allariz 13 Eb 42.11N 7.48W
All-Awash Island 51n Bb 12.55N 61.10W
Alldays 37 Dd 22.41S 29.06 E
Ålleberg 8 Ef 58.08N 13.36 E
Allegan 44 Ed 42.32N 85.51W
Allegheny Mountains 38 Lf 38.30N 80.00W
Allegheny Plateau 38 Le 41.30N 78.00W
Allegheny Reservoir 44 He 42.00N 78.56W
Allegheny River 43 Lc 40.27N 80.00W
Allègre, Pointe- 51e Ab 16.22N 61.45W
Allen 26 Hd 12.30N 124.17 E
Allen, Bog of- 9 Gh 53.20N 7.00W
Allen, Lough-/Loch Aillionn 9 Eg 54.08N 8.08W
Allendale 44 Gi 33.01N 81.19W
Allende 47 Dc 28.20N 100.51W
Allendorf (Eder) 12 Kc 51.02N 8.40 E
Allendorf (Lumda) 12 Kd 50.41N 8.50 E
Allentown 43 Lc 40.37N 75.30W
Alleppey 22 Ji 9.29N 76.19 E
Aller 10 Fd 52.57N 9.11 E
Allevard 11 Mi 45.24N 6.04 E
Allgäuer Alpen 10 Gi 47.20N 10.25 E
Alliance [Nb.-U.S.] 43 Gc 42.06N 102.52W
Alliance [Oh.-U.S.] 44 Ge 40.56N 81.06W
Allier 11 Ih 46.30N 3.00 E
Allier 5 Gf 46.57N 3.05 E
Al Līfīyah 23 Fc 30.35N 43.09 E
Al Liṣāfah 24 Li 27.37N 46.52 E
Alliston 44 Hc 44.09N 79.52W
Al Līth 23 Fe 20.09N 40.16 E
Alloa 9 Je 56.07N 3.49W
Allonnes 11 Gg 47.58N 0.09 E
Allos 11 Mj 44.14N 6.38 E
All Saints 51d Bb 17.03N 61.48W
Al Luḥayyah 23 Ff 15.43N 42.42 E
Al Luwaymī 24 Fd 27.54N 42.22 E
Alm 14 Hb 48.05N 13.55 E
Alma [Ga.-U.S.] 44 Fj 31.33N 82.28W
Alma [Mi.-U.S.] 44 Ed 43.23N 84.39W
Alma [Nb.-U.S.] 45 Gf 40.06N 99.22W
Alma [Que.-Can.] 42 Kg 48.32N 71.40W
Alma-Ata 22 Je 43.15N 76.57 E
Alma-Atinskaja Oblast 19 Hg 44.00N 77.00 E
Almada 13 Cf 38.41N 9.09W
Almadén 13 Hf 38.46N 4.50W
Al Madīnah [Iraq] 24 Lg 30.57N 47.16 E
Al Madīnah [Sau.Ar.] = Medina (EN) 22 Fg 24.28N 39.36 E
Al Madīnah al Fikrīyah 24 Di 27.56N 30.49 E
'Al Madow 35 Hc 10.59N 48.42 E
Al Mafraq 24 Gf 32.21N 36.12 E
Al Maghrib = Morocco (EN) 31 Ge 32.00N 5.50W
Almagro 13 If 38.53N 3.43W
Almagrundet 8 He 59.06N 19.00 E

Index Symbols

Independent Nation · State, Region · District, County · Municipality · Colony, Dependency · Continent · Physical Region · Historical or Cultural Region · Mount, Mountain · Volcano · Hill · Mountains, Mountain Range · Hills, Escarpment · Plateau, Upland · Pass, Gap · Plain, Lowland · Delta · Salt Flat · Valley, Canyon · Crater, Cave · Karst Features · Depression · Polder · Desert, Dunes · Forest, Woods · Heath, Steppe · Oasis · Cape, Point · Coast, Beach · Cliff · Peninsula · Isthmus · Sandbank · Island · Atoll · Rock, Reef · Islands, Archipelago · Rocks, Reefs · Coral Reef · Well, Spring · Geyser · River, Stream · Waterfall Rapids · River Mouth, Estuary · Lake · Salt Lake · Intermittent Lake · Reservoir · Swamp, Pond · Canal · Glacier · Ice Shelf, Pack Ice · Ocean · Sea · Gulf, Bay · Strait, Fjord · Lagoon · Bank · Seamount · Tablemount · Ridge · Shelf · Basin · Escarpment, Sea Scarp · Fracture · Trench, Abyss · National Park, Reserve · Point of Interest · Recreation Site · Cave, Cavern · Historic Site · Ruins · Wall, Walls · Church, Abbey · Temple · Scientific Station · Airport · Port · Lighthouse · Mine · Tunnel · Dam, Bridge

Al Maḥallah al Kubrā 33 Fc 30.58N 31.10 E
Al Maḥāriq 33 Fd 25.37N 30.39 E
Al Mahdiyah 32 Jb 35.30N 11.04 E
Al Mahdīyah [3] 32 Jb 35.35N 11.00 E
Al Maḥfid 33 Ig 14.03N 46.55 E
Al Mahrah 23 Hf 16.56N 52.15 E
Al Maḥras 32 Jc 34.32N 10.30 E
Al Majarr al Kabīr 24 Lg 31.34N 47.10 E
Almajului, Munţii- 15 Fe 44.43N 22.12 E
Al Maks al Qiblī 33 Fe 24.35N 30.38 E
Almalyk 19 Gg 40.49N 69.38 E
Al Manādir 24 Pk 23.10N 55.10 E
Al Manāmah = Manama (EN) 22 Hg 26.13N 50.35 E
Al Manāqil 35 Ec 14.15N 32.59 E
Almanor, Lake- 46 Ef 40.15N 121.08W
Almansa 13 Kf 38.52N 1.05W
Almansa, Puerto de- 13 Lf 38.49N 0.58W
Al Manshāh 33 Fd 26.28N 31.48 E
Almansor 13 Df 38.56N 8.54W
Al Manşūrah 33 Fc 31.03N 31.23 E
Al Manzilah 24 Dg 31.09N 31.56 E
Almanzor, Pico de- 13 Gd 40.15N 5.18W
Almanzora 13 Jg 37.21N 2.08W
Al Ma'qil 24 Lg 30.33N 47.48 E
Al Maqnah 24 Fh 28.24N 34.45 E
Al Maqta' 24 Pj 24.25N 54.29 E
Almar 13 Gd 40.54N 5.29W
Al Marāghah 24 Di 26.42N 31.36 E
Al Marsā 14 En 36.53N 10.20 E
Al Mary 31 Je 32.30N 20.54 E
Almaş 15 Gb 47.14N 23.19 E
Almas, Picos de- 52 Lg 13.33S 41.56W
Almas, Rio das- 54 If 14.35S 49.02W
'Al Maskād 35 Hc 11.18N 49.41 E
Al Maţarīyah 33 Fc 31.11N 32.02 E
Al Mawşil = Mosul (EN) 22 Gf 36.20N 43.08 E
Al Mayādīn 24 Ie 35.01N 40.27 E
Al Mayyāh 24 Ji 27.51N 42.47 E
Almazán 13 Jc 41.29N 2.32W
Al Mazār 24 Eg 31.23N 33.23 E
Almazny 20 Gd 62.19N 114.04 E
Almazora 13 Le 39.57N 0.03W
Al Mazra'ah 24 Fg 31.16N 35.31 E
Alme, Brilon- 12 Kc 51.27N 8.37 E
Almeida 13 Fd 41.16N 6.04W
Almeirim [Braz.] 54 Hd 1.32S 52.34W
Almeirim [Port.] 13 De 39.12N 8.38W
Al Mellem 35 Dd 9.49N 28.45 E
Almelo 11 Mb 52.21N 6.39 E
Almenara, Sierra de la- 13 Kg 37.35N 1.31W
Almendra, Embalse de- 13 Fc 41.13N 6.10W
Almendralejo 13 Ff 38.41N 6.24W
Almería [3] 13 Jg 37.10N 2.20W
Almería 6 Fh 36.50N 2.27W
Almería, Golfo de- 13 Jh 36.46N 2.30W
Almetjevsk 19 Fe 54.54N 52.20 E
Al Metlaoui 32 Ic 34.20N 8.24 E
Älmhult 7 Dh 56.33N 14.08 E
Almijara, Sierra de- 13 Ih 36.55N 3.55W
Almina, Punta- 13 Gi 35.54N 5.17W
Al Minyā [Eg.] 24 Dh 29.45N 31.18 E
Al Minyā [Eg.] 31 Kf 28.06N 30.45 E
Al Miqdādīyah 24 Kf 33.59N 44.56 E
Almirante 49 Fi 9.18N 82.24W
Almirante Brown 66 Qe 64.53S 62.53W
Almirós 15 Fj 39.11N 22.46 E
Almiroú, Órmos- 15 Hn 35.23N 24.20 E
Almodôvar 13 Dg 37.31N 8.04W
Almodóvar del Campo 13 Hf 38.43N 4.10W
Almodóvar del Rio 13 Gg 37.48N 5.01W
Almonte 13 Fg 37.15N 6.31W
Almonte 13 Fe 39.42N 6.28W
Almora 25 Fc 29.37N 79.40 E
Almoustarat 34 Fb 17.22N 0.07 E
Älmsta 8 He 59.58N 18.48 E
Al Mubarraz 23 Gd 25.25N 49.35 E
Al Mudawwarah 24 Fh 29.19N 35.59 E
Al Mudhari, Rujm- 24 Hf 32.45N 39.08 E
Al Mughayrā' [Sau.Ar.] 24 Gh 29.17N 37.41 E
Al Mughayrā' [U.A.E.] 24 Oj 24.05N 53.32 E
Al Muglad 31 Jg 11.02N 27.44 E
Al Muḥarraq 24 Ni 26.16N 50.37 E
Al Mukallā 22 Gh 14.32N 49.08 E
Al Mukhā 23 Fg 13.19N 43.15 E
Al Munastīr [3] 32 Jb 35.40N 10.50 E
Al Munastīr 32 Jb 35.47N 10.50 E
Almuñécar 13 Ih 36.43N 3.41W
Al Murabba' 24 Kj 25.43N 44.18 E
Almus 24 Gb 40.23N 36.55 E
Al Musannāh 24 Lh 29.02N 47.12 E
Al Muşawwarāt aş Şafra' 35 Eb 16.25N 33.22 E
Al Musayjīd 24 Hj 24.05N 39.06 E
Al Musayyib 24 Kf 32.47N 44.18 E
Al Mustawī 24 Kj 25.55N 44.40 E
Al Muthanna [3] 24 Kg 30.50N 45.20 E
Al Muwayh 33 He 22.45N 41.35 E
Al Muwaylih 24 Fi 27.41N 35.28 E
Alnön 8 Gb 62.25N 17.25 E
Alnwick 9 Lf 55.25N 1.42W
Ålö 8 Jd 60.20N 22.15 E
Aloândia 55 Hc 17.43S 49.29W
Alofi 58 Kf 19.03S 169.56W
Alofi, Ile- 57 Jf 14.19S 178.02W
Alofi Bay 64k Bb 19.01S 169.56W
Aloja 7 Fh 57.44N 24.59 E
Along 25 Ic 28.10N 94.46 E
Alönnisos 15 Gj 39.13N 23.55 E
Alonsa 45 Ga 50.47N 99.00W
Alonso, Rio- 55 Gg 24.05S 51.35W
Alor, Kepulauan- 26 Hh 8.15S 124.30 E
Alor, Pulau- 21 Oj 8.15S 124.45 E
Alora 13 Hh 36.48N 4.42W
Alor Setar 22 Mi 6.07N 100.22 E
Alost/Aalst 11 Kd 50.56N 4.02 E
Alotau 60 Ej 10.31S 150.43 E
Aloysius, Mount- 59 Fe 26.00S 128.34 E
Alpen = Alps (EN) 5 Gf 46.25N 10.00 E
Alpena 43 Kb 45.04N 83.26W
Alpera 13 Kf 38.58N 1.13W
Alpes = Alps (EN) 5 Gf 46.25N 10.00 E
Alpes Bernoises/Berner Alpen = Bernese Alps (EN) 14 Bd 46.25N 7.30 E
Alpes Cottiennes 14 Af 44.45N 7.00 E
Alpes de Haute-Provence [3] 11 Lj 44.10N 6.00 E
Alpes Grées/Alpi Graie 14 Be 45.30N 7.10 E
Alpes Mancelles 11 Ff 48.25N 0.10W
Alpes Maritimes 14 Bf 44.15N 7.10 E
Alpes-Maritimes [3] 11 Nk 44.00N 7.10 E
Alpes Pennines/Alpi Pennine 14 Bd 46.05N 7.50 E
Alpes Valaisannes/Walliser Alpen 14 Bd 46.10N 7.30 E
Alpha Cordillera (EN) 67 Re 85.30N 125.00W
Alphen aan der Rijn 12 Gb 52.08N 4.42 E
Alphonse Island 30 Mi 7.00S 52.45 E
Alpi = Alps (EN) 5 Gf 46.25N 10.00 E
Alpi Apuane 14 Ef 44.05N 10.20 E
Alpi Aurine 10 Hi 47.00N 11.55 E
Alpi Carniche 14 Gd 46.40N 13.00 E
Alpi Cozie 14 Af 44.45N 7.00 E
Alpi Graie/Alpes Grées 14 Be 45.30N 7.10 E
Alpi Lepontine 14 Cd 46.25N 8.40 E
Alpi Liguri 14 Cf 44.10N 8.05 E
Alpi Marittime 14 Bf 44.15N 7.10 E
Alpine [Az.-U.S.] 46 Kj 33.51N 109.09W
Alpine [Tx.-U.S.] 43 Ge 30.22N 103.40W
Alpine [Wy.-U.S.] 46 Je 43.15N 110.59W
Alpi Orobie 14 Dd 46.00N 10.00 E
Alpi Pennine/Alpes Pennines 14 Bd 46.05N 7.50 E
Alpi Retiche = Rhaetian Alps (EN) 14 Dd 46.30N 10.00 E
Alpi Ticinesi 14 Cd 46.20N 8.45 E
Alpi Venoste 10 Gj 46.45N 10.55 E
Alprech, Cap d'- 12 Dd 50.42N 1.34 E
Alps (EN) = Alpen 5 Gf 46.25N 10.00 E
Alps (EN) = Alpes 5 Gf 46.25N 10.00 E
Alps (EN) = Alpi 5 Gf 46.25N 10.00 E
Al qa 'Āmiyāt 35 Hb 18.50N 48.30 E
Al Qābil 24 Pk 23.56N 55.49 E
Al Qaḍārif 31 Kg 14.02N 35.24 E
Al Qaḍīmah 23 Ee 22.21N 39.09 E
Al Qādisīya [3] 24 Kg 31.50N 45.00 E
Al Qādisīya 24 Kg 31.42N 44.28 E
Al Qadmūs 24 Ge 35.05N 36.10 E
Al Qaffāy 24 Nj 24.35N 51.44 E
Al Qāhirah = Cairo (EN) 31 Ke 30.03N 31.15 E
Al Qāhirah-Imbabah 33 Fc 30.05N 31.13 E
Al Qāhirah-Mişr al Jadīdah 33 Fc 30.06N 31.20 E
Al Qā'iyah 24 Ki 26.27N 45.35 E
Al Qal'ah al Kubrā 14 Eo 35.52N 10.32 E
Al Qalībah 23 Ed 28.24N 37.42 E
Al Qāmishlī 23 Fb 37.02N 41.14 E
Al Qanţarah 33 Fc 30.52N 32.19 E
Al Qaryah ash Sharqīyah 33 Bc 30.24N 13.36 E
Al Qaryatayn 24 Ge 34.14N 37.14 E
Al Qaşab 24 Kj 25.18N 45.30 E
Al Qaşabāt 33 Bc 32.35N 14.03 E
Al Qa'şah 24 Ch 28.25N 28.56 E
Al Qash 35 Fb 16.48N 35.51 E
Al Qaşr 33 Ed 25.42N 28.53 E
Al Qaşrayn 32 Ib 35.11N 8.48 E
Al Qaşrayn [3] 32 Ib 35.15N 9.00 E
Al Qaţīf 24 Mi 26.33N 50.00 E
Al Qaţrānī 24 Gg 31.15N 36.03 E
Al Qaţrūn 33 Be 24.56N 14.38 E
Al Qay'īyah 23 Fe 24.18N 43.30 E
Al Qayrawān 32 Jb 35.41N 10.07 E
Al Qayrawān [3] 32 Ib 35.30N 10.00 E
Al Qayşūmah [Sau.Ar.] 24 Jh 29.11N 42.58 E
Al Qayşūmah [Sau.Ar.] 23 Gd 28.16N 46.03 E
Alqōsh 24 Jd 36.44N 43.06 E
Al Qubayyāt 24 Ge 34.34N 36.17 E
Al Qunayţirah 23 Ec 33.07N 35.49 E
Al Qunfudhah 23 Ff 19.08N 41.05 E
Al Qurayyah 24 Gh 28.45N 36.12 E
Al Qurnah 24 Lg 31.00N 47.26 E
Al Quşaymah 33 Fc 30.40N 34.22 E
Al Quşayr [Eg.] 31 Kf 26.06N 34.17 E
Al Quşayr [Syr.] 24 Ge 34.31N 36.35 E
Al Qūşīyah 33 Fd 27.26N 30.49 E
Al Quşūr 14 Co 35.54N 8.53 E
Al Quţayfah 24 Gf 33.44N 36.36 E
Al Quwārah 24 Ji 26.47N 43.28 E
Al Quwayr 24 Jd 36.03N 43.30 E
Al Quzah 35 Hb 15.06N 49.08 E
Als 8 Ci 55.00N 9.55 E
Alsace 11 Nf 48.30N 7.30 E
Alsace, Ballon d'- 11 Mg 47.50N 6.51 E
Alsasua 13 Jb 42.54N 2.10W
Alsdorf 12 Id 50.53N 6.10 E
Alsea River 46 Cd 44.26N 124.05W
Alsenz 12 Je 49.49N 7.51 E
Alsfeld 10 Ff 50.45N 9.16 E
Alsina, Laguna- 55 Am 36.52S 62.07W
Alsten 7 Cd 65.57N 12.36 E
Alsterån 8 Gh 56.55N 16.26 E
Alsunga 8 Ig 57.02N 21.28 E
Alta 7 Fb 69.58N 23.14 E
Altaelva 7 Fb 69.58N 23.23 E
Altafjorden 7 Fa 70.12N 23.06 E
Altagracia 54 Da 10.07N 71.14W
Alta Gracia 56 Hd 31.40S 64.26W
Altagracia de Orituco 50 Ch 9.52N 66.23W
Altai (EN) = Altay Shan 21 Le 46.30N 93.00 E
Altaj 22 Le 46.20N 96.17 E
Altaj 21 Kd 51.30N 90.00 E
Altajski 20 Df 51.58N 85.30 E
Altajski Kraj [3] 20 Df 52.00N 82.30 E
Altamaha River 43 Ke 31.19N 81.17W
Altamira 53 Kf 3.12S 52.12W
Altamira, Cuevas de- 13 Ha 43.23N 4.05W
Altamira, Sierra de- 13 Ge 39.35N 5.10W
Altamirano 48 Mi 16.53N 92.09W
Altamont 46 Ee 42.12N 121.44W
Altamura 14 Kj 40.49N 16.33 E
Altamura, Isla de- 48 Ee 25.00N 108.10W
Altan Bulag 27 Jc 44.19N 113.28 E
Altan-Emel → Xin Barag Youqi 27 Kb 48.41N 116.47 E
Altan Xiret → Ejin Horo Qi 27 Id 39.31N 109.45 E
Altar 48 Db 30.43N 111.44W
Altar, Desierto de- 38 Hf 31.50N 114.15W
Altar, Rio- 48 Db 30.39N 111.55W
Altar de los Sacrificios 49 Be 16.28N 90.32W
Altata 47 Cd 24.38N 107.55W
Alta Verapaz [3] 49 Bf 15.40N 90.00W
Altavista 44 Hg 37.07N 79.18W
Altay 22 Ke 47.52N 88.07 E
Altay Shan = Altai (EN) 21 Le 46.30N 93.00 E
Altdorf 14 Cd 46.53N 8.40 E
Altea 13 Lf 38.36N 0.03W
Altena 10 De 51.18N 7.40 E
Altenberge 12 Jb 52.03N 7.28 E
Altenburg 10 If 50.59N 12.27 E
Altenglan 12 Je 49.33N 7.28 E
Altenkirchen (Westerwald) 12 Jd 50.42N 7.39 E
Alter do Chão 13 Ee 39.12N 7.40W
Altevatnet 7 Eb 68.32N 19.30 E
Altındağ 24 Ec 39.56N 32.52 E
Altinoluk 15 Jj 39.34N 26.44 E
Altinova 15 Jj 39.13N 26.47 E
Altıntas 24 Dc 39.04N 30.07 E
Altinyayla 15 Mm 36.59N 29.33 E
Altkirch 11 Ng 47.37N 7.15 E
Altmark 10 Hd 52.40N 11.20 E
Altmühl 10 Hh 48.55N 11.52 E
Alto, Morro- 55 Ib 13.46S 46.50W
Alto, Pico- 54 Kd 4.20S 39.00W
Alto Alentejo 13 Ef 38.50N 7.40W
Alto Araguaia 54 Hg 17.19S 53.12W
Alto Coité 55 Eb 15.47S 54.20W
Alto Garças 55 Fc 16.56S 53.32W
Alto Longá 54 Je 5.15S 42.12W
Alto Molócuè 37 Fc 15.38S 37.42 E
Altomonte 14 Kk 39.42N 16.08 E
Alton [Eng.-U.K.] 12 Bc 51.08N 0.59W
Alton [Il.-U.S.] 43 Id 38.54N 90.10W
Altona, Hamburg- 10 Fc 53.33N 9.57 E
Altoona 43 Lc 40.32N 78.23W
Alto Paraguai 54 Gf 14.30S 56.31W
Alto Paraguay [3] 55 Ce 21.00S 59.00W
Alto Paraíso de Goiás 55 Ib 14.12S 47.38W
Alto Paraná [3] 55 Eg 25.00S 54.50W
Alto Parnaíba 54 Ie 9.06S 45.57W
Alto Purús, Rio- 54 De 9.34S 70.36W
Alto Rio Senguerr 56 Fg 45.02S 70.50W
Altos 54 Jd 5.03S 42.28W
Alto Sucuriú 55 Fd 19.19S 52.47W
Alttötting 10 Ih 48.14N 12.41 E
Alto Uruguai, Serra do- 55 Fh 27.35S 53.40W
Altun Ha 49 Ce 17.50N 88.20W
Āltūn Kūprī 24 Ke 35.45N 44.09 E
Altun Shan 21 Kf 38.00N 88.00 E
Alturas 43 Cc 41.29N 120.32W
Alturitas 49 Ki 9.45N 72.25W
Altus 43 He 34.38N 99.20W
Altynkan 18 Hd 41.03N 70.43 E
Altynkul 18 Bc 43.07N 58.55 E
Alu 63a Bb 7.05S 155.47 E
Al 'Ubaylah 35 Ia 21.59N 50.57 E
Al Ubayyiḍ 31 Kg 13.11N 30.13 E
Alucra 24 Hb 40.20N 38.46 E
Al 'Udaysāt 24 Ej 25.35N 32.29 E
Al Uḍayyah 35 Dc 12.03N 28.17 E
Alūksne/Aluksne 7 Gh 57.26N 27.01 E
Aluksne/Alūksne 7 Gh 57.26N 27.01 E
Aluksnes Ozero 8 Lg 57.22N 27.10 E
Aluksne Ozero/Alūksnes Ezers 8 Lg 57.22N 27.10 E
Alūksnes Ezers/Aluksne Ozero 8 Lg 57.22N 27.10 E
'Alūla 35 Ic 11.58N 50.48 E
Al 'Ulá 23 Ed 26.37N 37.52 E
Al Umm 33 Hf 18.18N 40.45 E
Alunda 8 Hd 60.04N 18.05 E
Alupka 19 Dg 44.24N 34.03 E
Al'Uqaylah 33 Cc 30.16N 19.12 E
Al 'Uqaylāt 14 Ii 26.43N 41.43 E
Al 'Uqayr 24 Nj 25.39N 50.13 E
Al Uqşur = Luxor (EN) 33 Fd 25.41N 32.39 E
Al Urayq 24 Hh 29.00N 39.10 E
Al Urdun = Jordan (EN) [1] 22 Ff 31.00N 36.00 E
Al 'Urūq al Mu'Tariḍah 35 Ia 21.00N 54.00 E
Ālūs 24 Ie 34.02N 42.26 E
Aluşta 19 Dg 44.42N 34.20 E
Al 'Uthmānīyah 24 Mj 25.15N 49.22 E
Al'Uwaynāt 33 Bd 25.48N 10.33 E
Al 'Uwaynidhīyah 24 Gi 26.38N 36.05 E
Al 'Uwayqīlah 24 Jg 30.21N 42.14 E
Al 'Uyūn 24 Hj 24.33N 39.35 E
Al Uzayin 24 Ke 34.02N 44.20 E
Al 'Uzayr 24 Lg 31.19N 47.25 E
Alva 43 Hd 36.48N 98.40W
Alva 13 Dd 40.18N 8.15W
Alvand, Kūh-e- 24 Me 34.41N 48.28 E
Älvängen 8 Eg 57.56N 12.09 E
Alvaro Obregón, Presa 48 Ed 28.00N 109.45W
Alvdal 7 Ce 62.07N 10.39 E
Älvdalen 8 Ed 60.30N 13.00 E
Älvdalen 7 Df 61.14N 14.02 E
Alvear 55 Di 29.06S 56.33W
Alvelos, Serra de- 13 De 39.55N 8.01W
Alvesta 7 Dh 56.54N 14.33 E
Alvik 8 Gb 62.25N 17.24 E
Älvik 7 Bf 60.26N 6.26 E
Alvin 45 Il 29.25N 95.15W
Älvkarleby 7 Df 60.34N 17.27 E
Alvord Valley 46 Fe 42.45N 118.25W
Alvøy 8 Ad 60.35N 4.50 E
Älvros 8 Fb 62.03N 14.35 E
Älvsborg [2] 7 Cg 58.00N 12.30 E
Älvsbyn 7 Ed 65.40N 21.00 E
Al Wāḥidī 23 Gg 14.20N 47.50 E
Al Wajh 22 Fg 26.14N 36.28 E
Al Wakrah 24 Nj 25.10N 51.36 E
Al Wannān 24 Mi 26.55N 48.24 E
Alwar 25 Fc 27.34N 76.36 E
Al Wari'ah 24 Li 27.50N 47.29 E
Al Wāsiţah 33 Fd 29.20N 31.12 E
Al Waslātīyah 14 Do 35.51N 9.35 E
Al Wati'ah 33 Bc 32.28N 11.46 E
Al Wazz 35 Eb 15.01N 30.10 E
Al Widyān 21 Gf 31.10N 40.45 E
Alxa Youqi (Ehen Hudag) 27 Hd 39.12N 101.40 E
Alxa Zuoqi (Bayan Hot) 27 Id 38.50N 105.32 E
Al Yaman = Yemen (EN) 22 Gh 15.00N 44.00 E
Al Yaman ad Dīmuqrāţīyah → Yemen (EN) 22 Gh 15.00N 44.00 E
Alyangula 59 Hb 13.50S 136.25 E
Alygdžer 20 Ef 53.38N 98.14 E
Alymka 17 Ng 59.01N 68.40 E
Alytus/Alitus 19 Ce 54.25N 24.08 E
Alz 10 Ih 48.10N 12.48 E
Alzamaj 20 Ee 55.33N 98.39 E
Alzey 10 Eg 49.45N 8.07 E
Alzira/Alcira 13 Le 39.09N 0.26W
Amachkalo Ahzar 34 Fb 15.30N 3.20 E
Amacuro, Rio- 54 Fb 8.32N 60.28W
Amada 33 Fe 22.45N 32.10 E
Amadeus, Lake- 57 Eg 24.50S 130.45 E
Amadi [Sud.] 35 Ed 5.31N 30.20 E
Amadi [Zaire] 36 Eb 3.35N 26.47 E
Amadjuak Lake 42 Kd 64.55N 71.00W
Amadora 13 Cf 38.45N 9.14W
Amadror 32 Ie 24.50N 6.25 E
Amadror 32 Id 26.00N 5.21W
Amagasaki 29 Dd 34.42N 135.25 E
Amager 8 Ei 55.35N 12.35 E
Amagi [Jap.] 29 Be 33.26N 130.39 E
Amagi [Jap.] 29b Bb 27.47N 128.52 E
Amagi-San 29 Fd 34.51N 139.00 E
Amaha 29 Fd 35.13N 139.51 E
Amahai 26 Ig 3.20S 128.55 E
Amain, Monts d'- 11 Gf 48.39N 0.20 E
Amajac, Rio- 48 Jg 21.15N 98.46W
Amakusa-Nada 28 Jh 32.25N 129.40 E
Amakusa-Shotō 28 Kh 32.22N 130.12 E
Amal 33 Dd 29.25N 21.10 E
Åmål 7 Cg 59.03N 12.42 E
Amalfi 14 Ij 40.38N 14.36 E
Amaliás 15 El 37.48N 21.21 E
Amalner 25 Fd 21.03N 75.04 E
Amambai 54 Gh 23.05S 55.13W
Amambai, Rio- 55 Ff 23.22S 53.56W
Amambai, Serra de- 55 Ef 23.10S 55.30W
Amambay [3] 55 Df 23.00S 56.00W
Amami Islands (EN) = Amami-Shotō 21 Og 28.16N 129.21 E
Amami-Ō-Shima 27 Mf 28.15N 129.20 E
Amami-Shotō = Amami Islands (EN) 21 Og 28.16N 129.21 E
Amān 8 Fc 61.12N 14.45 E
Amanã, Lago- 54 Fd 2.35S 64.40W
Amana, Rio- 50 Eh 9.45N 62.39W
Amanave 65c Cb 14.19S 170.49W
Amangeldy 19 Ge 50.10N 65.13 E
Amankaragaj 17 Lj 52.27N 64.08 E
Amantea 14 Kk 39.07N 16.08 E
Amanu Atoll 57 Mf 17.48S 140.46W
Amanzimtoti 37 Ef 30.05S 30.53 E
Amapá 53 Ke 2.03N 50.48W
Amapá, Territorio do- [2] 54 Hc 1.30N 52.00W
Amapala 49 Dg 13.17N 87.40W
Amara 15 Ke 44.37N 27.19 E
Amara 30 Kg 11.30N 37.45 E
Amaradia 15 Ge 44.22N 23.43 E
'Amara East 35 Ea 20.48N 30.23 E
Amarante [Braz.] 54 Je 6.14S 42.50W
Amarante [Port.] 13 Dc 41.16N 8.05W
Amaranth 45 Ga 50.36N 98.43W
Amargosa 46 Gh 36.18N 116.25W
Amargosa Desert 46 Gh 36.40N 116.30W
Amargosa Range 46 Gh 36.30N 116.45W
Amargosa River 46 Gh 36.13N 116.48W
Amarillo 39 If 35.13N 101.49W
Amárion 15 Hn 35.14N 24.39 E
Amarume 29 Fb 38.50N 139.54 E
Amasra 24 Eb 41.45N 32.34 E
Amasya 23 Ea 40.39N 35.51 E
Amathus 24 Ee 34.42N 33.08 E
Amatique, Bahia de- 49 Cf 15.55N 88.45W
Amatlán de Cañas 48 Gg 20.52N 104.27W
Amatrice 14 Hh 42.38N 13.17 E
Amaurilandia 55 Ff 22.35S 52.38W
Amay 12 Hd 50.33N 5.19 E
Amazar 20 Hf 53.54N 120.57 E
Amazon (EN) = Amazonas, Rio- (Solimões) 52 Lf 0.10S 49.00W
Amazon, Mouths of the- (EN) 52 Le 0.10S 49.00W
Amazonas [Braz.] [2] 54 Fd 5.00S 63.00W
Amazonas [Col.] [2] 54 Dd 1.00N 72.00W
Amazonas [Peru] [2] 54 Ce 5.00S 77.00W
Amazonas [Ven.] [2] 54 Ec 3.30N 66.00W
Amazonas, Rio- = Amazon (EN) 52 Lf 0.10S 49.00W
Amazonas, Rio- (Solimões) = Amazon (EN) 52 Lf 0.10S 49.00W
Amazon Cone (EN) 52 Ke 4.30N 52.00W
Amba Ferit 35 Fc 10.55N 38.55 E
Ambāla 25 Fb 30.21N 76.50 E
Ambalangoda 25 Gg 6.14N 80.03 E
Ambalavao 37 Hd 21.50S 46.57 E
Ambam 34 He 2.23N 11.17 E
Ambanja 37 Hb 13.39S 48.27 E
Ambarčik 22 Sc 69.39N 162.20 E
Ambarès-et-Lagrave 11 Fj 44.55N 0.29W
Ambargasta, Salinas de- 56 Hc 29.20S 64.30W
Ambarny 19 Db 65.54N 33.41 E
Ambasamudram 25 Fg 8.42N 77.28 E
Ambato 53 If 1.15S 78.37W
Ambato-Boéni 37 Hc 16.28S 46.40 E
Ambatofinandrahana 37 Hd 20.33S 46.47 E
Ambatolampy 37 Hc 19.23S 47.25 E
Ambatondrazaka 31 Lj 17.48S 48.26 E
Ambatosoratra 37 Hc 17.36S 48.32 E
Ambelau, Pulau- 26 Ig 3.51S 127.12 E
Amberg 10 Hg 49.27N 11.52 E
Ambergris Cay 49 Dd 18.03N 87.56W
Ambergris Cays 49 Lc 21.18N 71.37W
Ambérieu-en-Bugey 11 Li 45.57N 5.21 E
Amberley [Eng.-U.K.] 12 Bd 50.55N 0.32W
Amberley [N.Z.] 62 Ee 43.09S 172.45 E
Ambert 11 Ji 45.33N 3.45 E
Ambikāpur 25 Gd 23.07N 83.12 E
Ambila 37 Hd 21.58S 47.59 E
Ambilobe 37 Hb 13.11S 49.03 E
Ambitle 63a Aa 4.05S 153.40 E
Ambjörby 8 Ed 60.30N 13.10 E
Ambla 8 Ke 59.10N 25.44 E
Amblève 11 Ld 50.28N 5.36 E
Amblève/Amel 12 Id 50.21N 6.09 E
Ambo 54 Cf 10.07S 76.10W
Amboasary Sud 37 He 25.01S 46.23 E
Ambodifototra 37 Hc 16.58S 49.52 E
Ambohimahasoa 37 Hd 21.08S 47.12 E
Ambohimanarina 37 Hc 18.52S 47.29 E
Ambohitralanana 37 Ic 15.15S 50.28 E
Amboise 11 Gg 47.25N 0.59 E
Ambon 58 De 3.43S 128.12 E
Ambon, Pulau- 26 Ig 3.40S 128.10 E
Ambongo 37 Gc 16.50S 45.00 E
Amboseli, Lake- 36 Gc 2.37S 37.08 E
Ambositra 31 Lk 20.30S 47.14 E
Ambovombe 37 He 25.09S 46.06 E
Ambre, Cap d'- = Ambre, Cape d'- (EN) 30 Lj 11.57S 49.17 E
Ambre, Cape d'- (EN) = Ambre, Cap d'- 30 Lj 11.57S 49.17 E
Ambre, Montagne d'- 37 Hb 12.30S 49.10 E
Ambriz 31 Ii 7.50S 13.08 E
Ambrolauri 16 Mh 42.31N 43.05 E
Ambrym, Ile- 57 Hf 16.15S 168.07 E
Ambunti 60 Ch 4.14S 142.50 E
Āmbūr 25 Ff 12.47N 78.42 E
Amchitka 40a Bb 51.30N 179.00 E
Amchitka Pass 40a Cb 51.30N 179.30W
Am Dafok 35 Cc 10.28N 23.17 E
Am Dam 35 Cc 12.46N 20.29 E
Amded 32 He 22.10N 3.15 E
Amderma 19 Gb 69.45N 61.39 E
Am Djéména 35 Bc 13.06N 17.19 E
Amdo 27 Fe 32.29N 91.47 E
Ameca 47 Dd 20.33N 104.02W
Ameca, Rio- 48 Gg 20.41N 105.18W
Amel/Amblève 12 Id 50.21N 6.09 E
Ameland 12 Ha 53.26N 5.48 E
Ameland 11 La 53.25N 5.45 E
Ameland- Nes 12 Ha 53.26N 5.48 E
Amelia Island 44 Gj 30.37N 81.27W
Amélie-les-Bains-Palaloa 11 Il 42.28N 2.40 E
Amendola 14 Hh 42.59N 13.21 E
Amendolara 14 Kk 39.57N 16.35 E
'Āmerī 24 Nh 28.30N 51.05 E
Americana 55 If 22.45S 47.20W
American Falls 46 Ie 42.47N 112.51W
American Falls Reservoir 46 Ie 43.00N 113.00W
American Fork 46 Jf 40.23N 111.48W
American Highland 66 Ff 72.30S 78.00 E
American Samoa [5] 58 Kf 14.50S 170.00W
Americus 43 Ke 32.04N 84.14W
Amersfoort 11 Lb 52.09N 5.24 E
Amery Ice Shelf 66 Fe 69.30S 72.00 E
Ames 43 Ic 42.02N 93.37W
Amfilokhia 15 Ek 38.52N 21.10 E
Ámfissa 15 Fk 38.32N 22.23 E
Amfreville-la-Campagne 12 Ce 49.13N 0.57 E
Amga 20 Id 60.52N 131.50 E
Amga 21 Pc 62.40N 134.59 E
Amgalang → Xin Barag Zuoqi 27 Kb 48.13N 118.14 E
Am Géréda 35 Cc 12.52N 21.10 E
Amgu 28 Nb 45.51N 137.41 E
Amguema 20 Nc 68.03N 177.55W
Amguid 32 Id 26.30N 5.36 E
Amguid 31 Hf 26.26N 5.22 E
Amgun 21 Pd 52.56N 139.40 E
Amherst 42 Lg 45.49N 64.14W
Amherst, Mount- 59 Fc 18.11S 126.59 E
Amherst Island 44 Ic 44.12N 76.42W
Amiata, Monte- 14 Fh 42.53N 11.37 E
Amiens 6 Gf 49.54N 2.18 E
Āmij, Wādī- 24 If 33.48N 41.46 E
Amik Gölü 24 Gd 36.22N 36.17 E
Amik Oölü 24 Gd 36.15N 36.12 E
Amili 25 Jc 28.26N 95.52 E
Amindīvi Islands 25 Ef 11.23N 72.23 E
Aminuis 37 Bd 23.43S 19.21 E
'Āmir, Ra's- 30 Je 32.57N 21.43 E
Amirante Islands 30 Mi 6.00S 53.10 E
Amirante Trench (EN) 37 Bb 6.00S 52.30 E
Amisk Lake 42 Hf 54.35N 102.15W
Amistad, Presa de la- 45 Fl 28.34N 101.15W
Amistad Reservoir 43 Gf 28.34N 101.15W
Amite 45 Kk 30.44N 90.30W
Amlekhganj 25 Gc 27.17N 84.59 E
Amlia 40a Db 52.06N 173.30W
Amlwch 9 Ih 53.25N 4.20W

Index Symbols

- [1] Independent Nation
- [2] State, Region
- [3] District, County
- [4] Municipality
- [5] Colony, Dependency
- Continent
- Physical Region
- Historical or Cultural Region
- Mount, Mountain
- Volcano
- Hill
- Mountains, Mountain Range
- Hills, Escarpment
- Plateau, Upland
- Pass, Gap
- Plain, Lowland
- Delta
- Salt Flat
- Valley, Canyon
- Crater, Cave
- Karst Features
- Depression
- Polder
- Desert, Dunes
- Forest, Woods
- Heath, Steppe
- Oasis
- Cape, Point
- Coast, Beach
- Cliff
- Peninsula
- Isthmus
- Sandbank
- Island
- Atoll
- Rock, Reef
- Islands, Archipelago
- Rocks, Reefs
- Coral Reef
- Well, Spring
- Geyser
- River, Stream
- Waterfall Rapids
- River Mouth, Estuary
- Lake
- Salt Lake
- Intermittent Lake
- Reservoir
- Swamp, Pond
- Canal
- Glacier
- Ice Shelf, Pack Ice
- Ocean
- Sea
- Gulf, Bay
- Strait, Fjord
- Lagoon
- Bank
- Seamount
- Tablemount
- Ridge
- Shelf
- Basin
- Escarpment, Sea Scarp
- Fracture
- Trench, Abyss
- National Park, Reserve
- Point of Interest
- Recreation Site
- Cave, Cavern
- Historic Site
- Ruins
- Wall, Walls
- Church, Abbey
- Temple
- Scientific Station
- Airport
- Port
- Lighthouse
- Mine
- Tunnel
- Dam, Bridge

'Amm Adām 35 Fb 16.22N 36.09 E
'Ammān 22 Ff 31.57N 35.56 E
Ammanford 9 Jj 51.48N 3.59W
Ammarnäs 7 Dd 65.58N 16.12 E
Åmmeberg 8 Ff 58.52N 15.00 E
Ammer 10 Hi 47.57N 11.08 E
Ammerån 8 Ga 63.09N 16.13 E
Ammerland 10 Dc 53.15N 8.00 E
Ammersee 10 Hi 48.00N 11.08 E
Ammi-Moussa 13 Ni 35.52N 1.07 E
Ammokhostos → Famagusta (EN) 23 Dc 35.07N 33.57 E
Amnja 17 Me 63.45N 67.07 E
Amnok-kang 27 Ld 39.55N 124.20 E
Āmol 23 Hb 36.23N 52.20 E
Amolar 55 Dd 18.01S 57.30W
Amorgós 15 Im 36.50N 25.53 E
Amorgós 15 Im 36.50N 25.59 E
Amorinópolis 55 Gc 16.36S 51.08W
Amory 45 Lj 33.59N 88.29W
Amos 42 Jg 48.34N 78.07W
Amot [Nor.] 8 Be 59.35N 8.00 E
Amot [Nor.] 7 Bg 59.54N 9.54 E
Amotfors 8 Ee 59.46N 12.22 E
Amoucha 13 Rh 36.23N 5.25 E
Amouliani 15 Gi 40.20N 23.55 E
Amour, Djebel- 32 Hc 33.45N 1.45 E
Amourj 32 Ff 16.10N 7.35W
Ampanihy 37 Gd 24.40S 44.45 E
Amparafaravola 37 Hc 17.36S 48.12 E
Amparo 55 If 22.42S 46.47W
Amper 10 Hh 48.10N 11.50 E
Ampère Seamount (EN) 5 Eh 35.05N 12.13W
Amphitrite Point 46 Cb 48.56N 125.35W
Amposta 13 Md 40.43N 0.35 E
Ampthill 12 Bb 52.02N 0.29W
Ampurdán/L'Empordà 13 Ob 42.12N 2.45 E
Ampurias 13 Pb 42.10N 3.05 E
Amqui 44 Na 48.28N 67.26W
'Amrān 23 Ff 15.41N 43.55 E
Amrāvati 22 Jg 20.56N 77.45 E
Am-Raya 35 Bc 14.05N 16.30 E
Amritsar 22 Jf 31.35N 74.53 E
Amrum 8 Cj 54.40N 8.20 E
Amsaga 32 Ee 20.07N 14.10W
Amsittene, Jebel- 32 Fc 31.11N 9.40W
Amstel 12 Gb 52.22N 4.56 E
Amstelveen 12 Gb 52.18N 4.53 E
Amsterdam 30 Ol 37.57S 77.40 E
Amsterdam [Neth.] 6 Ge 52.22N 4.54 E
Amsterdam [N.Y.-U.S.] 44 Jd 42.56N 74.12W
Amsterdam-Rijnkanaal 12 Hc 51.57N 5.25 E
Amstetten 14 Ib 48.07N 14.52 E
Am Timan 31 Jg 11.02N 20.17 E
Amūd, Jabal al- 23 Ec 30.59N 39.20 E
Āmūdā 24 Id 37.05N 40.54 E
Amu-Darja 18 Ef 37.57N 65.15 E
Amudarja = Amu Darya (EN) 21 He 43.40N 59.01 E
Āmū Daryā = Amu Darya (EN) 21 He 43.40N 59.01 E
Amu Darya (EN) = Amudarja 21 He 43.40N 59.01 E
Amu Darya (EN) = Āmū Daryā 21 He 43.40N 59.01 E
Amudat 36 Fb 1.58N 34.56 E
Amukta Pass 40a Db 52.25N 172.00W
Amun 63a Ba 5.57S 154.45 E
Amund Ringnes 42 Ha 78.15N 97.00W
Amundsen Bay 66 Ee 66.55S 50.00 E
Amundsen Coast 66 Mg 85.30S 159.00W
Amundsen Glacier 66 Mg 85.35S 159.00W
Amundsen Gulf 38 Gb 71.00N 124.00W
Amundsen-Scott Station 66 Bg 90.00S 0.00
Amundsen Sea (EN) 66 Of 72.30S 112.00W
Amungen 8 Fc 61.10N 15.40 E
Amuntai 22 Nj 2.26S 115.15 E
Amur 21 Qd 52.56N 141.10 E
'Amūr, Wādī 35 Eb 18.56N 33.34 E
Amurang 26 Hf 1.11N 124.35 E
Amursk 20 If 50.16N 136.55 E
Amurskaja Oblast 20 Hf 54.00N 128.00 E
Amurzet 20 Ig 47.41N 131.07 E
Amvrakía, Gulf of- (EN) = Amvrakikós Kólpos 15 Dk 39.00N 21.00 E
Amvrakikós Kólpos = Amvrakía, Gulf of- (EN) 15 Dk 39.00N 21.00 E
Amvrosijevka 16 Kf 47.44N 38.31 E
Am Zoer 35 Cc 14.13N 21.23 E
Anaa Atoll 61 Lc 17.25S 145.30W
Anabar 64e Ba 0.29S 166.57 E
Anabar 21 Nb 73.08N 113.36 E
Anabarskoje Ploskogorje 21 Mc 70.00N 108.00 E
An Abhainn Dubh/Blackwater 9 Gh 53.39N 6.43W
An Abhainn Mhór/Blackwater [Ire.] 9 Fj 51.51N 7.50W
An Abhainn Mhór/Blackwater [N.Ire.-U.K.] 9 Gg 54.30N 6.35W
Anabuki 29 Dd 34.02N 134.11 E
Anacasti 56 Gc 28.49S 65.30W
Anaco 54 Fb 9.27N 64.28W
Anaconda 43 Eb 46.08N 112.57W
Anacortes 46 Db 48.30N 122.37W
Anadarko 45 Gi 35.04N 98.15W
Anadolu = Anatolia (EN) 21 Ff 39.00N 35.00 E
Anadyr 21 Tc 64.55N 176.05 E
Anadyr 22 Tc 64.45N 177.29 E
Anadyr Gulf (EN) = Anadyrski Zaliv 21 Uc 64.00N 179.00W
Anadyr Range (EN) = Anadyrskoje Ploskogorje 21 Tc 67.00N 174.00 E
Anadyrski Liman 20 Md 64.30N 178.00 E
Anadyrski Zaliv = Anadyr Gulf (EN) 21 Uc 64.00N 179.00W
Anadyrskoje Ploskogorje = Anadyr Range (EN) 21 Tc 67.00N 174.00 E
Anāfi 15 Im 36.22N 25.47 E
Anaghit 35 Fb 16.20N 38.39 E
Anagni 14 Hi 41.44N 13.09 E
'Ānah 23 Fc 34.28N 41.56 E
Anaheim 46 Gj 33.51N 117.57W
Anahola 65a Ba 22.09N 159.19W
Anáhuac 48 Id 27.14N 100.09W
Anahuac, Meseta de- 47 Dd 21.30N 101.00W
An Aird/Ards Peninsula 9 Hg 54.30N 5.30W
Anaj Mudi 21 Jh 10.10N 77.04 E
Anaktuvuk Pass 40 Ic 68.10N 151.50W
Analalava 37 Hb 14.38S 47.45 E
Analavelona 37 Gd 22.37S 44.10 E
Ana Maria, Golfo de- 49 Hc 21.25N 78.40W
Anambas, Kepulauan- = Ahambas Islands (EN) 21 Mi 3.00N 106.00 E
Anambas Islands (EN) = Anambas, Kepulauan- 21 Mi 3.00N 106.00 E
Anambra 34 Gd 6.30N 7.30 E
Anamé 63b De 20.08S 169.49 E
Anamizu 28 Nf 37.14N 136.54 E
Anamur 23 Db 36.06N 32.50 E
Anamur Burun 23 Db 36.03N 32.48 E
Anan [Jap.] 28 Mh 33.55N 134.39 E
Anan [Jap.] 29 Ed 35.19N 137.48 E
Anane, Djebel- 13 Mi 35.12N 0.47 E
Anánes 15 Hm 36.31N 24.08 E
Ananjev 16 Ff 47.43N 29.59 E
Anankwin 25 Je 15.41N 97.59 E
Anantapur 25 Ff 14.41N 77.36 E
Anantnāg (Islāmābād) 25 Fb 33.44N 75.09 E
Anapa 19 Dg 44.53N 37.19 E
Anapo 14 Jm 37.03N 15.16 E
Anápolis 53 Lg 16.20S 48.58W
Anapu, Rio- 54 Hd 2.15S 51.30W
Anār 23 Ic 30.53N 55.18 E
Anārak 23 Hc 33.20N 53.42 E
Anare Station 66 Jd 54.30S 158.55 E
Anaro, Rio- 49 Lj 7.48N 70.12W
Añasco 51a Ab 18.17N 67.10W
Anatahan Island 57 Fc 16.22N 145.40 E
Anatolia (EN) = Anadolu 21 Ff 39.00N 35.00 E
Anatoliki Rodhópi 15 Ih 41.44N 25.31 E
Añatuya 56 Hc 28.28S 62.50W
Anauá, Rio- 54 Fc 0.58N 61.21W
Anazarba 24 Fd 37.15N 35.45 E
An Baile Meánach/Ballymena 9 Gg 54.52N 6.17W
An Bhanna/Bann 9 Gf 55.10N 6.46W
An Bhearú/Barrow 9 Gi 52.10N 7.00W
An Bhinn Bhui/Benwee Head 9 Dg 54.21N 9.48W
An Bhograch/Boggeragh Mountains 9 Ei 52.05N 9.00W
An Bhóinn/Boyne 9 Gh 53.43N 6.15W
An Bhrosnach/Brosna 9 Fh 53.13N 7.58W
An Blascaod Mór/Great Blasket 9 Ci 52.05N 10.32W
Anbyŏn 28 Ie 39.02N 127.32 E
An Cabhán/Cavan 9 Fh 53.55N 7.30W
An Cabhán/Cavan 9 Fg 54.00N 7.21W
An Caisleán Nua/Newcastle 9 Hg 54.12N 5.54W
An Caisleán Nua/Newcastle West 9 Di 52.27N 9.03W
An Caisleán Riabhach/Castlerea 9 Eh 53.46N 8.29W
An Caoláire Rua/Killary Harbour 9 Dh 53.38N 9.55W
Ancares, Sierra de- 13 Fb 42.46N 6.54W
Ancash 54 Ce 9.30S 77.45W
Ancenis 11 Eg 47.22N 1.10W
An Chathair/Caher 9 Fi 52.22N 7.55W
An Cheacha/Caha Mountains 9 Dj 51.45N 9.45W
Anchorage 39 Ec 61.13N 149.53W
An Chorr Chriochach/Cookstown 9 Gg 54.39N 6.45W
Anci (Langfang) 27 Kd 39.29N 116.40 E
An Clár/Clare 9 Ei 52.50N 9.00W
An Cóbh/Cóbh 9 Ej 51.51N 8.17W
Ancohuma, Nevado- 54 Eg 15.51S 68.36W
Ancona 6 Hg 43.38N 13.30 E
Ancón de Sardinas, Bahía de- 54 Cc 1.30N 79.50W
Ancre 11 Ie 49.54N 2.28 E
Ancuabe 37 Fb 12.58S 39.51 E
Ancud 56 Ff 41.52S 73.50W
Ancud, Golfo de- 56 Ff 42.05S 73.00W
Anda 27 Mb 46.24N 125.20 E
Anda (Sartu) 28 Ha 46.35N 125.00 E
Andacollo [Arg.] 56 Fe 37.11S 70.41W
Andacollo [Chile] 56 Fd 30.14S 71.06W
Andahuaylas 54 Df 13.39S 73.23W
An Daingean/Dingle 9 Ci 52.08N 10.15W
Andalgalá 56 Gc 27.36S 66.19W
Åndalsnes 7 Be 62.34N 7.42 E
Andalucia = Andalusia (EN) 13 Hg 37.30N 4.30W
Andalucia = Andalusia (EN) 5 Fh 37.30N 4.30W
Andalusia 43 Je 31.19N 86.29W
Andalusia (EN) = Andalucia 13 Hg 37.30N 4.30W
Andalusia (EN) = Andalucia 5 Fh 37.30N 4.30W
Andaman and Nicobar 25 If 12.30N 92.45 E
Andaman Basin (EN) 21 Lh 10.00N 94.00 E
Andaman Islands 21 Lh 12.30N 92.43 E
Andaman Sea (EN) 21 Lh 10.00N 95.00 E
Andamooka 59 Hf 30.27S 137.12 E
'Andān, Wādī- 23 Ie 21.05N 58.23 E
Andant 55 Am 36.34S 62.07W
Andapa 37 Hb 14.38S 49.33 E
Andara 37 Cc 18.03S 21.27 E
Andelle 12 De 49.19N 1.14 E
Andenes 7 Db 69.19N 16.08 E
Andenne 12 Hd 50.29N 5.06 E
Andenne-Naméche 12 Hd 50.28N 5.00 E
Andéranboukane 34 Fb 15.26N 3.02 E
Anderlecht 12 Gd 50.50N 4.18 E
Anderlues 12 Gd 50.24N 4.16 E
Andermatt 14 Cd 46.38N 8.37 E
Andernach 10 Df 50.26N 7.24 E
Andernos-les-Bains 11 Ej 44.44N 1.06W
Anderson 42 Ec 69.42N 129.01W
Anderson [Ca.-U.S.] 46 Df 40.27N 122.18W
Anderson [In.-U.S.] 43 Jc 40.10N 85.41W
Anderson [S.C.-U.S.] 43 Ke 34.30N 82.39W
Anderstorp 8 Eg 57.17N 13.38 E
Andes (EN) = Andes, Cordillera de los- 52 Jh 20.00S 67.00W
Andes, Cordillera de los- = Andes (EN) 52 Jh 20.00S 67.00W
Andevoranto 37 Hc 18.48S 49.02 E
Andfjorden 7 Db 69.10N 16.20 E
Andhra Pradesh 25 Fe 16.00N 79.00 E
Andia, Sierra de- 13 Kb 42.45N 2.00W
Andikhásia Óri 15 Ej 39.47N 21.55 E
Andikira 15 Fk 38.23N 22.38 E
Andikithira = Andikithira (EN) 15 Gn 35.52N 23.18 E
Andikithira (EN) = Andikithira 15 Gn 35.52N 23.18 E
Andikithiron, Stenón- 15 Gn 35.45N 23.25 E
Andilamena 37 Hc 17.01S 48.32 E
Andilanatoby 37 Hc 17.56S 48.14 E
Andimeshk 24 Mf 32.27N 48.21 E
Andimilos 15 Hm 36.47N 24.14 E
Andiparos 15 Il 37.00N 25.03 E
Andipaxoi 15 Dj 39.08N 20.14 E
Andipsara 15 Ik 38.33N 25.24 E
Andir He 27 Dd 38.00N 83.36 E
Andırın 24 Gd 37.34N 36.20 E
Andirlangar 27 Dd 37.36N 83.50 E
Andirrion 15 Ek 38.20N 21.46 E
Anditilos 15 Km 36.22N 27.28 E
Andižan 22 Je 40.45N 72.22 E
Andižanskaja Oblast 19 Hg 40.45N 72.20 E
Andkhvoy 23 Kb 36.56N 65.08 E
Andŏng 27 Md 36.36N 128.44 E
Andorra (Valls d'Andorra) 6 Gg 42.30N 1.30 E
Andorra la Vella 6 Gg 42.31N 1.31 E
Andover 9 Lj 51.13N 1.28W
Andøya 7 Db 69.08N 15.54 E
Andradas 55 If 22.05S 46.35W
Andradina 56 Jb 20.54S 51.23W
Andraitx 13 Oe 39.35N 2.25 E
Andreanof Islands 38 Bd 52.00N 176.00W
Andreapol 7 Hh 56.39N 32.16 E
Andrées Land 41 Jd 73.20N 26.30W
Andrejevka [Kaz.-U.S.S.R.] 19 If 45.47N 80.35 E
Andrejevka [Ukr.-U.S.S.R.] 16 Je 49.32N 36.40 E
Andrejevo-Ivanovka 15 Nb 47.31N 30.21 E
Andrejevsk 20 Ge 58.10N 114.15 E
Andrelândia 55 Je 21.44S 44.18W
Andresito 55 Dk 33.08S 57.09W
Andrespol 10 Pe 51.43N 19.40 E
Andrews 45 Ej 32.19N 102.33W
Andria 14 Ki 41.13N 16.17 E
Andriamena 37 Hc 17.28S 47.29 E
Andriba 37 Hc 17.36S 46.53 E
Andrijevica 15 Cg 42.44N 19.48 E
Andringitra 30 Lk 22.20S 46.55 E
Andritsaina 15 El 37.29N 21.54 E
Androka 37 Gd 24.59S 44.04 E
Andropov → Rybinsk 6 Jd 58.03N 38.52 E
Ándros 5 Ih 37.50N 24.50 E
Andros 38 Lg 24.25N 78.00W
Ándros 15 Hl 37.50N 24.56 E
Androscoggin River 44 Md 43.55N 69.55W
Androssan 9 If 55.40N 4.55W
Andros Town 47 Id 24.43N 77.47W
Androth Island 25 Ef 10.50N 73.41 E
Androy 30 Lk 25.00S 45.40 E
Andruševka 16 Fe 49.59N 29.01 E
Andrychów 10 Pg 49.52N 19.21 E
Andselv 7 Eb 69.04N 18.30 E
Andudu 36 Eb 2.29N 28.41 E
Andújar 13 Hf 38.03N 4.04W
Andulo 36 Ce 11.28S 16.43 E
Andu Tan 26 Fe 7.35N 114.15 E
Anduze 11 Jj 44.03N 3.59 E
An Ea agail/Errigal 9 Ef 55.02N 8.07W
Aneby 8 Fg 57.50N 14.48 E
Anéfis 34 Fb 18.03N 0.36 E
Anegada 47 Le 18.45N 64.20W
Anegada, Bahía- 56 Hf 40.15S 62.15W
Anegada Passage 47 Le 18.30N 63.40W
Aného 34 Fd 6.14N 1.36 E
An Éirne/Erne 9 Eg 54.30N 8.15W
An Eithne/Inny 9 Fh 53.35N 7.50W
An Eoghanach/Annalee 9 Fg 54.02N 7.25W
Anet 12 Df 48.51N 1.26 E
Aneto, Pico de- 5 Gg 42.38N 0.40 E
Aney 34 Hb 19.24N 12.56 E
Aneytioum, Ile- 57 Hg 20.12S 169.49 E
An Feabhal 9 Ff 55.04N 7.15W
An Fhéil/Feale 9 Di 52.28N 9.40W
An Fheoir/Nore 9 Gi 52.25N 6.58W
Angamos, Punta- [Chile] 56 Fb 23.01S 70.32W
Angamos, Punta- [Pas.] 65d Bb 27.04S 109.17W
Angara 21 Ld 58.06N 93.00 E
Angarsk 22 Md 52.34N 103.54 E
Angarski, Pereval- 16 Ig 44.47N 34.25 E
Angarski Krjaž 20 Fe 57.30N 103.00 E
Angathonisi 15 Jl 37.28N 27.00 E
Angaur Island 57 Ed 6.54N 134.09 E
Ånge 7 De 62.31N 15.37 E
Änge 8 Fa 63.27N 14.03 E
An Gearran/Garron Point 9 Hf 55.05N 5.58W
Ángel, Cerro- 48 Hf 22.49N 102.34W
Ángel, Salto- = Angel Falls (EN) 52 Je 5.57N 62.30W
Angelburg 12 Kd 50.47N 8.25 E
Angel de la Guarda, Isla- 47 Bc 29.20N 113.25W
Angeles 26 Hc 15.09N 120.35 E
Angeles, Sierra de los- 48 Jf 23.10N 99.20W
Angel Falls (EN) = Ángel, Salto- 52 Je 5.57N 62.30W
Angel Falls (EN) = Churún Merú 52 Je 5.57N 62.30W
Ängelholm 7 Ch 56.15N 12.51 E
Angélica 55 Bj 31.33S 61.33W
Angeln 10 Fb 54.40N 9.45 E
Ängelsberg 8 Ge 59.58N 16.02 E
Anger 35 Fd 9.40N 36.06 E
Angereb 35 Fc 13.44N 36.28 E
Ångermanälven 5 Hc 62.48N 17.56 E
Angermünde 10 Jc 53.02N 14.00 E
Angers 6 Ff 47.28N 0.33W
Angkor 25 Kf 13.26N 103.52 E
Angikuni Lake 42 Hd 62.10N 99.55W
Angistrion 15 Gl 37.40N 23.20 E
Anglem, Mount- 62 Bg 46.44S 167.54 E
Anglés 13 Oc 41.57N 2.39 E
Anglesey 5 Fe 53.18N 4.20W
Anglet 11 Ek 43.29N 1.32W
Angleton 45 Il 29.10N 95.26W
Anglin 11 Gh 46.42N 0.52 E
Anglona 14 Cj 40.45N 8.45 E
Angmagssalik 67 Mc 65.45N 37.30W
Ango 36 Eb 4.02N 25.52 E
Angoche 31 Kj 16.12S 39.54 E
Angoche, Ilha- 30 Kj 16.20S 39.51 E
Angol 56 Fe 37.48S 72.43W
Angola 31 Ij 12.30S 18.30 E
Angola 44 Ee 41.38N 85.00W
Angola Basin (EN) 3 Ek 15.00S 3.00 E
Angoram 60 Ch 4.04S 144.04 E
Angostura 48 Ee 25.22N 108.11W
Angostura, Presa de la- 48 Mi 16.30N 92.30W
Angostura, Salto- 54 Dc 2.43N 70.57W
Angostura Reservoir 45 Ee 43.18N 103.27W
Angoulême 11 Gi 45.39N 0.09 E
Angoumois 11 Fi 45.30N 0.10W
Angra do Heroísmo 32 Bb 38.42N 27.15W
Angra do Heroísmo 31 Ee 38.39N 27.13W
Angra dos Reis 55 Jf 23.00S 44.18W
Angren 19 Hg 41.03N 70.10 E
Angu 36 Db 3.33N 24.28 E
Anguang 28 Gb 45.36N 123.48 E
Anguilla 39 Mh 18.15N 63.05W
Anguilla 38 Mh 18.15N 63.05W
Anguilla, Canal de l'- = Anguilla Channel (EN) 51b Ab 18.09N 63.04W
Anguilla Bank (EN) 51b Ab 18.30N 63.03W
Anguilla Cays 49 Hb 23.31N 78.33W
Anguilla Channel (EN) = Anguilla, Canal de l'- 51b Ab 18.09N 63.04W
Anguli Nur 28 Cd 41.23N 114.30 E
Anguo 28 Ce 38.25N 115.20 E
Anhanca 36 Cf 16.47S 15.33 E
Anhanguera 55 Hd 18.21S 48.17W
An Hoa 25 Le 15.46N 108.03 E
Anholt 7 Ch 56.40N 11.35 E
Anhua (Dongping) 27 Jf 28.27N 111.15 E
Anhui Sheng (An-hui Sheng) = Anhwei (EN) 27 Ke 32.00N 117.00 E
An-hui Sheng → Anhui Sheng = Anhwei (EN) 27 Ke 32.00N 117.00 E
Anhwei (EN) = Anhui Sheng (An-hui Sheng) 27 Ke 32.00N 117.00 E
Anhwei (EN) = An-hui Sheng → Anhui Sheng 27 Ke 32.00N 117.00 E
Ani 29 Gb 39.59N 140.25 E
Aniak 40 Hd 61.34N 159.30W
An Iarmhí/Westmeath 9 Fh 53.30N 7.30W
Anibare 64e Bb 0.32S 166.57 E
Anibare Bay 64e Bb 0.32S 166.57 E
Aniche 12 Fd 50.20N 3.15 E
Ánidros 15 Im 36.37N 25.41 E
Anié 34 Fd 7.45N 1.12 E
Anie, Pic d'- 11 Fl 42.57N 0.43W
Aniene 14 Gi 41.56N 12.30 E
Anijangying → Luanping 28 Dd 40.55N 117.19 E
Anikšćjaj/Anykščiai 7 Fi 55.31N 25.08 E
Animas Peak 45 Bk 31.35N 108.47W
Anina 15 Ed 45.05N 21.51 E
Anita Garibaldi 55 Gh 27.37S 51.05W
Anittepe 15 Kh 41.21N 27.42 E
Aniva 20 Jg 46.41N 142.35 E
Aniva, Zaliv- 20 Jg 46.20N 142.40 E
Anivorano Nord 37 Hb 12.43S 49.12 E
Aniwa, Ile- 57 Hf 19.16S 169.35 E
Anizy-le-Château 12 Fe 49.30N 3.27 E
Anjala 7 Gf 60.41N 26.50 E
Anji 28 Ei 30.39N 119.41 E
Anjiang → Qianyang 27 Jf 27.19N 110.13 E
Anjō 29 Ed 34.57N 137.05 E
Anjou 11 Fg 47.20N 0.30W
Anjou, Ostrova- = Anjou Islands (EN) 21 Qb 75.30N 143.00 E
Anjouan → Nzwani 30 Lj 12.15S 44.25 E
Anjou Islands (EN) = Anjou, Ostrova- 21 Qb 75.30N 143.00 E
Anjozorobe 37 Hc 18.24S 47.52 E
Anju 27 Md 39.37N 125.40 E
Anjuj 20 Ig 49.20N 136.20 E
Anjujski Hrebet 20 Lc 67.20N 166.00 E
Anjuou, Val d'- 11 Fg 47.25N 0.15W
Anka 34 Gc 12.07N 5.55 E
Ankang (Xing'an) 22 Mf 32.37N 109.03 E
Ankara 22 Ff 39.56N 32.52 E
Ankaratra 30 Lj 19.25S 47.12 E
Ankarsrum 7 Dh 57.42N 16.19 E
Ankavandra 37 Hc 18.45S 45.18 E
Ankazoabo 37 Gd 22.16S 44.30 E
Ankazobe 37 Hc 18.17S 47.05 E
Ankeny 45 Jf 41.44N 93.36W
Ankhor 35 Hc 10.47N 46.18 E
Anklam 10 Jc 53.52N 13.42 E
Ankober 35 Fd 9.40N 39.44 E
Ankoro 36 Ed 6.45S 26.57 E
Ankum 12 Jb 52.33N 7.53 E
An Laoi/Lee 9 Ej 51.55N 8.30W
Anlong 27 If 25.02N 105.30 E
An Longfort/Longford 9 Fh 53.40N 7.40W
An Longfort/Longford 9 Fh 53.44N 7.47W
An Lorgain/Lurgan 9 Gg 54.28N 6.20W
Anlu 27 Je 31.12N 113.46 E
An Mhi/Meath 9 Gh 53.35N 6.40W
An Mhuaidh/Moy 9 Dg 54.12N 9.08W
An Mhuir Cheilteach = Celtic Sea (EN) 5 Fe 51.00N 7.00W
An Muileann gCearr/Mullingar 9 Fh 53.32N 7.20W
An Muirthead/Mullet Peninsula 9 Cg 54.15N 10.04W
Ånn 7 Ce 63.15N 12.35 E
Ånn 8 Ea 63.19N 12.33 E
Ann, Cape- [Ant.] 66 Ee 66.10S 51.22 E
Ann, Cape- [Ma.-U.S.] 44 Ld 42.39N 70.38W
Anna [Il.-U.S.] 45 Lh 37.28N 89.15W
Anna [Nauru] 64e Ba 0.29S 166.56 E
Anna [R.S.F.S.R.] 19 Ee 51.29N 40.26 E
Annaba 31 He 36.54N 7.46 E
Annaba 32 Ib 35.35N 8.00 E
An Nabaṭīyah at Taḥtā 24 Gf 33.23N 35.29 E
Annaberg-Buchholz 10 If 50.34N 13.00 E
An Nabī Şāliḩ 24 Eh 28.38N 33.59 E
An Nabk 23 Ec 34.01N 36.44 E
An Nabk Abū Qaşr 24 Hg 30.21N 38.34 E
An Nafīdah 14 En 36.08N 10.23 E
An Nafūd 21 Gg 28.30N 41.00 E
An Najaf 22 Gf 31.59N 44.20 E
An Najaf 24 Kg 31.20N 44.07 E
An Nakhl 33 Fd 29.55N 33.45 E
Annalee/An Eoghanach 9 Fg 54.02N 7.25W
Annam (EN) = Trung Phan 21 Me 15.00N 108.00 E
Annamitique, Chaîne- 25 Le 17.00N 106.00 E
Annan 9 Jg 54.59N 3.16W
Annan 9 Jg 55.00N 3.16W
Anna Paulowna 12 Gb 52.52N 4.52 E
Anna Paulowna-Kleine Sluis 12 Gb 52.52N 4.52 E
Anna Point 64e Ba 0.29S 166.56 E
Annapolis 39 Lf 38.59N 76.30W
Annapolis Royal 44 Oc 44.45N 65.31W
Annapurna 21 Kg 28.34N 83.50 E
Ann Arbor 43 Kc 42.18N 83.45W
Anna Regina 50 Gi 7.16N 58.30W
An Nās/Naas 9 Gh 53.13N 6.39W
An Nashshāsh 24 Pk 23.05N 54.02 E
An Nashwah 24 Lg 30.49N 47.36 E
An Nāşirīyah 23 Gc 31.02N 46.16 E
An Nasser 24 Ej 24.36N 32.58 E
An Nawfalīyah 33 Cc 30.47N 17.50 E
Annecy 11 Mi 45.54N 6.07 E
Annecy, Lac d'- 11 Mi 45.51N 6.11 E
Annemasse 11 Mh 46.12N 6.15 E
Annevoie-Rouillon 12 Gd 50.21N 4.50 E
An Nīl 35 Ea 20.10N 33.00 E
An Nīl al Azraq 35 Ed 12.20N 34.15 E
Anning 27 Hg 24.58N 102.29 E
Anniston 43 Je 33.40N 85.50W
Annobón 30 Hi 1.32S 5.38 E
Annonay 11 Ki 45.14N 4.40 E
Annotto Bay 49 Id 18.16N 76.46W
An Nu'ayrīyah 24 Mi 27.28N 48.27 E
An Nuhūd 31 Jg 12.42N 28.26 E
An Nu' Mān 24 Fi 27.06N 35.46 E
An Nu'mānīyah 24 Kf 32.32N 45.25 E
Annweiler am Trifels 12 Je 49.12N 7.58 E
Anoia/Noya 13 Nc 41.28N 1.56 E
Anoka 45 Jd 45.11N 93.23W
An Ómaigh/Omagh 9 Fg 54.36N 7.18W
Anori 54 Fd 3.47S 61.38W
Anosyennes, Chaînes- 37 Hd 24.20S 47.00 E
Ânou Makarene 34 Gb 18.07N 7.35 E
Áno Viánnos 15 In 35.03N 25.25 E
Anóyia 15 Hn 35.15N 24.54 E
Anping [China] 28 Ce 38.13N 115.32 E
Anping [China] 28 Gd 41.10N 123.25 E
An Pointe/Warrenpoint 9 Gg 54.06N 6.15W
Anpu 27 Ig 21.30N 110.00 E
Anpu Gang 27 Ig 21.25N 109.40 E
Anqing 22 Nf 30.32N 116.59 E
Anqiu 28 Ef 36.25N 119.12 E
An Ráth/Ráth Luirc 9 Ei 52.21N 8.41W
An Ribhéar/Kenmare River 9 Dj 51.50N 9.50W
Anröchte 12 Kc 51.34N 8.20 E
Ans 12 Hd 50.39N 5.32 E
Anşāb 23 Fd 29.11N 44.43 E
Ansauvillers 12 Ee 49.34N 2.24 E
Ansbach 10 Gg 49.18N 10.35 E
An Sciobairín/Skibbereen 9 Dj 51.33N 9.15W
An Seancheann/Kinsale, Old Head of- 9 Ej 51.36N 8.32W
Anse-à-Veau 49 Kd 18.30N 73.19W
Anse-Bertrand 51e Ab 16.29N 61.31W
Anse-d'Hainault 49 Jd 18.30N 74.27W
Anse la Raye 51k Ab 13.57N 61.03W
Anshan 22 Oe 41.08N 122.59 E
Anshun 22 Mg 26.15N 105.58 E
Ansina 56 Id 31.54S 55.28W
Ansley 45 Gf 41.18N 99.23W
Anson Bay 59 Gb 13.20S 130.05 E
Ansongo 34 Fb 15.40N 0.31 E
An Srath Bán/Strabane 9 Fg 54.49N 7.27W
Anta 54 Df 13.29S 72.09W

Index Symbols

[1] Independent Nation
[2] State, Region
[3] District, County
[4] Municipality
[5] Colony, Dependency
Continent
Physical Region
Historical or Cultural Region
Mount, Mountain
Volcano
Hill
Mountains, Mountain Range
Hills, Escarpment
Plateau, Upland
Pass, Gap
Plain, Lowland
Delta
Salt Flat
Valley, Canyon
Crater, Cave
Karst Features
Depression
Polder
Desert, Dunes
Forest, Woods
Heath, Steppe
Oasis
Cape, Point
Coast, Beach
Cliff
Peninsula
Isthmus
Sandbank
Island
Atoll
Rock, Reef
Islands, Archipelago
Rocks, Reefs
Coral Reef
Well, Spring
Geyser
River, Stream
Waterfall Rapids
River Mouth, Estuary
Lake
Salt Lake
Intermittent Lake
Reservoir
Swamp, Pond
Canal
Glacier
Ice Shelf, Pack Ice
Ocean
Sea
Gulf, Bay
Strait, Fjord
Lagoon
Bank
Seamount
Tablemount
Ridge
Shelf
Basin
Escarpment, Sea Scarp
Fracture
Trench, Abyss
National Park, Reserve
Point of Interest
Recreation Site
Cave, Cavern
Historic Site
Ruins
Wall, Walls
Church, Abbey
Temple
Scientific Station
Airport
Port
Lighthouse
Mine
Tunnel
Dam, Bridge

Antabamba 54 Df 14.19S 72.55W
Antakya = Antioch (EN) 23 Eb 36.14N 36.07 E
Antalaha 31 Mj 14.55S 50.15 E
Antalya 22 Ff 36.53N 30.42 E
Antalya, Gulf of- (EN) = Antalya Körfezi 23 Db 36.30N 31.00 E
Antalya Körfezi = Antalya, Gulf of- (EN) 23 Db 36.30N 31.00 E
An Tan 25 Le 15.26N 108.39 E
Antananarivo 31 Lj 18.55S 47.30 E
Antananarivo [3] 37 Hc 19.00S 46.40 E
Antanimora 37 Hd 24.48S 45.39 E
An tAonach/Nenagh 9 Ei 52.52N 8.12W
Antarctica (EN) 66 Bg 90.00S 0.00
Antarctic Peninsula (EN) 66 Qe 69.30S 65.00W
Antas, Cachoeira das- 55 Ha 13.06S 48.09W
Antas, Rio das- 55 Gi 29.04S 51.21W
An Teampall Mór/Templemore 9 Fi 52.48N 7.50W
Antela, Laguna de- 13 Eb 42.07N 7.41W
Antelao 14 Gd 46.27N 12.16 E
Antelope Creek 46 Me 43.29N 105.23W
Anten 8 Ef 58.03N 12.30 E
Antequera [Par.] 55 Dg 24.08S 57.07W
Antequera [Sp.] 13 Hg 37.01N 4.33W
Anthony 45 Cj 32.00N 106.34W
Anti-Atlas 30 Ge 30.00N 8.30W
Antibes 11 Nk 43.35N 7.07 E
Antibes, Cap d'- 11 Nk 43.32N 7.07 E
Antica, Isla- 50 Eg 10.24N 62.43W
Anticosti, Ile d'- 38 Me 49.30N 63.00W
Antigo 45 Ld 45.09N 89.09W
Antigonish 42 Lg 45.37N 61.58W
Antigua 38 Mh 17.03N 61.48W
Antigua and Barbuda 39 Mh 17.03N 61.48W
Antigua Guatemala 47 Ff 14.34N 90.44W
Antiguo Cauce del Río Bermejo 56 Hc 25.39S 60.11W
Antiguo Morelos 48 Jf 22.30N 99.05W
Antilla 49 Jc 20.50N 75.45W
Antillas, Mar de las-/Caribe, Mar- = Caribbean Sea (EN) 38 Lh 15.00N 73.00W
Antillas Mayores = Greater Antilles (EN) 38 Lh 20.00N 74.00W
Antillas Menores = Lesser Antilles (EN) 38 Mh 15.00N 61.00W
Antilles, Mer des-/Caraïbe, Mer- = Caribbean Sea (EN) 38 Lh 15.00N 73.00W
An tInbhear Mór/Arklow 9 Gi 52.48N 6.09W
Antioch 46 Eg 38.00N 121.49W
Antioch (EN) = Antakya 23 Eb 36.14N 36.07 E
Antioche, Pertuis d'- 11 Eh 46.05N 1.20W
Antiope Reef 57 Kf 18.15S 168.40W
Antioquia [2] 54 Cb 7.00N 75.30W
Antipajëta 20 Cc 69.09N 77.00 E
Antipodes Islands 57 Ii 49.40S 178.50 E
Antiques, Pointe d'- 51e Ab 16.26N 61.33W
An t-Iúr/Newry 9 Gg 54.11N 6.20W
Antler River 45 Fb 49.08N 101.00W
Antlers 45 Ii 34.14N 95.37W
Antofagasta [2] 56 Gb 23.30S 69.00W
Antofagasta 53 Ih 23.39S 70.24W
Antofagasta de la Sierra 56 Gc 26.04S 67.25W
Antofalla, Salar de- 56 Gc 25.44S 67.45W
Antofalla, Volcán- 56 Gc 25.34S 67.55W
Antoing 12 Fd 50.34N 3.27 E
Antón 49 Gi 8.24N 80.16W
Anton Dohrn Seamount (EN) 9 Cd 57.30N 11.00W
Antongil, Baie d'- 30 Lj 15.45S 49.50 E
Antonina 56 Kc 25.27S 48.43W
Antônio João 55 Ef 23.15S 55.31W
Antonito 45 Dh 37.05N 106.00W
Antón Lizardo, Punta de- 48 Lh 19.03N 95.58W
Antony 12 Ef 48.45N 2.18 E
Antopol 10 Ud 52.12N 24.53 E
Antracit 16 Ke 48.06N 39.06 E
Antreff 12 Ld 50.52N 9.15 E
Antrim/Aontroim 9 Gg 54.43N 6.13W
Antrim Mountains 9 Gf 55.00N 6.10W
Antrodoco 14 Hh 42.25N 13.05 E
Antsakabary 37 Hc 15.03S 48.56 E
Antsalova 37 Gc 18.42S 44.33 E
Antseranana [3] 37 Hb 13.40S 49.15 E
An tSionainn/Shannon 5 Fe 52.36N 9.41W
Antsirabe 31 Lj 19.51S 47.01 E
Antsiranana 31 Lj 12.17S 49.17 E
An tSiúir/Suir 9 Gi 52.15N 7.00W
Antsla 7 Gh 57.52N 26.33 E
An tSláine/Slaney 9 Gi 52.21N 6.30W
Antsohihy 31 Lj 14.52S 47.58 E
An tSuca/Suck 9 Eh 53.16N 8.03W
Anttola 8 Lc 61.35N 27.39 E
Antu (Songjiang) 28 Jc 42.33N 128.20 E
An Tuc 25 Lf 13.57N 108.39 E
Antufash, Jazirat- 33 Hf 15.42N 42.25 E
An Tulach/Tullow 9 Gi 52.48N 6.44W
An Tulach Mhór/Tullamore 9 Fh 53.16N 7.30W
Antwerp (EN) = Antwerpen/Anvers 6 Ge 50.38N 5.34 E
Antwerp (EN) = Anvers/Antwerpen 6 Ge 50.38N 5.34 E
Antwerpen [3] 12 Gc 51.10N 4.30 E
Antwerpen/Anvers = Antwerp (EN) 6 Ge 50.38N 5.34 E
Antwerpen-Ekeren 11 Kc 51.17N 4.25 E
Antwerpen-Hoboken 12 Gc 51.10N 4.21 E
Antwerpen-Merksem 12 Gc 51.15N 4.27 E
Antykan 20 If 54.55N 135.13 E
An Uaimh/Navan 9 Gh 53.39N 6.41W
Anuradhapura 25 Gg 8.21N 80.23 E
Anuta Island 57 Hf 11.38S 169.50 E
Anvers/Antwerpen = Antwerp (EN) 6 Ge 50.38N 5.34 E
Anvers Island 66 Qe 64.33S 63.35W
Anvik 40 Gd 62.40N 160.12W
Anxi 22 Le 40.30N 96.00 E
Anxiang 27 Jf 29.26N 112.11 E
Anxin 28 Ce 38.55N 115.56 E
Anxious Bay 59 Gf 33.25S 134.35 E
Anyang (Zhangde) 22 Nf 36.01N 114.25 E
A'nyêmaqen Shan 21 Lf 34.30N 100.00 E
Anyi 28 Cj 28.50N 115.31 E
Anykščiai/Anikščjaj 7 Fi 55.31N 25.08 E
Anyva, Mys- 20 Jg 46.00N 143.25 E
Anza 14 Ce 46.00N 8.17 E
Anze 28 Bf 36.09N 112.14 E
Anzegem 12 Fd 50.50N 3.28 E
Anžero-Sudžensk 22 Kd 56.07N 86.00 E
Anzi 36 Dc 0.52S 23.24 E
Anzio 14 Gi 41.27N 12.37 E
Anzoátegui [2] 54 Fb 9.00N 64.30W
Anzob, Pereval- 18 Ge 39.07N 68.53 E
Aoba, Ile- 61 Cc 15.25S 167.50 E
Ao Ban Don 25 Jg 9.20N 99.25 E
Aoga-Shima 27 Oe 32.30N 139.50 E
Aohan Qi (Xinhui) 28 Ec 42.18N 119.53 E
Aoiz 13 Kb 42.47N 1.22W
Aoji 28 Kc 42.31N 130.24 E
Aola 63a Ec 9.32S 160.29 E
Aomen/Macau = Macao (EN) [5] 22 Ng 22.10N 113.33 E
Aomen/Macau = Macao (EN) 27 Jg 22.12N 113.33 E
Aomori 22 Qe 40.49N 140.45 E
Aomori Ken [2] 28 Pd 40.40N 140.40 E
Aono-Yama 29 Bd 34.27N 131.48 E
Aontroim/Antrim 9 Gg 54.43N 6.13W
Aopo 65c Aa 13.29S 172.30W
Aôral, Phnum- 25 Kf 12.02N 104.10 E
Aoré 63b Cb 15.35S 167.10 E
Aosta / Aoste 14 Be 45.44N 7.20 E
Aosta, Val d'- 14 Be 45.45N 7.20 E
Aoste / Aosta 14 Be 45.44N 7.20 E
Aouk, Bahr- 30 Ih 8.51N 18.53 E
Aoukalé 35 Cd 9.10N 20.30 E
Aoukâr [Afr.] 32 Ge 24.00N 2.30W
Aoukâr [Mtna.] 30 Gg 17.30N 9.30W
Aoulef 32 Hd 26.58N 1.05 E
Aoumou 63b Be 21.24S 165.49 E
Aourou 34 Cc 14.28N 11.34W
Aoya 29 Cd 35.32N 133.59 E
Aozou 31 If 21.49N 17.25 E
Apa, Rio- 56 Ib 22.06S 58.00W
Apača 20 Kf 52.50N 157.10 E
Apache 46 Kh 31.44N 109.07W
Apache Junction 46 Jj 33.26N 111.32W
Apahida 15 Gc 46.49N 23.45 E
Apakho 63c Bb 11.25S 166.32 E
Apalachee Bay 38 Kg 29.30N 84.00W
Apalachicola 44 Ek 29.44N 84.59W
Apalachicola River 44 Ek 29.44N 84.59W
Apan 48 Jh 19.43N 98.25W
Apaporis, Rio- 52 Jf 1.23S 69.25W
Aparecida do Taboado 54 Hg 20.05S 51.05W
Aparri 22 Oh 18.22N 121.39 E
Apataki Atoll 57 Mf 15.26S 146.20W
Apatin 15 Bd 45.40N 18.59 E
Apatity 6 Jb 67.34N 33.18 E
Apatzingán de la Constitucion 47 De 19.05N 102.21W
Apaxtla de Castrejón 48 Jh 18.09N 99.52W
Ape 7 Gh 57.32N 26.42 E
Apeldoorn 11 Lb 52.13N 5.58 E
Apeldoorn-Nieuw Milligen 12 Hb 52.14N 5.45 E
Apen 12 Ja 53.13N 7.48 E
Apennines (EN) = Appennini 5 Hg 43.00N 13.00 E
Apere, Rio- 54 Ef 13.44S 65.18W
Aphrodisias 24 Cd 37.45N 28.40 E
Api 21 Kf 30.00N 80.57 E
Api 36 Eb 3.40N 25.26 E
Apia 58 Jf 13.50S 171.44W
Apiacás, Serra dos- 54 Gf 10.15S 57.15W
Apio 63a Ec 9.39S 161.23 E
Apipé Grande, Isla- 55 Di 27.30S 56.54W
Apizaco 48 Jh 19.25N 98.09W
Aplao 54 Dg 16.05S 72.31W
Apo, Mount- 21 Oi 6.59N 125.16 E
Apodi 54 Ke 5.39S 37.48W
Apolda 10 He 51.01N 11.30 E
Apolima 65c Aa 13.49S 172.07W
Apolima Strait 65c Aa 13.50S 172.10W
Apollo Bay 59 Ig 38.45S 143.40 E
Apollonia [Alb.] 15 Ci 40.43N 19.27 E
Apollonia [Lib.] 33 Dc 32.54N 21.58 E
Apolo 54 Ef 14.43S 68.31W
Apón, Rio- 49 Kh 10.06N 72.23W
Apopka, Lake- 44 Gk 28.37N 81.38W
Aporé 55 Fd 18.58S 52.01W
Aporé, Rio- 52 Kg 19.27S 50.57W
Apostle Islands 43 Ib 46.50N 90.30W
Apostoles 56 Ic 27.55S 55.46W
Apostolovo 16 Hf 47.39N 33.43 E
Apoteri 54 Gc 4.02N 58.34W
Apôtres, Iles des- 30 Mm 45.40S 50.20 E
Appalachia 44 Fg 36.54N 82.48W
Appalachian Mountains 38 Lc 41.00N 77.00W
Äppelbo 8 Ed 60.30N 14.00 E
Appennini = Apennines (EN) 5 Hg 43.00N 13.00 E
Appennino Abruzzese 14 Hh 42.00N 13.55 E
Appennino Calabro 14 Kl 39.00N 16.30 E
Appennino Campano 14 Ii 40.50N 14.45 E
Appennino Ligure 14 Cf 44.30N 9.00 E
Appennino Lucano 14 Jj 40.30N 16.00 E
Appennino Tosco-Emiliano 14 Fg 44.00N 11.30 E
Appennino Umbro-Marchigiano 14 Gg 43.20N 12.55 E
Appenzell 14 Dc 47.20N 9.25 E
Appenzell Ausser-Rhoden [2] 14 Dc 47.20N 9.20 E
Appenzell Inner-Rhoden [2] 14 Dc 47.15N 9.25 E
Appingedam 12 Ia 53.19N 6.52 E
Appleby 9 Kg 54.36N 2.29W
Appleton 43 Jc 44.16N 88.25W
Appomattox 44 Hg 37.21N 78.51W
Apra Harbor 64c Bb 13.27N 144.38 E
Apricena 14 Ji 41.47N 15.27 E
Aprilia 14 Gi 41.36N 12.39 E
Apšeronsk 19 Dg 44.27N 39.44 E
Apšeronski Poluostrov = Apsheron Peninsula (EN) 5 Lg 41.00N 50.50 E
Apsheron Peninsula (EN) = Apšeronski Poluostrov 5 Lg 41.00N 50.50 E
Apt 11 Lk 43.53N 5.24 E
Apucarana 56 Jb 23.33S 51.29W
Apucarana, Serra da- 55 Gf 23.50S 51.20W
Apuka 20 Ld 60.23N 169.45 E
Apuka 20 Ld 60.25N 169.35 E
Apulia (EN) = Puglia [2] 14 Ki 41.15N 16.15 E
Apurashokoru 64a Ac 7.17N 134.18 E
Apure [2] 54 Eb 7.10N 68.50W
Apure, Rio- 52 Je 7.37N 66.25W
Apurimac [2] 54 Df 14.00S 73.00W
Apurimac, Rio- 52 Ig 12.17S 73.56W
Apurito 50 Bi 7.56N 68.27W
Apuseni, Munţii- = Apuseni Mountains (EN) 5 If 46.30N 22.30 E
Apuseni Mountains (EN) = Apuseni, Munţii- 5 If 46.30N 22.30 E
Āq 24 Kc 38.59N 45.27 E
Āqā 24 Me 35.00N 47.00 E
Aqaba (EN) = Al 'Aqabah 23 Dd 29.31N 35.00 E
Aqaba, Gulf of- (EN) = 'Aqabah, Khalīj al- 30 Kf 29.00N 34.40 E
Āqā Bāba 24 Md 36.20N 49.46 E
'Aqabah, Khalīj al- = Aqaba, Gulf of- (EN) 30 Kf 29.00N 34.40 E
Āqcheh 23 Kb 36.56N 66.11 E
'Aqdā 24 Of 32.26N 53.37 E
'Aqiq 35 Fb 18.14N 38.12 E
Aqitag 27 Fc 41.49N 90.38 E
Āqotāq 24 Ld 37.10N 47.05 E
Āq Qal'eh 24 Pd 37.01N 54.30 E
Aqqikkol Hu 27 Ed 37.00N 88.20 E
'Aqrah 24 Jd 36.45N 43.54 E
'Aqrin, Jabal- 24 Hg 31.32N 38.18 E
Āq Şū 24 Ke 34.35N 44.31 E
Aquidabã, Rio- 55 De 20.58S 57.50W
Aquidabán, Rio- 55 Df 23.11S 57.32W
Aquidauana 54 Gh 20.28S 55.48W
Aquidauana, Rio- 54 Gg 19.44S 56.50W
Aquidauana, Serra de- 55 Ee 20.50S 55.30W
Aquiles Serdán 48 Gc 28.36N 105.53W
Aquin 49 Kd 18.16N 73.24W
Aquitaine, Bassin d'- = Aquitaine Basin (EN) 5 Fg 44.00N 0.10W
Aquitaine Basin (EN) = Aquitaine, Bassin d'- 5 Fg 44.00N 0.10W
Ara 13 Mb 42.25N 0.09 E
'Arab, Baḩr al- 30 Jh 9.02N 29.28 E
'Arab, Khalīj al- 33 Ec 30.55N 29.05 E
'Arab, Shaţţ al- 21 Gf 30.28N 47.59 E
'Arabah, Wādī- 24 Eh 29.07N 32.39 E
'Arabah, Wādī al- 24 Fg 30.58N 32.24 E
Arabatskaja Strelka, Kosa- 16 Ig 45.40N 35.05 E
'Arabestān 24 Mg 30.30N 50.00 E
Arabian Basin (EN) 3 Gh 11.30N 65.00 E
Arabian Desert (EN) = Sharqīyah, Aş Şaḩrā' ash- 30 Kf 28.00N 32.00 E
Arabian Peninsula (EN) 21 Gg 25.00N 45.00 E
Arabian Sea (EN) 21 Ih 15.00N 65.00 E
Araç 24 Eb 41.15N 33.21 E
Aracá, Rio- 54 Fd 0.25S 62.55W
Aracaju 53 Mg 10.55S 37.04W
Aracataca 49 Jh 10.35N 74.13W
Aracati 54 Kd 4.34S 37.46W
Araçatuba 53 Kh 21.12S 50.25W
Aracena 13 Fg 37.53N 6.33W
Aracena, Sierra de- 13 Fg 37.56N 6.50W
Aracides, Cape- 63a Ec 8.39S 161.01 E
Aracruz 54 Jg 19.49S 40.16W
Araçuai 54 Jg 16.52S 42.04W
Arad 6 If 46.11N 21.19 E
'Arad 24 Fg 31.15N 35.13 E
Arad [2] 15 Ec 46.11N 21.25 E
Arada 35 Cb 15.01N 20.40 E
'Arādah 35 Ia 22.59N 53.26 E
Arafali 35 Fb 15.04N 39.45 E
Ara Fana 35 Gd 6.01N 41.11 E
Arafune-Yama 29 Fc 36.12N 138.38 E
Arafura, Laut- = Arafura Sea (EN) 57 Ee 9.00S 133.00 E
Arafura, Sea (EN) = Arafura, Laut- 57 Ee 9.00S 133.00 E
Aragac, Gora- 5 Kg 40.31N 44.10 E
Aragarças 53 Kg 15.55S 52.15W
Aragón 13 Kb 42.13N 1.44W
Aragón 5 Fg 41.00N 1.00W
Aragón 13 Lc 41.00N 1.00W
Aragona 14 Hm 37.24N 13.37 E
Aragua [2] 54 Eb 10.00N 67.10W
Araguacema 54 Ie 8.50S 49.34W
Aragua de Barcelona 50 Dh 9.28N 64.49W
Aragua de Maturín 50 Eh 9.58N 63.29W
Araguaia, Rio- 52 Lf 5.21S 48.41W
Araguaiana 55 Gb 16.49S 53.05W
Araguaina 54 Ie 7.12S 48.12W
Araguao, Boca- 54 Fb 9.17N 60.48W
Araguao, Caño- 50 Fh 9.15N 60.50W
Araguapiche, Punta- 50 Fh 9.29N 60.56W
Araguari 54 Ig 18.38S 48.11W
Araguari, Rio- [Braz.] 52 Le 1.15N 49.55W
Araguari, Rio- [Braz.] 55 Hd 18.21S 48.40W
Araguatins 54 Ie 5.38S 48.07W
'Arāguib 32 Ff 18.50N 7.45W
Aragvi 16 Ni 41.50N 44.43 E
Arai 28 Of 37.09N 138.06 E
Arainn/Inishmore 9 Dh 53.07N 9.45W
Árainn Mhór/Aran Island 9 Ef 55.00N 8.30W
Araioses 54 Jd 2.53S 41.55W
Arāk 22 Gf 34.05N 49.41 E
Arak 32 Hd 25.18N 3.45 E
Arakabesan 64a Ac 7.21N 134.27 E
Arakan [2] 25 Ie 19.00N 94.15 E
Arakan Yoma 21 Lh 19.00N 94.40 E
Arakawa 29 Fb 38.09N 139.25 E
Ara-Kawa [Jap.] 29 Fb 38.09N 139.23 E
Ara-Kawa [Jap.] 29 Fc 37.11N 138.15 E
Arakhthos 15 Ej 39.01N 21.03 E
Araks 21 Gf 39.56N 48.20 E
Aral [China] 27 Dc 40.38N 81.24 E
Aral [Kirg.-U.S.S.R.] 19 Hg 41.48N 74.25 E
Aral Sea (EN) = Aralskoje More 21 He 45.00N 60.00 E
Aralsk 22 Ie 46.48N 61.40 E
Aralskoje More = Aral Sea (EN) 21 He 45.00N 60.00 E
Aralsor, Ozero- 16 Pe 49.05N 48.15 E
Aralsulfat 19 Gf 46.50N 61.59 E
Aramac 59 Jd 22.59S 145.14 E
Arambaré 55 Gj 30.55S 51.29W
Arān 24 Ne 34.03N 51.30 E
Aranda de Duero 13 Ic 41.41N 3.41W
Arandelovac 15 De 44.18N 20.35 E
Arandilla 13 Ic 41.40N 3.41W
Aran Island/Arainn Mhór 9 Dh 53.07N 9.45W
Aran Islands 9 Ef 55.00N 8.30W
Aranjuez 13 Id 40.02N 3.36W
Aranos 37 Bd 24.09S 19.09 E
Arañuelo, Campo- 13 Ge 39.55N 5.30W
Aranuka Atoll 57 Id 0.11N 173.36 E
Arao 29 Be 32.59N 130.27 E
Araouane 31 Gg 18.53N 3.35W
Arapahoe 45 Gf 40.18N 99.54W
Arapey Grande, Rio- 55 Dj 30.55S 57.49W
Arapiraca 54 Ke 9.45S 36.39W
Arápis, Ákra- 15 Gi 40.27N 24.00 E
Arapkir 24 Hc 39.03N 38.30 E
Arapoim, Rio- 55 Kb 15.45S 43.39W
Arapongas 56 Jb 23.23S 51.27W
Arapoti 55 Hg 24.08S 49.50W
'Ar'ar 24 Ig 30.59N 41.02 E
'Ar'ar, Wādī 24 Jg 31.23N 42.26 E
Araranguá 56 Kc 28.56S 49.29W
Araraquara 53 Lh 21.47S 48.10W
Araras 55 If 22.22S 47.23W
Araras, Açude- 54 Jd 4.20S 40.30W
Araras, Serra das- 55 Fd 18.45S 53.30W
Ararat [Arm.-U.S.S.R.] 19 Eh 39.50N 44.43 E
Ararat [Austl.] 59 Ig 37.17S 142.56 E
Ararat, Mount- (EN) = Büyük Ağri Daği 21 Gf 39.40N 44.24 E
Arari 54 Jd 3.28S 44.47W
Arari, Lago- 54 Id 0.37S 49.07W
Aras 21 Gf 39.56N 48.20 E
Aras Dağları 24 Jc 40.00N 43.00 E
Aratika Atoll 57 Mf 15.32S 145.32W
Aratürük/Yiwu 27 Fc 43.15N 94.35 E
Arauca [2] 54 Db 6.30N 71.00W
Arauca 54 Db 7.03N 70.47W
Arauca, Rio- 52 Je 7.24N 66.35W
Araucania [2] 56 Fe 37.50S 73.15W
Arauco 56 Fe 37.15S 73.19W
Araure 50 Bh 9.38N 69.15W
Aravaca, Madrid- 13 Id 40.27N 3.47W
Aravis 11 Mi 45.53N 6.28 E
Arawalli Range 21 Jg 25.00N 73.30 E
Araxá 54 Ig 19.35S 46.55W
Araxos, Ákra- 15 Ek 38.10N 21.23 E
Araya 50 Dg 10.34N 64.15W
Araya, Peninsula de- 54 Fa 10.35N 64.00W
Arba 13 Kc 41.52N 1.18W
Arba'āt 35 Fb 19.50N 37.03 E
Arba'īn, Darb al- 24 Di 26.40N 30.50 E
Arbaj-Here 27 Hb 46.15N 102.48 E
Arba Minch 31 Kh 5.59N 37.38 E
'Arbat 24 Ke 35.25N 45.35 E
Arbatax 14 Dk 39.56N 9.42 E
Arboga 7 Dg 59.24N 15.50 E
Arbogaån 8 Ge 59.26N 16.04 E
Arbois 11 Lh 46.54N 5.46 E
Arboletes 49 Ii 8.52N 76.25W
Arbolito 55 Ek 32.39S 54.15W
Arbon 14 Dc 47.30N 9.25 E
Arbore 15 Ib 47.44N 25.56 E
Arborea 14 Ck 39.46N 8.35 E
Arborea 14 Ck 39.50N 8.50 E
Arborg 45 Ha 50.55N 97.15W
Arbrå 7 Dc 61.29N 16.23 E
Arbroath 9 Ke 56.34N 2.35W
Arbus 14 Ck 39.32N 8.36 E
Arc [Fr.] 11 Mi 45.34N 6.12 E
Arc [Fr.] 11 Lk 43.31N 5.07 E
Arcachon 11 Ej 44.39N 1.10W
Arcachon, Bassin d'- 11 Ej 44.42N 1.09W
Arcadia [Fl.-U.S.] 44 Gl 27.14N 81.52W
Arcadia [La.-U.S.] 45 Jj 32.33N 92.55W
Arcagly-Ajat 17 Jj 53.00N 61.50 E
Arcas, Cayos- 47 Fd 20.12N 91.58W
Arcata 46 Cf 40.52N 124.05W
Arcelia 48 Ih 18.17N 100.16W
Arcen, Areen en Velden- 12 Ic 51.28N 6.11 E
Arcevia 14 Gg 43.30N 12.56 E
Archangel (EN) = Arhangelsk 6 Kc 64.34N 40.32 E
Archaringa Creek 59 He 28.15S 135.15 E
Archer River 59 Ib 13.28S 141.41 E
Archer's Post 36 Gb 0.39N 37.41 E
Archidona 13 Hg 37.05N 4.23W
Arcidosso 14 Fh 42.52N 11.33 E
Arcipelago Campano 5 Hg 40.30N 13.20 E
Arcipelago Toscano = Tuscan Archipelago (EN) 5 Hg 42.45N 10.20 E
Arcis-sur-Aube 11 Kf 48.32N 4.08 E
Arciz 16 Fg 45.59N 29.27 E
Arco [Id.-U.S.] 46 Ie 43.38N 113.18W
Arco [It.] 14 Ee 45.55N 10.53 E
Arconce 11 Jh 46.27N 4.00 E
Arcos 55 Je 20.17S 45.32W
Arcos de Jalón 13 Jc 41.13N 2.16W
Arcos de la Frontera 13 Gh 36.45N 5.48W
Arcos de Valdevez 13 Dc 41.51N 8.25W
Arcoverde 53 Mf 8.25S 37.04W
Arctic Bay 39 Kb 73.02N 85.11W
Arctic Ocean 67 Be 85.00N 170.00 E
Arctic Ocean (EN) = Ishavet 67 Be 85.00N 170.00 E
Arctic Ocean (EN) = Severny Ledovity Okean 67 Be 85.00N 170.00 E
Arctic Red River 42 Ec 67.27N 133.45W
Arctic Red River 42 Ec 67.22N 133.30W
Arctic Village 40 Jc 68.08N 145.19W
Arda [Eur.] 15 Jh 41.39N 26.29 E
Arda [It.] 14 Ee 45.02N 10.02 E
Ardabīl [Iran] 22 Gf 38.15N 48.18 E
Ardabīl [Iraq] 24 Ie 34.24N 40.59 E
Ardahan 24 Jb 41.07N 42.41 E
Ardakāh 23 Hc 32.19N 53.59 E
Ardakān 24 Og 30.16N 52.01 E
Ardal 24 Ng 31.59N 50.39 E
Ardales 13 Hh 36.52N 4.51W
Årdalsfjorden 8 Bc 61.15N 7.30 E
Årdalstangen 7 Bf 61.14N 7.43 E
Ardanuç 24 Jb 41.08N 42.03 E
Ardatov [R.S.F.S.R.] 7 Ki 55.17N 43.12 E
Ardatov [R.S.F.S.R.] 7 Li 54.53N 46.13 E
'Arde 35 Hd 9.58N 46.04 E
Ardèche 11 Kj 44.16N 4.39 E
Ardèche [3] 11 Kj 44.40N 4.20 E
Ardee/Béal Átha Fhirdhia 9 Gh 53.52N 6.33W
Ardencaple Fjord 41 Jd 75.15N 20.10W
Ardenne, Plateau de l'-/Ardennen, Plateau van der- = Ardennes (EN) 5 Ge 50.10N 5.45 E
Ardennen, Plateau van der-/Ardenne, Plateau de l'- = Ardennes (EN) 5 Ge 50.10N 5.45 E
Ardennes [3] 11 Ke 49.40N 4.40 E
Ardennes (EN) = Ardenne, Plateau de l'-/Ardennen, Plateau van der- 5 Ge 50.10N 5.45 E
Ardennes (EN) = Ardennen, Plateau van der-/Ardenne, Plateau de l'- 5 Ge 50.10N 5.45 E
Ardennes, Canal des- 11 Ke 49.26N 4.02 E
Ardennes, Forêt des- 12 Ge 49.48N 4.50 E
Ardentes 11 Hh 46.45N 1.50 E
Ardeşen 24 Ib 41.12N 41.00 E
Ardestān 24 Of 33.22N 52.23 E
Ardhas 15 Jh 41.39N 26.29 E
Ardila 13 Ef 38.12N 7.28W
Ard Mhacha/Armagh 9 Gg 54.21N 6.39W
Ardmore 43 He 34.10N 97.08W
Ardnamurchan, Point of- 9 Ge 56.45N 6.30W
Ardon 16 Nh 43.07N 44.13 E
Ardooie 12 Fd 50.59N 3.12 E
Ardre 12 Fe 49.18N 3.40 E
Ardres 12 Dd 50.51N 1.59 E
Ards Peninsula/An Aird 9 Hg 54.30N 5.30W
Ar Dub'al Khālī 21 Hg 21.00N 51.00 E
Ardud 15 Fb 47.38N 22.53 E
Arebi 36 Eb 2.50N 29.38 E
Arecibo 47 Ke 18.28N 66.43W
Areen en Valden 12 Ic 51.28N 6.11 E
Areen en Velden-Arcen 12 Ic 51.28N 6.11 E
Arėgala/Ariogala 8 Ji 55.13N 23.30 E
Areia, Ribeirão da- 55 Jc 16.07S 45.52W
Areia Branca 54 Kd 4.57S 37.08W
Arekalong Peninsula 64a Bb 7.40N 134.38 E
Aremberg 12 Id 50.25N 6.49 E
Arena 26 He 9.14N 120.46 E
Arena, Point- 43 Cd 38.57N 123.44W
Arena, Punta- 47 Cd 23.30N 109.30W
Arena de la Ventana, Punta- 47 Cd 24.04N 109.52W
Arenápolis 54 Gf 14.26S 56.49W
Arenas, Cayo- 47 Fd 22.08N 91.24W
Arenas, Punta de- 56 Gh 53.09S 68.13W
Arenas de San Pedro 13 Gd 40.12N 5.05W
Arenberg 12 Jb 52.42N 7.20 E
Arendal 7 Bg 58.27N 8.48 E
Arendonk 12 Hc 51.19N 5.05 E
Arenys de Mar/Arenys de Mar 13 Oc 41.35N 2.33 E
Arenys de Mar/Arénys de Mar 13 Oc 41.35N 2.33 E
Areópolis 15 Fm 36.40N 22.23 E
Areq, Sebkha bou- 13 Ji 35.10N 2.45W
Arequipa 53 Ig 16.24S 71.33W
Arequipa [2] 54 Dg 16.00S 72.30W
Arequito 55 Bk 33.09S 61.28W
Arero 35 Fe 4.44N 38.50 E
Ares, Muela de- 13 Ld 40.28N 0.07W
Areskutan 8 Ea 63.26N 13.06 E
Åreskutan 7 Ce 63.24N 13.06 E
Arévalo 13 Hc 41.04N 4.43W
Arezzo 14 Fg 43.25N 11.53 E
Arga 13 Kb 42.18N 1.47W
Argajas 17 Ji 55.31N 60.55 E
Argamasilla de Alba 13 Ie 39.07N 3.06W
Argan 27 Ec 40.09N 88.22 E
Arganda 13 Id 40.18N 3.26W
Arga-Sala 20 Gc 68.37N 112.05 E
Argelès-Gazost 11 Fk 43.01N 0.06W
Argelès-sur-Mer 11 Jl 42.33N 3.01 E
Argens 11 Mk 43.24N 6.44 E

Index Symbols

[1] Independent Nation
[2] State, Region
[3] District, County
[4] Municipality
[5] Colony, Dependency
Continent
Physical Region
Historical or Cultural Region
Mount, Mountain
Volcano
Hill
Mountains, Mountain Range
Hills, Escarpment
Plateau, Upland
Pass, Gap
Plain, Lowland
Delta
Salt Flat
Valley, Canyon
Crater, Cave
Karst Features
Depression
Polder
Desert, Dunes
Forest, Woods
Heath, Steppe
Oasis
Cape, Point
Coast, Beach
Cliff
Peninsula
Isthmus
Sandbank
Island
Atoll
Rock, Reef
Islands, Archipelago
Rocks, Reefs
Coral Reef
Well, Spring
Geyser
River, Stream
Waterfall Rapids
River Mouth, Estuary
Lake
Salt Lake
Intermittent Lake
Reservoir
Swamp, Pond
Canal
Glacier
Ice Shelf, Pack Ice
Ocean
Sea
Gulf, Bay
Strait, Fjord
Lagoon
Bank
Seamount
Tablemount
Ridge
Shelf
Basin
Escarpment, Sea Scarp
Fracture
Trench, Abyss
National Park, Reserve
Point of Interest
Recreation Site
Cave, Cavern
Historic Site
Ruins
Wall, Walls
Church, Abbey
Temple
Scientific Station
Airport
Port
Lighthouse
Mine
Tunnel
Dam, Bridge

Argent, Côte d'- 11 Ej 44.00N 1.30W
Argenta 14 Ff 44.37N 11.50 E
Argentan 11 Ff 48.45N 0.01W
Argentario, Monte- 14 Fh 42.24N 11.09 E
Argentat 11 Hi 45.06N 1.56 E
Argentera 14 Bf 44.10N 7.18 E
Argenteuil 11 If 48.57N 2.15 E
Argentiera, Capo dell'- 14 Cj 40.44N 8.08 E
Argentina 55 Ai 29.33S 62.17W
Argentina [1] 53 Ji 34.00S 64.00W
Argentine Basin (EN) 3 Cn 45.00S 45.00W
Argentino, Lago- 52 Ik 50.13S 72.25W
Argentino, Mar- 52 Kj 46.00S 59.40W
Argenton 11 Fg 47.05N 0.13W
Argenton-Château 11 Fh 46.59N 0.27W
Argenton-sur-Creuse 11 Hh 46.35N 1.31 E
Arges 15 Jd 44.04N 26.37 E
Arges [2] 15 Hd 45.00N 24.50 E
Arghandāb 23 Jc 31.27N 64.23 E
Argo 35 Eb 19.31N 30.25 E
Argo Depth (EN) 3 Jk 12.10S 165.40W
Argolikós Kólpos = Argolis, Gulf of- (EN) 15 Fl 37.20N 22.55 E
Argolis, Gulf of- (EN) = Argolikós Kólpos 15 Fl 37.20N 22.55 E
Argonne 12 He 49.30N 5.00 E
Argonne 11 Ke 49.30N 5.00 E
Argos 15 Fl 37.38N 22.44 E
Árgos Orestikón 15 Ei 40.30N 21.16 E
Argostólion 15 Dk 38.11N 20.29 E
Arguedas 13 Kb 42.10N 1.36W
Argueil-Fry 12 De 49.37N 1.31 E
Arguello, Point- 46 Ei 34.35N 120.39W
Arguenon 11 Df 48.35N 2.13W
Argun 16 Nh 43.16N 45.52 E
Argun 21 Od 53.20N 121.28 E
Argungu 34 Fc 12.45N 4.31 E
Argyle 51n Ba 13.10N 61.10W
Argyle, Lake- 57 Df 16.15S 128.40 E
Argyll 9 Ie 56.20N 5.00W
Arhangelsk = Archangel (EN) 6 Kc 64.34N 40.32 E
Arhangelskaja Oblast [3] 19 Ec 63.30N 43.00 E
Arhara 20 Ig 49.30N 130.09 E
Arhavi 24 Ib 41.22N 41.16 E
Arholma 8 He 59.50N 19.05 E
Ar Horqin Qi (Tianshan) 27 Lc 43.55N 120.05 E
Århus [2] 8 Dh 56.10N 10.15 E
Århus 6 Hd 56.09N 10.13 E
Århus Bugt 8 Dh 56.10N 10.20 E
Arhust 27 Ib 47.42N 107.50 E
Ariadnoje 20 Ig 45.08N 134.25 E
Ariake-Kai 28 Kh 32.55N 130.27 E
Ariamsvlei 37 Be 28.08S 19.50 E
Ariano Irpino 14 Ji 41.09N 15.05 E
Ariari, Rio- 54 Dc 2.35N 72.47W
Arias 56 Hd 33.38S 62.25W
Ari Atoll 25a Bb 3.30N 72.45 E
Aribinda 34 Ec 14.14N 0.52W
Arica 53 Ig 18.29S 70.20W
Arica, Golfo de- 52 Ig 18.30S 70.30W
Arichuna 50 Ci 7.42N 67.08W
Arid, Cape- 59 Ef 34.00S 123.09 E
Arida 28 Mg 34.05N 135.07 E
Arida-Gawa 29 Dd 34.05N 135.06 E
Aridhaia 15 Fi 40.59N 22.04 E
Ariège 11 Hk 43.31N 1.25 E
Ariège [3] 11 Hk 43.00N 1.30 E
Ariel 55 Cm 36.32S 59.54W
Arieş 15 Gc 46.26N 23.59 E
Ariguani 54 Db 9.50N 74.01W
Ariguani, Rio- 49 Ki 9.35N 73.46W
Arīḥā [Jor.] 24 Fg 31.52N 35.27 E
Arīḥā [Syr.] 24 Ge 35.48N 36.36 E
Arikaree River 45 Ff 40.01N 101.56W
Arikawa 29 Ae 32.59N 129.07 E
Arilje 15 Df 43.45N 20.06 E
Arima 54 Fa 10.38N 61.17W
Arinos 55 Ib 15.55S 46.04W
Arinos, Rio- 52 Kg 10.25S 58.20W
Arinos Novo, Rio- 55 Db 14.14S 56.01W
Ariogala/Arėgala 8 Ji 55.13N 23.30 E
Aripuanã 54 Fe 9.10S 60.38W
Aripuanã, Rio- 52 Jf 5.07S 60.24W
Ariquemes 54 Fe 9.56S 63.04W
Arisa 35 Gc 11.11N 41.38 E
'Arish, Wādī al- 24 Eg 31.09N 33.49 E
Arismendi 49 Mi 8.29N 68.22W
Arita 29 Ae 33.11N 129.52 E
Aritzo 14 Dk 39.57N 9.12 E
Arixang/Wenquan 27 Dc 44.59N 81.04 E
Ariza 13 Jc 41.19N 2.03W
Arizaro, Salar de- 56 Gb 24.42S 67.45W
Arize, Massif de l'- 11 Hl 42.50N 1.30 E
Arizona [2] 43 Ee 34.00N 112.00W
Arizpe 48 Db 30.20N 110.10W
Årjäng 7 Cg 59.23N 12.08 E
Arjeplog 7 Dc 66.03N 17.54 E
Arjo 35 Fd 8.45N 36.30 E
Arjona 54 Ca 10.15N 75.21W
Arkadak 19 Ee 51.58N 43.28 E
Arkadelphia 43 Ie 34.07N 93.04W
Arkalyk 22 Id 50.13N 66.50 E
Arkansas 38 Jf 33.48N 91.04W
Arkansas [2] 43 Id 34.50N 93.40W
Arkansas City 43 Hd 37.04N 97.02W
Arkanū, Jabal- 33 De 22.15N 24.45 E
Arkatag 21 Kf 36.45N 89.10 E
Arkhángelos 15 Lm 36.12N 28.08 E
Arki 15 Jl 37.22N 26.45 E
Arklow/An tInbhear Mór 9 Gi 52.48N 6.09W
Arkona, Kap- 10 Jb 54.41N 13.26 E
Arkonam 25 Ff 13.06N 79.40 E
Arkösund 8 Gf 58.30N 16.56 E
Arkoúdhion 15 Dk 38.33N 20.43 E
Arktičeskoga Instituta, Ostrova- = Arkticheski Institut Islands (EN) 20 Da 75.20N 81.50 E
Arkticheski Institut Islands (EN) = Arktičeskoga Instituta, Ostrova- 20 Da 75.20N 81.50 E
Arlan, Gora- 16 Sj 39.43N 54.40 E
Arlanza 13 Hb 42.06N 4.09W
Arlanzón 13 Hb 42.03N 4.17W
Arlberg 14 Ec 47.08N 10.12 E
Arles 11 Kk 43.40N 4.38 E
Arlington [Or.-U.S.] 46 Ed 45.46N 120.13W
Arlington [Tx.-U.S.] 45 Hj 32.44N 97.07W
Arlington [Va.-U.S.] 43 Ld 38.52N 77.05W
Arlington Heights 45 Me 42.05N 87.59W
Arlit 31 Hg 19.00N 7.38 E
Arlon/Aarlen 11 Le 49.41N 5.49 E
Arlöv 8 Ei 55.39N 13.05 E
Arly 34 Fc 11.35N 1.28 E
Armagh/Ard Mhacha 9 Gg 54.21N 6.39W
Armagnac 11 Gk 43.45N 0.10 E
Armagnac, Collines de l'- 11 Gk 43.30N 0.30 E
Armah, Wādī- 23 Hf 18.12N 51.02 E
Arman 20 Ke 59.43N 150.12 E
Armançon 11 Jg 47.57N 3.30 E
Armandale, Perth- 59 Df 32.09S 116.00 E
Armant 33 Fd 25.37N 32.32 E
Armáthia 15 Jn 35.26N 26.52 E
Armavir 6 Kf 45.00N 41.08 E
Armenia 53 Ie 4.31N 75.41W
Armenia (EN) = Ermenistan 23 Fb 39.10N 43.00 E
Armenia (EN) = Ermenistan 21 Gf 39.10N 43.00 E
Armenian SSR (EN) = Armjanskaja SSR [2] 19 Eg 40.00N 45.00 E
Armentières 11 Id 50.41N 2.53 E
Armeria 48 Gh 18.56N 103.58W
Armi, Capo dell'- 14 Jm 37.57N 15.41 E
Armidale 58 Gh 30.31S 151.39 E
Armisvesi 8 Lb 62.30N 26.35 E
Armjansk 16 Hf 46.05N 33.41 E
Armjanskaja Sovetskaja Socialističeskaja Respublika [2] 19 Eg 40.00N 45.00 E
Armjanskaja SSR/Haikakan Sovetakan Socialistakan Respublika [2] 19 Eg 40.00N 45.00 E
Armjanskaja SSR = Armenian SSR (EN) [2] 19 Eg 40.00N 45.00 E
Armoricain, Massif- = Armorican Massif (EN) 5 Ff 48.00N 3.00W
Armorican Massif (EN) = Armoricain, Massif- 5 Ff 48.00N 3.00W
Armour 45 Ge 43.19N 98.21W
Arm River 46 Ma 50.46N 105.00W
Armstrong [Arg.] 55 Bk 32.47S 61.36W
Armstrong [B.C.-Can.] 46 Fa 50.27N 119.12W
Armstrong [Ont.-Can.] 42 If 50.18N 89.02W
Ārmūdiū 24 Qd 37.15N 56.05 E
Armutçuk Dağ 15 Ki 40.05N 27.23 E
Armutlu 15 Li 40.31N 28.50 E
Armutova 15 Jj 39.23N 26.50 E
Arnaia 15 Gi 40.29N 23.36 E
Arnaud 42 Kd 60.00N 69.55W
Arnautis, Akrōtērion- 24 Ee 35.06N 32.17 E
Arnay-le-Duc 11 Kg 47.08N 4.29 E
Arnedo 13 Jb 42.13N 2.06W
Årnes 7 Cf 60.09N 11.28 E
Arnhem 11 Lc 51.59N 5.55 E
Arnhem, Cape- 57 Ef 12.21S 136.21 E
Arnhem Bay 59 Hb 12.20S 136.10 E
Arnhem Land 57 Ef 13.10S 134.30 E
Arno 5 Hg 43.41N 10.17 E
Arno Atoll 57 Id 7.05N 171.41 E
Arnold 12 Aa 53.00N 1.08W
Arnon 11 Ig 47.13N 2.01 E
Arnøy 7 Ea 70.08N 20.36 E
Arnprior 44 Ic 45.26N 76.21W
Arnsberg 10 Ee 51.23N 8.05 E
Arnsberger Wald 12 Kc 51.26N 8.10 E
Arnsberg-Oeventrop 12 Kc 51.24N 8.08 E
Arnsburg 12 Kd 50.29N 8.48 E
Arnstadt 10 Gf 50.50N 10.57 E
Aro, Rio- 50 Di 8.01N 64.11W
Aroa 50 Bg 10.26N 68.54W
Aroa, Pointe- 65e Fc 17.28S 149.46W
Aroa, Rio- 50 Bg 10.41N 68.18W
Aroa, Sierra de- 50 Bg 10.15N 68.55W
Aroab 37 Be 26.47S 19.40 E
Aroánia Óri 15 Fl 37.57N 22.13 E
Aroche 13 Fg 37.57N 6.57W
Aroche, Pico de- 13 Ff 38.01N 6.56W
Aroeira 55 Ee 21.41S 54.25W
Arolsen 10 Ff 51.22N 9.01 E
Aroma 35 Fb 15.49N 36.08 E
Aron 11 Jh 46.50N 3.27 E
Arona 14 Ce 45.46N 8.34 E
Aroostook River 44 Nb 46.48N 67.45W
Arorae Island 57 Ie 2.38S 176.49 E
Arorangi 64p Bb 21.13S 159.49W
Aros, Rio- 48 Ec 29.30N 109.15W
Arosa 14 Dd 46.47N 9.40 E
Arosa, Ria de- 13 Db 42.28N 8.57W
Aros Papigochic, Rio- 48 Ec 29.09N 108.35W
Årøsund 8 Ci 55.15N 9.43 E
Arouca 13 Dd 40.56N 8.15W
Arpaçay 24 Jb 40.45N 43.25 E
Arpajon 11 If 48.35N 2.15 E
Arpino 14 Hi 41.39N 13.36 E
Arquata Scrivia 14 Cf 44.41N 8.53 E
Arque 54 Eg 17.48S 66.23W
Arques-la-Bataille 12 De 49.53N 1.08 E
Ar Rachidiya 32 Gc 31.55N 4.40W
Ar Rachidiya [3] 32 Gc 31.00N 4.00W
Ar Radīsīyah Baḥrī 33 Fe 24.57N 32.53 E
Arrah 25 Gc 25.34N 84.40 E
Ar Rahad 35 Ec 12.43N 30.39 E
Ar Rahad 30 Kg 14.28N 33.31 E
Arraias 54 If 12.56S 46.57W
Arraias, Rio- [Braz.] 54 Hf 11.10S 53.35W
Arraias, Rio- [Braz.] 55 Ia 12.28S 47.18W
Arraiolos 13 Ef 38.43N 7.59W
Ar Ramādī 23 Fc 33.25N 43.17 E
Ar Ramlah 24 Fh 29.32N 35.57 E
Ar Ramlī al Kabīr 33 Dd 26.30N 22.10 E
Arran, Island of- 9 Hf 55.35N 5.15W
Ar Rank 35 Ec 11.45N 32.48 E
Ar Raqqah 23 Eb 35.56N 39.01 E
Arras 11 Id 50.17N 2.47 E
Ar Rāshidah 24 Cj 25.35N 28.56 E
Ar Rass 24 Jj 25.52N 43.28 E
Ar Rastān 24 Ge 34.55N 36.44 E
Arrats 11 Gj 44.06N 0.52 E
Ar Rawḍah [Sau.Ar.] 33 He 21.16N 42.50 E
Ar Rawḍatayn 24 Lh 29.53N 47.44 E
Ar Rayḥānī 24 Pk 23.37N 55.58 E
Arrecife 32 Ed 28.57N 13.32W
Arrecife Alacrán 47 Gd 22.24N 89.42W
Arrecifes 56 Hd 34.05S 60.07W
Arrecifes, Rio- 55 Ck 33.46S 59.31W
Arrée, Montagnes d'- 11 Cf 48.26N 3.55W
Arresø 8 Ei 55.55N 12.05 E
Arriaga 48 Mi 16.14N 93.54W
Ar Rifā'ī 24 Lg 31.43N 46.07 E
Ar Rihāb 24 Kg 30.52N 45.30 E
Ar Rimāh 24 Lj 25.34N 47.09 E
Ar Rimāl 21 Hg 22.00N 52.50 E
Ar Riyāḍ = Riyadh (EN) 22 Gg 24.38N 46.43 E
Arrochar 9 Ie 56.12N 4.45W
Arroio Grande 55 Fk 32.14S 53.05W
Arrojado 55 Ja 13.29S 44.37W
Arrojado, Rio- 55 Ja 13.24S 44.20W
Arromanches-les-Bains 12 Be 49.20N 0.37W
Arros 11 Gk 43.40N 0.02 E
Arroscia 14 Cg 44.03N 8.11 E
Arroux 11 Jh 46.29N 3.58 E
Arrow, Lough-/Loch Arabhach 9 Eg 54.05N 8.20W
Arrowsmith, Mount- 61 Dh 43.21S 170.59 E
Arrowtown 62 Cf 44.56S 168.50 E
Arroyo Barú 55 Cj 31.52S 58.26W
Arroyo de la Luz 13 Fe 39.29N 6.35W
Arroyo Grande 46 Ei 35.07N 120.34W
Arroyos y Esteros 56 Dg 25.04S 57.06W
Arruda 55 Db 15.02S 56.07W
Arrufó 56 Hd 30.15S 61.45W
Ar Rumaythah 24 Kg 31.32N 45.12 E
Ar Ruq'ī 24 Lh 29.01N 46.33 E
Ar Ruṣāfah 24 He 35.02N 36.17 E
Ar Ruṣayriṣ 31 Kg 11.51N 34.23 E
Ar Ruṭbah 23 Fc 33.02N 40.17 E
Ar Ruwayḍah 24 Ki 26.23N 44.14 E
Ar Ruways [Qatar] 23 Hd 26.08N 51.13 E
Ar Ruways [U.A.E.] 23 He 24.08N 52.45 E
Ar Ruzayqāt 24 Ej 25.35N 32.28 E
Års 8 Ch 56.48N 9.32 E
Arsenjān 24 Oh 29.56N 53.18 E
Arsenjev 20 Ih 44.12N 133.20 E
Arsi [3] 35 Fd 7.10N 40.00 E
Arsk 7 Lh 56.07N 49.52 E
Årskogen 8 Gb 62.05N 17.20 E
Arslanköy 24 Fd 37.01N 34.17 E
Ars-sur-Moselle 12 Ie 49.05N 6.04 E
Arsuk 41 Hf 61.11N 48.30W
Årsunda 8 Gd 60.32N 16.44 E
Art 63b Ad 19.43S 163.39 E
Artá 13 Pe 39.42N 3.21 E
Arta 35 Gc 11.31N 42.50 E
Árta 15 Dj 39.09N 20.59 E
Artà, Cuevas de- 13 Pe 39.40N 3.24 E
Artašat 16 Nj 39.59N 44.33 E
Arteaga 48 Hh 18.28N 102.25W
Artem 20 Ih 43.23N 132.10 E
Artemisa 47 Hd 22.49N 82.46W
Artemón 15 Hm 36.57N 24.43 E
Artem-Ostrov 19 Fg 40.28N 50.18 E
Artemovsk [R.S.F.S.R.] 20 Ef 54.23N 93.30 E
Artemovsk [Ukr.-U.S.S.R.] 16 Ke 48.33N 38.03 E
Artemovski 17 Jh 57.25N 61.58 E
Artesa de Segre 13 Nc 41.54N 1.03 E
Artesia 43 Ge 32.51N 104.24W
Arthur 45 Ff 41.35N 101.31W
Arthur Creek 59 Hd 23.00S 136.58 E
Arthur River 59 Ih 41.00S 144.55 E
Arthur's Pass 61 Dh 42.57S 171.34 E
Arthur's Pass 62 De 42.54S 171.34 E
Arthur's Town 49 Ja 24.38N 75.32W
Arti 17 Ih 56.26N 58.32 E
Artibonite, Rivière de l'- 49 Kd 19.15N 72.47W
Artigas 56 Id 30.42S 56.28W
Artigas [2] 55 Dj 30.35S 57.00W
Artijarvi/Artsjö 8 Ld 60.45N 26.05 E
Artik 16 Mi 40.36N 43.58 E
Artillery Lake 42 Gd 63.08N 107.45W
Artois 11 Id 50.10N 2.30 E
Artois, Collines de l'- 11 Id 50.30N 2.15 E
Artoli 35 Eb 18.19N 33.54 E
Artsjö/Artijarvi 8 Ld 60.45N 26.05 E
Artux 27 Cd 39.40N 76.10 E
Artvin 23 Fa 41.11N 41.49 E
Artyk 20 Jd 64.12N 145.15 E
Aru 36 Fb 2.52N 30.51 E
Aru, Kepulauan- = Aru Islands (EN) 57 Ee 6.00S 134.30 E
Arua 31 Kh 3.01N 30.55 E
Aruanã 55 Gb 14.54S 51.05W
Aruba 54 Ea 12.30N 70.00W
Aruba 39 Lh 12.30N 71.00W
Aru Islands (EN) = Aru, Kepulauan 57 Ee 6.00S 134.30 E
Arukoron Point 64a Bb 7.43N 134.38 E
Arun 9 Mk 50.48N 0.33W
Arunāchal Pradesh [3] 25 Ic 27.50N 94.50 E
Arundel 12 Bd 50.51N 0.33W
Arun He 27 Lb 47.36N 124.06 E
Arun Qi 27 Lb 48.09N 123.29 E
Arus, Tanjung- 26 Hf 1.24N 125.06 E
Arusha [3] 36 Gc 3.30S 36.00 E
Arusha 31 Ki 3.22S 36.41 E
Arutua Atoll 61 Lc 15.18S 146.44W
Arutunga 61 Jc 18.52S 159.46W
Aruwimi 30 Jh 1.13N 23.36 E
Arvada [Co.-U.S.] 45 Dg 39.50N 105.05W
Arvada [Wy.-U.S.] 46 Ld 44.40N 106.03W
Arve 11 Mh 46.12N 6.08 E
Arvert, Presqu'île d'- 11 Ei 45.45N 1.05W
Arvida 42 Kg 48.26N 71.11W
Arvidsjaur 7 Ed 65.35N 19.10 E
Arvika 7 Cg 59.39N 12.36 E
Årviksand 7 Ea 70.12N 20.32 E
Arvin 46 Fi 35.12N 118.50W
Aryānah 14 En 36.52N 10.11 E
Arys 18 Gc 42.48N 68.15 E
Arys 19 Gg 42.26N 68.48 E
Arys, Ozero- 18 Fb 45.50N 66.20 E
Arz 11 Dg 47.39N 2.06W
Arzachena 14 Di 41.05N 9.23 E
Arzamas 19 Ed 55.23N 43.50 E
Arzanah 24 Oj 24.47N 52.34 E
Aržano 14 Kg 43.35N 16.59 E
Arzew 32 Gb 35.51N 0.19W
Arzew, Golfe d'- 13 Li 35.50N 0.10W
Arzew, Salines d'- 13 Li 35.42N 0.18W
Arzfeld 12 Id 50.05N 6.16 E
Arzgir 19 Ef 45.22N 44.13 E
Arzúa 13 Db 42.56N 8.09W
As 12 Hc 51.01N 5.35 E
Ås 8 De 59.40N 10.48 E
Aš 10 If 50.13N 12.12 E
Aša 19 Fd 55.02N 57.18 E
Aså 8 Dg 57.09N 10.25 E
Asab 37 Be 25.29S 17.59 E
Asaba 34 Gd 6.11N 6.45 E
Asad, Buḥayrat al- 24 He 35.57N 38.10 E
Asadābād [Afg.] 23 Lc 34.52N 71.09 E
Asadābād [Iran] 24 Me 34.47N 48.07 E
Asafik 35 Bc 13.10N 19.26 E
Asahi [Jap.] 29 Fb 38.15N 139.30 E
Asahi [Jap.] 29a Ca 44.08N 142.35 E
Asahi [Jap.] 29 Gd 35.43N 140.35 E
Asahi [Jap.] 29 Ec 36.57N 137.34 E
Asahi-Dake 29 Fb 38.16N 139.55 E
Asahi-Gawa 29 Cd 34.36N 133.58 E
Asahikawa 22 Qe 43.46N 142.22 E
Asaka-Drainage 29 Gc 37.30N 140.15 E
Asale, Lake- 35 Gc 14.00N 40.20 E
'Asalūyeh 24 Oi 27.28N 52.37 E
Asama-Yama 28 Of 36.27N 138.30 E
Asan-Man 28 If 36.56N 126.51 E
Asansol 22 Kg 23.41N 86.59 E
Asarna 7 De 62.39N 14.21 E
Asarum 8 Fh 56.12N 14.50 E
'Asäyr = Guardafui, Cape- (EN) 30 Mg 11.49N 51.15 E
Asayta 35 Gc 11.33N 41.27 E
Asbest 17 Jh 57.01N 61.31 E
Asbestos 44 Lc 45.46N 71.57W
Asbe Teferi 35 Gd 9.05N 40.51 E
Asbury Park 44 Je 40.14N 74.01W
Ascension 30 Fi 7.57S 14.22W
Ascensión, Bahía de la- 47 Ge 19.40N 87.30W
Ascensión, Bahía de la- 48 Ph 19.40N 87.30W
Ascensión, Laguna de la- 48 Fb 31.05N 107.55W
Aschaffenburg 10 Fg 49.59N 9.09 E
Ascheberg 12 Jc 51.47N 7.37 E
Aschendorf (Ems), Papenburg- 12 Ja 53.04N 7.22 E
Aschersleben 10 He 51.45N 11.28 E
Aščikol, Ozero- 18 Fb 45.05N 67.20 E
Aščiozek 16 Pe 49.12N 48.06 E
Ascoli Piceno 14 Hh 42.51N 13.34 E
Ascoli Satriano 14 Ji 41.12N 15.34 E
Ascot 12 Bc 51.24N 0.40W
Aseb 31 Lg 13.00N 42.44 E
Åseda 7 Dh 57.10N 15.20 E
Asedjrad 30 Hf 24.42N 1.40 E
Asekejevo 16 Rc 53.36N 52.51 E
Asela 31 Kh 7.58N 39.08 E
As Ela 35 Gc 11.06N 42.06 E
Åsele 7 Dd 64.10N 17.20 E
Åsen [Nor.] 7 Ce 63.36N 11.03 E
Åsen [Swe.] 7 Cf 61.17N 13.50 E
Asendabo 35 Fd 9.47N 37.36 E
Asendorf 12 Kb 52.46N 9.00 E
Asenovgrad 15 Hg 42.01N 24.52 E
Åsensbruk 8 Ef 58.48N 12.25 E
Åseral 8 Bf 58.37N 7.25 E
Aseri/Azeri 7 Gg 59.29N 26.51 E
Asfeld 12 Ge 49.28N 4.07 E
Aşfūn al Maṭā'inah 24 Ej 25.23N 32.32 E
Åsgårdstrand 8 De 59.21N 10.28 E
Ashabad 22 Hf 37.57N 58.23 E
Ašhabadskaja Oblast [3] 19 Fh 38.30N 59.00 E
Ashanti [3] 34 Ed 6.45N 1.30W
Ashburn 44 Fj 31.43N 83.39W
Ashburton 61 Dh 43.54S 171.45 E
Ashburton River 57 Cg 21.40S 114.56 E
Ashdod 24 Fg 31.49N 34.39 E
Ashdown 45 Ij 33.41N 94.08W
Asheboro 44 Hh 35.42N 79.49W
Asheroft 46 Ea 50.43N 121.17W
Asheville 43 Kd 35.34N 82.33W
Ashford 9 Nj 51.09N 0.53 E
Ashford Airport 12 Cc 51.10N 0.59 E
Ash Fork 46 Ii 35.13N 112.29W
Ashibetsu 28 Qc 43.31N 142.11 E
Ashikaga 29 Fc 36.21N 139.27 E
Ashington 9 Lf 55.11N 1.34W
Ashiro 29 Ga 40.06N 141.01 E
Ashiya 29 Be 33.53N 130.40 E
Ashizuri-Misaki 28 Lh 32.44N 133.01 E
Ashkal, Qar'at al- 14 Dm 37.10N 9.40 E
Āshkhāneh 24 Qd 37.28N 57.00 E
Ashland [Ks.-U.S.] 45 Gh 37.11N 99.46W
Ashland [Ky.-U.S.] 43 Kd 38.28N 82.38W
Ashland [Mt.-U.S.] 46 Ld 45.35N 106.16W
Ashland [Oh.-U.S.] 44 Fe 40.52N 82.19W
Ashland [Or.-U.S.] 43 Cc 42.12N 122.42W
Ashland [Wi.-U.S.] 43 Ib 46.35N 90.53W
Ashland, Mount- 46 De 42.05N 122.43W
Ashley 45 Gc 46.02N 99.22W
Ashmore Islands 57 Df 12.15S 123.05 E
Ashmūn 24 Dg 30.18N 30.58 E
Ashoro 29a Cb 43.14N 143.31 E
Ashqelon 24 Fg 31.40N 34.35 E
Ash Shabakah 24 Jg 30.49N 43.39 E
Ash Shabb 33 Ee 22.19N 29.46 E
Ash Shā'ib 24 Gh 28.59N 37.07 E
Ash Sha'm 23 Id 26.02N 56.05 E
Ash Shamālīyah [3] 35 Db 18.40N 30.00 E
Ash 'Shāmīyah 24 Kg 31.57N 44.36 E
Ash Shāmīyah 24 Lg 30.15N 46.55 E
Ash Shaqq 24 Lh 28.20N 47.30 E
Ash Shaqrā' 23 Gd 25.15N 45.15 E
Ash Sha'rā' 24 Kj 24.16N 44.11 E
Ash Sharīqah 23 Id 25.22N 55.23 E
Ash Sharqāṭ 23 Fb 35.27N 43.16 E
Ash Sharqī 32 Jc 34.45N 11.15 E
Ash Sharqī 24 Ge 34.00N 36.30 E
Ash Sharqīyah 23 Ie 22.15N 58.30 E
Ash Shatrah 24 Lg 31.25N 46.10 E
Ash Shawbak 24 Fg 30.32N 35.34 E
Ash Shaykh Ḥumayd 24 Fh 28.07N 34.34 E
Ash Shifā 24 Fh 28.30N 35.30 E
Ash Shiḥr 23 Gg 14.44N 49.35 E
Ash Shināfīyah 24 Kg 31.35N 44.39 E
Ash Shu'aybah [Kuw.] 24 Mh 29.03N 48.08 E
Ash Shu'aybah [Sau.Ar.] 24 Ji 27.53N 42.43 E
Ash Shu'bah 24 Kh 28.54N 44.44 E
Ash Shumlūl 24 Li 26.31N 47.20 E
Ash Shuqayq 23 Ff 17.44N 42.01 E
Ash Shurayk 35 Eb 18.48N 33.34 E
Ash Shuwayhāt 24 Oj 24.05N 52.28 E
Ash Shuwaykh 24 Lh 29.21N 47.55 E
Ashtabula 43 Kc 41.53N 80.47W
Ashtabula, Lake- 45 Hc 47.11N 97.58W
Ashtiyān 24 Me 34.30N 49.55 E
Ashton [Id.-U.S.] 46 Jd 44.04N 111.27W
Ashton [St.Vin.] 51n Bb 12.36N 61.27W
Ashuanipi 42 Kf 52.55N 66.00W
Ashuanipi Lake 42 Kf 52.45N 66.10W
Asia 21 Ke 40.00N 85.00 E
Asia, Kepulauan- 26 Jf 1.03N 131.18 E
Asiago 14 Fe 45.52N 11.30 E
Asiago, Altopiano di- 14 Fe 45.54N 11.30 E
Asilah 32 Fb 35.28N 6.02W
Asinara 5 Gg 41.04N 8.15 E
Asinara, Golfo dell'- 14 Cj 41.00N 8.35 E
Asino 20 De 56.58N 86.09 E
'Asīr 23 Ff 19.00N 42.00 E
Aškadar 17 Hi 53.37N 56.01 E
Aşkale 24 Ic 39.55N 40.42 E
Askanija-Nova 16 Hf 46.27N 33.52 E
Asker 8 De 59.50N 10.26 E
Askersund 7 Dg 58.53N 14.54 E
Askī Al Mawṣil 24 Jd 36.34N 42.42 E
Askim [Nor.] 8 De 59.35N 11.10 E
Askim [Swe.] 8 Dg 57.38N 11.56 E
Áskion Óros 15 Ei 40.22N 21.34 E
Askiz 20 Ef 53.08N 90.32 E
Askja 5 Eb 65.03N 16.48W
Askola 8 Kd 60.32N 25.36 E
Äsköping 8 Ge 59.09N 16.04 E
Askøy 8 Ad 60.30N 5.05 E
Askøy 8 Ad 60.24N 5.11 E
Askrova 8 Ac 61.30N 4.55 E
Askvoll 7 Af 61.21N 5.04 E
Asl 24 Eh 29.30N 32.43 E
Aslanapa 15 Mj 39.13N 29.52 E
Asmara (EN) = Asmera 31 Kg 15.19N 38.57 E
Asmera = Asmara (EN) 31 Kg 15.19N 38.57 E
Åsnen 8 Fh 56.40N 14.40 E
Asni 32 Fc 31.15N 7.59W
Asnières-sur-Seine 12 Ef 48.55N 2.17 E
Aso 14 Hg 43.06N 13.51 E
Aso 29 Be 32.58N 131.02 E
Asola 14 Ee 45.13N 10.24 E
Asosa 31 Kg 10.02N 34.32 E
Aso-San 29 Be 32.53N 131.06 E
Asoteriba, Jabal- 35 Fa 21.51N 36.30 E
Asouf Mellene 32 Hd 25.40N 2.08 E
Asō-Wan 29 Ad 34.20N 129.15 E
Āspās 24 Og 30.40N 52.24 E
Aspe 13 Lf 38.21N 0.46W
Aspen 43 Fd 39.11N 106.49W
Aspermont 45 Fj 33.08N 100.14W
Aspiring, Mount- 61 Ch 44.23S 168.44 E
Aspromonte 14 Jl 38.10N 16.00 E
Assa 32 Fd 28.37N 9.25W
Aş Şadr 23 He 24.40N 54.41 E
Aş Şaff 24 Dh 29.34N 31.17 E
Aş Şāfī 24 Fg 31.02N 35.28 E
As Safīrah 24 Gd 36.04N 37.22 E
Aş Şaḥm 24 Qj 24.10N 56.53 E
Assahoun 34 Fd 6.27N 0.55 E
Aş Şa'īd 30 Kf 26.00N 32.00 E
Assal, Lac- 35 Gc 11.40N 42.22 E
As Salamīyah [Sau.Ar.] 23 Ge 24.12N 47.23 E
As Salamīyah [Syr.] 24 Ge 35.01N 37.03 E
Aş Şāliḥīyah 24 Ie 34.44N 40.45 E
As Sallūm 31 Je 31.34N 25.09 E
As Salmān 24 Kg 30.26N 44.30 E
As Salt 24 Ff 32.03N 35.44 E
As Salwá 23 He 24.45N 50.49 E

Index Symbols

[1] Independent Nation
[2] State, Region
[3] District, County
[4] Municipality
[5] Colony, Dependency
Continent
Physical Region
Historical or Cultural Region
Mount, Mountain
Volcano
Hill
Mountains, Mountain Range
Hills, Escarpment
Plateau, Upland
Pass, Gap
Plain, Lowland
Delta
Salt Flat
Valley, Canyon
Crater, Cave
Karst Features
Depression
Polder
Desert, Dunes
Forest, Woods
Heath, Steppe
Oasis
Cape, Point
Coast, Beach
Cliff
Peninsula
Isthmus
Sandbank
Island
Atoll
Rock, Reef
Islands, Archipelago
Rocks, Reefs
Coral Reef
Well, Spring
Geyser
River, Stream
Waterfall Rapids
River Mouth, Estuary
Lake
Salt Lake
Intermittent Lake
Reservoir
Swamp, Pond
Canal
Glacier
Ice Shelf, Pack Ice
Ocean
Sea
Gulf, Bay
Strait, Fjord
Lagoon
Bank
Seamount
Tablemount
Ridge
Shelf
Basin
Escarpment, Sea Scarp
Fracture
Trench, Abyss
National Park, Reserve
Point of Interest
Recreation Site
Cave, Cavern
Historic Site
Ruins
Wall, Walls
Church, Abbey
Temple
Scientific Station
Airport
Port
Lighthouse
Mine
Tunnel
Dam, Bridge

Assam 21 Lg 26.50N 94.00 E
Assam 25 Ic 26.00N 93.00 E
Assamakka 34 Gb 19.21N 5.38 E
As Samawah 23 Gc 31.18N 45.17 E
As Sanām 35 Ia 22.00N 51.10 E
Assaouas 34 Gb 16.52N 7.27 E
As Sars 14 Dn 36.05N 9.01 E
As Sayl al Kabir 33 He 21.38N 40.25 E
Asse 12 Gd 50.56N 4.12 E
Asse 11 Lk 43.53N 5.53 E
Assebroek, Brugge- 12 Fc 51.12N 3.16 E
Assekkârai 34 Fb 15.50N 2.52 E
Assemini 14 Dk 39.17N 9.01 E
Assen 11 Ma 53.00N 6.34 E
Assenede 12 Fc 51.14N 3.45 E
Assens 8 Ci 55.16N 9.55 E
As Sībā'īyah 24 Ej 25.11N 32.41 E
As Sidr 31 Ie 30.39N 18.22 E
As Sidrah=Sirte Desert (EN) 30 Ie 30.30N 17.30 E
As Sila' 23 He 24.02N 51.46 E
As Simbillāwayn 24 Dg 30.53N 31.27 E
Assiniboia 42 Gg 49.38N 105.59W
Assiniboine 38 Je 49.53N 97.08W
Assiniboine, Mount- 38 Hd 50.52N 115.39W
Assis 56 Jb 22.40S 50.25W
Assisi 14 Gg 43.04N 12.37 E
Aßlar 12 Kd 50.36N 8.28 E
Assos 15 Jj 39.31N 26.20 E
As Sālimīyah 24 Mh 29.20N 48.04 E
As Subaykhah 14 Eo 35.56N 10.01 E
As Subū' 33 Fe 22.45N 32.34 E
As Sūdān=Sudan (EN) 31 Jg 15.00N 30.00 E
As Sudd 30 Kh 8.00N 31.00 E
As Sufāl 35 Hc 14.06N 48.43 E
Aş Şufuq 24 Nk 23.52N 51.45 E
Aş Şukhayrah 32 Jc 34.17N 10.06 E
As Sukhnah 24 He 34.52N 38.52 E
As Sulaymī 24 Ii 26.17N 41.21 E
As Sulayyil 23 Ge 20.27N 45.34 E
Aş Şulb 24 Mj 25.42N 48.25 E
Aş Sumayḩ 35 Dd 9.49N 27.39 E
Aş Şummān 33 Ie 23.00N 48.00 E
Aş Şummān 24 Li 27.00N 47.00 E
Assumption Island 30 Li 9.45S 46.30 E
As Sūq 33 He 21.54N 42.03 E
Assur 24 Je 35.25N 43.16 E
Aş Şuwār 24 Ie 35.30N 40.39 E
As Suwaydā' 23 Ec 32.42N 36.34 E
Aş Şuwayrah 24 Kf 32.55N 44.47 E
As Suways=Suez (EN) 31 Kf 29.58N 32.33 E
Astakidha 15 Jn 35.53N 26.50 E
Astakós 15 Ek 38.32N 21.05 E
Āstāneh [Iran] 24 Md 37.17N 49.59 E
Āstāneh [Iran] 24 Mf 33.53N 49.22 E
Āstārā 23 Gb 38.26N 48.52 E
Astara 6 Kh 38.28N 48.52 E
Aštarak 16 Ni 40.16N 44.18 E
Asten 12 Hc 51.24N 5.45 E
Asti 14 Cf 44.54N 8.12 E
Astico 14 Fe 45.37N 11.37 E
Astipálaia 15 Jm 36.33N 26.21 E
Astipálaia 15 Jm 36.35N 26.20 E
Asto, Monte- 11a Ba 42.30N 9.15 E
Astola Island 25 Cc 25.07N 63.51 E
Astorga 13 Fb 42.27N 6.03W
Astoria 43 Cb 46.11N 123.50W
Åstorp 8 Eh 56.08N 12.57 E
Astove Island 30 Lj 10.06S 47.45 E
Astrahan 6 Kf 46.21N 48.03 E
Astrahanskaja Oblast 19 Ef 47.10N 47.30 E
Astrolabe, Cape- 63a Ec 8.20S 160.34 E
Astrolabe, Récifs de l'- 57 Hf 19.49S 165.35 E
Astudillo 13 Hb 42.12N 4.18W
Asturias 13 Ga 43.20N 6.00W
Asuisui, Cape- 65c Aa 13.47S 172.29W
Asunción 53 Kh 25.16S 57.40W
Asunción, Bahía- 48 Bd 27.05N 114.10W
Asunción, Cerro de la- 48 Je 24.15N 99.56W
Asuncion Island 57 Fc 19.40N 145.24 E
Asunción Mita 49 Cf 14.20N 89.43W
Asunción Nochixtlán 48 Ki 17.28N 97.14W
Åsunden 8 Fg 58.00N 15.50 E
Åsunden 8 Eg 57.44N 13.22 E
Aswa 36 Fb 3.43N 31.55 E
Aswān 31 Kf 24.05N 32.53 E
Aswān, Sadd al-=First Cataract (EN) 30 Kf 24.01N 32.52 E
Asyūţ 31 Kf 27.11N 31.11 E
Asyūţī, Wādī al- 24 Di 27.10N 31.16 E
Aszód 10 Pi 47.39N 19.30 E
'Ata 65b Bc 21.03S 174.59W
Atacama 56 Gc 27.30S 70.00W
Atacama, Desierto de-=Atacama Desert (EN) 52 Jh 22.30S 69.15W
Atacama, Salar de- 52 Jh 23.30S 68.15W
Atacama Desert (EN)=Atacama, Desierto de- 52 Jh 22.30S 69.15W
Atacama Trench (EN) 3 Nm 30.00S 73.00W
Atafu Atoll 57 Je 8.33S 172.30W
Atagaj 20 Ee 55.06N 99.25 E
Ata Island 57 Jg 21.03S 175.00W
Atakor 30 Hf 23.13N 5.40 E
Atakora 34 Fc 10.00N 1.35 E
Atakora 34 Fc 10.45N 1.30 E
Atakpamé 31 Hh 7.32N 1.08 E
Atalaia do Norte 54 Dd 4.20S 70.12W
Atalándi 15 Fk 38.39N 23.00 E
Atalaya 54 Df 10.44S 73.45W
Atalayasa 13 Nf 38.55N 1.15 E
Atambua 26 Hh 9.07S 124.54 E
Atami 29 Fd 35.05N 139.02 E
Atangmik 41 Gf 64.53N 52.00W
Atār 31 Ff 20.30N 13.03W
Atas-Bogdo-Ula 27 Gc 43.20N 96.30 E
Atascadero 46 Ei 35.29N 120.41W
Atasu 19 Hf 48.42N 71.38 E
'Atata 65b Ac 21.03S 175.15W
Atatürk Barajı 24 Hd 37.30N 38.30 E
Atauro, Pulau 26 Ih 8.13S 125.35 E
Atáviros 15 Km 36.12N 27.52 E
Ataway 35 Bd 9.59N 18.38 E
Atbara 35 Eb 17.40N 33.56 E
'Atbarah 30 Kg 17.40N 33.56 E
'Atbarah 31 Kg 17.42N 33.59 E
Atbasar 22 Id 51.48N 68.20 E
At-Baši 19 Hg 41.08N 75.51 E
Atça 15 Ll 37.53N 28.13 E
Atchafalaya Bay 43 If 29.25N 91.20W
Atchison 43 Hd 39.34N 95.07W
Atebubu 34 Ed 7.45N 0.59W
Ateca 13 Kc 41.20N 1.47W
Aterno 14 Hh 42.11N 13.51 E
Atessa 14 Ih 42.04N 14.27 E
Ath/Aat 11 Jd 50.38N 3.47 E
Athabasca 38 Hd 58.40N 110.50W
Athabasca 42 Gf 54.43N 113.17W
Athabasca, Lake- 38 Id 59.07N 110.00W
Athamánon, Óri- 15 Ej 39.27N 21.08 E
Athamánon Óri 15 Ej 39.27N 21.08 E
Athens [Al.-U.S.] 44 Dh 34.48N 86.58W
Athens [Ga.-U.S.] 43 Ke 33.57N 83.23W
Athens [Oh.-U.S.] 44 Ff 39.20N 82.06W
Athens [Tn.-U.S.] 44 Eh 35.28N 84.35W
Athens [Tx.-U.S.] 45 Ij 32.12N 95.51W
Athens (EN) = Athínai 6 Ih 37.59N 23.44 E
Athéras 15 Jl 37.38N 26.15 E
Atherton 59 Jc 17.16S 145.29 E
Athi 36 Gc 2.59S 38.31 E
Athies-sous-Laon 12 Fe 49.34N 3.41 E
Athínai = Athens (EN) 6 Ih 37.59N 23.44 E
Athi River 36 Gc 1.27S 36.59 E
Athis-de-l'Orne 12 Bf 48.49N 0.30W
Athlone/Baile Átha Luain 9 Fh 53.25N 7.56W
Athol 44 Kd 42.36N 72.14W
Áthos 15 Hi 40.10N 24.20 E
Athos, Mount- (EN)=Áyion Óros 15 Hi 40.15N 24.15 E
Ath Thamad 24 Fh 29.41N 34.18 E
Ath Thumāmī 24 Ki 27.42N 44.59 E
Athus, Aubange- 12 He 49.34N 5.50 E
Athy 9 Gi 53.00N 7.00W
Ati 31 Ig 13.13N 18.20 E
Atiak 36 Fb 3.16N 32.07 E
Atiamuri 62 Gc 38.23S 176.02 E
Atibaia, Rio- 55 If 22.42S 47.17W
Atienza 13 Jc 41.12N 2.52W
Atikokan 42 Ig 48.45N 91.37W
Atikonak Lake 42 Lf 52.40N 64.35W
Atimoono 64n Bc 10.26S 160.58W
Atitlán, Lago de- 49 Bf 14.42N 91.12W
Atitlán, Volcán- 47 Ff 14.35N 91.11W
Atiu Island 57 Lg 20.02S 158.07W
'Atk, Wādī al- 24 Li 26.03N 46.30 E
Atka 38 Bd 52.15N 174.30W
Atka [Ak.-U.S.] 40a Db 52.12N 174.12W
Atka [R.S.F.S.R.] 20 Kd 60.49N 151.58 E
Atka Iceport 66 Bf 70.35S 7.45W
Atkarsk 19 Ee 51.52N 44.59 E
Atkasook 40 Hb 70.28N 157.24W
Atkinson 45 Ge 42.32N 98.59W
Atlacomulco de Fabela 48 Jh 19.48N 99.53W
Atlanta [Ga.-U.S.] 39 Kf 33.45N 84.23W
Atlanta [Mi.-U.S.] 44 Ec 45.00N 84.09W
Atlanta [Tx.-U.S.] 45 Ij 33.07N 94.10W
Atlanterhavet=Atlantic Ocean (EN) 3 Di 2.00N 25.00W
Atlantic [Ia.-U.S.] 45 If 41.24N 95.01W
Atlantic [N.C.-U.S.] 44 Ih 34.54N 76.20W
Atlantic City 39 Lf 39.27N 74.35W
Atlantic Coastal Plain 38 Lf 34.00N 79.00W
Atlantic-Indian Basin (EN) 3 Eo 60.00S 15.00 E
Atlantic-Indian Ridge (EN) 3 Eo 52.00S 25.00 E
Atlántico 54 Da 10.40N 75.00W
Atlántico, Océano-=Atlantic Ocean (EN) 3 Di 2.00N 25.00W
Atlântico, Oceano-=Atlantic Ocean (EN) 3 Di 2.00N 25.00W
Atlantic Ocean 3 Di 2.00N 25.00W
Atlantic Ocean (EN)=Atlanterhavet 3 Di 2.00N 25.00W
Atlantic Ocean (EN)=Atlântico, Oceano- 3 Di 2.00N 25.00W
Atlantic Ocean (EN)=Atlántico, Océano- 3 Di 2.00N 25.00W
Atlantic Ocean (EN)=Atlantiese Oseaan 3 Di 2.00N 25.00W
Atlantic Ocean (EN)=Atlantique, Océan- 3 Di 2.00N 25.00W
Atlantic Ocean (EN)=Atlantshaf 3 Di 2.00N 25.00W
Atlantic Ocean (EN)=Muhīt, Al Baḩr al- 3 Di 2.00N 25.00W
Atlántida 49 Df 15.30N 87.00W
Atlantiese Oseaan=Atlantic Ocean (EN) 3 Di 2.00N 25.00W
Atlantique 34 Fd 6.35N 2.15 E
Atlantique, Océan-=Atlantic Ocean (EN) 3 Di 2.00N 25.00W
Atlantshaf=Atlantic Ocean (EN) 3 Di 2.00N 25.00W
Atlas=Atlas Mountains (EN) 30 Ge 32.00N 2.00W
Atlas Mountains (EN)=Atlas 30 Ge 32.00N 2.00W
Atlasova, Ostrov- 20 Kf 50.50N 155.25 E
Atlasovo 20 Jg 46.00N 142.09 E
Atlas Saharien=Saharan Atlas (EN) 30 He 34.00N 2.00 E
Atlas Tellien=Tell Atlas (EN) 30 He 36.00N 2.00 E
Atlin 42 Ee 59.35N 133.42W
Atlin Lake 42 Ee 59.35N 133.43W
Atlixco 47 Ee 18.54N 98.26W
Atløy 8 Ac 61.20N 4.55 E
Atmore 44 Dj 31.02N 87.29W
Atna 8 Dc 61.44N 10.49 E
Atna Peak 42 Ef 53.57N 128.04W
Atō 29 Bd 34.24N 131.43 E
Atoka 45 Hi 34.23N 96.08W
Átokos 15 Dk 38.29N 20.49 E
Atotonilco el Alto 48 Hg 20.33N 102.31W
Atoui, Khatt- 32 De 20.04N 15.58W
Atouila, 'Erg- 30 Gf 21.15N 3.20W
Atoyac, Rio- 48 Ki 16.30N 97.31W
Atoyac de Alvarez 48 Ii 17.12N 100.26W
Atrak 21 Hf 37.23N 53.57 E
Ätran 7 Ch 56.53N 12.30 E
Atrato, Rio- 52 Ie 8.17N 76.58W
Atrek 21 Hf 37.23N 53.57 E
Atri 14 Hh 42.35N 13.59 E
Atsugi 29 Fd 35.26N 139.20 E
Atsukeshi 28 Rc 43.02N 144.51 E
Atsukeshi-Wan 29a Db 43.00N 144.45 E
Atsumi [Jap.] 28 Oe 38.37N 139.35 E
Atsumi [Jap.] 29 Ed 34.37N 137.05 E
Atsumi-Hantō 29 Ed 34.40N 137.15 E
Atsumi-Wan 29 Ed 34.45N 137.15 E
Atsuta 29a Bb 43.24N 141.25 E
Atsutoko 29a Db 43.15N 145.13 E
Aţ Ţaff 23 He 23.55N 54.25 E
Aţ Ţafīlah 24 Fg 30.50N 35.36 E
Aţ Ţā'if 22 Gg 21.16N 40.25 E
At Tāj 35 De 24.13N 23.18 E
Attalla 44 Dh 34.01N 86.05W
At Tallāb 35 De 24.01N 23.10 E
At Ta'mīm 24 Ke 36.00N 44.00 E
Attapu 25 Lf 14.48N 106.50 E
Aţ Ţārmīyah 24 Kf 33.40N 44.24 E
Attawapiskat 38 Kd 52.57N 82.18W
Attawapiskat 39 Kd 52.55N 82.26W
Attawapiskat Lake 42 If 52.15N 87.50W
At Ţawīl 24 Hh 29.20N 39.35 E
At Taysīyah 24 Jh 28.00N 44.00 E
Aţ Ţayyārah 35 Ec 13.12N 30.47 E
Attendorn 12 Jc 51.07N 7.54 E
Attersee 14 Hc 47.55N 13.33 E
Attert 12 Ie 49.49N 6.05 E
Attica 44 De 40.17N 87.15W
Attichy 12 Fe 49.25N 3.03 E
Attigny 12 Ge 49.29N 4.35 E
At Tīh Desert (EN)=Tīh, Şaḩrā' at- 33 Fc 30.05N 34.00 E
Attikamagen Lake 42 Ke 55.00N 66.30W
Attleboro 44 Le 41.56N 71.17W
Attleborough 12 Db 52.31N 1.01 E
Attre 12 Fd 50.37N 3.50 E
Attu 40a Ab 52.56N 173.15 E
Attu 40a Ab 52.55N 173.00 E
Aţ Ţulayhī 24 Ki 27.33N 44.08 E
Aţ Ţūr 24 Eh 28.14N 33.37 E
Aţ Ţurayf 23 Ec 31.44N 38.33 E
At Turbah 23 Fg 12.40N 43.30 E
Aţ Ţuwayshah 35 Dc 12.21N 26.32 E
Atuel, Rio- 52 Ji 36.17S 66.50W
Åtvidaberg 7 Dg 58.12N 16.00 E
Atwater 46 Eh 37.21N 120.36W
Atwood 45 Fg 39.45N 101.03W
Aua Island 57 Fe 1.27S 143.04 E
Auasbila 49 Ef 14.52N 84.40W
Auatu 35 Gd 7.17N 41.03 E
Auau Channel 65a Ec 20.51N 156.45W
Aubagne 11 Lk 43.17N 5.34 E
Aubange 12 He 49.35N 5.48 E
Aubange-Athus 12 He 49.34N 5.50 E
Aube 11 Jf 48.34N 3.43 E
Aube 11 Kf 48.15N 4.05 E
Aubel 12 Hd 50.42N 5.51 E
Aubenas 11 Kj 44.37N 4.23 E
Aubenton 12 Ge 49.50N 4.12 E
Aubetin 12 Ff 48.49N 3.01 E
Aubigny-en-Artois 12 Ed 50.21N 2.35 E
Aubigny-sur-Nère 11 Ig 47.29N 2.26 E
Aubin 11 Ij 44.32N 2.15 E
Aubrac, Monts d'- 11 Ij 44.38N 3.00 E
Aubry, Lake - 42 Ec 67.25N 126.30W
Auburn [Al.-U.S.] 44 Ei 32.36N 85.29W
Auburn [Ca.-U.S.] 46 Eg 38.54N 121.04W
Auburn [In.-U.S.] 44 Ee 41.22N 85.04W
Auburn [Me.-U.S.] 44 Lc 44.06N 70.14W
Auburn [Nb.-U.S.] 45 If 40.23N 95.51W
Auburn [N.Y.-U.S.] 44 Id 42.57N 76.34W
Auburn [Wa.-U.S.] 46 Dc 47.18N 122.13W
Auburn Range 59 Ke 25.10S 150.30 E
Aubusson 11 Ii 45.57N 2.10 E
Aucanquilcha, Cerro- 52 Jh 21.14S 68.28W
Auce 8 Jh 56.28N 22.50 E
Auch 11 Gk 43.39N 0.35 E
Auchel 12 Ed 50.30N 2.28 E
Auchi 34 Gd 7.04N 6.16 E
Auckland 58 Ih 36.52S 174.45 E
Auckland Islands 57 Hi 50.35S 166.00 E
Auckland Peninsula 62 Eb 36.15S 174.00 E
Aude 11 Jk 43.13N 3.14 E
Aude 11 Ik 43.05N 2.30 E
Auden 45 Ma 50.13N 87.47W
Audenarde/Oudenaarde 11 Jd 50.51N 3.36 E
Audierne 11 Bf 48.01N 4.32W
Audierne, Baie d'- 11 Bg 47.57N 4.28W
Audincourt 11 Mg 47.29N 6.50 E
Audo 35 Gd 6.09N 41.53 E
Audresselles 12 Dd 50.49N 1.35 E
Audru 8 Kf 58.24N 24.19 E
Audruicq 12 Ed 50.53N 2.05 E
Audubon 45 If 41.43N 94.55W
Audun-le-Roman 12 He 49.22N 5.53 E
Audun-le-Tiche 12 He 49.28N 5.57 E
Aue 10 If 50.35N 12.42 E
Aue [Ger.] 10 Fd 52.33N 9.05 E
Aue [Ger.] 12 Kb 52.16N 8.59 E
Auerbach 10 If 50.31N 12.24 E
Auezov 19 If 49.40N 81.40 E
Auffay 12 De 49.43N 1.06 E
Augathella 58 Fg 25.48S 146.35 E
Auge, Pays d'- 11 Ge 49.05N 0.10 E
Augpilagtoq 41 Gd 72.45N 55.35W
Augrabies Falls 30 Jk 28.35S 20.23 E
Augsburg 6 Hf 48.22N 10.53 E
Augusta [Ar.-U.S.] 45 Ki 35.17N 91.22W
Augusta [Austl.] 58 Ch 34.10S 115.10 E
Augusta [Ga.-U.S.] 39 Kf 33.29N 81.57W
Augusta [It.] 14 Jm 37.13N 15.13 E
Augusta [Ks.-U.S.] 45 Hh 37.41N 96.58W
Augusta [Me.-U.S.] 39 Me 44.19N 69.47W
Augusta [Mt.-U.S.] 46 Ic 47.30N 112.24W
Augusta, Golfo di- 14 Jm 37.10N 15.15 E
Augustów 10 Sc 53.51N 22.59 E
Augustowski, Kanał- 10 Tc 53.54N 23.26 E
Augustus, Mount- 57 Cg 24.20S 116.50 E
Auki 58 He 8.45S 160.42 E
Auld, Lake- 59 Ed 22.30S 123.45 E
Aulla 14 Df 44.12N 9.58 E
Aulne 11 Bf 48.17N 4.16W
Aulneau Peninsula 45 Ib 49.23N 94.29W
Aulnoye-Aymeries 12 Fd 50.12N 3.50 E
Aulong 64a Ac 7.17N 134.17 E
Ault 12 Dd 50.06N 1.27 E
Auluptagel 64a Ac 7.19N 134.29 E
Aulus-les-Bains 11 Hl 42.48N 1.20 E
Aumale 11 He 49.46N 1.45 E
Auna 34 Fc 10.11N 4.43 E
Aunay-sur-Odon 12 Be 49.01N 0.38W
Auneuil 12 Ee 49.22N 2.00 E
Auning 7 Ch 56.26N 10.23 E
Aunis 11 Fh 46.10N 1.00W
Aunuu 65c Cb 14.17S 170.33W
Auob 30 Jk 26.27S 20.38 E
Aura 8 Jd 60.36N 22.34 E
Aurangābād 25 Fe 19.53N 75.20 E
Aurari Bay 59 Gb 11.40S 133.40 E
Aur Atoll 57 Id 8.16N 171.06 E
Auray 11 Dg 47.40N 2.59W
Aurdal 7 Bf 60.56N 9.24 E
Aure 11 Ee 49.20N 1.07W
Aure [Nor.] 7 Be 63.13N 8.32 E
Aure [Nor.] 8 Bb 62.24N 6.36 E
Aurejärvi 8 Jb 62.05N 23.25 E
Aurès, Massif de l'- 30 He 35.14N 6.10 E
Aurich 10 Dc 53.28N 7.29 E
Aurillac 11 Ij 44.55N 2.27 E
Aurlandsfjorden 8 Bc 61.05N 7.05 E
Aurlandsvangen 7 Bf 60.54N 7.11 E
Auron 11 Mj 44.12N 6.56 E
Auron 11 Ig 47.06N 2.24 E
Aurora [Co.-U.S.] 43 Gd 39.44N 104.52W
Aurora [Il.-U.S.] 43 Jc 42.46N 88.19W
Aurora [Mo.-U.S.] 45 Jh 36.58N 93.43W
Aurora [Phil.] 26 He 7.57N 123.36 E
Aurora do Norte 55 Ia 12.38S 46.23W
Aursjøen 8 Cb 62.20N 8.40 E
Aursunden 8 Db 62.40N 11.40 E
Aurukun Mission 59 Ib 13.19S 141.45 E
Aurunci, Monti- 14 Hi 41.20N 13.40 E
Aus 37 Be 26.40S 16.15 E
Au Sable River 44 Fc 44.25N 83.20W
Ausangate, Nudo- 52 Ig 13.47S 71.13W
Ausiait/Egedesminde 67 Nc 68.50N 52.45W
Ausoni, Monti- 14 Hi 41.25N 13.20 E
Aust-Agder 7 Bg 58.50N 8.00 E
Austfonna 41 Oc 79.55N 25.00 E
Austin [Mn.-U.S.] 43 Ic 43.40N 92.59W
Austin [Nv.-U.S.] 43 Dd 39.30N 117.04W
Austin [Tx.-U.S.] 39 Jf 30.16N 97.45W
Austin, Lake- 59 De 27.40S 118.00 E
Austral, Chaco- 52 Jh 25.00S 61.00W
Australes, Iles-/Tubuai, Iles-=Tubuai Islands (EN) 57 Lg 23.00S 150.00W
Australia 57 Eg 25.00S 135.00 E
Australia 58 Eg 25.00S 135.00 E
Australian Alps 57 Fh 37.00S 148.00 E
Australian Capital Territory 59 Jg 35.30S 149.00 E
Austria (EN) = Österreich 6 Hf 47.30N 14.00 E
Austvågøy 7 Db 68.20N 14.36 E
Autazes 54 Gd 3.35S 59.08W
Autheuil-Authouillet 12 De 49.06N 1.17 E
Authie 11 Hd 50.21N 1.38 E
Autlán de Navarro 47 De 19.46N 104.22W
Autun 11 Kh 46.57N 4.18 E
Auve 12 Ge 49.02N 4.42 E
Auvergne 11 Ii 45.20N 3.00 E
Auvergne, Monts d'- 11 Ii 45.30N 2.45 E
Auvézère 11 Gi 45.12N 0.50 E
Auvillers-lès-Forges-Mon Idée 12 Ge 49.52N 4.21 E
Auxerre 11 Jg 47.48N 3.34 E
Auxi-le-Château 11 Id 50.14N 2.07 E
Auxois 11 Kg 47.20N 4.30 E
Auxonne 11 Lg 47.12N 5.23 E
Auyán-Tepuy 54 Fb 5.55N 62.32W
Auzances 11 Ih 46.01N 2.30 E
Avaavaroa Passage 64p Bc 21.16S 159.47W
Availles-Limouzine 11 Gh 46.07N 0.39 E
Avala 15 De 44.42N 20.31 E
Avaldsnes 8 Ae 59.21N 5.16 E
Avallon 11 Jg 47.29N 3.54 E
Avalon Peninsula 42 Mg 47.30N 53.30W
Avana 64p Cb 21.14S 159.41W
Avaré 55 Hf 23.05S 48.55W
Avarua 58 Lg 21.12S 159.46W
Avarua Harbour 64p Bb 21.11S 159.46W
Avatele 64k Bb 19.06S 169.55W
Avatele Bay 64k Bb 19.05S 169.56W
Avatiu 64p Bb 21.12S 159.47W
Avatiu Harbour 64p Bb 21.11S 159.47W
Avatolu, Passe- 64h Ab 13.19S 176.14W
Ávdhira 15 Hi 40.59N 24.57 E
Ave 13 Dc 41.20N 8.45W
Aveh 24 Ne 34.47N 50.25 E
Aveh, Gardaneh-ye- 24 Me 35.32N 49.09 E
Aveiro 13 Dd 40.45N 8.30W
Aveiro [Braz.] 54 Gd 3.15S 55.10W
Aveiro [Port.] 13 Dd 40.38N 8.39W
Āvej 24 Me 35.34N 49.13 E
Avelgem 12 Fd 50.46N 3.26 E
Avellaneda [Arg.] 56 Ic 29.07S 59.40W
Avellaneda [Arg.] 56 Id 34.39S 58.23W
Avellino 14 Ij 40.54N 14.47 E
Aven Armand 11 Jj 44.15N 3.22 E
Averbode 12 Gc 51.02N 4.59 E
Avereest 12 Ib 52.37N 6.27 E
Avereest-Dedemsvaart 12 Ib 52.37N 6.27 E
Averøya 7 Be 63.00N 7.35 E
Aversa 14 Ij 40.58N 14.12 E
Avesnes-le-Compte 12 Ed 50.17N 2.32 E
Avesnes-les-Aubert 12 Fd 50.12N 3.23 E
Avesnes-sur-Helpe 11 Jd 50.07N 3.56 E
Aves Ridge (EN) 47 Lf 14.00N 63.30W
Avesta 7 Df 60.09N 16.12 E
Aveyron 11 Hj 44.05N 1.16 E
Aveyron 11 Ij 44.15N 2.30 E
Avezzano 14 Hh 42.02N 13.25 E
Avgan 15 Mk 38.25N 29.24 E
Avgó [Grc.] 15 In 35.36N 25.34 E
Avgó [Grc.] 15 Jn 35.55N 26.30 E
Aviemore 9 Jd 57.12N 3.50W
Avigait 41 Gf 62.15N 50.00W
Avigliano 14 Jj 40.44N 15.43 E
Avignon 6 Gg 43.57N 4.49 E
Ávila 13 Hd 40.39N 4.42W
Ávila 13 Hd 40.35N 5.00W
Ávila, Sierra de- 13 Gd 40.35N 5.08W
Avilés 13 Ga 43.33N 5.55W
Avinurme 8 Lf 58.55N 26.50 E
Avion 12 Ed 50.24N 2.50 E
Ávios Theódhoros 15 Gn 35.32N 23.56 E
Avioth 12 He 49.34N 5.24 E
Avis 13 Ee 39.03N 7.53W
Avisio 14 Fd 46.07N 11.05 E
Avize 12 Gf 48.58N 4.01 E
Avlaka Burun 15 Ii 40.07N 25.40 E
Avola [B.C.-Can.] 46 Fa 51.47N 119.19W
Avola [It.] 14 Jn 36.54N 15.08 E
Avon 9 Kj 51.30N 2.30W
Avon [Eng.-U.K.] 9 Kj 51.59N 2.10W
Avon [Eng.-U.K.] 9 Kj 51.30N 2.43W
Avon [Eng.-U.K.] 9 Lk 50.43N 1.46W
Avon Downs 58 Eg 20.05S 137.30 E
Avon Park 44 Gl 27.36N 81.31W
Avon River 59 Df 31.40S 116.07 E
Avranches 11 Ef 48.41N 1.22W
Avre [Fr.] 11 Ie 49.53N 2.20 E
Avre [Fr.] 11 Hf 48.47N 1.22 E
Avrig 15 Hd 45.43N 24.23 E
Avron 11 Ki 45.15N 4.50 E
Avşa Adasi 15 Ki 40.30N 27.30 E
Avuavu 63a Ec 9.50S 160.23 E
Awaji 28 Mg 34.35N 135.01 E
Awaji-Shima 28 Mg 34.25N 134.50 E
'Awālī 24 Ni 26.05N 50.33 E
Awanui 61 Dg 35.03S 173.15 E
Awara Plain 36 Hb 3.45N 41.07 E
Aware 35 Gd 8.14N 44.10 E
Awarua Bay 62 Cf 44.20S 168.05 E
Awasa 31 Kh 7.02N 38.29 E
Awash 30 Lg 11.12N 41.40 E
Awash 35 Gd 8.59N 40.10 E
Awa-Shima 28 Oe 38.27N 139.14 E
Awaso 34 Ed 6.14N 2.16W
Awat 27 Dc 40.38N 80.22 E
Awata 35 Fe 4.45N 39.26 E
Awatere 62 Fd 41.36S 174.10 E
Awbārī 31 If 26.35N 12.46 E
Awbārī 33 Bd 26.35N 12.46 E
Awbārī, Şaḩrā' 30 If 27.30N 11.30 E
Awdēgle 35 Ge 1.58N 44.51 E
Awe, Loch- 9 He 56.15N 5.15W
Awjilah 31 Jf 29.06N 21.17 E
Axel 12 Fc 51.16N 3.54 E
Axel Heiberg 38 Ja 80.30N 92.00W
Axim 34 Ee 4.52N 2.14W
Axiós 15 Fi 40.35N 22.50 E
Axixá 54 Jd 2.51S 44.04W
Ax-les-Thermes 11 Hl 42.43N 1.50 E
Ayabaca 54 Cd 4.38S 79.43W
Ayabe 28 Mg 35.18N 135.15 E
Ayachi, Ari n'- 32 Gc 32.30N 4.50W
Ayacucho 54 Df 14.00S 74.00W
Ayacucho [Arg.] 56 Ie 37.09S 58.29W
Ayacucho [Peru] 53 Ig 13.07S 74.13W
Ayakita-Gawa 29 Bf 31.58N 131.23 E
Ayakkum Hū 27 Ed 37.30N 89.20 E
Ayamé 34 Ed 5.37N 3.11W
Ayamonte 13 Eg 37.13N 7.24W
Ayancık 24 Fb 41.57N 34.36 E
Ayangba 34 Gd 7.31N 7.08 E
Ayapel 54 Cb 8.18N 75.08W
Ayas 24 Eb 40.01N 32.21 E
Ayaviri 54 Df 14.52S 70.35W
Āybak 23 Kb 36.16N 68.01 E
Aybastı 24 Gb 40.41N 37.24 E
Aycliffe 9 Lg 54.36N 1.34W
'Aydim, Wādī- 35 Ib 18.08N 53.08 E
Aydın 23 Cb 37.51N 27.51 E
Aydıncık 24 Ed 36.08N 33.17 E
Aydın Dağları 24 Bc 38.00N 28.00 E
Aydingkol Hu 27 Ec 42.40N 89.15 E
Aydinkent 24 Ed 37.06N 31.36 E
Aydos Dağı 24 Fd 37.21N 34.22 E
Ayerbe 13 Lb 42.17N 0.41W
Ayer Hitam 26 Df 1.55N 103.11 E

Index Symbols

1 Independent Nation
2 State, Region
3 District, County
4 Municipality
5 Colony, Dependency
Continent
Physical Region
Historical or Cultural Region
Mount, Mountain
Volcano
Hill
Mountains, Mountain Range
Hills, Escarpment
Plateau, Upland
Pass, Gap
Plain, Lowland
Delta
Salt Flat
Valley, Canyon
Crater, Cave
Karst Features
Depression
Polder
Desert, Dunes
Forest, Woods
Heath, Steppe
Oasis
Cape, Point
Coast, Beach
Cliff
Peninsula
Isthmus
Sandbank
Island
Atoll
Rock, Reef
Islands, Archipelago
Rocks, Reefs
Coral Reef
Well, Spring
Geyser
River, Stream
Waterfall Rapids
River Mouth, Estuary
Lake
Salt Lake
Intermittent Lake
Reservoir
Swamp, Pond
Canal
Glacier
Ice Shelf, Pack Ice
Ocean
Sea
Gulf, Bay
Strait, Fjord
Lagoon
Bank
Seamount
Tablemount
Ridge
Shelf
Basin
Escarpment, Sea Scarp
Fracture
Trench, Abyss
National Park, Reserve
Point of Interest
Recreation Site
Cave, Cavern
Historic Site
Ruins
Wall, Walls
Church, Abbey
Temple
Scientific Station
Airport
Port
Lighthouse
Mine
Tunnel
Dam, Bridge

Name	Page	Grid	Lat.	Long.
Ayeyarwady	25	Ie	17.00N	95.00 E
Ayeyarwady = Irrawaddy (EN)	21	Lg	15.50N	95.06 E
Ayiá	15	Fj	39.43N	22.46 E
Ayia Marina	15	Jl	37.09N	26.52 E
Ayiásos	15	Jj	39.06N	26.22 E
Áyion Óros=Athos, Mount- (EN) [2]	15	Hi	40.15N	24.15 E
Áyios Evstrátios	15	Hj	39.31N	25.00 E
Áyios Ioánnis, Ákra-	15	In	35.20N	25.46 E
Áyios Kírikos	15	Jl	37.35N	26.14 E
Áyios Minás	15	Jl	37.36N	26.34 E
Áyios Nikólaos	15	In	35.11N	25.43 E
Áyios Yeóryios	15	Gl	37.28N	23.56 E
Aykota	35	Fb	15.10N	37.03 E
Aylesbury	9	Mj	51.50N	0.50W
Ayllón, Sierra de-	13	Ic	41.15N	3.25W
Aylmer Lake	42	Gd	64.05N	108.30W
Aylsham	12	Db	52.47N	1.15 E
Ayna	13	Jf	38.33N	2.05W
'Aynabo	35	Hd	8.57N	46.30 E
'Ayn ad Darāhim	14	Cn	36.47N	8.42 E
'Ayn al Baydā	24	Ge	34.32N	37.55 E
'Ayn al Ghazāl [Eg.]	24	Dj	25.46N	30.38 E
'Ayn al Ghazāl [Lib.]	31	Jf	21.50N	24.55 E
'Ayn al Shigi	24	Ci	27.01N	28.02 E
'Ayn al Wādī	24	Ci	27.23N	28.13 E
'Ayn Bū Sālim	14	Cn	36.37N	8.59 E
'Ayn Dāllah	33	Ed	27.19N	27.20 E
'Ayn Dār	24	Mj	25.58N	49.14 E
'Ayn Dīwār	24	Jd	37.17N	42.11 E
'Ayn Ilwān	24	Dj	25.44N	30.25 E
'Ayn Khalīfah	24	Bi	26.46N	27.47 E
'Ayn Sifnī	24	Jd	36.42N	43.21 E
'Ayn Sukhnah	33	Fd	29.30N	32.10 E
'Aynūnah	23	Ed	28.05N	35.08 E
Ayod	35	Ed	8.08N	31.24 E
Ayora	13	Ke	39.04N	1.03W
Ayorou	34	Fc	14.44N	0.55 E
'Ayoûn el 'Atroûs	31	Gg	16.38N	9.36W
Ayr	9	If	55.29N	4.28W
Ayr [Austl.]	59	Jc	19.35 S	147.24 E
Ayr [Scot.-U.K.]	9	If	55.28N	4.38W
Ayre, Point of-	9	Ig	54.26N	4.22W
Ayrolle, Étang de l'-	11	Jk	43.16N	3.30 E
Aysha	35	Gc	10.45N	42.35 E
Aytré	11	Eh	46.08N	1.06W
Ayutla	48	Gg	20.07N	104.22W
Ayutla de los Libres	48	Ji	16.54N	99.13W
Ayvacık	24	Gb	41.00N	36.45 E
Ayvacik	15	Jj	39.36N	26.24 E
Ayvalık	23	Cb	39.18N	26.41 E
Aywaille	12	Hd	50.28N	5.40 E
Āzādshahr	24	Pd	37.05N	55.08 E
'Azahar, Costa del-	13	Me	39.58N	0.01 E
Azaila	13	Lc	41.17N	0.29W
Azambuja	13	De	39.04N	8.52W
Azamgarh	25	Gc	26.04N	83.11 E
Azángaro	54	Df	14.55 S	70.13W
Azannes-et-Soumazannes	12	He	49.18N	5.28 E
Azaouâd=Azaouad (EN)	30	Gg	19.00N	3.00W
Azaouad (EN)=Azaouâd	30	Gg	19.00N	3.00W
Azaouak	34	Fb	15.30N	3.18 E
Azaouak	30	Hg	15.20N	4.55 E
Azaouak, Vallée de l'-	30	Hg	17.30N	3.40 E
Azar	34	Fb	16.02N	4.04 E
Āžarbāījān-e Gharbī [3]	23	Fb	37.00N	45.00 E
Āžarbāījān-e Sharqī [3]	23	Gb	37.00N	47.00 E
Azarbaijčan Sovet Socialistik Respublicasy/ Azerbajdžanskaja SSR [2]	19	Eg	40.30N	47.30 E
Azare	34	Hc	11.41N	10.12 E
Āzār Shahr	24	Kd	37.45N	45.59 E
Azay-le-Rideau	11	Gg	47.16N	0.28 E
A 'zāz	24	Gd	36.35N	37.03 E
Azazga	13	Qh	36.44N	4.22 E
Azbine/Aïr	30	Hg	18.00N	8.30 E
Azdaak, Gora-	16	Ni	40.13N	44.59 E
Azdavay	24	Eb	41.39N	33.18 E
Azefal	30	Ff	21.00N	14.45W
Azeffoun	13	Qh	36.53N	4.25 E
Azemmour	32	Fc	33.17N	8.21W
Azerbaijan (EN)	21	Gf	37.00N	46.00 E
Azerbaijan SSR (EN) = Azerbajdžanskaja SSR [2]	19	Eg	40.30N	47.30 E
Azerbajdžanskaja Sovetskaja Socialističeskaja Respublika [2]	19	Eg	40.30N	47.30 E
Azerbajdžanskaja SSR/ Azarbaijčan Sovet Socialistik Respublicasy [2]	19	Eg	40.30N	47.30 E
Azerbajdžanskaja SSR= Azerbaijan SSR (EN)	19	Eg	40.30N	47.30 E
Azeri/Aseri	7	Gg	59.29N	26.51 E
Azevedo Sodré	55	Ej	30.04S	54.36W
Azezo	35	Fc	12.33N	37.25 E
Azilal [3]	32	Fc	32.09N	6.05W
Azilal	32	Fc	31.58N	6.35W
Aznā	24	Mf	33.56N	49.24 E
Aznakajevo	7	Mi	54.56N	53.04 E
Azogues	54	Cd	2.44 S	78.48W
Azores (EN)=Açores [5]	31	Ee	38.30N	28.00W
Azores (EN)=Açores, Arquipélago dos-	30	Ee	38.30N	28.00W
Azores-Gibraltar Ridge (EN)	3	Df	37.00N	16.00W
Azoum, Bahr-	30	Jg	10.53N	20.15 E
Azov	19	Df	47.05N	39.25 E
Azov, Sea of- (EN)= Azovskoje More	5	Jf	46.00N	36.00 E
Azovskoje More=Azov, Sea of- (EN)	5	Jf	46.00N	36.00 E
Azpeitia	13	Ja	43.11N	2.16W
Azrak, Bahr-	35	Bc	10.50N	19.50 E
Azraq, Al Baḩr al-=Blue Nile (EN)	30	Kg	15.38N	32.31 E
Azraq ash Shīshān	24	Gg	31.50N	36.49 E
Azrou	32	Fc	33.26N	5.13W
Aztec	45	Ch	36.49N	107.59W
Aztec Ruins	46	Kh	36.51N	108.10W
Azua	49	Ld	18.27N	70.44W
Azuaga	13	Gf	38.16N	5.41W
Azuar	13	Ie	39.08N	3.36W
Azuero, Peninsula de-= Azuero Peninsula (EN)	38	Ki	7.40N	80.30W
Azuero Peninsula (EN)= Azuero, Peninsula de-	38	Ki	7.40N	80.30W
Azul	53	Ki	36.45 S	59.50W
Azul, Arroyo del-	55	Cm	36.15 S	59.07W
Azul, Cerro-	54a	Ab	0.54 S	91.21W
Azul, Cordillera-	54	Ce	8.30 S	76.00W
Azul, Rio-	48	Oi	17.54N	88.52W
Azul, Serra-	55	Eb	14.50 S	54.50W
Azul, Sierras del-	55	Cm	37.02 S	59.55W
Azūm	35	Cc	10.53N	20.15 E
Azuma-San	29	Gc	37.44N	140.08 E
Azur, Côte d'-	11	Mk	43.30N	7.00 E
Azurduy	54	Fg	19.59 S	64.29W
Azzaba	32	Ib	36.44N	7.06 E
Az Zāb al Kabīr	23	Fb	36.00N	43.21 E
Az Zāb aş Şaghīr	23	Fb	35.12N	43.25 E
Az Zabdānī	24	Gf	33.43N	36.05 E
Az Zabū	24	Ch	28.22N	28.56 E
Aẓ Ẓafir	23	Ff	19.57N	41.30 E
Az Zaghāwa	35	Cb	15.15N	23.14 E
Aẓ Ẓāhirah	24	Qk	23.30N	56.15 E
Az Zallāq	24	Ni	26.03N	50.29 E
Az Zaqāzīq	33	Fc	30.35N	31.31 E
Az Zarqā'	24	Oj	24.53N	53.04 E
Az Zarqā'	24	Gf	32.05N	36.06 E
Az Zāwiyah [3]	33	Bc	32.40N	12.10 E
Az Zāwiyah	33	Bc	32.45N	12.44 E
Az Zaytūn	33	Ed	29.09N	25.47 E
Azzel Matti, Sebkha-	30	Hf	26.00N	0.55 E
Az Zilfī	24	Ki	26.18N	44.48 E
Az Zubayr	24	Lg	30.23N	47.43 E

B

Name	Page	Grid	Lat.	Long.
Baa	26	Hi	10.43 S	123.03 E
Baaba	63b	Ae	20.03 S	163.58 E
Ba'ādwēyn	35	Hd	7.12N	47.24 E
Bá an Daingin/Dingle Bay	9	Ci	52.05N	10.15W
Baar	10	Ei	48.00N	8.30 E
Baarle-Hertog	12	Gc	51.27N	4.56 E
Baarn	12	Hb	52.14N	5.17 E
Baas, Bassure de-	12	Dd	50.30N	1.15 E
Bāb	24	Ok	23.55N	53.45 E
Baba	35	Bd	6.25N	17.07 E
Baba	15	Ei	40.55N	21.10 E
Baba Burun [Tur.]	24	Db	41.18N	31.26 E
Baba Burun [Tur.]	24	Bc	39.29N	26.04 E
Babadağ	15	Ll	37.48N	28.52 E
Baba Dağ	15	Mm	36.32N	29.10 E
Babadag	15	Le	44.54N	28.43 E
Babadag, Gora-	16	Pi	41.01N	48.29 E
Babaeski	24	Bb	41.26N	27.06 E
Bābā-Ḩeydar	24	Nf	32.20N	50.28 E
Babajevo	19	Dd	59.24N	35.55 E
Babajtag, Gora-	18	Hd	41.13N	70.16 E
Babajurt	16	Oh	43.35N	46.47 E
Bāb al Māndab=Bab el Mandeb (EN)	30	Lg	12.35N	43.25 E
Babanūsah	35	Dc	11.20N	27.48 E
Babao → Qilian	27	Hd	38.14N	100.15 E
Babaoyo	54	Cd	1.50 S	79.30W
Babar, Kepulauan-	26	Ih	7.50 S	129.45 E
Babar, Pulau-	57	De	7.55 S	129.45 E
Babase	63a	Aa	4.01 S	153.42 E
Babatag, Hrebet-	18	Ge	38.00N	68.10 E
Babati	36	Gc	4.13 S	35.45 E
Babbitt	45	Kc	47.43N	91.57W
B'abdā	24	Ff	33.50N	35.32 E
Bab el Mandeb (EN)=Bāb al Māndab	30	Lg	12.35N	43.25 E
Babelthuap Island	57	Ed	7.30N	134.36 E
Babenhausen [Ger.]	10	Gh	48.09N	10.15 E
Babenhausen [Ger.]	12	Ke	49.58N	8.57 E
Babeni	15	He	44.59N	24.15 E
Baberton	44	Ge	41.02N	81.38W
Bá Bheanntrai/Bantry Bay	9	Dj	51.38N	9.48W
Babian Jiang=Black River (EN)	21	Mg	20.17N	106.34 E
Babil [3]	24	Kf	32.40N	44.50 E
Babine Lake	42	Ef	54.45N	126.00W
Babino Polje	14	Lh	42.43N	17.33 E
Babit Point	51b	Ab	18.03N	63.02W
Babo	26	Jg	2.33 S	133.25 E
Bābol	23	Hb	36.34N	52.42 E
Babol Sar	24	Od	36.43N	52.39 E
Baboquivari Peak	46	Jk	31.46N	111.35W
Babor, Djebel-	13	Rh	36.32N	5.28 E
Baborigame	48	Fd	26.27N	107.16W
Baboua	35	Ad	5.48N	14.49 E
Babozero, Ozero-	7	Ic	66.30N	37.25 E
Babu → Hexian	27	Jg	24.28N	111.34 E
Babuna	15	Eh	41.30N	21.40 E
Babuyan	26	Hc	19.32N	121.57 E
Babuyan	26	Gd	10.01N	118.58 E
Babuyan Channel	26	Hc	18.44N	121.40 E
Babuyan Islands	21	Oh	19.15N	121.40 E
Babylon	23	Fc	32.32N	44.25 E
Bač	15	Cd	45.23N	19.14 E
Bacabachi	48	Ed	26.55N	109.24W
Bacabal	53	Lf	4.14 S	44.47W
Ba-Cagan	27	Gb	45.40N	99.30 E
Bacajá, Rio-	54	Hd	3.25 S	51.50W
Bacalar	48	Oh	18.43N	88.27W
Bacalar, Laguna de-	48	Oh	18.43N	88.22W
Bacalar Chico, Boca-	49	Dd	18.12N	87.53W
Bacan, Kepulauan-	26	Ig	0.35 S	127.30 E
Bacan, Pulau-	26	Ig	0.35 S	127.30 E
Bacău [2]	15	Jc	46.36N	27.00 E
Bacău	6	If	46.34N	26.54 E
Baccarat	11	Mf	48.27N	6.45 E
Bacchiglione	14	Ge	45.11N	12.14 E
Baceşti	15	Kc	46.51N	27.14 E
Bachaquero	49	Li	9.56N	71.08W
Bacharach	12	Jd	50.04N	7.46 E
Bacheli	25	Ge	18.40N	81.15 E
Bachiniva	48	Fc	28.45N	107.15W
Bachu/Maralwexi	27	Cd	39.46N	78.15 E
Back	38	Jd	67.15N	95.15W
Bačka	15	Cd	45.50N	19.30 E
Bac Kan	25	Ld	22.08N	105.49 E
Bačka Palanka	15	Cd	45.15N	19.22 E
Bačka Topola	15	Cd	45.49N	19.39 E
Bäckefors	8	Ef	58.48N	12.10 E
Bäckhammar	8	Fe	59.10N	14.11 E
Backnang	10	Fh	48.57N	9.26 E
Bačkovski Manastir	15	Hh	41.56N	24.51 E
Bac Lieu	25	Lg	9.17N	105.43 E
Bac Ninh	25	Ld	21.11N	106.03 E
Bacolet	51p	Bb	12.02N	61.41W
Bacolod	22	Oh	10.40N	122.57 E
Bac-Phan=Tonkin (EN)	21	Mg	22.00N	105.00 E
Bacqueville, Lac-	42	Ke	58.00N	74.00W
Bacqueville-en Caux	12	Ce	49.47N	1.00 E
Bácsalmás	10	Pj	46.08N	19.20 E
Bács-Kiskun [2]	10	Pj	46.30N	19.25 E
Bacton	12	Db	52.51N	1.28 E
Bād	23	Hc	33.41N	52.01 E
Badagara	25	Ff	11.36N	75.35 E
Badagri	34	Fd	6.25N	2.53 E
Badain Jaran Shamo	21	Me	40.20N	101.40 E
Badajós, Lago-	54	Fd	3.15 S	62.45W
Badajoz	6	Fh	38.53N	6.58W
Badajoz [3]	13	Ff	38.40N	6.10W
Badakhshan [3]	23	Lb	36.45N	72.00 E
Badalona	13	Oc	41.27N	2.15 E
Badanah	23	Fc	30.59N	41.02 E
Badaohao	28	Fd	41.50N	121.59 E
Badas, Kepulauan-	26	Ef	0.35N	107.06 E
Bad Aussee	14	Hc	47.36N	13.47 E
Bad Axe	44	Fd	43.48N	83.00W
Bad Bergzabern	10	Dg	49.06N	8.00 E
Bad Berleburg	12	Kc	51.04N	8.24 E
Bad Bertrich	12	Jd	50.03N	7.02 E
Bad Bramstedt	10	Fc	53.55N	9.53 E
Bad Brückenau	10	Ff	50.18N	9.45 E
Badda	35	Fd	7.55N	39.23 E
Baddo	25	Cc	27.59N	64.21 E
Bad Doberan	10	Hb	54.06N	11.54 E
Bad Driburg	12	Lc	51.44N	9.01 E
Bad Düben	10	Ie	51.36N	12.35 E
Bad Dürkheim	12	Ke	49.28N	8.12 E
Bade	26	Kh	7.10 S	139.35 E
Bademli	15	Lk	38.04N	28.04 E
Baden [Aus.]	14	Kb	48.01N	16.14 E
Baden [Switz.]	14	Cc	47.28N	8.18 E
Baden-Baden	10	Eh	48.45N	8.15 E
Badenoch	9	Je	56.50N	4.00W
Baden-Württemberg [2]	10	Eh	48.30N	9.00 E
Bad Essen	12	Kb	52.19N	8.20 E
Bad Freienwalde	10	Kd	52.47N	14.02 E
Badgastein	14	Hc	47.07N	13.08 E
Bādghīsat [3]	23	Jc	35.00N	63.45 E
Bad Gleichenberg	14	Jd	46.52N	15.54 E
Bad Godesberg, Bonn-	10	Df	50.41N	7.09 E
Bad Hall	14	Ib	48.02N	14.12 E
Bad Harzburg	10	Ge	51.53N	10.34 E
Bad Herrenalb	12	Kf	48.48N	8.25 E
Bad Hersfeld	10	Ff	50.52N	9.42 E
Bad Homburg	10	Ef	50.13N	8.37 E
Bad Honnef	12	Jd	50.38N	7.12 E
Bá Dhún na nGall/Donegal Bay	5	Fe	54.30N	8.30W
Badhyz	18	Cg	35.50N	62.00 E
Badiraguato	48	Fe	25.22N	107.31W
Bad Ischl	14	Hc	47.43N	13.37 E
Bad Kissingen	10	Gf	50.12N	10.05 E
Bad Kreuznach	10	Dg	49.50N	7.52 E
Badlands [S.D.-U.S.]	45	Ee	43.30N	102.20W
Badlands [U.S.]	43	Gb	46.45N	103.30W
Bad Langensalza	10	Ge	51.06N	10.39 E
Bad Lautenberg am Harz	10	Ge	51.38N	10.28 E
Bad Liebenwerda	10	Je	51.31N	13.24 E
Bad Liebenzel	12	Kf	48.46N	8.44 E
Bad Mergentheim	10	Fg	49.29N	9.46 E
Bad Mondorf/Mondorf-les-Bains	12	Ie	49.30N	6.17 E
Bad Münster am Stein Ebernburg	12	Je	49.49N	7.51 E
Bad Münstereifel	12	Id	50.34N	6.45 E
Bad Muskau	10	Ke	51.33N	14.43 E
Bad Nauheim	12	Kd	50.22N	8.45 E
Bad Neuenahr-Ahweiler	10	Df	50.33N	7.08 E
Bad Neustadt an der Saale	10	Gf	50.20N	10.13 E
Bad Oeynhausen	12	Kb	52.12N	8.48 E
Bad Oldesloe	10	Gc	53.49N	10.23 E
Ba Don	25	Le	17.45N	106.27 E
Badou [China]	28	Df	36.27N	117.56 E
Badou [Togo]	34	Fd	7.35N	0.36 E
Bad Pyrmont	10	Fe	51.59N	9.15 E
Bad Ragaz	14	Dc	47.00N	9.30 E
Badrah	24	Kf	33.06N	45.58 E
Bad Reichenhall	10	Ii	47.44N	12.53 E
Badr Ḩunayn	23	Ee	23.44N	38.46 E
Bad River	45	Fd	44.22N	100.22W
Bad Salzuflen	12	Kb	52.05N	8.46 E
Bad Salzungen	10	Gf	50.49N	10.14 E
Bad Schwartau	10	Gc	53.55N	10.42 E
Bad Segeberg	10	Gc	53.56N	10.19 E
Bad Tölz	10	Hi	47.46N	11.34 E
Badulla	25	Gg	6.59N	81.03 E
Bad Wildungen	10	Fe	51.07N	9.07 E
Bad Wimpfen	10	Fg	49.14N	9.08 E
Baena	13	Hg	37.37N	4.19W
Baeza [Ec.]	54	Cd	0.28 S	77.53W
Baeza [Sp.]	13	Ig	37.59N	3.28W
Baf/Paphos	24	Ee	34.50N	32.35 E
Bafang	34	Hd	5.09N	10.11 E
Bafatà	31	Fg	12.10N	14.40W
Bafélé	34	Cc	10.09N	10.08W
Baffin	38	Mc	68.00N	70.00W
Baffin Bay	38	Mb	73.00N	65.00W
Bafia	34	He	4.45N	11.14 E
Bafilo	34	Fd	9.21N	1.16 E
Bafing [Afr.]	30	Fg	13.49N	10.50W
Bafing [I.C.]	34	Dd	7.52N	7.07W
Bafoulabé	34	Cc	13.48N	10.50W
Bafoussam	31	Ih	5.28N	10.25 E
Bāfq	23	Ic	31.35N	55.24 E
Bāfq, Kūh-e-	24	Pg	31.20N	55.10 E
Bafra	23	Ea	41.34N	35.56 E
Bafra Burnu	24	Fb	41.44N	35.58 E
Bāft	24	Qh	29.14N	56.38 E
Bafwaboli	36	Eb	0.39N	26.10 E
Bafwasende	36	Eb	1.05N	27.16 E
Baga	34	Hc	13.06N	13.50 E
Bagaces	49	Eh	10.31N	85.15W
Bagagem, Rio-	55	Ha	13.58 S	48.21W
Bagajevski	16	Lf	47.19N	40.25 E
Bāgalkot	25	Fe	16.11N	75.42 E
Bagamoyo	36	Gd	6.26 S	38.54 E
Bagansiapi-Api	26	Df	2.09N	100.49 E
Bağarasi	15	Kl	37.42N	27.33 E
Baga Sola	35	Ac	13.32N	14.19 E
Bagata	36	Cc	3.44 S	17.57 E
Bagdad	48	Ke	25.57N	97.09W
Bagdarin	20	Gf	54.30N	113.36 E
Bağdere	24	Ic	38.10N	40.45 E
Bagé	53	Ki	31.20 S	54.06W
Bages et de Sigean, Étang de-	11	Jk	43.05N	3.01 E
Baggs	46	Lf	41.02N	107.39W
Bágh Baile na Sgealg/ Ballinskelligs Bay	9	Cj	51.50N	10.15W
Baghdād [3]	24	Kf	33.18N	44.36 E
Baghdād	22	Gf	33.21N	44.23 E
Baghdādī, Ra's-	24	Fj	24.40N	35.06 E
Bāgh-e Chenār	24	Qh	28.11N	56.54 E
Bāgh-e-Malek	24	Mg	31.32N	49.55 E
Bagheria	14	Hl	38.05N	13.30 E
Bāghīn	23	Ic	30.12N	56.48 E
Baghlān [3]	23	Kb	35.45N	69.00 E
Baghlān	23	Kb	36.13N	68.46 E
Bāglung	25	Gc	28.16N	83.36 E
Bagn	8	Cd	60.49N	9.34 E
Bagnara Calabra	14	Jl	38.17N	15.48 E
Bagnères-de-Bigorre	11	Gk	43.04N	0.09 E
Bagnères-de-Luchon	11	Gl	42.47N	0.36 E
Bagni di Lucca	14	Ef	44.01N	10.35 E
Bagno di Romagna	14	Fg	43.50N	11.57 E
Bagnolo Mella	14	Ee	45.26N	10.10 E
Bagnols-sur-Cèze	11	Kj	44.10N	4.37 E
Bago	22	Lh	17.30N	96.30 E
Bagoé	30	Gg	12.36N	6.34W
Bagolino	14	Ee	45.49N	10.28 E
Bagrationovsk	8	Ij	54.23N	20.40 E
Bagrax/Bohu	27	Ec	41.58N	86.29 E
Bagrax Hu/Bosten	21	Ke	42.00N	87.00 E
Bagua	54	Ce	5.40 S	78.31W
Baguio	22	Oh	16.25N	120.36 E
Baguirmi	30	Ig	11.40N	16.20 E
Bagzane, Monts-	30	Hg	17.43N	8.45 E
Bahama Islands	38	Lg	24.15N	76.00W
Bahamas [1]	39	Lg	24.15N	76.00W
Bahamas, Canal Viejo de-= Old Bahama Channel (EN)	49	Ib	22.30N	78.05W
Bahār	24	Me	34.54N	48.26 E
Baharampur	25	Hd	24.06N	88.15 E
Baharden	19	Fh	38.28N	57.28 E
Bahardok	19	Fh	38.51N	58.24 E
Baharīyah, Wāḩāt al-	33	Ed	28.10N	29.00 E
Bahariya Oasis (EN)= Baḩarīyah, Wāḩāt al-	33	Ed	28.15N	28.57 E
Bahaur	26	Fg	3.20N	114.00 E
Bahāwalnagar	25	Ec	29.59N	73.16 E
Bahāwalpur	22	Jg	29.24N	71.41 E
Bahčisaraj	16	Hg	44.45N	33.51 E
Bahę	24	Gd	37.14N	36.34 E
Bahi	36	Gd	5.39 S	35.19 E
Bahia [2]	54	Jf	12.00 S	42.00W
Bahía, Islas de la-	47	Ge	16.20N	86.30W
Bahía Blanca	53	Ji	38.44 S	62.16W
Bahía de Caráquez	54	Bd	0.37 S	80.25W
Bahia Kino	47	Bc	28.50N	111.55W
Bahía Negra	56	Ib	20.15 S	58.12W
Bahias, Cabo dos-	52	Jj	44.55 S	65.32W
Bahīj	24	Cg	30.56N	29.35 E
Bahinga	36	Ed	5.57 S	27.06 E
Bahi Swamp	36	Gd	6.05 S	35.10 E
Bahlui	15	Kb	47.08N	27.44 E
Bahmač	19	De	51.11N	32.50 E
Bahoruco, Sierra de-	49	Ld	18.10N	71.25W
Bahraich	25	Gc	27.35N	81.36 E
Bahrain (EN)=Al Baḩrayn [1]	22	Hg	26.00N	50.29 E
Baḩr al Ghazāl [3]	35	Dd	8.15N	26.50 E
Bahr ar Ramla al Kabīr	33	Ed	27.00N	26.00 E
Baḩrayn, Khalij al-	24	Nj	25.45N	50.40 E
Bahr Dar	31	Kg	11.36N	37.22 E
Bahta	20	Dd	62.20N	89.15 E
Bahusi	15	Jc	46.43N	26.42 E
Baia	15	Le	44.43N	28.40 E
Baia de Aramă	15	Fe	45.00N	22.50 E
Baia de Fier	15	Gd	45.10N	23.46 E
Baia dos Tigres	36	Bf	16.35 S	11.43 E
Baia Farta	36	Be	12.37 S	13.26 E
Baia Mare	15	Gb	47.40N	23.35 E
Baião	54	Id	2.41 S	49.41W
Baia Sprie	15	Gb	47.40N	23.42 E
Baibiene	55	Ci	29.36 S	58.10W
Baïbokoum	35	Bd	7.45N	15.41 E
Baicheng	22	Oe	45.34N	122.49 E
Baicheng/Bay	27	Dc	41.46N	81.52 E
Băicoi	15	Id	45.02N	25.51 E
Băiculeşti	15	Hd	45.04N	24.42 E
Baïdou	35	Cd	5.52N	20.41 E
Baie-Comeau	39	Me	49.13N	68.10W
Baie-Mahault	50	Fd	16.16N	61.35W
Baie-Saint-Paul	42	Kg	47.27N	70.30W
Baie-Trinité	44	Na	49.24N	67.19W
Baie Verte	42	Lg	49.55N	56.11W
Baiguan → Shangyu	28	Fi	30.01N	120.53 E
Baihe	27	Je	32.46N	110.06 E
Bai He [China]	28	Bh	32.10N	112.20 E
Bai He [China]	28	Dd	40.43N	116.33 E
Baikal, Lake- (EN)=Bajkal, Ozero-	21	Md	53.00N	107.40 E
Baikal Range (EN)= Bajkalski Hrebet	21	Md	55.00N	108.40 E
Baile an Chaistil/ Ballycastle	118	Gf	55.12N	6.15W
Baile an Róba/Ballinrobe	118	Dh	53.37N	9.13W
Baile Átha Cliath/Dublin [2]	9	Gh	53.20N	6.15W
Baile Átha Cliath/Dublin	6	Fe	53.20N	6.15W
Baile Átha Luain/Athlone	9	Fh	53.25N	7.56W
Baile Átha Troim/Trim	9	Gh	53.34N	6.47W
Băile Borşa	15	Hb	47.41N	24.43 E
Baile Brigín/Balbriggan	9	Gh	53.37N	6.11W
Băile Govora	15	Hd	45.05N	24.11 E
Baile Locha Riach/Loughrea	9	Eh	53.12N	8.34W
Baile Mhistéala/ Mitchelstown	9	Ei	52.16N	8.16W
Bailén	13	If	38.06N	3.46W
Baile na Mainistreach/ Newtownabbey	9	Hg	54.42N	5.54W
Baile Nua na hArda/ Newtownards	9	Hg	54.36N	5.41W
Băile Olăneşti	15	Hd	45.12N	24.14 E
Băileşti	15	Ge	44.01N	23.21 E
Bailleul	12	Ce	49.12N	0.26 E
Bailleul	12	Ed	50.44N	2.44 E
Ba Illi	35	Bc	10.31N	16.29 E
Bailong Jiang	27	Ie	32.42N	105.15 E
Bailundo	36	Ce	12.10 S	15.56 E
Baima	27	He	33.05N	100.29 E
Bain	12	Ba	53.04N	0.12W
Bainbridge	43	Ke	30.54N	84.34W
Bain-de-Bretagne	11	Eg	47.50N	1.41W
Baines Drift	37	Dd	22.30 S	28.43 E
Baing	26	Hi	10.14 S	120.34 E
Baingoin	27	Ee	31.36N	89.48 E
Baiquan	27	Mb	47.38N	126.04 E
Bā'ir	24	Gg	30.46N	36.41 E
Bā'ir, Wādī-	24	Gg	31.12N	37.31 E
Baird	45	Gj	32.24N	99.24W
Baird Inlet	40	Gd	60.45N	164.00W
Baird Mountains	40	Gc	67.35N	161.30W
Baird Peninsula	42	Jc	69.00N	75.15W
Bairiki	58	Id	1.20N	173.01 E
Bairin Youqi (Daban)	27	Kc	43.30N	118.37 E
Bairin Zuoqi (Lindong)	27	Kc	43.59N	119.22 E
Bairnsdale	58	Fh	37.50 S	147.38 E
Bais	26	He	9.35N	123.07 E
Bai Shan	27	Fc	40.53N	93.48 E
Baisogala/Bajsogala	8	Ji	55.35N	23.44 E
Baitou Shan	21	Oe	42.00N	128.00 E
Baitoushan Tian Chi	28	Jc	42.00N	128.03 E
Baixiang	28	Cf	37.29N	114.44 E
Baixo Alentejo	13	Dg	37.55N	8.10W
Baixo Guandu	54	Jg	19.31 S	41.01W
Baixo Longa	36	Cf	15.42 S	18.38 E
Baiyanghe	27	Ec	43.12N	88.28 E
Baiyü	27	Ge	31.13N	98.51 E
Baja	10	Oj	46.11N	18.58 E
Baja, Punta- [Mex.]	48	Dc	28.25N	111.45W
Baja, Punta- [Pas.]	65d	Ab	27.10 S	109.22W
Baja California=Lower California (EN)	38	Hg	28.00N	112.00W
Baja California Norte [2]	47	Ac	30.00N	115.00W
Baja California Sur [2]	47	Bd	25.50N	111.50W
Bājah [3]	32	Ib	36.30N	9.30 E
Bājah	32	Ib	36.44N	9.11 E
Bajalān	24	Md	37.18N	48.47 E
Bajan	27	Jb	49.15N	111.58 E
Bajanaul	19	He	50.47N	75.42 E
Bajandaj	20	Ff	53.04N	105.30 E
Bajan-Delger	27	Jb	45.55N	112.15 E
Bajangol	20	Ff	50.40N	103.25 E
Bajan-Hongor	22	Me	46.20N	100.40 E
Bajan-Ula [Mong.]	27	Jb	49.07N	112.45 E
Bajan-Ula [Mong.]	27	Gb	47.05N	95.15 E
Bajan-Under	27	Gc	44.45N	98.45 E
Baja Verapaz [3]	49	Bf	15.05N	90.20W
Bajawa	26	Hh	8.47 S	120.59 E
Bajčunas	16	Rf	47.17N	53.03 E
Bajdarackaja Guba	20	Bc	69.00N	67.30 E
Bajdarata	17	Nb	68.12N	68.18 E
Bajdrag Gol	27	Hb	45.10N	100.45 E
Bājgīrān	24	Rd	37.36N	58.24 E
Baj-Haak	20	Ef	51.07N	94.34 E
Bajiazi	28	Jc	42.41N	129.13 E
Bajina Bašta	15	Cf	43.58N	19.34 E
Bajkal	20	Ff	51.53N	104.47 E
Bajkal, Ozero-=Baikal, Lake- (EN)	21	Md	53.00N	107.40 E
Bajkalovo	17	Kh	57.24N	63.40 E
Bajkalsk	20	Ff	51.30N	104.05 E
Bajkalski Hrebet=Baikal Range (EN)	21	Md	55.00N	108.40 E
Bajkit	20	Ed	61.41N	96.25 E
Bajkonur	19	Gf	47.50N	66.07 E
Bajmak	19	Fe	52.36N	58.19 E
Bajmba, Mount-	59	Ke	29.20 S	152.05 E
Bajmok	15	Cd	45.58N	19.26 E
Bajo Baudó	54	Cc	4.58N	77.22W

Index Symbols

[1] Independent Nation
[2] State, Region
[3] District, County
[4] Municipality
[5] Colony, Dependency
Continent
Physical Region
Historical or Cultural Region
Mount, Mountain
Volcano
Hill
Mountains, Mountain Range
Hills, Escarpment
Plateau, Upland
Pass, Gap
Plain, Lowland
Delta
Salt Flat
Valley, Canyon
Crater, Cave
Karst Features
Depression
Polder
Desert, Dunes
Forest, Woods
Heath, Steppe
Oasis
Cape, Point
Coast, Beach
Cliff
Peninsula
Isthmus
Sandbank
Island
Atoll
Rock, Reef
Islands, Archipelago
Rocks, Reefs
Coral Reef
Well, Spring
Geyser
River, Stream
Waterfall Rapids
River Mouth, Estuary
Lake
Salt Lake
Intermittent Lake
Reservoir
Swamp, Pond
Canal
Glacier
Ice Shelf, Pack Ice
Ocean
Sea
Gulf, Bay
Strait, Fjord
Lagoon
Bank
Seamount
Tablemount
Ridge
Shelf
Basin
Escarpment, Sea Scarp
Fracture
Trench, Abyss
National Park, Reserve
Point of Interest
Recreation Site
Cave, Cavern
Historic Site
Ruins
Wall, Walls
Church, Abbey
Temple
Scientific Station
Airport
Port
Lighthouse
Mine
Tunnel
Dam, Bridge

Bajo Boquete 49 Fi 8.46N 82.26W
Bajram-Ali 19 Gh 37.39N 62.12 E
Bajram Curri 15 Dg 42.21N 20.04 E
Bajsogala/Baisogala 8 Ji 55.35N 23.44 E
Bajsun 18 Fe 38.14N 67.12 E
Bajun Islands 30 Li 0.50S 42.15 E
Bajžansaj 18 Gc 43.13N 69.56 E
Baka 35 Ee 4.33N 30.05 E
Bakacak 15 Ki 40.12N 27.05 E
Bakadžicite 15 Jg 42.25N 26.43 E
Bakal 19 Fe 54.56N 58.48 E
Bakala 35 Cd 6.11N 20.22 E
Bakanas 19 Hg 44.48N 76.15 E
Bakar 14 Ie 45.18N 14.32 E
Bakčar 20 De 57.01N 82.10 E
Bake 26 Dg 3.03S 100.16 E
Bakel 34 Cc 14.54N 12.27W
Baker [Ca.-U.S.] 46 Gi 35.15N 116.02W
Baker [La.-U.S.] 45 Kk 30.35N 91.10W
Baker [Mt.-U.S.] 43 Gb 46.22N 104.17W
Baker [Or.-U.S.] 43 Dc 44.47N 117.50W
Baker, Mount- 43 Cb 48.47N 121.49W
Baker Island 57 Jd 0.15N 176.27W
Baker Lake 39 Jc 64.10N 95.30W
Baker Lake 38 Jc 64.10N 95.30W
Bakersfield 39 Hf 35.23N 119.01W
Bā Kēv 25 Lf 13.42N 107.12 E
Bakhma 24 Kd 36.38N 44.17 E
Bakhtarān (Kermānshāh) 22 Gf 34.19N 47.04 E
Bakhtarān [3] 23 Gc 34.15N 47.20 E
Bakhtegān, Daryāchech-ye 24 Ph 29.20N 54.05 E
Bakhūn, Kūh-e- 23 Id 27.56N 56.18 E
Bakir 24 Bc 38.55N 27.00 E
Bakırköy, İstanbul 15 Li 40.59N 28.52 E
Baklan 15 Ml 37.58N 29.36 E
Bako 35 Fd 7.19N 35.08 E
Bako [Eth.] 35 Fd 9.05N 37.07 E
Bako [Eth.] 35 Fd 5.50N 36.37 E
Bakony=Bakony Mountains (EN) 5 Hf 47.15N 17.50 E
Bakony Mountains (EN)= Bakony 5 Hf 47.15N 17.50 E
Bakool [3] 35 Ge 4.10N 43.50 E
Bakouma 35 Cd 5.42N 22.47 E
Bakoye 34 Cc 13.49N 10.50W
Bakpulād 24 Qc 38.10N 57.00 E
Baksan 16 Mh 43.40N 43.28 E
Baksan 16 Nh 43.42N 44.03 E
Baku 6 Kg 40.23N 49.51 E
Bakum 12 Kb 52.44N 8.11 E
Bakungan 26 Cf 2.56N 97.30 E
Bakuriani 16 Mi 41.43N 43.31 E
Bakutis Coast 66 Of 74.45S 120.00W
Balā 24 Ec 39.34N 33.08 E
Bala, Cerros de- 54 Ef 14.30S 67.40W
Balabac 26 Ge 7.59N 117.04 E
Balabac 26 Ge 7.57N 117.01 E
Balabac, Selat-=Balabac Strait (EN) 21 Ni 7.40N 117.00 E
Balabac Strait (EN)= Balabac, Selat- 21 Ni 7.40N 117.00 E
Ba'labakk 24 Ge 34.00N 36.12 E
Balabalangan, Kepulauan- 26 Gg 2.20S 117.25 E
Balaban Daği 24 Hb 40.28N 39.15 E
Balabanovo 16 Jb 55.11N 36.40 E
Balabio 63b Be 20.07S 164.11 E
Balaci 15 He 44.21N 24.55 E
Bal'ad 35 He 2.22N 45.24 E
Balad 24 Ke 34.01N 44.01 E
Balādīn as Sakrān 24 Kj 25.12N 44.37 E
Baladiyat 'Adan=Aden (EN) 22 Gh 12.46N 45.01 E
Balad Rūz 24 Kf 33.42N 45.05 E
Balagannoje 20 Je 59.43N 149.15 E
Balagansk 20 Ff 53.58N 103.02 E
Bālāghāt 25 Gd 21.48N 80.11 E
Bālāghāt Range 25 Fe 18.45N 76.30 E
Balagne 11a Aa 42.35N 8.50 E
Balaguer 13 Mc 41.47N 0.49 E
Balahna 19 Ed 56.31N 43.37 E
Balahta 20 Ee 55.24N 91.37 E
Balaka 36 Fe 14.59S 34.57 E
Balaklava 16 Hg 44.31N 33.34 E
Balakleja 19 Df 49.27N 36.52 E
Balakovo 6 Ke 52.02N 47.45 E
Balama 37 Fb 13.16S 38.36 E
Balambangam, Pulau- 26 Ge 7.17N 116.55 E
Bālā Morghāb 23 Jb 35.35N 63.20 E
Balan Daği 15 Lm 36.52N 28.20 E
Balankanche 48 Og 20.45N 88.30W
Balasan 26 Hd 11.28N 123.05 E
Balasore → Bāleshwar 25 Hd 21.30N 86.56 E
Balašov 19 Ee 51.33N 43.10 E
Balassagyarmat 10 Ph 48.05N 19.18 E
Balāţ 33 Ed 25.33N 29.16 E
Balaton 5 Hf 46.50N 17.45 E
Balatonfüred 10 Nj 46.57N 17.53 E
Balatonkeresztúr 10 Nj 46.42N 17.23 E
Balaurin 26 Hh 8.15S 123.43 E
Băläuseri 15 Hc 46.24N 24.41 E
Balayan 26 Hd 13.57N 120.44 E
Balazote 13 Jf 38.53N 2.08W
Balbi, Mount- 60 Ei 5.55S 154.59 E
Balboa Heights 47 Ig 8.57N 79.33W
Balbriggan/Baile Brigin 9 Gh 53.37N 6.11W
Balby 8 Ei 55.40N 13.20 E
Balcarce 56 Ie 37.50S 58.15W
Balcarce, Sierras de- 55 Cm 37.50S 58.40W
Bălcesti 15 Ge 44.37N 23.57 E
Balčik 15 Lf 43.25N 28.10 E
Balclutha 61 Ci 46.14S 169.44 E
Bald Eagle Mountain 44 Ie 41.00N 77.45W
Bald Head 59 Dg 35.07S 118.01 E
Bald Knob 44 Hg 37.56N 79.51W
Bald Knob 45 Ki 35.19N 91.34W
Baldo, Monte- 14 Ee 45.40N 10.50 E
Baldock 12 Bc 51.59N 0.11W
Baldone 8 Kh 56.41N 24.22 E
Baldur 45 Gb 49.23N 99.15W
Baldwin 44 Ed 43.54N 85.51W
Baldy Peak 43 Fe 33.55N 109.35W
Bale [3] 35 Gd 6.00N 41.00 E
Bâle/Basel 6 Gf 47.30N 7.30 E
Baleares [3] 13 Oe 39.30N 3.00 E
Baleares, Islas-/Balears, Illes-=Balearic Islands (EN) 5 Gh 39.30N 3.00 E
Balearic Islands (EN)= Bàleares, Islas-/Balears, Illes- 5 Gh 39.30N 3.00 E
Balearic Islands (EN)= Balears, Illes-/Baleares, Islas- 5 Gh 39.30N 3.00 E
Balears, Illes-/Baleares, Islas-=Balearic Islands (EN) 5 Gh 39.30N 3.00 E
Balease, Gunung- 26 Hg 2.24S 120.33 E
Baleia, Ponta de- 52 Mg 17.40S 36.07W
Baleine, Rivière à la- 42 Ke 58.15N 67.38W
Balej 20 Gf 51.35N 116.38 E
Balen 12 Hc 51.10N 5.09 E
Baler 26 Hc 15.46N 121.34 E
Bāleshwar 25 Hd 21.30N 86.56 E
Balezino 19 Fd 57.59N 53.02 E
Balfate 49 Df 15.48N 86.25W
Bălgarija=Bulgaria (EN) [1] 6 Ig 43.00N 25.00 E
Balgazyn 20 Ef 50.58N 95.12 E
Balguntay 27 Ec 42.45N 86.18 E
Balḩāf 23 Fg 13.58N 48.11 E
Balhaš 22 Je 46.49N 74.59 E
Balhaš, Ozero-=Balkhash, Lake- (EN) 21 Je 46.00N 74.00 E
Balho 35 Gc 12.00N 42.10 E
Balholm 7 Bf 61.12N 6.33 E
Bali [3] 26 Gh 8.30S 115.00 E
Bali, Laut-=Bali Sea (EN) 21 Nj 7.45S 115.30 E
Bali, Pulau- 21 Nj 8.20S 115.00 E
Bali, Selat-=Bali Strait (EN) 26 Fh 8.18S 114.25 E
Baliceaux Island 51n Bb 12.57N 61.08W
Baliem 26 Kg 4.25S 138.59 E
Balige 26 Cf 2.20N 99.04 E
Balikesir 23 Cb 39.39N 27.53 E
Balık Gölü 24 Jc 39.45N 43.36 E
Balīkh, Nahr- 24 He 35.53N 39.10 E
Balikpapan 22 Nj 1.17S 116.50 E
Balimbing 26 Dh 5.55S 104.34 E
Balimo 60 Ci 8.03S 142.56 E
Balingen 10 Eh 48.17N 8.51 E
Balinqiao 28 Ec 43.16N 118.38 E
Balintang Channel 26 Hc 19.49N 121.40 E
Bali Sea (EN)=Bali, Laut- 21 Nj 7.45S 115.30 E
Bali Strait (EN)=Bali, Selat- 26 Fh 8.18S 114.25 E
Balitung, Palau- 21 Mj 2.50S 107.55 E
Baliza 55 Fc 16.15S 52.25W
Balk, Gaasterland- 12 Hb 52.54N 5.36 E
Balkan Mountains (EN) = Stara Planina 5 Ig 43.15N 25.00 E
Balkan Peninsula (EN) 5 Ig 41.30N 23.00 E
Balkašino 19 Ge 52.32N 68.46 E
Balkh 23 Kb 36.46N 66.54 E
Balkh [3] 23 Kb 36.30N 67.00 E
Balkhash, Lake- (EN)= Balhaš, Ozero- 21 Je 46.00N 74.00 E
Balladonia 59 Ef 32.27S 123.51 E
Ballagen 7 Db 68.20N 16.50 E
Ballaghaderreen/Bealach an Doirin 9 Eh 53.55N 8.35W
Ballantrae 9 If 55.06N 5.00W
Ballantyne Strait 42 Ga 77.30N 115.00W
Ballarat 58 Fh 37.34S 143.52 E
Ballard, Lake- 59 Ee 29.25S 120.55 E
Ballé 34 Db 15.20N 8.36W
Ballenas, Bahía- 48 Cd 26.45N 113.25W
Ballenas, Canal de- 48 Cc 29.10N 113.25W
Ballenero, Canal- 56 Fh 54.50S 71.00W
Ballenita, Punta- 56 Fc 25.46S 70.44W
Balleny Islands 66 Ke 66.35S 162.50 E
Balleroy 12 Be 49.11N 0.50W
Balleza 48 Fd 26.57N 106.21W
Balli 15 Ki 40.50N 27.03 E
Ballia 25 Gc 25.45N 84.10 E
Ballina 59 Ke 28.52S 153.33 E
Ballina/Béal an Átha 9 Dg 54.07N 9.09W
Ballinasloe/Béal Átha na Sluaighe 9 Eh 53.20N 8.13W
Ballinger 45 Gk 31.44N 99.57W
Ballinrobe/Baile an Róba 9 Dh 53.37N 9.13W
Ballinskelligs Bay/Bágh Baile na Sgealg 9 Cj 51.50N 10.15W
Ballshi 15 Ci 40.36N 19.44 E
Ball's Pyramid 57 Gh 31.45S 159.15 E
Ballycastle/Baile an Chaistil 9 Gf 55.12N 6.15W
Ballyhaunis/Béal Átha hAmhnais 9 Eh 53.46N 8.46W
Ballymena/An Baile Meánach 9 Gg 54.52N 6.17W
Ballyshannon/Béal Átha Seanaidh 9 Eg 54.30N 8.11W
Balmazújváros 10 Ri 47.37N 21.21 E
Balmoral Castle 9 Jd 57.02N 3.15W
Balneario Orense 55 Cn 38.49S 59.46W
Balneario Oriente 55 Bn 38.55S 60.32W
Balombo 36 Be 12.21S 14.43 E
Balonne River 57 Fg 28.47S 147.56 E
Balota, Virful- 15 Gd 45.18N 23.53 E
Balovale 31 Jj 13.33S 23.07 E
Balrāmpur 25 Gc 27.26N 82.11 E
Balranald 59 If 34.38S 143.33 E
Balş 15 He 44.21N 24.06 E
Balsas [Braz.] 54 Ie 7.31S 46.02W
Balsas [Mex.] 48 Jh 18.00N 99.47W
Balsas, Depresión del- 48 Ih 18.00N 100.10W
Balsas, Río- [Mex.] 38 Ih 17.55N 102.10W
Balsas, Río- [Pan.] 49 Ii 8.15N 77.59W
Balsas, Rio das- [Braz.] 54 Ie 9.58S 47.52W
Balsas, Rio das- [Braz.] 54 Je 7.14S 44.33W
Bålsta 8 Ge 59.35N 17.30 E
Balsthal 14 Bc 47.19N 7.42 E
Balta 16 Ff 47.57N 29.38 E
Baltanàs 13 Hc 41.56N 4.15W
Baltasar Brum 56 Id 30.44S 57.19W
Baltaţi 15 Kb 47.13N 27.09 E
Baltic Sea (EN)=Baltijas Jūra 5 Hd 57.00N 19.00 E
Baltic Sea (EN)=Baltijos Jura 5 Hd 57.00N 19.00 E
Baltic Sea (EN)=Balti Meri 5 Hd 57.00N 19.00 E
Baltic Sea- (EN)=Baltiskoje More 5 Hd 57.00N 19.00 E
Baltic Sea (EN)=Bałtyckie, Morze- 5 Hd 57.00N 19.00 E
Baltic Sea (EN)=Itämeri 5 Hd 57.00N 19.00 E
Baltic Sea (EN)= Östersjön 5 Hd 57.00N 19.00 E
Baltic Sea (EN)= Østersøen 5 Hd 57.00N 19.00 E
Baltic Sea (EN)=Ostsee 5 Hd 57.00N 19.00 E
Baltijas Jūra=Baltic Sea (EN) 5 Hd 57.00N 19.00 E
Baltijos Jura=Baltic Sea (EN) 5 Hd 57.00N 19.00 E
Baltijsk 19 Be 54.40N 19.58 E
Baltijskaja Grjada 7 Fi 55.00N 25.00 E
Baltim 33 Fc 31.33N 31.05 E
Balti Meri=Baltic Sea (EN) 5 Hd 57.00N 19.00 E
Baltimore 39 Lf 39.17N 76.37W
Baltiskoje More=Baltic Sea (EN) 5 Hd 57.00N 19.00 E
Baltit (Hunza) 25 Ea 36.20N 74.40 E
Baltoj Voke 8 Kj 54.24N 25.16 E
Baltrum 10 Dc 53.44N 7.23 E
Bałtyckie, Morze-=Baltic Sea (EN) 5 Hd 57.00N 19.00 E
Baluarte, Rio- 48 Ff 22.49N 106.02W
Baluchistān=Baluchistan (EN) 21 Ig 28.00N 63.00 E
Baluchistān=Baluchistan (EN) [3] 25 Cc 28.00N 63.00 E
Baluchistan (EN)= Baluchistān [3] 25 Cc 28.00N 63.00 E
Baluchistan (EN)= Baluchistān 21 Ig 28.00N 63.00 E
Balupe 8 Lh 56.54N 27.02 E
Balurghat 25 Hc 25.13N 88.46 E
Balvard 24 Qh 29.25N 56.06 E
Balve 12 Jc 51.20N 7.52 E
Balver Wald 12 Jc 51.21N 7.51 E
Balvi/Balvy 7 Gh 57.08N 27.20 E
Balvy/Balvi 7 Gh 57.08N 27.20 E
Balya 24 Bc 39.45N 27.35 E
Balygyčan 20 Kd 64.00N 154.10 E
Balykši 16 Qf 47.02N 51.55 E
Bām 24 Qd 36.58N 57.59 E
Bam 23 Id 29.06N 58.21 E
Bama 34 Hc 11.31N 13.41 E
Bamaji Lake 45 Ka 51.09N 91.25W
Bamako 31 Gg 12.38N 8.00W
Bamako [3] 34 Dc 13.00N 8.00W
Bamba 34 Eb 17.02N 1.24W
Bambama 36 Bc 2.32S 13.33 E
Bambana, Río- 49 Fg 13.27N 83.50W
Bambangando 36 Df 16.59S 20.57 E
Bambari 31 Jh 5.45N 20.40 E
Bamberg 10 Gg 49.42N 10.52 E
Bambesa 36 Eb 3.28N 25.43 E
Bambesi 35 Ed 9.45N 34.44 E
Bambey J4 Bc 14.42N 16.28W
Bambezi 37 Dc 19.57S 28.55 E
Bambili 36 Eb 3.39N 26.07 E
Bambio 35 Be 3.54N 16.59 E
Bamboi 34 Ed 8.10N 2.02W
Bambouti 35 Dd 5.24N 27.12 E
Bambouto, Monts- 30 Ih 5.44N 10.04 E
Bambui 55 Je 20.01S 45.58W
Bam Co 27 Fe 31.15N 90.32 E
Bamenda 34 Hd 5.56N 10.10 E
Bāmīān [3] 23 Kc 34.45N 67.15 E
Bāmīān 23 Kc 34.50N 67.50 E
Bamiancheng 28 Gc 43.15N 124.00 E
Bamiantong→Muling 28 Kb 44.55N 130.32 E
Bamingui 35 Cd 7.34N 20.11 E
Bamingui 30 Ih 8.33N 19.05 E
Bamingui-Bangoran [3] 35 Cd 7.50N 20.15 E
Bampūr 23 Jd 27.12N 60.27 E
Bampūr 23 Id 27.18N 59.06 E
Banaadir 30 Lh 1.00N 44.00 E
Banaadir [3] 35 He 2.00N 45.15 E
Banaba Island 57 He 0.52S 169.35 E
Banabuiú, Açude- 54 Ke 5.20S 39.00W
Banagi 36 Fc 2.16S 34.51 E
Banalia 36 Eb 1.33N 25.20 E
Banamba 34 Dc 13.32N 7.27W
Bananal, Ilha do- [Braz.] 52 Kg 11.30S 50.15W
Bananal, Ilha do- [Braz.] 55 Dc 17.05S 56.25W
Bananga 25 Ig 6.57N 93.54 E
Banarli 15 Kh 41.04N 27.20 E
Banās 25 Fc 25.54N 76.45 E
Banās, Ra's- 30 Kf 23.54N 35.48 E
Banat 5 If 45.30N 21.00 E
Banat 15 Dd 45.30N 21.00 E
Banaz 24 Cc 38.46N 29.46 E
Banaz 24 Cc 38.12N 29.14 E
Banbar 27 Fe 30.48N 94.52 E
Banbridge/Droichead na Banna 9 Gg 54.21N 6.16W
Banbury 9 Li 52.04N 1.20W
Banco, Punta- 49 Fi 8.23N 83.09W
Bancroft 44 Ic 45.03N 77.51W
Bānda 25 Gc 25.29N 80.20 E
Banda, Kepulauan-=Banda Islands (EN) 26 Ig 4.35S 129.55 E
Banda, Laut-=Banda Sea (EN) 57 De 5.00S 128.00 E
Banda, Punta- 48 Ab 31.45N 116.45W
Banda Aceh 22 Li 5.34N 95.20 E
Bandai-San 29 Gc 37.38N 140.04 E
Banda Islands (EN)=Banda, Kepulauan- 26 Ig 4.35S 129.55 E
Bandak 8 Ce 59.25N 8.15 E
Bandama 30 Gh 5.10N 4.58W
Bandama Blanc 34 Dd 6.54N 5.31W
Bandar Behestī 23 Jd 25.18N 60.37 E
Bandar-e 'Abbās 22 Hg 27.11N 56.17 E
Bandar-e Anzalī 23 Gb 37.28N 49.27 E
Bandar-e Būshehr 22 Hg 28.59N 50.50 E
Bandar-e Chīrū 24 Oi 26.43N 53.43 E
Bandar-e Deylam 23 Hg 30.05N 50.07 E
Bandar-e-Gaz 24 Od 36.47N 53.59 E
Bandar-e-Khomeynī 24 Mg 30.25N 49.08 E
Bandar-e Lengeh 23 Hd 26.33N 54.53 E
Bandar-e Māh Shahr 23 Gc 30.33N 49.12 E
Bandar-e Maqām 23 Hd 26.56N 53.29 E
Bandar-e Moghūyeh 24 Pi 26.35N 54.31 E
Bandar-e-Rīg 24 Nh 29.29N 50.38 E
Bandar-e-Torkeman 23 Gf 30.45N 51.33 E
Bandar Seri Begawan 22 Ni 4.53N 114.56 E
Banda Sea (EN)=Banda, Laut- 57 De 5.00S 128.00 E
Bande 13 Eb 42.02N 7.58W
Bandeira, Pico da- 52 Lh 20.26S 41.47W
Bandeirantes 55 Ga 13.41S 50.48W
Bandeirantes, Ilha dos- 55 Ff 23.22S 53.50W
Bandera 56 Hc 28.54S 62.16W
Bandera, Alto- 49 Ld 18.49N 70.37W
Banderas, Bahia de- 47 Cd 20.40N 105.25W
Bandiagara 34 Ec 14.20N 3.37W
Bandiat 11 Gi 45.46N 0.20 E
Bandırma 23 Ca 40.20N 27.58 E
Bandirma Körfezi 15 Ki 40.25N 28.00 E
Bandol 11 Lk 43.08N 5.45 E
Bandon 46 Ce 43.07N 124.25W
Bandon/Abhainn na Bandan 9 Ej 51.40N 8.30W
Bandon/Droichead na Bandan 9 Ej 51.45N 8.45W
Ban Don, Ao- 25 Jg 9.20N 99.25 E
Bandundu [2] 36 Cc 5.00S 17.00 E
Bandundu 31 Ii 3.18S 17.20 E
Bandung 22 Mj 6.54S 107.36 E
Bāneh 24 Ke 35.59N 45.53 E
Banes 47 Id 20.58N 75.43W
Banff [Alta.-Can.] 42 Ff 51.10N 115.34W
Banff [Scot.-U.K.] 9 Kd 57.40N 2.31W
Banfora 34 Ec 10.38N 4.46W
Banga 36 Dd 5.57S 20.28 E
Bangalore 22 Jh 12.59N 77.35 E
Bangangté 34 Hd 5.09N 10.31 E
Bangar 26 Gf 4.43N 115.04 E
Bangassou 31 Jh 4.44N 22.49 E
Bangeta, Mount- 60 Di 6.16S 147.04 E
Banggai 26 Hg 1.34S 123.30 E
Banggai, Kepulauan-= Banggai Archipelago (EN) 26 Hg 1.30S 123.15 E
Banggai, Selat- 26 Hg 1.55S 124.00 E
Banggai Archipelago (EN)= Banggai, Kepulauan- 26 Hg 1.30S 123.15 E
Banggi, Pulau- 26 Ge 7.17N 117.12 E
Banghāzī=Benghazi (EN) 31 Je 32.07N 20.04 E
Banghāzī=Benghazi (EN) [3] 33 Dd 27.00N 20.30 E
Bangka, Pulau- [Indon.] 26 If 1.48N 125.09 E
Bangka, Pulau- [Indon.] 21 Mj 2.15S 106.00 E
Bangka, Selat-=Bangka Strait (EN) 26 Eg 2.20S 105.45 E
Bangkalan 26 Fh 7.02S 112.44 E
Bangka Strait (EN)= Bangka, Selat- 26 Eg 2.20S 105.45 E
Bangkinang 26 Df 0.21N 101.02 E
Bangko 26 Dg 2.05S 102.17 E
Bangkok (EN)=Krung Thep 22 Mh 13.45N 100.31 E
Bangladesh [1] 22 Kg 24.00N 90.00 E
Bangli 26 Gh 8.27S 115.21 E
Bangolo 34 Dd 7.01N 7.09W
Bangong Co 27 Ce 33.45N 79.15 E
Bangor [Me.-U.S.] 43 Nc 44.49N 68.47W
Bangor [Wales-U.K.] 9 Ih 53.13N 4.08W
Bangor/Beannchar 9 Hg 54.40N 5.40W
Bangoran 35 Bd 8.42N 19.06 E
Bangsund 7 Cd 64.24N 11.24 E
Bangu 36 Dd 9.05S 23.44 E
Bangued 26 Hc 17.36N 120.37 E
Bangui [C.A.R.] 31 Ih 4.22N 18.35 E
Bangui [Phil.] 26 Hc 18.32N 120.46 E
Bangweulu, Lake- 30 Jj 11.05S 29.45 E
Bangweulu Swamps 36 Fe 11.30S 30.15 E
Banhā 33 Fc 30.28N 31.11 E
Ban Houayxay 25 Kd 20.18N 100.26 E
Bani 30 Gg 14.30N 4.12W
Baní 47 Je 18.17N 70.20W
Bani, Jbel- 30 Gf 28.30N 9.00W
Bani Bangou 34 Fb 15.03N 2.42 E
Banie 10 Kc 53.08N 14.38 E
Banifing 34 Dc 12.43N 6.25W
Banī Forūr, Jazīreh-ye- 24 Pi 26.07N 54.28 E
Banihal Pass 25 Fb 33.15N 75.09 E
Banija 14 Ke 45.10N 16.10 E
Banikoara 34 Fc 11.18N 2.26 E
Banī ma 'Ārid 33 Ie 20.42N 47.42 E
Banī Mazār 33 Fd 28.30N 30.48 E
Banī Muḩammadiyāt 24 Di 27.17N 31.05 E
Banī Suwayf 33 Fd 29.05N 31.05 E
Banī Tonb 24 Pi 26.12N 54.56 E
Banī Walīd 33 Bc 31.46N 13.59 E
Bāniyās 23 Ec 33.15N 35.41 E
Banja 15 Hg 42.33N 24.50 E
Banja Koviljača 15 Ce 44.30N 19.11 E
Banja Luka 14 Lf 44.46N 17.10 E
Banjarmasin 22 Nj 3.20S 114.35 E
Banjul 31 Fg 13.27N 16.35W
Bank 16 Pj 39.27N 49.14 E
Bankas 34 Ec 14.05N 3.31W
Bankeryd 8 Fg 57.51N 14.07 E
Banket 37 Ec 17.23S 30.24 E
Bankhead Lake 44 Di 33.30N 87.15W
Bankilaré 34 Fc 14.35N 0.44 E
Bankja 15 Gg 42.42N 23.08 E
Ban Kongmi 25 Lf 14.31N 106.55 E
Banks [Can.] 38 Gb 73.15N 121.30W
Banks [Can.] 42 Ef 53.25N 130.10W
Banks, Iles-=Banks Islands (EN) 57 Hf 13.50S 167.35 E
Banks Island 59 Ib 10.10S 142.15 E
Banks Islands (EN)=Banks, Iles- 57 Hf 13.50S 167.35 E
Banks Lake 46 Fc 47.45N 119.15W
Banks Peninsula 57 Ii 43.40S 172.40 E
Banks Strait 59 Jh 40.40S 148.10 E
Ban/An Bhanna 9 Gf 55.10N 6.46W
Ban Na San 25 Jg 8.53N 99.17 E
Bannerman Town 44 Im 24.09N 76.09W
Banning 46 Gj 33.56N 116.52W
Bannock Range 46 Ie 42.30N 112.20W
Bannu 25 Eb 32.59N 70.36 E
Bañolas/Banyoles 13 Ob 42.07N 2.46 E
Bánovce nad Bebravou 10 Oh 48.44N 18.15 E
Banqiao 27 Hf 25.28N 104.02 E
Banská Bystrica 10 Ph 48.44N 19.09 E
Banská Štiavnica 10 Oh 48.27N 18.55 E
Bansko 15 Gh 41.50N 23.29 E
Bānswāra 25 Ed 23.33N 74.27 E
Banta 35 Ge 1.13N 42.30 E
Bantenan, Tanjung- 26 Fh 8.47S 114.33 E
Bantry/Beanntrai 9 Dj 51.41N 9.27W
Bantry Bay/Bá Bheanntraí 9 Dj 51.38N 9.48W
Bañuela 13 Hf 38.24N 4.11W
Banyak, Kepulauan-= Banyak Islands (EN) 26 Cf 2.10N 97.15 E
Banyak Islands (EN)= Banyak, Kepulauan- 26 Cf 2.10N 97.15 E
Banyo 34 Hd 6.45N 11.49 E
Banyoles/Bañolas 13 Ob 42.07N 2.46 E
Banyuls-sur-Mer 11 Jl 42.29N 3.08 E
Banyuwangi 22 Nj 8.12S 114.21 E
Banzare Coast 66 Ie 67.00S 126.00 E
Banzare Seamounts (EN) 66 Df 58.50S 77.44 E
Banzart 32 Ib 37.00N 9.30 E
Banzart=Bizerte (EN) 31 He 37.17N 9.52 E
Banzart, Buḩayrat- 14 Dm 37.11N 9.52 E
Bao'an 27 Jg 22.35N 114.10 E
Bao'an→Zhidan 27 Id 36.48N 108.46 E
Baochang→Taibus Qi 27 Kc 41.55N 115.22 E
Baode 27 Jd 38.59N 111.07 E
Baodi 28 De 39.43N 117.18 E
Baoding 22 Nf 38.47N 115.30 E
Baofeng [China] 27 Je 33.48N 113.14 E
Baofeng [China] 28 Bh 33.52N 113.04 E
Baoji 22 Mf 34.26N 107.12 E
Baokang 27 Je 31.49N 111.13 E
Baokang→Horqin Zuoyi Zhongqi 27 Lc 44.06N 123.19 E
Bao Loc 25 Lf 11.32N 107.48 E
Baoqing 27 Nb 46.20N 132.11 E
Baoro 35 Bd 5.40N 15.58 E
Baoshan 22 Lg 25.09N 99.12 E
Baotou 22 Me 40.38N 110.00 E
Baoulé [Afr.] 30 Gg 12.35N 6.34W
Baoulé [Mali] 30 Gg 13.33N 9.54W
Baoying 28 Eh 33.15N 119.18 E
Bapaume 11 Id 50.06N 2.51 E
Baqên (Dartang) 27 Fe 31.58N 94.00 E
Bāqerābād 24 Ne 34.56N 50.50 E
Ba'qūbah 23 Fc 33.45N 44.38 E
Baquedano 56 Gb 23.20S 69.51W
Bar 12 Ge 49.42N 4.50 E
Bar [Ukr.-U.S.S.R.] 16 Ee 49.02N 27.40 E
Bar [Yugo.] 15 Cg 42.05N 19.06 E
Barabai 26 Gg 2.35S 115.23 E
Barabevú 55 Bk 33.20S 61.52W
Barabinsk 22 Jd 55.21N 78.21 E
Barabinskaja Step 20 Ce 55.00N 79.00 E
Baraboo 45 Le 43.28N 89.45W
Baracaldo 13 Ja 43.18N 2.59W
Baracoa 47 Jd 20.21N 74.30W
Bărăganului, Cîmpia- 15 Ke 44.55N 27.15 E
Baragoi 36 Gb 1.47N 36.47 E
Bārah 35 Ec 13.42N 30.22 E
Barahona 47 Je 18.12N 71.06W
Barak 24 Gd 36.51N 37.59 E
Baraka 35 Fb 18.13N 37.35 E
Barakah 35 Fb 18.13N 37.35 E
Barakāt 35 Ec 14.20N 33.36 E
Barakī Barak 23 Kc 33.58N 68.58 E
Baram 26 Ff 4.36N 113.59 E
Baram 26 Ff 4.36N 113.58 E
Baramanni 50 Gi 7.50N 59.13W
Barama River 50 Gi 7.40N 59.15W
Barāmūla 25 Eb 34.12N 74.21 E
Bāran 25 Fc 25.06N 76.31 E
Baran 7 Hi 54.29N 30.19 E
Baraniha 20 Lc 68.31N 168.25 E
Baranja 14 Me 46.00N 18.30 E
Baranoa 49 Jh 10.49N 75.03W
Baranof 40 Le 57.00N 135.00W

Index Symbols

[1] Independent Nation
[2] State, Region
[3] District, County
[4] Municipality
[5] Colony, Dependency
Continent
Physical Region
Historical or Cultural Region
Mount, Mountain
Volcano
Hill
Mountains, Mountain Range
Hills, Escarpment
Plateau, Upland
Pass, Gap
Plain, Lowland
Delta
Salt Flat
Valley, Canyon
Crater, Cave
Karst Features
Depression
Polder
Desert, Dunes
Forest, Woods
Heath, Steppe
Oasis
Cape, Point
Coast, Beach
Cliff
Peninsula
Isthmus
Sandbank
Island
Atoll
Rock, Reef
Islands, Archipelago
Rocks, Reefs
Coral Reef
Well, Spring
Geyser
River, Stream
Waterfall Rapids
River Mouth, Estuary
Lake
Salt Lake
Intermittent Lake
Reservoir
Swamp, Pond
Canal
Glacier
Ice Shelf, Pack Ice
Ocean
Sea
Gulf, Bay
Strait, Fjord
Lagoon
Bank
Seamount
Tablemount
Ridge
Shelf
Basin
Escarpment, Sea Scarp
Fracture
Trench, Abyss
National Park, Reserve
Point of Interest
Recreation Site
Cave, Cavern
Historic Site
Ruins
Wall, Walls
Church, Abbey
Temple
Scientific Station
Airport
Port
Lighthouse
Mine
Tunnel
Dam, Bridge

Name	Page	Grid	Lat.	Long.
Baranoviči	6	Ie	53.08N	26.02 E
Baranovka	16	Ed	50.18N	27.41 E
Baranya [2]	10	Oj	46.05N	18.15 E
Barão de Capanema	55	Da	13.19S	57.52W
Barão de Cotegipe	55	Fh	27.37S	52.23W
Barão de Grajaú	54	Je	6.45S	43.01W
Barão de Melgaço	54	Gg	16.13S	55.58W
Baraque de Fraiture	11	Ld	50.15N	5.45 E
Baratang	25	If	12.13N	92.45 E
Barataria Bay	45	Ll	29.22N	89.57W
Barat Daya, Kepulauan-	21	Oj	7.25S	128.00 E
Barāwe	31	Lh	1.09N	44.03 E
Barbacena	53	Lh	21.14S	43.46 E
Barbacoas [Ven.]	49	Li	9.49N	70.03W
Barbacoas [Ven.]	50	Ch	9.29N	66.58W
Barbacoas, Bahia de-	49	Jh	10.10N	75.35W
Barbado, Rio-	55	Cb	15.12S	58.58W
Barbados [1]	39	Nh	13.10N	59.32W
Barbados	38	Nh	13.10N	59.32W
Barbados Ridge (EN)	50	Gf	12.45N	59.35W
Barbagia	14	Dj	40.10N	9.10 E
Barbar	35	Eb	18.01N	33.59 E
Bárbara	54	Dd	0.52S	72.30W
Barbaros	15	Ki	40.54N	27.27 E
Barbas, Cabo-	32	De	22.18N	16.41W
Barbastro	13	Mb	42.02N	0.08 E
Barbate de Franco	13	Gh	36.12N	5.55W
Barbeau Peak	38	La	81.54N	75.01W
Barbeton	37	Ee	25.48S	31.03 E
Barbezieux	11	Fi	45.28N	0.09W
Barbourville	44	Fg	36.52N	83.53W
Barboza Ferraz	55	Fg	24.04S	52.03W
Barbuda	38	Mh	17.38N	61.48W
Barcaldine	58	Fg	23.33S	145.17 E
Barcarrota	13	Ff	38.31N	6.51W
Barcău	15	Ec	46.59N	21.07 E
Barcellona Pozzo di Gotto	14	Jl	38.09N	15.13 E
Barcelona [3]	13	Nc	41.40N	2.00 E
Barcelona [Sp.]	6	Gg	41.23N	2.11 E
Barcelona [Ven.]	54	Fa	10.08N	64.42W
Barcelonnette	11	Mj	44.23N	6.39 E
Barcelos [Braz.]	54	Fd	0.58S	62.57W
Barcelos [Port.]	13	Dc	41.32N	8.37W
Barcin	10	Nd	52.52N	17.57 E
Barcoo River	59	Ie	25.30S	142.50 E
Barcs	10	Nk	45.58N	17.28 E
Barda	16	Oi	40.25N	47.05 E
Bardagé	35	Ba	22.06N	16.28 E
Bardai	31	If	21.21N	16.59 E
Bardār Shāh	24	Ld	36.45N	47.15 E
Bārdaw	14	En	36.49N	10.08 E
Barddhamān	25	Hd	23.15N	87.51 E
Bardejov	10	Rg	49.18N	21.16 E
Bārḍēre	31	Lh	2.20N	42.20 E
Bardeskan	24	Qe	35.12N	57.58 E
Bardīyah	33	Ed	31.46N	25.06 E
Bardonecchia	14	Ae	45.05N	6.42 E
Bardsey	9	Ii	52.45N	4.45W
Bardstown	44	Eg	37.49N	85.28W
Barèda	31	Mg	11.52N	51.03 E
Bareilly	22	Jg	28.25N	79.23 E
Barencevo More=Barents Sea (EN)	67	Jd	74.00N	36.00 E
Barentin	11	Ge	49.33N	0.57 E
Barentsburg	67	Kd	78.04N	14.14 E
Barentshav=Barents Sea (EN)	67	Jd	74.00N	36.00 E
Barentsøya	41	Oc	78.27N	21.15 E
Barents Sea (EN)= Barencevo More	67	Jd	74.00N	36.00 E
Barents Sea (EN)= Barentshav	67	Jd	74.00N	36.00 E
Barents Trough (EN)	5	Ia	73.00N	29.00 E
Barentu	35	Fb	15.06N	37.36 E
Barfleur	11	Ee	49.40N	1.15W
Barfleur, Pointe de-	11	Ee	49.42N	1.16W
Barga	22	Kf	30.48N	81.17 E
Bārgāl	35	Ic	11.18N	51.07 E
Bargarh	25	Gd	21.20N	83.37 E
Barguelonne	11	Gj	44.07N	0.50 E
Barguzin	20	Ff	53.27N	108.58 E
Barguzinski Hrebet	20	Ff	54.30N	110.00 E
Bar Harbor	44	Mc	44.23N	68.13W
Barhi	25	Hd	24.18N	85.25 E
Bari [3]	35	Hd	10.00N	50.00 E
Bari	6	Hg	41.08N	16.51 E
Bari, Terra di-	14	Kj	41.05N	16.50 E
Ba Ria	25	Lf	10.30N	107.10 E
Barīdī, Ra's-	24	Gj	24.17N	37.31 E
Barika	13	Ri	35.22N	5.05 E
Barim	33	Hg	12.39N	43.25 E
Barima, Rio-	50	Fh	8.35N	60.25W
Barima River	50	Fh	8.35N	60.25W
Barinas	54	Db	8.38N	70.12W
Barinas [2]	54	Eb	8.10N	70.00W
Baring, Cape-	42	Fb	70.01N	117.28W
Baringa	36	Db	0.45N	20.52 E
Barinitas	49	Li	8.45N	70.25W
Baripāda	25	Hd	21.56N	86.43 E
Bariri	55	Hf	22.04S	48.44W
Bariri, Represa-	55	Hf	22.21S	48.39W
Bāris	33	Fe	24.40N	30.36 E
Bari Sādri	25	Ed	24.25N	74.28 E
Barisāl	25	Id	22.42N	90.22 E
Barisan, Pegunungan-= Barisan Mountains (EN)	21	Mj	3.00S	102.15 E
Barisan Mountains (EN)= Barisan, Pegunungan-	21	Mj	3.00S	102.15 E
Barito	21	Nj	3.32S	114.29 E
Barjols	11	Lk	43.33N	6.00 E
Barkā'	23	Ie	23.35N	57.55 E
Barkam	27	He	31.45N	102.32 E
Barkan, Ra's-e-	24	Mg	30.01N	49.35 E
Barkava	8	Lh	56.40N	26.45 E
Barkley, Lake-	43	Jd	36.40N	87.55W
Barkley Sound	46	Cb	48.53N	125.20W
Barkly East	37	Df	30.58S	27.33 E
Barkly Tableland	57	Ef	19.00S	138.00 E
Barkly West	37	Ce	28.05S	24.31 E
Barkol	27	Fc	43.35N	92.51 E
Barkol Hu	27	Fc	43.40N	92.39 E
Barlavento [3]	32	Cf	16.10N	24.40W
Bar-le-Duc	11	Lf	48.47N	5.10 E
Barlee, Lake-	57	Cg	29.10S	119.30 E
Barlee Range	59	Dd	23.35S	116.00 E
Barletta	14	Ki	41.19N	16.17 E
Barlinek	10	Lc	53.00N	15.12 E
Barlovento, Islas de-= Windward Islands (EN)	38	Mh	15.00N	61.00W
Barma	26	Jg	1.54S	133.00 E
Barmer	25	Ec	25.45N	71.23 E
Barmera	59	If	34.15S	140.28 E
Barmouth	9	Ii	52.43N	4.03W
Barnard Castle	9	Lg	54.33N	1.55W
Barnaul	22	Kd	53.22N	83.45 E
Barnes Ice Cap	42	Kc	70.00N	73.30W
Barnesville [Ga.-U.S.]	44	Ei	33.04N	84.09W
Barnesville [Mn.-U.S.]	45	Hc	46.39N	96.25W
Barnet, London-	12	Bc	51.39N	0.12W
Barneveld	12	Hb	52.08N	5.34 E
Barnim	10	Jd	52.40N	13.45 E
Barnsley	9	Lh	53.34N	1.28W
Barnstaple	9	Ij	51.05N	4.04W
Barnstaple (Bideford Bay)	9	Ij	51.05N	4.20W
Barnstorf	12	Kb	52.43N	8.30 E
Barntrup	12	Lc	51.59N	9.07 E
Barnwell	44	Gi	33.14N	81.21W
Baro	30	Kh	8.26N	33.14 E
Baro [Chad]	35	Bc	12.12N	18.58 E
Baro [Nig.]	34	Gd	8.36N	6.25 E
Baronnies	11	Lj	44.15N	5.30 E
Barora Fa	63a	Db	7.30S	158.20 E
Barora Ite	63a	Db	7.36S	158.24 E
Barotseland	36	Df	15.05S	24.00 E
Barqah=Cyrenaica (EN)	33	Dc	31.00N	22.30 E
Barqah=Cyrenaica (EN)	30	Je	31.00N	23.00 E
Barqah, Jabal al-	24	Ej	24.24N	32.34 E
Barqah al Bahrīyah= Marmarica (EN)	30	Je	31.40N	24.30 E
Barqū, Jabal-	14	Dn	36.04N	9.37 E
Barques, Pointe aux-	44	Fc	44.04N	82.58W
Barquisimeto	53	Jd	10.04N	69.19W
Barr	11	Nf	48.24N	7.27 E
Barr, Ra's al-	24	Nj	25.47N	50.34 E
Barra	53	Lg	11.05S	43.10W
Barra	9	Fd	57.00N	7.30W
Barra, Ponta da-	30	Kk	23.47S	35.32 E
Barra, Sound of-	9	Fd	57.10N	7.20W
Barraba	59	Kf	30.22S	150.36 E
Barra Bonita, Represa-	55	Hf	22.38S	48.20W
Barra de Navidad	47	De	19.12N	104.41W
Barra do Bugres	54	Gg	15.05S	57.11W
Barra do Corda	54	Ie	5.30S	45.15W
Barra do Cuanza	36	Bd	9.18S	13.09 E
Barra do Dande	36	Bd	8.28S	13.22 E
Barra do Garças	54	Hg	15.53S	52.15W
Barra Falsa, Ponta da-	30	Kk	22.55S	35.37 E
Barra Head	9	Fe	56.46N	7.36W
Barra Mansa	54	Jh	22.32S	44.11W
Barrāmīyah, Wādī al-	24	Ej	25.00N	33.23 E
Barranca	54	Cd	4.50S	76.42W
Barrancabermeja	53	Ie	7.03N	73.52W
Barrancas [Col.]	49	Kh	10.57N	72.50W
Barrancas [Ven.]	54	Fb	8.42N	62.11W
Barrancas, Arroyo-	55	Cj	30.19S	59.25W
Barranco	55	Db	15.56S	57.41W
Barrancos	13	Ff	38.08N	6.59W
Barranqueras	56	Ic	27.29S	58.56W
Barranquilla	53	Id	10.59N	74.48W
Barranquitas	51a	Bb	18.12N	66.23W
Barra Patuca	49	Ef	15.50N	84.17W
Barras	54	Jd	4.15S	42.18W
Barra Velha	55	Hh	26.39S	48.43W
Barre	44	Kc	44.12N	72.30W
Barreira	55	Db	15.24S	57.52W
Barreiras	53	Lg	12.08S	45.00W
Barreirinha	54	Gd	2.47S	57.03W
Barreirinhas	54	Jd	2.45S	42.50W
Barreiro	13	Cf	38.40N	9.04W
Barreiro, Rio-	55	Fb	15.43S	52.45W
Barreiro Grande	55	Jd	18.12S	45.10W
Barreiros	54	Ke	8.49S	35.12W
Barren	25	If	12.16N	93.51 E
Barren, Iles-	37	Gc	18.25S	43.40 E
Barren Islands	40	Ie	58.55N	152.15W
Barretos	56	Kb	20.33S	48.33W
Barrie	42	Jh	44.24N	79.40W
Barrier Bay	66	Ge	67.45S	81.10 E
Barrier Islands	63a	Db	7.44S	158.32 E
Barrington Tops	59	Kf	32.00S	151.28 E
Barro Alto	55	Hb	15.04S	48.58W
Barrois, Plateau du-	11	Kf	48.45N	5.00 E
Barros, Lagoa dos-	55	Gi	29.56S	50.23W
Barros, Tierra de-	13	Ff	38.40N	6.25W
Barroso	55	Ke	21.11S	43.58W
Barrouallie	51n	Ba	13.14N	61.17W
Barrow [Ak.-U.S.]	39	Db	71.17N	156.47W
Barrow [Arg.]	55	Bn	38.18S	60.14W
Barrow/An Bhearú	9	Gi	52.10N	7.00W
Barrow, Point-	38	Db	71.23N	156.30W
Barrow Creek	58	Eg	21.33S	133.53 E
Barrow-in-Furness	9	Jg	54.07N	3.14W
Barrow Island	57	Cg	20.50S	115.25 E
Barrow Range	59	Fe	26.05S	127.30 E
Barrow Strait	38	Jb	74.21N	94.10W
Barru	26	Gg	4.25S	119.37 E
Barry	9	Jj	51.24N	3.18W
Barrytown	62	De	42.14S	171.20 E
Barsakelmes, Ostrov-	18	Bb	45.40N	59.55 E
Barsalogo	34	Ec	13.25N	1.03W
Barsatas	19	Hf	48.13N	78.33 E
Baršć/Forst	10	Ke	51.44N	14.38 E
Bärsi	25	Fe	18.14N	75.42 E
Barsinghausen	10	Fd	52.18N	9.27 E
Barstow	43	De	34.54N	117.01W
Bar-sur-Aube	11	Kf	48.14N	4.43 E
Bar-sur-Seine	11	Kf	48.07N	4.22 E
Baršyn	19	Gf	49.45N	69.36 E
Bārta/Barta	8	Ih	56.57N	20.57 E
Barta/Bārta	8	Ih	56.57N	20.57 E
Bartallah	24	Jd	36.23N	43.25 E
Bartang	18	Hf	37.55N	71.33 E
Barth	10	Ib	54.22N	12.44 E
Bartholomew, Bayou-	45	Jj	32.43N	92.04W
Bartica	54	Gb	6.24N	58.37W
Bartın	24	Eb	41.38N	32.21 E
Bartle Frere, Mount-	57	Ff	17.23S	145.49 E
Bartlesville	43	Hd	36.45N	95.59W
Bartlett	45	Gf	41.53N	98.33W
Bartoszyce	10	Qb	54.16N	20.49 E
Bartow	44	Gl	27.54N	81.50W
Barú, Isla-	49	Jh	10.26N	75.35W
Barú, Volcán	47	Hg	8.48N	82.33W
Bārūd, Ra's-	24	Ei	26.47N	33.39 E
Barumini	14	Dk	39.42N	9.01 E
Barun-Bogdo-Ula	27	Hb	45.00N	100.20 E
Baruni	25	Hc	25.29N	85.59 E
Barun-Šabartuj, Gora-	20	Fg	49.43N	109.58 E
Barun-Urt	27	Jb	46.40N	113.12 E
Barwice	10	Mc	53.45N	16.22 E
Barwon River	57	Fg	30.00S	148.05 E
Barycz	10	Me	51.42N	16.15 E
Baryš	7	Lj	53.40N	47.08 E
Baryš	7	Li	54.35N	46.47 E
Bāsa'idū	24	Pi	26.39N	55.17 E
Basail	55	Ch	27.52S	59.18W
Basankusu	36	Cb	1.14N	19.48 E
Basaral, Ostrov-	18	Ib	45.25N	73.45 E
Basauri	13	Ja	43.13N	2.53W
Basavilbaso	55	Ck	32.22S	58.53W
Bas Champs	12	Dd	50.20N	1.41 E
Basco	26	Hb	20.27N	121.58 E
Bascuñán, Cabo-	56	Fc	28.51S	71.30W
Base	11	Gj	44.17N	0.18 E
Basel [2]	14	Bc	47.35N	7.40 E
Basel/Bâle	6	Gf	47.30N	7.30 E
Baselland [2]	14	Bc	47.30N	7.45 E
Basentello	14	Kj	40.40N	16.23 E
Basento	14	Kj	40.20N	16.49 E
Başeu	15	Kb	47.44N	27.15 E
Basey	26	Id	11.17N	125.04 E
Bashi Channel (EN)=Bashi Haixia	27	Lg	22.00N	121.00 E
Bashi Haixia=Bashi Channel (EN)	27	Lg	22.00N	121.00 E
Bāsht	24	Ng	30.21N	51.09 E
Ba Shui	28	Ci	30.25N	115.02 E
Basilan	21	Oi	6.34N	122.03 E
Basilan City (Isabela)	22	Oi	6.42N	121.58 E
Basilan Strait	26	He	6.49N	122.05 E
Basildon	9	Nj	51.34N	0.25 E
Basilicata [2]	14	Kj	40.30N	16.30 E
Basingstoke	9	Lj	51.16N	1.05W
Basjanovski	17	Jg	58.19N	60.44 E
Başkale	24	Jc	38.02N	44.00 E
Baskatong, Réservoir-	42	Jg	46.47N	75.50W
Baškaus	20	Df	51.09N	87.43 E
Baskil	24	Hc	38.35N	38.40 E
Baškirskaja ASSR [3]	19	Fe	55.00N	56.00 E
Baskunčak, Ozero-	16	Oe	48.10N	46.55 E
Bašmakovo	16	Mc	53.12N	43.03 E
Bāsmenj	24	Ld	37.59N	46.29 E
Basoko	36	Db	1.14N	23.36 E
Basongo	36	Dc	4.20S	20.24 E
Basque Provinces (EN)= Euzkadi/Vascongadas	13	Ja	43.00N	2.30W
Basque Provinces (EN)= Vascongadas/Euzkadi	13	Ja	43.00N	2.30W
Basra (EN)=Al Başrah	22	Gf	30.30N	47.47 E
Bas Rhin [3]	11	Nf	48.35N	7.40 E
Bass, Ilots de-	57	Mg	27.55S	143.26W
Bassano	46	Ia	50.47N	112.28W
Bassano del Grappa	14	Fe	45.46N	11.44 E
Bassar	34	Fd	9.15N	0.47 E
Bassas da India	30	Lk	21.25S	39.42 E
Bassein → Pathein	22	Lh	16.47N	94.44 E
Bassein→Vasai	25	Ee	19.21N	72.48 E
Basse-Kotto [3]	35	Ce	5.00N	21.30 E
Basse-Pointe	51h	Ab	14.52N	61.07W
Basses, Pointe des-	51e	Bc	15.52N	61.17W
Basse-Sambre	12	Gd	50.27N	4.37 E
Basse Santa Su	34	Cc	13.19N	14.13W
Basse-Terre	50	Fd	16.10N	61.40W
Basse-Terre	47	Le	16.00N	61.44W
Basseterre	47	Le	17.18N	62.43W
Bassett	45	Ge	42.35N	99.32W
Bassigny	11	Lf	48.00N	5.30 E
Bassikounou	32	Ff	15.52N	5.58W
Bassila	34	Fd	9.01N	1.40 E
Bass Islands	63c	Ba	9.58S	167.17 E
Basso, Plateau de-	30	Jg	17.20N	22.40 E
Bass Strait	57	Fh	39.20S	145.30 E
Bassum	12	Kb	52.51N	8.44 E
Basswood Lake	45	Kb	48.05N	91.35W
Båstad	7	Ch	56.26N	12.51 E
Bastak	24	Pi	27.14N	54.22 E
Bastām	24	Pd	36.29N	55.04 E
Bastenaken/Bastogne	11	Le	50.00N	5.43 E
Bastia [Fr.]	6	Gg	42.42N	9.27 E
Bastia [It.]	14	Gg	43.04N	12.33 E
Bastogne/Bastenaken	11	Le	50.00N	5.43 E
Bastrop	45	Kj	32.47N	91.55W
Basudan Ula	27	Fe	33.05N	91.00 E
Basuo→Dongfang	27	Ih	19.14N	108.39 E
Basuto	37	Dc	19.52S	26.32 E
Bas-Zaïre [2]	36	Bd	5.30S	14.30 E
Bata	31	Hh	1.51N	9.45 E
Batabanó, Golfo de-	47	Hd	22.15N	82.30W
Batagaj	20	Ic	67.38N	134.38 E
Batagaj-Alyta	20	Ic	67.53N	130.31 E
Bataguaçu	54	Hh	21.42S	52.22W
Bataiporã	55	Ff	22.20S	53.17W
Batajnica	15	De	44.54N	20.17 E
Batajsk	19	Df	47.05N	39.46 E
Batak	15	Hh	41.57N	24.13 E
Bataklık Gölü	24	Ed	37.42N	33.07 E
Batala	25	Fb	31.48N	75.12 E
Batalha	13	De	39.39N	8.50W
Batama	36	Eb	0.56N	26.39 E
Batamaj	20	Hd	63.30N	129.25 E
Batamšinski	19	Fe	50.36N	58.17 E
Batan	26	Hb	20.30N	121.50 E
Batang	27	Ge	30.02N	99.10 E
Batanga	36	Ac	0.21S	9.18 E
Batangafo	35	Bd	7.18N	18.18 E
Batangas	22	Oh	13.45N	121.03 E
Batanghari	26	Mj	1.00S	104.00 E
Batan Islands	21	Og	20.30N	121.50 E
Batanta, Pulau-	26	Jg	0.50S	130.40 E
Bátaszék	10	Oj	46.11N	18.44 E
Batatais	55	Ie	20.53S	47.37W
Batavia	44	Hd	43.00N	78.11W
Bat-Cengel	27	Hb	47.47N	101.58 E
Batchawana	44	Eb	46.58N	84.34W
Batchelor	59	Gb	13.04S	131.01 E
Bătdâmbâng	22	Mh	13.06N	103.12 E
Batéké, Plateaux-	36	Cc	3.30S	15.45 E
Batel, Esteros del-	55	Ci	28.30S	58.20W
Batemans Bay	59	Kg	35.43S	150.11 E
Batesburg	44	Gi	33.56N	81.33W
Batesville [Ar.-U.S.]	45	Ki	35.46N	91.39W
Batesville [Ms.-U.S.]	45	Li	34.18N	90.00W
Bath [Eng.-U.K.]	9	Kj	51.23N	2.22W
Bath [Me.-U.S.]	44	Md	43.55N	69.49W
Bath [N.B.-Can.]	44	Nb	46.32N	67.33W
Bath [St.C.N.]	51c	Ab	17.08N	62.37W
Batha	35	Bc	14.00N	19.00 E
Bathinda	25	Fb	30.12N	74.57 E
Bá Thrá Lí/Tralee Bay	9	Di	52.15N	9.59W
Bathsheba	50	Gf	13.13N	59.31W
Bá Thuath Reanna/ Liscannor Bay	9	Di	52.55N	9.25W
Bathurst	38	Ib	76.00N	100.30W
Bathurst [Austl.]	59	Jf	33.25S	149.35 E
Bathurst [N.B.-Can.]	39	Me	47.36N	65.39W
Bathurst, Cape-	38	Gb	70.35N	128.00W
Bathurst Inlet	38	Ic	68.10N	108.50W
Bathurst Inlet	39	Ic	66.50N	108.01W
Bathurst Island	57	Ef	11.35S	130.25 E
Bati	35	Gc	11.13N	40.01 E
Batié	34	Ed	9.53N	2.55W
Bāṭin, Wādī al-	23	Gc	30.25N	47.35 E
Batman	23	Fb	37.52N	41.07 E
Batman	24	Id	37.45N	41.00 E
Batna [3]	32	Ib	35.10N	6.00 E
Batna	31	He	35.34N	6.11 E
Ba To	25	Lf	14.46N	108.44 E
Bato Bato	26	Ge	5.06N	119.50 E
Batoka	36	Ef	16.47S	27.15 E
Baton Rouge	39	Jf	30.23N	91.11W
Batopilas	48	Fd	27.01N	107.44W
Batouri	34	He	4.26N	14.22 E
Batovi	55	Fb	15.53S	53.24W
Batovi, Coxilha de-	55	Ej	30.33S	54.27W
Båtsfjord	7	Ga	70.38N	29.44 E
Bat-Sumber	27	Ib	48.25N	106.42 E
Batticaloa	25	Gg	7.43N	81.42 E
Batti Maly	25	Ig	8.50N	92.51 E
Battipaglia	14	Ij	40.37N	14.58 E
Battle	12	Cd	50.55N	0.30 E
Battle	42	Gf	52.42N	108.15W
Battle Creek	46	Kb	48.36N	109.11W
Battle Creek	43	Jc	42.19N	85.11W
Battle Harbour	39	Nd	52.17N	55.35W
Battle Mountain	43	Dc	40.38N	116.56W
Battonya	10	Rj	46.17N	21.01 E
Battowia Island	51n	Bb	12.58N	61.09W
Batu	35	Fd	6.59N	39.37 E
Batu, Kepulauan-=Batu Islands (EN)	21	Lj	0.18S	98.28 E
Batuasa	26	Jg	3.32S	130.08 E
Batuata, Pulau-	26	Hh	6.12S	122.42 E
Batudaka, Pulau-	26	Hg	0.28S	121.48 E
Batui	26	Hg	1.17S	122.33 E
Batu Islands (EN)=Batu, Kepulauan-	21	Lj	0.18S	98.28 E
Batumi	6	Kg	41.38N	41.38 E
Batu Pahat	26	Df	1.51N	102.56 E
Baturaja	26	Dg	4.08S	104.10 E
Baturino	20	De	57.45N	85.12 E
Baturité	54	Kd	4.20S	38.53W
Batz, Ile de-	11	Bf	48.45N	4.01W
Bau	26	Ff	1.25N	110.09 E
Baubau	22	Oj	5.28S	122.38 E
Baucau	26	Ih	8.27S	126.27 E
Bauchi	31	Hg	10.19N	9.50 E
Bauchi [2]	34	Hc	10.40N	10.00 E
Bauchi Plateau	34	Gc	10.00N	9.30 E
Baud	11	Cg	47.52N	3.01W
Baudette	45	Ib	48.43N	94.36W
Baudo, Serrania de-	54	Cb	6.00N	77.05W
Baudour, Saint-Ghislain-	12	Fd	50.29N	3.49 E
Baugé	11	Fg	47.33N	0.06W
Bauges	11	Mi	45.38N	6.10 E
Baúl, Cerro-	48	Ii	17.38N	100.19W
Baula	26	Hg	4.09S	121.41 E
Bauld, Cape-	38	Nd	51.38N	55.25W
Bauman Fiord	42	Ia	77.45N	86.00W
Baume-les-Dames	11	Mg	47.21N	6.22 E
Baunach	10	Gg	49.59N	10.51 E
Baunani	63a	Ec	9.08S	160.51 E
Baunei	14	Dj	40.02N	9.40 E
Baures	54	Ff	13.35S	63.35W
Bauru	53	Lh	22.19S	49.04W
Baús	55	Fd	18.19S	53.10W
Baús, Serra dos-	55	Fd	18.20S	53.25W
Bauska	7	Fh	56.24N	24.13 E
Bautzen/Budyšin	10	Ke	51.11N	14.26 E
Bavaria (EN)=Bayern [2]	10	Hg	49.00N	11.30 E
Bavaria (EN)=Bayern	5	Hf	49.00N	11.30 E
Bavarian Forest (EN)= Bayerischer Wald	10	Ig	49.00N	12.55 E
Bavay	12	Fd	50.18N	3.47 E
Båven	8	Ge	59.00N	16.55 E
Bavispe	48	Eb	30.24N	108.50W
Bavispe, Rio de-	48	Ec	29.15N	109.11W
Bavly	7	Mi	54.26N	53.18 E
Bawah, Pulau-	26	Ef	2.31N	106.03 E
Bawal, Pulau-	26	Fg	2.44S	110.06 E
Bawe	58	Ee	2.59S	134.43 E
Bawean, Pulau-	26	Fh	5.46S	112.40 E
Bawku	34	Ec	11.03N	0.15W
Baxian	27	Kd	39.03N	116.24 E
Baxoi	27	Ge	30.07N	96.56 E
Bay [3]	35	Ge	2.50N	43.30 E
Bay/Baicheng	27	Dc	41.46N	81.52 E
Bayamo	47	Id	20.23N	76.39W
Bayamón	49	Nd	18.24N	66.09W
Bayan	28	Ia	46.05N	127.24 E
Bayanbulak	27	Dc	43.05N	84.05 E
Bayanga	35	Be	2.53N	16.19 E
Bayan Gol	27	Gd	37.18N	96.50 E
Bayan Gol→Dengkou	22	Me	40.25N	106.59 E
Bayan Har Shan	21	Lf	34.20N	97.00 E
Bayan Har Shankou	27	Ge	34.06N	97.38 E
Bayan Hot → Alxa Zuoqi	27	Id	38.50N	105.32 E
Bayan Hure→Chen Barag Qi	27	Kb	49.21N	119.25 E
Bayan Huxu→Horqin Youyi Zhongqi	27	Lb	45.04N	121.27 E
Bayano, Lago de-	49	Hi	9.00N	78.30W
Bayan Obo	27	Ic	41.50N	109.58 E
Bayan Qagan	28	Ga	46.11N	123.59 E
Bayan Qagan → Qahar Youyi Houqi	28	Bd	41.28N	113.10 E
Bayan Ul Hot→Xi Ujimqin Qi	27	Kc	44.31N	117.33 E
Bayas	48	Gf	23.32N	104.50W
Bayat	24	Fb	40.39N	34.15 E
Bayauca	55	Bl	34.51S	61.18W
Bayawan	26	He	9.20N	123.00 E
Bayāẓ	24	Pg	30.42N	55.28 E
Bayāzeh	24	Pf	30.42N	55.28 E
Baybay	26	Hd	10.41N	124.48 E
Bayburt	23	Fa	40.16N	40.15 E
Bay City [Mi.-U.S.]	43	Kc	43.36N	83.53W
Bay City [Tx.-U.S.]	43	Hf	29.09N	95.39W
Bayerische Alpen	10	Hi	47.30N	11.30 E
Bayerischer Wald=Bavarian Forest (EN)	10	Ig	49.00N	12.55 E
Bayern=Bavaria (EN)	5	Hf	49.00N	11.30 E
Bayern=Bavaria (EN) [2]	10	Hg	49.00N	11.30 E
Bayes, Cap-	63b	Be	20.57S	165.25 E
Bayeux	11	Fe	49.16N	0.42W
Bayfield	45	Kc	46.49N	90.49W
Bay Fiord	42	Ja	79.00N	84.00W
Baygorria	55	Dk	32.52S	56.44W
Baygorria, Lago Artificial de-	55	Dk	33.05S	57.00W
Bayhān al Qişāb	33	Ig	14.48N	45.44 E
Bayındır	24	Bc	38.13N	27.40 E
Bayjī	24	Je	34.56N	43.29 E
Bay Minette	44	Dj	30.53N	87.47W
Baynūnah	24	Ok	23.50N	52.50 E
Bayombong	26	Hc	16.29N	121.09 E
Bayona	13	Db	42.07N	8.51W
Bayonnaise Seamount (EN)	57	Jf	12.00S	179.30W
Bayonne	6	Fg	43.29N	1.29W
Bayou Bodcau Lake	45	Jj	32.58N	93.30W
Bayou D'Arbonne Lake	45	Jj	32.45N	92.27W
Bayramiç	15	Jj	39.48N	26.37 E
Bayreuth	10	Hg	49.57N	11.35 E
Bayrūt=Beirut (EN)	22	Ff	33.53N	35.30 E
Bay Saint Louis	45	Lk	30.19N	89.20W
Bay Springs	45	Lk	31.59N	89.17W
Bayt al Faqīh	23	Fg	14.31N	43.17 E
Baytik Shan	27	Fb	45.15N	90.50 E
Bayt Laḥm=Bethlehem (EN)	24	Fg	31.43N	35.12 E
Baytown	43	If	29.44N	94.58W
Bayuda Desert (EN)= Bayyūḍah, Ṣaḥrā'-	30	Kg	18.00N	33.00 E
Bayunglencir	26	Dg	2.03S	103.41 E
Bayview	46	Gc	48.00N	116.30W
Bay View	62	Gc	39.26S	176.52 E
Bayy al Kabīr	33	Cc	31.11N	15.53 E
Bayyūḍah, Ṣaḥrā'-=Bayuda Desert (EN)	30	Kg	18.00N	33.00 E
Baza	13	Jg	37.29N	2.46W
Baza, Sierra de-	13	Jg	37.15N	2.45W
Bazardjuzju, Gora-	5	Kg	41.13N	47.51 E
Bazaruto, Ilha do-	37	Fd	21.40S	35.25 E
Bazas	11	Fj	44.26N	0.13W
Bazhong	27	Ie	31.54N	106.42 E
Bazoches-sur-Vesle	12	Fe	49.19N	3.37 E
Baztán	13	Ka	43.09N	1.31W
Beach	43	Gb	46.55N	103.52W
Beachy Head	9	Nk	50.44N	0.16 E
Beacon	44	Ke	41.31N	73.59W
Beaconsfield [Austl.]	59	Jh	41.12S	146.48 E
Beaconsfield [Eng.-U.K.]	12	Bc	51.36N	0.38W
Beagle, Canal-	56	Gh	54.53S	68.10W
Beagle Gulf	59	Gb	12.00S	130.20 E
Bealach an Doirín/ Ballaghaderreen	9	Eh	53.55N	8.35W
Béalanana	37	Hb	14.33S	48.44 E
Béal an Átha/Ballina	9	Dg	54.07N	9.09W
Béal an Bheara/Gweebarra Bay	9	Eg	54.52N	8.20W
Béal Átha Fhirdhia/Ardee	9	Gh	53.52N	6.33W
Béal Átha hAmhnais/ Ballyhaunis	9	Eh	53.46N	8.46W

Index Symbols

[1] Independent Nation
[2] State, Region
[3] District, County
[4] Municipality
[5] Colony, Dependency
Continent
Physical Region
Historical or Cultural Region
Mount, Mountain
Volcano
Hill
Mountains, Mountain Range
Hills, Escarpment
Plateau, Upland
Pass, Gap
Plain, Lowland
Delta
Salt Flat
Valley, Canyon
Crater, Cave
Karst Features
Depression
Polder
Desert, Dunes
Forest, Woods
Heath, Steppe
Oasis
Cape, Point
Coast, Beach
Cliff
Peninsula
Isthmus
Sandbank
Island
Atoll
Rock, Reef
Islands, Archipelago
Rocks, Reefs
Coral Reef
Well, Spring
Geyser
River, Stream
Waterfall Rapids
River Mouth, Estuary
Lake
Salt Lake
Intermittent Lake
Reservoir
Swamp, Pond
Canal
Glacier
Ice Shelf, Pack Ice
Ocean
Sea
Gulf, Bay
Strait, Fjord
Lagoon
Bank
Seamount
Tablemount
Ridge
Shelf
Basin
Escarpment, Sea Scarp
Fracture
Trench, Abyss
National Park, Reserve
Point of Interest
Recreation Site
Cave, Cavern
Historic Site
Ruins
Wall, Walls
Church, Abbey
Temple
Scientific Station
Airport
Port
Lighthouse
Mine
Tunnel
Dam, Bridge

Béal Atha na Muice/ Swinford 9 Eh 53.57N 8.57W
Béal Atha na Sluaighe/ Ballinasloe 9 Eh 53.20N 8.13W
Béal Átha Seanaidh/ Ballyshannon 9 Eg 54.30N 8.11W
Beale, Cape- 46 Cb 48.44N 125.20W
Béal Easa/Foxford 9 Dh 53.59N 9.07W
Béal Feirste/Belfast 6 Fe 54.35N 5.55W
Beal Range 59 Ie 25.30S 141.30 E
Béal Tairbirt/Belturbet 9 Fg 54.06N 7.26W
Beanna Boirche/Mourne Mountains 9 Gg 54.10N 6.04W
Beannchar/Bangor 9 Hg 54.40N 5.40W
Beanntrai/Bantry 9 Dj 51.41N 9.27W
Bear Bay 42 Ia 75.45N 86.30W
Beardmore 45 Mb 49.36N 87.57W
Beardstown 45 Kg 39.59N 90.26W
Bear Island (EN)= Bjørnöya 5 Ha 74.30N 19.00 E
Bear Islands (EN)=Medveži, Ostrova- 21 Sb 70.52N 161.26 E
Bear Lake 43 Ec 42.00N 111.20W
Bear Lodge Mountains 45 Dd 44.35N 104.15W
Béarn [5] 11 Fk 43.20N 0.45W
Bearpaw Mountains 46 Kb 48.15N 109.30W
Bear Peninsula 66 Of 74.36S 110.50W
Bear River 46 If 41.30N 112.08W
Bearskin Lake 42 If 53.57N 90.59W
Beās 25 Eb 31.10N 74.59 E
Beas de Segura 13 Jf 38.15N 2.53W
Beata, Cabo- 47 Je 17.36N 71.25W
Beata, Isla- 49 Le 17.35N 71.31W
Beata Ridge (EN) 47 Je 16.00N 72.30W
Beatrice 43 Hc 40.16N 96.44W
Beatrice, Cape- 59 Hb 14.15S 137.00 E
Beatton 42 Fe 56.06N 120.22W
Beatton River 42 Fe 56.10N 120.25W
Beatty 43 Dd 36.54N 116.46W
Beattyville 44 Ia 48.52N 77.10W
Beatys Butte 46 Fe 42.23N 119.20W
Beau-Bassin 37a Bb 20.13S 57.27 E
Beaucaire 11 Kk 43.48N 4.38 E
Beaucamps-le-Vieux 12 De 49.50N 1.47 E
Beaucanton 44 Ha 49.05N 79.15W
Beauce 11 Hf 48.22N 1.50 E
Beaudesert 59 Ke 27.59S 153.00 E
Beaufort [Mala.] 26 Ge 5.20N 115.45 E
Beaufort [S.C.-U.S.] 44 Gi 32.26N 80.40W
Beaufort/Befort 12 Ie 49.50N 6.18 E
Beaufort, Massif de- 11 Mi 45.50N 6.40 E
Beaufort Island 66 Kf 76.57S 166.56 E
Beaufort Sea 67 Eb 73.00N 140.00W
Beaufort West 31 Jl 32.20S 22.33 E
Beaugency 11 Hg 47.47N 1.38 E
Beaujolais, Monts du- 11 Kh 46.00N 4.22 E
Beauly 9 Id 57.29N 4.29W
Beaumesnil 12 Ce 49.01N 0.43 E
Beaumetz-lès-Loges 12 Ed 50.14N 2.39 E
Beaumont [Bel.] 12 Gd 50.14N 4.14 E
Beaumont [Fr.] 11 Gj 44.46N 0.46 E
Beaumont [Fr.] 11 Ee 49.40N 1.51W
Beaumont [Fr.] 12 Hf 48.51N 5.47 E
Beaumont [Ms.-U.S.] 45 Lk 31.11N 88.55W
Beaumont [N.Z.] 62 Cf 45.49S 169.32 E
Beaumont [Tx.-U.S.] 39 Jf 30.05N 94.06W
Beaumont-de-Lomagne 11 Gk 43.53N 0.59 E
Beaumont-en-Argonne 12 He 49.32N 5.03 E
Beaumont-le-Roger 12 Ce 49.05N 0.47 E
Beaumont-sur-Oise 12 Ee 49.08N 2.17 E
Beaumont-sur-Sarthe 11 Gf 48.13N 0.08 E
Beaune 11 Kg 47.02N 4.50 E
Beaupré 44 Lb 47.03N 70.53W
Beauraing 12 Gd 50.07N 4.48 E
Beaurepaire 11 Li 45.20N 5.03 E
Beausejour 42 Hf 50.04N 96.33W
Beautemps Beaupré 63b Ce 20.25S 166.08 E
Beauvais 11 Ie 49.26N 2.05 E
Beauval 12 Ed 50.06N 2.20 E
Beauvoir-sur-Mer 11 Dh 46.55N 2.03W
Beaver [Ak.-U.S.] 40 Jc 66.22N 147.24W
Beaver [Ok.-U.S.] 45 Fh 36.48N 100.30W
Beaver [Ut.-U.S.] 43 Ed 38.17N 112.38W
Beaver Creek [Co.-U.S.] 45 Ef 40.20N 103.33W
Beaver Creek [U.S.] 45 Ec 47.20N 103.39W
Beaver Creek [U.S.] 45 Gf 40.04N 99.20W
Beaver Creek [U.S.] 45 Ee 43.25N 103.59W
Beaver Dam 45 Le 43.28N 88.50W
Beaver Falls 44 Ge 40.45N 80.21W
Beaverhead Mountains 46 Id 45.00N 113.20W
Beaver Island 44 Ec 45.40N 85.31W
Beaver Lake 45 Jh 36.20N 93.55W
Beaver River [U.S.] 45 Gh 36.10N 98.45W
Beaver River [Ut.-U.S.] 46 Ig 39.10N 112.57W
Beaverton 46 Dd 45.29N 122.48W
Beāwar 25 Ec 26.06N 74.19 E
Bebedouro 56 Kb 20.56S 48.28W
Becan 48 Oh 18.37N 89.35W
Becanchén 48 Oh 19.50N 89.22W
Beccles 9 Oi 52.28N 1.34 E
Bečej 15 Dd 45.37N 20.03 E
Beceni 15 Jd 45.23N 26.47 E
Becerreá 13 Eb 42.51N 7.10W
Becerro, Cayos- 49 Ff 15.57N 83.17W
Béchar 31 Ge 31.37N 2.13W
Béchar [3] 32 Gd 30.00N 2.00W
Becharof Lake 40 He 58.00N 156.30W
Bechet 15 Gf 43.46N 23.57 E
Bechevin Bay 40 Ge 55.00N 163.27W
Bechyně 10 Kg 49.18N 14.28 E
Beckingen 12 Ie 49.24N 6.42 E
Beckley 43 Kd 37.46N 81.12W
Beckum 10 Ee 51.45N 8.02 E
Beckumer Berge 12 Kc 51.43N 8.10 E
Beclean 15 Hb 47.11N 24.11 E
Bédarieux 11 Jk 43.37N 3.09 E
Bedburg-Hau 12 Ic 51.46N 6.11 E
Bedele 35 Fd 8.27N 36.22 E
Bedesa 35 Gd 8.53N 40.46 E
Bedford 9 Mi 52.10N 0.50W
Bedford [Eng.-U.K.] 9 Mi 52.08N 0.29W
Bedford [In.-U.S.] 44 Df 38.52N 86.29W
Bedford [Pa.-U.S.] 44 He 40.00N 78.31W
Bedford [Va.-U.S.] 44 Hg 37.20N 79.31W
Bedford Level 9 Ni 52.30N 0.05 E
Bedford Point 51p Bb 12.13N 61.36W
Bedfordshire [3] 9 Mi 52.05N 0.20W
Bednja 14 Kd 46.18N 16.45 E
Bednodemjanovsk 16 Mc 53.55N 43.12 E
Bedourie 59 Hd 24.21S 139.28 E
Bedum 12 Ia 53.18N 6.39 E
Beech Grove 44 Df 39.43N 86.03W
Beecroft Head 59 Kg 35.01S 150.50 E
Beef Island 51a Db 18.27N 64.31W
Beelitz 10 Id 52.14N 12.58 E
Beemster 12 Gb 52.34N 4.56 E
Beerfelden 12 Ke 49.34N 8.59 E
Beernem 12 Fc 51.09N 3.20 E
Beerse 12 Gc 51.19N 4.52 E
Beersel 12 Gd 50.46N 4.18 E
Beersheba (EN)=Be'er Sheva 23 Dc 31.14N 34.47 E
Be'er Sheva=Beersheba (EN) 23 Dc 31.14N 34.47 E
Beerze 12 Hc 51.36N 5.19 E
Beeskow 10 Kd 52.10N 14.14 E
Beestekraal 37 De 25.23S 27.38 E
Beeston 9 Li 52.56N 1.12W
Beethoven Peninsula 66 Qf 71.40S 73.45W
Beetsterzwaag, Opsterland- 12 Ia 53.03N 6.04 E
Beeville 43 Hf 28.24N 97.45W
Befale 36 Db 0.28N 20.58 E
Befandriana Nord 37 Hc 15.15S 48.32 E
Befandriana Sud 37 Gd 22.06S 43.54 E
Befori 36 Db 0.06N 22.17 E
Befort/Beaufort 12 Ie 49.50N 6.18 E
Bega 15 Dd 45.13N 20.19 E
Bega 58 Fh 36.40S 149.50 E
Bégard 11 Cf 48.38N 3.18W
Begejski kanal 15 Dd 45.27N 20.27 E
Beggars Point 51d Bb 17.10N 61.48W
Bègle 11 Fj 44.48N 0.32W
Begna 7 Bf 60.35N 10.00 E
Begoml 8 Mj 54.46N 28.14 E
Begunicy 8 Me 59.31N 29.30 E
Behābād 24 Pg 31.52N 55.57 E
Behbehān 23 Hc 30.35N 50.14 E
Behring Point 49 Ia 24.27N 77.43W
Behshahr 23 Hb 36.43N 53.34 E
Bei'an 22 Oe 48.16N 126.29 E
Beibu Wan=Tonkin, Gulf of- (EN) 21 Mh 20.00N 108.00 E
Beida He 27 Gc 40.18N 99.01 E
Beihai 22 Mg 21.31N 109.07 E
Bei Hulsan Hu 27 Gd 36.55N 95.55 E
Bei Jiang 27 Jg 23.02N 112.58 E
Beijing=Peking (EN) 22 Nf 39.55N 116.23 E
Beijing Shi (Pei-ching Shih) [4] 27 Kc 40.15N 116.30 E
Beila 32 Df 18.10N 15.53W
Beilen 12 Ib 52.52N 6.32 E
Beiliutang He 28 Eg 34.12N 119.33 E
Beilrstroom 12 Ib 52.41N 6.12 E
Beilsteim 12 Jd 50.07N 7.15 E
Beilu He 27 Fe 34.34N 94.00 E
Beinamar 35 Bd 8.40N 15.23 E
Beine-Nauroy 12 Ge 49.15N 4.13 E
Beipiao 27 Lc 41.49N 120.45 E
Beira 31 Kj 19.50S 34.52 E
Beira Alta 13 Ed 40.40N 7.35W
Beira Baixa 13 Ee 39.55N 7.30W
Beira Litoral 13 Dd 40.15N 8.25W
Beiru He 28 Bh 33.40N 113.35 E
Beirut (EN)=Bayrūt 22 Ff 33.53N 35.30 E
Bei Shan 21 Le 41.30N 96.00 E
Beitstad 7 Cd 64.05N 11.22 E
Beiuş 15 Fc 46.40N 22.21 E
Beiwei Tan 27 Kg 21.10N 116.10 E
Beizhen [China] 27 Kd 37.24N 117.59 E
Beizhen [China] 28 Fd 41.36N 121.47 E
Beja 13 Ef 38.01N 7.52W
Beja [2] 13 Eg 37.58N 7.50W
Bejaïa [3] 32 Ib 36.40N 5.10 E
Bejaïa 31 He 36.45N 5.05 E
Bejaia, Golfe de- 13 Rh 36.45N 5.20 E
Béjar 13 Gd 40.23N 5.46W
Beji 25 Dc 29.47N 67.58 E
Bejneu 19 Ff 45.15N 55.05 E
Bejsug 16 Kf 46.02N 38.35 E
Bejsugski Liman 16 Kf 46.05N 38.25 E
Bekabad 19 Gg 40.13N 69.14 E
Bekasi 26 Eh 6.14S 106.59 E
Bekdaš 19 Fg 41.31N 52.40 E
Békés 10 Rj 46.46N 21.08 E
Békés [2] 10 Qj 46.45N 21.00 E
Békéscsaba 10 Rj 46.41N 21.06 E
Bekilli 15 Mk 38.14N 29.26 E
Bekily 37 Hd 24.12S 45.18 E
Bekkai 29a Db 43.25N 145.07 E
Bekoji 35 Fd 7.32N 39.15 E
Bekopaka 37 Gc 19.08S 44.45 E
Bekovo 16 Mc 52.29N 43.45 E
Bela [India] 25 Gc 25.56N 81.59 E
Bela [Pak.] 25 Dc 26.14N 66.19 E
Bélabo 34 He 4.52N 13.10 E
Bela Crkva 15 Ee 44.54N 21.26 E
Bela Dila 25 Ge 18.40N 80.55 E
Bela Floresta 55 Ge 20.36S 51.16W
Belaga 26 Ff 2.42N 113.47 E
Belaja [R.S.F.S.R.] 20 Mc 65.30N 173.15 E
Belaja [R.S.F.S.R.] 5 Ld 56.00N 54.32 E
Belaja [R.S.F.S.R.] 16 Kg 45.03N 39.25 E
Belaja Cerkov 6 Jf 49.49N 30.07 E
Belaja Gora 20 Jc 68.30N 146.15 E
Belaja Holunica 19 Fd 58.53N 50.50 E
Belaja Kalitva 19 Ef 48.09N 40.49 E
Bela Krajina 14 Je 45.35N 15.15 E
Bela Lorena 55 Ib 15.13S 46.01W
Belang 26 Hf 0.57N 124.47 E
Bela Palanka 15 Ff 43.13N 22.19 E
Belarbi 13 Li 35.09N 0.27W
Belaruskaja Sovetskaja Socialistyčnaja Respublika /Belorusskaja SSR [2] 19 Ce 53.50N 28.00 E
Belasica 15 Fh 41.21N 22.50 E
Belau = Palau (EN) 14 Di 41.11N 9.23 E
Bela Vista [Braz.] 54 Gh 22.06S 56.31W
Bela Vista [Braz.] 55 Dc 17.37S 57.01W
Bela Vista [Moz.] 37 Ee 26.20S 32.40 E
Belawan 26 Cf 3.47N 98.41 E
Běła Woda/Weißwasser 10 Ke 51.31N 14.38 E
Belayan 26 Gg 0.14S 116.36 E
Belbo 14 Cf 44.54N 8.31 E
Bełchatow 10 Pe 51.22N 19.21 E
Belcher Channel 42 Ia 77.20N 94.30W
Belcher Islands 38 Ld 56.20N 79.30W
Belchite 13 Lc 41.18N 0.45W
Belcy 19 Cf 47.46N 27.55 E
Bełczyna 10 Ne 51.25N 17.50 E
Belebej 19 Fe 54.10N 54.07 E
Belecke, Warstein- 12 Kc 51.29N 8.20 E
Beled 10 Ni 47.28N 17.06 E
Beled Wéyne 31 Lh 4.47N 45.12 E
Bélel 34 Hd 7.03N 14.26 E
Belém [Moz.] 37 Fb 14.08S 35.58 E
Belém [Braz.] 53 Lf 1.27S 48.29W
Belem [Mex.] 48 Dd 27.45N 110.28W
Belém de São Francisco 54 Ke 8.46S 38.58W
Belen 43 Fe 34.40N 106.46W
Belén [Arg.] 56 Gc 27.39S 67.02W
Belén [Nic.] 49 Eh 11.30N 85.53W
Belén [Par.] 55 Df 23.30S 57.06W
Belén [Ur.] 55 Dj 30.47S 57.47W
Belén, Cuchilla de- 55 Dj 30.55S 56.30W
Belén de Escobar 55 Cl 34.21S 58.47W
Belene 15 If 43.39N 25.07 E
Belep, Iles- 57 Hf 19.45S 163.40 E
Beles 35 Fc 10.55N 35.10 E
Belev 16 Jc 53.50N 36.10 E
Beleye 35 Fc 11.24N 36.10 E
Belfast [Me.-U.S.] 44 Mc 44.27N 69.01W
Belfast [S.Afr.] 37 Ee 25.43S 30.03 E
Belfast/Béal Feirste 6 Fe 54.35N 5.55W
Belfast Lough/Loch Lao 9 Hg 54.40N 5.50W
Belfield 45 Ec 46.53N 103.12W
Belford 9 Lf 55.36N 1.49W
Belfort 11 Mg 47.45N 7.00 E
Belgaum 22 Jh 15.52N 74.30 E
Belgica Bank (EN) 67 Ld 78.28N 15.00W
Belgicafjella 66 Df 72.35S 31.10 E
België/Belgique=Belgium (EN) [1] 6 Ge 50.30N 4.30 E
Belgique/België=Belgium (EN) [1] 6 Ge 50.30N 4.30 E
Belgium (EN)=België/ Belgique [1] 6 Ge 50.30N 4.30 E
Belgium (EN)=Belgique/ België [1] 6 Ge 50.30N 4.30 E
Belgorod 6 Je 50.36N 36.35 E
Belgorod-Dnestrovski 19 Df 46.12N 30.17 E
Belgorodskaja Oblast [3] 19 De 50.45N 37.30 E
Belgrade (EN) = Beograd 6 Ig 44.50N 20.30 E
Bel Hairane 32 Ic 31.17N 6.20 E
Beli 34 Hd 7.52N 10.58 E
Belice 14 Gm 37.35N 12.52 E
Beli Drim 15 Dg 42.05N 20.20 E
Belidži 16 Pi 41.53N 48.20 E
Beli Lom 15 Jf 43.41N 26.00 E
Beli Manastir 14 Me 45.46N 18.37 E
Belimbegovo 15 Eh 42.00N 21.35 E
Belin 11 Fj 44.30N 0.47W
Belinga 36 Bb 1.04N 13.12 E
Belinski 16 Mc 52.58N 43.29 E
Belinyu 26 Eg 1.38S 105.46 E
Beliş 15 Gc 46.39N 23.02 E
Beli Timok 15 Ff 43.55N 22.18 E
Belize [1] 39 Kh 17.15N 88.45W
Belize (British Honduras) 47 Ge 17.35N 88.35W
Belize City 39 Kh 17.30N 88.12W
Belize River 49 Ce 17.32N 88.14W
Beljajevka 16 Gf 46.29N 30.14 E
Beljanica 15 Ee 44.07N 21.43 E
Belka 8 Mg 57.40N 29.47 E
Belkovski, Ostrov- 20 Ia 75.30N 136.00 E
Bellac 11 Hh 46.07N 1.03 E
Bella Coola 42 Ef 52.22N 126.46W
Bellagio 14 De 45.59N 9.15 E
Bellaire [Oh.-U.S.] 44 Ge 40.02N 80.46W
Bellaire [Tx.-U.S.] 45 Il 29.43N 95.28W
Bellaria-Igea Marina 14 Gf 44.09N 12.28 E
Bellary 22 Jh 15.09N 76.56 E
Bella Unión 55 Dj 30.15S 57.35W
Bella Vista [Arg.] 56 Ic 28.30S 59.03W
Bella Vista [Par.] 55 Df 22.08S 56.31W
Bellavista, Capo- 14 Dk 39.56N 9.43 E
Bell Bay 42 Jb 71.10N 84.55W
Belle-Anse 49 Kd 18.14N 72.04W
Belledonne 11 Mi 45.18N 6.08 E
Bellefontaine [Mart.] 51h Ab 14.40N 61.10W
Bellefontaine [Oh.-U.S.] 44 Fe 40.22N 83.45W
Belle Fourche 43 Gc 44.40N 103.51W
Belle Fourche River 45 Ed 44.26N 102.19W
Bellegarde 11 If 47.59N 2.26 E
Bellegarde-sur-Valserine 11 Lh 46.06N 5.49 E
Belle Glade 44 Gl 26.41N 80.40W
Belle Ile 5 Ff 47.19N 3.11W
Belle Isle 42 Lf 51.55N 55.20W
Belle Isle, Strait of- 38 Nd 51.35N 56.30W
Bellencombre 12 De 49.42N 1.14 E
Belleplaine 51q Ab 13.15N 59.34W
Belleville [Fr.] 11 Kh 46.06N 4.45 E
Belleville [Il.-U.S.] 45 Lg 38.31N 90.00W
Belleville [Ks.-U.S.] 45 Hg 39.49N 97.38W
Belleville [Ont.-Can.] 42 Jh 44.10N 77.23W
Bellevue [Nb.-U.S.] 45 If 41.09N 95.54W
Bellevue [Wa.-U.S.] 46 Dc 47.37N 122.12W
Belley 11 Li 45.46N 5.41 E
Bellheim 12 Ke 49.12N 8.17 E
Bellin → Kangirsuk 39 Lc 60.00N 70.01W
Bellingham [Eng.-U.K.] 9 Kf 55.09N 2.16W
Bellingham [Wa.-U.S.] 39 Ge 48.46N 122.29W
Bellingsfors 8 Ef 58.59N 12.15 E
Bellingshausen 66 Re 62.12S 58.56W
Bellingshausen Ice Shelf 66 Ce 71.00S 89.00W
Bellingshausen Sea (EN) 66 Pf 71.00S 85.00W
Bellinzona 14 Dd 46.11N 9.02 E
Bello 54 Cb 6.19N 75.34W
Bellocq 55 Bl 35.55S 61.32W
Bellona, Récifs- 57 Gg 21.00S 159.00 E
Bellona Island 60 Fj 11.17S 159.47 E
Bellot Strait 42 Ib 72.00N 94.30W
Bellow Falls 44 Kd 43.08N 72.28W
Bell Peninsula 42 Jd 63.45N 81.30W
Bell River 42 Jg 49.49N 77.39W
Bell Rock → Inchcape 9 Ke 56.26N 2.24W
Bellsund 41 Nc 77.39N 14.15 E
Belluno 14 Gd 46.09N 12.13 E
Bell Ville 56 Hd 32.37S 62.42W
Bellville 37 Bf 33.53S 18.36 E
Belmond 45 Je 42.51N 93.37W
Belmont 44 Hd 42.14N 78.02W
Belmonte [Braz.] 54 Kg 15.51S 38.54W
Belmonte [Port.] 13 Ed 40.21N 7.21W
Belmonte [Sp.] 13 Je 39.34N 2.42W
Belmopan 39 Kh 17.15N 88.46W
Beloeil 12 Fd 50.35N 3.43 E
Belogorsk [R.S.F.S.R.] 22 Od 50.57N 128.25 E
Belogorsk [Ukr.-U.S.S.R.] 16 Ig 45.01N 34.33 E
Belogradčik 15 Ff 43.38N 22.41 E
Belogradčiški 15 Ff 43.38N 22.28 E
Belo Horizonte 53 Lg 19.55S 43.56W
Beloit [Ks.-U.S.] 45 Gg 39.28N 98.06W
Beloit [Wi.-U.S.] 43 Jc 42.31N 89.02W
Belojarovo 20 Hf 51.35N 128.55 E
Belojarski 19 Gc 63.40N 66.45 E
Beloje More=White Sea (EN) 5 Kb 66.00N 44.00 E
Beloje Ozero=White Lake (EN) 5 Jc 60.11N 37.35 E
Belokany 16 Oi 41.43N 46.28 E
Belomorsk 6 Jc 64.29N 34.43 E
Belomorsko-Baltijski Kanal =White Sea-Baltic Canal (EN) 5 Jc 63.30N 34.48 E
Belomorsko-Kulojskoje Plato 7 Jd 65.20N 41.50 E
Beloozersk 16 Dc 52.28N 25.13 E
Belopolje 19 De 51.09N 34.18 E
Belorečensk 16 Kg 44.43N 39.52 E
Beloreck 19 Fe 53.58N 58.24 E
Belorusskaja Grjada 16 Ec 53.50N 27.00 E
Belorusskaja Sovetskaja Socialističeskaja Respublika [2] 19 Ce 53.50N 28.00 E
Belorusskaja SSR/ Belaruskaja Sovetskaja Socialistyčnaja Respublika [2] 19 Ce 53.50N 28.00 E
Belorusskaja SSR= Byelorussian SSR (EN) [2] 19 Ce 53.50N 28.00 E
Belo-sur-Mer 37 Gd 20.44S 44.00 E
Belo-sur-Tsiribihina 37 Gc 19.39S 44.32 E
Belot, Lac- 42 Ec 66.50N 126.20W
Belovo 20 Df 54.25N 86.18 E
Belovodsk 16 Ke 49.10N 39.33 E
Belovodskoe 18 Jc 42.47N 74.13 E
Belozersk 19 Dd 60.03N 37.48 E
Belper 12 Aa 53.02N 1.28W
Belted Range 46 Gh 37.25N 116.10W
Belton [Mo.-U.S.] 45 Ig 38.49N 94.32W
Belton [Tx.-U.S.] 45 Hk 31.04N 97.28W
Belton Lake 45 Hk 31.08N 97.32W
Belturbet/Béal Tairbirt 9 Fg 54.06N 7.26W
Beluha 21 Ke 49.48N 86.35 E
Belvedere Marittimo 14 Jk 39.37N 15.52 E
Belvidere 45 Le 42.15N 88.50W
Bely 7 Hi 55.50N 32.58 E
Bely, Ostrov-=Bely Island (EN) 21 Jb 73.10N 70.45 E
Belyando River 59 Jd 21.38S 146.50 E
Bely Čeremoš 15 Ia 48.06N 25.04 E
Bely Island (EN)=Bely, Ostrov- 21 Jb 73.10N 70.45 E
Bely Jar 20 De 58.26N 85.03 E
Belyje Berega 16 Ic 53.12N 34.42 E
Belz 16 Dd 50.23N 24.03 E
Bełżec 10 Tf 50.24N 23.26 E
Belzoni 45 Kj 33.11N 90.29W
Bełżyce 10 Se 51.11N 22.18 E
Bemaraha, Plateau de- 30 Lj 19.00S 45.15 E
Bembe 36 Bd 7.02S 14.18 E
Bembéréké 34 Fc 10.13N 2.40 E
Bembézar 13 Gg 37.45N 5.13W
Bembridge 12 Ad 50.41N 1.05W
Bemidji 43 Ib 47.29N 94.53W
Ben 24 Nf 32.32N 50.45 E
Benāb 23 Gb 37.18N 46.05 E
Benabarre/Benavarn 13 Mb 42.07N 0.29 E
Bena Dibele 36 Dc 4.07S 22.50 E
Bénaize 11 Hh 46.34N 1.04 E
Benalla 59 Jg 36.33S 145.59 E
Benares → Vārānasi 22 Kg 25.20N 83.00 E
Benasc/Benasque 13 Mb 42.36N 0.32 E
Benasque/Benasc 13 Mb 42.36N 0.32 E
Benavarn/Benabarre 13 Mb 42.07N 0.29 E
Benavente 13 Gc 42.00N 5.41W
Benbecula 9 Fd 57.27N 7.20W
Bencheng → Luannan 28 Ee 39.30N 118.42 E
Ben-Chicao, Col de- 13 Oh 36.12N 2.51 E
Bend 43 Cc 44.03N 121.19W
Bendaja 34 Cd 7.10N 11.15W
Bendel [2] 34 Gd 6.00N 5.50 E
Bendela 36 Cc 3.18S 17.36 E
Bender Bäyla 31 Mh 9.30N 50.30 E
Bendersiyada 35 Hc 11.14N 48.57 E
Bendery 19 Cf 46.48N 29.22 E
Bendigo 58 Fh 36.46S 144.17 E
Bendorf 12 Jd 50.26N 7.34 E
Bēne/Bene 8 Jh 56.28N 23.01 E
Bene/Bēne 8 Jh 56.28N 23.01 E
Bénéna 34 Ec 13.06N 4.22W
Benepú, Rada- 65d Ac 27.10S 109.25W
Benešov 10 Kg 49.47N 14.40 E
Benevento 14 Ii 41.08N 14.45 E
Bengal 21 Kg 24.00N 90.00 E
Bengal, Bay of- (EN) 21 Kh 15.00N 90.00 E
Bengamisa 36 Eb 0.57N 25.10 E
Bengbis 34 He 3.27N 12.27 E
Bengbu 22 Nf 32.47N 117.23 E
Benghazi (EN)=Banghāzī 31 Je 32.07N 20.04 E
Benghazi (EN)= Banghāzī [3] 33 Dd 27.00N 20.30 E
Benghisa Point 14 Io 35.50N 14.35 E
Bengkalis 26 Df 1.28N 102.08 E
Bengkulu [3] 26 Dg 3.48S 102.16 E
Bengkulu 22 Mj 3.48S 102.16 E
Bengo, Baia do- 30 Ii 8.43S 13.21 E
Bengo He 28 Eg 35.04N 118.22 E
Bengough 46 Mb 49.24N 105.08W
Bengtsfors 7 Cg 59.02N 12.13 E
Benguela 31 Ij 12.35S 13.26 E
Benguela [3] 36 Be 12.00S 15.00 E
Benguerir 32 Fc 32.14N 7.57W
Benguérua, Ilha- 37 Fd 21.53S 35.26 E
Bengue Viejo 49 Ce 17.05N 89.08W
Bengut, Cap- 32 Hb 36.55N 3.54 E
Beni 31 Jh 0.30N 29.28 E
Beni [2] 54 Ef 14.00S 65.30W
Beni, Río- 52 Jg 10.23S 65.24W
Beni Abbes 32 Gc 30.08N 2.10W
Beni Baufrah 13 Hi 35.05N 4.18W
Benicarló 13 Md 40.25N 0.26 E
Benicasim 13 Md 40.03N 0.04 E
Beni Chougran, Monts des- 13 Mi 35.30N 0.15 E
Benidorm 13 Lf 38.32N 0.08W
Beni Enzar 13 Ji 35.14N 2.57W
Beni Haoua 13 Nh 36.32N 1.34 E
Beni Mellal 31 Ge 32.20N 6.21W
Beni Mellal [3] 32 Fc 32.30N 6.30W
Benin 34 Gd 5.45N 5.04 E
Bénin=Benin (EN) [1] 31 Hh 9.30N 2.15 E
Bénin (Dahomey) [1] 31 Hh 9.30N 2.15 E
Benin (EN)=Bénin [1] 31 Hh 9.30N 2.15 E
Benin, Bight of- 30 Hh 5.30N 4.00 E
Benin City 31 Hh 6.20N 5.38 E
Beni Ounif 32 Gc 32.03N 1.15W
Benisa 13 Mf 38.43N 0.03 E
Beni Saf 13 Ki 35.19N 1.23W
Benisheikh 34 Hc 11.48N 12.29 E
Benito Juárez 48 Mi 17.50N 92.32W
Benito Juárez, Presa- 48 Li 16.27N 95.30W
Benjamen Island 37b Bb 5.27S 53.21 E
Benjamin 45 Gj 33.35N 99.48W
Benjamin Aceval 55 Dg 24.58S 57.34W
Benjamin Constant 53 If 4.22S 70.02W
Benjamin Hill 48 Db 30.10N 111.10W
Benkei-Misaki 29a Bb 42.50N 140.11 E
Benkelman 45 Ff 40.03N 101.32W
Benkovac 14 Jf 44.02N 15.37 E
Ben Mehidi 14 Bn 36.46N 7.54 E
Bennett, Lake- 59 Gd 23.50S 131.00 E
Bennett, Ostrov- 20 Ja 76.45N 149.00 E
Benneydale 62 Fc 38.31S 175.21 E
Bennichab 32 Df 19.26N 15.21W
Bennington 44 Kd 42.53N 73.12W
Benom 26 Df 3.50N 102.06 E
Benoni 31 Jk 26.19S 28.27 E
Bénoué=Benue (EN) 30 Hh 7.48N 6.46 E
Benoy 35 Bd 8.59N 16.19 E
Benrath 12 Ic 51.10N 6.52 E
Bensekrane 13 Ki 35.04N 1.13W
Bensheim 10 Eg 49.41N 8.37 E
Ben Slimane 32 Fc 33.37N 7.07W
Benson [Az.-U.S.] 46 Jk 31.58N 110.18W
Benson [Mn.-U.S.] 45 Id 45.19N 95.36W
Benson Point 64g Ab 1.56N 157.30W
Bent 23 Id 26.17N 59.31 E
Benteng [Indon.] 26 Hg 0.24S 121.59 E
Benteng [Indon.] 26 Hh 6.08N 120.27 E
Bentheim 10 Dd 52.19N 7.10 E
Bentiaba 36 Be 14.29S 12.50 E
Bentinck 25 Jf 11.45N 98.03 E
Bentinck Island 59 Hc 17.05S 139.30 E
Bentiu 35 Dd 9.14N 29.50 E
Bento Conçalves 56 Jc 29.10S 51.31W
Bento Gomes, Rio- 55 Dc 16.40S 57.12W
Benton [Ar.-U.S.] 45 Ji 34.34N 92.35W
Benton [Il.-U.S.] 45 Lg 38.01N 88.55W
Bentong 26 Df 3.32N 101.55 E
Benton Harbor 44 Dd 42.07N 86.27W
Bentonville 45 Ih 36.22N 94.13W
Benua, Pulau- 26 Ef 0.56N 107.27 E
Benue [2] 34 Gd 7.15N 8.20 E
Benue 30 Hh 7.48N 6.46 E
Benue (EN)=Bénoué 30 Hh 7.48N 6.46 E
Benwee Head/An Bhinn Bhuí 9 Dg 54.21N 9.48W
Benxi 22 Oe 41.16N 123.48 E
Beo 26 If 4.15N 126.48 E
Beograd = Belgrade (EN) 6 Ig 44.50N 20.30 E
Beograd-Krnjača 15 De 44.52N 20.28 E
Beograd-Zemun 15 De 44.53N 20.25 E
Béoumi 34 Dd 7.40N 5.34W

Index Symbols

[1] Independent Nation
[2] State, Region
[3] District, County
[4] Municipality
[5] Colony, Dependency
Continent
Physical Region
Historical or Cultural Region
Mount, Mountain
Volcano
Hill
Mountains, Mountain Range
Hills, Escarpment
Plateau, Upland
Pass, Gap
Plain, Lowland
Delta
Salt Flat
Valley, Canyon
Crater, Cave
Karst Features
Depression
Polder
Desert, Dunes
Forest, Woods
Heath, Steppe
Oasis
Cape, Point
Coast, Beach
Cliff
Peninsula
Isthmus
Sandbank
Island
Atoll
Rock, Reef
Islands, Archipelago
Rocks, Reefs
Coral Reef
Well, Spring
Geyser
River, Stream
Waterfall Rapids
River Mouth, Estuary
Lake
Salt Lake
Intermittent Lake
Reservoir
Swamp, Pond
Canal
Glacier
Ice Shelf, Pack Ice
Ocean
Sea
Gulf, Bay
Strait, Fjord
Lagoon
Bank
Seamount
Tablemount
Ridge
Shelf
Basin
Escarpment, Sea Scarp
Fracture
Trench, Abyss
National Park, Reserve
Point of Interest
Recreation Site
Cave, Cavern
Historic Site
Ruins
Wall, Walls
Church, Abbey
Temple
Scientific Station
Airport
Port
Lighthouse
Mine
Tunnel
Dam, Bridge

Beppu 27 Ne 33.17N 131.30 E
Beppu-Wan 29 Be 33.20N 131.35 E
Bequia Head 51n Ba 13.03N 61.12W
Bequia Island 50 Ff 13.01N 61.13W
Beraketa 37 Hd 24.11S 45.42 E
Berati 15 Ci 40.42N 19.57 E
Beratus, Gunung- 26 Gg 1.02S 116.20 E
Berau, Teluk-=McCluer Gulf (EN) 26 Jg 2.30S 132.30 E
Berberä 31 Lg 10.25N 45.02 E
Berbérati 31 Ih 4.16N 15.47 E
Berberia, Cabo- 13 Nf 38.38N 1.23 E
Berbice River 54 Gb 6.17N 57.32W
Berca 15 Jd 45.17N 26.41 E
Berchères-sur-Vesgre 12 Df 48.51N 1.33 E
Berchtesgaden 10 Ii 47.38N 13.00 E
Berck [Fr.] 12 Dd 50.24N 1.36 E
Berck [Fr.] 11 Hd 50.24N 1.34 E
Berck- Berck Plage 12 Dd 50.24N 1.34 E
Berck-Plage, Berck- 12 Dd 50.24N 1.34 E
Berda 16 Jf 46.47N 36.52 E
Berdāle 35 Hd 7.04N 47.51 E
Berdičev 19 Cf 49.53N 28.36 E
Berdigestjah 20 Hd 62.03N 126.50 E
Berdjansk 19 Df 46.43N 36.48 E
Berdsk 20 Df 54.47N 83.05 E
Beregomet 15 Ia 48.10N 25.24 E
Beregovo 19 Cf 48.13N 22.41 E
Bereku 36 Gc 4.27S 35.44 E
Berekua 50 Fe 15.14N 61.19W
Berekum 34 Ed 7.27N 2.35W
Berens 42 Hf 52.21N 97.01W
Berens River 42 Hf 52.22N 97.02W
Beresford 45 He 43.05N 96.47W
Berestečko 10 Vf 50.16N 25.14 E
Bereşti 15 Kc 46.06N 27.53 E
Berettyó 15 Ec 46.59N 21.07 E
Berettyóújfalu 10 Ri 47.13N 21.33 E
Bereza 19 Ce 52.33N 24.58 E
Berezan 16 Gd 50.19N 31.31 E
Berežany 16 De 49.29N 25.00 E
Berezina [Bye.-U.S.S.R.] 16 Dc 53.48N 25.59 E
Berezina [U.S.S.R.] 5 Je 52.33N 30.14 E
Berezino [Bye.-U.S.S.R.] 16 Fc 53.51N 29.00 E
Berezino [Bye.-U.S.S.R.] 8 Mj 54.55N 28.16 E
Berezino [Ukr.-U.S.S.R.] 15 Mc 46.16N 29.11 E
Bereznegovatoje 16 Hf 47.20N 32.49 E
Bereznik 19 Ec 62.53N 42.42 E
Berezniki 6 Ld 59.24N 56.46 E
Berezno 16 Ed 51.01N 26.45 E
Berezovka [Bye.-U.S.S.R.] 10 Vc 53.40N 25.37 E
Berezovka [R.S.F.S.R.] 17 Hd 64.59N 56.29 E
Berezovka [Ukr.-U.S.S.R.] 19 Df 47.12N 30.56 E
Berezovka Višerka 17 Hf 60.55N 56.50 E
Berezovo 19 Gc 63.58N 65.00 E
Berezovski [R.S.F.S.R.] 17 Jh 56.55N 60.50 E
Berezovski [R.S.F.S.R.] 20 De 55.39N 86.16 E
Berezovy 20 If 51.41N 135.52 E
Berga [Sp.] 13 Nb 42.06N 1.51 E
Berga [Swe.] 8 Gg 57.13N 16.02 E
Bergama 23 Cb 39.07N 27.10 E
Bergamo 14 De 45.41N 9.43 E
Bergantiños 13 Da 43.20N 8.45W
Bergby 7 Df 60.56N 17.02 E
Bergen [Ger.] 10 Jb 54.25N 13.26 E
Bergen [Neth.] 12 Gb 52.40N 4.42 E
Bergen [Nor.] 6 Gc 60.23N 5.20 E
Bergen/Mons 11 Jd 50.27N 3.56 E
Bergen aan Zee, Bergen- 12 Gb 52.40N 4.38 E
Bergen-Bergen aan Zee 12 Gb 52.40N 4.38 E
Bergen op Zoom 11 Kc 51.30N 4.17 E
Bergerac 11 Gj 44.51N 0.29 E
Bergeyk 12 Hc 51.19N 5.22 E
Bergh 12 Ic 51.53N 6.16 E
Bergheim 10 Cf 50.58N 6.39 E
Bergh-s'Heerenberg 12 Ic 51.53N 6.16 E
Bergisches Land 10 De 51.07N 7.10 E
Bergisch Gladbach 10 Df 50.59N 7.08 E
Bergkvara 8 Gh 56.23N 16.05 E
Bergneustadt 12 Jc 51.02N 7.39 E
Bergö 8 Ib 62.55N 21.10 E
Bergsjö 7 Df 61.59N 17.04 E
Bergslagen 8 Fd 60.05N 14.30 E
Bergstraße 12 Ke 49.40N 8.40 E
Bergues 12 Ed 50.58N 2.26 E
Bergum, Tietjerksteradeel- 12 Ha 53.12N 6.00 E
Bergviken 8 Gc 61.10N 16.45 E
Bergville 37 De 28.52S 29.18 E
Berh 27 Jb 47.45N 111.07 E
Berhala, Selat- 26 Dg 0.48S 104.25 E
Berici, Monti- 14 Fe 45.26N 11.31 E
Berīkān 24 Nh 28.17N 51.14 E
Berikulski 20 De 55.32N 88.08 E
Beringa, Ostrov-=Bering Island (EN) 20 Lf 55.00N 166.10 E
Beringen 12 Hc 51.03N 5.13 E
Bering Glacier 40 Kd 60.15N 143.30W
Bering Island (EN)= Beringa, Ostrov- 20 Lf 55.00N 166.10 E
Beringovo More=Bering Sea (EN) 38 Bd 60.00N 175.00W
Beringovski 22 Tc 63.07N 179.19 E
Bering Proliv=Bering Strait (EN) 38 Cc 65.30N 169.00W
Bering Sea 38 Bd 60.00N 175.00W
Bering Sea (EN)=Beringovo More 38 Bd 60.00N 175.00W
Bering Strait 38 Cc 65.30N 169.00W
Bering Strait (EN)=Bering Proliv 38 Cc 65.30N 169.00W
Berislav 16 Hf 46.51N 33.29 E
Berisso 55 Dl 34.52S 57.53W
Berit Dağı 24 Gc 38.01N 36.52 E
Berīzak 24 Qi 26.06N 57.15 E
Berja 13 Jh 36.51N 2.57W
Berkåk 7 Be 62.50N 10.00 E
Berkane 32 Gc 34.56N 2.20W
Berkel 10 Cd 52.09N 6.12 E
Berkeley 43 Cd 37.57N 122.18W
Berkhamsted 12 Bc 51.45N 0.33W
Berkner Island 66 Rf 79.30S 49.30W
Berkovica 15 Gf 43.14N 23.07 E
Berks 9 Lj 51.15N 1.20W
Berkshire 9 Lj 51.30N 1.10W
Berkshire Downs 9 Lj 51.35N 1.25W
Berkshire Hills 44 Kd 42.20N 73.10W
Berlaimont 12 Fd 50.12N 3.49 E
Berlanga de Duero 13 Jc 41.28N 2.51W
Berlengas, Ilhas- 13 Ce 39.25N 9.30W
Berlevåg 7 Ga 70.51N 29.06 E
Berlin [N.H.-U.S.] 43 Mc 44.29N 71.10W
Berlin [Ger.] 6 He 52.31N 13.24 E
Berlin (Ost) = Berlin 6 He 52.31N 13.24 E
Berlin (West) = Berlin 6 He 52.31N 12.24 E
Berlin-Pankow 10 Jd 52.34N 13.24 E
Bermeja, Sierra- 13 Gh 36.30N 5.15W
Bermejillo 47 Dc 25.53N 103.37W
Bermejito, Río- 55 Bg 25.39S 60.11W
Bermejo, Isla- 55 An 39.01S 62.01W
Bermejo, Paso-/Cumbre, Paso de la- 52 Ii 32.50S 70.05W
Bermejo, Río- [Arg.] 52 Ji 31.52S 67.22W
Bermejo, Río- [S.Amer.] 52 Kh 26.52S 58.23W
Bermen, lac- 42 Kf 53.35N 68.55W
Bermeo 13 Ja 43.26N 2.43W
Bermillo de Sayago 13 Fc 41.22N 6.06W
Bermuda 39 Mf 32.20N 64.45W
Bermuda Islands 39 Mf 32.20N 64.45W
Bermuda Rise (EN) 38 Mf 32.30N 65.00W
Bern 14 Bd 46.55N 7.40 E
Bern/Berne 6 Gf 46.55N 7.30 E
Bernalda 14 Kj 40.24N 16.41 E
Bernalillo 45 Ci 35.18N 106.33W
Bernard Islands 64d Bb 7.18N 151.32 E
Bernardo de Irigoyen 55 Bk 32.10S 61.09W
Bernardo do Irigoyen 56 Jc 26.15S 53.39W
Bernasconi 56 He 37.54S 63.43W
Bernau bei Berlin 10 Jd 52.40N 13.35 E
Bernaville 12 Ed 50.08N 2.10 E
Bernay 11 Ge 49.06N 0.36 E
Bernburg 10 He 51.48N 11.44 E
Berndorf 14 Kc 47.57N 16.06 E
Berne [Ger.] 12 Ka 53.11N 8.29 E
Berne [In.-U.S.] 44 Ee 40.39N 84.57W
Berne/Bern 6 Gf 46.55N 7.30 E
Berner Alpen/Alpes Bernoises=Bernese Alps (EN) 14 Bd 46.25N 7.30 E
Berneray 9 Fd 57.43N 7.15W
Bernese Alps (EN)=Alpes Bernoises/Berner Alpen 14 Bd 46.25N 7.30 E
Bernese Alps (EN)=Berner Alpen/Alpes Bernoises 14 Bd 46.25N 7.30 E
Bernesga 13 Gb 42.28N 5.31W
Bernesq 12 Be 49.16N 0.56W
Bernier Bay 42 Ib 71.08N 88.00W
Bernier Island 59 Cd 24.50S 113.10 E
Bernina 14 Ed 46.25N 10.01 E
Bernina 5 Gf 46.22N 9.50 E
Bernīnapaß 14 Ed 46.25N 10.01 E
Bernissart 12 Fd 50.28N 3.38 E
Bernkastel-Kues 10 Dg 49.55N 7.04 E
Bernstorffs Isfjord 41 Hf 63.10N 40.45W
Berón de Astrada 55 Dh 27.33S 57.32W
Beroroha 37 Hd 21.39S 45.10 E
Béroubouay 34 Fc 10.32N 2.44 E
Beroun 10 Kg 49.58N 14.04 E
Berounka 10 Kg 50.00N 14.24 E
Berovo 15 Fh 41.43N 22.51 E
Berre, Étang de- 11 Lk 43.27N 5.08 E
Berriane 32 Hc 32.50N 3.46 E
Berrouaghia 13 Oh 36.08N 2.55 E
Berry 11 Hh 47.00N 2.00 E
Berry-au-Bac 12 Fe 49.24N 3.54 E
Berryessa, Lake- 46 Dg 38.37N 122.16W
Berry Head 9 Jk 50.24N 3.29W
Berry Islands 47 Ic 25.34N 77.45W
Berry River 46 Ja 50.50N 111.36W
Beršad 19 Cf 48.23N 29.33 E
Berseba 37 Be 26.01S 17.41 E
Bersenbrück 12 Jb 52.33N 7.56 E
Berthierville 44 Kb 46.05N 73.11W
Bertincourt 12 Ed 50.05N 2.59 E
Bertogne 12 Hd 50.05N 5.40 E
Bertolinía 54 Je 7.38S 43.57W
Bertoua 31 Ih 4.35N 13.41 E
Bertraghboy Bay 9 Dh 53.23N 9.50W
Bertrix 12 He 49.51N 5.15 E
Beru Island 57 Ie 1.20S 176.00 E
Berwick-upon-Tweed 9 Lf 55.46N 2.00W
Berwyn 9 Ji 52.53N 3.24W
Besalampy 37 Gc 16.44S 44.24 E
Besançon 6 Gf 47.15N 6.02 E
Besar, Gunung- 26 Gg 1.25S 115.39 E
Besbre 11 Jh 46.33N 3.44 E
Besed 16 Gc 52.38N 31.11 E
Besikama 26 Hh 9.36S 124.57 E
Beskid Mountains (EN) 5 Hf 49.40N 20.00 E
Beskid Niski 10 Rg 49.20N 21.30 E
Beskid Średni 10 Pg 49.45N 19.20 E
Beskid Wysoki 10 Pg 49.32N 20.00 E
Beskidy Wschodnie 10 Sg 49.20N 22.30 E
Beskidy Zachodnie 10 Pg 49.30N 19.30 E
Beskol 18 Ma 46.06N 81.01 E
Beslan 19 Eg 43.10N 44.35 E
Besna Kobila 15 Fg 42.32N 22.14 E
Besni 24 Gd 37.41N 37.52 E
Besparmak Dağ 15 Kl 37.30N 27.35 E
Bessao 35 Bd 7.53N 15.59 E
Bessarabia (EN)= Bessarabija 15 Lb 47.00N 28.30 E
Bessarabija=Bessarabia (EN) 15 Lb 47.00N 28.30 E
Bessarabka 16 Ff 46.20N 28.59 E
Bessèges 11 Kj 44.17N 4.06 E
Bessemer 43 Je 33.25N 86.57W
Bessin 11 Fe 49.10N 1.00W
Bessines-sur-Gartempe 11 Hh 46.06N 1.22 E
Besšoki, Gora- 16 Rh 43.57N 52.30 E
Best 12 Hc 51.30N 5.24 E
Bestjah [R.S.F.S.R.] 20 Hc 66.00N 123.35 E
Bestjah [R.S.F.S.R.] 20 Hd 61.17N 128.50 E
Bestobe 19 He 52.30N 73.05 E
Bestwig 12 Kc 51.22N 8.24 E
Betafo 37 Hc 19.49S 46.50 E
Betanzos [Bol.] 54 Eg 19.34S 65.27W
Betanzos [Sp.] 13 Da 43.17N 8.12W
Betanzos, Ría de- 13 Da 43.23N 8.15W
Bétaré Oya 34 Hd 5.36N 14.05 E
Bétérou 34 Fd 9.12N 2.16 E
Beteta 13 Jd 40.34N 2.04W
Bethal 37 De 26.27S 29.28 E
Bethanien 37 Be 26.30S 17.00 E
Bethanien 31 Ik 26.32S 17.11 E
Bethany [Mo.-U.S.] 45 If 40.16N 94.02W
Bethany [Ok.-U.S.] 45 Hi 35.31N 97.38W
Bethel 39 Cc 60.48N 161.46W
Bétheniville 12 Ge 49.18N 4.22 E
Bethlehem [Pa.-U.S.] 44 Je 40.36N 75.22W
Bethlehem [S.Afr.] 31 Jk 28.15S 28.15 E
Bethlehem (EN)=Bayt Laḩm 24 Fg 31.43N 35.12 E
Bethulie 37 Df 30.32S 25.59 E
Béthune 11 Id 50.32N 2.38 E
Béthune 11 He 49.53N 1.09 E
Betioky 37 Gd 23.42S 44.22 E
Betong 25 Kg 5.45N 101.05 E
Betor 35 Fc 11.37N 39.00 E
Bétou 36 Cb 3.03N 18.31 E
Betpak-Dala 21 Ie 46.00N 70.00 E
Betroka 37 Hd 23.15S 46.05 E
Bet She'an 24 Ff 32.30N 35.30 E
Betsiamites, Rivière- 42 Kg 48.56N 68.38W
Betsiboka 30 Lj 16.03S 46.36 E
Bette 30 If 22.00N 19.12 E
Bettembourg/Bettemburg 12 Ie 49.31N 6.06 E
Bettemburg/Bettembourg 12 Ie 49.31N 6.06 E
Bettendorf 45 Kf 41.32N 90.30W
Bettles Field 40 Ic 66.53N 151.51W
Bettna 8 Gf 58.55N 16.38 E
Bettola 14 Df 44.47N 9.36 E
Betūl 25 Fd 21.55N 77.54 E
Betuwe 11 Lc 51.55N 5.30 E
Betwa 25 Hc 25.55N 80.12 E
Betz 12 Ee 49.09N 2.57 E
Betzdorf 10 Df 50.47N 7.53 E
Beulah 44 Dc 44.38N 86.06W
Beult 12 Cc 51.13N 0.26 E
Bèuvron 11 Hg 47.29N 1.15 E
Beuzeville 12 Ce 49.20N 0.21 E
Beveland 11 Jc 51.30N 3.40 E
Beveren 12 Gc 51.13N 4.15 E
Beveridge Reef 57 Kg 20.00S 168.00W
Beverley [Austl.] 59 Df 32.06S 116.56 E
Beverley [Eng.-U.K.] 9 Mh 53.51N 0.26W
Beverwijk 11 Kb 52.28N 4.40 E
Bewsher, Mount- 66 Ff 70.54S 65.28 E
Bexhill 9 Nk 50.50N 0.29 E
Bexley, London- 12 Cc 51.26N 0.09 E
Beyağaç 15 Ll 37.13N 28.57 E
Beyānlū 24 Ld 36.02N 47.53 E
Bey Dağı 24 Hc 38.15N 38.22 E
Bey Dağlari 23 Db 36.40N 30.15 E
Beykoz 24 Cb 41.08N 29.05 E
Beyla 34 Dd 8.41N 8.38W
Beyoğlu, İstanbul 15 Lh 41.02N 28.59 E
Beyoneisu-Retsugan 27 Oe 31.55N 139.55 E
Beypazari 24 Db 40.10N 31.55 E
Beyra 35 Hd 6.57N 47.19 E
Beyram 24 Oi 27.26N 53.31 E
Beyşehir 24 Dd 37.41N 31.43 E
Beyşehir Gölü 23 Db 37.40N 31.30 E
Bezaha 37 Gd 23.29S 44.30 E
Bežanickaja Vozvyšennost 7 Gh 56.45N 29.30 E
Bežanicy 7 Gh 56.58N 29.57 E
Bezdan 15 Bd 45.51N 18.56 E
Bezděz 10 Kf 50.32N 14.43 E
Bezdež 10 Vd 52.18N 25.20 E
Bežeck 19 Dd 57.50N 36.41 E
Bezenčuk 7 Lj 53.01N 49.24 E
Bezerra, Rio- 55 Ia 13.16S 47.31W
Bezerros 54 Ke 8.14S 35.45W
Beziers 11 Jk 43.21N 3.15 E
Bezmein 19 Fh 38.05N 58.12 E
Bežta 19 Eg 42.08N 46.08 E
Bhadrak 25 Hd 21.04N 86.30 E
Bhadrāvati 25 Ff 13.52N 75.43 E
Bhāgalpur 22 Kg 25.15N 87.00 E
Bhairawa 25 Gc 27.31N 83.24 E
Bhaironghati 25 Fb 31.01N 78.53 E
Bhakkar 25 Eb 31.38N 71.04 E
Bhamo 25 Jd 24.16N 97.14 E
Bhandāra 25 Fd 21.10N 79.39 E
Bhanjan 25 Gc 25.47N 83.36 E
Bhārat Juktarashtra=India (EN) 22 Jh 20.00N 77.00 E
Bharatpur 25 Fc 27.13N 77.29 E
Bharūch 25 Ed 21.46N 72.54 E
Bhatinda → Bathinda 25 Eb 30.12N 74.57 E
Bhātpāra 25 Hd 22.52N 88.24 E
Bhaunagar 22 Jg 21.46N 72.09 E
Bhera 25 Eb 32.29N 72.55 E
Bheri 25 Gc 28.44N 81.16 E
Bhīlwāra 25 Ec 25.21N 74.38 E
Bhīma 21 Jh 16.25N 77.17 E
Bhind 25 Fc 26.34N 78.48 E
Bhiwāni 25 Fc 28.47N 76.08 E
Bhopāl 22 Jg 23.16N 77.24 E
Bhubaneshwar 22 Kg 20.14N 85.50 E
Bhuj 25 Dd 23.16N 69.40 E
Bhusāwal 25 Fd 21.03N 75.46 E
Bhutan (Druk-Yul) 22 Lg 27.30N 90.30 E
Bia 34 Ed 5.21N 3.11W
Bia, Phou- 21 Mh 18.36N 103.01 E
Biá, Rio- 54 Ed 3.28S 67.23W
Bīābān, Kūh-e- 24 Qi 26.30N 57.25 E
Biabou 51n Ba 13.12N 61.09W
Biafra 30 Hh 5.00N 7.30 E
Biafra, Bight of- 30 Hh 3.20N 9.20 E
Biak 26 Kg 1.10S 136.06 E
Biak, Pulau- 57 Ee 1.00S 136.00 E
Biała Piska 10 Sc 53.37N 22.04 E
Biała Podlaska 10 Td 52.00N 23.05 E
Biała Podlaska 10 Td 52.02N 23.06 E
Białobrzegi 10 Qe 51.40N 20.57 E
Białogard 10 Lb 54.01N 16.00 E
Białostocka, Wysoczyzna- 10 Tc 53.23N 23.10 E
Białowieża 10 Td 52.41N 23.50 E
Białystok 6 Ie 53.09N 23.09 E
Białystok 10 Tc 53.10N 23.10 E
Biancavilla 14 Im 37.38N 14.52 E
Bianco 14 Kl 38.05N 16.09 E
Bianco, Monte- 5 Gf 45.50N 6.52 E
Biankouma 34 Dd 7.44N 7.37W
Biankouma 34 Dd 7.43N 7.40W
Bianzhuang → Cangshan 28 Eg 34.51N 118.03 E
Biaro, Pulau- 26 If 2.05N 125.20 E
Biarritz 11 Ek 43.29N 1.34W
Biasca 14 Cd 46.22N 8.57 E
Bibā 33 Fd 28.55N 30.59 E
Bibai 27 Pc 43.19N 141.52 E
Bibala 36 Be 14.50S 13.30 E
Biban, Chaine des- 13 Qh 36.12N 4.25 E
Bibbiena 14 Fg 43.42N 11.49 E
Biberach an der Riß 10 Fh 48.06N 9.48 E
Bibiani 34 Ed 6.28N 2.20W
Bic 44 Ma 48.22N 68.42W
Bicaj 15 Dh 41.59N 20.25 E
Bicas 55 Ke 21.43S 43.04W
Bicaz 15 Jc 46.55N 26.04 E
Bicaz, Pasul- 15 Ic 46.49N 25.52 E
Bičenekski, Pereval- 16 Nj 39.33N 45.48 E
Bicester 9 Lj 51.54N 1.09W
Bichena 35 Fc 10.21N 38.14 E
Bickerton Island 59 Hb 13.45S 136.10 E
Bicske 10 Oi 47.29N 18.38 E
Bičura 20 Ff 50.36N 107.35 E
Bīd 24 Qd 36.33N 57.35 E
Bida 31 Hh 9.05N 6.01 E
Bīdar 25 Fe 17.54N 77.33 E
Bidasoa 13 Ka 43.22N 1.47W
Biddeford 43 Mc 43.30N 70.26W
Bideford 9 Ij 51.01N 4.13W
Bideford Bay → Barnstaple 9 Ij 51.05N 4.20W
Bidon V/Poste Maurice Cortier 32 He 22.18N 1.05 E
Bié 36 Ce 13.00S 17.30 E
Bié, Planalto do- 30 Ij 13.30S 17.02 E
Biebrza 10 Sc 53.13N 22.28 E
Biecz 10 Rg 49.44N 21.14 E
Biedenkopf 10 Ef 50.55N 8.32 E
Biei 29a Cb 43.35N 142.28 E
Biel/Bienne 14 Bc 47.10N 7.15 E
Bielefeld 10 Ed 52.02N 8.32 E
Bielefeld-Brackwede 12 Kc 51.59N 8.31 E
Bielefeld-Sennestadt 12 Kc 51.57N 8.35 E
Biella 14 Ce 45.34N 8.03 E
Bielsk 10 Pd 52.40N 19.49 E
Bielska, Wysoczyzna- 10 Sd 52.35N 23.00 E
Bielsko 10 Og 49.50N 19.00 E
Bielsko-Biała 10 Pg 49.49N 19.02 E
Bielsk Podlaski 10 Td 52.47N 23.12 E
Bien Dong=South China Sea (EN) 21 Ni 10.00N 113.00 E
Bien Hoa 25 Lf 10.57N 106.49 E
Bienne 11 Lh 46.20N ·5.38 E
Bienne/Biel 14 Bc 47.10N 7.15 E
Bienvenida 13 Jd 40.30N 2.30W
Bienville, Lac - 42 Ke 55.20N 72.40W
Bierbeek 12 Gd 50.50N 4.46 E
Bieszczady 10 Sg 49.10N 22.35 E
Bièvre 12 He 49.56N 5.01 E
Biferno 14 Ji 41.59N 15.02 E
Bifoum 36 Bc 0.20S 10.23 E
Bifuka 28 Qb 44.29N 142.21 E
Biga 24 Bb 40.13N 27.14 E
Bigadiç 24 Cc 39.23N 28.08 E
Big Bald Mountain 44 Nb 47.37N 66.38W
Big Baldy Mountain 46 Jc 46.58N 110.37W
Big Bay [Mi.-U.S.] 44 Db 46.49N 87.44W
Big Bay [Van.] 63b Cb 15.05S 166.54 E
Big Beaver House 42 If 52.58N 89.57W
Big Belt Mountains 46 Jc 46.40N 111.25W
Big Black River 45 Kj 32.00N 91.05W
Big Blue River 43 Hd 39.11N 96.32W
Big Creek Peak 46 Id 44.28N 113.32W
Big Dry Creek 46 Lc 47.30N 106.19W
Big Falls 45 Jb 48.11N 93.46W
Biggar 42 Gf 52.04N 108.00W
Biggenden 59 Ke 25.30S 152.00 E
Biggleswade 9 Mi 52.05N 0.17W
Big Hatchet Peak 45 Bk 31.37N 108.20W
Big Hole River 46 Id 45.34N 112.20W
Bighorn Basin 43 Fc 44.15N 108.10W
Bighorn Lake 46 Kd 45.08N 108.10W
Bighorn Mountains 38 Ie 44.00N 107.30W
Bighorn River 43 Fb 46.09N 107.28W
Bight, Head of- 59 Gf 31.30S 131.10 E
Big Island 42 Kd 62.43N 70.40W
Big Lake 44 Nc 45.10N 67.40W
Big Lake 45 Fk 31.12N 101.28W
Big Lost River 46 Ie 43.50N 112.44W
Big Muddy Creek 46 Mb 48.08N 104.36W
Big Muddy Lake 46 Mb 49.08N 104.54W
Bignona 34 Bc 12.49N 16.14W
Bigorre 11 Gk 43.06N 0.05 E
Big Porcupine Creek 46 Lc 46.17N 106.47W
Big Quill Lake 42 Hf 51.51N 104.18W
Big Rapids 44 Ed 43.42N 85.29W
Big River 42 Gf 53.50N 107.01W
Big River 42 Fb 72.50N 125.00W
Big Sand Lake 42 He 57.45N 99.45W
Big Sandy 46 Jb 48.11N 110.07W
Big Sandy Creek 45 Eg 38.06N 102.29W
Big Sandy River [Az.-U.S.] 46 Ii 34.19N 113.31W
Big Sandy River [Wy.-U.S.] 46 Kf 41.50N 109.48W
Big Sheep Mountains 46 Mc 47.03N 105.43W
Big Sioux River 43 Hc 42.30N 96.25W
Big Smoky Valley 43 Dd 38.30N 117.15W
Big Snowy Mountains 46 Kc 46.50N 109.30W
Big Spring 39 If 32.15N 101.28W
Big Spruce Knob 44 Gf 38.16N 80.12W
Big Stone Lake 45 Hd 45.25N 96.40W
Big Timber 46 Kd 45.50N 109.57W
Big Trout Lake 42 If 53.45N 90.00W
Biguglia, Étang de- 11a Ba 42.36N 9.29 E
Big Wood Cay 49 Ia 24.21N 77.44W
Big Wood River 46 He 42.52N 114.55W
Bihać 14 Jf 44.49N 15.52 E
Bihār 25 Hd 25.00N 86.00 E
Bihār 25 Hc 25.11N 85.31 E
Biharamulo 36 Fc 2.38S 31.20 E
Bihor 15 Ec 47.00N 22.00 E
Bihoro 27 Pc 43.49N 144.07 E
Bihorului, Munţii- 15 Fc 46.40N 22.45 E
Bija 21 Kd 52.25N 85.05 E
Bijagós, Arquipélago dos-=Bijagos Islands (EN) 30 Fg 11.15N 16.05W
Bijagós Islands (EN)= Bijagós, Arquipélago dos- 30 Fg 11.15N 16.05W
Bijapur 25 Fe 16.50N 75.42 E
Bījār 23 Gb 35.52N 47.36 E
Bijeljina 14 Nf 44.45N 19.13 E
Bijelo Polje 15 Cf 43.02N 19.45 E
Bijiang (Zhiziluo) 27 Gf 26.39N 99.00 E
Bijie 27 If 27.15N 105.16 E
Bijlikol, Ozero- 18 Hc 43.05N 70.40 E
Bijou Creek 45 Ef 40.17N 103.52W
Bijoutier Island 37b Bb 7.04S 52.45 E
Bijsk 22 Kd 52.34N 85.15 E
Bīkāner 22 Jg 28.01N 73.18 E
Bikar Atoll 57 Ic 12.15N 170.06 E
Bikeqi 28 Ad 40.45N 111.17 E
Bikin 20 Ig 46.43N 134.02 E
Bikin 20 Ig 46.51N 134.02 E
Bikini Atoll 57 Hc 11.35N 165.23 E
Bikoro 31 Ii 0.45S 18.07 E
Bilād Ghāmid 33 Hf 19.58N 41.38 E
Bilād Zahrān 33 He 20.15N 41.15 E
Bilāspur 22 Kg 22.03N 82.10 E
Bilate 35 Fd 6.34N 38.01 E
Bilauktaung Range 21 Lh 13.00N 99.00 E
Bilbao 6 Fg 43.15N 2.58W
Bilbays 33 Fc 30.25N 31.34 E
Bileća 14 Mh 42.53N 18.26 E
Bilecik 23 Ca 40.09N 29.59 E
Bīlehsavār 24 Mc 39.28N 48.20 E
Bilé Karpaty=White Carpathians (EN) 10 Nh 48.55N 17.50 E
Bilesha Plain 36 Hb 0.35N 40.45 E
Biłgoraj 10 Sf 50.34N 22.43 E
Bili 36 Db 4.50N 22.29 E
Bili 36 Eb 4.09N 25.10 E
Bilibino 22 Sc 68.03N 166.20 E
Biliran 26 Hd 11.35N 124.28 E
Bilishti 15 Di 40.37N 20.59 E
Biliu He 28 Ge 39.30N 122.36 E
Bill Baileys Bank (EN) 9 Ca 60.40N 10.20W
Billerbeck 12 Jc 51.58N 7.18 E
Billericay 12 Cc 51.37N 0.35 E
Billingen 8 Ef 58.24N 13.45 E
Billings 39 Jf 37.04N 93.33W
Billings, Reprêsa- 55 If 23.45S 46.40W
Billingshurst 12 Bc 51.01N 0.27W
Bill Williams River 46 Hi 34.17N 114.03W
Billy Chinook, Lake- 46 Ed 44.33N 121.20W
Bilma 31 Ig 18.41N 12.56 E
Biloela 59 Kd 24.24S 150.30 E
Bilo Gora 14 Le 45.50N 17.10 E
Biloku 54 Gc 1.46N 58.33W
Biloxi 43 Je 30.24N 88.53W
Bilqās Qism Awwal 24 Dg 31.13N 31.21 E
Bîlteni 15 Ge 44.52N 23.17 E
Biltine 35 Cc 14.32N 20.55 E
Biltine 35 Cc 15.00N 21.00 E
Bilzen 12 Hd 50.51N 5.31 E
Bima 36 Eb 3.23N 25.09 E
Bimbān 24 Ej 24.26N 32.53 E
Bimberi Peak 59 Jg 35.40S 148.47 E
Bimbila 34 Fd 8.51N 0.04 E
Bimbo 35 Be 4.18N 18.33 E
Bimini Islands 47 Ic 25.44N 79.15W
Bināb 24 Md 36.35N 48.41 E
Binačka Morava 15 Eg 42.27N 21.47 E
Binaiya, Gunung- 26 Ig 3.11S 129.26 E
Binatang 26 Ff 2.10N 111.38 E
Bınboga Dağı 24 Gc 38.21N 36.32 E
Binche 12 Gd 50.24N 4.10 E
Binder 27 Jb 48.35N 110.36 E
Bindura 31 Kj 17.17S 31.20 E
Bine el Ouidane 32 Fc 32.08N 6.28W
Binéfar 13 Mc 41.51N 0.18 E
Binem 35 Bb 18.43N 19.40 E
Binga [Zaire] 36 Db 2.23N 20.30 E
Binga [Zimb.] 37 Dc 17.37S 27.20 E

Index Symbols

[1] Independent Nation
[2] State, Region
[3] District, County
[4] Municipality
[5] Colony, Dependency
Continent
Physical Region
Historical or Cultural Region
Mount, Mountain
Volcano
Hill
Mountains, Mountain Range
Hills, Escarpment
Plateau, Upland
Pass, Gap
Plain, Lowland
Delta
Salt Flat
Valley, Canyon
Crater, Cave
Karst Features
Depression
Polder
Desert, Dunes
Forest, Woods
Heath, Steppe
Oasis
Cape, Point
Coast, Beach
Cliff
Peninsula
Isthmus
Sandbank
Island
Atoll
Rock, Reef
Islands, Archipelago
Rocks, Reefs
Coral Reef
Well, Spring
Geyser
River, Stream
Waterfall Rapids
River Mouth, Estuary
Lake
Salt Lake
Intermittent Lake
Reservoir
Swamp, Pond
Canal
Glacier
Ice Shelf, Pack Ice
Ocean
Sea
Gulf, Bay
Strait, Fjord
Lagoon
Bank
Seamount
Tablemount
Ridge
Shelf
Basin
Escarpment, Sea Scarp
Fracture
Trench, Abyss
National Park, Reserve
Point of Interest
Recreation Site
Cave, Cavern
Historic Site
Ruins
Wall, Walls
Church, Abbey
Temple
Scientific Station
Airport
Port
Lighthouse
Mine
Tunnel
Dam, Bridge

Bingen 10 Dg 49.58N 7.54 E
Bingham [Me.-U.S.] 44 Mc 45.03N 69.53W
Bingham [N.M.-U.S.] 45 Cj 33.56N 106.17W
Binghamton 43 Lc 42.06N 75.55W
Bin Ghunaymah, Jabal- 30 If 25.00N 15.30 E
Bing Inlet 44 Gc 45.13N 80.30W
Bingöl 23 Fb 38.53N 40.29 E
Bingöl Dağları 24 Ic 39.20N 41.20 E
Binhai (Dongkan) 27 Ke 34.00N 119.52 E
Binjai 26 Cf 3.36N 98.30 E
Binkiliç 15 Lh 41.25N 28.11 E
Binongko, Pulau- 26 Hh 5.57S 124.02 E
Bin Qirdān 32 Jc 33.08N 11.13 E
Bintan, Pulau- 26 Df 1.05N 104.30 E
Bintuhan 26 Dg 4.48S 103.22 E
Bintulu 26 Ff 3.10N 113.02 E
Bin Walīd, Jabal- 14 En 36.52N 10.47 E
Binxian 28 Df 37.22N 117.57 E
Binxian (Binzhou) [China] 27 Mb 45.45N 127.27 E
Binxian (Binzhou) [China] 27 Id 35.02N 108.06 E
Binzhou → Binxian [China] 27 Id 35.02N 108.06 E
Binzhou → Binxian [China] 27 Mb 45.45N 127.27 E
Bioara 25 Fd 23.58N 76.55 E
Biobío 56 Fe 36.49S 73.10W
Bío Bío [2] 56 Fe 37.45S 72.00W
Biograd na Moru 14 Jg 43.57N 15.27 E
Bioko [3] 34 Ge 3.00N 8.40 E
Bioko 30 Hh 4.30N 9.30 E
Biokovo 14 Lg 43.18N 17.02 E
Biorra/Birr 9 Fh 53.05N 7.54W
Bippen 12 Jb 52.35N 7.44 E
Bir 25 Fe 18.59N 75.46 E
Bira 20 Ig 49.03N 132.27 E
Bi'r Abraq 33 Fe 23.35N 34.48 E
Bi'r Abū al Ḩuşayn 33 Ee 22.53N 29.55 E
Bi'r Abū Gharādiq 24 Cg 30.06N 28.06 E
Bi'r Abū Hashim 33 Fe 23.42N 34.08 E
Bi'r Abū Minqat 33 Ed 26.30N 27.35 E
Birah Kaprah 24 Kd 36.52N 44.01 E
Birāk 33 Bd 27.39N 14.17 E
Birakan 20 Ig 49.02N 131.40 E
Bi'r al 'Abd 24 Eg 31.22N 32.58 E
Bi'r al Ghuzaylah 33 Bd 28.50N 10.45 E
Bi'r al Ḩakim 33 Dc 31.36N 23.29 E
Bi'r al Hasa 35 Fa 22.58N 35.40 E
Bi'r al Khamsah 33 Ec 30.57N 25.46 E
Bi'r 'Allāq 33 Bc 31.10N 11.55 E
Bi'r al Mushayqīq 32 Jc 30.53N 10.18 E
Bi'r al Qurayyah 24 Ei 26.22N 33.01 E
Bi'r al Uzam 33 Dc 31.46N 23.59 E
Bi'r al Wa'r 31 Be 22.39N 14.10 E
Bi'r al Washkah 33 Cd 28.52N 15.35 E
Birao 31 Jg 10.17N 22.47 E
Bi'r 'Arjā' 24 Ij 25.17N 40.58 E
Bi'r ar Rāh 24 If 33.27N 40.25 E
Bi'r ar Rūmān 32 Ic 32.31N 8.21 E
Birātnagar 25 Hc 26.29N 87.17 E
Biratori 28 Qc 42.35N 142.12 E
Bi'r Bayli 33 Ec 30.32N 25.08 E
Bi'r Bayzaḩ 24 Fj 25.10N 34.05 E
Bi'r Bū Ḩawsh 33 Dd 24.34N 22.07 E
Bi'r Bū Zurayyq 33 Dd 24.32N 22.38 E
Birca 15 Gf 43.58N 23.37 E
Birch 42 Ge 58.28N 112.17W
Birch Mountains 42 Ge 57.20N 112.55W
Bird 42 Ie 56.30N 94.14W
Bi'r Dibs 33 Ee 22.12N 29.32 E
Bird Island [Gren.] 51p Bb 12.12N 61.33W
Bird Island [Sey.] 37b Ca 3.43S 55.12 E
Birdsville 59 He 25.54S 139.22 E
Birdum 59 Gc 15.39S 133.13 E
Birecik 24 Gd 37.02N 37.58 E
Bir El Ater 32 Ic 34.44N 8.03 E
Bir el Mrabba'ab 24 He 34.30N 39.07 E
Bir Enzarān 32 Ee 23.53N 14.32W
Bireuen 26 Ce 5.12N 96.41 E
Bi'r Fajr 24 Gh 28.54N 37.54 E
Bi'r Fu'ād 33 Ec 30.27N 26.27 E
Bir Gandūs 32 De 21.36N 16.30W
Birganj 25 Gc 27.00N 84.52 E
Bir Gara 35 Bc 13.11N 15.58 E
Bir-Ghbalou 13 Ph 36.16N 3.35 E
Birgi 15 Lk 38.15N 28.05 E
Bi'r Ḩasanah 24 Eg 30.28N 33.47 E
Bi'r Ḩaymir 24 Hj 24.41N 38.04 E
Bi'r Ḩulayyī 24 Fj 24.06N 34.32 E
Birigui 55 Ge 21.18S 50.19W
Biriliussy 20 Ee 57.07N 90.42 E
Birīn 24 Ge 35.01N 36.40 E
Birine 13 Pi 35.37N 3.13 E
Birjand 22 Hf 32.53N 59.13 E
Birjusa 21 Ld 57.43N 95.24 E
Birjusinsk 20 Ee 55.55N 97.55 E
Bi'r Karawayn 24 Ci 27.06N 28.32 E
Birkeland 7 Bg 58.20N 8.14 E
Birkenfeld 10 Dg 49.39N 7.11 E
Birkenhead 9 Jh 53.24N 3.02W
Birkerød 8 Ei 55.50N 12.26 E
Bi'r Khālidah 24 Bg 30.50N 27.15 E
Birksgate Range 59 Fe 27.10S 129.45 E
Birlad 15 Kc 46.14N 27.40 E
Birlad 15 Kc 45.36N 27.31 E
Bir Lehlū 32 Fd 26.21N 9.34W
Bi'r Ma'sūr 24 Fj 24.31N 34.12 E
Birmingham [Al.-U.S.] 39 Kf 33.31N 86.49W
Birmingham [Eng.-U.K.] 6 Fe 52.30N 1.50W
Bi'r Misāḩah 33 Ee 22.12N 27.57 E
Bi'r Murr 33 Fe 23.21N 30.05 E
Bi'r Murrah 33 Fe 22.32N 33.54 E
Bi'r Nāhid 33 Ec 30.13N 28.52 E
Bi'r Naşīf 23 Ee 24.51N 39.11 E
Birnie Atoll 57 Je 3.35S 171.31W
Birnin Gaouré 34 Fc 13.05N 2.54 E
Birnin Gwari 34 Gc 11.02N 6.47 E
Birnin Kebbi 34 Fc 12.28N 4.12 E
Birni Nkonni 31 Hg 13.48N 5.15 E
Birnin Kudu 34 Gc 11.27N 9.30 E
Birni Yauri 34 Fc 10.47N 4.49 E
Bi'r Nukhaylah 24 Dj 24.01N 30.52 E
Birobidžan 22 Pe 48.48N 132.57 E
Birr/Biorra 9 Fh 53.05N 7.54W
Birs 14 Bc 47.26N 7.33 E
Bi'r Şafājah 33 Fd 26.50N 34.54 E
Bi'r Sayyālah 24 Ei 26.07N 33.56 E
Bi'r Shalatayn 33 Ge 23.08N 35.36 E
Birsk 19 Fd 55.25N 55.32 E
Birštonas 8 Kj 54.33N 24.07 E
Bi'r Ţarfāwī 33 Ee 22.55N 28.53 E
Biru 27 Fe 31.30N 93.50 E
Bi'r Umm al 'Abbās 24 Ei 26.57N 32.34 E
Bi'r Umm Fawākhir 24 Ei 26.01N 33.38 E
Bi'r Umm Sa'īd 24 Eh 29.40N 33.34 E
Bi'r Umm Ţunaydibah 24 Ej 25.16N 33.06 E
Biruni 19 Gg 41.42N 60.45 E
Biržai/Biržaj 19 Cd 56.12N 24.48 E
Biržaj/Biržai 19 Cd 56.12N 24.48 E
Bîrzava 15 Ec 46.07N 21.59 E
Bîrzava 15 Dd 45.16N 20.49 E
Birzebbuga 14 Io 35.49N 14.32 E
Bisa, Pulau- 26 Ig 1.15S 127.28 E
Bisaccia 14 Ji 41.01N 15.22 E
Bisacquino 14 Hm 37.42N 13.15 E
Bisbee 43 Fe 31.27N 109.55W
Biscarrosse, Étang de- 11 Ej 44.21N 1.10W
Biscay, Bay of- (EN)= Gascogne, Golfe de- 5 Fg 44.00N 4.00W
Bisceglie 14 Ki 41.14N 16.30 E
Bischofslofen 10 Jc 47.25N 13.13 E
Bischofswerda/Biskopicy 10 Ke 51.07N 14.11 E
Biscoe Islands 66 Qe 66.00S 66.30W
Biscotasi Lake 44 Fb 47.20N 82.05W
Biscucuy 50 Bh 9.22N 69.59W
Bisert 17 Hh 56.39N 57.59 E
Bisert 19 Fd 56.52N 59.03 E
Biševiski Kanal 14 Kg 43.00N 16.03 E
Biševo 14 Kh 42.59N 16.01 E
Bisha 35 Fb 15.28N 37.33 E
Bishārah 33 De 22.58N 22.39 E
Bishāriyīn, Barq al- 35 Eb 19.26N 32.22 E
Bishnupur 25 Hd 23.05N 87.19 E
Bishop 43 Dd 37.22N 118.24W
Bishop Auckland 9 Lg 54.40N 1.40W
Bishop Rock 9 Gl 49.53N 6.25W
Bishop's Falls 42 Lg 49.01N 55.30W
Bishop's Stortford 9 Nj 51.53N 0.09 E
Bishop's Waltham 12 Ad 50.57N 1.13W
Bishri, Jabal- 24 He 35.20N 39.20 E
Bishui 27 La 52.07N 123.43 E
Biskopicy/Bischofswerda 10 Ke 51.07N 14.11 E
Biskra 31 He 34.51N 5.44 E
Biskra [3] 32 Ic 34.40N 6.00 E
Biskupiec 10 Qc 53.52N 20.27 E
Bislig 26 Ie 8.13N 126.19 E
Bismarck 39 Ie 46.48N 100.47W
Bismarck, Kap- 41 Kc 76.40N 18.40W
Bismarck Archipelago 57 Fe 5.00S 150.00 E
Bismarck Sea 60 Dh 4.00S 147.30 E
Bismark Range 60 Ci 5.30S 144.45 E
Bismil 24 Id 37.51N 40.40 E
Bison 45 Ed 45.31N 102.28W
Bisotūn 24 Le 34.23N 47.26 E
Bispfors 8 Ga 63.02N 16.37 E
Bissau 31 Fg 11.51N 15.35W
Bissaula 34 Hd 7.01N 10.27 E
Bissett 44 Hb 46.13N 78.02W
Bisson, Banc du- 37 Hb 12.00S 46.25 E
Bistcho Lake 42 Fe 59.45N 118.50W
Bistineau, Lake- 45 Jj 32.25N 93.22W
Bistra 15 Fd 45.29N 22.11 E
Bistra 15 Dh 41.37N 20.44 E
Bistreţ 15 Gf 43.54N 23.30 E
Bistrica 15 Dg 42.09N 20.59 E
Bistrica 15 Cf 43.28N 19.42 E
Bistriţa 15 Hb 47.08N 24.29 E
Bistriţa [Rom.] 15 Jc 46.30N 26.57 E
Bistriţa [Rom.] 15 Hb 47.04N 24.25 E
Bistriţa-Năsăud [2] 15 Hb 47.05N 24.35 E
Bitam 36 Bb 2.05N 11.29 E
Bitam 13 Ri 35.15N 5.11 E
Bitburg 12 Ie 49.58N 6.32 E
Bitche 11 Ne 49.03N 7.26 E
Bitéa 35 Cc 13.11N 20.10 E
Bithia 14 Cl 38.55N 8.52 E
Bithynia 15 Mi 40.20N 29.30 E
Bitjug 16 Kd 50.37N 39.55 E
Bitkine 35 Bc 11.59N 18.13 E
Bitlis 23 Fb 38.22N 42.06 E
Bitola 6 Ig 41.02N 21.20 E
Bitonto 14 Ki 41.06N 16.41 E
Bitterfeld 10 Ie 51.37N 12.19 E
Bitterfontein 31 Il 31.00S 18.32 E
Bitterroot Range 38 He 47.06N 115.10W
Bitterroot River 46 Hc 46.52N 114.06W
Bitti 14 Dj 40.29N 9.23 E
Bitung 26 If 1.27N 125.11 E
Biu 31 Ig 10.37N 12.12 E
Bivolari 15 Kb 47.32N 27.26 E
Bivolu, Virful- 15 Ib 47.15N 25.56 E
Bivona 14 Hm 37.37N 13.26 E
Biwa-ko 28 Ng 35.13N 136.05 E
Bixad [Rom.] 15 Ic 46.06N 25.52 E
Bixad [Rom.] 15 Gb 47.56N 23.24 E
Bixby 45 Ii 35.57N 95.53W
Biyalā 24 Dg 31.10N 31.13 E
Biyang 27 Je 32.40N 113.21 E
Biyārjomand 24 Pd 36.06N 55.53 E
Bizuljak 17 Gj 53.43N 54.16 E
Biže 18 Kb 45.10N 77.58 E
Bizen 28 Mg 34.44N 134.09 E
Bizerte (EN)= Banzart 31 He 37.17N 9.52 E
Bjala 15 If 43.27N 25.44 E
Bjala Slatina 15 Gf 43.28N 23.56 E
Bjargtangar 5 Db 65.30N 24.32W
Bjärna/Perniö 7 Ff 60.12N 23.08 E
Bjärnum 8 Eh 56.17N 13.42 E
Bjästa 8 Ha 63.12N 18.30 E
Bjelašnica [Yugo.] 14 Mg 43.43N 18.09 E
Bjelašnica [Yugo.] 14 Mh 42.51N 18.09 E
Bjelašnica [Yugo.] 14 Mg 43.09N 18.23 E
Bjelolasica 14 Ie 45.16N 14.58 E
Bjelovar 14 Ke 45.54N 16.51 E
Bjerkvik 7 Db 68.33N 17.34 E
Bjerringbro 8 Ch 56.23N 9.40 E
Bjervamoen 8 Ce 59.25N 9.04 E
Bjeshkët e Nemuna 15 Cg 42.30N 19.50 E
Björdo 8 Fd 60.28N 14.42 E
Bjørkelangen 8 De 59.53N 11.34 E
Björkfors 8 Ff 58.01N 15.54 E
Björklinge 8 Gd 60.02N 17.33 E
Björkö 7 Eg 59.55N 19.00 E
Björna 7 Ee 63.34N 18.33 E
Bjørnafjorden 8 Ad 60.05N 5.20 E
Björneborg 8 Fe 59.15N 14.15 E
Björneborg/Pori 6 Ic 61.29N 21.47 E
Bjorne Peninsula 42 Ia 77.30N 87.00W
Bjornesfjorden 8 Bd 60.10N 7.40 E
Bjørnevatn 7 Gb 69.40N 30.00 E
Bjørnøya 67 Kd 74.30N 19.00 E
Björnöya = Bear Island (EN) 5 Ha 74.30N 19.00 E
Bjurholm 7 Ee 63.56N 19.13 E
Bjuröklubb 7 Ed 64.28N 21.35 E
Bjuv 8 Eh 56.05N 12.54 E
Bla 34 Dc 12.56N 5.45W
Blace 15 Ef 43.18N 21.18 E
Blackall 58 Gf 24.25S 145.28 E
Black Bank (EN)= Zwarte Bank 12 Fa 53.15N 3.55 E
Black Bay 45 Lb 48.40N 88.30W
Blackburn 9 Kh 53.45N 2.29W
Blackburn, Mount- 38 Ec 61.44N 143.26W
Black Butte Lake 46 Dg 39.45N 122.20W
Black Coast 66 Qf 71.45S 62.00W
Blackdown Hills 9 Jk 50.57N 3.09W
Blackduck 45 Ic 47.44N 94.33W
Blackfoot 43 Ec 43.11N 112.20W
Blackfoot Reservoir 46 Je 42.55N 111.35W
Black Forest (EN)= Schwarzwald 5 Gf 48.00N 8.15 E
Black Head 9 Hk 50.01N 5.03W
Black Hills 38 Ie 44.00N 104.00W
Black Isle 9 Id 57.35N 4.20W
Black Lake 42 Ge 59.11N 105.20W
Blackman's 51q Ab 13.11N 59.32W
Black Mesa 46 Jh 36.35N 110.20W
Blackmoor 9 Ik 50.23N 4.50W
Black Mountain 43 Kd 36.54N 82.54W
Black Mountains [U.S.] 46 Hi 35.30N 114.30W
Black Mountains [Wales-U.K.] 9 Jj 51.57N 3.08W
Blackpool 9 Jh 53.50N 3.03W
Black Range 43 Fe 33.20N 107.50W
Black River 49 Id 18.01N 77.51W
Black River [Az.-U.S.] 46 Jj 33.44N 110.13W
Black River [Mi.-U.S.] 44 Fd 43.00N 82.25W
Black River [N.Y.-U.S.] 44 Id 43.59N 76.04W
Black River [U.S.] 45 Ki 35.38N 91.19W
Black River [Wi.-U.S.] 45 Ke 43.57N 91.22W
Black River (EN)= Babian Jiang 21 Mg 20.17N 106.34 E
Black River (EN)= Da, Sông- 21 Mg 20.17N 106.34 E
Black River Falls 45 Kd 44.16N 90.52W
Black Rock 56 Lh 53.39S 41.48W
Black Rock [Ire.] 9 Cg 54.05N 10.20W
Black Rock [Phil.] 26 Ge 8.48N 119.50 E
Black Rock Desert 43 Dc 41.10N 119.00W
Blacksburg 44 Gg 37.15N 80.25W
Black Sea (EN)= Černoje More 5 Jg 43.00N 35.00 E
Black Sea (EN)= Černo More 5 Jg 43.00N 35.00 E
Black Sea (EN)= Karadeniz 5 Jg 43.00N 35.00 E
Black Sea (EN)= Neagră, Marea- 5 Jg 43.00N 35.00 E
Blacksod Bay/Cuan an Fhóid Duibh 9 Dg 54.08N 10.00W
Blackstairs Mountains/Na Staighrí Dubha 9 Gi 52.33N 6.49W
Blackstone 44 Hg 37.04N 78.01W
Blackville 44 Ob 46.47N 65.54W
Black Volta 30 Gh 8.38N 1.30W
Black Volta (EN)= Volta Noire 30 Gh 8.38N 1.30W
Black Volta (EN)= Volta Noire [3] 34 Ec 12.30N 4.00W
Blackwater 12 Cc 51.43N 0.28 E
Blackwater/An Abhainn Dubh 9 Gh 53.39N 6.43W
Blackwater/An Abhainn Mhór [Ire.] 9 Fj 51.51N 7.50W
Blackwater/An Abhainn Mhór [N.Ire.-U.K.] 9 Gg 54.30N 6.35W
Blackwell 45 Hh 36.48N 97.17W
Blackwood River 59 Df 34.35S 115.02 E
Blagnac 11 Hk 43.38N 1.24 E
Blagodarny 16 Mg 45.04N 43.24 E
Blagojevgrad 15 Gg 42.01N 23.06 E
Blagojevgrad [2] 15 Gh 41.45N 23.25 E
Blagoveščenka 20 Cf 52.50N 79.55 E
Blagoveščensk [R.S.F.S.R.] 19 Fd 55.01N 55.59 E
Blagoveščensk [R.S.F.S.R.] 22 Od 50.17N 127.32 E
Blåhø 8 Cb 62.45N 9.19 E
Blain 11 Eg 47.29N 1.45W
Blaine [Mn.-U.S.] 45 Jd 45.11N 93.14W
Blaine [Wa.-U.S.] 46 Db 48.59N 122.44W
Blair 45 Hf 41.33N 96.08W
Blair Athol 59 Jd 22.42S 147.33 E
Blairgowrie 9 Je 56.36N 3.21W
Blairmore 46 Hb 49.36N 114.26W
Blaise 11 Kf 48.38N 4.43 E
Blaj 15 Gc 46.11N 23.55 E
Blake Basin (EN) 43 Mf 29.00N 76.00W
Blakely 44 Ej 31.23N 84.56W
Blakeney Point 9 Ni 52.59N 1.00 E
Blake Plateau (EN) 38 Lf 31.00N 79.00W
Blake Ridge (EN) 38 Lg 29.00N 73.30W
Blakstad 7 Bg 58.30N 8.39 E
Blanc, Cape- (EN)= Abyaḑ, Ra's al- 30 He 37.20N 9.50 E
Blanc, Cape- (EN)= Nouâdhibou, Râs- 30 Ff 20.46N 17.03W
Blanc, Lac- 44 Kb 47.45N 73.12W
Blanc, Mont- 5 Gf 45.50N 6.52 E
Blanca, Bahía- 52 Ji 38.55S 62.10W
Blanca, Cerro- 49 Gi 8.40N 80.35W
Blanca, Cordillera- 54 Ce 9.10S 77.35W
Blanca, Costa- 13 Lg 37.38N 0.40W
Blanca, Isla- 48 Pg 21.24N 86.50W
Blanca, Punta- 48 Bc 29.05N 114.45W
Blancagrande 55 Bm 36.32S 60.53W
Blanca Peak [Co.-U.S.] 43 Fd 37.34N 105.29W
Blanca Peak [U.S.] 38 If 37.35N 105.29W
Blanche, Lake- [Austl.] 59 Ed 22.25S 123.15 E
Blanche, Lake- [Austl.] 59 He 29.15S 139.40 E
Blanche, Point- 51b Ac 18.00N 63.03W
Blanche Channel 63a Cc 8.30S 157.30 E
Blanc-Nez, Cap- 12 Dd 50.56N 1.42 E
Blanco, Cabo- [C.R.] 47 Gg 9.33N 85.06W
Blanco, Cabo- [Sp.] 13 Oe 39.22N 2.46 E
Blanco, Cape- 43 Cc 42.50N 124.34W
Blanco, Cerro- 48 Fe 25.43N 107.39W
Blanco, Río- 54 Ff 12.30S 64.18W
Blanco del Sur, Cayo- 49 Gb 22.02N 81.24W
Blanda 7a Bb 65.39N 20.18W
Blanding 46 Kh 37.37N 109.29W
Blanes 13 Oc 41.41N 2.48 E
Blangy-le-Château 12 Ce 49.14N 0.17 E
Blangy-sur-Bresle 11 He 49.56N 1.38 E
Blanice [Czech.] 10 Kg 49.48N 14.58 E
Blanice [Czech.] 10 Kg 49.17N 14.09 E
Blankaholm 8 Gg 57.35N 16.31 E
Blankenberge 11 Jc 51.19N 3.08 E
Blankenheim 12 Id 50.26N 6.39 E
Blanquilla, Isla- 54 Fa 11.51N 64.37W
Blanquillo 55 Ek 32.55S 55.40W
Blansko 10 Mg 49.22N 16.39 E
Blantyre 31 Ki 15.47S 35.00 E
Blantyre-Limbe 36 Gf 15.49S 35.03 E
Blåskavlen 8 Bd 60.58N 7.18 E
Błaszki 10 Oe 51.39N 18.27 E
Blatná 10 Jg 49.26N 13.53 E
Blato 14 Kh 42.56N 16.48 E
Blåvands Huk 5 Gd 55.33N 8.05 E
Blavet [Fr.] 11 Cf 48.13N 3.10W
Blavet [Fr.] 11 Cg 47.46N 3.18W
Blaye 11 Fi 45.08N 0.40W
Blaye-les-Mines 11 Ij 44.01N 2.08 E
Bled 14 Id 46.22N 14.08 E
Blefjell 8 Ce 59.48N 9.10 E
Bleialf 12 Id 50.14N 6.17 E
Blekinge [2] 7 Dh 56.20N 15.20 E
Blenheim 58 Ii 41.31S 173.57 E
Bletchley 9 Mj 52.00N 0.46W
Bleus, Monts- 36 Fb 1.30N 30.30 E
Bihārshāh 25 Fe 19.50N 79.22 E
Blida [3] 32 Hb 36.35N 2.30 E
Blida 31 He 36.34N 2.55 E
Blidö 8 He 59.35N 18.55 E
Blidsberg 8 Eg 57.56N 13.29 E
Blies 12 Je 49.07N 7.04 E
Blieskastel 12 Je 49.14N 7.15 E
Bligh Water 63d Ab 17.00S 178.00 E
Blind River 42 Jg 46.10N 82.58W
Blitar 26 Fh 8.06S 112.09 E
Blitta 34 Fd 8.19N 0.59 E
Block Island 44 Le 41.11N 71.35W
Bloemfontein 31 Jk 29.12S 26.07 E
Bloemhof 37 De 27.38S 25.32 E
Blois 11 Hg 47.35N 1.20 E
Blokhus 8 Cg 57.15N 9.35 E
Blomberg 12 Lc 51.56N 9.05 E
Blönduós 7a Bb 65.40N 20.18W
Bloody Foreland/Cnoc Fola 9 Ef 55.09N 8.17W
Bloomfield [Ia.-U.S.] 45 Jf 40.45N 92.25W
Bloomfield [In.-U.S.] 44 Df 39.01N 86.56W
Bloomington [Il.-U.S.] 43 Jc 40.29N 88.59W
Bloomington [In.-U.S.] 43 Jd 39.10N 86.32W
Bloomington [Mn.-U.S.] 45 Jd 44.50N 93.17W
Bloomsburg 44 Ie 41.01N 76.27W
Blosseville Kyst 41 Je 68.45N 27.25W
Blötberget 8 Fd 60.07N 15.04 E
Blountstown 44 Ej 30.29N 85.03W
Bludenz 14 Dc 47.09N 9.49 E
Blue Earth 45 Ie 43.38N 94.06W
Bluefield 43 Kd 37.14N 81.17W
Bluefields 39 Kh 12.00N 83.45W
Bluefields, Bahía de- 49 Fg 12.02N 83.44W
Blue Mesa Reservoir 45 Cg 38.28N 107.15W
Blue Mountain 44 Ie 40.15N 77.30W
Blue Mountain [Or.-U.S.] 46 Ge 42.25N 117.50W
Blue Mountain [U.S.] 45 Ii 34.41N 94.03W
Blue Mountain Lake 44 Jd 43.53N 74.26W
Blue Mountain Pass 46 Ge 42.18N 117.45W
Blue Mountain Peak 47 Ie 18.03N 76.35W
Blue Mountains [Austl.] 59 Kf 33.35S 150.15 E
Blue Mountains [U.S.] 43 Ec 44.35N 118.25W
Blue Mud Bay 59 Hb 13.25S 135.55 E
Blue Nile (EN)= Abay 30 Kg 15.38N 32.31 E
Blue Nile (EN)= Azraq, Al Baḩr al- 30 Kg 15.38N 32.31 E
Bluenose Lake 42 Fc 68.00N 121.00W
Blue Ridge 44 Eh 34.52N 84.20W
Blue Ridge 38 Kf 37.00N 82.00W
Blue Stack/Na Cruacha 9 Eg 54.45N 8.06W
Bluestone Lake 44 Gg 37.30N 80.50W
Bluff [N.Z.] 61 Ci 46.36S 168.21 E
Bluff [Ut.-U.S.] 46 Kh 37.17N 109.33W
Bluff Point 59 Ce 27.50S 114.05 E
Bluffton 44 Ee 40.44N 85.11W
Blumberg 10 Ei 47.50N 8.32 E
Blumenau 56 Kc 26.56S 49.03W
Blyth 12 Db 52.19N 1.41 E
Blyth 9 Lf 55.07N 1.30W
Blythe 43 Ee 33.37N 114.36W
Blytheville 43 Jd 35.56N 89.55W
Bø 7 Bg 59.25N 9.04 E
Bo 31 Fh 7.58N 11.45W
Boa 34 Dd 8.26N 7.10W
Boac 26 Hd 12.28N 122.28 E
Boaco [3] 49 Eg 12.35N 85.25W
Boaco 49 Eg 12.28N 85.40W
Boa Esperança 55 Je 21.05S 45.34W
Boa Esperança, Reprêsa- 54 Je 6.50S 44.00W
Boa Esperançao, Serra da- 55 Je 20.57S 45.40W
Bo'ai 28 Bg 35.10N 113.03 E
Boal 13 Fa 43.26N 6.49W
Boali 35 Be 4.48N 18.07 E
Boano, Pulau- 26 Ig 2.56S 127.56 E
Boardman 46 Fd 45.51N 119.43W
Boa Sentença, Serra da- 55 Ed 19.13S 57.33W
Boa Vista 30 Eg 16.05N 22.50W
Boa Vista [Braz.] 55 Ec 17.51S 54.13W
Boa Vista [Braz.] 55 Ia 12.40S 46.51W
Boa Vista [Braz.] 53 Je 2.49N 60.40W
Bobai 27 Ig 22.15N 109.58 E
Bobali, Cerros de- 49 Ki 8.53N 73.28W
Bobali, Cerros de- 49 Ki 8.53N 73.28W
Bobbio 14 Df 44.46N 9.23 E
Bobigny 12 If 48.54N 2.27 E
Bobo Dioulasso 31 Gg 11.12N 4.18W
Bobojod, Gora- 18 Hd 40.50N 70.20 E
Bobolice 10 Mc 53.57N 16.36 E
Bobonong 37 Dd 21.58S 28.25 E
Bobovdol 15 Fg 42.22N 23.00 E
Bóbr 10 Ld 52.04N 15.04 E
Bobrik 16 Ec 52.08N 26.48 E
Bobrinec 16 He 48.04N 32.09 E
Bobrka 10 Ug 49.34N 24.20 E
Bobrov 19 Ee 51.06N 40.01 E
Bobrovica 16 Gd 50.43N 31.28 E
Bobrowniki 10 Tc 53.08N 23.50 E
Bobrujsk 6 Ie 53.09N 29.14 E
Bobures 54 Db 9.15N 71.11W
Boby, Pic- 37 Hd 22.12S 46.55 E
Boca del Río 48 Ee 25.20N 108.25W
Boca de Pozo 50 Dg 11.00N 64.23W
Boca do Acre 53 Jf 8.45S 67.23W
Bocage, Cap- 63b Be 21.12S 165.37 E
Bocăina 55 Db 15.16S 56.45W
Bocaiúva 55 Kc 17.07S 43.49W
Bocajá 55 Ef 22.45S 55.13W
Bocaranga 35 Bd 6.59N 15.39 E
Boca Raton 43 Kf 26.21N 80.05W
Bocas del Toro 47 Hg 9.20N 82.15W
Bocas del Toro [3] 49 Fi 8.50N 82.10W
Bocas del Toro, Archipiélago de- 49 Fi 9.20N 82.10W
Bocay 49 Ef 14.19N 85.10W
Bochaine 11 Lj 44.20N 5.50 E
Bochnia 10 Qg 49.58N 20.26 E
Bocholt [Bel.] 12 Hc 51.10N 5.35 E
Bocholt [Ger.] 10 Ce 51.50N 6.36 E
Bochum 10 De 51.29N 7.13 E
Bocognano 11a Ba 42.05N 9.04 E
Bocoio 36 Be 12.28S 14.08 E
Boconó 49 Li 9.15N 70.16W
Bocşa 15 Ed 45.23N 21.47 E
Boda 35 Be 4.19N 17.28 E
Boda 8 Fc 61.01N 15.13 E
Böda 8 Gg 57.15N 17.03 E
Bodafors 8 Fg 57.30N 14.42 E
Bodajbo 22 Nd 57.51N 114.10 E
Bodalangi 36 Db 3.14N 22.14 E
Bode 10 Hd 52.01N 11.12 E
Bödefeld-Freiheit, Schmallenberg- 12 Kc 51.15N 8.24 E
Bodegraven 12 Gb 52.06N 4.44 E
Bodélé 30 Ig 16.30N 17.30 E
Boden 6 Ib 65.50N 21.42 E
Bodenheim 12 Ke 49.56N 8.18 E
Bodensee = Constance, Lake- (EN) 5 Gf 47.35N 9.25 E
Boderg, Lough- 9 Fh 53.52N 8.00W
Bodmin 9 Ik 50.29N 4.43W
Bodmin Moor 9 Ik 50.35N 4.40W
Bodø 6 Hb 67.17N 14.23 E
Bodoquena 55 De 20.12S 56.48W
Bodoquena, Serra da- 54 Gh 21.00S 56.50W
Bodrog 10 Rh 48.07N 21.25 E
Bodrogköz 10 Rh 48.15N 21.45 E
Bodrum 23 Cb 37.02N 27.06 E
Bodrum Yarimadasi 15 Kl 37.05N 27.30 E
Bodva 10 Qh 48.12N 20.47 E
Boën 11 Ji 45.44N 4.00 E
Boende 31 Ji 0.13S 20.52 E
Boeo, Capo- (Lilibeo, Capo-) 14 Gm 37.34N 12.41 E
Boerne 45 Gl 29.47N 98.44W
Boesmanland = Bushman-land (EN) 37 Be 29.30S 19.00 E
Boffa 34 Cc 10.10N 14.02W
Boga 15 Cg 42.24N 19.38 E
Bogale 25 Je 16.17N 95.24 E
Bogalusa 45 Lk 30.47N 89.52W
Bogandé 34 Ec 12.59N 0.08W
Bogangolo 35 Bd 5.34N 18.15 E
Bogatić 15 Ce 44.51N 19.29 E
Bogatynia 10 Kf 50.55N 14.59 E
Boğazkale 24 Fb 40.01N 34.35 E
Boğazlıyan 24 Fc 39.12N 35.15 E
Bogbonga 36 Cb 1.35N 19.25 E

Index Symbols

[1] Independent Nation
[2] State, Region
[3] District, County
[4] Municipality
[5] Colony, Dependency
Continent
Physical Region
Historical or Cultural Region
Mount, Mountain
Volcano
Hill
Mountains, Mountain Range
Hills, Escarpment
Plateau, Upland
Pass, Gap
Plain, Lowland
Delta
Salt Flat
Valley, Canyon
Crater, Cave
Karst Features
Depression
Polder
Desert, Dunes
Forest, Woods
Heath, Steppe
Oasis
Cape, Point
Coast, Beach
Cliff
Peninsula
Isthmus
Sandbank
Island
Atoll
Rock, Reef
Islands, Archipelago
Rocks, Reefs
Coral Reef
Well, Spring
Geyser
River, Stream
Waterfall Rapids
River Mouth, Estuary
Lake
Salt Lake
Intermittent Lake
Reservoir
Swamp, Pond
Canal
Glacier
Ice Shelf, Pack Ice
Ocean
Sea
Gulf, Bay
Strait, Fjord
Lagoon
Bank
Seamount
Tablemount
Ridge
Shelf
Basin
Escarpment, Sea Scarp
Fracture
Trench, Abyss
National Park, Reserve
Point of Interest
Recreation Site
Cave, Cavern
Historic Site
Ruins
Wall, Walls
Church, Abbey
Temple
Scientific Station
Airport
Port
Lighthouse
Mine
Tunnel
Dam, Bridge

Bogcang Zangbo 27 Ee 31.56N 87.24 E
Bogda Feng 27 Ec 43.45N 88.32 E
Bogdan 15 Hg 42.37N 24.28 E
Bogdanovka 16 Mi 41.15N 43.36 E
Bogda Shan 21 Ke 43.35N 90.00 E
Bogen 7 Db 68.32N 17.00 E
Bogenfels 37 Be 27.23S 15.22 E
Bogense 8 Di 55.34N 10.06 E
Boggeragh Mountains/An Bhograch 9 Ei 52.05N 9.00W
Boggy Peak 51d Bb 17.03N 61.51W
Boghar 13 Oi 35.55N 2.43 E
Boghni 13 Ph 36.32N 3.57 E
Bogia 60 Ch 4.16S 144.58 E
Bognor Regis 12 Bd 50.47N 0.39W
Bogny-sur-Meuse 12 Ge 49.54N 4.43 E
Bogoduhov 16 Id 50.12N 35.31 E
Bogomila 15 Eh 41.36N 21.28 E
Bogor 22 Mj 6.35S 106.47 E
Bogoridick 19 De 53.50N 38.08 E
Bogorodčany 10 Uh 48.45N 24.40 E
Bogorodsk 7 Kh 56.09N 43.32 E
Bogorodskoje [R.S.F.S.R.] 7 Mh 57.51N 50.48 E
Bogorodskoje [R.S.F.S.R.] 20 Jf 52.22N 140.30 E
Bogotá 53 Ie 4.36N 74.05W
Bogotol 20 De 56.17N 89.43 E
Bogøy 7 Dc 67.54N 15.11 E
Bogra 25 Hd 24.51N 89.22 E
Bogučany 20 Ee 58.23N 97.39 E
Bogučar 16 Le 49.57N 40.33 E
Bogué 32 Ef 16.36N 14.15W
Boguševsk 7 Hi 54.50N 30.13 E
Boguslav 19 Df 49.33N 30.54 E
Bo Hai=Chihli, Gulf of- (EN) 21 Nf 38.30N 120.00 E
Bohai Haixia 27 Ld 38.00N 121.30 E
Bohain-en-Vermandois 12 Fe 49.59N 3.27 E
Bohemia (EN)=Čechy 5 Hf 50.00N 14.30 E
Bohemia (EN)=Čechy 10 Kf 50.00N 14.30 E
Bohemian Forest (EN)= Böhmerwald 5 Hf 49.00N 13.30 E
Bohemian Forest (EN)= Český Les 10 Ig 49.50N 12.30 E
Bohemian Forest (EN)= Oberpfälzer Wald 10 Ig 49.50N 12.30 E
Bohemian Forest (EN)= Šumava 5 Hf 49.00N 13.30 E
Bohicon 34 Fd 7.12N 2.04 E
Böhmerwald=Bohemian Forest (EN) 5 Hf 49.00N 13.30 E
Bohmte 12 Kb 52.22N 8.19 E
Bohodoyou 34 Dd 9.46N 9.04W
Bohol 21 Oi 9.50N 124.10 E
Böhönye 10 Nj 46.24N 17.24 E
Bohor 14 Jd 46.04N 15.26 E
Bohu/Bagrax 27 Ec 41.58N 86.29 E
Bohus 8 Eg 57.51N 12.01 E
Bohuslän 8 Df 58.15N 11.50 E
Boiaçu 54 Fd 0.27S 61.46W
Boiano 14 Ii 41.29N 14.29 E
Boina 30 Lj 16.00S 46.30 E
Bois, Lac des - 42 Ec 66.50N 125.15W
Bois, Rio dos- [Braz.] 55 Gd 18.35S 50.02W
Bois, Rio dos- [Braz.] 55 Ha 13.55S 49.51W
Bois Blanc Island 44 Ec 45.45N 84.28W
Boischaut 11 Hh 46.40N 1.45 E
Boise 39 He 43.37N 116.13W
Boise City 45 Eh 36.44N 102.31W
Boise River 46 Ge 43.49N 117.01W
Boissay 12 De 49.31N 1.21 E
Boissevain 42 Hg 49.14N 100.03W
Boizenburg 10 Gc 53.23N 10.43 E
Bojador, Cabo- 30 Ff 26.08N 14.30W
Bojana 15 Ch 41.52N 19.22 E
Bojanowo 10 Me 51.42N 16.44 E
Bojarka 19 De 50.19N 30.20 E
Bojčinovci 15 Gf 43.28N 23.20 E
Bojnūrd 23 Ib 37.28N 57.19 E
Bojonegoro 26 Fh 7.09S 111.52 E
Bojuru 55 Gj 31.38S 51.26W
Bokatola 36 Cc 0.38S 18.46 E
Boké 34 Cc 10.56N 14.13W
Bokhara River 59 Je 29.55S 146.42 E
Bokn 8 Ae 59.15N 5.25 E
Boknafjorden 5 Gd 59.10N 5.35 E
Boko 36 Bc 4.47S 14.38 E
Bokol Mayo 35 Ge 4.31N 41.32 E
Bokoro 35 Bc 12.23N 17.03 E
Bokote 36 Dc 0.05S 20.08 E
Bokpyin 25 Jf 11.16N 98.46 E
Boksitogorsk 19 Dd 59.29N 33.52 E
Bokungu 36 Dc 0.41S 22.19 E
Bol [Chad] 35 Ac 13.30N 14.41 E
Bol [Yugo.] 14 Kg 43.16N 16.40 E
Bola, Bahr- 35 Bd 9.50N 18.59 E
Bolama 34 Bc 11.35N 15.28W
Bolands 51d Bb 17.02N 61.53W
Bolaños, Rio- 48 Gg 21.14N 104.08W
Bolattau, Gora- 18 Ha 46.44N 71.54 E
Bolayir 15 Ji 40.31N 26.45 E
Bolbec 11 Ge 49.34N 0.29 E
Bolda 16 Pg 45.58N 48.35 E
Bole [Eth.] 35 Fd 6.37N 37.22 E
Bole [Ghana] 34 Ed 9.02N 2.29W
Bole/Bortala 27 Dc 44.59N 81.57 E
Bolehov 16 Ce 49.03N 23.50 E
Bolesławiec 10 Le 51.16N 15.34 E
Bolgatanga 31 Gg 10.47N 0.51W
Bolgrad 16 Fg 45.40N 28.38 E
Bolhov 19 De 53.30N 36.01 E
Boli 27 Nb 45.46N 130.31 E
Bolia 36 Cc 1.36S 18.23 E
Boliden 7 Ed 64.52N 20.23 E
Bolinao, Cape- 26 Gc 16.22N 119.50 E
Bolintin Vale 15 Ie 44.27N 25.46 E
Bolívar [Col.] 54 Db 9.00N 74.40W
Bolivar [Mo.-U.S.] 45 Jh 37.37N 93.25W
Bolivar [Tn.-U.S.] 44 Ch 35.15N 88.59W
Bolívar [Ven.] 54 Fb 6.20N 63.30W
Bolívar, Cerro- 54 Fb 7.28N 63.25W
Bolívar, Pico- 52 Ie 8.30N 71.02W
Bolivia 53 Jg 17.00S 65.00W
Bolivia, Altiplano de- 52 Jg 18.00S 68.00W
Boljevac 15 Ef 43.50N 21.58 E
Bollendorf 12 Ie 49.51N 6.22 E
Bollène 11 Kj 44.17N 4.45 E
Bollnäs 7 Df 61.21N 16.25 E
Bollon 59 Je 28.02S 147.28 E
Bollstabruk 8 Ga 63.00N 17.41 E
Bollullos par del Condado 13 Fg 37.20N 6.32W
Bolmen 7 Ch 56.55N 13.40 E
Bolnisi 16 Ni 41.28N 44.31 E
Bolobo 36 Cc 2.10S 16.14 E
Bolodek 20 If 53.43N 133.09 E
Bologna 6 Hg 44.29N 11.20 E
Bolognesi 54 Df 10.01S 74.05W
Bologoje 6 Jd 57.54N 34.02 E
Bolohovo 16 Jb 54.05N 37.52 E
Bolomba 36 Cb 0.29N 19.12 E
Bolombo 36 Dc 3.59S 21.22 E
Bolon 20 Ig 49.58N 136.04 E
Bolotnoje 20 De 55.41N 84.33 E
Bolovens, Plateau des- 25 Le 15.20N 106.20 E
Bolšaja Balahnja 20 Fb 73.37N 107.05 E
Bolšaja Berestovica 10 Uc 53.09N 24.02 E
Bolšaja Černigovka 7 Mj 52.08N 50.48 E
Bolšaja Glušica 7 Mj 52.24N 50.29 E
Bolšaja Ižora 8 Me 59.55N 29.40 E
Bolšaja Kinel 7 Mj 53.14N 50.32 E
Bolšaja Koksaga 7 Lh 56.07N 47.48 E
Bolšaja Kuonamka 20 Gc 70.50N 113.20 E
Bolšaja Oju 17 Jb 69.42N 60.42 E
Bolšaja Rogovaja 17 Jc 66.30N 60.40 E
Bolšaja Synja 17 Id 65.58N 58.01 E
Bolšaja Tap 17 Lg 59.55N 65.42 E
Bolšaja Ussurka 20 Ig 46.00N 133.30 E
Bolšaja Vladimirovka 19 He 50.53N 79.30 E
Bolšakovo 8 Ij 54.50N 21.36 E
Bolsena 14 Fh 42.39N 11.59 E
Bolsena, Lago di- 14 Fh 42.35N 11.55 E
Bolšerečje 19 Hd 56.06N 74.38 E
Bolšereck 20 Kf 52.22N 156.24 E
Bolšeustikinskoje 17 Ii 55.57N 58.20 E
Bolševik 20 Jd 62.40N 147.30 E
Bolševik, Ostrov-=Bolshevik Island (EN) 21 Mb 78.40N 102.30 E
Bolšezemelskaja Tundra 19 Fb 67.30N 58.30 E
Bolshevik Island (EN)= Bolševik, Ostrov- 21 Mb 78.40N 102.30 E
Bolšije Uki 19 Hd 56.57N 72.37 E
Bolšoj Anjuj 20 Lc 68.30N 160.50 E
Bolšoj Begičev, Ostrov- 20 Gb 74.20N 112.30 E
Bolšoj Berezovy, Ostrov- 8 Md 60.15N 28.35 E
Bolšoj Boktybaj, Gora- [Kaz.-U.S.S.R.] 19 Ff 48.30N 58.20 E
Bolšoj Boktybaj, Gora- [U.S.S.R.] 16 Ue 48.30N 58.25 E
Bolšoj Bolvanski Nos, Mys- 17 Ia 70.27N 59.05 E
Bolšoj Čeremšan 7 Li 54.12N 49.40 E
Bolšoje Muraškino 7 Ki 55.47N 44.46 E
Bolšoje Vlasjevo 20 Jf 53.25N 140.55 E
Bolšoje Zagorje 8 Mg 57.47N 28.58 E
Bolšoj Gašun 16 Mf 47.22N 42.42 E
Bolšoj Ik 17 Hj 51.47N 56.20 E
Bolšoj Irgiz 19 Ee 52.01N 47.24 E
Bolšoj Jenisej 20 Ef 51.40N 94.26 E
Bolšoj Jugan 19 Hc 60.55N 73.40 E
Bolšoj Kamen 20 Ih 43.08N 132.28 E
Bolšoj Klimecki, Ostrov- 7 Ie 62.00N 35.15 E
Bolšoj Kujalnik 16 Gf 46.46N 30.38 E
Bolšoj Kumak 16 Ud 51.22N 58.55 E
Bolšoj Ljahovski, Ostrov- 20 Jb 73.35N 142.00 E
Bolšoj Murta 20 Ee 56.55N 93.10 E
Bolšoj Nimnyr 20 He 58.08N 125.45 E
Bolšoj Pit 20 Ee 59.02N 91.40 E
Bolšoj Tjuters, Ostrov- 8 Le 59.50N 27.10 E
Bolšoj Uluj 20 Ee 56.45N 90.46 E
Bolšoj Uvat, Ozero- 17 Oh 57.35N 70.30 E
Bolšoj Uzen 5 Kf 48.50N 49.40 E
Bolsón, Cerro del- 52 Jh 27.13S 66.06W
Bolšovcy 10 Ug 49.08N 24.47 E
Bolsward 12 Ha 53.04N 5.30 E
Boltaña 13 Mb 42.27N 0.04 E
Bolton 9 Kh 53.35N 2.26W
Bolu 23 Da 40.44N 31.37 E
Bolu Dağları 24 Eb 41.05N 32.05 E
Bolungarvik 7a Aa 66.09N 23.15W
Boluntay 27 Fd 36.29N 92.18 E
Bolva 16 Ic 53.17N 34.20 E
Bolvadin 24 Dc 38.42N 31.04 E
Bolzano/Bozen 6 Hf 46.31N 11.22 E
Bom, Rio- 55 Gf 23.56S 51.44W
Boma 31 Ii 5.51S 13.03 E
Bomassa 36 Cb 2.12N 16.12 E
Bombala 59 Jg 36.54S 149.14 E
Bombarral 13 Ce 39.16N 9.09W
Bombay 22 Jh 18.58N 72.50 E
Bomberai, Jazirah- 26 Jg 3.00S 133.00 E
Bombo 36 Fb 0.35N 32.32 E
Bomboma 36 Cb 2.26N 18.57 E
Bom Comércio 54 Ee 9.45S 65.54W
Bom Conselho 54 Ke 9.10S 36.41W
Bom Despacho 54 Ig 19.43S 45.15W
Bomdila 25 Ic 27.16N 92.23 E
Bomi/Bowo 27 Ge 30.02N 95.39 E
Bomi Hills 31 Fh 6.52N 10.45W
Bomili 36 Eb 1.40N 27.01 E
Bom Jardim de Goiás 55 Fc 16.17S 52.07W
Bom Jardim de Minas 55 Je 21.57S 44.11W
Bom Jesus 55 Gi 28.42S 50.24W
Bom Jesus da Lapa 53 Lg 13.15S 43.25W
Bom Jesus de Goiás 55 Hd 18.12S 49.37W
Bømlafjorden 8 Ae 59.40N 5.20 E
Bømlo 7 Ag 59.45N 5.10 E
Bomokandi 36 Eb 3.30N 26.08 E
Bomongo 36 Cb 1.22N 18.21 E
Bom Retiro 55 Hh 27.48S 49.31W
Bom Sucesso 55 Je 21.02S 44.46W
Bomu 30 Jh 4.08N 22.26 E
Bomu (EN)=Mbomou 30 Jh 4.08N 22.26 E
Bomu (EN)=Mbomou 35 Cd 5.30N 23.30 E
Bon, Cape- (EN)=Țib, Ra's At- 30 Ie 37.05N 11.03 E
Bona, Mount- 40 Kd 61.20N 141.50W
Bonaire 54 Ea 12.10N 68.15W
Bonaire Basin (EN) 50 Cg 11.25N 67.30W
Bonampak 48 Ni 16.43N 91.05W
Bonanza 49 Ef 14.01N 84.35W
Bonanza Peak 46 Eb 48.14N 120.52W
Bonao 49 Ld 18.56N 70.25W
Bonaparte, Mount- 46 Fb 48.45N 119.08W
Bonaparte Archipelago 57 Df 14.20S 125.20 E
Bonaparte Lake 46 Ea 51.16N 120.35W
Bonaparte Rocks 51p Cb 12.24N 61.30W
Bonasse 50 Fg 10.05N 61.52W
Bonavista 42 Mg 48.39N 53.07W
Bonavista Bay 42 Mg 49.00N 53.20W
Bon-Cagan-Nur 27 Gb 45.35N 99.15 E
Bondeno 14 Ff 44.53N 11.25 E
Bondo 31 Jh 3.49N 23.40 E
Bondoukou 34 Ed 8.02N 2.48W
Bondoukou 34 Ed 8.20N 2.55W
Bondowoso 26 Fh 7.55S 113.49 E
Bone, Gulf of- (EN)=Bone, Teluk- 21 Oj 4.00S 120.40 E
Bone, Teluk-=Bone, Gulf of- (EN) 21 Oj 4.00S 120.40 E
Bone Bay 51a Db 18.45N 64.22W
Bonelohe 26 Hh 5.48S 120.27 E
Bönen 12 Jc 51.36N 7.46 E
Bone Rate, Kepulauan- 26 Hh 7.00S 121.00 E
Bone Rate, Pulau- 26 Hh 7.22S 121.08 E
Bonete, Cerro- 56 Gc 27.51S 68.47W
Bong 34 Cd 6.49N 10.19W
Bong 34 Dd 7.00N 9.40W
Bonga 35 Fd 7.16N 36.14 E
Bongabong 26 Hd 12.45N 121.29 E
Bongandanga 36 Db 1.30N 21.03 E
Bongo, Massif des- 30 Jh 8.40N 22.25 E
Bongolava 37 Hc 18.35S 45.20 E
Bongor 31 Ig 10.17N 15.22 E
Bongouanou 34 Ed 6.43N 4.12W
Bongouanou 34 Ed 6.39N 4.12W
Bonham 45 Hj 33.35N 96.11W
Bonheiden 12 Gc 51.02N 4.32 E
Bonhomme, Col du- 11 Nf 48.10N 7.06 E
Bonhomme, Pic- 49 Kd 19.05N 72.15W
Bonifacio 11a Bb 41.23N 9.09 E
Bonifacio, Bocche di-= Bonifacio, Strait of- (EN) 5 Gg 41.18N 9.15 E
Bonifacio, Strait of- (EN)= Bonifacio, Bocche di- 5 Gg 41.18N 9.15 E
Bonifati, Capo- 14 Jk 39.33N 15.52 E
Bonin Basin (EN) 60 Bb 29.00N 137.00 E
Bonin Islands (EN)= Ogasawara-Shotō 21 Qg 27.00N 142.10 E
Bonin Trench (EN) 3 If 30.00N 145.00 E
Bonita Springs 44 Gl 26.21N 81.47W
Bonito [Braz.] 55 Jb 15.20S 44.46W
Bonito [Braz.] 55 De 21.08S 56.28W
Bonito, Pico- 47 Ge 15.38N 86.55W
Bonito, Rio- [Braz.] 55 Hb 15.18S 49.36W
Bonito, Rio- [Braz.] 55 Gc 16.31S 51.23W
Bonn 6 Ge 50.44N 7.06 E
Bonn-Bad Godesberg 10 Df 50.41N 7.09 E
Bonnebosq 12 Ce 49.12N 0.05 E
Bonnechère River 44 Ic 45.31N 76.33W
Bonners Ferry 46 Gb 48.41N 116.18W
Bonnet, Lac du- 45 Ia 50.22N 95.55W
Bonnétable 11 Gf 48.11N 0.26 E
Bonnet Plume 42 Ec 65.53N 134.58W
Bonneval 11 Hf 48.11N 1.24 E
Bonneville 11 Mh 46.05N 6.25 E
Bonneville Salt Flats 46 If 40.45N 113.50W
Bonnières-sur-Seine 12 De 49.02N 1.35 E
Bonningues-lès-Ardres 12 Ed 50.47N 2.01 E
Bonny 34 Ge 4.25N 7.10 E
Bono 14 Dj 40.25N 9.02 E
Bō-no-Misaki 29 Bf 31.15N 130.13 E
Bonorva 14 Cj 40.25N 8.46 E
Bontang 26 Gf 0.08N 117.30 E
Bonthain 26 Gh 5.32S 119.56 E
Bonthe 34 Cd 7.32N 12.30W
Bontoc 26 Hc 17.05N 120.58 E
Bonyhád 10 Oj 46.18N 18.32 E
Boo, Kepulauan- 26 Ig 1.12S 129.24 E
Boola 34 Dd 8.22N 8.43W
Booligal 59 If 33.52S 144.53 E
Boone [Ia.-U.S.] 45 Je 42.04N 93.53W
Boone [N.C.-U.S.] 44 Gg 36.13N 81.41W
Booneville [Ar.-U.S.] 45 Ji 35.08N 93.55W
Booneville [Ms.-U.S.] 45 Li 34.39N 88.34W
Boon Point 51d Bb 17.10N 61.50W
Boonville [In.-U.S.] 44 Df 38.03N 87.16W
Boonville [Mo.-U.S.] 45 Jg 38.58N 92.44W
Boos 12 De 49.23N 1.12 E
Boothia, Gulf of- 38 Jb 71.00N 91.00W
Boothia Peninsula 38 Jb 70.30N 95.00W
Boot Reefs 60 Cj 10.00S 144.35 E
Booué 31 Ii 0.06S 11.56 E
Bophuthatswana 37 De 26.00S 25.30 E
Bopolu 34 Cd 7.04N 10.29W
Boppard 12 Jd 50.14N 7.36 E
Boquerón 55 Bf 23.00S 61.00W
Boquerón 51a Ab 18.03N 67.09W
Boquilla, Presa de la- 48 Gd 27.30N 105.30W
Boquillas del Carmen 48 Hc 29.17N 102.53W
Bor [Czech.] 10 Ig 49.43N 12.47 E
Bor [R.S.F.S.R.] 19 Ed 56.23N 44.07 E
Bor [Sud.] 31 Kh 6.12N 31.33 E
Bor [Swe.] 8 Fg 57.07N 14.10 E
Bor [Tur.] 24 Fd 37.54N 34.34 E
Bor [Yugo.] 15 Fe 44.06N 22.06 E
Bora-Bora, Ile- 57 Lf 16.30S 151.45W
Borah Peak 38 He 44.08N 113.14W
Boraldaj 18 Gc 42.30N 69.05 E
Bora Marina 14 Jm 37.56N 15.55 E
Bōramo 35 Gd 9.58N 43.07 E
Borås 7 Ch 57.43N 12.55 E
Borāzjān 24 Nh 29.16N 51.12 E
Borba [Braz.] 54 Gd 4.24S 59.35W
Borba [Port.] 13 Ef 38.48N 7.27W
Borborema, Planalto da- 52 Mf 7.00S 37.00W
Borca 15 Ib 47.11N 25.46 E
Borcea 15 Ke 44.20N 27.45 E
Borcea, Braţul- 15 Ke 44.40N 27.53 E
Borchgrevink Coast 66 Kf 73.00S 171.00 E
Borçka 24 Ib 41.22N 41.40 E
Borculo 12 Ib 52.07N 6.31 E
Borda da Mata, Serra- 55 Ie 21.18S 47.06W
Bordeaux 6 Fg 44.50N 0.34W
Borden 42 Ga 78.30N 110.30W
Borden Peninsula 38 Kb 73.00N 83.00W
Borders 9 Kf 55.35N 3.00W
Bordertown 58 Fh 36.19S 140.47 E
Bordighera 14 Bg 43.46N 7.39 E
Bordj Bou Arreridj 32 Hb 36.04N 4.46 E
Bordj el Emir Abdelkader 13 Oi 35.52N 2.16 E
Bordj Fly Sainte Marie 32 Gd 27.18N 2.59W
Bordj-Menaïel 13 Ph 36.44N 3.43 E
Bordj Messouda 32 Ic 30.12N 9.25 E
Bordj Moktar 31 Hf 21.20N 0.56 E
Bordj Omar Driss 31 Hf 28.09N 6.49 E
Bord Khūn-e Now 24 Nh 28.03N 51.28 E
Bordon Camp 12 Bc 51.07N 0.51W
Boreal, Chaco- 52 Kh 23.00S 60.00W
Boren 8 Ff 58.35N 15.10 E
Borensberg 8 Ff 58.34N 15.17 E
Borgå/Porvoo 7 Ff 60.24N 25.40 E
Borgarnes 7a Bb 64.32N 21.55W
Børgefjell 7 Cd 65.23N 13.50 E
Borgentreich 12 Lc 51.34N 9.15 E
Borger [Neth.] 12 Ib 52.55N 6.48 E
Borger [Tx.-U.S.] 43 Gd 35.39N 101.24W
Borgholm 7 Dh 56.53N 16.39 E
Borghorst, Steinfurt- 12 Jb 52.08N 7.25 E
Borgia 14 Kl 38.49N 16.30 E
Borgloon 12 Hd 50.48N 5.20 E
Borgomanero 14 Ce 45.42N 8.28 E
Borgorose 14 Hh 42.11N 13.15 E
Borgo San Dalmazzo 14 Bf 44.20N 7.30 E
Borgo San Lorenzo 14 Fg 43.57N 11.23 E
Borgosesia 14 Ce 45.43N 8.16 E
Borgou 34 Fc 10.30N 2.50 E
Borgo Val di Taro 14 Df 44.29N 9.46 E
Borgo Valsugana 14 Fd 46.03N 11.27 E
Borgu 30 Hg 10.35N 3.40 E
Borgworm/Waremme 11 Ld 50.42N 5.15 E
Bori 34 Ge 4.42N 7.21 E
Borinquen, Punta- 51a Ab 18.30N 67.10W
Borislav 19 Cf 49.18N 23.27 E
Borisoglebsk 6 Ke 51.23N 42.06 E
Borisov 19 Ce 54.15N 28.30 E
Borisovka 16 Jd 50.36N 36.06 E
Borispol 19 De 50.23N 30.59 E
Bo River 35 Dd 6.48N 27.55 E
Borja 14 Lf 44.31N 17.44 E
Borja [Peru] 54 Cd 4.26S 77.33W
Borja [Sp.] 13 Kc 41.50N 1.32W
Borjas Blancas/Les Borges Blanques 13 Mc 41.31N 0.52 E
Borken 10 Ce 51.51N 6.52 E
Borkou 30 Ig 18.15N 18.50 E
Borkou-Ennedi-Tibesti 35 Bb 18.00N 19.00 E
Borkoviči 8 Mi 55.38N 28.23 E
Borkum 10 Cc 53.35N 6.41 E
Borlänge 7 Df 60.29N 15.25 E
Borlu 24 Cc 38.44N 28.27 E
Bormida 14 Cf 44.56N 8.40 E
Bormio 14 Ed 46.28N 10.22 E
Born 11 Fj 44.30N 1.00W
Borna 10 Ie 51.07N 12.30 E
Borndiep 12 Ha 53.25N 5.35 E
Borne 12 Ib 52.18N 6.45 E
Borneo/Kalimantan 21 Ni 1.00N 114.00 E
Bornheim 12 Id 50.46N 7.00 E
Bornholm 5 Hd 55.10N 15.00 E
Bornholm 8 Fi 55.10N 15.00 E
Bornos 13 Gh 36.48N 5.44W
Bornova, İzmir- 26 Bc 38.27N 27.14 E
Bornu 34 Hc 12.00N 12.40 E
Bornu 30 Ig 12.30N 13.00 E
Boro 30 Jh 8.52N 26.11 E
Borodino [R.S.F.S.R.] 7 Ii 55.32N 35.49 E
Borodino [R.S.F.S.R.] 20 Ee 55.57N 95.03 E
Borodinskoje 8 Md 61.00N 29.29 E
Borogoncy 20 Id 62.39N 131.08 E
Borohoro Shan 21 Ke 44.20N 85.00 E
Boromo 34 Ec 11.45N 2.56W
Borongan 26 Id 11.37N 125.26 E
Borotou 34 Dd 8.44N 7.30W
Borovan 15 Gf 43.26N 23.45 E
Borovec 15 Gg 42.16N 23.35 E
Boroviči 19 Dd 58.24N 33.56 E
Borovici 8 Mg 57.58N 29.47 E
Borovljanka 20 Df 52.38N 84.35 E
Borovo 14 Me 45.24N 18.59 E
Borovski 19 Gd 57.03N 65.44 E
Borovskoj 19 Ge 53.48N 64.17 E
Borrachas, Islas- 50 Dg 10.18N 64.44W
Borrān 35 Hc 10.11N 48.53 E
Borrby 8 Fi 55.27N 14.10 E
Borroloola 58 Ef 16.04S 136.17 E
Borş 15 Eb 47.07N 21.49 E
Borşa 15 Hb 47.39N 24.40 E
Borščovočny Hrebet= Borshchovochny Range (EN) 20 Gf 52.00N 118.30 E
Borsec 15 Ic 46.57N 25.34 E
Borshchovochny Range (EN) =Borščovočny Hrebet 20 Gf 52.00N 118.30 E
Borsod-Abaúj-Zemplén 10 Qh 48.15N 21.00 E
Bortala/Bole 27 Dc 44.59N 81.57 E
Bortala He 27 Dc 44.53N 82.45 E
Bort-les-Orgues 11 Ii 45.24N 2.30 E
Borūjen 24 Ng 31.59N 51.18 E
Borūjerd 23 Gc 33.54N 48.46 E
Borzja 22 Nd 50.24N 116.31 E
Borzna 16 Hd 51.15N 32.29 E
Boržomi 16 Mi 41.50N 43.25 E
Borzsöny 10 Oi 47.55N 19.00 E
Borzyszkowy 10 Nb 54.03N 17.22 E
Bosa 14 Cj 40.18N 8.30 E
Bosanska Dubica 14 Ke 45.11N 16.48 E
Bosanska Gradiška 14 Le 45.09N 17.15 E
Bosanska Krupa 14 Kf 44.53N 16.10 E
Bosanski Brod 14 Me 45.08N 18.01 E
Bosanski Novi 14 Ke 45.03N 16.22 E
Bosanski Petrovac 14 Kf 44.34N 16.21 E
Bosanski Šamac 14 Me 45.04N 18.28 E
Bosansko Grahovo 23 Ff 44.11N 16.22 E
Bōsāso 31 Lg 11.13N 49.08 E
Bosavi, Mount- 59 Ia 6.35S 142.50 E
Bosbeek 12 Hc 51.06N 5.48 E
Bose 22 Mg 24.01N 106.32 E
Boshan 27 Kd 36.30N 117.50 E
Boshrūyeh 24 Qf 33.53N 57.26 E
Bosilegrad 15 Fg 42.30N 22.28 E
Bosingfeld, Extertal- 12 Lb 52.04N 9.07 E
Bosna 14 Me 45.04N 18.28 E
Bosna 15 Kg 42.11N 27.27 E
Bosna=Bosnia (EN) 5 Hg 44.00N 18.00 E
Bosna = Bosnia (EN) 14 Lf 44.00N 18.00 E
Bosna i Hercegovina = Bosnia-Hercegovina (EN) 14 Lf 44.15N 17.50 E
Bosnia (EN) = Bosna 14 Lf 44.00N 18.00 E
Bosnia (EN)=Bosna 5 Hg 44.00N 18.00 E
Bosnia-Hercegovina (EN) = Bosna i Hercegovina 14 Lf 44.15N 17.50 E
Bosnik 26 Kg 1.10S 136.14 E
Bošnjakovo 20 Jg 49.41N 142.10 E
Bosobolo 36 Cb 4.11N 19.54 E
Bōsō-Hantō 28 Pg 35.20N 140.10 E
Bosporus (EN)=İstanbul Boğazi 5 Ig 41.00N 29.00 E
Bosque Bonito 48 Gb 30.42N 105.06W
Bossangoa 31 Ih 6.29N 17.27 E
Bossé Bangou 34 Fc 13.21N 1.18 E
Bossembélé 35 Bd 5.16N 17.39 E
Bossemtélé II 35 Bd 5.41N 16.38 E
Bossier City 43 Ie 32.31N 93.43W
Bosso 34 Hc 13.42N 13.19 E
Bosso, Dallol- 30 Hg 12.25N 2.50 E
Bossut, Cape- 59 Ec 18.43S 121.38 E
Bostān 25 Db 30.26N 67.02 E
Bostānābād 24 Ld 37.50N 46.50 E
Bosten/Bagrax Hu 21 Ke 42.00N 87.00 E
Boston [Eng.-U.K.] 9 Mi 52.59N 0.01W
Boston [Ma.-U.S.] 39 Le 42.21N 71.04W
Boston Bar 46 Eb 49.52N 121.26W
Boston Deeps 12 Ca 53.00N 0.15 E
Boston Mountains 43 Id 35.50N 93.20W
Botan 24 Id 37.44N 41.48 E
Botas, Ribeirão das- 55 Fe 20.26S 53.43W
Botesdale 12 Db 52.20N 1.01 E
Botev 5 Ig 42.43N 24.55 E
Botevgrad 15 Gg 42.54N 23.47 E
Bothnia, Gulf of- (EN)= Bottniska viken 5 Hc 63.00N 20.00 E
Bothnia, Gulf of- (EN)= Pohjanlahti 5 Hc 63.00N 20.00 E
Boticas 13 Ec 41.41N 7.40W
Botletle 37 Cd 21.07S 24.42 E
Botlih 16 Oh 42.41N 46.13 E
Botna 15 Mc 46.48N 29.30 E
Botoşani 15 Jb 47.40N 26.43 E
Botoşani 15 Jb 47.45N 26.40 E
Botrange 11 Md 50.30N 6.08 E
Botswana 31 Jk 22.00S 24.00 E
Botte Donato 14 Kk 39.17N 16.27 E
Bottineau 43 Gb 48.50N 100.27W
Bottniska viken=Bothnia, Gulf of- (EN) 5 Hc 63.00N 20.00 E
Bottrop 10 Ce 51.31N 6.55 E
Botucatu 56 Kb 22.52S 48.26W
Botucatu, Serra de- 55 Hf 23.00S 48.20W
Botwood 42 Lg 49.08N 55.21W
Bouaflé 34 Dd 6.59N 5.45W
Bouaflé 34 Dd 7.03N 5.48W
Bouaké 31 Gh 7.41N 5.02W
Bouaké 34 Dd 7.45N 5.02W
Bou Anane 32 Gc 32.02N 3.03W
Bouar 31 Ih 5.57N 15.36 E
Bou Arfa 32 Gc 32.32N 1.57W
Boubin 10 Jh 48.58N 13.50 E
Bouca 31 Ih 6.30N 18.17 E
Bouchain 12 Fd 50.17N 3.19 E
Bouchegouf 14 Bn 36.28N 7.44 E
Bouche Island 51k Bb 13.57N 60.53W
Bouches-du-Rhône 11 Kk 43.30N 5.00 E
Boudenib 32 Gc 31.57N 3.36W
Boudeuse Cay 37b Bb 6.05S 52.51 E
Boû Djébéha 34 Eb 18.33N 2.45W
Bouenza 36 Bc 3.00S 13.00 E
Boufarik 13 Oh 36.34N 2.55 E
Bougaa 13 Rh 36.20N 5.05 E
Bougainville Island 57 Ge 6.00S 155.00 E
Bougainville Reef 59 Jc 15.30S 147.05 E
Bougainville Strait [Ocn.] 63a Cb 6.40S 156.10 E
Bougainville Strait [Van.] 63b Cb 15.50S 167.10 E
Bougouni 31 Gg 11.25N 7.28W

Index Symbols

Independent Nation
State, Region
District, County
Municipality
Colony, Dependency
Continent
Physical Region
Historical or Cultural Region
Mount, Mountain
Volcano
Hill
Mountains, Mountain Range
Hills, Escarpment
Plateau, Upland
Pass, Gap
Plain, Lowland
Delta
Salt Flat
Valley, Canyon
Crater, Cave
Karst Features
Depression
Polder
Desert, Dunes
Forest, Woods
Heath, Steppe
Oasis
Cape, Point
Coast, Beach
Cliff
Peninsula
Isthmus
Sandbank
Island
Atoll
Rock, Reef
Islands, Archipelago
Rocks, Reefs
Coral Reef
Well, Spring
Geyser
River, Stream
Waterfall Rapids
River Mouth, Estuary
Lake
Salt Lake
Intermittent Lake
Reservoir
Swamp, Pond
Canal
Glacier
Ice Shelf, Pack Ice
Ocean
Sea
Gulf, Bay
Strait, Fjord
Lagoon
Bank
Seamount
Tablemount
Ridge
Shelf
Basin
Escarpment, Sea Scarp
Fracture
Trench, Abyss
National Park, Reserve
Point of Interest
Recreation Site
Cave, Cavern
Historic Site
Ruins
Wall, Walls
Church, Abbey
Temple
Scientific Station
Airport
Port
Lighthouse
Mine
Tunnel
Dam, Bridge

Name	Page	Grid	Lat.	Long.
Bougtob	32	Hc	34.02N	0.05 E
Bouguenais	11	Eg	47.11N	1.37W
Bougzoul	13	Oi	35.42N	2.51 E
Bou Hadjar	14	Cn	36.30N	8.06 E
Bouhalla, Jbel-	13	Gi	35.06N	5.07W
Bou Hamed	13	Hi	35.19N	4.45W
Bouillante	51e	Ab	16.08N	61.46W
Bouillon	11	Le	49.48N	5.04 E
Bouira	32	Hb	36.23N	3.54 E
Bouira [3]	32	Hb	36.15N	4.10 E
Bou Ismail	13	Oh	36.38N	2.41 E
Bou Izakarn	32	Fd	29.10N	9.44W
Bou Kadir	13	Nh	36.04N	1.07 E
Boukombé	34	Fc	10.11N	1.06 E
Boû Lanouâr	32	De	21.16N	16.30W
Boulay-Moselle	12	Ie	49.11N	6.30 E
Boulder [Co.-U.S.]	39	Ie	40.01N	105.17W
Boulder [Mt.-U.S.]	46	Ic	46.14N	112.07W
Boulder City	46	Hi	35.59N	114.50W
Boulemane	32	Gc	33.22N	4.45W
Boulemane [3]	32	Gc	33.02N	4.04W
Boulevard Atlántico	55	Dn	38.19S	57.59W
Boulia	59	Hd	22.54S	139.54 E
Bouligny	11	Le	49.17N	5.45 E
Boulogne	11	Eg	47.05N	1.40W
Boulogne-Billancourt	11	If	48.50N	2.15 E
Boulogne-sur-Mer	11	Hd	50.43N	1.37 E
Boulonnais	11	Hd	50.42N	1.40 E
Bouloupari	63b	Ce	21.52S	166.03 E
Boulsa	34	Ec	12.39N	0.34W
Boultoum	34	Hc	14.40N	10.18 E
Bou Maad, Djebel-	13	Oh	36.26N	2.08 E
Boumba	34	Ie	2.02N	15.12 E
Boumdeid	32	Ef	17.26N	11.21W
Boum Kabir	35	Bc	10.11N	19.24 E
Boumort	13	Nb	42.14N	1.08 E
Bouna	31	Gh	9.16N	3.00W
Bouna [3]	34	Ed	9.15N	3.20W
Boû Nâga	32	Ef	19.00N	13.13W
Bou Nasser, Adrar-	32	Gc	33.35N	3.53W
Boundary Peak	46	Fh	37.51N	118.21W
Boundiali [3]	34	Dd	9.23N	6.32W
Boundiali	34	Dd	9.31N	6.29W
Boundji	36	Cc	1.03S	15.22 E
Boungou	35	Cd	6.45N	22.06 E
Bountiful	43	Ec	40.53N	111.53W
Bounty Bay	64q	Ab	25.03S	130.05W
Bounty Islands	57	Ii	47.45S	179.05 E
Bounty Trough (EN)	3	Jn	46.00S	178.00 E
Bourail	61	Cd	21.34S	165.30 E
Bourbon-Lancy	11	Jh	46.37N	3.47 E
Bourbonnais	11	Ih	46.30N	3.00 E
Bourbonne-les-Bains	11	Lg	47.57N	5.45 E
Bourbourg	12	Ed	50.57N	2.12 E
Bourbre	11	Li	45.47N	5.11 E
Bourem	34	Eb	16.58N	0.21W
Bouressa	34	Fa	20.01N	2.18 E
Bourg-Achard	12	Ce	49.21N	0.49 E
Bourganeuf	11	Hi	45.57N	1.45 E
Bourgar'oûn, Cap-	32	Ib	37.06N	6.28 E
Bourg-de-Péage	11	Li	45.02N	5.03 E
Bourg-en-Bresse	11	Lh	46.12N	5.13 E
Bourges	6	Gf	47.05N	2.24 E
Bourget, Lac du-	11	Li	45.44N	5.52 E
Bourgneuf, Baie de-	11	Dg	47.05N	2.13W
Bourgogne	12	Ge	49.21N	4.04 E
Bourgogne=Burgundy (EN)	5	Gf	47.00N	4.30 E
Bourgogne=Burgundy (EN)	11	Kg	47.00N	4.30 E
Bourgogne, Canal de-	11	Jg	47.58N	3.30 E
Bourgogne, Porte de-	11	Mg	47.38N	6.52 E
Bourgoin-Jallieu	11	Li	45.35N	5.17 E
Bourgtheroulde-Infreville	12	Ce	49.18N	0.53 E
Bourguébus	12	Be	49.07N	0.18W
Boû Rjeimat	32	Df	19.04N	15.08W
Bourke	58	Fh	30.05S	145.56 E
Bourne	12	Bb	52.46N	0.23W
Bournemouth	9	Lk	50.43N	1.54W
Bourtanger Moor	12	Jb	52.50N	7.06 E
Bourth	12	Cf	48.46N	0.49 E
Bou Saâda	32	Hb	35.12N	4.11 E
Bou Sellam	13	Qh	36.26N	4.34 E
Boussac	11	Ih	46.21N	2.13 E
Boussé	34	Ec	12.39N	1.53W
Boussens	11	Gk	43.11N	0.58 E
Bousso	35	Bc	10.29N	16.43 E
Bouthaleb, Djebel-	13	Ri	35.48N	5.12 E
Boutilimit	32	Ef	17.33N	14.42W
Bou-Tlélis	13	Li	35.34N	0.54W
Boutonne	11	Fi	45.55N	0.49W
Bouvet	66	Cd	54.26S	3.24 E
Bouxwiller	12	Jf	48.49N	7.29 E
Bouza	34	Gc	14.25N	6.02 E
Bouzanne	11	Hh	46.38N	1.28 E
Bouzghaia	13	Nh	36.20N	1.15 E
Bouzonville	12	Ie	49.18N	6.32 E
Bovalino	14	Kl	38.09N	16.11 E
Bovec	14	Hd	46.20N	13.33 E
Bovenkarspel	12	Hb	52.42N	5.17 E
Boves	12	Ee	49.51N	2.23 E
Bovino	14	Ji	41.15N	15.20 E
Bovril	55	Cj	31.21S	59.26W
Bowa → Muli	27	Hf	27.55N	101.13 E
Bowen [Arg.]	56	Ge	35.02S	67.31W
Bowen [Austl.]	58	Fg	20.01S	148.15 E
Bowers Bank (EN)	40a	Bb	54.00N	180.00
Bowers Ridge (EN)	40a	Bb	54.30N	180.00
Bowie	45	Hj	33.34N	97.51W
Bowkān	24	Ld	36.31N	46.12 E
Bowland, Forest of-	9	Kh	54.00N	2.35W
Bowling Green [Ky.-U.S.]	43	Jd	37.00N	86.27W
Bowling Green [Oh.-U.S.]	44	Fe	41.22N	83.40W
Bowman	43	Gb	46.11N	103.24W
Bowman Bay	42	Kc	65.33N	73.40W
Bowman Island	66	He	65.17S	103.08 E
Bowman, Mount-	46	Ea	51.10N	121.55W
Bowo/Bomi	27	Ge	30.02N	95.39 E
Bowokan, Kepulauan-	26	Hg	2.05S	123.35 E
Bowral	59	Kf	34.28S	150.25 E
Bow River	42	Gg	49.56N	111.42W
Box Elder Creek	46	Kc	46.57N	108.04W
Boxelder Creek	46	Nd	45.59N	103.57W
Boxholm	7	Dg	58.12N	15.03 E
Boxian	27	Ke	33.46N	115.44 E
Boxing	27	Kd	37.07N	118.04 E
Boxmeer	12	Hc	51.39N	5.57 E
Boxtel	11	Lc	51.35N	5.20 E
Boyabat	24	Fb	41.28N	34.47 E
Boyabo	36	Cb	3.43N	18.46 E
Boyacá [2]	54	Db	5.30N	72.50W
Boyang	27	Kf	29.00N	116.41 E
Boyer, Cap-	63b	De	21.37S	168.07 E
Boyer Ahmadī-e Kohkīlūyeh [3]	23	Hc	31.00N	50.30 E
Boyle/Mainistir na Búille	9	Eh	53.58N	8.18W
Boyne/An Bhóinn	9	Gh	53.43N	6.15W
Boyne City	44	Ec	45.13N	85.01W
Boynes, Iles de-	30	Nm	49.58S	69.59 E
Boynton Beach	44	Gl	26.32N	80.03W
Boysen Reservoir	46	Ke	43.19N	108.11W
Boz, Kūh-e-	24	Pi	27.46N	55.54 E
Bozburun	15	Li	40.32N	28.46 E
Bozburun	15	Lm	36.41N	28.04 E
Bozburun Dağı	24	Dd	37.18N	31.03 E
Bozcaada	24	Bc	39.50N	26.04 E
Bozcaada	24	Bc	39.49N	26.03 E
Bozdağ	15	Lk	38.20N	28.06 E
Boz Dağı [Tur.]	24	Cd	37.18N	29.12 E
Boz Dağı [Tur.]	24	Cc	38.19N	28.08 E
Boz Dağları	15	Kj	38.20N	27.45 E
Bozdoğan	15	Ll	37.40N	28.19 E
Bozeman	39	He	45.41N	111.02W
Bozen / Bolzano	6	Hf	46.31N	11.22 E
Bozene	36	Cb	2.56N	19.12 E
Bozhen	28	De	38.04N	116.34 E
Bozkol, Zaliv-	18	Cb	45.20N	61.45 E
Bozkurt	24	Fb	41.57N	34.01 E
Bozok Platosu	24	Fc	39.05N	35.05 E
Bozouls	11	Ij	44.28N	2.43 E
Bozoum	31	Ih	6.19N	16.23 E
Bozova	24	Hd	37.22N	38.31 E
Bozovici	15	Ee	44.56N	22.00 E
Bozqūsh, Kūh-e-	24	Ld	37.45N	47.40 E
Bra	14	Bf	44.42N	7.51 E
Braås	8	Fg	57.04N	15.03 E
Braathen, Cape-	66	Pf	71.48S	96.05W
Brabant	11	Lc	51.10N	5.05 E
Brabant [3]	12	Gd	50.45N	4.30 E
Brabant-les-Villers	12	Gf	48.51N	4.59 E
Brâbich	34	Eb	17.30N	3.00W
Brač	14	Kg	43.19N	16.40 E
Bracadale, Loch-	9	Gd	57.20N	6.35W
Bracciano	14	Gh	42.06N	12.40 E
Bracciano, Lago di-	14	Gh	42.05N	12.15 E
Bräcke	7	De	62.43N	15.27 E
Brackettville	45	Fl	29.19N	100.24W
Bracki Kanal	14	Kg	43.24N	16.40 E
Brackley	12	Ab	52.02N	1.09W
Bracknell	9	Mj	51.26N	0.46W
Brackwede, Bielefeld-	12	Kc	51.59N	8.31 E
Brad	15	Fc	46.08N	22.47 E
Bradano	14	Kj	40.23N	16.51 E
Bradenton	43	Kf	27.29N	82.34W
Bradford [Eng.-U.K.]	9	Lh	53.48N	1.45W
Bradford [Pa.-U.S.]	44	He	41.57N	78.39W
Bradley Reef	60	Gi	6.52S	160.48 E
Brady	43	He	31.08N	99.20W
Brady Mountains	45	Gk	31.20N	99.40W
Brædstrup	8	Ci	55.58N	9.37 E
Braemar	9	Jd	57.01N	3.24W
Braga [2]	13	Dc	41.35N	8.25W
Braga	6	Fg	41.33N	8.26W
Bragadiru	15	If	43.46N	25.31 E
Bragado	56	He	35.08S	60.30W
Bragança [2]	13	Fc	41.30N	6.45W
Bragança [Braz.]	53	Lf	1.03S	46.46W
Bragança [Port.]	13	Fc	41.49N	6.45W
Bragança Paulista	55	If	22.57S	46.34W
Brahestad/Raahe	7	Fd	64.41N	24.29 E
Brāhmanbāria	25	Id	23.59N	91.07 E
Brahmapur	22	Kh	19.19N	84.47 E
Brahmaputra	21	Lg	24.02N	90.59 E
Brăila [2]	15	Kd	45.13N	27.48 E
Brăila	6	If	45.16N	27.59 E
Brăilei, Balta-	15	Ke	45.00N	28.00 E
Braine	12	Fe	49.20N	3.32 E
Braine-l'Alleud/Eigenbrakel	12	Gd	50.41N	4.22 E
Brainerd	43	Ib	46.21N	94.12W
Braintree	12	Cc	51.53N	0.34 E
Braithwaite Point	59	Gb	11.58S	134.00 E
Brake (Unterweser)	10	Ec	53.20N	8.29 E
Brakel [Bel.]	12	Fd	50.47N	3.45 E
Brakel [Ger.]	12	Lc	51.43N	9.11 E
Brakna [3]	32	Ef	17.30N	13.30W
Brålanda	8	Ef	58.34N	12.22 E
Bralorne	46	Da	50.47N	122.49W
Bramming	8	Ci	55.28N	8.42 E
Brämön	8	Gb	62.10N	17.40 E
Brampton	44	Hd	43.41N	79.46W
Bramsche	10	Dd	52.24N	7.59 E
Bran, Pasul-	15	Id	45.26N	25.17 E
Branco	32	Cf	16.39N	24.41W
Branco, Cabo-	52	Mf	7.09S	34.47W
Branco, Rio- [Braz.]	52	Jf	1.24S	61.51W
Branco, Rio- [Braz.]	55	De	21.00S	57.48W
Branco ou Cabixi, Rio-	55	Ba	13.55S	60.10W
Brandberg	30	Ik	21.08S	14.35 E
Brandbu	7	Cf	60.26N	10.28 E
Brande	7	Bi	55.57N	9.07 E
Brandenburg	10	Id	52.25N	12.33 E
Brandenburg	10	Jd	52.10N	13.30 E
Brändö	8	Id	60.25N	21.05 E
Brandon [Eng.-U.K.]	12	Cb	52.27N	0.37 E
Brandon [Fl.-U.S.]	44	Fl	27.56N	82.17W
Brandon [Man.-Can.]	39	Je	49.50N	99.57W
Brandon [Vt.-U.S.]	44	Kd	43.47N	73.05W
Brandon Head/Na Machairí	9	Ci	52.16N	10.15W
Brandon Mount/Cnoc Bréanainn	9	Ci	52.14N	10.15W
Brandval	8	Ed	60.19N	12.02 E
Brandvlei	37	Cf	30.25S	20.30 E
Brandýs nad Labem-Stará Boleslav	10	Kf	50.11N	14.40 E
Brăneşti	15	Je	44.27N	26.20 E
Braniewo	10	Pb	54.24N	19.50 E
Bransby Point	51c	Bc	16.43N	62.14W
Bransfield Strait	66	Re	63.00S	59.00W
Brańsk	10	Sd	52.45N	22.51 E
Branson	45	Jh	36.39N	93.13W
Brantevik	8	Fi	55.31N	14.21 E
Brantford	42	Jh	43.08N	80.16W
Brantôme	11	Gi	45.22N	0.39 E
Bras d'Or Lake	42	Lg	45.50N	60.50W
Brasil=Brazil (EN) [1]	53	Kf	9.00S	53.00W
Brasil, Planalto do- = Brazilian Highlands (EN)	52	Lg	17.00S	45.00W
Brasiléia	54	Ef	11.00S	68.44W
Brasília	53	Lg	15.47S	47.55W
Brasília de Minas	55	Jc	16.12S	44.26W
Brasla	8	Kg	57.08N	24.50 E
Braslav	7	Gi	55.37N	27.05 E
Braşov [2]	15	Id	45.40N	25.10 E
Braşov	6	If	45.38N	25.35 E
Brass	34	Ge	4.19N	6.14 E
Brassac	11	Ik	43.38N	2.30 E
Brasschaat	12	Gc	51.17N	4.27 E
Brasstown Bald	44	Fh	34.52N	83.48W
Brastavăţu	15	Hf	43.55N	24.24 E
Brataj	15	Ci	40.16N	19.40 E
Bråte	8	De	59.43N	11.27 E
Bratea	15	Fc	46.56N	22.37 E
Bratislava	6	Hf	48.09N	17.07 E
Bratsk	22	Md	56.05N	101.48 E
Bratskoje Vodohranilišče = Bratsk Reservoir (EN)	20	Fe	56.30N	102.00 E
Bratsk Reservoir (EN) = Bratskoje Vodohranilišče	20	Fe	56.30N	102.00 E
Brattleboro	43	Mc	42.51N	72.36W
Brattvåg	8	Bb	62.36N	6.27 E
Braubach	12	Jd	50.17N	7.40 E
Braunau am Inn	14	Hb	48.16N	13.02 E
Braunschweig	10	Gd	52.16N	10.32 E
Brava	32	Cf	14.52N	24.43W
Brava, Costa-	13	Pc	41.45N	3.04 E
Bråviken	8	Gf	58.40N	16.30 E
Bravo del Norte, Rio- = Grande, Rio- (EN)	38	Jg	25.57N	97.09W
Brawley	43	De	32.59N	115.34W
Bray	42	Jc	69.20N	77.00W
Bray	37	Ce	25.26S	23.38 E
Bray/Brè	9	Gh	53.12N	6.06W
Bray, Pays de-	11	He	49.46N	1.26 E
Bray-Dunes	12	Ec	51.05N	2.31 E
Braye	11	Gg	47.45N	0.42 E
Bray Head	9	Cj	51.53N	10.25W
Bray-sur-Somme	12	Ee	49.56N	2.43 E
Brazi	15	Je	44.52N	26.01 E
Brazil	44	Df	39.32N	87.08W
Brazil (EN)=Brasil [1]	53	Kf	9.00S	53.00W
Brazil Basin (EN)	3	Dk	15.00S	25.00W
Brazilian Highlands (EN) = Brasil, Planalto do-	52	Lg	17.00S	45.00W
Brazos	38	Jg	28.53N	95.23W
Brazos Santiago Pass	45	Hm	26.05N	97.16W
Brazzaville	31	Ii	4.16S	15.17 E
Brčko	14	Mf	44.52N	18.49 E
Brda	10	Oc	53.07N	18.08 E
Brdy	10	Jg	49.35N	13.50 E
Bré/Bray	9	Gh	53.12N	6.06W
Brea, Punta-	51a	Bc	17.54N	66.55W
Breaden, Lake-	59	Fe	25.45S	125.40 E
Breaksea Sound	62	Bf	45.35S	166.40 E
Breaza [Rom.]	15	Id	45.11N	25.40 E
Breaza [Rom.]	15	Ib	47.37N	25.20 E
Breaza, Vîrful-	15	Hb	47.22N	24.02 E
Brebes	26	Eh	6.53S	109.03 E
Brêche	12	Ee	49.16N	2.30 E
Brechin	9	Ke	56.44N	2.40W
Brecht	12	Gc	51.21N	4.38 E
Brechte	12	Jb	52.15N	7.10 E
Breckenridge [Mn.-U.S.]	45	Hc	46.16N	96.35W
Breckenridge [Tx.-U.S.]	45	Gj	32.45N	98.54W
Breckland	9	Ni	52.30N	0.35 E
Břeclav	10	Mh	48.46N	16.54 E
Brecon	9	Jj	51.57N	3.24W
Brecon Beacons	9	Jj	51.53N	3.31W
Breda	11	Kc	51.35N	4.46 E
Bredaryd	8	Eg	57.10N	13.44 E
Bredasdorp	31	Jl	34.32S	20.02 E
Brede	12	Cd	50.55N	0.43 E
Bredene	12	Ec	51.14N	2.58 E
Bredstedt	10	Eb	54.37N	8.59 E
Bredy	19	Ge	52.26N	60.21 E
Bree	12	Hc	51.08N	5.36 E
Breg	10	Ei	47.57N	8.31 E
Bregalnica	15	Eh	41.36N	21.56 E
Bregenz	14	Dc	47.30N	9.46 E
Bréhat, Ile de-	11	Df	48.51N	3.00W
Breiðafjörður	5	Db	65.15N	23.15W
Breimsvatnet	8	Bc	61.40N	6.25 E
Breisach am Rhein	10	Dh	48.02N	7.35 E
Breisund	8	Ab	62.30N	6.00 E
Breit Bridge	37	Dd	22.12S	29.59 E
Breivikbotn	7	Fa	70.37N	22.29 E
Brejão	55	Ia	12.59S	46.28W
Brekken	7	Ce	62.39N	11.53 E
Brekstad	7	Be	63.41N	9.41 E
Bremangerlandet	7	Af	61.50N	5.00 E
Brembana, Val-	14	De	45.55N	9.40 E
Brembo	14	De	45.35N	9.32 E
Bremen [2]	10	Ec	53.05N	8.50 E
Bremen [Ger.]	6	Ge	53.05N	8.48 E
Bremen [In.-U.S.]	44	De	41.27N	86.09W
Bremerhaven	6	Ge	53.33N	8.35 E
Bremerton	43	Cb	47.34N	122.38W
Bremervörde	10	Fc	53.29N	9.08 E
Brendel	46	Kg	38.57N	109.50W
Brenham	45	Hk	30.10N	96.24W
Brenne	11	Hh	46.44N	1.14 E
Brennero, Passo del- = Brenner Pass (EN)	5	Hf	47.00N	11.30 E
Brennerpaß=Brenner Pass (EN)	5	Hf	47.00N	11.30 E
Brenner Pass (EN) = Brennero, Passo del-	5	Hf	47.00N	11.30 E
Brenner Pass (EN) = Brennerpaß	5	Hf	47.00N	11.30 E
Brenta	14	Ge	45.11N	12.18 E
Brentwood	9	Nj	51.38N	0.18 E
Brescia	6	Hf	45.33N	10.15 E
Breskens	12	Fc	51.24N	3.33 E
Breslau (EN)=Wrocław	6	He	51.06N	17.00 E
Bresle	11	Hd	50.04N	1.22 E
Bressanone / Brixen	14	Fd	46.43N	11.39 E
Bressay	9	La	60.08N	1.05W
Bresse	11	Lh	46.30N	5.15 E
Bressuire	11	Fh	46.51N	0.29W
Brest [Bye.-U.S.S.R.]	6	Ie	52.06N	23.42 E
Brest [Fr.]	6	Ff	48.24N	4.29W
Brestova	14	Ie	45.08N	14.14 E
Brestskaja Oblast [3]	19	Ce	52.20N	25.30 E
Bretagne=Brittany (EN)	11	Df	48.00N	3.00W
Bretagne=Brittany (EN)	5	Ff	48.00N	3.00W
Bretçu	15	Jc	46.03N	26.18 E
Breteuil [Fr.]	12	Cf	48.50N	0.55 E
Breteuil [Fr.]	11	Ie	49.38N	2.18 E
Breton, Marais-	11	Eh	46.56N	2.00W
Breton, Pertuis-	11	Eh	46.16N	1.22W
Breton Sound	45	Ll	29.30N	89.30W
Brett	12	Cc	51.58N	0.57 E
Brett, Cape-	62	Fa	35.10S	174.20 E
Bretten	12	Ke	49.03N	8.42 E
Bretteville-sur-Laize	12	Be	49.03N	0.20W
Breueh, Pulau-	26	Be	5.41N	95.05 E
Breuil Cervinia	14	Be	45.56N	7.38 E
Breukelen	12	Db	52.10N	5.01 E
Breuna	12	Lc	51.25N	9.11 E
Breves	54	Hd	1.40S	50.29W
Brevik	7	Bg	59.04N	9.42 E
Brevoort	42	Ld	63.30N	64.20W
Brewarrina	59	Je	29.57S	146.52 E
Brewerville	34	Cd	6.25N	10.47W
Brewster	46	Fb	48.06N	119.47W
Brewster, Kap-	67	Md	70.10N	21.30W
Brewton	43	Je	31.07N	87.04W
Brežice	14	Je	45.54N	15.35 E
Brézina	32	Hc	33.05N	1.16 E
Březnice	10	Jg	49.33N	13.57 E
Breznik	15	Fg	42.44N	22.54 E
Brezno	10	Ph	48.49N	19.39 E
Brezoi	15	Hd	45.21N	24.15 E
Brezolles	12	Df	48.41N	1.04 E
Brezovo	15	Ig	42.21N	25.05 E
Bria	31	Jh	6.32N	21.59 E
Briance	11	Hi	45.47N	1.12 E
Briançon	11	Mj	44.54N	6.39 E
Brianza	14	De	45.45N	9.15 E
Briare, Canal de-	11	If	48.02N	2.43 E
Bribie Island	59	Ke	27.00S	153.05 E
Bričany	15	Ka	48.18N	27.04 E
Bride	9	Fi	52.05N	7.50W
Bridgend	9	Jj	51.31N	3.35W
Bridgeport [Ca.-U.S.]	46	Fg	38.10N	119.13W
Bridgeport [Ct.-U.S.]	43	Mc	41.11N	73.11W
Bridgeport [Nb.-U.S.]	45	Ef	41.40N	103.06W
Bridge River	46	Ea	50.45N	121.55W
Bridger Peak	46	Lf	41.12N	107.02W
Bridges Point	64g	Bb	1.58N	157.28W
Bridgeton	44	Jf	39.26N	75.14W
Bridgetown [Austl.]	59	Df	33.57S	116.08 E
Bridgetown [Bar.]	39	Nh	13.06N	59.37W
Bridgewater	42	Lh	44.23N	64.31W
Bridgwater	9	Kj	51.08N	3.00W
Bridgwater Bay	9	Jj	51.16N	3.12W
Bridlington	9	Mg	54.05N	0.12W
Bridlington Bay	9	Mg	54.04N	0.08W
Bridport	9	Kk	50.44N	2.46W
Brie	11	Jf	48.40N	3.30 E
Brielle	12	Gc	51.54N	4.10 E
Brienzer-See	14	Bd	46.45N	7.55 E
Briey	11	Le	49.15N	5.56 E
Brig	14	Bd	46.20N	8.00 E
Brigach	10	Ei	47.58N	8.30 E
Brigham City	43	Ec	41.31N	112.01W
Brighstone	12	Ad	50.38N	1.23W
Bright	59	Jg	36.44S	146.58 E
Brightlingsea	12	Dc	51.48N	1.02 E
Brighton [Co.-U.S.]	45	Dg	39.59N	104.49W
Brighton [Eng.-U.K.]	6	Fe	50.50N	0.10W
Brignoles	11	Mk	43.24N	6.04 E
Brihuega	13	Jd	40.45N	2.52W
Brijuni	14	Hf	44.55N	13.46 E
Brikama	34	Bc	13.16N	16.39W
Brilhante, Rio-	54	Hh	21.58S	54.18W
Brilon	12	Kc	51.24N	8.35 E
Brilon-Alme	12	Kc	51.27N	8.37 E
Brimstone Hill	51c	Ab	17.21N	62.49W
Brindisi	6	Hg	40.38N	17.56 E
Brinkley	45	Ki	34.53N	91.12W
Brinkmann	55	Aj	30.52S	62.02W
Brionne	12	Ce	49.12N	0.43 E
Brioude	11	Ji	45.18N	3.24 E
Brisbane	58	Gg	27.28S	153.02 E
Brisighella	14	Ff	44.13N	11.46 E
Bristol	66	Ad	59.02S	26.31W
Bristol [Eng.-U.K.]	6	Fe	51.27N	2.35W
Bristol [Tn.-U.S.]	44	Fg	36.36N	82.11W
Bristol Bay	38	Dd	58.00N	159.00W
Bristol Channel	5	Fe	51.20N	4.00W
Bristol Lake	46	Hi	34.28N	115.41W
Bristow	45	Hi	35.50N	96.23W
Britannia Range	66	Jf	80.00S	158.00 E
British Columbia [3]	42	Fe	55.00N	125.00W
British Honduras → Belize	49	Ce	17.35N	88.35W
British Indian Ocean Territory [5]	22	Jj	7.00S	72.00 E
British Isles	5	Fd	54.00N	4.00W
British Mountains	40	Kc	69.20N	140.20W
British Solomon Islands → Solomon Islands [1]	58	Ge	8.00S	159.00 E
British Virgin Islands [5]	39	Mh	18.20N	64.50W
Brits	37	De	25.40S	27.46 E
Britstown	37	Cf	30.37S	23.30 E
Britt	45	Je	43.06N	93.48W
Brittany (EN)=Bretagne	5	Ff	48.00N	3.00W
Brittany (EN)=Bretagne	11	Df	48.00N	3.00W
Britton	45	Hd	45.48N	97.45W
Brive-la-Gaillarde	11	Hi	45.09N	1.32 E
Briviesca	13	Ib	42.33N	3.19W
Brixen / Bressanone	14	Fd	46.43N	11.39 E
Brixham	9	Jk	50.24N	3.30W
Brjansk	6	Je	53.15N	34.22 E
Brjanskaja Oblast [3]	19	De	52.50N	33.20 E
Brjuhoveckaja	16	Kg	45.46N	39.01 E
Brjukoviči	10	Jg	49.52N	24.00 E
Brno	6	Hf	49.12N	16.37 E
Broa, Ensenada de la-	49	Fb	22.35N	82.00W
Broad Bay	9	Gc	58.15N	6.15W
Broadford	9	Hd	57.14N	5.54W
Broad Sound	59	Jd	22.10S	149.45 E
Broadstairs	12	Dc	51.22N	1.27 E
Broadus	43	Fb	45.27N	105.25W
Brocēni/Broceny	8	Jh	56.41N	22.30 E
Broceny/Brocēni	8	Jh	56.41N	22.30 E
Brochet	42	He	57.53N	101.40W
Brochu, Lac-	44	Ja	48.26N	74.15W
Brock	42	Ga	77.55N	114.30W
Brocken	10	Ge	51.48N	10.36 E
Brockman, Mount-	59	Dd	22.28S	117.18 E
Brockton	44	Ld	42.05N	71.01W
Brockville	42	Jh	44.35N	75.41W
Brod	15	Eh	41.31N	21.14 E
Brodarevo	15	Cf	43.14N	19.43 E
Broderick Falls	36	Fb	0.37N	34.46 E
Brodeur Peninsula	38	Kb	73.00N	88.00W
Brodick	9	Hf	55.35N	5.09W
Brodnica	10	Pc	53.16N	19.23 E
Brody	16	Dd	50.04N	25.12 E
Broglie	12	Ce	49.01N	0.32 E
Brok	10	Rd	52.43N	21.52 E
Brok	10	Rd	52.38N	21.55 E
Broken Arrow	45	Ih	36.03N	95.48W
Broken Bow	45	Gf	41.24N	99.38W
Broken Bow Lake	45	Ii	34.10N	94.40W
Broken Hill	58	Fh	31.57S	141.27 E
Broken Ridge (EN)	3	Hm	31.30S	95.00 E
Brokind	8	Ff	58.13N	15.40 E
Brokopondo	54	Hb	5.04N	55.00W
Bromarv	8	Je	59.55N	23.00 E
Bromley, London-	12	Cc	51.25N	0.01 E
Bromölla	7	Dh	56.04N	14.28 E
Brønderslev	8	Cg	57.16N	9.58 E
Brong-Ahafo [3]	34	Ed	7.45N	1.30W
Bronnikovo	17	Ng	58.29N	68.27 E
Brønnøysund	7	Cd	65.28N	12.13 E
Bronte	14	Im	37.47N	14.50 E
Brooke's Point	26	Ge	8.47N	117.50 E
Brookfield	45	Jg	39.47N	93.04W
Brookhaven	45	Kk	31.35N	90.26W
Brookings [Or.-U.S.]	43	Cc	42.03N	124.17W
Brookings [S.D.-U.S.]	43	Hc	44.19N	96.48W
Brooks	42	Gf	50.35N	111.53W
Brooks Banks (EN)	60	Mc	24.05N	166.50W
Brooks Range	38	Dc	68.00N	154.00W
Brookston	45	Jc	46.50N	92.32W
Brooksville	44	Fk	28.33N	82.23W
Brookton	59	Df	32.22S	117.01 E
Brookville [In.-U.S.]	44	Ef	39.25N	85.01W
Brookville [Pa.-U.S.]	44	He	41.10N	79.06W
Broom	9	Hd	57.45N	5.05W
Broom, Loch-	9	Hd	57.55N	5.15W
Broome	58	Df	17.58S	122.14 E
Brora	9	Jc	58.00N	3.50W
Brora	9	Jc	58.01N	3.51W
Brosna/An Bhrosnach	9	Fh	53.13N	7.58W
Broşteni	15	Ib	47.14N	25.42 E
Brou	11	Hf	48.13N	1.11 E
Brough	9	Kg	54.32N	2.19W
Broughton Island	39	Mc	67.35N	63.50W
Broussard	45	Kk	30.09N	91.58W
Brovary	16	Gd	50.32N	30.48 E
Brovst	8	Cg	57.06N	9.32 E
Brown Bank (EN)=Bruine Bank	12	Fb	52.35N	3.20 E
Brownfield	43	Ge	33.11N	102.16W
Browning	46	Ib	48.34N	113.01W
Browns Bank (EN)	42	Kh	42.40N	66.05W
Brownsville [Tn.-U.S.]	44	Ch	35.36N	89.15W
Brownsville [Tx.-U.S.]	39	Jg	25.54N	97.30W
Brownwood	43	He	31.43N	98.59W
Browse Island	59	Eb	14.05S	123.35 E
Broye	14	Bd	46.55N	7.02 E
Bruay-en-Artois	11	Id	50.29N	2.33 E
Bruay-sur-l'Escaut	12	Fd	50.23N	3.32 E
Bruce	45	Lj	33.59N	89.21W
Bruce, Mount-	57	Cg	22.36S	118.08 E
Bruce Crossing	44	Cb	46.32N	89.10W
Bruce Peninsula	42	Jh	44.59N	81.20W
Bruce Rock	59	Df	31.53S	118.09 E
Bruche	11	Nf	48.34N	7.43 E

Index Symbols

[1] Independent Nation
[2] State, Region
[3] District, County
[4] Municipality
[5] Colony, Dependency
Continent
Physical Region

Historical or Cultural Region
Mount, Mountain
Volcano
Hill
Mountains, Mountain Range
Hills, Escarpment
Plateau, Upland

Pass, Gap
Plain, Lowland
Delta
Salt Flat
Valley, Canyon
Crater, Cave
Karst Features

Depression
Polder
Desert, Dunes
Forest, Woods
Heath, Steppe
Oasis
Cape, Point

Coast, Beach
Cliff
Peninsula
Isthmus
Sandbank
Island
Atoll

Rock, Reef
Islands, Archipelago
Rocks, Reefs
Coral Reef
Well, Spring
Geyser
River, Stream

Waterfall Rapids
River Mouth, Estuary
Lake
Salt Lake
Intermittent Lake
Reservoir
Swamp, Pond

Canal
Glacier
Ice Shelf, Pack Ice
Ocean
Sea
Gulf, Bay
Strait, Fjord

Lagoon
Bank
Seamount
Tablemount
Ridge
Shelf
Basin

Escarpment, Sea Scarp
Fracture
Trench, Abyss
National Park, Reserve
Point of Interest
Recreation Site
Cave, Cavern

Historic Site
Ruins
Wall, Walls
Church, Abbey
Temple
Scientific Station
Airport

Port
Lighthouse
Mine
Tunnel
Dam, Bridge

Bruchhausen Vilsen 12 Lb 52.50N 9.01 E
Bruchmühlbach Miesau 12 Je 49.23N 7.28 E
Bruchsal 10 Eg 49.08N 8.36 E
Bruck an der Leitha 14 Kb 48.01N 16.46 E
Bruck an der Mur 14 Jc 47.25N 15.17 E
Brue 9 Kj 51.13N 3.00W
Bruges/Brugge 11 Jc 51.13N 3.14 E
Brugg 14 Cc 47.29N 8.12 E
Brugge/Bruges 11 Jc 51.13N 3.14 E
Brugge-Assebroek 12 Fc 51.12N 3.16 E
Brüggen 12 Ic 51.15N 6.11 E
Brugge-Sint-Andries 12 Fc 51.12N 3.10 E
Brühl [Ger.] 12 Ke 49.24N 8.32 E
Brühl [Ger.] 12 Id 50.50N 6.54 E
Bruine Bank = Brown Bank (EN) 12 Fb 52.35N 3.20 E
Bruin Point 43 Ed 39.39N 110.22W
Brule River 44 Cc 45.57N 88.12W
Brumado 54 Jf 14.13S 41.40W
Brummen 12 Ib 52.06N 6.10 E
Brummo 8 Ef 58.50N 13.40 E
Brumunddal 7 Cf 60.53N 10.56 E
Bruna 14 Eh 42.45N 10.53 E
Brune 12 Fe 49.45N 3.47 E
Bruneau 46 He 42.53N 115.48W
Bruneau River 46 He 42.57N 115.58W
Bruneck / Brunico 14 Fd 46.48N 11.56 E
Brunehamel 12 Ge 49.46N 4.11 E
Brunei [5] 22 Ni 4.30N 114.40 E
Brunei, Teluk- 21 Ni 5.05N 115.18 E
Brunette Downs 59 Hc 18.38S 135.57 E
Brunflo 8 Fa 63.05N 14.49 E
Brunico / Bruneck 14 Fd 46.48N 11.56 E
Brunna 8 Ge 59.52N 17.25 E
Brunner 62 De 42.26S 171.19 E
Brunner, Lake- 62 De 42.35S 171.25 E
Brunnsberg 8 Ec 61.17N 13.55 E
Brunsbüttel 10 Fc 53.54N 9.07 E
Brunssum 12 Hd 50.57N 5.57 E
Brunswick [Ga.-U.S.] 43 Ke 31.10N 81.29W
Brunswick [Me.-U.S.] 43 Nc 43.55N 69.58W
Brunswick, Peninsula de- 52 Ik 53.30S 71.25W
Brunswick Lake 44 Fa 49.00N 83.23W
Bruntál 10 Ng 49.59N 17.28 E
Bruny Island 59 Jh 43.30S 147.05 E
Brus 15 Ef 43.23N 21.02 E
Brus, Laguna de- 49 Ef 15.50N 84.35W
Brush 43 Gc 40.15N 103.37W
Brus Laguna 49 Ef 15.47N 84.35W
Brusque 56 Kc 27.06S 48.56W
Brussel/Bruxelles = Brussels (EN) 6 Ge 50.50N 4.20 E
Brussels (EN) = Brussel/Bruxelles 6 Ge 50.50N 4.20 E
Brussels (EN) = Bruxelles/Brussel 6 Ge 50.50N 4.20 E
Brusset, 'Erg- 34 Hb 18.55N 10.30 E
Brusturi 15 Fb 47.09N 22.15 E
Brusy 10 Nc 53.53N 17.45 E
Bruxelles/Brussel = Brussels (EN) 6 Ge 50.50N 4.20 E
Bruzual 50 Bh 8.03N 69.19W
Bryan [Oh.-U.S.] 44 Ee 41.30N 84.34W
Bryan [Tx.-U.S.] 43 He 30.40N 96.22W
Bryan Coast 66 Pf 73.35S 84.00W
Bryne 7 Ag 58.44N 5.39 E
Brza Palanka 15 Fe 44.28N 22.27 E
Brzava kanal 15 Dd 45.16N 20.49 E
Brzeg 10 Nf 50.52N 17.27 E
Brzeg Dolny 10 Me 51.15N 16.40 E
Brzeziny 10 Pe 51.48N 19.46 E
Brzozów 10 Sg 49.42N 22.02 E
Bsharrī 24 Ge 34.15N 36.01 E
Bū 12 Df 48.48N 1.30 E
Bua 8 Eg 57.14N 12.07 E
Buada Lagoon 64e Ab 0.32S 166.54 E
Buala 58 Ge 8.10S 159.35 E
Bū al Ḩidān, Wādī- 33 Cd 27.25N 19.22 E
Buapinang 26 Hg 4.46S 121.34 E
Buatan 26 Df 0.44N 101.51 E
Bū aţ Ţifl 33 Dd 28.54N 22.30 E
Bua Yai 25 Ke 15.34N 102.24 E
Bu'ayrāt al Ḩasūn 33 Cc 31.24N 15.44 E
Bubanza 36 Ec 3.06S 29.23 E
Bubaque 34 Bc 11.17N 15.50W
Būbīyān 24 Mh 29.45N 48.15 E
Bubu 36 Gd 6.03S 35.19 E
Bubye 37 Ed 22.20S 31.07 E
Buca 15 Kk 38.22N 27.11 E
Bučač 16 De 49.04N 25.23 E
Bucačača 20 Gf 52.59N 116.55 E
Bucak 24 Dd 37.28N 30.36 E
Bucaramanga 53 Ie 7.08N 73.09W
Bucas Grande 26 Ie 9.40N 125.58 E
Buccament Bay 51n Ba 13.12N 61.17W
Buccaneer Archipelago 59 Ec 16.17S 123.20 E
Bucecea 15 Jb 47.46N 26.26 E
Buchanan 31 Fh 5.53N 10.03W
Buchanan, Lake- [Austl.] 59 Jd 21.30S 145.50 E
Buchanan, Lake- [Tx.-U.S.] 45 Gk 30.48N 98.25W
Buchanan Bay 42 Ka 78.55N 75.00W
Buchan Gulf 42 Kb 71.48N 74.06W
Buchardo 56 Hd 34.43S 63.31W
Bucharest (EN) = Bucureşti 6 Ig 44.26N 26.06 E
Buchen 10 Fg 49.31N 9.20 E
Buchholz in der Nordheide 10 Fc 53.20N 9.52 E
Buchon, Point- 46 Ei 35.15N 120.54W
Buchs 14 Dc 47.10N 9.30 E
Buchy 12 De 49.35N 1.22 E
Bückeburg 12 Lb 52.16N 9.03 E
Buckeye 46 Ij 33.22N 112.35W
Buckhaven 9 Je 56.11N 3.03W
Buckie 9 Kd 57.40N 2.58W
Buckingham [Eng.-U.K.] 12 Bb 52.00N 0.59W
Buckingham [Que.-Can.] 44 Jc 45.35N 75.25W
Buckingham Bay 59 Hb 12.10S 135.46 E
Buckinghamshire [3] 9 Mj 51.50N 0.55W
Buckland 40 Gc 66.16N 161.20W
Buckle Island 66 Ke 66.47S 163.14 E
Buckley Bay 66 Je 68.16S 148.12 E
Bucks 9 Mj 51.50N 0.55W
Bucksport 44 Mc 44.34N 68.48W
Buco Zau 36 Bc 4.50S 12.33 E
Bu Craa 32 Ed 26.17N 12.46W
Bucureşti [2] 15 Je 44.30N 26.05 E
Bucureşti = Bucharest (EN) 6 Ig 44.26N 26.06 E
Bucy-lès-Pierrepont 12 Fe 49.39N 3.54 E
Bucyrus 44 Fe 40.47N 82.57W
Bud 7 Be 62.55N 6.55 E
Budacu, Vîrful- 15 Ib 47.07N 25.41 E
Buda-Koševelo 16 Gc 52.43N 30.39 E
Budapest [2] 10 Pi 47.30N 19.05 E
Budapest 6 Hf 47.30N 19.05 E
Búdardalur 7a Bb 65.07N 21.46W
Budaun 25 Fc 28.03N 79.07 E
Budbud 35 He 4.13N 46.31 E
Budd Coast 66 He 66.30S 113.00 E
Buddusò 14 Di 40.35N 9.15 E
Bude [Eng.-U.K.] 9 Ik 50.50N 4.33W
Bude [Ms.-U.S.] 45 Kk 31.28N 90.51W
Bude Bay 9 Ik 50.50N 4.37W
Budel 12 Hc 51.16N 5.30 E
Budennovsk 19 Eg 44.45N 44.08 E
Budeşti 15 Je 44.14N 26.27 E
Budia 13 Jd 40.38N 2.45W
Büdingen 10 Ff 50.18N 9.07 E
Búdir 7a Cb 64.56N 14.01W
Budjala 36 Cb 2.39N 19.42 E
Budkowiczanka 10 Nf 50.52N 17.33 E
Budogošč 7 Hg 59.19N 32.29 E
Budrio 14 Ff 44.32N 11.32 E
Budslav 8 Lj 54.49N 27.32 E
Budva 15 Bg 42.17N 18.51 E
Budyšin/Bautzen 10 Ke 51.11N 14.26 E
Budžjak 15 Lc 46.15N 28.45 E
Buea 34 Ge 4.09N 9.14 E
Buech 11 Lj 44.12N 5.57 E
Buenaventura [Col.] 53 Ie 3.53N 77.04W
Buenaventura [Mex.] 47 Cc 29.51N 107.29W
Buenaventura, Bahía de- 54 Cc 3.45N 77.15W
Buenavista 48 Ef 23.39N 109.42W
Buena Vista [Co.-U.S.] 45 Cg 38.50N 106.08W
Buena Vista [Mex.] 48 Mi 16.05N 93.00W
Buena Vista [Mex.] 48 Bb 31.10N 115.40W
Buena Vista [Ven.] 50 Eh 9.02N 63.49W
Buenavista, Bahía de- 49 Hb 22.30N 79.08W
Buendía, Embalse de- 13 Jd 40.25N 2.43W
Buenópolis 55 Jc 17.54S 44.11W
Buenos Aires [2] 56 Ie 36.00S 60.00W
Buenos Aires [Arg.] 53 Ki 34.36S 58.27W
Buenos Aires [C.R.] 49 Fi 10.04N 84.26W
Buenos Aires, Lago- 52 Ij 46.30S 72.00W
Buffalo 42 Fe 60.52N 115.03W
Buffalo [N.Y.-U.S.] 39 Le 42.54N 78.53W
Buffalo [Ok.-U.S.] 45 Gh 36.50N 99.38W
Buffalo [S.D.-U.S.] 43 Gb 45.35N 103.33W
Buffalo [Tx.-U.S.] 45 Hk 31.28N 96.04W
Buffalo [Wy.-U.S.] 43 Fc 44.21N 106.42W
Buffalo Bill Reservoir 46 Kd 44.29N 109.13W
Buffalo Lake 42 Fd 60.12N 115.25W
Buffalo Narrows 42 Ge 55.51N 108.30W
Buffalo Pound Lake 46 Ma 50.38N 105.20W
Buffels 37 Be 29.41S 17.04 E
Bū Fishah 14 En 36.18N 10.28 E
Buford 44 Fh 34.07N 84.00W
Buftea 15 Ie 44.34N 25.57 E
Bug 5 Ie 52.31N 21.05 E
Buga 54 Cc 3.55N 76.18W
Bugarach, Pech de- 11 Il 42.52N 2.23 E
Bugeat 11 Hi 45.36N 1.56 E
Bugene 36 Fc 1.35S 31.08 E
Bugey 11 Li 45.48N 5.30 E
Bugojno 23 Ff 44.03N 17.27 E
Bugøynes 7 Gb 69.58N 29.39 E
Bugrino 17 Db 68.48N 49.09 E
Bugsuk 26 Ge 8.15N 117.18 E
Bugt 27 Lb 48.47N 121.55 E
Bugulma 19 Fe 54.33N 52.48 E
Bugun 18 Hc 43.22N 70.10 E
Bugun 18 Gc 42.56N 68.36 E
Bügür/Luntai 27 Dc 41.46N 84.10 E
Buguruslan 19 Fe 53.39N 52.30 E
Buhara 22 If 39.49N 64.25 E
Buharskaja Oblast [3] 19 Gg 41.20N 64.20 E
Bū Ḩaşā' 24 Ok 23.20N 53.20 E
Buhera 37 Ec 19.18S 31.29 E
Buh He 27 Gd 36.58N 99.48 E
Buhl 46 He 42.36N 114.46W
Bühl 10 Eh 48.42N 8.09 E
Bühödle 35 Hd 8.15N 46.20 E
Buhtarminskoje Vodohranilišče 19 If 49.10N 84.00 E
Bui Dam 34 Ed 8.22N 2.10W
Builth Wells 9 Ji 52.09N 3.24W
Buin [Chile] 56 Fd 33.44S 70.44W
Buin [Pap.N.Gui.] 60 Fi 6.50S 155.44 E
Buinsk 19 Ee 54.59N 48.17 E
Buir Nur 27 Kb 47.48N 117.42 E
Buitrago del Lozoya 13 Id 41.00N 3.38W
Buj 17 Gh 56.15N 54.12 E
Buj 19 Ed 58.29N 41.31 E
Bujalance 13 Hg 37.54N 4.22W
Bujanovac 15 Eg 42.28N 21.47 E
Bujaraloz 13 Lc 41.30N 0.09W
Buje 14 He 45.24N 13.40 E
Bujnaksk 19 Eg 42.49N 47.07 E
Bujukly 20 Jg 49.33N 142.55 E
Bujumbura 31 Ji 3.23S 29.22 E
Bujunda 20 Kd 62.00N 153.30 E
Buk 10 Md 52.22N 16.31 E
Bük 10 Mi 47.23N 16.45 E
Buk 10 Hb 54.10N 11.42 E
Buka Island 57 Ge 5.15S 154.35 E
Bukakata 36 Fc 0.18S 32.02 E
Bukama 31 Ji 9.12S 25.51 E
Buka Passage 63a Ba 5.25S 154.41 E
Bukavu 31 Ji 2.30S 28.52 E
Bukene 36 Fc 4.14S 32.53 E
Bukhā 24 Qi 26.10N 56.09 E
Bukit Besi 26 Df 4.46N 103.12 E
Bukit Mertajam 26 De 5.22N 100.28 E
Bukittinggi 22 Mj 0.19S 100.22 E
Bükk 10 Qh 48.05N 20.30 E
Bukoba 31 Ki 1.20S 31.49 E
Bukovina 15 Ia 48.00N 25.30 E
Bukowiec 10 Ld 52.23N 15.20 E
Bukuru 34 Gd 9.48N 8.52 E
Būl, Kūh-e- 23 Hc 30.48N 52.45 E
Bulajevo 19 He 54.53N 70.26 E
Bulan 26 Hd 12.40N 123.52 E
Bulanaš 17 Kh 57.16N 62.02 E
Bulancak 24 Hb 40.57N 38.14 E
Bulanık 24 Jc 39.05N 42.15 E
Būlāq 33 Fd 25.12N 30.32 E
Bulawayo 31 Jk 20.09S 28.34 E
Buldan 24 Cc 38.03N 28.51 E
Buldir 40a Bb 52.21N 175.54 E
Bulgan [Mong.] 27 Hc 44.05N 103.32 E
Bulgan [Mong.] 27 Hb 48.45N 103.34 E
Bulgan [Mong.] 27 Fb 46.05N 91.34 E
Bulgaria (EN) = Bălgarija [1] 6 Ig 43.00N 25.00 E
Buli 26 If 0.53N 128.18 E
Buli, Teluk- 26 If 0.45N 128.30 E
Buliluyan, Cape- 26 Ge 8.20N 117.11 E
Bulki 35 Fd 6.01N 36.36 E
Bullahār 35 Gc 10.23N 44.27 E
Bullange/Büllingen 12 Id 50.25N 6.16 E
Bullaque 13 Hf 38.59N 4.17W
Bulla Regia 14 Cn 36.33N 8.45 E
Bullas 13 Kf 38.03N 1.40W
Bulle 14 Bd 46.37N 7.04 E
Buller 62 Dd 41.44S 171.35 E
Bullfinch 59 Df 30.59S 119.06 E
Büllingen/Bullange 12 Id 50.25N 6.16 E
Bullion Mountains 46 Hi 34.25N 116.00W
Bulloo River 57 Fg 28.43S 142.30 E
Bull Point [Eng.-U.K.] 9 Ij 51.12N 4.10W
Bull Point [Falk.Is.] 56 Ih 52.19S 59.18W
Bulls 62 Fd 40.10S 175.23 E
Bulls Bay 44 Hi 32.59N 79.33W
Bull Shoals Lake 45 Jh 36.30N 92.50W
Bully Choop Mountain 46 Df 40.35N 122.45W
Bully-les-Mines 12 Ed 50.26N 2.43 E
Bulo Berde 35 He 3.52N 45.40 E
Bulolo 60 Di 7.12S 146.39 E
Bulqiza 15 Dh 41.30N 20.21 E
Bulter 45 Ig 38.16N 94.20W
Bultfontein 37 De 28.20S 26.05 E
Bulukumba 26 Hh 5.33S 120.11 E
Bulungu [Zaire] 36 Cc 4.33S 18.36 E
Bulungu [Zaire] 36 Dd 6.04S 21.54 E
Bumba 31 Jh 2.11N 22.28 E
Bumbah, Khalīj al- 33 Dc 32.25N 23.06 E
Buna 15 Ch 41.52N 19.22 E
Buna 36 Gb 2.47N 39.31 E
Bunbury 58 Ch 33.19S 115.38 E
Buncrana/Bun Cranncha 9 Ff 55.08N 7.27W
Bun Cranncha/Buncrana 9 Ff 55.08N 7.27W
Bunda 36 Fc 2.03S 33.52 E
Bundaberg 58 Gg 24.52S 152.21 E
Bünde 10 Ed 52.12N 8.35 E
Bundesrepublik Deutschland = Germany 6 Ge 51.00N 10.00 E
Bun Dobhráin/Bundoran 9 Eg 54.28N 8.17W
Bundoran/Bun Dobhráin 9 Eg 54.28N 8.17W
Bungay 12 Db 52.27N 1.27 E
Bungku 26 Hg 2.33S 121.58 E
Bungo 36 Cd 7.26S 15.24 E
Bungo Strait (EN) = Bungo-Suidō 28 Lh 32.40N 132.18 E
Bungo-Suidō = Bungo Strait (EN) 28 Lh 32.40N 132.18 E
Bungotakada 29 Be 33.33N 131.27 E
Bungsberg 10 Gb 54.12N 10.43 E
Buni 34 Hc 11.12N 12.02 E
Bunja 31 Kh 1.34N 30.15 E
Bunji 25 Ea 35.40N 74.36 E
Bunker 45 Kh 37.27N 91.13W
Bunker Group 59 Kd 23.50S 152.20 E
Bunkeya 36 Ee 10.24S 26.58 E
Bunkie 45 Jk 30.57N 92.11W
Bunnerfjällen 8 Ea 63.10N 12.34 E
Buñol 13 Le 39.25N 0.47W
Bunschoten 12 Hb 52.14N 5.24 E
Buntingford 12 Bc 51.57N 0.01W
Buntok 26 Fg 1.42S 114.48 E
Bünyan 24 Fc 38.51N 35.52 E
Bunyu, Pulau- 26 Gf 3.30N 117.50 E
Buon Me Thuot 25 Lf 12.40N 108.03 E
Buor-Haja, Guba- 20 Ib 71.00N 131.00 E
Buotama 20 Hd 61.17N 128.55 E
Buqayq 23 Gd 25.56N 49.40 E
Buqda Kōsār 35 Ge 4.31N 44.49 E
Bur 20 Hb 71.40N 123.40 E
Bura 36 Gc 1.06S 39.57 E
Buram 31 Jg 10.49N 25.10 E
Buran 19 If 48.04N 85.15 E
Burang 27 De 30.18N 81.08 E
Burāq 24 Gf 33.10N 36.29 E
Buras 45 Ll 29.21N 89.32W
Buraydah 22 Gg 26.20N 43.59 E
Burbach 12 Kd 50.43N 8.03 E
Būrdab 35 Hd 9.05N 46.30 E
Burdekin River 59 Jc 19.39S 147.30 E
Burdère 35 He 3.30N 45.37 E
Burdur 23 Db 37.43N 30.17 E
Burdur Gölü 24 Dd 37.44N 30.12 E
Burdwood Bank (EN) 56 Ih 54.15S 59.00W
Bure 12 Db 52.38N 1.45 E
Bure [Eth.] 35 Fd 8.20N 35.08 E
Bure [Eth.] 35 Fc 10.43N 37.03 E
Bureå 7 Ed 64.37N 21.12 E
Bureinski Hrebet = Bureya Range (EN) 21 Pd 50.40N 134.00 E
Bureja 20 Hg 49.43N 129.51 E
Bureja 21 Oe 49.25N 129.35 E
Büren 10 Ee 51.33N 8.34 E
Buren-Cogt 27 Jb 46.45N 111.30 E
Bureya Range (EN) = Bureinski Hrebet 21 Pd 50.40N 134.00 E
Burfjord 7 Fb 69.56N 22.03 E
Būr Gābo 35 Gf 1.10S 41.50 E
Burgas 6 Ig 42.30N 27.28 E
Burgas [2] 15 Kg 42.30N 27.20 E
Burgas, Gulf of- (EN) = Burgaski Zaliv 15 Kg 42.30N 27.33 E
Burgaski Zaliv = Burgas, Gulf of- (EN) 15 Kg 42.30N 27.33 E
Burg auf Fehmarn 10 Hb 54.26N 11.12 E
Burg auf Fehmarn-Puttgarden 10 Hb 54.30N 11.13 E
Burgaw 44 Ih 34.33N 77.56W
Burgaz Dağı 15 Mk 38.25N 29.46 E
Burg bei Magdeburg 10 Hd 52.16N 11.51 E
Burgdorf [Ger.] 10 Gd 52.27N 10.01 E
Burgdorf [Switz.] 14 Bc 47.04N 7.37 E
Burgenland [2] 14 Kc 47.30N 16.25 E
Burgersdorp 37 Df 31.00S 26.20 E
Burgess Hill 12 Bd 50.58N 0.08W
Burgfjället 7 Dd 64.56N 15.03 E
Burghausen 10 Ih 48.10N 12.50 E
Burghūth, Sabkhat al- 24 Ie 34.58N 41.06 E
Burglengenfeld 10 Ig 49.12N 12.02 E
Burgos [3] 13 Ib 42.20N 3.40W
Burgos [Mex.] 48 Je 24.57N 98.57W
Burgos [Sp.] 6 Fg 42.21N 3.42W
Burg-Reuland 12 Id 50.12N 6.09 E
Burgsvik 7 Eh 57.03N 18.16 E
Burgundy (EN) = Bourgogne 5 Gf 47.00N 4.30 E
Burgundy (EN) = Bourgogne 11 Kg 47.00N 4.30 E
Burgwald 12 Kd 50.57N 8.48 E
Bur Hakkaba 35 Ge 2.43N 44.10 E
Burhaniye 24 Bc 39.30N 26.58 E
Burhānpur 22 Jg 21.18N 76.14 E
Burias 26 Hd 12.57N 123.08 E
Buribaj 17 Ij 51.57N 58.11 E
Burica, Punta- 47 Hg 8.03N 82.53W
Burien 46 Dc 47.27N 122.21W
Burin Peninsula 42 Lg 47.00N 55.40W
Buriram 25 Kf 14.59N 103.08 E
Buriti, Rio- 55 Ca 12.50S 58.28W
Buriti Alegre 55 Hd 18.09S 49.03W
Buriti Bravo 54 Je 5.50S 43.50W
Buriti dos Lopes 54 Jd 3.10S 41.52W
Buritis 55 Ib 15.37S 46.26W
Burj al Ḩaţţābah 32 Ic 30.20N 9.30 E
Burjasot 13 Le 39.31N 0.25W
Burjatskaja ASSR [3] 20 Ff 53.00N 110.00 E
Burj Şāfitā 24 Ge 34.49N 36.07 E
Burkandja 20 Jd 63.27N 147.27 E
Burkburnett 45 Gi 34.06N 98.34W
Burke 45 Ge 43.11N 99.18W
Burke, Mount- 46 Ha 50.18N 114.30W
Burke Island 66 Of 73.08S 105.06W
Burke River 59 Hd 23.12S 139.33 E
Burketown 58 Ef 17.44S 139.22 E
Burkina Faso [1] 31 Gg 13.00N 2.00W
Burley 43 Ec 42.32N 113.48W
Burli 16 Rd 51.28N 52.44 E
Burlingame 45 Ig 38.45N 95.50W
Burlington [Co.-U.S.] 43 Gd 39.18N 102.16W
Burlington [Ia.-U.S.] 43 Ic 40.49N 91.07W
Burlington [Ks.-U.S.] 45 Ig 38.12N 95.45W
Burlington [N.C.-U.S.] 44 Hg 36.06N 79.26W
Burlington [Ont.-Can.] 44 Hd 43.19N 79.43W
Burlington [Vt.-U.S.] 43 Mc 44.28N 73.14W
Burlington [Wi.-U.S.] 45 Le 42.41N 88.17W
Burma [1] 22 Lg 22.00N 98.00 E
Burma [1] (Myanmar-Nainggan-Daw) 22 Lg 22.00N 98.00 E
Burnazului, Cîmpia- 15 Ie 44.10N 25.50 E
Burnett River 59 Kd 24.46S 152.25 E
Burney 46 Ef 40.53N 121.40W
Burnham Market 12 Cb 52.57N 0.44 E
Burnham-on-Crouch 12 Cc 51.37N 0.50 E
Burnie 59 Jh 41.04S 145.54 E
Burnley 9 Kh 53.48N 2.14W
Burns 43 Dc 43.35N 119.03W
Burnside 42 Gc 66.51N 108.04W
Burnside, Lake- 59 Ee 25.20S 123.10 E
Burns Lake 42 Ef 54.14N 125.46W
Burnsville 44 Fh 35.55N 82.18W
Burnt Lava Flow 46 Ef 41.35N 121.35W
Burnt River 44 Hc 44.35N 78.46W
Burntwood 42 He 56.08N 96.33W
Bur'o 31 Lh 9.30N 45.34 E
Burqin 27 Eb 47.43N 86.53 E
Burqin He 27 Eb 47.42N 86.50 E
Burqūm, Ḩarrat al- 33 He 20.54N 42.00 E
Burra 59 Hf 33.40S 138.56 E
Burragorang Lake 59 Kf 34.00S 150.25 E
Burreli 15 Ch 41.37N 20.00 E
Burrendong Reservoir 59 Jf 32.40S 149.10 E
Burriana 13 Le 39.53N 0.05W
Burro, Serranías del- 48 Ic 28.50N 101.35W
Burrow Head 9 Ig 54.41N 4.24W
Bursa 22 Ee 40.11N 29.04 E
Būr Sa'īd = Port Said (EN) 31 Ke 31.16N 32.18 E
Burscheid 12 Jc 51.06N 7.07 E
Bürstadt 12 Ke 49.38N 8.27 E
Burštyn 16 De 49.16N 24.37 E
Būr Sūdān = Port Sudan (EN) 31 Kg 19.37N 37.14 E
Burt Lake 44 Ec 45.27N 84.40W
Burtnieku, Ozero- 8 Kg 57.35N 25.10 E
Burtnieku, Ozero-/Burtnieku Ezers 8 Kg 57.35N 25.10 E
Burtnieku Ezers 8 Kg 57.35N 25.10 E
Burtnieku Ezers/Burtnieku, Ozero- 8 Kg 57.35N 25.10 E
Burton 44 Fd 43.02N 83.36W
Burton Latimer 12 Bb 52.21N 0.40W
Burton-upon-Trent 9 Li 52.49N 1.36W
Burträsk 7 Ed 64.31N 20.39 E
Buru, Pulau- 57 De 3.24S 126.40 E
Burullus, Buḩayrat al- 24 Dg 31.30N 30.50 E
Burultokay/Fuhai 27 Eb 47.06N 87.23 E
Burum Gana 34 Hc 13.00N 11.57 E
Burūn, Ra's- 24 Eg 31.14N 33.04 E
Burundaj 19 Hg 43.20N 76.49 E
Burundi [1] 31 Ki 3.15S 30.00 E
Bururi 36 Ec 3.57S 29.37 E
Burutu 34 Gd 5.21N 5.31 E
Bury 9 Kh 53.36N 2.17W
Burylbajtal 18 Ib 44.56N 73.59 E
Buryn 16 Hd 51.13N 33.48 E
Bury Saint Edmunds 9 Ni 52.15N 0.43 E
Burzil Pass 25 Ff 34.54N 75.06 E
Busalla 14 Cf 44.34N 8.57 E
Busanga [Zaire] 36 Ee 10.12S 25.23 E
Busanga [Zaire] 36 Dc 0.51S 22.04 E
Busanga Swamp 36 Ee 14.10S 25.50 E
Buşayrah 24 Ie 35.09N 40.26 E
Būsh 24 Dh 29.09N 31.08 E
Būshehr [3] 23 Hd 28.00N 52.00 E
Būshgān 24 Nh 28.48N 51.42 E
Bushimaie 29 Ji 6.02S 23.45 E
Bushmanland (EN) = Boesmanland 37 Be 29.30S 19.00 E
Busia 36 Fb 0.28N 34.06 E
Busigny 12 Fd 50.02N 3.28 E
Businga 36 Db 3.20N 20.53 E
Busira 30 Ii 0.15S 18.59 E
Busk 16 Dd 50.01N 24.37 E
Buskerud [2] 7 Bf 60.30N 9.10 E
Busko-Zdrój 10 Qf 50.28N 20.44 E
Busoga [3] 36 Fb 0.45N 33.30 E
Buşrá ash Shām 24 Gf 32.31N 36.29 E
Busselton 59 Df 33.39S 115.20 E
Bussum 11 Lb 52.16N 5.10 E
Bustamante, Bahía- 56 Gg 45.07S 66.27W
Buşteni 15 Id 45.24N 25.32 E
Busto Arsizio 14 Ce 45.37N 8.51 E
Buštyna 10 Th 48.03N 23.28 E
Busuanga 26 Hd 12.05N 120.05 E
Busu-Djanoa 36 Db 1.43N 21.23 E
Büsum 10 Eb 54.08N 8.51 E
Buta 31 Jh 2.48N 24.44 E
Butajira 35 Fd 8.08N 38.27 E
Buta Ranquil 56 Ge 37.03S 69.50W
Butare 36 Ec 2.36S 29.44 E
Butaritari Atoll 57 Id 3.03N 172.49 E
Bute, Island of- 9 Hf 55.50N 5.05W
Bute Inlet 46 Ca 50.37N 124.53W
Butembo 31 Jh 0.09N 29.17 E
Butera 14 Im 37.11N 14.11 E
Butere 36 Fb 0.13N 34.30 E
Butha Qi (Zalantum) 27 Lb 48.02N 122.42 E
Buthidaung 25 Id 20.52N 92.32 E
Butiá 56 Jd 30.07S 51.58W
Butiaba 36 Fb 1.49N 31.19 E
Butler 44 He 40.51N 79.55W
Butser Hill 12 Bd 50.57N 0.59W
Butte 39 He 46.00N 112.32W
Butterworth [Mala.] 26 Df 5.25N 100.24 E
Butterworth [S.Afr.] 37 Df 32.23S 28.04 E
Button Bay 42 Ie 58.45N 94.25W
Butuan 22 Oi 8.57N 125.33 E
Butung, Palau- 21 Oj 5.00S 122.55 E
Buturlinovka 16 Ld 50.48N 40.45 E
Butzbach 12 Kd 50.26N 8.41 E
Bützow 10 Hc 53.50N 11.59 E
Buxtehude 10 Fc 53.27N 9.42 E
Buxton [Eng.-U.K.] 9 Lh 53.15N 1.55W
Buxton [N.C.-U.S.] 44 Jh 35.16N 75.32W
Buyo 34 Dd 6.16N 7.03W
Büyük Ağrı Dağı = Ararat, Mount- (EN) 21 Gf 39.40N 44.24 E
Büyükanafarta 15 Ji 40.17N 26.22 E
Büyükçekmece 15 Lh 41.01N 28.34 E
Büyükkarıştıran 15 Kh 41.18N 27.32 E
Büyük Kemikli Burun 15 Ji 40.18N 26.14 E
Büyük Mahya 15 Kh 41.47N 27.36 E
Büyük Menderes 23 Cb 37.57N 28.58 E
Büyükorhan 15 Lj 39.45N 28.55 E
Buyun Shan 27 Lc 40.06N 122.42 E
Buzači, Poluostrov- 19 Ff 45.00N 52.00 E
Buzan 16 Pf 46.18N 49.06 E
Buzançais 11 Hh 46.53N 1.25 E
Buzancy 12 Ge 49.25N 4.57 E
Buzău [2] 15 Jd 45.09N 26.50 E
Buzău 15 Jd 45.09N 26.50 E
Buzău 15 Kd 45.26N 27.44 E
Buzaymah 33 De 24.55N 22.02 E
Buzen 29 Be 33.37N 131.08 E
Buzet 14 He 45.24N 13.59 E
Būzhān 24 Le 34.09N 47.05 E
Búzi 37 Ec 19.51S 34.30 E
Búzi 37 Ec 19.52S 34.46 E
Buziaş 15 Ed 45.39N 21.36 E
Búzios, Ilha dos- 55 Jf 23.48S 45.08W
Bužora, Gora- 10 Th 48.24N 23.15 E
Buzuluk 19 Fe 52.46N 52.17 E
Buzuluk [R.S.F.S.R.] 16 Md 50.13N 42.12 E
Buzuluk [R.S.F.S.R.] 16 Rc 52.47N 52.16 E
Buzzards Bay 44 Le 41.33N 70.47W

Index Symbols

[1] Independent Nation
[2] State, Region
[3] District, County
[4] Municipality
[5] Colony, Dependency
Continent
Physical Region
Historical or Cultural Region
Mount, Mountain
Volcano
Hill
Mountains, Mountain Range
Hills, Escarpment
Plateau, Upland
Pass, Gap
Plain, Lowland
Delta
Salt Flat
Valley, Canyon
Crater, Cave
Karst Features
Depression
Polder
Desert, Dunes
Forest, Woods
Heath, Steppe
Oasis
Cape, Point
Coast, Beach
Cliff
Peninsula
Isthmus
Sandbank
Island
Atoll
Rock, Reef
Islands, Archipelago
Rocks, Reefs
Coral Reef
Well, Spring
Geyser
River, Stream
Waterfall Rapids
River Mouth, Estuary
Lake
Salt Lake
Intermittent Lake
Reservoir
Swamp, Pond
Canal
Glacier
Ice Shelf, Pack Ice
Ocean
Sea
Gulf, Bay
Strait, Fjord
Lagoon
Bank
Seamount
Tablemount
Ridge
Shelf
Basin
Escarpment, Sea Scarp
Fracture
Trench, Abyss
National Park, Reserve
Point of Interest
Recreation Site
Cave, Cavern
Historic Site
Ruins
Wall, Walls
Church, Abbey
Temple
Scientific Station
Airport
Port
Lighthouse
Mine
Tunnel
Dam, Bridge

Bwagaoia 63a Ad 10.42S 152.50 E
Byälven 8 Ee 59.06N 12.54 E
Byam Martin 42 Ha 75.15N 104.15W
Byam Martin Channel 42 Ha 76.00N 105.00W
Bychawa 10 Se 51.01N 22.32 E
Byczyna 10 Oe 51.07N 18.11 E
Bydgoszcz [2] 10 Nc 53.10N 18.00 E
Bydgoszcz 6 He 53.08N 18.00 E
Byelorussian SSR (EN) = Belorusskaja SSR [2] 19 Ce 53.50N 28.00 E
Bygdin 8 Cc 61.20N 8.35 E
Bygland [Nor.] 7 Bg 58.51N 7.51 E
Bygland [Nor.] 8 Bf 58.41N 7.48 E
Byglandsfjorden 8 Bf 58.50N 7.50 E
Byhov 19 De 53.31N 30.15 E
Byk 15 Mc 46.55N 29.25 E
Bykovec 15 Lb 47.12N 28.18 E
Bykovo 16 Ne 49.47N 45.25 E
Bykovski 20 Hb 71.56N 129.05 E
Bylot 38 Lb 73.13N 78.34W
Byrd, Cape- 66 Qe 69.38S 76.07W
Byrdbreen 66 Df 71.35S 26.00 E
Byrd Glacier 66 Jg 80.15S 160.20 E
Byron, Cape- 57 Gg 28.39S 153.38 E
Byron Bay 42 Gc 68.55N 108.25W
Byron Bay 59 Ke 28.39S 153.37 E
Byrranga Gory = Byrranga Mountains (EN) 21 Mb 75.00N 104.00 E
Byrranga Mountains (EN) = Byrranga Gory 21 Mb 75.00N 104.00 E
Bystraja 20 Kf 52.40N 156.10 E
Bystreyca 10 Se 51.40N 22.33 E
Bystřice 10 Lf 50.11N 15.30 E
Bystrovka 18 Jc 42.45N 75.43 E
Bystrzyca [Pol.] 10 Se 51.16N 22.45 E
Bystrzyca [Pol.] 10 Me 51.13N 16.54 E
Bystrzyca Kłodzka 10 Mf 50.19N 16.39 E
Bytantaj 20 Ic 68.40N 134.50 E
Bytča 10 Og 49.14N 18.35 E
Byten 10 Vd 52.49N 25.33 E
Bytom 10 Of 50.22N 18.54 E
Bytów 10 Nb 54.11N 17.30 E
Byumba 36 Fc 1.35S 30.04 E
Byxelkrok 7 Dh 57.20N 17.00 E
Bzura 10 Qd 52.23N 20.09 E
Bzyb 16 Lh 43.12N 40.15 E

C

Cà, Sông- 25 Le 18.40N 105.40 E
Caacupé 56 Ic 25.23S 57.09W
Caadajevka 16 Nc 53.09N 45.56 E
Caaguazú 56 Ic 25.26S 56.02W
Caaguazú [3] 55 Eg 25.00S 55.45W
Caála 36 Ce 12.55S 15.35 E
Caapucú 55 Dh 26.13S 57.12W
Caarapó 55 Ef 22.38S 54.48W
Caatinga 54 Ig 17.10S 45.53W
Caatinga 52 Lf 9.00S 42.00W
Caatinga, Rio- 55 Jc 17.10S 45.52W
Caazapá [3] 55 Dh 26.10S 56.00W
Caazapá 56 Ic 26.09S 56.24W
Cabaçal, Rio- 55 Db 16.00S 57.42W
Cabadbaran 26 Ie 9.10N 125.38 E
Cabaiguán 49 Hb 22.05N 79.30W
Caballería, Cabo de- 13 Qd 40.05N 4.05 E
Caballo Cocha 54 Dd 3.54S 70.32W
Caballo Reservoir 45 Cj 32.58N 107.18W
Cabañas 13 Jg 37.40N 3.00W
Cabanatuan 22 Oh 15.29N 120.58 E
Cabano 44 Mb 47.41N 68.54W
Čabar 14 Ie 45.36N 14.39 E
Cabeceira do Apa 55 Ef 22.01S 55.46W
Cabeceiras 55 Ib 15.48S 46.59W
Cabeceiras de Basto 13 Ec 41.31N 7.59W
Cabeza, Arrecife- 48 Lh 19.04N 95.50W
Cabeza de Buey 13 Gf 38.43N 5.13W
Cabildo 55 Bn 38.29S 61.54W
Cabimas 53 Id 10.23N 71.28W
Cabinda 31 Ii 5.35S 12.13 E
Cabinda [3] 36 Bd 5.00S 12.30 E
Cabinet Mountains 46 Hb 48.08N 115.46W
Cabo Bojador 32 Ed 26.08N 14.30W
Cabo Frio 53 Lh 22.53S 42.01W
Cabo Gracias a Dios 47 Ff 14.59N 83.10W
Cabonga, Réservoir- 42 Jg 47.20N 76.35W
Caboolture 59 Ke 27.05S 152.50 E
Cabora Bassa, Dique de- 37 Ec 15.34S 32.42 E
Cabora Bassa, Lago- = Cabora Bassa, Lake-(EN) 30 Kj 15.40S 31.40 E
Cabora Bassa, Lake-(EN) = Cabora Bassa, Lago- 30 Kj 15.40S 31.40 E
Caborca 47 Bb 30.37N 112.06W
Cabot Strait 38 Ne 47.20N 59.30W
Cabourg 11 Fe 49.17N 0.08W
Cabo Verde = Cape Verde (EN) [1] 31 Eg 16.00N 24.00W
Cabo Verde, Ilhas do- = Cape Verde Islands (EN) 30 Eg 16.00N 24.10W
Cabra 13 Hg 37.28N 4.27W
Cabral, Serra do- 55 Jc 17.45S 44.22W
Cabras 14 Ck 39.56N 8.32 E
Cabras, Stagno di- 14 Ck 39.55N 8.30 E
Cabreira 13 Dc 41.39N 8.04W
Cabrejas, Puerto de- 13 Jd 40.08N 2.25W
Cabrera 49 Md 19.38N 69.54W
Cabrera, Isla- 13 Oe 39.09N 2.56 E
Cabrera, Sierra de la- 13 Fb 42.10N 6.25W
Cabri 46 Ka 50.37N 108.28W
Cabriel 13 Ke 39.14N 1.03W
Cabrit, Ilet 'a- 51e Ac 15.53N 61.36W
Cabrits, Ilet- 51h Bc 14.23N 60.52W
Cabrón, Cabo- 49 Md 19.22N 69.12W
Cabruta 50 Ci 7.38N 66.15W
Čabulja 14 Lg 43.30N 17.35 E
Cabure 49 Mh 11.08N 69.38W
Cacacas, Islas- 50 Dg 10.22N 64.26W
Caçador 56 Jc 26.47S 51.00W
Čačak 15 Df 43.54N 20.21 E
Caçapava dó Sul 56 Jd 30.30S 53.30W
Caccamo 14 Hm 37.56N 13.40 E
Caccia, Capo- 14 Cj 40.34N 8.09 E
Cacequi 55 Ei 29.53S 54.49W
Cáceres [3] 13 Ge 39.40N 6.00W
Cáceres [Braz.] 53 Kg 16.04S 57.41W
Cáceres [Sp.] 13 Fe 39.29N 6.22W
Cáceres, Laguna- 55 Dd 18.56S 57.48W
Cachari 56 Ie 36.24S 59.32W
Cache Peak 46 Ie 42.11N 113.40W
Cacheu 34 Bc 12.10N 16.21W
Cachimbo 53 Kf 9.08S 55.10W
Cachimbo, Serra do- 52 Kf 8.30S 55.50W
Cachimo 36 Dd 8.20S 21.21 E
Cáchira 49 Kj 7.46N 73.03W
Cáchira, Rio- 49 Kj 7.52N 73.40W
Cachoeira 54 Kf 12.36S 38.58W
Cachoeira Alta 55 Gd 18.48S 50.58W
Cachoeira de Goiás 55 Gc 16.44S 50.38W
Cachoeira do Arari 54 Id 1.01S 48.58W
Cachoeira do Sul 56 Jc 29.58S 52.54W
Cachoeira Dourada, Reprêsa de- 54 Ig 18.30S 49.00W
Cachoeirinha 55 Gi 29.57S 51.05W
Cachoeiro de Itapemirim 54 Jh 20.51S 41.06W
Cacinbinho 55 Ee 21.50S 55.43W
Căciulaţi 15 Je 44.38N 26.10 E
Cacolo 36 Ce 10.08S 19.18 E
Caconda 36 Ce 13.45S 15.05 E
Cacuaco 36 Bd 8.47S 13.21 E
Cacuchi 36 Ce 14.23S 16.59 E
Cacula 36 Be 14.29S 14.10 E
Caculé 54 Jf 14.30S 42.13W
Caculuvar 36 Bf 16.46S 14.56 E
Cacuso 36 Cd 9.26S 15.45 E
Čadan 20 Ef 51.17N 91.40 E
Cadaqués 13 Pb 42.17N 3.17 E
Čadca 10 Og 49.26N 18.48 E
Caddo Lake 45 Ij 32.42N 94.01W
Cadena Costero Catalana/ Serralada Litoral Catalana = Catalan Coastal Range (EN) 5 Gg 41.35N 1.40 E
Cadereyta Jiménez 48 Ie 25.36N 100.00W
Cadí, Serra del-/Cadí, Sierra del- 13 Nb 42.17N 1.42 E
Cadibarrawirracanna, Lake- 59 He 28.50S 135.25 E
Cadibona, Colle di- 14 Cf 44.20N 8.22 E
Cadillac [Fr.] 11 Fj 44.38N 0.19W
Cadillac [Mi.-U.S.] 43 Jc 44.15N 85.24W
Cadí, Sierra del/Cadí, Serra del- 13 Nb 42.17N 1.42 E
Cadiz 26 Hd 10.57N 123.18 E
Cádiz [3] 13 Gh 36.30N 5.45W
Cádiz 6 Fh 36.32N 6.18W
Cadiz [Ca.-U.S.] 46 Hi 34.30N 115.30W
Cadiz [Ky.-U.S.] 44 Dg 36.52N 87.50W
Cádiz, Bahía de- 13 Fh 36.32N 6.16W
Cádiz, Golfo de- 13 Fh 36.50N 7.10W
Cadiz Lake 46 Hi 34.18N 115.24W
Cadore 14 Gd 46.30N 12.20 E
Cadwell 43 Dc 43.40N 116.41W
Čadyr-Lunga 16 Ff 46.04N 28.52 E
Caen 6 Ff 49.11N 0.21W
Caen, Campagne de- 11 Fe 49.05N 0.20W
Caernarvon 9 Ih 53.08N 4.16W
Caernarvon Bay 9 Ih 53.05N 4.30W
Caerphilly 9 Jj 51.35N 3.14W
Caetité 54 Jf 14.04S 42.29W
Cafayate 56 Gc 26.05S 65.58W
Cafelândia [Braz.] 55 Fc 16.40S 53.25W
Cafelândia [Braz.] 55 Ie 21.49S 49.35W
Cafundó, Serra do- 55 Hb 14.40S 48.23W
Čagan 19 He 50.30N 79.10 E
Cagan-Aman 19 Ef 47.32N 46.43 E
Cagan-Nur [Mong.] 27 Eb 49.40N 89.55 E
Cagan-Nur [Mong.] 27 Ia 50.25N 105.15 E
Cagan-Ula 27 Gb 49.35N 98.25 E
Cagatá, Arroyo- 55 Df 23.26S 56.36W
Cagayan 26 Hc 18.22N 121.37 E
Cagayan de Oro 22 Oi 8.29N 124.39 E
Cagayan Islands 26 He 9.40N 121.16 E
Cagayan Sulu 26 Ge 7.01N 118.30 E
Čagda 20 Ie 58.42N 130.37 E
Cageri 16 Mh 42.39N 42.42 E
Çağiş 15 Lj 39.30N 28.01 E
Cagli 14 Gg 43.33N 12.39 E
Cagliari 6 Gh 39.13N 9.07 E
Cagliari, Golfo di- 14 Dk 39.10N 9.10 E
Cagliari, Stagno di- 14 Dk 39.15N 9.05 E
Čaglinka 17 Nj 53.59N 69.47 E
Cagnes-sur-Mer 11 Nk 43.40N 7.09 E
Čagoda 7 Ig 59.12N 35.13 E
Čagodošča 7 Ig 58.58N 36.37 E
Caguas 47 Ke 18.14N 66.02W
Čagyl 19 Fg 40.43N 55.25 E
Cahama 36 Bf 16.16S 14.17 E
Caha Mountains/An Cheacha 9 Dj 51.45N 9.45W
Caher/An Chathair 9 Fi 52.22N 7.55W
Cahersiveen/Cathair Saidhbhín 9 Cj 51.57N 10.13W
Cahore Point/Rinn Chathóir 9 Gi 52.34N 6.11W
Cahors 11 Hj 44.26N 1.26 E
Cai, Rio- 55 Gi 29.56S 51.16W
Caia 37 Fc 17.49S 35.20 E
Caia 13 Ef 38.50N 7.05W
Caiabis, Serra dos- 54 Gf 11.40S 56.30W
Caiapó, Rio- 55 Gb 15.49S 51.53W
Caiapó, Serra do- 52 Kg 17.00S 52.00W
Caiapônia 55 Gc 16.57S 51.49W
Caibarién 47 Id 22.31N 79.28W
Caiçara 55 Gb 15.34S 50.12W
Caicara 54 Eb 7.37N 66.10W
Caicara de Maturin 50 Eh 9.49N 63.36W
Caicó 54 Ke 6.27S 37.06W
Caicos Bank (EN) 47 Jd 21.35N 71.55W
Caicos Islands 38 Lg 21.45N 71.35W
Caicos Passage 47 Jd 22.00N 72.30W
Caille Island 51p Bb 12.17N 61.35W
Caimanera 49 Jd 19.59N 75.09W
Caine, Rio- 54 Eg 18.23S 65.21W
Cai Nuoc 25 Lg 8.56N 105.01 E
Caird Coast 66 Af 76.00S 24.30W
Cairngorms Mountains 9 Jd 57.06N 3.30W
Cairns 58 Ff 16.55S 145.46 E
Cairo [Ga.-U.S.] 44 Ej 30.53N 84.12W
Cairo [Il.-U.S.] 43 Jd 37.00N 89.11W
Cairo (EN) = Al Qāhirah 31 Ke 30.03N 31.15 E
Cairo Montenotte 14 Cf 44.24N 8.16 E
Caiseal/Cashel 9 Fi 52.31N 7.53W
Caisleán an Bharraigh/ Castlebar 9 Dh 53.52N 9.17W
Caister-on-Sea 12 Db 52.40N 1.45 E
Caiundo 36 Cf 15.42S 17.27 E
Caiúva, Lagoa- 55 Fk 32.24S 52.30W
Caiyuanzhen → Shengsi 28 Gi 30.42N 122.29 E
Caizi Hu 28 Di 30.48N 117.05 E
Čaja 20 De 58.17N 82.45 E
Cajabamba 54 Ce 7.58S 77.59W
Caja de Muertos, Isla- 51a Bc 17.53N 66.31W
Cajamarca 53 If 7.10S 78.31W
Cajamarca [2] 54 Ce 6.15S 78.50W
Cajapió 54 Jd 2.58S 44.48W
Cajarc 11 Hj 44.29N 1.51 E
Cajatambo 54 Cf 10.29S 77.02W
Čajkovski 19 Fd 56.47N 54.09 E
Çakırgöl Dağ 24 Hb 40.34N 39.42 E
Cakmak 24 Fd 37.37N 34.19 E
Çakmak Daği 24 Jc 39.46N 42.12 E
Čakor 15 Dg 42.40N 20.02 E
Čakovec 14 Kd 46.23N 16.26 E
Cakrani 15 Ci 40.36N 19.37 E
Çal 24 Cc 38.05N 29.24 E
Cal, Rio de la- 55 Cc 17.27S 58.15W
Calabar 31 Hh 4.57N 8.19 E
Calabozo 54 Eb 8.56N 67.26W
Calabozo, Ensenada de- 49 Lh 11.30N 71.45W
Calabria [2] 14 Kl 39.00N 16.30 E
Calaburras, Punta de- 13 Hh 36.30N 4.38W
Calacoto 54 Eg 17.18S 68.39W
Calaccucia 11a Ba 42.20N 9.01 E
Calaf 13 Nc 41.44N 1.31 E
Calafat 15 Ff 43.59N 22.56 E
Calafate 53 Ik 50.20S 72.16W
Cala Figuera, Cabo de- 13 Oe 39.27N 2.31 E
Calagua Islands 26 Hd 14.27N 122.55 E
Calahorra 13 Kb 42.18N 1.58W
Calai 36 Cf 17.50S 19.20 E
Calais [Fr.] 6 Ge 50.57N 1.50 E
Calais [Me.-U.S.] 44 Nc 45.11N 67.17W
Calais, Pas de- = Dover, Strait of- (EN) 5 Ge 51.00N 1.30 E
Calakmul 48 Oh 18.05N 89.55W
Calalaste, Sierra de- 56 Gc 25.30S 67.30W
Calama 53 Jh 22.28S 68.56W
Calamar 49 Jh 10.14N 74.56W
Calamian Group 21 Nh 12.00N 120.00 E
Calamocha 13 Kd 40.55N 1.18W
Călan 15 Fd 45.44N 22.59 E
Calanda 13 Ld 40.56N 0.14W
Calang 26 Cf 4.30N 95.40 E
Calangiánus 14 Dj 40.56N 9.11 E
Calapan 26 Hd 13.25N 121.10 E
Calar Alto 13 Jg 37.15N 2.25W
Călărași 15 Ke 44.12N 27.20 E
Cala Ratjada 13 Pe 39.42N 3.25 E
Calar del Mundo 13 Jf 38.31N 2.28W
Calatafimi 14 Gm 37.55N 12.52 E
Calatañazor 13 Jc 41.42N 2.49W
Calatayud 13 Kc 41.21N 1.38W
Calatrava 13 If 38.35N 3.48W
Calatrava, Campo de- 13 Hf 38.50N 4.15W
Calavà, Capo- 14 Il 38.10N 14.55 E
Calavon 11 Kk 43.51N 5.00 E
Calayan 26 Hc 19.20N 121.27 E
Calbayog 22 Oh 12.04N 124.36 E
Calchaqui 56 Hc 29.54S 60.18W
Calçoene 54 Hc 2.30N 50.57W
Calcutta 22 Kg 22.32N 88.22 E
Caldaro / Kaltern 14 Fd 46.25N 11.14 E
Caldas [2] 54 Cb 5.15N 75.30W
Caldas da Rainha 13 Ce 39.24N 9.08W
Caldas Novas 55 Hc 17.45S 48.38W
Caldeirão, Serra de- 13 Dg 37.19N 8.04W
Calder 9 Lh 53.44N 1.21W
Caldera 56 Fc 27.04S 70.50W
Calderina, Sierra de la- 13 Ie 39.19N 3.48W
Caldes de Mombúy 13 Oc 41.38N 2.10 E
Caldwell 44 Gf 39.44N 81.32W
Caledon 37 Bf 34.12S 19.23 E
Caledon 30 Jl 30.32S 26.05 E
Caledonia [Blz.] 49 Cd 18.14N 88.29W
Caledonia [Mn.-U.S.] 45 Ke 43.38N 91.29W
Caledonian Canal 9 Id 57.20N 4.30W
Calella 13 Oc 41.37N 2.40 E
Caleta Olivia 56 Gg 46.26S 67.32W
Calexico 46 Hj 32.40N 115.30W
Çalgal Dağı 24 Hc 39.06N 38.05 E
Calgary 39 Hd 51.03N 114.05W
Calhoun 44 Eh 34.30N 84.57W
Cali 53 Ie 3.27N 76.31W
Calicut (Kozhikode) 22 Jh 11.19N 75.46 E
Caliente 43 Ed 37.37N 114.31W
California [2] 43 Dd 37.30N 119.30W
California, Golfo de- = California, Gulf of- (EN) 38 Hg 28.00N 112.00W
California, Gulf of- (EN) = California, Golfo de- 38 Hg 28.00N 112.00W
Căliman, Munţii- 15 Ib 47.07N 25.03 E
Călimăneşti 15 Hd 45.14N 24.20 E
Calimere, Point- 25 Ff 10.18N 79.52 E
Calingasta 56 Gd 31.19S 69.25W
Calispell Peak 46 Gb 48.26N 117.30W
Calitri 14 Jj 40.54N 15.26 E
Calitzdorp 37 Cf 33.33S 21.42 E
Caliviny 51p Bb 12.01N 61.43W
Calixtlahuaca 48 Jh 19.15N 99.45W
Calka 16 Ni 41.35N 44.05 E
Calkini 48 Ng 20.22N 90.03W
Callabonna, Lake- 59 Ie 29.45S 140.05 E
Callac 11 Cf 48.24N 3.26W
Callaghan, Mount- 46 Gg 39.42N 116.57W
Callainn/Callan 9 Fi 52.33N 7.23W
Callan/Callainn 9 Fi 52.33N 7.23W
Callander [Ont.-Can.] 44 Hb 46.13N 79.23W
Callander [Scot.-U.K.] 9 Ie 56.15N 4.13W
Callantsoog 12 Gb 52.50N 4.41 E
Callao 53 Ig 12.02S 77.05W
Callao [2] 54 Cf 2.04S 77.09W
Calliaqua 51n Ba 13.08N 61.12W
Callosa de Ensarriá 13 Lf 38.39N 0.07W
Callosa de Segura 13 Lf 38.08N 0.52W
Calmalli 48 Cc 28.14N 113.33W
Călmăţui [Rom.] 15 If 43.46N 25.10 E
Călmăţui [Rom.] 15 Ke 44.50N 27.50 E
Calonne 12 Ce 49.17N 0.12 E
Calore 14 Ii 41.11N 14.28 E
Čalovo 10 Ni 47.52N 17.47 E
Calpe 13 Mf 38.39N 0.03 E
Caltabellotta 14 Hm 37.34N 13.13 E
Caltagirone 14 Im 37.14N 14.31 E
Caltanissetta 14 Im 37.29N 14.04 E
Caltilibük 15 Lj 39.57N 28.36 E
Çaltyr 16 Kf 47.17N 39.29 E
Caluago 36 Cd 8.15S 19.38 E
Calucinga 36 Ce 11.19S 16.13 E
Călugareni 15 Ie 44.11N 25.59 E
Calulo 36 Bd 9.59S 14.54 E
Caluquembe 36 Be 13.46S 14.41 E
Calvados [3] 11 Fe 49.10N 0.30W
Calvados, Côte du- 11 Fe 49.22N 0.30W
Calvert Island 46 Ba 51.35N 128.00W
Calvert River 59 Hc 16.17S 137.44 E
Calvi 11a Aa 42.34N 8.45 E
Calvillo 48 Hg 21.51N 102.43W
Calvinia 31 Il 31.25S 19.45 E
Calvitero 13 Gd 40.20N 5.43W
Cam 9 Ni 52.21N 0.15 E
Camabatela 36 Cd 8.13S 15.23 E
Camacá 54 Kg 15.24S 39.30W
Camacupa 36 Ce 12.01S 17.22 E
Camaguán 50 Ch 8.06N 67.36W
Camagüey [3] 49 Ic 21.30N 78.10W
Camagüey 39 Lg 21.23N 77.55W
Camagüey, Archipiélago de- 47 Id 22.18N 78.00W
Camaiore 14 Eg 43.56N 10.18 E
Camajuaní 49 Hb 22.28N 79.44W
Camamu 54 Kf 13.57S 39.07W
Camaná 54 Dg 16.37S 72.42W
Camapuã 55 Ed 19.30S 54.05W
Camapuã, Sertão de- 52 Kg 19.00S 51.30W
Camaquã 56 Jd 30.51S 51.49W
Camaquã, Rio- 55 Gj 31.17S 51.47W
Camarat, Cap- 11 Mk 43.12N 6.41 E
Camargo [Bol.] 54 Eh 20.39S 65.13W
Camargo [Sp.] 13 Ia 43.24N 3.54W
Camargos, Reprêsa- 55 Je 21.20S 44.30W
Camargue 11 Kk 43.31N 4.34 E
Camariñas 13 Ca 43.07N 9.10W
Camarón, Cabo- 47 He 16.00N 85.04W
Camarones 56 Gf 44.48S 65.42W
Camarones, Bahía- 56 Gf 44.45S 65.34W
Camas [Sp.] 13 Fg 37.24N 6.02W
Camas [Wa.-U.S.] 46 Dd 45.35N 122.24W
Camatagua, Embalse de- 50 Ch 9.48N 66.55W
Ca Mau, Mui- = Ca Mau Point (EN) 21 Mi 8.38N 104.44 E
Ca Mau Point (EN) = Ca Mau, Mui- 21 Mi 8.38N 104.44 E
Cambados 13 Db 42.30N 8.48W
Camberg 12 Kd 50.18N 8.16 E
Camberley 12 Bc 51.21N 0.44W
Cambo 36 Cd 7.40S 17.17 E
Cambodia (EN) = Kampuchea 22 Mh 13.00N 105.00 E
Cambo-les-Bains 11 Ek 43.22N 1.24W
Cambrai 11 Jd 50.10N 3.14 E
Cambremer 12 Ce 49.09N 0.03 E
Cambrésis 12 Fd 50.15N 3.05 E
Cambrian Mountains 5 Fe 52.35N 3.35W
Cambridge 9 Ni 52.25N 0.10 E
Cambridge [Eng.-U.K.] 9 Ni 52.12N 0.07 E
Cambridge [Id.-U.S.] 46 Gd 44.34N 116.41W
Cambridge [Ma.-U.S.] 44 Ld 42.22N 71.06W
Cambridge [Md.-U.S.] 44 If 38.34N 76.04W
Cambridge [Mn.-U.S.] 45 Jd 45.31N 93.14W
Cambridge [N.Z.] 62 Fb 37.53S 175.28 E
Cambridge [Oh.-U.S.] 44 Ge 40.02N 81.36W
Cambridge Airport 12 Cb 52.10N 0.08 E
Cambridge Bay 39 Ic 69.03N 105.05W
Cambridge Gulf 59 Fb 14.55S 128.15 E
Cambridgeshire [3] 9 Mi 52.25N 0.05W
Cambutal, Cerro- 49 Gj 7.16N 80.36W
Camden [Al.-U.S.] 44 Dj 32.00N 87.17W
Camden [Ar.-U.S.] 43 Ie 33.35N 92.50W
Camden [N.J.-U.S.] 44 Jf 39.57N 75.07W
Camden [S.C.-U.S.] 44 Gh 34.16N 80.36W
Camden [Tn.-U.S.] 44 Cg 36.04N 88.06W
Camden Bay 40 Kb 70.00N 145.00W
Camdenton 45 Jg 38.00N 92.45W
Camel 9 Ik 50.33N 4.55W
Çameli 24 Cd 37.05N 29.20 E
Camerino 14 Hg 43.08N 13.04 E
Cameron 42 Ha 76.15N 104.00W
Cameron [Az.-U.S.] 46 Ji 35.51N 111.25W
Cameron [La.-U.S.] 45 Jl 29.48N 93.19W
Cameron [Mo.-U.S.] 45 Ig 39.44N 94.14W
Cameron [Tx.-U.S.] 45 Hk 30.51N 96.59W
Cameron [Wi.-U.S.] 45 Kd 45.25N 91.44W
Cameron Hills 42 Fe 60.00N 118.00W
Cameron Mountains 62 Bf 46.00S 166.55 E
Cameroon (EN) = Cameroun [1] 31 Ih 6.00N 12.00 E
Cameroon, Mount- (EN) = Cameroun 30 Hh 4.12N 9.11 E
Camerota 14 Jj 40.02N 15.22 E
Cameroun = Cameroon (EN) [1] 31 Ih 6.00N 12.00 E
Cameroun = Cameroon, Mount-(EN) 30 Hh 4.12N 9.11 E
Cametá 54 Id 2.15S 49.30W
Camiguin [Phil.] 26 Hc 18.56N 121.55 E
Camiling 26 Hc 15.42N 120.24 E
Camilla 44 Ej 31.14N 84.12W
Caminha 13 Dc 41.52N 8.50W
Camissombo 36 Dd 8.10S 20.39 E
Camoapa 49 Eg 12.23N 85.31W
Camocim 53 Lf 2.54S 40.50W
Camonica, Val- 14 Ed 46.00N 10.20 E
Camooweal 59 Hc 19.55S 138.07 E
Camopi 54 Hc 3.13N 52.28W
Camorta 25 Ig 8.08N 93.30 E
Campagne-lès-Hesdin 12 Dd 50.24N 1.52 E
Campana 55 Cl 34.10S 58.57W
Campana, Isla- 52 Ij 48.20S 75.15W
Campanario 13 Gf 38.52N 5.37W
Campanário 55 Ef 22.48S 55.03W
Campania [2] 14 Ii 41.00N 14.30 E
Campanquiz, Cerros- 54 Cd 4.30S 77.40W
Campbell, Cape- 62 Fd 41.44S 174.16 E
Campbell Island 62 Ci 52.30S 169.10 E
Campbell Plateau (EN) 57 Ij 51.00S 170.00 E
Campbell River 42 Ef 50.01N 125.15W
Campbellsville 44 Eg 37.21N 85.20W
Campbellton 42 Kg 48.00N 66.40W
Campbelltown, Sydney- 59 Kf 34.05S 150.49 E
Campbeltown 9 Hf 55.26N 5.36W
Campeche 39 Jh 19.51N 90.32W
Campeche [2] 47 Fe 19.00N 90.30W
Campeche, Bahía de- = Campeche, Gulf of- (EN) 38 Jg 20.00N 94.00W
Campeche, Gulf of- (EN) = Campeche, Bahía de- 38 Jg 20.00N 94.00W
Campeche Bank (EN) 47 Fd 22.00N 90.00W
Campechuela 49 Ic 20.14N 77.17W
Camperdown 59 Ig 38.14S 143.09 E
Campidano 14 Ck 39.30N 8.45 E
Campiglia Marittima 14 Eg 43.03N 10.37 E
Campillos 13 Hg 37.03N 4.51W
Campina Grande 53 Mf 7.13S 35.53W
Campinas 53 Lh 22.54S 47.05W
Campina Verde 55 Hd 19.31S 49.28W
Campine/Kempen 11 Lc 51.10N 5.20 E
Campinorte 55 Hb 14.20S 49.08W
Campione d'Italia 14 Ce 45.59N 8.59 E
Campo 34 Ge 2.22N 9.49 E
Campo Alegre 50 Bh 9.15N 68.25W
Campo Alegre de Goiás 55 Ic 17.36S 47.46W
Campobasso 14 Ii 41.34N 14.39 E
Campo Belo 55 Je 20.53S 45.16W
Campo de Criptana 13 Ie 39.24N 3.07W
Campo de la Cruz 49 Jh 10.23N 74.52W
Campo del Cielo 55 Bh 27.53S 61.49W
Campo Florido 55 Hd 19.46S 48.34W
Campo Formoso 54 Jf 10.31S 40.20W
Campo Gallo 56 Hc 26.35S 62.51W
Campo Garay 55 Bi 29.41S 61.37W
Campo Grande [Arg.] 55 Eh 27.13S 54.58W
Campo Grande [Braz.] 53 Kh 20.27S 54.37W
Campo Largo [Arg.] 55 Bh 26.48S 60.50W
Campo Largo [Braz.] 55 Hg 25.26S 49.32W
Campo Maior [Braz.] 54 Jd 4.49S 42.10W
Campo Maior [Port.] 13 Ee 39.01N 7.04W
Campomarino 14 Ji 41.57N 15.02 E
Campo Mourão 56 Jb 24.03S 52.22W
Campos 53 Lh 21.45S 41.18W
Campos [Braz.] 52 Lg 15.00S 44.30W
Campos [Braz.] 52 Kh 21.00S 51.00W
Campos, Laguna- 55 Be 20.50S 61.31W
Campos, Tierra de- 13 Hb 42.10N 4.50W
Campos Altos 55 Id 19.41S 46.10W
Campos Belos 55 Ia 13.03S 46.53W
Campos do Jordão 55 Jf 22.44S 45.35W
Campos Novos 55 Gh 27.24S 51.12W
Campos Sales 54 Je 7.04S 40.23W
Campo Tures / Sand in Taufers 14 Fd 46.55N 11.57 E
Camp Verde 43 Ee 34.34N 111.51W
Cam Ranh 25 Lf 11.54N 109.13 E
Camrose 42 Gf 53.01N 112.50W
Camsell 42 Fc 65.40N 118.07W
Camsell Portage 42 Ge 59.38N 109.42W
Čan 24 Bb 40.02N 27.03 E
Canaan [Ct.-U.S.] 44 Kd 42.02N 73.20W
Canaan [Trin.] 50 Fg 11.09N 60.49W
Canaan Mountain 46 Jh 37.45N 111.51W
Cana Brava, Ribeirão- 55 Ic 16.35S 46.34W
Cana Brava, Rio- 55 Ib 14.40S 47.07W
Cana Brava, Rio- [Braz.] 55 Ha 12.12S 48.40W
Cana Brava, Rio- [Braz.] 55 Ha 13.11S 48.11W
Canada [1] 39 Jc 60.00N 95.00W
Cañada 13 Fb 42.50N 6.05W
Canada Basin (EN) 67 Ad 80.00N 145.00W
Cañada de Gomez 56 Hd 32.49S 61.24W
Canadian 45 Fi 35.55N 100.23W
Canadian River 38 Jf 35.27N 95.03W
Canaguá, Rio- 49 Mj 7.57N 69.36W
Canaima 54 Db 9.49N 70.56W

Index Symbols

[1] Independent Nation
[2] State, Region
[3] District, County
[4] Municipality
[5] Colony, Dependency
Continent
Physical Region
Historical or Cultural Region
Mount, Mountain
Volcano
Hill
Mountains, Mountain Range
Hills, Escarpment
Plateau, Upland
Pass, Gap
Plain, Lowland
Delta
Salt Flat
Valley, Canyon
Crater, Cave
Karst Features
Depression
Polder
Desert, Dunes
Forest, Woods
Heath, Steppe
Oasis
Cape, Point
Coast, Beach
Cliff
Peninsula
Isthmus
Sandbank
Island
Atoll
Rock, Reef
Islands, Archipelago
Rocks, Reefs
Coral Reef
Well, Spring
Geyser
River, Stream
Waterfall Rapids
River Mouth, Estuary
Lake
Salt Lake
Intermittent Lake
Reservoir
Swamp, Pond
Canal
Glacier
Ice Shelf, Pack Ice
Ocean
Sea
Gulf, Bay
Strait, Fjord
Lagoon
Bank
Seamount
Tablemount
Ridge
Shelf
Basin
Escarpment, Sea Scarp
Fracture
Trench, Abyss
National Park, Reserve
Point of Interest
Recreation Site
Cave, Cavern
Historic Site
Ruins
Wall, Walls
Church, Abbey
Temple
Scientific Station
Airport
Port
Lighthouse
Mine
Tunnel
Dam, Bridge

Canakkale Boğazi= Dardanelles (EN) 5 Ig 40.15N 26.25 E
Canala 63b Be 21.32S 165.57 E
Canandaigua 44 Id 42.53N 77.19W
Cananea 47 Bb 30.57N 110.18W
Cananéia 55 Ig 25.01S 47.57W
Canapolis 55 Hd 18.44S 49.13W
Canarias, Islas-=Canary Islands (EN) [5] 31 Ff 28.00N 15.30W
Canarias, Islas-=Canary Islands (EN) 30 Ff 28.00N 15.30W
Canaries 51k Ab 13.55N 61.04W
Canaronero, Laguna- 48 Ff 23.00N 106.15W
Canarreos, Archipiélago de los- 47 Hd 21.50N 82.30W
Canary Basin (EN) 3 Dg 30.00N 25.00W
Canary Islands (EN)= Canarias, Islas- 30 Ff 28.00N 15.30W
Canary Islands (EN)= Canarias, Islas- [5] 31 Ff 28.00N 15.30W
Cañas [C.R.] 49 Eh 10.25N 85.07W
Cañas [Pan.] 49 Gj 7.27N 80.16W
Canastra, Serra da- 55 Ie 20.00S 46.20W
Canatlán 48 Ge 24.31N 104.47W
Cañaveral 13 Fe 39.47N 6.23W
Canaveral, Cape- 38 Kg 28.30N 80.35W
Canavese 14 Be 45.20N 7.40 E
Canavieiras 54 Kg 15.39S 38.57W
Canazei 14 Fd 46.28N 11.46 E
Canberra 58 Fh 35.17S 149.08 E
Canby [Mn.-U.S.] 45 Hd 44.43N 96.16W
Canby [Or.-U.S.] 46 Dd 45.16N 122.42W
Cance 11 Ki 45.12N 4.48 E
Canche 11 Hd 50.31N 1.39 E
Cancon 11 Gj 44.32N 0.37 E
Cancún 47 Gd 21.05N 86.46W
Cancún, Isla- 48 Pg 21.05N 86.46W
Çandarli 15 Jk 38.56N 26.56 E
Çandarli Körfezi 15 Jk 38.52N 26.55 E
Candé 11 Eg 47.34N 1.02W
Candela 48 Id 26.50N 100.40W
Candelaria 48 Nh 18.18N 91.21W
Candelaria, Cerro- 48 Hf 23.25N 103.43W
Candelaria, Río- [Bol.] 55 Cc 17.17S 58.39W
Candelaria, Río- [Mex.] 48 Nh 18.38N 91.15W
Candelaro 14 Ji 41.34N 15.53 E
Cândido de Abreu 55 Gg 24.35S 51.20W
Cândido Mendes 54 Id 1.27S 45.43W
Candlemas Islands 66 Ad 57.03S 26.40W
Candói 55 Fg 25.43S 52.11W
Čandyr 16 Jj 38.13N 55.44 E
Canela 56 Jc 29.22S 50.50W
Canelli 14 Cf 44.43N 8.17 E
Canelones [2] 55 El 34.35S 56.00W
Canelones 55 Dl 34.32S 56.17W
Canendiyu [3] 55 Eg 24.20S 55.00W
Cañete [Chile] 56 Fe 37.48S 73.24W
Cañete [Sp.] 13 Kd 40.03N 1.39W
Cangallo 55 Cm 37.13S 58.42W
Cangamba 36 Ce 13.44S 19.53 E
Cangas 13 Db 42.16N 8.47W
Cangas de Narcea 13 Fa 43.11N 6.33W
Cangas de Onís 13 Ga 43.21N 5.07W
Cangola 36 Cd 7.58S 15.53 E
Cangombe 36 Ce 14.24S 19.59 E
Cangshan (Bianzhuang) 28 Eg 34.51N 118.03 E
Canguçu 55 Fj 31.24S 52.41W
Canguçu, Serra do- 55 Fj 31.20S 52.40W
Canguinha 55 Eb 14.42S 55.40W
Cangumbe 36 Ce 12.00S 19.09 E
Cangyuan 27 Gg 23.10N 99.15 E
Cangzhou 27 Kd 38.14N 116.58 E
Cani, Iles- 14 Em 37.21N 10.07 E
Caniapiscau 38 Md 57.40N 69.30W
Caniapiscau, Lac- 42 Kf 54.00N 70.10W
Canicattì 14 Hm 37.21N 13.51 E
Canigou, Pic du- 11 Il 42.31N 2.27 E
Canik Dağları 24 Gb 40.50N 37.10 E
Canim Lake 46 Ea 51.52N 120.45W
Canindé 54 Kd 4.22S 39.19W
Canindé, Rio- 54 Je 6.15S 42.52W
Cañitas de Felipe Pescador 48 Hf 23.36N 102.43W
Çankaya 24 Ec 39.56N 32.52 E
Çankırı 23 Da 40.36N 33.37 E
Canna 9 Gd 57.03N 6.33W
Cannac 63a Ac 9.15S 153.29 E
Çannakale 23 Ca 40.09N 26.24 E
Cannanore 25 Ff 11.51N 75.22 E
Cannanore Islands 25 Ef 10.05N 72.10 E
Cannes 11 Nk 43.33N 7.01 E
Cannich 9 Id 57.20N 4.45W
Canning Basin 59 Ed 20.10S 123.00 E
Cannobio 14 Cd 46.04N 8.42 E
Cannock 9 Ki 52.42N 2.01W
Cannonball River 45 Fc 46.26N 100.38W
Cann River 59 Jg 37.34S 149.10 E
Caño, Isla del- 49 Fi 8.44N 83.53W
Canoas 56 Jc 29.56S 51.11W
Canoas, Punta- 48 Bc 29.25N 115.10W
Canoas, Rio- 56 Jc 27.36S 51.25W
Canoeiros 54 Ig 18.02S 45.31W
Canoinhas 55 Gh 26.10S 50.24W
Canoinhas, Rio- 55 Gh 26.07S 50.22W
Cañoles 13 Le 39.02N 0.29W
Canon City 43 Fd 38.27N 105.14W
Canon Fiord 42 Ja 80.15N 83.00W
Canonnier, Pointe du- 51b Ab 18.04N 63.10W
Canora 42 Hf 51.37N 102.26W
Canosa di Puglia 14 Ki 41.13N 16.04 E
Canouan Island 50 Ff 12.43N 61.20W
Canourgue 11 Jj 44.25N 3.13 E
Canso, Strait of - 42 Lg 45.35N 61.23W
Canta 54 Cf 11.25S 76.38W
Cantabrian Mountains (EN) =Cantábrica, Cordillera- 5 Fg 43.00N 5.00W
Cantábrica, Cordillera-= Cantabrian Mountains (EN) 5 Fg 43.00N 5.00W
Cantal 5 Gf 45.10N 2.50 E
Cantal [3] 11 Ii 45.05N 2.40 E
Cantalejo 13 Ic 41.15N 3.55W
Cantanhede 13 Dd 40.21N 8.36W
Cantaura 54 Fb 9.19N 64.21W
Cantavieja 13 Ld 40.32N 0.24W
Cantavir 15 Cd 45.55N 19.46 E
Canterbury [2] 62 De 43.30S 171.50 E
Canterbury 9 Oj 51.17N 1.05 E
Canterbury Bight 57 Ii 44.10S 172.00 E
Can Tho 22 Mi 10.02N 105.47 E
Cantiles, Cayo- 49 Fc 21.36N 82.02W
Canto do Buriti 54 Je 8.07S 42.58W
Canton [Il.-U.S.] 45 Kf 40.33N 90.02W
Canton [Mo.-U.S.] 45 Kf 40.08N 91.32W
Canton [Ms.-U.S.] 45 Kj 32.37N 90.02W
Canton [N.Y.-U.S.] 44 Jc 44.37N 75.11W
Canton [Oh.-U.S.] 43 Kc 40.48N 81.23W
Canton [S.D.-U.S.] 45 He 43.18N 96.35W
Canton (EN)=Guangzhou 22 Ng 23.07N 113.18 E
Cantù 14 De 45.44N 9.08 E
Cantwell 40 Jd 63.23N 148.57W
Cañuelas 55 Cl 35.03S 58.44W
Canumã, Rio- 52 Kf 3.55S 59.10W
Canutama 54 Fe 6.32S 64.20W
Canvey 12 Cc 51.31N 0.36 E
Čany 20 Ce 55.19N 76.56 E
Čany, Ozero- 21 Jd 54.50N 77.30 E
Cany-Barville 12 Ce 49.47N 0.38 E
Canyon [Mn.-U.S.] 45 Jc 47.02N 92.29W
Canyon [Tx.-U.S.] 43 Ge 34.59N 101.55W
Canyon [Wy.-U.S.] 46 Jd 44.44N 110.30W
Canyon Lake 45 Gl 29.52N 98.16W
Canzar 36 Dd 7.36S 21.33 E
Cao Bang 25 Ld 22.40N 106.15 E
Caojiahe → Qichun 28 Ci 30.15N 115.26 E
Caojian 27 Gf 25.38N 99.07 E
Caombo 36 Cd 8.42S 16.33 E
Caorle 14 Ge 45.36N 12.53 E
Caoxian 28 Cg 34.49N 115.33 E
Caozhou → Heze 27 Kd 35.14N 115.28 E
Capaccio 14 Jj 40.25N 15.05 E
Čapajev 19 Fe 50.14N 51.08 E
Čapajevsk 19 Ee 53.01N 49.36 E
Capanaparo, Río- 54 Eb 7.01N 67.07W
Capanema [Braz.] 54 Id 1.12S 47.11W
Capanema [Braz.] 55 Fg 25.40S 53.48W
Capanema, Serra do- 55 Fh 26.05S 53.16W
Capão Alto 55 Gh 27.56S 50.30W
Capão Bonito 55 Hf 24.01S 48.20W
Capão Doce, Morro do- 55 Gh 26.43S 51.25W
Caparo, Río- 49 Lj 7.46N 70.23W
Capatárida 49 Lh 11.11N 70.37W
Capbreton 11 Ek 43.38N 1.26W
Cap Breton Canyon (EN) 11 Ek 43.40N 1.50W
Čapčama, Pereval- 18 Hd 41.34N 70.50 E
Cap-Chat 44 Na 49.06N 66.42W
Capcir 11 Il 42.45N 2.10 E
Cap-de-la-Madeleine 42 Kg 46.22N 72.32W
Capdenac-Gare 11 Ij 44.34N 2.05 E
Cape Barren Island 59 Jh 40.25S 148.10 E
Cape Basin (EN) 3 Em 37.00S 7.00 E
Cape Breton Island 38 Me 46.00N 60.30W
Cape Charles 44 Jg 37.17N 76.00W
Cape Coast 31 Gh 5.06N 1.15W
Cape Cod Bay 44 Le 41.52N 70.22W
Cape Coral 44 Gl 26.33N 81.58W
Cape Dorset 39 Lc 64.14N 76.32W
Cape Dyer 39 Mc 66.30N 61.18W
Cape Fear River 44 Ii 33.53N 78.00W
Cape Girardeau 43 Jd 37.19N 89.32W
Cape Johnson Tablemount (EN) 57 Jc 17.08N 177.15W
Capel 12 Bc 51.08N 0.19W
Cape Lisburne 40 Fc 68.52N 166.05W
Capelka 8 Mf 58.02N 29.07 E
Capelongo 36 Ce 14.54S 15.05 E
Capem 55 Ea 13.14S 55.14W
Cape May 44 Jf 38.56N 74.54W
Cape Mount [3] 34 Cd 7.05N 10.50W
Cape Province/ Kaapprovinsie [2] 37 Cf 32.00S 22.00 E
Cape Rise (EN) 3 En 42.00S 15.00 E
Cape Smith 42 Jd 60.44N 78.29W
Capesterre 51e Bc 15.54N 61.13W
Capesterre-Belle-Eau 50 Fd 16.03N 61.34W
Cape Town / Kaapstad 31 Il 33.55S 18.22 E
Cape Verde (EN)=Cabo Verde [1] 31 Eg 16.00N 24.00W
Cape Verde (EN)=Cap Vert [3] 34 Bc 14.45N 17.20W
Cape Verde Basin (EN) 3 Ch 15.00N 30.00W
Cape Verde Islands (EN)= Cabo Verde, Ilhas do- 30 Eg 16.00N 24.10W
Cape Yakataga 40 Kd 60.04N 142.26W
Cape York Peninsula 57 Ff 14.00S 142.30 E
Cap-Haïtien 39 Lh 19.45N 72.15W
Capiibary, Arroyo- 55 Dg 24.06S 56.26W
Capiibary, Río- 55 Eg 25.30S 55.33W
Capim, Rio- 52 Lf 1.40S 47.47W
Capinópolis 55 Hd 18.41S 49.35W
Capira 49 Hi 8.45N 79.53W
Capital Federal [2] 56 Id 34.36S 58.27W
Capitán Arturo Prat 66 Re 62.29S 59.39W
Capitán Bado 56 Ib 23.16S 55.32W
Capitán Bermúdez 55 Bk 32.49S 60.43W
Capitán Sarmiento 55 Cl 34.10S 59.48W
Capitão Noronha, Rio- 55 Ea 13.19S 54.36W
Capivara, Reprêsa da- 55 Gf 22.40S 50.57W
Capivari, Rio- 55 Dd 19.16S 57.10W
Capivarita 55 Fj 30.18S 52.19W
Cap Lopez, Baie du- 36 Ac 0.40S 9.00 E
Čaplygin 16 Kc 53.17N 39.59 E
Cappeln (Oldenburg) 12 Kb 52.49N 8.07 E
Cap Point 50 Fe 14.07N 60.57W
Capraia 14 Dg 43.05N 9.50 E
Caprara, Punta- 14 Ci 41.07N 8.19 E
Capreol 44 Gb 46.43N 80.56W
Caprera 14 Di 41.10N 9.30 E
Capri 14 Ij 40.35N 14.15 E
Capri 14 Ij 40.33N 14.14 E
Capricorn, Cape- 59 Kd 23.30S 151.15 E
Capricorn Channel 59 Kd 22.15S 151.30 E
Capricorn Group 57 Gg 23.30S 152.00 E
Caprivi Strip (EN)=Caprivi Zipfel 30 Jj 18.00S 23.00 E
Caprivi Zipfel=Caprivi Strip (EN) 30 Jj 18.00S 23.00 E
Captain Cook 65a Fd 19.30N 155.55W
Captains Flat 59 Jg 35.35S 149.27 E
Captieux 11 Fj 44.17N 0.15W
Capua 14 Ii 41.06N 14.12 E
Capuchin, Cape- 51g Ba 15.38N 61.28W
Capunda 36 Ce 10.41S 17.23 E
Cap Vert=Cape Verde (EN) [3] 34 Bc 14.45N 17.20W
Caquetá [2] 54 Dc 1.00N 74.00W
Čara 21 Oc 60.17N 120.40 E
Čara [R.S.F.S.R.] 20 Ge 56.58N 118.17 E
Čara [R.S.F.S.R.] 20 Ge 58.54N 118.12 E
Carabobo [2] 54 Ea 10.10N 68.05W
Caracal 15 He 44.07N 24.21 E
Caracaraí 54 Fc 1.50N 61.08W
Caracas 53 Jd 10.30N 66.56W
Carache 49 Li 9.38N 70.14W
Caracol 55 De 21.59S 57.02W
Caracol, Rio- 55 Df 22.13S 57.03W
Caracollo 54 Eg 17.39S 67.10W
Cara Droma Rúisc/Carrick-on-Shannon 9 Eh 53.57N 8.05W
Caraguatá, Cuchilla- 55 Ek 32.05S 54.54W
Caraguatatuba 55 Jf 23.37S 45.25W
Caraïbe, Mer-/Antilles, Mer des-=Caribbean Sea (EN) 38 Lh 15.00N 73.00W
Carajas, Serra dos- 54 He 6.00S 51.20W
Caramoan Peninsula 26 Hd 13.48N 123.40 E
Caramulo, Serra do- 13 Dd 40.34N 8.11W
Caraná, Rio- 55 Ca 13.20S 59.17W
Carandaí 55 Ke 20.57S 43.48W
Carandazal 55 Dd 19.50S 57.09W
Caransebeş 15 Fd 45.25N 22.13 E
Carapá, Río- 55 Eg 24.30S 54.20W
Carapelle 14 Ji 41.30N 15.55 E
Caraş 15 Ee 44.49N 21.20 E
Caraş Severin [2] 15 Ed 45.20N 22.00 E
Caratasca, Cayo- 49 Fe 16.02N 83.20W
Caratasca, Laguna de- 47 He 15.20N 83.50W
Caratinga 54 Jg 19.47S 42.08W
Carauari 54 Ed 4.52S 66.54W
Caraúbas 54 Ke 5.47S 37.34W
Caravaca 13 Kf 38.06N 1.51W
Caravelas 53 Mg 17.45S 39.15W
Caraveli 54 Dg 15.46S 73.22W
Caravelle, Presqu'île de la- 51h Bb 14.45N 60.55W
Caravelle, Rocher de la- 51h Bb 14.48N 60.53W
Caràzinho 56 Jc 28.18S 52.48W
Carazo [3] 49 Dh 11.45N 86.15W
Carballino 13 Db 42.26N 8.04W
Carballo 13 Da 43.13N 8.41W
Carberry 45 Gb 49.52N 99.20W
Carbet, Pitons du- 51h Ab 14.42N 61.07W
Carbon, Cap- [Alg.] 13 Rh 36.47N 5.06 E
Carbon, Cap- [Alg.] 13 Li 35.54N 0.20W
Carbonara, Capo- 14 Dk 39.06N 9.31 E
Carbondale [Il.-U.S.] 43 Jd 37.44N 89.13W
Carbondale [Pa.-U.S.] 44 Je 41.35N 75.31W
Carbonera, Cuchilla de la- 55 El 34.10S 54.00W
Carboneras 13 Kh 36.59N 1.54W
Carboneras, Cerro- 48 Ih 18.10N 101.10W
Carbones 13 Gg 37.36N 5.39W
Carbonia 14 Ck 39.10N 8.31 E
Carcans, Étang de- 11 Ei 45.06N 1.07W
Carcar 26 Hd 10.06N 123.38 E
Carcarañá, Río- 55 Bk 32.27S 60.48W
Carcassonne 11 Ik 43.13N 2.21 E
Carcross 42 Ed 60.10N 134.42W
Çardak [Tur.] 15 Ji 40.22N 26.43 E
Çardak [Tur.] 24 Cd 37.48N 29.40 E
Čardara 19 Gg 41.15N 68.01 E
Čardarinskoje Vodohranilišče 18 Gd 41.05N 68.15 E
Cárdenas [Cuba] 47 Hd 23.02N 81.12W
Cárdenas [Mex.] 47 Ed 22.00N 99.40W
Cárdenas [Mex.] 48 Mi 17.59N 93.22W
Cárdenas, Bahía de- 49 Gb 23.05N 81.10W
Cardener/Cardoner 13 Nc 41.41N 1.51 E
Cardiel, Lago- 56 Fg 48.55S 71.15W
Cardiff 6 Fe 51.30N 3.13W
Cardigan 9 Ii 52.06N 4.40W
Cardigan Bay 5 Fe 52.30N 4.20W
Cardona [Sp.] 13 Nc 41.55N 1.41 E
Cardona [Ur.] 55 Dk 33.54S 57.22W
Cardoner/Cardener 13 Nc 41.41N 1.51 E
Cardozo 55 Dk 32.38S 56.21W
Cardston 42 Gg 49.12N 113.18W
Čardžou 22 If 39.06N 63.34 E
Čardžouskaja Oblast [3] 19 Gh 39.00N 63.00 E
Carei 15 Fb 47.41N 22.28 E
Careiro 54 Gd 3.12S 59.45W
Carentan 11 Ee 49.18N 1.14W
Carey 46 Ie 43.20N 113.58W
Carey, Lake- 57 Dg 29.05S 122.15 E
Cargados Carajos Islands 30 Mj 16.35S 59.40 E
Cargese 11a Aa 42.08N 8.35 E
Carhaix-Plouguer 11 Cf 48.17N 3.35W
Cari 14 Hi 41.23N 13.50 E
Caria 15 Ll 37.30N 29.00 E
Cariacica 54 Jh 20.16S 40.25W
Cariaco 50 Eg 10.29N 63.33W
Cariaco, Golfo de- 50 Eg 10.30N 64.00W
Cariaco Basin (EN) 50 Dg 10.37N 65.10W
Cariati 14 Kk 39.30N 16.57 E
Caribana, Punta- 49 Ii 8.37N 76.52W
Caribbean Sea 38 Lh 15.00N 73.00W
Caribbean Sea (EN)= Antillas, Mar de las-/ Caribe, Mar- 38 Lh 15.00N 73.00W
Caribbean Sea (EN)= Antilles, Mer des-/Caraïbe, Mer- 38 Lh 15.00N 73.00W
Caribbean Sea (EN)= Caribe, Mar-/Antillas, Mar de las- 38 Lh 15.00N 73.00W
Caribe, Mar-/Antillas, Mar de las-=Caribbean Sea (EN) 38 Lh 15.00N 73.00W
Cariboo Mountains 42 Ff 53.00N 121.00W
Caribou 42 Ie 59.20N 94.45W
Caribou 44 Mb 46.52N 68.01W
Caribou Island 44 Eb 47.27N 85.52W
Caribou Lake 45 La 50.25N 89.00W
Caribou Mountains 38 Hd 59.12N 115.40W
Caribou Range 46 Je 43.05N 111.15W
Caričin Grad 15 Eg 42.57N 21.45 E
Carignan 11 Le 49.38N 5.10 E
Carignano 14 Bf 44.55N 7.40 E
Cariñena 13 Kc 41.20N 1.13W
Carinhanha 54 Jf 14.08S 43.47W
Carinhanha, Rio- 55 Kb 14.20S 43.47W
Carini 14 Hl 38.08N 13.11 E
Carinola 14 Hi 41.11N 13.58 E
Carinthia (EN) = Kärnten [2] 14 Hd 46.45N 14.00 E
Carinthia (EN) = Kärnten 14 Hd 46.45N 14.00 E
Caripe 50 Eg 10.21N 63.29W
Caripito 54 Fa 10.08N 63.06W
Caris, Rio- 50 Eh 8.09N 63.46W
Carlet 13 Le 39.14N 0.31W
Carleton Place 44 Ic 45.07N 76.08W
Carletonville 37 De 26.23S 27.22 E
Carlin 46 Gf 40.43N 116.07W
Carling 12 Ie 49.10N 6.43 E
Carlingford Lough/Loch Cairlinn 9 Gg 54.05N 6.14W
Carlinville 45 Lg 39.17N 89.53W
Carlisle [Eng.-U.K.] 6 Fe 54.54N 2.55W
Carlisle [Pa.-U.S.] 44 Ie 40.12N 77.12W
Carlisle Bay 51q Ab 13.05N 59.37W
Carloforte 14 Ck 39.08N 8.18 E
Carlos Beguerie 55 Ch 35.29S 59.06W
Carlos Casares 56 He 35.38S 61.21W
Carlos Chagas 54 Jg 17.43S 40.45W
Carlos Reyles 55 Dk 33.03S 56.29W
Carlos Tejedor 55 Al 35.23S 62.25W
Carlow/Ceatharlach 9 Gi 52.50N 6.55W
Carlow/Ceatharlach [2] 9 Gi 52.50N 7.00W
Carloway 9 Gc 58.17N 6.47W
Carlsbad [Ca.-U.S.] 46 Gj 33.10N 117.21W
Carlsbad [N.M.-U.S.] 39 If 32.25N 104.14W
Carlyle 42 Hg 49.38N 102.16W
Carlyle Lake 45 Lg 38.40N 89.18W
Carmacks 42 Dd 62.05N 136.18W
Carmagnola 14 Bf 44.51N 7.43 E
Carmarthen 9 Ij 51.52N 4.19W
Carmarthen Bay 9 Ij 51.40N 4.30W
Carmaux 11 Ij 44.03N 2.09 E
Carmel Head 9 Ih 53.24N 4.34W
Carmelita 49 Be 17.21N 90.10W
Carmelo 56 Id 34.00S 58.17W
Carmen 55 Dk 33.15S 56.01W
Carmen, Isla- 47 Bc 25.57N 111.12W
Carmen, Isla del- 48 Nh 18.42N 91.40W
Carmen, Laguna del- 48 Mh 18.15N 93.50W
Carmen, Río del- 48 Fb 30.42N 106.29W
Carmen, Sierra del- 48 Hc 29.00N 102.30W
Carmen de Patagones 56 Hf 40.48S 62.59W
Carmensa 56 Ge 35.08S 67.38W
Carmi 45 Lg 38.07N 88.10W
Carmichael 46 Eg 38.38N 121.19W
Carmo de Minas 55 Jf 22.07S 45.08W
Carmo do Paranaíba 55 Id 18.59S 46.21W
Carmona 13 Gg 37.28N 5.38W
Carnac 11 Cg 47.35N 3.05W
Carnamah 59 De 29.42S 115.53 E
Carnarvon [Austl.] 58 Cg 24.53S 113.40 E
Carnarvon [S.Afr.] 31 Jl 30.56S 22.08 E
Carnarvon Range 59 Ee 25.10S 121.00 E
Carnatic (EN) 21 Jh 10.30N 79.00 E
Carnegie, Lake- 57 Dg 26.10S 122.30 E
Carnegie Ridge (EN) 3 Nj 1.00S 85.00W
Carn Eige 9 Hd 57.30N 5.05W
Carney Island 66 Nf 73.57S 121.00W
Carnia 14 Gd 46.25N 13.00 E
Car Nicobar 25 Ig 9.10N 92.47 E
Carnot 35 Be 4.48N 16.03 E
Carnoustie 9 Ke 56.30N 2.44W
Carnsore Point/Ceann an Chairn 9 Gi 52.10N 6.22W
Carn Ui Néid/Mizen Head 5 Fe 51.27N 9.49W
Caro 44 Fd 43.29N 83.24W
Carol City 44 Gm 25.56N 80.16W
Carolina [Braz.] 53 Lf 7.20S 47.28W
Carolina [P.R.] 51a Cb 18.24N 65.57W
Carolina [S.Afr.] 37 Ee 26.05S 30.06 E
Carolina Beach 44 Ih 34.02N 77.54W
Carolinas, Puntan- 64b Bb 14.54N 145.38 E
Caroline Atoll 57 Le 9.58S 150.13W
Caroline Islands 57 Fd 8.00N 147.00 E
Carondelet Reef 57 Je 5.34S 173.51W
Caroni, Río- 52 Je 8.21N 62.43W
Caronie → Nebrodi 14 Im 37.55N 14.35 E
Carora 54 Da 10.11N 70.05W
Carpathian Mountains (EN) 5 If 48.00N 24.00 E
Carpathian Mountains (EN) = Carpații Occidentali 15 Fc 46.30N 22.10 E
Carpathian Mountains (EN) = Carpații Orientali 15 Ib 47.30N 25.30 E
Carpații Meridionali= Transylvanian Alps (EN) 5 If 45.30N 22.10 E
Carpații Occidentali = Carpathian Mountains (EN) 15 Fc 46.30N 22.10 E
Carpații Orientali= Carpathian Mountains (EN) 15 Ib 47.30N 25.30 E
Carpen 15 Ge 44.20N 23.15 E
Carpentaria, Gulf of- 57 Ef 14.00S 139.00 E
Carpentras 11 Lj 44.03N 5.03 E
Carpi 14 Ef 44.47N 10.53 E
Carpina 54 Ke 7.51S 35.15W
Carr, Cape- 66 Ie 66.07S 130.51 E
Carraig Fhearghais/ Carrickfergus 9 Hg 54.43N 5.44W
Carraig na Siúire/Carrick-on-Suir
Carrara 14 Ef 44.05N 10.06 E
Carrauntoohil 5 Fe 52.00N 9.45W
Carreiro, Rio- 55 Gi 29.07S 51.43W
Carreño 13 Ga 43.35N 5.46W
Carreta, Punta- 54 Cf 14.13S 76.18W
Carretero, Puerto- 13 Ig 37.28N 3.40W
Carriacou 50 Ff 12.30N 61.27W
Carrick 9 If 55.15N 4.40W
Carrickfergus/Carraig Fhearghais 9 Hg 54.43N 5.44W
Carrick-on-Shannon/cara Droma Rúisc 9 Eh 53.57N 8.05W
Carrick-on-Suir/Carraig na Siúire 9 Fi 52.21N 7.25W
Carrington 43 Hb 47.27N 99.08W
Carrión 13 Hc 41.53N 4.32W
Carrión de los Condes 13 Hb 42.20N 4.36W
Carrizal 49 Kh 11.58N 72.12W
Carrizo Peak 45 Dj 33.20N 105.38W
Carrizos 48 Gc 29.58N 105.16W
Carrizo Springs 45 Gl 28.31N 99.52W
Carrizo Wash 46 Ki 34.36N 109.26W
Carrizozo 45 Dj 33.38N 105.53W
Carroll 45 Ie 42.04N 94.52W
Carroll Inlet 66 Qf 73.18S 78.30W
Carrollton [Ga.-U.S.] 44 Ei 33.35N 85.05W
Carrollton [Il.-U.S.] 45 Kg 39.18N 90.24W
Carrollton [Ky.-U.S.] 44 Ef 38.41N 85.11W
Carrollton [Mo.-U.S.] 45 Jg 39.22N 93.30W
Carron, Loch- 9 Hd 57.30N 5.40W
Carrot 42 Hf 53.50N 101.18W
Carrowmore Lough 9 Dg 54.12N 9.47W
Çarşamba 24 Gb 41.12N 36.44 E
Çarşamba 24 Ed 37.53N 32.37 E
Čaršanga 19 Gh 37.31N 66.03 E
Čarsk 19 If 49.35N 81.05 E
Carson 46 Ed 45.44N 121.49W
Carson City 39 Hf 39.10N 119.46W
Carson Lake 46 Fg 39.19N 118.43W
Carson Sink 46 Fg 39.45N 118.30W
Cartagena [Col.] 53 Id 10.25N 75.32W
Cartagena [Sp.] 6 Fh 37.36N 0.59W
Cartago [3] 49 Fi 9.50N 83.45W
Cartago [Col.] 54 Cc 4.46N 75.56W
Cartago [C.R.] 47 Hg 9.52N 83.55W
Cartaxo 13 De 39.09N 8.47W
Carter, Mount- 59 Ib 13.05S 143.15 E
Carteret 11 Ee 49.23N 1.47W
Cartersville 44 Eh 34.10N 85.05W
Carterton 62 Fd 41.01S 175.31 E
Carthage [Mo.-U.S.] 45 Ih 37.11N 94.19W
Carthage [Tx.-U.S.] 45 Ij 32.09N 94.20W
Cartier 44 Gb 46.42N 81.32W
Cartier Island 57 Df 12.30S 123.30 E
Caruaru 53 Mf 8.17S 35.58W
Carúpano 54 Fa 10.40N 63.14W
Carutapera 54 Id 1.13S 46.01W
Čarvak 18 Gd 41.38N 69.56 E
Carvin 12 Ed 50.29N 2.58 E
Carvoeiro, Cabo- 13 Ce 39.21N 9.24W
Čaryn 18 Lc 43.50N 79.12 E
Čaryš 20 Df 52.22N 83.45 E
Casablanca [2] 32 Fc 33.37N 7.35W
Casablanca 31 Ge 33.36N 7.37W
Casa Branca 55 Ie 21.46S 47.05W
Casa Grande 43 Ee 32.53N 111.45W
Casalbordino 14 Ih 42.09N 14.35 E
Casale Monferrato 14 Ce 45.08N 8.27 E
Casalmaggiore 14 Ef 44.59N 10.26 E
Casalvasco 55 Cb 15.19S 59.59W
Casal Velino 14 Jj 40.11N 15.06 E
Casamance 34 Bc 12.33N 16.46W
Casamance [3] 34 Bc 12.50N 15.00W
Casanare [2] 54 Db 5.20N 72.00W
Casanare, Río- 54 Eb 6.02N 69.51W
Casanay 50 Eg 10.30N 63.25W
Casa Nova 54 Je 9.25S 41.08W
Casarano 14 Mj 40.00N 18.10 E
Casas Grandes, Río- 48 Eb 30.22N 107.31W
Casas-Ibáñez 13 Ke 39.17N 1.28W
Casca, Rio da- 55 Eb 14.52S 55.52W
Cascade 46 Hd 44.31N 115.59W
Cascade Point 62 Cf 44.01S 168.22 E
Cascade Range 38 Ge 45.00N 121.30W
Cascais 13 Cf 38.42N 9.25W
Cascavel 56 Jb 24.57S 53.28W
Cascia 14 Hh 42.43N 13.01 E
Casciana Terme 14 Eg 43.32N 10.38 E
Cascina 14 Eg 43.41N 10.33 E
Casentino 14 Fg 43.40N 11.50 E

Index Symbols

[1] Independent Nation
[2] State, Region
[3] District, County
[4] Municipality
[5] Colony, Dependency
Continent
Physical Region
Historical or Cultural Region
Mount, Mountain
Volcano
Hill
Mountains, Mountain Range
Hills, Escarpment
Plateau, Upland
Pass, Gap
Plain, Lowland
Delta
Salt Flat
Valley, Canyon
Crater, Cave
Karst Features
Depression
Polder
Desert, Dunes
Forest, Woods
Heath, Steppe
Oasis
Cape, Point
Coast, Beach
Cliff
Peninsula
Isthmus
Sandbank
Island
Atoll
Rock, Reef
Islands, Archipelago
Rocks, Reefs
Coral Reef
Well, Spring
Geyser
River, Stream
Waterfall Rapids
River Mouth, Estuary
Lake
Salt Lake
Intermittent Lake
Reservoir
Swamp, Pond
Canal
Glacier
Ice Shelf, Pack Ice
Ocean
Sea
Gulf, Bay
Strait, Fjord
Lagoon
Bank
Seamount
Tablemount
Ridge
Shelf
Basin
Escarpment, Sea Scarp
Fracture
Trench, Abyss
National Park, Reserve
Point of Interest
Recreation Site
Cave, Cavern
Historic Site
Ruins
Wall, Walls
Church, Abbey
Temple
Scientific Station
Airport
Port
Lighthouse
Mine
Tunnel
Dam, Bridge

Case-Pilote 51h Ab 14.38N 61.08W
Caserta 14 Ii 41.04N 14.20 E
Casey 66 He 66.17S 110.32 E
Casey Bay 66 Ee 67.00S 48.00 E
Cashel/Caiseal 9 Fi 52.31N 7.53W
Casigua 49 Ki 8.46N 72.30W
Casilda 56 Hd 33.03S 61.10W
Casimcea 15 Le 44.24N 28.33 E
Casino 59 Ke 28.52S 153.03 E
Casiquiare, Brazo- 54 Ec 2.01N 67.07W
Čáslav 10 Lg 49.55N 15.25 E
Casma 54 Ce 9.28S 78.19W
Časnačorr, Gora- 7 Hc 67.45N 33.29 E
Časniki 7 Gi 54.52N 29.08 E
Casoli 14 Ih 42.07N 14.18 E
Casoria 14 Ij 40.54N 14.17 E
Caspe 13 Lc 41.14N 0.02W
Casper 39 Ie 42.51N 106.19W
Caspian Depression (EN)= Prikaspijskaja Nizmennost 5 Lf 48.00N 52.00 E
Caspian Sea (EN)= Kaspijskoje More 5 Lg 42.00N 50.30 E
Caspian Sea (EN)= Māzandarān, Daryā-ye- 5 Lg 42.00N 50.30 E
Cassai 30 Ii 3.02S 16.57 E
Cassamba 36 De 13.04S 20.25 E
Cassange, Rio- 55 Dc 17.06S 57.23W
Cassano allo Ionio 14 Kk 39.47N 16.19 E
Cass City 44 Fd 43.36N 83.10W
Cassel 12 Ed 50.47N 2.29 E
Casselton 45 Hc 46.54N 97.13W
Cássia 55 Ie 20.36S 46.56W
Cassiar 42 Ee 59.16N 129.40W
Cassiar Mountains 38 Gd 59.00N 129.00W
Cassilândia 54 Hg 19.09S 51.45W
Cassino [Braz.] 55 Fk 32.11S 52.10W
Cassino [It.] 14 Hi 41.30N 13.49 E
Cassis 11 Lk 43.13N 5.32 E
Cass Lake 45 Ic 47.23N 94.36W
Cass River 44 Fd 43.23N 83.59W
Cassununga 55 Fc 16.03S 53.38W
Castagneto Carducci 14 Eg 43.10N 10.36 E
Castagniccia 11a Ba 42.25N 9.30 E
Castañar, Sierra del- 13 He 39.35N 4.10W
Castanhal 54 Id 1.18S 47.55W
Castaños 48 Id 26.47N 101.25W
Castelbuono 14 Im 37.56N 14.05 E
Castel di Sangro 14 Ii 41.47N 14.06 E
Castelfidardo 14 Hg 43.28N 13.33 E
Castelfranco Veneto 14 Fe 45.40N 11.55 E
Casteljaloux 11 Gj 44.19N 0.06 E
Castellabate 14 Ij 40.17N 14.57 E
Castellammare, Golfo di- 14 Gl 38.10N 12.55 E
Castellammare del Golfo 14 Gl 38.01N 12.53 E
Castellammare di Stabia 14 Ij 40.42N 14.29 E
Castellana Grotte 14 Lj 40.53N 17.10 E
Castellane 11 Mk 43.51N 6.31 E
Castellaneta 14 Kj 40.38N 16.56 E
Castelldefels 13 Nc 41.17N 1.58 E
Castelli [Arg.] 56 Hc 25.57S 60.37W
Castelli [Arg.] 55 Dm 36.06S 57.47W
Castelló de la Plana/ Castellón de la Plana 6 Fh 39.59N 0.02W
Castellón [3] 13 Ld 40.10N 0.10W
Castellón de la Plana/ Castelló de la Plana 6 Fh 39.59N 0.02W
Castellón de la Plana-El Grao 13 Me 39.58N 0.01 E
Castellote 13 Ld 40.48N 0.19W
Castelnaudary 11 Hk 43.19N 1.57 E
Castelnau-de-Médoc 11 Fi 45.02N 0.48W
Castelnovo ne' Monti 14 Ef 44.26N 10.24 E
Castelo Branco [2] 13 Ee 40.00N 7.30W
Castelo Branco 13 Ee 39.49N 7.30W
Castelo de Vide 13 Ee 39.25N 7.27W
Castelo do Piaui 54 Je 5.20S 41.33W
Castel San Giovanni 14 De 45.04N 9.26 E
Castelsardo 14 Cj 40.55N 8.43 E
Castelsarrasin 11 Hj 44.02N 1.06 E
Casteltermini 14 Hm 37.32N 13.39 E
Castelvetrano 14 Gm 37.41N 12.47 E
Castets 11 Ek 43.53N 1.09W
Castiglione del Lago 14 Gg 43.07N 12.03 E
Castiglione della Pescaia 14 Eh 42.46N 10.53 E
Castiglion Fiorentino 14 Fg 43.20N 11.55 E
Castilla la Nueva=New Castile (EN) 13 Id 40.00N 3.45W
Castilla la Vieja=Old Castile (EN) 13 Ic 41.30N 4.00W
Castillejo 13 Gc 41.14N 5.30W
Castillon-la-Bataille 11 Fj 44.51N 0.02W
Castillonnès 11 Gj 44.39N 0.36 E
Castillos 56 Jd 34.12S 53.50W
Castillos, Laguna de- 55 Fl 34.20S 53.54W
Castlebar/Caisleán an Bharraigh 9 Dh 53.52N 9.17W
Castle Bruce 51g Bb 15.26N 61.16W
Castle Dome Peak 46 Hj 33.05N 114.08W
Castle Douglas 9 Jg 54.57N 3.56W
Castlegar 42 Fg 49.19N 117.40W
Castleisland/Oileán Ciarraí 9 Di 52.14N 9.27W
Castlemaine 59 Ig 37.04S 144.13 E
Castle Peak 46 Hd 44.03N 114.32W
Castlepoint 62 Gd 40.55S 176.13 E
Castlepollard 9 Fh 53.41N 7.17W
Castlerea/An Caisleán Riabhach 9 Eh 53.46N 8.29W
Castlereagh Bay 59 Hb 12.10S 135.10 E
Castle Rock Butte 45 Ed 45.00N 103.27W
Castle Rock Lake 45 Le 43.56N 89.58W
Častoozerje 17 Mi 55.34N 67.53 E
Castor 46 Ja 52.13N 111.53W
Castres 11 Ik 43.36N 2.15 E
Castricum 12 Gb 52.33N 4.42 E
Castries 39 Mh 14.01N 61.00W
Castrignano del Capo 14 Mk 39.50N 18.20 E
Castro [Braz.] 56 Jb 24.47S 50.03W
Castro [Chile] 56 Ff 42.29S 73.46W
Castro Alves 54 Kf 12.45S 39.26W
Castrocaro Terme e Terra del Sole 14 Ff 44.10N 11.57 E
Castro Daire 13 Ed 40.54N 7.56W
Castro del Rio 13 Hg 37.41N 4.28W
Castrojeriz 13 Hb 42.17N 4.08W
Castropol 13 Ea 43.32N 7.02W
Castrop-Rauxel 12 Jc 51.33N 7.19 E
Castro Urdiales 13 Ia 43.23N 3.13W
Castro Verde 13 Dg 37.42N 8.05W
Castrovillari 14 Kk 39.49N 16.12 E
Castrovirreyna 54 Cf 13.16S 75.19W
Castuera 13 Gf 38.43N 5.33W
Častyje 17 Gh 57.19N 54.59 E
Casupá 55 El 34.09S 55.38W
Caswell Sound 62 Bf 45.00S 167.10 E
Çat 24 Ic 39.40N 41.02 E
Čata 10 Oi 47.58N 18.40 E
Catacamas 49 Ef 14.54N 85.56W
Catahoula Lake 45 Jk 31.30N 92.06W
Çatak 24 Jc 38.01N 43.07 E
Çatak 24 Jd 37.53N 42.39 E
Catalan Coastal Range (EN) =Cadena Costero Catalana /Serralada Litoral Catalana 5 Gg 41.35N 1.40 E
Catalan Coastal Range (EN) =Serralada Litoral Catalana/Cadena Costero Catalana 5 Gg 41.35N 1.40 E
Catalão 54 Ig 18.10S 47.57W
Çatal Balkan 15 Jg 42.46N 27.00 E
Çatalca 15 Lh 41.09N 28.27 E
Çatal Dağ 15 Lj 39.51N 28.20 E
Catalina 56 Gc 25.13S 69.43W
Catalina, Isla- 49 Md 18.21N 69.00W
Catalina, Punta- 56 Gh 52.32S 68.47W
Catalonia (EN)=Cataluña/ Catalunya 5 Gg 42.00N 2.00 E
Catalonia (EN)=Cataluña/ Catalunya 13 Nc 42.00N 2.00 E
Catalonia (EN)=Catalunya/ Cataluña 5 Gg 42.00N 2.00 E
Catalonia (EN)=Catalunya/ Cataluña 13 Nc 42.00N 2.00 E
Cataluña/Catalunya= Catalonia (EN) 5 Gg 42.00N 2.00 E
Cataluña/Catalunya= Catalonia (EN) 13 Nc 42.00N 2.00 E
Catalunya/Cataluña= Catalonia (EN) 13 Nc 42.00N 2.00 E
Catalunya/Cataluña= Catalonia (EN) 5 Gg 42.00N 2.00 E
Çatalzeytin 24 Fb 41.57N 34.13 E
Catamarca 53 Jh 28.30S 65.45W
Catamarca [2] 56 Gc 27.00S 67.00W
Catanduanes 21 Oh 13.45N 124.15 E
Catanduva 56 Kb 21.08S 48.58W
Catanduvas 55 Fg 25.12S 53.08W
Catania 6 Hh 37.30N 15.06 E
Catania, Golfo di- 14 Jm 37.25N 15.10 E
Catania, Piana di- 14 Im 37.25N 14.50 E
Catanzaro 6 Hh 38.54N 16.35 E
Catarman 26 Hd 12.30N 124.38 E
Catastrophe, Cape- 57 Eh 35.00S 136.00 E
Catatumbo, Rio- 49 Li 9.21N 71.45W
Catbalogan 26 Hd 11.46N 124.53 E
Catemaco, Lago- 48 Lh 18.25N 95.05W
Catete 36 Bd 9.07S 13.41 E
Cathair na Mart/Westport 9 Dh 53.48N 9.32W
Cathair Saidhbhín/ Cahersiveen 9 Cj 51.57N 10.13W
Cathcart 37 Df 32.18S 27.09 E
Catherine, Mount- 46 Ig 39.05N 112.04W
Catholic Island 51n Bb 12.40N 61.24W
Catio 34 Bc 11.17N 15.15W
Cat Island 18 Lg 24.30N 75.30W
Čatkal 18 Hd 41.36N 70.05 E
Čatkalski Hrebet 19 Hg 41.30N 70.50 E
Cat Lake 42 If 51.40N 91.52W
Catoche, Cabo- 38 Kg 21.36N 87.07W
Cato Island 57 Gg 23.15S 155.35 E
Catolé do Rocha 54 Ke 6.21S 37.45W
Catoute 13 Fb 42.45N 6.20W
Catria 14 Gg 43.28N 12.42 E
Catriló 56 He 36.26S 63.24W
Catrimani, Rio- 54 Fc 0.28N 61.44W
Catskill Mountains 44 Jd 42.10N 74.30W
Cattenom 12 Ie 49.25N 6.15 E
Cattolica 14 Gg 43.58N 12.44 E
Catu 54 Kf 12.21S 38.23W
Catuane 37 Ee 26.48S 32.14 E
Catumbela 36 Be 12.27S 13.29 E
Catur 37 Fb 13.45S 35.37 E
Catwick, Iles- 25 Lg 10.00N 109.00 E
Catwright 39 Nd 53.50N 56.45W
Catyrkël, Ozero- 18 Jd 40.35N 75.20 E
Čatyrtaš 18 Kd 40.52N 76.23 E
Cauca [2] 54 Cc 2.30N 77.00W
Cauca, Rio- 52 Ie 8.54N 74.28W
Caucasia 54 Cb 7.59N 75.13W
Caucasus (EN)=Kavkaz, Bolšoj- 5 Kg 42.30N 45.00 E
Caucete 56 Gd 31.38S 68.16W
Caudebec-en-Caux 12 Ce 49.32N 0.44 E
Caudete 13 Lf 38.42N 0.59W
Caudry 12 Fd 50.08N 3.25 E
Caulonia 14 Kl 38.23N 16.24 E
Caumont-l'Eventé 12 Be 49.05N 0.48W
Caungula 31 Ii 8.26S 18.37 E
Čaunskaja Guba 20 Lc 69.30N 170.00 E
Caupolican 54 Ef 13.30S 68.30W
Cauquenes 56 Fe 35.58S 72.21W
Caura, Rio- 52 Je 7.38N 64.53W
Causapscal 44 Na 48.22N 67.14W
Caussade 11 Hj 44.10N 1.32 E
Čausy 16 Gc 53.50N 30.59 E
Cauterets 11 Fl 42.53N 0.07W
Cauto, Rio- 49 Ic 20.33N 77.15W
Cauvery 21 Jh 11.09N 78.52 E
Caux, Pays de- 11 Ge 49.40N 0.40 E
Cávado 13 Dc 41.32N 8.48W
Cavaillon 11 Lk 43.50N 5.02 E
Cavalcante 55 Ia 13.48S 47.30W
Cavalese 14 Fd 46.17N 11.27 E
Cavalli Islands 62 Ea 35.00S 173.55 E
Cavallo, Isola- 11a Bb 41.22N 9.16 E
Cavallo Pass 45 Hl 28.25N 96.26W
Cavally 30 Gh 4.22N 7.32W
Cavan/An Cabhán 9 Fg 54.00N 7.21W
Cavan/An Cabhán [2] 9 Fh 53.55N 7.30W
Cavarzere 14 Ge 45.08N 12.05 E
Çavdarhisar 15 Mj 39.12N 29.37 E
Çavdir 15 Ml 37.09N 29.42 E
Caviana, Ilha- 54 Hc 0.10N 50.05W
Cavili 26 He 9.17N 120.50 E
Cavour, Canale- 14 Be 45.11N 7.54 E
Cavtat 14 Mh 42.35N 18.13 E
Caxambu 55 Je 21.59S 44.56W
Caxias 53 Lf 4.50S 43.21W
Caxias do Sul 53 Kh 29.10S 51.11W
Caxito 36 Bd 8.34S 13.40 E
Çay 24 Dc 38.35N 31.02 E
Cayambe 54 Cc 0.05N 78.08W
Cayambe, Volcán- 52 Ie 0.02N 77.59W
Cayastá 55 Bj 31.12S 60.10W
Cayce 44 Gi 33.59N 81.04W
Çaycuma 24 Eb 41.25N 32.05 E
Çayeli 24 Ib 41.05N 40.44 E
Cayenne 53 Ke 4.56N 52.20W
Cayeux-Sur-Mer 12 Dd 50.11N 1.29 E
Cayey 49 Nd 18.07N 66.10W
Çayırlı 24 Ic 39.48N 40.01 E
Çaykara 24 Ib 40.45N 40.19 E
Caylus 11 Hj 44.14N 1.47 E
Cayman Brac 47 Ie 19.43N 79.49W
Cayman Islands [5] 39 Kh 19.30N 80.30W
Cayman Islands 38 Kh 19.30N 80.30W
Cayman Ridge (EN) 47 He 19.30N 80.30W
Cayman Trench (EN) 3 Bh 19.00N 80.00W
Cayo 49 Ce 17.10N 88.50W
Cayon 51c Ab 17.21N 62.43W
Cayones, Cayos- 49 Fe 16.05N 83.12W
Cay Sal Bank 47 Hd 23.45N 80.00W
Cayuga Lake 44 Id 42.45N 76.45W
Cazalla de la Sierra 13 Gg 37.56N 5.45W
Caza Pava 55 Di 28.17S 56.07W
Cazaux, Étang de- 11 Ej 44.29N 1.10W
Cazombo 31 Jj 11.54S 22.53 E
Cazorla 13 Jg 37.55N 3.00W
Cazorla, Sierra de- 13 Jf 37.55N 2.55W
Cea 13 Gb 42.00N 5.36W
Ceahlău 15 Ib 47.03N 25.58 E
Ceanannas Mór/Kells 9 Gh 53.44N 6.53W
Ceanna Cailliġhe/Hags Head 9 Di 52.57N 9.28W
Ceann Acla/Achill Head 9 Ch 53.59N 10.13W
Ceann an Chairn/Carnsore Point 9 Gi 52.10N 6.22W
Ceann Chill Mhantáin/ Wicklow Head 9 Hi 52.58N 6.00W
Ceann Gólaim/Slyne Head 9 Ch 53.24N 10.13W
Ceann Iorrais/Erris Head 5 Fe 54.19N 10.00W
Ceann Léime/Loop Head 9 Di 52.34N 9.56W
Ceann Ros Eoghain/Rossan Point 9 Eg 54.42N 8.48W
Ceann Sléibhe/Slea Head 9 Ci 52.06N 10.27W
Ceann Toirc/Kanturk 9 Ei 52.10N 8.55W
Ceará [2] 54 Kd 5.00S 39.30W
Ceará-Mirim 54 Ke 5.38S 35.26W
Ceatharlach/Carlow [2] 9 Gi 52.50N 7.00W
Ceatharlach/Carlow 9 Gi 52.50N 6.55W
Cébaco, Isla- 49 Gj 7.32N 81.09W
Ceballos 48 Gd 26.32N 104.09W
Čebarkul 17 Ji 54.58N 60.25 E
Čeboksary 6 Kd 56.09N 47.15 E
Cebollati 55 Fk 33.16S 53.47W
Cebollati, Rio- 55 Fk 33.09S 53.38W
Cebollera, Sierra- 13 Jc 42.00N 2.40W
Ceboruco, Volcán- 48 Gg 21.09N 104.30W
Cebreros 13 Hd 40.27N 4.28W
Cebrikovo 15 Nb 47.09N 30.02 E
Cebu 21 Oh 10.20N 123.45 E
Cebu 22 Oh 10.18N 123.54 E
Cece 10 Oj 46.46N 18.39 E
Čečen, Ostrov- 16 Og 44.00N 47.45 E
Čečeno-Ingušskaja ASSR [3] 19 Eg 43.15N 45.30 E
Cecen-Ula 27 Gb 48.45N 95.55 E
Cecerleg 22 Me 47.30N 101.27 E
Čečersk 16 Gc 52.56N 30.58 E
Čechy=Bohemia (EN) 5 Hf 50.00N 14.30 E
Čechy=Bohemia (EN) 10 Kf 50.00N 14.30 E
Cecina 14 Eg 43.18N 10.29 E
Cecina 14 Eg 43.10N 10.31 E
Čečuisk 20 Fe 58.07N 108.32 E
Cedar City 39 Hf 37.41N 113.04W
Cedar Creek 45 Fc 46.07N 101.18W
Cedar Creek Reservoir 45 Hj 32.20N 96.10W
Cedar Falls 43 Ic 42.32N 92.27W
Cedar Grove 51d Bb 17.10N 61.49W
Cedar Lake 42 Hf 53.25N 100.00W
Cedar Rapids 39 Je 41.59N 91.40W
Cedar River [Nb.-U.S.] 45 Hf 41.22N 97.57W
Cedar River [U.S.] 43 Ic 41.17N 91.20W
Cedartown 44 Eh 34.01N 85.15W
Cedar-Tree Point 51d Ba 17.42N 61.53W
Cedeira 13 Da 43.39N 8.03W
Cedral 48 If 23.48N 100.44W
Cedrino 14 Dj 40.23N 9.44 E
Cedro 54 Ke 6.36S 39.03W
Cedrón 13 Ie 39.48N 3.33W
Cedros, Isla- [Mex.] 47 Ac 28.12N 115.15W
Cedros, Isla [Mex.] =Cedros Island (EN) 38 Hg 28.10N 115.15W
Cedros Island (EN)=Cedros, Isla [Mex.] 38 Hg 28.10N 115.15W
Cedros Trench (EN) 47 Ac 27.45N 115.45W
Ceduna 59 Gf 32.07S 133.40 E
Cedynia 10 Kd 52.50N 14.14 E
Cefalù 14 Il 38.02N 14.01 E
Cega 13 Hc 41.33N 4.46W
Čegdomyn 22 Pd 51.07N 133.05 E
Čegem 16 Mh 43.36N 43.48 E
Cegléd 10 Pi 47.10N 19.48 E
Ceglie Messapico 14 Lj 40.39N 17.31 E
Cehegin 13 Kf 38.06N 1.48W
Čehotina 15 Bf 43.31N 18.45 E
Čehov [R.S.F.S.R.] 7 Ii 55.11N 37.29 E
Čehov [R.S.F.S.R.] 20 Jg 47.24N 142.05 E
Ceica 15 Fc 46.51N 22.11 E
Çekerek 24 Fb 40.34N 35.46 E
Çekerek 24 Fb 40.04N 35.31 E
Čekmaguš 17 Gi 55.10N 54.40 E
Celano 14 Hh 42.05N 13.33 E
Celaya 47 Dd 20.31N 100.37W
Čelbas 16 Kf 46.06N 38.59 E
Célé 11 Hj 44.28N 1.38 E
Celebes/Sulawesi 21 Oj 2.00S 121.10 E
Celebes Basin (EN) 26 Hf 4.00N 122.00 E
Celebes Sea (EN)= Sulawesi, Laut- 21 Oi 3.00N 122.00 E
Čeleken 19 Fh 39.27N 53.10 E
Čeleken, Poluostrov- 16 Rj 39.25N 53.35 E
Celendin 54 Ce 6.52S 78.09W
Celerain, Punta- 48 Pg 20.16N 86.59W
Celeste 55 Dj 31.18S 57.04W
Celestún 48 Ng 20.52N 90.24W
Celinograd 22 Jd 51.10N 71.30 E
Celinogradskaja Oblast [3] 19 Gh 51.00N 70.00 E
Čeljabinsk 22 Id 55.10N 61.24 E
Čeljabinskaja Oblast [3] 19 Ge 54.00N 61.00 E
Celje 14 Jd 46.14N 15.16 E
Celjuskin, Mys- 21 Mb 77.45N 104.20 E
Čelkar 19 Ff 47.50N 59.29 E
Celldömölk 10 Ni 47.15N 17.09 E
Celle 10 Gd 52.37N 10.05 E
Celles 12 Fd 50.43N 3.27 E
Celles, Houyet- 12 Hd 50.19N 5.01 E
Cellina 14 Ge 46.02N 12.47 E
Celone 14 Ji 41.36N 15.41 E
Celorico da Beira 13 Ed 40.38N 7.23W
Celtic Sea 5 Fe 51.00N 7.00W
Celtic Sea (EN)=An Mhuir Cheilteach 5 Fe 51.00N 7.00W
Cerhaes Head 9 Ii 52.07N 4.44W
Čemal 20 Df 51.25N 86.05 E
Čemdalsk 20 Fe 59.45N 103.18 E
Cemernica 14 Lf 44.30N 17.15 E
Cemerno 15 Df 43.36N 20.26 E
Çemişkezek 24 Hc 39.04N 38.55 E
Cenajo, Embalse de- 13 Kf 38.20N 1.55W
Cenderawasih, Teluk- 26 Kg 2.25S 135.10 E
Cengel 27 Eb 48.56N 89.10 E
Çengel Geçidi 24 Kc 39.45N 44.02 E
Ceno 14 Ef 44.41N 10.05 E
Centenary 37 Ec 16.44S 31.07 E
Centennial 46 Lf 41.51N 106.07W
Centennial Lake 44 Ic 45.15N 77.00W
Centennial Mountains 46 Jd 44.35N 111.55W
Center 45 Ik 31.48N 94.11W
Center Hill Lake 44 Eg 36.00N 85.45W
Centerville 45 Jf 40.43N 92.52W
Centinela, Farallón- 50 Cg 10.49N 66.05W
Centinela, Picacho del- 47 Dc 29.07N 102.27W
Cento 14 Ff 44.43N 11.17 E
Centrafrique=Central African Republic (EN) [1] 31 Jh 7.00N 21.00 E
Central [Bots.] [3] 37 Dd 21.30S 26.00 E
Central [Ghana] [3] 34 Ed 5.30N 1.00W
Central [Kenya] [3] 36 Gc 0.45S 37.00 E
Central [Mwi.] [3] 36 Fe 13.30S 34.00 E
Central [Par.] [3] 55 Dg 25.30S 57.30W
Central [Scot.-U.K.] [3] 9 Ie 56.15N 4.10W
Central [Ug.] [3] 36 Fb 0.10N 32.05 E
Central [Zam.] [3] 36 Ee 15.00S 29.00 E
Central, Chaco- 52 Kh 25.00S 59.45W
Central, Cordillera- [Dom.Rep.] 47 Je 18.45N 70.30W
Central, Cordillera- [P.R.] 49 Nd 18.10N 66.35W
Central, Massif- 5 Gf 45.00N 3.10 E
Central, Meseta- 38 Ig 23.00N 103.00W
Central African Republic (EN)=Centrafrique [1] 31 Jh 7.00N 21.00 E
Central Auckland [2] 62 Fb 36.45S 174.40 E
Central Brāhui Range 25 Dc 29.20N 66.55 E
Central City 45 Hf 41.07N 98.00W
Centralia [Il.-U.S.] 45 Lg 38.31N 89.08W
Centralia [Wa.-U.S.] 43 Cb 46.43N 122.58W
Central Lowland 38 Ke 40.20N 90.00W
Central Makrān Range 21 Ig 26.40N 64.30 E
Centralno Tungusskoje Plato 20 Fd 61.15N 102.00 E
Centralny-Kospašski 17 Hg 59.03N 57.50 E
Central Pacific Basin (EN) 3 Ki 5.00N 175.00W
Central Plateau 64e Bb 0.32S 166.56 E
Central Point 46 De 42.23N 122.57W
Central Range 57 Fe 5.00S 142.30 E
Central Russian Uplands (EN)=Srednerusskaja Vozvyšennost 5 Je 52.00N 38.00 E
Central Siberian Uplands (EN)=Srednesibirskoje Ploskogorje 21 Mc 65.00N 105.00 E
Central Urals (EN)=Sredni Ural 5 Ld 58.00N 59.00 E
Centre [Togo] [3] 34 Fd 9.15N 1.00 E
Centre [U.V.] [3] 34 Ec 12.00N 1.00W
Centre, Canal du- 11 Jh 46.28N 3.59 E
Centre-Est [3] 34 Ec 11.30N 0.20W
Centre-Nord [3] 34 Ec 13.20N 0.55W
Centre-Ouest [3] 34 Ec 12.00N 2.20W
Centre-Sud [3] 34 He 3.30N 11.50 E
Centro, Cayo- 48 Ph 18.35N 87.20W
Centuripe 14 Im 37.37N 14.44 E
Čepca 19 Fd 58.35N 50.05 E
Čepelare 15 Hh 41.44N 24.41 E
Cephalonia (EN)= Kefallinía 5 Ih 38.15N 20.35 E
Čepin 14 Me 45.32N 18.34 E
Ceplenița 15 Jb 47.23N 26.58 E
Cepu 26 Fh 7.09S 111.35 E
Cer 15 Ce 44.37N 19.28 E
Ceram Sea (EN)=Seram, Laut- 57 De 2.30S 128.00 E
Cerbatana, Serranía de la- 54 Eb 6.50N 66.15W
Cerbicales, Iles- 11a Bb 41.33N 9.22 E
Cercal 13 Dg 37.47N 8.42W
Čerchov 10 Rg 49.10N 21.05 E
Čerdakly 7 Li 54.23N 48.51 E
Čerdyn 17 Hf 60.25N 56.29 E
Cère 11 Hj 44.55N 1.52 E
Čereha 7 Gh 57.47N 28.22 E
Čeremhovo 22 Md 53.09N 103.05 E
Čerepanovo 20 Df 54.13N 83.32 E
Čerepovec 6 Jd 59.08N 37.54 E
Ceres [Arg.] 56 Hc 29.53S 61.57W
Ceres [Braz.] 54 Ig 15.17S 49.35W
Ceres [S.Afr.] 37 Bf 33.21S 19.18 E
Céret 11 Il 42.29N 2.45 E
Ceretè 54 Cb 8.53N 75.47W
Cerf Island 30 Mi 9.31S 51.01 E
Cerfontaine 12 Gd 50.10N 4.25 E
Cergy 12 Ee 49.02N 2.04 E
Cerignola 14 Ji 41.16N 15.54 E
Čerikov 16 Gc 53.35N 31.25 E
Cérilly 11 Ih 46.37N 2.50 E
Čerkasskaja Oblast [3] 19 Df 49.15N 31.15 E
Čerkassy 19 Df 49.26N 32.04 E
Çerkeş 24 Eb 40.50N 32.54 E
Čerkessk 19 Eg 44.14N 42.04 E
Çerkezköy 15 Kh 41.17N 28.00 E
Čerlak 19 He 54.09N 74.58 E
Čerlakski 19 He 53.47N 74.31 E
Čermasàn 17 Gi 55.10N 55.20 E
Cermei 15 Ec 46.33N 21.51 E
Çermenika 15 Dh 41.03N 20.20 E
Čermoz 17 Hg 58.47N 56.10 E
Cerna [Rom.] 15 Ge 44.37N 23.57 E
Cerna [Rom.] 15 Fd 44.42N 22.25 E
Cerna [Rom.] 15 Fe 45.53N 22.58 E
Černaja 17 Hb 68.35N 56.31 E
Černaja [R.S.F.S.R.] 17 Hb 68.35N 56.30 E
Černaja [Ukr.-U.S.S.R.] 15 Mb 47.39N 29.11 E
Cerna Skala, Prohod- 15 Fg 42.02N 22.47 E
Černatica 15 Hh 41.53N 24.33 E
Černavčicy 10 Td 52.11N 23.47 E
Cernavoda 15 Le 44.22N 28.01 E
Cernay 11 Ng 47.49N 7.10 E
Cernay-en-Dormois 12 Ge 49.13N 4.46 E
Černevo 8 Mf 58.35N 28.23 E
Černigov 6 Je 51.30N 31.18 E
Černigovskaja Oblast [3] 19 De 51.20N 32.00 E
Černi Lom 15 If 43.33N 25.57 E
Černi vrăh 15 Gg 42.35N 23.15 E
Černjahovsk 19 Ce 54.38N 21.48 E
Černjanka 16 Jd 50.55N 37.49 E
Černobyl 19 De 51.17N 30.13 E
Černogorsk 20 Ef 53.45N 91.18 E
Černoje More=Black Sea (EN) 5 Jg 43.00N 35.00 E
Černo More=Black Sea (EN) 5 Jg 43.00N 35.00 E
Černomorskoje 16 Hg 45.31N 32.42 E
Černovcy 6 If 48.18N 25.56 E
Černovickaja Oblast [3] 19 Cf 48.20N 26.10 E
Černuška 19 Fd 56.31N 56.03 E
Černy Jar 16 Oe 48.03N 46.05 E
Černyje Zemli 16 Nf 45.55N 46.00 E
Černyševa, Grjada- 17 Ic 66.20N 59.45 E
Černyševa, Zaliv- 18 Bb 45.50N 59.10 E
Černyševsk 20 Gf 52.35N 117.02 E
Černyševski 20 Gd 62.58N 112.15 E
Černyškovski 16 Me 48.27N 42.14 E
Cérou 11 Hj 44.08N 1.52 E
Cerralvo 48 Jd 26.06N 99.37W
Cerralvo, Isla- 47 Cd 24.15N 109.55W
Cerredo, Torre de- 13 Ha 43.13N 4.50W
Cerriku 15 Ch 41.02N 19.57 E
Cerrito [Col.] 54 Db 6.51N 72.42W
Cerrito [Par.] 55 Dh 27.19S 57.40W
Cerritos 47 Dd 22.26N 100.17W
Cerro Azul 48 Kg 21.12N 97.44W
Cerro Azul 56 Kb 24.50S 49.15W
Cerro Chato 55 Ek 33.06S 55.08W
Cerro Colorado 55 Ek 33.52S 55.33W
Cerro de las Mesas 48 Kh 18.47N 96.05W
Cerro de Pasco 53 Ig 10.41S 76.16W
Cêrro Grande 55 Gj 30.36S 51.45W
Cerro Largo 56 Jc 28.09S 54.45W
Cerro Largo [2] 55 Ek 32.20S 54.20W
Cerron, Cerro- 49 Lh 10.19N 70.39W
Cerro San Valentín 52 Ij 46.36S 73.20W
Cerros Colorados, Embalse- 56 Ge 38.35S 68.40W
Cerro Vera 55 Dk 33.11S 57.28W
Cerrudo Cué 55 Dh 27.34S 57.57W
Čerski 22 Sc 68.45N 161.45 E
Čerskogo, Hrebet- [R.S.F.S.R.] 20 Gf 52.00N 114.00 E
Čerskogo, Hrebet- [R.S.F.S.R.]=Cherski Mountains (EN) 21 Qc 65.00N 145.00 E

Index Symbols

[1] Independent Nation
[2] State, Region
[3] District, County
[4] Municipality
[5] Colony, Dependency
Continent
Physical Region
Historical or Cultural Region
Mount, Mountain
Volcano
Hill
Mountains, Mountain Range
Hills, Escarpment
Plateau, Upland
Pass, Gap
Plain, Lowland
Delta
Salt Flat
Valley, Canyon
Crater, Cave
Karst Features
Depression
Polder
Desert, Dunes
Forest, Woods
Heath, Steppe
Oasis
Cape, Point
Coast, Beach
Cliff
Peninsula
Isthmus
Sandbank
Island
Atoll
Rock, Reef
Islands, Archipelago
Rocks, Reefs
Coral Reef
Well, Spring
Geyser
River, Stream
Waterfall Rapids
River Mouth, Estuary
Lake
Salt Lake
Intermittent Lake
Reservoir
Swamp, Pond
Canal
Glacier
Ice Shelf, Pack Ice
Ocean
Sea
Gulf, Bay
Strait, Fjord
Lagoon
Bank
Seamount
Tablemount
Ridge
Shelf
Basin
Escarpment, Sea Scarp
Fracture
Trench, Abyss
National Park, Reserve
Point of Interest
Recreation Site
Cave, Cavern
Historic Site
Ruins
Wall, Walls
Church, Abbey
Temple
Scientific Station
Airport
Port
Lighthouse
Mine
Tunnel
Dam, Bridge

Certaldo 14 Fg 43.33N 11.02 E
Čertkovo 16 Le 49.20N 40.12 E
Cervaro 14 Ji 41.30N 15.52 E
Cervati 14 Jj 40.17N 15.29 E
Červeh 15 Jf 43.37N 26.02 E
Červen 16 Fc 53.43N 28.29 E
Červen brjag 15 Hf 43.16N 24.06 E
Cervera 13 Nc 41.40N 1.17 E
Cervera del Rio Alhama 13 Kb 42.01N 1.57W
Cervera de Pisuerga 13 Hb 42.52N 4.30W
Cerveteri 14 Gh 42.00N 12.06 E
Cervia 14 Gf 44.15N 12.22 E
Cervin/Cervino 14 Be 45.58N 7.39 E
Cervino/Cervin 14 Be 45.58N 7.39 E
Cervione 11a Ba 42.20N 9.29 E
Červonoarmejsk 10 Vf 50.03N 25.18 E
Červonoarmejskoje 15 Ld 45.50N 28.38 E
Červonograd 19 Ce 50.24N 24.12 E
Cesano 14 Hg 43.45N 13.10 E
Cesar [2] 54 Db 9.50N 73.30W
César, Río- 49 Ki 9.00N 73.58W
Cesena 14 Gf 44.08N 12.15 E
Cesenatico 14 Gf 44.12N 12.24 E
Cēsis/Cesis 19 Cd 57.18N 25.18 E
Cesis/Cēsis 19 Cd 57.18N 25.18 E
Česká Lipa 10 Kf 50.42N 14.32 E
Česká Třebová 10 Mg 49.54N 16.27 E
České Budějovice 10 Kh 48.58N 14.29 E
České středohoří 10 Jf 50.35N 14.00 E
Ceské země [2] 10 Kg 49.45N 15.00 E
Českomoravská Vrchovina = Moravian Upland (EN) 5 Hf 49.20N 15.30 E
Československá Socialistická Republika (ČSSR) [1] 6 Hf 49.30N 17.00 E
Československo = Czechoslovakia (EN) [1] 6 Hf 49.30N 17.00 E
Český Krumlov 10 Kh 48.49N 14.19 E
Český Les=Bohemian Forest (EN) 10 Ig 49.50N 12.30 E
Cesma 14 Kf 45.35N 16.29 E
Česma 17 Jj 53.50N 60.40 E
Çeşme 24 Bc 38.18N 26.19 E
Çeşme Yarimadasi 15 Jk 38.30N 26.30 E
Češskaja Guba=Chesha Bay (EN) 5 Kb 67.20N 46.30 E
Cessnock 59 Kf 32.50S 151.21 E
Cestos 30 Gh 5.27N 9.35W
Cesvaine/Cesvajne 8 Lh 56.55N 26.20 E
Cesvajne/Cesvaine 8 Lh 56.55N 26.20 E
Cetate 15 Ge 44.06N 23.03 E
Cetina 14 Kg 43.27N 16.42 E
Cetinje 15 Bg 42.24N 18.55 E
Çetinkaya 24 Gc 39.15N 37.38 E
Cetraro 14 Jk 39.31N 15.56 E
Cetynia 10 Sd 52.33N 22.26 E
Ceuta [5] 31 Ge 35.53N 5.19W
Ceva-i-Ra (Conway Reef) 57 Ig 21.45S 174.35 E
Cevedale/Zufallspitze 14 Ed 46.27N 10.37 E
Cévennes 5 Gg 44.40N 4.00 E
Ceyhan 23 Eb 36.45N 35.42 E
Ceyhan 23 Eb 37.04N 35.47 E
Ceylanpınar 24 Id 36.51N 40.02 E
Ceylon→Srī Lanka [1] 22 Ki 7.40N 80.50 E
Cézallier 11 Ii 45.20N 3.00 E
Cèze 11 Kj 44.06N 4.42 E
Chaalis, Abbaye de- 12 Ee 49.10N 2.40 E
Cha-am 25 Jf 12.48N 99.58 E
Chabanais 11 Gi 45.52N 0.43 E
Chabjuwardoo Bay 59 Cd 22.55S 113.50 E
Chablais 11 Mh 46.20N 6.30 E
Chāboksar 24 Nd 36.58N 50.34 E
Chabówka 10 Pg 49.34N 19.58 E
Chacabuco 56 Hd 34.38S 60.29W
Chachan, Nevado- 54 Dg 16.12S 71.33W
Chachapoyas 54 Ce 6.13S 77.51W
Chachoengsao 25 Kf 13.41N 101.03 E
Chaco [2] 56 Hc 26.00S 60.30W
Chaco [3] 55 Bd 20.00S 60.30W
Chaco, Gran- 52 Jh 23.00S 60.00W
Chaco Mesa 45 Ci 35.50N 107.35W
Chaco River 45 Bh 36.46N 108.69W
Chad (EN)=Tchad [1] 31 Ig 15.00N 19.00 E
Chad, Lake- (EN)=Tchad, Lac- 30 Ig 13.20N 14.00 E
Chādegān 24 Nf 32.46N 50.38 E
Chadileuvú, Río- 56 Ee 38.49S 64.57W
Chadiza 36 Fe 14.04S 32.26 E
Chadron 43 Gc 42.50N 103.02W
Chaeryŏng 28 He 38.24N 125.37 E
Chafarinas, Islas- 13 Ji 35.11N 2.26W
Chāgai Hills 21 Ig 29.30N 64.15 E
Chagang-Do [2] 28 Ie 40.50N 126.30 E
Chaghcharān 22 If 34.31N 65.15 E
Chagny 11 Kh 46.55N 4.45 E
Chagos Archipelago 21 Jj 6.00S 72.00 E
Chagos-Laccadive Plateau (EN) 3 Gi 3.00N 73.00 E
Chagu, Serra do- 55 Fg 25.10S 52.40W
Chaguaramas 50 Ch 9.20N 66.16W
Chahār Borjak 23 Jc 30.17N 62.03 E
Chahār Mahāl-e Bakhtīārī [3] 23 Hc 32.00N 50.00 E
Chahbounia 13 Oi 35.33N 2.36 E
Ch'aho 28 Jd 40.12N 128.38 E
Chai Badan 25 Ke 15.05N 101.04 E
Chaibāsa 25 Hd 22.34N 85.49 E
Chaigoubu → Huai'an 28 Cd 40.40N 114.25 E
Chai He 28 Gc 42.20N 123.51 E
Chaillu, Massif du- 30 Ii 2.32S 11.10 E
Chainat 25 Ke 15.10N 100.10 E
Chaitén 56 Ff 42.55S 72.43W
Chaiyaphum 25 Ke 16.09N 102.02 E
Chajul 49 Bf 15.30N 91.02W
Chakari 37 Dc 18.09S 29.52 E
Chak Chak 35 Dd 8.40N 26.54 E
Chake Chake 31 Ki 5.15S 39.46 E
Chakhānsūr 23 Jc 31.10N 62.04 E
Chala 54 Dg 15.52S 74.16W
Chalais 11 Gi 45.17N 0.02 E
Chalaltenango 49 Cf 14.03N 88.56W
Chalan Kanoa 64b Ba 15.08N 145.43 E
Chālās 22 Gf 37.16N 49.36 E
Chalbi Desert 30 Kh 3.00N 37.20 E
Chalchuapa 49 Cg 13.59N 89.41W
Chalcidice (EN)= Khalkidhiki 5 Ig 40.25N 23.25 E
Chālesbān 24 Ne 35.18N 50.03 E
Chaleur Bay 42 Kg 47.50N 65.30W
Chalhuanca 54 Df 14.17S 73.15W
Chaling 27 Jf 26.47N 113.32 E
Chalky Inlet 62 Bg 46.05S 166.30 E
Challans 11 Eh 46.51N 1.53W
Challapata 54 Eg 18.54S 66.47W
Challis 46 Hd 44.30N 114.14W
Chalmette 45 Ll 29.56N 89.58W
Châlons-sur-Marne 11 Kf 48.57N 4.22 E
Chalon-sur-Saône 11 Kh 46.47N 4.51 E
Chaltubo 16 Mh 42.19N 42.34 E
Chālūs 23 Hb 36.38N 51.26 E
Châlus 11 Gi 45.39N 0.59 E
Cham 10 Ig 49.13N 12.40 E
Chama 36 Fe 11.12S 33.10 E
Chama, Rio- 45 Ch 36.03N 106.05W
Chama, Río- 49 Li 9.03N 71.37W
Chaman 25 Db 30.55N 66.27 E
Chaman Bīd 24 Qd 37.25N 56.38 E
Chamba [India] 25 Fb 32.34N 76.08 E
Chamba [Tan.] 36 Ge 11.35S 36.58 E
Chambal 21 Jg 26.29N 79.15 E
Chambaran, Plateau de- 11 Li 45.10N 5.20 E
Chambas 49 Hb 22.12N 78.55W
Chamberlain 45 Ge 43.49N 99.20W
Chamberlain Lake 44 Mb 46.17N 69.20W
Chamberlain River 59 Fc 15.35S 127.51 E
Chambersburg 44 If 39.57N 77.40W
Chambéry 11 Li 45.34N 5.56 E
Chambeshi 30 Jj 11.53S 29.48 E
Chambley-Bussières 12 He 49.03N 5.54 E
Chambly 12 Ee 49.10N 2.15 E
Chambois 12 Cf 48.48N 0.07 E
Chambon, Lac de- 11 Ih 45.35N 2.55 E
Chambord 11 Hg 47.37N 1.31 E
Chamchamal 24 Ke 35.32N 44.50 E
Chame, Punta- 49 Hi 8.39N 79.42W
Chamela 48 Gh 19.32N 105.05W
Chamela, Bahía- 48 Gh 19.30N 105.10W
Chamelecón, Río- 49 Df 15.51N 87.49W
Chamical 56 Gd 30.21S 66.19W
Chamiss Bay 46 Ba 50.07N 127.22W
Chamoli 25 Fb 30.24N 79.21 E
Chamonix-Mont-Blanc 11 Mi 45.55N 6.52 E
Chamouchouane, Rivière- 44 Ka 48.40N 72.20W
Champagne 5 Gf 49.00N 4.30 E
Champagne 11 Kf 49.00N 4.30 E
Champagne Berrichonne 11 Hh 47.00N 2.00 E
Champagne Humide 11 Kf 48.20N 4.30 E
Champagne Pouilleuse 11 Kf 48.40N 4.20 E
Champagnole 11 Lh 46.45N 5.55 E
Champaign 43 Jc 40.07N 88.14W
Champaqui, Cerro- 52 Ji 31.59S 64.56W
Champasak 25 Lf 14.53N 105.52 E
Champaubert 12 Ff 48.53N 3.47 E
Champdoré, Lac- 42 Ke 55.55N 65.45W
Champeigne 11 Gg 47.15N 0.50 E
Champerico 49 Bf 14.18N 91.55W
Champlain, Lake- 43 Mc 44.45N 73.15W
Champlitte-et-le-Prélot 11 Lg 47.37N 5.31 E
Champotón 47 Fe 19.21N 90.43W
Champsaur 11 Mj 44.45N 6.10 E
Chāmrājnagar 25 Ff 11.55N 76.57 E
Chañaral 56 Fc 26.21S 70.37W
Chança 13 Eg 37.33N 7.31W
Chan Chan 54 Ce 8.07S 79.02W
Chanco 56 Fe 35.44S 72.32W
Chandalar 40 Jc 66.36N 145.48W
Chandalar 40 Jc 67.30N 148.30W
Chandausi 25 Fc 28.27N 78.46 E
Chandeleur Islands 43 Jf 29.48N 88.51W
Chandeleur Sound 45 Ll 29.55N 89.10W
Chandīgarh 22 Jf 30.44N 76.55 E
Chandler 42 Lg 48.21N 64.41W
Chandless, Rio 54 Ee 9.08S 69.51W
Chāndpur 25 Id 23.13N 90.39 E
Chandragupta 25 Fe 16.11N 78.52 E
Chandrapur 22 Jh 19.57N 79.18 E
Chang, Ko- 25 Kf 12.00N 102.23 E
Changajn Nuruu → Hangaj, Hrebet-=Khangai Mountains (EN) 21 Le 47.30N 100.00 E
Chang'an → Rong'an 27 If 25.16N 109.23 E
Changane 30 Kk 24.43S 33.32 E
Changbai 28 Jd 41.25N 128.11 E
Changbai Shan 21 Oe 42.00N 128.00 E
Changchun 22 Oe 43.51N 125.20 E
Changdao(Sihou) 28 Ff 37.56N 120.42 E
Changde 22 Ng 29.04N 111.42 E
Ch'angdo 28 Ie 38.30N 127.45 E
Changfeng (Shuijiahu) 28 Dh 32.29N 117.10 E
Changge 28 Bg 34.12N 113.45 E
Changhang 28 If 36.01N 126.42 E
Chang He 28 Ei 31.21N 118.21 E
Changhowŏn 28 If 37.07N 127.38 E
Changhua 27 Lg 24.05N 120.32 E
Changhŭng 28 Ig 34.40N 126.54 E
Changji 27 Ec 44.01N 87.16 E
Chang Jiang 28 Dj 28.59N 116.42 E
Changjiang (Shiliu) 27 Ih 19.20N 109.03 E
Chang Jiang (Yangtze Kiang) 21 Of 31.48N 121.10 E
Changjiang Kou 27 Le 31.24N 121.59 E
Changjin-gang 28 Id 40.30N 127.12 E
Changjin-ho 28 Id 40.30N 127.12 E
Changjin-ŭp 27 Mc 40.23N 127.15 E
Changli 28 Ee 39.43N 119.10 E
Changling 27 Lc 44.15N 123.58 E
Changlung 25 Fb 34.56N 77.29 E
Changping 28 Dd 40.14N 116.13 E
Changsha 22 Ng 28.12N 113.02 E
Changshan 28 Ej 28.55N 118.31 E
Changshan Qundao 28 Ge 39.10N 122.34 E
Changshu 28 Fi 31.38N 120.44 E
Changsŏng 28 Ig 35.19N 126.48 E
Changting 28 Jb 44.27N 128.50 E
Changtu 28 Hc 42.47N 124.08 E
Changuillo 54 Cf 14.40S 75.12W
Changuinola 49 Fi 9.26N 82.31W
Changwu 27 Id 35.17N 107.52 E
Changxing 28 Ei 31.01N 119.55 E
Changxing Dao 28 Fe 39.35N 121.42 E
Changyi 28 Ef 36.52N 119.25 E
Changyŏn 27 Md 38.15N 125.05 E
Changyuan 28 Cg 35.12N 114.40 E
Changzhi 27 Jd 36.07N 113.10 E
Changzhou 28 Ei 31.46N 119.56 E
Channel Islands [5] 9 Kl 49.20N 2.20W
Channel Islands [Chan.Is.] 5 Ff 49.20N 2.20W
Channel Islands [U.S.] 38 Hf 34.00N 120.00W
Channel Port-aux-Basques 39 Ne 47.35N 59.11W
Channel Rock 49 Ib 23.00N 77.55W
Channing 45 Ei 35.41N 102.20W
Chantada 13 Eb 42.37N 7.46W
Chantengo, Laguna- 48 Ji 16.35N 99.10W
Chanthaburi 25 Kf 12.35N 102.06 E
Chantilly 11 Ie 49.12N 2.28 E
Chantonnay 11 Eh 46.41N 1.03W
Chantrey Inlet 38 Jc 67.48N 96.20W
Chanute 45 Ih 37.41N 95.27W
Chanza 13 Eg 37.33N 7.31W
Chao'an (Chaozhou) 27 Kg 23.41N 116.37 E
Chaobai Xinhe 28 De 39.07N 117.41 E
Chao He 28 Dd 40.36N 117.08 E
Chao Hu 28 Di 31.31N 117.33 E
Chao Phraya 21 Mh 13.32N 100.36 E
Chaor He 27 Lb 46.49N 123.45 E
Chaoxian 27 Ke 31.37N 117.49 E
Chaoyang [China] 22 Oe 41.35N 120.26 E
Chaoyang [China] 27 Kg 23.17N 116.37 E
Chaoyang → Huinan 28 Ic 42.41N 126.03 E
Chaoyang → Jiayin 27 Nb 48.52N 130.21 E
Chaoyangchuan 28 Jc 42.53N 129.23 E
Chaoyangcun 27 La 50.01N 124.22 E
Chaozhong 27 La 50.53N 121.23 E
Chaozhou → Chao'an 27 Kg 23.41N 116.37 E
Chapada dos Guimarães 54 Gg 15.26S 55.45W
Chapadinha 54 Jd 3.44S 43.21W
Chapais 44 Ja 49.47N 74.56W
Chapala 48 Hg 20.18N 103.12W
Chapala, Lago de- 38 Ig 20.15N 103.00W
Chaparral 54 Cc 3.43N 75.28W
Chapecó 56 Jc 27.06S 52.36W
Chapecó, Rio- 55 Fh 27.06S 53.01W
Chapecó, Serra do- 55 Gh 26.44S 51.54W
Chapel Hill 44 Hh 35.55N 79.04W
Chapicuy 55 Dj 31.40S 57.55W
Chapleau 42 Jg 47.50N 83.24W
Chaplin 46 La 50.28N 106.40W
Chaplin Lake 46 La 50.18N 106.35W
Chapman, Cape- 42 Ic 69.15N 89.27W
Chappell 45 Ef 41.06N 102.28W
Chāpra 25 Gc 25.46N 84.45 E
Chapultepec 48 Hf 23.27N 103.04W
Chaqui 54 Eg 19.36S 65.32W
Char 32 Ee 21.31N 12.51W
Charadai 55 Ch 27.38S 59.54W
Charagua 54 Fg 19.48S 63.13W
Charām 24 Ng 30.45N 50.44 E
Charaña 54 Eg 17.36S 69.28W
Charcas 48 If 23.08N 101.07W
Charco de la Aguja 48 Gc 28.25N 104.01W
Charcot Island 66 Qe 69.45S 75.15W
Chard [Alta.-Can.] 42 Ge 55.48N 111.10W
Chard [Eng.-U.K.] 9 Kk 50.53N 2.58W
Chardāvol 24 Lf 33.45N 46.38 E
Chardonnières 49 Jd 18.16N 74.10W
Charente [3] 11 Gi 45.40N 0.05 E
Charente 11 Ei 45.57N 1.05W
Charente-Maritime [3] 11 Fi 45.30N 0.45W
Charentonne 12 Ce 49.07N 0.44 E
Chari 30 Ig 12.58N 14.31 E
Chari-Baguirmi [3] 35 Bc 12.00N 17.00 E
Chārīkār 23 Kb 35.01N 69.11 E
Charing 12 Cc 51.12N 0.48 E
Chariton 45 Jf 41.00N 93.19W
Chariton River 45 Jg 39.19N 92.57W
Charity 54 Gb 7.24N 58.36W
Charleroi 11 Kd 50.25N 4.26 E
Charleroi-Jumet 11 Kd 50.27N 4.26 E
Charleroi-Marcinelle 12 Gd 50.25N 4.28 E
Charles 42 Kd 62.38N 74.15W
Charles, Cape- [Can.] 38 Nd 52.13N 55.40W
Charles, Cape- [Va.-U.S.] 43 Ld 37.08N 75.58W
Charles, Peak- 59 Ef 32.52S 121.11 E
Charlesbourg 44 Lb 46.52N 71.16W
Charles City 43 Ic 43.04N 92.40W
Charles de Gaulle, Aéroport- =Charles de Gaulle Airport (EN) 12 Ee 49.02N 2.35 E
Charles de Gaulle Airport (EN)=Charles de Gaulle, Aéroport- 12 Ee 49.02N 2.35 E
Charleston [Il.-U.S.] 45 Lg 39.30N 88.10W
Charleston [Mo.-U.S.] 45 Lh 36.55N 89.21W
Charleston [Ms.-U.S.] 45 Ki 34.01N 90.04W
Charleston [N.Z.] 62 Dd 41.54S 171.27 E
Charleston [S.C.-U.S.] 39 Lf 32.48N 79.57W
Charleston [W.V.-U.S.] 39 Kf 38.21N 81.38W
Charleston Peak 43 Dd 36.16N 115.42W
Charles Town 44 If 39.18N 77.52W
Charlestown 50 Ed 17.12N 62.35W
Charleval 12 De 49.22N 1.23 E
Charleville 58 Fg 26.24S 146.15 E
Charleville-Mézières 11 Ke 49.46N 4.43 E
Charleville Mézières-Mohon 12 Ge 49.46N 4.43 E
Charlevoix 44 Ec 45.19N 85.16W
Charlieu 11 Kh 46.09N 4.11 E
Charlotte [Mi.-U.S.] 44 Ed 42.36N 84.50W
Charlotte [N.C.-U.S.] 39 Kf 35.14N 80.50W
Charlotte Amalie 47 Le 18.21N 64.56W
Charlotte Bank (EN) 57 If 11.47S 173.13 E
Charlotte Harbor 44 Fl 26.45N 82.12W
Charlottenberg 8 Ee 59.53N 12.17 E
Charlottesville 43 Ld 38.02N 78.29W
Charlottetown 39 Me 46.14N 63.08W
Charlton 59 Ig 36.16S 143.21 E
Charlton 42 Jf 52.00N 79.26W
Charly 12 Ff 48.58N 3.17 E
Charmes 11 Mf 48.22N 6.17 E
Charnley River 59 Ec 16.20S 124.53 E
Charny-sur-Meuse 12 He 49.12N 5.22 E
Charollais 11 Kh 46.26N 4.16 E
Charouine 32 Gd 29.01N 0.16W
Charroux 11 Gh 46.09N 0.24 E
Chārsadda 25 Eb 34.09N 71.44 E
Charters Towers 58 Fg 20.05S 146.16 E
Chartres 11 Hf 48.27N 1.30 E
Charzykowskie, Jezioro- 10 Nc 53.47N 17.30 E
Chascomus 56 Ie 35.34S 58.01W
Chase 46 Fa 50.49N 119.41W
Chasŏng 28 Id 41.25N 126.35 E
Chassengue 36 Ce 10.26S 18.32 E
Chassezac 11 Kj 44.26N 4.19 E
Chassiron, Pointe de- 11 Eh 46.03N 1.24W
Chat 24 Pd 37.59N 55.16 E
Châtaigneraie 11 Ij 44.45N 2.20 E
Chātāl 24 Pd 37.40N 55.45 E
Château-Arnoux 11 Lj 44.06N 6.00 E
Chateaubelair 51n Ba 13.17N 61.15W
Châteaubriant 11 Eg 47.43N 1.23W
Château-Chinon 11 Jg 47.04N 3.56 E
Château-du-Loir 11 Gg 47.42N 0.25 E
Châteaudun 11 Hf 48.05N 1.20 E
Château-Gontier 11 Fg 47.50N 0.42W
Châteaulin 11 Bf 48.12N 4.05W
Châteaulin, Bassin de- 11 Cf 48.18N 3.50W
Châteaumeillant 11 Ih 46.34N 2.12 E
Châteauneuf-de-Randon 11 Jj 44.39N 3.04 E
Châteauneuf-sur-Cher 11 Ih 46.51N 2.19 E
Châteauneuf-sur-Loire 11 Ig 47.52N 2.14 E
Château-Porcien 12 Ge 49.32N 4.15 E
Châteaurenard 11 Kk 43.53N 4.51 E
Château-Renault 11 Gg 47.35N 0.54 E
Châteauroux 11 Hh 46.49N 1.42 E
Château-Salins 11 Mf 48.49N 6.30 E
Château-Thierry 11 Je 49.03N 3.24 E
Châteaux, Pointe des- 51e Bb 16.15N 61.11W
Châtelaillon-Plage 11 Eh 46.04N 1.05W
Châtelet 12 Gd 50.24N 4.31 E
Châtelguyon 11 Ji 45.55N 3.04 E
Châtellerault 11 Gh 46.48N 0.32 E
Chatelodo 55 De 21.19S 57.28W
Chatham [Eng.-U.K.] 9 Nj 51.23N 0.32 E
Chatham [N.B.-Can.] 42 Kg 47.02N 65.26W
Chatham [Ont.-Can.] 42 Jh 42.24N 82.11W
Chatham [Va.-U.S.] 44 Hg 36.49N 79.26W
Chatham Island 57 Ji 44.00S 176.30W
Chatham Islands 57 Ji 44.00S 176.30W
Chatham Rise (EN) 57 Ii 43.30S 180.00
Chatham Strait 40 Me 57.30N 134.45W
Châtillon-en-Bazois 11 Jg 47.03N 3.40 E
Châtillon-sur-Indre 11 Hh 46.59N 1.10 E
Châtillon-sur-Marne 12 Fe 49.06N 3.45 E
Châtillon-sur-Seine 11 Kg 47.51N 4.33 E
Chatom 44 Cj 31.28N 88.16W
Chatsworth 37 Ec 19.38S 30.50 E
Chattahoochee 44 Ej 30.42N 84.51W
Chattahoochee 38 Kf 30.52N 84.57W
Chattanooga 39 Kf 35.03N 85.19W
Chatteris 12 Cb 52.27N 0.03 E
Chaucas 55 Cc 16.46S 58.44W
Chaudfontaine 12 Hd 50.35N 5.38 E
Chaudière, Rivière- 44 Lb 46.43N 71.17W
Chauk 25 Id 20.53N 94.49 E
Chaulnes 12 Ee 49.49N 2.48 E
Chaumont 11 Lf 48.07N 5.08 E
Chaumont-en-Vexin 12 De 49.16N 1.53 E
Chaumont-Gistoux 12 Gd 50.41N 4.44 E
Chaumont-Porcien 12 Ge 49.39N 4.15 E
Chaumont-sur-Aire 12 Hf 48.56N 5.15 E
Chaumont-sur-Loire 11 Hg 47.29N 1.11 E
Chauny 11 Je 49.37N 3.13 E
Chau Phu 25 Lf 10.42N 105.07 E
Chausey, Iles- 11 Ef 48.53N 1.50W
Chauvigny 11 Gh 46.34N 0.39 E
Chavantina 54 Hf 14.40S 52.21W
Chavarria 55 Ci 28.57S 58.35W
Chaves [Braz.] 54 Id 0.10S 49.55W
Chaves [Port.] 13 Ec 41.44N 7.28W
Chavigny, Lac- 42 Je 58.00N 75.05W
Chavuma 36 De 13.05S 22.42 E
Chazelles-sur-Lyon 11 Ki 45.38N 4.23 E
Chbar 25 Lf 12.46N 107.10 E
Cheaha Mountain 44 Ei 33.30N 85.47W
Cheat River 44 Hf 39.45N 79.55W
Cheb 10 If 50.04N 12.23 E
Cheboygan 43 Kb 45.39N 84.29W
Chech, 'Erg- 30 Gf 25.00N 3.00W
Chechaouene [3] 32 Fb 35.00N 5.00W
Chechaouene 32 Fb 35.10N 5.16W
Checheng 27 Lg 22.05N 120.42 E
Che-Chiang Sheng → Zhejiang Sheng [2] 27 Kf 29.00N 120.00 E
Chech'ŏn 28 Jf 37.08N 128.12 E
Chęciny 10 Qf 50.48N 20.28 E
Cheddar Gorge 9 Kj 51.13N 2.47W
Cheduba 25 Ie 18.48N 93.38 E
Chée 12 Gf 48.45N 4.39 E
Cheektowaga 44 Hd 42.57N 78.38W
Chefu 37 Ed 22.27S 32.45 E
Chegga 31 Gf 25.22N 5.49W
Cheghelvandī 24 Mf 33.42N 48.25 E
Chehel Pāyeh 24 Qg 31.54N 57.14 E
Cheju 27 Me 33.31N 126.32 E
Cheju-Do 21 Of 33.25N 126.30 E
Cheju-Do [2] 28 Ih 33.25N 126.30 E
Cheju-Haehyŏp 28 Ih 33.40N 126.28 E
Chela, Serra da- 30 Ij 16.00S 13.10 E
Chelan 46 Ec 47.51N 120.01W
Chelan, Lake- 46 Eb 48.05N 120.30W
Chelforó, Arroyo- 55 Cm 36.55S 58.12W
Cheliff [3] 32 Hb 36.10N 1.45 E
Cheliff 30 He 36.02N 0.08 E
Cheliff 32 Hb 36.10N 1.20 E
Cheliff, Plaine du- 13 Mi 35.57N 0.45 E
Chellalat el Adhaouara 13 Pi 35.56N 3.25 E
Chelleh Khāneh, Kūh-e- 24 Md 36.52N 48.36 E
Chełm [2] 10 Te 51.10N 23.30 E
Chełm 10 Te 51.10N 23.28 E
Chelmer 12 Cc 51.44N 0.42 E
Chełmińskie, Pojezierze- 10 Oc 53.20N 19.00 E
Chełmno 10 Oc 53.22N 18.26 E
Chelmsford 9 Nj 51.44N 0.28 E
Chełmża 10 Oc 53.12N 18.37 E
Cheltenham 9 Kj 51.54N 2.04W
Chelva 13 Le 39.45N 0.59W
Chemainus 46 Db 48.55N 123.43W
Chemāma 32 Ef 16.50N 14.00 E
Chemba 37 Ec 17.09S 34.53 E
Chembe 36 Ee 11.58S 28.45 E
Chemillé 11 Fg 47.13N 0.43W
Chemnitz = Karl-Marx-Stadt 6 He 50.50N 12.55 E
Chemult 46 Ee 43.13N 121.47W
Chenachane 32 Gd 26.00N 4.15W
Chenārbāshi 24 Lf 33.20N 46.20 E
Chen Barag Qi (Bayan Hure) 27 Kb 49.21N 119.25 E
Chencha 35 Fd 6.17N 37.40 E
Chencoyi 48 Nh 19.48N 90.14W
Cheney 46 Gc 47.29N 117.34W
Cheney Reservoir 45 Hh 37.45N 97.50W
Cheng'an 28 Cf 36.27N 114.41 E
Chengde 27 Kc 41.00N 117.57 E
Chengdu 22 Mf 30.45N 104.04 E
Chengkou 27 Ie 31.54N 108.37 E
Chengmai 27 Ih 19.50N 109.59 E
Chengshan Jiao 27 Ld 37.24N 122.42 E
Chengxi Hu 28 Dh 32.22N 116.12 E
Chengzitan 27 Ld 39.31N 122.28 E
Chenisckali 16 Mh 42.06N 42.16 E
Chenjiagang 28 Eg 34.22N 119.48 E
Chenonceaux 11 Hg 47.20N 1.04 E
Chenxi 27 Jf 28.02N 110.15 E
Chenxian 27 Jf 25.49N 113.05 E
Chenying → Wannian 28 Dj 28.42N 117.04 E
Chépénéhé 63b Ce 20.47S 167.09 E
Chepes 56 Gd 31.21S 66.36W
Chepo 49 Hi 9.10N 79.06W
Cher [3] 11 Ig 47.00N 2.30 E
Cher 5 Gf 47.21N 0.29 E
Cheradi, Isole- 14 Lj 40.25N 17.10 E
Cherangany Hills 36 Gb 1.15N 35.27 E
Cheraw 44 Hh 34.42N 79.53W
Cherbaniani Reef 25 Ef 12.18N 71.53 E
Cherbourg 6 Ff 49.39N 1.39W
Cherchell 32 Hb 36.36N 2.12 E
Chère 11 Eg 47.42N 1.50W
Chergui, Chott Ech- 30 He 34.21N 0.30 E
Chéri 34 Hc 13.26N 11.21 E
Cherlen → Kerulen 21 Ne 48.48N 117.00 E
Cherokee 45 Ie 42.45N 95.33W
Cherokees, Lake O' the- 45 Ih 36.39N 94.49W
Cherski Mountains (EN)= Čerskogo, Hrebet- [R.S.F.S.R.] 21 Qc 65.00N 145.00 E
Chersterfield Inlet 39 Jc 63.21N 90.42W
Chertsey 12 Bc 51.23N 0.30W
Cherwell 9 Lj 51.44N 1.15W
Chesapeake 44 Ig 36.45N 76.15W
Chesapeake Bay 38 Lf 38.40N 76.25W
Chesapeake Bay Bridge-Tunnel 44 Ig 37.00N 76.02W
Chesha Bay (EN)=Češskaja Guba 5 Kb 67.20N 46.30 E
Chesham 12 Bc 51.42N 0.36W
Cheshire [3] 9 Kh 53.15N 2.30W
Cheshire Plain 9 Kh 53.20N 2.40W
Cheshunt 12 Bc 51.42N 0.02W
Chester 9 Kh 53.10N 2.55W
Chester [Eng.-U.K.] 9 Kh 53.12N 2.54W
Chester [Il.-U.S.] 45 Lh 37.55N 89.49W
Chester [Mt.-U.S.] 46 Jb 48.31N 110.58W
Chester [Pa.-U.S.] 44 Jf 39.50N 75.23W
Chester [S.C.-U.S.] 44 Gh 34.40N 81.12W
Chesterfield 9 Lh 53.15N 1.25W
Chesterfield, Ile- 37 Gc 16.20S 43.58 E
Chesterfield, Récifs et Iles- =Chesterfield Reefs and Islands (EN) 57 Gf 20.00S 159.00 E
Chesterfield Inlet 38 Jc 63.25N 90.45W
Chesterfield Reefs and Islands (EN)=Chesterfield, Récifs et Iles- 57 Gf 20.00S 159.00 E
Chesterton Range 59 Je 25.30S 147.30 E
Chestnut Ridge 44 He 40.10N 79.25W
Chesuncook Lake 44 Mb 46.00N 69.20W
Chetaibi 32 Ib 37.04N 7.23 E
Chetumal 39 Kh 18.35N 88.07W
Chetumal, Bahia de 47 Ge 18.20N 88.05W
Cheviot 62 Ee 42.49S 173.16 E
Chew Bahir=Stefanie, Lake- (EN) 30 Kh 4.38N 36.50 E
Chewelah 46 Gb 48.17N 117.43W
Cheyenne [Ok.-U.S.] 45 Gi 35.37N 99.40W

Index Symbols

- [1] Independent Nation
- [2] State, Region
- [3] District, County
- [4] Municipality
- [5] Colony, Dependency
- Continent
- Physical Region
- Historical or Cultural Region
- Mount, Mountain
- Volcano
- Hill
- Mountains, Mountain Range
- Hills, Escarpment
- Plateau, Upland
- Pass, Gap
- Plain, Lowland
- Delta
- Salt Flat
- Valley, Canyon
- Crater, Cave
- Karst Features
- Depression
- Polder
- Desert, Dunes
- Forest, Woods
- Heath, Steppe
- Oasis
- Cape, Point
- Coast, Beach
- Cliff
- Peninsula
- Isthmus
- Sandbank
- Island
- Atoll
- Rock, Reef
- Islands, Archipelago
- Rocks, Reefs
- Coral Reef
- Well, Spring
- Geyser
- River, Stream
- Waterfall Rapids
- River Mouth, Estuary
- Lake
- Salt Lake
- Intermittent Lake
- Reservoir
- Swamp, Pond
- Canal
- Glacier
- Ice Shelf, Pack Ice
- Ocean
- Sea
- Gulf, Bay
- Strait, Fjord
- Lagoon
- Bank
- Seamount
- Tablemount
- Ridge
- Shelf
- Basin
- Escarpment, Sea Scarp
- Fracture
- Trench, Abyss
- National Park, Reserve
- Point of Interest
- Recreation Site
- Cave, Cavern
- Historic Site
- Ruins
- Wall, Walls
- Church, Abbey
- Temple
- Scientific Station
- Airport
- Port
- Lighthouse
- Mine
- Tunnel
- Dam, Bridge

Cheyenne [Wy.-U.S.] 39 Ie 41.08N 104.49W
Cheyenne River 43 Gc 44.40N 101.15W
Cheyenne Wells 45 Eg 38.51N 102.11W
Cheyne Bay 59 Df 34.35S 118.50 E
Chhatarpur 25 Fd 24.54N 79.36 E
Chhindwāra 25 Fd 22.04N 78.56 E
Chi 25 Ke 15.11N 104.43 E
Chiamboni, Rās- 35 Gf 1.38S 41.36 E
Chiana, Val di- 14 Fg 43.15N 11.50 E
Chianciano Terme 14 Fg 43.02N 11.49 E
Chiang-hsi Sheng → Jangxi Sheng = Kiangsi (EN) [2] 27 Kf 28.00N 116.00 E
Chiang Mai 22 Lh 18.46N 98.58 E
Chiang Rai 22 Lh 19.54N 99.50 E
Chiang-su Sheng → Jiangsu Sheng = Kiangsu (EN) [2] 27 Ke 33.00N 120.00 E
Chiani 14 Gh 42.44N 12.07 E
Chianje 31 Ij 15.45S 13.54 E
Chianti 14 Fg 43.30N 11.25 E
Chiapa, Río- 48 Mj 16.30N 93.10W
Chiapas [2] 47 Fe 16.30N 92.30W
Chiapas, Meseta de- 47 Fe 16.30N 92.00W
Chiaramonte Gulfi 14 Im 37.02N 14.42 E
Chiaravalle 14 Hg 43.36N 13.19 E
Chiaromonte 14 Kj 40.07N 16.13 E
Chiautla de Tapia 48 Jh 18.17N 98.36W
Chiavari 14 Df 44.19N 9.19 E
Chiavenna 14 Dd 46.19N 9.24 E
Chiayi 27 Lg 23.29N 120.27 E
Chiba 27 Pd 35.36N 140.07 E
Chiba Ken [2] 28 Pg 35.40N 140.20 E
Chibemba 36 Bf 15.45S 14.06 E
Chibia 36 Bf 15.11S 13.41 E
Chibougamau 39 Le 49.53N 74.21W
Chibougamau, Lac- 44 Ja 49.50N 74.15W
Chibougamau, Rivière- 44 Ja 49.50N 74.25W
Chiburi-Jima 28 Lf 36.00N 133.02 E
Chibuto 37 Ed 24.42S 33.33 E
Chicago 39 Ke 41.53N 87.38W
Chicago Heights 45 Mf 41.30N 87.38W
Chicala 36 Ce 11.59S 19.30 E
Chicapa 30 Ji 6.25S 20.48 E
Chic-Chocs, Monts- 44 Na 48.55N 66.45W
Chicha 35 Bb 16.52N 18.33 E
Chichagof 40 Le 57.30N 135.30W
Chichancanab, Laguna de- 48 Oh 19.54N 88.46W
Chichaoua 32 Fc 31.32N 8.46W
Chichas, Cordillera de- 54 Eh 20.30S 66.30W
Chicheng 27 Kc 40.55N 115.47 E
Chichén Itzá 39 Kg 20.40N 88.35W
Chichester 9 Mk 50.50N 0.48W
Chichester Range 59 Dd 22.20S 119.20 E
Chichibu 28 Og 35.59N 139.05 E
Chichigalpa 49 Dg 12.34N 87.02W
Chichijma-Rettō 60 Cb 27.06N 142.12 E
Chichilla de Monte-Aragón 13 Kf 38.55N 1.43W
Chichiriviche 49 Mh 10.56N 68.16W
Chickasawhay River 45 Lk 31.00N 88.45W
Chickasha 43 Hd 35.02N 97.58W
Chicken 40 Kd 64.04N 141.56W
Chiclana de la Frontera 13 Fh 36.25N 6.08W
Chiclayo 53 If 6.46S 79.50W
Chico 43 Cd 39.44N 121.50W
Chico, Río- [Arg.] 52 Jj 43.48S 66.25W
Chico, Río- [Arg.] 52 Jj 49.56S 68.32W
Chicoana 56 Gc 25.06S 65.33W
Chicomo 37 Ed 24.31S 34.17 E
Chiconono 37 Fb 12.57S 35.45 E
Chicopee 44 Kd 42.10N 72.36W
Chicote 36 Df 16.01S 21.48 E
Chicoutimi 39 Le 48.26N 71.04W
Chicoutimi Nord 44 La 48.29N 71.02W
Chicualacuala 37 Ed 22.05S 31.42 E
Chidenguele 37 Ed 24.55S 34.10 E
Chidley, Cape- 38 Mc 60.25N 64.30W
Chiemsee 10 Ii 47.54N 12.29 E
Chiengi 36 Ed 8.39S 29.10 E
Chienti 14 Hg 43.18N 13.45 E
Chieri 14 Be 45.01N 7.49 E
Chiers 12 He 49.39N 5.00 E
Chiese 14 Ee 45.08N 10.25 E
Chieti 14 Ih 42.21N 14.10 E
Chièvres 12 Fd 50.35N 3.48 E
Chifeng/Ulanhad 27 Kc 42.16N 118.57 E
Chifumage 36 De 12.10S 22.30 E
Chifwefwe 36 Fe 13.35S 29.35 E
Chigasaki 29 Fd 35.19N 139.24 E
Chignik 40 He 56.18N 158.23W
Chigombe 37 Ed 23.26S 33.19 E
Chigorodó 49 Ij 7.41N 76.41W
Chigubo 37 Ed 22.50S 33.31 E
Chigu Co 27 Ff 28.40N 91.50 E
Chi He 28 Dh 32.51N 117.59 E
Chihli, Gulf of- (EN) = Bo Hai 21 Nf 38.30N 120.00 E
Chihuahua [2] 47 Cc 28.30N 106.00W
Chihuahua 39 Ig 28.38N 106.05W
Chii-san 28 Ig 35.20N 127.44 E
Chikaskia River 45 Hh 36.37N 97.15W
Chikugo 29 Be 33.13N 130.30 E
Chikugo-Gawa 29 Be 33.10N 130.21 E
Chikuma-Gawa 29 Fc 37.00N 138.35 E
Chikwana 36 Ff 16.03S 34.48 E
Chilapa de Alvarez 48 Ji 17.36N 99.10W
Chilās 25 Ea 35.26N 74.05 E
Chilaw 25 Fg 7.34N 79.47 E
Chilcotin 42 Ff 51.46N 122.22W
Childers 59 Ke 25.14S 152.17 E
Childress 43 Ge 34.25N 100.13W
Chile [1] 53 Ii 30.00S 71.00W
Chile Basin (EN) 3 Mm 33.00S 90.00W
Chile Chico 56 Fg 46.33S 71.44W
Chilecito [Arg.] 56 Gd 33.53S 69.03W
Chilecito [Arg.] 56 Gc 29.10S 67.30W
Chile Rise (EN) 3 Mm 40.00S 90.00W
Chili 35 Cb 16.44N 20.53 E
Chilia, Braţul- 15 Md 45.13N 29.43 E
Chililabombwe 36 Ee 12.22S 27.50 E
Chi-lin Sheng → Jilin Sheng = Kirin (EN) [2] 27 Mc 43.00N 126.00 E
Chilko Lake 46 Ca 51.20N 124.05W
Chilko River 46 Da 52.00N 123.40W
Chillán 53 Ii 36.36S 72.07W
Chillar 56 Ie 37.18S 59.59W
Chillicothe [Il.-U.S.] 45 Lf 40.55N 89.29W
Chillicothe [Mo.-U.S.] 45 Jg 39.48N 93.33W
Chillicothe [Oh.-U.S.] 43 Kd 38.20N 82.59W
Chilliwack 46 Eb 49.10N 121.57W
Chiloé, Isla de- 52 Ij 42.30S 73.55W
Chilón 48 Mi 17.14N 92.25W
Chiloquin 46 Ee 42.35N 121.52W
Chilpancingo de los Bravos 47 Ee 17.33N 99.30W
Chiltern Hills 9 Mj 51.42N 0.48W
Chilton 45 Ld 44.02N 88.10W
Chiluage 36 Dd 9.31S 21.46 E
Chilumba 36 Fe 10.27S 34.16 E
Chilwa, Lake- 36 Fc 15.12S 35.50 E
Chimala 36 Fd 8.51S 34.01 E
Chimaltenango 49 Bf 14.39N 90.49W
Chimaltenango [3] 49 Bf 14.40N 90.55W
Chimán 49 Hi 8.42N 78.37W
Chimanas, Islas- 50 Dg 10.17N 64.38W
Chimay 12 Gd 50.03N 4.19 E
Chimborazo, Volcán- 52 If 1.28S 78.48W
Chimbote 53 If 9.05S 78.36W
Chimichagua 49 Ki 9.16N 73.49W
Chimoio 37 Ec 19.00S 33.23 E
Chimorra 13 Hf 38.18N 4.53W
Chin [2] 25 Id 22.00N 93.30 E
China [Jap.] 29b Bb 27.20N 128.36 E
China [Mex.] 48 Je 25.42N 99.14W
China (EN) = Zhonghua Renmin Gongheguo [1] 22 Mf 35.00N 105.00 E
Chinacates 48 Ge 25.00N 105.13W
China Lake 46 Gi 35.46N 117.39W
Chinandega 47 Gf 12.37N 87.09W
Chinandega [3] 49 Dg 12.45N 87.05W
Chinati Peak 45 Dl 29.57N 104.29W
Chincha Alta 54 Cf 13.27S 76.08W
Chinchaga 42 Fe 58.52N 118.19W
Chinchilla 59 Ke 26.45S 150.38 E
Chinchón 13 Id 40.08N 3.25W
Chinchorro, Banco- 47 Ge 18.35N 87.20W
Chincoteague 44 Jg 37.55N 75.23W
Chinde 31 Kj 18.34S 36.27 E
Chin-Do 28 Ig 34.25N 126.15 E
Chindu 27 Ge 33.30N 96.31 E
Chindwinn 21 Lg 21.26N 95.15 E
Ch'ing-hai Sheng → Qinghai Sheng = Tsinghai (EN) [2] 27 Gd 36.00N 96.00 E
Chingil 35 Bc 10.33N 18.57 E
Chingola 31 Jj 12.32S 27.52 E
Chinguar 36 Ce 12.33S 16.22 E
Chinguetti 32 Ee 20.27N 12.21W
Chinguetti, Dahr de- 32 Ee 20.43N 12.20W
Chinhae 28 Jg 35.08N 128.40 E
Chiniot 25 Eb 31.43N 72.59 E
Chinipas 48 Ed 27.23N 108.32W
Chinju 27 Md 35.11N 128.05 E
Chinko 30 Jh 4.50N 23.53 E
Chinle 46 Kh 36.09N 109.33W
Chinle Creek 46 Kh 37.12N 109.43W
Chinmen 27 Kg 24.25N 118.25 E
Chino 27 Fd 36.00N 138.09 E
Chinon 11 Gg 47.10N 0.15 E
Chinook 46 Kb 48.35N 109.14W
Chinquila 48 Pg 21.30N 87.25W
Chinsali 36 Fe 10.33S 32.04 E
Chinteche 36 Fe 11.50S 34.10 E
Chinú 54 Cb 9.06N 75.24W
Chinvali 19 Eg 42.13N 43.57 E
Chiny 12 He 49.44N 5.20 E
Chinyŏng 28 Jg 35.18N 128.44 E
Chioco 37 Ec 16.25S 32.50 E
Chioggia 14 Ge 45.13N 12.17 E
Chios (EN) = Khios 5 Ih 38.22N 26.00 E
Chipata 31 Kj 13.39S 32.40 E
Chipepo 36 Ef 16.49S 27.50 E
Chipindo 36 Ce 13.48S 15.48 E
Chiping 28 Df 36.35N 116.16 E
Chipinge 37 Ed 20.12S 32.38 E
Chipman 44 Ob 46.11N 65.53W
Chippenham 9 Kj 51.28N 2.07W
Chippewa, Lake- 45 Kd 45.56N 91.13W
Chippewa Falls 43 Ic 44.56N 91.24W
Chippewa River [Wi.-U.S.] 45 Id 44.56N 95.44W
Chippewa River [U.S.] 45 Jd 44.25N 92.10W
Chipping Ongar 12 Cc 51.42N 0.15 E
Chiputneticook Lakes 44 Mc 45.45N 68.45W
Chiquián 54 Cf 10.09S 77.11W
Chiquimula [3] 49 Cf 14.40N 89.25W
Chiquimula 49 Cf 14.48N 89.33W
Chiquimulilla 49 Bf 14.05N 90.23W
Chiquinquirá 54 Db 5.37N 73.50W
Chiquitos, Llanos de- 54 Fg 18.00S 61.30W
Chirāla 25 Ge 15.49N 80.21 E
Chiran 29 Bf 31.22N 130.27 E
Chiredzi 31 Kk 21.03S 31.45 E
Chirfa 34 Ha 20.57N 12.21 E
Chirgua, Río- 50 Bh 8.30N 68.01W
Chiricahua Peak 43 Fe 31.52N 109.20W
Chiriguaná 49 Ki 9.22N 73.37W
Chirikof 40 He 55.50N 155.35W
Chiriqui [3] 49 Fi 8.30N 82.00W
Chiriqui, Golfo de- 38 Ki 8.00N 82.20W
Chiriquí, Laguna de- 47 Hg 9.03N 82.00W
Chiriquí Grande 49 Fi 8.57N 82.07W
Chirnogi 15 Je 44.07N 26.34 E
Chiromo 36 Gf 16.33S 35.08 E
Chirripó, Cerro- 49 Fi 9.29N 83.29W
Chirripó, Río- [C.R.] 49 Fh 10.03N 83.16W
Chirripó, Río- [C.R.] 49 Fh 10.41N 83.41W
Chirundu 37 Dc 15.59S 28.54 E
Chisamba 36 Ee 14.59S 28.23 E
Chisāpāni Garhi 25 Hc 27.34N 85.08 E
Chisenga 36 Fd 9.56S 33.26 E
Chisasibi 39 Ld 53.50N 79.00W
Chishui 27 If 28.30N 105.44 E
Chişineu Criş 15 Ec 46.32N 21.31 E
Chisone 14 Bf 44.49N 7.25 E
Chitado 36 Bf 17.18S 13.54 E
Chita-Hantō 29 Ed 34.50N 136.50 E
Chitati 35 Ac 14.40N 14.30 E
Chitato 31 Ji 7.22S 20.49 E
Chita-Wan 29 Ed 34.50N 136.55 E
Chitembo 36 Ce 13.31S 16.45 E
Chitina 40 Kd 61.31N 144.27W
Chitipa 36 Fd 9.43S 33.16 E
Chitorgarh 25 Ed 24.53N 74.38 E
Chitose 28 Pc 42.49N 141.39 E
Chitradurga 25 Ff 14.14N 76.24 E
Chitrāl 25 Ea 35.51N 71.47 E
Chitré 47 Hg 7.58N 80.26W
Chittagong 22 Lg 22.20N 91.50 E
Chittoor 25 Ff 13.12N 79.07 E
Chiumbe 30 Ji 6.59S 21.12 E
Chiume 36 Df 15.08S 21.12 E
Chiusi 14 Fg 43.01N 11.57 E
Chiusi, Lago di- 14 Fg 43.05N 12.00 E
Chiva 13 Le 39.28N 0.43W
Chivacoa 50 Bg 10.10N 68.54W
Chivapuri, Río- 50 Ci 6.25N 66.23W
Chivasso 14 Be 45.11N 7.53 E
Chivay 54 Dg 15.38S 71.36W
Chivilcoy 56 Hd 34.53S 60.01W
Chixoy o Negro, Río- 49 Be 16.28N 90.33W
Chizou → Guichi 27 Ke 30.38N 117.30 E
Chizu 29 Dd 35.15N 134.14 E
Chŏâm Khsant 25 Kf 14.13N 104.56 E
Choapa, Río- 56 Fd 31.38S 71.34W
Chobe 30 Jj 17.47S 25.10 E
Choc Bay 51k Ba 14.03N 60.59W
Choch'iwŏn 28 If 36.36N 127.18 E
Chocó [2] 54 Cb 6.00N 77.00W
Chocolate Mountains 46 Hj 33.25N 114.10W
Chodecz 10 Pd 52.24N 19.01 E
Chodov 10 If 50.15N 12.45 E
Chodzież 10 Md 52.59N 16.56 E
Choele-Choel 56 Ge 39.16S 65.41W
Choique 56 He 38.28S 62.43W
Choiseul 51k Ab 13.47N 61.03W
Choiseul Island 57 Ge 7.00S 157.00 E
Choix 48 Ed 26.43N 108.17W
Chojna 10 Kd 52.58N 14.28 E
Chojnice 10 Nc 53.42N 17.34 E
Chojnów 10 Le 51.17N 15.56 E
Chŏkai-San 28 Pe 39.10N 140.02 E
Choke 30 Kg 10.45N 37.35 E
Chŏkué 31 Kk 24.27S 32.55 E
Cho La 27 Ge 31.52N 98.51 E
Cholet 11 Fg 47.04N 0.53W
Chŏlla-Namdo [2] 28 Ig 34.45N 127.00 E
Chŏlla-Pukto [2] 28 Ig 35.45N 127.15 E
Cholo 36 Gf 16.04S 35.08 E
Cholula 48 Jh 19.04N 98.18W
Choluteca 47 Gf 13.18N 87.12W
Choluteca [3] 49 Dg 13.20N 87.10W
Choluteca, Río- 49 Dg 13.07N 87.19W
Choma 31 Jj 16.49S 26.59 E
Chomo/Yadong 27 Ef 27.38N 89.03 E
Chomo Lhari 27 Ef 27.50N 89.16 E
Chomutov 10 Jf 50.28N 13.25 E
Ch'ŏnan 27 Md 36.48N 127.09 E
Chon Buri 25 Kf 13.22N 100.59 E
Chone 54 Bd 0.42S 80.07W
Ch'ŏngch'ŏn-gang 28 He 39.35N 125.28 E
Ch'ŏngjin 22 Oe 41.46N 129.49 E
Ch'ŏngjin Si [2] 28 Jd 41.45N 129.45 E
Chŏngju 27 Md 39.51N 125.15 E
Ch'ŏngju 27 Md 36.38N 127.30 E
Chongli (Xiwanzi) 28 Cd 40.57N 115.12 E
Chongming 28 Fi 31.38N 121.24 E
Chongming Dao 28 Fi 31.36N 121.33 E
Chongoroi 36 Be 13.34S 13.55 E
Chongqing (Yuzhou) = Chungking (EN) 22 Mg 29.34N 106.27 E
Chongqing → Yuzhou = Chungking (EN) 22 Mg 29.34N 106.27 E
Ch'ŏngsan-Do 28 Ig 34.11N 126.54 E
Chŏngŭp 28 Ig 35.34N 126.51 E
Chongyang 28 Cj 29.32N 114.02 E
Chongzuo 27 Ig 22.29N 107.22 E
Chŏnju 27 Md 35.49N 127.09 E
Chonos, Archipiélago de los- 52 Ij 45.00S 74.00W
Chontaleña, Cordillera- 49 Eh 11.50N 85.00W
Chontales [3] 49 Eg 12.05N 85.10W
Chopim, Rio- 55 Fg 25.35S 53.05W
Chopinzinho 55 Fg 25.51S 52.30W
Chorito, Sierra del- 13 He 39.25N 4.25W
Choroszcz 10 Sc 53.09N 22.59 E
Chorreras, Cerro- 48 Fd 26.02N 106.21W
Ch'ŏrwŏn 27 Md 38.15N 127.13 E
Chorzele 10 Qc 53.16N 20.55 E
Chorzów 10 Of 50.19N 18.57 E
Ch'osan 28 Hd 40.45N 125.50 E
Choszebuz/Cottbus 10 Ke 51.46N 14.20 E
Chōshi 28 Pg 35.44N 140.50 E
Chos Malal 56 Fe 37.23S 70.16W
Chosŏn M.I.K. = North Korea (EN) [1] 22 Oe 40.00N 127.30 E
Chosŏn Minjuju-Inmin-Konghwaguk = Chosŏn M.I.K. [1] 22 Oe 40.00N 127.30 E
Choszczno 10 Lc 53.10N 15.26 E
Chota 54 Ce 6.33S 78.39W
Chotanagpur Plateau 21 Kg 22.00N 86.00 E
Choteau 46 Ic 47.49N 112.11W
Chotla, Cerro de- 48 Ii 17.55N 101.31W
Choukchot, Djebel- 13 Qh 36.01N 4.11 E
Choum 32 Ee 21.18N 12.59W
Chovd → Kobdo 27 Fb 48.06N 92.11 E
Chövsgöl nuur → Hubsugul Nur 21 Md 51.00N 100.30 E
Chowchilla 46 Eh 37.07N 120.16W
Chowra 25 Ig 8.27N 93.02 E
Chréa 13 Oh 36.25N 2.53 E
Chřiby 10 Ng 49.10N 17.20 E
Christchurch 58 Ii 43.32S 172.37 E
Christian, Cape - 42 Kb 70.32N 68.18W
Christian, Point- 64q Ab 25.04S 130.07W
Christiana 37 De 27.52S 25.08 E
Christian IV Gletscher 41 Ie 68.40N 30.20W
Christiansburg 44 Gg 37.07N 80.26W
Christiansfeld 8 Ci 55.21N 9.29 E
Christianshåb/Qasigiánguit 41 Ge 68.45N 51.30W
Christiansø 8 Fi 55.20N 15.10 E
Christian Sound 40 Me 55.56N 134.40W
Christiansted 50 Dd 17.45N 64.40W
Christiansted Harbor 51a Dc 17.46N 64.42W
Christie Bay 42 Gd 62.45N 110.15W
Christmas → Kiritimati Atoll 57 Ld 1.52N 157.20W
Christmas Creek 59 Fc 18.29S 125.23 E
Christmas Creek 59 Fc 18.53S 125.55 E
Christmas Island [5] 22 Mk 10.30S 105.40 E
Christmas Ridge (EN) 3 Ki 10.00N 165.00W
Chrudim 10 Lg 49.57N 15.47 E
Chrzanów 10 Pf 50.09N 19.24 E
Chrząstowa 10 Mc 53.35N 16.58 E
Chuansha 28 Fi 31.11N 121.42 E
Chūbar 24 Mc 38.11N 48.51 E
Chubut [2] 56 Gf 44.00S 69.00W
Chubut, Río- 52 Jj 43.20S 65.03W
Chucunaque, Río- 49 Ii 8.09N 77.44W
Chugach Mountains 40 Jd 61.00N 145.00W
Chuginadak 40 Ef 52.49N 169.50W
Chugoku-Sanchi 21 Pf 35.15N 133.30 E
Chu He 28 Eh 32.15N 119.03 E
Chuhuichupa 48 Ec 29.38N 108.22W
Chuí 55 Fk 33.41S 53.27W
Chuka 36 Gc 0.20S 37.39 E
Chukai 26 Df 4.15N 103.25 E
Chukchi Peninsula (EN) = Čukotski Poluostrov 21 Uc 66.00N 175.00W
Chukchi Plateau (EN) 67 Bd 78.00N 165.00W
Chukchi Sea 67 Bd 69.00N 171.00W
Chukchi Sea (EN) = Čukotskoje More 67 Bd 69.00N 171.00W
Chula Vista 46 Gj 32.39N 117.05W
Chulitna 40 Jd 62.55N 149.39W
Chullo 13 Jg 37.10N 2.57W
Chulucanas 54 Be 5.06S 80.10W
Chumbicha 56 Gc 28.52S 66.14W
Chumphon 25 Jf 10.32N 99.13 E
Chumunjin 28 Jf 37.53N 128.49 E
Ch'unch'ŏn 27 Md 37.52N 127.44 E
Chunga 36 Ef 15.03S 26.00 E
Ch'ungch'ŏng-Namdo [2] 28 If 36.30N 127.00 E
Ch'ungch'ŏng-Pukto [2] 28 Jf 36.45N 128.00 E
Ch'ungju 27 Md 36.58N 127.56 E
Chungking (EN) = Chongqing (Yuzhou) 22 Mg 29.34N 106.27 E
Chungking (EN) = Yuzhou → Chongqing 22 Mg 29.34N 106.27 E
Ch'ungmu 28 Jg 34.51N 128.26 E
Chunya 36 Fd 8.32S 33.25 E
Chuquibamba 54 Dg 15.50S 72.39W
Chuquibambilla 54 Df 14.07S 72.43W
Chuquicamata 56 Gb 22.19S 68.56W
Chuquisaca [2] 54 Fg 20.00S 64.20W
Chur/Cuera 14 Dd 46.50N 9.35 E
Churchill 39 Jd 58.46N 94.10W
Churchill [Can.] 38 Md 53.30N 60.10W
Churchill [Can.] 38 Jd 58.47N 94.12W
Churchill, Cape - 42 Ie 58.46N 93.12W
Churchill Falls 42 Lf 53.30N 64.10W
Churchill Lake 42 Ge 56.05N 108.15W
Churchill Peak 42 Ee 58.20N 125.02W
Churchill Range 66 Jg 81.30S 158.30 E
Chūru 25 Ec 28.18N 74.57 E
Churuguara 54 Ea 10.49N 69.32W
Churún Merú = Angel Falls (EN) 52 Je 5.57N 62.30W
Chuska Mountains 46 Kh 36.15N 108.50W
Chute-des Passes 42 Kg 49.50N 71.00W
Chuxian 27 Ke 32.16N 118.15 E
Chuxiong 27 Hf 25.02N 101.32 E
Chuy 55 Fk 33.41S 53.27W
Ciamis 26 Eh 7.20S 108.21 E
Cianjur 26 Eh 6.49S 107.08 E
Ciarraí/Kerry [2] 9 Di 52.10N 9.30W
Ćiatura 16 Mh 42.17N 43.15 E
Cibuta, Cerro- 48 Db 31.02N 110.58W
Ćićarija 14 He 45.28N 13.54 E
Ćićevac 15 Ef 43.43N 21.27 E
Cicicleja 15 Nb 47.23N 30.50 E
Cicolano 14 Hh 42.15N 13.10 E
Cidacos 13 Kb 42.19N 1.55W
Cide 24 Eb 41.54N 33.00 E
Cidlina 10 Lf 50.09N 15.12 E
Ciechanów 10 Qd 52.53N 20.38 E
Ciechanów [2] 10 Qd 52.55N 20.40 E
Ciechanowiec 10 Sd 52.42N 22.31 E
Ciechanowska, Wysoczyzna- 10 Qc 53.10N 20.30 E
Ciego de Ávila 47 Id 21.51N 78.46W
Ciego de Ávila [3] 49 Hb 22.00N 78.40W
Ciénaga 54 Da 11.00N 74.14W
Ciénaga de Flores 48 Ie 25.57N 100.11W
Ciénaga de Oro 49 Ji 8.53N 75.38W
Cieneguita 48 Fd 27.57N 106.59W
Cienfuegos [3] 49 Gb 22.15N 80.30W
Cienfuegos 39 Kg 22.09N 80.27W
Cies, Islas de- 13 Db 42.13N 8.54W
Cieszanów 10 Tf 50.16N 23.08 E
Cieza 13 Kf 38.14N 1.25W
Çifteler 24 Dc 39.22N 31.03 E
Cifuentes 13 Jd 40.47N 2.37W
Čiganak 19 Hf 45.05N 73.58 E
Čigirin 16 He 49.03N 32.42 E
Cigüela 13 Ie 39.08N 3.44W
Cihanbeyli 24 Ec 38.40N 32.56 E
Cihanbeyli Platosu 24 Ec 38.40N 32.45 E
Čihareši 16 Mh 42.47N 43.02 E
Cihuatlán 48 Gh 19.14N 104.35W
Čiily 19 Gg 44.13N 66.46 E
Cijara, Embalse de- 13 He 39.18N 4.52W
Cijulang 26 Eh 7.44S 108.27 E
Čik 15 Dd 45.42N 20.04 E
Čikoj 20 Ff 51.02N 106.39 E
Cikurački, Vulkan- 20 Kf 50.15N 155.29 E
Cilacap 26 Eh 7.44S 109.00 E
Çıldır 24 Jb 41.08N 43.07 E
Çıldır Gölü 24 Jb 41.04N 43.15 E
Cilento 14 Jj 40.20N 15.20 E
Čilik 18 Lc 43.42N 78.14 E
Čilik 19 Hg 43.35N 78.12 E
Cill Airne/Killarney 9 Di 52.03N 9.30W
Cill Chainnigh/Kilkenny 9 Fi 52.39N 7.15W
Cill Chainnigh/Kilkenny [2] 9 Fi 52.40N 7.20W
Cill Chaoi/Kilkee 9 Di 52.41N 9.38W
Cill Dara/Kildare [2] 9 Gh 53.15N 6.45W
Cill Dara/Kildare 9 Gh 53.10N 6.55W
Cill Mhantáin/Wicklow 9 Gi 52.59N 6.03W
Cill Mhantáin/Wicklow [2] 9 Gi 53.00N 6.30W
Cill Mocheallóg/Kilmallock 9 Ei 52.25N 8.35W
Cill Rois/Kilrush 9 Di 52.39N 9.29W
Cilma 17 Fd 65.25N 52.05 E
Cilo Daği 24 Kd 37.30N 44.00 E
Cimaltepec, Sierra- 47 Ee 16.00N 96.40W
Cimarron 38 Jf 36.10N 96.17W
Cimarron 45 Dh 36.31N 104.55W
Čimbaj 19 Fg 42.59N 59.47 E
Cimini, Monti- 14 Gh 42.24N 12.12 E
Čimišlija 16 Ff 46.32N 28.46 E
Čimkent 22 Ie 42.18N 69.36 E
Čimkentskaja Oblast [3] 19 Gg 43.00N 68.40 E
Cimljansk 19 Ef 47.37N 42.04 E
Cimljanskoje Vodohranilišče = Tsimlyansk Reservoir (EN) 5 Kf 48.00N 43.00 E
Cimone 5 Hg 44.12N 10.40 E
Cîmpeni 15 Gc 46.22N 23.03 E
Cîmpia Turzii 15 Gc 46.33N 23.53 E
Cîmpina 15 Id 45.08N 25.44 E
Cîmpulung 15 Id 45.16N 25.03 E
Cîmpulung Moldovenesc 15 Ib 47.32N 25.34 E
Čimtarga, Gora- 18 Ge 39.14N 68.12 E
Cina, Tanjung- 26 Dh 5.55S 104.35 E
Çınar 24 Id 37.39N 40.06 E
Cinarcik 15 Mi 40.39N 29.06 E
Cinaruco, Río- 50 Ci 6.41N 67.07W
Cina Selatan, Laut- = South China Sea (EN) 21 Ni 10.00N 113.00 E
Cinaz 18 Gd 40.56N 68.45 E
Cinca 13 Mc 41.26N 0.21 E
Cincar 14 Lg 43.54N 17.04 E
Cincinnati 39 Kf 39.06N 84.31W
Cinco Irmãos, Serra dos- 55 Ff 22.55S 52.50W
Cinco Saltos 56 Ge 38.49S 68.04W
Cindrelu, Vîrful- 15 Gd 45.35N 23.48 E
Çine 24 Cd 37.36N 28.04 E
Ĉine 15 Kl 37.46N 27.49 E
Ciney 11 Ld 50.18N 5.06 E
Cingirlau 19 Fe 51.07N 54.05 E
Cingoli 14 Hg 43.22N 13.13 E
Cintalapa de Figueroa 48 Mi 16.44N 93.43W
Cinto, Monte- 5 Gg 42.23N 8.56 E
Cintra, Golfo de- 32 De 23.00N 16.15W
Cinzas, Rio das- 55 Gf 22.56S 50.32W
Ciociaria 14 Hi 41.45N 13.15 E
Cionn Mhálanna/Malin Head 5 Fd 55.23N 7.24W
Cionn tSáile/Kinsale 9 Ej 51.42N 8.32W
Ciorani 15 Je 44.49N 26.25 E
Ćiovo 14 Kg 43.30N 16.18 E
Cipa 20 Ge 55.20N 115.55 E
Cipikan 20 Gf 54.58N 113.21 E
Cipó 54 Kf 11.06S 38.31W
Cipolletti 56 Ge 38.56S 67.59W
Ciprovci 15 Ff 43.23N 22.53 E
Cir 16 Me 48.35N 42.55 E
Circeo, Capo- 14 Hi 41.14N 13.03 E
Čirčik 19 Gg 41.28N 69.35 E
Circle [Ak.-U.S.] 40 Kc 65.50N 144.04W
Circle [Mt.-U.S.] 46 Mc 47.25N 105.35W
Circleville 47 Ff 39.36N 82.57W
Cirebon 22 Mj 6.44S 108.34 E
Cirencester 9 Lj 51.44N 1.59W
Ciriè 14 Be 45.14N 7.36 E
Čirinda 20 Fc 67.30N 100.35 E
Čirip, Vulkan- 20 Jg 45.20N 147.58 E
Čirka-Kem 7 Hd 64.45N 32.10 E
Cirò 14 Lk 39.23N 17.04 E
Cirò Marina 14 Lk 39.22N 17.08 E
Ciron 11 Fj 44.36N 0.18W
Čirpan 15 Ig 42.12N 25.20 E
Cirque Mountain 42 Le 58.55N 63.33W
Cisa, Passo della- 14 Df 44.28N 9.55 E
Ciscaucasia (EN) 5 Kf 45.00N 43.00 E
Cisco 45 Gj 32.23N 98.59W
Ciskei 37 Df 31.30S 26.40 E
Čišmy 19 Fe 54.35N 55.25 E
Cisnădie 15 Hd 45.43N 24.09 E
Cisne, Islas del- 47 He 17.22N 83.51W
Cistern Point 49 Ib 24.40N 77.45W
Cistierna 13 Gb 42.48N 5.07W
Čistoozernoje 20 Cf 54.43N 76.43 E
Čistopol 19 Fd 55.23N 50.39 E
Čita 22 Nd 52.03N 113.30 E
Çitak 15 Mk 38.08N 29.39 E

Index Symbols

[1] Independent Nation
[2] State, Region
[3] District, County
[4] Municipality
[5] Colony, Dependency
Continent
Physical Region
Historical or Cultural Region
Mount, Mountain
Volcano
Hill
Mountains, Mountain Range
Hills, Escarpment
Plateau, Upland
Pass, Gap
Plain, Lowland
Delta
Salt Flat
Valley, Canyon
Crater, Cave
Karst Features
Depression
Polder
Desert, Dunes
Forest, Woods
Heath, Steppe
Oasis
Cape, Point
Coast, Beach
Cliff
Peninsula
Isthmus
Sandbank
Island
Atoll
Rock, Reef
Islands, Archipelago
Rocks, Reefs
Coral Reef
Well, Spring
Geyser
River, Stream
Waterfall Rapids
River Mouth, Estuary
Lake
Salt Lake
Intermittent Lake
Reservoir
Swamp, Pond
Canal
Glacier
Ice Shelf, Pack Ice
Ocean
Sea
Gulf, Bay
Strait, Fjord
Lagoon
Bank
Seamount
Tablemount
Ridge
Shelf
Basin
Escarpment, Sea Scarp
Fracture
Trench, Abyss
National Park, Reserve
Point of Interest
Recreation Site
Cave, Cavern
Historic Site
Ruins
Wall, Walls
Church, Abbey
Temple
Scientific Station
Airport
Port
Lighthouse
Mine
Tunnel
Dam, Bridge

Citeli-Ckaro 16 Oi 41.28N 46.06 E
Čitinskaja Oblast [3] 20 Gf 52.30N 117.30 E
Citlaltépetl, Volcán- → Orizaba, Pico de- 38 Jh 19.01N 97.16W
Citrusdale 37 Bf 32.36S 19.00 E
Città del Vaticano = Vatican City (EN) [1] 6 Hg 41.54N 12.27 E
Città di Castello 14 Gg 43.27N 12.14 E
Cittanova 14 Kl 38.21N 16.05 E
Ciucaşu, Vîrful- 15 Id 45.31N 25.55 E
Ciucea 15 Fd 46.57N 22.49 E
Ciudad 48 Gf 23.44N 105.44W
Ciudad Acuña 47 Dc 29.18N 100.55W
Ciudad Altamirano 48 Ih 18.20N 100.40W
Ciudad Bolívar 53 Je 8.08N 63.33W
Ciudad Bolivia 54 Db 8.21N 70.34W
Ciudad Camargo [Mex.] 47 Ec 26.19N 98.50W
Ciudad Camargo [Mex.] 47 Cc 27.40N 105.10W
Ciudad Cuauhtémoc 48 Mj 15.37N 92.00W
Ciudad Darío 49 Dg 12.43N 86.08W
Ciudad de Areco 55 Cl 34.18S 59.46W
Ciudad de Dolores Hidalgo 48 Ig 21.10N 100.56W
Ciudad de la Habana [3] 49 Fb 23.10N 82.10W
Ciudad del Carmen 47 Fe 18.38N 91.50W
Ciudad del Maíz 48 Jf 22.24N 99.36W
Ciudad de México = Mexico City (EN) 39 Jh 19.24N 99.09W
Ciudad de Nutrias 54 Eb 8.07N 69.19W
Ciudad de Río Grande 47 Dd 23.50N 103.02W
Ciudadela/Ciutadella 13 Pd 40.02N 3.50 E
Ciudad Guayana 53 Je 8.22N 62.40W
Ciudad Guerrero 47 Cc 28.33N 107.30W
Ciudad Guzmán 47 De 19.41N 103.29W
Ciudad Hidalgo [Mex.] 48 Mj 14.41N 92.09W
Ciudad Hidalgo [Mex.] 48 Ih 19.41N 100.34W
Ciudad Juárez 39 If 31.44N 106.29W
Ciudad Lerdo 47 Dc 25.32N 103.32W
Ciudad Madero 39 Jg 22.16N 97.50W
Ciudad Mante 47 Ed 22.44N 98.57W
Ciudad Mendoza 48 Kh 18.48N 97.11W
Ciudad Obregón 39 Ig 27.59N 109.56W
Ciudad Ojeda 54 Da 10.12N 71.19W
Ciudad Piar 54 Fb 7.27N 63.19W
Ciudad Real 13 If 38.59N 3.56W
Ciudad Real [3] 13 If 39.00N 4.00W
Ciudad Río Bravo 47 Ec 25.59N 98.06W
Ciudad-Rodrigo 13 Fd 40.36N 6.32W
Ciudad Valles 47 Ed 21.59N 99.01W
Ciudad Victoria 39 Jg 23.44N 99.08W
Ciutadella/Ciudadela 13 Pd 40.02N 3.50 E
Civa Burnu 24 Gb 41.22N 36.35 E
Cividale del Friuli 14 Hd 46.06N 13.25 E
Civilsk 7 Li 55.53N 47.29 E
Civita Castellana 14 Gh 42.17N 12.25 E
Civitanova Marche 14 Hg 43.18N 13.44 E
Civitavecchia 14 Fh 42.06N 11.48 E
Civitella del Tronto 14 Hh 42.46N 13.40 E
Çivril 24 Cc 38.56N 29.35 E
Cixerri 14 Ck 39.17N 8.59 E
Cixi (Hushan) 28 Fi 30.10N 121.14 E
Cixian 28 Cf 36.22N 114.22 E
Čiža 19 Eb 67.06N 44.19 E
Cizre 23 Fb 37.20N 42.12 E
Cjurupinsk 16 Hf 46.37N 32.43 E
Čkalovsk 7 Kh 56.47N 43.17 E
Clacton-on-Sea 9 Oj 51.48N 1.09 E
Clain 11 Gh 46.47N 0.33 E
Claire, Côte- 66 Ie 66.30S 133.00 E
Claire, Lake - 42 Ge 58.30N 112.00W
Clair Engle Lake 46 Df 40.52N 122.43W
Claise 11 Gh 46.56N 0.42 E
Clamecy 11 Jg 47.27N 3.31 E
Clan Alpine Mountains 46 Gg 39.40N 117.55W
Clanton 44 Di 32.50N 86.38W
Clanwilliam 37 Bf 32.11S 18.54 E
Claraz 55 Cm 37.54S 59.17W
Clár Chlainne Mhuiris/ Claremorris 9 Eh 53.44N 9.00W
Clare [Austl.] 59 Hf 33.50S 138.36 E
Clare [Mi.-U.S.] 44 Ed 43.49N 84.46W
Clare/Abhainn an Chláir 9 Dh 53.20N 9.03W
Clare/An Clár [2] 9 Ei 52.50N 9.00W
Clare/Cliara 9 Dh 53.49N 10.00W
Claremont 44 Kd 43.23N 72.21W
Claremore 45 Ih 36.19N 95.36W
Claremorris/Clár Chlainne Mhuiris 9 Eh 53.44N 9.00W
Clarence 62 Ee 42.10S 173.57 E
Clarence 62 Ee 42.10S 173.56 E
Clarence, Cape - 42 Ib 73.55N 90.12W
Clarence Cannon Reservoir 45 Kg 39.31N 91.45W
Clarence Island 66 Re 61.12S 54.05W
Clarence River 59 Ke 29.25S 153.22 E
Clarence Strait [Ak.-U.S.] 40 Me 55.25N 132.00W
Clarence Strait [Austl.] 59 Gb 12.00S 131.00 E
Clarence Town 49 Jb 23.06N 74.59W
Clarendon 45 Fi 34.56N 100.53W
Clarenville 42 Mg 48.09N 53.58W
Claresholm 42 Gf 50.02N 113.35W
Clarinda 45 If 40.44N 95.02W
Clarines 50 Dh 9.56N 65.10W
Clarion, Isla- 47 Be 18.22N 114.44W
Clarion Fracture Zone (EN) 3 Lh 18.00N 130.00W
Clarion River 44 He 41.07N 79.41W
Clark 45 Hd 44.53N 97.44W
Clark, Lake- 40 Id 60.15N 154.15W
Clark, Mount - 42 Fd 64.25N 124.14W
Clarkdale 46 Ii 34.46N 112.03W
Clarke Range 59 Jd 20.50S 148.35 E
Clark Fork 38 He 48.09N 116.15W
Clark Hill Lake 44 Fi 33.50N 82.20W
Clark Mountain 46 Hi 35.32N 115.35W
Clarksburg 43 Kd 39.17N 80.21W
Clarksdale 43 Ie 34.12N 90.34W
Clarks Fork 46 Kd 45.39N 108.43W
Clark's Harbour 44 Od 43.26N 65.38W
Clarkston 46 Gc 46.30N 117.03W
Clarksville [Ar.-U.S.] 45 Ji 35.28N 93.28W
Clarksville [Tn.-U.S.] 43 Jd 36.32N 87.21W
Clarksville [Tx.-U.S.] 45 Ij 33.37N 95.03W
Claro, Rio- [Braz.] 54 Hg 19.08S 50.40W
Claro, Rio- [Braz.] 54 Hg 15.28S 51.45W
Clary 12 Fd 50.00N 3.24 E
Claude 45 Fi 35.07N 101.22W
Claustra/Klosters 14 Dd 46.52N 9.52 E
Clavering 41 Jd 74.20N 21.10W
Claxton 44 Gi 32.10N 81.55W
Clay Belt 38 Kd 51.50N 82.00W
Clay Center 45 Hg 39.23N 96.08W
Clay Cross 12 Aa 53.09N 1.25W
Claye Souilly 12 Ef 48.57N 2.42 E
Clayton 43 Gd 36.27N 103.11W
Clear, Cape- 9 Dj 51.26N 9.31W
Clear Boggy Creek 45 Ii 34.03N 95.47W
Clear Creek [Az.-U.S.] 46 Ji 34.59N 110.38W
Clear Creek [U.S.] 46 Ld 44.53N 106.04W
Clearfield [Pa.-U.S.] 44 He 41.02N 78.27W
Clearfield [Ut.-U.S.] 46 If 41.07N 112.01W
Clear Fork Brazos 45 Gj 33.01N 98.40W
Clear Lake 43 Cd 39.02N 122.50W
Clear Lake [Ia.-U.S.] 45 Je 43.08N 93.23W
Clear Lake [S.D.-U.S.] 45 Hd 44.45N 96.41W
Clear Lake Reservoir 46 Ef 41.52N 121.08W
Clearwater 42 Ge 56.45N 111.22W
Clearwater 43 Kf 27.58N 82.48W
Clearwater Mountains 43 Db 46.00N 115.30W
Clearwater River [Alta.-Can.] 46 Ha 52.23N 114.50W
Clearwater River [U.S.] 46 Gc 46.25N 117.02W
Cleburne 43 He 32.21N 97.23W
Clécy 12 Bf 48.55N 0.29W
Clee Hills 9 Ki 52.25N 2.35W
Cleethorpes 9 Mh 53.34N 0.02W
Clères 12 De 49.36N 1.07 E
Clerf/Clervaux 12 Id 50.03N 6.02 E
Clermont [Austl.] 59 Jd 22.49S 147.39 E
Clermont [Fr.] 11 Ie 49.23N 2.24 E
Clermont-en-Argonne 12 He 49.06N 5.04 E
Clermont-Ferrand 6 Gf 45.47N 3.05 E
Clermont-l'Hérault 11 Jk 43.37N 3.26 E
Clervaux/Clerf 12 Id 50.03N 6.02 E
Clervé 12 Ie 49.57N 6.01 E
Cles 14 Fd 46.22N 11.02 E
Clevedon 9 Kj 51.27N 2.51W
Cleveland 9 Lg 54.25N 1.05W
Cleveland [3] 9 Mg 54.40N 1.00W
Cleveland [Ms.-U.S.] 45 Kj 33.45N 90.50W
Cleveland [Oh.-U.S.] 39 Ke 41.30N 81.41W
Cleveland [Tn.-U.S.] 43 Kd 35.10N 84.53W
Cleveland [Tx.-U.S.] 45 Ik 30.21N 95.05W
Cleveland, Mount- 43 Eb 48.56N 113.51W
Cleveland Heights 44 Ge 41.30N 81.34W
Clevelândia 55 Fh 26.24S 52.21W
Cleveland Mountain 46 Ic 46.37N 113.47W
Clew Bay/Cuan Mó 9 Dh 53.50N 9.50W
Ciiara/Clare 9 Dh 53.49N 10.00W
Cliff 45 Bj 32.59N 108.36W
Clifton [Az.-U.S.] 43 Fe 33.03N 109.18W
Clifton [St.Vin.] 51n Bb 12.36N 61.26W
Clifton [Tx.-U.S.] 45 Hk 31.47N 97.35W
Clinch River 44 Eh 35.53N 84.29W
Cline, Mount- 46 Ga 52.10N 116.40W
Clines Corners 45 Di 35.01N 105.34W
Clingmans Dome 44 Fh 35.35N 83.30W
Clinton [Ar.-U.S.] 45 Ji 35.36N 92.28W
Clinton [B.C.-Can.] 42 Ff 51.05N 121.35W
Clinton [Ia.-U.S.] 43 Ic 41.51N 90.12W
Clinton [Il.-U.S.] 45 Lf 40.09N 88.57W
Clinton [Mo.-U.S.] 45 Jg 38.22N 93.46W
Clinton [Ms.-U.S.] 45 Kj 32.20N 90.20W
Clinton [N.C.-U.S.] 44 Hh 34.59N 78.20W
Clinton [N.Z.] 62 Cg 46.13S 169.23 E
Clinton [Ok.-U.S.] 43 Hd 35.31N 98.59W
Clinton-Colden Lake 42 Gd 63.55N 107.30W
Clintonville 45 Ld 44.37N 88.46W
Clipperton 38 Ih 10.17N 109.13W
Clipperton, Fracture Zone (EN) 3 Mi 10.00N 115.00W
Clisson 11 Eg 47.05N 1.17W
Cloates, Point- 59 Cd 22.45S 113.40 E
Clochán an Aifir/ Giant's Causeway 9 Gf 55.15N 6.35W
9 Gf 55.15N 6.35W
Clodomira 56 Hc 27.35S 64.08W
Cloich na Coillte/Clonakilty 9 Ej 51.37N 8.54W
Clonakilty/Cloich na Coillte 9 Ej 51.37N 8.54W
Cloncurry 58 Fg 20.42S 140.30 E
Clones/Cluain Eois 9 Fg 54.11N 7.14W
Clonmel/Cluain Meala 9 Fi 52.21N 7.42W
Cloppenburg 10 Ed 52.51N 8.02 E
Cloquet 43 Ib 46.43N 92.28W
Clorinda 53 Kh 25.20S 57.40W
Cloud Peak 43 Fc 44.25N 107.10W
Clouère 11 Gh 46.26N 0.17 E
Cloverdale 46 Dg 38.48N 123.01W
Clovis [Ca.-U.S.] 46 Fh 36.49N 119.42W
Clovis [N.M.-U.S.] 39 If 34.24N 103.12W
Cluain Meala/Clonmel 9 Fi 52.21N 7.42W
Cluan Eois/Clones 9 Fg 54.11N 7.14W
Cluj [2] 15 Gc 46.49N 23.35 E
Cluj Napoca 6 If 46.46N 23.36 E
Cluny 11 Kh 46.26N 4.39 E
Cluses 11 Mh 46.04N 6.36 E
Clusone 14 De 45.53N 9.57 E
Clutha 62 Cg 46.21S 169.48 E
Clwyd 9 Jh 53.20N 3.30W
Clwyd [3] 9 Jh 53.10N 3.15W
Clyde 9 If 55.56N 4.29W
Clyde [N.W.T.-Can.] 39 Mb 70.25N 68.30W
Clyde [N.Z.] 62 Cf 45.11S 169.19 E
Clyde, Firth of- 9 If 55.42N 5.00W
Clyde Inlet 42 Kb 70.20N 68.20W
Cna 5 Ke 54.32N 42.05 E
Cnoc Bréanainn/Brandon Mount 9 Ci 52.14N 10.15W
Cnoc Fola/Bloody Foreland 9 Ef 55.09N 8.17W
Cnoc Mhaoldonn/ Knockmealdown Mountains 9 Fi 52.15N 8.00W
Cnori 16 Ni 41.35N 45.59 E
Cnossus (EN) = Knosós 15 In 35.18N 25.10 E
Côa 13 Ec 41.05N 7.06W
Coachella Canal 46 Hj 33.34N 116.00W
Coahuayana 48 Hh 18.44N 103.41W
Coahuila [2] 47 Dc 27.20N 102.00W
Coalcomán, Sierra de- 47 De 18.30N 102.55W
Coalcomán de Matamoros 48 Hh 18.47N 103.09W
Coaldale 46 Ib 49.43N 112.37W
Coalgate 45 Hi 34.32N 96.13W
Coalinga 46 Eh 36.09N 120.21W
Coalville 9 Li 52.44N 1.20W
Coamo 49 Nd 18.05N 66.22W
Coari 54 Fd 4.05S 63.08W
Coari, Lago de- 54 Fd 4.15S 63.25W
Coari, Rio- 52 Jf 4.30S 63.33W
Coast [3] 36 Gc 3.00S 39.30 E
Coast Mountains 38 Gd 55.00N 129.00W
Coast Plain (EN) = Kustvlakte 11 Ic 51.00N 2.30 E
Coast Ranges 38 Ge 41.00N 123.30W
Coatbridge 9 If 55.52N 4.01W
Coatepec 48 Kh 19.27N 96.58W
Coatepel, Cerro- 48 Kh 18.25N 97.35W
Coatepeque 49 Bf 14.42N 91.52W
Coats 38 Kc 62.30N 83.00W
Coats Land (EN) 66 Af 77.00S 28.00W
Coatzacoalcos 39 Jh 18.09N 94.25W
Coatzacoalcos, Bahía- 48 Lh 18.10N 94.27W
Coatzacoalcos, Río- 48 Lh 18.09N 94.24W
Coba 47 Gd 20.36N 87.35W
Cobadin 15 Le 44.05N 28.13 E
Cobalt 42 Jg 47.24N 79.41W
Cobán 47 Fe 15.29N 90.19W
Cobar 59 Jf 31.30S 145.49 E
Cobb, Mount- 46 Dg 38.45N 122.40W
Cobb Seamount (EN) 38 Fe 46.46N 130.43W
Cóbh/An Cóbh 9 Ej 51.51N 8.17W
Cobija 54 Ef 11.02S 68.44W
Cobo 55 Dm 37.48S 57.38W
Cobourg 42 Jh 43.58N 78.10W
Cobourg Peninsula 59 Gb 11.20S 132.15 E
Cöbue 37 Eb 12.07S 34.52 E
Coburg 10 Gf 50.15N 10.58 E
Coburg 42 Ja 75.57N 79.00W
Coburn Mountain 44 Lc 45.28N 70.06W
Coca, Pizzo di- 14 Ed 46.04N 10.01 E
Cocalinho 55 Gb 14.22S 51.00W
Cocentaina 13 Lf 38.45N 0.26W
Cochabamba [2] 54 Eg 17.30S 65.40W
Cochabamba 53 Jg 17.24S 66.09W
Coche, Isla- 50 Eg 10.47N 63.56W
Cochem 10 Df 50.08N 7.09 E
Cochin 22 Ji 9.58N 76.14 E
Cochin China (EN) = Nam Phan 21 Mg 11.00N 107.00 E
Cochinos, Bahía de- = Pigs, Bay of- (EN) 49 Gb 22.07N 81.10W
Cochons, Ile aux- 30 Mm 46.05S 50.08 E
Cochran 44 Fi 32.23N 83.21W
Cochrane 42 He 57.55N 101.32W
Cochrane [Alta.-Can.] 46 Ha 51.11N 114.28W
Cochrane [Ont.-Can.] 39 Ke 49.04N 81.01W
Cockburn, Canal- 56 Fh 54.20S 71.30W
Cockburn, Mount- 59 Gd 22.46S 130.36 E
Cockburn Bank 9 El 49.40N 8.50W
Cockburn Island 44 Fc 45.55N 83.22W
Cockburn Town 49 Ja 24.02N 74.31W
Cockermouth 9 Jg 54.40N 3.21W
Coclé [3] 49 Gi 8.30N 80.15W
Coco, Cayo- 49 Hb 22.30N 78.28W
Coco, Ile- 51b Bc 11.52N 62.49W
Coco, Isla del- 38 Ki 5.32N 87.04W
Coco, Río-o Segovia, Río- 38 Kh 15.00N 83.08W
Cocoa 43 Kf 28.21N 80.44W
Cocoa Beach 44 Gk 28.19N 80.36W
Cocoa Point 51d Ba 17.33N 61.46W
Cocobeach 36 Ab 0.59N 9.36 E
Coco Channel 25 If 14.00N 93.00 E
Coco Islands 25 If 14.05N 93.18 E
Coconino Plateau 46 Ii 35.50N 112.30W
Cocorocuma, Cayos- 49 Ff 15.45N 83.00W
Cocos 64c Bb 13.14N 144.39 E
Cócos 55 Jb 14.10S 44.33W
Cocos Islands (Keeling Islands) 21 Lk 12.10S 96.55 E
Cocos Islands (Keeling Islands) [5] 22 Lk 12.10S 96.55 E
Cocos Ridge (EN) 3 Ni 5.30N 86.00W
Cocula 48 Hg 20.23N 103.50W
Cocuzzo 14 Kk 39.13N 16.08 E
Cod, Cape- 44 Me 41.50N 70.00W
Cod, Cape- 38 Le 41.42N 70.15W
Coda Cavallo, Capo- 14 Dj 40.51N 9.43 E
Codaeşti 15 Kc 46.52N 27.45 E
Codajás 54 Fd 3.50S 62.05W
Codera, Cabo- 50 Cg 10.35N 66.04W
Codfish Island 62 Bg 46.45S 167.40 E
Codigoro 14 Gf 44.49N 12.08 E
Codlea 15 Id 45.42N 25.27 E
Codó 54 Jd 4.29S 43.53W
Codogno 14 De 45.09N 9.42 E
Codrington 50 Fd 17.38N 61.50W
Codrington Lagoon 51d Ba 17.39N 61.51W
Codrului, Munţii- 15 Fc 46.35N 22.10 E
Cody 43 Fc 44.32N 109.05W
Coen 58 Ff 13.56S 143.12 E
Coesfeld 10 De 51.56N 7.09 E
Coetivy Island 30 Mi 7.08S 56.16 E
Coeur d'Alene 43 Db 47.41N 116.46W
Coevorden 11 Mb 52.40N 6.45 E
Coffeyville 45 Ih 37.02N 95.37W
Coffs Harbour 58 Gh 30.18S 153.08 E
Cofre de Perote, Cerro- (Nauhcampatépetl) 48 Kh 19.29N 97.08W
Cofrentes 13 Ke 39.14N 1.04W
Coggeshall 12 Cc 51.52N 0.41 E
Coghinas 14 Cj 40.56N 8.48 E
Coghinas, Lago del- 14 Dj 40.45N 9.05 E
Coglians 14 Gd 46.37N 12.53 E
Cognac 11 Fi 45.42N 0.20W
Cogne 14 Be 45.37N 7.21 E
Cogolludo 13 Id 40.57N 3.05W
Čograjskoje Vodohranilišče 16 Ng 45.30N 44.30 E
Coiba, Isla de- 47 Hg 7.27N 81.45W
Coig, Río- (Coyle) 56 Gh 50.58S 69.11W
Coihaique 56 Fg 45.34S 72.04W
Coimbatore 22 Jh 11.00N 76.58 E
Coimbra [2] 13 Dd 40.12N 8.25W
Coimbra [Braz.] 55 Dd 19.55S 57.47W
Coimbra [Port.] 13 Dd 40.12N 8.25W
Coin 13 Hh 36.40N 4.45W
Coipasa, Salar de- 54 Eg 19.30S 68.10W
Čojbalsan 22 Ne 48.04N 114.30 E
Cojedes 50 Bh 9.37N 68.55W
Cojedes [2] 54 Eb 9.20N 68.20W
Cojedes, Río- 50 Bh 8.44N 68.15W
Cojutepeque 49 Cg 13.43N 88.56W
Čoka 15 Dd 45.56N 20.09 E
Cokeville 46 Je 42.05N 110.55W
Cokover River 59 Ed 20.40S 120.45 E
Čokurdah 20 Jb 70.38N 147.55 E
Colac [Austl.] 59 Ig 38.20S 143.35 E
Colac [N.Z.] 62 Bg 46.22S 167.53 E
Colatina 53 Lg 19.32S 40.37W
Colbeck, Cape- 66 Mf 77.06S 157.48W
Colbitz-Letzlinger Heide 10 Hd 52.27N 11.35 E
Colby 45 Fg 39.24N 101.03W
Colchester 9 Nj 51.54N 0.54 E
Cold Bay 40 Ge 55.11N 162.30W
Cold Lake 42 Gf 54.27N 110.10W
Coldstream 9 Kf 55.39N 2.15W
Coldwater [Ks.-U.S.] 45 Gh 37.16N 99.19W
Coldwater [Mi.-U.S.] 44 Ee 41.57N 85.00W
Colebrook 44 Lc 44.53N 71.30W
Coleman 45 Gk 31.50N 99.26W
Coleman River 59 Ic 15.06S 141.38 E
Coleraine/Cúil Raithin 9 Gf 55.08N 6.40W
Coleridge, Lake- 62 De 43.20S 171.30 E
Coles, Punta- 54 Dg 17.42S 71.23W
Colesberg 37 Df 30.45S 25.05 E
Colfax [La.-U.S.] 45 Jk 31.31N 92.42W
Colfax [Wa.-U.S.] 46 Gc 46.53N 117.22W
Colfontaine 12 Fd 50.25N 3.50 E
Colhué Huapi, Lago- 56 Gg 45.30S 68.48W
Colibaşi 15 He 44.56N 24.54 E
Colibris, Pointe des- 51e Bb 16.17N 61.06W
Colima [2] 47 De 19.10N 104.00W
Colima 39 Ih 19.14N 103.43W
Colima, Nevado de- 38 Ih 19.33N 103.38W
Colinas 55 Hb 14.12S 48.03W
Coll 9 Ge 56.40N 6.35W
Collado Bajo 13 Kd 40.14N 1.50W
Collarada 13 Lb 42.43N 0.29W
Colle di Val d'Elsa 14 Fg 43.25N 11.07 E
Colleferro 14 Gi 41.44N 12.59 E
College 40 Jd 64.51N 147.47W
College Place 46 Fc 46.03N 118.23W
College Station 45 Hk 30.37N 96.21W
Collegno 14 Be 45.05N 7.34 E
Collie 59 Df 33.21S 116.09 E
Collier Bay 59 Ec 16.10S 124.15 E
Collierville 44 Ch 35.03N 89.40W
Collingwood [N.Z.] 61 Dh 40.41S 172.41 E
Collingwood [Ont.-Can.] 44 Gc 44.29N 80.13W
Collinson Peninsula 42 Hb 70.00N 101.10W
Collinsville 59 Jd 20.34S 147.51 E
Collmberg 10 Je 51.15N 13.02 E
Colmar 11 Nf 48.05N 7.22 E
Colmena 55 Bi 28.45S 60.06W
Colmenar 13 Hh 36.54N 4.20W
Colmenar Viejo 13 Id 40.40N 3.46W
Colne 12 Cc 51.51N 0.59 E
Colne Point 12 Dc 51.46N 1.03 E
Colnett, Punta- 48 Ab 31.00N 116.20W
Cologne (EN) = Köln 6 Ge 50.56N 6.57 E
Colombia [2] 53 Ie 4.00N 72.00W
Colombia 55 He 20.10S 48.40W
Colombian Basin (EN) 38 Lh 13.00N 76.00W
Colombier, Pointe à- 51b Bc 17.55N 62.53W
Colombo 22 Ji 6.56N 79.51 E
Colón [Arg.] 56 Hd 33.53S 61.07W
Colón [Arg.] 56 Id 32.13S 58.08W
Colón [Cuba] 47 Hd 22.43N 80.54W
Colón [Hond.] [3] 49 Ef 15.20N 84.30W
Colón [Pan.] [3] 49 Hi 9.30N 79.15W
Colón [Pan.] 39 Li 9.22N 79.54W
Colón [Ur.] 55 Ek 33.53S 54.43W
Colón, Archipiélago de-/ Galápagos, Islas- = Galapagos Islands (EN) 52 Gf 0.30S 90.30W
Colón, Montañas de- 49 Ef 14.55N 84.45W
Colona 59 Gf 31.38S 132.05 E
Colonarie 51n Ba 13.14N 61.08W
Colonarie 51n Ba 13.14N 61.08W
Colonel Hill 49 Jb 22.52N 74.15W
Colonia [2] 55 Dl 34.10S 57.30W
Colonia 60 Bf 9.31N 138.08 E
Colonia agricola de Turén 50 Bh 9.15N 69.05W
Colonia Carlos Pellegrini 55 Di 28.32S 57.10W
Colonia del Sacramento 56 Id 34.28S 57.51W
Colonia Elisa 55 Ch 26.56S 59.32W
Colonia Juárez 48 Eb 30.19N 108.05W
Colonia Las Heras 56 Gg 46.33S 68.57W
Colonia Lavalleja 56 Id 31.06S 57.01W
Colonial Heights 44 Ig 37.15N 77.25W
Colonia Morelos 48 Eb 30.50N 109.10W
Colonne, Capo- 14 Lk 39.02N 17.12 E
Colonsay 9 Ge 56.05N 6.10W
Colorado 49 Fh 10.46N 83.35W
Colorado [2] 43 Fd 39.30N 105.30W
Colorado, Cerro- 48 Bb 31.31N 115.31W
Colorado, Rio- [Arg.] 52 Ji 39.50S 62.08W
Colorado, Rio- [N.Amer.] 38 Hf 31.45N 114.40W
Colorado City 45 Fj 32.24N 100.52W
Colorado Plateau 38 Hf 36.30N 118.00W
Colorado River [N.Amer.] 38 Hf 31.45N 114.40W
Colorado River [U.S.] 38 Jg 28.36N 95.58W
Colorados, Archipiélago de los- 49 Eb 22.36N 84.20W
Colorado Springs 39 If 38.50N 104.49W
Colotlán 48 Hf 22.03N 103.16W
Colpon-Ata 18 Kc 42.39N 77.06 E
Coltishall 12 Db 52.44N 1.22 E
Colui 36 Cf 15.10S 16.40 E
Columbia 38 Ge 46.15N 124.05W
Columbia [Ky.-U.S.] 44 Eg 37.06N 85.18W
Columbia [Mo.-U.S.] 43 Id 38.57N 92.20W
Columbia [Ms.-U.S.] 45 Lk 31.15N 89.56W
Columbia [Pa.-U.S.] 44 Ie 40.02N 76.30W
Columbia [S.C.-U.S.] 39 Kf 34.00N 81.03W
Columbia [Tn.-U.S.] 44 Dh 35.37N 87.02W
Columbia, Cape- 38 La 83.08N 70.35W
Columbia, Mount- 38 Hd 57.00N 117.00W
Columbia Basin 43 Db 46.45N 119.05W
Columbia Falls 46 Hb 48.23N 114.11W
Columbia Mountains 38 Hd 52.00N 119.00W
Columbia Plateau 38 He 44.00N 117.30W
Columbia Seamount (EN) 54 Lh 20.40S 31.30W
Columbine, Cape- 30 Il 32.49S 17.51 E
Columbretes, Islas-/ Columbrets, Els- 13 Me 39.52N 0.40 E
Columbrets, Els-/ Columbretes, Islas- 13 Me 39.52N 0.40 E
Columbus [Ga.-U.S.] 39 Kf 32.29N 84.59W
Columbus [In.-U.S.] 43 Jd 39.13N 85.55W
Columbus [Ks.-U.S.] 45 Ih 37.10N 94.50W
Columbus [Ms.-U.S.] 43 Je 33.30N 88.25W
Columbus [Mt.-U.S.] 46 Kd 45.38N 109.15W
Columbus [Nb.-U.S.] 43 Hc 41.25N 97.22W
Columbus [N.M.-U.S.] 45 Ck 31.50N 107.38W
Columbus [Oh.-U.S.] 39 Kf 39.57N 83.00W
Columbus [Tx.-U.S.] 45 Hl 29.42N 96.33W
Columbus Point 49 Ja 24.08N 75.16W
Colville 38 Dc 70.25N 150.30W
Colville, Cape- 62 Fb 36.28S 175.21 E
Colville Channel 62 Fb 36.25S 175.30 E
Colville Lake 42 Ec 67.10N 126.00W
Colville Lake 42 Ec 67.06N 126.00W
Col Visentin 14 Gd 46.05N 12.20 E
Colwyn Bay 9 Jh 53.18N 3.43W
Coma 35 Fd 8.27N 36.55 E
Comacchio 14 Gf 44.42N 12.11 E
Comacchio, Valli di- 14 Gf 44.40N 12.05 E
Comai (Damxoi) 27 Ff 28.26N 91.32 E
Comala 48 Hh 19.19N 103.45W
Comalcalco 47 Fe 18.16N 93.13W
Coman, Mount- 66 Qf 73.49S 64.18W
Comanche [Mt.-U.S.] 46 Kc 46.02N 108.54W
Comanche [Tx.-U.S.] 45 Gk 31.54N 98.36W
Comandante Fontana 55 Cg 25.20S 59.41W
Comandău 15 Jd 45.46N 26.16 E
Comăneşti 15 Jc 46.25N 26.26 E
Comayagua 47 Gf 14.25N 87.37W
Comayagua [3] 49 Df 14.30N 87.40W
Combarbala 56 Fd 31.11S 71.02W
Combeaufontaine 11 Lg 47.43N 5.53 E
Combermere Bay 25 Ie 19.37N 93.34 E
Comblain-au-Pont 12 Hd 50.28N 5.35 E
Combles 12 Ed 50.01N 2.52 E
Combourg 11 Ef 48.25N 1.45W
Combraille 11 Ih 46.30N 3.10 E
Combrailles 11 Ih 46.15N 2.10 E
Comedero 48 Fe 24.37N 106.46W
Comendador 49 Ld 18.53N 71.42W
Comeragh Mountains/Na Comaraigh 9 Fi 52.13N 7.35W
Comerío 51a Bb 18.13N 66.16W
Comilla 25 Id 23.27N 91.12 E
Comines 12 Fd 50.46N 3.01 E
Comines/Komen 12 Ed 50.46N 2.59 E
Comino 14 In 36.00N 14.20 E
Comino, Capo- 14 Dj 40.32N 9.49 E
Comiso 14 In 36.56N 14.36 E
Comitán de Domínguez 47 Fe 16.15N 92.08W
Commentry 11 Ih 46.17N 2.45 E
Commerce 45 Ij 33.15N 95.54W
Commercy 11 Lf 48.45N 5.35 E
Commiges 11 Gk 43.15N 0.45 E
Committee Bay 38 Kc 68.30N 86.30W
Commonwealth Bay 66 Je 66.54S 142.40 E
Communism Peak (EN) = Kommunizma, Pik- 21 Jf 38.57N 72.08 E
Como [China] 27 Ee 33.26N 85.21 E
Como [It.] 14 De 45.47N 9.05 E
Como, Lago di- 14 Dd 46.00N 9.15 E
Comodoro 55 Bl 35.19S 60.31W
Comodoro Ravadavia 53 Jj 45.50S 67.30W
Comondú 47 Bc 26.03N 111.46W
Comores/Comoros [1] 31 Lj 12.10S 44.10 E
Comores, Archipel des- = Comoro Islands (EN) 30 Lj 12.10S 44.15 E
Comorin, Cape- 21 Ji 8.04N 77.34 E
Comoro Islands (EN) = Comores, Archipel des- 30 Lj 12.10S 44.15 E
Comoros/Comores [1] 31 Lj 12.10S 44.10 E
Comox 46 Cb 49.40N 124.55W
Compiègne 11 Ie 49.25N 2.50 E
Compostela 47 Dd 21.14N 104.55W
Comprida, Ilha- 55 Ig 24.50S 47.42W
Compton 46 Fj 33.54N 118.13W
Comstock 45 Fl 29.41N 101.11W
Comtal, Causse du- 11 Ij 44.26N 2.38 E

Index Symbols

[1] Independent Nation
[2] State, Region
[3] District, County
[4] Municipality
[5] Colony, Dependency
Continent
Physical Region
Historical or Cultural Region
Mount, Mountain
Volcano
Hill
Mountains, Mountain Range
Hills, Escarpment
Plateau, Upland
Pass, Gap
Plain, Lowland
Delta
Salt Flat
Valley, Canyon
Crater, Cave
Karst Features
Depression
Polder
Desert, Dunes
Forest, Woods
Heath, Steppe
Oasis
Cape, Point
Coast, Beach
Cliff
Peninsula
Isthmus
Sandbank
Island
Atoll
Rock, Reef
Islands, Archipelago
Rocks, Reefs
Coral Reef
Well, Spring
Geyser
River, Stream
Waterfall Rapids
River Mouth, Estuary
Lake
Salt Lake
Intermittent Lake
Reservoir
Swamp, Pond
Canal
Glacier
Ice Shelf, Pack Ice
Ocean
Sea
Gulf, Bay
Strait, Fjord
Lagoon
Bank
Seamount
Tablemount
Ridge
Shelf
Basin
Escarpment, Sea Scarp
Fracture
Trench, Abyss
National Park, Reserve
Point of Interest
Recreation Site
Cave, Cavern
Historic Site
Ruins
Wall, Walls
Church, Abbey
Temple
Scientific Station
Airport
Port
Lighthouse
Mine
Tunnel
Dam, Bridge

Čona 21 Mc 62.00N 110.00 E
Cona 27 Ff 28.01N 91.57 E
Co Nag 27 Fe 32.00N 91.25 E
Conakry 31 Fh 9.31N 13.43W
Conara Junction 59 Jh 41.50S 147.26 E
Concarneau 11 Cg 47.52N 3.55W
Conceição da Barra 54 Kg 18.35S 39.45W
Conceição do Araguaia 54 Ie 8.15S 49.17W
Conceição do Mato Dentro 55 Kd 19.01S 43.25W
Concepción [3] 55 Df 23.00S 57.00W
Concepción [Arg.] 56 Gc 27.20S 65.35W
Concepción [Arg.] 55 Di 28.23S 57.53W
Concepción [Bol.] 54 Fg 16.15S 62.04W
Concepción [Chile] 53 Ii 36.50S 73.03W
Concepción [Par.] 53 Kh 23.25S 57.17W
Concepción [Peru] 54 Cf 11.55S 75.17W
Concepción [Ven.] 49 Lh 10.25N 71.41W
Concepción, Bahía- 48 Dd 26.40N 111.48W
Concepción, Laguna- 54 Fg 17.30S 61.25W
Concepción, Punta- 48 Dd 26.50N 111.50W
Concepción, Río- 55 Ab 15.46S 62.10W
Concepción del Bermejo 55 Bh 26.36S 60.57W
Concepción del Oro 47 Dd 24.38N 101.25W
Concepción del Uruguay 56 Id 32.29S 58.14W
Conception, Point- 38 Gf 34.27N 120.27W
Conception Bay 42 Mg 48.00N 52.50W
Conception Island 49 Jb 23.52N 75.03W
Concha 49 Li 9.02N 71.45W
Conchas 55 Hf 23.01S 48.00W
Conchas Dam 45 Di 35.22N 104.11W
Conchas Lake 45 Di 35.25N 104.14W
Conches-en-Ouche 11 Gf 48.58N 0.56 E
Concho River 45 Gk 31.32N 99.43W
Conchos, Río- 38 Ig 29.35N 104.25W
Concoran 46 Fh 36.06N 119.33W
Concord [Ca.-U.S.] 46 Eh 37.59N 122.00W
Concord [N.H.-U.S.] 39 Le 43.12N 71.32W
Concordia [Arg.] 53 Ki 31.24S 58.02W
Concordia [Braz.] 55 Fh 27.14S 52.01W
Concordia [Ks.-U.S.] 45 Hg 39.34N 97.39W
Concordia [Mex.] 48 Ff 23.17N 106.04W
Concordia Baai 51c Aa 17.31N 62.58W
Con Cuong 25 Ke 19.02N 104.54 E
Conda 36 Be 11.06S 14.20 E
Condamine River 59 Je 27.00S 149.50 E
Condat 11 Ii 45.22N 2.46 E
Conde 54 Kf 11.49S 37.37W
Condé-en-Brie 12 Fe 49.01N 3.33 E
Condega 49 Dg 13.21N 86.24W
Condé-sur-l'Escaut 12 Fd 50.27N 3.35 E
Condé-sur-Marne 12 Ge 49.03N 4.11 E
Condé-sur-Noireau 11 Ff 48.51N 0.33W
Condobolin 59 Jf 33.05S 147.09 E
Condom 11 Gk 43.58N 0.22 E
Condon 46 Ed 45.14N 120.11W
Condor, Cordillera del- 54 Cd 4.20S 78.30W
Condroz/Condruzisch Plateau 11 Kd 50.25N 5.00 E
Condruzisch Plateau/Condroz 11 Kd 50.25N 5.00 E
Conecuh River 44 Dj 30.58N 87.14W
Conegliano 14 Ge 45.53N 12.18 E
Conejera, Isla- [Sp.] 13 Nf 38.59N 1.12 E
Conejera, Isla- [Sp.] 13 Oe 39.11N 2.57 E
Conejo 48 De 24.05N 111.00W
Conejo, Cerro- 48 Jg 21.24N 99.06W
Conero 14 Hg 43.33N 13.36 E
Conesa 55 Bk 33.36S 60.21W
Conference Island 51p Bb 12.09N 61.35W
Conflans-en-Jarnisy 12 He 49.10N 5.51 E
Conflans-Sainte-Honorine 12 Ef 48.59N 2.06 E
Confolens 11 Gh 46.01N 0.40 E
Confuso, Río- 55 Dg 25.09S 57.34W
Conghua 27 Jg 23.31N 113.30 E
Congo [1] 31 Ii 1.00S 15.00 E
Congo 30 Ii 6.04S 12.24 E
Congo, Dem. Rep. of the- → Zaire [1] 31 Ji 1.00S 25.00 E
Congo Basin (EN) 30 Ih 0.00 17.00 E
Congonhas 55 Ke 20.30S 43.52W
Conil de la Frontera 13 Fh 36.16N 6.05W
Coniston 44 Gb 46.29N 80.51W
Conn, Lough-/Loch Con 9 Dg 54.04N 9.20W
Connacht/Connaught 9 Eh 53.30N 9.00W
Connaught/Connacht 9 Eh 53.30N 9.00W
Conneaut 44 Ge 41.58N 80.34W
Connecticut [2] 43 Mc 41.45N 72.45W
Connecticut River 43 Mc 41.17N 72.21W
Connell 46 Fc 46.40N 118.52W
Connellsville 44 He 40.02N 79.38W
Connemara, Mountains of- 9 Dh 53.30N 9.45W
Connersville 44 Ef 39.39N 85.08W
Conn Lake 42 Kb 70.30N 73.30W
Connors Range 59 Jd 21.40S 149.10 E
Conon 9 Id 57.35N 4.30W
Conquista 55 Id 19.56S 47.33W
Conrad 46 Jb 48.10N 111.57W
Conroe 45 Ik 30.19N 95.27W
Conroe Lake 45 Ik 30.25N 95.37W
Conscripto Bernardi 55 Cj 31.03S 59.05W
Conselheiro Lafaiete 54 Jh 20.40S 43.48W
Conselice 14 Ff 44.31N 11.49 E
Consett 9 Lg 54.51N 1.49W
Consolación del Sur 49 Fb 22.30N 83.31W
Con Son 25 Lg 8.43N 106.36 E
Constance, Lake- (EN) = Bodensee 5 Gf 47.35N 9.25 E
Constanța [2] 15 Le 44.30N 28.30 E
Constanța 6 Ig 44.11N 28.39 E
Constantina 13 Gg 37.52N 5.37W
Constantine [3] 32 Ib 36.20N 6.35 E
Constantine 31 He 36.22N 6.37 E
Constantine, Cape- 40 He 58.25N 158.50W
Constitución [Chile] 56 Fe 35.20S 72.25W
Constitución [Ur.] 55 Dj 31.05S 57.50W
Consuegra 13 Ie 39.28N 3.36W
Consuelo Peak 57 Fg 24.58S 148.10 E
Contamana 54 De 7.15S 74.54W
Contas, Rio de- 52 Mg 14.17S 39.01W
Contoy, Isla- 48 Pg 21.30N 86.48W
Contraforte Central, Serra do- 55 Ic 17.15S 47.50W
Contramaestre 49 Ic 20.18N 76.15W
Contraviesa, Sierra- 13 Ih 36.50N 3.10W
Contreras, Embalse de- 13 Ke 39.32N 1.30W
Contreras, Islas- 49 Gj 7.50N 81.47W
Contreras, Puerto de- 13 Ke 39.32N 1.30W
Contres 11 Hg 47.25N 1.26 E
Contumazá 54 Ce 7.22S 78.49W
Contursi 14 Jj 40.39N 15.14 E
Contwig 12 Je 49.15N 7.26 E
Contwoyto Lake 42 Gc 65.40N 110.40W
Conty 12 Ee 49.44N 2.09 E
Convención 54 Db 8.28N 73.20W
Conversano 14 Lj 40.58N 17.07 E
Conway 9 Jh 53.17N 3.50W
Conway [Ar.-U.S.] 43 Id 35.05N 92.26W
Conway [N.H.-U.S.] 44 Ld 43.58N 71.07W
Conway [S.C.-U.S.] 44 Hi 33.51N 79.04W
Conway [Wales-U.K.] 9 Jh 53.17N 3.50W
Conway, Mount- 59 Gd 23.45S 133.25 E
Conway Reef → Ceva-i-Ra 57 Ig 21.45S 174.35 E
Conyers 44 Fi 33.40N 84.00W
Conza, Sella di- 14 Jj 40.50N 15.18 E
Coober Pedy 58 Eg 29.01S 134.43 E
Cooch Behār → Koch Bihār 25 Hc 26.19N 89.26 E
Cook 66 Ad 59.27S 27.10W
Cook 59 Gf 30.37S 130.25 E
Cook, Bahía- 56 Fi 55.10S 70.10W
Cook, Cap- 63b Dd 19.32S 169.30 E
Cook, Cape- 46 Ba 50.08N 127.55W
Cook, Mount- 57 Hi 43.36S 170.09 E
Cook, Récif de- 63b Ad 19.25S 163.50 E
Cooke, Mount- 59 Df 32.25S 116.18 E
Cookes Peak 45 Cj 32.32N 107.44W
Cookeville 44 Eg 36.10N 85.31W
Cook Ice Shelf 66 Je 68.40S 152.30 E
Cook Inlet 38 Dc 60.30N 152.00W
Cook Island 64g Bb 1.57N 157.28W
Cook Islands [5] 58 Lf 20.00S 158.00W
Cookstown/An Chorr Chríochach 9 Gg 54.39N 6.45W
Cook Strait 57 Ii 41.20S 174.25 E
Cooktown 58 Ff 15.28S 145.15 E
Coolgardie 59 Ef 30.57S 121.10 E
Coolidge [Az.-U.S.] 43 Ee 32.59N 111.31W
Coolidge [Ks.-U.S.] 45 Fg 38.03N 101.59W
Coolidge Dam 46 Jj 33.12N 110.32W
Cooma 59 Jg 36.14S 149.08 E
Coonabarabran 59 Jf 31.16S 149.17 E
Coonamble 59 Jf 30.57S 148.23 E
Coonoor 25 Ff 11.21N 76.49 E
Coon Rapids 45 Jd 45.09N 93.18W
Cooper 45 Ij 33.23N 95.35W
Cooper, Mount- 46 Ga 50.13N 117.12W
Cooper Creek 57 Eg 28.29S 137.46 E
Cooper's Town 44 Il 26.51N 77.31W
Cooperstown [N.D.-U.S.] 45 Gc 47.27N 98.07W
Cooperstown [N.Y.-U.S.] 44 Jd 42.43N 74.56W
Coosa River 44 Di 32.30N 86.16W
Coos Bay 43 Cc 43.22N 124.13W
Coos Bay 46 Ce 43.23N 124.16W
Cootamundra 59 Jf 34.39S 148.02 E
Čop 16 Ce 48.26N 22.14 E
Copaiapó, Río- 56 Fc 27.19S 70.56W
Copainalá 48 Mi 17.05N 93.12W
Copán [3] 49 Cf 14.50N 89.00W
Copan 39 Kh 14.50N 89.09W
Copán 49 Cf 14.50N 89.12W
Copenhagen (EN) = København 6 Hi 55.40N 12.35 E
Copertino 14 Mj 40.16N 18.03 E
Copetonas 55 Bn 38.43N 60.27W
Copiapó 53 Ih 27.22S 70.20W
Çöpköy 15 Jh 41.13N 26.49 E
Coporito 50 Fh 8.56N 62.00W
Coporolo 36 Be 12.56S 13.00 E
Copparo 14 Ff 44.54N 11.49 E
Copper 40 Kd 60.30N 144.50W
Copperbelt [3] 36 Ee 13.00S 28.00 E
Copper Center 40 Jd 61.58N 145.19W
Copper Cliff 42 Jg 46.28N 81.04W
Copper Harbor 44 Db 47.27N 87.53W
Coppermine 39 Hc 67.50N 115.05W
Coppermine 38 Hc 67.49N 115.04W
Coppermine Point 44 Eb 46.59N 84.47W
Copper Queen 37 Dc 17.31S 29.20 E
Coqên (Maindong) 27 Ee 31.15N 85.13 E
Coquet 9 Lf 55.22N 1.37W
Coquetá, Río- 52 Jf 3.08S 64.46W
Coquille 46 Ce 43.11N 124.11W
Coquimbo [2] 56 Fd 31.00S 71.00W
Coquimbo 53 Ih 29.58S 71.21W
Corabia 15 Hf 43.47N 24.30 E
Coracão de Jesus 55 Jc 16.42S 44.22W
Coradi o Cheradi, Isole- 14 Lj 40.27N 17.09 E
Corail 49 Kd 18.34N 73.53W
Corail, Mer de- = Coral Sea (EN) 57 Gf 20.00S 158.00 E
Coral, Cabeza de- 48 Ph 18.47N 87.19W
Coral Gables 43 Kf 25.45N 80.16W
Coral Harbour 39 Kc 64.08N 83.10W
Coral Sea 57 Gf 20.00S 158.00 E
Coral Sea (EN) = Corail, Mer de- 57 Gf 20.00S 158.00 E
Coral Sea Basin (EN) 57 Gf 14.00S 152.00 E
Coral Sea Islands Territory 59 Lc 18.00S 158.00 E
Coralville 45 Kf 41.40N 91.35W
Coralville Lake 45 Kf 41.47N 91.48W
Corantijn River 52 Ke 5.55N 57.05W
Corato 14 Ki 41.09N 16.25 E
Corbara, Lago di- 14 Gh 42.45N 12.15 E
Corbeil-Essones 11 If 48.36N 2.29 E
Corbie 12 Ee 49.55N 2.30 E
Corbières 11 Il 42.55N 2.38 E
Corbigny 11 Jg 47.15N 3.40 E
Corby 9 Mi 52.29N 0.40W
Corcaigh/Cork [2] 9 Ej 52.00N 8.30W
Corcaigh/Cork 6 Fe 51.54N 8.28W
Corcoran 46 Gi 35.45N 117.23W
Corcovado, Cerro- 48 Bb 30.40N 114.55W
Corcovado, Golfo 56 Ff 43.30S 73.30W
Corcovado, Golfo- 52 Ij 43.30S 73.30W
Corcovado, Volcán- 52 Ij 43.12S 72.48W
Corcubión 13 Cb 42.57N 9.11W
Corcubión, Ría de- 13 Cb 42.54N 9.09W
Cordele 43 Ke 31.58N 83.47W
Cordes 11 Hj 44.04N 1.57 E
Cordevole 14 Gd 46.05N 12.04 E
Cordilheiras, Serra das- 54 Ie 7.30S 48.30W
Cordillera [3] 55 Dg 25.15S 57.00W
Cordillera Central [Phil.] 26 Hc 17.20N 120.57 E
Cordillera Central [S.Amer.] 52 If 8.00S 77.00W
Cordillera Occidental 52 Ig 14.00S 74.00W
Cordillera Oriental 52 If 7.00S 76.00W
Córdoba [3] 13 Hf 38.00N 4.50W
Córdoba [Arg.] [2] 56 Hd 32.00S 64.00W
Córdoba [Arg.] 53 Ji 31.25S 64.10W
Córdoba [Col.] [2] 54 Cb 8.20N 75.40W
Córdoba [Mex.] 47 Ee 18.53N 96.56W
Córdoba [Sp.] 6 Fh 37.53N 4.46W
Córdoba, Sierras de- 52 Ji 31.15S 64.00W
Cordova 39 Ec 60.33N 145.46W
Corfu (EN) = Kérkira 5 Hh 39.40N 19.45 E
Corfu, Strait of- (EN) = Kerkiras, Stenón- 15 Dj 39.35N 20.05 E
Corguinho 55 Ed 19.53S 54.52W
Coria 13 Fe 39.59N 6.32W
Coria del Río 13 Fg 37.16N 6.03W
Coribe 55 Ja 13.50S 44.28W
Coricudgy, Mount- 59 Kf 32.50S 150.22 E
Corigliano Calabro 14 Kk 39.36N 16.31 E
Corigliano Islets 59 Jc 17.00S 150.00 E
Corinne 46 Ma 50.06N 104.32W
Corinth 43 Je 34.56N 88.31W
Corinth (EN) = Kórinthos 15 Fl 37.55N 22.53 E
Corinth, Gulf of- (EN) = Korinthiakós Kólpos 5 Ih 38.12N 22.30 E
Corinth Canal (EN) = Korinthou, Dhiórix- 15 Fl 37.57N 22.58 E
Corinto [Braz.] 54 Jg 18.21S 44.27W
Corinto [Nic.] 49 Dg 12.29N 87.10W
Corisco 34 Ge 0.55N 9.19 E
Cork/Corcaigh 6 Fe 51.54N 8.28W
Cork/Corcaigh [2] 9 Ej 52.00N 8.30W
Cork Harbour 9 Ej 51.45N 8.15W
Corleone 14 Hm 37.49N 13.18 E
Çorlu 23 Ca 41.09N 27.48 E
Çorlu 15 Kh 41.12N 27.28 E
Cormeilles 12 Ce 49.15N 0.23 E
Cormoran Reef 64a Bb 7.50N 134.32 E
Cornelio 48 Dc 29.55N 111.08W
Cornélio Procópio 56 Jb 23.08S 50.39W
Cornelius Grinnel Bay 42 Ld 63.20N 64.50W
Corner Brook 39 Ne 48.57N 57.57W
Corner Seamounts (EN) 38 Nf 35.30N 51.30W
Cornia 14 Eh 42.57N 10.33 E
Corning [Ar.-U.S.] 45 Kh 36.24N 90.35W
Corning [Ca.-U.S.] 46 Dg 39.56N 122.11W
Corning [N.Y.-U.S.] 44 Id 42.10N 77.04W
Corno Grande 14 Hh 42.28N 13.34 E
Cornouaille 11 Cg 48.00N 4.00W
Cornwall [3] 9 Ik 50.30N 4.30W
Cornwall 42 Kg 45.02N 74.44W
Cornwall 42 Ia 73.30N 95.00W
Cornwall 9 Hk 50.20N 5.05W
Cornwall 5 Fe 50.30N 4.40W
Cornwall, Cape- 9 Hk 50.08N 5.43W
Cornwallis 42 Ia 75.15N 95.00W
Coro 53 Jd 11.25N 69.41W
Coro, Golfete de- 49 Mh 11.34N 69.53W
Corocoro 54 Eg 17.12S 68.28W
Corocoro, Isla- 50 Fh 8.31N 60.05W
Corod 15 Kd 45.54N 27.37 E
Çoroh 23 Fa 41.36N 41.35 E
Coroico 54 Eg 16.10S 67.44W
Coromandel [Braz.] 55 Id 18.28S 47.13W
Coromandel [N.Z.] 62 Fb 36.46S 175.30 E
Coromandel Coast 21 Kh 14.00N 80.10 E
Coromandel Peninsula 61 Eg 36.50S 175.35 E
Coromandel Range 62 Fb 37.00S 175.40 E
Coron 26 Hd 12.00N 120.12 E
Corona 45 Di 34.15N 105.36W
Corona Bank (EN) 59 Db 12.20S 118.30 E
Coronado, Bahía de- 38 Ki 9.00N 83.50W
Coronado, Isla- 48 Aa 32.25N 117.15W
Coronados, Isla- 48 Dd 26.07N 111.17W
Coronation 66 Re 60.37S 45.35W
Coronation 46 Ja 52.05N 111.27W
Coronation, Cap- 63b Cf 22.15S 167.02 E
Coronation Gulf 38 Ic 68.25N 110.00W
Coronda 55 Bj 31.58S 60.55W
Coronda, Laguna- 55 Bk 32.06S 60.52W
Coronel 56 Fe 37.01S 73.08W
Coronel Bogado 56 Ic 27.11S 56.18W
Coronel Dorrego 56 He 38.42S 61.17W
Coronel du Graty 55 Bh 27.40S 60.56W
Coronel Fabriciano 54 Jg 19.31S 42.38W
Coronel Oviedo 56 Ic 25.25S 56.27W
Coronel Ponce 55 Eb 15.34S 55.01W
Coronel Pringles 56 He 37.58S 61.22W
Coronel Rodolfo Bunge 55 Bm 37.34S 60.08W
Coronel Suárez 56 He 37.28S 61.55W
Coronel Vidal 55 Dm 37.27S 57.43W
Coronel Vivida 55 Fg 25.58S 52.34W
Coropuna, Nudo- 52 Ig 15.30S 72.41W
Çorovoda 15 Di 40.30N 20.13 E
Corozal [Blz.] 49 Cd 18.24N 88.24W
Corozal [Blz.] 49 Cd 18.15N 88.17W
Corozal [Col.] 49 Ji 9.18N 75.17W
Corpus Christi 39 Jg 27.48N 97.24W
Corpus Christi, Lake- 45 Hl 28.10N 97.53W
Corpus Christi Bay 45 Hm 27.48N 97.20W
Corque 54 Eg 18.21S 67.42W
Corral de Bustos 55 Ak 33.17S 62.12W
Corrèggio 14 Ef 44.46N 10.47 E
Córrego do Ouro 55 Gc 16.18S 50.32W
Corrente 54 If 10.27S 45.10W
Corrente, Rio- [Braz.] 54 Hg 19.19S 50.50W
Corrente, Rio- [Braz.] 55 Ka 13.08S 43.28W
Corrente, Rio- [Braz.] 55 Ib 14.14S 46.58W
Correntes 55 Ec 17.37S 54.59W
Correntes, Rio- 55 Ec 17.38S 55.08W
Correnti, Capo delle- 5 Hh 36.40N 15.05 E
Correntina 54 Jf 13.20S 44.39W
Corrèze 11 Hi 45.10N 1.28 E
Corrèze [3] 11 Hi 45.15N 1.50 E
Corrib, Lough-/Loch Coirib 9 Dh 53.05N 9.10W
Corrientes [2] 56 Ic 29.00S 58.00W
Corrientes 53 Kh 27.30S 58.50W
Corrientes, Cabo- [Arg.] 55 Dn 38.01S 57.32W
Corrientes, Cabo- [Col.] 54 Cb 5.30N 77.34W
Corrientes, Cabo- [Cuba] 49 Ec 21.45N 84.31W
Corrientes, Cabo- [Mex.] 38 Ig 20.25N 105.42W
Corrientes, Ensenada de- 49 Ec 21.45N 84.31W
Corrientes, Rio- [Arg.] 55 Cj 30.21S 59.33W
Corrientes, Rio- [Peru] 54 Dd 3.43S 74.40W
Corrieyairack Pass 9 Id 57.05N 4.40W
Corrigan 45 Ik 31.00N 94.50W
Corrigin 59 Df 32.21S 117.52 E
Corry 44 He 41.56N 79.39W
Corryong 59 Jg 36.12S 147.54 E
Corse = Corsica (EN) 5 Gg 42.00N 9.00 E
Corse, Cap- 5 Gg 43.00N 9.23 E
Corse-du-Sud [3] 11a Ab 41.50N 9.00 E
Corsewall Point 9 Hf 55.02N 5.05W
Corsica (EN) = Corse 5 Gg 42.00N 9.00 E
Corsica, Canale di- 14 Dh 42.45N 9.45 E
Corsicana 43 He 32.06N 96.28W
Cort Adelaer, Kap- 41 Hf 61.45N 42.00W
Corte 11a Ba 42.18N 9.09 E
Cortegana 13 Fg 37.55N 6.49W
Cortés [3] 49 Cf 15.30N 88.00W
Cortes 13 Kc 41.55N 1.25W
Cortez 43 Fd 37.21N 108.35W
Cortina d'Ampezzo 14 Gd 46.32N 12.08 E
Čortkov 16 De 48.59N 25.50 E
Cortland 44 Id 42.36N 76.10W
Cortona 14 Fg 43.16N 11.59 E
Corubal 34 Bc 11.57N 15.06W
Coruche 13 Df 38.57N 8.31W
Çoruh 23 Fa 41.36N 41.35 E
Çorum 24 Fb 40.29N 35.36 E
Çorum 23 Da 40.33N 34.58 E
Corumbá 53 Kg 19.01S 57.39W
Corumbá, Rio- 54 Ig 18.19S 48.55W
Corumbá de Goiás 55 Hb 15.55S 48.48W
Corumbáiba 55 Hd 18.09S 48.34W
Corumo, Río- 50 Fi 6.49N 60.52W
Corvallis 43 Cc 44.34N 123.16W
Corvo 30 De 39.42N 31.06W
Corzuela 55 Bh 26.57S 60.58W
Cosalá 48 Fe 24.23N 106.41W
Cosamaloapan 48 Lh 18.22N 95.48W
Cosenza 6 Hh 39.18N 16.15 E
Coshocton 44 Ge 40.16N 81.53W
Cosigüina, Punta- 49 Dg 12.54N 87.41W
Cosmoledo Group 30 Li 9.43S 47.35 E
Cosne-sur-Loire 11 Ig 47.24N 2.55 E
Cosquín 56 Hd 31.15S 64.29W
Cossato 14 Ce 45.34N 8.10 E
Costa, Cordillera de la- 52 Je 9.50N 66.00W
Costa Rica [1] 39 Ki 10.00N 84.00W
Costa Verde 13 Ga 43.40N 5.40W
Costești 15 He 44.40N 24.53 E
Costiera, Catena- 14 Kk 39.25N 16.10 E
Coswig 10 Je 51.08N 13.35 E
Cotabato 26 He 7.13N 124.15 E
Cotagaita 54 Eh 20.50S 65.41W
Cotahuasi 54 Dg 15.12S 72.56W
Côte d'Ivoire = Ivory Coast (EN) [1] 31 Gh 8.00N 5.00W
Côte d'Or 11 Kg 47.10N 4.50 E
Côte-d'Or [3] 11 Kg 47.30N 4.50 E
Cotentin 5 Ff 49.30N 1.30W
Côtes-d'Armor 11 Df 48.25N 2.40W
Cotiella 13 Mb 42.31N 0.19 E
Cotmeana 15 He 44.24N 24.45 E
Cotmeana 15 He 44.58N 24.37 E
Cotonou 31 Hh 6.21N 2.26 E
Cotopaxi, Volcán- 52 If 0.40S 78.26W
Cotswold Hills 9 Kj 51.45N 2.10W
Cottage Grove 46 De 43.48N 123.03W
Cottbus/Chośebuz 10 Ke 51.46N 14.20 E
Cottenham 12 Cb 52.17N 0.08 E
Cottondale 44 Ej 30.48N 85.23W
Cottonwood Wash 46 Ji 35.05N 110.22W
Cotui 49 Ld 19.03N 70.09W
Cotulla 45 Gl 28.26N 99.14W
Coubre, Pointe de la- 11 Ei 45.42N 1.14W
Couburg 10 Gf 50.15N 10.58 E
Coucy-le-Château-Auffrique 12 Fe 49.31N 3.19 E
Coudekerque-Branche 12 Ec 51.02N 2.24 E
Coudersport 44 He 41.46N 78.01W
Couedic, Cape du- 59 Hg 36.10S 136.40 E
Couesnon 11 Ef 48.37N 1.31W
Couhé 11 Gh 46.18N 0.11 E
Couilly-Pont-aux-Dames 12 Ef 48.53N 2.52 E
Coulee Dam 46 Fb 48.00N 118.59W
Coulihaut 51g Bb 15.30N 61.29W
Coulman Island 66 Kf 73.28S 169.45 E
Coulogne 12 Dd 50.55N 1.53 E
Coulommiers 11 Jf 48.49N 3.05 E
Coulonge, Rivière- 44 Ic 45.51N 76.45W
Coulounieix-Chamiers 11 Gi 45.10N 0.42 E
Council 46 Gd 44.44N 116.26W
Council Bluffs 43 Hc 41.16N 95.52W
Courcelles 12 Gd 50.28N 4.22 E
Courcelles-Chaussy 12 Ie 49.07N 6.24 E
Courland (EN) = Kurzeme 5 Id 57.00N 20.30 E
Courmayeur 14 Ae 45.47N 6.58 E
Cours 11 Kh 46.06N 4.19 E
Courseulles-sur-Mer 12 Be 49.20N 0.27W
Courtenay 42 Fg 49.41N 125.00W
Courtisols 12 Gf 48.59N 4.31 E
Courtrai/Kortrijk 11 Jd 50.50N 3.16 E
Coushatta 45 Jj 32.00N 93.21W
Cousin 11 Kh 46.58N 4.15 E
Coutances 11 Ee 49.03N 1.26W
Couto de Magalhães, Rio- 55 Fa 13.37S 53.09W
Coutras 11 Fi 45.02N 0.08W
Couture, Lac- 42 Jd 60.05N 75.20W
Couvin 11 Kd 50.03N 4.20 E
Couvin-Mariembourg 12 Gd 50.06N 4.31 E
Covarrubias 13 Ib 42.04N 3.31W
Covasna [2] 15 Id 46.00N 26.00 E
Covasna 15 Jd 45.51N 26.11 E
Coveñas 49 Ji 9.25N 75.42W
Coventry 9 Li 52.25N 1.30W
Covilhã 13 Ed 40.17N 7.30W
Covington [Ga.-U.S.] 44 Fi 33.37N 83.51W
Covington [Ky.-U.S.] 43 Kd 39.05N 84.30W
Covington [La.-U.S.] 45 Kk 30.29N 90.06W
Covington [Tn.-U.S.] 44 Ch 35.34N 89.39W
Covington [Va.-U.S.] 44 Hg 37.48N 79.59W
Cowal 9 He 56.05N 5.10W
Cowan, Lake- 59 Ef 31.50S 121.50 E
Cowan Knob 45 Ji 35.52N 93.29W
Cowell 59 Hf 33.41S 136.55 E
Cowes 12 Ad 50.46N 1.18W
Cowichan Lake 46 Cb 48.54N 124.20W
Cowra 59 Jf 33.50S 148.41 E
Coxim 53 Kg 18.30S 54.45W
Coxim, Rio- 55 Ed 18.34S 54.46W
Cox's Bāzār 25 Id 21.26N 91.59 E
Coyah 34 Cd 9.43N 13.23W
Coyame 48 Gc 29.28N 105.06W
Coyanosa Draw 45 Ek 31.18N 103.06W
Coycoyan, Sierra de- 48 Ji 17.30N 98.20W
Coyle—Coig, Rio- 56 Gh 50.58S 69.11W
Coyote, Rio- 48 Cb 30.48N 112.35W
Coyotitán 48 Ff 23.47N 106.35W
Coyuca, Laguna de- 48 Ii 16.57N 100.05W
Cozia, Pasul- 15 Hd 45.15N 24.15 E
Cozumel 48 Pg 20.31N 86.55W
Cozumel, Isla de- 47 Gd 20.25N 86.55W
Cradock 31 Jl 32.08S 25.36 E
Craig [Ak.-U.S.] 40 Me 55.29N 133.09W
Craig [Co.-U.S.] 43 Fc 40.31N 107.33W
Craigmont 46 Gc 46.15N 116.28W
Craigs Range 59 Ke 26.40S 151.30 E
Crailsheim 10 Gg 49.09N 10.05 E
Craiova 6 Ig 44.19N 23.48 E
Cranbrook [Austl.] 59 Df 34.18S 117.32 E
Cranbrook [B.C.-Can.] 42 Fg 49.31N 115.46W
Cranbrook [Eng.-U.K.] 12 Cc 51.05N 0.32 E
Crandon 45 Ld 45.34N 88.54W
Crane [Or.-U.S.] 46 Fe 43.25N 118.35W
Crane [Tx.-U.S.] 45 Ek 31.24N 102.21W
Crane Lake 45 Jb 48.16N 92.28W
Crane Lake 46 Ka 50.06N 109.06W
Cranleigh 12 Bc 51.08N 0.29W
Craon 11 Fg 47.51N 0.57W
Craonne 12 Fe 49.26N 3.47 E
Crapaud, Puy- 11 Fh 46.40N 0.40W
Crary Mountains 66 Of 76.48S 117.40W
Crasna 15 Fa 48.09N 22.20 E
Crasna [Rom.] 15 Kc 46.31N 27.51 E
Crasna [Rom.] 15 Fb 47.10N 22.54 E
Crater Lake [Or.-U.S.] 43 Cc 42.56N 122.06W
Crater Lake [St.Vin.] 51n Ba 13.19N 61.11W
Crateús 53 Lf 5.10S 40.40W
Crati 14 Kk 39.43N 16.31 E
Crato [Braz.] 54 Ke 7.14S 39.23W
Crato [Port.] 13 Ee 39.17N 7.39W
Crau 11 Kk 43.36N 4.50 E
Crauford, Cape- 42 Jb 73.44N 84.51W
Cravo Norte 54 Db 6.17N 70.12W
Crawford 45 Ee 42.41N 103.25W
Crawfordsville 44 De 40.02N 86.54W
Crawley 9 Mj 51.07N 0.12W
Crazy Mountains 46 Jc 46.08N 110.20W
Crazy Peak 43 Eb 46.01N 110.16W
Creciente, Isla- 48 De 24.23N 111.37W
Crécy-en-Ponthieu 12 Dd 50.15N 1.53 E
Crécy-la-Chapelle 12 Ef 48.51N 2.55 E
Crécy-sur-Serre 12 Fe 49.42N 3.37 E
Crediton 9 Jk 50.47N 3.39W
Cree [Sask.-Can.] 42 Ge 58.50N 105.40W
Cree [Scot.-U.K.] 9 Ig 54.52N 4.20W
Creede 45 Ch 37.51N 106.56W
Creel 47 Cc 27.45N 107.38W
Cree Lake 42 Ge 57.30N 106.30W
Creglingen 10 Gg 49.28N 10.02 E
Creil 11 Ie 49.16N 2.29 E
Crema 14 De 45.22N 9.41 E
Cremenea, Brațul- 15 Ke 44.57N 27.54 E
Crémieu, Plateau de- 11 Li 45.40N 5.30 E
Cremona 14 Ee 45.07N 10.02 E
Crepaja 15 Dd 45.01N 20.39 E
Crepori, Rio- 54 Ge 5.42S 57.08W
Crépy-en-Valois 11 Ie 49.14N 2.54 E
Cres [Yugo.] 14 If 44.40N 14.25 E
Cres [Yugo.] 14 If 44.58N 14.24 E
Crescent 46 Ee 43.29N 121.41W
Crescent City 43 Cc 41.45N 124.12W
Crescent Lake 44 Gk 29.28N 81.30W
Crespo 55 Bk 32.02S 60.19W

Index Symbols

[1] Independent Nation
[2] State, Region
[3] District, County
[4] Municipality
[5] Colony, Dependency
Continent
Physical Region
Historical or Cultural Region
Mount, Mountain
Volcano
Hill
Mountains, Mountain Range
Hills, Escarpment
Plateau, Upland
Pass, Gap
Plain, Lowland
Delta
Salt Flat
Valley, Canyon
Crater, Cave
Karst Features
Depression
Polder
Desert, Dunes
Forest, Woods
Heath, Steppe
Oasis
Cape, Point
Coast, Beach
Cliff
Peninsula
Isthmus
Sandbank
Island
Atoll
Rock, Reef
Islands, Archipelago
Rocks, Reefs
Coral Reef
Well, Spring
Geyser
River, Stream
Waterfall Rapids
River Mouth, Estuary
Lake
Salt Lake
Intermittent Lake
Reservoir
Swamp, Pond
Canal
Glacier
Ice Shelf, Pack Ice
Ocean
Sea
Gulf, Bay
Strait, Fjord
Lagoon
Bank
Seamount
Tablemount
Ridge
Shelf
Basin
Escarpment, Sea Scarp
Fracture
Trench, Abyss
National Park, Reserve
Point of Interest
Recreation Site
Cave, Cavern
Historic Site
Ruins
Wall, Walls
Church, Abbey
Temple
Scientific Station
Airport
Port
Lighthouse
Mine
Tunnel
Dam, Bridge

Crest 11 Lj 44.44N 5.02 E
Crested Butte 45 Cg 38.52N 106.59W
Creston [B.C.-Can.] 46 Gb 49.06N 116.31W
Creston [Ia.-U.S.] 43 Ic 41.04N 94.22W
Crestone Peak 45 Dh 37.58N 105.36W
Crestview 43 Je 30.46N 86.34W
Creswell 44 Ih 35.52N 76.23W
Creswell Bay 42 Ib 72.40N 93.30W
Creswell Creek 59 Hc 18.10S 135.11 E
Crete 45 Hf 40.38N 96.58W
Crete (EN) = Kriti 5 Ih 35.15N 24.45 E
Crete (EN) = Kriti [2] 15 Hn 35.35N 25.00 E
Crete, Sea of- (EN) = Kritikón Pélagos 15 Hn 36.00N 25.00 E
Créteil 11 If 48.47N 2.28 E
Cretin, Cape- 60 Di 6.40S 147.52 E
Creus, Cabo de-/Creus, Cap de- 5 Gg 42.19N 3.19 E
Creus, Cap de-/Creus, Cabo de- 5 Gg 42.19N 3.19 E
Creuse [3] 11 Hh 46.05N 2.00 E
Creuse 11 Gg 47.00N 0.34 E
Creutzwald 11 Me 49.12N 6.41 E
Crevecoeur-en-Auge 12 Ce 49.07N 0.01 E
Crèvecoeur-le-Grand 12 Ee 49.36N 2.05 E
Crevillente 13 Lf 38.15N 0.48W
Crewe 9 Kh 53.05N 2.27W
Crézancy 12 Fe 49.03N 3.30 E
Criciúma 53 Lh 28.40S 49.23W
Cricket Mountains 46 Ig 38.50N 113.00W
Crieff 9 Je 56.23N 3.52W
Criel-sur-Mer 12 Dd 50.01N 1.19 E
Criel sur Mer-Mesnil Val 12 Dd 50.03N 1.20 E
Crikvenica 14 Ie 45.11N 14.42 E
Crillon 12 De 49.31N 1.56 E
Crimea (EN)=Krymski Poluostrov 5 Jf 45.00N 34.00 E
Crimean Mountains (EN)= Krymskije Gory 5 Jg 44.45N 34.30 E
Crimmitschau 10 If 50.49N 12.23 E
Criquetot-l'Esneval 12 Ce 49.39N 0.16 E
Crissolo 14 Bf 44.42N 7.09 E
Cristal, Monts de- 36 Bb 0.30N 10.30 E
Cristal, Sierra del- 49 Jc 20.33N 75.31W
Cristalândia 54 If 10.36S 49.11W
Cristalina 54 Ig 16.45S 47.36W
Cristalino, Rio- 54 Hf 12.40S 50.40W
Cristallo 14 Gd 46.34N 12.12 E
Cristóbal Colón, Pico 52 Id 10.50N 73.45W
Cristuru Secuiesc 15 Ic 46.35N 25.47 E
Crişu Alb 15 Ec 46.42N 21.16 E
Crişu Negru 15 Ec 46.42N 21.16 E
Crişu Repede 15 Dc 46.55N 20.59 E
Crixás 55 Hb 14.27S 49.58W
Crixás-Açu, Rio- 54 Hf 13.19S 50.36W
Crixás Mirim, Rio- 55 Ga 13.28S 50.36W
Crkvena Planina 15 Fg 42.48N 22.22 E
Crna Gora 15 Eg 42.16N 21.35 E
Crna Gora 15 Ce 44.05N 19.50 E
Crna Gora = Montenegro (EN) [2] 15 Cg 42.30N 19.18 E
Crna Gora=Montenegro (EN) 15 Cg 42.30N 19.18 E
Crna Reka 15 Ef 43.50N 21.55 E
Crna reka 15 Eh 41.33N 21.59 E
Crni Drim 15 Dg 42.05N 20.23 E
Crni Timok 15 Ff 43.55N 22.18 E
Crni Vrh 14 Jd 46.29N 15.14 E
Crni vrh 14 Kf 44.36N 16.30 E
Črnomelj 14 Je 45.34N 15.12 E
Croatia (EN) = Hrvatska [2] 14 Jf 45.00N 15.30 E
Croatia (EN) = Hrvatska 5 Hf 45.00N 15.30 E
Croatia (EN) = Hrvatska 14 Je 45.00N 15.30 E
Crocker, Banjaran- 26 Ge 5.40N 116.20 E
Crockett 45 Ik 31.19N 95.28W
Crocq 11 Ii 45.52N 2.22 E
Crocus Bay 51b Ab 18.13N 63.05W
Croisette, Cap- 11 Lk 43.13N 5.20 E
Croisic, Pointe du- 11 Dg 47.17N 2.33W
Croisilles 12 Ed 50.12N 2.53 E
Croissy-sur-Celle 12 Ee 49.42N 2.11 E
Croix, Lac la- 45 Jb 48.21N 92.05W
Croix-Haute, Col de la- 11 Lj 44.43N 5.40 E
Croker, Cape- 59 Gb 10.58S 132.35 E
Croker Bay 42 Jb 74.38N 83.15W
Croker Island 59 Gb 11.10S 132.30 E
Cromarty 9 Id 57.40N 4.02W
Cromer 9 Oi 52.56N 1.18 E
Cromwell 62 Cf 45.03S 169.14 E
Crooked Island 47 Jd 22.45N 74.13W
Crooked Island Passage 47 Jd 22.55N 74.35W
Crooked River 46 Ed 44.34N 121.16W
Crookston 43 Hb 47.47N 96.37W
Crosby [Mn.-U.S.] 45 Jc 46.28N 93.57W
Crosby [N.D.-U.S.] 45 Eb 48.55N 103.18W
Cross 34 Ge 4.55N 8.15 E
Cross City 44 Fk 29.32N 83.07W
Crossett 45 Kj 33.08N 91.58W
Cross Fell 9 Kg 54.42N 2.29W
Cross Lake 42 Hf 54.47N 97.22W
Crossman Peak 46 Hi 34.32N 114.07W
Cross River [2] 34 Gd 5.40N 8.10 E
Cross Sound 40 Le 58.10N 136.30W
Crotone 14 Lk 39.05N 17.08 E
Crotto 55 Bm 36.35S 60.10W
Crouch 12 Cc 51.37N 0.53 E
Crow Agency 46 Ld 45.36N 107.27W
Crowborough 12 Cc 51.03N 0.09 E
Crow Creek 45 Df 40.23N 104.29W
Crowell 45 Gj 33.59N 99.43W
Crow Lake 45 Jb 49.12N 93.57W
Crowley 45 Jk 30.13N 92.22W
Crowley, Lake- 46 Fh 37.37N 118.44W
Crowley Ridge 45 Ki 35.45N 90.45W
Crownpoint 45 Bi 35.42N 108.07W
Crown Prince Frederik 42 Ic 70.05N 86.40W
Crowsnest Pass 42 Gg 49.00N 114.30W
Crows Nest Peak 45 Ed 44.03N 103.58W
Croydon 59 Ic 18.12S 142.14 E
Croydon, London- 9 Mj 51.23N 0.07W
Crozet, Iles- 30 Mm 46.30S 51.00 E
Crozet Basin (EN) 3 Gm 39.00S 60.00 E
Crozet Ridge (EN) 3 Fn 45.00S 45.00 E
Crozon 11 Bf 48.15N 4.29W
Crozon, Presqu'île de- 11 Bf 48.15N 4.25W
Crucero, Cerro- 48 Gg 21.41N 104.25W
Cruces 49 Gb 22.21N 80.16W
Crump Lake 46 Fe 42.17N 119.50W
Crumpton Point 51g Ba 15.35N 61.19W
Cruz, Cabo- 47 Ie 19.51N 77.44W
Cruz Alta [Arg.] 55 Bk 33.01S 61.49W
Cruz Alta [Braz.] 53 Kh 28.39S 53.36W
Cruz del Eje 56 Hd 30.44S 64.48W
Cruzeiro do Oeste 56 Jb 23.46S 53.04W
Cruzeiro do Sul 53 If 7.38S 72.36W
Cruzen Island 66 Mf 74.47S 140.42W
Cruz Grande 48 Ji 16.44N 99.08W
Crvanj 14 Mg 43.25N 18.11 E
Crvenka 15 Cd 45.39N 19.28 E
Crystal Brook 59 Hf 33.21S 138.13 E
Crystal City [Man.-Can.] 45 Gb 49.08N 98.57W
Crystal City [Tx.-U.S.] 45 Gl 28.41N 99.50W
Crystal Falls 44 Cb 46.06N 88.20W
Crystal Springs 45 Kk 31.59N 90.21W
Csákvár 10 Oi 47.24N 18.27 E
Cserhat 10 Pi 47.55N 19.30 E
Csongrád [2] 10 Qj 46.25N 20.15 E
Csongrád 10 Qj 46.42N 20.09 E
Csorna 10 Ni 47.37N 17.15 E
ČSSR → Československá Socialistická Republika [1] 6 Hf 49.30N 17.00 E
Csurgó 10 Nj 46.16N 17.06 E
Ctesiphon 24 Kf 33.05N 44.35 E
Ču 21 Ie 45.00N 67.44 E
Ču 22 Je 43.33N 73.45 E
Cuajinicuilapa 48 Ji 16.28N 98.25W
Cuale 36 Cd 7.40S 17.01 E
Cuamba 31 Kj 14.49S 36.33 E
Cuan an Fhóid Duibh/ Blacksod Bay 9 Dg 54.08N 10.00W
Cuanavale 36 Cf 15.07S 19.14 E
Cuan Bhaile Átha Cliath/ Dublin Bay 9 Gh 53.20N 6.06W
Cuan Chill Ala/Killala Bay 9 Dg 54.15N 9.10W
Cuan Dhun Dealgan/ Dundalk Bay 9 Gh 53.57N 6.17W
Cuan Dhún Droma/Dundrum Bay 9 Hg 54.13N 5.45W
Cuando 30 Jj 18.27S 23.32 E
Cuando-Cubango [3] 36 Df 16.00S 20.30 E
Cuan Eochaille/Youghal Harbour 9 Fj 51.52N 7.50W
Cuangar 36 Cf 17.36S 18.37 E
Cuango 30 Ii 3.14S 17.22 E
Cuango [Ang.] 36 Cd 9.07S 18.05 E
Cuango [Ang.] 36 Cd 6.17S 16.41 E
Cuan Loch Garman/Wexford Harbour 9 Gi 52.20N 6.25W
Cuan Mó/Clew Bay 9 Dh 53.50N 9.50W
Cuan na Gaillimhe/Galway Bay 5 Fe 53.10N 9.15W
Cuan na gCaorach/Sheep Haven 9 Ff 55.10N 7.52W
Cuan Phort Láirge/ Waterford Harbour 9 Gi 52.10N 6.57W
Cuan Shligigh/Sligo Bay 9 Eg 54.20N 8.40W
Cuanza 30 Ii 9.19S 13.08 E
Cuanza Norte [3] 36 Bd 8.50S 14.30 E
Cuanza Sul [3] 36 Be 10.50S 14.50 E
Cuareim, Arroyo- 55 Dj 30.12S 57.36W
Cuaró 55 Dj 30.37S 56.54W
Cuaró Grande, Arroyo- 55 Dj 30.18S 57.12W
Cuarto, Río- 56 Hd 33.25S 63.02W
Cuatir 36 Cf 17.01S 18.09 E
Cuatro Ciénegas de Carranza 48 Hd 26.59N 102.05W
Cuauhtémoc 47 Cc 28.25N 106.52W
Cuautitlán 48 Jh 19.40N 99.11W
Cuay Grande 55 Di 28.40S 56.17W
Cuba 38 Lg 21.30N 80.00W
Cuba [1] 39 Lg 21.30N 80.00W
Cuba [Mo.-U.S.] 45 Kg 38.04N 91.24W
Cuba [N.M.-U.S.] 45 Ch 36.01N 107.04W
Cuba [Port.] 13 Ef 38.10N 7.53W
Cubabi, Cerro- 48 Cb 31.42N 112.46W
Cubagua, Isla- 50 Dg 10.49N 64.11W
Cubal 36 Be 13.03S 14.15 E
Cubal [Ang.] 36 Be 11.29S 13.48 E
Cubal [Ang.] 36 Bf 15.22S 12.39 E
Cubango 30 Jj 18.53S 22.24 E
Çubuk 24 Eb 40.59N 32.05 E
Čubukulah, Gora- 20 Kc 66.23N 153.59 E
Cucalón, Sierra de- 13 Kd 40.59N 1.10W
Cuchi 36 Ce 14.40S 16.52 E
Cuchi 30 Ij 15.28S 17.21 E
Cuchibi 36 De 15.00S 20.45 E
Cuchilla Áquila, Cerro- 48 Ig 21.27N 101.03W
Cuchivero, Río- 50 Di 7.40N 65.57W
Cuchumatanes, Sierra de los- 49 Bf 15.35N 91.25W
Cuckfield 12 Bc 51.01N 0.08W
Cuckmere 12 Cd 50.45N 0.09 E
Cucui 54 Ec 1.12N 66.50W
Cucumbi 36 Ce 10.17S 19.03 E
Cucurpe 48 Db 30.20N 110.43W
Cúcuta 53 Ie 7.54N 72.31W
Cudahy 45 Me 42.57N 87.52W
Cudalbi 15 Kd 45.47N 27.42 E
Cuddalore 21 Jh 11.45N 79.45 E
Cuddapah 25 Ff 14.28N 78.49 E
Čudovo 19 Dd 59.08N 31.41 E
Čudskoje Ozero=Peipus, Lake- (EN) 5 Id 58.45N 27.30 E
Cue 59 De 27.25S 117.54 E
Cuebe 36 Cf 15.48S 17.30 E
Cuelei 36 Cf 15.33S 17.21 E
Cuéllar 13 Hc 41.29N 4.19W
Cuemba 36 Ce 12.09S 18.07 E
Cuenca [3] 13 Jd 40.00N 2.00W
Cuenca [Ec.] 53 If 2.53S 78.59W
Cuenca [Sp.] 13 Jd 40.04N 2.08W
Cuenca, Serranía de- 5 Fg 40.10N 1.55W
Cuencamé de Ceniceros 48 He 24.53N 103.42W
Cuera/Chur 14 Dd 46.50N 9.35 E
Cuerda del Pozo, Embalse de la- 13 Jc 41.51N 2.44W
Cuernavaca 39 Jh 18.55N 99.15W
Cuero 45 Hl 29.06N 97.18W
Cuevas del Almanzora 13 Kg 37.18N 1.53W
Cugir 15 Gd 45.50N 23.22 E
Cugo 36 Cd 7.22S 17.06 E
Čugujev 16 Je 49.50N 36.41 E
Čugujevka 28 Mb 44.08N 133.53 E
Čuhloma 19 Ed 58.47N 42.41 E
Cuiabá 53 Kg 15.35S 56.05W
Cuiabá, Rio- 52 Kg 17.05S 56.36W
Cuiabá Mirim, Rio- 55 Ec 16.20S 55.55W
Cuidado, Punta- 65d Bb 27.08S 109.19W
Cuijk, Cuijk en Sint Agatha- 12 Hc 51.44N 5.52 E
Cuijk en Sint Agatha-Cuijk 12 Hc 51.44N 5.52 E
Cuilapa 49 Bf 14.17N 90.18W
Cuillin Hills 9 Gd 57.14N 6.15W
Cuilo 30 Ii 3.22S 17.22 E
Cúil Raithin/Coleraine 9 Gf 55.08N 6.40W
Cuiluan 27 Mb 47.39N 128.34 E
Cuima 36 Ce 13.14S 15.38 E
Cuito 30 Jj 18.01S 20.48 E
Cuito Cuanavale 31 Ij 15.13S 19.08 E
Cuitzeo, Lago de- 48 Ih 19.55N 101.05W
Cuiuni, Rio- 54 Fd 0.45S 63.07W
Cujmir 15 Fe 44.13N 22.56 E
Čukata 15 Ih 41.50N 25.15 E
Čukotski Nacionalny okrug [3] 20 Mc 66.00N 172.30 E
Čukotski Poluostrov= Chukchi Peninsula (EN) 21 Uc 66.00N 175.00W
Čukotskoje More=Chukchi Sea (EN) 67 Bd 69.00N 171.00W
Çukurca 24 Jd 37.15N 43.37 E
Çukurdağı 15 Ll 37.58N 28.44 E
Čulakkurgan 19 Gg 43.48N 69.12 E
Culan 11 Ih 46.33N 2.21 E
Cu Lao, Hon- 25 Lf 10.30N 109.13 E
Culasi 26 Hd 11.26N 122.03 E
Culbertson 46 Mb 48.09N 104.31W
Culebra, Isla de- 49 Od 18.19N 65.17W
Culebra, Sierra de la- 13 Fc 41.55N 6.20W
Culebra Peak 45 Dh 37.06N 105.10W
Culemborg 12 Hc 51.57N 5.14 E
Culiacán, Río de- 48 Fe 24.31N 107.41W
Culiacán Rosales 39 Ig 24.48N 107.24W
Culion 26 Gd 11.50N 119.55 E
Culion 26 Hd 11.53N 120.01 E
Culiseu, Rio- 54 Hf 12.14S 53.17W
Cullera 13 Le 39.10N 0.15W
Cullman 43 Je 34.11N 86.51W
Čulman 22 Od 56.52N 124.52 E
Culpeper 44 Hf 38.28N 78.01W
Culuene, Rio- 52 Kg 12.56S 52.51W
Culukidze 16 Mh 42.18N 42.25 E
Culver, Point- 59 Ef 32.54S 124.43 E
Culverden 62 Ee 42.46S 172.51 E
Čulym 20 De 55.06N 80.58 E
Čulym 21 Kd 57.40N 83.50 E
Čulyšman 20 Df 51.20N 87.45 E
Cuma 36 Ce 12.52S 15.04 E
Cumaná 53 Jd 10.28N 64.10W
Cumanacoa 50 Eg 10.15N 63.55W
Cumaovası 15 Kk 38.15N 27.09 E
Cumbal, Volcán- 54 Cc 0.57N 77.52W
Cumberland 9 Kg 54.40N 2.50W
Cumberland 38 Kf 37.09N 88.25W
Cumberland [B.C.-Can.] 46 Cb 49.37N 125.01W
Cumberland [Md.-U.S.] 43 Ld 39.39N 78.46W
Cumberland [Va.-U.S.] 44 Hg 37.31N 78.16W
Cumberland, Cap- 63b Cb 14.39S 166.37 E
Cumberland, Lake- 44 Eg 36.57N 84.55W
Cumberland Bay 51n Ba 13.16N 61.17W
Cumberland Island 44 Gj 30.51N 81.27W
Cumberland Islands 59 Jd 20.40S 149.10 E
Cumberland Lake 42 Hf 54.00N 102.20W
Cumberland Peninsula 38 Mc 66.50N 64.00W
Cumberland Plateau 38 Kf 36.00N 85.00W
Cumberland Sound 38 Mc 65.10N 65.30W
Cumbernauld 9 Jf 55.58N 3.59W
Cumbre, Paso de la-/ Bermejo, Paso- 52 Ii 32.50S 70.05W
Cumbria [3] 9 Kg 54.35N 2.45W
Cumbrian Mountains 9 Jg 54.30N 3.05W
Čumerna 15 Ig 42.47N 25.58 E
Čumikan 20 If 54.42N 135.19 E
Cummins 59 Hf 34.16S 135.44 E
Cumnock 9 If 55.27N 4.16W
Cumpas 48 Eb 30.02N 109.48W
Çumra 24 Ed 37.34N 32.48 E
Čumyš 20 Df 53.30N 83.10 E
Cuna 21 Ld 57.42N 95.35 E
Cunagua 49 Hb 22.05N 78.20W
Cuñapirú 55 Ej 31.32S 55.35W
Cuñapirú, Arroyo- 55 Ej 31.12S 55.31W
Cuñapirú, Cuchilla de- 55 Ej 31.12S 55.36W
Cunaviche, Río- 50 Ci 7.19N 67.11W
Cunderdin 59 Df 31.39S 117.15 E
Cundinamarca [2] 54 Db 5.00N 74.00W
Cundža 19 Hg 43.32N 79.28 E
Cunene [3] 36 Cf 16.30S 15.00 E
Cunene=Kunene (EN) 30 Ij 17.20S 11.50 E
Cuneo 14 Bf 44.23N 7.32 E
Čunja 21 Lc 61.30N 96.20 E
Cunnamulla 58 Fg 28.04S 145.41 E
Čunski [R.S.F.S.R.] 20 Ee 56.03N 99.48 E
Čunski [R.S.F.S.R.] 20 Ee 57.23N 97.40 E
Cuorgné 14 Be 45.23N 7.39 E
Čupa 19 Db 66.17N 33.01 E
Cupar 9 Je 56.19N 3.01W
Cupica, Golfo de- 54 Cb 6.35N 77.30W
Ćuprija 15 Ef 43.56N 21.22 E
Cupula, Pico- 48 De 24.47N 110.50W
Čur 7 Mh 57.11N 53.01 E
Curaçá 54 Ke 8.59S 39.54W
Curacao 52 Jd 12.11N 69.00W
Curacautín 56 Fe 38.26S 71.53W
Cura Malal, Sierra de- 55 Am 37.44S 62.16W
Curanilahue 56 Fe 37.28S 73.21W
Čurapča 20 Id 61.56N 132.18 E
Curaray, Río- 54 Dd 2.20S 74.05W
Curcubata, Vîrful- 15 Fc 46.25N 22.35 E
Curdimurka 58 Eg 29.30S 137.10 E
Curé 55 De 21.25S 56.25W
Cure 11 Jg 47.40N 3.41 E
Curepipe 37a Bb 20.19S 57.31 E
Curepto 56 Fe 35.05S 72.00W
Curiapo 54 Fb 8.33N 61.00W
Curicó 53 Ii 34.59S 71.14W
Curicuriari, Rio- 54 Ed 0.14S 66.48W
Curitabanos 56 Jc 27.18S 50.36W
Curitiba 53 Lh 25.25S 49.15W
Curoca 36 Bf 15.43S 11.55 E
Currais Novos 54 Ke 6.15S 36.31W
Curralinho 54 Id 1.48S 49.47W
Curral-Velho 32 Cf 15.59N 22.48W
Current River 45 Kh 36.15N 90.57W
Currie 59 Ig 39.56S 143.52 E
Curtea de Argeş 15 Hd 45.08N 24.41 E
Curtici 15 Ec 46.21N 21.18 E
Curtis 45 Ff 40.38N 100.31W
Curtis Channel 59 Kd 23.55S 152.05 E
Curtis Island 57 Jh 30.35S 178.36W
Curtis Island [Austl.] 59 Kd 23.40S 151.10 E
Curuá, Rio- [Braz.] 55 Ga 13.26S 51.24W
Curuá, Rio- [Braz.] 54 Gd 1.55S 55.07W
Curuá, Rio- [Braz.] 52 Kf 5.23S 54.22W
Curuçá 54 Id 0.43S 47.50W
Curuçá, Rio- 54 Dd 4.27S 71.23W
Curuguaty 56 Ib 24.31S 55.42W
Curuguaty, Arroyo- 55 Dg 24.06S 56.02W
Curup 26 Dg 3.28S 102.32 E
Curupira, Sierra de- 54 Fc 1.25N 64.30W
Cururupu 54 Jd 1.50S 44.52W
Curuzú Cuatiá 56 Ic 29.47S 58.03W
Curvelo 54 Jg 18.45S 44.25W
Cusco 53 Ig 13.31S 71.59W
Cushing 45 Hi 35.59N 96.46W
Cushing, Mount- 42 Ee 57.36N 126.51W
Čusovaja 5 Ld 58.13N 56.30 E
Čusovoj 19 Fd 58.17N 57.50 E
Cusset 11 Jh 46.08N 3.28 E
Cusseta 44 Ei 32.18N 84.47W
Čust 18 Hd 41.00N 71.15 E
Custer 45 Ee 43.46N 103.36W
Cutato 36 Ce 10.33S 16.48 E
Cut Bank 43 Eb 48.38N 112.20W
Cutervo 54 Ce 6.22S 78.51W
Cuthbert 44 Ej 31.46N 84.48W
Cutral Có 56 Ge 38.56S 69.14W
Cutro 14 Kk 39.02N 16.59 E
Cuttack 22 Kg 20.30N 85.50 E
Čuvašskaja ASSR [3] 19 Ed 55.30N 47.10 E
Cuvelai 36 Cf 15.40S 15.47 E
Cuvette [3] 36 Cc 0.10S 15.30 E
Cuvier Basin (EN) 59 Cd 22.00S 111.00 E
Cuvier Island 62 Fb 36.25S 175.45 E
Cuvo ou Queve 30 Ij 10.50S 13.47 E
Cuxhaven 10 Ec 53.53N 8.42 E
Cuya 56 Fa 19.07S 70.08W
Cuyahoga Falls 44 Ge 41.08N 81.55W
Cuyo Islands 26 Hd 11.04N 120.57 E
Cuyubini, Río- 50 Fh 8.20N 60.20W
Cuyuni, Río- 52 Kf 6.23N 58.41W
Cuyuni River 52 Kf 6.23N 58.41W
Cuyutlán, Laguna- 48 Gh 19.00N 104.10W
Cuzco [2] 54 Df 12.30S 72.30W
Cuzna 13 Hf 38.04N 4.41W
Čvikov 10 Kf 50.48N 14.40 E
Čvrsnica 14 Lg 43.35N 17.35 E
Cyangugu 36 Ec 2.29S 28.54 E
Cybinka 10 Kd 52.12N 14.48 E
Cyclades (EN) = Kikládhes 5 Ih 37.00N 25.10 E
Čyjyrčyk, Pereval- 18 Id 40.15N 73.20 E
Cypress Hills 38 Ie 49.40N 109.30W
Cypress Lake 46 Kb 49.28N 109.29W
Cyprus (EN)=Kıbrıs/ Kypros [1] 22 Ff 35.00N 33.00 E
Cyprus (EN)=Kıbrıs/ Kypros 21 Ff 35.00N 33.00 E
Cyprus (EN)=Kypros/ Kıbrıs [1] 22 Ff 35.00N 33.00 E
Cyprus (EN)=Kypros/ Kıbrıs 21 Ff 35.00N 33.00 E
Cyrenaica (EN)=Barqah 33 Dc 31.00N 22.30 E
Cyrenaica (EN)=Barqah 30 Je 31.00N 23.00 E
Cyrene 33 Dc 32.48N 21.59 E
Cyrus Field Bay 42 Ld 62.50N 65.00W
Cysoing 12 Fd 50.34N 3.13 E
Cythera (EN)=Kithira 15 Fm 36.09N 23.00 E
Czaplinek 10 Mc 53.34N 16.14 E
Czarna [Pol.] 10 Pe 51.12N 19.53 E
Czarna [Pol.] 10 Rf 50.30N 21.15 E
Czarna Białostocka 10 Tc 53.18N 23.19 E
Czarna Dąbrówka 10 Nb 54.20N 17.32 E
Czarna Hańcza 10 Tc 53.50N 23.47 E
Czarnków 10 Md 52.55N 16.34 E
Czchów 10 Qg 49.50N 20.39 E
Czechoslovakia (EN)= Československo [1] 6 Hf 49.30N 17.00 E
Czechowice-Dziedzice 10 Og 49.54N 19.00 E
Czeremcha 10 Td 52.32N 23.15 E
Czersk 10 Nc 53.48N 18.00 E
Częstochowa 6 He 50.49N 19.06 E
Częstochowa [2] 10 Pf 50.50N 19.05 E
Człopa 10 Mc 53.06N 16.08 E
Człuchów 10 Nc 53.41N 17.21 E

D

Da, Sông- = Black River (EN) 21 Mg 20.17N 106.34 E
Da'an (Dalai) 27 Lb 45.35N 124.16 E
Dabaga 36 Gd 8.07S 35.55 E
Dabakala 34 Ed 8.22N 4.26W
Dabakala [3] 34 Ed 8.27N 4.28W
Daban → Bairin Youqi 27 Kc 43.30N 118.37 E
Dabas 10 Pi 47.11N 19.19 E
Daba Shan 21 Mf 32.15N 109.00 E
Dabat 35 Fc 12.58N 37.45 E
Dabay Sima 35 Gc 12.43N 42.17 E
Dabba/Daocheng 27 Hf 29.01N 100.26 E
Dabbāgh, Jabal- 23 Ed 27.52N 35.45 E
Dabeiba 54 Cb 7.02N 76.16W
Dąbie 10 Od 52.05N 18.49 E
Dąbie, Jezioro- 10 Kc 53.29N 14.40 E
Dabie Shan 21 Nf 31.15N 115.00 E
Dabl, Wādī- [Sau.Ar.] 24 Gh 28.35N 39.04 E
Dabl, Wādī- [Sau.Ar.] 24 Gh 29.05N 36.14 E
Dabnou 34 Gc 14.09N 5.22 E
Dabola 34 Cc 10.45N 11.07W
Daborow 35 Hd 6.11N 48.22 E
Dabou 34 Ed 5.19N 4.23W
Dabqig → Uxin Qi 27 Id 38.27N 109.08 E
Dabraš 15 Gh 41.40N 23.50 E
Dąbrowa Białostocka 10 Tc 53.40N 23.20 E
Dąbrowa Górnicza 10 Pf 50.20N 19.11 E
Dąbrowa Tarnowska 10 Qf 50.11N 21.00 E
Dabsan Hu 27 Fd 36.58N 95.00 E
Dăbuleni 15 Hf 43.48N 24.05 E
Dabus 35 Fc 10.38N 35.10 E
Dacata 35 Gd 7.16N 42.15 E
Dacca → Dhaka 22 Lg 23.43N 90.25 E
Dachangzhen 28 Eh 32.13N 118.44 E
Dachau 10 Hh 48.16N 11.26 E
Dachen Dao 28 Fj 28.29N 121.53 E
Dachstein 14 Hc 47.30N 13.36 E
Dacia Seamount (EN) 5 Ei 31.10N 13.42W
Dačice 10 Lg 49.05N 15.26 E
Dac Lac, Caonguyen- 25 Lf 12.50N 108.05 E
Đacovica 15 Dg 42.23N 20.26 E
Dadali 63a Dc 8.07S 159.06 E
Dadanawa 54 Gc 2.50N 59.30W
Daday 24 Eb 41.28N 33.28 E
Dade City 44 Fk 28.22N 82.12W
Dadou 11 Hk 43.44N 1.49 E
Dādra and Nagar Haveli [3] 25 Ed 20.20N 72.50 E
Dadu 25 Dc 26.44N 67.47 E
Dadu He 21 Mg 29.32N 103.44 E
Dadukou 28 Di 30.30N 117.03 E
Dăeni 15 Le 44.50N 28.07 E
Daet 26 Hd 14.05N 122.55 E
Dafang 27 If 27.06N 105.32 E
Dafeng (Dazhongji) 28 Fh 33.11N 120.27 E
Dagana 34 Bb 16.31N 15.30W
Dagana 35 Bc 13.05N 16.00 E
Daga Post 35 Ed 9.13N 33.58 E
Dağardi 15 Lj 39.26N 29.00 E
Dagash 35 Eb 19.22N 33.24 E
Dagda 8 Lh 56.04N 27.36 E
Dagdan-Daba 27 Gb 48.20N 96.50 E
Dagéla 35 Bc 10.40N 18.26 E
Dagestanskaja [3] 19 Eg 43.00N 47.00 E
Dagestanskije Ogni 19 Eg 42.06N 48.12 E
Dagezhen → Fengning 28 Dd 41.12N 116.39 E
Dagu 28 De 38.58N 117.40 E
Daguan 27 Hf 27.48N 103.54 E
Dagu He 27 Ff 37.34N 121.17 E
Daguokui Shan 28 Jb 45.19N 129.50 E
Dagupan 26 Hc 16.03N 120.20 E
Dagxoi → Yidun 27 Ge 30.25N 99.28 E
Dagzê 27 Ff 29.41N 91.24 E
Dagzê Co 27 Ee 31.54N 87.29 E
Daheiding Shan 27 Mb 47.58N 129.10 E
Dahei He 28 Ad 40.34N 111.05 E
Da Hinggan Ling=Greater Khingan Range (EN) 21 Oe 49.00N 122.00 E
Dahlak Archipelago 30 Lg 15.40N 40.30 E
Dahlak Kebir 35 Gb 15.38N 40.11 E
Daḥl al Furayy 24 Li 26.45N 47.03 E
Dahlem 12 Id 50.23N 6.33 E
Dahlonega Plateau 44 Fh 34.30N 83.45W
Dahm, Ramlat- 33 If 16.25N 45.45 E
Dahme 10 Je 51.52N 13.26 E
Dahmouni 13 Ni 35.25N 1.29 E
Dahn 12 Je 49.09N 7.47 E
Dahomey → Bénin [1] 31 Hh 9.30N 2.15 E
Dahongliutan 27 Cd 36.00N 79.12 E
Dahra 13 Mh 36.18N 0.55 E
Dahra [Lib.] 33 Cd 29.40N 17.40 E
Dahra [Sen.] 34 Bb 15.21N 15.29W
Dahra, Massif de- 13 Oh 36.30N 2.05 E
Dahūk [3] 24 Jd 36.57N 43.00 E
Dahūk 24 Jd 36.52N 43.00 E
Dahushan 28 Gd 41.37N 122.09 E
Daḥy, Nafūd ad- 33 Ie 22.00N 45.25 E
Dai 63a Eb 7.53S 160.37 E
Daia 15 If 44.00N 25.59 E
Daïa, Région des- 32 Hc 33.30N 3.25 E
Daicheng 28 De 38.42N 116.37 E
Daigo 28 Pf 36.46N 140.21 E
Dai Hai 28 Bd 40.31N 112.43 E
Dailekh 25 Gc 28.50N 81.44 E
Daimanji-San 29 Cc 36.15N 133.19 E
Daimiel 13 Ie 39.04N 3.37W

Index Symbols

[1] Independent Nation
[2] State, Region
[3] District, County
[4] Municipality
[5] Colony, Dependency
Continent
Physical Region
Historical or Cultural Region
Mount, Mountain
Volcano
Hill
Mountains, Mountain Range
Hills, Escarpment
Plateau, Upland
Pass, Gap
Plain, Lowland
Delta
Salt Flat
Valley, Canyon
Crater, Cave
Karst Features
Depression
Polder
Desert, Dunes
Forest, Woods
Heath, Steppe
Oasis
Cape, Point
Coast, Beach
Cliff
Peninsula
Isthmus
Sandbank
Island
Atoll
Rock, Reef
Islands, Archipelago
Rocks, Reefs
Coral Reef
Well, Spring
Geyser
River, Stream
Waterfall Rapids
River Mouth, Estuary
Lake
Salt Lake
Intermittent Lake
Reservoir
Swamp, Pond
Canal
Glacier
Ice Shelf, Pack Ice
Ocean
Sea
Gulf, Bay
Strait, Fjord
Lagoon
Bank
Seamount
Tablemount
Ridge
Shelf
Basin
Escarpment, Sea Scarp
Fracture
Trench, Abyss
National Park, Reserve
Point of Interest
Recreation Site
Cave, Cavern
Historic Site
Ruins
Wall, Walls
Church, Abbey
Temple
Scientific Station
Airport
Port
Lighthouse
Mine
Tunnel
Dam, Bridge

Dainanji-San 29 Ec 36.36N 137.42 E
Dainichi-San 29 Ec 36.09N 136.30 E
Dainkog 27 Ge 32.31N 97.59 E
Daiō-Zaki 28 Ng 34.22N 136.53 E
Dairan (EN)=Dalian (Lüda) 22 Of 38.55N 121.39 E
Dairan (EN) = Lüda→Dalian 22 Of 38.55N 121.39 E
Dairbhre/Valentia 9 Cj 51.55N 10.20W
Daireaux 55 Bm 36.36 S 61.45W
Dai-Sen 29 Cd 35.24N 133.34 E
Daisengen-Dake 29a Bc 41.35N 140.09 E
Daishan (Gaotingzhen) 28 Gi 30.15N 122.13 E
Daitō [Jap.] 29 Cd 35.19N 132.58 E
Daitō [Jap.] 29 Gb 39.02N 141.22 E
Daito Islands (EN)=Daitō Shotō 21 Pg 25.00N 131.15 E
Daitō Shotō=Daito Islands (EN) 21 Pg 25.00N 131.15 E
Daitō-Zaki 29 Gd 35.18N 140.24 E
Daixian 28 Be 39.03N 112.57 E
Daiyue→Shanyin 28 Be 39.30N 112.48 E
Dajabón 49 Ld 19.33N 71.42W
Dajarra 58 Eg 21.42S 139.31 E
Dajtit, Mali i- 15 Ch 41.22N 19.55 E
Daka 34 Ed 8.19N 0.13W
Dakar 31 Fg 14.40N 17.26W
Dākhilah, Wāḥāt al-= Dakhla Oasis (EN) 30 Jf 25.30N 29.10 E
Dakhla Oasis (EN)= Dākhilah, Wāḥāt al- 30 Jf 25.30N 29.10 E
Dakhlet Nouâdhibou 32 De 20.30N 16.00W
Dakla 31 Ff 23.42N 15.56W
Dakoro 34 Gc 14.30N 6.25 E
Đakovo 14 Me 45.19N 18.25 E
Daksti 8 Kg 57.38N 25.32 E
Đak To 25 Lf 14.42N 107.51 E
Dal 8 Dd 60.15N 11.12 E
Dal, Jökulsá á- 7a Cb 65.40N 14.20W
Đala 15 Dc 46.09N 20.07 E
Dala [Ang.] 36 De 11.03S 20.17 E
Dala [Sol.Is.] 63a c 8.36S 160.41 E
Dalaba 34 Cc 10.42N 12.15W
Dalai → Da'an 27 Lb 45.35N 124.16 E
Dalai Nur 27 Kc 43.18N 116.15 E
Dala-Järna 8 Fd 60.33N 14.21 E
Dālakī 24 Nh 29.19N 51.06 E
Dalälven 5 Hc 60.38N 17.27 E
Dalaman 24 Cd 36.40N 28.45 E
Dalaman 15 Lm 36.44N 28.49 E
Dalāmī 35 Ec 11.52N 30.28 E
Dalān 24 Kj 24.15N 45.47 E
Dalan-Dzadgad 22 Me 43.47N 104.29 E
Dalane 8 Bf 58.35N 6.20 E
Dalarna 8 Fd 61.00N 14.05 E
Dalarö 8 He 59.08N 18.24 E
Da Lat 22 Mh 11.56N 108.25 E
Dālbandin 25 Cc 28.53N 64.25 E
Dalbosjön 8 Ef 58.45N 12.50 E
Dalboslätten 8 Ef 58.35N 12.25 E
Dalby 59 Ke 27.11S 151.16 E
Dale [Nor.] 7 Af 60.35N 5.49 E
Dale [Nor.] 7 Af 61.22N 5.25 E
Dale Hollow Lake 44 Eg 36.36N 85.19W
Dalen 7 Bg 59.27N 8.00 E
Dalfsen 12 Ib 52.30N 6.14 E
Dalgaranger, Mount- 59 De 27.51S 117.06 E
Dălgopol 15 Kf 43.03N 27.21 E
Dalhart 43 Gd 36.04N 102.31W
Dalhousie 42 Kg 48.04N 66.23W
Dalhousie, Cape - 42 Eb 70.15N 129.41W
Dali [China] 22 Mg 25.43N 100.07 E
Dali [China] 27 Ie 34.55N 110.00 E
Dalian (Lüda) = Dairan (EN) 22 Of 38.55N 121.39 E
Dalias 13 Jh 36.49N 2.52W
Daling He 28 Fd 40.56N 121.44 E
Dalizi 27 Mc 41.45N 126.50 E
Dalj 14 Me 45.29N 18.59 E
Daljā' 33 Fd 27.39N 30.42 E
Dalkowskie, Wzgórza- 10 Le 51.35N 15.50 E
Dall [Ak.-U.S.] 40 Mf 54.50N 132.55W
Dall [Can.] 2 Ef 55.00N 133.00W
Dallas [Or.-U.S.] 46 Dd 44.55N 123.19W
Dallas [Tx.-U.S.] 39 Jf 32.47N 96.48W
Dalmā' 24 Oj 24.30N 52.20 E
Dalmā', Qārat- 33 Dd 25.32N 23.57 E
Dalmacija 14 Kg 43.00N 17.00 E
Dalmacija = Dalmatia (EN) 5 Hg 43.00N 17.00 E
Dalmaj, Hawr- 24 Kf 32.20N 45.28 E
Dalmally 9 Ie 56.24N 4.58W
Dalmatia (EN) = Dalmacija 5 Hg 43.00N 17.00 E
Dalmatovo 17 Kh 56.16N 63.00 E
Dalnegorsk 22 Pe 44.31N 135.31 E
Dalnerečensk 22 Pe 45.55N 133.45 E
Dalni [R.S.F.S.R.] 20 Kf 53.15N 157.30 E
Dalni [R.S.F.S.R.] 20 Ih 44.57N 135.03 E
Dalnjaja, Gora- 20 Mc 68.08N 179.53 E
Daloa 34 Dd 6.58N 6.23W
Daloa 31 Gh 6.53N 6.27W
Dalou Shan 21 Mg 28.00N 106.40 E
Dalqū 35 Ea 20.07N 30.35 E
Dalrymple, Mount- 57 Fg 21.02S 148.38 E
Dalsbruk 8 Jd 60.02N 22.31 E
Dalsbruk/Taalintehdas 8 Jd 60.02N 22.31 E
Dalsfjorden 8 Ac 61.20N 5.05 E
Dalsjöfors 8 Eg 57.43N 13.05 E
Dalsland 8 Ef 58.35N 12.55 E
Dalslands kanal 8 Ef 58.50N 12.25 E
Dals Långed 7 Cg 58.55N 12.18 E
Dalton 44 Eh 34.47N 84.58W
Daltonganj 25 Gd 24.02N 84.04 E
Dalul 35 Gc 14.22N 40.21 E
Daluo 27 Hg 21.38N 100.15 E
Dalupiri 26 Hc 19.05N 121.12 E
Dalvik 7a Bb 65.58N 18.32W
Dalwallinu 59 Df 30.17S 116.40 E
Dalyan 15 Lm 36.50N 28.39 E
Daly Bay 42 Id 64.00N 89.40W
Daly City 46 Dh 37.42N 122.29W
Daly River 57 Ef 13.20S 130.19 E
Daly Waters 59 Gc 16.15S 133.22 E
Damā, Wādī- 24 Fi 27.09N 35.47 E
Damagarim 34 Gc 13.42N 9.00 E
Damān 25 Ed 20.10N 73.00 E
Damanhūr 33 Fc 31.02N 30.28 E
Damar, Pulau- 26 Ih 7.09S 128.40 E
Damara 35 Be 4.58N 18.42 E
Damaraland 37 Bd 21.00S 17.30 E
Damas Cays 49 Hb 23.58N 79.55W
Damascus (EN)=Dimashq 22 Ff 33.30N 36.15 E
Damāsh 24 Md 36.46N 49.46 E
Damaturu 34 Hc 11.45N 11.58 E
Damāvand 24 He 35.56N 52.08 E
Damāvand, Qolleh-ye- 21 Hf 35.56N 52.08 E
Damba 36 Cd 6.50S 15.07 E
Dambaslar 15 Kh 41.13N 27.14 E
Dame Marie, Cap- 47 Je 18.36N 74.26W
Damergou 30 Hg 15.00N 9.00 E
Dāmghān 24 Pd 36.09N 54.22 E
Damianópolis 55 Ib 14.33S 46.10W
Damiao 27 He 30.52N 104.38 E
Damietta (EN)=Dumyāṭ 31 Ke 31.25N 31.48 E
Daming 28 Cf 36.17N 115.09 E
Daming Shan 27 Ig 23.23N 108.30 E
Damīr Qābū 24 Id 36.54N 41.47 E
Dammartin en Goële 12 Ee 49.03N 2.41 E
Dammastock 14 Cd 46.38N 8.25 E
Damme [Bel.] 12 Fc 51.15N 3.17 E
Damme [Ger.] 12 Kb 52.31N 8.12 E
Dammer Berge 12 Kb 52.35N 8.17 E
Damoh 25 Fd 23.50N 79.27 E
Damongo 34 Ed 9.05N 1.49W
Damous 13 Nh 36.33N 1.42 E
Dampier 58 Cg 20.39S 116.45 E
Dampier, Selat-=Dampier Strait (EN) 26 Jg 0.40S 130.40 E
Dampier Archipelago 59 Dd 20.35S 116.35 E
Dampier Land 59 Ec 17.30S 122.55 E
Dampierre 12 Df 48.42N 1.59 E
Dampier Strait 59 Ja 5.36S 148.12 E
Dampier Strait (EN)= Dampier, Selat- 26 Jg 0.40S 130.40 E
Damqawt 23 Hf 16.34N 52.50 E
Damqog Kanbab/Maquan He 27 Df 29.36N 84.09 E
Dam Qu 27 Fe 33.56N 92.41 E
Damville 12 Df 48.52N 1.04 E
Damvillers 12 He 49.20N 5.24 E
Damwoude, Dantumadeel- 12 Ha 53.18N 5.59 E
Damxoi → Comai 27 Ff 28.26N 91.32 E
Damxung 27 Fe 30.34N 91.16 E
Danakil=Danakil Plain (EN) 30 Lg 12.25N 40.30 E
Danakil Plain (EN)= Danakil 30 Lg 12.25N 40.30 E
Danané 34 Dd 7.25N 8.10W
Danané 34 Dd 7.16N 8.09W
Da Nang 22 Mh 16.04N 108.13 E
Danba/Rongzhag 27 He 30.48N 101.54 E
Danbury 44 Ke 41.23N 73.27W
Danby Lake 46 Hi 34.14N 115.07W
Dancheng 28 Ch 33.36N 115.14 E
Dancheng→Xiangshan 27 Lf 29.29N 121.52 E
Dandarah 33 Fd 26.10N 32.39 E
Dandeldhura 25 Gc 29.18N 80.35 E
Dandenong, Melbourne- 59 Jg 37.59S 145.12 E
Dandong 22 Oe 40.10N 124.15 E
Daneborg 41 Jd 74.25N 20.10W
Danells Fjord 41 Hf 60.45N 42.45W
Daneţi 15 Hf 43.59N 24.03 E
Danfeng (Longjuzhai) 27 Je 33.44N 110.22 E
Danforth Hills 45 Cf 40.15N 108.00W
Danfu 63a Aa 4.12S 153.04 E
Dangara 19 Gh 38.09N 69.22 E
Dangchengwan → Subei 27 Fd 39.36N 94.58 E
Dang He 27 Fc 40.30N 94.42 E
Dangjin Shankou 21 Lf 39.15N 94.30 E
Dangla 35 Fc 11.16N 36.50 E
Dangla Shan→Tanggula Shan 21 Lf 33.00N 92.00 E
Dangoura, Mount- 35 Dd 6.12N 26.27 E
Dangrek Range (EN)=Dong Rak, Phanom- 21 Mh 14.25N 104.30 E
Dangshan 27 Ke 34.22N 116.21 E
Dangtu 28 Ei 31.33N 118.30 E
Dangu 12 De 49.15N 1.42 E
Dangyang 28 Ai 30.49N 111.47 E
Dan He 28 Bg 35.05N 112.59 E
Daniel 46 Je 42.52N 110.04W
Daniel, Serra- 55 Ea 13.40S 54.55W
Danielskuil 37 Ce 28.11S 23.33 E
Danilov 19 Ed 58.12N 40.13 E
Danilovgrad 15 Cg 42.33N 19.07 E
Danilovka 16 Nd 50.21N 44.06 E
Daning 27 Jd 36.31N 110.45 E
Danjiang → Junxian 27 Je 32.31N 111.32 E
Danjiangkou Shuiku 27 Je 32.37N 111.30 E
Danjo-Guntō 27 Me 32.00N 128.20 E
Dank 24 Qk 23.33N 56.16 E
Dankov 16 Kc 53.16N 39.07 E
Danli 49 Df 14.00N 86.35W
Danmark=Denmark (EN) 6 Gd 56.00N 10.00 E
Danmark Fjord 67 Me 81.10N 23.20W
Danmarks Havn 67 Ld 76.50N 18.30W
Danmarksstraedet= Denmark Strait (EN) 38 Qc 67.00N 25.00W
Dannenberg 10 Hc 53.06N 11.06 E
Dannevirke 62 Gd 40.12S 176.06 E
Danot 35 Hd 7.33N 45.17 E
Dantumadeel 12 Ha 53.18N 5.59 E
Dantumadeel-Damwoude 12 Ha 53.18N 5.59 E
Danube (EN)=Donau 5 If 45.20N 29.40 E
Danube (EN)=Duna 5 If 45.20N 29.40 E
Danube (EN)=Dunaj 5 If 45.20N 29.40 E
Danube (EN)=Dunărea 5 If 45.20N 29.40 E
Danube (EN)=Dunav 5 If 45.20N 29.40 E
Danube, Mouths of the- (EN) = Dunării, Delta- 5 If 45.30N 29.45 E
Danville [Ar.-U.S.] 45 Ji 35.03N 93.24W
Danville [Il.-U.S.] 43 Jc 40.08N 87.37W
Danville [In.-U.S.] 44 Df 39.46N 86.32W
Danville [Ky.-U.S.] 43 Kd 37.39N 84.46W
Danville [Va.-U.S.] 43 Ld 36.34N 79.25W
Danxian (Nada) 27 Ih 19.38N 109.32 E
Danyang 28 Eh 32.00N 119.33 E
Danzig (EN)=Gdańsk 6 He 54.23N 18.40 E
Dao 26 Hd 10.31N 121.57 E
Dāo 13 Dd 40.20N 8.11W
Daocheng/Dabba 27 Hf 29.01N 100.26 E
Daokou → Huaxian 28 Cg 35.33N 114.30 E
Daosa 25 Fc 26.53N 76.20 E
Dao Shui 28 Ci 30.42N 114.40 E
Dao Timni 34 Ha 20.38N 13.39 E
Daoura 32 Gd 29.03N 4.33W
Daoxian 27 Jf 25.37N 111.36 E
Dapaong 34 Fc 10.52N 0.12 E
Dapchi 34 Hc 12.29N 11.29 E
Daqing Shan 28 Ad 41.00N 111.00 E
Daqin Tal→Naiman Qi 27 Lc 42.49N 120.38 E
Daquing Shan 28 Ed 40.30N 119.38 E
Dar'ā 23 Ec 32.37N 36.06 E
Dārāb 24 Ph 28.45N 54.34 E
Darabani 15 Ja 48.11N 26.35 E
Daraçya Yarimadasi 15 Lm 36.40N 28.10 E
Darāfisah 35 Ec 13.23N 31.59 E
Dārān 24 Nf 32.59N 50.24 E
Darasun 20 Gf 51.39N 113.59 E
Đaravica 15 Dg 42.32N 20.08 E
Darāw 24 Ej 24.25N 32.56 E
Darazo 34 Hc 11.00N 10.25 E
Darband 23 Ic 31.38N 57.02 E
Darband, Kūh-e- 24 Qg 31.34N 57.08 E
Darbandī Khān, Sad ad- 24 Ke 35.07N 45.50 E
Darbat Alī, Ra's- 23 Hf 16.43N 53.33 E
Darbėnai/Darbenaj 8 Ih 56.02N 21.08 E
Dar Ben Karriche el Bahri 13 Gi 35.51N 5.21W
Darbhanga 25 Hc 26.10N 85.54 E
Dārboruk 35 Gd 9.44N 44.31 E
Darby 46 Hc 46.01N 114.11W
Darchan→Darhan 22 Me 49.33N 106.21 E
Darda 14 Me 45.38N 18.42 E
Dardanelle Lake 45 Ji 35.25N 93.20W
Dardanelles (EN)= Çanakkale Boğazi 5 Ig 40.15N 26.25 E
Dardo/Kangding 27 He 30.01N 101.58 E
Dar el Kouti 35 Cd 8.50N 21.50 E
Darende 24 Gc 38.34N 37.30 E
Dar es Salaam 36 Gd 6.50S 39.02 E
Dar es Salaam 31 Ki 6.48S 39.17 E
Darfield 62 Ee 43.29S 172.07 E
Darfo Boario Terme 14 Ee 45.53N 10.11 E
Dārfūr 30 Jg 12.40N 24.20 E
Dārfūr al Janūbīyah 35 Dc 11.30N 25.10 E
Dārfūr ash Shamālīyah 35 Db 16.00N 25.30 E
Dargan-Ata 19 Gg 40.29N 62.12 E
Dargaville 61 Dg 35.56S 173.52 E
Darhan (Darchan) 22 Me 49.33N 106.21 E
Darhan Muminggan Lianheqi 27 Jc 41.45N 110.24 E
Darica [Tur.] 15 Kj 40.00N 27.50 E
Darica [Tur.] 15 Mi 40.45N 29.23 E
Darién 47 Ig 8.30N 77.30W
Darien 44 Gj 31.22N 81.26W
Darién 49 Ii 8.10N 77.45W
Darién, Golfo de- 52 Ie 8.25N 76.53W
Darién, Serranía del- 47 Ig 8.30N 77.30W
Dariense, Cordillera- 49 Eg 12.55N 85.30W
Darja 18 Ee 38.13N 65.46 E
Darjeeling → Dārjiling 25 Hc 27.02N 88.16 E
Dārjiling 25 Hc 27.02N 88.16 E
Dar-Kebdani 13 Ii 35.07N 3.21W
Dark Head 51n Ba 13.17N 61.17W
Dārkhovin 24 Mg 30.45N 48.25 E
Darlag 27 Ge 33.49N 99.08 E
Darling 37 Bf 33.23S 18.23 E
Darling Downs 57 Fg 27.30S 150.30 E
Darling Range 57 Ch 32.00S 116.30 E
Darling River 57 Fh 34.07S 141.55 E
Darlington [Eng.-U.K.] 9 Lg 54.31N 1.34W
Darlington [S.C.-U.S.] 44 Hh 34.19N 79.53W
Darłowo 10 Mb 54.26N 16.23 E
Darmouth 9 Jk 50.21N 3.35W
Darmstadt 10 Eg 49.52N 8.39 E
Darnah 31 Je 32.46N 22.39 E
Darnah 33 Dc 31.00N 23.40 E
Darnétal 12 De 49.27N 1.09 E
Darney 11 Mf 48.05N 6.03 E
Darnley, Cape- 66 Fe 67.43S 69.30 E
Darnley Bay 42 Fc 69.45N 123.45W
Daroca 13 Kc 41.07N 1.25W
Darou Khoudos 34 Bb 15.06N 16.50W
Darovskoj 7 Lg 58.47N 47.59 E
Darrah, Mount- 46 Hb 49.28N 114.35W
Darregueira 56 He 37.42S 63.10W
Darrehshahr 24 Lf 33.10N 47.18 E
D'Arros Island 37b Bb 5.24S 53.18 E
Dar Rounga 30 Jg 10.45N 22.20 E
Dar Sila 35 Cc 12.11N 21.21 E
Darss 10 Ib 54.25N 12.31 E
Darßer Ort 10 Ib 54.29N 12.31 E
Dart 9 Jk 50.20N 3.33W
Dart, Cape- 66 Nf 73.06S 126.20W
D'Artagnan Bank (EN) 59 Eb 13.00S 121.00 E
Dartang → Baqên 27 Fe 31.58N 94.00 E
Dartford 12 Cc 51.27N 0.13 E
Dartmoor 9 Jk 50.35N 4.00W
Dartmouth 42 Lh 44.40N 63.34W
Dartuch, Cabo- 13 Pe 39.56N 3.48 E
Daru 60 Ci 9.04S 143.12 E
Daruneh 24 Qe 35.10N 57.18 E
Daruvar 14 Le 45.35N 17.14 E
Darvaza 19 Fg 40.15N 58.24 E
Darvel, Teluk- 26 Gf 4.50N 118.30 E
Darwin 58 Ef 12.28S 130.50 E
Darwin, Bahía- 56 Fg 45.27S 74.40W
Darwin, Isla- 54a Aa 1.39N 92.00W
Darwin, Port- 59 Gb 12.20S 130.40 E
Dar Zagaoua 35 Cb 15.15N 23.14 E
Dar Zebada 35 Bc 13.45N 18.50 E
Dās 24 Oj 25.09N 52.53 E
Dašava 10 Ug 49.13N 24.05 E
Daš-Balbar 27 Jb 49.31N 114.21 E
Dasha He 28 Ce 38.27N 114.39 E
Dashengtang Shan 28 Dc 42.07N 117.12 E
Dashennongjia 27 Je 31.47N 114.12 E
Dashennongjia 27 Je 31.26N 110.18 E
Dashiqiao → Yingkou 28 Gd 40.39N 122.31 E
Dashitou 28 Jc 43.18N 128.29 E
Dasht 24 Qd 37.17N 56.04 E
Dasht Āb 24 Qh 28.59N 56.32 E
Dashtak 24 Og 30.23N 52.30 E
Dasht-e-Āzādegan 24 Mg 31.32N 48.10 E
Daškesan 16 Oi 40.30N 46.03 E
Dasseneiland 37 Bf 33.26S 18.05 E
Dastgardān 24 Qe 34.19N 56.51 E
Dastjerd-e Qaddādeh 24 Nf 32.44N 51.32 E
Datça 24 Bd 36.45N 27.40 E
Date 28 Pc 42.27N 140.51 E
Dāth, Sha'īb ad- 24 Jj 25.45N 43.10 E
Datia 25 Fc 25.40N 78.28 E
Datian Ding 27 Jg 22.17N 111.13 E
Datil 45 Ci 34.09N 107.47W
Datong [China] 27 Hd 36.56N 101.40 E
Datong [China] 22 Ne 40.09N 113.17 E
Datteln 12 Jc 51.40N 7.23 E
Datteln-Hamm Kanal 12 Jc 51.39N 7.21 E
Datu 21 Mi 2.05N 109.39 E
Datu, Teluk 21 Ni 2.00N 111.00 E
Datu Plang 26 He 6.58N 124.40 E
Dāūd Khel 25 Eb 32.53N 71.34 E
Daudzeva 8 Kh 56.28N 25.18 E
Daugaard-Jensen Land 41 Fb 80.10N 63.30W
Daugaj/Daugai 8 Kj 54.20N 24.28 E
Daugava=Dvina(EN) 19 Cd 57.04N 24.03 E
Daugavpils 6 Id 55.53N 26.32 E
Daule 54 Cd 1.50S 79.57W
Daun 10 Cf 50.12N 6.50 E
Daung Kyun 25 Jf 12.14N 98.05 E
Daunia, Monti della- 14 Ji 41.25N 15.05 E
Dauphin 42 Hf 51.09N 100.03W
Dauphiné 11 Lj 44.50N 6.00 E
Dauphin Lake 42 Hf 51.15N 99.45W
Daura 34 Gc 13.02N 8.18 E
Dautphetal 12 Kd 50.52N 8.33 E
Dāvangere 25 Ff 14.28N 75.55 E
Davao 22 Oi 7.04N 125.36 E
Davao Gulf 21 Oi 6.40N 125.55 E
Dāvarān, Kūh-e- 24 Qg 30.40N 56.15 E
Dāvar Panāh 23 Jd 27.21N 62.21 E
Dāvarzan 24 Qd 36.23N 56.50 E
Đavat 15 Eh 41.04N 21.06 E
Davenport [Ia.-U.S.] 39 Je 41.32N 90.41W
Davenport [Wa.-U.S.] 46 Fc 47.39N 118.09W
Davenport Range 59 Gd 20.45S 134.50 E
Daventry 12 Ab 52.15N 1.10W
Davert 12 Jc 51.51N 7.36 E
Davey, Port- 59 Jh 43.20S 145.55 E
David 39 Ki 8.25N 82.27W
David City 45 Hf 41.15N 97.08W
David-Gorodok 16 Ec 52.03N 27.13 E
David Point 51p Bb 12.14N 61.39W
Davidson 46 Ma 51.18N 105.59W
Davidson Mountains 40 Kc 68.45N 142.10W
Davies, Mount- 59 Fe 26.14S 129.16 E
Davis 43 Cd 38.33N 121.44W
Davis 66 Fe 68.35S 77.58 E
Davis, Cape- 66 Ee 66.24S 56.50 E
Davis, Mount- 44 Hf 39.47N 79.10W
Davis Bay 66 Ie 66.08S 134.05 E
Davis Inlet 42 Le 56.00N 61.30W
Davis Mountains 45 Ek 30.35N 104.00W
Davis Sea (EN) 66 Ge 66.00S 92.00 E
Davisstrædet = Davis Strait (EN) 38 Nc 68.00N 58.00W
Davis Strait 38 Nc 68.00N 58.00W
Davis Strait (EN) = Davisstrædet 38 Nc 68.00N 58.00W
Davlekanovo 19 Fe 54.13N 55.03 E
Davo 34 Dd 5.00N 6.08W
Davos/Tavau 14 Dd 46.47N 9.50 E
Davutlar 15 Kl 37.43N 27.17 E
Dawa 28 Gd 40.58N 122.01 E
Dawanlē 35 Gc 11.06N 42.38 E
Dawāsir, Wādī ad- 21 Gg 20.24N 46.29 E
Dawei 22 Lh 14.05N 98.12 E
Dawen He 28 Dg 35.37N 116.23 E
Dawes Range 59 Kd 24.30S 151.10 E
Dawḥarab 33 Hf 16.17N 41.57 E
Dawson [Ga.-U.S.] 44 Ej 31.47N 84.26W
Dawson [Yuk.-Can.] 39 Fc 64.04N 139.25W
Dawson, Mount- 46 Ga 51.09N 117.25W
Dawson Creek 39 Gd 55.45N 120.07W
Dawson-Lambton Glacier 66 Af 76.15S 27.30W
Dawson Range 42 Dd 65.15N 137.45W
Dawson River 59 Jd 23.38S 149.46 E
Dawu 27 He 30.45N 101.11 E
Dawu (Erlangdian) 28 Ci 31.33N 114.07 E
Dawu→Maqên 27 He 34.29N 100.01 E
Dawukou → Shizuishan 27 Id 39.03N 106.24 E
Dax 11 Ek 43.43N 1.03W
Da Xi 27 Lf 28.10N 120.14 E
Daxian 27 Ie 31.15N 107.28 E
Daxin 27 Ig 22.52N 107.14 E
Daxing 28 De 39.45N 116.19 E
Daxinggou 28 Jc 43.23N 129.39 E
Daxue Shan 21 Mf 30.30N 101.30 E
Dayan→Lijiang 22 Mg 26.56N 100.15 E
Dayang He 28 Ge 39.52N 123.40 E
Dayao 27 Hf 25.49N 101.18 E
Daye 28 Ci 30.05N 114.58 E
Dayishan→Guanyun 28 Eg 34.18N 119.14 E
Daymán, Cuchilla del- 55 Dj 31.38S 57.10W
Daymán, Río- 55 Dj 31.40S 58.02W
Daym Zubayr 35 Dd 7.43N 26.13 E
Dayong 27 Jf 29.09N 110.30 E
Dayr, Jabal ad- 35 Ec 12.27N 30.45 E
Dayr az Zawr 22 Gf 35.20N 40.09 E
Dayr Ḥāfir 24 Gd 36.09N 37.42 E
Dayr Kātrīnā = Saint Catherine Monastery of- (EN) 33 Fd 28.31N 33.57 E
Dayr Mawās 24 Di 27.38N 30.51 E
Dayrūṭ 33 Fd 27.33N 30.49 E
Dayton [Oh.-U.S.] 39 Kf 39.45N 84.15W
Dayton [Wa.-U.S.] 46 Gc 46.19N 117.59W
Daytona Beach 39 Kg 29.12N 80.59W
Dayu 27 Jf 25.29N 114.22 E
Da Yunhe=Grand Canal (EN) 21 Nf 39.54N 116.44 E
Dayville 46 Fd 44.28N 119.32W
Dayyīnah 24 Oj 24.57N 52.24 E
Dazhongji → Dafeng 28 Fh 33.11N 120.27 E
Dazhu 27 Ie 30.42N 107.12 E
Dazjā 24 Pe 35.50N 55.46 E
Dazkırı 24 Cd 37.54N 29.42 E
De Aar 31 Jl 30.39S 24.00 E
Dead 9 Ei 52.40N 8.30W
Deadhorse 40 Jb 70.11N 148.27W
Deadmans Cay 49 Jb 23.14N 75.14W
Dead Sea (EN)=Mayyit, Al Baḥr al- 21 Ff 31.30N 35.30 E
Deadwood 45 Ed 44.23N 103.44W
Deal 12 Dc 51.13N 1.24 E
Dealu Mare 15 Jb 47.27N 26.40 E
De'an 28 Cj 29.18N 115.45 E
Deán Funes 56 Hd 30.26S 64.21W
Dearborn 44 Fd 42.18N 83.10W
Dearg, Beinn- 9 Id 57.48N 4.57W
Deary 46 Gc 46.52N 116.31W
Dease 42 Ee 59.55N 128.29W
Dease Arm 42 Fc 66.50N 120.00W
Dease Lake 39 Fd 58.35N 130.02W
Dease Strait 42 Gc 69.00N 107.00W
Death Valley 38 Hf 36.30N 117.00W
Death Valley 46 Gh 36.20N 116.50W
Deauville 11 Ge 49.22N 0.04 E
Debak 26 Ff 1.34N 111.25 E
Debalcevo 16 Ke 48.20N 38.29 E
Debao 27 Ig 23.17N 106.21 E
Debar 15 Dh 41.32N 20.32 E
Debark 35 Fc 13.08N 37.53 E
Debdou 32 Gc 33.59N 3.03W
Debed 16 Ni 41.22N 44.58 E
Deben 12 Db 52.01N 1.22 E
De Beque 45 Bg 39.20N 108.13W
Dębica 10 Rf 50.04N 21.24 E
De Bilt 12 Hb 52.06N 5.11 E
Debin 20 Kd 62.18N 150.47 E
Dęblin 10 Re 51.35N 21.50 E
Dębno 10 Kd 52.45N 14.40 E
Débo, Lac- 34 Eb 15.18N 4.09W
Deborah East, Lake- 59 Df 30.45S 119.10 E
Deborah West, Lake- 59 Df 30.45S 119.05 E
Deboyne Islands 57 Gf 10.43S 152.22 E
Debrc 15 Ce 44.37N 19.54 E
Debre Berhan 35 Fd 9.41N 39.33 E
Debrecen 6 If 47.32N 21.38 E
Debrecen 10 Ri 47.31N 21.40 E
Debre Libanos 35 Fd 9.43N 38.52 E
Debre Markos 31 Kg 10.10N 37.36 E
Debre Sina 35 Fd 9.51N 39.46 E
Debre Tabor 35 Fc 11.51N 38.00 E
Debre Zeyt 31 Kh 8.47N 39.00 E
De-Buka, Glacier- 66 Nf 76.00S 131.00W
Decatur [Al.-U.S.] 43 Je 34.36N 86.59W
Decatur [Ga.-U.S.] 44 Ei 33.46N 84.18W
Decatur [Il.-U.S.] 43 Jd 39.51N 89.32W
Decatur [In.-U.S.] 44 Ee 40.50N 84.56W
Decatur [Tx.-U.S.] 45 Hj 33.14N 97.35W
Decazeville 11 Ij 44.33N 2.15 E
Deccan 21 Jh 14.00N 77.00 E
Decelles, Reservoir- 44 Hb 47.40N 78.08W
Deception Bay 59 Ia 7.07S 144.05 E
Dechang 27 Hf 27.22N 102.12 E
Děčín 10 Kf 50.47N 14.13 E
Decize 11 Jh 46.50N 3.28 E
Decorah 45 Ke 43.18N 91.48W
Deda 15 Hc 46.56N 24.54 E
Dededo 64c Ba 13.31N 144.49 E
Dedegöl Daği 24 Dd 37.39N 31.17 E
Dedemsvaart, Avereest- 12 Ib 52.37N 6.27 E
Dédougou 34 Ec 12.28N 3.28W
Dedoviči 7 Gh 57.33N 29.58 E
Dedza 36 Fe 14.22S 34.20 E
Dee [Eng.-U.K.] 9 Jh 53.19N 3.11W
Dee [Scot.-U.K.] 9 Kd 57.08N 2.04W
Dee [Scot.-U.K.] 9 Ig 54.50N 4.03W
Deep Creek Range 46 If 40.00N 113.57W
Deering 40 Gc 66.05N 162.43W
Deer Isle 44 Mc 44.13N 68.41W
Deer Lake [Newf.-Can.] 42 Lg 49.10N 57.25W
Deer Lake [Ont.-Can.] 42 If 52.40N 94.30W
Deer Park 46 Gc 47.57N 117.28W
Defiance 44 Ee 41.17N 84.21W
Defla 13 Qi 35.14N 4.26 E
De Funiak Springs 44 Dj 30.43N 86.07W
Dega Ahmedo 35 Gd 7.50N 42.53 E
Dēgē 27 Ge 31.52N 98.36 E
Degebe 13 Ef 38.13N 7.29W
Degeh Bur 35 Gd 8.13N 43.34 E
Degema 34 Ge 4.45N 6.46 E
Degerby 8 Id 60.02N 20.23 E
Degerfors 7 Dg 59.14N 14.26 E
Degerhamn 7 Dh 56.21N 16.24 E
Deggendorf 10 Ih 48.50N 12.58 E

Index Symbols

1 Independent Nation
2 State, Region
3 District, County
4 Municipality
5 Colony, Dependency
Continent
Physical Region
Historical or Cultural Region
Mount, Mountain
Volcano
Hill
Mountains, Mountain Range
Hills, Escarpment
Plateau, Upland
Pass, Gap
Plain, Lowland
Delta
Salt Flat
Valley, Canyon
Crater, Cave
Karst Features
Depression
Polder
Desert, Dunes
Forest, Woods
Heath, Steppe
Oasis
Cape, Point
Coast, Beach
Cliff
Peninsula
Isthmus
Sandbank
Island
Atoll
Rock, Reef
Islands, Archipelago
Rocks, Reefs
Coral Reef
Well, Spring
Geyser
River, Stream
Waterfall Rapids
River Mouth, Estuary
Lake
Salt Lake
Intermittent Lake
Reservoir
Swamp, Pond
Canal
Glacier
Ice Shelf, Pack Ice
Ocean
Sea
Gulf, Bay
Strait, Fjord
Lagoon
Bank
Seamount
Tablemount
Ridge
Shelf
Basin
Escarpment, Sea Scarp
Fracture
Trench, Abyss
National Park, Reserve
Point of Interest
Recreation Site
Cave, Cavern
Historic Site
Ruins
Wall, Walls
Church, Abbey
Temple
Scientific Station
Airport
Port
Lighthouse
Mine
Tunnel
Dam, Bridge

Değirmendere 15 Kk 38.06N 27.09 E
De Gray Lake 45 Ji 34.15N 93.15W
De Grey River 59 Dd 20.12S 119.11 E
Degtarsk 17 Jh 56.42N 60.06 E
De Haan 12 Fc 51.16N 3.02 E
Dehaj 24 Pg 30.42N 54.53 E
Dehaq 24 Nf 32.55N 50.57 E
Deh Bārez 24 Qi 27.26N 57.12 E
Deh Bīd 24 Og 30.38N 53.13 E
Deh Dasht 24 Ng 30.47N 50.34 E
Dehdez 24 Ng 31.43N 50.17 E
Deh-e-Namak 24 Oe 35.25N 52.50 E
Deh-e Shīr 24 Og 31.29N 53.45 E
Deh-e Ziyār 24 Qg 30.40N 57.00 E
Dehgolān 24 Le 35.17N 47.25 E
Dehiwala-Mount Lavinia 25 Fg 6.50N 79.52 E
Dehlorān 24 Lf 32.41N 47.16 E
Deh Now 24 Qf 33.01N 57.41 E
Dehra Dūn 25 Fb 30.19N 78.02 E
Dehui 27 Mc 44.33N 125.38 E
Deinze 11 Jd 50.59N 3.32 E
Dej 15 Gb 47.09N 23.52 E
Deje 8 Ee 59.36N 13.28 E
Dejen 35 Fc 10.05N 38.11 E
Dejës, Mali i- 15 Dh 41.42N 20.10 E
Dejnau 19 Gh 39.18N 63.11 E
De Jongs, Tanjung- 26 Kh 6.56S 138.32 E
De Kalb 45 Lf 41.56N 88.45W
Dekar 37 Cd 21.30S 21.58 E
Dekese 31 Ji 3.27S 21.24 E
Dekina 34 Gd 7.42N 7.01 E
Dēkoa 35 Bd 6.19N 19.04 E
De Koog, Texel- 12 Ga 53.07N 4.46 E
De La Garma 55 Bm 37.58S 60.25W
De Land 44 Gk 29.02N 81.18W
Delano 43 Dd 35.41N 119.15W
Delano Peak 43 Ed 38.22N 112.23W
Delārām 23 Jc 32.11N 63.25 E
Delarof Islands 40a Cb 51.30N 178.45W
Delaware 44 Fe 40.18N 83.06W
Delaware 45 Ek 32.00N 104.00W
Delaware [2] 43 Jd 39.10N 75.30W
Delaware Bay 38 Lc 39.05N 75.15W
Delaware River 43 Ld 39.20N 75.25W
Delbrück 12 Kc 51.46N 8.34 E
Del Carril 55 Cl 35.31S 59.30W
Delčevo 15 Fh 41.58N 22.47 E
Del City 45 Hi 35.27N 97.27W
Delegate 59 Jg 37.03S 148.58 E
Delémont/Delsberg 14 Bc 47.22N 7.21 E
Delet/Teili 8 Id 60.15N 20.35 E
Delfinópolis 55 Ie 20.20S 46.51W
Delft 11 Kb 52.00N 4.21 E
Delfzijl 11 Ma 53.19N 6.56 E
Delgada, Punta- 52 Jj 42.46S 63.38W
Delgado, Cabo-=Delgado, Cape-(EN) 30 Lj 10.40S 40.38 E
Delgado, Cabo-=Delgado, Cape-(EN) [3] 37 Fb 12.30S 39.00 E
Delgado, Cape-(EN)= Delgado, Cabo- 30 Lj 10.40S 40.38 E
Delgado, Cape-(EN)= Delgado, Cabo- [3] 37 Fb 12.30S 39.00 E
Delger Muren 27 Hb 49.17N 100.40 E
Delhi [Co.-U.S.] 45 Eh 37.42N 103.58W
Delhi [India] 25 Jg 28.40N 77.13 E
Delhi [N.Y.-U.S.] 44 Jd 42.17N 74.57W
Deliblatska Peščara 15 Dd 45.00N 21.00 E
Delice 24 Fc 39.58N 34.02 E
Deliceırmak 24 Fb 40.28N 34.10 E
Delicias [Cuba] 49 Ic 21.11N 76.34W
Delicias [Mex.] 47 Cc 28.13N 105.28W
Delījān 24 Nf 33.59N 50.40 E
Delingha 27 Gd 37.26N 97.25 E
Dēliņkalns/Delinkalns, Gora- 8 Lg 57.30N 27.02 E
Delinkalns, Gora-/Dēliņkalns 8 Lg 57.30N 27.02 E
Delitzsch 10 Ie 51.32N 12.21 E
Deljatin 15 Ha 48.29N 24.45 E
Delle 11 Mg 47.30N 7.00 E
Dell Rapids 45 He 43.50N 96.43W
Dellys 32 Hb 36.55N 3.55 E
Delmarva Peninsula 38 Lf 38.50N 75.30W
Delme 12 Ka 53.05N 8.40 E
Delme 12 If 48.53N 6.24 E
Delmenhorst 10 Ec 53.03N 8.37 E
Delnice 14 Ie 45.24N 14.48 E
Delo 35 Fd 5.49N 37.57 E
De Long Strait (EN)= Longa, Proliv- 21 Tb 70.20N 178.00 E
De-Longa, Ostrova-=De Long Islands (EN) 21 Rb 76.30N 153.00 E
De Long Islands (EN)=De-Longa, Ostrova- 21 Rb 76.30N 153.00 E
De Long Mountains 40 Gc 68.20N 162.00W
Deloraine 59 Jh 41.31S 146.39 E
Delorme, Lac- 42 Kf 54.35N 69.55W
Delphi (EN) = Dhelfoi 15 Fk 38.29N 22.30 E
Del Rio 43 Gf 29.22N 100.54W
Delsberg/Delémont 14 Bc 47.22N 7.21 E
Delsbo 7 Dc 61.48N 16.35 E
Delta [Co.-U.S.] 43 Fd 38.44N 108.04W
Delta [Ut.-U.S.] 43 Ed 39.21N 112.35W
Delta Amacuro [2] 54 Fb 8.30N 61.30W
Delta Junction 40 Jd 64.02N 145.41W
Delvāda 25 Ed 20.46N 71.02 E
Del Valle 55 Bl 35.54S 60.43W
Delvina 15 Dj 39.57N 20.06 E
Dēma 17 Gi 54.42N 55.58 E
Demanda, Sierra de la- 13 Ib 42.15N 3.05W
Demba 36 Dd 5.30S 22.16 E
Dembi 35 Fd 8.05N 36.28 E
Dembia 35 Cd 5.07N 24.25 E
Dembi Dolo 35 Ed 8.32N 34.49 E
De Medinilla, Farallon- 57 Fc 16.01N 146.04 E
Demer 11 Kd 50.58N 4.45 E
Demerara Plateau (EN) 52 Le 4.30N 44.00W
Demerara River 50 Gi 6.48N 58.10W
Demidov 16 Gb 55.15N 31.29 E
Demidovka 10 Vf 50.20N 25.27 E
Deming 43 Fe 32.16N 107.45W
Demini, Rio- 54 Fd 0.46S 62.56W
Demirci 24 Cc 39.03N 28.40 E
Demir Kapija 15 Fh 41.25N 22.15 E
Demirköy 15 Kh 41.49N 27.15 E
Demirtaş 15 Mi 40.16N 29.06 E
Demjanka 19 Gd 59.34N 69.20 E
Demjansk 7 Hh 57.38N 32.29 E
Demjanskoje 19 Gd 59.36N 69.18 E
Demmin 10 Jc 53.54N 13.02 E
Demopolis 44 Di 32.31N 87.50W
Dempo, Gunung- 21 Mj 4.02S 103.09 E
Demta 26 Lg 2.20S 140.08 E
Denain 11 Jd 50.20N 3.23 E
Denan 35 Gd 6.30N 43.30 E
Denau 19 Gh 38.18N 67.55 E
Den Bosch/'s-Hertogenbosch 11 Lc 51.41N 5.19 E
Den Burg, Texel- 12 Ga 53.03N 4.47 E
Den Chai 25 Ke 17.59N 100.04 E
Dendang 26 Eg 3.05S 107.54 E
Dender/Dendre 11 Kc 51.02N 4.06 E
Dendermonde/Termonde 12 Gc 51.02N 4.07 E
Dendre/Dender 11 Kc 51.02N 4.06 E
Dendtler Island 66 Pf 72.58S 89.57W
Denekamp 12 Jb 52.23N 7.00 E
Denežkin Kamen, Gora- 19 Fc 60.25N 59.31 E
Dengarh 25 Hd 23.50N 81.42 E
Dêngkagoin→Têwo 27 He 34.03N 103.21 E
Dengkou (Bayan Gol) 22 Me 40.25N 106.59 E
Dêngqên 27 Ge 31.29N 95.32 E
Dengzhou→Penglai 27 Ld 37.44N 120.45 E
Den Haag/'s-Gravenhage= The Hague (EN) 6 Ge 52.06N 4.18 E
Den Ham 12 Ib 52.28N 6.32 E
Denham→Shak Bay 59 Ce 25.55S 113.32 E
Denham, Mount- 49 Id 18.13N 77.32W
Denham Range 59 Jd 21.55S 147.45 E
Denham Sound 59 Ce 25.40S 113.15 E
Den Helder 11 Kb 52.54N 4.45 E
Denia 13 Mf 38.51N 0.07 E
Deniliquin 59 Ig 35.32S 144.58 E
Denio 46 Ff 41.59N 118.39W
Denis Island 37b Ca 3.48S 55.40 E
Denison [Ia.-U.S.] 43 Hc 42.01N 95.20W
Denison [Tx.-U.S.] 43 He 33.45N 96.33W
Denison, Mount- 40 Ie 58.25N 154.27W
Denizli 23 Cb 37.46N 29.06 E
Denklingen, Reichshoft- 12 Jd 50.55N 7.39 E
Denman Glacier 66 Ge 66.45S 99.25 E
Denmark [Austl.] 59 Df 34.57S 117.21 E
Denmark [S.C.-U.S.] 44 Gi 33.19N 81.09W
Denmark (EN)=Danmark [1] 6 Gd 56.00N 10.00 E
Denmark Strait (EN)= Danmarksstraedet 38 Qc 67.00N 25.00W
Dennery 51k Bb 13.55N 60.54W
Den Oever, Wieringen- 12 Hb 52.56N 5.02 E
Denpasar 22 Nj 8.39S 115.13 E
Denton 43 He 33.13N 97.08W
D'Entrecasteaux, Point- 59 Df 34.50S 116.00 E
D'Entrecasteaux Islands 57 Ge 9.35S 150.40 E
Denver 39 If 39.43N 105.01W
Deoghar 25 Hd 24.29N 86.42 E
Deolāli 25 Ee 19.54N 73.50 E
De Pajaros, Farallon- 57 Fb 20.32N 144.54 E
De Panne/La Panne 12 Ec 51.06N 2.35 E
De Pere 45 Ld 44.27N 88.04W
Deputatski 20 Ic 69.13N 139.55 E
Dêqên 27 Gf 28.32N 98.50 E
Deqing 27 Jg 23.14N 111.42 E
De Queen 45 Ii 34.02N 94.21W
De Quincy 45 Jk 30.27N 93.26W
Dequing 28 Fi 30.34N 120.05 E
Dera, Lach- 35 Ge 0.15N 42.17 E
Dera, Lagh- 30 Lh 0.15N 42.17 E
Dera Bugti 25 Dc 29.02N 69.09 E
Dera Ghāzi Khān 22 Jf 30.03N 70.38 E
Dera Ismāīl Khān 25 Eb 31.50N 70.54 E
Derbent [R.S.F.S.R.] 6 Kg 42.00N 48.18 E
Derbent [Tur.] 15 Lk 38.11N 28.33 E
Derby 9 Lh 53.05N 1.40W
Derby [Austl.] 58 Df 17.18S 123.38 E
Derby [Eng.-U.K.] 9 Li 52.55N 1.30W
Derby [Ks.-U.S.] 45 Hh 37.33N 97.16W
Derbyshire [3] 9 Lh 53.10N 1.35W
Đerdap 15 Fe 44.41N 22.10 E
Derecske 10 Ri 47.21N 21.34 E
Dereköy 15 Kh 41.56N 27.21 E
Dereli 24 Hb 40.45N 38.27 E
Derg/Abhainn na Deirge 9 Fg 54.40N 7.25W
Derg, Lough-/Loch Deirgeirt 9 Ei 53.00N 8.20W
Dergači [R.S.F.S.R.] 16 Pd 51.13N 48.46 E
Dergači [Ukr.-U.S.S.R.] 16 Jd 50.09N 36.09 E
Der Grabow 10 Ib 54.23N 12.50 E
De Ridder 45 Jk 30.51N 93.17W
Derik 24 Id 37.22N 40.17 E
Derkul 16 Qd 51.17N 51.15 E
Dermott 45 Kj 33.32N 91.26W
Dernieres, Isles- 45 Kl 29.02N 90.47W
Derong 27 Gf 28.44N 99.18 E
De Rose Hill 59 Ge 26.25S 133.15 E
Déroute, Passage de la- 11 Ee 49.12N 1.51W
Dersa, Eglab- 32 Gd 26.45N 4.26W
Dersca 15 Jb 47.59N 26.12 E
Dersingham 12 Cb 52.51N 0.30 E
Derudeb 35 Fb 17.32N 36.06 E
Derventa 14 Lf 44.59N 17.55 E
Derwent [Eng.-U.K.] 9 Mg 54.10N 0.40W
Derwent [Eng.-U.K.] 12 Ab 52.53N 1.17W
Derwent River 59 Jh 43.03S 147.22 E
Deržavinsk 19 Ge 51.03N 66.19 E
Desaguadero, Rio- 52 Ji 34.13S 66.47W
Désappointement, Iles du- 57 Mf 14.10S 141.20W
Des Arc 45 Ki 34.58N 91.30W
Desborough 12 Bb 52.26N 0.49W
Descalvado 55 Ie 21.54S 47.37W
Descartes 11 Gh 46.58N 0.45 E
Deschambault Lake 42 Hf 54.50N 103.30W
Deschutes River 43 Cb 45.38N 120.54W
Descoberto, Rio- 55 Hc 16.20S 48.19W
Dese 31 Kg 11.07N 39.38 E
Deseado, Rio- 52 Jj 47.45S 65.54W
Desecheo, Isla- 51a Ab 18.25N 67.28W
Desengaño, Punta- 56 Gg 49.15S 67.37W
Desenzano del Garda 14 Ee 45.28N 10.32 E
Desert Center 46 Hj 33.42N 115.26W
Desert Peak 46 If 40.28N 112.38W
Deshaies [Guad.] 51e Ab 16.18N 61.48W
Deshaies [Guad.] 51e Ab 16.18N 61.47W
Desiderio, Rio- 55 Ja 12.20S 44.50W
Desmaraisville 44 Ia 49.31N 76.10W
De Smet 45 Hd 44.23N 97.33W
Desmochado 55 Ch 27.07S 58.06W
Des Moines 38 Je 40.22N 91.26W
Des Moines [Ia.-U.S.] 39 Je 41.35N 93.37W
Des Moines [N.M.-U.S.] 45 Eh 36.46N 103.50W
Desmoronado, Cerro- 47 Dd 20.21N 105.01W
Desna 5 Je 50.33N 30.32 E
Desnățui 15 Ge 43.53N 23.35 E
Desolación, Isla- 52 Ik 53.00S 74.10W
De Soto 45 Kg 38.08N 90.33W
Despeñaperros, Desfiladero de- 13 If 38.24N 3.30W
Des Roches, Ile- 37b Bb 5.41S 53.41 E
Dessau 10 Ie 51.50N 12.15 E
Destruction Bay 42 Dd 61.20N 139.00W
Desventuradas, Islas- 52 Ih 26.45S 80.00W
Desvres 11 Hd 50.40N 1.50 E
Deta 15 Ed 45.24N 21.14 E
Dete 37 Dc 18.37S 26.51 E
Detmold 10 Ee 51.56N 8.53 E
Detour, Point- 44 Dc 45.36N 86.37W
Detroit [Mi.-U.S.] 39 Ke 42.20N 83.03W
Detroit [Or.-U.S.] 46 Dd 44.42N 122.10W
Detroit Lakes 45 Ic 46.49N 95.51W
Dettifoss 7a Cb 65.49N 16.24W
Detva 10 Ph 48.34N 19.25 E
Deûle 12 Ed 50.44N 2.56 E
Deurdeur 13 Oh 36.14N 2.16 E
Deurne 12 Hc 51.28N 5.48 E
Deutsche Bucht 10 Db 54.30N 7.30 E
Deutsche Demokratische Republik = Germany 6 Ge 51.00N 10.00 E
Deutschlandsberg 14 Jd 46.49N 15.13 E
Deux-Bassins, Col des- 13 Ph 36.27N 3.18 E
Deux Sèvres [3] 11 Fh 46.30N 0.15W
Deva 15 Fd 45.53N 22.54 E
Dévaványa 10 Qi 47.02N 20.58 E
Deveci Dağları 24 Gb 40.05N 36.00 E
Devecser 10 Ni 47.06N 17.26 E
Develi 24 Fc 38.22N 35.06 E
Deventer 11 Mb 52.15N 6.10 E
Deverd, Cap- 63b Be 20.46S 164.22 E
Deveron 9 Kd 57.40N 2.30W
Devès, Monts du- 11 Jj 44.57N 3.46 E
Devetak 14 Mg 43.58N 19.00 E
Devil River Peak 62 Ed 40.58S 172.39 E
Devil's Hole 9 Ne 56.38N 0.40 E
Devil's Island (EN)=Diable, Ile du- 54 Hb 5.17N 52.35W
Devils Lake 43 Hb 48.07N 98.59W
Devils Lake 45 Gb 48.01N 98.52W
Devils Paw 40 Me 58.44N 133.50W
Devils River 45 Fl 29.39N 100.58W
Devils Tower 46 Md 44.31N 104.57W
Devin 15 Hh 41.45N 24.24 E
Devizes 9 Lj 51.22N 1.59W
Devnja 15 Kf 43.13N 27.33 E
Devodi Munda 25 Ge 17.37N 82.57 E
De Volet Point 51n Ba 13.22N 61.13W
Devolli 15 Ci 40.49N 19.51 E
Devolli 15 Di 40.30N 20.50 E
Dévoluy 11 Lj 44.39N 5.53 E
Devon [3] 9 Jk 50.50N 3.50W
Devon 9 Jk 50.50N 4.00W
Devon 38 Kb 75.00N 87.00W
Devon 12 Ba 53.04N 0.49W
Devonport 57 Fi 41.11S 146.21 E
Devoto 55 Aj 31.24S 62.19W
Devrek 24 Db 41.13N 31.57 E
Devrez 24 Fb 41.06N 34.25 E
Dewa 30 Lh 4.11N 42.06 E
Dewar Lakes 42 Kc 68.00N 73.00W
Dewās 25 Fd 22.58N 76.04 E
Dewa-Sanchi 29 Gb 39.30N 140.15 E
Dewey 45 Ih 36.48N 95.56W
De Witt 45 Ki 34.18N 91.20W
Dexemhare 35 Fb 15.04N 39.03 E
Dexing 28 Dj 28.55N 117.33 E
Dexter 45 Lh 36.48N 89.57W
Deyang 27 He 31.07N 104.25 E
Dey-Dey, Lake- 59 Ge 29.15S 131.05 E
Deyhük 24 Qf 33.17N 57.30 E
Deyyer 23 Hd 27.50N 51.55 E
Dez 24 Mg 31.39N 48.52 E
Dezfūl 22 Gf 32.23N 48.24 E
Dez Gerd 24 Ng 30.45N 51.57 E
Dezhou 27 Kd 37.28N 116.18 E
Dháfni 15 Fl 37.46N 22.02 E
Dhahab 33 Fd 28.29N 34.32 E
Dhaka 22 Lg 23.43N 90.25 E
Dhamār 23 Fg 14.37N 44.23 E
Dhamtari 25 Gd 20.41N 81.34 E
Dhānbād 25 Hd 23.48N 86.27 E
Dhanushkodi 25 Fg 9.11N 79.24 E
Dhaulagiri 21 Kg 28.44N 83.25 E
Dhekeleia 24 Ee 35.03N 33.40 E
Dhelfoi = Delphi (EN) 15 Fk 38.29N 22.30 E
Dhelvinákion 15 Dj 39.56N 20.28 E
Dhenkanal 25 Hd 20.40N 85.36 E
Dheskáti 15 Ej 39.55N 21.49 E
Dhespotikó 15 Hm 36.58N 25.00 E
Dhiapóndioi Nisoi 15 Cj 39.50N 19.25 E
Dhibān 24 Fg 31.30N 35.47 E
Dhidhimótikhon 15 Jh 41.21N 26.30 E
Dhikti Óros 15 In 35.15N 25.30 E
Dhílos 15 Il 37.24N 25.16 E
Dhílos 15 Il 37.24N 25.16 E
Dhimitsána 15 Fl 37.36N 22.03 E
Dhionisiádhes, Nísoi- 15 Jn 35.21N 26.10 E
Dhiórix Potidhaia 15 Gi 40.10N 23.20 E
Dhī-Qār [3] 24 Lg 31.10N 46.10 E
Dhī-Qār 24 Kf 32.14N 44.22 E
Dhírfis Óros 15 Gk 38.38N 23.50 E
Dhísoron Óros 15 Fh 41.11N 22.57 E
Dhivounia 15 Jn 35.50N 26.28 E
Dhodhekánisos = Dodecanese (EN) 15 Jm 36.20N 27.00 E
Dhodhóni = Dodona (EN) 15 Dj 39.33N 20.46 E
Dholpur 25 Fc 26.42N 77.54 E
Dhomokós 15 Fj 39.08N 22.18 E
Dhone 25 Fe 15.25N 77.53 E
Dhonoúsa 15 Il 37.10N 25.50 E
Dhorāji 25 Ed 21.44N 70.27 E
Dhoxáton 15 Hh 41.06N 24.14 E
Dhragónisos 15 Il 37.27N 25.29 E
Dhuburi 25 Hc 26.02N 89.58 E
Dhule 22 Jg 20.54N 74.47 E
Dhulián 25 Hd 24.41N 87.58 E
Dia 15 In 35.27N 25.13 E
Diable, Ile du-=Devil's Island (EN) 54 Hb 5.17N 52.35W
Diable, Morne au- 51g Ba 15.37N 61.27W
Diable, Pointe du- [Mart.] 51h Bb 14.47N 60.54W
Diable, Pointe du- [Van.] 63b Dc 16.01S 168.12 E
Diablo, Punta del- 55 Fl 34.22S 53.46W
Diablo, Puntan- 64b Ba 15.00N 145.34 E
Diablo Range 46 Eh 36.45N 121.20W
Diafarabé 34 Ec 14.10N 5.00W
Dialafara 34 Cc 13.27N 11.23W
Diamant, Pointe du- 51h Ac 14.27N 61.04W
Diamant, Rocher du- 51h Ac 14.27N 61.03W
Diamante [Arg.] 56 Hd 32.04S 60.39W
Diamante [It.] 14 Jk 39.41N 15.49 E
Diamante, Punta del- 48 Ji 16.47N 99.52W
Diamantina 54 Jg 18.15S 43.36W
Diamantina, Chapada- 52 Lg 11.30S 41.10W
Diamantina, Rio- 55 Fc 16.42S 52.45W
Diamantina Depth (EN) 3 Hm 33.30S 102.00 E
Diamantina Lakes 59 Id 23.46S 141.09 E
Diamantina River 57 Eg 26.45S 139.10 E
Diamantina Trench (EN) 3 Hm 36.00S 104.00 E
Diamantino 53 Kg 14.25S 56.27W
Diamantino, Rio- 55 Fc 16.08S 52.28W
Diamond Harbour 25 Hd 22.12N 88.12 E
Diamond Island 51p Bb 12.20N 61.35W
Diamond Jenness Peninsula 42 Fb 71.00N 117.00W
Diamond Peak [Nv.-U.S.] 46 Hg 39.40N 115.48W
Diamond Peak [Or.-U.S.] 46 De 43.33N 122.09W
Diamond Peak [U.S.] 46 Id 44.09N 113.05W
Diamond Peak [U.S.] 46 Gc 46.07N 117.32W
Diamou 34 Cc 14.05N 11.16W
Diana, Baie- 42 Kd 61.00N 70.00W
Dianbai 27 Jg 21.33N 110.58 E
Dianbu → Feidong 28 Di 31.53N 117.29 E
Diancang Shan 27 Hf 25.42N 100.02 E
Dian Chi 27 Hg 24.50N 102.45 E
Diane, Étang de- 11a Ba 42.07N 9.32 E
Dianjiang 27 Ie 30.19N 107.25 E
Diano Marina 14 Cg 43.54N 8.05 E
Dianópolis 54 If 11.38S 46.50W
Dianra 34 Dd 8.45N 6.18W
Diapaga 34 Fc 12.04N 1.47 E
Diaz 55 Bk 32.22S 61.05W
Dibā, Dawḥat- 24 Qk 25.38N 56.18 E
Dībagah 24 Je 35.52N 43.49 E
Dibang 25 Jc 27.50N 95.32 E
Dibaya 36 Dd 6.30S 22.57 E
Dibaya-Lubue 36 Cc 4.09S 19.52 E
Dibella 34 Hb 17.31N 12.59 E
Dibrugarh 22 Lg 27.29N 94.54 E
Dibs 24 Ke 35.40N 44.04 E
Dibsī Afnān 24 Ee 35.55N 38.16 E
Dickens 45 Fj 33.37N 100.50W
Dickinson 43 Gb 46.53N 102.47W
Dickins Seamount (EN) 40 Lf 54.30N 137.00W
Dickson 44 Dg 36.05N 87.23W
Dicle 24 Ic 38.22N 40.04 E
Dicle=Tigris (EN) 21 Gf 31.00N 47.25 E
Didam 12 Ic 51.56N 6.09 E
Didao 28 Kb 45.22N 130.48 E
Didcot 12 Ac 51.36N 1.15W
Didesa 35 Fd 9.30N 35.32 E
Didiéni 34 Dc 13.23N 8.05W
Didyma 15 Kl 37.21N 27.13 E
Die 11 Lj 44.45N 5.22 E
Dieburg 10 Eg 49.54N 8.51 E
Diecinueve de Abril 55 El 34.22S 54.04W
Dieciocho de Julio 55 Fk 33.41S 53.33W
Diefenbaker Lake 42 Gf 51.00N 107.00W
Diège 11 Ii 45.36N 2.16 E
Diego Garcia 21 Jj 6.20S 72.20 E
Diego Ramírez, Islas 56 Gi 56.30S 68.44W
Diekirch 11 Me 49.53N 6.10 E
Die Lewitz 10 Hc 53.30N 11.30 E
Diéma 34 Dc 14.33N 9.11W
Diemel 10 Fe 51.39N 9.27 E
Diemelsee 12 Kc 51.19N 8.43 E
Diemelstadt 12 Lc 51.27N 9.01 E
Dien Bien Phu 25 Kd 21.23N 103.01 E
Diepenbeek 12 Hd 50.54N 5.24 E
Diepholz 10 Ed 52.36N 8.22 E
Dieppe 11 He 49.56N 1.05 E
Dieppe Bay Town 51c Ab 17.25N 62.48W
Dierdorf 12 Jd 50.33N 7.40 E
Dieren, Rheden- 12 Ib 52.03N 6.08 E
Di'er Songhua Jiang 27 Lc 45.26N 124.39 E
Diest 12 Hd 50.59N 5.03 E
Dieulefit 11 Lj 44.31N 5.04 E
Dieulouard 12 If 48.51N 6.04 E
Dieuze 11 Mf 48.49N 6.43 E
Dieveniškes 8 Kj 54.10N 25.44 E
Die Ville 12 Id 50.40N 6.55 E
Diez 12 Kd 50.22N 8.01 E
Dif 36 Hb 0.59N 40.57 E
Diffa [2] 34 Hb 16.00N 13.30 E
Diffa 34 Hc 13.19N 12.37 E
Differdange/Differdingen 11 Le 49.32N 5.52 E
Differdingen/Differdange 11 Le 49.32N 5.52 E
Digby 42 Kh 44.40N 65.50W
Dighton 45 Fg 38.29N 100.28W
Digne 11 Mj 44.06N 6.14 E
Digoin 11 Jh 46.29N 3.59 E
Digora 16 Nh 43.07N 44.06 E
Digos 26 Ie 6.45N 125.20 E
Digranes 7a Ca 66.02N 14.45W
Digul 26 Kh 7.07S 138.42 E
Dihāng 25 Jc 27.48N 95.30 E
Dijar 16 Tf 46.33N 56.05 E
Dijlah=Tigris (EN) 21 Gf 31.00N 47.25 E
Dijle 11 Kd 50.53N 4.42 E
Dijon 6 Gf 47.19N 5.01 E
Dik 35 Bd 9.58N 17.31 E
Dikanäs 7 Dd 65.14N 16.00 E
Dikhil 35 Gc 11.06N 42.22 E
Dikili 24 Bc 39.04N 26.53 E
Dikli 8 Kg 57.30N 25.00 E
Diksmuide/Dixmude 11 Ic 51.02N 2.52 E
Dikson 22 Kb 73.30N 80.35 E
Dikwa 34 Hc 12.02N 13.55 E
Dila 35 Fd 6.23N 38.19 E
Dilbeek 12 Gd 50.51N 4.16 E
Dili 22 Oj 8.33S 125.34 E
Di Linh 25 Lf 11.35N 108.04 E
Diližan 16 Ni 40.46N 44.55 E
Dilj 14 Me 45.16N 18.01 E
Dill 12 Kd 50.33N 8.29 E
Dillenburg 10 Ef 50.44N 8.17 E
Dillia 30 Ig 14.09N 12.50 E
Dilling 31 Jg 12.03N 29.39 E
Dillingen (Saar) 12 Ie 49.21N 6.44 E
Dillingham 39 Dd 59.02N 158.29W
Dillon [Mt.-U.S.] 43 Eb 45.13N 112.38W
Dillon [S.C.-U.S.] 44 Hh 34.25N 79.22W
Dilly 34 Dc 14.57N 7.43W
Dilolo 31 Jj 10.42S 22.20 E
Dilsen 12 Hc 51.02N 5.44 E
Dimashq=Damascus (EN) 22 Ff 33.30N 36.15 E
Dimbelenge 36 Dd 5.30S 23.53 E
Dimbokro [3] 34 Ed 6.50N 4.45W
Dimbokro 34 Ed 6.39N 4.42W
Dimboola 59 Ig 36.27S 142.02 E
Dîmbovița 15 Je 44.14N 26.27 E
Dîmbovița [2] 15 Ie 44.55N 25.30 E
Dîmbovnic 15 Ie 44.20N 25.40 E
Dimitrovgrad [Bul.] 15 Ig 42.03N 25.36 E
Dimitrovgrad [R.S.F.S.R.] 19 Ee 54.14N 49.42 E
Dimitrovgrad [Yugo.] 15 Fg 43.01N 22.47 E
Dimmitt 45 Ei 34.33N 102.19W
Dimona 24 Fg 31.04N 35.02 E
Dimovo 15 Ff 43.44N 22.44 E
Dinagat 26 Id 10.12N 125.35 E
Dinājpur 25 Hc 25.38N 88.38 E
Dinan 11 Df 48.27N 2.02W
Dinangourou 34 Ec 14.27N 2.14W
Dinant 11 Kd 50.16N 4.55 E
Dinar 24 Dc 38.04N 30.10 E
Dīnar, Kūh-e- 24 Ng 30.50N 51.35 E
Dinara 14 Kf 44.04N 16.23 E
Dinara=Dinaric Alps (EN) 5 Hg 43.50N 16.35 E
Dinard 11 Df 48.38N 2.04W
Dinaric Alps (EN)= Dinara 5 Hg 43.50N 16.35 E
Dindar, Nahr ad- 35 Ec 14.06N 33.40 E
Dinder 35 Ec 14.06N 33.40 E
Dindigul 25 Ff 10.21N 77.57 E
Dindima 34 Hc 10.14N 10.09 E
Dinga 36 Cd 5.19S 16.34 E
Dingbian 27 Id 37.35N 107.37 E
Dingden, Hamminkeln- 12 Ic 51.46N 6.37 E
Dinggyê 27 Ef 28.25N 87.45 E
Dinghai 27 Le 30.05N 122.07 E
Dingle 8 Df 58.32N 11.34 E
Dingle/An Daingean 9 Ci 52.08N 10.15W
Dingle Bay/Bá an Daingin 9 Ci 52.05N 10.15W
Dingolfing 10 Ih 48.38N 12.30 E
Dingshuzhen 28 Ei 31.16N 119.50 E
Dingtao 28 Cg 35.04N 115.35 E
Dinguiraye 34 Cc 11.18N 10.43W
Dingwall 9 Id 57.35N 4.26W
Dingxi 27 Hd 35.33N 104.32 E
Dingxian 27 Jd 39.29N 115.00 E
Dingxiang 28 Be 38.32N 112.59 E
Dingxing 27 Kd 39.11N 115.48 E
Dingyuan 28 Dh 32.32N 117.41 E
Dingzi Gang 28 Ff 36.33N 120.59 E
Dinh, Mui- 21 Mh 11.22N 109.01 E
Dinkel 12 Ib 52.30N 6.58 E
Dinosaur 45 Bf 40.15N 109.01W
Dinskaja 16 Kg 45.09N 39.12 E
Dinslaken 12 Ic 51.34N 6.44 E
Dīnsōr 35 Ge 2.23N 42.58 E
Dintel 12 Gc 51.39N 4.24 E
Dinuba 46 Fh 36.36N 119.27W

Index Symbols

[1] Independent Nation
[2] State, Region
[3] District, County
[4] Municipality
[5] Colony, Dependency
Continent
Physical Region
Historical or Cultural Region
Mount, Mountain
Volcano
Hill
Mountains, Mountain Range
Hills, Escarpment
Plateau, Upland
Pass, Gap
Plain, Lowland
Delta
Salt Flat
Valley, Canyon
Crater, Cave
Karst Features
Depression
Polder
Desert, Dunes
Forest, Woods
Heath, Steppe
Oasis
Cape, Point
Coast, Beach
Cliff
Peninsula
Isthmus
Sandbank
Island
Atoll
Rock, Reef
Islands, Archipelago
Rocks, Reefs
Coral Reef
Well, Spring
Geyser
River, Stream
Waterfall Rapids
River Mouth, Estuary
Lake
Salt Lake
Intermittent Lake
Reservoir
Swamp, Pond
Canal
Glacier
Ice Shelf, Pack Ice
Ocean
Sea
Gulf, Bay
Strait, Fjord
Lagoon
Bank
Seamount
Tablemount
Ridge
Shelf
Basin
Escarpment, Sea Scarp
Fracture
Trench, Abyss
National Park, Reserve
Point of Interest
Recreation Site
Cave, Cavern
Historic Site
Ruins
Wall, Walls
Church, Abbey
Temple
Scientific Station
Airport
Port
Lighthouse
Mine
Tunnel
Dam, Bridge

Dinwiddie 44 Ig 37.05N 77.35W
Dioila 34 Dc 12.28N 6.47W
Diois, Massif du- 11 Lj 44.35N 5.20 E
Dion 34 Dc 10.12N 8.39W
Diorama 55 Gc 16.21S 51.14W
Dios 63a Ba 5.33S 154.58 E
Diosig 15 Eb 47.18N 22.00 E
Dioura 34 Dc 14.51N 5.15W
Diourbel [3] 34 Bc 14.45N 16.10W
Diourbel 34 Bc 14.40N 16.15W
Dipkarpas 24 Fe 35.36N 34.23 E
Dipolog 22 Oi 8.35N 123.20 E
Dir 25 Ea 35.12N 71.53 E
Dira, Djebel- 13 Ph 36.05N 3.38 E
Diré 34 Eb 16.15N 3.24W
Dire Dawa 31 Lh 9.35N 41.53 E
Diriamba 49 Dh 11.51N 86.14W
Dirico 36 Df 17.58S 20.45 E
Dirj 33 Bc 30.09N 10.26 E
Dirk Hartog Island 59 Ce 25.45S 113.00 E
Dirkou 34 Hb 19.01N 12.53 E
Dirranbandi 58 Fg 28.35S 148.14 E
Dirty Devil River 46 Jh 37.53N 110.24W
Disappointment, Cape- [B.A.T.] 56 Mh 54.53S 36.07W
Disappointment, Cape- [U.S.] 46 Cc 46.18N 124.03W
Disappointment, Lake- 57 Dg 23.30S 122.50 E
Discovery Tablemount (EN) 30 Hm 42.00S 0.10 E
Dishna 33 Fd 26.07N 32.28 E
Disko 67 Nc 69.50N 53.30W
Disko Bay (EN)=Disko Bugt 67 Nc 69.15N 52.30W
Disko Bugt=Disko Bay (EN) 67 Nc 69.15N 52.30W
Diskofjord 41 Ge 69.39N 53.45W
Disna 7 Gi 55.33N 28.12 E
Disna 7 Gi 55.34N 28.12 E
Disnaj, Ozero-/Dysnų Ežeras 7 Gi 55.35N 26.32 E
Dispur 25 Ic 26.07N 91.48 E
Diss 12 Db 52.23N 1.07 E
District of Columbia [2] 43 Ld 38.54N 77.01W
Distrito Federal [Braz.] [2] 54 Ig 15.45S 47.45W
Distrito Federal [Mex.] [2] 47 Ee 19.15N 99.10W
Disūq 24 Dg 31.08N 30.39 E
Dithmarschen 10 Fb 54.10N 9.15 E
Ditrău 15 Ic 46.49N 25.31 E
Dittaino 14 Im 37.25N 15.00 E
Diu [3] 25 Ed 20.42N 70.59 E
Divāndarreh 24 Le 35.55N 47.02 E
Divénié 36 Bc 2.41S 12.05 E
Divenskaja 8 Ne 59.09N 30.09 E
Dives 11 Fe 49.19N 0.05W
Dives-sur-Mer 12 Be 49.17N 0.06W
Diviaka 15 Ci 41.00N 19.32 E
Diviči 16 Pi 42.10N 49.01 E
Divin 10 Ue 51.57N 24.09 E
Divinópolis 53 Lh 20.09S 44.54W
Divion 12 Ed 50.28N 2.30 E
Divisões, Serra das- 54 Hg 16.40S 50.50W
Divisor, Serra de 54 De 8.00S 73.50W
Divnogorsk 20 Ee 55.58N 92.32 E
Divnoje 19 Ef 45.53N 43.22 E
Divo [3] 34 Dd 5.57N 5.15W
Divo 34 Dd 5.50N 5.22W
Divoká Orlice 10 Mf 50.09N 16.06 E
Divor 13 Df 38.59N 8.29W
Divriği 24 Hc 39.23N 38.07 E
Dīvrūd 24 Nd 36.52N 49.34 E
Dixmude/Diksmuide 11 Ic 51.02N 2.52 E
Dixon [Il.-U.S.] 45 Lf 41.50N 89.29W
Dixon [N.M.-U.S.] 45 Dh 36.11N 105.53W
Dixon Entrance 38 Fd 54.25N 132.30W
Diyālā [3] 21 Gf 33.14N 44.31 E
Diyālā [3] 24 Kf 34.00N 45.00 E
Diyarbakir 23 Fb 37.55N 40.14 E
Dizy 12 Fe 49.04N 3.58 E
Dizy-le-Gros 12 Ge 49.38N 4.01 E
Dja 30 Ih 2.02N 15.12 E
Djado 31 If 21.01N 12.18 E
Djado, Plateau du- 30 If 21.45N 12.50 E
Djakovo 10 Th 48.03N 23.01 E
Djamaa 32 Ic 33.32N 6.00 E
Djambala 31 Ii 2.33S 14.45 E
Djanet 31 Hf 24.34N 9.29 E
Djaret 32 Hd 26.35N 1.38 E
Djatkovo 19 De 53.36N 34.20 E
Djatlovo 16 Dc 53.31N 25.24 E
Djaul Island 60 Eh 2.56S 150.55 E
Djebel Țāriq, El Bōghâz-= Gibraltar, Strait of- (EN) 5 Fh 35.57N 5.36W
Djédaa 35 Bc 13.31N 18.34 E
Djedi 30 He 34.39N 5.55 E
Djedoug, Djebel- 13 Qi 35.53N 4.20 E
Djelfa 31 He 34.40N 3.15 E
Djelfa [3] 32 Hc 34.15N 3.30 E
Djéma 31 Jh 6.03N 25.19 E
Djember 35 Bc 10.25N 17.50 E
Djemila 32 Ib 36.19N 5.44 E
Djenane 13 Pi 35.43N 3.59 E
Djenné 34 Ec 13.55N 4.33W
Djerem 34 Hd 5.20N 13.24 E
Dji 35 Cd 6.47N 22.14 E
Djibo 34 Ec 14.06N 1.38W
Djibouti 31 Lg 11.35N 43.08 E
Djibouti (Afars and Issas) [1] 31 Lg 11.30N 43.00 E
Djokupunda 36 Dd 5.27S 20.58 E
Djolu 31 Jh 0.37N 22.21 E
Djoua 36 Bb 1.13N 13.12 E
Djougou 34 Fd 9.42N 1.40 E
Djoum 34 He 2.40N 12.40 E
Djourab, Erg du- [Chad] 35 Bb 17.00N 19.30 E
Djourab, Erg du- [Chad] 35 Bb 16.40N 18.50 E
Djugu 36 Fb 1.55N 30.30 E
Djultydag, Gora- 16 Oi 41.58N 46.56 E
Djup 8 Bd 60.50N 8.00 E
Djúpi vogur 7a Cb 64.39N 14.17W
Djurbeldžin 18 Jd 41.10N 74.59 E
Djurdjura, Djebel- 13 Qh 36.27N 4.15 E
Djurmo 8 Fd 60.33N 15.10 E
Djurö 8 Ef 58.50N 13.30 E
Djursholm 8 He 59.24N 18.05 E
Djursland 8 Dh 56.20N 10.45 E
Djurtjuli 19 Fd 55.29N 54.55 E
Dmitrija Lapteva, Proliv-= Dmitri Laptev Strait (EN) 21 Qb 73.00N 142.00 E
Dmitrijev-Lgovski 16 Ic 52.08N 35.05 E
Dmitri Laptev Strait (EN)= Dmitrija Lapteva, Proliv- 21 Qb 73.00N 142.00 E
Dmitrov 7 Ih 56.26N 37.31 E
Dmitrovsk-Orlovski 16 Ic 52.31N 35.09 E
Dnepr 5 Jf 46.30N 32.18 E
Dneprodzeržinsk 19 Df 48.30N 34.37 E
Dneprodzeržinskoje Vodohranilišče 16 Ie 48.45N 34.10 E
Dnepropetrovsk 6 Jf 48.27N 34.59 E
Dnepropetrovskaja Oblast [3] 19 Df 48.15N 35.00 E
Dneprorudnoje 16 If 47.23N 35.01 E
Dneprovski Liman 16 Gf 46.35N 31.55 E
Dneprovsko-Bugski Kanal 16 Dc 52.03N 25.10 E
Dnepr Upland (EN)= Pridneprovskaja Vozvyšennost 5 Jf 49.00N 32.00 E
Dnestr [U.S.S.R.] 5 Jf 46.18N 30.17 E
Dnestrovsk 15 Mc 46.39N 29.48 E
Dnestrovski Liman 16 Gf 46.15N 30.15 E
Dno 19 Cd 57.49N 29.59 E
Doany 37 Hb 14.22S 49.30 E
Doba 35 Bd 8.39N 16.51 E
Dobbiaco / Toblach 14 Gd 46.44N 12.14 E
Dobele 7 Fh 56.39N 23.16 E
Döbeln 10 Je 51.07N 13.07 E
Doberah, Jazirah- 26 Jg 1.30S 132.30 E
Dobo 26 Jh 5.46S 134.13 E
Doboj 14 Mf 44.44N 18.05 E
Dobra 10 Oe 51.54N 18.37 E
Dobre Miasto 10 Qc 53.59N 20.25 E
Dobreta Turnu Severin 6 Ig 44.38N 22.40 E
Dobrinka 16 Lc 52.08N 40.29 E
Dobříš 10 Kg 49.47N 14.10 E
Dobrjanka 19 Fd 58.29N 56.29 E
Dobrodzień 10 Of 50.44N 18.27 E
Dobrogea=Dobruja (EN) 15 Ke 44.00N 28.00 E
Dobrogea = Dobruja (EN) 5 Ig 44.00N 28.00 E
Dobrogean, Masivul- 15 Le 44.50N 28.30 E
Dobromil 10 Sg 49.34N 22.49 E
Dobropolje 16 Je 48.28N 37.02 E
Dobroteşti 15 He 44.17N 24.53 E
Dobrotvor 10 Uf 50.10N 24.27 E
Dobrudžansko Plato 15 Kf 43.32N 27.50 E
Dobruja (EN)=Dobrogea 15 Ke 44.00N 28.00 E
Dobruja (EN) = Dobrogea 5 Ig 44.00N 28.00 E
Dobruš 16 Gc 52.26N 31.19 E
Dobruška 10 Mf 50.18N 16.10 E
Dobrzyń nad Wisłą 10 Pd 52.38N 19.20 E
Dobrzyńskie, Pojezierze- 10 Pc 53.00N 19.20 E
Dobšiná 10 Qh 48.49N 20.22 E
Doce, Rio- [Braz.] 52 Mg 19.37S 39.49W
Doce, Rio- [Braz.] 55 Gd 18.28S 51.05W
Doce Leguas, Cayos de las- 49 Hc 20.55N 79.05W
Doce Leguas, Laberinto de las- 49 Hc 20.39N 78.35W
Docker River 59 Fd 24.58S 129.03 E
Docksta 8 Ha 63.03N 18.20 E
Doctor Arroyo 48 If 23.40N 100.11W
Doctor Cecilio Baez 55 Dg 25.03S 56.19W
Doctor Pedro P. Peña 56 Hb 22.26S 62.22W
Doctor Petru Groza 15 Fc 46.37N 22.25 E
Doda 25 Fb 33.08N 75.34 E
Doda Betta 25 Ff 11.24N 76.44 E
Dodecanese (EN) = Dhodhekánisos 15 Jm 36.20N 27.00 E
Dodecanese (EN)= Nótioi Sporádhes 5 Ih 36.00N 27.00 E
Dodge City 43 Gd 37.45N 100.00W
Dodgeville 45 Ke 42.58N 90.08W
Dodman Point 9 Ik 50.13N 4.48W
Dodoma [3] 36 Gd 6.00S 36.00 E
Dodoma 31 Ki 6.11S 35.45 E
Dodona (EN) = Dhodhóni 15 Dj 39.33N 20.46 E
Dodurga 15 Mj 39.48N 29.55 E
Doesburg 12 Ib 52.01N 6.08 E
Doetinchem 11 Mc 51.58N 6.17 E
Dofa 26 Ig 1.47S 125.22 E
Dogai Coring 27 Ee 34.30N 89.10 E
Doğanbey 15 Jk 38.04N 26.53 E
Doğanşehir 24 Gc 38.06N 37.53 E
Dog Creek 46 Da 51.35N 122.15W
Dogger Bank 5 Ge 55.00N 3.00 E
Dog Island 50 Ec 18.15N 63.13W
Dog Lake [Man.-Can.] 45 Ga 51.02N 98.30W
Dog Lake [Ont.-Can.] 44 Ea 48.18N 84.10W
Dog Lake [Ont.-Can.] 45 Lb 48.46N 89.32W
Dogliani 14 Bf 44.32N 7.56 E
Dōgo 28 Lf 36.15N 133.17 E
Dogonbadān 23 Hc 30.21N 50.48 E
Dogondoutchi 34 Fc 13.38N 4.02 E
Dōgo-San 29 Cd 35.04N 133.14 E
Dog Rocks 49 Ha 24.05N 79.51W
Doğubayazıt 24 Kc 39.32N 44.08 E
Dogwood Point 51c Ab 17.06N 62.38W
Doha (EN)=Ad Dawḩah 22 Hg 25.17N 51.32 E
Dohad 25 Ed 22.50N 74.16 E
Dohāzāri 25 Id 22.10N 92.04 E
Doi Luang Chiang Dao 25 Je 19.23N 98.54 E
Doilungdêqên 27 Ff 29.47N 90.49 E
Doire/Londonderry 6 Fd 55.00N 7.19W
Doire Baltée/Dora Baltea 14 Ce 45.11N 8.03 E
Doische 12 Gd 50.08N 4.45 E
Dojransko jezero 15 Fh 41.13N 22.44 E
Doka 35 Fc 13.31N 35.46 E
Dokhara, Dunes de- 32 Ic 32.50N 6.00 E
Dokka 8 Dd 60.49N 10.05 E
Dokka 7 Cf 60.50N 10.05 E
Dokkum 11 La 53.19N 6.00 E
Dokšicy 7 Gi 54.56N 27.46 E
Doksy 10 Kf 50.34N 14.40 E
Dokučajevsk 16 Jf 47.43N 37.47 E
Dolak, Pulau- 57 Ee 7.50S 138.30 E
Dolbeau 42 Kg 48.52N 72.14W
Dol-de-Bretagne 11 Ef 48.33N 1.45W
Dôle 11 Lg 47.06N 5.30 E
Doleib Hill 35 Ed 9.22N 31.36 E
Dolenjsko 14 Je 45.50N 15.10 E
Dolgaja, Kosa- 16 Jf 46.40N 37.45 E
Dolgellau 9 Ji 52.44N 3.53W
Dolgi, Ostrov- 17 Ib 69.15N 59.05 E
Dolgi Most 20 Ee 56.45N 96.58 E
Dolianova 14 Dk 39.22N 9.10 E
Dolina 16 De 48.58N 24.01 E
Dolinsk 20 Jg 47.20N 142.50 E
Dolinskaja 19 Df 48.07N 32.44 E
Dolinskoje 15 Mb 47.33N 29.50 E
Dolj [2] 15 Ge 44.10N 23.40 E
Dollart 11 Na 53.17N 7.10 E
Dolly Cays 49 Ib 23.39N 77.22W
Dolni Dăbnik 15 Hf 43.24N 24.26 E
Dolní Dvořiště 10 Kh 48.39N 14.27 E
Dolnomoravský úval 10 Nh 49.00N 17.15 E
Dolnośląskie, Bory- 10 Le 51.25N 15.20 E
Dolný Kubin 10 Pg 49.12N 19.17 E
Dolo 31 Lh 4.11N 42.05 E
Dolomites (EN) = Dolomiti 5 Hf 46.23N 11.51 E
Dolomiti = Dolomites (EN) 5 Hf 46.23N 11.51 E
Dolon, Pereval- 18 Jd 41.48N 75.45 E
Dolonnur/Duolun 27 Kc 42.10N 116.30 E
Dolores [Arg.] 56 Ie 36.20S 57.40W
Dolores [Guat.] 49 Ce 16.31N 89.25W
Dolores [Ur.] 56 Id 33.33S 58.13W
Dolores River 46 Kg 38.49N 109.17W
Dolphin, Cape- 56 Ih 51.15S 58.58W
Dolphin and Union Strait 42 Gc 69.00N 115.00W
Dom, Kūh-e- 24 Of 33.52N 53.00 E
Domačevo 10 Te 51.46N 23.37 E
Domaniç 24 Cc 39.48N 29.37 E
Domantai/Domantaj 8 Ji 55.57N 23.19 E
Domantaj/Domantai 8 Ji 55.57N 23.19 E
Domart-en-Ponthieu 12 Ed 50.04N 2.07 E
Domasa, údolná nádrž- 10 Rg 49.05N 21.47 E
Domažlice 10 Ig 49.27N 12.56 E
Dombaj-Ulgen, Gora- 16 Lh 43.14N 41.46 E
Dombarovski 19 Fe 50.47N 59.34 E
Dombås 6 Gc 62.05N 9.08 E
Dombe Grande 36 Be 12.56S 13.07 E
Dombes 11 Lh 46.00N 5.03 E
Dombóvár 10 Oj 46.23N 18.07 E
Dombrád 10 Rh 48.14N 21.56 E
Domburg 12 Fc 51.34N 3.30 E
Dôme, Monts- 11 Ii 45.45N 2.55 E
Dôme, Puy de- 11 Ii 45.47N 2.58 E
Domérat 11 Ih 46.21N 2.32 E
Domeyko, Cordillera- 52 Jh 24.30S 69.00W
Domfront 11 Ff 48.36N 0.39W
Domingo M. Irala 55 Eg 25.54S 54.43W
Domingos Martins 54 Jh 20.22S 40.40W
Dominica [1] 39 Mh 15.30N 61.20W
Dominica 38 Mh 15.30N 61.20W
Dominical 49 Fi 9.13N 83.51W
Dominicana, República-= Dominican Republic (EN) [1] 39 Lh 19.00N 70.40W
Dominican Republic (EN)= Dominicana, República- [1] 39 Lh 19.00N 70.40W
Dominica Passage 50 Fe 15.10N 61.15W
Dominica Passage (EN)= Dominique, Canal de la- 50 Fe 15.10N 61.15W
Dominion, Cape - 42 Kc 66.10N 74.30W
Dominique, Canal de la-= Dominica Passage (EN) 50 Fe 15.10N 61.15W
Domino 42 Lf 53.28N 55.46W
Domiongo 36 Dc 4.37S 21.15 E
Dommartin-Varimont 12 Gf 48.59N 4.46 E
Domme 11 Hj 44.48N 1.13 E
Dommel 11 Lc 51.40N 5.20 E
Domneşti 15 Hd 45.12N 24.50 E
Domo 35 Hd 7.57N 46.51 E
Domodedovo 7 Ii 55.27N 37.47 E
Domodossola 14 Cd 46.07N 8.17 E
Domont 12 Ee 49.02N 2.20 E
Dom Pedrito 56 Jd 30.59S 54.40W
Dom Pedro 54 Jd 5.00S 44.27W
Dompierre-sur-Besbre 11 Jh 46.31N 3.41 E
Dompu 26 Gh 8.32S 118.28 E
Domusnovas 14 Ck 39.19N 8.39 E
Domuyo, Volcán- 52 Ii 36.38S 70.26W
Don 48 Ed 26.26N 109.02W
Don [Eng.-U.K.] 9 Mh 53.39N 0.59W
Don [Fr.] 11 Eg 47.40N 1.56W
Don [R.S.F.S.R.] 5 Jf 47.04N 39.18 E
Don [Scot.-U.K.] 9 Kd 57.10N 2.04W
Donaldsonville 45 Kk 30.06N 90.59W
Donau=Danube (EN) 5 If 45.20N 29.40 E
Donaueschingen 10 Ei 47.57N 8.30 E
Donaumoos 10 Hh 48.40N 11.15 E
Donauried 10 Gh 48.35N 10.40 E
Donauwörth 10 Gh 48.42N 10.48 E
Don Benito 13 Gf 38.57N 5.52W
Doncaster 9 Lh 53.32N 1.07W
Dondjušany 15 Ka 48.11N 27.31 E
Dondo [Ang.] 31 Ii 9.40S 14.26 E
Dondo [Moz.] 37 Ec 19.36S 34.44 E
Dondra Head 21 Ki 5.55N 80.35 E
Donec 5 Kf 47.40N 40.50 E
Doneck [R.S.F.S.R.] 16 Ke 48.21N 39.59 E
Doneck [Ukr.-U.S.S.R.] 6 Jf 48.00N 37.48 E
Doneckaja Oblast [3] 19 Df 48.00N 37.45 E
Donecki Krjaž=Donec Ridge (EN) 5 Kh 48.15N 38.45 E
Donec Ridge (EN)=Donecki Krjaž 5 Kh 48.15N 38.45 E
Donegal/Dún na nGall 9 Eg 54.39N 8.06W
Donegal/Dún na nGall [2] 9 Fg 54.50N 8.00W
Donegal Bay/Bá Dhún na nGall 5 Fe 54.30N 8.30W
Donegal Mountains 9 Eg 54.50N 8.10W
Donga 34 Hd 8.19N 10.01 E
Dongara 59 Ce 29.15S 114.56 E
Dongbei Pingyuan 28 Gc 44.00N 124.00 E
Dongchuan (Tangdan) 27 Hf 26.07N 103.05 E
Dongcun → Lanxian 28 Ae 38.17N 111.38 E
Dong Dao 27 Jc 16.45N 113.00 E
Donge 12 Gc 51.41N 4.49 E
Dong'e (Tongcheng) 28 Df 36.19N 116.14 E
Dongen 12 Gc 51.37N 4.57 E
Donges 11 Dg 47.18N 2.04W
Dongfang (Basuo) 27 Ih 19.14N 108.39 E
Dongfanghong 28 La 46.15N 133.07 E
Dongfeng 28 Hc 42.41N 125.33 E
Donggala 26 Gg 0.40S 119.44 E
Donggou 27 Ld 39.55N 124.08 E
Dongguang 28 Df 37.54N 116.32 E
Dong Hai=East China Sea (EN) 21 Og 29.00N 125.00 E
Donghai Dao 27 Jg 21.00N 110.25 E
Dong He 27 Hc 42.12N 101.10 E
Dong Hoi 25 Le 17.29N 106.36 E
Dong Jang 21 Ng 23.02N 113.31 E
Dongkala 26 Hh 5.18S 122.03 E
Dongkan → Binhai 27 Ke 34.00N 119.52 E
Donglan 27 Ig 24.35N 107.22 E
Dongliao He 28 Gc 43.24N 123.42 E
Dongming 28 Cg 35.17N 115.04 E
Dongnan Qiuling 27 Jg 24.00N 113.00 E
Dongo 36 Ce 14.36S 15.43 E
Dongola (EN)=Dunqulah 31 Kg 19.10N 30.29 E
Dongou 36 Cb 2.02N 18.04 E
Dongoun → Haiyang 28 Ff 36.46N 121.09 E
Dongping 27 Kd 35.51N 116.15 E
Dongping → Anhua 27 Jf 28.27N 111.15 E
Dong Rak, Phanom-= Dangrek Range (EN) 21 Mh 14.25N 104.30 E
Dongsha Dao 27 Kg 20.45N 116.45 E
Dongsha Qundao 21 Ng 20.42N 116.43 E
Dongsheng 27 Id 39.48N 110.00 E
Dongtai 27 Le 32.47N 120.18 E
Dong Taijnar Hu 27 Fd 37.25N 94.00 E
Dongting Hu 21 Ng 29.18N 112.45 E
Dong Ujimqin Qi (Uliastai) 27 Kc 45.31N 116.58 E
Dongwe 36 De 13.56S 23.53 E
Dongxiang 28 Kf 28.15N 116.38 E
Dongyang 28 Fj 29.16N 120.14 E
Dongying 27 Kd 37.30N 118.30 E
Dongzhi (Yaodu) 28 Di 30.06N 117.01 E
Donington 12 Bb 52.54N 0.12W
Doniphan 45 Kh 36.37N 90.50W
Donja Brela 14 Kg 43.23N 16.55 E
Donji Miholjac 14 Me 45.45N 18.10 E
Donji Vakuf 14 Lf 44.08N 17.24 E
Dønna 7 Cc 66.06N 12.35 E
Donnacona 44 Lb 46.40N 71.47W
Donner Pass 43 Cd 39.19N 120.20W
Donnersberg 12 Je 49.38N 7.55 E
Donner und Blitzen River 46 Fe 43.17N 118.49W
Donnybrook 59 Df 33.35S 115.49 E
Donskaja Grjada=Don Upland (EN) 5 Kf 49.10N 42.00 E
Donskoj 16 Kb 54.01N 38.20 E
Don Upland (EN)=Donskaja Grjada 5 Kf 49.10N 42.00 E
Donuzlav, Ozero- 16 Hg 45.25N 33.10 E
Doolette Bay 66 Je 67.55S 147.00 E
Doon 9 If 55.26N 4.38W
Doonerak, Mount- 40 Ic 67.56N 150.37W
Doorn 12 Hb 52.02N 5.19 E
Doornik/Tournai 11 Jd 50.36N 3.23 E
Door Peninsula 45 Md 44.55N 87.20W
Do Qu 27 He 31.48N 102.09 E
Dora, Lake- 59 Ed 22.05S 122.56 E
Dora Baltea/Doire Baltée 14 Ce 45.11N 8.03 E
Dorada, Costa- 13 Nc 41.08N 1.10 E
Dora Riparia 14 Be 45.05N 7.44 E
Dorbiljin/Emin 27 Db 46.32N 83.39 E
Dorchester 9 Kk 50.43N 2.26W
Dorchester, Cape - 42 Jc 65.28N 77.30W
Dordabis 37 Bd 22.52S 17.38 E
Dordogne 5 Ff 45.02N 0.35W
Dordogne [3] 11 Gi 45.10N 0.50 E
Dordrecht [Neth.] 12 Gc 51.48N 4.40 E
Dordrecht [Neth.] 11 Kc 51.49N 4.40 E
Dordrecht [S.Afr.] 37 Df 31.20S 27.03 E
Dore 11 Ji 46.00N 3.28 E
Dore, Monts- 5 Gf 45.30N 2.45 E
Doré Lake 42 Gf 54.45N 107.20W
Dores do Indaia 54 Ig 19.27S 45.36W
Dorgali 14 Dj 40.17N 9.35 E
Dori 31 Gg 14.02N 0.02W
Doring 30 Il 31.52S 18.39 E
Dorking 12 Bc 51.13N 0.20W
Dormagen 12 Ic 51.06N 6.50 E
Dormans 11 Je 49.04N 3.38 E
Dormidontovka 20 Ig 47.45N 134.58 E
Dornbirn 14 Dc 47.25N 9.44 E
Dornoch 9 Id 57.52N 4.02W
Dornoch Firth 9 Id 57.52N 4.02W
Doro 34 Eb 16.09N 0.51W
Dorog 10 Oi 47.43N 18.44 E
Dorogobuž 16 Hb 54.56N 33.15 E
Dorohoi 15 Jb 47.57N 26.24 E
Dorotea 7 Dd 64.16N 16.24 E
Dorre Island 59 Ce 25.10S 113.05 E
Dorrigo 59 Kf 30.20S 152.45 E
Dorset [3] 9 Kk 50.50N 2.10W
Dorset 9 Kk 50.55N 2.15W
Dorsten 10 Ce 51.40N 6.58 E
Dortmund 6 Ge 51.31N 7.27 E
Dortmund-Ems-Kanal 10 Dd 51.32N 7.27 E
Do Rūd 23 Gc 33.28N 49.04 E
Doruma 36 Eb 4.44N 27.42 E
Dörverden 12 Lb 52.51N 9.14 E
Doseo, Bar- 35 Bd 9.01N 19.38 E
Dos Hermanas 13 Gg 37.17N 5.55W
Dos Lagunas 49 Ce 17.42N 89.36W
Dospat 15 Hh 41.39N 24.10 E
Dospat 15 Hh 41.23N 24.05 E
Dosse 10 Ic 53.13N 12.20 E
Dosso 31 Hg 13.03N 3.12 E
Dosso [2] 34 Fc 13.30N 3.30 E
Dossor 19 Ff 47.32N 53.01 E
Dostluk 18 Ef 37.45N 65.22 E
Dothan 43 Je 31.13N 85.24W
Dotnuva 8 Ji 55.18N 23.55 E
Dötyol 24 Gd 36.52N 36.12 E
Douai 11 Jd 50.22N 3.04 E
Douala 31 Hh 4.03N 9.42 E
Douaouir 34 Ea 20.45N 2.30W
Douarnenez 11 Bf 48.06N 4.20W
Douarnenez, Baie de- 11 Bf 48.10N 4.25W
Double Mountain Fork Brazos 45 Gj 33.15N 100.00W
Doubrava 10 Lf 50.03N 15.20 E
Doubs 11 Lh 46.54N 5.02 E
Doubs [3] 11 Mg 47.10N 6.25 E
Doubtful Sound 62 Bf 45.15S 166.50 E
Doubtless Bay 62 Ea 34.55S 173.25 E
Douchy-les-Mines 12 Fd 50.18N 3.23 E
Doudeville 12 Ce 49.43N 0.48 E
Doué-la-Fontaine 11 Fg 47.12N 0.17W
Douentza 34 Eb 15.03N 2.57W
Douera 13 Oh 36.40N 2.57 E
Dougga 32 Ib 36.24N 9.13 E
Douglas [Ak.-U.S.] 40 Me 58.16N 134.26W
Douglas [Az.-U.S.] 43 Fe 31.21N 109.33W
Douglas [Ga.-U.S.] 44 Fj 31.31N 82.51W
Douglas [S.Afr.] 37 Ce 29.04S 23.46 E
Douglas [U.K.] 9 Ig 54.09N 4.28W
Douglas [Wy.-U.S.] 43 Fc 42.45N 105.24W
Douglas Lake 44 Fh 36.00N 83.22W
Douglas Range 66 Qf 70.00S 69.35W
Doullens 11 Id 50.09N 2.21 E
Doumé 34 He 4.14N 13.27 E
Douna 34 Ec 14.39N 1.43W
Doupovské hory 10 Jf 50.13N 13.08 E
Dour 12 Fd 50.24N 3.47 E
Dourada, Serra- [Braz.] 55 Gb 16.00S 50.05W
Dourada, Serra- [Braz.] 55 Ha 13.10S 48.45W
Dourados 53 Kh 22.13S 54.48W
Dourados, Rio- [Braz.] 55 Ee 21.58S 54.18W
Dourados, Rio- [Braz.] 55 Id 18.17S 47.36W
Dourbali 35 Bc 11.49N 15.52 E
Dourdan 11 If 48.32N 2.01 E
Douro 5 Fg 41.08N 8.40W
Douro Litoral 13 Dc 41.05N 8.20W
Doushi → Gong'an 27 Je 30.05N 112.12 E
Douve 11 Ee 49.19N 1.44W
Douvres-la-Delivrande 12 Be 49.17N 0.23W
Douze 11 Fk 43.54N 0.30W
Douzy 12 He 49.40N 5.03 E
Dove 9 Li 52.50N 1.35W
Dove Bugt 41 Jd 76.25N 21.00W
Dove Creek 45 Bh 37.46N 108.54W
Dover [De.-U.S.] 39 Lf 39.10N 75.32W
Dover [Eng.-U.K.] 6 Ge 51.08N 1.19 E
Dover [N.H.-U.S.] 44 Ld 43.12N 70.55W
Dover [Oh.-U.S.] 44 Ge 40.32N 81.30W
Dover, Strait of- 5 Ge 51.00N 1.30 E
Dover, Strait of- (EN)= Calais, Pas de- 5 Ge 51.00N 1.30 E
Dover Foxcroft 44 Mc 45.11N 69.13W
Dovey 9 Ji 52.34N 3.59W
Dovre 8 Cc 61.59N 9.15 E
Dovrefjell 5 Gc 62.10N 9.25 E
Dowa 36 Fe 13.39S 33.56 E
Dowagiac 44 De 41.59N 86.06W
Dowlatābād 24 Qh 28.20N 57.13 E
Downey 46 Ie 42.26N 112.07W
Downham Market 12 Cb 52.36N 0.22 E
Downieville 46 Eg 39.34N 120.50W
Downpatrick / Dún Pádraig 9 Hg 54.20N 5.43W
Dow Sar 24 Me 35.06N 48.02 E
Dōzen 29 Cc 36.05N 132.59 E
Dozois, Reservoir- 44 Ib 47.30N 77.00W
Dozulé 12 Be 49.14N 0.03W
Drâa 30 Ff 28.40N 11.07W
Drâa, Cap- 32 Ed 28.44N 11.05W
Drâa, Hamada du- 30 Gf 28.30N 7.30W
Draa el Baguel 32 Ic 30.17N 6.25 E
Draa el Mizan 13 Ph 36.32N 3.50 E
Drac 11 Li 45.13N 5.41 E
Dracena 55 Ge 21.32S 51.29W
Drach, Cuevas del- 13 Pe 39.32N 3.15 E
Dragalina 15 Kc 44.26N 27.19 E
Dragan 7 Dd 64.00N 15.21 E
Drăgăneşti-Olt 15 He 44.09N 24.42 E
Drăgăneşti-Vlaşca 15 Ie 44.06N 25.36 E
Drăgăşani 15 He 44.39N 24.16 E
Dragobia 15 Cg 42.26N 19.59 E
Dragón, Bocas del-/ Dragon's Mouths 54 Fa 10.45N 61.46W
Dragonera, Isla-/Dragonera, Sa- 13 Oe 39.35N 2.19 E
Dragonera, Sa-/Dragonera, Isla- 13 Oe 39.35N 2.19 E

Index Symbols

[1] Independent Nation
[2] State, Region
[3] District, County
[4] Municipality
[5] Colony, Dependency
Continent
Physical Region
Historical or Cultural Region
Mount, Mountain
Volcano
Hill
Mountains, Mountain Range
Hills, Escarpment
Plateau, Upland
Pass, Gap
Plain, Lowland
Delta
Salt Flat
Valley, Canyon
Crater, Cave
Karst Features
Depression
Polder
Desert, Dunes
Forest, Woods
Heath, Steppe
Oasis
Cape, Point
Coast, Beach
Cliff
Peninsula
Isthmus
Sandbank
Island
Atoll
Rock, Reef
Islands, Archipelago
Rocks, Reefs
Coral Reef
Well, Spring
Geyser
River, Stream
Waterfall Rapids
River Mouth, Estuary
Lake
Salt Lake
Intermittent Lake
Reservoir
Swamp, Pond
Canal
Glacier
Ice Shelf, Pack Ice
Ocean
Sea
Gulf, Bay
Strait, Fjord
Lagoon
Bank
Seamount
Tablemount
Ridge
Shelf
Basin
Escarpment, Sea Scarp
Fracture
Trench, Abyss
National Park, Reserve
Point of Interest
Recreation Site
Cave, Cavern
Historic Site
Ruins
Wall, Walls
Church, Abbey
Temple
Scientific Station
Airport
Port
Lighthouse
Mine
Tunnel
Dam, Bridge

Dragon's Mouths/Dragón, Bocas del- 54 Fa 10.45N 61.46W
Dragør 8 Ei 55.36N 12.41 E
Draguignan 11 Mk 43.32N 6.28 E
Drahanska vrchovina 10 Mg 49.30N 16.45 E
Drain 46 De 43.40N 123.19W
Drake 45 Fc 47.55N 100.23W
Drake, Estrecho de- = Drake Passage (EN) 52 Jk 58.00S 70.00W
Drakensberg 30 Jk 29.00S 29.00 E
Drake Passage (EN) = Drake, Estrecho de- 52 Jk 58.00S 70.00W
Dráma 15 Hh 41.09N 24.09 E
Drammen 6 Hd 59.44N 10.15 E
Dramselva 8 De 59.44N 10.14 E
Drangajokull 7a Aa 66.09N 22.15W
Dranse 11 Mh 46.24N 6.30 E
Drau = Drava (EN) 5 Hf 45.33N 18.55 E
Dráva = Drava (EN) 5 Hf 45.33N 18.55 E
Drava (EN) = Drau 5 Hf 45.33N 18.55 E
Drava (EN) = Dráva 5 Hf 45.33N 18.55 E
Dravograd 14 Jd 46.35N 15.01 E
Drawa 10 Ld 52.52N 15.59 E
Drawno 10 Lc 53.13N 15.45 E
Drawsko, Jezioro- 10 Mc 53.33N 16.10 E
Drawsko Pomorskie 10 Lc 53.32N 15.48 E
Drayton Valley 42 Gf 53.13N 115.00W
Drean 14 Bn 36.41N 7.45 E
Dreieich 12 Ke 50.01N 8.43 E
Drenovci 14 Mf 44.55N 18.55 E
Drenthe [3] 12 Ib 52.45N 6.30 E
Dresden 6 He 51.03N 13.45 E
Dreux 11 Hf 48.44N 1.22 E
Drevsjø 7 Cf 61.54N 12.02 E
Drezdenko 10 Ld 52.51N 15.50 E
Dricēni/Driceni 8 Lh 56.39N 27.11 E
Driceni/Dricēni 8 Lh 56.39N 27.11 E
Driffield 9 Mg 54.01N 0.26W
Driggs 46 Je 43.44N 111.14W
Drina 5 Hg 44.53N 19.21 E
Drincea 15 Fe 44.07N 22.59 E
Drin Gulf (EN) = Drinit, Gjiri i- 15 Ch 41.45N 19.28 E
Drini 5 Hg 41.45N 19.34 E
Drini i Zi 15 Dg 42.05N 20.23 E
Drinit, Gjiri i- = Drin Gulf (EN) 15 Ch 41.45N 19.28 E
Drinjača 14 Nf 44.17N 19.10 E
Drinosi 15 Di 40.17N 20.02 E
Drissa 7 Gi 55.47N 27.57 E
Drisvjaty, Ozero-/Drūkšiu Ežeras 8 Lj 55.37N 26.45 E
Driva 8 Cb 62.40N 8.34 E
Drjanovo 15 Ig 42.58N 25.28 E
Drniš 14 Kg 43.52N 16.09 E
Drøbak 7 Cg 59.39N 10.39 E
Drocea, Vîrful- 15 Fc 46.12N 22.14 E
Drogheda/Droichead Átha 9 Gh 53.43N 6.21W
Drogičin 16 Dc 52.13N 25.10 E
Drogobyč 16 Ce 49.22N 23.33 E
Drohiczyn 10 Sd 52.24N 22.41 E
Droichead Átha/Drogheda 9 Gh 53.43N 6.21W
Droichead na Bandan/Bandon 9 Ej 51.45N 8.45W
Droichead na Banna/Banbridge 9 Gg 54.21N 6.16W
Drokija 16 Ee 48.01N 27.53 E
Drôme 12 Be 49.19N 0.45W
Drôme [3] 11 Lj 44.35N 5.10 E
Drömling 10 Hd 52.29N 11.04 E
Dronero 14 Bf 44.28N 7.22 E
Dronne 11 Fi 45.02N 0.09W
Dronning Fabiola-Fjella 66 Df 71.30S 35.40 E
Dronning Louise Land 41 Jc 76.45N 24.00W
Dronten 11 Lb 52.31N 5.42 E
Dropt 11 Fj 44.35N 0.06W
Drovjanoj 20 Cb 72.25N 72.45 E
Drowning River 45 Na 50.55N 84.35W
Druja 7 Gi 55.47N 27.29 E
Drūkšiu Ežeras/Drisvjaty, Ozero- 8 Lj 55.37N 26.45 E
Druk-Yul → Bhutan [1] 22 Lg 27.30N 90.30 E
Drulingen 12 Jf 48.52N 7.11 E
Drumheller 42 Gf 51.28N 112.42W
Drummond [Mt.-U.S.] 46 Ic 46.40N 113.09W
Drummond [Wi.-U.S.] 45 Kc 46.20N 91.15W
Drummond Island 44 Fb 46.00N 83.40W
Drummond Range 59 Jd 23.30S 147.15 E
Drummondville 42 Kg 45.50N 72.20W
Drummore 9 Ig 54.42N 4.54W
Drumochter, Pass of- 9 Ie 56.50N 4.12W
Drunen 12 Hc 51.41N 5.10 E
Druskininkai/Druskininkaj 7 Fi 54.04N 24.06 E
Druskininkaj/Druskininkai 7 Fi 54.04N 24.06 E
Drut 16 Gc 53.04N 30.35 E
Druten 12 Hc 51.54N 5.38 E
Družba 16 Hc 52.02N 33.59 E
Druzba 19 If 45.18N 82.29 E
Družkovka 16 Je 48.36N 37.33 E
Družnaja Gorka 8 Ne 59.11N 30.10 E
Družnino 17 Ih 56.48N 59.29 E
Družno, Jezioro- 10 Pb 54.08N 19.30 E
Drvar 14 Kf 44.22N 16.23 E
Drvenik 14 Lg 43.09N 17.15 E
Drwęca 10 Oc 53.00N 18.42 E
Dryden 42 Ig 49.47N 92.50W
Dry Fork 46 Me 43.30N 105.24W
Drygalski Ice Tongue 66 Kf 75.24S 163.30 E
Drygalski Island 66 Ge 65.45S 92.30 E
Drysdale River 59 Fb 13.59S 126.51 E
Dry Tortugas 43 Kg 24.38N 82.55W
Drzewica 10 Qe 51.27N 20.28 E
Drzewiczka 10 Qe 51.33N 20.35 E
Dschang 34 Hd 5.27N 10.04 E
Dua 36 Db 3.20N 20.53 E
Duaca 54 Ea 10.18N 69.10W
Duancun → Wuxiang 28 Bf 36.50N 112.51 E
Duarte, Pico- 38 Lh 19.00N 71.00W
Duartina 55 Hf 22.24S 49.25W
Dubawnt 42 Hd 64.30N 100.06W
Dubawnt Lake 38 Ic 63.08N 101.30W
Ḑubay'ah, Ra's- 24 Pj 24.20N 54.09 E
Dubayy 22 Hg 25.18N 55.18 E
Dubbo 58 Fh 32.15S 148.36 E
Dübener Heide 10 Ie 51.40N 12.40 E
Dubenski 16 Td 51.29N 56.38 E
Dubh Artach 9 Ge 56.08N 6.39W
Dubica 14 Ke 45.13N 16.48 E
Dublin 43 Ke 32.32N 82.54W
Dublin/Baile Átha Cliath [2] 9 Gh 53.20N 6.15W
Dublin/Baile Átha Cliath 6 Fe 53.20N 6.15W
Dublin Bay/Cuan Bhaile Átha Cliath 9 Gh 53.20N 6.06W
Dubljany 10 Tg 49.26N 23.16 E
Dublon 64d Bb 7.23N 151.53 E
Dubna 8 Lh 56.20N 26.31 E
Dubna 19 Dd 56.47N 37.10 E
Dubnica nad Váhom 10 Oh 48.58N 18.10 E
Dubno 19 Ce 50.29N 25.46 E
Du Bois 44 He 41.06N 78.46W
Dubois [Id.-U.S.] 46 Id 44.10N 112.14W
Dubois [Wy.-U.S.] 46 Ke 43.33N 109.38W
Dubossary 16 Ff 47.17N 29.10 E
Dubovka 19 Ef 49.03N 44.50 E
Dubovoje 10 Ih 48.08N 23.59 E
Dubreka 34 Cd 9.48N 13.31W
Dubrovica 16 Ed 51.34N 26.34 E
Dubrovnik 6 Hg 42.39N 18.07 E
Dubrovno 7 Hi 54.33N 30.41 E
Dubrovnoje 19 Gd 57.58N 69.25 E
Dubuque 43 Ic 42.30N 90.41W
Dubysa 8 Ji 55.02N 23.27 E
Duc de Gloucester, Iles du- = Duke of Gloucester, Islands (En) 57 Mg 20.38S 143.20W
Duchang 28 Dj 29.16N 116.11 E
Duchesne 46 Jf 40.10N 110.24W
Duchess 59 Hd 21.22S 139.52 E
Ducie Atoll 57 Og 24.40S 124.47W
Duck River 44 Dg 36.02N 87.52W
Duckwater Peak 46 Hg 38.58N 115.26W
Duclair 12 Ce 49.29N 0.53 E
Duc Lap 25 Lf 12.27N 107.38 E
Ducos 51h Bb 14.34N 60.58W
Dudelange/Düdelingen 12 Ie 49.28N 6.06 E
Duderstadt 10 Ge 51.31N 10.16 E
Dudinka 22 Kc 69.25N 86.15 E
Dudley 9 Ki 52.30N 2.05W
Ḑūdo 35 Id 9.20N 50.14 E
Dudub 35 Hd 6.55N 46.42 E
Dudune 63b Ce 21.21S 167.44 E
Dudváh 10 Ni 47.58N 17.50 E
Dudweiler, Saarbrücken- 12 Je 49.17N 7.02 E
Düdwëyn 35 Gd 9.19N 44.53 E
Dudypta 20 Db 70.55N 89.50 E
Duékoué 34 Dd 6.45N 7.21W
Dueodde 8 Fj 54.59N 15.05 E
Duerna 13 Gb 42.19N 5.54W
Duero 5 Fg 41.08N 8.40W
Dufek Coast 66 Lg 84.30S 179.00W
Duffer Peak 46 Ff 41.40N 118.44W
Duff Islands 57 He 9.50S 167.10 E
Dugi Otok 14 Ii 44.00N 15.00 E
Dugo Selo 14 Ke 45.48N 16.15 E
Du Gué, Rivière- 42 Ke 57.20N 70.46W
Duhovnickoje 16 Pc 52.29N 48.15 E
Duijan Yan 27 He 31.01N 103.28 E
Duiru → Wuchuan 27 If 28.28N 107.57 E
Duisburg 10 Ce 51.26N 6.45 E
Duitama 54 Db 5.50N 73.02W
Dujūma 35 Ge 1.14N 42.34 E
Dukagjini 15 Cg 42.18N 19.45 E
Dūkān 24 Ke 35.56N 44.58 E
Dukan, Sad ad- 24 Kd 36.10N 44.56 E
Dukat 15 Fg 42.26N 22.21 E
Duke of Gloucester Islands (EN) = Duc de Gloucester, Iles du- 57 Mg 20.38S 143.20W
Duke of York 63a Aa 4.10S 152.28 E
Duke of York Bay 42 Jc 65.25N 84.50W
Duk Fadiat 35 Ed 7.45N 31.25 E
Duk Faiwil 35 Ed 7.30N 31.29 E
Dukhān 23 Hd 25.25N 50.48 E
Dukielska, Przełecz- 10 Rg 49.25N 21.42 E
Dukku 34 Hc 10.49N 10.46 E
Dukla 10 Rg 49.34N 21.41 E
Dukou 22 Mg 26.31N 101.44 E
Dūkštas/Dukštas 8 Li 55.32N 26.28 E
Dukštas/Dūkštas 8 Li 55.32N 26.28 E
Dulan (Qagan Us) 22 Lf 36.29N 98.29 E
Dulce, Bahía- 48 Ji 16.30N 98.50W
Dulce, Golfo- 47 Hg 8.36N 83.15W
Dulce, Río- 52 Ji 30.31S 62.32W
Dulce Nombre de Culmí 49 Ef 15.09N 85.37W
Duldurga 20 Gf 50.38N 113.35 E
Dulgalah 21 Pc 67.30N 133.20 E
Dulia 36 Db 2.57N 24.08 E
Dülmen 10 De 51.50N 7.18 E
Dulovka 8 Mg 57.27N 28.29 E
Dulovo 15 Kf 43.49N 27.09 E
Duluth 39 Je 46.47N 92.06W
Dūmā 24 Gf 33.35N 36.24 E
Dumaguete 26 He 9.18N 123.18 E
Dumai 26 Df 1.41N 101.27 E
Dumaran 26 Gd 10.33N 119.51 E
Dumaresq River 59 Ke 28.40S 150.28 E
Dumas [Ar.-U.S.] 45 Kj 33.53N 91.29W
Dumas [Tx.-U.S.] 45 Fi 35.52N 101.58W
Dumayr 24 Gf 33.38N 36.40 E
Dumbarton 9 If 55.57N 4.35W
Dumbéa 63b Cf 22.09S 166.27 E
Dumbrăveni [Rom.] 15 Jb 47.39N 26.25 E
Dumbrăveni [Rom.] 15 Hc 46.14N 24.34 E
Dumfries 9 Jf 55.04N 3.37W
Dumfries and Galloway [3] 9 Jf 55.10N 3.35W
Dumka 25 Hd 24.16N 87.15 E
Dumlupinar 15 Mk 38.52N 30.00 E
Dümmer 10 Ed 52.31N 8.19 E
Dumoine, Lac- 44 Ib 46.52N 77.52W
Dumoine, Rivière- 44 Ib 46.13N 77.50W
Dumont d'Urville 66 Je 66.40S 140.01 E
Dumont D'Urville Sea (EN) 66 Je 63.00S 140.00 E
Dumpu 58 Fe 5.52S 145.46 E
Dümrek 15 Lk 38.40N 28.24 E
Dumuhe 28 La 46.21N 133.33 E
Dumyāţ = Damietta (EN) 31 Ke 31.25N 31.48 E
Dumyāţ, Maşabb- 24 Dg 31.27N 31.51 E
Duna = Danube (EN) 5 If 45.20N 29.40 E
Dunaföldvár 10 Oi 46.48N 18.56 E
Dunaharaszti 10 Pi 47.21N 19.05 E
Dunaj 20 Ih 42.57N 132.20 E
Dunaj = Danube (EN) 5 If 45.20N 29.40 E
Dunajec 10 Qf 50.15N 20.44 E
Dunajevcy 16 Ee 48.51N 26.44 E
Dunajská Streda 10 Ni 47.01N 17.38 E
Dunakeszi 10 Pi 47.38N 19.08 E
Dunántúl 10 Nj 47.00N 18.00 E
Dunărea = Danube (EN) 5 If 45.20N 29.40 E
Dunărea Veche 15 Ld 45.17N 28.02 E
Dunării, Delta- = Danube, Mouths of the- (EN) 5 If 45.30N 29.45 E
Duna-Tisza Köze 10 Pj 46.45N 19.30 E
Dunaújváros 10 Oj 46.58N 18.56 E
Dunav = Danube (EN) 5 If 45.20N 29.40 E
Dunavățu de Jos 15 Me 44.59N 29.13 E
Dunav-Tisa-Dunav kanal 15 Dd 45.10N 20.50 E
Dunback 62 Df 45.23S 170.38 E
Dunbar 9 Kf 56.00N 2.31W
Duncan [Az.-U.S.] 46 Kj 32.43N 109.06W
Duncan [B.C.-Can.] 46 Db 48.47N 123.42W
Duncan [Ok.-U.S.] 43 He 34.30N 97.57W
Duncan Passage 25 If 11.00N 92.00 E
Duncansby Head 5 Fd 58.39N 3.01W
Dundaga 8 Jg 57.31N 22.14 E
Dundalk 44 If 39.15N 76.31W
Dundalk/Dún Dealgan 9 Gg 54.01N 6.25W
Dundalk Bay/Cuan Dhun Dealgan 9 Gh 53.57N 6.17W
Dundas [Grld.] 41 Fc 76.30N 69.00W
Dundas [Ont.-Can.] 44 Hd 43.16N 79.58W
Dundas, Lake- 59 Ef 32.35S 121.50 E
Dundas Peninsula 42 Gb 74.40N 113.00W
Dundas Strait 59 Gb 11.20S 131.35 E
Dún Dealgan/Dundalk 9 Gg 54.01N 6.25W
Dundee [S.Afr.] 37 Ee 28.12S 30.16 E
Dundee [Scot.-U.K.] 6 Fd 56.28N 3.00W
Dund Hot → Zhenglan Qi 28 Cc 42.14N 115.59 E
Dundrum Bay/Cuan Dhún Droma 9 Hg 54.13N 5.45W
Dunedin [Fl.-U.S.] 44 Fk 28.02N 82.47W
Dunedin [N.Z.] 58 Ii 45.53S 170.31 E
Dunfanaghy 9 Ff 55.11N 7.59W
Dunfermline 9 Je 56.04N 3.29W
Dungannon/Dún Geanainn 9 Gg 54.31N 6.46W
Dún Garbhán/Dungarvan 9 Fi 52.05N 7.37W
Düngarpur 25 Ed 23.50N 73.43 E
Dungarvan/Dún Garbhán 9 Fi 52.05N 7.37W
Dungas 34 Gc 13.04N 9.20 E
Dungau 10 Ih 48.45N 12.30 E
Dún Geanainn/Dungannon 9 Gg 54.31N 6.46W
Dungeness 9 Nk 50.55N 0.58 E
Dungu 36 Eb 3.42N 28.40 E
Dungu 36 Eb 3.37N 28.34 E
Dunhua 27 Mc 43.22N 128.12 E
Dunhuang 27 Fc 40.10N 94.50 E
Dunkerque 11 Ic 51.03N 2.22 E
Dunkery Beacon 9 Jj 51.11N 3.35W
Dunkirk 43 Lc 42.29N 79.21W
Dunkwa 34 Ed 5.58N 1.47W
Dún Laoghaire 9 Gh 53.17N 6.08W
Dún Mánmhai/Dunmanway 9 Dj 51.43N 9.07W
Dunmanway/Dún Mánmhai 9 Dj 51.43N 9.07W
Dunn 44 Hh 35.19N 78.37W
Dún na nGall/Donegal [2] 9 Fg 54.50N 8.00W
Dún na nGall/Donegal 9 Eg 54.39N 8.06W
Dunnellon 44 Fk 29.03N 82.28W
Dunnet Head 9 Jc 58.39N 3.23W
Dunning 45 Ff 41.50N 100.06W
Dún Pádraig/Downpatrick 9 Hg 54.20N 5.43W
Dunqulah = Dongola (EN) 31 Kg 19.10N 30.29 E
Dunqulah al Qadīmah 35 Eb 18.13N 30.45 E
Dunqunāb 35 Fa 21.06N 37.05 E
Dunqunāb, Khalīj- 35 Fa 21.05N 37.08 E
Dunrankin 44 Fa 48.39N 83.04W
Duns 9 Kf 55.47N 2.20W
Dünsberg 12 Kd 50.39N 8.35 E
Dunsmuir 46 Df 41.13N 122.16W
Dunstable 12 Bc 51.53N 0.31W
Dunstan Mountains 62 Cf 44.55S 169.30 E
Dun-sur-Auron 11 Ih 46.53N 2.34 E
Dun-sur-Meuse 12 He 49.23N 5.11 E
Duntroon 62 Df 44.51S 170.41 E
Dunvegan 9 Gd 57.26N 6.35W
Duobukur 27 La 50.19N 124.57 E
Duolun/Dolonnur 27 Kc 42.10N 116.30 E
Duong Dong 25 Kf 10.13N 103.58 E
Dupree 45 Fd 45.03N 101.36W
Duqm 22 Hf 19.41N 57.32 E
Duque de Bragança, Quedas- 30 Ii 9.05S 16.10 E
Duque de Caxias 54 Jh 22.47S 43.18W
Duque de York, Isla- 56 Eh 50.40S 75.20W
Du Quoin 45 Lg 38.01N 89.14W
Durack Range 59 Fc 17.00S 128.00 E
Durack River 59 Fc 15.33S 127.52 E
Duragan 24 Fb 41.25N 35.04 E
Durance 5 Gg 43.55N 4.44 E
Durand 45 Kd 44.38N 91.58W
Durand, Récif- 63b Df 22.02S 168.39 E
Durango [2] 47 Dd 24.50N 104.50W
Durango [Co.-U.S.] 39 If 37.16N 107.53W
Durango [Sp.] 13 Ja 43.10N 2.37W
Durañona 55 Bm 37.15S 60.31W
Durant 43 He 33.59N 96.23W
Duras 11 Gj 44.40N 0.11 E
Duratón 13 Hc 41.37N 4.07W
Durazno 56 Id 33.22S 56.31W
Durazno [2] 55 Dk 33.05S 56.05W
Durazno, Cuchilla Grande del- 55 Dk 33.15S 56.15W
Durazzo (EN) = Durresi 15 Ch 41.19N 19.26 E
Durban 31 Kk 29.55S 30.56 E
Durbe 8 Ih 56.39N 21.14 E
Durbet-Daba, Pereval- 27 Eb 49.37N 89.25 E
Đurbo 35 Ic 11.30N 50.18 E
Durbuy 12 Hd 50.21N 5.28 E
Đurđevac 14 Ld 46.02N 17.04 E
Düren 10 Cf 50.48N 6.29 E
Durg 25 Gd 21.11N 81.17 E
Durgapur 25 Hd 23.30N 87.15 E
Durgen-Nur 27 Fb 47.40N 93.30 E
Durham 9 Lg 54.45N 1.45W
Durham [3] 9 Lg 54.45N 1.40W
Durham [Eng.-U.K.] 9 Lg 54.47N 1.34W
Durham [N.C.-U.S.] 43 Ld 35.59N 78.54W
Durkee 46 Gd 44.36N 117.28W
Durlas/Thurles 9 Fi 52.41N 7.49W
Durmā 23 Ge 24.37N 46.08 E
Durmersheim 12 Kf 48.56N 8.16 E
Durmitor 5 Hg 43.09N 19.02 E
Durnford, Punta- 32 De 23.37N 16.00W
Durresi = Durazzo (EN) 15 Ch 41.19N 19.26 E
Durrësit, Gjiri- 15 Ch 41.16N 19.28 E
Dursey/Oiléan Baoi 9 Cj 51.36N 10.12W
Dursunbey 24 Cc 39.35N 28.38 E
Durtal 11 Fg 47.40N 0.15W
Duru → Wuchuan 27 If 28.28N 107.57 E
Duruksi 35 Hd 8.29N 45.38 E
Durusu Gölü 15 Lh 41.20N 28.38 E
Durūz, Jabal ad- 24 Gf 32.40N 36.44 E
D'Urville Island 61 Dh 40.50S 173.50 E
Dušak 18 Cf 37.15N 60.01 E
Dusa Mareb 35 Hd 5.31N 46.24 E
Dušanbe 22 If 38.35N 68.48 E
Dušeti 16 Nh 42.05N 44.42 E
Dusetos 8 Li 55.42N 26.02 E
Dushan 22 Mg 25.55N 107.36 E
Dushan Hu 28 Dg 35.06N 116.48 E
Dusios Ežeras/Dusja, Ozero- 8 Jj 54.15N 23.45 E
Dusja, Ozero-/Dusios Ežeras 8 Jj 54.15N 23.45 E
Dusky Sound 62 Bf 45.45S 166.30 E
Düsseldorf 6 Ge 51.13N 6.46 E
Dusti 18 Gf 37.22N 68.43 E
Dutch Harbor 40a Eb 53.53N 166.32W
Dutlwe 37 Cd 23.58S 23.54 E
Dutton, Mount- 46 Ig 38.01N 112.13W
Duved 8 Ea 63.24N 12.52 E
Duvergé 49 Ld 18.22N 71.31W
Düvertepe 15 Lj 39.14N 28.27 E
Duvno 14 Lg 43.43N 17.14 E
Duwayhin 23 He 24.16N 51.20 E
Duwayhin, Khawr- 24 Nj 24.20N 51.25 E
Duyfken Point 59 Ib 12.35S 141.40 E
Duyun 27 If 26.20N 107.28 E
Düz 32 Ic 33.28N 9.01 E
Düzce 23 Da 40.50N 31.10 E
Dve Mogili 15 If 43.36N 25.52 E
Dvina (EN) = Daugava 19 Cd 57.04N 24.03 E
Dvina Gulf (EN) = Dvinskaja Guba 5 Jb 65.00N 39.45 E
Dvinskaja Guba = Dvina Gulf (EN) 5 Jb 65.00N 39.45 E
Dvor 14 Ke 45.04N 16.23 E
Dvuh Cirkov, Gora- 20 Lc 67.30N 168.20 E
Dvůr Králové nad Labem 10 Lf 50.26N 15.48 E
Dwārka 25 Dd 22.14N 68.58 E
Dworshak Reservoir 46 Hc 46.45N 116.00W
Dyer, Cape- 38 Mc 66.37N 61.18W
Dyero 34 Dc 12.50N 6.30W
Dyer Plateau 66 Qf 70.45S 65.30W
Dyersburg 43 Jd 36.03N 89.23W
Dyfed [3] 9 Ji 52.05N 4.00W
Dyhtau, Gora- 16 Mh 43.05N 43.12 E
Dyje 10 Mh 48.37N 16.56 E
Dyjsko-Svratecký úval 10 Mh 48.56N 16.25 E
Dyle 12 Gd 50.57N 4.40 E
Dylewska Góra 10 Pc 53.34N 19.57 E
Dynów 10 Sg 49.49N 22.14 E
Dyr, Djebel- 14 Cn 36.13N 8.46 E
Dyrhólaey 5 Ec 63.24N 19.08W
Dysnų Ežeras/Disnaj, Ozero- 7 Gi 55.35N 26.32 E
Dytike Rodhópi 15 Hh 41.45N 24.05 E
Dzabhan 21 Le 48.54N 93.23 E
Dzagdy, Hrebet- 20 If 53.40N 131.00 E
Džalagaš 19 Gf 45.05N 64.40 E
Džalal-Abad 18 Id 40.56N 73.05 E
Džalilabad 16 Oj 39.12N 48.31 E
Džalinda 20 Hf 53.31N 123.59 E
Džambejty 16 Rd 50.14N 52.38 E
Džambul [Kaz.-U.S.S.R.] 22 Je 42.54N 71.22 E
Džambul [Kaz.-U.S.S.R.] 19 Hf 47.17N 71.42 E
Džambulskaja Oblast [3] 19 Hg 44.30N 72.30 E
Dzamyn-Ud 27 Jb 43.50N 111.45 E
Džanak 16 Si 40.30N 55.35 E
Džanga 19 Fg 40.01N 53.10 E
Džankoj 19 Df 45.42N 34.22 E
Džansugurov 19 Hf 45.23N 79.29 E
Džanybek 19 Ef 49.24N 46.50 E
Dzaoudzi 31 Lj 12.47S 45.17 E
Džardžan 20 Hc 68.55N 124.05 E
Dzargalant 27 Gb 47.20N 99.35 E
Dzargalant 27 Ib 48.35N 105.50 E
Džarkurgan 19 Gh 37.29N 67.25 E
Džava 16 Mh 42.24N 43.53 E
Džebariki-Haja 20 Id 62.23N 135.50 E
Džebel [Bul.] 15 Ih 41.30N 25.18 E
Džebel [Tur.-U.S.S.R.] 16 Sj 39.37N 54.18 E
Džebrail 16 Oj 39.23N 47.01 E
Dzereg 27 Fb 47.08N 92.50 E
Džergalan 18 Lc 42.33N 79.02 E
Dzermuk 16 Nj 39.48N 45.39 E
Dzeržinsk [Bye.-U.S.S.R.] 16 Ec 53.44N 27.08 E
Dzeržinsk [R.S.F.S.R.] 19 Ed 56.16N 43.32 E
Dzeržinsk [Ukr.-U.S.S.R.] 16 Je 48.22N 37.50 E
Dzeržinskaja, Gora- 8 Lk 53.53N 27.10 E
Dzeržinskoje 20 Ee 56.49N 95.18 E
Džetygara 22 Id 52.11N 61.12 E
Džetysaj 18 Gd 40.49N 68.20 E
Džezkazgan [Kaz.-U.S.S.R.] 19 Gf 47.53N 67.27 E
Džezkazgan [Kaz.-U.S.S.R.] 22 Ie 47.47N 67.46 E
Džezkazganskaja Oblast [3] 19 Gf 47.30N 70.00 E
Dzhugdzhur Range (EN) = Džugdžur, Hrebet- 21 Pd 58.00N 136.00 E
Działdówka 10 Qd 52.58N 20.05 E
Działdowo 10 Qc 53.15N 20.10 E
Działoszyce 10 Qf 50.22N 20.21 E
Dzibalchén 48 Oh 19.31N 89.45W
Dzibilchaltún 48 Og 21.05N 89.36W
Dzierzgoń 10 Pc 53.56N 19.21 E
Dzierżoniów 10 Mf 50.44N 16.39 E
Džirgatal 18 He 39.13N 71.12 E
Džizak 19 Gg 40.07N 67.52 E
Džizakskaja Oblast [3] 19 Gg 40.20N 67.40 E
Džugdžur, Hrebet- = Dzhugdzhur Range (EN) 21 Pd 58.00N 136.00 E
Džūkste/Džukste 8 Jh 56.45N 23.10 E
Džukste/Džūkste 8 Jh 56.45N 23.10 E
Džulfa 16 Nj 38.59N 45.35 E
Džuma 18 Fe 39.44N 66.39 E
Dzun-Bajan 27 Jc 44.26N 110.03 E
Dzungarian Basin (EN) = Junggar Pendi 21 Ke 45.00N 88.00 E
Dzungarian Gate (EN) = Alataw Shankou 21 Ke 45.25N 82.25 E
Dzungarian Gate (EN) = Džungarskije Vorota 21 Ke 45.25N 82.25 E
Džungarski Alatau, Hrebet- 21 Ke 45.00N 81.00 E
Džungarskije Vorota = Dzungarian Gate (EN) 21 Ke 45.25N 82.25 E
Dzun-Hara 27 Ib 48.40N 106.40 E
Dzun-Mod 27 Ib 47.50N 106.57 E
Džurak-Sal 16 Mf 47.18N 43.36 E
Džusaly 19 Gf 45.29N 64.05 E
Džvari 16 Mh 42.42N 42.02 E

E

Éadan Doire/Edenderry 9 Fh 53.21N 7.03W
Eads 45 Eg 38.29N 102.47W
Eagle 40 Kd 64.46N 141.16W
Eagle 42 Lf 53.35N 57.25W
Eagle Creek 46 La 52.22N 107.24W
Eagle Lake 44 Mb 47.02N 68.36W
Eagle Lake [Ca.-U.S.] 46 Ef 40.39N 120.44W
Eagle Lake [Me.-U.S.] 44 Mb 46.20N 69.20W
Eagle Lake [Ont.-Can.] 45 Jb 49.42N 93.13W
Eagle Mountain 45 Kc 47.54N 90.33W
Eagle Nest 45 Dh 36.35N 105.14W
Eagle Pass 43 Gf 28.43N 100.30W
Eagle Peak [Ca.-U.S.] 43 Cc 41.17N 120.12W
Eagle Peak [Tx.-U.S.] 45 Dk 30.56N 105.01W
Eagle River [Ak.-U.S.] 40 Jd 61.19N 149.34W
Eagle River [Wi.-U.S.] 45 Ld 45.55N 89.15W
Eagle Summit 40 Jc 65.30N 145.38W
Ealing, London- 12 Bc 51.30N 0.19W
Ear Falls 45 Ja 50.38N 93.13W
Earn 9 Je 56.25N 3.30W
Earn, Loch- 9 Ie 56.28N 4.10W
Earnslaw, Mount- 62 Cf 44.37S 168.25 E
Easley 44 Fh 34.50N 82.36W
East Alligator River 59 Gb 12.08S 132.42 E
East Anglia 9 Ni 52.25N 1.00 E
East Angus 44 Lc 45.29N 71.40W
East Bay [Can.] 42 Jd 64.05N 81.30W
East Bay [U.S.] 45 Ll 29.05N 89.15W
East Berlin = Berlin 6 He 52.31N 13.24 E
Eastbourne [Eng.-U.K.] 9 Nk 50.46N 0.17 E
Eastbourne [N.Z.] 62 Fd 41.17S 174.54 E
East Caicos 49 Lc 21.41N 71.30W
East Cape [Fl.-U.S.] 44 Gm 25.07N 81.05W
East Cape [N.Z.] 57 Ih 37.41S 178.33 E
East Caroline Basin (EN) 3 Ii 4.00N 146.45 E
East Chicago 44 De 41.38N 87.27W
East China Sea (EN) = Dong Hai 21 Og 29.00N 125.00 E
East China Sea (EN) = Higashi-Shina-Kai 21 Og 29.00N 125.00 E
East Coast [2] 62 Gc 38.20S 177.50 E
East Dereham 9 Ni 52.41N 0.56 E
Eastend 46 Kb 49.31N 108.48W
East Entrance 64a Bb 7.50N 134.40 E
Easter Island (EN) = Pascua, Isla de-/Rapa Nui 57 Qg 27.07S 109.22W
Easter Island (EN) = Rapa Nui/Pascua, Isla de- 57 Qg 27.07S 109.22W
Eastern [Ghana] [3] 34 Ed 6.30N 0.30W
Eastern [Kenya] [3] 36 Gb 0.05N 38.00 E
Eastern [S.L.] [3] 34 Cd 8.15N 11.00W
Eastern [Ug.] [3] 36 Fb 1.30N 33.50 E
Eastern [Zam.] [3] 36 Fe 13.00S 32.15 E
Eastern Fields 60 Dj 10.03S 145.22 E

Index Symbols

[1] Independent Nation
[2] State, Region
[3] District, County
[4] Municipality
[5] Colony, Dependency
Continent
Physical Region
Historical or Cultural Region
Mount, Mountain
Volcano
Hill
Mountains, Mountain Range
Hills, Escarpment
Plateau, Upland
Pass, Gap
Plain, Lowland
Delta
Salt Flat
Valley, Canyon
Crater, Cave
Karst Features
Depression
Polder
Desert, Dunes
Forest, Woods
Heath, Steppe
Oasis
Cape, Point
Coast, Beach
Cliff
Peninsula
Isthmus
Sandbank
Island
Atoll
Rock, Reef
Islands, Archipelago
Rocks, Reefs
Coral Reef
Well, Spring
Geyser
River, Stream
Waterfall Rapids
River Mouth, Estuary
Lake
Salt Lake
Intermittent Lake
Reservoir
Swamp, Pond
Canal
Glacier
Ice Shelf, Pack Ice
Ocean
Sea
Gulf, Bay
Strait, Fjord
Lagoon
Bank
Seamount
Tablemount
Ridge
Shelf
Basin
Escarpment, Sea Scarp
Fracture
Trench, Abyss
National Park, Reserve
Point of Interest
Recreation Site
Cave, Cavern
Historic Site
Ruins
Wall, Walls
Church, Abbey
Temple
Scientific Station
Airport
Port
Lighthouse
Mine
Tunnel
Dam, Bridge

Eastern Ghats 21 Jh 14.00N 78.50 E
Eastern Point 51b Ab 18.07N 63.01W
Eastern Sayans (EN)= Vostočny Sajan 21 Ld 53.00N 97.00 E
Eastern Siberia (EN) 21 Rc 65.00N 155.00 E
Eastern Sierra Madre (EN)= Madre Oriental, Sierra- 38 Jg 22.00N 99.30W
Eastern Turkistan (EN) 21 Jf 40.00N 80.00 E
East Falkland/Soledad, Isla- 52 Kk 51.45S 58.50W
East Fork 45 Ie 42.41N 94.12W
East Friesland (EN)= Ostfriesland 10 Dc 53.20N 7.40 E
East Frisian Islands (EN)= Ostfriesische Inseln 10 Dc 53.45N 7.25 E
East Grand Forks 45 Hc 47.56N 97.01W
East Grand Rapids 44 Ed 42.56N 85.35W
East Greenland (EN)= Østgrønland [2] 41 Id 72.00N 35.00W
East Grinstead 9 Mj 51.08N 0.01W
East Ilsley 12 Ac 51.32N 1.17W
East Kilbride 9 If 55.46N 4.10W
East Lansing 44 Ed 42.44N 84.29W
East Las Vegas 46 Hh 36.07N 115.01W
Eastleigh 9 Lk 50.58N 1.22W
East London 31 Jl 33.00S 27.55 E
East Lynn Lake 44 Ff 38.05N 82.20W
Eastmain 42 Jf 52.15N 78.34W
Eastmain 42 Jf 52.14N 78.31W
Eastman 44 Fi 32.12N 83.11W
East Mariana Basin (EN) 3 Jh 12.00N 153.00 E
East Midlands Airport 12 Ab 52.50N 1.20W
East Novaya Zemlya Trough (EN) 67 Hd 73.30N 61.00 E
Easton 44 Je 40.41N 75.13W
East Pacific Rise (EN) 3 Ml 20.00S 110.00W
East Point 44 Ei 33.40N 84.27W
East Point [B.V.I.] 51a Db 18.43N 64.16W
East Point [V.I.U.S.] 51a Dc 17.46N 64.33W
Eastport 44 Nc 44.54N 67.00W
East Pryor Mountain 46 Kd 45.14N 108.30W
East Retford 9 Mh 53.19N 0.56W
East Road 12 Cd 51.00N 1.02 E
East Schelde (EN)= Oosterschelde 11 Jc 51.30N 4.00 E
East Scotia Basin (EN) 52 Mk 57.00S 35.00W
East Siberian Sea (EN)= Vostočno Sibirskoje More 67 Cd 74.00N 166.00 E
East St. Louis 43 Id 38.38N 90.05W
East Sussex [3] 9 Nk 50.55N 0.15 E
East Tavaputs Plateau 46 Kg 39.45N 109.30W
East Wear Bay 12 Dc 51.08N 1.18 E
Eaton 44 Ef 39.44N 84.37W
Eatonia 46 Ka 51.13N 109.23W
Eatonton 44 Fi 33.20N 83.23W
Eatonville 46 Dc 46.51N 122.17W
Eau Claire 43 Ic 44.49N 91.31W
Eau-Claire, Lac à l' - 42 Ke 56.20N 74.00W
Eauripik Atoll 57 Fd 6.42N 143.03 E
Eauripik Ridge (EN) 60 Cg 3.00N 142.00 E
Eauze 11 Gk 43.52N 0.06 E
Ebano 48 Jf 22.13N 98.24W
Ebbegebirge 10 De 51.10N 7.45 E
Ebbw Vale 9 Jj 51.47N 3.12W
Ebebiyin 34 He 2.09N 11.20 E
Ebeltoft 8 Dh 56.12N 10.41 E
Ebensburg 44 He 40.28N 78.44W
Ebensee 14 Hc 47.48N 13.46 E
Eberbach 10 Eg 49.28N 8.59 E
Eber Gölü 24 Dc 38.38N 31.12 E
Ebersbach 10 Ke 51.01N 14.35 E
Eberswalde 10 Jd 52.50N 13.50 E
Ebetsu 28 Pc 43.07N 141.34 E
Ebino 28 Kh 32.02N 130.47 E
Ebinur Hu 21 Ke 44.55N 82.55 E
Ebla 23 Eb 35.42N 36.50 E
Ebo 36 Ce 11.02S 14.40 E
Ebola 36 Db 3.20N 20.57 E
Eboli 14 Jj 40.36N 15.04 E
Ebolowa 31 Ih 2.54N 11.09 E
Ebombo 36 Ed 5.42S 26.07 E
Ebon Atoll 57 Hd 4.38N 168.43 E
Ebre/Ebro 5 Gg 40.43N 0.54 E
Ebre, Delta de l'-/Ebro, Delta del- 13 Md 40.43N 0.54 E
Ebril, Récif- 61 Od 22.40S 133.30W
Ebro/Ebre 5 Gg 40.43N 0.54 E
Ebro, Delta del-/Ebre, Delta de l'- 13 Md 40.43N 0.54 E
Ebro, Embalse del- 13 Ia 43.00N 3.58W
Ebschloß 10 Ef 50.58N 8.15 E
Ecaussines 12 Gd 50.34N 4.10 E
Ecbatana 24 Me 34.48N 48.30 E
Eceabat 15 Ji 40.11N 26.21 E
Echdeiria 32 Ed 27.14N 10.27W
Echegarate, Puerto de- 13 Jb 42.57N 2.14W
Echeng [China] 28 Ci 30.24N 114.52 E
Echeng [China] 27 Kd 36.10N 116.03 E
Echez 11 Gk 43.28N 0.02 E
Echigo-Sanmyaku 29 Fc 37.30N 139.15 E
Echizen-Misaki 29 Dd 35.59N 135.57 E
Echo Bay 39 Hc 66.04N 118.00W
Echo Seamount (EN) 32 Dd 25.23N 19.25W
Echt 12 Hc 51.06N 5.52 E
Echternach 12 Ie 49.49N 6.25 E
Echuca 59 Ig 36.10S 144.45 E
Echzell 12 Kd 50.23N 8.52 E
Ecija 13 Gg 37.32N 5.05W
Eckernförde 10 Fb 54.28N 9.50 E
Eckerö 7 Ef 60.15N 19.35 E
Eclipse Sound 42 Jb 72.40N 79.30W
Ečmiadzin 19 Eg 40.09N 44.18 E
Ecommoy 11 Gg 47.50N 0.16 E
Ecos 12 De 49.10N 1.39 E
Ecouis 12 De 49.19N 1.26 E
Écouves, Forêt d'- 11 Gf 48.32N 0.04 E
Écrin, Barre des- 11 Mj 44.55N 6.22 E
Ecuador [2] 53 If 2.00S 77.30W
Ecury-sur-Coole 12 Gf 48.54N 4.20 E
Ed 7 Cf 58.54N 11.56 E
Edam-Volendam 12 Hb 52.30N 5.03 E
Edane 8 Ee 59.38N 12.49 E
Eday 9 Kb 59.11N 2.47W
Edchera 32 Ed 27.02N 13.04W
Eddrachillis Bay 9 Hc 58.19N 5.15W
Eddystone Point 59 Jh 41.00S 148.20 E
Eddystone Rocks 9 Ik 50.15N 4.10W
Eddyville 44 Cg 37.03N 88.04W
Ede [Neth.] 11 Lb 52.03N 5.40 E
Ede [Nig.] 34 Fd 7.44N 4.26 E
Edéa 31 Ih 3.48N 10.08 E
Ed Edd 35 Gc 13.56N 41.40 E
Edefors 7 Ec 66.13N 20.54 E
Edéia 55 Hc 17.18S 49.55W
Edelény 10 Qh 48.18N 20.44 E
Eden 9 Jg 54.57N 3.01W
Eden [Austl.] 59 Jg 37.04S 149.54 E
Eden [Tx.-U.S.] 45 Gk 31.13N 99.51W
Edenburg 37 De 29.45S 25.56 E
Edenderry/Éadan Doire 9 Fh 53.21N 7.03W
Edenkoben 12 Ke 49.17N 8.09 E
Edenton 44 Ig 36.04N 76.39W
Eder 10 Fe 51.13N 9.27 E
Edersee 12 Lc 51.11N 9.03 E
Edertal 12 Lc 51.09N 9.09 E
Edewecht 12 Ja 53.08N 7.59 E
Edgar Ranges 59 Ec 18.43S 123.25 E
Edgartown 44 Le 41.23N 70.31W
Edgecumbe 62 Gb 37.58S 176.50 E
Edgeley 45 Gc 46.22N 98.43W
Edgell 42 Ld 61.50N 65.00W
Edgemont 45 Ee 43.18N 103.50W
Edgeøya 67 Jd 77.45N 22.30 E
Édhessa 15 Fi 40.48N 22.03 E
Edina 45 Jd 44.55N 93.20W
Edinburg 43 Hf 26.18N 98.10W
Edinburgh 6 Fd 55.57N 3.13W
Edinburgh, Arrecife- 49 Ff 14.50N 82.39W
Edincik 24 Bb 40.20N 27.51 E
Edingen/Enghien 12 Gd 50.42N 4.02 E
Edirne 24 Bb 41.40N 26.34 E
Edisto Island 44 Gi 32.35N 80.10W
Edisto River 44 Gi 32.39N 80.24W
Edith, Mount- 46 Jc 46.26N 111.11W
Edith Ronne Land (EN) 66 Qf 78.30S 61.00W
Edjeleh 32 Id 27.42N 9.53 E
Edjereh 32 He 24.35N 4.30 E
Édjérir 34 Fb 18.06N 0.50 E
Edmond 45 Hi 35.39N 97.29W
Edmonds 46 Dc 47.48N 122.22W
Edmonton 39 Hd 53.33N 113.28W
Edmundston 42 Kg 47.22N 68.20W
Edna 45 Hl 28.42N 96.39W
Edremit 23 Cb 39.35N 27.01 E
Edremit, Gulf of- (EN)= Edremit Körfezi 24 Bc 39.30N 26.45 E
Edremit Körfezi=Edremit, Gulf of- (EN) 24 Bc 39.30N 26.45 E
Edsbro 7 Eg 59.54N 18.29 E
Edsbruk 8 Gf 58.02N 16.28 E
Edsbyn 8 Fc 61.23N 15.49 E
Edson 42 Ff 53.35N 116.26W
Edsvalla 8 Ee 59.26N 13.13 E
Eduardo Castex 56 He 35.54S 64.18W
Eduni, Mount- 42 Ed 64.08N 128.10W
Edward, Lake- 30 Ji 0.25S 29.30 E
Edward, Lake- (EN)= Rutanzige, Lac- 30 Ji 0.25S 29.30 E
Edwards Creek 59 He 28.21S 135.51 E
Edwards Plateau 38 If 31.20N 101.00W
Edward VIII Bay 66 Ee 66.50S 57.00 E
Edward VII Peninsula 66 Mf 77.40S 155.00W
Edzo 42 Fd 62.47N 116.08W
Eeklo 11 Jc 51.11N 3.34 E
Eelde 12 Ia 53.08N 6.33 E
Eel River 43 Cc 40.40N 124.20W
Eem 12 Hb 52.16N 5.20 E
Eems 11 Na 53.19N 7.03 E
Eemskanaal 12 Ia 53.19N 6.57 E
Eenrum 12 Ia 53.23N 6.25 E
Eersel 12 Hc 51.22N 5.19 E
Eesti Nõukogude Socialistlik Vabarijk/Estonskaja SSR [2] 19 Cd 59.00N 26.00 E
Eesti NSV=Estonian SSR (EN) [2] 19 Cd 59.00N 26.00 E
Efaté, Ile- 57 Hf 17.40S 168.25 E
Eferding 14 Ib 48.19N 14.01 E
Efes = Ephesus (EN) 15 Kl 37.55N 27.20 E
Effingham 45 Lg 39.07N 88.33W
Eflâni 24 Eb 41.26N 32.57 E
Eforie 15 Le 44.01N 28.38 E
Ega 13 Kb 42.19N 1.55W
Egadi, Isole-=Egadi Islands (EN) 5 Hh 38.00N 12.15 E
Egadi Islands (EN)=Egadi, Isole- 5 Hh 38.00N 12.15 E
Egan Range 46 Hg 39.00N 115.00W
Eganville 44 Ic 47.33N 77.06W
Egbe 34 Gd 8.13N 5.31 E
Ege Denizi=Aegean Sea (EN) 5 Ih 39.00N 25.00 E
Egedesminde/Ausiait 67 Nc 68.50N 52.45W
Egegik 40 He 58.13N 157.22W
Egentliga Finland/Varsinais-Suomi 8 Jd 60.40N 22.30 E
Eger 10 Kf 50.32N 14.08 E
Eger 10 Qi 47.54N 20.23 E
Egersund 7 Ag 58.27N 6.00 E
Egerton, Mount- 59 Dd 24.45S 117.45 E
Egeskov 8 Di 55.10N 10.30 E
Eggegebirge 10 Ee 51.40N 8.55 E
Eggenfelden 10 Ih 48.24N 12.46 E
Eggenstein Leopoldshafen 12 Ke 49.05N 8.23 E
Eggum 7 Cb 68.19N 13.42 E
Eghezée 12 Gd 50.36N 4.56 E
Egijn-Gol 27 Ha 49.24N 103.36 E
Egletons 11 Ii 45.24N 2.03 E
Eglinton 42 Fa 75.45N 118.50W
Egmont, Cape- 61 Dg 39.17S 173.45 E
Egmont, Mount- 62 Fc 39.18S 174.04 E
Egnazia 14 Lj 40.50N 17.25 E
Eğridir 24 Dd 37.52N 30.51 E
Eğridir Gölü 23 Db 38.02N 30.53 E
Eğrigöz Dağ 15 Mj 39.21N 29.07 E
Egtved 8 Ci 55.37N 9.18 E
Éguas ou Correntina, Rio das- 55 Ja 13.26S 44.14W
Eguey 30 Ig 16.10N 16.10 E
Egvekinot 22 Tc 66.19N 179.10 E
Egypt (EN)=Mişr [1] 31 Jf 27.00N 30.00 E
Eha Amufu 34 Gd 6.40N 7.46 E
Ehen Hudag → Alxa Youqi 27 Hd 39.12N 101.40 E
Ehime Ken [2] 28 Lh 33.35N 132.40 E
Ehingen 10 Fh 48.17N 9.44 E
Ehrang, Trier- 12 Ie 49.49N 6.41 E
Ehrwald 14 Ec 47.24N 10.55 E
Ei 29 Bf 31.13N 130.30 E
Eiao, Ile- 57 Me 8.00S 140.40W
Eibar 13 Ja 43.11N 2.28W
Eibergen 12 Ib 52.07N 6.40 E
Eichsfeld 10 Ge 51.25N 10.20 E
Eichstätt 10 Hh 48.53N 11.11 E
Eickelborn, Lippetal- 12 Kc 51.39N 8.13 E
Eide 8 Bb 62.55N 7.26 E
Eider 10 Eb 54.19N 8.58 E
Eiderstedt 10 Eb 54.22N 8.50 E
Eidet 7 Cd 64.27N 13.37 E
Eidfjord 7 Bf 60.28N 7.05 E
Eidfjorden 8 Bd 60.25N 6.45 E
Eidslandet 8 Ad 60.44N 5.45 E
Eidsvåg 7 Be 62.47N 8.03 E
Eidsvoll 7 Cf 60.19N 11.14 E
Eidsvollfiellet 41 Nc 79.00N 13.00 E
Eierlandse Gat 12 Ga 53.12N 4.52 E
Eifel 10 Cf 50.15N 6.45 E
Eiffel Flats 37 Dc 18.15S 29.59 E
Eigenbrakel/Braine-l'Alleud 12 Gd 50.41N 4.22 E
Eigerøya 8 Af 58.25N 5.55 E
Eigg 9 Ge 56.54N 6.10W
Eight Degree Channel 21 Ji 8.00N 73.00 E
Eights Coast 66 Pf 73.30S 96.00W
Eighty Mile Beach 59 Ec 19.45S 121.00 E
Eigrim, Jabal- 35 Fb 19.22N 35.18 E
Eijsden 12 Hd 50.46N 5.42 E
Eikeren 8 Ce 59.40N 10.00 E
Eikesdalsvatnet 8 Cb 62.35N 8.10 E
'Eilai 35 Eb 16.33N 30.54 E
Eildon, Lake- 59 Jg 37.10S 145.50 E
Eilenburg 10 Ie 51.28N 12.37 E
Eiler Rasmussen, Kap- 41 Kb 82.40N 20.00W
Eil Malk 64a Ac 7.09N 134.22 E
Eina 8 Dd 60.38N 10.36 E
Einasleigh 59 Ic 18.31S 144.05 E
Einasleigh River 59 Ic 17.30S 142.17 E
Einbeck 10 Fe 51.49N 9.52 E
Eindhoven 11 Lc 51.26N 5.28 E
Einsiedeln 14 Cc 47.08N 8.45 E
Éire/Ireland [1] 6 Fe 53.00N 8.00W
Eiríksjökull 7a Bb 64.46N 20.24W
Eirunepé 53 Jf 6.40S 69.52W
Eisack/Isarco 14 Fd 46.27N 11.18 E
Eisacktal/Isarco, Valle- 14 Fd 46.45N 11.35 E
Eisacktal/Valle Isarco 14 Fd 46.45N 11.35 E
Eisenach 10 Gf 50.59N 10.19 E
Eisenberg 10 Hf 50.58N 11.54 E
Eisenberg 12 Kc 51.15N 8.50 E
Eisenberg (Pfalz) 12 Ke 49.33N 8.06 E
Eisenerz 14 Ic 47.32N 14.53 E
Eisenerzer Alpen 14 Ic 47.30N 14.40 E
Eisenhüttenstadt 10 Kd 52.10N 14.42 E
Eisenstadt 14 Kc 47.51N 16.31 E
Eisenwurzen 14 Jc 47.56N 15.02 E
Eišiškės/Ejšiškes 7 Fi 54.14N 25.02 E
Eisleben 10 He 51.32N 11.33 E
Eitorf 12 Jd 50.46N 7.27 E
Eivissa/Ibiza=Iviza (EN) 5 Gh 39.00N 1.25 E
Eje, Sierra del- 13 Fb 42.20N 6.55W
Ejea de los Caballeros 13 Kb 42.08N 1.08W
Ejeda 37 Gd 24.19S 44.21 E
Ejido 54 Db 8.33N 71.14W
Ejido Insurgentes 48 De 25.12N 111.45W
Ejin Horo Qi (Altan Xiret) 27 Id 39.31N 109.45 E
Ejin Qi 22 Me 41.50N 100.50 E
Ejšiškes/Eišiškės 7 Fi 54.14N 25.02 E
Ejura 34 Ed 7.23N 1.22W
Ejutla de Crespo 47 Ee 16.34N 96.44W
Ekalaka 46 Md 45.53N 104.33W
Ekecek Dağı 24 Fc 38.39N 34.03 E
Ekenäs/Tammisaari 7 Fg 59.58N 23.26 E
Ekeren, Antwerpen- 11 Kc 51.17N 4.25 E
Eket 34 Ge 4.39N 7.56 E
Eketahuna 62 Fd 40.39S 175.44 E
Ekhinádhes Nísoi 15 Ek 38.25N 21.02 E
Ekiatapski Hrebet 20 Mc 68.40N 177.50 E
Ekibastuz 19 He 51.42N 75.22 E
Ekimčan 20 If 53.07N 133.02 E
Ekoli 36 Dc 0.23S 24.16 E
Ekoln 8 Ge 59.45N 17.35 E
Ekombe 36 Db 1.16N 21.36 E
Ekonda 20 Fc 65.47N 105.17 E
Eksjö 7 Dh 57.40N 14.57 E
Ekuma 37 Bc 18.10S 15.47 E
Ekwan 42 Jf 53.12N 82.15W
El Aaiún 31 Ff 27.10N 13.12W
El Aargub 32 De 23.37N 15.52W
El Aatf 32 De 23.30N 15.30W
El Abadia 13 Nh 36.13N 1.40 E
El-Abd 13 Mi 35.29N 0.42 E
El Abiodh Sidi Cheikh 32 Hc 32.53N 0.34 E
El 'Açâba [3] 32 Ef 16.30N 12.00W
El 'Açâba 30 Fg 16.49N 12.05W
El Adeb Larache 32 Id 27.22N 8.52 E
El Affroun 13 Oh 36.28N 2.37 E
Elafónisi Channel (EN) = Elafonísou, Stenón- 15 Fm 36.25N 23.00 E
Elafónisos 15 Fm 36.29N 22.58 E
Elafonísou Stenón-= Elafónisi Channel (EN) 15 Fm 36.25N 23.00 E
El Agreb 32 Ic 30.48N 5.30 E
El Aguilar 56 Gb 32.12S 65.42W
El Álamo 48 Ab 31.34N 116.02W
El Alia 32 Ic 32.42N 5.26 E
El-Amria 13 Ki 35.32N 1.01W
Elan 15 Lc 46.06N 28.04 E
El Andévalo 13 Fg 37.40N 7.00W
El Aouinet 14 Bo 35.52N 7.54 E
El Arahal 13 Gg 37.16N 5.33W
El Aricha 32 Gc 34.13N 1.16W
Elása 15 Jn 35.17N 26.20 E
Elassón 15 Fj 39.54N 22.11 E
Elat 22 Fg 29.33N 34.57 E
Eláti 15 Dk 38.43N 20.39 E
Elato Atoll 57 Fd 7.28N 146.10 E
El Attaf 13 Nh 36.13N 1.40 E
Elâzığ 23 Eb 38.41N 39.14 E
El Azúcar, Presa de- 48 Jd 26.15N 99.00W
Elba 44 Dj 31.25N 86.04W
Elba 5 Hg 42.45N 10.15 E
Elban 20 If 50.05N 136.30 E
El Banco 54 Db 9.01N 73.58W
El Barco de Ávila 13 Gd 40.21N 5.31W
El Barco de Valdeorras 13 Fb 42.25N 6.59W
Elbasani 15 Dh 41.06N 20.05 E
El Baúl 54 Eb 8.57N 68.17W
El Bayadh 32 Hc 33.41N 1.01 E
Elbe 5 Ge 53.50N 9.00 E
Elbe (EN)=Labe 5 Ge 53.50N 9.00 E
Elbe-Lübeck-Kanal 10 Gc 53.50N 10.36 E
Elbert, Mount- 38 If 39.07N 106.27W
Elberton 44 Fh 34.07N 82.52W
Elbe-Seitenkanal 10 Gd 52.22N 10.34 E
Elbeuf 11 Ge 49.17N 1.00 E
Elbeyl 23 Eb 36.41N 37.26 E
El Bierzo 13 Fb 42.40N 6.50W
Elbıstan 24 Gc 38.13N 37.12 E
Elbląg [2] 10 Pb 54.10N 19.25 E
Elbląg 6 He 54.10N 19.25 E
Elbląski, Kanał- 10 Pc 53.43N 19.53 E
El Bolsón 56 Ff 41.58S 71.31W
El Bonillo 13 Jf 38.57N 2.32W
Elbow 46 La 51.07N 106.35W
Elbow Cays 49 Gb 23.57N 80.29W
Elbow Lake 45 Id 46.00N 95.58W
Elbrus 5 Kg 43.21N 42.26 E
Elbsandsteingebirge 10 Kf 50.50N 14.12 E
'Ēlbūr 35 He 4.40N 46.40 E
Elburg 11 Lb 52.26N 5.50 E
El Burgo de Osma 13 Ic 41.35N 3.04W
Elburgon 36 Gc .0.18S 35.49 E
El Burro 48 Ic 29.16N 101.55W
Elburz Mountains (EN)= Alborz, Reshteh-ye Kūhhā-ye- 21 Hf 36.00N 53.00 E
El Cajon 43 De 32.48N 116.58W
El Callao 54 Fb 7.21N 61.49W
El Calvario 50 Ch 8.59N 67.00W
El Campo 45 Hl 29.12N 96.16W
El Canelo 48 Ie 24.19N 100.23W
El Cármen 55 Cd 18.49S 58.33W
El Carmen de Bolivar 54 Cb 9.43N 75.07W
El Casco 48 Ge 25.34N 104.35W
El Castillo 49 Eh 11.01N 84.24W
El Centro 43 De 32.48N 115.34W
El Cerro 54 Fg 17.31S 61.34W
El Chaparro 50 Dh 9.10N 65.01W
Elche 13 Lf 38.15N 0.42W
Elcho Island 59 Hb 11.55S 135.45 E
El Cury 56 Ge 39.56S 68.20W
Elda 13 Lf 38.29N 0.47W
Ēldab 35 Hd 8.58N 46.38 E
Elde 10 Ic 53.17N 12.40 E
'Ēl Ḍēre 31 Lh 3.55N 47.10 E
El Dere 35 Gd 5.07N 43.12 E
El Descanso 48 Aa 32.12N 116.55W
El Desemboque 47 Bb 30.30N 112.59W
El Dificíl 49 Ji 9.51N 74.14W
Eldikan 20 Id 60.38N 135.07 E
El Djouf 30 Gf 21.25N 6.40W
El Doncello 54 Cc 1.43N 75.17W
Eldorado 45 Fk 30.52N 100.36W
Eldorado 56 Jc 26.24S 54.38W
El Dorado [Ar.-U.S.] 43 Ie 33.13N 92.40W
El Dorado [Ks.-U.S.] 43 Hd 37.49N 96.52W
El Dorado [Mex.] 47 Cd 24.17N 107.31W
El Dorado [Ven.] 53 Je 6.44N 61.38W
Eldorado Paulista 55 Hg 24.32S 48.06W
El Dorado Springs 45 Ih 37.52N 94.01W
Eldoret 36 Gb 0.31N 35.17 E
Eldsberga 8 Eh 56.36N 12.59 E
'Ēl Ḍubbo 35 Ge 3.52N 44.45 E
Eldžik 18 De 39.25N 63.01 E
Elefantes, Rio dos- 37 Ed 24.03S 32.40 E
El Eglab 30 Gf 26.30N 5.00W
Elēja/Eleja 7 Fh 56.28N 23.41 E
Eleja/Elēja 7 Fh 56.28N 23.41 E
Elektrénai/Elektrenaj 8 Kj 54.46N 24.47 E
Elektrenaj/Elektrénai 8 Kj 54.46N 24.47 E
Elektrostal 19 Dd 55.48N 38.29 E
Elele 34 Gd 5.06N 6.49 E
Elena 15 Ig 42.56N 25.53 E
El Encanto [Bol.] 55 Cc 16.57S 59.24W
El Encanto [Col.] 54 Dd 1.37S 73.13W
Elephant Butte Reservoir 45 Cj 33.19N 107.10W
Elephant Island 66 Re 61.10S 55.14W
Elephant Mountain 45 Ek 30.02N 103.30W
Elesbão Veloso 54 Je 6.13S 42.08W
El Escorial 13 Hd 40.35N 4.10W
Eleşkirt 24 Jc 39.49N 42.40 E
El Estor 49 Cf 15.32N 89.21W
Eleuthera 38 Lg 25.15N 76.20W
Elevsís 15 Gk 38.02N 23.32 E
Elevtheroúpolis 15 Hi 40.55N 24.15 E
El Fendek 13 Gi 35.34N 5.35W
El Ferrol del Caudillo 13 Da 43.29N 8.14W
El Fud 35 Gd 7.15N 42.51 E
El Fuerte [Mex.] 48 Hf 23.50N 103.06W
El Fuerte [Mex.] 47 Cc 26.25N 108.39W
Elgåhogna 8 Eb 62.09N 12.04 E
'Ēl Gāl 35 Ic 11.23N 50.23 E
El Galhak 35 Ec 11.03N 32.42 E
El Gassi 32 Ic 30.55N 5.50 E
Elgen 20 Kd 62.45N 150.40 E
Elgepiggen 7 Ce 62.10N 11.22 E
El Ghomri 13 Mi 35.41N 0.12 E
Elgi 20 Jd 64.20N 142.05 E
Elgin [Il.-U.S.] 43 Jc 42.02N 88.17W
Elgin [N.D.-U.S.] 45 Fc 46.24N 101.51W
Elgin [Or.-U.S.] 46 Gd 45.34N 117.55W
Elgin [Scot.-U.K.] 9 Jd 57.39N 3.20W
Elginski 20 Jd 64.48N 141.50 E
Elgjaij 20 Gd 62.28N 117.37 E
El Goléa 31 He 30.34N 2.53 E
Elgon, Mont- 30 Kh 1.08N 34.33 E
Elgoran 35 Gd 5.04N 44.22 E
El Grao, Castellón de la Plana- 13 Me 39.58N 0.01 E
El Grao, Valencia- 13 Le 39.27N 0.20W
El Guapo 50 Dg 10.09N 65.58W
El Guayabo 49 Ki 8.37N 72.20W
El Hadjar 14 Bn 36.48N 7.45 E
El Hajeb 32 Fc 33.42N 5.22W
El-Ham 13 Qi 35.42N 4.52 E
El Hammam 13 Li 35.50N 0.15W
'Ēl Ḥamurre 35 Hd 7.11N 48.55 E
El Hank 30 Gf 24.00N 6.30W
El Harrach, Al Jazā'ir- 13 Ph 36.43N 3.08 E
Elhotovo 16 Nh 43.20N 44.13 E
Elhovo 15 Jg 42.10N 26.34 E
El Huecú 56 Fe 37.37S 70.36W
Elida 45 Ej 33.57N 103.39W
Èliki, Vallée d'- 34 Gc 14.45N 7.15 E
Elila 36 Ec 2.43S 25.53 E
Elila 30 Ji 2.45S 25.53 E
Elimäki 8 Ld 60.43N 26.28 E
Elin Pelin 15 Gg 42.40N 23.36 E
Elisejna 15 Gf 43.05N 23.29 E
Elisenvaara 8 Mc 61.19N 29.47 E
Elista 6 Kf 46.16N 44.14 E
Elizabeth [Austl.] 58 Eh 34.45S 138.39 E
Elizabeth [N.J.-U.S.] 44 Je 40.40N 74.13W
Elizabeth, Cape- 46 Cc 47.22N 124.22W
Elizabeth City 43 Ld 36.18N 76.14W
Elizabeth Reef 57 Gg 29.55S 159.05 E
Elizabethton 44 Fg 36.21N 82.13W
Elizabethtown [Ky.-U.S.] 44 Eg 37.42N 85.52W
Elizabethtown [N.C.-U.S.] 44 Hh 34.38N 78.37W
El Jadida [3] 32 Fc 32.54N 8.30W
El Jadida 31 Ge 33.15N 8.30W
El Jicaro 49 Dg 13.43N 86.08W
'Ēl Jilib 35 He 3.48N 47.07 E
Ełk 10 Sc 53.50N 22.22 E
Ełk 10 Sc 53.32N 22.47 E
El Kala 32 Ib 36.54N 8.27 E
El Kantara 32 Ib 35.13N 5.43 E
El-Karimia 13 Nh 36.07N 1.33 E
Elk City [Id.-U.S.] 46 Hd 45.51N 115.29W
Elk City [Ok.-U.S.] 45 Gi 35.25N 99.25W
El Kelaa des Srarhna [3] 32 Fc 32.03N 7.30W
El Kelaa des Srarhna 32 Fc 32.03N 7.24W
El Kere 35 Gd 5.51N 42.06 E
Elkhart [In.-U.S.] 43 Jc 41.41N 85.58W
Elkhart [Ks.-U.S.] 45 Fh 37.00N 101.54W
El Khatt 32 Ef 19.00N 12.25W
Elkhead Mountains 45 Cf 40.50N 107.05W
El Khnâchîch 34 Ea 21.20N 3.45W
Elkhorn River 45 Hf 41.07N 96.19W
Elkins 44 Hf 38.56N 79.53W
Elk Lake 44 Gb 47.42N 80.11W
Elk Mountain 46 Lf 41.38N 106.32W
Elk Mountains 45 Cg 38.55N 106.50W
Elko 39 He 40.50N 115.46W
Elk Peak 46 Jc 46.27N 110.46W
Elk River 44 Gf 38.21N 81.38W
Elk River 45 Jd 45.18N 93.35W
Elku Kalns 8 Kg 57.04N 25.23 E
Ell, Lake- 59 Fe 29.15S 127.45 E
Ellás=Greece (EN) [1] 6 Ih 39.00N 22.00 E
Ellé 11 Cg 47.52N 3.32W
Ellef Ringnes 38 Ib 78.30N 104.00W
Ellen, Mount- 43 Ed 38.07N 110.49W
Ellendale 43 Hb 46.06N 98.32W
Ellensburg 43 Cb 46.40N 120.32W
Ellenville 44 Je 41.43N 74.23W
Ellesmere 38 Kb 79.00N 82.00W
Ellesmere, Lake- 62 Ee 43.45S 172.30 E
Ellice 42 Hc 68.02N 103.25W
Ellice Islands → Tuvalu [1] 58 Ie 8.00S 178.00 E
Elliot [Austl.] 59 Gc 17.35S 133.35 E
Elliot [S.Afr.] 37 Df 31.18S 27.50 E
Elliot, Mount- 59 Jc 19.29S 146.58 E
Elliot Lake 42 Jg 46.23N 82.39W
Ellisras 37 Dd 23.40S 27.46 E
Elliston 59 Gf 33.39S 134.55 E
Ellisville 45 Lk 31.36N 89.12W
Ellmau 14 Gc 47.31N 12.18 E
Ellös 7 Cg 58.11N 11.27 E
Ellsworth [Ks.-U.S.] 45 Gg 38.44N 98.14W
Ellsworth [Me.-U.S.] 44 Mc 44.33N 68.26W
Ellsworth [Nb.-U.S.] 45 Ee 42.04N 102.15W
Ellsworth, Lake- 45 Gi 34.48N 98.20W
Ellsworth Land (EN) 66 Pf 75.30S 80.00W
Ellsworth Mountains 66 Pf 78.30S 85.00W
Ellwangen 10 Gh 48.57N 10.08 E

Index Symbols

[1] Independent Nation
[2] State, Region
[3] District, County
[4] Municipality
[5] Colony, Dependency
Continent
Physical Region
Historical or Cultural Region
Mount, Mountain
Volcano
Hill
Mountains, Mountain Range
Hills, Escarpment
Plateau, Upland
Pass, Gap
Plain, Lowland
Delta
Salt Flat
Valley, Canyon
Crater, Cave
Karst Features
Depression
Polder
Desert, Dunes
Forest, Woods
Heath, Steppe
Oasis
Cape, Point
Coast, Beach
Cliff
Peninsula
Isthmus
Sandbank
Island
Atoll
Rock, Reef
Islands, Archipelago
Rocks, Reefs
Coral Reef
Well, Spring
Geyser
River, Stream
Waterfall Rapids
River Mouth, Estuary
Lake
Salt Lake
Intermittent Lake
Reservoir
Swamp, Pond
Canal
Glacier
Ice Shelf, Pack Ice
Ocean
Sea
Gulf, Bay
Strait, Fjord
Lagoon
Bank
Seamount
Tablemount
Ridge
Shelf
Basin
Escarpment, Sea Scarp
Fracture
Trench, Abyss
National Park, Reserve
Point of Interest
Recreation Site
Cave, Cavern
Historic Site
Ruins
Wall, Walls
Church, Abbey
Temple
Scientific Station
Airport
Port
Lighthouse
Mine
Tunnel
Dam, Bridge

Name	Page	Key	Lat.	Long.
Elm	10	Gd	52.09N	10.53 E
El Macao	49	Md	18.46N	68.33W
Elmadağ	24	Ec	39.55N	33.15 E
Elma Daği	15	Mk	38.46N	29.32 E
El Maestrat/El Maestrazgo	13	Ld	40.30N	0.10W
El Maestrazgo/El Maestrat	13	Ld	40.30N	0.10W
El Mahia	34	Ea	22.30N	2.30W
El Maitén	56	Ff	42.03S	71.10W
Elmaki	34	Gb	17.55N	8.20 E
El Malah	13	Ph	36.18N	3.14 E
Elmalı	24	Ic	39.25N	40.35 E
Elmali	24	Cd	36.44N	29.56 E
El Manteco	50	Ei	7.27N	62.32W
El Marfil	55	Bb	15.35S	60.19W
El Marsa	13	Mh	36.24N	0.55 E
El Medo	35	Gd	5.41N	41.46 E
El Meghaïer	32	Ic	33.57N	5.56 E
Elmhurst	45	Mf	41.53N	87.56W
El Milagro	56	Gd	31.01S	65.59W
Elmira	43	Lc	42.06N	76.50W
El Mrâyer	32	Fe	21.30N	8.10W
El Mreïti	32	Fe	23.29N	7.52W
El Mreyyé	30	Gg	19.30N	7.00W
Elmshorn	10	Fc	53.45N	9.39 E
Elmstein	12	Je	49.22N	7.56 E
Elne	11	Il	42.36N	2.58 E
El Nevado, Cerro-	56	Ge	35.35S	68.30W
El Niabo	35	Fe	4.33N	39.59 E
El Nihuil	56	Gd	34.58S	68.40W
El Novillo	48	Ec	28.40N	109.30W
El Novillo, Presa-	48	Ec	29.05N	109.45W
El Ochenta y Uno	48	Kg	21.35N	97.57W
Elorn	11	Bf	48.27N	4.16W
Elortondo	55	Bk	33.42S	61.37W
Elorza	54	Eb	7.03N	69.31W
Elota, Río-	48	Ff	23.52N	106.56W
El Oued	32	Ic	33.20N	6.53 E
Eloy	46	Jj	32.45N	111.33W
El Palmar	50	Fh	8.01N	61.53W
El Palmito	48	Ge	25.40N	104.59W
El Panadés/El Penedès	13	Nc	41.25N	1.30 E
El Pao [Ven.]	50	Eh	8.06N	62.33W
El Pao [Ven.]	50	Bh	9.38N	68.08W
El Paraiso	49	Df	14.10N	86.30W
El Paraíso	49	Dg	13.51N	86.34W
El Páramo	13	Gb	42.25N	5.45W
El Pardo, Madrid-	13	Id	40.32N	3.46W
El Paso [Il.-U.S.]	45	Lf	40.44N	89.01W
El Paso [Tx.-U.S.]	39	If	31.45N	106.29W
El Penedès/El Panadés	13	Nc	41.25N	1.30 E
El Perú	50	Fi	7.19N	61.49W
El Pico	54	Fg	15.57S	64.42W
El Pilar	50	Eg	10.32N	63.09W
El Pintado	56	Hb	24.38S	61.27W
El Porvenir [Hond.]	49	Df	14.41N	87.11W
El Porvenir [Pan.]	49	Hi	9.12N	80.08W
El Porvenir [Ven.]	50	Bi	6.55N	68.42W
El Potosí	48	Ie	24.51N	100.19W
El Prat de Llobregat/Prat de Llobregat	13	Oc	41.20N	2.06 E
El Priorat/El Priorato	13	Mc	41.10N	1.00 E
El Priorato/El Priorat	13	Mc	41.10N	1.00 E
El Progreso	49	Cf	14.50N	90.00W
El Progreso [Guat.]	49	Bf	14.51N	90.04W
El Progreso [Hond.]	47	Ge	15.21N	87.49W
El Puente del Arzobispo	13	Ge	39.48N	5.10W
El Puerto	48	Dc	28.45N	111.20W
El Puerto de Santa María	13	Fh	36.36N	6.13W
El Rastro	50	Ch	9.03N	67.27W
El Real de Santa María	49	Ii	8.08N	77.43W
El Reno	43	Hd	35.32N	97.57W
El Ribeiro	13	Db	42.25N	8.10W
Elrose	46	Ka	51.13N	108.01W
El Saler	13	Le	39.23N	0.20W
El Salto	47	Cd	23.47N	105.23W
El Salvador	39	Kh	13.50N	88.55W
El Samán de Apure	50	Bi	7.55N	68.44W
El Sauce [Mex.]	48	De	24.34N	111.29W
El Sauce [Nic.]	49	Dg	12.53N	86.32W
El Sáuz	48	Fc	29.03N	106.15W
Elsberry	45	Kg	39.10N	90.47W
Elsdorf	12	Id	50.56N	6.34 E
Else	12	Kb	52.12N	8.40 E
El Seibo	49	Md	18.46N	68.52W
Elsen, Paderborn-	12	Kc	51.44N	8.41 E
Elsen Nur	27	Fd	35.08N	92.20 E
'Ēl Shāma	35	Ge	2.46N	41.03 E
El Socorro	50	Dh	8.59N	65.44W
El Sombrero	54	Eb	9.23N	67.03W
Elst	12	Hc	51.55N	5.52 E
Elsterwerda	10	Je	51.27N	13.32 E
El Sueco	47	Cc	29.54N	106.24W
El-Taht	13	Mi	35.27N	0.46 E
El Tajin	47	Ed	20.27N	97.23W
El Tala	56	Gc	26.07S	65.17W
Eltanin Bay	66	Pf	73.40S	82.00W
Eltham	62	Fc	39.26S	174.18 E
El Tigre	53	Je	8.55N	64.15W
El Tigre, Isla-	49	Dg	13.16N	87.38W
El Toboso	13	Je	39.31N	3.00W
El Tocuyo	54	Eb	9.47N	69.48W
Elton	16	Oe	49.08N	46.50 E
Elton, Ozero-	19	Ef	49.10N	46.40 E
El Torcal	13	Hh	36.55N	4.35W
El Trébol	55	Bk	32.12S	61.42W
El Trigo	55	Cl	35.52S	59.24W
El Triunfo [Hond.]	49	Dg	13.06N	87.00W
El Triunfo [Mex.]	48	Df	23.47N	110.08W
El Tuito	48	Gg	20.19N	105.22W
El Turbio	56	Fh	51.41S	72.05W
Eltville am Rhein	12	Kd	50.02N	8.07 E
Eltz	12	Jd	50.12N	7.18 E
Elūru	25	Ge	17.05N	82.15 E
Elva	7	Gg	58.13N	26.25 E
El Valle	49	Gi	8.31N	80.08W
El Valles/Valles	13	Oc	41.35N	2.15 E
Elvas	13	Ef	38.53N	7.10W
El Vejo, Cerro-	54	Db	7.30N	73.05W
El Venado, Isla-	49	Fh	11.57N	83.44W
El Vendrell/Vendrell	13	Nc	41.13N	1.32 E
Elverum	7	Cf	60.53N	11.34 E
El Viejo	49	Dg	12.40N	87.10W
El Viejo, Volcán	38	Kh	12.38N	87.11W
El Vigia	49	Li	8.38N	71.39W
El Vigia, Cerro-	48	Gg	21.25N	104.00W
El Wak	36	Hb	2.49N	40.56 E
Elwell, Lake-	46	Jb	48.22N	111.17W
Elwood	44	Ee	40.17N	85.50W
Ely [Eng.-U.K.]	9	Ni	52.24N	0.16 E
Ely [Mn.-U.S.]	43	Ib	47.54N	91.51W
Ely [Nv.-U.S.]	39	Hf	39.15N	114.53W
Elyria	44	Fe	41.22N	82.06W
El Yunque	51a	Cb	18.18N	65.47W
Elz	12	Kd	50.25N	8.02 E
Elzbach	12	Jd	50.12N	7.22 E
Emaé	63b	Dc	17.04S	168.22 E
Ema Jōgi/Emajygi	8	Lf	58.20N	27.15 E
Emajygi/Ema Jōgi	8	Lf	58.20N	27.15 E
Emali	36	Gc	2.05S	37.28 E
Emāmshahr [Iran]	23	Ib	36.25N	55.01 E
Emāmshahr [Iran]	22	Hf	36.50N	54.29 E
Emāmzādeh 'Abbās	24	Lf	32.25N	47.55 E
Emån	7	Dh	57.08N	16.30 E
Emba	19	Ff	48.50N	58.10 E
Emba	5	Lf	46.38N	53.04 E
Embaracai, Rio-	55	Ff	23.27S	53.58W
Embarcación	56	Hb	23.13S	64.06W
Embarras Portage	42	Ge	58.25N	111.27W
Embarras River	45	Mg	38.39N	87.37W
Embira, Rio-	54	De	7.19S	70.15W
Embrun	11	Mj	44.34N	6.30 E
Embu	36	Gc	0.32S	37.27 E
Emden	10	Dc	53.22N	7.13 E
Emeldžak	20	He	58.27N	126.57 E
Emerald	58	Fg	23.32S	148.10 E
Emerald	42	Ga	76.50N	114.00W
Emerson	45	Hb	49.00N	97.12W
Emet	24	Cc	39.20N	29.15 E
Emiliano Zapata	48	Ni	17.45N	91.46W
Emilia-Romagna	14	Ef	44.45N	11.00 E
Emilio R. Coni	55	Cj	30.04S	58.16W
Emili Rock	52	Hh	29.40S	87.25W
Emin/Dorbiljin	27	Db	46.32N	83.39 E
Emine, Nos-	15	Kg	42.42N	27.54 E
Emira Island	60	Dh	1.40S	150.00 E
Emirdağ	24	Dc	39.01N	31.10 E
Emisu, Tarso-	30	If	21.13N	18.32 E
Emlichheim	10	Cd	52.37N	6.51 E
Emmaboda	7	Dh	56.38N	15.32 E
Emmaste	7	Fg	58.43N	22.36 E
Emme	14	Bd	47.10N	7.35 E
Emmeloord, Noordoostpolder-	12	Hb	52.42N	5.44 E
Emmelshausen	12	Jd	50.09N	7.34 E
Emmen	11	Mb	52.47N	6.55 E
Emmendingen	10	Dh	48.08N	7.51 E
Emmen-Emmer-Compascuum	12	Jb	52.49N	7.03 E
Emmen-Klazienaveen	12	Jb	52.44N	7.01 E
Emmen-Nieuw Weerdinge	12	Jb	52.52N	7.01 E
Emmental	14	Bd	46.55N	7.45 E
Emmen-Weerdinge	12	Ib	52.49N	6.57 E
Emmer	12	Lb	52.03N	9.23 E
Emmer-Compascuum, Emmen-	12	Jb	52.49N	7.03 E
Emmerich	10	Ce	51.50N	6.15 E
Emmet	59	Id	24.40S	144.28 E
Emmetsburg	45	Ie	43.07N	94.41W
Emmett	46	Ge	43.52N	116.30W
Emmonak	40	Gd	62.46N	164.30W
Emőd	10	Qi	47.56N	20.49 E
Emory	46	Jf	41.05N	111.16W
Emory Peak	43	Gf	29.13N	103.17W
Empalme	47	Bc	27.58N	110.51W
Empangeni	37	Ee	28.50S	31.48 E
Empedrado	56	Ic	27.57S	58.48W
Emperor Seamounts (EN)	3	Je	40.00N	171.00 E
Empoli	14	Eg	43.43N	10.57 E
Emporia [Ks.-U.S.]	43	Hd	38.24N	96.11W
Emporia [Va.-U.S.]	44	Ig	36.42N	77.33W
Emporium	44	He	41.31N	78.14W
Empress Augusta Bay	63a	Bb	6.25S	155.05 E
Empress Mine	37	Dc	18.27S	29.27 E
Ems	11	Na	53.19N	7.03 E
Emsbach	12	Kd	50.24N	8.06 E
Emsdetten	10	Dd	52.11N	7.32 E
Ems-Jade-Kanal	10	Dc	53.19N	7.10 E
Emsland	10	Dd	52.50N	7.20 E
Emstek	12	Kb	52.50N	8.09 E
Emumägi/Emumjagi	8	Lf	58.54N	26.23 E
Emumjagi/Emumägi	8	Lf	58.54N	26.23 E
Ena	29	Ed	35.27N	137.24 E
Enånger	7	Df	61.32N	17.00 E
Enaratoli	26	Kg	3.55S	136.21 E
Enard Bay	9	Hc	58.06N	5.20W
Ena-San	29	Ed	35.26N	137.36 E
Enbetsu	28	Pb	44.44N	141.47 E
Encantada, Cerro de la-	38	Hf	31.00N	115.23W
Encantada, Sierra de la-	48	Hc	28.30N	102.20W
Encantadas, Serra das	55	Fj	30.40S	53.00W
Encantado, Cerro-	47	Bc	27.03N	112.30W
Encarnación	53	Kh	27.20S	55.54W
Encarnación de Díaz	48	Hg	21.31N	102.14W
Enchi	34	Ed	5.49N	2.49W
Encinal	45	Gl	28.02N	99.21W
Encinasola	13	Ff	38.08N	6.52W
Encontrados	54	Db	8.46N	72.30W
Encounter Bay	59	Hg	35.35S	138.45 E
Encrucijada	49	Hb	22.37N	79.52W
Encruzilhada do Sul	55	Fj	30.32S	52.31W
Encs	10	Rh	48.20N	21.08 E
Ende	22	Oj	8.50S	121.39 E
Endeavour Strait	59	Ib	10.50S	142.15 E
Endelave	8	Di	55.45N	10.15 E
Enderbury Atoll	57	Je	3.08S	171.05W
Enderby	46	Fa	50.33N	119.08W
Enderby Land	66	Ee	67.30S	53.00 E
Endicott Mountains	40	Ic	67.50N	152.00W
Ené, Río-	54	Df	11.09S	74.19W
Energetik	19	Fe	51.44N	58.48 E
Enez	24	Bb	40.44N	26.04 E
Enez Körfezı	15	Ii	40.45N	26.00 E
Enfer, Portes d'-	36	Ed	5.05S	27.30 E
Enfield	44	Ig	36.11N	77.47W
Enfield, London-	12	Bc	51.40N	0.04W
Engadin/Engiadin'ota/Engadina	14	Dd	46.35N	10.00 E
Engadina/Engadin/Engiadin'ota	14	Dd	46.35N	10.00 E
Engaño, Cabo-	47	Ke	18.37N	68.20W
Engaru	28	Qb	44.03N	143.31 E
Engelberg	14	Cd	46.50N	8.24 E
Engelhard	44	Jh	35.31N	76.00W
Engels	6	Ke	51.30N	46.07 E
Engelskirchen	12	Jd	50.59N	7.24 E
Engenho	55	Db	15.10S	56.25W
Enger	12	Kb	52.08N	8.34 E
Engeren	8	Ec	61.35N	12.05 E
Engershatu	35	Fb	16.34N	38.15 E
Enggano, Pulau-	21	Mj	5.24S	102.16 E
Enghien/Edingen	12	Gd	50.42N	4.02 E
Engiadin'ota/Engadina/Engadin	14	Dd	46.35N	10.00 E
England	5	Fe	52.30N	1.30W
England	9	Li	52.30N	1.30W
Englehart	42	Jg	47.49N	79.52W
Englewood	45	Dg	39.39N	104.59W
English	44	Df	38.20N	86.28W
English Channel	5	Fe	50.20N	1.00W
English Coast	66	Qf	73.30S	73.00W
English River	45	Ia	50.12N	95.00W
English River	45	Kb	49.13N	90.58W
Engozero, Ozero-	7	Hd	65.45N	33.30 E
Enguera	13	Lf	38.59N	0.41W
Engure/Engures	8	Jg	57.09N	23.06 E
Engures/Engure	8	Jg	57.09N	23.06 E
Engures, Ozero-/Engures Ezers	8	Jg	57.15N	23.10 E
Engures Ezers/Engures, Ozero-	8	Jg	57.15N	23.10 E
Enh-Gajvan	27	Gb	48.05N	97.35 E
Enid	39	Jf	36.19N	97.48W
Enid Lake	45	Li	34.10N	89.50W
Eniwa	28	Pc	42.53N	141.14 E
Eniwa-Dake	29a	Bb	42.47N	141.17 E
Eniwetok Atoll	57	Hc	11.30N	162.15 E
Enkenbach Alsenborn	12	Je	49.29N	7.53 E
Enkhuizen	11	Lb	52.42N	5.17 E
Enklinge	8	Id	60.20N	20.45 E
Enköping	7	Dg	59.38N	17.04 E
Enna	14	Im	37.34N	14.16 E
Ennadai	42	Hd	61.10N	101.00W
Ennadei Lake	42	Hd	60.55N	101.20W
Enné	35	Bc	14.24N	18.45 E
Ennedi	30	Jg	17.15N	22.00 E
Ennell, Lough-/Loch Ainninn	9	Fh	53.28N	7.24W
Ennepetal	12	Jc	51.18N	7.21 E
Ennigerloh	12	Kc	51.50N	8.01 E
Enning	45	Ed	44.37N	102.31W
Ennis [Mt.-U.S.]	46	Jd	45.21N	111.44W
Ennis [Tx.-U.S.]	45	Hj	32.20N	96.38W
Ennis/Inis	9	Ei	52.50N	8.59W
Enniscorthy/Inis Córthaidh	9	Gi	52.30N	6.34W
Enniskillen/Inis Ceithleann	9	Fg	54.21N	7.38W
Ennistymon/Inis Diomáin	9	Di	52.57N	9.13W
Enns	14	Ib	48.12N	14.28 E
Enns	5	Hf	48.14N	14.30 E
Ennstaler Alpen	14	Ic	47.37N	14.35 E
Eno	7	He	62.48N	30.09 E
Enontiekö	7	Fb	68.23N	23.38 E
Enonvesi [Fin.]	8	Mb	62.10N	28.55 E
Enonvesi [Fin.]	8	Lc	61.20N	26.30 E
Enozero, Ozero-	7	Ib	68.10N	38.00 E
Enrekang	26	Gg	3.34S	119.47 E
Enrique Carbó	55	Ck	33.08S	59.14W
Enriquillo	49	Le	17.54N	71.14W
Enriquillo, Lago-	47	Je	18.27N	71.39W
Enschede	11	Mb	52.12N	6.53 E
Ensenada [Arg.]	55	Dl	34.51S	57.55W
Ensenada [Mex.]	39	Hf	31.52N	116.37W
Enshi	27	Ie	30.16N	109.26 E
Enshū-Nada	29	Ed	34.30N	138.00 E
Entebbe	31	Kh	0.04N	32.28 E
Entenbühl	10	Ig	49.46N	12.24 E
Enterprise [Al.-U.S.]	44	Ej	31.19N	85.51W
Enterprise [N.W.T.-Can.]	42	Fd	60.39N	116.08W
Enterprise [Or.-U.S.]	46	Gd	45.25N	117.17W
Entinas, Punta-	13	Jh	36.41N	2.46W
Entrada, Punta-	47	Ab	30.22N	115.59W
Entraygues-sur-Truyère	11	Ij	44.39N	2.34 E
Entrecasteaux, Récifs d'-	57	Hf	18.20S	163.00 E
Entrepeñas, Embalse de-	13	Jd	40.34N	2.42W
Entre Rios	56	Id	32.00S	59.00W
Entre Rios	54	Fh	21.32S	64.12W
Entre Rios de Minas	55	Je	20.41S	44.04W
Entrevaux	11	Mk	43.57N	6.49 E
Entroncamento	13	De	39.28N	8.28W
Enugu	31	Hh	6.26N	7.29 E
Enugu Ezike	34	Gd	6.59N	7.27 E
Envermeu	12	De	49.54N	1.16 E
Envigado	54	Cb	6.08N	75.39W
Envira	54	De	7.18S	70.13W
Enyamba	36	Dc	3.40S	24.58 E
Enyélé	36	Cb	2.49N	18.06 E
Enz	10	Fh	49.00N	9.10 E
Enza	14	Ef	44.54N	10.31 E
Enzan	28	Og	34.52N	138.44 E
Enzgau	12	Kf	48.48N	8.37 E
Eo	13	Ea	43.28N	7.03W
Eochaill/Youghal	9	Fj	51.57N	7.50W
Eolie o Lipari, Isole-=Lipari Islands (EN)	5	Hh	38.35N	14.55 E
Epanomí	15	Fi	40.26N	22.56 E
Epazote, Cerro-	47	Cd	24.35N	105.07W
Epe [Neth.]	12	Hb	52.21N	5.59 E
Epe [Nig.]	34	Fd	6.35N	3.59 E
Epéna	36	Cb	1.22N	17.29 E
Épernay	11	Je	49.03N	3.57 E
Epe-Vaassen	12	Hb	52.17N	5.58 E
Ephesus (EN)=Efes	15	Kl	37.55N	27.20 E
Ephraim	46	Jg	39.22N	111.35W
Ephrata	46	Fc	47.19N	119.33W
Epi, Ile-	57	Hf	16.43S	168.15 E
Epidamnus	15	Ch	41.19N	19.26 E
Epidaurus (EN) = Epídhavros	15	Gl	37.38N	23.09 E
Epídhavros = Epidaurus (EN)	15	Gl	37.38N	23.09 E
Epila	13	Kc	41.36N	1.17W
Épinal	11	Mf	48.11N	6.27 E
Epirus (EN)=Ipiros	5	Ih	39.30N	20.40 E
Epirus (EN)=Ipiros	15	Dj	39.30N	20.40 E
Episkopi	24	Ee	34.40N	32.54 E
Epping	12	Cc	51.42N	0.07 E
Eppingen	12	Ke	49.08N	8.54 E
Epsom	9	Mj	51.20N	0.16W
Epte	11	He	49.04N	1.31 E
Epukiro	37	Bd	21.41S	19.08 E
Epukiro	37	Bd	21.28S	19.59 E
Epulu	36	Eb	1.15N	28.21 E
Eqlīd	23	Hc	30.55N	52.39 E
Équateur=Equator (EN)	36	Eb	1.00N	20.00 E
Equator (EN)=Équateur	36	Eb	1.00N	20.00 E
Equatorial Guinea (EN)=Guinea Ecuatorial	1	Hh	2.00N	9.00 E
Equinox Mountain	44	Kd	43.15N	73.10W
Era [It.]	14	Eg	43.40N	10.38 E
Era [Sud.]	35	Dd	5.30N	29.50 E
Eraclea	14	Kj	40.15N	16.40 E
Eraclea Minoa	14	Hm	37.25N	13.18 E
Eradaka	63b	Dc	17.39S	168.08 E
Eräjärvi	8	Kc	61.35N	24.34 E
Eratiní	15	Fk	38.22N	22.14 E
Erbaa	24	Gb	40.42N	36.36 E
Erbach	10	Eg	49.39N	9.00 E
Erbeskopf	10	Dg	49.44N	7.05 E
Erbīl	24	Je	36.10N	44.00 E
Erbīl	22	Gf	36.11N	44.01 E
Ercek	24	Jc	38.39N	43.36 E
Erçek Gölü	24	Jc	38.39N	43.32 E
Erciş	24	Jc	39.00N	43.19 E
Erciyas Daği	21	Ff	38.32N	35.28 E
Ercolano	14	Ij	40.48N	14.21 E
Ercsi	10	Oi	47.15N	18.54 E
Érd	10	Oi	47.22N	18.56 E
Erdaobaihe	27	Mc	42.28N	128.05 E
Erdao Jiang	28	Ic	42.35N	127.10 E
Erdek	24	Bb	40.24N	27.48 E
Erdek Körfezi	24	Bb	40.25N	27.45 E
Erdemli	24	Fd	36.37N	34.18 E
Erdene-Cagan	27	Kb	45.55N	115.30 E
Erdene-Dalaj	27	Hb	46.02N	104.55 E
Erdene-Mandal	27	Hb	48.30N	101.21 E
Erdi	30	Jg	19.05N	22.40 E
Erdi Ma	35	Cb	18.35N	23.30 E
Erding	10	Hh	48.18N	11.56 E
Erdinger Moos	10	Hh	48.20N	11.50 E
Erdre	11	Eg	47.13N	1.32W
Erebus, Mount-	66	Kf	77.32S	167.09 E
Erechim	56	Jc	27.38S	52.17W
Ereğli [Tur.]	23	Db	37.31N	34.04 E
Ereğli [Tur.]	23	Da	41.17N	31.25 E
Erei, Monti-	14	Im	37.35N	14.20 E
Ereke	26	Hg	4.45S	123.10 E
Eren	24	Dd	37.25N	30.05 E
Erenhot	22	Ne	43.35N	112.00 E
Erepecu, Lago do-	54	Gd	1.20S	56.35W
Eresma	13	Hc	41.26N	4.45W
Erétria	15	Gk	38.25N	23.48 E
Erfelek	24	Fb	41.55N	34.57 E
Erfengshan	28	Ag	35.50N	111.47 E
Erfoud	32	Gc	31.26N	4.14W
Erft	10	Ce	51.11N	6.44 E
Erftstadt	12	Id	50.48N	6.49 E
Erfurt	6	He	50.59N	11.02 E
Ergani	24	Hc	38.17N	39.46 E
Ergene	24	Bb	41.01N	26.22 E
Erges	13	Ee	39.40N	7.01W
Ergig, Bahr-	35	Bc	11.22N	15.24 E
Ērgļi/Ergli	7	Fh	56.55N	25.41 E
Ergli/Ērgļi	7	Fh	56.55N	25.41 E
Ergun He	21	Od	53.20N	121.28 E
Ergun Youqi (Labudalin)	27	La	50.16N	120.09 E
Ergun Zuoqi (Genhe)	22	Od	50.47N	121.32 E
Er Hai	27	Hf	25.45N	100.10 E
Eria	13	Gb	42.03N	5.44W
Eriba	35	Fb	16.37N	36.04 E
Eriboll, Loch-	9	Ic	58.30N	4.40W
Eric	42	Kf	51.52N	65.45W
Erice	14	Gl	38.02N	12.35 E
Ericeira	13	Cf	38.59N	9.25W
Erichsen Lake	42	Jb	70.38N	80.20W
Ericht, Loch-	9	Ie	56.50N	4.25W
Erick	45	Gi	35.13N	99.52W
Eridu	24	Lg	36.00N	44.00 E
Erie	39	Ke	42.08N	80.04W
Erie, Lake-	38	Ke	42.15N	81.00W
'Erigābo	35	Hc	10.37N	47.24 E
Erîgât	30	Gg	19.40N	4.50W
Erikoússa	15	Cj	39.53N	19.35 E
Eriksdale	45	Ga	50.52N	98.06W
Eriksenstretet	41	Oc	79.00N	26.00 E
Erikub Atoll	57	Id	9.08N	170.02 E
Erímanthos Óros	15	El	37.58N	21.48 E
Erimo-Misaki	27	Pc	41.55N	143.15 E
Eriskay	9	Fd	57.04N	7.13W
Eritrea	30	Kg	15.00N	40.00 E
Eritrea	35	Fb	15.00N	39.00 E
Eritrea	35	Fb	15.00N	40.00 E
Erjas	13	Ee	39.40N	7.01W
Erkelenz	12	Ic	51.05N	6.19 E
Erken	8	He	59.50N	18.35 E
Erkowit	35	Fb	18.46N	37.07 E
Erlangdian → Dawu	28	Ci	31.33N	114.07 E
Erlangen	10	Hg	49.36N	11.01 E
Erlang Shan	27	Hf	29.58N	102.20 E
Erlauf	14	Jb	48.12N	15.11 E
Erldunda	59	Ge	25.14S	133.12 E
Erlenbach	12	Ke	49.07N	8.11 E
Erlong Shan	27	Mc	43.30N	128.44 E
Ermelo [Neth.]	12	Hb	52.19N	5.37 E
Ermelo [S.Afr.]	37	De	26.34S	29.58 E
Ermenek	24	Ed	36.38N	32.54 E
Ermenistan=Armenia (EN)	23	Fb	39.10N	43.00 E
Ermenistan=Armenia (EN)	21	Gf	39.10N	43.00 E
Ermenonville	12	Ee	49.08N	2.42 E
Ermesinde	13	Dc	41.13N	8.33W
Ermoúpolis	15	Hl	37.27N	24.56 E
Erndtebrück	12	Kd	50.59N	8.16 E
Erne/An Éirne	9	Eg	54.30N	8.15W
Ernée	11	Ff	48.18N	0.56W
Ernest Legouvé Reef	57	Lh	35.12S	150.35W
Ernici, Monti-	14	Hi	41.50N	13.20 E
Erode	25	Ff	11.21N	77.44 E
Eromanga	59	Ie	26.40S	143.16 E
Erongoberg	37	Bd	21.40S	15.40 E
Erpengdianzi	28	Hd	41.12N	125.29 E
Errego	37	Fc	16.02S	37.10 E
Errigal/An Ea agail	9	Ef	55.02N	8.07W
Erris Head/Ceann Iorrais	5	Fe	54.19N	10.00W
Erromango, Ile-	57	Hf	18.48S	169.05 E
Erseka	15	Di	40.20N	20.41 E
Erstein	11	Nf	48.26N	7.40 E
Ertai	27	Fb	46.02N	90.10 E
Ertil	19	Ee	51.50N	40.51 E
Ertix He	21	Ke	47.52N	84.16 E
Erts	37	De	25.08S	29.55 E
Ertvågøy	8	Ca	63.15N	8.25 E
Eruh	24	Jd	37.46N	42.15 E
Ervânia	55	Ee	21.43S	55.32W
Erve	11	Fg	47.50N	0.20W
Ervy-le-Châtel	11	Jf	48.02N	3.55 E
Erwin	44	Fg	36.09N	82.25W
Erwitte	12	Kc	51.37N	8.21 E
Eryuan	27	Gf	26.09N	99.56 E
Erzeni	15	Ch	41.26N	19.27 E
Erzgebirge=Ore Mountains (EN)	5	He	50.30N	13.15 E
Erzin	20	Ef	50.17N	95.10 E
Erzincan	23	Eb	39.44N	39.29 E
Erzurum	22	Gf	39.55N	41.17 E
Esan-Misaki	28	Pd	41.48N	141.12 E
Esashi [Jap.]	28	Pd	41.52N	140.07 E
Esashi [Jap.]	28	Qb	44.56N	142.35 E
Esashi [Jap.]	28	Pe	39.12N	141.09 E
Esbjerg	6	Gd	55.28N	8.27 E
Esbo/Espoo	7	Ff	60.13N	24.40 E
Escalante	46	Jh	37.47N	111.36W
Escalante Desert	46	Ih	37.50N	113.30W
Escalante River	46	Jh	37.17N	110.53W
Escalaplano	14	Dk	39.37N	9.21 E
Escalón	47	Dc	26.45N	104.20W
Escalona	13	Hd	40.10N	4.24W
Escanaba	39	Ke	45.45N	87.04W
Escanaba River	44	Dc	45.47N	87.04W
Escandón, Puerto de-	13	Ld	40.17N	1.00W
Escandorgue	11	Jk	43.46N	3.14 E
Escarpada Point	21	Oh	18.31N	122.13 E
Escarpé, Cap-	63b		20.41S	167.13 E
Escatrón	13	Lc	41.17N	0.19W
Escaut=Schelde (EN)	11	Kc	51.22N	4.15 E
Esch an der Alzette/Esch-sur-Alzette	11	Le	49.30N	5.59 E
Eschkopf	12	Je	49.19N	7.51 E
Esch-sur-Alzette/Esch an der Alzette	11	Le	49.30N	5.59 E
Eschwege	10	Ge	51.11N	10.04 E
Eschweiler	10	Cf	50.49N	6.17 E
Escocesa, Bahía-	49	Md	19.25N	69.45W
Escondida, Punta-	48	Kj	15.49N	97.03W
Escondido	46	Gj	33.07N	117.05W
Escondido, Río-	49	Fg	12.04N	83.45W
Escravos	34	Gd	5.36N	5.11 E
Escudo, Puerto del-	13	Ia	43.05N	3.50W
Escudo de Veraguas, Isla-	49	Gi	9.06N	81.33W
Escuintla	49	Bf	14.10N	91.00W
Escuintla [Guat.]	47	Ff	14.18N	90.47W
Escuintla [Mex.]	48	Mj	15.20N	92.38W
Escuro, Rio- [Braz.]	55	Ic	17.31S	46.39W
Escuro, Rio- [Braz.]	55	Ha	12.50S	49.28W
Ese	36	Eb	4.04N	26.40 E
Ese-Hajja	20	Ic	67.35N	134.55 E
Eséka	34	He	3.39N	10.46 E
Eşen	24	Cd	36.27N	29.16 E
Esendere	24	Kd	37.46N	44.40 E
Esera	13	Mb	42.06N	0.15 E
Esfahān	23	Hc	32.50N	51.50 E
Eşfahān=Isfahan (EN)	22	Hf	32.40N	51.38 E
Esfandārān	24	Og	31.52N	52.32 E
Esfarāyen, Reshteh-ye-	24	Qd	36.46N	57.10 E
Esgueva	13	Hc	41.40N	4.43W

Index Symbols

- Independent Nation
- State, Region
- District, County
- Municipality
- Colony, Dependency
- Continent
- Physical Region
- Historical or Cultural Region
- Mount, Mountain
- Volcano
- Hill
- Mountains, Mountain Range
- Hills, Escarpment
- Plateau, Upland
- Pass, Gap
- Plain, Lowland
- Delta
- Salt Flat
- Valley, Canyon
- Crater, Cave
- Karst Features
- Depression
- Polder
- Desert, Dunes
- Forest, Woods
- Heath, Steppe
- Oasis
- Cape, Point
- Coast, Beach
- Cliff
- Peninsula
- Isthmus
- Sandbank
- Island
- Atoll
- Rock, Reef
- Islands, Archipelago
- Rocks, Reefs
- Coral Reef
- Well, Spring
- Geyser
- River, Stream
- Waterfall Rapids
- River Mouth, Estuary
- Lake
- Salt Lake
- Intermittent Lake
- Reservoir
- Swamp, Pond
- Canal
- Glacier
- Ice Shelf, Pack Ice
- Ocean
- Sea
- Gulf, Bay
- Strait, Fjord
- Lagoon
- Bank
- Seamount
- Tablemount
- Ridge
- Shelf
- Basin
- Escarpment, Sea Scarp
- Fracture
- Trench, Abyss
- National Park, Reserve
- Point of Interest
- Recreation Site
- Cave, Cavern
- Historic Site
- Ruins
- Wall, Walls
- Church, Abbey
- Temple
- Scientific Station
- Airport
- Port
- Lighthouse
- Mine
- Tunnel
- Dam, Bridge

Eshowe 37 Ee 28.50S 31.29 E
Eshetehärd 24 Ne 35.44N 50.23 E
Esigodini 37 Dd 20.18S 28.56 E
Esino 14 Hg 43.39N 13.22 E
Esk 9 Jg 54.58N 3.04W
Eskifjördur 7a Cb 65.04N 14.01W
Eskilstuna 7 Dg 59.22N 16.30 E
Eskimo Point 39 Jc 61.07N 94.03W
Eskişehir 22 Ff 39.46N 30.32 E
Esla 13 Fc 41.29N 6.03W
Eslāmābād 23 Gc 34.11N 46.35 E
Eşler Daği 15 Ml 37.24N 29.43 E
Eslohe (Sauerland) 12 Kc 51.15N 8.10 E
Eslöv 7 Ci 55.50N 13.20 E
Eşme 24 Cc 38.24N 28.59 E
Esmeralda [Braz.] 55 Gi 28.03S 51.12W
Esmeralda [Cuba] 49 Hc 21.51N 78.07W
Esmeralda, Isla- 56 Eg 48.57S 75.25W
Esmeralda Bank (EN) 65b Ab 14.57N 145.15 E
Esmeraldas 53 Ie 0.59N 79.42W
Esnagami Lake 45 Ma 50.21N 86.48W
Esneux 12 Hd 50.32N 5.34 E
Espada, Punta- 49 Lg 12.05N 71.07W
Espagnol Point 51n Ba 13.22N 61.09W
Espalion 11 Ij 44.31N 2.46 E
Espalmador, Isla- 13 Nf 38.47N 1.26 E
España=Spain (EN) [1] 6 Fg 40.00N 4.00W
Espanola [N.M.-U.S.] 45 Ch 36.06N 106.02W
Espanola [Ont.-Can.] 44 Gb 46.15N 81.46W
Española, Isla- 54a Bb 1.25S 89.42W
Espardell, Isla- 13 Nf 38.47N 1.27 E
Esparta 49 Ei 9.59N 84.40W
Espeland 8 Ad 60.23N 5.28 E
Espelkamp 10 Ed 52.25N 8.37 E
Esperance 58 Dh 33.51S 121.53 E
Esperance, Cape- 63a Dc 9.15S 159.43 E
Esperance Bay 59 Ef 33.50S 121.55 E
Esperance Harbour 51k Ba 14.04N 60.55W
Esperancita 55 Bc 16.55S 60.06W
Esperantina 54 Jd 3.54S 42.14W
Esperanza 66 Re 63.26S 57.00W
Esperanza [Arg.] 56 Hd 31.27S 60.56W
Esperanza [Mex.] 48 Ed 27.35N 109.56W
Esperanza [P.R.] 51a Cb 18.06N 65.29W
Esperanza, Sierra la- 49 Ef 15.40N 85.45W
Espevær 7 Ag 59.36N 5.10 E
Espichel, Cabo- 13 Cf 38.25N 9.13W
Espiel 13 Gf 38.12N 5.01W
Espigão Serra do- 55 Gh 26.55S 50.25W
Espinal [Bol.] 55 Cc 17.13S 58.43W
Espinal [Col.] 54 Dc 4.10N 74.54W
Espinazo del Diablo, Sierra- 48 Ff 24.00N 106.00W
Espinhaço, Serra do- 52 Lg 17.30S 43.30W
Espinho 13 Dc 41.01N 8.38W
Espinilho, Serra do- 55 Ei 28.30S 55.06W
Espinillo 55 Cg 24.58S 58.34W
Espino 50 Dh 8.34N 66.01W
Espinosa 54 Jf 14.56S 42.50W
Espinouse 11 Ik 43.32N 2.46 E
Espirito Santo [2] 54 Jg 20.00S 40.30W
Espiritu Santo, Bahia del- 48 Ph 19.20N 87.35W
Espiritu Santo, Isla- 48 De 24.30N 110.22W
Espita 48 Og 21.01N 88.19W
Esplanada 54 Kf 11.47S 37.57W
Espoo/Esbo 7 Ff 60.13N 24.40 E
Espoo-Tapiola 8 Kd 60.11N 24.49 E
Esposende 13 Dc 41.32N 8.47W
Espumoso 55 Fi 28.44S 52.51W
Espuña, Sierra de- 13 Kg 37.52N 1.34W
Espungabera 37 Ed 20.28S 32.46 E
Esquel 53 Ij 42.55S 71.20W
Esquina 56 Id 30.01S 59.32W
Esquinapa de Hidalgo 47 Cd 22.51N 105.48W
Esquipular 49 Cf 14.34N 89.21W
Essandsjøen 8 Da 63.05N 12.00 E
Essaouira 31 Ge 31.31N 9.46W
Essaouira [3] 32 Fc 31.04N 9.03W
Essen [Bel.] 12 Gc 51.28N 4.28 E
Essen [Ger.] 6 Ge 51.27N 7.01 E
Essen (Oldenburg) 12 Jb 52.42N 7.55 E
Essendon, Mount- 59 Ed 24.59S 120.28 E
Essequibo River 52 Ke 6.50N 58.30W
Essex 46 Hi 34.42N 115.12W
Essex 9 Nj 51.50N 0.30 E
Essex [3] 9 Mj 51.50N 0.35W
Essex Mountain 46 Ke 42.02N 109.13W
Esslingen am Neckar 10 Fh 48.45N 9.18 E
Esso 20 Ke 55.55N 158.40 E
Essonne 11 If 48.37N 2.29 E
Essonne [3] 11 If 48.36N 2.20 E
Est [Cam.] [3] 34 He 4.00N 14.00 E
Est [U.V.] [3] 34 Fc 12.00N 1.00 E
Est, Canal de l'- 11 Lf 48.45N 5.35 E
Est, Cap- 37 Ic 15.16S 50.29 E
Est, Ile de l'- 30 Mm 46.15S 52.05 E
Est, Pointe de l'- 42 Lg 49.08N 61.41W
Estaca de Bares, Punta de la- 5 Fg 43.46N 7.42W
Estados, Isla de los-=Staten Island (EN) 52 Jk 54.47S 64.15W
Estados Unidos Mexicanos [1] 39 Ig 23.00N 102.00W
Eşţahbān 24 Ph 29.08N 54.04 E
Estaimpuis 12 Fd 50.42N 3.15 E
Estância 54 Kf 11.16S 37.26W
Estancias, Sierra de las- 13 Jg 37.35N 2.20W
Estanislao del Campo 55 Bg 25.03S 60.06W
Estarreja 13 Dd 40.45N 8.34W
Estats, Pica d'- 11 Hn 42.40N 1.24 E
Estats, Pica d'-/Estats, Pico d'- 11 Hn 42.40N 1.24 E
Estats, Pic d'- 11 Hn 42.40N 1.24 E
Estats, Pico d'- 11 Hn 42.40N 1.24 E
Estats, Pico d'-/Estats, Pica d'- 11 Hn 42.40N 1.24 E
Estcourt 37 De 29.01S 29.52 E
Este 14 Fe 45.14N 11.39 E
Este, Punta- 51a Cb 18.08N 65.16W
Este, Punta del- 56 Jd 34.59S 54.57W
Esteban Rams 55 Bi 29.47S 61.29W
Esteli 47 Gf 13.05N 86.23W
Esteli [3] 49 Dg 13.10N 86.20W
Estella 13 Jb 42.40N 2.02W
Estepa 13 Hg 37.18N 4.54W
Estepona 13 Gh 36.26N 5.08W
Estérel 11 Mk 43.30N 6.50 E
Esternay 12 Ff 48.44N 3.34 E
Esterri d'Aneu/Esterri de Aneu 13 Nb 42.38N 1.08 E
Esterri de Aneu/Esterri d'Aneu 13 Nb 42.38N 1.08 E
Esterwegen 12 Jb 52.59N 7.37 E
Estes Park 45 Df 40.23N 105.31W
Este Sudeste, Cayos del- 47 Hf 12.26N 81.27W
Estevan 42 Hg 49.07N 103.05W
Estherville 45 Ie 43.24N 94.50W
Estissac 11 Jf 48.16N 3.49 E
Eston 46 Ka 51.10N 108.46W
Estonia (EN) 5 Id 59.00N 26.00 E
Estonian SSR (EN)=Eesti NSV [2] 19 Cd 59.00N 26.00 E
Estonskaja Sovetskaja Socialističeskaja Respublika [2] 19 Cd 59.00N 26.00 E
Estonskaja SSR/Eesti Nõukogude Socialistlik Vabariik [2] 19 Cd 59.00N 26.00 E
Estoril 13 Cf 38.42N 9.24W
Estrées-Saint-Denis 12 Ee 49.26N 2.39 E
Estreito 55 Gj 31.50S 51.44W
Estreito, Represa do- 55 Ie 20.15S 47.09W
Estrêla [Braz.] 55 Gi 29.29S 51.58W
Estrêla [Braz.] 55 Gj 31.15S 21.45W
Estrela, Arroyo- 55 Df 22.05S 56.25W
Estrela, Serra da- 55 Fc 16.27S 53.24W
Estrela, Serra da- 5 Fg 40.20N 7.38W
Estrêla do Sul 55 Id 18.21S 47.49W
Estrella 13 If 38.28N 3.35W
Estrella, Punta- 48 Bb 30.55N 114.40W
Estrema, Serra da- 55 Jc 16.50S 45.07W
Estremadura 13 Ce 39.15N 9.10W
Estremoz 13 Ef 38.51N 7.35W
Estrondo, Serra do- 54 Ie 9.00S 48.45W
Estry 12 Bf 48.54N 0.44W
Estuaire [3] 36 Ab 0.10N 10.00 E
Esztergom 10 Oi 47.48N 18.45 E
Etah 41 Ec 78.19N 72.38W
Étain 12 He 49.13N 5.38 E
Etajima 29 Cd 34.15N 132.29 E
Étalle 12 He 49.41N 5.36 E
Étampes 11 If 48.26N 2.09 E
Étaples 11 Hd 50.31N 1.39 E
Etāwah 25 Fc 26.46N 79.02 E
Ethe, Virton- 12 He 49.35N 5.35 E
Ethel Reefs 63d Ab 16.56S 177.13 E
Ethiopia (EN)=Ityopya [1] 31 Kh 9.00N 39.00 E
Ethiopian Plateau (EN) 30 Kg 10.00N 38.10 E
Etive, Loch- 9 He 56.35N 5.15W
Etna 8 Dd 60.50N 10.03 E
Etna 5 Hh 37.50N 14.55 E
Etne 8 Ae 59.40N 5.56 E
Etoile Cay 37b Bb 5.53S 53.01 E
Etolin Island 40 Me 56.08N 132.26W
Etolin Strait 40 Fd 60.20N 165.15W
Etomo-Misaki 29a Bb 42.20N 140.55 E
Etorofu Tō/Iturup, Ostrov- 21 Qe 44.54N 147.30 E
Etosha Pan 30 Ij 18.50S 16.20 E
Etoumbi 36 Bb 0.01N 14.57 E
Etrépagny 12 De 49.18N 1.37 E
Étretat 11 Ge 49.42N 0.12 E
Etropole 15 Gg 42.50N 24.00 E
Etruria 56 Hd 32.56S 63.15W
Etsch/Adige 5 Hf 45.10N 12.20 E
Ettelbrüch/Ettelbruck 12 Ie 49.51N 6.07 E
Ettelbruck/Ettelbrüch 12 Ie 49.51N 6.07 E
Etten-Leur 12 Gc 51.35N 4.39 E
Ettersberg 10 He 51.03N 11.15 E
Ettlingen 12 Kf 48.57N 8.24 E
Etzna Tixmucuy •48 Nh 19.35N 90.13W
Eu 11 Hd 50.03N 1.25 E
'Eua Iki 65b Bc 21.07S 174.59W
Eua Island 61 Gd 21.22S 174.56W
Euboea (EN)=Évvoia 5 Ih 38.30N 24.00 E
Eucla 58 Dh 31.43S 128.52 E
Euclid 44 Ge 41.34N 81.33W
Euclides da Cunha 54 Kf 10.31S 39.01W
Eucumbene, Lake- 59 Jg 36.05S 148.45 E
Eudora 45 Kj 33.07N 91.16W
Eufaula 45 Ij 31.54N 85.09W
Eufaula Lake 45 Ii 35.17N 95.31W
Euganei, Colli- 14 Fe 45.19N 11.40 E
Eugene 39 Ge 44.02N 123.05W
Eugenia, Punta- 38 Hg 27.50N 115.03W
Eugênio Penzo 55 Ef 22.13S 55.53W
Eugmo 7 Fe 63.49N 22.45 E
Eume 13 Da 43.25N 8.08W
Eunice [La.-U.S.] 45 Jk 30.30N 92.26W
Eunice [N.M.-U.S.] 45 Ej 32.26N 103.09W
Eupen 11 Md 50.38N 6.02 E
Euphrates (EN)=Al Furāt 21 Gf 31.00N 47.25 E
Euphrates (EN)=Firat 21 Gf 31.00N 47.25 E
Eupora 45 Lj 33.32N 89.16W
Eura 7 Ff 61.08N 22.08 E
Eurajoki 8 Ic 61.12N 21.44 E
Eurasia Basin (EN) 67 Ge 87.00N 80.00 E
Eure [3] 11 Ge 49.10N 1.00 E
Eure 11 He 49.18N 1.12 E
Eure-et-Loir [3] 11 Hf 48.30N 1.30 E
Eureka [Ca.-U.S.] 39 Ge 40.47N 124.09W
Eureka [Ks.-U.S.] 45 Hh 37.49N 96.17W
Eureka [Mt.-U.S.] 46 Hb 48.53N 115.03W
Eureka [Nv.-U.S.] 43 Dd 39.31N 115.58W
Eureka [N.W.T.-Can.] 42 Ia 80.00N 85.59W
Eureka [S.D.-U.S.] 45 Gd 45.46N 99.38W
Eureka [Ut.-U.S.] 46 Ig 39.57N 112.07W
Eureka Sound 42 Ia 79.00N 87.00W
Europa 30 Lk 22.20S 40.22 E
Europa, Picos de- 5 Fg 43.12N 4.48W
Europe 5 Ie 50.00N 20.00 E
Europoort 11 Jc 51.58N 4.00 E
Euskirchen 10 Cf 50.40N 6.47 E
Eustis 44 Gk 28.51N 81.41W
Eutaw 44 Di 32.50N 87.53W
Eutin 10 Gb 54.08N 10.37 E
Euzkadi/Vascongadas=Basque Provinces (EN) 13 Ja 43.00N 2.30W
Evale 36 Cf 16.33S 15.44 E
Evans, Lac- 42 Jf 50.50N 77.00W
Evans, Mount- 46 Ic 46.05N 113.07W
Evans Strait 42 Jd 63.20N 82.00W
Evanston [Il.-U.S.] 45 Me 42.03N 87.42W
Evanston [Wy.-U.S.] 43 Ec 41.16N 110.58 E
Evansville 39 Kf 37.58N 87.35W
Evant 45 Gk 31.29N 98.09W
Evart 44 Ed 43.54N 85.14W
Evaux-les-Bains 11 Ih 46.10N 2.29 E
Evaz 24 Oi 27.46N 53.59 E
Evciler [Tur.] 15 Jj 39.46N 26.46 E
Evciler [Tur.] 15 Mk 38.03N 29.54 E
Evelyn, Mount- 59 Gb 13.36S 132.53 E
Evenkijski Nac. okrug [3] 20 Ed 65.00N 98.00 E
Evensk 22 Rc 61.57N 159.14 E
Everard, Lake- 59 Hf 31.25S 135.05 E
Everard Ranges 59 Ge 27.05S 132.30 E
Everest, Mount- (EN)=Qomolangma Feng 21 Kg 27.59N 86.56 E
Everest, Mount- (EN)=Saragmatha 21 Kg 27.59N 86.56 E
Everett 43 Cb 47.59N 122.13W
Everett Mountains 42 Kd 62.45N 67.10W
Evergem 12 Fc 51.07N 3.42 E
Evergem-Sleidinge 12 Fc 51.08N 3.41 E
Everglades City 44 Gm 25.52N 81.23W
Evergreen 44 Dj 31.26N 86.57W
Evertsberg 8 Ec 61.08N 13.57 E
Evesham 9 Li 52.05N 1.56W
Evesham, Vale of- 9 Li 52.05N 1.50W
Evian-les-Bains 11 Mh 46.23N 6.35 E
Evijärvi 7 Fe 63.22N 23.29 E
Evinayong 34 He 1.27N 10.34 E
Évinos 15 Ek 38.19N 21.32 E
Evje 7 Bg 58.36N 7.51 E
Évora 6 Fh 38.34N 7.54W
Évora [2] 13 Ef 38.35N 7.50W
Evoron 20 If 51.23N 136.23 E
Evowghlī 24 Kc 38.43N 45.13 E
Evre 11 Eg 47.22N 1.02W
Evrecy 12 Be 49.06N 0.30W
Evreux 11 He 49.01N 1.09 E
Evron 11 Ff 48.10N 0.24W
Évros 15 Ji 40.52N 26.12 E
Evrótas 15 Fm 36.48N 22.41 E
Evry 11 If 48.38N 2.27 E
Évvoia=Euboea (EN) 5 Ih 38.30N 24.00 E
Évvoia, Gulf of- (EN)=Vórios Evvoïkós Kólpos 15 Gk 38.45N 23.10 E
Evzonoi 15 Fh 41.06N 22.33 E
Ewa Beach 65a Cb 21.19N 158.00W
Ewing Seamount (EN) 30 Hk 23.20S 8.45 E
Ewo 36 Bc 0.55S 14.49 E
Excelsior Mountain 46 Fg 38.02N 119.18W
Excelsior Mountains 46 Fg 38.10N 118.30W
Excelsior Springs 45 Ig 39.20N 94.13W
Exe 9 Jk 50.37N 3.25W
Executive Committee Range 66 Nf 76.50S 126.00W
Exeter [Eng.-U.K.] 6 Fe 50.43N 3.31W
Exeter [N.H.-U.S.] 44 Ld 42.59N 70.56W
Exeter Sound 42 Lc 66.10N 62.00W
Exmoor 9 Jj 51.10N 3.45W
Exmouth [Austl.] 59 Cd 21.55S 114.07 E
Exmouth [Eng.-U.K.] 9 Jk 50.37N 3.25W
Exmouth Gulf 57 Cg 22.00S 114.20 E
Exmouth Plateau (EN) 59 Cc 16.00S 114.00 E
Expedition Range 59 Jd 24.30S 149.05 E
Explorer Tablemount (EN) 47 He 16.55N 83.15W
Externsteine 12 Kc 51.52N 8.55 E
Extertal 12 Lb 52.04N 9.07 E
Extertal-Bösingfeld 12 Lb 52.04N 9.07 E
Extremadura 13 Ge 39.00N 6.00W
Exuma Cays 47 Id 24.00N 76.20W
Exuma Cays 49 Ia 24.20N 76.40W
Exuma Sound 47 Id 24.15N 76.00W
Eyasi, Lake- 30 Ki 3.40S 35.05 E
Eydehavn 8 Cf 58.31N 8.53 E
Eye 12 Db 52.19N 1.09 E
Eyemouth 9 Kf 55.52N 2.06W
Eye Peninsula 9 Gc 58.13N 6.05W
Eygurande 11 Ii 45.40N 2.28 E
Eyjafjallajökull 7a Bc 63.38N 19.36W
Eyl 31 Lh 8.00N 49.51 E
Eymoutiers 11 Hi 45.44N 1.44 E
Eynesil 24 Hb 41.03N 39.08 E
Eyrarbakki 7a Bc 63.52N 21.09W
Eyre 59 Ff 32.15S 126.18 E
Eyre, Lake- 57 Eg 28.43S 137.11 E
Eyre Creek 57 Eg 26.40S 139.00 E
Eyre Mountains 62 Cf 45.20S 168.20 E
Eyre North, Lake- 59 He 28.40S 137.10 E
Eyre Peninsula 57 Ef 34.00S 135.45 E
Eyre South, Lake- 59 He 29.30S 137.20 E
Eyrieux 11 Kj 44.48N 4.48 E
Eystrup 12 Lb 52.47N 9.13 E
Eythorne 12 Dc 51.11N 1.17 E
Eyvānakī 24 Oe 35.24N 51.56 E
Ezequiel Ramos Mexia, Embalse- 56 Ge 39.30S 69.00W
Ezere 8 Jh 56.27N 22.17 E
Ežerelis 8 Jj 54.50N 23.38 E
Ezine 24 Bc 39.47N 26.20 E
Eznas/Jieznas 8 Kj 54.34N 24.17 E
Ežva 17 Ef 61.47N 50.40 E

F

Faaa 65e Fc 17.33S 149.36W
Faaite Atoll 61 Lc 16.45S 145.14W
Fabens 45 Ck 31.30N 106.10W
Fåberg 8 Dc 61.10N 10.24 E
Faber Lake 42 Fd 63.55N 117.15W
Fåborg 7 Ci 55.06N 10.15 E
Fabriano 14 Gg 43.20N 12.54 E
Făcăeni 15 Ke 44.34N 27.54 E
Facatativá 54 Dc 4.49N 74.22W
Facha 33 Cd 29.30N 17.20 E
Fachi 31 Ig 18.06N 11.34 E
Facpi Point 64c Bb 13.20N 144.38 E
Fada 31 Jg 17.14N 21.33 E
Fada N'Gourma 31 Hg 12.04N 0.21 E
Faddeja, Zaliv- 20 Fa 76.30N 107.30 E
Faddejevski, Ostrov- 20 Ja 75.30N 144.00 E
Fadiffolu Atoll 25a Ba 5.25N 73.30 E
Fāğilī 24 Mi 26.58N 49.15 E
Faeara, Pointe- 65e Fc 17.52S 149.11W
Faenza 14 Ff 44.17N 11.53 E
Færœ Bank (EN) 9 Ea 60.55N 8.40W
Faeroe-Iceland Ridge (EN) 5 Fc 64.00N 10.00W
Faeroe Islands (EN)=Færøerne/Føroyar 5 Fc 62.00N 7.00W
Faeroe Islands (EN)=Færøerne/Føroyar [5] 6 Fc 62.00N 7.00W
Faeroe Islands (EN)=Föroyar/Færøerne [5] 6 Fc 62.00N 7.00W
Faeroe Islands (EN)=Föroyar/Færøerne 5 Fc 62.00N 7.00W
Færøerne/Føroyar=Faeroe Islands (EN) 5 Fc 62.00N 7.00W
Færøerne/Föroyar=Faeroe Islands (EN) [5] 6 Fc 62.00N 7.00W
Fafa 35 Bd 7.18N 18.16 E
Fafe 13 Dc 41.27N 8.10W
Fafen 30 Lh 5.47N 44.11 E
Faga 34 Fc 13.45N 0.58 E
Fagaloa Bay 65c Ba 13.54S 171.28W
Fagamalo 65c Aa 13.25S 172.21W
Făgăraş 15 Hd 45.51N 24.58 E
Făgărasului, Munţii- 15 Hd 45.35N 25.00 E
Fagataufa Atoll 57 Ng 22.14S 138.45W
Fågelmara 8 Fh 56.15N 15.57 E
Fagerhult 8 Fg 57.09N 15.40 E
Fagernes 7 Bf 60.59N 9.15 E
Fagersta 7 Df 60.00N 15.47 E
Făget 15 Fd 45.51N 22.11 E
Fagita 26 Jg 1.48S 130.25 E
Fagnano, Lago- 56 Gh 54.38S 68.00W
Fagne 11 Kd 50.10N 4.25 E
Faguibine, Lac- 30 Gg 16.45N 3.54W
Fahliān 24 Ng 30.12N 51.28 E
Fahner Höhe 10 Ge 51.10N 10.45 E
Faial 30 Ee 38.34N 28.42W
Fā'id 24 Eg 30.19N 32.19 E
Faioa 64h Bc 13.23S 176.08W
Fairbairn Reservoir 59 Jd 23.40S 148.00 E
Fairbanks 39 Ec 64.51N 147.43W
Fairborn 44 Ef 39.48N 84.03W
Fairbury 43 Hc 40.08N 97.11W
Fairchild 45 Kd 44.36N 90.58W
Fairfield [Al.-U.S.] 44 Di 33.29N 86.55W
Fairfield [Ca.-U.S.] 46 Dg 38.15N 122.01W
Fairfield [Ia.-U.S.] 45 Kf 40.59N 91.57W
Fairfield [Id.-U.S.] 46 He 43.21N 114.48W
Fairfield [Il.-U.S.] 45 Lg 38.23N 88.22W
Fair Isle 9 Lb 59.30N 1.40W
Fairlie 62 Df 44.06S 170.50 E
Fairmont [Mn.-U.S.] 43 Ic 43.39N 94.28W
Fairmont [W.V.-U.S.] 43 Ld 39.28N 80.08W
Fair Ness 42 Kd 63.24N 72.05W
Fairview [Mt.-U.S.] 46 Mc 47.51N 104.03W
Fairview [Ok.-U.S.] 45 Gh 36.16N 98.29W
Fairview Peak 46 De 43.35N 122.39W
Fairweather, Mount- 38 Fd 58.54N 137.32W
Fais Island 57 Fd 9.46N 140.31 E
Faistós 15 Hn 35.03N 24.48 E
Faith 43 Gb 45.02N 102.02W
Faizābād 25 Gc 26.47N 82.08 E
Fajardo 49 Od 18.20N 65.39W
Fajou, Ilet 'a- 51e Ab 16.21N 61.35W
Fakahina Atoll 57 Mf 15.59S 140.08W
Fakaofo Atoll 57 Je 9.22S 171.14W
Fakarava Atoll 57 Mf 16.20S 145.37W
Fakaura 29 Fa 40.38N 139.55 E
Fakel 7 Mh 57.40N 53.05 E
Fakenham 12 Cb 52.50N 0.50 E
Fakfak 26 Jg 2.55S 132.18 E
Fakhr 24 Pg 31.25N 54.01 E
Fakse Bugt 8 Ei 55.10N 12.15 E
Faksefjell 8 Ec 61.20N 12.52 E
Fakse Ladeplads 8 Ei 55.15N 12.08 E
Faku 28 Gc 42.30N 123.24 E
Falaba 34 Cd 9.51N 11.19W
Fala-Beguets 64d Bb 7.21N 151.40 E
Falaise 11 Ff 48.54N 0.12W
Falaise de Tiguidit 34 Gb 16.22N 7.45 E
Falakrón Óros 5 Gh 41.19N 24.00 E
Falalu 4d Ba 7.38N 151.41 E
Falam 25 Id 22.55N 93.41 E
Falas 64d Ba 7.32N 151.46 E
Fălciu 15 Lc 46.18N 28.08 E
Falcón [2] 54 Ea 11.00N 69.50W
Falcon, Cap 13 Li 35.46N 0.48W
Falcon, Presa- 45 Gm 26.37N 99.11W
Falconara Marittima 14 Hg 43.37N 13.24 E
Falcone, Punta- 14 Cj 40.58N 8.12 E
Falcon Reservoir 43 Hf 26.37N 99.11W
Faléa 34 Cc 12.16N 11.15W
Faleallej Pass 64d Bb 7.26N 151.34 E
Falealupo 65c Aa 13.30S 172.48W
Falelima 65c Aa 13.32S 172.41W
Falémé 30 Fg 14.46N 12.14W
Falenki 7 Mg 58.23N 51.36 E
Falerum 8 Gf 58.09N 16.13 E
Faleşty 16 Ef 47.35N 27.44 E
Falevai 65c Ba 13.55S 171.59W
Falfurrias 43 Hf 27.14N 98.09W
Falkenberg 7 Ch 56.54N 12.28 E
Falkensee 10 Jd 52.34N 13.05 E
Falkirk 9 Jf 56.00N 3.48W
Falkland Islands/Malvinas, Islas- [5] 53 Kk 51.45S 59.00W
Falkland Islands/Malvinas, Islas- 52 Kk 51.45S 59.00W
Falkland Plateau (EN) 52 Lk 51.00S 50.00W
Falkland Sound 56 Ih 51.45S 59.25W
Falkonéra 15 Gm 36.50N 23.53 E
Falköping 7 Cg 58.10N 13.31 E
Fallingbostel 10 Fd 52.52N 9.42 E
Fallon [Mt.-U.S.] 46 Mc 46.48N 105.00W
Fallon [Nv.-U.S.] 46 Fg 39.28N 118.47W
Fall River 43 Mc 41.43N 71.08W
Falls City 45 Ic 40.03N 95.36W
Falmouth [Atg.] 51d Bb 17.01N 61.46W
Falmouth [Eng.-U.K.] 9 Hk 50.08N 5.04W
Falmouth [Jam.] 49 Id 18.30N 77.39W
Falmouth [Ky.-U.S.] 44 Ef 38.40N 84.20W
Falmouth Bay 9 Hk 50.10N 5.05W
Falmouth Harbour 51d Bb 17.01N 61.46W
Falo 64d Bb 7.29N 151.53 E
False Bay 30 Il 34.15S 18.35 E
False Pass 40 Gf 54.52N 163.24W
Falset 13 Mc 41.08N 0.49 E
Falso, Cabo- [Dom.Rep.] 49 Le 17.47N 71.41W
Falso, Cabo- [Hond.] 49 Ff 15.12N 83.20W
Falso, Cabo- [Mex.] 47 Cd 22.52N 109.58W
Falso Cabo de Hornos 56 Gi 55.43S 68.05W
Falster 7 Ci 54.50N 12.00 E
Falsterbo 8 Ei 55.24N 12.50 E
Falterona 14 Fg 43.52N 11.42 E
Fälticeni 15 Jb 47.27N 26.18 E
Falun 6 Hc 60.36N 15.38 E
Fama 35 Cb 15.22N 20.34 E
Famagusta (EN)=Gazimağusa 23 Dc 35.07N 33.57 E
Famatina, Nevados de- 56 Gc 29.00S 67.51W
Famenne 11 Ld 50.15N 5.15 E
Fana 34 Dc 12.45N 6.57W
Fanan 64d Bb 7.11N 151.59 E
Fanchang 27 Ke 31.00N 118.11 E
Fancy 51n Ba 13.22N 61.12W
Fandriana 37 Hd 20.13S 47.20 E
Fangak 35 Ed 9.04N 30.53 E
Fangatau Atoll 57 Mf 15.50S 140.52W
Fangcheng 27 Je 33.09N 113.05 E
Fangliao 27 Lg 22.22N 120.25 E
Fangshan 28 Ce 39.43N 115.58 E
Fangxian 27 Je 32.03N 110.41 E
Fangzheng 27 Mb 45.50N 128.49 E
Fangzi 28 Ef 36.36N 119.08 E
Fanjiatun 28 Hc 43.42N 125.05 E
Fanjing Shan 27 If 27.57N 108.50 E
Fannaråken 8 Bc 61.31N 7.55 E
Fanning→Tabuaeran Atoll 57 Ld 3.52N 159.20W
Fano 14 Hg 43.50N 13.01 E
Fanø 8 Ci 55.25N 8.25 E
Fanø Bugt 8 Ci 55.25N 8.10 E
Fanshi 28 Be 39.11N 113.16 E
Fan Si Pan 21 Mg 22.15N 103.50 E
Fan Si Pan 25 Kd 22.18N 103.46 E
Fanuatapu 65c Ba 13.59S 171.20W
Fanxian 28 Cg 35.53N 115.29 E
Faqūs 24 Dg 30.44N 31.48 E
Farab 18 De 39.12N 63.38 E
Faraba 34 Cc 12.52N 11.23W
Faraday 66 Qe 65.15S 64.15W
Faraday Seamounts (EN) 5 Df 49.30N 28.30W
Faradje 36 Eb 3.44N 29.43 E
Faradofay 31 Lk 25.01S 46.59 E
Farafangana 37 Hd 22.48S 47.50 E
Farāfirah, Wāḩāt al-=Farafra Oasis (EN) 30 Jf 27.15N 28.10 E
Farafra Oasis (EN)=Farāfirah, Wāḩāt al- 30 Jf 27.15N 28.10 E
Farāh 21 If 31.29N 61.24 E
Farāh 22 If 32.22N 62.07 E
Farāh [3] 23 Jc 33.00N 62.30 E
Far'ah, Wādī al- 24 Hj 24.02N 38.09 E
Farahābād 24 Od 36.47N 53.06 E
Faranah 34 Cc 10.02N 10.44W
Farasan 23 Ff 16.42N 42.00 E
Farasan, Jazā'ir- 23 Ff 16.48N 41.54 E
Farasān al Kabir 33 Hf 16.42N 42.00 E
Faraulep Atoll 57 Fd 8.36N 144.33 E
Farcău, Vîrful- 15 Hb 47.55N 24.27 E
Farciennes 12 Gd 50.26N 4.33 E
Fardes 13 Jg 37.35N 3.00W
Fare 65e Db 16.42S 151.01W
Fareham 9 Lk 50.51N 1.10W
Farewell, Cape- 57 Ii 40.30S 172.43 E
Farewell Spit 62 Ed 40.30S 172.50 E
Färgelanda 8 Df 58.34N 11.59 E
Fargo 39 Je 46.52N 96.48W
Faribault 45 Jd 44.18N 93.16W
Faribault, Lac- 42 Ke 58.00N 72.00W

Index Symbols

[1] Independent Nation
[2] State, Region
[3] District, County
[4] Municipality
[5] Colony, Dependency
Continent
Physical Region
Historical or Cultural Region
Mount, Mountain
Volcano
Hill
Mountains, Mountain Range
Hills, Escarpment
Plateau, Upland
Pass, Gap
Plain, Lowland
Delta
Salt Flat
Valley, Canyon
Crater, Cave
Karst Features
Depression
Polder
Desert, Dunes
Forest, Woods
Heath, Steppe
Oasis
Cape, Point
Coast, Beach
Cliff
Peninsula
Isthmus
Sandbank
Island
Atoll
Rock, Reef
Islands, Archipelago
Rocks, Reefs
Coral Reef
Well, Spring
Geyser
River, Stream
Waterfall Rapids
River Mouth, Estuary
Lake
Salt Lake
Intermittent Lake
Reservoir
Swamp, Pond
Canal
Glacier
Ice Shelf, Pack Ice
Ocean
Sea
Gulf, Bay
Strait, Fjord
Lagoon
Bank
Seamount
Tablemount
Ridge
Shelf
Basin
Escarpment, Sea Scarp
Fracture
Trench, Abyss
National Park, Reserve
Point of Interest
Recreation Site
Cave, Cavern
Historic Site
Ruins
Wall, Walls
Church, Abbey
Temple
Scientific Station
Airport
Port
Lighthouse
Mine
Tunnel
Dam, Bridge

Farīd, Qārat al- 24 Ch 28.43N 28.21 E
Faridpur 25 Hd 23.36N 89.50 E
Färila 7 Df 61.48N 15.51 E
Farilhões, Ilhas- 13 Ce 39.28N 9.34W
Farim 34 Bc 12.29N 15.13W
Farini d'Olmo 14 Df 44.43N 9.34 E
Fāris 24 Ej 24.37N 32.54 E
Farīš 18 Fd 40.33N 66.52 E
Fāris 35 Ia 20.11N 50.56 E
Faris Seamount (EN) 40 Jf 54.30N 147.15W
Färjestaden 7 Dh 56.39N 16.27 E
Farkadhón 15 Fj 39.36N 22.04 E
Farmahīn 24 Me 34.30N 49.41 E
Farmakonisi 15 Kl 37.18N 27.08 E
Farmerville 45 Jj 32.47N 92.24W
Farmington [Me.-U.S.] 44 Lc 44.40N 70.09W
Farmington [Mo.-U.S.] 45 Kh 37.47N 90.25W
Farmington [N.M.-U.S.] 43 Fd 36.44N 108.12W
Farmville 44 Hg 37.17N 78.25W
Färnäs 8 Fc 61.00N 14.38 E
Farnborough 12 Bc 51.16N 0.44W
Farne Deep 9 Mf 55.30N 0.50W
Farne Islands 9 Lf 55.38N 1.38W
Farnham [Eng.-U.K.] 12 Bc 51.12N 0.48W
Farnham [Que.-Can.] 44 Kc 45.17N 72.59W
Farnham, Mount- 46 Ga 50.29N 116.30W
Fårö 7 Eh 57.55N 19.10 E
Faro 34 Hd 9.21N 12.55 E
Faro [2] 13 Dg 37.12N 8.10W
Faro 6 Fh 37.01N 7.56W
Faro, Punta- 49 Jh 11.07N 74.51W
Faro, Sierra del- 13 Eb 42.37N 7.55W
Faro de Avión 13 Db 42.18N 8.16W
Faro de Chantada 13 Eb 42.37N 7.55W
Farofa, Serra da- 55 Gh 28.00S 50.10W
Farosund 8 Hg 57.55N 19.05 E
Fårösund 7 Eh 57.52N 19.03 E
Farquhar, Cape- 59 Cd 23.35S 113.35 E
Farquhar Group 30 Mj 10.10S 51.10 E
Farrar 9 Id 57.27N 4.35W
Farrāshband 24 Oh 28.53N 52.06 E
Farris 8 Ce 59.05N 10.00 E
Farruch, Cabo- 13 Pe 39.47N 3.21 E
Farrukhābād 25 Fc 27.24N 79.34 E
Fārs 21 Hg 29.00N 53.00 E
Fārs [3] 23 Hd 29.00N 53.00 E
Fārsābād 24 Mc 39.30N 48.05 E
Fársala 15 Fj 39.18N 22.23 E
Farshūț 24 Ei 26.03N 32.09 E
Farsø 8 Ch 56.47N 9.21 E
Farsund 7 Bg 58.05N 6.48 E
Fartak, Ra's- 23 Hf 15.38N 52.15 E
Fartura, Rio- 55 Gc 16.29S 50.33W
Fartura, Serra da- [Braz.] 55 Hf 23.20S 49.25W
Fartura, Serra da- [Braz.] 55 Fh 26.21S 52.52W
Fārūj 24 Rd 37.14N 58.14 E
Farvel, Kap-/Ūmánarssuaq 67 Nb 59.50N 43.50W
Farwell Island 66 Pf 72.49S 91.10W
Fāryāb [3] 23 Jb 36.00N 65.00 E
Fasā 24 Oh 28.56N 53.42 E
Fasano 14 Lj 40.50N 17.22 E
Fastnet Rock 9 Dj 51.24N 9.35W
Fastov 19 De 50.06N 30.01 E
Fataka Island 57 If 11.55S 170.12 E
Fatala 34 Cc 10.13N 14.00W
Fatehpur 25 Ed 28.01N 74.58 E
Fatež 16 Ic 52.06N 35.52 E
Father Lake 44 Ja 49.24N 75.18W
Fatick 34 Bc 14.20N 16.25W
Fátima 13 De 39.37N 8.39W
Fatīrah, Wādī- 24 Ei 26.39N 32.58 E
Fatsa 24 Gb 40.59N 37.24 E
Fatu Hiva, Ile- 57 Nf 10.28S 138.38W
Fatu Hutu, Ile- 57 Ne 9.00S 138.50W
Fatumanini, Passe- 64h Ab 13.14S 176.13W
Fatunda 36 Cc 4.08S 17.13 E
Fauabu 63a Ec 8.34S 160.43 E
Faucigny 11 Mh 46.05N 6.35 E
Faucille, Col de la- 11 Mh 46.22N 6.02 E
Faulkton 45 Gd 45.02N 99.08W
Faulquemont 12 Ie 49.03N 6.36 E
Fauquembergues 12 Ed 50.36N 2.05 E
Făurei 15 Kd 45.04N 27.14 E
Fauro 63a Cb 6.55S 156.07 E
Fauske 7 Dc 67.15N 15.24 E
Fauville-en-Caux 12 Ce 49.39N 0.35 E
Faux-Lap 37 He 25.32S 45.30 E
Fåvang 8 Dc 61.26N 10.13 E
Favara 14 Hm 37.19N 13.39 E
Faversham 12 Cc 51.19N 0.54 E
Favignana 14 Gm 37.55N 12.19 E
Favignana 14 Gm 37.56N 12.20 E
Favorite 12 Kf 48.49N 8.16 E
Fawley 12 Ad 50.49N 1.21W
Fawn 42 Ie 55.22N 88.20W
Fa'w Qiblī 24 Ei 26.07N 32.24 E
Faxaflói 5 Dc 64.24N 23.00W
Faxinal 55 Gf 23.59S 51.22W
Faya-Largeau 31 Ig 17.55N 19.07 E
Fayaoué 63b Ce 20.39S 166.32 E
Fayd 24 Ji 27.07N 42.31 E
Fayette [Al.-U.S.] 44 Di 33.42N 87.50W
Fayette [Oh.-U.S.] 44 Ee 41.41N 84.20W
Fayetteville [Ar.-U.S.] 43 Id 36.04N 94.10W
Fayetteville [N.C.-U.S.] 39 Lf 35.03N 78.54W
Fayetteville [Tn.-U.S.] 44 Dh 35.09N 86.35W
Faylakah, Jazīrat- 24 Mh 29.27N 48.20 E
Faysh Khābūr 24 Jd 37.04N 42.23 E
Fayu Island 57 Gd 8.35N 151.22 E
Fazenda de Cima 55 Db 15.56S 56.37W
Fazenda Nova 55 Gc 16.11S 50.48W
Fāzilka 25 Eb 30.24N 74.02 E
Fazrān 24 Mi 26.13N 49.12 E
Fazzān=Fezzan (EN) 33 Bd 25.30N 14.00 E
Fazzān=Fezzan (EN) 30 If 26.00N 14.00 E
Fdérick 31 Ff 22.39N 12.43W
Feale/An Fhéil 9 Di 52.28N 9.40W
Fear, Cape- 43 Le 33.50N 77.58W
Featherston 62 Fd 41.07S 175.19 E
Feathertop, Mount- 59 Jg 36.54S 147.08 E
Fécamp 11 Ge 49.45N 0.22 E
Fecht 11 Nf 48.11N 7.26 E
Federacion 56 Id 31.00S 57.54W
Federal 56 Id 30.55S 58.45W
Federated States of Micronesia [5] 58 Gd 6.30N 152.00 E
Federovka [Kaz.-U.S.S.R.] 19 Ge 53.38N 62.42 E
Federovka [R.S.F.S.R.] 17 Gj 53.10N 55.10 E
Federsee 10 Fh 48.05N 9.38 E
Fedje 7 Af 60.47N 4.42 E
Fedorovka 16 Qd 51.16N 52.00 E
Fefan 64d Bb 7.21N 151.51 E
Fegen 8 Eg 57.11N 13.09 E
Fegen 8 Eg 57.06N 13.02 E
Fehérgyarmat 10 Si 47.59N 22.31 E
Fehmarn 10 Hb 54.30N 11.10 E
Fehmarnbelt 8 Dj 54.35N 11.15 E
Fehrbellin 10 Id 52.48N 12.46 E
Feicheng 28 Df 36.15N 116.46 E
Feidong (Dianbu) 28 Di 31.53N 117.29 E
Fei Huang He 28 Fg 34.15N 120.17 E
Feijó 54 De 8.09S 70.21W
Feilding 61 Eh 40.12S 175.35 E
Feira 36 Ff 15.37S 30.25 E
Feira de Santana 53 Mg 12.15S 38.57W
Feiran Oasis 24 Eh 28.42N 33.38 E
Feistritz 14 Kc 47.01N 16.08 E
Feixi (Shangpaihe) 28 Di 31.42N 117.09 E
Feixian 28 Dg 35.16N 117.59 E
Feixiang 28 Cf 36.32N 114.47 E
Fejão Prêto ou Furtado, Rio- 55 Dc 17.33S 57.23W
Fejér [2] 10 Oi 47.10N 18.35 E
Fejø 8 Dj 54.55N 11.25 E
Feke 24 Fd 37.53N 35.58 E
Fekete-viz 10 Ok 45.47N 18.13 E
Felanitx 13 Pe 39.28N 3.08 E
Feldbach 14 Jd 46.57N 15.53 E
Feldioara 15 Id 45.49N 25.36 E
Feldkirch 14 Dc 47.14N 9.36 E
Feldkirchen 14 Id 46.43N 14.06 E
Feliciano, Arroyo- 55 Cj 31.06S 59.54W
Felidu Atoll 25a Bb 3.30N 73.30 E
Felipe Carrillo Puerto 47 Ge 19.35N 88.03W
Felix, Cape - 42 Hc 69.55N 97.47W
Felixlândia 55 Jd 18.47S 44.55W
Felixstowe 9 Oj 51.58N 1.20 E
Felletin 11 Ii 45.53N 2.11 E
Feltre 14 Fd 46.01N 11.54 E
Femer Bælt 8 Dj 54.35N 11.15 E
Femø 8 Dj 54.55N 11.35 E
Femund 7 Ce 62.15N 11.50 E
Fena Valley Reservoir 64c Bb 13.20N 144.45 E
Fener Burnu 24 Hb 41.07N 39.25 E
Fénérive 37 Hc 17.22S 49.25 E
Fenerwa 35 Fc 13.05N 39.01 E
Fénétrange 12 Jf 48.51N 7.01 E
Fengcheng [China] 27 Lc 40.28N 124.01 E
Fengcheng [China] 28 Cj 28.11N 115.47 E
Fengdu 27 If 29.58N 107.39 E
Fenghua 28 Fj 29.40N 121.24 E
Fengjie 27 He 31.06N 104.30 E
Fenglingdu 27 Je 34.40N 110.19 E
Fengnan (Xugezhuang) 28 Ee 39.34N 118.05 E
Fengning (Dagezhen) 28 Dd 41.12N 116.39 E
Fengqing 27 Gg 24.41N 99.53 E
Fengqiu 28 Cg 35.02N 114.24 E
Fengrun 28 Ee 39.50N 118.09 E
Fengshui Shan 27 La 52.15N 123.30 E
Fengtai [China] 28 Dh 32.43N 116.43 E
Fengtai [China] 28 De 39.51N 116.17 E
Fengweiba → Zhenkang 27 Gg 23.54N 99.00 E
Fengxian 28 Dg 34.42N 116.35 E
Fengxian (Nanqiao) 28 Fi 30.55N 121.27 E
Fengxiang 27 Ie 34.32N 107.34 E
Fengxiang → Luobei 27 Nb 47.36N 130.58 E
Fengxin 28 Cj 28.42N 115.23 E
Fengyang 28 Dh 32.53N 117.33 E
Fengzhen 27 Jc 40.28N 113.09 E
Fen He [China] 27 Jd 35.36N 110.42 E
Fen He [China] 28 Ae 38.06N 111.52 E
Feni Islands 57 Ge 4.05S 153.42 E
Fennimore 45 Ke 42.59N 90.39W
Fensfjorden 8 Ad 60.50N 4.50 E
Fenshui Guan 27 Kf 27.56N 117.50 E
Fenton 44 Fd 42.48N 83.42W
Fenua Fu 64h Ac 13.23S 176.11W
Fenualoa 63c Bb 10.16S 166.15 E
Fenyang 27 Jd 37.17N 111.45 E
Feodosija 19 Df 45.02N 35.23 E
Fer, Cap de- 32 Ib 37.05N 7.10 E
Fer, Point au- 45 Kl 29.20N 91.21W
Feragen 8 Db 62.30N 11.55 E
Férai 15 Ji 40.54N 26.10 E
Ferdows 23 Ic 34.00N 58.09 E
Fère-Champenoise 11 Jf 48.45N 3.59 E
Fère-en-Tardenois 12 Fe 49.12N 3.31 E
Feren 8 Da 63.34N 11.50 E
Ferentino 14 Hi 41.42N 13.15 E
Ferfer [Eth.] 35 Hd 5.06N 45.09 E
Ferfer [Som.] 35 Hd 5.07N 45.07 E
Fergana 22 Je 40.23N 71.46 E
Fergana 21 Je 40.30N 71.00 E
Ferganskaja Oblast [3] 19 Hg 40.30N 71.20 E
Ferganski Hrebet 19 Hg 41.00N 74.00 E
Fergus Falls 43 Hb 46.17N 96.04W
Ferguson Lake 42 Hc 69.00N 105.00W
Fergusson Island 60 Ei 9.30S 150.40 E
Ferkéssédougou [3] 34 Ed 9.20N 4.55W
Ferkéssédougou 34 Dd 9.36N 5.12W
Ferlo 30 Fg 15.00N 14.00W
Ferlo 30 Fg 15.42N 15.30W
Fermo 14 Hg 43.09N 13.43 E
Fermoselle 13 Fc 41.19N 6.23W
Fermoy/Mainistir Fhear Mai 9 Ei 52.08N 8.16W
Fernandina, Isla- 52 Gf 0.25S 91.30W
Fernandina Beach 44 Gj 30.40N 81.27W
Fernando de Noronha, Ilha- 52 Mf 3.51S 32.25W
Fernando de Noronha, Território de- [2] 54 Ld 3.50S 33.00W
Fernandópolis 56 Kb 20.16S 50.00W
Fernán-Núñez 13 Hg 37.40N 4.43W
Fernelmont 12 Hd 50.35N 5.02 E
Fernie 46 Hb 49.30N 115.03W
Ferrandina 14 Kj 40.29N 16.27 E
Ferrara 14 Ff 44.50N 11.35 E
Ferrat, Cap- 13 Li 35.54N 0.23W
Ferrato, Capo- 14 Dk 39.18N 9.38 E
Ferré 55 Bl 34.08S 61.08W
Ferré, Cap- 51h Bc 14.28N 60.49W
Ferreira do Alentejo 13 Df 38.03N 8.07W
Ferreñafe 54 Ce 6.38S 79.48W
Ferret, Cap- 11 Ej 44.37N 1.15W
Ferriday 45 Kk 31.38N 91.33W
Ferrières 12 Hd 50.24N 5.36 E
Ferro, Capo- 14 Di 41.09N 9.31 E
Ferro, Rio- 55 Ea 12.27S 54.31W
Ferru, Monte- 14 Cj 40.08N 8.36 E
Ferry, Pointe- 51e Ab 16.17N 61.49W
Fertilia 14 Cj 40.36N 8.17 E
Fertő → Neusiedler See 10 Mi 47.50N 16.45 E
Fès 31 Ge 34.02N 4.59W
Fès [3] 32 Gc 34.00N 5.00W
Feshi 36 Cd 6.07S 18.10 E
Fessenden 45 Gc 47.39N 99.38W
Festieux 12 Fe 49.31N 3.45 E
Festus 45 Kg 38.13N 90.24W
Fetești 15 Ke 44.23N 27.50 E
Fethiye 23 Cb 36.37N 29.07 E
Fethiye Körfezi 24 Cd 36.40N 29.00 E
Fetlar 9 Ma 60.37N 0.52W
Fetsund 7 Cg 59.56N 11.10 E
Feuchtwangen 10 Gg 49.10N 10.20 E
Feuilles, Baie aux - 42 Ke 58.55N 69.15W
Feuilles, Rivière aux- 42 Ke 58.46N 70.05W
Feurs 11 Ki 45.45N 4.14 E
Fevik 8 Cf 58.23N 8.42 E
Feyzābād 22 Jf 37.06N 70.34 E
Fezzan (EN)=Fazzān 33 Bd 25.30N 14.00 E
Fezzan (EN)=Fazzān 30 If 26.00N 14.00 E
Fezzane, Emi- 34 Ha 21.42N 14.15 E
Ffestiniog 9 Ji 52.58N 3.55W
Fiambalá 56 Gc 27.41S 67.38W
Fianarantsoa 31 Lk 21.28S 47.05 E
Fianarantsoa [3] 37 Hd 21.30S 47.05 E
Fianga 35 Bd 9.55N 15.09 E
Fiche 35 Fd 9.48N 38.44 E
Fichtelgebirge 5 He 50.00N 12.00 E
Ficksburg 37 De 28.57S 27.50 E
Fidenza 14 Ef 44.52N 10.03 E
Fieni 15 Id 45.08N 25.25 E
Fier 15 Ci 40.43N 19.34 E
Fier 11 Li 45.56N 5.50 E
Fieri 15 Ci 40.43N 19.34 E
Fife [3] 9 Je 56.05N 3.15W
Fife Ness 9 Ke 56.17N 2.36W
Fiffa 34 Dc 11.27N 9.52W
Fifth Cataract (EN)= Khāmis, Ash Shallāl al- 30 Kg 18.23N 33.47 E
Figalo, Cap- 13 Ki 35.35N 1.12W
Figeac 11 Ij 44.36N 2.02 E
Figeholm 8 Gg 57.22N 16.33 E
Figtree 37 Dd 20.22S 28.20 E
Figueira, Baia da- 55 Dc 16.33S 57.25W
Figueira da Foz 13 Dd 40.09N 8.52W
Figueira de Castelo Rodrigo 13 Fd 40.54N 6.58W
Figueras 13 Ob 42.16N 2.58 E
Figueras/Figueres 13 Ob 42.16N 2.58 E
Figueres 13 Ob 42.16N 2.58 E
Figueres/Figueras 13 Ob 42.16N 2.58 E
Figuig [3] 32 Gc 33.00N 2.01W
Figuig 31 Ge 32.06N 1.14W
Fiherenana 37 Gd 23.19S 43.37 E
Fijāj, Shatt al- 32 Ic 33.55N 9.10 E
Fiji [1] 58 If 18.00S 178.00 E
Fiji Islands 57 If 18.00S 178.00 E
Fik 35 Gd 8.08N 42.18 E
Filabres, Sierra de los- 13 Jg 37.15N 2.20W
Filabusi 37 Dd 20.32S 29.16 E
Filadélfia 54 Ie 7.21S 47.30W
Filadelfia [C.R.] 49 Eh 10.26N 85.34W
Filadelfia [It.] 14 Kl 38.47N 16.17 E
Filakara 63b Dc 16.49S 168.24 E
Filákovo 10 Ph 48.16N 19.50 E
Filamana 34 Dc 10.30N 7.57W
Filatova Gora 8 Mg 57.39N 28.21 E
Filchner Ice Shelf 66 Af 79.00S 40.00W
Filey 9 Mg 54.12N 0.17W
Filiași 15 Ge 44.33N 23.31 E
Filiátai 15 Dj 39.36N 20.49 E
Filiatrá 15 El 37.09N 21.35 E
Filicudi 14 Il 38.35N 14.35 E
Filingué 34 Fc 14.21N 3.19 E
Filiouri 15 Ii 40.57N 25.20 E
Filippiás 15 Dj 39.12N 20.53 E
Filippoi 15 Hh 41.02N 24.20 E
Filippoi = Philippi (EN) 15 Hh 41.02N 24.18 E
Filipstad 7 Dg 59.43N 14.10 E
Fillefjell 8 Cc 61.09N 8.15 E
Filliévres 12 Ed 50.19N 2.10 E
Fillmore 46 Ig 38.58N 112.20W
Fils 10 Fh 48.35N 9.29 E
Filtu 35 Gd 5.06N 40.40 E
Fimaina 15 Jl 37.35N 26.26 E
Fimi 30 Ii 3.01S 16.58 E
Fin [Iran] 24 Pi 27.38N 55.55 E
Fin [Iran] 24 Nf 33.57N 51.24 E
Finale Emilia 14 Ff 44.50N 11.17 E
Finale Ligure 14 Cf 44.10N 8.20 E
Findhorn 9 Jd 57.41N 3.32W
Fındıklı 24 Ib 41.17N 41.09 E
Findlay 43 Kc 41.02N 83.40W
Findlay, Mount- 46 Ga 50.04N 116.28W
Findlay Group 42 Ha 77.15N 104.00W
Fineveke 64h Ab 13.19S 176.12W
Fingoé 37 Ec 15.10S 31.53 E
Finike 24 Dd 36.18N 30.09 E
Finistère [3] 11 Cf 48.20N 4.00W
Finisterre, Cabo de- 5 Fg 42.53N 9.16W
Finisterre Range 59 Ja 5.50S 146.05 E
Finke 58 Eg 25.34S 134.35 E
Finke, Mount- 59 Gf 30.55S 134.02 E
Finke River 57 Eg 27.00S 136.10 E
Finland/Suomi [1] 6 Ic 64.00N 26.00 E
Finland, Gulf of- (EN)= Finski Zaliv 5 Ic 60.00N 27.00 E
Finland, Gulf of- (EN)= Soomenlaht 5 Ic 60.00N 27.00 E
Finland, Gulf of- (EN)= Suomenlahti 5 Ic 60.00N 27.00 E
Finlay 42 Fe 55.59N 123.50W
Finlay Mountains 45 Dk 31.30N 105.35W
Finne 10 He 51.13N 11.19 E
Finngrunden 8 Hc 60.59N 18.19 E
Finnigan, Mount- 59 Jc 15.50S 145.20 E
Finniss, Cape- 59 Gf 33.38S 134.51 E
Finnmark 8 Fc 61.40N 14.45 E
Finnmark [3] 7 Fb 69.50N 24.10 E
Finnmarksvidda 5 Ib 69.30N 24.20 E
Finnøy 8 Ae 59.10N 5.50 E
Finnskogen 8 Ed 60.40N 12.40 E
Finnsnes 7 Eb 69.14N 18.02 E
Finnveden 8 Eh 56.50N 13.40 E
Finote Selam 35 Fc 10.42N 37.12 E
Finschhafen 59 Ja 6.35S 147.50 E
Finse 8 Bd 60.36N 7.30 E
Finski Zaliv=Finland, Gulf of- (EN) 5 Ic 60.00N 27.00 E
Finspång 7 Dg 58.43N 15.47 E
Finstadåa 8 Dc 61.47N 11.10 E
Finsteraarhorn 14 Cd 46.32N 8.08 E
Finsterwalde 10 Je 51.38N 13.43 E
Finström 8 Hd 60.16N 19.50 E
Fiora 14 Fh 42.20N 11.34 E
Fiorenzuola d'Arda 14 Df 44.56N 9.55 E
Firat=Euphrates (EN) 21 Gf 31.00N 47.25 E
Firenze = Florence (EN) 6 Hg 43.46N 11.15 E
Firenzuola 14 Ff 44.07N 11.23 E
Firmat 55 Bk 33.27S 61.29W
Firminópolis 55 Gc 16.40S 50.19W
Firminy 11 Ki 45.23N 4.18 E
Fīrozābād 25 Fc 27.09N 78.25 E
Fīrozpur 25 Eb 30.55N 74.36 E
First Cataract (EN)=Aswān, Sadd al- 30 Kf 24.01N 32.52 E
Fīrūzābād 24 Oh 28.50N 52.36 E
Fīrūzābād 24 Pg 31.59N 54.20 E
Fīrūzābād 24 Le 34.09N 46.25 E
Fīrūz Kūk 24 Oe 35.45N 52.47 E
Fischbach 12 Je 49.44N 7.24 E
Fischbacher Alpen 14 Jc 47.25N 15.30 E
Fischland 10 Ib 54.22N 12.25 E
Fish [Nam.] 30 Ik 17.11S 28.08 E
Fish [S.Afr.] 37 Cf 31.14S 20.15 E
Fisher Glacier 66 Ef 73.15S 66.00 E
Fisher Peak 44 Gg 36.33N 80.50W
Fisher Strait 42 Jd 63.00N 84.00W
Fishguard 6 Fe 51.59N 4.59W
Fish River' Canyon 37 Be 27.35S 17.35 E
Fiskárdhon 15 Dk 38.28N 20.35 E
Fiskenaes Bank (EN) 41 Gf 63.18N 52.10W
Fiskenæsset 41 Gf 63.10N 50.45W
Fismes 11 Je 49.18N 3.41 E
Fišt, Gora- 19 Dg 43.57N 39.55 E
Fitchburg 44 Ld 42.35N 71.48W
Fitjar 7 Ag 59.55N 5.20 E
Fito, Mount- 65c Ba 13.55S 171.44W
Fitri, Lac- 35 Bc 12.50N 17.28 E
Fitzcarrald 54 Df 11.49S 71.48W
Fitzgerald [Alta.-Can.] 42 Ge 59.52N 111.40W
Fitzgerald [Ga.-U.S.] 44 Fj 31.43N 83.15W
Fitzroy Crossing 59 Fc 18.11S 125.35 E
Fitzroy River [Austl.] 59 Kc 23.32S 150.52 E
Fitzroy River [Austl.] 57 Df 17.31S 123.35 E
Fitzwilliam Island 44 Gc 45.30N 81.45W
Fiuggi 14 Hi 41.48N 13.13 E
Fiumicino 14 Gi 41.46N 12.14 E
Five Island Harbour 51d Bb 17.06N 61.54W
Fivizzano 14 Ef 44.14N 10.08 E
Fizi 31 Ji 4.18S 28.57 E
Fizuli 16 Eh 39.35N 47.11 E
Fjærlandsfjorden 8 Bc 61.15N 6.40 E
Fjällbacka 8 Df 58.36N 11.17 E
Fjärås 7 Ch 57.26N 12.09 E
Fjerritslev 8 Cg 57.05N 9.16 E
Fjöllum, Jökulsá á- 7a Ca 66.02N 16.27W
Fjugesta 8 Fe 59.10N 14.52 E
Flacq 37a Bb 20.12S 57.43 E
Flade Isblink 41 Kb 81.25N 16.00W
Fladen 8 Dg 57.07N 11.35 E
Fladen 8 Dg 57.10N 11.45 E
Flagler 45 Eg 39.18N 103.04W
Flagstaff 39 Hf 35.12N 111.39W
Flåm 7 Bf 60.50N 7.07 E
Flamborough Head 9 Mg 54.07N 0.04W
Fläming 10 Ie 52.00N 13.00 E
Flaming Gorge Reservoir 46 Kf 41.15N 109.30W
Flamingo 44 Gm 25.09N 80.56W
Flamingo, Teluk- 26 Kh 5.33S 138.00 E
Flanders (EN)=Flandres/Vlaanderen 5 Ge 51.00N 3.20 E
Flanders (EN)=Flandres/Vlaanderen 11 Jc 51.00N 3.20 E
Flanders (EN)=Vlaanderen/Flandres 5 Ge 51.00N 3.20 E
Flanders (EN)=Vlaanderen/Flandres 11 Jc 51.00N 3.20 E
Flanders Plain (EN)= Flandres, Plaine des- 11 Id 50.40N 2.50 E
Flanders Plain (EN)= Vlamse Vlakte 11 Id 50.40N 2.50 E
Flandreau 45 Hd 44.03N 96.36W
Flandres/Vlaanderen= Flanders (EN) 11 Jc 51.00N 3.20 E
Flandres/Vlaanderen= Flanders (EN) 5 Ge 51.00N 3.20 E
Flandres, Plaine des-= Flanders Plain (EN) 11 Id 50.40N 2.50 E
Flannan Isles 9 Fc 58.20N 7.35W
Flåren 8 Fh 57.00N 14.05 E
Flasher 45 Fc 46.27N 101.14W
Fläsjön 7 Dd 64.06N 15.51 E
Flat 40 Hd 62.27N 158.01W
Flatey 7a Ab 65.22N 22.56W
Flateyri 7a Aa 66.03N 23.31W
Flathead Lake 43 Eb 47.52N 114.08W
Flathead Range 46 Ib 48.05N 113.28W
Flathead River 46 Hc 47.22N 114.47W
Flat Point 51b Ab 18.15N 63.05W
Flat River 45 Kh 37.51N 90.31W
Flattery, Cape- 38 Ge 48.23N 124.43W
Flåvatnet 8 Ce 59.20N 8.50 E
Flaxton 45 Eb 48.54N 102.24W
Flaygreen Lake 42 Hf 53.50N 97.20W
Fleckenstein, Château de- 12 Je 49.05N 7.48 E
Fleet 12 Bc 51.17N 0.50W
Fleetwood 9 Jh 53.56N 3.01W
Flekkefjord 7 Bg 58.17N 6.41 E
Flémalle 12 Hd 50.36N 5.29 E
Flemish Bight [Eur.] 11 Dc 51.44N 2.30W
Flemish Bight [U.K.] 9 Pi 52.10N 2.50 E
Flemish Cap (EN) 38 Oe 47.00N 45.00W
Flemsøya 8 Bb 62.40N 6.20 E
Flen 7 Dg 59.04N 16.35 E
Flensborg Fjord 8 Cj 54.50N 9.45 E
Flensburg 6 Ge 54.47N 9.26 E
Flensburger Förde 8 Cj 54.50N 9.45 E
Flers 11 Ff 48.45N 0.34W
Flesberg 8 Ce 59.51N 9.27 E
Fleurance 11 Gk 43.50N 0.40 E
Fleury-sur-Andelle 12 De 49.22N 1.21 E
Fleuve [3] 34 Cb 16.00N 13.50W
Flevoland 11 Lb 52.25N 5.30 E
Flian 8 Ef 58.27N 13.05 E
Flims 14 Dd 46.50N 9.16 E
Flinders Bay 59 Df 34.25S 115.19 E
Flinders Island 57 Fi 40.00S 148.00 E
Flinders Passage 59 Jc 18.50S 149.00 E
Flinders Ranges 57 Eh 31.25S 138.45 E
Flinders Reefs 57 Ff 17.40S 148.30 E
Flinders River 57 Ff 17.36S 140.36 E
Flin Flon 39 Id 54.56N 101.53W
Flint [Mi.-U.S.] 39 Ke 43.01N 83.41W
Flint [Wales-U.K.] 9 Jh 53.15N 3.07W
Flint Hills 45 Hh 37.20N 96.35W
Flint Island 57 Lf 11.26S 151.48W
Flint River 43 Ke 30.52N 84.38W
Flisa 7 Cf 60.37N 12.04 E
Flisa 8 Ed 60.36N 12.01 E
Flisegga 8 Be 59.50N 7.50 E
Flitwick 12 Bb 52.00N 0.29W
Flix 13 Mc 41.14N 0.33 E
Flixecourt 12 Ed 50.01N 2.05 E
Flize 12 Ge 49.42N 4.46 E
Flobecq/Vloesberg 12 Fd 50.44N 3.44 E
Floby 8 Ef 58.08N 13.20 E
Floda [Swe.] 8 Fd 60.26N 14.49 E
Floda [Swe.] 8 Eg 57.48N 12.22 E
Flood Range 66 Nf 76.03S 134.00W
Flora [Il.-U.S.] 45 Lg 38.40N 88.29W
Flora [Nor.] 7 Af 61.36N 5.00 E
Florac 11 Jj 44.19N 3.36 E
Florala 44 Dj 31.00N 86.20W
Florange 12 Ie 49.20N 6.07 E
Florence [Al.-U.S.] 43 Je 34.49N 87.40W
Florence [Ks.-U.S.] 45 Hg 38.15N 96.56W
Florence [Or.-U.S.] 46 Cd 44.01N 124.07W
Florence [S.C.-U.S.] 43 Le 34.12N 79.44W
Florence (EN) = Firenze 6 Hg 43.46N 11.15 E
Florencia [Arg.] 55 Ci 28.02S 59.15W
Florencia [Col.] 53 Ie 1.36N 75.36W
Florencio Sánchez 55 Dk 33.53S 57.24W
Florennes 12 Gd 50.15N 4.37 E
Florentino Ameghino, Embalse- 56 Gf 43.48S 66.25W
Florenville 11 Le 49.42N 5.18 E
Flores [2] 55 Dk 33.35S 56.50W
Flores 30 De 39.26N 31.13W
Flores [Guat.] 49 Ce 16.56N 89.53W
Flores [Guat.] 47 Ge 16.58N 89.50W
Flores, Arroyo de las- 55 Cl 35.36S 59.01W
Flores, Laut-=Flores Sea (EN) 21 Oj 8.00S 121.00 E
Flores, Pulau- 21 Oj 8.30S 121.00 E
Flores Island 46 Bb 49.20N 126.10W
Flores Sea (EN)=Flores, Laut- 21 Oj 8.00S 121.00 E
Floreşty 16 Ff 47.55N 28.18 E
Floriano 53 Lf 6.47S 43.01W
Florianópolis 53 Lh 27.35S 48.34W
Florida 38 Kg 28.00N 82.00W
Florida [Braz.] 55 Ei 29.15S 54.36W
Florida [Cuba] 47 Id 21.32N 78.14W
Florida [U.S.] [2] 43 Kf 28.00N 82.00W
Florida [Ur.] [2] 55 Ek 33.50S 55.55W
Florida [Ur.] 56 Id 34.06S 56.13W
Florida, Estrecho de-= Florida, Straits of- (EN) 38 Kg 24.00N 81.00W
Florida, Straits of- 38 Kg 24.00N 81.00W
Florida, Straits of- (EN)= Florida, Estrecho de- 38 Kg 24.00N 81.00W
Florida Bay 44 Gm 25.00N 80.45W
Floridablanca 54 Db 7.04N 73.06W

Index Symbols

[1] Independent Nation
[2] State, Region
[3] District, County
[4] Municipality
[5] Colony, Dependency
Continent
Physical Region
Historical or Cultural Region
Mount, Mountain
Volcano
Hill
Mountains, Mountain Range
Hills, Escarpment
Plateau, Upland
Pass, Gap
Plain, Lowland
Delta
Salt Flat
Valley, Canyon
Crater, Cave
Karst Features
Depression
Polder
Desert, Dunes
Forest, Woods
Heath, Steppe
Oasis
Cape, Point
Coast, Beach
Cliff
Peninsula
Isthmus
Sandbank
Island
Atoll
Rock, Reef
Islands, Archipelago
Rocks, Reefs
Coral Reef
Well, Spring
Geyser
River, Stream
Waterfall Rapids
River Mouth, Estuary
Lake
Salt Lake
Intermittent Lake
Reservoir
Swamp, Pond
Canal
Glacier
Ice Shelf, Pack Ice
Ocean
Sea
Gulf, Bay
Strait, Fjord
Lagoon
Bank
Seamount
Tablemount
Ridge
Shelf
Basin
Escarpment, Sea Scarp
Fracture
Trench, Abyss
National Park, Reserve
Point of Interest
Recreation Site
Cave, Cavern
Historic Site
Ruins
Wall, Walls
Church, Abbey
Temple
Scientific Station
Airport
Port
Lighthouse
Mine
Tunnel
Dam, Bridge

Name	Page	Grid	Lat.	Long.
Florida City	44	Gm	25.27N	80.29W
Florida Islands	60	Gi	9.00S	160.10 E
Florida Keys	43	Kg	24.45N	81.00W
Floridia	14	Jm	37.05N	15.09 E
Florido, Rio-	48	Gd	27.43N	105.10W
Flórina	15	Ei	40.47N	21.24 E
Flörsheim	12	Kd	50.01N	8.26 E
Flotte, Cap de-	63b	Ce	21.11S	167.24 E
Floydada	45	Fj	33.59N	101.20W
Fluessen	11	Lb	52.57N	5.30 E
Flumen	13	Lc	41.43N	0.09W
Flumendosa	14	Dk	39.26N	9.37 E
Fluminimaggiore	14	Ck	39.26N	8.30 E
Flumini Mannu	14	Ck	39.16N	9.00 E
Flums	14	Dc	47.05N	9.20 E
Fluvià	13	Pb	42.12N	3.07 E
Flying Fish, Cape-	66	Of	72.06S	102.29W
Fly River	57	Fe	8.00S	142.21 E
Fnideq	13	Gi	35.50N	5.22W
Fnjóská	7a	Bb	65.54N	18.07W
Foa	65b	Ba	19.45S	174.18W
Foam Lake	46	Na	51.39N	103.33W
Foça	15	Jk	38.39N	26.46 E
Foča	14	Mg	43.31N	18.47 E
Fochi	15	Bb	18.25N	15.40 E
Fochi	35	Bb	18.56N	15.57 E
Focşani	15	Kd	45.42N	27.11 E
Fodda	13	Nh	36.14N	1.33 E
Fodé	35	Cd	5.29N	23.18 E
Føeringehavn	41	Gf	63.45N	51.28W
Foga, Dallol-	34	Fc	12.05N	3.32 E
Foggaret ez Zoua	32	Hd	27.22N	2.50 E
Foggia	6	Hg	41.27N	15.34 E
Foggo	34	Gc	11.23N	9.57 E
Foglia	14	Gg	43.55N	12.54 E
Föglö	8	Ie	60.00N	20.25 E
Fogo [Can.]	42	Mg	49.40N	54.10W
Fogo [C.V.]	30	Eg	14.55N	24.25W
Fohnsdorf	14	Ic	47.12N	14.41 E
Föhr	10	Eb	54.45N	8.30 E
Föhren	12	Ie	49.51N	6.46 E
Foix	11	Hl	42.58N	1.36 E
Fojnica	23	Fg	43.58N	17.54 E
Fokino	16	Ic	53.27N	34.26 E
Folda	7	Dc	67.36N	14.50 E
Folégandros	15	Hm	36.38N	24.54 E
Foley	42	Kc	68.30N	75.00W
Foleyet	42	Jg	48.16N	82.30W
Folgefonni	7	Bf	60.00N	6.20 E
Foligno	14	Gh	42.57N	12.42 E
Folkestone	9	Oj	51.05N	1.11 E
Folkingham	12	Bb	52.52N	0.24W
Folkston	44	Fj	30.50N	82.01W
Folldals verk	7	Bb	62.08N	10.00 E
Follebu	7	Cf	61.14N	10.17 E
Föllinge	7	De	63.40N	14.37 E
Follo	8	De	59.55N	10.55 E
Follonica	14	Eh	42.55N	10.45 E
Follonica, Golfo di-	14	Eh	42.55N	10.40 E
Folschviller	12	Ie	49.04N	6.41 E
Fomboni	37	Gb	12.16S	43.45 E
Fomento	49	Hb	22.06N	79.43W
Fond d'Or Bay	51k	Bb	13.56N	60.54W
Fond-du-Lac	42	Ge	59.19N	107.10W
Fond-du-Lac	42	Ge	59.17N	106.00W
Fond du Lac	43	Jc	43.47N	88.27W
Fondi	14	Hi	41.21N	13.25 E
Fongen	8	Da	63.11N	11.38 E
Fongoro	35	Cc	11.30N	22.25 E
Fonni	14	Dj	40.07N	9.15 E
Fonoifua	65b	Bb	20.17S	174.38W
Fonsagrada	13	Ea	43.08N	7.04W
Fonseca	54	Da	10.53N	72.50W
Fonseca, Golfo de-	38	Kh	13.08N	87.40W
Fonsecas, Serra dos-	55	Jc	17.02S	44.13W
Fontaine-Bellenger	12	De	49.11N	1.16 E
Fontainebleau	11	If	48.24N	2.42 E
Fontaine-Henry, Château de-	12	Be	49.17N	0.27W
Fontaine-le-Dun	12	Ce	49.49N	0.51 E
Fontaine-l'Evêque	12	Gd	50.25N	4.19 E
Fontas	42	Fe	58.17N	121.46W
Fonte Boa	54	Ed	2.32S	66.01W
Fontenay-le-Comte	11	Fh	46.28N	0.49W
Fontenay Trésigny	12	Ef	48.42N	2.52 E
Fontenelle Reservoir	46	Je	42.05N	110.06W
Fontevraud-l'Abbaye	11	Gg	47.11N	0.03 E
Fontur	5	Eb	66.23N	14.32W
Fonuafo'ou Falcon	61	Fd	20.19S	175.25W
Fonualei Island	57	Jf	18.01S	174.19W
Fonyód	10	Nj	46.44N	17.33 E
Foraker, Mount-	40	Id	62.56N	151.26W
Forbach	11	Me	49.11N	6.54 E
Forbes	59	Jf	33.23S	148.01 E
Forbes, Mount-	46	Ga	51.52N	116.56W
Forcados	34	Gd	5.23N	5.19 E
Forcados	34	Gd	5.21N	5.25 E
Forcalquier	11	Lk	43.58N	5.47 E
Forchheim	10	Hg	49.43N	11.04 E
Ford City	46	Fi	35.09N	119.27W
Førde	7	Af	61.27N	5.52 E
Førdefjorden	8	Ac	61.30N	5.40 E
Ford Ranges	66	Mf	77.00S	145.00W
Fordyce	45	Jj	33.49N	92.25W
Forécariah	34	Cd	9.26N	13.06W
Forel, Mont-	67	Mc	67.05N	36.55W
Forelshogna	8	Db	62.41N	10.47 E
Forest	45	Lj	32.22N	89.28W
Forest Park	44	Ei	33.37N	84.22W
Forestville	44	Ma	48.45N	69.06W
Forez, Monts du-	11	Ji	45.35N	3.48 E
Forez, Plaine du-	11	Ki	45.50N	4.10 E
Forfar	9	Ke	56.38N	2.54W
Forges-les-Eaux	11	He	49.37N	1.33 E
Forggensee	10	Gi	47.36N	10.44 E
Forks	46	Cc	47.57N	124.23W
Forlì	14	Gf	44.13N	12.03 E
Forlì, Bocca di-	14	Ii	41.45N	14.10 E
Formby Point	9	Jh	53.33N	3.06W
Formentera	5	Gh	38.42N	1.28 E
Formentor, Cabo de-/Formentor, Cap de-	13	Pe	39.58N	3.12 E
Formentor, Cap de-/Formentor, Cabo de-	13	Pe	39.58N	3.12 E
Formerie	12	De	49.39N	1.44 E
Formia	14	Hi	41.15N	13.37 E
Formiga	54	Ih	20.27S	45.25W
Formigas	32	Cb	37.16N	24.47W
Formosa [2]	56	Ib	25.00S	60.00W
Formosa [Arg.]	53	Kh	26.10S	58.11W
Formosa [Braz.]	54	Ig	15.32S	47.20W
Formosa [Gui. Bis.]	34	Bc	11.45N	16.05W
Formosa [Tai.] → Taiwan	21	Og	23.30N	121.00 E
Formosa, Serra-	52	Kg	12.00S	55.00W
Formosa Bay	36	Hc	2.45S	40.20 E
Formosa Strait (EN) = Taiwan Haixia	21	Ng	24.00N	119.00 E
Formoso [Braz.]	55	Ib	14.57S	46.14W
Formoso [Braz.]	55	Ha	13.37S	48.54W
Formoso, Rio- [Braz.]	55	Ja	13.26S	44.14W
Formoso, Rio- [Braz.]	54	If	10.34S	49.59W
Formoso, Rio- [Braz.]	55	Fd	18.25S	52.28W
Fornæs	7	Ch	56.27N	10.58 E
Fornosovo	8	Ne	59.31N	30.45 E
Fornovo di Taro	14	Ef	44.42N	10.06 E
Föroyar/Færøerne = Faeroe Islands (EN) [5]	6	Fc	62.00N	7.00W
Föroyar/Færøerne = Faeroe Islands (EN)	5	Fc	62.00N	7.00W
Forres	9	Jd	57.37N	3.38W
Forrest	59	Ff	30.51S	128.06 E
Forrest City	45	Ki	35.01N	90.47W
Forrester Island	66	Nf	74.06S	132.00W
Forsayth	59	Ic	18.35S	143.36 E
Forsbacka	8	Gd	60.37N	16.53 E
Forserum	8	Fg	57.42N	14.28 E
Forshaga	7	Cg	59.32N	13.28 E
Forsnäs	7	Ec	66.14N	18.39 E
Forssa	7	Ff	60.49N	23.38 E
Forst/Baršć	10	Ke	51.44N	14.38 E
Forsyth	46	Lc	46.16N	106.41W
Fort Albany	39	Kd	52.15N	81.37W
Fortaleza	53	Mf	3.43S	38.30W
Fortaleza, Ribeirão-	55	Fd	19.50S	53.25W
Fort Augustus	9	Id	57.09N	4.41W
Fort Beaufort	37	Df	32.46S	26.40 E
Fort Benton	43	Eb	47.49N	110.40W
Fort Bragg	43	Cd	39.26N	123.48W
Fort Bridger	46	Jf	41.19N	110.23W
Fort-Carnot	37	Hd	21.53S	48.26 E
Fort Chipewyan	42	Ge	58.42N	111.08W
Fort Cobb Reservoir	45	Gi	35.12N	98.29W
Fort Collins	43	Fc	40.35N	105.05W
Fort Collinson	42	Fb	71.37N	117.57W
Fort Coulonge	44	Ic	45.51N	76.44W
Fort Davis	45	Ek	30.35N	103.54W
Fort-de-France	39	Mh	14.36N	61.05W
Fort-de-France, Baie de-	51h	Ab	14.34N	61.04W
Fort Dodge	43	Ic	42.30N	94.10W
Forte	55	Ib	14.16S	47.17W
Forte dei Marmi	14	Eg	43.57N	10.10 E
Fortescue River	57	Cg	21.00S	116.06 E
Fort Frances	39	Je	48.36N	93.24W
Fort Franklin	42	Fc	65.12N	123.26W
Fort Garland	45	Dh	37.26N	105.26W
Fort Gibson Lake	45	Ih	36.00N	95.18W
Fort Good-Hope	39	Gc	66.15N	128.38W
Forth	9	Je	56.04N	3.42W
Forth, Firth of-	5	Fd	56.05N	2.55W
Fort Hall	36	Gc	0.43S	37.09 E
Fort Hope	42	If	51.32N	88.00W
Fortin Avalos Sanchez	55	Bf	23.28S	60.07W
Fortín Boquerón	55	Cf	22.47S	59.57W
Fortín Buenos Aires	55	Bf	22.57S	61.51W
Fortín Cadete Pastor Pando	55	Cg	24.20S	58.54W
Fortín Capitán Figari	55	Cf	23.12S	59.32W
Fortín Carlos A. Lopez	55	Ce	21.19S	59.44W
Fortín Comandante Nowak	55	Cg	24.51S	58.15W
Fortín Coronel Bogado	55	Ce	20.46S	59.09W
Fortín Coronel Eugenio Garay	56	Hb	20.31S	62.08W
Fortín Coronel Hermosa	55	Bf	22.33S	60.01W
Fortín Coronel Martínez	55	Cf	22.15S	59.09W
Fortín Florida	55	Ce	20.45S	59.17W
Fortín Galpón	55	Cd	19.51S	58.16W
Fortín Gaspar Rodriguez de Francia	55	Cf	23.01S	59.57W
Fortín General Caballero	55	Cg	24.08S	59.30W
Fortín General Delgado	55	Cg	24.28S	59.15W
Fortín General Diaz	56	Hb	23.31S	60.34W
Fortín Guarani	55	Cf	22.44S	59.30W
Fortín Hernandarias	55	Be	21.58S	61.30W
Fortín José M. López	55	Be	20.07S	60.15W
Fortín Lagerenza	55	Be	20.06S	61.03W
Fortín Madrejón	55	Ce	20.38S	59.52W
Fortín Mariscal López	55	Cf	23.39S	59.44W
Fortín Max Paredes	55	Cd	19.16S	59.58W
Fortín May Alberto Gardel	55	Af	22.46S	62.12W
Fortín Mayor Long	55	Ae	20.33S	62.01W
Fortín Mayor R. Santacruz	55	Be	20.15S	60.37W
Fortín Nueva Asunción	55	Be	20.42S	61.55W
Fortín Pikyrenda	55	Be	20.05S	61.48W
Fortín Pilcomayo [Par.]	55	Bf	23.44S	60.51W
Fortín Pilcomayo [Arg.]	55	Bf	23.52S	60.53W
Fortín Pratts Gill	55	Bf	22.41S	61.33W
Fortín Presidente Ayala	55	Cf	23.30S	59.46W
Fortín Ravelo	55	Bd	19.18S	60.35W
Fortín Suarez Arana	55	Bd	18.40S	60.09W
Fortín Teniente 1° Alfredo Stroessner	55	Bf	22.45S	61.32W
Fortín Teniente 1° H. Mendoza	55	Cd	19.54S	59.47W
Fortín Teniente 1° M. Cabello	55	Bf	23.28S	61.19W
Fortín Teniente 1° Ramiro Espinola	55	Be	21.28S	61.18W
Fortín Teniente Acosta	55	Bf	22.41S	60.32W
Fortín Teniente Agripino Enciso	55	Be	21.12S	61.34W
Fortín Teniente Américo Picco	55	Cd	19.35S	59.43W
Fortín Teniente Aristigueta	55	Bf	22.21S	60.38W
Fortín Teniente E. Ochoa	55	Be	21.42S	61.02W
Fortín Teniente Esteban Martinez	55	Cg	24.02S	59.51W
Fortín Teniente Juan E. López	55	Be	21.05S	61.48W
Fortín Teniente Montania	55	Cf	22.04S	59.57W
Fortín Teniente R. Rueda	55	Be	21.49S	60.49W
Fortín Toledo	55	Bf	22.20S	60.21W
Fortín Torres	55	Ce	21.01S	59.30W
Fortín Vanguardia	55	Cd	19.39S	58.10W
Fortín Vitiones	55	Cd	19.30S	58.06W
Fortín Zenteno	55	Cf	23.10S	59.59W
Fort Jeuedy, Point of-	51p	Bb	12.00N	61.42W
Fort Kent	44	Mb	47.15N	68.36W
Fort Knox	44	Eg	37.53N	85.55W
Fort Lamy → N'djamena	31	Ig	12.07N	15.03 E
Fort Lauderdale	43	Kf	26.07N	80.08W
Fort Liard	39	Gc	60.15N	123.28W
Fort-Liberté	49	Ld	19.38N	71.57W
Fort MacKay	42	Ge	57.08N	111.42W
Fort Macleod	42	Gg	49.43N	113.25W
Fort Mac Mahon	32	Hd	29.46N	1.37 E
Fort Madison	45	Kf	40.38N	91.21W
Fort-Mahon-Plage	12	Dd	50.21N	1.34 E
Fort McMurray	39	Hd	56.44N	111.23W
Fort McPherson	39	Fc	67.27N	134.53W
Fort Miribel	32	Hd	29.26N	3.00 E
Fort Morgan	45	Ef	40.15N	103.48W
Fort Myers	39	Kg	26.37N	81.54W
Fort Myers Beach	44	Gl	26.27N	81.57W
Fort Nelson	39	Gd	58.49N	122.39W
Fort Nelson	42	Fe	59.33N	124.01W
Fort Norman	42	Ed	64.56N	125.22W
Fortore	14	Ji	41.55N	15.17 E
Fort Payne	44	Eh	34.27N	85.43W
Fort Peck	46	Lb	48.01N	106.27W
Fort Peck Lake	43	Fb	47.45N	106.50W
Fort Pierce	43	Kf	27.27N	80.20W
Fort Pierre	43	Gc	44.21N	100.22W
Fort Portal	36	Fb	0.39N	30.17 E
Fort Providence	39	Hc	61.21N	117.39W
Fort Qu'Appelle	46	Na	50.56N	103.09W
Fort Resolution	42	Gd	61.10N	113.40W
Fortrose	62	Cg	46.34S	168.48 E
Fort Saint James	42	Ff	54.26N	124.15W
Fort Saint John	39	Gd	56.15N	120.51W
Fort Sandeman	25	Db	31.20N	69.27 E
Fort Saskatchewan	42	Gf	53.43N	113.13W
Fort Scott	45	Ih	37.50N	94.42W
Fort-Ševčenko	19	Fg	44.30N	50.14 E
Fort Severn	39	Kd	56.00N	87.38W
Fort Simpson	39	Gc	61.52N	121.23W
Fort Smith [Ar.-U.S.]	39	Jf	35.23N	94.25W
Fort Smith [N.W.T.-Can.]	39	Hd	60.00N	111.53W
Fort Stockton	43	Ge	30.53N	102.53W
Fort Sumner	45	Di	34.28N	104.15W
Fortuna	46	Cf	40.36N	124.09W
Fortuna, Rio de la-	55	Cc	16.36S	58.46W
Fortune Bay	42	Lg	47.15N	55.40W
Fort Vermilion	42	Fe	58.24N	116.00W
Fort Walton Beach	43	Je	30.25N	86.36W
Fort Washakie	46	Ke	43.00N	108.53W
Fort Wayne	39	Ke	41.04N	85.09W
Fort William	9	He	56.49N	5.07W
Fort Worth	39	Jf	32.45N	97.20W
Fort Yates	45	Fc	46.05N	100.38W
Fort Yukon	39	Ec	66.34N	145.17W
Forūr, Jazīreh-ye-	24	Pi	26.17N	54.32 E
Foshan	22	Ng	22.59N	113.05 E
Fosheim Peninsula	42	Ja	80.00N	84.30W
Fosnavåg	8	Ab	62.21N	5.39 E
Fosnøy	8	Ad	60.45N	4.55 E
Fossacesia	14	Ih	42.15N	14.29 E
Fossano	14	Bf	44.33N	7.43 E
Fossato, Colle di-	14	Gg	43.20N	12.49 E
Fossberg	8	Cc	61.50N	8.34 E
Fossil	46	Ed	44.59N	120.13W
Fossil Bluff	66	Qf	71.20S	68.17W
Fossombrone	14	Gg	43.41N	12.48 E
Fosston	45	Ic	47.35N	95.45W
Fos-sur-Mer	11	Kk	43.26N	4.57 E
Foster	59	Jg	38.39S	146.12 E
Foster, Mount-	40	Le	59.48N	135.29W
Foster Bugt	41	Jd	73.40N	21.40W
Fostoria	44	Fe	41.10N	83.25W
Fotuha'a	65b	Ba	19.49S	174.44W
Foucarmont	12	De	49.51N	1.34 E
Fougamou	36	Bc	1.13S	10.36 E
Fougères	11	Ef	48.21N	1.12W
Foul, Khalīj-	33	Ge	23.30N	35.40 E
Foula	9	Ka	60.10N	2.05W
Foul Bay	51q	Bb	13.06N	59.27W
Fouligny	12	Ie	49.06N	6.30 E
Foulness	9	Nj	51.36N	0.55 E
Foulness Point	12	Cc	51.37N	0.57 E
Foulwind, Cape-	62	Dd	41.45S	171.28 E
Foumban	34	Hd	5.43N	10.55 E
Foumbouni	37	Gb	11.50S	43.30 E
Foum Zguid	32	Fc	30.05N	6.52W
Foundation Ice Stream	66	Qg	83.15S	60.00W
Fountains Abbey	9	Lg	54.07N	1.34W
Fouquet Island	37b	Bb	5.25S	53.20 E
Fourchambault	11	Jg	47.01N	3.05 E
Fourchue, Ile-	51b	Bc	17.57N	62.55W
Fourmies	11	Kd	50.00N	4.03 E
Four Mountains, Islands of the-	40a	Db	52.50N	170.00W
Foúrnoi	15	Jl	37.34N	26.30 E
Fouron/Voeren	12	Hd	50.45N	5.48 E
Fours	11	Jh	46.49N	3.43 E
Fourth Cataract (EN) = Rabi', Ash Shallāl ar-	30	Kg	18.47N	32.03 E
Fous, Pointe des-	51g	Bb	15.12N	61.20W
Fouta	34	Cb	16.18N	14.48W
Fouta Djalon	30	Fg	11.30N	12.30W
Foutouna, Ile-	57	If	19.32S	170.13 E
Foux, Cap-à-	49	Kd	19.45N	73.27W
Fouzon	11	Hg	47.16N	1.27 E
Foveaux Strait	57	Hi	46.40S	168.10 E
Fowler [Co.-U.S.]	45	Eg	38.08N	104.00W
Fowler [In.-U.S.]	44	De	40.37N	87.19W
Fowlers Bay	59	Gf	32.00S	132.25 E
Fowman	24	Md	37.13N	49.19 E
Foxe Basin	38	Lc	68.25N	77.00W
Foxe Channel	38	Lc	64.30N	80.00W
Foxen	8	De	59.25N	11.55 E
Foxe Peninsula	38	Lc	65.00N	76.00W
Foxford/Béal Easa	9	Dh	53.59N	9.07W
Fox Glacier	61	Ch	43.28S	170.00 E
Fox Islands	38	Cd	54.00N	168.00W
Fox Peak	62	De	43.50S	170.47 E
Fox River	45	Lf	41.21N	88.50W
Foxton	62	Fd	40.28S	175.17 E
Fox Valley	46	Ka	50.29N	109.28W
Foyle	9	Ff	55.04N	7.15W
Foyle, Lough-/Loch Feabhail	9	Ff	55.05N	7.10W
Foz do Cunene	36	Bf	17.15S	11.48 E
Foz do Iguaçu	53	Kh	25.33S	54.35W
Fraga	13	Mc	41.31N	0.21 E
Fragoso, Cayo	49	Hb	22.44N	79.30W
Fraire, Walcourt-	12	Gd	50.16N	4.30 E
Fram	55	Eh	27.06S	55.58W
Fram Basin (EN)	67	He	88.00N	80.00 E
Framlingham	12	Db	52.13N	1.20 E
Franca	56	Kb	20.32S	47.24W
Franca-Josifa, Zemlja- = Franz Joseph Land (EN)	21	Ha	81.00N	55.00 E
Francavilla al Mare	14	Ih	42.25N	14.17 E
Francavilla Fontana	14	Lj	40.31N	17.35 E
France [1]	6	Gf	46.00N	2.00 E
Frances	42	Ed	60.16N	129.11W
Francés, Punta-	49	Fc	21.38N	83.12W
Francesi, Punta di li-	14	Di	41.08N	9.02 E
Francés Viejo, Cabo-	49	Md	19.39N	69.55W
Franceville	31	Ii	1.38S	13.35 E
Franche-Comté	11	Lh	47.00N	6.00 E
Franches Montagnes/Freiberge	14	Ac	47.15N	7.00 E
Francia	55	Dk	32.34S	36.38W
Francia, Sierra de-	13	Fd	40.35N	6.05W
Francis Case, Lake-	38	Je	43.15N	99.00W
Francisco Beltrão	56	Jc	26.05S	53.04W
Francisco Escárcega	48	Nh	18.37N	90.43W
Francisco I. Madero	48	Ge	24.32N	104.22W
Francisco Madero	55	Al	35.52S	62.03W
Francisco Morazán [3]	49	Df	14.15N	87.15W
Francisco Sá	54	Jg	16.28S	43.30W
Franciscus Bay	37	Ae	25.00S	14.50 E
Francistown	31	Jk	21.09S	27.31 E
Francofonte	14	Im	37.14N	14.53 E
Franconian Jura (EN) = Fränkische Alb	5	Hf	49.00N	11.30 E
Francs Peak	43	Fc	43.58N	109.20W
Franeker	11	La	53.11N	5.32 E
Frankenau	12	Kc	51.06N	8.56 E
Frankenberg (Eder)	10	Ee	51.04N	8.40 E
Frankenhöhe	10	Gg	49.15N	10.15 E
Frankenthal (Pfalz)	12	Ke	49.32N	8.21 E
Frankenwald	10	Hf	50.18N	11.36 E
Frankfort [In.-U.S.]	44	De	40.17N	86.31W
Frankfort [Ky.-U.S.]	39	Kf	38.12N	84.52W
Frankfort [Mi.-U.S.]	44	Dc	44.38N	86.14W
Frankfort on the Main (EN) = Frankfurt am Main	6	Ge	50.07N	8.41 E
Frankfurt	10	Kd	52.21N	14.33 E
Frankfurt am Main = Frankfort on the Main (EN)	6	Ge	50.07N	8.41 E
Fränkische Alb = Franconian Jura(EN)	5	Hf	49.00N	11.30 E
Fränkische Saale	10	Ff	50.03N	9.42 E
Fränkische Schweiz	10	Hg	49.45N	11.20 E
Franklin [In.-U.S.]	44	Df	39.29N	86.03W
Franklin [Ky.-U.S.]	44	Dg	36.43N	86.35W
Franklin [La.-U.S.]	45	Kl	29.48N	91.30W
Franklin [N.C.-U.S.]	44	Fh	35.11N	83.23W
Franklin [N.H.-U.S.]	44	Ld	43.27N	71.39W
Franklin [Pa.-U.S.]	44	He	41.24N	79.49W
Franklin [Tn.-U.S.]	44	Dh	35.55N	86.52W
Franklin, District of- [3]	42	Hb	72.00N	96.00W
Franklin Bay	38	Gc	68.45N	125.35W
Franklin Delano Roosevelt Lake	43	Db	48.20N	118.10W
Franklin Island	66	Kf	76.05S	168.11 E
Franklin Lake [Nv.-U.S.]	46	Hf	40.24N	115.12W
Franklin Lake [N.W.T.-Can.]	42	Hc	66.55N	96.05W
Franklin Mountains	38	Gc	63.15N	123.30W
Franklin Strait	42	Hb	71.30N	96.30W
Fransfontein	37	Bd	20.12S	15.01 E
Fränsta	8	Gb	62.30N	16.09 E
Franz Josef Glacier	62	De	43.23S	170.11 E
Franz Joseph Land (EN) = Franca-Josifa, Zemlja-	21	Ha	81.00N	55.00 E
Frascati	14	Gi	41.48N	12.41 E
Fraser [Can.]	38	Ge	49.09N	123.12W
Fraser [Newf.-Can.]	42	Le	56.39N	63.08W
Fraserburg	37	Cf	31.55S	21.30 E
Fraserburgh	9	Ld	57.42N	2.00W
Fraser[illegible]	42	Jg	49.51N	81.38W
Fraser Island	57	Gg	25.15S	153.10 E
Fraser Plateau	38	Gd	51.30N	122.00W
Fraser Range	59	Ef	32.03S	122.48 E
Frasertown	62	Gc	38.58S	177.24 E
Frasnes-les-Anvaing	12	Fd	50.40N	3.36 E
Frauenfeld	14	Cc	47.35N	8.54 E
Fray Bentos	56	Id	33.08S	58.18W
Frechen	12	Id	50.55N	6.49 E
Frechilla	13	Hb	42.08N	4.50W
Fredericia	7	Bi	55.35N	9.46 E
Frederick [Md.-U.S.]	44	If	39.25N	77.25W
Frederick [Ok.-U.S.]	45	Gi	34.23N	99.01W
Frederick E. Hyde Fjord	41	Jb	82.40N	25.45W
Frederick Reef	57	Gg	21.00S	154.25 E
Fredericksburg [Tx.-U.S.]	45	Gk	30.17N	98.52W
Fredericksburg [Va.-U.S.]	44	If	38.18N	77.30W
Fredericktown	45	Kh	37.33N	90.18W
Frederico Westphalen	55	Fh	27.22S	53.24W
Fredericton	39	Me	45.58N	66.39W
Frederiksborg [2]	8	Ei	55.55N	12.15 E
Frederiksdal	41	Hf	60.15N	45.30W
Frederikshåb/Påmiut	41	Hf	62.00N	49.45W
Frederikshåbs Bank (EN)	41	Hf	62.16N	49.45W
Frederikshavn	6	Hd	57.26N	10.32 E
Frederikssund	8	Ei	55.50N	12.04 E
Frederiksted	50	Dd	17.42N	64.48W
Frederiksværk	8	Ei	55.58N	12.02 E
Fredonia	46	Ih	36.57N	112.32W
Fredrika	7	Ed	64.05N	18.24 E
Fredriksberg	7	Df	60.08N	14.23 E
Fredrikshamn/Hamina	7	Gf	60.34N	27.12 E
Fredrikstad	7	Cg	59.13N	10.57 E
Fredvang	7	Cb	68.05N	13.10 E
Freeling Heights	59	Hf	30.10S	139.25 E
Freels, Cape-	42	Mg	49.13N	53.29W
Freeport [Bah.]	47	Ic	26.30N	78.45W
Freeport [Il.-U.S.]	43	Jc	42.17N	89.36W
Freeport [N.Y.-U.S.]	44	Ke	40.40N	73.35W
Freeport [Tx.-U.S.]	43	Hf	28.55N	95.22W
Freer	45	Gm	27.53N	98.37W
Freetown [Atg.]	51d	Bb	17.03N	61.42W
Freetown [S.L.]	31	Fh	8.30N	13.15W
Fregenal de la Sierra	13	Ff	38.10N	6.39W
Fregene	14	Gi	41.51N	12.12 E
Frei	8	Ba	63.01N	7.48 E
Freiberg	10	Jf	50.55N	13.22 E
Freiberge/Franches Montagnes	14	Ac	47.15N	7.00 E
Freiberger Mulde	10	Ie	51.10N	12.48 E
Freiburg/Fribourg	14	Bd	46.50N	7.10 E
Freiburg im Breisgau	6	Gf	48.00N	7.51 E
Freilassing	10	Ii	47.51N	12.59 E
Freirina	56	Fc	28.30S	71.06W
Freisen	12	Je	49.33N	7.15 E
Freising	10	Hh	48.24N	11.44 E
Freistadt	14	Ib	48.30N	14.30 E
Freital	10	Je	51.01N	13.39 E
Fréjus	11	Mk	43.26N	6.44 E
Fréjus, Col du-	11	Mi	45.07N	6.40 E
Fremantle, Perth-	59	Df	32.03S	115.45 E
Fremont [Ca.-U.S.]	43	Cd	37.34N	122.01W
Fremont [Nb.-U.S.]	43	Hc	41.26N	96.30W
Fremont [Oh.-U.S.]	44	Fe	41.21N	83.08W
Fremont River	46	Jg	38.24N	110.42W
French Frigate Shoals	57	Kb	23.45N	166.10W
French Guiana (EN) = Guyane Française [5]	53	Ke	4.00N	53.00W
French Lick	44	Df	38.33N	86.37W
Frenchman Creek	45	Ff	40.13N	100.50W
Frenchman River	43	Fb	48.24N	107.05W
French Pass	62	Ed	40.55S	173.50 E
French Plain (EN)	5	Gf	47.00N	1.00 E
French Polynesia (EN) = Polynésie Française [5]	58	Mf	16.00S	145.00W
French River	44	Gc	45.56N	80.54W
Frenda	32	Hb	35.04N	1.02 E
Frénel, Cap-	11	Df	48.42N	2.19W
Frentani, Monti dei-	14	Ii	41.55N	14.30 E
Freren	12	Jb	52.29N	7.33 E
Fresco	34	Dd	5.05N	5.34W
Fresco, Rio-	54	He	6.39S	52.00W
Freshfield, Cape-	66	Je	68.22S	151.05 E
Fresnes-en-Woëvre	12	He	49.06N	5.37 E
Fresnillo de Gonzales Echeverria	47	Dd	23.10N	102.53W
Fresno	39	Hf	36.45N	119.45W
Fresno, Portillo del-	13	Ib	42.35N	3.40W
Fresno River	46	Eh	37.05N	120.33W
Fresquel	11	Ik	43.14N	2.24 E
Fresvikbreen	8	Bc	61.02N	6.45 E
Freu, Cabo-	13	Pe	39.45N	3.27 E
Freudenberg	12	Jd	50.54N	7.52 E
Freudenstadt	10	Eh	48.26N	8.25 E
Frévent	11	Id	50.16N	2.17 E
Freycinet Estuary	59	Ce	26.25S	113.45 E
Freycinet Peninsula	59	Jh	42.15S	148.20 E
Freyming-Merlebach	12	Ie	49.09N	6.47 E
Freyre	55	Aj	31.10S	62.02W
Freyung	10	Jh	48.48N	13.33 E
Fri	15	Jn	35.25N	26.56 E
Fria	34	Cc	10.27N	13.32W
Fria, Cape-	30	Ij	18.27S	12.01 E
Frias	56	Gc	28.39S	65.09W
Fribourg [2]	14	Bd	46.40N	7.10 E
Fribourg/Freiburg	14	Bd	46.50N	7.10 E
Fridtjof Nansen, Mount-	66	Lg	85.21S	167.33W
Friedberg [Aus.]	14	Kc	47.26N	16.03 E
Friedberg [F.R.G.]	10	Ef	50.21N	8.46 E
Friedrichshafen	10	Fi	47.39N	9.29 E
Friedrichsthal	12	Je	49.19N	7.06 E
Friesach	14	Id	46.57N	14.24 E
Friese Gat	12	Ia	53.30N	6.05 E
Friese Wad	12	Ha	53.25N	5.50 E
Friese Wad	12	Ha	53.24N	5.45 E
Friesland [3]	12	Ha	53.03N	5.45 E
Friesland	11	La	53.05N	6.00 E
Friesland	5	Ge	53.05N	6.00 E

Index Symbols

[1] Independent Nation
[2] State, Region
[3] District, County
[4] Municipality
[5] Colony, Dependency
Continent
Physical Region

Historical or Cultural Region
Mount, Mountain
Volcano
Hill
Mountains, Mountain Range
Hills, Escarpment
Plateau, Upland

Pass, Gap
Plain, Lowland
Delta
Salt Flat
Valley, Canyon
Crater, Cave
Karst Features

Depression
Polder
Desert, Dunes
Forest, Woods
Heath, Steppe
Oasis
Cape, Point

Coast, Beach
Cliff
Peninsula
Isthmus
Sandbank
Island
Atoll

Rock, Reef
Islands, Archipelago
Rocks, Reefs
Coral Reef
Well, Spring
Geyser
River, Stream

Waterfall Rapids
River Mouth, Estuary
Lake
Salt Lake
Intermittent Lake
Reservoir
Swamp, Pond

Canal
Glacier
Ice Shelf, Pack Ice
Ocean
Sea
Gulf, Bay
Strait, Fjord

Lagoon
Bank
Seamount
Tablemount
Ridge
Shelf
Basin

Escarpment, Sea Scarp
Fracture
Trench, Abyss
National Park, Reserve
Point of Interest
Recreation Site
Cave, Cavern

Historic Site
Ruins
Wall, Walls
Church, Abbey
Temple
Scientific Station
Airport

Port
Lighthouse
Mine
Tunnel
Dam, Bridge

Friesoythe 10 Dc 53.01N 7.51 E
Frigate Island 51p Cb 12.25N 61.29W
Friggesund 8 Gc 61.54N 16.32 E
Frignano 14 Ef 44.20N 10.50 E
Frindsbury Reef 63a Da 5.00S 159.07 E
Frinnaryd 8 Fg 57.56N 14.49 E
Frinton-on-Sea 12 Dc 51.50N 1.15 E
Frio, Cabo- 52 Lh 22.53S 42.00W
Frio, Rio- 49 Eh 11.08N 84.46W
Frio Draw 45 Ei 34.50N 102.08W
Friona 45 Ei 34.38N 102.43W
Frio River 45 Gl 28.30N 98.10W
Frisco Peak 46 Ig 38.31N 113.14W
Frisian Islands (EN) 5 Ge 54.00N 7.00 E
Fristad 8 Eg 57.50N 13.01 E
Fritsla 8 Eg 57.33N 12.47 E
Fritzlar 10 Fe 51.08N 9.17 E
Friuli 14 Ge 46.00N 13.00 E
Friuli-Venezia Giulia [2] 14 Gd 46.00N 13.00 E
Frobisher Bay 38 Mc 62.30N 66.00W
Frobisher Lake 42 Ge 56.20N 108.20W
Froidchapelle 12 Gd 50.09N 4.20 E
Froissy 12 Ee 49.34N 2.13 E
Frolovo 19 Ef 49.45N 43.39 E
Fromberg 46 Kd 45.23N 108.54W
Frombork 10 Pb 54.22N 19.41 E
Frome 9 Kj 51.14N 2.20W
Frome, Lake- 57 Eh 30.50S 139.50 E
Frondenberg 12 Jc 51.28N 7.46 E
Fronteira 13 Ee 39.03N 7.39W
Fronteiras 54 Je 7.05S 40.37W
Frontera 48 Mh 18.32N 92.38W
Frontera, Punta- 48 Mh 19.36N 92.42W
Fronteras 48 Eb 30.56N 109.31W
Frontignan 11 Jk 43.27N 3.45 E
Frontino, Paramo- 54 Cb 6.28N 76.04W
Front Range 38 If 39.45N 105.45W
Front Royal 44 Hf 38.56N 78.13W
Frosinone 14 Hi 41.38N 13.19 E
Frösö 8 Fa 63.11N 14.32 E
Frostburg 44 Hf 39.39N 78.56W
Frost Glacier 66 Ie 67.05S 129.00 E
Frövi 8 Fe 59.28N 15.22 E
Frøya 7 Be 63.43N 8.42 E
Frøysjøen 8 Ac 61.50N 5.05 E
Frozen Strait 42 Jc 65.50N 84.30W
Fruges 11 Id 50.31N 2.08 E
Frunze [Kirg.-U.S.S.R.] 18 Hd 40.06N 71.45 E
Frunze [Kirg.-U.S.S.R.] 22 Je 42.54N 74.36 E
Frunzovka 15 Mb 47.20N 29.37 E
Fruška Gora 15 Cd 45.10N 19.35 E
Frutal 54 Ih 20.02S 48.55W
Frutigen 14 Bd 46.35N 7.40 E
Fry Canyon 46 Jh 37.38N 110.08W
Frýdek Místek 10 Og 49.41N 18.22 E
Frylinckspan 37 Ce 26.46S 22.28 E
Fteri 15 Ej 39.09N 21.33 E
Fua'amotu 65b Ac 21.15S 175.08W
Fua Mulaku Island 25a Bc 0.15S 73.30 E
Fu'an 27 Kf 27.10N 119.44 E
Fu-chien Sheng → Fujian Sheng = Fukien (EN) [2] 27 Kf 26.00N 118.00 E
Fuchskauten 10 Ef 50.40N 8.05 E
Fuchū [Jap.] 29 Cd 34.34N 133.14 E
Fuchū [Jap.] 29 Fd 35.41N 139.28 E
Fuchun-Jiang 28 Fi 30.15N 120.15 E
Fuchunjiang-Shuiku 28 Ej 29.29N 119.31 E
Fucino, Conca del- 14 Hj 42.01N 13.31 E
Fudai 29 Ga 40.01N 141.52 E
Fuding 27 Lf 27.19N 120.08 E
Fuengirola 13 Hh 36.32N 4.37W
Fuente Alto 56 Fd 33.37S 70.35W
Fuente del Maestre 13 Ff 38.32N 6.27W
Fuente-Obejuna 13 Gf 38.16N 5.25W
Fuentesaúco 13 Gc 41.14N 5.30W
Fuentes de Andalucía 13 Gg 37.28N 5.21W
Fuentes de Cantos 13 Ff 38.15N 6.18W
Fuerte 47 Cc 25.54N 109.22W
Fuerte, Isla- 49 Ii 9.23N 76.11W
Fuerte, Sierra del- 48 Hd 27.30N 102.45W
Fuerte Olimpo 56 Ib 21.02S 57.54W
Fuerteventura 30 Ff 28.20N 14.00W
Fuga 26 Hc 18.52N 121.22 E
Fugong 27 Gf 27.03N 98.57 E
Fugou 28 Cg 34.04N 114.23 E
Fugu 27 Jd 39.02N 111.03 E
Fuguo → Zhanhua 28 Ef 37.42N 118.08 E
Fuhai/Burultokay 27 Eb 47.06N 87.23 E
Fuhayrī, Wādī- 23 Hf 16.04N 52.11 E
Fu He 28 Dj 28.36N 116.04 E
Fuji 28 Og 35.09N 138.38 E
Fujian Sheng (Fu-chien Sheng) = Fukien (EN) [2] 27 Kf 26.00N 118.00 E
Fujieda 29 Fd 34.51N 138.15 E
Fuji-Gawa 29 Fd 35.07N 138.38 E
Fujin 27 Nb 47.15N 132.01 E
Fujinomiya 29 Fd 35.12N 138.38 E
Fujioka 29 Fc 36.15N 139.03 E
Fuji-San 21 Pf 35.26N 138.43 E
Fujisawa 29 Fd 35.21N 139.27 E
Fuji-yoshida 29 Fd 35.29N 138.47 E
Fukagawa 27 Pc 43.43N 142.03 E
Fūkah 24 Bg 31.04N 27.55 E
Fukang 27 Ec 44.10N 87.59 E
Fuka-Shima 29 Be 32.43N 131.56 E
Fukiage 29 Bf 31.30N 130.20 E
Fukien (EN) = Fu-chien Sheng → Fujian Sheng [2] 27 Kf 26.00N 118.00 E
Fukien (EN) = Fujian Sheng (Fu-chien Sheng) [2] 27 Kf 26.00N 118.00 E
Fukuchiyama 28 Mg 35.18N 135.07 E
Fukue 28 Jh 32.41N 128.50 E
Fukueichiao 27 Lf 25.19N 121.34 E
Fukue-Jima 28 Jh 32.41N 128.48 E
Fukui 27 Od 36.04N 136.13 E
Fukui Ken [2] 28 Ng 36.00N 136.20 E
Fukuma 29 Be 33.47N 130.28 E
Fukuoka 22 Pf 33.35N 130.24 E
Fukuoka Ken [2] 28 Kh 33.28N 130.45 E
Fukuroi 29 Ed 34.45N 137.54 E
Fukushima [Jap.] 27 Pd 37.45N 140.28 E
Fukushima [Jap.] 27 Pc 41.29N 140.15 E
Fukushima Ken [2] 28 Pf 37.25N 140.10 E
Fukuyama 27 Ne 34.29N 133.22 E
Fūlādī, Kūh-e- 23 Kc 34.38N 67.32 E
Fūlād Mahalleh 24 Od 36.02N 53.44 E
Fulanga 63d Cc 19.08S 178.34W
Fulda 5 Ge 51.25N 9.39 E
Fulda 10 Ff 50.33N 9.40 E
Fuliji 28 Dh 33.47N 116.59 E
Fulin → Hanyuan 27 Hf 29.25N 102.12 E
Fuling 27 If 29.40N 107.21 E
Fullerton 45 Hf 41.22N 97.58W
Fulton [Arg.] 55 Cm 37.25S 58.48W
Fulton [Il.-U.S.] 45 Kf 41.52N 90.11W
Fulton [Ky.-U.S.] 44 Cg 36.30N 88.53W
Fulton [Mo.-U.S.] 45 Kg 38.52N 91.57W
Fulton [N.Y.-U.S.] 44 Id 43.20N 76.26W
Fulufjället 8 Ec 61.33N 12.43 E
Fumaiolo 14 Gg 43.47N 12.04 E
Fumay 11 Kd 50.00N 4.42 E
Fumel 11 Gj 44.30N 0.58 E
Funabasi 28 Og 35.42N 139.59 E
Funabiki 29 Gc 37.26N 140.35 E
Funafuti 58 Ie 8.01S 178.00 E
Funafuti Atoll 57 Ie 8.31S 179.08 E
Funagata 29 Gb 38.42N 140.18 E
Funagata-Yama 29 Gb 38.27N 140.37 E
Funakoshi-Wan 29 Hb 39.25N 142.00 E
Funan 28 Ch 32.38N 115.35 E
Funäsdalen 7 Ce 62.32N 12.33 E
Funchal 31 Fe 32.38N 16.54W
Fundación 54 Da 10.29N 74.12W
Fundão 13 Ed 40.08N 7.30W
Fundy, Bay of- 38 Me 45.00N 66.00W
Funeral Peak 46 Gh 36.08N 116.37W
Fungalei 64h Bb 13.17S 176.07W
Funhalouro 37 Ed 23.05S 34.24 E
Funing [China] 27 Ig 23.39N 105.33 E
Funing [China] 28 Eh 33.48N 119.47 E
Funing [China] 28 Ee 39.56N 119.15 E
Funiu Shan 27 Je 33.40N 112.10 E
Funtua 34 Gc 11.32N 7.19 E
Fuping 28 Ce 38.49N 114.15 E
Fuqing 27 Kf 25.47N 119.24 E
Furancungo 37 Eb 14.54S 33.37 E
Furano 28 Qc 43.21N 142.23 E
Füren 29a Ca 44.17N 142.25 E
Furenai 29a Cb 42.43N 142.15 E
Füren-Ko 29a Db 43.20N 145.20 E
Fürg 24 Ph 28.18N 55.13 E
Fur Jiang 28 Hc 42.37N 125.33 E
Furmanov 7 Jh 57.16N 41.07 E
Furnas, Represa de- 54 Ih 21.20S 45.50W
Furnas, Serra das- 55 Fb 15.45S 53.20W
Furneaux Group 57 Fi 40.10S 148.05 E
Furnes/Veurne 11 Ic 51.04N 2.40 E
Furqlus 24 Ge 34.36N 37.05 E
Furrīyānah 32 Ic 34.57N 8.34 E
Fürstenau 12 Jb 52.31N 7.43 E
Furstenauer Berge 12 Jb 52.35N 7.45 E
Fürstenfeld 14 Kc 47.03N 16.05 E
Fürstenfeldbruck 10 Hh 48.11N 11.15 E
Furstenlager 12 Ke 49.42N 8.38 E
Fürstenwalde 10 Kd 52.22N 14.04 E
Fürth [Ger.] 10 Gg 49.28N 11.00 E
Fürth [Ger.] 12 Ke 49.39N 8.47 E
Furth im Wald 10 Ig 49.18N 12.51 E
Furubira 29a Bb 43.16N 140.39 E
Furudal 7 Df 61.10N 15.08 E
Furukawa 27 Pd 38.34N 140.58 E
Furusund 8 He 59.40N 18.55 E
Fury and Hecla Strait 42 Jc 69.55N 84.00W
Fushan [China] 28 Ff 37.30N 121.15 E
Fushan [China] 28 Ag 35.58N 111.51 E
Fushë-Arëzi 15 Dg 42.04N 20.02 E
Fushë-Lura 15 Dh 41.48N 20.13 E
Fu Shui 28 Cj 29.52N 115.26 E
Fushun 22 Oe 41.46N 123.56 E
Fusong 27 Mc 42.20N 127.17 E
Füsselberg 12 Je 49.32N 7.14 E
Füssen 10 Gi 47.34N 10.42 E
Futa, Passo della- 14 Ff 44.05N 11.17 E
Futago-Yama 29 Be 33.35N 131.38 E
Futaoi-Jima 29 Bd 34.06N 130.47 E
Futog 15 Cd 45.15N 19.42 E
Futuna, Ile- 57 Jf 14.17S 178.09W
Fuwah 24 Dg 31.12N 30.33 E
Fuxian (Wafangdian) 27 Ld 39.38N 121.59 E
Fuxian Hu 27 Hg 24.30N 102.55 E
Fuxin 22 Oe 41.59N 121.38 E
Fuxin Monggolzu Zizhixian 28 Fc 42.06N 121.46 E
Fuyang 27 Ke 32.47N 115.46 E
Fuyang He 28 Dg 38.14N 116.05 E
Fuyang Zhan 28 Ch 32.56N 115.53 E
Fuyu [China] 27 Lb 45.10N 124.52 E
Fuyu [China] 27 Lb 47.48N 124.26 E
Fuyuan [China] 27 Lc 42.44N 124.57 E
Fuyuan [China] 27 Nb 48.21N 134.18 E
Fuyuan [China] 27 Hf 25.43N 104.20 E
Fuyun/Koktokay 22 Ke 47.13N 89.39 E
Füzesabony 10 Qi 47.45N 20.25 E
Fuzhou [China] 22 Ng 26.10N 119.20 E
Fuzhou [China] 27 Kf 27.58N 116.20 E
Fuzhou He 28 Fe 39.36N 121.35 E
Fyllas Bank (EN) 41 Gf 64.00N 53.00W
Fyn 5 Hd 55.20N 10.30 E
Fyn [2] 8 Di 55.20N 10.30 E
Fyne, Loch- 9 He 56.10N 5.20W
Fyresdal 7 Bg 59.11N 8.06 E
Fyresvatn 8 Ce 59.05N 8.10 E
Fzåra, Gara'et- 14 Bn 36.47N 7.30 E

G

Gaasbeek 12 Gd 50.48N 4.10 E
Gaasterland 12 Hb 52.54N 5.36 E
Gaasterland 12 Hb 52.53N 5.35 E
Gaasterland-Balk 12 Hb 52.54N 5.36 E
Gabaru Reef 64a Bb 7.53N 134.31 E
Gabas 11 Fk 43.46N 0.42W
Gabba' 35 Id 8.02N 50.08 E
Gabbs 46 Gg 38.52N 117.55W
Gabela 31 Ij 10.52S 14.23 E
Gabès, Gulf of-(EN) = Qābis, Khalīj- 30 Ie 34.00N 10.25 E
Gabon 36 Ab 0.25N 9.20 E
Gabon [1] 31 Ii 1.00S 11.45 E
Gaborone 31 Jk 24.40S 25.55 E
Gabras 35 Dc 10.16N 26.14 E
Gabriel Strait 42 Kd 61.50N 65.40W
Gabriel y Galán, Embalse de- 13 Fd 40.15N 6.15W
Gabrovo 15 Ig 42.52N 25.19 E
Gabrovo [2] 15 Ig 42.52N 25.19 E
Gacé 11 Gf 48.48N 0.18 E
Gachsārān 24 Ng 30.12N 50.47 E
Gackle 45 Gc 46.38N 99.09W
Gacko 14 Mg 43.10N 18.32 E
Gadag 25 Fe 15.25N 75.37 E
Gäddede 7 Dd 64.30N 14.09 E
Gadê 27 Ge 34.13N 99.29 E
Gadjač 16 Id 50.22N 34.01 E
Gádor, Sierra de- 13 Jh 36.55N 2.45W
Gadsden 43 Je 34.02N 86.02W
Gadūk, Gardaneh-ye- 24 Oe 35.55N 52.55 E
Gadzi 35 Be 4.47N 16.42 E
Gael Hamkes Bugt 41 Jd 74.00N 22.00W
Găeşti 15 Ie 44.43N 25.19 E
Gaeta 14 Hi 41.12N 13.35 E
Gaeta, Golfo di- 14 Hi 41.05N 13.30 E
Gaferut Island 57 Fd 9.14N 145.23 E
Gaffney 44 Gh 35.05N 81.39W
Gagan 63a Ba 5.14S 154.37 E
Gagarin [R.S.F.S.R.] 19 Dd 55.35N 35.01 E
Gagarin [Uzb.-U.S.S.R.] 18 Gd 40.40N 68.05 E
Gagévésouva, Pointe- 63b Ca 13.04S 166.32 E
Gaggenau 12 Kf 48.48N 8.20 E
Gagnef 7 Df 60.35N 15.04 E
Gagnoa 31 Gh 6.08N 5.56W
Gagnoa [3] 34 Dd 6.03N 6.00W
Gagnon 42 Kf 51.55N 68.10W
Gagra 19 Eg 43.17N 40.15 E
Gahkom 24 Ph 28.12N 55.50 E
Gahkom, Kūh-e- 24 Ph 28.10N 55.57 E
Gaiba, Laguna- 55 Dc 17.45S 57.43W
Gail 14 Hd 46.36N 13.53 E
Gaillac 11 Hk 43.54N 1.55 E
Gaillefontaine 12 De 49.39N 1.37 E
Gaillimh/Galway 6 Fe 53.16N 9.03W
Gaillimh/Galway [2] 9 Eh 53.20N 9.00W
Gaillon 12 De 49.10N 1.20 E
Gailtaler Alpen 14 Gd 46.40N 13.00 E
Gaiman 56 Gf 43.17S 65.29W
Găineşti 15 Ib 47.25N 25.55 E
Gainesville [Fl.-U.S.] 39 Kg 29.40N 82.20W
Gainesville [Ga.-U.S.] 43 Ke 34.18N 83.50W
Gainesville [Mo.-U.S.] 45 Jh 36.36N 92.26W
Gainesville [Tx.-U.S.] 43 He 33.37N 97.08W
Gainsborough 9 Mh 53.24N 0.46W
Gairdner, Lake- 57 Eh 31.35S 136.00 E
Gairloch 9 Hd 57.43N 5.40W
Gaizina Kalns/Gajzinkalns 8 Kh 56.50N 25.59 E
Gaj 19 Fe 51.31N 58.30 E
Gajny 19 Fc 60.20N 54.15 E
Gajsin 19 Cf 48.50N 29.27 E
Gajvoron 16 Fe 48.22N 29.52 E
Gajzinkalns/Gaizina Kalns 8 Kh 56.50N 25.59 E
Galaasija 18 Ee 39.52N 64.27 E
Gălăbovo 15 Ig 42.08N 25.51 E
Gala Gölü 15 Ji 40.45N 26.12 E
Galaico, Macizo- 13 Eb 42.30N 7.20W
Galán, Cerro- 56 Gc 25.55S 66.52W
Galana 30 Li 3.09S 40.08 E
Galanta 10 Nh 48.12N 17.44 E
Galap 64a Bb 7.38N 134.39 E
Galápagos, Islas-/Colón, Archipiélago de- = Galapagos Islands (EN) 52 Gf 0.30S 90.30W
Galapagos Fracture Zone (EN) 3 Mi 0.00 100.00W
Galapagos Islands (EN) = Colon, Archipiélago de-/Galápagos, Islas- 52 Gf 0.30S 90.30W
Galapagos Islands (EN) = Galápagos, Islas-/Colón, Archipiélago de- 52 Gf 0.30S 90.30W
Galarza 55 Di 28.06S 56.41W
Galashiels 9 Kf 55.37N 2.49W
Galaţi 15 Kd 45.33N 27.56 E
Galaţi [2] 6 If 45.27N 28.03 E
Galatina 14 Mj 40.10N 18.10 E
Galatone 14 Mj 40.09N 18.04 E
Galatzó 13 Oe 39.38N 2.29 E
Galdar 32 Dd 28.09N 15.39W
Galdhøpiggen 7 Bf 61.37N 8.17 E
Galeana [Mex.] 48 Fb 30.07N 107.38W
Galeana [Mex.] 48 Ie 24.50N 100.04W
Galeh Dār 24 Oi 27.38N 52.42 E
Galela 58 Dd 1.50N 127.50 E
Galena [Ak.-U.S.] 40 Hd 64.44N 156.57W
Galena [Il.-U.S.] 45 Ke 42.25N 90.26W
Galeota Point 50 Fg 10.08N 60.59W
Galera, Punta- 56 Fe 39.59S 73.43W
Galera, Rio- 55 Bb 14.25S 60.07W
Galera Point 50 Fg 10.49N 60.55W
Galesburg 43 Ic 40.57N 90.22W
Galga 10 Pi 47.33N 19.43 E
Gal Gaduud [3] 35 Hd 5.00N 47.00 E
Galheirão, Rio- 55 Ja 12.23S 45.05W
Galheiros 55 Ia 13.18S 46.25W
Gali 16 Lh 42.36N 41.42 E
Galič [R.S.F.S.R.] 19 Ed 58.23N 42.21 E
Galič [Ukr.-U.S.S.R.] 16 De 49.06N 24.43 E
Galicea Mare 15 Ge 44.06N 23.18 E
Galicia 5 Fg 43.00N 8.00W
Galicia 13 Eb 43.00N 8.00W
Galicia (EN) = Galicija 5 If 49.50N 21.00 E
Galicia (EN) = Galicija [Eur.] 10 Qg 49.50N 21.00 E
Galicia (EN) = Galicja 10 Qg 49.50N 21.00 E
Galicia (EN) = Galicja 5 If 49.50N 21.00 E
Galicija [Eur.] = Galicia (EN) 10 Qg 49.50N 21.00 E
Galicija [Ukr.-U.S.S.R.] 10 Jg 49.00N 24.00 E
Galicija = Galicia (EN) 5 If 49.50N 21.00 E
Galicja = Galicia (EN) 5 If 49.50N 21.00 E
Galicja = Galicia (EN) 10 Qg 49.50N 21.00 E
Galilee, Lake- 59 Jd 22.20S 145.55 E
Galimy 20 Kd 62.19N 156.00 E
Galina Point 49 Id 18.24N 76.53W
Galion 44 Fe 40.44N 82.46W
Galion, Baie du- 51h Bb 14.44N 60.57W
Galiton 14 Cm 37.30N 8.52 E
Galiuro Mountains 46 Jj 32.40N 110.20W
Gālka'yo 31 Lh 6.49N 47.23 E
Galkino 17 Ki 55.40N 62.55 E
Gallarate 14 Ce 45.40N 8.47 E
Gallatin 44 Dg 36.24N 86.27W
Gallatin Range 46 Jd 45.15N 111.05W
Gallatin River 46 Jd 45.56N 111.29W
Galle 22 Ki 6.02N 80.13 E
Gállego 13 Lc 41.39N 0.51W
Gallegos, Rio- 52 Jk 51.36S 68.59W
Gallinas, Punta- 52 Id 12.25N 71.40W
Gallinas Peak 45 Di 34.15N 105.45W
Gallipoli 14 Lj 40.03N 17.58 E
Gallipoli Peninsula (EN) = Gelibolu Yarimadası 15 Ji 40.20N 26.30 E
Gallipolis 44 Ff 38.49N 82.14W
Gällivare 6 Ib 67.08N 20.42 E
Galljaaral 18 Fd 40.02N 67.35 E
Gallo 13 Jd 40.48N 2.09W
Gällö 7 De 62.55N 15.14 E
Gallo, Capo- 14 Hl 38.15N 13.19 E
Gallo Mountains 45 Bi 34.00N 108.15W
Galloway 9 If 55.00N 4.25W
Galloway, Mull of- 9 Ig 54.38N 4.50W
Gallup 39 If 35.32N 108.44W
Gallur 13 Kc 41.52N 1.19W
Gallura 14 Dj 41.00N 9.15 E
Galmaarden/Gammerages 12 Fd 50.45N 3.58 E
Galole 36 Hc 1.30S 40.02 E
Galt 44 Gd 43.22N 80.19W
Gal Tardo 35 He 3.37N 45.58 E
Galtasen 8 Eg 57.48N 13.30 E
Galty Mountains/Na Gaibhlte 9 Ei 52.23N 8.11W
Galut 17 Hb 46.43N 100.08 E
Galveston 39 Jg 29.18N 94.48W
Galveston Bay 38 Jg 29.36N 94.57W
Galveston Island 45 Il 29.13N 94.55W
Gálvez 56 Hd 32.02S 61.13W
Galway/Gaillimh [2] 9 Eh 53.20N 9.00W
Galway/Gaillimh 6 Fe 53.16N 9.03W
Galway Bay/Cuan na Gaillimhe 5 Fe 53.10N 9.15W
Gamaches 12 De 49.59N 1.33 E
Gamagōri 29 Ed 34.49N 137.13 E
Gamarra 54 Db 8.19N 73.44W
Gamba [China] 27 Ef 28.17N 88.31 E
Gamba [Gabon] 36 Ac 2.37S 10.00 E
Gambaga 34 Ec 10.32N 0.26W
Gambela 31 Kh 8.15N 34.36 E
Gambell 40 Ed 63.46N 171.46W
Gambia 30 Fg 13.28N 16.34W
Gambia [1] 31 Fg 13.25N 16.00W
Gambie 34 Bc 13.28N 16.34W
Gambier, Iles- = Gambier Islands (EN) 57 Ng 23.09S 134.58W
Gambier Islands (EN) = Gambier, Iles- 57 Ng 23.09S 134.58W
Gambo 35 Ce 4.39N 22.16 E
Gamboma 36 Cc 1.53S 15.51 E
Gamboula 35 Be 4.08N 15.09 E
Gamda → Zamtang 27 He 32.23N 101.05 E
Gamelão 55 Db 15.29S 57.50W
Gamkonora, Gunung- 26 If 1.21N 127.31 E
Gamlakarleby/Kokkola 6 Ic 63.50N 23.07 E
Gamla Uppsala 8 Ge 59.54N 17.38 E
Gamleby 7 Dh 57.54N 16.24 E
Gamo Gofa [3] 35 Fd 5.45N 37.20 E
Gamua 64h Bb 13.15S 176.08W
Gamud 35 Fe 4.05N 38.06 E
Gamvik 7 Ga 71.03N 28.14 E
Ganāne, Webi- = Juba (EN) 30 Lh 0.15S 42.38 E
Gananoque 44 Ic 44.20N 76.10W
Ganāveh 24 Nh 29.32N 50.31 E
Gancedo 55 Bh 27.30S 61.42W
Ganceviči 16 Ec 52.45N 26.29 E
Gand/Gent = Ghent (EN) 11 Jc 51.03N 3.43 E
Ganda 36 Be 12.59S 14.40 E
Gandadiwata, Bulu- 26 Gg 2.42S 119.27 E
Gandajika 36 Dd 6.45S 23.57 E
Gandak 25 Hc 25.39N 85.13 E
Gander 39 Ne 48.57N 54.34W
Ganderkesee 12 Ka 53.04N 8.33 E
Gandesa 13 Mc 41.03N 0.26 E
Gandhinagar 22 Jg 23.21N 72.40 E
Gāndhi Sāgar 25 Fd 24.30N 75.30 E
Gandia 13 Lf 38.58N 0.11W
Gandia-Grao de Gandia 13 Lf 38.59N 0.09W
Gandisê Shan 21 Kf 31.00N 83.00 E
Gandu 54 Kf 13.45S 39.30W
Ganetti 35 Eb 17.58N 31.13 E
Ganga = Ganges (EN) 21 Lg 23.20N 90.30 E
Gangaw 25 Id 22.10N 94.08 E
Gangca (Shaliuhe) 27 Hd 37.30N 100.14 E
Ganges 11 Jk 43.56N 3.42 E
Ganges (EN) = Ganga 21 Lg 23.20N 90.30 E
Ganges, Mouths of the- (EN) 21 Lg 23.20N 90.30 E
Gangi 14 Im 37.48N 14.12 E
Gango 36 Cd 9.48S 15.40 E
Gangtok 22 Kg 27.20N 88.37 E
Gangu 27 Ie 34.45N 105.12 E
Gangziyao 28 Cf 36.17N 114.06 E
Gan He 27 Mb 49.12N 125.14 E
Ganhe 27 La 50.43N 123.00 E
Gani 26 Ig 0.47S 128.13 E
Ganjgah 24 Md 37.42N 48.16 E
Gan Jiang 21 Ng 29.12N 116.00 E
Ganjig → Horqin Zuoyi Houqi 27 Lc 42.57N 122.14 E
Gannan 27 Lb 47.53N 123.26 E
Gannat 11 Jh 46.06N 3.12 E
Gannett Peak 38 Ie 43.10N 109.40W
Gansbaai 37 Bf 34.35S 19.22 E
Gansu Sheng (Kan-su Sheng) = Kansu (EN) [2] 27 Hd 38.00N 102.00 E
Ganta 34 Dd 7.14N 8.59W
Gantang → Taiping 28 Ei 30.18N 118.07 E
Ganyu (Qingkou) 28 Eg 34.50N 119.07 E
Ganzhou 22 Ng 25.49N 114.56 E
Gao [3] 34 Eb 18.15N 1.00W
Gao [Mali] 31 Hg 16.15N 0.01 E
Gao [Niger] 34 Gb 15.25N 5.45 E
Gao'an 27 Kf 28.27N 115.24 E
Gaobeidian → Xincheng 28 Ce 39.20N 115.50 E
Gaocheng 28 Ce 38.02N 114.50 E
Gaolan (Shidongsi) 27 Hd 36.23N 103.55 E
Gaoliangjian → Hongze 27 Ke 33.10N 119.58 E
Gaoligong Shan 27 Gf 25.45N 98.45 E
Gaolou Ling 27 Ig 24.47N 106.48 E
Gaomi 28 Ef 36.23N 119.45 E
Gaoping 27 Jd 35.46N 112.55 E
Gaoqing (Tianzhen) 28 Df 37.10N 117.50 E
Gaotai 27 Gd 39.20N 99.58 E
Gaotingzhen → Daishan 28 Gi 30.15N 122.13 E
Gaoua 34 Ec 10.20N 3.11W
Gaoual 34 Cc 11.45N 13.12W
Gaoyang 28 Ce 38.42N 115.47 E
Gaoyi 28 Cf 37.37N 114.37 E
Gaoyou 28 Eh 32.46N 119.27 E
Gaoyou Hu 27 Ke 32.50N 119.15 E
Gaozhou 27 Jg 21.56N 110.47 E
Gap 11 Mj 44.34N 6.05 E
Gar 27 Ce 32.12N 79.57 E
Gara, Lough-/Loch Ui Ghadra 9 Eh 53.55N 8.30W
Gara'ad 35 Hd 6.54N 49.20 E
Garabato 55 Bi 28.56S 60.09W
Garachiné 49 Hi 8.04N 78.22W
Garachiné, Punta- 49 Hi 8.06N 78.25W
Gara Dragoman 15 Fg 42.55N 22.56 E
Ga'raet el Oubeira 14 Cn 36.50N 8.23 E
Gara Kostenec 15 Gg 42.18N 23.52 E
Garalo 34 Dc 11.00N 7.26W
Gara Muleta 35 Gd 9.05N 41.43 E
Garanhuns 53 Mf 8.54S 36.29W
Garapan 64b Ba 15.12N 145.43 E
Garapuava 55 Ic 16.06S 46.33W
Garavuti 18 Gf 37.36N 68.29 E
Garba 35 Cd 9.12N 20.30 E
Garbahārrey 35 Ge 3.20N 42.17 E
Garberville 46 Df 40.06N 123.48W
Gārbosh, Kūh-e- 24 Nf 32.36N 50.04 E
Garça 55 Hf 22.14S 49.37W
Garças, Rio das- 55 Fb 15.54S 52.16W
Garcias 55 Fe 20.34S 52.13W
Gard [3] 11 Jj 44.00N 4.00 E
Gard 11 Kk 43.51N 4.37 E
Garda 14 Ee 45.34N 10.42 E
Garda, Lago di- = Garda, Lake- (EN) 5 Hf 45.35N 10.35 E
Garda, Lake- (EN) = Garda, Lago di- 5 Hf 45.35N 10.35 E
Gardabani 16 Ni 41.29N 45.05 E
Garde, Cap de- 14 Bn 36.58N 7.47 E
Gardelegen 10 Hd 52.32N 11.22 E
Garden City [Ga.-U.S.] 44 Gi 32.06N 81.09W
Garden City [Ks.-U.S.] 43 Gd 37.58N 100.53W
Garden Grove 46 Gj 33.46N 117.57W
Garden Peninsula 44 Dc 45.40N 86.35W
Gardermoen 8 Dd 60.13N 11.06 E
Gardey 55 Cm 37.17S 59.21W
Gardēz 23 Kc 33.37N 69.07 E
Gardiner 46 Jd 45.02N 110.42W
Gardiner Range 59 Fc 19.15S 128.50 E
Gardner → Nikumaroro Atoll 57 Je 4.40S 174.32W
Gardner Pinnacles 57 Kb 25.00N 167.55W
Gardno, Jezioro- 10 Nb 54.43N 17.05 E
Gardone Riviera 14 Ee 45.37N 10.34 E
Gardždai/Gargždaj 7 Ei 55.43N 21.24 E
Gareloi 40a Cb 51.47N 178.48W
Garessio 14 Cf 44.12N 8.02 E
Garfagnana 14 Ef 44.05N 10.30 E
Gargaliánoi 15 El 37.04N 21.38 E
Gargano 5 Hg 41.50N 16.00 E
Gargano, Testa del- 14 Ki 41.35N 16.12 E
Gargantua, Cape- 44 Eb 47.36N 85.02W
Gargždaj/Gargždai 7 Ei 55.43N 21.24 E
Gari 19 Gd 59.28N 62.25 E
Garibaldi 55 Gi 29.15S 51.32W
Garibaldi, Mount- 46 Db 49.51N 123.01W
Garies 37 Bf 30.30S 18.00 E
Garigliano 14 Hi 41.13N 13.45 E
Garimpo 55 Ed 18.41S 54.50W
Garissa 31 Ki 0.28S 39.38 E

Index Symbols

[1] Independent Nation
[2] State, Region
[3] District, County
[4] Municipality
[5] Colony, Dependency
Continent
Physical Region
Historical or Cultural Region
Mount, Mountain
Volcano
Hill
Mountains, Mountain Range
Hills, Escarpment
Plateau, Upland
Pass, Gap
Plain, Lowland
Delta
Salt Flat
Valley, Canyon
Crater, Cave
Karst Features
Depression
Polder
Desert, Dunes
Forest, Woods
Heath, Steppe
Oasis
Cape, Point
Coast, Beach
Cliff
Peninsula
Isthmus
Sandbank
Island
Atoll
Rock, Reef
Islands, Archipelago
Rocks, Reefs
Coral Reef
Well, Spring
Geyser
River, Stream
Waterfall Rapids
River Mouth, Estuary
Lake
Salt Lake
Intermittent Lake
Reservoir
Swamp, Pond
Canal
Glacier
Ice Shelf, Pack Ice
Ocean
Sea
Gulf, Bay
Strait, Fjord
Lagoon
Bank
Seamount
Tablemount
Ridge
Shelf
Basin
Escarpment, Sea Scarp
Fracture
Trench, Abyss
National Park, Reserve
Point of Interest
Recreation Site
Cave, Cavern
Historic Site
Ruins
Wall, Walls
Church, Abbey
Temple
Scientific Station
Airport
Port
Lighthouse
Mine
Tunnel
Dam, Bridge

Name	Map	Grid	Lat.	Long.
Garkida	34	Hc	10.25N	12.34 E
Garland	45	Hj	32.54N	96.39W
Garlasco	14	Ce	45.12N	8.55 E
Garliava/Garljava	8	Jj	54.46N	23.55 E
Garljava/Garliava	8	Jj	54.46N	23.55 E
Garm	18	He	39.02N	70.18 E
Garmisch-Partenkirchen	10	Hi	47.30N	11.06 E
Garmsar	24	Oe	35.20N	52.13 E
Garnet Bank (EN)	55	Hk	33.05S	49.25W
Garnet Range	46	Ic	46.45N	113.15W
Garnett	45	Ig	38.17N	95.14W
Garonne	5	Ff	45.02N	0.36W
Garonne, Canal latéral à la-	11	Fj	44.34N	0.09W
Garopába	55	Hi	28.04S	48.40W
Garoua	31	Ih	9.18N	13.24 E
Garoua Boulaï	35	Ad	5.53N	14.33 E
Garoubi	34	Fc	13.07N	2.18 E
Garōwe	31	Lh	8.25N	48.33 E
Garpenberg	8	Gd	60.19N	16.12 E
Garphyttan	8	Fe	59.19N	14.56 E
Garrel	12	Kb	52.57N	8.01 E
Garreru	64a	Bc	7.20N	134.33 E
Garri, Kūh-e-	24	Mf	33.59N	48.25 E
Garrigues	11	Kj	44.10N	4.30 E
Garrison	45	Fc	47.40N	101.25W
Garron Point/An Gearran	9	Hf	55.05N	5.58W
Garrovillas	13	Fe	39.43N	6.33W
Garruchos	55	Ei	28.11S	55.39W
Garry	9	Je	56.45N	3.45W
Garry Bay	42	Ic	69.00N	85.10W
Garry Lake	38	Jc	66.00N	100.00W
Garsen	36	Hc	2.16S	40.07 E
Gartar/Qianning	27	He	30.27N	101.29 E
Gartempe	11	Gh	46.47N	0.50 E
Gartog → Markam	27	Gf	29.32N	98.33 E
Garut	26	Eh	7.13S	107.54 E
Garuva	55	Hh	26.01S	48.51W
Garvie Mountains	62	Cf	45.30S	168.50 E
Garwa	25	Gd	24.11N	83.49 E
Garwolin	10	Re	51.54N	21.37 E
Gary	43	Jc	41.36N	87.20W
Garyarsa	27	De	31.40N	80.26 E
Garzê	27	Ge	31.42N	99.58 E
Garzón [Col.]	54	Cc	2.13N	75.38W
Garzón [Ur.]	56	Jd	34.36S	54.33W
Gasan-Kuli	19	Fh	37.29N	53.59 E
Gascogne = Gascony (EN)	11	Gk	43.30N	0.10 E
Gasconade River	45	Kg	38.40N	91.33W
Gascony (EN) = Gascogne	11	Gk	43.30N	0.10 E
Gascoyne Junction	59	De	25.03S	115.12 E
Gascoyne River	57	Cg	24.52S	113.37 E
Gasefjord	41	Je	70.00N	27.30W
Gaseland	41	Jd	70.20N	29.00W
Gash	30	Kg	16.48N	35.51 E
Gas Hu	27	Fd	38.08N	90.45 E
Gashua	31	Ig	12.52N	11.03 E
Gaspar Strait (EN)=Kelasa, Selat-	26	Eg	2.40S	107.15 E
Gaspé	39	Me	48.50N	64.29W
Gaspé, Cap de -	42	Lg	48.45N	64.10W
Gaspé, Péninsule de-= Gaspe Peninsula (EN)	38	Me	48.30N	65.00W
Gaspe Peninsula (EN)= Gaspé, Péninsule de-	38	Me	48.30N	65.00W
Gassan	29	Gb	38.34N	140.01 E
Gassol	34	Hd	8.32N	10.28 E
Gaston, Lake-	44	Ig	36.35N	78.00W
Gastonia	43	Kd	35.16N	81.11W
Gastoúni	15	El	37.51N	21.15 E
Gastre	56	Gf	42.17S	69.14W
Gästrikland	8	Gd	60.30N	16.30 E
Gata, Akrōtērion-	24	Ee	34.34N	33.02 E
Gata, Cabo de-	5	Fh	36.43N	2.12W
Gata, Sierra de-	13	Fd	40.15N	6.45W
Gătaia	15	Ed	45.26N	21.26 E
Gatčina	19	Dd	59.34N	30.09 E
Gate	45	Fh	36.51N	100.01W
Gate City	44	Fg	36.38N	82.37W
Gateshead	9	Lg	54.58N	1.37W
Gateshead	42	Hb	70.35N	100.15W
Gathemo	12	Bf	48.46N	0.58W
Gâtinais	11	If	48.00N	2.20 E
Gâtine, Hauteurs de-	11	Fh	46.38N	0.38W
Gatineau, Rivière-	42	Jg	45.27N	75.42W
Gatlinburg	44	Fh	35.43N	83.31W
Gato, Cumbres del-	48	Fd	27.00N	106.35W
Gattinara	14	Ce	45.37N	8.22 E
Gatún	49	Hi	9.16N	79.55W
Gatún, Lago-=Gatun Lake (EN)	47	Ig	9.12N	79.55W
Gatun Lake (EN)=Gatún, Lago-	47	Ig	9.12N	79.55W
Gatvand	24	Mf	32.15N	48.50 E
Gatwich Airport	12	Bc	51.08N	0.12W
Gaucín	13	Gh	36.31N	5.19W
Gauhati → Guwāhāti	22	Lg	26.11N	91.44 E
Gauiena/Gaujiena	8	Lg	57.25N	26.28 E
Gauja	7	Fh	57.10N	24.16 E
Gaujiena/Gauiena	8	Lg	57.25N	26.28 E
Gaula [Nor.]	8	Da	63.21N	10.14 E
Gaula [Nor.]	8	Ac	61.22N	5.41 E
Gauldalen	8	Db	63.00N	11.00 E
Gauley River	44	Gf	38.10N	81.12W
Gau-Odernheim	12	Ke	49.46N	8.12 E
Gaurdak	19	Gh	37.49N	66.01 E
Gausdal	8	Cc	61.20N	9.55 E
Gausta	7	Bg	59.50N	8.39 E
Gāvbandī	24	Oi	27.12N	53.04 E
Gāvbūs, Kūh-e-	24	Oi	27.10N	54.00 E
Gavdhopoúla	15	Go	34.56N	24.00 E
Gávdhos	5	Ii	34.50N	24.05 E
Gāveh	24	Le	35.00N	46.58 E
Gavere	12	Fd	50.56N	3.40 E
Gavkhūnī, Bātlāq-e-	24	Of	32.06N	52.52 E
Gāv Kosh	24	Le	34.00N	48.00 E
Gävle	6	Hc	60.40N	17.10 E
Gävleborg [2]	7	Df	61.30N	16.15 E
Gävlebukten	8	Gd	60.40N	17.20 E
Gavorrano	14	Eh	42.55N	10.54 E
Gavri	8	Lh	56.49N	27.58 E
Gavrilov-Jam	7	Jh	57.19N	39.51 E
Gāw Koshi	23	Id	28.38N	57.12 E
Gawler	59	Hf	34.37S	138.44 E
Gawler Ranges	57	Eh	32.30S	136.00 E
Gaxun Nur	21	Me	42.25N	101.00 E
Gaya [India]	22	Kg	24.47N	85.00 E
Gaya [Niger]	34	Fc	11.53N	3.27 E
Gaya He	28	Jc	42.58N	129.52 E
Gaylord	44	Ec	45.02N	84.40W
Gayndah	59	Ke	25.37S	151.36 E
Gaz	24	Nf	32.48N	51.37 E
Gaza [3]	37	Ed	23.30S	33.00 E
Gaz-Ačak	19	Gg	41.11N	61.27 E
Gazalkent	18	Gd	41.33N	69.46 E
Gazaoua	34	Gc	13.32N	7.55 E
Gazelle, Récif de la-	63b	Be	20.11S	165.27 E
Gaziantep	22	Ff	37.05N	37.22 E
Gaziemir	15	Kk	38.19N	27.10 E
Gazimağusa = Famagusta (EN)	23	Dc	35.07N	33.57 E
Gazipaşa	24	Ed	36.17N	32.20 E
Gazli	19	Gg	40.09N	63.23 E
Gbarnga	31	Gh	7.00N	9.29W
Gboko	34	Gd	7.21N	8.58 E
Gbon	34	Dd	9.50N	6.27W
Gdańsk [2]	10	Ob	54.25N	18.40 E
Gdańsk=Danzig (EN)	6	He	54.23N	18.40 E
Gdansk, Gulf of- (EN)= Gdanska, Zatoka-	5	He	54.40N	19.15 E
Gdov	7	Gg	58.47N	27.54 E
Gdynia	6	He	54.32N	18.33 E
Gearhart Mountain	46	Ee	42.30N	120.53W
Gêba	34	Bc	11.58N	15.00W
Gebe, Pulau-	26	Ig	0.05S	129.20 E
Gebze	24	Cb	40.48N	29.25 E
Gecha	35	Fd	7.29N	35.25 E
Geçitkale	25	Ee	35.15N	33.45 E
Gedi	36	Hc	3.18S	40.01 E
Gedinne	12	Ge	49.59N	4.56 E
Gediz	24	Cc	39.02N	29.25 E
Gedo	35	Ge	2.20N	41.20 E
Gedo [3]	35	Ge	3.00N	42.00 E
Gedo	35	Fd	9.00N	37.29 E
Gedser, Sydfalster-	7	Ci	54.35N	11.57 E
Gedser Odde	8	Dj	54.34N	11.59 E
Geel	11	Kc	51.10N	5.00 E
Geelong	58	Fh	38.08S	144.21 E
Geelvink Channel	59	Ce	28.30S	114.10 E
Geer	12	Hd	50.51N	5.42 E
Geeste	12	Jb	52.36N	7.16 E
Geesthacht	10	Gc	53.26N	10.22 E
Gê'gyai	27	De	32.29N	80.52 E
Ge Hu	28	Ei	31.36N	119.51 E
Geidam	34	Hc	12.53N	11.56 E
Geigar	35	Ec	11.59N	32.46 E
Geihoku	29	Cd	34.44N	132.17 E
Geikie	42	He	57.48N	103.46W
Geilo	7	Bf	60.31N	8.12 E
Geiranger	8	Bb	62.06N	7.12 E
Geisenheim	12	Je	49.59N	7.58 E
Geislingen an der Steige	10	Fh	48.37N	9.51 E
Geita	36	Fc	2.52S	32.10 E
Geithus	7	Bg	59.57N	9.59 E
Geiyo-Shotō	29	Cd	34.15N	132.45 E
Gejiu	22	Mg	23.22N	103.14 E
Gel [Sud.]	30	Jh	7.46N	29.36 E
Gel [Sud.]	35	Ed	6.08N	31.17 E
Gela	14	Im	37.04N	14.15 E
Gela, Golfo di-	14	Im	37.05N	14.10 E
Geladi	35	Hd	6.57N	46.25 E
Geldenaken/Jodoigne	12	Gd	50.43N	4.52 E
Gelderland [3]	12	Hb	52.10N	5.50 E
Geldermalsen	12	Hc	51.53N	5.19 E
Geldern	10	Ce	51.31N	6.20 E
Geldrop	12	Hc	51.25N	5.33 E
Geleen	11	Ld	50.58N	5.52 E
Gelembé	15	Kj	39.10N	27.50 E
Gelemso	35	Gd	8.48N	40.32 E
Gelendžik	19	Dg	44.33N	38.06 E
Gélengdeng	35	Bc	10.56N	15.32 E
Gelgaudiškis	8	Ji	55.02N	22.58 E
Gelibolu	24	Bb	40.24N	26.40 E
Gelibolu Yarimadası = Gallipoli Peninsula (EN)	15	Ji	40.20N	26.30 E
Gélise	11	Gj	44.11N	0.17 E
Gellinsör	35	Hd	6.24N	46.46 E
Gelnhausen	10	Ff	50.12N	9.11 E
Gelsenkirken	10	De	51.31N	7.06 E
Gemena	31	Ih	3.15N	19.46 E
Gemerek	24	Gc	39.11N	36.05 E
Gemert	12	Hc	51.33N	5.41 E
Gemi, Jabal-	35	Ed	9.01N	34.09 E
Gemlik	24	Cb	40.26N	29.09 E
Gemlik Körfezi	24	Cb	40.25N	28.55 E
Gemona del Friuli	14	Hd	46.16N	13.09 E
Gemünden (Felda)	12	Ld	50.42N	9.03 E
Gemünden (Wohra)	12	Kd	50.58N	8.58 E
Gemünden am Main	10	Ff	50.03N	9.42 E
Genale	30	Lh	0.15S	42.38 E
Genç	24	Ic	38.46N	40.35 E
Gendringen	12	Ic	51.52N	6.23 E
Gendringen-Ulft	12	Ic	51.54N	6.24 E
Genemuiden	12	Ib	52.37N	6.02 E
General Acha	56	He	37.23S	64.36W
General Alvear [Arg.]	56	Gd	34.58S	67.42W
General Alvear [Arg.]	56	He	36.03S	60.01W
General Arenales	55	Bl	34.18S	61.18W
General Artigas	55	Dh	26.53S	56.17W
General Belgrano	56	Ie	35.46S	58.30W
General Belgrano Station	66	Af	77.50S	38.00W
General Bernardo O'Higgins	66	Re	63.19S	57.54W
General Bravo	48	Je	25.48N	99.10W
General Cabrera	56	Hd	32.48S	63.52W
General Capdevila	55	Bh	27.26S	61.28W
General Carneiro	55	Gh	26.28S	51.25W
General Carrera, Lago-	52	Ij	46.30S	72.00W
General Cepeda	48	Ie	25.23N	101.27W
General Conesa [Arg.]	55	Dm	36.30S	57.20W
General Conesa [Arg.]	56	Hf	40.06S	64.26W
General Enrique Martínez	55	Fk	33.12S	53.50W
General Galarza	55	Ck	32.43S	59.24W
General Güemes	56	Hb	24.40S	65.00W
General Guide	56	Ie	36.40S	57.46W
General José de San Martín	55	Ch	26.33S	59.21W
General Juan Madariaga	56	Ie	37.00S	57.09W
General La Madrid	56	He	37.16S	61.17W
General Lavalle	56	Ie	36.24S	56.58W
General Manuel Belgrano, Cerro-	52	Jh	29.01S	67.49W
General O'Brien	55	Bl	34.54S	60.45W
General Pico	56	He	35.40S	63.44W
General Pinedo	56	Hc	27.19S	61.17W
General Pinto	55	Bl	34.46S	61.53W
General Pirán	55	Dm	37.16S	57.45W
General Roca	56	Ge	39.02S	67.35W
General Salgado	55	Ge	20.39S	50.22W
General Santos	22	Oi	6.05N	125.10 E
General Sarmiento	55	Cl	34.33S	58.43W
General Terán	48	Je	25.16N	99.41W
General-Toševo	15	Lf	43.42N	28.02 E
General Treviño	48	Jd	26.14N	99.29W
General Trías	48	Fc	28.21N	106.22W
General Vargas	55	Ei	29.42S	54.40W
General Viamonte	55	Bl	35.01S	61.01W
General Villegas	56	He	35.02S	63.01W
Genesee River	44	Id	43.16N	77.36W
Geneseo	44	Id	42.46N	77.49W
Geneva [Al.-U.S.]	44	Ej	31.02N	85.52W
Geneva [Nb.-U.S.]	45	Hf	40.32N	97.36W
Geneva [N.Y.-U.S.]	44	Id	42.53N	76.59W
Geneva (EN) = Genève	6	Gf	46.10N	6.10 E
Geneva, Lake- (EN) = Léman, Lac-	5	Gf	46.25N	6.30 E
Genève [2]	14	Ad	46.10N	6.15 E
Genève = Geneva (EN)	6	Gf	46.10N	6.10 E
Genevois	11	Mh	46.00N	6.10 E
Genhe → Ergun Zuoqi	22	Od	50.47N	121.32 E
Geni	35	Ed	8.31N	33.10 E
Geničesk	19	Df	46.12N	34.48 E
Genil	13	Gg	37.42N	5.19W
Genk	11	Ld	50.58N	5.30 E
Genkai-Nada	29	Ae	33.45N	130.00 E
Gennargentu	5	Gg	40.00N	9.20 E
Gennep	12	Hc	51.42N	5.59 E
Genoa (EN) = Genova	6	Gg	44.25N	8.57 E
Genoa, Gulf of- (EN) = Genova, Golfo di-	5	Gg	44.10N	8.55 E
Genova = Genoa (EN)	6	Gg	44.25N	8.57 E
Genova, Golfo di- = Genoa, Gulf of- (EN)	5	Gg	44.10N	8.55 E
Genova-Nervi	14	Df	44.23N	9.02 E
Genova-Voltri	14	Cf	44.26N	8.45 E
Genovesa, Isla-	54a	Ba	0.20N	89.58W
Gent/Gand=Ghent (EN)	11	Jc	51.03N	3.43 E
Gentbrugge, Gent-	12	Fc	51.03N	3.45 E
Gent-Gentbrugge	12	Fc	51.03N	3.45 E
Genthin	10	Id	52.24N	12.10 E
Gent-Sint-Amandsberg	12	Fc	51.04N	3.45 E
Genū, Kūhhā-ye-	23	Id	27.25N	56.09 E
Genyem	26	Lg	2.46S	140.12 E
Genzano di Lucania	14	Kj	40.51N	16.02 E
Genzano di Roma	14	Fi	41.42N	11.41 E
Geographe Bay	57	Ch	33.35S	115.15 E
Geographe Channel	59	Cd	24.40S	113.20 E
Geographical Society Øer	41	Jd	72.40N	22.20W
Geokčaj	16	Oi	40.40N	47.42 E
Geok-Tepe	19	Fh	38.10N	57.58 E
Geomagnetic Pole (1975) (EN)	66	Hf	78.40S	109.33 E
Georga, Zemlja-	21	Ga	80.30N	49.00 E
George	38	Md	58.30N	66.00W
George	37	Cf	33.58S	22.24 E
George, Lake- [Austl.]	59	Jg	35.05S	149.25 E
George, Lake- [Fl.-U.S.]	44	Gk	29.17N	81.36W
George, Lake- [Ug.]	36	Fc	0.00	30.12 E
George, Lake- [U.S.]	44	Kd	43.35N	73.35W
George Gill Range	59	Gd	24.15S	131.35 E
Georges Bank (EN)	43	Nc	41.15N	67.30W
George Sound	62	Bf	44.50S	167.20 E
George Town	58	Fi	41.06S	146.50 E
Georgetown	45	Hk	30.38N	97.41W
George Town	22	Mi	5.25N	100.20 E
Georgetown [Austl.]	58	Ff	18.18S	143.33 E
Georgetown [Bah.]	49	Jb	23.30N	75.46W
Georgetown [Cay.Is.]	47	He	19.18N	81.23W
Georgetown [De.-U.S.]	44	Jf	38.42N	75.23W
Georgetown [Gam.]	31	Fg	13.32N	14.46W
Georgetown [Guy.]	53	Ke	6.48N	58.10W
Georgetown [Ky.-U.S.]	44	Ef	38.13N	84.33W
Georgetown [Oh.-U.S.]	44	Ff	38.52N	83.54W
Georgetown [S.C.-U.S.]	43	Le	33.23N	79.18W
Georgetown [St.Hel.]	31	Fi	7.56S	14.25W
Georgetown [St.Vin.]	50	Ff	13.16N	61.08W
George V Coast	66	Je	68.30S	147.30 E
George VI Sound	66	Qf	71.00S	68.00W
George West	45	Gl	28.20N	98.07W
Georgia [2]	43	Ke	32.50N	83.15W
Georgia (EN)	5	Kg	42.00N	44.00 E
Georgia, Strait of -	42	Fg	49.00N	123.20W
Georgia del Sur, Islas-/ South Georgia	66	Ad	54.15S	36.45W
Georgian Bay	38	Ke	45.15N	80.50W
Georgian SSR (EN)= Gruzinskaja SSR [2]	19	Eg	42.00N	44.00 E
Georgijevka [Kaz.-U.S.S.R.]	19	Hg	43.02N	74.43 E
Georgijevka [Kaz.-U.S.S.R.]	19	If	49.19N	81.35 E
Georgijevsk	16	Mg	44.09N	43.28 E
Georgina River	57	Eg	23.30S	139.47 E
Georgsmarienhütte	10	Ed	52.16N	8.02 E
Gera	10	Ge	51.08N	10.56 E
Gera	10	If	50.52N	12.05 E
Geraardsbergen/Grammont	12	Fd	50.46N	3.52 E
Gerais, Chapadão dos-	55	Jc	17.40S	45.35W
Geral, Serra- [Braz.]	55	Gi	29.10S	50.15W
Geral, Serra- [Braz.]	52	Kh	26.30S	50.30W
Geral, Serra- [Braz.]	55	Gf	23.54S	50.46W
Geral da Serra, Coxilha-	55	Ej	30.20S	55.15W
Geral de Goiás, Serra-	52	Lg	13.00S	46.15W
Geraldine	62	Df	44.05S	171.15 E
Geral do Paraná, Serra-	55	Ib	14.45S	47.30W
Geraldton [Austl.]	58	Cg	28.46S	114.36 E
Geraldton [Ont.-Can.]	42	Ig	49.44N	86.57W
Gérardmer	11	Mf	48.04N	6.53 E
Gerāsh	24	Pi	27.40N	54.06 E
Gerbiči, Gora-	20	Fc	66.39N	105.02 E
Gerca	15	Ja	48.10N	26.17 E
Gercüş	24	Id	37.34N	41.23 E
Gerecse	10	Oi	47.41N	18.29 E
Gerede	24	Eb	40.52N	32.39 E
Gerede	24	Eb	40.48N	32.12 E
Gerês, Serra do-	13	Ec	41.48N	8.00W
Gereshk	23	Jc	31.48N	64.34 E
Gérgal	13	Jg	37.07N	2.33W
Gering	45	Ef	41.50N	103.40W
Gerlachovský štít	10	Qg	49.12N	20.09 E
Gerlogubi	35	Hd	6.56N	45.03 E
Gerlos	14	Gc	47.14N	12.02 E
Gerlovo	15	Kf	43.03N	27.35 E
German Democratic Republic = Germany	6	Ge	51.00N	10.00 E
Germania	55	Al	34.34S	62.03W
Germania Land	41	Kc	76.50N	20.00W
Germany, Federal Republic of = Germany	6	Ge	51.00N	10.00 E
Germencik	15	Kl	37.51N	27.37 E
Germersheim	12	Ke	49.13N	8.22 E
Germī	23	Hc	33.32N	54.58 E
Germi	24	Mc	39.01N	48.03 E
Germiston	37	De	26.15S	28.05 E
Gernsbach	12	Kf	48.46N	8.19 E
Gernsheim	12	Ke	49.45N	8.29 E
Gero	28	Ng	35.48N	137.14 E
Gerolstein	12	Id	50.13N	6.40 E
Gerona [3]	13	Ob	42.10N	2.40 E
Gerona/Girona	13	Oc	41.59N	2.49 E
Gerpinnes	12	Gd	50.20N	4.31 E
Gers	11	Gj	44.09N	0.39 E
Gers [3]	11	Gk	43.40N	0.30 E
Gersprenz	12	Le	49.59N	9.04 E
Gêrzê	27	De	32.20N	84.04 E
Gerze	24	Fb	41.48N	35.12 E
Gescher	12	Jc	51.57N	7.00 E
Geseke	12	Kc	51.39N	8.31 E
Geser	26	Jg	3.53S	130.54 E
Gesunda	8	Fd	60.54N	14.32 E
Gesunden	8	Fa	63.10N	15.55 E
Geta	7	Ef	60.23N	19.50 E
Getafe	13	Id	40.18N	3.43W
Gete	11	Ld	50.55N	5.08 E
Getinge	7	Ch	56.49N	12.44 E
Gettysburg	45	Gd	45.01N	99.57W
Gettysburg Seamount (EN)	32	Eb	36.32N	11.37W
Getúlio Vargas	55	Fh	27.50S	52.16W
Getz Ice Shelf	66	Nf	74.15S	125.00W
Geul	12	Hd	50.40N	5.43 E
Gévaudan	11	Jj	44.27N	3.30 E
Gevelsberg	12	Jc	51.19N	7.20 E
Gevgelija	15	Fh	41.08N	22.31 E
Gévora	13	Ff	38.53N	6.57W
Gevsjön	8	Ea	63.25N	12.40 E
Gewane	35	Gc	10.10N	40.39 E
Gex	11	Mh	46.20N	6.04 E
Gexianzhuang → Qinghe	28	Cf	37.03N	115.39 E
Geyersberg	10	Fg	49.50N	9.30 E
Geyik Dağı	24	Ed	36.54N	32.10 E
Geyikli	15	Jj	39.48N	26.12 E
Geyser, Banc du-	37	Hb	12.25S	46.25 E
Geysir	5	Dc	64.19N	20.18W
Geyve	24	Db	40.30N	30.18 E
Ghabāri, Darb al-	24	Cj	25.10N	29.50 E
Ghadāmis	31	He	30.08N	9.30 E
Ghadduwah	33	Bd	26.26N	14.18 E
Ghaghara	21	Kg	24.52N	84.55 E
Ghaghe	63a	Db	7.23S	158.12 E
Ghallah, Wādī al-	30	Jg	10.25N	27.32 E
Ghamrah, Wādī al-	24	Hj	25.47N	38.45 E
Ghana [1]	31	Gh	8.00N	2.00W
Ghanzi	31	Jk	21.42S	21.38 E
Ghanzi [3]	37	Cd	22.00S	23.00 E
Ghār ad Dimā'	14	Cn	36.27N	8.26 E
Gharaqābād	24	Me	35.06N	49.50 E
Gharbī, Al Hajar al-	24	Qj	24.10N	56.15 E
Gharbīyah, Aş Şahrā' al-= Western Desert (EN)	30	Jf	27.30N	28.00 E
Ghardaïa	31	He	32.29N	3.40 E
Ghārib, Jabal-	33	Fd	28.07N	32.54 E
Gharrāf, Shaţţ al-	24	Kf	32.30N	45.48 E
Gharsah, Shaţţ al-	32	Ic	34.06N	7.50 E
Gharyān	33	Bc	32.10N	13.01 E
Gharyān [3]	33	Bc	30.35N	12.00 E
Ghāt	31	If	24.58N	10.11 E
Ghatere	63a	Db	7.58S	159.01 E
Ghaţţī	24	Gg	31.16N	37.31 E
Ghazāl, Baḩr al-	35	Ed	9.31N	30.25 E
Ghazal, Bahr el-	30	Ig	13.01N	15.28 E
Ghazal, Bahr el-	35	Bc	14.00N	16.30 E
Ghazaouet	32	Gb	35.06N	1.51W
Ghazipur	25	Gc	25.35N	83.34 E
Ghaznī	22	If	33.33N	68.26 E
Ghāznī [3]	23	Kc	33.00N	68.00 E
Ghent (EN)=Gand/Gent	11	Jc	51.03N	3.43 E
Ghent (EN)=Gent/Gand	11	Jc	51.03N	3.43 E
Gheorghe Gheorghiu-Dej	15	Jc	46.12N	26.46 E
Gheorghieni	15	Ic	46.43N	25.37 E
Gheorghiu-Dej	19	De	51.00N	39.31 E
Gherla	15	Gb	47.02N	23.55 E
Ghidigeni	15	Kc	46.03N	27.30 E
Ghidole (EN)=Gidole	35	Fd	5.37N	37.29 E
Ghilarza	14	Cj	40.07N	8.50 E
Ghimeş, Pasul-	15	Jc	46.33N	26.07 E
Ghisonaccia	11a	Ba	42.00N	9.24 E
Ghizunabeana Islands	63a	Db	7.33S	158.45 E
Ghowr [3]	23	Jc	34.00N	65.00 E
Ghriss	13	Mi	35.15N	0.10 E
Ghubbat al Qamar	21	Hh	16.00N	52.30 E
Ghudāf, Wādī al-	24	Jf	32.56N	43.30 E
Ghurāb, Jabal al-	24	Hf	34.00N	38.42 E
Ghurayrah	33	Hf	18.37N	42.41 E
Ghūrīān	23	Jc	34.21N	61.30 E
Ghurraḩ, Jabal al-	14	Cn	36.36N	8.23 E
Ghuzayyil, Sabkhat-	33	Dd	29.50N	19.45 E
Giaginskaja	16	Lg	44.47N	40.05 E
Giala, Jabal-	24	Ei	27.20N	32.57 E
Gialo Oasis (EN)=Jālū, Wāḩāt-	30	Jf	29.00N	21.20 E
Gialoúsa	24	Fe	35.35N	34.15 E
Gia Nghia	25	Lf	11.59N	107.42 E
Giannutri	14	Fh	42.15N	11.05 E
Giant's Causeway/Clochán an Aifir	9	Gf	55.15N	6.35W
Giarre	14	Jm	37.43N	15.11 E
Gibara	49	Ic	21.07N	76.08W
Gibbon Point	51b	Bb	18.14N	63.00W
Gibb River	59	Fc	16.25S	126.25 E
Gibbs Islands	66	Re	61.30S	55.31W
Gibellina	14	Gm	37.47N	12.58 E
Gibeon [3]	37	Bd	25.00S	18.30 E
Gibeon	37	Be	25.09S	17.43 E
Gibostad	7	Db	69.21N	18.00 E
Gibraleón	13	Fg	37.23N	6.58W
Gibraltar	6	Fh	36.11N	5.22W
Gibraltar [5]	6	Fh	36.11N	5.22W
Gibraltar, Estrecho de-= Gibraltar, Strait of- (EN)	5	Fh	35.57N	5.36W
Gibraltar, Strait of- (EN)= Djebel Ţāriq, El Bōghāz-	5	Fh	35.57N	5.36W
Gibraltar, Strait of- (EN)= Gibraltar, Estrecho de-	5	Fh	35.57N	5.36W
Gibson Desert	57	Dg	24.30S	126.00 E
Gidami	35	Ed	8.58N	34.40 E
Giddings	45	Hk	30.11N	96.56W
Gidigič	15	Lb	47.04N	28.38 E
Gidole=Ghidole (EN)	35	Fd	5.37N	37.29 E
Gien	11	Ig	47.42N	2.38 E
Giens, Presqu'île de-	11	Mk	43.02N	6.08 E
Gier	11	Ki	45.35N	4.46 E
Gießen	10	Ef	50.35N	8.39 E
Gieten	12	Ia	53.01N	6.48 E
Giethoorn	12	Ib	52.43N	6.07 E
Gifford	42	Jb	70.21N	83.05W
Gifford Seamount (EN)	52	Hi	39.00S	82.00W
Gifhorn	10	Gd	52.29N	10.33 E
Gift Lake	42	Fe	55.49N	115.57W
Gifu	22	Pf	35.25N	136.45 E
Gifu Ken [2]	28	Ng	35.50N	137.00 E
Gigant	16	Lf	46.29N	41.20 E
Giganta, Cerro-	47	Bc	26.07N	111.36W
Giganta, Sierra de la-	47	Bc	26.18N	111.39W
Gigante	54	Cc	2.24N	75.34W
Gigen	15	Hf	43.42N	24.29 E
Gigha	9	Hf	55.41N	5.44W
Giglio	14	Eh	42.20N	10.55 E
Gijón	6	Fg	43.32N	5.40W
Gikongoro	36	Ec	2.30S	29.35 E
Gila Bend	46	Ij	32.57N	112.43W
Gila Bend Mountains	46	Ij	33.10N	113.10W
Gīlān [3]	23	Gb	37.00N	49.50 E
Gīlān-e-Gharb	24	Ke	34.08N	45.55 E
Gila River	43	Ee	32.43N	114.33W
Gilbert, Mount-	46	Ca	50.51N	124.20W
Gilbert River	59	Ic	16.35S	141.15 E
Gilbert Seamount (EN)	40	If	52.50N	150.10W
Gilbués	54	Ie	9.50S	45.21W
Gilé	37	Fc	16.09S	38.19 E
Giles Meteorological Station	59	Fe	25.02S	128.18 E
Gilford Island	46	Ba	50.45N	126.25W
Gilgandra	59	Jf	31.42S	148.39 E
Gilğau	15	Gb	47.17N	23.43 E
Gilgil	36	Gc	0.30S	36.19 E
Gilgit	25	Ea	35.44N	74.38 E
Gilgit	22	Jf	35.55N	74.18 E
Giljuj	20	Hf	54.17N	127.05 E
Gillam	42	Ie	56.21N	94.43W
Gilleleje	8	Eh	56.07N	12.19 E
Gillen, Lake-	59	Ee	26.10S	124.40 E
Gillenfeld	12	Id	50.07N	6.54 E
Gillette	43	Fc	44.18N	105.30W
Gillian, Lake -	42	Jc	69.30N	75.30W
Gillingham	9	Nj	51.24N	0.33 E
Gilo	35	Ed	8.10N	33.15 E
Gilort	15	Ge	44.36N	23.27 E
Gilroy	46	Eh	37.00N	121.34W
Giluwe, Mount-	60	Ci	6.04S	143.53 E
Gīlvān	24	Md	36.47N	49.08 E
Gimån	8	Gb	62.28N	16.20 E
Gimbi	35	Fd	9.10N	35.51 E
Gimie, Mount-	50	Ff	13.52N	61.01W
Gimli	42	Hf	50.39N	97.00W
Gimo	8	Hd	60.11N	18.11 E
Gimolskoje, Ozero-	7	He	63.00N	32.15 E
Gimone	11	Hk	44.00N	1.06 E
Ginda	35	Fb	15.27N	39.06 E
Ginetu	63a	Ac	9.30S	152.43 E

Index Symbols

[1] Independent Nation
[2] State, Region
[3] District, County
[4] Municipality
[5] Colony, Dependency
Continent
Physical Region
Historical or Cultural Region
Mount, Mountain
Volcano
Hill
Mountains, Mountain Range
Hills, Escarpment
Plateau, Upland
Pass, Gap
Plain, Lowland
Delta
Salt Flat
Valley, Canyon
Crater, Cave
Karst Features
Depression
Polder
Desert, Dunes
Forest, Woods
Heath, Steppe
Oasis
Cape, Point
Coast, Beach
Cliff
Peninsula
Isthmus
Sandbank
Island
Atoll
Rock, Reef
Islands, Archipelago
Rocks, Reefs
Coral Reef
Well, Spring
Geyser
River, Stream
Waterfall Rapids
River Mouth, Estuary
Lake
Salt Lake
Intermittent Lake
Reservoir
Swamp, Pond
Canal
Glacier
Ice Shelf, Pack Ice
Ocean
Sea
Gulf, Bay
Strait, Fjord
Lagoon
Bank
Seamount
Tablemount
Ridge
Shelf
Basin
Escarpment, Sea Scarp
Fracture
Trench, Abyss
National Park, Reserve
Point of Interest
Recreation Site
Cave, Cavern
Historic Site
Ruins
Wall, Walls
Church, Abbey
Temple
Scientific Station
Airport
Port
Lighthouse
Mine
Tunnel
Dam, Bridge

Gin Gin 59 Kd 25.00S 151.58 E
Gingin 59 Df 31.21S 115.42 E
Gingoog 26 Ie 8.50N 125.07 E
Ginir 35 Gd 7.08N 40.43 E
Ginosa 14 Kj 40.35N 16.45 E
Ginowan 29b Ab 26.17N 127.45 E
Ginzo de Limia 13 Eb 42.03N 7.43W
Giofra Oasis (EN)=Jufrah, Wāḥāt al- 30 If 29.10N 16.00 E
Gioia, Golfo di- 14 Jl 38.30N 15.45 E
Gioia del Colle 14 Kj 40.48N 16.55 E
Gioia Tauro 14 Jl 38.25N 15.54 E
Gion 35 Fd 8.24N 37.55 E
Gióna Óros 15 Fk 38.35N 22.15 E
Giovi, Passo dei- 14 Cf 44.33N 8.57 E
Giraltovce 10 Rg 49.07N 21.31 E
Girardot 54 Dc 4.18N 74.49W
Girdle Ness 9 Kd 57.08N 2.02W
Giresun 23 Ea 40.55N 38.24 E
Giresun Dağları 24 Hb 40.40N 38.10 E
Giri 36 Cb 0.28N 17.59 E
Giridih 25 Hd 24.11N 86.18 E
Giriftu 36 Gb 2.00N 39.45 E
Girne 24 Ee 35.20N 33.19 E
Girón 54 Cd 3.10S 79.09W
Girona/Gerona 13 Oc 41.59N 2.49 E
Gironde [3] 11 Fj 44.55N 0.30W
Gironde 5 Ff 45.35N 1.03W
Gironella 13 Nb 42.02N 1.53 E
Girou 11 Hk 43.46N 1.23 E
Girvan 9 If 55.15N 4.51W
Girvas 7 He 62.31N 33.44 E
Gisborne 58 Ih 38.39S 178.01 E
Gisenyi 36 Ec 1.42S 29.15 E
Gislaved 8 Eg 57.18N 13.32 E
Gisors 11 He 49.17N 1.47 E
Gissar 18 Ge 38.31N 68.36 E
Gissarski Hrebet 18 Ge 39.00N 68.40 E
Gistad 8 Ff 58.27N 15.55 E
Gistel 12 Ec 51.10N 2.57 E
Gistral 13 Ea 43.28N 7.35W
Gitarama 36 Ec 2.05S 29.16 E
Gitega 36 Ec 3.26S 29.56 E
Gitu 24 Me 35.20N 48.05 E
Giudicarie, Valli- 14 Ed 46.00N 10.40 E
Giulianova 14 Hh 42.45N 13.57 E
Giumalău, Vîrful- 15 Ib 47.26N 25.29 E
Giurgeni 15 Ke 44.35N 27.48 E
Giurgiu 15 If 43.53N 25.58 E
Give 8 Ci 55.51N 9.15 E
Givors 11 Ki 45.35N 4.46 E
Givry-en-Argonne 12 Gf 48.57N 4.53 E
Givry Island 64d Bb 7.07N 151.53 E
Giwa 34 Gc 11.18N 7.27 E
Giza (EN)=Al Jīzah 31 Ke 30.01N 31.13 E
Gižduvan 19 Gg 40.06N 64.40 E
Gižiga 20 Ld 62.03N 160.30 E
Gižiginskaja Guba 20 Kd 61.10N 158.30 E
Gizo 63a Cc 8.07S 156.50 E
Gizo 60 Fi 8.06S 156.51 E
Giżycko 10 Rb 54.03N 21.47 E
Gjalicës, Mali i- 15 Dg 42.01N 20.28 E
Gjamyš, Gora- 16 Oi 40.20N 46.25 E
Gjandža 6 Kg 40.40N 46.22 E
Gjerstad 8 Cf 58.52N 9.00 E
Gjevilvatn 8 Cb 62.40N 9.25 E
Gjirokastra 15 Di 40.05N 20.10 E
Gjoa Haven 39 Jc 68.38N 95.57W
Gjøvik 6 Hc 60.48N 10.42 E
Gjuhës, Kep i- 15 Ci 40.25N 19.18 E
Glace Bay 42 Lg 46.12N 59.57W
Glacier Bay 40 Le 58.40N 136.00W
Glacier Peak 43 Cb 48.07N 121.07W
Glacier Strait 42 Ja 76.15N 79.00W
Gladbeck 12 Ic 51.34N 6.59 E
Gladenbach 12 Kd 50.46N 8.34 E
Gladewater 45 Ij 32.33N 94.56W
Gladstone [Austl.] 58 Gg 23.51S 151.16 E
Gladstone [Man.-Can.] 45 Ga 50.15N 98.50W
Gladstone [Mi.-U.S.] 44 Dc 45.51N 87.03W
Gladstone [Mo.-U.S.] 45 Ig 39.13N 94.34W
Glafsfjorden 8 Ee 59.35N 12.35 E
Glåma 5 Hd 59.12N 10.57 E
Gláma 7a Ab 65.48N 23.00W
Glamis Castle 9 Ke 56.37N 3.00W
Glamoč 23 Ff 44.03N 16.51 E
Glan 7 Dg 58.35N 15.55 E
Glan [Aus.] 14 Id 46.36N 14.25 E
Glan [Ger.] 10 Dg 49.47N 7.43 E
Glan-Münchweiler 12 Je 49.28N 7.26 E
Glarner Alpen 14 Cd 46.55N 9.00 E
Glärnisch 14 Cd 47.00N 9.00 E
Glarus [2] 14 Dd 46.55N 9.05 E
Glarus 14 Dc 47.03N 9.04 E
Glasgow [Ky.-U.S.] 44 Eg 37.00N 85.55W
Glasgow [Mt.-U.S.] 43 Fb 48.12N 106.38W
Glasgow [Scot.-U.K.] 6 Fd 55.53N 4.15W
Glashütte 10 Jf 50.51N 13.47 E
Glass 9 Id 57.25N 4.30W
Glassboro 44 Jf 39.42N 75.06W
Glass Mountains 45 Ek 30.25N 103.15W
Glastonbury 9 Kj 51.09N 2.43W
Glauchau 10 If 50.49N 12.32 E
Glava 8 Ee 59.33N 12.34 E
Glazov 6 Ld 58.09N 52.40 E
Gleann Dá Loch/Glendalough 9 Gh 53.00N 6.20W
Gledićske Planine 15 Df 43.49N 20.55 E
Gleinalpe 14 Jc 47.10N 15.05 E
Gleisdorf 14 Jc 47.06N 15.43 E
Glen 12 Bb 52.50N 0.07W
Glénan, Iles de- 11 Cg 47.43N 4.00W
Glen Arbor 44 Ec 44.53N 85.58W
Glenavy 62 Df 44.55S 171.06 E
Glen Canyon 46 Jh 37.05N 111.41W
Glencoe [Mn.-U.S.] 45 Id 44.46N 94.09W
Glencoe [S.Afr.] 37 Ee 28.12S 30.07 E
Glendale [Az.-U.S.] 43 Ee 33.32N 112.11W
Glendale [Ca.-U.S.] 43 De 34.10N 118.17W
Glendalough/Gleann Dá Loch 9 Gh 53.00N 6.20W
Glendive 43 Gb 47.06N 104.43W
Glendo Reservoir 46 Me 42.31N 104.58W
Glenhope 61 Dh 41.39S 172.39 E
Glen Innes 58 Gg 29.44S 151.44 E
Glennallen 40 Jd 62.07N 145.33W
Glenner 14 Dd 46.46N 9.12 E
Glenns Ferry 46 He 42.57N 115.18W
Glenorchy 62 Cf 44.52S 168.24 E
Glenrock 46 Me 42.52N 105.52W
Glen Rose 45 Hj 32.14N 97.45W
Glenrothes 9 Je 56.12N 3.05W
Glens Falls 44 Kd 43.17N 73.41W
Glenville 44 Gf 38.57N 80.51W
Glenwood [Ia.-U.S.] 45 If 41.03N 95.45W
Glenwood [Mn.-U.S.] 45 Id 45.39N 95.23W
Glenwood Springs 43 Fd 39.32N 107.19W
Glibokaja 15 Ja 48.05N 26.00 E
Glina 14 Ke 45.20N 16.06 E
Glinjany 10 Ug 49.46N 24.33 E
Glittertinden 5 Gc 61.39N 8.33 E
Gliwice 10 Of 50.17N 18.40 E
Globe 43 Ee 33.24N 110.47W
Globino 16 He 49.24N 33.18 E
Głogów 10 Me 51.40N 16.05 E
Glomfjord 7 Cc 66.49N 13.58 E
Glommersträsk 7 Ed 65.16N 19.38 E
Glonn 10 Hh 48.11N 11.45 E
Glorieuses, Iles- 30 Lj 11.30S 47.20 E
Glottof, Mount- 40 Ie 57.30N 153.30W
Gloucester [*] 9 Kj 51.55N 2.15W
Gloucester [Eng.-U.K.] 9 Kj 51.53N 2.14W
Gloucester [Ma.-U.S.] 44 Ld 42.41N 70.39W
Gloucester, Cape- 60 Di 5.27S 148.25 E
Gloucestershire [3] 9 Lj 51.50N 1.55W
Glover Island 51p Bb 11.59N 61.47W
Glover's Reef 49 De 16.49N 87.48W
Gloversville 44 Jd 43.03N 74.21W
Głowno 10 Pe 51.58N 19.44 E
Głubczyce 10 Nf 50.13N 17.49 E
Glubokoje [Bye.-U.S.S.R.] 19 Cd 55.08N 27.41 E
Glubokoje [Kaz.-U.S.S.R.] 19 Ie 50.06N 82.19 E
Glubokoje, Ozero- 8 Md 60.30N 29.25 E
Głuchołazy 10 Nf 50.20N 17.22 E
Glücksburg 10 Fb 54.50N 9.33 E
Glückstadt 10 Fc 53.47N 9.25 E
Gluhov 19 De 51.43N 33.57 E
Gluša 16 Fc 53.06N 28.52 E
Glyngøre 8 Ch 56.46N 8.52 E
Gmünd [Aus.] 14 Hd 46.54N 13.32 E
Gmünd [Aus.] 14 Ib 48.46N 14.59 E
Gmunden 14 Hc 47.55N 13.48 E
Gnarp 7 De 62.03N 17.16 E
Gnesta 7 Dg 59.03N 17.18 E
Gniben 8 Dh 56.01N 11.18 E
Gniew 10 Oc 53.51N 18.49 E
Gniewkowo 10 Od 52.54N 18.25 E
Gniezno 10 Nd 52.31N 17.37 E
Gnjilane 15 Eg 42.28N 21.29 E
Gnosjö 7 Ch 57.22N 13.44 E
Gnowangerup 59 Df 33.56S 117.50 E
Goa, Damān and Diu [3] 25 Ee 15.35N 74.00 E
Goageb 37 Be 26.44S 17.15 E
Goālpāra 25 Ic 26.10N 90.37 E
Goat 63b Dd 18.42S 169.17 E
Goat Island 51d Ba 17.44N 61.51W
Goat Point 51d Ba 17.44N 61.51W
Goba 31 Kh 7.01N 39.59 E
Gobabis 31 Ik 22.30S 18.58 E
Gobabis [3] 37 Bd 22.00S 19.00 E
Göbel 15 Lj 40.00N 28.09 E
Gober 34 Gc 13.48N 6.51 E
Gobernador Gregores 56 Fg 48.46S 70.15W
Gobernador Ingeniero Valentin Virasoro 56 Ic 28.03S 56.02W
Gobernador Mansilla 55 Ck 32.33S 59.22W
Gobi, Pustynja-=Gobi Desert (EN) 21 Me 43.00N 106.00 E
Gobi Altai (EN)=Gobijski Altaj 21 Me 44.00N 102.00 E
Gobi Desert (EN)=Gobi, Pustynja- 21 Me 43.00N 106.00 E
Gobijski Altaj=Gobi Altai (EN) 21 Me 44.00N 102.00 E
Gobō 28 Mh 33.53N 135.10 E
Göçbeyli 15 Kj 39.13N 27.25 E
Goceano 14 Dj 40.30N 9.15 E
Goceano, Catena del- 14 Cj 40.30N 9.00 E
Goce Delčev 15 Gh 41.33N 23.42 E
Goch 10 Ce 51.40N 6.10 E
Gochas 37 Bd 24.55S 18.55 E
Goczałkowickie, Jezioro- 10 Og 49.53N 18.50 E
Göd 10 Pi 47.42N 19.08 E
Godafoss 7a Cb 65.41N 17.33W
Godalming 12 Bc 51.11N 0.36W
Godār 24 Qh 29.45N 57.30 E
Godār-e Shah 24 Me 34.45N 48.10 E
Godāvari 21 Kh 17.00N 81.45 E
Godbout, Rivière- 44 Na 49.21N 67.42W
Gode 35 Gd 5.55N 43.40 E
Godeč 15 Gf 43.01N 23.03 E
Godelbukta Breidvika 66 Df 70.15S 24.15 E
Goderich 44 Gd 43.45N 81.43W
Goderville 12 Ce 49.39N 0.22 E
Godhavn/Qeqertarssuaq 67 Nc 69.20N 53.35W
Godhra 25 Ed 22.45N 73.38 E
Godinlabe 35 Hd 5.54N 46.40 E
Gödöllő 10 Pi 47.36N 19.22 E
Godoy Cruz 56 Gd 32.55S 68.50W
Gods Lake 42 If 54.40N 94.09W
Gods Lake 42 If 54.40N 94.20W
Gods Mercy, Bay of- 42 Id 63.30N 86.10W
Gods River 42 Ie 56.22N 92.52W
Godthåb/Nûk 67 Nc 64.15N 51.40W
Godthåbfjord 41 Gf 64.20N 51.30W
Godwin Austen (EN)=K2 21 Jf 35.53N 76.30 E
Godwin Austen (EN)=Qogir Feng 21 Jf 35.53N 76.30 E
Goedereede 12 Fc 51.49N 3.58 E
Goéland, Lac au- 42 Jg 49.45N 76.50W
Goélands, Lac aux- 42 Le 55.30N 64.30W
Goële 12 Ee 49.10N 2.40 E
Goelette Island 37b Bc 10.13S 51.08 E
Goeree 11 Jc 51.50N 3.55 E
Goes 11 Jc 51.30N 3.54 E
Gogama 42 Jg 47.40N 81.43W
Gō-Gawa 29 Cd 35.01N 132.13 E
Gogebic Range 44 Cb 46.45N 89.25W
Gogland, Ostrov- 7 Gf 60.05N 27.00 E
Gog Magog Hills 12 Cb 52.09N 0.11 E
Gogounou 34 Fc 10.50N 2.50 E
Gogrial 35 Dd 8.32N 28.07 E
Gogu, Vîrful- 15 Fd 45.12N 22.30 E
Gogui 34 Db 15.39N 9.21W
Goğu Karadeniz Dağları 24 Ib 40.40N 40.00 E
Gohelle 12 Ed 50.28N 2.45 E
Goiandira 54 Ig 18.08S 48.06W
Goianésia 54 Ig 15.19S 49.04W
Goiânia 53 Lg 16.40S 49.16W
Goianinha 54 Ke 6.16S 35.12W
Goiás [2] 54 If 12.00S 48.00W
Goiás 54 Hg 15.56S 50.08W
Goiatuba 54 Ig 18.01S 49.22W
Goikul 64a Bc 7.22N 134.36 E
Göinge 8 Eh 56.20N 13.50 E
Goio-Erê 56 Jb 24.12S 53.01W
Goioxim 55 Gg 25.14S 52.01W
Goirle 12 Hc 51.34N 5.05 E
Góis 13 Dd 40.09N 8.07W
Goito 14 Ee 45.15N 10.40 E
Gojam [3] 35 Fc 10.33N 37.35 E
Gojō 29 Dd 34.21N 135.42 E
Gojōme 29 Gb 39.56N 140.07 E
Gojra 25 Eb 31.09N 72.41 E
Gojthski, Pereval- 16 Kg 44.15N 39.18 E
Gokase-Gawa 28 Be 32.35N 131.42 E
Gokasho-Wan 29 Ed 34.20N 136.40 E
Gökbel Dağı 15 Kl 37.28N 28.00 E
Gökçay 24 Ed 36.36N 33.23 E
Gökçeada 24 Ac 40.10N 25.50 E
Gökçeören 15 Lk 38.35N 28.32 E
Gökçeyazi 15 Kj 39.38N 27.39 E
Gökdere 24 Ed 36.39N 33.35 E
Gökırmak 24 Fb 41.24N 35.08 E
Göksu [Tur.] 24 Fd 36.20N 34.05 E
Göksu [Tur.] 24 Fd 37.37N 35.35 E
Göksu [Tur.] 15 Mi 40.23N 29.58 E
Göksun 24 Gc 38.03N 36.30 E
Gök Tepe 15 Mm 36.53N 29.17 E
Göktepe 15 Ll 37.16N 28.36 E
Gokwe 37 Dc 18.13S 28.55 E
Gol 7 Bf 60.42N 8.57 E
Golāghāt 25 Ic 26.31N 93.58 E
Golaja Pristan 16 Hf 46.29N 32.31 E
Gołańcz 10 Nd 52.57N 17.18 E
Golconda [Il.-U.S.] 45 Lh 37.22N 88.29W
Golconda [Nv.-U.S.] 46 Gf 40.57N 117.30W
Gölcük 24 Cb 40.44N 29.44 E
Golčův Jenikov 10 Lg 49.49N 15.30 E
Goldap 10 Sb 54.19N 22.19 E
Gold Beach 46 Ce 42.25N 124.25W
Gold Coast 58 Gg 27.58S 153.25 E
Gold Coast 30 Gh 5.20N 0.45W
Golden [B.C.-Can.] 42 Ff 51.18N 116.58W
Golden [Co.-U.S.] 45 Dg 39.46N 105.13W
Golden Bay 62 Ed 40.50S 172.50 E
Goldendale 46 Ed 45.49N 120.50W
Goldene Aue 10 Ge 51.25N 11.00 E
Golden Gate 46 Dh 37.49N 122.29W
Golden Hinde 42 Eg 49.39N 125.44W
Golden Meadow 45 Kl 29.23N 90.16W
Golden Vale/Machaire na Mumhan 9 Fi 52.30N 8.00W
Goldfield 46 Gh 37.42N 117.14W
Gold River 46 Bb 49.41N 126.08W
Goldsboro 43 Ld 35.23N 77.59W
Goldsworthy 59 Dd 20.20S 119.30 E
Göle 24 Jb 40.48N 42.36 E
Golegã 13 De 39.24N 8.29W
Goleniów 10 Kc 53.36N 14.50 E
Golešnica 15 Eh 41.42N 21.33 E
Goleta, Cerro- 48 Ih 18.38N 100.04W
Golfito 47 Hg 8.38N 83.11W
Golfo Aranci 14 Dj 41.00N 9.37 E
Gölgeli Dağları 15 Ml 37.15N 29.06 E
Gölhisar 15 Ml 37.08N 29.30 E
Goliad 45 Hl 28.40N 97.23W
Golija [Yugo.] 15 Df 43.19N 20.18 E
Golija [Yugo.] 15 Bf 43.02N 18.47 E
Goljak 15 Eg 42.44N 21.31 E
Goljama Kamčija 15 Kf 43.03N 27.29 E
Goljama Sjutkja 15 Hh 41.54N 24.01 E
Goljamo Konare 15 Hg 42.16N 24.33 E
Goljam Perelik 15 Hh 41.36N 24.34 E
Goljam Persenk 15 Hh 41.49N 24.33 E
Gölköy 24 Gb 40.15N 37.26 E
Gölkük 15 Kj 39.19N 27.59 E
Göllheim 12 Ke 49.35N 8.03 E
Gölmarmara 15 Kk 38.42N 27.56 E
Golmud He 27 Gd 36.54N 95.11 E
Golo 11a Ba 42.31N 9.32 E
Goloby 10 Ve 51.06N 25.06 E
Gologory 10 Ug 49.35N 24.30 E
Golocha 35 Gd 8.12N 40.05 E
Golovin 40 Gd 64.33N 163.02W
Golovnin Seamount (EN) 20 Kg 46.50N 157.00 E
Gölpāyegān 23 Hc 33.27N 50.18 E
Gölpazarı 24 Db 40.17N 30.19 E
Golšanka 10 Kb 54.00N 26.16 E
Golspie 9 Jd 57.58N 3.58W
Gol Tappeh 24 Kd 36.35N 45.45 E
Golubac 15 Ee 44.39N 21.38 E
Golub-Dobrzyń 10 Pc 53.08N 19.02 E
Golungo Alto 36 Bd 9.08S 14.47 E
Golyšmanovo 19 Gd 56.23N 68.23 E
Goma 31 Ji 1.37S 29.12 E
Gómara 13 Jc 41.37N 2.13W
Gombe 31 Ig 10.17N 11.10 E
Gombi 34 Hc 10.10N 12.44 E
Gomel 6 Je 52.25N 31.00 E
Gomelskaja Oblast [3] 19 Ce 52.20N 29.40 E
Gomera 30 Ff 28.06N 17.08W
Gómez Farías 48 Ie 24.57N 101.02W
Gómez Palacio 47 Dc 25.34N 103.30W
Gomo Co 27 Ee 33.45N 85.35 E
Goms 14 Cd 46.25N 8.10 E
Gonābād 23 Ic 34.20N 58.42 E
Gonaïves 47 Je 19.27N 72.43W
Gonam 20 Ie 57.18N 131.20 E
Gonâve, Golfe de la- 47 Je 19.00N 73.30W
Gonâve, Ile de la- 47 Je 18.51N 73.03W
Gonbad-e Qābūs 23 Ib 37.15N 55.09 E
Gonda 25 Gc 27.08N 81.56 E
Gonder [3] 35 Fc 12.00N 38.00 E
Gonder 31 Kg 12.38N 37.27 E
Gondia 25 Gd 21.27N 80.12 E
Gondo 30 Gg 14.20N 3.10W
Gondomar 13 Dc 41.09N 8.32W
Gondwana 21 Kg 23.00N 81.00 E
Gönen 24 Bb 40.06N 27.39 E
Gönen 24 Bb 40.06N 27.36 E
Gonfreville-l'Orcher 12 Ce 49.30N 0.14 E
Gong'an (Doushi) 27 Je 30.05N 112.12 E
Gongbo'gyamda 27 Ff 29.59N 93.25 E
Gonggar 27 Ff 29.17N 90.50 E
Gongga Shan 21 Mg 29.34N 101.53 E
Gonghe 27 Hd 36.21N 100.47 E
Gongliu/Tokkuztara 27 Dc 43.30N 82.15 E
Gongola 30 Ih 9.30N 12.04 E
Gongola [2] 34 Hd 8.40N 11.20 E
Gongpoquan 27 Gc 41.50N 97.00 E
Gongshan 27 Gf 27.39N 98.35 E
Gongxian 27 Kf 26.05N 119.32 E
Gongzian (Xiaoyi) 28 Bg 34.46N 112.57 E
Gongzhuling → Huaide 27 Lc 43.30N 124.52 E
Goñi 55 Dk 33.31S 56.24W
Goniądz 10 Sc 53.30N 22.45 E
Gonīshān 24 Pd 37.04N 54.06 E
Gonjo 27 Ge 30.52N 98.20 E
Gonohe 29 Ga 40.31N 141.19 E
Go-no-ura 29 Ae 33.45N 129.41 E
Gönük 24 Ic 39.00N 40.41 E
Gonzales 45 Hl 29.30N 97.27W
Gonzáles, Riacho- 55 Df 22.48S 57.54W
González 48 Jf 22.50N 98.27W
Goodenough, Cape- 66 Ie 66.16S 126.10 E
Goodenough Bay 59 Ja 9.55S 150.00 E
Goodenough Island 60 Ei 9.22S 150.16 E
Good Hope, Cape of-/Groeie Hoop, Kaap die- 30 Il 34.21S 18.28 E
Goodhouse 37 Be 28.57S 18.13 E
Gooding 46 He 42.56N 114.43W
Goodland 43 Gd 39.21N 101.43W
Goodnews Bay 40 Ge 59.07N 161.35W
Goodsir, Mount- 46 Ga 51.12N 116.20W
Good Spirit Lake 46 Na 51.34N 102.40W
Goodwin Sands 12 Dc 51.15N 1.35 E
Goodyear 46 Ij 33.26N 112.21W
Goole 9 Mh 53.42N 0.52W
Goomalling 59 Df 31.19S 116.49 E
Goondiwindi 58 Gg 28.32S 150.19 E
Goonyella 59 Jd 21.43S 147.58 E
Goor 12 Ib 52.14N 6.37 E
Goose Lake 43 Cc 41.57N 120.25W
Goose River 45 Hc 47.28N 96.52W
Gopło, Jezioro- 10 Od 52.35N 18.20 E
Göppingen 10 Fh 48.42N 9.40 E
Góra 10 Me 51.40N 16.33 E
Gora 10 Di 40.40N 20.30 E
Góra Kalwaria 10 Re 51.59N 21.12 E
Gorakhpur 22 Kg 26.45N 83.22 E
Goransko 15 Bf 43.07N 18.50 E
Gorata 15 Ih 41.45N 25.55 E
Goražde 14 Mg 43.40N 18.59 E
Gorda 13 De 39.24N 8.29W
Gorda, Cayo 49 Ff 15.55N 82.15W
Gorda, Punta- [Ca.-U.S.] 46 Cf 40.16N 124.20W
Gorda, Punta- [Cuba] 49 Fb 22.24N 82.10W
Gorda, Punta- [Nic.] 49 Ff 14.21N 83.12W
Gördes 15 Lk 38.54N 28.18 E
Gördes 15 Kj 38.46N 27.58 E
Gordil 35 Cd 9.44N 21.35 E
Gordior 24 Ec 39.37N 32.00 E
Gordon [Nb.-U.S.] 45 Ee 42.48N 102.12W
Gordon [Wi.-U.S.] 45 Kc 46.15N 91.47W
Gordon, Lake- 59 Jh 43.05S 146.05 E
Gordon Horne Peak 46 Fa 51.46N 118.50W
Gordonvale 59 Jc 17.05S 145.47 E
Goré 35 Bd 7.55N 16.38 E
Gore [Eth.] 35 Fd 8.09N 35.34 E
Gore [N.Z.] 62 Cg 46.06S 168.56 E
Görele 24 Hb 41.02N 39.00 E
Görenez Dağı 15 Lk 39.00N 28.01 E
Gorenjsko 14 Id 46.20N 14.10 E
Gorey/Guaire 9 Gi 52.40N 6.18W
Gorgān 24 Pd 36.59N 54.05 E
Gorgān 24 Jf 33.21N 43.40 E
Gorgān, Khalīj-e- 24 Od 36.40N 53.50 E
Gorgany 10 Jh 48.30N 24.15 E
Gorgin 24 Ld 36.15N 47.55 E
Gorgol [3] 32 Ef 15.45N 13.00W
Gorgol el Abiod 32 Ef 16.14N 12.58W
Gorgona 14 Dg 43.25N 9.55 E
Gorgona, Isla- 54 Cc 2.59N 78.12W
Gorgora 35 Fc 12.14N 37.17 E
Gorham 44 Lc 44.23N 71.11W
Gori 19 Eg 42.00N 44.02 E
Gorinchem 11 Kc 51.50N 5.00 E
Goring 12 Ac 51.31N 1.08W
Goris 16 Oj 39.31N 46.22 E
Gorizia 14 He 45.57N 13.38 E
Gorj [2] 15 Gd 45.00N 23.20 E
Gorjačegorsk 20 De 55.24N 88.55 E
Gorjači Ključ 16 Kg 44.36N 39.07 E
Gorjanci 14 Je 45.45N 15.20 E
Gorki [Bye.-U.S.S.R.] 16 Gb 54.17N 31.00 E
Gorki [R.S.F.S.R.] → Nižnij Novgorod 6 Kd 57.38N 45.05 E
Gorki [R.S.F.S.R.] 20 Bc 65.05N 65.15 E
Gorkovskaja Oblast [3] 19 Ed 56.15N 44.45 E
Gorkovskoje Vodohranilišče =Gorky Reservoir (EN) 5 Kd 57.00N 43.10 E
Gorkum 10 Hf 50.10N 11.08 E
Gorky Reservoir (EN)= Gorkovskoje Vodohr. 5 Kd 57.00N 43.10 E
Gørlev 8 Di 55.32N 11.14 E
Gorlice 10 Rg 49.40N 21.10 E
Görlitz 10 Ke 51.10N 15.00 E
Gorlovka 6 Jf 48.18N 38.03 E
Gornalunga 14 Jm 37.24N 15.03 E
Gorna Orjahovica 15 If 43.07N 25.41 E
Gornjak [R.S.F.S.R.] 20 Df 51.00N 81.29 E
Gornjak [Ukr.-U.S.S.R.] 10 Uf 50.16N 24.13 E
Gornji Milanovac 15 De 44.02N 20.27 E
Gornji Vakuf 23 Fg 43.56N 17.36 E
Gorno-Altajsk 22 Kd 51.58N 85.58 E
Gorno-Altajskaja Avtonomnaja Oblast [3] 20 Df 51.00N 87.00 E
Gorno-Badahšanskaja Avtonomnaja Oblast [3] 19 Hh 38.15N 73.00 E
Gorno-Čujski 20 Ge 57.40N 111.40 E
Gornozavodsk [R.S.F.S.R.] 20 Jg 46.30N 141.55 E
Gornozavodsk [R.S.F.S.R.] 17 Ig 58.25N 58.20 E
Gorny [R.S.F.S.R.] 20 Ih 44.50N 133.56 E
Gorny [R.S.F.S.R.] 16 Pd 51.45N 48.34 E
Gorny [R.S.F.S.R.] 20 If 50.48N 136.26 E
Gornyje Ključi 28 Lb 45.15N 133.30 E
Gorochan 35 Fd 9.26N 37.05 E
Gorodec [R.S.F.S.R.] 19 Ed 56.40N 43.30 E
Gorodec [R.S.F.S.R.] 8 Mf 58.30N 29.55 E
Gorodenka 16 De 48.42N 25.32 E
Gorodišče [Bye.-U.S.S.R.] 10 Vc 53.16N 26.03 E
Gorodišče [R.S.F.S.R.] 16 Nc 53.16N 45.42 E
Gorodišče [Ukr.-U.S.S.R.] 16 Ge 49.17N 31.27 E
Gorodnica 16 Ed 50.49N 27.22 E
Gorodnja 16 Gd 51.55N 31.31 E
Gorodok [Bye.-U.S.S.R.] 19 Cd 55.26N 29.59 E
Gorodok [Ukr.-U.S.S.R.] 16 Ee 49.10N 26.31 E
Gorodok [Ukr.-U.S.S.R.] 16 Ce 49.47N 23.39 E
Gorodovikovsk 19 Ef 46.05N 41.59 E
Gorohov 10 Uf 50.28N 24.47 E
Gorohovec 7 Kh 56.12N 42.42 E
Goroka 58 Fe 6.02S 145.22 E
Gorom-Gorom 34 Ec 14.26N 0.14W
Gorong, Kepulauan- 26 Jg 4.05S 131.20 E
Gorongosa, Serra da- 37 Ec 18.24S 34.06 E
Gorontalo 22 Oi 0.33N 123.03 E
Goroual 34 Fc 14.42N 0.53 E
Górowo Iławeckie 10 Qb 54.17N 20.30 E
Gorron 11 Ff 48.25N 0.49W
Goršečnoje 16 Kd 51.33N 38.09 E
Gorski Kotar 14 Ie 45.26N 14.40 E
Gorssel 12 Ib 52.12N 6.13 E
Gort 9 Eh 53.04N 8.50W
Goru, Vîrful- 15 Jd 45.48N 26.25 E
Görükle 15 Li 40.14N 28.50 E
Goryn 19 Ce 52.09N 27.17 E
Gorzów [2] 10 Ld 54.25N 15.15 E
Gorzów Wielkopolski 10 Ld 52.44N 15.15 E
Goschen Strait 59 Kb 10.09S 150.56 E
Gosen 28 Of 37.44N 139.11 E
Gosford 59 Kf 33.26S 151.21 E
Goshen 44 Ee 41.35N 85.50W
Goshogawara 28 Pd 40.48N 140.27 E
Gosier 51e Bb 16.12N 61.30W
Goslar 10 Ge 51.54N 10.26 E
Gospić 14 Jf 44.33N 15.23 E
Gosport 9 Lk 50.48N 1.08W
Gossen 8 Bb 62.50N 6.55 E
Gossi 34 Eb 15.47N 1.15W
Gossinga 35 Dd 8.39N 25.59 E
Gostivar 15 Dh 41.48N 20.54 E
Gostyń 10 Me 51.53N 17.00 E
Gostynin 10 Pd 52.26N 19.29 E
Gota älv 5 Hd 57.42N 11.52 E
Göta Kanal 5 Hd 58.50N 13.58 E
Götaland 5 Hd 57.30N 14.30 E
Götaland 7 Dg 57.30N 14.30 E
Göteborg 6 Hd 57.43N 11.58 E
Göteborg och Bohus [2] 7 Cg 58.30N 11.30 E
Gotel Mountains 30 Ih 7.00N 11.40 E
Gotemba 29 Fd 35.18N 138.56 E
Götene 7 Cg 58.32N 13.29 E
Gotha 10 Gf 50.57N 10.43 E
Gothenburg 45 Ff 40.56N 100.09W
Gothèye 34 Fc 13.52N 1.34 E
Gotland [2] 7 Eh 57.30N 18.30 E
Gotland 5 Hd 57.30N 18.30 E
Gotō-Nada 29 Ae 32.45N 129.30 E
Gotō-Rettō 27 Me 32.50N 129.00 E
Gotowasi 26 If 0.38N 128.26 E
Gotska Sandön 7 Eg 58.25N 19.15 E
Gōtsu 28 Lg 35.00N 132.14 E
Göttingen 10 Fe 51.32N 9.56 E
Gottwaldov 10 Ng 49.13N 17.39 E
Goubangzi 28 Fd 41.23N 121.48 E
Gouda 11 Kc 52.01N 4.43 E
Goudiri 34 Cc 14.11N 12.43W
Gouet 11 Df 48.32N 2.45W
Gough Island 30 Gm 40.20S 10.00W
Gough Lake 46 Ia 52.02N 112.28W
Gouin, Réservoir- 42 Kg 48.35N 74.50W
Goulbin Kaba 34 Gc 13.42N 6.19 E
Goulburn 58 Fh 34.45S 149.43 E

Index Symbols

[1] Independent Nation
[2] State, Region
[3] District, County
[4] Municipality
[5] Colony, Dependency
Continent
Physical Region
Historical or Cultural Region
Mount, Mountain
Volcano
Hill
Mountains, Mountain Range
Hills, Escarpment
Plateau, Upland
Pass, Gap
Plain, Lowland
Delta
Salt Flat
Valley, Canyon
Crater, Cave
Karst Features
Depression
Polder
Desert, Dunes
Forest, Woods
Heath, Steppe
Oasis
Cape, Point
Coast, Beach
Cliff
Peninsula
Isthmus
Sandbank
Island
Atoll
Rock, Reef
Islands, Archipelago
Rocks, Reefs
Coral Reef
Well, Spring
Geyser
River, Stream
Waterfall Rapids
River Mouth, Estuary
Lake
Salt Lake
Intermittent Lake
Reservoir
Swamp, Pond
Canal
Glacier
Ice Shelf, Pack Ice
Ocean
Sea
Gulf, Bay
Strait, Fjord
Lagoon
Bank
Seamount
Tablemount
Ridge
Shelf
Basin
Escarpment, Sea Scarp
Fracture
Trench, Abyss
National Park, Reserve
Point of Interest
Recreation Site
Cave, Cavern
Historic Site
Ruins
Wall, Walls
Church, Abbey
Temple
Scientific Station
Airport
Port
Lighthouse
Mine
Tunnel
Dam, Bridge

Name	Page	Grid	Lat.	Long.
Goulburn Islands	59	Gb	11.50S	133.30 E
Gould Bay	66	Rf	78.10S	44.00W
Gould Coast	66	Mg	84.30S	150.00W
Goulia	34	Dc	10.01N	7.11W
Goulimine	32	Ed	28.59N	10.04W
Gouménissa	15	Fi	40.57N	22.27 E
Gouna	34	Hd	8.32N	13.34 E
Gounda	35	Cd	9.09N	21.15 E
Goundam	34	Eb	16.24N	3.38W
Goundi	35	Bd	9.22N	17.22 E
Goundoumaria	34	Hc	13.42N	11.10 E
Gounou Gaya	35	Bd	9.38N	15.31 E
Gourara	32	Hd	29.30N	0.40 E
Gouraya	13	Nh	36.34N	1.55 E
Gourcy	34	Ec	13.13N	2.21W
Gourdon	11	Hj	44.44N	1.23 E
Gouré	31	Ig	13.58N	10.18 E
Gourin	11	Cf	48.08N	3.36W
Gourma [Mali]	30	Gg	15.45N	2.00W
Gourma [U.V.]	30	Hg	12.20N	1.30 E
Gourma-Rharous	34	Eb	16.52N	1.55W
Gournay-en-Bray	11	He	49.29N	1.44 E
Gourniá	15	In	35.06N	25.48 E
Gouro	35	Bb	19.40N	19.28 E
Gourrama	32	Gc	32.20N	4.05W
Goussainville	12	Ee	49.01N	2.28 E
Gouyave	51p	Bb	12.10N	61.44W
Gouzeaucourt	12	Fd	50.03N	3.07 E
Gouzon	11	Ih	46.11N	2.14 E
Govena, Mys-	20	Le	59.47N	166.02 E
Gove Peninsula	59	Hb	13.02S	136.50 E
Goverla, Gora-	19	Cf	48.10N	24.32 E
Governador Valadares	53	Lg	18.51S	41.56W
Governor's Harbour	47	Ic	25.10N	76.14W
Gowanda	44	Hd	42.28N	78.57W
Gower	9	Ij	51.36N	4.10W
Gowganda	44	Gb	47.38N	80.46W
Goya	53	Kh	29.10S	59.20W
Goyave	51e	Ab	16.08N	61.34W
Goyaves, Ilets 'a-	51e	Ab	16.10N	61.48W
Goyder River	59	Hb	12.38S	135.05 E
Göynücek	24	Fb	40.24N	35.32 E
Göynük	15	Ni	40.20N	30.05 E
Göynük	24	Db	40.24N	30.47 E
Gozaisho-Yama	29	Ed	35.01N	136.24 E
Goz Arian	35	Bc	14.35N	20.00 E
Goz Beida	35	Cc	12.13N	21.25 E
Gozha Co	27	De	34.59N	81.06 E
Goz Kerki	35	Bb	15.30N	18.50 E
Gözlü Baba Dağı	15	Lk	38.15N	28.28 E
Gozo	5	Hh	36.05N	14.15 E
Graaff-Reinet	37	Cf	32.14S	24.32 E
Graafschap	11	Mb	52.05N	6.30 E
Graben Neudorf	12	Ke	49.10N	8.28 E
Grabia	10	Oe	51.26N	18.56 E
Grabière Point	51g	Bb	15.30N	61.29W
Grabowa	10	Mb	54.26N	16.20 E
Gračac	14	Jf	44.18N	15.51 E
Gračanica	14	Mf	44.42N	18.18 E
Gračanica, Manastir-	15	Eg	42.36N	21.12 E
Gracias	49	Cf	14.35N	88.35W
Gracias a Dios	49	Ef	15.20N	84.20W
Gracias a Dios, Cabo	38	Kh	15.00N	83.08W
Graciosa [Azr.]	32	Ee	39.04N	28.00W
Graciosa [Can.Is.]	32	Ed	29.15N	13.30W
Gradačac	14	Mf	44.53N	18.26 E
Gradaús, Serra dos-	52	Kf	8.00S	50.45W
Grado [It.]	14	He	45.40N	13.23 E
Grado [Sp.]	13	Fa	43.23N	6.04W
Grænalon	7a	Cb	64.10N	17.24W
Grænlandshaf=Greenland Sea (EN)	67	Ld	77.00N	1.00W
Grafenau	10	Jh	48.51N	13.24 E
Grafham Water	12	Bb	52.19N	0.10W
Grafing bei München	10	Hh	48.03N	11.58 E
Grafschaft Bentheim	12	Jb	52.30N	7.05 E
Grafton [Austl.]	59	Ke	29.41S	152.56 E
Grafton [N.D.-U.S.]	43	Hb	48.25N	97.25W
Grafton [W.V.-U.S.]	44	Hf	39.21N	80.00W
Grafton, Mount-	46	Hg	38.40N	114.45W
Graham	42	Ef	53.40N	132.30W
Graham [N.C.-U.S.]	44	Hg	36.05N	79.25W
Graham [Tx.-U.S.]	45	Gj	33.06N	98.35W
Graham, Mount-	43	Fe	32.42N	109.52W
Graham Land (EN)	66	Qe	66.00S	63.30W
Graham Moore, Cape	42	Jb	72.51N	76.05W
Grahamstown	31	Jl	33.19S	26.31 E
Grain Coast	30	Gh	5.00N	9.00W
Graisivaudan	11	Li	45.15N	5.50 E
Grajaú	54	Ie	5.49S	46.08W
Grajaú, Rio-	54	Jd	3.41S	44.48W
Grajewo	10	Sc	53.39N	22.27 E
Gram	8	Ci	55.17N	9.04 E
Gramalote	49	Kj	7.54N	72.48W
Gramat	11	Hj	44.47N	1.43 E
Gramat, Causse de-	11	Hj	44.40N	1.50 E
Graminha, Represa da-	55	Ie	21.33S	46.38W
Grammeneges/Galmaarden	12	Fd	50.45N	3.58 E
Grammichele	14	Im	37.13N	14.38 E
Grammont/Geraardsbergen	12	Fd	50.46N	3.52 E
Grámmos Óros	15	Di	40.20N	20.45 E
Grampian	9	Kd	57.25N	2.35W
Grampian Mountains	5	Fd	56.45N	4.00W
Gramshi	15	Di	40.52N	20.11 E
Gran	8	Dd	60.22N	10.34 E
Granada [Col.]	54	Dc	3.33N	73.44W
Granada [Nic.]	49	Eh	11.50N	86.00W
Granada [Nic.]	47	Gf	11.56N	85.57W
Granada [Sp.]	13	Ig	37.15N	3.15W
Granada [Sp.]	6	Fh	37.13N	3.41W
Granada, Vega de-	13	Ig	37.15N	4.00W
Gránard/Granard	9	Fh	53.47N	7.30W
Granard/Gránard	9	Fh	53.47N	7.30W
Granby	42	Kg	45.24N	72.43W
Gran Canaria	30	Ff	28.00N	15.36W
Gran Chaco	52	Jh	23.00S	60.00W
Grand Anse Bay	51p	Bb	12.02N	61.45W
Grand Bahama	38	Lg	26.40N	78.20W
Grand Ballon	11	Ng	47.55N	7.08 E
Grand Bank	42	Lg	47.06N	55.47W
Grand Banks (EN)	38	Oe	45.00N	50.00W
Grand Bassa	34	Dd	6.10N	9.40W
Grand-Bassam	31	Gh	5.12N	3.44W
Grand Bay	51g	Bb	15.14N	61.19W
Grand Bay	51p	Cb	12.29N	61.23W
Grand-Béréby	34	De	4.38N	6.55W
Grand-Bourg	50	Fe	15.53N	61.19W
Grand Cache	42	Ff	53.14N	119.00W
Grand Caille Point	51k	Ab	13.52N	61.05W
Grandcamp-Maisy	12	Ae	49.23N	1.02W
Grand Canal	9	Gh	53.21N	6.14W
Grand Canal (EN)=Da Yunhe	21	Nf	39.54N	116.44 E
Grand Canyon	43	Ed	36.03N	112.09W
Grand Canyon	38	Hc	36.10N	112.45W
Grand' Case	51b	Ab	18.06N	63.03W
Grand Cayman	47	He	19.20N	81.15W
Grand Cess	34	De	4.24N	8.13W
Grand Chartreuse	11	Li	45.22N	5.50 E
Grand Colombier	11	Li	45.54N	5.46 E
Grand Coulee	46	Fc	47.56N	119.00W
Grand-Couronne	12	De	49.21N	1.01 E
Grandcourt	12	De	49.55N	1.30 E
Grand Cul de Sac Bay	51k	Ab	13.59N	61.02W
Grand Cul-de-Sac Marin	51e	Ab	16.20N	61.35W
Grande, Arroyo-	55	Dm	37.32S	57.34W
Grande, Bahía-	52	Jk	50.45S	68.45W
Grande, Boca-	54	Fb	8.45N	60.35W
Grande, Cachoeira-	55	Gb	15.37S	51.48W
Grande, Cerro-	48	If	23.40N	100.40W
Grande, Ciénaga-	49	Ji	9.13N	75.46W
Grande, Corixa-	55	Cc	17.10S	58.20W
Grande, Cuchilla- [Arg.]	55	Cj	31.45S	58.35W
Grande, Cuchilla- [Ur.]	52	Ki	33.15S	55.07W
Grande, Ile-	11	Cf	48.48N	3.35W
Grande, Ilha	54	Jh	23.10S	44.10W
Grande, Rio- [Ven.]	54	Fb	8.39N	60.59W
Grande, Rio- [Braz.]	52	Lg	11.05S	43.09W
Grande, Rio- [N.Amer.]	38	Jg	25.57N	97.09W
Grande, Rio- (EN)=Bravo del Norte, Rio-	38	Jg	25.57N	97.09W
Grande, Rio- o Guapay, Rio-	52	Jg	15.51S	64.39W
Grande, Serra-	52	Lf	6.00S	40.52W
Grande, Sierra-	48	Gc	29.40N	104.55W
Grande-Anse	51e	Bb	16.18N	61.04W
Grande Anse	51k	Ba	14.01N	60.54W
Grande Briere	11	Dg	47.22N	2.15W
Grande Casse	11	Mi	45.24N	6.50 E
Grande Cayemite	49	Kd	18.37N	73.45W
Grande Comore → Njazidja	30	Lj	11.35S	43.20 E
Grande de Santa Marta, Ciénaga-	49	Jh	10.50N	74.25W
Grande de Santiago, Rio-	38	Ig	21.36N	105.26W
Grande do Gurupa, Ilha-	54	Hd	1.00S	51.30W
Grande Inferior, Cuchilla-	55	Dk	33.50S	56.10W
Grande Kabylie	13	Ph	36.45N	4.00 E
Grande ou Sete Quedas, Ilha-	55	Ef	23.45S	54.03W
Grande Pointe [Guad.]	51b	Bc	17.50N	62.50W
Grande Pointe [Guad.]	51e	Ac	15.59N	61.38W
Grande Prairie	39	Hd	55.10N	118.48W
Grand Erg de Bilma	30	Ig	18.30N	13.50 E
Grand Erg Occidental	30	He	30.20N	0.01 E
Grand Erg Oriental	30	He	30.00N	7.00 E
Grande Rio-	52	Kh	20.06S	51.04W
Grande Rivière à Goyaves	51e	Ab	16.18N	61.37W
Grande Rivière de la Baleine	38	Ld	55.15N	77.45W
Grande Rivière du Nord	49	Kd	19.35N	72.11W
Grande Ronde River	46	Gc	46.05N	116.59W
Grandes, Salinas-	52	Ji	30.05S	65.05W
Grandes Sebkha d'Oran	13	Li	35.32N	0.48W
Grandes Rousse	11	Mi	45.06N	6.07 E
Grande-Synthe	12	Ec	51.01N	2.17 E
Grand Etang	51p	Bb	12.06N	61.42W
Grande-Terre	50	Fd	16.20N	61.25W
Grande Vigie, Pointe de la-	51e	Ba	16.31N	61.28W
Grand Falls [N.B.-Can.]	42	Kg	47.03N	67.44W
Grand Falls [Newf.-Can.]	39	Ne	48.56N	55.40W
Grand Forks [B.C.-Can.]	46	Fb	49.02N	118.27W
Grand Forks [N.D.-U.S.]	39	Je	47.55N	97.03W
Grand Found, Anse du-	51b	Bc	17.53N	62.49W
Grand Gedeh	34	Dd	5.45N	8.05W
Grand Haven	44	Dd	43.04N	86.10W
Grand Ilet	51e	Ac	15.50N	61.36W
Grand Island	39	Je	40.55N	98.21W
Grand Junction	39	If	39.05N	108.33W
Grand-Lahou	34	Dd	5.08N	5.01W
Grand Lake [La.-U.S.]	45	Kl	29.55N	91.35W
Grand Lake [La.-U.S.]	45	Jl	29.55N	92.47W
Grand Lake [N.B.-Can.]	44	Nc	45.42N	66.05W
Grand Lake [Newf.-Can.]	42	Lg	49.00N	57.20W
Grand Lake [Oh.-U.S.]	44	Ee	40.30N	84.32W
Grand Lake Victoria	44	Ib	47.35N	77.33W
Grand Lieu, Lac de-	11	Eg	47.05N	1.40W
Grand Manan Channel	44	Nc	44.45N	66.52W
Grand Manan Island	42	Kh	44.40N	66.50W
Grand Marais [Mi.-U.S.]	44	Eb	46.40N	85.59W
Grand Marais [Mn.-U.S.]	45	Kc	47.45N	90.20W
Grand-Mère	44	Kb	46.37N	72.41W
Grand Morin	11	If	48.54N	2.50 E
Grândola	13	Df	38.10N	8.34W
Grândola, Serra de-	13	Df	38.06N	8.38W
Grand Passage	63b	Ad	18.45S	163.10 E
Grand-Popo	34	Fd	6.17N	1.50 E
Grand Portage	45	Lc	47.58N	89.41W
Grand Prairie	45	Hj	32.45N	96.59W
Grandpré	12	Ge	49.20N	4.52 E
Grand Rapids [Man.-Can.]	42	Hf	53.10N	99.17W
Grand Rapids [Mi.-U.S.]	39	Ke	42.58N	85.40W
Grand Rapids [Mn.-U.S.]	43	Ib	47.14N	93.31W
Grand Récif Sud	61	Cd	22.38S	167.00 E
Grand River [Mi.-U.S.]	44	Dd	43.04N	86.15W
Grand River [Mo.-U.S.]	45	Jg	39.23N	93.06W
Grand River [Ont.-Can.]	44	Hd	42.51N	79.34W
Grand River [S.D.-U.S.]	45	Fd	45.40N	100.32W
Grand'Rivière	51h	Ab	14.52N	61.11W
Grand Roy	51p	Bb	12.08N	61.45W
Grand-Sans-Toucher	51e	Ab	16.06N	61.41W
Grand Teton	43	Ec	43.44N	110.48W
Grand Traverse Bay	43	Jb	45.02N	85.30W
Grand Turk	49	Lc	21.30N	71.10W
Grand Turk	47	Jd	21.28N	71.09W
Grand Union Canal	12	Bc	51.30N	0.02W
Grand Valley	45	Bg	39.27N	108.03W
Grandview [Man.-Can.]	45	Fa	51.10N	100.45W
Grandview [Mo.-U.S.]	45	Ig	38.53N	94.32W
Grandvilliers	12	De	49.40N	1.56 E
Grand Wash Cliffs	46	Ii	35.45N	113.45W
Grand Wintersberg	11	Ne	48.59N	7.37 E
Granger	46	Ee	46.21N	120.11W
Grängesberg	8	Fd	60.05N	14.59 E
Grangeville	46	Gd	45.56N	116.07W
Gran Guardia	56	Ic	25.52S	58.53W
Granite City	45	Kg	38.42N	90.09W
Granite Falls	45	Id	44.49N	95.33W
Granite Pass	46	Ld	44.38N	107.30W
Granite Peak [Nv.-U.S.]	43	Dc	41.40N	117.35W
Granite Peak [U.S.]	43	Fb	45.10N	109.48W
Granite Range	46	Ff	41.00N	119.35W
Granitola, Punta-	14	Gm	37.34N	12.41 E
Grankulla/Kauniainen	8	Kd	60.13N	24.45 E
Granma	49	Ic	20.30N	77.00W
Gran Malvina, Isla-/West Falkland	52	Kk	51.40S	60.00W
Gran Morelos [Mex.]	48	Eb	30.40N	108.35W
Gran Morelos [Mex.]	48	Fc	28.15N	106.30W
Gränna	8	Ff	58.01N	14.28 E
Granollers/Granollérs	13	Oc	41.37N	2.18 E
Granollérs/Granollers	13	Oc	41.37N	2.18 E
Gran Paradis/Gran Paradiso	14	Be	45.32N	7.16 E
Gran Paradiso/Gran Paradis	14	Be	45.32N	7.16 E
Gran Pilastro/Hochfeiler	14	Fd	46.58N	11.44 E
Gran San Bernardo	14	Be	45.50N	7.10 E
Gran Sasso d'Italia	5	Hg	42.25N	13.40 E
Grant	45	Ff	40.50N	101.56W
Grant, Mount-	46	Fg	38.34N	118.48W
Gran Tarajal	32	Ed	28.12N	14.01W
Grantham	9	Mi	52.54N	0.38W
Grant Island	66	Nf	74.24S	131.20W
Grantown-on-Spey	9	Jd	57.20N	3.38W
Grant Range	46	Hg	38.25N	115.30W
Grants	43	Fd	35.09N	107.52W
Grantsburg	45	Jd	45.47N	92.41W
Grants Pass	43	Cc	42.26N	123.19W
Granville	11	Ef	48.50N	1.36W
Granville Lake	42	He	56.00N	100.20W
Granvin	8	Bd	60.33N	6.43 E
Grao de Gandia, Gandia-	13	Lf	38.59N	0.09W
Grao de Sagunto, Sagunto-	13	Le	39.40N	0.16W
Grappa, Monte-	14	Fe	45.52N	11.48 E
Grappler Bank (EN)	51a	Cc	17.48N	65.55W
Graskop	37	Ed	24.58S	30.49 E
Gräsmark	8	Ee	59.57N	12.55 E
Gräsö	7	Ef	60.25N	18.25 E
Grasse	11	Mk	43.40N	6.55 E
Grasset,Lac-	44	Ha	49.58N	78.10W
Grassrange	46	Kc	47.01N	108.48W
Gråsten	7	Bi	54.55N	9.36 E
Grästorp	8	Ef	58.20N	12.40 E
Graubünden	14	Dd	46.35N	9.35 E
Graulhet	11	Hk	43.46N	2.00 E
Graus	13	Mb	42.11N	0.20 E
Grave	12	Hc	51.45N	5.45 E
Grave, Pointe de-	11	Ei	45.34N	1.04W
Gravedona	14	Dd	46.09N	9.18 E
Gravelbourg	42	Gg	49.53N	106.34W
Gravelines	11	Id	50.59N	2.07 E
Gravenhurst	44	Hc	44.55N	79.22W
Gravenor Bay	51d	Ba	17.33N	61.45W
Graves	11	Fj	44.35N	0.30W
Gravesend	9	Nj	51.27N	0.24 E
Gravesend-Tilbury	9	Nj	51.28N	0.23 E
Gravina in Puglia	14	Kj	40.49N	16.25 E
Gravone	11a	Ab	41.55N	8.47 E
Gray	11	Lg	47.27N	5.35 E
Gray Feather Bank (EN)	60	Df	8.00N	148.40 E
Grayling	44	Ec	44.40N	84.43W
Grays Harbor	46	Cc	46.56N	124.05W
Grayson	44	Ff	38.20N	82.57W
Grays Peak	43	Fd	39.37N	105.45W
Graz	6	Hf	47.04N	15.27 E
Grazalema	13	Gh	36.46N	5.22W
Grdelica	15	Fg	42.54N	22.04 E
Greåker	8	De	59.16N	11.02 E
Great	51p	Bb	12.10N	61.38W
Great Artesian Basin	57	Fg	25.00S	143.00 E
Great Astrolabe Reef	63d	Bc	18.52S	178.31 E
Great Australian Bight	57	Eh	35.00S	130.00 E
Great Bacolet Point	51p	Bb	12.05N	61.37W
Great Bahama Bank (EN)	38	Lg	23.15N	78.00W
Great Bardfield	12	Cc	51.56N	0.29 E
Great Barrier Island	57	Ih	36.10S	175.25 E
Great Barrier Reef	57	Ff	19.10S	149.00 E
Great Basin	38	Hf	40.00N	117.00W
Great Bay	44	Jf	39.30N	74.23W
Great Bear	42	Ed	64.54N	125.35W
Great Bear Lake	38	Hc	66.00N	120.00W
Great Belt (EN)=Store Bælt	5	Hd	55.30N	11.00 E
Great Bend	43	Hd	38.22N	98.46W
Great Blasket/An Blascaod Mór	9	Ci	52.05N	10.32W
Great Britain	5	Fd	54.00N	3.00W
Great Central Lake	46	Cb	49.27N	125.12W
Great Channel	21	Li	6.00N	94.00 E
Great Chesterford	12	Cb	52.04N	0.12 E
Great Dismal Swamp	44	Ig	36.30N	76.30W
Great Dividing Range	57	Fg	25.00S	147.00 E
Great Dunmow	12	Cc	51.53N	0.22 E
Greater Accra	34	Fd	5.45N	0.10 E
Greater Antilles (EN)=Antillas Mayores	38	Lh	20.00N	74.00W
Greater Khingan Range (EN)=Da Hinggan Ling	21	Oe	49.00N	122.00 E
Greater London	9	Mj	51.35N	0.05W
Greater Manchester	9	Kh	53.35N	2.10W
Greater Sunda Islands (EN)	21	Nj	3.52S	111.20 E
Great Exhibition Bay	61	Df	34.40S	173.00 E
Great Exuma Island	47	Id	23.32N	75.50W
Great Falls	39	He	47.30N	111.17W
Great Harbour Cay	44	Im	25.45N	77.52W
Great Inagua	38	Lg	21.02N	73.20W
Great Indian Desert/Thar	21	Ig	27.00N	70.00 E
Great Karasberge (EN)=Groot-Karasberge	30	Ik	27.20S	18.45 E
Great Karroo (EN)=Groot Karoo	30	Jl	33.00S	22.00 E
Great Lake	59	Jh	41.52S	146.45 E
Great Namaland/Groot Namaland	37	Be	26.00S	17.00 E
Great Nicobar	21	Li	7.00N	93.50 E
Great North East Channel	59	Ia	9.30S	143.25 E
Great Ormes Head	9	Jh	53.21N	3.52W
Great Ouse	9	Ni	52.44N	0.23 E
Great Plain of the Koukdjuak	42	Kc	66.25N	72.50W
Great Plains	38	Je	42.00N	100.00W
Great Reef	63c	Bb	10.14S	166.02 E
Great Ruaha	30	Ki	7.56S	37.52 E
Great Sacandaga Lake	44	Jd	43.08N	74.10W
Great Sale Cay	44	Hl	27.00N	78.12W
Great Salt Lake	38	He	41.10N	112.30W
Great Salt Lake Desert	43	Ec	40.40N	113.30W
Great Salt Plains Lake	45	Gh	36.44N	98.12W
Great Salt Pond	51c	Ab	17.15N	62.38W
Great Sandy Desert [Austl.]	57	Dg	21.30S	125.00 E
Great Sandy Desert [U.S.]	43	Cc	43.35N	120.15W
Great Sea Reef	63d	Bb	16.15S	178.33 E
Great Shelford	12	Cb	52.07N	0.08 E
Great Sitkin	40a	Cb	52.03N	176.07W
Great Slave Lake	38	Hd	61.30N	114.00W
Great Smoky Mountains	44	Fh	35.35N	83.30W
Great Stour	9	Oj	51.19N	1.15 E
Great Valley [U.S.]	44	Ie	40.15N	76.50W
Great Valley [U.S.]	43	Kd	36.30N	82.00W
Great Victoria Desert	57	Dg	28.30S	127.45 E
Great Yarmouth	9	Oi	52.37N	1.44 E
Grebbestad	7	Cg	58.42N	11.15 E
Grebenka	16	Hd	50.07N	32.25 E
Gréboun, Mont-	34	Gb	20.00N	8.35 E
Greci	15	Ld	45.11N	28.14 E
Gredos, Sierra de-	13	Gd	40.20N	5.05W
Greece (EN)=Ellás	6	Ih	39.00N	22.00 E
Greeley [Co.-U.S.]	43	Gc	40.25N	104.42W
Greeley [Nb.-U.S.]	45	Gf	41.33N	98.32W
Greely Fiord	42	Ja	80.40N	85.00W
Greem-Bell	21	Ia	81.10N	64.00 E
Green	46	De	43.07N	123.28W
Green Bay	43	Jb	45.00N	87.30W
Green Bay	39	Ke	44.30N	88.01W
Greencastle	44	Df	39.38N	86.52W
Green Cay	49	Ia	24.02N	77.11W
Greeneville	44	Fg	36.10N	82.50W
Greenfield [In.-U.S.]	44	Ef	39.47N	85.46W
Greenfield [Ma.-U.S.]	44	Kd	42.36N	72.36W
Greenhorn Mountain	45	Dh	37.57N	105.00W
Green Island	62	Df	45.54S	170.26 E
Green Island [Atg.]	51d	Bb	17.03N	61.40W
Green Island [Gren.]	51p	Bb	12.14N	61.35W
Green Islands	57	Ge	4.30S	154.10 E
Greenland	51q	Ab	13.15N	59.34W
Greenland (EN)=Grønland/Kalaallit Nunaat	38	Pb	70.00N	40.00W
Greenland (EN)=Grønland/Kalaallit Nunaat	39	Pb	70.00N	40.00W
Greenland (EN)=Kalaallit Nunaat/Grønland	38	Pb	70.00N	40.00W
Greenland (EN)=Kalaallit Nunaat/Grønland	39	Pb	70.00N	40.00W
Greenland Basin (EN)	3	Gb	77.00N	0.00
Greenland Sea (EN)=Grænlandshaf	67	Ld	77.00N	1.00W
Greenland Sea (EN)=Grønlandshavet	67	Ld	77.00N	1.00W
Green Lookout Mountain	46	Dd	45.52N	122.08W
Green Mountains	38	Le	43.45N	72.45W
Greenock	9	If	55.57N	4.45W
Greenough River	59	Ce	28.51S	114.38 E
Green Peter Lake	46	Dd	44.28N	122.30W
Green River [U.S.]	44	Dg	37.55N	87.30W
Green River [U.S.]	38	If	38.11N	109.53W
Green River [Ut.-U.S.]	43	Ed	38.59N	110.10W
Green River [Wy.-U.S.]	43	Fc	41.32N	109.28W
Green River Lake	44	Eg	37.15N	85.15W
Greensboro	39	Lf	36.04N	79.47W
Greensburg [In.-U.S.]	44	Ef	39.20N	85.29W
Greensburg [Ks.-U.S.]	45	Gh	37.36N	99.18W
Greensburg [La.-U.S.]	45	Kk	30.51N	90.42W
Greenstone Point	9	Hd	57.55N	5.40W
Greenvale	59	Jc	18.55S	145.05 E
Greenville [Al.-U.S.]	44	Dj	31.50N	86.38W
Greenville [Il.-U.S.]	45	Lg	38.53N	89.25W
Greenville [Lbr.]	31	Gh	4.59N	9.02W
Greenville [Me.-U.S.]	44	Mc	45.28N	69.35W
Greenville [Ms.-U.S.]	43	Ie	33.25N	91.05W
Greenville [N.C.-U.S.]	43	Ld	35.37N	77.23W
Greenville [Oh.-U.S.]	44	Ee	40.06N	84.37W
Greenville [Pa.-U.S.]	44	Ge	41.24N	80.24W
Greenville [S.C.-U.S.]	39	Kf	34.51N	82.23W
Greenville [Tx.-U.S.]	43	He	33.08N	96.07W
Greenwich	44	Fe	41.02N	82.32W
Greenwich, London-	9	Mj	51.28N	0.00
Greenwood [Ms.-U.S.]	43	Ie	33.31N	90.11W
Greenwood [S.C.-U.S.]	44	Fh	34.12N	82.10W
Greenwood, Lake-	44	Gh	34.15N	82.00W
Greer	44	Fh	34.55N	82.14W
Greers Ferry Lake	45	Ji	35.30N	92.10W
Greeson, Lake-	45	Ji	34.10N	93.45W
Grefrath	12	Ic	51.18N	6.19 E
Gregoria Pérez de Denis	55	Bi	28.14S	61.32W
Gregorio, Rio-	54	De	6.50S	70.46W
Gregório, Rio-	55	Ha	13.42S	49.58W
Gregory, Lake-	59	He	28.55S	139.00 E
Gregory Lake	59	Fd	20.10S	127.20 E
Gregory Range	57	Ff	19.00S	143.00 E
Gregory River	59	Hc	17.53S	139.17 E
Greifenburg	14	Hd	46.45N	13.11 E
Greifswald	10	Jb	54.06N	13.23 E
Greifswalder Bodden	10	Jb	54.15N	13.35 E
Greifswalder Oie	10	Jb	54.14N	13.55 E
Grein	14	Ib	48.13N	14.51 E
Greiz	10	If	50.39N	12.12 E
Grēko, Akrōtērion-	24	Fe	34.56N	34.05 E
Gremiha	6	Jb	68.03N	39.29 E
Gremjačinsk	17	Hg	58.34N	57.51 E
Grenå	7	Ch	56.25N	10.53 E
Grenada	39	Mh	12.07N	61.40W
Grenada	38	Mh	12.07N	61.40W
Grenada	45	Lj	33.47N	89.55W
Grenada Basin (EN)	47	Lf	13.30N	62.00W
Grenada Lake	45	Lj	33.50N	89.40W
Grenadines	47	Lf	12.40N	61.15W
Grenchen	14	Bc	47.11N	7.25 E
Grenen	5	Hd	57.44N	10.40 E
Grenfell	45	Ea	50.25N	102.56W
Grenoble	6	Gf	45.10N	5.43 E
Grenora	45	Eb	48.37N	103.56W
Grense-Jakobselv	7	Hb	69.47N	30.50 E
Grenville	50	Ff	12.07N	61.37W
Grenville, Cape-	59	Ib	12.00S	143.15 E
Gréoux-les-Bains	11	Lk	43.45N	5.53 E
Gresham	46	Dd	45.30N	122.26W
Gresik	26	Fh	7.09S	112.38 E
Gressoney-la-Trinité	14	Be	45.50N	7.49 E
Gretas Klackar	8	Gc	61.34N	17.50 E
Gretna	45	Kl	29.55N	90.03W
Grevelingen	12	Fc	51.45N	4.00 E
Greven	10	Dd	52.06N	7.37 E
Grevená	15	Ei	40.05N	21.25 E
Grevenbroich	12	Ce	51.05N	6.35 E
Grevenbrück, Lennestadt-	12	Kc	51.08N	8.01 E
Grevenmacher	12	Ie	49.41N	6.27 E
Grevesmühlen	10	Hc	53.52N	11.11 E
Grey	62	De	42.26S	171.11 E
Greybull	46	Kd	44.30N	108.03W
Greybull River	46	Kd	44.28N	108.03W
Grey Islands	42	Lf	50.50N	55.35W
Greymouth	61	Dh	42.27S	171.12 E
Grey Range	57	Fg	27.00S	143.35 E
Greystones/Na Clocha Liatha	9	Gh	53.09N	6.04W
Greytow	37	Ee	29.07S	30.30 E
Greytown	62	Fd	41.05S	175.28 E
Gribanovski	16	Ld	51.29N	41.58 E
Gribb Bank (EN)	66	Ge	63.00S	90.30 E
Gribès, Mali i-	15	Ci	40.34N	19.34 E
Gribingui	35	Bd	7.00N	19.30 E
Gribingui	35	Bd	8.33N	19.05 E
Griend	12	Ha	53.15N	5.20 E
Griesheim	12	Ke	49.52N	8.33 E
Grieskirchen	14	Hb	48.14N	13.50 E
Griffin	43	Ke	33.15N	84.16W
Griffith	59	Jf	34.17S	146.03 E
Grigoriopol	15	Mb	47.09N	29.13 E
Grijalva	38	Jh	18.36N	92.39W
Grim, Cape-	59	Ih	40.41S	144.41 E
Grimari	35	Cd	5.44N	20.03 E
Grimbergen	12	Gd	50.56N	4.23 E
Grimma	10	Ie	51.14N	12.43 E
Grimmen	10	Jb	54.06N	13.03 E
Grimsby	9	Mh	53.35N	0.05W
Grimsey	7a	Ca	66.33N	18.00W
Grimsstadir	7a	Cb	65.39N	16.07W
Grimstad	7	Bg	58.20N	8.36 E
Grimsvötn	7a	Cb	64.24N	17.22W
Grindavík	7a	Ac	63.50N	22.30W
Grindelwald	14	Cd	46.38N	8.03 E
Grindsted	7	Bi	55.45N	8.56 E
Grinnell	45	Jf	41.45N	92.43W
Grinnel Peninsula	42	Ia	76.40N	95.00W
Grintavec	14	Id	46.22N	14.32 E
Griquatown	37	Ce	28.49S	23.15 E
Grise Fiord	39	Kb	76.10N	83.15W
Gris-Nez, Cap-	11	Hd	50.52N	1.35 E
Grisslehamn	8	Hd	60.06N	18.50 E
Grjazi	19	De	52.29N	39.57 E
Grjazovec	19	Ed	58.53N	40.15 E
Grmeč	14	Kf	44.43N	16.15 E
Grobiņa/Grobinja	7	Eh	56.33N	21.11 E
Grobinja/Grobiņa	7	Eh	56.33N	21.11 E
Groblersdal	37	De	25.15S	29.25 E
Grocka	15	De	44.41N	20.43 E
Grodk/Spremberg	10	Ke	51.33N	14.22 E
Grodków	10	Nf	50.43N	17.22 E
Grodnenskaja Oblast	19	Ce	53.45N	25.10 E
Grodno	6	Ie	53.42N	23.50 E
Grodzisk Mazowiecki	10	Qd	52.07N	20.37 E
Grodzjanka	16	Fc	53.34N	28.48 E
Groeie Hoop, Kaap die-/Good Hope, Cape of-	30	Il	34.21S	18.28 E

Index Symbols

[1] Independent Nation
[2] State, Region
[3] District, County
[4] Municipality
[5] Colony, Dependency
Continent
Physical Region

Historical or Cultural Region
Mount, Mountain
Volcano
Hill
Mountains, Mountain Range
Hills, Escarpment
Plateau, Upland

Pass, Gap
Plain, Lowland
Delta
Salt Flat
Valley, Canyon
Crater, Cave
Karst Features

Depression
Polder
Desert, Dunes
Forest, Woods
Heath, Steppe
Oasis
Cape, Point

Coast, Beach
Cliff
Peninsula
Isthmus
Sandbank
Island
Atoll

Rock, Reef
Islands, Archipelago
Rocks, Reefs
Coral Reef
Well, Spring
Geyser
River, Stream

Waterfall Rapids
River Mouth, Estuary
Lake
Salt Lake
Intermittent Lake
Reservoir
Swamp, Pond

Canal
Glacier
Ice Shelf, Pack Ice
Ocean
Sea
Gulf, Bay
Strait, Fjord

Lagoon
Bank
Seamount
Tablemount
Ridge
Shelf
Basin

Escarpment, Sea Scarp
Fracture
Trench, Abyss
National Park, Reserve
Point of Interest
Recreation Site
Cave, Cavern

Historic Site
Ruins
Wall, Walls
Church, Abbey
Temple
Scientific Station
Airport

Port
Lighthouse
Mine
Tunnel
Dam, Bridge

Name	Page	Key	Lat.	Long.
Groenlo	12	Ib	52.04N	6.39 E
Groesbeek	12	Hc	51.47N	5.56 E
Grofa, Gora-	15	Ha	48.34N	24.03 E
Groix	11	Cg	47.38N	3.28W
Groix, Ile de-	11	Cg	47.38N	3.28W
Grójec	10	Qe	51.52N	20.52 E
Gröll Seamount (EN)	54	Lf	14.00S	32.00W
Gromnik	10	Nf	50.42N	17.07 E
Gronau (Westfalen)	10	Dd	52.12N	7.02 E
Grong	7	Cd	64.30N	12.27 E
Groningen [3]	12	Ia	53.13N	6.33 E
Groningen [Neth.]	6	Ge	53.13N	6.33 E
Groningen [Sur.]	54	Gb	5.48N	55.28W
Groninger-wad	12	Ia	53.27N	6.25 E
Groningerwad	12	Ia	53.25N	6.30 E
Grønland/Kalaallit Nunaat= Greenland (EN)	38	Pb	70.00N	40.00W
Grønland/Kalaallit Nunaat= Greenland (EN) [5]	67	Nd	70.00N	40.00W
Grønlandshavet=Greenland Sea (EN)	67	Ld	77.00N	1.00W
Grønnedal	41	Hf	61.20N	47.45W
Grönskara	8	Fg	57.05N	15.44 E
Groot	30	Jl	33.45S	24.58 E
Groot Baai	51b	Ab	18.01N	63.04W
Groote Eylandt	57	Ef	14.00S	136.40 E
Grootfontein	31	Ij	19.32S	18.05 E
Grootfontein [3]	37	Bc	19.00S	19.00 E
Groot-Karasberge=Great Karasberge (EN)	30	Ik	27.20S	18.45 E
Groot Karoo=Great Karroo (EN)	30	Jl	33.00S	22.00 E
Grootlaagte	37	Cd	20.55S	21.27 E
Groot Namaland/Great Namaland	37	Be	26.00S	17.00 E
Grootvloer	37	Ce	30.00S	20.40 E
Gropeni	15	Kd	45.05N	27.54 E
Gros Caps, Pointe des-	51e	Bb	16.28N	61.25W
Gros Islet Bay	51k	Ba	14.05N	60.58W
Gros Islets	51k	Ba	14.05N	60.58W
Gros-Morne	51h	Ab	14.43N	61.01W
Gros-Morne	42	Lg	49.00N	57.22W
Grosne	11	Kh	46.42N	4.56 E
Gros Piton	51k	Ab	13.49N	61.04W
Große Aa	12	Jb	52.25N	7.23 E
Große Aue	12	Kb	52.30N	8.38 E
Großefehn	12	Ja	53.24N	7.33 E
Große Laaber	10	Ih	48.50N	12.30 E
Großenhain	10	Je	51.17N	13.33 E
Großenkneten	12	Kb	52.57N	8.16 E
Grosse Pointe	51e	Bb	16.01N	61.17W
Großer Arber	10	Jg	49.07N	13.07 E
Großer Gleichberg	10	Gf	50.23N	10.35 E
Großer Inselsberg	10	Gf	50.52N	10.28 E
Grosseto	14	Fh	42.46N	11.08 E
Grosseto, Formiche di-	14	Eh	42.40N	10.55 E
Groß-Gerau	10	Eg	49.55N	8.29 E
Großglockner	5	Hf	47.04N	12.42 E
Großräschen	10	Je	51.35N	14.00 E
Groß-Umstadt	12	Ke	49.52N	8.56 E
Großvenediger	14	Gc	47.06N	12.21 E
Grostenquin	12	If	48.59N	6.44 E
Gros Ventre Range	46	Je	43.30N	110.15W
Groswater Bay	38	Nd	54.20N	57.30W
Grøtavær	7	Db	68.58N	16.16 E
Grote Nete	12	Gc	51.07N	4.34 E
Grotli	7	Be	62.01N	7.40 E
Grottaglie	14	Lj	40.32N	17.26 E
Grottammare	14	Hh	42.59N	13.52 E
Groumania	34	Ed	7.55N	4.00W
Groundhog River	44	Ga	49.43N	81.58W
Grouse Creek Montains	46	If	41.55N	113.50W
Grove Mountains	66	Ff	72.53S	74.53 E
Groves	45	Jl	29.57N	93.55W
Grovfjord	7	Db	68.41N	17.09 E
Grow, Idaarderadeel-	12	Ha	53.06N	5.50 E
Grozny	6	Kg	43.20N	45.42 E
Grubišno Polje	14	Le	45.42N	17.10 E
Grudovo	15	Kg	42.21N	27.10 E
Grudziądz	10	Oc	53.29N	18.45 E
Grumento Nova	14	Jj	40.17N	15.53 E
Grumo Appula	14	Ki	41.01N	16.42 E
Grums	8	Ee	59.21N	13.06 E
Grünau	37	Be	27.47S	18.23 E
Grünberg	12	Kd	50.36N	8.57 E
Gründau	12	Ld	50.14N	9.05 E
Grundy	44	Fg	37.17N	82.06W
Grunidera	48	Ie	24.15N	101.58W
Grünstadt	12	Ke	49.34N	8.10 E
Grunwald	10	Qc	53.30N	20.05 E
Gruppo di Brenta	14	Ed	46.10N	10.55 E
Gruyère	14	Bd	46.40N	7.10 E
Gruža	15	Df	43.54N	20.47 E
Gruzinskaja Sovetskaja Socialističeskaja Respublika [2]	19	Eg	42.00N	44.00 E
Gruzinskaja SSR/ Sakartvelos Sabčata Socialisturi Respublika [2]	19	Eg	42.00N	44.00 E
Gruzinskaja SSR=Georgian SSR (EN) [2]	19	Eg	42.00N	44.00 E
Grybów	10	Qg	49.38N	20.56 E
Gryckbo	8	Fd	60.41N	15.28 E
Gryfice	10	Lc	53.56N	15.12 E
Gryfino	10	Kc	53.15N	14.30 E
Grythyttan	8	Fe	59.42N	14.32 E
Grytviken	66	Ad	54.17S	36.31W
Gstaad	14	Bd	46.28N	7.17 E
Guacanayabo, Golfo de-	47	Id	20.28N	77.30W
Guacara	50	Cg	10.14N	67.53W
Guaçu	55	Ef	22.11S	54.31W
Guadaioz	13	Hg	37.50N	4.51W
Guadaira	13	Fg	37.20N	6.01W
Guadalajara [3]	13	Jd	40.50N	2.30W
Guadalajara [Mex.]	39	Ig	20.40N	103.20W
Guadalajara [Sp.]	13	Id	40.38N	3.10W
Guadalaviar	13	Kd	40.21N	1.08W
Guadalbullón	13	Ig	37.59N	3.47W
Guadalcanal	13	Gf	38.06N	5.49W
Guadalcanal Island	57	He	9.32S	160.12 E
Guadalén	13	If	38.05N	3.32W
Guadalentín o Sangonera	13	Kg	37.59N	1.04W
Guadalete	13	Fh	36.35N	6.13W
Guadalfeo	13	Ih	36.43N	3.35W
Guadalimar	13	Ig	37.59N	3.44W
Guadalmena	13	Jf	38.20N	2.55W
Guadalmez	13	Gf	38.46N	5.04W
Guadalope	13	Lc	41.15N	0.03W
Guadalquivir	5	Fh	36.47N	6.22W
Guadalupe [Mex.]	47	Dc	25.41N	100.15W
Guadalupe [Mex.]	48	Hf	22.45N	102.31W
Guadalupe [Mex.]	48	Id	26.12N	101.23W
Guadalupe [Sp.]	13	Ge	39.27N	5.19W
Guadalupe, Isla de-	38	Hg	29.00N	118.16W
Guadalupe, Sierra de-	13	Ge	39.25N	5.25W
Guadalupe Bravos	48	Fb	31.23N	106.07W
Guadalupe Mountains	45	Dj	32.20N	105.00W
Guadalupe Peak	43	Ge	31.50N	104.52W
Guadalupe River	45	Hl	28.30N	96.53W
Guadalupe Victoria, Presa-	48	Gf	23.50N	104.55W
Guadalupe y Calvo	48	Fd	26.06N	106.58W
Guadarrama	13	He	39.53N	4.10W
Guadarrama, Puerto de-	13	Hd	40.43N	4.10W
Guadarrama, Sierra de-	13	Id	40.55N	4.00W
Guadazaón	13	Ke	39.42N	1.36W
Guadeloupe	38	Mh	16.15N	61.35W
Guadeloupe [5]	39	Mh	16.15N	61.35W
Guadeloupe, Canal de la-= Guadeloupe Passage (EN)	47	Le	16.40N	61.50W
Guadeloupe Passage	50	Fd	16.40N	61.50W
Guadeloupe Passage (EN)= Guadeloupe, Canal de la-	47	Le	16.40N	61.50W
Guadiana	5	Fh	37.14N	7.22W
Guadiana, Canal del-	13	Ie	39.20N	3.20W
Guadiana, Ojos del-	13	Ie	39.08N	3.31W
Guadiana Menor	13	Ig	37.56N	3.15W
Guadiaro	13	Gh	36.17N	5.17W
Guadiela	13	Jd	40.22N	2.49W
Guadix	13	Ig	37.18N	3.08W
Guafo, Boca del-	56	Ff	43.40S	74.15W
Guafo, Isla-	56	Ff	43.36S	74.43W
Guaiba	56	Jd	30.06S	51.19W
Guaiba, Rio-	55	Gj	30.15S	51.12W
Guaimaca	49	Df	14.52N	86.51W
Guaimorato, Laguna de-	49	Ef	15.58N	85.55W
Guainía [2]	54	Ec	2.30N	69.00W
Guainia, Rio-	52	Je	2.01N	67.07W
Guaiquinima, Cerro-	54	Fb	5.49N	63.40W
Guaíra [3]	56	Dg	25.45S	56.30W
Guaíra [Braz.]	56	Jb	24.04S	54.15W
Guaíra [Braz.]	55	He	20.19S	48.18W
Guaíra Falls (EN) = Sete Quedas, Saltos das-	56	Jb	24.02S	54.16W
Guairas	55	Ja	12.39S	44.16W
Guaire/Gorey	9	Gi	52.40N	6.18W
Guaitecas, Islas-	56	Ff	43.57S	73.50W
Guajaba, Cayo-	49	Ic	21.50N	77.30W
Guajará Mirim	53	Jg	10.48S	65.22W
Guajira, Peninsula de la-	52	Id	12.00N	71.30W
Guajolotes, Sierra del-	48	Ge	26.00N	105.15W
Guakolak, Tanjung-	26	Eh	6.50S	105.14 E
Gualaco	49	Df	15.06N	86.07W
Gualán	49	Cf	15.08N	89.22W
Gualdo Tadino	14	Gg	43.14N	12.47 E
Gualeguay	55	Ck	33.09S	59.20W
Gualeguay, Rio-	55	Ck	33.19S	59.39W
Gualeguaychu	56	Id	33.01S	58.31W
Gualeguaychú, Rio-	55	Ck	33.05S	58.25W
Gualicho, Salina del-	56	Gf	40.24S	65.15W
Guam [5]	58	Fc	13.28N	144.47 E
Guam	57	Fc	13.28N	144.47 E
Guamini	56	He	37.02S	62.25W
Guampi, Sierra de-	54	Eb	6.00N	65.35W
Guamuchil	47	Cc	25.22N	108.22W
Gua Musang	26	Df	4.53N	101.58 E
Gu'an	28	De	39.24N	116.10 E
Guanabacoa	49	Fb	23.07N	82.18W
Guanabara, Baia de-	55	Kf	22.50S	43.10W
Guanacaste [3]	49	Eh	10.30N	85.15W
Guanacaste, Cordillera de-	49	Eh	10.45N	85.05W
Guanacevi	48	Ge	25.56N	105.57W
Guanahacabibes, Golfo de-	49	Eb	22.08N	84.35W
Guanahacabibes, Peninsula de-	49	Ec	21.57N	84.35W
Guana Island	51a	Db	18.29N	64.34W
Guanaja	49	Ee	16.27N	85.54W
Guanaja, Isla de-	49	Ee	16.30N	85.55W
Guanajay	49	Fb	22.55N	82.42W
Guanajibo	51a	Ab	18.10N	67.09W
Guanajibo, Punta-	51a	Ab	18.12N	67.10W
Guanajuato	47	Dd	21.01N	101.15W
Guanajuato [2]	47	Dd	21.00N	101.00W
Guanambi	54	Jf	14.13S	42.47W
Guanare	54	Eb	9.03N	69.45W
Guanare, Rio-	50	Ch	8.13N	67.46W
Guanare Viejo, Rio-	49	Mi	8.19N	68.10W
Guanarito	50	Bh	8.42N	69.12W
Guandacol	56	Gc	29.31S	68.32W
Guandi Shan	27	Jd	38.09N	111.27 E
Guane	47	Hd	22.12N	84.05W
Guangde	27	Ke	30.51N	119.26 E
Guangdong Sheng (Kuang-tung Sheng)= Kwangtung (EN) [2]	27	Jg	23.00N	113.00 E
Guangfeng	28	Ej	28.27N	118.12 E
Guanghua	27	Je	32.18N	111.45 E
Guangji (Wuxue)	27	Kf	29.58N	115.32 E
Guangling	28	Ce	39.46N	114.16 E
Guangmao Shan	27	Hf	26.48N	100.56 E
Guangming Ding	28	Ei	30.09N	118.11 E
Guangnan	27	Ig	24.02N	105.04 E
Guangrao	28	Ef	37.03N	118.25 E
Guangshan	28	Ci	32.02N	114.53 E
Guangshui	28	Ci	31.37N	114.01 E
Guangxi Zhuangzu Zizhiqu (Kuang-hsi-chuang-tsu Tzu-chih-ch'ü)=Kwangsi Chuang (EN) [2]	27	Ig	24.00N	109.00 E
Guangyuan	22	Mf	32.27N	105.55 E
Guangzhou=Canton (EN)	22	Ng	23.07N	113.18 E
Guan He	28	Ch	32.18N	115.44 E
Guánica	51a	Bc	17.59N	66.56W
Guanipa, Rio-	50	Eh	9.56N	62.26W
Guannan (Xin'anzhen)	28	Eg	34.04N	119.21 E
Guantánamo [3]	49	Jc	20.10N	75.00W
Guantanamo	39	Lg	20.08N	75.12W
Guantánamo, Bahia de-	49	Jd	20.00N	75.10W
Guantánamo Bay	47	Id	20.00N	75.10W
Guantanamo Bay Naval Station	49	Jd	20.00N	75.08W
Guantao (Nanguantao)	28	Cf	36.33N	115.18 E
Guanting Shuiku	28	Cd	40.13N	115.36 E
Guanxian	22	Mf	31.00N	103.38 E
Guanyun (Dayishan)	28	Eg	34.18N	119.14 E
Guapé	55	Je	20.47S	45.55W
Guapi	54	Cc	2.35N	77.55W
Guápiles	49	Fh	10.13N	83.46W
Guapó	55	Hc	16.51S	49.33W
Guaporé	55	Gi	29.10S	51.54W
Guaporé	56	Jc	28.51S	51.54W
Guaporé, Rio-	52	Jg	11.55S	65.04W
Guaqui	54	Eg	16.35S	68.51W
Guará	55	Gg	25.23S	51.17W
Guara, Sierra de-	13	Lb	42.17N	0.10W
Guarabira	54	Ke	6.51S	35.29W
Guaranda	54	Cd	1.35S	78.59W
Guaraniacu	56	Jc	25.06S	52.52W
Guarani de Goiás	55	Ia	13.57S	46.28W
Guarapiche, Rio-	50	Eh	9.57N	62.52W
Guarapuava	56	Jc	25.23S	51.27W
Guaraqueçaba	55	Hg	25.17S	48.21W
Guararapes	55	Ge	21.15S	50.38W
Guaratinguetá	55	Jf	22.49S	45.13W
Guaratuba	55	Hg	25.54S	48.34W
Guarayos, Rio-	55	Bb	14.38S	62.11W
Guarda	13	Ed	40.32N	7.16W
Guarda [2]	13	Ed	40.40N	7.10W
Guardafui, Cape-(EN)= 'Asäyr	30	Mg	11.49N	51.15 E
Guardal	13	Jg	37.36N	2.45W
Guarda-Mor	55	Ic	17.47S	47.06W
Guardiagrele	14	Ih	42.11N	14.13 E
Guardian Seamount (EN)	38	Ki	9.32N	87.40W
Guardo	13	Hb	42.47N	4.50W
Guardunha, Serra da-	13	Ed	40.05N	7.31W
Guarei, Rio-	55	Ff	22.40S	53.34W
Guareña	13	Gc	41.29N	5.23W
Guarenas	50	Cg	10.28N	66.37W
Guaribas, Rio-	55	Jc	16.22S	45.03W
Guaribe, Rio-	50	Dh	9.53N	65.11W
Guárico [2]	54	Eb	8.40N	66.35W
Guárico, Embalse del-	50	Ch	9.00N	67.20W
Guarico, Rio-	54	Eb	7.55N	67.23W
Guariquito, Rio-	50	Ci	7.40N	66.18W
Guarita, Rio-	55	Fh	27.11S	53.44W
Guaritico, Caño-	50	Bi	7.52N	68.53W
Guaritire, Rio-	55	Ba	13.43S	60.38W
Guarujá	55	If	24.00S	46.16W
Guarulhos	56	Kb	23.28S	46.32W
Guasave	47	Cc	25.34N	108.27W
Guasdualito	54	Db	7.15N	70.44W
Guasipati	54	Fb	7.28N	61.54W
Guasopa	63a	Ac	9.14S	152.55 E
Guastalla	14	Ef	44.55N	10.39 E
Guatemala	39	Jh	14.38N	90.31W
Guatemala [3]	49	Bf	14.40N	90.30W
Guatemala [1]	39	Jh	14.38N	90.31W
Guatemala Basin (EN)	3	Mh	11.00N	95.00W
Guateque [Col.]	54	Db	5.05N	73.30W
Guateque [Col.]	54	Db	5.00N	73.28W
Guatimozin	55	Ak	33.27S	62.27W
Guatisimiña	54	Fc	4.33N	63.57W
Guatraché	56	He	37.40S	63.32W
Guaviare, Rio-	52	Je	4.03N	67.44W
Guaviravi	55	Di	29.22S	56.50W
Guaxupé	55	Ie	21.18S	46.42W
Guayabal [Cuba]	49	Ic	20.42N	77.36W
Guayabal [Ven.]	50	Ci	8.00N	67.24W
Guayabero, Rio-	52	Je	4.03N	67.44W
Guayalejo, Rio-	48	Kf	22.13N	97.52W
Guayama	49	Ne	17.59N	66.07W
Guayana, Macizo de la-= Guiana Highlands (EN)	52	Ke	5.00N	60.00W
Guayana Basin (EN)	3	Ci	10.00N	52.00W
Guayaneco, Archipiélago-	56	Eg	47.45S	75.10W
Guayanés, Punta-	51a	Cb	18.04N	65.48W
Guayanilla	51a	Bb	18.02N	66.47W
Guayanilla, Bahia de-	51a	Bc	17.58N	66.45W
Guayape, Rio-	49	Df	14.26N	86.02W
Guayaquil	53	If	2.10S	79.50W
Guayaquil, Golfo de-	52	Hf	3.00S	80.30W
Guaycurú, Rio-	55	Ch	27.19S	58.45W
Guaymas	39	Hg	27.56N	110.54W
Guayquiraró, Rio-	55	Cj	30.10S	58.34W
Guba [Eth.]	35	Fc	11.15N	35.20 E
Guba [Zaire]	36	Ee	10.38S	26.25 E
Guba Dolgaja	19	Fa	70.19N	58.45 E
Gubaha	19	Fd	58.52N	57.36 E
Guban	30	Lg	10.15N	44.26 E
Gubbio	14	Gg	43.21N	12.25 E
Gubdor	17	Hf	60.15N	56.35 E
Guber	10	Rb	54.13N	21.02 E
Gubin	10	Ke	51.56N	14.45 E
Gubio	34	Hc	12.30N	12.47 E
Gubkin	19	De	51.17N	37.33 E
Güdar, Sierra de-	13	Ld	40.27N	0.42W
Gudara	19	Hh	38.23N	72.42 E
Gudauta	16	Lh	43.07N	40.37 E
Gudbrandsdalen	7	Bf	61.30N	10.00 E
Gudenå	8	Dh	56.29N	10.13 E
Gudermes	19	Eg	43.22N	46.08 E
Gudivāda	25	Ge	16.27N	80.59 E
Gudiyāttam	25	Ff	12.57N	78.52 E
Gudou Shan	27	Jg	22.12N	112.57 E
Güdül	24	Eb	40.13N	32.15 E
Güdür	25	Ff	14.08N	79.51 E
Gudvangen	8	Bd	60.52N	6.50 E
Guebwiller	11	Ng	47.55N	7.12 E
Guéckédou	34	Cd	8.33N	10.09W
Guelma [3]	32	Ib	36.15N	7.30 E
Guelma	32	Ib	36.28N	7.26 E
Guelph	42	Jh	43.33N	80.15W
Guelta Zemmur	32	Ed	25.08N	12.22W
Guemar	32	Ic	33.29N	6.48 E
Guéméné-Penfao	11	Eg	47.38N	1.50W
Guénange	12	Ie	49.18N	6.11 E
Guéné	34	Fc	11.44N	3.13 E
Guer	11	Dg	47.54N	2.07W
Guéra [3]	35	Bc	11.30N	18.30 E
Güera	32	De	20.52N	17.03W
Guéra, Massif de-	30	Ig	11.55N	18.12 E
Guérande	11	Dg	47.20N	2.26W
Guerara	32	Hc	32.48N	4.30 E
Guercif	32	Gc	34.14N	3.22W
Guerdjoumane, Djebel-	13	Oh	36.25N	2.51 E
Güere, Rio-	50	Dh	9.50N	65.08W
Guéréda	35	Cc	14.31N	22.05 E
Guéret	11	Hh	46.10N	1.52 E
Guérin-Kouka	34	Fd	9.41N	0.37 E
Guernica y Luno	13	Ja	43.19N	2.41W
Guernsey	9	Kl	49.27N	2.35W
Guerrero [2]	47	De	17.40N	100.00W
Guerrero	48	Ic	28.20N	100.26W
Guessou-Sud	34	Fc	10.03N	2.38 E
Guest Peninsula	66	Mf	76.18S	148.00W
Guge	35	Fd	6.12N	37.30 E
Gügerd, Küh-e-	24	Oe	34.50N	53.00 E
Guglionesi	14	Ii	41.55N	14.55 E
Guguan Island	57	Fc	17.19N	145.51 E
Guia	55	Db	15.22S	56.14W
Guia Lopes da Laguna	55	De	21.26S	56.07W
Guiana Highlands (EN) = Guayana, Macizo de la-	52	Ke	5.00N	60.00W
Guiana Island	51d	Bb	17.06N	61.44W
Guichi (Chizhou)	27	Ke	30.38N	117.30 E
Guichón	55	Dk	32.21S	57.12W
Guide	27	Hd	36.00N	101.30 E
Guider	34	Hd	9.56N	13.57 E
Guidimaka [3]	32	Ef	15.30N	12.00W
Guidimouni	34	Gc	13.42N	9.30 E
Guiding	27	If	26.33N	107.16 E
Guidong	27	Jf	26.11N	113.58 E
Guiers	11	Li	45.37N	5.37 E
Guiglo	34	Dd	6.33N	7.29W
Guiglo [3]	34	Dd	6.30N	7.40W
Guijá	37	Ed	24.29S	33.00 E
Güija, Lago de-	49	Cf	14.13N	89.34W
Gui Jiang	21	Ng	23.28N	111.18 E
Guijk en Sint Agatha	12	Hc	51.44N	5.52 E
Guijuelo	13	Gd	40.33N	5.40W
Guil	11	Mj	44.40N	6.36 E
Guildford	9	Mj	51.14N	0.35W
Guiler Gol	28	Ga	46.03N	122.06 E
Guilin	22	Ng	25.21N	110.15 E
Guillaume Delisle, Lac-	42	Je	56.25N	76.00W
Guillestre	11	Mj	44.40N	6.39 E
Guilvinec	11	Bg	47.47N	4.17W
Guimarães [Braz.]	54	Jd	2.08S	44.36W
Guimarães [Port.]	13	Dc	41.27N	8.18W
Guimaras	26	Hd	10.35N	122.37 E
Guinchos Cay	49	Hb	22.45N	78.06W
Guinea (EN)=Guinée [1]	31	Fg	11.00N	10.00W
Guinea, Gulf of-	30	Hh	2.00N	2.30 E
Guinea, Gulf of- (EN)= Guinée, Golfe de-	30	Hh	2.00N	2.30 E
Guinea Basin (EN)	3	Di	0.00	5.00W
Guinea-Bissau (EN)=Guiné-Bissau [1]	31	Fg	12.00N	15.00W
Guinea Ecuatorial= Equatorial Guinea (EN) [1]	31	Hh	2.00N	9.00 E
Guinea Rise (EN)	3	Dj	4.00S	0.00
Guiné-Bissau=Guinea-Bissau (EN) [1]	31	Fg	12.00N	15.00W
Guinée=Guinea (EN) [1]	31	Fg	11.00N	10.00W
Guinée, Golfe de-=Guinea, Gulf of- (EN)	30	Hh	2.00N	2.30 E
Guinée Forestière [3]	34	Dd	8.40N	9.50W
Guinée Maritime [3]	34	Cc	10.00N	14.00W
Guînes	12	Dd	50.52N	1.52 E
Güines	47	Hd	22.50N	82.02W
Guingamp	11	Cf	48.33N	3.09W
Guinguinéo	34	Bc	14.16N	15.57W
Guiones, Punta-	49	Eh	9.54N	85.41W
Guiping	27	Ig	23.23N	110.00 E
Guipúzcoa [3]	13	Ja	43.10N	2.10W
Guir, Hamada du-	30	Ge	31.00N	3.20W
Güira de Melena	49	Fb	22.48N	82.30W
Guiratinga	54	Hg	16.21S	53.45W
Güiria	54	Fa	10.34N	62.18W
Guiscard	12	Fe	49.39N	3.03 E
Guise	11	Je	49.54N	3.38 E
Guitiriz	13	Ea	43.11N	7.54W
Guiuan	26	Id	11.02N	125.43 E
Guixi	27	Kf	28.18N	117.15 E
Guixian	27	Ig	23.10N	109.35 E
Guiyang	22	Mg	26.38N	106.43 E
Guizhou Sheng (Kuei-chou Sheng)=Kweichow (EN) [2]	27	If	27.00N	107.00 E
Gujan-Mestras	11	Ej	44.38N	1.04W
Gujarāt [3]	25	Ed	22.51N	71.30 E
Gujarāt	21	Jg	22.51N	71.30 E
Gujranwala	22	Jf	32.09N	74.11 E
Gujrāt	25	Eb	32.34N	74.05 E
Gukovo	16	Ke	48.04N	39.58 E
Gulang	27	Hd	37.30N	102.54 E
Gulbarga	22	Jh	17.20N	76.50 E
Gulbene	19	Cd	57.12N	26.49 E
Gulča	19	Hg	40.19N	73.33 E
Gulf	55	Ad	19.08S	62.01W
Gulf Breeze	44	Dj	30.22N	87.07W
Gulf Coastal Plain	38	Jf	31.00N	92.00W
Gulfport	43	Je	30.22N	89.06W
Gulian	27	La	52.58N	122.09 E
Gulin	27	If	28.02N	105.47 E
Gulistan	19	Gg	40.30N	68.45 E
Guliya Shan	27	Lb	49.48N	122.25 E
Gulja	20	Hf	54.43N	121.03 E
Gulja/Yining	27	Dc	43.54N	81.21 E
Guljajpole	16	Jf	47.37N	36.18 E
Gulkana	40	Jd	62.16N	145.23W
Gulkeviči	16	Lg	45.19N	40.44 E
Gull Bay	45	Lb	49.47N	89.02W
Gulleråsen	8	Fc	61.04N	15.11 E
Gullfoss	7a	Bb	64.20N	20.08W
Gullkronafjärd	8	Jd	60.05N	22.15 E
Gull Lake	42	Gf	50.08N	108.27W
Gullringen	8	Fg	57.48N	15.42 E
Gull River	45	Lb	49.50N	89.04W
Gullspång	8	Ff	58.59N	14.06 E
Güllü	15	Mk	38.16N	29.07 E
Güllük	24	Bd	37.14N	27.36 E
Gülpinar	15	Jj	39.32N	26.07 E
Gülşehir	24	Fc	38.45N	34.38 E
Gulstav	8	Dj	54.43N	10.41 E
Gulu	31	Kh	2.47N	32.18 E
Guma /Pishan	27	Cd	37.38N	78.19 E
Gumbiri, Jabal-	35	Ee	4.18N	30.57 E
Gumel	34	Gc	12.38N	9.23 E
Gummersbach	10	De	51.02N	7.33 E
Gummi	34	Gc	12.09N	5.07 E
Gümüşçey	15	Ki	40.17N	27.17 E
Gümüşhacıköy	24	Fb	40.53N	35.14 E
Gümüşhane	23	Ea	40.27N	39.29 E
Gümüşsu	15	Nk	38.14N	30.01 E
Guna	35	Fc	11.44N	38.15 E
Guna	25	Fd	24.19N	77.19 E
Gundagai	59	Jg	35.04S	148.07 E
Gundji	36	Db	2.05N	21.27 E
Gündoğdu	15	Ki	40.15N	27.07 E
Gündoğmuş	24	Ed	36.48N	32.01 E
Güney	15	Mk	38.09N	29.05 E
Güneydoğu Toroslar	21	Gf	38.30N	41.00 E
Gungu	36	Cd	5.44S	19.19 E
Gunma Ken [2]	28	Of	36.20N	139.05 E
Gunnar	42	Ge	59.23N	108.53W
Gunnbjørns Fjeld	67	Mc	68.55N	29.20W
Gunnedah	59	Kf	30.59S	150.15 E
Gunnison	43	Fd	38.33N	106.56W
Gunt	18	Hf	37.30N	71.03 E
Guntakal	25	Fe	15.10N	77.23 E
Guntersville	44	Dh	34.21N	86.18W
Guntersville Lake	44	Dh	34.45N	86.03W
Guntür	22	Kh	16.18N	80.27 E
Gunungapi, Pulau-	26	Ih	6.38S	126.40 E
Gunungsitoli	26	Cf	1.17N	97.37 E
Günz	10	Gh	48.27N	10.16 E
Günzburg	10	Gh	48.27N	10.16 E
Gunzenhausen	10	Gg	49.06N	10.45 E
Guo He	28	Dh	32.58N	117.13 E
Guojiadian	28	Hc	43.20N	124.37 E
Guoyang	28	Dh	33.31N	116.12 E
Guozhen	28	Bj	29.24N	113.09 E
Gurahont	15	Fc	46.16N	22.21 E
Gura Humorului	15	Ib	47.33N	25.54 E
Gurban Obo	27	Jc	43.06N	112.28 E
Gurbantünggüt Shamo	27	Eb	45.30N	87.30 E
Gurdžaani	16	Ni	41.43N	45.48 E
Güre	15	Mk	38.39N	29.10 E
Gurgei, Jabal-	35	Cc	13.50N	24.19 E
Gurghiului, Munţii-	15	Ic	46.41N	25.12 E
Gurgueia, Rio-	52	Lf	6.50S	43.24W
Guri — Raúl Leoni, Represa-	54	Fb	7.30N	63.00W
Gurjev	6	Lf	47.07N	51.56 E
Gurjevsk	20	Df	54.20N	86.00 E
Gurjevskaja Oblast [3]	19	Ff	47.30N	52.00 E
Gurk	14	Id	46.36N	14.31 E
Gurk	14	Id	46.52N	14.18 E
Gurktaler Alpen	14	Hd	46.55N	14.00 E
Guro	37	Ec	17.26S	33.20 E
Gurpınar	24	Jc	38.18N	43.25 E
Gurskoje	20	If	50.20N	138.05 E
Gurskøy	7	Ae	62.15N	5.40 E
Gürsu	15	Mi	40.13N	29.12 E
Gurué	37	Fc	15.28S	36.59 E
Gurumeti	36	Fc	2.05S	33.57 E
Gürün	24	Gc	38.43N	37.17 E
Gurupá	54	Hd	1.25S	51.39W
Gurupi	53	Lg	11.43S	49.04W
Gurupi, Rio-	52	Lf	1.13S	46.06W
Gurupi, Serra do-	54	Id	5.00S	47.30W
Guru Sikhar	25	Ed	24.39N	72.46 E
Gus	7	Ji	55.00N	41.12 E
Gusau	31	Hg	12.10N	6.40 E
Gusev	19	Ce	54.37N	22.12 E
Gushan	28	Ge	39.54N	123.36 E
Gushi	27	Ke	32.02N	115.39 E
Gushikawa	29b	Ab	26.21N	127.52 E
Gushk	24	Ph	28.13N	55.52 E
Gus-Hrustalny	7	Ji	55.38N	40.40 E
Gusinaja, Guba-	20	Kb	72.00N	150.00 E
Gusinaja Zemlja, Poluostrov-	19	Fa	71.50N	52.00 E
Gusinje	15	Cg	42.34N	19.50 E
Gusinoozersk	20	Ff	51.17N	106.30 E
Guspini	14	Ck	39.32N	8.37 E
Güssing	14	Kc	47.04N	16.20 E
Gustav Holm, Kap-	41	Ie	66.45N	34.00W
Gustavia	51b	Bc	17.54N	62.52W

Index Symbols

[1] Independent Nation
[2] State, Region
[3] District, County
[4] Municipality
[5] Colony, Dependency
Continent
Physical Region
Historical or Cultural Region
Mount, Mountain
Volcano
Hill
Mountains, Mountain Range
Hills, Escarpment
Plateau, Upland
Pass, Gap
Plain, Lowland
Delta
Salt Flat
Valley, Canyon
Crater, Cave
Karst Features
Depression
Polder
Desert, Dunes
Forest, Woods
Heath, Steppe
Oasis
Cape, Point
Coast, Beach
Cliff
Peninsula
Isthmus
Sandbank
Island
Atoll
Rock, Reef
Islands, Archipelago
Rocks, Reefs
Coral Reef
Well, Spring
Geyser
River, Stream
Waterfall Rapids
River Mouth, Estuary
Lake
Salt Lake
Intermittent Lake
Reservoir
Swamp, Pond
Canal
Glacier
Ice Shelf, Pack Ice
Ocean
Sea
Gulf, Bay
Strait, Fjord
Lagoon
Bank
Seamount
Tablemount
Ridge
Shelf
Basin
Escarpment, Sea Scarp
Fracture
Trench, Abyss
National Park, Reserve
Point of Interest
Recreation Site
Cave, Cavern
Historic Site
Ruins
Wall, Walls
Church, Abbey
Temple
Scientific Station
Airport
Port
Lighthouse
Mine
Tunnel
Dam, Bridge

Gustavs/Kustavi 8 Id 60.30N 21.25 E
Gustavs/Kustavi 8 Id 60.33N 21.21 E
Gustavsfors 8 Ee 59.12N 12.06 E
Gustavus 40 Le 58.25N 135.44W
Güstrow 10 Ic 53.48N 12.10 E
Gusum 8 Gf 58.16N 16.29 E
Gütersloh 10 Ee 51.54N 8.23 E
Guthrie [Ok.-U.S.] 45 Hi 35.53N 97.25W
Guthrie [Tx.-U.S.] 45 Fj 33.37N 100.19W
Gutian 27 Kf 26.40N 118.42 E
Gutiérrez Zamora 48 Kg 20.27N 97.05W
Gutii, Vîrful- 15 Gb 47.42N 23.52 E
Guting → Yutai 28 Dg 35.00N 116.40 E
Gutu 37 Ec 19.39S 31.10 E
Guwāhāti 22 Lg 26.11N 91.44 E
Guyana 53 Ke 5.00N 59.00W
Guyane Française = French Guiana (EN) 53 Ke 4.00N 53.00W
Guyang 27 Jc 41.02N 110.04 E
Guyenne 11 Gj 44.35N 1.00 E
Guymon 43 Gd 36.41N 101.29W
Guyonneau, Anse- 51e Ab 16.14N 61.47W
Guyuan 27 Id 36.01N 106.17 E
Guyuan (Pingdingbu) 28 Cd 41.40N 115.41 E
Guzar 18 Fe 38.37N 66.18 E
Güzelyurt 24 Ee 35.12N 32.59 E
Gūzhān 24 Le 34.20N 46.57 E
Guzhen 28 Dh 33.20N 117.19 E
Guzhou → Rongjiang 27 If 25.58N 108.30 E
Guzmán, Laguna de- 48 Fb 31.20N 107.30W
Gvardejsk 7 Ei 54.40N 21.03 E
Gvardejskoje 16 Hg 45.06N 33.59 E
Gvary 8 Ce 59.23N 9.09 E
Gwa 25 Ie 17.36N 94.35 E
Gwadabawa 34 Gc 13.22N 5.14 E
Gwādar 22 Ig 25.07N 62.19 E
Gwai 30 Jj 17.59S 26.52 E
Gwai 37 Dc 19.17S 27.39 E
Gwalior 22 Jg 26.13N 78.10 E
Gwanda 37 Dd 20.56S 29.00 E
Gwane 36 Eb 4.43N 25.50 E
Gwda 10 Mc 53.04N 16.44 E
Gweebarra Bay/Béal an Bheara 9 Eg 54.52N 8.20W
Gwent 9 Kj 51.45N 2.55W
Gweru 31 Jj 19.27S 29.49 E
Gweta 37 Dd 20.13S 25.14 E
Gwydir River 59 Je 29.27S 149.48 E
Gwynedd 9 Ji 52.50N 3.50W
Gyaca 27 Ff 29.09N 92.38 E
Gya'gya → Saga 27 Ef 29.22N 85.15 E
Gyai Qu 27 Fe 31.30N 94.40 E
Gyaisi/Jiulong 27 Hf 28.58N 101.33 E
Gya La 27 Gf 29.05N 98.41 E
Gyala Shankou 27 Gf 29.05N 98.41 E
Gyangzê 27 Ef 29.00N 89.38 E
Gyaring Co 27 Ee 31.10N 88.15 E
Gyaring Hu 27 Ge 34.55N 98.00 E
Gyda 20 Cb 70.52N 78.30 E
Gydanskaja Guba 20 Cb 71.20N 76.30 E
Gydanski Poluostrov = Gyda Peninsula (EN) 21 Jb 70.50N 79.00 E
Gyda Peninsula (EN) = Gydanski Poluostrov 21 Jb 70.50N 79.00 E
Gyigang → Zayü 27 Gf 28.43N 97.25 E
Gyirong (Zongga) 27 Ef 28.57N 85.12 E
Gyldenløves Fjord 41 Hf 64.10N 40.30W
Gyldenløves Høj 8 Di 55.33N 11.52 E
Gympie 58 Gg 26.11S 152.40 E
Gyoma 10 Qj 46.56N 20.50 E
Gyöngyös 10 Pi 47.47N 19.56 E
Györ 6 Hf 47.41N 17.38 E
Györ 10 Ni 47.40N 17.39 E
Györ-Sopron 10 Ni 47.40N 17.15 E
Gypsumville 42 Hf 51.45N 98.35W
Gysinge 8 Gd 60.17N 16.53 E
Gyttorp 8 Fe 59.31N 14.58 E
Gyula 10 Rj 46.39N 21.17 E

H

Haacht 12 Gd 50.59N 4.38 E
Häädemeeste/Hjademeeste 8 Uf 58.00N 24.28 E
Ha'afeva 65b Ba 19.57S 174.43W
Haafusia 64h Bb 13.18S 176.09W
Haag, Mount- 66 Qf 77.40S 79.00W
Haaksbergen 12 Ib 52.09N 6.45 E
Haamstede, Westerschouwen- 12 Fc 51.42N 3.45 E
Haanja Kõrgustik 8 Lg 57.30N 27.30 E
Ha'ano 65b Ba 19.40S 174.17W
Ha'apai Group 57 Jf 19.47S 174.27W
Haapajärvi 7 Fe 63.45N 25.20 E
Haapamäki 8 Kb 62.15N 24.28 E
Haapasaari 8 Ld 60.15N 27.10 E
Haapaselkä [Fin.] 8 Mc 61.35N 28.15 E
Haapaselkä [Fin.] 8 Mb 62.10N 28.10 E
Haapiti 65e Fc 17.34S 149.52W
Haapsalu 19 Cd 58.57N 23.32 E
Ḩa'arava 24 Fg 30.58N 32.24 E
Haardt 10 Dg 49.15N 8.00 E
Haardtkopf 12 Je 49.51N 7.04 E
Haaren, Wünnenberg- 12 Kc 51.34N 8.44 E
Haarlem 11 Kb 52.23N 4.38 E
Haarlemmermeer 12 Gb 52.20N 4.41 E
Haarlerberg 12 Ib 52.20N 6.25 E
Haarstrang 12 Kc 51.30N 8.20 E
Haast 58 Hi 43.52S 169.01 E
Haast Pass 62 Cf 44.06S 169.21 E
Habahe/Kaba 27 Eb 47.53N 86.12 E
Habarovsk 22 Pe 48.27N 135.06 E
Habarovski Kraj 20 If 53.00N 137.00 E
Ḩabarūt 23 Hf 17.22N 52.42 E
Ḩabashiyah, Jabal- 35 Ib 16.45N 50.05 E
Habaswein 36 Gb 1.01N 39.29 E
Habay [Alta.-Can.] 42 Fe 58.52N 118.45W
Habay [Bel.] 12 He 49.45N 5.38 E
Habay [Som.] 35 Ge 1.08N 43.46 E
Ḩabbān 35 Hc 14.21N 47.05 E
Ḩabbānīyah, Hawr al- 24 Jf 33.17N 43.29 E
Habibas, Iles- 13 Ki 35.44N 1.08W
Habichtswald 10 Fe 51.20N 9.25 E
Habo 8 Fg 57.55N 14.04 E
Haboro 27 Pc 44.22N 141.42 E
Ḩabshān 24 Ok 23.50N 53.37 E
Hache 10 Ec 53.05N 8.50 E
Hachenburg 12 Jd 50.39N 7.50 E
Hachijō 29 Fe 35.15N 139.45 E
Hachijō-Fuji 29 Fe 33.08N 139.46 E
Hachijō-Jima 27 Oe 33.05N 139.50 E
Hachiman 29 Ed 35.46N 136.57 E
Hachimori 29 Fa 40.22N 140.00 E
Hachinohe 22 Qe 40.30N 141.29 E
Hachiōji 29 Fd 35.39N 139.18 E
Hachiro-Gata 29 Fa 40.00N 140.00 E
Hacibey De 24 Kd 36.58N 44.18 E
Hackar Dağı 24 Ib 40.50N 41.10 E
Hackås 7 De 62.55N 14.31 E
Håckren 8 Ea 63.10N 13.35 E
Hačmas 19 Eg 41.25N 48.52 E
Hadagang 28 Kb 45.24N 131.12 E
Hadamar 12 Kd 50.27N 8.03 E
Ḩaḑan, Ḩarrat- 33 He 21.30N 41.23 E
Hadano 29 Fd 35.22N 139.14 E
Ḩadāribah, Ra's al- 35 Fa 22.04N 36.54 E
Hadd, Ra's al- 21 Hg 22.32N 59.59 E
Haddad 30 Ig 14.40N 18.46 E
Ḩadded 35 Hc 10.10N 48.28 E
Haddington 9 Kf 55.58N 2.47W
Haddummati Atoll 25a Bb 1.45N 73.30 E
Hadejia 34 Hc 12.27N 10.03 E
Hadejia 34 Hc 12.50N 10.51 E
Hadeland 8 Dd 60.25N 10.35 E
Hadeln 10 Ec 53.45N 8.45 E
Hadera 24 Ff 32.26N 34.55 E
Haderslev 7 Bi 55.15N 9.30 E
Hadībah 23 Hg 12.39N 54.02 E
Hadim 24 Ed 36.59N 32.28 E
Hadimköy 24 Cb 41.09N 28.37 E
Hadīyah 23 Ed 25.34N 38.41 E
Hadjer el Hamis 35 Ac 12.51N 14.50 E
Hadjout 13 Oh 36.31N 2.25 E
Hadleigh 12 Cb 52.03N 0.56 E
Hadley Bay 42 Gb 72.30N 108.30W
Ha Dong 25 Ld 20.58N 105.46 E
Ḩaḑramawt 21 Gh 15.00N 50.00 E
Hadrian's Wall 9 Kg 54.59N 2.26W
Hadsten 8 Dh 56.20N 10.03 E
Hadsund 8 Dh 56.43N 10.07 E
Hadytajaha 17 Nc 66.57N 69.12 E
Hadyženski 16 Kg 44.25N 39.31 E
Hadzibeiski Liman 15 Nc 46.40N 30.30 E
Haedo, Cuchilla de- 55 Dj 31.40S 56.18W
Haeju 28 He 38.02N 125.42 E
Haena 60 Oc 22.13N 159.34W
Ḩafar al 'Atk 24 Lj 25.56N 46.47 E
Ḩafar al Bāṭin 23 Gd 28.27N 46.00 E
Haffner Bjerg 41 Fc 76.30N 63.00W
Ḩaffūz 14 Do 35.38N 9.40 E
Hafik 24 Gc 39.52N 37.24 E
Ḩafirat al 'Aydā 23 Ed 26.26N 39.12 E
Ḩafit 24 Pk 23.59N 55.49 E
Ḩafit, Jabal- 24 Pj 24.03N 55.46 E
Hafnarfjördur 7a Bb 64.04N 21.57W
Haft Gel 24 Mg 31.27N 49.27 E
Hāfūn 35 Ic 10.10N 51.05 E
Hāfūn, Rās- = Hafun, Ras- (EN) 30 Mg 10.27N 51.24 E
Hafun, Ras- (EN) = Hāfūn, Rās- 30 Mg 10.27N 51.24 E
Hāfūn Bay North 35 Ic 10.37N 51.15 E
Hāfūn Bay South 35 Ic 10.15N 51.05 E
Hagadera 36 Hb 0.02N 40.17 E
Hagby 8 Gh 56.33N 16.10 E
Hageland 12 Gd 50.55N 4.45 E
Hagemeister 40 Ge 58.40N 161.00W
Hagen 10 De 51.21N 7.28 E
Hagenow 10 Hc 53.26N 11.12 E
Hagere Hiywet 35 Fd 8.58N 37.53 E
Hagerman 46 He 42.49N 114.54W
Hagerstown 43 Ld 39.39N 77.43W
Hagetmau 11 Fk 43.40N 0.35W
Hagfors 7 Cf 60.02N 13.42 E
Häggenås 8 Fa 63.24N 14.55 E
Hagi 28 Kg 34.24N 131.25 E
Ha Giang 25 Kd 22.50N 104.59 E
Hágios Theódóros 24 Fe 35.20N 34.01 E
Hagman, Puntan- 64b Ba 15.09N 145.48 E
Hagondange 11 Me 49.15N 6.10 E
Hags Head/Ceanna Cailighe 9 Di 52.57N 9.28W
Hague, Cap de la- 5 Ff 49.43N 1.57W
Haguenau 11 Nf 48.49N 7.47 E
Hagunia 32 Ed 27.26N 12.24W
Hahajima-Rettō 60 Cb 26.37N 142.10 E
Hahns Peak 45 Cf 40.56N 107.01W
Hahót 10 Mj 46.38N 16.56 E
Hai'an 28 Fh 32.33N 120.26 E
Haicheng 27 Lc 40.51N 122.43 E
Haidenaab 10 Ig 49.35N 12.08 E
Hai Duong 25 Ld 20.56N 106.19 E
Haifa (EN) = Hefa 22 Ff 32.50N 35.00 E
Haifeng 27 Kg 22.58N 115.21 E
Haiger 12 Kd 50.45N 8.13 E
Hai He 28 De 38.57N 117.43 E
Haikakan Sovetakan Socialistakan Respublika/Armjanskaja SSR 19 Eg 40.00N 45.00 E
Haikang (Leizhou) 27 Jg 20.56N 110.06 E
Haikou 22 Ng 20.05N 110.20 E
Ḩā'il 22 Gg 27.33N 41.42 E
Hailang He 28 Jb 44.33N 129.33 E
Hailar 22 Ne 49.14N 119.42 E
Hailar He 21 Ne 49.30N 117.50 E
Hailin 27 Mc 44.35N 129.22 E
Hailong (Meihekou) 27 Mc 42.32N 125.37 E
Hailsham 12 Cd 50.52N 0.16 E
Hailun 27 Mb 47.29N 126.55 E
Hailuoto/Karlö 5 Ib 65.02N 24.42 E
Haima Tan 27 Kd 10.52N 116.53 E
Haimen [China] 28 Fi 31.53N 121.10 E
Haimen [China] 28 Fj 28.40N 121.27 E
Haina 12 Kc 51.03N 8.56 E
Hainan Dao 21 Mh 19.00N 109.00 E
Hainaut 11 Jd 50.20N 3.50 E
Hainaut 12 Fd 50.30N 4.00 E
Hainburg an der Donau 14 Kb 48.09N 16.56 E
Haines 39 Fd 59.14N 135.27W
Haines Junction 42 Dd 60.45N 137.30W
Hainich 10 Ge 51.05N 10.27 E
Hainleite 10 Ge 51.20N 10.48 E
Hai Phong 22 Mg 20.52N 106.41 E
Haïti = Haiti (EN) 39 Lh 19.00N 72.25W
Haiti (EN) = Haïti 39 Lh 19.00N 72.25W
Haixing (Suji) 28 De 38.10N 117.29 E
Haixin Shan 27 Hd 37.00N 100.03 E
Haiyan (Sanjiaocheng) 27 Hd 36.58N 100.50 E
Haiyan (Wuyuanzhen) 28 Fi 30.31N 120.56 E
Haiyang (Dongcun) 28 Ff 36.46N 121.09 E
Haiyang Dao 28 Ge 39.03N 123.12 E
Haiyou → Sanmen 27 Lf 29.08N 121.22 E
Haiyuan 27 Id 36.35N 105.40 E
Haizhou 28 Eg 34.34N 119.08 E
Haizhou Wan 21 Nf 35.00N 119.30 E
Ḩajar Banga 35 Cc 11.30N 23.00 E
Hajdarken 19 Hh 39.55N 71.24 E
Hajdú-Bihar 10 Ri 47.25N 21.30 E
Hajdúböszörmény 10 Ri 47.40N 21.31 E
Hajdúhadház 10 Ri 47.41N 21.40 E
Hajdúnánás 10 Ri 47.51N 21.26 E
Hajdúság 10 Ri 47.35N 21.30 E
Hajdúszoboszló 10 Ri 47.27N 21.24 E
Hajihi-Zaki 29 Fb 38.19N 138.31 E
Ḩājjīābād [Iran] 24 Ph 28.19N 55.55 E
Ḩājjīābād [Iran] 24 Ph 28.21N 54.27 E
Ḩājjīābād-e Māsīleh 24 Ne 34.49N 51.13 E
Hajnówka 10 Td 52.45N 23.36 E
Hajós 10 Pj 46.24N 19.07 E
Hajpudyrskaja Guba 17 Ib 68.40N 59.30 E
Hakase-Yama 29 Fc 37.22N 139.43 E
Hakasskaja Avtonomnaja Oblast 20 Df 53.30N 90.00 E
Hakata-Wan 29 Be 33.40N 130.20 E
Hakefjord 8 Dg 57.41N 11.44 E
Hakha 25 Id 22.39N 93.37 E
Hakkâri 23 Fb 37.34N 43.45 E
Hakken-Zan 29 Dd 34.10N 135.54 E
Hakkōda San 29 Ga 40.40N 140.53 E
Hako-Dake 29a Ca 44.40N 142.25 E
Hakodate 22 Qe 41.45N 140.43 E
Hakone-Yama 29 Fd 35.13N 139.00 E
Hakui 28 Nf 36.53N 136.47 E
Hakupu 64k Bb 19.06S 169.50W
Haku-San 29 Ec 36.09N 136.45 E
Hal/Halle 11 Kd 50.44N 4.14 E
Halab 24 Md 36.17N 48.03 E
Ḩalab = Aleppo (EN) 22 Ff 36.12N 37.10 E
Ḩalabjah 24 Ke 35.10N 45.59 E
Halač 19 Gh 39.04N 64.53 E
Halachó 48 Ng 20.29N 90.05W
Halahei 28 Gb 46.11N 122.46 E
Ḩalā'ib 31 Kf 22.13N 36.38 E
Halalii Lake 65a Ab 21.52N 160.11W
Halangingie Point 64k Bb 19.03S 169.58W
Hålaveden 8 Ff 58.05N 14.45 E
Halawa 65a Eb 21.10N 156.44W
Halawa, Cape- 65a Eb 21.10N 156.43W
Ḩalbā 24 Ge 34.33N 36.05 E
Halberstadt 10 He 51.54N 11.03 E
Halcon, Mount- 26 Hd 13.16N 121.00 E
Haldean-Sogotyn-Daba 27 Gb 49.05N 97.55 E
Halden 7 Cg 59.09N 11.23 E
Haldensleben 10 Hd 52.18N 11.25 E
Haldia 25 Hd 22.08N 88.05 E
Haldwani 25 Fc 29.13N 79.31 E
Hale, Mount- 59 De 26.00S 117.10 E
Haleakala Crater 65a Ec 20.43N 156.12W
Haleiwa 65a Cb 21.36N 158.06W
Halemaumau 65a Fd 19.24N 155.17W
Hale River 59 Hd 24.56S 135.53 E
Halesworth 12 Db 52.21N 1.30 E
Haleyville 44 Dh 34.14N 87.37W
Halfā al Gadida 35 Fb 15.19N 35.34 E
Half Assini 34 Ed 5.03N 2.53W
Halfeti 24 Gd 37.15N 37.52 E
Halfway 42 Fe 56.13N 121.26W
Halh-Gol 27 Kb 48.01N 118.10 E
Haliburton 44 Hc 45.03N 78.33W
Halifax 39 Me 44.39N 63.36W
Halifax, Mount- 59 Jc 19.05S 146.20 E
Halifax Bay 59 Jc 18.50S 146.30 E
Ḩalīl 23 Id 27.28N 58.44 E
Ḩalīleh, Ra's-e- 24 Nh 28.46N 50.56 E
Halilovo 16 Ud 51.27N 58.10 E
Ḩalin 35 Hd 9.08N 48.47 E
Haliut → Urad Zhonghou Lianheqi 27 Ic 41.34N 108.32 E
Haljala 8 Le 59.22N 26.09 E
Haljasavej 20 Cd 63.20N 78.30 E
Hall 40 Ed 60.40N 173.05W
Halladale 9 Jc 58.30N 3.50W
Hallam Peak 46 Fa 52.11N 118.46W
Halland 8 Eh 57.00N 12.45 E
Halland 7 Ch 56.45N 13.00 E
Hallandsås 8 Eh 56.23N 13.00 E
Halla-san 28 Ih 33.22N 126.32 E
Ḩallat 'Ammār 24 Gh 29.08N 36.02 E
Hall Beach 42 Jc 68.10N 81.56W
Halle 10 He 51.30N 12.00 E
Halle/Hal 11 Kd 50.44N 4.14 E
Halle (Westfalen) 12 Kb 52.05N 8.22 E
Halleberg 8 Ef 58.23N 12.25 E
Hällefors 8 Fe 59.47N 14.30 E
Hälleforsnäs 8 Ge 59.10N 16.30 E
Halleim 14 Hc 47.41N 13.06 E
Hällekis 8 Ef 58.38N 13.25 E
Hallen 7 De 63.11N 14.05 E
Hallenberg 12 Kc 51.07N 8.38 E
Hallencourt 12 De 49.59N 1.53 E
Halle-Neustadt 10 He 51.31N 11.53 E
Hallertau 10 Hh 48.35N 11.50 E
Hällestad 8 Ff 58.44N 15.34 E
Hallettsville 45 Hl 29.27N 96.57W
Halley Bay 66 Af 75.31S 26.38W
Halli 8 Kc 61.52N 24.50 E
Hallie-Jackson Bank (EN) 63c Ba 9.45S 166.10 E
Halligen 10 Eb 54.35N 8.35 E
Hallingdal 7 Bf 60.40N 9.15 E
Hallingdalselva 8 Cd 60.23N 9.35 E
Hallingskarvet 5 Gc 60.37N 7.45 E
Hall Islands 57 Gd 8.37N 152.00 E
Halliste Jõgi 8 Kf 58.23N 24.25 E
Hall Lake 42 Jc 68.40N 82.20W
Hall Land 41 Fb 81.12N 61.10W
Hallock 45 Hb 48.47N 96.57W
Hall Peninsula 38 Mc 63.30N 66.00W
Hallsberg 7 Dg 59.04N 15.07 E
Halls Creek 58 Df 18.13S 127.40 E
Hallstahammar 7 Dg 59.37N 16.13 E
Hallstatt 14 Hb 47.33N 13.39 E
Hallstavik 7 Ef 60.03N 18.36 E
Halluin 12 Fd 50.47N 3.08 E
Halmahera 57 Dd 1.00N 128.00 E
Halmahera, Laut- = Halmahera Sea (EN) 57 De 1.00S 129.00 E
Halmahera Sea (EN) = Halmahera, Laut- 57 De 1.00S 129.00 E
Halmer-Ju 19 Gb 67.58N 64.40 E
Halmeu 15 Gb 47.58N 23.01 E
Halmstad 6 Hd 56.39N 12.50 E
Haloze 14 Jd 46.20N 15.50 E
Ḩalq al Wādī 32 Jb 36.49N 10.18 E
Hals 7 Cg 57.00N 10.19 E
Hälsingland 8 Gc 61.30N 17.00 E
Halsön 8 Ib 62.50N 21.10 E
Halstead 12 Cc 51.57N 0.38 E
Halsteren 12 Gc 51.32N 4.16 E
Haltang He 27 Fd 39.00N 94.40 E
Halten Bank (EN) 7 Bd 64.45N 8.45 E
Haltern 12 Jc 51.44N 7.11 E
Haltiatunturi 7 Eb 69.18N 21.16 E
Haltom City 45 Hj 32.48N 97.16W
Halturin 19 Ed 58.35N 48.55 E
Ḩālūl 24 Oj 25.40N 52.25 E
Halver 12 Jc 51.12N 7.29 E
Ham 11 Je 49.45N 3.04 E
Ham, Roches de- 12 Ae 49.02N 1.02W
Hamada 29 Cd 34.53N 132.03 E
Hamadān 22 Gf 34.48N 48.30 E
Hamadān 23 Gb 35.00N 48.40 E
Hamadia 13 Ni 35.28N 1.52 E
Hamaguir 32 Gc 30.54N 3.02W
Hamāh 23 Eb 35.08N 36.45 E
Hamakita 29 Ed 34.49N 137.45 E
Hamamasu 28 Pc 43.36N 141.21 E
Hamamatsu 27 Oe 34.42N 137.44 E
Hamanaka 29a Db 43.05N 145.05 E
Hamanaka-Wan 29a Db 43.07N 145.10 E
Hamana-Ko 29 Ed 34.45N 137.34 E
Hamanen, Oued el- 32 Hd 25.52N 1.26 E
Hamaoka 29 Fd 34.39N 138.07 E
Hamar 6 Hc 60.48N 11.06 E
Hamar-Daran, Hrebet- 20 Ff 51.10N 105.00 E
Hamasaka 29 Dd 35.38N 134.27 E
Ḩamāṭah, Jabal- 33 Ge 24.12N 35.00 E
Hamatonbetsu 28 Qb 45.07N 142.23 E
Hambantota 25 Gg 6.10N 81.07 E
Hambre, Cayos del- 49 Fb 22.15N 82.47W
Hamburg 10 Fc 53.35N 10.00 E
Hamburg [Ger.] 6 Ge 53.33N 10.00 E
Hamburg [S.Afr.] 37 Df 33.18S 27.28 E
Hamburg-Altona 10 Fc 53.33N 9.57 E
Hamburg-Harburg 10 Fc 53.28N 10.00 E
Hamburgsund 8 Df 58.33N 11.16 E
Ḩamdah 33 Hf 19.02N 43.36 E
Ḩamḑh, Wādī al- 21 Fg 25.58N 36.42 E
Häme 7 Ff 61.30N 24.30 E
Häme 8 Kc 61.30N 25.30 E
Hämeenkangas 8 Jc 61.45N 22.40 E
Hämeenlinna/Tavastehus 7 Ff 61.00N 24.27 E
Hämeenselkä 8 Kb 62.30N 25.00 E
Hamelin Pool 59 Ce 26.15S 114.05 E
Hameln 10 Fd 52.06N 9.21 E
Hamero Hadad 35 Gd 7.28N 42.13 E
Hamersley Range 59 Dd 21.55S 116.45 E
Hamgyŏng-Namdo 28 Id 40.00N 127.30 E
Hamgyŏng-Pukto 28 Jd 41.45N 129.50 E
Hamgyŏng-Sanmaek 28 Jd 41.00N 128.45 E
Hamhŭng 22 Of 39.54N 127.32 E
Hami/Kumul 22 Le 42.48N 93.27 E
Ḩamīdīyeh 24 Mg 31.29N 48.26 E
Hamilton [Austl.] 59 Ig 37.45S 142.02 E
Hamilton [Ber.] 39 Mf 32.17N 64.46W
Hamilton [Mt.-U.S.] 43 Eb 46.15N 114.09W
Hamilton [N.Z.] 58 Ih 37.47S 175.17 E
Hamilton [Oh.-U.S.] 43 Kd 39.23N 84.33W
Hamilton [Ont.-Can.] 39 Le 43.15N 79.51W
Hamilton [Scot.-U.K.] 9 If 55.47N 4.03W
Hamilton [Tx.-U.S.] 45 Gk 31.42N 98.07W
Hamilton, Lake- 45 Ji 34.30N 93.05W
Hamilton, Mount- 46 Hg 39.14N 115.32W
Hamilton River 59 Hd 23.30S 139.47 E
Ḩamīn, Wādī al- 33 Dc 30.28N 22.00 E
Hamina/Fredrikshamn 7 Gf 60.34N 27.12 E
Hamm 10 De 51.41N 7.48 E
Ḩammām al 'Alīl 24 Jd 36.10N 43.16 E
Ḩammām al Anf 32 Jb 36.44N 10.20 E
Ḩammāmāt 32 Jb 36.24N 10.37 E
Ḩammāmāt, Khalīj- 32 Jb 36.05N 10.40 E
Hammam Bou Hadjar 13 Li 35.23N 0.58W
Hammami 30 Ff 23.03N 11.30W
Hammam Righa 13 Oh 36.23N 2.24 E
Ḩammār, Hawr al- 23 Gc 30.50N 47.10 E
Hammarstrand 8 Ga 63.06N 16.21 E
Hamme 12 Gc 51.06N 4.08 E
Hammelburg 10 Ff 50.07N 9.54 E
Hammerdal 7 De 63.36N 15.21 E
Hammeren 8 Fi 55.18N 14.47 E
Hammerfest 6 Ia 70.40N 23.45 E
Hamminkeln 12 Ic 51.44N 6.35 E
Hamminkeln-Dingden 12 Ic 51.46N 6.37 E
Hammond [In.-U.S.] 44 De 41.36N 87.30W
Hammond [La.-U.S.] 43 Ie 30.30N 90.28W
Hammonton 44 Jf 39.38N 74.48W
Hamont,-Hamont-Achel- 12 Hc 51.15N 5.33 E
Hamont-Achel 12 Hc 51.15N 5.33 E
Hamont-Achel-Hamont 12 Hc 51.15N 5.33 E
Hamoyet, Jabal- 30 Kg 17.33N 38.02 E
Hampden 62 Df 45.20S 170.49 E
Hampshire 9 Lk 51.00N 1.10W
Hampshire Downs 9 Lj 51.15N 1.15W
Hampton [Ia.-U.S.] 45 Je 42.45N 93.12W
Hampton [Va.-U.S.] 44 Ig 37.02N 76.23W
Hampton Butte 46 Ee 43.46N 120.17W
Hamp'yong 28 Ig 35.04N 126.31 E
Ḩamrā' 35 Dc 10.54N 29.54 E
Hamra [R.S.F.S.R.] 20 Gd 60.17N 114.10 E
Hamra [Swe.] 7 Fc 61.39N 15.00 E
Ḩamrā', Al Ḩamādah al- 30 If 29.30N 12.00 E
Hamra, Saguia el- 30 Ff 27.24N 13.43W
Hamrān 24 Kd 36.22N 45.44 E
Ḩamrat ash Shaykh 35 Dc 14.35N 27.58 E
Ḩamrīn, Jabal- 24 Ke 34.30N 44.30 E
Hāmūn-e Hirmand, Daryācheh-ye- 23 Jc 31.30N 61.20 E
Han 34 Ec 10.41N 2.27W
Hana 60 Oc 20.45N 155.59W
Hanahan 44 Hi 32.55N 80.00W
Hanaizum 29 Gb 38.51N 141.12 E
Ḩanak 23 Ed 25.33N 36.56 E
Hanalei 65a Ba 22.13N 159.30W
Hanamaki 28 Pe 39.23N 141.07 E
Hanang 30 Ki 4.26S 35.24 E
Hanaoka 29 Ga 40.21N 140.34 E
Hanapepe 65a Bb 21.55N 159.35W
Hanau 10 Ef 50.08N 8.55 E
Han-Bogdo 27 Ic 43.12N 107.10 E
Hanceville 42 Ff 51.55N 123.02W
Hancheng 27 Jd 35.30N 110.25 E
Hanchuan 28 Bi 30.39N 113.46 E
Hancock 44 Cb 47.07N 88.35W
Handa 29 Ed 34.53N 136.56 E
Handan 22 Nf 36.35N 114.28 E
Handen 8 He 59.10N 18.08 E
Handeni 36 Gd 5.26S 38.01 E
Handlová 10 Oh 48.44N 18.46 E
Handöl 8 Ea 63.16N 12.26 E
Handyga 22 Pc 62.40N 135.36 E
Hānegev = Negev Desert (EN) 24 Fg 30.30N 34.55 E
Hanford 46 Fh 36.20N 119.39W
Hangaj, Hrebet- (Changajn Nuruu) = Khangai Mountains (EN) 21 Le 47.30N 100.00 E
Han-gang 27 Md 37.45N 126.11 E
Hanga Roa 65d Ab 27.09S 109.26W
Hang'bu He 28 Di 31.33N 117.05 E
Hanggin Houqi (Xamba) 27 Ic 40.59N 107.07 E
Hanggin Qi (Xin Zhen) 27 Id 39.54N 108.55 E
Hangö/Hanko 7 Fg 59.50N 22.57 E
Hangöudde/Hankoniemi 8 Je 59.50N 23.10 E
Hangu 28 De 39.16N 117.50 E
Hangzhou 22 Of 30.18N 120.11 E
Hangzhou Wan 28 Fi 30.25N 121.00 E
Ḩanīsh 33 Hg 13.45N 42.45 E
Ḩanīsh al Kabīr, Jazīrat al- 33 Hg 13.43N 42.45 E
Hanja, Vozvyšennost- 8 Lg 57.30N 27.30 E
Ḩanjūrah, Ra's- 24 Pj 24.44N 54.39 E
Hanka, Ozero- = Khanka Lake (EN) 21 Pe 45.00N 132.24 E
Hankasalmi 8 Lb 62.23N 26.26 E
Hankensbüttel 10 Gd 52.44N 10.36 E
Hanko/Hangö 7 Fg 59.50N 22.57 E
Hankoniemi/Hangöudde 8 Je 59.50N 23.10 E
Hankou, Wuhan- 28 Ci 30.35N 114.16 E
Hanksville 46 Jg 38.25N 110.10W
Hanlar 16 Oi 40.34N 46.20 E
Hanmej, Gora- 17 Lc 67.08N 66.00 E
Hanmer Springs 62 Ee 42.31S 172.50 E
Hann, Mount- 59 Fc 15.50S 125.50 E
Hanna [Alta.-Can.] 42 Gf 51.38N 111.54W
Hanna [Wy.-U.S.] 46 Lf 41.52N 106.34W
Hannah Bay 42 Jf 51.15N 79.50W
Hannibal 43 Id 39.42N 91.22W
Hanningfield Reservoir 12 Cc 51.37N 0.28 E
Hannō 29 Fd 35.53N 139.17 E
Hannover 6 Ge 52.22N 9.43 E
Hann River 59 Fc 17.10S 126.10 E
Hannuit/Hannut 12 Hd 50.40N 5.05 E
Hannut/Hannuit 12 Hd 50.40N 5.05 E
Hano 8 Fi 56.00N 14.50 E
Hanöbukten 8 Fi 55.45N 14.30 E
Ha Noi 22 Mg 21.02N 105.51 E
Hanover [N.H.-U.S.] 44 Kd 43.42N 72.17W
Hanover [Ont.-Can.] 44 Gc 44.09N 81.02W
Hanover [Pa.-U.S.] 44 If 39.47N 76.59W
Hanover [S.Afr.] 37 Cf 31.04S 24.29 E
Hanover, Isla- 56 Fh 51.00S 74.40W
Hanpan, Cape- 59 Ka 5.01S 154.37 E
Han Pijesak 14 Mf 44.05N 18.57 E

Index Symbols

[1] Independent Nation
[2] State, Region
[3] District, County
[4] Municipality
[5] Colony, Dependency
Continent
Physical Region
Historical or Cultural Region
Mount, Mountain
Volcano
Hill
Mountains, Mountain Range
Hills, Escarpment
Plateau, Upland
Pass, Gap
Plain, Lowland
Delta
Salt Flat
Valley, Canyon
Crater, Cave
Karst Features
Depression
Polder
Desert, Dunes
Forest, Woods
Heath, Steppe
Oasis
Cape, Point
Coast, Beach
Cliff
Peninsula
Isthmus
Sandbank
Island
Atoll
Rock, Reef
Islands, Archipelago
Rocks, Reefs
Coral Reef
Well, Spring
Geyser
River, Stream
Waterfall Rapids
River Mouth, Estuary
Lake
Salt Lake
Intermittent Lake
Reservoir
Swamp, Pond
Canal
Glacier
Ice Shelf, Pack Ice
Ocean
Sea
Gulf, Bay
Strait, Fjord
Lagoon
Bank
Seamount
Tablemount
Ridge
Shelf
Basin
Escarpment, Sea Scarp
Fracture
Trench, Abyss
National Park, Reserve
Point of Interest
Recreation Site
Cave, Cavern
Historic Site
Ruins
Wall, Walls
Church, Abbey
Temple
Scientific Station
Airport
Port
Lighthouse
Mine
Tunnel
Dam, Bridge

Hansen Mountains 66 Ee 68.16S 58.47 E
Hanshan 28 Ei 31.43N 118.07 E
Hanshou 28 Aj 28.55N 111.58 E
Han Shui 21 Nf 30.34N 114.17 E
Hanstholm 8 Cg 57.07N 8.38 E
Han Sum 28 Eb 44.33N 119.58 E
Han-sur-Lesse, Rochefort- 12 Hd 50.08N 5.11 E
Han-sur-Nied 12 If 48.59N 6.26 E
Hantajskoje, Ozero- 20 Ec 68.25N 91.00 E
Hantau 19 Hg 44.13N 73.48 E
Hantengri Feng 27 Dc 42.03N 80.11 E
Hants 9 Lj 51.10N 1.10W
Hanty-Mansijsk 22 Ic 61.00N 69.06 E
Hanty-Mansijski Nacionalny Okrug [3] 19 Hc 62.00N 72.30 E
Hantzsch 42 Kc 67.32N 72.26W
Hanušovice 10 Mf 50.05N 16.55 E
Hanwang 27 He 31.25N 104.13 E
Hanyang 28 Ci 30.34N 114.01 E
Hanyang, Wuhan- 28 Ci 30.33N 114.16 E
Hanyü 29 Fc 36.11N 139.32 E
Hanyuan (Fulin) 27 Hf 29.25N 102.12 E
Hanzhong [China] 22 Mf 32.59N 107.11 E
Hanzhong [China] 27 Ie 33.07N 107.00 E
Hanzhuang 28 Dg 34.38N 117.23 E
Hao Atoll 57 Mf 18.15S 140.54W
Hāora 24 Kg 22.35N 88.20 E
Haoud el Hamra 32 Ic 31.58N 5.59 E
Haoxue 28 Bi 30.02N 112.25 E
Haparanda 7 Fd 65.50N 24.10 E
Hapčeranga 20 Gg 49.42N 112.20 E
Happy Valley-Goose Bay 39 Md 53.19N 60.24W
Hapsu 28 Jd 41.13N 128.51 E
Ḩaql 24 Fh 29.18N 34.57 E
Ḩaql al Barqan 24 Lh 28.55N 47.57 E
Ḩaql al Manāqish 24 Lh 29.02N 47.32 E
Ḩaql as Şābirīyah 24 Lh 29.48N 47.50 E
Hara, Zaliv-/Hara Laht 8 Ke 59.35N 25.30 E
Hara-Ajrag 27 Ib 45.50N 109.20 E
Harabali 19 Ef 47.25N 47.16 E
Ḩaraḑ 23 Ge 24.14N 49.11 E
Haraiki Atoll 57 Mf 17.28S 143.27W
Hara Laht/Hara, Zaliv- 8 Ke 59.35N 25.30 E
Haramachi 28 Pf 37.38N 140.58 E
Haram Dāgh 23 Gb 37.35N 46.43 E
Harami, Pereval- 16 Oh 42.48N 46.12 E
Harand 24 Of 32.34N 52.26 E
Harani'ia Point 63a Ed 10.21S 161.16 E
Hara Nur 27 Fb 48.05N 93.12 E
Ḩarardēre 35 He 4.32N 47.53 E
Harare 31 Kj 17.50S 31.10 E
Harat 35 Fb 16.05N 39.28 E
Hara-Tas, Krjaž- 20 Fb 72.00N 107.00 E
Haratini 64n Bc 10.28S 160.58W
Ḩarat Zuwayyah 31 Jf 24.14N 21.59 E
Hara-Us-Nur 27 Fb 48.00N 92.10 E
Haraz 35 Bc 13.57N 19.26 E
Harāz 24 Od 36.40N 52.43 E
Harāzah, Jabal- 35 Eb 15.03N 30.27 E
Haraze 35 Cd 9.55N 20.48 E
Harbel 34 Cd 6.16N 10.21W
Harbin 22 Oe 45.45N 126.37 E
Harbor Beach 44 Fd 43.51N 82.39W
Harbor Breton 42 Lg 47.29N 55.50W
Harbour Grace 42 Mg 47.41N 53.15W
Harburg, Hamburg- 10 Fc 53.28N 10.00 E
Harcourt 44 Ob 46.30N 65.15W
Harcuvar Mountains 46 Ii 34.00N 113.30W
Harcyzsk 16 Kf 47.59N 38.11 E
Hardanger 8 Bd 60.20N 6.30 E
Hardangerfjorden 5 Gc 60.10N 6.00 E
Hardangerjøkulen 8 Bd 60.35N 7.25 E
Hardangervidda 7 Bf 60.20N 7.30 E
Hardelot Plage, Neufchâtel Hardelot- 12 Dd 50.38N 1.35 E
Hardenberg 12 Ib 52.34N 6.37 E
Harderwijk 11 Lb 52.21N 5.36 E
Hardin 43 Fb 45.44N 107.37W
Harding 37 Df 30.34S 29.58 E
Hardinsburg 44 Dg 37.47N 86.28W
Härdler 12 Kc 51.06N 8.14 E
Hardoi 25 Gc 27.25N 80.07 E
Hardy, Peninsula- 56 Gi 55.25S 68.30W
Hareid 8 Bb 62.22N 6.02 E
Hareidlandet 7 Ae 62.20N 5.55 E
Hare Indian 42 Ec 66.18N 128.38W
Harelbeke 12 Fd 50.51N 3.18 E
Haren 12 Ia 53.11N 6.38 E
Haren (Ems) 12 Jb 52.47N 7.14 E
Harer 31 Lh 9.18N 42.08 E
Harerge [3] 35 Gd 9.00N 41.30 E
Harēri Mālinwarfā 35 He 4.34N 47.21 E
Harewa 35 Gd 9.54N 41.58 E
Harfleur 12 Ce 49.30N 0.12 E
Harg 8 Hd 60.11N 18.24 E
Hargeysa 31 Lh 9.30N 44.03 E
Harghiţa [2] 15 Ic 46.25N 25.45 E
Harghita, Munţii- 15 Ic 46.31N 25.33 E
Harghita, Vîrful- 15 Ic 46.27N 25.35 E
Hargla 8 Lg 57.31N 26.25 E
Harhorin 27 Hb 47.13N 102.50 E
Har Hu 38.15N 97.40 E
Ḩarīb 23 Gg 14.56N 45.30 E
Haridwār 25 Fc 29.58N 78.10 E
Harihari 62 De 43.09S 170.34 E
Hari Kurk 8 Je 59.00N 22.50 E
Harim 24 Gd 36.12N 36.31 E
Harīm, Jabal al- 24 Qj 25.58N 56.14 E
Harima-Nada 29 Dd 34.30N 134.35 E
Haringey, London- 12 Bc 51.36N 0.06W
Harīrūd 21 If 37.24N 60.38 E
Härjångsfjallet 8 Ea 63.01N 12.35 E
Harjavalta 7 Ff 61.19N 22.08 E
Härjedalen 8 Eb 62.20N 13.05 E
Härjehågna 8 Ec 61.44N 12.08 E
Hårkan 8 Fa 63.20N 14.55 E
Harkov 6 Je 50.00N 36.15 E
Harkovskaja Oblast [3] 19 Df 49.40N 36.30 E
Harlan [Ia.-U.S.] 45 If 41.39N 95.19W
Harlan [Ky.-U.S.] 44 Fg 36.51N 83.19W
Harlan County Lake 45 Gf 40.04N 99.16W
Harlech Castle 9 Ii 52.52N 4.07W
Harlem 46 Kb 48.32N 108.47W
Harleston 12 Db 52.24N 1.18 E
Harlingen [Neth.] 11 La 53.10N 5.24 E
Harlingen [Tx.-U.S.] 43 Hf 26.11N 97.42W
Harlovka 7 Ib 68.47N 37.20 E
Harlovka 7 Ib 68.47N 37.15 E
Harlow 9 Nj 51.47N 0.08 E
Harlowton 46 Kc 46.26N 109.50W
Harlu 7 Hf 61.51N 30.54 E
Hărman 15 Id 45.43N 25.41 E
Harmancık 24 Cc 39.41N 29.10 E
Harmånger 7 Df 61.56N 17.13 E
Harmanli 15 Ih 41.56N 25.54 E
Harmil 35 Gb 16.30N 40.12 E
Harmony 45 Ke 43.33N 91.59W
Harnai 25 Ee 17.48N 73.06 E
Harney Basin 38 Ge 43.15N 120.40W
Harney Lake 46 Dc 43.14N 119.07W
Harney Peak 43 Gc 44.00N 103.30W
Härnön 8 Gb 62.35N 18.00 E
Härnösand 6 Hc 62.38N 17.56 E
Haro 13 Jb 42.35N 2.51W
Harovsk 19 Ed 59.59N 40.11 E
Harøya 8 Bb 62.45N 6.45 E
Harøyfjorden 8 Bb 62.45N 6.35 E
Harpenden 12 Bc 51.48N 0.21W
Harper [Ks.-U.S.] 45 Gh 37.17N 98.01W
Harper [Lbr.] 31 Gh 4.22N 7.43W
Harper, Mount- 40 Kd 64.14N 143.50W
Harper Pass 62 De 42.44S 171.53 E
Harplinge 8 Eh 56.45N 12.43 E
Harqin Qi (Jinshan) 28 Ed 41.57N 118.40 E
Harqin Zuoyi Monggolzu Zizhixian 28 Ed 41.05N 119.40 E
Ḩarrah 23 Hg 14.57N 50.19 E
Ḩarrat al 'Uwayrid 23 Ed 27.00N 37.30 E
Harricana 42 Jf 51.10N 79.47W
Harricana, Rivière- 44 Ha 51.10N 79.45W
Harrington-Harbour 42 Lf 50.26N 59.30W
Harris 9 Gd 57.53N 6.55W
Harris 51c Bc 16.28N 62.10W
Harris, Lake- 44 Gk 28.46N 81.49W
Harris, Sound of- 9 Fd 57.45N 7.08W
Harrisburg 39 Le 40.16N 76.52W
Harrismith 37 De 28.18S 29.03 E
Harrison [Ar.-U.S.] 45 Jh 36.14N 93.07W
Harrison [Mi.-U.S.] 44 Ec 44.01N 84.48W
Harrison [Nb.-U.S.] 45 Ee 42.41N 103.53W
Harrison, Cape- 42 Lf 54.56N 57.55W
Harrison Bay 40 Ib 70.30N 151.30W
Harrisonburg 44 Hf 38.27N 78.54W
Harrison Lake 46 Eb 49.31N 121.59W
Harrison Point 51q Ab 13.18N 59.38W
Harrisonville 45 Ig 38.39N 94.21W
Harrisville [Mi.-U.S.] 44 Fc 44.39N 83.17W
Harrisville [W.V.-U.S.] 44 Gf 39.13N 81.04W
Harrodsburg 44 Eg 37.46N 84.51W
Harrogate 9 Lh 54.00N 1.33W
Harrow, London- 12 Bc 51.36N 0.20W
Harry S. Truman Reservoir 45 Jg 38.00N 93.45W
Har Sai Shan 27 Gd 35.26N 97.41 E
Harsewinkel 12 Kc 51.58N 8.14 E
Harshō 35 Hc 11.17N 47.30 E
Harsim 24 Lf 33.48N 46.50 E
Harsīn 24 Le 34.16N 47.35 E
Harstad 7 Db 68.47N 16.30 E
Harsvik 7 Cd 64.03N 10.02 E
Hart 44 Dd 43.42N 86.22W
Hart 42 Dc 65.51N 136.22W
Hartao 28 Gc 42.30N 122.08 E
Hartbees 30 Jk 28.45S 20.33 E
Hartberg 14 Jc 47.17N 15.58 E
Hårteigen 8 Bd 60.12N 7.04 E
Hartford [Ct.-U.S.] 39 Le 41.46N 72.41W
Hartford [Ky.-U.S.] 44 Dg 37.27N 86.55W
Hartford City 44 Ee 40.29N 85.23W
Hartington 45 He 42.37N 97.16W
Hartland 44 Nb 46.18N 67.32W
Hartland Point 9 Ij 51.02N 4.31W
Hartlepool 9 Lg 54.42N 1.11W
Hartmannberge 37 Ac 17.30S 12.23 E
Hartola 7 Gf 61.35N 26.01 E
Harts 28.24S 24.18 E
Hartselle 44 Dh 34.27N 86.56W
Harts Range 59 Gd 23.05S 134.55 E
Hartsville 44 Gh 34.23N 80.04W
Hartwell 44 Fh 34.21N 82.56W
Hartwell Lake 44 Fh 34.30N 82.55W
Harun, Bukit- 26 Gf 4.06N 115.46 E
Haruno 29 Ce 33.30N 133.30 E
Harves Bank (EN) 51c Ac 16.52N 62.35W
Harvey [Austl.] 59 Df 33.05S 115.54 E
Harvey [N.D.-U.S.] 43 Hb 47.47N 99.56W
Harvey Bay 59 Kd 25.00S 153.00 E
Harwich 9 Oj 51.57N 1.17 E
Haryana [3] 25 Fc 29.30N 76.30 E
Harz 5 He 51.45N 10.30 E
Hasaki 29 Gd 35.44N 140.48 E
Hasama 29 Gb 38.42N 141.13 E
Hasan 20 Ih 42.26N 130.39 E
Ḩasanābād [Iran] 24 Ph 28.47N 54.19 E
Ḩasanābād [Iran] 24 Nd 36.28N 50.17 E
Hasan Daği 23 Db 38.08N 34.12 E
Ḩasan Langī 24 Qi 27.22N 56.52 E
Hasavjurt 16 Oh 43.16N 46.35 E
Hāsbayyā 24 Ff 33.43N 33.52 E
Hasdo 25 Hd 21.44N 82.44 E
Hase 10 Dd 52.41N 7.18 E
Hasekijata 15 Kg 42.08N 27.30 E
Hasenkamp 55 Cj 31.31S 59.51W
Hashimoto 29 Dd 34.19N 135.37 E
Hashtpar 24 Md 37.48N 48.55 E
Hasi Hausert 32 Ee 22.35N 14.18W
Haskell 43 He 33.10N 99.44W
Haskerland 12 Hb 52.58N 5.47 E
Haskerland-Joure 12 Hb 52.58N 5.47 E
Haskovo 15 Ih 41.56N 25.33 E
Haskovo [2] 15 Ih 41.50N 25.55 E
Hasle 8 Fi 55.11N 14.43 E
Haslemere 9 Mj 51.06N 0.43W
Haslev 8 Di 55.20N 11.58 E
Hăşmaşu Mare, Vîrful- 15 Ic 46.30N 25.50 E
Haspengouws Plateau/Hesbaye 11 Ld 50.35N 5.10 E
Haspres 12 Fd 50.15N 3.25 E
Hassa 24 Gd 36.50N 36.29 E
Hassan 25 Ff 13.00N 76.05 E
Hassberge 10 Gf 50.12N 10.29 E
Hassela 7 De 62.07N 16.42 E
Hassel Sound 42 Ha 78.30N 99.00W
Hasselt 11 Ld 50.56N 5.20 E
Hassi Bel Guebbour 32 Id 28.30N 6.41 E
Hassi el Ghella 13 Ki 35.27N 1.03W
Hassi-Mamèche 13 Mi 35.51N 0.04 E
Hassi Messaoud 31 He 31.43N 6.03 E
Hassi R'mel 32 Hc 32.55N 3.16 E
Hassi Serouenout 32 Ie 24.00N 7.50 E
Hässleholm 7 Ch 56.09N 13.46 E
Hasslö 8 Fh 56.05N 15.25 E
Haßloch 12 Ke 49.23N 8.16 E
Hastière 12 Gd 50.13N 4.50 E
Hastière-Hastière par-delà 12 Gd 50.13N 4.50 E
Hastière-par-delà, Hastière- 12 Gd 50.13N 4.50 E
Hastings [Bar.] 51q Ab 13.04N 59.35W
Hastings [Eng.-U.K.] 9 Nk 50.51N 0.36 E
Hastings [Mi.-U.S.] 44 Ed 42.39N 85.17W
Hastings [Mn.-U.S.] 45 Jd 44.44N 92.51W
Hastings [Nb.-U.S.] 43 Hc 40.35N 98.23W
Hastings [N.Z.] 61 Eg 39.38S 176.50 E
Hästveda 8 Eh 56.16N 13.56 E
Hašuri 16 Mi 41.59N 43.33 E
Hasvik 7 Fa 70.29N 22.09 E
Ḩasy al Qaţţār 33 Ec 30.14N 27.11 E
Ḩasy Hague 33 Bd 26.17N 10.31 E
Hat'ae-Do 28 Hg 34.23N 125.17 E
Hatanga 22 Mb 71.58N 102.30 E
Hatanga 21 Mb 72.55N 106.00 E
Hatch 45 Cj 32.40N 107.09W
Hatches Creek 59 Hd 20.56S 135.12 E
Haţeg 15 Fd 45.37N 22.57 E
Hatgal 27 Ha 50.26N 100.09 E
Ḩāţibah, Ra's- 23 Ee 21.59N 38.55 E
Ha Tien 25 Kf 10.23N 104.29 E
Ha Tinh 25 Le 18.20N 105.54 E
Hato Mayor 49 Md 18.46N 69.15W
Ḩattā, Jabal- 24 Qj 24.45N 56.04 E
Hattem 12 Ib 52.28N 6.06 E
Hatten 12 Ka 53.03N 8.23 E
Hatteras, Cape- 38 Lf 35.13N 75.32W
Hatteras Inlet 44 Jh 35.00N 75.40W
Hatteras Island 43 Ld 35.25N 75.30W
Hattfjelldal 7 Cd 65.36N 14.00 E
Hattiesburg 43 Je 31.19N 89.16W
Hattingen 12 Jc 51.24N 7.10 E
Hatu Iti, Ile- 61 Ma 8.42S 140.43W
Hatutaa, Ile- 57 Me 7.30S 140.38W
Hatvan 10 Pi 47.40N 19.41 E
Hat Yai 25 Kg 7.01N 100.27 E
Hatyrka 20 Md 62.03N 175.05 E
Hau Bon 25 Lf 13.24N 108.27 E
Haubourdin 12 Ed 50.36N 2.59 E
Hauge 7 Bg 58.21N 6.17 E
Haugesund 6 Gd 59.25N 5.18 E
Hauho 8 Kc 61.10N 24.33 E
Hauhungaroa Range 62 Fc 38.40S 175.35 E
Haukeligrend 7 Bg 59.51N 7.11 E
Haukipudas 7 Fd 65.15N 25.28 E
Haukivesi 5 Ic 62.05N 28.30 E
Haukivuori 8 Lb 62.01N 27.13 E
Hauraha 63a Ed 10.49S 161.57 E
Hauraki Gulf 61 Eg 36.35S 175.00 E
Hauroko, Lake- 62 Bf 45.55S 167.20 E
Hausa 32 Ed 27.06N 11.01W
Hausruck 14 Hb 48.07N 13.35 E
Haut, Isle au- 44 Mc 44.03N 68.38W
Haut Atlas=High Atlas (EN) 30 Ge 32.00N 6.00W
Haute-Champagne 12 Ge 49.18N 4.15 E
Haute-Corse [3] 11a Aa 42.30N 9.00 E
Haute-Garonne [3] 11 Hk 43.25N 1.30 E
Haute-Guinée [3] 34 Dc 11.30N 10.00W
Haute-Kotto [3] 35 Cd 7.00N 23.00 E
Haute-Loire [3] 11 Ji 45.05N 4.00 E
Haute-Marne [3] 11 Lf 48.05N 5.10 E
Hauterive 44 Ma 49.11N 68.16W
Hautes-Alpes [3] 11 Mj 44.40N 6.30 E
Haute-Sangha [3] 35 Be 4.30N 16.00 E
Haute-Saône [3] 11 Mg 47.40N 6.10 E
Haute-Saône, Plateau de- 11 Lg 47.50N 6.00 E
Haute-Savoie [3] 11 Mi 46.00N 6.20 E
Hautes Fagnes/Hoge Venen 10 Bf 50.30N 6.00 E
Hautes-Pyrénées [3] 11 Gk 43.00N 0.10 E
Haute Vienne [3] 11 Hi 45.50N 1.10 E
Haute Volta→Burkina Faso 31 Gg 13.00N 2.00W
Haut-Mbomou [3] 35 Dd 6.00N 26.00 E
Hautmont 11 Jd 50.15N 3.56 E
Haut-Ogooué [3] 36 Bc 2.00S 14.00 E
Haut Rhin [3] 11 Ng 48.00N 7.20 E
Hauts-Bassins [3] 34 Ec 12.30N 4.30W
Hauts-de-Seine [3] 11 If 48.50N 2.11 E
Hauts-Plateaux 30 He 34.00N 0.01 E
Haut-Zaire [2] 36 Eb 2.30N 25.30 E
Hauula 65a 21.36N 157.54W
Hauz-Han 18 Cf 37.16N 61.15 E
Hauz-Hanskoje Vodohr. 18 Cf 37.10N 61.20 E
Havana 45 Kf 40.18N 90.04W
Havana (EN)=La Habana 39 Kg 23.08N 82.22W
Havant 9 Mk 50.51N 0.59W
Havast 18 Gd 40.16N 68.51 E
Havasu, Lake- 46 Hi 34.30N 114.20W
Havel 10 Hd 52.53N 11.58 E
Havelange 12 Hd 50.23N 5.14 E
Havelange-Méan 12 Hd 50.22N 5.20 E
Havelberg 10 Id 52.49N 12.05 E
Havelland 10 Id 52.25N 12.45 E
Havelländisches Luch 10 Id 52.40N 12.40 E
Havelock [N.C.-U.S.] 44 Ih 34.53N 76.54W
Havelock [N.Z.] 62 Ed 41.17S 173.46 E
Havelock North 62 Gc 39.40S 176.53 E
Havelte 12 Ib 52.46N 6.16 E
Haverfordwest 9 Ij 51.49N 4.58W
Haverhill [Eng.-U.K.] 9 Ni 52.05N 0.26 E
Haverhill [Ma.-U.S.] 44 Ld 42.47N 71.05W
Havering, London- 12 Cc 51.36N 0.11 E
Havířov 10 Og 49.48N 18.27 E
Havlíčkův Brod 10 Lg 49.36N 15.34 E
Havøysund 7 Fa 71.03N 24.40 E
Havran 24 Bc 39.33N 27.06 E
Havre 39 Ie 48.33N 109.41W
Havre-Saint-Pierre 39 Md 50.15N 63.36W
Havsa 15 Jh 41.33N 26.49 E
Havza 24 Fb 41.05N 35.45 E
Hawaii [2] 58 Kb 24.00N 167.00W
Hawaiian Islands 57 Kb 24.00N 167.00W
Hawaiian Ridge (EN) 3 Kg 24.00N 165.00W
Hawaii Island 57 Lc 19.30N 155.30W
Ḩawallī 23 Gd 29.19N 48.02 E
Ḩawār 24 Nj 25.40N 50.45 E
Hawarden 62 Ee 42.56S 172.39 E
Ḩawashīyah, Wādī- 24 Eh 28.31N 32.58 E
Hawaymī, Sha'īb al- 24 Kg 30.58N 44.15 E
Hawd 30 Lh 7.40N 47.43 E
Ḩawḑ Al Waqf 24 Ei 26.03N 32.22 E
Hawea, Lake- 62 Cf 44.30S 169.20 E
Hawera 61 Dg 39.35S 174.17 E
Hawi 58 Lb 20.14N 155.50W
Hawick 9 Kf 55.25N 2.47W
Ḩawīzah, Hawr al- 24 Lg 31.35N 47.38 E
Hawkdun Range 62 Cf 44.50S 170.00 E
Hawke Bay 61 Eg 39.25S 177.20 E
Hawke Harbour 42 Lf 53.01N 55.50W
Hawker 59 Hf 31.53S 138.25 E
Hawkes, Mount- 66 Rg 83.55S 56.05W
Hawke's Bay [2] 62 Gc 39.30S 176.40 E
Hawkesbury 44 Jc 45.36N 74.37W
Hawkhurst 12 Cc 51.02N 0.30 E
Hawkinsville 44 Fi 32.17N 83.28W
Hawksbill 44 Hf 38.33N 78.23W
Hawk Springs 46 Mf 41.48N 104.09W
Ḩawmat as Sūq 32 Jc 33.53N 10.51 E
Hawng Tuk 25 Jd 20.28N 99.56 E
Ḩawrā' 35 Hb 15.43N 48.18 E
Hawrān, Wādī al- 23 Fc 33.58N 42.34 E
Ḩawsh 'Īsá 24 Dg 30.55N 30.17 E
Hawthorne 43 Dd 38.32N 118.38W
Hawthorne, Mount- 66 Pf 72.10S 98.39W
Haxtun 45 Ef 40.39N 102.38W
Hay 58 Fh 34.30S 144.51 E
Hay 38 Hc 60.51N 115.44W
Hayachine-San 29 Gb 39.34N 141.29 E
Hayakita 29a Bb 42.45N 141.48 E
Hayange 11 Me 49.20N 6.03 E
Hayasui-no-Seto 28 Kh 33.20N 132.00 E
Hayato 29 Bf 31.45N 130.43 E
Haybān 35 Ec 11.13N 30.31 E
Haybān, Jabal- 35 Ec 11.15N 30.31 E
Hayden 46 Jj 33.00N 110.47W
Hayes [Man.-Can.] 42 Ie 57.00N 92.15W
Hayes [N.W.T.-Can.] 42 Hc 67.20N 95.02W
Hayes, Mount- 40 Jd 63.37N 146.43W
Hayes Halvø=Hayes Peninsula (EN) 67 Od 77.40N 64.30W
Hayes Peninsula (EN)= Hayes Halvø 67 Od 77.40N 64.30W
Hayl 24 Qj 24.33N 56.06 E
Hayl, Wādī al- 24 He 34.47N 39.18 E
Hayling Island 12 Bd 50.48N 0.58W
Haymana 24 Ec 39.27N 32.30 E
Haymana Platosu 24 Ec 39.25N 32.45 E
Haynin 23 Gf 15.50N 48.18 E
Hayrabolu 24 Bb 41.12N 27.06 E
Ḩayrān 33 Hf 16.02N 42.49 E
Hay River 59 Hd 25.00S 138.00 E
Hay River 39 Hc 60.51N 115.40W
Hayrüt 35 Ib 15.59N 52.09 E
Hays 43 Hd 38.53N 99.20W
Hay Springs 45 Ee 42.41N 102.41W
Haystack Peak 46 Ig 39.50N 113.55W
Hayward [Ca.-U.S.] 46 Dh 37.40N 122.05W
Hayward [Wi.-U.S.] 45 Kc 46.01N 91.29W
Haywards Heath 12 Bc 51.00N 0.06W
Hazar, Wādī- 35 Hb 17.50N 49.07 E
Hazarasp 18 Cd 41.19N 61.08 E
Hazard 44 Fg 37.15N 83.12W
Hazar Gölü 24 Hc 38.30N 39.25 E
Hazārībāgh 25 Hd 23.59N 85.21 E
Hazebrouck 11 Id 50.43N 2.32 E
Hazelton 42 Ee 55.15N 127.40W
Hazen 45 Fc 47.18N 101.38W
Hazen Strait 42 Ga 77.15N 110.00W
Ḩaẕeva 24 Fg 30.48N 35.15 E
Hazlehurst [Ga.-U.S.] 44 Fj 31.52N 82.36W
Hazlehurst [Ms.-U.S.] 45 Kk 31.52N 90.24W
Hazleton 44 Je 40.58N 76.00W
Hazlett, Lake- 59 Fd 21.30S 128.50 E
Hazrah, Ra's al- 24 Nj 24.22N 51.36 E
Hazro 24 Ic 38.15N 40.47 E
Heacham 12 Cb 52.55N 0.29 E
Headley 12 Bc 51.07N 0.49W
Healdsburg 46 Dg 38.37N 122.52W
Heanor 12 Aa 53.00N 1.18W
Heard Island 30 On 53.00S 73.35 E
Hearne 45 Hk 30.53N 96.36W
Hearst 42 Jg 49.41N 83.40W
Heart River 45 Fc 46.47N 100.51W
Heathrow Airport London 12 Bc 51.28N 0.30W
Hebbronville 45 Gm 27.18N 98.41W
Hebei Sheng (Ho-pei Sheng) =Hopeh (EN) [2] 27 Kd 39.00N 116.00 E
Heber City 46 Jf 40.30N 111.25W
Hebi 27 Jd 35.53N 114.09 E
Hebian 27 Jd 38.35N 113.06 E
Hebiji 28 Cf 36.00N 114.08 E
Hebrides 5 Fd 57.00N 6.30W
Hebrides, Sea of the- 9 Ge 57.00N 7.00W
Hebron [N.D.-U.S.] 45 Ec 46.54N 102.03W
Hebron [Newf.-Can.] 42 Le 58.15N 62.35W
Heby 8 Ge 59.56N 16.53 E
Hecate Strait 42 Ef 53.20N 131.00W
Hecelchakán 48 Ng 20.10N 90.08W
Hechi (Jnchengjiang) 27 Ig 24.44N 108.02 E
Hechingen 10 Eh 48.21N 8.59 E
Hechuan 27 Ie 30.07N 106.15 E
Hecla 45 Gd 45.43N 98.09W
Hecla and Griper Bay 42 Ga 76.00N 111.30W
Hecla Island 45 Ha 51.08N 96.45W
Heddalsvatnet 8 Ce 59.30N 9.15 E
Hede 7 Ce 62.25N 13.30 E
Hede → Sheyang 28 Fh 33.47N 120.15 E
Hedemarken 8 Dd 60.50N 11.20 E
Hedemora 7 Df 60.17N 15.59 E
Hedensted 8 Ci 55.46N 9.42 E
Hedesunda 7 Df 60.25N 17.00 E
Hedesunda fjärdarna 8 Gd 60.20N 17.00 E
Hedmark [2] 7 Cf 61.30N 11.45 E
Hedo-Misaki 29b Bb 26.52N 128.16 E
Heemskerk 12 Gb 52.30N 4.42 E
Heemstede 12 Gb 52.21N 4.37 E
Heerenveen 11 Lb 52.57N 5.55 E
Heerhugowaard 12 Gb 52.40N 4.50 E
Heerlen 11 Ld 50.54N 5.59 E
Hefa=Haifa (EN) 22 Ff 32.50N 35.00 E
Hefei 22 Nf 31.47N 117.15 E
Hefeng 27 Jf 29.49N 110.01 E
Hegang 22 Pe 47.20N 130.12 E
Hegau 10 Ei 47.50N 8.45 E
Hegura Jima 27 Od 37.50N 136.55 E
Heide 10 Fb 54.12N 9.06 E
Heidelberg 10 Eg 49.25N 8.42 E
Heidenheim an der Brenz 10 Gh 48.41N 10.09 E
Heidenreichstein 14 Jb 48.52N 15.07 E
Hei-Gawa 29 Gb 39.38N 141.58 E
Heigun-Tō 29 Ce 33.47N 132.15 E
Hei He 27 Hd 38.15N 100.15 E
Heihe→Aihui 22 Od 50.13N 127.26 E
Heilbron 37 De 27.21S 27.58 E
Heilbronn 10 Fg 49.08N 9.13 E
Heiligenblut 14 Gd 47.02N 12.50 E
Heiligenhafen 10 Gb 54.22N 10.59 E
Heiligenhaus 12 Ic 51.19N 6.58 E
Heiligenstadt 10 Ge 51.23N 10.08 E
Heilinzi 28 Ib 44.33N 126.41 E
Heilong Jiang 21 Qd 52.56N 141.10 E
Heilongjiang Sheng (Hei-lung-chiang Sheng)= Heilungkiang (EN) [2] 27 Mb 48.00N 128.00 E
Heiloo 12 Gb 52.36N 4.43 E
Hei-lung-chiang Sheng→Heilongjiang Sheng=Heilungkiang (EN) [2] 27 Mb 48.00N 128.00 E
Heilungkiang (EN)= Heilongjiang Sheng (Hei-lung-chiang Sheng) [2] 27 Mb 48.00N 128.00 E
Heilungkiang (EN)=Hei-lung-chiang Sheng→Heilongjiang Sheng [2] 27 Mb 48.00N 128.00 E
Heimæy 7a c 63.26N 20.17W
Heimbach 12 Id 50.38N 6.29 E
Heimdal 7 Ce 63.21N 10.22 E
Heimsheim 12 Kf 48.48N 8.51 E
Heinävesi 7 Ge 62.26N 28.36 E
Heinola 7 Gf 61.13N 26.02 E
Heinsberg 12 Ic 51.04N 6.05 E
Heishan 28 Gd 41.42N 122.07 E
Heishan Xia 27 Hd 37.18N 104.39 E
Heishui [China] 28 Ec 42.06N 119.22 E
Heishui [China] 27 He 32.03N 103.05 E
Heist, Knokke- 12 Fc 51.21N 3.15 E
Heist-op-den-Berg 12 Gc 51.05N 4.43 E
Hei-Zaki 29 Hb 39.39N 142.00 E
Hejgijaha 17 Pd 65.27N 72.50 E
Hejian 28 De 38.27N 116.05 E
Hejing 27 Ec 42.18N 86.18 E
Hejjaha 17 Kb 68.18N 62.32 E
Hekimhan 24 Gc 38.49N 37.56 E
Hekinan 29 Ed 34.52N 136.58 E
Hekla 5 Ec 64.00N 19.40W
Hekou 28 Ci 31.20N 114.25 E
Hekou → Yanshan 28 Dj 28.18N 117.41 E
Hel 10 Ob 54.37N 18.48 E
Helagsfjället 7 Ce 62.55N 12.27 E
Helan 27 Id 38.35N 106.18 E
Helan Shan 27 Id 39.00N 106.00 E
Helden's Point 51c Ab 17.24N 62.50W
Helena [Ar.-U.S.] 43 Ie 34.32N 90.35W
Helena [Guy.] 54 Gb 6.41N 57.55W
Helena [Mt.-U.S.] 39 He 46.36N 112.01W
Helen Glacier 66 Ge 66.40S 93.55 E
Helen Reef 57 Ed 2.35N 131.47 E
Helensburgh 9 Ie 56.01N 4.44W
Helensville 62 Fb 36.40S 174.27 E
Helgaå 8 Fi 55.53N 14.08 E
Helgasjön 8 Fh 56.55N 14.45 E
Helgeland 7 Cd 66.15N 13.05 E
Helgoland 10 Db 54.12N 7.53 E

Index Symbols

[1] Independent Nation
[2] State, Region
[3] District, County
[4] Municipality
[5] Colony, Dependency
Continent
Physical Region
Historical or Cultural Region
Mount, Mountain
Volcano
Hill
Mountains, Mountain Range
Hills, Escarpment
Plateau, Upland
Pass, Gap
Plain, Lowland
Delta
Salt Flat
Valley, Canyon
Crater, Cave
Karst Features
Depression
Polder
Desert, Dunes
Forest, Woods
Heath, Steppe
Oasis
Cape, Point
Coast, Beach
Cliff
Peninsula
Isthmus
Sandbank
Island
Atoll
Rock, Reef
Islands, Archipelago
Rocks, Reefs
Coral Reef
Well, Spring
Geyser
River, Stream
Waterfall Rapids
River Mouth, Estuary
Lake
Salt Lake
Intermittent Lake
Reservoir
Swamp, Pond
Canal
Glacier
Ice Shelf, Pack Ice
Ocean
Sea
Gulf, Bay
Strait, Fjord
Lagoon
Bank
Seamount
Tablemount
Ridge
Shelf
Basin
Escarpment, Sea Scarp
Fracture
Trench, Abyss
National Park, Reserve
Point of Interest
Recreation Site
Cave, Cavern
Historic Site
Ruins
Wall, Walls
Church, Abbey
Temple
Scientific Station
Airport
Port
Lighthouse
Mine
Tunnel
Dam, Bridge

Helgoländer Bucht 10 Eb 54.10N 8.04 E
Helikón Óros 15 Fk 38.20N 22.50 E
Helixi 28 Ei 30.39N 119.01 E
Heljulja 8 Nc 61.37N 30.38 E
Hella 7a Bc 63.50N 20.24W
Hellberge 10 Hd 52.34N 11.17 E
Hélleh 24 Nh 29.10N 50.40 E
Hellendoorn 11 Mb 52.24N 6.26 E
Hellendoorn-Nijverdal 12 Ib 52.22N 6.27 E
Hellenic Trough (EN) 5 Ii 35.00N 24.00 E
Hellental 12 Id 50.29N 6.26 E
Hellesylt 7 Be 62.05N 6.54 E
Hellin 13 Kf 38.31N 1.41W
Hells Canyon 43 Db 45.20N 116.45W
Hellweg 12 Kc 51.40N 8.00 E
Helmand 21 If 31.12N 61.34 E
Helmand 23 Jc 31.00N 64.00 E
Helme 10 He 51.20N 11.20 E
Helmeringhausen 37 Be 25.54S 16.57 E
Helmond 11 Lc 51.29N 5.40 E
Helmsdale 9 Jc 58.10N 3.40W
Helmsdale 9 Jc 58.07N 3.40W
Helmstedt 10 Gd 52.14N 11.00 E
Helong 27 Mc 42.32N 129.00 E
Helpe Majeure 12 Fd 50.11N 3.47 E
Helpringham 12 Bb 52.56N 0.18W
Helpter Berge 10 Jc 53.30N 13.36 E
Helsingborg 6 Hd 56.03N 12.42 E
Helsinge 8 Eh 56.01N 12.12 E
Helsingfors/Helsinki 6 Ic 60.10N 24.58 E
Helsingør 7 Ch 56.02N 12.37 E
Helsinki/Helsingfors 6 Ic 60.10N 24.58 E
Helska, Mierzeja- 10 Ob 54.45N 18.39 E
Helston 9 Hk 50.05N 5.16W
Helvecia 55 Bj 31.06S 60.05W
Helwân (EN)=Ḩulwān 33 Fd 29.51N 31.20 E
Ḩemār 24 Qg 31.42N 57.31 E
Hemčik 20 Ef 51.40N 92.10 E
Hemel Hempstead 9 Mj 51.46N 0.28W
Hemer 12 Jc 51.23N 7.46 E
Hemnesberget 7 Cc 66.14N 13.38 E
Hemsby 12 Db 52.41N 1.42 E
Hemse 8 Hg 57.14N 18.22 E
Hemsedal 8 Cd 60.50N 8.40 E
Hemsö 7 Ee 62.45N 18.05 E
Hen 8 Dd 60.13N 10.14 E
Henan 27 He 34.33N 101.55 E
Hen and Chickens Islands 62 Fa 35.55S 174.45 E
Henan Sheng (Ho-nan Sheng)=Honan (EN) 27 Je 34.00N 114.00 E
Henares 13 Id 40.24N 3.30W
Henashi-Zaki 29 Fa 40.37N 139.51 E
Henbury 59 Gd 24.35S 133.15 E
Hendaye 11 Ek 43.22N 1.47W
Hendek 24 Db 40.48N 30.45 E
Henderson [Arg.] 55 Bm 36.18S 61.43W
Henderson [Ky.-U.S.] 44 Dg 37.50N 87.35W
Henderson [N.C.-U.S.] 44 Hg 36.20N 78.25W
Henderson [Nv.-U.S.] 43 Dd 36.02N 115.01W
Henderson [Tx.-U.S.] 45 Ij 32.09N 94.48W
Henderson Island 57 Og 24.22S 128.19W
Henderson Seamount (EN) 43 Df 25.34N 119.33W
Hendersonville [N.C.-U.S.] 44 Fh 35.19N 82.28W
Hendersonville [Tn.-U.S.] 44 Dg 36.18N 86.37W
Hendījān 24 Mg 30.14N 49.43 E
Hendorābī, Jazīreh-ye- 24 Oi 26.40N 53.37 E
Hendrik Verwderddam 30 Km 46.36S 37.55 E
Hengām, Jazīreh-ye- 24 Pi 26.39N 55.53 E
Hengduan Shan 21 Lg 27.30N 99.00 E
Hengelo [Neth.] 11 Mb 52.15N 6.45 E
Hengelo [Neth.] 12 Ib 52.03N 6.20 E
Heng Shan [China] 27 Jd 39.42N 113.45 E
Hengshan [China] 27 Jf 27.16N 112.51 E
Heng Shan [China] 27 Jf 27.18N 112.41 E
Hengshan [China] 27 Id 37.51N 109.20 E
Hengshan [China] 28 Kb 45.24N 131.01 E
Hengshui 27 Kd 37.39N 115.46 E
Hengxian 27 Ig 22.46N 109.15 E
Hengyang 22 Ng 26.56N 112.35 E
Henik Lakes 42 Hd 61.05N 97.20W
Hénin-Liétard 11 Id 50.25N 2.56 E
Henley-on-Thames 12 Bc 51.32N 0.54W
Hennan 8 Fb 62.05N 15.45 E
Hennan 7 De 62.02N 15.54 E
Hennebont 11 Cg 47.48N 3.17W
Hennef (Sieg) 12 Jd 50.47N 7.17 E
Hennigsdorf bei Berlin 10 Jd 52.38N 13.12 E
Henrietta Maria, Cape - 42 Je 55.09N 82.19W
Henrietty, Ostrov- 20 Ka 77.00N 157.00 E
Henry, Mount- 46 Hb 48.53N 115.31W
Henry Bay 66 Ie 66.40S 120.40 E
Henryetta 45 Ii 35.27N 95.59W
Henry Kater Peninsula 42 Kk 69.15N 67.30W
Henry Mountains 46 Jh 37.55N 110.50W
Henrys Fork River 46 Je 43.45N 111.56W
Henslow, Cape- 63a Ec 9.56S 160.38 E
Hentej 21 Me 48.50N 109.00 E
Hentiesbaai 37 Ad 22.08S 14.18 E
Henzada 22 Lh 17.38N 95.28 E
Heping → Yanhe 27 If 28.31N 108.28 E
Heppenheim (Bergstraße) 12 Ke 49.38N 8.39 E
Heppner 46 Fd 45.21N 119.33W
Hepu (Lianzhou) 27 Ig 21.40N 109.12 E
Hequ 27 Jd 39.22N 111.15 E
Herakol Dağı 24 Id 37.45N 42.35 E
Heralds Cays 59 Jc 16.55S 149.10 E
Herāt 23 Jc 34.30N 62.00 E
Herāt 22 If 34.20N 62.12 E
Hérault 11 Jk 43.40N 3.30 E
Hérault 11 Jk 43.17N 3.26 E
Herbert [N.Z.] 62 Df 45.13S 170.46 E
Herbert [Sask.-Can.] 46 La 50.26N 107.12W
Herberton 59 Jc 17.23S 145.23 E
Herbert River 59 Jc 18.32S 146.17 E
Herborn 10 Ef 50.41N 8.19 E
Herby 10 Of 50.45N 18.40 E
Hercegnovi 15 Bg 42.27N 18.32 E
Hercegovina 14 Lg 43.00N 17.50 E
Hercegovina 5 Hg 43.00N 17.50 E
Herdubreid 7a Cb 65.11N 16.21W
Heredia 49 Fh 10.30N 84.00W
Heredia 47 Hf 10.00N 84.07W
Hereford 9 Ki 52.15N 2.50W
Hereford [Eng.-U.K.] 9 Ki 52.04N 2.43W
Hereford [Tx.-U.S.] 43 Ge 34.49N 102.24W
Hereford and Worcester 9 Ki 52.10N 2.35W
Hereheretue Atoll 57 Mf 19.54S 144.58W
Hereke 15 Mi 40.48N 29.39 E
Herekino 62 Ea 35.16S 173.13 E
Herent 12 Gd 50.54N 4.40 E
Herentals 12 Gc 51.11N 4.50 E
Herfølge 8 Ei 55.25N 12.10 E
Herford 10 Ed 52.08N 8.41 E
Héricourt 11 Mg 47.35N 6.45 E
Herington 45 Hg 38.40N 96.57W
Heriot 61 Ci 45.51S 169.16 E
Heris 24 Lc 38.14N 47.07 E
Herisau 14 Dc 47.24N 9.16 E
Herk 12 Hd 50.58N 5.07 E
Herk-de-Stad 12 Hd 50.56N 5.10 E
Herkimer 44 Jd 43.02N 74.59W
Herlen He 27 Kb 48.48N 117.00 E
Hermagor 14 Hd 46.37N 13.22 E
Hermanas 48 Id 27.14N 101.14W
Herma Ness 9 Ma 60.50N 0.54W
Hermano Peak 45 Bh 37.17N 108.48W
Hermansverk 8 Bc 61.11N 6.51 E
Hermanus 37 Bf 34.25S 19.16 E
Hermeskeil 12 Ie 49.39N 6.57 E
Hermiston 46 Fd 45.51N 119.17W
Hermitage 62 De 43.44S 170.05 E
Hermit Islands 57 Fe 1.32S 145.05 E
Hermosa de Santa Rosa, Sierra- 48 Id 28.00N 101.45W
Hermosillo 39 Hg 29.04N 110.58W
Hermoso Campo 55 Bh 27.36S 61.21W
Hérnad 10 Qh 48.00N 20.58 E
Hernandarias 56 Jc 25.22S 54.45W
Hernández [Arg.] 55 Bk 32.21S 60.02W
Hernández [Mex.] 48 Hf 23.02N 102.02W
Hernani 13 Ka 43.16N 1.58W
Herne 10 De 51.33N 7.13 E
Herne Bay 9 Oj 51.23N 1.08 E
Herning 6 Gd 56.08N 8.59 E
Heroica Alvarado 48 Lh 18.46N 95.46W
Heroica Tlapacoyan 48 Kh 19.58N 97.13W
Heroica Zitácuaro 48 Ih 19.24N 100.22W
Herouville-Saint-Clair 12 Be 49.12N 0.19W
Herowābād 24 Md 37.37N 48.32 E
Herradura 55 Ch 26.29S 58.18W
Herre 8 Ce 59.06N 9.34 E
Herrera 55 Ck 32.26S 58.38W
Herrera 49 Gj 7.54N 80.38W
Herrera del Duque 13 Ge 39.10N 5.03W
Herrera de Pisuerga 13 Hb 42.36N 4.20W
Herrero, Punta- 48 Ph 19.10N 87.30W
Herrljunga 8 Ef 58.05N 13.02 E
Hers 11 Hk 43.47N 1.20 E
Herschel 42 Dc 69.35N 139.05W
Herselt 12 Gc 51.03N 4.53 E
Herserange 12 He 49.31N 5.47 E
Hershey 44 Ie 40.17N 76.39W
Hersilia 55 Bj 30.00S 61.51W
Herson 6 Jf 46.38N 32.35 E
Hersonesskij, Mys- 16 Hg 44.33N 33.25 E
Hersonskaja Oblast 19 Df 46.40N 33.30 E
Herstal 11 Ld 50.40N 5.38 E
Herten 12 Jc 51.36N 7.08 E
Hertford 9 Mj 51.50N 0.05W
Hertford 9 Mj 51.48N 0.05W
Hertfordshire 9 Mj 51.45N 0.20W
Hertugen Af Orleans Land 41 Jc 78.15N 21.12W
Hervás 13 Gd 40.16N 5.51W
Herve 12 Hd 50.38N 5.48 E
Herve, Plateau van-/Herveland 12 Hd 50.40N 5.50 E
Herveland/Herve, Plateau van- 12 Hd 50.40N 5.50 E
Hervey Bay 59 Ke 25.15S 152.50 E
Herzberg 10 Je 51.41N 13.14 E
Herzberg am Harz 10 Ge 51.39N 10.20 E
Herzebrock 12 Kc 51.53N 8.15 E
Herzele 12 Fd 50.53N 3.53 E
Herzliyya 24 Ff 32.10N 34.51 E
Herzogenrath 12 Id 50.52N 6.06 E
Herzog-Ernst-Bucht (Vahsel Bay) 66 Af 77.48S 34.39W
Hesāmābād 24 Me 35.52N 48.25 E
Hesbaye/Haspengouws Plateau 11 Ld 50.35N 5.10 E
Hesdin 11 Id 50.22N 2.02 E
Hesel 12 Ja 53.18N 7.36 E
Heshi 24 Md 37.30N 48.15 E
Heshun 27 Jd 37.18N 113.32 E
Hesse (EN)=Hessen 10 Ff 50.30N 9.15 E
Hesselberg 10 Gg 49.05N 10.35 E
Hesselø 8 Dh 56.10N 11.45 E
Hessen 12 Ke 49.47N 8.08 E
Hessen=Hesse (EN) 10 Ff 50.30N 9.15 E
Hess Tablemount (EN) 57 Jc 17.50N 174.15W
Heta 21 Mb 71.54N 102.00 E
Heta 20 Eb 71.35N 99.45 E
Hettange-Grande 12 Ie 49.24N 6.09 E
Hettinger 45 Ec 46.00N 102.39W
Heuberg 10 Eh 48.06N 8.55 E
Heuchin 12 Ed 50.28N 2.16 E
Heuru 63a Ed 10.12S 161.25 E
Hève, Cap de la- 11 Fe 49.31N 0.04W
Heves 10 Qi 47.36N 20.17 E
Heves 10 Qi 47.50N 20.15 E
Hexham 9 Kg 54.58N 2.06W
Hexi 27 Hf 27.44N 102.09 E
Hexian 28 Ei 31.43N 118.22 E
Hexian (Babu) 27 Jg 24.28N 111.34 E
Hexigten Qi (Jingfeng) 27 Kc 43.15N 117.31 E
Heydarābād 24 Kd 37.06N 45.27 E
Heysham 9 Kg 54.02N 2.54W
Heyuan 27 Jg 23.41N 114.43 E
Heywood 59 Ig 38.08S 141.38 E
Heze (Caozhou) 27 Kd 35.14N 115.28 E
Hezuo 27 Hd 35.02N 102.57 E
Hialeah 44 Gm 25.49N 80.17W
Hiawatha 45 Ig 39.51N 95.32W
Hibara-Ko 29 Gc 37.42N 140.03 E
Hibbing 43 Ib 47.25N 92.56W
Hibernia Reef 59 Eb 12.00S 123.25 E
Hibiki-Nada 29 Bd 34.15N 130.40 E
Hibiny 7 Hc 67.40N 33.35 E
Hiburi-Jima 29 Ce 33.10N 132.18 E
Hickman 44 Cg 36.34N 89.11W
Hickory 44 Gh 35.44N 81.21W
Hick's Cay 49 Ce 17.39N 88.08W
Hida-Gawa 29 Ed 35.25N 137.03 E
Hidaka [Jap.] 28 Qc 42.53N 142.28 E
Hidaka [Jap.] 29 Dd 35.28N 134.47 E
Hidaka-Gawa 29 De 33.53N 135.08 E
Hidaka Sanmyaku 28 Qc 42.25N 142.50 E
Hidalgo 47 Ed 20.30N 99.00W
Hidalgo [Mex.] 47 Ed 24.15N 99.26W
Hidalgo [Mex.] 48 Jd 27.47N 99.52W
Hidalgo del Parral 39 Ig 26.56N 105.40W
Hida-Sanchi 29 Ec 36.20N 137.00 E
Hida-Sanmyaku 28 Nf 36.10N 137.30 E
Hiddensee 10 Jb 54.33N 13.07 E
Hidra 8 Bf 58.15N 6.35 E
Hidrolândia 55 Hc 16.58S 49.16W
Hidrolina 55 Hb 14.37S 49.25W
Hieflau 14 Ic 47.36N 14.44 E
Hiei-Zan 29 Dd 35.05N 135.50 E
Hienghène 61 Cd 20.35S 164.56 E
Hierro 30 Ff 27.45N 18.00W
Higashi 29b b 26.38N 128.08 E
Higashihiroshima 29 Cd 34.25N 132.43 E
Higashi-izu 29 Fd 34.48N 139.02 E
Higashi-matsuyama 29 Fc 36.02N 139.22 E
Higashimuroran 29a Bb 42.21N 141.02 E
Higashine 28 Pe 38.26N 140.24 E
Higashiōsaka 29 Dd 34.40N 135.37 E
Higashi Rishiri 29a Ba 45.16N 141.15 E
Higashi-Shina-Kai=East China Sea (EN) 21 Og 29.00N 125.00 E
Higgins 45 Fh 36.07N 100.02W
Higham Ferrers 12 Bb 52.18N 0.35W
High Atlas (EN)=Haut Atlas 30 Ge 32.00N 6.00W
Highland 9 Id 57.30N 5.00W
Highland Park 45 Me 42.11N 87.48W
High Level 42 Fe 58.30N 117.05W
Highmore 45 Gd 44.31N 99.27W
High Plains 38 If 38.30N 103.00W
High Point 43 Ld 35.58N 79.59W
High Prairie 42 Fe 55.27N 116.30W
High River 42 Gf 50.35N 113.52W
Highrock Lake 42 He 55.49N 100.23W
High Springs 44 Fk 29.50N 82.36W
High Tatra (EN)=Vysoké Tatry 10 Pg 49.10N 20.00 E
High Willhays 9 Jk 50.41N 3.59W
Highwood Mountains 46 Jc 47.25N 110.30W
High Wycombe 9 Mj 51.38N 0.46W
Higuera de Zaragoza 48 Ee 25.59N 109.16W
Higüero, Punta- 49 Nd 18.22N 67.16W
Higuerote 50 Cg 10.29N 66.06W
Higüey 49 Md 18.37N 68.43W
Hiidenvesi 8 Kd 60.20N 24.10 E
Hii-Gawa 29 Cd 35.26N 132.52 E
Hiiraan 35 He 4.00N 45.30 E
Hiitola 7 Gf 61.16N 29.42 E
Hiiumaa/Hiuma 5 Id 58.50N 22.40 E
Hijar 13 Lc 41.10N 0.27W
Ḩijāz 23 Ee 24.30N 38.30 E
Ḩijāz, Jabal al- 33 Hf 19.45N 41.55 E
Hiji 29 Be 33.22N 131.32 E
Hiji-Gawa 29 Ce 33.36N 132.29 E
Hikami 29 Dd 35.11N 135.02 E
Hikari 28 Kh 33.58N 131.56 E
Hiketa 29 Dd 34.13N 134.24 E
Hikiä 8 Kd 60.45N 24.55 E
Hiki-Gawa 29 De 33.35N 135.26 E
Ḩikmah, Ra's al- 24 Bg 31.17N 27.44 E
Hikone 28 Ng 35.15N 136.15 E
Hiko-San 29 Be 33.29N 130.56 E
Hikueru Atoll 61 Mc 17.36S 142.37W
Hikurangi 62 Hb 37.55S 178.04 E
Hikurangi 62 Fa 35.36S 174.17 E
Hila 26 Ih 7.35S 127.24 E
Hilāl, Ra's al- 33 Dc 32.55N 22.11 E
Hiland 46 Le 43.08N 107.18W
Hilchenbach 12 Kc 51.00N 8.06 E
Hildburghausen 10 Gf 50.25N 10.45 E
Hilden 12 Ic 51.10N 6.56 E
Hildesheim 10 Fd 52.09N 9.58 E
Hillaby, Mount- 50 Gf 13.12N 59.35W
Hillared 8 Eg 57.38N 13.09 E
Hillary Coast 66 Kf 79.00S 161.00 E
Hill Bank 49 Ce 17.35N 88.42W
Hill City 45 Gg 39.22N 99.51W
Hillcrest Center 46 Fi 35.23N 118.57W
Hille 12 Kb 52.20N 8.45 E
Hillegom 12 Gb 52.18N 4.35 E
Hillekrog 8 Dj 54.36N 11.30 E
Hillerød 8 Ei 55.56N 12.19 E
Hillerstorp 8 Eg 57.19N 13.52 E
Hillesheim 12 Id 50.19N 6.41 E
Hillingdon, London- 12 Bc 51.31N 0.27W
Hillsboro [Il.-U.S.] 45 Lg 39.09N 89.29W
Hillsboro [N.D.-U.S.] 45 Hc 47.26N 97.03W
Hillsboro [Oh.-U.S.] 44 Ff 39.12N 83.37W
Hillsboro [Or.-U.S.] 46 Dd 45.31N 122.59W
Hillsboro [Tx.-U.S.] 45 Hj 32.01N 97.08W
Hillsborough 51p Cb 12.29N 61.26W
Hillsdale 44 Ee 41.55N 84.38W
Hillsville 44 Gg 36.46N 80.44W
Hillswich 9 La 60.28N 1.30W
Hilo 58 Lc 19.44N 155.05W
Hilo Bay 65a Fd 19.44N 155.05W
Hilok 21 Md 51.19N 106.59 E
Hilok 20 Gf 51.22N 110.30 E
Hilton Head Island 44 Gi 32.12N 80.45W
Hiltrup, Münster- 12 Jc 51.54N 7.38 E
Hilvan 24 Hd 37.30N 38.58 E
Hilvarenbeek 12 Hc 51.29N 5.08 E
Hilversum 11 Lb 52.14N 5.10 E
Himāchal Prādesh 25 Fb 31.00N 78.00 E
Himalaya=Himalayas (EN) 21 Kg 29.00N 83.00 E
Himalayas (EN)=Himalaya 21 Kg 29.00N 83.00 E
Himara 15 Ci 40.07N 19.44 E
Himeji 27 Ne 34.49N 134.42 E
Hime-Jima 29 Be 33.43N 131.40 E
Hime-Kawa 29 Ec 37.02N 137.50 E
Hime-Shima 29 Ae 32.49N 128.41 E
Hime-Zaki 29 Fb 38.05N 138.34 E
Himi 28 Nf 36.51N 136.59 E
Himki 7 Ii 55.56N 37.28 E
Himmelbjerget 8 Ch 56.06N 9.42 E
Himmerfjärden 8 Ge 59.00N 17.43 E
Himmerland 8 Ch 56.50N 9.38 E
Himo 36 Gc 3.23S 37.33 E
Ḩimş=Homs (E) 22 Ff 34.44N 36.43 E
Ḩims, Bahrat- 24 Ge 34.39N 36.34 E
Hinai 29 Ga 40.13N 140.35 E
Hinca Renancó 56 Hd 34.50S 64.23W
Hinche 49 Kd 19.09N 72.01W
Hinchinbrook 40 Jd 60.22N 146.30W
Hinchinbrook Island 59 Jc 18.25S 146.15 E
Hinckley 12 Ab 52.32N 1.22W
Hindås 8 Eg 57.42N 12.27 E
Hindhead 12 Bc 51.06N 0.44W
Ḩindī, Badwëynta-=Indian Ocean (EN) 3 Gl 21.00S 82.00 E
Hindmarsh, Lake- 59 Ig 36.05S 141.55 E
Hinds 62 Df 44.00S 171.34 E
Hindsholm 8 Di 55.33N 10.40 E
Hindukush 21 Jf 35.00N 71.00 E
Hindustan 21 Jg 25.00N 79.00 E
Hinesville 44 Gj 31.51N 81.36W
Hinganghāt 25 Fd 20.34N 78.50 E
Hınıs 24 Ic 39.22N 41.44 E
Hınıs 24 Jc 39.18N 42.12 E
Hinlopenstretet 41 Oc 79.15N 21.00 E
Hinnøya 5 Hb 68.30N 16.00 E
Hino-Gawa 29 Cd 35.27N 133.22 E
Hinojosa del Duque 13 Gf 38.30N 5.09W
Hinokage 29 Be 32.39N 131.24 E
Hi-no-Misaki 29 Cd 35.26N 132.38 E
Hino-Misaki 29 De 33.53N 135.04 E
Hinterrhein 14 Dd 46.49N 9.25 E
Hinton 42 Ff 53.25N 117.34W
Hi-Numa 29 Gc 36.16N 140.30 E
Hınzır Burun 24 Fb 36.22N 35.45 E
Hiou 63b Ca 13.08S 166.33 E
Hipólito 48 Ie 25.41N 101.26W
Hippolytushoef, Wieringen- 12 Gb 52.54N 4.59 E
Hippone 14 Bn 36.52N 7.44 E
Hirado 28 Jh 33.22N 129.33 E
Hirado-Shima 28 Jh 33.19N 129.32 E
Hiraka 29 Gb 39.16N 140.29 E
Hirakata 29 Dd 34.48N 135.38 E
Hirākud 25 Gd 21.15N 84.15 E
Hiraman 36 Gc 1.07S 39.55 E
Hiranai 29a Bc 40.54N 140.57 E
Hirara 27 Mg 24.48N 125.17 E
Hira-Shima 29 Ae 33.01N 129.15 E
Hirata 29 Cd 35.26N 132.49 E
Hiratsuka 29 Fd 35.19N 139.19 E
Hirfanlı barajı Gölü 24 Ec 39.10N 33.32 E
Hirgis 27 Fb 49.32N 93.48 E
Hirgis-Nur 21 Le 49.12N 93.24 E
Hirhafok 32 Ie 23.29N 5.45 E
Hîrlău 15 Jb 47.26N 26.54 E
Hiromi 29 Ce 33.15N 132.38 E
Hiroo 27 Pc 42.17N 143.19 E
Hirosaki 27 Pc 40.35N 140.28 E
Hiroshima 22 Pf 34.24N 132.27 E
Hiroshima Ken 28 Lg 34.35N 132.50 E
Hiroshima-Wan 29 Cd 34.10N 132.20 E
Hirschhorn (Neckar) 12 Ke 49.27N 8.54 E
Hirson 11 Ke 49.55N 4.05 E
Hîrşova 15 Ke 44.41N 27.56 E
Hîrtibaciu 15 Hd 45.44N 24.14 E
Hirtshals 7 Bh 57.35N 9.58 E
Hirvensalmi 8 Lc 61.38N 26.48 E
Hīs 35 Hc 10.50N 46.54 E
Hisai 29 Ed 34.40N 136.28 E
Hisaka-Shima 29 Ae 32.48N 128.52 E
Hisar 15 Jg 42.35N 27.00 E
Hisar 25 Fc 29.10N 75.43 E
Hisarcık 15 Mj 39.15N 29.15 E
Hisarja 15 Hg 42.30N 24.42 E
Ḩismā 24 Fh 28.30N 35.50 E
Ḩişn al 'Abr 33 If 16.08N 47.14 E
Ḩişn as Şaḩābī 33 Dc 30.01N 20.48 E
Hispaniola (EN)=La Española 38 Lh 19.00N 71.00W
Histon 12 Cb 52.15N 0.06 E
Histria 15 Le 44.30N 28.45 E
Hit 24 Jf 33.38N 42.49 E
Hita 28 Kh 33.19N 130.56 E
Hitachi 28 Pf 36.36N 140.39 E
Hitachi-ōta 29 Gc 36.32N 140.31 E
Hitchin 12 Bc 51.57N 0.16W
Hitiaa 65e Fc 17.36S 149.18W
Hitotsuse-Gawa 29 Be 32.03N 131.31 E
Hitoyoshi 28 Kh 32.15N 130.45 E
Hitra 5 Gc 63.30N 8.45 E
Hiuchi-ga-Take 29 Fc 36.57N 139.17 E
Hiuchi-Nada 29 Cd 34.05N 133.15 E
Hiuma/Hiiumaa 5 Id 58.50N 22.40 E
Hiv 16 Oi 41.46N 47.57 E
Hiva 19 Gg 41.25N 60.23 E
Hiva Oa, Ile- 57 Ne 9.45S 139.00W
Hiw 24 Ei 26.01N 32.16 E
Hjademeste/Häädemeeste 8 Uf 58.00N 24.28 E
Hjallerup 8 Dg 57.10N 10.09 E
Hjälmare kanal 8 Fe 59.25N 15.55 E
Hjälmaren 5 Hd 59.15N 15.45 E
Hjelm 8 Dh 56.10N 10.50 E
Hjelmelandsvågen 7 Bg 59.15N 6.10 E
Hjelmsøya 7 Fa 71.05N 24.43 E
Hjerkinn 8 Cb 62.13N 9.32 E
Hjo 7 Dg 58.18N 14.17 E
Hjørring 7 Bh 57.28N 9.59 E
Hlatikulu 37 Ee 26.58S 31.19 E
Hlavní město Praha 10 Kf 50.05N 14.25 E
Hlavní město SSR Bratislava 10 Nh 48.10N 17.10 E
Hlinsko 10 Lg 49.46N 15.54 E
Hlohovec 10 Nh 48.25N 17.48 E
Hluhluwe 37 Ee 28.02S 32.17 E
Hmelnickaja Oblast 19 Cf 49.30N 27.00 E
Hmelnicki 19 Cf 49.24N 26.57 E
Hmelnik 16 Ee 49.33N 27.59 E
Hnilec 10 Rh 48.53N 21.01 E
Ho 34 Fd 6.36N 0.28 E
Hoa Binh 25 Ld 20.50N 105.20 E
Hoai Nhon 25 Lf 14.26N 109.01 E
Hoanib 37 Ac 19.23S 13.06 E
Hoare Bay 42 Lc 65.30N 63.10W
Hoback Peak 46 Je 43.10N 110.33W
Hobart [Austl.] 58 Fi 42.53S 147.19 E
Hobart [Ok.-U.S.] 45 Gi 35.01N 99.06W
Hobbs 43 Ge 32.42N 103.08W
Hobbs Coast 66 Nf 74.50S 131.00W
Hobda 16 Sd 50.55N 54.38 E
Hoboken, Antwerpen- 12 Gc 51.10N 4.21 E
Hoboksar 27 Eb 46.47N 85.43 E
Hobq Shamo 27 Ic 40.30N 108.00 E
Hobro 7 Bh 56.38N 9.48 E
Hoburgen 7 Eh 56.55N 18.07 E
Hobyā 31 Lh 5.20N 48.38 E
Hocalar 15 Mk 38.37N 29.57 E
Hochalmspitze 14 Hc 47.01N 13.19 E
Hochfeiler/Gran Pilastro 14 Fd 46.58N 11.44 E
Hochgolling 14 Hc 47.16N 13.45 E
Hochschwab 14 Jc 47.36N 15.05 E
Höchstadt an der Aisch 10 Gg 49.42N 10.44 E
Hochstetters Forland 41 Kc 75.45N 20.00W
Höchst im Odenwald 12 Ke 49.48N 9.00 E
Hochtor 14 Gc 47.05N 12.48 E
Hockenheim 12 Ke 49.19N 8.33 E
Hodaka-Dake 29 Ec 36.17N 137.39 E
Hodda 35 Ic 11.30N 50.45 E
Hoddesdon 12 Cc 51.45N 0.00
Hodgenville 44 Eg 37.34N 85.44W
Hodh 30 Gg 16.10N 8.40W
Hodh ech Chargui 32 Ff 17.00N 7.15W
Hodh el Gharbi 32 Ff 16.30N 10.00W
Hódmezővásárhely 10 Qj 46.25N 20.20 E
Hodna, Chott el- 32 Hb 35.25N 4.45 E
Hodna, Monts du- 32 Hb 35.50N 4.50 E
Hodna, Plaine du- 13 Qi 35.35N 4.35 E
Hodonín 10 Nh 48.52N 17.08 E
Hodorov 16 De 49.25N 24.18 E
Hodžambas 18 Ee 38.06N 65.01 E
Hodža-Pirjah, Gora- 18 Fe 38.47N 67.35 E
Hodželi 19 Fg 42.23N 59.20 E
Hœdic, Ile de- 11 Dg 47.20N 2.52W
Hoegaarden 12 Gd 50.47N 4.53 E
Hoei/Huy 12 Hd 50.31N 5.14 E
Hoë Karoo 30 Jl 30.00S 21.30 E
Hoek van Holland 11 Kc 51.59N 4.09 E
Hoeselt 12 Hd 50.51N 5.29 E
Hof 10 Hf 50.19N 11.55 E
Höfdakaupstadur 7a Bb 65.50N 20.19W
Hofgeismar 10 Fe 51.29N 9.24 E
Hofheim 12 Kd 50.05N 8.27 E
Hofmeyr 37 Df 31.39S 25.50 E
Höfn 7a Cb 64.15N 15.13W
Hofsjökull 5 Ec 64.49N 18.48W
Höfu 28 Kg 34.03N 131.34 E
Höganäs 8 Eh 56.12N 12.33 E
Hogarth, Mount- 59 Hd 21.48S 136.58 E
Hogback Mountain 46 Id 44.54N 112.07W
Hog Cliffs 51d Ba 17.38N 61.44W
Hoge Venen/Hautes Fagnes 10 Bf 50.30N 6.00 E
Högfors/Karkkila 7 Ff 60.32N 24.11 E
Hog Island 51p Bb 12.00N 61.44W
Hogne, Somme-Leuze- 12 Hd 50.15N 5.17 E
Hog Point 51d Ba 17.43N 61.48W
Högsby 7 Dh 57.10N 16.02 E
Høgste Breakulen 8 Bc 61.41N 7.02 E
Høgstegia 8 Db 62.23N 10.08 E
Hogsty Reef 49 Kc 21.41N 73.49W
Höhang-nyŏng 28 Jd 41.48N 128.20 E
Hohe Acht 10 Cf 50.23N 7.00 E
Hohe Eifel 12 Id 50.16N 6.50 E
Hohenau 55 Eh 27.05S 55.45W
Hohenems 14 Dc 47.22N 9.41 E
Hohenloher Ebene 10 Fg 49.20N 9.40 E
Hohes Venn 10 Bf 50.30N 6.00 E
Hohe Tauern 14 Gc 47.10N 12.30 E
Hohhot 22 Ne 40.51N 111.38 E
Höhoku 29 Bd 34.17N 130.57 E
Höhr-Grenzhausen 12 Jd 50.26N 7.40 E
Höhtiäinen 8 Mb 62.50N 29.40 E
Hoh Xil Hu 27 Fd 35.35N 91.06 E
Hoh Xil Shan 21 Lf 35.20N 91.00 E
Hoi An 25 Le 15.52N 108.19 E

Index Symbols

[1] Independent Nation
[2] State, Region
[3] District, County
[4] Municipality
[5] Colony, Dependency
Continent
Physical Region
Historical or Cultural Region
Mount, Mountain
Volcano
Hill
Mountains, Mountain Range
Hills, Escarpment
Plateau, Upland
Pass, Gap
Plain, Lowland
Delta
Salt Flat
Valley, Canyon
Crater, Cave
Karst Features
Depression
Polder
Desert, Dunes
Forest, Woods
Heath, Steppe
Oasis
Cape, Point
Coast, Beach
Cliff
Peninsula
Isthmus
Sandbank
Island
Atoll
Rock, Reef
Islands, Archipelago
Rocks, Reefs
Coral Reef
Well, Spring
Geyser
River, Stream
Waterfall Rapids
River Mouth, Estuary
Lake
Salt Lake
Intermittent Lake
Reservoir
Swamp, Pond
Canal
Glacier
Ice Shelf, Pack Ice
Ocean
Sea
Gulf, Bay
Strait, Fjord
Lagoon
Bank
Seamount
Tablemount
Ridge
Shelf
Basin
Escarpment, Sea Scarp
Fracture
Trench, Abyss
National Park, Reserve
Point of Interest
Recreation Site
Cave, Cavern
Historic Site
Ruins
Wall, Walls
Temple
Church, Abbey
Scientific Station
Airport
Port
Lighthouse
Mine
Tunnel
Dam, Bridge

Hoima 36 Fb 1.26N 31.21 E
Hoisington 45 Gg 38.31N 98.47W
Hoj, Vozvyšennost- 17 Ob 68.50N 71.30 E
Højer 8 Cj 54.58N 8.43 E
Hojniki 19 Ce 51.54N 29.56 E
Hōjō 28 Lh 33.58N 132.46 E
Hökensås 8 Ff 58.11N 14.08 E
Hokianga Harbour 62 Ea 35.30S 173.20 E
Hokitika 58 Ii 42.43S 170.58 E
Hok-Kai=Okhotsk, Sea of- (EN) 21 Qd 53.00N 150.00 E
Hokkaidō 21 Qe 43.00N 143.00 E
Hokkaidō Ken [2] 28 Qc 43.00N 143.00 E
Hokksund 7 Bg 59.47N 9.59 E
Hokmābād 24 Qd 36.37N 57.36 E
Hokota 29 Gc 36.10N 140.30 E
Hol 8 Cd 60.36N 8.22 E
Holap 64d Ba 7.39N 151.54 E
Holbæk 8 Di 55.43N 11.43 E
Holbeach 12 Cb 52.48N 0.01 E
Holbeach Marsh 12 Cb 52.52N 0.02 E
Holbox, Isla- 48 Pg 21.33N 87.15W
Holbrook 43 Ee 34.54N 110.10W
Holdenville 45 Hi 35.05N 96.24W
Holderness 9 Mh 53.47N 0.10W
Holdrege 45 Gf 40.26N 99.22W
Hold With Hope 41 Jd 73.40N 21.45W
Hole in the Wall 44 Im 25.51N 77.12W
Hølen 8 De 59.32N 10.45 E
Holešov 10 Ng 49.20N 17.33 E
Holetown 51q Ab 13.11N 59.39W
Holguín 39 Lg 20.53N 76.15W
Holguín [3] 49 Jc 20.40N 75.50W
Hol Hol 35 Gc 11.20N 42.50 E
Holitna 40 Hd 61.40N 157.12W
Höljes 7 Cf 60.54N 12.36 E
Hollabrunn 14 Kb 48.33N 16.05 E
Holland 44 Dd 42.47N 86.07W
Holland [Eng.-U.K.] 12 Bb 52.52N 0.10W
Holland [Neth.] 5 Ge 52.20N 4.45 E
Hollandale 45 Kj 33.10N 90.58W
Hollandsbird Island 37 Ad 24.45S 14.34 E
Hollands Diep 12 Gc 51.40N 4.30 E
Hollesley Bay 12 Db 52.04N 1.33 E
Hollick-Kenyon Plateau 66 Pf 79.00S 97.00W
Hollis 45 Gi 34.41N 99.55W
Hollister [Ca.-U.S.] 46 Eh 36.51N 121.24W
Hollister [Id.-U.S.] 46 He 42.23N 114.35W
Hollola 8 Kc 61.03N 25.26 E
Höllviksnäs 8 Ei 55.25N 12.57 E
Holly Springs 45 Li 34.41N 89.26W
Hollywood 43 Kf 26.00N 80.09W
Holm 7 Hh 57.09N 31.12 E
Holma 34 Hd 9.54N 13.03 E
Holman Island 42 Fb 70.40N 117.35W
Hólmavík 7a Bb 65.43N 21.41W
Holmes Reefs 57 Ff 16.30S 148.00 E
Holmestrand 8 De 59.29N 10.18 E
Holm Land 41 Kb 80.16N 18.20W
Holms 41 Gd 74.30N 57.00W
Holmsjö 8 Fh 56.25N 15.32 E
Holmsjön [Swe.] 7 De 62.25N 15.20 E
Holmsjön [Swe.] 8 Gb 62.40N 16.35 E
Holmsk 20 Jg 47.00N 142.03 E
Holmski 16 Kg 44.50N 38.24 E
Holmsland Klit 8 Ch 56.00N 8.10 E
Holmsund 7 Ee 63.42N 20.21 E
Holmsveden 8 Gc 61.07N 16.43 E
Holmudden 8 Hg 57.57N 19.21 E
Holod 15 Fc 46.47N 22.08 E
Holohit, Punta- 48 Og 21.37N 88.08W
Holothuria Banks (EN) 59 Fb 13.25S 126.00 E
Holsnøy 8 Ad 60.35N 5.05 E
Holstebro 7 Bh 56.21N 8.38 E
Holsted 8 Ci 55.30N 8.55 E
Holstein 45 Ie 42.29N 95.33W
Holsteinsborg/ Sisimiut 67 Nc 67.05N 53.45W
Holt 12 Db 52.54N 1.05 E
Holten 12 Ib 52.17N 6.27 E
Holton 45 Ig 39.28N 95.44W
Holtoson 20 Ff 50.18N 103.20 E
Holtyn-Daba 27 Ib 47.40N 107.20 E
Holwerd, Westdongeradeel- 12 Ha 53.22N 5.54 E
Holy Cross 40 Hd 62.12N 159.47W
Holyhead 9 Ih 53.20N 4.38W
Holy Island [Eng.-U.K.] 9 Lf 55.41N 1.48W
Holy Island [Wales-U.K.] 9 Ih 53.18N 4.37W
Holyoke [Co.-U.S.] 45 Ef 40.35N 102.18W
Holyoke [Ma.-U.S.] 44 Kd 42.12N 72.37W
Holýšov 10 Jg 49.36N 13.07 E
Homa Bay 36 Fc 0.31S 34.27 E
Homalin 25 Id 24.52N 94.55 E
Homathko River 46 Ca 50.55N 124.50W
Homberg (Ohm) 12 Kd 50.44N 8.59 E
Hombori 34 Eb 15.17N 1.42W
Hombre Muerto, Salar del- 56 Gc 25.23S 67.06W
Homburg 10 Dg 49.19N 7.20 E
Home Bay 38 Mc 68.45N 67.10W
Homecourt 12 He 49.14N 5.59 E
Home Hill 59 Jc 19.40S 147.25 E
Homer [Ak.-U.S.] 39 Dd 59.39N 151.33W
Homer [La.-U.S.] 45 Jj 32.48N 93.04W
Homert 12 Kc 51.16N 8.06 E
Homerville 44 Fj 31.02N 82.45W
Homestead 44 Gm 25.29N 80.29W
Homewood 44 Di 33.29N 86.48W
Hommelstø 7 Cd 65.25N 12.30 E
Hommersåk 8 Af 58.55N 5.50 E
Homoine 37 Fd 23.52S 35.08 E
Homoljske Planina 15 Ee 44.20N 21.45 E
Homonhon 26 Id 10.44N 125.43 E
Homosassa 44 Fk 28.47N 82.37W
Homs (EN)=Ḩimş 22 Ff 34.44N 36.43 E
Honan (EN)=Henan Sheng (Ho-nan Sheng) [2] 27 Je 34.00N 114.00 E
Honan (EN)=Ho-nan Sheng→Henan Sheng [2] 27 Je 34.00N 114.00 E
Ho-nan Sheng→Henan Sheng=Honan (EN) [2] 27 Je 34.00N 114.00 E
Honaz 15 Ml 37.45N 29.17 E
Honaz Daği 15 Ml 37.41N 29.18 E
Honbetsu 28 Qc 43.18N 143.33 E
Honda 54 Db 5.13N 74.45W
Honda, Bahía- 49 Lg 12.21N 71.47W
Hondeklipbaai 37 Bf 30.20S 17.18 E
Hòn Diên, Núi- 25 Lf 11.33N 108.38 E
Hondo 47 Ge 18.29N 88.19W
Hondo [Jap.] 28 Kh 32.27N 130.12 E
Hondo [N.M.-U.S.] 45 Dj 33.23N 105.16W
Hondo [Tx.-U.S.] 45 Gl 29.21N 99.09W
Hondo, Río- 45 Dj 33.22N 104.24W
Hondschoote 12 Ed 50.59N 2.35 E
Hondsrug 11 Mb 52.50N 6.50 E
Honduras [1] 39 Kh 15.00N 86.30W
Honduras, Cabo de- 49 De 16.01N 86.01W
Honduras, Golfo de-= Honduras, Gulf of- (EN) 38 Kh 16.10N 87.50W
Honduras, Gulf of- 38 Kh 16.10N 87.50W
Honduras, Gulf of- (EN)= Honduras, Golfo de- 38 Kh 16.10N 87.50W
Hønefoss 7 Cf 60.10N 10.18 E
Honey Lake 46 Ef 40.16N 120.19W
Honfleur 12 Ge 49.25N 0.14 E
Hông, Sông-=Red River (EN) 21 Mg 20.17N 106.34 E
Hong'an (Huang'an) 28 Ci 31.17N 114.37 E
Hongch'ŏn 28 If 37.41N 127.52 E
Hong-Do 28 Hg 34.41N 125.13 E
Hong He 28 Ch 32.24N 115.32 E
Honghton Lake 44 Ec 44.22N 84.43W
Hong Hu 27 Je 30.00N 113.25 E
Honghu (Xindi) 28 Bj 29.50N 113.28 E
Honghui 27 Id 36.46N 105.05 E
Hong Kong/Xianggang [5] 22 Ng 22.15N 114.10 E
Hongliuyuan 27 Gc 41.02N 95.24 E
Hongluoxian 28 Fd 41.01N 120.52 E
Hongning → Wulian 28 Eg 35.45N 119.13 E
Hongor 28 Bb 45.48N 112.45 E
Hongqizhen 27 Ih 18.48N 109.30 E
Hongshui He 21 Mg 23.47N 109.33 E
Hongsŏng 28 If 36.36N 126.40 E
Hongtong 28 Af 36.15N 111.41 E
Hongū 29 De 33.50N 135.46 E
Hongwedo, Détroit d'- 42 Lg 49.30N 65.00W
Hongwansi → Sunan 27 Gd 38.59N 99.25 E
Hongwŏn 28 Id 40.02N 127.58 E
Hongyuan (Hurama) 27 He 32.45N 102.38 E
Hongze (Gaoliangjian) 27 Ke 33.10N 119.58 E
Hongze Hu 28 Eh 33.20N 118.40 E
Honiara 58 Ge 9.27S 159.57 E
Honikulu, Passe- 64h Ac 13.23S 176.11W
Honiton 9 Jk 50.48N 3.13W
Honjō 28 Pe 39.23N 140.03 E
Honkajoki 8 Jb 61.59N 22.16 E
Hon-kawane 29 Fd 35.07N 138.06 E
Honningsvåg 7 Ga 70.59N 26.01 E
Hönö 8 Dg 57.42N 11.39 E
Honokaa 65a Fc 20.05N 155.28W
Honokohau 65a Eb 21.01N 156.37W
Honolulu 58 Lb 21.19N 157.52W
Honomu 65a Fd 19.52N 155.07W
Honrubia 13 Je 39.37N 2.16W
Honshū 21 Pf 36.00N 136.00 E
Hontenisse 12 Gc 51.23N 4.00 E
Hontenisse-Kloosterzande 12 Gc 51.23N 4.00 E
Honuapo Bay 65a Fd 19.05N 155.33W
Honuu 20 Jc 66.27N 143.06 E
Honyō 29 Fc 36.14N 139.10 E
Hood 42 Gc 67.25N 108.53W
Hood, Mount- 38 Ge 45.23N 121.41W
Hood Point 59 Df 34.23S 119.34 E
Hood River 46 Ed 45.43N 121.31W
Hoogeveen 11 Mb 52.43N 6.29 E
Hoogezand-Sappemeer 12 Ia 53.09N 6.48 E
Hooglede 12 Fd 50.59N 3.05 E
Hoogstraten 12 Gc 51.24N 4.46 E
Hooker 45 Fh 36.52N 101.13W
Hooker, Cape- 66 Kf 70.38S 166.45 E
Hook Head/Rinn Dúain 9 Gi 52.07N 6.55W
Hook Island 59 Jc 20.10S 148.55 E
Hoolehua 65a Db 21.10N 157.05W
Hoonah 40 Le 58.07N 135.26W
Hooper, Cape- 42 Kc 68.24N 66.43W
Hooper Bay 40 Fd 61.31N 166.06W
Hoopeston 45 Mf 40.28N 87.40W
Höör 8 Ei 55.56N 13.32 E
Hoorn 11 Lb 52.38N 5.04 E
Hoornaar 12 Gc 51.53N 4.57 E
Hoover Dam 46 Hi 36.00N 114.27W
Hopa 24 Ib 41.25N 41.24 E
Hope [Ar.-U.S.] 45 Jj 33.40N 93.36W
Hope [Az.-U.S.] 46 Ij 33.44N 113.42W
Hope [B.C.-Can.] 46 Eb 49.23N 121.26W
Hope, Ben- 9 Ic 58.24N 4.36W
Hope, Lake- 59 Ef 32.50S 121.40 E
Hope, Point- 38 Cc 68.21N 166.50W
Hopedale 42 Le 55.50N 60.10W
Hopefield 37 Bf 33.04S 18.21 E
Hopeh (EN)=Hebei Sheng (Ho-pei Sheng) [2] 27 Kd 39.00N 116.00 E
Hopeh (EN)=Ho-pei Sheng→Hebei Sheng [2] 27 Kd 39.00N 116.00 E
Hopeh (EN)=Hu-pei Sheng→Hubei Sheng [2] 27 Je 31.00N 112.00 E
Ho-pei Sheng→Hebei Sheng =Hopeh (EN) [2] 27 Kd 39.00N 116.00 E
Hopelchén 48 Oh 19.46N 89.51W
Hopen 41 Oc 76.35N 25.10 E
Hopër 5 Kf 49.36N 42.19 E
Hopes Advance, Cap - 42 Kd 61.05N 69.33W
Hopetoun [Austl.] 59 Ig 35.44S 142.22 E
Hopetoun [Austl.] 58 Dh 33.57S 120.07 E
Hopetown 37 Ce 29.34S 24.03 E
Hopewell 44 Ig 37.17N 77.19W
Hopewell Islands 42 Je 58.20N 78.10W
Hopin 25 Jd 24.59N 96.31 E
Hopkins, Lake- 59 Fd 24.15S 128.50 E
Hopkinsville 43 Jd 36.52N 87.29W
Hopsten 12 Jb 52.23N 7.37 E
Hoptrup 8 Ci 55.11N 9.28 E
Hoquiam 43 Cb 46.59N 123.53W
Hor 20 Ig 47.48N 134.43 E
Hor 20 Ig 47.55N 135.01 E
Hōrai 29 Ed 34.55N 137.34 E
Hōrai-San 29 Dd 35.13N 135.53 E
Horasan 24 Jb 40.03N 42.11 E
Horaždovice 10 Jg 49.20N 13.42 E
Horb am Neckar 10 Eh 48.26N 8.41 E
Horconcitos 49 Fi 8.19N 82.10W
Hordaland [2] 7 Bf 60.15N 6.30 E
Hordogoj 20 Gd 62.32N 115.38 E
Horezmskaja Oblast [3] 19 Gg 41.30N 60.40 E
Horfors 7 Df 60.33N 16.17 E
Horgen 14 Cc 47.15N 8.36 E
Horgoš 15 Cc 46.09N 19.58 E
Horgos 19 Ig 44.10N 80.20 E
Hořice 10 Lf 50.22N 15.38 E
Horinger 28 Ad 40.24N 111.46 E
Horizon Tablemount (EN) 57 Kc 19.40N 168.30W
Horizontina 55 Eh 27.37S 54.19W
Horley 12 Bc 51.10N 0.10W
Horlick Mountains 66 Og 85.23S 121.00W
Hormigas 48 Gc 29.12N 105.45W
Hormoz [Iran] 24 Pi 27.32N 54.57 E
Hormoz [Iran] 23 Id 27.06N 56.28 E
Hormoz, Kūh-e- 23 Id 27.27N 55.10 E
Hormoz, Tangeh-ye-= Hormuz, Strait of- (EN) 21 Hg 26.34N 56.15 E
Hormozgān [3] 23 Id 27.30N 56.00 E
Hormūd-e Bāgh 24 Pi 27.30N 54.18 E
Hormuz, Strait of- (EN)= Hormoz, Tangeh-ye- 21 Hg 26.34N 56.15 E
Horn 42 Fd 61.30N 118.00W
Horn 5 Db 66.28N 22.30W
Horn [Aus.] 14 Jb 48.39N 15.39 E
Horn [Swe.] 8 Fg 57.54N 15.50 E
Horn, Cape- (EN)=Hornos, Cabo de- 52 Jk 55.59N 67.16W
Hornád 10 Qh 48.00N 20.58 E
Hornaday 42 Fc 69.22N 123.56W
Hornavan 7 Dc 66.14N 17.30 E
Hornbach 12 Je 49.12N 7.22 E
Horn-Bad Meinberg 12 Kc 51.54N 8.57 E
Hornby Bay 42 Fc 66.35N 117.50W
Horncastle 9 Mh 53.13N 0.07W
Horndal 8 Gd 60.18N 16.25 E
Horndean 12 Bd 50.55N 0.59W
Hörnefors 7 Ee 63.38N 19.54 E
Hornell 44 Id 42.19N 77.39W
Hornepayne 42 Jg 49.13N 84.47W
Hornindalsvatn 8 Bc 61.55N 6.25 E
Hornisgrinde 10 Eh 48.36N 8.12 E
Horn Islands (EN)=Horne, Iles de- 57 Jf 14.19S 178.05W
Hörnli 14 Cc 47.23N 8.56 E
Hornomoravský úval 10 Ng 49.25N 17.20 E
Hornos, Cabo de-=Horn, Cape- (EN) 52 Jk 55.59S 67.16W
Hornoy-le-Bourg 12 De 49.51N 1.54 E
Horn Plateau 42 Fd 62.10N 119.30W
Hornsea 9 Mh 53.55N 0.10W
Hornslandet 8 Gc 61.40N 17.30 E
Horns Rev 8 Bi 55.30N 8.00 E
Horns Rev 8 Bi 55.30N 7.45 E
Hornsund 41 Nc 76.58N 15.28 E
Hornsundtind 41 Nc 76.55N 16.10 E
Horog 22 Jf 37.31N 71.33 E
Horokanai 29a Ca 44.02N 142.09 E
Horol 16 He 49.29N 33.49 E
Horol [R.S.F.S.R.] 28 Lb 44.30N 132.03 E
Horol [Ukr.-U.S.S.R.] 16 He 49.47N 33.16 E
Horonobe 28 Pb 45.00N 141.51 E
Hořovice 10 Jg 49.50N 13.54 E
Horqin Youyi Qianqi (Ulan Hot) 22 Oe 46.04N 122.00 E
Horqin Youyi Zhongqi (Bayan Huxu) 27 Lb 45.04N 121.27 E
Horqin Zuoyi Houqi (Ganjig) 27 Lc 42.57N 122.14 E
Horqin Zuoyi Zhongqi (Baokang) 27 Lc 44.06N 123.19 E
Horqueta 56 Ib 23.24S 56.53W
Horred 8 Eg 57.21N 12.28 E
Horse Creek [Co.-U.S.] 45 Eg 38.05N 103.19W
Horse Creek [U.S.] 46 Nf 41.57N 103.58W
Horsehead Lake 45 Gc 47.02N 99.47W
Horsens 7 Bi 55.52N 9.52 E
Horsham [Austl.] 58 Fh 36.43S 142.13 E
Horsham [Eng.-U.K.] 9 Mj 51.04N 0.21W
Hørsholm 8 Ei 55.53N 12.30 E
Horšovský Týn 10 Ig 49.32N 12.57 E
Horst 12 Gd 50.56N 4.47 E
Horst 12 Ic 51.28N 6.03 E
Hörstel 12 Jb 52.19N 7.35 E
Horstmar 12 Jb 52.05N 7.19 E
Horsunlu 15 Ll 37.55N 28.36 E
Horta 38 Bb 38.32N 28.28W
Horta [3] 32 Bb 38.35N 28.40W
Horten 8 De 59.25N 10.30 E
Horton 42 Ec 70.01N 126.42W
Hörvik 8 Fh 56.03N 14.46 E
Ḫorvot 'Avedat 24 Fg 30.48N 34.46 E
Ḫorvot Meẓada 24 Fg 31.19N 35.21 E
Horwood Lake 44 Fa 48.03N 82.20W
Hosaina 35 Fd 7.33N 37.52 E
Hose Mountains 26 Ff 2.00N 114.10 E
Hosenofu 33 De 23.34N 21.15 E
Hoseynābād [Iran] 24 Ne 34.30N 50.59 E
Hoseynābād [Iran] 24 Le 35.33N 47.08 E
Hoseynīyeh 24 Mg 32.42N 48.14 E
Hoshāb 25 Cc 26.01N 63.56 E
Hosingen 12 Id 50.01N 6.05 E
Hoskins 60 Ei 5.30S 150.32 E
Hospet 25 Fe 15.16N 76.24 E
Hospital, Cuchilla del- 55 Ej 31.40S 54.53W
Hospitalet 13 Oc 41.22N 2.08 E
Hospitalet del Infante/ L'Hospitalet de l'Infant 13 Md 40.59N 0.56 E
Hoste, Isla- 52 Jk 55.15S 69.00W
Hot 25 Je 18.06N 98.35 E
Hotagen 7 De 63.53N 14.29 E
Hotaka 29 Ec 36.20N 137.53 E
Hotan 22 Jf 37.07N 79.55 E
Hotan He 21 Ke 40.30N 80.48 E
Hotazel 37 Ce 27.15S 23.00 E
Hotin 16 Ee 48.29N 26.29 E
Hoting 7 Dd 64.07N 16.10 E
Hotkovo 7 Ih 56.18N 38.00 E
Hotont 27 Hb 47.23N 102.30 E
Hot Springs 43 Gc 43.26N 103.29W
Hot Springs→Truth or Consequences 43 Fe 33.08N 107.15W
Hot Springs National Park 39 Jf 34.30N 93.03W
Hot Springs Peak 46 Gf 41.22N 117.26W
Hotspur Seamount (EN) 54 Kg 18.00S 36.00W
Hottah Lake 42 Fc 65.05N 118.36W
Hottentot Bay 37 Ae 26.07S 14.57 E
Hotton 12 Hd 50.16N 5.27 E
Hottstedt 10 He 51.39N 11.30 E
Houaïlou 61 Cd 21.17S 165.38 E
Houat, Ile de- 11 Dg 47.24N 2.58W
Houdan 11 Hf 48.47N 1.36 E
Houeillès 11 Gj 44.12N 0.02 E
Houffalize 12 Hd 50.08N 5.47 E
Houghton 43 Jb 47.06N 88.34W
Houillères, Canal des- 12 If 48.42N 6.55 E
Houji → Liangshan 28 Dg 35.48N 116.07 E
Houlgate 12 Be 49.18N 0.04W
Houlton 43 Nb 46.08N 67.51W
Houma [China] 27 Jd 35.36N 111.23 E
Houma [La.-U.S.] 43 If 29.36N 90.43W
Houndé 34 Ec 11.30N 3.31W
Hourtin, Étang d'- 11 Ei 45.10N 1.06W
House Range 46 Ig 39.30N 113.15W
Houston [Mo.-U.S.] 45 Kh 37.22N 91.58W
Houston [Tx.-U.S.] 39 Jg 29.46N 95.22W
Houthalen-Helchteren 12 Hc 51.02N 5.22 E
Houthulst 12 Ed 50.59N 2.57 E
Houthulst-Merkem 12 Ed 50.57N 2.51 E
Houtman Abrolhos 59 Ce 28.40S 113.50 E
Houtskär/Houtskari 8 Id 60.15N 21.20 E
Houtskari/Houtskär 8 Id 60.15N 21.20 E
Houyet 12 Hd 50.11N 5.01 E
Houyet-Celles 12 Hd 50.19N 5.01 E
Hov 8 Di 55.55N 10.16 E
Hova 8 Ff 58.52N 14.13 E
Hovden 8 Ac 61.40N 4.50 E
Hovden 8 Be 59.32N 7.21 E
Hove 9 Mk 50.49N 0.10W
Hovgaard 41 Kc 80.00N 18.45W
Hovmantorp 8 Fh 56.47N 15.08 E
Hovu-Aksy 20 Ef 51.01N 93.43 E
Howa 35 Db 17.30N 27.08 E
Howar 30 Jg 17.30N 27.08 E
Howard 45 Hd 44.01N 97.32W
Howe, Cape- 57 Fh 37.31S 149.59 E
Howell 44 Fd 42.36N 83.55W
Howick [N.Z.] 62 Fb 36.54S 174.56 E
Howick [S.Afr.] 37 Ee 29.28S 30.14 E
Howland 44 Mc 45.14N 68.40W
Howland Island 57 Jd 0.48N 176.38W
Howrah → Hāora 22 Kg 22.35N 88.20 E
Howth 9 Gh 53.23N 6.04W
Howz Soltān 24 Ne 35.06N 51.06 E
Hoxie 45 Fg 39.21N 100.26W
Höxter 10 Fe 51.46N 9.23 E
Hoxud 27 Ec 42.16N 86.51 E
Hoy 9 Jc 58.52N 3.18W
Hoya 12 Lb 52.48N 9.09 E
Høyanger 7 Bf 61.13N 6.05 E
Hoyerswerda/Wojerecy 10 Ke 51.26N 14.15 E
Hoyos 13 Fd 40.10N 6.43W
Hōyo-Shotō 29 Ce 33.50N 132.30 E
Hoytiäinen 7 Ge 62.48N 29.39 E
Hozat 24 Hc 39.07N 39.14 E
Hpunhpu 25 Jc 26.42N 97.17 E
Hradec Králové 10 Lf 50.13N 15.50 E
Hradiště 10 Jf 50.13N 13.08 E
Hrami 16 Ni 41.20N 45.07 E
Hrastnik 14 Jd 46.09N 15.06 E
Hřebeny 10 Kg 49.50N 14.10 E
Hristinovka 16 Fe 48.53N 29.56 E
Hroma 20 Jb 71.30N 144.49 E
Hromtau 19 Fe 50.18N 58.35 E
Hron 10 Oi 47.49N 18.45 E
Hrubieszów 10 Tf 50.49N 23.55 E
Hrubý-Jeseník 10 Nf 50.05N 17.10 E
Hrustalny 20 Ih 44.24N 135.06 E
Hrvatska = Croatia (EN) [2] 14 Jf 45.00N 15.30 E
Hrvatska = Croatia (EN) 14 Je 45.00N 15.30 E
Hrvatska = Croatia (EN) 5 Hf 45.00N 15.30 E
Ḫrvot Shivta 24 Fg 30.53N 34.38 E
Hsin-chiang-wei-wu-erh Tzu-chih-ch'ü→Xinjiang Uygur Zizhiqu=Sinkiang (EN) [2] 27 Ec 42.00N 86.00 E
Hsinchu 27 Lg 24.48N 120.58 E
Hsinying 27 Lg 23.25N 120.20 E
Hsipaw 25 Jd 22.37N 97.18 E
Hsi-tsang Tzu-chih-ch'ü→Xizang Zizhiqu [2] 27 Ee 32.00N 90.00 E
Hsuphāng 25 Jd 20.18N 98.42 E
Huab 37 Ad 20.49S 13.24 E
Huabei Pingyuan 21 Nf 37.00N 117.00 E
Huachacalla 54 Eg 18.45S 68.17W
Huachinera 48 Eb 30.15N 108.50W
Huacho 54 Cf 11.07S 77.37W
Huaco 56 Gd 30.09S 68.31W
Huacrachuco 54 Ce 8.39S 77.05W
Huade 27 Jc 41.50N 114.00 E
Huadian 27 Mc 42.59N 126.38 E
Hua Hin 25 Jf 12.34N 99.58 E
Huahine, Iles- 57 Lf 16.45S 151.00W
Huahine Iti 65e Eb 16.45S 151.00W
Huahine Nui 65e Eb 16.43S 151.00W
Huahuapán 48 Ge 24.31N 105.57W
Huai'an 28 Eh 33.30N 119.08 E
Huai'an (Chaigoubu) 28 Cd 40.40N 114.25 E
Huaibei 27 Ke 33.56N 116.48 E
Huaibin (Wulongji) 28 Ci 32.27N 115.23 E
Huaide (Gongzhuling) 27 Lc 43.30N 124.52 E
Huaidian → Shenqiu 27 Ke 33.27N 115.05 E
Huai He 21 Nf 33.12N 118.33 E
Huaiji 27 Jg 23.57N 112.12 E
Huailai (Shacheng) 27 Kc 40.29N 115.30 E
Huainan 22 Nf 32.32N 116.59 E
Huaining (Shipai) 28 Di 30.25N 116.39 E
Huairen 27 Jd 39.50N 113.07 E
Huairou 28 Dd 40.20N 116.37 E
Huaiyang 28 Ch 33.44N 114.52 E
Huaiyin (Wangying) 28 Eh 33.35N 119.02 E
Huaiyuan 28 Dh 32.58N 117.10 E
Huajuapan de León 47 Ee 17.48N 97.46W
Hualalai 65a Fd 19.41N 155.52W
Hualapai Mountains 46 Ii 34.40N 113.45W
Hualien 27 Lg 23.58N 121.36 E
Huallaga, Río- 52 If 5.07S 75.30W
Huallanca 54 Ce 8.49S 77.52W
Huamachuco 54 Ce 7.48S 78.04W
Huamahuaca 56 Gb 23.13S 65.23W
Huambo [3] 36 Ce 12.30S 15.40 E
Huambo 31 Ij 12.47S 15.43 E
Huanan 27 Nb 46.14N 130.33 E
Huancabamba [Peru] 54 Cf 10.21S 75.32W
Huancabamba [Peru] 54 Ce 5.14S 79.28W
Huancané 54 Eg 15.12S 69.46W
Huancapi 54 Df 13.41S 74.04W
Huancavelica [2] 54 Df 13.00S 75.00W
Huancavelica 53 Ig 12.46S 75.02W
Huancayo 53 Ig 12.04S 75.14W
Huanchaca, Serranía- 55 Bb 14.30S 60.39W
Huang'an→Hong'an 28 Ci 31.17N 114.37 E
Huangcaoba→Xingyi 27 Hf 25.03N 104.55 E
Huangchuan 27 Ke 32.00N 115.02 E
Huanggang 28 Ci 30.27N 114.53 E
Huanggangliang 27 Kc 43.33N 117.32 E
Huanggang Shan 27 Kf 27.50N 117.47 E
Huanggi Hai 28 Bd 40.51N 113.17 E
Huang Hai=Yellow Sea (EN) 21 Of 36.00N 124.00 E
Huang He=Yellow River (EN) 21 Nf 37.32N 118.19 E
Huanghe Kou 28 Ef 37.54N 118.48 E
Huangheyan→Madoi 22 Lf 35.00N 98.56 E
Huanghua 28 De 38.23N 117.21 E
Huanghuashi 28 Bj 28.14N 113.11 E
Huangliu 27 Ih 18.41N 108.46 E
Huangmao Jian 27 Kf 27.55N 119.11 E
Huangmei 28 Ci 30.05N 115.56 E
Huangnihe 28 Ic 43.33N 127.28 E
Huangpi 28 Ci 30.53N 114.22 E
Huangpu 27 Jg 23.05N 113.25 E
Huang Shan 27 Ke 30.10N 118.10 E
Huangshi 22 Nf 30.12N 115.00 E
Huang Shui 27 Hd 36.05N 103.20 E
Huangtu Gaoyuan 21 Mf 37.00N 108.00 E
Huanguelén 55 Bm 37.02S 61.57W
Huangxian 27 Ld 37.32N 120.30 E
Huangyan 27 Lf 28.39N 121.17 E
Huangyuan 27 Hd 36.40N 101.12 E
Huangzhai → Yangqu 28 Be 38.05N 112.37 E
Huangzhong 27 Hd 36.30N 101.30 E
Huanren 27 Mc 41.16N 125.22 E
Huan Shui 28 Ci 30.40N 114.21 E
Huanta 54 Df 12.56S 74.15W
Huantai (Suozhen) 28 Ef 36.57N 118.05 E
Huánuco [2] 54 Ce 9.30S 75.50W
Huánuco 53 If 9.55S 76.14W
Huanxian 27 Id 36.36N 107.06 E
Huaráz 53 If 9.32S 77.32W
Huarmey 54 Cf 10.04S 78.10W
Huarong 28 Bj 29.31N 112.33 E
Huascarán, Nevado- 52 If 9.07S 77.37W
Hua Shan 27 Je 34.27N 110.05 E
Huatabampo 47 Cc 26.50N 109.38W
Huatong 28 Fd 40.03N 121.56 E
Huatusco de Chiquellar 48 Kh 19.09N 96.57W
Huauchinango 48 Jg 20.11N 98.03W
Huautla de Jiménez 48 Kh 18.08N 96.51W
Huaxian (Daokou) 28 Cg 35.33N 114.30 E
Huayllay 54 Cf 11.01S 76.21W
Huaynamota, Río- 48 Gg 21.51N 104.42W
Huaytara 54 Cf 13.36S 75.22W
Hubbard Creek Lake 45 Gj 32.45N 99.00W
Hubbard Lake 44 Fc 44.49N 83.34W
Hubei Sheng (Hu-pei Sheng) = Hupeh (EN) [2] 27 Je 31.00N 112.00 E
Hubli-Dhārwār 22 Jh 15.21N 75.10 E
Hubsugul Nur (Chövsgöl nuur) 21 Md 51.00N 100.30 E
Hückelhoven 12 Ic 51.03N 6.13 E
Hückeswagen 12 Jc 51.09N 7.21 E
Hucknall 9 Lh 53.02N 1.11W
Hucqueliers 12 Dd 55.03N 1.54 E
Huczwa 10 Tf 50.49N 23.59 E
Hudat [Abz.-U.S.S.R.] 16 Pi 41.34N 48.43 E
Hudat [Eth.] 35 Fe 4.45N 39.27 E
Huddersfield 9 Lh 53.39N 1.47W
Huddinge 8 Ge 59.14N 17.59 E
Ḥuddun 35 Hd 9.08N 47.32 E
Huddur Hadama 35 Ge 4.07N 43.55 E

Index Symbols

[1] Independent Nation
[2] State, Region
[3] District, County
[4] Municipality
[5] Colony, Dependency
Continent
Physical Region
Historical or Cultural Region
Mount, Mountain
Volcano
Hill
Mountains, Mountain Range
Hills, Escarpment
Plateau, Upland
Pass, Gap
Plain, Lowland
Delta
Salt Flat
Valley, Canyon
Crater, Cave
Karst Features
Depression
Polder
Desert, Dunes
Forest, Woods
Heath, Steppe
Oasis
Cape, Point
Coast, Beach
Cliff
Peninsula
Isthmus
Sandbank
Island
Atoll
Rock, Reef
Islands, Archipelago
Rocks, Reefs
Coral Reef
Well, Spring
Geyser
River, Stream
Waterfall Rapids
River Mouth, Estuary
Lake
Salt Lake
Intermittent Lake
Reservoir
Swamp, Pond
Canal
Glacier
Ice Shelf, Pack Ice
Ocean
Sea
Gulf, Bay
Strait, Fjord
Lagoon
Bank
Seamount
Tablemount
Ridge
Shelf
Basin
Escarpment, Sea Scarp
Fracture
Trench, Abyss
National Park, Reserve
Point of Interest
Recreation Site
Cave, Cavern
Historic Site
Ruins
Wall, Walls
Church, Abbey
Temple
Scientific Station
Airport
Port
Lighthouse
Mine
Tunnel
Dam, Bridge

Hude (Oldenburg) 12 Ka 53.07N 8.28 E
Huder 27 Lb 49.59N 121.30 E
Hudiksvall 6 Hc 61.44N 17.07 E
Hudson 38 Le 40.42N 74.02W
Hudson [Fl.-U.S.] 44 Fk 28.22N 82.42W
Hudson [N.Y.-U.S.] 44 Kd 42.15N 73.47W
Hudson, Lake- 45 Ih 36.20N 95.05W
Hudson Bay 42 Hf 52.52N 102.23W
Hudson Bay 38 Kd 60.00N 86.00W
Hudson Canyon (EN) 44 Kf 39.27N 72.12W
Hudson Hope 42 Fe 56.02N 121.55W
Hudson Land 41 Jd 73.45N 22.30W
Hudson Mountains 66 Pf 74.32S 99.20W
Hudson Strait 38 Lc 62.30N 72.00W
Hudžirt 27 Hb 47.05N 102.45 E
Hue 22 Mh 16.28N 107.36 E
Huebra 13 Fc 41.02N 6.48W
Huechucuicui, Punta- 56 Ff 41.47S 74.02W
Hueco Montains 45 Dj 32.05N 105.55W
Huedin 15 Gc 46.52N 23.03 E
Huehuetenango [3] 49 Bf 15.40N 91.35W
Huehuetenango 47 Fe 15.20N 91.28W
Huejutla de Reyes 48 Jg 21.08N 98.25W
Huelgoat 11 Cf 48.22N 3.45W
Huelma 13 Ig 37.39N 3.27W
Huelva [3] 13 Fg 37.40N 7.00W
Huelva 6 Fh 37.16N 6.57W
Huelva, Ribera de- 13 Gg 37.27N 6.00W
Huércal Overa 13 Kg 37.23N 1.57W
Huerfano Mountain 45 Bh 36.30N 108.10W
Huertas, Cabo de- 13 Lf 38.21N 0.24W
Huerva 13 Lc 41.39N 0.52W
Huesca 13 Lb 42.08N 0.25W
Huesca [3] 13 Lb 42.10N 0.10W
Huéscar 13 Jg 37.49N 2.32W
Hueso, Sierra del- 48 Gb 30.15N 105.20W
Huesos, Arroyo de los- 55 Cm 36.30S 59.09W
Huetamo de Núñez 48 Ih 18.35N 100.53W
Huete 13 Jd 40.08N 2.41W
Ḩufrat an Naḩās 35 Cd 9.45N 24.19 E
Huftarøy 8 Ad 60.05N 5.15 E
Hugh Butler Lake 45 Ff 40.22N 100.42W
Hughenden 58 Fg 20.51S 144.12 E
Hughes 40 Ic 66.03N 154.16W
Hughes Range 46 Hb 49.55N 115.28W
Hugo 45 Ii 34.01N 95.31W
Huguan 28 Bf 36.05N 113.12 E
Huhur He 28 Fc 43.55N 120.47 E
Hui'an 27 Kf 25.07N 118.47 E
Huiarau Range 62 Gc 38.35S 177.10 E
Huib-Hochplato 37 Be 27.10S 16.50 E
Huichang 27 Kf 25.33N 115.45 E
Huicheng → Shexian 28 Ej 29.53N 118.27 E
Huicholes, Sierra de los- 48 Gf 22.00N 104.00W
Huich'ŏn 27 Mc 40.10N 126.17 E
Huifa He 28 Ic 43.06N 126.53 E
Hui He [China] 27 Kb 48.51N 119.12 E
Hui He [China] 28 Be 39.21N 112.37 E
Huiji He 28 Ch 33.53N 115.37 E
Huila [2] 54 Cc 2.30N 75.45W
Huila [3] 36 Ce 15.00S 15.00 E
Huila, Nevado del- 52 Ie 3.00N 76.00W
Huilai 27 Kg 23.05N 116.18 E
Huili 27 Hf 26.37N 102.19 E
Huimanguillo 48 Mi 17.51N 93.23W
Huimin 27 Kd 37.29N 117.30 E
Huinan (Chaoyang) 28 Ic 42.41N 126.03 E
Huisne 11 Gg 47.59N 0.11 E
Huissen 12 Hc 51.56N 5.55 E
Huiten Nur 27 Fd 35.30N 91.55 E
Huittinen 8 Jc 61.11N 22.42 E
Huivuilay, Isla de- 48 Dd 27.03N 110.01W
Huixian [China] 28 Bg 35.27N 113.47 E
Huixian [China] 27 Ie 33.46N 106.06 E
Huixtla 47 Fe 15.09N 92.28W
Huize 27 Hf 26.28N 103.18 E
Huizen 12 Hb 52.18N 5.16 E
Huizhou 27 Jg 23.02N 114.28 E
Hukou 28 Dj 29.44N 116.14 E
Hu Kou 27 Jd 36.09N 110.20 E
Hüksan-Chedo 27 Me 34.30N 125.20 E
Hukuntsi 37 Cd 23.59S 21.44 E
Hulan 27 Mb 46.03N 126.36 E
Hulan He 27 Mb 45.54N 126.42 E
Ḩulayfā' 23 Fd 26.00N 40.47 E
Hulett 46 Md 44.41N 104.36W
Hulga 17 Jd 64.15N 60.58 E
Hulin 27 Nb 45.52N 132.58 E
Hulin He 28 Hb 45.19N 124.06 E
Hull 42 Jg 45.26N 75.43W
Hull → Kingston-upon-Hull 6 Fe 53.45N 0.20W
Hull → Orona Atoll 57 Je 4.29S 172.10W
Hull Bay 66 Nf 74.55S 137.40W
Hull Glacier 66 Nf 75.05S 137.15W
Hull Mountain 46 Dg 39.31N 122.59W
Hüls, Krefeld- 12 Ic 51.22N 6.31 E
Hultsfred 7 Dh 57.29N 15.50 E
Huludao 27 Lc 40.44N 120.59 E
Hulun Nur 21 Ne 49.00N 117.30 E
Ḩulwān = Helwān (EN) 33 Fd 29.51N 31.20 E
Hulwāt, Qūr al- 24 Hh 28.49N 38.50 E
Huma [China] 27 Ma 51.44N 126.36 E
Huma [Ton.] 65b Bc 21.19S 174.56W
Humacao 49 Od 18.09N 65.50W
Huma He 27 Ma 51.42N 126.42 E
Humaitá [Braz.] 53 Jf 7.31S 63.02W
Humaitá [Par.] 56 Ic 27.03S 58.33W
Humansdorp 37 Cf 34.02S 24.46 E
Humbe 36 Bf 16.42S 14.54 E
Humber 5 Fe 53.40N 0.10W
Humberside [3] 9 Mh 53.55N 0.30W
Humbolat River 38 He 40.02N 118.31W
Humboldt 57 Cd 21.53S 166.25 E
Humboldt [Ia.-U.S.] 45 Ie 42.43N 94.13W
Humboldt [Nb.-U.S.] 45 If 40.10N 95.57W
Humboldt [Sask.-Can.] 42 Gf 52.12N 105.07W
Humboldt [Tn.-U.S.] 44 Ch 35.49N 88.55W
Humboldt Gletscher 41 Fc 79.40N 63.45W
Humboldt Range 46 Ff 40.15N 118.10W
Hume, Lake- 59 Jg 36.05S 147.05 E
Humenné 10 Rh 48.56N 21.55 E
Hummelfjell 8 Db 62.27N 11.17 E
Hümmling, Der- 10 Dd 52.52N 7.31 E
Humphreys Peak 38 Hf 35.20N 111.40W
Humppila 7 Ff 60.56N 23.22 E
Humuya, Rio- 49 Df 15.13N 87.57W
Hün 31 If 29.07N 15.56 E
Húnaflói 5 Db 65.50N 20.50W
Hunan Sheng (Hu-nan Sheng) [3] 27 Jf 28.00N 112.00 E
Hu-nan Sheng → Hunan Sheng [3] 27 Jf 28.00N 112.00 E
Hunchun 28 Kc 42.52N 130.21 E
Hundested 8 Di 55.58N 11.52 E
Hunedoara [2] 15 Fd 45.45N 22.52 E
Hünfeld 10 Ff 50.40N 9.46 E
Hünfelden 12 Kd 50.19N 8.11 E
Hunga Ha'apai 65b Ab 20.33S 175.24W
Hungary (EN) = Magyarország [1] 6 Hf 47.00N 20.00 E
Hunga Tonga 65b Ab 20.32S 175.23W
Hungen 12 Kd 50.28N 8.54 E
Hüngnam 27 Md 39.50N 127.38 E
Hungry Horse Reservoir 46 Ib 48.15N 113.50W
Hun He [China] 28 Be 39.47N 113.15 E
Hun He [China] 28 Gd 40.41N 122.12 E
Hunhedoara 15 Fd 45.45N 22.54 E
Hunish, Rubha- 9 Gd 57.43N 6.20W
Hun Jiang 28 Hd 40.52N 125.42 E
Hunjiang 27 Mc 41.55N 126.27 E
Hunneberg 8 Ef 58.20N 12.27 E
Hunnebostrand 8 Df 58.27N 11.18 E
Hunsrück 10 Cg 49.50N 6.40 E
Hunstanton 9 Ni 52.57N 0.30 E
Hunte 10 Ed 52.30N 8.19 E
Hunter, Ile- 57 Ig 22.24S 172.03 E
Hunter Island 59 Ih 40.30S 144.45 E
Hunter Ridge (EN) 57 Ig 21.30S 174.30 E
Hunter River 59 Kf 32.30S 151.42 E
Hunterville 62 Fc 39.56S 175.34 E
Huntingdon 9 Mi 52.30N 0.10W
Huntingdon [Eng.-U.K.] 9 Mi 52.20N 0.12W
Huntingdon [Pa.-U.S.] 44 He 40.31N 78.02W
Huntingdon [Que.-Can.] 44 Jc 45.05N 74.08W
Huntington [In.-U.S.] 44 Ee 40.53N 85.30W
Huntington [W.V.-U.S.] 43 Kd 38.24N 82.26W
Huntly [N.Z.] 62 Fb 37.33S 175.10 E
Huntly [Scot.-U.K.] 9 Kd 57.27N 2.47W
Huntsville [Al.-U.S.] 39 Kf 34.44N 86.35W
Huntsville [Ont.-Can.] 42 Jg 45.20N 79.13W
Huntsville [Tx.-U.S.] 43 He 30.43N 95.33W
Hunucmá 48 Og 21.01N 89.52W
Hünxe 12 Ic 51.39N 6.47 E
Hunyani 37 Ec 15.37S 30.39 E
Hunyuan 27 Jd 39.38N 113.44 E
Hunza → Baltit 25 Ea 36.20N 74.40 E
Hunze 11 Ma 53.13N 6.40 E
Huocheng (Shuiding) 27 Dc 44.03N 80.49 E
Huojia 28 Bg 35.16N 113.39 E
Huolongmen 27 Mb 49.49N 125.49 E
Huolu 28 Ce 38.05N 114.18 E
Huon, Ile- 57 Hf 18.01S 162.57 E
Huon Gulf 59 Ja 7.10S 147.25 E
Huon Peninsula 60 Di 6.25S 147.30 E
Huonville 59 Jh 43.01S 147.02 E
Huoqin 28 Dh 32.21N 116.17 E
Huoshan 27 Ke 31.19N 116.20 E
Huo Shan [China] 27 Jd 37.00N 111.52 E
Huo Shan [China] 27 Ke 31.06N 116.12 E
Huoxian 27 Jd 36.39N 111.47 E
Hupeh (EN) = Hubei Sheng (Hu-pei Sheng) [2] 27 Je 31.00N 112.00 E
Hu-pei Sheng → Hubei Sheng = Hopeh (EN) [2] 27 Je 31.00N 112.00 E
Hür 24 Qg 30.50N 57.07 E
Hurama → Hongyuan 27 He 32.45N 102.38 E
Huránd 24 Lc 38.40N 47.20 E
Hurd, Cape- 44 Gc 45.13N 81.44W
Hurdalssjøen 8 Dd 60.20N 11.05 E
Hurd Deep = La Grande Trench (EN) 9 Kl 49.40N 3.00W
Hurdiyo 35 Ic 10.32N 51.08 E
Hurepoix 11 If 48.30N 2.10 E
Hure Qi 28 Fc 42.44N 121.44 E
Hurkett 45 Lb 48.50N 88.29W
Hurmuli 20 If 51.01N 136.56 E
Huroizumi 29a Cb 42.01N 143.07 E
Huron 43 Hc 44.22N 98.13W
Huron, Lake- 38 Ke 44.30N 82.15W
Huron Mountains 44 Db 46.45N 87.45W
Hurricane 46 Ih 37.11N 113.17W
Hurricane Cliffs 46 Ih 37.00N 113.05W
Hurrungane 8 Bc 61.27N 7.51 E
Hursley 12 Ac 51.01N 1.24W
Hurst 45 Hj 32.49N 97.09W
Hurstpierpoint 12 Bd 50.55N 0.10W
Hürth 10 Cf 50.52N 6.52 E
Hurum 8 De 59.35N 10.35 E
Hurunui 62 Ee 42.54S 173.18 E
Hurup 8 Ch 56.45N 8.25 E
Huş 15 Lc 46.41N 28.04 E
Húsavík 7a Ca 66.03N 17.21W
Hushan → Cixi 28 Fi 30.10N 121.14 E
Huskvarna 8 Fg 57.48N 14.16 E
Huslia 40 Hc 65.42N 156.25W
Husnes 8 Ae 59.52N 5.46 E
Husnesfjorden 8 Ae 59.50N 5.35 E
Hussigny-Godbrange 12 He 49.29N 5.52 E
Hust 16 Ce 48.10N 23.27 E
Hustadvika 8 Ba 63.00N 7.05 E
Husum [Ger.] 10 Fb 54.28N 9.03 E
Husum [Swe.] 7 Ee 63.20N 19.10 E
Hutag 27 Hb 49.23N 102.43 E
Hutchinson [Ks.-U.S.] 43 Hd 38.05N 97.56W
Hutchinson [Mn.-U.S.] 45 Id 44.54N 94.22W
Hutch Mountain 46 Ji 34.47N 111.22W
Hüth 33 Hf 16.14N 43.58 E
Hutou 27 Nb 46.00N 133.36 E
Hutte Sauvage, Lac de la- 42 Ke 55.57N 65.45W
Hutton, Mount- 59 Je 25.51S 148.20 E
Hutubi 27 Ec 44.07N 86.57 E
Hutuiti, Caleta- 65d Bb 27.07S 109.17W
Hutuo He 28 De 38.14N 116.05 E
Huvhojtun, Gora- 20 Le 57.44N 160.45 E
Huxley, Mount- 62 Cf 44.04S 169.41 E
Huy 10 Ge 51.55N 10.55 E
Huy/Hoei 11 Ld 50.31N 5.14 E
Huzhou → Wuxing 27 Le 30.47N 120.07 E
Hvaler 8 De 59.05N 11.00 E
Hvalynsk 19 Ee 52.30N 48.07 E
Hvammstangi 7a Bb 65.24N 20.57W
Hvannadalshnúkur 5 Ec 64.01N 16.41W
Hvar 14 Kg 43.07N 16.45 E
Hvar 14 Kg 43.11N 16.27 E
Hvarski kanal 14 Kg 43.15N 16.37 E
Hvatovka 16 Oc 52.21N 46.36 E
Hveragerdi 7a Bb 64.00N 21.12W
Hveravellir 7a Bb 64.54N 19.35W
Hvide Sande 8 Ci 55.59N 8.08 E
Hvitá [Ice.] 7a Bb 64.35N 21.46W
Hvitá [Ice.] 7a Bb 64.00N 20.58W
Hvittingfoss 8 De 59.29N 10.01 E
Hvojnaja 7 Ig 58.56N 34.31 E
Hwach'on-ni 28 Ie 38.58N 126.02 E
Hwang-Hae = Yellow Sea (EN) 21 Of 36.00N 124.00 E
Hwanghae-Namdo [2] 28 He 38.15N 125.30 E
Hwanghae-Pukto [2] 28 Ie 38.30N 126.25 E
Hwangju 28 He 38.40N 125.45 E
Hyannis [Ma.-U.S.] 44 Le 41.39N 70.17W
Hyannis [Nb.-U.S.] 45 Ff 42.00N 101.44W
Hybo 8 Gc 61.48N 16.12 E
Hyde Park 50 Gi 6.30N 58.16W
Hyderābād [India] 22 Jh 17.23N 78.28 E
Hyderābād [Pak.] 22 Ig 25.22N 68.22 E
Hyères 11 Mk 43.07N 6.07 E
Hyères, Iles d'- 11 Ml 43.00N 6.20 E
Hyesan 27 Mc 41.24N 128.10 E
Hyltebruk 7 Ch 57.00N 13.14 E
Hyndman Peak 46 He 43.50N 114.10W
Hyōgo Ken [2] 28 Mg 34.50N 134.48 E
Hyrov 10 Sg 49.32N 22.48 E
Hyrulä 8 Kd 60.24N 25.02 E
Hyrum 46 Jf 41.38N 111.51W
Hyrynsalmi 7 Gd 64.40N 28.32 E
Hysham 46 Lc 46.18N 107.14W
Hythe [Eng.-U.K.] 12 Ad 50.52N 1.24W
Hythe [Eng.-U.K.] 9 Oj 51.05N 1.05 E
Hyūga 28 Kh 32.25N 131.38 E
Hyūga-Nada 29 Be 32.25N 131.45 E
Hyvinge/Hyvinkää 7 Ff 60.38N 24.52 E
Hyvinkää/Hyvinge 7 Ff 60.38N 24.52 E

I

Iaco, Rio- 54 Ee 9.03S 68.35W
Iacobeni 15 Ib 47.26N 25.19 E
Iakora 37 Hd 23.08S 46.38 E
Ialomiţa [2] 15 Ke 44.30N 27.30 E
Ialomiţa 15 Ke 44.42N 27.51 E
Ialomiţei, Balta- 15 Ke 44.30N 28.00 E
Iapó, Rio- 55 Gg 24.30S 50.24W
Iaşi 6 If 47.10N 27.36 E
Iaşi [2] 15 Kb 47.07N 27.39 E
Iba 26 Gc 15.20N 119.58 E
Ibadan 31 Hh 7.23N 3.54 E
Ibague 53 Ie 4.27N 75.14W
Ibaiti 56 Jb 23.50S 50.10W
Iballja 15 Cg 42.11N 20.00 E
Ibans, Laguna de- 49 Ef 15.53N 84.52W
Ibar 15 Df 43.44N 20.45 E
Ibara 29 Cd 34.36N 133.28 E
Ibaraki 29 Dd 34.49N 135.34 E
Ibaraki Ken [2] 28 Pf 36.25N 140.30 E
Ibaré 55 Ej 30.49S 54.16W
Ibarra 53 Ie 0.21N 78.07W
Ibarreta 56 Ic 25.13S 59.51W
Ibb 22 Gh 13.58N 44.12 E
Ibba 35 De 4.48N 29.06 E
Ibba 35 Dd 7.09N 28.41 E
Ibbenbüren 10 Dd 52.16N 7.44 E
Ibdekkene 34 Fb 18.28N 0.38 E
Ibembo 36 Db 2.38N 23.37 E
Ibenga 36 Cb 2.20N 18.08 E
Iberá, Esteros del- 55 Di 28.05S 57.05W
Iberá, Laguna- 55 Di 28.30S 57.09W
Iberian Basin (EN) 3 De 40.00N 16.00W
Iberian Mountains (EN) = Sistema Ibérico 5 Fg 41.30N 2.30W
Iberian Peninsula (EN) = Peninsula Ibérica 5 Fg 40.00N 4.00W
Iberville, Lac d'- 42 Ke 56.00N 73.10W
Ibestad 7 Db 68.48N 17.08 E
Ibi [Nig.] 34 Gd 8.11N 9.45 E
Ibi [Sp.] 13 Lf 38.38N 0.34W
Ibiá 54 Ig 19.29S 46.32W
Ibiagui 55 Ja 13.03S 44.12W
Ibiai 55 Jc 16.51S 44.55W
Ibibobo 54 Fh 21.35S 62.58W
Ibicarai 54 Kf 14.51S 39.36W
Ibicui, Rio- 52 Kh 29.25S 56.47W
Ibicui da Armada, Rio- 55 Ej 30.16S 54.54W
Ibicuy 55 Ck 33.44S 59.10W
Ibicuy, Rio- 55 Ck 33.48S 59.10W
Ibigawa 29 Ed 35.29N 136.34 E
Ibipetuba 54 Jf 11.00S 44.32W
Ibiraiaras 55 Gi 28.22S 51.39W
Ibirama 55 Hh 27.04S 49.31W
Ibirapuitã, Rio- 55 Ei 29.22S 55.57W
Ibirocai, Arroio- 55 Di 29.26S 56.43W
Ibiruba 55 Fi 28.38S 53.06W
Ibitinga 55 He 21.45S 48.49W
Ibitinga, Represa- 55 He 21.41S 49.05W
Ibity 37 Hd 20.10S 46.58 E
Ibiza 13 Nf 38.54N 1.26 E
Ibiza/Eivissa = Iviza (EN) 5 Gh 39.00N 1.25 E
Iblei, Monti- 14 Im 37.10N 14.55 E
Ibn Hāni', Ra's- 24 Fe 35.35N 35.43 E
Ibn Qawrah 35 Ib 15.43N 50.32 E
Ibo 37 Gb 12.22S 40.36 E
Ibo-Gawa 29 Dd 34.46N 134.35 E
Iboundji, Mont- 36 Bc 1.08S 11.48 E
Ibrā' 23 Ie 22.38N 58.40 E
Ibrah 35 Dc 10.36N 25.20 E
Ibrāhīm, Jabal- 21 Gg 20.27N 41.09 E
Ibresi 7 Li 55.18N 47.05 E
'Ibrī 23 Ie 23.16N 56.32 E
Ibrim 33 Fe 22.39N 32.05 E
Ibshawāy 24 Dh 29.22N 30.41 E
Ibuki-Sanchi 29 Ed 35.35N 136.25 E
Ibuki-Yama 29 Ed 35.25N 136.24 E
Ibusuki 28 Ki 31.16N 130.39 E
Iča 20 Ke 55.28N 155.58 E
Ica [2] 54 Cf 14.20S 75.30W
Ica 53 Ig 14.04S 75.42W
Iça, Rio- 52 Jf 3.07S 67.58W
Icaiché 48 Oh 18.05N 89.10W
Icamaquã, Rio- 55 Ei 28.34S 56.00W
Icana, Rio- 54 Ec 0.26N 67.19W
Icara 55 Hi 28.42S 49.18W
Icaraíma 55 Ff 23.23S 53.41W
İçel 23 Db 36.48N 34.38 E
Iceland (EN) = Island 5 Eb 65.00N 18.00W
Iceland Basin (EN) 3 Dc 60.00N 20.00W
Ichalkaranji 25 Ee 16.42N 74.28 E
Ichibusa-Yama 29 Be 32.19N 131.06 E
Ichihara 28 Pg 35.31N 140.05 E
Ichi-Kawa 29 Dd 34.46N 134.43 E
Ichikawa 29 Fd 35.44N 139.55 E
Ichinohe 28 Pd 40.13N 141.17 E
Ichinomiya 28 Ng 35.18N 136.48 E
Ichinoseki 28 Pe 38.55N 141.08 E
Ich'ŏn [N.Kor.] 28 Ie 38.29N 126.53 E
Ich'ŏn [S.Kor.] 28 If 37.17N 127.27 E
Ichtegem 12 Fc 51.06N 3.00 E
Ičigemski Hrebet 20 Ld 63.30N 164.00 E
Ičinskaja Sopka, Vulkan- 21 Rd 55.39N 157.40 E
Ičnja 19 De 50.52N 32.25 E
Icó 54 Ke 6.24S 38.51W
Icy Cape 40 Gb 70.20N 161.52W
Idaarderadeel 12 Ha 53.06N 5.50 E
Idaarderadeel-Grow 12 Ha 53.06N 5.50 E
Idabel 45 Ij 33.54N 94.50W
Idah 34 Gd 7.06N 6.44 E
Idaho [2] 43 Ec 45.00N 115.00W
Idaho Falls 39 He 43.30N 112.02W
Idalia 45 Eg 39.43N 102.14W
Idān 35 Hd 6.03N 49.01 E
Idanha-a-Nova 13 Ee 39.55N 7.14W
Idar-Oberstein 10 Dg 49.42N 7.18 E
Idarwald 12 Je 49.50N 7.13 E
Idel 7 Id 64.08N 34.12 E
Ideles 32 Ie 23.49N 5.55 E
Ider 27 Hb 49.16N 100.41 E
Idfū 33 Fe 24.58N 32.52 E
Idhi Óros 5 Ih 35.15N 24.45 E
Idhra 15 Gl 37.20N 23.30 E
Idhra 15 Gl 37.21N 23.28 E
Idhras, Kólpos- 15 Gl 37.22N 23.22 E
Idice 14 Ff 44.35N 11.49 E
Idil 24 Id 37.21N 41.54 E
Idini 32 Df 17.58N 15.40W
Idiofa 36 Cc 4.59S 19.36 E
Idjil, Kédia d'- 32 Ee 22.38N 12.33W
Idkerberget 8 Fd 60.23N 15.14 E
Idle 9 Mh 53.27N 0.48W
Idlib 23 Eb 35.55N 36.38 E
Idokogo 36 Ab 0.35N 9.19 E
Idolo, Isla del- 48 Kg 21.25N 97.27W
Idre 8 Ec 61.52N 12.43 E
Idrica 8 Mh 56.18N 28.55 E
Idrija 14 Id 46.00N 14.02 E
Idro, Lago d'- 14 Ee 45.47N 10.30 E
Idstein 10 Ef 50.14N 8.16 E
Iddževan 16 Ni 40.52N 45.04 E
Iecava 8 Jh 56.40N 23.40 E
Iecava 8 Kh 56.33N 24.11 E
Iepê 55 Gf 22.40S 51.05W
Ieper/Ypres 11 Id 50.51N 2.53 E
Ierápetra 15 In 35.01N 25.45 E
Ierisós 15 Gi 40.24N 23.53 E
Ierisoú, Kólpos- 15 Gi 40.26N 23.55 E
Iernut 15 Hc 46.27N 24.15 E
Ie-Shima 29b Ab 26.43N 127.47 E
Ieshima-Shotō 29 Dd 34.40N 134.30 E
Iesolo 14 Ge 45.32N 12.38 E
Iezerul, Virful- 15 Hd 45.28N 24.57 E
Ifakara 36 Gd 8.08S 36.41 E
Ifaki 34 Gd 7.48N 5.14 E
'Ifāl, Wādī al- 24 Fh 28.07N 35.02 E
Ifalik Atoll 57 Fd 7.15N 144.27 E
Ifanadiana 37 Hd 21.17S 47.35 E
Ife 34 Fd 7.28N 4.34 E
Iferouâne 31 Hg 19.04N 8.24 E
Ifetesene 32 Hd 25.30N 4.33 E
Ifni 32 Ed 29.15N 10.08W
Ifon 34 Gd 6.58N 5.55 E
Iforas, Adrar des- 30 Hg 19.00N 2.00 E
Iga 29 Ed 34.49N 136.12 E
Igal 10 Nj 46.32N 17.57 E
Iganga 36 Fb 0.37N 33.29 E
Igara Paraná, Rio- 54 Dd 2.09N 71.47W
Igarapava 55 Ie 20.03S 47.47W
Igarapé-Açu 54 Id 1.07S 47.37W
Igarapé-Miri 54 Id 1.59S 48.58W
Igarka 22 Kc 67.28N 86.35 E
Igatimi 56 Ib 24.05S 55.30W
Igawa 36 Fd 8.46S 34.23 E
Igbetti 34 Fd 8.45N 4.08 E
Iğdır 24 Kc 39.56N 44.02 E
Iggesund 7 Df 61.38N 17.04 E
Iglesias 14 Ck 39.19N 8.32 E
Iglesiente 14 Ck 39.20N 8.32 E
Igli 32 Gc 30.27N 2.18W
Iglim al Janūbīyah = Southern Region (EN) [2] 35 Dd 6.00N 30.00 E
Iglino 17 Hi 54.50N 56.28 E
Igloolik 39 Kc 69.24N 81.49W
Ignace 42 Ig 49.26N 91.41W
Ignalina 7 Gi 55.22N 26.13 E
Ignatovo 7 If 60.49N 37.48 E
Iğneada 24 Bb 41.50N 27.58 E
Iğneada Burun 15 Lh 41.54N 28.03 E
Igombe 36 Fc 4.25S 31.58 E
Igoumenitsa 15 Dj 39.30N 20.16 E
Igra 19 Fd 57.33N 53.10 E
Igreja, Morro de- 55 Hi 28.08S 49.30W
Igren 16 Ie 48.29N 35.13 E
Igrim 19 Gc 63.12N 64.29 E
Iguaçu, Rio- 52 Kh 25.36S 54.36W
Igualada 13 Nc 41.35N 1.38 E
Iguala de la Independencia 47 Ee 18.21N 99.32W
Iguana, Sierra de la- 48 Id 26.30N 100.15W
Iguape 55 Ig 24.43S 47.33W
Iguariaça, Serra do- 55 Ei 29.03S 55.15W
Iguassu Falls (EN) = Iguazú, Cataratas del- 52 Kh 25.41S 54.26W
Iguatemi 54 If 14.35S 49.02W
Iguatemi, Rio- 55 Ef 23.55S 54.10W
Iguatu 53 Mf 6.22S 39.18W
Iguazú, Cataratas del- = Iguassu Falls (EN) 52 Kh 25.41S 54.26W
Iguéla 36 Ac 1.55S 9.19 E
Iguidi, 'Erg- 30 Gf 27.00N 6.00W
Ihavandiffulu Atoll 25a Ba 7.00N 72.55 E
Iheya-Jima 29b Ab 27.03N 127.57 E
Ih-Hajrhan 27 Ib 46.56N 105.56 E
Ihiala 34 Gd 5.51N 6.51 E
Ihirene 32 He 20.28N 4.37 E
Ihnāsiyat al Madīnah 24 Dh 29.05N 30.56 E
Ih-Obo-Ula 27 Gc 44.55N 95.20 E
Ihosy 31 Lk 22.25S 46.07 E
Ihotry, Lac- 37 Gd 21.56S 43.41 E
Ihrhove, Westoverledingen- 12 Ja 53.10N 7.27 E
Ihsaniye 24 Dc 36.55N 34.46 E
Ihtiman 15 Gg 42.26N 23.49 E
Ih-Ula 27 Hb 49.27N 101.27 E
Ii 7 Fd 65.19N 25.27 E
Iida 28 Ng 35.31N 137.50 E
Iide-San 29 Fc 37.52N 139.41 E
Iijoki 7 Fd 65.20N 25.17 E
Iisaku/Isaku 8 Le 59.14N 27.41 E
Iisalmi 7 Ge 63.34N 27.11 E
Iisvesi 8 Lb 62.45N 26.50 E
Iittala 8 Kc 61.04N 24.10 E
Iivaara 7 Gd 65.47N 29.40 E
Iiyama 29 Fc 36.52N 138.20 E
Iizuka 29 Be 33.38N 130.41 E
Ija 20 Fe 55.02N 101.00 E
Ijebu Ode 34 Fd 6.49N 3.56 E
IJmuiden, Velsen- 12 Gb 52.28N 4.35 E
Ijoubbâne, 'Erg- 34 Da 22.30N 6.00W
IJssel 11 Lb 52.30N 6.00 E
IJsselmeer 11 Lb 52.45N 5.25 E
IJsselmuiden 12 Hb 52.34N 5.56 E
IJsselstein 12 Hb 52.01N 5.02 E
Ijuí 56 Jc 28.23S 53.55W
Ijuí, Rio- 55 Eh 27.58S 55.20W
Ijūin 29 Bf 31.37N 130.24 E
Ijuizinho, Rio- 55 Ei 28.20S 54.28W
Ijuw 64e Bb 0.31S 166.57 E
IJzendijke 12 Fc 51.20N 3.37 E
IJzer 11 Ic 51.09N 2.43 E
Ik [R.S.F.S.R.] 5 Ld 55.55N 52.36 E
Ikaalinen 7 Ff 61.46N 23.03 E
Ikalamavony 37 Hd 21.10S 46.32 E
Ikamatua 62 De 42.17S 171.42 E
Ikaria 15 Jl 37.35N 26.10 E
Ikarion Pélagos 15 Jl 37.30N 26.35 E
Ikast 8 Ch 56.08N 9.10 E
Ikatski Hrebet 20 Gf 54.00N 111.15 E
Ikawa 29 Fd 35.13N 138.14 E
Ikeda [Jap.] 29 Cd 34.01N 133.48 E
Ikeda [Jap.] 27 Pc 42.55N 143.27 E
Ikeda-Ko 29 Bf 31.14N 130.34 E
Ikej 20 Ff 54.12N 100.04 E
Ikeja 34 Fd 6.36N 3.21 E
Ikela 31 Ji 1.11S 23.16 E
Ikelemba 36 Cb 0.07N 18.17 E
Ikerre 34 Gd 7.30N 5.14 E
Ikerssuaq 41 Ie 65.10N 39.45W
Iki 29 Ae 33.45N 129.45 E
Iki-Kaikyō 28 Jh 33.45N 129.50 E
Ikitsuki-Shima 29 Ae 33.25N 129.25 E
Ikizdere 24 Ib 40.47N 40.33 E
Ikom 34 Gd 5.58N 8.42 E
Ikongo 36 Gd 9.04S 36.51 E
Ikopa 37 Hc 16.50S 46.50 E
Ikot Ekpene 34 Gd 5.10N 7.43 E
Ikuno 29 Dd 35.10N 134.48 E
Ikurangi, Mount- 64p Bb 21.12S 159.45W
Ila 34 Fd 7.40N 4.40 E
Ilaferh 32 He 21.50N 1.20 E
Ilagan 22 Oh 17.10N 121.54 E
Ilām 15 Hc 26.54N 87.56 E
Ilam 23 Gc 33.38N 46.26 E
Ilām 23 Gc 33.00N 47.00 E
Ilan 27 Lg 24.45N 121.44 E
Ilanski 20 Ee 56.10N 96.03 E
Ilaro 34 Fd 6.53N 3.01 E
Iława 10 Pc 53.37N 19.33 E

Index Symbols

[1] Independent Nation
[2] State, Region
[3] District, County
[4] Municipality
[5] Colony, Dependency
Continent
Physical Region
Historical or Cultural Region
Mount, Mountain
Volcano
Hill
Mountains, Mountain Range
Hills, Escarpment
Plateau, Upland
Pass, Gap
Plain, Lowland
Delta
Salt Flat
Valley, Canyon
Crater, Cave
Karst Features
Depression
Polder
Desert, Dunes
Forest, Woods
Heath, Steppe
Oasis
Cape, Point
Coast, Beach
Cliff
Peninsula
Isthmus
Sandbank
Island
Atoll
Rock, Reef
Islands, Archipelago
Rocks, Reefs
Coral Reef
Well, Spring
Geyser
River, Stream
Waterfall Rapids
River Mouth, Estuary
Lake
Salt Lake
Intermittent Lake
Reservoir
Swamp, Pond
Canal
Glacier
Ice Shelf, Pack Ice
Ocean
Sea
Gulf, Bay
Strait, Fjord
Lagoon
Bank
Seamount
Tablemount
Ridge
Shelf
Basin
Escarpment, Sea Scarp
Fracture
Trench, Abyss
National Park, Reserve
Point of Interest
Recreation Site
Cave, Cavern
Historic Site
Ruins
Wall, Walls
Church, Abbey
Temple
Scientific Station
Airport
Port
Lighthouse
Mine
Tunnel
Dam, Bridge

Ilbengja 20 Hd 62.55N 124.10 E
Ile-à-la-Crosse 42 Ge 55.27N 107.53W
Ilebo 31 Ji 4.44S 20.33 E
Ile de France 11 Ie 49.00N 2.20 E
Ile de France 41 Kc 77.45N 27.45W
Ile de France, Côte de l'- 11 Jf 48.55N 3.50 E
Ilek 19 Fe 51.32N 53.27 E
Ilek 5 Le 51.30N 53.20 E
Ileksa 7 Ie 62.30N 36.57 E
Ilerh 32 He 21.40N 2.22 E
Ileša 7 Le 62.37N 46.35 E
Ilesha [Nig.] 34 Fd 8.55N 3.25 E
Ilesha [Nig.] 34 Fd 7.37N 4.44 E
Ilet 7 Li 55.57N 48.14 E
Ilfov [2] 15 Je 44.30N 26.20 E
Ilfracombe 9 Ij 51.13N 4.08W
Ilgaz 24 Eb 40.56N 33.38 E
Ilgaz Dağları 24 Eb 41.00N 33.35 E
Ilgın 24 Dc 38.17N 31.55 E
Ilha Grande 54 Ed 0.27S 65.02W
Ilha Grande, Baia da- 55 Jf 23.09S 44.30W
Ilhas Desertas 32 Dc 32.30N 16.30W
Ilhavo 13 Dd 40.36N 8.40W
Ilhéus 53 Mg 14.49S 39.02W
Ili 21 Je 45.24N 74.08 E
Ilia 15 Fd 45.56N 22.39 E
Iliamna 40 Ie 59.45N 154.54W
Iliamna Lake 40 He 59.30N 155.00W
İliç 24 Hc 39.28N 38.34 E
Ilič 18 Gd 40.55N 68.29 E
Ilica 15 Kj 39.52N 27.46 E
Iličevsk [Abz.-U.S.S.R.] 16 Nj 39.33N 44.59 E
Iličevsk [Ukr.-U.S.S.R.] 19 Df 46.18N 30.37 E
Ilidža 14 Mg 43.50N 18.19 E
Iligan 22 Oi 8.14N 124.14 E
Iligan Bay 26 He 8.25N 124.05 E
Ilim 20 Fe 56.50N 103.25 E
Ilimskoje Vodohranilišče 20 Fe 57.20N 102.30 E
Ilinski [R.S.F.S.R.] 7 Hf 61.02N 32.42 E
Ilinski [R.S.F.S.R.] 20 Jg 47.59N 142.21 E
Ilinski [R.S.F.S.R.] 17 Gg 58.35N 55.41 E
Ilion 44 Jd 43.01N 75.04W
Ilio Point 65a Db 21.13N 157.16W
Ilir 20 Fe 55.13N 100.45 E
Ilirska Bistrica 14 Ie 45.34N 14.16 E
Iljaly 18 Bd 41.53N 59.40 E
Ilkal 25 Fe 15.58N 76.08 E
Ilkeston 12 Ab 52.58N 1.18W
Ill 11 Nf 48.40N 7.53 E
Illampu, Nevado del- 54 Eg 15.50S 68.34W
Illana Bay 26 He 7.25N 123.45 E
Illapel 56 Fd 31.38S 71.10W
Illbillee, Mount- 59 Ge 27.02S 132.30 E
Ille 11 Ef 48.08N 1.40W
Ille-et-Vilaine [3] 11 Ef 48.10N 1.30W
Illéla 34 Gc 14.28N 5.15 E
Iller 10 Fh 48.23N 9.58 E
Illescas 13 Id 40.07N 3.50W
Ille-sur-Têt 11 Il 42.40N 2.37 E
Illi, Ba- 35 Bc 10.44N 16.21 E
Illimani, Nevado del- 52 Jg 16.39S 67.48W
Illingen 12 Je 49.22N 7.03 E
Illinois 38 Jf 38.58N 90.27W
Illinois [2] 43 Jd 40.00N 89.00W
Illinois Peak 46 Hc 47.02N 115.04W
Illizi 31 Hf 26.29N 8.28 E
Ilm 10 He 51.07N 11.40 E
Ilmajoki 8 Jb 62.44N 22.34 E
Ilmen, Ozero- 5 Jd 58.20N 31.20 E
Ilmenau 10 Gf 50.41N 10.54 E
Ilmenau 10 Gc 53.23N 10.10 E
Il Montello 14 Ge 45.49N 12.07 E
Ilo 54 Dg 17.38S 71.20W
Iloilo 22 Oh 10.42N 122.34 E
Ilok 14 Ne 45.13N 19.23 E
Ilomantsi 7 He 62.40N 30.55 E
Ilorin 31 Hh 8.30N 4.33 E
Iloron, Cerro- 48 Gg 20.57N 104.22W
Ilova 14 Ke 45.25N 16.45 E
Ilovik 14 If 44.27N 14.33 E
Ilovlja 16 Ne 49.18N 44.01 E
Ilovlja 16 Me 49.14N 43.54 E
Ilpyrski 20 Le 59.52N 164.12 E
Ilski 16 Kg 44.51N 38.32 E
Iltin 20 Nc 67.52N 178.48W
Ilubabor [3] 35 Ed 7.50N 35.00 E
Ilūkste/Ilukste 8 Li 55.58N 26.26 E
Ilukste/Ilūkste 8 Li 55.58N 26.26 E
Ilulissat/Jakobshavn 67 Nc 69.20N 50.50W
Ilwaki 26 Ih 7.56S 126.26 E
Ilyč 17 He 62.32N 56.40 E
Ilz 10 Jh 48.35N 13.30 E
Ilžanka 10 Re 51.14N 21.47 E
Imabari 28 Lg 34.03N 133.00 E
Imagane 28 Pc 42.26N 140.01 E
Imaichi 28 Of 36.43N 139.41 E
Imán, Sierra del- 55 Eh 27.42S 55.28W
Imanburluk 17 Mj 53.40N 67.15 E
Imandra, Ozero- 5 Jb 67.30N 33.00 E
Imano-Yama 29 Ce 32.51N 132.49 E
Imari 28 Jh 33.16N 129.53 E
Imaruí 55 Hi 28.21S 48.49W
Imataca, Serranía de- 50 Fi 7.45N 61.00W
Imatra 7 Gf 61.10N 28.46 E
Imazu 29 Ed 35.24N 136.01 E
Imbabah, Al Qāhirah- 33 Fc 30.05N 31.13 E
Imba-Numa 29 Gd 35.45N 140.14 E
Imbert 49 Ld 19.45N 70.50W
Imbituba 56 Kc 28.14S 48.40W
Imeni 26 Bakinskih Komissarov [Abz.-U.S.S.R.] 19 Eh 39.19N 49.12 E
Imeni 26 Bakinskih Komissarov [Tur.-U.S.S.R.] 19 Fh 39.21N 54.12 E
İmeni Gastello 20 Jd 61.35N 147.59 E
Imeni Karla Liebknechta 16 Id 51.38N 35.29 E
İmeni Mariny Raskovoj 20 Jd 62.05N 146.30 E
İmeni Poliny Osipenko 20 If 52.23N 136.25 E
Imi 31 Lh 6.28N 42.11 E
Imilili 32 De 22.50N 15.54W
Imi n'Tanout 32 Fc 31.03N 8.08W
Imišli 19 Eh 39.53N 48.03 E
Imjin-gang 28 If 37.47N 126.40 E
Imlay 46 Ff 40.42N 118.07W
Immenstadt im Allgäu 10 Gi 47.34N 10.13 E
Imo [2] 34 Gd 5.30N 7.20 E
Imola 14 Ff 44.21N 11.42 E
Imotski 14 Lg 43.27N 17.13 E
Imperatriz 53 Lf 5.32S 47.29W
Imperia 14 Cg 43.53N 8.03 E
Imperial 45 Ff 40.31N 101.39W
Imperial de Aragón, Canal- 13 Kb 42.02N 1.33W
Imperial Valley 46 Hj 32.50N 115.30W
Impfondo 31 Ih 1.37N 18.04 E
Imphāl 22 Lg 24.49N 93.57 E
Imphy 11 Jh 46.56N 3.15 E
Impilanti 7 Hf 61.41N 31.12 E
Imrali Adasi 15 Li 40.32N 28.32 E
Imst 14 Ec 47.14N 10.44 E
Imtan 24 Gf 32.24N 36.49 E
Imuris 48 Db 30.47N 110.52W
Im-Zouren 13 Ii 35.04N 3.50W
Ina 28 Ng 35.50N 137.57 E
Ina 10 Kc 53.32N 14.38 E
I-n-Abanrherit 34 Gb 17.58N 6.05 E
Inabu 29 Ed 35.13N 137.30 E
Inaccessible Islands 66 Re 60.34S 46.44W
Inaccessible Island 30 Fi 37.17S 12.45W
I-n-Afaleleh 32 Ie 23.34N 9.12 E
I Naftan, Puntan- 64b Ba 15.05N 145.45 E
Ina-Gawa 29 Fc 37.23N 139.18 E
I-n-Amenas 31 Hf 28.03N 9.33 E
Inami 29 De 33.48N 135.12 E
Inanba-Jima 29 Fe 33.39N 139.18 E
Inangahua Junction 62 Dd 41.52S 171.56 E
Inanwatan 26 Jg 2.08S 132.10 E
Iñapari 54 Ef 10.57S 69.35W
Inarajan 64c Bb 13.16N 144.45 E
I-n-Arhâta 34 Ea 21.09N 0.18W
Inari 6 Ib 68.54N 27.01 E
Inari, Lake- (EN)= Inarijärvi 5 Ib 69.00N 28.00 E
Inarijärvi=Inari, Lake- (EN) 5 Ib 69.00N 28.00 E
Inawashiro 29 Gc 37.34N 140.05 E
Inawashiro-Ko 28 Pf 37.30N 140.03 E
I-n Azaoua 34 Ga 20.47N 7.31 E
I-n-Azaoua 34 Ga 20.54N 7.28 E
Inazawa 29 Ed 35.15N 136.47 E
Inca 13 Oe 39.43N 2.54 E
Inca de Oro 56 Gc 26.45S 69.54W
Incaguasi 56 Fc 29.13S 71.03W
Ince Burun 15 Ki 40.28N 27.16 E
İnce Burun 23 Da 42.07N 34.56 E
İncekum Burun 24 Ed 36.13N 33.58 E
Inceler 15 Ml 37.42N 29.35 E
I-n-Chaouâg 34 Fb 16.23N 0.10 E
Inchcape (Bell Rock) 9 Ke 56.26N 2.24W
Inchiri [3] 32 Df 20.00N 15.00W
Inch'ŏn 22 Of 37.28N 126.38 E
Incirliova 15 Kl 37.50N 27.43 E
Incudine 11a Bb 41.51N 9.12 E
Indaiá, Rio- 55 Jd 18.27S 45.22W
Indaia Grande, Ribeirão- 55 Fd 19.31S 52.29W
Indaiatuba 55 If 23.05S 47.14W
Indal 8 Gb 62.34N 17.06 E
Indalsälven 7 De 62.31N 17.27 E
Inda Selase 35 Fc 14.06N 38.17 E
Indawgyi 25 Jc 25.08N 96.20 E
Indefatigable Banks 9 Ph 53.35N 2.20 E
Independence [Ca.-U.S.] 46 Fh 36.48N 118.12W
Independence [Ia.-U.S.] 45 Ke 42.28N 91.54W
Independence [Ks.-U.S.] 43 Hd 37.13N 95.42W
Independence [Mo.-U.S.] 45 Ig 39.05N 94.04W
Independence [Va.-U.S.] 44 Gg 36.38N 81.11W
Independence Fjord 67 Me 82.00N 30.25W
Independence Mountains 46 Gf 41.15N 116.05W
Independência [Braz.] 54 Je 5.23S 40.19W
Independência [Braz.] 55 Fa 13.34S 53.57W
Independenta 15 Kd 45.29N 27.45 E
Inder → Jalaid Qi 27 Lb 46.41N 122.52 E
Inder, Ozero- 16 Qe 48.25N 51.55 E
Inderborski 6 Lf 48.32N 51.47 E
India (EN) 21 Jh 20.00N 77.00 E
India (EN)=Bhārat Juktarashtra [1] 22 Jh 20.00N 77.00 E
India Muerta, Arroyo de la- 55 Fk 33.40S 54.04W
Indiana [2] 43 Jc 40.00N 86.15W
Indiana 44 He 40.39N 79.11W
Indianapolis 39 Kf 39.46N 86.09W
Indian Church 49 Ce 17.45N 88.40W
Indian Creek Point 51d Bb 17.00N 61.43W
Indian Harbour 42 Lf 54.27N 57.13W
Indian Head 42 Hf 50.32N 103.40W
Indian Ocean 3 Gl 21.00S 82.00 E
Indian Ocean (EN)=Ḥindī, Badwēynta- 3 Gl 21.00S 82.00 E
Indian Ocean (EN)=Indico, Oceano- 3 Gl 21.00S 82.00 E
Indian Ocean (EN)=Indien, Océan- 3 Gl 21.00S 82.00 E
Indian Ocean (EN)=Indiese Oseaan- 3 Gl 21.00S 82.00 E
Indian Ocean (EN)= Indonesia, Samudera- 3 Gl 21.00S 82.00 E
Indianola 45 Kj 33.27N 90.39W
Indianópolis 55 Id 19.02S 47.55W
Indian Peak 46 Ig 38.16N 113.53W
Indian Rock 46 Ec 46.01N 120.49W
Indian Springs 43 Dd 36.34N 115.40W
Indiantown 44 Gl 27.01N 80.28W
Indian Town Point 51d Bb 17.06N 61.40W
Indiapora 55 Gd 19.57S 50.17W
Indias Occidentales=West Indies (EN) 47 Je 19.00N 70.00W
Indico, Oceano-=Indian Ocean (EN) 3 Gl 21.00S 82.00 E
Indien, Océan-=Indian Ocean (EN) 3 Gl 21.00S 82.00 E
Indiese, Oseaan-=Indian Ocean (EN) 3 Gl 21.00S 82.00 E
Indiga 19 Eb 67.41N 49.00 E
Indigirka 21 Qb 70.48N 148.54 E
Indigskaja Guba 17 Dc 67.45N 48.20 E
Inđija 15 Dd 45.03N 20.05 E
Indio 43 De 33.43N 116.13W
Indio, Rio- 49 Fh 10.57N 83.44W
Indio Rico 55 Bn 38.19S 60.53W
Indispensable Reefs 57 Hf 12.40S 160.25 E
Indispensable Strait 63a Ec 9.00S 160.30 E
Indochina (EN) 21 Mh 16.00N 107.00 E
Indonesia [1] 22 Nj 5.00S 120.00 E
Indonesia, Samudera-= Indian Ocean (EN) 3 Gl 21.00S 82.00 E
Indore 22 Jg 22.43N 75.50 E
Indra 8 Li 55.53N 27.40 E
Indragiri 26 Dg 0.22S 103.26 E
Indramayu 26 Eh 6.20S 108.19 E
Indrāvati 25 Ge 18.44N 80.16 E
Indre 11 Gg 47.14N 0.11 E
Indre [3] 11 Hh 46.50N 1.40 E
Indre Arna 8 Ad 60.26N 5.30 E
Indre-et-Loire [3] 11 Gg 47.15N 0.45 E
Indus 21 Ig 24.20N 67.47 E
İnebolu 23 Da 41.58N 33.46 E
Inece 15 Kh 41.41N 27.04 E
Inecik 15 Ki 40.56N 27.16 E
İnegöl 23 Ca 40.05N 29.31 E
Inés Indart 55 Bl 34.24S 60.33W
Ineu 15 Ec 46.26N 21.51 E
Ineu, Vîrful- 15 Hb 47.32N 24.53 E
Inezgane 32 Fc 30.21N 9.32W
I-n-Ezzane 32 Je 23.29N 11.15 E
Inferior, Laguna- 48 Li 16.15N 94.45W
Infiernillo, Presa del- 47 De 18.35N 101.45W
Infiesto 13 Ga 43.21N 5.22W
Infreschi, Punta degli- 14 Jk 39.59N 15.25 E
Ingá 54 Ke 7.17S 35.36W
Inga 36 Bd 5.39S 13.39 E
Ingå/Inkoo 7 Ff 60.03N 24.01 E
Ingabu 25 Je 17.49N 95.16 E
Ingai, Rio- 55 Je 21.10S 44.52W
I-n Gall 34 Gb 16.47N 6.56 E
Ingarö 8 He 59.15N 18.30 E
Ingavi 55 Bb 15.02S 60.29W
Ingelheim am Rhein 12 Ke 49.59N 8.02 E
Ingelmunster 12 Fd 50.55N 3.15 E
Ingelstad 8 Fh 56.45N 14.55 E
Ingende 36 Cc 0.15S 18.57 E
Ingeniero Guillermo N. Juarez 56 Hb 23.54S 61.51W
Ingeniero Jacobacci 56 Gf 41.18S 69.35W
Ingeniero Luiggi 56 He 35.25S 64.29W
Ingenio Santa Ana 56 Gc 27.28S 65.41W
Ingermanland (EN) 5 Id 59.00N 30.00 E
Ingham 58 Ff 18.39S 146.10 E
Ingička 18 Ee 39.47N 65.58 E
Inglefield Bredning 41 Fc 77.40N 65.00W
Inglefield Land 41 Fc 78.44N 68.20W
Inglewood [Austl.] 59 Ke 28.25S 151.05 E
Inglewood [Ca.-U.S.] 46 Fj 33.58N 118.21W
Inglewood [N.Z.] 62 Fc 39.09S 174.12 E
Ingolf Fjord 41 Kb 80.35N 17.35W
Ingólfshöfði 7a Cc 63.48N 16.39W
Ingolstadt 10 Hh 48.46N 11.26 E
Ingrāj Bāzār 25 Hc 25.00N 88.09 E
I-n-Guezzâm 31 Hg 19.32N 5.42 E
Ingul 16 Gf 47.02N 31.59 E
Ingulec 16 Hf 46.41N 32.48 E
Ingulec 19 Df 47.43N 33.10 E
Inguri 16 Lh 42.24N 41.32 E
Inhaca, Ilha da- 30 Kk 26.02S 32.58 E
Inhambane 31 Kk 23.52S 35.23 E
Inhambane [3] 37 Ed 23.00S 34.30 E
Inhambane, Baía de- 37 Fd 23.50S 35.20 E
Inhaminga 37 Fc 18.25S 35.01 E
Inhandui-Guaçu, Rio- 55 Fe 21.37S 52.59W
Inhanduizinho, Rio- 55 Fe 21.34S 53.36W
Inharrime 37 Fd 24.28S 35.01 E
Inhassoro 37 Fd 21.32S 35.12 E
Inhaúma 55 Ja 13.01S 44.39W
I-n-Hihaou 32 He 23.00N 2.00 E
Inhobi, Rio- 55 Ef 23.45S 54.40W
Inhumas 54 Ig 16.22S 49.30W
Iniö 8 Id 60.25N 21.25 E
Inirida, Rio- 52 Je 3.55N 67.52W
Inis/Ennis 9 Ei 52.50N 8.59W
Inis Airc/Inishark 9 Ch 53.37N 10.16W
Inis Bó Finne/Inishbofin 9 Ch 53.38N 10.12W
Inis Ceithleann/Enniskillen 9 Fg 54.21N 7.38W
Inis Córthaidh/Enniscorthy 9 Gi 52.30N 6.34W
Inis Díomáin/Ennistymon 9 Di 52.57N 9.13W
Inis Eoghain/Inishowen Peninsula 9 Ff 55.15N 7.20W
Inishark/Inis Airc 9 Ch 53.37N 10.16W
Inishbofin/Inis Bó Finne 9 Ch 53.38N 10.12W
Inisheer/Inis Oírr 9 Dh 53.03N 9.31W
Inishkea 9 Cg 54.08N 10.11W
Inishmaan/Inis Meáin 9 Dh 53.05N 9.35W
Inishmore/Árainn 9 Dh 53.07N 9.45W
Inishmurray/Inis Muirigh 9 Eg 54.26N 8.40W
Inishowen Peninsula/Inis Eoghain 9 Ff 55.15N 7.20W
Inishtrahull 9 Ff 55.27N 7.14W
Inishturk/Inis Toirc 9 Ch 53.43N 10.05W
Inis Meáin/Inishmaan 9 Dh 53.05N 9.35W
Inis Muirigh/Inishmurray 9 Eg 54.26N 8.40W
Inis Oírr/Inisheer 9 Dh 53.03N 9.31W
Inis Toirc/Inishturk 9 Ch 53.43N 10.05W
Inja 20 Je 59.22N 144.50 E
Inja [R.S.F.S.R.] 20 Je 59.30N 144.48 E
Inja [R.S.F.S.R.] 20 Df 50.27N 86.42 E
Injeŭp 28 Je 38.04N 128.10 E
Injibara 35 Fc 10.55N 36.58 E
Injune 59 Je 25.51S 148.34 E
I-n-Kak 34 Fb 16.20N 0.17 E
Inkisi 36 Bc 4.46S 14.52 E
Inkoo/Ingå 7 Ff 60.03N 24.01 E
Inland Kaikoura Range 62 Ee 42.00S 173.35 E
Inland Sea (EN)= Setonaikai 21 Pf 34.10N 133.00 E
Inn 5 Hf 48.35N 13.28 E
Innamincka 59 Ie 27.45S 140.44 E
Inner Hebrides 9 Ge 57.00N 6.45W
Inner Mongolia (EN)=Nei Monggol Zizhiqu (Nei-meng-ku Tzu-chih-ch'ü) [2] 27 Jc 44.00N 112.00 E
Inner Silver Pit 9 Nh 53.30N 0.40 E
Inner Sound 9 Hd 57.30N 5.55W
Innerste 10 Fd 52.15N 9.50 E
Innisfail [Alta.-Can.] 46 Ia 52.02N 113.57W
Innisfail [Austl.] 59 Jc 17.32S 146.02 E
Innokentjevka 20 Ig 49.42N 136.55 E
Innokentjevski 20 Jg 48.38N 140.12 E
Innoko 40 Hd 62.14N 159.45W
Innsbruck 6 Hf 47.16N 11.24 E
Innuksuac 42 Je 58.27N 78.08W
Innviertel 14 Hb 48.15N 13.15 E
Innvikfjorden 8 Bc 61.50N 6.35 E
Inny/An Eithne 9 Fh 53.35N 7.50W
Ino 29 Ce 33.33N 133.26 E
Inobonto 26 Hf 0.52N 123.57 E
Inongo 31 Ii 1.57S 18.16 E
Inoni 36 Cc 3.04S 15.39 E
Inönü 15 Nj 39.48N 30.09 E
I-n-Ouagar 34 Gb 16.12N 6.54 E
I-n-Ouzzal 32 He 21.34N 1.59 E
Inowrocław 10 Od 52.48N 18.15 E
I-n-Salah 31 Hf 27.13N 2.28 E
Insar 7 Ki 54.42N 45.18 E
Insar 7 Kj 53.52N 44.23 E
Inscription, Cape- 57 Cg 25.30S 112.59 E
Insjön 8 Fd 60.41N 15.05 E
Insko 10 Lc 53.27N 15.33 E
Instruč 8 Ij 54.39N 21.48 E
Insurăţei 15 Ke 44.55N 27.36 E
Inta 6 Mb 66.05N 60.08 E
I-n-Tabezas 34 Fb 17.54N 1.50 E
I-n-Tallak 34 Fb 16.19N 3.15 E
Intepe 15 Ji 40.00N 26.20 E
Interlaken 14 Bd 46.41N 7.52 E
International Falls 43 Ib 48.36N 93.25W
Interview 25 If 12.55N 92.43 E
Inthanon, Doi- 25 Je 18.35N 98.29 E
Intibucá [3] 49 Cf 14.20N 88.15W
Intiyaco 56 Hc 28.39S 60.05W
Intorsura Buzaului 15 Jd 45.41N 26.02 E
Intracoastal Waterway 45 Im 28.45N 95.40W
Inubō-Zaki 29 Gd 35.42N 140.52 E
Inukjuak 39 Ld 58.30N 78.15W
Inutil, Bahía- 56 Fh 52.45S 71.24W
Inuvik 39 Fc 68.25N 133.30W
Inuyama 29 Ed 35.23N 136.56 E
Inva 17 Gg 58.59N 55.40 E
Inveraray 9 He 56.13N 5.05W
Invercargill 58 Hi 46.25S 168.21 E
Inverell 59 Ke 29.47S 151.07 E
Inverness 6 Fd 57.27N 4.15W
Inverurie 9 Kd 57.17N 2.23W
Investigator Group 57 Eh 33.45S 134.30 E
Investigator Strait 59 Hg 35.25S 137.10 E
Inyangani 30 Kj 18.18S 32.51 E
Inyangani 37 Ec 18.13S 32.46 E
Inyati 37 Dc 19.40S 28.51 E
Inyazura 37 Ec 18.43S 32.10 E
Inyo Mountains 46 Gh 36.50N 117.45W
Inza 19 Ee 53.53N 46.28 E
Inzá 54 Cc 2.33N 76.04W
Inžavino 16 Mc 52.19N 42.31 E
Inzer 17 Hi 54.30N 56.28 E
Inzer 17 Hi 54.14N 57.34 E
Inzia 36 Cc 3.45S 17.57 E
Iō/Kazan-Rettō=Volcano Islands (EN) 21 Qg 25.00N 141.00 E
Ioánnina 6 Ih 39.40N 20.50 E
Ioanninon, Limni- 15 Dj 39.40N 20.53 E
Iokanga 7 Jb 68.03N 39.40 E
Iola 45 Ih 37.55N 95.24W
Iolotan 19 Gh 37.18N 62.21 E
Iona 9 Ge 56.19N 6.25W
Iona 36 Bf 16.52S 12.34 E
Ionava/Jonava 7 Fi 55.05N 24.17 E
Ion Corvin 15 Ke 44.07N 27.48 E
Ione 46 Eg 38.21N 120.56W
Ionia 44 Ed 42.59N 85.04W
Ionian Basin (EN) 5 Hh 36.00N 20.00 E
Ionian Islands (EN)=Iónioi Nisoi 5 Ih 38.30N 20.30 E
Ionian Sea (EN)=Ionio, Mar- 5 Hh 39.00N 19.00 E
Ionian Sea (EN)=Iónion Pélagos 5 Hh 39.00N 19.00 E
Ionio, Mar-=Ionian Sea (EN) 5 Hh 39.00N 19.00 E
Iónioi Nisoi [2] 15 Dk 38.40N 20.10 E
Iónioi Nisoi=Ionian Islands (EN) 5 Ih 38.30N 20.30 E
Iónion Pélagos=Ionian Sea (EN) 5 Hh 39.00N 19.00 E
Ioniškelis/Joniškėlis 8 Ki 56.00N 24.14 E
Ioniškis/Joniškis 7 Fh 56.16N 23.37 E
Iony, Ostrov- 20 Je 56.15N 143.20 E
Iori 16 Oi 41.03N 46.27 E
Ios 15 Im 36.44N 25.18 E
Ios 15 Im 36.42N 25.20 E
Iō-Shima 28 Ki 31.51N 130.13 E
Iowa [2] 43 Ic 42.15N 93.15W
Iowa City 43 Ic 41.40N 91.32W
Iowa Falls 45 Je 42.31N 93.16W
Iowa Park 45 Gj 33.57N 98.40W
Iowa River 45 Kf 41.10N 91.02W
Iō-Yama 29a Da 44.10N 145.10 E
Ipa 16 Fc 52.07N 29.12 E
Ipameri 54 Ig 17.43S 48.09W
Ipatovo 19 Ef 45.43N 42.53 E
Ipaumirim 54 Ke 6.47S 38.43W
Ipel' 10 Oi 47.49N 18.52 E
Ipiales 54 Cc 0.50N 77.37W
Ipiaú 54 Kf 14.08S 39.44W
Ipiranga 55 Gg 25.01S 50.35W
Ipiros [2] 15 Dj 39.30N 20.40 E
Ipiros=Epirus (EN) 15 Dj 39.30N 20.40 E
Ipiros=Epirus (EN) 5 Ih 39.30N 20.40 E
Ipixuma, Rio- 54 Fe 5.50S 63.00W
Ipixuna 54 De 7.34S 72.36W
Ipoh 22 Mi 4.35N 101.05 E
Ipoly 10 Oi 47.49N 18.52 E
Iporã 55 Ff 23.59S 53.37W
Iporá 54 Hg 16.28S 51.07W
Ippy 35 Cd 6.15N 21.12 E
Ipsala 24 Bb 40.55N 26.23 E
Ipsizonos Óros 15 Gi 40.28N 23.34 E
Ipswich [Austl.] 58 Gg 27.36S 152.46 E
Ipswich [Eng.-U.K.] 6 Ge 52.04N 1.10 E
Ipswich [S.D.-U.S.] 45 Gd 45.27N 99.02W
Ipu 54 Jd 4.20S 40.42W
Iqaluit 39 Mc 63.44N 68.28W
Iquique 53 Ih 20.13S 70.10W
Iquitos 53 If 3.50S 73.15W
Iraan 45 Fk 30.54N 101.54W
Ira Banda 35 Cd 5.57N 22.06 E
Irabu-Jima 27 Mg 24.50N 125.10 E
Iracoubo 54 Hb 5.29N 53.13W
Iraël 17 Gd 64.27N 55.08 E
Irago-Suidō 29 Ed 34.35N 136.55 E
Irago-Zaki 29 Ed 34.35N 137.01 E
Iráklia 15 Gh 41.10N 23.16 E
Iráklia 15 Im 36.50N 25.26 E
Iráklion 6 Ih 35.20N 25.08 E
Irān=Iran (EN) [1] 22 Hf 32.00N 53.00 E
Iran (EN)=Irān [1] 22 Hf 32.00N 53.00 E
Iran, Pegunungan-=Iran Mountains (EN) 21 Ni 2.05N 114.55 E
Iran, Plateau of- (EN) 21 Hf 32.00N 56.00 E
Irani, Serra do- 55 Fh 27.00S 52.12W
Iran Mountains (EN)=Iran, Pegunungan- 21 Ni 2.05N 114.55 E
Irānshahr 22 Ig 27.13N 60.41 E
Irapa 50 Eg 10.34N 62.35W
Irapuá, Arroio- 55 Fj 30.15S 53.10W
Irapuato 39 Ig 20.41N 101.28W
Iraq (EN)=Al 'Irāq [1] 22 Gf 33.00N 44.00 E
'Irāq al 'Arabi 24 Kg 31.50N 45.50 E
Irati 13 Kb 42.35N 1.16W
Irati 56 Jc 25.27S 50.39W
Irazú, Volcán- 38 Ki 9.59N 83.51W
Irbeni Väin 8 Ig 57.48N 22.05 E
Irbid 23 Ec 32.33N 35.51 E
Irbiktepe 15 Jh 41.00N 26.30 E
Irbit 17 Kh 57.42N 63.07 E
Irbit 19 Gd 57.41N 63.03 E
Irebu 36 Cc 0.37S 17.45 E
Irecê 54 Jf 11.18S 41.52W
Iregua 13 Jb 42.27N 2.24W
Ireland 5 Fe 53.00N 8.00W
Ireland/Éire [1] 6 Fe 53.00N 8.00W
Ireland Trough (EN) 5 Ed 55.00N 12.40W
Iren 17 Hh 57.27N 56.59 E
Ireng River 54 Gc 3.33N 59.51W
Irês Corações 54 Ih 21.42S 45.16W
Iretama 55 Fg 24.27S 52.02W
Irgiz 19 Gf 48.13N 62.08 E
Irgiz 19 Gf 48.36N 61.16 E
Irharhar [Alg.] 30 Hf 28.00N 6.15 E
Irharhar [Alg.] 32 Ie 21.01N 6.01 E
Irherm 32 Fc 30.04N 8.26W
Iri 28 Ig 35.56N 126.57 E
Iriba 31 Jg 15.07N 22.15 E
Irīgui 30 Gg 16.43N 5.30W
Iriklinski 16 Ud 51.39N 58.38 E
Iriklinskoje Vodohranilišče 16 Ud 51.45N 58.45 E
Iringa [3] 36 Gd 8.00S 35.30 E
Iringa 31 Ki 7.46S 35.42 E
Irinja, Gora- 20 Fe 58.20N 104.30 E
Iriomote Jima 27 Lg 24.20N 123.50 E
Iriona 49 Ef 15.57N 85.11W
Iriri, Rio- 52 Kf 3.52S 52.37W
Irish Sea 5 Fe 53.30N 5.20W
Irish Sea (EN)=Muir Eireann 5 Fe 53.30N 5.20W
Irituia 54 Id 1.46S 47.26W
Irkeštam 18 Ie 39.38N 73.55 E
Irkutsk 22 Md 52.16N 104.20 E
Irkutskaja Oblast [3] 20 Fe 56.00N 104.00 E
Irlir, Gora- 18 Dc 42.40N 63.30 E
Irminio 14 In 36.46N 14.36 E
Irnijärvi 7 Gd 65.36N 29.05 E
Iro, Lac- 35 Bc 10.06N 19.25 E
Iroise 11 Bf 48.15N 4.55W
Iron Gate (EN) = Portile de Fier 5 Ig 44.41N 22.31 E
Iron Knob 59 Hf 32.44S 137.08 E
Iron Mountain 43 Jb 45.49N 88.04W
Iron Mountains 9 Fg 54.15N 7.50W
Iron River [Mi.-U.S.] 43 Jb 46.05N 88.39W
Iron River [Wi.-U.S.] 45 Kc 46.34N 91.24W
Ironside Mountain 46 Fd 44.15N 118.08W
Ironton [Mo.-U.S.] 45 Kh 37.36N 90.38W
Ironton [Oh.-U.S.] 44 Ff 38.32N 82.40W
Ironwood 43 Ib 46.27N 90.10W
Iroquois Falls 42 Jg 48.46N 80.41W
Irō-Zaki 28 Og 34.35N 138.55 E

Index Symbols

[1] Independent Nation
[2] State, Region
[3] District, County
[4] Municipality
[5] Colony, Dependency
Continent
Physical Region
Historical or Cultural Region
Mount, Mountain
Volcano
Hill
Mountains, Mountain Range
Hills, Escarpment
Plateau, Upland
Pass, Gap
Plain, Lowland
Delta
Salt Flat
Valley, Canyon
Crater, Cave
Karst Features
Depression
Polder
Desert, Dunes
Forest, Woods
Heath, Steppe
Oasis
Cape, Point
Coast, Beach
Cliff
Peninsula
Isthmus
Sandbank
Island
Atoll
Rock, Reef
Islands, Archipelago
Rocks, Reefs
Coral Reef
Well, Spring
Geyser
River, Stream
Waterfall Rapids
River Mouth, Estuary
Lake
Salt Lake
Intermittent Lake
Reservoir
Swamp, Pond
Canal
Glacier
Ice Shelf, Pack Ice
Ocean
Sea
Gulf, Bay
Strait, Fjord
Lagoon
Bank
Seamount
Tablemount
Ridge
Shelf
Basin
Escarpment, Sea Scarp
Fracture
Trench, Abyss
National Park, Reserve
Point of Interest
Recreation Site
Cave, Cavern
Historic Site
Ruins
Wall, Walls
Church, Abbey
Temple
Scientific Station
Airport
Port
Lighthouse
Mine
Tunnel
Dam, Bridge

Irpen 19 De 50.31N 30.16 E
Irpinia 14 Ij 40.55N 15.00 E
Irrawaddy → Ayeyarwady 25 Ie 17.00N 95.00 E
Irrawaddy (EN) = Ayeyarwady 21 Lg 15.50N 95.06 E
Irrel 12 Ie 49.51N 6.28 E
Irsãva 10 Th 48.15N 23.05 E
Irsina 14 Kj 40.45N 16.14 E
Irtek 16 Rd 51.29N 52.42 E
Irthlingborough 12 Bb 52.19N 0.36W
Irtyš 21 Ic 61.04N 68.52 E
Irtyšsk 19 He 53.21N 75.27 E
Irumu 36 Eb 1.27N 29.52 E
Irún 13 Ka 43.21N 1.47W
Irurzun 13 Kb 42.55N 1.50W
Irves Šaurums 8 Ig 57.48N 22.05 E
Irvine 9 If 55.37N 4.40W
Irving 45 Hj 32.49N 96.56W
Is, Jabal- 35 Fa 21.49N 35.39 E
Isa, Ra's- 33 Hf 15.11N 42.39 E
Isabel 45 Fd 45.24N 101.26W
Isabel, Bahia- 54a Ab 0.38S 91.25W
Isabela 51a Ab 18.31N 67.07W
Isabela → Basilan City 26 He 6.42N 121.58 E
Isabela, Cabo- 49 Ld 19.56N 71.01W
Isabela, Isla- [Ec.] 52 Gf 0.30S 91.06W
Isabela, Isla- [Mex.] 48 Gg 21.51N 105.55W
Isabella, Cordillera- 47 Gf 13.30N 85.30W
Isabel Segunda 49 Od 18.09N 65.27W
Isabey 15 Ml 38.00N 29.24 E
Isaccea 15 Ld 45.16N 28.28 E
Isachsen 39 Ib 78.50N 103.30W
Isafjörður 6 Db 66.03N 23.09W
Isahaya 28 Jh 32.50N 130.03 E
Isakov, Seamount (EN) 57 Ga 31.35N 151.07 E
Isana, Rio- 54 Ec 0.26N 67.19W
Isandja 36 Dc 2.59S 22.00 E
Isanga 36 Dc 1.26S 22.18 E
Isangi 36 Db 0.46N 24.15 E
Isanlu Makutu 34 Gd 8.16N 5.48 E
Isaouane-n-Irarraren 32 Id 27.15N 8.00 E
Isaouane-n-Tifernine 32 Id 27.00N 7.30 E
Isar 10 Ih 48.49N 12.58 E
Isarco/Eisack 14 Fd 46.27N 11.18 E
Isarco, Valle-/Eisacktal 14 Fd 46.45N 11.35 E
Isbergues 12 Ed 50.37N 2.27 E
Iscayachi 54 Eh 21.31S 65.03W
Ischgl 14 Ec 47.01N 10.17 E
Ischia 14 Hj 40.45N 13.55 E
Ischia 14 Hj 40.44N 13.57 E
Ise 27 Oe 34.29N 136.42 E
Isefjord 8 Di 55.50N 11.50 E
Isejevka 7 Li 54.28N 48.17 E
Isen 10 Ih 48.20N 12.45 E
Isenach 12 Ke 49.38N 8.28 E
Isen-Zaki 29b Bb 27.39N 128.55 E
Iseo, Lago d'- 14 Ee 45.45N 10.05 E
Iseran, Col de l'- 11 Ni 45.25N 7.02 E
Isère 11 Kj 44.59N 4.51 E
Isère [3] 11 Li 45.10N 5.50 E
Išerit, Gora- 17 If 61.08N 59.10 E
Iserlohn 10 De 51.22N 7.42 E
Isernia 14 Ii 41.36N 14.14 E
Isesaki 29 Fc 36.19N 139.12 E
Iset 21 Id 56.36N 66.24 E
Isetskoje 17 Lh 56.29N 65.21 E
Ise-Wan 28 Ng 34.40N 136.42 E
Iseyin 34 Fd 7.58N 3.36 E
Isfahan (EN) = Esfahān 22 Hf 32.40N 51.38 E
Isfana 18 Ge 39.51N 69.32 E
Isfara 18 Hd 40.07N 70.38 E
Isfendiyar Dağları 23 Da 41.45N 34.10 E
Isfjorden 41 Nc 78.15N 15.00 E
Isha Baydabo 31 Lh 3.04N 43.48 E
Ishasha River 36 Ec 0.50S 29.40 E
Ishavet = Arctic Ocean (EN) 67 Be 85.00N 170.00 E
Isherton 54 Gc 2.19N 59.22W
Ishigaki 27 Lg 24.20N 124.09 E
Ishikari 29a Bb 43.13N 141.18 E
Ishikari-Dake 29a Cb 43.33N 143.00 E
Ishikari-Gawa 29a Bb 43.15N 141.20 E
Ishikari-Heiya 29a Bb 43.00N 141.40 E
Ishikari-Wan 27 Pc 43.25N 141.00 E
Ishikawa [Jap.] 27 Mf 26.27N 127.50 E
Ishikawa [Jap.] 29 Gc 37.09N 140.27 E
Ishikawa Ken [2] 28 Nf 36.35N 136.40 E
Ishim Steppe (EN) = Išimskaja Step 21 Id 55.00N 67.30 E
Ishinomaki 27 Pd 38.25N 141.18 E
Ishinomaki-Wan 29 Gb 38.20N 141.15 E
Ishioka 28 Pf 36.11N 140.16 E
Ishitate-San 29 De 33.44N 134.03 E
Ishizuchi-Yama 29 Ce 33.45N 133.05 E
Ishodnaja, Gora- 20 Nd 64.50N 173.26W
Ishpeming 44 Db 46.30N 87.40W
Isidro Alves 55 Ee 20.09S 55.12W
Isigny-sur-Mer 11 Ee 49.19N 1.06W
Isii 29 Dd 34.04N 134.26 E
Işıklar Dağı 24 Bb 40.50N 27.05 E
Işıklı 15 Mk 38.19N 29.51 E
Işıklı Göl 15 Mk 38.14N 29.55 E
Isili 14 Dk 39.44N 9.06 E
Isilkul 19 He 54.55N 71.16 E
Išim 22 Id 56.09N 69.27 E
Išim 21 Jd 57.45N 71.12 E
Išimbaj 19 Fe 53.28N 56.02 E
Išimskaja Step = Ishim Steppe (EN) 21 Id 55.00N 67.30 E
Isinga 20 Gf 52.55N 112.00 E
Isiolo 36 Gb 0.21N 37.35 E
Isiro 31 Jh 2.48N 27.41 E
Isisford 59 Id 24.16S 144.26 E
Isjangulovo 17 Hj 52.12N 56.36 E
Iskandar 18 Gd 41.35N 69.43 E
Iskăr 15 Hf 43.44N 24.27 E
Iskăr, Jazovir- 15 Gg 42.25N 23.35 E
Iškašim 19 Hh 36.44N 71.39 E
İskenderun = Alexandretta (EN) 22 Ff 36.37N 36.07 E
İskenderun Körfezi = Alexandretta, Gulf of- (EN) 23 Eb 36.30N 35.40 E
İskilip 24 Fb 40.45N 34.29 E
Iski-Naukat 18 Id 40.14N 72.41 E
Iskininski 16 Rf 47.13N 52.36 E
Iskitim 20 Df 54.38N 83.18 E
Iskushuban 35 Ic 10.13N 50.14 E
Iskut 42 Ee 56.45N 131.48W
Isla-Cristina 13 Eg 37.12N 7.19W
İslâhiye 24 Gd 37.26N 36.41 E
Islāmābād 22 Jf 33.42N 73.10 E
Islāmābād → Anantnāg 25 Fb 33.44N 75.09 E
Isla Mujeres 48 Pg 21.12N 86.43W
Island = Iceland (EN) [1] 6 Eb 65.00N 18.00W
Island = Iceland (EN) 5 Eb 65.00N 18.00W
Island Harbour 51b Ab 18.16N 63.02W
Island Lagoon 59 Hf 31.30S 136.40 E
Island Lake 42 If 53.45N 94.30W
Island Lake 42 If 53.58N 94.46W
Island Pond 44 Lc 44.50N 71.53W
Islands, Bay of - [Can.] 42 Lg 49.10N 58.15W
Islands, Bay of- [N.Z.] 62 Fa 35.10S 174.10 E
Islao, Massif de l'- 30 Lk 22.30S 45.20 E
Islas de la Bahía [3] 49 De 16.20N 86.30W
Islay 5 Fd 55.46N 6.10W
Islaz 15 Hf 43.44N 24.45 E
Isle 11 Fj 44.55N 0.15W
Isle of Man [5] 9 Ig 54.15N 4.30W
Isle of Wight [3] 9 Lk 50.40N 1.15W
Isleta 45 Ci 34.55N 106.42W
Isle-Verte 44 Ma 48.01N 69.22W
Ismael Cortinas 55 Dk 33.56S 57.08W
Ismailia (EN) = Al Ismā'īlīyah 33 Fc 30.35N 32.16 E
Ismailly 16 Pi 40.47N 48.13 E
Ismantorps Borg 8 Gh 56.45N 16.40 E
Isnā 31 Kf 25.18N 32.33 E
Isny im Allgäu 10 Gi 47.42N 10.02 E
Isojärvi 8 Ic 61.45N 21.45 E
Isojoki 7 Ee 62.07N 21.58 E
Isojoki/Storå 7 Ee 62.07N 21.58 E
Isoka 36 Fe 10.08S 32.38 E
Isola del Liri 14 Hi 41.41N 13.34 E
Isola di Capo Rizzuto 14 Ll 38.58N 17.05 E
Isonzo 14 He 45.43N 13.33 E
Isonzo (EN) = Soča 14 He 45.43N 13.33 E
Isosyöte 7 Gd 65.37N 27.35 E
Isparta 23 Db 37.46N 30.33 E
Isperih 15 Jf 43.43N 26.50 E
Ispica 14 In 36.47N 14.55 E
İspir 24 Ib 40.29N 41.00 E
Ispiriz Dağı 24 Jc 38.03N 43.55 E
Israel (EN) = Yisra'el [1] 22 Ff 31.30N 35.00 E
Isratu 35 Fb 16.20N 39.55 E
Issa 8 Mh 56.55N 28.50 E
Issano 54 Gb 5.49N 59.25W
Issaran, Ra's- 24 Eh 28.50N 32.56 E
Issel 10 Cd 52.00N 6.10 E
Isser 13 Ph 36.51N 3.40 E
Issia [3] 34 Dd 6.30N 6.35W
Issia 34 Dd 6.29N 6.35W
Issoire 11 Ji 45.33N 3.15 E
Issoudun 11 Hh 46.57N 2.00 E
Issyk 18 Kc 43.20N 77.28 E
Issyk-Kul, Ozero- 21 Je 42.25N 77.15 E
Issyk-Kulskaja Oblast [3] 19 Hg 42.10N 78.00 E
Ist 14 If 44.17N 14.47 E
İstanbul 22 Ee 41.01N 28.58 E
İstanbul-Bakırköy 15 Li 40.59N 28.52 E
İstanbul-Beyoğlu 15 Lh 41.02N 28.59 E
İstanbul Boğazi = Bosporus (EN) 5 Ig 41.00N 29.00 E
İstanbul-Kadıköy 15 Mi 40.59N 29.01 E
Isteren 8 Db 62.00N 11.50 E
Istgāh-e Eqbālīyeh 24 Ne 35.50N 50.45 E
Isthilart 55 Dj 31.11S 57.58W
Istiaia 15 Gk 38.57N 23.09 E
Istisu 16 Nj 39.57N 46.00 E
Istmina 54 Cb 5.09N 76.42W
Isto, Mount- 38 Ec 69.12N 143.48W
Istok 15 Dg 42.47N 20.29 E
Istokpoga, Lake- 44 Gl 27.22N 81.17W
Istra = Istria (EN) 5 Hf 45.00N 14.00 E
Istres 11 Kk 43.31N 4.59 E
Istria 15 Le 44.34N 28.43 E
Istria (EN) = Istra 5 Hf 45.00N 14.00 E
Isulan 26 He 7.02N 124.29 E
Itabaiana 54 Kf 10.41S 37.26W
Itabaianinha 54 Kf 11.16S 37.47W
Itaberá 55 Hf 23.51S 49.09W
Itaberaba 54 Jf 12.32S 40.18W
Itaberai 54 Ig 16.02S 49.48W
Itabira 54 Jg 19.37S 43.13W
Itabirito 55 Ke 20.15S 43.48W
Itabuna 53 Mg 14.48S 39.16W
Itacaiúna, Rio- 54 Ie 5.21S 49.08W
Itacarambi 55 Jb 15.01S 44.03W
Itacoatiara 53 Kf 3.08S 58.25W
Itacolomi, Pico do- 55 Ke 20.26S 43.29W
Itacuai, Rio- 54 Dd 4.20S 70.12W
Itacumbi 55 Ei 28.44S 55.08W
Itacurubi del Rosario 55 Dg 24.29S 56.41W
Itaguari, Rio- 55 Jb 14.11S 44.40W
Itaguaru 55 Hb 15.44S 49.37W
Itaguí 54 Cb 6.12N 75.40W
Itaimbézinho 55 Gi 28.38S 50.34W
Itaituba 53 Kf 4.17S 55.59W
Itajai 53 Lh 26.53S 48.39W
Itajai Açu, Rio- 55 Hh 26.54S 48.33W
Itajubá 54 Ih 22.26S 45.27W
Itajuípe 54 Kf 14.41S 39.22W
Itaka 20 Gf 53.54N 118.42 E
Italia = Italy (EN) [1] 6 Hg 42.50N 12.50 E
Itálica 13 Fg 37.25N 6.05W
Italy (EN) = Italia [1] 6 Hg 42.50N 12.50 E
Itambacuri 54 Jg 18.01S 41.42W
Itambé, Pico de- 52 Lg 18.23S 43.21W
Itämeri = Baltic, Sea (EN) 5 Hd 57.00N 19.00 E
Itampolo 37 Gd 24.41S 43.57 E
Itanagar 25 Ic 26.57N 93.15 E
Itanará, Rio- 55 Eg 24.00S 55.53W
Itanhaém 56 Kb 24.11S 46.47W
Itano 29 Dd 34.09N 134.28 E
Itapaci 55 Hb 14.57S 49.34W
Itapagé 54 Kd 3.41S 39.34W
Itapajipe 55 Hd 19.54S 49.22W
Itaparaná, Rio- 54 Fe 5.47S 63.03W
Itapebi 54 Kg 15.56S 39.32W
Itapecerica 55 Je 20.28S 45.07W
Itapecuru-Mirim 54 Jd 3.24S 44.20W
Itaperimirim 54 Jh 21.01S 40.50W
Itaperina, Pointe- 30 Lk 24.59S 47.06 E
Itaperuna 54 Jh 21.12S 41.54W
Itapetinga 54 Jg 15.15S 40.15W
Itapetininga 56 Kb 23.36S 48.03W
Itapetininga, Rio- 55 Hf 23.35S 48.27W
Itapeva 55 Hf 23.58S 48.52W
Itapeva, Lagoa- 55 Hi 29.30S 49.55W
Itapicuru, Rio- [Braz.] 54 Kf 11.47S 37.32W
Itapicuru, Rio- [Braz.] 52 Lf 2.52S 44.12W
Itapipoca 54 Kd 3.31S 39.33W
Itapiranga [Braz.] 54 Gd 2.45S 58.01W
Itapiranga [Braz.] 55 Fh 27.08S 53.43W
Itapirapuã, Pico- 55 Hg 24.17S 49.12W
Itápolis 55 He 21.35S 48.46W
Itaporã 55 Ef 22.01S 54.54W
Itaporanga [Braz.] 55 Hf 23.42S 49.29W
Itaporanga [Braz.] 54 Ke 7.18S 38.10W
Itapúa [3] 55 Eh 26.50S 55.50W
Itapuã 55 Gj 30.16S 51.01W
Itapuranga 54 Ig 15.35S 49.59W
Itaqui 56 Ic 29.08S 56.33W
Itaquyry 55 Eg 24.56S 55.13W
Itararé 55 Hg 24.07S 49.20W
Itararé, Rio- 55 Hf 23.10S 49.42W
Itārsi 25 Fd 22.37N 77.45 E
Itarumã 55 Gd 18.42S 51.25W
Itati 55 Ch 27.16S 58.15W
Itatinga 55 Hf 23.07S 48.36W
Itatski 20 De 56.07N 89.20 E
Itaum 55 Ef 22.00S 55.20W
Itaúna 54 Jh 20.04S 44.34W
Itaya-Tōge 29 Gc 37.50N 140.13 E
Itbāy 30 Kf 22.00N 35.30 E
Itbayat 26 Hb 20.46N 121.50 E
Itchen 12 Ad 50.57N 1.22W
Ite 54 Dg 17.50S 70.58W
Itéa 15 Fk 38.26N 22.25 E
Ithaca 43 Lc 42.26N 76.30W
Ithaca (EN) = Itháki 15 Dk 38.24N 20.40 E
Itháki 15 Dk 38.22N 20.43 E
Itháki = Ithaca (EN) 15 Dk 38.24N 20.40 E
Ith Hils 10 Fd 52.05N 9.35 E
Ithnayn, Harrat- 24 Ii 26.40N 40.10 E
Itigi 36 Fd 5.42S 34.29 E
Itimbiri 30 Jh 2.02N 22.44 E
Itiopya = Ethiopia (EN) [1] 31 Kh 9.00N 39.00 E
Itiquira 54 Hg 17.05S 54.56W
Itiquira, Rio- 52 Kg 17.18S 56.44W
Itirapina 55 If 22.15S 47.49W
Itiúba 54 Kf 10.43S 39.51W
Itivdleq 41 Ge 66.38N 53.51W
Itō 28 Og 34.58N 139.05 E
Itoigawa 28 Nf 37.02N 137.51 E
Itoko 36 Dc 1.00S 21.45 E
Itoman 29b Ab 26.07N 127.40 E
Iton 11 Hf 49.09N 1.12 E
Itremo, Massif de l'- 37 Hd 20.45S 46.30 E
Itsā 24 Dh 29.15N 30.48 E
Itsukaichi 29 Cd 34.22N 132.22 E
Itsuki 29 Be 32.24N 130.50 E
Ittiri 14 Cj 40.36N 8.34 E
Itu [Braz.] 55 If 23.16S 47.19W
Itu [Nig.] 34 Gd 5.12N 7.59 E
Itu, Rio- 55 Ei 29.25S 55.51W
Itui, Rio- 54 Dd 4.38S 70.19W
Ituiutaba 54 Ig 18.58S 49.28W
Itula 36 Ec 3.29S 27.52 E
Itumbiara 54 Ig 18.25S 49.13W
Itumkale 16 Nh 42.43N 45.35 E
Ituna 46 Na 51.10N 103.30W
Itungi Port 36 Fd 9.35S 33.56 E
Itupiranga 54 Ie 5.09S 49.20W
Iturama 55 Gd 19.44S 50.11W
Iturbide 48 Oh 19.40N 89.37W
Ituri 30 Jh 1.40N 27.01 E
Iturregui 55 Bm 36.50S 61.08W
Iturup, Ostrov- 21 Qe 44.54N 147.30 E
Iturup, Ostrov-/Etorofu Tō 21 Qe 44.54N 147.30 E
Itutinga 55 Je 21.18S 44.40W
Ituverava 56 Kb 20.20S 47.47W
Ituxi, Rio- 54 Ee 7.18S 64.51W
Ituzaingó 55 Dh 27.36S 56.41W
Itz 10 Gg 49.58N 10.52 E
Itzehoe 10 Fc 53.55N 9.31 E
Ivacevići 16 Dc 52.43N 25.21 E
Ivai 55 Gg 25.01S 50.52W
Ivai, Rio- [Braz.] 55 Fi 29.08S 53.16W
Ivai, Rio- [Braz.] 52 Kh 23.18S 53.42W
Ivaiporã 55 Gg 24.15S 51.45W
Ivajlovgrad 15 Jh 41.32N 26.08 E
Ivakoany, Massif de l'- 37 Hd 23.50S 46.25 E
Ivalojoki 7 Gc 68.43N 27.36 E
Ivančice 10 Mg 49.06N 16.22 E
Ivangorod 7 Gg 59.23N 28.20 E
Ivangrad 15 Cg 42.51N 19.52 E
Ivanhoe 58 Fh 32.54S 144.18 E
Ivanić-Grad 14 Ke 45.42N 16.24 E
Ivaniči 10 Uf 50.38N 24.24 E
Ivanjica 15 Df 43.35N 20.14 E
Ivanjska 14 Lf 44.55N 17.04 E
Ivankov 16 Fd 50.57N 29.58 E
Ivano-Frankovo 10 Tg 49.52N 23.46 E
Ivano-Frankovsk 6 If 48.55N 24.43 E
Ivano-Frankovskaja Oblast [3] 19 Cf 48.40N 24.40 E
Ivanovka [R.S.F.S.R.] 20 Hf 50.18N 127.59 E
Ivanovka [Ukr.-U.S.S.R.] 16 Gf 46.57N 30.28 E
Ivanovo [Bye.-U.S.S.R.] 16 Dc 52.10N 25.32 E
Ivanovo [R.S.F.S.R.] 6 Kd 57.00N 40.59 E
Ivanovskaja Oblast [3] 19 Ed 57.00N 41.50 E
Ivanovskoje 8 Me 59.12N 28.59 E
Ivanščica 14 Kd 46.11N 16.10 E
Ivdel 19 Gc 60.42N 60.28 E
Ivenec 8 Lk 53.55N 26.49 E
Ivigtut 41 Hf 61.15N 48.00W
Ivindo 30 Ii 0.09S 12.09 E
Ivinheima 55 Ff 22.10S 53.37W
Ivinheima, Rio- 54 Hh 23.14S 53.42W
Ivinski razliv 7 If 61.10N 35.00 E
Iviza (EN) = Eivissa/Ibiza 5 Gh 39.00N 1.25 E
Iviza (EN) = Ibiza/Eivissa 5 Gh 39.00N 1.25 E
Ivje 10 Vc 53.55N 25.51 E
Ivohibe 37 Hd 22.29S 46.52 E
Ivoire, Côte d'- = Ivory Coast (EN) 30 Gh 5.00N 5.00W
Ivolândia 55 Gc 16.34S 50.51W
Ivory Coast (EN) = Côte d'Ivoire [1] 31 Gh 8.00N 5.00W
Ivory Coast (EN) = Ivoire, Côte d'- 30 Gh 5.00N 5.00W
Ivösjön 8 Fh 56.05N 14.25 E
Ivrea 14 Be 45.28N 7.52 E
Ivrindi 15 Kj 39.34N 27.29 E
Ivry-la-Bataille 12 Df 48.53N 1.28 E
Ivry-sur-Seine 12 Ef 48.49N 2.23 E
Ivujivik 39 Lc 62.25N 77.54W
Iwai-Shima 29 Be 33.47N 131.58 E
Iwaizumi 28 Pe 39.50N 141.48 E
Iwaki 22 Qf 36.55N 140.48 E
Iwaki-Gawa 29 Ga 41.01N 140.22 E
Iwaki-Hisanohama 29 Gc 37.09N 140.59 E
Iwaki-Jōban 29 Gc 37.02N 140.50 E
Iwaki-Kawamae 29 Gc 37.12N 140.45 E
Iwaki-Miwa 29 Gc 37.09N 140.42 E
Iwaki-Nakoso 29 Gc 36.56N 140.48 E
Iwaki-Onahama 29 Gc 36.57N 140.53 E
Iwaki-San 29 Ga 40.40N 140.20 E
Iwaki-Taira 29 Gc 37.05N 140.55 E
Iwaki-Uchigō 29 Gc 37.04N 140.50 E
Iwaki-Yoshima 29 Gc 37.05N 140.50 E
Iwaki-Yotsukura 29 Gc 37.07N 140.58 E
Iwakuni 27 Ne 34.09N 132.11 E
Iwami 29 Dd 35.35N 134.20 E
Iwami-Kōgen 29 Cd 35.00N 132.30 E
Iwamizawa 27 Pc 43.12N 141.46 E
Iwanai 28 Pc 42.58N 140.30 E
Iwanuma 29 Gb 38.07N 140.52 E
Iwase 29 Gc 36.21N 140.06 E
Iwasuge-Yama 29 Fc 36.44N 138.32 E
Iwata 29 Ed 34.42N 137.48 E
Iwate 28 Pe 39.30N 141.30 E
Iwate Ken [2] 28 Pe 39.30N 141.15 E
Iwate San 28 Pe 39.49N 141.26 E
Iwo 34 Fd 7.38N 4.11 E
Iwŏn 27 Mc 40.19N 128.37 E
Iwuy 12 Fd 50.14N 3.19 E
Ixiamas 54 Ef 13.45S 68.09W
Ixmiquilpan 48 Jg 20.29N 99.14W
Ixopo 37 Ef 30.08S 30.00 E
Ixtapa, Punta- 48 Ii 17.39N 101.40W
Ixtepec 47 Ee 16.34N 95.06W
Ixtlahuacán del Rio 48 Hg 20.52N 103.15W
Ixtlán del Rio 47 Dd 21.02N 104.22W
Iyah 35 Hd 9.00N 49.38 E
Iyo 28 Lh 33.46N 132.42 E
Iyo-mishima 29 Ce 33.58N 133.33 E
Iyo-Nada 29 Ce 33.40N 132.15 E
Iž 7 Mh 56.00N 52.41 E
Iž 14 Jf 44.03N 15.06 E
Izabal [3] 49 Cf 15.30N 89.00W
Izabal, Lago de- 47 Ge 15.30N 89.10W
Izad Khvāst 24 Og 31.31N 52.07 E
Izamal 47 Gd 20.56N 89.01W
Izamal 48 Og 20.56N 89.01W
Izapa 47 Ff 14.55N 92.10W
'Izbat al Jājah 24 Dj 24.48N 30.35 E
'Izbat Dush 24 Dj 24.34N 30.42 E
Izberbaš 19 Eg 42.33N 47.52 E
Izbiceni 15 Hf 43.50N 24.39 E
Izborsk 8 Mg 57.39N 28.01 E
Izegem 12 Fd 50.55N 3.12 E
Izeh 24 Mg 31.50N 49.50 E
Izena-Shima 29b Ab 26.56N 127.56 E
Iževsk 6 Ld 56.51N 53.14 E
Izjaslav 16 Ed 50.09N 26.51 E
Izjum 19 Df 49.12N 37.17 E
Izki 23 Ie 22.57N 57.49 E
Ižma 5 Lb 65.19N 52.54 E
Ižma 17 Fd 65.02N 53.55 E
Izmail 6 If 45.21N 28.50 E
İzmir = Smyrna (EN) 22 Ef 38.25N 27.09 E
İzmir, Gulf of- (EN) = İzmir Körfezi 24 Bc 38.30N 26.50 E
İzmir-Bornova 24 Bc 38.27N 27.14 E
İzmir Körfezi = Izmir, Gulf of- (EN) 24 Bc 38.30N 26.50 E
İzmit 22 Ee 40.46N 29.55 E
İzmit Körfezi 24 Cb 40.45N 29.35 E
İzmor 24 Ab 40.11N 25.55 E
Iznajar, Embalse de- 13 Hg 37.15N 4.30W
Iznalloz 13 Ig 37.23N 3.31W
İznik 24 Cb 40.26N 29.43 E
İznik Gölü 23 Ca 40.26N 29.30 E
Izobilny 16 Lg 45.19N 41.42 E
Izola 14 He 45.32N 13.40 E
Izōrskaja Vozvyšennost 8 Me 59.35N 29.30 E
Izozog, Bañados del- 54 Fg 18.50S 62.10W
Izra' 24 Gf 32.51N 36.15 E
Izsák 10 Pj 46.48N 19.22 E
Iztočni Rodopi 15 Ih 41.44N 25.31 E
Izúcar de Matamoros 48 Jh 18.36N 98.28W
Izu-Hantō 28 Og 34.55N 138.55 E
Izuhara 28 Jg 34.12N 129.17 E
Izu Islands (EN) = Izu-shotō 21 Pf 32.00N 140.00 E
Izumi [Jap.] 28 Kh 32.05N 130.22 E
Izumi [Jap.] 29 Dd 34.29N 135.26 E
Izumi [Jap.] 29 Gb 38.19N 140.51 E
Izumi-sano 29 Dd 34.24N 135.18 E
Izumo 28 Lg 35.22N 132.46 E
Izu-Shotō = Izu Islands (EN) 21 Pf 32.00N 140.00 E
Izvesti CIK, Ostrova- = Izvestiya Tsik Islands (EN) 20 Da 75.55N 82.30 E
Izvestiya Tsik Islands (EN) = Izvesti CIK, Ostrova- 20 Da 75.55N 82.30 E

J

Jaala 8 Lc 61.03N 26.29 E
Jaama/Jama 8 Lf 58.59N 27.45 E
Jääsjärvi 8 Lc 61.35N 26.05 E
Jaba 24 Qe 35.55N 56.35 E
Jabal, Baḥr al- = Mountain Nile (EN) 30 Kh 9.30N 30.30 E
Jabal Abū Rujmayn 24 Ge 34.50N 37.56 E
Jabal al Awliyā' 35 Eb 15.14N 32.30 E
Jabal az Zannah 24 Oj 24.11N 52.38 E
Jabalón 13 Hf 38.53N 4.05W
Jabalpur 22 Jg 23.10N 79.57 E
Jabal Şabāyā 33 Hf 18.35N 41.03 E
Jabālyah 24 Fg 31.32N 34.29 E
Jabal Zuqar, Jazīrat- 33 Hg 14.00N 42.45 E
Jabbārah 33 Hf 19.27N 40.03 E
Jabbeke 12 Fc 51.11N 3.05 E
Jabjabah, Wādī- 35 Ea 22.37N 33.17 E
Jablah 24 Fe 35.21N 35.55 E
Jablanac 14 If 44.43N 14.53 E
Jablanica 15 Dh 41.15N 20.30 E
Jablanica [Bul.] 15 Hf 43.01N 24.06 E
Jablanica [Yugo.] 14 Lg 43.39N 17.45 E
Jabločny 20 Jg 47.09N 142.03 E
Jablonec nad Nisou 10 Lf 50.44N 15.10 E
Jablonicki, Pereval- 5 If 48.18N 24.28 E
Jablonovo 20 Gf 51.51N 112.50 E
Jablonovy Hrebet = Yablonovy Range (EN) 21 Nd 53.30N 115.00 E
Jablunkovský průsmyk 10 Og 49.31N 18.45 E
Jaboatão 54 Ke 8.07S 35.01W
Jaboti 55 De 20.48S 56.23W
Jabrīn 24 Ni 27.51N 51.26 E
Jabuka 14 Jg 43.05N 15.28 E
Jabung, Tanjung- 26 Dg 1.01S 104.22 E
Jabuticabal 56 Kb 21.16S 48.19W
Jabuticatubas 55 Kd 19.30S 43.45W
Jaca 13 Lb 42.34N 0.33W
Jacaltenango 49 Bf 15.40N 91.44W
Jacaré, Rio- 55 Je 21.03S 45.16W
Jacarei 55 Jf 23.19S 45.58W
Jacarezinho 56 Kb 23.09S 49.59W
Jáchal, Rio- 52 Ji 30.44S 68.08W
Jaciara [Braz.] 55 Ib 14.12S 46.41W
Jaciara [Braz.] 55 Eb 15.59S 54.57W
Jackman 44 Lc 45.38N 70.16W
Jack Mountain 46 Eb 48.47N 120.57W
Jackpot 46 Hf 41.59N 114.09W
Jacksboro 45 Gj 33.13N 98.10W
Jacks Mountain 44 Ie 40.45N 77.30W
Jackson [Al.-U.S.] 44 Dj 31.31N 87.53W
Jackson [Bar.] 51q Ab 13.10N 59.43W
Jackson [Ky.-U.S.] 44 Fg 37.33N 83.23W
Jackson [Mi.-U.S.] 43 Kc 42.15N 84.24W
Jackson [Mn.-U.S.] 45 Ie 43.37N 94.59W
Jackson [Mo.-U.S.] 45 Lh 37.23N 89.40W
Jackson [Ms.-U.S.] 39 Jf 32.18N 90.12W
Jackson [Oh.-U.S.] 44 Ff 39.03N 82.40W
Jackson [Tn.-U.S.] 43 Jd 35.37N 88.49W
Jackson [Wy.-U.S.] 46 Je 43.29N 110.38W
Jackson, Cape- 62 Fd 40.59S 174.19 E
Jackson, Mount- [Ant.] 66 Qf 71.23S 63.22W
Jackson, Mount- [Austl.] 59 Df 30.15S 119.16 E
Jackson Bay 62 Ce 43.55S 168.40 E
Jackson Head 62 Ce 43.58S 168.37 E
Jackson Lake 46 Je 43.55N 110.40W
Jacksonville [Ar.-U.S.] 45 Ji 34.52N 92.07W
Jacksonville [Fl.-U.S.] 39 Kf 30.20N 81.40W
Jacksonville [Il.-U.S.] 45 Kg 39.44N 90.14W
Jacksonville [N.C.-U.S.] 43 Le 34.45N 77.26W
Jacksonville [Tx.-U.S.] 45 Ih 31.58N 95.17W
Jacksonville Beach 43 Ke 30.18N 81.24W
Jacmel 47 Je 18.14N 72.32W
Jacobābād 25 Dc 28.17N 68.26 E
Jacobina 54 Jf 11.11S 40.31W
Jacob Lake 46 Ih 36.45N 112.13W
Jacobs 45 La 50.15N 89.46W
Jacona de Plancarte 48 Hh 19.57N 102.16W
Jacques-Cartier, Détroit de- 42 Lg 50.00N 63.30W
Jacques Cartier, Mont- 42 Kg 48.58N 65.57W
Jacuba, Rio- 55 Fd 18.25S 52.28W
Jacuí, Rio- 52 Ki 30.02S 51.15W
Jacuí-Mirim, Rio- 55 Fi 28.51S 53.07W
Jacundá 54 Id 4.33S 49.28W
Jacundá, Rio- 54 Hd 1.57S 50.26W
Jacupiranga 56 Kb 24.42S 48.00W
Jada 34 Hd 8.46N 12.09 E
Jadal 34 Fb 18.37N 5.00 E

Index Symbols

[1] Independent Nation
[2] State, Region
[3] District, County
[4] Municipality
[5] Colony, Dependency
Continent
Physical Region
Historical or Cultural Region
Mount, Mountain
Volcano
Hill
Mountains, Mountain Range
Hills, Escarpment
Plateau, Upland
Pass, Gap
Plain, Lowland
Delta
Salt Flat
Valley, Canyon
Crater, Cave
Karst Features
Depression
Polder
Desert, Dunes
Forest, Woods
Heath, Steppe
Oasis
Cape, Point
Coast, Beach
Cliff
Peninsula
Isthmus
Sandbank
Island
Atoll
Rock, Reef
Islands, Archipelago
Rocks, Reefs
Coral Reef
Well, Spring
Geyser
River, Stream
Waterfall Rapids
River Mouth, Estuary
Lake
Salt Lake
Intermittent Lake
Reservoir
Swamp, Pond
Canal
Glacier
Ice Shelf, Pack Ice
Ocean
Sea
Gulf, Bay
Strait, Fjord
Lagoon
Bank
Seamount
Tablemount
Ridge
Shelf
Basin
Escarpment, Sea Scarp
Fracture
Trench, Abyss
National Park, Reserve
Point of Interest
Recreation Site
Cave, Cavern
Historic Site
Ruins
Wall, Walls
Church, Abbey
Temple
Scientific Station
Airport
Port
Lighthouse
Mine
Tunnel
Dam, Bridge

Jadar [Yugo.] 15 Ce 44.38N 19.16 E
Jaddi, Rās- 25 Cc 25.14N 63.31 E
Jade 10 Ec 53.25N 8.05 E
Jadebusen 10 Ec 53.30N 8.10 E
Jadid Ra's al Fil 35 Dc 12.40N 25.43 E
Jadito Wash 46 Ji 35.22N 110.50W
J.A.D. Jensens Nunatakker 41 Hf 62.45N 48.20W
Jädraås 8 Gd 60.51N 16.28 E
Jadransko More=Adriatic Sea (EN) 5 Hg 43.00N 16.00 E
Jadrin 7 Li 55.57N 46.11 E
Jādū 33 Bc 31.57N 12.01 E
Ja'ēl 35 Ic 10.56N 51.09 E
Jaén [3] 13 If 38.00N 3.30W
Jaén 13 Ig 37.46N 3.47W
Jæren 8 Af 58.45N 5.45 E
Jærens rev 8 Af 58.45N 5.29 E
Jaffa, Cape- 59 Hg 36.58S 139.40 E
Jaffna 22 Ji 9.40N 80.00 E
Jafr, Qā' al- 24 Gg 30.17N 36.20 E
Jägala Jõgi 8 Ke 59.28N 25.04 E
Jagdalpur 22 Kh 19.04N 82.02 E
Jagdaqi 27 La 50.26N 124.02 E
Jaghbūb, Wāḥāt al-=Jarabub Oasis (EN) 30 Jf 29.41N 24.43 E
Jagotin 16 Gd 50.17N 31.47 E
Jagst 10 Fg 49.14N 9.11 E
Jaguapitã 55 Gf 23.07S 51.33W
Jaguaquara 54 Kf 13.32S 39.58W
Jaguarão 56 Jd 32.34S 53.23W
Jaguarão, Rio- 55 Fk 32.39S 53.12W
Jaguarari 54 Jf 10.16S 40.12W
Jaguari 55 Ei 29.30S 54.41W
Jaguari, Rio- [Braz.] 55 Ei 29.42S 55.07W
Jaguari, Rio- [Braz.] 55 If 22.41S 47.17W
Jaguariaiva 56 Kb 24.15S 49.42W
Jaguaribe 54 Ke 5.53S 38.37W
Jaguaribe, Rio 52 Mf 4.25S 37.45W
Jaguaruana 54 Kd 4.50S 37.47W
Jagüey Grande 49 Gb 22.32N 81.08W
Jahadyjaha 17 Pc 67.03N 72.01 E
Jahām, 'Irq- 24 Li 26.12N 47.00 E
Jahorina 14 Mg 43.42N 18.35 E
Jahrom 23 Hd 28.31N 53.33 E
Jahroma 7 Ih 56.20N 37.29 E
Jaice 23 Ff 44.21N 17.17 E
Jaicoa, Cordillera- 51a Ab 18.25N 67.05W
Jaicós 54 Je 7.21S 41.08W
Jailolo 26 If 1.05N 127.30 E
Jailolo, Selat- 26 If 0.05N 129.05 E
Jaina, Isla de- 48 Ng 20.14N 90.40W
Jainca 27 Hd 35.57N 102.00 E
Jaipur 22 Jg 26.55N 75.49 E
Jaisalmer 25 Ec 26.55N 70.54 E
Jaja 20 De 56.12N 86.26 E
Jäjarm 24 Qd 36.58N 56.27 E
Jajdúdorog 10 Ri 47.49N 21.30 E
Jajere 34 Hc 11.59N 11.26 E
Jajpan 18 Hd 40.23N 70.50 E
Jajsan 16 Td 50.51N 56.14 E
Jajva 19 Fd 59.20N 57.16 E
Jajva 17 Hg 59.16N 56.42 E
Jakarta 22 Mj 6.10S 106.46 E
Jakobshavn/Ilulissat 67 Nc 69.20N 50.50W
Jakobstad/Pietarsaari 7 Fe 63.40N 22.42 E
Jakoruda 15 Gg 42.02N 23.40 E
Jakupica 15 Eh 41.43N 21.26 E
Jakutsk 22 Oc 62.13N 129.49 E
Jakutskaja ASSR [3] 20 Hc 67.00N 130.00 E
Jal 45 Ej 32.07N 103.12W
Jalaid Qi (Inder) 27 Lb 46.41N 122.52 E
Jalājil 24 Kj 25.41N 45.28 E
Jalālābād 23 Lc 34.26N 70.28 E
Jalālah al Baḥrīyah, Jabal al- 24 Eh 29.20N 32.20 E
Jalālah al Qiblīyah, Jabal al- 24 Eh 28.42N 32.22 E
Jalán, Río- 49 Df 15.43N 87.34W
Jalandhar 22 Jf 31.19N 75.34 E
Jalapa [3] 49 Cf 14.35N 89.55W
Jalapa [Guat.] 47 Gf 14.38N 89.59W
Jalapa [Mex.] 48 Mi 17.43N 92.49W
Jalapa [Nic.] 47 Gf 13.55N 86.08W
Jalapa Enriquez 39 Jh 19.32N 96.55W
Jalasjarvi 7 Fe 62.30N 22.45 E
Jales 55 Ge 20.16S 50.33W
Jälgaon 25 Fd 21.01N 75.34 E
Jalhay 12 Hd 50.34N 5.58 E
Jalibah 24 Lg 30.35N 46.32 E
Jalib Shahab 24 Lg 30.23N 46.09 E
Jalingo 34 Hd 8.53N 11.22 E
Jalisco [2] 47 Dd 20.20N 103.40W
Jāliṭah=La Galite (EN) 30 He 37.32N 8.56 E
Jāliṭah, Canal de- 14 Cm 37.20N 9.00 E
Jallas 13 Cb 42.54N 9.08W
Jālna 25 Fe 19.50N 75.53 E
Jalón 13 Kc 41.47N 1.04W
Jalostotitlán 48 Hg 21.12N 102.28W
Jalpa 48 Hg 21.38N 102.58W
Jalpaiguri 25 Hc 26.31N 88.44 E
Jalpan 48 Jg 21.14N 99.29W
Jalpug, Ozero- 16 Fg 45.25N 28.40 E
Jalta 19 Dg 44.30N 34.10 E
Jaltepec, Rio- 48 Li 17.26N 94.59W
Jālū 33 Dd 28.30N 21.05 E
Jālū, Wāḥāt-=Gialo Oasis (EN) 30 Jf 29.00N 21.20 E
Jaluit Atoll 57 Hd 6.00N 169.35 E
Jalūlā' 24 Ke 34.16N 45.10 E
Jalutorovsk 19 Gd 56.40N 66.18 E
Jam [Iran] 24 Pe 35.45N 55.02 E
Jam [Iran] 24 Oi 27.50N 52.22 E
Jama/Jaama 8 Lf 58.59N 27.45 E
Jamaari 30 Ig 12.06N 10.14 E
Jamaica 49 Jc 20.12N 75.09W
Jamaica 38 Lh 18.15N 77.30W
Jamaica [1] 39 Lh 18.15N 77.30W
Jamaica Channel 47 Ie 18.00N 75.30W
Jamaica Channel (EN)=Jamaïque, Canal de- 49 Jd 18.00N 75.30W
Jamaïque, Canal de-=Jamaica Channel (EN) 49 Jd 18.00N 75.30W
Jamal, Poluostrov-=Yamal Peninsula (EN) 21 Ib 70.00N 70.00 E
Jamalo-Nenecki Nacionalny okrug [3] 20 Cc 67.00N 75.00 E
Jamālpur 25 Hd 24.55N 89.56 E
Jamāme 31 Lh 0.04N 42.46 E
Jamantau, Gora- 5 Le 54.15N 58.06 E
Jamanxim, Rio- 52 Kf 4.43S 56.18W
Jamari, Rio- 54 Fe 8.27S 63.30W
Jamarovka 20 Gf 50.38N 110.16 E
Jambi 22 Oj 1.38S 123.42 E
Jambi [3] 26 Dg 1.36S 103.37 E
Jambol [2] 15 Jg 42.15N 26.35 E
Jambol 15 Jg 42.29N 26.30 E
Jambongan, Pulau- 26 Ge 6.41N 117.25 E
Jambuair, Tanjung- 26 Ce 5.16N 97.30 E
Jambusar 25 Ed 22.03N 72.48 E
James Bay 38 Kd 51.00N 80.30W
Jameson Land 41 Jd 70.45N 23.45W
James River [U.S.] 38 Je 42.52N 97.18W
James River [U.S.] 44 Ig 36.56N 76.27W
James Ross 66 Re 64.15S 57.45W
James Ross Strait 42 Hc 69.50N 96.30W
Jamestown [Austl.] 59 Hf 33.12S 138.36 E
Jamestown [N.D.-U.S.] 43 Hb 46.54N 98.42W
Jamestown [N.Y.-U.S.] 43 Lc 42.05N 79.15W
Jamestown [St.Hel.] 31 Gj 15.56S 5.43W
Jamestown Reservoir 45 Gc 47.15N 98.40W
Jamm 8 Mf 58.24N 28.15 E
Jammer Bugt 7 Bh 57.20N 9.30 E
Jammu 22 Jf 32.44N 74.52 E
Jammu and Kashmir [3] 25 Fb 34.00N 76.00 E
Jāmnagar 22 Jg 22.28N 70.04 E
Jamno, Jezioro- 10 Mb 54.15N 16.10 E
Jampol 16 Fe 48.16N 28.17 E
Jämsä 7 Ff 61.52N 25.12 E
Jamsah 24 Ei 27.38N 33.35 E
Jämsänkoski 8 Kc 61.55N 25.11 E
Jamshedpur 22 Kg 22.48N 86.11 E
Jamsk 20 Ke 59.37N 154.10 E
Jämtland [2] 7 De 63.00N 14.40 E
Jämtland 8 Fa 63.25N 14.05 E
Janā 24 Mi 27.22N 49.54 E
Jana 21 Pb 71.31N 136.32 E
Janakpur 25 Hc 26.42N 85.55 E
Janaucu, Ilha- 54 Hc 0.30N 50.10W
Janaul 17 Gh 56.16N 54.59 E
Janda, Laguna de la- 13 Gh 36.15N 5.51W
Jandaia 55 Gc 17.06S 50.07W
Jandaq 24 Pe 34.02N 54.26 E
Jandiatuba, Rio- 54 Ed 3.28S 68.42W
Jandowae 59 Ke 26.47S 151.06 E
Jandula 13 Hf 38.03N 4.06W
Jane Peak 62 Cf 45.20S 168.19 E
Janesville 43 Jc 42.41N 89.01W
Jangada 55 Db 15.14S 56.29W
Jangada, Rio- 55 Db 15.12S 56.24W
Jangao Shan 27 Gf 25.31N 98.08 E
Jange 27 Ie 31.59N 105.28 E
Jangijer 18 Gd 40.18N 68.50 E
Jangijul 19 Gg 41.07N 69.03 E
Jangirabad 18 Ed 40.03N 65.59 E
Jango 55 Ee 20.27S 55.29W
Jangxi Sheng (Chiang-hsi Sheng)=Kiangsi (EN) [2] 27 Kf 28.00N 116.00 E
Jangy-Bazar 18 Hd 41.40N 70.52 E
Janikowo 10 Od 52.45N 18.07 E
Janin 24 Ff 32.28N 35.18 E
Janisjarvi, Ozero- 7 He 62.00N 31.00 E
Janja 14 Nf 44.40N 19.19 E
Jan Mayen 5 Fa 71.00N 8.30W
Jan Mayen Ridge (EN) 5 Fb 69.00N 8.00W
Jano-Indigirskaja Nizmennost 20 Ib 71.00N 139.30 E
Janos 47 Cb 30.56N 108.08W
Jánoshalma 10 Pj 46.18N 19.20 E
Jánosháza 10 Ni 47.07N 17.10 E
Janów Lubelski 10 Sf 50.43N 22.24 E
Janów Podlaski 10 Td 52.11N 23.11 E
Jansenville 37 Cf 32.56S 24.40 E
Jansha Jang 21 Mg 28.46N 104.38 E
Janski Zaliv 21 Pb 72.00N 136.00 E
Jantarny 8 Hj 54.53N 19.55 E
Jantra 15 If 43.38N 25.34 E
Januária 54 Jg 15.29S 44.22W
Janūbīyah, Aṣ Ṣaḥrā' al-=Southern Desert (EN) 30 Jf 24.00N 30.00 E
Janykurgan 19 Gg 43.55N 67.14 E
Janzhang Ansha 27 Ke 9.30N 116.59 E
Japan (EN) 21 Pf 35.00N 135.00 E
Japan (EN)=Nippon [1] 22 Pf 38.00N 137.00 E
Japan, Sea of- (EN)=Japonskoje More 21 Pf 40.00N 134.00 E
Japan, Sea of- (EN)=Nippon Kai 21 Pf 40.00N 134.00 E
Japan, Sea of- (EN)=Tong-Hae 21 Pf 40.00N 134.00 E
Japan Basin (EN) 27 Nc 40.00N 135.00 E
Japan Trench (EN) 3 If 37.00N 143.00 E
Japiim 54 De 7.37S 72.54W
Japonskoje More=Japan, Sea of- (EN) 21 Pf 40.00N 134.00 E
Jäppilä 8 Lb 62.23N 27.26 E
Japtiksale 17 Pb 69.25N 72.29 E
Japurá 54 Ed 1.24S 69.25W
Japurá, Rio- 52 Jf 3.08S 64.46W
Jaqué 49 Hj 7.31N 78.10W
Jaquet, Point- 51g Ba 15.38N 61.26W
Jaquirana 55 Gi 28.54S 50.23W
Jar 7 Mg 58.17N 52.06 E
Jarabub Oasis (EN)=Jaghbūb, Wāḥāt al- 30 Jf 29.41N 24.43 E
Jarābulus 24 Hd 36.49N 38.01 E
Jaraguá [Braz.] 55 Hb 15.45S 49.20W
Jaraguá [Braz.] 55 Hh 26.29S 49.04W
Jaraguá, Serra do- 55 Hh 26.40S 49.15W
Jaraguari 55 Ee 20.09S 54.25W
Jaraiz de la Vera 13 Gd 40.04N 5.45W
Jarama 13 Id 40.02N 3.39W
Jaramillo 56 Gg 47.11S 67.09W
Jarandilla 13 Gd 40.08N 5.39W
Jaransk 19 Ed 57.18N 47.55 E
Jarānwāla 25 Eb 31.20N 73.26 E
Jarash 24 Ff 32.17N 35.54 E
Jarau, Cêrro do- 55 Dj 30.18S 56.32W
Jarbah 30 Ie 33.48N 10.54 E
Järbo 7 Df 60.43N 16.36 E
Jarcevo [R.S.F.S.R.] 16 Hb 55.05N 32.45 E
Jarcevo [R.S.F.S.R.] 20 Ed 60.15N 90.10 E
Jardāwīyah 24 Jj 25.24N 42.42 E
Jardim 54 Gh 21.28S 56.09W
Jardine River 59 Ib 11.10S 142.30 E
Jardines de la Reina, Archipiélago de los- 47 Id 20.50N 78.55W
Jardinópolis 55 Ie 21.02S 47.46W
Jarega 17 Fe 63.27N 53.31 E
Jaremča 16 De 48.31N 24.33 E
Jarenga 7 Le 62.08N 49.03 E
Jarez de Garcías Salinas 47 Dd 22.39N 103.00W
Järfälla 8 Ge 59.24N 17.50 E
Jargava 15 Lc 46.27N 28.27 E
Jari, Rio- 52 Kf 1.09S 51.54W
Jarid, Shaṭṭ al- 30 He 33.42N 8.26 E
Jarīr, Wādī- 24 Jj 25.38N 42.30 E
Jarjis 32 Jc 33.30N 11.07 E
Jarkovo 17 Mh 57.26N 67.05 E
Jarmah 33 Bd 26.32N 13.04 E
Järna 8 Ge 59.06N 17.34 E
Jarnac 11 Fi 45.41N 0.10W
Järnlunden 8 Ff 58.10N 15.40 E
Jarny 11 Le 49.09N 5.53 E
Jarocin 10 Ne 51.59N 17.31 E
Jaroměř 10 Lf 50.21N 15.55 E
Jaroměřice nad Rokytnou 10 Lg 49.06N 15.54 E
Jaroslavl 6 Jd 57.37N 39.52 E
Jaroslavskaja Oblast [3] 19 Dd 57.45N 39.15 E
Jaroslavski 28 Lb 44.10N 132.13 E
Jarosław 10 Sf 50.02N 22.42 E
Järpen 8 Ea 63.21N 13.29 E
Jarrāḥī 24 Mg 30.44N 48.46 E
Jarroto, Ozero- 17 Oc 67.55N 71.40 E
Jar-Sale 20 Cc 66.50N 70.50 E
Jartai 27 Id 39.45N 105.46 E
Jartai Yanchi 27 Id 39.45N 105.40 E
Jarudej 17 Od 65.50N 71.50 E
Jarud Qi (Lubei) 27 Lc 44.30N 120.55 E
Järva-Jaani/Jarva-Jani 8 Ke 59.00N 25.49 E
Jarva-Jani/Järva-Jaani 8 Ke 59.00N 25.49 E
Järvakandi/Jarvakandi 8 Kf 58.45N 24.44 E
Jarvakandi/Järvakandi 8 Kf 58.45N 24.44 E
Järvenpää 7 Ff 60.28N 25.06 E
Jarvis Island 57 Ke 0.23S 160.01W
Järvsö 7 Df 61.43N 16.10 E
Jaščera 8 Ne 59.05N 30.00 E
Jaselda 16 Ec 52.07N 26.29 E
Jasień 10 Le 51.46N 15.01 E
Jasikan 34 Fd 7.24N 0.28 E
Jasinja 10 Uh 48.14N 24.31 E
Jasinovataja 16 Je 48.05N 37.57 E
Jasiołka 10 Rg 49.47N 21.30 E
Jasīra 35 He 1.57N 45.16 E
Jasīred Mayd 35 Hc 11.12N 47.13 E
Jāsk 23 Id 25.38N 57.46 E
Jaškul 16 Nf 46.17N 45.10 E
Jaškul 16 Nf 46.11N 45.17 E
Jasło 10 Rg 49.45N 21.29 E
Jasmund 10 Jb 54.32N 13.35 E
Jasnogorsk 16 Jb 54.29N 37.42 E
Jasny [R.S.F.S.R.] 19 Fe 51.01N 59.59 E
Jasny [R.S.F.S.R.] 20 Hf 53.18N 128.03 E
Jason Islands 56 Hh 51.00S 61.00W
Jasper [Alta.-Can.] 39 Hd 52.53N 118.05W
Jasper [Al.-U.S.] 43 Je 33.50N 87.17W
Jasper [Fl.-U.S.] 44 Fj 30.31N 82.57W
Jasper [In.-U.S.] 44 Df 38.24N 86.56W
Jasper [Tn.-U.S.] 44 Eh 35.04N 85.38W
Jasper [Tx.-U.S.] 45 Jk 30.55N 93.59W
Jasper Seamount (EN) 38 Gf 30.32N 122.42W
Jaşşān 24 Kf 32.58N 45.53 E
Jastrebarsko 14 Je 45.40N 15.39 E
Jastrowie 10 Mc 53.26N 16.49 E
Jastrzebie Zdrój 10 Og 49.58N 18.34 E
Jászapáti 10 Qi 47.31N 20.09 E
Jászárokszállás 10 Pi 47.38N 19.59 E
Jászberény 10 Pi 47.30N 19.55 E
Jászság 10 Pi 47.25N 20.00 E
Jat, Uad el- 30 Ff 26.47N 13.03W
Jatai 53 Kg 17.53S 51.43W
Jatapu, Rio- 54 Gd 2.30S 58.17W
Játiva/Xátiva 13 Lf 38.59N 0.31W
Jatobá, Rio- 55 Ea 12.23S 54.07W
Jaú 56 Kb 22.18S 48.33W
Jaú, Rio- 54 Fd 1.55S 61.25W
Jaua, Cerro- 54 Fc 4.48N 64.26W
Jauaperi, Rio- 52 Jf 1.26S 61.35W
Jauja 54 Cf 11.48S 75.30W
Jaumave 48 Jf 23.25N 99.23W
Jaunanna 8 Lg 57.13N 27.10 E
Jaunelgava/Jaunjelgava 7 Fh 56.37N 25.06 E
Jaunfeld 14 Id 46.35N 14.45 E
Jaungulbene 8 Lh 57.00N 26.42 E
Jaunjelgava/Jaunelgava 7 Fh 56.37N 25.06 E
Jaunpiebalga 8 Lg 57.05N 26.03 E
Jaunpur 25 Gc 25.44N 82.41 E
Jauru 55 Ed 18.35S 54.17W
Jauru, Rio- [Braz.] 54 Hg 18.40S 54.36W
Jauru, Rio- [Braz.] 55 Dc 16.22S 57.46W
Java (EN)=Jawa 21 Mj 7.20S 110.00 E
Javalambre 13 Ld 40.06N 1.00W
Javalambre, Sierra de- 13 Ld 40.05N 1.00W
Javan 18 Ge 38.19N 69.01 E
Javānrūd 24 Le 34.48N 46.30 E
Javari, Rio- 52 If 4.21S 70.02W
Java Sea (EN)=Jawa, Laut- 21 Mj 5.00S 110.00 E
Java Trench (EN) 3 Hk 10.30S 110.00 E
Jávea 13 Mf 38.47N 0.10 E
Javier 13 Kb 42.36N 1.13W
Javor 14 Mf 44.07N 18.59 E
Javorie 10 Ph 48.27N 19.18 E
Javornik 10 Jh 48.10N 13.35 E
Javorniky 10 Og 49.20N 18.20 E
Javorov 16 Cd 50.00N 23.27 E
Javorová skála 10 Kg 49.31N 14.30 E
Jävre 7 Ed 65.09N 21.29 E
Jawa=Java (EN) 21 Mj 7.20S 110.00 E
Jawa, Laut-=Java Sea (EN) 21 Mj 5.00S 110.00 E
Jawa Barat [3] 26 Eh 7.00S 107.00 E
Jawa Tengah [3] 26 Eh 7.30S 110.00 E
Jawa Timur [3] 26 Fh 8.00S 113.00 E
Jawf, Wādī- 33 If 15.50N 45.30 E
Jawor 10 Me 51.03N 16.11 E
Jaworzno 10 Pf 50.13N 19.15 E
Jaya, Puncak- 57 Ee 4.10S 137.00 E
Jayapura 58 Fe 2.32S 140.42 E
Jayawijaya, Pegunungan- 26 Kg 4.30S 139.30 E
Jāyezān 24 Mg 30.50N 49.52 E
Jaypur 25 He 18.51N 82.35 E
Jazāyer va Banāder-e Khalīj-e Fārs va Daryā-ye Omān→Hormozgān 23 Id 27.30N 56.00 E
Jaz Mūrīān, Hāmūn-e- 23 Id 27.20N 58.55 E
Jazva 17 Hf 60.23N 56.50 E
Jazvān 24 Md 36.58N 48.40 E
Jazykovo 7 Li 54.20N 47.22 E
Jazzīn 24 Ff 33.32N 35.34 E
Jdiouia 13 Mi 35.56N 0.50 E
Jeannetty, Ostrov- 20 Ka 76.45N 158.25 E
Jean-Rabel 49 Kd 19.52N 73.11W
Jebala 13 Gi 35.25N 5.30W
Jebal Bārez, Kūh-e- 23 Id 28.30N 58.20 E
Jebba 34 Fd 9.08N 4.50 E
Jebel 15 Ed 45.33N 21.14 E
Jebha 13 Hi 35.13N 4.40W
Jedincy 16 Ee 48.06N 27.19 E
Jedisa 16 Nh 42.32N 44.14 E
Jędrzejów 10 Qf 50.39N 20.18 E
Jeetze 10 Hc 53.09N 11.04 E
Jefferson 45 Ie 42.01N 94.23W
Jefferson, Mount- [Nv.-U.S.] 43 Dd 38.46N 116.55W
Jefferson, Mount- [Or.-U.S.] 46 Ed 44.40N 121.47W
Jefferson City 39 Jf 38.34N 92.10W
Jefferson River 46 Jd 45.56N 111.30W
Jeffersonville 44 Ef 38.17N 85.44W
Jef-Jef el Kebir 35 Ca 20.30N 21.25 E
Jefremov 19 De 53.11N 38.07 E
Jega 34 Fc 12.13N 4.23 E
Jegersfontein 37 De 29.44S 25.29 E
Jegorjevsk 7 Ji 55.25N 39.07 E
Jegorlyk 16 Lf 46.32N 41.52 E
Jegorlykskaja 16 Lf 46.34N 40.44 E
Jehegnadzor 16 Nj 39.47N 45.18 E
Jeja 16 Kf 46.39N 38.36 E
Jejsk 19 Df 46.40N 38.15 E
Jejuí Guazú, Rio- 55 Dg 24.13S 57.09W
Jēkabpils/Jekabpils 19 Cd 56.30N 25.59 E
Jekaterinovka 16 Nc 52.04N 44.30 E
Jekkevarre 7 Eb 69.28N 20.00 E
Jelabuga 19 Fd 55.48N 52.05 E
Jelai 26 Fg 2.59S 110.45 E
Jelan 16 Md 50.57N 43.43 E
Jelancy 20 Ff 52.44N 106.27 E
Jelanec 16 Gf 47.42N 31.50 E
Jelcz 10 Ne 51.01N 17.18 E
Jelec 6 Je 52.37N 38.30 E
Jeleckj 17 Lc 67.03N 64.15 E
Jelenia Góra 10 Lf 50.55N 15.46 E
Jelenia Góra [2] 10 Lf 50.55N 15.45 E
Jelgava 19 Cd 56.39N 23.41 E
Jelica 15 Df 43.47N 20.20 E
Jelin vrh 15 Cf 43.02N 19.27 E
Jelizavety, Mys- 5 Qd 54.30N 142.40 E
Jelizovo [Bye.-U.S.S.R.] 16 Fc 53.24N 29.00 E
Jelizovo [R.S.F.S.R.] 20 Kf 53.06N 158.20 E
Jelling 8 Ci 55.45N 9.26 E
Jelnja 16 Hb 54.35N 33.12 E
Jeloguj 20 Dd 63.10N 87.45 E
Jelow Gir 24 Lf 32.58N 47.48 E
Jeløy 8 De 58.30N 10.40 E
Jelsk 16 Fd 51.49N 29.13 E
Jelva 17 Ee 63.05N 50.50 E
Jemaja, Pulau- 26 Ef 2.55N 105.45 E
Jemanželinsk 19 Ge 54.45N 61.20 E
Jember 26 Fh 8.10S 113.42 E
Jemca 7 Je 63.32N 41.56 E
Jemca 7 Je 63.04N 40.18 E
Jemeppe-sur-Sambre 12 Gd 50.28N 4.40 E
Jeminay 27 Eb 47.28N 85.48 E
Jemnice 10 Lg 49.01N 15.35 E
Jena 10 Hf 50.56N 11.35 E
Jenakijevo 16 Ke 48.12N 38.18 E
Jenašimski Polkan, Gora- 20 Ee 59.50N 92.45 E
Jendyr 17 Mf 61.38N 67.20 E
Jeneponto 26 Gh 5.41S 119.42 E
Jenisej=Yenisey (EN) 21 Kb 71.50N 82.40 E
Jenisejsk 20 Ee 58.27N 92.10 E
Jenisejski Krjaž=Yenisey Ridge (EN) 21 Ld 59.00N 92.30 E
Jenisejski Zaliv=Yenisey Bay (EN) 20 Db 72.00N 81.00 E
Jennersdorf 14 Kd 46.56N 16.08 E
Jennings 45 Jk 30.13N 92.39W
Jenny Lind 42 Hc 68.50N 101.30W
Jenny Point 51g Bb 15.28N 61.15W
Jensen 46 Kf 40.22N 109.17W
Jens Munk 42 Jc 69.40N 79.40W
Jequié 53 Lg 13.51S 40.05W
Jequitai 55 Jc 17.15S 44.28W
Jequitai, Rio 55 Jc 17.04S 44.50W
Jequitinhonha, Rio- 52 Mg 15.51S 38.53W
Jerada 32 Gc 34.19N 2.09W
Jeralijev 19 Fg 43.12N 51.43 E
Jerbogačen 20 Fd 61.15N 107.57 E
Jérémie 47 Je 18.39N 74.08W
Jeremoabo 54 Kf 10.04S 38.21W
Jerer 35 Gd 7.40N 43.48 E
Jerevan 6 Kg 40.11N 44.30 E
Jerez, Punta- 48 Kf 22.54N 97.46W
Jerez de la Frontera 13 Fh 36.41N 6.08W
Jerez de los Caballeros 13 Ff 38.19N 6.46W
Jergeni 5 Kf 47.00N 44.00 E
Jericho 59 Jd 23.36S 146.08 E
Jermak 19 He 52.02N 76.55 E
Jermakovskoje 20 Ef 53.16N 92.24 E
Jermentau 19 He 51.38N 73.10 E
Jermolajevo 17 Gj 52.43N 55.48 E
Jeroaquara 55 Gb 15.23S 50.25W
Jerofej Pavlovič 20 Hf 53.58N 121.57 E
Jerome 46 He 42.43N 114.31W
Jersa 17 Fc 66.19N 52.32 E
Jersey 9 Kl 49.15N 2.10W
Jersey City 43 Mc 40.44N 74.04W
Jerseyville 45 Kg 39.07N 90.20W
Jeršov 19 Ee 51.20N 48.17 E
Jertarski 17 Lh 56.47N 64.25 E
Jerte 13 Fe 39.58N 6.17W
Jerusalem (EN)=Yerushalayim 22 Ff 31.46N 35.14 E
Jeruslan 16 Od 50.20N 46.25 E
Jervis Bay 59 Kg 35.05S 150.44 E
Jerzu 14 Dk 39.47N 9.31 E
Jesberg 12 Lc 51.00N 9.09 E
Jesenice [Yugo.] 14 If 44.14N 15.34 E
Jesenice [Yugo.] 14 Id 46.27N 14.04 E
Jesenik 10 Nf 50.14N 17.12 E
Jesi 14 Hg 43.31N 13.14 E
Jesil 19 Ge 51.58N 66.24 E
Jeskianhor, Kanal- 18 Fe 39.15N 66.00 E
Jessej 20 Fc 68.29N 102.10 E
Jessentuki 16 Mg 44.03N 42.51 E
Jessheim 7 Cf 60.09N 11.11 E
Jessore 25 Hd 23.10N 89.13 E
Ještěd 10 Kf 50.42N 14.59 E
Jestro, Wabe- 30 Lh 4.11N 42.09 E
Jesup 43 Ke 31.36N 81.53W
Jesús Carranza 48 Li 17.26N 95.02W
Jesús Maria 56 Hd 30.59S 64.06W
Jesús Maria, Boca de- 48 Ke 24.29N 97.40W
Jesús Maria, Rio- 48 Gg 21.55N 104.30W
Jetmore 45 Gg 38.03N 99.54W
Jever 10 Dc 53.35N 7.54 E
Jevgenjevka 18 Kc 43.27N 77.40 E
Jevišovka 10 Mh 48.52N 16.36 E
Jevlah 19 Eg 40.35N 47.10 E
Jevnaker 7 Cf 60.15N 10.28 E
Jevpatorija 19 Df 45.12N 33.18 E
Jevrejskaja Avtonomnaja Oblast 20 Ig 48.30N 132.00 E
Jeyḥūn 24 Pi 27.16N 55.12 E
Jeypore → Jaypur 25 He 18.51N 82.35 E
Jezercës 5 Hg 42.26N 19.49 E
Jezero 14 Lf 44.21N 17.10 E
Jeziorak, Jezioro- 10 Pc 53.50N 19.35 E
Jeziorany 10 Qc 53.58N 20.46 E
Jeziorka 10 Rd 52.10N 21.06 E
Jhang Sadar 25 Eb 31.16N 72.19 E
Jhānsi 22 Jg 25.26N 78.35 E
Jhelum 25 Eb 32.56N 73.44 E
Jhelum 21 Jf 31.12N 72.08 E
Jiaji → Qionghai 27 Jh 19.25N 110.28 E
Jialing Jiang 21 Mg 29.34N 106.35 E
Jiamusi 22 Pe 46.49N 130.21 E
Ji'an [China] 27 Mc 41.08N 126.10 E
Ji'an [China] 22 Ng 27.12N 114.59 E
Jianchang 28 Ed 40.49N 119.46 E
Jianchuan 27 Gf 26.32N 99.53 E
Jiande (Baisha) 27 Kf 29.31N 119.17 E
Jiang'an 27 If 28.40N 105.07 E
Jiangao Shan 27 Gf 25.31N 98.08 E
Jiangbiancun 27 Kf 27.13N 115.57 E
Jiangcheng 27 Hg 22.37N 101.48 E
Jiangdu (Xiannümiao) 28 Eh 32.30N 119.33 E
Jianghua (Shuikou) 27 Jg 24.58N 111.56 E
Jiangjin 27 If 29.15N 106.18 E
Jiangle 27 Kf 26.48N 117.29 E
Jiangling (Jingzhou) 27 Je 30.21N 112.10 E
Jiangmen 27 Jg 22.35N 113.02 E
Jiangpu 28 Eh 32.03N 118.37 E
Jiangshan 28 Ej 28.45N 118.37 E
Jiangsu Sheng (Chiang-su Sheng)=Kiangsu (EN) [2] 27 Ke 33.00N 120.00 E
Jiangyou (Zhongba) 27 He 31.48N 104.39 E
Jianhu 28 Eh 33.28N 119.47 E
Jianli 27 Jf 29.50N 112.55 E
Jian'ou 27 Kf 27.08N 118.20 E
Jianping (Yebaishou) 27 Kc 41.55N 119.37 E
Jianshi 27 Ie 30.32N 109.43 E
Jianshui 27 Hg 23.39N 102.46 E
Jianyang 27 Kf 27.23N 118.03 E
Jiaocheng 27 Jd 37.32N 112.09 E
Jiaoding Shan 27 Lc 41.11N 120.01 E
Jiaohe [China] 27 Mc 43.43N 127.20 E
Jiaohe [China] 28 De 38.01N 116.17 E
Jiaolai He [China] 28 Ef 37.07N 119.35 E
Jiaolai He [China] 28 Fc 43.02N 120.48 E
Jiaoliu He 28 Gb 45.21N 122.48 E
Jiaonan (Wanggezhuang) 28 Eg 35.53N 119.58 E

Index Symbols

[1] Independent Nation
[2] State, Region
[3] District, County
[4] Municipality
[5] Colony, Dependency
Continent
Physical Region
Historical or Cultural Region
Mount, Mountain
Volcano
Hill
Mountains, Mountain Range
Hills, Escarpment
Plateau, Upland
Pass, Gap
Plain, Lowland
Delta
Salt Flat
Valley, Canyon
Crater, Cave
Karst Features
Depression
Polder
Desert, Dunes
Forest, Woods
Heath, Steppe
Oasis
Cape, Point
Coast, Beach
Cliff
Peninsula
Isthmus
Sandbank
Island
Atoll
Rock, Reef
Islands, Archipelago
Rocks, Reefs
Coral Reef
Well, Spring
Geyser
River, Stream
Waterfall Rapids
River Mouth, Estuary
Lake
Salt Lake
Intermittent Lake
Reservoir
Swamp, Pond
Canal
Glacier
Ice Shelf, Pack Ice
Ocean
Sea
Gulf, Bay
Strait, Fjord
Lagoon
Bank
Seamount
Tablemount
Ridge
Shelf
Basin
Escarpment, Sea Scarp
Fracture
Trench, Abyss
National Park, Reserve
Point of Interest
Recreation Site
Cave, Cavern
Historic Site
Ruins
Wall, Walls
Church, Abbey
Temple
Scientific Station
Airport
Port
Lighthouse
Mine
Tunnel
Dam, Bridge

Jiaoxian 27 Kd 36.20N 120.00 E
Jiaozhou-Wan 28 Ff 36.10N 120.15 E
Jiaozuo 22 Nf 35.15N 113.18 E
Jiashan 28 Fi 30.51N 120.54 E
Jiashan (Mingguang) 28 Dh 32.47N 118.00 E
Jiashi/Payzawat 27 Cd 39.29N 76.39 E
Jiawang 28 Dg 34.27N 117.26 E
Jiaxian 28 Bh 33.58N 113.13 E
Jiaxing 27 Le 30.44N 120.46 E
Jiayin (Chaoyang) 27 Nb 48.52N 130.21 E
Jiayu 27 Jf 30.00N 113.57 E
Jiayuguan 27 Gd 39.49N 98.18 E
Jibalei 35 Ic 10.07N 50.47 E
Jibão, Serra do- 55 Jb 14.48S 45.15W
Jibiya 34 Gc 13.06N 7.14 E
Jibou 15 Gb 47.16N 23.15 E
Jicarón, Isla- 49 Gj 7.16N 81.47W
Jičín 10 Lf 50.26N 15.22 E
Jiddah 22 Fg 21.29N 39.12 E
Jiddat al Ḩarāsīs 23 Ie 20.05N 56.00 E
Jiehu → Yinan 28 Eg 35.33N 118.27 E
Jieshou 28 Ch 33.17N 115.22 E
Jiesjjavrre 7 Fb 69.40N 24.12 E
Jiexiu 27 Jd 37.00N 112.00 E
Jieyang 27 Kg 23.32N 116.25 E
Jieznas/Eznas 8 Kj 54.34N 24.17 E
Jifn, Wādī al- 24 Jj 25.48N 42.15 E
Jiftūn, Jazā'ir- 24 Ei 27.13N 33.56 E
Jigley 35 He 4.25N 45.22 E
Jiguaní 49 Ic 20.22N 76.26W
Jigüey, Bahia de- 49 Hb 22.08N 78.05W
Jigzhi 27 He 33.28N 101.29 E
Jihlava 10 Mh 48.55N 16.37 E
Jihlava 10 Lg 49.24N 15.34 E
Jihlavské vrchy 10 Lg 49.15N 15.20 E
Jihočeský kraj [3] 10 Kg 49.05N 14.30 E
Jihomoravský kraj [3] 10 Mg 49.10N 16.40 E
Jijel 32 Ib 36.48N 5.46 E
Jijel [3] 32 Ib 36.45N 5.45 E
Jijia 15 Lc 46.54N 28.05 E
Jijiga 35 Gd 9.21N 42.48 E
Jijona 13 Lf 38.32N 0.30W
Jikharrah 33 Dd 29.17N 21.38 E
Jilava 15 Je 44.20N 26.05 E
Jilf al Kabīr, Haḑabat al- 33 Ee 23.30N 26.00 E
Jilib 31 Lh 0.29N 42.47 E
Jilin 27 Mc 43.51N 126.33 E
Jilin Sheng (Chi-lin Sheng) =Kirin (EN) [2] 27 Mc 43.00N 126.00 E
Jiliu He 27 La 52.02N 120.41 E
Jiloca 13 Kc 41.21N 1.39W
Jima=Jimma (EN) 31 Kh 7.39N 36.49 E
Jimāl, Wādī- 24 Fj 24.40N 35.06 E
Jimani 49 Ld 18.28N 71.51W
Jimbe 36 De 11.05S 24.00 E
Jimbolia 15 Dd 45.48N 20.43 E
Jimena 13 Ig 37.50N 3.28W
Jimena de la Frontera 13 Gh 36.26N 5.27W
Jiménez 47 Dc 27.08N 104.55W
Jiménez del Teul 48 Gf 23.10N 104.05W
Jimma (EN)=Jima 31 Kh 7.39N 36.49 E
Jimo 28 Ff 36.24N 120.27 E
Jimsar 27 Ec 43.59N 89.04 E
Jimulco 48 He 25.20N 103.10W
Jināh 24 Dj 25.20N 30.31 E
Jinan=Tsinan (EN) 22 Nf 36.35N 117.00 E
Jincheng [China] 27 Jd 35.32N 112.53 E
Jincheng [China] 28 Fd 41.12N 121.25 E
Jinchuan /Quqên 27 He 31.02N 102.02 E
Jind 25 Fc 29.19N 76.19 E
Jindřichův Hradec 10 Kg 49.09N 15.00 E
Jinfo Shan 27 If 29.01N 107.14 E
Jing/Jinghe 27 Dc 44.39N 82.50 E
Jing'an 28 Cj 28.51N 115.21 E
Jingbian (Zhangjiapan) 27 Id 37.32N 108.45 E
Jingde 28 Ei 30.18N 118.30 E
Jingdezhen 22 Ng 29.18N 117.18 E
Jingfeng → Hexigten Qi 27 Kc 43.15N 117.31 E
Jinggang Shan 27 Jf 26.42N 114.07 E
Jinggu 27 Hg 23.28N 100.39 E
Jinghai 28 De 38.57N 116.56 E
Jinghe/Jing 27 Dc 44.39N 82.50 E
Jinghong (Yunjinghong) 27 Hg 21.59N 100.48 E
Jinghong Dao 27 Je 9.45N 114.28 E
Jingjiang 28 Fh 32.01N 120.15 E
Jingle 28 Ae 38.22N 111.56 E
Jingmen 27 Je 31.00N 112.11 E
Jingning 27 Id 35.30N 105.45 E
Jingping → Pinglu 28 Be 39.32N 112.14 E
Jingpo Hu 28 Jc 43.50N 128.53 E
Jingshan 28 Bi 31.04N 113.08 E
Jingtai 27 Hd 37.10N 104.08 E
Jingxian [China] 27 If 26.40N 109.37 E
Jingxian [China] 27 Ke 30.41N 118.29 E
Jingxing (Weishui) 28 Ce 38.03N 114.09 E
Jingyu 28 Ic 42.25N 126.48 E
Jingyuan 27 Hd 36.35N 104.40 E
Jingzhi 28 Ef 36.18N 119.22 E
Jingzhou → Jiangling 27 Je 30.21N 112.10 E
Jinhu (Licheng) 28 Eh 33.01N 119.01 E
Jinhua 27 Kf 29.09N 119.38 E
Jining [China] 22 Nf 37.26N 116.36 E
Jining [China] 22 Ne 41.02N 113.07 E
Jinja 31 Kh 0.26N 33.13 E
Jin Jiang 28 Cj 28.23N 115.48 E
Jinkou 28 Ci 30.20N 114.07 E
Jinotega [3] 49 Eg 14.00N 85.25W
Jinotega 47 Gf 13.06N 86.00W
Jinotepe 47 Gf 11.51N 86.12W
Jinping 27 Hg 22.45N 103.15 E
Jinsha 27 If 27.18N 106.16 E
Jinsha → Nantong 28 Fh 32.06N 120.52 E
Jinshan 28 Fi 30.54N 121.09 E
Jinshan → Harqin Qi 28 Ed 41.57N 118.40 E
Jinshi 28 Aj 29.03N 111.52 E
Jinta 27 Gc 40.00N 99.00 E
Jintan 28 Ei 31.45N 119.34 E
Jinxi 27 Lc 40.46N 120.50 E
Jinxian [China] 27 Ld 39.06N 121.44 E
Jinxian [China] 28 Dj 28.21N 116.16 E
Jinxiang 28 Dg 35.04N 116.19 E
Jinyang 27 Hf 27.39N 103.12 E
Jinyun 28 Fj 28.39N 120.05 E
Jinzhai (Meishan) 28 Ci 31.40N 115.52 E
Jinzhou 22 Oe 41.09N 121.08 E
Jinzū-Gawa 29 Ec 36.45N 137.13 E
Jiparaná, Rio- 52 Jf 8.03S 62.52W
Jipijapa 54 Bd 1.22S 80.34W
Jiquilisco 49 Cg 13.19N 88.35W
Jiquilisco, Bahia de- 49 Cg 13.10N 88.28W
Jirjā 33 Fd 26.20N 31.53 E
Jishou 27 If 28.18N 109.43 E
Jishu 28 Ib 44.16N 126.50 E
Jisr ash Shughur 24 Ge 35.48N 36.19 E
Jiu 15 Gd 43.47N 23.48 E
Jiucai Ling 27 Jf 25.33N 111.18 E
Jiucheng → Wucheng 28 Df 37.12N 116.04 E
Jiujiang 22 Ng 29.39N 116.00 E
Jiuling Shan 27 Jf 28.55N 114.50 E
Jiulong/Gyaisi 27 Hf 28.58N 101.33 E
Jiuquan (Suzhou) 22 Lf 39.46N 98.34 E
Jiurongcheng 28 Gf 37.22N 122.33 E
Jiutai 27 Mc 44.10N 125.50 E
Jīwani, Rās- 25 Cc 25.01N 61.44 E
Jixi [China] 28 Ei 30.04N 118.36 E
Jixi [China] 22 Pe 45.15N 130.55 E
Jixian [China] 28 Cg 35.23N 114.04 E
Jixian [China] 28 Cf 37.34N 115.34 E
Jixian [China] 28 Dd 40.03N 117.24 E
Jiyang 28 Df 36.59N 117.11 E
Jiyuan 28 Bg 35.06N 112.35 E
Jiyun He 28 De 39.05N 117.45 E
Jiz, Wādī al- 35 Ib 16.12N 52.14 E
Jīzān 22 Gh 16.54N 42.32 E
Jize 28 Cf 36.54N 114.52 E
Jizera 10 Kf 50.10N 14.43 E
Jizerské Hory 10 Lf 50.50N 15.13 E
Jizl, Wādī al- 24 Hj 25.39N 38.25 E
Jizō-Zaki 28 Lg 35.33N 133.18 E
Jmbe 36 De 10.20S 16.40 E
Jnchengjiang → Hechi 27 Ig 24.44N 108.02 E
Joaçaba 55 Gh 27.10S 51.30W
Joal-Fadiout 34 Bc 14.10N 16.51W
João Câmara 54 Ke 5.32S 35.48W
João Monlevade 55 Kd 19.50S 43.08W
João Pessoa 53 Mf 7.07S 34.52W
João Pinheiro 54 Ig 17.45S 46.10W
Joaquin V. González 56 Hb 25.00S 64.11W
Jobado 49 Ic 20.54N 77.17W
Jódar 13 Ig 37.50N 3.21W
Jodhpur 22 Jg 26.17N 73.02 E
Jodoigne/Geldenaken 12 Gd 50.43N 4.52 E
Joensuu 6 Ic 62.36N 29.46 E
Joerg Plateau 66 Qf 75.00S 69.30W
Joes Hill 64g Bb 1.48N 157.19W
Jõetsu 27 Od 37.06N 138.15 E
Joeuf 12 Ie 49.14N 6.01 E
Jöf di Montasio 14 Hd 46.26N 13.26 E
Joffre, Mount- 46 Ha 50.32N 115.13W
Jogbani 25 Hc 26.25N 87.15 E
Jõgeva/Jygeva 7 Gg 58.46N 26.26 E
Joghatāy 24 Qd 36.36N 57.01 E
Joghatāy, Kūh-e- 24 Qd 36.30N 57.00 E
Jōhana 29 Ec 36.31N 136.54 E
Johannesburg 31 Jk 26.15S 28.00 E
Jöhen 29 Ce 32.57N 132.35 E
John Day 46 Fd 44.25N 118.57W
John Day River 43 Cb 45.44N 120.39W
John H. Kerr Reservoir 44 Hg 36.31N 78.18W
John Martin Reservoir 45 Eg 38.05N 103.02W
John o' Groat's 9 Jc 58.38N 3.05W
Johnson 45 Fh 37.34N 101.45W
Johnson, Pico de- 48 Cc 29.13N 112.07W
Johnson City [Tn.-U.S.] 43 Kd 36.19N 82.21W
Johnson City [Tx.-U.S.] 45 Gk 30.17N 98.25W
Johnsons Crossing 42 Ed 60.29N 133.17W
Johnsons Point 51d Bb 17.02N 61.53W
Johnstone, Lake- 59 Ef 32.20S 120.40 E
Johnstone Strait 46 Ca 50.25N 126.00W
Johnston Island 57 Kc 17.00N 168.30W
Johnston Island [5] 58 Kc 17.00N 168.30W
Johnstown [N.Y.-U.S.] 44 Jd 43.01N 74.22W
Johnstown [Pa.-U.S.] 43 Lc 40.20N 78.56W
Johor Baharu 22 Mi 1.28N 103.45 E
Joia 55 Ei 28.39S 54.08W
Joigny 11 Jg 47.59N 3.24 E
Joinvile 53 Lh 26.18S 48.50W
Joinville 11 Lf 48.27N 5.08 E
Joinville Island 66 Re 63.15S 55.45W
Jokau 35 Ed 8.24N 33.49 E
Jokela 8 Kd 60.33N 24.59 E
Jokelbugten 41 Kc 78.25N 19.00W
Jokioinen 8 Jd 60.49N 23.28 E
Jokkmokk 7 Ec 66.36N 19.51 E
Jøkuleggi 8 Cc 61.03N 8.12 E
Jolfā 24 Kc 38.57N 45.38 E
Joliet 43 Jc 41.32N 88.05W
Joliette 42 Kg 46.01N 73.26W
Jolo 26 He 6.00N 121.00 E
Jolo Group 21 Oi 6.00N 121.09 E
Jølstravatnet 8 Bc 61.30N 6.15 E
Jomala 8 Hd 60.09N 19.58 E
Jombang 26 Fh 7.33S 112.14 E
Jomda 27 Ge 31.37N 98.20 E
Jönåker 8 Gf 58.44N 16.40 E
Jonava/Ionava 7 Fi 55.05N 24.17 E
Jonê 27 He 34.35N 103.32 E
Jones Bank 9 Fl 49.50N 8.00W
Jonesboro [Ar.-U.S.] 43 Id 35.50N 90.42W
Jonesboro [La.-U.S.] 45 Jj 32.15N 92.43W
Jones Mountains 66 Pf 73.32S 94.00W
Jones Sound 38 Kb 76.00N 85.00W
Jonesville 44 Fg 36.41N 83.06W
Jonglei [3] 35 Ed 7.20N 32.00 E
Jonglei 35 Ed 6.50N 31.18 E
Jonglei, Tur'ah-=Jonglei Canal (EN) 35 Ed 9.22N 31.30 E
Jonglei Canal (EN)=Jonglei, Tur'ah- 35 Ed 9.22N 31.30 E
Joniškėlis/Ioniškelis 8 Ki 56.00N 24.14 E
Joniškis/Ioniškis 7 Fh 56.16N 23.37 E
Jönköping 6 Hd 57.47N 14.11 E
Jönköping [2] 7 Dh 57.30N 14.30 E
Jonquière 42 Kg 48.25N 71.15W
Jonuta 48 Mh 18.05N 92.08W
Jonzac 11 Fi 45.27N 0.26W
Joplin 39 Jf 37.06N 94.31W
Jordan 43 Fb 47.19N 106.55W
Jordan 23 Ec 31.46N 35.33 E
Jordan (EN)=Al Urdun [1] 22 Ff 31.00N 36.00 E
Jordan Valley 46 Ge 42.58N 117.03W
Jordão, Rio- 55 Fg 25.46S 52.07W
Jorhāt 22 Lg 26.45N 94.13 E
Jörn 7 Ed 65.04N 20.02 E
Joroinen 7 Ge 62.11N 27.50 E
Jørpeland 7 Bg 59.01N 6.03 E
Jos 31 Hh 9.55N 8.54 E
José A. Guisasola 55 Bn 38.40S 61.05W
José Battle y Ordóñez 55 Ek 33.28S 55.07W
José Bonifácio 55 He 21.03S 49.41W
José de San Martin 56 Ff 44.02S 70.29W
Joselandia 55 Dc 16.32S 56.12W
José Otávio 55 Ej 31.17S 54.07W
José Pedro Varela 55 Ek 33.27S 54.32W
Joseph, Lake- 44 Hc 45.14N 79.45W
Joseph Bonaparte Gulf 57 Df 14.55S 128.15 E
Josephine Seamount (EN) 5 Eh 36.52N 14.20W
Joseph Lake 42 Kf 52.48N 65.17W
Joshimath 25 Fb 30.34N 79.34 E
Joškar-Ola 6 Kd 56.40N 47.55 E
Jos Plateau 30 Hh 10.00N 9.30 E
Josselin 11 Dg 47.57N 2.33W
Jostedalen 8 Bc 61.35N 7.20 E
Jostedalsbreen 7 Bf 61.40N 7.00 E
Jostefonn 8 Bc 61.26N 6.33 E
Jost Van Dyke 51a Db 18.28N 64.45W
Jotunheimen 5 Gc 61.40N 8.20 E
Joubertberge 37 Ac 18.45S 13.55 E
Joué-lès-Tours 11 Gg 47.21N 0.40 E
Jouquara, Rio- 55 Db 15.06S 57.06W
Joure, Haskerland- 12 Hb 52.58N 5.47 E
Joutsa 7 Gf 61.44N 26.07 E
Joutseno 7 Gf 61.06N 28.30 E
Jovan, Deli- 15 Fe 44.15N 22.13 E
Jovellanos 49 Gb 22.48N 81.12W
Joviânia 55 Hc 17.49S 49.30W
Jowhar 31 Lh 2.46N 45.32 E
Jow Kār 24 Me 34.26N 48.42 E
Jowzjān [3] 23 Kb 36.30N 66.00 E
Joya, Laguna de la- 48 Mj 15.55N 93.40W
Jreida 32 Df 18.19N 16.03W
Jrian Jaya [3] 26 Kg 3.55S 138.00 E
Juan Aldama 47 Dd 24.19N 103.21W
Juana Ramirez, Isla- 48 Kg 21.50N 97.40W
Juan Blanquier 55 Cl 35.46S 59.18W
Juancheng 28 Cg 35.33N 115.30 E
Juan de Fuca, Strait of- 38 Ge 48.20N 124.00W
Juan de Nova, Ile- 30 Lj 17.03S 42.45 E
Juan E. Barra 55 Bm 37.48S 60.29W
Juan Fernández, Archipielago-=Juan Fernández, Islands (EN) 52 Ii 33.00S 80.00W
Juan Fernandez Islands (EN)=Juan Fernández, Archipielago- 52 Ii 33.00S 80.00W
Juan G. Bazán 55 Bg 24.33S 60.50W
Juangriego 50 Eg 11.05N 63.57W
Juanjuy 54 Ce 7.11S 76.45W
Juan L. Lacaze 55 Dl 34.26S 57.27W
Juárez [Arg.] 56 Ie 37.40S 59.48W
Juárez [Mex.] 48 Id 27.37N 100.44W
Juárez, Sierra de- 48 Bb 32.00N 115.50W
Juarzohn 34 Dd 5.20N 8.58W
Juàzeirinho 54 Ke 7.04S 36.35W
Juàzeiro 53 Lf 9.25S 40.30W
Juàzeiro do Norte 53 Mf 7.12S 39.20W
Jūbā 31 Kh 4.51N 31.37 E
Juba (EN)=Ganāne, Webi- 30 Lh 0.15S 42.38 E
Juba, Rio- 55 Db 14.59S 57.44W
Jūbāl, Maḑiq- 24 Ei 27.40N 33.55 E
Jubaland (EN) 30 Lh 1.00N 42.00 E
Jubayl [Eg.] 24 Eh 28.12N 33.38 E
Jubayl [Leb.] 24 Fe 34.07N 35.39 E
Jubayt [Sud.] 35 Fb 18.57N 36.50 E
Jubayt [Sud.] 35 Fa 20.59N 36.18 E
Jubbada Dhexe [3] 35 Ge 1.15N 42.30 E
Jubbada Hoose [3] 35 Gf 0.30S 42.00 E
Jubbah 24 Ih 28.02N 40.56 E
Jubilee Lake 59 Fe 29.10S 126.40 E
Juby, Cap- 30 Ff 27.57N 12.55W
Júcar/Xúquer 5 Fh 39.09N 0.14W
Juçara 55 Gb 15.53S 50.51W
Jucaro 49 Hc 21.37N 78.51W
Jüchen 12 Ic 51.06N 6.30 E
Juchipila 48 Hg 21.25N 103.07W
Juchipila, Rio- 48 Hg 21.03N 103.25W
Juchitán de Zaragoza 39 Jh 16.26N 95.01W
Jučjugej 20 Jd 63.20N 142.15 E
Judas, Punta- 49 Ei 9.31N 84.32W
Judayyidat 'Ar'ar 23 Fc 31.22N 41.26 E
Judenburg 14 Ic 47.10N 14.40 E
Juding Shan 27 He 31.30N 104.00 E
Judith Mountains 46 Kc 47.12N 109.15W
Judith River 46 Kc 47.44N 109.38W
Judoma 20 Ie 59.08N 135.03 E
Judomski Hrebet 20 Jd 61.05N 141.30 E
Juegang → Rudong 28 Fh 32.19N 121.11 E
Juelsminde 8 Di 55.43N 10.01 E
Jufrah, Wāḩāt al-=Giofra Oasis (EN) 30 If 29.10N 16.00 E
Jug 5 Kc 60.45N 46.20 E
Jug 17 Hh 57.43N 56.12 E
Jugo-Osetinskaja Avtonomnaja Oblast [3] 19 Eg 42.20N 44.05 E
Jugorski Poluostrov 17 Kb 69.30N 62.30 E
Jugorski Šar, Proliv- 19 Gb 69.45N 60.35 E
Jugoslavija = Yugoslavia (EN) [1] 6 Hg 44.00N 19.00 E
Jugo-Tala 20 Kc 66.03N 151.05 E
Jugydjan 17 Gf 61.42N 54.58 E
Juhaym 24 Kh 29.36N 45.24 E
Juhnov 16 Ib 54.43N 35.12 E
Juhor 15 Ef 43.50N 21.15 E
Juhoslovenská nížina 10 Ph 48.10N 19.40 E
Juhua Dao 28 Fd 40.32N 120.48 E
Juigalpa 49 Eg 12.05N 85.24W
Juina, Rio- 55 Ca 12.36S 58.57W
Juine 11 If 48.32N 2.23 E
Juininha, Rio- 55 Ca 12.55S 59.13W
Juist 10 Cc 53.40N 7.00 E
Juiz de Fora 53 Lh 21.45S 43.20W
Jujuy [2] 56 Gb 23.00S 66.00W
Jukagirskoje Ploskogorje 20 Kc 66.00N 155.30 E
Jukonda 17 Mg 59.38N 67.20 E
Juksejevo 17 Gg 59.52N 54.16 E
Jula 7 Ke 63.48N 44.44 E
Juldybajevo 17 Hj 52.20N 57.52 E
Julesburg 45 Ef 40.59N 102.16W
Juli 54 Eg 16.13S 69.27W
Juliaca 54 Dg 15.30S 70.08W
Julia Creek 59 Id 20.39S 141.45 E
Julian Alps (EN)=Julijske Alpe 14 Hd 46.20N 13.45 E
Juliana Top 54 Gc 3.41N 56.32W
Julianehåb/Qaqortoq 67 Nc 60.50N 46.10W
Jülich 10 Cf 50.56N 6.22 E
Jülicher Borde 12 Id 50.50N 6.30 E
Julijske Alpe=Julian Alps (EN) 14 Hd 46.20N 13.45 E
Julimes 48 Gc 28.25N 105.27W
Júlio de Castilhos 55 Fi 29.14S 53.41W
Jullundur → Jalandhar 22 Jf 31.19N 75.34 E
Julong/New Kowloon 22 Ng 22.20N 114.09 E
Julu 28 Cf 37.13N 115.02 E
Juma 7 Hd 65.05N 33.13 E
Juma He 28 De 39.31N 116.08 E
Jumet, Charleroi- 11 Kd 50.27N 4.26 E
Jumièges 12 Ce 49.26N 0.49 E
Jumilla 13 Kf 38.29N 1.17W
Jümme 12 Ja 53.13N 7.31 E
Junāgadh 25 Ed 21.31N 70.28 E
Junan (Shizilu) 28 Eg 35.10N 118.50 E
Junaynah, Ra's al- 24 Eh 29.01N 33.58 E
Juncal 48 De 24.50N 111.47W
Juncos 51a Cb 18.13N 65.55W
Junction [Tx.-U.S.] 45 Gk 30.29N 99.46W
Junction [Ut.-U.S.] 46 Ig 38.14N 112.13W
Junction City 43 Hd 39.02N 96.50W
Jundiai 56 Kb 23.11S 46.52W
Jundiai do Sul 55 Gf 23.27S 50.17W
Jundūbah 32 Ib 36.30N 8.45 E
Jundūbah [3] 32 Ib 36.28N 8.41 E
Juneau 39 Fd 57.20N 134.27W
Junee 59 Jf 34.52S 147.35 E
Jungar Qi (Shagedu) 27 Jd 39.37N 110.58 E
Jungfrau 14 Bd 46.32N 7.58 E
Junggar Pendi=Dzungarian Basin 21 Ke 45.00N 88.00 E
Junin [2] 54 Df 11.30S 75.00W
Junin [Arg.] 53 Ji 34.35S 60.57W
Junín [Peru] 54 Cf 11.10S 76.00W
Junin, Lago de- 54 Cf 11.02S 76.05W
Junin de los Andes 56 Fe 39.56S 71.05W
Juniville 12 Ge 49.24N 4.23 E
Jūnīyah 24 Ff 33.59N 35.38 E
Junjaha 17 Jc 66.25N 62.00 E
Junlian 27 Hf 28.12N 104.34 E
Junsele 7 De 63.41N 16.54 E
Juntura 46 Fe 43.45N 118.05W
Junxian (Danjiang) 27 Je 32.31N 111.32 E
Juodupė 8 Kh 56.03N 25.44 E
Juojärvi 8 Mb 62.45N 28.35 E
Juoksengi 7 Fc 66.34N 23.51 E
Jupiá, Represa de- 56 Jb 20.47S 51.39W
Juquiá 55 Ig 24.19S 47.38W
Juquiá, Rio- 55 Ig 24.22S 47.49W
Juquiá, Serra do- 55 Gg 25.10S 52.00W
Jur 20 Ie 59.48N 137.29 E
Jur 30 Jh 8.39N 29.18 E
Jura [2] 14 Ac 47.25N 6.15 E
Jura 5 Gf 46.45N 6.30 E
Jura [3] 11 Lh 46.50N 5.50 E
Jura 9 Hf 56.00N 5.50W
Jura/Jūra 7 Fi 55.03N 22.10 E
Jūra/Jura 7 Fi 55.03N 22.10 E
Jura, Sound of- 9 Hf 55.55N 5.22W
Juradó 54 Cb 7.07N 77.46W
Juratiški 8 Kj 54.02N 26.00 E
Juraybī'āt 24 Lh 29.50N 46.03 E
Juraybīyāt 24 Kh 29.08N 45.33 E
Jurbarkas 7 Fi 55.08N 22.47 E
Jurdī, Wādī- 24 Ei 26.33N 32.44 E
Jurga 20 De 55.42N 84.55 E
Jurgamyš 17 Li 55.25N 64.28 E
Juribej 17 Nb 68.55N 69.05 E
Jurien Bay 59 Cf 30.15S 115.00 E
Jurigue, Rio- 55 Ec 16.29S 54.37W
Jurilovca 15 Le 44.46N 28.52 E
Jurja 7 Lg 59.03N 49.20 E
Jurjaha 17 Gc 66.42N 56.00 E
Jurjevec 7 Kh 57.22N 43.06 E
Jurjev-Polski 7 Jh 56.31N 39.44 E
Jurjuzan 17 Hi 55.43N 56.57 E
Jurjuzan 17 Ii 54.52N 58.28 E
Jurla 17 Gg 59.20N 54.16 E
Jurmala/Jūrmala 19 Cd 56.59N 23.38 E
Jūrmala/Jurmala 19 Cd 56.59N 23.38 E
Jurmo 8 Ie 59.50N 21.35 E
Jurong 28 Ei 31.56N 119.10 E
Juruá 54 Ed 3.27S 66.03W
Juruá, Rio- 52 Jf 2.37S 65.44W
Juruena, Rio- 52 Kf 7.20S 58.03W
Jurumirim, Represa de- 56 Kb 23.20S 49.00W
Juruti 54 Gd 2.09S 56.04W
Jurva 8 Ib 62.41N 21.59 E
Jusan-Kō 29a Bc 41.00N 140.20 E
Jusayrah 24 Nj 25.53N 50.36 E
Jusheng 27 Mb 48.44N 126.37 E
Ju Shui 28 Ci 31.09N 114.52 E
Juškozero 19 Dc 64.45N 32.08 E
Jussarö 8 Je 59.50N 23.35 E
Justo Daract 56 Gd 33.52S 65.11W
Jusva 17 Gg 58.59N 54.57 E
Jutai 54 Ee 5.11S 68.54W
Jutai, Rio- 52 Jf 2.43S 66.57W
Jüterbg 10 Je 51.59N 13.05 E
Juti 55 Ef 22.52S 54.37W
Jutiapa [3] 49 Bf 14.10N 89.50W
Jutiapa [Guat.] 47 Gf 14.17N 89.54W
Jutiapa [Hond.] 49 Df 15.46N 86.34W
Juticalpa 47 Gf 14.42N 86.15W
Jutland (EN)=Jylland 5 Gd 56.00N 9.15 E
Juuka 7 Ge 63.14N 29.15 E
Juva 7 Gf 61.54N 27.51 E
Juventud, Isla de la-=Pines, Isle of- (EN) 38 Kg 21.40N 82.50W
Juxian 27 Kd 35.33N 118.45 E
Jüybār 24 Od 36.38N 52.53 E
Juye 28 Dg 35.23N 116.05 E
Jūyom 24 Oh 28.10N 54.02 E
Juža 7 Kh 56.36N 42.01 E
Južnaja Keltma 17 Gf 60.30N 55.40 E
Južna Morava 15 Ef 43.41N 21.24 E
Južni Rodopi 15 Ih 41.15N 25.30 E
Južnoje 20 Jg 46.13N 143.27 E
Južno-Jenisejski 20 Ee 58.48N 94.45 E
Južno-Kurilsk 20 Jh 44.05N 145.52 E
Južno-Sahalinsk 22 Qe 46.58N 142.42 E
Južno-Uralsk 19 Ge 54.26N 61.15 E
Južny, Mys- 20 Ke 57.42N 156.55 E
Južny Bug 5 Jf 46.59N 31.58 E
Južny Ural=Southern Urals (EN) 5 Le 54.00N 58.30 E
Jygeva/Jõgeva 7 Gg 58.46N 26.26 E
Jylland=Jutland (EN) 5 Gd 56.00N 9.15 E
Jylland Bank 8 Bh 56.55N 7.20 E
Jyske Ås 8 Dg 57.15N 10.14 E
Jyväskylä 6 Ic 62.14N 25.44 E

K

K2=Godwin Austen (EN) 21 Jf 35.53N 76.30 E
Ka 34 Fc 11.39N 4.11 E
Kaabong 36 Fb 3.31N 34.09 E
Kaahka 19 Fh 37.21N 59.38 E
Kaala 65a Cb 21.31N 158.09W
Kaala-Gomén 63b Be 20.40S 164.24 E
Kaalualu Bay 65a Fe 18.58N 155.37W
Kaamanen 7 Gb 69.06N 27.12 E
Kaap Kruis 37 Ad 21.46S 13.58 E
Kaap Plateau (EN)=Kaapplato 30 Jk 27.30S 23.45 E
Kaapplato=Kaap Plateau (EN) 30 Jk 27.30S 23.45 E
Kaapprovinsie/Cape Province [2] 37 Cf 32.00S 22.00 E
Kaapstad / Cape Town 31 Il 33.55S 18.22 E
Kaarst 12 Ic 51.15N 6.37 E
Kaarta 34 Cc 14.35N 10.00W
Kaba/Habahe 27 Eb 47.53N 86.12 E
Kabaena, Pulau- 26 Hh 5.15S 121.55 E
Kabah 48 Og 20.07N 89.29W
Kabala 34 Cd 9.35N 11.33W
Kabale 36 Ec 1.15S 29.59 E
Kabalega Falls 36 Fb 2.17N 31.41 E
Kabalo 31 Ji 6.03S 26.55 E
Kabaman 63a Aa 4.38S 152.42 E
Kabambare 36 Ec 4.16S 27.07 E
Kabamet 36 Gb 0.30N 35.45 E
Kabanjahe 26 Cf 3.06N 98.30 E
Kabardino-Balkarskaja ASSR [3] 19 Eg 43.30N 43.30 E
Kabare 36 Ec 2.29S 28.48 E
Kabasalan 26 He 7.48N 122.45 E
Kaba-Shima [Jap.] 29 Ae 32.45N 129.00 E
Kaba-Shima [Jap.] 29 Ae 32.34N 129.47 E
Kabba 34 Gd 7.50N 6.04 E
Kābdalis 7 Ec 66.09N 20.00 E
Kaberamaido 36 Fb 1.45N 33.10 E
Kabetogama Lake 45 Jb 48.28N 92.59W
Kabhegy 10 Ni 47.03N 17.39 E
Kabinakagami Lake 44 Ea 48.58N 84.25W
Kabinda 31 Ji 6.08S 24.29 E
Kabīr, Wādī al- 14 Dn 36.23N 9.52 E
Kabīr Kūh 24 Lf 33.25N 46.45 E
Kabkābīyah 35 Cc 13.39N 24.05 E
Kableškovo 15 Kg 42.39N 27.34 E
Kabna 35 Eb 19.10N 32.41 E
Kabo 35 Bd 7.35N 18.38 E
Kābol 22 If 34.31N 69.12 E
Kābol 23 Kc 34.30N 69.00 E
Kabompo 36 De 13.36S 24.12 E
Kabompo 30 Jj 14.11S 23.11 E
Kabondo Dianda 36 Ed 8.53S 25.40 E
Kabongo 36 Ed 7.19S 25.35 E
Kabou 34 Fd 9.27N 0.49 E
Kabūdiyāh, Ra's- 32 Jb 35.14N 11.10 E
Kabūd Rāhang 24 Me 35.12N 48.44 E
Kābul 21 Jf 33.55N 72.14 E
Kabunda 36 Ee 12.13S 29.23 E

Index Symbols

[1] Independent Nation
[2] State, Region
[3] District, County
[4] Municipality
[5] Colony, Dependency
Continent
Physical Region
Historical or Cultural Region
Mount, Mountain
Volcano
Hill
Mountains, Mountain Range
Hills, Escarpment
Plateau, Upland
Pass, Gap
Plain, Lowland
Delta
Salt Flat
Valley, Canyon
Crater, Cave
Karst Features
Depression
Polder
Desert, Dunes
Forest, Woods
Heath, Steppe
Oasis
Cape, Point
Coast, Beach
Cliff
Peninsula
Isthmus
Sandbank
Island
Atoll
Rock, Reef
Islands, Archipelago
Rocks, Reefs
Coral Reef
Well, Spring
Geyser
River, Stream
Waterfall Rapids
River Mouth, Estuary
Lake
Salt Lake
Intermittent Lake
Reservoir
Swamp, Pond
Canal
Glacier
Ice Shelf, Pack Ice
Ocean
Sea
Gulf, Bay
Strait, Fjord
Lagoon
Bank
Seamount
Tablemount
Ridge
Shelf
Basin
Escarpment, Sea Scarp
Fracture
Trench, Abyss
National Park, Reserve
Point of Interest
Recreation Site
Cave, Cavern
Historic Site
Ruins
Wall, Walls
Church, Abbey
Temple
Scientific Station
Airport
Port
Lighthouse
Mine
Tunnel
Dam, Bridge

Kabunga 36 Ec 1.42S 28.08 E
Kaburuang, Pulau- 26 If 3.48N 126.48 E
Kabwe 31 Jj 14.27S 28.27 E
Kača 16 Hg 44.44N 33.32 E
Kačanik 15 Eg 42.14N 21.15 E
Kačanovo 8 Lg 57.24N 27.53 E
Kačergine 8 Jj 54.53N 23.49 E
Kachchh, Gulf of 21 Ig 22.36N 69.30 E
Kachchh, Rann of 25 Dd 23.51N 70.30 E
Kachia 34 Gd 9.52N 7.57 E
Kachikau 37 Cc 18.09S 24.29 E
Kachin [2] 25 Jc 26.00N 97.30 E
Kačiry 19 He 53.04N 76.07 E
Kačkanar 19 Fd 58.42N 59.35 E
Kačug 20 Ff 54.00N 105.52 E
Kaczawa 10 Me 51.18N 16.27 E
Kadada 16 Oc 53.09N 46.01 E
Kadaň 10 Jf 50.23N 13.16 E
Kadan Kyun 25 Jf 12.30N 98.22 E
Kadeï 30 Ih 3.31N 16.03 E
Kadijevka 19 Df 48.32N 38.40 E
Kadiköy 24 Bb 40.51N 26.50 E
Kadıköy, İstanbul 15 Mi 40.59N 29.01 E
Kadina 59 Hf 33.58S 137.43 E
Kadınhanı 24 Ec 38.15N 32.14 E
Kadiolo 34 Dc 10.34N 5.45W
Kadiri 25 Ff 14.07N 78.10 E
Kadirli 23 Eb 37.23N 36.05 E
Kadja 35 Cc 12.02N 22.28 E
Kadmat Island 25 Ef 11.14N 72.47 E
Kadnikov 7 Jg 59.30N 40.24 E
Kadoka 45 Fe 43.50N 101.31W
Kaduj 7 Ig 59.14N 37.09 E
Kaduna [2] 34 Gc 11.00N 7.30 E
Kaduna 30 Hh 8.45N 5.48 E
Kaduna 31 Hg 10.31N 7.26 E
Kāduqlī 31 Jg 11.01N 29.43 E
Kadykčan 20 Jd 63.05N 146.58 E
Kadžaran 16 Oj 39.11N 46.10 E
Kadžerom 17 Gd 64.41N 55.54 E
Kadži-Saj 18 Kc 42.08N 77.10 E
Kaech'ŏn 28 He 39.42N 125.53 E
Kaédi 31 Fg 16.08N 13.31W
Kaélé 34 Hc 10.07N 14.27 E
Kaena Point 65a Cb 21.35N 158.17W
Kaeo 62 Ea 35.06S 173.47 E
Kaesŏng 22 Of 37.58N 126.33 E
Kaesŏng Si [2] 28 Ie 38.05N 126.30 E
Kāf 24 Gg 31.24N 37.29 E
Kafakumba 36 Dd 9.41S 23.44 E
Kafan 19 Eh 39.12N 46.28 E
Kafanchan 34 Gd 9.35N 8.18 E
Kaffrine 34 Bc 14.06N 15.33W
Kafia Kingi 35 Cd 9.16N 24.25 E
Kafiréos, Dhiékplous- 15 Hl 38.00N 24.40 E
Kafirévs, Ákra- 15 Hk 38.10N 24.35 E
Kafr ad Dawwār 24 Dg 31.08N 30.07 E
Kafr ash Shaykh 33 Fc 31.07N 30.56 E
Kafta 35 Fc 13.54N 37.11 E
Kafu 36 Fb 1.39N 32.05 E
Kafue 30 Ef 15.56S 28.55 E
Kafue 31 Jj 15.47S 28.11 E
Kafue Dam 36 Ef 15.45S 28.28 E
Kafue Flats 36 Ef 15.40S 26.25 E
Kafufu 36 Fd 7.12S 31.31 E
Kaga 28 Nf 36.18N 136.18 E
Kaga Bandoro 35 Bd 7.02N 19.13 E
Kagalaska 40a Cb 51.47N 176.23W
Kagalnik 16 Kf 47.04N 39.18 E
Kagami 29 Be 32.34N 130.40 E
Kagan 19 Gh 39.43N 64.32 E
Kagarlyk 16 Ge 49.53N 30.56 E
Kagawa Ken [2] 28 Mg 34.15N 134.15 E
Kagera 30 Ki 0.57S 31.47 E
Kağızman 24 Jb 40.09N 43.07 E
Kagoshima 22 Pf 31.36N 130.33 E
Kagoshima Bay (EN)=
Kagoshima-Wan 28 Ki 31.27N 130.40 E
Kagoshima Ken [2] 28 Ki 31.45N 130.40 E
Kagoshima-Taniyama 29 Bf 31.31N 130.31 E
Kagoshima-Wan=
Kagoshima Bay (EN) 28 Ki 31.27N 130.40 E
Kagul 15 Ld 45.32N 28.27 E
Kagul 19 Cf 45.53N 28.14 E
Kahal Tabelbala 32 Gd 28.45N 2.15W
Kahama 36 Fc 3.50S 32.36 E
Kahemba 31 Ii 7.17S 19.00 E
Kahi 16 Oi 41.23N 46.59 E
Kahiu Point 65a Eb 21.13N 156.58W
Kahler Asten 10 Ee 51.11N 8.29 E
Kahnūj 24 Qi 27.58N 57.47 E
Kahoku 29 Gb 38.30N 141.20 E
Kahoku-Gata 29 Ec 36.40N 136.40 E
Kahoolawe Island 57 Lb 20.33N 156.35W
Kahouanne, Ilet à- 51e Ab 16.22N 61.47W
Kahovka 19 Df 46.47N 33.32 E
Kahovskoje Vodohranilišče
=Kakhovka Reservoir (EN)
5 Jf 47.25N 34.10 E
Kahramanmaraş 23 Eb 37.36N 36.55 E
Kahrūyeh 24 Ng 31.43N 51.48 E
Kâhta 24 Hd 37.46N 38.36 E
Kahuku 65a Db 21.41N 157.57W
Kahuku Point 65a Db 21.43N 157.59W
Kahului 65a Ec 20.53N 156.27W
Kahului Bay 65a Ec 20.55N 156.30W
Kahurangi Point 62 Ed 40.46S 172.13 E
Kai, Kepulauan- 57 Ee 5.35S 132.45 E
Kaiama 34 Fd 9.36N 3.57 E
Kaiapoi 62 Ee 43.23S 172.39 E
Kaibab Plateau 46 Ih 36.30N 112.15W
Kai Besar 26 Jh 5.35S 133.00 E
Kaidu He/Karaxabar He 27 Ec 41.55N 86.38 E
Kaieteur Falls 54 Gc 5.10N 59.28W
Kaifeng 22 Nf 34.45N 114.25 E
Kaihua 28 Ej 29.10N 118.24 E
Kai Kecil 26 Jh 5.45S 132.40 E
Kaikohe 62 Ea 35.24S 173.48 E
Kaikoura 61 Dh 42.25S 173.41 E
Kaili 27 If 26.35N 107.59 E
Kailu 27 Lc 43.37N 121.19 E
Kailua [Hi.-U.S.] 65a Fd 19.39N 155.59W
Kailua [Hi.-U.S.] 65a Db 21.23N 157.44W
Kaimana 26 Jg 3.39S 133.45 E
Kaimanawa Mountains 62 Fc 39.15S 176.00 E
Kaimon-Dake 29 Bf 31.10N 130.32 E
Kain, Tournai- 12 Fd 50.38N 3.22 E
Kainach 14 Jd 46.54N 15.31 E
Kainan [Jap.] 29 Dd 34.09N 135.12 E
Kainan [Jap.] 29 De 33.36N 134.22 E
Kainantu 60 Di 6.15S 145.53 E
Kainji Dam 34 Fd 9.55N 4.40 E
Kainji Reservoir 34 Fc 10.30N 4.35 E
Kaipara Harbour 62 Fb 36.25S 174.15 E
Kaiparowits Plateau 46 Jh 37.20N 111.15W
Kaiser Franz Josephs
Fjord 41 Jd 73.30N 24.00W
Kaisersesch 12 Jd 50.14N 7.09 E
Kaiserslautern 10 Dg 49.27N 7.45 E
Kaiserstuhl 10 Dh 48.06N 7.40 E
Kaishantun 27 Mc 42.43N 129.37 E
Kaišiadorys/Kajšjadoris 7 Fi 54.53N 24.31 E
Kaita 29 Cd 34.20N 132.32 E
Kaitaia 62 Ea 35.07S 173.14 E
Kaitangata 62 Cg 46.17S 169.51 E
Kaithal 25 Fc 29.48N 76.23 E
Kaitong → Tongyu 27 Lc 44.47N 123.05 E
Kaituma River 50 Gh 8.11N 59.41W
Kaiwaka 61 Dg 36.10S 174.26 E
Kaiwi Channel 60 Oc 21.13N 157.30W
Kaixian 27 Ie 31.10N 108.25 E
Kaiyuan [China] 27 Lc 42.33N 124.04 E
Kaiyuan [China] 27 Hg 23.47N 103.15 E
Kaiyuh Mountains 40 Hd 64.00N 158.00W
Kaja 30 Jg 12.02N 22.28 E
Kajaani 6 Ic 64.14N 27.41 E
Kajaapu 26 Dh 5.26S 102.24 E
Kajabbi 58 Fg 20.02S 140.02 E
Kajak 20 Fb 71.30N 103.15 E
Kajang 26 Df 2.59N 101.47 E
Kajdak, Sor- 16 Rg 44.40N 53.30 E
Kajerkan 20 Dc 69.25N 87.30 E
Kajiado 36 Gc 1.51S 36.47 E
Kajiki 29 Bf 31.44N 130.40 E
Kajmakčalan 15 Ei 40.58N 21.48 E
Kajnar 15 Lb 47.50N 28.06 E
Kajo Kaji 35 Ee 3.53N 31.40 E
Kajrakkumskoje
Vodohranilišče 18 Hd 40.20N 70.05 E
Kajrakty 19 Hf 48.31N 73.14 E
Kajšjadoris/Kaišiadorys 7 Fi 54.53N 24.31 E
Kajuru 34 Gc 10.19N 7.41 E
Kaka 35 Fd 7.28N 39.06 E
Kākā 35 Ec 10.36N 32.11 E
Kakagi Lake 45 Jb 49.13N 93.52W
Kakamas 37 Ce 28.45S 20.33 E
Kakamega 36 Fb 0.17N 34.45 E
Kakamigahara 29 Ed 35.25N 136.50 E
Kakanj 14 Mf 44.08N 18.05 E
Kaka Point 65a Ec 20.32N 156.33W
Kakata 34 Cd 6.32N 10.21W
Kake 29 Cd 34.36N 132.19 E
Kakegawa 29 Ed 34.46N 138.00 E
Kakenge 36 Dc 4.51S 21.55 E
Kakeroma-Jima 29b Ba 28.08N 129.15 E
Kakhovka Reservoir (EN)=
Kahovskoje
Vodohranilišče 5 Jf 47.25N 34.10 E
Kākī 24 Nh 28.19N 51.34 E
Kākināda 22 Kh 16.56N 82.13 E
Kakisa Lake 42 Fd 60.55N 117.40W
Kakizaki 29 Fc 37.16N 138.22 E
Kaklkan 24 Cd 36.15N 29.24 E
Kakogawa 29 Dd 34.46N 134.51 E
Kakpin 34 Ed 8.39N 3.48W
Kaktovik 40 Kb 70.08N 143.37W
Kakuda 29 Gc 37.58N 140.47 E
Kakuma 36 Fb 3.43N 34.52 E
Kakunodate 28 Pe 39.40N 140.32 E
Kakva 17 Jg 59.37N 60.50 E
Kakya 36 Gc 1.36S 39.02 E
Kalaa 13 Mi 35.35N 0.20 E
Kalaa Khasba 14 Co 35.38N 8.36 E
Kalaallit Nunaat/Grønland=
Greenland (EN) [5] 39 Pb 70.00N 40.00W
Kalaallit Nunaat/Grønland=
Greenland (EN) 38 Pb 70.00N 40.00W
Kalabahi 26 Hh 8.13S 124.31 E
Kalabáka 15 Ej 39.42N 21.38 E
Kalabera 64b Ba 15.14N 145.48 E
Kalabo 36 De 14.58S 22.41 E
Kalâbsha 33 Fe 23.33N 32.50 E
Kalač 19 Ee 50.23N 41.01 E
Kalačinsk 19 Hd 55.03N 74.34 E
Kalač-na-Donu 19 Ef 48.43N 43.32 E
Kaladan 25 Id 20.09N 92.57 E
Ka Lae 60 Od 18.55N 155.41W
Kalahari Desert 30 Jk 23.00S 22.00 E
Kalaheo 65a Bb 21.56N 159.32W
Kalai-Mor 19 Gh 35.37N 62.31 E
Kalaj Humo 18 He 38.25N 70.47 E
Kalajoki 7 Fd 64.15N 23.57 E
Kalakan 20 Ge 55.10N 116.45 E
Kalaldi 34 Hd 6.30N 14.04 E
Kalāleh 24 Pd 37.25N 55.40 E
Kalámai 6 Ih 37.02N 22.07 E
Kalamákion 15 Gl 37.55N 23.43 E
Kalamazoo 43 Jc 42.17N 85.32W
Kalambo Falls 36 Fd 8.36S 31.14 E
Kalamitski Zaliv 16 Hg 45.00N 33.25 E
Kálamos 15 Dk 38.37N 20.55 E
Kalamunda,
Perth- 59 Df 31.57S 116.03 E
Kalan 23 Eb 39.07N 39.32 E
Kalanshiyū, Sarīr- 30 Jf 27.00N 21.30 E
Kalao, Pulau- 26 Hh 7.18S 120.58 E
Kalaotoa, Pulau- 26 Hh 7.22S 121.47 E
Kalapana 65a Gd 19.21N 154.59W
Kalaraš 16 Ff 47.16N 28.16 E
Kälarne 8 Gb 62.59N 16.05 E
Kalarski Hrebet 20 Ge 56.30N 118.50 E
Kalasin [Indon.] 26 Ff 0.12N 114.16 E
Kalasin [Thai.] 25 Ke 16.29N 103.31 E
Kalāt 25 Dc 29.02N 66.35 E
Kalāteh 24 Pd 36.29N 54.10 E
Kalau 65b Bc 21.28S 174.57W
Kalaupapa 65a Eb 21.12N 156.59W
Kalaus 16 Ng 45.43N 44.07 E
Kalavárdha 15 Km 36.20N 27.57 E
Kálavrita 15 Fk 38.02N 22.07 E
Kalbā' 24 Qj 25.03N 56.21 E
Kalbīyah, Sabkhat al- 14 Eo 35.51N 10.17 E
Kaldbakur 7a Ab 65.49N 23.39W
Kaldygajty 16 Re 49.20N 52.38 E
Kale [Tur.] 24 Cd 37.26N 28.51 E
Kale [Tur.] 24 Cd 36.14N 29.59 E
Kalecik 24 Eb 40.06N 33.25 E
Kalehe 36 Ec 2.06S 28.55 E
Kalemie 31 Ji 5.56S 29.12 E
Kāl-e Shur 23 Jb 35.05N 60.59 E
Kalevala 19 Db 65.12N 31.10 E
Kalewa 25 Id 23.12N 94.18 E
Kaleybar 24 Lc 38.47N 47.02 E
Kalgoorlie 58 Dh 30.45S 121.28 E
Kaliakoúdha 15 Ek 38.48N 21.46 E
Kaliakra, Nos- 15 Lf 43.18N 28.30 E
Kalibo 26 Hd 11.43N 122.22 E
Kalí Límni 15 Kn 35.35N 27.08 E
Kalima 31 Ji 2.34S 26.37 E
Kalimantan/Borneo 21 Ni 1.00N 114.00 E
Kalimantan Barat [3] 26 Ff 0.01N 110.30 E
Kalimantan Selatan [3] 26 Gg 2.30S 115.30 E
Kalimantan Tengah [3] 26 Fg 2.00S 113.30 E
Kalimantan Timur [3] 26 Gf 1.30N 116.30 E
Kálimnos 15 Jm 36.57N 26.59 E
Kalinin [R.S.F.S.R.] →
Tver' 6 Jd 56.52N 35.55 E
Kalinin [Tur.- U.S.S.R.] 19 Fg 42.07N 59.40 E
Kalininabad 18 Gf 37.53N 68.57 E
Kaliningrad [R.S.F.S.R.] 6 Ie 54.43N 20.30 E
Kaliningrad [R.S.F.S.R.] 7 Ii 55.55N 37.57 E
Kaliningradskaja Oblast [3] 19 Ce 54.45N 21.20 E
Kalinino [Arm.-U.S.S.R.] 16 Ni 41.08N 44.14 E
Kalinino [R.S.F.S.R.] 16 Kg 45.05N 38.59 E
Kalininsk [Mold.-U.S.S.R.] 15 Ka 48.07N 27.16 E
Kalininsk [R.S.F.S.R.] 16 Nd 51.30N 44.30 E
Kalininskaja Oblast [3] 19 Dd 57.20N 34.40 E
Kalinkoviči 19 Ce 52.07N 29.23 E
Kalino 17 Hg 58.15N 57.35 E
Kalinovik 14 Mg 43.31N 18.26 E
Kalinovka 16 Fe 49.29N 28.32 E
Kaliro 36 Fb 0.54N 33.30 E
Kalispell 39 He 48.12N 114.19W
Kalisz [2] 10 Of 51.45N 18.05 E
Kalisz 10 Oe 51.46N 18.06 E
Kalisz Pomorski 10 Lc 53.19N 15.54 E
Kalitva 16 Le 48.10N 40.46 E
Kaliua 36 Fd 5.04S 31.48 E
Kalix 7 Fd 65.51N 23.08 E
Kalixälven 7 Fd 65.47N 23.13 E
Kalja 17 Jf 60.20N 60.01 E
Kaljazin 19 Dd 57.15N 37.55 E
Kalkandere 24 Ib 40.55N 40.28 E
Kalkar 12 Ic 51.44N 6.18 E
Kalkaska 44 Ec 44.44N 85.11W
Kalkfeld 37 Bd 20.53S 16.11 E
Kalkfontein 37 Cd 22.07S 20.54 E
Kalkim 15 Kj 39.48N 27.13 E
Kalkrand 37 Bd 24.03S 17.33 E
Kall 7 Ce 63.28N 13.15 E
Kållands Halvö 8 Ef 58.35N 13.05 E
Kållandsö 8 Ef 58.40N 13.10 E
Kallaste 7 Gg 58.41N 27.08 E
Kallavesi 5 Ic 62.50N 27.45 E
Kalletal 12 Kb 52.08N 8.57 E
Kallhäll 8 Ge 59.27N 17.48 E
Kallídhromon Óros 15 Fk 38.44N 22.34 E
Kallinge 7 Dh 56.14N 15.17 E
Kallonís, Kolpos- 15 Jj 39.07N 26.08 E
Kallsjön 7 Ce 63.35N 13.00 E
Kalmar 6 Hd 56.40N 16.22 E
Kalmar [2] 7 Dh 57.20N 16.00 E
Kalmarsund 7 Dh 56.40N 16.25 E
Kalmit 12 Ke 49.19N 8.05 E
Kalmius 16 Jf 47.03N 37.34 E
Kalmthout 12 Gc 51.23N 4.28 E
Kalmyckaja ASSR [3] 19 Ef 46.30N 45.30 E
Kalmykovo 16 Qe 49.05N 51.47 E
Kalnciems 8 Jh 56.48N 23.34 E
Kalnik 14 Kd 46.10N 16.30 E
Kalocsa 10 Oj 46.32N 19.00 E
Kalofer 15 Hg 42.37N 24.59 E
Kalohi Channel 65a Ec 21.00N 156.56W
Kaloko 36 Ed 6.47S 25.47 E
Kalole 36 Ec 3.42S 27.22 E
Kaloli Point 65a Gd 19.37N 154.57W
Kalomo 36 Ef 17.02S 26.30 E
Kalpa 25 Fb 31.37N 78.10 E
Kalpákion 15 Dj 39.53N 20.35 E
Kalpeni Island 25 Ef 10.05N 73.38 E
Kalpin 27 Cc 40.31N 79.03 E
Kalsūbai 21 Jh 19.36N 73.43 E
Kaltern/Caldaro 14 Fd 46.25N 11.14 E
Kaltungo 34 Hd 9.49N 11.19 E
Kaluga 6 Je 54.31N 36.16 E
Kalulushi 36 Ee 12.50S 28.05 E
Kalumburu Mission 59 Fb 14.18S 126.39 E
Kalundborg 7 Ci 55.41N 11.06 E
Kaluš 19 Cf 49.03N 24.23 E
Kałuszyn 10 Rd 52.13N 21.49 E
Kalužskaja Oblast [3] 19 De 54.20N 35.30 E
Kalvåg 8 Ac 61.46N 4.53 E
Kalvarija 7 Fi 54.27N 23.14 E
Kalya 36 Fd 6.28S 30.03 E
Kalyān 25 Ee 19.15N 73.09 E
Kám 10 Mi 47.06N 16.53 E
Kama 36 Ec 3.32S 27.07 E
Kama [R.S.F.S.R.] 17 Nf 60.27N 69.00 E
Kama [U.S.S.R.] 5 Ld 55.45N 52.00 E
Kamae 29 Be 32.48N 131.56 E
Kamaï 35 Ba 21.12N 17.30 E
Kamaing 25 Jc 25.31N 96.44 E
Kamaishi 28 Pe 39.16N 141.53 E
Kamakou 65a Eb 21.07N 156.52W
Kamakura 29 Fd 35.19N 139.32 E
Kamālia 25 Eb 30.44N 72.39 E
Kamalo 65a Eb 21.03N 156.53W
Kaman 24 Ec 39.25N 33.45 E
Kamand, Āb-e- 24 Mf 33.28N 49.04 E
Kamanjab 37 Ac 19.35S 14.51 E
Kamanyola 36 Ec 2.46S 29.00 E
Kamaran 23 Ff 15.12N 42.35 E
Kamarang 54 Fb 5.53N 60.35W
Kama Reservoir (EN)=
Kamskoje
Vodohranilišče 5 Ld 58.50N 56.15 E
Kamaši 19 Gh 38.48N 66.29 E
Kamativi 37 Dc 18.19S 27.03 E
Kambalda 59 Ef 31.10S 121.37 E
Kambalnaja Sopka, Vulkan-
20 Kf 51.17N 156.57 E
Kambara 29 Fd 35.07N 138.36 E
Kambara 63d Cc 18.57S 178.57W
Kambarka 7 Nh 56.18N 54.14 E
Kambia 34 Cd 9.07N 12.55W
Kambja 8 Lf 58.11N 26.43 E
Kambove 36 Ee 10.52S 26.35 E
Kamčatka 20 Le 56.10N 162.30 E
Kamčatka, Poluostrov-=
Kamchatka Peninsula (EN)
21 Rd 56.00N 160.00 E
Kamčatskaja Oblast [3] 20 Kf 54.50N 159.00 E
Kamčatski Zaliv 20 Le 55.30N 163.00 E
Kamchatka Peninsula (EN)
=Kamčatka, Poluostrov-
21 Rd 56.00N 160.00 E
Kamčija 15 Kf 43.02N 27.53 E
Kamčijska Plato 15 Kg 42.56N 27.32 E
Kameda [Jap.] 29 Fc 37.52N 139.06 E
Kameda [Jap.] 29a Bc 41.49N 140.46 E
Kameda-Hantō 29a Bc 41.45N 141.00 E
Kámeiros 15 Km 36.18N 27.56 E
Kamelik 16 Pc 52.06N 49.30 E
Kamen 12 Jc 51.36N 7.40 E
Kaménai 15 Im 36.25N 25.25 E
Kamende 36 Dd 6.28S 24.33 E
Kamenec 10 Td 52.23N 23.49 E
Kamenec-Podolski 19 Cf 48.39N 26.33 E
Kamenijak, Rt- 14 Hf 44.46N 13.56 E
Kamenka [Kaz.-U.S.S.R.] 16 Qd 51.07N 50.20 E
Kamenka [Mold.-U.S.S.R.] 16 Fe 48.03N 28.45 E
Kamenka [R.S.F.S.R.] 16 Kd 50.43N 39.25 E
Kamenka [R.S.F.S.R.] 19 Ee 53.13N 44.03 E
Kamenka [R.S.F.S.R.] 7 Kd 65.54N 44.04 E
Kamenka [R.S.F.S.R.] 28 Nb 44.28N 136.01 E
Kamenka [Ukr.-U.S.S.R.] 19 Df 49.03N 32.06 E
Kamenka-Bugskaja 10 Uf 50.01N 24.25 E
Kamenka-Dneprovskaja 16 If 47.29N 34.29 E
Kamen-Kaširski 16 Dd 51.36N 24.59 E
Kamen-na-Obi 20 Df 53.47N 81.20 E
Kamennogorsk 7 Gf 60.59N 29.12 E
Kamennoje, Ozero- 7 Hd 64.30N 30.15 E
Kamennomostski 16 Lg 44.17N 40.12 E
Kamen-Rybolov 28 Kb 44.45N 132.04 E
Kamenskoje 20 Ld 62.30N 166.12 E
Kamensk-Šahtinski 16 Le 48.18N 40.16 E
Kamensk-Uralski 22 Id 56.28N 61.54 E
Kamenz/Kamjenc 10 Ke 51.16N 14.06 E
Kameoka 29 Dd 35.00N 135.35 E
Kameškovo 7 Jh 56.22N 41.01 E
Kamet 25 Fd 30.55N 79.35 E
Kameyama 29 Ed 34.51N 136.27 E
Kami-Agata 29 Ad 34.38N 129.25 E
Kamiah 46 Gc 46.14N 116.02W
Kamicharo 29a Cb 43.11N 143.52 E
Kamienna 10 Re 51.06N 21.47 E
Kamienna Góra 10 Mf 50.47N 16.01 E
Kamień Pomorski 10 Kc 53.58N 14.46 E
Kamiénsk 10 Pe 51.12N 19.30 E
Kamieskroon 37 Bf 30.09S 17.56 E
Kami-furano 29a Cb 43.29N 142.27 E
Kamiiso 28 Pd 41.49N 140.39 E
Kamiita 29 Dd 34.08N 134.24 E
Kamiji 36 Dd 6.39S 23.17 E
Kamikawa 29a Cb 43.50N 142.47 E
Kami-Koshiki-Jima 29 Af 31.50N 129.55 E
Kamina 31 Ji 8.44S 24.59 E
Kaminak Lake 42 Id 62.13N 95.00W
Kaminokuni 29a Bc 41.48N 140.05 E
Kamino-Shima 29 Ad 34.30N 129.25 E
Kaminoyama 28 Pe 38.09N 140.17 E
Kaminuriak Lake 42 Hd 63.00N 95.45W
Kamioka 28 Nf 36.16N 137.18 E
Kami-shihoro 29a Cb 43.13N 143.16 E
Kamisunagawa 29a Bb 43.28N 141.58 E
Kamitsushima 29 Ad 34.39N 129.28 E
Kamituga 36 Ec 3.04S 28.11 E
Kamiyama 29 De 33.58N 134.21 E
Kami-yūbetsu 29a Ca 44.11N 143.34 E
Kamjenc/Kamenz 10 Ke 51.16N 14.06 E
Kamloops 39 Gd 50.40N 120.20W
Kamloops Plateau 46 Ea 50.10N 120.35W
Kamnik 14 Id 46.14N 14.37 E
Kamo [Arm.-U.S.S.R.] 16 Ni 40.22N 45.05 E
Kamo [Jap.] 29 Fc 37.39N 139.03 E
Kamo [N.Z.] 62 Fa 35.41S 174.17 E
Kamōda-Misaki 29 De 33.50N 134.45 E
Kamogawa 29 Gd 35.06N 140.05 E
Kamp 14 Jb 48.23N 15.48 E
Kampala 31 Kh 0.19N 32.35 E
Kampar 26 Df 4.18N 101.09 E
Kampar 26 Mi 0.32N 103.08 E
Kampen 11 Lb 52.33N 5.54 E
Kampene 36 Ec 3.36S 26.40 E
Kamphaeng Phet 25 Je 16.26N 99.33 E
Kamp-Lintford 12 Ic 51.30N 6.32 E
Kamp'o 28 Jg 35.48N 129.30 E
Kâmpóng Cham 22 Mh 12.00N 105.27 E
Kâmpóng Chhnăng 25 Kf 12.15N 104.40 E
Kâmpóng Saôm 22 Mh 10.38N 103.30 E
Kâmpóng Saôm, Chhâk- 25 Kf 10.50N 103.32 E
Kâmpóng Thum 25 Kf 12.42N 104.54 E
Kâmpôt 25 Kf 10.37N 104.11 E
Kampti 34 Ec 10.08N 3.27W
Kampuchea → Cambodia 22 Mh 13.00N 105.00 E
Kamrau, Teluk- 26 Jg 3.32S 133.37 E
Kamsack 42 Hf 51.34N 101.54W
Kamsar 34 Cc 10.40N 14.36W
Kamskoje Ustje 7 Li 55.14N 49.16 E
Kamskoje Vodohranilišče=
Kama Reservoir (EN) 5 Ld 58.50N 56.15 E
Kam Summa 35 Ge 0.21N 42.44 E
Kamuenai 29a Bb 43.08N 140.26 E
Kamui-Dake 29a Cb 42.25N 142.52 E
Kamui-Misaki 27 Pc 43.20N 140.20 E
Kámuk, Cerro- 49 Fi 9.17N 83.04W
Kamvoúnia Óri 15 Ei 40.00N 21.52 E
Kāmyārān 24 Le 34.47N 46.56 E
Kamyšin 6 Ke 50.06N 45.24 E
Kamyšlov 19 Gd 56.52N 62.43 E
Kamyšovaja Buhta 16 Hg 44.31N 33.33 E
Kamysty-Ajat 17 Jj 53.01N 61.35 E
Kamyzjak 19 Ef 46.06N 48.05 E
Kan 24 Ne 35.45N 51.16 E
Kan 20 Ee 56.31N 93.47 E
Kana 37 Dc 18.32S 27.24 E
Kanaaupscow 42 Jf 54.01N 76.32W
Kanaaupscow 42 Jf 53.40N 77.08W
Kanab 43 Ed 37.03N 112.32W
Kanab Creek 46 Ih 36.24N 112.38W
Kanaga 40a Cb 51.45N 177.10W
Kanagawa Ken [2] 28 Og 35.30N 139.10 E
Kanaliasem 26 Dg 1.44S 103.35 E
Kanami-Zaki 29b Bb 27.53N 128.58 E
Kananga 31 Ji 5.54S 22.25 E
Kanariktok 42 Le 55.03N 60.10W
Kanaš 7 Li 55.31N 47.31 E
Kanathea 63d Cb 17.16S 179.09W
Kanaya 29 Fd 34.48N 138.07 E
Kanayama 29 Ed 35.39N 137.09 E
Kanazawa 22 Pf 36.34N 136.39 E
Kanbalu 25 Jd 23.12N 95.31 E
Kanbe 25 Je 16.42N 96.01 E
Kanchanaburi 25 Jf 14.02N 99.33 E
Kānchenjunga 21 Kg 27.42N 88.08 E
Kānchipuram 25 Ff 12.50N 79.43 E
Kandalakša 6 Jb 67.09N 32.21 E
Kandalaksha, Gulf of- (EN)
=Kandalakšski Zaliv
5 Jb 66.35N 32.45 E
Kandalakšski Zaliv=
Kandalaksha, Gulf of- (EN)
5 Jb 66.35N 32.45 E
Kandangan 26 Gg 2.47S 115.16 E
Kándanos 15 Gn 35.20N 23.44 E
Kandava 7 Fh 57.03N 22.46 E
Kandavu Island 57 If 19.00S 178.13 E
Kandavu Passage 63d Ac 18.45S 178.00 E
Kandel 12 Ke 49.05N 8.12 E
Kandel 10 Eh 48.04N 8.01 E
Kandhelioúsa 15 Jm 36.30N 26.58 E
Kandi 31 Hg 11.08N 2.56 E
Kandıra 24 Db 41.04N 30.09 E
Kandla 25 Ed 23.02N 70.14 E
Kando-Gawa 29 Cd 35.22N 132.40 E
Kandovān, Gardaneh-ye- 24 Nd 36.09N 51.18 E
Kandrian 60 Di 6.13S 149.33 E
Kandry 17 Gi 54.34N 54.10 E
Kandy 22 Ki 7.18N 80.38 E
Kane 44 He 41.40N 78.48W
Kane Bassin 67 Od 79.35N 67.00W
Kaneh 24 Pi 27.04N 54.18 E
Kanem [3] 35 Bc 15.00N 16.00 E
Kanem 30 Ig 14.45N 15.30 E
Kaneohe 60 Oc 21.25N 157.48W
Kaneohe Bay 65a Db 21.28N 157.48W
Kánestron, Ákra- 15 Gj 39.56N 23.45 E
Kanev 16 Ge 49.42N 31.29 E
Kanevskaja 19 Df 46.06N 38.58 E
Kaneyama 29 Fc 37.27N 139.30 E
Kang 37 Cd 23.44S 22.50 E
Kangaba 34 Dc 11.56N 8.25W
Kangal 24 Gc 39.15N 37.24 E
Kangalassy 20 Hd 62.17N 129.58 E
Kangâmiut 41 Ge 65.39N 53.55W
Kangān [Iran] 24 Oi 27.50N 52.03 E
Kangān [Iran] 24 Qj 25.48N 57.28 E
Kangar 26 De 6.26N 100.12 E
Kangaré 34 Dc 11.37N 8.08W
Kangaroo Island 57 Eh 35.50S 137.05 E
Kangasala 8 Kc 61.28N 24.05 E
Kangasniemi 7 Gf 61.59N 26.38 E
Kangâtsiaq 41 Ge 68.20N 53.18W
Kangāvar 24 Le 34.30N 47.58 E
Kangbao 28 Cd 41.51N 114.37 E
Kangding/Dardo 27 He 30.01N 101.58 E
Kangean, Kepulauan-=
Kangean Islands (EN) 26 Gh 6.55S 115.30 E
Kangean, Pulau- 26 Gh 6.54S 115.20 E
Kangean Islands (EN)=
Kangean, Kepulauan- 26 Gh 6.55S 115.30 E
Kangeeak Point 42 Lc 68.01N 64.45W
Kangen 30 Kh 6.47N 33.09 E
Kangerdlugssuaq 41 Ie 68.20N 31.40W
Kangetet 36 Gb 1.58N 36.06 E

Index Symbols

- [1] Independent Nation
- [2] State, Region
- [3] District, County
- [4] Municipality
- [5] Colony, Dependency
- Continent
- Physical Region
- Historical or Cultural Region
- Mount, Mountain
- Volcano
- Hill
- Mountains, Mountain Range
- Hills, Escarpment
- Plateau, Upland
- Pass, Gap
- Plain, Lowland
- Delta
- Salt Flat
- Valley, Canyon
- Crater, Cave
- Karst Features
- Depression
- Polder
- Desert, Dunes
- Forest, Woods
- Heath, Steppe
- Oasis
- Cape, Point
- Coast, Beach
- Cliff
- Peninsula
- Isthmus
- Sandbank
- Island
- Atoll
- Rock, Reef
- Islands, Archipelago
- Rocks, Reefs
- Coral Reef
- Well, Spring
- Geyser
- River, Stream
- Waterfall Rapids
- River Mouth, Estuary
- Lake
- Salt Lake
- Intermittent Lake
- Reservoir
- Swamp, Pond
- Canal
- Glacier
- Ice Shelf, Pack Ice
- Ocean
- Sea
- Gulf, Bay
- Strait, Fjord
- Lagoon
- Bank
- Seamount
- Tablemount
- Ridge
- Shelf
- Basin
- Escarpment, Sea Scarp
- Fracture
- Trench, Abyss
- National Park, Reserve
- Point of Interest
- Recreation Site
- Cave, Cavern
- Historic Site
- Ruins
- Wall, Walls
- Church, Abbey
- Temple
- Scientific Station
- Airport
- Port
- Lighthouse
- Mine
- Tunnel
- Dam, Bridge

Kanggup'o 28 Id 41.07N 127.31 E
Kanggye 27 Mc 40.58N 126.36 E
Kangi 35 Dd 8.10N 27.39 E
Kangjin 28 Ig 34.38N 126.46 E
Kangiqsualujjuaq 39 Md 58.35N 65.59W
Kangiqsujuaq 42 Kd 61.36N 71.57W
Kangirsuk 39 Lc 60.00N 70.01W
Kangmar 27 Ef 28.32N 89.43 E
Kangnüng 27 Md 37.44N 128.54 E
Kango 36 Bb 0.09N 10.08 E
Kangondu 36 Gc 1.06S 37.42 E
Kangping 28 Gc 42.45N 123.20 E
Kangrinboqê Feng 27 De 31.04N 81.30 E
Kangto 25 Ic 27.52N 92.30 E
Kangwŏn-Do [N.Kor.] [2] 28 Ie 38.45N 127.35 E
Kangwŏn-Do [S.Kor.] [2] 28 Jf 37.45N 128.15 E
Kani 34 Dd 8.29N 6.36W
Kaniama 36 Dd 7.31S 24.11 E
Kanibadam 18 Hd 40.17N 70.25 E
Kaniet Islands 57 Fe 0.53S 145.30 E
Kanija 15 Lc 46.16N 28.13 E
Kanimeh 18 Ed 40.18N 65.09 E
Kanina 15 Ci 40.26N 19.31 E
Kanin Kamen 17 Bb 68.15N 45.15 E
Kanin Nos 19 Eb 68.39N 43.14 E
Kanin Nos, Mys- 5 Kb 68.39N 43.16 E
Kanin Peninsula (EN)= Kanin Poluostrov 5 Kb 68.00N 45.00 E
Kanin Poluostrov=Kanin Peninsula (EN) 5 Kb 68.00N 45.00 E
Kanioumé 34 Eb 15.46N 3.09W
Kanita 29a Bc 41.02N 140.38 E
Kanjiža 15 Dc 46.04N 20.03 E
Kankaanpää 7 Ff 61.48N 22.25 E
Kankakee 43 Jc 41.07N 87.52W
Kankakee River 45 Lf 41.23N 88.16W
Kankalabé 34 Cc 11.00N 12.00W
Kankan 31 Gg 10.23N 9.18W
Kanker 25 Gd 20.17N 81.29 E
Kankesanturai 25 Gg 9.49N 80.02 E
Kankossa 32 Ef 15.55N 11.31W
Kankunski 20 He 57.39N 126.25 E
Kanla 10 Hf 50.48N 11.35 E
Kanmav Kyun 25 Jf 11.40N 98.28 E
Kanmon-Kaikyō 29 Bd 33.56N 130.57 E
Kanmuri-Yama 29 Cd 34.28N 132.05 E
Kannapolis 43 Kd 35.30N 80.37W
Kannone-Jima 28 Jj 28.51N 128.58 E
Kannonkoski 8 Kb 62.58N 25.15 E
Kannus 7 Fe 63.54N 23.54 E
Kano [2] 34 Gc 12.00N 9.00 E
Kano 31 Hg 12.00N 8.31 E
Kanona 36 Fe 13.04S 30.38 E
Kan'onji 28 Lg 34.07N 133.39 E
Kanoya 28 Ki 31.23N 130.51 E
Kanozero, Ozero- 7 Ic 67.00N 34.05 E
Kānpur 22 Kg 26.28N 80.21 E
Kansas 38 Jf 39.07N 94.36W
Kansas [2] 43 Hd 38.45N 98.15W
Kansas City [Ks.-U.S.] 39 Jf 39.07N 94.39W
Kansas City [Mo.-U.S.] 39 Jf 39.05N 94.35W
Kanshi 27 Kg 24.57N 116.52 E
Kansk 22 Ld 56.13N 95.41 E
Kansŏng 28 Je 38.22N 128.28 E
Kansu (EN)=Gansu Sheng (Kan-su Sheng) [2] 27 Hd 38.00N 102.00 E
Kansu (EN)=Kan-su Sheng→Gansu Sheng [2] 27 Hd 38.00N 102.00 E
Kan-su Sheng→Gansu Sheng=Kansu (EN) [2] 27 Hd 38.00N 102.00 E
Kansyat 26 Kg 2.15S 138.51 E
Kant 18 Jc 42.52N 74.50 E
Kantang 25 Jg 7.23N 99.32 E
Kantchari 34 Fc 12.29N 1.31 E
Kanté 34 Fd 9.57N 1.03 E
Kantemirovka 19 Df 49.45N 39.53 E
Kantō-Heiya 29 Fc 36.00N 139.30 E
Kanton Atoll 57 Je 2.50S 171.41W
Kantō-Sanchi 29 Fc 36.00N 138.45 E
Kantubek 18 Bb 45.06N 59.16 E
Kanturk/Ceann Toirc 9 Ei 52.10N 8.55W
Kanuma 29 Fc 36.34N 139.45 E
Kanye 31 Jk 24.58S 25.21 E
Kanyu 37 Cd 20.04S 24.36 E
Kanzenze 36 Ee 10.31S 25.12 E
Kao 65b Aa 19.40S 175.01W
Kaohsiung 22 Og 22.38N 120.17 E
Kaôk Nhêk 25 Lf 13.05N 107.04 E
Kaoko Otavi 37 Ac 18.15S 13.37 E
Kaokoveld [3] 37 Ac 18.00S 13.00 E
Kaokoveld 30 Ij 19.30S 13.30 E
Kaolack 31 Fg 14.09N 16.04W
Kao Neua, Col de- 25 Le 18.23N 105.10 E
Kaouadja 35 Cd 8.00N 23.14 E
Kaouar 34 Hb 19.05N 12.52 E
Kapaa 65a Ba 22.05N 159.19W
Kapanga 31 Ji 8.21S 22.35 E
Kapar 24 Ld 36.32N 47.30 E
Kapčagaj 19 Hg 43.52N 77.03 E
Kapčagajskoje Vodohranilišče 19 Hg 43.45N 78.00 E
Kapchorwa 36 Fb 1.24N 34.27 E
Kap Dan 41 Ie 65.32N 37.30W
Kapelle 12 Fc 51.39N 3.57 E
Kapellskär 8 He 59.43N 19.04 E
Kapena 36 Ee 10.47S 28.20 E
Kapenguria 36 Gb 1.14N 35.07 E
Kapfenberg 14 Jc 47.26N 15.18 E
Kapıdağı Yarimadası 15 Ki 40.28N 27.50 E
Kapiri Mposhi 36 Ee 13.58S 28.41 E
Kāpīsā [3] 23 Kc 34.45N 69.30 E
Kapit 26 Ff 2.01N 112.56 E
Kapiti Island 62 Fd 40.50S 174.55 E
Kapka, Massif du- 35 Cb 15.07N 21.45 E
Kapoeta 31 Kh 4.47N 33.35 E
Kapona 36 Ed 7.11S 29.09 E
Kapos 10 Oj 46.44N 18.29 E
Kaposvár 10 Nj 46.22N 17.48 E
Kapp 8 Dd 60.42N 10.52 E
Kappeln 10 Fb 54.40N 9.56 E
Kapša 7 Hg 59.52N 33.45 E
Kapsan 28 Jd 41.05N 128.18 E
Kapsukas 7 Fi 54.33N 23.23 E
Kapuas [Indon.] 26 Mj 0.25S 109.40 E
Kapuas [Indon.] 26 Fg 3.01S 114.20 E
Kapuas Hulu, Pegunungan-=Kapuas Mountains (EN) 26 Ff 1.25N 113.15 E
Kapuas Mountains (EN)= Kapuas Hulu, Pegunungan 26 Ff 1.25N 113.15 E
Kapugargin 15 Lm 36.40N 28.50 E
Kapušany 10 Rg 49.03N 21.21 E
Kapuskasing 39 Ke 49.25N 82.26W
Kapustin Jar 16 Ne 48.35N 45.45 E
Kapustoje 7 Ic 67.17N 34.12 E
Kaputdžuh, Gora- 16 Oj 39.12N 46.01 E
Kapuvár 10 Ni 47.36N 17.02 E
Kara 17 Lb 69.10N 64.45 E
Kara 34 Fd 9.33N 1.12 E
Kara [3] 34 Fd 9.35N 1.05 E
Kara Ada [Tur.] 15 Km 36.58N 27.28 E
Kara Ada [Tur.] 15 Jk 38.25N 26.20 E
Kara-Balta 19 Hg 42.49N 73.57 E
Karabas 19 Hf 49.30N 73.00 E
Karabaš 17 Ji 55.29N 60.13 E
Karabekaul 19 Gh 38.28N 64.10 E
Karabiga 15 Ki 40.24N 27.18 E
Karabil, Vozvyšennost- 18 Df 36.20N 63.30 E
Kara-Bogaz-Gol 19 Fg 41.01N 52.59 E
Kara-Bogaz-Gol, proliv- 16 Ri 41.04N 52.59 E
Kara-Bogaz-Gol, Zaliv- 5 Lg 41.00N 53.15 E
Karabuk 23 Da 41.12N 32.37 E
Karabulak [Kaz.-U.S.S.R.] 18 Lb 44.54N 78.29 E
Karabulak [Kaz.-U.S.S.R.] 19 Gg 42.31N 69.47 E
Kara Burun 15 Km 36.32N 27.58 E
Karaburun [Tur.] 24 Cb 41.21N 28.40 E
Karaburun [Tur.] 24 Bc 38.37N 26.31 E
Karabutak 19 Gf 49.57N 60.08 E
Karacabey 24 Cb 40.13N 28.21 E
Karaca Dağ 24 Hd 37.40N 39.50 E
Karačajevo-Čerkesskaja Avtonomnaja Oblast [3] 19 Eg 43.45N 41.45 E
Karačajevsk 16 Lh 43.44N 41.58 E
Karacaköy 24 Cb 41.22N 28.30 E
Karacaoğlan 15 Kh 41.32N 27.04 E
Karacasu 24 Cd 37.43N 28.37 E
Karačev 19 De 53.04N 34.59 E
Karāchi 22 Ig 24.52N 67.03 E
Kara Dağ [Tur.] 24 Jd 37.40N 43.42 E
Kara Dağ [Tur.] 24 Ed 37.23N 33.10 E
Karadah 16 Oh 42.29N 46.54 E
Karadeniz=Black Sea (EN) 5 Jg 43.00N 35.00 E
Kara Dong 27 Dd 38.26N 81.50 E
Karagajly 19 Hf 49.20N 75.48 E
Karaganda 22 Je 49.50N 73.10 E
Karagandinskaja Oblast [3] 19 Hf 50.00N 74.00 E
Karaginski, Ostrov- 21 Sd 58.48N 164.05 E
Karaginski Zaliv 21 Sd 58.50N 164.00 E
Kara Gölü 15 Mm 36.42N 29.50 E
Karagoš, Gora- 20 Df 51.44N 89.24 E
Karahalli 15 Mk 38.20N 29.32 E
Karaidelski 17 Hi 55.49N 57.05 E
Kara-Irtyš 21 Ke 47.52N 84.16 E
Karaisali 24 Fd 37.16N 35.03 E
Karaj 24 Ne 35.48N 50.59 E
Karaj 24 Ne 35.07N 51.35 E
Karak, Gora- 19 Gg 44.59N 63.05 E
Kara-Kala 19 Fh 38.28N 56.18 E
Karakalpak ASSR (EN)= Karakalpakskaja ASSR [3] 19 Fg 43.30N 59.00 E
Karakalpakskaja ASSR= Karakalpak ASSR (EN) [3] 19 Fg 43.30N 59.00 E
Karakax/Moyu 27 Cd 37.17N 79.42 E
Karakax He 27 Dd 38.06N 80.24 E
Karakaya Baraji 24 Hc 38.25N 38.45 E
Karakeçi 24 Hd 37.26N 39.26 E
Karakelong, Pulau- 26 If 4.15N 126.48 E
Karakoçan 24 Ic 38.02N 40.07 E
Karakoin, Ozero- 18 Ga 46.10N 68.40 E
Karakojsu 16 Oh 42.30N 47.05 E
Karakolka 18 Kd 41.29N 77.24 E
Karakoram 21 Jf 34.00N 78.00 E
Karakoram Pass 21 Jf 35.30N 77.50 E
Karakore 35 Gc 10.25N 40.01 E
Karakoro 34 Cc 14.43N 12.03 E
Karakorum Shan 27 Cd 36.00N 76.00 E
Karakorum Shankou 27 Cd 35.30N 77.50 E
Karaköy 24 Ic 39.04N 41.42 E
Kara-Kul 18 Id 41.34N 72.47 E
Karakul, Ozero- 19 Hh 39.05N 73.25 E
Karakumski kanal imeni V.I. Lenina 19 Gh 37.42N 64.20 E
Karakumy 21 Hf 39.00N 60.00 E
Karakuwisa 37 Bc 18.56S 19.40 E
Karam 20 Fe 55.09N 107.37 E
Karama 26 Gg 2.18S 119.06 E
Karaman 23 Db 37.11N 33.14 E
Karamanli 15 Ml 37.22N 29.49 E
Karamay 22 Ke 45.30N 84.55 E
Karamea 61 Dh 41.15S 172.06 E
Karamea Bight 62 Dd 41.25S 171.50 E
Karamet-Nijaz 19 Gh 37.43N 64.31 E
Karamiran He 27 Dd 37.50N 84.35 E
Karamiran Shankou 27 Ed 36.15N 87.05 E
Karamiševo 8 Mg 57.44N 28.50 E
Karamoja [3] 36 Fb 2.45N 34.15 E
Karamürsel 15 Mi 40.42N 29.36 E
Kara-myk 19 Hh 39.30N 71.51 E
Karamyš 16 Nd 51.18N 45.00 E
Karān 24 Mi 27.43N 49.49 E
Karaova 15 Kl 37.05N 27.40 E
Karapınar 24 Ed 37.43N 33.33 E
Kara-Saki 29 Ad 34.40N 129.29 E
Kara-Sal 16 Mf 47.18N 43.36 E
Karasay 27 Dd 36.48N 83.48 E
Karasburg 31 Ik 28.00S 18.43 E
Kara Sea (EN)=Karskoje More 67 Hd 76.00N 80.00 E
Karašica 14 Me 45.36N 18.36 E
Karasjok 7 Fb 69.27N 25.30 E
Kara Strait (EN)=Karskije Vorota, Proliv- 21 Hb 70.30N 58.00 E
Karasu 24 Db 41.04N 30.47 E
Karasu [Tur.] 21 Ff 38.52N 38.48 E
Karasu [Tur.] 24 Ic 38.49N 41.28 E
Karasu [Tur.] 24 Jc 38.32N 43.10 E
Karasu Dağları 24 Ic 39.30N 40.45 E
Karasuk 20 Cf 53.44N 78.08 E
Karasuk 20 Cf 53.35N 77.30 E
Karasuyama 29 Gc 36.39N 140.08 E
Karatá, Laguna- 49 Fg 13.56N 83.30W
Karatal 19 Hf 46.26N 77.10 E
Karataş [Tur.] 24 Fd 36.36N 35.21 E
Karataş [Tur.] 15 Lk 38.34N 28.17 E
Karataş Burun 24 Fb 36.35N 35.22 E
Karatau 19 Hg 43.10N 70.29 E
Karatau, Hrebet- 21 Ie 43.40N 69.00 E
Karatj 7 Ec 66.43N 18.33 E
Karatobe 16 Re 49.42N 53.33 E
Karaton 19 Ff 46.25N 53.34 E
Karatsu 28 Jh 33.26N 130.00 E
Karatsu-Wan 29 Be 33.30N 130.00 E
Kara-Turgaj 21 Ie 48.01N 62.45 E
Karaul [Kaz.-U.S.S.R.] 19 Hf 49.00N 79.20 E
Karaul [R.S.F.S.R.] 20 Db 70.10N 83.08 E
Karaulbazar 18 Ee 39.29N 64.47 E
Karaulkala 18 Bc 42.18N 58.41 E
Karava 15 Ej 39.19N 21.36 E
Karavanke 14 Id 46.25N 14.25 E
Karavastase, Gjiri i- 15 Ci 40.55N 19.30 E
Karavastase, Laguna e- 15 Ci 40.55N 19.30 E
Karávi 15 Gm 36.45N 23.35 E
Karavonisia 15 Jn 35.59N 26.26 E
Karawa 36 Db 3.20N 20.18 E
Karaxabar He/Kaidu He 27 Ec 41.55N 86.38 E
Karažal 19 Hf 47.59N 70.53 E
Karbalā' 22 Gf 32.36N 44.02 E
Karbalā [3] 24 Jf 32.30N 43.45 E
Kårbole 7 Df 61.59N 15.19 E
Karcag 10 Qi 47.19N 20.56 E
Kardhámaina 15 Km 36.47N 27.09 E
Kardhámila 15 Jk 38.31N 26.06 E
Kardhiotissa 15 Im 36.38N 25.01 E
Kardhítsa 15 Ej 39.22N 21.55 E
Kärdla/Kjardla 7 Fg 59.01N 22.42 E
Kărdžali 15 Ih 41.39N 25.22 E
Kărdžali [2] 15 Ih 41.30N 25.30 E
Kareha, Jbel- 13 Gi 35.15N 5.30W
Karelia (EN) 5 Jc 64.00N 32.00 E
Karelskaja ASSR [3] 19 Dc 63.30N 33.30 E
Karema 36 Fd 6.49S 30.26 E
Karen → Kayin 25 Je 17.30N 97.45 E
Karen 25 If 12.51N 92.53 E
Karesuando 7 Fb 68.27N 22.29 E
Karët 30 Gf 24.00N 7.30W
Kärevere/Kjarevere 8 Lf 58.23N 26.30 E
Kargala 16 Sd 51.59N 55.10 E
Kargapazarı Dağı 24 Ib 40.07N 41.35 E
Kargapolje 17 Li 55.57N 64.27 E
Kargasok 20 De 59.07N 81.01 E
Kargat 20 De 55.10N 80.17 E
Kargı 24 Fb 41.08N 34.30 E
Kargil 25 Fb 34.34N 76.06 E
Kargilik/Yecheng 22 Jf 37.54N 77.26 E
Kargopol 19 Dc 61.32N 38.58 E
Karhula 7 Gf 60.31N 26.57 E
Kari 34 Hc 11.14N 10.34 E
Kariai 6 Ig 40.15N 24.15 E
Kariba 31 Jj 16.30S 28.45 E
Kariba, Lake- 30 Jj 17.00S 28.00 E
Kariba-Dake 29a Ab 42.37N 139.56 E
Kariba Dam 37 Dc 16.30S 28.50 E
Karibib 31 Ik 21.58S 15.51 E
Karibib [3] 37 Bd 22.00S 16.00 E
Kariet-Arkmane 13 Ji 35.06N 2.45W
Karigasniemi 7 Fb 69.24N 25.50 E
Karijärvi 8 Jc 61.35N 22.30 E
Karikachi Tōge 29a Cb 43.10N 142.40 E
Kārikāl 25 Ff 10.55N 79.50 E
Karikari, Cape- 62 Ea 34.47S 173.24 E
Karima (EN)=Kuraymah 31 Kg 18.33N 31.51 E
Karimama 34 Fc 12.04N 3.11 E
Karimata, Kepulauan-= Karimata Islands (EN) 26 Eg 1.25S 109.05 E
Karimata, Pulau- 26 Eg 1.36S 108.55 E
Karimata, Selat-=Karimata Strait (EN) 21 Mj 2.05S 108.40 E
Karimata Islands (EN)= Karimata, Kepulauan- 26 Eg 1.25S 109.05 E
Karimata Strait (EN)= Karimata, Selat- 21 Mj 2.05S 108.40 E
Karīmganj 25 Id 24.42N 92.33 E
Karīmnagar 25 Fe 18.26N 79.09 E
Karimunjawa, Kepulauan-= Karimunjawa Islands (EN) 26 Fh 5.50S 110.25 E
Karimunjawa Islands (EN)= Karimunjawa, Kepulauan- 26 Fh 5.50S 110.25 E
Karin [Som.] 35 Hc 10.59N 49.13 E
Karin [Som.] 35 Hc 10.51N 45.45 E
Karis/Karjaa 7 Ff 60.05N 23.40 E
Karisimbi 30 Ji 1.30S 29.27 E
Káristos 15 Hk 38.01N 24.25 E
Karjaa/Karis 7 Ff 60.05N 23.40 E
Karkār 35 Hd 9.57N 49.20 E
Karkaralinsk 19 Hf 49.23N 75.31 E
Karkar Island 57 Fe 4.40S 146.00 E
Karkas, Kūh-e 24 Nf 33.27N 51.48 E
Karkheh 23 Gc 31.31N 47.55 E
Karkinitski zaliv 5 Jf 45.55N 33.00 E
Karkkila/Högfors 7 Ff 60.32N 24.11 E
Karkku 8 Jc 61.25N 23.01 E
Kärkölä 8 Kd 60.55N 25.15 E
Kärla/Kjarla 8 Jf 58.16N 22.05 E
Karlholm 8 Gd 60.31N 17.37 E
Karlik Shan 21 Le 43.00N 94.30 E
Karlino 10 Lb 54.03N 15.51 E
Karliova 24 Ic 39.18N 41.01 E
Karl Marx, Pik- 19 Hh 37.08N 72.29 E
Karl-Marx-Stadt — Chemnitz 6 He 50.50N 12.55 E
Karlö/Hailuoto 5 Ib 65.02N 24.42 E
Karlobag 14 Jf 44.32N 15.05 E
Karlovac 14 Je 45.29N 15.33 E
Karlovka 16 Ie 49.28N 35.08 E
Karlovo 15 Hg 42.38N 24.48 E
Karlovy Vary 10 If 50.14N 12.52 E
Karlsbad 12 Kf 48.55N 8.35 E
Karlsborg 7 Df 58.32N 14.31 E
Karlshamn 7 Dh 56.10N 14.51 E
Karlskoga 7 Dg 59.20N 14.31 E
Karlskrona 6 Hd 56.10N 15.35 E
Karlsöarna 8 Gg 57.15N 18.00 E
Karlsruhe 10 Eg 49.01N 8.24 E
Karlstad [Mn.-U.S.] 45 Hb 48.35N 96.31W
Karlstad [Swe.] 6 Hd 59.22N 13.30 E
Karluk 40 Ie 57.34N 154.28W
Karmah=Kerma (EN) 35 Eb 19.38N 30.25 E
Karmana 18 Ed 40.09N 65.15 E
Karmøy 7 Ag 59.15N 5.15 E
Karnāli 25 Gc 28.45N 81.16 E
Karnataka (Mysore) [3] 25 Ff 13.30N 76.00 E
Karnobat 15 Jg 42.39N 26.59 E
Kärnten = Carinthia (EN) [2] 14 Hd 46.45N 14.00 E
Kärnten = Carinthia (EN) 14 Hd 46.45N 14.00 E
Karoi 37 Dc 16.50S 29.40 E
Karonga 31 Ki 9.56S 33.56 E
Karora 35 Fb 17.39N 38.22 E
Káros 15 Im 36.53N 25.39 E
Kárpathos 15 Kn 35.30N 27.14 E
Kárpathos=Karpathos (EN) 5 Ih 35.40N 27.10 E
Karpathos (EN)= Kárpathos 5 Ih 35.40N 27.10 E
Karpáthou, Stenón- 15 Kn 35.50N 27.30 E
Karpenision 15 Ek 38.55N 21.47 E
Karpinsk 17 Jg 59.45N 60.01 E
Karpuzlu 15 Kl 37.33N 27.50 E
Kars 23 Fa 40.37N 43.05 E
Karsakpaj 19 Gf 47.48N 66.45 E
Kärsämäki 7 Fe 64.00N 25.46 E
Karsava/Kársava 7 Gh 56.47N 27.42 E
Kársava/Karsava 7 Gh 56.47N 27.42 E
Karši 22 If 38.53N 65.48 E
Karşiyaka 15 Ki 40.26N 28.00 E
Karsiyaka 15 Kk 38.27N 27.07 E
Karskije Vorota, Proliv-= Kara Strait (EN) 21 Hb 70.30N 58.00 E
Karskoje More=Kara Sea (EN) 67 Hd 76.00N 80.00 E
Kars Platosu 24 Jb 40.40N 43.07 E
Karst (EN)=Kras 5 Hf 45.48N 14.00 E
Kårsta 8 He 59.39N 18.14 E
Karstula 7 Fe 62.52N 24.47 E
Kartal 24 Cb 40.53N 29.10 E
Kartaly 19 Ge 53.03N 60.40 E
Kartaly-Ajat 17 Jj 53.01N 61.50 E
Karttula 8 Lb 62.53N 26.58 E
Kartuzy 10 Ob 54.20N 18.12 E
Karumai 29 Ga 40.20N 141.28 E
Karumba 59 Ic 17.29S 140.50 E
Karūn 21 Gf 30.25N 48.12 E
Karungi 7 Fc 66.03N 23.57 E
Karungu 36 Fc 0.51S 34.09 E
Karunki 7 Fc 66.02N 24.01 E
Karūr 25 Ff 10.57N 78.05 E
Karvia 7 Fe 62.08N 22.34 E
Karviná 10 Og 49.51N 18.32 E
Kārwār 25 Ef 14.48N 74.08 E
Karwendel Gebirge 14 Fc 47.28N 11.20 E
Karymskoje 20 Gf 51.37N 114.21 E
Kas 35 Cc 12.34N 24.17 E
Kaş 24 Cd 36.12N 29.38 E
Kasaba [Tur.] 15 Mm 36.18N 29.44 E
Kasaba [Zam.] 36 Ee 10.44S 29.43 E
Kasado-Shima 29 Be 33.57N 131.50 E
Kasah 16 Mi 40.03N 43.52 E
Kasai 29 Dd 34.56N 134.49 E
Kasai 30 Ii 3.02S 16.57 E
Kasai Occidental [2] 36 Dc 5.00S 21.30 E
Kasai Oriental [2] 36 Dc 3.00S 23.00 E
Kasaji 36 De 10.22S 23.27 E
Kasaku 36 Ec 1.55S 25.50 E
Kasama [Jap.] 29 Gc 36.22N 140.16 E
Kasama [Zam.] 31 Kj 10.13S 31.12 E
Kasan 18 Ee 39.01N 65.35 E
Kasane 31 Jj 17.48S 25.09 E
Kasanga 36 Fd 8.28S 31.09 E
Kasangulu 36 Bc 4.36S 15.10 E
Kasansaj 18 Hd 41.10N 71.32 E
Kasaoka 29 Cd 34.30N 133.29 E
Kāsaragod 25 Ef 12.30N 75.00 E
Kasari 29b Ba 28.27N 129.41 E
Kasary 16 Le 49.02N 41.03 E
Kasatori-Yama 29 Ce 33.33N 132.55 E
Kasba Lake 42 Hd 60.20N 102.10W
Kasba Tatla 32 Fc 32.36N 6.16W
Kaseda 28 Ki 31.25N 130.19 E
Kasempa 36 Ee 13.27S 25.50 E
Kasenga 31 Jj 10.22S 28.37 E
Kasenye 36 Fb 1.24N 30.26 E
Kasese [Ug.] 36 Fb 0.10N 30.05 E
Kasese [Zaire] 36 Ec 1.38S 27.07 E
Kashaf 23 Jb 35.58N 61.07 E
Kāshān 22 Hf 33.59N 51.29 E
Kashi 22 Jf 39.29N 75.58 E
Kashihara 29 Dd 34.31N 135.47 E
Kashima [Jap.] 29 Cd 35.31N 132.59 E
Kashima [Jap.] 29 Gd 35.58N 140.38 E
Kashima [Jap.] 29 Be 33.07N 130.07 E
Kashima-Nada 29 Gc 36.30N 140.45 E
Kashiobwe 36 Ed 9.39S 28.37 E
Kashiwazaki 28 Of 37.25N 138.30 E
Kashkū'īyeh 24 Qh 28.58N 56.37 E
Kāshmar 23 Ib 35.12N 58.27 E
Kashmir 21 Jf 34.00N 76.00 E
Kashmor 25 Dc 28.26N 69.35 E
Kasimov 19 Ee 54.59N 41.28 E
Kašin 19 Dd 57.23N 37.37 E
Kasindi 36 Eb 0.02N 29.43 E
Kašira 7 Ji 54.52N 38.11 E
Kasiruta, Pulau- 26 Ig 0.25S 127.12 E
Kasisty 20 Fb 73.40N 109.45 E
Kaškadarinskaja Oblast [3] 19 Gh 38.50N 66.10 E
Kaškadarja 18 Ee 39.35N 64.38 E
Kaskaskia River 45 Lh 37.59N 89.56W
Kaskelen 19 Hg 43.09N 76.37 E
Kaskö/Kaskinen 7 Ee 62.23N 21.13 E
Kasli 17 Ji 55.53N 60.48 E
Kaslo 46 Gb 49.55N 116.55W
Kasongo 31 Ji 4.27S 26.40 E
Kasongo-Lunda 36 Cd 6.28S 16.49 E
Kásos 15 Jn 35.25N 26.55 E
Kásou, Stenón- 15 Jn 35.25N 26.35 E
Kaspi 16 Ni 41.58N 44.25 E
Kaspičan 15 Kf 43.18N 27.11 E
Kaspijsk 19 Eg 42.57N 47.35 E
Kaspijski 19 Ef 45.25N 47.22 E
Kaspijskoje More=Caspian Sea (EN) 5 Lg 42.00N 50.30 E
Kasplja 16 Gb 55.24N 30.43 E
Kasr, Ra's- 35 Fb 18.04N 38.33 E
Kassaar/Kassar 8 Jf 58.47N 22.40 E
Kassalā 31 Kg 15.28N 36.24 E
Kassalā [3] 35 Fc 14.40N 35.30 E
Kassándra 15 Gi 40.00N 23.30 E
Kassandra, Gulf of- (EN) = Kassándras, Kólpos- 15 Gi 40.05N 23.30 E
Kassándras, Ákra- 15 Gj 39.57N 23.21 E
Kassándras, Kólpos- = Kassandra, Gulf of- (EN) 15 Gi 40.05N 23.30 E
Kassel 10 Fe 51.19N 9.30 E
Kassiópi 15 Cj 39.47N 19.55 E
Kastamonu 23 Da 41.22N 33.47 E
Kastanéai 15 Jh 41.39N 26.28 E
Kastellaun 12 Jd 50.04N 7.27 E
Kastéllion [Grc.] 15 In 35.12N 25.20 E
Kastéllion [Grc.] 15 Gn 35.30N 23.39 E
Kastéllos, Ákra- 15 Kn 35.23N 27.09 E
Kasterlee 12 Gc 51.15N 4.57 E
Kastlösa 8 Gh 56.28N 16.25 E
Kastoria 15 Ei 40.31N 21.16 E
Kastorías, Límni- 15 Ei 40.31N 21.18 E
Kastornoje 16 Kd 51.51N 38.07 E
Kastós 15 Dk 38.35N 20.55 E
Kasuga 29 Be 33.32N 130.27 E
Kasugai 29 Ed 35.14N 136.58 E
Kasulu 36 Fc 4.34S 30.06 E
Kasumbalesa 36 Ee 12.13S 27.48 E
Kasumi 29 Dd 35.38N 134.38 E
Kasumi-ga-Ura 28 Pf 36.00N 140.25 E
Kasumkent 16 Pi 41.42N 48.10 E
Kasungan 26 Fg 1.58S 113.24 E
Kasungu 36 Fe 13.02S 33.29 E
Kasupe 36 Gf 15.10S 35.18 E
Kasūr 25 Eb 31.07N 74.27 E
Kaszuby 10 Ob 54.10N 18.15 E
Kataba 31 Jj 16.05S 25.10 E
Katahdin, Mount- 43 Nb 45.55N 68.55W
Katajsk 17 Kh 56.18N 62.35 E
Katako-Kombe 36 Dc 3.24S 24.25 E
Katanga 36 Ed 10.00S 25.30 E
Katanga 20 Fd 60.10N 102.10 E
Katangli 20 Jf 51.43N 143.16 E
Katanning 59 Df 33.42S 117.33 E
Katav-Ivanovsk 17 Ii 54.47N 58.15 E
Katchall 25 Ig 7.57N 93.22 E
Katchi 32 Ef 17.00N 13.55W
Katende, Chutes de- 36 Dd 6.30S 22.10 E
Katerini 15 Fi 40.16N 22.30 E
Katesh 36 Gc 4.31S 35.23 E
Katete 36 Fe 14.06S 32.05 E
Katha 25 Jd 24.11N 96.21 E
Katherine 58 Ef 14.28S 132.16 E
Katherine River 59 Gb 14.39S 131.42 E
Kāthiāwār 21 Jg 21.58N 70.30 E
Kāthmāndāū = Kathmandu (EN) 22 Kg 27.43N 85.19 E
Kathmandu → Kāthmāndāū 22 Kg 27.43N 85.19 E
Kathua 36 Gc 1.17S 39.03 E
Kati 34 Dc 12.43N 8.05W
Katihār 25 Hc 25.32N 87.35 E
Katiki, Volcán- 65d Bb 27.06S 109.16W
Katima Mulilo 36 Df 17.28S 24.14 E
Katiola 34 Dd 8.08N 5.06W
Katiola [3] 34 Dd 8.13N 5.02W
Katiu Atoll 61 Mc 16.26S 144.22W
Katla 7a Bc 63.36N 18.58W
Katlabuh, Ozero- 15 Ld 45.25N 29.00 E
Katlanovo 15 Eh 41.54N 21.41 E
Katmai, Mount- 40 Ie 58.17N 154.56W
Káto Akhaia 15 Ek 38.09N 21.33 E
Katofio 36 Ee 11.02S 28.01 E
Katompi 36 Ed 6.11S 26.20 E
Katonga 36 Fb 0.10N 30.40 E
Katon-Karagaj 19 If 49.11N 85.37 E
Káto Ólimbos 15 Fj 39.55N 22.28 E
Katoomba 59 Kf 33.42S 150.18 E
Katopasa, Gunung- 26 Hg 1.14S 121.25 E

Index Symbols

[1] Independent Nation
[2] State, Region
[3] District, County
[4] Municipality
[5] Colony, Dependency
Continent
Physical Region
Historical or Cultural Region
Mount, Mountain
Volcano
Hill
Mountains, Mountain Range
Hills, Escarpment
Plateau, Upland
Pass, Gap
Plain, Lowland
Delta
Salt Flat
Valley, Canyon
Crater, Cave
Karst Features
Depression
Polder
Desert, Dunes
Forest, Woods
Heath, Steppe
Oasis
Cape, Point
Coast, Beach
Cliff
Peninsula
Isthmus
Sandbank
Island
Atoll
Rock, Reef
Islands, Archipelago
Rocks, Reefs
Coral Reef
Well, Spring
Geyser
River, Stream
Waterfall Rapids
River Mouth, Estuary
Lake
Salt Lake
Intermittent Lake
Reservoir
Swamp, Pond
Canal
Glacier
Ice Shelf, Pack Ice
Ocean
Sea
Gulf, Bay
Strait, Fjord
Lagoon
Bank
Seamount
Tablemount
Ridge
Shelf
Basin
Escarpment, Sea Scarp
Fracture
Trench, Abyss
National Park, Reserve
Point of Interest
Recreation Site
Cave, Cavern
Historic Site
Ruins
Wall, Walls
Church, Abbey
Temple
Scientific Station
Airport
Port
Lighthouse
Mine
Tunnel
Dam, Bridge

Katowice [2] 10 Of 50.15N 19.00 E
Katowice 6 He 50.16N 19.00 E
Katrancık Dağı 24 Dd 37.27N 30.25 E
Kātrīnā, Jabal- 30 Kf 28.31N 33.57 E
Katrineholm 7 Dg 59.00N 16.12 E
Katsina 31 Hg 13.00N 7.36 E
Katsina Ala 34 Gd 7.48N 8.52 E
Katsumoto 28 Jh 33.51N 129.42 E
Katsuta 28 Pf 36.24N 140.32 E
Katsuura 28 Pg 35.08N 140.18 E
Katsuyama [Jap.] 28 Nf 36.03N 136.30 E
Katsuyama [Jap.] 29 Cd 35.06N 133.41 E
Kattakurgan 19 Gh 39.55N 66.15 E
Kattavia 15 Kn 35.57N 27.46 E
Kattegat 5 Hd 57.00N 11.00 E
Katthammarsvik 8 Hg 57.26N 18.50 E
Katulo, Lagh- 36 Hb 2.08N 40.56 E
Katumbi 36 Fe 10.49S 33.32 E
Katun 21 Kd 52.25N 85.05 E
Katwijk aan Zee 11 Kb 52.13N 4.24 E
Katwijk aan Zee, Katwijk-Katwijk aan Zee 12 Gb 52.12N 4.25 E
Katwijk-Katwijk aan Zee 12 Gb 52.12N 4.25 E
Katzenelnbogen 12 Jd 50.17N 7.57 E
Kau 26 If 1.11N 127.54 E
Kauai Channel 60 Oc 21.45N 158.50W
Kauai Island 57 Lb 22.03N 159.30W
Kaub 12 Jd 50.05N 7.46 E
Kauehi Atoll 61 Lc 15.51S 145.09W
Kaufbeuren 10 Gi 47.53N 10.37 E
Kauhajoki 7 Fe 62.26N 22.11 E
Kauhava 7 Fe 63.06N 23.05 E
Kauiki Head 60 Oc 20.46N 155.59W
Kaukauna 45 Ld 44.17N 88.17W
Kaukauveld 30 Jk 20.00S 21.50 E
Kaukonen 7 Fc 67.29N 24.54 E
Kaukura Atoll 57 Mf 15.45S 146.42W
Kaula Island 57 Kb 21.40N 160.32W
Kaulakahi Channel 65a Ba 22.02N 159.53W
Kaumalapau 65a Ec 20.47N 156.59W
Kaunakakai 60 Oc 21.05N 157.02W
Kaunas 6 Ie 54.54N 23.54 E
Kaunasskoje Vodohranilišče /Kauno Marios 8 Kj 54.50N 24.15 E
Kauniainen/Grankulla 8 Kd 60.13N 24.45 E
Kauno Marios/Kaunasskoje Vodohranilišče 8 Kj 54.50N 24.15 E
Kaunos 15 Lm 36.50N 28.35 E
Kaupanger 7 Bf 61.11N 7.14 E
Kau Paulatmada, Gunung- 26 Ig 3.15S 126.09 E
Kaura Namoda 34 Gc 12.36N 6.35 E
Kauriāla Ghāt 25 Gc 28.27N 80.59 E
Kaušany 16 Ff 46.39N 29.25 E
Kaustinen 7 Fe 63.32N 23.42 E
Kautokeino 7 Fb 68.59N 23.08 E
Kavacik 15 Lj 39.40N 28.30 E
Kavadarci 15 Fh 41.26N 22.01 E
Kavaja 15 Ch 41.11N 19.33 E
Kavak [Tur.] 15 Ji 40.36N 26.54 E
Kavak [Tur.] 24 Gb 41.05N 36.03 E
Kavaklidere 15 Ll 37.26N 28.22 E
Kavála 6 Ig 40.56N 24.25 E
Kaválas, Kólpos- 15 Hi 40.52N 24.25 E
Kavalerovo 20 Ih 44.19N 135.05 E
Kavali 25 Ff 14.55N 79.59 E
Kavār 24 Oh 29.11N 52.44 E
Kavaratti 22 Jh 10.33N 72.38 E
Kavaratti Island 25 Ef 10.33N 72.38 E
Kavarna 15 Lf 43.25N 28.20 E
Kavarskas/Kovarskas 8 Ki 55.24N 25.03 E
Kavendou, Mont- 30 Fg 10.41N 12.12W
Kavieng 60 Eh 2.34S 150.48 E
Kavīr, Dasht-e- 21 Hf 34.40N 54.30 E
Kavkaz 16 Jg 45.21N 36.12 E
Kavkaz, Bolšoj-=Caucasus (EN) 5 Kg 42.30N 45.00 E
Kävlinge 8 Ei 55.48N 13.06 E
Kävlingeån 8 Ei 55.47N 13.06 E
Kawa 35 Eb 19.10N 30.39 E
Kawabe 29 Gb 39.39N 140.15 E
Kawachi-nagano 29 Dd 34.27N 135.34 E
Kawagoe 29 Fd 35.55N 139.28 E
Kawaguchi 29 Fd 35.48N 139.42 E
Kawaihae Bay 65a Fc 20.02N 155.51W
Kawaihoa Point 65a Ab 21.47N 160.12W
Kawakawa 62 Fa 35.23S 174.04 E
Kawalusu, Pulau- 26 If 4.15N 125.19 E
Kawamata 29 Gc 37.40N 140.36 E
Kawambwa 36 Ed 9.47S 29.05 E
Kawaminami 29 Be 32.12N 131.32 E
Kawamoto 29 Cd 34.59N 132.29 E
Kawanishi 29 Gc 37.59N 140.03 E
Kawanoe 29 Cd 34.01N 133.34 E
Kawartha Lakes 44 Hc 44.32N 78.30W
Kawasaki [Jap.] 29 Gb 38.10N 140.38 E
Kawasaki [Jap.] 28 Og 35.32N 139.43 E
Kawashiri-Misaki 29 Bd 34.26N 130.58 E
Kawauchi 29a Bc 41.12N 141.00 E
Kawau Island 62 Fb 36.25S 174.50 E
Kawaura 29 Be 32.21N 130.05 E
Kawerau 62 Gc 38.05S 176.42 E
Kawhia 62 Fc 38.04S 174.49 E
Kawich Range 46 Gh 37.40N 116.30W
Kawio, Kepulauan- 26 If 4.30N 125.30 E
Kawkareik 25 Je 16.33N 98.14 E
Kawm Umbū 33 Fe 24.28N 32.57 E
Kawthaung 25 Jg 9.59N 98.33 E
Kaxgar He 21 Jf 39.46N 78.15 E
Kax He 27 Dc 43.37N 81.48 E
Kaya 34 Ec 13.05N 1.05W
Kayah [2] 25 Je 19.15N 97.15 E
Kayak 40 Ke 59.52N 144.30W
Kayali Dağı 15 Jj 39.58N 26.58 E
Kayan 21 Ni 2.55N 117.35 E
Kayanga 34 Bc 11.58N 15.00W
Kayangel Islands 57 Ed 8.04N 134.43 E
Kayangel Passage 64a Ba 8.01N 134.42 E
Kaycee 46 Le 43.43N 106.38W
Kayenta 46 Jh 36.44N 110.17W
Kayes [3] 34 Cc 14.00N 11.00W
Kayes 31 Fg 14.26N 11.27W
Kayin 25 Je 17.30N 97.45 E
Kayoa, Pulau- 26 Ig 0.05S 127.25 E
Kayseri 22 Ff 38.43N 35.30 E
Kayuagung 26 Dg 3.24S 104.50 E
Kayu Ara, Pulau- 26 Ef 1.31N 106.26 E
Kazačje 20 Ib 70.40N 136.13 E
Kazah 16 Ni 41.05N 45.22 E
Kazahskaja Sovetskaja Socialističeskaja Respublika [2] 19 Gf 48.00N 68.00 E
Kazahskaja SSR/Kazak Sovettik Socialistik Respublikasy [2] 19 Gf 48.00N 68.00 E
Kazahskaja SSR=Kazakh SSR (EN) [2] 19 Gf 48.00N 68.00 E
Kazahski Melkosopočnik=Kazakh Hills (EN) 21 Je 49.00N 73.00 E
Kazahski Zaliv 16 Rh 42.40N 52.25 E
Kazakh Hills (EN)=Kazahski Melkosopočnik 21 Je 49.00N 73.00 E
Kazakh SSR (EN)=Kazahskaja SSR [2] 19 Gf 48.00N 68.00 E
Kazakhstan (EN) 21 Hd 51.11N 52.52 E
Kazaklija 15 Lc 46.05N 28.38 E
Kazak Sovettik Socialistik Respublikasy [2] 19 Gf 48.00N 68.00 E
Kazalak 15 Ke 44.03N 27.24 E
Kazalinsk 19 Gf 45.46N 62.07 E
Kazan 6 Kd 55.45N 49.08 E
Kazan 38 Jc 64.02N 95.30W
Kazandžik 19 Fh 39.17N 55.34 E
Kazanka 7 Li 55.48N 49.05 E
Kazanka 16 Hf 47.50N 32.49 E
Kazanlăk 15 Ig 42.37N 25.24 E
Kazan-Rettō/Iō=Volcano Islands (EN) 21 Qg 25.00N 141.00 E
Kazanskoje 19 Gd 55.38N 69.14 E
Kazarman 19 Hg 41.20N 74.02 E
Kazatin 19 Cf 49.43N 28.50 E
Kazbek, Gora- 5 Kg 42.42N 44.31 E
Kaz Daği 23 Cb 39.42N 26.50 E
Kaz Daği 15 Mk 38.35N 29.15 E
Kāzerūn 22 Hg 29.37N 51.38 E
Kažim 17 Ef 60.20N 51.32 E
Kazi-Magomed 16 Pi 40.02N 48.56 E
Kazimierza Wielka 10 Qf 50.16N 20.30 E
Kâzımkarabekir 24 Ed 37.14N 32.59 E
Kazincbarcika 10 Qh 48.15N 20.38 E
Kazinga Channel 36 Ec 0.13S 29.53 E
Kazly-Rūda/Kazlu-Ruda 8 Jj 54.42N 23.32 E
Kazo 29 Fc 36.08N 139.36 E
Kaztalovka 16 Pe 49.46N 48.44 E
Kazumba 36 Dd 6.25S 22.02 E
Kazuno 28 Pd 40.14N 140.48 E
Kazym 19 Gc 63.54N 65.50 E
Kazyr 20 Ef 53.50N 92.53 E
Kcynia 10 Nd 53.00N 17.30 E
Kdyně 10 Jg 49.24N 13.02 E
Ké 35 Bb 18.32N 17.55 E
Kéa 15 Hl 37.37N 24.20 E
Kéa 15 Hl 37.39N 24.20 E
Keaau 65a Fd 19.37N 155.03W
Keahole Point 65a Ed 19.44N 156.04W
Kealaikahiki Channel 65a Ec 20.37N 156.50W
Kealaikahiki Point 65a Ec 20.32N 156.42W
Kealakekua Bay 65a Fd 19.28N 155.56W
Keams Canyon 46 Ji 35.49N 110.12W
Keanae 65a Ec 20.52N 156.09W
Keanapapa Point 65a Dc 20.54N 157.04W
Kearney 43 Hc 40.42N 99.05W
Kearns 46 Jf 40.39N 111.59W
Kéas, Stenón- 15 Hl 37.40N 24.12 E
Keats Bank (EN) 57 Id 5.23S 173.28 E
Keb 8 Mg 57.44N 28.38 E
Keban Baraji 24 Hc 38.53N 39.00 E
Kébémer 34 Bb 15.22N 16.27W
Kebir, Oued el- 14 Bn 36.51N 7.57 E
Kebnekaise 5 Hb 67.53N 18.33 E
Kebri Dehar 31 Lh 6.45N 44.17 E
Kebumen 26 Eh 7.40S 109.39 E
Kecel 10 Pj 46.32N 19.16 E
Kechika 42 Ee 59.38N 127.09W
Kecskemét 10 Pj 46.54N 19.42 E
Kėdainiai/Kedajnjaj 7 Fi 55.18N 23.59 E
Kedajnjaj/Kėdainiai 7 Fi 55.18N 23.59 E
Kedgwick 44 Nb 47.39N 67.21W
Kediri 22 Nj 7.49S 112.01 E
Kédougou 34 Cc 12.33N 12.11W
Kedva 17 Fd 64.14N 53.30 E
Kędzierzyn-Koźle 10 Of 50.20N 18.10 E
Keele 42 Fd 64.24N 124.47W
Keele Peak 38 Fc 63.26N 130.19W
Keeling Islands→Cocos Islands 21 Lk 12.10S 96.55 E
Keeling Islands→Cocos Islands [5] 22 Lk 12.10S 96.55 E
Keelung 22 Og 25.08N 121.44 E
Keene 44 Kd 42.55N 72.17W
Keer-Weer, Cape- 59 Ib 13.58S 141.30 E
Keetmanshoop 31 Ik 26.36S 18.08 E
Keetmanshoop [3] 37 Be 26.30S 18.30 E
Keewatin 42 Ig 49.46N 94.34W
Keewatin, District of- [3] 42 Hd 64.00N 96.00W
Kefa [3] 35 Fd 7.00N 36.00 E
Kefallinia=Cephalonia (EN) 5 Ih 38.15N 20.35 E
Kefamenanu 26 Hh 9.27S 124.29 E
Kefar Sava 24 Ff 32.10N 34.54 E
Keffi 34 Gd 8.51N 7.52 E
Keflavík 7a Ab 64.01N 22.34W
Kegen 19 Hg 42.58N 79.12 E
Kegums 8 Kh 56.41N 24.44 E
Kehdingen 10 Fc 53.45N 9.20 E
Kehl 10 Dh 48.35N 7.49 E
Kehra 7 Fg 59.19N 25.18 E
Keighley 9 Lh 53.52N 1.54W
Keila/Kejla 7 Fg 59.19N 24.27 E
Keila Jõgi/Kejla 8 Ke 59.25N 24.15 E
Keimoes 37 Ce 28.41S 21.00 E
Keipel Bank (EN) 59 Le 25.15S 159.30E
Keita 34 Gc 14.46N 5.46 E
Kéita, Bahr- 35 Bd 9.14N 18.21 E
Keitele 5 Ic 62.55N 26.00 E
Keith [Austl.] 59 Ig 36.06S 140.21 E
Keith [Scot.-U.K.] 9 Kd 57.32N 2.57W
Keith Arm 42 Fc 65.20N 122.00W
Keiyasi 63d Ab 17.53S 177.45 E
Kejla/Keila 7 Fg 59.19N 24.27 E
Kejla/Keila Jõgi 8 Ke 59.25N 24.15 E
Kejvy 7 Ic 67.30N 37.45 E
Kekaha 65a Bb 21.58N 159.43W
Kekerengu 62 Ee 42.00S 174.00 E
Kékes 10 Qi 47.52N 20.01 E
Keklau 64a Bb 7.35N 134.39 E
Kelafo 35 Gd 5.37N 44.13 E
Kelakam 34 Hc 13.35N 11.44 E
Kela Met 35 Fb 15.50N 38.23 E
Kelan 27 Jd 38.44N 111.34 E
Kelang 22 Mi 3.02N 101.27 E
Kelasa, Selat-=Gaspar Strait (EN) 26 Eg 2.40S 107.15 E
Kelberg 12 Id 50.18N 6.55 E
Kelcyra 15 Di 40.19N 20.11 E
Kelefesia 65b Bb 20.30S 174.44W
Kelekçi 15 Ml 37.14N 29.28 E
Kelem 35 Fe 4.49N 35.59 E
Keles 15 Mj 39.55N 29.14 E
Keles 18 Gd 41.02N 68.37 E
Kelheim 10 Hh 48.55N 11.52 E
Kelifely, Causse du- 37 Hc 17.15S 45.30 E
Kelifski Uzboj 18 Ef 37.45N 64.40 E
Keli Hāji Ibrāhīm 24 Kd 36.42N 45.00 E
Kelkheim 12 Kd 50.08N 8.27 E
Kelkit 23 Ea 36.32N 40.46 E
Kelkit 24 Hb 40.08N 39.27 E
Kellé 36 Bc 0.06S 14.33 E
Kellerberrin 59 Df 31.38S 117.43 E
Kellerwald 10 Fe 51.03N 9.10 E
Kellett, Cape- 42 Eb 72.57N 125.27W
Kellett Strait 42 Fa 75.50N 117.40W
Kellog 20 Dd 62.27N 86.35 E
Kellogg 43 Db 47.32N 116.07W
Kelloselkä 7 Gc 66.56N 29.00 E
Kells/Ceanannas Mór 9 Gh 53.44N 6.53W
Kelmé/Kelme 7 Fi 55.39N 22.58 E
Kelme/Kelmé 7 Fi 55.39N 22.58 E
Kelmency 15 Ja 48.27N 26.47 E
Kelmis/La Calamine 12 Hd 50.43N 6.00 E
Kélo 35 Bd 9.15N 15.48 E
Kelowna 39 He 49.53N 119.29W
Kelsey 42 He 56.00N 97.00W
Kelsey Bay 42 Ef 50.24N 125.57W
Kelso 46 Dc 46.09N 122.54W
Kelso Bank 59 Ld 24.10S 159.10 E
Kelso Bank (EN) 59 Ld 24.10S 159.30 E
Kel Tepe [Tur.] 24 Eb 41.05N 32.27 E
Kel Tepe [Tur.] 15 Ni 40.39N 30.06 E
Keltie, Mount- 66 Jf 79.15S 159.00 E
Keluang 26 Df 2.02N 103.19 E
Kelvin Seamount (EN) 43 Od 38.50N 64.00W
Kelyehēd 35 Hd 8.44N 49.10 E
Kem 19 Dc 64.57N 34.31 E
Kema 7 If 60.19N 37.15 E
Ke Macina 34 Dc 13.57N 5.23W
Kemah 24 Hc 39.36N 39.02 E
Kemaliye 24 Hc 39.16N 38.29 E
Kemalpaşa 24 Cc 40.00N 28.20 E
Kemalpaşa 15 Kk 38.25N 27.26 E
Kembé 35 Ce 4.36N 21.54 E
Kemer [Tur.] 15 Mm 36.28N 29.21 E
Kemer [Tur.] 24 Dd 36.36N 30.34 E
Kemer Baraji 15 Ll 37.30N 28.35 E
Kemeri/Ķemeri 8 Jh 56.56N 23.25 E
Ķemeri/Kemeri 8 Jh 56.56N 23.25 E
Kemerovo 22 Kd 55.20N 86.05 E
Kemerovskaja Oblast [3] 20 De 55.00N 87.00 E
Kemi 6 Ib 65.44N 24.34 E
Kemijärvi 7 Gc 66.40N 27.25 E
Kemijärvi=Kenni, Lake- (EN) 7 Gc 66.36N 27.24 E
Kemijoki 5 Ib 65.47N 24.30 E
Kemiö 8 Jd 60.10N 22.40 E
Kemiö/Kimito 8 Jd 60.10N 22.40 E
Kemlja 7 Ki 54.43N 45.15 E
Kemmerer 46 Jf 41.48N 110.32W
Kémo-Gribingui [3] 35 Bd 6.00N 19.00 E
Kemp, Lake- 45 Gj 33.45N 99.13W
Kempaž 17 Jd 64.03N 61.02 E
Kempele 7 Fd 64.55N 25.30 E
Kempen 11 Lc 51.22N 6.25 E
Kempen/Campine 11 Lc 51.10N 5.20 E
Kempendjaj 20 Gd 62.02N 118.42 E
Kempenich 12 Jd 50.25N 7.08 E
Kemp Land 66 Ee 67.10S 58.00 E
Kemps Bay 49 Ia 24.02N 77.33W
Kempsey 59 Kf 31.05S 152.50 E
Kempston 12 Bb 52.06N 0.29W
Kempt, Lac- 42 Kg 47.25N 74.15W
Kempten 10 Gi 47.43N 10.19 E
Ken 25 Hc 25.46N 80.31 E
Ken, Loch- 9 If 55.02N 4.02W
Kena 7 Je 62.06N 39.05 E
Kenadsa 32 Gc 31.34N 2.26W
Kenai 39 Dc 60.33N 151.15W
Kenai Mountains 40 Ie 60.00N 150.00W
Kenai Peninsula 38 Ed 60.10N 150.00W
Kendal 9 Kg 54.20N 2.45W
Kendall 44 Gm 25.41N 80.19W
Kendall, Cape- 42 Id 63.36N 87.13W
Kendallville 44 Ee 41.27N 85.16W
Kendari 22 Oj 3.57S 122.35 E
Kendawangan 26 Fg 2.32S 110.12 E
Kenema 31 Fh 7.52N 11.12W
Kenge 31 Ii 4.52S 16.59 E
Kengere 36 Ee 11.10S 25.28 E
Keng Tung 25 Jd 21.17N 99.36 E
Kenhardt 37 Ce 29.19S 21.12 E
Kéniéba 34 Cc 12.50N 11.14W
Keningau 26 Ge 5.20N 116.10 E
Kenitra 31 Ge 34.16N 6.36W
Kenitra [3] 32 Fc 34.00N 6.00W
Kenli (Xishuanghe) 28 Ef 37.35N 118.30 E
Kenmare 43 Gb 48.40N 102.05W
Kenmare/Neidin 9 Dj 51.53N 9.35W
Kenmare River/An Ribhéar 9 Dj 51.50N 9.50W
Kennebunk 44 Ld 43.23N 70.33W
Kennedy Peak 25 Id 23.19N 93.46 E
Kennedy Range 59 Cd 24.30S 115.00 E
Kenner 45 Ki 29.59N 90.15W
Kennet 9 Mj 51.28N 0.57W
Kennett 45 Kh 36.14N 90.03W
Kennewick 46 Fc 46.12N 119.07W
Kenni, Lake- (EN)=Kemijärvi 7 Gc 66.36N 27.24 E
Kennington 12 Cc 51.09N 0.53 E
Kenn Reef 57 Gg 21.10S 155.50 E
Kénogami 44 La 48.26N 71.14W
Kénogami, Lac- 44 La 48.21N 71.28W
Kenogami River 42 Jf 51.06N 84.29W
Keno Hill 42 Dd 63.54N 135.18W
Kenora 39 Je 49.47N 94.29W
Kenosha 43 Jc 42.35N 87.49W
Kent 9 Nj 51.10N 0.55 E
Kent [3] 9 Nj 51.20N 0.55 E
Kent [S.L.] 34 Cd 8.10N 13.10W
Kent [Wa.-U.S.] 46 Dc 47.23N 122.14W
Kent, Vale of- 9 Nj 51.10N 0.30 E
Kentau 19 Gg 43.32N 68.33 E
Kent Group 59 Jg 39.30S 147.20 E
Kenton 44 Fe 40.38N 83.38W
Kent Peninsula 42 Gc 68.30N 107.00W
Kentucky [2] 43 Jd 37.30N 85.15W
Kentucky Lake 43 Jd 36.25N 88.05W
Kentucky River 44 Ef 38.41N 85.11W
Kenya [1] 31 Kh 1.00N 38.00 E
Kenya, Mount-/Kirinyaga 30 Ki 0.10S 37.20 E
Keokea 65a Ec 20.42N 156.21W
Keokuk 43 Ic 40.24N 91.24W
Keonjhargarh 25 Hd 21.38N 85.35 E
Keowee, Lake- 44 Fh 34.55N 82.50W
Kepe 7 Hd 65.09N 32.08 E
Kepi 26 Kh 6.32S 139.19 E
Kępno 10 Ne 51.17N 17.59 E
Kepsut 24 Cc 39.41N 28.09 E
Kerala [3] 25 Ff 11.00N 76.30 E
Kerama-Rettō 29b Ab 26.10N 127.15 E
Kerang 59 Ig 35.44S 143.55 E
Keratéa 15 Gl 37.48N 23.59 E
Kerava/Kervo 8 Kd 60.24N 25.07 E
Kerč 6 Jf 45.22N 36.27 E
Kerčenski Poluostrov 16 Ig 45.15N 36.00 E
Kerčenski Proliv 5 Jf 45.22N 36.38 E
Kerdhilion Óros 15 Gi 40.47N 23.39 E
Kerema 60 Di 7.58S 145.46 E
Keren 35 Fb 15.47N 38.27 E
Keret, Ozero- 7 Hd 65.50N 32.50 E
Kerewan 34 Bc 13.29N 16.06W
Kerguélen 30 Nm 49.20S 69.30 E
Kerguélen, Iles- 30 Nm 49.15S 69.10 E
Kerguelen Plateau (EN) 3 Go 55.00S 75.00 E
Kericho 36 Gc 0.22S 35.17 E
Keri Kera 35 Ec 12.21N 32.46 E
Kerimäki 8 Mc 61.55N 29.17 E
Kerinci, Gunung- 21 Mj 1.42S 101.16 E
Kerio 30 Kh 2.59N 36.07 E
Kerion 15 Dl 37.40N 20.49 E
Keriya/Yutian 22 Kf 36.52N 81.42 E
Keriya He 27 Dd 38.30N 82.10 E
Keriya Shankou 27 Dd 35.12N 81.44 E
Kerka 10 Mj 46.28N 16.36 E
Kerken 12 Ic 51.27N 6.26 E
Kerkennah Islands (EN)=Qarqannah, Juzur- 30 Ie 34.44N 11.12 E
Kerketevs Óros 15 Jl 37.44N 26.38 E
Kerki 19 Gh 37.50N 65.13 E
Kerkini Óros 15 Fh 41.21N 22.50 E
Kérkira 15 Cj 39.36N 19.55 E
Kérkira=Corfu (EN) 5 Hh 39.40N 19.45 E
Kerkiras, Stenón-=Corfu, Strait of- (EN) 15 Dj 39.35N 20.05 E
Kerkrade 12 Id 50.52N 6.04 E
Kerma (EN)=Karmah 35 Eb 19.38N 30.25 E
Kermadec Islands 57 Jh 30.00S 178.30W
Kermadec Ridge (EN) 57 Jh 30.30S 178.30W
Kermadec Trench (EN) 3 Km 30.00S 177.00W
Kermajarvi 8 Mb 62.30N 28.40 E
Kermān [3] 23 Ic 30.50N 57.50 E
Kermān 22 Hf 30.17N 57.05 E
Kermānshāh→Bakhtarān 22 Gf 34.19N 47.04 E
Kermānshāhān 24 Pg 31.17N 54.55 E
Kerme 15 Kl 37.02N 28.00 E
Kerme Körfezi 24 Bd 36.50N 28.00 E
Kermit 45 Ek 31.51N 103.06W
Kern River 46 Fi 35.13N 119.17W
Kérouané 34 Dd 9.16N 9.01W
Kerpen 12 Id 50.52N 6.41 E
Kerrobert 42 Gf 51.55N 109.08W
Kerrville 43 He 30.03N 99.08W
Kerry/Ciarraí [2] 9 Di 52.10N 9.30W
Kerry, Mountains of- 9 Dj 51.55N 9.50W
Kertamulya 26 Eg 0.23N 109.09 E
Kerteh 26 Df 4.31N 103.27 E
Kerteminde 8 Di 55.27N 10.40 E
Kerulen (Cherlen) 21 Ne 48.48N 117.00 E
Kervo/Kerava 8 Kd 60.24N 25.07 E
Kerzaz 32 Gd 29.27N 1.25W
Keržence 7 Kh 56.04N 45.01 E
Kesagami Lake 42 Jf 50.23N 80.10W
Kesälahti 8 Mc 61.54N 29.50 E
Keşan 23 Ca 40.51N 26.37 E
Keşap 24 Hb 40.55N 38.31 E
Kesen'numa 28 Pe 38.54N 141.35 E
Kesen'numa-Wan 29 Gb 38.50N 141.35 E
Keshan 27 Mb 48.04N 125.51 E
Keskastel 12 Jf 48.58N 7.02 E
Keskin 24 Ec 39.41N 33.37 E
Keski-Suomi [2] 7 Fe 62.30N 25.30 E
Kestenga 7 Hd 65.53N 31.45 E
Keswick 9 Jg 54.37N 3.08W
Keszthely 10 Nj 46.46N 17.15 E
Ket 21 Kd 58.55N 81.32 E
Kéta 34 Fd 5.55N 0.59 E
Keta, Ozero- 20 Dc 68.45N 90.00 E
Ketanda 20 Jd 60.38N 141.30 E
Ketapang 22 Mj 1.52S 109.59 E
Ketchikan 39 Fd 55.21N 131.35W
Ketchum 43 Ec 43.41N 114.22W
Ketchum Mountain 45 Fk 31.15N 101.00W
Kete Krachi 34 Ed 7.46N 0.03W
Ketelmeer 12 Hb 52.35N 5.45 E
Ketlī, Jbel- 13 Gi 35.22N 5.17W
Ketmen, Hrebet- 18 Lc 43.20N 80.00 E
Kétou 34 Fd 7.22N 2.36 E
Kętrzyn 10 Rb 54.06N 21.23 E
Kettering [Eng.-U.K.] 9 Mi 52.24N 0.44W
Kettering [Oh.-U.S.] 44 Ef 39.41N 84.10W
Kettle River 46 Fb 48.42N 118.07W
Kettle River Range 46 Fb 48.30N 118.40W
Keuka Lake 44 Id 42.27N 77.10W
Keur Massène 32 Df 16.33N 16.14W
Keuruu 7 Fe 62.16N 24.42 E
Keuruunselkä 8 Kb 62.10N 24.40 E
Kevelaer 12 Ic 51.35N 6.15 E
Kew 21 Ae 21.54N 72.02W
Kewanee 43 Jc 41.14N 89.56W
Keweenaw Bay 44 Cb 46.56N 88.23W
Keweenaw Peninsula 43 Jb 47.12N 88.25W
Key, Lough-/Loch Cé 9 Eg 54.00N 8.15W
Keya Paha River 45 Ge 42.54N 99.00W
Keyhole Reservoir 46 Md 44.21N 104.51W
Key Largo 44 Gm 25.04N 80.28W
Keypel Bank (EN) 59 Le 25.15S 159.30 E
Keystone Lake 45 Hh 36.15N 96.25W
Key West 39 Kg 24.33N 81.48W
Kez 7 Mh 57.56N 53.43 E
Kezi 37 Dd 20.55S 28.29 E
Kežma 20 Fe 59.02N 101.09 E
Kežmarok 10 Qg 49.08N 20.25 E
Kgalagadi [3] 37 Ce 25.00S 22.00 E
Kgatleng [3] 37 Dd 24.28S 26.05 E
Kghoti 37 Cd 24.55S 21.59 E
Khabr, Kūh-e- 23 Id 28.50N 56.26 E
Khābūr, Nahr al- 24 Ie 35.08N 40.26 E
Khadari, Wādī al- 35 Dc 10.29N 27.00 E
Khādim, Shūshat al- 24 Bh 28.35N 27.43 E
Khadki (Kirkee) 25 Ee 18.34N 73.52 E
Khadra 13 Mh 36.15N 0.35 E
Khafs Banbān 24 Lj 25.31N 46.27 E
Khairónia 15 Fk 38.30N 22.51 E
Khairpur 25 Dc 27.32N 68.46 E
Khāiz, Kūh-e- 24 Ng 30.27N 50.55 E
Khakhea 37 Cd 24.42S 23.30 E
Khalatse 25 Fb 34.20N 76.49 E
Khalīj-e Fārs=Persian Gulf (EN) 21 Hg 27.00N 51.00 E
Khálki 15 Km 36.13N 27.37 E
Khálki 15 Km 36.14N 27.36 E
Khalkidhiki=Chalcidice (EN) 5 Ig 40.25N 23.25 E
Khalkis 15 Gk 38.28N 23.36 E
Khaluf 23 Ie 20.29N 57.59 E
Khambhāt 25 Ed 22.18N 72.37 E
Khambhāt, Gulf of- 21 Jg 21.00N 72.30 E
Khāmgaon 25 Fd 20.41N 76.34 E
Khamili 15 Jn 35.52N 26.14 E
Khamir 23 Ff 15.59N 43.57 E
Khāmis, Ash Shallāl al-=Fifth Cataract (EN) 30 Kg 18.23N 33.47 E
Khamīs Mushayţ 23 Ff 18.18N 42.44 E
Khammam 25 Ge 17.15N 80.09 E
Khamseh 24 Md 36.40N 48.50 E
Khan 37 Ad 22.42S 14.54 E
Khān 24 Qj 24.13N 56.20 E
Khānābād 23 Kb 36.41N 69.07 E
Khān al Baghdādī 24 Jf 33.51N 42.33 E
Khān al Hammād 24 Kf 32.19N 44.17 E
Khānaqīn 23 Gc 34.21N 45.22 E
Khān az Zabīb 24 Gg 31.28N 36.06 E
Khandwa 25 Fd 21.50N 76.20 E
Khāneh Sorkh, Gardaneh-ye- 24 Qh 29.49N 56.06 E
Khānewāl 25 Eb 30.18N 71.56 E
Khangai Mountains (EN)=Changajn Nuruu→Hangaj, Hrebet- 21 Le 47.30N 100.00 E
Khangai Mountains (EN)=Hangaj, Hrebet- (Changajn Nuruu) 21 Le 47.30N 100.00 E
Khánia 6 Ih 35.31N 24.02 E
Khanion, Kólpos- 15 Gn 35.35N 23.50 E
Khanka, Lake- (EN)=Hanka, Ozero- 21 Pe 45.00N 132.24 E
Khanka Lake (EN)=Xingkai Hu 21 Pe 45.00N 132.24 E
Khānpur 25 Ec 28.39N 70.39 E
Khān Shaykhūn 24 Ge 35.26N 36.38 E
Khān Takhtī 24 Kc 38.09N 44.55 E
Khān Yūnus 24 Fg 31.21N 34.19 E
Khānzīr, Rās- 35 Hc 10.50N 45.50 E

Index Symbols

[1] Independent Nation
[2] State, Region
[3] District, County
[4] Municipality
[5] Colony, Dependency
Continent
Physical Region
Historical or Cultural Region
Mount, Mountain
Volcano
Hill
Mountains, Mountain Range
Hills, Escarpment
Plateau, Upland
Pass, Gap
Plain, Lowland
Delta
Salt Flat
Valley, Canyon
Crater, Cave
Karst Features
Depression
Polder
Desert, Dunes
Forest, Woods
Heath, Steppe
Oasis
Cape, Point
Coast, beach
Cliff
Peninsula
Isthmus
Sandbank
Island
Atoll
Rock, Reef
Islands, Archipelago
Rocks, Reefs
Coral Reef
Well, Spring
Geyser
River, Stream
Waterfall Rapids
River Mouth, Estuary
Lake
Salt Lake
Intermittent Lake
Reservoir
Swamp, Pond
Canal
Glacier
Ice Shelf, Pack Ice
Ocean
Sea
Gulf, Bay
Strait, Fjord
Lagoon
Bank
Seamount
Tablemount
Ridge
Shelf
Basin
Escarpment, Sea Scarp
Fracture
Trench, Abyss
National Park, Reserve
Point of Interest
Recreation Site
Cave, Cavern
Historic Site
Ruins
Wall, Walls
Church, Abbey
Temple
Scientific Station
Airport
Port
Lighthouse
Mine
Tunnel
Dam, Bridge

Khao Laem 25 Kf 14.19N 101.11 E
Khao Miang 25 Ke 17.42N 101.01 E
Khao Mokochu 25 Je 15.56N 99.06 E
Khao Saming 25 Kf 12.16N 102.26 E
Khar 24 Me 35.53N 48.55 E
Kharagpur 22 Kg 22.20N 87.20 E
Khárakas 15 In 35.01N 25.07 E
Khārān 24 Qh 28.55N 57.09 E
Kharānaq 24 Pf 32.20N 54.39 E
Kharānaq, Kūh-e- 24 Pf 32.10N 54.39 E
Kharga Oasis (EN)=
Khārijah, Waḥāt al- 30 Kf 25.20N 30.35 E
Khārijah, Wāḥāt al-=
Kharga Oasis (EN) 30 Kf 25.20N 30.35 E
Kharīt, Wādī al- 24 Ej 24.26N 33.03 E
Kharīṭah, Shiqqat al- 33 If 17.10N 47.50 E
Khārk 24 Nh 29.15N 50.20 E
Khārk, Jazīreh-ye- 23 Hd 29.15N 50.20 E
Khār Khū 24 Og 31.39N 53.46 E
Kharmān, Kūh-e- 23 Hd 29.13N 53.35 E
Kharshah, Qārat al- 24 Bg 30.35N 27.25 E
Khartoum (EN)=Al
Kharṭūm [3] 35 Eb 15.50N 33.00 E
Khartoum (EN)=Al
Kharṭūm 31 Kg 15.36N 32.32 E
Khartoum North (EN)=Al
Kharṭūm Baḥrī 31 Kg 15.38N 32.33 E
Khāsh 23 Jc 31.31N 62.52 E
Khāsh 23 Jc 31.11N 62.05 E
Khashm al Qirbah 35 Fc 14.58N 35.55 E
Khāsi Jaintia 21 Lg 25.35N 91.38 E
Khatikhon, Yam-=
Mediterranean Sea (EN) 5 Hh 35.00N 20.00 E
Khaṭṭ 33 Dd 28.40N 22.40 E
Khātūn, Kūh-e- 24 Og 30.25N 53.38 E
Khawr al Fakkān 24 Qk 25.21N 56.22 E
Khawr āl Juḥaysh 35 Ia 20.36N 50.59 E
Khawr al Mufattaḥ 24 Mh 28.40N 48.25 E
Khawr Umm Qasr 24 Lg 30.02N 47.56 E
Khay' 23 Ff 18.45N 41.24 E
Khaybar 23 Ed 25.42N 39.31 E
Khaybar, Ḥarrat- 24 Hj 25.30N 39.45 E
Khazzī, Qārat- 30 Jf 21.26N 24.30 E
Khemis 13 Qh 36.10N 4.04 E
Khemis Anjra 13 Gi 35.41N 5.32W
Khemis Beni Arouss 13 Gi 35.19N 5.38W
Khemis Miliana 32 Hb 36.16N 2.13 E
Khemissat 32 Fc 33.49N 6.04W
Khemisset [3] 32 Fc 33.49N 6.00W
Khemmarat 25 Ke 16.03N 105.11 E
Khenchela 32 Ib 35.26N 7.08 E
Khenifra 32 Fc 32.56N 5.40W
Khenifra [3] 32 Fc 33.00N 5.08W
Kherāmeh 24 Oh 29.32N 53.21 E
Khersan 24 Ng 31.33N 50.22 E
Khersónisos Akrotiri 15 Hn 35.35N 24.10 E
Kheyrābād [Iran] 24 Mg 31.49N 48.23 E
Kheyrābād [Iran] 24 Ph 29.26N 55.19 E
Khiónótripa 15 Hh 41.18N 24.05 E
Khios 15 Jk 38.22N 26.08 E
Khios=Chios (EN) 5 Ih 38.22N 26.00 E
Khirbat Isrīyah 24 Ge 35.21N 37.46 E
Khirr, Nahr al- 24 Kf 33.17N 44.21 E
Khlomón Óros 15 Fk 38.36N 23.00 E
Khlong Yai 25 Kf 11.46N 102.53 E
Khokhropār 25 Ec 25.42N 70.12 E
Khok Kloi 25 Jg 8.17N 98.19 E
Khok Samrong 25 Ke 15.03N 100.44 E
Kholm 23 Kb 36.42N 67.41 E
Khomām 24 Md 37.22N 49.40 E
Khomas Highland (EN)=
Khomas Hochland 30 Ik 22.40S 16.20 E
Khomas Hochland=Khomas
Highland (EN) 30 Ik 22.40S 16.20 E
Khomeyn 24 Nf 33.38N 50.04 E
Khomeynīshahr 23 Hc 32.42N 51.27 E
Khon Kaen 25 Ke 16.26N 102.50 E
Khonsār 24 Nf 33.21N 50.19 E
Khóra 15 El 37.03N 21.43 E
Khor Anghar 35 Gc 12.27N 43.18 E
Khorāsān 21 Hf 34.00N 56.00 E
Khorāsān [3] 23 Ic 35.00N 58.00 E
Khorāsānī, Godār-e 24 Qg 30.44N 57.03 E
Khóra Sfakíon 15 Hn 35.12N 24.09 E
Khormūj, Kūh-e- 23 Hd 28.43N 51.22 E
Khorof Harar 36 Hb 2.14N 40.44 E
Khorramābād 23 Gc 33.30N 48.20 E
Khorramshahr 23 Gc 30.25N 48.11 E
Khorsābād 24 Jd 36.38N 43.17 E
Khoshyeylāq 24 Pd 36.53N 55.15 E
Khosrowābād 24 Mg 30.00N 48.25 E
Khosrowshah 24 Ld 37.57N 46.03 E
Khouribga [3] 32 Fc 32.56N 6.36W
Khouribga 32 Fc 32.53N 6.54W
Khowst 23 Kc 33.22N 69.57 E
Khrisi 15 Io 34.52N 25.42 E
Khrisoúpolis 15 Hi 40.59N 24.42 E
Khristianá 15 Im 36.14N 25.13 E
Khu Dağı 24 Jc 38.35N 43.40 E
Khuff [Lib.] 33 Cd 28.17N 18.20 E
Khuff [Sau.Ar.] 23 Ed 25.20N 37.20 E
Khulna 22 Kg 22.48N 89.33 E
Khūrān 24 Pi 26.50N 55.40 E
Khurayş 23 Gd 25.05N 48.02 E
Khurayt 35 Dc 13.57N 26.02 E
Khurīyā Murīyā, Jazā'ir-=
Kuria Muria Islands (EN)
21 Hh 17.30N 56.00 E
Khurr, Wādī al- 24 Jg 30.52N 42.10 E
Khursaniyah 24 Mi 27.18N 49.16 E
Khūshābar 24 Md 37.59N 48.54 E
Khutse 37 Cd 23.20S 24.34 E
Khuwayy 35 Dc 13.05N 29.14 E
Khuzdār 25 Dc 27.48N 66.37 E
Khūzestān [3] 23 Gc 32.00N 48.30 E
Khūzestān 21 Gf 30.33N 50.00 E
Khvojeh Lāk, Kūh-e- 24 Le 35.43N 46.29 E
Khvor 24 Pf 33.47N 55.03 E
Khvorāsgān 24 Nf 32.39N 51.45 E
Khvormūj 24 Nh 28.39N 51.23 E
Khvoshkūh 24 Qi 27.37N 56.41 E
Khvoy 24 Kc 38.33N 44.58 E
Khyber Pass 25 Eb 34.05N 71.10 E
Kia 63a Db 7.32S 158.26 E
Kia 63d Bb 16.14S 179.05 E
Kiamba 26 He 5.59N 124.37 E
Kiambi 36 Ed 7.20S 28.01 E
Kiamichi River 45 Ij 33.57N 95.14W
Kiangarow, Mount- 59 Ke 26.49S 151.33 E
Kiangsi (EN)=Chiang-hsi
Sheng→Jangxi Sheng [2] 27 Kf 28.00N 116.00 E
Kiangsi (EN)=Jangxi Sheng
(Chiang-hsi Sheng) [2] 27 Kf 28.00N 116.00 E
Kiangsu (EN)=Chiang-su
Sheng→Jiangsu Sheng [2] 27 Ke 33.00N 120.00 E
Kiangsu (EN)=Jiangsu
Sheng (Chiang-su Sheng)
[2] 27 Ke 33.00N 120.00 E
Kiantajärvi 7 Gd 65.03N 29.07 E
Kiáton 15 Fk 38.01N 22.45 E
Kibali 36 Eb 3.37N 28.34 E
Kibangou 36 Bc 3.27S 12.21 E
Kibartaj/Kybartai 8 Jj 54.38N 22.44 E
Kibasira Swamp 36 Gd 8.20S 36.18 E
Kibau 36 Gd 8.35S 35.17 E
Kibaya 36 Gd 5.18S 36.34 E
Kibbish 35 Fe 4.40N 35.53 E
Kiberg 7 Ha 70.17N 31.00 E
Kibikogen 29 Cd 34.45N 133.15 E
Kiboko 36 Gc 2.15S 37.42 E
Kibombo 36 Ec 3.54S 25.55 E
Kibondo 36 Fc 3.35S 30.42 E
Kibre Mengist 35 Fd 5.58N 39.00 E
Kıbrıs/Kypros=Cyprus (EN)
[1] 22 Ff 35.00N 33.00 E
Kıbrıs/Kypros=Cyprus (EN)
21 Ff 35.00N 33.00 E
Kibungo 36 Fc 2.10S 30.32 E
Kibuye 36 Ec 2.03S 29.21 E
Kibwezi 36 Gc 2.25S 37.58 E
Kičevo 15 Dh 41.31N 20.58 E
Kichi Kichi 35 Bb 17.36N 17.19 E
Kicking Horse Pass 42 Ff 51.50N 116.30W
Kidal 31 Hg 18.26N 1.24 E
Kidapawan 26 Ie 7.01N 125.03 E
Kidatu 36 Gd 7.42S 36.57 E
Kidira 34 Cc 14.28N 12.13W
Kidnappers, Cape- 62 Gc 39.38S 177.06 E
Kiekie 65a Ab 21.53N 160.13W
Kiel 6 He 54.20N 10.08 E
Kiel Canal (EN)=Nord-
Ostsee Kanal 5 Ge 53.53N 9.08 E
Kielce 6 Ie 50.52N 20.37 E
Kielce [2] 10 Qf 50.50N 20.35 E
Kieler Bucht 10 Gb 54.35N 10.35 E
Kienge 36 Ee 10.33S 27.33 E
Kierspe 12 Jc 51.08N 7.35 E
Kieta 58 Ge 6.15S 155.37 E
Kietrz 10 Of 50.05N 18.01 E
Kiev (EN)=Kijev 6 Je 50.26N 30.31 E
Kiev Reservoir (EN)=
Kijevskoje
Vodohranilišče 5 Je 51.00N 30.25 E
Kiffa 31 Fg 16.36N 11.23W
Kifisiá 15 Gk 38.04N 23.49 E
Kifisós 15 Gk 38.26N 23.15 E
Kifrī 24 Ke 34.42N 44.58 E
Kigač 16 Pf 46.28N 49.08 E
Kigali 31 Ki 1.57S 30.04 E
Kiğı 24 Ic 39.19N 40.21 E
Kigille 35 Ed 8.40N 34.02 E
Kigoma 31 Ji 4.52S 29.38 E
Kigoma [3] 36 Fc 4.50S 30.05 E
Kigosi 36 Fc 4.40S 31.27 E
Kihelkonna 8 If 58.20N 21.54 E
Kihniö 8 Jb 62.12N 23.11 E
Kihnu 7 Fg 58.10N 24.00 E
Kiholo 65a Fd 19.51N 155.55W
Kiholo Bay 65a Fd 19.52N 155.56W
Kihti/Skiftet 8 Id 60.15N 21.05 E
Kii-Hantō 27 Oe 34.00N 135.45 E
Kiikka 8 Jc 61.20N 22.46 E
Kiil 16 Se 49.27N 54.50 E
Kiiminki 7 Fd 65.08N 25.44 E
Kii-Sanchi 29 Dd 34.15N 135.50 E
Kii-Suido 28 Mh 34.00N 134.55 E
Kija 20 De 56.52N 86.40 E
Kijev=Kiev (EN) 6 Je 50.26N 30.31 E
Kijevka 19 He 50.16N 71.34 E
Kijevskaja Oblast [3] 19 De 50.20N 30.45 E
Kijevskoje Vodohranilišče=
Kiev Reservoir (EN) 5 Je 51.00N 30.25 E
Kijma 19 Ge 51.35N 67.34 E
Kikai-Jima 27 Mf 28.15N 130.00 E
Kikerino 8 Me 59.23N 29.38 E
Kikinda 15 Dd 45.50N 20.29 E
Kikládhes = Cyclades (EN)
5 Ih 37.00N 25.10 E
Kikonai 28 Pd 41.40N 140.26 E
Kikori 58 Fe 7.25S 144.13 E
Kikori River 57 Fe 7.23S 144.16 E
Kikuchi 29 Be 32.59N 130.49 E
Kikuma 29 Cd 34.03N 132.51 E
Kikvidze 16 Md 50.44N 43.03 E
Kikwit 31 Ii 5.02S 18.49 E
Kil [Nor.] 8 Cf 58.52N 9.19 E
Kil [Swe.] 7 Cg 59.30N 13.19 E
Kilafors 7 Df 61.15N 16.33 E
Kilambé, Cerro- 49 Eg 13.34N 85.42W
Kilauea 65a Ba 22.13N 159.25W
Kilauea Crater 65a Fd 19.24N 155.17W
Kilauea Point 65a Ba 22.14N 159.24W
Kilbrannan Sound 9 Hf 55.40N 5.25W
Kilbuck Mountains 40 Hd 60.30N 159.45W
Kilchu 27 Mc 40.58N 129.20 E
Kilcoy 59 Ke 26.57S 152.33 E
Kildare/Cill Dara [2] 9 Gh 53.15N 6.45W
Kildare/Cill Dara 9 Gh 53.10N 6.55W
Kildin, Ostrov- 7 Ib 69.20N 34.10 E
Kilembe 36 Cd 5.42S 19.55 E
Kilgore 45 Ij 32.23N 94.53W
Kilgoris 36 Fc 1.00S 34.53 E
Kiliao He 21 Oe 43.24N 123.42 E
Kiliç 15 Mi 40.40N 29.23 E
Kilifi 36 Gc 3.38S 39.51 E
Kili Island 57 Hd 5.39N 169.04 E
Kilija 19 Cf 45.27N 29.14 E
Kilijskoje girlo 15 Md 45.13N 29.43 E
Kilimanjaro [3] 36 Gc 4.00S 37.40 E
Kilimanjaro, Mount- 30 Ki 3.04S 37.22 E
Kilimli 24 Db 41.29N 31.50 E
Kilinailau Islands 60 Fh 4.45S 155.20 E
Kilindoni 31 Ki 7.55S 39.39 E
Kilingi-Nõmme/Kilingi-
Nymme 7 Fg 58.08N 24.59 E
Kilingi-Nymme/Kilingi-
Nõmme 7 Fg 58.08N 24.59 E
Kilis 23 Eb 36.44N 37.05 E
Kilitbahir 24 Bb 40.12N 26.20 E
Kilkee/Cill Chaoi 9 Di 52.41N 9.38W
Kilkenny/Cill Chainnigh 9 Fi 52.39N 7.15W
Kilkenny/Cill Chainnigh [2] 9 Fi 52.40N 7.20W
Kilkieran Bay 9 Dh 53.15N 9.45W
Kilkis 15 Fi 41.00N 22.52 E
Killala Bay/Cuan Chill
Ala 9 Dg 54.15N 9.10W
Killarney/Cill Airne 9 Di 52.03N 9.30W
Killary Harbour/An Caoláire
Rua 9 Dh 53.38N 9.55W
Killdeer 45 Ec 47.22N 102.45W
Killeen 43 He 31.08N 97.44W
Killinek Island 42 Ld 60.25N 64.40W
Killini 15 El 37.56N 21.09 E
Killini Óros 15 Fl 37.55N 22.26 E
Kilmallock/Cill Mocheallóg 9 Ei 52.25N 8.35W
Kilmarnock 9 If 55.37N 4.30W
Kilmez 7 Mh 56.58N 50.29 E
Kilmez 7 Mh 57.03N 51.24 E
Kilmore 59 Ig 37.18S 144.57 E
Kilombero 36 Gd 8.31S 37.22 E
Kilosa 31 Ki 6.50S 36.59 E
Kilpisjärvi 7 Eb 69.03N 20.48 E
Kilp-Javr 7 Hb 69.07N 32.28 E
Kilrush/Cill Rois 9 Di 52.39N 9.29W
Kilsbergen 8 Fe 59.20N 14.45 E
Kiltān Island 25 Ef 11.29N 73.00 E
Kilwa 36 Ed 9.17S 28.20 E
Kilwa Kisiwani 31 Ki 8.58S 39.30 E
Kilwa Kivinje 36 Gd 8.45S 39.24 E
Kilwa Masoko 36 Gd 8.56S 39.31 E
Kilyos → Kumköy 15 Mh 41.15N 29.02 E
Kim 45 Eh 37.15N 103.21W
Kimamba 36 Gd 6.47S 37.08 E
Kimba 59 Hf 33.09S 136.25 E
Kimball [Nb.-U.S.] 45 Ef 41.14N 103.40W
Kimball [S.D.-U.S.] 45 Ge 43.45N 98.57W
Kimball, Mount- 40 Kd 63.14N 144.39W
Kimbe 59 Ka 5.31S 150.12 E
Kimbe Bay 60 Ei 5.30S 150.30 E
Kimberley 57 Df 16.00S 126.00 E
Kimberley [B.C.-Can.] 42 Fg 49.41N 115.59W
Kimberley [S.Afr.] 31 Jk 28.43S 24.46 E
Kimberley Plateau 59 Fc 17.00S 127.00 E
Kimch'aek (Sŏngjin) 27 Mc 40.41N 129.12 E
Kimch'ŏn 27 Md 36.07N 128.07 E
Kimhandu 30 Ki 7.05S 37.35 E
Kimi 15 Hk 38.38N 24.06 E
Kimito 8 Jd 60.10N 22.40 E
Kimito/Kemiö 8 Jd 60.10N 22.40 E
Kimje 28 Ig 35.48N 126.53 E
Kimobetsu 29a Bb 42.47N 140.56 E
Kimolos 15 Hm 36.48N 24.34 E
Kimongo 36 Bc 4.29S 12.58 E
Kimovsk 19 De 54.01N 38.36 E
Kimpu-San 29 Fd 35.52N 138.37 E
Kimry 19 Dd 56.52N 37.24 E
Kimvula 36 Cd 5.44S 15.58 E
Kinabalu, Gunong- 21 Ni 6.05N 116.33 E
Kinabatangan 26 Ge 5.42N 118.23 E
Kinango 36 Gc 4.08S 39.19 E
Kinaros 15 Jm 36.59N 26.17 E
Kincardine 42 Jh 44.11N 81.38W
Kind 8 Eg 57.35N 13.25 E
Kinda 36 Ed 9.18S 25.04 E
Kinda 8 Ff 58.05N 15.40 E
Kindamba 36 Bc 3.44S 14.31 E
Kinder 45 Jk 30.29N 92.51W
Kinder Scout 9 Lh 53.23N 1.52W
Kindersley 42 Gf 51.27N 109.10W
Kindi 34 Ec 12.26N 2.01W
Kindia 31 Fg 10.04N 12.51W
Kindu 31 Ji 2.57S 25.56 E
Kinel 7 Mj 53.14N 50.40 E
Kinesi 36 Fc 1.28S 33.52 E
Kinešma 19 Ed 57.28N 42.16 E
King 63a Aa 4.24S 152.43 E
King, Cayos- 49 Fg 12.45N 83.20W
Kingaroy 59 Ke 26.33S 151.50 E
King Christian 42 Ha 77.45N 102.00W
King Christian IX Land (EN)
= Kong Christian IX
Land 67 Mc 68.00N 36.30W
King Christian X Land (EN)
= Kong Christian X
Land 67 Md 72.20N 32.30W
King City 43 Cd 36.13N 121.08W
King Edward River 59 Fb 14.14S 126.35 E
Kingfisher 45 Hi 35.52N 97.56W
King Frederik VI Coast (EN)
=Kong Frederik VI
Kyst 67 Nc 63.00N 43.30W
King Frederik VIII Land (EN)
= Kong Frederik VIII
Land 67 Md 78.30N 28.00W
King George Island 66 Re 62.00S 58.15W
King George Islands 42 Je 57.15N 78.30W
King George Sound 59 Dg 35.10S 118.10 E
Kingisepp 7 Gg 59.23N 28.37 E
Kingisepp/Kingissepp 19 Cd 58.17N 22.29 E
King Island 57 Fh 39.50S 144.00 E
Kingissepp/Kingisepp 19 Cd 58.17N 22.29 E
King Lear Peak 46 Ff 41.12N 118.34W
King Leopold
Ranges 59 Fc 17.30S 125.45 E
Kingman [Az.-U.S.] 43 Ed 35.12N 114.04W
Kingman [Ks.-U.S.] 45 Gh 37.39N 98.07W
Kingman Reef 57 Kd 6.19N 162.28W
Kingombe [Zaire] 36 Ec 2.35S 26.37 E
Kingombe [Zaire] 36 Ec 3.52S 26.35 E
Kingoome Inlet 46 Ba 50.49N 126.13W
Kingoonya 58 Eh 30.54S 135.18 E
King Peninsula 66 Of 73.12S 101.00W
Kingscliere 12 Ac 51.19N 1.15W
Kingscote 59 Hg 35.40S 137.38 E
King's Lynn 9 Ni 52.45N 0.24 E
King Sound 57 Df 17.00S 123.30 E
Kings Peak [Ca.-U.S.] 46 Cf 40.10N 124.08W
Kings Peak [U.S.] 38 He 40.46N 110.22W
Kingsport 43 Kd 36.32N 82.33W
Kings River 46 Fh 36.03N 119.49W
Kingston [Jam.] 39 Lh 18.00N 76.50W
Kingston [Nor.I.] 58 Hg 29.04S 167.58 E
Kingston [N.Y.-U.S.] 43 Mc 41.55N 74.00W
Kingston [N.Z.] 61 Ci 45.20S 168.43 E
Kingston [Ont.-Can.] 39 Le 44.14N 76.30W
Kingston Peak 46 Hi 35.42N 115.52W
Kingston South East 58 Eh 36.50S 139.51 E
Kingston-upon-Hull (Hull) 6 Fe 53.45N 0.20W
Kingston-upon-Thames,
London- 9 Mj 51.28N 0.19W
Kingstown 39 Mh 13.09N 61.14W
Kingsville 43 Hf 27.31N 97.52W
Kings Worthy 12 Ac 51.05N 1.18W
Kingussie 9 Id 57.05N 4.04W
King William 38 Jc 69.00N 97.30W
King William's Town 31 Jl 32.51S 27.22 E
Kiniama 36 Ee 11.26S 28.19 E
Kınık 24 Bc 39.05N 27.23 E
Kinkala 36 Bc 4.22S 14.46 E
Kinlochleven 9 Ie 56.43N 4.58W
Kinna 8 Eg 57.30N 12.41 E
Kinnairds Head 9 Ld 57.42N 2.00W
Kinnared 8 Eg 57.02N 13.06 E
Kinnekulle 8 Ef 58.35N 13.23 E
Kinneret, Yam- 24 Ff 32.48N 35.35 E
Kino-Kawa 29 Dd 34.13N 135.08 E
Kinomoto 29 Ed 35.31N 136.13 E
Kinoosao 42 He 57.06N 102.01W
Kinós Kefalai 15 Fj 39.25N 22.34 E
Kinross 9 Je 56.13N 3.27W
Kinsale/cionn tSáile 9 Ej 51.42N 8.32W
Kinsale, Old Head of-/An
Seancheann 9 Ej 51.36N 8.32W
Kinsangire 36 Gd 7.26S 38.35 E
Kinsarvik 7 Bf 60.23N 6.43 E
Kinshasa [2] 36 Cc 4.00S 16.00 E
Kinshasa (Leopoldville) 31 Ii 4.18S 15.18 E
Kinsley 45 Gh 37.55N 99.25W
Kinston 43 Ld 35.16N 77.35W
Kintampo 34 Ed 8.03N 1.43W
Kintap 26 Gg 3.51S 115.13 E
Kintyre 9 Hf 55.32N 5.35W
Kin-Wan 29b Ab 26.25N 127.54 E
Kinyan 34 Dc 11.51N 6.01W
Kinyeti 30 Kh 3.57N 32.54 E
Kinzig [Eur.] 10 Dh 48.37N 7.49 E
Kinzig [Ger.] 10 Ef 50.08N 8.54 E
Kioa 63d Bb 16.39S 179.55 E
Kipaka 36 Ec 4.09S 26.30 E
Kiparissia 15 El 37.15N 21.40 E
Kiparissia, Gulf of- (EN) =
Kiparissiakós Kólpos 15 El 37.30N 21.25 E
Kiparissiakós Kólpos =
Kiparissia, Gulf of- (EN) 15 El 37.30N 21.25 E
Kipawa, Lac- 42 Jg 46.55N 79.00W
Kipembawe 36 Fd 7.39S 33.24 E
Kipengere Range 30 Ki 9.10S 34.15 E
Kiperčeny 15 Lb 47.32N 28.40 E
Kipili 36 Fd 7.26S 30.36 E
Kipini 36 Hc 2.32S 40.31 E
Kipling 45 Ea 50.10N 102.38W
Kippure 9 Gh 53.11N 6.20W
Kiprarenukk, Mys-/Undva
Neem 8 If 58.25N 21.45 E
Kipros = Cyprus (EN) 23 Db 35.01N 33.00 E
Kipushi 36 Ee 11.46S 27.14 E
Kirakira 58 Hf 10.27S 161.56 E
Kiraz 24 Cc 39.21N 27.25 E
Kirazlı 24 Bb 40.01N 26.40 E
Kirbla 8 Jf 58.42N 23.49 E
Kircasalih 15 Jh 41.23N 26.48 E
Kirchberg (Hunsrück) 12 Je 49.57N 7.24 E
Kirchhain 12 Kd 50.49N 8.58 E
Kirchheimbolanden 12 Ke 49.40N 8.01 E
Kirchheim unter Teck 10 Fh 48.39N 9.27 E
Kirchhundem 12 Kc 51.06N 8.06 E
Kirchhundem-Rahrbach 12 Jc 51.02N 7.59 E
Kirchlengern 12 Kb 52.12N 8.38 E
Kirdimi 35 Bb 18.11N 18.38 E
Kireç 15 Lj 39.33N 28.22 E
Kirenga 21 Md 57.47N 107.59 E
Kirensk 22 Md 57.46N 108.08 E
Kirghiz SSR (EN)=
Kirgizskaja SSR [2] 19 Hg 41.30N 75.00 E
Kirghiz Steppe (EN) 5 Lf 49.30N 50.30 E
Kirgizskaja Sovetskaja
Socialističeskaja
Respublika [2] 19 Hg 41.30N 75.00 E
Kirgizskaja SSR/Kyrgyz
Sovetik Socialistik
Respublikasy [2] 19 Hg 41.30N 75.00 E
Kirgizskaja SSR=Kirghiz
SSR (EN) [2] 19 Hg 41.30N 75.00 E
Kirgizski Hrebet 19 Hg 42.30N 74.00 E
Kiri 36 Cc 1.27S 19.00 E
Kiribati [1] 58 Je 0.01S 174.00 E
Kirikhan 24 Gd 36.32N 36.19 E
Kırıkkale 23 Db 39.50N 33.31 E
Kirillov 7 Jg 59.54N 38.27 E
Kirillovskoje 8 Md 60.28N 29.28 E
Kirin (EN)=Chi-lin
Sheng→Jilin Sheng [2] 27 Mc 43.00N 126.00 E
Kirin (EN)=Jilin Sheng
(Chi-lin Sheng) [2] 27 Mc 43.00N 126.00 E
Kirinyaga/Kenya, Mount- 30 Ki 0.10S 37.20 E
Kirishima-Yama 29 Bf 31.56N 130.52 E
Kiriši 19 Dd 59.27N 32.02 E
Kiritimati Atoll (Christmas)
57 Ld 1.52N 157.20W
Kirja 7 Li 55.05N 46.52 E
Kirkağaç 24 Bc 39.06N 27.40 E
Kirkby Lonsdale 9 Kg 54.13N 2.36W
Kirkcaldy 9 Je 56.07N 3.10W
Kirkcudbright 9 Ig 54.50N 4.03W
Kirkee→Khadki 25 Ee 18.34N 73.52 E
Kirkenær 7 Cf 60.28N 12.03 E
Kirkenes 6 Jb 69.43N 30.03 E
Kirkjubæjarklaustur 7a Bc 63.47N 18.04W
Kirkkonummi/Kyrkslätt 8 Kd 60.07N 24.26 E
Kirkland 46 Dc 47.41N 122.12W
Kirkland Lake 39 Ke 48.09N 80.02W
Kirklareli 23 Ca 41.44N 27.12 E
Kirkpatrick, Mont- 66 Kg 84.20S 166.19 E
Kirkpınar Dağı 24 Fd 37.14N 34.15 E
Kirksville 43 Ic 40.12N 92.35W
Kirkūk 22 Gf 35.28N 44.23 E
Kirkwall 9 Kc 58.59N 2.58W
Kirkwood [Mo.-U.S.] 45 Kg 38.35N 90.24W
Kirkwood [S.Afr.] 37 Df 33.22S 25.15 E
Kırlangıç Burun 24 Dd 36.13N 30.25 E
Kirn 10 Dg 49.47N 7.27 E
Kirobasi 24 Ed 36.43N 33.52 E
Kirov [R.S.F.S.R.] 19 De 54.03N 34.21 E
Kirov [R.S.F.S.R.] 6 Kd 58.33N 49.42 E
Kirova, Zaliv- 16 Pj 39.05N 49.05 E
Kirovabad → Gjandža 6 Kg 40.40N 46.22 E
Kirovaken 19 Eg 40.48N 44.28 E
Kirovgrad 17 Jh 57.26N 60.04 E
Kirovo 18 Hd 40.28N 70.34 E
Kirovo-Čepeck 19 Fd 58.35N 50.03 E
Kirovograd 6 Jf 48.30N 32.18 E
Kirovogradskaja Oblast [3] 19 Df 48.20N 31.50 E
Kirovsk [R.S.F.S.R.] 19 Db 67.37N 33.37 E
Kirovsk [R.S.F.S.R.] 7 Hg 59.53N 31.01 E
Kirovsk [Tur.-U.S.S.R.] 18 Cf 37.43N 60.24 E
Kirovskaja Oblast [3] 19 Ed 58.30N 50.00 E
Kirovski [Kaz.-U.S.S.R.] 19 Hg 44.53N 78.12 E
Kirovski [R.S.F.S.R.] 20 Ig 45.05N 133.27 E
Kirovski [R.S.F.S.R.] 16 Pg 45.48N 48.08 E
Kirovski [R.S.F.S.R.] 20 Kf 54.25N 155.37 E
Kirovski [R.S.F.S.R.] 20 Hf 54.26N 127.00 E
Kirovskoje 18 Hc 42.39N 71.35 E
Kirpilski Liman 16 Kg 45.50N 38.05 E
Kirriemuir 9 Je 56.41N 3.01W
Kirs 19 Fd 59.21N 52.18 E
Kirsanov 16 Mc 52.41N 42.45 E
Kırşehir 23 Db 39.09N 34.10 E
Kirthar Range 21 Ig 27.00N 67.20 E
Kirton 12 Bb 52.55N 0.03W
Kiruna 6 Ib 67.51N 20.13 E
Kirundu 36 Ec 0.44S 25.32 E
Kiryū 29 Fc 36.25N 139.20 E
Kiržač 7 Jh 56.11N 38.53 E
Kisa 7 Dh 57.59N 15.37 E
Kisabi 36 Ed 8.03S 29.11 E
Kisač 15 Cd 45.21N 19.44 E
Kisakata 29 Fb 39.14N 139.54 E
Kisaki 36 Gd 7.28S 37.36 E
Kisalföld 10 Mi 47.30N 17.00 E
Kisangani 31 Jh 0.25N 25.12 E
Kisarazu 29 Fd 35.23N 139.55 E
Kisbér 10 Oi 47.30N 18.02 E
Kiselevsk 20 Df 54.03N 86.49 E
Kiserawe 36 Gd 6.54S 39.05 E
Kishangarh 25 Ec 26.34N 74.52 E
Kishb, Harrat al- 33 He 22.47N 41.30 E
Kishi 34 Fd 9.05N 3.51 E
Kishiwada 28 Mg 34.28N 135.22 E
Kisii 36 Fc 0.41S 34.46 E
Kisiju 36 Gd 7.24S 39.20 E
Kišinev 6 If 46.59N 28.52 E
Kısır Dağı 24 Jb 40.58N 43.04 E
Kiska 40a Bb 52.00N 177.30 E
Kiska Volcano 40a Bb 52.07N 177.36 E
Kisko 8 Jd 60.14N 23.29 E
Kiskörei Víztároló 10 Qi 47.44N 20.40 E
Kiskörös 10 Pj 46.37N 19.18 E
Kiskunfélegyháza 10 Pj 46.43N 19.51 E
Kiskunhalas 10 Pj 46.26N 19.30 E
Kiskunmajsa 10 Pj 46.29N 19.45 E
Kiskunság 10 Pj 46.35N 19.15 E
Kislovodsk 19 Eg 43.54N 42.42 E
Kismanyo 31 Li 0.22S 42.32 E
Kisofukushima 29 Ed 35.51N 137.41 E
Kiso-Gawa 28 Ng 35.05N 136.45 E
Kisoro 36 Ec 1.17S 29.41 E
Kiso-Sanmyaku 29 Ed 35.45N 137.45 E
Kisria, Daiet el- 13 Oi 35.44N 2.47 E
Kissámou, Kólpos- 15 Gn 35.35N 23.40 E
Kissidougou 34 Cd 9.11N 10.06W
Kissimmee 44 Gk 28.18N 81.24W
Kissimmee, Lake- 44 Gl 27.55N 81.16W
Kissū, Jabal- 35 Da 21.35N 25.09 E
Kistelek 10 Pj 46.28N 19.59 E
Kisterenye 10 Ph 48.01N 19.50 E

Index Symbols

[1] Independent Nation
[2] State, Region
[3] District, County
[4] Municipality
[5] Colony, Dependency
Continent
Physical Region
Historical or Cultural Region
Mount, Mountain
Volcano
Hill
Mountains, Mountain Range
Hills, Escarpment
Plateau, Upland
Pass, Gap
Plain, Lowland
Delta
Salt Flat
Valley, Canyon
Crater, Cave
Karst Features
Depression
Polder
Desert, Dunes
Forest, Woods
Heath, Steppe
Oasis
Cape, Point
Coast, Beach
Cliff
Peninsula
Isthmus
Sandbank
Island
Atoll
Rock, Reef
Islands, Archipelago
Rocks, Reefs
Coral Reef
Well, Spring
Geyser
River, Stream
Waterfall Rapids
River Mouth, Estuary
Lake
Salt Lake
Intermittent Lake
Reservoir
Swamp, Pond
Canal
Glacier
Ice Shelf, Pack Ice
Ocean
Sea
Gulf, Bay
Strait, Fjord
Lagoon
Bank
Seamount
Tablemount
Ridge
Shelf
Basin
Escarpment, Sea Scarp
Fracture
Trench, Abyss
National Park, Reserve
Point of Interest
Recreation Site
Cave, Cavern
Historic Site
Ruins
Wall, Walls
Church, Abbey
Temple
Scientific Station
Airport
Port
Lighthouse
Mine
Tunnel
Dam, Bridge

Kisújszállás 10 Qi 47.13N 20.46 E
Kisuki 29 Cd 35.17N 132.54 E
Kisumu 31 Ki 0.06S 34.45 E
Kisvárda 10 Sh 48.13N 22.05 E
Kita 31 Gg 13.03N 9.30W
Kitab 19 Gh 39.08N 66.54 E
Kita-Daitō-Jima 27 Nf 25.55N 131.20 E
Kitaibaraki 28 Pf 36.48N 140.45 E
Kita-Iō-Jima 60 Cb 25.26N 141.17 E
Kitaj, Ozero- 15 Md 45.35N 29.15 E
Kitakami 27 Pd 39.30N 141.10 E
Kitakami-Gawa 29 Gb 38.25N 141.19 E
Kitakami-Sanchi 29 Gb 39.30N 141.30 E
Kitakata 28 Of 37.39N 139.52 E
Kitakyushū 22 Pf 33.53N 130.50 E
Kitale 31 Kh 1.01N 35.00 E
Kitamaiaioi 29a Cb 43.33N 143.57 E
Kitami 27 Pc 43.48N 143.54 E
Kitami-Fuji 29a Cb 43.42N 143.14 E
Kitami-Sanchi 28 Qb 44.30N 142.30 E
Kitami Tōge 29a Cb 43.55N 142.55 E
Kitan-Kaikyō 29 Dd 34.15N 135.00 E
Kita-Taiheyō=Pacific Ocean (EN) 60 Ch 22.00N 167.00 E
Kita-Ura 29 Gc 36.00N 140.34 E
Kit Carson 45 Eg 38.46N 102.48W
Kitchener 42 Jh 43.27N 80.29W
Kitee 7 He 62.06N 30.09 E
Kitessa 35 Dd 5.22N 25.22 E
Kitgum 36 Fb 3.19N 32.53 E
Kíthira=Cythera (EN) 15 Fm 36.09N 23.00 E
Kíthira=Kythera (EN) 5 Ih 36.15N 23.00 E
Kithira Channel (EN)= Kithíron Dhiékplous 15 Fm 36.00N 23.00 E
Kithíron, Dhiékplous-= Kithira Channel (EN) 15 Fm 36.00N 23.00 E
Kíthnos 15 Hl 37.25N 24.26 E
Kíthnos 15 Hl 37.23N 24.25 E
Kíthnou, Stenón- 15 Hl 37.25N 24.30 E
Kitimat 39 Gd 54.05N 128.38W
Kitimat Ranges 42 Ef 53.58N 128.39W
Kitoushi-Yama 29a Cb 43.27N 143.25 E
Kitrianí 15 Hm 36.54N 24.44 E
Kitridge Point 51q Bb 13.09N 59.25W
Kítros 15 Fi 40.22N 22.35 E
Kitsuki 29 Be 33.25N 131.37 E
Kittanning 44 He 40.49N 79.31W
Kittery 44 Ld 43.05N 70.45W
Kittilä 7 Fc 67.40N 24.54 E
Kitui 31 Ki 1.22S 38.01 E
Kitunda 36 Fd 6.48S 33.13 E
Kitutu 36 Ec 3.17S 28.05 E
Kitwe-Nkana 31 Jj 12.49S 28.13 E
Kitzbühel 14 Gc 47.27N 12.23 E
Kitzbüheler Alpen 14 Gc 47.20N 12.20 E
Kitzingen 10 Gg 49.44N 10.10 E
Kiunga [Kenya] 36 Hc 1.45S 41.29 E
Kiunga [Pap.N.Gui.] 60 Ci 6.07S 141.18 E
Kiuruvesi 7 Ge 63.39N 26.37 E
Kivalina 40 Gc 67.59N 164.33W
Kivercy 16 Dd 50.50N 25.31 E
Kivijärvi [Fin.] 8 Ld 60.55N 27.40 E
Kivijärvi [Fin.] 7 Fe 63.10N 25.09 E
Kivik 7 Di 55.41N 14.15 E
Kiviõli/Kiviyli 7 Gg 59.23N 26.59 E
Kiviyli/Kiviõli 7 Gg 59.23N 26.59 E
Kivu 36 Ec 2.30S 27.30 E
Kivu, Lac-=Kivu, Lake- (EN) 30 Ii 2.00S 29.10 E
Kivu, Lake- (EN)=Kivu, Lac- 30 Ii 2.00S 29.10 E
Kiwai Island 60 Ci 8.30S 143.25 E
Kīyāmakī Dāgh 24 Kc 38.47N 45.51 E
Kiyiköy 24 Cb 41.25N 28.01 E
Kiyosato 29a Db 43.51N 144.35 E
Kizel 19 Fd 59.03N 57.40 E
Kizema 7 Kf 61.09N 44.46 E
Kizilcabölük 15 Ml 37.37N 29.01 E
Kızılca Dağı 24 Cd 36.55N 29.52 E
Kızılcahaman 24 Eb 40.28N 32.39 E
Kızıl Dağ 24 Ed 36.25N 32.42 E
Kizilhisar 15 Ml 37.33N 29.18 E
Kizilirmak 21 Fe 41.45N 35.59 E
Kızılırmak 24 Eb 40.22N 33.59 E
Kiziljurt 16 Oh 43.13N 46.55 E
Kizilskoje 17 Ij 52.44N 58.54 E
Kızıltepe 24 Id 37.12N 40.36 E
Kizimen, Vulkan- 20 Le 55.03N 160.27 E
Kižinga 20 Ff 51.51N 109.55 E
Kizir 20 Ef 54.10N 93.30 E
Kizljar 19 Eg 43.50N 46.42 E
Kizljarski Zaliv 16 Og 44.35N 46.55 E
Kizukuri 29a Bc 40.48N 140.22 E
Kizyl-Arvat 19 Fh 39.01N 56.20 E
Kizyl-Atrek 19 Fh 37.38N 54.47 E
Kizyl-Su 19 Fh 39.46N 53.01 E
Kjahta 20 Ff 50.26N 106.25 E
Kjalvaz 16 Pj 38.38N 48.20 E
Kjardla/Kärdla 7 Fg 59.01N 22.42 E
Kjarevere/Kärevere 8 Lf 58.23N 26.30 E
Kjarla/Kärla 8 Jf 58.16N 22.05 E
Kjellerup 8 Ch 56.17N 9.26 E
Kjøllefjord 7 Ga 70.56N 27.27 E
Kjölur 7a Bb 64.50N 19.25W
Kjøpsvik 7 Db 68.06N 16.21 E
Kjubjume 20 Jd 63.28N 140.30 E
Kjurdamir 19 Eg 40.20N 48.07 E
Kjusjur 20 Hb 70.35N 127.45 E
Kjustendil 15 Fg 42.17N 22.41 E
Kjustendil 15 Fg 42.17N 22.41 E
Kjyosumi-Yama 29 Gd 35.10N 140.09 E
Klabat, Gunung- 26 If 1.28N 125.02 E
Kladanj 23 Gf 44.14N 18.42 E
Kladno 10 Kf 50.09N 14.07 E
Kladovo 15 Fe 44.37N 22.37 E
Klagenfurt 6 Hf 46.38N 14.18 E
Klaipėda/Klajpeda 6 Id 55.43N 21.07 E
Klajpeda/Klaipėda 6 Id 55.43N 21.07 E
Klamath 46 Cf 41.32N 124.02W
Klamath Falls 39 Ge 42.13N 121.46W
Klamath Mountains 43 Cc 41.40N 123.20W
Klamath River 46 Cf 41.33N 124.04W
Klamono 26 Jg 1.08S 131.30 E
Klarälven 5 Hd 59.23N 13.32 E
Klaten 26 Fh 7.42S 110.35 E
Klatovy 10 Jg 49.24N 13.19 E
Klavreström 8 Fg 57.08N 15.08 E
Klawer 37 Bf 31.44S 18.36 E
Klazienaveen, Emmen- 12 Jb 52.44N 7.01 E
Kleck 16 Ec 53.03N 26.40 E
Kłecko 10 Nd 52.38N 17.26 E
Kleinblittersdorf 12 Je 49.09N 7.02 E
Kleine Nete 12 Gc 51.08N 4.34 E
Kleine Sluis, Anna Paulowna- 12 Gb 52.52N 4.52 E
Klein-Karoo=Little Karroo (EN) 37 Cf 33.42S 21.20 E
Kleinsee 37 Be 29.40S 17.05 E
Klekovača 14 Kf 44.26N 16.31 E
Kléla 34 Dc 11.40N 5.40W
Kleppe 8 Af 58.46N 5.40 E
Klerksdorp 37 De 26.58S 26.39 E
Kletnja 19 De 53.27N 33.17 E
Kletski 16 Me 49.19N 43.04 E
Kleve 10 Ce 51.47N 6.09 E
Klibreck, Ben- 9 Ic 58.19N 4.30W
Klička 20 Gf 50.24N 118.01 E
Klimoviči 19 De 53.37N 32.01 E
Klimovo 16 Hc 52.23N 32.16 E
Klin 19 Dd 56.20N 36.42 E
Klina 15 Dg 42.37N 20.35 E
Klincy 19 De 52.46N 32.17 E
Klingbach 12 Ke 49.11N 8.24 E
Klingenthal 10 If 50.22N 12.28 E
Klínovec 10 If 50.24N 12.58 E
Klintehamn 7 Eh 57.24N 18.12 E
Klippan 8 Eh 56.08N 13.06 E
Klipplaat 37 Cf 33.02S 24.21 E
Kliškovcy 15 Ja 48.23N 26.13 E
Klisura 15 Hg 42.42N 24.27 E
Klitmøller 8 Cg 57.02N 8.31 E
Kljazma 5 Kd 56.10N 42.58 E
Ključevskaja Sopka, Vulkan- 21 Sd 56.04N 160.38 E
Kljuci 20 Le 56.14N 160.58 E
Kłobuck 10 Of 50.55N 18.57 E
Kłodawa 10 Od 52.16N 18.55 E
Kłodzka, Kotlina- 10 Mf 50.30N 16.35 E
Kłodzko 10 Mf 50.28N 16.40 E
Kløfta 8 Dd 60.04N 11.09 E
Kloga/Klooga 8 Ke 59.24N 24.10 E
Kłomnice 10 Pf 50.56N 19.21 E
Klondike Plateau 42 Dd 63.10N 139.55W
Klondike River 42 Dd 64.03N 139.26W
Klooga/Kloga 8 Ke 59.24N 24.10 E
Kloosteezande, Hontenisse- 12 Gc 51.23N 4.00 E
Klosi 15 Dh 41.29N 20.06 E
Klosterneuburg 14 Kb 48.18N 16.19 E
Klosters/Claustra 14 Dd 46.52N 9.52 E
Kloten 14 Cc 47.27N 8.35 E
Klotz, Lac - 42 Kd 60.40N 73.00W
Kluane Lake 42 Dd 61.15N 138.40W
Kluczbork 10 Of 50.59N 18.13 E
Knaben 8 Bf 58.39N 7.04 E
Knäred 8 Eh 56.32N 13.19 E
Kneža 15 Hf 43.30N 24.05 E
Knife River 45 Fc 47.20N 101.23W
Knin 14 Kf 44.02N 16.12 E
Knislinge 8 Fh 56.11N 14.05 E
Knittelfeld 14 Ic 47.13N 14.49 E
Knivsta 8 Ge 59.43N 17.48 E
Knjaževac 15 Ff 43.34N 22.15 E
Knobly Mountain 44 Hf 39.15N 79.05W
Knockmealdown Mountains/ Cnoc Mhaoldonn 9 Fi 52.15N 8.00W
Knokke-Heist [Bel.] 12 Fc 51.21N 3.15 E
Knokke-Heist [Bel.] 11 Jc 51.21N 3.17 E
Knokke-Westkapelle 12 Fc 51.19N 3.18 E
Knolls grund 8 Gg 57.30N 17.30 E
Knøsen 8 Dg 57.12N 10.18 E
Knosós = Cnossus (EN) 15 In 35.18N 25.10 E
Knox, Cape - 42 Ef 54.11N 133.05W
Knox Coast 66 He 66.30S 105.00 E
Knoxville [Ia.-U.S.] 45 Jf 41.19N 93.06W
Knoxville [Tn.-U.S.] 39 Kf 35.58N 83.56W
Knud Rasmussen Land 67 Nd 80.00N 55.00W
Knüllgebirge 10 Ff 50.50N 9.30 E
Knutsholstind 8 Cc 61.26N 8.34 E
Knysna 31 Jl 34.02S 23.02 E
Ko, Kut 25 Kf 11.40N 102.35 E
Koartac 42 Kd 60.50N 69.30W
Koba 26 Eg 2.29S 106.24 E
Koba, Pulau- 26 Jh 6.25S 134.28 E
Kobar Sink 35 Gc 14.00N 40.30 E
Kobayashi 28 Ki 31.59N 130.59 E
Kobdo 22 Le 48.01N 91.38 E
Kobdo (Chovd) 27 Fb 48.06N 92.11 E
Kōbe 22 Pf 34.41N 135.10 E
Kobeljaki 16 Ie 49.08N 34.12 E
København 8 Ei 55.40N 12.10 E
København=Copenhagen (EN) 6 Hi 55.40N 12.35 E
Kobenni 32 Ff 15.55N 9.05W
Kobern-Gondorf 12 Jd 50.19N 7.28 E
Kobjaj 20 Hd 63.30N 126.26 E
Koblenz 10 Df 50.21N 7.36 E
Kobo 35 Fc 12.09N 39.39 E
Koboldo 20 If 52.58N 132.42 E
Kobra 7 Mg 59.19N 50.54 E
Kobrin 19 Ce 52.13N 24.23 E
Kobrinskoje 8 Ne 59.22N 30.14 E
Kobroor, Pulau- 26 Jh 6.12S 134.32 E
Kobuk 38 Cc 66.45N 161.00W
Kobuleti 16 Li 41.47N 41.45 E
Koca 24 Eb 41.41N 32.15 E
Kocabaş 24 Bb 40.22N 27.19 E
Koca Çay 15 Lj 38.43N 28.30 E
Koca Çay [Tur.] 24 Bb 40.08N 27.57 E
Koca Çay [Tur.] 24 Cd 36.17N 29.16 E
Koca Çay/Orhaneli 15 Lj 39.56N 28.32 E
Kočani 15 Fh 41.55N 22.25 E
Kocasu 15 Mj 39.42N 29.31 E
Kočečum 20 Fd 64.17N 100.10 E
Kočetovka 16 Lc 53.01N 40.31 E
Kočevje 14 Ie 45.39N 14.51 E
Kočevski rog 14 Ie 45.41N 15.00 E
Koch 42 Jc 69.35N 78.20W
Kŏch'ang 28 Ig 35.41N 127.55 E
Ko Chang 25 Kf 12.00N 102.23 E
Koch Bihār 25 Hc 26.19N 89.26 E
Kochi 27 Ne 33.33N 133.33 E
Kōchi Ken 28 Lh 33.20N 133.30 E
Kochisar Ovası 24 Ec 38.50N 33.30 E
Kock 10 Se 51.39N 22.27 E
Kočkorka 18 Jc 42.11N 75.45 E
Kočmar 15 Kf 43.41N 27.28 E
Kočubej 19 Eg 44.23N 46.31 E
Kočubejevskoje 16 Lg 44.41N 41.50 E
Kodiak 39 Dd 57.48N 152.23W
Kodiak 38 Dd 57.30N 153.30W
Kodino 7 Je 63.44N 39.40 E
Kodok 35 Ed 9.53N 32.07 E
Kodomari 29a Bc 41.08N 140.18 E
Kodori 16 Lh 42.49N 41.10 E
Kodry 15 Lb 47.15N 28.15 E
Kodyma 16 Ge 48.01N 30.48 E
Kodža Balkan 15 Jg 42.50N 27.00 E
Koekenaap 37 Bf 31.29S 18.19 E
Koes 37 Be 25.59S 19.08 E
Kofa Mountains 46 Ij 33.20N 114.00W
Koţarli 15 Kl 37.45N 27.42 E
Kofąz 24 Bb 41.58N 27.12 E
Koffiefontein 37 Ce 29.30S 25.00 E
Kofiau, Pulau- 26 Ig 1.11S 129.50 E
Köflach 14 Jc 47.04N 15.05 E
Koforidua 31 Gh 6.05N 0.15W
Kōfu [Jap.] 29 Cd 35.18N 133.29 E
Kōfu [Jap.] 27 Od 35.39N 138.35 E
Koga 29 Fc 36.12N 139.42 E
Kogaluc 42 Je 59.38N 77.30W
Kōge 29 Dd 35.24N 134.15 E
Køge 7 Ci 55.27N 12.11 E
Køge Bugt 8 Ei 55.30N 12.20 E
Kogel 17 He 62.38N 57.07 E
Kogilnik 15 Md 45.51N 29.38 E
Kogilnik (Kunduk) 15 Md 45.51N 29.38 E
Kogon 34 Cc 11.09N 14.42W
Kogota 29 Gb 38.32N 141.01 E
Kohala Mountains 65a Fc 20.05N 155.43W
Kohāt 25 Eb 33.35N 71.26 E
Kohila 8 Ke 59.11N 24.40 E
Kohima 25 Ic 25.40N 94.07 E
Koh-i Mārān 25 Dc 29.05N 66.50 E
Kohinggo 63a Cc 8.13S 157.10 E
Kohma 7 Jh 56.57N 41.07 E
Kohtla-Jarve/Kohtla-Järve 19 Cd 59.25N 27.14 E
Kohu Daği 15 Mm 36.30N 29.50 E
Kohunlich 48 Oh 18.30N 88.55W
Koide 29 Fc 37.14N 138.57 E
Koigi/Kojgi 8 Kf 58.49N 25.40 E
Koin 17 Ee 63.10N 51.15 E
Koindu 34 Cd 8.28N 10.20W
Koitere 7 He 62.58N 30.45 E
Kojā 23 Jd 25:34N 61.13 E
Kojandytau 18 Lb 44.20N 78.45 E
Kojda 7 Kc 66.23N 42.31 E
Koje-Do 28 Jg 34.52N 128.37 E
Kojetín 10 Ng 49.21N 17.20 E
Kojgi/Koigi 8 Kf 58.49N 25.40 E
Ko-Jima [Jap.] 29 Fe 33.07N 139.40 E
Ko-Jima [Jap.] 28 Od 41.22N 139.47 E
Kojŏ 27 Md 38.57N 127.52 E
Kojonup 59 Df 33.50S 117.09 E
Kojtaš 18 Fd 40.14N 67.22 E
Kojtezek, Pereval- 18 If 37.29N 72.45 E
Kojur 24 Nd 36.23N 51.43 E
Kojva 17 Ig 58.15N 58.14 E
Kokab 35 Cc 10.03N 22.04 E
Kokai-Gawa 29 Gd 35.52N 140.08 E
Kokand 22 Je 40.33N 70.57 E
Kökar 7 Eg 59.55N 20.55 E
Kökarsfjärden 8 Ie 59.55N 20.45 E
Kokas 26 Jg 2.42S 132.26 E
Kokava nad Rimavicou 10 Ph 48.34N 19.50 E
Kokawa 29 Dd 34.17N 135.26 E
Kokčetav 22 Id 53.17N 69.25 E
Kokčetavskaja Oblast 19 Ge 53.30N 70.00 E
Kokemäenjoki 8 Ic 61.33N 21.42 E
Kokemäki/Kumo 7 Ff 61.15N 22.21 E
Kok-Jangak 19 Hg 40.59N 73.15 E
Kokkina 24 Ee 35.10N 32.36 E
Kokkola/Gamlaklarleby 6 Ic 63.50N 23.07 E
Koko [Eth.] 35 Fc 10.20N 36.04 E
Koko [Nig.] 34 Fc 11.26N 4.30 E
Kokomo 43 Jc 40.29N 86.08W
Kokonau 26 Kg 4.43S 136.26 E
Kokong 37 Cd 24.27S 23.03 E
Koko Nor (EN)=Qinghai Hu 21 Mf 37.00N 100.20 E
Kokpekty 19 If 48.45N 82.24 E
Kokšaal-Tau, Hrebet- 19 Hg 41.00N 78.00 E
Kokšenga 7 Kf 61.27N 42.38 E
Koksijde 12 Ec 51.06N 2.39 E
Koksoak 42 Ke 58.31N 68.11W
Kokstad 31 Jl 30.32S 29.29 E
Koktal 18 Lb 44.05N 79.44 E
Koktokay/Fuyun 22 Ke 47.13N 89.39 E
Kokubu 28 Ki 31.44N 130.46 E
Kola 19 Db 68.53N 33.01 E
Kola, Pulau- 26 Jh 5.30S 134.35 E
Kolahun 34 Cd 8.17N 10.05W
Kolaka 26 Hg 4.03S 121.36 E
Kolamadulu Atoll 25a Bb 2.25N 73.10 E
Kola Peninsula (EN)=Kolski Poluostrov 5 Jb 67.30N 37.00 E
Kolār Gold Fields 25 Ff 12.55N 78.17 E
Kolari 7 Fc 67.20N 23.48 E
Kólarovo 10 Ni 47.55N 18.00 E
Kolašin 15 Cg 42.49N 19.32 E
Kolbäck 8 Ge 59.34N 16.15 E
Kolbäcksån 8 Ge 59.32N 16.16 E
Kolbio 36 Hc 1.09S 41.12 E
Kolbuszowa 10 Rf 50.15N 21.47 E
Kolby 8 Di 55.48N 10.33 E
Kolčugino 7 Jh 56.16N 39.23 E
Kolda 34 Cc 12.53N 14.57W
Kolding 6 Gd 55.31N 9.29 E
Kole [Zaire] 36 Dc 3.31S 22.27 E
Kole [Zaire] 36 Eb 2.07N 25.26 E
Koléa 13 Oh 36.38N 2.46 E
Kolendo 20 Jf 53.43N 142.57 E
Kolente 34 Cd 8.55N 13.08W
Kolesnoje 15 Mc 46.04N 29.45 E
Kolga 8 Ke 59.28N 25.29 E
Kolga, Zaliv-/Kolga Laht 8 Ke 59.30N 25.15 E
Kolga Laht/Kolga, Zaliv- 8 Ke 59.30N 25.15 E
Kolgompja, Mys- 8 Me 59.44N 28.35 E
Kolgujev, Ostrov- 5 Kb 69.05N 49.15 E
Kolhāpur 22 Jh 16.42N 74.13 E
Kolhozabad 18 Gf 37.35N 68.39 E
Kolhozbentskoje, Vodohranilišče- 18 Df 37.10N 62.30 E
Koli 7 Ge 63.06N 29.53 E
Kolimbiné 34 Cc 14.45N 11.00 E
Kolín 10 Lf 50.02N 15.13 E
Kolito 35 Fd 7.25N 38.07 E
Koljučinskaja Guba 20 Nc 66.50N 174.30W
Kolka 8 Jg 57.44N 22.27 E
Kolkasrags 7 Fh 57.46N 22.37 E
Kolki 16 Dd 51.07N 25.42 E
Kollinai 15 Fl 37.17N 22.22 E
Kollumúli 7a Cb 65.47N 14.21W
Kolmården 8 Gf 58.41N 16.35 E
Köln=Cologne (EN) 6 Ge 50.56N 6.57 E
Köln-Lövenich 12 Id 50.57N 6.50 E
Kolno 10 Rc 53.25N 21.56 E
Köln-Porz 10 Df 50.53N 7.03 E
Koło 10 Od 52.12N 18.38 E
Koloa 65a Bb 21.54N 159.28W
Kołobrzeg 10 Lb 54.12N 15.33 E
Kolodnja 16 Hb 54.49N 32.11 E
Kologriv 7 Kg 58.51N 44.17 E
Kolokani 34 Dc 13.34N 8.03W
Koloko 34 Dc 11.05N 5.19W
Kolokolkova Guba 17 Fb 68.30N 52.30 E
Kololo 35 Gd 7.27N 41.59 E
Kolombangara Island 60 Fi 8.00S 157.05 E
Kolomna 6 Jd 55.05N 38.49 E
Kolomyja 19 Cf 48.32N 25.01 E
Kolondiéba 34 Dc 11.06N 6.53W
Kolonga 65b Ac 21.08S 175.04W
Kolonodale 26 Hg 2.00S 121.19 E
Kolosovka 19 Hd 56.28N 73.36 E
Kolossa 34 Dc 13.52N 7.35W
Kolovai 65b Ac 21.06S 175.20W
Kolozero, Ozero- 7 Hb 68.15N 33.15 E
Kolp 7 Ig 59.20N 36.50 E
Kolpaševo 22 Kd 58.20N 82.50 E
Kolpino 7 Hg 59.45N 30.33 E
Kolpny 16 Jc 52.16N 37.00 E
Kolski Poluostrov=Kola Peninsula (EN) 5 Jb 67.30N 37.00 E
Koltubanovski 16 Rc 52.57N 52.02 E
Kolubara 15 De 44.40N 20.15 E
Koluszki 10 Pe 51.44N 19.49 E
Koluton 19 Ge 51.42N 69.25 E
Kolva [R.S.F.S.R.] 19 Fb 65.55N 57.20 E
Kolva [R.S.F.S.R.] 17 Hf 60.22N 56.33 E
Kolvickoje, Ozero- 7 Hc 67.05N 33.30 E
Kölvrå 8 Ch 56.18N 9.08 E
Kolwezi 31 Jj 10.43S 25.28 E
Kolyma 21 Sc 69.30N 161.00 E
Kolyma Plain (EN) = Kolymskaja Nizmennost 21 Rc 68.30N 154.00 E
Kolyma Range (EN)= Kolymskoje Nagorje 21 Rc 62.30N 155.00 E
Kolymskaja Nizmennost= Kolyma Plain (EN) 21 Rc 68.30N 154.00 E
Kolymskoje Nagorje= Kolyma Range (EN) 21 Rc 62.30N 155.00 E
Kolyšlej 16 Nc 52.40N 44.31 E
Kolžat 19 Ig 43.29N 80.37 E
Kom 15 Gf 43.10N 23.03 E
Kom 36 Gb 1.05N 38.02 E
Komádi 10 Rj 47.00N 21.30 E
Komadugu Gana 34 Hc 13.05N 12.24 E
Komadugu Yobe 30 Ig 13.42N 13.24 E
Komagane 29 Ed 35.43N 137.54 E
Koma-ga-Take [Jap.] 29 Fd 35.45N 138.13 E
Koma-ga-Take [Jap.] 29 Gb 39.47N 140.50 E
Koma-ga-Take [Jap.] 29a Bb 42.04N 140.40 E
Komandorski Islands (EN) =Komandorskije Ostrova 21 Sd 55.00N 167.00 E
Komandorskije Ostrova= Komandorski Islands (EN) 21 Sd 55.00N 167.00 E
Komandorskiye Basin (EN) 20 Le 57.00N 168.00 E
Komarin 16 Gd 51.27N 30.32 E
Komarno 10 Tg 49.34N 23.43 E
Komárno 10 Oi 47.46N 18.09 E
Komárom 10 Oi 47.40N 18.15 E
Komárom 10 Oi 47.44N 18.07 E
Komatipoort 37 Ee 25.25S 31.55 E
Komatsu 27 Od 36.24N 136.37 E
Komatsujima 29 Dd 34.01N 134.35 E
Komba, Pulau- 26 Hh 7.47S 123.35 E
Kombissiri 34 Ec 12.04N 1.20W
Kombolcha 35 Fc 11.05N 39.45 E
Komebail Lagoon 64a Ac 7.24N 134.27 E
Komen/Comines 12 Ed 50.46N 2.59 E
Komi ASSR 19 Fc 64.00N 55.00 E
Komi-Permjacki Nacionalny Okrug 19 Fd 60.00N 54.30 E
Komló 10 Oj 46.12N 18.16 E
Kommunarsk 16 Ke 48.27N 38.52 E
Kommunary 8 Nd 60.55N 30.10 E
Kommunizma, Pik-= Communism Peak (EN) 21 Jf 38.57N 72.08 E
Komodo, Pulau- 26 Gh 8.36S 119.30 E
Komoé 30 Gh 5.12N 3.44W
Komoé 34 Ec 10.25N 4.20W
Komono 36 Bc 3.15S 13.14 E
Komoran, Pulau- 26 Kh 8.18S 138.45 E
Komoro 29 Fc 36.19N 138.24 E
Komotiní 15 Ih 41.07N 25.24 E
Komovi 15 Cg 42.41N 19.39 E
Kompasberg 30 Jl 31.46S 24.32 E
Komrat 16 Ff 46.17N 28.38 E
Komsa 20 Dd 61.40N 89.25 E
Komsomoleć 17 Kj 53.45N 62.02 E
Komsomolec, Ostrov- 21 La 80.30N 95.00 E
Komsomolec, Zaliv- 16 Rg 45.30N 52.45 E
Komsomolsk [R.S.F.S.R.] 7 Jh 57.02N 40.22 E
Komsomolsk [R.S.F.S.R.] 20 De 57.25N 86.02 E
Komsomolsk [Tur.-U.S.S.R.] 19 Gh 39.02N 63.36 E
Komsomolski [Kaz.-U.S.S.R.] 19 Ff 47.20N 53.44 E
Komsomolski [R.S.F.S.R.] 16 Og 45.22N 46.01 E
Komsomolski [R.S.F.S.R.] 7 Ki 54.27N 45.45 E
Komsomolski [R.S.F.S.R.] 19 Gb 67.35N 63.47 E
Komsomolski [R.S.F.S.R.] 17 Kf 61.20N 63.15 E
Komsomolski [R.S.F.S.R.] 20 Mc 69.12N 172.55 E
Komsomolsk-na-Amure 22 Pd 50.36N 137.02 E
Komsomolsk-na-Ustjurte 19 Fg 44.07N 58.17 E
Komsomolskoje [Ukr.-U.S.S.R.] 16 Je 49.36N 36.33 E
Komsomolskoje [Ukr.-U.S.S.R.] 16 Kf 47.37N 38.05 E
Komsomolskoj Pravdy, Ostrova- 20 Fa 77.15N 107.30 E
Kŏmun-Do 28 Ig 34.02N 127.19 E
Kömür Burun 15 Jk 38.39N 26.25 E
Komusan 27 Mc 42.07N 129.42 E
Kona 34 Ec 14.57N 3.53W
Kona Coast 65a Fd 19.35N 155.56W
Konakovo 19 Dd 56.42N 36.46 E
Konar 23 Lc 34.25N 70.32 E
Konārak 25 Hh 19.54N 86.07 E
Konarha 23 Lb 35.15N 71.00 E
Konda 19 Gc 60.40N 69.46 E
Kondagaon 25 Ge 19.36N 81.40 E
Kondinin 59 Df 32.30S 118.16 E
Kondinskoje 17 Mg 59.40N 67.25 E
Kondoa 31 Ki 4.54S 35.47 E
Kondopoga 6 Jc 62.13N 34.17 E
Kondratjevo 8 Md 60.36N 28.02 E
Kondrovo 19 De 54.49N 35.55 E
Kondurča 7 Mj 53.31N 50.24 E
Koné 61 Bd 21.04S 164.52 E
Konečnaja 19 He 50.45N 78.27 E
Konevic, Ostrov- 8 Nd 60.50N 30.45 E
Kong 34 Ed 9.09N 4.37W
Kŏng 25 Lf 13.32N 105.58 E
Kŏng, Kaôh- 25 Kf 11.20N 103.00 E
Konga/Koonga 8 Jf 58.34N 24.00 E
Kongauru 64a Ac 7.04N 134.17 E
Kong Christian IX Land = King Christian IX Land (EN) 67 Mc 68.00N 36.30W
Kong Christian X Land = King Christian X Land (EN) 67 Md 72.20N 32.30W
Kongeå 8 Ci 55.23N 8.39 E
Kong Frederik VIII Land = King Frederik VIII Land (EN) 67 Md 78.30N 28.00W
Kong Frederik VI Kyst = King Frederik VI Coast (EN) 67 Nc 63.00N 43.30W
Konginkangas 8 Kb 62.46N 25.48 E
Kongju 28 If 36.27N 127.08 E
Kong Karls Land 41 Oc 78.50N 28.00 E
Kong Kong 35 Ed 7.26N 33.14 E
Kongolo 31 Ji 5.23S 27.00 E
Kongor 35 Ed 7.10N 31.21 E
Kong Oscars Fjord 67 Md 72.20N 23.00W
Kongoussi 34 Ec 13.19N 1.32W
Kongsberg 7 Bg 59.39N 9.39 E
Kongsøya 41 Oc 78.55N 28.40 E
Kongsvinger 7 Cf 60.12N 12.00 E
Kongur Shan 21 Jf 38.40N 75.21 E
Kongwa 36 Gd 6.12S 36.25 E
Kong Wilhelms Land 41 Jc 75.48N 23.15W
Koniecpol 10 Pf 50.48N 19.41 E
Königslutter am Elm 10 Gd 52.15N 10.49 E
Konigswinter 12 Jd 50.41N 7.11 E
Königs Wusterhausen 10 Jd 52.17N 13.37 E
Konin 10 Od 52.13N 18.16 E
Konin 10 Od 52.15N 18.15 E
Konispoli 15 Dj 39.39N 20.10 E
Kónitsa 15 Di 40.03N 20.45 E
Konj 14 Kg 43.43N 16.55 E
Konjed Jān 24 Nf 33.30N 50.27 E
Konjic 14 Lg 43.39N 17.58 E
Konjuh 14 Mf 44.18N 18.33 E
Konkan 25 Ee 18.05N 73.25 E
Konkiep 37 Be 28.00S 17.23 E
Konko 36 Ed 10.12S 27.27 E
Konkouré 34 Cd 9.58N 13.42W
Konnevesi 8 Lb 62.40N 26.35 E
Konnevesi 8 Lb 62.37N 26.19 E
Konnivesi 8 Lc 61.10N 26.10 E
Konoša 6 Kc 60.58N 40.15 E

Index Symbols

Independent Nation
State, Region
District, County
Municipality
Colony, Dependency
Continent
Physical Region
Historical or Cultural Region
Mount, Mountain
Volcano
Hill
Mountains, Mountain Range
Hills, Escarpment
Plateau, Upland
Pass, Gap
Plain, Lowland
Delta
Salt Flat
Valley, Canyon
Crater, Cave
Karst Features
Depression
Polder
Desert, Dunes
Forest, Woods
Heath, Steppe
Oasis
Cape, Point
Coast, Beach
Cliff
Peninsula
Isthmus
Sandbank
Island
Atoll
Rock, Reef
Islands, Archipelago
Rocks, Reefs
Coral Reef
Well, Spring
Geyser
River, Stream
Waterfall Rapids
River Mouth, Estuary
Lake
Salt Lake
Intermittent Lake
Reservoir
Swamp, Pond
Canal
Glacier
Ice Shelf, Pack Ice
Ocean
Sea
Gulf, Bay
Strait, Fjord
Lagoon
Bank
Seamount
Tablemount
Ridge
Shelf
Basin
Escarpment, Sea Scarp
Fracture
Trench, Abyss
National Park, Reserve
Point of Interest
Recreation Site
Cave, Cavern
Historic Site
Ruins
Wall, Walls
Church, Abbey
Temple
Scientific Station
Airport
Port
Lighthouse
Mine
Tunnel
Dam, Bridge

Kōnosu 29 Fc 36.04N 139.30 E
Konotop 6 Je 51.14N 33.12 E
Konqi He 21 Ke 41.48N 86.47 E
Konrei 64a Bb 7.43N 134.37 E
Konsei-Tōge 29 Fc 36.52N 139.22 E
Konsen-Daichi 29a Db 43.20N 144.50 E
Końskie 10 Qe 51.12N 20.26 E
Konstantinovka 16 Je 48.29N 37.43 E
Konstantinovsk 16 Lf 47.35N 41.05 E
Konstanz 10 Fi 47.40N 9.11 E
Kontagora 31 Hg 10.24N 5.29 E
Kontcha 34 Hd 7.58N 12.14 E
Kontich 12 Gc 51.08N 4.27 E
Kontiolahti 7 Ge 62.46N 29.51 E
Kontiomäki 7 Gd 64.21N 28.09 E
Kontum 25 Lf 14.21N 108.00 E
Kontum, Plateau de- 25 Lf 13.55N 108.05 E
Konusin, Mys- 7 Kc 67.10N 43.50 E
Konya 22 Ff 37.52N 32.31 E
Konya Ovası 24 Ed 37.30N 33.20 E
Konz 12 Ie 49.42N 6.35 E
Konza 36 Gc 1.45 S 37.07 E
Konžakovski Kamen, Gora- 5 Ld 59.38N 59.08 E
Koocanusa, Lake- 46 Hb 48.45N 115.15W
Kook, Punta- 65d Ab 27.08 S 109.26W
Koolau Range 65a Db 21.21N 157.47W
Koonga/Konga 8 Jf 58.34N 24.00 E
Koorda 59 Df 30.50 S 117.29 E
Koosa 8 Lf 58.33N 27.07 E
Kootenay Lake 46 Gb 49.35N 116.50W
Kootenay River 38 He 49.15N 117.39W
Kopa 18 Jc 43.31N 75.48 E
Kopaonik 15 Df 43.15N 20.50 E
Kópasker 7a Ca 66.18N 16.27W
Kópavogur 7a Bb 64.06N 21.55W
Kopejsk 19 Gd 55.08N 61.39 E
Koper 14 He 45.33N 13.44 E
Kopervik 7 Ag 59.17N 5.18 E
Kopetdag, Hrebet- 21 Hf 37.45N 58.15 E
Kop Geçidi 24 Ib 40.01N 40.28 E
Ko Phangan 25 Jg 9.45N 100.00 E
Köping 7 Dg 59.31N 16.00 E
Köpingsvik 8 Gh 56.53N 16.43 E
Kopjevo 20 Df 54.59N 89.55 E
Kopliku 15 Cg 42.13N 19.26 E
Köpmanholmen 7 Ee 63.10N 18.34 E
Koporje 8 Me 59.40N 29.08 E
Koporski Zaliv 8 Me 59.45N 28.45 E
Koppal 25 Fe 15.21N 76.09 E
Koppang 7 Cf 61.34N 11.04 E
Koppány 10 Oj 46.35N 18.26 E
Kopparberg 8 Fe 59.52N 14.59 E
Kopparberg [2] 7 Df 61.00N 14.30 E
Kopparstenarna 8 Hf 58.32N 19.20 E
Koppom 8 Ee 59.43N 12.09 E
Koprivnica 14 Kd 46.10N 16.50 E
Kopru 24 Dd 36.49N 31.10 E
Köprüören 15 Mj 39.30N 29.47 E
Korab 5 Ig 41.44N 20.32 E
Korablino 7 Jj 53.57N 40.00 E
Korahe 35 Gd 6.36N 44.16 E
Korak 64a Bc 7.21N 134.34 E
Koralpe 14 Id 46.45N 15.00 E
Koramlik 27 Ed 37.32N 85.42 E
Korana 14 Je 45.30N 15.35 E
Korangi 25 Dd 24.47N 67.08 E
Koraput 25 Ge 18.49N 82.43 E
Korba 25 Gd 22.21N 82.41 E
Korbach 10 Ee 51.17N 8.52 E
Körby 8 Ei 55.51N 13.39 E
Korça 15 Di 40.37N 20.46 E
Korčula 14 Kh 42.57N 16.55 E
Korčula 14 Lh 42.58N 17.08 E
Korčulanski Kanal 14 Kg 43.03N 16.40 E
Kordān 24 Ne 35.56N 50.50 E
Kordel 12 Ie 49.50N 6.38 E
Kordestān [3] 23 Gb 35.30N 47.00 E
Kord Kūy 23 Hb 36.48N 54.07 E
Kordun 14 Je 45.10N 15.35 E
Korea Bay (EN)=Sŏjosŏn-man 21 Of 39.15N 125.00 E
Korean Peninsula (EN) 21 Of 35.30N 125.30 E
Korea Strait (EN)=Taehan-Haehyŏp 21 Of 34.40N 129.00 E
Korea Strait (EN)=Tsushima-Kaikyō 21 Of 34.40N 129.00 E
Korec 16 Ed 50.37N 27.10 E
Korem 35 Fc 12.30N 39.32 E
Korenovsk 19 Df 45.28N 39.28 E
Korf 20 Ld 60.18N 166.01 E
Korfovski 20 Ig 48.11N 135.04 E
Korgen 7 Cc 66.05N 13.50 E
Kõrgesaare/Kyrgesare 8 Je 59.00N 22.25 E
Korhogo 31 Gh 9.27N 5.38W
Korhogo [3] 34 Dd 9.35N 5.55W
Koribundu 34 Cd 7.43N 11.42W
Korienzé 34 Eb 15.24N 3.47W
Korinthiakós Kólpos=Corinth, Gulf of- (EN) 5 Ih 38.12N 22.30 E
Kórinthos 15 Fl 37.55N 22.53 E
Kórinthos = Corinth (EN) 15 Fl 37.55N 22.53 E
Korínthou, Dhiórix- = Corinth Canal (EN) 15 Fl 37.57N 22.58 E
Koriolei 31 Lh 1.48N 44.30 E
Kőrishegy 10 Ni 47.12N 17.49 E
Koritnik 15 Dg 42.05N 20.34 E
Kōriyama 27 Pd 37.24N 140.23 E
Korjakskaja Sopka, Vulkan- 21 Rd 53.20N 158.47 E
Korjakski Nacionalny okrug [3] 20 Le 60.00N 163.00 E
Korjakskoje Nagorje=Koryak Range (EN) 21 Tc 62.30N 172.00 E
Korjažma 19 Ec 61.18N 47.07 E
Korjukovka 16 Hd 51.47N 32.17 E
Korkino 17 Ji 54.54N 61.25 E
Korkodon 20 Kd 64.43N 154.05 E
Korkuteli 24 Dd 37.04N 30.13 E
Korla 22 Ke 41.44N 86.09 E
Körmend 10 Mi 47.01N 16.36 E
Kormy, Gora- 20 Fd 62.15N 106.08 E
Kornati 14 Jg 43.49N 15.20 E
Kornejevka 17 Ni 54.01N 68.27 E
Kornešty 15 Kb 47.23N 28.00 E
Korneuburg 14 Kb 48.21N 16.20 E
Kórnik 10 Nd 52.17N 17.04 E
Kornsjø 7 Cg 58.57N 11.39 E
Koro 34 Ec 14.05N 3.04W
Koroba 59 Ia 5.40 S 142.45 E
Koroča 16 Jd 50.50N 37.13 E
Köroğlu Dağları 23 Da 40.40N 32.35 E
Köroğlu Tepe 24 Db 40.31N 31.53 E
Korogwe 36 Gd 5.09 S 38.29 E
Koro Island 57 If 17.32 S 179.42 E
Koroit 59 Ig 38.17 S 142.22 E
Korolevo 10 Th 48.08N 23.07 E
Korolevu 63d Ac 18.12 S 177.53 E
Korom, Bahr 35 Bc 10.35N 19.45 E
Koromiri 64p Cc 21.15 S 159.43W
Koronadal 26 He 6.12N 125.01 E
Korónia, Límni- 15 Gi 40.40N 23.10 E
Koronowo 10 Nc 53.19N 17.57 E
Koronowski e, Jezioro- 10 Nc 53.22N 17.55 E
Koror 57 Ed 7.20N 134.30 E
Koror 58 Ed 7.20N 134.29 E
Körös 10 Qj 46.43N 20.12 E
Koro Sea 61 Ec 18.00 S 180.00
Korosten 6 Ie 50.57N 28.39 E
Korostyšev 16 Fd 50.18N 29.05 E
Korotaiha 17 Jb 68.55N 60.55 E
Koro Toro 31 Ig 16.05N 18.30 E
Korovin Volcano 40a Db 52.22N 174.10W
Korpijärvi 8 Lc 61.15N 27.10 E
Korpilahti 7 Fe 62.01N 25.33 E
Korpo/Korppoo 8 Id 60.10N 21.35 E
Korppoo/Korpo 8 Id 60.10N 21.35 E
Korsakov 20 Jg 46.37N 142.51 E
Korshäs 7 Ee 62.47N 21.12 E
Korsholm/Mustasaari 8 Ia 63.05N 21.43 E
Korso 8 Kd 60.21N 25.06 E
Korsør 7 Ci 55.20N 11.09 E
Korsun-Ševčenkovski 16 Ge 49.26N 31.18 E
Korsze 10 Rb 54.10N 21.09 E
Kortemark 12 Fc 51.02N 3.02 E
Kortrijk/Courtrai 11 Jd 50.50N 3.16 E
Koruçam Burnu 24 Ee 35.24N 32.56 E
Korucu 15 Kj 39.28N 27.22 E
Koru Dağ 15 Ji 40.42N 26.45 E
Koryak Range (EN)=Korjakskoje Nagorje 21 Tc 62.30N 172.00 E
Korzybie 10 Mb 54.18N 16.50 E
Kos 15 Km 36.53N 27.18 E
Kos 15 Km 36.50N 27.10 E
Kosa 17 Gg 59.56N 55.01 E
Kosa 17 Gf 60.11N 55.10 E
Kosai 29 Ed 34.43N 137.30 E
Kosaja Gora 16 Jb 54.09N 37.31 E
Kosaka 29 Ga 40.20N 140.44 E
Kō-Saki 29 Ad 34.05N 129.13 E
Ko Samui 25 Jg 9.30N 99.58 E
Kosan-ŭp 27 Md 38.51N 127.25 E
Koscagyl 16 Rf 46.52N 53.47 E
Kościan 10 Md 52.06N 16.38 E
Kościerzyna 10 Nb 54.08N 18.00 E
Kosciusko 45 Lj 32.58N 89.35W
Kosciusko, Mount- 57 Fg 36.27 S 148.16 E
Kose/Koze 8 Ke 59.11N 25.05 E
Köse Dağ 24 Gb 40.06N 37.58 E
Kosha 35 Ea 20.49N 30.32 E
Koshigaya 29 Fd 35.55N 139.45 E
Koshiji 29 Fc 37.24N 138.45 E
Koshiki-Kaikyō 29 Bf 31.45N 130.05 E
Koshiki Rettō 27 Me 31.45N 129.45 E
Koshimizu 29a Db 43.51N 144.25 E
Kōshoku 28 Of 36.38N 138.06 E
Kōshyū Seamount (EN) 29 Df 31.35N 135.50 E
Košice 6 If 48.43N 21.15 E
Kosjerić 15 Cf 44.00N 19.55 E
Kosju 17 Ic 66.18N 59.53 E
Kosju 17 Id 65.38N 58.59 E
Köşk 15 Ll 37.51N 28.03 E
Koski 8 Jd 60.39N 23.09 E
Koskolovo 8 Me 59.34N 28.30 E
Koslan 19 Ec 63.29N 48.52 E
Kosma 17 Dd 65.43N 49.50 E
Kosmaj 15 De 44.28N 20.33 E
Kosŏng 27 Md 38.40N 128.19 E
Kosov 15 Ia 48.15N 25.08 E
Kosovo 15 Eg 42.40N 21.05 E
Kosovo [3] 15 Dg 42.35N 21.00 E
Kosovska Mitrovica 15 Dg 42.53N 20.52 E
Kosrae (Kusaie) 57 Hd 5.19N 162.59 E
Kossol Passage 64a Bb 7.52N 134.36 E
Kossol Reef 64a Bb 7.57N 134.41 E
Kossou, Barrage de- 34 Dd 7.01N 5.29W
Kossovo 16 Dc 52.47N 25.10 E
Kostajnica 14 Ke 45.13N 16.33 E
Kostenec 15 Gg 42.16N 23.49 E
Koster 37 De 25.57 S 26.42 E
Kosteröarna 8 Df 58.55N 11.05 E
Kostjukoviči 16 Hc 53.23N 32.06 E
Kostjukovka 16 Gc 52.32N 30.58 E
Kostolac 15 Ee 44.44N 21.12 E
Kostopol 16 Ed 50.53N 26.29 E
Kostriževka 15 Ia 48.31N 25.45 E
Kostroma 6 Kd 57.47N 40.59 E
Kostromskaja Oblast [3] 19 Ed 58.30N 44.00 E
Kostrzyń 10 Nd 52.25N 17.14 E
Kostrzyn 10 Kd 52.37N 14.39 E
Kosva 17 Hg 58.50N 56.45 E
Koszalin 10 Mb 54.12N 16.09 E
Koszalin [2] 10 Mb 54.10N 16.10 E
Kőszeg 10 Mi 47.23N 16.33 E
Kota 22 Jg 25.16N 75.55 E
Kotaagung 26 Dh 5.30 S 104.38 E
Kota Baharu 22 Mi 6.08N 102.15 E
Kotabaru 26 Gg 3.14 S 116.13 E
Kotabumi 22 Mj 4.50 S 104.54 E
Kotadabok 26 Dg 0.30 S 104.33 E
Kota Kinabalu 22 Ni 5.59N 116.04 E
Kotamobagu 26 Hf 0.46N 124.19 E
Ko Tao 25 Jf 10.05N 99.52 E
Kotari 14 Jf 44.05N 15.30 E
Ko Tarutau 25 Jg 6.35N 99.40 E
Kota Tinggi 26 Df 1.44N 103.54 E
Kotel 15 Jg 42.53N 26.27 E
Kotelnič 19 Ed 58.20N 48.20 E
Kotelnikovo 16 Mf 47.38N 43.09 E
Kotelny, Ostrov- 21 Pb 75.45N 138.44 E
Kotelva 16 Id 50.03N 34.45 E
Köthen 10 He 51.45N 11.58 E
Kotido 36 Fb 3.00N 34.09 E
Kotjužany 29 Gb 47.50N 28.27 E
Kotka 7 Gf 60.28N 26.55 E
Kot Kapūra 25 Eb 30.35N 74.54 E
Kotlas 6 Kc 61.16N 46.35 E
Kotlenik 15 Df 43.51N 20.42 E
Kotlenski prohod 15 Jg 42.53N 26.27 E
Kotlik 40 Gd 63.02N 163.33W
Kotlin, Ostrov- 8 Md 60.00N 29.45 E
Kotly 8 Me 59.30N 28.48 E
Kotobi 34 Ed 6.42N 4.08W
Kotohira 29 Cd 34.11N 133.48 E
Koton Karifi 34 Gd 8.06N 6.48 E
Kotor 15 Bg 42.25N 18.46 E
Kotorosl 7 Jh 57.38N 39.57 E
Kotorska, Boka- 15 Bg 42.25N 18.40 E
Kotor Varoš 14 Lf 44.37N 17.22 E
Kotouba 34 Ed 8.41N 3.12W
Kotovo 19 Ee 50.18N 44.48 E
Kotovsk [Mold.-U.S.S.R.] 16 Ff 46.49N 28.33 E
Kotovsk [R.S.F.S.R.] 19 Ee 52.35N 41.32 E
Kotovsk [Ukr.-U.S.S.R.] 19 Cf 47.43N 29.33 E
Kotra 10 Uc 53.32N 24.17 E
Kotri 25 Dc 25.22N 68.18 E
Kötschach 14 Gd 46.40N 13.00 E
Kottayam 25 Fg 9.35N 76.31 E
Kotto 30 Jh 4.14N 22.02 E
Kotton 35 Id 9.37N 50.32 E
Kotu 65b Ba 19.57 S 174.48W
Kotu Group 57 Jg 20.00 S 174.45W
Kotuj 21 Mb 71.55N 102.05 E
Kotujkan 20 Fb 70.40N 103.25 E
Koturdepe 16 Rj 39.26N 53.40 E
Kotzebue 39 Cc 66.53N 162.39W
Kotzebue Sound 38 Cc 66.20N 163.00W
Kouandé 34 Fc 10.20N 1.42 E
Kouango 35 Be 4.58N 19.59 E
Kouba Modounga 35 Bb 15.40N 18.15 E
Koudougou 31 Gg 11.44N 4.31W
Kouéré 34 Ec 10.27N 3.59W
Koufália 15 Fi 40.47N 22.35 E
Koufonísion [Grc.] 15 Jo 34.56N 26.10 E
Koufonísion [Grc.] 15 Im 36.55N 25.35 E
Koufonísiou, Stenón- 15 Jo 35.00N 26.10 E
Kouilou [3] 36 Bc 4.00 S 12.00 E
Kouilou 30 Ii 4.28 S 11.41 E
Koukdjuak 42 Kc 66.47N 73.10W
Kouki 35 Bd 7.10N 17.18 E
Koukourou 35 Cd 7.12N 20.02 E
Koulamoutou 36 Bc 1.08 S 12.29 E
Koulikoro 34 Dc 12.51N 7.34W
Koulountou 34 Cc 13.15N 13.37W
Koumac 58 Hg 20.30 S 164.12 E
Koumac, Grand Récif de- 63b Be 20.32 S 164.04 E
Koumbi-Saleh 32 Ff 15.47N 7.58W
Koumi 29 Fc 36.05N 138.28 E
Koumpentoum 34 Cc 13.59N 14.34W
Koumra 35 Bd 8.55N 17.33 E
Koundara 31 Fg 12.29N 13.18W
Koundian 34 Cc 13.08N 10.42W
Kounoúpoi 15 Jm 36.32N 26.27 E
Kounradski 19 Hf 46.57N 75.01 E
Kounta 34 Eb 17.30N 0.40W
Koupéla 34 Ec 12.11N 0.21W
Kouqian → Yongji 28 Ic 43.40N 126.30 E
Kourou 54 Hb 5.09N 52.39W
Kouroussa 34 Dc 10.39N 9.53W
Koury 34 Ec 12.10N 4.48W
Koussané 34 Cc 14.52N 11.15W
Kousséri 34 Ic 12.05N 15.02 E
Koussi, Emi- 30 Ig 19.55N 18.30 E
Koutiala 31 Gg 12.23N 5.27W
Koutoumo 63b Cf 22.40 S 167.32 E
Koutous 34 Hc 14.30N 10.00 E
Kouvola 7 Gf 60.52N 26.42 E
Kouyou 36 Cc 0.45 S 16.38 E
Kova 20 Fe 58.20N 100.20 E
Kovač 15 Cf 43.31N 19.07 E
Kovačica 15 Dd 45.06N 20.38 E
Koval 10 Pd 52.31N 19.10 E
Kovalevka 15 Nc 46.42N 30.31 E
Kovarskas/Kavarskas 8 Ki 55.24N 25.03 E
Kovdor 19 Db 67.33N 30.25 E
Kovdozero, Ozero- 7 Hc 66.47N 32.00 E
Kovel 19 Ce 51.13N 24.43 E
Kovenskaja 17 Mf 61.24N 67.39 E
Kovin 15 De 44.45N 20.59 E
Kovinskaja Grjada 20 Fe 57.15N 101.00 E
Kovrov 19 Ed 56.24N 41.20 E
Kovylkino 7 Ki 54.02N 43.58 E
Kowŏn 27 Md 39.26N 127.15 E
Kowtal-e Do Rāh 23 Lb 36.07N 71.15 E
Kowt-e 'Ashrow 23 Kc 34.27N 68.48 E
Kōyama 29 Bf 31.19N 130.57 E
Köyceğiz 24 Cd 36.55N 28.43 E
Köycegiz Gölü 15 Lm 36.55N 28.40 E
Koyoshi-Gawa 29 Gb 39.24N 140.01 E
Koyuk 40 Gd 64.56N 161.08W
Koyukuk 38 Dc 64.56N 157.30W
Kozaklı 24 Fc 39.13N 34.49 E
Kozan 24 Fd 37.27N 35.49 E
Kozáni 15 Ei 40.18N 21.47 E
Kozara 14 Ke 45.00N 16.55 E
Kozawa 29a Bb 42.58N 140.40 E
Koze/Kose 8 Ke 59.11N 25.05 E
Kozelsk 19 De 54.01N 35.46 E
Koževnikovo 20 De 56.18N 84.00 E
Kozhikode → Calicut 22 Jh 11.19N 75.46 E
Kozienice 10 Re 51.35N 21.33 E
Kožim 17 Id 65.43N 59.31 E
Kožim 17 Id 65.45N 59.15 E
Kozima 14 He 45.37N 13.56 E
Kozjak 15 Eh 41.06N 21.54 E
Kozloduj 15 Gf 43.47N 23.44 E
Kozlovka 7 Li 55.52N 48.13 E
Kozlovščina 10 Vc 53.14N 25.20 E
Kozlu 24 Db 41.25N 31.46 E
Kozluk 24 Ic 38.11N 41.29 E
Koźmin 10 Ne 51.50N 17.28 E
Kozmodemjansk 7 Lh 56.20N 46.36 E
Kožozero, Ozero- 7 Je 63.05N 38.05 E
Kożuchów 10 Le 51.45N 15.35 E
Kožuf 15 Fh 41.09N 22.10 E
Kōzu-Shima 27 Oe 34.15N 139.10 E
Kožva 17 Hd 65.07N 56.57 E
Kožva 17 Hd 65.10N 57.00 E
Kozyrevsk 20 Ke 55.59N 159.59 E
Kpalimé 34 Fd 6.54N 0.38 E
Kpandu 34 Fd 7.00N 0.18 E
Kpessi 34 Fd 8.04N 1.16 E
Kra, Isthmus of- (EN)=Kra, Khokhok- 21 Lh 10.20N 99.00 E
Kra, Khokhok-=Kra, Isthmus of- (EN) 21 Lh 10.20N 99.00 E
Kraba 15 Ch 41.12N 19.59 E
Krabbfjärden 8 Gf 58.45N 17.40 E
Krabi 25 Jg 8.05N 98.53 E
Krabit, Mali i- 15 Cg 42.07N 19.59 E
Kra Buri 25 Jf 10.24N 98.47 E
Krâchéh 22 Mh 12.29N 106.01 E
Kragerø 7 Bg 58.52N 9.25 E
Kragujevac 15 De 44.01N 20.55 E
Kraichbach 12 Ke 49.22N 8.31 E
Kraichgau 10 Eg 49.10N 8.50 E
Kraichtal 12 Ke 49.07N 8.46 E
Krajina 14 Kf 44.45N 16.35 E
Krajina 15 Fe 44.10N 22.30 E
Krajište 15 Fg 42.35N 22.25 E
Krajnovka 16 Oh 43.57N 47.24 E
Kråka 8 Ca 63.28N 9.00 E
Krakatau, Gunung- 21 Mj 6.07 S 105.24 E
Krak des Chevaliers 24 Ge 34.46N 36.19 E
Krakovec 10 Tg 49.56N 23.13 E
Kraków [2] 10 Pf 50.05N 20.00 E
Kraków 6 He 50.03N 19.58 E
Kraków-Nowa Huta 10 Qf 50.04N 20.05 E
Krakowsko-Częstochowska, Wyżyna- 10 Pf 50.50N 19.15 E
Kralendijk 50 Bf 12.10N 68.16W
Kraljevica 14 Ie 45.16N 14.34 E
Kraljevo 15 Df 43.44N 20.43 E
Kralupy nad Vltavou 10 Kf 50.14N 14.19 E
Kramatorsk 16 Je 48.43N 37.32 E
Kramfors 7 De 62.56N 17.47 E
Krammer 12 Gc 51.38N 4.15 E
Kranenburg 12 Ic 51.47N 6.01 E
Kranídhion 15 Gl 37.23N 23.09 E
Kranj 14 Id 46.14N 14.22 E
Krapina 14 Jd 46.10N 15.53 E
Krapkowice 10 Nf 50.29N 17.56 E
Kras=Karst (EN) 5 Hf 45.48N 14.00 E
Krasavino 19 Ec 60.59N 46.28 E
Krasiczyn 10 Sg 49.48N 22.39 E
Krasilov 16 Ee 49.37N 26.59 E
Kraskino 28 Kc 42.44N 130.48 E
Kraslava/Krāslava 7 Gi 55.54N 27.10 E
Krāslava/Kraslava 7 Gi 55.54N 27.10 E
Krasnaja Poljana 16 Lh 43.40N 40.12 E
Kraśnik 10 Sf 50.56N 22.13 E
Kraśnik Fabryczny, Kraśnik- 10 Sf 50.58N 22.12 E
Kraśnik-Kraśnik Fabryczny 10 Sf 50.58N 22.12 E
Krasnoarmejsk [Kaz.-U.S.S.R.] 19 Ge 53.57N 69.43 E
Krasnoarmejsk [R.S.F.S.R.] 19 Ee 51.02N 45.42 E
Krasnoarmejsk [Ukr.-U.S.S.R.] 16 Je 48.11N 37.12 E
Krasnoarmejski 20 Mc 69.37N 172.02 E
Krasnodar 6 Jf 45.02N 39.00 E
Krasnodarski Kraj [3] 19 Df 45.20N 39.30 E
Krasnodon 16 Ke 48.17N 39.44 E
Krasnogorodskoje 8 Mh 56.47N 28.18 E
Krasnogorsk [R.S.F.S.R.] 20 Jg 48.26N 142.10 E
Krasnogorsk [R.S.F.S.R.] 7 Ii 55.51N 37.20 E
Krasnogorski 17 Ji 54.36N 61.15 E
Krasnograd 19 Df 49.22N 35.27 E
Krasnogvardejsk 18 Fe 39.45N 67.16 E
Krasnogvardejskoje 16 Lg 45.49N 41.31 E
Krasnoholmski 17 Gh 56.02N 55.05 E
Krasnoilsk 15 Ia 48.02N 25.48 E
Krasnojarsk 22 Ld 56.01N 92.50 E
Krasnojarski 17 Ij 51.58N 59.57 E
Krasnojarski Kraj [3] 20 Ee 57.30N 95.00 E
Krasnojarskoje Vodohranilišče 20 Ee 55.05N 91.30 E
Krasnoje 10 Ug 49.49N 24.39 E
Krasnoje Selo 7 Hg 59.43N 30.03 E
Krasnoje Znamja 18 Df 36.50N 62.29 E
Krasnokamensk 20 Gf 50.00N 118.05 E
Krasnokamsk 19 Fd 58.04N 55.45 E
Krasnokutsk 19 He 52.59N 75.59 E
Krasnolesje 8 Jj 54.23N 22.25 E
Krasnolesny 16 Kd 51.52N 39.35 E
Krasnooktjabrski [Kirg.-U.S.S.R.] 18 Jc 42.45N 74.20 E
Krasnooktjabrski [R.S.F.S.R.] 7 Lh 56.43N 47.37 E
Krasnooskolskoje Vodohranilišče 16 Je 49.25N 37.35 E
Krasnoostrovski 8 Md 60.12N 28.39 E
Krasnoperekopsk 19 Df 45.57N 33.47 E
Krasnorečenski 28 Mb 44.38N 135.15 E
Krasnoščelje 7 Ic 67.23N 37.02 E
Krasnoselki 10 Uc 53.14N 24.30 E
Krasnoselkup 20 Dc 65.41N 82.28 E
Krasnoslobodsk [R.S.F.S.R.] 16 Ne 48.40N 44.31 E
Krasnoslobodsk [R.S.F.S.R.] 7 Ki 54.27N 43.47 E
Krasnoturinsk 19 Gd 59.46N 60.18 E
Krasnoufimsk 19 Fd 56.37N 57.46 E
Krasnouralsk 19 Gd 58.24N 60.03 E
Krasnousolski 19 Fe 53.54N 56.29 E
Krasnovišersk 19 Fc 60.23N 57.03 E
Krasnovodsk 22 He 40.00N 53.00 E
Krasnovodskaja Oblast [3] 19 Fh 39.50N 55.00 E
Krasnovodski Poluostrov 16 Rc 40.30N 53.15 E
Krasnovodski Zaliv 16 Rj 39.50N 53.15 E
Krasnozatonski 19 Fc 61.41N 51.01 E
Krasnozavodsk 7 Jh 56.29N 38.13 E
Krasnoznamensk [Kaz.-U.S.S.R.] 19 Ge 51.03N 69.30 E
Krasnoznamensk [R.S.F.S.R.] 8 Jj 54.52N 22.27 E
Krasny Čikoj 20 Ff 50.25N 108.45 E
Krasny Holm 7 Ig 58.04N 37.09 E
Krasny Jar [R.S.F.S.R.] 20 De 57.07N 84.40 E
Krasny Jar [R.S.F.S.R.] 19 Hd 55.14N 72.56 E
Krasnyje Barrikady 16 Of 46.13N 47.50 E
Krasnyje Okny 15 Mb 47.34N 29.23 E
Krasny Kut 19 Ee 50.58N 46.58 E
Krasny Liman 16 Je 48.59N 37.47 E
Krasny Luč 16 Ke 48.09N 38.57 E
Krasny Oktjabr 19 Gd 55.37N 64.48 E
Krasny Profintern 7 Jh 57.47N 40.29 E
Krasnystaw 10 Tf 50.59N 23.10 E
Krasny Sulin 16 Lf 47.53N 40.09 E
Kratovo 15 Fg 42.05N 22.12 E
Kraulshavn 41 Gd 74.10N 57.00W
Krâvanh, Chuŏr Phnum- 21 Mh 12.00N 103.15 E
Krawang 26 Eh 6.19 S 107.17 E
Krefeld 10 Ce 51.20N 6.34 E
Krefeld-Hüls 12 Ic 51.22N 6.31 E
Kremastá, Límni- 15 Ek 38.50N 21.30 E
Kremenchug Reservoir (EN) =Kremenčugskoje Vodohranilišče 5 Jf 49.20N 32.30 E
Kremenčug 6 Jf 49.04N 33.25 E
Kremenčugskoje Vodohranilišče=Kremenchug Reservoir (EN) 5 Jf 49.20N 32.30 E
Kremenec 16 Dd 50.06N 25.43 E
Kremennaja 16 Ke 49.03N 38.14 E
Kremmling 45 Cf 40.03N 106.24W
Krems 14 Jb 48.25N 15.36 E
Krems an der Donau 14 Jb 48.25N 15.36 E
Kremsmünster 14 Ib 48.03N 14.08 E
Krenitzin Islands 40a Eb 54.08N 166.00W
Kresta, Zaliv- 20 Nc 65.30N 179.00W
Krestcy 7 Hg 58.15N 32.31 E
Krestovy, Pereval- 16 Nh 42.32N 44.30 E
Kretek 26 Fh 7.59 S 110.19 E
Kretinga 7 Ei 55.55N 21.17 E
Kreuzau 12 Id 50.45N 6.29 E
Kreuzberg 10 Ff 50.22N 9.58 E
Kreuzlingen 14 Dc 47.39N 9.10 E
Kreuztal 10 Df 50.58N 7.59 E
Kria Vrisi 15 Fi 40.41N 22.18 E
Kribi 31 Hh 2.57N 9.55 E
Kričev 19 De 53.43N 31.43 E
Kričim 15 Hg 42.08N 24.31 E
Krim 14 Ie 45.56N 14.28 E
Krimml 14 Gc 47.13N 12.11 E
Krimpen aan den IJssel 12 Gc 51.55N 4.35 E
Kriós, Ákra- 5 Ih 35.14N 23.35 E
Krishna 21 Kh 15.57N 80.59 E
Krishnanagar 25 Hd 23.24N 88.30 E
Kristdala 8 Gg 57.24N 16.11 E
Kristiansand 6 Gd 58.10N 8.00 E
Kristianstad 7 Dh 56.02N 14.08 E
Kristianstad [2] 7 Ch 56.15N 14.00 E
Kristiansund 6 Gc 63.07N 7.45 E
Kristiinankaupunki/Kristinestad 7 Ee 62.17N 21.23 E
Kristineberg 7 Ed 65.04N 18.35 E
Kristinehamn 7 Dg 59.20N 14.07 E
Kristinestad/Kristiinankaupunki 7 Ee 62.17N 21.23 E
Kríti = Crete (EN) 5 Ih 35.15N 24.45 E
Kríti = Crete (EN) [2] 15 Hn 35.35N 25.00 E
Kritikón Pélagos = Crete, Sea of- (EN) 15 Hn 36.00N 25.00 E
Krivaja 14 Mf 44.27N 18.10 E
Kriva Palanka 15 Fg 42.12N 22.21 E
Kriviči 8 Lj 54.44N 27.20 E
Krivodol 15 Gf 43.23N 23.29 E
Krivoje Ozero 16 Gf 47.57N 30.21 E
Krivoj Rog 6 Jf 47.54N 33.21 E
Križevci 14 Kd 46.02N 16.32 E
Krk 14 Ie 45.05N 14.35 E
Krk 14 Ie 45.02N 14.35 E
Krka [Yugo.] 14 Jg 43.43N 15.51 E
Krka [Yugo.] 14 Je 45.53N 15.36 E
Krkonoše 10 Lf 50.46N 15.35 E
Krn 14 Hd 46.16N 13.40 E
Krndija 14 Le 45.27N 17.55 E
Krnjača, Beograd- 15 De 44.52N 20.28 E
Krnov 10 Nf 50.05N 17.41 E
Krobia 10 Me 51.47N 16.58 E
Krøderen 8 Cd 60.15N 9.40 E
Krokeaí 15 Fm 36.53N 22.33 E
Krokek 8 Gf 58.40N 16.24 E
Kroken 7 Dd 65.22N 14.16 E

Index Symbols

[1] Independent Nation
[2] State, Region
[3] District, County
[4] Municipality
[5] Colony, Dependency
Continent
Physical Region
Historical or Cultural Region
Mount, Mountain
Volcano
Hill
Mountains, Mountain Range
Hills, Escarpment
Plateau, Upland
Pass, Gap
Plain, Lowland
Delta
Salt Flat
Valley, Canyon
Crater, Cave
Karst Features
Depression
Polder
Desert, Dunes
Forest, Woods
Heath, Steppe
Oasis
Cape, Point
Coast, Beach
Cliff
Peninsula
Isthmus
Sandbank
Island
Atoll
Rock, Reef
Islands, Archipelago
Rocks, Reefs
Coral Reef
Well, Spring
Geyser
River, Stream
Waterfall Rapids
River Mouth, Estuary
Lake
Salt Lake
Intermittent Lake
Reservoir
Swamp, Pond
Canal
Glacier
Ice Shelf, Pack Ice
Ocean
Sea
Gulf, Bay
Strait, Fjord
Lagoon
Bank
Seamount
Tablemount
Ridge
Shelf
Basin
Escarpment, Sea Scarp
Fracture
Trench, Abyss
National Park, Reserve
Point of Interest
Recreation Site
Cave, Cavern
Historic Site
Ruins
Wall, Walls
Church, Abbey
Temple
Scientific Station
Airport
Port
Lighthouse
Mine
Tunnel
Dam, Bridge

Krokom 7 De 63.20N 14.28 E
Krolevec 16 Hd 51.32N 33.30 E
Kroměříž 10 Ng 49.18N 17.22 E
Krompachy 10 Qh 48.56N 20.52 E
Kronach 10 Hf 50.14N 11.19 E
Krŏng Kaôh Kŏng 25 Kf 11.37N 102.59 E
Kronoberg [2] 7 Dh 56.40N 14.40 E
Kronockaja Sopka, Vulkan- 20 Lf 54.47N 160.35 E
Kronocki, Mys- 20 Lf 54.43N 162.07 E
Kronocki Zaliv 20 Lf 54.00N 161.00 E
Kronoki 20 Lf 54.33N 161.14 E
Kronprins Christian Land 41 Jb 80.45N 22.00W
Kronprinsesse Mærtha Kyst 66 Bf 72.00S 7.30W
Kronprins Frederiks Bjerge 41 Ie 67.20N 34.00W
Kronprins Olav Kyst 66 Ee 68.30S 42.30 E
Kronštadt 19 Cc 60.01N 29.44 E
Kroonstad 31 Jk 27.46S 27.12 E
Kropotkin [R.S.F.S.R.] 19 Ef 45.26N 40.34 E
Kropotkin [R.S.F.S.R.] 20 Ge 58.36N 115.27 E
Kroppefjäll 8 Ef 58.40N 12.13 E
Krośniewice 10 Pd 52.16N 19.10 E
Krosno 10 Rg 49.42N 21.46 E
Krosno [2] 10 Rg 49.40N 21.45 E
Krosno Odrzańskie 10 Ld 52.04N 15.05 E
Krossfjorden 8 Ad 60.10N 5.05 E
Krotoszyn 10 Ne 51.42N 17.26 E
Kroviga, Gora- 20 Ed 60.40N 91.30 E
Krško 14 Je 45.58N 15.28 E
Krstača 15 Dg 42.58N 20.08 E
Krugersdorp 31 Jk 26.05S 27.35 E
Krui 26 Dh 5.11S 103.56 E
Kruibeke 12 Gc 50.10N 4.19 E
Kruiningen 12 Gc 51.27N 4.02 E
Kruja 15 Ch 41.30N 19.48 E
Kruleviščina 8 Li 55.03N 27.52 E
Krumbach 10 Gh 48.15N 10.22 E
Krumovgrad 15 Ih 41.28N 25.39 E
Krung Thep=Bangkok (EN) 22 Mh 13.45N 100.31 E
Krupanj 15 Ce 44.22N 19.22 E
Krupinica 10 Oh 48.05N 18.54 E
Krupinská vrchovina 10 Ph 48.20N 19.15 E
Kruså 8 Cj 54.50N 9.25 E
Krušedol 15 Cd 45.07N 19.57 E
Kruševac 15 Ef 43.35N 21.20 E
Kruševo 15 Eh 41.22N 21.15 E
Krušné Hory=Ore Mountains (EN) 5 He 50.30N 13.15 E
Krustpils 8 Lh 56.29N 26.00 E
Kruzof 40 Le 57.10N 135.40W
Krym 16 Jg 45.23N 36.36 E
Krymsk 19 Dg 44.54N 37.57 E
Krymskaja Oblast [3] 19 Dg 45.15N 34.20 E
Krymskije Gory=Crimean Mountains (EN) 5 Jg 44.45N 34.30 E
Krymski Poluostrov=Crimea (EN) 5 Jf 45.00N 34.00 E
Krynica 10 Qg 49.25N 20.56 E
Krzemieniucha 10 Sb 54.12N 22.54 E
Krzepice 10 Of 50.58N 18.44 E
Krzna 10 Td 52.08N 23.31 E
Krzywiń 10 Me 51.58N 16.49 E
Krzyż 10 Md 52.53N 16.01 E
Ksar el Boukhari 32 Hb 35.53N 2.45 E
Ksar el Kebir 32 Fc 35.00N 5.59W
Ksar es Srhir 13 Gi 35.51N 5.34W
Ksenjevka 20 Gf 53.34N 118.44 E
Kšenski 16 Jd 51.52N 37.44 E
Ksour, Monts des- 32 Gc 32.45N 0.10W
Kū', Wādī al- 35 Dc 12.12N 25.43 E
Kuai He 28 Dh 33.09N 117.32 E
Kuala Belait 26 Ff 4.35N 114.11 E
Kuala Dungun 26 Df 4.47N 103.26 E
Kuala Kangsar 26 Df 4.46N 100.56 E
Kualakapuas 26 Fg 3.01S 114.21 E
Kuala Kerai 26 De 5.32N 102.12 E
Kualakurun 26 Fg 1.07S 113.53 E
Kualalangsa 26 Cf 4.32N 98.01 E
Kuala Lipis 26 Df 4.11N 102.03 E
Kuala Lumpur 22 Mi 3.10N 101.42 E
Kuala Pilah 26 Df 2.44N 102.15 E
Kuala Rompin 26 Df 2.49N 103.29 E
Kuala Terengganu 22 Mi 5.20N 103.08 E
Kuancheng 28 Ed 40.37N 118.31 E
Kuandang 26 Hf 0.52N 122.55 E
Kuandian 27 Lc 40.45N 124.48 E
Kuang-hsi-chuang-tsu Tzu-chih-ch'ü→Guangxi Zhuangzu Zizhiqu=Kwangsi Chuang (EN) [2] 27 Ig 24.00N 109.00 E
Kuang-tun Sheng→Guangdong Sheng=Kwangtung (EN) [2] 27 Jg 23.00N 113.00 E
Kuantan 26 Df 3.48N 103.20 E
Kuba 19 Eg 41.20N 48.35 E
Kuban 5 Jf 45.20N 37.30 E
Kuba-Shima 29b b 26.10N 127.15 E
Kubaysah 24 Jf 33.35N 42.37 E
Kubbum 35 Cc 11.47N 23.47 E
Kubena 7 Jg 59.37N 39.48 E
Kubenskoje, Ozero- 7 Jg 59.40N 39.30 E
Kubnja 7 Li 55.32N 48.28 E
Kubokawa 28 Lh 33.12N 133.08 E
Kubolta 15 Lb 47.48N 28.03 E
Kubrat 15 Jf 43.48N 26.30 E
Kubumesaai 26 Gf 1.31N 115.06 E
Kučaj 15 Ef 43.53N 21.44 E
Kučevo 15 Ee 44.29N 21.41 E
Kuching 22 Ni 1.33N 110.20 E
Kuchinoerabu-Shima 28 Ki 30.28N 130.10 E
Kuchinotsu 29 Be 32.36N 130.12 E
Kuçukçekmece 15 Li 40.59N 28.46 E
Küçükerenköy 24 Ee 35.22N 33.45 E
Küçükkuyu 15 Jj 39.32N 26.36 E
Küçuk Menderes 15 Kl 37.57N 27.16 E
Kučurgan 15 Mc 46.35N 29.55 E
Kudaka-Jima 29b Ab 26.10N 127.54 E
Kudamatsu 29 Bd 34.01N 131.53 E
Kudat 26 Ge 6.53N 116.50 E
Kudeb 8 Mg 57.30N 28.16 E
Kudirkos-Naumestis 8 Jj 54.43N 22.49 E
Kudowa-Zdrój 10 Mf 50.27N 16.20 E
Kudremukh 25 Ff 13.08N 75.16 E
Kudus 26 Fh 6.48S 110.50 E
Kudymkar 19 Fd 59.01N 54.37 E
Kuee Ruins 65a Fd 19.12N 155.23W
Kuei-chou Sheng→Guizhou Sheng=Kweichow (EN) [2] 27 If 27.00N 107.00 E
Kufi 24 Cc 38.10N 29.43 E
Kufrah, Wāḥāt al-=Kufra Oasis (EN) 30 Jf 24.10N 23.15 E
Kufra Oasis (EN)=Kufrah, Wāḥāt al- 30 Jf 24.10N 23.15 E
Kufstein 14 Gc 47.35N 12.10 E
Kuganavolok 7 Ie 62.16N 36.55 E
Kugmallit Bay 42 Ek 69.30N 133.20W
Kugojeja 16 Kf 46.33N 39.38 E
Kūh, Ra's al- 23 Id 25.48N 57.19 E
Kuḩaylī 35 Eb 19.29N 32.49 E
Kūhbonān 24 Qg 31.23N 56.19 E
Kūhdasht 24 Lf 33.32N 47.36 E
Kūh-e Būrh 24 Pi 27.22N 54.40 E
Kūh-e Gāvbūs 24 Oi 27.10N 54.00 E
Kūh-e Karkas 24 Nf 33.27N 51.48 E
Kūh-e Kārūn 24 Ng 31.27N 50.18 E
Kūhestak 24 Qi 26.47N 57.02 E
Kūhīn, Gardaneh-ye- 24 Md 36.23N 49.37 E
Kühlungsborn 10 Hb 54.09N 11.43 E
Kuhmo 7 Gd 64.08N 29.31 E
Kuhmoinen 8 Kc 61.34N 25.11 E
Kuhn 41 Kd 74.45N 19.45W
Kūhpāyeh 23 Ic 30.35N 57.15 E
Kūhpāyeh [Iran] 24 Of 32.43N 52.26 E
Kūhpāyeh [Iran] 24 Qg 30.43N 57.30 E
Kührān, Kūh-e- 23 Id 26.46N 58.12 E
Kuhtuj 20 Je 59.23N 143.10 E
Kuhva 8 Mg 57.17N 28.17 E
Kuiseb 37 Ad 23.00S 14.33 E
Kuishan Ding 27 Ig 22.32N 109.52 E
Kuito 31 Ij 12.23S 16.56 E
Kuiu 40 Me 57.45N 134.10W
Kuivaniemi 7 Fd 65.35N 25.11 E
Kujang 27 Md 39.52N 126.01 E
Kujawy 10 Od 52.45N 18.30 E
Kujawy 10 Od 52.45N 18.35 E
Kujbyšev 6 Le 53.12N 50.09 E
Kujbyšev [R.S.F.S.R.] 7 Li 55.01N 49.06 E
Kujbyšev [R.S.F.S.R.] 20 Ce 55.27N 78.29 E
Kujbyševskaja Oblast [3] 19 Fe 53.20N 50.30 E
Kujbyševski [Kaz.-U.S.S.R.] 19 Ge 53.15N 66.51 E
Kujbyševski [Tad.-U.S.S.R.] 18 Gf 37.53N 68.44 E
Kujbyševskoje Vodohranilišče=Kuybyshev Reservoir (EN) 5 Ke 53.50N 49.00 E
Kujeda 17 Gh 56.26N 55.35 E
Kujgan 19 Hf 45.22N 74.10 E
Kuji 28 Pd 40.11N 141.46 E
Kuji-Gawa 29 Gc 36.30N 140.37 E
Kujtun 20 Ff 54.21N 101.35 E
Kujūkuri-Hama 29 Gd 35.40N 140.30 E
Kujū-San 28 Kh 33.09N 131.15 E
Kūkalār, Kūh-e- 24 Ng 31.50N 50.53 E
Kukalaya, Rio- 49 Fg 13.39N 83.37W
Kukësi 15 Dg 42.05N 20.24 E
Kukkia 8 Kc 61.20N 24.40 E
Kukmor 7 Mh 56.13N 50.52 E
Kükürt Dağı 24 Ib 41.07N 41.27 E
Kula [Bul.] 15 Ff 43.53N 22.31 E
Kula [Tur.] 24 Cc 38.30N 28.40 E
Kula [Yugo.] 15 Cd 45.37N 19.32 E
Kulai 26 Df 1.40N 103.36 E
Kulanak 18 Jd 41.18N 75.34 E
Kulandy 19 Ff 46.08N 59.31 E
Kular 20 Ib 70.32N 134.26 E
Kular, Hrebet- 20 Ic 69.00N 133.30 E
Kulata 15 Gh 41.23N 23.22 E
Kulautuva 8 Jj 54.55N 23.43 E
Kulbus 35 Cc 14.24N 22.31 E
Kuldīga/Kuldiga 19 Cd 56.59N 21.59 E
Kuldiga/Kuldīga 19 Cd 56.59N 21.59 E
Kuldur 20 Ig 49.10N 131.40 E
Kulebaki 7 Ki 55.26N 42.32 E
Kulenjin 24 Me 35.40N 49.30 E
Kulen Vakuf 14 Kf 44.33N 16.06 E
Kulgera 58 Eg 25.50S 133.18 E
Kulikovo 10 Ug 49.55N 24.06 E
Kulim 26 De 5.22N 100.34 E
Kuljab 19 Gh 37.55N 69.47 E
Kuljabskaja Oblast [3] 19 Gh 38.00N 69.40 E
Kullaa 8 Jc 61.28N 22.10 E
Kullen 7 Ch 56.18N 12.26 E
Kulmasa 34 Ed 9.35N 2.27W
Kulmbach 10 Hf 50.06N 11.27 E
Kuloj 7 Kf 61.03N 42.30 E
Kuloj [R.S.F.S.R.] 19 Eb 66.00N 43.30 E
Kuloj [R.S.F.S.R.] 7 Kf 61.01N 42.12 E
Kulp 24 Ic 38.30N 41.02 E
Kulsary 19 Ff 46.57N 54.02 E
Kultuk 20 Ff 51.44N 103.42 E
Kulu 20 Jd 62.15N 147.45 E
Kulu [India] 25 Fb 31.58N 77.06 E
Kulu [Tur.] 24 Ec 39.06N 33.05 E
Kulumadau 63a Ac 9.03S 152.43 E
Kulunda 20 Cf 52.35N 78.57 E
Kulundinskaja Step 20 Cf 52.45N 79.00 E
Kulundinskoje, Ozero- 20 Cf 53.00N 79.30 E
Kum 24 Bc 38.38N 27.32 E
Kum, Kūh-e- 24 Oh 29.55N 53.45 E
Kuma 29 Ce 33.39N 132.54 E
Kuma [R.S.F.S.R.] 17 Mg 59.33N 66.40 E
Kuma [R.S.F.S.R.] 7 Hc 66.15N 31.02 E
Kuma [U.S.S.R.] 5 Kg 44.56N 47.00 E
Kumagaya 28 Of 36.08N 139.23 E
Kumai [Indon.] 26 Fg 2.44S 111.43 E
Kumai [Indon.] 26 Fg 3.23S 112.33 E
Kumaishi 29a Ab 42.08N 139.59 E
Kumak 16 Vd 51.13N 60.08 E
Kumamoto 22 Pf 32.48N 130.43 E
Kumamoto Ken [2] 28 Kh 32.30N 130.50 E
Kumano 28 Nh 33.54N 136.05 E
Kumano-Gawa 29 De 33.45N 135.59 E
Kumano-Nada 29 Ee 34.00N 136.30 E
Kumanovo 15 Eg 42.08N 21.43 E
Kumara [N.Z.] 62 De 42.38S 171.11 E
Kumara [R.S.F.S.R.] 20 Hf 51.35N 126.45 E
Kumasi 31 Gh 6.41N 1.37W
Kumba 34 Ge 4.38N 9.25 E
Kumbakonam 25 Ff 10.58N 79.23 E
Kumbe 26 Lh 8.21S 140.13 E
Kumbo 34 Hd 6.12N 10.40 E
Kumboro Cape 63a Cb 7.18S 157.32 E
Kümch'ŏn 28 Ie 38.10N 126.30 E
Kum-Dag 19 Fh 39.13N 54.40 E
Kumdah 33 Ie 20.23N 45.05 E
Kume-Jima [Jap.] 27 Mf 26.20N 126.45 E
Kumertau 19 Fe 52.46N 55.47 E
Kumhwa 28 Ie 38.17N 127.28 E
Kumihama 29 Dd 35.36N 134.54 E
Kuminski 19 Gd 58.40N 65.55 E
Kumköy (Kilyos) 15 Mh 41.15N 29.02 E
Kumkuduk 27 Fc 40.15N 91.55 E
Kumkurgan 18 Ff 37.50N 67.35 E
Kumla 7 Dg 59.08N 15.08 E
Kumlinge 8 Id 60.15N 20.45 E
Kumluca 24 Dd 36.22N 30.18 E
Kummerower See 10 Ic 53.49N 12.52 E
Kumo/Kokemäki 7 Ff 61.15N 22.21 E
Kumo-Manyčski Kanal 16 Ng 45.27N 44.38 E
Kumon Taung 21 Lg 26.30N 96.50 E
Kumora 20 Ge 55.56N 111.13 E
Kumru 24 Gb 40.53N 37.17 E
Kumu 36 Eb 3.04N 25.09 E
Kumuh 16 Oh 42.11N 47.07 E
Kumukahi, Cape- 60 Od 19.31N 154.49W
Kumul/Hami 22 Le 42.48N 93.27 E
Kümüx 27 Ec 42.15N 88.10 E
Kumzār 24 Qj 26.20N 56.25 E
Kunashiri-Tō/Kunašir, Ostrov- 21 Qe 44.05N 145.51 E
Kunašir, Ostrov-/Kunashiri-Tō 21 Qe 44.05N 145.51 E
Kunašírski Proliv=Nemuro Strait (EN) 20 Jh 43.50N 145.30 E
Kunchaung 25 Jd 23.50N 96.35 E
Kunda 7 Gg 59.30N 26.30 E
Kunda Jõgi 8 Le 59.25N 26.27 E
Kundelungu, Monts- 36 Ed 9.30S 28.00 E
Kundiawa 59 Ia 6.00S 145.00 E
Kunduchi 36 Gd 6.40S 39.13 E
Kunduk 15 Md 45.51N 29.38 E
Kunduk→Kogilnik 15 Md 45.51N 29.38 E
Kunduk→Sasyk, Ozero- 16 Fg 45.45N 29.40 E
Kunene 30 Ij 17.20S 11.50 E
Kunene (EN)=Cunene 30 Ij 17.20S 11.50 E
Künes/Xinyuan 27 Dc 43.24N 83.18 E
Künes He 27 Dc 43.32N 82.29 E
Kungälv 7 Ch 57.52N 11.58 E
Kungej-Alatau, Hrebet- 19 Hg 42.50N 77.15 E
Kungmiut 41 Ie 65.50N 36.45W
Kungrad 19 Fg 43.06N 58.54 E
Kungsbacka 7 Ch 57.29N 12.04 E
Kungsbackafjorden 8 Eg 57.25N 12.04 E
Kungshamn 8 Df 58.21N 11.15 E
Kungsör 8 Ge 59.25N 16.05 E
Kungu 36 Cb 2.47N 19.12 E
Kungur 19 Fd 57.25N 56.57 E
Kunhegyes 10 Qi 47.22N 20.38 E
Kunhing 25 Jd 21.18N 98.26 E
Kunigami 29b Bb 26.45N 128.11 E
Kunigami-Misaki 29b Bb 27.26N 128.43 E
Kunimi-Dake 29 Be 32.33N 131.01 E
Kunisaki 29 Be 33.34N 131.45 E
Kunisaki-Hantō 29 Be 33.30N 131.40 E
Kunja 7 Hh 57.09N 31.10 E
Kunja-Urgenč 19 Fg 42.20N 59.12 E
Kunlong 25 Jd 23.25N 98.39 E
Kunlun Guan 27 Ig 23.06N 108.40 E
Kunlun Shan 21 Kf 36.00N 84.00 E
Kunlun Shankou 27 Fd 35.40N 94.03 E
Kunming 22 Mg 25.08N 102.43 E
Kunnui 29a Bb 42.26N 140.19 E
Kunovat 17 Ld 64.59N 65.35 E
Kunsan 27 Md 35.59N 126.43 E
Kunshan 28 Fi 31.22N 120.57 E
Kuntaur 34 Cc 13.40N 14.53W
Kununurra 59 Fc 15.47S 128.44 E
Kunyao 36 Gb 1.47N 35.03 E
Kunyu Shan 28 Ff 37.15N 121.46 E
Künzelsau 10 Fg 49.17N 9.41 E
Kuohijärvi 8 Kc 61.15N 24.55 E
Kuolimo 8 Lc 61.15N 27.35 E
Kuop Atoll 64d Bb 7.03N 151.56 E
Kuopio [2] 7 Ge 63.20N 27.35 E
Kuopio 6 Ic 62.54N 27.41 E
Kuorboaivi 7 Gb 69.41N 27.45 E
Kuortane 8 Jb 62.48N 23.30 E
Kupa 14 Ke 45.28N 16.24 E
Kupang 22 Ok 10.10S 123.35 E
Kupiano 60 Dj 10.10S 148.02 E
Kupičev 10 Uf 50.58N 24.52 E
Kupino 20 Cf 54.22N 77.18 E
Kupiškis 7 Fi 55.49N 25.01 E
Kupjansk 19 Df 49.42N 37.37 E
Kupjansk-Uzlovoj 16 Je 49.39N 37.45 E
Küplü [Tur.] 15 Jh 41.07N 26.21 E
Küplü [Tur.] 15 Mi 40.06N 30.00 E
Kuppenheim 12 Kf 48.50N 8.15 E
Kupreanof 40 Me 56.50N 133.30W
Kuqa 22 Ke 41.43N 82.57 E
Kura [R.S.F.S.R.] 16 Mh 44.05N 44.45 E
Kura [U.S.S.R.] 5 Kh 39.20N 49.25 E
Kuragaty 18 Ic 43.55N 73.34 E
Kuragino 20 Ef 53.53N 92.40 E
Kurahashi-Jima 29 Cd 34.08N 132.30 E
Kuraminski Hrebet 18 Hd 40.50N 70.30 E
Kurashiki 28 Lg 34.35N 133.46 E
Kurashiki-Kojima 29 Cd 34.28N 133.48 E
Kurashiki-Tamashima 29 Cd 34.33N 133.40 E
Kura-Take 29 Be 32.27N 130.20 E
Kuraymah=Karima (EN) 31 Kg 18.33N 31.51 E
Kurayoshi 28 Lg 35.28N 133.49 E
Kurbneshi 15 Dh 41.47N 20.05 E
Kurčatov 16 Id 51.41N 35.42 E
Kurdaj 18 Jc 43.18N 74.59 E
Kurdistan 21 Gf 37.00N 44.00 E
Kurdistan 23 Fb 37.00N 44.00 E
Kurdufān 30 Jg 13.00N 30.00 E
Kurdufān al Janūbīyah [3] 35 Dc 11.00N 29.30 E
Kurdufān ash Shamālīyah [3] 35 Dc 14.50N 29.40 E
Kure 28 Lg 34.14N 132.34 E
Küre 24 Eb 41.48N 33.43 E
Kure Island 57 Jb 28.25N 178.25W
Kurejka 21 Kc 66.25N 87.12 E
Kurgaldžinski 19 He 50.30N 70.03 E
Kurgalski, Mys- 8 Me 59.39N 28.03 E
Kurgan 22 Id 55.26N 65.18 E
Kurganinsk 16 Lg 44.57N 40.35 E
Kurganskaja Oblast [3] 19 Gd 55.00N 65.00 E
Kurgan-Tjube 19 Gh 37.51N 68.46 E
Kurgan-Tjubinskaja Oblast [3] 19 Gh 37.30N 68.30 E
Kuria Island 57 Id 0.14N 173.25 E
Kuria Muria Islands (EN)=Khurīyā Murīyā, Jazā'ir 21 Hh 17.30N 56.00 E
Kuri Bay 59 Ec 15.35S 124.50 E
Kurikka 7 Fe 62.37N 22.25 E
Kurikoma 29 Gb 38.50N 140.59 E
Kurikoma-Yama 29 Gb 38.57N 140.47 E
Kuril Basin (EN) 20 Jg 47.00N 150.00 E
Kuril Islands (EN)=Kurilskije Ostrova 21 Re 46.10N 152.00 E
Kurilo 15 Gg 42.49N 23.21 E
Kurilsk 20 Jg 45.16N 147.58 E
Kurilskije Ostrova=Kuril Islands (EN) 21 Re 46.10N 152.00 E
Kuril Trench (EN) 3 Je 47.00N 155.00 E
Kuring Kuru 37 Bc 17.38S 18.33 E
Kurino 29 Bf 31.57N 130.43 E
Kurinskaja Kosa 16 Pj 39.05N 49.10 E
Kurinwás, Río- 49 Fg 12.49N 83.41W
Kuriyama 29a Bb 43.03N 141.45 E
Kūrkhūd, Kūh-e- 24 Qd 37.15N 56.30 E
Kurkosa 16 Pj 38.59N 49.08 E
Kurkūmā, Ra's- 24 Gj 25.51N 36.39 E
Kurkur 24 Ek 23.54N 32.19 E
Kurlovski 7 Ji 55.29N 40.39 E
Kurmuk 35 Ec 10.33N 34.17 E
Kurnool 22 Jh 15.50N 78.03 E
Kurobe 28 Nf 36.51N 137.26 E
Kurobe-Gawa 29 Ec 36.55N 137.26 E
Kurogi 29 Be 33.14N 130.40 E
Kuroishi 28 Pd 40.38N 140.36 E
Kuroiso 28 Pf 36.58N 140.03 E
Kuromatsunai 28 Pc 42.43N 140.20 E
Kurono-Seto 29 Be 32.05N 130.10 E
Kurort Družba 15 Kf 43.12N 28.00 E
Kurort Slănčev brjag 15 Kg 42.40N 27.42 E
Kurort Zlatni pjasăci 15 Lf 43.16N 28.02 E
Kuro-Shima 28 Ji 31.52N 129.58 E
Kurovskoje 7 Ji 55.35N 38.59 E
Kurow 61 Dh 44.44S 170.28 E
Kurów 10 Se 51.25N 22.10 E
Kurpiowska, Puszcza- 10 Rc 53.20N 21.30 E
Kuršėnai/Kuršėnaj 19 Cd 56.03N 22.58 E
Kuršėnaj/Kuršėnai 19 Cd 56.03N 22.58 E
Kuršiu užūrekis 8 Ii 55.05N 21.00 E
Kursk 6 Je 51.42N 36.12 E
Kurskaja Kosa 7 Ei 55.18N 21.00 E
Kurskaja Oblast [3] 19 De 51.45N 36.15 E
Kurski zaliv 7 Ei 55.05N 21.00 E
Kuršumlija 15 Ef 43.09N 21.16 E
Kurtalan 24 Id 37.57N 41.42 E
Kurtamyš 19 Ge 54.55N 64.27 E
Kūrtī 31 Kg 18.07N 31.33 E
Kurtistown 65 Fd 19.36N 155.04W
Kurty 18 Kb 44.19N 76.42 E
Kuru 8 Jc 61.52N 23.44 E
Kuru 35 Dd 9.08N 26.57 E
Kuruçaşile 24 Eb 41.51N 32.43 E
Kuruktag 27 Ec 41.30N 89.00 E
Kuruman 30 Jk 26.56S 20.39 E
Kuruman 31 Jk 27.28S 23.28 E
Kurume 28 Kh 33.19N 130.31 E
Kurunegala 25 Gg 7.29N 80.22 E
Kurur, Jabal- 35 Ea 20.31N 31.32 E
Kurzeme=Courland (EN) 8 Ih 56.50N 22.00 E
Kurzemes Augstiene/Kurzemskaja Vozvyšennost 8 Jh 56.45N 22.15 E
Kurzemskaja Vozvyšennost/Kurzemes Augstiene 8 Jh 56.45N 22.15 E
Kusa 17 Ii 55.20N 59.29 E
Kuşada Körfezi 15 Kl 37.50N 27.08 E
Kuşadasi 24 Bd 37.51N 27.15 E
Kusagaki-Guntō 27 Me 31.00N 129.00 E
Kusaie→Kosrae 57 Hd 5.19N 162.59 E
Kusalu/Kuusalu 8 Ke 59.23N 25.25 E
Kusary 16 Pi 41.24N 48.29 E
Kusatsu [Jap.] 29 Fc 36.37N 138.35 E
Kusatsu [Jap.] 29 Dd 35.03N 135.59 E
Kuščevskaja 16 Kf 46.33N 39.37 E
Kuščinski 16 Oi 40.33N 46.06 E
Kusel 12 Je 49.33N 7.24 E
Kuş Gölü 24 Bb 40.10N 27.59 E
Kushida-Gawa 29 Ed 34.36N 136.34 E
Kushikino 28 Ki 31.44N 130.16 E
Kushima 28 Ki 31.29N 131.14 E
Kushimoto 28 Mh 33.28N 135.47 E
Kushiro 22 Qe 42.58N 144.23 E
Kushiro-Gawa 29a Db 42.59N 144.23 E
Kushtia 25 Hd 23.55N 89.07 E
Kuška 18 Dg 35.16N 62.18 E
Kuskokwim 38 Cc 60.17N 162.27W
Kuskokwim Bay 38 Cd 59.45N 162.25W
Kuskokwim Mountains 38 Dc 62.30N 156.00W
Kušmurun 19 Ge 52.27N 64.40 E
Kušmurun, Ozero- 19 Ge 52.40N 64.45 E
Kušnarenkovo 17 Gi 55.06N 55.22 E
Kušnica 16 Ce 48.29N 23.20 E
Kusŏng 27 Md 39.59N 125.16 E
Kussharo Ko 28 Rc 43.35N 144.15 E
Kustanaj 22 Id 53.10N 63.35 E
Kustanajskaja Oblast [3] 19 Ge 53.00N 64.00 E
Kustavi 8 Id 60.30N 21.25 E
Kustavi/Gustavs 8 Id 60.30N 21.25 E
Küstenkanal 10 Dd 52.57N 7.18 E
Kūstī 31 Kg 13.10N 32.40 E
Kustvlakte=Coast Plain (EN) 11 Ic 51.00N 2.30 E
Kusu 29 Be 33.16N 131.09 E
Kušva 19 Fd 58.18N 59.45 E
Kut, Ko- 25 Kf 11.40N 102.35 E
Kūt 'Abdollāh 24 Mg 31.13N 48.39 E
Kutacane 26 Cf 3.30N 97.48 E
Kutahya 23 Cb 39.25N 29.59 E
Kutaisi 6 Kg 42.15N 42.40 E
Kutch, Gulf of-→Kachchh, Gulf of 21 Ig 22.36N 60.30 E
Kutch, Rann of- 25 Ed 24.05N 70.10 E
Kutchan 28 Pc 42.54N 140.45 E
Kutcharo-Ko 29a Ca 45.10N 142.20 E
Kutina 14 Ke 45.29N 16.47 E
Kutkai 25 Jd 23.27N 97.56 E
Kutkašen 16 Oi 40.58N 47.52 E
Kutná Hora 10 Lg 49.57N 15.16 E
Kutno 10 Pd 52.15N 19.23 E
Kutse, Gora-/Kuutse Mägi 8 Lg 57.58N 26.24 E
Kuttara-Ko 29a Bb 42.30N 141.10 E
Kutu 31 Ii 2.44S 18.09 E
Kutum 35 Cc 14.12N 24.40 E
Kúty 10 Nh 48.40N 17.01 E
Kuty 15 Ia 48.13N 25.15 E
Kuujjuaq 39 Md 58.10N 68.30W
Kuujjuarapik 42 Je 55.20N 76.50W
Kuuli-Majak 19 Fg 40.16N 52.45 E
Kuurne 12 Fd 50.51N 3.17 E
Kuusalu/Kusalu 8 Ke 59.23N 25.25 E
Kuusamo 6 Ib 66.00N 29.11 E
Kuusankoski 8 Ld 60.54N 26.38 E
Kuutse Mägi/Kutse, Gora- 8 Lg 57.58N 26.24 E
Kuvandyk 16 Td 51.29N 57.28 E
Kuvdlorssuaq 41 Gd 74.38N 56.40W
Kuvšinovo 7 Ih 57.03N 34.13 E
Kuwait (EN)=Al Kuwayt [1] 22 Gg 29.30N 47.45 E
Kuwait (EN)=Al Kuwayt 22 Gg 29.20N 47.59 E
Kuwana 29 Ed 35.04N 136.39 E
Kuybyshev Reservoir (EN)=Kujbyševskoje Vodohranilišče 5 Ke 53.50N 49.00 E
Kūysanjaq 24 Kd 36.05N 44.38 E
Kuytun 27 Dc 44.25N 84.58 E
Kuyucak 15 Ll 37.55N 28.28 E
Kuzey Kibris = North Cyprus 23 Db 35.15N 33.40 E
Kuzneck 19 Ee 53.07N 46.36 E
Kuznecki Alatau 21 Kd 54.45N 88.00 E
Kuznečnoje 8 Mc 61.04N 29.58 E
Kuźnia Raciborska 10 Of 50.11N 18.15 E
Kuzomen 19 Db 66.18N 36.49 E
Kuzovatovo 7 Lj 53.33N 47.41 E
Kuzumaki 29 Ga 40.02N 141.26 E
Kuzuryū-Gawa 29 Ec 36.13N 136.08 E
Kvænangen 7 Ea 70.05N 21.13 E
Kvaløy 7 Eb 69.40N 18.30 E
Kvaløya 7 Fa 70.37N 23.52 E
Kvalsund 7 Fa 70.30N 24.00 E
Kvam 8 Cc 61.40N 9.42 E
Kvareli 16 Ni 41.57N 45.47 E
Kvarkeno 17 Ij 52.05N 59.40 E
Kvarnbergsvattnet 7 Dd 64.36N 14.03 E
Kvarner 14 If 44.45N 14.15 E
Kvarnerić 14 If 44.45N 14.35 E
Kvichak Bay 40 He 58.48N 157.30W
Kvemo-Kedi 16 Oi 41.22N 46.31 E
Kvenna 8 Bd 60.01N 7.56 E
Kvichak 40 He 59.10N 156.40W
Kvikkjokk 7 Dc 66.57N 17.47 E
Kvina 8 Bf 58.17N 6.56 E
Kvinesdal 7 Bg 58.19N 6.57 E
Kvissleby 8 Gb 62.17N 17.21 E
Kviteggia 8 Bb 62.05N 6.40 E
Kviteseid 8 Ce 59.24N 8.30 E
Kvitøya 67 Je 80.08N 32.35 E
Kwa 30 Ii 3.10S 16.11 E
Kwahu Plateau 34 Ed 6.30N 0.30W
Kwailibesi 63a Ec 8.20S 160.40 E
Kwajalein Atoll 57 Hd 9.05N 167.20 E
Kwakoegron 54 Gb 5.15N 55.20W
Kwale [Kenya] 36 Gc 4.11S 39.27 E
Kwale [Nig.] 34 Gd 5.45N 6.25 E
Kwamouth 36 Cc 3.10S 16.12 E
Kwa Mtoro 36 Gd 5.14S 35.26 E
Kwando 36 Df 18.27S 23.32 E
Kwangdae-ri 27 Mc 40.34N 127.33 E
Kwangju 22 Of 35.09N 126.55 E
Kwango 30 Ii 3.14S 17.22 E

Index Symbols

[1] Independent Nation
[2] State, Region
[3] District, County
[4] Municipality
[5] Colony, Dependency
Continent
Physical Region
Historical or Cultural Region
Mount, Mountain
Volcano
Hill
Mountains, Mountain Range
Hills, Escarpment
Plateau, Upland
Pass, Gap
Plain, Lowland
Delta
Salt Flat
Valley, Canyon
Crater, Cave
Karst Features
Depression
Polder
Desert, Dunes
Forest, Woods
Heath, Steppe
Oasis
Cape, Point
Coast, Beach
Cliff
Peninsula
Isthmus
Sandbank
Island
Atoll
Rock, Reef
Islands, Archipelago
Rocks, Reefs
Coral Reef
Well, Spring
Geyser
River, Stream
Waterfall Rapids
River Mouth, Estuary
Lake
Salt Lake
Intermittent Lake
Reservoir
Swamp, Pond
Canal
Glacier
Ice Shelf, Pack Ice
Ocean
Sea
Gulf, Bay
Strait, Fjord
Lagoon
Bank
Seamount
Tablemount
Ridge
Shelf
Basin
Escarpment, Sea Scarp
Fracture
Trench, Abyss
National Park, Reserve
Point of Interest
Recreation Site
Cave, Cavern
Historic Site
Ruins
Wall, Walls
Church, Abbey
Temple
Scientific Station
Airport
Port
Lighthouse
Mine
Tunnel
Dam, Bridge

Kwangsi Chuang (EN)= Guangxi Zhuangzu Zizhiqu (Kuang-hsi-chuang-tsu Tzu-chih-ch'ü) [2] 27 Ig 24.00N 109.00 E
Kwangsi Chuang (EN)= Kuang-hsi-chuang-tsu Tzu-chih-ch'ü→Guangxi Zhuangzu Zizhiqu [2] 27 Ig 24.00N 109.00 E
Kwangtung (EN)= Guangdong Sheng (Kuang-tung Sheng) [2] 27 Jg 23.00N 113.00 E
Kwangtung (EN)=Kuang-tun Sheng→Guangdong Sheng [2] 27 Jg 23.00N 113.00 E
Kwanmo-bong 28 Jd 41.42N 129.13 E
Kwara [2] 34 Fd 8.30N 5.00 E
Kweichow (EN)=Guizhou Sheng (Kuei-chou Sheng) [2] 27 If 27.00N 107.00 E
Kweichow (EN) = Kuei-chou Sheng → Guizhou Sheng 27 If 27.00N 107.00 E
Kwekwe 31 Jj 18.55S 29.49 E
Kweneng [3] 37 Cd 24.00S 24.00 E
Kwenge 30 Ii 4.50S 18.44 E
Kwethluk 40 Gd 60.49N 161.27W
Kwidzyn 10 Oc 53.45N 18.56 E
Kwigillingok 40 Ge 59.51N 163.08W
Kwilu 30 Ii 3.22S 17.22 E
Kwisa 10 Le 51.35N 15.25 E
Kwoka, Gunung- 26 Jg 0.31S 132.27 E
Kyabé 31 Ih 9.27N 18.57 E
Kyabram 59 Jg 36.19S 145.03 E
Kyaikkami 25 Je 16.04N 97.34 E
Kyaikto 25 Je 17.18N 97.01 E
Kyaka 36 Fc 1.16S 31.25 E
Kyancutta 58 Eh 33.08S 135.34 E
Kyan-Zaki 29b Ab 26.05N 127.40 E
Kyaukpyu 25 Id 20.51N 92.58 E
Kyaukse 25 Jd 21.36N 96.08 E
Kybartai/Kibartaj 8 Jj 54.38N 22.44 E
Kyeintali 25 Ie 18.00N 94.29 E
Kyelang 25 Fb 32.35N 77.02 E
Kyfhauser 10 He 51.25N 11.10 E
Kyjov 10 Ng 49.01N 17.08 E
Kyle, Lake- 37 Ed 20.12S 31.00 E
Kyle of Lochalsh 9 Hd 57.17N 5.43W
Kyll 10 Cg 49.48N 6.42 E
Kyllburg 12 Id 50.02N 6.35 E
Kyma 7 Ld 64.48N 47.31 E
Kymi [2] 7 Gf 61.00N 28.00 E
Kymijoki 8 Ld 60.30N 26.52 E
Kyn 17 Ih 57.52N 58.32 E
Kynnefjäll 8 Df 58.42N 11.41 E
Kynsivesi 8 Lb 62.25N 26.10 E
Kyoga, Lake- 30 Kh 1.30N 33.00 E
Kyōga-Dake 29 Be 33.00N 130.05 E
Kyōga-Misaki 28 Mg 35.45N 135.11 E
Kyonan 29 Fd 35.07N 139.49 E
Kyŏnggi-Do [2] 28 If 37.30N 127.15 E
Kyŏnggi-man 28 Hf 37.25N 126.00 E
Kyŏngju 27 Md 35.50N 129.13 E
Kyŏngsang-Namdo [2] 28 Jg 35.15N 128.30 E
Kyŏngsang-Pukto [2] 28 Jf 36.20N 128.40 E
Kyŏngsŏng 28 Jd 41.40N 129.40 E
Kyōto 22 Pf 35.00N 135.45 E
Kyōto Fu 28 Mg 35.25N 135.15 E
Kypros → Kipros = Cyprus (EN) 23 Db 35.01N 33.00 E
Kyra 20 Gg 49.36N 111.58 E
Kyren 20 Ef 51.41N 102.10 E
Kyrenia 24 Ee 35.20N 33.19 E
Kyrgesaare/Kõrgesaare 8 Je 59.00N 22.25 E
Kyrgyz Sovetik Socialistik Respublikasy/Kirgizskaja SSR [2] 19 Hg 41.30N 75.00 E
Kyritz 10 Id 52.57N 12.24 E
Kyrkheden 8 Ed 60.10N 13.29 E
Kyrksæterora 7 Be 63.17N 9.06 E
Kyrkslätt/Kirkkonummi 8 Kd 60.07N 24.26 E
Kyrö 8 Jd 60.42N 22.45 E
Kyrönjoki 8 Ia 63.14N 21.45 E
Kyrösjärvi 8 Jc 61.45N 23.10 E
Kyröskoski 8 Jc 61.40N 23.11 E
Kyštym 19 Gd 55.42N 60.34 E
Kysucké Nové Mesto 10 Og 49.18N 18.48 E
Kythera (EN)=Kíthira 5 Ih 36.15N 23.00 E
Kythraia 24 Ee 35.15N 33.29 E
Kyuquot Sound 46 Bb 49.55N 127.25W
Kyūshū 21 Pf 32.50N 131.00 E
Kyushu-Palau Ridge (EN) 3 Ih 20.00N 136.00 E
Kyushū-Sanchi 29 Be 32.40N 131.10 E
Kyyjärvi 7 Fe 63.02N 24.34 E
Kyyvesi 8 Lc 61.55N 27.05 E
Kyzikos 24 Bb 40.28N 27.47 E
Kyzyl 22 Ld 51.42N 94.27 E
Kyzylart, Pereval- 19 Hh 39.22N 73.20 E
Kyzyl-Kija 19 Hg 40.14N 72.12 E
Kyzylkum 21 Ie 42.00N 64.00 E
Kyzylrabot 19 Hh 37.28N 74.45 E
Kyzylsu [U.S.S.R.] 18 Gf 37.22N 69.22 E
Kyzylsu [U.S.S.R.] 18 He 39.17N 71.25 E
Kyzylžar 19 Gf 48.17N 69.49 E
Kzyl-Orda 22 Ie 44.48N 65.28 E
Kzyl-Ordinskaja Oblast [3] 19 Gf 45.00N 65.00 E
Kzyltu 19 He 53.41N 72.15 E

L

Laa an der Thaya 14 Kb 48.43N 16.23 E
Laakdal 12 Gc 51.05N 4.59 E
La Alberca 13 Fd 40.29N 6.06W
La Alcarria 13 Jd 40.31N 2.45W
La Almunia de Doña Godina 13 Kc 41.29N 1.22W
La Ametlla de Mar 13 Md 40.54N 0.48 E
La Ardilla, Cerro- 48 Hf 22.15N 102.40W
La Armuña 13 Gc 41.05N 5.35W
Laasphe 12 Kd 50.56N 8.24 E
La Asunción 54 Fa 11.02N 63.53W
Laau Point 65a Db 21.06N 157.16W
Laayoune 13 Ni 35.42N 2.00 E
Lab 15 Eg 42.45N 21.01 E
Laba 16 Kg 45.10N 39.40 E
La Babia 48 Hc 28.34N 102.04W
Laba Daği 15 Kl 37.22N 27.33 E
Labaddey 35 Ge 0.32N 42.45 E
Labadie Bank 9 Ek 50.30N 8.15W
La Banda 56 Hc 27.44S 64.15W
La Bañeza 13 Gb 42.18N 5.54W
La Barca 48 Hg 20.17N 102.34W
Labardén 55 Cm 36.57S 58.06W
La Barge 46 Je 42.16N 110.12W
La Barra, Punta- 49 Lh 11.30N 70.10W
La-Barre-en-Ouche 12 Cf 48.57N 0.40 E
La Baule-Escoublac 11 Dg 47.17N 2.24W
Labbezanga 34 Fc 14.59N 0.43 E
Labé 31 Fg 11.19N 12.17W
Labe=Elbe (EN) 5 Ge 53.50N 9.00 E
La Belle 44 Gl 26.46N 81.26W
Labelle 44 Jb 46.17N 74.45W
La Berzosa 13 Fd 40.35N 6.40W
Labin 14 Ie 45.05N 14.08 E
Labinsk 19 Eg 44.35N 40.44 E
Labis 26 Df 2.23N 103.02 E
La Bisbal/La Bisbal d'Empordà 13 Pc 41.57N 3.03 E
La Bisbal d'Empordà/La Bisbal 13 Pc 41.57N 3.03 E
La Blanca, Laguna- 55 Bj 30.14S 60.38W
Laboe 10 Gb 54.24N 10.13 E
Laborec 10 Rh 48.31N 21.54 E
Laborie 51k Bb 13.45N 61.00W
Labota 26 Hg 2.52S 122.10 E
Labouheyre 11 Fj 44.13N 0.55W
Laboulaye 56 Hd 34.07S 63.24W
Labra, Peña- 13 Ha 43.03N 4.26W
Labrador 38 Md 55.00N 70.00W
Labrador, Coast of- 38 Me 56.00N 60.35W
Labrador Basin (EN) 3 Dd 53.00N 48.00W
Labrador City 39 Md 52.57N 66.54W
Labrador Sea 38 Nd 57.00N 53.00W
Labrang→Xiahe 27 Hd 35.18N 102.30 E
Lábrea 53 Jf 7.16S 64.46W
Labrieville 44 Ma 49.19N 69.34W
Labrit 11 Fj 44.06N 0.33W
Labuan, Pulau- 26 Ge 5.19N 115.13 E
Labudalin→Ergun Youqi 27 La 50.16N 120.09 E
Labuha 26 Ig 0.37S 127.29 E
Labuhan 26 Eh 6.22S 105.50 E
Labuhanbajo 26 Gh 8.29S 119.54 E
Labuhanbilik 26 Df 2.31N 100.10 E
Labuk, Teluk- 26 Ge 6.10N 117.50 E
La Bureba 13 Ib 42.36N 3.24W
Labutta 25 Ie 16.09N 94.46 E
Labytnangi 22 Ic 66.39N 66.21 E
Lac [3] 35 Ac 13.30N 14.20 E
Lača, Ozero- 7 Jf 61.20N 38.50 E
La Cadena 48 Ge 25.53N 104.12W
La Calamine/Kelmis 12 Hd 50.43N 6.00 E
La Calandria 55 Cj 30.48S 58.39W
Lac Allard 42 Lf 50.30N 63.30W
La Campiña 13 Hg 37.45N 4.45W
Lacanau 11 Ej 44.59N 1.05W
Lacanau, Étang de- 11 Ej 44.58N 1.07W
Lacanau-Océan 11 Ei 45.00N 1.12W
Lacantún, Río- 48 Ni 16.36N 90.39W
La-Capelle 11 Je 49.58N 3.55 E
Laćarak 15 Ce 45.00N 19.34 E
La Carlota [Arg.] 56 Hd 33.26S 63.18W
La Carlota [Phil.] 26 Hd 10.25N 122.55 E
La Carlota [Sp.] 13 Hg 37.40N 4.56W
La Carolina 13 If 38.15N 3.37W
Lacaune 11 Ik 43.43N 2.42 E
Lacaune, Monts de- 11 Ik 43.40N 2.36 E
Laccadive Islands→Lakshadweep 21 Jh 11.00N 72.00 E
La Ceiba [Hond.] 39 Kh 15.47N 86.50W
La Ceiba [Ven.] 49 Li 9.28N 71.04W
Lacepede Bay 59 Hg 36.45S 139.45 E
Lacepede Islands 59 Ec 16.50S 122.10 E
La Cerdaña/La Cerdanya 13 Nb 42.24N 1.40 E
La Cerdanya/La Cerdaña 13 Nb 42.24N 1.40 E
Lacey 46 Dc 47.07N 122.49W
Lac Giao → Buon Me Thuot 25 Lf 12.40N 108.03 E
La Chaise-Dieu 11 Ji 45.19N 3.42 E
La Charité-sur-Loire 11 Jg 47.11N 3.01 E
La Châtre 11 Hh 46.35N 1.59 E
La Chaux-de-Fonds 14 Ac 47.06N 6.50 E
Lachay, Punta- 54 Cf 11.18S 77.39W
La China, Sierra- 55 Bm 36.47S 60.34W
Lachine 44 Kc 45.26N 73.40W
Lachlan River 57 Fh 34.21S 143.57 E
La Chorrera [Col.] 54 Dd 0.45S 73.00W
La Chorrera [Pan.] 47 Ig 8.53N 79.47W
Laçi 15 Ch 41.38N 19.43 E
Lačin 16 Oj 39.39N 46.33 E
La Ciotat 11 Lk 43.10N 5.36 E
Łąck 10 Pd 52.28N 19.40 E
Lackawanna 44 Hd 42.49N 78.49W
Lac La Biche 42 Gf 54.46N 111.58W
Lac la Martre 42 Fd 63.21N 117.00W
Lac Mégantic 42 Kg 45.35N 70.53W
La Colina 55 Bm 37.20S 61.32W
La Coloma 49 Fb 22.15N 83.34W
La Colorada 48 Dc 28.41N 110.25W
Lacombe 42 Gf 52.28N 113.44W
Lacon 45 Lf 41.02N 89.24W
La Concepción [Pan.] 49 Fi 8.31N 82.37W
La Concepción [Ven.] 49 Lh 10.48N 71.46W
La Concha 48 Gg 21.46N 105.29W
Laconi 14 Dk 39.51N 9.03 E
Laconia 43 Mc 43.32N 71.29W
Laconia, Gulf of- (EN) = Lakonikós Kólpos 15 Fm 36.35N 22.40 E
La Coronilla 55 Fk 33.44S 53.31W
La Coruña 6 Fg 43.22N 8.23W
La Coruña [3] 13 Da 43.10N 8.25W
La Côte-Saint-André 11 Li 45.23N 5.15 E
La Couronne 11 Gi 45.37N 0.06 E
La Courtine-le-Trucq 11 Ii 45.42N 2.16 E
Lacq 11 Fk 43.25N 0.38W
Lacroix-sur-Meuse 12 Hf 48.58N 5.31 E
La Crosse [Ks.-U.S.] 45 Gg 38.32N 99.18W
La Crosse [Wi.-U.S.] 39 Je 43.49N 91.15W
La Cruz [Arg.] 56 Ic 29.10S 56.38W
La Cruz [C.R.] 49 Eh 11.04N 85.39W
La Cruz [Mex.] 47 Cd 23.55N 106.54W
La Cruz [Ur.] 56 Id 33.56S 56.15W
La Cruz de Río Grande 49 Eg 13.06N 84.10W
La Cruz de Taratara 49 Mh 11.03N 69.44W
La Cuesta 48 Hc 28.45N 102.25W
La Cumbre 56 Hd 30.58S 64.30W
Lac Yora 35 Cb 19.08N 20.35 E
Ladário 55 Dd 19.01S 57.35W
Ladbergen 12 Jb 52.08N 7.45 E
Lądek-Zdrój 10 Mf 50.21N 16.50 E
Ladenburg 12 Ke 49.28N 8.37 E
La Désirade 50 Fd 16.19N 61.03W
La Digue Island 37b Ca 4.21S 55.50 E
Lādik 24 Fb 40.36N 36.45 E
Ladismith 37 Cf 33.30S 21.16 E
Ladispoli 14 Gi 41.56N 12.05 E
Lado, Jabal- 35 Ed 5.06N 31.35 E
Ladoga, Lake- (EN)= Ladožkoje Ozero 5 Jc 61.00N 31.00 E
Ladong 27 Ig 24.49N 109.34 E
La Dorada 54 Db 5.22N 74.42W
Ladožkoje Ozero=Ladoga, Lake (EN) 5 Jc 61.00N 31.00 E
Ladrones, Islas- 49 Fj 7.52N 82.26W
Laduškin 8 Ij 54.35N 20.10 E
Ladva-Vetka 7 If 61.20N 34.29 E
Lady Ann Strait 42 Ja 75.45N 80.00W
Ladybrand 37 De 29.19S 27.25 E
Lady Evelyn Lake 44 Gb 47.20N 80.10W
Lady Newnes Ice Shelf 66 Kf 73.40S 167.30 E
Ladysmith [B.C.-Can.] 46 Db 48.58N 123.49W
Ladysmith [S.Afr.] 31 Jk 28.34S 29.45 E
Ladysmith [Wi.-U.S.] 43 Ib 45.28N 91.07W
Ladyžin 16 Fe 48.40N 29.13 E
Lae 58 Fe 6.43S 147.01 E
Lae Atoll 57 Hd 8.56N 166.14 E
La Eduvigis 55 Ch 26.50S 59.05W
Laem, Khao- 25 Kf 14.19N 101.11 E
Laer [Ger.] 12 Jb 52.04N 7.21 E
Laer [Ger.] 12 Kb 52.06N 8.05 E
Lærdalsøyri 7 Bf 61.06N 7.29 E
La Escala/L'Escala 13 Pb 42.07N 3.08 E
La Esmeralda 54 Ec 3.10N 65.33W
Læsø 7 Bh 57.15N 10.00 E
Læsø Rende 8 Dg 57.15N 10.45 E
La Española=Hispaniola (EN) 38 Lh 19.00N 71.00W
La Esperanza [Bol.] 54 Ff 14.34S 62.10W
La Esperanza [Hond.] 49 Cf 14.20N 88.10W
La Estrada 13 Db 42.41N 8.29W
Lafayette [Al.-U.S.] 44 Ei 32.54N 85.24W
Lafayette [In.-U.S.] 43 Jc 40.25N 86.53W
Lafayette [La.-U.S.] 39 Jf 30.14N 92.01W
La Fère 12 Fe 49.40N 3.22 E
La Ferrière-sur-Risle 12 Cf 48.59N 0.48 E
La Ferté-Bernard 11 Gf 48.11N 0.40 E
La Ferté-Frênel 12 Cf 48.50N 0.30 E
La Ferté-Macé 11 Ff 48.36N 0.22W
La Ferté-Milon 12 Fe 49.10N 3.07 E
La Ferté-Saint-Aubin 11 Hg 47.43N 1.56 E
La Ferté-sous-Jouarre 11 Jf 48.57N 3.08 E
Laffān, Ra's- 24 Nj 25.54N 51.35 E
Lafia 34 Gd 8.29N 8.31 E
Lafiagi 34 Gd 8.52N 5.15 E
La Flèche 11 Fg 47.42N 0.05W
Lafnitz 14 Kd 46.57N 16.16 E
La Foa 63b Be 21.43S 165.49 E
La Follette 44 Eg 36.23N 84.07W
La Fría 49 Ki 8.13N 72.15W
Laft 24 Pi 26.54N 55.46 E
La Fuente de San Esteban 13 Fd 40.48N 6.15W
Laga, Monti della- 14 Hh 42.45N 13.35 E
La Galite (EN)=Jālițah 30 He 37.32N 8.56 E
La Gallareta 55 Bi 29.34S 60.23W
Lagamar 55 Id 18.13S 46.48W
Lagan 8 Eh 56.33N 12.56 E
Lagan 8 Eh 56.55N 13.59 E
Lagan/Abhainn an Lagáin 9 Hg 54.37N 5.53W
Lagarina, Val- 14 Fe 45.50N 11.10 E
La Garita Mountains 45 Ch 38.00N 106.40W
Lagarto 54 Kf 10.54S 37.41W
Lagash 24 Lg 31.27N 46.13 E
Lagawe 26 Hc 16.49N 121.06 E
Lage 12 Kc 51.59N 8.48 E
Lågen 7 Cf 61.08N 10.25 E
Lagh Bogal 36 Gb 0.42N 40.55 E
Laghmān [3] 23 Lb 35.00N 70.15 E
Laghouat 31 He 33.48N 2.53 E
Laghouat [3] 32 Hc 33.30N 3.15 E
La Gloria 49 Ki 8.38N 73.48W
Lagny 11 If 48.52N 2.43 E
Lagoa 13 Dg 37.08N 8.27W
Lagôa 55 Eb 14.08S 55.20W
Lagoa da Prata 55 Je 20.01S 45.33W
Lagoa Vermelha 56 Jc 28.13S 51.32W
Lagodehi 16 Oi 41.50N 46.14 E
La Gomera 49 Bf 14.05N 91.03W
Lagonegro 14 Jj 40.07N 15.46 E
Lagonoy Gulf 26 Hd 13.35N 123.45 E
Lagoon 64n Ab 10.23S 161.05W
Lagos 13 Dg 37.06N 8.40W
Lagos 31 Hh 6.27N 3.23 E
Lágos 15 Ih 41.01N 25.07 E
Lagos [2] 34 Fd 6.30N 3.30 E
Lagos, Baia de- 13 Dg 37.06N 8.39W
Lagosa 36 Ed 5.57S 29.53 E
Lagos de Moreno 47 Dd 21.21N 101.55W
La Grand-Combe 11 Kj 44.13N 4.02 E
La Grande 43 Db 45.20N 118.05W
La Grande Fosse 9 Kl 49.40N 3.00W
La Grande-Motte 11 Kk 43.34N 4.07 E
La Grande Rivière 38 Ld 53.50N 79.00W
La Grande Trench (EN)= Hurd Deep 9 Kl 49.40N 3.00W
La Grange 44 Ef 38.24N 85.23W
Lagrange 44 Ee 41.39N 85.25W
La Grange [Ga.-U.S.] 43 Je 33.02N 85.02W
La Grange [Tx.-U.S.] 45 Hl 29.54N 96.52W
La Gran Sabana 54 Fb 5.30N 61.30W
La Grita 54 Db 8.08N 71.59W
Lagskär 8 He 59.50N 20.00 E
La Guaira 53 Jd 10.36N 66.56W
La Guajira [2] 54 Da 11.30N 72.30W
Lagua Lichan, Puntan- 64b Ba 15.16N 145.50 E
Laguardia 13 Jb 42.33N 2.35W
La Guardia [Sp.] 13 Dc 41.54N 8.53W
La Guardia [Sp.] 13 Ie 39.47N 3.29W
La Guasima 48 Kg 21.06N 97.49W
La Guerche-sur-l'Aubois 11 Ih 46.57N 2.57 E
Laguiole 11 Ij 44.41N 2.51 E
Laguna 56 Kc 28.29S 48.47W
Laguna Alsina 55 Am 36.49S 62.13W
Laguna Beach 46 Gj 33.33N 117.51W
Laguna Blanca 55 Cg 25.08S 58.15W
Laguna de Bay 26 Hd 14.23N 121.15 E
Laguna Limpia 55 Ch 26.29S 59.41W
Laguna Mountains 46 Gj 32.55N 116.25W
Laguna Paiva 56 Hd 31.19S 60.39W
Laguna Superior 47 Fe 16.20N 94.25W
Laguna Veneta 14 Ge 45.25N 12.20 E
Laguna Yema 55 Bg 24.15S 61.15W
Lagunillas [Bol.] 54 Fg 19.38S 63.43W
Lagunillas [Mex.] 48 Ii 17.50N 101.44W
Lagunillas [Ven.] 49 Lh 10.08N 71.16W
Lagunillas [Ven.] 49 Li 8.31N 71.24W
Laha 27 Lb 48.13N 124.36 E
La Habana [3] 49 Fb 22.45N 82.10W
La Habana=Havana (EN) 39 Kg 23.08N 82.22W
Lahad Datu 26 Ge 5.02N 118.19 E
Laham 34 Fc 14.54N 4.25 E
Lahat 26 Dg 3.48S 103.32 E
Lahdenpohja 7 Hf 61.33N 30.13 E
Lahewa 26 Cf 1.24N 97.11 E
Lahij 23 Fg 13.04N 44.53 E
Lāhijān 23 Hb 37.12N 50.01 E
Lahn 10 Df 50.18N 7.37 E
Lahnstein 12 Jd 50.20N 7.29 E
Laholm 7 Ch 56.31N 13.02 E
Laholmsbukten 8 Eh 56.35N 12.50 E
Lahore 22 Jf 31.35N 74.18 E
Lahr 10 Dh 48.20N 7.52 E
Lahti 6 Ic 60.58N 25.40 E
Laï 31 Ih 9.24N 16.18 E
Laiagam 60 Ci 5.31S 143.39 E
Lai'an 28 Eh 32.28N 118.26 E
Lai Chau 25 Kd 22.02N 103.10 E
Laich o'Moray 9 Jd 57.40N 3.30W
Laie 65a Db 21.39N 157.56W
Laifeng 27 If 29.31N 109.23 E
Laighean/Leinster 9 Gh 53.00N 7.00W
L'Aigle 11 Gf 48.45N 0.38 E
Laignes 11 Kg 47.50N 4.22 E
Laihia 7 Fe 62.58N 22.01 E
Lainioälven 7 Fc 67.22N 22.39 E
Lairg 9 Ic 58.01N 4.25W
Lairi 35 Bc 10.49N 17.06 E
Lairi, Batha de- 35 Bc 12.28N 16.45 E
Lais 26 Dg 3.32S 102.03 E
La Isabela 49 Gb 22.57N 80.01W
Laisamis 36 Gb 1.36N 37.48 E
Laiševo 7 Li 55.26N 49.32 E
Laishui 28 Ce 39.23N 115.42 E
Laisvall 7 Dc 66.08N 17.10 E
Laitila 7 Ef 60.53N 21.41 E
Laiwu 28 Df 36.12N 117.40 E
Laiwui 26 Ig 1.22S 127.40 E
Laixi (Shuiji) 28 Ff 36.52N 120.31 E
Laiyang 27 Ld 36.59N 120.39 E
Laiyuan 27 Jd 39.19N 114.43 E
Laizhou Wan 28 Ef 37.30N 119.30 E
Laja 56 Fe 37.16S 72.42W
Laja 17 Hc 66.20N 56.16 E
La Jara 13 He 39.40N 4.55W
Lajeado 55 Gi 29.27S 51.58W
Lajeado, Serra do- 55 Hd 19.08S 49.56W
Lājerd 24 Oe 35.24N 53.04 E
Lajes [Braz.] 54 Ke 5.41S 36.14W
Lajes [Braz.] 53 Kh 27.48S 50.19W
Lajes do Pico 32 Bb 38.23N 28.16W
Lajosmizse 10 Pi 47.01N 19.33 E
La Junta [Co.-U.S.] 43 Gd 37.59N 103.33W
La Junta [Mex.] 48 Fc 28.28N 107.20W
Lak Bor 36 Hb 1.18N 40.40 E
Lake Cargelligo 59 Jf 33.18S 146.23 E
Lake Charles 39 Jf 30.12N 93.12W
Lake City 43 Ke 30.12N 82.38W
Lake District 9 Jg 54.30N 3.10W
Lake Fork Creek 46 Jf 40.13N 110.07W
Lake Geneva 45 Le 42.36N 88.26W
Lake George 44 Kd 43.25N 73.45W
Lake Grace 59 Df 33.06S 118.28 E
Lake Harbour 42 Kd 62.51N 69.53W
Lake Havasu City 46 Hi 34.27N 114.22W
Lake Itasca 45 Ic 46.51N 95.13W
Lake Jackson 45 Il 29.02N 95.27W
Lake King 59 Df 33.05S 119.40 E
Lakeland 43 Kf 28.03N 81.57W
Lake Louise 46 Ga 51.26N 116.11W
Lakemba 63d Cc 18.13S 178.47W
Lakemba Passage 63d Cb 17.53S 178.32W
Lake Mills 45 Je 43.25N 93.32W
Lake Minchumina 40 Ia 63.53N 152.19W
Lake Murray 60 Ci 6.54S 141.28 E
Lake Oswego 46 Dd 45.26N 122.39W
Lake Placid 44 Kc 44.18N 73.59W
Lake Providence 45 Kj 32.48N 91.11W
Lake Pukaki 62 Df 44.11S 170.08 E
Lake Range 46 Ff 40.15N 119.25W
Lake River 42 Jf 54.28N 82.30W
Lakes Entrance 59 Jg 37.53S 147.59 E
Lakeside 46 If 41.13N 112.57W
Lake Tekapo 62 Df 44.00S 170.29 E
Lakeview 43 Cc 42.11N 120.21W
Lakeville 45 Jd 44.39N 93.14W
Lake Wales 44 Gl 27.55N 81.35W
Lakewood [Co.-U.S.] 45 Dg 39.44N 105.06W
Lakewood [Oh.-U.S.] 44 Ge 41.29N 81.50W
Lake Worth 44 Gl 26.37N 80.03W
Lakhdar, Chergui Kef- 13 Pi 35.57N 3.16 E
Lakhdaria 13 Ph 36.34N 3.35 E
Lāki 15 Hh 41.50N 24.50 E
Lakin 45 Fh 37.58N 101.15W
Lakinsk 7 Jh 56.04N 39.58 E
Lákmos Óros 15 Ej 39.40N 21.07 E
Lakon, Ile- 57 Hf 14.17S 167.30 E
Lakonikós Kólpos = Laconia, Gulf of- (EN) 15 Fm 36.35N 22.40 E
Lakota [3] 34 Dd 5.53N 5.42W
Lakota [I.C.] 34 Dd 5.51N 5.41W
Lakota [N.D.-U.S.] 45 Gb 48.02N 98.21W
Laksefjorden 7 Ga 70.58N 27.00 E
Lakselv 7 Fa 70.03N 25.01 E
Lakshadweep [3] 25 Ef 11.00N 72.00 E
La Laguna 55 Bb 14.30S 61.06W
Lalanna 37 Hd 23.28S 45.05 E
Lalapaşa 15 Jh 41.50N 26.44 E
Lāleh Zār, Kūh-e- 21 Hg 29.24N 56.46 E
La Leonesa 55 Ch 27.03S 58.43W
Lālī 24 Mf 32.21N 49.06 E
Lalibela 35 Fc 12.00N 39.04 E
La Libertad [2] 54 Ce 8.00S 78.30W
La Libertad [ElSal.] 47 Gf 13.29N 89.16W
La Libertad [Guat.] 49 Be 16.47N 90.07W
La Libertad [Guat.] 49 Bf 15.30N 91.50W
La Libertad [Hond.] 49 Df 14.43N 87.36W
La Ligua 56 Fd 32.27S 71.14W
Lalin 13 Db 42.39N 8.07W
La Linea 13 Gh 36.10N 5.19W
Lalin He 28 Hb 45.28N 125.43 E
Lalitpur 25 Fd 24.41N 78.25 E
Lalla Khedidja 13 Qh 36.27N 4.14 E
Lālmanir Hāt 25 Hc 25.54N 89.27 E
La Loche 42 Ge 56.29N 109.27W
La Loupe 11 Hf 48.28N 1.01 E
La Louvière 11 Kd 50.29N 4.11 E
L'Alpe-d'Huez 11 Mi 45.06N 6.04 E
La Lucila 55 Bj 30.25S 61.01W
Lalzit, Gjiri i- 15 Ch 41.31N 19.29 E
La Machine 11 Jh 46.53N 3.28 E
La Maddalena 14 Di 41.13N 9.24 E
La Maiella 5 Hg 42.05N 14.07 E
La Maladeta/Maladitos, Montes- 13 Mb 42.40N 0.50 E
La Malbaie 42 Kg 47.39N 70.10W
La Mancha 5 Fh 39.05N 3.00W
La Manche 5 Fe 50.20N 1.00W
Lamap 61 Cc 16.26S 167.43 E
Lamar 43 Gd 38.05N 102.37W
La Maragateria 13 Fb 42.25N 6.10W
La Marina 13 Lf 38.35N 0.05W
La Marmora 14 Dk 39.59N 9.20 E
La Marque 45 Il 29.22N 94.58W
Lamas 54 Ce 6.25S 76.35W
Lamastre 11 Kj 44.59N 4.35 E
Lamawan 28 Ad 40.05N 111.25 E
Lambach 14 Hb 48.05N 13.53 E
Lamballe 11 Df 48.28N 2.31W
Lambar, Rio- 55 Jd 19.30S 45.00W
Lambaréné 31 Ii 0.42S 10.13 E
Lambari 55 Je 21.58S 45.21W
Lambasa 61 Ec 16.26S 179.24 E
Lambay/Reachrainn 9 Gh 53.29N 6.01W
Lambayeque [2] 54 Ce 6.20S 80.00W
Lambayeque 54 Ce 6.42S 79.55W
Lambert Glacier 66 Ff 71.00S 70.00 E
Lambert Land 41 Jc 79.10N 21.00W
Lamberts Bay 31 Il 32.05S 18.17 E
Lambro 14 De 45.08N 9.32 E
Lambsheim 12 Ke 49.31N 8.17 E
Lambton, Cape- 42 Fb 71.04N 123.08W
Lamé 35 Ad 9.15N 14.32 E
Lame Deer 46 Ld 45.37N 106.40W
Lamego 13 Ec 41.06N 7.49W
Lamentin 51e Ab 16.16N 61.38W
La Mesa 46 Gj 32.46N 117.01W
Lamesa 43 Ge 32.44N 101.57W
La Meta 14 Hj 41.41N 13.56 E
Lamezia Terme 14 Kl 38.59N 16.17 E
Lamia 15 Fk 38.54N 22.26 E
Lamina 55 De 20.34S 56.14W
Lamlam, Mount- 64c Bb 13.20N 144.40 E
Lammermuir Hills 9 Kf 55.52N 2.40W
Lammhult 8 Fg 57.10N 14.35 E
Lammi 7 Ff 61.05N 25.01 E
Lamoil 64d Ba 7.39N 151.41 E
Lamon Bay 21 Oh 14.25N 122.00 E
Lamone 14 Gf 44.29N 12.08 E
Lamoni 45 Jf 40.37N 93.56W
Lamont 44 Fj 30.21N 83.50W
La Montaña 52 If 10.00S 72.50W
La Moraña 13 Hd 40.45N 4.55W
La Mosquitia 49 Ef 15.00N 84.20W
La Mothe-Achard 11 Eh 46.37N 1.40W
Lamotrek Atoll 57 Fd 7.30N 146.20 E

Index Symbols

[1] Independent Nation
[2] State, Region
[3] District, County
[4] Municipality
[5] Colony, Dependency
Continent
Physical Region
Historical or Cultural Region
Mount, Mountain
Volcano
Hill
Mountains, Mountain Range
Hills, Escarpment
Plateau, Upland
Pass, Gap
Plain, Lowland
Delta
Salt Flat
Valley, Canyon
Crater, Cave
Karst Features
Depression
Polder
Desert, Dunes
Forest, Woods
Heath, Steppe
Oasis
Cape, Point
Coast, Beach
Cliff
Peninsula
Isthmus
Sandbank
Island
Atoll
Rock, Reef
Islands, Archipelago
Rocks, Reefs
Coral Reef
Well, Spring
Geyser
River, Stream
Waterfall Rapids
River Mouth, Estuary
Lake
Salt Lake
Intermittent Lake
Reservoir
Swamp, Pond
Canal
Glacier
Ice Shelf, Pack Ice
Ocean
Sea
Gulf, Bay
Strait, Fjord
Lagoon
Bank
Seamount
Tablemount
Ridge
Shelf
Basin
Escarpment, Sea Scarp
Fracture
Trench, Abyss
National Park, Reserve
Point of Interest
Recreation Site
Cave, Cavern
Historic Site
Ruins
Wall, Walls
Church, Abbey
Temple
Scientific Station
Airport
Port
Lighthouse
Mine
Tunnel
Dam, Bridge

Lamotte-Beuvron 11 Ig 47.36N 2.01 E
La Moure 45 Gc 46.21N 98.18W
Lampang 25 Je 18.16N 99.34 E
Lampasas 45 Gk 31.03N 98.12W
Lampazos de Naranjo 48 Id 27.01N 100.31W
Lampedusa 14 Go 35.30N 12.35 E
Lampertheim 10 Eg 49.36N 8.28 E
Lampeter 9 Ii 52.07N 4.05W
Lamphun 25 Je 18.35N 99.00 E
Lampione 14 Go 35.35N 12.20 E
Lampung [3] 26 Dg 5.00S 105.00 E
Lamu 31 Li 2.16S 40.54 E
Lamud 54 Ce 6.09S 77.55W
La Mure 11 Lj 44.54N 5.47 E
Lan 16 Ec 52.09N 27.18 E
Lana 14 Fd 46.37N 11.09 E
Lana, Rio de la- 48 Li 17.49N 95.09W
Lanai City 65a Ec 20.50N 156.55W
Lanaihale 65a Ec 20.49N 156.52W
Lanai Island 57 Lb 20.50N 156.55W
Lanaken 12 Hd 50.53N 5.39 E
Lanark 9 Jf 55.41N 3.48W
Lanbi Kyun 25 Jf 10.50N 98.15 E
Lancang (Menglangba) 27 Gg 22.37N 99.57 E
Lancang Jiang = Mekong (EN) 21 Mh 10.15N 105.55 E
Lancashire [3] 9 Kh 53.55N 2.40W
Lancashire Plain 9 Kh 53.40N 2.45W
Lancaster 9 Kh 53.45N 2.50W
Lancaster [Ca.-U.S.] 43 De 34.42N 118.08W
Lancaster [Eng.-U.K.] 9 Kg 54.03N 2.48W
Lancaster [Mo.-U.S.] 45 Jf 40.31N 92.32W
Lancaster [N.H.-U.S.] 44 Lc 44.29N 71.34W
Lancaster [Oh.-U.S.] 44 Ff 39.43N 82.37W
Lancaster [Ont.-Can.] 44 Jc 45.12N 74.30W
Lancaster [Pa.-U.S.] 43 Lc 40.01N 76.19W
Lancaster [S.C.-U.S.] 44 Gh 34.43N 80.47W
Lancaster Sound 38 Kb 74.13N 84.00W
Lançeiro 55 Fe 20.59S 53.43W
Lancelin 59 Df 31.01S 115.19 E
Lanciano 14 Ih 42.14N 14.23 E
Lančin 15 Ha 48.31N 24.49 E
Lancun 28 Ff 36.25N 120.11 E
Łańcut 10 Sf 50.05N 22.13 E
Land 8 Cd 60.45N 10.00 E
Låndana 36 Bd 5.15S 12.10 E
Landau an der Isar 10 Ih 48.41N 12.41 E
Landau in der Pfalz 10 Eg 49.12N 8.07 E
Land Bay 66 Mf 75.25S 141.45W
Landeck 14 Ec 47.08N 10.34 E
Landen 12 Hd 50.45N 5.05 E
Lander 43 Fc 42.50N 108.44W
Landerneau 11 Bf 48.27N 4.15W
Lander River 59 Gd 20.25S 132.00 E
Landeryd 8 Eg 57.05N 13.16 E
Landes 11 Fj 44.15N 1.00W
Landes [3] 11 Fj 44.00N 0.50W
Landesbergen 12 Lb 52.34N 9.08 E
Landeta 55 Ak 32.01S 62.04W
Landete 13 Ke 39.54N 1.22W
Landfallis 25 If 13.40N 93.02 E
Land Glacier 66 Mf 75.40S 141.45W
Landi Kotal 25 Eb 34.06N 71.09 E
Landless Corner 36 Ee 14.53S 28.04 E
Landrecies 12 Fd 50.08N 3.42 E
Landsberg am Lech 10 Gh 48.03N 10.52 E
Landsbro 8 Fg 57.22N 14.54 E
Land's End 5 Fe 50.03N 5.44W
Lands End 42 Fa 76.25N 122.45W
Landshut 10 Ih 48.32N 12.09 E
Landskrona 8 Ei 55.52N 12.50 E
Landsort 8 Gf 58.45N 17.50 E
Landsortsdjupet 8 Hf 58.40N 18.30 E
Landstuhl 12 Je 49.25N 7.34 E
Landusky 46 Kc 47.54N 108.37W
La Neuve-Lyre 12 Cf 48.54N 0.45 E
Lanfeng → Lankao 28 Cg 34.49N 114.48 E
Lang 46 Mb 49.56N 104.23W
La'nga Co 27 De 30.41N 81.17 E
Langadhás 15 Gi 40.45N 23.04 E
Langádhia 15 Fl 37.39N 22.03 E
Långan 7 De 63.19N 14.44 E
Langano, Lake- 35 Fd 7.36N 38.43 E
Langao 27 Ie 32.20N 108.53 E
Langara 26 Hg 4.02S 123.00 E
Langarfoss 7a Cb 65.35N 14.15W
Langasian 26 Ie 8.16N 125.39 E
Langdon 45 Gb 48.46N 98.22W
Langeac 11 Ji 45.06N 3.29 E
Langeais 11 Gg 47.20N 0.24 E
Langeb 35 Fb 17.46N 36.41 E
Langebaan 37 Bf 33.06S 18.02 E
Langeberg 37 Cf 33.56S 20.45 E
Langedijk 12 Gb 52.42N 4.48 E
Langeland 7 Ci 55.00N 10.50 E
Langelands Bælt 8 Dj 54.50N 10.55 E
Längelmävesi 8 Kc 61.30N 24.20 E
Langen 12 Ke 49.59N 8.40 E
Langenberg 12 Kc 51.17N 8.34 E
Langenburg 45 Fa 50.50N 101.43W
Langenfeld (Rheinland) 12 Ic 51.06N 6.57 E
Langenhagen 10 Fd 52.27N 9.45 E
Langenselbold 12 Ld 50.11N 9.02 E
Langenthal 14 Bc 47.13N 7.49 E
Langeoog 10 Dc 53.46N 7.32 E
Langeri 20 Jf 50.08N 143.20 E
Langesund 8 Ce 59.00N 9.45 E
Langesundsfjorden 8 Cf 59.00N 9.48 E
Langevåg 8 Bb 62.27N 6.12 E
Langfang → Anci 27 Kd 39.29N 116.40 E
Långfjället 8 Eb 62.10N 12.20 E
Langfjorden 8 Bb 62.45N 7.30 E
Langhe 14 Bf 44.30N 8.00 E
Langholm 9 Kf 55.09N 3.00W
Langjökull 5 Ec 64.39N 20.00W
Langkawi, Pulau- 26 Ce 6.22N 99.48 E
Langkon 26 Ge 6.32N 116.42 E
Langlade 44 Ja 48.12N 75.57W
Langnau im Emmental 14 Bd 46.56N 7.46 E
Langogne 11 Jj 44.43N 3.51 E
Langon 11 Fj 44.33N 0.15W
Langorüd 24 Md 37.11N 50.10 E
Langøya 7 Db 68.44N 14.50 E
Langreo 13 Ga 43.18N 5.41W
Langres 11 Lg 47.52N 5.20 E
Langres, Plateau de- 5 Gf 47.41N 5.03 E
Langrune-sur-Mer 12 Be 49.19N 0.22W
Langsa 22 Li 4.28N 97.58 E
Långsele 8 Ga 63.11N 17.04 E
Långshyttan 8 Gd 60.27N 16.01 E
Lang Son 25 Ld 21.50N 106.44 E
Lang Suan 25 Jg 9.55N 99.07 E
Languedoc 5 Gg 44.00N 4.00 E
Languedoc 11 Jj 44.00N 4.00 E
Langueyú, Arroyo- 55 Cm 36.39S 58.27W
Langwedel 12 Lb 52.58N 9.13 E
Langxi 28 Ei 31.08N 119.11 E
Langzhong 27 Ie 31.40N 106.04 E
Lan Hsu 27 Lg 22.00N 121.30 E
Laniel 44 Hb 47.06N 79.15W
Lanin, Volcán- 52 Ii 39.38S 71.30W
Lankao 27 Cd 35.12N 79.50 E
Lankao (Lanfeng) 27 Kg 21.00N 116.00 E
Lankao (Lanfeng) 28 Cg 34.49N 114.48 E
Länkipohja 8 Kc 61.44N 24.48 E
Lannemezan 11 Gk 43.08N 0.23 E
Lannemezan, Plateau de- 11 Gk 43.09N 0.27 E
Lannion 11 Cf 48.44N 3.28W
Lannion, Baie de- 11 Cf 48.43N 3.34W
La Noria 56 Gb 20.23S 69.53W
Lansdowne House 42 If 52.13N 87.53W
L'Anse 44 Cb 46.45N 88.27W
Lansing [Ia.-U.S.] 45 Ke 43.22N 91.13W
Lansing [Mi.-U.S.] 39 Ke 42.43N 84.34W
Lansjärv 7 Fc 66.39N 22.12 E
Łańskie, Jezioro- 10 Qc 53.33N 20.30 E
Lantar 20 Ie 56.05N 137.35 E
Lanta Yai, Ko- 25 Jg 7.35N 99.03 E
Lanteri 55 Ci 28.50S 59.39W
Lanterne 11 Mg 47.44N 6.03 E
Lanús 55 Cl 34.43S 58.24W
Lanusei 14 Dk 39.53N 9.32 E
Lanvaux, Landes de- 11 Dg 47.47N 2.36W
Lanxi [China] 28 Ej 29.13N 119.28 E
Lanxi [China] 28 Ha 46.15N 126.16 E
Lanxian (Dongcun) 28 Ae 38.17N 111.38 E
Lanyi He 28 Ae 38.40N 110.53 E
Lanzarote 30 Ff 29.00N 13.40W
Lanzhou 22 Mf 36.03N 103.41 E
Lanzo Torinese 14 Be 45.16N 7.28 E
Lao 14 Jk 39.47N 15.48 E
Laoag 22 Oh 18.12N 120.36 E
Laoang 26 Id 12.34N 125.00 E
Lao Cai 22 Mg 22.30N 103.57 E
Laocheng 28 Hc 42.37N 124.04 E
Laoha He 27 Lc 43.24N 120.39 E
Lao He 28 Cj 29.02N 115.47 E
Laohuanghe Kou 28 Ef 37.39N 119.02 E
Laois [2] 9 Fi 53.00N 7.30W
Laojunmiao → Yumen 22 Lf 39.50N 97.44 E
Laojun Shan 27 Je 33.45N 111.38 E
Lao Ling 28 Id 41.24N 126.10 E
Laon 11 Je 49.34N 3.37 E
Laona 45 Ld 45.34N 88.40W
Laonnois 12 Fe 49.35N 3.40 E
La Orchila, Isla- 54 Ea 11.48N 66.10W
La Oroya 53 Ig 11.32S 75.57W
Laos [1] 22 Mh 18.00N 105.00 E
Laoshan (Licun) 28 Ff 36.10N 120.25 E
Laotougou 28 Jc 42.54N 129.09 E
Laou 13 Gi 35.26N 5.05W
Laoye Ling 28 Kb 44.50N 130.10 E
Lapa 56 Kc 25.45S 49.42W
Lapai 34 Gd 9.03N 6.43 E
Lapalisse 11 Jh 46.15N 3.38 E
La Palma 30 Ff 28.40N 17.52W
La Palma [ElSal.] 49 Cf 14.19N 89.11W
La Palma [Pan.] 47 Ig 8.25N 78.09W
La Palma del Condado 13 Fg 37.23N 6.33W
La Paloma 55 El 34.40S 54.10W
La Pampa [2] 56 Ge 37.00S 66.00W
La Panne/De Panne 12 Ec 51.06N 2.35 E
La Paragua 54 Fb 6.50N 63.20W
La Partida, Isla- 48 De 24.30N 110.25W
La Paz [3] 49 Df 14.15N 87.50W
La Paz [2] 54 Eg 15.00S 68.00W
La Paz [Arg.] 56 Id 30.45S 59.39W
La Paz [Arg.] 56 Gd 33.28S 67.33W
La Paz [Bol.] 53 Jg 16.30S 68.09W
La Paz [Col.] 49 Kh 10.23N 73.10W
La Paz [Hond.] 47 Gf 14.16N 87.40W
La Paz [Mex.] 39 Hg 24.10N 110.18W
La Paz [Ur.] 55 Dl 34.46S 56.13W
La Paz [Ven.] 49 Lh 10.41N 72.00W
La Paz, Bahia de- 47 Bd 24.09N 110.25W
La Paz, Llano de- 48 De 24.00N 110.30W
La Paz Centro 49 Dg 12.20N 86.41W
La Pedrera 54 Ed 1.18S 69.40W
Lapeer 44 Fd 43.03N 83.19W
La Pelada 55 Bj 30.52S 60.59W
La Pérouse, Bahia- 65d Bb 27.04S 109.18W
La Perouse Strait (EN) = Laperuza, Proliv- 21 Qe 45.30N 142.00 E
La Perouse Strait (EN) = Sōya-Kaikyō 21 Qe 45.30N 142.00 E
Laperuza, Proliv- = La Perouse Strait (EN) 21 Qe 45.30N 142.00 E
La Pesca 47 Ed 23.47N 97.47W
La Petite Pierre 12 Jf 48.52N 7.19 E
La Picasa, Laguna- 55 Al 34.20S 62.14W
La Piedad Cavadas 48 Hg 20.21N 102.00W
La Pine 46 Ee 43.40N 121.30W
Lapinjärvi/Lappträsk 8 Ld 60.36N 26.09 E
Lapinlahti 7 Ge 63.22N 27.30 E
La Plaine 51g Bb 15.20N 61.15W
La Plana 13 Ld 40.00N 0.05W
Lapland (EN) = Lappi 5 Ib 66.50N 22.00 E
Lapland (EN) = Lappland 5 Ib 66.50N 22.00 E
La Plant 45 Fd 45.10N 100.38W
La Plata 53 Ki 34.55S 57.57W
La Pobla de Lillet 13 Nb 42.15N 1.59 E
La Pobla de Segur/Pobla de Segur 13 Mb 42.15N 0.58 E
La Pocatièr 44 Lb 47.21N 70.02W
La Porte 44 De 41.36N 86.43W
Lapovo 15 Ee 44.11N 21.06 E
Lappajärvi 7 Fe 63.08N 23.40 E
Lappeenranta/Villmanstrand 6 Ic 61.04N 28.11 E
Lappfjärd/Lapväärtti 8 Ib 62.15N 21.32 E
Lappi [2] 7 Gc 67.40N 26.30 E
Lappi 8 Ic 61.06N 21.50 E
Lappi = Lapland (EN) 5 Ib 66.50N 22.00 E
Lappo/Lapua 7 Fe 62.57N 23.00 E
Lappträsk/Lapinjärvi 8 Ld 60.36N 26.09 E
Lapri 20 He 55.45N 124.59 E
Laprida 56 He 37.33S 60.49W
Lâpseki 24 Bb 40.20N 26.31 E
Lapta 24 Ee 35.20N 33.10 E
Laptev Sea (EN) = Laptevyh, More- 67 Fd 76.00N 126.00 E
Laptevyh, More- = Laptev Sea (EN) 67 Fd 76.00N 126.00 E
Lapua/Lappo 7 Fe 62.57N 23.00 E
La Puebla 13 Pe 39.46N 3.01 E
La Puebla de Cazalla 13 Gg 37.14N 5.19W
Lapuna 55 Ba 13.19S 60.28W
La Puntilla 52 Hf 2.11S 81.01W
La Purisima 48 Cd 26.10N 112.04W
Lâpuş 15 Hb 47.30N 24.01 E
Lâpuş 15 Gb 47.39N 23.24 E
La Push 46 Cc 47.55N 124.38W
Lapväärtti/Lappfjärd 8 Ib 62.15N 21.32 E
Łapy 10 Sd 53.00N 22.53 E
Laqiyat al Arba'in 35 Da 20.03N 28.02 E
La Quemada 48 Hf 22.27N 102.45W
La Quiaca 56 Gb 22.06S 65.37W
L'Aquila 6 Hg 42.22N 13.22 E
Lar 23 Hd 27.41N 54.17 E
Lara [2] 54 Ea 10.10N 69.50W
Larache 32 Fb 35.12N 6.09W
Laragne-Montéglin 11 Lj 44.19N 5.49 E
Lārak 23 Id 26.52N 56.22 E
La Rambla 13 Hg 37.36N 4.44W
Laramie 39 Ie 41.19N 105.35W
Laramie Mountains 43 Fc 42.00N 105.40W
Laramie Peak 46 Me 42.17N 105.27W
Laramie River 46 Me 42.12N 104.32W
Laranjal, Rio- 55 Ff 23.12S 53.45W
Laranjeiras do Sul 56 Jc 25.25S 52.25W
Larantuka 26 Hh 8.21S 122.59 E
Larat 26 Jh 7.09S 131.45 E
Larat, Pulau- 26 Jh 7.10S 131.50 E
La Raya 49 Ji 8.20N 74.34W
L'Arba 13 Ph 36.34N 3.09 E
L'Arbaa-Naït-Irathen 13 Qh 36.38N 4.12 E
L'Arbresle 11 Ki 45.50N 4.37 E
Lärbro 7 Eh 57.47N 18.47 E
Larche, Col de- 11 Mj 44.25N 6.53 E
Larde 37 Fc 16.28S 39.43 E
Larderello 14 Eg 43.14N 10.53 E
La Réale 11 Fj 44.35N 0.02W
Laredo [Sp.] 13 Ia 43.24N 3.25W
Laredo [Tx.-U.S.] 39 Jg 27.31N 99.30W
Laren 12 Hb 52.16N 5.16 E
Larestān 21 Hg 27.00N 55.30 E
Larestan 24 Pi 27.00N 55.30 E
Large Island 51p Cb 12.24N 61.30W
Largentière 11 Kj 44.32N 4.18 E
L'Argentière-la-Bessée 11 Mj 44.47N 6.33 E
Largo, Cayo- 49 Gc 21.38N 81.28W
Largs 9 If 55.48N 4.52W
La Ribagorça/Ribagorza 13 Mb 42.15N 0.30 E
La Ribera 13 Kb 42.30N 2.00W
Larimore 45 Hc 47.54N 97.38W
Larino 14 Ii 41.48N 14.54 E
La Rioja [2] 56 Gc 30.00S 67.30W
La Rioja 13 Jb 42.20N 2.20W
La Rioja 53 Jh 29.25S 66.50W
Lárisa 6 Ih 39.38N 22.25 E
La Rivière-Thibouville, Nassandres- 12 Ce 49.07N 0.44 E
Lärkäna 25 Dc 27.33N 68.13 E
Larmor-Plage 11 Cg 47.42N 3.23W
Larnaka/Lárnax 23 Dc 34.55N 33.38 E
Lárnax/Larnaka 23 Dc 34.55N 33.38 E
Larne/Latharna 9 Hg 54.51N 5.49W
Larned 45 Gg 38.11N 99.06W
La Robla 13 Gb 42.48N 5.37W
La Roche 63b De 21.28S 168.02 E
La Roche-en-Ardenne 11 Ld 50.11N 5.35 E
La Rochefoucauld 11 Gi 45.44N 0.23 E
La Roche-Guyon 12 De 49.05N 1.38 E
La Rochelle 6 Ff 46.10N 1.09W
La Roche-sur-Yon 11 Eh 46.40N 1.26W
La Roda 13 Je 39.13N 2.09W
La Romana 47 Ke 18.25N 68.58W
La Ronge 42 Ge 55.06N 105.17W
La Ronge, Lac- 38 Id 55.05N 104.59W
Larose 45 Kl 29.35N 90.23W
La Rosita 48 Ic 28.24N 101.43W
Larouco 13 Ec 41.56N 7.40W
Larreynaga 49 Dg 12.40N 86.34W
Larrey Point 59 Dc 20.00S 119.10 E
Larrimah 58 Ef 15.35S 133.12 E
Larsa 24 Kg 31.16N 45.49 E
Lars Christensen Kyst 66 Fe 69.30S 68.00 E
Larsen, Mount- 66 Kf 74.51S 162.12 E
Larsen Ice Shelf 66 Qe 68.30S 62.30W
Lartijas Padomju Socialistiska Respublika/Latvijskaja SSR [2] 19 Cd 57.00N 25.00 E
La Rumorosa 48 Aa 32.34N 116.06W
Laruns 11 Fk 43.00N 0.25W
Larvik 7 Bg 59.04N 10.00 E
La Sabana [Arg.] 55 Ch 27.52S 59.57W
La Sabana [Col.] 54 Ec 2.20N 68.32W
Las Adjuntas, Presa de- 48 Jf 23.55N 98.45W
La Sagra 13 Id 40.05N 4.00W
La Sagra 13 Jg 37.57N 2.34W
La Salle 45 Lf 41.20N 89.06W
La Salle, Pic- 47 Je 18.22N 71.59W
La Sal Mountains 46 Kg 38.30N 109.10W
Las Alpujarras 13 Ih 36.50N 3.25W
La Sanabria 13 Fb 42.08N 6.30W
Las Animas 45 Eg 38.04N 103.13W
Lās 'ānōd 35 Hd 8.26N 47.24 E
La Sarre 42 Jg 48.48N 79.12W
Las Aves, Islas- 54 Ea 11.58N 67.33W
Las Avispas 55 Bi 29.53S 61.18W
Las Bardenas 13 Kb 42.10N 1.25W
Las Bonitas 50 Di 7.52N 65.40W
Las Breñas 56 Hc 27.05S 61.05W
Las Cabezas de San Juan 13 Gh 36.59N 5.56W
Lascahobas 49 Ld 18.50N 71.56W
Lascano 55 Ek 33.40S 54.12W
Las Casitas, Cerro- 47 Cd 23.31N 109.53W
Lascaux, Grotte de- 11 Hi 45.03N 1.11 E
Las Cejas 56 Hc 26.53S 64.44W
Las Chilcas, Arroyo- 55 Cm 37.16S 58.26W
Las Choapas 47 Fe 17.55N 94.05W
Las Cinco Villas 13 Kb 42.05N 1.07W
Las Cruces 43 Fe 32.23N 106.29W
Läsdäred 35 Hc 10.10N 46.01 E
Läs Dawa'o 35 Hc 10.22N 49.03 E
La Segarra 13 Nc 41.30N 1.10 E
La Selva 13 Oc 41.40N 2.50 E
La Serena 13 Gf 38.45N 5.30W
La Serena 53 Ih 29.54S 71.16W
La Seu d'Urgell/Seo de Urgel 13 Nb 42.21N 1.28 E
La-Seyne-sur-Mer 11 Lk 43.06N 5.53 E
Las Flores 56 Ie 36.03S 59.07W
Lāsh-e Joveyn 23 Jc 31.43N 61.37 E
Las Heras 56 Gd 32.51S 68.49W
Lashkar Gāh 22 If 31.35N 64.21 E
Las Hurdes 13 Fd 40.20N 6.20W
La Sila 5 Hh 39.15N 16.30 E
Łasin 10 Pc 53.32N 19.05 E
Łask 10 Pe 51.36N 19.07 E
Las Lajas 56 Fe 38.31S 70.22W
Las Lomitas 56 Hb 24.42S 60.36W
Las Margaritas 48 Ni 16.19N 91.59W
Las Mariñas 13 Da 43.20N 8.15W
Las Marismas 13 Fg 37.00N 6.15W
Las Mercedes 54 Eb 9.07N 66.24W
Las Mestenas 48 Gc 28.13N 104.35W
Las Minas, Cerro- 47 Gf 14.33N 88.39W
Las Minas, Sierra de- 47 Ge 15.05N 90.00W
Las Mixtecas, Sierra del- 48 Ki 17.45N 97.15W
La Sola, Isla- 54 Fa 11.20N 63.34W
La Solana 13 If 38.56N 3.14W
Lasolo 26 Hg 3.29S 122.04 E
La Sorcière 51k Bb 13.59N 60.56W
La Souterraine 11 Hh 46.14N 1.29 E
Las Palmas [3] 32 Ed 28.20N 14.20W
Las Palmas de Gran Canaria 31 Ff 28.06N 15.24W
Las Petas 55 Cc 16.23S 59.11W
La Spezia 6 Gg 44.07N 9.50 E
Las Piedras 56 Id 34.45S 56.13W
Las Plumas 53 Jj 43.40S 67.15W
Lās Qoray 35 Hc 11.15N 48.22 E
Las Rosas 55 Bk 32.28S 61.34W
Lassen Peak 43 Cc 40.29N 121.31W
Lassigny 12 Ee 49.35N 2.51 E
Laßnitz 14 Jd 46.46N 15.32 E
Lasso 64b Ba 15.02N 145.38 E
Las Tablas 49 Gj 7.46N 80.17W
Last Mountain Lake 42 Gf 51.10N 105.15W
Las Toscas 55 Ci 28.21S 59.17W
Lastoursville 36 Bc 0.49S 12.42 E
Lastovo 14 Kh 42.46N 16.55 E
Lastovo 14 Kh 42.45N 16.50 E
Lastovski kanal 14 Kh 42.50N 16.59 E
Las Tres Virgenes, Volcán- 47 Bc 27.27N 112.34W
Las Tunas [3] 49 Ic 21.00N 77.00W
Las Tunas, Punta- 51a Bb 18.30N 66.37W
Las Varillas 56 Hd 31.52S 62.43W
Las Vegas [N.M.-U.S.] 43 Fd 35.36N 105.13W
Las Vegas [Nv.-U.S.] 39 Hf 36.11N 115.08W
Las Villuercas 13 Ge 39.33N 5.27W
Łaszczów 10 Tf 50.32N 23.40 E
Lata 65c Db 14.14S 169.29W
Latacunga 54 Cd 0.55S 78.37W
La Tagua 54 Dd 0.03S 74.40W
Latakia (EN) = Al Lādhiqīyah 22 Ff 35.31N 35.07 E
Latarc, Causse du- 11 Jk 43.57N 3.11 E
Late Island 61 Gc 18.48S 174.39W
Laterza 14 Kj 40.37N 16.48 E
La Teste 11 Ej 44.38N 1.09W
Latgale [2] 8 Lh 56.45N 27.30 E
Latgales Augstiene/Latgalskaja Vozvyšennost 8 Lh 56.10N 27.30 E
Latgalskaja Vozvyšennost/Latgales Augstiene 8 Lh 56.10N 27.30 E
Latharna/Larne 9 Hg 54.51N 5.49W
Lathen 12 Jb 52.52N 7.19 E
La Tigra 55 Bh 27.06S 60.34W
Latina 14 Gi 41.28N 12.52 E
Latisana 14 Ge 45.47N 13.00 E
Latium (EN) = Lazio [2] 14 Gh 42.02N 12.23 E
La Toja 13 Db 42.27N 8.50W
La Toma 56 Gd 33.03S 65.37W
La Tontouta 63b Ce 22.00S 166.15 E
Latorica 10 Rh 48.28N 21.50 E
La Tortuga, Isla- 54 Ea 10.56N 65.20W
La-Tour-du-Pin 11 Li 45.34N 5.27 E
La Trimouille 11 Hh 46.28N 1.03 E
La Trinidad 49 Dg 12.58N 86.14W
La Trinidad de Orichuna 50 Bi 7.07N 69.45W
La Trinité 50 Fe 14.44N 60.58W
Latronico 14 Kj 40.05N 16.01 E
Lattari, Monti- 14 Ij 40.40N 14.30 E
La Tuque 42 Kg 47.27N 72.47W
Lätür 25 Fe 18.24N 76.35 E
Latvian SSR (EN) = Latvijas PSR [2] 19 Cd 57.00N 25.00 E
Latvijas PSR = Latvian SSR (EN) [2] 19 Cd 57.00N 25.00 E
Latvijskaja Sovetskaja Socialističeskaja Respublika [2] 19 Cd 57.00N 25.00 E
Latvijskaja SSR/Latvijas Padomju Socialistiska Respublika [2] 19 Cd 57.00N 25.00 E
Lau 30 Kh 6.56N 30.16 E
Laubach 12 Kd 50.33N 8.59 E
Lauchert 10 Fh 48.05N 9.15 E
Lauchhammer 10 Je 51.30N 13.48 E
Lauenburg 10 Gc 53.22N 10.34 E
Lauf an der Pegnitz 10 Hg 49.31N 11.17 E
Laughlan Islands 63a Ac 9.15S 153.40 E
Laughlin Peak 45 Dh 36.38N 104.12W
Lau Group 57 Jf 18.20S 178.30W
Lauhanvuori 8 Jb 62.10N 22.10 E
Laujar de Andarax 13 Jh 36.59N 2.51W
Laukaa 7 Fe 62.25N 25.57 E
Laukuva 8 Ji 55.35N 22.08 E
Laulau, Bahia- 64b Ba 15.08N 145.46 E
Launceston [Austl.] 58 Fi 41.26S 147.08 E
Launceston [Eng.-U.K.] 9 Ik 50.38N 4.21W
La Unión [Bol.] 55 Bb 15.18S 61.05W
La Unión [Chile] 56 Ff 40.17S 73.05W
La Unión [Col.] 54 Cc 1.37N 77.08W
La Unión [ElSal.] 47 Gf 13.20N 87.51W
La Unión [Mex.] 48 Ii 17.58N 101.49W
La Unión [Peru] 54 Ce 9.46S 76.48W
La Unión [Sp.] 13 Lg 37.37N 0.52W
La Unión [Ven.] 49 Ni 8.13N 67.46W
Laura 59 Ic 15.34S 144.28 E
La Urbana 50 Ci 7.08N 66.56W
Laurel [Ms.-U.S.] 43 Je 31.42N 89.08W
Laurel [Mt.-U.S.] 43 Fb 45.40N 108.46W
Laureles 55 Ej 31.23S 55.52W
Laurel Hill 44 He 40.02N 79.17W
Laurel Mountain 44 Hf 39.20N 79.50W
Laurens 44 Fh 34.30N 82.01W
Laurentian Plateau (EN) = Laurentien, Plateau- 38 Md 50.00N 70.00W
Laurentian Scarp 44 Ic 45.50N 76.15W
Laurentide Scarp 44 Kb 46.38N 73.00W
Laurentien, Plateau- = Laurentian Plateau (EN) 38 Md 50.00N 70.00W
Lauria 14 Jj 40.02N 15.50 E
Lau Ridge (EN) 3 Kl 25.00S 179.00 E
Laurie River 42 He 56.00N 100.58W
Laurinburg 44 Hh 34.47N 79.27W
Laurium 44 Cb 47.14N 88.26W
Lauro Muller 55 Hi 28.24S 49.23W
Lausanne 6 Gf 46.30N 6.40 E
Lausitzer Gebirge 10 Kf 50.48N 14.40 E
Lausitzer Neiße 10 Kd 52.04N 14.46 E
Laut, Pulau- 26 Ef 4.43N 107.59 E
Laut, Pulau- 21 Nj 3.40S 116.10 E
Lautaret, Col du- 11 Mi 45.02N 6.24 E
Lautaro 56 Fe 38.31S 72.27W
Lautém 26 Ih 8.22S 126.54 E
Lauter 10 Eg 48.58N 8.11 E
Lauterbach 10 Ff 50.38N 9.24 E
Lauterbourg 12 Kf 48.59N 8.11 E
Lauterecken 12 Je 49.39N 7.36 E
Lauthala 63d Cb 16.45S 179.41W
Laut Kecil, Kepulauan- 26 Gg 4.50S 115.45 E
Lautoka 61 Ec 17.37S 177.27 E
Lauvergne Island 64d Cb 7.00N 152.00 E
Lauwersmeer 12 Ia 53.25N 6.15 E
Lauzerte 11 Hj 44.15N 1.08 E
Lauzon 44 Lb 46.50N 71.10W
Lauzoue 11 Gj 44.03N 0.15 E
Lava 10 Rb 54.37N 21.14 E
Lava, Nosy- [Mad.] 37 Hb 12.49S 48.41 E
Lava, Nosy- [Mad.] 37 Hb 14.33S 47.36 E
Lavaca River 45 Hl 28.50N 96.36W
Lava Flow 45 Bi 34.45N 108.20W
Laval 11 Ff 48.01N 0.46W
Lavalle 55 Ci 29.01S 59.11W
Lavalleja [2] 55 El 34.00S 55.00W
Lāvān, Jazīreh-ye- 23 Hd 26.48N 53.00 E
Lavanggu 63a Ed 11.37S 160.15 E
Lavant 14 Id 46.38N 14.56 E
Lavapié, Punta- 52 Ii 37.09S 73.35W
Lävar Meydän 24 Pg 30.20N 54.30 E
Lavassaare 8 Kf 58.29N 24.16 E
Lavaur 11 Hk 43.42N 1.49 E
La Vecilla 13 Gb 42.51N 5.24W
La Vega 47 Je 19.13N 70.31W
La Vela de Coro 49 Mh 11.27N 69.34W
Lavelanet 11 Hl 42.56N 1.51 E
Lavello 14 Ji 41.03N 15.48 E
La Venta 47 Fe 18.08N 94.03W
Laventie 12 Ed 50.38N 2.46 E
La Ventura 48 Ie 24.37N 100.54W
La Vera 13 Gd 40.05N 5.30W
L'Averdy, Cape- 63a Ba 5.33S 155.04 E
Laverton 59 Ee 28.38S 122.25 E
Lavia 7 Ff 61.36N 22.36 E
La Victoria 54 Ea 10.14N 67.20W
La Vila Jojosa/Villajoyosa 13 Lf 38.30N 0.14W
La Villita, Presa- 48 Hh 18.05N 102.05W
La Viña 54 Ce 6.54S 79.28W

Index Symbols

[1] Independent Nation
[2] State, Region
[3] District, County
[4] Municipality
[5] Colony, Dependency
Continent
Physical Region
Historical or Cultural Region
Mount, Mountain
Volcano
Hill
Mountains, Mountain Range
Hills, Escarpment
Plateau, Upland
Pass, Gap
Plain, Lowland
Delta
Salt Flat
Valley, Canyon
Crater, Cave
Karst Features
Depression
Polder
Desert, Dunes
Forest, Woods
Heath, Steppe
Oasis
Cape, Point
Coast, Beach
Cliff
Peninsula
Isthmus
Sandbank
Island
Atoll
Rock, Reef
Islands, Archipelago
Rocks, Reefs
Coral Reef
Well, Spring
Geyser
River, Stream
Waterfall Rapids
River Mouth, Estuary
Lake
Salt Lake
Intermittent Lake
Reservoir
Swamp, Pond
Canal
Glacier
Ice Shelf, Pack Ice
Ocean
Sea
Gulf, Bay
Strait, Fjord
Lagoon
Bank
Seamount
Tablemount
Ridge
Shelf
Basin
Escarpment, Sea Scarp
Fracture
Trench, Abyss
National Park, Reserve
Point of Interest
Recreation Site
Cave, Cavern
Historic Site
Ruins
Wall, Walls
Church, Abbey
Temple
Scientific Station
Airport
Port
Lighthouse
Mine
Tunnel
Dam, Bridge

La Vôge 11 Mf 48.05N 6.05 E
Lavoisier Island 66 Qe 66.12S 66.44W
Lavougba 35 Cd 5.37N 23.19 E
La Voulte-sur-Rhône 11 Kj 44.48N 4.47 E
Lavouras 55 Db 14.59S 56.47W
Lavras 54 Jh 21.14S 45.00W
Lavras do Sul 55 Fj 30.49S 53.55W
Lavrentija 20 Nc 65.33N 171.02W
Lávrion 15 Hl 37.43N 24.03 E
Lavumisa 37 Ee 27.15S 31.55 E
Lawas 26 Gf 4.51N 115.24 E
Lawdar 23 Gg 13.53N 45.52 E
Lawe 12 Ed 50.38N 2.42 E
Lawers, Ben- 9 Ie 56.33N 4.15W
Lawit, Gunong- 26 Ff 1.23N 112.55 E
Lawqah 24 Jh 29.49N 42.45 E
Lawra 34 Ec 10.39N 2.52W
Lawrence [Ks.-U.S.] 43 Hd 38.58N 95.14W
Lawrence [Ma.-U.S.] 43 Mc 42.42N 71.09W
Lawrence [N.Z.] 62 Cf 45.55S 169.42 E
Lawrenceburg [Ky.-U.S.] 44 Ef 38.02N 84.54W
Lawrenceburg [Tn.-U.S.] 44 Dh 35.15N 87.20W
Lawson, Mount- 59 Ja 7.44S 146.37 E
Lawton 39 Jf 34.37N 98.25W
Lawu, Gunung- 21 Nj 7.38S 111.11 E
Lawz, Jabal al- 24 Fh 28.41N 35.18 E
Laxå 7 Dg 58.59N 14.37 E
Lay 11 Eh 46.18N 1.17W
Laylá 23 Ge 22.17N 46.45 E
Layon 11 Fg 47.20N 0.45W
Layou 51g Bb 15.23N 61.26W
Layou 51n Ba 13.12N 61.17W
Laysan Island 57 Jb 25.50N 171.50W
Layton 46 Jf 41.04N 111.58W
La Zarca 48 Ge 25.50N 104.44W
Lazarev 20 Jf 52.13N 141.35 E
Lazarevac 15 De 44.23N 20.16 E
Lázaro Cárdenas, Presa- 48 Ge 25.35N 105.05W
Lazdijai/Lazdijaj 7 Fi 54.13N 23.33 E
Lazdijaj/Lazdijai 7 Fi 54.13N 23.33 E
Lāzeh 24 Oi 26.48N 53.22 E
Lazio = Latium (EN) [2] 14 Gh 42.02N 12.23 E
Lazo 28 Mc 43.25N 134.01 E
Lazovsk 16 Ff 47.38N 28.12 E
Łazy 10 Pf 50.27N 19.26 E
Lea 9 Nj 51.30N 0.01 E
Lead 43 Gc 44.21N 103.46W
Leader 46 Ka 50.53N 109.31W
Lead Hill 45 Jh 37.06N 92.38W
Leadville 43 Fd 39.15N 106.20W
Leaf River 45 Lk 31.00N 88.45W
League City 45 Il 29.31N 95.05W
Leamington 44 Fd 42.03N 82.36W
Leandro N. Alem 55 Bl 34.30S 61.24W
Leane, Lough-/Loch Léin 9 Di 52.05N 9.35W
Le'an Jiang 28 Dj 28.58N 116.41 E
Learmonth 59 Cd 22.13S 114.04 E
Leavenworth [Ks.-U.S.] 45 Ig 39.19N 94.55W
Leavenworth [Wa.-U.S.] 46 Ec 47.36N 120.40W
Łeba 10 Nb 54.47N 17.33 E
Łeba 10 Nb 54.43N 17.25 E
Lebach 12 Ie 49.24N 6.55 E
Lébamba 36 Bc 2.12S 11.30 E
Lebanon [In.-U.S.] 44 De 40.03N 86.28W
Lebanon [Ky.-U.S.] 44 Eg 37.34N 85.15W
Lebanon [Mo.-U.S.] 45 Jh 37.41N 92.40W
Lebanon [N.H.-U.S.] 44 Kd 43.38N 72.15W
Lebanon [Or.-U.S.] 46 Dd 44.32N 122.54W
Lebanon [Pa.-U.S.] 44 Ie 40.21N 76.25W
Lebanon [Tn.-U.S.] 44 Dg 36.12N 86.18W
Lebanon (EN) = Lubnān [1] 22 Ff 33.50N 35.50 E
Lebanon Mountains (EN) = Lubnān, Jabal- 23 Ec 34.00N 36.30 E
Lebap 18 Cd 41.02N 61.54 E
Le Bec-Hellouin 12 Ce 49.14N 0.43 E
Lebedin 19 De 50.36N 34.30 E
Lebediny 20 He 58.25N 125.58 E
Lebedjan 19 De 53.02N 39.07 E
Le Bény-Bocage 12 Bf 48.56N 0.50W
Lebjažje [Kaz.-U.S.S.R.] 19 He 51.28N 77.46 E
Lebjažje [R.S.F.S.R.] 17 Mi 55.16N 66.29 E
Le Blanc 11 Hh 46.38N 1.04 E
Lebo 36 Db 4.29N 23.57 E
Lebomboberge 30 Kk 26.15S 32.00 E
Lebombo Mountains 30 Kk 26.15S 32.00 E
Lębork 10 Nb 54.33N 17.44 E
Le Bourget 12 Ef 48.56N 2.25 E
Lebrija 13 Fh 36.55N 6.04W
Łebsko, Jezioro- 10 Nb 54.44N 17.24 E
Lebu 56 Fe 37.37S 73.39W
Le Carbet 51h Ab 14.43N 61.11W
Le Cateau 12 Fd 50.06N 3.33 E
Le Catelet 12 Fd 50.01N 3.15 E
Lecce 6 Hg 40.23N 18.11 E
Lecco 14 De 45.51N 9.23 E
Lech 10 Gh 48.44N 10.56 E
Lech 14 Ec 47.12N 10.09 E
Le Champ du Feu 11 Nf 48.24N 7.15 E
Lechang 27 Jf 25.15N 113.25 E
Le Château-d'Oléron 11 Ei 45.54N 1.12W
Le Chesne 11 Ke 49.31N 4.46 E
Le Cheylard 11 Kj 44.54N 4.25 E
Lechfeld 10 Gh 48.10N 10.50 E
Lechiguiri, Cerro- 48 Li 16.43N 95.30W
Lechtaler Alpen 14 Ec 47.15N 10.30 E
Léconi 36 Bc 1.11S 13.16 E
Léconi 36 Bc 1.35S 14.14 E
Le Cornate 14 Eg 43.10N 10.58 E
Le Coudray-Saint-Germer 12 De 49.25N 1.50 E
Le Creusot 11 Kh 46.48N 4.26 E
Le Croisic 11 Dg 47.18N 2.30W
Le Crotoy 12 Dd 50.13N 1.37 E
Łęczna 10 Se 51.19N 22.52 E
Łęczyca 10 Pd 52.04N 19.13 E
Led 7 Ke 62.20N 43.00 E
Lede 12 Fd 50.57N 3.59 E
Ledesma 13 Gc 41.05N 6.00W
Le Diamant 51h Ac 14.29N 61.02W
Ledjanaja, Gora- [R.S.F.S.R.] 21 Tc 61.45N 171.15 E
Ledjanaja, Gora- [R.S.F.S.R.] 21 Qe 49.28N 142.45 E
Lednik Entuziastov 66 Cf 70.30S 16.00 E
Lednik Mušketova 66 Cf 72.00S 14.00 E
Ledo, Cabo- 36 Bd 9.41S 13.12 E
Ledolom Tajmyrski 66 Ge 66.00S 83.00 E
Le Donjon 11 Jh 46.21N 3.48 E
Le Dorat 11 Hh 46.13N 1.05 E
Lędyczek 10 Mc 53.33N 16.58 E
Lee/An Laoi 9 Ej 51.55N 8.30W
Leech Lake 43 Ib 47.09N 94.23W
Leeds [Al.-U.S.] 44 Di 33.33N 86.33W
Leeds [Eng.-U.K.] 6 Fe 53.50N 1.35W
Leeds [N.D.-U.S.] 45 Gb 48.17N 99.27W
Leek 12 Ia 53.10N 6.24 E
Leer 10 Dc 53.14N 7.26 E
Leer (Ostfriesland) 10 Dc 53.14N 7.26 E
Leerdam 12 Hc 51.53N 5.06 E
Lées 11 Fk 43.38N 0.14W
Leesburg 43 Kf 29.49N 81.53W
Leeste, Weyhe- 12 Kb 52.59N 8.50 E
Leesville 45 Jk 31.08N 93.16W
Leeuwarden 11 La 53.12N 5.46 E
Leeuwarderadeel 12 Ha 53.16N 5.46 E
Leeuwarderadeel-Stiens 12 Ha 53.16N 5.46 E
Leeuwin, Cape- 59 Cf 34.25S 115.00 E
Leeward Islands 47 Le 17.00N 63.00W
Leeward Islands (EN) = Sous le Vent, Iles- 57 Lf 16.38S 151.30W
Léfini 36 Cc 2.57S 16.10 E
Lefka 15 Jh 41.52N 26.16 E
Lefke 24 Ee 35.07N 32.51 E
Lefkoşa/Levkosía = Nicosia (EN) 22 Ff 35.10N 33.22 E
Le François 51h Bb 14.37N 60.54W
Lefroy, Lake- 59 Ef 31.15S 121.40 E
Łeg 10 Rf 50.38N 21.49 E
Leganés 13 Id 40.19N 3.45W
Legazpi 22 Oh 13.09N 123.44 E
Legden 12 Jb 52.02N 7.06 E
Legges Tor 59 Jh 41.32S 147.40 E
Leggett 46 Dg 39.52N 123.43W
Leghorn (EN) = Livorno 6 Hg 43.33N 10.19 E
Legionowo 10 Qd 52.25N 20.56 E
Léglise 12 He 49.48N 5.32 E
Legnago 14 Fe 45.11N 11.18 E
Legnano 14 Ce 45.36N 8.54 E
Legnica [2] 10 Me 51.15N 16.10 E
Legnica 10 Me 51.13N 16.09 E
Le Grand-Quevilly 12 De 49.25N 1.02 E
Le Grand Veymont 11 Lj 44.52N 5.32 E
Le Grau-du-Roi 11 Kk 43.32N 4.08 E
Léguer 11 Cf 48.44N 3.32W
Leh 25 Fb 34.10N 77.35 E
Le Havre 6 Gf 49.30N 0.08 E
Lehi 46 Jf 40.24N 111.51W
Lehmann 55 Bj 31.08S 61.27W
Le Hohneck 11 Nf 48.02N 7.01 E
Le Houlme 12 De 49.31N 1.02 E
Lehrte 10 Fd 52.23N 9.58 E
Lehtimäki 8 Jb 62.47N 23.55 E
Lehua Island 65a Aa 22.01N 160.06W
Lehututu 37 Cd 23.53S 21.49 E
Leibnitz 14 Jd 46.46N 15.32 E
Leibo 27 Hf 28.13N 103.34 E
Leicester 6 Fe 52.38N 1.05W
Leicester 9 Mi 52.40N 1.00W
Leicestershire [3] 9 Mi 52.38N 1.00W
Leichhardt Range 59 Jd 20.40S 147.05 E
Leichhardt River 59 Hc 17.35S 139.48 E
Leiden 11 Kc 52.09N 4.30 E
Leidschendam 12 Gb 52.05N 4.26 E
Leie 11 Jc 51.03N 3.43 E
Leifear/Lifford 9 Fg 54.50N 7.29W
Leigh Creek 58 Eh 30.28S 138.25 E
Leighton Buzzard 12 Bc 51.55N 0.39W
Leigong Shan 27 If 26.23N 108.15 E
Leikanger 7 Ae 62.07N 5.20 E
Léim an Mhadaidh/Limavady 9 Gf 55.03N 6.57W
Leimen 12 Ke 49.21N 8.41 E
Leimus 49 Ef 14.44N 84.07W
Leine 10 Fd 52.43N 9.40 E
Leinster/Laighean 9 Gh 53.00N 7.00W
Leipzig 6 He 51.18N 12.20 E
Leira 8 Cd 60.58N 9.18 E
Leiria [2] 13 De 39.40N 8.50W
Leiria 13 De 39.45N 8.48W
Leirvik 7 Ag 59.47N 5.30 E
Leisi/Lejsi 8 Jf 58.33N 22.30 E
Leisler, Mount- 59 Fd 23.30S 129.20 E
Leiston 12 Db 52.12N 1.34 E
Leitariegos, Puerto de- 13 Fa 43.00N 6.25W
Leitha 14 Lc 47.52N 17.18 E
Leithagebirge 14 Kc 47.58N 16.40 E
Leitir Ceanainn/Letterkenny 9 Fg 54.57N 7.44W
Leitrim/Liatroim [3] 9 Eg 54.20N 8.20W
Leiva, Cerro- 54 Dc 2.54N 74.48W
Leiyang 27 Jf 26.30N 112.57 E
Leizhou → Haikang 27 Jg 20.56N 110.06 E
Leizhou Bandao 21 Ng 20.40N 110.05 E
Lejasciems 8 Lg 57.08N 26.36 E
Lejsi/Leisi 8 Jf 58.33N 22.30 E
Lek 11 Lc 52.00N 6.00 E
Leka 7 Cd 65.05N 11.37 E
Lékana 36 Cc 2.19S 14.36 E
Leketi, Monts de la- 30 Ii 2.34S 14.17 E
Lekhainá 15 El 37.56N 21.16 E
Lekhal 13 Ph 36.20N 3.51 E
Lekitobi 26 Hg 1.58S 124.33 E
Lekki Lagoon 34 Fd 6.30N 4.07 E
Leknes 7 Cb 68.10N 13.42 E
Łęknica 10 Ke 51.32N 14.48 E
Lékoumou [3] 36 Bc 3.00S 13.50 E
Leksand 7 Df 60.44N 15.01 E
Leksozero, Ozero- 7 He 63.45N 31.00 E
Leksula 26 Ig 3.46S 126.31 E
Leksvik 7 Ce 63.40N 10.37 E
Le Lamentin 50 Fe 14.37N 61.01W
Leland 45 Kj 33.24N 90.54W
Lelång 8 Ee 59.10N 12.10 E
Le Lavandou 11 Mk 43.08N 6.22 E
Lelčicy 16 Fd 51.49N 28.21 E
Leleiwi Point 65a Gd 19.44N 155.00W
Lelepa 63b Dc 17.36S 168.13 E
Leleque 56 Ff 42.23S 71.03W
Leli 63a Ec 8.45S 161.02 E
Leli → Tianlin 27 Ig 24.22N 106.11 E
Lelija 14 Mg 43.26N 18.29 E
Leling 28 Df 37.44N 117.13 E
Léliogat 63b Ce 21.18S 167.35 E
Lelle 7 Fg 58.53N 25.00 E
Le Locle 14 Ac 47.05N 6.45 E
Le Lorrain 51h Ab 14.50N 61.04W
Lelystad 11 Lb 52.31N 5.27 E
Le Madonie 14 Hm 37.50N 14.00 E
Le Maire, Estrecho de- 56 Hh 54.50S 65.00W
Léman, Lac- = Geneva, Lake- (EN) 5 Gf 46.25N 6.30 E
Leman Bank 9 Oh 53.10N 1.58 E
Lemankoa 63a Ba 5.03S 154.34 E
Le Mans 6 Gf 48.00N 0.12 E
Le Marin 51h Bc 14.28N 60.52W
Le Mars 45 He 42.47N 96.10W
Le Mas-d'Azil 11 Hk 43.05N 1.22 E
Lembach 12 Je 49.00N 7.48 E
Lembeck 12 Ic 51.44N 6.59 E
Lemberg 12 Je 49.00N 7.23 E
Lembolovskaja Vozvyšennost 8 Md 60.50N 30.15 E
Lembruch 12 Kb 52.32N 8.21 E
Leme 55 If 22.12S 47.24W
Lemelerberg 12 Ib 52.29N 6.23 E
Lemesós/Limassol 23 Dc 34.40N 33.02 E
Lemgo 10 Ed 52.02N 8.54 E
Lemhi Range 46 Id 44.30N 113.25W
Lemieux Islands 42 Ld 64.00N 64.20W
Lemju 17 He 63.50N 56.57 E
Lemland 8 Id 60.05N 20.10 E
Lemmer, Lemsterland- 12 Hb 52.51N 5.42 E
Lemmon 43 Gb 45.56N 102.10W
Lemmon, Mount- 46 Jj 32.26N 110.47W
Lemnos (EN) = Límnos 5 Ih 39.55N 25.15 E
Le-Molay-Littry 12 Be 49.15N 0.53W
Le-Mont-Saint-Michel 11 Ef 48.38N 1.30W
Le Morne Rouge 51h Ab 14.46N 61.08W
Lemotol Bay 64d Bb 7.21N 151.35 E
Le Moyne, Lac- 42 Ke 57.00N 68.00W
Lempa, Río- 47 Gf 13.14N 88.49W
Lempäälä 8 Jc 61.19N 23.45 E
Lempira [3] 49 Cf 14.20N 88.40W
L'Empordà/Ampurdán 13 Ob 42.12N 2.45 E
Lemro 25 Id 20.25N 93.20 E
Lemsid 32 Ed 26.33N 13.51W
Lemsterland 12 Hb 52.51N 5.42 E
Lemsterland-Lemmer 12 Hb 52.51N 5.42 E
Le Murge 5 Hg 40.50N 16.40 E
Le Muy 11 Mk 43.28N 6.33 E
Lemvig 8 Ch 56.32N 8.18 E
Lemya 17 Jc 66.30N 62.00 E
Lena 21 Ob 72.25N 126.40 E
Lena, Mount- 46 Kf 40.50N 109.27W
Lénakel 63b Dd 19.32S 169.16 E
Lena Mountains (EN) = Prilenskoje Plato 21 Oc 60.45N 125.00 E
Lena Tablemount (EN) 30 Ln 53.00S 45.00 E
Lençóis Paulista 55 Hf 22.36S 48.47W
Lendava 14 Kd 46.34N 16.27 E
Lendery 7 He 63.26N 31.12 E
Lendinara 14 Fe 45.05N 11.36 E
Le Neubourg 12 Ce 49.09N 0.55 E
Lenger 19 Gg 42.10N 69.55 E
Lengerich 10 Dd 52.11N 7.52 E
Lengoué 36 Cb 0.49N 15.47 E
Lengshuijiang 27 Jf 27.41N 111.28 E
Lengua de Vaca, Punta- 56 Fd 30.14S 71.38W
Lengulu 36 Eb 3.15N 26.30 E
Lenhovda 7 Dh 57.00N 15.17 E
Lenina, Pik- = Lenin Peak (EN) 21 Jf 39.19N 73.01 E
Leninabad 22 Ie 40.17N 69.37 E
Leninabadskaja Oblast [3] 19 Gh 40.00N 69.10 E
Leninakan 6 Kg 40.47N 43.50 E
Lenin Canal (EN) = Volgo-Donskoj sudohodny kanal imeni V. I. Lenina 5 Kf 48.40N 43.37 E
Leningrad 6 Jc 59.55N 30.15 E
Leningradskaja 66 Je 69.30S 159.23 E
Leningradskaja 16 Kf 46.17N 39.25 E
Leningradskaja Oblast [3] 19 Dd 60.00N 31.40 E
Leningradski [R.S.F.S.R.] 20 Mc 69.17N 178.10 E
Leningradski [Tad.-U.S.S.R.] 19 Hh 38.09N 70.01 E
Lenino 16 Ig 45.17N 35.44 E
Leninogorsk [Kaz.-U.S.S.R.] 22 Kd 50.27N 83.32 E
Leninogorsk [R.S.F.S.R.] 19 Fe 54.38N 52.30 E
Lenin Peak (EN) = Lenina, Pik- 21 Jf 39.19N 73.01 E
Leninsk [R.S.F.S.R.] 16 Ne 48.42N 45.11 E
Leninsk [Tur.-U.S.S.R.] 18 Bc 42.04N 59.24 E
Leninsk [Uzb.-U.S.S.R.] 18 Id 40.40N 72.20 E
Leninski [Kaz.-U.S.S.R.] 19 He 52.13N 76.50 E
Leninski [Mold.-U.S.S.R.] 15 Lb 47.50N 28.16 E
Leninski [R.S.F.S.R.] 20 He 58.02N 125.58 E
Leninsk-Kuzneckí 22 Kd 54.38N 86.10 E
Leninskoje [Kaz.-U.S.S.R.] 19 Ge 54.05N 65.23 E
Leninskoje [R.S.F.S.R.] 7 Lg 58.21N 47.07 E
Leninskoje [R.S.F.S.R.] 20 Ig 47.59N 132.38 E
Leninváros 10 Ri 47.56N 21.05 E
Lenkoran 6 Kh 38.44N 48.50 E
Lenne 10 De 51.25N 7.30 E
Lenne 12 Jc 51.15N 7.50 E
Lennestadt 12 Kc 51.08N 8.01 E
Lennestadt-Grevenbrück 12 Kc 51.08N 8.01 E
Lennox Hills 9 Ie 56.05N 4.10W
Leno-Angarskoje Plato 20 Fe 55.00N 104.30 E
Lenoir 44 Gh 35.55N 81.32W
Le Nouvion-en-Thiérache 12 Fd 50.01N 3.47 E
Lens 11 Id 50.26N 2.50 E
Lensk 22 Nc 61.00N 114.50 E
Lenti 10 Mi 46.37N 16.33 E
Lentiira 7 Gd 64.21N 29.50 E
Lentini 14 Jm 37.17N 15.01 E
Lentua 7 Gd 64.14N 29.36 E
Lentvaris 8 Kj 54.38N 25.13 E
Léo 34 Ec 11.06N 2.06W
Leoben 14 Jc 47.23N 15.06 E
Léogâne 49 Kd 18.31N 72.38W
Leok 26 Hf 1.11N 121.26 E
Leola 45 Gd 45.43N 98.56W
Leominster 9 Ki 52.14N 2.45W
León 13 Gc 42.00N 6.00W
Léon 11 Ek 43.53N 1.18W
León [Mex.] 39 Ig 21.10N 101.42W
León [Nic.] [3] 49 Dg 12.35N 86.35W
León [Nic.] 39 Kh 12.26N 86.54W
León [Sp.] 6 Fg 42.36N 5.34W
León [Sp.] [3] 13 Gb 42.40N 6.00W
León, Montes de- 13 Fb 42.30N 6.20W
León, Puerto del- 13 Hh 36.50N 4.21W
Leonardville 37 Bd 23.29S 18.49 E
Leonberg 12 Kf 48.48N 9.01 E
Leone, Monte- 14 Cd 46.15N 8.10 E
Leones 55 Ak 32.39S 62.18W
Leonessa 14 Gh 42.34N 12.58 E
Leonforte 14 Im 37.38N 14.23 E
Leonidhion 15 Fl 37.10N 22.52 E
Leonora 58 Dg 28.53S 121.20 E
Leon River 45 Hk 30.59N 97.24W
Leopold and Astrid Coast 66 Ge 67.10S 84.10 E
Leopoldina 54 Jh 21.32S 42.38W
Leopold McClintock, Cape - 42 Fa 77.38N 116.20W
Leopoldo de Bulhões 55 Hc 16.37S 48.46W
Leopoldsburg 12 Hc 51.07N 5.15 E
Leopoldville → Kinshasa 31 Ii 4.18S 15.18 E
Leova 16 Ff 46.29N 28.15 E
Lepa 65c Bb 14.01S 171.28W
Le Palais 11 Cg 47.21N 3.09W
Lepar, Pulau- 26 Eg 2.57S 106.50 E
Le Parcq 12 Ed 50.23N 2.06 E
Lepaterique 49 Df 14.02N 87.27W
Lepe 13 Eg 37.15N 7.12W
Lepel 19 Ce 54.53N 28.46 E
Lepenica 15 Ee 44.10N 21.08 E
Le Petit Caux 12 De 49.55N 1.20 E
Le Petit-Couronne 12 De 49.23N 1.01 E
Le Petit-Quevilly 12 De 49.26N 1.02 E
Lephepe 37 Dd 23.22S 25.52 E
Leping 27 Kf 28.59N 117.07 E
Lepini, Monti- 14 Gi 41.35N 13.00 E
Le Plessis-Belleville 12 Ee 49.06N 2.46 E
Le Pont-de-Claix 11 Li 45.07N 5.42 E
Le Portel 12 Dd 50.42N 1.34 E
Leppävesi 8 Kb 62.15N 25.55 E
Leppävirta 8 Lb 62.29N 27.47 E
Le Prêcheur 51h Ab 14.48N 61.14W
Lepsøya 8 Bb 62.35N 6.10 E
Lepsy 18 La 46.18N 78.20 E
Lepsy 19 Hf 46.12N 78.55 E
Leptis Magna 33 Bc 32.38N 14.18 E
Le Puy 11 Ji 45.02N 3.53 E
Leqemt (EN) = Nekemt 31 Kh 9.05N 36.33 E
Le Quesnoy 12 Fd 50.15N 3.38 E
Lercara Friddi 14 Hm 37.45N 13.36 E
Lerchenfeld Glacier 66 Af 77.50S 34.50W
Lere 34 Gc 10.23N 8.35 E
Léré 35 Ad 9.39N 14.13 E
Lérida 54 Dc 0.06N 70.43W
Lérida [3] 13 Nc 42.00N 1.10 E
Lérida/Lleida 13 Mc 41.37N 0.37 E
Lérins, Iles de- 11 Nk 43.31N 7.03 E
Lerma 13 Ib 42.02N 3.45W
Lerma, Río- 48 Hg 20.13N 102.46W
Lermontov 16 Mg 44.06N 42.45 E
Le Robert 51h Bb 14.41N 60.57W
Léros 15 Jl 37.08N 26.50 E
Lerum 7 Ch 57.46N 12.16 E
Lerwick 9 La 60.09N 1.09W
Léry 12 De 49.17N 1.13 E
Les Abrets 11 Li 45.32N 5.35 E
Le Saint-Esprit 51h Bb 14.34N 60.57W
Les Alberes/Albères, Montes- 11 In 42.28N 2.56 E
Les Allobroges 63b Dc 16.47S 168.09 E
Les Andelys 11 He 49.15N 1.25 E
Les Anses-d'Arlets 51h Ac 14.29N 61.05W
Les-Baux-de-Provence 11 Kk 43.45N 4.48 E
Les Borges Blanques/Borjas Blancas 13 Mc 41.31N 0.52 E
Lesbos (EN) = Lésvos 5 Ih 39.10N 26.32 E
L'Escala/La Escala 13 Pb 42.07N 3.08 E
Les Cayes 47 Je 18.12N 73.45W
Les Coëvrons 11 Ff 48.12N 0.10W
Le Serre 14 Kl 38.30N 16.30 E
Les Escoumins 44 Ma 48.25N 69.29W
Les Eyzies-de-Tayac 11 Hj 44.56N 1.01 E
Les Falaises 12 Ce 49.44N 0.21 E
Leshan 27 Hf 29.34N 103.45 E
Les Herbiers 11 Eh 46.52N 1.01W
Lesina, Lago di- 14 Ji 41.55N 15.25 E
Lesja 8 Cb 62.07N 8.52 E
Lesjöfors 7 Dg 59.59N 14.11 E
Leskino 20 Cb 72.25N 79.40 E
Lesko 10 Sg 49.29N 22.21 E
Leskov 66 Ad 56.40S 28.10W
Leskovac 15 Eg 42.59N 21.57 E
Leskoviku 15 Di 40.09N 20.35 E
Les Mangles 51e Ab 16.23N 61.27W
Les Mauges 11 Fg 47.10N 1.00W
Les Minquiers 9 Km 48.58N 2.08W
Les Monédières 11 Hi 45.30N 1.52 E
Les Mureaux 12 Df 49.00N 1.55 E
Lesnaja 10 Vd 52.55N 25.52 E
Lesnaja 16 Cc 52.11N 23.30 E
Lesneven 11 Bf 48.34N 4.19W
Lešnica 15 Ce 44.39N 19.19 E
Lesnoj [R.S.F.S.R.] 19 Gd 57.01N 67.50 E
Lesnoj [R.S.F.S.R.] 19 Fd 59.49N 52.10 E
Lesnoj, Ostrov- 8 Md 60.02N 28.20 E
Lesný 10 If 50.02N 12.37 E
Lesogorski 8 Mc 61.01N 28.51 E
Lesosibirsk 22 Ld 58.15N 92.30 E
Lesotho [1] 31 Jk 29.30S 28.30 E
Lesozavodsk 20 Ig 45.26N 133.25 E
Lesozavodski 7 Hc 66.45N 32.50 E
Lesparre-Médoc 11 Fi 45.18N 0.56W
L'Espérance Rock 57 Jh 31.26S 178.54W
Les Ponts-de-Cé 11 Fg 47.25N 0.31W
Les Posets 13 Mb 42.39N 0.25 E
Les Sables-d'Olonne 11 Eh 46.30N 1.47W
Lessay 11 Ee 49.13N 1.32W
Lesse 11 Kd 50.14N 4.54 E
Lessebo 7 Dh 56.45N 15.16 E
Lessen/Lessines 12 Fd 50.43N 3.50 E
Les Sept Iles 11 Cf 48.53N 3.28W
Lesser Antilles (EN) = Antillas Menores 38 Mh 15.00N 61.00W
Lesser Caucasus (EN) = Maly Kavkaz 5 Kg 41.00N 44.35 E
Lesser Khingan Range (EN) = Xiao Hinggan Ling 21 Oe 48.45N 127.00 E
Lesser Slave Lake 38 Hd 55.25N 115.30W
Lesser Sunda Islands (EN) 21 Oj 9.13S 121.12 E
Lessines/Lessen 12 Fd 50.43N 3.50 E
Lessini 14 Fe 45.41N 11.13 E
Les Tantes 51p Bb 12.19N 61.33W
Les Thilliers-en-Vexin 12 De 49.14N 1.36 E
Les Triagoz 11 Cf 48.53N 3.40W
Les Trois-Ilets 51h Ab 14.33N 61.03W
Lešukonskoje 7 Kd 64.52N 45.40 E
Lésvos = Lesbos (EN) 5 Ih 39.10N 26.32 E
Leszno [2] 10 Me 51.50N 16.35 E
Leszno 10 Me 51.51N 16.35 E
Letälven 8 Fe 59.05N 14.20 E
Le Tanargue 11 Kj 44.37N 4.09 E
Letchworth 12 Bc 51.58N 0.13W
Letea, Ostrovul- 15 Md 45.20N 29.20 E
Le Teil 11 Kj 44.33N 4.41 E
Letenye 10 Mj 46.26N 16.44 E
Lethbridge 39 He 49.42N 110.50W
Lethem 53 Ke 3.20N 59.50W
Le Thillot 11 Mg 47.53N 6.46 E
Leti, Kepulauan- = Leti Islands (EN) 26 Ih 8.13S 127.50 E
Letiahau 30 Jk 21.04S 24.25 E
Leticia 53 Jf 4.09S 69.57W
Leti Islands (EN) = Leti, Kepulauan- 26 Ih 8.13S 127.50 E
Leting 28 Ee 39.25N 118.55 E
Letka 7 Mg 58.59N 50.14 E
Letlhakane 37 Dd 21.25S 25.36 E
Letnerečenski 7 Id 64.19N 34.25 E
Letni Bereg 7 Jd 64.50N 38.20 E
Letohrad 10 Mf 50.03N 16.31 E
Le Touquet-Paris-Plage 11 Hd 50.31N 1.35 E
Letovice 10 Mg 49.33N 16.36 E
Letpadan 25 Je 17.47N 95.45 E
Le Translay 12 De 49.58N 1.41 E
Le Tréport 11 Hd 50.04N 1.22 E
Letsôk-aw Kyun 25 Jf 11.37N 98.15 E
Letterkenny/Leitir Ceanainn 9 Fg 54.57N 7.44W
Leu 15 Ge 44.11N 24.00 E
Leuca 14 Mk 39.48N 18.21 E
Leucas (EN) = Levkás 15 Dk 38.43N 20.38 E
Leucate 11 Jl 42.55N 3.02 E
Leucate, Étang de- 11 Il 42.51N 3.00 E
Leuk 14 Bd 46.20N 7.38 E
Leukónoikon 24 Ee 35.15N 33.42 E
Leulumoega 65c Ba 13.49S 171.55W
Leuna 10 Ie 51.19N 12.01 E
Leušeny 15 Lc 46.51N 28.11 E
Leuser, Gunung- 21 Li 3.45N 97.11 E
Leutkirch im Allgäu 10 Gi 47.50N 10.02 E
Leuven/Louvain 11 Kd 50.53N 4.42 E
Leuze-en-Hainaut 12 Fd 50.36N 3.36 E
Levádhia 15 Fk 38.26N 22.53 E
Levaja Hetta 20 Cc 65.15N 73.20 E
Levanger 7 Ce 63.45N 11.18 E
Levante, Riviera di- 14 Df 44.15N 9.30 E
Levanzo 14 Gm 38.00N 12.20 E
Levaši 16 Oh 42.27N 47.20 E
Le Vauclin 51h Bb 14.33N 60.51W
Levelland 45 Ej 33.35N 102.23W
Lévêque, Cape- 59 Ec 16.25S 122.55 E
Le Verdon-sur-Mer 11 Ei 45.33N 1.04W
Leverkusen 10 Ce 51.01N 6.59 E
Leverkusen-Opladen 10 De 51.04N 7.01 E
Lévézou 11 Ij 44.09N 2.53 E
Levice 10 Oh 48.13N 18.37 E
Levico Terme 14 Fd 46.01N 11.18 E
Le Vigan 11 Jk 43.59N 3.36 E
Levin 61 Eh 40.37S 175.17 E
Lévis 42 Kg 46.48N 71.10W
Levisa Fork 44 Ff 38.06N 82.37W
Levitha 15 Jm 37.00N 26.28 E
Levittown 44 Je 40.09N 74.50W
Levká Óri 15 Gn 35.20N 24.00 E
Levkás 15 Dk 38.50N 20.42 E
Levkás = Leucas (EN) 15 Dk 38.43N 20.38 E

Index Symbols

[1] Independent Nation
[2] State, Region
[3] District, County
[4] Municipality
[5] Colony, Dependency
Continent
Physical Region
Historical or Cultural Region
Mount, Mountain
Volcano
Hill
Mountains, Mountain Range
Hills, Escarpment
Plateau, Upland
Pass, Gap
Plain, Lowland
Delta
Salt Flat
Valley, Canyon
Crater, Cave
Karst Features
Depression
Polder
Desert, Dunes
Forest, Woods
Heath, Steppe
Oasis
Cape, Point
Coast, Beach
Cliff
Peninsula
Isthmus
Sandbank
Island
Atoll
Rock, Reef
Islands, Archipelago
Rocks, Reefs
Coral Reef
Well, Spring
Geyser
River, Stream
Waterfall Rapids
River Mouth, Estuary
Lake
Salt Lake
Intermittent Lake
Reservoir
Swamp, Pond
Canal
Glacier
Ice Shelf, Pack Ice
Ocean
Sea
Gulf, Bay
Strait, Fjord
Lagoon
Bank
Seamount
Tablemount
Ridge
Shelf
Basin
Escarpment, Sea Scarp
Fracture
Trench, Abyss
National Park, Reserve
Point of Interest
Recreation Site
Cave, Cavern
Historic Site
Ruins
Wall, Walls
Church, Abbey
Temple
Scientific Station
Airport
Port
Lighthouse
Mine
Tunnel
Dam, Bridge

Levkōsia/Lefkosa=Nicosia (EN) 22 Ff 35.10N 33.22 E
Levoča 10 Qg 49.02N 20.35 E
Levroux 11 Hh 46.59N 1.37 E
Levski 15 If 43.22N 25.08 E
Lev Tolstoj 16 Kc 53.12N 39.28 E
Levuka 63d Bb 17.41S 178.50 E
Levuo/Lévuo 8 Kh 56.02N 24.28 E
Lévuo/Levuo 8 Kh 56.02N 24.28 E
Lewes [De.-U.S.] 44 Jf 38.47N 75.08W
Lewes [Eng.-U.K.] 9 Nk 50.52N 0.01 E
Lewin Brzeski 10 Nf 50.46N 17.37 E
Lewis, Butt of- 9 Gc 58.31N 6.15W
Lewis, Isle of- 5 Fd 58.10N 6.40W
Lewis and Clark Lake 45 He 42.50N 97.45W
Lewisburg 44 Gg 37.49N 80.28W
Lewis Pass 62 Ee 42.24S 172.24 E
Lewis Range 38 He 48.30N 113.15W
Lewis River 46 Dd 45.51N 122.48W
Lewis Smith Lake 44 Dh 34.00N 87.07W
Lewiston [Id.-U.S.] 39 He 46.25N 117.01W
Lewiston [Me.-U.S.] 43 Mc 44.06N 70.13W
Lewistown [Mt.-U.S.] 43 Fb 47.04N 109.26W
Lewistown [Pa.-U.S.] 44 Ie 40.37N 77.36W
Lewisville 45 Jj 33.22N 93.35W
Lexington [Ky.-U.S.] 39 Kf 38.03N 84.30W
Lexington [Nb.-U.S.] 43 Hc 40.47N 99.45W
Lexington [N.C.-U.S.] 44 Gh 35.49N 80.15W
Lexington [Ok.-U.S.] 45 Hi 35.01N 97.20W
Lexington [Va.-U.S.] 44 Hg 37.47N 79.27W
Leygues, Iles- 30 Nm 48.45S 69.30 E
Leyre 11 Ej 44.39N 1.01W
Leysdown-on-Sea 12 Cc 51.23N 0.55 E
Leyte 21 Oh 10.50N 124.50 E
Lez 11 Kj 44.13N 4.43 E
Leżajsk 10 Sf 50.16N 22.24 E
Lézard, Pointe à- 51e Ab 16.08N 61.47W
Lézarde, Rivière- 51h Ab 14.36N 61.01W
Lezha 15 Ch 41.47N 19.39 E
Lézignan-Corbières 11 Ik 43.12N 2.46 E
Lgov 19 De 51.41N 35.17 E
Lhari 27 Fe 30.48N 93.25 E
Lhasa 22 Lg 29.42N 91.07 E
Lhazê 27 Ef 29.13N 87.44 E
Lhazhong 27 Ee 31.28N 86.36 E
Lhokseumawe 26 Ce 5.10N 97.08 E
Lhoksukon 26 Ce 5.03N 97.19 E
L'Hôpital 12 Ie 49.10N 6.44 E
Lhorong 27 Ge 30.45N 95.48 E
L'Hospitalet de l'Infant/Hospitalet del Infante 13 Md 40.59N 0.56 E
Lhozhag 27 Ff 28.18N 90.51 E
Lhünzhub (Poindo) 27 Fe 30.17N 91.20 E
Liádhi 15 Jm 36.55N 26.10 E
Liákoura 15 Fk 38.32N 22.37 E
Liamone 11a Aa 42.04N 8.43 E
Liancheng 27 Kf 25.48N 116.48 E
Liancourt 12 Ee 49.20N 2.28 E
Liane 12 Dd 50.43N 1.36 E
Liangcheng 28 Bd 40.32N 112.28 E
Liangpran, Gunung- 26 Ff 1.04N 114.23 E
Liangshan (Houji) 28 Dg 35.48N 116.07 E
Liangzhou → Wuwei 22 Mf 37.58N 102.48 E
Liangzi Hu 27 Je 30.15N 114.32 E
Lianjiang 27 Jg 21.42N 110.14 E
Lianshui 28 Eh 33.47N 119.16 E
Lianxian 27 Jg 24.48N 112.26 E
Lianyin 27 La 53.26N 123.50 E
Lianyungang 27 Ke 34.38N 119.27 E
Lianyungang (Xinpu) 22 Nf 34.34N 119.15 E
Lianzhou → Hepu 27 Ig 21.40N 109.12 E
Lianzhushan 28 Kb 45.28N 131.45 E
Liaocheng 27 Kd 36.27N 115.58 E
Liaodong Bandao=Liaotung Peninsula (EN) 21 Of 40.00N 122.20 E
Liaodong Wan=Liaotung, Gulf of- (EN) 27 Lc 40.00N 121.30 E
Liao He 21 Oe 40.39N 122.12 E
Liaoning Sheng (Liao-ning Sheng) [2] 27 Lc 41.00N 123.00 E
Liao-ning Sheng → Liaoning Sheng [2] 27 Lc 41.00N 123.00 E
Liaotung, Gulf of- (EN)=Liaodong Wan 27 Lc 40.00N 121.30 E
Liaotung Peninsula (EN)=Liaodong Bandao 21 Of 40.00N 122.20 E
Liaoyang 27 Lc 41.16N 123.10 E
Liaoyuan 22 Oe 42.55N 125.09 E
Liaozhong 28 Gd 41.30N 122.42 E
Liard 38 Gc 61.52N 121.18W
Liard River 42 Ee 59.15N 126.09W
Liat, Pulau- 26 Eg 2.53S 107.05 E
Liatorp 8 Fh 56.40N 14.16 E
Liatroim/Leitrim [2] 9 Eg 54.20N 8.20W
Liban 30 Lh 5.05N 40.05 E
Libano 55 Bm 37.32S 61.18W
Libby 46 Hb 48.23N 115.33W
Libenge 31 Ih 3.39N 18.38 E
Libengé 36 Cb 3.39N 18.38 E
Liberal 43 Gd 37.02N 100.55W
Liberec 10 Lf 50.46N 15.03 E
Liberia 47 Gf 10.38N 85.27W
Liberia [1] 31 Fh 6.00N 10.00W
Libertad [Ur.] 55 Dl 34.38S 56.39W
Libertad [Ven.] 49 Li 8.08N 71.28W
Libertad [Ven.] 54 Eb 8.20N 69.37W
Libertade, Rio- 54 He 9.35S 52.17W
Libertador General Bernardo O'Higgins [2] 56 Fd 33.35S 70.45W
Libertador Gen. San Martin 56 Hb 23.48S 64.48W
Libertador General San Martin, Cumbre del- 52 Jh 24.55S 66.40W
Liberty [Mo.-U.S.] 45 Ig 39.15N 94.25W
Liberty [Tx.-U.S.] 45 Ik 30.03N 94.47W
Lībiyā=Libya (EN) [1] 31 If 27.00N 17.00 E
Lībīyah, Aş Şaḩrā' al-=Libyan Desert (EN) 30 Jf 24.00N 25.00 E
Libo 27 If 25.28N 107.52 E
Libobo, Tanjung- 26 Ig 0.54S 128.28 E
Liboi 36 Hb 0.24N 40.57 E
Libourne 11 Fj 44.55N 0.14W
Libramont-Chevigny 12 He 49.55N 5.23 E
Librazhdi 15 Dh 41.11N 20.19 E
Libreville 31 Hh 0.23N 9.27 E
Libro Point 26 Gd 11.26N 119.29 E
Libya (EN)=Lībiyā [1] 31 If 27.00N 17.00 E
Libyan Desert (EN)=Lībīyah, Aş Şaḩrā' al- 30 Jf 24.00N 25.00 E
Licantén 56 Fe 34.59S 72.00W
Licata 14 Hm 37.06N 13.56 E
Lice 24 Ic 38.28N 40.39 E
Licenciado Matienzo 55 Cm 37.55S 58.54W
Lich 12 Kd 50.31N 8.50 E
Licheng → Jinhu 28 Eh 33.01N 119.01 E
Lichfield 9 Li 52.42N 1.48W
Lichinga 31 Kj 13.20S 35.20 E
Lichtenau 12 Kc 51.37N 8.54 E
Lichtenburg 37 De 26.08S 26.08 E
Lichtenfels 10 Hf 50.09N 11.04 E
Lichtenvoorde 12 Ic 51.59N 6.34 E
Licking River 44 Ef 39.06N 84.30W
Licosa, Punta- 14 Ij 40.15N 14.54 E
Licuare 37 Fc 17.54S 36.49 E
Licun → Laoshan 28 Ff 36.10N 120.25 E
Licungo 37 Fc 17.40S 37.22 E
Lida 19 Ce 53.56N 25.18 E
Lidan 8 Ef 58.31N 13.09 E
Liddel 9 Kf 55.04N 2.57W
Liddon Gulf 42 Gb 75.00N 113.30W
Liden 7 De 62.42N 16.48 E
Lidhorikion 15 Fk 38.32N 22.12 E
Lidhult 8 Eh 56.50N 13.26 E
Lidingö 7 Eg 59.22N 18.08 E
Lidköping 7 Cg 58.30N 13.10 E
Lido 34 Fc 12.54N 3.44 E
Lido, Venezia- 14 Ge 45.25N 12.22 E
Lido di Ostia 14 Gi 41.44N 12.16 E
Lidzbark 10 Pc 53.17N 19.49 E
Lidzbark Warmiński 10 Qb 54.09N 20.35 E
Lié 11 Df 48.00N 2.40W
Liebenau 12 Lb 52.36N 9.06 E
Liebig, Mount- 59 Gd 23.15S 131.20 E
Liechtenstein [1] 6 Gf 47.10N 9.30 E
Liège [3] 12 Hd 50.30N 5.40 E
Liège/Luik 6 Ge 50.38N 5.34 E
Lieksa 7 He 63.19N 30.01 E
Lielupė 7 Fh 57.03N 23.56 E
Lielvarde/Lielvārde 8 Kh 56.40N 24.49 E
Lielvārde/Lielvarde 8 Kh 56.40N 24.49 E
Lienen 12 Jb 52.09N 7.59 E
Lienz 14 Gd 46.50N 12.47 E
Liepaja/Liepāja 6 Id 56.35N 21.01 E
Liepāja/Liepaja 6 Id 56.35N 21.01 E
Liepajas, Ozero-/Liepājas Ezers 8 Ih 56.35N 20.35 E
Liepājas ezers/Liepaja, Ozero- 8 Ih 56.35N 20.35 E
Liepna 8 Lg 57.16N 27.35 E
Liepupe 8 Kg 57.22N 24.22 E
Lier/Lierre 11 Kc 51.08N 4.34 E
Lierbyen 8 De 59.47N 10.14 E
Lierneux 12 Hd 50.17N 5.48 E
Lierre/Lier 11 Kc 51.08N 4.34 E
Liesborn, Wadersloh- 12 Kc 51.43N 8.16 E
Lieser 10 Dg 49.55N 7.01 E
Liesing 14 Jc 47.20N 15.02 E
Liestal 14 Bc 47.29N 7.44 E
Lieşti 15 Kd 45.37N 27.31 E
Lieto 8 Jd 60.30N 22.27 E
Lietuvos Tarybu Socialistine Respublika/Litovskaja SSR [2] 19 Cd 56.00N 24.00 E
Lietuvos TSR=Lithuanian SSR (EN) [2] 19 Cd 56.00N 24.00 E
Lietvesi 8 Lc 61.30N 28.00 E
Lieurey 12 Ce 49.14N 0.29 E
Lieuvin 11 Ge 49.10N 0.30 E
Lievestuoreenjärvi 8 Lb 62.20N 26.10 E
Liévin 11 Id 50.25N 2.46 E
Lievre, Rivière du- 44 Jc 45.35N 75.25W
Liezen 14 Ic 47.34N 14.14 E
Lifford/Leifear 9 Fg 54.50N 7.29W
Li Fiord 42 Ia 80.17N 94.35W
Lifjell 8 Ce 59.30N 8.52 E
Lifou, Ile- 57 Hg 20.53S 167.13 E
Lifuka 65b Ba 19.48S 174.21W
Līgatne/Ligatne 8 Kg 57.07N 25.00 E
Ligatne/Līgatne 8 Kg 57.07N 25.00 E
Lighthouse Reef 49 De 17.20N 87.32W
Lignano Sabbiadoro 14 He 45.52N 13.09 E
Lignières 11 Ih 46.45N 2.10 E
Lignon 11 Ki 45.44N 4.08 E
Ligny-en-Barrois 11 Lf 48.41N 5.20 E
Ligonha 37 Fc 16.51S 39.09 E
Ligure, Mar-=Ligurian Sea (EN) 5 Gg 43.30N 9.00 E
Liguria [2] 14 Cf 44.30N 8.50 E
Ligurian Sea (EN)=Ligure, Mar- 5 Gg 43.30N 9.00 E
Lihir Group 57 Ge 3.05S 152.40 E
Lihme 8 Ch 56.36N 8.44 E
Lihoslavl 7 Ih 57.09N 35.29 E
Lihou Reefs and Cays 57 Gf 17.25S 151.40 E
Lihue 60 Oc 21.59N 159.22W
Lihula 7 Fg 58.44N 23.49 E
Liinahamari 7 Hb 69.40N 31.22 E
Lijiang (Dayan) 22 Mg 26.56N 100.15 E
Lijin 28 Ef 37.29N 118.15 E
Lika 14 Jf 44.46N 15.10 E
Lika 14 Jf 44.30N 15.30 E
Likasi 31 Jj 10.59S 26.43 E
Likati 36 Db 2.53N 24.03 E
Likati 36 Db 3.21N 23.53 E
Likėnai/Likenaj 8 Kh 56.11N 24.42 E
Likenaj/Likėnai 8 Kh 56.11N 24.42 E
Likenäs 8 Ed 60.37N 13.02 E
Likhapani 25 Jc 27.19N 95.54 E
Likiep Atoll 57 Hc 9.53N 169.09 E
Likolo 36 Cc 0.43S 19.40 E
Likoma Island 36 Fe 12.04S 34.44 E
Likoto 36 Dc 1.10S 24.45 E
Likouala [3] 36 Cb 2.00N 17.30 E
Likouala 36 Cc 1.13S 16.48 E
Likouala aux Herbes 36 Cc 0.50S 17.11 E
Liku 64k Bb 19.02S 169.47W
L'Ile Rousse 11a Aa 42.38N 8.56 E
Lilibeo, Capo- → Boeo, Capo- 14 Gm 37.34N 12.41 E
Lilienfeld 14 Jb 48.01N 15.38 E
Lilienthal 12 Ka 53.08N 8.55 E
Lilla Edet 7 Cg 58.08N 12.08 E
Lille [Bel.] 12 Gc 51.14N 4.50 E
Lille [Fr.] 6 Ge 50.38N 3.04 E
Lille Bælt=Little Belt (EN) 5 Gd 55.20N 9.45 E
Lillebonne 11 Ge 49.31N 0.33 E
Lille Fiskebanke 8 Bh 56.56N 6.20 E
Lillehammer 7 Cf 61.08N 10.30 E
Lille Hellefiske Bank (EN) 41 Ge 65.05N 54.00W
Lillers 11 Id 50.34N 2.29 E
Lillesand 7 Bg 58.15N 8.24 E
Lillestrøm 8 De 59.57N 11.05 E
Lillhärdal 7 Df 61.51N 14.04 E
Lillie Glacier 66 Kf 70.45S 163.55 E
Lillo 13 Ie 39.43N 3.18W
Lillooet 42 Ff 50.42N 121.56W
Lillooet Range 46 Eb 50.00N 121.45W
Lillooet River 42 Fg 49.45N 122.10W
Lilongwe 31 Kj 13.59S 33.47 E
Liloy 26 He 8.08N 122.40 E
Lim [Afr.] 35 Bd 7.54N 15.46 E
Lim [Yugo.] 14 Ng 43.45N 19.13 E
Lima 13 Dc 41.41N 8.50W
Lima [2] 54 Cf 12.00S 76.35W
Lima [Mt.-U.S.] 46 Id 44.38N 112.36W
Lima [Oh.-U.S.] 43 Kc 40.43N 84.06W
Lima [Par.] 55 Df 23.54S 56.20W
Lima [Peru] 53 Ig 12.03S 77.03W
Lima [Swe.] 8 Ed 60.56N 13.21 E
Lima, Pulau-Pulau- 26 Gg 3.03S 107.24 E
Limagne 11 Jh 46.00N 3.20 E
Līmah 24 Qj 25.56N 56.25 E
Liman [R.S.F.S.R.] 16 Og 45.45N 47.14 E
Liman [Ukr.-U.S.S.R.] 15 Md 45.42N 29.46 E
Limanskoje 15 Mc 46.38N 29.54 E
Limari, Río- 56 Fd 30.44S 71.43W
Limassol/Lemesós 23 Dc 34.40N 33.02 E
Limavady/Léim an Mhadaidh 9 Gf 55.03N 6.57W
Limay 12 Df 48.59N 1.44 E
Limay, Río- 52 Ji 38.59S 68.00W
Limbara 14 Dj 40.51N 9.10 E
Limbaži 7 Fh 57.31N 24.47 E
Limbé 49 Kd 19.42N 72.24W
Limbe, Blantyre- 36 Gf 15.49S 35.03 E
Limbot 63b Cb 14.12S 167.34 E
Limboto 26 Hf 0.37N 122.57 E
Limbourg 12 Hd 50.37N 5.56 E
Limbourg/Limburg 11 Lc 51.05N 5.40 E
Limburg [Bel.] [3] 12 Hc 51.00N 5.30 E
Limburg [Neth.] [3] 12 Hc 51.14N 5.50 E
Limburg/Limbourg 11 Lc 51.05N 5.40 E
Limburg an der Lahn 10 Ef 50.23N 8.03 E
Limedsforsen 8 Ed 60.54N 13.23 E
Limeira 56 Kb 22.34S 47.24W
Limerick/Luimneach [2] 9 Ei 52.30N 9.00W
Limerick/Luimneach 6 Fe 52.40N 8.38W
Limestone, Haḑabat- 33 Fe 24.50N 32.00 E
Limfjorden 5 Gd 56.55N 9.10 E
Limia 13 Dc 41.41N 8.50W
Limingen 7 Cd 64.47N 13.36 E
Liminka 7 Fd 64.49N 25.29 E
Limmat 14 Cc 47.30N 8.15 E
Limmen Bight 59 Hb 14.45S 135.40 E
Limmen Bight River 59 Hc 15.15S 135.30 E
Límni 15 Gk 38.46N 23.19 E
Límnos=Lemnos (EN) 5 Ih 39.55N 25.15 E
Limoeiro 54 Ke 7.52S 35.27W
Limoges 6 Gf 45.51N 1.15 E
Limogne, Causse de- 11 Hj 44.20N 1.55 E
Limon 43 Gd 39.16N 103.41W
Limón [3] 49 Fi 10.00N 83.15W
Limón [C.R.] 39 Kh 10.00N 83.02W
Limón [Hond.] 49 Ef 15.52N 85.33W
Limone Piemonte 14 Bf 44.12N 7.34 E
Limousin 11 Hi 45.30N 1.50 E
Limousin, Plateau du- 11 Hi 45.50N 1.10 E
Limoux 11 Ik 43.04N 2.14 E
Limpopo 30 Jk 25.12S 33.32 E
Limu Ling 27 Ie 19.02N 109.43 E
Limuru 36 Gc 1.06S 36.39 E
Līnah 24 Jh 28.42N 43.48 E
Lin'an 27 Ke 30.14N 119.39 E
Linapacan 26 Gd 11.27N 119.49 E
Linares [Chile] 53 Ii 35.51S 71.36W
Linares [Mex.] 47 Ed 24.52N 99.34W
Linares [Sp.] 13 If 38.05N 3.38W
Linares Viejo 55 Bf 23.09S 61.46W
Linaro, Capo- 14 Fh 42.02N 11.50 E
Lincang 22 Mg 23.48N 100.04 E
Lincheng 28 Cf 37.26N 114.34 E
Lincheng → Xuecheng 28 Dg 34.48N 117.14 E
Lincoln 9 Mh 53.20N 0.30W
Lincoln [Arg.] 56 Hd 34.52S 61.32W
Lincoln [Eng.-U.K.] 9 Mh 53.14N 0.33W
Lincoln [Il.-U.S.] 45 Lf 40.09N 89.22W
Lincoln [Nb.-U.S.] 39 Je 40.48N 96.42W
Lincoln [N.Z.] 62 Ee 43.38S 172.29 E
Lincoln, Mount- 45 Cg 39.21N 106.07W
Lincoln City 46 Cd 44.59N 124.01W
Lincoln Sea 67 Ne 83.00N 56.00W
Lincolnshire [3] 9 Mh 53.00N 0.10W
Lindashalvøya 8 Ad 60.40N 5.15 E
Lindau 10 Fi 47.33N 9.41 E
Linde [Neth.] 12 Hb 52.49N 5.52 E
Linde [R.S.F.S.R.] 20 Hd 64.59N 124.36 E
Linden [Guy.] 54 Gb 6.00N 58.18W
Linden [Tn.-U.S.] 44 Dh 35.37N 87.50W
Lindenows Fjord 41 Hf 60.25N 43.00W
Linderödsšasen 8 Ei 55.53N 13.56 E
Lindesberg 7 Dg 59.35N 15.15 E
Lindesnes 5 Gd 58.00N 7.02 E
Lindhorst 12 Lb 52.22N 9.17 E
Líndhos 15 Lm 36.06N 28.04 E
Lindi [3] 36 Gd 9.30S 38.20 E
Lindi 31 Ki 10.00S 39.43 E
Lindi 30 Jh 0.33N 25.05 E
Lindis Pass 62 Cf 44.35S 169.39 E
Lindlar 12 Jc 51.01N 7.23 E
Lindome 8 Eg 57.34N 12.05 E
Lindong → Bairin Zuoqi 27 Kc 43.59N 119.22 E
Lindsay [Ca.-U.S.] 46 Fh 36.12N 119.05W
Lindsay [Ont.-Can.] 44 Hc 44.21N 78.44W
Lindsdal 8 Gh 56.44N 16.18 E
Line Islands 57 Le 0.01S 157.00W
Linfen 27 Jd 36.03N 111.32 E
Lingayen 22 Oh 16.01N 120.14 E
Lingayen Gulf 26 Hc 16.15N 120.14 E
Lingbi 28 Dh 33.33N 117.33 E
Lingbo 7 Df 61.03N 16.41 E
Lingchuan 28 Bg 35.46N 113.16 E
Lingen (Ems) 10 Dd 52.31N 7.19 E
Lingfield 12 Bc 51.10N 0.01W
Lingga, Kepulauan-=Lingga Archipelago (EN) 21 Mj 0.02S 104.35 E
Lingga, Pulau- 26 Dg 0.12S 104.35 E
Lingga Archipelago (EN)=Lingga, Kepulauan- 21 Mj 0.02S 104.35 E
Linghed 8 Fd 60.47N 15.51 E
Lingling 27 Jf 26.24N 111.41 E
Lingomo 36 Db 0.38N 21.59 E
Lingqiu 28 Ce 39.26N 114.14 E
Lingshan 27 Ig 22.30N 109.17 E
Lingshan Dao 28 Fg 35.45N 120.10 E
Lingshi 28 Af 36.50N 111.46 E
Lingshou 28 Ce 38.18N 114.22 E
Linguère 31 Fg 15.24N 15.07W
Lingwu 27 Id 38.05N 106.20 E
Lingxian 28 Df 37.20N 116.35 E
Lingyuan 28 Ed 41.15N 119.23 E
Linh, Ngoc- 21 Mh 15.04N 107.59 E
Linhai 27 La 51.36N 124.22 E
Linhai (Taizhou) 27 Lf 28.52N 121.08 E
Linhares 54 Jg 19.25S 40.04W
Linhe 27 Ic 40.49N 107.28 E
Linhuaiguan 28 Dh 32.54N 117.39 E
Linjiang 28 Id 41.49N 126.55 E
Linköping 6 Hd 58.25N 15.37 E
Linkou 27 Nb 45.18N 130.18 E
Linkuva 8 Jh 56.02N 23.58 E
Linlü Shan 28 Bf 36.02N 113.42 E
Linn, Mount- 46 Df 40.03N 122.48W
Linneryd 8 Fh 56.40N 15.07 E
Linnhe, Loch- 9 He 56.37N 5.25W
Linnich 12 Id 50.59N 6.16 E
Linosa 14 Go 35.50N 12.50 E
Linovo 10 Ud 52.28N 24.35 E
Linqing 27 Kd 36.48N 115.49 E
Linqu 28 Ef 36.31N 118.32 E
Linquan 28 Ch 33.04N 115.16 E
Linru 28 Bg 34.10N 112.51 E
Lins 56 Kb 21.40S 49.45W
Linsell 8 Eb 62.09N 13.53 E
Linshu (Xiazhuang) 28 Eg 34.56N 118.38 E
Linslade 12 Bc 51.55N 0.40W
Linta 37 Ge 25.02S 44.05 E
Lintao 27 Hd 35.20N 104.00 E
Linthal 14 Cd 46.55N 9.00 E
Linton [Eng.-U.K.] 12 Cb 52.06N 0.16 E
Linton [N.D.-U.S.] 45 Fc 46.16N 100.14W
Linxi [China] 22 Ne 43.36N 118.02 E
Linxi [China] 28 Ee 39.42N 118.26 E
Linxia 22 Mf 35.28N 102.59 E
Linxian 27 Jd 37.57N 111.00 E
Linxiang 28 Bj 29.29N 113.28 E
Linyi [China] 28 Df 37.11N 116.51 E
Linyi [China]' 27 Kd 35.09N 118.15 E
Linz 6 Hf 48.18N 14.18 E
Linze (Shahezhen) 27 Hd 39.10N 100.21 E
Lion, Golfe du-=Lion, Gulf of- (EN) 5 Gg 43.00N 4.00 E
Lion, Gulf of- (EN)=Lion, Golfe du- 5 Gg 43.00N 4.00 E
Lions Den 37 Ec 17.16S 30.02 E
Lion-sur-Mer 12 Be 49.18N 0.19W
Lioppa 26 Ih 7.40S 126.00 E
Lios Mór/Lismore 9 Fi 52.08N 7.55W
Lios na gCearrbhach/Lisburn 9 Gg 54.31N 6.03W
Lios Tuathail/Listovel 9 Di 52.27N 9.29W
Liouesso 36 Cb 1.02N 15.43 E
Lipa 26 Hd 13.57N 121.10 E
Lipany 10 Qg 49.10N 20.58 E
Lipari 14 Il 38.30N 14.55 E
Lipari 14 Il 38.28N 14.57 E
Lipari Islands (EN)=Eolie o Lipari, Isole- 5 Hh 38.35N 14.55 E
Lipeck 6 Je 52.37N 39.35 E
Lipeckaja Oblast [3] 19 De 52.45N 39.10 E
Lipenská přehradní nádrž 10 Kh 48.45N 14.05 E
Liperi 7 Ge 62.32N 29.22 E
Lipez, Cordillera de- 54 Eh 22.00S 66.45W
Liphook 12 Bc 51.04N 0.48W
Lipkani 15 Ja 48.13N 26.48 E
Lipljan 15 Eg 42.32N 21.08 E
Lipno 10 Pd 52.51N 19.10 E
Lipova 15 Ec 46.05N 21.42 E
Lipovcy 20 Ih 44.15N 131.45 E
Lippborg, Lippetal- 12 Kc 51.40N 8.02 E
Lippe 10 Ce 51.39N 6.38 E
Lipper Bergland 12 Kb 52.05N 8.57 E
Lippetal 12 Kc 51.40N 8.13 E
Lippetal-Eickelborn 12 Kc 51.39N 8.13 E
Lippetal-Lippborg 12 Kc 51.40N 8.02 E
Lippischer Wald 12 Kc 51.56N 8.45 E
Lippstadt 10 Ee 51.40N 8.21 E
Lipsko 10 Re 51.09N 21.39 E
Lipsoí 15 Jl 37.20N 26.45 E
Liptako 30 Hg 14.15N 0.02 E
Liptovský Mikuláš 10 Pg 49.05N 19.38 E
Lira 36 Fb 2.15N 32.54 E
Liranga 36 Cc 0.40S 17.36 E
Liri 14 Hi 41.25N 13.52 E
Liria 13 Le 39.38N 0.36W
Lís 13 De 39.53N 8.58W
Lisa 15 Cf 43.08N 19.42 E
Lisac 15 Eg 42.45N 21.56 E
Lisakovsk 19 Ge 52.33N 62.28 E
Lisala 31 Jh 2.09N 21.31 E
Lisboa [2] 13 Ce 39.00N 9.08W
Lisboa=Lisbon (EN) 6 Fh 38.43N 9.08W
Lisbon 45 Hc 46.27N 97.41W
Lisbon (EN)=Lisboa 6 Fh 38.43N 9.08W
Lisbon Canyon (EN) 13 Cf 38.20N 9.20W
Lisburn/Lios na gCearrbhach 9 Gg 54.31N 6.03W
Lisburne, Cape- 40 Fc 68.52N 166.14W
Liscannor Bay/Bá Thuath Reanna 9 Di 52.55N 9.25W
Lisec 10 Uh 48.48N 24.45 E
Li Shan 28 Ag 35.25N 111.58 E
Lishi 27 Jd 37.29N 111.08 E
Lishu 28 Hc 43.19N 124.20 E
Lishui 27 Kf 28.30N 119.55 E
Lisianski Island 57 Jb 26.02N 174.00W
Lisičansk 19 Df 48.53N 38.28 E
Lisieux 11 Ge 49.09N 0.14 E
Liska 15 Dh 41.19N 20.58 E
L'Isle-Adam 12 Ee 49.07N 2.14 E
L'Isle-Jourdain 11 Hk 43.37N 1.05 E
L'Isle sur-la-Sorgue 11 Lk 43.55N 5.03 E
Lismore 58 Gg 28.48S 153.17 E
Lismore/Lios Mór 9 Fi 52.08N 7.55W
Liss 24 Hg 31.14N 38.31 E
Liss 12 Bc 51.02N 0.54W
List 10 Ea 55.01N 8.26 E
Lista 8 Bf 58.10N 6.40 E
Listafjorden 8 Bf 58.10N 6.35 E
Lister, Mount- 66 Kf 78.04S 162.41 E
Lištica 14 Lg 43.23N 17.39 E
Listovel/Lios Tuathail 9 Di 52.27N 9.29W
Listowel 44 Gd 43.44N 80.57W
Liswarta 10 Pe 51.06N 19.01 E
Lit 8 Fa 63.19N 14.49 E
Litang [China] 27 Ig 23.12N 109.05 E
Litang [China] 27 He 30.02N 100.18 E
Litani Rivier 54 Hc 3.18N 54.06W
Litchfield 45 Id 45.08N 94.31W
Lithgow 58 Gh 33.29S 150.09 E
Líthinon, Ákra- 15 Ho 34.55N 24.44 E
Lithuania (EN) 5 Id 56.00N 24.00 E
Lithuanian SSR (EN)=Lietuvos TSR [2] 19 Cd 56.00N 24.00 E
Litókhoron 15 Fi 40.06N 22.30 E
Litoměřice 10 Kf 50.32N 14.08 E
Litovel 10 Ng 49.43N 17.05 E
Litovko 20 Ig 49.17N 135.10 E
Litovskaja Sovetskaja Socialističeskaja Respublika [2] 19 Cd 56.00N 24.00 E
Litovskaja SSR/Lietuvos Tarybu Socialistine Respublika [2] 19 Cd 56.00N 24.00 E
Little Abaco Island 47 Ic 26.53N 77.43W
Little Abitibi River 44 Ha 49.29N 79.32W
Little Aden 23 Fg 12.45N 44.52 E
Little America 46 Kf 41.32N 109.47W
Little Andaman 21 Lh 10.45N 92.30 E
Little Bahama Bank (EN) 47 Ic 26.30N 78.00W
Little Barrier Island 62 Fb 36.10S 175.05 E
Little Beaver Creek 45 Ec 46.17N 103.56W
Little Belt (EN)=Lille Bælt 5 Gd 55.20N 9.45 E
Little Belt Mountains 46 Jc 46.45N 110.35W
Little Blue River 45 Hg 39.41N 96.40W
Little Bow River 46 Ib 49.53N 112.29W
Little Carpathians (EN) = Malé Karpaty 10 Nh 48.30N 17.20 E
Little Cayman 47 He 19.41N 80.03W
Little Colorado River 38 Hc 36.11N 111.48W
Little Current 42 Jg 45.58N 81.56W
Little Current 42 Jf 50.57N 84.36W
Little Dry Creek 46 Lc 47.21N 106.22W
Little Exuma Island 49 Jb 23.27N 75.37W
Little Falls 43 Ib 45.59N 94.21W
Littlefield 45 Ej 33.55N 102.20W
Little Fort 46 Ea 51.25N 120.12W
Little Grand Rapids 42 Hf 52.02N 95.25W
Little Halibut Bank 9 Lc 58.20N 1.15W
Littlehampton 12 Bd 50.48N 0.32W
Little Inagua Island 47 Jd 21.30N 73.00W
Little Karroo (EN)=Klein-Karoo 37 Cf 33.42S 21.20 E
Little Missouri 38 Ie 47.30N 102.25W
Little Namaland (EN)=Namakwaland 37 Be 29.00S 17.00 E
Little Nicobar 25 Ig 7.20N 93.40 E
Little Ouse 9 Ni 52.30N 0.22 E
Littleport 12 Cb 52.27N 0.18 E
Little Powder River 46 Md 45.28N 105.20W
Little Quill Lake 46 Ma 51.55N 104.05W
Little River 62 Ee 43.46S 172.47 E
Little Rock 39 Jf 34.44N 92.15W
Little Rocky Mountains 46 Kb 48.00N 108.45W

Index Symbols

[1] Independent Nation
[2] State, Region
[3] District, County
[4] Municipality
[5] Colony, Dependency
Continent
Physical Region
Historical or Cultural Region
Mount, Mountain
Volcano
Hill
Mountains, Mountain Range
Hills, Escarpment
Plateau, Upland
Pass, Gap
Plain, Lowland
Delta
Salt Flat
Valley, Canyon
Crater, Cave
Karst Features
Depression
Polder
Desert, Dunes
Forest, Woods
Heath, Steppe
Oasis
Cape, Point
Coast, Beach
Cliff
Peninsula
Isthmus
Sandbank
Island
Atoll
Rock, Reef
Islands, Archipelago
Rocks, Reefs
Coral Reef
Well, Spring
Geyser
River, Stream
Waterfall Rapids
River Mouth, Estuary
Lake
Salt Lake
Intermittent Lake
Reservoir
Swamp, Pond
Canal
Glacier
Ice Shelf, Pack Ice
Ocean
Sea
Gulf, Bay
Strait, Fjord
Lagoon
Bank
Seamount
Tablemount
Ridge
Shelf
Basin
Escarpment, Sea Scarp
Fracture
Trench, Abyss
National Park, Reserve
Point of Interest
Recreation Site
Cave, Cavern
Historic Site
Ruins
Wall, Walls
Church, Abbey
Temple
Scientific Station
Airport
Port
Lighthouse
Mine
Tunnel
Dam, Bridge

Little Scarcies 34 Cd 8.51N 13.09W
Little Sioux River 45 Hf 41.49N 96.04W
Little Sitkin 40a Cb 51.55N 178.30 E
Little Smoky 42 Fe 55.39N 117.37W
Little Snake River 45 Bf 40.27N 108.26W
Littleton [Co.-U.S.] 45 Dg 39.37N 105.01W
Littleton [N.H.-U.S.] 44 Lc 44.18N 71.46W
Little White River [Ont.-Can.] 44 Fb 46.15N 83.00W
Little White River [S.D.-U.S.] 45 Fe 43.44N 100.40W
Littoral [3] 34 He 4.30N 10.00 E
Litvinov 10 Jf 50.36N 13.36 E
Liuba 27 Ie 33.39N 106.53 E
Liuhe 27 Mc 42.16N 125.45 E
Liu He [China] 28 Gd 41.48N 122.43 E
Liu He [China] 28 Ic 42.46N 126.13 E
Liuheng Dao 28 Gj 29.43N 122.08 E
Liujia Xia 27 Hd 35.50N 103.00 E
Liukang Tenggaja, Kepulauan- 26 Gh 6.45S 118.50 E
Liupai → Tian'e 27 If 25.05N 107.12 E
Liupan Shan 27 Id 35.40N 106.15 E
Liuqu He 27 Fd 40.10N 120.15 E
Liuwa Plain 36 De 14.27S 22.25 E
Liuyang 28 Bj 28.09N 113.38 E
Liuzhangzhen → Yuanqu 27 Jd 35.19N 111.44 E
Liuzhou 22 Mg 24.22N 109.20 E
Līvāni/Livány 7 Gh 56.22N 26.12 E
Livanjsko Polje 14 Kg 43.51N 16.50 E
Livany/Līvāni 7 Gh 56.22N 26.12 E
Livarot 12 Ce 49.01N 0.09 E
Livengood 40 Jc 65.32N 148.33W
Livenza 14 Ge 45.35N 12.51 E
Livenzi 15 Ge 44.14N 23.47 E
Live Oak 44 Fj 30.18N 82.59W
Livermore 46 Eh 37.41N 121.46W
Livermore, Mount- 45 Dk 30.37N 104.08W
Liverpool [Eng.-U.K.] 6 Fe 53.25N 2.55W
Liverpool [N.S.-Can.] 42 Lh 44.02N 64.43W
Liverpool, Cape- 42 Jb 73.38N 78.05W
Liverpool Bay [Can.] 42 Ec 70.00N 129.00W
Liverpool Bay [Eng.-U.K.] 9 Jh 53.30N 3.16W
Liverpool Range 59 Kf 31.40S 150.30 E
Liverpool River 59 Gb 12.00S 134.00 E
Livigno 14 Ed 46.32N 10.04 E
Livingston [Guat.] 49 Cf 15.50N 88.45W
Livingston [Mt.-U.S.] 43 Eb 45.40N 110.34W
Livingston [Newf.-Can.] 42 Kf 53.40N 66.10W
Livingston [Tn.-U.S.] 44 Eg 36.23N 85.19W
Livingston [Tx.-U.S.] 45 Ik 30.43N 94.56W
Livingston, Lake- 45 Ik 30.45N 95.15W
Livingstone, Chutes de-= Livingstone Falls (EN) 30 Ii 4.50S 14.30 E
Livingstone Falls (EN)= Livingstone, Chutes de- 30 Ii 4.50S 14.30 E
Livingstone Memorial 36 Fe 12.19S 30.18 E
Livingstone Mountains 36 Fd 9.45S 34.20 E
Livingstonia 36 Fe 10.36S 34.07 E
Livingston Island 66 Qe 62.36S 60.30W
Livno 14 Lg 43.50N 17.01 E
Livny 19 De 52.28N 37.37 E
Livonia 44 Fd 42.25N 83.23W
Livonia (EN)=Livonija 5 Id 58.50N 27.30 E
Livonija=Livonia (EN) 5 Id 58.50N 27.30 E
Livorno=Leghorn (EN) 6 Hg 43.33N 10.19 E
Livradois, Monts du- 11 Ji 45.30N 3.33 E
Livramento do Brumado 54 Jf 13.39S 41.50W
Livron-sur-Drôme 11 Kj 44.46N 4.51 E
Liwale 36 Gd 9.46S 37.56 E
Liwiec 10 Rd 52.35N 21.33 E
Liwonde 36 Gf 15.01S 35.13 E
Lixi 27 Hf 26.21N 102.03 E
Lixian [China] 27 Ie 34.11N 105.02 E
Lixian [China] 27 Jf 29.40N 111.45 E
Lixian [China] 28 Ce 38.29N 115.34 E
Lixin 28 Dh 33.09N 116.12 E
Lixoúrion 15 Dk 38.12N 20.26 E
Liyang 28 Ei 31.26N 119.29 E
Lizard 9 Hl 49.57N 5.13W
Lizard Point 5 Ff 49.56N 5.13W
Lizhu 28 Fj 29.58N 120.26 E
Lizy sur Ourcq 12 Fe 49.01N 3.02 E
Ljady 8 Mf 58.35N 28.55 E
Ljahoviči 16 Ec 53.04N 26.15 E
Ljahovskije Ostrova= Lyakhov Islands (EN) 21 Qb 73.30N 141.00 E
Ljalja 17 Jg 59.10N 61.30 E
Ljamin 17 Of 61.18N 71.45 E
Ljangar 18 Ed 40.23N 65.59 E
Ljangasovo 7 Lg 58.33N 49.29 E
Ljapin 17 Je 63.38N 61.58 E
Ljaskelja 8 Nc 61.39N 31.03 E
Ljaskovec 15 If 43.06N 25.43 E
Ljig 15 De 44.14N 20.15 E
Ljuban [Bye.-U.S.S.R.] 16 Ec 52.48N 27.59 E
Ljuban [R.S.F.S.R.] 7 Hg 59.22N 31.13 E
Ljubar 16 Ee 49.55N 27.44 E
Ljubaševka 15 Nb 47.50N 30.07 E
Ljubelj 14 Id 46.26N 14.16 E
Ljubercy 19 Dd 55.40N 37.55 E
Ljubešov 10 Ve 51.45N 25.37 E
Ljubim 7 Jg 58.22N 40.41 E
Ljubimec 15 Jh 41.50N 26.05 E
Ljubinje 14 Mh 42.57N 18.06 E
Ljubišnja 15 Cf 43.20N 19.07 E
Ljubljana 6 Hf 46.02N 14.30 E
Ljuboml 10 Cd 51.15N 23.59 E
Ljubotin 16 Ie 49.59N 35.55 E
Ljubovija 15 Ce 44.12N 19.22 E
Ljubuški 14 Lg 43.12N 17.33 E
Ljubytino 7 Hg 58.50N 33.25 E
Ljudinovo 19 De 53.51N 34.28 E
Ljugarn 7 Eh 57.19N 18.42 E
Ljungan 5 Hc 62.19N 17.23 E
Ljungaverk 8 Gb 62.29N 16.03 E
Ljungby 7 Ch 56.50N 13.56 E
Ljungbyholm 8 Gh 56.38N 16.10 E
Ljungdalen 7 Ce 62.51N 12.47 E
Ljungsbro 8 Ff 58.31N 15.30 E
Ljungskile 8 Df 58.14N 11.55 E
Ljusdal 7 Df 61.50N 16.05 E
Ljusnan 5 Hc 61.12N 17.08 E
Ljusne 7 Df 61.13N 17.08 E
Ljusterö 8 He 59.30N 18.35 E
Ljuta 8 Mf 58.33N 28.45 E
Llandilo 9 Jj 51.53N 3.59W
Llandovery 9 Jj 51.59N 3.48W
Llandrindod Wells 9 Ji 52.15N 3.23W
Llandudno 9 Jh 53.19N 3.49W
Llanelli 9 Ij 51.42N 4.10W
Llanes 13 Ha 43.25N 4.45W
Llangefni 9 Ih 53.16N 4.18W
Llangollen 9 Ji 52.58N 3.10W
Llano 45 Gk 30.45N 98.41W
Llano Estacado 38 If 33.30N 102.40W
Llano River 45 Gk 30.35N 98.25W
Llanos 52 Je 5.00N 70.00W
Llanos de Sonora 47 Bc 28.20N 111.00W
Llanquihue, Lago- 56 Ff 41.08S 72.48W
Llata 54 Ce 9.25S 76.47W
Lleida/Lérida 13 Mc 41.37N 0.37 E
Llerena 13 Ff 38.14N 6.01W
Lleyn 9 Ii 52.54N 4.30W
Llica 54 Eg 19.52S 68.16W
Llivia 13 Nb 42.28N 1.59 E
Llobregat 13 Oc 41.19N 2.09 E
Lloret de Mar 13 Oc 41.42N 2.51 E
Llorona, Punta- 49 Fi 8.37N 83.44W
Llorri/Orri, Pic d'- 13 Nb 42.23N 1.12 E
Lloydminster 42 Gf 53.17N 110.00W
Lluchmayor 13 Oe 39.29N 2.54 E
Llullaillaco, Volcán- 52 Jh 24.43S 68.33W
Lo 63b Ca 13.21S 166.38 E
Loa 46 Jg 38.24N 111.38W
Loa, Rio- 56 Fb 21.26S 70.04W
Loanatit, Pointe- 63b Dd 19.21S 169.14 E
Loange 30 Ji 4.17S 20.02 E
Loango 36 Bc 4.39S 11.48 E
Loano 14 Cf 44.08N 8.15 E
Loban 7 Mh 56.59N 51.12 E
Lobatse 31 Jk 25.13S 25.41 E
Löbau/Lubij 10 Ke 51.06N 14.40 E
Lobaye 30 Ih 3.41N 18.35 E
Lobaye [3] 35 Be 4.00N 17.40 E
Lobenstein 10 Hf 50.27N 11.39 E
Loberia 56 Ie 38.09S 58.47W
Łobez 10 Lc 53.39N 15.36 E
Lobito 31 Ij 12.22S 13.34 E
Lobo 34 Dd 6.02N 6.47W
Lobos 56 Ie 35.11S 59.06W
Lobos 32 Ed 28.45N 13.49W
Lobos, Cabo- 48 Cc 29.55N 112.45W
Lobos, Cay- 49 Ib 22.24N 77.32W
Lobos, Cayo- 48 Ph 18.22N 87.24W
Lobos, Isla- 48 Dd 27.20N 110.36W
Lobos, Islas de- 48 Kg 21.27N 97.15W
Lobos de Afuera, Islas- 54 Be 6.57S 80.42W
Lobos de Tierra, Isla- 54 Be 6.27S 80.52W
Lobva 19 Gd 59.12N 60.30 E
Łobżonka 10 Nc 53.07N 17.18 E
Locana 14 Be 45.25N 7.27 E
Locarno 14 Cd 46.10N 8.48 E
Loch Aillionn/Allen, Lough- 9 Eg 54.08N 8.08W
Loch Arabhach/Arrow, Lough- 9 Eg 54.05N 8.20W
Lochboisdale 9 Fd 57.09N 7.19W
Loch Cairlinn/Carlingford Lough 9 Gg 54.05N 6.14W
Loch Ce/Key, Lough- 9 Eg 54.00N 8.15W
Loch Coirib/Corrib, Lough 9 Dh 53.05N 9.10W
Loch Con/Conn, Lough- 9 Dg 54.04N 9.20W
Loch Cuan/Strangford Lough 9 Hg 54.26N 5.36W
Loch Deirgeirt/Derg, Lough- 9 Ei 53.00N 8.20W
Lochearnhead 9 Ie 56.23N 4.18W
Loch Éirne Íochtair/Lower Lough Erne 9 Fg 54.30N 7.50W
Loch Éirne Uachtair/Upper Lough Erne 9 Fg 54.20N 7.30W
Lochem 12 Ib 52.10N 6.25 E
Loches 11 Gg 47.08N 1.00 E
Loch Feabhail/Foyle, Lough- 9 Ff 55.05N 7.10W
Loch Garman/Wexford 6 Fe 52.20N 6.27W
Loch Garman/Wexford [2] 9 Gi 52.20N 6.40W
Lochgilphead 9 He 56.03N 5.26W
Loch Hinninn/Ennell, Lough- 9 Fh 53.28N 7.24W
Lochinver 9 Hc 58.09N 5.15W
Loch Lao/Belfast Lough 9 Hg 54.40N 5.50W
Loch Léin/Leane, Lough- 9 Di 52.05N 9.35W
Loch Leven 9 Je 56.13N 3.10W
Loch Long 9 Ie 56.04N 4.50W
Lochmaddy 9 Fd 57.36N 7.10W
Loch Measca/Mask, Lough- 9 Dh 53.35N 9.20W
Lochnagar 9 Je 56.55N 3.10W
Loch nEathach/Neagh, Lough- 5 Fe 54.38N 6.24W
Loch Ness 9 Id 57.15N 4.30W
Łochów 10 Rd 52.32N 21.48 E
Loch Pholl an Phúca/ Poulaphuca Reservoir 9 Gh 53.10N 6.30W
Loch Rí/Ree, Lough- 9 Fh 53.35N 8.00W
Lochsa River 46 Hc 46.08N 115.36W
Loch Sileann/Sheelin, Lough- 9 Fh 53.48N 7.20W
Loch Súilí/Swilly, Lough- 9 Ff 55.10N 7.38W
Loch Uí Ghadra/Gara, Lough- 9 Eh 53.55N 8.30W
Lochy 9 He 56.49N 5.06W
Lochy, Loch- 9 Ie 56.55N 4.55W
Lockerbie 9 Jf 55.07N 3.22W
Lockhart 45 Hl 29.53N 97.41W
Lock Haven 44 Ie 41.09N 77.28W
Löcknitz 10 Hc 53.07N 11.16 E
Lockport 44 Hd 43.11N 78.39W
Locminé 11 Dg 47.53N 2.50W
Locri 14 Kl 38.14N 16.16 E
Lod 24 Fg 31.58N 34.54 E
Lodalskåpa 7 Bf 61.47N 7.12 E
Loddon 12 Db 52.32N 1.29 E
Loddon River 59 Ig 36.41S 143.55 E
Lodejnoje Pole 19 Dc 60.44N 33.33 E
Lodève 11 Jk 43.43N 3.19 E
Lodi [Ca.-U.S.] 46 Eg 38.08N 121.16W
Lodi [It.] 14 De 45.19N 9.30 E
Lødingen 7 Db 68.25N 16.00 E
Lodja 31 Ji 3.29S 23.26 E
Lodosa 13 Jb 42.25N 2.05W
Lödöse 8 Ef 58.02N 12.08 E
Lodwar 31 Kh 3.07N 35.36 E
Łódź 6 He 51.46N 19.30 E
Łódź [2] 10 Pe 51.45N 19.30 E
Loei 25 Ke 17.32N 101.34 E
Loeriesfontein 37 Bf 30.56S 19.26 E
Lofanga 65b Ba 19.50S 174.33W
Loffa 30 Fh 6.36N 11.05W
Loffa [3] 34 Dd 7.45N 10.00W
Lofoten 5 Hb 68.30N 15.00 E
Lofoten Basin (EN) 5 Ga 70.00N 4.00 E
Lofsdalen 8 Eb 62.07N 13.16 E
Loftahammar 8 Gg 57.52N 16.40 E
Loga 34 Fc 13.37N 3.14 E
Logan [N.M.-U.S.] 45 Ei 35.22N 103.25W
Logan [Oh.-U.S.] 44 Ff 39.32N 82.24W
Logan [Ut.-U.S.] 43 Ec 41.44N 111.50W
Logan [W.V.-U.S.] 44 Gg 37.52N 81.58W
Logan, Mount- [Can.] 38 Ec 60.34N 140.24W
Logan, Mount- [Wa.-U.S.] 46 Eb 48.32N 120.57W
Logan Martin Lake 44 Di 33.40N 86.15W
Logan Mountains 42 Ed 61.00N 128.00W
Logansport 44 De 40.45N 86.21W
Loge 30 Ii 7.49S 13.06 E
Logojsk 8 Lj 54.12N 27.57 E
Logone 30 Ig 12.06N 15.02 E
Logone Birni 34 Ic 11.47N 15.06 E
Logone Occidental [3] 35 Bd 8.40N 16.00 E
Logone Occidental 35 Bd 9.07N 16.26 E
Logone Oriental [3] 35 Bd 8.20N 16.30 E
Logone Oriental 35 Bd 9.07N 16.26 E
Logroño [3] 13 Jb 42.15N 2.30W
Logroño [Arg.] 55 Bi 29.30S 61.42W
Logroño [Sp.] 13 Jb 42.28N 2.27W
Logrosán 13 Ge 39.20N 5.29W
Løgstør 7 Bh 56.58N 9.15 E
Logudoro 14 Cj 40.35N 8.40 E
Løgumkloster 8 Ci 55.03N 8.57 E
Lögurinn 7a Cb 65.15N 14.30W
Lohja/Lojo 7 Ff 60.15N 24.05 E
Lohjanjärvi 8 Jd 60.15N 23.55 E
Lohjanselkä/Lojo åsen 8 Kd 60.15N 24.10 E
Löhme 12 Kc 51.41N 8.42 E
Löhne 10 Ed 52.11N 8.41 E
Lohne 12 Kb 52.40N 8.14 E
Lohra 12 Kd 50.44N 8.38 E
Lohr am Main 10 Ff 49.59N 9.35 E
Lohusuu/Lokusu 8 Lf 58.53N 27.01 E
Lohvica 16 Hd 50.22N 33.15 E
Loi, Phou- 25 Kd 20.16N 103.12 E
Loi-Kaw 25 Je 19.41N 97.13 E
Loile 36 Dc 0.52S 20.12 E
Loimaa 7 Ff 60.51N 23.03 E
Loimijoki 8 Jc 61.13N 22.38 E
Loing 11 If 48.23N 2.48 E
Loir 11 Fg 47.33N 0.32W
Loir, Vaux du- 11 Gg 47.45N 0.25 E
Loire [3] 11 Ji 45.30N 4.00 E
Loire 5 Ff 47.16N 2.11W
Loire, Canal latéral à la- 11 Jh 46.29N 3.59 E
Loire, Val de- 11 Hg 47.40N 1.35 E
Loire-Atlantique [3] 11 Eg 47.15N 1.50W
Loiret [3] 11 Ig 47.55N 2.20 E
Loir-et-Cher [3] 11 Hg 47.30N 1.30 E
Loisach 10 Hi 47.56N 11.27 E
Loison 12 He 49.30N 5.17 E
Loja [Ec.] 53 If 4.00S 79.13W
Loja [Sp.] 13 Hg 37.10N 4.09W
Lojo/Lohja 7 Ff 60.15N 24.05 E
Lojo åsen/Lohjanselkä 8 Kd 60.15N 24.10 E
Loka 35 Ee 4.16N 31.01 E
Lokači 10 Uf 50.43N 24.44 E
Lokalahti 8 Id 60.41N 21.28 E
Lokandu 36 Ec 2.31S 25.47 E
Lokantekojärvi 7 Gc 68.56N 27.40 E
Lokbatan 16 Pi 40.21N 49.42 E
Lokčim 17 Ef 61.48N 51.45 E
Løken 8 De 59.48N 11.29 E
Lokeren 11 Jc 51.06N 4.00 E
Lokichar 36 Gb 2.23N 35.39 E
Lokichokio 36 Fb 4.12N 34.21 E
Lokitaung 36 Gb 4.16N 35.45 E
Løkken [Den.] 8 Cg 57.22N 9.43 E
Løkken [Nor.] 7 Be 63.05N 9.36 E
Loknja 7 Hh 56.49N 30.09 E
Loko 34 Gd 8.00N 7.50 E
Lokoja 34 Gd 7.48N 6.44 E
Lokomo 34 Ie 2.41N 15.19 E
Lokoro 36 Cc 1.43S 18.23 E
Lokossa 34 Fd 6.38N 1.43 E
Lokot 16 Ic 52.33N 34.31 E
Lokoti 34 Hd 8.22N 14.20 E
Loksa 7 Fg 59.34N 25.44 E
Loks Land 42 Ld 62.27N 64.30W
Lokuru 63a Cc 8.35S 157.20 E
Lokusu/Lohusuu 8 Lf 58.53N 27.01 E
Lokwa Kangole 36 Gb 3.32N 35.54 E
Lol 30 Jh 9.13N 28.59 E
Lola 34 Dd 7.48N 8.32W
Lolimi 35 Ee 4.35N 33.59 E
Loliondo 36 Gc 2.03S 35.37 E
Lolland 5 He 54.45N 11.30 E
Lollar 12 Kd 50.38N 8.42 E
Lolo 36 Db 2.13N 23.00 E
Lolo 36 Bc 0.40S 12.28 E
Lolodorf 34 He 3.14N 10.44 E
Lolo Pass 46 Hc 46.40N 114.33W
Loloway 63b Cb 15.17S 167.58 E
Lom 15 Gf 43.49N 23.14 E
Lom [Afr.] 34 Hd 5.20N 13.24 E
Lom [Bul.] 15 Gf 43.50N 23.15 E
Loma Bonita 48 Lh 18.07N 95.53W
Lomaloma 63d Cb 17.17S 178.59W
Lomami 30 Jh 0.46N 24.16 E
Loma Mountains 30 Fh 9.10N 11.07W
Lomas de Vallejos 55 Dh 27.44S 57.56W
Loma Verde 55 Cl 35.16S 58.24W
Lomba 36 Df 15.36S 21.32 E
Lombarda, Serra- 54 Hc 2.50N 51.50W
Lombarde, Prealpi- 14 De 46.00N 9.30 E
Lombardia = Lombardy (EN) [2] 14 De 45.40N 9.30 E
Lombardy (EN) = Lombardia [2] 14 De 45.40N 9.30 E
Lomblen, Pulau- 21 Oj 8.25S 123.30 E
Lombok, Pulau- 21 Nj 8.45S 116.30 E
Lombok, Selat- 26 Gh 8.30S 115.50 E
Lomé 31 Hh 6.08N 1.13 E
Lomela 31 Ji 2.18S 23.17 E
Lomela 30 Ji 0.14S 20.42 E
Lomellina 14 Ce 45.15N 8.45 E
Loméméti 63b Dd 19.30S 169.27 E
Lomié 34 He 3.10N 13.37 E
Lomlom 63c Bb 10.19S 166.16 E
Lomma 8 Ei 55.41N 13.05 E
Lomme 12 Hd 50.08N 5.10 E
Lommel 11 Lc 51.14N 5.18 E
Lomnica 10 Ug 49.02N 24.47 E
Lomond, Loch- 9 Ie 56.08N 4.38W
Lomonosov 19 Cd 59.55N 29.40 E
Lomonosovki 19 Ge 52.50N 66.28 E
Lomonosov Ridge (EN) 67 De 88.00N 140.00 E
Lomont 11 Mg 47.21N 6.36 E
Lompobatang, Gunung- 26 Gh 5.20S 119.55 E
Lompoc 43 Ce 34.38N 120.27W
Lomsegga 8 Cc 61.49N 8.22 E
Łomża 10 Sc 53.11N 22.05 E
Łomża [2] 10 Sc 53.10N 22.05 E
Lønahorg 8 Bd 60.42N 6.25 E
Loncoche 56 Fe 39.22S 72.38W
Londa 25 Ee 15.28N 74.31 E
Londerzeel 12 Gc 51.01N 4.18 E
Londiani 36 Gc 0.10S 35.36 E
Londinières 12 De 49.50N 1.24 E
London [Eng.-U.K.] 6 Fe 51.30N 0.10W
London [Kir.] 64g Bb 1.58N 157.29W
London [Ky.-U.S.] 44 Eg 37.08N 84.05W
London [Ont.-Can.] 39 Ke 42.59N 81.14W
London-Barnet 12 Bc 51.39N 0.12W
London-Bexley 12 Cc 51.26N 0.09 E
London Bridge 51p Bb 12.17N 61.35W
London-Bromley 12 Cc 51.25N 0.01 E
London-Croydon 9 Mj 51.23N 0.07W
Londonderry/Doire 6 Fd 55.00N 7.19W
Londonderry, Cape- 59 Fb 13.45S 126.55 E
London-Ealing 12 Bc 51.30N 0.19W
London-Enfield 12 Bc 51.40N 0.04W
London-Greenwich 9 Mj 51.28N 0.00
London-Haringey 12 Bc 51.36N 0.06W
London-Harrow 12 Bc 51.36N 0.20W
London-Havering 12 Cc 51.36N 0.11 E
London-Hillingdon 12 Bc 51.31N 0.27W
London-Kingston-upon-Thames 9 Mj 51.28N 0.19W
London-Redbridge 12 Cc 51.35N 0.08 E
London-Sutton 12 Bc 51.21N 0.12W
London-Wandsworth 12 Bc 51.27N 0.12W
London-Westminster 12 Bc 51.30N 0.08W
Londrina 53 Kh 23.18S 51.09W
Lone Pine 46 Fh 36.36N 118.04W
Longa 36 Ce 14.41S 18.29 E
Longa [Ang.] 36 Cf 16.25S 19.04 E
Longa [Ang.] 36 Be 10.15S 13.30 E
Longa, Proliv- = De Long Strait (EN) 21 Tb 70.20N 178.00 E
Longá, Rio- 54 Jd 3.09S 41.56W
Long Akah 26 Ff 3.19N 114.47 E
Longarone 14 Gd 46.16N 12.18 E
Longbangun 26 Gf 0.36N 115.11 E
Long Bay [Bar.] 51q Bb 13.04N 59.29W
Long Bay [S.C.-U.S.] 43 Le 33.35N 78.45W
Long Beach [Ca.-U.S.] 39 Hf 33.46N 118.11W
Long Beach [N.Y.-U.S.] 44 Ke 40.35N 73.40W
Long Beach [Wa.-U.S.] 46 Cc 46.21N 124.03W
Long Branch 43 Mc 40.18N 74.00W
Long Buckby 12 Ab 52.18N 1.04W
Long Cay 49 Jb 22.37N 74.20W
Longchuan 27 Kg 24.10N 115.17 E
Long Creek 46 Nb 49.07N 103.00W
Long Eaton 12 Ab 52.54N 1.16W
Longfeng 28 Ha 46.31N 125.02 E
Longford/An Longfort [2] 9 Fh 53.40N 7.40W
Longford/An Longfort 9 Fh 53.44N 7.47W
Long Forties 9 Nd 57.10N 0.05 E
Long Hu 28 Dj 29.37N 116.12 E
Longhua 28 Dd 41.18N 117.44 E
Longido 36 Gc 2.44S 36.41 E
Long Island [Atg.] 51d Bb 17.08N 61.45W
Long Island [Bah.] 38 Lg 23.10N 75.10W
Long Island [Can.] 42 Jf 54.50N 79.20W
Long Island [Can.] 44 Nc 44.20N 66.15W
Long Island [Pap.N.Gui.] 57 Fe 5.36S 148.00 E
Long Island [U.S.] 38 Le 40.50N 73.00W
Long Island Sound 44 Ke 41.05N 72.58W
Longjiang 27 Lb 47.20N 123.09 E
Longjuzhai → Danfeng 27 Je 33.44N 110.22 E
Longkou 27 Ld 37.39N 120.20 E
Longlac 42 Ig 49.50N 86.32W
Long Lake [N.D.-U.S.] 45 Fc 46.43N 100.07W
Long Lake [Ont.-Can.] 45 Mb 49.32N 86.45W
Longmalinau 26 Gf 3.30N 116.31 E
Long Men 27 Je 34.40N 110.30 E
Longmont 45 Df 40.10N 105.06W
Longnan 27 Jg 24.54N 114.48 E
Longobucco 14 Kk 39.27N 16.37 E
Longoz 15 Kf 43.02N 27.41 E
Longping → Luodian 27 If 25.26N 106.47 E
Long Point 44 Gd 42.34N 80.15W
Long Point Bay 44 Gd 42.40N 80.14W
Longpujungan 26 Gf 2.34N 115.40 E
Longquan 27 Kf 28.06N 119.05 E
Long Range Mountains 42 Lg 48.00N 58.30W
Longreach 58 Fg 23.26S 144.15 E
Long Sand 12 Dc 51.37N 1.10 E
Longs Peak 38 Ie 40.15N 105.37W
Long Sutton 12 Cb 52.47N 0.08 E
Longtan 28 Eh 32.10N 119.03 E
Longtown 9 Kf 55.01N 2.58W
Longué 11 Fg 47.23N 0.07W
Longueau 12 Ee 49.52N 2.21 E
Longueville-sur-Scie 12 De 49.48N 1.06 E
Longuyon 11 Le 49.26N 5.36 E
Long Valley 46 Ji 34.37N 111.16W
Longview [Tx.-U.S.] 43 Ie 32.30N 94.44W
Longview [Wa.-U.S.] 43 Cb 46.08N 122.57W
Longwu 27 Hg 24.07N 102.18 E
Longwy 11 Le 49.31N 5.46 E
Longxi 27 Hd 35.01N 104.38 E
Longxian 27 Id 35.00N 106.53 E
Longxian → Wengyuan 27 Jg 24.21N 114.13 E
Longxi Shan 27 Kf 26.35N 117.17 E
Long Xuyen 25 Lf 10.23N 105.25 E
Longyan 27 Kf 25.06N 117.01 E
Longyao 28 Cf 37.21N 114.46 E
Longyearbyen 67 Kd 78.13N 15.38 E
Longyou 28 Ej 29.01N 119.10 E
Longzhou 27 Ig 22.23N 106.49 E
Lonigo 14 Fe 45.23N 11.23 E
Löningen 10 Dd 52.44N 7.46 E
Lonja 14 Ke 45.27N 16.41 E
Lonjsko Polje 14 Ke 45.24N 16.42 E
Lönsboda 8 Fh 56.24N 14.19 E
Lons-le-Saunier 11 Lh 46.40N 5.33 E
Lontra, Ribeirão- 55 Fe 21.28S 53.37W
Lookout, Cape- [N.C.-U.S.] 43 Le 34.35N 76.32W
Lookout, Cape- [Or.-U.S.] 46 Dd 45.20N 124.00W
Lookout Mountain 44 Eh 34.40N 85.20W
Lookout Pass 43 Db 47.27N 115.42W
Loolmalasin 36 Gc 3.03S 35.49 E
Loop Head/Ceann Léime 9 Di 52.34N 9.56W
Loosdrechtse Plassen 12 Hb 52.10N 5.08 E
Lop 27 Dd 37.01N 80.16 E
Lopatina, Gora- 21 Qd 50.52N 143.10 E
Lopatino 16 Nc 52.37N 45.47 E
Lopatka, Mys- 21 Rd 50.52N 156.40 E
Lop Buri 25 Kf 14.48N 100.37 E
Lopča 20 He 55.44N 122.45 E
Lopévi 63b Dc 16.30S 168.21 E
Lopez, Cap-=Lopez, Cape-(EN) 30 Hi 0.37S 8.43 E
Lopez, Cape-(EN)=Lopez, Cap- 30 Hi 0.37S 8.43 E
Lop Nur 21 Le 40.30N 90.30 E
Lopnur/Yuli 27 Ec 41.22N 86.09 E
Lopori 30 Ih 1.14N 19.49 E
Loppersum 12 Ia 53.19N 6.45 E
Lopphavet 7 Ea 70.25N 22.00 E
Loppi 8 Kd 60.43N 24.27 E
Lopud 14 Lh 42.41N 17.57 E
Łopuszno 10 Qf 50.57N 20.15 E
Lora del Río 13 Gg 37.39N 5.32W
Lorain 43 Kc 41.28N 82.11W
Lorán, Boca- 54 Fb 9.00N 60.45W
Lorca 13 Kg 37.40N 1.42W
Lorch 12 Jd 50.03N 7.49 E
Lord Howe Island 57 Gh 31.35S 159.05 E
Lord Howe Rise (EN) 3 Jm 32.00S 162.00 E
Lord Mayor Bay 42 Ic 69.45N 92.00W
Lordsburg 45 Bj 32.21N 108.43W
Loreley 12 Jd 50.08N 7.43 E
Lorena 55 Jf 22.44S 45.08W
Lorengau 60 Dh 2.01S 147.17 E
Lorestān [3] 23 Gc 33.30N 48.40 E
Loreto [2] 54 Dd 5.00S 75.00W
Loreto [Arg.] 55 Dh 27.46S 57.17W
Loreto [Bol.] 54 Fg 15.13S 64.40W
Loreto [Braz.] 54 Ie 7.05S 45.09W
Loreto [It.] 14 Hg 43.26N 13.36 E
Loreto [Mex.] 48 If 22.16N 101.58W
Loreto [Mex.] 47 Bc 26.01N 111.21W
Loreto [Par.] 56 Ib 23.16S 57.11W
Loreto Aprutino 14 Hh 42.26N 13.59 E
Lorica 54 Cb 9.14N 75.49W
Lorient 6 Ff 47.45N 3.22W
Lőrinci 10 Pi 47.44N 19.41 E
Lorn, Firth of- 9 He 56.20N 5.40W
Lorne 59 Ig 38.33S 143.59 E
Lörrach 10 Di 47.37N 7.40 E
Lorrain, Plateau- 11 Me 49.00N 6.30 E
Lorrain, Rivière du- 51h Ab 14.50N 61.03W
Lorraine 11 Lf 49.00N 6.00 E
Lorraine, Plaine- 11 Lf 48.10N 5.50 E
Lorsch 12 Ke 49.39N 8.34 E
Los 7 Df 61.44N 15.10 E
Los, Iles de-= Los Islands (EN) 34 Cd 9.30N 13.48W

Index Symbols

[1] Independent Nation
[2] State, Region
[3] District, County
[4] Municipality
[5] Colony, Dependency
Continent
Physical Region
Historical or Cultural Region
Mount, Mountain
Volcano
Hill
Mountains, Mountain Range
Hills, Escarpment
Plateau, Upland
Pass, Gap
Plain, Lowland
Delta
Salt Flat
Valley, Canyon
Crater, Cave
Karst Features
Depression
Polder
Desert, Dunes
Forest, Woods
Heath, Steppe
Oasis
Cape, Point
Coast, Beach
Cliff
Peninsula
Isthmus
Sandbank
Island
Atoll
Rock, Reef
Islands, Archipelago
Rocks, Reefs
Coral Reef
Well, Spring
Geyser
River, Stream
Waterfall Rapids
River Mouth, Estuary
Lake
Salt Lake
Intermittent Lake
Reservoir
Swamp, Pond
Canal
Glacier
Ice Shelf, Pack Ice
Ocean
Sea
Gulf, Bay
Strait, Fjord
Lagoon
Bank
Seamount
Tablemount
Ridge
Shelf
Basin
Escarpment, Sea Scarp
Fracture
Trench, Abyss
National Park, Reserve
Point of Interest
Recreation Site
Cave, Cavern
Historic Site
Ruins
Wall, Walls
Church, Abbey
Temple
Scientific Station
Airport
Port
Lighthouse
Mine
Tunnel
Dam, Bridge

Los Alamos 39 If 35.53N 106.19W
Los Amates 49 Cf 15.16N 89.06W
Los Amores 55 Ci 28.06S 59.59W
Los Angeles 39 Hf 34.03N 118.15W
Los Ángeles 53 Ii 37.28S 72.21W
Los Angeles Aqueduct 46 Fi 35.22N 118.05W
Losap Atoll 57 Gd 6.54N 152.44 E
Los Banos 46 Eh 37.04N 120.51W
Los Blancos 56 Hb 23.36S 62.36W
Los Charrúas 55 Cj 31.10S 58.11W
Los Chiles 49 Eh 11.02N 84.43W
Los Conquistadores 55 Cj 30.36S 58.28W
Los Frailes, Islas- 50 Eg 11.12N 63.45W
Los Frentones 55 Bh 26.25S 61.25W
Los Gatos 46 Eh 37.14N 121.59W
Losheim 12 Ie 49.31N 6.45 E
Los Hermanos, Islas- 54 Fa 11.45N 64.25W
Łosice 10 Sd 52.14N 22.43 E
Lošinj 14 If 44.35N 14.28 E
Los Islands (EN)=Los, Iles de- 34 Cd 9.30N 13.48W
Los Juries 55 Ai 28.28S 62.06W
Los Lagos 56 Fe 39.51S 72.50W
Los Lagos [2] 56 Ff 41.20S 73.00W
Los Llanos de Aridane 32 Dd 28.39N 17.54W
Los Médanos, Istmo de- 49 Mh 11.35N 69.45W
Los Mochis 39 Ig 25.45N 108.53W
Los Monegros 13 Lc 41.29N 0.03W
Los Monjes, Islas- 54 Da 12.25N 70.55W
Los Navalmorales 13 He 39.43N 4.38W
Loso 36 Ec 1.10S 27.10 E
Los Palacios 49 Fb 22.35N 83.12W
Los Palacios y Villafranca 13 Gg 37.10N 5.56W
Los Pedroches 13 Hf 38.27N 4.45W
Los Pirpintos 55 Ah 26.08S 62.05W
Los Remedios, Río de- 48 Fe 24.41N 106.28W
Los Reyes de Salgado 48 Hh 19.35N 102.29W
Los Roques, Islas- 54 Ea 11.50N 66.45W
Los Roques Basin (EN) 50 Cf 12.20N 67.40W
Los Santos [3] 49 Gj 7.45N 80.30W
Los Santos 49 Gj 7.56N 80.25W
Losser 12 Jb 52.16N 7.01 E
Lossiemouth 9 Jd 57.43N 3.18W
Lossnen 8 Eb 62.30N 12.50 E
Los Taques 49 Lh 11.50N 70.16W
Los Telares 56 Hc 28.59S 63.26W
Los Teques 54 Ea 10.21N 67.02W
Los Testigos, Islas- 54 Fa 11.23N 63.06W
Lost River 46 Ef 41.56N 121.30W
Lost River Range 46 Id 44.10N 113.35W
Lost Trail Pass 43 Eb 45.41N 113.57W
Los Vilos 56 Fd 31.55S 71.31W
Lot 5 Gg 44.18N 0.20 E
Lot [3] 11 Hj 44.30N 1.30 E
Lota 56 Fe 37.05S 73.10W
Lotagipi Swamp 35 Ee 4.36N 34.55 E
Løten 8 Dd 60.49N 11.19 E
Lot-et-Garonne [3] 11 Gj 44.20N 0.30 E
Lothair 37 Ee 26.26S 30.27 E
Lothian [3] 9 Jf 55.55N 3.30W
Lothian 9 Jf 55.55N 3.05W
Loto 36 Dc 2.47S 22.30 E
Lotofaga 65c Ba 13.59S 171.50W
Lotoi 36 Cc 1.35S 18.30 E
Lotru 15 Hd 45.20N 24.16 E
Lotrului, Munţii- 15 Gd 45.30N 23.52 E
Lotta 7 Hb 68.39N 30.20 E
Lottefors 8 Gc 61.25N 16.24 E
Löttorp 8 Gg 57.10N 16.59 E
Lotuke, Jabal- 35 Ee 4.07N 33.48 E
Louang Namtha 25 Kd 20.57N 101.25 E
Louangphrabang 22 Mh 19.52N 102.08 E
Loubomo 31 Ii 4.12S 12.41 E
Loučná 10 Lf 50.06N 15.48 E
Loudéac 11 Df 48.10N 2.45W
Loudima 36 Bc 4.07S 13.04 E
Loudon 44 Eh 35.44N 84.20W
Loudun 11 Gh 47.00N 0.04 E
Loué 11 Fg 48.00N 0.09W
Loue 11 Lg 47.01N 5.27 E
Loufan 28 Ae 38.04N 111.47 E
Louga 34 Bb 15.37N 16.13W
Louga [3] 34 Bb 15.00N 15.30W
Louge 11 Hk 43.27N 1.20 E
Loughborough 9 Li 52.47N 1.11W
Lougheed 42 Ha 77.30N 105.00W
Loughrea/Baile Locha Riach 9 Eh 53.12N 8.34W
Louhans 11 Lh 46.38N 5.13 E
Louhi 19 Db 66.04N 33.01 E
Louisa 44 Ff 38.07N 82.36W
Louiseville 44 Kb 46.16N 72.57W
Louisiade Archipelago 57 Gf 11.00S 153.00 E
Louisiana 45 Kg 39.27N 91.03W
Louisiana [2] 43 Ie 31.15N 92.15W
Louis Trichardt 37 Dd 23.01S 29.43 E
Louisville [Ky.-U.S.] 39 Kf 38.16N 85.45W
Louisville [Ms.-U.S.] 45 Lj 33.07N 89.03W
Louis-XIV, Pointe- 42 Jf 54.50N 79.30W
Loukoléla 36 Cc 1.02S 17.07 E
Loulan Yiji 27 Ec 40.32N 89.50 E
Loulé 13 Dg 37.08N 8.02W
Loum 34 Ge 4.43N 9.44 E
Lount Lake 45 Ia 50.10N 94.20W
Louny 10 Jf 50.22N 13.49 E
Loup City 45 Gf 41.17N 98.58W
Loup River 43 Hc 41.24N 97.19W
Loups Marins, Lacs des- 42 Ke 56.40N 74.00W
Lourdes 11 Fk 43.06N 0.03W
Lourenço Marques→Maputo 31 Kk 25.58S 32.34 E
Lousa, Serra da- 13 Dd 40.04N 8.13W
Loushan Guan 27 If 28.02N 106.51 E
Louštín 10 Jf 50.12N 13.48 E
Louth [Austl.] 59 Jf 30.32S 145.07 E
Louth [Eng.-U.K.] 9 Mh 53.22N 0.01W
Louth/Lú [2] 9 Gh 53.55N 6.30W
Loutrá Aidhipsoú 15 Gk 38.51N 23.03 E
Loutrá Killínis 15 El 37.52N 21.07 E
Loutrákion 15 Fl 37.59N 23.00 E
Louvain/Leuven 11 Kd 50.53N 4.42 E
Louvet Point 51k Bb 13.58N 60.53W
Louviers 11 He 49.13N 1.10 E
Lövånger 7 Ed 64.22N 21.18 E
Lovászi 10 Mj 46.33N 16.34 E
Lovat 5 Jd 58.14N 31.28 E
Lovćen 15 Bg 42.24N 18.49 E
Loveč [2] 15 Hf 43.08N 24.43 E
Loveč 15 Hf 43.08N 24.43 E
Loveland 45 Df 40.24N 105.05W
Lovell 43 Fc 44.50N 108.24W
Lovelock 43 Dc 40.11N 118.28W
Lövenich, Köln- 12 Id 50.57N 6.50 E
Lovenske Gorice 14 Jd 46.40N 16.00 E
Lovere 14 Ee 45.49N 10.04 E
Loviisa 7 Gf 60.27N 26.14 E
Loviisa/Lovisa 7 Gf 60.27N 26.14 E
Loving 45 Dj 32.17N 104.06W
Lovington 43 Ge 33.27N 103.21W
Lovisa 7 Gf 60.27N 26.14 E
Lovisa/Loviisa 7 Gf 60.27N 26.14 E
Lovoi 36 Ed 8.05S 26.40 E
Lovosice 10 Kf 50.31N 14.03 E
Lovozero 7 Ib 68.01N 35.01 E
Lovozero, Ozero- 7 Ic 67.50N 35.10 E
Lövstabruk 8 Gd 60.24N 17.53 E
Lövstabukten 8 Gd 60.35N 17.45 E
Lovua 36 Dd 6.07S 20.35 E
Lovua 36 De 11.31S 23.35 E
Low, Cape- 42 Id 63.06N 85.18W
Lowa 30 Ji 1.24S 25.52 E
Lowell 43 Mc 42.39N 71.18W
Löwenberg in der Mark 10 Jd 52.53N 13.09 E
Lower Arrow Lake 46 Fb 49.40N 118.08W
Lower Austria (EN) = Niederösterreich [2] 14 Jb 48.30N 15.45 E
Lower California (EN)=Baja California 38 Hg 28.00N 112.00W
Lower Hutt 62 Fd 41.13S 174.55 E
Lower Lake 46 Ef 41.15N 120.02W
Lower Lake 46 Dg 38.55N 122.36W
Lower Lough Erne/Loch Éirne Iochtair 9 Fg 54.30N 7.50W
Lower Post 42 Ee 59.55N 128.30W
Lower Red Lake 45 Ic 48.00N 94.50W
Lower Rhine (EN) = Neder-Rijn 11 Mc 51.59N 6.20 E
Lower Saxony (EN)= Niedersachsen [2] 10 Fd 52.00N 10.00 E
Lower Trajan's Wall (EN)= Nižni Trajanov Val 15 Ld 45.45N 28.30 E
Lower Tunguska (EN)= Nižnjaja Tunguska 21 Kc 65.48N 88.04 E
Lowestoft 9 Oi 52.29N 1.45 E
Lowestoft Ness 9 Oi 52.28N 1.44 E
Lowgar [3] 23 Kc 33.50N 69.00 E
Łowicz 10 Pd 52.07N 19.56 E
Lowlands 9 Jf 56.00N 4.00W
Lowrah 21 If 31.33N 66.33 E
Lowshān 24 Md 36.39N 49.32 E
Low Tatra (EN) = Nízke Tatry 10 Ph 48.54N 19.40 E
Lowther 42 Hb 74.35N 97.40W
Lowville 44 Jd 43.47N 75.30W
Loxton [Austl.] 59 If 34.27S 140.35 E
Loxton [S.Afr.] 37 Cf 31.30S 22.22 E
Loyalty Islands (EN)= Loyauté, Iles- 57 Hg 21.00S 167.00 E
Loyauté, Iles-=Loyalty Islands (EN) 57 Hg 21.00S 167.00 E
Loyoro 36 Fb 3.21N 34.17 E
Lozère [3] 11 Jj 44.30N 3.30 E
Lozère, Mont- 11 Jj 44.25N 3.46 E
Loznica 15 Ce 44.32N 19.13 E
Lozovaja 19 Df 48.53N 36.15 E
Lozva 19 Gd 59.36N 62.20 E
Lú/Louth [2] 9 Gh 53.55N 6.30W
Lua 36 Cb 2.46N 18.26 E
Luacano 36 De 11.16S 21.38 E
Luachimo 36 Dd 6.33S 20.59 E
Luaha-Sibuha 26 Cg 0.31S 98.28 E
Luahoko 65b Ba 19.40S 174.24W
Luala 37 Fc 17.57S 36.30 E
Lualaba 29 Jh 0.26N 25.20 E
Luama 36 Ec 4.46S 26.53 E
Lua Makika 65a Ec 20.35N 156.34W
Luampa 36 De 14.32S 24.10 E
Lu'an 27 Ke 31.44N 116.30 E
Luanda 31 Ii 8.50S 13.15 E
Luanda [3] 36 Bd 8.30S 13.20 E
Luando 30 Ij 10.19S 16.40 E
Luang, Khao- 25 Jg 8.31N 99.47 E
Luang, Thale- 25 Kg 7.30N 100.15 E
Luang Chiang Dao, Doi- 25 Je 19.23N 98.54 E
Luanginga 30 Jj 15.11S 22.55 E
Luang Prabang Range 25 Ke 18.30N 101.15 E
Luangue 36 Dc 4.17S 20.01 E
Luangwa 30 Kj 15.36S 30.25 E
Luan He 21 Nf 39.20N 119.10 E
Luaniva 64h Bb 13.16S 176.07W
Luannan (Bencheng) 28 Ee 39.30N 118.42 E
Luanping (Anjiangying) 28 Dd 40.55N 117.19 E
Luanshya 31 Jj 13.08S 28.25 E
Luanxian 27 Kd 39.45N 118.44 E
Luanza 36 Ed 8.40S 28.40 E
Luapula 30 Ji 9.26S 28.33 E
Luapula [3] 36 Ee 10.40S 29.15 E
Luarca 13 Fa 43.32N 6.32W
Luashi 36 De 10.56S 23.37 E
Luba 34 Ge 3.28N 8.40 E
Lubaantum 49 Ce 16.17N 88.58W
Lubaczów 10 Tf 50.10N 23.07 E
Lubaczówka 10 Sf 50.08N 22.35 E
Lubalo 36 Cd 7.22S 19.20 E
Lubalo 36 Cd 9.07S 19.15 E
Lubamba 36 Ed 5.14S 26.02 E
Lubań 10 Le 51.08N 15.18 E
Lubāna/Lubana 8 Lh 56.49N 26.49 E
Lubana/Lubāna 8 Lh 56.49N 26.49 E
Lubānas, Ozero-/Lubānas Ezers 8 Lh 56.40N 27.00 E
Lubānas Ezers/Lubanas, Ozero- 8 Lh 56.40N 27.00 E
Lubang Islands 26 Hd 13.45N 120.15 E
Lubango 31 Ij 14.55S 13.28 E
Lubao 31 Ji 5.22S 25.45 E
Lubartów 10 Se 51.28N 22.46 E
Lubawa 10 Pc 53.30N 19.45 E
Lübbecke 10 Ed 52.18N 8.37 E
Lubbeek 12 Gd 50.53N 4.50 E
Lübben/Lubin 10 Je 51.57N 13.54 E
Lübbenau/Lubnjow 10 Je 51.52N 13.58 E
Lubbock 39 If 33.35N 101.51W
Lübeck 6 He 53.52N 10.42 E
Lübecker Bucht 10 Gb 54.00N 10.55 E
Lübeck-Travemünde 10 Gc 53.57N 10.52 E
Lubefu 36 Dc 4.10S 23.00 E
Lubefu 36 Dc 4.43S 24.25 E
Lubei→Jarud Qi 27 Lc 44.30N 120.55 E
Lubelska, Wyżyna- 10 Sf 51.00N 23.00 E
Lubenec 10 Jf 50.08N 13.20 E
Lubenka 16 Sd 50.28N 54.06 E
Lubero 36 Ec 0.06S 29.06 E
Lubéron, Montagne du- 11 Lk 43.48N 5.22 E
Lubi 36 Dc 4.59S 23.26 E
Lubie, Jezioro- 10 Lc 53.30N 15.50 E
Lubień Kujawski 10 Pd 52.25N 19.10 E
Lubij/Löbau 10 Ke 51.06N 14.40 E
Lubilash 29 Ji 6.02S 23.45 E
Lubin 10 Me 51.24N 16.13 E
Lubin/Lübben 10 Je 51.57N 13.54 E
Lublin 6 Ie 51.15N 22.35 E
Lublin [2] 10 Se 51.15N 22.35 E
Lubliniec 10 Of 50.40N 18.41 E
Lubnān=Lebanon (EN) [1] 22 Ff 33.50N 35.50 E
Lubnān, Jabal-=Lebanon Mountains (EN) 23 Ec 34.00N 36.30 E
Lubnjow/Lübbenau 10 Je 51.52N 13.58 E
Lubny 19 De 50.01N 33.00 E
Luboń 10 Md 52.23N 16.54 E
Lubraniec 10 Od 52.33N 18.50 E
Lubsko 10 Ke 51.46N 14.59 E
Lubsza 10 Ke 51.55N 14.45 E
Lubudi 29 Ji 9.13S 25.38 E
Lubudi 36 Ed 9.57S 25.58 E
Lubue 36 Cc 4.10S 19.53 E
Lubuklinggau 26 Dg 3.10S 102.52 E
Lubuksikaping 26 Df 0.08N 100.10 E
Lubumba 36 Ec 3.58S 29.06 E
Lubumbashi 31 Jj 11.40S 27.30 E
Lubuskie, Pojezierze- 10 Ld 52.18N 15.20 E
Lubutu 31 Ji 0.44S 26.35 E
Lucala 36 Bd 6.38S 12.34 E
Lucala 36 Cd 9.16S 15.16 E
Lucania, Mount- 42 Dd 61.01N 140.29W
Lucas 55 Ea 13.05S 55.56W
Lucca 14 Eg 43.50N 10.29 E
Lucea 49 Hd 18.27N 78.10W
Luce Bay 9 Ig 54.47N 4.50W
Lucedale 45 Lk 30.55N 88.35W
Lučegorsk 20 Ig 46.25N 134.20 E
Lucélia 55 Ge 21.44S 51.01W
Lucena [Phil.] 26 Hd 13.56N 121.37 E
Lucena [Sp.] 13 Hg 37.24N 4.29W
Lucena del Cid 13 Ld 40.08N 0.17W
Luc-en-Diois 11 Lj 44.37N 5.27 E
Lučenec 10 Ph 48.20N 19.41 E
Lucera 14 Ji 41.30N 15.20 E
Lucerne (EN) = Luzern 14 Cc 47.05N 8.20 E
Lucerne, Lake- (EN) = Vierwaldstätter-See 14 Cc 47.00N 8.30 E
Lucero 48 Fb 30.49N 106.30W
Lucheng 28 Bf 36.18N 113.15 E
Lucheringo 37 Fb 11.43S 36.15 E
Lucheux 12 Ed 50.12N 2.25 E
Luchico 30 Lj 12.15S 44.25 E
Luchico 36 Cd 6.12S 19.42 E
Lüchow 10 Hd 52.58N 11.09 E
Lüchun 27 Hg 23.02N 102.19 E
Lucipara, Kepulauan- 26 Ih 5.30S 127.33 E
Lucira 36 Be 13.52S 12.32 E
Luck 19 Ce 50.47N 25.20 E
Luckau 10 Je 51.51N 13.43 E
Luckenwalde 10 Jd 52.05N 13.10 E
Lucknow 22 Kg 26.51N 80.55 E
Luçon 11 Eh 46.27N 1.10W
Lucrecia, Cabo- 49 Jc 21.04N 75.37W
Luc-sur-Mer 12 Be 49.18N 0.21W
Lucunga 36 Bd 6.49S 14.35 E
Lucusse 36 De 12.33S 20.51 E
Lüda→Dalian=Dairan (EN) 22 Of 38.55N 121.39 E
Luda Kamčija 15 Kg 43.03N 27.29 E
Ludbreg 14 Kd 46.15N 16.37 E
Lüdenscheid 10 De 51.13N 7.37 E
Lüderitz 31 Ik 26.38S 15.10 E
Lüderitz [3] 37 Be 26.00S 15.00 E
Lüderitz Bay 37 Be 26.35S 15.10 E
Ludhiāna 22 Jf 30.54N 75.51 E
Lüdinghausen 10 De 51.46N 7.28 E
Ludington 43 Jc 43.57N 86.27W
Ludlow 9 Ki 52.22N 2.43W
Ludogorije 15 Jf 43.46N 26.56 E
Ludogorsko Plato 15 Kf 43.36N 27.03 E
Luduş 15 Hc 46.29N 24.06 E
Ludvika 7 Df 60.09N 15.11 E
Ludwigsburg 10 Fh 48.54N 9.11 E
Ludwigshafen am Rhein 10 Eg 49.29N 8.27 E
Ludwigslust 10 Hc 53.19N 11.30 E
Ludza 7 Gh 56.32N 27.45 E
Luebo 31 Ji 5.21S 21.25 E
Lueki 36 Ec 3.24S 25.57 E
Lueki 36 Ec 3.22S 25.51 E
Luele 36 Dd 7.55S 20.00 E
Luembé 36 Dd 6.43S 24.11 E
Luembe 36 Dd 6.37S 21.06 E
Luena [Ang.] 36 De 12.31S 22.34 E
Luena [Ang.] 31 Ij 11.48S 19.55 E
Luena [Zaire] 36 Ed 9.27S 25.47 E
Luena [Zam.] 36 Df 15.20S 23.30 E
Luengué 36 Df 16.54S 21.52 E
Luenha 37 Ec 16.24S 33.48 E
Luera Peak 45 Cj 33.47N 107.49W
Lueta 36 Dd 7.04S 21.40 E
Lueyang 27 Ie 33.25N 106.14 E
Lufeng 27 Kg 22.57N 115.41 E
Lufico 36 Bd 6.22S 13.30 E
Lufira 29 Ji 8.16S 26.27 E
Lufira, Chutes de la- 36 Ed 9.50S 27.30 E
Lufkin 43 Ie 31.20N 94.44W
Lug 15 De 44.23N 20.45 E
Luga 19 Cd 59.43N 28.18 E
Luga 19 Cd 58.44N 29.50 E
Lugano 14 Cd 46.00N 8.57 E
Lugano, Lago di- 14 Cd 46.00N 9.00 E
Lugansk = Vorošilovgrad 6 Jf 48.34N 39.20 E
Luganville 58 Hf 15.32S 167.10 E
Lügde 12 Lc 51.57N 9.15 E
Lugela 37 Fc 16.26S 36.39 E
Lugenda 30 Kj 11.26S 38.33 E
Lugnaquillia 5 Fe 52.58N 6.27W
Lugo [3] 13 Eb 43.00N 7.30W
Lugo [It.] 14 Ff 44.25N 11.54 E
Lugo [Sp.] 13 Ea 43.00N 7.34W
Lugoj 15 Ed 45.41N 21.55 E
Lugovoj [Kaz.-U.S.S.R.] 19 Hg 42.55N 72.47 E
Lugovoj [R.S.F.S.R.] 19 Gd 59.44N 65.55 E
Lugovski 20 Ge 58.05N 112.55 E
Lugulu 36 Ec 2.17S 26.32 E
Luh 7 Kh 56.14N 42.28 E
Luhe 10 Gc 53.18N 10.11 E
Luhe 28 Eh 32.21N 118.50 E
Luhin Sum 27 Kb 46.41N 118.38 E
Luhit 25 Jc 27.48N 95.28 E
Luhovicy 7 Ji 54.59N 39.02 E
Luhuo 27 He 31.21N 100.40 E
Lui 36 Cd 8.41S 17.56 E
Luia 36 Dd 8.26S 21.45 E
Luiana 36 Df 17.22S 22.59 E
Luiana 30 Jj 17.27S 23.14 E
Luie 36 Ce 4.33S 17.41 E
Luik/Liège 6 Ge 50.38N 5.34 E
Luilaka 30 Ii 0.52S 20.12 E
Luilu 36 Dd 6.22S 23.50 E
Luimneach/Limerick 6 Fe 52.40N 8.38W
Luimneach/Limerick [2] 9 Ei 52.30N 9.00W
Luing 9 He 56.13N 5.39W
Luino 14 Cd 46.00N 8.44 E
Luio 36 De 13.15S 21.39 E
Lui Pătru, Vîrful- 15 Gd 45.30N 23.30 E
Luis Correia 54 Jd 2.53S 41.40W
Luishia 36 Ee 11.13S 27.07 E
Luitpold Coast 66 Af 78.30S 32.00W
Luiza 36 Dd 7.12S 22.25 E
Luján [Arg.] 56 Gd 32.22S 65.57W
Luján [Arg.] 56 Id 34.34S 59.07W
Lujiang 28 Di 31.15N 117.17 E
Lukafu 36 Ee 10.30S 27.33 E
Lukanga Swamp 36 Ee 14.25S 27.45 E
Lukavac 14 Mf 44.33N 18.32 E
Lukengo 36 Ed 5.46S 29.06 E
Lukenie 30 Ii 2.44S 18.09 E
Lukeville 46 Ik 31.57N 112.50W
Lukojanov 19 Ed 55.02N 44.30 E
Lukolela 36 Cc 1.03S 17.12 E
Lukonzolwa 36 Ed 8.47S 28.39 E
Lukov 10 Se 51.14N 24.25 E
Lukovit 15 Hf 43.12N 24.10 E
Łuków 10 Se 51.56N 22.23 E
Lukuga 30 Ji 5.40S 26.55 E
Lukula 36 Bd 5.23S 12.57 E
Lukulu 36 De 14.23S 23.15 E
Lukusashi 36 Fe 14.38S 30.00 E
Luleå 6 Ib 65.34N 22.10 E
Luleälven 5 Ib 65.35N 22.03 E
Lüleburgaz 23 Ca 41.24N 27.21 E
Lüliang Shan 21 Nf 37.45N 111.25 E
Lulimba 36 Ec 4.42S 28.38 E
Luling 45 Hl 29.41N 97.39W
Lulong 28 Ee 39.53N 118.52 E
Lulonga 36 Cb 0.37N 18.23 E
Lulonga 30 Ih 0.43N 18.23 E
Lulua 30 Ji 5.02S 21.07 E
Lulu Fakahega, Mount- 64h Bb 13.16S 176.10W
Luma 65c Db 14.14S 169.32W
Lumajang 26 Fh 8.08S 113.13 E
Lumajangdong Co 27 De 34.00N 81.37 E
Lumbala Kaquengue 31 Jj 14.06S 21.25 E
Lumbala N'guimbo 36 De 12.39S 22.32 E
Lumberton 43 Le 34.37N 79.00W
Lumbo 37 Gc 15.00S 40.44 E
Lumbrales 13 Fd 40.56N 6.43W
Lumbres 12 Ed 50.42N 2.08 E
Lumby 46 Fa 50.15N 118.58W
Lumding 25 Ic 25.45N 93.10 E
Lumege 36 De 11.34S 20.48 E
Lumesule 36 Ge 11.14S 38.06 E
Lumi 60 Ch 3.29S 142.03 E
Lummen 12 Hd 50.59N 5.15 E
Lumparland 8 Id 60.10N 20.15 E
Lumphât 25 Lf 13.30N 106.59 E
Lumsden [N.Z.] 62 Cf 45.44S 168.26 E
Lumsden [Sask.-Can.] 46 Ma 50.34N 104.53W
Lumuna 36 Ec 3.46S 26.24 E
Lumut 26 Df 4.14N 100.38 E
Luna 13 Gb 42.40N 5.49W
Luna, Laguna de- 55 Di 28.06S 56.46W
Lunan Shan 27 Hf 27.00N 102.30 E
Lunayyir, Harrat- 24 Gj 25.10N 37.50 E
Lunca Ilvei 15 Hb 47.22N 24.59 E
Lund 7 Ci 55.42N 13.11 E
Lunda [3] 36 Cd 9.30S 20.00 E
Lundazi 31 Kj 12.19S 33.13 E
Lunde 8 Gb 62.53N 17.51 E
Lundevatn 8 Bf 58.20N 6.35 E
Lundi 30 Kk 21.19S 32.24 E
Lundu 26 Ef 1.40N 109.51 E
Lundy Island 9 Ij 51.10N 4.40W
Lüneburg 10 Gc 53.15N 10.24 E
Lüneburger Heide 10 Gc 53.10N 10.20 E
Lunel 11 Kk 43.41N 4.08 E
Lünen 10 De 51.37N 7.31 E
Lunéville 11 Mf 48.36N 6.30 E
Lunga 30 Jj 14.34S 26.26 E
Lungué-Bungo 37 Jj 28.38S 16.27 E
Lungwebungu 36 De 14.19S 23.14 E
Lūni 25 Ed 24.41N 71.14 E
Lūni 25 Ec 26.00N 73.00 E
Lunigiana 14 Df 44.20N 9.55 E
Luninec 19 Ce 52.16N 26.50 E
Lunino 16 Nc 53.35N 45.14 E
Lunsemfwa 36 Fe 14.54S 30.12 E
Luntai/Bügür 27 Dc 41.46N 84.10 E
Luobei (Fengxiang) 27 Nb 47.36N 130.58 E
Luobuzhuang 27 Ed 39.30N 88.15 E
Luocheng 27 Ig 24.51N 108.53 E
Luodian (Longping) 27 If 25.26N 106.47 E
Luoding 27 Jg 22.43N 111.33 E
Luohe 27 Je 33.30N 114.08 E
Luo He 27 Id 32.18N 109.12 E
Luoma Hu 28 Eg 34.10N 118.12 E
Luonteri 8 Lc 61.35N 27.45 E
Luoping 27 Hg 24.58N 104.19 E
Luopioinen 8 Kc 61.22N 24.40 E
Luoshan 28 Ch 32.13N 114.32 E
Luotian 28 Ci 30.48N 115.23 E
Luoxiao Shan 27 Jf 26.35N 114.00 E
Luoyang 22 Nf 34.41N 112.25 E
Luoyuan 27 Kf 26.31N 119.32 E
Luozi 36 Bc 4.57S 14.08 E
Lupa 36 Fd 8.39S 33.12 E
Lupane 37 Dc 18.56S 27.48 E
Łupawa 10 Nb 54.42N 17.07 E
Lupeni 15 Gd 45.21N 23.14 E
Luperón 49 Ld 19.54N 70.57W
Łupków 10 Sg 49.12N 22.06 E
Luputa 36 Dd 7.10S 23.42 E
Lūq 31 Lh 3.56N 42.32 E
Luqiao 28 Fj 28.39N 120.05 E
Luqu 27 He 34.36N 102.30 E
Luque 56 Ic 25.16S 57.34W
Luquillo 51a Cb 18.22N 65.43W
Luray 44 Hf 38.40N 78.28W
Lure 11 Mg 47.41N 6.30 E
Lure, Montagne de- 11 Lj 44.07N 5.47 E
Luremo 36 Cd 8.30S 17.51 E
Lurgan/An Lorgain 9 Gg 54.28N 6.20W
Lurín 54 Cf 12.17S 76.52W
Lúrio 37 Gb 13.32S 40.30 E
Lúrio 30 Lj 13.31S 40.42 E
Lusaka 31 Jj 15.25S 28.17 E
Lusambo 31 Ji 4.58S 23.27 E
Lusanga 36 Cc 4.44S 18.58 E
Lusangi 36 Ec 4.37S 27.08 E
Lu Shan 27 Kf 29.30N 115.55 E
Lushan [China] 28 Cj 29.33N 115.58 E
Lushan [China] 28 Bh 33.44N 112.54 E
Lushi 27 Je 34.04N 111.02 E
Lushiko 36 Cd 6.12S 19.42 E
Lushnja 15 Ci 40.56N 19.42 E
Lushoto 36 Gc 4.47S 38.17 E
Lu Shui 28 Bj 29.54N 113.39 E
Lushui (Luzhangjie) 27 Gf 26.00N 98.50 E
Lüshun=Port Arthur (EN) 27 Ld 38.50N 121.13 E
Lusignan 11 Gh 46.26N 0.07 E
Lusk 43 Gc 42.46N 104.27W
Lussac-les-Châteaux 11 Gh 46.24N 0.43 E
Lustrafjorden 8 Bc 61.20N 7.20 E
Lūt, Dasht-e-=Lut, Dasht-i- (EN) 21 Hf 33.00N 57.00 E
Lut, Dasht-i- (EN)=Lūt, Dasht-e- 21 Hf 33.00N 57.00 E
Lu Tao 27 Lg 22.35N 121.30 E
Lutembo 36 De 13.28S 21.22 E
Luti 63a Cb 7.14S 157.00 E
Lütjenburg 10 Gb 54.17N 10.35 E
Luton 9 Mj 51.53N 0.25W
Luton Airport 12 Bc 51.50N 0.22W
Lutong 26 Ff 4.28N 114.00 E
Lutshima 36 Cd 5.22S 18.59 E
Lutshima 36 Cd 5.22S 18.59 E
Lutterworth 12 Ab 52.27N 1.12W
Lutuai 36 De 12.40S 20.12 E
Lutugino 16 Ke 48.23N 39.13 E
Lützow-Holmbukta 66 De 69.10S 37.30 E
Lutzputs 37 Ce 28.22S 20.37 E
Luuk 26 He 5.58N 121.18 E
Luverne 45 He 43.39N 96.13W
Luvidjo 36 Ed 6.26S 26.59 E
Luvua 30 Ji 6.46S 26.58 E
Luvuei 36 De 13.06S 21.12 E
Luwegu 30 Ki 8.31S 37.23 E
Luwingu 36 Ee 10.16S 29.54 E
Luwuk 26 Hg 0.56S 122.47 E
Luxembourg [3] 12 He 50.00N 5.30 E
Luxembourg/Luxemburg [1] 6 Gf 49.45N 6.05 E
Luxembourg/Luxemburg 6 Gf 49.45N 6.05 E
Luxemburg/Luxembourg 6 Gf 49.45N 6.05 E
Luxemburg/Luxembourg [1] 6 Gf 49.45N 6.05 E
Luxeuil-les-Bains 11 Mg 47.49N 6.23 E
Luxi 22 Mg 24.34N 103.44 E
Luxi (Mangshi) 27 Gg 24.29N 98.40 E
Luxor (EN)=Al Uqşur 33 Fd 25.41N 32.39 E
Luy 11 Ek 43.39N 1.08W
Luy de Béarn 11 Fk 43.38N 0.47W

Index Symbols

[1] Independent Nation
[2] State, Region
[3] District, County
[4] Municipality
[5] Colony, Dependency
Continent
Physical Region
Historical or Cultural Region
Mount, Mountain
Volcano
Hill
Mountains, Mountain Range
Hills, Escarpment
Plateau, Upland
Pass, Gap
Plain, Lowland
Delta
Salt Flat
Valley, Canyon
Crater, Cave
Karst Features
Depression
Polder
Desert, Dunes
Forest, Woods
Heath, Steppe
Oasis
Cape, Point
Coast, Beach
Cliff
Peninsula
Isthmus
Sandbank
Island
Atoll
Rock, Reef
Islands, Archipelago
Rocks, Reefs
Coral Reef
Well, Spring
Geyser
River, Stream
Waterfall Rapids
River Mouth, Estuary
Lake
Salt Lake
Intermittent Lake
Reservoir
Swamp, Pond
Canal
Glacier
Ice Shelf, Pack Ice
Ocean
Sea
Gulf, Bay
Strait, Fjord
Lagoon
Bank
Seamount
Tablemount
Ridge
Shelf
Basin
Escarpment, Sea Scarp
Fracture
Trench, Abyss
National Park, Reserve
Point of Interest
Recreation Site
Cave, Cavern
Historic Site
Ruins
Wall, Walls
Church, Abbey
Temple
Scientific Station
Airport
Port
Lighthouse
Mine
Tunnel
Dam, Bridge

Luy de France 11 Fk 43.38N 0.47W
Luyi 28 Ch 33.51N 115.28 E
Luz 55 Jd 19.48S 45.41W
Luz, Costa de la- 13 Fh 36.40N 6.20W
Luza 19 Ec 60.39N 47.15 E
Luza 5 Kc 60.40N 46.25 E
Luzarches 12 Ee 49.07N 2.25 E
Luzern 14 Cc 47.05N 8.10 E
Luzern = Lucerne (EN) 14 Cc 47.05N 8.20 E
Luzhai 27 Ig 24.31N 109.46 E
Luzhangjie → Lushui 27 Gf 26.00N 98.50 E
Luzhou 22 Mg 28.55N 105.20 E
Luziânia 54 Ig 16.15S 47.56W
Lužická Nisa 10 Kd 52.04N 14.46 E
Luzilândia 54 Jd 3.28S 42.22W
Lužnice 10 Kg 49.16N 14.25 E
Luzon 21 Oh 16.00N 121.00 E
Luzon Sea 26 Gd 12.30N 119.00 E
Luzon Strait (EN) 21 Og 21.00N 122.00 E
Luz-Saint-Sauveur 11 Gl 42.52N 0.01 E
Lužskaja Guba 8 Me 59.35N 28.25 E
Lužskaja Vozvyšennost 8 Mf 58.15N 28.45 E
Luzy 11 Jh 46.47N 3.58 E
Łużyca 10 Oe 51.33N 18.15 E
Lvov 6 If 49.50N 24.00 E
Lvovskaja Oblast 19 Cf 49.45N 24.00 E
Lwowa 60 Hj 10.44S 165.45 E
Lwówek 10 Md 52.28N 16.10 E
Lwówek Śląski 10 Le 51.07N 15.35 E
Lyakhov Islands (EN) = Ljahovskije Ostrova 21 Qb 73.30N 141.00 E
Lyall, Mount- 62 Bf 45.17S 167.33 E
Lyallpur 22 Jf 31.25N 73.05 E
Lychsele 7 Ed 64.36N 18.40 E
Lycia 15 Mm 36.30N 29.30 E
Lyckeby 8 Fh 56.12N 15.39 E
Lyckebyån 8 Fh 56.11N 15.40 E
Lyčkovo 7 Hh 57.57N 32.24 E
Lydd 9 Nk 50.57N 0.55 E
Lydd Airport 12 Cd 50.58N 0.56 E
Lydenburg 37 Ee 25.10S 30.29 E
Lydia 15 Lk 38.35N 28.30 E
Lygna 8 Bf 58.10N 7.02 E
Lygnern 8 Eg 57.29N 12.20 E
Lyme Bay 9 Kk 50.38N 3.00W
Lyminge 12 Dc 51.07N 1.05 E
Lymington 9 Lk 50.46N 1.33W
Łyna 10 Rb 54.37N 21.14 E
Lynchburg 43 Ld 37.24N 79.09W
Lynd 58 Ff 18.56S 144.30 E
Lynden 46 Db 48.57N 122.27W
Lyndon River 59 Cd 23.29S 114.06 E
Lyngdal 7 Bg 58.08N 7.05 E
Lyngen 7 Eb 69.58N 20.30 E
Lyngør 8 Cf 58.38N 9.10 E
Lyngseidet 7 Eb 69.35N 20.13 E
Lynn 44 Ld 42.28N 70.57W
Lynnaj, Gora- 20 Ld 62.55N 163.58 E
Lynn Canal 40 Le 58.50N 135.15W
Lynn Deeps 12 Cb 52.58N 0.20 E
Lynn Lake 39 Id 56.51N 101.03W
Lyntupy 8 Li 55.02N 26.27 E
Lynx Lake 42 Gd 62.25N 106.20W
Lyon 6 Gf 45.45N 4.51 E
Lyon Inlet 42 Jc 66.20N 83.40W
Lyonnais, Monts du- 11 Ki 45.40N 4.30 E
Lyon River 59 De 25.00S 115.20 E
Lyons [Ga.-U.S.] 44 Fi 32.12N 82.19W
Lyons [Ks.-U.S.] 45 Gg 38.21N 98.12W
Lyons, Forêt de- 12 De 49.25N 1.30 E
Lyons-la-Forêt 12 De 49.24N 1.28 E
Lyra Reef 60 Eh 1.50S 153.35 E
Lys 11 Jc 51.03N 3.43 E
Łysa Góra 10 Nd 52.07N 17.33 E
Lysaja, Gora- 8 Lj 54.12N 27.40 E
Lysá nad Labem 10 Kf 50.12N 14.50 E
Lysefjorden 8 Be 59.00N 6.14 E
Lysekil 7 Cf 58.16N 11.26 E
Lyskovo 19 Ed 56.03N 45.03 E
Lyss 14 Bc 47.04N 7.37 E
Lysva 19 Fd 58.07N 57.47 E
Lytham Saint Anne's 9 Jh 53.45N 3.01W
Lyttelton 62 Ee 43.36S 172.43 E
Lytton 46 Ea 50.14N 121.34W
Lyža 17 Hd 65.42N 56.40 E

M

Ma, Oued el- 32 Fe 24.03N 9.10W
Ma, Song 25 Le 19.45N 105.55 E
Maâdis, Djebel- 13 Qi 35.52N 4.44 E
Maalaea Bay 65a Ec 20.47N 156.29W
Ma'āmir 24 Mg 30.04N 48.20 E
Ma'ān 23 Ec 30.12N 35.44 E
Ma'āniyah 24 Jg 30.44N 43.00 E
Maanselkä 5 Ib 68.07N 28.29 E
Maanselkä 7 Ge 63.54N 28.30 E
Ma'anshan 27 Ke 31.38N 118.30 E
Maardu 8 Ke 59.28N 24.56 E
Maarianhamina/Mariehamn 7 Ef 60.06N 19.57 E
Ma 'arrat an Nu 'mān 24 Ge 35.38N 36.40 E
Maarssen 12 Hb 52.08N 5.03 E
Maas = Meuse (EN) 5 Ge 51.49N 5.01 E
Maaseik 11 Lc 51.06N 5.48 E
Maaseik-Neeroeteren 12 Hc 51.05N 5.42 E
Maasin 26 Hd 10.08N 124.50 E
Maasmechelen/Mechelen 12 Hd 50.57N 5.40 E
Maassluis 12 Gc 51.55N 4.17 E
Maastricht 11 Ld 50.52N 5.43 E
Maasupa 63a Ec 9.18S 161.15 E
Ma'āzah, Al Haḍabat al- 33 Fd 27.44N 31.44 E
Mabalane 37 Ed 23.38S 32.31 E
Mabaruma 50 Gh 8.12N 59.47W
Mabechi-Gawa 29 Ga 40.31N 141.31 E
Mabella 45 Lb 48.37N 89.58W
Mabel Lake 46 Fa 50.35N 118.44W
Mablethorpe 9 Nh 53.21N 0.15 E
Mabote 37 Ed 22.03S 34.08 E
Ma'būs Yūsuf 31 Jf 25.45N 21.00 E
Maçaão 13 Ee 39.33N 8.00W
McAdam 42 Kg 45.36N 67.20W
Macajaí, Rio- 54 Fc 2.25N 60.50W
McAllen 43 Hf 26.12N 98.15W
Macaloge 37 Fb 12.25S 35.25 E
Mac Alpine Lake 42 Hc 66.40N 102.50W
Macambará 55 Di 29.08S 56.03W
Macamic 44 Ha 48.48N 79.01W
Macamic, Lac- 44 Ha 48.46N 79.00W
Macao (EN) = Aomen/Macau 22 Ng 22.10N 113.33 E
Macao (EN) = Aomen/Macau 27 Jg 22.12N 113.33 E
Macao (EN) = Macau/Aomen 22 Ng 22.10N 113.33 E
Macao (EN) = Macau/Aomen 27 Jg 22.12N 113.33 E
Macapá 53 Ke 0.02N 51.03W
Macará 54 Cd 4.21S 79.56W
Macaracas 49 Gj 7.44N 80.33W
Macareo, Caño- 54 Fb 9.47N 61.36W
McArthur 44 Ff 39.14N 82.29W
Mc Arthur River 59 Hc 15.54S 136.40 E
Maçãs 13 Fc 41.29N 6.39W
Macas 54 Cd 2.18S 78.06W
Macatete, Sierra de- 48 Dd 28.00N 110.05W
Macau 53 Mf 5.07S 36.38W
Macau/Aomen = Macao (EN) 27 Jg 22.12N 113.33 E
Macau/Aomen = Macao (EN) 22 Ng 22.10N 113.33 E
Macaúbas 54 Jf 13.02S 42.42W
Macauley Island 57 Ih 30.13S 178.33W
Macaya, Pic de- 47 Je 18.23N 74.02W
McBeth Fiord 42 Kc 69.43N 69.20W
McCamey 45 Ek 31.08N 102.13W
McCammon 46 Ie 42.39N 112.12W
Mc Carthy 40 Kd 61.26N 142.55W
McClellanville 44 Hi 33.06N 79.28W
McClenny 44 Fj 30.18N 82.07W
Macclesfield 9 Kh 53.16N 2.07W
Macclesfield Bank (EN) 26 Fc 15.50N 114.20 E
McClintock 42 Ie 57.48N 94.12W
McClintock, Mount- 66 Jg 80.13S 157.26 E
Mc Clintock Channel 38 Ib 71.00N 101.00W
McCluer Gulf (EN) = Berau, Teluk- 26 Jg 2.30S 132.30 E
Mc Clure Strait 38 Hb 74.30N 116.00W
McClusky 45 Fc 47.29N 100.27W
McComb 43 Ie 31.14N 90.27W
McConaughy, Lake- 45 Ff 41.18N 101.46W
McConnelsville 44 Gf 39.39N 81.51W
McCook 43 Gc 40.12N 100.38W
McCormick 44 Fi 33.55N 82.19W
McDame 42 Ee 59.13N 129.14W
McDermitt 46 Gf 41.59N 117.36W
Macdhui, Ben- 9 Jd 57.04N 3.40W
Macdonald, Lake- 59 Fd 23.30S 129.00 E
Mc Donald Islands 30 On 52.59S 72.50 E
McDonald Peak [Ca.-U.S.] 46 Ef 40.58N 120.26W
McDonald Peak [Mt.-U.S.] 46 Ic 47.29N 113.46W
Macdonald Range 46 Hb 49.12N 114.46W
Macdonnell Ranges 57 Eg 23.45S 132.20 E
McDouglas Sound 42 Hd 75.15N 97.30W
Macduff 9 Kd 57.40N 2.29W
Macedo de Cavaleiros 13 Fc 41.32N 6.58W
Macedonia (EN) = Makedhonia 5 Ig 41.00N 23.00 E
Macedonia (EN) = Makedhonia 15 Fh 41.00N 23.00 E
Macedonia (EN) = Makedonija 15 Eh 41.50N 22.00 E
Macedonia (EN) = Makedonija 5 Ig 41.00N 23.00 E
Macedonia (EN) = Makedonija 15 Fh 41.00N 23.00 E
Maceió 53 Mf 9.40S 35.43W
Macenta 34 Dd 8.33N 9.28W
Macerata 14 Hg 43.18N 13.27 E
McGehee 45 Kj 33.38N 91.24W
McGill 46 Hg 39.23N 114.47W
Macgillycuddy's Reeks/Na Cruacha Dubha 9 Di 52.00N 9.50W
McGrath 40 Hd 62.58N 155.38W
MacGregor 45 Gb 49.57N 98.49W
McGregor 45 Jc 46.36N 93.19W
McGregor Lake 46 Ia 50.31N 112.53W
Mc Gregor Range 59 Ie 26.40S 142.45 E
McGuire, Mount- 46 Hd 45.10N 114.36W
Machachi 54 Cd 0.30S 78.34W
Machado 55 Je 21.41S 45.56W
Machagai 56 Hc 26.56S 60.03W
Machaila 37 Ed 22.15S 32.58 E
Machaire na Mumhan/Golden Vale 9 Fi 52.30N 8.00W
Machaire Rátha/Maghera 9 Gg 54.51N 6.40W
Machakos 36 Gc 1.31S 37.16 E
Machala 54 Cd 3.16S 79.58W
Machaneng 37 Dd 23.12S 27.30 E
Machareti 54 Fh 20.49S 63.24W
Machar Marshes 35 Ed 9.20N 33.10 E
Machattie, Lake- 59 Hd 24.50S 139.48 E
Machault 12 Ge 49.21N 4.30 E
Macheke 37 Ec 18.05S 31.51 E
Macheng 27 Je 31.10N 115.00 E
Machias 44 Nc 44.43N 67.28W
Machida 29 Fd 35.32N 139.27 E
Machilipatnam (Bandar) 25 Ge 16.10N 81.08 E
Machiques 54 Da 10.04N 72.34W
Machona, Laguna- 48 Mh 18.20N 93.40W
Machów 10 Rf 50.34N 21.40 E
Machupicchu 53 Ig 13.07S 72.34W
Macia 37 Ef 25.02S 33.06 E
Mc Ilwraith Range 59 Ib 13.45S 143.20 E
Mâcin 15 Ld 45.15N 28.09 E
Macina 30 Gg 14.30N 5.00W
McIntosh 45 Fd 45.55N 101.21W
Macintyre River 59 Je 29.25S 148.45 E
Maçka 24 Hb 40.50N 39.38 E
Mackay [Austl.] 58 Fg 21.09S 149.11 E
Mackay [Id.-U.S.] 46 Ie 43.55N 113.37W
Mackay, Lake- 57 Dg 22.30S 129.00 E
McKay Lake 45 Mb 49.35N 86.22W
McKean Atoll 57 Je 3.36S 174.08W
McKeand 42 Kd 63.00N 65.05W
McKeesport 44 He 40.21N 79.52W
Mackenzie 38 Fc 69.15N 134.08W
McKenzie 44 Cg 36.08N 88.31W
Mackenzie, District of- 42 Gd 65.00N 115.00W
Mackenzie Bay [Ant.] 66 Fe 68.20S 71.15 E
Mackenzie Bay [Can.] 38 Fc 69.00N 136.30W
McKenzie Island 42 If 51.05N 93.48W
Mackenzie King 38 Hb 77.45N 111.00W
Mackenzie Mountains 38 Gc 64.00N 130.00W
McKenzie River 46 Dd 44.07N 123.06W
Mackenzie River 59 Jd 24.00S 149.55 E
McKerrow, Lake- 62 Cf 44.25S 168.05 E
Mackinac, Straits of- 43 Kb 45.49N 84.45W
Mackinaw City 44 Ec 45.47N 84.44W
McKinley, Mount- 38 Dc 63.30N 151.00W
McKinley Park 40 Jd 63.44N 148.54W
McKinney 45 Hj 33.12N 96.37W
Mackinnon Road 36 Gc 3.44S 39.03 E
McLaughlin 45 Fd 45.49N 100.49W
McLean 45 Fi 35.14N 100.36W
McLeans Town 44 Il 26.39N 77.59W
Maclean Strait 42 Ha 77.30N 103.10W
Maclear 37 Df 31.02S 28.23 E
Macleay River 59 Kf 30.52S 153.01 E
Mc Leod, Lake- 57 Cg 24.10S 113.35 E
McLeod Bay 42 Gd 62.53N 110.15W
McLeod Lake 42 Ff 54.59N 123.02W
McLoughlin, Mount- 46 De 42.27N 122.19W
McLure 46 Ea 51.03N 120.14W
Macmillan 42 Dd 62.52N 135.55W
McMillan, Lake- 45 Dj 32.40N 104.20W
McMillan Pass 42 Ed 63.00N 130.00W
McMinnville [Or.-U.S.] 46 Dd 45.13N 123.12W
McMinnville [Tn.-U.S.] 44 Eh 35.41N 85.46W
McMurdo 66 Kf 77.51S 166.37 E
McNaughton Lake 42 Ff 52.00N 117.50W
Macomb 45 Kf 40.27N 90.40W
Macomer 14 Cj 40.16N 8.47 E
Macomia 37 Gb 12.15S 40.08 E
Mâcon 11 Kh 46.18N 4.50 E
Macon [Ga.-U.S.] 39 Kf 32.50N 83.38W
Macon [Mo.-U.S.] 45 Jg 39.44N 92.28W
Macon [Ms.-U.S.] 45 Lj 33.07N 88.34W
Macondo 36 De 12.36S 23.43 E
Mâconnais, Monts du- 11 Kh 46.18N 4.45 E
Macoris, Cabo- 49 Ld 19.47N 70.28W
Macouba 51h Ab 14.52N 61.09W
McPherson 43 Hd 38.22N 97.40W
Mc Pherson Range 59 Ke 28.20S 153.00 E
Macquarie 66 Jd 54.30S 158.30 E
Macquarie Harbour 59 Jh 42.20S 145.25 E
Macquarie Ridge (EN) 3 Jo 57.00S 159.00 E
Macquarie River 57 Fh 30.07S 147.24 E
Mac Robertson Land 66 Fe 70.00S 65.00 E
Macroom/Maigh Chromtha 9 Ej 51.54N 8.57W
Macugnaga 14 Be 45.58N 7.58 E
Macujer 54 Dc 0.24N 73.07W
Macuro 50 Fg 10.39N 61.56W
Macusani 54 Df 14.05S 70.26W
Macuspana 48 Mi 17.48N 92.36W
Mačva 15 Ce 44.49N 19.30 E
McVicar Arm 42 Fc 65.10N 120.30W
Ma'dabā 24 Fg 31.43N 35.48 E
Madagali 34 Hc 10.53N 13.38 E
Madagascar 30 Lj 20.00S 47.00 E
Madagascar (EN) = Madagasikara 31 Lj 19.00S 46.00 E
Madagascar Basin (EN) 3 Fl 27.00S 53.00 E
Madagascar Plateau (EN) 3 Fm 30.00S 45.00 E
Madagasikara = Madagascar (EN) 31 Lj 19.00S 46.00 E
Madā'in Ṣāliḥ 24 Gi 26.48N 37.53 E
Madalai 64a Ac 7.20N 134.28 E
Madama 34 Ha 21.58N 13.39 E
Madan 15 Hh 41.30N 24.57 E
Madang 58 Fe 5.13S 145.48 E
Madaniyin 31 Ie 33.21N 10.30 E
Madanīyīn 32 Jc 33.00N 10.45 E
Madaoua 34 Gc 14.05N 5.58 E
Madara 15 Kf 43.17N 27.06 E
Madara-Shima 29 Ae 33.35N 129.45 E
Madaroumfa 34 Gc 13.18N 7.09 E
Madau 63a Ac 9.00S 152.26 E
Madawaska Highlands 44 Hc 45.20N 78.15W
Maddalena 14 Di 41.15N 9.25 E
Maddalena, Colle della- 11 Mj 44.25N 6.53 E
Maddaloni 14 Ii 41.02N 14.23 E
Made, Made en Drimmelen- 12 Gc 51.41N 4.48 E
Made en Drimmelen 12 Gc 51.41N 4.48 E
Made en Drimmelen-Made 12 Gc 51.41N 4.48 E
Madeir 35 Dd 7.50N 29.12 E
Madeira 31 Fe 32.40N 16.45W
Madeira 30 Fe 32.44N 17.00W
Madeira, Arquipélago da- = Madeira Islands (EN) 30 Fe 32.40N 16.45W
Madeira, Rio- 52 Kf 3.22S 58.45W
Madeira Islands (EN) = Madeira, Arquipélago da- 30 Fe 32.40N 16.45W
Madeleine, Ile de la- 42 Lg 47.26N 61.44W
Madeleine, Monts de la- 11 Jh 46.03N 3.50 E
Maden 24 Hc 38.23N 39.40 E
Madenassa Veld 30 Jj 19.00S 25.30 E
Madera [Ca.-U.S.] 46 Eh 36.57N 120.03W
Madera [Mex.] 47 Cc 29.12N 108.07W
Mader-Chih 13 Ri 35.26N 5.07 E
Madero, Puerto del- 13 Jc 41.48N 2.05W
Madesimo 14 Dd 46.26N 9.21 E
Madgaon 25 Ee 15.22N 73.49 E
Madhya Pradesh 25 Fd 22.00N 79.00 E
Madimba 36 Cc 4.58S 15.08 E
Madina do Boé 34 Cc 11.45N 14.13W
Madinani 34 Dd 9.37N 6.57W
Madinat al Abyār 33 Dc 32.11N 20.36 E
Madinat ash Sha'b 22 Gh 12.50N 44.56 E
Madingo-Kayes 36 Bc 4.10S 12.18 E
Madingou 36 Bc 4.09S 13.34 E
Madirovalo 37 Hc 16.29S 46.30 E
Madison [Fl.-U.S.] 44 Fj 30.28N 83.25W
Madison [In.-U.S.] 44 Ef 38.44N 85.23W
Madison [Mn.-U.S.] 45 Hd 45.01N 96.11W
Madison [S.D.-U.S.] 45 He 44.00N 97.07W
Madison [Wi.-U.S.] 39 Ke 43.05N 89.22W
Madison [W.V.-U.S.] 44 Gf 38.03N 81.50W
Madison Range 46 Jd 45.15N 111.20W
Madison River 46 Jd 45.56N 111.30W
Madisonville 43 Jd 37.20N 87.30W
Madiun 26 Fh 7.37S 111.31 E
Mado Gashi 36 Gb 0.44N 39.10 E
Madoi (Huangheyan) 22 Lf 35.00N 98.56 E
Madon 11 Mf 48.36N 6.06 E
Madona 7 Gh 56.53N 26.20 E
Madra Dağı 15 Kj 39.23N 27.12 E
Madrakah, Ra's al- 23 If 18.59N 57.45 E
Madranbaba Dağı 15 Ll 37.38N 28.12 E
Madras [India] 22 Kh 13.05N 80.17 E
Madras [Or.-U.S.] 46 Ed 44.38N 121.08W
Madre, Laguna- [Mex.] 47 Ed 25.00N 97.40W
Madre, Laguna- [Tx.-U.S.] 43 Hf 27.00N 97.35W
Madre, Sierra- 38 Jh 15.20N 92.20W
Madre de Dios 54 Df 12.00S 70.15W
Madre de Dios 54 Df 12.36S 69.59W
Madre de Dios, Isla- 52 Ik 50.15S 75.05W
Madre de Dios, Rio- 52 Jg 10.59S 66.08W
Madre del Sur, Sierra- = Southern Sierra Madre (EN) 38 Jj 17.00N 100.00W
Madre Occidental, Sierra- = Western Sierra Madre (EN) 38 Ig 25.00N 105.00W
Madre Oriental, Sierra- = Eastern Sierra Madre (EN) 38 Jg 22.00N 99.30W
Madrid 13 Id 40.30N 3.40W
Madrid 6 Fg 40.24N 3.41W
Madrid-Aravaca 13 Id 40.27N 3.47W
Madridejos 13 Ie 39.28N 3.32W
Madrid-El Pardo 13 Id 40.32N 3.46W
Madrid-Vallecas 13 Id 40.23N 3.37W
Madrid-Villaverde 13 Id 40.21N 3.42W
Madrigal de las Altas Torres 13 Hc 41.05N 5.00W
Mad River 46 Cf 40.57N 124.07W
Madriz 49 Dg 13.30N 86.30W
Madrona, Sierra- 13 Hf 38.25N 4.10W
Madula 36 Eb 0.28N 25.23 E
Madura, Palau- 21 Nj 7.00S 113.20 E
Madurai 22 Ji 9.56N 78.07 E
Madvār, Kūh-e- 23 Hc 30.36N 54.52 E
Madwin 33 Cd 28.42N 17.31 E
Madyan 21 Fg 27.40N 35.35 E
Madžalis 16 Oh 42.08N 47.50 E
Maebara 29 Be 33.34N 130.13 E
Maebashi 27 Od 36.23N 139.04 E
Mae Hong Son 25 Je 19.16N 97.56 E
Mæl 8 Ce 59.56N 8.48 E
Mae Nam Khong = Mekong (EN) 21 Mh 10.15N 105.55 E
Maesawa 29 Gb 39.03N 141.07 E
Mae Sot 25 Je 16.40N 98.35 E
Maestra, Sierra- 38 Lh 20.00N 76.45W
Maevatanana 37 Hc 16.56S 46.49 E
Maéwo, Ile- 57 Hf 15.10S 168.10 E
Mafeteng 37 De 29.45S 27.18 E
Mafia Channel 36 Gd 7.50S 39.35 E
Mafia Island 30 Ki 7.50S 39.50 E
Mafikeng 31 Jk 25.53S 25.39 E
Mafra [Braz.] 56 Kc 26.07S 49.49W
Mafra [Port.] 13 Cf 38.56N 9.20W
Magadan 22 Rd 59.34N 150.48 E
Magadanskaja Oblast 20 Kd 62.30N 154.00 E
Magadi 36 Gc 1.54S 36.17 E
Magallanes, Estrecho de- = Magellan, Strait of- (EN) 52 Ik 54.00S 71.00W
Magallanes y Antártica Chilena 56 Fh 51.30S 73.30W
Magangué 54 Db 9.14N 74.46W
Maganik 15 Cg 42.44N 19.16 E
Maganoy 26 He 6.51N 124.31 E
Magaria 34 Gc 12.59N 8.50 E
Magazine Mountain 45 Ji 35.10N 93.38W
Magdagači 20 Hf 53.29N 125.55 E
Magdala 55 Bm 36.06S 61.42W
Magdalena 54 Db 10.00N 74.15W
Magdalena [Arg.] 55 Dl 35.04S 57.32W
Magdalena [Bol.] 54 Ff 13.20S 64.08W
Magdalena [Mex.] 47 Bb 30.38N 110.57W
Magdalena [N.M.-U.S.] 45 Ci 34.07N 107.14W
Magdalena, Bahía- 48 Ce 24.35N 112.00W
Magdalena, Isla- 47 Bd 24.55N 112.15W
Magdalena, Llano de la- 47 Bd 24.30N 111.40W
Magdalena, Rio- [Col.] 52 Id 11.06N 74.51W
Magdalena, Rio- [Mex.] 48 Cb 30.48N 112.32W
Magda Plateau 42 Jb 72.18N 82.55W
Magdeburg 6 He 52.10N 11.40 E
Magdeburger Börde 10 Hd 52.00N 11.30 E
Magdelaine Cays 57 Gf 16.35S 150.15 E
Magee 45 Lk 31.52N 89.44W
Magee, Island-/Oileán Mhic Aodha 9 Hg 54.50N 5.50W
Magelang 26 Fh 7.28S 110.13 E
Magellan, Strait of- (EN) = Magallanes, Estrecho de- 52 Ik 54.00S 71.00W
Magellan Seamounts (EN) 57 Gc 17.30N 152.00 E
Magenta 14 Ce 45.28N 8.53 E
Magerøya 7 Fa 71.03N 25.45 E
Magetan 26 Fh 7.39S 111.20 E
Maggiorasca 14 Df 44.33N 9.29 E
Maggiore, Lago- 14 Ce 45.55N 8.40 E
Maghāghah 33 Fd 28.39N 30.50 E
Maghama 32 Ef 15.31N 12.50W
Maghera/Machaire Rátha 9 Gg 54.51N 6.40W
Maghnia 32 Gc 34.51N 1.44W
Magic Reservoir 46 He 43.20N 114.18W
Māgina, Sierra- 13 Ig 37.45N 3.30W
Magistralny 20 Fe 56.03N 107.35 E
Maglaj 14 Mf 44.33N 18.06 E
Măglenik 15 Ih 41.20N 25.45 E
Maglie 14 Mj 40.07N 18.18 E
Magliž 15 Ig 42.36N 25.33 E
Magnetawan River 44 Gc 45.46N 80.37W
Magnetic Island 59 Jc 19.10S 146.50 E
Magnitka 17 Ii 55.21N 59.43 E
Magnitnaja, Gora- 17 Ij 53.10N 59.10 E
Magnitogorsk 6 Le 53.27N 59.04 E
Magnolia 45 Jj 33.16N 93.14W
Magnor 7 Cg 59.57N 12.12 E
Magny-en-Vexin 11 He 49.09N 1.47 E
Mago 20 Jf 53.18N 140.20 E
Màgoé 37 Ec 15.48S 31.43 E
Magoebaskloof 37 Ed 23.51S 30.02 E
Magog 44 Kc 45.16N 72.09W
Magosa = Famagusta (EN) 23 Dc 35.07N 33.57 E
Magra [Alg.] 13 Qi 35.29N 4.58 E
Magra [It.] 14 Df 44.03N 9.58 E
Magtā Lahjar 32 Ef 17.50N 13.20W
Maguarinho, Cabo- 54 Id 0.20S 48.20W
Magude 37 Ee 25.02S 32.40 E
Magumeri 34 Hc 12.07N 12.49 E
Magura, Gora- 10 Th 48.50N 23.44 E
Magway 25 Jd 20.00N 95.00 E
Magway 22 Lg 20.09N 94.55 E
Magyarország = Hungary (EN) 6 Hf 47.00N 20.00 E
Mahābād 23 Gb 36.45N 45.53 E
Mahabalipuram 25 Gf 12.37N 80.12 E
Mahabe 37 Hc 17.05S 45.20 E
Mahabo 37 Gd 20.21S 44.39 E
Mahačkala 6 Kg 42.58N 47.30 E
Mahadday Wēyne 35 He 3.00N 45.32 E
Mahādeo Range 25 Ee 17.50N 74.15 E
Mahafaly, Plateau- 37 Gd 24.30S 44.00 E
Mahagi 36 Fb 2.18N 30.59 E
Mahajamba 37 Hc 15.33S 47.08 E
Mahājan 25 Ec 28.47N 73.50 E
Mahajanga 31 Lj 15.17S 46.43 E
Mahajanga 37 Hc 16.30S 47.00 E
Mahajilo 37 Hc 19.42S 45.22 E
Mahakam 21 Nj 0.35S 117.17 E
Mahalapye 37 Dd 23.07S 26.46 E
Mahalevona 37 Hc 15.26S 49.55 E
Mahallāt 24 Nf 33.55N 50.27 E
Mahamid 35 Cb 15.09N 20.25 E
Māhān 24 Qg 30.05N 57.19 E
Mahānadi 21 Kg 20.19N 86.45 E
Mahanoro 37 Hc 19.53S 48.49 E
Maharadze 19 Eg 41.53N 42.01 E
Mahārāshtra 25 Ee 18.00N 75.00 E
Mahārlū, Daryācheh-ye- 24 Oh 29.25N 52.50 E
Mahās 35 He 4.24N 46.07 E
Maha Sarakham 25 Ke 16.12N 103.16 E
Mahavavy 30 Lj 15.57S 45.54 E
Mahbés 32 Dd 27.10N 9.50W
Maḥḍah 24 Pj 24.24N 55.59 E
Mahdia 54 Gb 5.16N 59.09W
Mahe 25 Ff 11.42N 75.32 E
Mahébourg 37a Bb 20.24S 57.42 E
Mahé Island 30 Mi 4.40S 55.28 E
Mahendra Giri 25 Ge 18.58N 84.21 E
Mahenge 31 Ki 8.41S 36.43W
Maheno 62 Df 45.10S 170.50 E
Mahesāna 25 Ed 23.36N 72.24 E
Mahi 25 Ed 22.16N 72.58 E
Mahia Peninsula 61 Eg 39.10S 177.55 E
Mahmudābād 24 Lc 39.25N 47.15 E
Mahmūdābād 24 Od 36.38N 52.15 E
Mahmūd-e 'Erāqī 23 Kb 35.01N 69.20 E
Mahmudiye 24 Dc 39.30N 31.00 E
Mahmutşevketpaşa 15 Mh 41.09N 29.11 E
Māhneshān 24 Ld 36.45N 47.38 E
Mahnevo 17 Jg 58.27N 61.42 E
Mahnomen 45 Ic 47.19N 95.59W
Mahón/Mao 13 Qe 39.53N 4.15 E
Mahoré/Mayotte 30 Lj 12.50S 45.10 E
Mahrāt, Jabal- 35 Ib 17.00N 52.00 E
Mahuan Dao 27 Kd 10.50N 115.47 E
Mahua Point 63a Fd 10.28S 162.05 E
Maiana Atoll 57 Id 0.55N 173.00 E
Maiao, Ile- (Tubai-Manu) 57 Lf 17.34S 150.35W
Maicao 54 Da 11.23N 72.15W
Maicasagi, Lac- 44 Ia 49.52N 76.48W
Maîche 11 Mg 47.15N 6.48 E
Maicuru, Rio- 54 Hd 2.10S 54.17W
Maidenhead 12 Bc 51.31N 0.42W
Maidstone 9 Nj 51.17N 0.32 E
Maiduguri 31 Ig 11.51N 13.09 E
Maigh Chromtha/Macroom 9 Ej 51.54N 8.57W
Maigudo 35 Fd 7.26N 37.10 E
Maihara 29 Ed 35.20N 136.18 E
Maikala Range 25 Gd 22.30N 81.30 E
Maiko 36 Eb 0.14N 25.33 E
Maikona 36 Gb 2.56N 37.38 E
Maikoor, Pulau- 26 Jh 6.15S 134.15 E
Main 10 Ef 50.00N 8.18 E
Mainalon Óros 15 Fl 37.40N 22.15 E

Index Symbols

1 Independent Nation
2 State, Region
3 District, County
4 Municipality
5 Colony, Dependency
Continent
Physical Region
Historical or Cultural Region
Mount, Mountain
Volcano
Hill
Mountains, Mountain Range
Hills, Escarpment
Plateau, Upland
Pass, Gap
Plain, Lowland
Delta
Salt Flat
Valley, Canyon
Crater, Cave
Karst Features
Depression
Polder
Desert, Dunes
Forest, Woods
Heath, Steppe
Oasis
Cape, Point
Coast, Beach
Cliff
Peninsula
Isthmus
Sandbank
Island
Atoll
Rock, Reef
Islands, Archipelago
Rocks, Reefs
Coral Reef
Well, Spring
Geyser
River, Stream
Waterfall Rapids
River Mouth, Estuary
Lake
Salt Lake
Intermittent Lake
Reservoir
Swamp, Pond
Canal
Glacier
Ice Shelf, Pack Ice
Ocean
Sea
Gulf, Bay
Strait, Fjord
Lagoon
Bank
Seamount
Tablemount
Ridge
Shelf
Basin
Escarpment, Sea Scarp
Fracture
Trench, Abyss
National Park, Reserve
Point of Interest
Recreation Site
Cave, Cavern
Historic Site
Ruins
Wall, Walls
Church, Abbey
Temple
Scientific Station
Airport
Port
Lighthouse
Mine
Tunnel
Dam, Bridge

Main Barrier Range 59 If 31.25S 141.25 E
Mainburg 10 Hh 48.39N 11.47 E
Main Camp 64g Ba 2.01N 157.25W
Main Channel 44 Gc 45.22N 81.50W
Mai-Ndombe, Lac- 30 Ii 2.10S 18.15 E
Main-Donau-Kanal 10 Gg 49.55N 10.50 E
Maindong → Coqên 27 Ee 31.15N 85.13 E
Maine 11 Ff 48.15N 0.10W
Maine [2] 43 Nb 45.15N 69.15W
Maine [Fr.] 11 Fg 47.25N 0.37W
Maine [Fr.] 11 Eg 47.09N 1.27W
Maine, Gulf of- 38 Me 43.00N 68.00W
Maine-et-Loire [3] 11 Fg 47.30N 0.20W
Maïné-Soroa 34 Hc 13.18N 12.02 E
Mainistir Fhear Maí/Fermoy 9 Ei 52.08N 8.16W
Mainistir na Búille/Boyle 9 Eh 53.58N 8.18W
Mainistir na Corann/Midleton 9 Ej 51.55N 8.10W
Mainistir na Féile/Abbeyfeale 9 Di 52.24N 9.18W
Mainit, Lake- 26 Ie 9.26N 125.32 E
Mainland [Scot.-U.K.] 5 Fc 60.20N 1.22W
Mainland [Scot.-U.K.] 5 Fd 59.00N 3.10W
Maintal 12 Kd 50.08N 8.51 E
Maintenon 11 Hf 48.35N 1.35 E
Maintirano 31 Lj 18.03S 44.03 E
Mainz 10 Eg 50.00N 8.15 E
Maio 32 Cf 23.10N 15.10W
Maio 30 Eg 15.15N 23.10W
Maipo, Volcán- 52 Ji 34.10S 69.50W
Maipú 56 Ie 36.52S 57.52W
Maiquetia 54 Ea 10.36N 66.57W
Maira 14 Bf 44.49N 7.38 E
Mairi 54 Jf 11.43S 40.08W
Mairipotaba 55 Hc 17.21S 49.31W
Maisān [3] 24 Lg 32.00N 47.00 E
Maisí, Punta- 47 Jd 20.15N 74.09W
Maišiagala/Maišjagala 8 Kj 54.51N 25.14 E
Maišjagala/Maišiagala 8 Kj 54.51N 25.14 E
Maiter 13 Qi 35.23N 4.17 E
Maitland [Austl.] 59 Hf 34.22S 137.40 E
Maitland [Austl.] 58 Gh 32.44S 151.33 E
Maíz, Isla Grande del- 49 Fg 12.10N 83.03W
Maíz, Isla Pequeña del- 49 Fg 12.18N 82.59W
Maíz, Islas del- 47 Hf 12.15N 83.00W
Maizhokunggar 27 Ff 29.50N 91.40 E
Maizières-lès-Metz 12 Ie 49.13N 6.09 E
Maizuru 28 Mg 35.27N 135.20 E
Maizuru-Nishimaizuru 29 Dd 35.28N 135.19 E
Maizuru-Wan 29 Dd 35.30N 135.20 E
Maja 21 Pd 60.17N 134.41 E
Majagual 49 Ji 8.35N 74.37W
Majakovski 16 Mh 42.02N 42.47 E
Majangat 27 Fb 48.20N 91.58 E
Majardah, Wādī- 14 Em 37.07N 10.13 E
Majāz al Bāb 14 Dn 36.39N 9.37 E
Majdanpek 15 Ee 44.25N 21.56 E
Majene 22 Nj 3.33S 118.57 E
Majërtën=Mijirtein (EN) 30 Lh 9.00N 50.00 E
Majevica 14 Mf 44.40N 18.40 E
Maji 35 Fd 6.10N 35.35 E
Majia He 27 Kd 38.09N 117.53 E
Majja 20 Id 61.38N 130.25 E
Majkain 19 He 51.27N 75.52 E
Majkamys 18 Ka 46.34N 77.37 E
Majkop 6 Kg 44.35N 40.07 E
Majli-Saj 18 Id 41.15N 72.30 E
Majma'ah 24 Kj 25.54N 45.20 E
Majmak 19 Hg 42.40N 71.14 E
Majmakan 20 Ie 57.30N 135.23 E
Majmeča 20 Fb 71.20N 104.15 E
Majn 20 Mc 65.03N 172.10 E
Majna [R.S.F.S.R.] 20 Ef 53.00N 91.28 E
Majna [R.S.F.S.R.] 7 Li 54.09N 47.37 E
Major, Puig- 13 Oe 39.48N 2.48 E
Major, Puig-/Mayor, Puig- 13 Oe 39.48N 2.48 E
Majorca (EN)=Mallorca 5 Gh 39.30N 3.00 E
Majrur 35 Db 16.40N 26.53 E
Majski [R.S.F.S.R.] 16 Nh 43.36N 44.03 E
Majski [R.S.F.S.R.] 20 Hf 52.18N 129.38 E
Maju, Pulau 26 If 1.20N 126.25 E
Majuro Atoll 57 Id 7.09N 171.12 E
Makabana 31 Ii 3.28S 12.36 E
Makaha 65a Cb 21.29N 158.13W
Makahuena Point 65a Bb 21.52N 159.27W
Makalamabedi 37 Cd 20.20S 23.53 E
Makale 26 Gg 3.06S 119.51 E
Makallé 56 Ic 27.13S 59.17W
Makalondi 34 Fc 12.50N 1.41 E
Makamby, Nosy- 37 Hc 15.42S 45.54 E
Makanči 19 If 46.51N 81.57 E
Makanza 36 Cb 1.36N 19.07 E
Makapala 65a Fc 20.13N 155.45W
Makapu Point 64k Ba 18.59S 169.55W
Makapuu Head 65a Db 21.18N 157.39W
Makara, Prohod- 15 Ih 41.16N 25.26 E
Makares 15 Il 37.05N 25.42 E
Makarfi 34 Gc 11.23N 7.53 E
Makari 34 Hc 12.35N 14.28 E
Makari Mountains 36 Ed 6.05S 29.50 E
Makarjev 7 Kh 57.57N 43.49 E
Makarov 20 Jg 48.39N 142.51 E
Makarov Basin (EN) 67 Ce 87.00N 170.00 E
Makarov Seamount (EN) 57 Gb 29.30N 153.30 E
Makarska 14 Lg 43.18N 17.02 E
Makā Rūd 24 Nd 36.21N 51.16 E
Makasar → Ujung Pandang 22 Nj 5.07S 119.24 E
Makasar, Selat-=Makassar Strait (EN) 21 Nj 2.00S 117.30 E
Makassar Strait (EN)=Makasar, Selat- 21 Nj 2.00S 117.30 E
Makat 6 Lf 47.40N 53.28 E
Makatea, Ile- 57 Mf 15.50S 148.15W
Makaw 25 Jc 26.27N 96.42 E
Makawao 65a Ec 20.51N 156.19W
Makay, Massif du- 37 Hd 21.15S 45.15 E
Makedhonia [2] 15 Fi 40.40N 22.30 E
Makedhonia=Macedonia (EN) 15 Fh 41.00N 23.00 E
Makedhonia=Macedonia (EN) 5 Ig 41.00N 23.00 E
Makedonija=Macedonia (EN) 5 Ig 41.00N 23.00 E
Makedonija = Macedonia (EN) [2] 15 Eh 41.50N 22.00 E
Makedonija=Macedonia (EN) 15 Fh 41.00N 23.00 E
Makejevka 16 Jf 48.00N 37.58 E
Makelulu, Mount- 64a Bb 7.34N 134.35 E
Makemo Atoll 57 Mf 16.35S 143.40W
Makeni 31 Fh 8.53N 12.03W
Makgadikgadi Pans 30 Jk 20.50S 25.30 E
Makhfar al Buşayyah 24 Lg 30.08N 46.07 E
Makhfar al Hammām 24 He 35.51N 38.45 E
Makhmūr 24 Je 35.46N 43.35 E
Makhyah, Wādī- 23 Gf 17.40N 49.01 E
Maki 29 Fc 37.45N 138.52 E
Makian, Pulau- 26 If 0.20N 127.25 E
Makikihi 62 Df 44.38S 171.09 E
Makinsk 19 He 52.40N 70.26 E
Makkah=Mecca (EN) 22 Fg 21.27N 39.49 E
Makkovik 42 Le 55.05N 59.11W
Maknassy 32 Ic 34.37N 9.36 E
Makó 10 Qj 46.13N 20.29 E
Makokou 31 Ih 0.34N 12.52 E
Makongai 63d Bb 17.27S 178.58 E
Makongolosi 36 Fd 8.24S 33.09 E
Makorako 62 Gc 39.09S 176.03 E
Makoua 31 Ih 0.01N 15.39 E
Makoura 63b Dc 17.08S 168.26 E
Makov 10 Og 49.22N 18.29 E
Maków Mazowiecki 10 Rd 52.52N 21.06 E
Makrá 15 Im 36.16N 25.53 E
Makrān 21 Hg 26.00N 60.00 E
Makrónisos 15 Hl 37.42N 24.07 E
Maksatiha 7 Ih 57.48N 35.55 E
Makteir 30 Ff 21.50N 11.40W
Makthar 14 Do 35.50N 9.13 E
Makthar 32 Ib 35.51N 9.12 E
Makū 23 Hd 27.52N 52.26 E
Mākū 24 Kc 39.17N 44.31 E
Makubetsu 29a Cb 42.54N 143.19 E
Makumbato 36 Fd 8.51S 34.50 E
Makumbi 36 Dd 5.51S 20.41 E
Makunduchi 36 Gd 6.25S 39.33 E
Makung 27 Kg 23.35N 119.35 E
Makurazaki 28 Ki 31.16N 139.19 E
Makurdi 31 Hh 7.44N 8.32 E
Makushin Volcano 40a Eb 53.53N 166.50W
Makušino 19 Gd 55.13N 67.13 E
Makuyuni 36 Gc 3.33S 36.06 E
Malå 7 Ed 65.11N 18.44 E
Mala/Mallow 9 Ei 52.08N 8.39W
Mala, Punta- 47 Ig 7.28N 80.00W
Malabang 26 He 7.38N 124.03 E
Malabar Coast 21 Jh 10.00N 76.15 E
Malabo 31 Hh 3.45N 8.47 E
Malabrigo 55 Ci 29.20S 59.58W
Malacca, Strait of- (EN)=Melaka, Selat- 21 Mi 2.30N 101.20 E
Malacky 10 Nh 48.27N 17.01 E
Malad City 46 Ie 42.12N 112.15W
Malá Fatra 10 Og 49.08N 18.50 E
Málaga [3] 13 Hh 36.48N 4.45W
Málaga [Col.] 54 Db 6.42N 72.44W
Málaga [Sp.] 6 Fh 36.43N 4.25W
Malagarasi 30 Ji 5.12S 29.47 E
Malagón 13 Ie 39.10N 3.51W
Malaimbandi 37 Hd 20.20S 45.36 E
Malaita Island 57 He 9.00S 161.00 E
Malaja Kuonamka 20 Gb 70.50N 113.20 E
Malaja Ob 20 Bc 66.08N 65.50 E
Malaja Sosva 19 Gc 63.10N 64.22 E
Malaja Višera 19 Dd 58.52N 32.14 E
Malaja Viska 16 Ge 48.39N 31.38 E
Malakāl 31 Kh 9.31N 31.39 E
Malakal Harbor 64a Ac 7.20N 134.26 E
Malakal Pass 64a Ac 7.17N 134.28 E
Malakand 14 Jf 44.55N 15.28 E
Malakobi 63a Db 7.19S 158.07 E
Mallamalla Range 25 Fe 16.17N 79.29 E
Malang 22 Nj 7.59S 112.37 E
Malangen 7 Eb 69.30N 18.20 E
Malanje 36 Cd 9.30S 16.30 E
Malanje 31 Ii 9.33S 16.22 E
Malanville 34 Fc 11.52N 3.23 E
Malao 63b Cb 15.10S 166.51 E
Mała Panew 10 Nf 50.44N 17.52 E
Mälaren 5 Hd 59.30N 17.15 E
Malargüe 56 Ge 35.28S 69.35W
Malartic, Lac- 44 Ha 48.15N 78.05W
Malaspina Glacier 40 Ke 59.50N 140.30W
Malatya 22 Ff 38.21N 38.19 E
Malāvi 24 Lf 33.10N 47.50 E
Malawi [1] 31 Kj 13.30S 34.00 E
Malawi, Lake- 30 Kj 12.00S 34.30 E
Malaya 26 Df 4.00N 102.00 E
Malaybalay 26 Ie 8.09N 125.05 E
Malāyer 24 Me 34.16N 48.12 E
Malāyer 23 Gc 34.17N 48.50 E
Malay Peninsula (EN) 21 Mi 6.00N 102.00 E
Malaysia [1] 22 Mi 4.00N 102.00 E
Malaysia, Semenanjung- [2] 26 Df 4.00N 102.00 E
Malazgirt 24 Jc 39.09N 42.31 E
Malberg 12 Id 50.03N 6.35 E
Malbor 24 Og 30.45N 52.05 E
Malbork 10 Pb 54.02N 19.01 E
Malbrán 56 Hc 29.21S 62.27W
Malchin 10 Ic 53.44N 12.47 E
Maldegem 12 Fc 51.13N 3.27 E
Malden 45 Lh 36.34N 89.57W
Malden Island 57 Le 4.03S 154.59W
Malditos, Montes-/La Maladeta 13 Mb 42.40N 0.50 E
Maldive Islands 21 Ji 3.15N 73.00 E
Mal di Ventre 14 Ck 40.00N 8.20 E
Maldives [1] 22 Ji 3.15N 73.00 E
Maldon 9 Nj 51.45N 0.40 E
Maldonado [2] 55 El 34.40S 54.55W
Maldonado 56 Jd 34.54S 54.57W
Maldonado, Punta- 48 Ji 16.20N 98.35W
Male 22 Ji 4.10N 73.30 E
Malé 14 Ed 46.21N 10.55 E
Mâle, Lac du- 44 Ja 48.30N 75.30W
Malea, Cape- (EN)=Maléas, Ákra- 15 Gm 36.26N 23.12 E
Maléas, Ákra- = Malea, Cape- (EN) 15 Gm 36.26N 23.12 E
Male Atoll 21 Ji 4.29N 73.30 E
Malebo, Pool- 30 Ii 4.17S 15.20 E
Mälegaon 25 Ed 20.33N 74.32 E
Maléha 34 Dc 11.48N 9.43W
Malek 35 Ed 6.04N 31.36 E
Malé Karpaty = Little Carpathians (EN) 10 Nh 48.30N 17.20 E
Malek Kandī 24 Ld 37.09N 46.06 E
Malékoula, Ile 57 Hf 16.15S 167.30 E
Malema 37 Fb 14.57S 37.25 E
Malemba Nkulu 36 Ed 8.02S 26.48 E
Malenga 7 Ie 63.50N 36.25 E
Măleruş 15 Id 45.54N 25.32 E
Malesherbes 11 If 48.18N 2.25 E
Malgobek 16 Nh 43.32N 44.34 E
Malgomaj 7 Dd 64.47N 16.12 E
Malhada 55 Kb 14.21S 43.47W
Malhanski Hrebet 20 Ff 50.30N 109.00 E
Malhão da Estrêla 13 Ed 40.19N 7.37W
Malha Wells 35 Db 15.08N 26.12 E
Malheur Lake 43 Dc 43.20N 118.45W
Malheur River 46 Gd 44.03N 116.59W
Mali [1] 31 Gg 17.00N 4.00W
Mali 34 Cc 12.05N 12.18W
Mali 25 Jc 25.42N 97.30 E
Mali 63d Bb 16.20S 179.21 E
Mália 15 In 35.17N 25.28 E
Maliakós Kólpos 15 Fk 38.52N 22.38 E
Malik, Wādī al- 30 Kg 18.02N 30.58 E
Mali kanal 15 Cd 45.42N 19.19 E
Malik Siah, Kūh-i- 23 Jd 29.51N 60.52 E
Målilla 8 Fg 57.23N 15.48 E
Mali Lošinj 14 If 44.32N 14.28 E
Malimba, Monts- 36 Ed 7.32S 29.30 E
Malin 16 Fd 50.46N 29.14 E
Malinalco 48 Jh 18.57N 99.30W
Malinaltepec 48 Ji 17.03N 98.40W
Malindi 31 Li 3.13S 40.07 E
Malines/Mechelen 11 Kc 51.02N 4.29 E
Malin Head/Cionn Mhálanna 5 Fd 55.23N 7.24W
Malino, Bukit- 26 Hf 0.45N 120.47 E
Malinovoje Ozero 20 Cf 51.40N 79.55 E
Malinyi 36 Gd 8.56S 36.08 E
Malipo 27 Hg 23.07N 104.42 E
Maliqi 15 Di 40.43N 20.41 E
Malita 26 Ie 6.25N 125.36 E
Maljen 15 De 44.07N 20.03 E
Maljovica 15 Gg 42.11N 23.22 E
Malka 16 Nh 43.44N 44.15 E
Malkara 24 Bb 40.53N 26.54 E
Malki Lom 15 Jf 43.39N 26.04 E
Malko Tărnovo 15 Kh 41.59N 27.32 E
Mallacoota 59 Jg 37.30S 149.50 E
Mallaig 9 Hd 57.00N 5.50W
Mallāq, Wādī- 14 Cn 36.32N 8.51 E
Mallawī 33 Fd 27.44N 30.50 E
Mallery Lake 42 Hd 64.00N 98.00W
Malles Venosta / Mals 14 Ed 46.41N 10.32 E
Mallet 55 Gg 25.55S 50.50W
Mallorca=Majorca (EN) 5 Gh 39.30N 3.00 E
Mallow/Mala 9 Ei 52.08N 8.39W
Malm 7 Cd 64.04N 11.13 E
Malmbäck 8 Fg 57.35N 14.28 E
Malmberget 7 Ec 67.10N 20.40 E
Malmédy 11 Md 50.26N 6.02 E
Malmesbury 37 Bf 33.28S 18.44 E
Malmö 6 Hd 55.36N 13.00 E
Malmöhus [2] 7 Ci 55.45N 13.30 E
Malmön 8 Df 58.21N 11.20 E
Malmslätt 8 Ff 58.25N 15.30 E
Malmyž 19 Fd 56.31N 50.41 E
Malo 63b Cb 15.41S 167.10 E
Maloarhangelsk 16 Jc 52.26N 36.29 E
Maloelap 57 Id 8.45N 171.03 E
Maloggia/Malojapaß 14 Dd 46.24N 9.41 E
Malojapaß/Maloggia 14 Dd 46.24N 9.41 E
Malojaroslavec 16 Jb 55.02N 36.28 E
Maloje Polesje 10 Jf 50.10N 24.30 E
Malolo 63d Ab 17.45S 177.10 E
Malolos 26 Hd 14.51N 120.49 E
Malombe, Lake- 36 Ge 14.38S 35.12 E
Malone 44 Jc 44.52N 74.19W
Malonga 36 De 10.24S 23.10 E
Małopolska 10 Pf 50.45N 20.00 E
Malorita 16 Dd 51.48N 24.05 E
Malošujka 7 Ie 63.47N 37.22 E
Måløy 7 Af 61.56N 5.07 E
Malozemelskaja Tundra 17 Ec 68.00N 52.00 E
Malpaso 48 Mi 17.20N 93.30W
Malpelo, Isla de- 52 He 3.59N 81.35W
Malprabha 25 Fe 16.12N 76.03 E
Mals / Malles Venosta 14 Ed 46.41N 10.32 E
Malsch 12 Kf 48.53N 8.20 E
Malše 10 Kh 48.59N 14.29 E
Malta 5 Hh 35.54N 14.31 E
Malta [1] 6 Hh 35.50N 14.30 E
Malta [Lat.-U.S.S.R.] 8 Lh 56.18N 27.15 E
Malta [Mt.-U.S.] 43 Fb 48.21N 107.52W
Malta, Canale di- [Eur.] = Malta Channel (EN) 14 In 36.30N 14.30 E
Malta Channel (EN)=Malta, Canale di- [Eur.] 14 In 36.30N 14.30 E
Maltahöhe [3] 37 Bd 25.00S 16.30 E
Maltahöhe 31 Ik 24.50S 17.00 E
Maltepe 15 Mi 40.55N 29.08 E
Malton 9 Mg 54.08N 0.48W
Maluku [3] 26 Ig 4.00S 128.00 E
Maluku, Kepulauan-=Moluccas (EN) 57 De 2.00S 128.00 E
Maluku, Laut-=Molucca Sea (EN) 21 Oj 0.05S 125.00 E
Malumfashi 34 Gc 11.48N 7.37 E
Malunda 26 Gg 3.00S 118.50 E
Malung 7 Cf 60.40N 13.44 E
Malungsfors 8 Ed 60.44N 13.33 E
Malūţ 35 Ec 10.26N 32.12 E
Maluu 63a Ec 8.21S 160.38 E
Malvern [Ar.-U.S.] 45 Ji 34.22N 92.49W
Malvern [Eng.-U.K.] 9 Ki 52.07N 2.19W
Malvinas 55 Ci 29.37S 58.59W
Malvinas, Islas-/Falkland Islands [5] 53 Kk 51.45S 59.00W
Malvinas, Islas-/Falkland Islands 52 Kk 51.45S 59.00W
Maly, Ostrov- 8 Ld 60.02N 27.58 E
Malya 36 Fc 2.59S 33.31 E
Maly Anjuj 20 Lc 68.35N 161.03 E
Malý Čeremšan 7 Mi 54.20N 50.01 E
Malý Dunaj 10 Nh 48.08N 17.09 E
Malygina, Proliv- 20 Cb 73.00N 70.30 E
Maly Jenisej 20 Ef 51.40N 94.26 E
Maly Kavkaz=Lesser Caucasus (EN) 5 Kg 41.00N 44.35 E
Maly Ljahovski, Ostrov- 20 Jb 74.07N 140.36 E
Maly Tajmyr, Ostrov- 20 Fa 78.08N 107.08 E
Maly Uzen 5 Kf 48.50N 49.38 E
Mama 20 Ge 58.20N 112.54 E
Mamadyš 7 Mi 55.45N 51.24 E
Mamagota 63a Bb 6.46S 155.24 E
Mamaia 15 Le 44.17N 28.37 E
Mamakan 20 Ge 57.48N 114.05 E
Mamantel 48 Nh 18.33N 91.05W
Mamanutha Group 63d Ab 17.34S 177.04 E
Mamaqān 24 Kd 37.51N 45.59 E
Mambaj 55 Ib 14.28S 46.07W
Mambajao 26 He 9.15N 124.43 E
Mambasa 36 Eb 1.21N 29.03 E
Mambéré 35 Be 3.31N 16.03 E
Mambili 36 Cb 0.07N 16.08 E
Mamborê 55 Fg 24.18S 52.32W
Mambova 36 Ef 17.44S 25.11 E
Mambrui 36 Hc 3.07S 40.09 E
Mamburao 26 Hd 13.14N 120.35 E
Mamedkala 16 Ph 42.12N 48.06 E
Mamer 12 Ie 49.38N 6.02 E
Mamers 11 Gf 48.21N 0.23 E
Mamfe 34 Gd 5.46N 9.17 E
Mamiá, Lago- 54 Fd 4.15S 63.05W
Mamisonski, Pereval- 16 Mh 42.43N 43.45 E
Mamljutka 19 Ge 54.57N 68.35 E
Mammoth Cave 44 Dg 37.10N 86.08W
Mammoth Hot Springs 46 Jd 44.59N 110.43W
Mamoré, Rio- 52 Jg 10.23S 65.53W
Mamou 31 Fg 10.23N 12.05W
Mampikony 37 Hc 16.05S 47.37 E
Mampodre, Picos de- 13 Ga 43.02N 5.12W
Mampong 34 Ed 7.04N 1.24W
Mamry, Jezioro- 10 Rb 54.08N 21.42 E
Mamuju 26 Gg 2.41S 118.54 E
Mamuno 37 Cd 22.17S 20.02 E
Ma'murah, Ra's al- 14 En 36.27N 10.49 E
Mamurokawa 29 Gb 38.54N 140.15 E
Mamutzu 37 Hb 12.47S 45.14 E
Man 31 Gh 7.24N 7.33W
Man [3] 34 Dd 7.13N 7.41W
Man, Calf of- 9 Ig 54.03N 4.48W
Man, Isle of- 5 Fe 54.15N 4.30W
Mana 60 Oc 22.02N 159.46W
Mana 20 Ee 55.57N 92.28 E
Manacapuru 54 Fd 3.18S 60.37W
Manacor 13 Pe 39.34N 3.12 E
Manado 22 Oi 1.29N 124.51 E
Managua 39 Kh 12.09N 86.17W
Managua [3] 49 Dg 12.05N 86.20W
Managua, Lago de- 47 Gf 12.20N 86.20W
Manakara 31 Lk 22.07S 48.00 E
Manama (EN)=Al Manāmah 22 Hg 26.13N 50.35 E
Manambolo 37 Gc 19.19S 44.17 E
Manam Island 57 Fe 4.05S 145.03 E
Manamo, Caño- 54 Fb 9.55N 62.16W
Mananara 37 Hc 16.10S 49.45 E
Mananara 37 Hd 23.21S 47.42 E
Mananjary 31 Lk 21.14S 48.17 E
Manankoro 34 Dc 10.28N 7.25W
Manantenina 37 Hd 24.17S 47.18 E
Manaoba 63a Ec 8.19S 160.47 E
Manapire, Rio- 50 Ci 7.42N 66.07W
Manapouri 58 Hi 45.34S 167.36 E
Manapouri, Lake- 62 Bf 45.30S 167.30 E
Manār, Jabal- 33 Hg 14.10N 44.17 E
Manas 22 Ke 44.18N 86.13 E
Manas, Gora- 18 Hc 42.18N 71.06 E
Manas He 27 Eb 45.38N 85.12 E
Manas Hu 27 Eb 45.45N 85.55 E
Manasija, Manastir- 15 Ee 44.06N 21.28 E
Manati 49 Ic 21.19N 76.56W
Manati 49 Nd 18.26N 66.29W
Manatuto 26 Ih 8.30S 126.01 E
Manaure 49 Kh 11.46N 72.28W
Manaus 53 Jf 3.08S 60.01W
Manavgat 24 Dd 36.47N 31.26 E
Manbij 24 Gd 36.31N 37.57 E
Manbūbnagar 25 Fe 16.44N 77.59 E
Mancelona 44 Ec 44.54N 85.04W
Mancha Real 13 Ig 37.47N 3.37W
Manche [3] 11 Ee 49.00N 1.10W
Mancheng 28 Ce 38.57N 115.19 E
Manchester [Ct.-U.S.] 44 Ke 41.47N 72.31W
Manchester [Eng.-U.K.] 6 Fe 53.30N 2.15W
Manchester [Ia.-U.S.] 45 Ke 42.29N 91.27W
Manchester [Ky.-U.S.] 44 Fg 37.09N 83.46W
Manchester [N.H.-U.S.] 43 Mc 42.59N 71.28W
Manchester [Tn.-U.S.] 44 Dh 35.29N 86.05W
Manchok 34 Gd 9.40N 8.31 E
Manchuria (EN) 22 Oe 47.00N 125.00 E
Manciano 14 Fh 42.35N 11.31 E
Mand 23 Hd 28.11N 51.17 E
Manda [Chad] 35 Bd 9.11N 18.13 E
Manda [Tan.] 36 Fe 10.28S 34.35 E
Manda, Jabal- 35 Cd 8.39N 24.27 E
Mandabe 37 Gd 21.02S 44.56 E
Mandaguari 56 Jb 23.32S 51.42W
Manda Island 36 Hc 2.17S 40.57 E
Mandal 7 Bg 58.02N 7.27 E
Mandalay [3] 25 Jd 21.00N 96.00 E
Mandalay 22 Lg 22.00N 96.05 E
Mandal-Gobi 27 Ib 45.45N 106.12 E
Mandali 24 Kf 33.45N 45.32 E
Mandalselva 8 Bf 58.02N 7.28 E
Mandalt → Sonid Zuoqi 27 Kc 43.50N 116.45 E
Mandalya körfezi 24 Bd 37.12N 27.20 E
Mandan 43 Gb 46.50N 100.54W
Mandaon 26 Hd 12.13N 123.17 E
Mandara, Monts-=Mandara Mountains (EN) 34 Hc 10.45N 13.40 E
Mandara Mountains (EN)=Mandara, Monts- 34 Hc 10.45N 13.40 E
Mandas 14 Dk 39.38N 9.07 E
Mandasor 25 Fd 24.04N 75.04 E
Mandera 31 Lh 3.56N 41.52 E
Manderscheid 12 Id 50.06N 6.49 E
Mandeville 49 Id 18.02N 77.30W
Mandi 25 Fb 31.43N 76.55 E
Mandiana 34 Dc 10.38N 8.41W
Mandimba 37 Fb 14.21S 35.39 E
Mandingues, Monts- 34 Cc 13.00N 11.00W
Mandioli, Pulau- 26 Ig 0.44S 127.14 E
Mandioré, Laguna- 55 Dd 18.08S 57.33W
Mandirituba 55 Hg 25.46S 49.19W
Mandji 36 Bc 1.42S 10.24 E
Mandla 25 Gd 22.36N 80.23 E
Mandø 8 Ci 55.15N 8.35 E
Mandoúdhion 15 Gk 38.48N 23.29 E
Mandrákion 15 Km 36.36N 27.08 E
Mandritsara 37 Hc 15.49S 48.48 E
Mandurah 59 Df 32.32S 115.43 E
Manduria 14 Lj 40.24N 17.38 E
Māndvi 25 Dd 22.50N 69.22 E
Mandya 25 Ff 12.33N 76.54 E
Måne 8 Ce 59.56N 8.48 E
Măneciu Ungureni 15 Id 45.19N 25.59 E
Manendragarh 25 Gd 23.10N 82.35 E
Maneromango 36 Gd 7.16S 38.46 E
Manevičí 16 Dd 51.19N 25.33 E
Manfalūţ 33 Fd 27.19N 30.58 E
Manfredonia 14 Ji 41.38N 15.55 E
Manfredonia, Golfo di- 14 Ki 41.35N 16.05 E
Manga [Afr.] 30 Ig 15.00N 14.00 E
Manga [Braz.] 54 Jf 14.46S 43.56W
Mangabeiras, Chapada das- 52 Lg 10.00S 46.30W
Mangai 36 Cc 4.03S 19.35 E
Mangaia Island 57 Lg 21.55S 157.55W
Mangakino 62 Fc 38.22S 175.46 E
Mangalia 15 Lf 43.48N 28.35 E
Mangalmé 35 Bc 12.21N 19.37 E
Mangalore 22 Jh 12.52N 74.53 E
Mangareva, Ile- 57 Ng 23.07S 134.57W
Mangfall 10 Ii 47.51N 12.08 E
Manggar 26 Eg 2.53S 108.16 E
Manggautu 63a Dd 11.30S 159.59 E
Mangin Yoma 25 Jd 24.20N 95.42 E
Mangistau 16 Qg 44.03N 51.57 E
Mangit 19 Gg 42.07N 60.01 E
Mangkalihat, Tanjung- 26 Gf 1.02N 118.59 E
Manglares, Cabo- 54 Cc 1.36N 79.02W
Mangnai 27 Fd 37.48N 91.55 E
Mangniu He 28 Ib 45.10N 126.58 E
Mango [Fiji] 63d Cb 17.27S 179.09W
Mango [Ton.] 65b Bb 20.20S 174.43W
Mangoche 36 Ge 14.28S 35.16 E
Mangoky [Mad.] 37 Hd 23.27S 45.13 E
Mangoky [Mad.] 30 Lk 21.29S 43.41 E
Mangole, Pulau- 26 Ig 1.53S 125.50 E
Mangonui 62 Ea 34.59S 173.32 E
Mangrove Cay 49 Ia 24.51N 76.14W
Mangrullo, Cuchilla- 55 Fk 32.27S 53.50W
Mangshi → Luxi 27 Gg 24.29N 98.40 E
Mangualde 13 Ed 40.36N 7.46W
Mangueira, Lagoa- 56 Jd 33.06S 52.48W
Mangueni, Plateau de- 30 If 22.35N 12.40 E
Mangui 27 La 52.03N 122.09 E
Mangula 37 Ec 16.52S 30.08 E
Mangum 45 Gi 34.53N 99.30W
Manguredjipa 36 Eb 0.21N 28.44 E
Mangyšlak 19 Fg 43.40N 51.15 E
Mangyšlak, Plato- 19 Fg 43.25N 53.00 E
Mangyšlakskaja Oblast [3] 19 Fg 44.00N 53.30 E
Mangyšlakski Zaliv 16 Qg 44.45N 51.00 E
Manhattan 43 Hd 39.11N 96.35W
Manhiça 37 Ee 25.24S 32.48 E
Manica 36 Ed 6.27S 25.20 E
Mani 54 Dc 4.49N 72.17W
Mani 27 Ee 34.16N 87.20 E
Mānī', Wādī al- 24 Ie 34.16N 41.02 E
Mania 37 Hc 19.42S 45.22 E
Maniago 14 Gd 46.10N 12.43 E
Manica [3] 37 Ec 19.00S 33.20 E
Manica 37 Ec 18.56S 32.53 E
Manicaland [3] 37 Ec 19.00S 32.30 E
Manicoré 53 Jf 5.49S 61.17W

Index Symbols

[1] Independent Nation
[2] State, Region
[3] District, County
[4] Municipality
[5] Colony, Dependency
Continent
Physical Region

Historical or Cultural Region
Mount, Mountain
Volcano
Hill
Mountains, Mountain Range
Hills, Escarpment
Plateau, Upland

Pass, Gap
Plain, Lowland
Delta
Salt Flat
Valley, Canyon
Crater, Cave
Karst Features

Depression
Polder
Desert, Dunes
Forest, Woods
Heath, Steppe
Oasis
Cape, Point

Coast, Beach
Cliff
Peninsula
Isthmus
Sandbank
Island
Atoll

Rock, Reef
Islands, Archipelago
Rocks, Reefs
Coral Reef
Well, Spring
Geyser
River, Stream

Waterfall Rapids
River Mouth, Estuary
Lake
Salt Lake
Intermittent Lake
Reservoir
Swamp, Pond

Canal
Glacier
Ice Shelf, Pack Ice
Ocean
Sea
Gulf, Bay
Strait, Fjord

Lagoon
Bank
Seamount
Tablemount
Ridge
Shelf
Basin

Escarpment, Sea Scarp
Fracture
Trench, Abyss
National Park, Reserve
Point of Interest
Recreation Site
Cave, Cavern

Historic Site
Ruins
Wall, Walls
Church, Abbey
Temple
Scientific Station
Airport

Port
Lighthouse
Mine
Tunnel
Dam, Bridge

Manicoré, Rio- 54 Fe 5.51S 61.19W
Manicouagan 42 Kg 49.10N 68.15W
Manicouagan 42 Kf 51.00N 68.20W
Manicouagan, Réservoir- 38 Md 51.30N 68.19W
Manigotagan 45 Ha 51.06N 96.18W
Manihi Atoll 57 Mf 14.24S 145.56W
Manihiki Anchorage 64n Ab 10.23S 161.03W
Manihiki Atoll 57 Kf 10.24S 161.01W
Manika, Plateau de la- 36 Ed 10.00S 26.00 E
Manila [Phil.] 22 Oh 14.35N 121.00 E
Manila [Ut.-U.S.] 46 Kf 40.59N 109.43W
Manila Bay 21 Oh 14.30N 120.45 E
Manilaid/Manilajd 8 Kf 58.08N 24.03 E
Manilajd/Manilaid 8 Kf 58.08N 24.03 E
Manily 20 Ld 62.30N 165.20 E
Maningrida Settlement 59 Gb 12.05S 134.10 E
Maniouro, Pointe- 63b Dc 17.41S 168.35 E
Manipa, Selat- 26 Ig 3.20S 127.23 E
Manipur [3] 25 Id 25.00N 94.00 E
Manipur 25 Id 22.52N 94.05 E
Manisa 23 Cb 38.36N 27.26 E
Manisa Dağı 15 Kk 38.33N 27.28 E
Manises 13 Le 39.29N 0.27W
Manissau a-Missu, Rio- 54 Hf 10.58S 53.20W
Manistee 44 Dc 44.15N 86.18W
Manistee River 44 Dc 44.15N 86.21W
Manistique 43 Jb 45.57N 86.15W
Manitique Lake 44 Eb 46.15N 85.45W
Manitoba [3] 42 Hf 55.00N 97.00W
Manitoba, Lake- 38 Jd 51.00N 98.45W
Manitou Islands 44 Ec 45.10N 86.00W
Manitou Lake 44 Gc 45.48N 82.00W
Manitoulin Island 42 Jg 45.45N 82.30W
Manitou Springs 45 Dg 38.52N 104.55W
Manitouwadge 45 Nb 49.08N 85.47W
Manitowoc 43 Jc 44.06N 87.40W
Manitsoq/Sukkertoppen 41 Ge 65.25N 53.00W
Maniwaki 42 Jg 46.23N 75.58W
Manizales 53 Ie 5.05N 75.32W
Manja 17 Jd 64.23N 60.50 E
Manja 37 Gd 21.23S 44.20 E
Manjača 14 Lf 44.35N 17.05 E
Manjacaze 37 Ed 24.42S 33.33 E
Manjakandriana 37 Hc 18.55S 47.47 E
Manji 29a Bb 43.09N 141.59 E
Manjimup 59 Df 34.14S 116.09 E
Mānjra 25 Fe 18.49N 77.52 E
Mān Kāt 25 Jd 22.05N 98.01 E
Mankato [Ks.-U.S.] 45 Gg 39.47N 98.12W
Mankato [Mn.-U.S.] 43 Ic 44.10N 94.01W
Mankono 34 Dd 8.04N 6.12W
Mankono [3] 34 Dd 7.58N 6.02W
Mankoya 31 Jj 14.50S 25.00 E
Manley Hot Springs 40 Ic 65.00N 150.37W
Manlleu 13 Ob 42.00N 2.17 E
Manmād 25 Ed 20.15N 74.27 E
Manmanoc, Mount- 26 Hc 17.40N 121.06 E
Manna 26 Dh 4.27S 102.55 E
Mannahill 59 Hf 32.26S 139.59 E
Mannar 25 Fg 8.59N 79.54 E
Mannar, Gulf of- 21 Ji 8.30N 79.00 E
Mannheim 6 Gf 49.29N 8.28 E
Manning [Alta.-Can.] 42 Fe 56.55N 117.33W
Manning [S.C.-U.S.] 44 Gi 33.42N 80.12W
Manning, Cape- 64g Ba 2.02N 157.26W
Manning Strait 63a Db 7.24S 158.04 E
Manningtree 12 Dc 51.57N 1.04 E
Mann Ranges 59 Fe 26.00S 129.30 E
Mann River 59 Gb 12.20S 134.07 E
Mannu, Capo- 14 Cj 40.02N 8.22 E
Mannu, Rio- [It.] 14 Cj 40.50N 8.23 E
Mannu, Rio- [It.] 14 Cj 40.41N 8.59 E
Mano 34 Cd 6.56N 11.31W
Mano [Jap.] 29 Fc 37.58N 138.20 E
Mano [S.L.] 34 Cd 7.55N 12.00W
Manoa 54 Ee 9.40S 65.27W
Man of War, Cayos- 49 Fg 13.02N 83.22W
Manokwari 58 Ee 2.30S 134.36 E
Manombo 37 Gd 22.55S 43.28 E
Manompana 37 Hc 16.41S 49.45 E
Manonga 36 Fc 4.08S 34.12 E
Manono 31 Ji 7.18S 27.25 E
Manono 65c Aa 13.50S 172.05W
Manosque 11 Lk 43.50N 5.47 E
Manouane, Lac- 42 Kf 50.40N 70.45W
Manō-Wan 29 Fc 37.55N 138.15 E
Manp'ojin 28 Id 41.09N 126.17 E
Manra Atoll (Sydney) 57 Je 4.27S 171.15W
Manresa 13 Nc 41.44N 1.50 E
Mansa 31 Jj 11.12S 28.53 E
Mansa Konko 34 Bc 13.28N 15.33W
Mansel 38 Lc 62.00N 79.50W
Mansfield [Austl.] 59 Jg 37.03S 146.05 E
Mansfield [Eng.-U.K.] 9 Lh 53.09N 1.11W
Mansfield [La.-U.S.] 45 Jj 32.02N 93.43W
Mansfield [Oh.-U.S.] 43 Kc 40.46N 82.31W
Mansfield [Pa.-U.S.] 44 Ie 41.47N 77.05W
Mansfield, Mount- 44 Kc 44.33N 72.49W
Mansle 11 Gi 45.52N 0.11 E
Manso, Rio- 55 Db 14.42S 56.16W
Manso, Rio- ou Mortes, Rio das- 52 Kg 11.45S 50.44W
Mansôa 34 Bc 12.04N 15.19W
Mansourah 13 Qh 36.04N 4.28 E
Mansourah, Djebel- 13 Qh 36.02N 4.28 E
Manta 54 Bd 0.57S 80.42W
Manta, Bahía de- 54 Bd 0.50S 80.40W
Mantalingajan, Mount- 26 Ge 8.48N 117.40 E
Manteca 46 Eh 37.48N 121.13W
Mantecal [Ven.] 50 Di 6.52N 65.38W
Mantecal [Ven.] 50 Bi 7.33N 69.09W
Manteigas 13 Ed 40.24N 7.32W
Manteo 44 Jh 35.55N 75.40W
Mantes-la-Jolie 11 Hf 48.59N 1.43 E
Manti 46 Jg 39.16N 111.38W
Mantiqueira, Serra da- 52 Lh 22.00S 44.45W
Manto 49 Df 14.55N 86.23W
Manton 44 Ec 44.24N 85.24W
Mantova 14 Ee 45.09N 10.48 E
Mäntsälä 8 Kd 60.38N 25.20 E
Mänttä 7 Fe 62.02N 24.38 E
Mantua 49 Eb 22.17N 84.17W
Manturovo 19 Ed 58.22N 44.44 E
Mäntyharju 7 Gf 61.25N 26.53 E
Mäntyluoto 8 Ic 61.35N 21.29 E
Manu 54 Df 12.15S 70.50W
Manuae Atoll 57 Lf 19.21S 158.56W
Manua Islands 57 Kf 14.13S 169.35W
Manuangi Atoll 57 Mf 19.12S 141.16W
Manūbah 14 Dn 36.48N 10.06 E
Manuel 48 Jf 22.44N 98.19W
Manuel Alves, Rio- 54 If 11.19S 48.28W
Manuel Bonavides 48 Hc 29.05N 103.55W
Manuel Derqui 55 Ch 27.50S 58.48W
Manuel J. Cobo 55 Dl 35.49S 57.54W
Manuel Ocampo 55 Bk 33.46S 60.39W
Manuga Reefs 63a Ad 11.00S 153.21 E
Manui, Pulau- 26 Hg 3.35S 123.08 E
Manujān 24 Qi 27.24N 57.32 E
Mānūk, Tell- 24 Hf 33.10N 38.50 E
Manukau 58 Ih 36.56S 174.56 E
Manulu Lagoon 64g Bb 1.56N 157.20W
Manus Island 57 Fe 2.05S 147.00 E
Many 45 Jk 31.34N 93.29W
Manyara, Lake- 36 Gc 3.35S 35.50 E
Manyas 24 Bb 40.02N 27.58 E
Manyč 5 Kf 47.15N 40.00 E
Manyč-Gudilo, Ozero- 5 Kf 46.25N 42.35 E
Manyoni 36 Fd 5.45S 34.50 E
Manzanal, Puerto del- 13 Fb 42.32N 6.10W
Manzanares 13 Ie 39.00N 3.22W
Manzaneda, Cabeza de- 13 Eb 42.20N 7.15W
Manzanilla 13 Fg 37.23N 6.25W
Manzanillo [Cuba] 39 Lg 20.21N 77.07W
Manzanillo [Mex.] 39 Ih 19.03N 104.20W
Manzanillo, Bahía de- [Dom.Rep.] 49 Ld 19.45N 71.46W
Manzanillo, Bahía de- [Mex.] 48 Gh 19.04N 104.25W
Manzanillo, Punta- 49 Hi 9.38N 79.32W
Manzano Mountains 45 Ci 34.45N 106.20W
Manzhouli 22 Ne 49.33N 117.28 E
Manzilah, Buḥayrat al- 24 Eg 31.15N 32.00 E
Manzil Bū Ruqaybah 32 Ib 37.10N 9.48 E
Manzil bū Zalafah 14 En 36.41N 10.35 E
Manzil Tamīn 14 En 36.47N 10.59 E
Manzini 37 Ee 26.29S 31.22 E
Mao 63b Dc 17.29S 168.29 E
Mao [Chad] 31 Ig 14.07N 15.19 E
Mao [Dom.Rep.] 47 Je 19.34N 71.05W
Mao/Mahón 13 Qe 39.53N 4.15 E
Maoke, Pegunungan- 57 Ee 4.00S 138.00 E
Maomao Shan 27 Hd 37.12N 103.10 E
Maoming 22 Ng 21.41N 110.52 E
Maoniu Shan 27 He 32.50N 104.12 E
Maotou Shan 27 Hg 24.31N 100.38 E
Maouri, Dallol- 34 Fc 12.05N 3.32 E
Mapai 37 Ed 22.51S 31.58 E
Mapanda 36 Dd 9.32S 24.16 E
Mapati 36 Bc 3.38S 13.21 E
Mapi 58 Ee 7.07S 139.23 E
Mapi 26 Kh 7.00S 139.16 E
Mapia, Kepulauan- 26 Jf 0.50N 134.20 E
Mapimí, Bolsón de- 38 Ig 27.30N 103.15W
Mapinhane 37 Fd 22.15S 35.07 E
Mapire 50 Di 7.45N 64.42W
Mapiri 54 Eg 15.15S 68.10W
Maple Creek 42 Gg 49.55N 109.27W
Maprik 60 Ch 3.38S 143.03 E
Mapuera, Rio- 54 Gd 1.05S 57.02W
Maputo [3] 37 Ee 26.00S 32.30 E
Maputo (Lourenço Marques) 31 Kk 25.58S 32.34 E
Maputo, Baia de- 30 Kk 26.05S 33.00 E
Maqèn (Dawu) 27 He 34.29N 100.01 E
Maqran, Wādī al- 33 Ie 20.55N 47.12 E
Maqu 27 He 34.05N 101.45 E
Maquan He/Damqog Kanbab 27 Df 29.36N 84.09 E
Maquela do Zombo 31 Ii 6.03S 15.08 E
Maquinchao 56 Gf 41.15S 68.44W
Maquoketa 45 Ke 42.04N 90.40W
Mar, Serra do- 52 Lh 25.00S 48.00W
Mara 36 Fc 1.31S 33.56 E
Mara [3] 36 Fc 2.30S 34.00 E
Maraā 54 Ed 1.50S 65.22W
Marab 35 Fc 14.54N 37.55 E
Marabá 54 Ie 5.21S 49.07W
Marabahan 26 Fg 3.00S 114.45 E
Marabá Paulista 55 Gf 22.06S 51.56W
Maraca, Ilha de- 54 Hc 2.05N 50.25W
Maracaibo 53 Id 10.40N 71.37W
Maracaibo, Lago de- = Maracaibo, Lake- (EN) 52 Ie 9.50N 71.30W
Maracaibo, Lake- (EN) = Maracaibo, Lago de- 52 Ie 9.50N 71.30W
Maracaju 54 Gh 21.38S 55.09W
Maracaju, Serra de- [Braz.] 52 Kh 21.00S 55.00W
Maracaju, Serra de- [S.Amer.] 55 Ef 23.57S 55.01W
Maracanã 54 Id 0.46S 47.27W
Maracás 54 Jf 13.26S 40.27W
Maracay 53 Jd 10.15N 67.36W
Marādah 33 Cd 29.14N 19.13 E
Maradi 31 Hg 13.29N 7.06 E
Maradi [3] 34 Gc 14.15N 7.15 E
Marāgheh 23 Gb 37.23N 46.40 E
Marāh 23 Gd 25.04N 45.28 E
Maraho 35 Bb 18.21N 17.28 E
Marahuaca, Cerro- 52 Je 3.34N 65.27W
Marajó, Baia de- 52 Lf 1.00S 48.30W
Marajó, Ilha de- 52 Lf 1.00S 49.30W
Marakei Atoll 57 Id 1.58N 173.25 E
Maralal 36 Gb 1.06N 36.42 E
Maralinga 59 Gf 30.13S 131.35 E
Maralwexi/Bachu 27 Cd 39.46N 78.15 E
Maramag 26 He 7.46N 125.00 E
Maramasike Island 60 Gi 9.30S 161.25 E
Maramba 31 Jj 17.51S 25.52 E
Marampa 34 Cd 8.41N 12.28W
Maramureş [2] 15 Gb 47.40N 24.00 E
Maranchón 13 Jc 41.03N 2.12W
Marand 23 Gb 38.26N 45.46 E
Marang 26 De 5.12N 103.13 E
Maranhão [2] 54 Je 5.00S 45.00W
Maranhão, Rio- 54 If 14.34S 49.02W
Marano, Laguna di- 14 He 45.44N 13.10 E
Maranoa River 59 Je 27.50S 148.37 E
Marañón, Rio- 52 If 4.30S 73.35W
Marans 11 Fh 46.18N 1.00W
Marão 37 Ed 24.18S 34.07 E
Marão, Serra do- 13 Ec 41.15N 7.55W
Maraoué 34 Dd 6.54N 5.31W
Marapanim 54 Id 0.42S 47.42W
Marapi, Gunung- 26 Dg 0.23S 100.28 E
Marargiu, Capo- 14 Cj 40.20N 8.23 E
Marari, Serra do- 55 Gh 27.30S 51.00W
Mara Rosa 55 Ha 13.58S 49.09W
Mărăşeşti 15 Kd 45.53N 27.14 E
Maratea 14 Jk 39.59N 15.43 E
Marathón 15 Gk 38.09N 23.58 E
Marathon 45 Ek 30.12N 103.15W
Marathon 42 Ig 48.46N 86.26W
Maratua, Pulau- 26 Gf 2.15N 118.36 E
Marau 55 Fi 28.27S 52.12W
Maravari 63a Cb 7.54S 156.44 E
Marāveh Tappeh 24 Pd 37.55N 55.57 E
Maravilha 55 Fh 26.47S 53.09W
Maravillas Creek 45 El 29.34N 102.47W
Maravovo 63a Dc 9.17S 159.38 E
Marāwah 33 Dc 32.29N 21.25 E
Marawi 26 He 8.13N 124.15 E
Marawī 35 Eb 18.29N 31.49 E
Marāwiḥ 24 Oj 24.18N 53.18 E
Marayes 56 Gd 31.29S 67.20W
Marbella 13 Hh 36.31N 4.53W
Marble Bar 59 Dd 21.11S 119.44 E
Marble Canyon 46 Jh 36.30N 111.50W
Marble Falls 45 Gk 30.34N 98.17W
Marble Hall 37 Dd 24.57S 29.13 E
Marburg an der Lahn 10 Ef 50.49N 8.46 E
Marca, Ponta da- 30 Ij 16.31S 11.42 E
Marcal 10 Ni 47.38N 17.32 E
Marcala 49 Df 14.07N 88.00W
Marçal Dağları 15 Kl 37.09N 28.00 E
Marcali 10 Nj 46.35N 17.25 E
March 10 Mh 48.10N 16.59 E
March 9 Ni 52.33N 0.06 E
Marche 11 Hh 46.10N 1.30 E
Marche = Marches (EN) [2] 14 Hh 43.30N 13.15 E
Marche, Plateau de la- 11 Hh 46.16N 1.30 E
Marche-en-Famenne 11 Ld 50.14N 5.20 E
Marchena 13 Gg 37.20N 5.24W
Marchena, Isla- 54a Aa 0.20N 90.30W
Marches (EN) = Marche [2] 14 Hh 43.30N 13.15 E
Marchesato 14 Kk 39.05N 17.00 E
Marchfeld 14 Kb 48.15N 16.40 E
Mar Chiquita, Laguna- 55 Dm 37.37S 57.24W
Mar Chiquita, Laguna- 52 Ji 30.42S 62.36W
Marciana Marina 14 Eh 42.48N 10.12 E
Marcigny 11 Kh 46.16N 4.02 E
Marcilly-sur-Eure 12 Df 48.49N 1.21 E
Marcinelle, Charleroi- 12 Gd 50.25N 4.28 E
Marck 12 Dd 50.57N 1.57 E
Marcoing 12 Fd 50.07N 3.11 E
Marcos Juaréz 56 Hd 32.42S 62.06W
Marcus Baker, Mount- 40 Jd 61.26N 147.45W
Marcus Island (EN) = Minami-Tori-Shima 57 Gb 26.32N 142.09 E
Marcy, Mount- 43 Mc 44.07N 73.56W
Mardakert 16 Oi 40.12N 46.52 E
Mardakjan 16 Qi 40.29N 50.12 E
Mardān 25 Eb 34.09N 72.02 E
Mardarovka 15 Mb 47.30N 29.40 E
Mar del Plata 53 Ki 38.01S 57.35W
Marden 12 Cc 51.10N 0.30 E
Mardin 23 Fb 37.18N 40.44 E
Mardin Dağları 24 Id 37.20N 41.00 E
Maré, Ile- 57 Hg 21.30S 168.00 E
Mare, Muntele- 15 Gc 46.29N 23.14 E
Marechal Cândido Rondon 55 Eg 24.34S 54.04W
Maree, Loch- 9 Hd 57.40N 5.30W
Mareeba 59 Jc 17.00S 145.26 E
Mareg 35 He 3.47N 47.18 E
Maremma 14 Fh 42.30N 11.30 E
Marennes 11 Ei 45.49N 1.07W
Marettimo 14 Gm 37.56N 12.05 E
Mareuil-en-Brie 12 Ff 48.57N 3.45 E
Marfa 43 Ge 30.18N 104.01W
Marfil, Laguna- 55 Bb 15.30S 60.20W
Margai Caka 27 Ed 35.10N 86.55 E
Marganec 19 Df 47.38N 34.40 E
Margaret River 59 Df 33.57S 115.04 E
Margarida 55 De 21.41S 56.44W
Margarita, Isla de- 54 Fa 11.00N 64.00W
Margarita Belén 55 Ch 27.16S 58.58W
Margarition 15 Dj 39.21N 20.26 E
Margate [Eng.-U.K.] 9 Oj 51.24N 1.24 E
Margate [S.Afr.] 37 Ef 30.55S 30.15 E
Marghera, Venezia- 14 Ge 45.28N 12.44 E
Margherita 30 Jh 0.23N 29.54 E
Margherita di Savoia 14 Ki 41.22N 16.09 E
Marghine, Catena del- 14 Cj 40.20N 8.50 E
Marghita 15 Fb 47.21N 22.20 E
Marghūb, Kūh-e- 24 Qf 33.06N 57.30 E
Margilan 19 Hg 40.28N 71.46 E
Margina 15 Fd 45.51N 22.16 E
Marguerite Bay 66 Qe 68.30S 68.30W
Margut 12 He 49.35N 5.16 E
Marha 20 Hd 60.35N 123.10 E
Marha 21 Nc 63.20N 118.50 E
Mari 24 Ie 34.39N 40.53 E
Mari 24 Ee 34.44N 33.18 E
Maria Atoll [W.F.] 57 Ng 22.00S 136.10W
Maria Atoll [W.F.] 57 Lg 21.48S 154.41W
Maria Cleofas, Isla- 48 Fg 21.16N 106.14W
Maria Elena 56 Gb 22.21S 69.40W
Mariager 8 Ch 56.39N 10.00 E
Mariager Fjord 8 Dh 56.40N 10.20 E
Maria Grande, Arroyo- 55 Ci 29.21S 58.45W
Maria Ignacia 55 Cm 37.24S 59.30W
Maria Island [Austl.] 59 Jh 42.40S 148.05 E
Maria Island [Austl.] 59 Hb 14.55S 135.40 E
Maria Island [St.Luc.] 51k Bb 13.44N 60.56W
Mariakani 36 Gc 3.52S 39.28 E
Maria Laach 12 Jd 50.25N 7.15 E
Maria Madre, Isla- 48 Fg 21.35N 106.33W
Maria Magdalena, Isla- 48 Fg 21.25N 106.25W
Mariana Islands 57 Fc 16.00N 145.30 E
Marianao 47 Hd 23.05N 82.26W
Mariana Trench (EN) 3 Ih 14.00N 147.30 E
Marianna [Ar.-U.S.] 45 Ki 34.46N 90.46W
Marianna [Fl.-U.S.] 44 Ej 30.47N 85.14W
Mariannelund 8 Fg 57.37N 15.34 E
Mariano I. Loza 55 Ci 29.22S 58.12W
Mariánské Lázně 10 Ig 49.58N 12.43 E
Marías, Islas- 38 Ig 21.25N 106.28W
Marias Pass 46 Ib 48.19N 113.21W
Marias River 43 Eb 47.56N 110.30W
Maria Theresa Reef 57 Lh 36.58S 151.23W
Mariato, Punta- 47 Hg 7.13N 80.53W
Maria van Diemen, Cape- 62 Ea 34.29S 172.39 E
Mariazell 14 Jc 47.46N 15.19 E
Ma'rib 23 Gf 15.30N 45.21 E
Maribo 8 Dj 54.46N 11.31 E
Maribor 14 Jd 46.33N 15.39 E
Marica 5 Ig 40.52N 26.12 E
Marica 15 Ig 42.02N 25.50 E
Maricao 51a Bb 18.10N 66.58W
Maricopa 46 Ij 33.04N 112.03W
Marīdī 35 Dd 6.05N 29.24 E
Marīdī 35 De 4.55N 29.28 E
Marié, Rio- 54 Ed 0.25S 66.26W
Marie Byrd Land (EN) 66 Nf 80.00S 120.00W
Mariec 7 Lh 56.31N 49.51 E
Marie Galante 47 Le 15.56N 61.16W
Marie-Galante, Canal de- 51e Bc 15.55N 61.25W
Mariehamn / Maarianhamina 7 Ef 60.06N 19.57 E
Marie Louise Island 37b Bb 6.11S 53.09 E
Mariembourg, Couvin- 12 Gd 50.06N 4.31 E
Marienburg 12 Jd 50.04N 7.08 E
Marienmünster 12 Lc 51.50N 9.13 E
Marienstatt 12 Jd 50.40N 7.49 E
Mariental 31 Ik 24.36S 17.59 E
Mariestad 7 Cg 58.43N 13.51 E
Marietta [Ga.-U.S.] 43 Ke 33.57N 84.33W
Marietta [Oh.-U.S.] 44 Gf 39.26N 81.27W
Mariga 34 Gd 9.36N 5.57 E
Marignac 11 Gl 42.55N 0.39 E
Marignane 11 Lk 43.25N 5.13 E
Marigot [Dom.] 50 Fe 15.32N 61.18W
Marigot [Guad.] 50 Ec 18.04N 63.06W
Marigot [Haiti] 49 Kd 18.14N 72.19W
Marigot [Mart.] 51h Ab 14.49N 61.02W
Marigot [St.Luc.] 51k Ab 13.58N 61.02W
Mariinsk 20 De 56.13N 87.45 E
Mariinskij Posad 7 Lh 56.08N 47.48 E
Mariinskoje 20 Jf 51.43N 140.19 E
Marijovo 15 Eh 41.04N 21.45 E
Marijskaja ASSR [3] 19 Ed 56.40N 48.00 E
Marilia 56 Jb 22.13S 50.01W
Mariluz 55 Fg 24.02S 53.13W
Marimba 36 Cd 8.22S 17.02 E
Marimbondo, Cachoeira do- 55 He 20.18S 49.10W
Marin 13 Db 42.23N 8.42W
Marin, Cul-de-Sac du- 51h Bc 14.27N 60.53W
Marina di Catanzaro 14 Kl 38.49N 16.36 E
Marina di Gioiosa Ionica 14 Kl 38.18N 16.20 E
Marina di Pisa 14 Eg 43.40N 10.16 E
Marina di Ravenna 14 Gf 44.29N 12.17 E
Marina Gorka 19 Ce 53.31N 28.12 E
Marinduque 26 Hd 13.24N 121.58 E
Marineland 44 Gk 29.43N 81.12W
Marines 12 De 49.09N 1.59 E
Marinette 43 Jb 45.06N 87.38W
Maringá 53 Kh 23.25S 51.55W
Maringa 30 Ih 1.14N 19.48 E
Marinha Grande 13 De 39.45N 8.56W
Marino [It.] 14 Gi 41.46N 12.39 E
Marino [Van.] 63b Db 14.59S 168.03 E
Marins, Pico dos- 55 Jf 22.27S 45.10W
Marinsko 8 Mf 58.46N 28.39 E
Marion 30 Km 46.36S 37.55 E
Marion [Al.-U.S.] 44 Di 32.32N 87.26W
Marion [Ia.-U.S.] 45 Ke 42.02N 91.36W
Marion [Il.-U.S.] 45 Lh 37.44N 88.56W
Marion [In.-U.S.] 44 Ee 40.33N 85.40W
Marion [Oh.-U.S.] 43 Kc 40.35N 83.08W
Marion [S.C.-U.S.] 44 Hh 34.11N 79.23W
Marion [Va.-U.S.] 44 Gg 36.51N 81.30W
Marion, Lake- 44 Gi 33.30N 80.25W
Marion Reefs 57 Gf 19.10S 152.20 E
Maripa 54 Ea 7.26N 65.09W
Mariposa 46 Fh 37.29N 119.58W
Mariquita, Cerro- 48 Jf 23.13N 98.22W
Marisa 26 Hf 0.28N 121.56 E
Mariscala 55 El 34.03S 54.47W
Mariscal Estigarribia 56 Hb 22.02S 60.38W
Mariupol' 6 Jf 47.06N 37.33 E
Mariusa, Caño 50 Fh 9.43N 61.26W
Mariusa, Isla- 50 Fh 9.39N 61.19W
Marīvan 24 Le 35.31N 46.10 E
Märjamaa/Marjamaa 8 Kf 58.54N 24.21 E
Marjamaa/Märjamaa 8 Kf 58.54N 24.21 E
Marjanovka [R.S.F.S.R.] 19 He 54.58N 72.38 E
Marjanovka [Ukr.-U.S.S.R.] 10 Uf 50.23N 24.55 E
Mark 12 Gc 51.39N 4.39 E
Mark [Ger.] 12 Jc 51.13N 7.36 E
Mark [Swe.] 8 Eg 57.35N 12.35 E
Marka 31 Lh 1.43N 44.46 E
Markakol, Ozero- 19 If 48.45N 85.50 E
Markam (Gartog) 27 Gf 29.32N 98.33 E
Markaryd 7 Ch 56.26N 13.36 E
Markazi [3] 23 Hb 35.30N 51.30 E
Marken 12 Hb 52.27N 5.05 E
Markerwaard 12 Hb 52.31N 5.15 E
Market Deeping 12 Bb 52.40N 0.18W
Market Harborough 9 Mi 52.29N 0.55W
Markham, Mount- 66 Kg 82.51S 161.21 E
Markham Bay 42 Kd 63.30N 71.40W
Markham River 59 Ja 6.35S 146.25 E
Marki 10 Rd 52.20N 21.07 E
Märkische Schweiz 10 Jd 52.35N 14.00 E
Markit 27 Cd 38.53N 77.35 E
Markounda 35 Bd 7.37N 16.59 E
Markovac 15 Ee 44.14N 21.06 E
Markovka 16 Ke 49.31N 39.32 E
Markovo 22 Tc 64.40N 170.25 E
Markoye 34 Fc 14.39N 0.02 E
Marksburg 12 Jd 50.16N 7.40 E
Marksville 45 Jk 31.08N 92.04W
Marktoberdorf 10 Gi 47.47N 10.37 E
Marktredwitz 10 If 50.00N 12.05 E
Markulešty 15 Lb 47.51N 28.07 E
Marl 10 De 51.39N 7.05 E
Marlagne 12 Gd 50.25N 4.40 E
Marlborough [2] 62 Ed 41.50S 173.40 E
Marlborough [Austl.] 59 Jd 22.49S 149.53 E
Marlborough [Guy.] 50 Gi 7.29N 58.38W
Marle 11 Je 49.44N 3.46 E
Marlin 45 Hk 31.18N 96.53W
Marlinton 44 Gf 38.14N 80.06W
Marlow [Eng.-U.K.] 12 Bc 51.34N 0.46W
Marlow [Ok.-U.S.] 45 Hi 34.39N 97.57W
Marmande 11 Gj 44.30N 0.10 E
Marmara 24 Bb 40.35N 27.33 E
Marmara, Sea of- (EN) = Marmara Denizi 5 Ig 40.40N 28.15 E
Marmara Adasi 24 Bb 40.38N 27.37 E
Marmara Denizi = Marmara, Sea of- (EN) 5 Ig 40.40N 28.15 E
Marmara Ereğlisi 15 Ki 40.58N 27.57 E
Marmara Gölü 15 Lk 38.37N 28.02 E
Marmarica (EN) = Barqah al Bahrīyah 30 Je 31.40N 24.30 E
Marmaris 23 Cb 36.51N 28.16 E
Marmelos, Rio- 54 Fe 6.08S 61.47W
Marmion Lake 45 Kb 48.54N 91.30W
Marmolada 14 Fd 46.26N 11.51 E
Marmora 44 Ic 44.29N 77.41W
Marmore, Cascata delle- 14 Gh 42.35N 12.45 E
Marne 10 Ec 53.57N 9.00 E
Marne 5 Gf 48.49N 2.24 E
Marne [3] 11 Kf 48.55N 4.10 E
Marne à la Saône, Canal de la- 11 Kf 48.44N 4.36 E
Marne au Rhin, Canal de la- 11 Nf 48.35N 7.47 E
Mårnes 7 Dc 67.09N 14.06 E
Marneuli 16 Ni 41.29N 44.45 E
Maro 35 Bd 8.25N 18.46 E
Maro 35 Bb 19.23N 16.38 E
Maroa 54 Ec 2.43N 67.33W
Maroantsetra 31 Lj 15.27S 49.44 E
Marokau Atoll 61 Mc 18.02S 142.17W
Marolambo 37 Hd 20.04S 48.08 E
Maromandia 37 Hb 14.11S 48.06 E
Maromme 11 He 49.28N 1.02 E
Maromokotro 37 Hb 14.01S 48.58 E
Maroni, Fleuve- 52 Ke 5.45N 53.58W
Marònia 15 Ii 40.55N 25.31 E
Maronne 11 Hi 45.04N 1.56 E
Maroochydore 59 Ke 26.39S 153.06 E
Maro Reef 57 Jb 25.25N 170.35W
Maros 15 Dc 46.15N 20.12 E
Maros 26 Gg 5.00S 119.34 E
Maroua 31 Ig 10.36N 14.20 E
Marovoay 37 Hc 16.06S 46.37 E
Marowijne River 54 Hb 5.45N 53.58W
Marqādah 24 Ie 35.44N 40.46 E
Mar Qu 27 He 31.58N 101.54 E
Marquard 37 De 28.54S 27.28 E
Marquenterre 12 Dd 50.20N 1.41 E
Marquesas Islands (EN) = Marquises, Iles- 57 Ne 9.00S 139.30W
Marquette 43 Jb 46.33N 87.24W
Marquion 12 Fd 50.13N 3.05 E
Marquis [Gren.] 51p Bb 12.06N 61.37W
Marquis [St.Luc.] 51k Ba 14.02N 60.55W
Marquis, Cape- 51k Ba 14.03N 60.54W
Marquise 12 Dd 50.49N 1.42 E
Marquises, Iles- = Marquesas Islands (EN) 57 Ne 9.00S 139.30W
Marracuene 37 Ee 25.44S 32.41 E
Marradi 14 Ff 44.04N 11.37 E
Marrah, Jabal- 30 Jg 13.04N 24.21 E
Marrak 33 Hf 16.26N 41.54 E
Marrakech 31 Ge 31.38N 8.00W
Marrakech [3] 32 Fc 32.00N 8.00W
Marrawah 59 Ih 40.56S 144.41 E
Marree 59 Eg 29.39S 138.04 E
Marreh, Kūh-e- 24 Oh 29.15N 52.20 E
Marrero 45 Kl 29.54N 90.07W
Marresalja 17 Mb 69.44N 66.59 E
Marresalskije Koški, Ostrova- 17 Mb 69.30N 67.10 E
Marromeu 37 Fc 18.17S 35.56 E
Marrti 7 Gc 67.28N 28.22 E
Marrupa 37 Fb 13.12S 37.30 E
Marsá al 'Alam 33 Fd 25.05N 34.54 E
Marsá al Burayqah 33 Cc 30.25N 19.35 E

Index Symbols

[1] Independent Nation
[2] State, Region
[3] District, County
[4] Municipality
[5] Colony, Dependency
Continent
Physical Region
Historical or Cultural Region
Mount, Mountain
Volcano
Hill
Mountains, Mountain Range
Hills, Escarpment
Plateau, Upland
Pass, Gap
Plain, Lowland
Delta
Salt Flat
Valley, Canyon
Crater, Cave
Karst Features
Depression
Polder
Desert, Dunes
Forest, Woods
Heath, Steppe
Oasis
Cape, Point
Coast, Beach
Cliff
Peninsula
Isthmus
Sandbank
Island
Atoll
Rock, Reef
Islands, Archipelago
Rocks, Reefs
Coral Reef
Well, Spring
Geyser
River, Stream
Waterfall Rapids
River Mouth, Estuary
Lake
Salt Lake
Intermittent Lake
Reservoir
Swamp, Pond
Canal
Glacier
Ice Shelf, Pack Ice
Ocean
Sea
Gulf, Bay
Strait, Fjord
Lagoon
Bank
Seamount
Tablemount
Ridge
Shelf
Basin
Escarpment, Sea Scarp
Fracture
Trench, Abyss
National Park, Reserve
Point of Interest
Recreation Site
Cave, Cavern
Historic Site
Ruins
Wall, Walls
Church, Abbey
Temple
Scientific Station
Airport
Port
Lighthouse
Mine
Tunnel
Dam, Bridge

Marsá al Uwayjah 33 Cc 30.55N 17.52 E
Marsa Ben Mehidi 13 Ji 35.05N 2.11W
Marsabit 31 Kh 2.20N 37.59 E
Marsala 14 Gm 37.48N 12.26 E
Marsá Sha'b 35 Fa 22.52N 35.47 E
Marsá Umm Ghayj 24 Fj 25.38N 34.30 E
Marsberg 10 Ee 51.27N 8.51 E
Marsciano 14 Gh 42.54N 12.20 E
Marsdiep 12 Gb 52.58N 4.45 E
Marseille=Marseilles (EN) 6 Gg 43.18N 5.24 E
Marseille-en-Beauvaisis 11 He 49.35N 1.57 E
Marseilles (EN)=Marseille 6 Gg 43.18N 5.24 E
Marshall [Ak.-U.S.] 40 Gd 61.52N 162.04W
Marshall [Ar.-U.S.] 45 Ji 35.55N 92.38W
Marshall [Il.-U.S.] 45 Mg 39.23N 87.42W
Marshall [Lbr.] 34 Cd 6.09N 10.23W
Marshall [Mn.-U.S.] 43 Hc 44.27N 95.47W
Marshall [Mo.-U.S.] 45 Jg 39.07N 93.12W
Marshall [Tx.-U.S.] 43 Ie 32.33N 94.23W
Marshall Islands 58 Hd 9.00N 168.00 E
Marshall Islands 57 Hd 9.00N 168.00 E
Marshall River 59 Hd 22.59S 136.59 E
Marshalltown 43 Ic 42.03N 92.54W
Marshfield 45 Kd 44.40N 90.10W
Marsh Harbour 47 Ic 26.33N 77.03W
Mārshinān, Kūh-e- 24 Of 32.53N 52.24 E
Marsh Island 45 Kl 29.35N 91.53W
Marsica 14 Hi 41.55N 13.35 E
Marsico Nuovo 14 Jj 40.25N 15.44 E
Marsjaty 17 Jf 60.05N 60.29 E
Marsland 45 Ee 42.29N 103.16W
Mars-la-Tour 12 He 49.06N 5.54 E
Marson 12 Gf 48.55N 4.32 E
Märsta 8 Ge 59.37N 17.51 E
Marstal 8 Dj 54.51N 10.31 E
Marstrand 8 Dg 57.53N 11.35 E
Marta 14 Fh 42.14N 11.42 E
Martaban 25 Je 16.32N 97.37 E
Martaban, Gulf of- (EN) 21 Lh 16.30N 97.00 E
Martap 34 Hd 6.54N 13.03 E
Martapura [Indon.] 26 Dg 4.19S 104.22 E
Martapura [Indon.] 26 Fg 3.25S 114.51 E
Martelange/Martelingen 12 He 49.50N 5.44 E
Martelingen/Martelange 12 He 49.50N 5.44 E
Martés, Sierra de- 13 Le 39.20N 0.57W
Martha's Vineyard 43 Mc 41.25N 70.40W
Martigny 14 Bd 46.06N 7.05 E
Martigues 11 Lk 43.24N 5.03 E
Martil 13 Gi 35.37N 5.17W
Martim Vaz, Ilhas- 52 Nh 20.30S 28.51W
Martin 13 Lc 41.18N 0.19W
Martin [Czech.] 10 Og 49.04N 18.55 E
Martin [S.D.-U.S.] 43 Gc 43.10N 101.44W
Martin [Tn.-U.S.] 44 Cg 36.21N 88.51W
Martina Franca 14 Lj 40.42N 17.20 E
Martinez de Hoz 55 Bl 35.19S 61.37W
Martínez de la Torre 48 Kg 20.04N 97.03W
Martin Garcia, Isla- 55 Cl 34.11S 58.15W
Martin Hills 66 Pg 82.04S 88.01W
Martinho Campos 55 Jd 19.20S 45.13W
Martinique 38 Mh 14.40N 61.00W
Martinique 39 Mh 14.40N 61.00W
Martinique, Canal de la-= Martinique Passage (EN) 47 Le 15.10N 61.20W
Martinique Passage 50 Fe 15.10N 61.20W
Martinique Passage (EN)= Martinique, Canal de la- 47 Le 15.10N 61.20W
Martin Lake 44 Ei 32.50N 85.55W
Martin Peninsula 66 Of 74.25S 114.10W
Martinsburg 44 If 39.28N 77.59W
Martins Ferry 44 Ge 40.07N 80.45W
Martinsville [In.-U.S.] 44 Df 39.26N 86.25W
Martinsville [Va.-U.S.] 43 Ld 36.43N 79.53W
Marton 62 Fd 40.05S 175.23 E
Martos 13 Ig 37.43N 3.58W
Martre, Lac la- 42 Fd 63.20N 118.00W
Martuk 19 Fe 50.47N 56.31 E
Martuni 16 Ni 40.06N 45.18 E
Maru 34 Gc 12.21N 6.24 E
Marud 25 Ee 18.19N 72.58 E
Marudi 26 Ff 4.11N 114.19 E
Marudu, Teluk- 26 Ge 6.45N 116.55 E
Marugame 29 Cd 34.18N 133.47 E
Maruko 29 Fc 36.19N 138.15 E
Mārūn 24 Mg 31.02N 49.36 E
Marungu, Monts- 30 Ji 7.42S 30.00 E
Maruoka 29 Ec 36.09N 136.16 E
Maruseppu 29a Ca 44.01N 143.19 E
Marutea Atoll [W.F.] 57 Ng 21.30S 135.34W
Marutea Atoll [W.F.] 57 Mf 17.00S 143.10W
Maruyama-Gawa 29 Dd 35.40N 134.50 E
Marvão 13 Ee 39.24N 7.23W
Marvast 24 Pg 30.30N 54.15 E
Marvast, Kavīr-e- 24 Pg 30.20N 54.25 E
Mårvatn 8 Cd 60.10N 8.15 E
Marv-Dasht 23 Hd 29.50N 52.40 E
Marvejols 11 Jj 44.33N 3.17 E
Marvine, Mount- 46 Jg 38.40N 111.39W
Marx 16 Od 51.42N 46.46 E
Mary 22 If 37.36N 61.50 E
Maryborough [Austl.] 58 Gg 25.32S 152.42 E
Maryborough [Austl.] 59 Ig 37.03S 143.45 E
Marydale 37 Ce 29.23S 22.05 E
Maryjskaja Oblast 19 Gh 37.15N 62.30 E
Maryland 43 Ld 39.00N 76.45W
Maryland 34 De 4.45N 8.00W
Maryport 9 Jg 54.43N 3.30W
Mary River 59 Gb 12.53S 131.38 E
Marysville [Ca.-U.S.] 46 Eg 39.09N 121.35W
Marysville [Ks.-U.S.] 45 Hg 39.51N 96.39W
Marysville [N.B.-Can.] 44 Nc 45.59N 66.35W
Marysville [Oh.-U.S.] 44 Fe 40.13N 83.22W
Marysville [Wa.-U.S.] 46 Db 48.03N 122.11W
Maryville [Mo.-U.S.] 43 Ic 40.21N 94.52W
Maryville [Tn.-U.S.] 44 Fh 35.46N 83.58W
Marzūq 31 If 25.55N 13.55 E
Marzūq, Ḥamādat- 33 Bd 26.00N 12.30 E
Marzuq, Ṣaḥrā'- 30 If 24.30N 13.00 E
Masachapa 49 Dh 11.47N 86.31W
Masāhim, Kūh-e- 24 Pg 30.21N 55.20 E
Masai Steppe 30 Ki 4.45S 37.00 E
Masaka 36 Fc 0.20S 31.44 E
Masākin 32 Jb 35.44N 10.35 E
Masalembo, Kepulauan- 26 Fh 5.30S 114.26 E
Masally 19 Eh 39.01N 48.40 E
Masalog, Puntan- 64b Ba 15.01N 145.41 E
Masan 27 Md 35.11N 128.24 E
Masasi 31 Kj 10.43S 38.48 E
Masaya 49 Dh 12.00N 86.10W
Masaya 47 Gf 11.58N 86.06W
Masbate 21 Oh 12.15N 123.30 E
Masbate 26 Hd 12.10N 123.35 E
Mascara 32 Hb 35.24N 0.08 E
Mascara 32 Hb 35.30N 0.15 E
Mascareignes, Iles-/ Mascarene Islands 30 Mk 21.00S 57.00 E
Mascarene Basin (EN) 3 Fk 15.00S 56.00 E
Mascarene Islands/ Mascareignes, Iles- 30 Mk 21.00S 57.00 E
Mascarene Plateau (EN) 3 Gk 10.00S 60.00 E
Mascota 48 Gg 20.32N 104.49W
Masela, Pulau- 26 Ih 8.09S 129.50 E
Maseru 31 Jk 29.28S 27.29 E
Maşfūţ 24 Qk 24.48N 56.06 E
Mashābih 24 Gj 25.37N 36.32 E
Mashan 28 Kb 45.12N 130.32 E
Mashava 37 Ed 20.02S 30.29 E
Mashhad 22 Hf 36.18N 59.36 E
Mashike 28 Pc 43.51N 141.31 E
Mashiki 29 Be 32.47N 130.50 E
Mashīz 24 Qh 29.56N 56.37 E
Mashkel 21 Ig 28.02N 63.25 E
Mashonaland North 37 Ec 17.00S 31.00 E
Mashonaland South 37 Ec 18.00S 31.00 E
Mashra' ar Raqq 35 Dd 8.25N 29.16 E
Mashū-Ko 29a Db 43.35N 144.30 E
Masiaca 48 Ed 26.45N 109.18W
Masīlah, Wādī al- 21 Hh 15.10N 51.08 E
Masi-Manimba 36 Cc 4.46S 17.55 E
Masindi 36 Fb 1.42N 31.43 E
Maşīrah, Jazīrat- 21 Hg 20.29N 58.33 E
Maşīrah, Khalīj- 21 Hg 20.15N 57.40 E
Masisi 36 Ec 1.24S 28.49 E
Masjed-Soleymān 23 Gc 31.58N 49.18 E
Mask, Lough-/Loch Measca 9 Dh 53.35N 9.20W
Maskanah 24 Hd 36.01N 38.05 E
Maskelynes, Iles- 63b Cc 16.32S 167.49 E
Maslovare 14 Lf 44.34N 17.33 E
Masoala, Cap- 30 Mj 15.59S 50.13 E
Masoala, Presqu'île de- 37 Ic 15.40S 50.12 E
Mason 45 Gk 30.45N 99.14W
Mason Bay 62 Bg 46.55S 167.45 E
Mason City 39 Je 43.09N 93.12W
Masovia (EN)= Mazowsze 5 Ie 52.40N 20.20 E
Masparro, Rio- 49 Mi 8.04N 69.26W
Masqaṭ=Muscat (EN) 22 Hg 23.29N 58.33 E
Massa 14 Ef 44.01N 10.09 E
Massachusetts 43 Mc 42.15N 71.50W
Massachusetts Bay 44 Ld 42.20N 70.50W
Massaciuccoli, Lago di- 14 Eg 43.50N 10.20 E
Massafra 14 Lj 40.35N 17.07 E
Massaguet 35 Bc 12.28N 15.26 E
Massakori 35 Bc 13.00N 15.44 E
Massa Marittima 14 Eg 43.03N 10.53 E
Massangano 36 Bd 9.37S 14.17 E
Massangena 37 Ed 21.32S 32.57 E
Massapê 54 Jd 3.31S 40.19W
Massawa (EN)=Mitsiwa 31 Kg 15.37N 39.39 E
Massena 43 Mc 44.56N 74.57W
Massénya 35 Bc 11.24N 16.10 E
Masset 42 Ef 54.02N 132.09W
Masseube 11 Gk 43.26N 0.35 E
Massey Sound 42 Ia 78.00N 94.00W
Massiac 11 Ji 45.15N 3.13 E
Massiaru 8 Kg 57.52N 24.27 E
Massillon 44 Ge 40.48N 81.32W
Massinga 37 Fd 23.20S 35.22 E
Masson Island 66 Ge 66.08S 96.34 E
Massuma 36 De 14.05S 22.00 E
Mastābah 33 Ge 20.49N 39.26 E
Maštaga 16 Pi 40.32N 49.59 E
Masterton 61 Eh 40.57S 175.39 E
Mastūrah 33 Ge 23.06N 38.50 E
Masuda 27 Ne 34.40N 131.51 E
Māsūleh 24 Md 37.10N 48.59 E
Masurai, Gunung- 26 Dg 2.30S 101.51 E
Masuria (EN) 5 Ie 53.50N 21.30 E
Masurian Lakes (EN) 5 Ie 53.45N 21.45 E
Maşyāf 24 Ge 35.03N 36.21 E
Maszewo 10 Lc 53.29N 15.02 E
Mataabé, Cap- 63b Cb 15.38S 166.46 E
Matabeleland North 37 Dc 19.00S 27.30 E
Matabeleland South 37 Dd 21.00S 29.30 E
Matachel 13 Ff 38.50N 6.17W
Matachewan 42 Jg 47.56N 80.39W
Matacu 55 Bc 17.21S 61.28W
Matadi 31 Ii 5.49S 13.27 E
Matador 45 Fi 34.01N 100.49W
Matagalpa 49 Eg 13.00N 85.30W
Matagalpa 39 Kh 12.53N 85.57W
Matagami 42 Jg 49.45N 77.35W
Matagami, Lac- 44 Ia 49.54N 77.32W
Mata Gassile 35 Ge 2.30N 42.16 E
Matagorda Bay 45 Hl 28.35N 96.20W
Matagorda Island 45 Hl 28.15N 96.30W
Matagorda Peninsula 45 Hl 28.32N 96.07W
Mataiea 65e Fc 17.46S 149.25W
Mataiva Atoll 57 Mf 14.53S 148.40W
Mataj 19 Hf 45.51N 78.43 E
Matak, Pulau- 26 Ef 3.18N 106.16 E
Matakana Island 62 Gb 37.35S 176.05 E
Matala 36 Ce 14.43S 15.02 E
Matalaa, Pointe- 64h Bc 13.20S 176.08W
Matale 25 Gg 7.28N 80.37 E
Mataliele 37 Df 30.24S 28.43 E
Matam 34 Cb 15.40N 13.15W
Matamey 34 Gc 13.26N 8.28 E
Matamoros [Mex.] 47 Dc 25.32N 103.15W
Matamoros [Mex.] 39 Jg 25.53N 97.30W
Matana, Danau- 26 Hg 2.28S 121.20 E
Ma'ṭan as Sarra 33 De 21.41N 21.52 E
Matancita 48 De 25.09N 111.59W
Matane 42 Kg 48.51N 67.32W
Matankari 34 Fc 13.46N 4.01 E
Matanza 55 Cl 34.33S 58.35W
Matanzas 39 Kg 23.03N 81.35W
Matanzas 49 Gb 22.40N 81.10W
Matão 55 He 21.35S 48.22W
Matapalo, Cabo- 49 Fi 8.23N 83.19W
Matapan, Cape- (EN)= Tainaron, Ákra- 5 Ih 36.23N 22.29 E
Matape, Rio- 48 Dc 28.17N 110.41W
Mata Point 64k Bb 19.07S 169.50W
Matara 35 Fc 14.35N 39.28 E
Matara 25 Gg 5.56N 80.33 E
Mataram 22 Nj 8.35S 116.07 E
Mataranka 59 Gb 14.56S 133.07 E
Mataró 13 Oc 41.32N 2.27 E
Matarraña/Matarranya 13 Mc 41.14N 0.22 E
Matarranya/Matarraña 13 Mc 41.14N 0.22 E
Mataso 63b Dc 17.15S 168.25 E
Matatula, Cape- 65c Cb 14.15S 170.34W
Mataura 62 Cg 46.34S 168.44 E
Mataura 62 Cg 46.12S 168.52 E
Mata-Utu 58 Jf 13.17S 176.08W
Mata-Utu, Baie de- 64h Bb 13.19S 176.07W
Matavai 61 Gb 13.28S 172.35W
Matavera 64p Cb 21.13S 159.44W
Mataverj 65d Ab 27.10S 109.27W
Matawai 62 Gc 38.21S 177.32 E
Matawin, Réservoir- 44 Kb 46.45N 73.50W
Matawin, Rivière- 44 Kb 46.55N 72.55W
Maṭāy 24 Dh 28.25N 30.46 E
Maṭbakhayn 33 Hf 17.29N 41.48 E
Matca 15 Kd 45.51N 27.32 E
Matemo, Ilha- 37 Gb 12.13S 40.36 E
Matera 14 Kj 40.40N 16.36 E
Matese 14 Ii 41.25N 14.20 E
Mátészalka 10 Si 47.57N 22.20 E
Matfors 7 De 62.21N 17.02 E
Matha 11 Fi 45.52N 0.19W
Mathematicians Seamounts (EN) 47 Be 15.30N 111.00W
Matheson 44 Ga 48.32N 80.28W
Mathis 45 Hl 28.06N 97.50W
Mathrákion 15 Cj 39.46N 19.31 E
Mathura 25 Fc 27.30N 77.41 E
Mati 15 Ch 41.39N 19.34 E
Mati 26 Ie 6.57N 126.13 E
Matias Cardoso 55 Kb 14.52S 43.56W
Matias Romero 47 Ee 16.53N 95.02W
Maticora, Rio- 49 Lh 11.01N 71.09W
Matina 49 Fh 10.05N 83.17W
Matinha 54 Id 3.06S 45.02W
Māṭir 32 Ib 37.03N 9.40 E
Matiyure, Rio- 50 Ci 7.36N 67.39W
Matkaselkja 8 Nc 61.57N 30.33 E
Mātmāṭah 32 Ic 33.33N 9.58 E
Matnog 26 Hd 12.35N 124.05 E
Mato, Cerro- 50 Di 7.15N 65.14W
Mato, Rio- 50 Di 7.09N 65.07W
Matočkin Šar, Proliv- 19 Fa 73.30N 54.55 E
Mato Grosso 54 Gf 14.00S 56.00W
Mato Grosso [Braz.] 55 Dd 18.18S 57.20W
Mato Grosso [Braz.] 53 Kg 15.00S 59.57W
Mato Grosso, Planalto do- = Mato Grosso, Plateau of- (EN) 52 Kg 15.30S 56.00W
Mato Grosso, Plateau of- (EN) = Mato Grosso, Planalto do- 52 Kg 15.30S 56.00W
Mato Grosso do Sul 54 Hg 20.00S 55.00W
Matos Costa 55 Gh 26.27S 51.09W
Matosinhos 13 Dc 41.11N 8.42W
Matou 28 Cj 29.50N 115.32 E
Matov→Qiuxian 28 Cf 36.47N 114.30 E
Mátra 5 Hf 47.53N 19.57 E
Maţrah 23 Ie 23.29N 58.31 E
Matrei in Osttirol 14 Gc 47.00N 12.32 E
Maţrūḩ 31 Je 31.21N 27.14 E
Matsiatra 37 Hd 21.25S 45.33 E
Matsudo 28 Og 35.48N 139.55 E
Matsue 27 Nd 35.28N 133.04 E
Matsukawa [Jap.] 29 Gc 37.40N 140.28 E
Matsukawa [Jap.] 29 Ed 35.36N 137.53 E
Matsu Liehtao 27 Kf 26.05N 119.56 E
Matsumae 29a Bc 41.26N 140.07 E
Matsumae-Hantō 29a Bc 41.40N 140.15 E
Matsumoto 27 Od 36.14N 137.58 E
Matsuo 29 Gb 39.58N 141.02 E
Matsu-Ōminato 29a Bc 41.16N 141.09 E
Matsusaka 28 Ng 34.34N 136.32 E
Matsushima 29 Gb 38.22N 141.04 E
Matsutō 29 Ec 36.31N 136.33 E
Matsuura 29 Ae 33.22N 129.42 E
Matsuyama 22 Pf 33.50N 132.45 E
Matsuzaki 29 Fd 34.44N 138.45 E
Mattagami Lake 44 Gb 47.57N 81.35W
Mattagami River 42 Jf 50.43N 81.30W
Mattawa 42 Jg 46.19N 78.42W
Matterhorn [Eur.] 14 Be 45.58N 7.39 E
Matterhorn [Nv.-U.S.] 46 Hf 41.49N 115.23W
Matthew, Ile- 57 Ig 22.20S 171.20 E
Matthews Ridge 54 Fb 7.30N 60.10W
Matthew Town 47 Jd 20.57N 73.40W
Maṭṭī, Sabkhat- 35 Ia 23.30N 52.00 E
Mattighofen 14 Hb 48.06N 13.09 E
Mattoon 45 Lg 39.29N 88.22W
Matua, Ostrov- 20 Kg 48.00N 153.10 E
Matucana 54 Cf 11.51S 76.24W
Matuku Island 61 Ec 19.10S 179.46 E
Matundu 36 Db 4.21N 23.40 E
Matundu 36 Gd 8.50S 39.30 E
Maturín 53 Je 9.45N 63.11W
Matvejev Kurgan 16 Kf 47.34N 38.55 E
Maúa 37 Fb 13.52S 37.09 E
Maubeuge 11 Jd 50.17N 3.58 E
Ma-ubin 25 Je 16.44N 95.39 E
Maudheimvidda 66 Bf 74.00S 8.00W
Maud Seamount (EN) 66 Ce 65.00S 2.35 E
Maués 54 Gd 3.24S 57.42W
Maués, Rio- 54 Gd 3.22S 57.44W
Mau Escarpment 36 Gc 0.40S 36.02 E
Maug Islands 57 Fb 20.01N 145.13 E
Maui Island 57 Lb 20.45N 156.20W
Mauke Island 57 Lg 20.09S 157.23W
Mau Kyun 25 Jf 12.45N 98.20 E
Mauldre 12 Df 48.59N 1.49 E
Maule 56 Fe 35.45S 72.15W
Mauléon 11 Fh 46.55N 0.45W
Mauléon-Licharre 11 Fk 43.14N 0.53W
Maullín 56 Ff 41.38S 73.37W
Maumee 44 Fe 41.34N 83.39W
Maumere 26 Hh 8.37S 122.14 E
Maun 31 Jj 19.58S 23.26 E
Maun 14 If 44.26N 14.55 E
Mauna Kea 57 Lc 19.50N 155.28W
Maunaloa 65a Db 21.08N 157.13W
Mauna Loa 65a Fd 19.28N 155.36W
Maunath 25 Gc 25.40N 82.38 E
Maunawili 65a Db 21.21N 157.47W
Maunga Roa 64p Bb 21.13S 159.48W
Maungdaw 25 Id 20.49N 92.22 E
Maunoir, Lac- 42 Fc 67.30N 125.00W
Maupihaa Atoll (Mopelia, Atoll-) 57 Lf 16.50S 153.55W
Maupin 46 Ed 45.11N 121.05W
Maupiti, Ile- 57 Lf 16.27S 152.15W
Maurepas, Lake- 45 Kk 30.15N 90.30W
Maures 11 Mk 43.16N 6.23 E
Mauriac 11 Ii 45.13N 2.20 E
Maurice, Lake- 59 Ge 29.30S 131.00 E
Maurienne 11 Mi 45.13N 6.30 E
Mauritania (EN)= Mūrītāniyā 31 Fg 20.00N 12.00W
Mauriti 54 Ke 7.23S 38.46W
Mauritius 30 Mk 20.17S 57.33 E
Mauritius 31 Mj 18.00S 57.40 E
Mauron 11 Df 48.05N 2.18W
Maurs 11 Ij 44.43N 2.12 E
Mauston 45 Ke 43.48N 90.05W
Mauthausen 14 Ib 48.14N 14.31 E
Mauzé-sur-le-Mignon 11 Fh 46.12N 0.40W
Mavinga 36 Df 15.47S 20.24 E
Mavita 37 Ec 19.32S 33.09 E
Mavrovoúni [Grc.] 15 Fj 39.37N 22.47 E
Mavrovoúni [Grc.] 15 Gh 41.07N 23.08 E
Mawchi 25 Je 18.49N 97.09 E
Mawei 27 Kf 26.02N 119.30 E
Mawlaik 25 Id 23.38N 94.25 E
Mawlamyine 22 Le 16.30N 97.38 E
Mawqaq 24 Ii 27.25N 41.08 E
Mawr, Wādī- 23 Ff 15.41N 42.42 E
Mawson 66 Fe 67.36S 62.53 E
Mawson Coast 66 Fe 67.40S 63.30 E
Mawson Escarpment 66 Ff 73.05S 68.10 E
Maxcanú 47 Fd 20.35N 90.01W
Maxixe 37 Fd 23.51S 35.21 E
Maxwell Bay 42 Ib 74.32N 89.00W
May, Isle of- 9 Ke 56.10N 2.30W
Maya, Pulau- 26 Eg 1.10S 109.35 E
Mayaguana Island 47 Jd 22.23N 72.57W
Mayaguana Passage 49 Kb 22.32N 73.15W
Mayagüez 47 Ke 18.12N 67.09W
Mayahi 34 Gc 13.58N 7.40 E
Mayama 36 Bc 3.51S 14.54 E
Mayāmey 24 Pd 36.24N 55.42 E
Maya Mountains 47 Ge 16.40N 88.50W
Mayapan 47 Gd 20.38N 89.27W
Mayari 49 Jc 20.40N 75.41W
Maybell 45 Bf 40.31N 108.05W
Maychew 35 Fc 12.46N 39.34 E
Mayḍ 35 Hc 10.57N 47.06 E
Maydān 24 Ke 34.55N 45.37 E
Maydena 59 Jh 42.55S 146.30 E
Maydī 23 Ff 16.18N 42.48 E
Mayen 10 Df 50.20N 7.13 E
Mayenne 11 Ff 48.18N 0.37W
Mayenne 11 Fg 47.30N 0.32W
Mayenne 11 Ff 48.05N 0.40W
Mayfa'ah 35 Hc 14.16N 47.35 E
Mayfield 44 Cg 36.44N 88.38W
May Glacier 66 Ie 67.00S 130.00 E
Mayi He 28 Jb 45.52N 128.46 E
Maymyo 25 Jd 22.02N 96.28 E
Maynas 54 Dd 3.00S 75.00W
Mayo 39 Fc 63.35N 135.54W
Mayo/Muigheo 9 Dh 53.50N 9.30W
Mayo, Mountains of- 9 Dg 54.05N 9.30W
Mayo, Rio- 48 Ed 26.45N 109.47W
Mayo Darlé 34 Hd 6.30N 11.55 E
Mayo-Kébbi 35 Ad 9.18N 13.33 E
Mayo-Kébbi 35 Bd 10.00N 15.30 E
Mayoko 36 Bc 2.18S 12.49 E
Mayon, Mount- 21 Oh 13.15N 123.41 E
Mayor, Puig-/Major, Puig- 13 Oe 39.48N 2.48 E
Mayor Island 62 Gb 37.15S 176.15 E
Mayor Pablo Lagerenza 56 Ha 19.58S 60.45W
Mayotte 31 Lj 12.50S 45.10 E
Mayotte/Mahoré 30 Lj 12.50S 45.10 E
May Pen 47 Ie 17.58N 77.14W
Mayraira Point 26 Hc 18.39N 120.51 E
Mayran, Laguna de- 48 He 25.45N 102.45W
Mayreau Island 51n Bb 12.39N 61.23W
May-sur-Orne 12 Be 49.06N 0.22W
Maysville 44 Ff 38.39N 83.46W
Mayumba [Gabon] 31 Ii 3.25S 10.39 E
Mayumba [Zaire] 36 Ed 7.16S 27.03 E
Mayum La 27 De 30.35N 82.27 E
Mayville 44 Hd 42.15N 79.32W
Mayyit, Al Baḥr al-=Dead Sea (EN) 21 Ff 31.30N 35.30 E
Mazabuka 36 Ef 15.51S 27.46 E
Mazagão 54 Hd 0.07S 51.17W
Mazamet 11 Ik 43.30N 2.24 E
Māzandarān 23 Hb 36.00N 54.00 E
Māzandarān, Daryā-ye-= Caspian Sea (EN) 5 Lg 42.00N 50.30 E
Mazar 27 Cd 36.27N 77.03 E
Mazara del Vallo 14 Gm 37.39N 12.35 E
Mazār-e Sharīf 22 If 36.42N 67.06 E
Mazarrón, Golfo de- 13 Kg 37.30N 1.18W
Mazartag 27 Dd 38.29N 80.50 E
Mazaruni River 54 Gb 6.25N 58.38W
Mazatenango 47 Ff 14.32N 91.30W
Mazatlán 39 Ig 23.13N 106.25W
Mažeikiai/Mažejkjaj 7 Fh 56.20N 22.22 E
Mažejkjaj/Mažeikiai 7 Fh 56.20N 22.22 E
Mazḥafah, Jabal- 24 Fh 28.48N 34.57 E
Mazḥūr, 'Irq al- 24 Ji 27.25N 43.55 E
Mazinga 51c Ab 17.29N 62.58W
Mazirbe 8 Jg 57.40N 22.10 E
Mazoe 37 Ec 17.30S 30.58 E
Mazoe 30 Kj 16.32S 33.25 E
Mazomeno 36 Ec 4.55S 27.13 E
Mazong Shan 27 Gc 41.33N 97.10 E
Mazowsze 10 Qd 52.40N 20.20 E
Mazowsze=Masovia (EN) 5 Ie 52.40N 20.20 E
Mazsalaca 8 Kg 57.45N 24.59 E
Mazunga 37 Dd 21.44S 29.52 E
Mazurskie, Pojezierze- 10 Qc 53.40N 21.00 E
Mazzarino 14 Im 37.18N 14.13 E
Mba 63d Ab 17.33S 177.42 E
Mbabane 31 Kk 26.18S 31.07 E
Mbabo, Tchabal- 34 Hd 7.16N 12.09 E
Mbacké 34 Bc 14.48N 15.55W
Mbaéré 35 Be 3.47N 17.31 E
Mbaïki 31 Ih 3.53N 18.00 E
Mbakaou 34 Hd 6.19N 12.49 E
Mbakaou, Barrage de- 34 Hd 6.25N 13.00 E
Mbala 31 Ki 8.50S 31.22 E
Mbalam 34 He 2.13N 13.49 E
Mbale 31 Kh 1.05N 34.10 E
Mbali 35 Be 4.27N 18.20 E
Mbalmayo 34 He 3.31N 11.30 E
Mbam 30 Ih 4.24N 11.17 E
Mbamba Bay 36 Fe 11.17S 34.46 E
Mbandaka 31 Ih 0.04N 18.16 E
Mbanga 34 Ge 4.30N 9.34 E
Mbanika 63a Ec 9.05S 159.12 E
M'banza Congo 36 Bd 6.16S 14.15 E
Mbanza-Ngungu 31 Ii 5.35S 14.47 E
Mbarangandu 36 Gd 8.57S 37.24 E
Mbarara 36 Fc 0.36S 30.38 E
Mbari 35 Ce 4.34N 22.43 E
Mbatiki 63d Bb 17.46S 179.08 E
Mbava 63a Cb 7.49S 156.37 E
Mbé 34 Hd 7.51N 13.36 E
Mbengga 63d Bc 18.23S 178.08 E
Mbengwi 34 Hd 6.01N 10.00 E
Mbéré 35 Bd 9.07N 16.26 E
Mbeya 31 Ki 8.54S 33.27 E
Mbeya 36 Fd 8.00S 33.30 E
Mbi 35 Be 4.28N 18.07 E
Mbigou 36 Bc 1.53S 11.56 E
Mbinda 31 Ii 2.07S 12.52 E
Mbinga 36 Ge 10.56S 35.01 E
Mbingué 34 Dc 10.00N 5.54W
Mbini 34 Ge 1.34N 9.37 E
Mbini 34 He 1.30N 10.00 E
Mbini 30 Ih 1.30N 10.30 E
Mboki 35 Dd 5.19N 25.58 E
Mbokonimbeti 63a Ec 8.57S 160.05 E
Mbomo 36 Bb 0.24N 14.44 E
Mbomou=Bomu (EN) 35 Cd 5.30N 23.30 E
Mbomou=Bomu (EN) 30 Jh 4.08N 22.26 E
Mborokua 63a Dc 9.02S 158.44 E
Mbour 34 Bc 14.24N 16.58W
Mbout 32 Ef 16.01N 12.35W
Mbozi 36 Fd 9.02S 32.56 E
Mbrés 35 Bd 6.40N 19.48 E
M'Bridge 36 Bd 7.14S 12.52 E
Mbua 63d Bb 16.48S 178.37 E
Mbuji-Mayi 31 Ji 6.09S 23.33 E
Mbulo 63a Dc 8.46S 158.21 E
Mbulu 36 Gc 3.51S 35.32 E
Mburucuyá 55 Ci 28.03S 58.14W
Mbutha 63d Bb 16.39S 179.51 E
Mbuyuni 36 Gd 7.23S 36.32 E
Mbwemburu 36 Gd 9.29S 39.39 E
Mcalester 43 He 34.56N 95.46W
Mcensk 19 De 53.17N 36.32 E
M'Chedallah 13 Qh 36.22N 4.16 E
Mcherrah 32 Gd 27.00N 4.30W
Mchinga 36 Gd 9.44S 39.42 E
Mchinji 36 Fe 13.48S 32.54 E
Mdandu 36 Fd 9.09S 34.42 E
M'Daourouch 14 Bn 36.05N 7.49 E
Mdennah 32 Gd 25.00N 4.50W
Mdiq 13 Gi 35.41N 5.19W
Mead 44 Fa 49.29N 83.50W
Mead, Lake- 43 Ed 36.05N 114.25W
Meade 40 Hb 70.50N 156.25W
Meade 45 Fh 37.17N 100.20W
Meade Peak 46 Je 42.30N 111.15W
Meadow Lake 42 Gf 54.07N 108.20W
Meadville 44 Ge 41.38N 80.10W
Me-akan-Dake 29a Cb 43.23N 143.59 E
Mealhada 13 Dd 40.22N 8.27W

Index Symbols

1 Independent Nation
2 State, Region
3 District, County
4 Municipality
5 Colony, Dependency
Continent
Physical Region

Historical or Cultural Region
Mount, Mountain
Volcano
Hill
Mountains, Mountain Range
Hills, Escarpment
Plateau, Upland

Pass, Gap
Plain, Lowland
Delta
Salt Flat
Valley, Canyon
Crater, Cave
Karst Features

Depression
Polder
Desert, Dunes
Forest, Woods
Heath, Steppe
Oasis
Cape, Point

Coast, Beach
Cliff
Peninsula
Isthmus
Sandbank
Island
Atoll

Rock, Reef
Islands, Archipelago
Rocks, Reefs
Coral Reef
Well, Spring
Geyser
River, Stream

Waterfall Rapids
River Mouth, Estuary
Lake
Salt Lake
Intermittent Lake
Reservoir
Swamp, Pond

Canal
Glacier
Ice Shelf, Pack Ice
Ocean
Sea
Gulf, Bay
Strait, Fjord

Lagoon
Bank
Seamount
Tablemount
Ridge
Shelf
Basin

Escarpment, Sea Scarp
Fracture
Trench, Abyss
National Park, Reserve
Point of Interest
Recreation Site
Cave, Cavern

Historic Site
Ruins
Wall, Walls
Church, Abbey
Temple
Scientific Station
Airport

Port
Lighthouse
Mine
Tunnel
Dam, Bridge

Mealy Mountains 42 Lf 53.20N 59.30W
Meama 65b Ba 19.45S 174.34W
Méan, Havelange- 12 Hd 50.22N 5.20 E
Meander Reef 26 Ge 8.09N 119.14 E
Meander River 42 Fe 59.02N 117.42W
Meanguera, Isla- 49 Dg 13.12N 87.43W
Mearim, Rio- 52 Lf 3.04S 44.35W
Meath/An Mhí [2] 9 Gh 53.35N 6.40W
Meaux 11 If 48.57N 2.52 E
Mecca (EN)=Makkah 22 Fe 21.27N 39.49 E
Mechara 35 Gd 8.34N 40.28 E
Mechelen/Maasmechelen 12 Hd 50.57N 5.40 E
Mechelen/Malines 11 Kc 51.02N 4.29 E
Mecheraa-Asfa 13 Ni 35.24N 1.03 E
Mecheria 32 Gc 33.33N 0.17W
Mechernich 12 Id 50.36N 6.39 E
Mechongué 55 Cn 38.09S 58.13W
Mecidiye 15 Ji 40.38N 26.32 E
Mecitözü 24 Fb 40.31N 35.19 E
Mecklemburgischer Höhenrücken 10 Ic 53.40N 12.10 E
Mecklenburg 10 Hc 53.30N 12.00 E
Mecklenburger Bucht 10 Hb 54.20N 11.40 E
Mecklenburger Schweiz 10 Ic 53.45N 12.35 E
Mecoacán, Laguna- 48 Mh 18.20N 93.10W
Meconta 37 Fb 14.59S 39.50 E
Mecsek 10 Oj 46.10N 18.18 E
Mecubúri 37 Gb 14.10S 40.31 E
Mecúfi 37 Gb 13.17S 40.33 E
Mecula 37 Fb 12.05S 37.39 E
Médala 32 Ff 15.30N 5.37W
Medan 22 Li 3.35N 98.40 E
Médanos [Arg.] 56 He 38.50S 62.41W
Médanos [Arg.] 55 Ck 33.24S 59.05W
Medanosa, Punta- 56 Gg 48.06S 65.55W
Mede 14 Ce 45.06N 8.44 E
Médéa 32 Hb 36.16N 2.45 E
Médéa [3] 32 Hb 36.20N 3.25 E
Medebach 12 Kc 51.12N 8.43 E
Medellín 26 Hd 11.08N 123.58 E
Medellín 53 Ie 6.15N 75.35W
Medelpad 8 Gb 62.35N 16.15 E
Medemblik 12 Hb 52.46N 5.06 E
Medenica 10 Tg 49.21N 23.45 E
Mederdra 32 Df 16.54N 15.40W
Medetziz 24 Fd 37.25N 34.40 E
Medford [Or.-U.S.] 39 Ge 42.19N 122.52W
Medford [Wi.-U.S.] 45 Kd 45.09N 90.20W
Medgidia 15 Le 44.15N 28.17 E
Medi 35 Ed 5.06N 30.44 E
Media Luna, Arrecife de la- 49 Ff 15.13N 82.36W
Medianeira 55 Eg 25.17S 54.05W
Mediaş 15 Hc 46.10N 24.21 E
Medical Lake 46 Gc 47.34N 117.41W
Medicine Bow 46 Lf 41.54N 106.12W
Medicine Bow Mountains 46 Lf 41.10N 106.25W
Medicine Butte 46 Jf 41.29N 110.48W
Medicine Hat 39 Hd 50.03N 110.40W
Medicine Lake 46 Mb 48.28N 104.24W
Medicine Lodge 45 Gh 37.17N 98.35W
Medimurje 14 Kd 46.25N 16.30 E
Medina (EN)=Al Madīnah [Sau.Ar.] 22 Fg 24.28N 39.36 E
Medina Az-Zahra 13 Hg 37.52N 4.50W
Medinaceli 13 Jc 41.10N 2.26W
Medina del Campo 13 Hc 41.18N 4.55W
Medina de Rioseco 13 Gc 41.53N 5.02W
Medina-Sidonia 13 Gh 36.27N 5.55W
Medininkai/Medininkaj 8 Kj 54.32N 25.46 E
Medinīpur 25 Hd 22.26N 87.20 E
Medio, Arroyo del- 55 Bk 33.16S 60.15W
Mediterranean Sea (EN)= Akdeniz 5 Hh 35.00N 20.00 E
Mediterranean Sea (EN)= Khatikhon, Yam- 5 Hh 35.00N 20.00 E
Mediterranean Sea (EN)= Méditerranée, Mer- 5 Hh 35.00N 20.00 E
Mediterranean Sea (EN)= Mediterraneo, Mar- 5 Hh 35.00N 20.00 E
Mediterranean Sea (EN)= Mediterráneo, Mar- 5 Hh 35.00N 20.00 E
Mediterranean Sea (EN)= Mesoyéios Thálassa 5 Hh 35.00N 20.00 E
Mediterranean Sea (EN)= Mutawassiţ, Al Baḩr al- 5 Hh 35.00N 20.00 E
Méditerranée, Mer-= Mediterranean Sea (EN) 5 Hh 35.00N 20.00 E
Mediterráneo, Mar-= Mediterranean Sea (EN) 5 Hh 35.00N 20.00 E
Mediterraneo, Mar-= Mediterranean Sea (EN) 5 Hh 35.00N 20.00 E
Medje 36 Eb 2.25N 27.18 E
Medjerda, Monts de la- 32 Ib 36.35N 8.15 E
Mednogorsk 19 Fe 51.26N 57.40 E
Medny, Ostrov- 20 Lf 54.40N 167.50 E
Médoc 11 Fi 45.00N 1.00W
Mêdog 27 Gf 29.18N 95.27 E
Médouneu 36 Bb 1.01N 10.48 E
Medveđa 15 Eg 42.51N 21.36 E
Medvedica [R.S.F.S.R.] 5 Kf 49.35N 42.41 E
Medvedica [R.S.F.S.R.] 7 Ih 57.05N 37.31 E
Medvednica 14 Je 45.55N 15.58 E
Medvedok 7 Mh 57.24N 50.06 E
Medvenka 16 Jd 51.27N 36.08 E
Medveži, Ostrova-=Bear Islands (EN) 21 Sb 70.52N 161.26 E
Medvežjegorsk 19 Dc 62.56N 34.29 E
Medway 12 Cc 51.23N 0.31 E
Medzilaborce 10 Rg 49.16N 21.55 E
Meekatharra 58 Cg 26.36S 118.29 E
Meeker 45 Cf 40.02N 107.55W
Meerane 10 If 50.51N 12.28 E
Meerbusch 12 Ic 51.16N 6.40 E
Meerut 25 Fc 28.59N 77.42 E
Meeteetse 46 Kd 44.09N 108.52W
Mefarlane, Lake- 59 Hf 32.00S 136.40 E
Mega [Eth.] 31 Kh 4.03N 38.20 E
Mega [Indon.] 26 Jg 0.41S 131.53 E
Mega, Pulau- 26 Dg 4.00S 101.02 E
Megalo 35 Gd 6.52N 40.47 E
Megálon Khorion 15 Km 36.27N 27.21 E
Megalópolis 15 Fl 37.24N 22.08 E
Megálo Sofráno 15 Jm 36.04N 26.25 E
Meganísion 15 Dk 38.38N 20.43 E
Meganom, Mys- 16 Ig 44.48N 35.05 E
Mégara 15 Gk 38.00N 23.21 E
Megève 11 Mi 45.52N 6.37 E
Meghalaya [3] 25 Ic 26.00N 91.00 E
Megid 33 Dd 28.35N 22.10 E
Megion 19 Hc 61.00N 76.15 E
Megiscane, Lac- 44 Ia 48.30N 76.04W
Megri 16 Oj 38.55N 46.15 E
Mehadia 15 Fe 44.54N 22.22 E
Mehaigne 12 Hd 50.32N 5.13 E
Meharry, Mount- 59 Dd 23.00S 118.35 E
Mehdia 13 Ni 35.25N 1.45 E
Mehdīshahr 24 Oe 35.44N 53.22 E
Mehedinţi [2] 15 Fe 44.30N 23.00 E
Mehetia, Ile- 61 Lc 17.52S 148.03W
Mehrabān 24 Lc 38.05N 47.08 E
Mehrān 24 Pi 26.52N 55.24 E
Mehrān 24 Lf 33.07N 46.10 E
Mehrenga 7 Je 63.17N 41.20 E
Mehrīz 24 Pg 31.35N 54.28 E
Mehtar Lām 23 Lc 34.39N 70.10 E
Mehun-sur-Yèvre 11 Ig 47.09N 2.13 E
Meia Meia 36 Gd 5.49S 35.48 E
Meia Ponte, Rio- 54 Ig 18.32S 49.36W
Meiganga 34 Hd 6.31N 14.18 E
Meighen 42 Ha 79.55N 99.00W
Meihekou→Hailong 27 Mc 42.32N 125.37 E
Meiktila 25 Jd 20.52N 95.52 E
Meilü→Wuchuan 27 Jg 21.28N 110.44 E
Meinerzhagen 12 Jc 51.07N 7.39 E
Meiningen 10 Gf 50.33N 10.25 E
Meio, Rio do- 55 Ja 13.20S 44.34W
Meisenheim 12 Je 49.43N 7.40 E
Meishan [China] 27 He 30.05N 103.48 E
Meishan [China] 28 Ei 31.06N 119.43 E
Meishan → Jinzhai 28 Ci 31.40N 115.52 E
Meißen 10 Je 51.09N 13.29 E
Meißner 12 Le 51.12N 9.50 E
Meitan (Yiquan) 27 If 27.48N 107.32 E
Meixian 27 Kg 24.21N 116.07 E
Meiyukou 28 Bd 40.01N 113.08 E
Méjean, Causse- 11 Jj 44.16N 3.22 E
Mejillones 56 Fb 23.06S 70.27W
Mékambo 36 Bb 1.01N 13.56 E
Mekdela 35 Fc 11.28N 39.20 E
Mekele=Meqele (EN) 31 Kg 13.30N 39.28 E
Mékhé 34 Bb 15.07N 16.38W
Mekherrhane, Sebkha- 30 Hf 26.22N 1.20 E
Meknès [3] 32 Fc 33.00N 5.30W
Meknès 31 Ge 33.54N 5.32W
Mekong (EN)=Lancang Jiang 21 Mh 10.15N 105.55 E
Mekong (EN)=Mae Nam Khong 21 Mh 10.15N 105.55 E
Mekong (EN)=Mékôngk 21 Mh 10.15N 105.55 E
Mekong (EN)=Mènam Khong 21 Mh 10.15N 105.55 E
Mekong Delta (EN) 21 Mi 10.20N 106.40 E
Mekongga, Gunung- 26 Hg 3.35S 121.15 E
Mékôngk=Mekong (EN) 21 Mh 10.15N 105.55 E
Mekoryuk 40 Fd 60.23N 166.12W
Mékrou 34 Fc 12.24N 2.49 E
Mel, Ilha do- 55 Hg 25.31S 48.20W
Melaab 13 Ni 35.43N 1.20 E
Mēladēn 35 Hc 10.25N 49.52 E
Melaka 22 Mi 2.12N 102.15 E
Melaka, Selat-=Malacca, Strait of- (EN) 21 Mi 2.30N 101.20 E
Melamo, Cabo- 30 Lj 14.24S 40.49 E
Melanesia 57 Hf 13.00S 164.00 E
Melanesian Basin (EN) 3 Jj 0.05S 160.35 E
Melawi 26 Ff 0.05N 111.29 E
Melbourne [Ar.-U.S.] 45 Kh 36.04N 91.54W
Melbourne [Austl.] 58 Fh 37.49S 144.58 E
Melbourne [Eng.-U.K.] 12 Ab 52.49N 1.26W
Melbourne [Fl.-U.S.] 43 Kf 28.05N 80.37W
Melbourne-Dandenong 59 Jg 37.59S 145.12 E
Melchor Múzquiz 47 Dc 27.53N 101.31W
Melchor Ocampo 48 Hi 17.59N 102.11W
Meldorf 10 Fb 54.05N 9.05 E
Mele, Capo- 14 Cg 43.57N 8.10 E
Melekeiok 64a Bc 7.29N 134.38 E
Melela 37 Fc 17.04S 38.36 E
Melenci 15 Dd 45.31N 20.19 E
Melenki 17 Ed 55.23N 41.42 E
Meleto Dağı 24 Ic 38.35N 41.32 E
Meleuz 19 Fe 52.58N 55.59 E
Mélèzes, Rivière aux- 42 Ke 57.00N 69.00W
Melfa 14 Hi 41.30N 13.35 E
Melfi [Chad] 35 Bc 11.04N 17.56 E
Melfi [It.] 14 Jj 41.00N 15.39 E
Melfort 42 Hf 52.52N 104.36W
Melgaço 54 Hd 1.47S 50.44W
Melibocus 10 Eg 49.42N 8.40 E
Melilla [5] 31 Ge 35.19N 2.58W
Melincué, Laguna- 55 Bk 33.42S 61.28W
Melipilla 56 Fd 33.42S 71.13W
Melita 45 Fb 49.16N 101.00W
Meliti 15 Ei 40.50N 21.35 E
Melito di Porto Salvo 14 Jm 37.55N 15.47 E
Melito di Porto Salvo, Punta di- 14 Jm 37.57N 15.45 E
Melitopol 6 Jf 46.50N 35.22 E
Melk 14 Jb 48.13N 15.19 E
Mella 14 Ee 45.13N 10.13 E
Mellakou 13 Ni 35.15N 1.14 E
Mellanfryken 8 Ee 59.40N 13.15 E
Melle [Fr.] 11 Fh 46.13N 0.08W
Melle [Ger.] 12 Kb 52.12N 8.21 E
Mellen 45 Kc 46.20N 90.40W
Mellerud 7 Cg 58.42N 12.28 E
Mellish Reef 59 Lc 17.25S 155.50 E
Mellish Seamount (EN) 57 Ia 34.00N 178.15 E
Mellit 35 Dc 14.08N 25.33 E
Mělník 10 Kf 50.21N 14.30 E
Melnik 15 Gh 41.31N 23.24 E
Melo 53 Ki 32.22S 54.11W
Melo, Rio- 55 De 21.25S 57.55W
Melrhir, Chott- 30 He 34.20N 6.20 E
Melrose 46 Id 45.38N 112.40W
Melsungen 10 Fe 51.08N 9.33 E
Meltaus 7 Fc 66.54N 25.22 E
Melton Constable 12 Db 52.51N 1.02 E
Melton Mowbray 9 Mi 52.46N 0.53W
Meluco 37 Fb 12.33S 39.37 E
Meluli 37 Fc 16.28S 39.44 E
Melun 11 If 48.32N 2.40 E
Melville 38 Ib 75.15N 110.00W
Melville 46 Na 50.55N 102.48W
Melville, Cape- 59 Ib 14.10S 144.30 E
Melville, Lake- 42 Lf 53.42N 59.30W
Melville Bay 59 Hb 12.05S 136.45 E
Melville Bay (EN)=Melville Bugt 67 Od 75.35N 62.30W
Melville Bugt=Melville Bay (EN) 67 Od 75.35N 62.30W
Melville Hills 42 Fc 69.20N 123.00W
Melville Island 57 Ef 11.40S 131.00 E
Melville Peninsula 38 Kc 68.00N 84.00W
Melville Sound 42 Gc 68.05N 107.30W
Melvin, Lough- 9 Eg 54.25N 8.10W
Mélykút 10 Pj 46.13N 19.23 E
Memaliaj 15 Ci 40.20N 19.58 E
Memambetsu 29a Db 43.55N 144.11 E
Memba, Baia de- 37 Gb 14.11S 40.35 E
Memberamo 26 Kg 1.28S 137.52 E
Memboro 26 Gh 9.22S 119.32 E
Mēmele 8 Kh 56.24N 24.10 E
Memmert 10 Cc 53.39N 6.53 E
Memmingen 10 Gi 47.59N 10.10 E
Mempawah 26 Ef 0.22N 108.58 E
Memphis 33 Fd 29.52N 31.15 E
Memphis [Mo.-U.S.] 45 Jf 40.28N 92.10W
Memphis [Tn.-U.S.] 39 Jf 35.08N 90.03W
Memphis [Tx.-U.S.] 45 Fi 34.44N 100.32W
Memrut Dağı 24 Jc 38.40N 42.12 E
Memuro 28 Qc 42.55N 143.03 E
Memuro-Dake 29a Cb 42.52N 142.45 E
Mena 35 Gd 5.30N 41.06 E
Mena [Ar.-U.S.] 45 Ii 34.35N 94.15W
Mena [Ukr.-U.S.S.R.] 19 De 51.33N 32.14 E
Menabe 30 Lk 20.00S 44.40 E
Menai Strait 9 Ih 53.12N 4.12W
Ménaka 31 Hg 15.55N 2.26 E
Mènam Khong=Mekong (EN) 21 Mh 10.15N 105.55 E
Menangalaku 26 Gh 9.36S 119.01 E
Menard 45 Gk 30.55N 99.47W
Menawashei 35 Dc 12.40N 25.01 E
Menčul, Gora- 10 Th 48.16N 23.49 E
Mendala, Puncak- 26 Lg 4.44S 140.20 E
Mendanau, Pulau- 26 Eg 2.51S 107.26 E
Mendanha 55 Kd 18.06S 43.30W
Mende 11 Jj 44.31N 3.30 E
Mendebo 30 Kh 6.50N 39.40 E
Mendelejevsk 7 Mi 55.57N 52.22 E
Menden (Sauerland) 10 De 51.26N 7.48 E
Mendes 13 Mi 35.39N 0.52 E
Méndez 48 Je 25.07N 98.34W
Mendi [Eth.] 35 Fd 9.48N 35.05 E
Mendi [Pap.N.Gui.] 60 Ci 6.10S 143.40 E
Mendig 12 Jd 50.22N 7.16 E
Mendip Hills 9 Kj 51.15N 2.40W
Mendocino 46 Dg 39.19N 123.48W
Mendocino, Cape- 38 Ge 40.25N 124.25W
Mendocino Fracture Zone (EN) 3 Lf 40.00N 145.00W
Mendota [Ca.-U.S.] 46 Eh 36.45N 120.23W
Mendota [Il.-U.S.] 45 Lf 41.33N 89.07W
Mendoza 53 Ji 32.54S 68.50W
Mendoza [2] 56 Gd 34.30S 68.30W
Mené, Landes du- 11 Df 48.15N 2.32W
Mene de Mauroa 49 Lh 10.43N 71.01W
Mene Grande 54 Db 9.49S 70.56W
Menemen 24 Bc 38.36N 27.04 E
Menen/Menin 11 Jd 50.48N 3.07 E
Meneng Point 64e Bb 0.33S 166.57 E
Meneses 55 Dj 30.53S 56.30W
Ménez Hom 11 Bf 48.13N 4.16W
Menfi 14 Gm 37.36N 12.58 E
Mengcheng 27 Ke 33.11N 116.30 E
Mengdingjie 27 Gg 23.31N 99.07 E
Menggala 26 Eg 4.28S 105.17 E
Mengibar 13 Ig 37.58N 3.48W
Mengjin 28 Bg 34.50N 112.26 E
Mengla 27 Hg 21.30N 101.35 E
Menglangba → Lancang 27 Gg 22.37N 99.57 E
Menglian 27 Gg 22.20N 99.27 E
Mengoun Huizu Zizhixian 28 De 38.04N 117.06 E
Mengyin 28 Dg 35.42N 117.56 E
Mengzi 22 Mg 23.23N 103.34 E
Menihek Lakes 42 Kf 54.00N 66.30W
Menin/Menen 11 Jd 50.48N 3.07 E
Menindee 59 If 32.24S 142.26 E
Menindee Lake 59 If 22.00S 142.23 E
Meningie 59 Hg 35.42S 139.20 E
Menjapa, Gunung- 26 Gf 1.05N 116.05 E
Menno 45 He 43.14N 97.34W
Menoikion Óros 15 Gh 41.11N 23.48 E
Menominee 44 Dc 45.07N 87.39W
Menongue 31 Ij 14.40S 17.39 E
Menor, Mar- 13 Lg 37.43N 0.48W
Menorca=Minorca (EN) 5 Gg 40.00N 4.00 E
Menor do Araguaia, Braço- ou Javaes 54 He 9.50S 50.12W
Mentana 14 Gh 42.02N 12.38 E
Mentasta Lake 40 Kd 62.55N 143.45W
Mentawai, Kepulauan-= Mentawai Islands (EN) 21 Lj 2.00S 99.30 E
Mentawai, Selat- 21 Lj 2.00S 99.30 E
Mentawai Islands (EN)= Mentawai, Kepulauan- 21 Lj 2.00S 99.30 E
Menton 11 Nk 43.47N 7.30 E
Mentougou 28 De 39.56N 116.02 E
Menyuan 27 Hd 37.30N 101.35 E
Menzelinsk 7 Mi 55.45N 53.09 E
Menzies 59 Ee 29.41S 121.02 E
Menzies, Mount- 66 Ff 73.30S 61.50 E
Meon 12 Ad 50.49N 1.15W
Meoqui 47 Cc 28.17N 105.29W
Meponda 37 Eb 13.25S 34.52 E
Meppel 11 Mb 52.42N 6.11 E
Meppen 10 Dd 52.41N 7.19 E
Meqele(EN)=Mekele 31 Kg 13.30N 39.28 E
Mê Qu 27 He 33.58N 102.10 E
Mequinenza, Pantà de-/ Mequinenza, Embalse de- 13 Lc 41.15N 0.02W
Mequinenza, Embalse de-/ Mequinenza, Pantà de- 13 Lc 41.15N 0.02W
Mera 14 Dd 46.11N 9.25 E
Merabello, Gulf of- (EN) = Merabéllou, Kólpos- 15 In 35.14N 25.47 E
Merabéllou, Kólpos- = Merabello, Gulf of- (EN) 15 In 35.14N 25.47 E
Merak 26 Eh 5.56S 106.00 E
Meråker 7 Ce 63.26N 11.45 E
Méralab 63b Db 14.27S 168.03 E
Meramangye, Lake- 59 Ge 28.25S 132.15 E
Meran / Merano 14 Fd 46.40N 11.09 E
Merano / Meran 14 Fd 46.40N 11.09 E
Meratus, Pegunungan- 26 Gg 2.45S 115.40 E
Merauke 58 Fe 8.28S 140.20 E
Mercadal 13 Qe 39.59N 4.05 E
Mercato Saraceno 14 Gg 43.57N 12.12 E
Merced 43 Cd 37.18N 120.29W
Mercedario, Cerro- 52 Ii 31.59S 70.14W
Mercedes [Arg.] 56 Id 34.39S 59.27W
Mercedes [Arg.] 56 Ic 29.12S 58.05W
Mercedes [Arg.] 53 Ji 33.40S 65.30W
Mercedes [Ur.] 53 Ki 33.16S 58.01W
Merchants Bay 42 Lc 67.10N 62.50W
Merchtem 12 Gd 50.58N 4.14 E
Mercury Islands 62 Fb 36.35S 175.50 E
Mercy, Cape- 42 Ld 64.56N 63.40W
Mercy Bay 42 Fb 74.15N 118.10W
Meredith, Cape- 56 Hh 52.12S 60.38W
Meredith, Lake- 45 Fi 35.36N 101.42W
Meredoua 32 Hd 25.20N 2.05 E
Merefa 19 Df 49.51N 36.00 E
Merelbeke 12 Fd 51.00N 3.45 E
Merenga 20 Kd 61.43N 156.05 E
Mergui 22 Lh 12.26N 98.36 E
Mergui Archipelago 21 Lh 12.00N 98.00 E
Méri 34 Hc 10.47N 14.06 E
Meriç 15 Jh 41.11N 26.25 E
Meriç 24 Bb 40.52N 26.12 E
Mérida [2] 54 Db 8.30N 71.10W
Mérida [Mex.] 39 Kg 20.58N 89.37W
Mérida [Sp.] 13 Ff 38.55N 6.20W
Mérida [Ven.] 53 Ie 8.36N 71.08W
Mérida, Cordillera de- 52 Ie 8.40N 71.00W
Meridian 39 Kf 32.22N 88.42W
Mérig 63b Cb 14.19S 167.48 E
Mérignac 11 Fj 44.50N 0.38W
Merikarvia 7 Ef 61.51N 21.30 E
Merín, Laguna- 56 Jd 32.45S 52.50W
Meringur 59 If 34.24S 141.29 E
Merir Island 57 Ed 4.19N 132.19 E
Merizo 64c Bb 13.16N 144.40 E
Merke 18 Ic 42.52N 73.12 E
Merkem, Houthulst- 12 Ed 50.57N 2.51 E
Merkine/Merkinė 8 Kj 54.07N 24.20 E
Merkinė/Merkine 8 Kj 54.07N 24.20 E
Merkis/Merkys 7 Fi 54.10N 24.11 E
Merksem, Antwerpen- 12 Gc 51.15N 4.27 E
Merksplas 12 Gc 51.22N 4.52 E
Merkys/Merkis 7 Fi 54.10N 24.11 E
Meroe 35 Eb 16.56N 33.59 E
Meroe 35 Eb 16.05N 33.55 E
Merouane, Chott- 32 Ic 34.00N 6.02 E
Merredin 59 Df 31.29S 118.16 E
Merrick 9 If 55.08N 4.29W
Merrill 43 Jb 45.11N 89.41W
Merriman 45 Fe 42.55N 101.42W
Merritt 42 Ff 50.07N 120.47W
Merritt Island 43 Kf 28.21N 80.42W
Merritt Reservoir 45 Fe 42.35N 100.55W
Mersa Fatma 35 Gc 14.53N 40.19 E
Mersa Teklay 35 Fb 17.25N 38.45 E
Mersea Island 12 Cc 51.47N 0.57 E
Merseburg 10 He 51.22N 12.00 E
Mers el Kebir 13 Li 35.44N 0.43W
Mersey 9 Kh 53.25N 3.00W
Merseyside [3] 9 Kh 53.30N 3.00W
Mersin → Içel 23 Db 36.48N 34.38 E
Mersing 26 Df 2.26N 103.50 E
Mers-les-Bains 12 Dd 50.04N 1.23 E
Mērsrags/Mersrags 8 Jg 57.19N 23.01 E
Mersrags/Mērsrags 8 Jg 57.19N 23.01 E
Merta 25 Ec 26.39N 74.02 E
Merta Road 25 Ec 26.43N 73.55 E
Mertert 12 Ie 49.42N 6.29 E
Merthyr Tydfil 9 Jj 51.46N 3.23W
Merti 36 Gb 1.04N 38.40 E
Mértola 13 Eg 37.38N 7.40W
Mertule Maryam 35 Fc 10.50N 38.15 E
Mertvy Kultuk, Sor- 16 Rg 45.30N 53.40 E
Mertz Glacier 66 Je 67.40S 144.45 E
Meru 36 Gb 0.03N 37.39 E
Méru 11 Ie 49.14N 2.08 E
Meru, Mount- 36 Gc 3.14S 36.45 E
Merure 55 Fb 15.33S 53.05W
Merville 12 Ed 50.38N 2.38 E
Merzifon 23 Ea 40.53N 35.29 E
Merzig 10 Cg 49.27N 6.38 E
Meša 7 Li 55.34N 49.24 E
Mesa [Az.-U.S.] 39 Hf 33.25N 111.50W
Mesa [Co.-U.S.] 45 Bg 39.14N 108.08W
Mesabi Range 45 Jc 47.30N 92.50W
Mesagne 14 Lj 40.34N 17.48 E
Mescalero 45 Dj 33.09N 105.46W
Meščera=Moscow Basin 5 Kd 55.00N 40.30 E
Meschede 10 Ee 51.21N 8.17 E
Mescit Dağı 24 Ib 40.22N 41.11 E
Meščovsk 16 Ib 54.19N 35.18 E
Mesegon 64d Bb 7.09N 151.55 E
Mesfinto 35 Fc 13.28N 37.23 E
Me-Shima 28 Jh 32.01N 128.25 E
Meshkīnshahr 24 Lc 38.24N 47.40 E
Mesima 14 Jl 38.30N 15.55 E
Mesjagutovo 17 Ii 55.35N 58.20 E
Meskiana 14 Bo 35.38N 7.40 E
Meskiana, Oued- 14 Bo 35.48N 7.53 E
Meslo 35 Fd 6.22N 39.50 E
Mesnil-Val, Criel-sur-Mer- 12 Dd 50.03N 1.20 E
Mesola 14 Gf 44.55N 12.14 E
Mesolóngion 15 Ek 38.22N 21.26 E
Mesopotamia 52 Kh 30.00S 58.00W
Mesopotamia (EN) 23 Fc 34.00N 44.00 E
Mesoyéios Thálassa= Mediterranean Sea (EN) 5 Hh 35.00N 20.00 E
Mesquite [Nv.-U.S.] 46 Hh 36.48N 114.04W
Mesquite [Tx.-U.S.] 45 Hj 32.46N 96.36W
Mesra 13 Mi 35.50N 0.10 E
Messaad 32 Hc 34.10N 3.30 E
Messalo 30 Lj 11.40S 40.46 E
Messará, Órmos- 15 Ho 35.00N 24.40 E
Messina [It.] 6 Hh 38.11N 15.34 E
Messina [S.Afr.] 31 Kk 22.23S 30.00 E
Messina, Strait of- (EN) = Messina, Stretto di- 5 Hh 38.15N 15.35 E
Messina, Stretto di- = Messina, Strait of- (EN) 5 Hh 38.15N 15.35 E
Messini 15 El 37.15N 21.50 E
Messíni 15 Fl 37.03N 22.01 E
Messiniakós Kólpos 15 Fm 36.45N 22.10 E
Messojaha 20 Cc 67.52N 77.27 E
Mesta 15 Hi 40.51N 24.44 E
Mestecăniş, Pasul- 15 Ib 47.28N 25.20 E
Mesters Vig 41 Jd 72.15N 24.20W
Mestia 16 Mh 43.03N 42.43 E
Mestre, Espigão- 54 If 12.30S 46.00W
Mestre, Venezia- 14 Ge 45.29N 12.14 E
Mesuji 26 Eg 4.08S 105.52 E
Meta [2] 54 Dc 3.30N 73.00W
Meta, Rio- 52 Je 6.12N 67.28W
Meta Incognita Peninsula 38 Mc 62.40N 68.00W
Metairie 45 Kl 29.59N 90.09W
Metaliferi, Munţii- 15 Fc 46.10N 22.50 E
Metallifere, Colline- 14 Eg 43.10N 10.55 E
Metán 56 Hc 25.29S 64.57W
Metangula 37 Eb 12.43S 34.49 E
Metaponto 14 Kj 40.20N 16.50 E
Metauro 14 Hg 43.50N 13.03 E
Metautu 65c Ba 13.57S 171.54W
Meteghan 44 Nc 44.11N 66.10W
Metelen 12 Jb 52.09N 7.12 E
Metéora 15 Ej 39.43N 21.40 E
Meteor Seamount (EN) 30 Hm 48.00S 8.30 E
Meteor Trench (EN) 3 Do 55.00S 27.00 E
Méthana 15 Gl 37.35N 23.23 E
Methánon, Khersónisos- 15 Gl 37.36N 23.22 E
Methven 62 De 43.38S 171.38 E
Methwold 12 Cb 52.31N 0.33 E
Metković 14 Lg 43.03N 17.39 E
Metlakatla 40 Me 55.08N 131.35W
Metlika 14 Je 45.39N 15.19 E
Metlili Chaamba 32 Hc 32.16N 3.38 E
Metmárfag 32 Ed 26.26N 13.26W
Metohija 15 Dg 42.40N 20.27 E
Metro 26 Eh 5.05S 105.20 E
Metropolis 45 Lh 37.09N 88.44W
Métsovon 15 Ej 39.46N 21.11 E
Métsovon, Zigós- = Métsovon Pass (EN) 15 Ej 39.47N 21.15 E
Métsovon Pass (EN) = Métsovon, Zigós- 15 Ej 39.47N 21.15 E
Mettet 12 Gd 50.19N 4.40 E
Mettingen 12 Jb 52.19N 7.47 E
Mettlach 12 Ie 49.30N 6.36 E
Mettmann 12 Ic 51.15N 6.58 E
Metu 31 Kh 8.20N 35.38 E
Metuje 10 Lf 50.20N 15.55 E
Metz 6 Gf 49.08N 6.10 E
Metzervisse 12 Ie 49.19N 6.17 E
Meu 11 Ef 48.02N 1.47W
Meulaboh 26 Cf 4.09N 96.08 E
Meulan 12 De 49.01N 1.54 E
Meulebeke 12 Fd 50.57N 3.17 E
Meureudu 26 Ce 5.16N 96.16 E
Meurthe 11 Mf 48.47N 6.09 E
Meurthe-et-Moselle [3] 11 Mf 48.35N 6.10 E
Meuse [3] 11 Lf 49.00N 5.30 E
Meuse 5 Ge 51.49N 5.01 E
Meuse (EN)=Maas 5 Ge 51.49N 5.01 E
Meuse, Côtes de- 11 Le 49.10N 5.30 E
Meuzenti 35 Bb 18.14N 17.06 E
Mexia 45 Hk 31.41N 96.29W
Mexiana, Ilha 54 Ic 0.00 49.35W
Mexicali 39 Hf 32.40N 115.29W
Mexicana, Altiplanicie- = Mexico, Plateau of- (EN) 38 Ig 25.30N 104.00W
Mexican Hat 46 Kh 37.09N 109.52W
Mexicanos, Laguna de los- 48 Fc 28.09N 106.57W
Mexico 45 Kg 39.10N 91.53W
México [1] 39 Ig 23.00N 102.00W

Index Symbols

[1] Independent Nation
[2] State, Region
[3] District, County
[4] Municipality
[5] Colony, Dependency
Continent
Physical Region
Historical or Cultural Region
Mount, Mountain
Volcano
Hill
Mountains, Mountain Range
Hills, Escarpment
Plateau, Upland
Pass, Gap
Plain, Lowland
Delta
Salt Flat
Valley, Canyon
Crater, Cave
Karst Features
Depression
Polder
Desert, Dunes
Forest, Woods
Heath, Steppe
Oasis
Cape, Point
Coast, Beach
Cliff
Peninsula
Isthmus
Sandbank
Island
Atoll
Rock, Reef
Islands, Archipelago
Rocks, Reefs
Coral Reef
Well, Spring
Geyser
River, Stream
Waterfall Rapids
River Mouth, Estuary
Lake
Salt Lake
Intermittent Lake
Reservoir
Swamp, Pond
Canal
Glacier
Ice Shelf, Pack Ice
Ocean
Sea
Gulf, Bay
Strait, Fjord
Lagoon
Bank
Seamount
Tablemount
Ridge
Shelf
Basin
Escarpment, Sea Scarp
Fracture
Trench, Abyss
National Park, Reserve
Point of Interest
Recreation Site
Cave, Cavern
Historic Site
Ruins
Wall, Walls
Church, Abbey
Temple
Scientific Station
Airport
Port
Lighthouse
Mine
Tunnel
Dam, Bridge

México [2] 47 Ee 19.20N 99.30W
México, Golfo de-=Mexico, Gulf of- (EN) 38 Kg 25.00N 90.00W
Mexico, Gulf of- (EN)= México, Golfo de- 38 Kg 25.00N 90.00W
Mexico, Plateau of- (EN)= Mexicana, Altiplanicie- 38 Ig 25.30N 104.00W
Mexico Basin (EN) 3 Bg 25.00N 92.00W
Mexico City (EN)=Ciudad de México 39 Jh 19.24N 99.09W
Meybod 24 Of 32.16N 53.59 E
Meydān-e Gel 24 Ph 29.04N 54.50 E
Meyisti 15 Mm 36.08N 29.34 E
Meyisti 15 Mm 36.09N 29.40 E
Meymaneh 22 If 35.55N 64.47 E
Meymeh 24 Nf 33.27N 51.10 E
Meymeh 24 Lf 32.05N 47.16 E
Meža 7 Hi 55.43N 31.30 E
Mezcala 48 Ji 17.56N 99.37W
Mezcalapa, Río- 48 Mh 18.36N 92.39W
Mezdra 15 Gf 43.09N 23.42 E
Meždurečenski 19 Gd 59.36N 65.53 E
Meždušarski, Ostrov- 19 Fa 71.20N 53.00 E
Mèze 11 Jk 43.25N 3.36 E
Mezen 5 Kb 66.00N 43.59 E
Mezen 6 Kb 65.50N 44.13 E
Mézenc, Mont- 11 Kj 44.55N 4.11 E
Meženin 10 Sc 53.07N 22.29 E
Mezenskaja Guba 5 Kb 66.40N 43.45 E
Mezenskaja Pižma 7 Ld 64.30N 48.32 E
Mežgorje 10 Th 48.30N 23.37 E
Mežica 14 Id 46.31N 14.52 E
Mézidon-Canon 12 Be 49.05N 0.04W
Mézin 11 Gj 44.03N 0.16 E
Mezöberény 10 Rj 46.49N 21.02 E
Mezőcsát 10 Qi 47.49N 20.55 E
Mezőföld 10 Oj 46.55N 18.35 E
Mezőkovácsháza 10 Qj 46.24N 20.55 E
Mezőkövesd 10 Qi 47.49N 20.35 E
Mezőtúr 10 Qi 47.00N 20.38 E
Mežozerny 17 Ii 54.10N 59.25 E
Mežpjanje 7 Ki 55.25N 45.00 E
Mezquital 48 Gf 23.29N 104.23W
Mezquital, Río- 48 Gf 22.55N 104.54W
Mezquitic 48 Hf 22.23N 103.41W
Mgači 20 Jf 51.02N 142.18 E
Mglin 16 Hc 53.04N 32.53 E
Mhow 25 Fd 22.33N 75.46 E
Miahuatlán de Porfirio Díaz 48 Ki 16.20N 96.36W
Miajadas 13 Ge 39.09N 5.54W
Miaméré 35 Bd 9.02N 19.55 E
Miami [Az.-U.S.] 46 Jj 33.24N 110.52W
Miami [Fl.-U.S.] 39 Kg 25.46N 80.12W
Miami [Ok.-U.S.] 43 Id 36.53N 94.53W
Miami Beach 43 Kf 25.47N 80.08W
Miānābād 24 Qd 37.02N 57.27 E
Miāndowāb 23 Gb 36.58N 46.06 E
Miandrivazo 37 Hc 19.30S 45.28 E
Miānduhe 27 Lb 49.12N 121.09 E
Miāneh 23 Gb 37.26N 47.42 E
Miang, Khao- 25 Ke 17.42N 101.01 E
Miangas, Pulau- 26 Ie 5.35N 126.35 E
Mianning 27 Hf 28.31N 102.10 E
Miānwāli 25 Eb 32.35N 71.33 E
Mianyang 27 He 31.23N 104.49 E
Mianyang (Xiantaozhen) 28 Bi 30.22N 113.27 E
Miaodao Qundao 27 Ld 38.10N 120.45 E
Miao'er Shan 27 Jf 25.50N 110.22 E
Miao Ling 27 If 26.05N 108.00 E
Miarinarivo 37 Hc 18.56S 46.54 E
Miass 19 Gd 55.01N 60.06 E
Miass 19 Gd 56.06N 64.30 E
Miasskoje 17 Ji 55.15N 61.55 E
Miasteczko Krajeńskie 10 Nc 53.06N 17.01 E
Miastko 10 Mb 54.01N 17.00 E
Michael, Mount- 59 Ja 6.25S 145.20 E
Michajlova Island 66 Ge 66.30S 85.00 E
Michalovce 10 Rh 48.46N 21.55 E
Michelstadt 12 Le 49.41N 9.01 E
Miches 49 Md 18.59N 69.03W
Michigan [2] 43 Jc 44.00N 85.00W
Michigan, Lake- 38 Ke 44.00N 87.00W
Michigan City 43 Jc 41.43N 86.54W
Michipicoten Bay 44 Eb 47.55N 84.56W
Michipicoten Island 42 Ig 47.45N 85.45W
Michoacán [2] 47 De 19.10N 101.50W
Michów 10 Se 51.32N 22.19 E
Mico, Río- 49 Eg 12.11N 84.16W
Micoud 51k Bb 13.50N 60.54W
Micronesia 57 Gc 11.00N 159.00 E
Micronesia, Federated States of- [5] 58 Gd 6.30N 152.00 E
Mičurin 15 Kg 42.10N 27.51 E
Mičurinsk 6 Ke 52.54N 40.31 E
Midai, Pulau- 26 Ef 3.00N 107.47 E
Midar 32 Gc 34.57N 3.32W
Mid-Atlantic Ridge (EN) 3 Di 0.00 20.00W
Middelburg [Neth.] 11 Jc 51.30N 3.37 E
Middelburg [S.Afr.] 37 Cf 31.30S 25.00 E
Middelburg [S.Afr.] 37 De 25.47S 29.28 E
Middelfart 7 Bi 55.30N 9.45 E
Middelharnis 12 Gc 51.45N 4.12 E
Middelkerke 12 Ec 51.11N 2.49 E
Middelkerke-Westende 12 Ec 51.10N 2.46 E
Middle Alkali Lake 46 Ef 41.28N 120.04W
Middle America Trench (EN) 3 Mh 15.00N 95.00W
Middle Andaman 25 If 12.30N 92.50 E
Middle Atlas (EN)=Moyen Atlas 30 Ge 33.30N 4.30W
Middlebury 44 Kc 44.01N 73.10W
Middle Caicos 49 Lc 21.47N 71.43W
Middle Fork Feather River 46 Eg 38.47N 121.36W
Middle Island 37b Ab 9.22S 46.21 E
Middle Loup River 45 Gf 41.17N 98.23W
Middlemarch 62 Df 45.30S 170.07 E
Middle Reef 63a Ee 12.35S 160.30 E
Middlesboro 43 Kd 36.36N 83.43W
Middlesbrough 9 Lg 54.35N 1.14W
Middlesex 49 Ce 17.02N 88.31W
Middlesex 12 Bc 51.35N 0.10W
Middlesex 9 Mj 51.30N 0.05W
Middleton 40 Je 59.25N 146.25W
Middleton Reef 57 Gg 29.30S 159.10 E
Middletown [Ct.-U.S.] 44 Ke 41.33N 72.39W
Middletown [N.Y.-U.S.] 44 Je 41.26N 74.26W
Middletown [Oh.-U.S.] 44 Ef 39.31N 84.25W
Midelt 32 Gc 32.41N 4.45W
Mid Glamorgan [3] 9 Jj 51.35N 3.35W
Midhordland 8 Ad 60.15N 5.55 E
Midhurst 12 Bd 50.59N 0.44W
Midi, Canal du- 5 Gg 43.36N 1.25 E
Midi de Bigorre, Pic du- 11 Gl 42.56N 0.08 E
Midi d'Ossau, Pic du- 11 Fl 42.51N 0.26W
Mid-Indian Basin (EN) 3 Gj 10.00S 80.00 E
Mid-Indian Ridge (EN) 3 Gj 3.00S 75.00 E
Midland [Mi.-U.S.] 44 Ed 43.37N 84.14W
Midland [Ont.-Can.] 42 Jh 44.45N 79.53W
Midland [S.D.-U.S.] 45 Fd 44.04N 101.10W
Midland [Tx.-U.S.] 43 Ge 32.00N 102.05W
Midlands [3] 37 Dc 19.00S 30.00 E
Midlands 9 Li 52.40N 1.50W
Midleton/Mainistir na Corann 9 Ej 51.55N 8.10W
Midnapore → Medinīpur 25 Hd 22.26N 87.20 E
Midongy du Sud 37 Hd 23.34N 47.01 E
Midou 11 Fk 43.54N 0.30W
Midouze 11 Fk 43.48N 0.51W
Mid-Pacific Mountains (EN) 3 Jg 20.00N 170.00 E
Midway Islands [5] 58 Jb 28.13N 177.22W
Midway Islands 57 Jb 28.13N 177.22W
Midwest 46 Le 43.25N 106.16W
Midwest City 45 Hi 35.27N 97.24W
Midyat 24 Id 37.25N 41.23 E
Midžor 5 Ig 43.24N 22.40 E
Miechów 10 Qf 50.23N 20.01 E
Miedwie, Jezioro- 10 Kc 53.15N 14.55 E
Międzychód 10 Ld 52.36N 15.53 E
Międzylesie 10 Mf 50.10N 16.40 E
Międzyrzec Podlaski 10 Se 52.00N 22.47 E
Międzyrzecz 10 Ld 52.27N 15.34 E
Międzyrzecze Łomżyńskie 10 Rd 52.45N 21.45 E
Miehikkälä 8 Ld 60.40N 27.42 E
Mie Ken [2] 28 Ng 34.35N 136.25 E
Miekojärvi 7 Fc 66.36N 24.23 E
Mielan 11 Gk 43.26N 0.19 E
Mielec 10 Rf 50.18N 21.25 E
Mielno 10 Mb 54.16N 16.01 E
Mien 8 Fh 56.25N 14.50 E
Mier 48 Jd 26.26N 99.09W
Miercurea Ciuc 15 Ic 46.21N 25.48 E
Mieres 13 Ga 43.15N 5.46W
Miersig 15 Ec 46.53N 21.51 E
Mier y Noriega 48 If 23.25N 100.07W
Miesbach 10 Hi 47.47N 11.50 E
Mieso 35 Gd 9.15N 40.45 E
Mifune 29 Be 32.43N 130.48 E
Migang Shan 27 Id 35.32N 106.13 E
Miguel Alamán, Presa- 48 Kh 18.13N 96.32W
Miguel Auza 48 He 24.18N 103.25W
Miguel Hidalgo, Presa- 48 Ed 26.40N 108.45W
Miha Chakaja 19 Eg 42.17N 42.02 E
Mihăileşti 15 Ie 44.20N 25.54 E
Mihail Kogălniceanu 15 Le 44.22N 28.27 E
Mihajlov 19 De 54.16N 39.03 E
Mihajlovgrad 15 Gf 43.25N 23.13 E
Mihajlovgrad [2] 15 Gf 43.25N 23.13 E
Mihajlovka [Kaz.-U.S.S.R.] 18 Hc 43.01N 71.31 E
Mihajlovka [R.S.F.S.R.] 19 Ee 50.05N 43.15 E
Mihajlovsk 17 Ih 56.29N 59.07 E
Mihalıççık 24 Dc 39.52N 31.30 E
Mihara 29 Cd 34.24N 133.05 E
Mihara-Yama 29 Fd 34.43N 139.23 E
Mi He 28 Ef 37.12N 119.10 E
Mihonoseki 29 Cd 35.34N 133.18 E
Miho-Wan 29 Cd 35.30N 133.20 E
Miiraku 29 Ae 32.45N 128.40 E
Mijaly 16 Re 48.54N 53.50 E
Mijares/Millars 13 Le 39.55N 0.01W
Mijdaḥah 35 Hc 14.00N 48.26 E
Mijdrecht 12 Gb 52.12N 4.52 E
Mijirtein (EN)=Majērtēn 30 Lh 9.00N 50.00 E
Mikasa 28 Pc 43.20N 141.40 E
Mikata 29 Dd 35.34N 135.54 E
Miki 29 Dd 34.17N 134.07 E
Mikinai = Mycenae (EN) 15 Fl 37.43N 22.45 E
Mikindani 36 Ge 10.17S 40.07 E
Mikkeli [2] 7 Ge 62.00N 27.30 E
Mikkeli/Sankt Michel 6 Ic 61.41N 27.15 E
Mikomoto-Jima 29 Fd 34.34N 138.56 E
Mikonos 15 Il 37.27N 25.23 E
Mikonos 15 Il 37.27N 25.20 E
Mikonou, Stenón- 15 Il 37.30N 25.20 E
Mikrá Préspa, Límni- 15 Ei 40.45N 21.06 E
Mikre 15 Hf 43.02N 24.31 E
Mikró Sofráno 15 Jm 36.05N 26.24 E
Mikulov 10 Mh 48.49N 16.39 E
Mikumi 36 Gd 7.24S 36.59 E
Mikun 19 Fc 62.21N 50.05 E
Mikuni 29 Ec 36.13N 136.09 E
Mikuni-Sanmyaku 28 Of 36.15N 138.40 E
Mikuni-Tōge 29 Fc 36.46N 138.50 E
Mikuni-Yama 29 Dd 35.21N 134.01 E
Mikura-Jima 27 Oe 33.50N 139.35 E
Milaca 45 Jd 45.45N 93.39W
Miladummadulu Atoll 25a Ba 6.15N 73.15 E
Milagro 54 Cd 2.07S 79.36W
Milājerd 24 Me 34.37N 49.12 E
Milan [Mo.-U.S.] 45 Jf 40.12N 93.07W
Milan [Tn.-U.S.] 44 Ch 35.55N 88.46W
Milan (EN) = Milano 6 Gf 45.28N 9.12 E
Milange 37 Fc 16.05S 35.47 E
Milano = Milan (EN) 6 Gf 45.28N 9.12 E
Milâs 24 Bd 37.19N 27.47 E
Milazzo 14 Jl 38.13N 15.14 E
Milazzo, Capo di- 14 Jl 38.16N 15.14 E
Milazzo, Golfo di- 14 Jl 38.15N 15.20 E
Milbank 43 Hb 45.13N 96.38W
Mildenhall 12 Cb 52.21N 0.31 E
Mildura 58 Fh 34.12S 142.09 E
Mile 27 Hg 24.28N 103.26 E
Mile 35 Gc 11.08N 40.55 E
Miléai 15 Gj 39.20N 23.09 E
Miles 58 Gg 26.40S 150.11 E
Miles City 43 Fb 46.25N 105.51W
Milet = Miletus (EN) 15 Kl 37.30N 27.16 E
Miletus (EN) = Milet 15 Kl 37.30N 27.16 E
Milevec 15 Fg 42.34N 22.27 E
Milevsko 10 Kg 49.27N 14.22 E
Milford 46 Ig 38.24N 113.01W
Milford Haven 9 Hj 51.44N 5.02W
Milford Lake 45 Hg 39.15N 97.00W
Milford Sound 61 Ch 44.40S 167.55 E
Milford Sound 62 Bf 44.35S 167.50 E
Milgis 36 Gb 1.48N 38.06 E
Milḥ, Baḩr al- 23 Fc 32.40N 43.35 E
Milḥ, Ra's al- 33 Ec 31.55N 25.02 E
Miliana 13 Oh 36.17N 2.14 E
Mili Atoll 57 Id 6.08N 171.55 E
Milicz 10 Ne 51.32N 17.17 E
Milkovo 20 Kf 54.43N 158.43 E
Milk River 43 Eb 49.09N 112.05W
Milk River 46 Ib 49.09N 112.05W
Milkūh 23 Jc 32.45N 61.55 E
Mill 42 Jd 63.57N 78.00W
Millars/Mijares 13 Le 39.55N 0.01W
Millau 11 Jj 44.06N 3.05 E
Milledgeville 44 Fi 33.04N 83.14W
Mille Lacs, Lac des- 42 Ig 48.50N 90.30W
Mille Lacs Lake 43 Ib 46.15N 93.40W
Millen 44 Gi 32.48N 81.57W
Miller [Nb.-U.S.] 45 Gf 40.57N 99.26W
Miller [S.D.-U.S.] 45 Gd 44.31N 98.59W
Millerovo 19 Ef 48.52N 40.25 E
Miller Seamount (EN) 40 Kf 53.30N 144.20W
Millerton 62 Dd 41.38S 171.52 E
Millevaches, Plateau de- 11 Ii 45.45N 2.11 E
Millicent 59 Ig 37.36S 140.22 E
Millington 44 Ch 35.20N 89.54W
Millinocket 44 Mc 45.39N 68.43W
Mill Island 66 He 65.30S 100.40 E
Millmerran 59 Ke 27.52S 151.16 E
Mills Lake 42 Fd 61.28N 118.15W
Millstatt 14 Hd 46.48N 13.35 E
Millville 44 Jf 39.24N 75.02W
Millwood Lake 45 Jj 33.45N 94.00W
Milne Land 41 Jd 71.20N 27.30W
Milo 30 Gg 11.04N 9.14W
Milolii 65a Fd 19.11N 155.55W
Milos 15 Hm 36.45N 24.26 E
Milos = Milos (EN) 15 Hm 36.41N 24.25 E
Milos (EN) = Milos 15 Hm 36.41N 24.25 E
Milparinka 59 Ie 29.44S 141.53 E
Miltenberg 10 Fg 49.42N 9.15 E
Milton [Fl.-U.S.] 44 Dj 30.38N 87.03W
Milton [N.Z.] 62 Cg 46.07S 169.58 E
Milton-Freewater 46 Fd 45.56N 118.23W
Milton Keynes 9 Mi 52.03N 0.42W
Miltou 35 Bc 10.14N 17.26 E
Milumbe, Monts- 36 Ed 8.00S 27.30 E
Miluo 28 Bj 28.51N 113.05 E
Miluo Jiang 27 Jf 28.51N 112.59 E
Milwaukee 39 Ke 43.02N 87.55W
Milwaukee Depth (EN) 3 Do 55.10S 26.00W
Milwaukee Seamounts (EN) 57 Ia 32.28N 171.55 E
Milwaukie 46 Dd 45.27N 122.38W
Mimi-Gawa 29 Be 32.20N 131.37 E
Mimizan 11 Ej 44.12N 1.14W
Mimoń 10 Kf 50.40N 14.44 E
Mimongo 36 Bc 1.38S 11.39 E
Mimoso 55 Hb 15.10S 48.05W
Mina 13 Mi 35.58N 0.31 E
Mina [Mex.] 48 Id 26.01N 100.32W
Mina [Nv.-U.S.] 46 Fg 38.24N 118.07W
Mina, Cerro- 49 Ki 8.21N 73.10W
Mīnā' Abd Allāh 24 Mh 29.01N 48.10 E
Mīnā' al Aḩmadī 24 Mh 29.04N 48.09 E
Mīnāb 24 Qi 27.09N 57.05 E
Mīnāb 24 Qi 27.01N 56.53 E
Mīnā' Barānis 33 Ge 23.55N 35.28 E
Minahassa=Minahassa Peninsula (EN) 21 Oi 1.00N 124.35 E
Minahassa Peninsula (EN)= Minahassa 21 Oi 1.00N 124.35 E
Minakuchi 29 Ed 34.59N 136.11 E
Minamata 28 Kh 32.13N 130.24 E
Minami-Daitō-Jima 27 Nf 25.50N 131.15 E
Minami-furano 29a Cb 43.10N 142.32 E
Minami-Iō-Jima 60 Cc 24.14N 141.28 E
Minami-kayabe 29a Bc 41.53N 141.01 E
Minami-Tori-Shima=Marcus Island (EN) 57 Gb 26.32N 142.09 E
Minas [Cuba] 49 Ic 21.29N 77.37W
Minas [Indon.] 26 Df 0.50N 101.29 E
Minas [Ur.] 53 Ki 34.23S 55.14W
Minas de Riotinto 13 Fg 37.42N 6.35W
Minas Gerais [2] 54 Jg 18.00S 44.30W
Minā' Su'ūd 24 Mh 28.44N 48.24 E
Minatitlán [Mex.] 47 Fe 17.59N 94.31W
Minatitlán [Mex.] 48 Gh 19.22N 104.04W
Minaya 13 Je 39.17N 2.19W
Minbu 25 Id 20.11N 94.53 E
Minbya 25 Id 20.22N 93.16 E
Minchinmávida, Volcán- 56 Ff 42.49S 72.28W
Mincio 14 Ee 45.04N 10.59 E
Mindanao 21 Oi 8.00N 125.00 E
Mindanao Sea 21 Oi 9.15N 123.40 E
Mindel 10 Gh 48.31N 10.23 E
Mindelheim 10 Gh 48.03N 10.29 E
Mindelo 31 Eg 16.53N 25.00W
Minden [Ger.] 10 Ed 52.17N 8.55 E
Minden [La.-U.S.] 45 Jj 32.37N 93.17W
Minden [Nb.-U.S.] 45 Gf 40.30N 98.57W
Mindif 34 Hc 10.24N 14.26 E
Mindoro 21 Oh 12.50N 121.05 E
Mindoro Strait 26 Hd 12.20N 120.40 E
Mindouli 36 Bc 4.17S 14.21 E
Mindszent 10 Qj 46.32N 20.12 E
Mine 29 Bd 34.12N 131.11 E
Minehead 9 Jj 51.13N 3.29W
Mine Head 9 Fj 52.00N 7.35W
Mineiros 54 Hg 17.34S 52.34W
Mineral del Monte 48 Jg 20.08N 98.40W
Mineralnyje Vody 19 Eg 44.12N 43.08 E
Mineral Wells 43 He 32.48N 98.07W
Minerva Reefs 57 Jg 23.50S 179.00W
Minervino Murge 14 Ki 41.05N 16.05 E
Minervois 11 Ik 43.25N 2.45 E
Minfeng/Niya 27 Dd 37.04N 82.46 E
Minga 36 Ee 11.08S 27.56 E
Mingala 35 Cd 5.06N 21.49 E
Mingan 42 Lf 50.18N 64.01W
Mingečaur 16 Oi 40.46N 47.02 E
Mingečaurskoje Vodohranilišče 16 Oi 40.55N 46.45 E
Mingenew 59 De 29.11S 115.26 E
Minggang 28 Ci 32.27N 114.02 E
Mingguang → Jiashan 28 Dh 32.47N 118.00 E
Ming He 28 Cf 37.14N 114.47 E
Minglanilla 13 Ke 39.32N 1.36W
Mingoyo 36 Ge 10.06S 39.38 E
Mingshui 27 Mb 47.15N 125.53 E
Mingshui → Zhangqiu 28 Df 36.44N 117.33 E
Mingteke 27 Bd 37.09N 74.58 E
Mingteke Daban 27 Bd 37.00N 74.50 E
Minguez, Puerto- 13 Ld 40.50N 0.59W
Mingulay 9 Fe 56.50N 7.40W
Mingyuegou 28 Jc 43.08N 128.55 E
Minhe 27 Hd 36.20N 102.50 E
Minho 13 Dc 41.52N 8.51W
Minho 13 Dc 41.40N 8.30W
Minicoy Island 21 Ji 8.17N 73.02 E
Minigwal, Lake- 59 Ee 29.35S 123.10 E
Minija 8 Ii 55.20N 21.12 E
Minilya 59 Cd 23.51S 113.58 E
Minilya River 59 Cd 23.56S 113.51 E
Minipi Lake 42 Lf 52.28N 60.50W
Ministra, Sierra- 13 Jc 41.07N 2.30W
Minjar 17 Hi 55.04N 57.33 E
Min Jiang 27 Kf 26.05N 119.32 E
Minmaya 28 Pd 41.10N 140.28 E
Minna 31 Hh 9.37N 6.33 E
Minna Bluff 66 Kf 78.32S 166.30 E
Minneapolis [Ks.-U.S.] 45 Hg 39.08N 97.42W
Minneapolis [Mn.-U.S.] 39 Je 44.59N 93.13W
Minnedosa 42 Hf 50.14N 99.51W
Minnedosa River 45 Fb 49.53N 100.08W
Minnesota [2] 43 Ib 46.00N 94.15W
Minnesota River 43 Ic 44.54N 93.10W
Miño 5 Fg 41.52N 8.51W
Mino 29 Ed 35.32N 136.54 E
Minobu 29 Fd 35.22N 138.24 E
Minobu-Sanchi 29 Fd 35.15N 138.20 E
Minokamo 29 Ed 35.26N 137.00 E
Mino-Mikawa-Kōgen 29 Ed 35.10N 137.25 E
Minorca (EN)=Menorca 5 Gg 40.00N 4.00 E
Minot 39 Ie 48.14N 101.18W
Minqin 27 Hd 38.42N 103.11 E
Minqing 27 Kf 26.15N 118.52 E
Minquan 28 Cg 34.39N 115.08 E
Min Shan 27 He 33.35N 103.00 E
Minsk 6 Ie 53.54N 27.34 E
Minskaja Oblast [3] 19 Ce 53.50N 27.40 E
Minskaja Vozvyšennost 8 Lj 54.00N 27.10 E
Mińsk Mazowiecki 10 Rd 52.11N 21.34 E
Minta 34 He 4.35N 12.48 E
Minto, Lac- 42 Ke 57.15N 74.50W
Minto, Mount- 66 Kf 71.47S 168.45 E
Minto Inlet 42 Fb 71.19N 117.00W
Minto Reef 57 Gd 8.08N 154.17 E
Minturn 45 Cg 39.35N 106.26W
Minūdasht 24 Pd 37.10N 55.25 E
Minuf 24 Dg 30.28N 30.56 E
Minusinsk 20 Ef 53.43N 91.48 E
Minvoul 36 Bb 2.09N 12.08 E
Minwakh 35 Hb 16.48N 48.06 E
Minxian 27 He 34.26N 104.02 E
Miory 7 Gi 55.39N 27.41 E
Mios Num 26 Kg 1.30S 135.10 E
Miquan 27 Ec 44.05N 87.33 E
Miquelon 42 Jg 49.00N 76.00W
Mira 13 Dg 37.43N 8.47W
Mira [It.] 14 Ge 45.26N 12.08 E
Mira [Port.] 13 Dd 40.26N 8.44W
Mira, Peña- 13 Fc 41.55N 6.28W
Mirābād 23 Jc 30.25N 61.50 E
Mirabela 55 Jc 16.15S 44.11W
Miracatu 55 Ig 24.17S 47.28W
Miracema 54 Jh 21.25S 42.11W
Mirador, Serra do- 55 Hh 26.45S 49.50W
Miraflores [Col.] 54 Db 5.12N 73.12W
Miraflores [Col.] 54 Dc 1.30N 72.16W
Mirah, Wādī al- 24 If 32.26N 41.42 E
Miraj 25 Ee 16.50N 74.38 E
Miramar 56 Ie 38.16S 57.51W
Miramar, Laguna- 48 Ni 16.20N 91.20W
Miramas 11 Kk 43.35N 5.00 E
Mirambeau 11 Fi 45.22N 0.34W
Miramichi Bay 42 Kg 47.07N 65.10W
Miramont-de-Guyenne 11 Gj 44.36N 0.22 E
Miran 27 Ed 39.15N 88.50 E
Miranda [2] 54 Ea 10.15N 66.25W
Miranda [Arg.] 55 Cm 36.32S 59.09W
Miranda [Braz.] 54 Gh 20.14S 56.22W
Miranda de Corvo 13 Dd 40.06N 8.20W
Miranda de Ebro 13 Jb 42.41N 2.57W
Miranda do Douro 13 Fc 41.30N 6.16W
Mirande 11 Gk 43.31N 0.25 E
Mirandela 13 Ec 41.29N 7.11W
Mirandola 14 Ff 44.53N 11.04 E
Mirandópolis 55 Ge 21.09S 51.06W
Mirante do Paranapanema 55 Gf 22.17S 51.54W
Mira Por Vos 49 Jb 22.04N 74.38W
Mirapuxi, Rio- 55 Ga 13.06S 51.10W
Mirassol 55 He 20.46S 49.28W
Miravalles 13 Fb 42.45N 6.53W
Miravalles, Volcán- 38 Kh 10.45N 85.10W
Miravete, Puerto de- 13 Ge 39.43N 5.43W
Mir-Bašir 16 Oi 40.19N 46.58 E
Mirbāţ 23 Hf 16.58N 54.50 E
Mirdita 15 Ch 41.49N 19.56 E
Mirebalais 49 Kd 18.50N 72.06W
Mirebeau 11 Gh 46.47N 0.11 E
Mirecourt 11 Mf 48.18N 6.08 E
Mirepoix 11 Hk 43.05N 1.53 E
Mirgorod 19 Df 50.00N 33.40 E
Miri 22 Ni 4.23N 113.59 E
Miria 34 Gc 13.43N 9.07 E
Mirim, Lagoa- 52 Ki 32.45S 52.50W
Mirina 15 Ij 39.52N 25.04 E
Miriñay, Esteros del- 55 Di 28.49S 57.10W
Miriñay, Rio- 55 Dj 30.10S 57.39W
Mirny 66 Ge 66.33S 93.01 E
Mirny 22 Nc 62.33N 113.53 E
Mironovka 16 Ge 49.40N 31.01 E
Mirosławiec 10 Mc 53.21N 16.05 E
Mirpur 25 Eb 33.11N 73.46 E
Mirpur Khās 22 Ig 25.32N 69.00 E
Mirqah Sūr 24 Kd 36.50N 44.19 E
Mirsāle 35 Hd 5.58N 47.54 E
Mirşani 15 He 44.01N 24.01 E
Mirtóön Pélagos 15 Gm 37.00N 24.00 E
Miryang 28 Jg 35.29N 128.45 E
Mirzāpur 25 Gc 25.09N 82.35 E
Misaki 29 Ce 33.23N 132.07 E
Misawa 28 Pd 40.41N 141.24 E
Misery, Mount- 51c Ab 17.22N 62.48W
Mishan 27 Nb 45.34N 131.50 E
Mishawaka 44 De 41.40N 86.11W
Mi-Shima 28 Kg 34.47N 131.10 E
Mishima 29 Fd 35.07N 138.54 E
Mishraq, Khashm- 24 Lj 24.13N 46.18 E
Misilmeri 14 Hl 38.02N 13.27 E
Misima Island 60 Fj 10.40S 152.45 E
Misiones [3] 55 Dh 27.00S 57.00W
Misiones [2] 56 Jc 27.00S 55.00W
Misiones, Sierra de- 55 Eh 26.45S 54.20W
Miski, Enneri- 35 Bb 18.10N 17.45 E
Miškino 17 Ki 55.20N 63.55 E
Miskitos, Cayos- 47 Hf 14.23N 82.46W
Miskolc [2] 10 Qh 48.06N 20.43 E
Miskolc 6 If 48.06N 20.47 E
Mismār 35 Fb 18.13N 35.38 E
Misool, Pulau- 26 Jg 1.52S 130.10 E
Misquah Hills 43 Ib 47.17N 92.00W
Mişr=Egypt (EN) [1] 31 Jf 27.00N 30.00 E
Mişr al Jadīdah, Al Qāhirah- 33 Fc 30.06N 31.20 E
Mişrātah 31 Ie 32.23N 15.06 E
Mişrātah [3] 33 Cd 29.00N 16.00 E
Mişrātah, Ra's- 30 Ie 32.25N 15.05 E
Misserghin 13 Li 35.37N 0.44W
Missinaibi 42 Jf 50.44N 81.30W
Missinaibi Lake 44 Fa 48.23N 83.40W
Missinipe 42 He 55.36N 104.45W
Mission [S.D.-U.S.] 45 Fe 43.18N 100.40W
Mission [Tx.-U.S.] 45 Gm 26.13N 98.20W
Mission City 46 Db 49.08N 122.18W
Mission Range 46 Ic 47.30N 113.55W
Mississippi 38 Kg 29.00N 89.15W
Mississippi [2] 43 Je 32.50N 89.30W
Mississippi Delta 38 Kg 29.10N 89.15W
Mississippi Fan (EN) 43 Jf 26.45N 88.30W
Mississippi River 44 Ic 45.26N 76.16W
Mississippi Sound 45 Lk 30.15N 89.00W
Misso 8 Lg 57.33N 27.23 E
Missoula 39 He 46.52N 114.01W
Missour 32 Gc 33.03N 3.59W
Missouri 38 Jf 38.50N 90.08W
Missouri [2] 43 Id 38.30N 93.30W
Missouri, Coteau du- 45 Gc 46.00N 99.30W
Missouri Valley 45 If 41.33N 95.53W
Mistassibi 42 Kg 48.53N 72.13W
Mistassini 44 Ka 48.58N 72.40 E
Mistassini 42 Kf 50.30N 74.00W
Mistassini, Rivière- 42 Kg 48.42N 72.20W
Mistelbach an der Zaya 14 Kb 48.34N 16.34 E
Misterhult 8 Gg 57.28N 16.33 E
Mistrás 15 Fl 37.04N 22.22 E
Mistretta 14 Im 37.56N 14.22 E
Misugi 29 Ed 34.33N 136.15 E
Misumi [Jap.] 29 Bd 34.46N 131.58 E
Misumi [Jap.] 29 Be 32.37N 130.29 E
Mita, Punta- 48 Gg 32.04N 105.33W
Mitare, Rio- 49 Mh 11.28N 69.56W
Mitchell [Austl.] 59 Je 26.29S 147.58 E
Mitchell [Or.-U.S.] 46 Ed 44.34N 120.09W
Mitchell [S.D.-U.S.] 43 Hc 43.40N 98.01W
Mitchell, Mount- 38 Kf 35.46N 82.16W
Mitchell Range 59 Hb 12.50S 135.35 E
Mitchell River 57 Ff 15.12S 141.35 E
Mitchell River Mission 59 Ic 15.28S 141.44 E
Mitchelstown/Baile Mhistéala 9 Ei 52.16N 8.16W
Mithimna 15 Jj 39.22N 26.10 E
Mitiaro Island 57 Lf 19.49S 157.43W
Mitidja, Plaine de la- 13 Oh 36.36N 3.00 E
Mitilini 15 Jj 39.06N 26.33 E
Mitilinis, Stenón- 15 Jj 39.10N 26.35 E
Mitla 47 Ee 16.55N 96.17W
Mitla, Laguna- 48 Ii 17.03N 100.25W
Mito 27 Pd 36.22N 140.28 E
Mitomoni 36 Ge 11.32S 35.19 E

Index Symbols

[1] Independent Nation
[2] State, Region
[3] District, County
[4] Municipality
[5] Colony, Dependency
Continent
Physical Region
Historical or Cultural Region
Mount, Mountain
Volcano
Hill
Mountains, Mountain Range
Hills, Escarpment
Plateau, Upland
Pass, Gap
Plain, Lowland
Delta
Salt Flat
Valley, Canyon
Crater, Cave
Karst Features
Depression
Polder
Desert, Dunes
Forest, Woods
Heath, Steppe
Oasis
Cape, Point
Coast, Beach
Cliff
Peninsula
Isthmus
Sandbank
Island
Atoll
Rock, Reef
Islands, Archipelago
Rocks, Reefs
Coral Reef
Well, Spring
Geyser
River, Stream
Waterfall Rapids
River Mouth, Estuary
Lake
Salt Lake
Intermittent Lake
Reservoir
Swamp, Pond
Canal
Glacier
Ice Shelf, Pack Ice
Ocean
Sea
Gulf, Bay
Strait, Fjord
Lagoon
Bank
Seamount
Tablemount
Ridge
Shelf
Basin
Escarpment, Sea Scarp
Fracture
Trench, Abyss
National Park, Reserve
Point of Interest
Recreation Site
Cave, Cavern
Historic Site
Ruins
Wall, Walls
Church, Abbey
Temple
Scientific Station
Airport
Port
Lighthouse
Mine
Tunnel
Dam, Bridge

Mitsamiouli 37 Gb 11.23S 43.18 E
Mitsinjo 37 Hc 16.00S 45.52 E
Mitsio, Nosy- 37 Hb 12.54S 48.36 E
Mitsiwa=Massawa (EN) 31 Kg 15.37N 39.39 E
Mitsiwa Channel 35 Fb 15.30N 40.00 E
Mitsuishi 29a Cb 42.15N 142.33 E
Mitsukaido 29 Fc 36.01N 139.59 E
Mitsuke 29 Fc 37.32N 138.56 E
Mitsushima 29 Ad 34.16N 129.20 E
Mittelfranken 10 Gg 49.20N 10.40 E
Mittelland 14 Bd 46.50N 7.05 E
Mittellandkanal 5 He 52.16N 11.41 E
Mittelmark 10 Jd 52.20N 13.20 E
Mittenwald 10 Hi 47.27N 11.15 E
Mittersheim 12 If 48.52N 6.56 E
Mittersill 14 Gc 47.16N 12.29 E
Mittweida 10 If 50.59N 12.59 E
Mitú 53 Ie 1.08N 70.03W
Mitumba, Monts-=Mitumba Range (EN) 30 Ji 6.00S 29.00 E
Mitumba Range (EN)= Mitumba, Monts- 30 Ji 6.00S 29.00 E
Mituva 8 Jj 55.00N 22.45 E
Mitwaba 36 Ed 8.38S 27.20 E
Mitzic 36 Bb 0.47N 11.34 E
Miura 29 Fd 35.08N 139.37 E
Miura-Hantō 29 Fd 35.15N 139.40 E
Mixco Viejo 49 Bf 14.52N 90.40W
Mixian 28 Bg 34.31N 113.22 E
Mixteco, Rio- 48 Jh 18.11N 98.30W
Miya-Gawa 29 Ed 34.32N 136.42 E
Miyagi Ken [2] 28 Pe 38.30N 140.50 E
Miyagusuku-Jima 29b Ab 26.22N 127.59 E
Miyāh, Wādī al- (Eg.) 24 Ej 25.00N 33.23 E
Miyāh, Wādī al- (Sau. Ar.) 24 Gi 26.06N 36.31 E
Miyāh, Wādī al- (Syr.) 24 He 34.44N 39.57 E
Miyake-Jima 27 Oe 34.05N 139.30 E
Miyako 27 Pd 39.38N 141.57 E
Miyako-Jima 27 Mg 24.45N 125.20 E
Miyakonojō 28 Ki 31.44N 131.04 E
Miyako-Rettō 27 Lg 24.25N 125.00 E
Miyako-Wan 29 Hb 39.40N 142.00 E
Miyama 29 Dd 35.17N 135.34 E
Miyanojō 29 Bf 31.54N 130.27 E
Miyanoura-Dake 28 Ki 30.20N 130.29 E
Miyata 29 Be 33.45N 130.45 E
Miyazaki 27 Ne 31.54N 131.26 E
Miyazaki Ken [2] 28 Kh 32.05N 131.20 E
Miyazu 28 Mg 35.32N 135.11 E
Miyazuka-Yama 29 Fd 34.24N 139.16 E
Miyazu-Wan 29 Dd 35.35N 135.13 E
Miyoshi 28 Lg 34.48N 132.51 E
Miyun 27 Kc 40.22N 116.53 E
Miyun Shuiku 28 Dd 40.31N 116.58 E
Mizan Teferi 35 Fd 6.53N 35.28 E
Mizdah 33 Bc 31.26N 12.59 E
Mizen Head/Carn Ui Néid 5 Fe 51.27N 9.49W
Mizil 15 Je 45.01N 26.27 E
Mizorām [3] 25 Id 23.00N 93.00 E
Mizque 54 Eg 17.56S 65.19W
Mizuho 29 Cd 34.50N 132.29 E
Mizuho 66 Ef 70.43S 40.20 E
Mizunami 29 Ed 35.22N 137.15 E
Mizusawa 28 Pe 39.08N 141.08 E
Mjadel 8 Lj 54.54N 27.03 E
Mjakiševo 8 Mh 56.30N 28.54 E
Mjakit 20 Kd 61.23N 152.10 E
Mjällom 8 Ha 62.59N 18.26 E
Mjaundža 20 Jd 63.02N 147.13 E
Mjölby 7 Dg 58.19N 15.08 E
Mjøndalen 8 De 59.45N 10.01 E
Mjorn 8 Eg 57.54N 12.25 E
Mjøsa 5 Hc 60.40N 11.00 E
Mkoani 36 Gd 5.22S 39.39 E
Mkokotoni 36 Gd 5.52S 39.15 E
Mkushi Bona 36 Ee 13.37S 29.23 E
Mkushi River 36 Fe 13.33S 29.40 E
Mkuze 37 Ee 27.10S 32.00 E
Mladá Boleslav 10 Kf 50.21N 14.54 E
Mladenovac 15 De 44.26N 20.42 E
Mlava 15 Ee 44.45N 21.14 E
Mława 10 Qc 53.06N 20.23 E
Mljet 14 Lh 42.45N 17.30 E
Mljetski kanal 14 Lh 42.48N 17.35 E
Mmadinare 37 Dd 21.53S 27.45 E
Mnichovo Hradiště 10 Kf 50.32N 14.59 E
Mnogoveršinny 20 If 53.55N 139.50 E
Moa 49 Jc 20.40N 74.56W
Moa 34 Cd 6.59N 11.36W
Moa, Pulau- 26 Ih 8.10S 127.56 E
Moab 43 Fd 38.35N 109.33W
Moabi 36 Bc 2.24S 10.59 E
Moala 63d Bc 18.36S 179.53 E
Moamba 37 Ee 25.36S 32.15 E
Moanda (Gabon) 36 Bc 1.34S 13.11 E
Moanda (Zaire) 36 Bd 5.56S 12.21 E
Moatize 37 Ec 16.10S 33.46 E
Moba 31 Ji 7.03S 29.47 E
Mobara 29 Gd 35.25N 140.17 E
Mobārakeh 24 Nf 32.20N 51.30 E
Mobaye 31 Jh 4.19N 21.11 E
Mobayi-Mbongo 36 Db 4.18N 21.11 E
Mobeka 36 Cb 1.53N 19.46 E
Moberly 43 Id 39.25N 92.26W
Mobile 39 Kf 30.42N 88.05W
Mobile Bay 43 Je 30.25N 88.00W
Mobridge 43 Gb 45.32N 100.26W
Mobuto Sese Seko, Lac-= Albert, Lake- (EN) 30 Kh 1.40N 31.00 E
Moca 49 Ld 19.24N 70.31W
Moçambique= Mozambique (EN) [1] 31 Kj 18.15S 35.00 E
Moçambique= Mozambique (EN) 31 Lk 15.03S 40.45 E
Moçambique, Canal de-= Mozambique Channel (EN) 30 Lk 20.00S 43.00 E
Moçâmedes → Namibe 36 Bf 15.20S 12.30 E
Moçâmedes → Namibe 31 Ij 15.12S 12.10 E
Mocapra, Rio- 50 Ci 7.56N 66.46W
Mocha, Isla- 56 Fe 38.22S 73.56W
Moc Hoa 25 Lf 10.46N 105.56 E
Mochudi 37 Dd 24.23S 26.08 E
Mocímboa da Praia 31 Lj 11.20S 40.21 E
Möckeln 8 Fh 56.40N 14.10 E
Mockfjärd 8 Fd 60.30N 14.58 E
Môco, Serra- 30 Ij 12.28S 15.10 E
Mocoa 54 Cc 1.09N 76.38W
Mococa 55 Ie 21.28S 47.01W
Mocovi 55 Ci 28.24S 59.42W
Moctezuma (Mex.) 47 Cc 29.48N 109.42W
Moctezuma (Mex.) 48 If 22.45N 101.05W
Moctezuma (Mex.) 48 Fb 30.12N 106.26W
Moctezuma, Rio (Mex.) 48 Ec 29.09N 109.40W
Moctezuma, Rio- (Mex.) 48 Jg 21.59N 98.34W
Mocuba 31 Kj 16.51S 36.56 E
Mocubúri 37 Fb 14.39S 38.54 E
Močurica 15 Jg 42.31N 26.32 E
Modane 11 Mi 45.12N 6.40 E
Modderrivier 37 Ce 29.02S 24.37 E
Modena (It.) 14 Ef 44.40N 10.55 E
Modena (Ut.-U.S.) 46 Ih 37.49N 113.55W
Moder 11 Of 48.49N 8.06 E
Modesto 43 Cd 37.39N 120.59W
Modica 14 In 36.52N 14.46 E
Modjamboli 36 Db 2.28N 22.06 E
Modjigo 34 Hb 17.09N 13.12 E
Mödling 14 Kb 48.05N 16.28 E
Modriča 14 Mf 44.58N 18.18 E
Modum 8 Ce 59.55N 10.00 E
Moe 59 Jg 38.10S 146.15 E
Moelv 7 Cf 60.56N 10.42 E
Moen 64d Bb 7.26N 151.52 E
Moengo 54 Hb 5.37N 54.24W
Moen-jo-Daro 25 Dc 27.19N 68.07 E
Moenkopi Wash 46 Ji 35.54N 111.26W
Moerbeke 12 Fc 51.10N 3.56 E
Moers 10 Ce 51.27N 6.39 E
Moeskroen/Mouscron 11 Jd 50.44N 3.13 E
Moffat 9 Jf 55.20N 3.27W
Moga 36 Ec 2.21S 26.49 E
Mogadishu (EN)= Muqdisho 31 Lh 2.03N 45.22 E
Mogadouro 13 Fc 41.20N 6.43W
Mogadouro, Serra do- 13 Fc 41.19N 6.40W
Mogāl 24 Nd 36.35N 50.35 E
Mogalakwena 37 Dd 22.27S 28.55 E
Mogami 29 Gb 38.45N 140.30 E
Mogami-Gawa 28 Oe 38.54N 139.50 E
Mogami Trench (EN) 29 Fb 39.00N 139.00 E
Mogaung 25 Jc 25.18N 96.56 E
Mogho 35 Ge 4.49N 40.19 E
Mogielnica 10 Qe 51.42N 20.43 E
Mogilev 6 Je 53.56N 30.18 E
Mogilev-Podolski 16 Ee 48.27N 27.48 E
Mogilevskaja Oblast [3] 19 De 53.45N 30.30 E
Mogilno 10 Nd 52.40N 17.58 E
Mogincual 37 Gc 15.34S 40.24 E
Mogoča 22 Nd 53.44N 119.44 E
Mogočin 20 De 57.43N 83.40 E
Mogogh 35 Ed 8.26N 31.19 E
Mogojto 20 Gf 54.25N 110.27 E
Mogojtuj 20 Gf 51.15N 114.58 E
Mogok 25 Jd 22.55N 96.30 E
Mogollon Rim 43 Ee 34.20N 111.00W
Mogotes, Punta- 55 Dn 38.06S 57.33W
Mogotón, Pico- 49 Dg 13.45N 86.23W
Mogrein 31 Ff 25.13N 11.34W
Mogroum 35 Bc 11.06N 15.25 E
Moguer 13 Fg 37.16N 6.50W
Mogzon 20 Gf 51.42N 111.59 E
Mohács 10 Ok 45.59N 18.42 E
Mohaka 62 Gc 39.07S 177.12 E
Mohaka 62 Gc 39.07S 177.12 E
Mohales Hoek 37 Df 30.15S 27.25 E
Mohall 45 Fb 48.46N 101.31W
Moḥammadābād 24 Pg 31.47N 54.27 E
Mohammadia 13 Mi 35.35N 0.04 E
Mohammedia 32 Fc 33.42N 7.24W
Mohanganj 25 Id 24.54N 90.59 E
Mohang-ni 28 If 36.46N 126.08 E
Mohave, Lake- 43 Ed 35.25N 114.38W
Mohawk Mountains 46 Ij 32.25N 113.25W
Mohe 22 Od 53.27N 122.18 E
Moheda 8 Fh 57.00N 14.34 E
Mohéli → Mwali 30 Lj 12.15S 43.45 E
Moher, Cliffs of-/Aillte an Mhothair 9 Di 52.58N 9.27W
Mohican, Cape- 40 Fd 60.12N 167.28W
Mohinora 38 Ig 26.06N 107.04W
Möhnesee 12 Kc 51.29N 8.05 E
Mohns Ridge (EN) 5 Ga 73.00N 5.00 E
Moholm 8 Ff 58.37N 14.02 E
Mohon, Charleville-Mézières- 12 Ge 49.46N 4.43 E
Mohon Peak 46 Ii 34.57N 113.15W
Mohoro 36 Gd 8.08S 39.10 E
Mohotani, Ile- 61 Na 9.59S 138.49W
Mohovaja 20 Kf 53.01N 158.38 E
Moi 8 Bf 58.28N 6.32 E
Moikovac 15 Cg 42.58N 19.35 E
Moimenta da Beira 13 Ed 40.59N 7.37W
Moindou 63b Be 21.42S 165.41 E
Moineşti 15 Jc 46.28N 26.29 E
Moirai 15 Hn 35.03N 24.52 E
Mo i Rana 6 Hb 66.18N 14.08 E
Mõisaküla/Myjzakjula 7 Fg 58.07N 25.10 E
Moisés Ville 55 Bj 30.43S 61.29W
Moisie 42 Kf 50.13N 66.06W
Moisie 42 Kf 50.11N 66.06W
Moissac 11 Hj 44.06N 1.05 E
Moïssala 35 Bd 8.21N 17.46 E
Moitaco 50 Dh 8.01N 61.21W
Möja 8 He 59.25N 18.55 E
Mojácar 13 Kg 37.08N 1.51W
Mojada, Sierra- 48 Hd 27.15N 103.45W
Mojana, Caño- 49 Ji 9.02N 74.46W
Mojave 43 Dd 35.03N 118.10W
Mojave Desert 38 Hf 35.00N 117.00W
Mojiguaçu, Rio- 55 He 20.53S 48.10W
Moji Mirim 55 If 22.26S 46.57W
Mojjero 20 Fc 68.44N 103.30 E
Mojo 35 Fd 8.36N 39.09 E
Mojo 35 Gd 8.00N 41.50 E
Mojos, Llanos de- 52 Jg 15.00S 65.00W
Moju, Rio- 54 Id 1.40S 48.25W
Mojynty 19 Hf 47.10N 73.18 E
Mokambo 36 Ee 12.25S 28.21 E
Mokapu Peninsula 65a Db 21.26N 157.45W
Mokau 62 Fc 38.42S 174.35 E
Mokau 61 Dg 38.41S 174.37 E
Mokhotlong 37 De 29.17S 29.05 E
Mokil Atoll 57 Gd 6.40N 159.47 E
Moklakan 20 Gf 54.48N 118.56 E
Möklinta 8 Gd 60.05N 16.32 E
Mokochu, Khao- 25 Je 15.56N 99.06 E
Mokohinau Islands 62 Fa 35.55S 175.05 E
Mokolo 34 Hc 10.45N 13.48 E
Mokp'o 22 Of 34.47N 126.23 E
Mokra Gora 15 Dg 42.50N 20.25 E
Mokrany 10 Ue 51.48N 24.23 E
Mokrin 15 Dd 45.56N 20.25 E
Mokša 5 Ke 54.44N 41.53 E
Mokwa 34 Gd 9.17N 5.03 E
Mol 11 Lc 51.11N 5.07 E
Mola di Bari 14 Li 41.04N 17.05 E
Molango 48 Jg 20.47N 98.43W
Moláoi 15 Fm 36.48N 22.51 E
Molara 14 Dj 40.50N 9.45 E
Molas, Punta- 48 Pg 20.35N 86.44W
Molat 14 If 44.13N 14.50 E
Molatón 13 Kf 38.59N 1.24W
Moldau (EN)=Vltava 5 He 50.21N 14.30 E
Moldava nad Bodvou 10 Qh 48.37N 21.00 E
Moldavia (EN) = Moldova 15 Jc 46.30N 27.00 E
Moldavia (EN)=Moldova 5 If 46.30N 27.00 E
Moldavian SSR (EN)= Moldavskaja SSR [2] 19 Cf 47.00N 29.00 E
Moldavskaja Sovetskaja Socialističeskaja Respublika [2] 19 Cf 47.00N 29.00 E
Moldavskaja SSR/ Respublika Sovetike Socialiste Moldovenjaske [2] 19 Cf 47.00N 29.00 E
Moldavskaja SSR= Moldavian SSR (EN) [2] 19 Cf 47.00N 29.00 E
Molde 6 Gc 62.44N 7.11 E
Moldefjorden 8 Bb 62.45N 7.05 E
Moldotau, Hrebet- 18 Jd 40.00N 74.50 E
Moldova 15 Jc 46.54N 26.58 E
Moldova = Moldavia (EN) 15 Jc 46.30N 27.00 E
Moldova = Moldavia (EN) 5 If 46.30N 27.00 E
Moldova Nouă 15 Ee 44.44N 21.41 E
Moldoveanu, Virful- 5 If 45.36N 24.44 E
Moldoviţa 15 Ib 47.41N 25.32 E
Mole 12 Bc 51.24N 0.20W
Molène, Ile de- 11 Bf 48.24N 4.58W
Molens van Kinderdijk 12 Gc 51.52N 4.40 E
Molepolole 31 Jk 24.25S 25.30 E
Môle Saint-Nicolas 49 Kd 19.47N 73.22W
Moletai/Moletaj 8 Ki 55.13N 25.36 E
Moletaj/Moletai 8 Ki 55.13N 25.36 E
Molfetta 14 Ki 41.12N 16.36 E
Molihong Shan 28 Hc 42.11N 124.43 E
Molina, Parameras de- 13 Jd 40.55N 2.01W
Molina de Aragón 13 Kd 40.51N 1.53W
Molina de Segura 13 Kf 38.03N 1.12W
Moline 45 Kf 41.30N 90.31W
Moliniere Point 51p Bb 12.05N 61.45W
Molise [2] 14 Ii 41.40N 14.30 E
Molkābād 24 Oe 34.32N 52.35 E
Molkom 8 Ee 59.36N 13.43 E
Möll 14 Hd 46.50N 13.26 E
Moll 55 Cl 35.04S 59.39W
Mollafeneri 15 Mi 40.54N 29.30 E
Mölle 8 Eh 56.17N 12.29 E
Mollendo 53 Ig 17.02S 72.01W
Molliens-Dreuil 12 Ee 49.52N 2.01 E
Mölln 10 Gc 53.38N 10.41 E
Möllösund 8 Df 58.04N 11.28 E
Mölndal 7 Ch 57.39N 12.01 E
Mölnlycke 8 Ef 57.39N 12.09 E
Moločansk 16 If 47.10N 35.36 E
Moločny, Liman- 16 If 46.30N 35.20 E
Molócuè 37 Fc 17.03S 38.52 E
Molodečno 19 Ce 54.19N 26.53 E
Molodežnaja 66 Ee 67.40S 45.51 E
Molodi 8 Mf 58.00N 28.52 E
Molodogvardejskoje 19 He 54.07N 70.50 E
Mologa 5 Jd 58.50N 37.11 E
Molokai Island 57 Lb 21.08N 157.00W
Moloma 7 Lg 58.20N 48.28 E
Molong 9 Jf 33.06S 148.52 E
Molopo 30 Jk 28.31S 20.13 E
Molounbou 34 Ie 2.02N 15.13 E
Molteno 37 Df 31.24S 26.22 E
Molu, Pulau- 26 Jh 6.45S 131.33 E
Moluccas (EN)=Maluku, Kepulauan- 57 De 2.00S 128.00 E
Molucca Sea (EN)=Maluku, Laut- 21 Oj 0.05S 125.00 E
Molygino 20 Ee 58.11N 94.45 E
Moma 20 Jc 66.20N 143.06 E
Moma 37 Fc 16.44S 39.14 E
Mombaça 54 Ke 5.45S 39.28W
Mombasa 31 Ki 4.03S 39.40 E
Mombo 36 Gc 4.53S 38.17 E
Momboyo 36 Cc 0.16S 19.00 E
Mombuca, Serra da- 55 Fd 18.15S 52.26W
Momčilgrad 15 Ih 41.32N 25.25 E
Mömling 12 Le 49.50N 9.09 E
Momotombo, Volcán- 49 Dg 12.26N 86.33W
Mompono 36 Db 0.04N 21.48 E
Mompós 54 Db 9.14N 74.27W
Momski Hrebet 20 Jc 66.00N 145.00 E
Mon [2] 25 Je 17.22N 97.20 E
Møn 7 Ci 55.00N 12.20 E
Mona, Canal de la-=Mona Passage (EN) 38 Mh 18.30N 67.45W
Mona, Isla- 47 Ke 18.05N 67.54W
Mona, Punta- 49 Fi 9.38N 82.37W
Monach Islands 9 Fd 57.32N 7.40W
Monaco [1] 6 Gg 43.42N 7.23 E
Monadhliath Mountains 9 Id 57.15N 4.10W
Monagas [2] 54 Fb 9.20N 63.00W
Monaghan/Muineachán [2] 9 Gg 54.10N 7.00W
Monaghan/Muineachán 9 Gg 54.15N 6.58W
Monahans 45 Ek 31.36N 102.54W
Mona Passage (EN)=Mona, Canal de la- 38 Mh 18.30N 67.45W
Monapo 37 Gb 14.55S 40.18 E
Monarch Mountain 42 Ef 51.54N 125.54W
Monashee Mountains 42 Ff 51.00N 118.43W
Monastyrščina 16 Gb 54.19N 31.48 E
Monatélé 34 He 4.16N 11.12 E
Monbetsu (Jap.) 28 Qc 42.28N 142.07 E
Monbetsu (Jap.) 27 Pc 44.21N 143.22 E
Monbetsu-Shokotsu 29a Ca 44.23N 143.16 E
Moncalieri 14 Be 45.00N 7.41 E
Moncalvo 14 Ce 45.03N 8.16 E
Monção (Braz.) 54 Id 3.30S 45.15W
Monção (Port.) 13 Db 42.05N 8.29W
Moncayo 13 Kc 41.46N 1.50W
Moncayo, Sierra del- 13 Kc 41.45N 1.50W
Mončegorsk 19 Db 67.56N 32.58 E
Mönchengladbach 10 Ce 51.12N 6.26 E
Mönchengladbach-Rheydt 12 Ic 51.10N 6.27 E
Mönchengladbach-Wickrath 12 Ic 51.08N 6.25 E
Mönchgut 10 Jb 54.20N 13.40 E
Monchique 13 Dg 37.19N 8.33W
Monchique, Serra de- 13 Dg 37.19N 8.36W
Monclova 39 Ig 26.54N 101.25W
Moncton 39 Me 46.06N 64.07W
Mondai 55 Fh 27.05S 53.25W
Mondego 13 Dd 40.09N 8.52W
Mondego, Cabo- 13 Dd 40.11N 8.55W
Mondeville 12 Be 49.10N 0.19W
Mondjoko 36 Dc 1.41S 21.12 E
Mondo 35 Bc 13.43N 15.32 E
Mondoñedo 13 Ea 43.26N 7.22W
Mondorf-les-Bains/Bad Mondorf 12 Ie 49.30N 6.17 E
Mondoubleau 11 Gg 47.59N 0.54 E
Mondovì 14 Bf 44.23N 7.49 E
Mondragone 14 Hi 41.07N 13.53 E
Mondy 20 Ff 51.40N 100.59 E
Monemvasia 15 Gm 36.41N 23.03 E
Monessen 44 He 40.09N 79.53W
Monett 45 Jh 36.55N 93.55W
Monfalcone 14 He 45.49N 13.32 E
Monferrato 14 Cf 44.55N 8.05 E
Monforte 13 Ee 39.03N 7.26W
Monforte de Lemos 13 Eb 42.31N 7.30W
Monga 36 Db 4.12N 22.49 E
Mongala 36 Cb 1.53N 19.46 E
Mongalla 35 Ed 5.12N 31.46 E
Mongbwalu 36 Fb 1.57N 30.02 E
Mong Cai 25 Ld 21.32N 107.58 E
Monger, Lake- 59 De 29.15S 117.05 E
Mongga 63a Cb 7.57S 156.59 E
Monggolküre/Zhaosu 27 Dc 43.10N 81.07 E
Monghyr → Munger 25 Hc 25.23N 86.28 E
Monginevro, Colle del- 11 Mj 44.56N 6.44 E
Mongo 31 Ig 12.11N 18.42 E
Mongo 34 Cd 9.34N 12.11W
Mongol Altajn Nuruu → Mongolski Altaj= Mongolian Altai (EN) 21 Le 46.30N 93.00 E
Mongol Ard-Uls=Mongolia (EN) [1] 22 Me 47.00N 104.00 E
Mongolia (EN)=Mongol Ard-Uls [1] 22 Me 47.00N 104.00 E
Mongolian Altai (EN)= Mongol Altajn Nuruu → Mongolski Altaj 21 Le 46.30N 93.00 E
Mongolian Altai (EN)= Mongolski Altaj (Mongol Altajn Nuruu) 21 Le 46.30N 93.00 E
Mongolski Altaj (Mongol Altajn Nuruu)=Mongolian Altai (EN) 21 Le 46.30N 93.00 E
Mongonu 34 Hc 12.41N 13.36 E
Mongororo 35 Cc 12.01N 22.28 E
Mongoumba 35 Be 3.38N 18.36 E
Mŏng Pan 25 Jd 20.19N 98.22 E
Mongrove, Punta- 48 Hi 17.56N 102.11W
Mongu 31 Jj 15.17S 23.08 E
Monguel 32 Ef 16.25N 13.08W
Mŏng Yai 25 Jd 22.25N 98.02 E
Monheim 12 Ic 51.05N 6.53 E
Mönichkirchen 14 Kc 47.30N 16.02 E
Mon Idée, Auvillers-lès-Forges- 12 Ge 49.52N 4.21 E
Monigotes 55 Bj 30.30S 61.39W
Moní Hosiou Loukā 15 Fk 38.24N 22.49 E
Monistrol-sur-Loire 11 Ki 45.17N 4.10 E
Monito, Isla- 51a Ab 18.09N 67.56W
Monitor Peak 46 Gg 38.50N 116.32W
Monitor Range 46 Gg 38.45N 116.40W
Monjolos 55 Jd 18.18S 44.05W
Monkayo 26 Ie 7.50N 126.00 E
Monkey Bay 36 Fe 14.05S 34.55 E
Monkey Point 49 Fg 11.36N 83.39W
Monkey River 49 Ce 16.22N 88.29W
Mońki 10 Sc 53.24N 22.49 E
Monkoto 36 Dc 1.38S 20.39 E
Monmouth (Il.-U.S.) 45 Kf 40.55N 90.39W
Monmouth 9 Kj 51.45N 3.00W
Monmouth (Or.-U.S.) 46 Dd 44.51N 123.14W
Monmouth (Wales-U.K.) 9 Kj 51.50N 2.43W
Monmouth Mountain 46 Da 51.00N 123.47W
Mönne 10 De 51.28N 7.30 E
Monnikendam 12 Hb 52.27N 5.02 E
Monnow 9 Kj 51.48N 2.42W
Mono 63a Bb 7.20S 155.35 E
Mono [3] 34 Fd 6.45N 1.50 E
Monobe-Gawa 29 Ce 33.32N 133.42 E
Mono Lake 43 Dd 38.00N 119.00W
Monólithos 15 Km 36.07N 27.45 E
Monopoli 14 Lj 40.57N 17.18 E
Monor 10 Pi 47.21N 19.27 E
Monou 35 Cb 16.24N 22.11 E
Monóvar 13 Lf 38.26N 0.50W
Monowai, Lake- 62 Bf 45.55S 167.25 E
Monreal 12 Jd 50.18N 7.10 E
Monreal del Campo 13 Kd 40.47N 1.21W
Monreale 14 Hl 38.05N 13.17 E
Monroe (Ga.-U.S.) 44 Fi 33.47N 83.43W
Monroe (La.-U.S.) 39 Jf 32.33N 92.07W
Monroe (Mi.-U.S.) 44 Fe 41.55N 83.24W
Monroe (N.C.-U.S.) 44 Gh 34.59N 80.33W
Monroe (Or.-U.S.) 46 Dd 44.19N 123.18W
Monroe (Wi.-U.S.) 45 Le 42.36N 89.38W
Monroe, Lake- 44 Df 39.05N 86.25W
Monroe City 45 Kg 39.39N 91.44W
Monroeville 44 Dj 31.31N 87.20W
Monrovia 31 Fh 6.19N 10.48W
Mons/Bergen 11 Jd 50.27N 3.56 E
Monsanto 13 Ed 40.02N 7.07W
Monschau 10 Cf 50.33N 6.15 E
Monselice 14 Fe 45.14N 11.45 E
Monserrate, Isla- 48 De 25.41N 111.05W
Monsheim 12 Ke 49.38N 8.12 E
Møns Klint 8 Ej 54.58N 12.33 E
Mönsterås 7 Dh 57.02N 16.26 E
Montabaur 10 Df 50.26N 7.50 E
Montagna Grande 14 Gm 37.56N 12.44 E
Montagne 11 Jh 46.10N 3.40 E
Montagu 66 Ad 58.25S 26.20W
Montague 40 Je 60.00N 147.30W
Montague, Isla- 48 Bb 31.45N 114.48W
Montaigu 11 Eh 46.59N 1.19W
Montalbán 13 Ld 40.50N 0.48W
Montalbano Ionico 14 Kj 40.17N 16.34 E
Montalcino 14 Fg 43.03N 11.29 E
Montalegre 13 Ec 41.49N 7.48W
Montalto di Castro 14 Fh 42.21N 11.37 E
Montalto Uffugo 14 Kk 39.24N 16.09 E
Montalvânia 55 Jb 14.28S 44.32W
Montana [2] 43 Eb 47.00N 110.00W
Montana 14 Bd 46.18N 7.30 E
Montánchez 13 Fe 39.13N 6.09W
Montánchez, Sierra de- 13 Ge 39.15N 5.55W
Montargis 11 Ig 48.00N 2.45 E
Montataire 12 Ee 49.16N 2.26 E
Montauban (Fr.) 11 Hj 44.01N 1.21 E
Montauban (Fr.) 11 Df 48.12N 2.03W
Montauk Point 44 Le 41.04N 71.52W
Montbard 11 Kg 47.37N 4.20 E
Montbéliard 11 Mg 47.31N 6.48 E
Montblanc 13 Nc 41.22N 1.10 E
Mont Blanc 5 Gf 45.50N 6.52 E
Montbrison 11 Ki 45.36N 4.03 E
Montceau-les-Mines 11 Kh 46.40N 4.22 E
Mont Cenis, Col du- 5 Gf 45.15N 6.54 E
Montchanin 11 Kh 46.45N 4.27 E
Mont Darwin 37 Ec 16.46S 31.35 E
Mont-de-Marsan 11 Fk 43.53N 0.30W
Montdidier 11 Ie 49.39N 2.34 E
Mont Dore 11 Ii 45.34N 2.49 E
Mont-Dore 63b Cf 22.17S 166.35 E
Monte, Laguna del- 55 Am 37.00S 62.28W
Monteagudo 54 Fg 19.49S 63.59W
Monte Alban 39 Jh 17.02N 96.45W
Monte Alegre 54 Hd 2.01S 54.04W
Monte Alegre, Rio- 55 Gc 17.16S 50.41W
Monte Alegre de Goiás 55 Ia 13.14S 47.10W
Montealegre del Castillo 13 Kf 38.47N 1.19W
Monte Alegre de Minas 55 Hd 18.52S 48.52W
Monte Azul 54 Jg 15.09S 42.53W
Montebello 44 Jc 45.39N 74.56W
Monte Bello Islands 59 Dd 20.25S 115.30 E
Monte Carlo 11 Nk 43.44N 7.25 E
Montecarlo 55 Eh 26.34S 54.47W
Monte Carmelo 55 Id 18.43S 47.29W
Monte Caseros 56 Id 30.15S 57.39W
Montecatini Terme 14 Eg 43.23N 10.45 E
Montecchio Maggiore 14 Fe 45.30N 11.24 E
Monte Comán 56 Gd 34.36S 67.54W
Montecristi 49 Ld 19.52N 71.39W
Montecristo 14 Eh 42.20N 10.20 E
Monte Cristo 55 Bb 14.43S 61.14W
Monte Ermoso 55 Bn 38.55S 61.33W
Monte Escobedo 48 Hf 22.18N 103.35W
Montefalco 14 Gh 42.52N 12.39 E
Montefeltro 14 Gg 43.55N 12.15 E
Montefiascone 14 Gh 42.32N 12.02 E
Montefrio 13 Hg 37.19N 4.01W
Montego Bay 39 Lh 18.30N 77.55W
Monteiro 54 Ke 7.53S 37.07W
Montelíbano 49 Ji 8.02N 75.29W
Montélimar 11 Kj 44.34N 4.45 E
Monte Lindo, Arroyo- 55 Cg 25.28S 59.25W
Monte Lindo, Rio- 56 Ib 23.56S 57.12W
Monte Lindo Chico, Riacho- 55 Dg 25.53S 57.53W

Index Symbols

[1] Independent Nation
[2] State, Region
[3] District, County
[4] Municipality
[5] Colony, Dependency
Continent
Physical Region
Historical or Cultural Region
Mount, Mountain
Volcano
Hill
Mountains, Mountain Range
Hills, Escarpment
Plateau, Upland
Pass, Gap
Plain, Lowland
Delta
Salt Flat
Valley, Canyon
Crater, Cave
Karst Features
Depression
Polder
Desert, Dunes
Forest, Woods
Heath, Steppe
Oasis
Cape, Point
Coast, Beach
Cliff
Peninsula
Isthmus
Sandbank
Island
Atoll
Rock, Reef
Islands, Archipelago
Rocks, Reefs
Coral Reef
Well, Spring
Geyser
River, Stream
Waterfall Rapids
River Mouth, Estuary
Lake
Salt Lake
Intermittent Lake
Reservoir
Swamp, Pond
Canal
Glacier
Ice Shelf, Pack Ice
Ocean
Sea
Gulf, Bay
Strait, Fjord
Lagoon
Bank
Seamount
Tablemount
Ridge
Shelf
Basin
Escarpment, Sea Scarp
Fracture
Trench, Abyss
National Park, Reserve
Point of Interest
Recreation Site
Cave, Cavern
Historic Site
Ruins
Wall, Walls
Church, Abbey
Temple
Scientific Station
Airport
Port
Lighthouse
Mine
Tunnel
Dam, Bridge

Monte Lindo Grande, Riacho- 55 Cg 25.45S 58.06W
Montello [Nv.-U.S.] 46 Hf 41.16N 114.12W
Montello [Wi.-U.S.] 45 Le 43.48N 89.20W
Montemorelos 47 Ec 25.12N 99.49W
Montemor-o-Novo 13 Df 38.39N 8.13W
Montemor-o-Velho 13 Dd 40.10N 8.41W
Montemuro, Serra de- 13 Dc 40.58N 8.01W
Montenegro 56 Jc 29.42S 51.28W
Montenegro (EN) = Crna Gora [2] 15 Cg 42.30N 19.18 E
Montenegro (EN)=Crna Gora 15 Cg 42.30N 19.18 E
Monte Plata 49 Md 18.48N 69.47W
Montepuez 37 Gb 12.32S 40.27 E
Montepuez 37 Fb 13.07S 39.00 E
Montepulciano 14 Fg 43.05N 11.47 E
Monte Quemado 56 Hc 25.48S 62.52W
Monte Real 13 De 39.51N 8.52W
Montereale, Passo di- 14 Hh 42.31N 13.13 E
Montereau-Faut-Yonne 11 If 48.23N 2.57 E
Monterey 43 Cd 36.37N 121.55W
Monterey Bay 43 Cd 36.45N 121.55W
Monteria 53 Ie 8.46N 75.53W
Montero 54 Fg 17.20S 63.15W
Monteros 56 Gc 27.10S 65.30W
Monterotondo 14 Gh 42.03N 12.37 E
Monterrey 39 Ig 25.40N 100.19W
Montesano 46 Dc 46.59N 123.36W
Monte San Savino 14 Fg 43.20N 11.43 E
Monte Sant'Angelo 14 Ji 41.42N 15.57 E
Monte Santu, Capo di- 14 Dj 45.05N 9.44 E
Montes Claros 53 Lg 16.43S 43.52W
Montes Claros de Goiás 55 Gb 15.54S 51.13W
Montesilvano 14 Ih 42.31N 14.09 E
Montevarchi 14 Fg 43.31N 11.34 E
Montevideo [2] 55 Dl 34.50S 56.10W
Montevideo [Mn.-U.S.] 45 Id 44.57N 95.43W
Montevideo [Ur.] 53 Ki 34.53S 56.11W
Monte Vista 45 Ch 37.35N 106.09W
Montfaucon 12 He 49.17N 5.08 E
Montfort-l'Amaury 12 Df 48.47N 1.49 E
Montfort-sur-Risle 12 Ce 49.18N 0.40 E
Montgenèvre, Col de- 11 Mj 44.56N 6.44 E
Montgomery 39 Kf 32.23N 86.18W
Montgomery Pass 46 Fh 38.00N 118.20W
Montguyon 11 Fi 45.13N 0.11W
Monthermé 12 Ge 49.53N 4.44 E
Monthey 14 Ad 46.15N 6.56 E
Monthois 12 Ge 49.19N 4.43 E
Monticello [Ar.-U.S.] 45 Kj 33.38N 91.47W
Monticello [Fl.-U.S.] 44 Fj 30.33N 83.52W
Monticello [Ia.-U.S.] 45 Ke 42.15N 91.12W
Monticello [In.-U.S.] 44 De 40.45N 86.46W
Monticello [Ky.-U.S.] 44 Eg 36.50N 84.51W
Monticello [N.Y.-U.S.] 44 Je 41.39N 74.41W
Monticello [Ut.-U.S.] 43 Fd 37.52N 109.21W
Montiel 13 Jf 38.42N 2.52W
Montiel, Campo de- 13 Jf 38.46N 2.44W
Montiel, Cuchilla de- 55 Cj 31.05S 59.10W
Montignac 11 Hi 45.04N 1.10 E
Montigny-le-Roi 11 Lf 48.00N 5.30 E
Montigny-les-Metz 11 Me 49.06N 6.09 E
Montigny-le-Tilleul 12 Gd 50.23N 4.22 E
Montijo [Pan.] 49 Gj 7.59N 81.03W
Montijo [Port.] 13 Df 38.42N 8.58W
Montijo [Sp.] 13 Ff 38.55N 6.37W
Montijo, Golfo de- 49 Gj 7.40N 81.07W
Montilla 13 Hg 37.35N 4.38W
Montividiu 55 Gc 17.24S 51.14W
Montivilliers 11 Ge 49.33N 0.12 E
Mont Joli 42 Kg 48.35N 68.11W
Mont-Laurier 42 Jg 46.33N 75.30W
Mont Louis 44 Oa 49.15N 65.43W
Mont-Louis 11 Il 42.31N 2.07 E
Montluçon 11 Ih 46.20N 2.36 E
Montmagny 42 Kg 46.59N 70.33W
Montmarault 11 Ih 46.19N 2.57 E
Montmédy 11 Le 49.31N 5.22 E
Montmirail 11 Jf 48.52N 3.32 E
Montmorency 12 Ef 49.00N 2.20 E
Montmorillon 11 Gh 46.26N 0.52 E
Montmort-Lucy 12 Ff 48.55N 3.49 E
Monto 59 Kd 24.52S 151.07 E
Montoire-sur-le-Loir 11 Gg 47.45N 0.52 E
Montone 14 Gf 44.24N 12.14 E
Montoro 13 Hf 38.01N 4.23W
Montpelier [Id.-U.S.] 43 Ec 42.19N 111.18W
Montpelier [Vt.-U.S.] 39 Le 44.16N 72.35W
Montpellier 6 Gg 43.36N 3.53 E
Montpon-Ménestérol 11 Gi 45.01N 0.10 E
Montréal 39 Le 45.31N 73.34W
Montreal Lake 42 Gf 54.20N 105.40W
Montreal River 44 Hb 47.08N 79.27W
Montréjeau 11 Gk 43.05N 0.35 E
Montreuil [Fr.] 11 Hd 50.28N 1.46 E
Montreuil [Fr.] 12 Ef 48.52N 2.26 E
Montreuil-l'Argillé 12 Cf 48.56N 0.29 E
Montreux 14 Ad 46.26N 6.55 E
Montrose [Co.-U.S.] 43 Fd 38.29N 107.53W
Montrose [Scot.-U.K.] 9 Ke 56.43N 2.29W
Monts, Pointe des- 44 Na 49.19N 67.23W
Mont-Saint-Aignan 12 De 49.28N 1.05 E
Mont-Saint-Michel, Baie du- 11 Ef 48.40N 1.40W
Montsalvy 11 Ij 44.42N 2.30 E
Montsant, Serra del-/ Montsant, Sierra de- 13 Mc 41.17N 0.50 E
Montsant, Sierra de-/ Montsant, Serra del- 13 Mc 41.17N 0.50 E
Montsec, Serra del-/ Montsech, Sierra del- 13 Mb 42.02N 0.50 E
Montsech, Sierra del-/ Montsec, Serra del- 13 Mb 42.02N 0.50 E
Montseny/Pallars, Montsent de- 13 Nb 42.29N 1.02 E
Montseny, Sierra de- 13 Oc 41.48N 2.24 E
Montserrado [3] 34 Cd 6.35N 10.35W
Montserrat [5] 39 Mh 16.45N 62.12W
Montserrat, Monasterio de- 13 Nc 41.35N 1.49 E
Montserrat, Monasterio de-/ Montserrat, Monèstir de- 13 Nc 41.35N 1.49 E
Montserrat, Monèstir de- 13 Nc 41.35N 1.49 E
Montserrat, Monèstir de-/ Montserrat, Monasterio de- 13 Nc 41.35N 1.49 E
Montuosa, Isla- 49 Fj 7.28N 82.14W
Montville 12 De 49.33N 1.07 E
Monument Peak 46 He 42.07N 114.14W
Monument Valley 46 Jh 36.50N 110.20W
Monveda 36 Db 2.57N 21.27 E
Monviso 5 Gg 44.40N 7.07 E
Monywa 25 Jd 22.07N 95.08 E
Monza 14 De 45.35N 9.16 E
Monze 36 Ef 16.16S 27.29 E
Monzen 29 Ec 37.17N 136.46 E
Monzón 13 Mc 41.55N 0.12 E
Mo'oka 29 Fc 36.27N 139.59 E
Moonbeam 44 Fa 49.25N 82.11W
Moonie 59 Ke 27.40S 150.19 E
Moonie River 59 Je 29.19S 148.43 E
Moonta 59 Hf 34.04S 137.35 E
Moora 58 Ch 30.39S 116.00 E
Moorcroft 46 Md 44.16N 104.57W
Moore 45 Hi 35.20N 97.29W
Moore, Lake- 57 Cg 29.50S 117.35 E
Moorea, Ile- 57 Mf 17.32S 149.50W
Moore's Island 44 Il 26.18N 77.33W
Moorhead 43 Hb 46.53N 96.45W
Moormerland 12 Ja 53.18N 7.26 E
Moormerland-Neermoor 12 Ja 53.18N 7.26 E
Moorreesburg 37 Bf 33.09S 18.40 E
Moosburg an der Isar 10 Hh 48.28N 11.56 E
Moose 38 Kd 50.48N 81.18W
Moosehead Lake 43 Nb 45.40N 69.40W
Moose Jaw 39 Id 50.23N 105.32W
Moose Jaw River 46 Ma 50.34N 105.17W
Moose Lake 45 Jc 46.25N 92.45W
Mooselookmeguntic Lake 44 Lc 44.53N 70.48W
Moose Mountain 45 Eb 49.45N 102.37W
Moose Mountain Creek 45 Eb 49.12N 102.10W
Moosomin 42 Hf 50.09N 101.40W
Moosonee 39 Kd 51.17N 80.39W
Mopeia 37 Fc 17.59S 35.43 E
Mopelia, Atoll- → Maupihaa Atoll 57 Lf 16.50S 153.55W
Mopti 31 Gg 14.30N 4.12W
Mopti [3] 34 Ec 14.40N 4.15W
Moqokorei 35 He 4.04N 46.08 E
Moquegua [2] 54 Dg 16.50S 70.55W
Moquegua 54 Dg 17.12S 70.56W
Mór 10 Oi 47.23N 18.12 E
Mor, Glen- 9 Id 57.10N 4.40W
Mora [Cam.] 34 Hc 11.03N 14.09 E
Mora [Port.] 13 Df 38.56N 8.10W
Mora [Sp.] 13 Ie 39.41N 3.46W
Mora [Swe.] 7 Df 61.00N 14.33 E
Morača 15 Cg 42.16N 19.09 E
Morača, Manastir- 15 Cg 42.46N 19.24 E
Morādābād 22 Jg 28.50N 78.47 E
Morada Nova de Minas 55 Jd 18.25S 45.22W
Móra d'Ebre/Mora de Ebro 13 Mc 41.05N 0.38 E
Mora de Ebro/Móra d'Ebre 13 Mc 41.05N 0.38 E
Mora de Rubielos 13 Ld 40.15N 0.45W
Morafenobe 37 Gc 17.49S 44.55 E
Morąg 10 Pc 53.56N 19.56 E
Mórahalom 10 Pj 46.13N 19.53 E
Moraleda, Canal- 56 Ff 44.30S 73.30W
Moraleja 13 Fd 40.04N 6.39W
Morales [Col.] 49 Ki 8.17N 73.52W
Morales [Guat.] 49 Cf 15.29N 88.49W
Morales, Laguna- 48 Kf 23.35N 97.45W
Moramanga 37 Hc 18.57S 48.11 E
Moran 46 Je 43.50N 110.28W
Morane Atoll 57 Ng 23.10S 137.07W
Morangas, Ribeirão- 55 Fd 19.39S 52.19W
Morant Bay 49 Ie 17.53N 76.25W
Morant Cays 47 Ie 17.24N 75.59W
Morant Point 49 Ie 17.55N 76.10W
Morar, Loch- 9 He 56.58N 5.45W
Morarano 37 Hc 17.46S 48.10 E
Mora River 45 Di 35.44N 104.23W
Moraska, Góra- 10 Md 52.30N 16.52 E
Morat/Murten 14 Bd 46.56N 7.08 E
Morata, Puerto de- 13 Kc 41.29N 1.31W
Moratalla 13 Kf 38.12N 1.53W
Moratuwa 25 Fg 6.46N 79.53 E
Morava 5 Hf 48.10N 16.59 E
Morava=Moravia (EN) 5 Hf 49.30N 17.00 E
Morava=Moravia (EN) 10 Mg 49.30N 17.00 E
Moravia (EN)=Morava 5 Hf 49.30N 17.00 E
Moravia (EN)=Morava 10 Mg 49.30N 17.00 E
Moravian Gate (EN)= Moravská Brána 5 Hf 49.33N 17.42 E
Moravian Upland (EN)= Českomoravská Vrchovina 5 Hf 49.20N 15.30 E
Moravica 15 Df 43.51N 20.05 E
Moravská Brána=Moravian Gate(EN) 5 Hf 49.33N 17.42 E
Moravské Budějovice 10 Lg 49.03N 15.49 E
Morawa 59 De 29.13S 116.00 E
Morawhanna 54 Gb 8.16N 59.45W
Moray Firth 5 Fd 57.50N 3.30W
Morbach 12 Je 49.49N 7.07 E
Morbihan [3] 11 Dg 47.55N 2.50W
Morbihan 11 Dg 47.35N 2.48W
Morbylånga 7 Dh 56.31N 16.23 E
Morcenx 11 Fj 44.02N 0.55W
Mordāb 24 Md 37.26N 49.25 E
Mordaga 27 La 51.14N 120.43 E
Morden 42 Hg 49.11N 98.05W
Mordovo 16 Lc 52.05N 40.46 E
Mordovskaja ASSR [3] 19 Ee 54.20N 44.30 E
Möre 8 Fh 56.25N 15.55 E
More, Ben- 9 Ie 56.23N 4.31W
Morea 37 Bd 22.41S 15.54 E
More Assynt, Ben- 9 Ic 58.07N 4.51W
Moreau River 43 Gb 45.18N 100.43W
Morecambe 9 Kg 54.04N 2.53W
Morecambe Bay 9 Kg 54.07N 3.00W
Moree 58 Fg 29.28S 149.51 E
Morehead [Ky.-U.S.] 44 Ff 38.11N 83.25W
Morehead [Pap.N.Gui.] 60 Ci 8.50S 141.57 E
Morehead City 39 Lf 34.43N 76.43W
Moreiz, Gora- 19 Gb 69.30N 62.05 E
Moreju 17 Ib 68.20N 59.45 E
Morelia 39 Ih 19.42N 101.07W
Morella 13 Ld 40.37N 0.06W
Morelos 48 Ic 28.25N 100.53W
Morelos [2] 47 Ee 18.45N 99.00W
Morena, Sierra- 5 Fh 38.00N 5.00W
Moreni 15 Ie 44.59N 25.39 E
Møre og Romsdal [2] 7 Be 62.40N 7.50 E
Moresby 42 Ef 52.45N 131.50W
Moreton Bay 59 Ke 27.20S 153.15 E
Moreton Island 59 Ke 27.10S 153.25 E
Moret-sur-Loing 11 If 48.22N 2.49 E
Moreuil 11 Ie 49.46N 2.29 E
Morez 11 Mh 46.31N 6.02 E
Morezu 15 Hd 45.09N 24.01 E
Mörfelden 12 Ke 49.59N 8.34 E
Morgan City 45 Kl 29.42N 91.12W
Morganfield 44 Dg 37.41N 87.55W
Morganton 44 Gh 35.45N 81.41W
Morgantown [Ky.-U.S.] 44 Dg 37.14N 86.41W
Morgantown [W.V.-U.S.] 44 Hf 39.38N 79.57W
Morges 14 Ad 46.31N 6.30 E
Morghāb 23 Jb 38.18N 61.12 E
Morhange 11 Mf 48.55N 6.38 E
Mori [China] 27 Fc 43.49N 90.11 E
Mori [Jap.] 28 Pc 42.06N 140.35 E
Moriarty 45 Ci 34.59N 106.03W
Morichal Largo, Río- 50 Eh 9.27N 62.25W
Moriguchi 29 Dd 34.44N 135.34 E
Morin Dawa (Nirji) 27 Lb 48.30N 124.28 E
Morioka 22 Qf 39.42N 141.09 E
Moriyoshi 29 Ga 40.07N 140.22 E
Moriyoshi-Yama 29 Gb 39.59N 140.33 E
Morjärv 7 Fc 66.04N 22.43 E
Morki 7 Lh 56.28N 49.00 E
Morko 8 Gf 59.00N 17.40 E
Morkoka 20 Gc 65.03N 115.40 E
Mørkøv 8 Di 55.40N 11.32 E
Morlaix 11 Cf 48.35N 3.50W
Morlanwelz 12 Gd 50.27N 4.14 E
Mörlunda 8 Fg 57.19N 15.51 E
Mormanno 14 Jk 39.53N 15.59 E
Morne-à-l'Eau 50 Fd 16.21N 61.31W
Morne Diablotin 47 Le 15.30N 61.24W
Mornington, Isla- 56 Eg 49.45S 75.23W
Mornington Island 59 Hc 16.35S 139.24 E
Moro 46 Ed 45.29N 120.44W
Morobe 58 Fe 7.45S 147.37 E
Morocco (EN)=Al Maghrib [1] 31 Ge 32.00N 5.50W
Morogoro 31 Ki 6.49S 37.40 E
Morogoro [3] 36 Gd 8.20S 37.00 E
Moro Gulf 26 He 6.51N 123.00 E
Moroleón 48 Ig 20.08N 101.12W
Morombe 31 Lk 21.44S 43.23 E
Morón [Arg.] 55 Cl 34.39S 58.37W
Morón [Cuba] 47 Id 22.06N 78.38W
Morón [Ven.] 54 Ea 10.29N 68.11W
Morona, Río- 54 Cd 4.45S 77.04W
Morondava 31 Lk 20.15S 44.17 E
Morón de la Frontera 13 Gg 37.08N 5.27W
Morones, Sierra- 48 Hg 21.55N 103.05W
Moroni 31 Lj 11.41S 43.16 E
Moron Us He 21 Lf 34.42N 94.50 E
Morotai, Pulau- 57 Dd 2.20N 128.25 E
Moroto 31 Kh 2.32N 34.39 E
Morovita 15 Ed 45.16N 21.16 E
Morozov 15 Ig 42.30N 25.10 E
Morozovsk 19 Ef 48.20N 41.50 E
Morpeth 9 Lf 55.10N 1.41W
Morphou → Güzelyurt 24 Ee 35.12N 32.59 E
Morrilton 45 Ji 35.09N 92.45W
Morrinhos 54 Ig 17.44S 49.07W
Morrinsville 62 Fb 37.39S 175.32 E
Morris [Il.-U.S.] 45 Lf 41.22N 88.26W
Morris [Man.-Can.] 42 Hg 49.21N 97.22W
Morris [Mn.-U.S.] 45 Id 45.35N 95.55W
Morris, Mount- 59 Ge 26.09S 131.04 E
Morrisburg 44 Jc 44.54N 75.11W
Morris Jesup, Kap- 67 Me 83.45N 35.50W
Morrison Dennis Cays 49 Ff 14.28N 82.53W
Morristown 44 Fg 36.13N 83.18W
Morrito 49 Eh 11.37N 85.05W
Morro, Punta del- 48 Kh 19.51N 96.27W
Morro Bay 43 Cd 35.22N 120.51W
Morro do Chapéu 54 Jf 11.33S 41.09W
Morrosquillo, Golfo de- 49 Ji 9.35N 75.40W
Morro Vermelho, Serra do- 55 Jc 17.45S 45.20W
Mörrum 8 Fh 56.11N 14.45 E
Morrumbala 37 Fc 17.20S 35.35 E
Morrumbene 37 Fd 23.39S 35.20 E
Mörrumsån 8 Fh 56.09N 14.44 E
Mors 8 Ch 56.50N 8.45 E
Moršansk 19 Ee 53.26N 41.49 E
Morsbach 12 Jd 50.52N 7.45 E
Morsberg 12 Ke 49.43N 8.54 E
Morsil 7 Ce 63.19N 13.38 E
Mörskom/Myrskylä 8 Kd 60.40N 25.51 E
Morsott 14 Co 35.40N 8.01 E
Mortagne 11 Mf 48.33N 6.27 E
Mortagne-au-Perche 11 Gf 48.31N 0.33 E
Mortagne-sur-Sèvre 11 Fg 47.00N 0.57W
Mortain 11 Ff 48.39N 0.56W
Mortara 14 Ce 45.15N 8.44 E
Mortcha 30 Jg 16.00N 21.10 E
Morteau 11 Mg 47.04N 6.37 E
Morteaux-Couliboeuf 12 Bf 48.56N 0.04W
Morteros 56 Hd 30.42S 62.00W
Mortes, Rio das- 55 Je 21.09S 44.53W
Mortesoro 35 Ec 10.12N 34.09 E
Mortlock Islands 57 Gd 5.27N 153.40 E
Morton 46 Dc 46.33N 122.17W
Mortsel 12 Gc 51.10N 4.28 E
Morumbi 55 Ef 23.46S 54.06W
Morvan 11 Jg 47.05N 4.00 E
Morven 59 Je 26.25S 147.07 E
Morvern 9 He 56.35N 5.50W
Morvi 25 Ed 22.49N 70.50 E
Morwell 58 Fh 38.14S 146.24 E
Morzine 11 Mh 46.11N 6.43 E
Moržovec, Ostrov- 7 Kc 66.45N 42.35 E
Moša 7 Je 62.25N 39.48 E
Mosbach 10 Fg 49.21N 9.09 E
Mosby 8 Bf 58.14N 7.54 E
Mošćny, Ostrov- 7 Gg 60.00N 27.50 E
Mosconi 55 Bl 35.44S 60.34W
Moscos Islands 25 Jf 14.00N 97.45 E
Moscow [Id.-U.S.] 43 Db 46.44N 116.59W
Moscow (EN)=Moskva 5 Jd 55.08N 38.50 E
Moscow (EN)=Moskva [R.S.F.S.R.] 6 Jd 55.45N 37.35 E
Moscow Basin (EN)= Meščera 5 Kd 55.00N 40.30 E
Moscow Canal (EN)= Moskvy, kanal imeni- 5 Jd 56.43N 37.08 E
Moscow Upland (EN)= Moskovskaja Vozvyšennost 5 Jd 56.30N 37.30 E
Mosel=Moselle (EN) 5 Ge 50.22N 7.36 E
Moselberge 12 Ie 49.57N 6.56 E
Moselle [3] 11 Me 49.00N 6.30 E
Moselle 5 Ge 50.22N 7.36 E
Moselle (EN)=Mosel 5 Ge 50.22N 7.36 E
Moses Lake 43 Db 47.08N 119.17W
Mosgiel 61 Di 45.53S 170.22 E
Moshi 31 Ki 3.21S 37.20 E
Mosina 10 Md 52.16N 16.51 E
Mosjøen 7 Cd 65.50N 13.12 E
Moskalvo 20 Jf 53.39N 142.37 E
Moskenesøy 7 Cc 67.59N 13.00 E
Moskovskaja Oblast [3] 19 Dd 55.45N 37.45 E
Moskovskaja Vozvyšennost =Moscow Upland (EN) 5 Jd 56.30N 37.30 E
Moskovski 18 Gf 37.40N 69.39 E
Moskva [R.S.F.S.R.] = Moscow (EN) 6 Jd 55.45N 37.35 E
Moskva [Tur.-U.S.S.R.] 18 Ee 38.27N 64.24 E
Moskva=Moscow (EN) 5 Jd 55.08N 38.50 E
Moskva, Pik- 18 He 38.55N 71.52 E
Moskvy, kanal imeni- = Moscow Canal (EN) 5 Jd 56.43N 37.08 E
Moslavačka Gora 14 Ke 45.38N 16.42 E
Moso 63b Dc 17.32S 168.15 E
Mosomane 37 Dd 24.01S 26.19 E
Mosoni-Duna 10 Ni 47.44N 17.47 E
Mosonmagyaróvár 10 Ni 47.52N 17.17 E
Mosor 14 Kg 43.30N 16.40 E
Mosquero 45 Ei 35.47N 103.58W
Mosquito, Baie - 42 Jd 60.40N 78.00W
Mosquito Coast (EN)= Mosquitos, Costa de- 38 Kh 13.00N 83.45W
Mosquito, Riacho- 55 Cf 22.12S 57.57W
Mosquitos, Costa de- = Mosquito Coast (EN) 38 Kh 13.00N 83.45W
Mosquitos, Golfo de los- 38 Ki 9.00N 81.20W
Moss 6 Hd 59.26N 10.42 E
Mossaka 36 Cc 1.13S 16.48 E
Mossâmedes 55 Gc 16.07S 50.11W
Mossbank 46 Mb 49.55N 105.59W
Mossburn 61 Ci 45.41S 168.15 E
Mosselbaai 31 Jl 34.11S 22.08 E
Mossendjo 36 Bc 2.57S 12.44 E
Mossman 58 Ff 16.28S 145.22 E
Mosso 8 Ch 56.05N 9.50 E
Mossoró 53 Mf 5.11S 37.20W
Moss Point 45 Lk 30.25N 88.29W
Mossuril 37 Gb 14.58S 40.40 E
Most 10 Jf 50.32N 13.39 E
Mostaganem [3] 32 Hb 35.40N 0.30 E
Mostaganem 31 He 35.56N 0.05 E
Mostar 14 Lg 43.21N 17.49 E
Mostardas 55 Gj 31.06S 50.57W
Møsting, Kap- 41 Hf 63.45N 41.00W
Mostiska 16 Ce 49.48N 23.09 E
Mostiştea 15 Je 44.15N 26.54 E
Most na Soci 14 Hd 46.09N 13.45 E
Mostovskoj 16 Lg 44.22N 40.48 E
Mosty 19 Ce 53.27N 24.33 E
Mosul (EN)=Al Mawşil 22 Gf 36.20N 43.08 E
Møsvatn 7 Bg 59.50N 8.05 E
Mota 63b Ca 13.40S 167.42 E
Mota 35 Fc 11.05N 37.53 E
Motaba 36 Cb 2.03N 18.03 E
Motacusito 55 Bc 17.35S 61.31W
Mota del Marques 13 Gc 41.38N 5.10W
Motagua 38 Kh 15.44N 88.14W
Motajica 14 Le 45.04N 17.40 E
Motala 7 Dg 58.33N 15.03 E
Motala ström 8 Gf 58.38N 16.10 E
Motatán 49 Li 9.24N 70.36W
Motatán, Río- 49 Li 9.32N 71.02W
Motegi 29 Gc 36.32N 140.10 E
Motehuala 47 Dd 23.39N 100.39W
Mothe 63d Cc 18.40S 178.30W
Motherwell 9 Jf 55.48N 4.00W
Motīhāri 25 Gc 26.39N 84.55 E
Motilla del Palancar 13 Ke 39.34N 1.53W
Motiti Island 62 Gb 37.40S 176.25 E
Motlav 63b Ca 13.40S 167.40 E
Motobu 29b Ab 26.40N 127.55 E
Motol 10 Vd 52.17N 25.40 E
Motovski Zaliv 7 Hb 69.30N 32.30 E
Motoyoshi 29 Gb 38.48N 141.31 E
Motozintla de Mendoza 48 Mj 15.22N 92.14W
Motril 13 Ih 36.45N 3.31W
Motru 15 Ge 44.33N 23.27 E
Motru 15 Fe 44.48N 23.00 E
Motsuta-Misaki 29a Ab 42.36N 139.49 E
Mott 45 Ec 46.22N 102.20W
Motteville 12 Ce 49.38N 0.51 E
Motu 62 Gb 37.51S 177.35 E
Motueka 62 Ed 41.07S 173.01 E
Motuhora Island 62 Gb 37.50S 177.00 E
Motu-Iti 65d Ac 27.11S 109.27W
Motu-Iti → Tupai Atoll 61 Kc 16.17S 151.50W
Motul 47 Gd 21.06N 89.17W
Motu-Nui 65d Ac 27.12S 109.28W
Motu One Atoll 57 Lf 15.48S 154.33W
Motupae 64n Ac 10.27S 161.02W
Motupena Point 63a Bb 6.32S 155.09 E
Moturiki 63d Bb 17.46S 178.45 E
Motutapu 64p Cb 21.14S 159.43W
Motu Tautara 65d Ab 27.05S 109.26W
Motutunga Atoll 57 Mf 17.06S 144.22W
Moubray Bay 66 Kf 72.11S 170.15 E
Mouchard 11 Lh 46.58N 5.48 E
Mouchoir Bank (EN) 47 Jd 20.57N 70.42W
Mouchoir Passage 49 Lc 21.10N 71.00W
Moudjéria 32 Ef 17.52N 12.20W
Mouila 31 Ii 1.52S 11.01 E
Mouka 35 Cd 7.16N 21.52 E
Moul 34 Hb 15.03N 13.18 E
Mould Bay 39 Hb 76.15N 119.30W
Moule 50 Fd 16.20N 61.21W
Moule à Chique, Cap- 51k Bb 13.43N 60.57W
Moulins 11 Jh 46.34N 3.20 E
Moulmein → Mawlamyine 22 Le 16.30N 97.38 E
Moulouya 30 Ge 35.06N 2.20W
Moult 12 Be 49.07N 0.10W
Moultrie 44 Fj 31.11N 83.47W
Moultrie, Lake- 44 Gi 33.20N 80.05W
Mouly, Pointe de- 63b Ce 20.43S 166.23 E
Moúnda, Ákra- 15 Dk 38.03N 20.47 E
Moundou 31 Ih 8.34N 16.05 E
Moundsville 44 Gf 39.54N 80.44W
Mo'unga'one 65b Ba 19.38S 174.29W
Moungoudou 36 Bc 2.40S 12.41 E
Mountainair 45 Ci 34.31N 106.15W
Mountain Grove 45 Jh 37.08N 92.16W
Mountain Home [Ar.-U.S.] 45 Jh 36.21N 92.23W
Mountain Home [Id.-U.S.] 43 Dc 43.08N 115.41W
Mountain Nile (EN)=Jabal, Baḩr al- 30 Kh 9.30N 30.30 E
Mountain Village 40 Gd 62.05N 163.44W
Mount Airy 44 Gg 36.31N 80.37W
Mount Barker 59 Df 34.38S 117.40 E
Mount Carmel 45 Mf 38.25N 87.46W
Mount Desert Island 44 Mc 44.20N 68.20W
Mount Douglas 58 Fg 21.30S 146.50 E
Mount Eba 59 Hf 30.12S 135.40 E
Mount Forest 44 Gd 43.59N 80.44W
Mount Frere 37 Df 31.00S 28.58 E
Mount Gambier 58 Fh 37.50S 140.46 E
Mount Hagen 60 Ci 5.52S 144.13 E
Mount Hope 59 Hf 34.07S 135.23 E
Mount Isa 58 Eg 20.44S 139.30 E
Mountlake Terrace 46 Dc 47.47N 122.18W
Mount Lebanon 44 Ge 40.23N 80.03W
Mount Lofty Ranges 59 Hg 35.15S 138.50 E
Mount Magnet 58 Cg 28.04S 117.49 E
Mount Maunganui 61 Eg 37.38S 176.12 E
Mount Morgan 59 Kd 23.39S 150.23 E
Mountnorris Bay 59 Gb 11.20S 132.45 E
Mount Peck 46 Ha 50.10N 115.02W
Mount Pleasant [Ia.-U.S.] 45 Kf 40.58N 91.33W
Mount Pleasant [Mi.-U.S.] 44 Ed 43.35N 84.47W
Mount Pleasant [S.C.-U.S.] 44 Hi 32.47N 79.52W
Mount Pleasant [Tx.-U.S.] 45 Ij 33.09N 94.58W
Mount Pleasant [Ut.-U.S.] 46 Jg 39.33N 111.27W
Mount's Bay 9 Hk 50.03N 5.25W
Mount Somers 62 De 43.42S 171.25 E
Mount Sterling [Il.-U.S.] 45 Kg 39.59N 90.45W
Mount Sterling [Ky.-U.S.] 44 Ff 38.04N 83.56W
Mount Vancouver 42 Dd 60.20N 139.41W
Mount Vernon [Al.-U.S.] 44 Cj 31.05N 88.01W
Mount Vernon [Austl.] 59 Dd 24.13S 118.14 E
Mount Vernon [Il.-U.S.] 43 Jd 38.19N 88.55W
Mount Vernon [In.-U.S.] 44 Dg 37.56N 87.54W
Mount Vernon [Ky.-U.S.] 44 Eg 37.21N 84.20W
Mount Vernon [Oh.-U.S.] 44 Fe 40.23N 82.30W
Mount Vernon [Wa.-U.S.] 43 Cb 48.25N 122.20W
Moura [Austl.] 59 Jd 24.35S 150.00 E
Moura [Port.] 13 Ef 38.08N 7.27W
Mourão 13 Ef 38.23N 7.21W
Mourdi 35 Cb 17.50N 22.25 E
Mourdi, Dépression du-= Mourdi Depression (EN) 30 Jg 18.10N 23.00 E
Mourdiah 34 Dc 14.26N 7.31W
Mourdi Depression (EN)= Mourdi, Dépression du- 30 Jg 18.10N 23.00 E
Mourmelon-le-Grand 12 Ge 49.08N 4.22 E
Mourne Mountains/Beanna Boirche 9 Gg 54.10N 6.04W
Mouscron/Moeskroen 11 Jd 50.44N 3.13 E
Moussoro 31 Ig 13.39N 16.29 E
Moustiers-Sainte-Marie 11 Mk 43.51N 6.13 E
Moutier/Münster 14 Bc 47.16N 7.22 E
Moutiers 11 Mi 45.29N 6.32 E
Moutong 26 Hf 0.28N 121.13 E
Mouy 12 Ee 49.19N 2.19 E
Mouydir 30 Hf 25.00N 4.10 E
Mouyondzi 36 Bc 3.58S 13.57 E
Mouzaia 13 Oh 36.28N 2.41 E
Mouzon 12 He 49.36N 5.05 E
Movas 48 Ec 28.10N 109.25W

Index Symbols

[1] Independent Nation
[2] State, Region
[3] District, County
[4] Municipality
[5] Colony, Dependency
Continent
Physical Region
Historical or Cultural Region
Mount, Mountain
Volcano
Hill
Mountains, Mountain Range
Hills, Escarpment
Plateau, Upland
Pass, Gap
Plain, Lowland
Delta
Salt Flat
Valley, Canyon
Crater, Cave
Karst Features
Depression
Polder
Desert, Dunes
Forest, Woods
Heath, Steppe
Oasis
Cape, Point
Coast, Beach
Cliff
Peninsula
Isthmus
Sandbank
Island
Atoll
Rock, Reef
Islands, Archipelago
Rocks, Reefs
Coral Reef
Well, Spring
Geyser
River, Stream
Waterfall Rapids
River Mouth, Estuary
Lake
Salt Lake
Intermittent Lake
Reservoir
Swamp, Pond
Canal
Glacier
Ice Shelf, Pack Ice
Ocean
Sea
Gulf, Bay
Strait, Fjord
Lagoon
Bank
Seamount
Tablemount
Ridge
Shelf
Basin
Escarpment, Sea Scarp
Fracture
Trench, Abyss
National Park, Reserve
Point of Interest
Recreation Site
Cave, Cavern
Historic Site
Ruins
Wall, Walls
Church, Abbey
Temple
Scientific Station
Airport
Port
Lighthouse
Mine
Tunnel
Dam, Bridge

Moxico [3] 36 De 12.00S 20.00 E
Moxico 36 De 11.51S 20.01 E
Moy/An Mhuaidh 9 Dg 54.12N 9.08W
Moyahua 48 Hg 21.16N 103.10W
Moyale [Eth.] 31 Kh 3.32N 39.04 E
Moyale [Kenya] 36 Gb 3.32N 39.03 E
Moyamba 34 Cd 8.10N 12.26W
Moÿ-de-l'Aisne 12 Fe 49.45N 3.22 E
Moyen Atlas=Middle Atlas (EN) 30 Ge 33.30N 4.30W
Moyen-Chari [3] 35 Bd 9.00N 18.00 E
Moyenne Guinée [3] 34 Cc 11.15N 12.30W
Moyenneville 12 Dd 50.04N 1.45 E
Moyen-Ogooué [3] 36 Bc 0.30S 10.30 E
Moyeuvre-Grande 12 Ie 49.15N 6.02 E
Moyo 36 Fb 3.40N 31.43 E
Moyo, Pulau- 26 Gh 8.15S 117.34 E
Moyobamba 53 If 6.02S 76.58W
Moyowosi 36 Fc 4.50S 31.24 E
Moyto 35 Bc 12.35N 16.33 E
Moyu/Karakax 27 Cd 37.17N 79.42 E
Možajsk 7 Ii 55.32N 36.02 E
Mozambique (EN)= Moçambique [1] 31 Kj 18.15S 35.00 E
Mozambique (EN)= Moçambique 31 Lk 15.03S 40.45 E
Mozambique, Canal de-= Mozambique Channel (EN) 30 Lk 20.00S 43.00 E
Mozambique Channel (EN) =Moçambique, Canal de- 30 Lk 20.00S 43.00 E
Mozambique Channel (EN) =Mozambique, Canal de- 30 Lk 20.00S 43.00 E
Mozambique Plateau (EN) 30 Kl 32.00S 35.00 E
Mozdok 19 Eg 43.44N 44.38 E
Možga 19 Fd 56.28N 52.13 E
Mozuli 8 Mh 56.32N 28.14 E
Mozyr 19 Ce 52.02N 29.16 E
Mpala 36 Ed 6.45S 29.31 E
Mpanda 31 Ki 6.22S 31.02 E
Mpigi 36 Fb 0.15N 32.20 E
Mpika 31 Kj 11.50S 31.27 E
Mpoko 35 Be 4.19N 18.33 E
Mporokoso 36 Fd 9.23S 30.08 E
Mpouia 36 Cc 2.37S 16.13 E
Mpui 36 Fd 8.21S 31.50 E
Mpulungu 36 Fd 8.46S 31.07 E
Mpwapwa 36 Gd 6.21S 36.29 E
Mrągowo 10 Rc 53.52N 21.19 E
Mrakovo 17 Hj 52.43N 56.38 E
Mrkonjić Grad 14 Lf 44.25N 17.06 E
Mrocza 10 Nc 53.14N 17.36 E
Mroga 10 Pd 52.09N 19.42 E
Msangesi 36 Ge 11.40S 36.45 E
Msid, Djebel- 14 Cn 36.25N 8.04 E
Msif 13 Qi 35.23N 4.45 E
M'Sila 13 Qi 35.31N 4.30 E
M'Sila [3] 32 Hb 35.00N 4.30 E
M'Sila 32 Hb 35.42N 4.33 E
Mšinskaja 8 Nf 58.55N 30.03 E
Msta 5 Jd 58.25N 31.20 E
Mstislavl 16 Gc 53.59N 31.45 E
Mszana Dolna 10 Qg 49.42N 20.05 E
Mtakuja 36 Fd 7.22S 30.37 E
Mtama 36 Ge 10.18S 39.22 E
Mtelo 36 Gb 1.39N 35.23 E
Mtera Reservoir 36 Gd 7.01S 35.55 E
Mtito Andei 36 Gc 2.41S 38.10 E
Mtubatuba 37 Ee 28.30S 32.08 E
Mtwara [3] 36 Ge 10.40S 39.00 E
Mtwara 31 Lj 10.16S 40.11 E
Mu, Cerro- 49 Ki 9.29N 73.07W
Mua 64h Ac 13.21S 176.10W
Mu'a 65b Ac 21.11S 175.07W
Mua, Baie de- 64h Bc 13.23S 176.09W
Muaná 54 Id 1.32S 49.13W
Muang Huon 25 Kd 20.09N 101.27 E
Muang Khammouan 25 Ke 17.24N 104.48 E
Muang Không 25 Lf 14.07N 105.51 E
Muang Khôngxédôn 25 Le 15.34N 105.49 E
Muang Khoua 25 Kd 21.05N 102.31 E
Muang Pak Lay 25 Ke 18.12N 101.25 E
Muang Pakxan 25 Ke 18.22N 103.39 E
Muang Pakxong 25 Le 15.11N 106.14 E
Muang Sing 25 Kd 21.11N 101.09 E
Muang Tahoi 25 Le 16.10N 106.38 E
Muang Thai=Thailand (EN) [1] 22 Lh 15.00N 100.00 E
Muang Vangviang 25 Ke 18.56N 102.27 E
Muang Xaignabouri 25 Ke 19.15N 101.45 E
Muang Xay 25 Kd 20.42N 101.59 E
Muang Xépôn 25 Le 16.41N 106.14 E
Muanzanza 36 Dd 6.32S 20.51 E
Muar 26 Df 2.02N 102.34 E
Muaraaman 26 Dg 3.07S 102.12 E
Muarabungo 26 Dg 1.28S 102.07 E
Muaraenim 26 Dg 3.39S 103.48 E
Muaralasan 26 Gf 1.48N 117.12 E
Muarapajang 26 Gg 1.32S 115.48 E
Muarasiberut 26 Cg 1.36S 99.11 E
Muarasiram 26 Gg 0.46S 116.11 E
Muaratebo 26 Dg 1.30S 102.26 E
Muaratewe 26 Fg 0.57S 114.53 E
Muarawahau 26 Gf 1.02N 116.52 E
Mubarek 18 Ee 39.16N 65.07 E
Mubende 36 Fb 0.35N 31.23 E
Mubi 31 Ig 10.16N 13.16 E
Much 12 Jd 50.55N 7.24 E
Muchinga Escarpment 36 Fe 13.40S 34.00 E
Muchinga Mountains 30 Kj 12.00S 31.45 E
Muck 9 Ge 56.50N 6.14W
Mücke 12 Ld 50.37N 9.02 E
Mucojo 37 Gb 12.04S 40.28 E
Muconda 36 De 10.34S 21.20 E
Mucua 37 Ee 18.09S 34.58 E
Mucubela 37 Fc 16.54S 37.49 E
Mucuchies 49 Li 8.45N 70.55W
Mucumbura 37 Ec 16.10S 31.42 E
Mucur 24 Fc 39.04N 34.23 E
Mucusso 36 Df 18.00S 21.25 E
Mudan Jang 21 Oe 46.18N 129.31 E
Mudanjiang 22 Oe 44.35N 129.34 E
Mudanya 24 Cb 40.22N 28.52 E
Muddy Gap 46 Le 42.22N 107.27W
Mudgee 59 Jf 32.36S 149.35 E
Mud Lake 46 Ie 43.53N 112.24W
Mud Lake 46 Gh 37.55N 117.05W
Mudon 25 Je 16.15N 97.44 E
Mudug [3] 35 Hd 6.30N 48.00 E
Mudug 35 Hd 6.20N 47.00 E
Mudurnu 24 Db 40.28N 31.13 E
Muecate 37 Fb 14.53S 39.38 E
Mueda 37 Fb 11.39S 39.33 E
Muerto, Cayo- 49 Ff 14.34N 82.44W
Muerto, Mar- 48 Li 16.10N 94.10W
Mufulira 31 Jj 12.33S 28.14 E
Mufu Shan 27 Jf 29.15N 114.20 E
Mufu Shan 27 Jf 29.00N 113.50 E
Mugello 14 Fg 43.55N 11.25 E
Múggia 14 He 45.36N 13.46 E
Mughshin, Wādī- 35 Ib 19.44N 55.00 E
Mugi 29 De 33.40N 134.25 E
Mu Gia, Deo- 25 Le 17.40N 105.47 E
Mugila, Monts- 36 Ed 6.49S 29.08 E
Muğla 23 Cb 37.12N 28.22 E
Mugodžary 21 He 49.00N 58.40 E
Mugur an Na'ām 24 Ig 31.56N 40.30 E
Muhaiwir 24 If 33.28N 40.59 E
Muḥammad, Ra's- 33 Fd 27.42N 34.13 E
Muḥammad Oawl 35 Fa 20.54N 37.05 E
Muhen 20 Ig 48.10N 136.08 E
Muheza 36 Gd 5.10S 38.47 E
Muhīt, Al Baḥr al-=Atlantic Ocean (EN) 3 Di 2.00N 25.00W
Mühlacker 10 Eh 48.57N 8.50 E
Mühldorf am Inn 10 Ih 48.15N 12.32 E
Mühlhausen in Thüringen 10 Ge 51.13N 10.27 E
Mühlig-Hofmann Gebirge 66 Cf 72.00S 5.20 E
Mühlviertel 14 Ib 48.30N 14.10 E
Muhoršibir 20 Ff 51.01N 107.50 E
Muhos 7 Gd 64.50N 26.01 E
Muhu 7 Fg 58.35N 23.15 E
Muhu 8 Jf 58.37N 23.05 E
Muhu, Proliv-/Muhu Väin 8 Jf 58.45N 23.15 E
Muhulu 36 Ec 1.03S 27.17 E
Muhu Väin/Muhu, Proliv- 8 Jf 58.45N 23.15 E
Muhuwesi 36 Ge 11.16S 37.58 E
Muiderslot 12 Hb 52.20N 5.06 E
Muigheo/Mayo [2] 9 Dh 53.50N 9.30W
Muikamachi 28 Of 37.04N 138.53 E
Muineachán/Monaghan [2] 9 Gg 54.10N 7.00W
Muineachán/Monaghan 9 Gg 54.15N 6.58W
Muine Bheag 9 Gi 52.42N 6.57W
Muir Bhreatan=Saint George's Channel (EN) 5 Fe 52.00N 6.00W
Muir Eireann=Irish Sea (EN) 5 Fe 53.30N 5.20W
Muiron Islands 59 Cd 21.35S 114.20 E
Muir Seamount (EN) 38 Mf 33.41N 63.32W
Muite 37 Fb 14.02S 39.02 E
Mujeres, Isla- 48 Pg 21.13N 86.43W
Mujezerski 7 He 63.57N 32.01 E
Muji 27 Cd 37.27N 78.33 E
Mujnak 19 Fg 43.44N 59.02 E
Mujnakski Zaliv 18 Bc 43.50N 58.40 E
Mujunkum, Peski- 21 Je 44.00N 70.30 E
Mukačevo 19 Cf 48.26N 22.45 E
Mukah 26 Ff 2.54N 112.06 E
Mukawa 29a Bb 42.35N 141.55 E
Mu-Kawa 29a Bb 42.33N 141.53 E
Mukawwar 35 Fa 20.48N 37.13 E
Mukdahan 25 Ke 16.31N 104.42 E
Mukden→Shenyang 22 Oe 41.48N 123.24 E
Mukeru 64a Bc 7.25N 134.30 E
Mukho 28 Jf 37.33N 129.07 E
Mukinbudin 59 Df 30.54S 118.13 E
Mukojima-Rettō 60 Cb 27.37N 142.10 E
Mukomuko 26 Dg 2.35S 101.07 E
Muksu 18 He 39.17N 71.25 E
Mula 25 Dc 27.57N 67.36 E
Mula 13 Kf 38.03N 1.30W
Mulainagiri 25 Ff 13.24N 75.43 E
Mulaku Atoll 25a Bb 2.57N 73.34 E
Mulaly 19 Hf 45.27N 78.20 E
Mulan 27 Mb 46.00N 128.02 E
Mulanje 36 Gf 16.03S 35.31 E
Mulanje 36 Gf 16.02S 35.30 E
Mulatre, Point- 51g Bb 15.17N 61.15W
Mulatupo Sasardi 49 Ii 8.57N 77.45W
Mulchatna 40 Hd 59.39N 157.08W
Mulchén 56 Fe 37.34S 72.14W
Mulda 17 Kc 67.28N 63.34 E
Mulde 10 Ie 51.48N 12.10 E
Mulebreen 66 Ee 67.28S 59.21 E
Mulegé 47 Bc 26.53N 112.01W
Mulegé, Sierra de- 47 Bc 27.30N 112.40W
Mulenda 36 Dc 4.18S 24.58 E
Muleshoe 45 Ei 34.13N 102.43W
Mulgrave Island 59 Ib 10.05S 142.10 E
Mulhacén 5 Fh 37.03N 3.19W
Mülheim an der Ruhr 12 Ic 51.26N 6.53 E
Mülheim-Kärlich 12 Jd 50.23N 7.30 E
Mulhouse 6 Gf 47.45N 7.20 E
Muli (Bowa) 27 Hf 27.55N 101.13 E
Mulifanua 65c Aa 13.50S 172.02W
Muling 28 Kb 44.34N 130.12 E
Muling (Bamiantong) 28 Kb 44.55N 130.32 E
Muling Guan 28 Ef 36.10N 118.46 E
Muling He 28 Lb 45.53N 133.30 E
Mull, Island of- 5 Fd 56.27N 6.00W
Mull, Sound of- 9 He 56.35N 5.50W
Mullen 45 Fe 42.03N 101.01W
Mullens 44 Gg 37.35N 81.25W
Muller, Pegunungan- 26 Ff 0.40N 113.50 E
Mullet Peninsula/An Muirthead 9 Cg 54.15N 10.04W
Mullett Lake 44 Ec 45.30N 84.30W
Mullewa 59 De 28.33S 115.31 E
Müllheim 10 Di 47.48N 7.38 E
Mullingar/An Muileann gCearr 9 Fh 53.32N 7.20W
Mullsjö 8 Eg 57.55N 13.53 E
Mulobezi 36 Ef 16.47S 25.10 E
Mulock Glacier 66 Jf 79.03S 159.10 E
Mulongo 36 Ed 7.50S 26.57 E
Multān 22 Jf 30.11N 71.29 E
Multé 48 Ni 17.41N 91.24W
Multia 8 Kb 62.25N 24.47 E
Multien 12 Ee 49.05N 2.55 E
Mulu, Gunong- 26 Ff 4.03N 114.56 E
Mulvane 45 Hh 37.29N 97.14W
Mulymja 17 Lf 60.12N 64.32 E
Mumbué 36 Ce 13.53S 17.19 E
Mumbwa 36 Ee 14.59S 27.04 E
Mumhan/Munster 9 Ei 52.30N 9.00W
Mumra 16 Og 45.43N 47.41 E
Mun 21 Mh 15.19N 105.30 E
Muna 48 Og 20.29N 89.43W
Muna 21 Oc 67.52N 123.10 E
Muna, Pulau- 26 Hg 5.00S 122.30 E
Munābāo 25 Ec 25.45N 70.17 E
Munamägi/Munamjagi 8 Lg 57.38N 27.10 E
Munaybarah, Sharm- 24 Gi 26.04N 36.38 E
Muncar 26 Fh 8.29S 114.21 E
Münchberg 10 Hf 50.12N 11.47 E
München=Munich (EN) 6 Hf 48.09N 11.35 E
Münchhausen 12 Kd 50.57N 8.43 E
Muncho Lake 42 Ee 58.56N 125.46W
Munch'ŏn 28 Ie 39.14N 127.22 E
Muncie 43 Jc 40.11N 85.23W
Munda 63a Cc 8.19S 157.15 E
Mundaring, Perth- 59 Df 31.54S 116.10 E
Munday 45 Gj 33.27N 99.38W
Mundemba 34 Ge 4.59N 8.40 E
Münden 10 Fe 51.25N 9.41 E
Mundesley 12 Db 52.52N 1.25 E
Mundford 12 Cb 52.30N 0.39 E
Mundiwindi 58 Dg 23.52S 120.09 E
Mundo 13 Kf 38.19N 1.40W
Mundo Novo 54 Jf 11.52S 40.28W
Munellës, Mali i- 15 Dh 41.58N 20.06 E
Munera 13 Je 39.02N 2.28W
Mungana 59 Ic 17.07S 144.24 E
Mungbere 31 Jh 2.38N 28.30 E
Munger 25 Hc 25.23N 86.28 E
Mungindi 59 Je 28.58S 148.59 E
Munhango 36 Ce 12.10S 18.34 E
Munh-Hajrhan-Ula 21 Le 46.40N 91.30 E
Munich (EN)=München 6 Hf 48.09N 11.35 E
Muniesa 13 Lc 41.02N 0.48W
Munīfah 23 Gd 27.38N 49.00 E
Munising 44 Db 46.25N 86.40W
Munkedal 7 Cg 58.29N 11.41 E
Munkfors 7 Cg 59.50N 13.32 E
Munku Sardik, Gora- 21 Md 51.45N 100.20 E
Muñoz Gamero, Peninsula- 56 Fh 52.30S 73.10W
Munsan 28 If 37.55N 126.22 E
Münsingen 10 Fh 48.25N 9.30 E
Munster 11 Nf 48.03N 7.08 E
Münster [Ger.] 10 De 51.58N 7.38 E
Münster [Ger.] 12 Ke 49.55N 8.52 E
Münster/Moutier 14 Bc 47.16N 7.22 E
Munster/Mumhan 9 Ei 52.30N 9.00W
Münster-Hiltrup 12 Jc 51.54N 7.38 E
Münsterland [Ger.] 10 De 52.00N 7.30 E
Münsterland [Ger.] 12 Kb 52.45N 8.10 E
Münstermaifeld 12 Jd 50.15N 7.22 E
Muntenia 15 Ie 44.00N 26.00 E
Munteni Buzău 15 Je 44.38N 26.59 E
Muntok 26 Eg 2.04S 105.11 E
Munzur Dağları 24 Hc 39.30N 39.10 E
Muojärvi 7 Gd 65.56N 28.36 E
Muong Sen 25 Ke 19.24N 104.08 E
Muonio 6 Ib 67.57N 23.42 E
Muonioälven Muonionjoki 6 Ib 67.11N 23.34 E
Muping 28 Ff 37.23N 121.36 E
Muqaddam 35 Eb 18.04N 31.30 E
Muqayshiṭ 24 Oj 24.10N 53.45 E
Muqdisho=Mogadishu (EN) 31 Lh 2.03N 45.22 E
Mur 5 Hf 46.18N 16.55 E
Mura 5 Hf 46.18N 16.55 E
Muradiye [Tur.] 15 Kk 38.39N 27.24 E
Muradiye [Tur.] 24 Jc 39.00N 43.43 E
Murafa 16 Fe 48.13N 28.14 E
Murakami 28 Oe 38.14N 139.29 E
Murallón, Cerro- 52 Ij 49.48S 73.25W
Murān 10 Qh 48.45N 20.02 E
Mur'aryo 35 Ic 11.41N 50.27 E
Murași 19 Ed 59.24N 48.59 E
Murat 21 Ff 38.52N 38.48 E
Murat 11 Ii 45.07N 2.52 E
Murat Dağı 23 Cb 38.55N 29.43 E
Muratlı [Tur.] 24 Ib 41.29N 41.41 E
Muratlı [Tur.] 15 Kh 41.10N 27.30 E
Murau 14 Ic 47.06N 14.10 E
Muravera 14 Dk 39.25N 9.34 E
Murayama 29 Gb 38.29N 140.23 E
Mürchen Khvort 24 Nf 33.06N 51.30 E
Murchison 62 Ed 41.48S 172.20 E
Murchison, Mount- [Austl.] 59 De 26.46S 116.25 E
Murchison, Mount- [N.Z.] 62 De 43.01S 171.17 E
Murchison River 57 Cg 27.50S 114.00 E
Murcia 6 Fh 37.59N 1.07W
Murcia [3] 13 Kg 38.00N 1.30W
Murcia 13 Kf 38.30N 1.45W
Mur-de-Barrez 11 Ij 44.51N 2.39 E
Murdo 45 Fe 43.53N 100.43W
Mürefte 15 Ki 40.40N 27.14 E
Muren 22 Me 49.38N 100.10 E
Mureș 5 If 46.15N 20.12 E
Mureș [2] 15 Hc 46.30N 24.40 E
Muret 11 Hk 43.28N 1.21 E
Murfreesboro 43 Jd 35.51N 86.23W
Murg 10 Eh 48.55N 8.10 E
Murgab 21 If 38.18N 61.12 E
Murgab [Tad.-U.S.S.R.] 19 Hh 38.10N 73.59 E
Murgab [Tur.-U.S.S.R.] 18 Df 37.32N 62.01 E
Murgaš 15 Gg 42.50N 23.40 E
Murgeni 15 Lc 46.12N 28.01 E
Murgon 59 Ke 26.15S 151.57 E
Muri 64p Cc 21.15S 159.43W
Muriaé 54 Jh 21.08S 42.22W
Murici 54 Ke 9.19S 35.56W
Muriege 36 Dd 9.53S 21.13 E
Murihiti 64n Ab 10.23S 161.02W
Murilo Atoll 57 Gd 8.40N 152.11 E
Mūrītāniyā=Mauritania (EN) [1] 31 Fg 20.00N 12.00W
Müritz 10 Ic 53.25N 12.43 E
Murkong Selek 25 Jc 27.44N 95.18 E
Murmansk 6 Jb 68.58N 33.05 E
Murmanskaja Oblast [3] 19 Db 68.00N 35.30 E
Murmaši 19 Db 68.49N 32.49 E
Murnau 10 Hi 47.41N 11.12 E
Muro 13 Pe 39.44N 3.03 E
Muro, Capo di- 11a Ab 41.44N 8.40 E
Muro Lucano 14 Jj 40.45N 15.29 E
Murom 6 Kd 55.34N 42.02 E
Muromcevo 19 Hd 56.23N 75.14 E
Muroran 22 Qe 42.18N 140.59 E
Muros 13 Cb 42.47N 9.02W
Muros y Noya, Ria de- 13 Db 42.45N 9.00W
Muroto 27 Ne 33.18N 134.09 E
Muroto Zaki 28 Mh 33.16N 134.10 E
Murowana Goślina 10 Nd 52.35N 17.01 E
Murphy [Id.-U.S.] 46 Ge 43.13N 116.33W
Murphy [N.C.-U.S.] 44 Eh 35.05N 84.01W
Murphysboro 45 Lh 37.46N 89.20W
Murrah al Kubrā, Al Buḥayrah al- 24 Eg 30.20N 32.23 E
Murray [Ky.-U.S.] 44 Cg 36.37N 88.19W
Murray [Ut.-U.S.] 46 Jf 40.40N 111.53W
Murray, Lake- [Pap.N.Gui.] 60 Ci 7.00S 141.30 E
Murray, Lake- [S.C.-U.S.] 44 Gh 34.04N 81.23W
Murray Bridge 59 Hg 35.07S 139.17 E
Murray Fracture zone (EN) 3 Lf 34.00N 135.00W
Murray Islands 59 Ia 9.55S 144.05 E
Murray Ridge (EN) 3 Gg 21.00N 61.50 E
Murray River 57 Eh 35.22S 139.22 E
Murraysburg 37 Cf 31.58S 23.47 E
Murro di Porco, Capo- 14 Jm 37.00N 15.20 E
Murrumbidgee River 57 Fh 34.43S 143.12 E
Murrupula 37 Fc 15.27S 38.47 E
Murska Sobota 14 Kd 46.40N 16.10 E
Murten/Morat 14 Bd 46.56N 7.08 E
Murter 14 Jg 43.47N 15.37 E
Murtle Lake 46 Fa 52.08N 119.38W
Murud, Gunong- 26 Gf 3.52N 115.30 E
Murupara 62 Gc 38.27S 176.42 E
Mururoa Atoll 57 Ng 21.52S 138.55W
Murwāra 25 Gd 23.51N 80.24 E
Murwillumbah 59 Ke 28.19S 153.24 E
Mürz 14 Jc 47.24N 15.17 E
Mürzzuschlag 14 Jc 47.36N 15.41 E
Muş 23 Fb 38.44N 41.30 E
Muša/Mūša 7 Fh 56.24N 24.12 E
Mūša/Muša 7 Fh 56.24N 24.12 E
Mūsa, Jabal-=Sinai, Mount- (EN) 24 Eh 28.32N 33.59 E
Musa Ali 35 Gc 12.30N 42.27 E
Musāfi 24 Qk 25.18N 56.10 E
Musā'id 33 Ed 31.36N 25.03 E
Musala 5 Ig 42.11N 23.34 E
Musallam 24 Lg 31.53N 46.56 E
Musan 27 Mc 42.14N 129.13 E
Musandam Peninsula 24 Qi 26.18N 56.24 E
Musay'id 24 Nj 25.00N 51.33 E
Musaymir 33 Hg 13.27N 44.37 E
Muscat (EN)=Masqaṭ 22 Hg 23.29N 58.33 E
Muscat and Oman (EN) →Oman (EN) [1] 22 Hg 21.00N 57.00 E
Muscatine 45 Kf 41.25N 91.03W
Musgrave 58 Ff 14.47S 143.30 E
Musgrave Ranges 57 Eg 26.10S 131.50 E
Mūshā 24 Di 27.07N 31.14 E
Mus-Haja, Gora- 21 Qc 62.35N 140.50 E
Mushāsh al 'Ashawī 24 Mj 24.12N 48.50 E
Mushāsh Ramlān 24 Mj 24.25N 49.15 E
Mushayrib, Ra's- 24 Nj 24.18N 51.44 E
Mushie 36 Cc 3.01S 16.54 E
Müsi 25 Ge 15.20N 80.06 E
Musi 21 Mj 2.20S 104.56 E
Mūsiān 24 Lf 32.28N 47.26 E
Musicians Seamounts (EN) 57 Kb 29.00N 162.00W
Muskegon 43 Jc 43.14N 86.16W
Muskegon Heights 44 Dd 43.12N 86.12W
Muskegon River 44 Dd 43.14N 86.20W
Muskö 8 He 59.00N 18.05 E
Muskogee 43 Hd 35.45N 95.22W
Muskoka, Lake- 44 Hc 45.00N 79.25W
Musoma 31 Ki 1.30S 33.48 E
Musone 14 Hg 43.28N 13.38 E
Mussaṭṭaḥah, Al Jazīrah al- 14 Em 37.11N 10.20 E
Mussau Island 60 Dh 1.25S 149.38 E
Musselkanaal, Stadskanaal- 12 Jb 52.56N 7.02 E
Musselshell River 43 Fb 47.21N 107.58W
Mussende 36 Ce 10.31S 16.02 E
Mussidan 11 Gi 45.02N 0.22 E
Mussömeli 14 Hm 37.35N 13.45 E
Must 27 Fb 46.40N 92.40 E
Muṣṭafá, Ra's- 14 Fn 36.50N 11.07 E
Mustafakemalpaşa 24 Cb 40.02N 28.24 E
Mustahil 35 Gd 5.15N 44.44 E
Mustang 25 Gc 29.11N 83.58 E
Mustang Draw 45 Fj 32.00N 101.40W
Mustang Island 45 Hm 28.00N 96.55W
Mustasaari/Korsholm 8 Ia 63.05N 21.43 E
Musters, Lago- 56 Gg 45.27S 69.13W
Mustique Island 50 Ff 12.39N 61.15W
Mustjala 8 Jf 58.25N 22.04 E
Mustla 7 Fg 58.14N 25.52 E
Mustvee 7 Gg 58.52N 26.59 E
Musu-dan 28 Jd 40.50N 129.43 E
Muswellbrook 59 Kf 32.16S 150.53 E
Muszyna 10 Qg 49.21N 20.54 E
Mut 24 Ed 36.39N 33.27 E
Mūṭ 33 Ed 25.29N 28.59 E
Mūtaf, Ra's al- 23 Hd 27.41N 51.27 E
Mutalau 64k Ba 18.56S 169.50W
Mutarara 31 Kj 17.27S 35.04 E
Mutatá 54 Cb 7.16N 76.32W
Mutawassiṭ, Al Baḥr al-= Mediterranean Sea (EN) 5 Hh 35.00N 20.00 E
Mutha 36 Gc 1.48S 38.26 E
Muting 26 Lh 7.23S 140.20 E
Mutis, Gunung- 26 Hh 9.35S 124.14 E
Mutoraj 20 Fd 61.20N 100.20 E
Mutsamudu 31 Lj 12.09S 44.25 E
Mutshatsha 36 De 10.39S 24.27 E
Mutsu 27 Pc 41.05N 140.55 E
Mutsu-Wan 28 Pd 41.10N 140.55 E
Mutthaburra 59 Id 22.36S 144.33 E
Mutterstadt 12 Ke 49.27N 8.21 E
Mutton/Oileán Coarach 9 Di 52.49N 9.31W
Mutton Bird Islands 62 Bg 47.15S 167.25 E
Mutuali 37 Fb 14.53S 37.00 E
Mutún 55 Dd 19.10S 57.54W
Mutunópolis 55 Ha 13.40S 49.15W
Mutusjärvi 7 Gb 69.31N 26.57 E
Muurame 8 Kb 62.08N 25.40 E
Mu Us Shamo=Ordos Desert (EN) 21 Mf 38.45N 109.10 E
Muxima 36 Bd 9.32S 13.57 E
Muyinga 36 Fc 2.51S 30.20 E
Muy Muy 49 Eg 12.46N 85.38W
Muzaffarābād 25 Eb 34.22N 73.28 E
Muzaffargarh 25 Eb 30.04N 71.12 E
Muzaffarnagar 25 Fc 29.28N 77.41 E
Muzaffarpur 25 Hc 26.07N 85.24 E
Muzambinho 55 Ie 21.22S 46.32W
Muzat He 27 Dc 41.15N 83.27 E
Muži 20 Bc 65.27N 64.40 E
Muzillac 11 Dg 47.33N 2.29W
Mužlja 15 Dd 45.21N 20.25 E
Muztag [China] 21 Kf 35.55N 80.20 E
Muztag [China] 21 Kf 36.25N 87.25 E
Muztagata 27 Cd 38.17N 75.07 E
Mvolo 35 Dd 6.03N 29.56 E
Mvomero 36 Gd 6.20S 37.25 E
Mvoung 36 Bb 0.04N 12.18 E
Mwadingusha 36 Ee 10.45S 27.15 E
Mwali 30 Lj 12.15S 43.45 E
Mwanza [3] 36 Fc 2.30S 32.30 E
Mwanza [Mwi.] 36 Ff 15.37S 34.31 E
Mwanza [Tan.] 31 Ki 2.31S 32.54 E
Mwanza [Zaire] 36 Ed 7.54S 26.45 E
Mwatate 36 Gc 3.30S 38.23 E
Mweelrea 9 Dh 53.38N 9.50W
Mweka 31 Ji 4.51S 21.34 E
Mwene Ditu 31 Ji 7.03S 23.27 E
Mwenga 36 Ec 3.02S 28.26 E
Mweru, Lake- 30 Ji 9.00S 28.45 E
Mweru Wantipa, Lake- 36 Ed 8.42S 29.46 E
Mwimbi 36 Fd 8.39S 31.40 E
Mwinilunga 36 De 11.44S 24.26 E
Mya 30 He 31.40N 5.15 E
Myaing 25 Id 21.37N 94.51 E
Myanaung 25 Je 18.17N 95.19 E
Myanmar-Nainggan-Daw→Burma [1] 22 Lg 22.00N 98.00 E
Myaungmya 25 Ie 16.36N 94.56 E
Mycenae (EN)=Mikinai 15 Fl 37.43N 22.45 E
Myebon 25 Id 20.03N 93.22 E
Myingyan 22 Lg 21.28N 95.23 E
Myinmoletkat Taung 25 Jf 13.28N 98.48 E
Myitta 25 Jf 14.10N 98.31 E
Myjava 10 Mh 48.33N 16.58 E
Myjzakjula/Mõisaküla 7 Fg 58.07N 25.10 E
Mykulkin, Mys- 17 Cc 67.48N 46.40 E
Mylius Erichsens Land 41 Jb 81.40N 24.00W
Myltkyinā 22 Lg 25.23N 97.24 E
Mymensingh 25 Id 24.45N 90.24 E
Mynämäki 7 Ef 60.40N 22.00 E
Mynaral 19 Hf 45.22N 73.39 E
Myökö-Zan 29 Fc 36.52N 138.06 E
Mýrdalsjökull 7a Bc 63.40N 19.06W
Myre 7 Db 68.51N 15.05 E
Myrskylä/Mörskom 8 Kd 60.40N 25.51 E
Myrtle Beach 43 Le 33.42N 78.54W
Myrtle Point 46 Ce 43.04N 124.08W
Mysen 7 Cg 59.33N 11.20 E
Mysia 15 Kj 39.30N 28.00 E
Myśla 10 Kd 52.40N 14.29 E
Myślenice 10 Pg 49.51N 19.56 E
Myślibórz 10 Kd 52.55N 14.52 E
Mysore 22 Jh 12.18N 76.39 E
Mysore→Karnataka [3] 25 Ff 13.30N 76.00 E
Mys Saryč 16 Hg 44.23N 33.45 E
Myszków 10 Pf 50.36N 19.20 E
Myszyniec 10 Rc 53.24N 21.21 E
My Tho 22 Mh 10.21N 106.21 E
Mytišči 7 Ii 55.56N 37.46 E
Mývatn 7a Cb 65.36N 17.00W

Index Symbols

[1] Independent Nation
[2] State, Region
[3] District, County
[4] Municipality
[5] Colony, Dependency
Continent
Physical Region
Historical or Cultural Region
Mount, Mountain
Volcano
Hill
Mountains, Mountain Range
Hills, Escarpment
Plateau, Upland
Pass, Gap
Plain, Lowland
Delta
Salt Flat
Valley, Canyon
Crater, Cave
Karst Features
Depression
Polder
Desert, Dunes
Forest, Woods
Heath, Steppe
Oasis
Cape, Point
Coast, Beach
Cliff
Peninsula
Isthmus
Sandbank
Island
Atoll
Rock, Reef
Islands, Archipelago
Rocks, Reefs
Coral Reef
Well, Spring
Geyser
River, Stream
Waterfall Rapids
River Mouth, Estuary
Lake
Salt Lake
Intermittent Lake
Reservoir
Swamp, Pond
Canal
Glacier
Ice Shelf, Pack Ice
Ocean
Sea
Gulf, Bay
Strait, Fjord
Lagoon
Bank
Seamount
Tablemount
Ridge
Shelf
Basin
Escarpment, Sea Scarp
Fracture
Trench, Abyss
National Park, Reserve
Point of Interest
Recreation Site
Cave, Cavern
Historic Site
Ruins
Wall, Walls
Church, Abbey
Temple
Scientific Station
Airport
Port
Lighthouse
Mine
Tunnel
Dam, Bridge

Myzeqeja 15 Ci 41.01N 19.36 E
M'Zab 32 Hc 32.35N 3.20 E
Mže 10 Jg 49.46N 13.24 E
Mziha 36 Gd 5.54S 37.47 E
Mzimba 36 Fe 11.54S 33.36 E
Mzuzu 31 Kj 11.27S 33.55 E

N

Naab 10 Ig 49.01N 12.02 E
Naaldwijk 12 Gc 51.59N 4.12 E
Naalehu 65a Fd 19.04N 155.35W
Naantali/Nådendal 7 Ff 60.27N 22.02 E
Naarden 12 Hb 52.18N 5.10 E
Naas/An Nás 9 Gh 53.13N 6.39W
Nabadid 35 Gd 9.38N 43.29 E
Nabão 13 De 39.31N 8.21W
Nabari 29 Ed 34.37N 136.05 E
Naberera 36 Gc 4.12S 38.56 E
Naberežnyje Čelny 6 Ld 55.42N 52.19 E
Nabileque, Rio- 55 De 20.55S 57.49W
Nabire 58 Ee 3.22S 135.29 E
Nabī Shu'ayb, Jabal an- 21 Gh 15.17N 43.59 E
Nabq 24 Fh 28.04N 34.25 E
Nābul 31 Ie 36.27N 10.44 E
Nābul [3] 32 Jb 36.45N 10.45 E
Nābulus 24 Ff 32.13N 35.16 E
Nabusanke 36 Fb 0.01N 32.03 E
Nacala 37 Gb 14.33S 40.40 E
Nacala-a-Velha 31 Lj 14.33S 40.36 E
Nacaome 49 Dg 13.31N 87.30W
Nacaroa 37 Fb 14.23S 39.55 E
Nacereddine 13 Ph 36.08N 3.26 E
Nachikatsuura 29 De 33.39N 135.55 E
Nachingwea 36 Ge 10.23S 38.46 E
Nachi-San 29 De 33.42N 135.51 E
Náchod 10 Mf 50.26N 16.10 E
Nachuge 25 If 10.35N 92.28 E
Nachvak Fiord 42 Le 59.03N 63.45W
Nacka 7 Ee 59.18N 18.10 E
Ná Clocha Liatha/
Greystones 9 Gh 53.09N 6.04W
Nacogdoches 45 Ik 31.36N 94.39W
Na Comaraigh/Comeragh
Mountains 9 Fi 52.13N 7.35W
Nacori, Sierra- 48 Ec 29.50N 108.50W
Nacozari, Rio- 48 Ec 29.48N 109.42W
Nacozari de García 47 Cb 30.24N 109.39W
Na Cruacha/Blue Stack 9 Eg 54.45N 8.06W
Na Cruacha Dubha/
Macgillycuddy's Reeks 9 Di 52.00N 9.50W
Nacunday, Río- 55 Eh 26.03S 54.45W
Nada → Danxian 27 Ih 19.38N 109.32 E
Nådendal/Naantali 7 Ff 60.27N 22.02 E
Nadiād 25 Ed 22.42N 72.52 E
Nădlac 15 Dc 46.10N 20.45 E
Nador [3] 32 Gb 35.00N 3.00W
Nador 32 Gb 35.11N 2.56W
Nádusa 15 Fi 40.38N 22.04 E
Nadvoicy 19 Dc 63.52N 34.20 E
Nadvornaja 16 De 48.38N 24.34 E
Nadym 22 Jc 65.35N 72.42 E
Naeba-San 29 Fc 36.51N 138.41 E
Nærbø 8 Af 58.40N 5.39 E
Næstved 7 Ci 55.14N 11.46 E
Nafada 34 Hc 11.06N 11.20 E
Näfels 14 Dc 47.06N 9.04 E
Naftah 14 Dn 36.57N 9.04 E
Naftan Rock 64b Bb 14.50N 145.32 E
Naft-e-Safid 24 Mg 31.40N 49.17 E
Naft-e-Shāh 24 Kf 33.59N 45.30 E
Naft Khāneh 24 Ke 34.02N 45.28 E
Nafūsah, Jabal- 30 Ie 31.50N 12.00 E
Näg 25 Dc 27.24N 65.08 E
Naga 22 Oh 13.28N 123.39 E
Nāga, Kreb en- 32 Fe 24.00N 6.00W
Nagagami Lake 44 Ea 49.28N 85.02W
Nagagami River 45 Na 50.25N 84.20W
Nagahama [Jap.] 29 Ed 35.23N 136.16 E
Nagahama [Jap.] 29 Ce 33.36N 132.29 E
Nagai 29 Gb 38.06N 140.02 E
Nagai 40 Ge 55.11N 159.55W
Na Gaibhlte/Galty
Mountains 9 Ei 52.23N 8.11W
Nāgāland [3] 25 Ic 26.30N 94.00 E
Nagano 22 Pf 36.39N 138.11 E
Nagano Ken [2] 28 Nf 36.10N 138.00 E
Nagano-Matsushiro 29 Fc 36.34N 138.10 E
Nagano-Shinonoi 29 Fc 36.35N 138.06 E
Nagaoka 27 Od 37.27N 138.51 E
Nāgappattinam 25 Ff 10.46N 79.50 E
Nagara-Gawa 29 Ed 35.02N 136.43 E
Nagarote 49 Dg 12.16N 86.34W
Nagarzê 27 Ff 28.59N 90.28 E
Nagasaki 22 Of 32.47N 129.56 E
Nagasaki-Hantō 29 Ae 32.40N 129.45 E
Nagasaki Ken [2] 28 Jh 33.00N 129.50 E
Naga-Shima 29 Ce 33.50N 132.05 E
Nagashima 29 Ed 34.12N 136.19 E
Nagashima 29 Be 32.10N 130.10 E
Naga-Shima-Kaikyō 29 Be 32.15N 130.10 E
Nagato 28 Kg 34.21N 131.10 E
Nagayo 29 Ae 32.50N 129.52 E
Nāgda 25 Fd 23.27N 75.25 E
Nāgercoil 25 Fg 8.10N 77.26 E
Naghora Point 60 Gj 10.50S 162.24 E
Nagichot 35 Ee 4.16N 33.34 E
Nagi-San 29 Dd 35.10N 134.10 E
Nagiso 29 Ed 35.36N 137.36 E
Nago 27 Mf 26.35N 128.01 E
Nagold 10 Eh 48.52N 8.42 E
Nagorno-Karabahskaja
Avtonomnaja Oblast [3] 19 Eh 39.55N 46.45 E
Nagorny [R.S.F.S.R.] 20 He 55.45N 124.58 E
Nagorny [R.S.F.S.R.] 20 Md 63.10N 179.05 E
Nagorsk 7 Mg 59.21N 50.48 E
Nago-Wan 29b Ab 26.35N 127.55 E
Nagoya 22 Pf 35.10N 136.55 E
Nāgpur 22 Jg 21.09N 79.06 E
Nagqu 22 Lf 31.30N 92.00 E
Nag's Head 51c Ab 17.13N 62.38W
Nagua 49 Md 19.23N 69.50W
Naguabo 51a Cb 18.13N 65.44W
Nagyatád 10 Nj 46.13N 17.22 E
Nagybajom 10 Mj 46.23N 16.31 E
Nagyecsed 10 Si 47.52N 22.24 E
Nagyhalász 10 Rh 48.08N 21.46 E
Nagykálló 10 Ri 47.53N 21.51 E
Nagykanizsa 10 Mj 46.27N 16.59 E
Nagykáta 10 Pi 47.25N 19.45 E
Nagykőrös 10 Pi 47.02N 19.47 E
Nagykunság 10 Qj 46.55N 20.15 E
Nagy-Milic 10 Rh 48.35N 21.28 E
Naha 22 Og 26.13N 127.40 E
Nahanni Butte 42 Fd 61.04N 123.24W
Nahari 29 De 33.25N 134.01 E
Naharyya 24 Ff 33.00N 35.05 E
Nahāvand 23 Gc 34.12N 48.22 E
Nahe 10 Dg 49.58N 7.57 E
Nahičevan 6 Kh 39.13N 45.27 E
Nahičevanskaja ASSR [3] 19 Eh 39.15N 45.35 E
Na'hīmābād 24 Qg 30.51N 56.31 E
Nahodka 22 Pe 42.48N 132.52 E
Nahr al 'Āṣī = Orontes (EN)
(symbol) 23 Eb 36.02N 35.58 E
Nahr Quassel 13 Oi 35.45N 2.46 E
Nahuala, Laguna- 48 Ji 16.50N 99.40W
Nahuel Huapi, Lago- 56 Ff 40.58S 71.30W
Nahunta 44 Gj 31.12N 81.59W
Naie 29a Bb 43.24N 141.52 E
Naiguatá, Pico- 54 Ea 10.33N 66.46W
Naila 10 Hf 50.19N 11.42 E
Naiman Qi (Daqin Tal) 27 Lc 42.49N 120.38 E
Nain 39 Md 57.00N 61.40W
Nā'īn 24 Of 32.52N 53.05 E
Na'inābād 24 Pd 36.14N 54.39 E
Nairai 63d Bb 17.49S 179.24 E
Nairn 9 Jd 57.35N 3.53W
Nairobi 31 Ki 1.17S 36.49 E
Nairobi [3] 36 Gc 1.17S 36.50 E
Naissaar/Najssar 8 Ke 59.35N 24.25 E
Naitamba 63d Cb 17.01S 179.17W
Naizishan 28 Ic 43.41N 127.27 E
Najafābād 23 Hc 32.37N 51.21 E
Najd 23 Fe 25.00N 44.30 E
Najd 21 Gg 25.00N 44.30 E
Nājera 13 Jb 42.25N 2.44W
Najerilla 13 Jb 42.31N 2.42W
Naj' Ḥammādī 33 Fd 26.03N 32.15 E
Najibābād 25 Fc 29.58N 78.10 E
Najin 27 Nc 42.15N 130.18 E
Najō 29 Ec 35.47N 136.12 E
Najrān 33 Hf 17.30N 44.10 E
Najrān 33 Hf 17.30N 44.10 E
Najssaar/Naissaar 8 Ke 59.35N 24.25 E
Najstenjarvi 7 He 62.18N 32.42 E
Naju 28 Ig 35.02N 126.43 E
Najzataš, Pereval- 18 If 37.52N 73.46 E
Nakadōri-Jima 28 Jh 32.58N 129.05 E
Nakagawa 29a Ca 44.47N 142.05 E
Naka-Gawa [Jap.] 29 Gc 36.20N 140.36 E
Naka-Gawa [Jap.] 29 De 33.56N 134.42 E
Nakagusuku-Wan 29b Ab 26.15N 127.50 E
Nakahechi 29 De 33.47N 135.29 E
Naka-Iō-Jima 60 Cc 24.47N 141.20 E
Naka-Jima 29 Ce 33.58N 132.37 E
Nakajō 28 Oe 38.03N 139.24 E
Naka-Koshiki-Jima 29 Af 31.48N 129.50 E
Nakalele Point 65a Eb 21.02N 156.35W
Nakama 29 Be 33.50N 130.43 E
Nakaminato 29 Gc 36.22N 140.36 E
Nakamura 28 Lh 32.59N 132.56 E
Nakanai Mountains 59 Ka 5.35S 151.10 E
Nakano 29 Fc 36.45N 138.22 E
Nakano-Dake 29 Fc 37.04N 139.06 E
Nakanojō 29 Fc 36.35N 138.51 E
Naka-no-Shima 28 Lf 36.05N 133.04 E
Naka-no-Shima 27 Mf 29.50N 129.50 E
Nakasato 29a Bc 40.58N 140.26 E
Naka-satsunai 29a Cb 42.42N 143.08 E
Nakashibetsu 28 Rc 43.36N 145.00 E
Nakasongola 36 Fb 1.19N 32.28 E
Nakatonbetsu 29a Ca 44.58N 142.17 E
Nakatsu 28 Kh 33.34N 131.13 E
Nakatsugawa 28 Ng 35.29N 137.30 E
Nakfa 35 Fb 16.40N 38.30 E
Nakhon Pathom 25 Kf 13.49N 100.06 E
Nakhon Phanom 25 Mh 17.22N 104.46 E
Nakhon Ratchasima 22 Mh 14.57N 102.09 E
Nakhon Sawan 22 Mh 15.42N 100.06 E
Nakhon Si Thammarat 22 Li 8.26N 99.58 E
Nakijin 29b Ab 26.42N 127.59 E
Nakina 39 Kd 50.10N 86.42W
Nakkila 8 Ic 61.22N 22.00 E
Nakło nad Notecia 10 Nc 53.08N 17.35 E
Naknek 40 He 58.44N 157.02W
Nakonde 36 Fd 9.19S 32.46 E
Nakskov 7 Ci 54.50N 11.09 E
Näkten 8 Fb 62.50N 14.40 E
Naktong-gang 28 Jg 35.07N 128.57 E
Nakuru 31 Ki 0.20S 35.56 E
Nakusp 46 Ga 50.15N 117.48W
Nāl 25 Dc 26.02N 65.29 E
Nalajch → Nalajha 27 Ib 47.45N 107.16 E
Nalajha (Nalajch) 27 Ib 47.45N 107.16 E
Nalčik 6 Kg 43.29N 43.37 E
Nallıhan 24 Db 40.11N 31.21 E
Nalón 13 Fa 43.32N 6.04W
Nālūt 31 Ie 31.52N 10.59 E
Nalwasha 36 Gc 0.43S 36.26 E
Na Machairi/Brandon
Head 9 Ci 52.16N 10.15W
Namacurra 37 Fc 17.29S 37.01 E
Namai Bay 64a Bb 7.32N 134.39 E
Namak, Daryācheh-ye- =
Namak Lake (EN) 21 Hf 34.45N 51.36 E
Namak Lake (EN)=
Namak, Daryācheh-ye- 21 Hf 34.45N 51.36 E
Namakan Lake 45 Jb 48.27N 92.35W
Namak-e Mighān, Kavīr-e-
(symbol) 24 Me 34.13N 49.49 E
Namakia 37 Hc 15.56S 45.48 E
Namakwaland = Little
Namamland (EN) 37 Be 29.00S 17.00 E
Namanga 36 Gc 2.33S 36.47 E
Namangan 22 Je 41.00N 71.40 E
Namanganskaja Oblast [3] 19 Hg 41.00N 71.20 E
Namanyere 36 Fd 7.31S 31.03 E
Namapa 37 Fb 13.43S 39.50 E
Namaqua Seamount (EN)
(symbol) 37 Af 31.30S 11.20 E
Namarrói 37 Fc 15.57S 36.51 E
Namasagali 36 Fb 1.01N 32.57 E
Namasale 36 Fb 1.30N 32.37 E
Namatanai 60 Eh 3.40S 152.27 E
Namathu 63d Bb 17.21S 179.26 E
Nambavatu 63d Bb 16.36S 178.55 E
Namber 26 Jg 1.04S 134.49 E
Nambour 59 Ke 26.38S 152.58 E
Nambouwalu 61 Ec 16.59S 178.42 E
Nam Can 25 Kg 8.46N 104.59 E
Namche Bazar 25 Hc 27.49N 86.43 E
Nam Co 21 Lf 30.45N 90.35 E
Namčy 20 Hd 62.35N 129.40 E
Namdalen 7 Cd 64.38N 12.35 E
Nam Dinh 22 Mg 20.25N 106.10 E
Nämdö 8 He 59.10N 18.40 E
Nam Du, Quan Dao- 25 Kg 9.42N 104.22 E
Namêche, Andenne- 12 Hd 50.28N 5.00 E
Namelakl Passage 64a Bc 7.24N 134.38 E
Namen/Namur 11 Kd 50.28N 4.52 E
Namerikawa 29 Ec 36.45N 137.20 E
Náměšt nad Oslavou 10 Mg 49.12N 16.09 E
Nametil 37 Fc 15.43S 39.21 E
Namib Desert/
Namibwoestyn 30 Ik 23.00S 15.00 E
Namibia (South West
Africa) 31 Ik 22.00S 17.00 E
Namibe 31 Ij 15.12S 12.10 E
Namibe 36 Bf 15.20S 12.30 E
Namie 28 Pf 37.29N 140.59 E
Namīn 24 Mc 38.25N 48.30 E
Namioka 29 Ga 40.42N 140.35 E
Namiquipa 48 Fc 29.15N 107.40W
Namiranga 37 Gb 10.33S 40.30 E
Namjagbarwa Feng 21 Lg 29.38N 95.04 E
Namja La 27 Df 29.58N 82.34 E
Namkham 25 Jd 23.50N 97.41 E
Namlea 26 Ig 3.18S 127.06 E
Namling 27 Ef 29.44N 89.05 E
Namnoi, Khao- 27 Jf 10.36N 98.38 E
Namoi River 59 Je 30.00S 148.07 E
Namoluk Island 57 Gd 5.55N 153.08 E
Namonuito Atoll 57 Gd 8.46N 150.02 E
Namorik Atoll 57 Hd 5.36N 168.07 E
Namous 32 Gc 30.28N 0.14W
Nampa 43 Dc 43.34N 116.34W
Nampala 34 Db 15.17N 5.33W
Nam Phan = Cochin China
(EN) 21 Mg 11.00N 107.00 E
Nam Phong 25 Ke 16.45N 102.52 E
Nampi 28 De 38.02N 116.42 E
Namp'o 27 Md 38.44N 125.25 E
Nampula [3] 37 Fb 15.00S 39.30 E
Nampula 31 Kj 15.07S 39.15 E
Namsê Shankou 27 Df 29.58N 82.34 E
Namsos 6 Hc 64.30N 11.30 E
Namtu 25 Jd 23.05N 97.24 E
Namu 46 Ba 51.49N 127.52W
Namu Atoll 57 Hd 8.00N 168.10 E
Namuka-I-Lau 63d Cc 18.51S 178.38W
Namūli, Serra- 30 Kj 15.21S 37.00 E
Namuno 37 Fb 13.37S 38.48 E
Namur [3] 12 Gd 50.20N 4.50 E
Namur/Namen 11 Kd 50.28N 4.52 E
Namur-Saint Servais 12 Gd 50.28N 4.50 E
Namuruputh 36 Gb 4.34N 35.57 E
Namur-Wépion 12 Gd 50.25N 4.52 E
Namutoni 37 Bc 18.30S 17.55 E
Namwala 36 Ef 15.45S 26.26 E
Namwŏn 28 Ig 35.24N 127.23 E
Namysłów 10 Ne 51.05N 17.42 E
Nan 21 Mh 15.42N 100.09 E
Nan 25 Ke 18.48N 100.46 E
Nana 35 Bd 5.00N 15.50 E
Nana Barya 35 Bd 7.59N 17.43 E
Nanae 29a Bc 41.53N 140.41 E
Nanāimo 42 Fg 49.10N 123.56W
Nanakuli 65a Cb 21.23N 158.08W
Nana-Mambéré [3] 35 Bd 6.00N 16.00 E
Nanango 59 Ke 26.40S 152.00 E
Nanao 27 Od 37.03N 136.58 E
Nanao-Wan 29 Ec 37.10N 137.00 E
Nanatsu-Shima 29 Ec 37.35N 136.50 E
Nancha 27 Mb 47.08N 129.09 E
Nanchang 22 Ng 28.40N 115.58 E
Nancheng 27 Kf 27.32N 116.36 E
Nanchong 22 Mf 30.47N 106.03 E
Nancowry 25 Ig 7.59N 93.32 E
Nancy 6 Gf 48.41N 6.12 E
Nanda Devi 21 Jf 30.23N 79.59 E
Nandaime 49 Dh 11.46N 86.03W
Nandan [China] 27 Ig 24.59N 107.31 E
Nandan [Jap.] 28 Mg 34.15N 134.43 E
Nandaran → Qingyuan 28 Ce 38.46N 115.29 E
Nanded 22 Jh 19.09N 77.20 E
Nandewar Range 59 Kf 30.40S 151.10 E
Nandi 61 Ec 17.48S 177.25 E
Nandu Jiang 27 Jg 20.04N 110.22 E
Nanduri 63d Bb 16.27S 179.09 E
Nandyāl 25 Fe 15.29N 78.29 E
Nanfen 28 Gd 41.06N 123.45 E
Nanfeng 27 Kf 27.15N 116.30 E
Nanga-Eboko 34 He 4.41N 12.22 E
Nanga Parbat 21 Jf 35.15N 74.36 E
Nangapinoh 26 Fg 0.20S 111.44 E
Nangarhār [3] 23 Lc 34.15N 70.30 E
Nangatayap 26 Fg 1.32S 110.34 E
Nangis 11 If 48.33N 3.00 E
Nangnim-san 28 Id 40.21N 126.55 E
Nangnim-Sanmaek 28 Id 40.30N 127.00 E
Nangong 27 Kd 37.22N 115.23 E
Nangqên 27 Ge 32.15N 96.13 E
Nanguan 28 Af 36.42N 111.41 E
Nanguantao → Guantao 28 Cf 36.33N 115.18 E
Nangweshi 36 Df 16.26S 23.20 E
Nan Hai=South China Sea
(EN) 21 Ni 10.00N 113.00 E
Nanhaoqian → Shangyi 28 Bd 41.06N 113.58 E
Nanhe 28 Cf 36.58N 114.41 E
Nanhua 27 Hf 25.16N 101.18 E
Nanhui 28 Fi 31.03N 121.46 E
Nan Hulsan Hu 27 Gd 36.45N 95.45 E
Nanjian 27 Hf 25.05N 100.32 E
Nanjiang 27 Ie 32.22N 106.45 E
Nanjing=Nanking (EN) 22 Nf 31.59N 118.51 E
Nankai Trough (EN) 27 Ne 32.00N 135.00 E
Nanking (EN)=Nanjing 22 Nf 31.59N 118.51 E
Nankoku 28 Lh 33.39N 133.44 E
Nanle 28 Cf 36.06N 115.12 E
Nanling 28 Ei 30.55N 118.19 E
Nan Ling 21 Ng 25.00N 112.00 E
Nanlou Shan 28 Ic 43.24N 126.40 E
Nanma → Yiyuan 28 Ef 36.11N 118.10 E
Nanning 22 Mg 22.50N 108.18 E
Nannup 59 Df 33.59S 115.45 E
Nanortalik 41 Hf 60.32N 45.45W
Nanpan Jiang 27 Ig 24.56N 106.12 E
Nānpāra 25 Gc 27.52N 81.30 E
Nanping [China] 22 Ng 26.42N 118.09 E
Nanping [China] 27 He 33.15N 104.13 E
Nanpu 28 Ee 39.16N 118.12 E
Nanqiao → Fengxian 28 Fi 30.55N 121.27 E
Nansei-Shotō=Ryukyu
Islands (EN) 21 Og 26.30N 128.00 E
Nansen Cordillera (EN) 67 Ge 87.00N 90.00 E
Nansen Land 41 Hb 83.20N 46.00W
Nanshan Islands (EN)=
Nansha Qundao 21 Ni 9.40N 113.30 E
Nansha Qundao=
Nanshan Islands (EN) 21 Ni 9.40N 113.30E
Nansio 36 Fc 2.08S 33.03 E
Nant 11 Jj 44.01N 3.18 E
Nantais, Lac - 42 Kd 61.00N 73.50W
Nanterre 11 If 48.54N 2.12 E
Nantes 6 Ff 47.13N 1.33W
Nantes à Brest, Can. de- 11 Bf 48.12N 4.06W
Nanteuil-le-Haudouin 12 Ee 49.08N 2.48 E
Nanticoke 44 Je 41.13N 76.00W
Nantō 29 Ed 34.17N 136.29 E
Nantong 27 Le 32.00N 120.52 E
Nantong (Jinsha) 28 Fh 32.06N 120.52 E
Nantou 27 Lg 23.54N 120.51 E
Nantua 11 Lh 46.09N 5.37 E
Nantucket 44 Le 41.17N 70.06W
Nantucket Island 43 Mc 41.16N 70.03W
Nantucket Sound 44 Le 41.30N 70.15W
Nanuku Passage 63d Cb 16.45S 179.15W
Nanuku Reef 63d Cb 16.40S 179.26W
Nanumanga Island 57 Ie 6.18S 176.20 E
Nanumea Atoll 57 Ie 5.43S 176.00 E
Nanuque 54 Jg 17.50S 40.21W
Nanusa, Pulau-Pulau- 26 If 4.42N 127.06 E
Nanwan Shuiku 28 Bh 32.02N 113.57 E
Nanwei Dao 27 Je 8.42N 111.40 E
Nanweng He 27 Ma 51.10N 125.59 E
Nanxian 28 Bj 29.22N 112.25 E
Nanxiang 28 Fi 31.18N 121.17 E
Nanxiong 27 Jf 25.13N 114.18 E
Nanxun 28 Fi 30.53N 120.26 E
Nanyandang Shan 27 Lf 27.37N 120.06 E
Nanyang 22 Nf 32.56N 112.32 E
Nanyang Hu 28 Dg 35.15N 116.39 E
Nanyō 28 Pe 38.03N 140.10 E
Nanyuki 31 Kh 0.01N 37.04 E
Nanzhang 27 Je 31.45N 111.53 E
Nanzhao 27 Je 33.28N 112.29 E
Nao, Cabo de la- 5 Gh 38.44N 0.14 E
Naococane, Lac- 42 Kf 52.50N 70.40W
Naoero/Nauru [1] 58 He 0.31S 166.56 E
Naoetsu 29 Fc 37.11N 138.14 E
Não-me-Toque 55 Fi 28.28S 52.49W
Naours, Souterrains de- 12 Ed 50.05N 2.17 E
Napa 46 Dg 38.18N 122.17W
Napanee 44 Ic 44.15N 76.57W
Napassoq 41 Ge 65.45N 52.38W
Napata 35 Eb 18.29N 31.51 E
Na-Peng 25 Lg 23.10N 98.26 E
Napf 14 Bc 47.01N 7.57 E
Napier 58 Ih 39.30S 176.54 E
Napier, Mount- 59 Fc 17.32S 129.10 E
Napier Mountains 66 Ee 66.30S 53.40 E
Naples [Fl.-U.S.] 43 Kf 26.08N 81.48W
Naples [Id.-U.S.] 46 Gb 48.34N 116.24W
Naples (EN) = Napoli 6 Hg 40.50N 14.15 E
Naples, Gulf of- (EN) =
Napoli, Golfo di- 14 Ij 40.45N 14.10 E
Napo 27 Ig 23.25N 105.49 E
Napo, Rio- 52 If 3.20S 72.40W
Napoleon 45 Gc 46.30N 99.46W
Napoli = Naples (EN) 6 Hg 40.50N 14.15 E
Napoli, Golfo di- = Naples,
Gulf of- (EN) 14 Ij 40.45N 14.10 E
Napostá 55 An 38.26S 62.15W
Napuka, Ile- 57 Mf 14.12S 141.15W
Naqa 35 Eb 16.16N 33.17 E
Naqadeh 23 Gb 36.57N 45.23 E
Naqsh-e-Rostam 24 Og 30.01N 52.50 E
Nar 9 Ni 52.45N 0.24 E
Nära 25 Dc 24.07N 69.07 E
Nara [Jap.] 27 Oe 34.41N 135.50 E
Nara [Mali] 34 Db 15.11N 7.15W
Naračenskibani 15 Hh 41.54N 24.45 E
Naracoorte 59 Ig 36.58S 140.44 E
Nara-Ken [2] 28 Mg 34.20N 135.55 E
Naranjo 48 Ee 25.48N 108.31W
Naranjos [Bol.] 55 Cd 18.38S 59.09W
Naranjos [Mex.] 48 Kg 21.21N 97.41W
Narao 29 Ae 32.52N 129.04 E
Narathiwat 25 Kg 6.25N 101.48 E
Nārāyanganj 25 Id 23.37N 90.30 E
Narbonne 11 Ik 43.11N 3.00 E
Narca, Ponta da- 36 Bd 6.07S 12.16 E
Narcea 13 Fa 43.28N 6.06W
Narcondam 25 If 13.15N 94.30 E
Nardò 14 Mj 40.11N 18.02 E
Naré 55 Bj 30.58S 60.28W
Nares Land 41 Hb 82.25N 47.30W
Nares Strait 38 Lb 78.50N 73.00W
Narew 10 Td 52.55N 23.29 E
Narew 10 Qd 52.26N 20.42 E
Narian, Pointe- 63b Be 20.05S 164.00 E
Narin Gol 27 Fd 36.54N 92.51 E
Nariño [2] 54 Cc 1.30N 78.00W
Narita 29 Gd 35.47N 140.18 E
Narjan-Mar 6 Lb 67.39N 53.00 E
Närke 8 Ff 59.05N 15.05 E
Narlı 24 Gd 37.27N 37.09 E
Narmada 21 Jg 21.38N 72.36 E
Narman 24 Ib 40.21N 41.52 E
Närnaul 25 Fc 28.03N 76.06 E
Narni 14 Gh 42.31N 12.31 E
Naroč 8 Lj 54.27N 26.45 E
Naroč 8 Lj 54.57N 26.49 E
Naroč, Ozero- 16 Eb 54.50N 26.45 E
Naroda 17 Jd 64.15N 61.00 E
Narodnaja, Gora- 5 Mb 65.04N 60.09 E
Naro-Fominsk 19 Dd 55.24N 36.43 E
Narok 36 Gc 1.05S 35.52 E
Narovlja 16 Fd 51.48N 29.31 E
Närpes/Närpio 8 Ib 62.28N 21.20 E
Närpio/Närpes 8 Ib 62.28N 21.20 E
Narrabri 59 Jf 30.19S 149.47 E
Narrandera 59 Jf 34.45S 146.33 E
Narrogin 59 Df 32.56S 117.10 E
Narromine 59 Jf 32.14S 148.15 E
Narrows, The- 51c Ab 17.12N 62.38W
Narryer, Mount- 59 De 26.30S 116.25 E
Narsimhapur 25 Fd 22.57N 79.12 E
Narssalik 41 Hf 61.42N 49.11W
Narssaq [Grld.] 41 Hf 61.00N 46.00W
Narssaq [Grld.] 41 Gf 64.00N 51.33W
Narssarssuaq 41 Hf 61.10N 45.15W
Narthákion 15 Fj 39.14N 22.22 E
Nartkala 16 Mh 43.32N 43.47 E
Narubis 37 Be 26.55S 18.35 E
Narugo 29 Gb 38.44N 140.43 E
Nāruja 25 Jd 45.50N 26.47 E
Naru-Shima 29 Ae 32.50N 128.56 E
Naruto 28 Mg 34.11N 134.37 E
Naruto-Kaikyō 29 Dd 34.15N 134.40 E
Narva 7 Gg 59.29N 28.02 E
Narva 6 Id 59.23N 28.11 E
Narva Jõesuu/Narva-Jyesuu 8 Me 59.21N 28.04 E
Narva-Jyesuu/Narva Jõesuu 8 Me 59.21N 28.04 E
Narva laht 7 Gg 59.30N 27.40 E
Narvik 6 Hb 68.26N 17.25 E
Narvski Zaliv 7 Gg 59.30N 27.40 E
Narvskoje Vodohranilišče 8 Me 59.10N 28.30 E
Narym 20 De 58.58N 81.40 E
Naryn 21 Je 40.54N 71.45 E
Naryn 22 Je 41.26N 75.59 E
Naryncol 19 Ig 42.43N 80.08 E
Narynskaja Oblast [3] 19 Hg 41.20N 75.40 E
Nås 7 Df 60.27N 14.29 E
Na Sailti/Saltee Islands 9 Gi 52.07N 6.36W
Näsåker 7 De 63.23N 16.54 E
Nasarawa 34 Gd 8.32N 7.43 E
Năsăud 15 Hb 47.17N 24.24 E
Nasawa 63b Db 15.12S 168.06 E
Na Sceirí/Skerries 9 Gh 53.35N 6.07W
Nāshik 22 Jg 20.05N 73.48 E
Nash Point 9 Jj 51.24N 3.27W
Nashtārud 24 Nd 36.45N 51.02 E
Nashua 44 Ld 42.44N 71.28W
Nashville [Ar.-U.S.] 45 Jj 33.57N 93.51W
Nashville [Ga.-U.S.] 44 Fj 31.12N 83.15W
Nashville [Il.-U.S.] 45 Lg 38.21N 89.23W
Nashville [In.-U.S.] 44 Df 39.12N 86.15W
Nashville [Tn.-U.S.] 39 Kf 36.09N 86.48W
Nashville Seamount (EN) 38 Nf 35.00N 57.20W
Našice 14 Me 45.30N 18.06 E
Nasielsk 10 Qd 52.36N 20.48 E
Näsijärvi 5 Ic 61.35N 23.40 E
Nāşir 35 Ed 8.36N 33.04 E
Naskaupi 42 Lf 53.47N 60.51W
Nasorolevu 63d Bb 16.38S 179.24 E
Naşr [Eg.] 24 Dg 30.36N 30.23 E
Naşr [Lib.] 33 Dd 28.59N 21.13 E
Naşrābād 24 Of 32.09N 52.08 E
Nass 42 Ee 55.00N 129.50W
Nassandres 12 Ce 49.07N 0.44 E
Nassandres-La Rivière
Thibouville 12 Ce 49.07N 0.44 E
Nassau [Bah.] 39 Lg 25.05N 77.21W
Nassau [Ger.] 12 Jd 50.19N 7.48 E
Nassau, Bahía- 56 Gi 55.25S 67.40W
Nassau Island 57 Kf 11.33S 165.25W
Nassau River 59 Ic 15.58S 141.30 E
Nasser, Birkat- = Nasser,
Lake-(EN) 30 Kf 22.40N 32.00 E

Index Symbols

[1] Independent Nation
[2] State, Region
[3] District, County
[4] Municipality
[5] Colony, Dependency
Continent
Physical Region
Historical or Cultural Region
Mount, Mountain
Volcano
Hill
Mountains, Mountain Range
Hills, Escarpment
Plateau, Upland
Pass, Gap
Plain, Lowland
Delta
Salt Flat
Valley, Canyon
Crater, Cave
Karst Features
Depression
Polder
Desert, Dunes
Forest, Woods
Heath, Steppe
Oasis
Cape, Point
Coast, Beach
Cliff
Peninsula
Isthmus
Sandbank
Island
Atoll
Rock, Reef
Islands, Archipelago
Rocks, Reefs
Coral Reef
Well, Spring
Geyser
River, Stream
Waterfall Rapids
River Mouth, Estuary
Lake
Salt Lake
Intermittent Lake
Reservoir
Swamp, Pond
Canal
Glacier
Ice Shelf, Pack Ice
Ocean
Sea
Gulf, Bay
Strait, Fjord
Lagoon
Bank
Seamount
Tablemount
Ridge
Shelf
Basin
Escarpment, Sea Scarp
Fracture
Trench, Abyss
National Park, Reserve
Point of Interest
Recreation Site
Cave, Cavern
Historic Site
Ruins
Wall, Walls
Church, Abbey
Temple
Scientific Station
Airport
Port
Lighthouse
Mine
Tunnel
Dam, Bridge

Nasser, Lake-(EN)=Nasser, Birkat- 30 Kf 22.40N 32.00 E
Nassian 34 Ed 9.24N 4.29W
Nässjö 7 Dh 57.39N 14.41 E
Nassogne 12 Hd 50.08N 5.21 E
Na Staighri Dubha/Blackstairs Mountains 9 Gi 52.33N 6.49W
Nastapoka Islands 42 Je 56.50N 76.50W
Nastätten 12 Jd 50.12N 7.52 E
Nastola 8 Kd 60.57N 25.56 E
Nasu 29 Gc 37.02N 140.06 E
Nasu-Dake 29 Fc 37.07N 139.58 E
Näsviken 8 Gc 61.45N 16.52 E
Natá 49 Gi 8.20N 80.31W
Nata 30 Jk 20.14S 26.10 E
Nata 37 Dd 20.13S 26.11 E
Natal [2] 37 Ee 29.00S 30.00 E
Natal [B.C.-Can.] 46 Hb 49.44N 114.50W
Natal [Braz.] 53 Mf 5.47S 35.13W
Natal [Indon.] 26 Cf 0.33N 99.07 E
Natal Basin (EN) 3 Fm 30.00S 40.00 E
Natanz 24 Nf 33.31N 51.54 E
Natashquan 42 Lf 50.09N 61.37W
Natashquan 42 Lf 50.11N 61.49W
Natchez 43 Ie 31.34N 91.23W
Natchitoches 43 Ie 31.46N 93.05W
Natewa Bay 63d Bb 16.35S 179.40 E
Nathorsts Land 41 Jd 72.20N 27.00W
Nathula 63d Ab 16.53S 177.25 E
Natitingou 31 Hg 10.19N 1.22 E
Natityāy, Jabal- 33 Fe 23.01N 34.22 E
Natividad, Isla- 48 Bd 27.55N 115.10W
Natividade 54 If 11.43S 47.47W
Natori 28 Pe 38.11N 140.58 E
Natron, Lake- 30 Ki 2.25S 36.00 E
Natrūn, Wādī an- 24 Dg 30.25N 30.13 E
Natsudomari-Zaki 29a Bc 41.00N 140.53 E
Nättarö 8 Hf 58.50N 18.10 E
Nättraby 8 Fh 56.12N 15.31 E
Natuna Besar, Pulau- 26 Ef 4.00N 108.15 E
Natuna Islands (EN)= Bunguran, Kepulauan- 21 Mi 2.45N 109.00 E
Naturaliste, Cape- 57 Ch 33.32S 115.01 E
Naturaliste Channel 59 Ce 25.25S 113.00 E
Naturita 45 Bg 38.14N 108.34W
Naturno / Naturns 14 Ed 46.39N 11.00 E
Naturns / Naturno 14 Ed 46.39N 11.00 E
Nau 18 Gd 40.09N 69.22 E
Nau, Cap de la-/Nao, Cabo de la- 5 Gh 38.44N 0.14 E
Naucelle 11 Ij 44.12N 2.21 E
Nauëji-Akmjane/Naujoji-Akmenė 7 Fh 56.21N 22.50 E
Naugo/Nauvo 8 Id 60.10N 21.50 E
Nauhcampatépetl→Cofre de Perote, Cerro- 48 Kh 19.29N 97.08W
Nauja Bay 42 Kc 68.58N 75.00W
Naujamiestis/Naujamiestis 8 Ki 55.41N 24.09 E
Naujamiestis/Naujamiestis 8 Ki 55.41N 24.09 E
Naujoji-Akmenė/Nauëji-Akmjane 7 Fh 56.21N 22.50 E
Naukluft 37 Bd 24.10S 16.10 E
Naumburg [Ger.] 12 Lc 51.15N 9.10 E
Naumburg [Ger.] 10 He 51.09N 11.49 E
Nā'ūr 24 Fg 31.53N 35.50 E
Nauru 57 He 0.31S 166.56 E
Nauru/Naoero [1] 58 He 0.31S 166.56 E
Nauški 20 Ff 50.28N 106.07 E
Nausori 61 Ec 18.02S 178.32 E
Nauta 54 Dd 4.32S 73.33W
Nautanwa 25 Gc 27.26N 83.25 E
Nautla 48 Kg 20.13N 96.47W
Nauvo/Naugo 8 Id 60.10N 21.50 E
Nava 48 Ic 28.25N 100.45W
Navacerrada, Puerto de- 13 Id 40.47N 4.00W
Nava del Rey 13 Gc 41.20N 5.05W
Navahermosa 13 He 39.38N 4.28W
Navajo Mountain 46 Jh 37.02N 110.52W
Navajo Reservoir 45 Ch 36.55N 107.30W
Navalmoral de la Mata 13 Ge 39.54N 5.32W
Navan/An Uaimh 9 Gh 53.39N 6.41W
Navarin, Mys- 21 Tc 62.16N 179.10 E
Navarino, Isla- 52 Jk 55.05S 67.40W
Navarra [3] 13 Kb 42.45N 1.40W
Navarra=Navarre (EN) 13 Kb 43.00N 1.30W
Navarre (EN)=Navarra 13 Kb 43.00N 1.30W
Navarro 55 Cl 35.01S 59.16W
Navarro Mills Lake 45 Hk 31.56N 96.45W
Navašino 7 Ki 55.33N 42.12 E
Navasota 45 Hk 30.23N 96.05W
Navasota River 45 Hk 30.20N 96.09W
Navassa 47 Ie 18.24N 75.01W
Navaste Jõgi/Navesti 8 Kf 58.56N 24.58 E
Nävekvarn 8 Gf 58.38N 16.49 E
Naver 9 Ic 58.30N 4.15W
Navesti/Navaste Jõgi 8 Kf 58.56N 24.58 E
Navia 13 Fa 43.32N 6.43W
Navia 13 Fa 43.33N 6.44W
Navidad, Bahia de- 48 Gh 19.10N 104.45W
Navidad Bank (EN) 49 Mc 20.00N 68.50W
Naviti 63d Ab 17.07S 177.15 E
Navlja 16 Ic 52.42N 34.03 E
Navlja 19 De 52.50N 34.31 E
Năvodari 15 Le 44.19N 28.36 E
Navoi 19 Gg 40.10N 65.15 E
Navoja 47 Cc 27.06N 109.26W
Navolato 48 Fe 24.47N 107.42W
Navoloki 7 Jh 57.28N 41.59 E
Návpaktos 15 Ek 38.24N 21.50 E
Návplion 15 Fl 37.34N 22.48 E
Navrongo 34 Ec 10.54N 1.06W
Navsāri 25 Ed 20.55N 72.55 E
Navtilos 15 Gn 35.57N 23.13 E
Navua 63d Bc 18.13S 178.10 E
Navy Board Inlet 42 Jb 73.30N 81.00W
Nawa 24 Gf 32.53N 36.03 E
Nawābshāh 25 Dc 26.15N 68.25 E
Nawāşif, Ḩarrat- 33 He 21.20N 42.10 E
Nāws, Ra's- 23 If 17.18N 55.16 E
Náxos 15 Il 37.06N 25.23 E
Naxos 14 Jm 37.49N 15.15 E
Náxos=Naxos (EN) 5 Ih 37.02N 25.35 E
Naxos (EN)=Náxos 5 Ih 37.02N 25.35 E
Nayarit [2] 47 Cd 22.00N 105.00W
Nayarit, Sierra- 47 Dd 22.00N 103.50W
Nayau 63d Cb 17.58S 179.03W
Nāy Band [Iran] 24 Oi 27.23N 52.38 E
Nāy Band [Iran] 24 Qf 32.20N 57.34 E
Nāy Band, Ra's-e- 24 Oi 27.23N 52.34 E
Nayoro 27 Pc 44.21N 142.28 E
Nazaré [Braz.] 54 Kf 13.02S 39.00W
Nazaré [Port.] 13 Ce 39.36N 9.04W
Nazareth (EN)=Nazerat 24 Ff 32.42N 35.18 E
Nazarovo 20 Ee 56.01N 90.36 E
Nazas 48 Ge 25.14N 104.08W
Nazas, Rio- 38 Ig 25.35N 105.00W
Nazca 53 Ig 14.50S 74.55W
Nazca Ridge (EN) 3 Nl 22.00S 82.00W
Naze 27 Mf 28.23N 129.30 E
Nazerat=Nazareth (EN) 24 Ff 32.42N 35.18 E
Nazilli 23 Cb 37.55N 28.21 E
Nazimiye 24 Hc 39.11N 39.50 E
Nazimovo 20 Ee 59.30N 90.58 E
Nazino 20 Cd 60.15N 78.58 E
Nazlū 24 Kd 37.42N 45.16 E
Nazran 16 Nh 43.15N 44.46 E
Nazret 35 Fd 8.34N 39.18 E
Nazw'a 23 Ie 22.54N 57.31 E
Nazym 17 Nf 61.12N 68.57 E
Nazyvajevsk 19 Hd 55.34N 71.21 E
Nbâk 32 Ef 17.15N 14.59W
Nchanga 36 Ee 12.31S 27.52 E
Ncheu 36 Fe 14.49S 34.38 E
Ndala 36 Fc 4.46S 33.16 E
N'dalatando 36 Bd 9.18S 14.54 E
Ndali 34 Fd 9.51N 2.43 E
Ndélé 31 Jh 8.24N 20.39 E
Ndélélé 34 He 4.02N 14.56 E
Ndendé 36 Bc 2.23S 11.23 E
Ndindi 36 Bc 3.46S 11.09 E
N'Djamena (Fort-Lamy) 31 Ig 12.07N 15.03 E
Ndola 31 Jj 12.58S 28.38 E
Ndouana, Pointe- 63b Dc 16.35S 168.09 E
Ndrhamcha, Sebkha de- 32 Df 18.45N 15.48W
Nduindui 60 Fi 9.48S 159.58 E
Ndui Ndui 63b Cb 15.24S 167.46 E
Né 11 Fi 45.40N 0.23W
Nea 63c Ab 10.51S 165.47 E
Nea 7 Ce 63.13N 11.02 E
Néa Alikarnassós 15 In 35.20N 25.09 E
Néa Artáki 15 Gk 38.31N 23.38 E
Neagari 29 Ec 36.26N 136.26 E
Neagh, Lough-/Loch nEathach 5 Fe 54.38N 6.24W
Neagră, Marea-=Black Sea (EN) 5 Jg 43.00N 35.00 E
Neah Bay 46 Cb 48.22N 124.37W
Néa Ionia 15 Fj 39.23N 22.56 E
Neajlov 15 Je 44.11N 26.12 E
Neale, Lake- 59 Fd 24.20S 130.00 E
Neamţ [2] 15 Jb 47.00N 26.20 E
Neápolis [Grc.] 15 In 35.15N 25.37 E
Neápolis [Grc.] 15 Ei 40.19N 21.23 E
Neápolis [Grc.] 15 Gm 36.31N 23.04 E
Near Islands 38 Bd 52.40N 173.30W
Neath 9 Jj 51.37N 3.50W
Neath 9 Jj 51.40N 3.48W
Néa Zikhni 15 Gh 41.02N 23.50 E
Néba 63b Ae 20.09S 163.55 E
Nebaj 49 Bf 15.24N 91.08W
Nebbou 34 Ec 11.18N 1.53W
Nebit-Dag 22 Hf 39.30N 54.22 E
Neblina, Pico da- 52 Je 1.08N 66.10W
Nebo 59 Jd 21.40S 148.39 E
Nebo, Mount- 46 Jg 39.49N 111.46W
Nebolči 7 Hg 59.08N 33.21 E
Nebraska [2] 43 Gc 41.30N 100.00W
Nebraska City 43 Hc 40.41N 95.52W
Nebrodi (Caronie) 14 Im 37.55N 14.35 E
Necedah 45 Kd 44.02N 90.03W
Nechako 42 Ff 53.55N 122.44W
Nechako Reservoir 42 Ef 53.00N 126.10W
Nechar, Djebel- 13 Qi 35.52N 4.59 E
Neches River 45 Jl 29.55N 93.52W
Nechí 49 Jj 8.07N 74.46W
Nechí, Río- 49 Ji 8.08N 74.46W
Neckako Plateau 42 Ff 53.25N 124.40W
Neckar 10 Eg 49.31N 8.26 E
Neckarsulm 10 Fg 49.11N 9.14 E
Necker Island 57 Kb 23.35N 164.42W
Necochea 53 Ki 38.34S 58.45W
Necy 12 Bf 48.50N 0.07W
Nedeley 35 Bb 15.34N 18.10 E
Nederland 45 Jl 29.58N 93.59W
Nederland=Netherlands (EN) [1] 6 Ge 52.15N 5.30 E
Nederlandse Antillen [5] 50 Ec 18.06N 63.10W
Nederlandse Antillen = Netherlands Antilles (EN) [5] 53 Jd 12.15N 69.00W
Neder-Rijn = Lower Rhine (EN) 11 Mc 51.59N 6.20 E
Nēdong 22 Lg 29.14N 91.46 E
Nedstrand 8 Ae 59.21N 5.51 E
Nedstrandefjorden 8 Ae 59.20N 5.50 E
Neede 12 Ib 52.08N 6.37 E
Needham Market 12 Db 52.09N 1.02 E
Needham's Point 51q Ab 13.05N 59.36W
Needles 43 Ee 34.51N 114.37W
Neembucú [3] 55 Dh 27.00S 58.00W
Neenah 45 Ld 44.11N 88.28W
Neepawa 45 Ga 50.13N 99.29W
Neermoor, Moormerland- 12 Ja 53.18N 7.26 E
Neeroeteren, Maaseik- 12 Hc 51.05N 5.42 E
Neerpelt 12 Hc 51.13N 5.25 E
Nefasit 35 Fb 15.18N 39.04 E
Nefedova 19 Hd 58.48N 72.34 E
Né Finn/Nephin 9 Dg 54.01N 9.22W
Neftah 32 Ic 33.52N 7.53 E
Neftečala 16 Pj 39.19N 49.13 E
Neftegorsk [R.S.F.S.R.] 16 Kg 44.22N 39.42 E
Neftegorsk [R.S.F.S.R.] 20 Jf 53.00N 143.00 E
Neftegorsk [R.S.F.S.R.] 19 Fe 52.45N 51.13 E
Neftejugansk 19 Hc 61.05N 72.45 E
Neftekamsk 19 Fd 56.06N 54.17 E
Neftekumsk 19 Eg 44.43N 44.59 E
Neftjanyje Kamin 16 Qi 40.15N 50.49 E
Negage 36 Cd 7.46S 15.18 E
Negara 26 Fh 8.22S 114.37 E
Negele=Neghelle (EN) 31 Kh 5.20N 39.37 E
Negev Desert (EN)= Hānegev 24 Fg 30.30N 34.55 E
Neghelle (EN)=Negele 31 Kh 5.20N 39.37 E
Negla, Arroyo- 55 Df 22.52S 56.41W
Negola 36 Be 14.10S 14.30 E
Negomano 37 Fb 11.26S 38.33 E
Negombo 25 Fg 7.13N 79.50 E
Negonego Atoll 57 Mf 18.47S 141.48W
Negotin 15 Fe 44.13N 22.32 E
Negotino 15 Fh 41.29N 22.06 E
Negra, Cordillera- 54 Ce 9.25S 77.40W
Negra, Coxilha- 55 Ej 31.02S 55.45W
Negra, Peña- 13 Fb 42.11N 6.30W
Negra, Ponta- 55 Jf 23.21S 44.36W
Negra, Punta- 52 Hf 6.06S 81.10W
Negra, Serra- 55 Fc 16.30S 52.10W
Negra o de los Difuntos, Laguna- 55 Fl 34.03S 53.40W
Negreira 13 Db 42.54N 8.44W
Negreni 15 He 44.34N 24.36 E
Negreşti 15 Gb 47.52N 23.26 E
Negrine 32 Ic 34.29N 7.31 E
Negrinho, Rio- 55 Ed 19.20S 55.05W
Negro, Cabo- 13 Gi 35.41N 5.17W
Negro, Rio- [Arg.] 55 Ch 27.27S 58.54W
Negro, Rio- [Arg.] 52 Jj 41.02S 62.47W
Negro, Rio- [Bol.] 54 Ff 14.11S 63.07W
Negro, Rio- [Braz.] 54 Gg 19.13S 57.17W
Negro, Rio- [Braz.] 56 Jc 26.01S 50.30W
Negro, Rio- [Par.] 56 Ib 24.23S 57.11W
Negro, Rio- [S.Amer.] 52 Kf 3.08S 59.55W
Negro, Rio- [S.Amer.] 55 Ce 20.11S 58.10W
Negro, Rio- [Ur.] 52 Ki 33.24S 58.22W
Negros 21 Oi 10.00N 123.00 E
Negru, Rîu- 15 Id 45.45N 25.46 E
Negru Vodă 15 Lf 43.49N 28.12 E
Nehajevski 16 Ld 50.27N 41.46 E
Nehalem River 46 Dd 45.40N 123.56W
Nehāvand 24 Me 35.56N 49.31 E
Nehe 27 Lb 48.28N 124.53 E
Nehoiu 15 Jd 45.26N 26.17 E
Néhoué, Baie de- 63b Be 20.21S 164.09 E
Neiba 49 Ld 18.28N 71.25W
Neiba, Bahia de- 49 Ld 18.15N 71.02W
Neidin/Kenmare 9 Dj 51.53N 9.35W
Neige, Crêt de la- 11 Lh 46.16N 5.56 E
Neiges, Piton des- 30 Mk 21.05S 55.29 E
Neijiang 22 Mg 29.38N 104.58 E
Neilton 46 Dc 47.25N 123.52W
Nei-meng-ku Tzu-chih-ch'ü→Nei Monggol Zizhiqu [2] 27 Jc 44.00N 112.00 E
Nei Monggol Gaoyuan 21 Ne 42.00N 111.00 E
Nei Monggol Zizhiqu (Nei-meng-ku Tzu-chih-ch'ü)=Inner Mongolia (EN) [2] 27 Jc 44.00N 112.00 E
Neiqiu 28 Cf 37.17N 114.30 E
Neiva 53 Ie 2.56N 75.18W
Neja 19 Ed 58.19N 43.52 E
Nejanilini Lake 42 He 59.30N 97.50W
Nejdek 10 If 50.19N 12.44 E
Nejo 35 Fd 9.30N 35.32 E
Nejva 17 Kh 57.54N 62.18 E
Nekemt=Leqemt (EN) 31 Kh 9.05N 36.33 E
Neksø 8 Fi 55.04N 15.09 E
Nelemnoje 20 Kc 65.23N 151.08 E
Nelgese 20 Ic 66.40N 136.30 E
Nelichu 35 Ed 6.08N 34.25 E
Nelidovo 19 Dd 56.13N 32.50 E
Neligh 45 Ge 42.08N 98.02W
Neljaty 20 Ge 56.29N 115.50 E
Nelkan 20 Jd 64.15N 143.03 E
Nellore 22 Jh 12.56N 79.08 E
Nelma 20 Ig 47.40N 139.08 E
Nelson [2] 62 Ed 41.45S 172.30 E
Nelson 38 Jd 57.04N 92.30W
Nelson [B.C.-Can.] 42 Fg 49.29N 117.17W
Nelson [N.Z.] 58 Ii 41.16S 173.15 E
Nelson, Cape- [Austl.] 57 Fh 38.26S 141.33 E
Nelson, Cape- [Pap.N.Gui.] 59 Ja 9.00S 149.15 E
Nelson Island 40 Gd 60.35N 164.45W
Nelson's Dockyard 51d Bb 17.00N 61.46W
Nelspruit 31 Kk 25.30S 30.58 E
Néma 31 Gg 16.36N 7.15W
Néma, Dahr- 32 Ff 16.14N 7.30W
Neman 5 Id 55.18N 21.23 E
Neman 7 Fi 55.03N 22.01 E
Nembrala 26 Hi 10.53S 122.50 E
Nemda 7 Kh 57.31N 43.15 E
Neméa 15 Fl 37.49N 22.39 E
Neméa 15 Fl 37.49N 22.40 E
Neměçkes, Mali i- 15 Di 40.08N 20.24 E
Nemenčinė 8 Kj 54.50N 25.29 E
Nemërçkës, Mali i- 15 Di 40.08N 20.24 E
Nemira, Vîrful- 15 Jc 46.15N 26.19 E
Nemirov [Ukr.-U.S.S.R.] 10 Tf 50.08N 23.28 E
Nemirov [Ukr.-U.S.S.R.] 16 Fe 48.59N 28.50 E
Némiscau 42 Jf 51.30N 77.00W
Nemjuga 7 Kd 65.29N 43.40 E
Nemours 11 If 48.16N 2.42 E
Nemunas 5 Id 55.18N 21.23 E
Nemunėlis 8 Kh 56.24N 24.10 E
Nemuro 27 Qc 43.20N 145.35 E
Nemuro-Hantō 29a Db 43.20N 145.35 E
Nemuro-Kaikyō=Nemuro Strait (EN) 20 Jh 43.50N 145.30 E
Nemuro Strait (EN)= Kunaširski Proliv 20 Jh 43.50N 145.30 E
Nemuro Strait (EN)= Nemuro-Kaikyō 20 Jh 43.50N 145.30 E
Nemuro-Wan 29a Db 43.25N 145.25 E
Nenagh/An tAonach 9 Ei 52.52N 8.12W
Nenana 40 Jd 64.30N 149.00W
Nenana 40 Jd 64.34N 149.07W
Nendo Island 57 Hf 10.40S 165.54 E
Nene 9 Ni 52.48N 0.13 E
Nenecki Nacionalny Okrug [3] 19 Fb 67.30N 54.00 E
Nenjiang 22 Oe 49.10N 125.12 E
Nen Jiang 21 Oe 45.26N 124.39 E
Neo 29 Ed 35.38N 136.37 E
Neodesha 45 Ih 37.25N 95.41W
Néon Karlovásion 15 Jl 37.47N 26.42 E
Neosho 45 Ih 36.52N 94.22W
Neosho River 45 Ih 35.48N 95.18W
Néouvielle, Massif de- 11 Gl 42.51N 0.07 E
Nepal 22 Kg 28.00N 84.00 E
Nepalganj 25 Gc 28.03N 81.37 E
Nephi 43 Ed 39.43N 111.50W
Nephin/Né Finn 9 Dg 54.01N 9.22W
Nepisiguit River 44 Ob 47.37N 65.38W
Nepoko 30 Jh 1.40N 27.01 E
Nepomuk 10 Jg 49.29N 13.34 E
Ner 10 Od 52.10N 18.40 E
Nera [It.] 14 Gh 42.26N 12.24 E
Nera [Rom.] 15 Ee 44.49N 21.22 E
Nérac 11 Gj 44.08N 0.21 E
Neratovice 10 Kf 50.16N 14.31 E
Nerău 15 Dd 45.58N 20.34 E
Nerča 20 Gf 51.54N 116.30 E
Nerčinsk 20 Gf 51.58N 116.35 E
Nerčinski Zavod 20 Gf 51.17N 119.30 E
Nerehta 19 Ed 57.28N 40.34 E
Nereju 15 Jd 45.42N 26.43 E
Nereta 8 Kh 56.12N 25.24 E
Neretva 14 Lg 43.02N 17.27 E
Neretvanski kanal 14 Lg 43.03N 17.11 E
Nerica 17 Fd 65.20N 52.45 E
Neringa 7 Ei 55.24N 21.05 E
Neringa 7 Ei 55.18N 21.00 E
Neringa-Juodkrante/Neringa-Juodkrantė 8 Ii 55.35N 21.01 E
Neringa-Juodkrantė/Neringa-Juodkrante 8 Ii 55.35N 21.01 E
Neringa-Nida 8 Ii 55.18N 20.53 E
Neringa-Preila/Neringa-Prejla 8 Ii 55.20N 20.59 E
Neringa-Prejla/Neringa-Preila 8 Ii 55.20N 20.59 E
Nerinquinha 36 Df 15.45S 21.33 E
Neris/Njaris 8 Kj 54.55N 25.45 E
Nerja 13 Ih 36.44N 3.52W
Nerjungri 20 He 56.40N 124.47 E
Nerl [R.S.F.S.R.] 7 Jh 56.11N 40.34 E
Nerl [R.S.F.S.R.] 7 Ih 57.07N 37.39 E
Nerpio 13 Jf 38.09N 2.18W
Nerussa 16 Hc 52.33N 33.47 E
Nerva 13 Fg 37.42N 6.32W
Nervi, Genova- 14 Df 44.23N 9.02 E
Nervión 13 Ja 43.14N 2.53W
Nes 8 Cd 60.34N 9.59 E
Nes, Ameland- 12 Ha 53.26N 5.48 E
Nesbyen 7 Bf 60.34N 9.06 E
Nesebăr 15 Kg 42.39N 27.44 E
Nesjøen 8 Db 63.00N 12.00 E
Neskaupstaður 7a Db 65.09N 13.42W
Nesle 12 Ee 49.46N 2.45 E
Nesna 7 Cc 66.12N 13.02 E
Ness City 45 Gg 38.27N 99.54W
Nesterov [R.S.F.S.R.] 7 Fi 54.42N 22.34 E
Nesterov [Ukr.-U.S.S.R.] 16 Cd 50.03N 24.00 E
Néstos 15 Hi 40.51N 24.44 E
Nesttun 8 Ad 60.19N 5.20 E
Nesviž 16 Ec 53.13N 26.39 E
Netanya 24 Ff 32.20N 34.51 E
Netcong 44 Je 40.54N 74.43W
Nete 11 Kc 51.10N 4.15 E
Nethe 12 Lc 51.44N 9.23 E
Netherdale 59 Jd 21.08S 148.32 E
Netherlands (EN)= Nederland [1] 6 Ge 52.15N 5.30 E
Netherlands Antilles (EN) = Nederlandse Antillen [5] 53 Jd 12.15N 69.00W
Neto 14 Lk 39.12N 17.09 E
Netphen 12 Kd 50.55N 8.06 E
Nettebach 12 Jd 50.26N 7.28 E
Nettersheim 12 Id 50.30N 6.38 E
Nettetal 12 Ic 51.18N 6.12 E
Nettiling Lake 38 Lc 66.30N 70.40W
Nettuno 14 Gi 41.27N 12.39 E
Netzahualcóyotl, Presa- 48 Mi 17.00N 93.30W
Neubourg, Campagne du- 11 Ge 49.08N 1.00 E
Neubrandenburg 10 Jc 53.34N 13.16 E
Neuburg an der Donau 10 Hh 48.44N 11.11 E
Neuchâtel [2] 14 Ac 47.05N 6.50 E
Neuchâtel/Neuenburg 14 Ad 46.59N 6.56 E
Neuchâtel, Lac de-/Neuenburger See 14 Ad 46.55N 6.55 E
Neuenbürg 12 Kf 48.50N 8.35 E
Neuenburg/Neuchâtel 14 Ad 46.59N 6.56 E
Neuenburger See/Neuchâtel, Lac de- 14 Ad 46.55N 6.55 E
Neuenhaus 12 Ib 52.30N 6.58 E
Neuenkirchen 12 Jb 52.15N 7.22 E
Neuerburg 12 Id 50.01N 6.18 E
Neufchâteau [Bel.] 11 Le 49.51N 5.26 E
Neufchâteau [Fr.] 11 Lf 48.21N 5.42 E
Neufchâtel-en-Bray 11 He 49.44N 1.27 E
Neufchâtel-Hardelot 12 Dd 50.37N 1.38 E
Neufchâtel Hardelot-Hardelot Plage 12 Dd 50.38N 1.35 E
Neufchâtel-sur-Aisne 12 Ge 49.26N 4.02 E
Neuffossé, Canal de- 12 Ed 50.45N 2.15 E
Neuhaus am Rennweg 10 Hf 50.31N 11.09 E
Neuilly-en-Thelle 12 Ee 49.13N 2.17 E
Neuilly-Saint-Front 12 Fe 49.10N 3.16 E
Neu-Isenburg 12 Kd 50.03N 8.42 E
Neukirchen-Vluyn 12 Ic 51.27N 6.34 E
Neum 14 Lh 42.55N 17.38 E
Neumagen Dhron 12 Ie 49.51N 6.54 E
Neumarkter Sattel 14 Id 47.06N 14.22 E
Neumarkt in der Oberpfalz 10 Hg 49.17N 11.28 E
Neumünster 10 Fb 54.04N 9.59 E
Neunkirchen [Aus.] 14 Kc 47.43N 16.05 E
Neunkirchen [Ger.] 10 Dg 49.21N 7.11 E
Neunkirchen [Ger.] 12 Kd 50.48N 8.00 E
Neunkirchen [Ger.] 12 Jd 50.51N 7.20 E
Neuquén 53 Ji 39.00S 68.05W
Neuquén [2] 56 Ge 39.00S 70.00W
Neuquén, Rio- 52 Ji 38.59S 68.00W
Neurupping 10 Ic 52.56N 12.48 E
Neuse River 44 Ih 35.06N 76.30W
Neusiedl am See 14 Kc 47.56N 16.50 E
Neusiedler See (Fertő) 10 Mi 47.50N 16.45 E
Neuß 10 Ce 51.12N 6.42 E
Neustadt (Hessen) 12 Ld 50.51N 9.07 E
Neustadt am Rübenberge 10 Fd 52.30N 9.28 E
Neustadt an der Aisch 10 Gg 49.35N 10.36 E
Neustadt an der Orla 10 Hf 50.44N 11.45 E
Neustadt an der Weinstraße 10 Eg 49.21N 8.09 E
Neustadt bei Coubyrg 10 Hf 50.19N 11.07 E
Neustadt in Holstein 10 Gb 54.06N 10.49 E
Neustrelitz 10 Jc 53.22N 13.05 E
Neu-Ulm 10 Gh 48.24N 10.01 E
Neuville-les-Dieppe 12 De 49.55N 1.06 E
Neuville-sur-Saône 11 Ki 45.52N 4.51 E
Neuwerk 10 Ec 53.55N 8.30 E
Neuwied 10 Df 50.26N 7.28 E
Neva 5 Jd 59.55N 30.15 E
Nevada [2] 43 Dd 39.00N 117.00W
Nevada [Ia.-U.S.] 45 Je 42.01N 93.27W
Nevada [Mo.-U.S.] 43 Id 37.51N 94.22W
Nevada, Sierra- [Sp.] 5 Fh 37.05N 3.10W
Nevada, Sierra- [U.S.] 38 Hf 38.00N 119.15W
Nevada del Cocuy, Sierra- 52 Ie 6.10N 72.15W
Nevada de Santa Marta, Sierra- 52 Id 10.50N 73.40W
Nevado, Cerro- 52 Ie 3.59N 74.04W
Nevado de Ampato 52 Ig 15.50S 71.52W
Neve, Serra da- 30 Ij 13.52S 13.26 E
Nevel 19 Cd 56.02N 29.55 E
Nevele 12 Fc 51.02N 3.33 E
Nevelsk 20 Jg 46.37N 141.57 E
Neverkino 16 Oc 52.47N 46.48 E
Nevers 11 Jg 46.59N 3.10 E
Nevesinje 14 Mg 43.16N 18.07 E
Nevinnomyssk 19 Eg 44.38N 41.58 E
Nevis 47 Le 17.10N 62.34W
Nevis, Ben- 5 Fd 56.48N 5.01W
Nevis Peak 51c Ab 17.10N 62.34W
Nevjansk 19 Gd 57.32N 60.13 E
Nevşehir 23 Db 38.38N 34.43 E
Nevskoje 28 Lb 45.42N 133.40 E
Newala 36 Ge 10.56S 39.18 E
New Albany [In.-U.S.] 43 Jd 38.18N 85.49W
New Albany [Ms.-U.S.] 45 Li 34.29N 89.00W
New Alresford 12 Ac 51.05N 1.10W
New Amsterdam 53 Ke 6.17N 57.36W
Newark [De.-U.S.] 44 Jf 39.41N 75.45W
Newark [N.J.-U.S.] 43 Mc 40.44N 74.11W
Newark [N.Y.-U.S.] 44 Id 43.03N 77.06W
Newark [Oh.-U.S.] 43 Kc 40.03N 82.25W
Newark-on-Trent 9 Mh 53.05N 0.49W
New Bedford 43 Mc 41.38N 70.56W
New Bern 43 Ld 35.07N 77.03W
Newberry [Mi.-U.S.] 44 Eb 46.21N 85.30W
Newberry [S.C.-U.S.] 44 Gh 34.17N 81.37W
New Braunfels 43 Hf 29.42N 98.08W
New Britain 44 Ke 41.40N 72.47W
New Britain Island 57 Ge 5.40S 151.00 E
New Britain Trench (EN) 60 Ei 6.00S 153.00 E
New Brunswick 44 Je 40.29N 74.27W
New Brunswick [3] 42 Kg 46.30N 66.45W
New Buckenham 12 Db 52.28N 1.05 E
New Buffalo 44 De 41.47N 86.45W
Newburgh 43 Mc 41.30N 74.00W
Newbury 9 Lj 51.25N 1.20W
New Caledonia (EN) = Nouvelle-Calédonie [5] 58 Hg 21.30S 165.30 E
New Caledonia (EN)= Nouvelle-Calédonie 57 Hg 21.30S 165.30 E
New Caledonia Basin (EN) 3 Jm 30.00S 165.00 E
New Carlisle 44 Oa 48.01N 65.20W
New Castile (EN)=Castilla la Nueva 13 Id 40.00N 3.45W
New Castle [In.-U.S.] 44 Ef 39.55N 85.22W
New Castle [Pa.-U.S.] 43 Kc 41.00N 80.22W
Newcastle [Austl.] 58 Gh 32.56S 151.46 E
Newcastle [N.B.-Can.] 42 Kg 47.00N 65.34W
Newcastle [N.Ire.-U.K.] 9 Hg 54.12N 5.54W
Newcastle [S.Afr.] 37 De 27.49S 29.55 E
Newcastle [St.C.N.] 51c Ab 17.13N 62.34W
Newcastle/An Caisleán Nua 9 Hg 54.12N 5.54W
Newcastle Creek 59 Gc 17.20S 133.23 E
Newcastle-under-Lyme 9 Kh 53.00N 2.14W

Index Symbols

[1] Independent Nation
[2] State, Region
[3] District, County
[4] Municipality
[5] Colony, Dependency
Continent
Physical Region
Historical or Cultural Region
Mount, Mountain
Volcano
Hill
Mountains, Mountain Range
Hills, Escarpment
Plateau, Upland
Pass, Gap
Plain, Lowland
Delta
Salt Flat
Valley, Canyon
Crater, Cave
Karst Features
Depression
Polder
Desert, Dunes
Forest, Woods
Heath, Steppe
Oasis
Cape, Point
Coast, Beach
Cliff
Peninsula
Isthmus
Sandbank
Island
Atoll
Rock, Reef
Islands, Archipelago
Rocks, Reefs
Coral Reef
Well, Spring
Geyser
River, Stream
Waterfall Rapids
River Mouth, Estuary
Lake
Salt Lake
Intermittent Lake
Reservoir
Swamp, Pond
Canal
Glacier
Ice Shelf, Pack Ice
Ocean
Sea
Gulf, Bay
Strait, Fjord
Lagoon
Bank
Seamount
Tablemount
Ridge
Shelf
Basin
Escarpment, Sea Scarp
Fracture
Trench, Abyss
National Park, Reserve
Point of Interest
Recreation Site
Cave, Cavern
Historic Site
Ruins
Wall, Walls
Church, Abbey
Temple
Scientific Station
Airport
Port
Lighthouse
Mine
Tunnel
Dam, Bridge

Name	Page	Grid	Lat.	Long.
Newcastle-upon-Tyne	6	Fd	54.59N	1.35W
Newcastle Waters	58	Ef	17.24S	133.24 E
Newcastle West/An Caisleán Nua	9	Di	52.27N	9.03W
New Delhi	22	Jg	28.36N	77.12 E
New Denver	46	Ga	50.00N	117.22W
Newell	45	Ed	44.43N	103.25W
Newell, Lake-	46	Ja	50.25N	111.56W
New England	38	Le	44.00N	71.20W
New England Range	57	Gh	30.00S	151.50 E
New England Seamounts (EN)	38	Mf	38.00N	61.00W
Newenham, Cape-	40	Ge	58.37N	162.12W
New Forest	9	Lk	50.55N	1.35W
Newfoundland [3]	42	Lf	52.00N	56.00W
Newfoundland, Island of-	38	Ne	48.30N	56.00W
Newfoundland Basin (EN)	3	De	45.00N	40.00W
New Galloway	9	If	55.05N	4.10W
New Georgia	57	Ge	8.30S	157.20 E
New Georgia Island	60	Fi	8.15S	157.30 E
New Georgia Sound (The Slot)	60	Fi	8.00S	158.10 E
New Glasgow	42	Lg	45.35N	62.39W
New Guinea/Pulau Irian	57	Fe	5.00S	140.00 E
New Guinea Trench (EN)	60	Bg	0.05N	135.50 E
New Hampshire [2]	43	Mc	43.35N	71.40W
New Hampton	45	Je	43.03N	92.19W
New Hanover Island	57	Ge	2.30S	150.15 E
New Harmony	44	Df	38.08N	87.56W
New Haven	39	Le	41.18N	72.56W
Newhaven	9	Nk	50.47N	0.03 E
New Hebrides/Nouvelles Hébrides	57	Hf	16.01S	167.01 E
New Hebrides Trench (EN)	3	Jl	20.00S	168.00 E
New Iberia	43	If	30.00N	91.49W
New Ireland Island	57	Ge	3.20S	152.00 E
New Jersey [2]	43	Mc	40.15N	74.30W
New Kowloon/Julong	22	Ng	22.20N	114.09 E
New Liskeard	42	Jg	47.30N	79.40W
New London	43	Mc	41.21N	72.07W
New Madrid	45	Lh	36.36N	89.32W
Newman	59	Dd	23.15S	119.35 E
Newmarket [Eng.-U.K.]	9	Ni	52.15N	0.25 E
Newmarket [Ont.-Can.]	44	Hc	44.03N	79.28W
New Martinsville	44	Gf	39.39N	80.52W
New Meadows	46	Gd	44.58N	116.32W
New Mexico [2]	43	Fe	34.30N	106.00W
Newnan	44	Ei	33.23N	84.48W
New Norfolk	59	Jh	42.47S	147.03 E
New Orleans	39	Jg	29.58N	90.07W
New Philadelphia	44	Ge	40.30N	81.27W
New Pine Creek	46	Ee	42.01N	120.18W
New-Plymouth	58	Ih	39.04S	174.04 E
Newport [Ar.-U.S.]	45	Ki	35.37N	91.17W
Newport [Eng.-U.K.]	12	Cc	51.59N	0.15 E
Newport [Eng.-U.K.]	9	Lk	50.42N	1.18W
Newport [Fl.-U.S.]	44	Ej	30.14N	84.12W
Newport [Or.-U.S.]	43	Cc	44.38N	124.03W
Newport [R.I.-U.S.]	44	Le	41.30N	71.19W
Newport [Tn.-U.S.]	44	Fh	35.58N	83.11W
Newport [Vt.-U.S.]	44	Kc	44.56N	72.13W
Newport [Wales-U.K.]	9	Kj	51.35N	3.00W
Newport [Wa.-U.S.]	46	Gb	48.11N	117.03W
Newport Beach	43	De	33.37N	117.54W
Newport News	39	Lf	37.04N	76.28W
Newport Pagnell	12	Bb	52.05N	0.43W
New Providence Island	47	Ic	25.02N	77.24W
Newquay	9	Hk	50.25N	5.05W
New Quebec Crater (EN) = Nouveau-Québec, Cratère du-	42	Kd	61.30N	73.55W
New Richmond [Oh.-U.S.]	44	Ef	38.57N	84.16W
New Richmond [Que.-Can.]	44	Oa	48.10N	65.52W
New River [Blz.]	49	Cd	18.22N	88.24W
New River [Guy.]	54	Gc	3.23N	57.36W
New River [U.S.]	44	Ff	38.50N	82.06W
New Rockford	45	Gc	47.41N	99.15W
New Romney	12	Cd	50.59N	0.56 E
New Ross/Ros Mhic Thriúin	9	Gi	52.24N	6.56W
Newry/an t-Iúr	9	Gg	54.11N	6.20W
New Salem	45	Fc	46.51N	101.25W
New Sandy Bay	51n	Ba	13.20N	61.08W
New Schwabenland (EN)	66	Cf	72.30S	1.00 E
New Siberia (EN)=Novaja Sibir, Ostrov-	21	Qb	75.00N	149.00 E
New Siberian Islands (EN) =Novosibirskije Ostrova	21	Qb	75.00N	142.00 E
New Smyrna Beach	44	Gk	29.02N	80.56W
New South Wales	59	Jf	33.00S	146.00 E
Newton [Ia.-U.S.]	45	Jf	41.42N	93.03W
Newton [Il.-U.S.]	45	Lg	38.59N	88.10W
Newton [Ks.-U.S.]	43	Hd	38.03N	97.21W
Newton [Ma.-U.S.]	44	Ld	42.21N	71.13W
Newton [Ms.-U.S.]	45	Lj	32.19N	89.10W
Newton [N.J.-U.S.]	44	Je	41.03N	74.45W
Newton Abbot	9	Jk	50.32N	3.36W
Newton Stewart	9	Ig	54.57N	4.29W
Newtontoppen	67	Kd	72.02N	17.30 E
New Town	45	Ec	47.59N	102.30W
Newtown	9	Ji	52.32N	3.19W
Newtownabbey/Baile na Mainistreach	9	Hg	54.42N	5.54W
Newtownards/Baile Nua na hArda	9	Hg	54.36N	5.41W
New Ulm	43	Ic	44.19N	94.28W
New Westminster	42	Fg	49.12N	122.55W
New York	39	Le	40.43N	74.01W
New York [2]	43	Lc	43.00N	75.00W
New York State Barge Canal	44	Hd	43.05N	78.43W
New Zealand [1]	58	Ii	41.00S	174.00 E
New Zealand	57	Ii	41.00S	174.00 E
Nexpa, Río-	48	Hh	18.05N	102.46W
Neyagawa	29	Dd	34.46N	135.36 E
Neyrīz	24	Ph	29.12N	54.19 E
Neyshābūr	23	Ib	36.12N	58.50 E
Nežárka	10	Kg	49.11N	14.43 E
Nežin	19	De	51.02N	31.57 E
Ngabé	36	Cc	3.12S	16.11 E
Ngahere	62	De	42.24S	171.26 E
Ngajangel	64a	Ba	8.05N	134.43 E
Ngala	34	Hc	12.20N	14.11 E
Ngaliema, Chutes-=Stanley Falls (EN)	30	Jh	0.30N	25.30 E
Ngamegei Passage	64a	Bb	7.44N	134.34 E
Ngami, Lake-	37	Cd	20.37S	22.40 E
Ngamiland [3]	37	Cc	19.09S	22.47 E
Ngamring	27	Ef	29.14N	87.12 E
Ngangala	35	Ee	4.42N	31.55 E
Ngangerabeli Plain	36	Hc	1.30S	40.15 E
Ngangla Ringco	27	De	31.40N	83.00 E
Nganglong Kangri	27	De	32.45N	81.12 E
Nganglong Kangri	21	Kf	32.00N	83.00 E
Ngangzê Co	27	Ee	31.00N	86.55 E
Ngao	25	Je	18.45N	99.59 E
Ngaoundéré	31	Ih	7.19N	13.35 E
Ngapara	62	Df	44.57S	170.45 E
Ngara	36	Fc	2.28S	30.39 E
Ngardmau	64a	Bb	7.37N	134.35 E
Ngardmau Bay	64a	Bb	7.39N	134.35 E
Ngardololok	64a	Ac	7.00N	134.16 E
Ngaregur	64a	Bb	7.45N	134.38 E
Ngarekeukl	64a	Ac	7.00N	134.14 E
Ngariungs	64a	Ba	8.03N	134.43 E
Ngaruangl	64a	Ba	8.10N	134.39 E
Ngaruangl Passage	64a	Ba	8.07N	134.40 E
Ngaruawahia	62	Fb	37.40S	175.09 E
Ngaruroro	62	Gc	39.34S	176.55 E
Ngatangiia	64p	Cb	21.14S	159.43W
Ngatangiia Harbour	64p	Cb	21.14S	159.43W
Ngateguil, Point-	64a	Bc	7.26N	134.37 E
Ngatik Atoll	57	Gd	5.51N	157.16 E
Ngatpang	64a	Bc	7.28N	134.32 E
Ngau Island	63d	Bc	18.02S	179.18 E
Ngauruhoe	62	Fc	39.09S	175.38 E
Ngawa/Aba	27	He	32.55N	101.45 E
Ngayu	36	Eb	1.35N	27.13 E
Ngemelis Islands	64a	Ac	7.07N	134.15 E
Ngeregong	64a	Ac	7.07N	134.22 E
Ngergoi	64a	Ac	7.05N	134.17 E
Ngesebus	64a	Ac	7.03N	134.16 E
Nggamea	63d	Cb	16.46S	179.46W
Nggatokae	63a	Dc	8.46S	158.11 E
Nggela Pile	63a	Ec	9.08S	160.20 E
Nggela Sule	63a	Ec	9.03S	160.12 E
Nggelelevu	63d	Cb	16.05S	179.09W
Ngidinga	36	Cd	5.37S	15.17 E
Ngiro, Ewaso-	36	Gb	0.28N	39.55 E
Ngo	36	Cc	2.29S	15.45 E
Ngoangoa	35	Dd	5.58N	25.10 E
Ngobasangel	64a	Ac	7.16N	134.20 E
Ngoko	36	Cb	1.40N	16.03 E
Ngola Shankou	27	Gd	35.30N	99.36 E
Ngoma	36	Ef	15.58S	25.56 E
Ngoring Hu	27	Gd	35.00N	97.30 E
Ngorongoro Crater	30	Ki	3.10S	35.35 E
Ngoui	34	Cb	16.09N	13.55W
Ngouna	63b	Dc	17.26S	168.21 E
Ngounié [3]	36	Bc	2.00S	11.00 E
Ngounié	36	Bc	0.37S	10.18 E
Ngoura	35	Bc	12.52N	16.27 E
Ngouri	35	Bc	13.38N	15.22 E
Ngourti	34	Hb	15.19N	13.12 E
Ngousouboot, Pointe-	63b	Ca	13.58S	167.27 E
Ngudu	36	Fc	2.58S	33.20 E
Nguigmi	31	Ig	14.15N	13.07 E
Ngulu Atoll	57	Ed	8.18N	137.29 E
Nguni	36	Gc	0.50S	38.20 E
Nguru	31	Ig	12.53N	10.28 E
Ngwaketse	37	Cd	24.50S	24.00 E
Nhachengue	37	Fd	22.51S	35.11 E
Nhamundá	54	Gd	2.14S	56.43W
Nhamundá, Rio-	54	Gd	2.12S	56.41W
Nhandeara	55	Ge	20.40S	50.02W
Nhandutiba	55	Jb	14.37S	44.12W
Nharea	36	Ce	11.28S	16.53 E
Nha Trang	22	Mh	12.15N	109.11 E
Nhecolândia	55	Dd	19.16S	57.04W
Nhia	36	Be	10.15S	14.12 E
Nhulunbuy	58	Ef	12.00S	35.58 E
Niafounké	34	Eb	15.56N	4.00W
Niagara Escarpment	44	Gc	44.30N	80.35W
Niagara Falls	38	Le	43.05N	79.04W
Niagara Falls [N.Y.-U.S.]	43	Lc	43.06N	79.02W
Niagara Falls [Ont.-Can.]	42	Jh	43.06N	79.04W
Niagara River	44	Hd	43.15N	79.04W
Niagassola	34	Dc	12.19N	9.07W
Niah	26	Ff	3.52N	113.44 E
Niakaramandougou	34	Dd	8.40N	5.17W
Niamey	31	Hg	13.31N	2.07 E
Niamey [2]	34	Fc	14.00N	2.00 E
Niandan	34	Dc	10.35N	9.45W
Niangara	31	Jh	3.42N	27.52 E
Niangay, Lac-	34	Eb	15.50N	3.00W
Niangoloko	34	Ec	10.17N	4.55W
Nia-Nia	36	Eb	1.24N	27.36 E
Nianzishan	27	Lb	47.31N	122.50 E
Niao Dao	27	Gd	37.20N	99.50 E
Niaoshu Shan	27	He	34.54N	104.04 E
Niari [3]	36	Bc	4.30S	13.00 E
Niari	36	Bc	3.56S	12.12 E
Nias, Palau-	21	Li	1.05N	97.35 E
Niassa [3]	37	Fb	13.00S	36.00 E
Niassa, Lago-=Nyasa, Lake- (EN)	30	Kj	12.00S	34.30 E
Niau, Ile-	57	Mf	16.09S	146.21W
Nibāk	24	Nj	24.24N	50.50 E
Nibe	8	Ch	56.59N	9.38 E
Nica	17	Lh	57.29N	64.33 E
Nīca/Nica	8	Ih	56.25N	20.56 E
Nica/Nīca	8	Ih	56.25N	20.56 E
Nicanor Olivera	55	Cn	38.17S	59.12W
Nicaragua [1]	39	Kh	13.00N	85.00W
Nicaragua, Lago de-= Nicaragua, Lake- (EN)	38	Kh	11.35N	85.25W
Nicaragua, Lake- (EN)= Nicaragua, Lago de-	38	Kh	11.35N	85.25W
Nicastro	14	Kl	38.59N	16.19 E
Nice	6	Gg	43.42N	7.15 E
Niceville	44	Dj	30.31N	86.29W
Nichicum, Lac-	42	Kf	53.08N	70.55W
Nichinan [Jap.]	29	Cd	35.10N	133.16 E
Nichinan [Jap.]	28	Ki	31.36N	131.23 E
Nicholas Channel	49	Gb	23.25N	80.05W
Nicholas Channel (EN)= Nicolás, Canal-	47	Hd	23.25N	80.05W
Nicholasville	44	Eg	37.53N	84.34W
Nicholls Town	49	Ia	25.08N	78.00W
Nicholson Range	59	De	27.15S	116.45 E
Nicholson River	57	Ef	17.31S	139.36 E
Nickerson Ice Shelf	66	Mf	75.45S	145.00W
Nickol Bay	59	Dd	20.40S	116.50 E
Nicobar Islands	21	Li	8.00N	93.30 E
Nicoclí	49	Ii	8.26N	76.48W
Nicolajevka	15	Nb	47.33N	30.41 E
Nicola River	46	Ea	50.25N	121.18W
Nicolás, Canal-=Nicholas Channel (EN)	47	Hd	23.25N	80.05W
Nicolet	44	Kb	46.14N	72.37W
Nicopolis (EN) = Nikópolis	15	Dj	39.00N	20.45 E
Nicosia	14	Im	37.45N	14.24 E
Nicosia (EN)=Lefkosa/ Levkōsia	22	Ff	35.10N	33.22 E
Nicosia (EN)=Levkōsia/ Lefkosa	22	Ff	35.10N	33.22 E
Nicotera	14	Jl	38.33N	15.56 E
Nicoya	47	Gf	10.09N	85.27W
Nicoya, Golfo de-	47	Hg	9.47N	84.48W
Nicoya, Peninsula de-= Nicoya Peninsula (EN)	38	Ki	10.00N	85.25W
Nicoya Peninsula (EN)= Nicoya, Península de-	38	Ki	10.00N	85.25W
Nicuadala	37	Fc	17.37S	36.50 E
Niculiţel	15	Ld	45.11N	28.29 E
Nida	10	Qf	50.18N	20.52 E
Nidda	12	Ld	50.25N	9.00 E
Nidda	10	Ef	50.06N	8.34 E
Nidder	12	Kd	50.12N	8.47 E
Nideggen	12	Id	50.42N	6.29 E
Nidelva [Nor.]	8	Cf	58.24N	8.48 E
Nidelva [Nor.]	8	Da	63.26N	10.25 E
Nido, Sierra del-	48	Fc	29.30N	106.45W
Nidže	15	Ei	41.00N	21.50 E
Nidzica	10	Qf	50.12N	20.40 E
Nidzica	10	Qc	53.22N	20.26 E
Nidzkie, Jezioro-	10	Rc	53.37N	21.30 E
Niebüll	10	Eb	54.48N	8.50 E
Nied	12	Ie	49.23N	6.40 E
Nieddu	14	Dj	40.44N	9.34 E
Niederbayern	10	Ih	48.35N	12.30 E
Niederbronn-les-Bains	11	Nf	48.58N	7.38 E
Niedere Tauern	14	Hc	47.20N	14.00 E
Niederlausitz	10	Ke	51.40N	14.15 E
Nieder-Olm	12	Ke	49.54N	8.13 E
Niederösterreich = Lower Austria (EN) [2]	14	Jb	48.30N	15.45 E
Niedersachsen=Lower Saxony (EN) [2]	10	Fd	52.00N	10.00 E
Niederwald	10	Df	50.10N	8.00 E
Niederzier	12	Id	50.53N	6.28 E
Niefang	34	He	1.50N	10.14 E
Niegocin, Jezioro-	10	Rb	54.00N	21.50 E
Niel	12	Gc	51.07N	4.20 E
Nielfa, Puerto de-	13	Hf	38.32N	4.23W
Niéllé	34	Dc	10.12N	5.38W
Niellim	35	Bd	9.42N	17.49 E
Niemba	36	Ed	5.57S	28.26 E
Niemba	36	Ed	5.57S	28.26 E
Niemodlin	10	Nf	50.39N	17.37 E
Niéna	34	Dc	11.25N	6.20W
Nienburg (Weser)	10	Fd	52.38N	9.13 E
Niepołomice	10	Qf	50.03N	20.13 E
Niermalak, Pointe-	63b	Cb	14.21S	167.24 E
Niers	10	Be	51.43N	5.57 E
Nierstein	12	Ke	49.53N	8.20 E
Niesky/Niska	10	Ke	51.18N	14.49 E
Nieszawa	10	Od	52.50N	18.55 E
Nieuport/Nieuwpoort	11	Ic	51.08N	2.45 E
Nieuw Amsterdam	54	Gb	5.53N	55.05W
Nieuwe-Pekela	12	Ia	53.04N	6.59 E
Nieuweschans	12	Ja	53.11N	7.15 E
Nieuw Milligen, Apeldoorn-	12	Hb	52.14N	5.45 E
Nieuw Nickerie	53	Ke	5.57N	56.59W
Nieuwolda	12	Ia	53.14N	6.59 E
Nieuwoudtville	37	Bf	31.22S	19.06 E
Nieuwpoort/Nieuport	11	Ic	51.08N	2.45 E
Nieuw Weerdinge, Emmen-	12	Jb	52.52N	7.01 E
Nieves	48	He	24.00N	103.01W
Nièvre [3]	11	Jg	47.05N	3.30 E
Nièvre	11	Jh	46.59N	3.10 E
Nigata	28	Lg	34.13N	132.29 E
Niğde	23	Db	37.59N	34.42 E
Nigenān	24	Qe	34.13N	57.19 E
Niger [1]	31	Hg	16.00N	8.00 E
Niger	30	Hh	5.33N	6.33 E
Niger [2]	34	Gd	9.40N	6.00 E
Niger Basin (EN)	30	Gg	15.00N	2.00 E
Niger Delta	30	Hh	4.50N	6.00 E
Nigeria [1]	31	Hh	10.00N	8.00 E
Night Hawk Lake	44	Ga	48.28N	81.00W
Nightingale Island	30	Fi	37.24S	12.28W
Nigrita	15	Gi	40.54N	23.30 E
Nihiru Atoll	57	Mf	16.42S	142.50W
Nihoa Island	57	Kb	23.06N	161.58W
Nihonmatsu	28	Pf	37.35N	140.26 E
Nihuil, Embalse del-	56	Ge	35.05S	68.45W
Niigata	22	Pf	37.55N	139.03 E
Niigata Ken [2]	28	Of	37.30N	138.50 E
Niihama	28	Lh	33.58N	133.16 E
Niihau Island	57	Kb	21.55N	160.10W
Nii-Jima	27	Oe	34.20N	139.15 E
Niikappu-Gawa	29a	Cb	42.22N	142.16 E
Niimi	28	Lg	34.59N	133.28 E
Niisato	29	Gb	39.36N	141.49 E
Niitsu	28	Of	37.48N	139.07 E
Nijar	13	Jh	36.58N	2.12W
Nijkerk	12	Hb	52.14N	5.29 E
Nijlen	12	Gc	51.10N	4.39 E
Nijmegen	11	Lc	51.50N	5.50 E
Nijvel/Nivelles	11	Kd	50.36N	4.20 E
Nijverdal, Hellendoorn-	12	Ib	52.22N	6.27 E
Nikel	19	Db	69.24N	30.13 E
Níki	15	Ei	40.55N	21.25 E
Nikitin Seamount (EN)	21	Kj	3.00S	83.00 E
Nikki	34	Fd	9.56N	3.12 E
Nikkō	29	Fc	36.44N	139.35 E
Nikolajev [Ukr.-U.S.S.R.]	16	Ce	49.32N	23.58 E
Nikolajev [Ukr.-U.S.S.R.]	6	Jf	46.58N	32.00 E
Nikolajevka	18	Kc	43.37N	77.01 E
Nikolajevo	8	Mf	58.14N	29.32 E
Nikolajevsk	19	Ee	50.02N	45.31 E
Nikolajevskaja Oblast [3]	19	Df	47.20N	32.00 E
Nikolajevski	20	Hf	54.50N	129.25 E
Nikolajevsk-na-Amure	22	Qd	53.08N	140.44 E
Nikolsk [R.S.F.S.R.]	19	Ee	53.42N	46.03 E
Nikolsk [R.S.F.S.R.]	19	Ed	59.33N	45.31 E
Nikolski [Ak.-U.S.]	40a	Eb	53.15N	168.22W
Nikolski [Kaz.-U.S.S.R.]	19	Gf	47.55N	67.33 E
Nikonga	36	Fc	4.40S	31.28 E
Nikopol [Bul.]	15	Hf	43.42N	24.54 E
Nikopol [Ukr.-U.S.S.R.]	19	Df	47.35N	34.25 E
Nikópolis = Nicopolis (EN)	15	Dj	39.00N	20.45 E
Nīkpey	24	Md	36.50N	48.10 E
Niksar	24	Gb	40.36N	36.58 E
Nikšić	15	Bg	42.46N	18.58 E
Nikumaroro Atoll (Gardner)	57	Je	4.40S	174.32W
Nikunau Island	57	Ie	1.23S	176.26 E
Nīl, Kūh-e-	24	Ng	30.52N	50.49 E
Nīl, Nahr an-=Nile (EN)	30	Ke	30.10N	31.06 E
Nila, Pulau-	26	Ih	6.44S	129.31 E
Nilakka	7	Ge	63.07N	26.33 E
Niland	46	Hj	33.14N	115.31W
Nilandu Atoll	25a	Bb	3.00N	72.55 E
Nile [3]	36	Fb	3.00N	31.30 E
Nile (EN)=Nīl, Nahr an-	30	Ke	30.10N	31.06 E
Nile Delta (EN)	30	Ke	31.20N	31.00 E
Nīleh, Kūh-e-	24	Nf	32.59N	50.32 E
Niles	44	De	41.50N	86.15W
Nilka	27	Dc	43.47N	82.20 E
Nīl Kowtal	23	Kc	34.48N	67.22 E
Nilsiä	7	Ge	63.12N	28.05 E
Nilüfer	15	Li	40.18N	28.27 E
Nimba [3]	34	Dd	6.45N	8.45W
Nimba, Monts-=Nimba Mountains (EN)	30	Gh	7.35N	8.28W
Nimba Mountains (EN)= Nimba, Monts-	30	Gh	7.35N	8.28W
Nîmes	6	Gg	43.50N	4.21 E
Nimjad	32	Df	17.25N	15.41W
Nimmitabel	59	Jg	36.31S	149.16 E
Nimpkish River	46	Ba	50.32N	126.59W
Nimrode Glacier	66	Kg	82.27S	161.00 E
Nimrud	24	Jd	36.06N	43.20 E
Nīmrūz [3]	23	Jc	30.30N	62.00 E
Nims	12	Ie	49.51N	6.28 E
Nimule	31	Kh	3.36N	32.03 E
Nimún, Punta-	48	Ng	20.46N	90.25W
Nin	14	Jf	44.14N	15.11 E
Nina	37	Bd	22.57S	18.14 E
Nīnawā [3]	24	Je	35.45N	42.45 E
Nīnawā=Nineveh (EN)	23	Fb	36.22N	43.09 E
Nine Degree Channel	21	Ji	9.00N	73.00 E
Ninetyeast Ridge (EN)	3	Gj	10.00S	90.00 E
Ninety Mile Beach [Austl.]	59	Jg	38.15S	147.25 E
Ninety Mile Beach [N.Z.]	62	Ea	34.45S	173.00 E
Nineveh (EN)=Nīnawā	23	Fb	36.22N	43.09 E
Ning'an	27	Mc	44.22N	129.23 E
Ningbo	22	Og	29.55N	121.28 E
Ningcheng (Tianyi)	27	Kc	41.34N	119.25 E
Ningde	27	Kf	26.44N	119.29 E
Ningdu	27	Kf	26.31N	115.59 E
Ningguo	28	Ei	30.39N	119.00 E
Ninghai	28	Fj	29.19N	121.26 E
Ning-hsia-hui-tsu Tzu-chih-ch'ü → Ningxia Huizu Zizhiqu=Ningsia Hui (EN) [2]	27	Id	37.00N	106.00 E
Ningjin [China]	28	Df	37.39N	116.48 E
Ningjin [China]	28	Cf	37.37N	114.55 E
Ningjing Shan	27	Ge	31.45N	97.15 E
Ninglang	27	Hf	27.17N	100.52 E
Ningling	28	Cg	34.27N	115.18 E
Ningnan	27	Hf	27.05N	102.44 E
Ningqiang	27	Ie	32.48N	106.15 E
Ningsia Hui (EN)=Ning-hsia-hui-tsu Tzu-chih-ch'ü → Ningxia Huizu Zizhiqu [2]	27	Id	37.00N	106.00 E
Ningsia Hui (EN)=Ningxia Huizu Zizhiqu (Ning-hsia-hui-tsu Tzu-chih-ch'ü) [2]	27	Id	37.00N	106.00 E
Ningwu	27	Jd	38.59N	112.14 E
Ningxia Huizu Zizhiqu (Ning-hsia-hui-tsu Tzu-chih-ch'ü)=Ningsia Hui (EN) [2]	27	Id	37.00N	106.00 E
Ningxian	27	Id	35.27N	107.50 E
Ningxiang	28	Bj	28.16N	112.33 E
Ningyang	28	Dg	35.45N	116.48 E
Ningyō-Tōge	29	Cd	35.19N	133.56 E
Ninh Binh	25	Ld	20.15N	105.59 E
Ninh Hoa	25	Lf	12.29N	109.08 E
Ninigo Group	57	Fe	1.15S	144.15 E
Niniva	65b	Ba	19.46S	174.38W
Ninnis Glacier	66	Je	68.12S	147.12 E
Ninohe	27	Pc	40.16N	141.18 E
Ninove	12	Fd	50.50N	4.00 E
Nioaque	54	Gh	21.08S	55.48W
Niobrara	38	Je	42.45N	98.00W
Niobrara	45	He	42.25N	98.00W
Nioghalvfjerdsfjorden	41	Kc	79.30N	18.45W
Nioki	36	Cc	2.43S	17.41 E
Niono	34	Dc	14.15N	6.00W
Nioro du Rip	34	Bc	13.45N	15.48W
Nioro du Sahel	31	Gg	15.14N	9.37W
Niort	11	Fh	46.19N	0.28W
Nipawin	42	Hf	53.22N	104.00W
Nipe, Bahía de-	49	Jc	20.47N	75.42W
Nipesotsu-Yama	29a	Cb	43.27N	143.02 E
Nipigon	39	Ke	49.01N	88.16W
Nipigon, Lake-	38	Ke	49.50N	88.30W
Nipigon Bay	45	Mb	48.53N	87.50W
Nipissing, Lake-	38	Le	46.17N	80.00W
Nippon=Japan (EN) [1]	22	Pf	38.00N	137.00 E
Nippon-Kai=Japan, Sea of- (EN)	21	Pf	40.00N	134.00 E
Nippur	24	Kf	32.10N	45.10 E
Niquelândia	54	If	14.27S	48.27W
Niquero	49	Ic	20.03N	77.35W
Niquitao, Teta de-	49	Li	9.07N	70.30W
Niquivil	56	Gd	30.25S	68.42W
Nīr	24	Lc	38.02N	47.59 E
Nirasaki	29	Fd	35.43N	138.27 E
Nirji → Morin Dawa	27	Lb	48.30N	124.28 E
Nirmal	25	Fe	19.06N	78.21 E
Niš	6	Ig	43.19N	21.54 E
Nisa	13	Ee	39.31N	7.39W
Nīşāb	23	Gg	14.24N	46.38 E
Nisāh, Sha'īb-	24	Lj	24.11N	47.11 E
Nišava	15	Ef	43.22N	21.46 E
Niscemi	14	Im	37.09N	14.23 E
Nishibetsu-Gawa	29a	Db	43.23N	145.17 E
Nishikawa	29	Gb	38.26N	140.08 E
Nishiki	29	Bd	34.16N	131.57 E
Nishinomiya	29	Dd	34.43N	135.20 E
Nishino'omote	27	Ne	30.44N	131.00 E
Nishino-Shima	60	Cb	27.30N	140.53 E
Nishi-No-Shima	28	Lf	36.06N	133.00 E
Nishiokoppe	29a	Ca	44.20N	142.57 E
Nishi-Sonogi-Hantō	29	Ae	32.55N	129.45 E
Nishiwaki	29	Dd	34.59N	134.58 E
Nísiros	15	Km	36.35N	27.10 E
Niska/Niesky	10	Ke	51.18N	14.49 E
Niška Banja	15	Ff	43.18N	22.01 E
Nisko	10	Sf	50.31N	22.09 E
Nismes, Viroinval-	12	Gd	50.05N	4.33 E
Nísoi Aiyaiou [2]	15	Il	37.40N	25.40 E
Nisporeny	16	Ff	47.06N	28.10 E
Nissan	8	Eh	56.40N	12.51 E
Nissan	63a	Ba	4.30S	154.14 E
Nisser	8	Ce	59.10N	8.30 E
Nissum Bredning	8	Ch	56.40N	8.20 E
Nissum Fjord	8	Ch	56.20N	8.15 E
Nita	29	Cd	35.12N	133.00 E
Nitchequon	42	Kf	53.15N	70.44W
Niterói	53	Lh	22.53S	43.07W
Nith	9	Jf	55.00N	3.35W
Nitra	10	Oi	47.46N	18.10 E
Nitra	10	Oh	48.19N	18.05 E
Niuafo'ou Island	57	Jf	15.35S	175.38W
Niuatoputapu Island	57	Jf	15.57S	173.45W
Niue [5]	58	Kf	19.02S	169.55W
Niue Island	57	Kf	19.02S	169.55W
Niu'erhe	27	La	51.30N	121.40 E
Niufu	29a	Ca	44.35N	142.35 E
Niulakita Island	57	If	10.45S	179.30 E
Niutaca, Corrente-	55	De	20.42S	57.37W
Niutao Island	57	Ie	6.06S	177.16 E
Niutg, Gunung-	26	Ef	1.00N	109.55 E
Niutoushan	27	Ke	31.00N	119.35 E
Niuzhuang	28	Gd	40.57N	122.30 E
Nivala	7	Fe	63.58N	25.01 E
Nive	11	Ek	43.30N	1.29W
Nivelles/Nijvel	11	Kd	50.36N	4.20 E
Nivernais	11	Jg	47.00N	3.30 E
Nivernais, Canal du-	11	Jg	47.40N	3.40 E
Nivernais, Côtes du-	11	Jg	47.10N	3.30 E
Nivillers	12	Ee	49.28N	2.10 E
Nixon	45	Hl	29.16N	97.46W
Niya/Minfeng	27	Dd	37.04N	82.46 E
Nīyābād	24	Le	35.12N	46.20 E
Niyodo-Gawa	29	Ce	33.28N	133.29 E
Nīza	24	Ph	28.25N	55.55 E
Nizāmābad	25	Fe	18.40N	78.07 E
Nižankoviči	10	Sg	49.40N	22.48 E
Nizip	23	Eb	37.01N	37.46 E
Nízke Tatry = Low Tatra (EN)	10	Ph	48.54N	19.40 E
Nízký-Jeseník	10	Ng	49.50N	17.30 E
Nižná	10	Pg	49.19N	19.32 E
Nižneangarsk	22	Md	55.47N	109.33 E
Nižnegorski	16	Ig	45.27N	34.44 E
Nižnejansk	20	Ib	71.24N	136.00 E
Nižnekamsk	19	Fd	55.38N	51.49 E
Nižnekolymsk	20	Lc	68.38N	160.56 E
Nižnetroicki	17	Fi	54.20N	53.41 E
Nižneudinsk	20	Ef	54.54N	99.03 E
Nižnevartovsk	22	Jc	61.00N	77.00 E
Nižni Baskunčak	19	Ef	48.13N	46.50 E
Nižni Bestjah	20	Hd	61.48N	129.55 E
Nižni Casučej	20	Gf	50.27N	115.08 E
Nižnije Serogozy	16	If	46.49N	34.24 E
Nižni Kuranah	20	He	58.40N	125.48 E
Nižni Lomov	19	Ee	53.32N	43.41 E
Nižni Odes	17	Ge	63.40N	54.52 E

Index Symbols

[1] Independent Nation
[2] State, Region
[3] District, County
[4] Municipality
[5] Colony, Dependency
Continent
Physical Region
Historical or Cultural Region
Mount, Mountain
Volcano
Hill
Mountains, Mountain Range
Hills, Escarpment
Plateau, Upland
Pass, Gap
Plain, Lowland
Delta
Salt Flat
Valley, Canyon
Crater, Cave
Karst Features
Depression
Polder
Desert, Dunes
Forest, Woods
Heath, Steppe
Oasis
Cape, Point
Coast, Beach
Cliff
Peninsula
Isthmus
Sandbank
Island
Atoll
Rock, Reef
Islands, Archipelago
Rocks, Reefs
Coral Reef
Well, Spring
Geyser
River, Stream
Waterfall Rapids
River Mouth, Estuary
Lake
Salt Lake
Intermittent Lake
Reservoir
Swamp, Pond
Canal
Glacier
Ice Shelf, Pack Ice
Ocean
Sea
Gulf, Bay
Strait, Fjord
Lagoon
Bank
Seamount
Tablemount
Ridge
Shelf
Basin
Escarpment, Sea Scarp
Fracture
Trench, Abyss
National Park, Reserve
Point of Interest
Recreation Site
Cave, Cavern
Historic Site
Ruins
Wall, Walls
Church, Abbey
Temple
Scientific Station
Airport
Port
Lighthouse
Mine
Tunnel
Dam, Bridge

Nižni Oseredok, Ostrov- 16 Pg 45.45N 48.35 E
Nižni Tagil 6 Ld 57.55N 59.57 E
Nižni Trajanov Val = Lower Trajan's Wall (EN) 15 Ld 45.45N 28.30 E
Nižnjaja Omra 17 Ge 62.46N 55.46 E
Nižnjaja Peša 19 Eb 66.43N 47.36 E
Nižnjaja Pojma 20 Ee 56.08N 97.18 E
Nižnjaja Salda 17 Jg 58.05N 60.48 E
Nižnjaja Tavda 19 Gd 57.40N 66.12 E
Nižnjaja Tojma 7 Ke 62.22N 44.15 E
Nižnjaja Tunguska = Lower Tunguska (EN) 21 Kc 65.48N 88.04 E
Nižnjaja Tura 17 Ig 58.37N 59.49 E
Nižnjaja Zolotica 7 Jd 65.41N 40.13 E
Nižny Pjandž 18 Gf 37.14N 68.35 E
Nizza Monferrato 14 Cf 44.46N 8.21 E
Njajs 17 Je 62.25N 60.47 E
Njamunas 5 Id 55.18N 21.23 E
Njandoma 19 Ec 61.43N 40.12 E
Njaris/Neris 8 Kj 54.55N 25.45 E
Njazepetrovsk 17 Ih 56.03N 59.38 E
Njazidja 30 Lj 11.35 S 43.20 E
Njegoš 15 Bg 42.53N 18.45 E
Njinjo 36 Gd 8.48 S 38.54 E
Njombe 30 Ki 6.56 S 35.06 E
Njombe 31 Ki 9.20 S 34.46 E
Njudung 8 Fg 57.25N 14.50 E
Njuja 20 Gd 60.32N 116.25 E
Njuk, Ozero- 7 Hd 64.25N 31.45 E
Njuksenica 7 Kf 60.28N 44.15 E
Njukža 20 He 56.30N 121.40 E
Njunes 7 Eb 68.45N 19.30 E
Njurba 22 Nc 63.17N 118.20 E
Njurundabommen 7 De 62.16N 17.22 E
Njutånger 8 Gc 61.37N 17.03 E
Njuvčim 17 Ef 61.22N 50.42 E
Nkambe 34 Hd 6.38N 10.40 E
Nkawkaw 34 Ed 6.33N 0.46W
Nkayi [Con.] 31 Ii 4.05S 13.18 E
Nkayi [Zimb.] 37 Dc 19.00S 28.54 E
Nkhata Bay 36 Fe 11.36 S 34.18 E
Nkongsamba 31 Hh 4.57N 9.56 E
Nkota Kota 31 Kj 12.55 S 34.18 E
Nkululu 36 Fd 6.26 S 32.49 E
Nkusi 36 Fb 1.07N 30.40 E
Nkwalini 37 Ee 28.45 S 31.30 E
'Nmai 25 Jc 25.42N 97.30 E
Nmaki 24 Pg 31.16N 55.29 E
Nnewi 34 Gd 6.01N 6.55 E
Nō 29 Ec 37.05N 137.59 E
Noailles 12 Ee 49.20N 2.12 E
Noākhāli 25 Id 22.49N 91.06 E
Noatak 40 Gc 67.34N 162.59W
Nobel 44 Gc 45.25N 80.06W
Nobeoka 27 Ne 32.35N 131.40 E
Noblesville 44 Ee 40.03N 86.00W
Noboribetsu 28 Pc 42.25N 141.11 E
Noce 14 Fd 46.09N 11.04 E
Nocra 35 Fc 15.40N 39.55 E
Nodaway River 45 Ig 39.54N 94.58W
Noën 27 Hc 43.15N 102.20 E
Noeuf, Ile des- 37b Bb 6.14S 53.03 E
Noeux-les-Mines 12 Ed 50.29N 2.40 E
Nogajskaja Step 16 Ng 44.15N 46.00 E
Nogales [Az.-U.S.] 43 Ee 31.21N 110.55W
Nogales [Mex.] 39 Hf 31.20N 110.56W
Nogaro 11 Fk 43.46N 0.02W
Nogat 10 Pb 54.11N 19.15 E
Nōgata 29 Be 33.44N 130.44 E
Nogent-le-Rotrou 11 Gf 48.19N 0.50 E
Nogent-sur-Marne 12 Ef 48.50N 2.29 E
Nogent-sur-Oise 12 Ee 49.16N 2.28 E
Nogent-sur-Seine 11 Jf 48.29N 3.30 E
Noginsk [R.S.F.S.R.] 20 Ed 64.25N 91.10 E
Noginsk [R.S.F.S.R.] 19 Dd 55.54N 38.28 E
Nogliki 20 Jf 51.45N 143.15 E
Nōgō-Hakusan 29 Ed 35.46N 136.31 E
Nogoyá 56 Id 32.24S 59.48W
Nogoya, Arroyo- 55 Ck 32.55 S 59.59W
Nógrád [2] 10 Ph 48.00N 19.35 E
Nogueira, Serra da- 13 Fc 41.42N 6.52W
Noguera Pallaresa 13 Mb 42.15N 0.54 E
Noguera Ribagorçana/Noguera Ribagorzana 13 Mc 41.40N 0.43 E
Noguera Ribagorzana/Noguera Ribagorçana 13 Mc 41.40N 0.43 E
Noh, Laguna- 48 Nh 18.40N 90.20W
Nohain 11 Ig 47.24N 2.55 E
Noheji 28 Pd 40.52N 141.08 E
Nohfelden 12 Je 49.35N 7.09 E
Noidore, Rio- 55 Fb 14.50S 52.34W
Noir, Causse- 11 Jj 44.09N 3.15 E
Noire, Montagne- 11 Ik 43.28N 2.18 E
Noires, Montagnes- 11 Cf 48.09N 3.40W
Noirétable 11 Ji 45.49N 3.46 E
Noirmoutier, Ile de- 11 Dh 46.58N 2.12W
Noirmoutier-en-l'Ile 11 Dg 47.00N 2.15W
Nojima-Zaki 29 Fd 34.54N 139.50 E
Nojiri-Ko 29 Fc 36.49N 138.13 E
Noka 63c Bb 10.40S 166.03 E
Nokaneng 37 Cc 19.40S 22.12 E
Nokia 7 Ff 61.28N 23.30 E
Nok Kundi 25 Cc 28.48N 62.46 E
Nokomis 46 Ma 51.30N 105.00W
Nokou 35 Ac 14.35N 14.47 E
Nokra 35 Fb 15.42N 39.56 E
Nol 8 Eg 57.55N 12.03 E
Nola [C.A.R.] 35 Be 3.32N 16.04 E
Nola [It.] 14 Ij 40.55N 14.33 E
Nolin Lake 44 Dg 37.20N 86.10W
Nolinsk 19 Ed 57.33N 50.00 E
Nomad 58 Fe 6.21S 142.12 E
Noma Omuramba 37 Cc 19.10S 22.16 E
Noma-Zaki 29 Bf 31.25N 130.06 E
Nombre de Dios 48 Gf 23.51N 104.14W
Nome 39 Cc 64.30N 165.24W
Nomeny 12 If 48.54N 6.14 E
Nomo-Saki 29 Ae 32.35N 129.45 E
Nomozaki 29 Ae 32.35N 129.45 E
Nomuka 65b Bb 20.15S 174.48W
Nomuka Group 57 Jg 20.20S 174.45W
Nomuka Iki 65b Bb 20.17S 174.49W
Nomwin Atoll 57 Gd 8.32N 151.47 E
Nonacho Lake 42 Gd 62.40N 109.30W
Nonancourt 12 Df 48.46N 1.12 E
Nonette 12 Ee 49.12N 2.24 E
Nong'an 27 Mc 44.24N 125.08 E
Nong Han 25 Ke 17.21N 103.06 E
Nong Khai 22 Mh 17.52N 102.45 E
Nongoma 37 Ee 27.53S 31.38 E
Nonoava 48 Fd 27.28N 106.44W
Nonouti Atoll 57 Ie 0.40S 174.21 E
Nonsan 28 If 36.12N 127.05 E
Nonsuch Bay 51d Bb 17.03N 61.42W
Nontron 11 Gi 45.32N 0.40 E
Noord-Beveland 12 Fc 51.35N 3.45 E
Noord-Brabant [3] 12 Gc 51.30N 5.00 E
Noord-Holland [3] 12 Gb 52.40N 4.50 E
Noordhollandskanaal 11 Kb 52.55N 4.50 E
Noordoewer 37 Be 28.45S 17.37 E
Noordoostpolder 11 Lb 52.42N 5.45 E
Noordoostpolder 12 Hb 52.42N 5.44 E
Noordoostpolder-Emmeloord 12 Hb 52.42N 5.44 E
Noordwijk aan Zee 11 Kb 52.14N 4.26 E
Noordwijk aan Zee, Noordwijk- 12 Gb 52.14N 4.26 E
Noordwijk-Noordwijk aan Zee 12 Gb 52.14N 4.26 E
Noordzee = North Sea (EN) 5 Gd 55.20N 3.00 E
Noordzeekanaal 11 Kb 52.30N 4.35 E
Noormarkku/Norrmark 8 Ic 61.35N 21.52 E
Noorvik 40 Gc 66.50N 161.12W
Nootka Island 46 Bb 49.32N 126.42W
Nootka Sound 46 Bb 49.33N 126.38W
Nóqui 36 Bd 5.50S 13.27 E
Nora [It.] 14 Dk 39.00N 9.02 E
Nora [Swe.] 7 Dg 59.31N 15.02 E
Noraskog 8 Fe 59.40N 14.50 E
Norberg 8 Fd 60.04N 15.56 E
Norcia 14 Hh 42.48N 13.05 E
Nord 41 Kb 81.45N 17.30W
Nord [Cam.] [3] 34 Hd 9.00N 13.50 E
Nord [Fr.] [3] 11 Jd 50.20N 3.40 E
Nord [U.V.] [3] 34 Ec 13.40N 2.50W
Nord, Canal du- 11 Id 49.57N 2.55 E
Nord, Mer du- = North Sea (EN) 5 Gd 55.20N 3.00 E
Nordausques 12 Ed 50.49N 2.05 E
Nordaustlandet 67 Jd 79.48N 22.24 E
Nordborg 8 Ci 55.03N 9.45 E
Nordby 8 Ci 55.27N 8.25 E
Norddeutsches Tiefland = North German Plain (EN) 5 He 53.00N 11.00 E
Norden 10 Dc 53.36N 7.12 E
Nordenham 10 Ec 53.39N 8.29 E
Nordenskjölda, Ostrova- = Nordenskjöld, Archipelago (EN) 20 Ea 76.50N 96.00 E
Nordenskjöld Archipelago (EN) = Nordenskjölda, Ostrova- 20 Ea 76.50N 96.00 E
Norderney 10 Dc 53.42N 7.10 E
Norderstedt 10 Fc 53.41N 9.58 E
Nordfjord 8 Bc 61.50N 6.15 E
Nordfjord 7 Af 61.55N 5.10 E
Nordfjordeid 7 Af 61.54N 6.00 E
Nordfold 7 Dc 67.46N 15.12 E
Nordfriesische Inseln = North Frisian Islands (EN) 10 Ea 54.50N 8.30 E
Nordfriesland 10 Eb 54.40N 8.55 E
Nordgau 10 Hg 49.15N 11.50 E
Nordgrønland = North Greenland (EN) [2] 41 Gc 79.30N 50.00W
Nordhausen 10 Ge 51.31N 10.48 E
Nordhordland 8 Ad 60.50N 5.50 E
Nordhorn 10 Dd 52.26N 7.05 E
Nord-Jylland [2] 8 Cg 57.15N 10.00 E
Nordkapp [Nor.] = North Cape (EN) 5 Ia 71.11N 25.48 E
Nordkapp [Sval.] 41 Nb 80.31N 20.00 E
Nordkinn 5 Ia 71.08N 27.39 E
Nordkinnhalvøya 7 Ga 70.55N 27.45 E
Nord-Kvaløy 7 Ea 70.10N 19.11 E
Nordland [3] 7 Cc 67.06N 13.20 E
Nördlingen 10 Gh 48.51N 10.30 E
Nordloher Tief 10 Ja 53.10N 7.45 E
Nordmark 8 Fe 59.50N 14.06 E
Nordmøre 8 Ca 63.00N 8.30 E
Nordostrundingen 67 Le 81.30N 11.00W
Nord-Ostsee Kanal = Kiel Canal (EN) 5 Ge 53.53N 9.08 E
Nord-Ouest [3] 34 Hd 6.30N 10.30 E
Nordøyane 8 Bb 62.40N 6.15 E
Nordreisa 7 Eb 69.46N 21.03 E
Nordre Rønner 8 Dg 57.22N 10.56 E
Nordrhein-Westfalen = North Rhine-Westphalia (EN) [2] 10 De 51.30N 7.30 E
Nordsee = North Sea (EN) 5 Gd 55.20N 3.00 E
Nordsjøen = North Sea (EN) 5 Gd 55.20N 3.00 E
Nordskjobotn 7 Eb 69.13N 19.34 E
Nordsøen = North Sea (EN) 5 Gd 55.20N 3.00 E
Nord Strand 10 Eb 54.30N 8.55 E
Nordtiroler Kalkalpen 10 Hi 47.30N 11.30 E
Nord-Trøndelag [2] 7 Cd 64.25N 12.00 E
Nordwestfjord 41 Jd 71.30N 26.30W
Nore/An Fheoir 9 Gi 52.25N 6.58W
Norefjell 8 Cd 60.16N 9.29 E
Norefjorden 8 Cd 60.10N 9.00 E
Norfolk 9 Oi 52.40N 1.05 E
Norfolk [3] 9 Mi 52.45N 0.40W
Norfolk [Nb.-U.S.] 43 Hc 42.02N 97.25W
Norfolk [Va.-U.S.] 39 Lf 38.40N 76.14W
Norfolk Island [5] 58 Hg 29.05S 167.59 E
Norfolk Island 57 Hg 29.05S 167.59 E
Norfolk Ridge (EN) 57 Hg 29.00S 168.00 E
Norfork Lake 45 Jh 36.25N 92.10W
Norg 12 Ia 53.04N 6.32 E
Norge = Norway (EN) [1] 6 Gc 62.00N 10.00 E
Norheimsund 7 Bf 60.22N 6.08 E
Norikura-Dake 29 Ec 36.06N 137.33 E
Norilsk 22 Kc 69.20N 88.06 E
Normal 45 Lf 40.31N 88.59W
Norman 43 Hd 35.15N 97.26W
Norman, Lake- 44 Gh 35.35N 81.00W
Normanby Island 60 Ej 10.00S 151.00 E
Normanby River 59 Ib 14.25S 144.08 E
Normand, Bocage- 11 Ef 49.00N 1.10W
Normandie = Normandy (EN) 11 Gf 49.00N 0.10 E
Normandie = Normandy (EN) 5 Gf 49.00N 0.10 E
Normandie, Collines de- = Normandy Hills (EN) 5 Ff 48.50N 0.40W
Normandin 44 Ka 48.52N 72.30W
Normandy (EN) = Normandie 11 Gf 49.00N 0.10 E
Normandy (EN) = Normandie 5 Gf 49.00N 0.10 E
Normandy Hills (EN) = Normandie, Collines de- 5 Ff 48.50N 0.40W
Norman Island 51a Db 18.20N 64.37W
Norman River 59 Ic 17.28S 140.39 E
Normanton 58 Ff 17.40S 141.05 E
Norman Wells 39 Gc 65.17N 126.51W
Norquinco 56 Ff 41.51S 70.54W
Norra Dellen 8 Gc 61.55N 16.40 E
Norrahammar 8 Fg 57.42N 14.06 E
Norrala 8 Gc 61.22N 16.59 E
Norra Midsjöbanken 8 Gh 56.10N 17.30 E
Norra Ny 7 Cf 60.24N 13.15 E
Norra Storfjället 7 Dd 65.53N 15.14 E
Norrbotten [2] 7 Ec 67.26N 19.35 E
Nørre Åby 8 Ci 55.27N 9.54 E
Nørre Alslev 8 Dj 54.54N 11.54 E
Nørre-Nebel 8 Ci 55.47N 8.18 E
Norrent-Fontes 12 Ed 50.35N 2.24 E
Nørresundby 7 Bh 57.04N 9.55 E
Norrhult 7 Dh 57.08N 15.10 E
Norris Lake 44 Fg 36.20N 83.55W
Norristown 44 Je 40.07N 75.20W
Norrköping 6 Hd 58.36N 16.11 E
Norrland 5 Hc 64.27N 17.20 E
Norrland 7 Dd 65.00N 18.00 E
Norrmark/Noormarkku 8 Ic 61.35N 21.52 E
Norrsundet 8 Gd 60.56N 17.08 E
Norrtälje 7 Eg 59.46N 18.42 E
Norseman 58 Dh 32.12S 121.46 E
Norsewood 62 Gd 40.04S 176.13 E
Norsjö 7 Ed 64.55N 19.29 E
Norsjø 8 Ce 59.20N 9.20 E
Norsk 20 Hf 52.20N 129.59 E
Norske Havet = Norwegian Sea (EN) 5 Gc 70.00N 2.00 E
Norske Øer 41 Kc 79.00N 18.00W
Norsoup 63b Cc 16.04S 167.23 E
Norte, Baía- 55 Hh 27.30S 48.35W
Norte, Cabo- [Braz.] 54 Ic 1.40N 50.00W
Norte, Cabo- [Pas.] 65d Ab 27.03S 109.24W
Norte, Canal do- 54 Hc 0.30N 50.30W
Norte, Punta- 56 Hf 42.04S 63.45W
Norte, Serra do- 54 Gf 11.00S 59.00W
Norte del Cabo San Antonio, Punta- 56 Ie 36.17S 56.47W
Norte de Santander [2] 54 Db 8.00N 73.00W
Nortelândia 54 Gf 14.25S 56.48W
North, Cape- 42 Lg 47.02N 60.25W
North Adams 44 Kd 42.42N 73.02W
Northallerton 9 Lg 54.20N 1.26W
Northam [Austl.] 58 Ch 31.39S 116.40 E
Northam [S.Afr.] 37 Dd 24.58S 27.11 E
North America 38 Jf 40.00N 95.00W
North American Basin (EN) 3 Cf 30.00N 60.00W
Northampton 9 Mi 52.30N 1.00W
Northampton [Austl.] 59 Ce 28.21S 114.37 E
Northampton [Eng.-U.K.] 9 Mi 52.14N 0.54W
Northampton [Ma.-U.S.] 44 Kd 42.19N 72.38W
Northampton Seamounts (EN) 57 Jb 25.20N 172.04W
Northamptonshire [3] 9 Mi 52.25N 0.55W
North Andaman 25 If 13.15N 92.55 E
North Arm 42 Gd 62.00N 114.30W
North Astrolabe Reef 63d Bc 18.39S 178.32 E
North Augusta 44 Gi 33.30N 81.58W
North Aulatsivik 42 Le 59.45N 64.04W
North Australian Basin (EN) 3 Hk 14.30S 116.30 E
North Battleford 39 Id 52.47N 108.17W
North Bay 39 Le 46.19N 79.28W
North Belcher Islands 42 Je 56.45N 79.45W
North Berwick 9 Ke 56.04N 2.44W
North Buganda [3] 36 Fb 0.50N 32.10 E
North Caicos 49 Lc 21.56N 71.59W
North Canadian River 43 Hd 35.17N 95.31W
North Cape 57 Ih 34.25S 173.03 E
North Cape (EN) = Nordkapp [Nor.] 5 Ia 71.11N 25.48 E
North Caribou Lake 42 If 52.48N 90.45W
North Carolina [2] 43 Ld 35.30N 80.00W
North Channel 42 Jg 46.02N 82.50W
North Channel/Sruth na Maoile 5 Fd 55.10N 5.40W
Northchapel 12 Bc 51.03N 0.38W
North Charleston 44 Hi 32.53N 80.00W
North Chicago 45 Me 42.20N 87.51W
North Cove 46 Cc 46.47N 124.06W
North Cyprus 22 Ff 35.15N 33.40 E
North Dakota 43 Gb 47.30N 100.15W
North Downs 9 Nj 51.20N 0.10 E
North East 44 Hd 42.13N 79.51W
North-East [3] 37 Dd 21.00S 27.30 E
Northeast Cape 40 Fd 63.18N 168.42W
North-Eastern [3] 36 Hb 1.00N 40.15 E
Northeast Islands 64d Ba 7.36N 151.57 E
Northeast Pacific Basin (EN) 3 Lg 20.00N 140.00W
Northeast Pass 64d Ba 7.30N 151.59 E
North East Point 64g Bb 1.57N 157.16W
Northeast Point [Bah.] 49 Kc 21.18N 72.54W
Northeast Point [Bah.] 49 Kb 22.43N 73.50W
Northeast Providence Channel 47 Ic 25.40N 77.09W
Northeim 10 Fe 51.42N 10.00 E
North Entrance 64a Bb 7.59N 134.37 E
Northern [Ghana] [3] 34 Ed 9.30N 1.00W
Northern [Mwi.] [3] 36 Fe 11.00S 34.00 E
Northern [S.L.] [3] 34 Cd 9.15N 11.45W
Northern [Ug.] [3] 36 Fb 2.45N 32.45 E
Northern [Zam.] [3] 36 Fe 11.00S 31.00 E
Northern Cay 49 De 17.27N 87.28W
Northern Cook Islands 57 Kf 10.00S 161.00W
Northern Dvina (EN) = Severnaja Dvina 5 Kc 64.32N 40.30 E
Northern Guinea 30 Gh 8.30N 1.00W
Northern Indian Lake 42 He 57.20N 97.17W
Northern Ireland [2] 9 Gg 54.40N 6.45W
Northern Mariana Islands [5] 58 Fc 16.00N 145.30 E
Northern Sporades (EN) = Vórioi Sporádhes, Nisoi- 5 Ih 39.15N 23.55 E
Northern Territory 59 Gc 20.00S 134.00 E
Northern Urals (EN) = Severny Ural 5 Lc 62.00N 59.00 E
Northern Uvals (EN) = Severnyje Uvaly 5 Kd 59.30N 49.00 E
Northfield 45 Jd 44.27N 93.09W
North Fiji Basin (EN) 3 Jk 16.00S 174.00 E
North Foreland 9 Oj 51.23N 1.27 E
North Fork Grand River 45 Ed 45.47N 102.16W
North Fork John Day River 46 Fd 44.45N 119.38W
North Fork Moreau River 45 Ed 45.09N 102.50W
North Fork Pass 42 Dd 64.00N 138.00W
North Fork Powder River 46 Le 43.40N 106.30W
North Fork Red 45 Gi 34.25N 99.14W
North Fort Myers 44 Gl 26.40N 81.54W
North Frisian Islands (EN) = Nordfriesische Inseln 10 Ea 54.50N 8.30 E
North German Plain (EN) = Norddeutsches Tiefland 5 He 53.00N 11.00 E
North Greenland (EN) = Nordgrønland [2] 41 Gc 79.30N 50.00W
North Highlands 46 Eg 38.40N 121.23W
North Horr 36 Gb 3.19N 37.04 E
North Island [N.Z.] 57 Ih 39.00S 176.00 E
North Island [Sey.] 37b Bc 10.07S 51.11 E
North Kent 42 Ia 76.40N 90.15W
North Korea (EN) = Chosŏn M.I.K. [1] 22 Oe 40.00N 127.30 E
North Lakhimpur 25 Ic 27.14N 94.07 E
Northland [2] 62 Ea 35.30S 173.40 E
North Las Vegas 46 Hh 36.12N 115.07W
North Lincoln Land 42 Ja 76.15N 80.00W
North Little Rock 43 Ie 34.46N 92.14W
North Loup River 45 Gf 41.17N 98.23W
North Magnetic Pole (1980) 67 Qd 77.03N 101.08W
North Malosmadulu Atoll 25a Ba 5.35N 72.55 E
North Mamm Peak 45 Cg 39.23N 107.52W
North Mayreau Channel 51n Bb 12.41N 61.20W
North Miami 44 Gm 25.56N 80.09W
North Minch 5 Fd 58.05N 5.55W
North Palisade 46 Fh 37.10N 118.38W
North Pass [F.S.M.] 64d Ba 7.41N 151.48 E
North Pass [U.S.] 45 Ll 29.10N 89.15W
North Platte 43 Gc 41.08N 100.46W
North Platte 38 Ie 41.15N 100.45W
North Point [N.Z.] 64n Ab 10.22S 161.02W
North Point [Bar.] 51q Ab 13.20N 59.36W
North Pole 67 Ge 90.00N 0.00
Northport 44 Di 33.14N 87.35W
North Powder 46 Gd 45.03N 117.55W
North Raccoon River 45 Jf 41.35N 93.31W
North Reef 63a Ee 12.13S 160.04 E
North Rhine-Westphalia (EN) = Nordrhein-Westfalen [2] 10 De 51.30N 7.30 E
North Rim 46 Ih 36.12N 112.03W
North River 42 Ie 58.53N 94.42W
North Rona 9 Hb 59.10N 5.40W
North Ronaldsay 9 Kb 59.25N 2.30W
North Saskatchewan 38 Id 53.15N 105.06W
North Sea 5 Gd 55.20N 3.00 E
North Sea (EN) = Noordzee 5 Gd 55.20N 3.00 E
North Sea (EN) = Nord, Mer du- 5 Gd 55.20N 3.00 E
North Sea (EN) = Nordsee 5 Gd 55.20N 3.00 E
North Sea (EN) = Nordsjøen 5 Gd 55.20N 3.00 E
North Sea (EN) = Nordsøen 5 Gd 55.20N 3.00 E
North Sentinel 25 If 11.33N 92.15 E
North Shoshone Peak 46 Gg 39.10N 117.29W
North Siberian Plain (EN) = Severo-Sibirskaja Niz. 21 Mb 72.00N 104.00 E
North Sound 51d Bb 17.07N 61.45W
North Sound 49 Gd 19.25N 81.26W
North Stradbroke Island 59 Ke 27.35S 153.30 E
North Taranaki Bight 62 Fc 38.50S 174.25 E
North Thompson 42 Ff 50.41N 120.11W
North Tokelau Trough (EN) 3 Kj 3.00S 165.00W
North Tonawanda 44 Hd 43.02N 78.54W
North Trap 62 Bg 47.20S 167.55 E
North Tyne 9 Kg 54.59N 2.08W
North Uist 9 Fd 57.37N 7.22W
Northumberland [3] 9 Kf 55.15N 2.10W
Northumberland 9 Kf 55.15N 2.05W
Northumberland Islands 57 Gg 21.40S 150.00 E
Northumberland Strait 42 Lg 46.00N 63.30W
North Umpqua River 46 De 43.16N 123.27W
North Vancouver 46 Db 49.19N 123.04W
North Walsham 12 Db 52.49N 1.23 E
Northway 40 Kd 62.59N 141.43W
North West Bluff 51c Bc 16.49N 62.12W
North West Cape 57 Cg 21.45S 114.10 E
North-Western [3] 36 Ee 13.00S 25.00 E
Northwest Frontier [3] 25 Eb 33.00N 70.30 E
North West Highlands 5 Fd 57.30N 5.00W
Northwest Pacific Basin (EN) 3 Je 40.00N 155.00 E
North West Point 64g Ab 2.02N 157.30W
Northwest Providence Channel 44 Hl 26.10N 78.20W
Northwest Reef 64a Bb 7.59N 134.33 E
North West River 42 Lf 53.32N 60.09W
Northwest Territories [3] 42 Hc 66.00N 102.00W
Northwich 9 Kh 53.16N 2.32W
North York Moors 9 Mg 54.25N 0.50W
North Yorkshire [3] 9 Lg 54.15N 1.40W
Norton [Ks.-U.S.] 43 Gd 39.50N 100.01W
Norton [Va.-U.S.] 44 Fg 36.56N 82.37W
Norton [Zimb.] 37 Ec 17.53S 30.41 E
Norton Bay 40 Gd 64.45N 161.15W
Norton Sound 38 Cc 64.45N 161.15W
Norvegia, Kapp- 66 Bf 71.25S 12.18W
Norwalk [Ct.-U.S.] 44 Ke 41.07N 73.27W
Norwalk [Oh.-U.S.] 44 Fe 41.14N 82.37W
Norway 44 Dc 45.47N 87.55W
Norway (EN) = Norge [1] 6 Gc 62.00N 10.00 E
Norway Bay 42 Hb 71.00N 104.35W
Norway House 42 Hf 53.58N 97.50W
Norwegian Basin (EN) 3 Dc 68.00N 2.00W
Norwegian Bay 42 Ij 77.45N 90.30W
Norwegian Sea (EN) = Norske Havet 5 Gc 70.00N 2.00 E
Norwegian Trench (EN) 5 Gd 59.00N 4.30 E
Norwich [Ct.-U.S.] 44 Ke 41.32N 72.05W
Norwich [Eng.-U.K.] 6 Ge 52.38N 1.18 E
Norwich [N.Y.-U.S.] 44 Jd 42.33N 75.33W
Norwich Airport 12 Db 52.40N 1.18 E
Norwood 44 Ef 39.10N 84.28W
Nosappu-Misaki 29a Db 43.23N 145.47 E
Noshappu-Misaki 29a Ba 45.27N 141.39 E
Noshiro 27 Pc 40.12N 140.02 E
Nosovaja 19 Fb 68.15N 54.31 E
Nosovka 19 De 50.54N 31.37 E
Nosratābād 23 Id 29.54N 59.59 E
Nossa Senhora das Candeias 54 Kf 12.40S 38.33W
Nossa Senhora do Livramento 55 Db 15.48S 56.22W
Noss Head 9 Jc 58.30N 3.05W
Nossob 30 Jk 26.55S 20.40 E
Nossop 37 Ce 26.55S 20.40 E
Nosy-Be 30 Lj 13.20S 48.15 E
Nosy-Be 31 Lj 13.22S 48.16 E
Nosy-Varika 37 Hd 20.35S 48.30 E
Nota 7 Hb 68.07N 30.10 E
Notch Peak 46 Ig 39.08N 113.24W
Noteć 10 Ld 52.44N 15.26 E
Notecka, Puszcza- 10 Ld 52.45N 16.00 E
Note Kemopla 63c b 10.55S 165.51 E
Notengo, Laguna de- 48 Ji 16.15N 98.10W
Notia Pindhos 15 Ej 39.30N 21.20 E
Nótioi Sporádhes = Dodecanese (EN) 5 Ih 36.00N 27.00 E
Nótios Evvoïkós Kólpos 15 Gk 38.20N 23.50 E
Nötö 8 Ie 60.00N 21.45 E
Noto [It.] 14 Jn 36.53N 15.04 E
Noto [Jap.] 28 Nf 37.18N 137.09 E
Noto, Golfo di- 14 Jn 36.50N 15.10 E
Notodden 7 Bg 59.34N 9.17 E
Noto-Hantō 27 Od 37.20N 137.00 E
Noto-Jima 29 Ec 37.07N 137.00 E
Notoro-Ko 29a Da 44.05N 144.10 E
Notoro-Misaki 29a Da 44.07N 144.15 E
Notranjsko 14 Ie 45.46N 14.26 E
Notre-Dame, Monts- 38 Me 48.00N 69.00W
Notre Dame Bay 42 Mg 49.50N 55.00W
Notre-Dame-de-Courson 12 Cf 48.59N 0.16 E
Notre-Dame-de-Gravenchon 12 Ce 49.29N 0.35 E
Notre Dame-du-Lac 44 Mb 47.38N 68.49W
Notre-Dame-du-Nord 44 Hb 47.36N 79.29W
Notsé 34 Fd 6.59N 1.12 E
Notsuke-Zaki 29a Db 43.34N 145.19 E
Nottawasaga Bay 44 Gc 44.40N 80.30W
Nottaway 38 Ld 51.25N 79.50W
Notterøy 8 De 59.15N 10.25 E
Nottingham 6 Fe 52.58N 1.10W
Nottingham 42 Jd 63.20N 78.00W
Nottingham 9 Mh 53.05N 1.00W
Nottinghamshire [3] 9 Mh 53.10N 0.55W
Nottoway River 44 Ig 36.33N 76.55W
Nottuln 12 Jc 51.56N 7.21 E
Notukeu Creek 46 Lb 49.55N 106.30W
Nouâdhibou 31 Ff 20.54N 17.01W
Nouâdhibou, Dahklet- 32 De 21.00N 16.50W
Nouâdhibou, Râs- = Blanc Cape- (EN) 30 Ff 20.46N 17.03W
Nouakchott 31 Fg 18.07N 15.59W
Nouakchott, District de- [3] 32 Df 18.06N 15.57W
Nouamrhar 32 Df 19.22N 16.31W
Nouméa 58 Hg 22.16S 166.26 E
Nouna 34 Ec 12.44N 3.52W
Noupoort 37 Cf 31.10S 24.57 E

Index Symbols

[1] Independent Nation; [2] State, Region; [3] District, County; [4] Municipality; [5] Colony, Dependency; Continent; Physical Region; Historical or Cultural Region; Mount, Mountain; Volcano; Hill; Mountains, Mountain Range; Hills, Escarpment; Plateau, Upland; Pass, Gap; Plain, Lowland; Delta; Salt Flat; Valley, Canyon; Crater, Cave; Karst Features; Depression; Polder; Desert, Dunes; Forest, Woods; Heath, Steppe; Oasis; Cape, Point; Coast, Beach; Cliff; Peninsula; Isthmus; Sandbank; Island; Atoll; Rock, Reef; Islands, Archipelago; Rocks, Reefs; Coral Reef; Well, Spring; Geyser; River, Stream; Waterfall Rapids; River Mouth, Estuary; Lake; Salt Lake; Intermittent Lake; Reservoir; Swamp, Pond; Canal; Glacier; Ice Shelf, Pack Ice; Ocean; Sea; Gulf, Bay; Strait, Fjord; Lagoon; Bank; Seamount; Tablemount; Ridge; Shelf; Basin; Escarpment, Sea Scarp; Fracture; Trench, Abyss; National Park, Reserve; Point of Interest; Recreation Site; Cave, Cavern; Historic Site; Ruins; Wall, Walls; Church, Abbey; Temple; Scientific Station; Airport; Port; Lighthouse; Mine; Tunnel; Dam, Bridge

Nouveau-Comptoir 42 Jf 52.35N 78.40W
Nouveau-Québec, Cratère du- = New Quebec Crater (EN) 42 Kd 61.30N 73.55W
Nouvelle-Calédonie = New Caledonia (EN) [5] 58 Hg 21.30S 165.30 E
Nouvelle-Calédonie=New Caledonia (EN) 57 Hg 21.30S 165.30 E
Nouvelle-France, Cap de - 42 Kd 62.33N 73.35W
Nouvelles Hébrides/New Hebrides 57 Hf 16.01S 167.01 E
Nouvion 12 Dd 50.12N 1.47 E
Nouzonville 11 Ke 49.49N 4.45 E
Novabad 18 He 39.01N 70.09 E
Nová Baňa 10 Oh 48.26N 18.39 E
Nová Bystřice 10 Lg 49.02N 15.06 E
Nova Cruz 54 Ke 6.28S 35.26W
Nova Esperança 55 Ff 23.08S 52.13W
Nova Friburgo 54 Jh 22.16S 42.32W
Nova Gaia 36 Ce 10.05S 17.32 E
Nova Gorica 14 He 45.57N 13.39 E
Nova Gradiška 14 Le 45.16N 17.23 E
Nova Granada 55 He 20.29S 49.19W
Nova Iguaçu 53 Lh 22.45S 43.27W
Novaja Igirma 20 Fe 57.10N 103.55 E
Novaja-Ivanovka 15 Md 45.59N 29.04 E
Novaja Kahovka 16 Hf 46.43N 33.23 E
Novaja Kazanka 16 Pe 48.58N 49.37 E
Novaja Ladoga 7 Hf 60.05N 32.16 E
Novaja Ljalja 19 Gd 59.03N 60.36 E
Novaja Odessa 16 Gf 47.18N 31.47 E
Novaja Sibir, Ostrov-=New Siberia (EN) 21 Qb 75.00N 149.00 E
Novaja Vodolaga 16 Ie 49.45N 35.52 E
Novaja Zemlja=Novaya Zemlya (EN) 21 Hb 74.00N 57.00 E
Nova Lamego 34 Cc 12.17N 14.13W
Nova Lima 54 Jh 19.59S 43.51W
Nova Londrina 55 Ff 22.45S 53.00W
Nova Mambone 37 Fd 20.58S 35.00 E
Nova Olinda do Norte 54 Gd 3.45S 59.03W
Nová Paka 10 Lf 50.29N 15.31 E
Nova Prata 55 Gi 28.47S 51.36W
Novara 14 Ce 45.28N 8.38 E
Nova Roma 55 Ia 13.51S 46.57W
Nova Russas 54 Jd 4.42S 40.34W
Nova Scotia [3] 42 Lh 45.00N 63.00W
Nova Scotia 38 Me 45.00N 63.00W
Nova Sintra 32 Cf 14.54N 24.40W
Nova Sofala 37 Ed 20.10S 34.44 E
Novato 46 Dg 38.06N 122.34W
Nova Varoš 15 Cf 43.28N 19.49 E
Nova Venécia 54 Jg 18.43S 40.24W
Novaya Zemlya (EN)= Novaja Zemlja 21 Hb 74.00N 57.00 E
Nova Zagora 15 Jg 42.29N 26.01 E
Novelda 13 Lf 38.23N 0.46W
Novellara 14 Ef 44.51N 10.44 E
Nové Mesto nad Váhom 10 Nh 48.46N 17.50 E
Nové Zámky 10 Oi 47.59N 18.11 E
Novgorod 6 Jd 58.31N 31.17 E
Novgorodka 8 Mg 57.00N 28.37 E
Novgorod-Severski 19 De 52.01N 33.16 E
Novgorodskaja Oblast [3] 19 Dd 58.20N 32.40 E
Novi Bečej 15 Dd 45.36N 20.08 E
Novigrad [Yugo.] 14 He 45.19N 13.34 E
Novigrad [Yugo.] 14 Jf 44.11N 15.33 E
Novi Kričim 15 Hg 42.03N 24.28 E
Novi Ligure 14 Cf 44.46N 8.47 E
Novillero 48 Gf 22.21N 105.39W
Novion-Porcien 12 Ge 49.36N 4.25 E
Novi Pazar [Bul.] 15 Kf 43.21N 27.12 E
Novi Pazar [Yugo.] 15 Df 43.08N 20.31 E
Novi Sad 6 Hf 45.15N 19.50 E
Novi Travnik 14 Lf 44.10N 17.39 E
Novi Vinodolski 14 Ie 45.08N 14.47 E
Novoaleksandrovsk 16 Lg 45.24N 41.14 E
Novoaleksejevka [Kaz.-U.S.S.R.] 16 Sd 50.08N 55.42 E
Novoaleksejevka [Ukr.-U.S.S.R.] 16 If 46.16N 34.39 E
Novoaltajsk 20 Df 53.24N 83.58 E
Novoanninski 19 Ee 50.31N 42.45 E
Novoarhangelsk 16 Ge 48.39N 30.50 E
Novo Aripuanã 54 Fe 5.08S 60.22W
Novoazovsk 16 Kf 47.05N 38.05 E
Novobirjusinski 20 Ee 56.58N 97.55 E
Novobogdanovka 16 If 47.05N 35.18 E
Novočeboksarsk 7 Lh 56.08N 47.29 E
Novočeremšansk 7 Mi 54.23N 50.10 E
Novočerkassk 19 Ef 47.25N 40.03 E
Novodevičje 7 Lj 53.35N 48.51 E
Novograd-Volynski 19 Ce 50.36N 27.36 E
Novogrudok 16 Dc 53.37N 25.50 E
Nôvo Hamburgo 56 Jc 29.41S 51.08W
Novohopërsk 16 Ld 51.06N 41.37 E
Novo Horizonte 55 He 21.28S 49.13W
Novoizborsk 8 Mg 57.43N 28.05 E
Novojenisejsk 20 Ee 58.19N 92.27 E
Novojerudinski 20 Ee 59.47N 93.30 E
Novokačalinsk 20 Ig 45.05N 131.59 E
Novokazalinsk 22 Ie 45.50N 62.10 E
Novokubansk 16 Lg 45.06N 41.01 E
Novokujbyševsk 19 Ee 53.08N 49.58 E
Novokuzneck 22 Kd 53.45N 87.06 E
Novolazarevskaja 66 Cf 70.46S 11.50 E
Novolukoml 7 Gi 54.38N 29.07 E
Novo Mesto 14 Je 45.48N 15.10 E
Novomičurinsk 7 Ji 54.02N 39.48 E
Novomihajlovka 20 Ih 44.17N 133.50 E
Novo Miloševo 15 Dd 45.43N 20.18 E
Novomirgorod 16 Ge 48.45N 31.39 E
Novomoskovsk [R.S.F.S.R.] 6 Je 54.05N 38.13 E
Novomoskovsk [Ukr.-U.S.S.R.] 19 Df 48.37N 35.16 E
Novonikolajevski 16 Md 50.55N 42.24 E
Novoorsk 19 Fe 51.24N 58.59 E
Novopokrovskaja 16 Lg 45.56N 40.42 E
Novopolock 19 Cd 55.31N 28.40 E
Novorossijsk 6 Jg 44.45N 37.45 E
Novorybnaja 20 Fb 72.50N 105.45 E
Novoržev 19 Cd 57.02N 29.20 E
Novo-Šahtinsk 19 Df 47.47N 39.54 E
Novoselica 15 Ja 48.13N 26.17 E
Novoselje 8 Mf 58.05N 29.00 E
Novoselki 10 Ud 52.04N 24.25 E
Novoselovo 20 Ef 54.55N 91.00 E
Novosergijevka 19 Fe 52.03N 53.39 E
Novosibirsk 22 Kd 55.02N 82.55 E
Novosibirskaja Oblast [3] 20 Ce 55.30N 80.00 E
Novosibirskije Ostrova= New Siberian Islands (EN) 21 Qb 75.00N 142.00 E
Novosibirskoje Vodohranilišče 20 Df 54.40N 82.35 E
Novosil 16 Jc 52.59N 37.01 E
Novosineglazovski 17 Ji 55.05N 61.25 E
Novosokolniki 19 Dd 56.19N 30.12 E
Novospasskoje 7 Lj 53.09N 47.44 E
Novotroick 19 Fe 51.12N 58.35 E
Novotroickoje 19 Hg 43.39N 73.45 E
Novoukrainka 16 Ge 48.19N 31.32 E
Novouljanovsk 7 Li 54.10N 48.23 E
Novouzensk 19 Ee 50.29N 48.08 E
Novovjatsk 7 Lg 58.31N 49.43 E
Novovolynsk 19 Ce 50.46N 24.09 E
Novovoronežski 16 Kd 51.17N 39.16 E
Novozybkov 19 De 52.32N 32.00 E
Novska 14 Ke 45.20N 16.59 E
Novy Bug 16 Hf 47.43N 32.29 E
Nový Bydžov 10 Lf 50.15N 15.29 E
Novy Jaričev 10 Ug 49.50N 24.21 E
Novyje Aneny 15 Mc 46.53N 29.13 E
Novyje Burasy 16 Oc 52.06N 46.06 E
Nový Jičin 10 Og 49.36N 18.01 E
Novy Oskol 19 De 50.43N 37.54 E
Novy Pogost 8 Li 55.30N 27.32 E
Novy Port 22 Jc 67.40N 72.52 E
Novy Tap 17 Mh 56.55N 67.15 E
Novy Terek 16 Oh 43.37N 47.25 E
Novy Uzen 19 Fg 43.19N 52.55 E
Novy Vasjugan 20 Ce 58.34N 76.29 E
Novy Zaj 7 Mi 55.17N 52.02 E
Nowa Dęba 10 Rf 50.26N 21.46 E
Nowa Huta, Kraków- 10 Qf 50.04N 20.05 E
Nowa Ruda 10 Mf 50.35N 16.31 E
Nowa Sarzyna 10 Sf 50.23N 22.22 E
Nowa Sól 10 Le 51.48N 15.44 E
Now Bandegān 24 Oh 28.52N 53.53 E
Nowbarān 24 Me 35.08N 49.42 E
Nowdesheh 24 Le 35.11N 46.15 E
Nowe 10 Oc 53.40N 18.43 E
Nowe Miasto Lubawskie 10 Pc 53.27N 19.35 E
Nowe Miasto-nad-Pilicą 10 Qe 51.38N 20.35 E
Nowe Warpno 10 Kc 53.44N 14.20 E
Nowfel low Shātow 24 Ne 34.27N 50.55 E
Nowgong 25 Ic 26.21N 92.40 E
Nowogard 10 Lc 53.40N 15.08 E
Nowogród 10 Rc 53.15N 21.53 E
Nowood River 46 Ld 44.17N 107.58W
Nowra 59 Kf 34.53S 150.36 E
Nowshahr 24 Nd 36.39N 51.31 E
Nowy Dwór Gdański 10 Pb 54.13N 19.06 E
Nowy Dwór Mazowiecki 10 Qd 52.26N 20.43 E
Nowy Korczyn 10 Qf 50.20N 20.50 E
Nowy Sącz [2] 10 Qg 49.40N 20.40 E
Nowy Sącz 10 Qg 49.38N 20.42 E
Nowy Targ 10 Qg 49.29N 20.02 E
Nowy Tomyśl 10 Md 52.20N 16.07 E
Noya 13 Db 42.47N 8.53W
Noya/Anoia 13 Nc 41.28N 1.56 E
Noyant 11 Gg 47.31N 0.08 E
Noyon 11 Ie 49.35N 3.00 E
Nozaki-Jima 29 Ae 33.11N 129.08 E
Nozay 11 Eg 47.34N 1.38W
Nsanje 36 Gf 16.55S 35.16 E
Nsawan 34 Ed 5.48N 0.21W
Nschodnia 10 Rf 50.30N 21.18 E
Nsefu 36 Fe 13.03S 32.07 E
Nsukka 34 Gd 6.52N 7.23 E
Ntadembele 36 Cc 2.11S 17.08 E
Ntchisi 36 Fe 13.22S 34.00 E
Ntem 30 Hh 2.10N 9.57 E
Ntoum 36 Ab 0.22N 9.47 E
Ntui 34 He 4.27N 11.38 E
Ntusi 36 Fb 0.03N 31.13 E
Nuageuses, Iles- 30 Nm 48.40S 68.58 E
Nuanetsi 30 Kk 22.40S 31.49 E
Nūbah, Jibāl an- 30 Kg 12.00N 30.45 E
Nubian Desert (EN)= Nūbiyah, Aş Şaḩrā' an- 30 Kf 20.30N 33.00 E
Nūbiyah, Aş Şaḩrā' an-= Nubian Desert (EN) 30 Kf 20.30N 33.00 E
Nudha 63a Ec 9.32S 160.48 E
Nueces Plain 43 Hf 28.30N 99.15W
Nueces River 43 Hf 27.50N 97.30W
Nueltin Lake 38 Jc 60.50N 99.30W
Nü'er He 28 Fd 41.06N 121.09 E
Nueva Asunción [3] 55 Be 21.00S 60.20W
Nueva Ciudad Guerrero 48 Jd 26.35N 99.15W
Nueva Esparta [2] 54 Fa 11.00N 64.00W
Nueva Germania 55 Df 23.54S 56.34W
Nueva Gerona 47 Hd 21.53N 82.48W
Nueva Imperial 56 Fe 38.44S 72.57W
Nueva Italia de Ruiz 48 Hh 19.01N 102.06W
Nueva Ocotepeque 49 Cf 14.24N 89.13W
Nueva Palmira 55 Ck 33.53S 58.25W
Nueva Rosita 39 Ig 27.57N 101.13W
Nueva San Salvador 47 Gf 13.41N 89.17W
Nueva Segovia [3] 49 Dg 13.40N 86.10W
Nueve de Julio 56 He 35.27S 60.52W
Nuevitas 47 Id 21.33N 77.16W
Nuevitas, Bahía de- 49 Ic 21.30N 77.12W
Nuevo, Cayo- 48 Mg 21.51N 92.05W
Nuevo, Golfo- 52 Jj 42.42S 64.36W
Nuevo Berlín 55 Ck 32.59S 58.03W
Nuevo Casas Grandes 39 If 30.25N 107.55W
Nuevo Laredo 39 Jg 27.30N 99.31W
Nuevo León [2] 47 Ec 25.40N 100.00W
Nuevo Mundo, Cerro- 54 Eh 21.55S 66.53W
Nuevo Rocafuerte 54 Cd 0.56S 75.25W
Nugaal [3] 35 Hd 8.30N 48.00 E
Nugālēd, Dēh- 30 Lh 7.58N 49.51 E
Nugālēd, Dōḥo- 35 Hd 8.35N 48.35 E
Nûgâtsiaq 41 Gd 71.39N 53.45W
Nugget Point 62 Cg 46.27S 169.49 E
Nûgssuaq 41 Gd 70.30N 51.30W
Nuguria Islands 57 Ge 3.20S 154.45 E
Nuguš 17 Gj 53.05N 56.00 E
Nuhaka 62 Gc 39.02S 177.45 E
Nui Atoll 57 Ie 7.15S 177.10 E
Nuijama 8 Md 60.58N 28.32 E
Nuiqsut 40 Ib 70.20N 151.00W
Nu Jang 21 Lh 16.31N 97.37 E
Nûk/Godthåb 67 Nc 64.15N 51.40W
Nukapu 63c Ab 10.07S 165.59 E
Nukey Bluff 59 Hf 32.35S 135.40 E
Nukhayb 23 Fc 32.02N 42.15 E
Nukhaylak 31 Jg 19.08N 26.20 E
Nukiki 63a Cb 6.45S 156.29 E
Nukuaéta 64h Ac 13.22S 176.11W
Nuku'alofa 58 Jg 21.08S 175.12W
Nukufetau Atoll 57 Ie 8.00S 178.22 E
Nukufotu 64h Bb 13.11S 176.10W
Nukuhifala 64h Bb 13.17S 176.05W
Nukuhione 64h Bb 13.16S 176.06W
Nuku Hiva, Ile- 57 Me 8.54S 140.06W
Nukulaelae Atoll 57 Ie 9.23S 179.52 E
Nukuloa 64h Bb 13.11S 176.09W
Nukumanu Islands 57 Ge 4.30S 159.30 E
Nukumbasanga 63d Cb 16.18S 179.15W
Nukunonu Atoll 57 Je 9.10S 171.53W
Nukuoro Atoll 57 Gd 3.51N 154.58 E
Nukus 22 He 42.50N 59.29 E
Nukutapu 64h Bb 13.13S 176.08W
Nukuteatea 64h Bb 13.12S 176.08W
Nulato 40 Hd 64.43N 158.06W
Nules 13 Le 39.51N 0.09W
Nullagine 58 Dg 21.53S 120.06 E
Nullagine River 59 Ed 20.43S 120.33 E
Nullarbor 59 Gf 31.26S 130.55 E
Nullarbor Plain 57 Dh 31.00S 129.00 E
Nulu'erhu Shan 27 Kc 41.40N 119.50 E
Numakawa 29a Ba 45.15N 141.51 E
Numan 34 Hd 9.28N 12.02 E
Numancia [Phil.] 26 Ie 9.52N 125.58 E
Numancia [Sp.] 13 Jc 41.47N 2.30W
Numanohata 29a Bb 42.40N 141.41 E
Numata [Jap.] 29a Bb 43.49N 141.55 E
Numata [Jap.] 28 Of 36.38N 139.03 E
Numatinna 35 Dd 7.14N 27.37 E
Numazu 28 Og 35.06N 138.52 E
Nümbrecht 12 Jd 50.54N 7.33 E
Numedal 7 Bf 60.05N 9.05 E
Numena 36 Ee 11.46S 26.31 E
Número Cinco, Canal- 55 Cm 37.14S 58.06W
Número Doce, Canal- 55 Cm 36.30S 59.08W
Número Dos, Canal- 55 Cm 36.51S 58.03W
Número Nueve, Canal- 55 Cm 36.08S 58.36W
Número Once, Canal- 55 Bm 36.28S 60.01W
Número Quince, Canal- 55 Dl 35.55S 57.45W
Número Uno, Canal- 55 Cm 36.40S 58.35W
Numfoor, Pulau- 26 Jg 1.03S 134.54 E
Nuneaton 9 Li 52.32N 1.28W
Nungarin 59 Df 31.11S 118.06 E
Nungnain Sum 27 Kb 45.45N 118.56 E
Nungo 37 Fb 13.25S 37.46 E
Nunivak 38 Cd 60.00N 166.30W
Nunkirchen, Wadern- 12 Ie 49.32N 6.53 E
Nunn 45 Df 40.45N 104.46W
Nunspeet 12 Hb 52.22N 5.46 E
Nunukan Timur, Pulau- 26 Gf 4.05N 117.40 E
Nuomin He 27 Lb 48.21N 124.32 E
Nuorgam 7 Ga 70.05N 27.51 E
Nuoro 6 Gg 40.19N 9.20 E
Nupani 63c Ab 10.04S 165.40 E
Nūq 24 Pg 30.55N 55.35 E
Nuqayr 24 Mi 27.48N 48.21 E
Nuqrah 24 Ij 25.34N 41.24 E
Nuqruş, Jabal- 33 Fe 24.49N 34.36 E
Nuquí 54 Cb 5.43N 77.16W
Nūr 24 Od 36.15N 52.20 E
Nūr 24 Pg 31.25N 54.20 E
Nura 19 Gf 48.57N 62.20 E
Nura 21 Id 50.30N 69.59 E
Nūrābād 24 Ng 30.48N 51.27 E
Nuraghe Santu Antine 14 Cj 40.29N 8.45 E
Nurata 19 Gg 40.34N 65.35 E
Nur Dağları 24 Gd 36.45N 36.20 E
Nure 14 De 45.03N 9.49 E
Nurek 19 Gh 38.25N 69.20 E
Nurhak Dağı 23 Eb 38.04N 37.29 E
Nūrī 35 Eb 18.30N 32.02 E
Nurki 20 Ie 56.42N 138.28 E
Nurlat 19 Fe 54.28N 50.48 E
Nurlati 7 Li 55.38N 48.17 E
Nurmes 7 Ge 63.33N 29.07 E
Nurmijärvi 8 Kd 60.28N 24.48 E
Nurmo 8 Jb 62.50N 22.54 E
Nürnberg 6 Hf 49.27N 11.05 E
Nurra 14 Cj 40.45N 8.15 E
Nurri, Mount- 59 Jf 31.42S 146.02 E
Nurugas 37 Bc 19.11S 18.54 E
Nurzec 10 Sd 52.33N 22.28 E
Nusa Tenggara Barat [3] 26 Gh 8.50S 117.30 E
Nusa Tenggara Timur [3] 26 Hh 9.30S 122.00 E
Nusaybin 24 Id 37.03N 41.13 E
Nushagak 40 He 58.57N 158.29W
Nushan 27 Gf 25.00N 99.00 E
Nu-Shima 29 Dd 34.10N 134.50 E
Nutak 42 Le 57.31N 62.00W
Nuttal 25 Dc 28.45N 68.08 E
Nuutele 65c Bb 14.02S 171.22W
Nuwākot 25 Gc 28.08N 83.53 E
Nuwara 25 Gg 6.58N 80.46 E
Nuwaybi 'al Muzayyinah 33 Fd 28.58N 34.39 E
Nyabing 59 Df 33.32S 118.09 E
Nyagquka/Yajiang 27 He 30.07N 100.58 E
Nyagrong/Xinlong 27 He 30.57N 100.12 E
Nyahanga 36 Fc 2.23S 33.33 E
Nyahua 36 Fc 4.58S 33.34 E
Nyainqêntanglha Feng 27 Fe 30.12N 90.33 E
Nyainqêntanglha Shan 21 Kf 30.10N 90.00 E
Nyakanazi 36 Fc 3.00S 31.15 E
Nyala 31 Jg 12.03N 24.53 E
Nyalam 27 Ef 28.15N 85.55 E
Ny-Ålesund 41 Nc 78.56N 11.57 E
Nyalikungu 36 Fc 3.11S 33.47 E
Nyamandhlovu 37 Dc 19.51S 28.16 E
Nyamapanda 37 Ec 16.55S 32.52 E
Nyamlell 35 Dd 9.07N 26.58 E
Nyamtumbo 36 Ge 10.30S 36.06 E
Nyanding 35 Ed 8.40N 32.41 E
Nyanga 30 Ii 2.58S 10.15 E
Nyanga [3] 36 Bc 3.00S 11.00 E
Nyanza [3] 36 Fc 0.30S 34.30 E
Nyanza-Lac 36 Ec 4.21S 29.36 E
Nyasa, Lake- (EN)=Niassa, Lago- 30 Kj 12.00S 34.30 E
Nyaunglebin 25 Je 17.57N 96.44 E
Nyborg 7 Ci 55.19N 10.48 E
Nybro 7 Dh 56.45N 15.54 E
Nyda 17 Pc 66.40N 72.50 E
Nyda 20 Cc 66.36N 72.54 E
Nyeboe Land 41 Gb 81.45N 56.40W
Nyêmo 27 Ff 29.30N 90.07 E
Nyeri 36 Gc 0.25S 36.57 E
Nyerol 35 Ed 8.41N 32.02 E
Ny Friesland 41 Nc 79.30N 17.00 E
Nyhammar 8 Fd 60.17N 14.58 E
Nyhem 8 Fb 62.54N 15.40 E
Nyika 30 Ki 2.37S 38.44 E
Nyika Plateau 30 Kj 10.40S 33.50 E
Nyikog Qu 27 He 30.24N 100.40 E
Nyimba 36 Fe 14.33S 30.48 E
Nyingchi 27 Ff 29.38N 94.23 E
Nyírbátor 10 Si 47.50N 22.08 E
Nyíregyháza 10 Ri 47.57N 21.43 E
Nyiri Desert 36 Gc 2.20S 37.20 E
Nyiro, Mount- 36 Gb 2.08N 36.51 E
Nyírség 10 Ri 47.50N 21.55 E
Nykøbing [Den.] 7 Ci 54.46N 11.53 E
Nykøbing [Den.] 7 Ci 55.55N 11.41 E
Nykøbing [Den.] 8 Ch 56.48N 8.52 E
Nyköping 7 Dg 58.45N 17.00 E
Nyköpingsån 8 Gf 58.45N 17.01 E
Nykroppa 8 Fe 59.38N 14.18 E
Nyland 8 Ga 63.00N 17.46 E
Nylstroom 37 Dd 24.42S 28.20 E
Nymburk 10 Lf 50.11N 15.03 E
Nymphe Bank (EN) 9 Fj 51.30N 7.05W
Nynäshamn 7 Dg 58.54N 17.57 E
Nyngan 58 Fh 31.34S 147.11 E
Nyon 14 Ad 46.23N 6.15 E
Nyong 30 Hh 3.17N 9.54 E
Nyonga 36 Fd 6.43S 32.04 E
Nyons 11 Lj 44.22N 5.08 E
Nýřany 10 Jg 49.43N 13.13 E
Nyrob 17 Hf 60.42N 56.45 E
Nyš 20 Jf 51.30N 142.49 E
Nysa 10 Nf 50.29N 17.20 E
Nysa Kłodzka 10 Nf 50.49N 17.50 E
Nysa Łużycka 10 Kd 52.04N 14.46 E
Nyslott/Savonlinna 7 Gf 61.52N 28.53 E
Nyssa 46 Ge 43.53N 117.00W
Nystad/Uusikaupunki 7 Ef 60.48N 21.25 E
Nysted 8 Dj 54.40N 11.45 E
Nytva 19 Fd 57.56N 55.20 E
Nyūdō-Zaki 28 Od 40.00N 139.35 E
Nyunzu 36 Ed 5.57S 28.01 E
Nyūzen 29 Ec 36.56N 137.30 E
Nzambi 36 Bc 3.58S 11.16 E
Nzara 35 De 4.40N 28.14 E
Nzega 36 Fc 4.13S 33.11 E
Nzérékoré 31 Gh 7.45N 8.49W
N'zeto 36 Bd 7.05S 12.50 E
Nzi 30 Gh 5.57N 4.50W
Nzilo, Barrage de- 36 Ee 10.35S 25.30 E
Nzo 34 Dd 6.16N 7.03W
Nzoro 36 Eb 3.18N 29.26 E
Nzwani 30 Lj 12.15S 44.25 E

O

Oa, Mull of- 9 Gf 55.35N 6.20W
Oahe, Lake- 38 Ie 45.30N 100.25W
Oahu Island 57 Lb 21.30N 158.00W
O-akan-Dake 29a Db 43.27N 144.10 E
Oakdale [Ca.-U.S.] 46 Eh 37.46N 120.51W
Oakdale [La.-U.S.] 45 Jk 30.49N 92.40W
Oakham 9 Mi 52.40N 0.44W
Oak Harbor 46 Db 48.18N 122.39W
Oak Lake 45 Fb 49.40N 100.45W
Oakland [Ca.-U.S.] 39 Gf 37.47N 122.13W
Oakland [Md.-U.S.] 44 Hf 39.25N 79.24W
Oakley [Id.-U.S.] 46 Ie 42.15N 113.53W
Oakley [Ks.-U.S.] 43 Gd 39.08N 100.51W
Oak Park 45 Mf 41.53N 87.48W
Oak Ridge 43 Kd 36.01N 84.16W
Oakridge 46 De 43.45N 122.28W
Oakville 44 Hd 43.27N 79.41W
Oamaru 61 Di 45.05S 170.59 E
Oancea 15 Ld 45.55N 28.06 E
Oani-Gawa 29 Ga 40.12N 140.16 E
Ōarai 29 Gc 36.18N 140.33 E
Oaro 62 Ee 42.31S 173.30 E
Oasis 46 Hf 41.01N 114.37W
Oasis 32 Hd 26.00N 5.00 E
Oates Coast 66 Jf 70.00S 160.00 E
Oaxaca [2] 47 Ee 17.00N 96.30W
Oaxaca, Sierra Madre de- 48 Ki 17.30N 96.30W
Oaxaca de Juárez 39 Jh 17.03N 96.43W
Ob 21 Ic 66.45N 69.30 E
Oba 42 Jg 48.55N 84.17W
Obala 34 He 4.10N 11.32 E
Obama [Jap.] 28 Mg 35.30N 135.45 E
Obama [Jap.] 29 Be 32.43N 130.13 E
Obama-Wan 29 Dd 35.30N 135.40 E
Oban [N.Z.] 61 Ci 46.52S 168.10 E
Oban [Scot.-U.K.] 9 He 56.25N 5.29W
Obanazawa 28 Pe 38.36N 140.24 E
Obando 53 Je 4.07N 67.45W
Oban Hills 34 Gd 5.30N 8.35 E
Obeliai/Obeljaj 8 Ki 55.58N 25.59 E
Obeljaj/Obeliai 8 Ki 55.58N 25.59 E
Oberá 56 Ic 27.29S 55.08W
Oberbayern 10 Hi 47.50N 11.50 E
Oberderdingen 12 Ke 49.04N 8.48 E
Oberfranken 10 Hf 50.10N 11.30 E
Oberhausen 10 Ce 51.28N 6.51 E
Oberkirchen, Schmallenberg- 12 Kc 51.09N 8.18 E
Oberland [Switz.] 14 Bd 46.35N 7.30 E
Oberland [Switz.] 14 Dd 46.45N 9.05 E
Oberlausitz 10 Ke 51.15N 14.30 E
Oberlin 45 Fg 39.49N 100.32W
Obermoschel 12 Je 49.44N 7.46 E
Obernkirchen 12 Lb 52.16N 9.08 E
Oberösterreich=Upper Austria (EN) [2] 14 Hb 48.15N 14.00 E
Oberpfalz 10 Ig 49.30N 12.10 E
Oberpfälzer Wald= Bohemian Forest (EN) 10 Ig 49.50N 12.30 E
Oberpullendorf 14 Kc 47.30N 16.31 E
Ober-Ramstadt 12 Ke 49.50N 8.45 E
Oberstdorf 10 Gi 47.24N 10.16 E
Oberursel (Taunus) 12 Kd 50.12N 8.35 E
Obervellach 14 Hd 46.56N 13.12 E
Oberwesel 12 Jd 50.06N 7.44 E
Ob Gulf (EN)=Obskaja Guba 21 Jc 69.00N 73.00 E
Obi, Kepulauan- 26 Ig 1.30S 127.45 E
Obi, Pulau- 57 De 1.30S 127.45 E
Obi, Selat- 26 Ig 0.52S 127.33 E
Óbidos [Braz.] 53 Kf 1.55S 55.31W
Óbidos [Port.] 13 Ce 39.22N 9.09W
Obihiro 27 Pc 42.55N 143.12 E
Obilić 15 Eg 42.41N 21.05 E
Obira 29a Ba 44.01N 141.38 E
Obispos 49 Li 8.36N 70.05W
Obispo Trejo 56 Hd 30.46S 63.25W
Obitočnaja Kosa 16 Jf 46.35N 36.15 E
Oblučje 20 Ig 48.59N 131.05 E
Obninsk 19 Dd 55.05N 36.37 E
Obo 31 Jh 5.24N 26.30 E
Obock 35 Gc 11.57N 43.17 E
Obojan 19 De 51.13N 36.16 E
Obokote 36 Ec 0.52S 26.19 E
Obol 7 Gi 55.24N 29.01 E
Oborniki 10 Md 52.39N 16.51 E
Obouya 36 Cc 0.56S 15.43 E
Obozerski 19 Ec 63.28N 40.20 E
Obra 10 Ld 52.36N 15.28 E
Obrenovac 15 De 44.39N 20.12 E
Obrovac 14 Jf 44.12N 15.41 E
Obrovo 10 Vd 52.27N 25.43 E
Obruchev Rise (EN) 20 Lf 52.30N 166.00 E
Obruk Platosu 24 Ec 38.02N 33.30 E
Obšči Syrt 5 Le 51.50N 51.00 E
Obskaja Guba=Ob Gulf (EN) 21 Jc 69.00N 73.00 E
Ob' Tablemount (EN) 30 Ln 52.30S 42.00 E
Ōbu 29 Ed 35.01N 136.58 E
Obuasi 34 Ed 6.12N 1.40W
Obudu 34 Gd 6.40N 9.10 E
Obuhov 16 Gd 50.07N 30.37 E
Obva 17 Gg 58.35N 55.25 E
Obzor 15 Kg 42.49N 27.53 E
Oca 13 Ib 42.46N 3.26W
Oca, Montes de- 13 Ib 42.20N 3.15W
Očakov 19 Df 46.38N 31.33 E
Ocala 43 Kf 29.11N 82.07W
Očamcira 16 Lh 42.46N 41.27 E
Ocampo [Mex.] 48 Hd 27.20N 102.21W
Ocampo [Mex.] 48 Ec 28.11N 108.23W
Ocaña [Col.] 54 Db 8.15N 73.20W
Ocaña [Sp.] 13 Ie 39.56N 3.31W
Occhito, Lago di- 14 Ii 41.35N 14.55 E
Ocean Bight 49 Kc 21.15N 73.15W
Ocean City [Md.-U.S.] 43 Ld 38.20N 75.05W
Ocean City [N.J.-U.S.] 44 Jf 39.16N 74.35W
Ocean Falls 42 Ef 52.21N 127.40W
Oceania 57 Ie 5.00S 175.00 E
Ocean Point 44 Il 26.16N 77.03W
Oceanside 43 De 33.12N 117.23W
Ocean Springs 45 Lk 30.25N 88.50W
Ocejón, Pico- 13 Ic 41.07N 3.15W
Očenyrd, Gora- 17 Mb 68.05N 66.20 E
Očer 19 Fd 57.53N 54.45 E
Ochagavia 13 Kb 42.55N 1.05W
Ochiai 29 Cd 35.02N 133.45 E
Ochi-Gata 29 Ec 36.55N 136.48 E
Ochiishi-Misaki 29a Db 43.10N 145.28 E
Ochil Hills 9 Je 56.23N 3.35W
Och'onjang 28 Jd 40.55N 128.50 E
Ocho Rios 49 Id 18.25N 77.07W
Ochsenfurt 10 Gg 49.39N 10.05 E
Ochtrup 12 Jb 52.13N 7.11 E
Ockelbo 7 Dd 60.53N 16.43 E
Öckerö 8 Dg 57.43N 11.39 E
Ocmulgee River 44 Fj 31.58N 82.32W
Ocna Mureş 15 Gc 46.23N 23.51 E

Index Symbols

[1] Independent Nation
[2] State, Region
[3] District, County
[4] Municipality
[5] Colony, Dependency
Continent
Physical Region
Historical or Cultural Region
Mount, Mountain
Volcano
Hill
Mountains, Mountain Range
Hills, Escarpment
Plateau, Upland
Pass, Gap
Plain, Lowland
Delta
Salt Flat
Valley, Canyon
Crater, Cave
Karst Features
Depression
Polder
Desert, Dunes
Forest, Woods
Heath, Steppe
Oasis
Cape, Point
Coast, Beach
Cliff
Peninsula
Isthmus
Sandbank
Island
Atoll
Rock, Reef
Islands, Archipelago
Rocks, Reefs
Coral Reef
Well, Spring
Geyser
River, Stream
Waterfall Rapids
River Mouth, Estuary
Lake
Salt Lake
Intermittent Lake
Reservoir
Swamp, Pond
Canal
Glacier
Ice Shelf, Pack Ice
Ocean
Sea
Gulf, Bay
Strait, Fjord
Lagoon
Bank
Seamount
Tablemount
Ridge
Shelf
Basin
Escarpment, Sea Scarp
Fracture
Trench, Abyss
National Park, Reserve
Point of Interest
Recreation Site
Cave, Cavern
Historic Site
Ruins
Wall, Walls
Church, Abbey
Temple
Scientific Station
Airport
Port
Lighthouse
Mine
Tunnel
Dam, Bridge

Ocna Sibiului 15 Hc 45.53N 24.03 E
Ocoa, Bahía de- 49 Ld 18.22N 70.39W
Oconee River 44 Fj 31.58N 82.32W
Oconto 45 Md 44.55N 87.52W
Ocosingo 48 Mi 17.04N 92.15W
Ocotal 49 Dg 13.38N 86.29W
Ocotepeque [3] 49 Cf 14.30N 89.00W
Ocotlán 47 Dd 20.21N 102.46W
Ocotlán de Morelos 48 Ki 16.48N 96.43W
Ocracoke Inlet 44 Ih 35.10N 76.05W
Ocracoke Island 44 Jh 35.09N 75.53W
Ocreza 13 Ee 39.32N 7.50W
Octeville-sur-Mer 12 Ce 49.33N 0.07 E
October Revolution Island (EN)=Oktjabrskoj Revoljuci, Ostrov- 21 Lb 79.30N 97.00 E
Ocú 49 Gj 7.57N 80.47W
Ocumare del Tuy 50 Cg 10.07N 66.46W
Oda [Ghana] 34 Ed 5.55N 0.59W
Oda [Jap.] 29 Ce 33.34N 132.48 E
Ōda 28 Lg 35.11N 132.30 E
Oda, Jabal- 35 Fa 20.21N 36.39 E
Ódáðahraun 7a Cb 65.09N 17.00W
Ōdai 29 Ed 34.24N 136.24 E
Odaigahara-San 29 Ed 34.11N 136.06 E
Odalen 8 Dd 60.15N 11.40 E
Ōdate 28 Pd 40.16N 140.34 E
Odawara 28 Og 35.15N 139.10 E
Odda 7 Bf 60.04N 6.33 E
Odder 8 Di 55.58N 10.10 E
Odeleite 13 Eg 37.21N 7.27W
Odemira 13 Dg 37.36N 8.38W
Ödemiş 24 Bc 38.13N 27.59 E
Odendaalsrus 37 De 27.48S 26.45 E
Odense 6 Hd 55.24N 10.23 E
Odenthal 12 Jc 51.02N 7.07 E
Odenwald 10 Eg 49.40N 9.00 E
Oder [Eur.] 5 He 53.40N 14.33 E
Oder [Ger.] 10 Ge 51.40N 10.02 E
Oderbruch 10 Kd 52.40N 14.15 E
Oderské vrchy 10 Ng 49.40N 17.45 E
Oderzo 14 Ge 45.47N 12.29 E
Ödeshög 7 Dg 58.14N 14.39 E
Odessa [Tx.-U.S.] 39 If 31.51N 102.22W
Odessa [Ukr.-U.S.S.R.] 6 Jf 46.28N 30.44 E
Odessa [Wa.-U.S.] 46 Fc 47.20N 118.41W
Odesskaja Oblast [3] 19 Df 46.45N 30.30 E
Odet 11 Bg 47.52N 4.06W
Odiel 13 Fg 37.10N 6.54W
Odienné 31 Gh 9.30N 7.34W
Odienné [3] 34 Dd 9.45N 7.45W
Odivelas 13 Df 38.12N 8.18W
Ödmården 8 Gc 61.05N 16.40 E
Odobeşti 15 Kd 45.46N 27.03 E
Ödöngk 25 Kf 11.48N 104.45 E
Odoorn 12 Ib 52.51N 6.50 E
Odorheiu Secuiesc 15 Ic 46.18N 25.18 E
Ōdose-Zaki 29a Bc 40.46N 140.03 E
Odra 5 He 53.40N 14.33 E
Ōdwēyne 35 Hd 9.23N 45.04 E
Odžaci 15 Cd 45.31N 19.16 E
Odžak 14 Me 45.01N 18.18 E
Odzi 37 Ec 19.47S 32.24 E
Oeiras 13 Eg 37.38N 7.40W
Oeiras [Braz.] 54 Je 7.01S 42.08W
Oeiras [Port.] 13 Cf 38.41N 9.19W
Oelde 12 Kc 51.49N 8.09 E
Oelerbeek 12 Ib 52.21N 6.38 E
Oelrichs 45 Ee 43.15N 103.10W
Oelsnitz 10 If 50.25N 12.10 E
Oelwein 45 Ke 42.41N 91.55W
Oeno Island 57 Ng 23.56S 130.44W
Oer-Erkenschwick 12 Jc 51.38N 7.15 E
Oeste, Punta- 51a Ab 18.05N 67.57W
Oeventrop, Arnsberg- 12 Kc 51.24N 8.08 E
Ōe-Yama 29 Dd 35.27N 135.06 E
Of 24 Ib 40.57N 40.16 E
O'Fallon Creek 46 Mc 46.50N 105.09W
Ofanto 14 Ki 41.21N 16.13 E
Ofaqim 24 Fg 31.17N 34.37 E
Offa 34 Fd 8.09N 4.43 E
Offaly/Uíbh Fhailí [2] 9 Fh 53.20N 7.30W
Offenbach am Main 10 Ef 50.06N 8.46 E
Offenbach-Hundheim 12 Je 49.37N 7.33 E
Offenburg 10 Dh 48.29N 7.56 E
Offida 14 Hh 42.56N 13.41 E
Offoué 36 Bc 0.04S 11.44 E
Offranville 12 De 49.52N 1.03 E
Ofidhoúsa 15 Jm 36.33N 26.09 E
Ofolanga 65b Ba 19.36S 174.27W
Ofu 65c Db 14.11S 169.42W
Ōfunato 28 Pe 39.04N 141.43 E
Oga 28 Oe 40.43N 141.18 E
Ogachi 29 Gb 39.05N 140.28 E
Ogaden 30 Lh 7.30N 45.00 E
Oga-Hantō 28 Oe 39.55N 139.50 E
Ōgaki 28 Ng 35.21N 136.37 E
Ogallala 43 Gc 41.08N 101.43W
Ogasawara-Shotō=Bonin Islands (EN) 21 Qg 27.00N 142.10 E
Ogawara-Ko 29a Bc 40.45N 141.20 E
Ogbomosho 31 Hh 8.08N 4.16 E
Ogden 39 He 41.14N 111.58W
Ogdensburg 44 Jc 44.42N 75.31W
Ogeechee River 44 Gj 31.51N 81.06W
Oghāsh 24 Lc 39.10N 46.55 E
Ogi 29 Fc 37.50N 138.16 E
Ogilvie Mountains 42 Dc 65.00N 140.00W
Ogi-no-Sen 29 Dd 35.26N 134.26 E
Oginski Kanal 16 Dc 52.20N 25.55 E
Oglanly 16 Sj 39.50N 54.33 E
Oglethorpe 44 Ei 31.28N 84.04W
Ogliastra 14 Dk 39.55N 9.35 E
Oglio 14 Ee 45.02N 10.39 E
Ognon 11 Lg 47.20N 5.29 E
Ogo 35 Hd 9.48N 45.35 E
Ogoamas, Bulu- 26 Hf 0.40N 120.12 E
Ogodža 20 If 52.48N 132.40 E
Ogoja 34 Gd 6.40N 8.48 E
Ogoki 42 If 51.38N 85.56W
Ogoki 42 If 51.38N 85.55W
Ogoki Reservoir 42 If 51.35N 86.00W
Ogonëk 20 Ie 59.40N 138.01 E
Ogooué 30 Hi 0.49S 9.00 E
Ogooué-Ivindo [3] 36 Bb 0.30N 13.00 E
Ogooué-Lolo [3] 36 Bc 1.00S 13.00 E
Ogooué-Maritime [3] 36 Ac 2.00S 9.30 E
Ogōri [Jap.] 29 Bd 34.06N 131.25 E
Ogōri [Jap.] 29 Be 33.24N 130.34 E
Ogosta 15 Gf 43.45N 23.51 E
Ograđden 15 Fh 41.30N 22.55 E
Ogre 8 Kh 56.42N 24.33 E
Ogre 7 Fh 56.50N 24.39 E
Ogulin 14 Je 45.16N 15.14 E
Ogun [2] 34 Fd 7.00N 3.40 E
Oguni [Jap.] 29 Fb 38.04N 139.45 E
Oguni [Jap.] 29 Be 33.07N 131.04 E
Ogurčinski, Ostrov- 16 Rj 38.55N 53.05 E
Oğuzeli 24 Gd 37.00N 37.30 E
Oha 22 Qd 53.34N 142.56 E
Ohai 62 Bf 45.56S 167.57 E
Ohakune 62 Fc 39.25S 175.25 E
Ohanet 32 Id 28.40N 8.50 E
Ohansk 17 Gh 57.42N 55.25 E
Ōhara 29 Gd 35.15N 140.23 E
Ōhasama 29 Gb 39.28N 141.17 E
Ohata 20 Je 59.20N 143.05 E
Ōhata 28 Pd 41.24N 141.10 E
Ohau, Lake- 62 Cf 44.15S 169.50 E
Ohey 12 Hd 50.26N 5.08 E
O'Higgins, Cabo- 65d Bb 27.05S 109.15W
Ohio 38 Kf 36.59N 89.08W
Ohio [2] 43 Kc 40.15N 82.45W
Ohm 10 Ef 50.51N 8.48 E
Ohmberge 10 Ge 51.30N 10.28 E
'Ohonua 65b Bc 21.20S 174.57W
Ohopoho 31 Ij 18.03S 13.45 E
Ohotsk 22 Qd 59.23N 143.18 E
Ohotskoje More=Okhotsk, Sea of- (EN) 21 Qd 53.00N 150.00 E
Ohre 10 Hd 52.18N 11.47 E
Ohře 10 Kf 50.32N 14.08 E
Ohrid 15 Dh 41.07N 20.48 E
Ohrid, Lake- (EN) = Ohridsko Jezero 5 Ig 41.00N 20.45 E
Ohrid, Lake- (EN) = Ohrit, Liqen i- 5 Ig 41.00N 20.45 E
Ohridsko Jezero=Ohrid, Lake- (EN) 5 Ig 41.00N 20.45 E
Öhringen 10 Fg 49.12N 9.30 E
Ohrit, Liqen i- = Ohrid, Lake- (EN) 5 Ig 41.00N 20.45 E
Ohura 62 Fc 38.51S 174.59 E
Oiapoque 54 Hc 3.50N 51.50W
Oich 9 Id 57.10N 4.45W
Oi-Gawa 29 Fd 34.46N 138.17 E
Oil City 44 He 41.26N 79.44W
Oildale 46 Fi 35.25N 119.01W
Oileán Baoi/Dursey 9 Cj 51.36N 10.12W
Oileán Ciarraí/Castleisland 9 Di 52.14N 9.27W
Oileán Coarach/Mutton 9 Di 52.49N 9.31W
Oileán Mhic Aodha/Magee, Island- 9 Hg 54.50N 5.50W
Oinoúsai 15 Jk 38.32N 26.13 E
Oinoúsai, Nisoi- 15 Jk 38.31N 26.14 E
Oirschot 12 Hc 51.30N 5.18 E
Oisans 11 Mi 45.02N 6.02 E
Oise [3] 11 Ie 49.30N 2.30 E
Oise 11 Ie 49.00N 2.04 E
Oise à l'Aisne, Canal de l'- 11 Je 49.36N 3.11 E
Oisemont 12 De 49.57N 1.46 E
Oissel 12 De 49.20N 1.06 E
Oisterwijk 12 Hc 51.35N 5.11 E
Oistins 51q Ab 13.04N 59.32W
Oistins Bay 51q Ab 13.03N 59.33W
Ōita 27 Ne 33.14N 131.36 E
Ōita Ken [2] 28 Kh 33.15N 131.20 E
Oiti Óros 15 Fk 38.49N 22.17 E
Oituz, Pasul- 15 Jc 46.03N 26.23 E
Oiwake 29a Bb 42.52N 141.48 E
Ojat 7 Hf 60.31N 33.05 E
Oje 8 Ed 60.49N 13.51 E
Ojestos de Jalisco 48 Ig 21.50N 101.35W
Ojika-Jima 29 Ae 33.13N 129.03 E
O-Jima 29 Be 34.00N 130.45 E
Ojinaga 47 Dc 29.34N 104.25W
Ojiya 28 Of 37.18N 138.48 E
Ojmjakon 20 Jd 63.28N 142.49 E
Ojocaliente 48 Hf 22.34N 102.15W
Ojo Caliente 48 Fb 30.25N 106.33W
Ojos del Salado, Nevado- 52 Jh 27.06S 68.32W
Ojos Negros 13 Kd 40.44N 1.30W
Ojtal 19 Hg 42.54N 73.21 E
Oka [R.S.F.S.R.] 21 Md 55.00N 102.03 E
Oka [U.S.S.R.] 5 Kd 56.20N 43.59 E
Okaba 26 Kh 8.06S 139.42 E
Okahandja [3] 37 Bd 21.30S 17.30 E
Okahandja 31 Ik 21.59S 16.58 E
Okahukura 62 Fc 38.47S 175.14 E
Okaihau 62 Ea 35.19S 173.46 E
Okak Islands 42 Le 57.28N 61.48W
Okanagan Lake 42 Fg 49.55N 119.30W
Okano 36 Bc 0.05S 10.57 E
Okanogan River 43 Db 48.06N 119.43W
Okapa 59 Ja 6.31S 145.32 E
Okāra 25 Eb 30.49N 73.27 E
Okarem 19 Fh 38.07N 54.05 E
Okato 62 Ec 39.12S 173.53 E
Okaukuejo 37 Bc 19.10S 15.54 E
Okavango 30 Jj 18.53N 22.24 E
Okavango [3] 37 Cc 18.00S 21.00 E
Okavango Swamp 30 Jj 19.30S 23.00 E
Ōkawa 29 Be 33.12N 130.23 E
Okaya 28 Of 36.03N 138.03 E
Okayama 22 Pf 34.39N 133.55 E
Okayama Ken [2] 28 Lg 34.50N 133.45 E
Okazaki 28 Ng 34.57N 137.10 E
Okeechobee 44 Gl 27.15N 80.50W
Okeechobee, Lake- 38 Kg 26.55N 80.45W
Okefenokee Swamp 44 Fj 30.42N 82.20W
Okehampton 9 Jk 50.44N 4.00W
Okene 34 Gd 7.33N 6.14 E
Oker 10 Gd 52.30N 10.22 E
Oketo 29a Cb 43.41N 143.32 E
Okha 25 Dd 22.27N 69.04 E
Ókhi Óros 15 Hk 38.04N 24.28 E
Okhotsk, Sea of- (EN)= Hok-Kai 21 Qd 53.00N 150.00 E
Okhotsk, Sea of- (EN)= Ohotskoje More 21 Qd 53.00N 150.00 E
Okhthonia, Ákra- 15 Hk 38.32N 24.14 E
Oki-Daitō-Jima 27 Ng 24.30N 131.00 E
Okiep 37 Be 29.39S 17.53 E
Okinawa 29b Ab 26.20N 127.47 E
Okinawa Islands (EN)= Okinawa-Shotō 21 Og 26.40N 128.00 E
Okinawa-Jima 27 Mf 26.40N 128.20 E
Okinawa Ken [2] 29b Ab 26.31N 127.59 E
Okinawa-Shotō=Okinawa Islands (EN) 21 Og 26.40N 128.00 E
Okinoerabu-Jima 27 Mf 27.20N 128.35 E
Okino-Shima [Jap.] 29 Ce 32.44N 132.33 E
Okino-Shima [Jap.] 29 Bd 34.15N 130.08 E
Okino-Tori-Shima 21 Pg 20.25N 136.00 E
Oki Ridge (EN) 28 Mf 37.00N 135.00 E
Oki-Shotō 27 Nd 36.00N 132.50 E
Okitipupa 34 Fd 6.30N 4.48 E
Oki Trench (EN) 29 Dc 37.00N 135.30 E
Oklahoma [2] 43 Hd 35.30N 98.00W
Oklahoma City 39 Jf 35.28N 97.32W
Okmulgee 45 Ii 35.37N 95.58W
Oknica 15 Ka 48.22N 27.24 E
Oko 35 Fa 22.20N 35.56 E
Okoko 36 Fb 2.06N 33.53 E
Okolo 36 Fb 2.40N 31.09 E
Okolona 44 Ef 38.08N 85.41W
Okondja 36 Bc 0.41S 13.47 E
Okonek 10 Mc 53.33N 16.50 E
Okoppe 28 Qb 44.28N 143.08 E
Okotoks 46 Ia 50.44N 113.59W
Okoyo 36 Cc 1.28S 15.04 E
Okrzeika 10 Re 51.40N 21.30 E
Øksfjord 7 Fa 70.14N 22.22 E
Oksino 17 Fc 67.33N 52.10 E
Okstindane 5 Hb 66.02N 14.10 E
Oktemberjan 16 Ni 40.09N 44.03 E
Oktjabrsk [Kaz.-U.S.S.R.] 6 Lf 48.40N 57.11 E
Oktjabrsk [R.S.F.S.R.] 7 Lj 53.13N 48.40 E
Oktjabrski [Bye.-U.S.S.R.] 16 Fc 52.38N 28.54 E
Oktjabrski [Kaz.-U.S.S.R.] 17 Kj 52.37N 62.43 E
Oktjabrski [R.S.F.S.R.] 20 Ee 56.05N 99.25 E
Oktjabrski [R.S.F.S.R.] 19 Fe 54.31N 53.28 E
Oktjabrski [R.S.F.S.R.] 17 Hh 56.31N 57.12 E
Oktjabrski [R.S.F.S.R.] 7 Kf 61.05N 43.08 E
Oktjabrski [R.S.F.S.R.] 20 Hf 53.00N 128.42 E
Oktjabrski [R.S.F.S.R.] 20 Kf 52.38N 156.15 E
Oktjabrski [R.S.F.S.R.] 16 Mf 47.56N 43.38 E
Oktjabrskoje 19 Gc 62.28N 66.01 E
Oktjabrskoj Revoljuci, Ostrov- = October Revolution Island (EN) 21 Lb 79.30N 97.00 E
Oku 29b Bb 26.50N 128.17 E
Ōkuchi 28 Kh 32.04N 130.37 E
Okulovka 7 Hg 58.24N 33.18 E
Okushiri 28 Oc 42.09N 139.29 E
Okushiri-Kaikyō 29a Ab 42.15N 139.40 E
Okushiri-Tō 27 Oc 42.10N 139.25 E
Okuta 34 Fd 9.13N 3.11 E
Oku Tango-Hantō 29 Dd 35.40N 135.10 E
Okwa 30 Jk 22.26S 22.58 E
Ola 20 Ke 59.37N 151.20 E
Ólafsfjördur 7a Ba 66.04N 18.39W
Ólafsvík 7a Ab 64.53N 23.43W
Ola Grande, Punta- 51a Bc 17.55N 66.08W
Olaine/Olajne 7 Fh 56.49N 23.59 E
Olajne/Olaine 7 Fh 56.49N 23.59 E
Olancha 46 Gh 36.17N 117.59W
Olanchito 49 Df 15.30N 86.35W
Olancho [3] 49 Ef 14.45N 86.00W
Öland 5 Hd 56.45N 16.40 E
Ölands norra udde 8 Gg 57.22N 17.05 E
Ölands södra grund 8 Gh 55.40N 17.25 E
Ölands södra udde 8 Gh 56.11N 16.24 E
Olanga 7 Hc 66.08N 30.38 E
Olathe 45 Ig 38.53N 94.49W
Olavarría 53 Ji 36.53S 60.20W
Oława 10 Nf 50.57N 17.17 E
Oława 10 Nf 50.57N 17.17 E
Olbernhau 10 Jf 50.40N 13.20 E
Olbia 6 Gg 40.55N 9.31 E
Olbia, Golfo di- 14 Dj 40.55N 9.40 E
Old Bahama Channel 49 Ib 22.30N 78.05W
Old Bahama Channel (EN)= Bahamas, Canal Viejo de- 49 Ib 22.30N 78.05W
Old Castile (EN)=Castilla la Vieja 13 Ic 41.30N 4.00W
Old Crow 39 Fc 67.35N 139.50W
Oldeani 36 Gc 3.21S 35.33 E
Oldebroek 12 Hb 52.26N 5.53 E
Oldenburg 10 Ec 53.10N 8.12 E
Oldenburg in Holstein 10 Gb 54.18N 10.53 E
Oldenzaal 11 Mb 52.19N 6.56 E
Old Faithful Geyser 46 Jd 44.30N 110.45W
Old Fletton 12 Bb 52.34N 0.15W
Oldham 9 Kh 53.33N 2.07W
Old Hickory Lake 44 Dg 36.18N 86.30W
Oldman River 46 Jb 49.56N 111.42W
Old Marsh Bed 59 Gd 20.55S 130.30 E
Old Mkuski 36 Ee 14.22S 29.22 E
Old Road 51d Bb 17.01N 61.50W
Old Road Town 51c Ab 17.19N 62.48W
Olds 42 Gf 51.47N 114.06W
Old Town 44 Mc 44.56N 68.39W
Old Wives Lake 46 Ma 50.06N 106.00W
Olean 44 Hd 42.05N 78.26W
Olecko 10 Sb 54.03N 22.30 E
Oleiros 13 Ee 39.55N 7.55W
Olëkma 21 Oc 60.22N 120.42 E
Olëkminsk 22 Oc 60.30N 120.15 E
Olëkminski Stanovik 20 Gf 54.00N 119.00 E
Ølen 7 Ag 59.36N 5.48 E
Olenegorsk 19 Db 68.10N 33.13 E
Olenëk 21 Nb 73.00N 119.55 E
Olenëkski Zaliv 20 Hb 73.10N 121.00 E
Olenica 7 Ic 66.29N 35.19 E
Olenj, Ostrov- 20 Cb 72.25N 77.45 E
Olenty 16 Re 49.45N 52.10 E
Oléron, Ile d'- 5 Ff 45.56N 1.18W
Olesko 10 Ug 49.53N 24.58 E
Oleśnica 10 Ne 51.13N 17.23 E
Olesno 10 Of 50.53N 18.25 E
Olevsk 16 Ed 51.13N 27.41 E
Olga 20 Ih 43.46N 135.21 E
Olga, Mount- 59 Ge 25.19S 130.46 E
Olgastretet 41 Oc 78.30N 24.00 E
Ølgod 8 Ci 55.49N 8.37 E
Olhão 13 Eg 37.02N 7.50W
Olhovatka 16 Kd 50.17N 39.17 E
Oli 34 Fd 9.40N 4.29 E
Oliana 13 Nb 42.04N 1.19 E
Olib 14 If 44.23N 14.47 E
Oliena 14 Dj 40.16N 9.24 E
Olifants [Afr.] 30 Kk 24.03S 32.40 E
Olifants [Nam.] 37 Be 25.30S 19.30 E
Olifantshoek 37 Ce 27.57S 22.42 E
Olimarao Atoll 57 Fd 7.42N 145.53 E
Olimbía 15 El 37.39N 21.38 E
Ólimbos 15 Kn 35.44N 27.13 E
Ólimbos, Óros-=Olympus, Mount- (EN) 5 Ig 40.05N 22.21 E
Ólimbos Óros 15 Jj 39.05N 26.20 E
Olímpia 55 He 20.44S 48.54W
Olinda 54 Le 8.01S 34.51W
Olite 13 Kb 42.29N 1.39W
Oliva [Arg.] 56 Hd 32.03S 63.34W
Oliva [Sp.] 13 Lf 38.55N 0.07W
Oliva, Monasterio de la- 13 Kb 42.20N 1.25W
Oliva de la Frontera 13 Ff 38.16N 6.55W
Oliveira 55 Je 20.41S 44.49W
Oliveira dos Brejinhos 54 Jf 12.19S 42.54W
Olivença 37 Fb 11.46S 35.13 E
Olivenza 13 Ef 38.41N 7.06W
Oliver 46 Fb 49.11N 119.33W
Olivet 11 Hg 47.52N 1.54 E
Olivia 45 Id 44.46N 94.59W
Olja 16 Og 45.47N 47.35 E
Olji Moron He 28 Fb 44.16N 121.42 E
Oljutorski, Mys- 21 Td 59.55N 170.25 E
Oljutorski Zaliv 20 Ld 60.00N 168.00 E
Olkusz 10 Pf 50.17N 19.35 E
Ollan 64d Bb 7.14N 151.38 E
Ollerton 12 Aa 53.13N 1.01W
Olmedo 13 Hc 41.17N 4.41W
Olmos 54 Ce 5.59S 79.46W
Olney [Eng.-U.K.] 12 Bb 52.09N 0.42W
Olney [Il.-U.S.] 45 Lg 38.44N 88.05W
Olney [Tx.-U.S.] 45 Gj 33.22N 98.45W
Oloči 20 Gf 51.20N 119.53 E
Olofström 7 Dh 56.16N 14.30 E
Oloitokitok 36 Gc 2.56S 37.30 E
Oloj 20 Kc 66.20N 159.29 E
Olojski Hrebet 20 Lc 65.50N 162.30 E
Olombo 36 Cc 1.18S 15.53 E
Olomburi 63a Ec 8.59S 161.09 E
Olomouc 10 Ng 49.36N 17.16 E
Olona 14 De 45.06N 9.21 E
Olonec 19 Dc 61.01N 32.58 E
Olonešty 15 Mc 46.29N 29.52 E
Olongapo 22 Oh 14.50N 120.16 E
Oloron, Gave d'- 11 Ek 43.33N 1.05W
Oloron-Sainte-Marie 11 Fk 43.12N 0.36W
Olosega 65c Db 14.11S 169.39W
Olot 13 Ob 42.11N 2.29 E
Olovjannaja 20 Gf 50.56N 115.35 E
Olovo 14 Mf 44.07N 18.35 E
Olpe 10 De 51.02N 7.51 E
Olpoy 63b Cb 14.52S 166.33 E
Olroyd River 59 Ib 14.10S 141.50 E
Olsberg 12 Kc 51.21N 8.30 E
Olshammar 8 Ff 58.45N 14.48 E
Olst 12 Ib 52.20N 6.08 E
Olsztyn 6 Ie 53.48N 20.29 E
Olsztyn [2] 10 Qc 53.50N 20.30 E
Olsztynek 10 Qc 53.36N 20.17 E
Olt [2] 15 He 44.25N 24.30 E
Olt 5 If 43.43N 24.51 E
Olten 8 Bf 58.50N 6.02 E
Oltedal 14 Bc 47.22N 7.55 E
Olteni 15 Ie 44.11N 25.17 E
Oltenia 15 Ge 44.30N 23.30 E
Olteniţa 15 Je 44.05N 26.38 E
Olteţ 15 He 44.14N 24.27 E
Oltu 24 Ib 40.33N 41.59 E
Oluanpi 21 Og 21.54N 120.51 E
Olutanga 26 He 7.22N 122.52 E
Olvera 13 Gh 36.56N 5.16W
Olym 16 Kc 52.27N 38.05 E
Olympia 39 Ge 47.03N 122.53W
Olympic Mountains 46 Dc 47.50N 123.45W
Olympus, Mount- 38 Ge 47.48N 123.43W
Olympus, Mount- (EN)= Ólimbos, Óros- 5 Ig 40.05N 22.21 E
Om 20 Cf 54.59N 73.22 E
Ōma 29a Bc 41.30N 140.55 E
Oma 17 Cc 66.45N 46.20 E
Ōmachi 28 Nf 36.30N 137.52 E
Omae-Zaki 29 Fd 34.36N 138.14 E
Ōmagari 28 Pe 39.27N 140.29 E
Omagh/An Ómaigh 9 Fg 54.36N 7.18W
Omaha 39 Je 41.16N 95.57W
Omak 46 Fb 48.24N 119.31W
Omakau 62 Cf 45.06S 169.36 E
Omak Lake 46 Fb 48.16N 119.23W
Oman (EN)='Umān [1] 22 Hg 21.00N 57.00 E
Oman, Gulf of- (EN)= 'Umān, Khalīj- 21 Hg 25.00N 58.00 E
Omarama 61 Ch 44.29S 169.58 E
Omar Gambon 35 He 3.10N 45.47 E
Omaru-Gawa 29 Be 32.07N 131.34 E
Omaruru 37 Bd 21.28S 15.56 E
Omaruru [3] 37 Bd 21.30S 15.00 E
Omatako 37 Bd 21.07S 16.43 E
Omatako, Omuramba- 30 Jj 17.57S 20.25 E
Omate 54 Dg 16.41S 70.59W
Ōma-Zaki 29a Bc 41.32N 140.55 E
Ombai, Selat- 26 Hh 8.30S 125.00 E
Ombella-Mpoko [3] 35 Bd 5.00N 18.00 E
Omberg 8 Ff 58.20N 14.39 E
Ombo 8 Ae 59.15N 6.00 E
Omboué 36 Ac 1.34S 9.15 E
Ombrone 14 Fh 42.39N 11.01 E
Ombu 27 Ee 31.18N 86.33 E
Omčak 20 Jd 61.38N 147.55 E
Omdurman (EN)=Umm Durmān 31 Kg 15.38N 32.30 E
Ōme 29 Fd 35.47N 139.15 E
Omegna 14 Ce 45.53N 8.24 E
Omeo 59 Jg 37.06S 147.36 E
Ömerköy 15 Lj 39.50N 28.04 E
Ometepe, Isla de- 47 Gf 11.30N 85.35W
Ometepec 47 Ee 16.41N 98.25W
Omhajer 35 Fc 14.19N 36.40 E
Ōmihachiman 29 Ed 35.08N 136.05 E
Omihi 62 Ee 43.01S 172.51 E
Omineca 42 Fe 56.05N 124.05W
Omineca Mountains 42 Ee 56.35N 125.55W
Omiš 14 Kg 43.27N 16.42 E
Ōmi-Shima [Jap.] 29 Bd 34.25N 131.15 E
Ōmi-Shima [Jap.] 29 Cd 34.15N 133.00 E
Omitara 37 Bd 22.18S 18.01 E
Ōmiya 27 Od 35.54N 139.38 E
Ommanney Bay 42 Hb 73.00N 101.00W
Omme Å 8 Ci 55.55N 8.25 E
Ommen 12 Ib 52.31N 6.25 E
Omo 30 Kh 4.32N 36.04 E
Omø 8 Di 55.10N 11.10 E
Omoa, Bahía de- 49 Cf 15.50N 88.10W
Omodeo, Lago- 14 Cj 40.10N 8.55 E
Omoloj 20 Ib 71.08N 132.01 E
Omolon 21 Rc 68.42N 158.36 E
Omolon 20 Lc 65.12N 160.27 E
Omono-Gawa 29 Gb 39.44N 140.04 E
Omont 12 Ge 49.36N 4.44 E
Omoto-Gawa 29 Gb 39.51N 141.58 E
Omsk 22 Jd 55.00N 73.24 E
Omskaja Oblast [3] 19 Hd 56.00N 72.30 E
Omsukčan 20 Kd 62.27N 155.50 E
Omsukčanski Hrebet 20 Kd 63.00N 155.10 E
Ōmu 28 Qb 44.34N 142.58 E
Omu, Vîrful- 15 Id 45.26N 25.25 E
Omulew 10 Rc 53.05N 21.32 E
Ōmura 28 Jh 32.54N 129.57 E
Ōmura-Wan 29 Ae 33.00N 129.50 E
Omurtag 15 Jf 43.06N 26.25 E
Ōmuta 28 Kh 33.02N 130.27 E
Omutinski 19 Gd 56.31N 67.45 E
Omutninsk 19 Fd 58.43N 52.12 E
Oña 13 Ib 42.44N 3.24W
Onagawa 29 Gb 38.26N 141.27 E
Onakayale 37 Bc 17.30S 15.01 E
Onaman Lake 45 Ma 50.00N 87.29W
Onamia 45 Jc 46.04N 93.40W
Onamue 64d Bb 7.21N 151.31 E
Onaping Lake 44 Gb 46.57N 81.30W
Onatchiway, Lac- 44 La 49.03N 71.03W
Onawa 45 He 42.02N 96.06W
Onch'ŏn 28 He 38.49N 125.13 E
Oncócua 36 Bf 16.40S 13.24 E
Onda 13 Le 39.58N 0.15W
Ondangua 31 Ij 17.55S 16.00 E
Ondárroa 13 Ja 43.19N 2.25W
Ondava 10 Rh 48.27N 21.48 E
Ondo [2] 34 Gd 7.00N 5.00 E
Ondo [Jap.] 29 Cd 34.12N 132.32 E
Ondo [Nig.] 34 Fd 7.06N 4.50 E
Ondor Sum 28 Bc 42.30N 113.00 E
Ondozero, Ozero- 7 He 63.40N 33.15 E
One and Half Degree Channel 21 Ji 1.30N 73.10 E
Oneata 63d Cc 18.27S 178.29W
Oneata Passage 63d Cc 18.32S 178.28W
Onega 6 Jc 63.57N 38.05 E
Onega 5 Jc 63.58N 37.55 E
Onega, Lake- (EN)= Onežskoje Ozero 5 Jc 61.30N 35.45 E
Onega Peninsula (EN)= Onežski Poluostrov 5 Jc 64.35N 38.00 E
One Hundred Mile House 42 Ff 51.38N 121.16W
Oneida 44 Jd 43.04N 75.40W
Oneida Lake 44 Jd 43.13N 76.00W
O'Neil 43 Hc 42.27N 98.39W
Onejime 29 Bf 31.14N 130.47 E
Onekotan, Ostrov- 21 Re 49.25N 154.45 E
Oneonta [Al.-U.S.] 44 Di 33.57N 86.29W
Oneonta [N.Y.-U.S.] 44 Jd 42.28N 75.04W
Oneroa 64p Cb 21.15S 159.43W
Onežskaja Guba 5 Jc 64.20N 36.30 E
Onežski Poluostrov=Onega Peninsula (EN) 5 Jc 64.35N 38.00 E
Onežskoje Ozero=Onega, Lake- (EN) 5 Jc 61.30N 35.45 E
Ongea Levu 63d Cc 19.08S 178.24W

Index Symbols

[1] Independent Nation
[2] State, Region
[3] District, County
[4] Municipality
[5] Colony, Dependency
Continent
Physical Region
Historical or Cultural Region
Mount, Mountain
Volcano
Hill
Mountains, Mountain Range
Hills, Escarpment
Plateau, Upland
Pass, Gap
Plain, Lowland
Delta
Salt Flat
Valley, Canyon
Crater, Cave
Karst Features
Depression
Polder
Desert, Dunes
Forest, Woods
Heath, Steppe
Oasis
Cape, Point
Coast, Beach
Cliff
Peninsula
Isthmus
Sandbank
Island
Atoll
Rock, Reef
Islands, Archipelago
Rocks, Reefs
Coral Reef
Well, Spring
Geyser
River, Stream
Waterfall Rapids
River Mouth, Estuary
Lake
Salt Lake
Intermittent Lake
Reservoir
Swamp, Pond
Canal
Glacier
Ice Shelf, Pack Ice
Ocean
Sea
Gulf, Bay
Strait, Fjord
Lagoon
Bank
Seamount
Tablemount
Ridge
Shelf
Basin
Escarpment, Sea Scarp
Fracture
Trench, Abyss
National Park, Reserve
Point of Interest
Recreation Site
Cave, Cavern
Historic Site
Ruins
Wall, Walls
Church, Abbey
Temple
Scientific Station
Airport
Port
Lighthouse
Mine
Tunnel
Dam, Bridge

Ongijn-Gol 27 Hc 44.30N 103.40 E
Ongjin 27 Md 37.56N 125.22 E
Ongniud Qi (Wudan) 27 Kc 42.58N 119.01 E
Ongole 25 Ge 15.30N 80.03 E
Ongon 27 Jb 45.49N 113.08 E
Onhaye 12 Gd 50.15N 4.50 E
Oni 16 Mh 42.35N 43.27 E
Onigajō-Yama 29 Ce 33.07N 132.41 E
Onilany 30 Lk 23.34S 43.45 E
Onishibetsu 29a Ca 45.21N 142.06 E
Onitsha 31 Hh 6.10N 6.47 E
Ono 29 Dd 34.51N 134.57 E
Ono 63d Bc 18.54S 178.29 E
Ōno [Jap.] 28 Ng 35.59N 136.29 E
Ōno [Jap.] 29 Cd 34.18N 132.17 E
Onoda 29 Be 33.59N 131.11 E
Ōno-Gawa 29 Be 33.15N 131.43 E
Ōnohara-Jima 29 Fd 34.02N 139.23 E
Onohoj 20 Ff 51.55N 108.01 E
Ono-i-Lau Islands 57 Jg 20.39S 178.42W
Onojō 29 Be 33.34N 130.29 E
Onomichi 28 Lg 34.25N 133.12 E
Onon 21 Nd 51.42N 115.50 E
Onoto 50 Dh 9.36N 65.12W
Onotoa Atoll 57 Ie 1.52S 175.34 E
Ons, Isla de- 13 Db 42.23N 8.56W
Onsala 7 Ch 57.25N 12.01 E
Onseepkans 37 Be 28.45S 19.17 E
Onslow 58 Cg 21.39S 115.06 E
Onslow Bay 43 Le 34.20N 77.20W
On-Take 29 Bf 31.35N 130.39 E
Ontake-San 29 Ed 35.53N 137.29 E
Ontario [3] 42 If 50.00N 86.00W
Ontario [Ca.-U.S.] 46 Gi 34.04N 117.39W
Ontario [Or.-U.S.] 43 Dc 44.02N 116.58W
Ontario, Lake- 38 Le 43.40N 78.00W
Ontario Peninsula 38 Ke 43.50N 81.00W
Onteniente/Ontinyent 13 Lf 38.49N 0.37W
Ontinyent/Onteniente 13 Lf 38.49N 0.37W
Ontojärvi 7 Gd 64.08N 29.09 E
Ontonagon 44 Cb 46.52N 89.19W
Ontong Java Atoll 57 Ge 5.20S 159.30 E
Ō-Numa 29a Bc 41.59N 140.41 E
Oodnadatta 58 Eg 27.33S 135.28 E
Ooidonk 12 Fc 51.01N 3.35 E
Ookala 65a Fc 20.01N 155.17W
Ooldea 58 Eh 30.27S 131.50 E
Oologah Lake 45 Ih 36.39N 95.36W
Ooltgensplaat, Oostflakkee- 12 Gc 51.41N 4.21 E
Oostburg 12 Fc 51.20N 3.30 E
Oostelijk Flevoland 12 Hb 52.30N 5.40 E
Oostende/Ostende 11 Ic 51.14N 2.55 E
Oosterhout 11 Kc 51.38N 4.51 E
Oosterschelde=East Schelde (EN) 11 Jc 51.30N 4.00 E
Oosterwolde, Ooststellingwerf- 12 Ha 53.00N 6.18 E
Oosterzele 12 Fd 50.57N 3.48 E
Oostflakkee 12 Gc 51.41N 4.21 E
Oostflakkee-Ooltgensplaat 12 Gc 51.41N 4.21 E
Oostkamp 12 Fc 51.09N 3.14 E
Oost-Souburg, Vlissingen- 12 Fc 51.28N 3.36 E
Ooststellingwerf 12 Ib 53.00N 6.18 E
Ooststellingwerf-Oosterwolde 12 Ha 53.00N 6.18 E
Oost Vieland, Vieland- 12 Ha 53.17N 5.06 E
Oost-Vlaanderen [3] 12 Fc 51.00N 3.40 E
Ootmarsum 12 Ib 52.25N 6.54 E
Opala 36 Dc 0.37S 24.21 E
Opalenica 10 Md 52.19N 16.23 E
Opanake 25 Gg 6.36N 80.37 E
Opari 35 Ee 3.56N 32.03 E
Oparino 7 Lg 59.53N 48.25 E
Opasatika 44 Fa 49.31N 82.58W
Opasatika Lake 44 Fa 49.06N 83.08W
Opasatika River 44 Fa 50.15N 82.25W
Opatija 14 Ie 45.20N 14.19 E
Opatów 10 Rf 50.49N 21.26 E
Opatówka 10 Rf 50.42N 21.50 E
Opava 10 Ng 49.57N 17.54 E
Opava 10 Og 49.51N 18.17 E
Opelika 43 Je 32.39N 85.23W
Opelousas 45 Jk 30.32N 92.05W
Opémisca, Lac- 44 Ja 49.58N 74.57W
Opheim 46 Lb 48.51N 106.24W
Ophir 40 Hd 63.10N 156.31W
Ophthalmia Range 59 Dd 23.15S 119.30 E
Opienge 36 Eb 0.12N 27.30 E
Opihikao 65a Gd 19.26N 154.53W
Opinaca 42 Jf 52.14N 78.02W
Opiscotéo, Lac- 42 Kf 53.09N 68.10W
Opladen, Leverkusen- 10 De 51.04N 7.01 E
Opobo 34 Ge 4.34N 7.27 E
Opočka 19 Cd 56.42N 28.41 E
Opoczno 10 Qe 51.23N 20.17 E
Opole [2] 10 Nf 50.40N 17.55 E
Opole 10 Nf 50.41N 17.55 E
Opole Lubelskie 10 Re 51.09N 21.58 E
Oporny 19 Ff 46.13N 54.29 E
Opotiki 62 Gc 38.01S 177.17 E
Opp 44 Dj 31.17N 86.22W
Oppa-Wan 29 Gb 38.35N 141.30 E
Oppdal 7 Be 62.36N 9.40 E
Oppenheim 10 Eg 49.51N 8.21 E
Oppland [2] 7 Bf 61.10N 9.40 E
Opportunity 46 Gc 47.39N 117.15W
Opsa 8 Li 55.31N 26.54 E
Opsterland 12 Ia 53.03N 6.04 E
Opsterland-Beetsterzwaag 12 Ia 53.03N 6.04 E
Opua 61 Dg 35.18S 174.07 E
Opunake 62 Ec 39.27S 173.51 E
Oputo 48 Eb 30.03N 109.20W
Oquossoc 44 Lc 45.04N 70.44W
Or 16 Ud 51.12N 58.33 E
Ōra 33 Cd 28.20N 19.35 E
Oradea 6 If 47.04N 21.56 E
Orahovac 15 Dg 42.24N 20.40 E
Orahovica 14 Le 45.32N 17.53 E
Orai 25 Fc 25.59N 79.28 E
Oraibi Wash 46 Ji 35.26N 110.49W
Oran 31 Ge 35.42N 0.38W
Oran [3] 32 Gb 36.00N 0.35W
Orange [Austl.] 58 Fh 33.17S 149.06 E
Orange [Fr.] 11 Kj 44.08N 4.48 E
Orange [Tx.-U.S.] 43 Ie 30.01N 93.44W
Orange [Va.-U.S.] 44 Hf 38.14N 78.07W
Orange/Oranje 30 Ik 28.38N 16.27 E
Orange, Cabo- 52 Ke 4.24N 51.33W
Orangeburg 43 Ke 33.30N 80.52W
Orange Free State/Oranje Vrystaat [2] 37 De 29.00S 26.00 E
Orange Lake 44 Fk 29.25N 82.13W
Orange Park 44 Gj 30.10N 81.42W
Orangeville 44 Gd 43.55N 80.06W
Orange Walk 47 Ge 18.06N 88.33W
Orango 30 Fg 11.05N 16.08W
Oranienburg 10 Jd 52.45N 13.14 E
Oranje/Orange 30 Ik 28.38N 16.27 E
Oranje Gebergte 54 Hc 3.00N 55.00W
Oranjemund 37 Be 28.38S 16.24 E
Oranjestad 54 Db 12.33N 70.06W
Oranje Vrystaat/Orange Free State [2] 37 De 29.00S 26.00 E
Oranžerei 16 Og 45.50N 47.36 E
Orapa 37 Dd 21.16S 25.22 E
Orăştie 15 Gd 45.50N 23.12 E
Orava 10 Pg 49.08N 19.10 E
Oravița 15 Ed 45.02N 21.42 E
Orayská Priehradni Nádrž 10 Pg 49.20N 19.35 E
Orb 11 Jk 43.15N 3.18 E
Orba 14 Cf 44.53N 8.37 E
Orba Co 27 De 34.33N 81.06 E
Ørbæk 8 Di 55.16N 10.41 E
Orbec 12 Ce 49.01N 0.25 E
Orbetello 14 Fh 42.27N 11.13 E
Orbetello, Laguna di- 14 Fh 42.25N 11.15 E
Orbigo 13 Gc 41.58N 5.40W
Orbiquet 12 Ce 49.09N 0.14 E
Orbost 59 Jg 37.42S 148.27 E
Örbyhus 8 Gd 60.14N 17.42 E
Orcadas 66 Re 60.40S 44.30W
Orcas Island 46 Db 48.39N 122.55W
Orchies 12 Fd 50.28N 3.14 E
Orchon→Orhon 21 Md 50.21N 106.05 E
Orcia 14 Fh 42.58N 11.21 E
Orco 14 Be 45.10N 7.52 E
Ord, Mount- 59 Fc 17.20S 125.35 E
Ordenes 13 Da 43.04N 8.24W
Ordos Desert (EN)=Mu Us Shamo 21 Mf 38.45N 109.10 E
Ord River 57 Df 15.30S 128.21 E
Ordu 23 Ea 41.00N 37.53 E
Ordubad 16 Oj 38.55N 46.01 E
Ordynskoje 20 Df 54.22N 81.58 E
Ordžonikidze [Ukr.-U.S.S.R.] 16 If 47.40N 34.04 E
Ordžonikidze [Kaz.-U.S.S.R.] 17 Jj 52.25N 61.45 E
Ordžonikidze [R.S.F.S.R.] 6 Kg 43.03N 44.40 E
Ordžonikidzeabad 19 Gh 38.34N 69.02 E
Ore älv 8 Fc 61.08N 14.35 E
Orebić 14 Lh 42.58N 17.11 E
Örebro 6 Hd 59.17N 15.13 E
Örebro [2] 7 Dg 59.30N 15.00 E
Oredež 8 Nf 58.50N 30.13 E
Oregon 44 Fe 41.38N 83.28W
Oregon [2] 43 Cc 44.00N 121.00W
Oregon City 43 Cb 45.21N 122.36W
Oregon Inlet 44 Jh 35.50N 75.35W
Öregrund 8 Hd 60.20N 18.26 E
Orehov 16 If 47.34N 35.47 E
Orehovo-Zujevo 6 Jd 55.49N 38.59 E
Orel 6 Je 52.59N 36.05 E
Orel 16 Ie 48.31N 34.55 E
Orel, Gora- 20 Jf 53.55N 140.01 E
Orellana [Peru] 54 Ce 6.54S 75.04W
Orellana [Peru] 54 Cd 4.40S 78.10W
Orem 43 Ec 40.19N 111.42W
Ore Mountains (EN)=Erzgebirge 5 He 50.30N 13.15 E
Ore Mountains (EN)=Krušné Hory 5 He 50.30N 13.15 E
Ören 24 Bd 37.18N 29.17 E
Orenbel 24 Hb 40.00N 39.10 E
Orenburg 6 Le 51.54N 55.06 E
Orenburgskaja Oblast [3] 19 Fe 52.00N 55.00 E
Örencik 24 Cc 39.16N 29.34 E
Orense [3] 13 Eb 42.10N 7.30W
Orense [Arg.] 56 Ie 38.40S 59.47W
Orense [Sp.] 13 Eb 42.20N 7.51W
Oreón, Dhiavlos- 15 Fk 38.54N 22.55 E
Orepuki 62 Bg 46.17S 167.44 E
Orestiás 15 Jh 41.30N 26.31 E
Øresund 5 Hd 55.50N 12.40 E
Oreti 62 Cg 46.28S 168.17 E
Orewa 62 Fb 36.35S 174.42 E
Orford 12 Db 52.05N 1.32 E
Orford Ness 9 Oi 52.05N 1.34 E
Organá/Organyà 13 Nb 42.13N 1.20 E
Organ Needle 45 Cj 32.21N 106.33W
Organyà/Organá 13 Nb 42.13N 1.20 E
Orgaz 13 Ie 39.39N 3.54W
Orgejev 19 Cf 47.23N 28.50 E
Orgelet 11 Lh 46.31N 5.37 E
Orgon Tal 28 Bc 43.20N 112.40 E
Orgosolo 14 Dj 40.12N 9.21 E
Orgün 23 Kc 32.57N 69.11 E
Orhaneli 15 Lj 39.54N 29.00 E
Orhaneli/Koca Çay 15 Lj 39.56N 28.32 E
Orhangazi 15 Mi 40.30N 29.18 E
Orhomenós 15 Fk 38.35N 22.54 E
Orhon (Orchon) 21 Md 50.21N 106.05 E
Orhy, Pico de- 13 La 42.59N 1.00W
Oria 13 Ja 43.17N 2.08W
Orichuna, Río- 50 Bi 7.30N 68.13W
Orick 46 Cf 41.17N 124.04W
Oriental 48 Kh 19.22N 97.37W
Oriental, Cordillera- 49 Md 18.55N 69.15W
Oriente 56 He 38.44S 60.37W
Orihuela 13 Lf 38.05N 0.57W
Oriku 15 Ci 40.17N 19.25 E
Öri Lekánis 15 Hh 41.08N 24.33 E
Orillia 42 Jh 44.37N 79.25W
Orimattila 7 Ff 60.48N 25.45 E
Orinoco, Río- 52 Je 8.37N 62.15W
Oripää 8 Jd 60.51N 22.41 E
Orissa [3] 25 Gd 21.00N 84.00 E
Orissaare/Orissare 7 Fg 58.34N 23.05 E
Orissare/Orissaare 7 Fg 58.34N 23.05 E
Oristano 14 Ck 39.54N 8.36 E
Oristano, Golfo di- 14 Ck 39.50N 8.30 E
Orituco, Río- 50 Ch 8.45N 67.27W
Orivesi 5 Ic 62.15N 29.25 E
Orivesi 7 Ff 61.41N 24.21 E
Oriximiná 54 Gd 1.45S 55.52W
Orizaba 39 Jh 18.51N 97.06W
Orizaba, Pico de- (Citlaltépetl, Volcán-) 38 Jh 19.01N 97.16W
Orizona 55 Hc 17.03S 48.18W
Orjahovo 15 Gf 43.44N 23.58 E
Ørje 8 De 59.29N 11.39 E
Orjen 15 Bg 42.34N 18.33 E
Orjiva 13 Ih 36.54N 3.25W
Orkanger 7 Be 63.19N 9.52 E
Orkdalen 8 Ca 63.15N 9.50 E
Örkelljunga 8 Eh 56.17N 13.17 E
Orkla 8 Ca 63.18N 9.50 E
Orkney 37 De 27.00S 26.39 E
Orkney [3] 9 Kb 59.00N 3.00W
Orkney Islands 5 Fd 59.00N 3.00W
Orlândia 55 Ie 20.43S 47.53W
Orlando 39 Kg 28.32N 81.23W
Orlando, Capo d'- 14 Il 38.10N 14.45 E
Orlanka 10 Td 52.52N 23.12 E
Orléanais 11 Hf 48.40N 1.20 E
Orléans 6 Gf 47.55N 1.54 E
Orlice 10 Lf 50.12N 15.49 E
Orlické Hory 10 Mf 50.10N 16.30 E
Orlik 20 Ef 52.30N 99.55 E
Orlovskaja Oblast [3] 19 De 52.45N 36.30 E
Orlovski 16 Mf 46.52N 42.06 E
Orlovski, mys- 7 Jc 67.16N 41.18 E
Orly 11 If 48.45N 2.24 E
Ormāra 25 Cc 25.12N 64.38 E
Ormes 12 Ce 49.03N 0.59 E
Ormoc 26 Hd 11.00N 124.37 E
Ormond 62 Gc 38.33S 177.55 E
Ormond Beach 44 Gk 29.17N 81.02W
Ornain 11 Kf 48.46N 4.47 E
Ornans 11 Mg 47.06N 6.09 E
Ornäs 8 Fd 60.31N 15.32 E
Orne [3] 11 Gf 48.40N 0.05 E
Orne [Fr.] 11 Ie 49.17N 6.11 E
Orne [Fr.] 11 Be 49.19N 0.14W
Orne Seamount (EN) 61 Je 27.30S 157.30W
Orneta 10 Qb 54.08N 20.08 E
Ornö 7 Eg 59.05N 18.25 E
Örnsköldsvik 7 Ee 63.18N 18.43 E
Oro 28 Id 40.01N 127.27 E
Oro, Río de- 55 Ch 27.04S 58.34W
Oro, Río del- 48 Ge 25.35N 105.03W
Orocué 54 Dc 4.48N 71.20W
Orodara 34 Ec 10.59N 4.55W
Orofino 46 Gc 46.29N 116.15W
Orogrande 45 Cj 32.23N 106.08W
Orohena, Mont- 65e Fc 17.31S 149.28W
Oroluk Atoll 57 Gd 7.32N 155.18 E
Orom 36 Fb 3.20N 33.40 E
Oromocto 42 Kg 45.51N 66.29W
Oron 34 Ge 4.50N 8.14 E
Orona Atoll (Hull) 57 Je 4.29S 172.10W
Orongo 65d Ac 27.10S 109.26W
Oronsay 9 Ge 56.01N 6.14W
Orontes (EN)=Nahr al 'Āṣī 23 Eb 36.02N 35.58 E
Oropesa [Sp.] 13 Ge 39.55N 5.10W
Oropesa [Sp.] 13 Ld 40.06N 0.09W
Oroqen Zizhiqi (Alihe) 27 La 50.35N 123.42 E
Oroquieta 26 He 8.29N 123.48 E
Orós 54 Ke 6.15S 38.55W
Orós, Açude- 54 Ke 6.15S 39.05W
Orosei 14 Dj 40.23N 9.42 E
Orosei, Golfo di- 14 Dj 40.15N 9.45 E
Orosháza 10 Qj 46.34N 20.40 E
Oro-Shima 29 Be 33.52N 130.02 E
Oroszlány 10 Oi 47.29N 18.19 E
Orote Peninsula 64c Bb 13.26N 144.38 E
Orote Point 64c Bb 13.27N 144.37 E
Orotukan 20 Kd 62.17N 151.50 E
Oroville [Ca.-U.S.] 46 Eg 39.31N 121.33W
Oroville [Wa.-U.S.] 46 Fb 48.56N 119.26W
Orp-Jauche 12 Gd 50.40N 4.57 E
Orqohan 27 Lb 49.36N 121.23 E
Orr 45 Jb 48.03N 92.50W
Orrefors 8 Fh 56.50N 15.45 E
Orri, Pic d'-/Llorri 13 Nb 42.23N 1.12 E
Orša 6 Je 54.30N 30.24 E
Orsa 7 Df 61.07N 14.37 E
Orsasjön 8 Fc 61.05N 14.35 E
Orsay 12 Ef 48.42N 2.11 E
Orsjön 8 Gc 61.35N 16.20 E
Orsk 6 Le 51.12N 58.34 E
Orşova 15 Fe 44.42N 22.25 E
Ørsta 7 Be 62.12N 6.09 E
Örsundsbro 8 Ge 59.44N 17.18 E
Orta, Lago d'- 14 Ce 45.50N 8.25 E
Ortaca 24 Cd 36.49N 28.47 E
Ortakent 15 Kl 37.02N 27.21 E
Ortaklar 15 Kl 37.53N 27.30 E
Orta Nova 14 Ji 41.19N 15.42 E
Orte 14 Gh 42.27N 12.23 E
Ortegal, Cabo- 13 Ea 43.45N 7.53W
Ortenberg 12 Ld 50.21N 9.03 E
Orthez 11 Fk 43.29N 0.46W
Orthon, Río- 54 Ef 10.50S 66.04W
Ortigueira [Braz.] 56 Jb 24.12S 50.55W
Ortigueira [Sp.] 13 Fa 43.34N 6.44W
Ortisei / Sankt Ulrich 14 Fd 46.34N 11.40 E
Ortiz [Mex.] 48 Dc 28.15N 110.43W
Ortiz [Ven.] 50 Ch 9.37N 67.17W
Ortlergruppe/Ortles 14 Ed 46.30N 10.40 E
Ortles/Ortlergruppe 14 Ed 46.30N 10.40 E
Ortolo 11a Ab 41.30N 8.55 E
Ortona 14 Ih 42.21N 14.24 E
Ortonville 45 Hd 45.19N 96.27W
Orto-Tokoj 18 Kc 42.20N 76.02 E
Örtze 10 Fd 52.40N 9.57 E
Orukuizu 64a Ac 7.10N 134.17 E
Orūmīyeh 22 Gf 37.33N 45.04 E
Orūmīyeh, Daryācheh-ye-=Urmia, Lake- (EN) 21 Gf 37.40N 45.30 E
Oruro [2] 54 Eg 18.40S 67.30W
Oruro 53 Jg 17.59S 67.09W
Orust 8 Df 58.10N 11.38 E
Orūzgān [3] 23 Kc 33.15N 66.00 E
Orūzgān 23 Kc 32.56N 66.38 E
Orval, Abbaye d'- 12 He 49.38N 5.22 E
Orvault 11 Eg 47.16N 1.37W
Orvieto 14 Gh 42.43N 12.07 E
Orville Escarpment 66 Qf 75.45S 65.30W
Orvilos, Óros- 15 Gh 41.23N 23.36 E
Orwell 12 Dc 51.58N 1.18 E
Orxois 12 Fe 49.08N 3.12 E
Orz 10 Rd 52.50N 21.30 E
Orzinuovi 14 De 45.24N 9.55 E
Orzyc 10 Rd 52.47N 21.13 E
Orzysz 10 Rc 53.49N 21.56 E
Oš 19 Hg 40.32N 72.50 E
Os 7 Ce 62.30N 11.12 E
Osa 19 Fd 57.17N 55.26 E
Oša 8 Lh 56.21N 26.29 E
Osa 10 Oc 53.33N 18.45 E
Osa, Peninsula de- 47 Hg 8.35N 83.33W
Osage 45 Je 43.17N 92.49W
Osage River 43 Id 38.35N 91.57W
Osaka 29 Ed 35.57N 137.14 E
Ōsaka 22 Pf 34.40N 135.30 E
Osaka Bay (EN)=Ōsaka-Wan 28 Mg 34.36N 135.27 E
Ōsaka-Fu [2] 28 Mg 34.45N 135.35 E
Osakarovka 19 He 50.32N 72.39 E
Ōsaka-Wan=Osaka Bay (EN) 28 Mg 34.36N 135.27 E
Osăm 15 Hf 43.42N 24.51 E
Osan 28 If 37.09N 127.04 E
Osasco 55 If 23.32S 46.46W
Osat 14 Nf 44.02N 19.20 E
Osawatomie 45 Ig 38.31N 94.57W
Osborne 45 Gg 39.26N 98.42W
Osburger Hochwald 12 Ie 49.40N 6.50 E
Osby 7 Ch 56.22N 13.59 E
Osceola [Ar.-U.S.] 45 Li 35.42N 89.58W
Osceola [Ia.-U.S.] 43 Ic 41.02N 93.46W
Osceola [Mo.-U.S.] 45 Jh 38.03N 93.42W
Oschatz 10 Je 51.18N 13.07 E
Oschersleben 10 Hd 52.02N 11.15 E
Oschiri 14 Dj 40.43N 9.06 E
Osen 7 Cd 64.18N 10.31 E
Osered 16 Ld 50.01N 40.48 E
Osetr 16 Kb 55.00N 38.45 E
Ōse-Zaki 28 Jh 32.38N 128.42 E
Oshamanbe 28 Pc 42.30N 140.22 E
Oshawa 42 Jh 43.54N 78.51W
Oshekehia Lake 37 Bc 18.08S 15.45 E
Oshika 29 Gb 38.17N 141.31 E
Oshika-Hantō 28 Pe 38.22N 141.27 E
Oshikango 37 Bc 17.22S 15.55 E
Oshima 29 Ce 33.55N 132.11 E
Ō-Shima [Jap.] 29 De 33.28N 135.50 E
Ō-Shima [Jap.] 29 Ae 33.30N 129.33 E
Ō-Shima [Jap.] 29 Ae 32.34N 128.54 E
Ō-Shima [Jap.] 29 Be 33.54N 130.27 E
Ō-Shima [Jap.] 27 Oe 34.45N 139.30 E
Ōshima [Jap.] 29 Fd 34.44N 139.20 E
Ō-Shima [Jap.] 29 Bf 31.32N 131.25 E
Ō-Shima [Jap.] 29 De 33.38N 134.30 E
Ō-Shima [Jap.] 29 Cd 34.10N 133.05 E
Ōshima [Jap.] 29 Ae 33.04N 129.36 E
Ō-Shima [Jap.] 28 Od 41.30N 139.15 E
Ō-Shima [Jap.] 28 Jh 32.04N 128.26 E
Oshima-Hantō 28 Pd 41.40N 140.30 E
Ōshima-Kaikyō 29b Ba 28.10N 129.15 E
Oshkosh [Nb.-U.S.] 45 Ef 41.24N 102.21W
Oshkosh [Wi.-U.S.] 43 Jc 44.01N 88.33W
Oshnaviyeh 24 Kd 37.02N 45.06 E
Oshogbo 31 Hh 7.46N 4.34 E
Oshtorān Kūh 23 Gc 33.20N 49.16 E
Oshtorīnān 24 Me 34.01N 48.38 E
Oshwe 36 Cc 3.24S 19.30 E
Osich'ŏn-ni 28 Jd 41.25N 128.16 E
Osijek 6 Hf 45.33N 18.42 E
Osilo 14 Cj 40.45N 8.40 E
Osimo 14 Hg 43.28N 13.29 E
Osinki 7 Lj 52.52N 49.31 E
Osinniki 20 Df 53.37N 87.31 E
Osipaonica 15 Ee 44.33N 21.04 E
Osipoviči 16 Fc 53.19N 28.40 E
Osječenica 14 Kf 44.29N 16.17 E
Oskaloosa 45 Jf 41.18N 92.39W
Oskarshamn 7 Dh 57.16N 16.26 E
Oskarström 8 Eh 56.48N 12.58 E
Oskélanéo 44 Ja 48.08N 75.05W
Oskino 20 Fd 60.48N 107.58 E
Öskjuvatn 7a Cb 65.02N 16.45W
Oskol 16 Je 49.06N 37.25 E
Osku 24 Ld 37.55N 46.06 E
Oslava 10 Mg 49.05N 16.22 E
Ösling 11 Le 49.55N 6.00 E
Osljanka, Gora- 17 Ig 59.10N 58.33 E
Oslo [2] 7 Cg 59.55N 10.45 E
Oslo 6 Hd 59.55N 10.45 E
Oslofjorden 5 Hd 59.20N 10.35 E
Osmānābād 25 Fe 18.10N 76.03 E
Osmancık 24 Fb 40.59N 34.49 E
Osmaneli 15 Ni 40.22N 30.01 E
Osmaniye 23 Eb 37.05N 36.14 E
Osmino 8 Mf 58.54N 29.15 E
Ošmjanskaja Vozvyšennost 8 Kj 54.30N 26.00 E
Ošmjany 16 Db 54.27N 25.57 E
Ösmo 8 Gf 58.59N 17.54 E
Osmussaar/Osmussar 8 Je 59.20N 23.15 E
Osmussar/Osmussaar 8 Je 59.20N 23.15 E
Osnabrück 6 Ge 52.16N 8.03 E
Osning 12 Kb 52.10N 8.05 E
Oso, Sierra del- 48 Gd 26.00N 105.25W
Osobloga 10 Nf 50.27N 17.58 E
Osogovske Planine 15 Fg 42.10N 22.30 E
Osor 14 If 44.42N 14.24 E
Osório 56 Jc 29.54S 50.16W
Osorno 53 Ij 40.34S 73.09W
Osoyoos 42 Fg 49.02N 119.28W
Osøyra 7 Af 60.11N 5.28 E
Ospino 50 Bh 9.18N 69.27W
Osprey Reef 57 Ff 13.55S 146.40 E
Oss 11 Lc 51.46N 5.31 E
Ossa, Mount- 57 Fi 41.54S 146.01 E
Óssa, Óros- 15 Fj 39.49N 22.40 E
Ossabaw Island 44 Gj 31.47N 81.06W
Ossa de Montiel 13 Jf 38.58N 2.45W
Osse 11 Gj 44.07N 0.17 E
Ossining 44 Ke 41.10N 73.52W
Ossjøen 8 Dc 61.15N 11.55 E
Ošskaja Oblast [3] 19 Hg 40.45N 73.20 E
Ossora 20 Le 59.15N 163.02 E
Östanvik 8 Fc 61.10N 15.13 E
Ostaškov 19 Dd 57.09N 33.07 E
Ostbevern 12 Jb 52.03N 7.51 E
Oste 10 Fc 53.33N 9.10 E
Ostende/Oostende 11 Ic 51.14N 2.55 E
Oster 16 Gd 50.55N 30.57 E
Oster [Ukr.-U.S.S.R.] 16 Gd 50.53N 30.55 E
Oster [U.S.S.R.] 16 Gc 53.47N 31.45 E
Osterburg in der Altmark 10 Hd 52.47N 11.44 E
Österbybruk 8 Gd 60.12N 17.54 E
Österdalälven 7 Df 60.33N 15.08 E
Østerdalen 7 Cf 62.00N 10.40 E
Osterfjorden 8 Ad 60.30N 5.20 E
Österforse 8 Ga 63.09N 17.01 E
Östergarnsholm 8 Hg 57.25N 19.00 E
Östergötland 8 Ff 58.25N 15.35 E
Östergötland [2] 7 Dg 58.25N 15.45 E
Osterholz Scharmbeck 10 Ec 53.14N 8.48 E
Österlen 8 Fi 55.30N 14.10 E
Ostermark/Teuva 7 Ee 62.29N 21.44 E
Osterode am Harz 10 Ge 51.44N 10.11 E
Osterøya 7 Af 60.35N 5.35 E
Österreich = Austria (EN) [1] 6 Hf 47.30N 14.00 E
Östersjön=Baltic Sea (EN) 5 Hd 57.00N 19.00 E
Østersøen=Baltic Sea (EN) 5 Hd 57.00N 19.00 E
Östersund 6 Hc 63.11N 14.39 E
Osterwick, Rosendahl- 12 Jb 52.01N 7.12 E
Østfold [2] 7 Cg 59.20N 11.30 E
Ostfriesische Inseln=East Frisian Islands (EN) 10 Dc 53.45N 7.25 E
Ostfriesland=East Friesland (EN) 10 Dc 53.20N 7.40 E
Østgrønland=East Greenland (EN) [2] 41 Id 72.00N 35.00W
Östhammar 7 Ed 60.16N 18.22 E
Osthofen 12 Ke 49.42N 8.20 E
Østmark 8 Ed 60.17N 12.45 E
Ostrach 10 Fh 48.05N 9.25 E
Östra Silen 8 Ee 59.15N 12.20 E
Ostrava 6 Hf 49.50N 18.17 E
Ostrhauderfehn 12 Ja 53.08N 7.37 E
Ostróda 10 Pc 53.43N 19.59 E
Ostrog 16 Ed 50.19N 26.32 E
Ostrogožsk 19 De 50.52N 39.05 E
Ostrołęka [2] 10 Rc 53.05N 21.35 E
Ostrołęka 10 Rc 53.06N 21.34 E
Ostrošicki Gorodok 8 Lj 54.03N 27.46 E
Ostrov [Bye.-U.S.S.R.] 10 Vd 52.48N 26.01 E
Ostrov [Czech.] 10 If 50.18N 12.57 E
Ostrov [Rom.] 15 Ke 44.07N 27.22 E
Ostrov [R.S.F.S.R.] 19 Cd 57.23N 28.22 E
Ostrov [R.S.F.S.R.] 8 Mf 58.28N 28.44 E
Ostrovec 8 Lj 54.38N 26.06 E
Ostrovicës, Mali i- 15 Di 40.34N 20.27 E
Ostrovskoje 7 Kh 57.50N 42.13 E
Ostrov Zmeiny 16 Gg 45.15N 30.12 E
Ostrowiec Świętokrzyski 10 Rf 50.57N 21.23 E
Ostrów Lubelski 10 Se 51.30N 22.52 E
Ostrów Mazowiecka 10 Rd 52.49N 21.54 E
Ostrów Wielkopolski 10 Ne 51.39N 17.49 E
Ostryna 10 Uc 53.41N 24.37 E
Ostrzeszów 10 Ne 51.25N 17.57 E
Ostsee=Baltic Sea (EN) 5 Hd 57.00N 19.00 E
Oststeirisches Hügelland 14 Jd 47.00N 15.45 E
Osttirol 14 Gd 46.55N 12.30 E
Ostuni 14 Lj 40.44N 17.35 E
Osumi 15 Ci 40.48N 19.52 E
Ōsumi 29 Bf 31.36N 130.59 E
Ōsumi-Hantō 29 Bf 31.15N 130.50 E
Osumi Islands (EN)=Ōsumi-Shotō 21 Pf 30.35N 130.59 E
Ōsumi-Shotō=Osumi Islands (EN) 21 Pf 30.35N 130.59 E
Osuna 13 Gg 37.14N 5.07W
Osveja 8 Mi 55.59N 28.10 E
Osvejskoje, Ozero- 8 Mh 56.00N 28.15 E
Oswego 43 Lc 43.27N 76.31W
Oswestry 9 Ji 52.52N 3.04W

Index Symbols

[1] Independent Nation
[2] State, Region
[3] District, County
[4] Municipality
[5] Colony, Dependency
Continent
Physical Region
Historical or Cultural Region
Mount, Mountain
Volcano
Hill
Mountains, Mountain Range
Hills, Escarpment
Plateau, Upland
Pass, Gap
Plain, Lowland
Delta
Salt Flat
Valley, Canyon
Crater, Cave
Karst Features
Depression
Polder
Desert, Dunes
Forest, Woods
Heath, Steppe
Oasis
Cape, Point
Coast, Beach
Cliff
Peninsula
Isthmus
Sandbank
Island
Atoll
Rock, Reef
Islands, Archipelago
Rocks, Reefs
Coral Reef
Well, Spring
Geyser
River, Stream
Waterfall Rapids
River Mouth, Estuary
Lake
Salt Lake
Intermittent Lake
Reservoir
Swamp, Pond
Canal
Glacier
Ice Shelf, Pack Ice
Ocean
Sea
Gulf, Bay
Strait, Fjord
Lagoon
Bank
Seamount
Tablemount
Ridge
Shelf
Basin
Escarpment, Sea Scarp
Fracture
Trench, Abyss
National Park, Reserve
Point of Interest
Recreation Site
Cave, Cavern
Historic Site
Ruins
Wall, Walls
Church, Abbey
Temple
Scientific Station
Airport
Port
Lighthouse
Mine
Tunnel
Dam, Bridge

Oświęcim 10 Pf 50.03N 19.12 E
Osyka 45 Kk 31.00N 90.28W
Ōta 29 Fc 36.18N 139.22 E
Ota 29 Ec 35.56N 136.03 E
Otago [2] 62 Cf 45.00S 169.10 E
Otago Peninsula 62 Df 45.50S 170.45 E
Ōtake 28 Lg 34.12N 132.13 E
Otakeho 62 Fc 39.33S 174.03 E
Otaki 62 Fd 40.45S 175.08 E
Ōtakime-Yama 29 Gc 37.22N 140.42 E
Otanoshike 29a Db 43.01N 144.16 E
Otar 19 Hg 43.31N 75.12 E
Otaru 27 Pc 43.13N 141.00 E
Otautau 62 Bg 46.09S 168.00 E
Otava 10 Kg 49.26N 14.12 E
Otava 8 Lc 61.39N 27.04 E
Otavi 37 Bc 19.39S 17.20 E
Ōtawara 28 Pf 36.52N 140.02 E
Otelu Roşu 15 Fd 45.32N 22.22 E
Otematata 62 Df 44.37S 170.11 E
Otepää/Otepja 7 Gg 58.03N 26.30 E
Otepää, Vozvyšennost-/Otepää Kõrgustik 8 Lf 58.00N 26.40 E
Otepää Kõrgustik/Otepää, Vozvyšennost- 8 Lf 58.00N 26.40 E
Otepja/Otepää 7 Gg 58.03N 26.30 E
Oteros 47 Cc 26.55N 108.30W
Othain 12 He 49.31N 5.23 E
Othello 46 Fc 46.50N 119.10W
Othonoi 15 Cj 39.50N 19.25 E
Óthris Óros 15 Fj 39.02N 22.37 E
Oti 30 Hh 7.48N 0.08 E
Otira 62 De 42.51S 171.33 E
Otish, Monts- 38 Md 52.45N 69.15W
Otjikondo 37 Bc 19.50S 15.23 E
Otjimbingwe 37 Bd 22.21S 16.08 E
Otjiwarongo 31 Ik 20.29S 16.36 E
Otjiwarongo [3] 37 Bd 20.30S 17.30 E
Otjosondjou, Omuramba- 30 Ij 19.55S 20.00 E
Otjosondu 37 Bd 21.12S 17.58 E
Otmuchowskie, Jezioro- 10 Nf 50.27N 17.15 E
Otnes 7 Cf 61.46N 11.12 E
Otobe 29a Bc 41.57N 140.08 E
Otočac 14 Jf 44.52N 15.14 E
Otofuke 29a Cb 42.59N 143.10 E
Otofuke-Gawa 29a Cb 42.56N 143.12 E
Otog Qi (Ulan) 27 Id 39.07N 108.00 E
Otoineppu 29a Ca 44.43N 142.16 E
Otok 14 Me 45.09N 18.53 E
Otopeni 15 Je 44.33N 26.04 E
Otorohanga 62 Fc 38.11S 175.12 E
Otorten, Gora- 17 If 61.50N 59.13 E
Ōtoyo 29 Ce 33.46N 133.40 E
Otra 5 Gd 58.09N 8.00 E
Otradnaja 16 Lg 44.23N 41.31 E
Otradnoje, Ozero- 8 Nd 60.50N 30.25 E
Otradny 7 Mj 53.23N 51.24 E
Otranto 14 Mj 40.09N 18.30 E
Otranto, Canale d'-= Otranto, Strait of- (EN) 5 Hg 40.00N 19.00 E
Otranto, Capo d'- 14 Mj 40.06N 18.31 E
Otranto, Strait of- (EN)= Otranto, Canale d'- 5 Hg 40.00N 19.00 E
Otranto, Strait of- (EN)= Otrantos, Kanali i- 15 Bi 40.00N 19.00 E
Otranto, Terra d'- 14 Mj 40.20N 18.15 E
Otrantos, Kanali i-=Otranto, Strait of- (EN) 15 Bi 40.00N 19.00 E
Ötscher 14 Jc 47.51N 15.12 E
Ōtsu 28 Mg 35.00N 135.52 E
Ōtsuchi 28 Pe 39.21N 141.54 E
Ōtsuki [Jap.] 29 Fd 35.36N 138.54 E
Ōtsuki [Jap.] 29 Ce 32.50N 132.41 E
Otta 8 Cc 61.46N 9.31 E
Otta 7 Bf 61.46N 9.32 E
Otta 64d Bb 7.09N 151.54 E
Ottadalen 8 Bc 61.55N 8.00 E
Ottana 14 Dj 40.15N 9.05 E
Otta Pass 64d Bb 7.09N 151.53 E
Ottawa [Il.-U.S.] 45 Lf 41.21N 88.51W
Ottawa [Ks.-U.S.] 43 Hd 38.37N 95.16W
Ottawa [Oh.-U.S.] 44 Ee 41.02N 84.03W
Ottawa [Ont.-Can.] 39 Le 45.25N 75.42W
Ottawa Islands 38 Kd 59.30N 80.10W
Ottawa River 38 Le 45.20N 73.58W
Ottemby 7 Dh 56.16N 16.24 E
Otterberg 12 Je 49.30N 7.46 E
Otter Creek 44 Fk 29.19N 82.48W
Otterndorf 10 Ec 53.48N 8.54 E
Otteroy 8 Bb 62.40N 6.50 E
Otter Rapids 44 Ga 50.15N 81.45W
Otterup 8 Di 55.31N 10.24 E
Ottumwa 43 Ic 41.01N 92.25W
Ottweiler 12 Je 49.23N 7.10 E
Otukpa 34 Gd 7.05N 7.40 E
Otumpa 55 Ah 27.19S 62.13W
Otuquis, Bañados de- 54 Gg 19.20S 58.30W
Otuquis, Rio- 55 Cd 19.41S 58.20W
Oturkpo 34 Gd 7.13N 8.09 E
Otu Tolu Group 65b Bb 20.21S 174.32W
Otuzco 54 Ce 7.54S 78.35W
Otway, Cape- 59 Ig 38.52S 143.31 E
Otwock 10 Rd 52.07N 21.16 E
Otynja 10 Uh 48.40N 24.57 E
Ötz 14 Ec 47.12N 10.54 E
Ötztaler Ache 14 Ec 47.14N 10.50 E
Ötztaler Alpen 10 Gi 46.45N 10.55 E
Ou 25 Kd 20.04N 102.13 E
'O'ua 65b Bb 20.02S 174.41W
Oua 63b Ce 21.14S 167.05 E
Ouachita, Lake- 45 Ji 34.40N 93.25W
Ouachita Mountains 38 Jf 34.40N 94.25W
Ouachita River 43 Ie 31.38N 91.49W
Ouadane 31 Ff 20.57N 11.35W
Ouaddai [3] 35 Cc 13.00N 21.00 E
Ouaddai 30 Jg 13.00N 21.00 E
Ouagadougou 31 Gg 12.22N 1.31W
Ouahigouya 31 Gg 13.35N 2.25W
Ouaka [3] 35 Cd 6.00N 21.00 E
Ouaka 30 Ih 4.59N 19.56 E
Oualata 32 Ff 17.18N 7.00W
Oualata, Dahr- 32 Ff 17.48N 7.24W
Oualidia 32 Fc 32.44N 9.02W
Ouallam 34 Fc 14.19N 2.05 E
Ouallene 32 He 24.35N 1.17 E
Ouanda-Djallé 35 Cd 8.54N 22.48 E
Ouandjia 35 Cd 8.35N 23.12 E
Ouandjia 35 Cd 9.35N 21.43 E
Ouango 35 Ce 4.19N 22.33 E
Ouangolodougou 34 Dd 9.58N 5.09W
Ouanne 11 Ig 47.57N 2.47 E
Ouarane 30 Ff 21.00N 10.00W
Ouargaye 34 Fc 11.32N 0.01 E
Ouargla 31 He 31.57N 5.20 E
Ouargla [3] 32 Id 30.00N 6.30 E
Ouarkziz, Jbel- 30 Gf 28.00N 8.20W
Ouarra 30 Jh 5.05N 24.26 E
Ouarsenis, Djebel- 13 Ni 35.53N 1.38 E
Ouarsenis, Massif de l'- 32 Hb 35.50N 2.05 E
Ouarzazate [3] 32 Fc 31.00N 6.30W
Ouarzazate 32 Fc 30.55N 6.55W
Oubangui 30 Ii 0.30S 17.42 E
Ouborré, Pointe- 63b Dd 18.47S 169.16 E
Ouche, Pays d'- 11 Gf 48.55N 0.45 E
Ouchi 29 Gb 39.27N 140.06 E
Oud Beijerland 12 Gc 51.50N 4.26 E
Oude IJssel 12 Ic 52.00N 6.10 E
Oudenaarde/Audenarde 11 Jd 50.51N 3.36 E
Oudenbosch 12 Gc 51.35N 4.34 E
Oude Rijn 11 Kb 52.05N 4.20 E
Oudon 11 Fg 47.37N 0.42W
Oudtshoorn 31 Jl 33.35S 22.14 E
Oued Ben Tili 32 Fd 25.48N 9.32W
Oued el Abtal 13 Mi 35.27N 0.41 E
Oued Fodda 13 Nh 36.11N 1.32 E
Oued Lili 13 Ni 35.31N 1.16 E
Oued Rhiou 32 Hb 35.58N 0.55 E
Oued-Taria 13 Mi 35.07N 0.05 E
Oued Tlelat 13 Li 35.33N 0.27W
Oued Zem 32 Gc 32.52N 6.34W
Ouégoa 63b Be 20.21S 164.26 E
Ouéllé 34 Ed 7.18N 4.01W
Ouémé 30 Hh 6.29N 2.32 E
Ouémé [3] 34 Fd 7.00N 2.35 E
Ouen 63b Cf 22.26S 166.48 E
Ouenza 32 Ib 35.57N 8.07 E
Ouenza, Djebel- 14 Co 35.57N 8.05 E
Ouessa 34 Ec 11.03N 2.47W
Ouessant, Ile d'- 11 Af 48.28N 5.05W
Ouesso 31 Ih 1.37N 16.04 E
Ouest [3] 34 Hd 5.20N 10.30 E
Ouest, Baie de l'- 64h Ab 13.15S 176.13W
Ouezzane 32 Fc 34.48N 5.36W
Oughter, Lough- 9 Fg 54.00N 7.29W
Ouham [3] 35 Bd 7.00N 18.00 E
Ouham 30 Ih 9.18N 18.14 E
Ouham-Pendé [3] 35 Bd 7.00N 16.00 E
Ouidah 34 Fd 6.22N 2.05 E
Ouistreham 11 Fe 49.17N 0.15W
Ouistreham-Riva Bella 12 Be 49.17N 0.16W
Oujda [3] 32 Gc 33.00N 2.00W
Oujda 31 Ge 34.40N 1.54W
Oujeft 32 Ee 20.02N 13.03W
Oulainen 7 Fd 64.16N 24.57 E
Oulchy-le-Château 12 Fe 49.12N 3.21 E
Ouled Djellal 32 Ic 34.25N 5.04 E
Ouled Naïl, Monts des- 32 Hc 34.40N 3.25 E
Oulou, Bahr- 35 Cd 9.48N 21.32 E
Oulu [2] 7 Gd 65.00N 27.00 E
Oulu/Uleåborg 6 Ib 65.01N 25.30 E
Oulu, Lake- (EN)= Oulujärvi 5 Ic 64.20N 27.15 E
Oulujärvi=Oulu, Lake- (EN) 5 Ic 64.20N 27.15 E
Oulujoki 5 Ib 65.01N 25.25 E
Oum Chalouba 31 Jg 15.48N 20.46 E
Oumé [3] 34 Dd 6.25N 5.30W
Oumé 34 Dd 6.23N 5.25W
Oum el Bouaghi [3] 32 Ib 35.30N 7.10 E
Oum el Bouaghi 32 Ib 35.53N 7.07 E
Oum er Rbia 30 Ge 33.19N 8.20W
Oum Hadjer 35 Bc 13.18N 19.41 E
Oumm ed Droûs Guebli, Sebkhet- 32 Ee 24.03N 11.45W
Oumm ed Droûs Telli, Sebkhet- 32 Ee 24.20N 11.30W
Ounasjoki 5 Ib 66.30N 25.45 E
Oundle 12 Bb 52.29N 0.28W
Ounianga [3] 35 Cb 19.10N 20.30 E
Ounianga Kébir 31 Jg 19.04N 20.29 E
Ountivou 34 Fd 7.21N 1.34 E
Ouolossébougou 34 Dc 12.00N 7.55W
Oupeye 12 Hd 50.42N 5.39 E
Oupu 27 Ma 52.45N 126.00 E
Our 12 Ie 49.53N 6.18 E
Ouray 45 Cg 38.01N 107.40W
Ouray, Mount- 45 Cg 38.25N 106.14W
Ource 11 Kf 48.06N 4.23 E
Ourcq 11 Je 49.01N 3.01 E
Ourcq, Canal de l'- 11 If 48.51N 2.22 E
Ourém 54 Id 1.33S 47.06W
Ouricuri 54 Je 7.35S 40.05W
Ourinhos 53 Lh 22.59S 49.52W
Ouro, Rio do- 55 Ha 13.20S 48.59W
Ouro Fino 55 If 22.17S 46.22W
Ouro Prêto 54 Jh 20.23S 43.30W
Ourthe [Bel.] 11 Ld 50.38N 5.35 E
Ourville-en-Caux 12 Ce 49.44N 0.36 E
Ous 19 Gc 60.55N 61.31 E
Ou-Sanmyaku 28 Pe 39.00N 141.00 E
Ouse [Eng.-U.K.] 9 Nk 50.47N 0.03 E
Ouse [Eng.-U.K.] 9 Mh 53.42N 0.41W
Oust 11 Dg 47.35N 2.06W
Outagouna 34 Fb 15.11N 0.43 E
Outaouais, Rivière- 38 Le 45.20N 73.58W
Outardes, Rivière aux- 42 Kg 49.05N 68.23W
Outat Oulad El Hajj 32 Gc 33.21N 3.42W
Outer Dowsing 9 Oh 53.25N 1.05 E
Outer Hebrides 9 Fd 57.50N 7.32W
Outer Santa Barbara Passage 46 Fj 33.10N 118.30W
Outer Silver Pit 9 Og 54.05N 2.00 E
Outjo 31 Ik 20.08S 16.08 E
Outjo [3] 37 Ac 19.30S 14.30 E
Outlook 46 La 51.30N 107.03W
Outokumpu 7 Ge 62.44N 29.01 E
Outram Mountain 46 Eb 49.19N 121.05W
Outreau 12 Dd 50.42N 1.35 E
Out Skerries 9 Ma 60.30N 0.50W
Outwell 12 Cb 52.37N 0.14 E
Ouvéa, Ile- 57 Hg 20.35S 166.35 E
Ouvèze 11 Kk 43.59N 4.51 E
Ouxian 28 Ej 28.58N 118.53 E
Ouyen 59 Ig 35.04S 142.20 E
Ouyou Bézédinga 34 Hb 16.32N 13.15 E
Ouzera 13 Oh 36.15N 2.51 E
Ovacık [Tur.] 24 Ed 36.11N 33.40 E
Ovacık [Tur.] 24 Hc 39.22N 39.13 E
Ovada 14 Cf 44.38N 8.38 E
Ova Gölü 15 Mm 36.16N 29.22 E
Ovakent 15 Lk 38.06N 28.02 E
Ovalau Island 63d Bb 17.40S 178.48 E
Ovalle 53 Ii 30.36S 71.12W
Oval Peak 46 Eb 48.15N 120.25W
Ovamboland 37 Bc 18.30S 16.00 E
Ovamboland [3] 37 Bc 18.00S 16.00 E
Ovan 36 Bb 0.30N 12.10 E
Ovanåker 7 Df 61.21N 15.54 E
Ovar 13 Dd 40.52N 8.38W
Ovau 63a Cb 6.48S 156.02 E
Ovejas 49 Ji 9.32N 75.14W
Overath 12 Jd 50.57N 7.18 E
Øverbygd 7 Eb 69.01N 19.18 E
Overflakkee 11 Kc 51.45N 4.10 E
Overhalla 7 Cd 64.30N 12.00 E
Overija 12 Gd 50.46N 4.32 E
Overijssel [3] 12 Ib 52.25N 6.30 E
Överkalix 7 Fc 66.19N 22.50 E
Overland Park 45 Ig 38.59N 94.40W
Övermark/Ylimarkku 8 Ib 62.37N 21.28 E
Overpelt 12 Hc 51.12N 5.25 E
Overri 34 Gd 5.29N 7.02 E
Overton 46 Hh 36.33N 114.27W
Övertorneå 7 Fc 66.23N 23.40 E
Överum 8 Gg 57.59N 16.19 E
Ovidiu 15 Le 44.16N 28.34 E
Oviedo [3] 13 Ga 43.20N 6.00W
Oviedo [Dom.Rep.] 49 Le 17.47N 71.22W
Oviedo [Sp.] 6 Fg 43.22N 5.50W
Oviši 8 Ig 57.34N 21.35 E
Ovo, Capo dell'- 14 Lj 40.18N 17.30 E
Øvre Årdal 7 Bf 61.19N 7.48 E
Övre Fryken 8 Ed 60.00N 13.05 E
Övre Soppero 7 Eb 68.05N 21.41 E
Ovruč 19 Ce 51.19N 28.50 E
Ovsjanka 20 Hf 53.32N 126.58 E
Owaka 62 Cg 46.27S 169.40 E
Owando 31 Ii 0.29S 15.55 E
Owani 28 Pd 40.31N 140.35 E
Owase 28 Ng 34.04N 136.12 E
Owatonna 43 Ic 44.05N 93.14W
Owego 44 Id 42.06N 76.16W
Owen, Mount- 62 Ed 41.33S 172.32 E
Owendo 36 Ab 0.17N 9.30 E
Owen Falls Dam 36 Fb 0.24N 33.11 E
Owensboro 43 Jd 37.46N 87.07W
Owens Lake 46 Gh 36.25N 117.56W
Owen Sound 42 Jh 44.34N 80.56W
Owens River 46 Gh 36.31N 117.57W
Owen Stanley Range 57 Fe 9.20S 148.00 E
Owl Creek Mountains 46 Ke 43.30N 108.35W
Ownay, Kowlal-e- 23 Kc 34.27N 68.22 E
Owo 34 Gd 7.11N 5.35 E
Owosso 44 Ed 43.00N 84.10W
Owyhee 46 Gf 41.57N 116.06W
Owyhee, Lake- 46 Ge 43.28N 117.20W
Owyhee Mountains 46 Ge 43.00N 116.45W
Owyhee River [U.S.] 46 Ge 43.40N 117.16W
Owyhee River [U.S.] 43 Dc 43.46N 117.02W
Oxberg 8 Fc 61.07N 14.10 E
Oxbow 45 Eb 49.14N 102.11W
Oxelösund 7 Dg 58.40N 17.06 E
Oxford 9 Lj 51.50N 1.30W
Oxford [Eng.-U.K.] 6 Fe 51.46N 1.15W
Oxford [Ms.-U.S.] 45 Li 34.22N 89.32W
Oxford [N.C.-U.S.] 44 Hg 36.19N 78.35W
Oxford [N.Z.] 62 Ee 43.17S 172.11 E
Oxford Lake 42 Hf 54.50N 95.35W
Oxfordshire [3] 9 Lj 51.50N 1.20W
Oxia 15 Ek 38.18N 21.06 E
Oxkutzcab 48 Og 20.18N 89.25W
Oxnard 43 De 34.12N 119.11W
Ox or Slieve Gamph Mountains/Sliabh Gamh 9 Eg 54.10N 8.50W
Oxted 12 Bc 51.14N 0.01W
Oyabe 29 Ec 36.40N 136.52 E
Oyahue 53 Jh 21.08S 68.45W
O-Yama 29 Fd 34.04N 139.31 E
Oyama 28 Of 36.21N 139.50 E
Oyama 29 Ec 36.35N 137.18 E
Ōyano 29 Be 32.35N 130.27 E
Oyapock, Fleuve- 52 Ke 4.08N 51.40W
Oyem 31 Ih 1.37N 11.35 E
Oyen 46 Ja 51.22N 110.28W
Øyeren 8 De 59.50N 11.14 E
Oykel 9 Id 57.50N 4.25W
Oyo [2] 34 Fd 8.00N 3.50 E
Oyo [Nig.] 34 Fd 7.51N 3.56 E
Oyo [Sud.] 35 Fa 21.55N 36.06 E
Oyodo-Gawa 29 Bf 31.55N 131.28 E
Oyonnax 11 Lh 46.15N 5.40 E
Oyster Bay 59 Jh 42.10S 148.10 E
Øystese 8 Bd 60.23N 6.13 E
Özalp 24 Jc 38.39N 43.59 E
Ozamiz 26 He 8.08N 123.50 E
Ozark 44 Ej 31.28N 85.38W
Ozark Plateau 38 Jf 37.00N 93.00W
Ozark Reservoir 45 Ii 35.25N 94.05W
Ozarks, Lake of the- 43 Id 37.39N 92.50W
Ózd 10 Qh 48.13N 20.18 E
Ozeblin 14 Jf 44.35N 15.53 E
Ozernoj, Zaliv- 20 Le 57.00N 163.20 E
Ozernovski 20 Kf 51.21N 156.32 E
Ozerny 16 Vd 51.08N 60.55 E
Ozersk 8 Ij 54.24N 21.59 E
Ozery [Bye.-U.S.S.R.] 10 Uc 53.38N 24.18 E
Ozery [R.S.F.S.R.] 7 Ji 54.54N 38.32 E
Ožeždy 19 Gf 48.03N 67.09 E
Ozieri 14 Cj 40.35N 9.00 E
Ozinki 19 Ee 51.12N 49.47 E
Ožogina 20 Kc 66.12N 151.05 E
Ozona 43 Ge 30.43N 101.12W
Ozorków 10 Pe 51.58N 19.19 E
Ozouri 36 Ac 0.55S 8.55 E
Ozren [Yugo.] 14 Mf 44.37N 18.15 E
Ozren [Yugo.] 14 Mg 43.59N 18.30 E
Ozren [Yugo.] 15 Ef 43.36N 21.54 E
Ōzu [Jap.] 29 Be 32.52N 130.52 E
Ōzu [Jap.] 28 Lh 33.30N 132.23 E

P

Pääjärvi 8 Kb 62.50N 24.45 E
Paama 63b Dc 16.28S 168.13 E
Pa-an → Pha-an 25 Je 16.53N 97.38 E
Paar 10 Hh 48.45N 11.35 E
Paarl 31 Il 33.45S 18.56 E
Paauilo 65a Fc 20.03N 155.22W
Paavola 7 Fd 64.36N 25.12 E
Pabbay 9 Fd 57.47N 7.20W
Pabellón, Ensenada del- 48 Fe 24.27N 107.36W
Pabianice 10 Pe 51.40N 19.22 E
Pābna 25 Hd 24.00N 89.15 E
Pabradé/Pabrade 7 Fi 54.59N 25.50 E
Pabrade/Pabradé 7 Fi 54.59N 25.50 E
Pacaás Novos, Serra dos- 54 Ff 10.50S 64.00W
Pacajá, Rio- 54 Hd 1.56S 50.55W
Pacajus 54 Kd 4.10S 38.28W
Pacaraima, Serra- 52 Je 4.30N 60.40W
Pacasmayo 54 Ce 7.24S 79.34W
Paceco 14 Gm 37.59N 12.33 E
Pachala 35 Ed 7.10N 34.06 E
Pacheco 48 Eb 30.06N 108.21W
Pachino 14 Jn 36.43N 15.05 E
Pachitea, Rio- 54 De 8.46S 74.32W
Pachuca de Soto 47 Ed 20.07N 98.44W
Pacific-Antarctic Ridge (EN) 3 Kp 62.00S 157.00W
Pacific City 46 Dd 45.12N 123.57W
Pacific Grove 46 Eh 36.38N 121.56W
Pacific Islands, Trust Territory of the- 58 Ed 7.30N 134.30 E
Pacifico, Océano- = Pacific Ocean (EN) 3 Ki 5.00N 155.00W
Pacific Ocean 3 Ki 5.00N 155.00W
Pacific Ocean (EN)=Kita-Taiheiyō 60 Ch 22.00N 167.00 E
Pacific Ocean (EN)= Pacifico, Océano- 3 Ki 5.00N 155.00W
Pacific Ocean (EN)= Pacifique, Océan- 3 Ki 5.00N 155.00W
Pacific Ocean (EN)= Taiheiyō 3 Ki 5.00N 155.00W
Pacific Ocean (EN)=Tihi Okean 3 Ki 5.00N 155.00W
Pacific Ranges 42 Ef 50.55N 125.10W
Pacifique, Océan-=Pacific Ocean (EN) 3 Ki 5.00N 155.00W
Packsattel 14 Id 46.58N 14.58 E
Pacui, Rio- 55 Jc 16.46S 45.01W
Pacuneiro, Rio- 55 Fa 13.02S 53.25W
Pacy-sur-Eure 12 De 49.01N 1.23 E
Paczków 10 Mf 50.27N 17.00 E
Padana, Pianura-=Po Valley (EN) 5 Gf 45.20N 10.00 E
Padang 22 Mj 0.57S 100.21 E
Padangsidempuan 26 Cf 1.22N 99.16 E
Padangtikar, Pulau- 26 Eg 0.50S 109.30 E
Padany 7 He 63.19N 33.25 E
Padasjoki 8 Kc 61.21N 25.17 E
Padauiri, Rio- 54 Fd 0.15S 64.05W
Paddle Prairie 42 Fe 58.02N 117.50W
Paderborn 10 Ee 51.43N 8.46 E
Paderborn-Elsen 12 Kc 51.44N 8.41 E
Paderborn-Schloß Neuhaus 12 Kc 51.44N 8.42 E
Padeş, Vîrful- 15 Fd 45.40N 22.20 E
Padilla 54 Fg 19.19S 64.20W
Padina 15 Ke 44.50N 27.07 E
Padornelo, Portillo del- 13 Fb 42.03N 6.50W
Padova = Padua (EN) 14 Fe 45.25N 11.53 E
Padre, Morro do- 55 Ic 16.48S 47.35W
Padre Bernardo 55 Hb 15.21S 48.30W
Padre Island 43 Hf 27.00N 97.15W
Padrón 13 Db 42.44N 8.40W
Padua (EN) = Padova 14 Fe 45.25N 11.53 E
Paducah [Ky.-U.S.] 39 Kf 37.05N 88.36W
Paducah [Tx.-U.S.] 45 Fi 34.01N 100.18W
Padula 14 Jj 40.20N 15.39 E
Paea 65e Fc 17.41S 149.35W
Paegam-san 28 Id 40.35N 126.15 E
Paengnyong-Do 27 Ld 38.00N 124.40 E
Paeroa 61 Eg 37.23S 175.41 E
Paestum 14 Jj 40.25N 15.01 E
Paeu 63c Bb 11.22S 166.50 E
Pafuri 37 Ed 22.26S 31.20 E
Pag 14 Jf 44.27N 15.03 E
Pag 14 If 44.30N 15.00 E
Pagadian 26 He 7.49N 123.25 E
Pagai, Kepulauan-=Pagai Islands (EN) 21 Lj 2.45S 100.00 E
Pagai Selatan 26 Dg 3.00S 100.20 E
Pagai Utara 26 Cg 2.42S 100.07 E
Pagan Island 57 Fc 18.07N 145.46 E
Pagasitikós Kólpos 15 Fj 39.15N 23.00 E
Pagatan 26 Gg 3.36S 115.56 E
Pagat Point 64c Bb 13.30N 144.53 E
Page 46 Jh 36.57N 111.27W
Pagėgiai 8 Ii 55.09N 21.54 E
Paget, Mount- 66 Ad 54.26S 36.33W
Pagi Islands (EN)=Pagai, Kepulauan- 21 Lj 2.45S 100.00 E
Paglia 14 Gh 42.42N 12.11 E
Pago Bay 64c Bb 13.25N 144.48 E
Pagoda Point 21 Lh 15.57N 94.15 E
Pāgodār 24 Qh 28.10N 57.22 E
Pago Pago 58 Jf 14.16S 170.42W
Pago Pago Harbor 65c Cb 14.17S 170.40W
Pago Redondo 55 Ci 29.35S 59.13W
Pagosa Springs 45 Ch 37.16N 107.01W
Pagoua Bay 51g Ba 15.32N 61.17W
Pagwa River 45 Na 50.01N 85.10W
Paháči 20 Ld 60.30N 169.00 E
Pahala 65a Fd 19.12N 155.29W
Pāhara, Laguna- 49 Ff 14.18N 83.15W
Pahiatua 62 Fd 40.27S 175.50 E
Pahkäing Bum 21 Lg 26.00N 95.30 E
Pahoa 65a Gd 19.30N 154.57W
Pahokee 44 Gl 26.49N 80.40W
Pahtakor 18 Fd 40.16N 67.55 E
Pahute Mesa 46 Gh 37.20N 116.40W
Paia 63b Dc 16.35S 168.12 E
Paide/Pajde 7 Fg 58.57N 25.35 E
Paignton 9 Jk 50.28N 3.30W
Päijänne 5 Ic 61.35N 23.30 E
Paikon Óros 15 Fi 40.56N 22.21 E
Paila 48 He 25.39N 102.07W
Pailin 25 Kf 12.51N 102.36 E
Pailitas 49 Ki 8.58N 73.38W
Pailolo Channel 65a Eb 21.05N 156.42W
Paimio/Pemar 8 Jd 60.27N 22.42 E
Paimionjoki 8 Jd 60.25N 22.40 E
Paimpol 11 Cf 48.46N 3.03W
Painan 26 Dg 1.21S 100.34 E
Paine, Mount- 66 Mg 86.46S 147.32W
Painel 55 Gh 27.55S 50.06W
Painesville 44 Ge 41.43N 81.15W
Painted Desert 43 Ed 36.00N 111.20W
Paintsville 44 Fg 37.49N 82.48W
Pais do Vinho 13 Ec 41.15N 7.55W
Paisley 9 If 55.50N 4.26W
Paita 54 Be 5.06S 81.07W
Paita 63b Cf 22.08S 166.22 E
Paiva 13 Dc 41.04N 8.16W
Paj 7 If 61.43N 34.28 E
Pajala 7 Fc 67.12N 23.22 E
Pajares, Puerto de- 13 Ga 43.00N 5.46W
Pajaros, Punta- 48 Ph 19.36N 87.25W
Pajaros Point 51a Db 18.31N 64.18W
Pajatén 54 Ce 7.29S 77.22W
Pajde/Paide 7 Fg 58.57N 25.35 E
Pajęczno 10 Oe 51.09N 19.00 E
Pajer, Gora- 19 Gb 66.40N 64.20 E
Paj-Hoj 5 Mb 69.00N 62.30 E
Pajule 36 Fb 2.58N 32.56 E
Pakanbaru 22 Mi 0.32N 101.27 E
Pakaraima Mountains 54 Fb 4.05N 61.30W
Pakch'on 28 He 39.44N 125.35 E
Pakhiá 15 Im 36.16N 25.50 E
Pakhna 24 Ee 34.46N 32.48 E
Pákhnes 15 Gn 35.18N 23.58 E
Paki 34 Gc 11.30N 8.09 E
Pakima 36 Dc 3.21S 24.06 E
Pakin Atoll 57 Gd 7.04N 157.48 E
Pakistan [1] 22 Ig 30.00N 70.00 E
Pakleni Otoci 14 Kg 43.10N 16.23 E
Pakokku 25 Jd 21.17N 95.06 E
Pakowki Lake 46 Jb 49.22N 110.57W
Pak Phanang 25 Kg 8.21N 100.12 E
Pakrac 14 Le 45.26N 17.12 E
Pakruojis/Pakruojo 7 Fi 55.57N 23.50 E
Pakruojo/Pakruojis 7 Fi 55.57N 23.50 E
Paks 10 Oj 46.38N 18.52 E
Paktiā [3] 23 Kc 33.30N 69.30 E
Pakwach 36 Fb 2.28N 31.30 E
Pakxé 22 Mh 15.07N 105.47 E
Pakxèng 25 Kd 20.10N 102.40 E
Pala 35 Ad 9.22N 14.54 E
Palacca Point 49 Kc 21.15N 73.26W
Palacios [Arg.] 55 Bj 30.43S 61.37W
Palacios [Tx.-U.S.] 45 Hl 28.42N 96.13W
Palafrugell 13 Pc 41.55N 3.10 E
Palagruža 14 Kh 42.24N 16.15 E
Palaiokastritsa 15 Cj 39.40N 19.41 E
Palaiokhóra 15 Gn 35.14N 23.41 E
Palaiseau 12 Ef 48.43N 2.15 E
Palamás 15 Fj 39.28N 22.05 E
Palamós 13 Pc 41.51N 3.08 E
Palamuse/Palamuze 8 Lf 58.39N 26.35 E
Palamut 15 Kk 38.59N 27.41 E
Palamuze/Palamuse 8 Lf 58.39N 26.35 E
Palana 22 Rd 59.07N 159.58 E
Palancia 13 Le 39.40N 0.12W
Palanga 19 Cd 55.57N 21.05 E
Palangkaraya 26 Fg 2.16S 113.56 E
Pālanpur 25 Ed 24.10N 72.26 E

Index Symbols

[1] Independent Nation
[2] State, Region
[3] District, County
[4] Municipality
[5] Colony, Dependency
Continent
Physical Region
Historical or Cultural Region
Mount, Mountain
Volcano
Hill
Mountains, Mountain Range
Hills, Escarpment
Plateau, Upland
Pass, Gap
Plain, Lowland
Delta
Salt Flat
Valley, Canyon
Crater, Cave
Karst Features
Depression
Polder
Desert, Dunes
Forest, Woods
Heath, Steppe
Oasis
Cape, Point
Coast, Beach
Cliff
Peninsula
Isthmus
Sandbank
Island
Atoll
Rock, Reef
Islands, Archipelago
Rocks, Reefs
Coral Reef
Well, Spring
Geyser
River, Stream
Waterfall Rapids
River Mouth, Estuary
Lake
Salt Lake
Intermittent Lake
Reservoir
Swamp, Pond
Canal
Glacier
Ice Shelf, Pack Ice
Ocean
Sea
Gulf, Bay
Strait, Fjord
Lagoon
Bank
Seamount
Tablemount
Ridge
Shelf
Basin
Escarpment, Sea Scarp
Fracture
Trench, Abyss
National Park, Reserve
Point of Interest
Recreation Site
Cave, Cavern
Historic Site
Ruins
Wall, Walls
Church, Abbey
Temple
Scientific Station
Airport
Port
Lighthouse
Mine
Tunnel
Dam, Bridge

Palaoa Point 65a Ec 20.44N 156.58W
Palapye 31 Jk 22.33S 27.08 E
Palasa 26 Hf 0.29N 120.24 E
Palatka [Fl.-U.S.] 43 Kf 29.39N 81.38W
Palatka [R.S.F.S.R.] 20 Kd 60.05N 151.00 E
Palau (EN) = Belau 14 Di 41.11N 9.23 E
Palau [5] 58 Ed 7.30N 134.30 E
Palau Islands 57 Ed 7.30N 134.30 E
Palauli 65c Aa 13.44S 172.16W
Palauli Bay 65c Aa 13.47S 172.14W
Palau Trench (EN) 60 Af 6.30N 134.30 E
Palavas-les-Flots 11 Jk 43.32N 3.56 E
Palaw 25 Jf 12.58N 98.39 E
Palawan 21 Ni 9.30N 118.30 E
Palawan Passage 26 Gd 10.00N 118.00 E
Palayan 26 Hc 15.33N 121.06 E
Pālayankottai 25 Fg 8.43N 77.44 E
Palazzo, Punta- 11a Aa 42.22N 8.33 E
Palazzolo Acreide 14 Im 37.04N 14.54 E
Palazzolo sull'Oglio 14 De 45.36N 9.53 E
Paldiski 19 Cd 59.20N 24.06 E
Pale di San Martino 14 Fd 46.14N 11.53 E
Paleleh 26 Hf 1.04N 121.57 E
Palembang 22 Mj 2.55S 104.45 E
Palena 14 Ii 41.59N 14.08 E
Palencia [3] 13 Hb 42.25N 4.30W
Palencia 13 Hb 42.01N 4.32W
Palen Lake 46 Hj 33.46N 115.12W
Palenque 39 Jh 17.30N 92.00W
Palenque [Mex.] 48 Ni 17.31N 91.58W
Palenque [Pan.] 49 Hi 9.13N 79.41W
Palenque, Punta- 49 Ld 18.14N 70.09W
Palermo 6 Hh 38.07N 13.22 E
Palermo, Golfo di- 14 Hl 38.10N 13.25 E
Palestine 45 He 31.46N 95.38W
Palestine (EN) 23 Dc 32.15N 34.47 E
Palestrina 14 Gi 41.50N 12.53 E
Pālghāt 25 Ff 10.47N 76.39 E
Palgrave Point 37 Ad 20.28S 13.16 E
Palhoça 55 Hh 27.38S 48.40W
Pāli 25 Ec 25.46N 73.20 E
Palinuro 14 Jj 40.02N 15.17 E
Palinuro, Capo- 14 Jj 40.02N 15.16 E
Palisades Reservoir 46 Je 43.04N 111.26W
Paliseul 12 He 49.54N 5.08 E
Palivere 8 Jf 59.00N 23.45 E
Palizada 48 Mh 18.15N 92.05W
Paljakka 7 Gd 64.45N 28.07 E
Paljavaam 20 Mc 68.50N 170.50 E
Paljenik 5 Hg 44.15N 17.36 E
Pälkäne 8 Kc 61.20N 24.16 E
Palkino 8 Mg 57.29N 28.10 E
Palk Strait 25 Ff 10.00N 79.45 E
Palla Bianca/Weißkugel 14 Ed 46.48N 10.44 E
Pallars 13 Mb 42.25N 0.55 E
Pallars, Montsent de-/Montseny 13 Nb 42.29N 1.02 E
Pallasovka 19 Ee 50.03N 46.55 E
Pallastunturi 7 Fb 68.06N 24.02 E
Palliser, Cape- 61 Eh 41.37S 175.16 E
Palliser, Iles- 57 Mf 15.30S 146.30W
Palma [Moz.] 37 Gb 10.46S 40.28 E
Palma [Sp.] 6 Gh 39.34N 2.39 E
Palma, Badia de-/Palma, Bahia de- 13 Oe 39.27N 2.35 E
Palma, Bahia de-/Palma, Badia de- 13 Oe 39.27N 2.35 E
Palma, Rio- 54 If 12.33S 47.52W
Palma, Sierra de la- 48 Id 26.00N 101.35W
Palma del Rio 13 Gg 37.42N 5.17W
Palma di Montechiaro 14 Hm 37.11N 13.46 E
Palmar, Laguna del- 55 Bi 29.35S 60.42W
Palmar, Rio- 49 Lh 10.11N 71.52W
Palmar, Salto- 55 Cg 24.18S 59.18W
Palmares 54 Ke 8.41S 35.36W
Palmares do Sul 55 Gj 30.16S 50.31W
Palmarito 54 Db 7.37N 70.10W
Palmarola 14 Gj 40.55N 12.50 E
Palmar Sur 47 Hg 8.58N 83.29W
Palmas 56 Jc 26.30S 52.00W
Palmas, Cape- 30 Gh 4.22N 7.44W
Palmas, Golfo di- 14 Cl 39.00N 8.30 E
Palmas Bellas 49 Gi 9.14N 80.05W
Palma Soriano 47 Id 20.13N 76.00W
Palm Bay 44 Gk 28.01N 80.35W
Palm Beach 43 Kf 26.42N 80.02W
Palmdale 46 Fi 34.35N 118.07W
Palmeira 55 Gg 25.25S 50.00W
Palmeira das Missões 56 Jc 27.55S 53.17W
Palmeira dos Indios 54 Ke 9.25S 36.37W
Palmeirais 54 Je 5.58S 43.04W
Palmeiras, Rio- 55 Gb 15.25S 51.10W
Palmeiras de Goiás 55 Hc 16.47S 49.53W
Palmeirinhas, Ponta das- 30 Ii 9.05S 13.00 E
Palmela 13 Df 38.34N 8.54W
Palmer 40 Jd 61.36N 149.07W
Palmer Archipelago 66 Qe 64.10S 62.00W
Palmer Land (EN) 66 Qf 71.30S 65.00W
Palmer Station 66 Qe 64.46S 64.05W
Palmerston 62 Df 45.29S 170.43 E
Palmerston Atoll 57 Kf 18.04S 163.10W
Palmerston North 58 Ii 40.28S 175.17 E
Palmetto Point 51d Ba 17.35N 61.52W
Palmi 14 Jl 38.21N 15.51 E
Palmira [Col.] 53 Ie 3.32N 76.16W
Palmira [Cuba] 49 Gb 22.14N 80.23W
Palm Islands 59 Jc 18.40S 146.30 E
Palmital 55 Fg 24.39S 52.16W
Palmitas 55 Dk 33.27S 57.48W
Palmito 55 Cd 18.53S 58.22W
Palmitos 55 Fh 27.05S 53.08W
Palm Springs 43 De 33.50N 116.33W
Palmyra 23 Ec 34.33N 38.17 E
Palmyra Atoll 57 Kd 5.52N 162.06W
Palo Alto 43 Cd 37.27N 122.09W
Paloh 26 Ef 1.43N 109.18 E
Paloich 35 Ec 10.28N 32.32 E
Palomani, Nevado- 52 Jg 14.38S 69.14W
Palomar Mountain 43 De 33.22N 116.50W
Palomera, Sierra- 13 Kd 40.40N 1.12W
Palopo 22 Oj 3.00S 120.12 E
Palos, Cabo de- 5 Fh 37.38N 0.41W
Palo Santo 55 Cg 25.34S 59.21W
Palotina 55 Fg 24.17S 53.50W
Palouse River 46 Fc 46.35N 118.13W
Palpa 54 Cf 14.32S 75.11W
Palsa 8 Lg 57.23N 26.24 E
Pålsboda 8 Fe 59.04N 15.20 E
Paltamo 7 Gd 64.25N 27.50 E
Palu [Indon.] 22 Nj 0.53S 119.53 E
Palu [Tur.] 24 Hc 38.42N 39.57 E
Palu, Pulau- 26 Hh 8.20S 121.43 E
Pam 63b Be 20.15S 164.17 E
Pama 34 Fc 11.15N 0.42 E
Påmark/Pomarkku 8 Ic 61.42N 22.00 E
Pambarra 37 Fd 21.56S 35.06 E
Pambeguwa 34 Gc 10.40N 8.17 E
Pamekasan 26 Fh 7.10S 113.28 E
Pamiers 11 Hk 43.07N 1.36 E
Pamir 21 Jf 38.00N 73.00 E
Pamir 19 Hh 37.01N 72.41 E
Påmiut/Frederikshåb 41 Hf 62.00N 49.45W
Pamlico Sound 43 Ld 35.20N 75.55W
Pampa 43 Gd 35.32N 100.58W
Pampa del Indio 55 Ch 26.02S 59.55W
Pampa del Infierno 55 Bh 26.31S 61.10W
Pampa de los Guanacos 56 Hc 26.14S 61.51W
Pampas 54 Df 12.24S 74.54W
Pampas 52 Ji 35.00S 63.00W
Pampeiro 55 Ej 30.38S 55.16W
Pamplona [Col.] 54 Db 7.23N 72.38W
Pamplona [Sp.] 6 Fg 42.49N 1.38W
Pamukkale 15 Ml 37.47N 29.04 E
Pamukova 15 Ni 40.31N 30.09 E
Pamunkey River 44 Ig 37.32N 76.48W
Pan, Tierra del- 13 Gc 41.50N 6.00W
Pana 36 Bc 1.41S 12.39 E
Panagjurište 15 Hg 42.30N 24.11 E
Panaitan, Pulau- 26 Eh 6.36S 105.12 E
Panaitolikón Óros 15 Ek 38.43N 21.39 E
Panaji (Panjim) 22 Jh 15.29N 73.50 E
Panakhaïkón Óros 15 Ek 38.12N 21.54 E
Panamá [1] 39 Li 9.00N 80.00W
Panamá = Panama (EN) [3] 49 Hi 9.00N 79.00W
Panamá = Panama City (EN) 39 Li 8.58N 79.31W
Panama (EN) = Panamá [3] 49 Hi 9.00N 79.00W
Panamá, Bahía de- 49 Hi 8.50N 79.15W
Panamá, Canal de- = Panama Canal (EN) 47 Ig 9.20N 79.55W
Panamá, Golfo de- = Panama, Gulf of- (EN) 38 Li 8.00N 79.10W
Panama, Gulf of- (EN) = Panamá, Golfo de- 38 Li 8.00N 79.10W
Panama, Isthmus of- (EN) = Panamá, Istmo de- 38 Li 9.20N 79.30W
Panamá, Istmo de- = Panama, Isthmus of- (EN) 38 Li 9.20N 79.30W
Panama Canal (EN) = Panamá, Canal de- 47 Ig 9.20N 79.55W
Panama City [La.-U.S.] 39 Kf 30.10N 85.41W
Panama City (EN) = Panamá 39 Li 8.58N 79.31W
Panamá La Vieja 49 Hi 9.00N 79.29W
Panambi 55 Fi 28.18S 53.30W
Panamint Range 46 Gh 36.30N 117.20W
Panao 54 Ce 9.45S 76.00W
Panarea 14 Jl 38.40N 15.05 E
Panaro 14 Ff 44.55N 11.25 E
Pana Tinai 63a Ad 11.14S 153.10 E
Pana-Wina 63a Ad 11.11S 153.01 E
Panay 21 Oh 11.15N 122.30 E
Pancake Range 46 Hg 39.00N 115.45W
Pančevo 15 De 44.52N 20.39 E
Pančičev vrh 15 Df 43.15N 20.45 E
Panciu 15 Kd 45.54N 27.05 E
Pancros 63b Db 15.58S 168.12 E
Panda 37 Ed 24.03S 34.43 E
Panda ma Tenga 37 Dc 18.32S 25.38 E
Pandan 26 Hd 11.43N 122.06 E
Pan de Azúcar 55 El 34.48S 55.14W
Pandeiros, Ribeirão- 55 Jb 15.42S 44.36W
Pandelis/Pandėlys 8 Kh 56.01N 25.21 E
Pandėlys/Pandelis 8 Kh 56.01N 25.21 E
Pandharpur 25 Fe 17.40N 75.20 E
Pandheon 15 Fi 40.05N 22.20 E
Pāndhurna 25 Fd 21.36N 78.31 E
Pandivere Kõrgustik/Pandivere Vozvyšennost 8 Le 59.00N 26.15 E
Pandivere Vozvyšennost/Pandivere Kõrgustik 8 Le 59.00N 26.15 E
Pando 56 Id 34.43S 55.57W
Pando [2] 54 Ef 11.20S 67.40W
Pandokrátor 15 Cj 39.45N 19.52 E
Pandora 49 Fi 9.45N 82.57W
Pandrup 8 Cg 57.14N 9.41 E
Pandu 36 Cb 4.59N 19.16 E
Panevėžis/Panevėžys 19 Cd 55.44N 24.22 E
Panevėžys/Panevežis 19 Cd 55.44N 24.22 E
Panfilov 19 Ig 44.08N 80.01 E
Panga 36 Eb 1.51N 26.25 E
Pangai 65b Ba 19.48S 174.21W
Pangaion Óros 15 Hi 40.50N 24.05 E
Panganes, Canal de- 30 Lk 22.48S 47.50 E
Pangani 36 Gd 5.26S 38.58 E
Pangani or Ruvu 36 Gc 5.26S 38.58 E
Pange 12 Ie 49.05N 6.22 E
Panggoe 58 Ge 7.01S 157.05 E
Pangi 36 Ec 3.11S 26.38 E
Pangkajene 26 Gg 4.50S 119.32 E
Pangkalanberandan 26 Cf 4.01N 98.17 E
Pangkalanbuun 26 Fg 2.41S 111.37 E
Pangkalanseang, Tanjung- 26 Hg 0.42S 123.26 E
Pangkalpinang 26 Eg 2.08S 106.08 E
Pangnirtung 39 Mc 66.08N 65.44W
Pang-Pang 63b Dc 17.41S 168.32 E
Panguitch 43 Ed 37.49N 112.26W
Panguma 34 Cd 8.24N 11.13W
Pangutaran Group 26 He 6.15N 120.30 E
Panhandle 45 Fi 35.21N 101.23W
Pania Mutombo 36 Dd 5.11S 23.51 E
Paniau 65a Ab 21.57N 160.05W
Panié, Mont- 61 Bd 20.36S 164.46 E
Pānīpat 25 Fc 29.23N 76.58 E
Paniza, Puerto de- 13 Kc 41.15N 1.20W
Panjang 26 Eh 5.29S 105.18 E
Panjang, Pulau- 26 Ef 2.44N 108.55 E
Panjgūr 25 Cc 26.58N 64.06 E
Panjim → Panaji 22 Jh 15.29N 73.50 E
Panjwin 24 Ke 35.36N 45.58 E
Pankow, Berlin- 10 Jd 52.34N 13.24 E
Pankshin 34 Gd 9.20N 9.27 E
P'anmunjŏm 28 If 37.57N 126.40 E
Panopah 26 Fg 1.56S 111.11 E
Panorama 56 Jb 21.21S 51.51W
Panshan 28 Gd 41.12N 122.03 E
Panshi 27 Mc 42.56N 126.02 E
Pant 12 Cc 51.53N 0.39 E
Pantanal 52 Kg 18.00S 56.00W
Pantar, Pulau- 26 Hh 8.25S 124.07 E
Pantego 44 Ih 35.34N 76.36W
Pantelleria 14 Fn 36.50N 11.57 E
Pantelleria 5 Hh 36.45N 12.00 E
Pantelleria, Canale di- 14 Fn 36.40N 11.46 E
Pante Makassar 26 Hh 9.12S 124.23 E
Pantoja 54 Cd 0.58S 75.10W
Pánuco 48 Jf 22.03N 98.10W
Pánuco 38 Jg 22.16N 97.47W
Panxian 27 Hf 25.45N 104.39 E
Panyam 34 Gd 9.25N 9.13 E
Panzi 36 Cd 7.13S 17.58 E
Panzós 49 Cf 15.24N 89.40W
Pao, Rio- [Ven.] 50 Bh 8.33N 68.01W
Pao, Rio- [Ven.] 50 Dh 8.06N 64.17W
Paola [It.] 14 Kk 39.21N 16.03 E
Paola [Ks.-U.S.] 45 Ig 38.35N 94.53W
Paoli 44 Df 38.33N 86.28W
Paopao 65e Fc 17.30S 149.49W
Paoua 35 Bd 7.15N 16.26 E
Pápa 10 Ni 47.20N 17.28 E
Papa 65a Fd 19.13N 155.52W
Papaaloa 65a Fd 19.59N 155.13W
Papagaios 55 Jd 19.32S 44.45W
Papagayo, Golfo del- 47 Gf 10.45N 85.45W
Papaikou 65a Fd 19.47N 155.06W
Papakura 62 Fb 37.03S 174.57 E
Papaloapan, Rio- 48 Lh 18.42N 95.38W
Papanduva 55 Gh 26.25S 50.09W
Papangpanjang 26 Dg 0.27S 100.25 E
Papantla de Olarte 47 Ed 20.27N 97.19W
Papar 26 Ge 5.44N 115.56 E
Paparoa Range 62 De 42.05S 171.35 E
Papa Stour 9 La 60.30N 1.40W
Papa Westray 9 Kb 59.22N 2.54W
Papeete 58 Mf 17.32S 149.34W
Papenburg 10 Dc 53.04N 7.24 E
Papenburg-Aschendorf (Ems) 12 Ja 53.04N 7.22 E
Papenoo 65e Fc 17.30S 149.25W
Papes Ezers/Papes Ozero 8 Ih 56.15N 20.55 E
Papes Ozero/Papes Ezers 8 Ih 56.15N 20.55 E
Papetoai 65e Fc 17.30S 149.52W
Papey 7a Cb 64.36N 14.11W
Paphos/Baf 24 Ee 34.50N 32.35 E
Papija 15 Kg 42.07N 27.51 E
Papikion Óros 15 Ih 41.15N 25.18 E
Papilé/Papile 8 Jh 56.09N 22.45 E
Papile/Papilé 8 Jh 56.09N 22.45 E
Papillion 45 Hf 41.09N 96.03W
Papua, Gulf of- 57 Fe 8.32S 145.00 E
Papua New Guinea [1] 58 Fe 6.00S 150.00 E
Papua Passage 64p Bc 21.15S 159.47W
Papuk 14 Le 45.31N 17.39 E
Papun 25 Je 18.04N 97.27 E
Para 7 Ji 54.23N 40.53 E
Pará [2] 54 Hd 4.00S 53.00W
Pará, Rio- 55 Jd 19.13S 45.07W
Para, Rio- 52 Lf 1.30S 48.55W
Parabel 20 De 58.40N 81.30 E
Parabel 20 De 58.43N 81.31 E
Paraburdoo 59 Dd 23.15S 117.45 E
Paracas 54 Cf 13.49S 76.16W
Paracatu 54 Ig 17.13S 46.52W
Paracatu, Rio- [Braz.] 55 Ic 17.30S 46.32W
Paracatu, Rio- [Braz.] 55 Jc 16.30S 45.04W
Paracel Islands (EN) = Xisha Qundao 21 Nh 16.30N 112.15 E
Pārachinār 25 Eb 33.54N 70.06 E
Paraćin 15 Ef 43.52N 21.25 E
Paracuru 54 Kd 3.24S 39.04W
Parada Km 329 55 Ek 32.30S 55.25W
Paradip 25 Hd 20.19N 86.42 E
Paradise [Ca.-U.S.] 46 Eg 39.46N 121.37W
Paradise [Mi.-U.S.] 44 Eb 46.38N 85.03W
Paragould 45 Kh 36.03N 90.29W
Paragua, Rio- 54 Fb 6.55N 62.55W
Paraguá, Rio- 54 Ff 13.34S 61.53W
Paraguaçu, Rio- 52 Mg 12.45S 38.54W
Paraguaçu Paulista 55 Gf 22.25S 50.34W
Paraguai, Rio- 52 Kh 27.18S 58.38W
Paraguaipoa 49 Lh 11.21N 71.57W
Paraguaná, Peninsula de- 52 Jd 11.55N 70.00W
Paraguarí [3] 55 Dg 26.00S 57.10W
Paraguarí 56 Ic 25.38S 57.09W
Paraguay [1] 53 Kh 23.00S 58.00W
Paraguay, Rio- 52 Kh 27.18S 58.38W
Paraíba [2] 54 Ke 7.10S 36.30W
Paraíba do Sul, Rio- 52 Lh 21.37S 41.03W
Paraibuna, Represa do- 55 Jf 23.25S 45.35W
Paraibuna, Rio- 55 Jf 23.22S 45.40W
Parainen/Pargas 7 Ff 60.18N 22.18 E
Paraiso [Braz.] 55 Fd 19.03S 52.59W
Paraiso [Mex.] 48 Mh 18.24N 93.14W
Paraiso, Rio- 55 Bb 15.08S 61.52W
Parakou 31 Hh 9.21N 2.37 E
Param 64d Bb 7.22N 151.48 E
Paramaribo 53 Ke 5.50N 55.10W
Paramera, Sierra de la- 13 Hd 40.30N 4.46W
Paramithiá 15 Dj 39.28N 20.31 E
Paramušir, Ostrov- 21 Rd 50.25N 155.50 E
Paraná 53 Ji 31.45S 60.30W
Paraná [2] 56 Jb 24.00S 51.00W
Paraná, Pico- 55 Hg 25.14S 48.48W
Paraná, Rio- 52 Ki 33.43S 59.15W
Paranã, Rio- 52 Lg 12.30S 48.14W
Paraná de las Palmas, Rio- 55 Cl 34.18S 58.33W
Paranaguá 53 Lh 25.31S 48.30W
Paraná-Guazú, Rio- 55 Ck 34.00S 58.25W
Paranaiba 54 Hg 19.40S 51.11W
Paranaíba, Rio- 52 Kh 20.07S 51.05W
Paranaiguara 55 Gd 18.53S 50.28W
Paranapanema, Rio- 52 Kh 22.40S 53.09W
Paranapiacaba, Serra do- 52 Lh 24.20S 49.00W
Paranapuã-Guaçu, Ponta do- 55 Ig 24.24S 47.00W
Paranavai 56 Jb 23.04S 52.28W
Parandak 24 Ne 35.21N 50.42 E
Paranéstion 15 Hh 41.16N 24.30 E
Paranhos 55 Ef 23.55S 55.25W
Paraoa Atoll 57 Mf 19.09S 140.43W
Paraopeba 55 Jd 19.18S 44.25W
Paraopeba, Rio- 55 Jd 18.50S 45.11W
Parapara 63b Ca 13.32S 167.20 E
Paraparaumu 62 Fd 40.55S 175.00 E
Paraspóri 15 Kn 35.54N 27.14 E
Parati 55 Jf 23.13S 44.43W
Paratodos, Serra- 55 Jb 14.40S 44.50W
Paratunka 20 Kf 52.52N 158.12 E
Parāu, Kūh-e- 24 Le 34.37N 47.05 E
Paraúna 55 Gc 17.02S 50.26W
Paravae 64n Bc 10.27S 160.58W
Paray-le-Monial 11 Kh 46.27N 4.07 E
Parbati 25 Fc 25.51N 76.36 E
Parbhani 25 Fe 19.16N 76.47 E
Parchim 10 Hc 53.26N 11.51 E
Parczew 10 Se 51.39N 22.54 E
Pardo 55 Cm 36.15S 59.22W
Pardo, Rio- [Braz.] 55 Fi 29.59S 52.23W
Pardo, Rio- [Braz.] 54 Hh 21.46S 52.09W
Pardo, Rio- [Braz.] 55 He 20.10S 48.38W
Pardo, Rio- [Braz.] 55 Hf 22.55S 49.58W
Pardo, Rio- [Braz.] 55 Jb 15.48S 44.48W
Pardo, Rio- [Braz.] 54 Kg 15.39S 38.57W
Pardubice 10 Lf 50.02N 15.45 E
Parea 65e Eb 16.49S 150.58W
Parecis, Chapada dos- 52 Kg 13.00S 60.00W
Parecis, Rio- 55 Da 12.56S 56.43W
Paredes de Nava 13 Hb 42.09N 4.41W
Parelhas 54 Ke 6.41S 36.39W
Paren 20 Ld 62.28N 163.05 E
Parent 42 Kg 47.55N 74.37W
Parentis-en-Born 11 Ej 44.21N 1.04W
Pareora 62 Df 44.29S 171.13 E
Parepare 22 Nj 4.01S 119.38 E
Párga 15 Dj 39.17N 20.24 E
Pargas/Parainen 7 Ff 60.18N 22.18 E
Pargolovo 8 Nd 60.03N 30.30 E
Parham 51d Bb 17.05N 61.46W
Parhar 19 Gh 37.31N 69.23 E
Pari, Rio- 55 Db 15.36S 56.08W
Paria, Golfo de-/Paria, Gulf of- 54 Fa 10.20N 62.00W
Paria, Gulf of-/Paria, Golfo de- 54 Fa 10.20N 62.00W
Paria, Peninsula de- 50 Eg 10.40N 62.30W
Pariaguán 54 Fb 8.51N 64.43W
Pariaman 26 Dg 0.38S 100.08 E
Paria River 46 Jh 36.52N 111.36W
Paricutín, Volcán- 48 Hh 19.28N 102.15W
Parida, Isla- 49 Fi 8.07N 82.20W
Pari das Pedras 55 Ja 12.45S 44.47W
Parigi 26 Hg 0.48S 120.10 E
Parika 54 Gb 6.52N 58.25W
Parikkala 7 Gf 61.33N 29.30 E
Parima, Serra- 52 Je 3.00N 64.20W
Parinacota 54 Eg 18.12S 69.16W
Pariñas, Punta- 52 Hf 4.40S 81.20W
Paringul Mare, Vîrful- 15 Gd 45.20N 23.30 E
Parintins 53 Kf 2.36S 56.44W
Paris [Fr.] 6 Gf 48.52N 2.20 E
Paris [Il.-U.S.] 45 Mg 39.36N 87.42W
Paris [Kir.] 64g Ab 1.56N 157.29W
Paris [Ky.-U.S.] 44 Ef 38.13N 84.14W
Paris [Tn.-U.S.] 44 Cg 36.19N 88.20W
Paris [Tx.-U.S.] 43 He 33.40N 95.33W
Paris Basin (EN) = Parisien, Bassin- 5 Gf 49.00N 2.00 E
Parisien, Bassin- = Paris Basin (EN) 5 Gf 49.00N 2.00 E
Parita 49 Gi 8.00N 80.31W
Parita, Bahía de- 49 Gi 8.08N 80.24W
Parit Buntar 26 De 5.07N 100.30 E
Parkano 7 Fe 62.01N 23.01 E
Parkent 18 Gd 41.18N 69.40 E
Parker 46 Hi 34.09N 114.17W
Parker, Mount- 59 Fc 17.10S 128.20 E
Parkersburg 43 Kd 39.17N 81.33W
Parker Seamount (EN) 40 If 52.35N 151.15W
Parkes 58 Fh 33.08S 148.11 E
Park Falls 45 Kd 45.56N 90.32W
Parkland 46 Dc 47.09N 122.26W
Park Range 45 Fc 40.00N 106.30W
Park Rapids 45 Ic 46.55N 95.04W
Park River 45 Hb 48.24N 97.45W
Park Valley 46 If 41.50N 113.21W
Parma 14 Ef 44.56N 10.26 E
Parma [It.] 6 Hg 44.48N 10.20 E
Parma [Oh.-U.S.] 44 Ge 41.24N 81.44W
Parnaguá 54 Jf 10.13S 44.38W
Parnaiba 53 Lf 2.54S 41.47W
Parnaíba, Rio- 52 Lf 3.00S 41.50W
Parnamirim [Braz.] 54 Ke 8.05S 39.34W
Parnamirim [Braz.] 54 Ke 5.55S 35.15W
Parnarama 54 Je 5.41S 43.06W
Parnassós Óros = Parnassus (EN) 5 Ih 38.30N 22.37 E
Parnassus 62 Ee 42.43S 173.17 E
Parnassus (EN) = Parnassós Óros 5 Ih 38.30N 22.37 E
Párnis Óros 15 Gk 38.10N 23.40 E
Párnon Óros 15 Fl 37.12N 22.38 E
Pärnu/Pjarnu 6 Id 58.24N 24.32 E
Pärnu-Jaagupi/Pjarnu-Jagupi 8 Kf 58.36N 24.25 E
Pärnu Jõgi/Pjarnu 7 Fg 58.23N 24.34 E
Pärnu Laht/Pjarnu, Zaliv- 7 Fg 58.15N 24.25 E
Parola 8 Kc 61.03N 24.22 E
Paroo River 57 Fh 31.28S 143.32 E
Paropamisus/Salseleh-ye Safīd Kūh 21 If 34.30N 63.30 E
Páros 15 Il 37.05N 25.09 E
Páros 15 Il 37.06N 25.12 E
Parowan 46 Ih 37.51N 112.57W
Parpaillon 11 Mj 44.35N 6.40 E
Parque Industrial 55 Jd 19.57S 44.01W
Parral 56 Fe 36.09S 71.50W
Parral, Rio- 48 Gd 27.35N 105.25W
Parras, Sierra de- 48 He 25.25N 102.00W
Parras de la Fuente 47 Dc 25.25N 102.11W
Parravicini 55 Dm 36.27S 57.46W
Parrett 9 Jj 51.13N 3.01W
Parrita 49 Ei 9.30N 84.19W
Parry, Cape - 42 Fb 70.12N 124.35W
Parry, Kap- [Grld.] 41 Jd 72.28N 22.00W
Parry, Kap- [Grld.] 41 Ec 77.00N 71.00W
Parry Bay 42 Jc 68.00N 82.00W
Parry Islands 38 Ib 76.00N 110.00W
Parry Peninsula 42 Fc 69.45N 124.35W
Parry Sound 42 Jg 45.21N 80.02W
Parsęta 10 Lb 54.12N 15.33 E
Parsons [Ks.-U.S.] 43 Hd 37.20N 95.16W
Parsons [W.V.-U.S.] 44 Hf 39.06N 79.43W
Parsons Range 59 Hb 13.30S 135.15 E
Partanna 14 Gm 37.43N 12.53 E
Parthenay 11 Fh 46.39N 0.15W
Partille 8 Eg 57.44N 12.07 E
Partinico 14 Hl 38.03N 13.07 E
Partizansk 20 Ih 43.13N 133.05 E
Partizánske 10 Oh 48.38N 18.23 E
Partizanskoje 20 Ee 55.30N 94.30 E
Paru, Rio- 52 Kf 1.33S 52.38W
Paru de Este, Rio- 54 Hc 1.10N 54.40W
Paru de Oeste, Rio- 52 Kf 1.30S 56.00W
Paruru 63a Ec 9.51S 160.49 E
Parvān [3] 23 Kb 35.15N 69.30 E
Pårvomaj 15 Ig 42.06N 25.13 E
Parys 37 De 27.04S 27.16 E
Paša 7 Hf 60.28N 32.55 E
Pasadena [Ca.-U.S.] 39 Hf 34.09N 118.09W
Pasadena [Tx.-U.S.] 45 Il 29.42N 95.13W
Paşaeli Yarimadası 15 Lh 41.20N 28.25 E
Paşalimani Adası 15 Ki 40.28N 27.37 E
Pasangkaju 26 Gg 1.10S 119.20 E
Pāsārgād 24 Og 30.17N 52.55 E
Pasarwajo 26 Hh 5.29S 122.50 E
Pascagoula 43 Je 30.23N 88.31W
Paşcani 15 Jb 47.15N 26.44 E
Pasco 43 Db 46.14N 119.06W
Pasco [2] 54 Cf 10.30S 75.15W
Pascoal 55 Ba 13.38S 61.06W
Pascoal, Monte- 54 Kg 16.54S 39.24W
Pascua, Isla de-/Rapa Nui = Easter Island (EN) 57 Qg 27.07S 109.22W
Pas-de-Calais [3] 11 Id 50.30N 2.20 E
Pas-en-Artois 12 Ed 50.09N 2.30 E
Pasewalk 10 Jc 53.31N 13.59 E
Pasinler 24 Ib 40.00N 41.41 E
Pašino 20 De 55.11N 83.02 E
Pasión, Rio de la- 49 Be 16.28N 90.33W
Pasir Mas 26 De 6.02N 102.08 E
Pasirpengarayan 26 Df 0.51N 100.16 E
Pasir Puteh 26 De 5.50N 102.24 E
Påskallavik 8 Gg 57.10N 16.27 E
Paškovski 16 Kg 45.01N 39.05 E
Pasłęk 10 Pb 54.05N 19.39 E
Pasłęka 10 Pb 54.25N 19.50 E
Pašman 14 Jg 43.57N 15.21 E
Pasni 22 Ig 25.16N 63.28 E
Paso de Indios 56 Gf 43.52S 69.06W
Paso del Cerro 55 Ej 31.31S 55.46W
Paso de los Libres 56 Ic 29.43S 57.05W
Paso de los Toros 56 Id 32.49S 56.31W
Paso Tranqueras 55 Ej 31.12S 55.45W
Passamaquoddy Bay 44 Nc 45.06N 66.59W
Passa Três, Serra- 55 Hb 14.40S 49.30W
Passau 10 Jh 48.35N 13.29 E
Passero, Capo- 14 Jn 36.40N 15.10 E
Passo Fundo 53 Kh 28.15S 52.24W
Passo Fundo, Rio- 55 Fh 27.16S 52.42W
Passos 54 Ig 20.43S 46.37W
Pastaza, Rio- 52 If 4.50S 76.25W
Pasteur 56 He 35.08S 62.14W
Pasto 53 Ie 1.13N 77.17W
Pastora Peak 46 Kh 36.47N 109.10W
Pastoria, Laguna de- 48 Ki 16.00N 97.40W
Pastos Bons 54 Je 6.36S 44.05W
Pastrana 13 Jd 40.25N 2.55W
Paštrik 15 Dg 42.14N 20.32 E
Pasubio 14 Fe 45.47N 11.10 E
Pasvalis/Pasvalys 7 Fh 56.02N 24.28 E
Pasvalys/Pasvalis 7 Fh 56.02N 24.28 E
Pásztó 10 Pi 47.55N 19.42 E

Index Symbols

[1] Independent Nation
[2] State, Region
[3] District, County
[4] Municipality
[5] Colony, Dependency
Continent
Physical Region
Historical or Cultural Region
Mount, Mountain
Volcano
Hill
Mountains, Mountain Range
Hills, Escarpment
Plateau, Upland
Pass, Gap
Plain, Lowland
Delta
Salt Flat
Valley, Canyon
Crater, Cave
Karst Features
Depression
Polder
Desert, Dunes
Forest, Woods
Heath, Steppe
Oasis
Cape, Point
Coast, Beach
Cliff
Peninsula
Isthmus
Sandbank
Island
Atoll
Rock, Reef
Islands, Archipelago
Rocks, Reefs
Coral Reef
Well, Spring
Geyser
River, Stream
Waterfall Rapids
River Mouth, Estuary
Lake
Salt Lake
Intermittent Lake
Reservoir
Swamp, Pond
Canal
Glacier
Ice Shelf, Pack Ice
Ocean
Sea
Gulf, Bay
Strait, Fjord
Lagoon
Bank
Seamount
Tablemount
Ridge
Shelf
Basin
Escarpment, Sea Scarp
Fracture
Trench, Abyss
National Park, Reserve
Point of Interest
Recreation Site
Cave, Cavern
Historic Site
Ruins
Wall, Walls
Church, Abbey
Temple
Scientific Station
Airport
Port
Lighthouse
Mine
Tunnel
Dam, Bridge

Patagonia 52 Jj 44.00S 68.00W
Patagonica, Cordillera- 52 Ij 46.00S 71.30W
Patan 25 Hc 27.40N 85.20 E
Pātan 25 Ed 23.50N 72.07 E
Patani 26 If 0.18N 128.48 E
Pata Peninsula 64d Bb 7.23N 151.35 E
Patchogue 44 Ke 40.46N 73.01W
Pate 36 Hc 2.08S 41.00 E
Patea 62 Fc 39.46S 174.29 E
Patea 62 Fc 39.46S 174.30 E
Pategi 34 Gd 8.44N 5.45 E
Patensie 37 Cf 33.46S 24.49 E
Paternò 14 Jm 37.34N 15.54 E
Paterson 43 Mc 40.55N 74.10W
Paterson Inlet 62 Bg 46.55S 168.00 E
Paterson Range 59 Ed 21.45S 122.05 E
Pathānkot 25 Fb 32.17N 75.39 E
Pathein 22 Lh 16.47N 94.44 E
Pathfinder Reservoir 46 Le 42.30N 106.50W
Pathfinder Seamount (EN) 40 Kf 50.55N 143.15W
Pathiu 25 Jf 10.41N 99.20 E
Patía, Río- 54 Cc 2.13N 78.40W
Patiāla 25 Fb 30.19N 76.24 E
Patiño, Estero- 55 Cg 24.05S 59.55W
Patio 65e Db 16.35S 151.29W
Pati Point 64c Ba 13.36N 144.57 E
Pătîrlagele 15 Jd 45.19N 26.21 E
Pativilca 54 Cf 10.42S 77.47W
Pátmos 15 Jl 37.19N 26.34 E
Pátmos 15 Jl 37.20N 26.33 E
Patna 22 Kg 25.36N 85.07 E
Patnos 24 Jc 39.14N 42.52 E
Pato Branco 56 Jc 26.13S 52.40W
Patom Plateau (EN) =
Patomskoje Nagorje 20 Ge 59.00N 115.30 E
Patomskoje Nagorje = Patom Plateau (EN) 20 Ge 59.00N 115.30 E
Patos 53 Mf 7.01S 37.16W
Patos, Isla de- 50 Fg 10.38N 61.52W
Patos, Lagoa dos- 52 Ki 31.06S 51.15W
Patos, Laguna de los- 55 Aj 30.25S 62.15W
Patos, Ribeirão dos- 55 Gd 18.58S 50.30W
Patos, Rio dos- [Braz.] 55 Da 13.33S 56.29W
Patos, Rio dos- [Braz.] 55 Hb 14.59S 48.46W
Patos de Minas 55 Lg 18.35S 46.32W
Patosi 15 Ci 40.38N 19.39 E
Patquía 56 Gd 30.03S 66.53W
Pátrai 6 Ih 38.15N 21.44 E
Patrai, Gulf of- (EN) =
Patraïkós Kólpos 15 Ek 38.15N 21.30 E
Patraïkós Kólpos = Patrai, Gulf of- (EN) 15 Ek 38.15N 21.30 E
Patricio Lynch, Isla- 56 Eg 48.36S 75.26W
Patricios 55 Bl 35.27S 60.42W
Patrocínio 54 Ig 18.57S 46.59W
Patta Island 30 Li 2.07S 41.03 E
Pattani 25 Kg 6.51N 101.16 E
Patteson, Passage- 63b Db 15.26S 168.09 E
Patti 14 Il 38.08N 14.58 E
Patti, Golfo di- 14 Jl 38.10N 15.05 E
Patton Seamount (EN) 38 Dd 54.40N 150.30W
Pattullo, Mount- 42 Ee 56.14N 129.39W
Patu 54 Ke 6.06S 37.38W
Patuākhāli 25 Id 22.16N 90.18 E
Patuca, Punta- 49 Ef 15.51N 84.18W
Patuca, Río- 47 He 15.50N 84.18W
Pătulele 15 Fe 44.21N 22.47 E
Patutahi 62 Gc 38.37S 177.53 E
Patuxent Range 66 Qg 84.43S 64.30W
Pátzcuaro 48 Ih 19.31N 101.36W
Pau 11 Fk 43.18N 0.22W
Pau, Gave de- 11 Ek 43.33N 1.12W
Paucartambo 54 Df 13.18S 71.40W
Paucerne, Rio- 55 Ba 13.34S 61.14W
Pau dos Ferros 54 Ke 6.07S 38.10W
Pauillac 11 Fi 45.12N 0.45W
Pauini 54 Ee 7.40S 66.58W
Pauini, Rio- 54 Ee 7.47S 67.15W
Pauksa Taung 25 Ie 19.55N 94.18 E
Paulatuk 39 Gc 69.23N 124.00W
Paulaya, Rio- 49 Ef 15.51N 85.06W
Paulding Bay 66 Ie 66.35S 123.00 E
Paulina Peak 46 Ee 43.41N 121.15W
Păuliş 15 Ec 46.07N 21.35 E
Paulistana 54 Je 8.09S 41.09W
Paulo Afonso 53 Mf 9.21S 38.14W
Paulo Afonso, Cachoeira de- 52 Mf 9.24S 38.12W
Pauls Valley 45 Hi 34.44N 97.13W
Paungde 25 Je 18.29N 95.30 E
Pavant Range 46 Ig 39.00N 112.15W
Pāveh 24 Le 35.03N 46.22 E
Pavia 14 De 45.10N 9.10 E
Pavilly 12 Ce 49.34N 0.58 E
Pāvilosta/Pavilosta 7 Eh 56.55N 21.13 E
Pavilosta/Pāvilosta 7 Eh 56.55N 21.13 E
Pavlikeni 15 If 43.14N 25.18 E
Pavlodar 22 Jd 52.18N 76.57 E
Pavlodarskaja Oblast [3] 19 He 52.00N 76.30 E
Pavlof Islands 40 Ge 55.15N 161.20W
Pavlof Volcano 40 Ge 55.24N 161.55W
Pavlograd 16 Ie 48.32N 35.53 E
Pavlovka 17 Hi 55.25N 56.33 E
Pavlovo 19 Ed 55.58N 43.04 E
Pavlov Seamount (EN) 20 Lf 50.40N 162.00 E
Pavlovsk 16 Ld 50.27N 40.08 E
Pavlovskaja 19 Df 46.06N 39.48 E
Pavullo nel Frignano 14 Ef 44.20N 10.50 E
Pavuvu 63a Dc 9.04S 159.08 E
Pawa 63a Ed 10.15S 161.44 E
Pawhuska 45 Hh 36.40N 96.20W
Pawnee 45 Hh 36.20N 96.48W
Pawnee River 45 Gg 38.10N 99.06W
Pawtucket 44 Le 41.53N 71.23W
Paximádhia, Nisídhes- 15 Ho 35.00N 24.35 E
Paxoí 15 Dj 39.12N 20.10 E
Paxson 40 Jd 63.02N 145.30W
Payakumbuk 26 Dg 0.14S 100.38 E
Payas, Cerro- 49 Ef 15.50N 85.00W
Payerne 14 Ad 46.49N 6.58 E
Payette 46 Gd 44.05N 116.57W
Payette 43 Dc 44.05N 116.56W
Payne, Baie- 42 Ke 59.55N 69.35W
Payne, Lac- 42 Ke 59.30N 74.00W
Paysandú [2] 55 Dk 32.00S 57.15W
Paysandú 53 Ki 32.19S 58.05W
Pays de Léon 11 Bf 48.28N 4.30W
Pays d'Othe 11 Jf 48.06N 3.37 E
Payson [Az.-U.S.] 46 Ji 34.14N 111.20W
Payson [Ut.-U.S.] 46 Jf 40.03N 111.44W
Payzawat/Jiashi 27 Cd 39.29N 76.39 E
Pāzanān 24 Mg 30.35N 49.59 E
Pazar 24 Ib 41.11N 40.53 E
Pazarbası Burun 24 Db 41.13N 30.17 E
Pazarcık 24 Gd 37.31N 37.19 E
Pazardžik 15 Hg 42.12N 24.20 E
Pazardžik [2] 15 Hg 42.12N 24.20 E
Pazarköy 15 Kj 39.51N 27.24 E
Pazaryeri 24 Cc 40.00N 29.54 E
Pazin 14 He 45.14N 13.56 E
Pčinja 15 Eh 41.49N 21.40 E
Pea 65b Ac 21.11S 175.14W
Peabirú 55 Ff 23.54S 52.20W
Peace Point 42 Ge 59.12N 112.33W
Peace River 39 Hd 56.14N 117.17W
Peace River [Can.] 38 Hd 56.14N 117.17W
Peace River [Fl.-U.S.] 44 Fl 26.55N 82.05W
Peachland 46 Fb 49.46N 119.44W
Peach Springs 46 Ii 35.32N 113.25W
Peacock Hills 42 Gc 66.05N 110.00W
Peak District 9 Lh 53.17N 1.45W
Peake Creek 59 He 28.05S 136.07 E
Peaked Mountain 44 Mb 46.34N 68.49W
Peale, Mount- 43 Fd 38.26N 109.14W
Pearl 45 Lb 48.42N 88.44W
Pearland 45 Il 29.34N 95.17W
Pearl and Hermes Reef 57 Jb 27.55N 175.45W
Pearl City 65a Db 21.23N 157.58W
Pearl Harbor 65a Cb 21.20N 158.00W
Pearl River 43 Je 30.11N 89.32W
Pearsall 45 Gl 28.53N 99.06W
Pearsoll Peak 46 De 42.18N 123.50W
Peary Channel 42 Ha 79.25N 101.00W
Peary Land 67 Me 82.40N 30.00W
Pease River 45 Gi 34.12N 99.07W
Pebane 37 Fc 17.14S 38.10 E
Pebas 54 Dd 3.20S 71.49W
Peć 15 Dg 42.39N 20.18 E
Peca 14 Id 46.29N 14.48 E
Peças, Ilha das- 55 Hg 25.26S 48.19W
Pecatonica River 45 Le 42.29N 89.03W
Pečeneżskoje Vodohranilišče 16 Jd 50.05N 36.50 E
Pečenga 6 Jb 69.33N 31.07 E
Pečenga 7 Hb 69.39N 31.27 E
Pechea 15 Kd 45.38N 27.48 E
Pechora (EN) = Pečora 5 Lb 68.13N 54.10 E
Pechora (EN) = Pečora 6 Lb 65.10N 57.11 E
Pechora Bay (EN) = Pečorskaja Guba 19 Fb 68.40N 54.45 E
Pechora Sea (EN) = Pečorskoje More 19 Fb 69.45N 54.30 E
Pecica 15 Ec 46.10N 21.04 E
Peçin 15 Kl 37.19N 27.45 E
Peckelsheim, Willebadessen- 12 Lc 51.36N 9.08 E
Pečora = Pechora (EN) 6 Lb 65.10N 57.11 E
Pečora = Pechora (EN) 5 Lb 68.13N 54.10 E
Pecora, Capo- 14 Ck 39.27N 8.23 E
Pečorskaja Guba = Pechora Bay (EN) 19 Fb 68.40N 54.45 E
Pečorskoje More = Pechora Sea (EN) 19 Fb 69.45N 54.30 E
Pečory 7 Gh 57.49N 27.38 E
Pecos 43 Ge 31.25N 103.30W
Pecos 38 Ig 29.42N 101.22W
Pecos Plain 43 Ge 33.20N 104.30W
Pécs 6 Hf 46.05N 18.14 E
Pécs [2] 10 Oj 46.06N 18.15 E
Pedasí 49 Gj 7.32N 80.02W
Pedder, Lake- 59 Jh 43.00S 146.15 E
Peddie 37 Df 33.14S 27.07 E
Pededze 8 Lh 56.53N 27.01 E
Pedernales [Dom.Rep.] 49 Ld 18.02N 71.45W
Pedernales [Ven.] 50 Eh 9.58N 62.16W
Pedernales, Salar de- 56 Gc 26.15S 69.10W
Pedja Jõgi 8 Lf 58.20N 26.10 E
Pědo Shankou 27 Df 29.12N 83.26 E
Pedra Azul 54 Jg 16.01S 41.16W
Pedra Branca 54 Ke 5.27S 39.43W
Pedra do Sino 55 Kf 22.27S 43.03W
Pedra Lume 32 Cf 16.46N 22.54W
Pedras, Rio das- 55 Ia 13.30S 47.09W
Pedras Altas, Coxilha- 55 Fj 31.45S 53.35W
Pedregal 54 Da 11.01N 70.08W
Pedreiras 54 Jd 4.34S 44.39W
Pedriceña 48 He 25.06N 103.47W
Pedrizas, Puerto de las- 13 Hh 36.55N 4.30W
Pedro Afonso 54 Ie 8.59S 48.11W
Pedro Bank (EN) 49 He 17.00N 78.30W
Pedro Betancourt 49 Gb 22.44N 81.17W
Pedro Cays 47 Ie 17.00N 77.50W
Pedro de Valdivia 56 Gb 22.37S 69.38W
Pedro Gomes 55 Ed 18.04S 54.32W
Pedro Gonzáles, Isla- 49 Hi 8.24N 79.06W
Pedro II 54 Jd 4.25S 41.28W
Pedro II, Ilha- 54 Ec 1.10N 66.44W
Pedro Juan Caballero 56 Ib 22.34S 55.37W
Pedro Leopoldo 55 Jd 19.38S 44.03W
Pedro Luro 56 He 39.29S 62.41W
Pedro Lustoza 55 Gg 25.49S 51.51W
Pedro Montoya 48 Jg 21.38N 99.49W
Pedro Osorio 56 Jd 31.51S 52.45W
Pedro R. Fernández 55 Ci 28.45S 58.39W
Pedro Severo 55 Ec 17.40S 54.02W
Pedroso, Sierra del- 13 Gf 38.35N 5.35W
Peebles 9 Jf 55.39N 3.12W
Pee Dee River 38 Lf 33.21N 79.16W
Peekskill 44 Ke 41.18N 73.56W
Peel 38 Fc 67.37N 134.40W
Peel 11 Lc 51.25N 5.50 E
Peel 9 Ig 54.13N 4.40W
Peel Sound 42 Hb 73.00N 96.00W
Peene 10 Jb 54.09N 13.46 E
Peer 12 Hc 51.08N 5.28 E
Peera Peera Poolanna Lake 59 He 26.30S 138.00 E
Peetz 45 Ef 40.58N 103.07W
Pegasus, Port- 62 Bg 47.10S 167.40 E
Pegasus Bay 61 Dh 43.20S 172.50 E
Pegnitz 10 Gg 49.29N 11.00 E
Pegnitz 10 Hg 49.45N 11.33 E
Pego 13 Lf 38.51N 0.07W
Pegtymel 20 Mc 69.47N 174.00 E
Pegu → Bago 22 Lh 17.30N 96.30 E
Pegu Yoma 21 Lh 19.00N 95.50 E
Pegwell Bay 12 Dc 51.18N 1.23 E
Pehčevo 15 Fh 41.46N 22.54 E
Pehlivanköy 15 Jh 41.21N 26.55 E
Pehuajó 56 He 35.48S 61.53W
Pei-ching Shih → Beijing Shi [4] 27 Kc 40.15N 116.30 E
Peine 10 Gd 52.19N 10.14 E
Peipsi järv = Peipus, Lake- (EN) 5 Id 58.45N 27.30 E
Peipus, Lake- (EN) = Čudskoje Ozero 5 Id 58.45N 27.30 E
Peipus, Lake- (EN) = Peipsi järv 5 Id 58.45N 27.30 E
Peixe 54 If 12.03S 48.32W
Peixe, Lagoa do- 55 Gj 31.18S 51.00W
Peixe, Rio do- [Braz.] 55 Ge 21.31S 51.58W
Peixe, Rio do- [Braz.] 55 Gb 14.06S 50.51W
Peixe, Rio do- [Braz.] 55 Hc 17.37S 48.29W
Peixe, Rio do- [Braz.] 55 Fc 16.32S 52.38W
Peixe, Rio do- [Braz.] 55 Gh 27.27S 51.54W
Peixe de Couro, Rio- 55 Ec 17.21S 55.29W
Peixes, Rio dos- 55 Hb 15.10S 49.30W
Peixian (Yunhe) 28 Dg 34.44N 116.56 E
Peixoto, Represa de- 54 Ih 20.30S 46.30W
Pejantan, Pulau- 26 Ef 0.07N 107.14 E
Pëjde/Pöide 8 Jf 58.30N 22.50 E
Pek 15 Ee 44.46N 21.33 E
Pekalongan 26 Eh 6.53S 109.40 E
Pekan 26 Df 3.30N 103.25 E
Pekin 43 Jc 40.35N 89.40W
Peking (EN) = Beijing 22 Nf 39.55N 116.23 E
Pekulnei, Hrebet- 20 Mc 66.30N 176.00 E
Pelabuhanratu 26 Eh 6.59S 106.33 E
Pelagie, Isole- 5 Hh 35.40N 12.40 E
Pelagonija 15 Eh 41.05N 21.30 E
Pélagos 15 Hj 39.20N 24.05 E
Pelaihari 26 Fg 3.48S 114.45 E
Pelat, Mont- 11 Mj 44.16N 6.42 E
Pelawanbesar 26 Gf 1.10N 117.54 E
Pélé 63b Dc 17.30S 168.24 E
Peleaga, Vîrful- 15 Fd 45.22N 22.53 E
Peleduj 20 Ge 59.40N 112.38 E
Pelée, Montagne- 47 Le 14.48N 61.10W
Pelee, Point- 44 Fe 41.54N 82.30W
Pelee Island 44 Fe 41.46N 82.39W
Peleliu Island 57 Ed 7.01N 134.15 E
Peleng, Pulau- 26 Hg 1.20S 123.10 E
Pelhřimov 10 Lg 49.26N 15.13 E
Pelican Lake 45 Gb 49.20N 99.35W
Pelicanpunt 37 Ad 22.54S 14.26 E
Peligre, Lac de- 49 Ld 18.52N 71.56W
Pelinaion Óros 15 Ik 38.32N 26.00 E
Pelješac 14 Lh 42.55N 17.25 E
Pelkosenniemi 7 Gc 67.07N 27.30 E
Pella 45 Jf 41.25N 92.55W
Pélla 15 Fi 40.46N 22.34 E
Pellegrini 56 He 36.16S 63.09W
Pellice 14 Bf 44.50N 7.38 E
Pellinge/Pellinki 8 Kd 60.15N 25.50 E
Pellinki/Pellinge 8 Kd 60.15N 25.50 E
Pello 7 Fc 66.47N 24.01 E
Pellworm 10 Eb 54.30N 8.40 E
Pelly 38 Fc 62.47N 137.19W
Pelly Bay 42 Ic 68.50N 90.10W
Pelly Bay 39 Kc 68.52N 89.55W
Pelly Crossing 42 Dd 62.50N 136.35W
Pelly Mountains 42 Ed 61.30N 132.00W
Peloncillo Mountains 46 Kj 32.15N 109.10W
Pelón de Nado, Cerro- 48 Jg 20.05N 99.55W
Peloponnesus (EN) = Pelopónnisos 5 Ih 37.40N 22.00 E
Peloponnesus (EN) = Pelopónnisos 15 El 37.40N 22.00 E
Pelopónnisos [2] 15 El 37.40N 22.00 E
Pelopónnisos = Peloponnesus (EN) 15 El 37.40N 22.00 E
Pelopónnisos = Peloponnesus (EN) 5 Ih 37.40N 22.00 E
Peloritani 14 Jl 38.05N 15.20 E
Peloro, Capo- o Faro, Punta del- 14 Jl 38.16N 15.39 E
Pelotas 53 Ki 31.46S 52.20W
Pelotas, Rio- 56 Jc 27.28S 51.55W
Pelplin 10 Oc 53.56N 18.42 E
Pelvoux, Massif du- 5 Gg 44.55N 6.20 E
Pelym 19 Gd 59.40N 63.05 E
Pelymski Tuman, Ozero- 17 Kf 60.05N 63.05 E
Pemalang 26 Eh 6.54S 109.22 E
Pemar/Paimio 8 Jd 60.27N 22.42 E
Pematangsiantar 22 Li 2.57N 99.03 E
Pemba [3] 36 Hd 5.02S 40.00 E
Pemba [Moz.] 31 Lj 12.57S 40.30 E
Pemba [Zam.] 36 Ef 16.31S 27.22 E
Pemba Channel 36 Gd 5.10S 39.20 E
Pemba Island 30 Ki 5.10S 39.48 E
Pemberton [Austl.] 59 Df 34.28S 116.01 E
Pemberton [B.C.-Can.] 46 Da 50.20N 122.48W
Pembina 42 Gf 54.45N 114.17W
Pembina 43 Hb 48.58N 97.15W
Pembina River 43 Hb 48.56N 97.15W
Pembroke [Ont.-Can.] 42 Jg 45.49N 77.07W
Pembroke [Wales-U.K.] 9 Ij 51.41N 4.55W
Pembuang 26 Fg 3.24S 112.33 E
Peña, Sierra de la- 13 Lb 42.31N 0.38W
Penafiel 13 Dc 41.12N 8.17W
Peñafiel 13 Hc 41.36N 4.07W
Peñagolosa/Penyagolosa 13 Ld 40.13N 0.21W
Peña Gorda, Cerro- 48 Gg 20.40N 104.55W
Peñalara 13 Id 40.51N 3.57W
Penalva 54 Id 3.18S 45.10W
Penamacor 13 Ed 40.10N 7.10W
Peña Nevada, Cerro- 38 Jg 23.46N 99.52W
Penápolis 55 Ge 21.24S 50.04W
Peñaranda de Bracamonte 13 Gd 40.54N 5.12W
Peñarroya 13 Ld 40.28N 0.43W
Peñarroya-Pueblonuevo 13 Gf 38.18N 5.16W
Peñas, Cabo de- 5 Fg 43.39N 5.51W
Penas, Golfo de- 52 Ij 47.22S 74.50W
Peñas, Punta- 54 Fa 10.44N 61.51W
Peñasco, Rio- 45 Dj 32.45N 104.19W
Pendé 35 Ad 9.07N 16.26 E
Pendembu [S.L.] 34 Cd 9.06N 12.12W
Pendembu [S.L.] 34 Cd 8.06N 10.42W
Pendik 15 Mi 40.53N 29.13 E
Pendjari 34 Fc 10.54N 0.51 E
Pendle Hill 9 Kh 53.52N 2.17W
Pendleton 39 He 45.40N 118.47W
Pendolo 26 Hg 2.05S 120.42 E
Pend Oreille Lake 43 Db 48.10N 116.11W
Pend Oreille River 43 Db 49.04N 117.37W
Pendžikent 19 Gh 39.29N 67.38 E
Peneda 13 Dc 41.58N 8.15W
Penedo 54 Kf 10.17S 36.36W
Penetanguishene 44 Hc 44.47N 79.55W
Penganga 25 Fe 19.53N 79.09 E
Pengcheng 27 Jd 36.25N 114.08 E
Penge 36 Dd 5.31S 24.37 E
Pengho Jiao 27 Jc 16.03N 112.35 E
Penghu Liehtao = Pescadores (EN) 27 Kg 23.30N 119.30 E
Penglai (Dengzhou) 27 Ld 37.44N 120.45 E
Pengshui 27 If 29.17N 108.13 E
Pengze 27 Kf 29.52N 116.34 E
Penha 55 Hh 26.46S 48.39W
Penhalonga 37 Ec 18.54S 32.40 E
Penibético, Sistema- 13 Ig 37.00N 3.30W
Peniche 13 Ce 39.21N 9.23W
Penicuik 9 Jf 55.50N 3.14W
Penida, Nusa- 26 Gh 8.44S 115.32 E
Peninsula Ibérica = Iberian Peninsula (EN) 5 Fg 40.00N 4.00W
Peñíscola 13 Md 40.21N 0.25 E
Penisola Salentina = Salentine Peninsula (EN) 5 Hg 40.30N 18.00 E
Penitente, Serra do- 54 Ie 8.45S 46.20W
Pénjamo 48 Ig 20.26N 101.44W
Penju, Kepulauan- 26 Ih 5.22S 127.46 E
Penmarch, Pointe de- 11 Bg 47.48N 4.22W
Penne 14 Hh 42.27N 13.55 E
Penne, Punta- 14 Lj 40.41N 17.56 E
Pennell Coast 66 Kf 71.00S 167.00 E
Penner 21 Kh 14.35N 80.10 E
Penn Hills 44 He 40.28N 79.53W
Pennines 5 Fe 54.10N 2.05W
Pennsylvania [2] 43 Lc 40.45N 77.30W
Penn Yan 44 Id 42.41N 77.03W
Penny Ice Cap 42 Kc 67.00N 65.10W
Penny Strait 42 Ha 76.35N 97.10W
Peno 7 Hh 56.57N 32.45 E
Penobscot Bay 44 Mc 44.15N 68.52W
Penobscot River 43 Nc 44.30N 68.50W
Penola 59 Ig 37.23S 140.50 E
Peñón del Rosario, Cerro- 48 Jh 19.40N 98.12W
Penong 58 Eh 31.55S 133.01 E
Penonomé 47 Hg 8.31N 80.22W
Pénot, Mont- 63b Cc 16.20S 167.31 E
Penrhyn Atoll 57 Le 9.00S 158.00W
Penrith 9 Kg 54.40N 2.44W
Penrith, Sydney- 59 Kf 33.45S 150.42 E
Pensacola 39 Kf 30.25N 87.13W
Pensacola Mountains 66 Rg 83.45S 55.00W
Pensacola Seamount (EN) 57 Lc 18.17N 157.20W
Pensamiento 55 Bb 14.44S 61.35W
Pensiangan 26 Gf 4.33N 116.19 E
Pentecôte, Ile- 57 Hf 15.45S 168.10 E
Penticton 42 Fg 49.30N 119.35W
Pentland 59 Jd 20.32S 145.24 E
Pentland Firth 9 Jc 58.44N 3.13W
Pentland Hills 9 Jf 55.48N 3.23W
Penwith 9 Hk 50.13N 5.40W
Penyagolosa/Peñagolosa 13 Ld 40.13N 0.21W
Penza 6 Ke 53.13N 45.00 E
Penzance 6 Ff 50.07N 5.33W
Penzenskaja Oblast [3] 19 Ee 53.15N 44.40 E
Penzhina Bay (EN) = Penžinskaja Guba 20 Ld 61.00N 163.00 E
Penžina 21 Sc 62.28N 165.18 E
Penžinskaja Guba = Penzhina Bay (EN) 20 Ld 61.00N 163.00 E
Penžinski Hrebet 20 Ld 62.15N 166.35 E
Peoples Creek 46 Kb 48.24N 108.19W
Peoria 39 Ke 40.42N 89.36W
Peoúia 24 Ee 34.53N 32.23 E
Pepa 36 Ed 7.42S 29.47 E
Pepel 34 Cd 8.35N 13.03W
Peperiguaçu, Rio- 55 Fh 27.10S 53.50W
Peqini 15 Ch 41.03N 19.45 E
Pequena, Lagoa- 55 Fj 31.36S 52.04W
Pequiri, Rio- 54 Gg 17.23S 55.38W
Perabumulih 26 Dg 3.27S 104.15 E
Perälä 8 Ib 62.28N 21.36 E
Perales, Puerto de- 13 Fd 40.15N 6.41W
Pérama 15 Hn 35.22N 24.42 E
Peräseinäjoki 8 Jb 62.34N 23.04 E
Perche, Col de la- 11 Il 42.30N 2.06 E
Perche, Collines du- 11 Gf 48.25N 0.40 E
Percival Lakes 59 Ed 21.25S 125.00 E
Percy Islands 59 Kd 21.40S 150.15 E
Perdasdefogu 14 Dk 39.41N 9.26 E
Perdida, Sierra- 48 Hd 27.30N 103.30W
Perdido, Monte- 5 Gg 42.40N 0.05 E
Perdido, Rio- 55 Df 22.10S 57.33W
Perdizes 55 Id 19.21S 47.17W
Perečin 10 Sh 48.44N 22.29 E
Pereginskoje 16 De 48.49N 24.12 E
Pereira 54 Cc 4.48N 75.42W
Pereira Barreto 56 Jb 20.38S 51.07W
Perejaslav-Hmelnicki 16 Gd 50.04N 31.27 E
Perejil, Isla de- 13 Ig 35.55N 5.26W
Pereljub 16 Qd 51.52N 50.20 E
Peremennyj, Cape- 66 He 66.08S 105.30 E
Peremyšliany 10 Ug 49.38N 24.35 E
Perenjori 59 De 29.26S 116.17 E
Pereščepino 16 Ie 48.59N 35.22 E
Pereslavl-Zalesski 7 Jh 56.45N 38.55 E
Peretu 15 Ie 44.03N 25.05 E
Peretyčiha 20 Ig 47.10N 138.35 E
Perevolocki 16 Sd 51.51N 54.15 E
Pergamino 56 Hd 33.53S 60.35W
Pergamon 15 Kj 39.08N 27.13 E
Perge 24 Dd 37.00N 30.10 E
Pergine Valsugana 14 Fd 46.04N 11.14 E
Pergola 14 Gg 43.34N 12.50 E
Perham 45 Ic 46.36N 95.34W
Perho 7 Fe 63.13N 24.25 E
Periam 15 Dc 46.03N 20.52 E
Péribonca, Rivière- 42 Kg 48.44N 72.06W
Perico 56 Hb 24.23S 65.00W
Pericos 48 Fe 25.03N 107.42W
Périgord 11 Gi 45.00N 0.30 E
Perigoso, Canal- 54 Ic 0.05N 49.40W
Périgueux 11 Gi 45.11N 0.43 E
Perijá, Sierra de- 52 Ie 10.00N 73.00W
Peristerá 15 Gj 39.12N 23.59 E
Perito Moreno 53 Ij 46.36S 70.56W
Perkam, Tanjung- = Urville, Cape d'- (EN) 26 Kg 1.28S 137.54 E
Perković 14 Kg 43.41N 16.06 E
Perlas, Archipiélago de las- 47 Ig 8.25N 79.00W
Perlas, Cayos de- 49 Fg 12.28N 83.28W
Perlas, Laguna de- 49 Fg 12.30N 83.40W
Perlas, Punta de- 49 Fg 12.23N 83.30W
Perleberg 10 Hc 53.04N 11.52 E
Perlez 15 Dd 45.12N 20.23 E
Perm 6 Ld 58.00N 56.15 E
Përmeti 15 Di 40.14N 20.21 E
Permskaja Oblast [3] 19 Fd 59.00N 57.00 E
Pernambuco [2] 54 Ke 8.30S 37.30W
Pernik 15 Gg 42.36N 23.02 E
Pernik [2] 15 Fg 42.35N 22.50 E
Perniö/Bjärna 7 Ff 60.12N 23.08 E
Péronne 11 Ie 49.56N 2.56 E
Perote 48 Kh 19.34N 97.14W
Perpignan 6 Gg 42.41N 2.53 E
Perro, Laguna del- 45 Di 34.40N 105.57W
Perros-Guirec 11 Cf 48.49N 3.27W
Perry [Fl.-U.S.] 44 Fj 30.07N 83.35W
Perry [Ga.-U.S.] 44 Fi 32.27N 83.44W
Perry [Ia.-U.S.] 45 If 41.50N 94.06W
Perry [Ok.-U.S.] 45 Hh 36.17N 97.17W
Perry Lake 45 Ig 39.20N 95.30W
Perryton 45 Fh 36.24N 100.48W
Perryville 40 He 55.54N 159.10W
Persan 12 Ee 49.09N 2.16 E
Perşani, Munţii- 15 Id 45.40N 25.15 E
Persberg 8 Fe 59.45N 14.15 E
Persembe 24 Gb 41.04N 37.46 E
Persepolis 24 Oh 29.57N 52.52 E
Perseverancia 54 Ff 14.44S 62.48W
Persian Gulf (EN) = Al-Khalīj al-'Arabī 21 Hg 27.00N 51.00 E
Persian Gulf (EN) = Khalīj-e Fārs 21 Hg 27.00N 51.00 E
Perstorp 8 Eh 56.08N 13.23 E
Pertek 24 Hc 38.50N 39.22 E
Perth [Austl.] 58 Ch 31.56S 115.50 E
Perth [Ont.-Can.] 44 Ic 44.54N 76.15W
Perth [Scot.-U.K.] 9 Je 56.24N 3.28W
Perth Amboy 44 Je 40.32N 74.17W
Perth-Andover 44 Nb 46.44N 67.42W
Perth-Armadale 59 Df 32.09S 116.00 E
Perth-Fremantle 59 Df 32.03S 115.45 E
Perth-Kalamunda 59 Df 31.57S 116.03 E
Perth-Mundaring 59 Df 31.54S 116.10 E
Perthus, Col de-/Portús, Coll del- 13 Ob 42.28N 2.51 E
Perthus, Col du- 13 Ob 42.28N 2.51 E
Pertuis 11 Lk 43.41N 5.30 E
Pertusato, Capo- 11a Bb 41.21N 9.11 E
Perú [1] 53 Ig 10.00S 76.00W
Peru [Il.-U.S.] 45 Lf 41.20N 89.08W
Peru [In.-U.S.] 44 De 40.45N 86.04W
Perú, Altiplano del- 54 Df 15.00S 72.00W
Peruaçu, Rio- 55 Jb 15.11S 44.07W
Peru Basin (EN) 3 Mk 17.00S 90.00W
Peru-Chile Trench (EN) 3 Nl 20.00S 73.00W
Perugia 6 Hg 43.08N 12.22 E
Perugorria 55 Ci 29.20S 58.37W
Peruibe 55 Ib 24.19S 47.00W
Perušić 14 Jf 44.39N 15.22 E
Péruwelz 12 Fd 50.31N 3.35 E

Index Symbols

[1] Independent Nation
[2] State, Region
[3] District, County
[4] Municipality
[5] Colony, Dependency
Continent
Physical Region
Historical or Cultural Region
Mount, Mountain
Volcano
Hill
Mountains, Mountain Range
Hills, Escarpment
Plateau, Upland
Pass, Gap
Plain, Lowland
Delta
Salt Flat
Valley, Canyon
Crater, Cave
Karst Features
Depression
Polder
Desert, Dunes
Forest, Woods
Heath, Steppe
Oasis
Cape, Point
Coast, Beach
Cliff
Peninsula
Isthmus
Sandbank
Island
Atoll
Rock, Reef
Islands, Archipelago
Rocks, Reefs
Coral Reef
Well, Spring
Geyser
River, Stream
Waterfall Rapids
River Mouth, Estuary
Lake
Salt Lake
Intermittent Lake
Reservoir
Swamp, Pond
Canal
Glacier
Ice Shelf, Pack Ice
Ocean
Sea
Gulf, Bay
Strait, Fjord
Lagoon
Bank
Seamount
Tablemount
Ridge
Shelf
Basin
Escarpment, Sea Scarp
Fracture
Trench, Abyss
National Park, Reserve
Point of Interest
Recreation Site
Cave, Cavern
Historic Site
Ruins
Wall, Walls
Church, Abbey
Temple
Scientific Station
Airport
Port
Lighthouse
Mine
Tunnel
Dam, Bridge

Pervari 24 Jd 37.54N 42.36 E
Pervomajsk [R.S.F.S.R.] 19 Ee 54.52N 43.48 E
Pervomajsk [Ukr.-U.S.S.R.] 16 Ke 48.36N 38.32 E
Pervomajsk [Ukr.-U.S.S.R.] 19 Df 48.03N 30.52 E
Pervomajski [Bye.-U.S.S.R.] 10 Vc 53.52N 25.33 E
Pervomajski [Kaz.-U.S.S.R.] 19 Ie 50.15N 81.59 E
Pervomajski [R.S.F.S.R.] 16 Lc 53.18N 40.15 E
Pervomajski [R.S.F.S.R.] 19 Ec 64.26N 40.48 E
Pervomajski [R.S.F.S.R.] 17 Ji 54.52N 61.08 E
Pervomajski [R.S.F.S.R.] 16 Sd 51.34N 54.59 E
Pervomajski [Ukr.-U.S.S.R.] 16 Je 49.24N 36.15 E
Pervouralsk 19 Fd 57.00N 60.00 E
Pervy Kurilski Proliv 20 Kf 50.50N 156.50 E
Perwez/Perwijs 12 Gd 50.37N 4.49 E
Perwijs/Perwez 12 Gd 50.37N 4.49 E
Pes 7 Ig 59.10N 35.18 E
Peša 17 Cc 66.50N 47.32 E
Pesaro 14 Gg 43.54N 12.55 E
Pescadores (EN)=Penghu Liehtao 27 Kg 23.30N 119.30 E
Pescadores, Punta- 48 Ef 23.45N 109.45W
Pesčany, Mys- 16 Qh 43.10N 51.18 E
Pesčany, Ostrov 20 Gb 74.20N 115.55 E
Pescara 14 Ih 42.28N 14.13 E
Pescara 6 Hg 42.28N 14.13 E
Pescasseroli 14 Hi 41.48N 13.47 E
Peschici 14 Ki 41.57N 16.01 E
Pescia 14 Eg 43.54N 10.41 E
Pescocostanzo 14 Ii 41.53N 14.04 E
Peshāwar 22 Jf 34.01N 71.33 E
Peshkopia 15 Dh 41.41N 20.26 E
Pesio 14 Bf 44.28N 7.53 E
Peskovka 7 Mg 59.03N 52.22 E
Pesmes 11 Lg 47.17N 5.34 E
Pesočny 8 Nd 60.05N 30.20 E
Peso da Régua 13 Ec 41.10N 7.47W
Pesqueira 54 Ke 8.22S 36.42W
Pesqueria, Rio- 48 Je 25.54N 99.11W
Pessac 11 Fj 44.48N 0.37W
Pest [2] 10 Pi 47.25N 19.20 E
Pešter 15 Df 43.05N 20.02 E
Peštera 15 Hg 42.02N 24.18 E
Pestovo 19 Dd 58.36N 35.47 E
Petacalco, Bahía de- 47 De 17.57N 102.05W
Petah Tiqwa 24 Ff 32.05N 34.53 E
Petäjävesi 8 Kb 62.15N 25.12 E
Petal 45 Lk 31.21N 89.17W
Petalioí 15 Hl 38.01N 24.17 E
Petalioí, Gulf of- (EN) = Petalión, Kólpos- 15 Hk 38.00N 24.05 E
Petalión, Kólpos- = Petalioi, Gulf of- (EN) 15 Hk 38.00N 24.05 E
Petaluma 46 Dg 38.14N 122.39W
Pétange/Petingen 12 He 49.33N 5.53 E
Petare 54 Ea 10.29N 66.49W
Petatlán 48 Ii 17.31N 101.16W
Petatlán, Rio- 48 Fd 26.09N 107.45W
Petauke 36 Fe 14.15S 31.20 E
Petén 47 Fe 16.15N 89.50W
Petén [3] 49 Be 16.50N 90.00W
Petén Itzá, Lago- 49 Ce 16.59N 89.50W
Petenwell Lake 45 Ld 44.05N 89.45W
Peterborough [Austl.] 59 Hf 32.58S 138.50 E
Peterborough [Eng.-U.K.] 9 Mi 52.35N 0.15W
Peterborough [Ont.-Can.] 42 Jh 44.18N 78.19W
Peterhead 9 Ld 57.30N 1.46W
Peter I, Oy- 66 Pe 68.47S 90.35W
Peter Island 51a Db 18.22N 64.35W
Peterlee 9 Lg 54.46N 1.19W
Petermann Gletscher 41 Fb 80.45N 61.00W
Petermann Ranges 59 Fd 25.00S 129.45 E
Petermanns Bjerg 67 Md 73.10N 28.00W
Peter Pond Lake 42 Ge 55.55N 108.40W
Petersberg 10 He 51.35N 11.57 E
Petersburg [Ak.-U.S.] 40 Me 56.49N 132.57W
Petersburg [In.-U.S.] 44 Df 38.30N 87.16W
Petersburg [Va.-U.S.] 43 Ld 37.14N 77.24W
Petersburg [W.V.-U.S.] 44 Hf 39.01N 79.09W
Petersfield 9 Mk 51.00N 0.56W
Petershagen 12 Kb 52.23N 8.58 E
Peter the Great Bay (EN)= Petra Velikogo, Zaliv- 21 Pe 42.40N 132.00 E
Petilia Policastro 14 Kk 39.07N 16.47 E
Petingen/Pétange 12 He 49.33N 5.53 E
Petit-Bourg 51eAb 16.12N 61.36W
Petit-Canal 51eBb 16.23N 61.29W
Petit Canouan 51nBb 12.47N 61.17W
Petit Cul-de-Sac Marin 51eAb 16.12N 61.33W
Petite Kabylie 13 Rh 36.35N 5.25 E
Petite Rivière de l'Artibonite 49 Kd 19.08N 72.29W
Petites Pyrénées 11 Hk 43.05N 1.10 E
Petite-Terre, Iles de la- 51eBb 16.10N 61.07W
Petit-Goâve 49 Kd 18.26N 72.52W
Petit Martinique Island 51p Ca 12.32N 61.22W
Petit-Mécatina, Rivière du- 42 Lf 50.39N 59.25W
Petit Morin 11 Jf 48.56N 3.07 E
Petit Mustique Island 51nBb 12.51N 61.13W
Petit Nevis Island 51nBb 12.58N 61.15W
Petitot 42 Fd 60.14N 123.29W
Petit Saint-Bernard, Col du- 14 Ae 45.40N 6.55 E
Petit Saint Vincent Island 51nBb 12.33N 61.23W
Petit Savanne 51gBb 15.15N 61.17W
Petitsikapau Lake 42 Kf 54.40N 66.25W
Petkula 7 Gc 67.40N 26.41 E
Petlalcingo 48 Kh 18.05N 97.54W
Peto 47 Gd 20.08N 88.55W
Petorca 56 Fd 32.15S 71.00W
Petoskey 44 Ec 45.22N 84.57W
Petra 24 Fg 30.19N 35.29 E
Petralia Soprana 14 Im 37.47N 14.06 E
Petra Pervogo, Hrebet- 18 He 39.00N 71.10 E
Petra Velikogo, Zaliv-= Peter the Great Bay (EN) 21 Pe 42.40N 132.00 E
Petre, Point- 44 Id 43.50N 77.09W
Petre Bay 62 Je 43.55S 176.40W
Petrel 66 Re 63.28S 56.17W
Petrela 15 Ch 41.15N 19.51 E
Petrella Tifernina 14 Ii 41.41N 14.42 E
Petrič 15 Gh 41.24N 23.13 E
Pétrie, Récif- 61 Bc 18.30S 164.20 E
Petrikov 16 Fc 52.08N 28.31 E
Petrila 15 Gd 45.27N 23.25 E
Petrinja 14 Ke 45.27N 16.17 E
Petrodvorec 7 Gg 59.53N 29.50 E
Petrólea 54 Db 8.30N 72.35W
Petrolia 44 Fd 42.52N 82.09W
Petrolina 54 Je 9.24S 40.30W
Petrolina de Goiás 55 Hc 16.06S 49.20W
Petronanski prohod 15 Gf 43.08N 23.08 E
Petronell 14 Kb 48.07N 16.51 E
Petropavlovka 20 Ff 50.38N 105.19 E
Petropavlovsk 22 Id 54.54N 69.06 E
Petropavlovsk-Kamčatski 22 Rd 53.01N 158.39 E
Petrópolis 53 Lh 22.31S 43.10W
Petroşani 15 Gd 45.25N 23.22 E
Petrovac [Yugo.] 15 Bg 42.12N 18.57 E
Petrovac [Yugo.] 15 Ee 44.22N 21.25 E
Petrova Gora 14 Je 45.17N 15.47 E
Petrovaradin 15 Cd 45.15N 19.53 E
Petrovka 15 Nc 46.55N 30.40 E
Petrovsk 19 Ee 52.18N 45.23 E
Petrovski Jam 7 Ie 63.18N 35.15 E
Petrovsk-Zabajkalski 22 Md 51.17N 108.50 E
Petrov Val 16 Nd 50.10N 45.12 E
Petrozavodsk 6 Jc 61.47N 34.20 E
Petuhovo 19 Gd 55.06N 67.58 E
Petuški 7 Ji 55.59N 39.28 E
Petworth 12 Bd 50.59N 0.36W
Peuetsagoe, Gunung- 26 Cf 4.55N 96.20 E
Peumo 56 Fd 34.24S 71.10W
Peureulak 26 Cf 4.48N 97.53 E
Pevek 22 Tc 69.42N 170.17 E
Pevensey 12 Cd 50.48N 0.21 E
Pevensey Bay 12 Cd 50.48N 0.22 E
Peza 7 Kd 65.34N 44.33 E
Pézenas 11 Jk 43.27N 3.25 E
Pezinok 10 Nh 48.18N 17.16 E
Pfaffenhofen an der Ilm 10 Hh 48.32N 11.31 E
Pfaffenhoffen 12 Jf 48.51N 7.37 E
Pfalz 12 Je 49.20N 7.57 E
Pfalzel, Trier- 12 Ie 49.46N 6.41 E
Pfälzer Bergland 10 Dg 49.35N 7.30 E
Pfälzer Wald 10 Dg 49.15N 7.50 E
Pfarrkirchen 10 Ih 48.26N 12.52 E
Pfinz 12 Ke 49.11N 8.25 E
Pfinztal 12 Ke 49.02N 8.30 E
Pforzheim an der Enz 10 Eh 48.53N 8.42 E
Pfrimm 12 Ke 49.39N 8.22 E
Pfullendorf 10 Fi 47.55N 9.15 E
Pfunds 14 Ed 46.58N 10.33 E
Pfungstadt 12 Ke 49.48N 8.36 E
Phalaborwa 37 Ed 23.55S 31.13 E
Phalodi 25 Ec 27.08N 72.22 E
Pha-an 25 Je 16.53N 97.38 E
Phangnga 25 Jg 8.28N 98.32 E
Phan Ly Cham 25 Lf 11.13N 108.31 E
Phanom 25 Jg 8.49N 98.50 E
Phan Rang 25 Lf 11.34N 108.59 E
Phan Thiet 25 Lf 10.56N 108.06 E
Pharr 45 Gm 26.12N 98.11W
Phatthalung 25 Kg 7.38N 100.04 E
Phayao 25 Ke 18.07N 100.11 E
Phenix City 43 Je 32.29N 85.01W
Phet Buri 25 Jf 13.06N 99.56 E
Phetchabun, Thiu Khao- 25 Ke 16.20N 100.55 E
Phichit 25 Ke 16.24N 100.21 E
Philadelphia [Ms.-U.S.] 45 Lj 32.46N 89.07W
Philadelphia [Pa.-U.S.] 39 Lf 39.57N 75.07W
Philae 33 Fe 23.35N 32.52 E
Philip 45 Fd 44.02N 101.40W
Philippeville 11 Kd 50.12N 4.33 E
Philippi 44 Gf 39.08N 80.03W
Philippi (EN) = Filippoi 15 Hh 41.02N 24.18 E
Philippi, Lake- 59 Hd 24.20S 139.00 E
Philippi Glacier 66 Ge 66.45S 88.20 E
Philippine Basin (EN) 3 Ih 17.00N 132.00 E
Philippine Islands (EN)= Pilipinas 21 Oh 13.00N 122.00 E
Philippines (EN)=Pilipinas [1] 22 Oh 13.00N 122.00 E
Philippine Sea (EN) 21 Oh 20.00N 130.00 E
Philippine Trench (EN) 3 Ii 9.00N 127.00 E
Philippsburg 12 Ke 49.14N 8.27 E
Philipsburg [Mt.-U.S.] 46 Ic 46.20N 113.08W
Philipsburg [Neth.Ant.] 50 Ec 18.01N 63.04W
Philip Smith Mountains 40 Jc 68.30N 148.00W
Philipstown 37 Cf 30.26S 24.29 E
Phillipsburg 45 Gg 39.45N 99.19W
Philpots 42 Jb 74.55N 80.00W
Phitsanulok 22 Mh 16.49N 100.15 E
Phnom Penh (EN)=Phnum Pénh 22 Mh 11.33N 104.55 E
Phnum Penh=Phnom Penh (EN) 22 Mh 11.33N 104.55 E
Phoenix 39 Hf 33.27N 112.05W
Phoenix → Rawaki Atoll 57 Je 3.43S 170.43W
Phoenix Islands 57 Je 4.00S 172.00W
Phôngsali 25 Kd 21.41N 102.06 E
Phrae 25 Ke 18.07N 100.11 E
Phra Nakhom Si Ayutthaya 22 Mh 14.21N 100.33 E
Phrygia 15 Mk 38.30N 29.50 E
Phu Cuong 25 Lf 10.58N 106.39 E
Phuket 22 Li 7.54N 98.24 E
Phuket, Ko- 21 Li 8.00N 98.20 E
Phulbani 25 Gd 20.28N 84.14 E
Phumĭ Mlu Prey 25 Lf 13.48N 105.16 E
Phumĭ Sâmraông 25 Kf 14.11N 103.31 E
Phu My 25 Lf 14.10N 109.03 E
Phuoc Binh 25 Lf 11.50N 106.58 E
Phu Quoc, Dao- 25 Kf 10.12N 104.00 E
Phu Tho 25 Ld 21.24N 105.13 E
Phu Vinh → Tra Vinh 25 Lg 9.56N 106.20 E
Piaanu Pass 64d Ab 7.20N 151.26 E
Piacenza 14 De 45.01N 9.40 E
Piana degli Albanesi 14 Hm 37.59N 13.17 E
Piana Mwanga 36 Ed 7.40S 28.10 E
Piancó 54 Ke 7.12S 37.57W
Pianguan 27 Jd 39.28N 111.32 E
Pianosa [It.] 14 Jh 42.15N 15.45 E
Pianosa [It.] 14 Eh 42.35N 10.05 E
Piaseczno 10 Rd 52.05N 21.01 E
Piaski 10 Se 51.08N 22.51 E
Piątek 10 Pd 52.05N 19.28 E
Piatra 15 If 43.49N 25.10 E
Piatra Neamţ 15 Jc 46.55N 26.20 E
Piatra Olt 15 He 44.22N 24.16 E
Piauí [2] 54 Je 7.00S 43.00W
Piauí, Rio- 52 Lf 6.38S 42.42W
Piave 5 Hf 45.32N 12.44 E
Piaxtla, Punta- 48 Ff 23.38N 106.50W
Piaxtla, Rio- 48 Ff 23.42N 106.49W
Piazza Armerina 14 Im 37.23N 14.22 E
Pibor 35 Ed 8.26N 33.13 E
Pibor Post 35 Ed 6.48N 33.08 E
Pica 56 Gb 20.30S 69.21W
Picachos, Cerro dos- 48 Bc 29.25N 114.10W
Picardie = Picardy (EN) 11 Je 50.00N 3.30 E
Picardy (EN) = Picardie 11 Je 50.00N 3.30 E
Picayune 45 Lk 30.26N 89.41W
Picentini, Monti- 14 Jj 40.45N 15.10 E
Pichanal 53 Jh 23.20S 64.15W
Pichilemu 56 Fd 34.23S 72.00W
Pichilingue 48 De 24.20N 110.20W
Pichna 10 Oe 51.50N 18.40 E
Pichones, Cayos- 49 Ff 15.45N 82.55W
Pichucalco 48 Mi 17.31N 93.04W
Pickering 9 Mg 54.14N 0.46W
Pickering, Vale of- 9 Mg 54.10N 0.45W
Pickle Lake 42 If 51.29N 90.10W
Pickwick Lake 44 Ch 34.55N 88.10W
Pico 30 Ee 38.28N 28.20W
Picos 53 Lf 7.05S 41.28W
Pico Truncado 56 Gg 46.48S 67.58W
Picquigny 11 Ie 49.57N 2.09 E
Picton 61 Dh 41.18S 174.00 E
Pictou 42 Lg 45.41N 62.43W
Picunda 16 Lh 43.12N 40.21 E
Pidurutalagala 21 Ki 7.00N 80.46 E
Piedecuesta 54 Db 6.59N 73.03W
Piedimonte Matese 14 Ii 41.20N 14.22 E
Piedmont [Al.-U.S.] 44 Ei 33.55N 85.37W
Piedmont [Mo.-U.S.] 45 Kh 37.09N 90.42W
Piedmont (EN) = Piemonte [2] 14 Be 45.00N 8.00 E
Piedmont Plateau 43 Kf 35.00N 81.00W
Piedra 13 Kc 41.19N 1.48W
Piedra, Monasterio de- 13 Kc 41.10N 1.50W
Piedrabuena 13 He 39.02N 4.10W
Piedrafita, Puerto de- 13 Fb 42.36N 6.57W
Piedrahita 13 Gd 40.28N 5.19W
Piedras 54 Cd 3.38S 79.54W
Piedras, Punta- 56 Ie 35.25S 57.08W
Piedras, Rio de las- 54 Ef 12.30S 69.14W
Piedras Negras 39 Ig 28.42N 100.31W
Piedras Negras 49 Be 17.12N 91.15W
Piedra Sola 56 Id 32.04S 56.21W
Piekary Śląskie 10 Of 50.24N 18.58 E
Pieksämäki 7 Ge 62.18N 27.08 E
Pielach 14 Jb 48.15N 15.22 E
Pielavesi 7 Ge 63.14N 26.45 E
Pielinen 5 Ic 63.15N 29.40 E
Piemonte = Piedmont (EN) [2] 14 Be 45.00N 8.00 E
Pieniężno 10 Qb 54.15N 20.08 E
Pieni Salpausselkä 8 Lc 61.10N 27.20 E
Piennes 12 He 49.19N 5.47 E
Pienza 14 Fg 43.04N 11.41 E
Pierce 46 Hc 46.29N 115.48W
Piéria Óri 15 Fi 40.12N 22.07 E
Pierre 39 Ie 44.22N 100.21W
Pierrefitte-sur-Aire 12 Hf 48.54N 5.20 E
Pierrefonds 12 Ee 49.21N 2.59 E
Pierrelatte 11 Kj 44.23N 4.42 E
Pieskehaure 7 Dc 66.57N 16.30 E
Piešt'any 10 Nh 48.36N 17.50 E
Pietarsaari/Jakobstad 7 Fe 63.40N 22.42 E
Pietermaritzburg 31 Kk 29.37S 30.16 E
Pietersburg 31 Jk 23.54S 29.25 E
Pietraperzia 14 Im 37.25N 14.08 E
Pietrasanta 14 Eg 43.57N 10.14 E
Piet Retief 37 Ee 27.01S 30.50 E
Pietrii, Virful- 15 Fd 45.23N 22.40 E
Pietroşani 15 If 43.43N 25.38 E
Pietrosu, Virful- [Rom.] 15 Ib 47.08N 25.11 E
Pietrosu, Virful- [Rom.] 5 If 47.23N 25.33 E
Pieve di Cadore 14 Gd 46.26N 12.22 E
Pigeon Island 51k Ba 14.06N 60.58W
Pigeon River 45 Lb 48.02N 89.41W
Piggott 45 Kh 36.23N 90.11W
Pigg's Peak 37 Ee 25.58S 31.15 E
Pigs, Bay of- (EN)= Cochinos, Bahía de- 49 Gb 22.07N 81.10W
Pigüé 55 Am 37.37S 62.25W
Pi He 28 Dh 32.26N 116.34 E
Pihkva järv=Pskov, Lake- (EN) 7 Gg 58.00N 28.00 E
Pihlajavesi 7 Gf 61.45N 28.45 E
Pihlava 8 Ic 61.33N 21.36 E
Pihtipudas 7 Fe 63.23N 25.34 E
Piikkiö 8 Jd 60.26N 22.31 E
Piirisaar/Pirissar 8 Lf 58.23N 27.40 E
Pijijiapan 48 Mj 15.42N 93.14W
Pijol, Pico- 49 Df 15.06N 87.35W
Pikalevo 7 Ig 59.32N 34.03 E
Pikangikum 42 If 51.49N 94.00W
Pikelot Island 57 Fd 8.05N 147.38 E
Pikes Peak 43 Fd 38.51N 105.03W
Piketberg 37 Bf 32.54S 18.46 E
Pikiutdleq 41 Hf 64.45N 40.10W
Pikou 28 Ge 39.24N 122.21 E
Pikounda 36 Cb 0.33N 16.42 E
Piła 10 Mc 53.10N 16.44 E
Piła [2] 10 Mc 53.10N 16.45 E
Pila 55 Cm 36.01S 58.08W
Pila, Sierra de la- 13 Kf 38.16N 1.11W
Pilar [Arg.] 55 Bj 31.27S 61.15W
Pilar [Braz.] 54 Ke 9.36S 35.56W
Pilar [Par.] 56 Ic 26.52S 58.23W
Pilas Group 26 He 6.45N 121.35 E
Pilat, Mont- 11 Ki 45.23N 4.35 E
Pilatus 14 Cd 46.59N 8.20 E
Pilaya, Rio- 54 Fh 20.55S 64.04W
Pilcaniyeu 56 Ff 41.08S 70.40W
Pilcomayo, Rio- 52 Kh 25.21S 57.42W
Pile, Jezioro- 10 Mc 53.35N 16.30 E
Píli 15 Ej 39.28N 21.37 E
Pilibhit 25 Fc 28.38N 79.48 E
Pilica 10 Re 51.52N 21.17 E
Pílion Óros 15 Gj 39.24N 23.05 E
Pilipinas=Philippine Islands (EN) 21 Oh 13.00N 122.00 E
Pilipinas=Philippines (EN) [1] 22 Oh 13.00N 122.00 E
Pilis 10 Oi 47.41N 18.53 E
Pillahuincó, Sierra de- 55 Bn 38.18S 60.45W
Pillar, Cape- 59 Jh 43.15S 148.00 E
Pilna 7 Ki 55.33N 45.55 E
Pilões, Rio- 55 Gc 16.14S 50.54W
Pilões, Serra dos- 55 Ic 17.50S 47.13W
Pilón, Rio- 48 Je 25.32N 99.32W
Pilos 15 Em 36.55N 21.42 E
Pilos = Pylos (EN) 15 Em 36.56N 21.40 E
Pilot Peak 46 Hf 41.02N 114.06W
Pilot Rock 46 Fd 45.29N 118.50W
Pilsen (EN)=Plzeň 6 Hf 49.45N 13.24 E
Piltene 7 Eh 57.15N 21.42 E
Pilzno 10 Rg 49.59N 21.17 E
Pim 19 Hc 61.18N 71.57 E
Pimba 59 Hf 31.15S 136.47 E
Pimenteiras 54 Je 6.14S 41.25W
Pimža Jõgi 8 Lg 57.57N 27.59 E
Pina 13 Lc 41.29N 0.32W
Pinacate, Cerro- 48 Cb 31.45N 113.31W
Pinaki Atoll 57 Nf 19.22S 138.44W
Pinamar 55 Dm 37.07S 56.50W
Piñami, Arroyo- 48 Cd 27.44N 113.47W
Pinar 13 Gh 36.46N 5.26W
Pinarbaşi 24 Gc 38.50N 36.30 E
Pinar del Rio 39 Kg 22.25N 83.42W
Pinar del Rio [3] 49 Eb 22.35N 83.40W
Pinarello 11a Bb 41.41N 9.22 E
Pinarhisar 15 Kh 41.37N 27.30 E
Pinchbeck 12 Bb 52.48N 0.09W
Pincher Creek 42 Gg 49.30N 113.48W
Pinçon, Mont- 11 Ff 48.58N 0.37W
Pîncota 15 Ec 46.20N 21.42 E
Pindaíba, Ribeirão 55 Gb 14.48S 52.00W
Pindaré, Rio- 54 Jd 3.17S 44.47W
Pindaré-Mirim 54 Id 3.38S 45.21W
Pindaval 55 Dc 17.08S 56.09W
Pindhos Óros=Pindus Mountains (EN) 5 Ih 39.45N 21.30 E
Pindus Mountains (EN)= Pindhos Óros 5 Ih 39.45N 21.30 E
Pine Bluff 43 Ie 34.13N 92.01W
Pine Bluffs 46 Mf 41.11N 104.04W
Pine Creek 59 Gb 13.49S 131.49 E
Pine Falls 42 Hf 50.35N 96.15W
Pinega 19 Ec 64.42N 43.22 E
Pinega 5 Kc 64.08N 41.54 E
Pine Island Glacier 66 Of 75.00S 101.00W
Pineland 45 Jk 31.15N 93.58W
Pine Mountain [Ga.-U.S.] 44 Ei 32.51N 84.47W
Pine Mountain [U.S.] 44 Fg 36.55N 83.20W
Pine Pass 42 Fe 55.50N 122.30W
Pine Point 39 Hc 61.01N 114.15W
Pine Ridge 45 Ee 43.02N 102.33W
Pinerolo 14 Bf 44.53N 7.21 E
Pines, Isle of- (EN)= Juventud, Isla de la- 38 Kg 21.40N 82.50W
Pines, Isle of- (EN)=Pins, Ile des- 57 Hg 22.37S 167.30 E
Pines, Lake O' The 45 Ij 32.46N 94.35W
Pinetown 37 Ee 29.52S 30.46 E
Ping 21 Mh 15.42N 100.09 E
Pingbian 27 Hg 22.56N 103.46 E
Pingchang 27 Ie 31.38N 107.06 E
Pingding 28 Bf 37.48N 113.37 E
Pingdingbu → Guyuan 28 Cd 41.40N 115.41 E
Pingding Shan 28 Mb 46.39N 128.30 E
Pingdingshan 27 Je 33.41N 113.27 E
Pingdu 28 Ef 36.47N 119.57 E
Pingelap Atoll 57 Hd 6.13N 160.42 E
Pingelly 59 Df 32.32S 117.05 E
Pinggu 28 Dd 40.08N 117.07 E
Pingguo 27 Ig 23.21N 107.34 E
Pinghu 28 Fi 30.42N 121.02 E
Pingjiang 28 Bj 28.45N 113.37 E
Pingle 27 Jg 24.43N 110.42 E
Pingli 27 Ie 32.27N 109.21 E
Pingliang 22 Mf 35.32N 106.41 E
Pinglu (Jingping) 28 Be 39.32N 112.14 E
Pingluo 22 Mf 38.56N 106.34 E
Pingma → Tiandong 27 Ig 23.40N 107.09 E
Pingnan 27 Jg 23.38N 110.23 E
Pingouins, Ile des- 30 Mm 46.25S 50.19 E
Pingquan 27 Kc 41.00N 118.36 E
Pingshan 28 Ce 38.21N 114.01 E
Pingshun 28 Bf 36.12N 113.26 E
Pingtan 27 Kf 25.31N 119.48 E
Pingtung 27 Lg 22.40N 120.29 E
Pingüicas, Cerro- 48 Jg 21.10N 99.42W
Pingvallavatn 7a Bb 64.15N 21.09W
Pingvellir 7a Bb 64.17N 21.03W
Pingwu 27 He 32.27N 104.35 E
Pingxiang [China] 27 Ig 22.11N 106.46 E
Pingxiang [China] 27 Jf 27.43N 113.48 E
Pingyang 27 Lf 27.40N 120.30 E
Pingyao 27 Jd 37.12N 112.13 E
Pingyi 28 Dg 35.30N 117.38 E
Pingyin 28 Df 36.17N 116.26 E
Pingyu 28 Ci 32.58N 114.36 E
Pingyuan 28 Df 37.10N 116.25 E
Pinhal 55 If 22.12S 46.45W
Pinhão 55 Gg 25.43S 51.38W
Pinheir Machado 55 Fj 31.34S 53.23W
Pinhel 13 Ed 40.46N 7.04W
Pini, Pulau- 26 Cf 0.08N 98.40 E
Piniós [Grc.] 15 Fj 39.53N 22.44 E
Piniós [Grc.] 15 El 37.48N 21.14 E
Pinipel 63a Ba 4.24S 154.08 E
Pinjug 7 Lf 60.16N 47.54 E
Pinka 10 Mi 47.00N 16.35 E
Pink Mountain 42 Fe 56.06N 122.35W
Pinnaroo 59 Ig 35.16S 140.55 E
Pinneberg 10 Fc 53.39N 9.48 E
Pinnes, Ákra- 15 Hi 40.07N 24.18 E
Pinolosean 26 Hf 0.23N 124.07 E
Pinos 48 If 22.18N 101.34W
Pinos, Mount- 38 Hf 34.50N 119.09W
Pinos-Puente 13 Ig 37.15N 3.45W
Pinrang 26 Gg 3.48S 119.38 E
Pins, Cap des- 63b Ce 21.04S 167.28 E
Pins, Ile des-=Pines, Isle of- (EN) 57 Hg 22.37S 167.30 E
Pins, Pointe aux- 44 Gd 42.15N 81.51W
Pinsk 19 Ce 52.08N 26.06 E
Pinta, Isla- 54a Aa 0.35N 90.44W
Pintas, Sierra de las- 48 Bb 31.40N 115.10W
Pinto [Arg.] 56 Hc 29.09S 62.39W
Pinto [Sp.] 13 Id 40.14N 3.41W
Pintwater Range 46 Hh 36.55N 115.30W
Pio 63a Ed 10.12S 161.42 E
Pioche 46 Hh 37.56N 114.27W
Piombino 14 Eh 42.55N 10.32 E
Piombino, Canale di- 14 Eh 42.55N 10.30 E
Pioneer Mountains 46 Id 45.40N 113.00W
Pioner, Ostrov- 21 Lb 79.50N 92.30 E
Pionerski [R.S.F.S.R.] 19 Gc 61.12N 62.57 E
Pionerski [R.S.F.S.R.] 7 Ei 54.57N 20.13 E
Pionki 10 Re 51.30N 21.27 E
Piorini, Lago- 54 Fd 3.35S 63.15W
Piorini, Rio- 54 Fd 3.23S 63.30W
Piotrków [2] 10 Pe 51.25N 19.40 E
Piotrków Trybunalski 10 Pe 51.25N 19.42 E
Piove di Sacco 14 Ge 45.18N 12.02 E
Pipa Dingzi 27 Mc 43.57N 128.14 E
Pipéri 15 Hj 39.19N 24.21 E
Pipestone 45 Hd 44.01N 96.19W
Pipestone Creek 45 Fb 49.42N 100.45W
Pipi 35 Cd 7.27N 22.48 E
Pipinas 55 Dl 35.32S 57.20W
Pipmouacan, Réservoir- 42 Kg 49.40N 70.20W
Piqan → Shanshan 27 Fc 42.52N 90.10 E
Piqua 44 Ee 40.08N 84.14W
Piqueras, Puerto de- 13 Jb 42.03N 2.32W
Piquiri, Rio- 56 Jb 24.03S 54.14W
Piquiri, Serra do- 55 Fg 24.53S 52.25W
Piracanjuba 55 Hc 17.18S 49.01W
Piracanjuba, Rio- [Braz.] 55 Hd 18.14S 48.48W
Piracanjuba, Rio- [Braz.] 55 Hc 17.18S 48.13W
Piracema 55 Je 20.31S 44.29W
Piracicaba 56 Kb 22.43S 47.38W
Piracicaba, Rio- 55 Hf 22.36S 48.19W
Piraçununga 55 Ie 21.59S 47.25W
Piracuruca 54 Jd 3.56S 41.42W
Piraeus (EN) = Piraiévs 6 Ih 37.57N 23.38 E
Pirai do Sul 55 Hg 24.31S 49.56W
Piraiévs = Piraeus (EN) 6 Ih 37.57N 23.38 E
Piraju 55 Hf 23.12S 49.23W
Pirajui 55 He 21.59S 49.29W
Piramide, Cerro- 52 Ij 49.01S 73.32W
Piran 14 He 45.32N 13.34 E
Pirané 56 Ic 25.43S 59.06W
Piranhas 55 Gc 16.31S 51.51W
Piranhas, Rio- 55 Gc 16.01S 51.52W
Pirān Shahr 24 Kd 36.40N 45.05 E
Pirapora 53 Lg 17.21S 44.56W
Piraraja 56 Jd 33.44S 54.45W
Pirate Well 49 Kb 22.26N 73.04W
Piratini 55 Fj 31.27S 53.06W
Piratini, Rio- 55 Fk 32.01S 52.25W
Piratinim, Rio- 55 Ei 28.06S 55.27W
Pirdop 15 Hg 42.42N 24.11 E
Pirenópolis 55 Hb 15.51S 48.57W
Pires do Rio 54 Ig 17.18S 48.17W
Pirgos 15 El 37.41N 21.27 E
Pirgós 15 Fi 40.38N 22.44 E
Piriápolis 55 El 34.54S 55.17W
Pirin 15 Gh 41.40N 23.30 E
Pirineos=Pyrenees (EN) 5 Gg 42.40N 1.00 E
Pirineus, Serra dos- 55 Hc 16.15S 49.10W
Piripiri 54 Jd 4.16S 41.47W
Pirissar/Piirisaar 8 Lf 58.23N 27.40 E
Piritu 50 Bh 9.23N 69.12W
Piritu, Islas- 50 Dg 10.10N 64.56W
Pirizal 55 Dc 16.16S 56.23W
Pirjatin 16 Hd 50.14N 32.30 E
Pirmasens 10 Dg 49.12N 7.36 E
Pirna 10 Jf 50.58N 13.56 E
Piron 63a Ad 11.20S 153.27 E
Pirón 13 Hc 41.23N 4.31W
Pirot 15 Ff 43.09N 22.36 E
Pirre, Cerro- 49 Ij 7.49N 77.43W
Pirrit Hills 66 Pg 81.17S 85.21W
Pirsagat 16 Pj 39.53N 49.19 E
Pīr Tāj 24 Me 35.45N 48.07 E
Pirttikyla/Pörtom 8 Ib 62.42N 21.37 E
Piru 26 Ig 3.04S 128.12 E
Pis 64d Ba 7.41N 151.46 E
Pisa 14 Eg 43.43N 10.23 E
Pisa 10 Rc 53.15N 21.52 E
Pisagua 56 Fa 19.36S 70.13W

Index Symbols

[1] Independent Nation
[2] State, Region
[3] District, County
[4] Municipality
[5] Colony, Dependency
Continent
Physical Region
Historical or Cultural Region
Mount, Mountain
Volcano
Hill
Mountains, Mountain Range
Hills, Escarpment
Plateau, Upland
Pass, Gap
Plain, Lowland
Delta
Salt Flat
Valley, Canyon
Crater, Cave
Karst Features
Depression
Polder
Desert, Dunes
Forest, Woods
Heath, Steppe
Oasis
Cape, Point
Coast, Beach
Cliff
Peninsula
Isthmus
Sandbank
Island
Atoll
Rock, Reef
Islands, Archipelago
Rocks, Reefs
Coral Reef
Well, Spring
Geyser
River, Stream
Waterfall Rapids
River Mouth, Estuary
Lake
Salt Lake
Intermittent Lake
Reservoir
Swamp, Pond
Canal
Glacier
Ice Shelf, Pack Ice
Ocean
Sea
Gulf, Bay
Strait, Fjord
Lagoon
Bank
Seamount
Tablemount
Ridge
Shelf
Basin
Escarpment, Sea Scarp
Fracture
Trench, Abyss
National Park, Reserve
Point of Interest
Recreation Site
Cave, Cavern
Historic Site
Ruins
Wall, Walls
Church, Abbey
Temple
Scientific Station
Airport
Port
Lighthouse
Mine
Tunnel
Dam, Bridge

Pisano 14 Eg 43.46N 10.33 E
Pisar 64d Cb 7.19N 152.01 E
Pisciotta 14 Jj 40.06N 15.14 E
Pisco 53 Ig 13.42 S 76.13W
Pişcolt 15 Fb 47.35N 22.18 E
Písek 10 Kg 49.19N 14.10 E
Pishan/Guma 27 Cd 37.38N 78.19 E
Pīsh Qal'eh 24 Qd 37.35N 57.05 E
Pīshvā 24 Ne 35.18N 51.44 E
Piso Firme 55 Ba 13.41 S 61.52W
Pissa 7 Ei 54.39N 21.50 E
Pisshiri-Dake 29a Ba 44.20N 141.55 E
Pista 7 Hd 65.28N 30.45 E
Pisticci 14 Kj 40.23N 16.33 E
Pistoia 14 Eg 43.55N 10.54 E
Pisuerga 13 Hc 41.33N 4.52W
Pisz 10 Rc 53.38N 21.49 E
Pita 34 Cc 11.05N 12.24W
Pitalito 54 Cc 1.53N 76.02W
Pitanga 56 Jb 24.46 S 51.44W
Pitanga, Serra da- 55 Gg 24.52 S 51.48W
Pitangui 55 Jd 19.40 S 44.54W
Pitcairn 58 Og 24.00 S 129.00W
Pitcairn Island 57 Na 25.04 S 130.05W
Piteå 7 Ed 65.20N 21.30 E
Piteälven 5 Ib 65.14N 21.32 E
Piteşti 6 Ig 44.51N 24.52 E
Pithiviers 11 If 48.10N 2.15 E
Pithorāgarh 25 Gc 29.35N 80.13 E
Piti 36 Fd 7.00 S 32.44 E
Piti 64c Bb 13.28N 144.41 E
Pitiquito 48 Cb 30.42N 112.02W
Pitkjaranta 19 Dc 61.35N 31.31 E
Pitkkala 8 Jc 61.28N 23.34 E
Pitljar 20 Bc 65.52N 65.55 E
Pitlochry 9 Je 56.43N 3.45W
Pitomača 14 Le 45.57N 17.14 E
Piton, Pointe du- 51e Ba 16.30N 61.27W
Pit River 43 Cc 40.45N 122.22W
Pitrufquén 56 Fe 38.59 S 72.39W
Pitt 42 Ef 53.40N 129.50W
Pitt Island 57 Ji 44.20 S 176.10W
Pittsburg 43 Id 37.25N 94.42W
Pittsburgh 39 Le 40.26N 80.00W
Pittsfield [Il.-U.S.] 45 Kg 39.36N 90.48W
Pittsfield [Ma.-U.S.] 44 Kd 42.27N 73.15W
Pittsfield [Me.-U.S.] 44 Mc 44.47N 69.23W
Pitt Strait 62 Jf 44.10 S 176.20W
Pitu 26 If 1.41N 128.01 E
Piũí 55 Je 20.28 S 45.58W
Piura 53 Hf 5.12 S 80.38W
Piura 54 Be 5.00 S 80.20W
Piuthān 25 Gc 28.06N 82.52 E
Piva 15 Bf 43.21N 18.51 E
Pivan 20 If 50.27N 137.05 E
Pivijay 49 Jh 10.28N 74.38W
Pižma [R.S.F.S.R.] 7 Lh 57.36N 48.58 E
Pižma [R.S.F.S.R.] 17 Fd 65.24N 52.05 E
Pizzo 14 Kl 38.44N 16.40 E
Pjakupur 20 Cd 65.00N 77.48 E
Pjalica 7 Jc 66.12N 39.32 E
Pjalma 19 Dc 62.27N 35.53 E
Pjana 7 Ki 55.37N 45.58 E
Pjandž 19 Gh 37.15N 69.07 E
Pjandž 21 If 37.06N 68.20 E
Pjaozero, Ozero- 5 Jb 66.05N 30.55 E
Pjarnu/Pärnu 6 Id 58.24N 24.32 E
Pjarnu/Pärnu Jõgi 7 Fg 58.23N 24.34 E
Pjarnu, Zaliv-/Pärnu Laht 7 Fg 58.15N 24.25 E
Pjarnu-Jagupi/Pärnu-Jaagupi 8 Kf 58.36N 24.25 E
Pjasina 21 Kb 73.47N 87.01 E
Pjasino, Ozero- 20 Dc 69.45N 87.30 E
Pjasinski Zaliv 20 Db 74.00N 85.00 E
Pjatigorsk 6 Kg 44.03N 43.04 E
Pjatihatki 16 He 48.27N 33.40 E
Pjórsá 5 Dc 63.45N 20.50W
Pjussi/Püssi 8 Le 59.17N 26.57 E
Pkulagalid 64a Bb 7.36N 134.33 E
Pkulagasemieg 64a Ac 7.08N 134.23 E
Pkurengel 64a Ac 7.27N 134.28 E
Plá 55 Bl 35.07 S 60.13W
Placentia 42 Mg 47.14N 53.58W
Placentia Bay 38 Ne 47.15N 54.30W
Placer 26 Hd 11.52N 123.55 E
Placerville 46 Eg 38.43N 120.48W
Placetas 47 Id 22.19N 79.40W
Plácido Rosas 55 Fk 32.45 S 53.44W
Plačkovci 15 Ig 42.49N 25.28 E
Plačkovica 15 Fh 41.46N 22.32 E
Plainfield 44 Je 40.37N 74.25W
Plains [Mt.-U.S.] 46 Hc 47.27N 114.53W
Plains [Tx.-U.S.] 45 Ej 33.11N 102.50W
Plainview [Nb.-U.S.] 45 He 42.21N 97.47W
Plainview [Tx.-U.S.] 43 Ge 34.11N 101.43W
Plainville 45 Gg 39.14N 99.18W
Pláka, Akra- 15 Ii 40.02N 25.25 E
Plake 15 Eh 41.14N 21.02 E
Plampang 26 Gh 8.48 S 117.48 E
Planá 10 Ig 49.52N 12.44 E
Plana Cays 49 Kb 22.37N 73.33W
Plana o Nueva Tabarca, Isla- 13 Lf 38.10N 0.28W
Planco, Peñón- 48 Ge 24.35N 104.15W
Plane, Ile- 13 Li 35.46N 0.54W
Planeta Rica 54 Cb 8.25N 75.35W
Planet Depth (EN) 3 Hi 10.20 S 110.30 E
Planézes 11 Ij 45.00N 2.50 E
Plankinton 45 Ge 43.43N 98.29W
Plantation 44 Gl 26.05N 80.14W
Plantaurel 11 Hk 43.04N 1.30 E
Plant City 44 Fk 28.01N 82.08W
Plasencia 13 Fd 40.02N 6.05W
Plast 19 Ge 54.22N 60.55 E
Plaster Rock 44 Nb 46.54N 67.24W
Plastun 20 Ih 44.48N 136.17 E
Plasy 10 Jg 49.56N 13.24 E
Plata, Rio de la- [P.R.] 51a Bb 18.30N 66.14W
Plata, Rio de la- [S.Amer.] 52 Ki 35.00 S 57.00W
Plataiai 15 Gk 38.13N 23.16 E
Platani 14 Hm 37.24N 13.16 E
Plateau 34 Gd 8.50N 9.00 E
Plateau 36 Cc 2.10 S 15.00 E
Plateau, Khorat- 21 Mh 15.30N 102.50 E
Plateaux 34 Fd 7.30N 1.10 E
Platen, Kapp- 41 Ob 80.31N 22.48 E
Plati 15 Fi 40.39N 22.32 E
Plato 54 Db 9.47N 74.47W
Platte 45 Ge 43.23N 98.51W
Platte 38 Je 43.23N 98.51W
Platte Island 30 Mi 5.52 S 55.23 E
Platte River 45 Ig 39.16N 94.50W
Platteville 45 Ke 42.44N 90.29W
Plattsburgh 43 Mc 44.42N 73.29W
Plattsmouth 45 If 41.01N 95.53W
Plau 10 Ic 53.27N 12.16 E
Plauen 10 If 50.30N 12.08 E
Plauer See 10 Ic 53.30N 12.20 E
Plav 15 Cg 42.36N 19.57 E
Plavecký Mikuláš 10 Nh 48.30N 17.18 E
Pļaviņas/Pljavinjas 7 Fh 56.38N 25.46 E
Plavsk 16 Jc 53.43N 37.18 E
Playa Azul 47 De 17.59N 102.24W
Playa Noriega, Laguna- 48 Dc 29.10N 111.50W
Playa Vicente 48 Li 17.50N 95.49W
Playón Chico 49 Hi 9.18N 78.14W
Pleasanton [Ks.-U.S.] 45 Ig 38.11N 94.43W
Pleasanton [Tx.-U.S.] 45 Gl 28.58N 98.29W
Pleasant Point 62 Df 44.16 S 171.08 E
Pleasant Valley 45 Fi 35.15N 101.48W
Plechý 10 Jh 48.49N 13.53 E
Pleiku 25 Lf 13.59N 108.00 E
Pleiße 10 Ie 51.20N 12.22 E
Plekinge 8 Fh 56.20N 15.05 E
Pleniţa 15 Ge 44.13N 23.11 E
Plenty, Bay of- 57 Ih 37.45 S 177.10 E
Plentywood 43 Gb 48.47N 104.34W
Plešcenicy 16 Eb 54.29N 27.55 E
Plesseck 19 Ec 62.44N 40.18 E
Plešivec 10 Qh 48.33N 20.25 E
Pleşu, Vîrful- 15 Fc 46.32N 22.11 E
Pleszew 10 Ne 51.54N 17.48 E
Plétipi, Lac- 42 Kf 51.42N 70.08W
Plettenberg 12 Jc 51.13N 7.53 E
Plettenbergbaai 37 Cf 34.03 S 23.22 E
Pleven 15 Hf 43.25N 24.37 E
Pleven 6 Ig 43.25N 24.37 E
Plibo 34 De 4.35N 7.40W
Pliska 15 Kf 43.22N 27.07 E
Pliszka 10 Kd 52.15N 14.40 E
Plitvice 14 Jf 44.54N 15.36 E
Pljavinjas/Pļaviņas 7 Fh 56.38N 25.46 E
Plješevica 14 Jf 44.45N 15.45 E
Pljevlja 15 Cf 43.21N 19.21 E
Pljusa 7 Gg 58.25N 29.20 E
Pljusa 7 Gg 59.13N 28.11 E
Ploča, Rt- 14 Jg 43.30N 15.58 E
Plóce 14 Lg 43.04N 17.26 E
Płock 10 Pd 52.35N 19.45 E
Płock 10 Pd 52.33N 19.43 E
Ploërmel 11 Dg 47.56N 2.24W
Ploieşti 6 Ig 44.57N 26.01 E
Plomárion 15 Jk 38.59N 26.22 E
Plomb du Cantal 11 Ii 45.03N 2.46 E
Plön 10 Gb 54.10N 10.26 E
Płonia 10 Kc 53.25N 14.36 E
Płońka 10 Qd 52.37N 20.30 E
Płońsk 10 Qd 52.38N 20.23 E
Plopana 15 Kc 46.41N 27.13 E
Płoty 10 Lc 53.50N 15.16 E
Plouguerneau 11 Bf 48.36N 4.30W
Plovdiv 15 Hg 42.09N 24.45 E
Plovdiv 6 Ig 42.09N 24.45 E
Plummer 46 Gc 47.20N 116.53W
Plumridge Lakes 59 Fe 29.30 S 125.25 E
Plumtree 37 Dd 20.31 S 27.48 E
Plungė/Plunge 7 Ei 55.56N 21.48 E
Plunge/Plungė 7 Ei 55.56N 21.48 E
Plymouth [Eng.-U.K.] 6 Fe 50.23N 4.10W
Plymouth [In.-U.S.] 44 De 41.21N 86.19W
Plymouth [Ma.-U.S.] 44 Le 41.58N 70.41W
Plymouth [Mont.] 47 Le 16.42N 62.13W
Plymouth Sound 9 Ik 50.26N 4.05W
Plzeň=Pilsen (EN) 6 Hf 49.45N 13.24 E
Plzeňská pahorkatina 10 Jg 49.50N 13.15 E
Pniewy 10 Md 52.31N 16.15 E
Pô 34 Ec 11.10N 1.09W
Po 5 Hg 44.57N 12.05 E
Po, Colline del- 14 Be 45.05N 7.50 E
Po, Foci del-=Po, Mouths of the- (EN) 14 Gf 44.52N 12.30 E
Po, Mouths of the- (EN)=Po, Foci del- 14 Gf 44.52N 12.30 E
Poarta de Fier a Transilvaniei, Pasul- 15 Fd 45.25N 22.40 E
Poarta Orientală, Pasul- 15 Fd 45.08N 22.20 E
Poás, Volcán- 49 Eh 10.11N 84.13W
Pobé 34 Fd 6.58N 2.41 E
Pobeda, Gora- 21 Qc 65.12N 146.12 E
Pobeda Ice Island 66 Ge 64.30 S 97.00 E
Pobedy, Pik- 21 Ke 42.02N 80.05 E
Pobla de Segur/La Pobla de Segur 13 Mb 42.15N 0.58 E
Poblet, Monasterio de-/Poblet, Monèstir de- 13 Nc 41.20N 1.05 E
Poblet, Monèstir de-/Poblet, Monasterio de- 13 Nc 41.20N 1.05 E
Pobrežije 15 Jf 43.56N 26.21 E
Pocahontas 45 Kh 36.16N 90.58W
Pocatello 39 He 42.52N 112.27W
Počep 16 Hc 52.57N 33.28 E
Pocerina 15 Ce 44.38N 19.35 E
Počinok 19 De 54.23N 32.29 E
Počitelj 14 Lg 43.08N 17.44 E
Pocito, Sierra del- 13 He 39.20N 4.05W
Pocito Casas 48 Dc 28.32N 111.06W
Pocklington Reef 60 Fj 11.00 S 155.00 E
Poções 54 Jf 14.31 S 40.21W
Poço Fundo, Cachoeira- 55 Jc 16.10 S 45.51W
Poconé 54 Gg 16.15 S 56.37W
Pocono Mountains 44 Je 41.10N 75.20W
Poços de Caldas 54 Ih 21.48 S 46.34W
Pocri 49 Gj 7.40N 80.07W
Podborovje [R.S.F.S.R.] 8 Mg 57.51N 28.46 E
Podborovje [R.S.F.S.R.] 7 Ig 59.32N 35.01 E
Podbrezová 10 Ph 48.49N 19.31 E
Podčerje 17 He 63.55N 57.30 E
Poděbrady 10 Lf 50.09N 15.07 E
Podgajcy 10 Vg 49.12N 25.12 E
Podgorina 15 Ce 44.15N 19.56 E
Po di Volano 14 Gf 44.49N 12.15 E
Podjuga 7 Jf 61.07N 40.54 E
Podkamennaja Tunguska=Stony Tunguska (EN) 21 Lc 61.36N 90.18 E
Podlasie 10 Sd 52.30N 23.00 E
Podlaska, Nizina- 10 Sc 53.00N 22.45 E
Podlužje 15 Ce 44.45N 19.55 E
Podolia (EN)=Podolskaja Vozvyšennost 5 If 49.00N 28.00 E
Podolsk 19 Dd 55.27N 37.33 E
Podolskaja Vozvyšennost=Podolia (EN) 5 If 49.00N 28.00 E
Podor 34 Cb 16.40N 14.57W
Podporožje 19 Dc 60.54N 34.09 E
Podravina 14 Le 45.40N 17.40 E
Podravska Slatina 14 Le 45.42N 17.42 E
Podrima 15 Dg 42.24N 20.33 E
Podromanija 14 Mg 43.54N 18.46 E
Podsvilje 8 Mi 55.09N 28.01 E
Podujevo 15 Eg 42.55N 21.12 E
Podunajská nižina 10 Nh 48.00N 17.40 E
Podvološino 20 Fe 58.15N 108.25 E
Poel 10 Hb 54.00N 11.26 E
Poeniţa, Vîrful- 15 Gc 46.15N 23.20 E
Pofadder 37 Be 29.10 S 19.22 E
Pogăniş 15 Ed 45.41N 21.21 E
Pogar 16 Hc 52.33N 33.16 E
Poggibonsi 14 Fg 43.28N 11.09 E
Pöggstall 14 Jb 48.19N 15.11 E
Pogibi 20 Jf 52.15N 141.45 E
Pogny 12 Gf 48.52N 4.29 E
Pogoanele 15 Je 44.55N 27.00 E
Pogórze Karpackie 10 Qg 49.52N 21.00 E
Pogradeci 15 Di 40.54N 20.39 E
Pograničny 20 Ih 44.26N 131.20 E
Pogrebišče 16 Fe 49.29N 29.14 E
Poguba Xoréu, Rio- 55 Ec 16.29 S 54.58W
P'ohang 27 Md 36.02N 129.22 E
Pohja/Pojo 8 Jd 60.06N 23.31 E
Pohjankangas 8 Jc 62.00N 22.30 E
Pohjanlahti=Bothnia, Gulf of- (EN) 5 Hc 63.00N 20.00 E
Pohjanmaa 8 Jb 63.00N 22.30 E
Pohjois-Karjala 7 Ge 63.00N 30.00 E
Pohlheim 12 Kd 50.32N 8.42 E
Pohorje 14 Jd 46.32N 15.28 E
Po Hu 28 Di 30.15N 116.32 E
Pohue Bay 65a Fd 19.01N 155.48W
Pohvistnevo 19 Fe 53.40N 52.08 E
Poiana Mare 15 Gf 43.55N 23.04 E
Poiana Ruscă, Munţii 15 Fd 45.41N 22.30 E
Pöide/Pejde 8 Jf 58.30N 22.50 E
Poie 36 Dc 2.55 S 23.10 E
Poindimié 61 Cd 20.56 S 165.20 E
Poindo → Lhünzhub 27 Fe 30.17N 91.20 E
Poinsett, Cape- 66 He 65.42 S 113.18 E
Poinsett, Lake- 45 Hd 44.34N 97.05W
Point Arena 46 Dg 38.55N 123.41W
Point au Fer Island 45 Kl 29.15N 91.15W
Pointe-à-Pitre 47 Le 16.14N 61.32W
Pointe Duble 51e Bb 16.20N 61.00W
Pointe-Noire 51e Ab 16.14N 61.47W
Pointe Noire 31 Ii 4.48 S 11.51 E
Point Hope 40 Fc 68.21N 166.41W
Point Lake 42 Gc 65.15N 113.00W
Point Lay 40 Gc 69.45N 163.03W
Point Pleasant [N.J.-U.S.] 44 Je 40.06N 74.02W
Point Pleasant [W.V.-U.S.] 44 Ff 38.53N 82.07W
Poisson-Blanc, Lac- 44 Jc 46.00N 75.44W
Poissonnier Point 59 Dc 20.00 S 119.10 E
Poissy 11 If 48.56N 2.03 E
Poitevin, Marais- 11 Eh 46.22N 1.06W
Poitiers 6 Gf 46.35N 0.20 E
Poitou 11 Fh 46.40N 0.30W
Poitou, Plaines et Seuil du- 11 Gh 46.26N 0.17 E
Poivre Islands 37b Bb 5.46 S 53.19 E
Poix-de-Picardie 11 He 49.47N 1.59 E
Poix-Terron 12 Ge 49.39N 4.39 E
Pojarkovo 20 Hg 49.42N 128.50 E
Pojkovski 19 Hc 60.59N 72.00 E
Pojo/Pohja 8 Jd 60.06N 23.31 E
Pojuba, Rio- 55 Ec 16.30 S 54.59W
Pokaran 25 Ec 26.55N 71.55 E
Pokhara 25 Gc 28.14N 83.59 E
Poko 36 Eb 3.09N 26.53 E
Pokoinu 64p Bb 21.12 S 159.49W
Pokój 10 Nf 50.56N 17.50 E
Pokrovka 18 Lc 42.19N 78.01 E
Pokrovsk 20 Hd 61.29N 129.10 E
Pokrovskoje [R.S.F.S.R.] 16 Jc 52.38N 36.51 E
Pokrovskoje [Ukr.-U.S.S.R.] 16 Jf 47.59N 36.13 E
Pokšenga 7 Kd 64.01N 44.15 E
Pokutje 15 Ia 48.20N 25.05 E
Pola 7 Hg 58.05N 31.40 E
Polabi 10 Lf 50.10N 15.10 E
Polacca 46 Ji 35.50N 110.23W
Pola de Laviana 13 Ga 43.15N 5.34W
Pola de Lena 13 Ga 43.10N 5.49W
Pola de Siero 13 Ga 43.23N 5.40W
Polanco 55 Ek 33.54 S 55.09W
Poland 64g Ab 1.52N 157.33W
Poland (EN)=Polska 6 He 52.00N 19.00 E
Polanów 10 Mb 54.08N 16.39 E
Polar Plateau 66 Cg 90.00 S 0.00
Polar Urals (EN)=Poljarny Ural 5 Mb 66.55N 64.30 E
Polatlı 23 Db 39.36N 32.09 E
Polch 12 Jd 50.18N 7.19 E
Połczyn Zdrój 10 Mc 53.46N 16.06 E
Pol-e Khomrī 23 Kb 35.56N 68.43 E
Pole of Inaccessibility (EN) 66 Eg 82.06 S 54.58 E
Pol-e-Safīd 24 Od 36.06N 53.01 E
Polesella 14 Ff 44.58N 11.45 E
Polesie Lubelskie 10 Te 51.30N 23.20 E
Polesine 14 Fe 45.00N 11.45 E
Polesje=Polesye (EN) 5 Ie 52.00N 27.00 E
Polessk 8 Ij 54.51N 21.02 E
Polesskoje 16 Fd 51.16N 29.27 E
Polesye (EN)=Polesje 5 Ie 52.00N 27.00 E
Polevskoj 19 Gd 56.28N 60.11 E
Polewali 26 Gg 3.25 S 119.20 E
Poležan 15 Gh 41.43N 23.30 E
Polgár 10 Ri 47.52N 21.07 E
Pŏlgyo 28 Ig 34.51N 127.21 E
Poli 34 Hd 8.29N 13.15 E
Poliaigos 15 Hm 36.46N 24.38 E
Poliçani 15 Di 40.08N 20.21 E
Policastro, Golfo di- 14 Jk 40.00N 15.35 E
Police 10 Kc 53.33N 14.35 E
Policoro 14 Kj 40.13N 16.41 E
Poligny 11 Lh 46.50N 5.43 E
Poligus 20 Ed 61.58N 94.40 E
Polikastron 15 Fh 41.00N 22.34 E
Polikhnitos 15 Jj 39.05N 26.11 E
Polillo Islands 21 Oh 14.50N 122.05 E
Pólis 24 Ee 35.02N 32.25 E
Polist 7 Hg 58.07N 31.32 E
Polistena 14 Kl 38.24N 16.04 E
Políyiros 15 Gi 40.23N 23.27 E
Poljarny [R.S.F.S.R.] 19 Db 69.13N 33.28 E
Poljarny [R.S.F.S.R.] 20 Mc 69.01N 178.45 E
Poljarny Ural=Polar Urals (EN) 5 Mb 66.55N 64.30 E
Polkowice 10 Me 51.32N 16.06 E
Pöllau 14 Jc 47.18N 15.50 E
Polle 64d Bb 7.20N 151.15 E
Pollença/Pollensa 13 Pe 39.53N 3.01 E
Pollensa/Pollença 13 Pe 39.53N 3.01 E
Pollino 5 Hh 39.55N 16.10 E
Polochic, Rio- 49 Cf 15.28N 89.22W
Polock 19 Cd 55.29N 28.52 E
Polog 15 Dh 42.00N 21.00 E
Pologi 19 Df 47.28N 36.15 E
Polonina 10 Jh 48.30N 23.30 E
Polonnaruwa 25 Gg 7.56N 81.00 E
Polonnoje 16 Ed 50.06N 27.29 E
Polousny Krjaž 20 Jc 69.30N 144.00 E
Polska=Poland (EN) 6 He 52.00N 19.00 E
Polski Gradec 15 Jg 42.11N 26.06 E
Polski Trămbeš 15 If 43.22N 25.38 E
Polson 46 Hc 47.41N 114.09W
Poltár 10 Ph 48.27N 19.48 E
Poltava 6 Jf 49.35N 34.34 E
Poltavka 19 He 54.22N 71.45 E
Poltavskaja Oblast 19 Df 49.45N 33.50 E
Põltsamaa/Pyltsamaa 8 Lf 58.23N 26.08 E
Põltsamaa/Pyltsamaa 7 Fg 58.39N 25.59 E
Polujj 20 Bc 66.30N 66.31 E
Polunočnoje 19 Gc 60.52N 60.25 E
Polür 24 Oe 32.52N 52.03 E
Põlva/Pylva 7 Gg 58.04N 27.06 E
Polvijärvi 8 Nb 62.51N 29.22 E
Polynesia 57 Le 4.00 S 156.00W
Polynésie Française=French Polynesia (EN) 58 Mf 16.00 S 145.00W
Pom, Laguna de- 48 Mh 18.35N 92.15W
Pomarance 14 Eg 43.18N 10.52 E
Pomarkku/Påmark 8 Ic 61.42N 22.00 E
Pombal [Braz.] 54 Ke 6.46 S 37.47W
Pombal [Port.] 13 De 39.55N 8.38W
Pombo, Rio- 55 Fe 20.53 S 52.23W
Pomerania (EN)=Pommern 5 He 54.00N 16.00 E
Pomerania (EN)=Pommern 10 Lc 54.00N 16.00 E
Pomeranian Bay (EN)=Pommersche Bucht 10 Kb 54.20N 14.20 E
Pomeranian Bay (EN)=Pomorska, Zatoka- 10 Kb 54.20N 14.20 E
Pomeroy 44 Ff 39.03N 82.03W
Pomio 58 Ge 5.32 S 151.30 E
Pomme de Terre Reservoir 45 Jh 37.51N 93.19W
Pommern=Pomerania (EN) 10 Lc 54.00N 16.00 E
Pommern=Pomerania (EN) 5 He 54.00N 16.00 E
Pommersche Bucht=Pomeranian Bay (EN) 10 Kb 54.20N 14.20 E
Pommersfelden 10 Gg 49.46N 10.49 E
Pomona 46 Gi 34.04N 117.45W
Pomona Lake 45 Ig 38.40N 95.35W
Pomorije 15 Kg 42.33N 27.39 E
Pomorska, Zatoka-=Pomeranian Bay (EN) 10 Kb 54.20N 14.20 E
Pomorski Bereg 7 Id 64.00N 36.15 E
Pomorskie, Pojezierze- 10 Mc 53.30N 16.30 E
Pomorski Proliv 19 Eb 68.40N 50.00 E
Pomošnaja 16 Ge 48.14N 31.29 E
Pompano Beach 44 Gl 26.15N 80.07W
Pompei 14 Ij 40.45N 14.30 E
Pompeu 55 Jd 19.12 S 44.59W
Ponape 58 Gd 6.52N 158.15 E
Ponape Island 57 Gd 6.55N 158.15 E
Ponca City 43 Hd 36.42N 97.05W
Ponce 39 Mh 18.01N 66.37W
Poncheville, Lac- 44 Ia 50.12N 76.55W
Pondcreek 45 Hh 36.40N 97.48W
Pondicherry 25 Ff 11.56N 79.53 E
Pondicherry 25 Ff 11.55N 79.45 E
Pond Inlet 39 Lb 72.41N 78.00W
Pond Inlet 42 Jb 72.48N 77.00W
Ponea 64n Ac 10.28 S 161.01W
Ponente, Riviera di- 14 Cf 44.10N 8.20 E
Ponérihouen 63b Be 21.05 S 165.24 E
Pones 64d Bb 7.12N 151.59 E
Ponferrada 13 Fb 42.33N 6.35W
Pongaroa 62 Gd 40.33 S 176.11 E
Pongo 30 Jh 8.42N 27.40 E
Pongola 37 Ee 26.52 S 32.20 E
Pong Qu 27 Ef 26.49N 87.09 E
Poniatowa 10 Se 51.11N 22.05 E
Ponoj 6 Kb 67.05N 41.07 E
Ponoj 5 Kb 66.59N 41.10 E
Ponomarevka 16 Sc 53.09N 54.12 E
Ponorogo 26 Fh 7.52 S 111.27 E
Pons 11 Fi 45.35N 0.33W
Pons/Ponts 13 Nc 41.55N 1.12 E
Ponsul 13 Ee 39.40N 7.31W
Pont-à-Celles 12 Gd 50.30N 4.21 E
Ponta Delgada 31 Ee 37.44N 25.40W
Ponta Delgada 32 Bb 37.48N 25.30W
Ponta Grossa 53 Kh 25.05 S 50.09W
Pont-à-Mousson 11 Mf 48.54N 6.04 E
Ponta Porá 53 Kh 22.32 S 55.43W
Pontarlier 11 Mh 46.54N 6.22 E
Pontassieve 14 Fg 43.46N 11.26 E
Pont-Audemer 11 Ge 49.21N 0.31 E
Pontaut 55 Bm 37.44 S 61.20W
Pontávert 12 Fe 49.25N 3.49 E
Pontchartrain, Lake- 43 Ie 30.10N 90.10W
Pontchâteau 11 Dg 47.26N 2.05W
Pont-de-l'Arche 12 De 49.18N 1.10 E
Pont de Suert 13 Mb 42.24N 0.45 E
Pont-de-Vaux 11 Kh 46.26N 4.56 E
Ponte Alta 55 Gh 27.29 S 50.23W
Ponte Alta, Serra da- 55 Id 19.42 S 47.40W
Ponte Branca 55 Fc 16.27 S 52.40W
Pontecorvo 14 Hi 42.27N 13.40 E
Ponte de Lima 13 Dc 41.46N 8.35W
Ponte de Pedra 55 Ec 17.06 S 54.23W
Ponte de Pedrã 55 Da 13.35 S 57.21W
Pontedera 14 Eg 43.40N 10.38 E
Ponte de Sor 13 De 39.15N 8.01W
Ponte Firme, Chapada da- 55 Id 18.05 S 46.25W
Ponteix 46 Lb 49.49N 107.30W
Ponte Nova 54 Jh 20.24 S 42.54W
Pontés e Lacerda 55 Cb 15.11 S 59.21W
Pontevedra 13 Db 42.30N 8.30W
Pontevedra 13 Db 42.26N 8.38W
Pontevedra, Ria de- 13 Db 42.22N 8.45W
Ponte Vermelha 55 Ed 19.29 S 54.25W
Pont-Farcy 12 Af 48.56N 1.02W
Pontfaverger-Moronvilliers 12 Ge 49.18N 4.19 E
Ponthieu 11 Hd 50.10N 1.55 E
Pontiac [Il.-U.S.] 45 Lf 40.53N 88.38W
Pontiac [Mi.-U.S.] 44 Fd 42.37N 83.18W
Pontianak 22 Mj 0.02 S 109.20 E
Pontian Kechil 26 Df 1.29N 103.23 E
Pontine Islands (EN)=Ponziane, Isole- 14 Gj 40.55N 13.00 E
Pontivy 11 Df 48.04N 2.59W
Pontivy, Pays de- 11 Dg 48.00N 3.00W
Pont-l'Abbé 11 Bg 47.52N 4.13W
Pont-l'Evêque 12 Ce 49.18N 0.11 E
Pontoise 11 Ie 49.03N 2.06 E
Pontorson 11 Ef 48.33N 1.31W
Pontremoli 14 Df 44.22N 9.53 E
Pontresina 14 Dd 46.28N 9.53 E
Ponts/Pons 13 Nc 41.55N 1.12 E
Pont-Sainte-Maxence 12 Ee 49.18N 2.36 E
Pont-Saint-Esprit 11 Kj 44.15N 4.39 E
Pontypool 9 Jj 51.43N 3.02W
Ponza 14 Gj 40.54N 12.58 E
Ponza 14 Gj 40.55N 12.55 E
Ponziane, Isole-=Pontine Islands (EN) 14 Gj 40.55N 13.00 E
Pool 36 Bc 3.30 S 15.00 E
Poole 9 Lk 50.43N 1.59W
Poona → Pune 22 Jh 18.32N 73.52 E
Poopó 54 Eg 18.23 S 66.59W
Poopó, Lago de-=Poopó, Lake- (EN) 52 Jg 18.45 S 67.07W
Poopó, Lake- (EN)=Poopó, Lago de- 52 Jg 18.45 S 67.07W
Poor Knights Islands 62 Fa 35.30 S 174.45 E
Pöösaspea Neem/Pyzaspea Neem 8 Je 59.15N 23.25 E
Popakai 54 Gc 3.22N 55.25W
Popayán 53 Ie 2.27N 76.36W
Poperinge 11 Id 50.51N 2.43 E
Poperinge-Watou 12 Ed 50.51N 2.37 E
Popigaj 20 Gb 71.55N 110.47 E
Popigaj 20 Fb 72.55N 106.00 E
Poplar 46 Mb 48.07N 105.12W
Poplar 42 Hf 53.00N 97.18W
Poplar Bluff 43 Id 36.45N 90.24W
Poplar River 46 Mb 48.05N 105.11W
Popocatépetl, Volcán- 38 Jh 19.02N 98.38W
Popokabaka 36 Cd 5.42 S 16.35 E
Popoli 14 Hh 42.10N 13.50 E
Popomanaseu, Mount- 63a Ec 9.42 S 160.03 E
Popondetta 60 Di 8.46 S 148.14 E
Popovo 15 Jf 43.21N 26.14 E
Poppberg 10 Hg 49.20N 11.45 E
Poppel, Ravels- 12 Hc 51.27N 5.02 E
Poprad 10 Qg 49.38N 20.42 E
Poprad 6 If 49.03N 20.19 E
Poptún 49 Ce 16.21N 89.26W
Por 10 Tf 50.48N 23.01 E
Porangahau 62 Gd 40.18 S 176.38 E

Index Symbols

Independent Nation
State, Region
District, County
Municipality
Colony, Dependency
Continent
Physical Region
Historical or Cultural Region
Mount, Mountain
Volcano
Hill
Mountains, Mountain Range
Hills, Escarpment
Plateau, Upland
Pass, Gap
Plain, Lowland
Delta
Salt Flat
Valley, Canyon
Crater, Cave
Karst Features
Depression
Polder
Desert, Dunes
Forest, Woods
Heath, Steppe
Oasis
Cape, Point
Coast, Beach
Cliff
Peninsula
Isthmus
Sandbank
Island
Atoll
Rock, Reef
Islands, Archipelago
Rocks, Reefs
Coral Reef
Well, Spring
Geyser
River, Stream
Waterfall Rapids
River Mouth, Estuary
Lake
Salt Lake
Intermittent Lake
Reservoir
Swamp, Pond
Canal
Glacier
Ice Shelf, Pack Ice
Ocean
Sea
Gulf, Bay
Strait, Fjord
Lagoon
Bank
Seamount
Tablemount
Ridge
Shelf
Basin
Escarpment, Sea Scarp
Fracture
Trench, Abyss
National Park, Reserve
Point of Interest
Recreation Site
Cave, Cavern
Historic Site
Ruins
Wall, Walls
Church, Abbey
Temple
Scientific Station
Airport
Port
Lighthouse
Mine
Tunnel
Dam, Bridge

Name	Ref.	Lat.	Long.
Porangatu	55 Ha	13.26S	49.10W
Porbandar	25 Dd	21.38N	69.36E
Porcien	12 Ge	49.40N	4.20E
Porcos, Rio dos-	55 Ja	12.42S	45.07W
Porcuna	13 Hg	37.52N	4.11W
Porcupine	38 Ec	66.35N	145.15W
Porcupine	44 Ga	48.32N	81.10W
Porcupine Bank (EN)	5 Ee	53.20N	13.30W
Porcupine Hills	46 Ha	50.05N	114.10W
Porcupine Plain	42 Dc	67.30N	137.30W
Pordenone	14 Ge	45.57N	12.39E
Poreč	14 He	45.13N	13.37E
Poreč	15 Fe	44.20N	22.05E
Porecatú	55 Gf	22.43S	51.24W
Porečje	8 Kk	53.53N	24.08E
Poreckoje	7 Li	55.13N	46.19E
Porhov	19 Cd	57.45N	29.32E
Pori/Björneborg	6 Ic	61.29N	21.47E
Porion	15 Gn	35.58N	23.16E
Porirua	61 Dh	41.08S	174.50E
Pörisvatn	7a Bb	64.20N	18.55W
Porjus	7 Ec	66.57N	19.49E
Porkkala	8 Ke	59.55N	24.25E
Porlamar	54 Fa	10.57N	63.51W
Porma	13 Gb	42.29N	5.28W
Pornic	11 Dg	47.07N	2.06W
Poronajsk	22 Qe	49.14N	143.04E
Poronin	10 Qg	49.20N	20.04E
Pòros	15 Gl	37.30N	23.31E
Póros	15 Gl	37.30N	23.27E
Poroshiri-Dake	28 Qc	42.42N	142.35E
Porosozero	7 He	62.44N	32.42E
Porozovo	10 Ud	52.54N	24.27E
Porpoise Bay	66 Ie	66.30S	128.30E
Porquis Junction	44 Ga	48.43N	80.52W
Porrentruy	14 Bc	47.25N	7.10E
Porreras	13 Oe	39.31N	3.00E
Porretta, Passo della-	14 Ef	44.02N	10.56E
Porretta Terme	14 Ef	44.09N	10.59E
Porsangen	5 Ia	70.50N	26.00E
Porsangerhalvøya	7 Fa	70.50N	25.00E
Porsgrunn	7 Bg	59.09N	9.40E
Pórshöfn	7a Ca	66.10N	15.20W
Porsuk	24 Dc	39.42N	31.59E
Portachuelo	54 Fg	17.21S	63.24W
Portadown/Port an Dúnáin	9 Gg	54.26N	6.27W
Portage	45 Le	43.33N	89.28W
Portage la Prairie	42 Hg	49.57N	98.18W
Port Alberni	42 Fg	49.14N	124.48W
Portalegre	13 Ee	39.17N	7.26W
Portalegre [2]	13 Ee	39.15N	7.35W
Portales	43 Ge	34.11N	103.20W
Port-Alfred	42 Kg	48.20N	70.53W
Port Alfred	37 Df	33.36S	26.55E
Port Alice	42 Ef	50.23N	127.27W
Port Allegany	44 He	41.48N	78.18W
Port an Dúnáin/Portadown	9 Gg	54.26N	6.27W
Port Angeles	43 Cb	48.07N	123.27W
Port Antonio	47 Ie	18.11N	76.28W
Port Arthur [Austl.]	59 Jh	43.09S	147.51E
Port Arthur [Tx.-U.S.]	39 Jg	29.55N	93.55W
Port Arthur (EN)=Lüshun	27 Ld	38.50N	121.13E
Port Augusta	58 Eh	32.30S	137.46E
Port-Au-Prince	39 Lh	18.32N	72.20W
Port-au-Prince, Baie de-	49 Kd	18.40N	72.30W
Port Austin	44 Fc	44.03N	83.01W
Port aux Français	31 Om	49.25S	70.10E
Porta Westfalica	12 Kb	52.15N	8.56E
Port-Bergé-Vao Vao	37 Hc	15.33S	47.38E
Port Blair	22 Lh	11.36N	92.45E
Port-Bou/Portbou	13 Pb	42.25N	3.10E
Portbou/Port-Bou	13 Pb	42.25N	3.10E
Port Burwell [Newf.-Can.]	39 Mc	60.25N	64.49W
Port Burwell [Ont.-Can.]	44 Gd	42.39N	80.49W
Port-Cartier	42 Kf	50.01N	66.53W
Port Chalmers	62 Df	45.49S	170.37E
Port Charlotte	43 Kf	26.59N	82.06W
Port Clinton	44 Fe	41.30N	82.58W
Port Coquitlam	46 Db	49.16N	122.46W
Port-de-Bouc	11 Kk	43.24N	4.59E
Port-de-Paix	49 Kd	19.57N	72.50W
Port Dickson	26 Df	2.31N	101.48E
Port Edward	37 Ef	31.03S	30.13E
Portel [Braz.]	54 Hd	1.57S	50.49W
Portel [Port.]	13 Ef	38.18N	7.42W
Port Elgin	44 Gc	44.26N	81.24W
Port Elizabeth [S.Afr.]	31 Jl	33.58S	25.40E
Port Elizabeth [St.Vin.]	51n Ba	13.00N	61.16W
Port Ellen	9 Gf	55.39N	6.12W
Port-en-Bessin-Huppain	11 Fe	49.21N	0.45W
Port Erin	9 Ig	54.05N	4.43W
Porter Point	51n Ba	13.23N	61.11W
Porterville [Ca.-U.S.]	43 Dd	36.04N	119.01W
Porterville [S.Afr.]	37 Bf	33.00S	19.00E
Portete, Bahía de-	49 Lg	12.13N	71.55W
Port Fairy	59 Ig	38.23S	142.14E
Port Fitzroy	62 Fb	36.10S	175.21E
Port-Gentil	31 Hi	0.43S	8.47E
Port Gibson	45 Kk	31.58N	90.58W
Port Harcourt	31 Hh	4.46N	7.01E
Port Hardy	42 Ef	50.43N	127.29W
Port Hawkesbury	42 Lg	45.37N	61.21W
Porthcawl	9 Jj	51.29N	3.43W
Port Hedland	58 Cg	20.19S	118.34E
Port Heiden	40 He	56.55N	158.41W
Port Hope Simpson	42 Lf	52.30N	56.17W
Port Huron	43 Kc	42.58N	82.27W
Portile de Fier = Iron Gate (EN)	5 Ig	44.41N	22.31E
Port-Ilič	16 Pj	38.53N	48.51E
Portimão	13 Dg	37.08N	8.32W
Port Isabel	45 Hm	26.04N	97.13W
Portița	15 Le	44.41N	29.00E
Port Láirge/Waterford [2]	9 Fi	52.10N	7.40W
Port Láirge/Waterford	6 Fe	52.15N	7.06W
Portland [Austl.]	59 Ig	38.21S	141.36E
Portland [Eng.-U.K.]	9 Kk	50.33N	2.27W
Portland [In.-U.S.]	44 Ee	40.26N	84.59W
Portland [Me.-U.S.]	39 Le	43.39N	70.17W
Portland [N.D.-U.S.]	45 Hc	47.30N	97.22W
Portland [N.Z.]	62 Fa	35.48S	174.20E
Portland [Or.-U.S.]	39 Ge	45.33N	122.36W
Portland [Tx.-U.S.]	45 Hm	27.53N	97.20W
Portland, Bill of-	9 Kk	50.31N	2.28W
Portland, Promontoire -	42 Je	58.41N	78.33W
Portland Bight	49 Ie	17.57N	77.08W
Portland Island	62 Gc	39.20S	177.50E
Portland Point	49 Ie	17.42N	77.11W
Port-la-Nouvelle	11 Jk	43.01N	3.03E
Portlaoise/Port Laoise	9 Fh	53.02N	7.17W
Port Laoise/Portlaoise	9 Fh	53.02N	7.17W
Port Lavaca	43 Hf	28.37N	96.38W
Port Lincoln	58 Eh	34.44S	135.52E
Port Loko	34 Cd	8.46N	12.47W
Port Louis	50 Fd	16.25N	61.32W
Port-Louis	31 Mk	20.10S	57.30E
Port Macquarie	59 Kf	31.26S	152.44E
Portmadoc	9 Ii	52.55N	4.08W
Port Maria	49 Id	18.22N	76.54W
Port-Menier	42 Lg	49.49N	64.20W
Port Moller	40 Ge	55.59N	160.34W
Port Moody	46 Db	49.17N	122.51W
Port Moresby	58 Fe	9.30S	147.07E
Port Nelson	42 Ie	57.04N	92.30W
Portneuf, Rivière-	44 Ma	48.37N	69.05W
Port Nolloth	31 Ik	29.17S	16.51E
Porto [2]	13 Dc	41.15N	8.20W
Porto [Fr.]	11a Aa	42.16N	8.42E
Porto [Port.]	6 Fg	41.09N	8.37W
Porto, Golfe de-	11a Aa	42.16N	8.37E
Pôrto Acre	54 Ee	9.34S	67.31W
Porto Alegre [Braz.]	53 Ki	30.04S	51.11W
Porto Alegre [SaoT.P.]	34 Ge	0.02N	6.32E
Porto Amboim	31 Ij	10.44S	13.45E
Porto Azzurro	14 Eh	42.46N	10.24E
Portobelo	49 Hi	9.33N	79.39W
Pôrto Cedro	55 Ed	18.17S	55.02W
Porto Cervo	14 Di	41.08N	9.35E
Porto Curupai	55 Ff	22.50S	53.53W
Porto de Moz	53 Kf	1.45S	52.14W
Porto Empedocle	14 Hm	37.17N	13.32E
Porto Esperança [Braz.]	55 Dd	19.37S	57.27W
Porto Esperança [Braz.]	55 Db	14.02S	56.06W
Porto Esperança [Braz.]	55 Dc	17.47S	57.07W
Porto Esperidião	55 Cb	15.51S	58.28W
Pôrto Estrêla	55 Db	15.20S	57.14W
Portoferraio	14 Eh	42.49N	10.19E
Port of Ness	9 Gc	58.30N	6.15W
Pôrto Franco	54 Ie	6.20S	47.24W
Port of Spain	53 Jd	10.39N	61.31W
Porto Fundação	55 Ea	13.39S	55.18W
Portogruaro	14 Ge	45.47N	12.50E
Porto Lucena	55 Eh	27.51S	55.01W
Pörtom/Pirttikyla	8 Ib	62.42N	21.37E
Portomaggiore	14 Ff	44.42N	11.48E
Porto Mendes	55 Eg	24.30S	54.20W
Porto Moniz	32 Dc	32.51N	17.10W
Porto Moroco	55 Ea	13.24S	55.35W
Porto Morrinho	55 Dc	16.38S	57.49W
Porto Murtinho	53 Kh	21.42S	57.52W
Porto Novo [Ben.]	31 Hh	6.29N	2.37E
Porto Novo [C.V.]	32 Bf	17.07N	25.04W
Port Orford	46 Ce	42.45N	124.30W
Porto San Giorgio	14 Hg	43.11N	13.48E
Pôrto Santana	54 Hd	0.03S	51.11W
Porto Sant'Elpidio	14 Hg	43.15N	13.45E
Porto Santo	30 Fe	33.04N	16.20W
Porto Santo Stefano	14 Fh	42.26N	11.07E
Portoscuso	14 Ck	39.12N	8.23E
Pôrto Seguro	54 Kg	16.26S	39.05W
Porto Tolle	14 Gf	44.56N	12.22E
Porto Torres	14 Cj	40.50N	8.24E
Porto União	55 Gh	26.15S	51.05W
Pôrto Válter	54 De	8.15S	72.45W
Porto Vecchio	11a Bb	41.35N	9.17E
Porto Velho	53 Jf	8.46S	63.54W
Portoviejo	53 Hf	1.03S	80.27W
Porto Xavier	55 Eh	27.54S	55.08W
Port Phillip Bay	59 Ig	38.05S	144.50E
Port Pirie	58 Eh	33.11S	138.01E
Portree	9 Gd	57.24N	6.12W
Port Renfrew	46 Cb	48.33N	124.25W
Port Rois/Portrush	9 Gf	55.12N	6.40W
Port Royal	44 If	38.10N	77.12W
Portrush/Port Rois	9 Gf	55.12N	6.40W
Port Said (EN)=Būr Sa'īd	31 Ke	31.16N	32.18E
Port Saint Joe	43 Jf	29.49N	85.18W
Port Saint Johns	37 Df	31.38S	29.33E
Port-Saint-Louis-du-Rhône	11 Kk	43.23N	4.48E
Port-Salut	49 Kd	18.05N	73.55W
Port Saunders	42 Lf	50.39N	57.18W
Port Shepstone	31 Kl	30.46S	30.22E
Portsmouth [Dom.]	50 Fe	15.35N	61.28W
Portsmouth [Eng.-U.K.]	9 Lk	50.48N	1.05W
Portsmouth [N.H.-U.S.]	43 Mc	43.03N	70.47W
Portsmouth [Oh.-U.S.]	43 Kd	38.45N	82.59W
Portsmouth [Va.-U.S.]	43 Ld	36.50N	76.26W
Portsmouth City Airport	12 Ad	50.46N	1.04W
Port Sudan (EN)=Būr Sūdān	31 Kg	19.37N	37.14E
Port Sulphur	45 Ll	29.29N	89.42W
Port Talbot	9 Jj	51.36N	3.47W
Porttipahdantekojärvi	7 Gb	68.06N	26.33E
Port Townsend	46 Db	48.07N	122.46W
Portugal [1]	6 Fh	39.30N	8.00W
Portugalete	13 Ia	43.19N	3.01W
Portuguesa [2]	54 Eb	9.10N	69.15W
Portuguesa, Rio-	54 Eb	7.57N	67.32W
Portuguesa, Sierra de-	50 Bh	9.35N	69.45W
Portuguese Guinea (EN) → Guinea Bissau (EN) [1]	31 Fg	12.00N	15.00W
Portús, Coll del-/Perthus, Col de-	13 Ob	42.28N	2.51E
Port-Vendres	11 Jl	42.31N	3.07E
Port-Vila	58 Hf	17.44S	168.19E
Port Wakefield	59 Hf	34.11S	138.09E
Port Washington	45 Me	43.23N	87.53W
Porvenir [Bol.]	54 Ef	11.15S	68.41W
Porvenir [Bol.]	55 Ba	13.59S	61.39W
Porvenir [Chile]	56 Fh	53.18S	70.22W
Porvenir [Ur.]	55 Dk	32.23S	57.59W
Porvoo/Borgå	7 Ff	60.24N	25.40E
Porvoonjoki	8 Kd	60.23N	25.40E
Porz, Köln-	10 Df	50.53N	7.03E
Posada, Fiume di-	14 Dj	40.39N	9.45E
Posadas [Arg.]	53 Kh	27.25S	55.50W
Posadas [Sp.]	13 Gg	37.48N	5.06W
Posavina	15 De	44.33N	20.04E
Poschiavo	14 Ed	46.20N	10.04E
Pošehonje-Volodarsk	7 Jg	58.30N	39.08E
Posht-e Bādām	24 Pf	33.02N	55.23E
Posio	7 Gc	66.06N	28.09E
Posjet	28 Kc	42.39N	130.48E
Poskam/Zepu	27 Cd	38.12N	77.18E
Poso	22 Oj	1.23S	120.44E
Poso, Danau-	26 Hg	1.52S	120.35E
Posof	24 Jb	41.31N	42.42E
Posŏng	28 Ig	34.46N	127.05E
Pospeliha	20 Df	52.02N	81.56E
Posse	54 If	14.05S	46.22W
Possession, Ile de la-	30 Mm	46.14S	49.55E
Possession Island	37 Be	27.01S	15.30E
Pößneck	10 Hf	50.42N	11.36E
Post	45 Fj	33.12N	101.23W
Posta de San Martin	55 Bk	33.09S	60.31W
Postavy	19 Cd	55.07N	26.50E
Poste Maurice Cortier/Bidon V	32 He	22.18N	1.05E
Poste Weygand	32 He	24.29N	0.40E
Postmasburg	37 Ce	28.18S	23.05E
Postojna	14 Ie	45.47N	14.14E
Posto Simões Lopes	55 Eb	14.14S	54.41W
Postville [Ia.-U.S.]	45 Ke	43.05N	91.34W
Postville [Newf.-Can.]	42 Lf	54.55N	59.58W
Potchefstroom	37 De	26.46S	27.01E
Poteau	45 Ii	35.03N	94.37W
Potenza	14 Hg	43.25N	13.40E
Potenza	14 Jj	40.38N	15.48E
Poteriteri, Lake-	62 Bg	46.05S	167.05E
Potes	13 Ha	43.09N	4.37W
Potgietersrus	37 Dd	24.15S	28.55E
Potholes Reservoir	46 Fc	47.01N	119.19W
Poti	6 Kg	42.08N	41.39E
Poti, Rio-	54 Je	5.02S	42.50W
Potigny	12 Bf	48.58N	0.14W
Potiskum	31 Ig	11.43N	11.04E
Potnarhvin	63b Dd	18.45S	169.12E
Potomac	38 Lf	38.00N	76.18W
Potosí [2]	54 Eh	20.40S	67.00W
Potosí [Bol.]	53 Jg	19.35S	65.45W
Potosí [Mex.]	47 Dd	24.51N	100.19W
Potosi, Bahía-	48 Ii	17.35N	101.30W
Potosi, Cerro-	48 Ie	24.52N	100.13W
Pototan	26 Hd	10.55N	122.40E
Potrerillos	56 Gc	26.26S	69.29W
Potrero, Río-	55 Bc	17.32S	61.35W
Potsdam [Ger.]	10 Jd	52.24N	13.04E
Potsdam [N.Y.-U.S.]	44 Jc	44.40N	75.01W
Pott	63b Ad	19.35S	163.36E
Potters Bar	12 Bc	51.41N	0.10W
Pottstown	44 Je	40.15N	75.38W
Pottsville	44 Ie	40.42N	76.13W
Pouancé	11 Eg	47.45N	1.10W
Pouébo	63b Be	20.24S	164.34E
Pouembout	63b Be	21.08S	164.54E
Poughkeepsie	44 Ke	41.43N	73.56W
Poulaphouca Reservoir/Loch Pholl an Phúca	9 Gh	53.10N	6.30W
Poum	63b Be	20.14S	164.01E
Pourtalé	55 Bm	37.02S	60.36W
Pouso Alegre	54 Ih	22.13S	45.56W
Pouss	34 Ic	10.51N	15.03E
Poutasi	65c Bb	14.01S	171.41W
Poŭthĭsăt	25 Kf	12.32N	103.55E
Poutrincourt, Lac-	44 Ja	49.13N	74.04W
Po Valley (EN)=Padana, Pianura-	5 Gf	45.20N	10.00E
Považská Bystrica	10 Og	49.07N	18.28E
Považský Inovec	10 Nh	48.35N	18.00E
Povenec	7 Ie	62.51N	34.45E
Poverty Bay	62 Gc	38.45S	178.00E
Povlen	15 Ce	44.09N	19.44E
Póvoa de Varzim	13 Dc	41.23N	8.46W
Povorino	16 Md	51.12N	42.17E
Povungnituk	42 Jd	60.03N	77.16W
Povungnituk	39 Lc	60.02N	77.10W
Powassan	44 Hb	46.05N	79.22W
Powder River [U.S.]	43 Fb	46.44N	105.26W
Powder River [Or.-U.S.]	46 Gd	44.45N	117.03W
Powell	46 Kd	44.45N	108.46W
Powell, Lake- [U.S.]	43 Ed	37.25N	110.45W
Powell Lake [Can.]	46 Ca	50.11N	124.24W
Powell River	42 Fg	49.52N	124.33W
Powers	44 Dc	45.39N	87.32W
Powers Lake	45 Eb	48.34N	102.39W
Powidzkie, Jezioro-	10 Nc	52.24N	17.57E
Powys [3]	9 Ji	52.25N	3.20W
Poxoréu	54 Hg	15.50S	54.23W
Poxoréu, Rio- [Braz.]	55 Ec	16.32S	54.46W
Poxoréu, Rio- [Braz.]	55 Ec	16.08S	54.14W
Poya	63b Be	21.21S	165.09E
Poyang Hu	21 Ng	29.00N	116.25E
Poza de la Sal	13 Ib	42.40N	3.30W
Pozanti	24 Fd	37.25N	34.52E
Požarevac	15 Ee	44.37N	21.12E
Poza Rica de Hidalgo	39 Jg	20.33N	97.27W
Požarskoje	28 Ma	46.16N	134.04E
Požega	15 Df	43.51N	20.02E
Poznań [2]	10 Pd	52.25N	19.55E
Poznań	6 He	52.25N	16.55E
Pozoblanco	13 Hf	38.22N	4.51W
Pozo Borrado	55 Bi	28.56S	61.41W
Pozo Colorado	55 Cf	23.22S	58.55W
Pozo del Mortero	55 Bg	24.24S	61.02W
Pozo del Tigre	55 Bc	17.34S	61.59W
Pozo Dulce	55 Ai	29.04S	62.02W
Pozos, Punta-	56 Gg	47.57S	65.47W
Pozuelos	54 Fa	10.11N	64.39W
Pozzallo	14 In	36.43N	14.51E
Pozzuoli	14 Ij	40.49N	14.07E
Pra [Ghana]	34 Ed	6.27N	1.47W
Pra [R.S.F.S.R.]	7 Ji	54.45N	41.01E
Prabuty	10 Pc	53.46N	19.10E
Prachatice	10 Jg	49.01N	14.00E
Prachin Buri	25 Kf	14.02N	101.22E
Prachuap Khiri Khan	25 Jf	11.48N	99.47E
Praděd	10 Nf	50.06N	17.14E
Prades	11 Il	42.37N	2.26E
Prado	54 Kg	17.21S	39.13W
Præstø	8 Ei	55.07N	12.03E
Prague (EN)=Praha	6 He	50.05N	14.26E
Praha=Prague (EN)	6 He	50.05N	14.26E
Prahova [2]	15 Id	45.10N	26.00E
Praia	31 Eg	14.55N	23.31W
Praia a Mare	14 Jk	39.54N	15.47E
Praia da Rocha	13 Dg	37.07N	8.32W
Praia Rica	55 Eb	14.51S	55.33W
Praid	15 Ic	46.33N	25.08E
Prainha	54 Hd	1.48S	53.29W
Prairie Dog Town Fork	45 Gi	34.26N	99.21W
Prairie du Chien	45 Ke	43.03N	91.09W
Prangli	8 Ke	59.38N	24.50E
Pránhita	25 Fe	18.49N	79.55E
Prapat	26 Cf	2.40N	98.56E
Prasat	25 Kf	14.38N	103.24E
Praslin	51k Bb	13.53N	60.54W
Praslin, Port-	51k Bb	13.53N	60.54W
Praslin Island	37b Ca	4.19S	55.44E
Prasonisi	15 Kn	35.52N	27.46E
Prat, Isla-	56 Fg	48.15S	75.00W
Prata	54 Ig	19.18S	48.55W
Prata, Rio da-	55 Hd	18.49S	49.54W
Pratapgarh	25 Ed	24.02N	74.47E
Prat de Llobregat/El Prat de Llobregat	13 Oc	41.20N	2.06E
Prato	14 Fg	43.53N	11.06E
Pratomagno	14 Fg	43.40N	11.40E
Pratt	43 Hd	37.39N	98.44W
Prättigau	14 Dd	46.55N	9.40E
Pratt Seamount (EN)	40 Ke	56.10N	142.30W
Prattville	44 Di	32.28N	86.29W
Pratudinho, Rio-	55 Ja	13.58S	45.10W
Pravda	18 Cf	36.50N	60.33E
Pravda Coast	66 Ge	67.00S	94.00E
Pravdinsk [R.S.F.S.R.]	8 Ij	54.28N	21.00E
Pravdinsk [R.S.F.S.R.]	7 Kh	56.33N	43.33E
Pravia	13 Fa	43.29N	6.07W
Praxedis G. Guerrero	48 Gb	31.22N	106.00W
Praya	26 Gh	8.42S	116.17E
Prealpi Venete	14 Fd	46.25N	11.50E
Predazzo	14 Fd	46.19N	11.36E
Predeal	15 Id	45.30N	25.34E
Predeal, Pasul-	15 Id	45.28N	25.36E
Predel	14 Hd	46.25N	13.35E
Predivinsk	20 Ee	57.04N	93.37E
Predporožny	20 Jd	65.00N	143.20E
Pré-en-Pail	11 Ff	48.27N	0.12W
Preetz	10 Gb	54.14N	10.17E
Pregolia	7 Ei	54.42N	20.24E
Pregradnaja	16 Lh	43.58N	41.12E
Preilj/Prejli	7 Gh	56.19N	26.48E
Preissac, Lac-	44 Ha	48.25N	78.28W
Prejli/Preilj	7 Gh	56.19N	26.48E
Prekmurje	14 Kd	46.45N	16.15E
Prekornica	15 Cg	42.40N	19.12E
Prekule/Priekulė	8 Ii	55.36N	21.12E
Přelouč	10 Lf	50.02N	15.33E
Premià de Mar/Premiá de Mar	13 Oc	41.29N	2.22E
Premiá de Mar/Premià de Mar	13 Oc	41.29N	2.22E
Premnitz	10 Id	52.32N	12.20E
Premuda	14 If	44.21N	14.37E
Prenaj/Prienai	7 Fi	54.39N	23.59E
Prenj	14 Lg	43.32N	17.52E
Prenjasi	15 Dh	41.04N	20.32E
Prentice	45 Kd	45.33N	90.17W
Prentiss	45 Lk	31.36N	89.52W
Prenzlau	10 Jc	53.19N	13.52E
Preobraženije	20 Ih	42.58N	133.55E
Preobraženka	20 Fd	60.04N	107.58E
Preparis Island	25 If	14.52N	93.41E
Preparis North Channel	25 Ie	15.27N	94.05E
Preparis South Channel	25 If	14.45N	94.05E
Přerov	10 Ng	49.27N	17.27E
Prescelly, Mynydd-	9 Ij	51.58N	4.42W
Prescott [Ar.-U.S.]	45 Jj	33.48N	93.23W
Prescott [Az.-U.S.]	43 Ee	34.33N	112.28W
Preševo	15 Eg	42.19N	21.39E
Presho	45 Fe	43.53N	100.04W
Presicce	14 Mk	39.54N	18.16E
Presidencia Roque Sáenz Peña	53 Jh	26.50S	60.30W
Presidente Epitácio	56 Jb	21.46S	52.06W
Presidente Frei	66 Re	62.12S	58.55W
Presidente Hayes [3]	55 Cf	24.00S	59.00W
Presidente Juscelino	55 Jd	18.39S	44.05W
Presidente Murtinho	55 Fb	15.39S	53.54W
Presidente Olegário	55 Id	18.25S	46.25W
Presidente Prudente	56 Jb	22.07S	51.22W
Presidente Venceslau	55 Ge	21.52S	51.50W
President Thiers Seamount (EN)	57 Lg	24.39S	145.51W
Presidio	43 Gf	29.33N	104.23W
Presidio, Rio del-	48 Ff	23.06N	106.17W
Preslav	15 Jf	43.10N	26.49E
Presnovka	17 Mi	54.40N	67.09E
Prešov	10 Rh	49.00N	21.14E
Prespa	15 Hh	41.43N	24.53E
Prespa, Lake- (EN)=Prespansko jezero	5 Ig	40.55N	21.00E
Prespansko jezero=Prespa, Lake- (EN)	5 Ig	40.55N	21.00E
Presque Isle	43 Nb	46.41N	68.01W
Prestea	34 Ed	5.26N	2.09W
Přeštice	10 Jg	49.35N	13.21E
Preston [Eng.-U.K.]	9 Kh	53.46N	2.42W
Preston [Id.-U.S.]	43 Ec	42.06N	111.53W
Preston [Ont.-Can.]	44 Gd	43.23N	80.21W
Prestonsburg	44 Fg	37.40N	82.46W
Preststranda	8 Ce	59.06N	9.04E
Prestwick	9 If	55.30N	4.37W
Prêto, Rio- [Braz.]	54 Jf	11.21S	43.52W
Prêto, Rio- [Braz.]	55 Gd	18.44S	50.23W
Prêto, Rio- [Braz.]	55 Ic	17.00S	46.12W
Prêto, Rio- [Braz.]	55 Ha	13.37S	48.06W
Preto do Igapó Açu, Rio-	54 Gd	4.26S	59.48W
Pretoria	31 Jk	25.45S	28.10E
Pretty Rock Butte	45 Fc	46.10N	101.42W
Preußisch-Oldendorf	12 Kb	52.18N	8.30E
Préveza	15 Dk	38.57N	20.45E
Prey	12 Df	48.58N	1.13E
Prey Vêng	25 Lf	11.29N	105.19E
Priangarskoje Plato	20 Ee	57.30N	97.00E
Priargunsk	20 Gf	50.27N	119.00E
Pribelski	17 Hi	54.24N	56.29E
Pribilof Islands	38 Cd	57.00N	170.00W
Priboj	15 Cf	43.35N	19.32E
Příbram	10 Kg	49.42N	14.01E
Price [Que.-Can.]	44 Ma	48.39N	68.12W
Price [Ut.-U.S.]	46 Jg	39.36N	110.48W
Price River	46 Jg	39.10N	110.06W
Prichard	44 Cj	30.44N	88.05W
Prickly Pear Cays	51b Ab	18.16N	63.11W
Prickly Point	51p Bc	11.59N	61.45W
Pridneprovskaja Vozvyšennost=Dnepr Upland (EN)	5 Jf	49.00N	32.00E
Priego	13 Jd	40.27N	2.18W
Priego de Córdoba	13 Hg	37.26N	4.11W
Priei, Măgura-	15 Fc	46.58N	22.50E
Priekule	7 Eh	56.29N	21.37E
Priekulė/Prekule	8 Ii	55.36N	21.12E
Prienai/Prenaj	7 Fi	54.39N	23.59E
Priene	24 Bd	37.40N	27.13E
Prieska	31 Jk	29.40S	22.42E
Priest Lake	46 Gb	48.34N	116.52W
Prieta, Peña-	13 Ha	43.01N	4.44W
Prieta, Sierra-	48 Cb	31.15N	112.55W
Prievidza	10 Oh	48.46N	18.39E
Prignitz	10 Hc	53.00N	12.00E
Prijedor	14 Kf	44.59N	16.42E
Prijepolje	15 Cf	43.24N	19.39E
Prijutovo	19 Fe	53.58N	53.58E
Prikaspijskaja Nizmennost=Caspian Depression (EN)	5 Lf	48.00N	52.00E
Prilenskoje Plato = Lena Mountains (EN)	21 Oc	60.45N	125.00E
Prilep	15 Eh	41.21N	21.34E
Priluki	19 De	50.36N	32.24E
Primavera	66 Qe	64.09S	60.57W
Primeira Cruz	54 Jd	2.30S	43.26W
Primorje	8 Hj	54.56N	20.00E
Primorsk [R.S.F.S.R.]	7 Gf	60.22N	28.36E
Primorsk [Ukr.-U.S.S.R.]	16 Jf	46.43N	36.22E
Primorski Hrebet	20 Ff	52.30N	106.00E
Primorski Kraj [3]	20 Ig	45.30N	135.30E
Primorsko	15 Kg	42.16N	27.46E
Primorsko-Ahtarsk	19 Df	46.03N	38.11E
Primorskoje [R.S.F.S.R.]	8 Ld	60.32N	27.56E
Primorskoje [Ukr.-U.S.S.R.]	15 Nd	45.59N	30.15E
Primošten	14 Jg	43.36N	15.55E
Primrose Lake	42 Gf	54.55N	109.45W
Prims	10 Cg	49.20N	6.44E
Prince Albert	39 Id	53.12N	104.46W
Prince Albert Mountains	66 Jf	76.00S	161.30E
Prince Albert Peninsula	42 Fb	72.30N	116.00W
Prince Albert Road	37 Cf	33.13S	22.02E
Prince Albert Sound	42 Gb	70.25N	115.00W
Prince Alfred, Cape-	42 Fb	74.05N	124.29W
Prince Charles	38 Lc	67.50N	76.00W
Prince Charles Mountains	66 Ff	72.00S	67.00E
Prince-de-Galles, Cap -	42 Kd	61.36N	71.30W
Prince Edward	30 Km	46.33S	37.57E
Prince Edward Island [3]	42 Lg	46.30N	63.00W
Prince Edward Island	38 Me	46.30N	63.00W
Prince Edward Islands	30 Km	46.35S	37.56E
Prince George	39 Gd	53.55N	122.49W
Prince Gustaf Adolf Sea	38 Ib	78.30N	107.00W
Prince of Wales [Ak.-U.S.]	40 Me	55.47N	132.50W
Prince of Wales [Can.]	38 Jb	72.40N	99.00W
Prince of Wales, Cape-	38 Cc	65.40N	168.05W
Prince of Wales Island	59 Ib	10.40S	142.10E
Prince of Wales Mountains	42 Ja	77.45N	78.00W
Prince of Wales Strait	42 Fb	72.45N	118.00W
Prince Patrick	38 Hb	76.45N	119.30W
Prince Regent Inlet	42 Ib	72.45N	90.30W
Prince Rupert	39 Fd	54.19N	130.19W
Prince Rupert Bay	51g Ba	15.34N	61.29W
Prince Rupert Bluff	51g Ba	15.35N	61.29W
Princes Risborough	12 Bc	51.43N	0.49W
Princess Anne	44 Jf	38.12N	75.41W
Princess Charlotte Bay	59 Ib	14.25S	144.00E
Princess Elizabeth Land	66 Ff	70.00S	80.00E

Index Symbols

[1] Independent Nation
[2] State, Region
[3] District, County
[4] Municipality
[5] Colony, Dependency
Continent
Physical Region
Historical or Cultural Region
Mount, Mountain
Volcano
Hill
Mountains, Mountain Range
Hills, Escarpment
Plateau, Upland
Pass, Gap
Plain, Lowland
Delta
Salt Flat
Valley, Canyon
Crater, Cave
Karst Features
Depression
Polder
Desert, Dunes
Forest, Woods
Heath, Steppe
Oasis
Cape, Point
Coast, Beach
Cliff
Peninsula
Isthmus
Sandbank
Island
Atoll
Rock, Reef
Islands, Archipelago
Rocks, Reefs
Coral Reef
Well, Spring
Geyser
River, Stream
Waterfall Rapids
River Mouth, Estuary
Lake
Salt Lake
Intermittent Lake
Reservoir
Swamp, Pond
Canal
Glacier
Ice Shelf, Pack Ice
Ocean
Sea
Gulf, Bay
Strait, Fjord
Lagoon
Bank
Seamount
Tablemount
Ridge
Shelf
Basin
Escarpment, Sea Scarp
Fracture
Trench, Abyss
National Park, Reserve
Point of Interest
Recreation Site
Cave, Cavern
Historic Site
Ruins
Wall, Walls
Church, Abbey
Temple
Scientific Station
Airport
Port
Lighthouse
Mine
Tunnel
Dam, Bridge

Princess Margaret Range 42 Ia 79.00N 88.30W
Princess Royal 42 Ef 52.55N 128.50W
Princeton [B.C.-Can.] 42 Fg 49.27N 120.31W
Princeton [Il.-U.S.] 45 Lf 41.23N 89.28W
Princeton [In.-U.S.] 44 Df 38.21N 87.34W
Princeton [Ky.-U.S.] 44 Dg 37.07N 87.53W
Princeton [Mo.-U.S.] 45 Jf 40.24N 93.35W
Prince William Sound 38 Ec 60.40N 147.00W
Principe 30 Hh 1.37N 7.25 E
Prineville 46 Ed 44.18N 120.51W
Prineville Reservoir 46 Ed 44.08N 120.42W
Prins Christians Sund 41 Hf 60.00N 43.10W
Prinsesse Astrid Kyst 66 Cf 70.45S 12.30 E
Prinsesse Ragnhild Kyst 66 Df 70.15S 27.30 E
Prins Harald Kyst 66 De 69.30S 36.00 E
Prins Karls Forland 41 Nc 78.32N 11.10 E
Prinzapolka 47 Hf 13.24N 83.34W
Prinzapolka, Rio- 49 Fg 13.24N 83.34W
Priora, Mount- 59 Ja 6.51S 145.58 E
Priozersk 19 Dc 61.04N 30.07 E
Pripet Marshes (EN) 5 Ie 52.00N 27.00 E
Pripjat 5 Je 51.21N 30.09 E
Pripoljarny Ural=Subpolar Urals (EN) 5 Lb 65.00N 60.00 E
Prirečny 19 Db 69.02N 30.15 E
Prišib 16 Pj 39.06N 48.38 E
Prislop, Pasul- 15 Hb 47.37N 24.55 E
Pristan-Prževalsk 18 Lc 42.33N 78.18 E
Pristen 16 Jd 51.15N 36.42 E
Priština 15 Eg 42.40N 21.10 E
Pritzwalk 10 Ic 53.09N 12.11 E
Privas 11 Kj 44.44N 4.36 E
Priverno 14 Hi 41.28N 13.11 E
Privolžkaja Vozvyšennost=Volga Hills (EN) 5 Ke 52.00N 46.00 E
Privolžsk 7 Jh 57.27N 41.16 E
Privolžski 16 Od 51.23N 46.02 E
Prizren 15 Dg 42.13N 20.43 E
Prizzi 14 Hm 37.43N 13.26 E
Prjaža 7 Hf 61.43N 33.37 E
Prnjavor 14 Lf 44.52N 17.40 E
Probolinggo 26 Fh 7.45S 113.13 E
Prochowice 10 Me 51.17N 16.22 E
Procida 14 Hj 40.45N 14.00 E
Proctor Reservoir 45 Gj 32.02N 98.32W
Proddatur 25 Ff 14.44N 78.33 E
Profitis Ilias [Grc.] 15 Fm 36.53N 22.22 E
Profitis Ilias [Grc.] 15 Fj 39.50N 22.38 E
Profondeville 12 Gd 50.23N 4.52 E
Progonati 15 Ci 40.13N 19.56 E
Prograničnik 18 Dg 35.43N 63.12 E
Progreso [Mex.] 39 Kg 21.17N 89.40W
Progreso [Mex.] 48 Id 27.28N 101.04W
Progress 20 Hg 49.41N 129.40 E
Prohladny 16 Nh 43.45N 44.01 E
Prohorovka 16 Jd 51.02N 36.42 E
Prokopjevsk 22 Kd 53.53N 86.45 E
Prokuplje 15 Ef 43.15N 21.36 E
Proletari 7 Hg 58.26N 31.43 E
Proletarsk [R.S.F.S.R.] 19 Ef 46.41N 41.44 E
Proletarsk [Tad.-U.S.S.R.] 18 Gd 40.10N 69.31 E
Proletarski 16 Id 50.51N 35.46 E
Proletarskoje Vodohranilišče 16 Mf 46.30N 42.10 E
Proliv Soela/Soela Väin 8 Jf 58.40N 22.30 E
Prome 22 Lh 18.49N 95.13 E
Promissão, Represa- 56 Kb 21.32S 49.52W
Promissão 55 He 21.32S 49.52W
Promyšlenny 17 Kc 67.35N 63.55 E
Pronja [Bye.-U.S.S.R.] 16 Gc 53.27N 31.03 E
Pronja [U.S.S.R.] 16 Lb 54.21N 40.24 E
Pronsfeld 12 Id 50.10N 6.20 E
Prophet 42 Fe 58.46N 122.45W
Propriá 54 Kf 10.13S 36.51W
Propriano 11a Ab 41.40N 8.54 E
Prorva 16 Rg 45.57N 53.13 E
Proserpine 59 Jd 20.24S 148.34 E
Prosna 10 Nd 52.10N 17.39 E
Prosotsáni 15 Gh 41.11N 23.59 E
Prosperidad 26 Ie 8.34N 125.52 E
Prospihino 20 Ee 58.37N 99.20 E
Prosser 46 Fc 46.12N 119.46W
Prostějov 10 Ng 49.29N 17.07 E
Proszowice 10 Qf 50.12N 20.18 E
Próti 15 El 37.03N 21.33 E
Protoka 16 Jg 45.43N 37.46 E
Protva 7 Ii 54.51N 37.16 E
Provadija 15 Kf 43.11N 27.26 E
Prøven 41 Gd 72.15N 55.40W
Provence 11 Lk 44.00N 6.00 E
Provence 5 Gg 44.00N 6.00 E
Providence [Ky.-U.S.] 44 Dg 37.24N 87.39W
Providence [R.I.-U.S.] 39 Le 41.50N 71.25W
Providence, Cape- 62 Bg 46.01S 166.28 E
Providence Bay 44 Fc 45.44N 82.18W
Providence Island 30 Mi 9.14S 51.02 E
Providencia, Isla de- 47 Hf 13.21N 81.22W
Providenciales 49 Kc 21.49N 72.15W
Providenija 22 Uc 64.23N 173.18W
Provincetown 44 Ld 42.03N 70.11W
Provins 11 Jf 48.33N 3.18 E
Provo 39 He 40.14N 111.39W
Prozor 14 Lg 43.49N 17.37 E
Prudentópolis 55 Gg 25.12S 50.57W
Prudhoe Bay 39 Eb 70.20N 148.25W
Prudnik 10 Nf 50.19N 17.34 E
Prüm 12 Ie 49.49N 6.28 E
Prüm 10 Cf 50.13N 6.25 E
Prune Island 51n Bb 12.35N 61.24W
Prussia (EN) 10 Pc 53.45N 20.00 E
Pruszcz Gdański 10 Ob 54.16N 18.36 E
Pruszków 10 Qd 52.11N 20.48 E
Prut 5 If 45.28N 28.14 E
Pružany 19 Ce 52.36N 24.28 E
Prvić 14 If 44.54N 14.48 E
Prydz Bay 66 Fe 69.00S 76.00 E
Pryor 45 Ih 36.19N 95.19W
Przasnysz 10 Qc 53.01N 20.55 E
Przedbórz 10 Pe 51.06N 19.53 E
Przemyśl [2] 10 Sg 49.47N 22.45 E
Przemyśl 10 Sg 49.47N 22.47 E
Prževalsk 22 Je 42.29N 78.24 E
Przeworsk 10 Sf 50.05N 22.29 E
Przysucha 10 Qe 51.22N 20.38 E
Psakhná 15 Gk 38.35N 23.38 E
Psará 15 Ik 38.35N 25.37 E
Psathoúra 15 Hj 39.30N 24.11 E
Pščiš 16 Kg 45.03N 39.25 E
Psebaj 16 Lg 44.07N 40.47 E
Psël 5 Jf 49.05N 33.30 E
Psérimos 15 Km 36.56N 27.09 E
Psina 10 Of 50.02N 18.16 E
Pšiš, Gora- 16 Lh 43.24N 41.14 E
Pskem 18 Hd 41.38N 70.01 E
Pskent 18 Gd 40.54N 69.23 E
Pskov 6 Id 57.50N 28.20 E
Pskov, Lake- (EN)=Pihkva järv 7 Gg 58.00N 28.00 E
Pskov, Lake- (EN)=Pskovskoje Ozero 5 Id 58.00N 28.00 E
Pskova 8 Mg 57.47N 28.30 E
Pskovskaja Oblast [3] 19 Cd 57.20N 29.20 E
Pskovskoje Ozero=Pskov, Lake- (EN) 5 Id 58.00N 28.00 E
Psunj 14 Le 45.24N 17.20 E
Ptič 16 Fc 52.09N 28.52 E
Ptolemais 15 Ei 40.31N 21.41 E
Ptuj 14 Jd 46.25N 15.52 E
Pua-a, Cape- 65c Aa 13.26S 172.43W
Puah, Pulau- 26 Hg 0.30S 122.34 E
Puapua 65c Aa 13.34S 172.09W
Pucallpa 53 If 8.20S 74.30W
Pučež 7 Kh 56.59N 43.11 E
Pucheng [China] 27 Kf 27.55N 118.30 E
Pucheng [China] 27 Id 35.00N 109.38 E
Pucho 36 Cf 17.35S 16.30 E
Pucioasa 15 Id 45.05N 25.25 E
Pučišća 14 Kg 43.21N 16.44 E
Puck 10 Ob 54.44N 18.27 E
Pucka, Zatoka- 10 Ob 54.40N 18.35 E
Pudasjärvi 7 Gd 65.23N 27.00 E
Pudož 19 Dc 61.50N 36.32 E
Pudukkottai 25 Ff 10.23N 78.49 E
Puebla [2] 47 Ee 18.50N 98.00W
Puebla, Sierra de- 48 Kh 19.50N 97.00W
Puebla de Alcocer 13 Gf 38.59N 5.15W
Puebla de Don Fabrique 13 Jg 37.58N 2.26W
Puebla de Guzmán 13 Eg 37.37N 7.15W
Puebla de Sanabria 13 Fb 42.03N 6.38W
Puebla de Trives 13 Eb 42.20N 7.15W
Puebla de Zaragoza 39 Jh 19.03N 98.12W
Pueblo 39 If 38.16N 104.37W
Pueblo Libertador 55 Cj 30.13S 59.23W
Pueblo Nuevo [Mex.] 48 Gf 23.23N 105.23W
Pueblo Nuevo [Ven.] 49 Mh 11.58N 69.55W
Pueblo Nuevo Tiquisate 49 Bf 14.17N 91.22W
Pueblo Viejo, Laguna de- 48 Kf 22.10N 97.55W
Puelches 56 Ge 38.09S 65.55W
Puenteáreas 13 Db 42.11N 8.30W
Puente de la Reina 13 Kb 42.40N 1.49W
Puentedeume 13 Da 43.24N 8.10W
Puente-Genil 13 Hg 37.23N 4.47W
Puentelarrá 13 Ib 42.45N 3.03W
Pueo Point 65a Ab 21.54N 160.04W
Pu'er 27 Hg 23.00N 101.00 E
Puerca, Punta- 51a Cb 18.15N 65.35W
Puerco, Rio- 45 Ci 34.22N 107.50W
Puerco River 46 Ji 34.52N 110.05W
Puerto Abente 55 Df 22.55S 57.43W
Puerto Acosta 54 Eg 15.32S 69.15W
Puerto Adela 55 Eg 24.33S 54.22W
Puerto Aisén 53 Ij 45.24S 72.42W
Puerto Alegre 54 Ff 13.53S 61.36W
Puerto Ángel 47 Ee 15.40N 96.29W
Puerto Arista 48 Mj 15.56N 93.48W
Puerto Armuelles 47 Hg 8.17N 82.52W
Puerto Asís 54 Cc 0.29N 76.32W
Puerto Ayacucho 53 Je 5.40N 67.35W
Puerto Ayora 54a Ab 0.45S 90.23W
Puerto Barrios 39 Kh 15.43N 88.36W
Puerto Bermejo 55 Ch 26.56S 58.30W
Puerto Berrio 54 Db 6.30N 74.25W
Puerto Boyacá 54 Db 5.45N 74.29W
Puerto Caballo 55 Ce 20.12S 58.12W
Puerto Cabello 53 Jd 10.28N 68.01W
Puerto Cabezas 47 Hf 14.02N 83.23W
Puerto Carreño 53 Je 6.12N 67.22W
Puerto Casado 56 Ib 20.20S 57.55W
Puerto Colombia 49 Jh 10.59N 74.57W
Puerto Colón 55 Df 23.11S 57.33W
Puerto Constanza 55 Ck 33.50S 59.03W
Puerto Cooper 56 Ib 23.03S 57.43W
Puerto Cortés [C.R.] 49 Fi 8.58N 83.32W
Puerto Cortés [Hond.] 39 Kh 15.48N 87.56W
Puerto Cumarebo 54 Ea 11.29N 69.21W
Puerto de Eten 54 Ce 6.56S 79.52W
Puerto de la Cruz 32 Dd 28.23N 16.33W
Puerto de Lajas, Cerro- 47 Cc 28.59N 107.02W
Puerto del Rosario 32 Ed 28.30N 13.52W
Puerto de Mazarrón 13 Kg 37.34N 1.15W
Puerto de San José 47 Ff 13.55N 90.49W
Puerto Deseado 53 Jj 47.45S 65.55W
Puerto de Sóller 13 Oe 39.48N 2.41 E
Puerto Escondido [Mex.] 47 Ee 15.48N 96.57W
Puerto Escondido [Mex.] 48 De 25.48N 111.20W
Puerto Esperanza [Arg.] 55 Eh 26.01S 54.39W
Puerto Esperanza [Par.] 55 Ce 20.26S 58.06W
Puerto Estrella 49 Lg 12.14N 71.13W
Puerto Fonciere 55 Df 22.29S 57.48W
Puerto Francisco de Orellana 54 Cd 0.27S 76.57W
Puerto Frey 55 Bb 14.42S 61.10W
Puerto Gaitán 54 Dc 4.20N 72.10W
Puerto General Diaz 55 Eg 25.12S 54.32W
Puerto Goya 55 Ci 29.09S 59.20W
Puerto Grether 54 Fg 17.12S 64.21W
Puerto Guarani 55 De 21.18S 57.55W
Puerto Heath 54 Ef 12.30S 68.40W
Puerto Huasco 56 Fc 28.28S 71.14W
Puerto Huitoto 54 Dc 0.18N 74.03W
Puerto Iguazú 56 Jc 25.34S 54.34W
Puerto Indio 55 Eg 24.52S 54.29W
Puerto Ingeniero Ibañez 56 Fg 46.18S 71.56W
Puerto Isabel 55 Dd 18.11S 57.37W
Puerto Jesús 49 Eh 10.07N 85.16W
Puerto Juárez 39 Kg 21.11N 86.49W
Puerto la Concordia 54 Dc 2.38N 72.47W
Puerto la Cruz 53 Jd 10.13N 64.38W
Puerto Leguizamo 53 If 0.12S 74.46W
Puerto Lempira 49 Ff 15.15N 83.46W
Puerto Libertad 47 Bc 29.55N 112.43W
Puerto Limón [Col.] 54 Cc 1.02N 76.32W
Puerto Limón [Col.] 54 Dc 3.23N 73.30W
Puertollano 13 Hf 38.41N 4.07W
Puerto Lopez 54 Dc 4.06N 72.58W
Puerto López 49 Lh 11.56N 71.17W
Puerto Lumbreras 13 Kg 37.34N 1.49W
Puerto Madero 48 Mj 14.44N 92.25W
Puerto Madryn 56 Gf 42.46S 65.03W
Puerto Magdalena 48 Ce 24.35N 112.05W
Puerto Maldonado 53 Jg 12.36S 69.11W
Puerto Marangatú 55 Eg 24.39S 54.21W
Puerto Mayor Otaño 55 Eh 26.19S 54.44W
Puerto Mihanovich 55 De 20.52S 57.59W
Puerto Monte Lindo 55 Df 23.57S 57.12W
Puerto Montt 53 Ij 41.28S 72.57W
Puerto Morelos 48 Pg 20.50N 86.52W
Puerto Mutis 54 Cb 6.14N 77.25W
Puerto Naranjito 55 Eh 26.57S 55.18W
Puerto Nariño 54 Ec 4.56N 67.48W
Puerto Natales 53 Ik 51.44S 72.31W
Puerto Nuevo 55 Ce 20.33S 58.03W
Puerto Nuevo, Punta- 51a Bb 18.30N 66.21W
Puerto Ordaz 54 Fb 8.22N 62.41W
Puerto Padre 49 Ic 21.12N 76.36W
Puerto Páez 54 Eb 6.13N 67.28W
Puerto Peñasco 47 Bb 31.20N 113.33W
Puerto Piña 49 Hj 7.35N 78.10W
Puerto Pinasco 56 Ib 22.43S 57.50W
Puerto Piritu 50 Dg 10.04N 65.03W
Puerto Plata 47 Je 19.48N 70.41W
Puerto Presidente Stroessner 55 Eg 25.33S 54.39W
Puerto Princesa 22 Ni 9.44N 118.44 E
Puerto Quijarro 55 Dc 17.47S 57.46W
Puerto Real 13 Fh 36.32N 6.11W
Puerto Rico [5] 39 Mh 18.15N 66.30W
Puerto Rico 38 Mh 18.15N 66.30W
Puerto Rico [Arg.] 56 Jc 26.48S 54.59W
Puerto Rico [Bol.] 54 Ef 11.05S 67.38W
Puerto Rico [Col.] 54 Cc 1.54N 75.10W
Puerto Rico Trench (EN) 3 Bg 20.00N 66.00W
Puerto Rondón 54 Db 6.18N 71.06W
Puerto San José 55 Eg 26.32S 54.50W
Puerto Santa Cruz 53 Jk 50.09S 68.30W
Puerto Sastre 56 Ib 22.06S 57.59W
Puerto Siles 54 Ef 12.48S 65.05W
Puerto Suárez 53 Kg 18.57S 57.51W
Puerto Tacurú Pytá 55 Df 23.49S 57.09W
Puerto Tirol 55 Ch 27.23S 59.05W
Puerto Tres Palmas 55 De 21.43S 57.58W
Puerto Triunfo 55 Eg 26.45S 55.06W
Puerto Vallarta 47 Cd 20.37N 105.15W
Puerto Varas 56 Ff 41.19S 72.59W
Puerto Victoria 55 Eh 26.20S 54.39W
Puerto Viejo 49 Eh 10.26N 83.59W
Puerto Villamizar 49 Ki 8.19N 72.26W
Puerto Villazón 55 Ba 13.32S 61.57W
Puerto Wilches 54 Db 7.20N 73.54W
Puerto Ybapobó 55 Df 23.42S 57.12W
Pueu 65e Fc 17.44S 149.13W
Pugačev 19 Ee 52.03N 48.48 E
Puget Sound 46 Dc 48.00N 122.30W
Puglia=Apulia (EN) [2] 14 Ki 41.15N 16.15 E
Pu He 28 Gd 41.21N 122.47 E
Puhja 8 Lf 58.13N 26.17 E
Puigcerdá 13 Nb 42.26N 1.56 E
Puigmal 13 Ob 42.23N 2.07 E
Puir 20 Jf 53.10N 141.25 E
Puisaye, Collines de la- 11 Jg 47.35N 3.18 E
Puisieux 12 Ed 50.07N 2.42 E
Pujehum 34 Cd 7.21N 11.42W
Pujeşti 15 Kc 46.25N 27.29 E
Puji → Wugong 27 Ie 34.15N 108.14 E
Pujiang 28 Ei 29.28N 119.53 E
Pujili 54 Cd 0.57S 78.42W
Puka 15 Cg 42.03N 19.54 E
Pukaki, Lake- 62 Df 44.05S 170.10 E
Pukalani 65a Ec 20.50N 156.21W
Pukapuka Atoll 57 Kf 10.53S 165.49W
Pukapuka Atoll [W.F.] 57 Nf 14.49S 138.48W
Pukaruha Atoll 57 Nf 18.20S 137.02W
Pukatawagan 42 He 55.44N 101.19W
Pukchin 28 Hd 40.12N 125.45 E
Pukch'ŏng 27 Mc 40.14N 128.19 E
Pukega, Pointe- 64h Ab 13.17S 176.13W
Pukekohe 62 Fb 37.12S 174.54 E
Pukemiro 62 Fb 37.37S 175.01 E
Pukeuri Junction 62 Df 45.02S 171.02 E
Pukšenga 7 Je 63.36N 41.55 E
Puksoozero 19 Ec 62.38N 40.32 E
Puksubaek-san 28 Id 40.42N 127.15 E
Pula [It.] 14 Ck 39.01N 9.00 E
Pula [Yugo.] 14 Hf 44.52N 13.50 E
Pula, Capo di- 14 Dl 38.59N 9.01 E
Pulandian → Xinjin 27 Ld 39.24N 121.59 E
Pulap Atoll 57 Fd 7.39N 149.25 E
Pulaski [Tn.-U.S.] 44 Dh 35.12N 87.02W
Pulaski [Va.-U.S.] 44 Gg 37.03N 80.47W
Pulau 26 Kh 5.50S 138.15 E
Pulau Halura 26 Hi 10.19S 120.11 E
Pulau Irian/New Guinea 57 Fe 5.00S 140.00 E
Pulau Sapudi 26 Fh 7.06S 114.20 E
Puławy 10 Re 51.25N 21.57 E
Pulborough 12 Bd 50.57N 0.31W
Pulheim 12 Ic 51.00N 6.48 E
Pulkau 14 Kb 48.43N 16.21 E
Pulkkila 7 Fd 64.16N 25.52 E
Pullman 43 Db 46.44N 117.10W
Pulo Anna Island 57 Ed 4.40N 131.58 E
Pulog, Mount- 21 Oh 16.36N 120.54 E
Pulpito, Punta- 48 Dd 26.30N 111.30W
Pulsano 14 Lj 40.23N 17.21 E
Pułtusk 10 Rd 52.43N 21.05 E
Pülümür 24 Hc 39.30N 39.54 E
Pulusuk Island 57 Fd 6.42N 149.19 E
Puluwat Atoll 57 Fd 7.22N 149.11 E
Puma Yumco 27 Ff 28.35N 90.20 E
Pumpénai/Pumpenaj 8 Ki 55.53N 24.25 E
Pumpenaj/Pumpénai 8 Ki 55.53N 24.25 E
Pumpkin Creek 46 Mc 46.15N 105.45W
Puná, Isla- 54 Bd 2.50S 80.10W
Punākha 25 Hc 27.37N 89.52 E
Punaluu 65a Fd 19.08N 155.30W
Pünch 25 Eb 33.46N 74.06 E
Punda Milia 37 Ed 22.40S 31.05 E
Pune (Poona) 22 Jh 18.32N 73.52 E
Pünel 24 Md 37.33N 49.07 E
Pungan 18 Hd 40.45N 70.50 E
P'unggi 28 Jf 36.52N 128.32 E
Pungoé 37 Ec 19.50S 34.48 E
P'ungsan 28 Jd 40.40N 128.05 E
Punia 36 Ec 1.28S 26.27 E
Punitaqui 56 Fd 30.50S 71.16W
Punjab [3] 25 Fb 31.00N 76.00 E
Punjab 21 Jf 30.00N 74.00 E
Punjad [3] 25 Eb 30.00N 74.00 E
Punkaharju 8 Mc 61.48N 29.24 E
Punkalaidun 8 Jc 61.07N 23.06 E
Puno 53 Ig 15.50S 70.02W
Puno [2] 54 Ef 15.00S 70.00W
Punta, Cerro de- 47 Ke 18.10N 66.36W
Punta Alta 53 Ji 38.53S 62.04W
Punta Arenas 53 Ik 53.09S 70.55W
Punta Cardón 54 Da 11.38N 70.14W
Punta de Mata 50 Eh 9.43N 63.38W
Punta Gorda [Blz.] 47 Ge 16.07N 88.48W
Punta Gorda [Fl.-U.S.] 44 Fl 26.56N 82.03W
Punta Gorda [Nic.] 49 Fh 11.31N 83.47W
Punta Gorda, Bahía de- 49 Fh 11.15N 83.45W
Punta Gorda, Río- 49 Fh 11.30N 83.47W
Punta Indio 55 Dl 35.16S 57.14W
Punta Prieta 47 Bc 28.58N 114.17W
Puntarenas [3] 49 Ei 9.00N 83.15W
Puntarenas 39 Ki 9.58N 84.50W
Punta Róbalo 49 Fi 9.02N 82.15W
Punto Fijo 54 Da 11.42N 70.13W
Puolanka 7 Gd 64.52N 27.40 E
Puolo Point 65a Bb 21.54N 159.36W
Puqi 27 Jf 29.43N 113.52 E
Puquio 54 Df 14.42S 74.08W
Purace, Volcán- 54 Cc 2.21N 76.23W
Purari 60 Ci 7.52S 145.10 E
Purcell Mountains 42 Fg 49.55N 116.15W
Purdy Islands 57 Fe 2.53S 146.20 E
Purgatoire River 45 Eg 38.04N 103.10W
Puri 25 He 19.48N 85.51 E
Purificación 47 Ed 23.58N 98.42W
Purikari Neem/Purikarinem 8 Ke 59.36N 25.35 E
Purikarinem/Purikari Neem 8 Ke 59.36N 25.35 E
Purmani/Puurmani 8 Lf 58.30N 26.14 E
Purmerend 11 Kb 52.31N 4.57 E
Purna [India] 25 Fe 19.07N 77.02 E
Purna [India] 25 Fd 21.05N 76.00 E
Purnač 7 Jc 67.00N 40.15 E
Pūrnia 25 Hc 25.47N 87.28 E
Purukcahu 26 Fg 0.35S 114.35 E
Purulya 25 Hd 23.20N 86.22 E
Puruni River 50 Gi 6.00N 59.12W
Purus, Rio- 52 Jf 3.42S 61.28W
Puruvesi 7 Gf 61.50N 29.25 E
Purwakarta 26 Eh 6.34S 107.26 E
Purwokerto 26 Eh 7.25S 109.14 E
Pusala Daği 24 Ed 37.12N 32.54 E
Pusan 22 Of 35.06N 129.03 E
Pusan Si [2] 28 Jg 35.10N 129.05 E
Pushi He 28 Hd 40.17N 124.43 E
Puškin 19 Dd 59.43N 30.24 E
Puškino [Azb.-U.S.S.R.] 16 Pj 39.28N 48.33 E
Puškino [R.S.F.S.R.] 16 Od 51.14N 46.59 E
Puškino [R.S.F.S.R.] 7 Ih 56.02N 37.53 E
Puškinskije Gory 8 Mh 56.59N 28.59 E
Pušlahta 7 Id 64.48N 36.33 E
Püspökladány 10 Ri 47.19N 21.07 E
Püssi/Pjussi 8 Le 59.17N 26.57 E
Pusteci 15 Di 40.47N 20.54 E
Pusteria, Val-/Pustertal 14 Gd 46.45N 12.20 E
Pustertal/Pusteria, Val- 14 Gd 46.45N 12.20 E
Pustomyty 10 Tg 49.37N 23.59 E
Pustoška 7 Gh 56.20N 29.22 E
Putao 25 Jc 27.21N 97.24 E
Putaruru 62 Fc 38.03S 175.47 E
Putian 27 Kf 25.32N 119.01 E
Putignano 14 Lj 40.51N 17.07 E
Putila 15 Ip 48.00N 25.07 E
Putivl 16 Hd 51.22N 33.55 E
Putjatin 28 Lc 42.52N 132.25 E
Putla de Guerrero 48 Ki 17.02N 97.56W
Putna 15 Kd 45.34N 27.30 E
Putna 15 Ib 47.52N 25.37 E
Putnok 10 Qh 48.18N 20.26 E
Puto 63a Ba 5.41S 154.43 E
Putorana, Plato-=Putoran Mountains (EN) 21 Lc 69.00N 95.00 E
Putoran Mountains (EN)=Putorana, Plato- 21 Lc 69.00N 95.00 E
Puttalam 25 Fg 8.02N 79.49 E
Putte 12 Gc 51.04N 4.38 E
Puttelange-aux-Lacs 12 Ie 49.03N 6.56 E
Putten 12 Hb 52.16N 5.35 E
Putten 12 Gc 51.50N 4.15 E
Puttgarden, Burg auf Fehmarn- 10 Hb 54.30N 11.13 E
Püttlingen 12 Ie 49.17N 6.53 E
Putumayo [2] 54 Cc 0.30N 76.00W
Putumayo, Rio- 52 Jf 3.07S 67.58W
Putuo (Shenjiamen) 28 Gj 29.57N 122.18 E
Putussibau 26 Ff 0.50N 112.56 E
Puu Kukui 65a Ec 20.54N 156.35W
Puulavesi 5 Ic 61.50N 26.40 E
Puumala 7 Gf 61.32N 28.11 E
Puu o Umi 65a Fc 20.05N 155.42W
Puurmani/Purmani 8 Lf 58.30N 26.14 E
Puurs 12 Gc 51.05N 4.17 E
Puuwai 65a Ab 21.54N 160.12W
Puyallup 46 Dc 47.11N 122.18W
Puyang 27 Jd 35.41N 115.00 E
Puy-de-Dôme [3] 11 Ii 45.40N 3.00 E
Puy-l'Évêque 11 Hj 44.30N 1.08 E
Puymorens, Col de- 11 Hl 42.34N 1.49 E
Puyo 54 Cd 1.29S 77.58W
Puysegur Point 62 Bg 46.10S 166.37 E
Pwani [3] 36 Gd 7.30S 39.00 E
Pweto 31 Ji 8.28S 28.54 E
Pwllheli 9 Ii 52.53N 4.25W
Pyapon 25 Je 16.17N 95.41 E
Pyhäjärvi 7 Fe 63.40N 25.59 E
Pyhäjärvi [Fin.] 7 Ff 61.00N 22.20 E
Pyhäjärvi [Fin.] 7 Fe 63.35N 25.57 E
Pyhäjärvi [Fin.] 8 Kc 62.45N 25.25 E
Pyhäjärvi [Fin.] 8 Jc 61.30N 23.35 E
Pyhäjoki 7 Fd 64.28N 24.13 E
Pyhäjoki 7 Fd 64.28N 24.14 E
Pyhäntä 7 Gd 64.06N 26.19 E
Pyhäranta 8 Id 60.57N 21.27 E
Pyhäselkä 7 Ge 62.30N 29.40 E
Pyhäselkä 8 Mb 62.26N 29.58 E
Pyhätunturi 7 Gc 67.01N 27.09 E
Pyhävesi 8 Lc 61.25N 26.35 E
Pyhävuori 8 Ib 62.17N 21.38 E
Pyhrnpaß 14 Ic 47.38N 14.18 E
Pyhtää/Pyttis 7 Gf 60.29N 26.32 E
Pyinmana 22 Lh 19.44N 96.13 E
Pylos (EN)=Pilos 15 Em 36.56N 21.40 E
Pyltsamaa/Põltsamaa 8 Lf 58.23N 26.08 E
Pyltsamaa/Põltsamaa 7 Fg 58.39N 25.59 E
Pylva/Põlva 7 Gg 58.04N 27.06 E
Pymatuning Reservoir 44 Ge 41.37N 80.30W
P'yŏngan-Namdo [2] 28 Ie 39.20N 126.00 E
P'yŏngan-Pukto [2] 28 Hd 40.00N 125.15 E
P'yŏnggang 27 Md 38.25N 127.17 E
P'yŏngsan 27 Md 38.20N 126.24 E
P'yongt'aek 28 If 36.59N 127.05 E
P'yŏngyang 22 Of 39.01N 125.45 E
P'yŏngyang Si [2] 28 He 39.04N 125.50 E
Pyramiden 41 Nc 77.54N 16.41 E
Pyramid Lake 43 Dc 40.00N 119.35W
Pyramid Mountains 45 Bj 32.00N 108.30W
Pyrénées=Pyrenees (EN) 5 Gg 42.40N 1.00 E
Pyrenees (EN)=Pirineos 5 Gg 42.40N 1.00 E
Pyrenees (EN)=Pyrénées 5 Gg 42.40N 1.00 E
Pyrenees (EN)=Serralada Pirinenca 5 Gg 42.40N 1.00 E
Pyrénées-Atlantiques [3] 11 Fk 43.15N 0.50W
Pyrénées-Orientales [3] 11 Il 42.30N 2.20 E
Pyrzyce 10 Kc 53.10N 14.55 E
Pyšma 19 Gd 57.08N 66.18 E
Pytalovo 7 Gh 57.06N 27.59 E
Pyttegga 8 Bd 62.13N 7.42 E
Pyttis/Pyhtää 7 Gf 60.29N 26.32 E
Pyu 25 Je 18.29N 96.26 E
Pyzaspea/Pöösaspea Neem 8 Je 59.15N 23.25 E
Pyzdry 10 Nd 52.11N 17.41 E

Q

Qā', Wādī al- 24 Hi 27.04N 38.34 E
Qābis [3] 32 Ic 33.00N 9.30 E
Qābis 31 Ie 33.53N 10.07 E
Qābis, Khalīj-=Gabès, Gulf of-(EN) 30 Ie 34.00N 10.25 E
Qabr Hūd 35 Hb 16.09N 49.34 E
Qāderābād 24 Og 30.17N 53.16 E
Qādir Karam 24 Ke 35.12N 44.53 E
Qādub 23 Hg 12.38N 53.57 E
Qā'emshahr 24 Od 36.30N 52.55 E
Qafşah 31 He 34.25N 8.48 E
Qafşah [3] 32 Ic 34.30N 9.00 E
Qa'fūr 14 Dn 36.20N 9.19 E
Qagan 27 Kb 49.16N 118.04 E
Qagan Moron He 28 Ec 43.13N 119.02 E
Qagan Nur 27 Jc 43.20N 112.58 E
Qagan Nur [China] 28 Bd 41.33N 113.48 E
Qagan Nur [China] 27 Jc 43.25N 114.50 E
Qagan Nur [China] 28 Hb 45.14N 124.17 E
Qagan Nur → Zhengxiangbai Qi 27 Jc 42.16N 114.59 E
Qagan Us → Dulan 22 Lf 36.29N 98.29 E
Qagchêng/Xiangcheng 27 Gf 28.56N 99.46 E
Qahar Youyi Houqi (Bayan Qagan) 28 Bd 41.28N 113.10 E
Qahar Youyi Qianqi (Togrog Ul) 28 Bd 40.46N 113.13 E
Qahar Youyi Zhongqi 28 Bd 41.15N 112.36 E
Qahd, Wādī- 24 Ii 26.13N 40.49 E
Qaidam He 27 Gd 36.48N 95.50 E
Qaidam Pendi=Tsaidam Basin (EN) 27 Fd 37.00N 95.00 E

Index Symbols

[1] Independent Nation
[2] State, Region
[3] District, County
[4] Municipality
[5] Colony, Dependency
Continent
Physical Region

Historical or Cultural Region
Mount, Mountain
Volcano
Hill
Mountains, Mountain Range
Hills, Escarpment
Plateau, Upland

Pass, Gap
Plain, Lowland
Delta
Salt Flat
Valley, Canyon
Crater, Cave
Karst Features

Depression
Polder
Desert, Dunes
Forest, Woods
Heath, Steppe
Oasis
Cape, Point

Coast, Beach
Cliff
Peninsula
Isthmus
Sandbank
Island
Atoll

Rock, Reef
Islands, Archipelago
Rocks, Reefs
Coral Reef
Well, Spring
Geyser
River, Stream

Waterfall Rapids
River Mouth, Estuary
Lake
Salt Lake
Intermittent Lake
Reservoir
Swamp, Pond

Canal
Glacier
Ice Shelf, Pack Ice
Ocean
Sea
Gulf, Bay
Strait, Fjord

Lagoon
Bank
Seamount
Tablemount
Ridge
Shelf
Basin

Escarpment, Sea Scarp
Fracture
Trench, Abyss
National Park, Reserve
Point of Interest
Recreation Site
Cave, Cavern

Historic Site
Ruins
Wall, Walls
Church, Abbey
Temple
Scientific Station
Airport

Port
Lighthouse
Mine
Tunnel
Dam, Bridge

Qala'an Naḫl 35 Ec 13.38N 34.57 E
Qalāt 23 Kc 32.07N 66.54 E
Qal'at Abū Ghār 24 Lg 30.25N 46.09 E
Qal'at al Akhḑar 23 Ed 28.06N 37.05 E
Qal 'at al Marqab 24 Fe 35.09N 35.57 E
Qal'at al Mu'aẓẓam 24 Gi 27.45N 37.31 E
Qal'at aş Şanam 14 Co 35.46N 8.21 E
Qal'at Bishah 22 Gh 20.00N 42.36 E
Qal'at Dīzah 24 Kd 36.11N 45.07 E
Qal'at Şāliḩ 24 Lg 31.31N 47.16 E
Qal'at Sukkar 24 Lg 31.53N 46.56 E
Qal'eh Asgar 24 Qh 29.30N 56.35 E
Qal'eh Kūh 24 Mf 33.00N 49.10 E
Qal'eh Mūreh 24 Pe 35.35N 55.58 E
Qal'eh-ye Now 23 Jc 34.59N 63.08 E
Qal'eh-ye Sahar 24 Mg 31.40N 48.33 E
Qalib ash Shuyūkh 23 Gd 29.12N 47.55 E
Qallābāt 35 Fc 12.58N 36.09 E
Qalmarz, Godār-e- 24 Qf 33.26N 56.14 E
Qalyūb 24 Dg 30.11N 31.13 E
Qamata 37 Df 31.58S 27.24 E
Qamdo 22 Lf 31.15N 97.12 E
Qamīnis 33 Dc 31.40N 20.01 E
Qamsar 24 Nf 33.45N 51.26 E
Qamūdah 32 Ic 35.00N 9.21 E
Qamūdah [3] 32 Ic 34.50N 9.20 E
Qânâq/Thule 67 Od 77.35N 69.40W
Qandahār [3] 23 Kc 31.00N 65.45 E
Qandahār 22 If 31.35N 65.45 E
Qandala 35 Hc 11.23N 49.53 E
Qangdin Gol 28 Cc 43.27N 115.03 E
Qanţarat al Fahş 14 Dn 36.23N 9.54 E
Qapqal 27 Dc 43.48N 80.47 E
Qaqortoq/Julianehåb 67 Nc 60.50N 46.10W
Qarā Dāgh 24 Lc 38.48N 47.13 E
Qārah 33 Ed 29.37N 26.30 E
Qarah Būlāq 24 Ke 34.32N 45.12 E
Qarah Dagh 24 Jd 37.00N 43.30 E
Qarah Tappah 24 Ke 34.25N 44.56 E
Qarānqū 24 Ld 37.23N 47.43 E
Qardo 31 Lh 9.30N 49.03 E
Qareh Āghāj 24 Ld 36.46N 48.46 E
Qareh Sū [Iran] 23 Ib 37.00N 56.50 E
Qareh Sū [Iran] 23 Hc 34.52N 51.25 E
Qareh Ẕīā'Od Dīn 24 Kc 38.53N 45.02 E
Qarkilik/Ruoqiang 22 Kf 39.02N 88.00 E
Qarnayn, Jazīrat al- 24 Oj 24.56N 52.52 E
Qarnayt, Jabal- 23 Fe 21.02N 40.22 E
Qarqan/Qiemo 22 Kf 38.08N 85.32 E
Qarqan He 21 Kf 39.30N 88.15 E
Qarqannah, Juzur-=
Kerkennah Islands (EN) 30 Ie 34.44N 11.12 E
Qartājannah 14 En 36.51N 10.20 E
Qārūn, Birkat- 33 Fd 29.28N 30.40 E
Qaryat Abū Nujaym 33 Cc 30.35N 15.24 E
Qaryat al Gharab 24 Kg 31.27N 44.48 E
Qaryat al Qaddāḩiyah 33 Cc 31.22N 15.14 E
Qaryat al 'Ulyā 23 Gd 27.33N 47.42 E
Qaryat az Zarrūq 33 Cc 32.22N 15.09 E
Qaryat az Zuwaytīnah 33 Dc 30.58N 20.07 E
Qaşabah, Ra's al- 24 Fh 28.02N 34.38 E
Qaşabāt, Hanshīr al- 14 Dn 36.24N 9.54 E
Qasigiánguit/Christianshåb 41 Ge 68.45N 51.30W
Qaşr al Azraq 24 Gg 31.53N 36.49 E
Qasr Al Hayr 24 Ge 34.23N 37.36 E
Qaşr al Qarahbullī 33 Bc 32.45N 13.43 E
Qaşr 'Amij 24 If 33.30N 41.45 E
Qaşr Bū Hādī 33 Cc 31.03N 16.40 E
Qaşr Burqu' 24 Gf 32.37N 37.58 E
Qasr-e Shīrīn 23 Gc 34.31N 45.35 E
Qaşr Farāfirah 31 Jf 27.15N 28.10 E
Qasr Ḩamān 23 Ge 20.50N 45.50 E
Qaşr Qārūn 24 Dh 29.25N 30.25 E
Qaşş Abū Sa'īd 24 Bi 27.00N 27.35 E
Qatana 24 Gf 33.26N 36.05 E
Qatar 21 Hg 25.30N 51.15 E
Qatar [1] 22 Hg 25.30N 51.15 E
Qatīfish 24 Qd 37.50N 57.19 E
Qaţrānī, Jabal- 24 Dh 29.41N 30.35 E
Qatrūyeh 24 Ph 29.09N 54.43 E
Qattara Depression (EN)=
Qaţţārah, Munkhafaḑ al- 30 Je 30.00N 27.30 E
Qaţţārah, Munkhafaḑ al-=
Qattara Depression (EN) 30 Je 30.00N 27.30 E
Qawām al Hamzah 24 Kg 31.43N 44.58 E
Qawz Abu Ḑulū' 35 Eb 16.55N 32.30 E
Qawz Rajab 35 Fb 16.04N 35.34 E
Qaysān 35 Ec 10.45N 34.48 E
Qayyārah 24 Je 35.48N 43.17 E
Qazvīn [Iran] 22 Gf 36.16N 50.00 E
Qazvīn [Iraq] 24 Je 34.21N 42.05 E
Qeqertarssuaq/Godhavn 67 Nc 69.20N 53.35W
Qeshm 24 Qi 26.58N 56.16 E
Qeshm 23 Id 26.45N 55.45 E
Qeydār 24 Md 36.07N 48.35 E
Qeys, Jazīreh-ye- 23 Hd 26.32N 53.58 E
Qezel Owzan 23 Gb 36.45N 49.22 E
Qian'an [China] 28 Ed 40.01N 118.42 E
Qian'an [China] 28 Hb 44.58N 124.01 E
Qianfangzi 28 Ad 40.01N 111.23 E
Qian Gorlos (Quianguozhen) 27 Lb 45.05N 124.52 E
Qian He 28 Dh 32.55N 117.10 E
Qianjiang [China] 27 Ig 23.37N 108.58 E
Qianjiang [China] 28 Bi 30.25N 112.54 E
Qianjiang [China] 27 If 29.30N 108.45 E
Qianning/Gartar 27 He 30.27N 101.29 E
Qian Shan 27 Lc 40.35N 123.00 E
Qiansuo 27 Hf 25.27N 100.41 E
Qianwei 27 Hf 29.08N 103.56 E
Qianxi [China] 27 If 27.03N 106.04 E
Qianxi [China] 28 Ed 40.08N 118.19 E
Qianyang (Anjiang) 27 Jf 27.19N 110.13 E
Qiaojia 27 Hf 27.00N 103.00 E
Qiaowan 27 Gc 40.36N 96.42 E
Qibili 32 Ic 33.42N 8.58 E
Qichun (Caojiahe) 28 Ci 30.15N 115.26 E
Qidaogou 28 Id 41.31N 126.18 E
Qidong 28 Fi 31.48N 121.39 E
Qiemo/Qarqan 22 Kf 38.08N 85.32 E
Qift 24 Ei 26.00N 32.49 E
Qijiang 27 If 29.00N 106.39 E
Qijiaojing 27 Fc 43.28N 91.36 E
Qike → Xunke 27 Mb 49.34N 128.28 E
Qili → Shitai 28 Di 30.12N 117.28 E
Qilian (Babao) 27 Hd 38.14N 100.15 E
Qilian Shan 27 Gd 39.12N 98.35 E
Qilian Shan 21 Lf 38.30N 100.00 E
Qimantag 27 Fd 37.00N 91.00 E
Qimen 27 Kf 29.57N 117.39 E
Qinā 31 Kf 26.10N 32.43 E
Qinā, Wādī- 24 Ei 26.12N 32.44 E
Qin'an 27 Ie 34.50N 105.35 E
Qingchengzi 28 Gd 40.44N 123.36 E
Qingchuan 27 Ie 32.32N 105.11 E
Qingdao=Tsingtao (EN) 22 Of 36.05N 120.21 E
Qingduizi 28 Fd 41.27N 121.52 E
Qingfeng 28 Cg 35.54N 115.07 E
Qinggang 27 Mb 46.41N 126.03 E
Qinggil/Qinghe 27 Fb 46.43N 90.24 E
Qinghai Hu=Koko Nor (EN) 21 Mf 37.00N 100.20 E
Qinghai Sheng (Ch'ing-hai Sheng)=Tsinghai (EN) [2] 27 Gd 36.00N 96.00 E
Qing He 28 Hc 42.16N 124.10 E
Qinghe/Qinggil 27 Fb 46.43N 90.24 E
Qinghe (Gexianzhuang) 28 Cf 37.03N 115.39 E
Qinghemen 28 Fd 41.45N 121.25 E
Qingjian 27 Jd 37.10N 110.09 E
Qingjiang 22 Nf 33.31N 119.03 E
Qing Jiang 27 Je 30.24N 111.30 E
Qingjiang (Zhangshuzhen) 27 Kf 28.02N 115.31 E
Qingkou → Ganyu 28 Eg 34.50N 119.07 E
Qinglong 28 Ed 40.26N 118.58 E
Qinglong He 28 Ee 39.51N 118.51 E
Qingshan 28 Ci 30.39N 114.27 E
Qingshuihe 27 Jd 39.56N 111.41 E
Qingshui Jiang 27 If 27.11N 109.48 E
Qingtian 27 Lf 28.12N 120.17 E
Qingxian 28 De 38.35N 116.48 E
Qingxu 28 Bf 37.36N 112.21 E
Qingyang [China] 27 Id 36.01N 107.48 E
Qingyang [China] 28 Di 30.38N 117.50 E
Qingyuan 27 Lc 42.06N 124.56 E
Qingyuan (Nandaran) 28 Ce 38.46N 115.29 E
Qingyuan (Xiejiaji) 28 Df 37.46N 117.22 E
Qing Zang Gaoyuan=Tibet, Plateau of- (EN) 21 Kf 32.30N 87.00 E
Qin He 28 Bg 35.01N 113.25 E
Qinhuangdao 27 Kg 40.00N 119.32 E
Qin Ling 21 Mf 34.00N 108.00 E
Qinshui 28 Bg 35.41N 112.10 E
Qintong 28 Fh 32.39N 120.06 E
Qinxian 28 Bf 36.46N 112.42 E
Qinyang 28 Bg 35.05N 112.56 E
Qinyuan 28 Bf 36.29N 112.20 E
Qinzhou 27 Ig 22.02N 108.30 E
Qionghai (Jiaji) 27 Jh 19.25N 110.28 E
Qionglai 27 He 30.24N 103.28 E
Qiongzhou Haixia 21 Ng 20.10N 110.15 E
Qipan Guan 27 Ie 32.45N 106.11 E
Qiqihar 22 Oe 47.21N 123.58 E
Qīr 24 Oh 28.29N 53.04 E
Qira 27 Dd 37.02N 80.53 E
Qiryat Gat 24 Fg 31.36N 34.46 E
Qiryat Shemona 24 Ff 33.13N 35.34 E
Qiryat Yam 24 Ff 32.51N 35.04 E
Qishn 23 Hf 15.26N 51.40 E
Qi Shui 28 Ci 30.09N 115.22 E
Qishuyan 28 Fi 31.41N 120.04 E
Qitai 22 Ke 44.01N 89.28 E
Qitaihe 27 Nb 45.49N 130.51 E
Qiuxian (Matou) 28 Cf 36.50N 115.10 E
Qixia 28 Ff 37.18N 120.50 E
Qixian [China] 28 Bf 37.23N 112.21 E
Qixian [China] 28 Cg 34.33N 114.46 E
Qixian (Zhaoge) 28 Cg 35.35N 114.12 E
Qiyang 27 Jf 26.44N 111.50 E
Qizhou 28 Ci 30.04N 115.20 E
Qogir Feng=Godwin Austen (EN) 21 Jf 35.53N 76.30 E
Qog Qi 27 Ic 41.31N 107.00 E
Qog Ul 27 Kc 44.50N 116.19 E
Qohrūd, Kūhhā-ye- 21 Hf 32.40N 53.00 E
Qoltag 27 Ec 42.20N 88.45 E
Qom 23 Hc 34.39N 50.54 E
Qom 24 Ne 34.48N 51.02 E
Qomolangma Feng=Everest, Mount- (EN) 21 Kg 27.59N 86.56 E
Qomrud 24 Ne 34.43N 51.04 E
Qomsheh 23 Hc 32.00N 51.50 E
Qondūz [3] 23 Kb 36.45N 68.30 E
Qondūz 22 If 36.45N 68.51 E
Qondūz 23 Kb 37.00N 68.16 E
Qoqek/Tacheng 22 Ke 46.45N 82.57 E
Qōrnoq 41 Gf 64.30N 51.19W
Qorveh 24 Le 35.10N 47.48 E
Qoşbeh-ye Naşşār 23 Gc 30.02N 48.27 E
Qoţbābād [Iran] 24 Oh 28.39N 53.37 E
Qoţbābād [Iran] 24 Qi 27.46N 56.06 E
Qoţūr 24 Kc 38.28N 44.25 E
Qotūr 24 Kc 38.46N 45.16 E
Quadda 31 Jh 8.04N 22.24 E
Quadros, Lagoa dos- 55 Gi 29.42S 50.05W
Quairading 59 Df 32.01S 117.25 E
Quakenbrück 10 Dd 52.41N 7.57 E
Quanah 45 Gi 34.18N 99.44W
Quanbao Shan 27 Je 34.08N 111.26 E
Quang Ngai 25 Le 15.07N 108.48 E
Quang Tri 25 Le 21.02N 106.29 E
Quan He 28 Ch 32.55N 115.52 E
Quanjiao 28 Eh 32.09N 118.16 E
Quan Long 25 Lg 9.11N 105.08 E
Quanzhou [China] 22 Ng 24.57N 118.35 E
Quanzhou [China] 27 Jf 26.01N 111.04 E
Qu'Appelle River 42 Hf 50.27N 101.19W
Quaraí 56 Id 30.23S 56.27W
Quarai, Rio- 55 Dj 30.12S 57.36W
Quaregnon 12 Fd 50.26N 3.51 E
Quartu Sant'Elena 14 Dk 39.14N 9.11 E
Quartz Lake 42 Jb 70.57N 80.40W
Quartz Mountain 46 De 43.10N 122.40W
Quartzsite 46 Hj 33.40N 114.13W
Quatre, Isle- 51n Bb 12.57N 61.15W
Quatsino Sound 46 Aa 50.25N 128.10W
Qūchān 22 Hf 37.06N 58.30 E
Qué 36 Ce 14.43S 15.06 E
Queanbeyan 59 Jg 35.21S 149.14 E
Québec 39 Le 46.49N 71.13W
Québec [3] 42 Kf 54.00N 72.00W
Quebó 55 Db 14.36S 56.04W
Quebra Anzol, Rio- 55 Id 19.09S 47.38W
Quebracho 55 Dj 31.57S 57.57W
Quebradillas 51a Bb 18.28N 66.56W
Quedas do Iguaçu 55 Fg 25.31S 52.54W
Quedlinburg 10 He 51.47N 11.09 E
Queen, Cape- 42 Jd 64.43N 78.18W
Queen Alexandra Range 66 Jg 84.00S 168.00 E
Queen Bess, Mount- 42 Ff 51.18N 124.33W
Queenborough 12 Cc 51.25N 0.46 E
Queen Charlotte Islands 38 Gd 51.30N 129.00W
Queen Charlotte Sound 42 Ef 51.30N 129.30W
Queen Charlotte Strait 38 Gd 50.40N 127.25W
Queen Elizabeth Islands 38 Ib 79.00N 105.00W
Queen Elizabeth Range 66 Kg 83.20S 162.00 E
Queen Mary Land 66 Ge 69.00S 96.00 E
Queen Maud Gulf 38 Ic 68.25N 102.30W
Queen Maud Land (EN) 66 Cf 72.30S 12.00 E
Queen Maud Range 66 Lg 86.00S 160.00W
Queens Channel [Austl.] 59 Fb 14.45S 129.25 E
Queens Channel [N.W.T.-Can.] 42 Ha 76.11N 96.00W
Queensland 59 Id 22.00S 145.00 E
Queenstown [Austl.] 59 Jh 42.05S 145.33 E
Queenstown [Guy.] 50 Gi 7.12N 58.29W
Queenstown [N.Z.] 62 Cf 45.02S 168.40 E
Queenstown [S.Afr.] 31 Jl 31.52S 26.52 E
Queguay, Cuchilla del- 55 Dj 31.50S 57.30W
Queguay Grande, Rio- 55 Ck 32.09S 58.09W
Queich 12 Ke 49.14N 8.23 E
Queimadas 54 Kf 10.58S 39.38W
Queiros 55 Ge 21.49S 50.13W
Quela 36 Cd 9.15S 17.05 E
Quelimane 31 Kj 17.51S 36.52 E
Quemado 45 Bi 34.20N 108.30W
Quemado de Güines 49 Gb 22.48N 80.15W
Quembo 36 De 14.57S 20.22 E
Quemú-Quemú 56 He 36.03S 63.33W
Quepos 49 Ei 9.25N 84.09W
Quequén 56 Ie 38.32S 58.42W
Quequén Grande, Rio- 55 Cn 38.34S 58.43W
Quequén Salado, Rio- 55 Bn 38.56S 60.31W
Quercy 11 Hj 44.15N 1.15 E
Querétaro [2] 47 Ed 21.00N 99.55W
Querétaro 39 Ig 20.36N 100.23W
Querobabi 48 Db 30.03N 111.01W
Quesada [C.R.] 49 Eh 10.19N 84.26W
Quesada [Sp.] 13 Ig 37.51N 3.04W
Queshan 27 Je 32.42N 114.04 E
Quesnel 42 Ff 52.59N 122.30W
Quesnel Lake 42 Ff 52.32N 121.05W
Questa 45 Dh 36.42N 105.36W
Quetena 54 Eh 22.10S 67.25W
Quetico Lake 45 Kb 48.37N 91.52W
Quetta 22 If 30.12N 67.00 E
Quevas, Cerro- 48 Dc 29.15N 111.20W
Quevedo 54 Cd 1.02S 79.27W
Queyras 11 Mj 44.44N 6.49 E
Quezaltenango 39 Jh 14.50N 91.31W
Quezaltenango [3] 49 Bf 14.45N 91.40W
Quezon 26 Ge 9.14N 117.56 E
Quezon City 22 Oh 14.38N 121.00 E
Qufu 28 Dg 35.35N 116.59 E
Quianguoshen → Qian Gorlos 27 Lb 45.05N 124.52 E
Quianshan 28 Di 30.38N 116.35 E
Quibala 36 Be 10.44S 14.59 E
Quibaxe 36 Bd 8.30S 14.36 E
Quibdó 54 Cb 5.42N 76.39W
Quiberon, Baie de- 11 Dg 47.32N 3.00W
Quiberon, Presqu'île de- 11 Cg 47.30N 3.08W
Quibor 49 Mi 9.56N 69.37W
Quiché [3] 49 Bf 15.30N 90.55W
Quierschied 12 Je 49.19N 7.03 E
Quiha 35 Fc 13.28N 39.33 E
Quiindy 55 Dh 25.58S 57.16W
Quijarro 55 Cd 19.26S 58.08W
Quilá 48 Fe 24.23N 107.13W
Quilàn, Cabo- 56 Ff 43.16S 74.23W
Quillabamba 54 Df 12.49S 72.43W
Quillacollo 54 Eg 17.26S 66.17W
Quillagua 56 Gb 21.39S 69.33W
Quillan 11 Il 42.52N 2.11 E
Quillebeuf-sur-Seine 12 Ce 49.28N 0.31 E
Quillota 56 Fd 32.53S 71.16W
Quilnes 56 Id 34.43S 58.16W
Quilon 25 Fg 8.53N 76.36 E
Quilpie 59 Ie 26.37S 144.15 E
Quilqué 56 Fd 33.03S 71.27W
Quimari, Alto de- 49 Ii 8.07N 76.23W
Quimbele 36 Cd 6.30S 16.14 E
Quimili 56 Hc 27.38S 62.25W
Quimome 55 Bc 17.42S 61.16W
Quimome, Rio- 55 Bc 17.36S 61.09W
Quimper 11 Bf 48.00N 4.06W
Quimperlé 11 Cg 47.52N 3.33W
Quinault River 46 Cc 47.23N 124.18W
Quincy [Ca.-U.S.] 46 Eg 39.56N 120.57W
Quincy [Fl.-U.S.] 44 Ej 30.37N 84.32W
Quincy [Il.-U.S.] 43 Id 39.56N 91.23W
Quincy [Ma.-U.S.] 44 Ld 42.15N 71.01W
Quincy [Wa.-U.S.] 46 Fc 47.14N 119.51W
Quindío [2] 54 Cc 4.30N 75.40W
Quingey 11 Lg 47.06N 5.53 E
Quinhagak 40 Ge 59.45N 161.43W
Qui Nhon 22 Mh 13.46N 109.14 E
Quiñihual 55 Bm 37.47S 61.36W
Quiniluban Group 26 Hd 11.27N 120.48 E
Quinn River 46 Ff 40.25N 119.00W
Quiñones 48 De 24.22N 111.25W
Quintanar de la Orden 13 Ie 39.34N 3.03W
Quintana Roo [2] 47 Ge 19.40N 88.30W
Quinze, Lac des- 44 Hb 47.30N 79.00W
Quionga 37 Gb 10.35S 40.33 E
Quipungo 36 Be 14.45S 14.05 E
Quirigua 49 Cf 15.18N 89.07W
Quirihue 56 Fe 36.17S 72.32W
Quirima 36 Ce 10.48S 18.09 E
Quirinópolis 54 Hg 18.32S 50.30W
Quiroga 13 Eb 42.29N 7.16W
Quiros, Cap- 63b Cb 14.56S 167.01 E
Quisiro 49 Lh 10.53N 71.17W
Quissanga 37 Gb 12.25S 40.29 E
Quissico 37 Ed 24.43S 34.45 E
Quita Sueno Bank 47 Hf 14.20N 81.15W
Quitengues 36 Be 14.06S 14.05 E
Quiterage 37 Gb 11.45S 40.27 E
Quitéria, Rio- 55 Ge 20.16S 51.08W
Quitilipi 55 Bh 26.52S 60.13W
Quitman [Ga.-U.S.] 44 Fj 30.47N 83.33W
Quitman [Ms.-U.S.] 45 Lj 32.03N 88.43W
Quito 53 If 0.13S 78.30W
Quitovac 48 Cb 31.32N 112.42W
Quixadá 54 Kd 4.58S 39.01W
Quixeramobim 54 Ke 5.12S 39.17W
Qujiang 28 Cj 28.14N 115.46 E
Qu Jiang [China] 27 Kf 29.32N 119.31 E
Qu Jiang [China] 27 Ie 30.01N 106.24 E
Qujing 27 Hf 25.31N 103.45 E
Qul'ān, Jazā'ir- 24 Fj 24.22N 35.23 E
Qulansiyah 23 Hg 12.41N 53.29 E
Qulaybiah 32 Jb 36.51N 11.06 E
Qulbān al 'Isāwiyah 24 Gg 30.38N 37.53 E
Qulbān an Nabk al Gharbī 24 Gg 31.15N 37.26 E
Qumar He 21 Lf 34.42N 94.50 E
Qumarlêb 27 Ge 34.35N 95.18 E
Qunayfidhah, Nafūd- 24 Kj 24.45N 45.30 E
Quoi 64d Ba 7.32N 151.59 E
Quoich 42 Id 63.56N 93.25W
Quorn 59 Hf 32.21S 138.03 E
Quqên/Jinchuan 27 He 31.02N 102.02 E
Quraitu 24 Ke 34.36N 45.30 E
Qurayyāt, Juzur- 32 Jb 35.48N 11.02 E
Qurbah 14 En 36.35N 10.52 E
Qurdūd 35 Dc 10.17N 29.56 E
Qūr Laban 24 Cg 30.23N 28.59 E
Qurunbāliyah 14 En 36.36N 10.30 E
Qūş 33 Fd 25.55N 32.45 E
Quşay'ir 35 Ic 14.55N 50.20 E
Qutdligssat 41 Gd 70.12N 53.00W
Quthing 37 Df 30.24S 27.42 E
Quţū 33 Hf 18.30N 41.04 E
Quwaiz 33 He 20.27N 44.53 E
Quxian 27 Kf 28.54N 118.53 E
Qüxü 27 Ff 29.23N 90.45 E
Quyang 28 Ce 38.37N 114.41 E
Quy Chau 25 Le 19.33N 105.06 E
Quzhou 28 Cf 36.47N 114.56 E
Qyteti Stalin 15 Ci 40.48N 19.54 E

R

Raab 10 Ni 47.41N 17.38 E
Raahe/Brahestad 7 Fd 64.41N 24.29 E
Rääkkylä 8 Mb 62.19N 29.37 E
Raalte 12 Ib 52.23N 6.17 E
Raamsdonk 12 Gc 51.41N 4.54 E
Raanes Peninsula 42 Ia 78.20N 86.20W
Raasay, Island of- 9 Gd 57.25N 6.04W
Raasay, Sound of- 9 Gd 57.25N 6.05W
Raasiku/Raziku 8 Ke 59.22N 25.11 E
Rab 14 If 44.46N 14.46 E
Rab 14 If 44.45N 14.46 E
Rába 10 Ni 47.41N 17.38 E
Raba 10 Qf 50.09N 20.30 E
Raba 22 Nj 8.27S 118.46 E
Rabāble 35 Hd 8.14N 48.18 E
Rabaçal 13 Ec 41.30N 7.12W
Rabat [Malta] 14 Io 35.50N 14.29 E
Rabat [Mor.] 31 Ge 34.02N 6.50W
Rabat-Salé [2] 32 Fc 34.02N 6.50W
Rabaul 58 Ge 4.12S 152.12 E
Rábca 10 Ni 47.41N 17.37 E
Rabenau 12 Kd 50.40N 8.52 E
Rabī', Ash Shallāl ar-=
Fourth Cataract (EN) 30 Kg 18.47N 32.03 E
Rābiah 24 Jd 36.47N 42.07 E
Rábida, Monasterio de- 13 Fg 37.12N 6.55W
Rābigh 23 Ee 22.48N 39.02 E
Rabinal 49 Bf 15.06N 90.27W
Rabka 10 Pg 49.36N 19.56 E
Raboćeostrovsk 7 Id 64.59N 34.44 E
Rabyānah, Şaḩrā'- 30 Jf 24.30N 21.00 E
Rabyānah, Wāḩāt al-=
Rebiana Oasis (EN) 33 De 24.14N 21.59 E
Răcăciuni 15 Jc 46.20N 26.59 E
Racalmuto 14 Hm 37.24N 13.44 E
Răcăşdia 15 Ee 44.59N 21.38 E
Racconigi 14 Bf 44.46N 7.46 E
Race, Cape- 38 Ne 46.40N 53.10W
Race Point 44 Ld 42.04N 70.14W
Rach Gia 22 Mh 10.01N 105.05 E
Rachid 32 Ef 18.48N 11.41W
Raciąż 10 Qd 52.47N 20.06 E
Racibórz 10 Of 50.06N 18.13 E
Racine 43 Jc 42.43N 87.48W
Ráckeve 10 Oi 47.10N 18.57 E
Racos 15 Ic 46.03N 25.30 E
Råda 8 Ed 60.00N 13.36 E
Radama, Iles- 37 Hb 14.00S 47.47 E
Radan 15 Ef 43.02N 21.30 E
Rădăuţi 15 Ib 47.51N 25.55 E
Radbuza 10 Jg 49.46N 13.24 E
Radeberg 10 Je 51.07N 13.55 E
Radebeul 10 Je 51.06N 13.39 E
Radeče 14 Jd 46.04N 15.11 E
Radehov 10 Uf 50.13N 24.43 E
Radenthein 14 Hd 46.48N 13.43 E
Radevormwald 12 Jc 51.12N 7.22 E
Radew 10 Lb 54.07N 15.50 E
Radford 44 Gg 37.07N 80.34W
Radnevo 15 Ig 42.18N 25.56 E
Radolfzell 10 Ei 47.44N 8.58 E
Radom [2] 10 Re 51.25N 21.10 E
Radom 6 Ie 51.25N 21.10 E
Radomir 15 Fg 42.33N 22.58 E
Radomka 10 Re 51.43N 21.26 E
Radomsko 10 Pe 51.05N 19.25 E
Radomyšl 16 Fd 50.29N 29.14 E
Radomyśl Wielki 10 Rf 50.12N 21.16 E
Radoškoviči 8 Lj 54.12N 27.17 E
Radotín 10 Kg 49.59N 14.22 E
Radovanu 15 Je 44.12N 26.31 E
Radoviš 15 Fh 41.38N 22.28 E
Radøy 8 Ad 60.40N 5.00 E
Radstadt 14 Hc 47.23N 13.27 E
Radun 10 Vb 54.02N 25.07 E
Radunia 10 Ob 54.25N 18.45 E
Raduša 14 Lg 43.52N 17.29 E
Radvaniči 10 Ue 51.59N 24.09 E
Radviliškis 7 Fi 55.50N 23.33 E
Radymno 10 Sg 49.57N 22.48 E
Radziejów 10 Od 52.38N 18.32 E
Radzyń Podlaski 10 Se 51.48N 22.38 E
Rae 42 Fd 62.50N 116.00W
Rāe Bareli 25 Gc 26.13N 81.14 E
Rae Isthmus 42 Ic 66.55N 86.10W
Raesfeld 12 Ic 51.46N 6.51 E
Raeside, Lake- 59 Ee 29.30S 121.50 E
Raetihi 62 Fc 39.26S 175.17 E
Raevavae, Ile- 57 Mg 23.52S 147.40W
Raevski, Groupe- 61 Mc 16.45S 144.14W
Rāf, Jabal- 24 Hh 29.12N 39.48 E
Rafaela 53 Ji 31.17S 61.30W
Rafai 35 Ce 4.58N 23.56 E
Rafḩā' 23 Fd 29.42N 43.30 E
Rafi 34 Fc 13.28N 4.10 E
Rāfkā 24 Qe 35.55N 57.36 E
Rafsanjān 23 Ic 30.24N 56.01 E
Rāfsö/Reposaari 8 Ic 61.37N 21.27 E
Raga 31 Jh 8.28N 25.41 E
Ragay Gulf 26 Hd 13.30N 122.45 E
Ragged Island 49 Jb 22.12N 75.44W
Ragged Island Range 47 Id 22.42N 75.55W
Ragged Point 51q Bb 13.10N 59.25W
Raglan 62 Fb 37.48S 174.52 E
Raguencau 44 Ma 49.04N 68.32W
Ragusa 14 In 36.55N 14.44 E
Raguva 8 Ki 55.30N 24.45 E
Raha 26 Hg 4.51S 122.43 E
Raḩā, Ḩarrat ar- 24 Gi 27.40N 36.40 E
Rahad al Bardī 35 Cc 11.18N 23.53 E
Rahama 34 Gc 10.25N 8.41 E
Raḩaţ, Ḩarrat- 33 He 23.00N 40.05 E
Rahat Daği 15 Ml 37.08N 29.49 E
Rahden 12 Kb 52.26N 8.37 E
Rāhgāmāti 25 Id 22.38N 92.12 E
Rahīmyār Khan 25 Ec 28.25N 70.18 E
Rahmanovskije Ključi 19 If 49.35N 86.35 E
Rahmet 19 Gf 49.19N 65.16 E
Råholt 8 Dd 60.16N 11.11 E
Rahouia 13 Ni 35.32N 1.01 E
Rahov 16 De 48.02N 24.18 E
Rahrbach, Kirchhundem- 12 Jc 51.02N 7.59 E
Raia 13 Df 39.00N 8.17W
Raiatea, Ile- 57 Lf 16.50S 151.25W
Raices 55 Cj 31.54S 59.16W
Rāichūr 22 Jh 16.12N 77.22 E
Raiganj 25 Hc 25.37N 88.07 E
Raigarh 25 Gd 21.54N 83.24 E
Raijua, Pulau- 26 Hi 10.37S 121.36 E
Rainbow Peak 46 Hd 44.55N 115.17W
Rainier, Mount- 38 Ge 46.52N 121.46W
Rainy Lake 43 Ib 48.42N 93.10W
Rainy River 45 Ib 48.43N 94.29W
Rainy River 45 Ib 48.50N 94.41W
Raipur 22 Kg 21.14N 81.38 E
Raisi, Punta- 14 Hl 38.11N 13.06 E
Raisio/Reso 7 Ff 60.29N 22.11 E
Raita Bank (EN) 60 Mb 25.25N 169.30W
Raja Ampat, Kepulauan- 26 Jg 0.50S 130.25 E
Rājahmundry 22 Kh 16.59N 81.47 E
Rajakoski 7 Gb 68.59N 29.07 E
Rajang 21 Ni 2.07N 111.12 E
Rājapālaiyam 25 Fg 9.27N 77.34 E
Rājasthān [3] 25 Ec 26.00N 74.00 E
Rājasthān Canal 25 Eb 31.10N 75.00 E
Rajbiraj 25 Hc 26.30N 86.50 E
Rajčihinsk 20 Hg 49.43N 129.27 E
Rajevski 17 Gi 54.04N 54.56 E
Rājgarh 25 Fc 28.38N 75.23 E
Rajgródzkie, Jezioro- 10 Sc 53.45N 22.38 E
Rajka 10 Ni 48.00N 17.12 E
Rajkot 22 Jg 22.18N 70.47 E
Raj Nāndgaon 25 Gd 21.06N 81.02 E
Rajony Respublikanskogo Podčinenija [Kirg.-U.S.S.R.] [3] 19 Hg 42.30N 73.50 E
Rajony Respublikanskogo Podčinenija [Tad.-U.S.S.R.] [3] 19 Gh 38.50N 69.30 E

Index Symbols

[1] Independent Nation
[2] State, Region
[3] District, County
[4] Municipality
[5] Colony, Dependency
Continent
Physical Region
Historical or Cultural Region
Mount, Mountain
Volcano
Hill
Mountains, Mountain Range
Hills, Escarpment
Plateau, Upland
Pass, Gap
Plain, Lowland
Delta
Salt Flat
Valley, Canyon
Crater, Cave
Karst Features
Depression
Polder
Desert, Dunes
Forest, Woods
Heath, Steppe
Oasis
Cape, Point
Coast, Beach
Cliff
Peninsula
Isthmus
Sandbank
Island
Atoll
Rock, Reef
Islands, Archipelago
Rocks, Reefs
Coral Reef
Well, Spring
Geyser
River, Stream
Waterfall Rapids
River Mouth, Estuary
Lake
Salt Lake
Intermittent Lake
Reservoir
Swamp, Pond
Canal
Glacier
Ice Shelf, Pack Ice
Ocean
Sea
Gulf, Bay
Strait, Fjord
Lagoon
Bank
Seamount
Tablemount
Ridge
Shelf
Basin
Escarpment, Sea Scarp
Fracture
Trench, Abyss
National Park, Reserve
Point of Interest
Recreation Site
Cave, Cavern
Historic Site
Ruins
Wall, Walls
Church, Abbey
Temple
Scientific Station
Airport
Port
Lighthouse
Mine
Tunnel
Dam, Bridge

Name	Map	Grid	Lat.	Long.
Rājshāhi	25	Hd	24.22N	88.36 E
Rakahanga Atoll	57	Kl	10.02S	161.05W
Rakaia	62	Ee	43.54S	172.13 E
Rakaia	62	Ee	43.45S	172.01 E
Rakan, Ra's-	24	Ni	26.10N	51.13 E
Rakata, Pulau-	26	Eh	6.10S	105.26 E
Raka Zangbo	27	Ef	29.24N	87.58 E
Rakhawt, Wādī-	35	Ib	18.16N	51.50 E
Rakht-e Shāh	24	Mf	33.17N	49.23 E
Rakitnoje	28	Mb	45.36N	134.17 E
Rakitovo	15	Hh	41.59N	24.05 E
Rakkestad	8	De	59.26N	11.21 E
Rakoniewice	10	Md	52.10N	16.16 E
Rakops	37	Cd	21.01S	24.20 E
Rakovnicka panev	10	Jf	50.10N	13.30 E
Rakovník	10	Jf	50.06N	13.43 E
Rakovski	15	Hg	42.18N	24.58 E
Raków	10	Rf	50.42N	21.03 E
Rakušečny, Mys-	16	Qh	42.52N	51.55 E
Råkvåg	7	Ce	63.46N	10.05 E
Rakvere	7	Gg	59.22N	26.22 E
Raleigh [N.C.-U.S.]	39	Lf	35.47N	78.39W
Raleigh [Ont.-Can.]	45	Kb	49.31N	91.56W
Raleigh Bay	44	Ih	35.00N	76.20W
Ralik Chain	57	Hd	8.00N	167.00 E
Rama	47	Hf	12.09N	84.15W
Rama, Río-	49	Eg	12.08N	84.13W
Ramādah	32	Jc	32.19N	10.24 E
Ramaḏīn, Wādī-	24	Ej	24.57N	32.34 E
Ramales de la Victoria	13	Ia	43.15N	3.27W
Ramalho, Serra do-	55	Ja	13.45S	44.00W
Ramapo Bank (EN)	57	Fb	27.15N	145.10 E
Ramatlabama	37	De	25.37S	25.30 E
Ramberg	10	He	51.45N	11.05 E
Rambervillers	11	Mf	48.21N	6.38 E
Rambi	63d	Cb	16.30S	179.59W
Rambouillet	11	Hf	48.39N	1.50 E
Rambutyo Island	57	Fe	2.18S	147.48 E
Rāmhormoz	24	Mg	31.16N	49.36 E
Ramigala/Ramygala	8	Ki	55.28N	24.23 E
Ramis	35	Gd	8.02N	41.36 E
Ramla	24	Fg	31.55N	34.52 E
Ramlīyah, 'Aqabat ar-	24	Di	26.01N	30.42 E
Ramlu	35	Gc	13.20N	41.45 E
Ramm, Jabal-	24	Fh	29.35N	35.24 E
Rammāk, Ghurd ar-	24	Ch	29.40N	29.20 E
Rāmnagar	25	Fc	29.24N	79.07 E
Ramnäs	8	Ge	59.46N	16.12 E
Ramón Santamarina	55	Cn	38.26S	59.20W
Ramos	63a	Ec	8.16S	160.11 E
Ramos, Río-	48	Ge	25.35N	105.03W
Ramotswa	37	Dd	24.52S	25.50 E
Rāmpur	25	Fc	28.49N	79.02 E
Ramree	25	Ie	19.06N	93.48 E
Rams	24	Qj	25.53N	56.02 E
Ramsele	7	De	63.33N	16.29 E
Ramsey [Eng.-U.K.]	12	Bb	52.27N	0.07W
Ramsey [Ont.-Can.]	44	Fb	47.29N	82.24W
Ramsey [U.K.]	9	Ig	54.20N	4.21W
Ramsey Lake	42	Jg	47.20N	83.00W
Ramsgate	9	Oj	51.20N	1.25 E
Rāmshīr	24	Mg	30.50N	49.30 E
Ramsjö	7	De	62.11N	15.39 E
Ramstein-Miesenbach	12	Je	49.27N	7.32 E
Ramsund	7	Db	68.29N	16.32 E
Ramu	60	Di	4.02S	144.41 E
Ramu	36	Hb	3.56N	41.13 E
Ramvik	7	De	62.49N	17.51 E
Ramville, Ilet-	51h	Bb	14.42N	60.53W
Ramygala/Ramigala	8	Ki	55.28N	24.23 E
Rana	7	Dc	66.20N	14.08 E
Rañadoiro, Sierra del-	13	Fa	43.20N	6.45W
Ranai	26	Ef	3.55N	108.23 E
Ranakah, Potjo-	26	Hh	8.38S	120.31 E
Rana Kao, Volcán-	65d	Ac	27.11S	109.27W
Rana Roi, Volcán-	65d	Ab	27.05S	109.23W
Rana Roraka, Volcán-	65d	Bb	27.07S	109.18W
Ranau	26	Ge	5.58N	116.41 E
Ranča	14	Lf	44.24N	17.22 E
Rancagua	53	Ii	34.10S	70.45W
Rance	11	Ef	48.31N	1.59W
Rance, Sivry-Rance-	12	Gd	50.09N	4.16 E
Rancharia	55	Gf	22.15S	50.55W
Rancheria, Río-	49	Kh	11.34N	72.54W
Rānchī	22	Kg	23.21N	85.20 E
Ranchos	55	Cl	35.32S	58.22W
Ranco, Lago-	56	Ff	40.14S	72.24W
Randa	35	Gc	11.51N	42.40 E
Randaberg	8	Ae	59.00N	5.36 E
Randazzo	14	Im	37.53N	14.57 E
Randers	7	Ch	56.28N	10.03 E
Randers Fjord	8	Dh	56.35N	10.20 E
Randijaure	7	Ec	66.42N	19.18 E
Randow	10	Kc	53.41N	14.04 E
Randsfjorden	7	Cf	60.25N	10.25 E
Ranérou	34	Cb	15.18N	13.58W
Ranfurly	62	Df	45.08S	170.06 E
Rangasa, Tanjung-	26	Gg	3.33S	118.56 E
Ranger	45	Gj	32.28N	98.41W
Rangiora	62	Ee	43.18S	172.36 E
Rangiroa Atoll	57	Mf	15.10S	147.35W
Rangitaiki	62	Gb	37.55S	176.53 E
Rangitata	62	Df	44.10S	171.30 E
Rangitikei	62	Fd	40.17S	175.13 E
Rangkasbitung	26	Eh	6.21S	106.15 E
Rangoon (EN) = Yangon	22	Lh	16.47N	96.10 E
Rangpur	25	Hc	25.44N	89.16 E
Rāniyah	24	Kd	36.15N	44.53 E
Rankin Inlet	39	Jc	62.45N	92.10W
Rankoshi	29a	Bb	42.47N	140.31 E
Rannoch, Loch-	9	Ie	56.41N	4.20W
Ranobe	37	Gc	17.10S	44.08 E
Ranon	63b	Dc	16.09S	168.07 E
Ranong	25	Jg	9.59N	98.40 E
Ranongga Island	60	Fi	8.05S	156.34 E
Ranova	16	Lb	54.07N	40.14 E
Ransaren	7	Dd	65.14N	14.59 E
Rantabe	37	Hc	15.42S	49.39 E
Rantasalmi	8	Mb	62.04N	28.18 E
Rantaupanjang	26	Fg	1.23S	112.04 E
Rantauprapat	26	Cf	2.06N	99.50 E
Rantekombola, Bulu-	21	Oj	3.21S	120.01 E
Rantoul	45	Lf	40.19N	88.09W
Ranua	7	Gd	65.55N	26.32 E
Ranyah, Wādī-	33	He	21.18N	43.20 E
Raohe	27	Nb	46.48N	133.58 E
Raon-l'Étape	11	Mf	48.24N	6.51 E
Raoui, Erg er-	32	Gd	29.15N	2.45W
Raoul Island	57	Jg	29.15S	177.52W
Raoyang	28	Ce	38.14N	115.44 E
Raoyang He	28	Gd	41.13N	122.12 E
Rapa, Ile-	57	Mg	27.36S	144.20W
Rapallo	14	Df	44.21N	9.14 E
Rapang	26	Gg	3.50S	119.48 E
Rapa Nui/Pascua, Isla de-= Easter Island (EN)	57	Qg	27.07S	109.22W
Raper, Cape -	42	Kc	69.41N	67.24W
Rapid City	39	Ie	44.05N	103.14W
Rapid Creek	45	Ee	43.54N	102.37W
Rapid River	44	Dc	45.58N	86.59W
Räpina/Rjapina	8	Lf	58.03N	27.35 E
Rapla	7	Fg	59.02N	24.47 E
Rappahannock River	44	Ig	37.34N	76.18W
Rápulo, Río-	52	Jg	13.43S	65.32W
Rāqūbah	31	If	28.58N	19.02 E
Raraka Atoll	57	Mf	16.10S	144.54W
Raroia Atoll	57	Mf	16.05S	142.26W
Rarotonga Island	57	Lg	21.14S	159.46W
Rasa, Punta-	52	Jj	40.51S	62.19W
Ra's Abū Daraj	24	Eh	29.23N	32.33 E
Ra's Abū Rudays	24	Eh	28.53N	33.11 E
Ra's Abū Shajarah	35	Fa	21.04N	37.14 E
Ra's Ajdīr	33	Bc	33.09N	11.34 E
Ra's al 'Ayn	24	Id	36.51N	40.04 E
Ra's al-Barr	24	Dg	31.31N	31.50 E
Ra's al Ḥikmah	24	Bg	31.08N	27.50 E
Ra's al Jabal	14	Em	37.13N	10.08 E
Ra's al Khafjī	24	Mh	28.25N	48.30 E
Ra's al Khaymah	23	Id	25.47N	55.57 E
Ra's al Mish'āb	24	Mh	28.12N	48.37 E
Ra's al Unūf	33	Cc	30.31N	18.34 E
Ra's an Naqb	24	Fh	30.00N	35.29 E
Ra's as Sidr	24	Eh	29.36N	32.40 E
Ra's at Tannūrah	24	Ni	26.42N	50.10 E
Ras Beddouza	30	Ge	32.22N	9.18W
Ras Dashan	30	Kg	13.19N	38.20 E
Raseiniai/Rasejnjaj	7	Fi	55.23N	23.07 E
Rasejnjaj/Raseiniai	7	Fi	55.23N	23.07 E
Râs el Mâ	34	Eb	16.37N	4.27W
Ras-el-Ma	13	Ji	35.08N	2.29W
Ras el Oued	13	Ri	35.57N	5.02 E
Ra's Ghārib	33	Fd	28.21N	33.06 E
Rashād	35	Ec	11.51N	31.04 E
Rāshayyā	24	Ff	33.30N	35.51 E
Rashīd = Rosetta (EN)	33	Fc	31.24N	30.25 E
Rashīd, Maşabb-	24	Dg	31.30N	30.20 E
Rasht	22	Gf	37.16N	49.36 E
Rāsiga 'Alūla	35	Ic	11.59N	50.50 E
Rās Jumbo	35	Gf	1.37S	41.31 E
Raška	15	Df	43.18N	20.38 E
Ra's Madhar, Jabal-	24	Gj	25.46N	37.32 E
Ra's Matārimah	24	Eh	29.27N	32.43 E
Rasmussen Basin	42	Hc	67.56N	95.15W
Rason Lake	59	Ee	28.45S	124.20 E
Rasskazovo	19	Ee	52.39N	41.57 E
Rassua, Ostrov-	20	Kg	47.40N	153.00 E
Rassvet	20	Ee	57.00N	91.32 E
Ras-Tarf, Cap-	13	Ii	35.17N	3.41W
Rastatt	10	Eh	48.51N	8.12 E
Rastede	12	Ka	53.15N	8.12 E
Rastigaissa	7	Ga	70.03N	26.18 E
Råstojaure	7	Eb	68.45N	20.30 E
Ra's Ţurunbī	24	Fj	25.40N	34.35 E
Rasūl	24	Pi	27.10N	55.30 E
Ra's Zayt	33	Fd	27.56N	33.31 E
Rat	40a	Bb	51.55N	178.20 E
Ratak Chain	57	Id	9.00N	171.00 E
Ratangarh	25	Ec	28.05N	74.36 E
Rätansbyn	7	De	62.29N	14.32 E
Rat Buri	25	Jf	13.32N	99.49 E
Rathbun Lake	45	Jf	40.54N	93.05W
Ráth Droma/Rathdrum	9	Gi	52.56N	6.13W
Rathdrum/Ráth Droma	9	Gi	52.56N	6.13W
Rathenow	10	Id	52.36N	12.20 E
Rathlin Island/Reachlainn	9	Gf	55.18N	6.13W
Ráth Luirc/An Ráth	9	Ei	52.21N	8.41W
Rathor, Pik-	18	If	37.55N	72.14 E
Rätikon	14	Dc	47.03N	9.40 E
Ratingen	12	Ic	51.18N	6.51 E
Rätische Alpen = Rhaetian Alps (EN)	14	Dd	46.30N	10.00 E
Rat Islands	38	Ad	52.00N	178.00 E
Ratlām	25	Fd	23.19N	75.04 E
Ratmanova, Ostrov-	20	Lc	35.45N	169.00W
Ratnāgiri	25	Ee	16.59N	73.18 E
Ratnapura	25	Gg	6.41N	80.24 E
Ratno	16	Dd	51.42N	24.31 E
Raton	43	Gd	36.54N	104.24W
Ratqh, Wādī ar-	24	Ie	34.25N	40.55 E
Rätta	20	Dd	63.35N	84.05 E
Rattlesnake Hills	46	Le	42.45N	107.10W
Rattray Head	9	Ld	57.38N	1.46W
Rättvik	7	Df	60.53N	15.06 E
Ratz, Mount-	38	Fd	57.23N	132.19W
Ratzeburg	10	Gc	53.42N	10.46 E
Raub	26	Df	3.48N	101.52 E
Rauch	56	Ie	36.46S	59.06W
Raucourt-et-Flaba	12	Ge	49.36N	4.57 E
Raudeberg	8	Ab	61.59N	5.09 E
Rauer Islands	66	Fe	68.51S	77.50 E
Raufarhöfn	7a	Ca	66.27N	15.57W
Raufjellet	8	Dc	61.15N	11.00 E
Raufoss	7	Cf	60.43N	10.37 E
Raukotaha	64n	Ac	10.28S	161.01W
Raukumara Range	62	Gc	38.00S	178.00 E
Rauland	8	Be	59.44N	8.00 E
Raúl Leoni, Represa- (Guri)	54	Fb	7.30N	63.00W
Rauma	7	Be	62.33N	7.43 E
Rauma/Raumo	7	Ef	61.08N	21.30 E
Raumo/Rauma	7	Ef	61.08N	21.30 E
Rauna	8	Kg	57.14N	25.39 E
Raunds	12	Bb	52.20N	0.32W
Raurimu	62	Fc	39.07S	175.24 E
Raurkela	22	Kg	22.13N	84.53 E
Rausu	28	Rb	44.01N	145.12 E
Rausu-Dake	29a	Da	44.06N	145.07 E
Rautalampi	8	Lb	62.38N	26.50 E
Ravahere Atoll	57	Mf	18.14S	142.09W
Ravan	14	Mf	44.15N	18.16 E
Ravanica, Manastir-	15	Ef	43.58N	21.30 E
Ravānsar	24	Le	34.43N	46.40 E
Ravanusa	14	Hm	37.16N	13.58 E
Rāvar	24	Qg	31.12N	56.53 E
Rava-Russkaja	16	Cd	50.13N	23.37 E
Ravels	12	Gc	51.22N	4.59 E
Ravelsbach	14	Jb	48.30N	15.50 E
Ravels-Poppel	12	Hc	51.27N	5.02 E
Ravenna [It.]	14	Gf	44.25N	12.12 E
Ravenna [Nb.-U.S.]	45	Gf	41.02N	98.55W
Ravensburg	10	Fi	47.47N	9.37 E
Ravenshoe	58	Ff	17.37S	145.29 E
Ravensthorpe	59	Ef	33.35S	120.02 E
Ravi	21	Jf	30.35N	71.49 E
Ravnina	19	Gh	37.57N	62.42 E
Rawaki Atoll (Phoenix)	57	Je	3.43S	170.43W
Rāwalpindi	22	Jf	33.35N	73.03 E
Rawa Mazowiecka	10	Qe	51.46N	20.16 E
Rawāndūz	24	Kd	36.37N	44.31 E
Rawdah	24	Ie	35.15N	41.05 E
Rawene	62	Ea	35.24S	173.30 E
Rawicz	10	Me	51.37N	16.52 E
Rawka	10	Qd	52.07N	20.08 E
Rawlinna	58	Dh	31.01S	125.20 E
Rawlins	43	Fc	41.47N	107.14W
Rawlinson Range	59	Fd	24.50S	128.00 E
Rawson [Arg.]	55	Bl	34.36S	60.04W
Rawson [Arg.]	53	Jj	43.18S	65.06W
Rawura, Ras-	36	He	10.20S	40.30 E
Raxaul	25	Gc	26.59N	84.51 E
Ray, Cape -	42	Lg	47.37N	59.19W
Raya, Bukit-	21	Nj	1.32S	111.05 E
Rayadrug	25	Ff	14.42N	76.52 E
Rayāt	24	Kd	36.40N	44.58 E
Rayleigh	12	Cc	51.35N	0.37 E
Raymond [Alta.-Can.]	46	Ib	49.27N	112.39W
Raymond [Wa.-U.S.]	46	Dc	46.41N	123.44W
Raymondville	43	Hf	26.29N	97.47W
Rayne	45	Jk	30.14N	92.16W
Rayón [Mex.]	48	Jg	21.51N	99.40W
Rayón [Mex.]	48	Dc	29.43N	110.35W
Rayones	48	Ie	25.01N	100.05W
Rayong	25	Kf	12.40N	101.17 E
Raysūt	23	Hf	16.54N	54.02 E
Raytown	45	Ig	39.00N	94.28W
Raz, Pointe du-	11	Bf	48.02N	4.44W
Razan	24	Me	35.23N	49.02 E
Razdan	16	Ni	40.28N	44.43 E
Razdelnaja	16	Gf	46.50N	30.05 E
Razdolinsk	20	Ee	58.25N	94.44 E
Razdolnaja	28	Kc	43.20N	131.49 E
Razdolnoje [R.S.F.S.R.]	28	Kc	43.33N	131.55 E
Razdolnoje [Ukr.-U.S.S.R.]	16	Hg	45.47N	33.30 E
Razgrad	15	Jf	43.32N	26.31 E
Razgrad	15	Jf	43.32N	26.31 E
Razī	24	Mc	38.32N	48.08 E
Raziku/Raasiku	8	Ke	59.22N	25.11 E
Razlog	15	Gh	41.53N	23.28 E
Razo	32	Cf	16.37N	24.36W
Ré, Ile de-	5	Ff	46.12N	1.25W
Reachlainn	9	Gf	55.18N	6.13W
Reachlainn/Rathlin Island	9	Gf	55.18N	6.13W
Reachrainn/Lambay	9	Gh	53.29N	6.01W
Read	42	Gc	69.12N	114.30W
Reading [Eng.-U.K.]	9	Mj	51.28N	0.59W
Reading [Pa.-U.S.]	43	Lc	40.20N	75.55W
Real, Cordillera- [Bol.]	54	Eg	16.30S	68.30W
Real, Cordillera- [Ec.]	52	If	3.00S	78.00W
Real Audiencia	55	Cm	36.11S	58.35W
Real del Castillo	48	Aa	31.58N	116.19W
Realicó	56	He	35.02S	64.15W
Réalmont	11	Ik	43.47N	2.12 E
Reao Atoll	57	Nf	18.31S	136.23W
Reatini, Monti-	14	Gh	42.35N	12.50 E
Rebais	12	Ff	48.51N	3.14 E
Rebecca, Lake-	59	Ee	29.55S	122.10 E
Rebiana Oasis (EN) = Rabyānah, Wāḩāt al-	33	De	24.14N	21.59 E
Rebollera	13	Hf	38.25N	4.02W
Reboly	7	He	63.52N	30.47 E
Rebord Manamblen	37	Hd	24.05S	46.30 E
Rebun	28	Pb	45.23N	141.02 E
Rebun-Dake	29a	Ba	45.22N	141.01 E
Rebun-Suidō	29a	Ba	45.15N	141.05 E
Rebun-Tō	27	Pb	45.23N	141.10 E
Recalde	55	Bm	36.39S	61.05W
Recanati	14	Hg	43.24N	13.32 E
Recaş	15	Ed	45.48N	21.30 E
Recherche, Archipelago of the-	57	Dh	34.06S	122.45 E
Rečica	19	De	52.22N	30.25 E
Recife	53	Mf	8.03S	34.54W
Recife, Cape-	30	Jl	34.02S	25.45 E
Recke	12	Jb	52.23N	7.43 E
Recklinghausen	10	De	51.37N	7.12 E
Recknitz	10	Ib	54.14N	12.28 E
Recoaro Terme	14	Fe	45.42N	11.13 E
Reconquista	56	Ic	29.09S	59.39W
Recovery Glacier	66	Ag	81.10S	28.00W
Recreo	56	Gc	29.16S	65.04W
Recz	10	Lc	53.16N	15.33 E
Reda	10	Ob	54.38N	18.30 E
Redange	12	He	49.46N	5.54 E
Red Bank	44	Eh	35.07N	85.17W
Red Bay	42	Lf	51.44N	56.25W
Red Bluff	43	Cc	40.11N	122.15W
Red Bluff Reservoir	45	Ek	31.57N	103.56W
Redbridge, London-	12	Cc	51.35N	0.08 E
Red Butte	46	Ii	35.55N	112.03W
Redcar	9	Lg	54.37N	1.04W
Red Cliff	51c	Ab	17.05N	62.32W
Redcliff	37	Dc	19.02S	29.50 E
Redcliffe, Mount-	59	Ee	28.25S	121.32 E
Red Cloud	45	Gf	40.05N	98.32W
Red Deer	39	Hd	52.16N	113.48W
Red Deer [Can.]	42	Hf	52.55N	101.27W
Red Deer [Can.]	38	Id	50.56N	109.54W
Redding	39	Ge	40.35N	122.24W
Redditch	9	Li	52.19N	1.56W
Rede	9	Kf	55.08N	2.13W
Redenção	54	Kd	4.13S	38.43W
Redfield	43	Hc	44.53N	98.31W
Red Hill	65a	Ec	20.43N	156.15W
Red Hills	45	Gh	37.25N	99.25W
Redkino	7	Ih	56.40N	36.19 E
Red Lake	42	If	51.05N	93.55W
Red Lake	42	If	51.03N	93.49W
Red Lake River	45	Hc	47.55N	97.01W
Red Lakes	43	Ib	48.05N	94.45W
Redlands	46	Gi	34.03N	117.11W
Red Lodge	46	Kd	45.11N	109.15W
Redmond	43	Cc	44.17N	121.11W
Red Mountain [Ca.-U.S.]	46	Df	41.35N	123.06W
Red Mountain [Mt.-U.S.]	46	Ic	47.07N	112.44W
Red Oak	45	If	41.01N	95.14W
Redon	11	Dg	47.39N	2.05W
Redonda	50	Ed	16.55N	62.19W
Redondela	13	Db	42.17N	8.36W
Redondo	13	Ef	38.39N	7.33W
Redondo Beach	46	Fj	33.51N	118.23W
Redoubt Volcano	38	Dc	60.29N	152.45W
Red River [N.Amer.]	38	Jd	50.24N	96.48W
Red River [U.S.]	38	Jf	31.00N	91.40W
Red River (EN) = Hông, Sông-	21	Mg	20.17N	106.34 E
Red River (EN) = Yuan Jiang [Asia]	21	Mg	20.17N	106.34 E
Red Rock, Lake-	45	Jf	41.30N	93.20W
Red Rock River	46	Id	44.59N	112.52W
Redruth	9	Hk	50.13N	5.14W
Red Sea (EN) = Aḩmar, Al Baḩr al-	30	Kf	25.00N	38.00 E
Redstone	42	Fd	64.17N	124.33W
Redstone	46	Da	52.08N	123.42W
Red Volta (EN) = Volta Rouge	30	Gh	10.34N	0.30W
Redwater Creek	46	Mb	48.03N	105.13W
Red Wing	43	Ic	44.34N	92.31W
Redwood City	46	Dh	37.29N	122.13W
Redwood Falls	45	Id	44.32N	95.07W
Ree, Lough-/Loch Rí	9	Fh	53.35N	8.00W
Reed City	44	Ed	43.53N	85.31W
Reedley	46	Fh	36.24N	119.37W
Reeds Peak	45	Cj	33.09N	107.51W
Reedsport	43	Cc	43.42N	124.06W
Reedy Glacier	66	Ng	85.30S	134.00W
Reef Islands	57	Hf	10.15S	166.10 E
Reefton	62	De	42.07S	171.52 E
Reepham	12	Db	52.45N	1.07 E
Rees	12	Ic	51.46N	6.24 E
Reese River	46	Gf	40.39N	116.54W
Refahiye	24	Hc	39.54N	38.46 E
Reforma, Río-	48	Ed	26.56N	108.12W
Reftele	8	Eg	57.11N	13.35 E
Reftinski	17	Jh	57.10N	61.43 E
Refugio	45	Hl	28.18N	97.17W
Refugio, Punta-	48	Cc	29.30N	113.30W
Rega	10	Lb	54.10N	15.18 E
Regar	19	Gh	38.34N	68.13 E
Regen	10	Jh	48.58N	13.08 E
Regen	10	Ig	49.01N	12.06 E
Regensburg	6	Hf	49.01N	12.06 E
Reggane	31	Hf	26.42N	0.10 E
Regge	12	Ib	52.26N	6.29 E
Reggio di Calabria	6	Hh	38.06N	15.39 E
Reggio nell'Emilia	14	Ef	44.43N	10.36 E
Reghin	15	Hc	46.46N	24.42 E
Regina [Fr.Gui.]	54	Hc	4.19N	52.08W
Regina [Sask.-Can.]	39	Id	50.25N	104.39W
Registan (EN) = Rīgestān	21	If	31.00N	65.00 E
Registro	55	Ig	24.30S	47.50W
Registro do Araguaia	55	Gb	15.44S	51.50W
Regnitz	10	Gg	49.54N	10.49 E
Regocijo	48	Gf	23.35N	105.11W
Reguengos de Monsaraz	13	Ef	38.25N	7.32W
Rehburg-Loccum	12	Lb	52.28N	9.14 E
Rehoboth	37	Bd	23.50S	17.00 E
Rehoboth	37	Bd	23.18S	17.03 E
Reḩovot	24	Fg	31.54N	34.49 E
Reichelsheim (Odenwald)	12	Ke	49.43N	8.51 E
Reichenbach	10	If	50.37N	12.18 E
Reichshoffen	12	Jf	48.56N	7.40 E
Reichshoft	12	Jd	50.55N	7.39 E
Reichshoft-Denklingen	12	Jd	50.55N	7.39 E
Reidsville	44	Hg	36.21N	79.40W
Reigate	9	Mj	51.14N	0.13W
Reims	6	Gf	49.15N	4.02 E
Rein = Rhine (EN)	5	Ge	51.52N	6.02 E
Reina Adelaida, Archipiélago-	52	Ik	52.10S	74.25W
Reindeer	42	He	55.34N	103.10W
Reindeer Bank (EN)	51p	Ac	11.50N	62.05W
Reindeer Lake	38	Id	57.15N	102.40W
Reineskarvet	8	Cd	60.47N	8.13 E
Reinga, Cape-	62	Ea	34.25S	172.41 E
Reinhardswald	10	Fe	51.30N	9.30 E
Reinheim	12	Je	49.08N	7.11 E
Reinosa	13	Ha	43.00N	4.08W
Reisa	7	Eb	69.48N	21.00 E
Reitoru Atoll	57	Mf	17.52S	143.05W
Reitz	37	De	27.53S	28.31 E
Rejmyra	8	Ff	58.50N	15.55 E
Rejowiec Fabryczny	10	Te	51.08N	23.13 E
Reka Devnja	15	Kf	43.13N	27.36 E
Rekarne	8	Ge	59.20N	16.25 E
Reken	12	Jc	51.48N	7.03 E
Reliance	39	Ic	62.42N	109.08W
Relizane	32	Hb	35.45N	0.33 E
Remagen	12	Jd	50.34N	7.14 E
Remarkable, Mount-	59	Hf	32.48S	138.10 E
Rembang	26	Fh	6.42S	111.20 E
Remedios	49	Gi	8.14N	81.51W
Remedios, Punta-	49	Cg	13.31N	89.49W
Remedios, Río-	49	Mh	11.01N	69.15W
Remich	12	Ie	49.32N	6.22 E
Rémire	54	Hc	4.53N	52.17W
Remiremont	11	Mf	48.01N	6.35 E
Remire Reef	37b	Bb	5.05S	53.22 E
Remontnoje	16	Mf	46.33N	43.40 E
Remoulins	11	Kk	43.56N	4.34 E
Remscheid	10	De	51.11N	7.12 E
Rena	7	Cf	61.08N	11.22 E
Rena	8	Dc	61.08N	11.23 E
Renaix/Ronse	11	Jd	50.45N	3.36 E
Renana, Fossa-	5	Gf	48.40N	7.50 E
Renard Islands	63a	Ad	10.50S	153.00 E
Renaud Island	66	Qe	65.40S	66.00W
Rende	14	Kk	39.20N	16.11 E
Rendezvous Bay	51b	Ab	18.10N	63.07W
Rend Lake	45	Lg	38.05N	88.58W
Rendova Island	60	Fi	8.32S	157.20 E
Rendsburg	10	Fb	54.18N	9.40 E
Renfrew	42	Jg	45.28N	76.41W
Rengat	26	Dg	0.24S	102.33 E
Rengo	56	Fd	34.25S	70.52W
Reni	16	Fg	45.29N	28.18 E
Renko	8	Kd	60.54N	24.17 E
Renkum	12	Hc	51.58N	5.45 E
Renland	41	Jd	71.15N	27.20W
Renmark	58	Fh	34.11S	140.45 E
Rennell, Islas-	56	Fh	52.00S	74.00W
Rennell Island	57	Hf	11.40S	160.10 E
Rennes	6	Ff	48.05N	1.41W
Rennes, Bassin de-	11	Ef	48.05N	1.40W
Rennesøy	8	Ae	59.05N	5.40 E
Rennick Glacier	66	Kf	70.30S	161.45 E
Rennie Lake	42	Gd	61.10N	105.30W
Reno	39	Hf	39.31N	119.48W
Reno	14	Gf	44.38N	12.16 E
Renqiu	28	De	38.42N	116.06 E
Rensselaer [In.-U.S.]	44	De	40.57N	87.09W
Rensselaer [N.Y.-U.S.]	44	Kd	42.37N	73.44W
Renterria	13	Ka	43.19N	1.54W
Renton	46	Dc	47.30N	122.11W
Renwez	12	Ge	49.50N	4.36 E
Renxian	28	Cf	37.07N	114.41 E
Reo	26	Hh	8.19S	120.30 E
Repartimento, Serra do-	55	Jc	17.40S	44.50W
Répce	10	Ni	47.41N	17.02 E
Repino	8	Md	60.10N	29.58 E
Repong, Pulau-	26	Ef	2.22N	105.53 E
Reposaari/Räfsö	8	Ic	61.37N	21.27 E
Republic	46	Fb	48.39N	118.44W
Republican	38	Jf	39.03N	96.48W
Repulse Bay	39	Kc	66.32N	86.15W
Repulse Bay [Austl.]	59	Jd	20.35S	148.45 E
Repulse Bay [Can.]	42	Ic	66.20N	86.00W
Repvåg	7	Fa	70.45N	25.41 E
Requena [Peru]	54	Dd	5.00S	73.50W
Requena [Sp.]	13	Ke	39.29N	1.06W
Requin Bay	51p	Bb	12.02N	61.38W
Réquista	11	Ij	44.02N	2.32 E
Reşadiye Yarimadası	15	Km	36.40N	27.45 E
Reschenpass/Resia, Passo di-	14	Ed	46.50N	10.30 E
Resen	15	Eh	41.05N	21.01 E
Reserva	55	Gg	24.38S	50.52W
Reserve	45	Bj	33.43N	108.45W
Rešetilovka	16	Ie	49.33N	34.05 E
Reshui	27	Hd	37.38N	100.30 E
Resia, Passo di-/Reschenpass	14	Ed	46.50N	10.30 E
Resistencia	53	Kh	27.30S	58.59W
Reşiţa	15	Ed	45.18N	21.55 E
Resko	10	Lc	53.47N	15.25 E
Reso/Raisio	7	Ff	60.29N	22.11 E
Resolute	39	Jb	74.41N	94.54W
Resolution	38	Mc	61.30N	65.00W
Resolution Island	42	Ld	61.35N	64.39W
Resolution Island	62	Bf	45.40S	166.35 E
Respublikai Soveth Socialisti Todžikiston/Tadžikskaja SSR	19	Hh	39.00N	71.00 E
Respublika Sovetike Sočialiste Moldovenjaske/Moldavskaja SSR	19	Cf	47.00N	29.00 E
Ressa	16	Ib	54.45N	35.10 E
Ressons-sur-Matz	12	Ee	49.33N	2.45 E
Restigouche River	44	Na	48.04N	66.20W
Restinga de Sefton, Isla-	52	Hi	37.00S	83.50W
Restinga Sêca	55	Fi	29.49S	53.23W
Reszel	10	Rb	54.04N	21.09 E
Retalhuleu	49	Bf	14.20N	91.50W
Retalhuleu	47	Ff	14.32N	91.41W
Retavas/Rietavas	8	Ii	55.43N	21.49 E
Retezatului, Munţii-	15	Fd	45.25N	23.00 E
Rethel	11	Ke	49.31N	4.22 E
Rethem (Aller)	12	Lb	52.47N	9.23 E
Réthinnon	15	Hn	35.22N	24.28 E
Retie	12	Hc	51.17N	5.05 E

Index Symbols

- Independent Nation
- State, Region
- District, County
- Municipality
- Colony, Dependency
- Continent
- Physical Region
- Historical or Cultural Region
- Mount, Mountain
- Volcano
- Hill
- Mountains, Mountain Range
- Hills, Escarpment
- Plateau, Upland
- Pass, Gap
- Plain, Lowland
- Delta
- Salt Flat
- Valley, Canyon
- Crater, Cave
- Karst Features
- Depression
- Polder
- Desert, Dunes
- Forest, Woods
- Heath, Steppe
- Oasis
- Cape, Point
- Coast, Beach
- Cliff
- Peninsula
- Isthmus
- Sandbank
- Island
- Atoll
- Rock, Reef
- Islands, Archipelago
- Rocks, Reefs
- Coral Reef
- Well, Spring
- Geyser
- River, Stream
- Waterfall Rapids
- River Mouth, Estuary
- Lake
- Salt Lake
- Intermittent Lake
- Reservoir
- Swamp, Pond
- Canal
- Glacier
- Ice Shelf, Pack Ice
- Ocean
- Sea
- Gulf, Bay
- Strait, Fjord
- Lagoon
- Bank
- Seamount
- Tablemount
- Ridge
- Shelf
- Basin
- Escarpment, Sea Scarp
- Fracture
- Trench, Abyss
- National Park, Reserve
- Point of Interest
- Recreation Site
- Cave, Cavern
- Historic Site
- Ruins
- Wall, Walls
- Church, Abbey
- Temple
- Scientific Station
- Airport
- Port
- Lighthouse
- Mine
- Tunnel
- Dam, Bridge

Retourne 12 Ge 49.26N 4.02 E
Rétság 10 Pi 47.56N 19.08 E
Rettihovka 28 Lb 44.10N 132.45 E
Retz 14 Jc 48.45N 15.57 E
Retz, Pays de- 11 Eg 47.07N 1.58W
Réunion=Reunion (EN) 30 Mk 21.06S 55.36 E
Réunion=Reunion (EN) 31 Mk 21.06S 55.36 E
Reunion (EN)=Réunion 30 Mk 21.06S 55.36 E
Reunion (EN)=Réunion 31 Mk 21.06S 55.36 E
Reus 13 Nc 41.09N 1.07 E
Reusel 12 Hc 51.22N 5.10 E
Reuss 14 Cc 47.28N 8.14 E
Reut 16 Ff 47.15N 29.09 E
Reutlingen 10 Fh 48.29N 9.13 E
Reutte 14 Ec 47.29N 10.43 E
Revda [R.S.F.S.R.] 17 Ih 56.48N 59.57 E
Revda [R.S.F.S.R.] 7 Ic 67.57N 34.32 E
Revel 11 Hk 43.28N 2.00 E
Revelstoke 42 Ff 50.59N 118.12W
Revermont 11 Lh 46.27N 5.25 E
Revillagigedo 40 Me 55.35N 131.23W
Revillagigedo, Islas- 38 Hh 19.00N 111.30W
Revin 11 Ke 49.56N 4.38 E
Revoljucii, Pik- 18 Ie 38.33N 72.28 E
Revsundssjön 8 Fb 62.50N 15.15 E
Rewa 63d Bc 18.08S 178.33 E
Rewa 25 Gd 24.32N 81.18 E
Rewāri 25 Fc 28.11N 76.37 E
Rex, Mount- 66 Qf 74.54S 75.57W
Rexburg 46 Je 43.49N 111.47W
Rexpoëde 12 Ed 50.56N 2.32 E
Rey 23 Hb 35.35N 51.25 E
Rey, Arroyo del- 55 Ci 29.12S 59.36W
Rey, Isla del- 47 Ig 8.22N 78.55W
Rey, Laguna del- 48 Hd 27.00N 103.25W
Rey Bouba 34 Hd 8.40N 14.11 E
Reyes, Point- 46 Dg 38.00N 123.01W
Reyhanli 24 Gd 36.18N 36.32 E
Reykjalid 7a Cb 65.39N 16.55W
Reykjanes 5 Dc 63.49N 22.43W
Reykjanes Ridge (EN) 3 Dc 62.00N 27.00W
Reykjavik 6 Dc 64.09N 21.57W
Reynolds Range 59 Gd 22.20S 132.50 E
Reynosa 39 Jg 26.07N 98.18W
Reyssouze 11 Kh 46.27N 4.54 E
Rež 17 Kh 57.54N 62.20 E
Rež 17 Jh 57.23N 61.24 E
Rezé 11 Eg 47.12N 1.34W
Rezekne/Rēzekne 6 Id 56.30N 27.19 E
Rēzekne/Rezekne 6 Id 56.30N 27.19 E
Rezelm, Lacul- 15 Le 44.54N 28.57 E
Rezina 16 Ff 47.43N 28.58 E
Reznas, Ozero-/Rēznas Ezers 8 Lh 56.20N 27.30 E
Rēznas Ezers/Reznas, Ozero- 8 Lh 56.20N 27.30 E
Rezovo 15 Lh 41.59N 28.02 E
Rezvān 24 Qi 27.34N 56.06 E
Rezve 15 Lh 41.59N 28.01 E
Rgotina 15 Fe 44.01N 22.17 E
Rhaetian Alps (EN)=Alpi Retiche 14 Dd 46.30N 10.00 E
Rhaetian Alps (EN)= Rätische Alpen 14 Dd 46.30N 10.00 E
Rhallamane 30 Ff 23.15N 10.00W
Rhauderfehn 12 Ja 53.08N 7.34 E
Rhaunen 12 Je 49.51N 7.21 E
Rheda-Wiedenbrück 10 Ee 51.51N 8.18 E
Rheden 12 Ib 52.01N 6.01 E
Rheden-Dieren 12 Ib 52.03N 6.08 E
Rheider Land 12 Ja 53.13N 7.18 E
Rhein 12 Ke 49.52N 8.07 E
Rhein=Rhine (EN) 5 Ge 51.52N 6.02 E
Rheinberg 12 Ic 51.33N 6.36 E
Rheine 10 Dd 52.17N 7.27 E
Rheinfall 14 Cc 47.41N 8.38 E
Rheinfelden 10 Di 47.34N 7.48 E
Rheingaugebirge 12 Jd 50.05N 8.00 E
Rheinisches Schiefergebirge =Rhenish Slate Mountains (EN) 5 Ge 50.25N 7.10 E
Rheinland-Pfalz=Rhineland-Palatinate (EN) 10 Cf 50.00N 7.00 E
Rheinsberg 10 Ic 53.06N 12.53 E
Rheinstetten 12 Kf 48.58N 8.18 E
Rhenen 12 Hc 51.58N 5.35 E
Rhenish Slate Mountains (EN)=Rheinisches Schiefergebirge 5 Ge 50.25N 7.10 E
Rheris 32 Gc 30.41N 4.57W
Rheydt, Mönchengladbach- 12 Ic 51.10N 6.27 E
Rhin=Rhine (EN) 5 Ge 51.52N 6.02 E
Rhine (EN)=Rein 5 Ge 51.52N 6.02 E
Rhine (EN)=Rhein 5 Ge 51.52N 6.02 E
Rhine (EN)=Rhin 5 Ge 51.52N 6.02 E
Rhine (EN)=Rijn 5 Ge 51.52N 6.02 E
Rhine Bank (EN) 56 Ji 50.30S 53.30W
Rhineland-Palatinate (EN)= Rheinland Pfalz 10 Cf 50.00N 7.00 E
Rhinelander 43 Jb 45.38N 89.25W
Rhinluch 10 Id 52.50N 12.50 E
Rhino Camp 36 Fb 2.58N 31.24 E
Rhiou 13 Mi 35.59N 0.53 E
Rhir, Cap- 32 Fc 30.38N 9.54W
Rho 14 De 45.32N 9.02 E
Rhode Island 43 Mc 41.40N 71.30W
Rhode Island Sound 44 Le 41.25N 71.15W
Rhodes (EN) = Ródhos 6 Ih 36.26N 28.13 E
Rhodes (EN) = Ródhos 5 Ih 36.10N 28.00 E
Rhodesia→Zimbabwe 31 Jj 20.00S 30.00 E
Rhodes Peak 46 Hc 46.41N 114.47W
Rhodope Mountains (EN) = Rodopi 5 Ig 41.30N 24.30 E
Rhomara 13 Hi 35.10N 4.57W
Rhön 10 Gf 50.25N 10.05 E
Rhondda 9 Jj 51.40N 3.30W
Rhône 5 Gg 43.20N 4.50 E
Rhône 11 Ki 46.00N 4.30 E
Rhône au Rhin, Canal du- 11 Lg 47.06N 5.19 E
Rhourd el Baguel 32 Ic 31.24N 6.57 E
Rhue 11 Ii 45.23N 2.29 E
Rhum 9 Ge 57.00N 6.20W
Rhyl 9 Jh 53.19N 3.29W
Riaba 34 Ge 3.24N 8.42 E
Riacho de Santana 54 Jf 13.37S 42.57W
Riangnom 35 Ed 9.55N 30.01 E
Riaño 13 Gb 42.58N 5.01W
Riánsares 13 Ie 39.32N 3.18W
Říany 10 Kg 50.00N 14.39 E
Rias Altas 13 Da 43.30N 8.30W
Rias Bajas 13 Db 42.30N 9.00W
Riau 26 Df 1.00N 102.00 E
Riau Archipelago (EN)= Riau, Kepulauan- 21 Mi 1.00N 104.30 E
Riau Kepulauan-=Riau Archipelago (EN) 21 Mi 1.00N 104.30 E
Riaza 13 Ic 41.17N 3.28W
Riaza 13 Ic 41.42N 3.55W
Ribadavia 13 Db 42.17N 8.08W
Ribadeo 13 Ea 43.32N 7.02W
Ribadesella 13 Ga 43.28N 5.04W
Ribagorza/La Ribagorça 13 Mb 42.15N 0.30 E
Ribamar 54 Jd 2.33S 44.03W
Ribas do Rio Pardo 55 Fe 20.27S 53.46W
Ribatejo 13 De 39.15N 8.30W
Ribáuè 37 Fb 14.57S 38.17 E
Ribble 9 Kh 53.44N 2.50W
Ribe 7 Bi 55.21N 8.46 E
Ribe 8 Ci 55.35N 8.45 E
Ribécourt-Dreslincourt 12 Ee 49.31N 2.55 E
Ribeira [Braz.] 55 Hg 24.39S 49.00W
Ribeira [Sp.] 13 Db 42.33N 9.00W
Ribeira, Rio- 55 Ig 24.40S 47.24W
Ribeira Brava 32 Cf 16.37N 24.18W
Ribeira Grande 32 Bf 17.11N 25.04W
Ribeirão Prêto 53 Lh 21.10S 47.48W
Ribeirãozinho 55 Fc 16.22S 52.36W
Ribeiro Gonçalves 54 Ie 7.32S 45.14W
Ribemont 12 Fe 49.48N 3.28 E
Ribera 14 Hm 37.30N 13.16 E
Ribérac 11 Gi 45.15N 0.20 E
Riberalta 53 Jg 10.59S 66.06W
Ribnica 14 Ie 45.44N 14.44 E
Ribnitz-Damgarten 10 Ib 54.15N 12.28 E
Ricardo Flores Magón 48 Fc 29.58N 106.58W
Riccia 14 Ii 41.29N 14.50 E
Riccione 14 Gg 43.59N 12.39 E
Rice Lake 44 Hc 44.08N 78.13W
Rich 32 Gc 32.15N 4.30W
Richan 45 Jb 49.59N 92.49W
Richard Collinson Inlet 42 Gb 72.45N 113.00W
Richards 42 Ec 69.20N 134.35W
Richard's Bay 31 Kk 28.47S 32.06 E
Richardson 45 Hj 32.57N 96.44W
Richardson Mountains 38 Fc 66.00N 135.20W
Richard Toll 34 Bb 16.28N 15.41W
Richât, Guel er- 32 Ee 21.07N 11.24W
Richel 12 Ha 53.18N 5.10 E
Richel Griend 12 Ha 53.18N 5.15 E
Richelieu 11 Gg 47.01N 0.19 E
Richer 45 Hb 49.39N 96.28W
Richey 46 Mc 47.39N 105.04W
Richfield 43 Ed 38.46N 112.05W
Richibucto 44 Ob 46.41N 64.52W
Richland 43 Db 46.17N 119.18W
Richland Center 45 Ke 43.22N 90.21W
Richmond [Austl.] 59 Id 20.44S 143.08 E
Richmond [Ca.-U.S.] 43 Cd 37.57N 122.22W
Richmond [Eng.-U.K.] 9 Lg 54.24N 1.44W
Richmond [In.-U.S.] 43 Kd 39.50N 84.54W
Richmond [Ky.-U.S.] 43 Kd 37.45N 84.18W
Richmond [N.Z.] 62 Ed 41.21S 173.11 E
Richmond [S.Afr.] 37 Cf 31.23S 23.56 E
Richmond [Tx.-U.S.] 45 Il 29.35N 95.46W
Richmond [Va.-U.S.] 39 Lf 37.30N 77.28W
Richmond, Mount- 62 Ed 41.28S 173.24 E
Richmond Hill 44 Hd 43.52N 79.27W
Richmond Peak 51n Ba 13.17N 61.13W
Richtofen, Mount- 45 Df 40.29N 105.57W
Rickmansworth 12 Bc 51.38N 0.28W
Ricobayo, Embalse de- 13 Gc 41.35N 5.50W
Ridā' 33 Hg 14.25N 44.50 E
Ridderkerk 12 Gc 51.52N 4.36 E
Ridgecrest 46 Gi 35.38N 117.36W
Ridgway 44 He 41.25N 78.45W
Riding Mountain 45 Fa 50.55N 100.25W
Riecito, Rio- 50 Bi 6.50N 68.51W
Ried 12 Ke 49.50N 8.25 E
Ried im Innkreis 14 Hb 48.13N 13.30 E
Riedlingen 10 Fh 48.09N 9.28 E
Riemst 12 Hd 50.48N 5.36 E
Ries 10 Gh 48.55N 10.40 E
Riesa 10 Je 51.18N 13.18 E
Riesco, Isla- 56 Fh 53.00S 72.30W
Riesi 14 Im 37.17N 14.05 E
Riet 30 Jk 29.00S 23.53 E
Rietavas/Retavas 8 Ii 55.43N 21.49 E
Rietberg 12 Kc 51.48N 8.26 E
Rietbron 37 Cf 32.54S 23.09 E
Rietfontein [Nam.] 37 Cd 21.58S 20.58 E
Rietfontein [S.Afr.] 37 Ce 26.44S 20.01 E
Rieti 14 Gh 42.24N 12.51 E
Rif 30 Ge 35.00N 4.00W
Rifle 45 Cg 39.32N 107.47W
Rifstangi 5 Eb 66.32N 16.12W
Rift Valley 36 Gb 0.30N 36.00 E
Rift Valley 30 Kh 0.30N 36.00 E
Riga/Rīga 6 Id 56.57N 24.06 E
Rīga/Riga 6 Id 56.57N 24.06 E
Riga, Gulf of- (EN)=Rīgas Jūras Līcis 5 Id 57.30N 23.35 E
Riga, Gulf of- (EN)=Riia Laht 5 Id 57.30N 23.35 E
Riga, Gulf of- (EN)=Rižski Zaliv 5 Id 57.30N 23.35 E
Rigachikum 34 Gc 10.38N 7.28 E
Rigas Jūras Līcis=Riga, Gulf of- (EN) 5 Id 57.30N 23.35 E
Rigestān=Registan (EN) 21 If 31.00N 65.00 E
Riggins 46 Gd 45.25N 116.19W
Rigolet 42 Lf 54.10N 58.26W
Rig-Rig 35 Ac 14.16N 14.21 E
Rihand Sagar 25 Hd 24.05N 83.05 E
Riia Laht=Riga, Gulf of- (EN) 5 Id 57.30N 23.35 E
Riihimäki 7 Ff 60.45N 24.46 E
Riiser-Larsen-Halvøya 66 De 68.55S 34.00 E
Riito 48 Ba 32.10N 114.45W
Riječki zaljev = Rijeka, Gulf of- (EN) 14 Ie 45.15N 14.25 E
Rijeka 6 Hf 45.21N 14.24 E
Rijeka, Gulf of- (EN)= Riječki zaljev 14 Ie 45.15N 14.25 E
Rijksmuseum Kröller-Müller 12 Hb 52.06N 5.47 E
Rijn=Rhine (EN) 5 Ge 51.52N 6.02 E
Rijssen 12 Ib 52.18N 6.37 E
Rijswijk 12 Gb 52.03N 4.21 E
Rika 10 Th 48.08N 23.22 E
Rikā, Wādī ar- 33 He 22.25N 44.50 E
Rikubetsu 29a Cb 43.28N 143.43 E
Rikuzentakada 28 Pe 39.01N 141.38 E
Rila 15 Gh 42.08N 23.33 E
Rila 15 Gg 42.08N 23.08 E
Riley 46 Fe 43.32N 119.29W
Riley, Mount- 45 Ck 31.58N 107.05W
Rilski Manastir 15 Gg 42.08N 23.20 E
Rima 30 Hg 13.04N 5.10 E
Rimatara, Ile- 57 Lg 22.38S 152.51W
Rimava 10 Qh 48.15N 20.21 E
Rimavská Sobota 10 Qh 48.23N 20.01 E
Rimbo 7 Eg 59.45N 18.22 E
Rimé 35 Bc 14.02N 18.03 E
Rimforsa 8 Ff 58.08N 15.40 E
Rimini 14 Gf 44.04N 12.34 E
Rimito/Rymättylä 8 Jd 60.25N 21.55 E
Rîmnic 15 Kd 45.32N 27.31 E
Rîmnicu Sărat 15 Kd 45.23N 27.03 E
Rîmnicu Vîlcea 15 Hd 45.06N 24.22 E
Rimouski 39 Me 48.27N 68.32W
Rimše/Rimšė 8 Li 55.30N 26.33 E
Rimšė/Rimše 8 Li 55.30N 26.33 E
Rinbung 27 Ef 29.15N 89.52 E
Rincon 50 Bf 12.14N 68.20W
Rincón 51a Ab 18.21N 67.16W
Rincón, Bahia de- 51a Bc 17.57N 66.19W
Rincón del Bonete, Lago Artificial de- 56 Id 32.45S 56.00W
Rincón de Romos 48 Hf 22.14N 102.18W
Rindal 7 Be 63.03N 9.13 E
Ringe 8 Di 55.14N 10.29 E
Ringebu 8 Dc 61.31N 10.10 E
Ringerike 8 Dd 60.05N 10.15 E
Ringgold Isles 57 Jf 16.15S 179.25W
Ringim 34 Gc 12.09N 9.10 E
Ringkøbing 8 Ch 56.10N 8.45 E
Ringkøbing 7 Bh 56.05N 8.15 E
Ringkøbing Fjord 7 Bi 56.00N 8.15 E
Ringlådes 15 Dj 39.25N 20.04 E
Ringsjön 8 Ei 55.50N 13.30 E
Ringsted 7 Ci 55.27N 11.49 E
Ringvassøy 7 Eb 69.55N 19.15 E
Rinia 15 Il 37.25N 25.13 E
Rinjani, Gunung- 26 Gh 8.24S 116.28 E
Rinn Chathóir/Cahore Point 9 Gi 52.34N 6.11W
Rinn Dúain/Hook Head 9 Gi 52.07N 6.55W
Rinteln 10 Fd 52.11N 9.05 E
Rinya 10 Nk 45.57N 17.27 E
Rio Azul 55 Gg 25.43S 50.47W
Riobamba 53 If 1.40S 78.38W
Rio Branco 53 Jf 9.58S 67.48W
Rio Branco 55 Fk 32.34S 53.25W
Rio Branco do Sul 55 Hg 25.10S 49.18W
Rio Brilhante 54 Hh 21.48S 54.33W
Rio Bueno 56 Ff 40.19S 72.58W
Rio Caribe 54 Fa 10.42N 63.07W
Rio Chico 50 Dg 10.19N 65.59W
Rio Claro [Braz.] 55 If 22.24S 47.33W
Rio Claro [Trin.] 50 Fg 10.18N 61.11W
Rio Colorado 56 He 39.01S 64.05W
Rio Cuarto 53 Ji 33.08S 64.20W
Rio de Janeiro 53 Lh 22.54S 43.15W
Rio de Janeiro 54 Jh 22.30S 42.30W
Rio de Jesús 49 Gj 7.59N 81.10W
Rio de Oro 32 Ee 24.00N 14.00W
Rio de Oro 49 Ki 8.57N 73.23W
Rio de Oro, Bahia de- 32 De 23.45N 15.50W
Rio do Sul 56 Kc 27.13S 49.39W
Rio Fortuna 55 Hi 28.06S 49.07W
Rio Gallegos 53 Jk 51.37S 69.10W
Rio Grande 53 Ki 32.02S 52.05W
Rio Grande [Arg.] 56 Gh 53.47S 67.42W
Rio Grande [Nic.] 49 Dg 12.59N 86.34W
Rio Grande [P.R.] 51a Cb 18.23N 65.50W
Rio Grande City 45 Gm 26.23N 98.49W
Rio Grande de Añasco 51a Ab 18.17N 67.10W
Rio Grande de Manati 51a Bb 18.29N 66.32W
Rio Grande de Matagalpa 47 Hf 12.54N 83.32W
Rio Grande do Norte 54 Ke 5.40S 36.00W
Rio Grande do Sul 56 Jc 30.00S 54.00W
Rio Grande Rise (EN) 3 Cm 31.00S 35.00W
Riohacha 54 Da 11.32N 72.54W
Rio Hato 49 Gi 8.23N 80.10W
Rio Lagartos 48 Og 21.36N 88.10W
Rio Largo 54 Ke 9.29S 35.51W
Riom 11 Ji 45.54N 3.07 E
Rio Maior 13 De 39.20N 8.56W
Rio Mayo 56 Fg 45.41S 70.16W
Riom-ès-Montagnes 11 Ii 45.17N 2.40 E
Rio Miranda 54 Gg 19.25S 57.20W
Rio Mulatos 54 Eg 19.42S 66.47W
Rion 15 Ek 38.18N 21.47 E
Rio Negro [Chile] 56 Ff 40.47S 73.14W
Rio Negro [Arg.] 56 Gf 40.00S 67.00W
Rio Negro [Braz.] 56 Kc 26.06S 49.48W
Rio Negro [Braz.] 55 Dd 19.33S 56.32W
Rio Negro [Ur.] 55 Dk 32.45S 57.20W
Rio Negro, Pantanal do- 54 Gg 18.50S 56.00W
Rionero in Vulture 14 Jj 40.56N 15.40 E
Rioni 16 Lh 42.10N 41.38 E
Rio Novo 55 Dc 16.28S 56.30W
Rio Pardo 56 Jc 29.59S 52.22W
Rio Prêto, Serra do- 55 Gd 18.18S 50.42W
Rio San Juan 49 Eh 11.10N 84.30W
Rio Segundo 56 Hd 31.40S 63.55W
Riosucio 54 Cb 7.27N 77.07W
Rio Tercero 56 Hd 32.11S 64.06W
Rio Tinto 54 Ke 6.48S 35.05W
Rioverde 47 Dd 21.56N 100.01W
Rio Verde 54 Hg 17.43S 50.56W
Rio Verde, Serra do- 55 Fc 17.32S 52.25W
Rio Verde de Mato Grosso 54 Hg 18.56S 54.52W
Rio Verde do Sul 55 Ef 22.54S 55.27W
Rioz 11 Mg 47.25N 6.04 E
Řip 10 Kf 50.24N 14.18 E
Ripanj 15 De 44.38N 20.32 E
Ripley [Eng.-U.K.] 12 Aa 53.02N 1.24W
Ripley [Tn.-U.S.] 44 Ch 35.44N 89.33W
Ripley [W.V.-U.S.] 44 Gf 38.49N 81.44W
Ripoll 13 Ob 42.12N 2.12 E
Ripon 9 Lg 54.08N 1.31W
Riposto 14 Jm 37.44N 15.12 E
Ripple Mountain 46 Gb 49.02N 117.05W
Risan 15 Bg 42.31N 18.42 E
Risaralda 54 Cb 5.00N 75.45W
Risbäck 7 Dd 64.42N 15.32 E
Rishah, Wādi- 24 Kj 25.33N 44.05 E
Ri Shahr 24 Nh 28.55N 50.50 E
Rishiri 28 Pb 45.11N 141.15 E
Rishiri-Suidō 29a Ba 45.10N 141.30 E
Rishiri-Tō 27 Pb 45.11N 141.15 E
Rishiri-Yama 29a Ba 45.11N 141.15 E
Rishmūk 24 Ng 31.15N 50.20 E
Rishon Leẕiyyon 24 Fg 31.58N 34.48 E
Rising Star 45 Gj 32.06N 98.58W
Risle 11 Ge 49.26N 0.23 E
Risnjak 14 Ie 45.26N 14.37 E
Rîşnov 15 Id 45.35N 25.27 E
Risør 7 Bg 58.43N 9.14 E
Risoux, Mont- 11 Mh 46.36N 6.10 E
Risøyhamn 7 Db 69.00N 15.45 E
Riß 10 Fh 48.17N 9.49 E
Risti 7 Fg 59.03N 24.01 E
Ristiina 8 Lc 61.30N 27.16 E
Ristijarvi 7 Gd 64.30N 28.13 E
Ristna, Mys-/Ristna Neem 8 If 58.55N 21.55 E
Ristna Neem/Ristna, Mys- 8 If 58.55N 21.55 E
Risū 24 Qf 33.52N 57.28 E
Ritchie's Archipelago 25 If 12.14N 93.10 E
Ritidian Point 64c Ba 13.39N 144.51 E
Ritscher-Hochland 66 Bf 73.20S 9.30W
Ritter, Mount- 43 Dd 37.42N 119.20W
Ritterhude 12 Ka 53.11N 8.45 E
Rituerto 13 Jc 41.36N 2.22W
Ritzville 46 Fc 47.08N 118.23W
Riva-Bella, Ouistreham- 12 Be 49.17N 0.16W
Rivadavia [Arg.] 56 Hb 24.11S 62.53W
Rivadavia [Arg.] 56 Gd 33.11S 68.28W
Riva del Garda 14 Ee 45.53N 10.50 E
Rivas 39 Kh 11.26N 85.51W
Rivas 49 Eh 11.25N 85.50W
Rive-de-Gier 11 Ki 45.22N 4.37 E
Rivellata, Punta di a- 11a Aa 42.35N 8.40 E
Rivera 55 Ej 31.30S 55.15W
Rivera [Arg.] 56 He 37.12S 63.14W
Rivera [Ur.] 53 Ki 30.54S 55.31W
River Cess 34 Dd 5.27N 9.35W
Riverdale 45 Fc 47.30N 101.22W
Riverina 59 Jg 35.25S 145.30 E
River Inlet 42 Ef 51.41N 127.15W
Rivers 34 Ge 4.50N 6.30 E
Rivers, Lake of the- 46 Mb 49.45N 105.45W
Riversdale [N.Z.] 62 Cf 45.54S 168.44 E
Riversdale [S.Afr.] 37 Cf 34.07S 21.15 E
Riverside 43 De 33.59N 117.22W
Riverton [N.Z.] 62 Bg 46.21S 168.00 E
Riverton [Wy.-U.S.] 43 Fc 43.02N 108.23W
Rivesaltes 11 Il 42.46N 2.52 E
Riviera Beach 44 Ge 26.47N 80.04W
Rivière-à-Pierre 44 Kb 46.58N 72.11W
Rivière-du-Loup 42 Kg 47.50N 69.32W
Rivière-Pilote 51h Bc 14.29N 60.54W
Rivière-Salée 51h Bb 14.32N 60.59W
Rivoli 14 Be 45.04N 7.31 E
Rivungo 36 Df 16.15S 22.00 E
Riwaka 62 Ed 41.05S 173.00 E
Riwoqê 27 Ge 31.13N 96.29 E
Rixensart 12 Gd 50.43N 4.35 E
Riyadh (EN)=Ar Riyāḑ 22 Gg 24.38N 46.43 E
Rize 23 Fa 41.02N 40.31 E
Rize, Gora- 18 Bf 37.48N 58.13 E
Rize Dağları 24 Ib 40.30N 40.50 E
Rizhao 27 Kd 35.27N 119.28 E
Rizokarpásso → Dipkarpas 24 Fe 35.36N 34.23 E
Rižski Zaliv = Riga, Gulf of- (EN) 5 Id 57.30N 23.35 E
Rizzuto, Capo- 14 Ll 38.53N 17.05 E
Rjabovo 8 Md 60.17N 29.01 E
Rjapina/Räpina 8 Lf 58.03N 27.35 E
Rjazan 6 Je 54.38N 39.44 E
Rjazanovski 7 Ji 55.08N 39.35 E
Rjazanskaja Oblast 19 Ee 54.30N 40.40 E
Rjažsk 6 Ke 53.43N 40.04 E
Rjukan 7 Bg 59.52N 8.34 E
Rjuven 8 Be 59.13N 7.10 E
Rkiz 32 Df 16.50N 15.20W
Rldal 8 Be 59.49N 6.48 E
Roa [Nor.] 8 Dd 60.17N 10.37 E
Roa [Sp.] 13 Ic 41.42N 3.55W
Road Town 47 Le 18.27N 64.37W
Roag, Loch- 9 Gc 58.16N 6.50W
Roan Antelope 36 Ee 13.08S 28.24 E
Roannais 11 Kh 46.05N 4.10 E
Roanne 11 Kh 46.02N 4.04 E
Roanoke 38 Lf 35.56N 76.43W
Roanoke [Al.-U.S.] 44 Ei 33.09N 85.22W
Roanoke [Va.-U.S.] 39 Lf 37.16N 79.57W
Roanoke Rapids 44 Ig 36.28N 77.40W
Roan Plateau 46 Kg 39.35N 108.55W
Roaringwater Bay 9 Dj 51.25N 9.30W
Roatán 49 De 16.18N 86.35W
Roatán, Isla de- 49 De 16.23N 86.30W
Robāṭ [Iran] 24 Qd 37.55N 57.42 E
Robāṭ [Iran] 24 Pg 30.04N 54.49 E
Robāt-e-Khān 23 Ic 33.21N 56.02 E
Robāt-e-Kord 24 Qf 33.45N 56.37 E
Robāt Karīm 24 Ne 35.28N 51.05 E
Robbie Bank (EN) 61 Fb 11.03S 176.53W
Robe, Mount- 59 If 31.40S 141.20 E
Röbel 10 Ic 53.23N 12.36 E
Robert Lee 45 Fk 31.54N 100.29W
Roberts 55 Bl 35.09S 61.57W
Roberts, Mount- 59 Ke 28.13S 152.28 E
Roberts Creek Mountain 46 Gg 39.52N 116.18W
Robertsfors 7 Ed 64.11N 20.51 E
Robert S. Kerr Lake 45 Ii 35.25N 95.00W
Robertson 37 Bf 33.46S 19.50 E
Robertson Bay 66 Kf 71.25S 170.00 E
Robertson Range 59 Ed 23.10S 121.00 E
Robertsport 34 Cd 6.45N 11.22W
Roberval 42 Kg 48.31N 72.13W
Robi 35 Fd 7.38N 39.52 E
Robinson Crusoe (EN) = Robinson Crusoe, Isla- 52 Ii 33.38S 78.52W
Robinson Crusoe, Isla- = Robinson Crusoe (EN) 52 Ii 33.38S 78.52W
Robinson Range 59 De 25.45S 119.00 E
Robinson River 59 Hc 16.03S 137.16 E
Roboré 53 Kg 18.20S 59.45W
Rob Roy 63a Cb 7.23S 157.36 E
Robson, Mount- 38 Hd 53.07N 119.09W
Robstown 45 Hm 27.27N 97.40W
Roby 45 Fj 32.45N 100.23W
Roca, Cabo da- 5 Fh 38.47N 9.30W
Rocamadour 11 Hj 44.48N 1.38 E
Roca Partida, Isla- 47 Be 19.01N 112.02W
Roca Partida, Punta- 48 Lh 18.42N 95.10W
Rocas, Atol das- 52 Mf 3.52S 33.49W
Roccaraso 14 Ii 41.51N 14.05 E
Ročegda 19 Ec 62.42N 43.23 E
Rocha 55 Fk 34.00S 54.00W
Rocha 56 Jd 34.29S 54.20W
Rochdale 9 Kh 53.38N 2.09W
Rochechouart 11 Gi 45.49N 0.49 E
Rochedo 55 Ed 19.57S 54.52W
Rochefort [Bel.] 11 Ld 50.10N 5.13 E
Rochefort [Fr.] 11 Fi 45.56N 0.59W
Rochefort-Han-sur-Lesse 12 Hd 50.08N 5.11 E
Rochelle 45 Lf 41.56N 89.04W
Rocher River 42 Gd 61.23N 112.45W
Rocher's Bluff 51c c 16.42N 62.09W
Rochester [Eng.-U.K.] 9 Nj 51.24N 0.30 E
Rochester [In.-U.S.] 44 De 41.04N 86.13W
Rochester [Mn.-U.S.] 43 Ic 44.02N 92.29W
Rochester [N.H.-U.S.] 44 Ld 43.18N 70.59W
Rochester [N.Y.-U.S.] 39 Le 43.10N 77.36W
Rochlitzer Berg 10 Ie 51.05N 12.48 E
Rocigalgo 13 He 39.35N 4.35W
Rockall 5 Ed 57.35N 13.48W
Rockall Rise (EN) 5 Ed 57.00N 14.00W
Rock Creek Butte 46 Fd 44.49N 118.07W
Rockefeller Plateau 66 Ng 80.00S 135.00W
Rockenhausen 12 Je 49.38N 7.50 E
Rockford 43 Jc 42.17N 89.06W
Rockglen 46 Mb 49.10N 105.57W
Rockhampton 58 Gg 23.23S 150.31 E
Rock Hill 43 Ke 34.55N 81.01W
Rockingham [Austl.] 59 Df 32.17S 115.44 E
Rockingham [N.C.-U.S.] 44 Hh 34.56N 79.46W
Rock Island 43 Ic 41.30N 90.34W
Rockland 43 Nc 44.06N 69.06W
Rocklands Reservoir 59 Ig 37.15S 142.00 E
Rockledge 44 Gk 28.20N 80.43W
Rockneby 8 Gh 56.49N 16.20 E
Rockport 45 Hl 28.01N 97.04W
Rock River 45 Kf 41.29N 90.37W
Rock Sound 44 Im 24.53N 76.09W
Rock Spring 43 Fc 41.35N 109.13W
Rocksprings 45 Fk 30.01N 100.13W
Rockville [In.-U.S.] 44 Df 39.45N 87.15W
Rockville [Md.-U.S.] 44 If 39.05N 77.09W
Rockwood 44 Eh 35.52N 84.41W
Rocky Ford 45 Eg 38.03N 103.43W
Rocky Island Lake 44 Fb 46.56N 83.04W
Rocky Mount 43 Ld 35.56N 77.48W
Rocky Mountain 43 Eb 47.49N 112.49W
Rocky Mountain House 42 Gf 52.22N 114.55W
Rocky Mountains 38 He 48.00N 116.00W
Rocky Point [Blz.] 49 Cd 18.22N 88.06W
Rocky Point [Nam.] 37 Ac 19.01S 12.29 E
Rocroi 12 Ge 49.55N 4.31 E
Rodach 10 Gf 50.08N 10.52 E
Rodalben 12 Je 49.14N 7.38 E
Roda Velha, Rio- 55 Ja 12.27S 45.33W
Rødberg 8 Cd 60.16N 8.58 E
Rødby 8 Dj 54.42N 11.24 E
Rødby Havn, Rødby- 7 Ci 54.39N 11.21 E
Rødby-Rødby Havn 7 Ci 54.39N 11.21 E
Roddickton 42 Lf 50.51N 56.07W
Rødding 8 Ci 55.22N 9.04 E

Index Symbols

Independent Nation
State, Region
District, County
Municipality
Colony, Dependency
Continent
Physical Region
Historical or Cultural Region
Mount, Mountain
Volcano
Hill
Mountains, Mountain Range
Hills, Escarpment
Plateau, Upland
Pass, Gap
Plain, Lowland
Delta
Salt Flat
Valley, Canyon
Crater, Cave
Karst Features
Depression
Polder
Desert, Dunes
Forest, Woods
Heath, Steppe
Oasis
Cape, Point
Coast, Beach
Cliff
Peninsula
Isthmus
Sandbank
Island
Atoll
Rock, Reef
Islands, Archipelago
Rocks, Reefs
Coral Reef
Well, Spring
Geyser
River, Stream
Waterfall Rapids
River Mouth, Estuary
Lake
Salt Lake
Intermittent Lake
Reservoir
Swamp, Pond
Canal
Glacier
Ice Shelf, Pack Ice
Ocean
Sea
Gulf, Bay
Strait, Fjord
Lagoon
Bank
Seamount
Tablemount
Ridge
Shelf
Basin
Escarpment, Sea Scarp
Fracture
Trench, Abyss
National Park, Reserve
Point of Interest
Recreation Site
Cave, Cavern
Historic Site
Ruins
Wall, Walls
Church, Abbey
Temple
Scientific Station
Airport
Port
Lighthouse
Mine
Tunnel
Dam, Bridge

Rödeby 8 Fh 56.15N 15.36 E
Rodeio Bonito 55 Fh 27.28S 53.10W
Roden 12 Ia 53.09N 6.26 E
Rodeo [Arg.] 56 Gd 30.12S 69.06W
Rodeo [Mex.] 48 Ge 25.11N 104.34W
Rodeo [N.M.-U.S.] 45 Bk 31.50N 109.02W
Röder 10 Je 51.30N 13.25 E
Rodez 11 Ij 44.20N 2.34 E
Rodgau 12 Kd 50.01N 8.53 E
Rodholivos 15 Gi 40.56N 23.59 E
Ródhos = Rhodes (EN) 6 Ih 36.26N 28.13 E
Ródhos = Rhodes (EN) 5 Ih 36.10N 28.00 E
Rodi Garganico 14 Ji 41.55N 15.53 E
Roding 9 Nj 51.31N 0.06 E
Rodna 15 Hb 47.25N 24.49 E
Rodnei, Munţii- 15 Hb 47.35N 24.40 E
Rodney, Cape- 40 Fd 64.39N 166.24W
Rodniki 7 Jh 57.07N 41.48 E
Rodonit, Gjiri i- 15 Ch 41.35N 19.30 E
Rodonit, Kep i- 15 Ch 41.35N 19.27 E
Rodopi=Rhodope Mountains (EN) 5 Ig 41.30N 24.30 E
Rodrigues Island 30 Nj 19.42S 63.25 E
Roebourne 59 Dd 20.47S 117.09 E
Roebuck Bay 59 Ec 18.04S 122.15 E
Roer 10 Be 51.12N 5.59 E
Roermond 11 Lc 51.12N 6.00 E
Roeselare/Roulers 11 Jd 50.57N 3.08 E
Roes Welcome Sound 42 Id 64.30N 86.45W
Roetgen 12 Id 50.39N 6.12 E
Rogačev 16 Gc 53.09N 30.06 E
Rogačevka 16 Kd 51.31N 39.34 E
Rogagua, Laguna- 54 Ef 13.45S 66.55W
Rogaguado, Laguna- 54 Ef 12.55S 65.45W
Rogaland [2] 7 Bg 59.00N 6.15 E
Rogaška Slatina 14 Jd 46.15N 15.38 E
Rogatica 14 Ng 43.48N 19.01 E
Rogatin 10 Ug 49.19N 24.40 E
Rogers 45 Ih 36.20N 94.07W
Rogers, Mount- 44 Gg 36.39N 81.33W
Rogers City 44 Fc 45.25N 83.49W
Rogers Lake 46 Gi 34.52N 117.51W
Rogers Peak 46 Jg 38.04N 111.32W
Rogersville 44 Fg 36.25N 82.59W
Roggan 42 Jf 54.24N 79.30W
Roggeveldberge 37 Bf 31.50S 19.50 E
Roggewein, Cabo- 65d Bb 27.07S 109.15W
Rognan 7 Dc 67.06N 15.23 E
Rogozhina 15 Ch 41.05N 19.40 E
Rogozna 15 Df 43.04N 20.40 E
Rogoźno 10 Md 52.46N 17.00 E
Rogue River 46 Ce 42.26N 124.25W
Rohan, Plateau de- 11 Df 48.10N 3.00W
Rohl 35 Dd 7.05N 29.46 E
Rohrbach in Oberösterreich 14 Hb 48.34N 13.59 E
Rohrbach-lès-Bitche 12 Je 49.03N 7.16 E
Rohri 25 Dc 27.41N 68.54 E
Rohtak 25 Fc 28.54N 76.34 E
Roi, Le Bois du- 11 Kh 46.59N 4.02 E
Roi Et 25 Ke 16.05N 103.42 E
Roi Georges, Iles du- 57 Mf 14.32S 145.08W
Roine 8 Kc 61.25N 24.05 E
Roisel 12 Fe 49.57N 3.06 E
Roja 7 Fh 57.30N 22.51 E
Rojas 56 Hd 34.12S 60.44W
Rojo, Cabo- [Mex.] 47 Ed 21.33N 97.20W
Rojo, Cabo- [P.R.] 49 Nd 18.01N 67.15W
Rokan 26 Df 2.00N 100.52 E
Rokiškis 7 Fi 55.59N 25.37 E
Rokitnoje 16 Ed 51.21N 27.14 E
Rokkasho 29a Bc 40.58N 141.21 E
Rokycany 10 Jg 49.45N 13.36 E
Rokytná 10 Mg 49.05N 16.21 E
Rola Co 27 Ed 35.25N 88.25 E
Rolândia 55 Gf 23.18S 51.22W
Rolla [Mo.-U.S.] 43 Id 37.57N 91.46W
Rolla [N.D.-U.S.] 45 Gb 48.52N 99.37W
Rolleston 62 Ee 43.35S 172.23 E
Rolvsøya 7 Fa 71.00N 24.00 E
Roma [Austl.] 58 Fg 26.35S 148.47 E
Roma [It.] = Rome (EN) 6 Hg 41.54N 12.29 E
Roma [Swe.] 7 Eh 57.32N 18.26 E
Romagna 14 Gf 44.30N 12.15 E
Romaine 42 Lf 50.18N 63.48W
Roman 15 Jc 46.55N 26.55 E
Romanche 11 Li 45.05N 5.43 E
Romanche Gap (EN) 3 Dj 0.10S 18.15W
Romang 55 Ci 29.30S 59.46W
Romang, Pulau- 26 Ih 7.35S 127.26 E
România=Romania (EN) 6 If 46.00N 25.30 E
Romania (EN)=România 6 If 46.00N 25.30 E
Romanija 14 Mg 43.51N 18.43 E
Roman Koš, Gora- 19 Dg 44.36N 34.16 E
Romano, Cayo- 49 Ib 22.04N 77.50W
Romanovka 20 Gf 53.14N 112.46 E
Romans-sur-Isère 11 Li 45.03N 5.03 E
Romanzof, Cape- 38 Cc 61.49N 166.09W
Romanzof Mountains 40 Kc 69.00N 144.00W
Rombas 12 Ie 49.15N 6.05 E
Romblon 26 Hd 12.35N 122.15 E
Rome [Ga.-U.S.] 43 Je 34.16N 85.11W
Rome [N.Y.-U.S.] 43 Lc 43.13N 75.28W
Rome [Or.-U.S.] 46 Ge 42.50N 117.37W
Rome (EN) = Roma [It.] 6 Hg 41.54N 12.29 E
Romeleåsen 8 Ei 55.34N 13.33 E
Romerike 8 Dd 60.05N 11.10 E
Romilly-sur-Seine 11 Jf 48.31N 3.43 E
Rommani 32 Fc 33.32N 6.36W
Romme 8 Fd 60.26N 15.30 E
Rommerskirchen 12 Ic 51.02N 6.41 E
Romney Marsh 12 Cc 51.02N 0.55 E
Romny 19 De 50.45N 33.29 E
Rømø 7 Bi 55.10N 8.30 E
Romodanovo 7 Ki 54.28N 45.18 E
Romont 14 Ad 46.42N 6.55 E
Romorantin-Lanthenay 11 Hg 47.22N 1.45 E
Romsdal 8 Bb 62.35N 7.50 E
Romsdalen 8 Bb 62.30N 7.55 E
Romsdalsfjorden 8 Bb 62.40N 7.15 E
Romsdalshorn 8 Bd 62.29N 7.50 E
Romsey 9 Lk 50.59N 1.30W
Ronas Hill 9 La 60.38N 1.20W
Ronave 64e Ba 0.29S 166.56 E
Roncador, Cayos de- 47 Hf 13.32N 80.03W
Roncador, Serra do- 52 Kg 13.00S 51.50W
Roncador Reef 57 Ge 6.13S 159.22 E
Roncesvalles 13 Ka 43.01N 1.19W
Roncesvalles o Ibañeta, Puerto de- 13 Ka 43.01N 1.19W
Ronciglione 14 Gh 42.17N 12.13 E
Ronco 14 Gf 44.24N 12.12 E
Ronda 13 Gh 36.44N 5.10W
Ronda, Serranía de- 13 Gh 36.45N 5.05W
Ronda do Sul 55 Cb 15.57S 59.42W
Rondane 7 Bf 61.55N 9.45 E
Rønde 7 Ch 56.18N 10.29 E
Ronde, Point- 51g Ba 15.33N 61.29W
Ronde Island 50 Ff 12.18N 61.31W
Rondeslottet 8 Cc 61.55N 9.46 E
Rondon 55 Ff 23.23S 52.48W
Rondón, Pico- 54 Fc 1.36N 63.08W
Rondônia 53 Jg 10.52S 61.57W
Rondônia, Território de- [2] 54 Ff 11.00S 63.00W
Rondonópolis 53 Kg 16.28S 54.38W
Rong'an (Chang'an) 27 If 25.16N 109.23 E
Rongcheng 28 Ce 39.03N 115.52 E
Rongcheng (Yatou) 28 Gf 37.10N 122.25 E
Rongelap Atoll 57 Hc 11.09N 166.50 E
Rongerik Atoll 57 Hc 11.21N 167.26 E
Rongjiang (Guzhou) 27 If 25.58N 108.30 E
Rongxian 27 Jg 22.48N 110.30 E
Rongzhag/Danba 27 He 30.48N 101.54 E
Rønne 7 Di 55.06N 14.42 E
Ronne Bay 66 Qf 72.30S 74.00W
Ronneby 7 Dh 56.12N 15.18 E
Ronnebyån 8 Fh 56.10N 15.18 E
Ronne Ice Shelf 66 Qf 78.30S 61.00W
Ronse/Renaix 11 Jd 50.45N 3.36 E
Ronuro, Rio- 52 Kg 11.56S 53.33W
Roodepoort 37 De 26.11S 27.54 E
Roof Butte 43 Fd 36.28N 109.05W
Rooiboklaagte 37 Cd 20.20S 21.15 E
Roon, Pulau- 26 Jg 2.23S 134.33 E
Rooniu, Mont- 65e c 17.49S 149.12W
Roorkee 25 Fc 29.52N 77.53 E
Roosendaal 11 Kc 51.32N 4.28 E
Roosevelt [Az.-U.S.] 46 Jj 33.40N 111.09W
Roosevelt [Ut.-U.S.] 46 Kf 40.18N 109.59W
Roosevelt, Mount- 42 Ee 58.23N 125.04W
Roosevelt, Rio- 52 Jf 7.35S 60.20W
Roosevelt Island 66 Lf 79.30S 162.00W
Root Portage 45 Ka 50.53N 91.18W
Ropa 10 Rg 49.46N 21.29 E
Ropar 25 Fb 30.58N 76.20 E
Ropaži 8 Kh 56.58N 24.26 E
Ropczyce 10 Rf 50.03N 21.37 E
Rope, The- 64q Ab 25.04S 130.05W
Roper River 57 Ef 14.43S 135.27 E
Roquefort 11 Fj 44.02N 0.19W
Roque Pérez 55 Cl 35.25S 59.20W
Roquetas de Mar 13 Jh 36.46N 2.36W
Roraima, Monte- 52 Je 5.12N 60.44W
Roraima, Território de- [2] 54 Fc 1.30N 61.00W
Røros 7 Ce 62.35N 11.24 E
Rorschach 14 Dc 47.30N 9.30 E
Rørvik 7 Cd 64.51N 11.14 E
Ros 16 Ge 49.39N 31.35 E
Rosa, Cap- 14 Cn 36.57N 8.14 E
Rosa, Lake- 49 Kc 20.55N 73.20W
Rosa, Monte- 5 Gf 45.55N 7.53 E
Rošal 7 Ji 55.41N 39.55 E
Rosala 8 Je 59.50N 22.25 E
Rosalia 46 Gc 47.14N 117.22W
Rosalia, Punta- 65d Bb 27.03S 109.19W
Rosalie 51g Bb 15.22N 61.16W
Rosalind Bank (EN) 49 Ge 16.30N 80.30W
Rosamond Lake 46 Fi 34.50N 118.04W
Rosamorada 48 Gf 22.08N 105.12W
Rosana 55 Ff 22.36S 53.01W
Rosario [Arg.] 53 Ji 32.57S 60.40W
Rosario [Braz.] 54 Jd 2.57S 44.14W
Rosario [Mex.] 48 Dd 26.27N 111.38W
Rosario [Mex.] 47 Cd 23.00N 105.52W
Rosario [Par.] 56 Ib 24.27S 57.03W
Rosario [Ven.] 49 Kh 10.19N 72.19W
Rosario, Arroyo- 48 Bb 30.03N 115.45W
Rosario, Bahía- 48 Bc 29.50N 115.45W
Rosario, Cayo del- 49 Gc 21.38N 81.53W
Rosario, Islas de- 49 Jh 10.10N 75.46W
Rosario, Sierra del- 48 He 25.35N 103.50W
Rosario de Arriba 47 Ab 30.01N 115.40W
Rosario de la Frontera 56 Hc 25.48S 64.58W
Rosario de Lerma 56 Gb 24.59S 65.35W
Rosario del Tala 55 Ck 32.18S 59.09W
Rosário do Sul 56 Jd 30.15S 54.55W
Rosário Oeste 54 Gf 14.50S 56.25W
Rosarito 48 Bc 28.38N 114.04W
Rosarno 14 Jl 38.29N 15.58 E
Rosas/Roses 13 Pb 42.16N 3.11 E
Rosas, Golfo de-/Roses, Golf de- 13 Pb 42.10N 3.15 E
Rosa Seamount (EN) 47 Bc 26.12N 114.58W
Rosa Zarate 54 Cc 0.18N 79.27W
Roščino 8 Md 60.13N 29.43 E
Roscoe Glacier 66 Ge 66.30S 95.20 E
Ros Comáin/Roscommon [2] 9 Eh 53.40N 8.30W
Ros Comáin/Roscommon 9 Eh 53.38N 8.11W
Roscommon 44 Ec 44.30N 84.35W
Roscommon/Ros Comáin 9 Eh 53.38N 8.11W
Roscommon/Ros Comáin [2] 9 Eh 53.40N 8.30W
Ros Cré/Roscrea 9 Fi 52.57N 7.47W
Roscrea/Ros Cré 9 Fi 52.57N 7.47W
Rose, Pointe de la- 51h Bb 14.33N 61.03W
Roseau [Dom.] 39 Mh 15.18N 61.24W
Roseau [Dom.] 51g Bb 15.18N 61.24W
Roseau [Mn.-U.S.] 45 Ib 48.51N 95.46W
Roseau [St.Luc.] 51k Ab 13.58N 61.02W
Roseau River 45 Hb 49.08N 97.14W
Rosebery 59 Jh 41.46S 145.32 E
Rosebud 46 Lc 46.16N 106.27W
Rosebud Creek 46 Lc 46.16N 106.28W
Rosebud River 46 Ia 51.25N 112.37W
Roseburg 43 Cc 43.13N 123.20W
Rosemary Bank (EN) 9 Cb 59.15N 10.10W
Rosenberg 43 Hf 29.33N 95.48W
Rosendahl 12 Jb 52.01N 7.12 E
Rosendahl-Osterwick 12 Jb 52.01N 7.12 E
Rosendal 7 Bf 59.59N 6.01 E
Rosenheim 10 Ii 47.51N 12.08 E
Rosental 14 Id 46.33N 14.15 E
Roses/Rosas 13 Pb 42.16N 3.11 E
Roses, Golf de-/Rosas, Golfo de- 13 Pb 42.10N 3.15 E
Roseţi 15 Ke 44.13N 27.26 E
Roseto degli Abruzzi 14 Ih 42.41N 14.01 E
Rosetown 42 Gf 51.33N 108.00W
Rosetta (EN)=Rashīd 33 Fc 31.24N 30.25 E
Roseville 46 Eg 38.45N 121.17W
Roshage 7 Bh 57.07N 8.38 E
Rosica 15 If 43.15N 25.42 E
Rosières-en-Santerre 12 Ee 49.49N 2.43 E
Rosignano Solvay 14 Eg 43.23N 10.26 E
Rosignol 54 Gb 6.17N 57.32W
Roşiori de Vede 15 He 44.07N 24.59 E
Roskilde [2] 8 Ei 55.35N 12.10 E
Roskilde 7 Ci 55.39N 12.05 E
Roslagen 8 He 59.30N 18.40 E
Ros Láir/Rosslare 9 Gi 52.17N 6.23W
Roslavl 19 De 53.58N 32.53 E
Roslyn 46 Ec 47.13N 120.59W
Ros Mhic Thriúin/New Ross 9 Gi 52.24N 6.56W
Rosnæs 8 Di 55.45N 10.55 E
Rosny-sur-Seine 12 Df 49.00N 1.38 E
Rösrath 12 Jd 50.54N 7.12 E
Ross 42 Ed 62.00N 132.25W
Ross [Austl.] 59 Jh 42.02S 147.29 E
Ross [Bye.-U.S.S.R.] 10 Uc 53.16N 24.29 E
Ross [N.Z.] 62 De 42.54S 170.49 E
Ross, Cape- 26 Gd 10.56N 119.13 E
Ross, Mount- 30 Nm 49.25S 69.08 E
Rossano 14 Kk 39.34N 16.38 E
Rossan Point/Ceann Ros Eoghain 9 Eg 54.42N 8.48W
Ross Barnett Reservoir 45 Lj 32.30N 90.00W
Rosseau Lake 44 Hc 45.10N 79.35W
Rossel Island 57 Gf 11.26S 154.07 E
Rossell, Cap- 63b Ce 20.23S 166.36 E
Ross Ice Shelf 66 Lg 81.30S 175.00W
Rossijskaja Sovetskaja Federativnaja Socialističeskaja Respublika (RSFSR) [2] 19 Jc 60.00N 100.00 E
Ross Island 66 Kf 77.30S 168.00 E
Ross Lake 46 Eb 48.53N 121.04W
Rossland 46 Gb 49.05N 117.48W
Rosslare/Ros Láir 9 Gi 52.17N 6.23W
Roßlau 10 Ie 51.53N 12.15 E
Rosso 31 Fg 16.31N 15.49W
Ross-on-Wye 9 Kj 51.55N 2.35W
Rossony 8 Mi 55.53N 28.49 E
Rossoš 19 De 50.11N 39.39 E
Ross River 42 Ed 61.59N 132.27W
Ross Sea (EN) 66 Lf 76.00S 175.00W
Røssvatn 7 Cd 65.45N 14.00 E
Røst 7 Cc 67.31N 12.07 E
Rosta 7 Eb 69.02N 18.40 E
Rostamī 24 Nh 28.52N 51.02 E
Rostan Kalā 24 Od 36.42N 53.27 E
Rösterkopf 12 Ie 49.40N 6.50 E
Rosthern 42 Gf 52.40N 106.20W
Rostock 6 He 54.05N 12.08 E
Rostock-Warnemünde 10 Ib 54.10N 12.05 E
Rostov 19 Dd 57.13N 39.25 E
Rostov-na-Donu 6 Jf 47.14N 39.42 E
Rostovskaja Oblast [3] 19 Ef 47.45N 41.15 E
Roswell [Ga.-U.S.] 44 Eh 34.03N 84.22W
Roswell [N.M.-U.S.] 39 If 33.24N 104.32W
Rot 8 Fc 61.15N 14.02 E
Rota 13 Fh 36.37N 6.21W
Rota Island 57 Fc 14.10N 145.12 E
Rotenburg (Wümme) 10 Fc 53.07N 9.24 E
Rotenburg an der Fulda 10 Ff 50.59N 9.43 E
Roter Main 10 Hf 50.03N 11.27 E
Roth 10 Hg 49.15N 11.06 E
Rothaargebirge 10 Ee 51.05N 8.15 E
Rothenburg ob der Tauber 10 Gg 49.23N 10.11 E
Rother [Eng.-U.K.] 9 Nk 50.57N 0.45 E
Rother [Eng.-U.K.] 12 Bd 50.57N 0.22W
Rothera 66 Qe 67.46S 68.54W
Rotherham 9 Lh 53.26N 1.20W
Rothesay 9 Hf 55.51N 5.03W
Rothorn 14 Cd 46.47N 8.03 E
Rothschild Island 66 Qe 69.25S 72.30W
Rothwell 12 Bb 52.25N 0.48W
Roti, Pulau- 21 Ok 10.45S 123.10 E
Roti, Selat- 26 Hi 10.25S 123.25 E
Rotja, Punta- 13 Nf 38.38N 1.34 E
Rotnes 8 Dd 60.04N 10.53 E
Roto 59 Jf 33.03S 145.29 E
Rotoiti, Lake- 62 Ed 41.50S 172.50 E
Rotondella 14 Kj 40.10N 16.31 E
Rotondo, Monte- 11a Ba 42.13N 9.03 E
Rotoroa, Lake- 62 Ed 41.50S 172.40 E
Rotorua 61 Eg 38.09S 176.15 E
Rotorua, Lake- 62 Gc 38.05S 176.15 E
Rotselaar 12 Gd 50.57N 4.43 E
Rott 10 Jh 48.25N 13.20 E
Rottenburg am Neckar 10 Eh 48.28N 8.56 E
Rotterdam 6 Ge 51.55N 4.28 E
Rottnaälven 8 Ed 59.48N 13.07 E
Rottnen 8 Fh 56.45N 15.05 E
Rottneros 8 Ee 59.48N 13.07 E
Rottnest Island 59 Df 32.00S 115.30 E
Rottumerplaat 11 Ma 53.35N 6.30 E
Rottweil 10 Eh 48.10N 8.37 E
Rotuma Island 57 If 12.30S 177.05 E
Roubaix 11 Jd 50.42N 3.10 E
Roubion 11 Kj 44.31N 4.42 E
Roudnice nad Labem 10 Kf 50.26N 14.16 E
Rouen 6 Gf 49.26N 1.05 E
Rouergue 11 Ij 44.30N 2.56 E
Rouge, Rivière- 44 Jc 45.38N 74.42W
Rouillac 11 Fi 45.47N 0.04W
Roulers/Roeselare 11 Jd 50.57N 3.08 E
Roumois 11 Ge 49.30N 0.30 E
Roundup 43 Fb 46.27N 108.33W
Rousay 9 Jb 59.01N 3.02W
Roussillon 11 Ki 45.22N 4.49 E
Roussillon 11 Il 42.30N 2.30 E
Roussin, Cap- 63b Ce 21.21S 167.59 E
Routot 12 Ce 49.23N 0.44 E
Rouyn-Noranda 39 Le 48.14N 79.01W
Rovaniemi 6 Ib 66.30N 25.43 E
Rovenskaja Oblast [3] 19 Ce 51.00N 26.30 E
Rovereto 14 Fe 45.53N 11.02 E
Rovigo 14 Fe 45.04N 11.47 E
Rovinari 15 Ge 44.55N 23.11 E
Rovinj 14 He 45.05N 13.38 E
Rovkulskoje, Ozero- 7 Hd 64.00N 31.00 E
Rovno 6 Ie 50.37N 26.15 E
Rovnoje 16 Od 50.47N 46.05 E
Rovuma=Ruvuma (EN) 30 Lj 10.29S 40.28 E
Rowa, Iles- 63b Ca 13.37S 167.32 E
Rowley 42 Jc 69.05N 78.55W
Rowley Shoals 57 Cf 17.30S 119.00 E
Roxas [Phil.] 26 Gd 10.28N 119.30 E
Roxas [Phil.] 26 Hd 11.35N 122.45 E
Roxboro 44 Hg 36.24N 78.59W
Roxburgh 62 Cf 45.33S 169.19 E
Roxen 8 Ff 58.30N 15.40 E
Roxo, Cap- 30 Fg 12.20N 16.43W
Roy [N.M.-U.S.] 45 Di 35.57N 104.12W
Roy [Ut.-U.S.] 46 If 41.10N 112.02W
Roya 11 Nk 43.48N 7.35 E
Royal Canal 9 Gh 53.21N 6.15W
Royale, Isle- 43 Jb 48.00N 89.00W
Royal Leamington Spa 9 Li 52.18N 1.31W
Royal Society Range 66 Jf 78.10S 162.36 E
Royal Tunbridge Wells 9 Nj 51.08N 0.16 E
Royan 11 Ei 45.38N 1.02W
Royat 11 Ji 45.46N 3.03 E
Royaumont, Abbaye de- 12 Ee 49.17N 2.28 E
Roye 11 Ie 49.42N 2.48 E
Roy Hill 59 Dd 22.38S 119.57 E
Røyken 8 De 59.45N 10.23 E
Royston 9 Mi 52.03N 0.01W
Rožaj 15 Dg 42.51N 20.10 E
Rożan 10 Rd 52.53N 21.25 E
Rozdol 10 Ug 49.24N 24.08 E
Rozewie, Przylądek- 10 Ob 54.51N 18.21 E
Rožišče 16 Dd 50.54N 25.19 E
Rožňava 10 Qh 48.40N 20.32 E
Rožniatov 10 Uh 48.51N 24.14 E
Roznov 15 Jc 46.50N 26.31 E
Rožnov pod Radhoštěm 10 Og 49.28N 18.09 E
Rożnów 10 Qg 49.46N 20.42 E
Rożnowskie, Jezioro- 10 Qg 49.48N 20.45 E
Rozoy-sur-Serre 12 Ge 49.43N 4.08 E
Roztocze 5 Ie 50.30N 23.20 E
Rrësheni 15 Ch 41.47N 19.54 E
RSFSR=Russian SFSR (EN) [2] 19 Jc 60.00N 100.00 E
RSFSR→Rossijskaja Sovetskaja Federativnaja Socialističeskaja Respublika [2] 19 Jc 60.00N 100.00 E
Rtanj 15 Ef 43.47N 21.54 E
Rtiščevo 19 Ee 52.16N 43.52 E
Ruacana, Quedas- 30 Jj 17.23S 14.15 E
Ruahine Range 62 Gc 39.50S 176.05 E
Ruapehu 57 Ih 39.17S 175.34 E
Ruapuke Island 61 Ci 46.45S 168.30 E
Rua Sura 63a Ec 9.30S 160.36 E
Ruatahuna 62 Gc 38.38S 176.58 E
Rubbestadneset 8 Ae 59.49N 5.17 E
Rubcovsk 22 Kd 51.33N 81.10 E
Rubeho Mountains 36 Gd 6.55S 36.30 E
Rubeshibe 28 Qc 43.47N 143.38 E
Rubežnoje 16 Ke 48.59N 38.26 E
Rubi 36 Db 2.48N 23.54 E
Rubiataba 55 Hb 15.08S 49.48W
Rubiku 15 Ch 41.46N 19.45 E
Rubio 54 Db 7.43N 72.22W
Rubio 13 Ic 41.26N 3.47W
Ruby 40 Hd 64.44N 155.30W
Ruby Lake 46 Hf 40.15N 115.30W
Ruby Mountains 46 Hf 40.25N 115.35W
Ruby Range 46 Id 45.15N 112.15W
Rucăr 15 Id 45.24N 25.10 E
Rucava 8 Ih 56.10N 21.10 E
Ruciane Nida 10 Rc 53.39N 21.35 E
Ruda 10 Of 50.18N 18.18 E
Rudabánya 10 Qh 48.23N 20.38 E
Rūdak 24 Nh 35.51N 51.33 E
Rūdān 24 Qi 27.17N 57.13 E
Ruda Śląska 10 Of 50.18N 18.51 E
Rūdbār [Afg.] 23 Jc 30.09N 62.36 E
Rūdbār [Iran] 24 Md 36.48N 49.24 E
Rüdersdorf bei Berlin 10 Jd 52.27N 13.47 E
Rüdesheim am Rhein 12 Je 49.59N 7.55 E
Rudiškes/Rūdiškės 8 Kj 54.30N 24.58 E
Rūdiškės/Rudiškes 8 Kj 54.30N 24.58 E
Rudki 10 Tg 49.34N 23.30 E
Rudkøbing 7 Ci 54.56N 10.43 E
Rudnaja-Pristan 20 Ih 44.25N 135.49 E
Rudničny 7 Mg 59.38N 52.29 E
Rudnik 15 De 44.08N 20.30 E
Rudnik [Bul.] 15 Kg 42.57N 27.46 E
Rudnik [Pol.] 10 Sf 50.28N 22.15 E
Rudnik [Yugo.] 15 De 44.08N 20.31 E
Rudnja [R.S.F.S.R.] 16 Nd 50.49N 44.36 E
Rudnja [R.S.F.S.R.] 19 De 54.57N 31.07 E
Rudno 10 Tg 49.44N 23.57 E
Rudny [Kaz.-U.S.S.R.] 19 Ge 52.57N 63.07 E
Rudny [R.S.F.S.R.] 28 Mb 44.28N 135.00 E
Rudolf, Lake-/Turkana, Lake- 30 Kh 3.30N 36.00 E
Rudolstadt 10 Hf 50.43N 11.20 E
Rudong (Juegang) 28 Fh 32.19N 121.11 E
Rudozem 15 Hh 41.29N 24.51 E
Rūd Sar 23 Hb 37.08N 50.18 E
Rudyard 46 Jb 48.34N 110.33W
Rue 11 Hd 50.16N 1.40 E
Ruecas 13 Ge 39.00N 5.55W
Ruelle-sur-Touvre 11 Gi 45.41N 0.14 E
Rufā'ah 35 Ec 14.46N 33.22 E
Ruffec 11 Gh 46.01N 0.12 E
Ruffing Point 51a Db 18.45N 64.25W
Rufiji 30 Ki 8.00S 39.20 E
Rufino 56 Hd 34.16S 62.42W
Rufisque 34 Bc 14.43N 17.17W
Rufunsa 36 Ef 15.05S 29.40 E
Rugao 28 Fh 32.24N 120.34 E
Rugby [Eng.-U.K.] 9 Li 52.23N 1.15W
Rugby [N.D.-U.S.] 43 Gb 48.22N 99.59W
Rügen 5 He 54.25N 13.24 E
Rugles 12 Cf 48.49N 0.42 E
Ru He 28 Ch 32.55N 114.24 E
Ruhea 25 Hc 26.10N 88.25 E
Ruhengeri 36 Ec 1.30S 29.38 E
Rühlertwist 12 Jb 52.39N 7.06 E
Ruhner Berge 10 Hc 53.17N 11.55 E
Ruhnu, Ostrov-/Ruhnu Saar 7 Fh 57.50N 23.15 E
Ruhnu Saar/Ruhnu, Ostrov- 7 Fh 57.50N 23.15 E
Ruhr 10 Ce 51.27N 6.44 E
Rui'an 27 Lf 27.48N 120.38 E
Ruichang 28 Cj 29.41N 115.38 E
Ruiena/Rūjiena 7 Fh 57.54N 25.17 E
Ruijin 27 Kf 25.59N 116.03 E
Ruili 27 Gg 24.03N 97.46 E
Ruiselede 12 Fc 51.03N 3.24 E
Ruiz 48 Gg 21.57N 105.09W
Ruiz, Nevado del- 54 Cc 4.54N 75.18W
Ruj 15 Fg 42.51N 22.35 E
Ruja/Rūja 8 Kg 57.38N 25.10 E
Rūja/Ruja 8 Kg 57.38N 25.10 E
Rujan 15 Eg 42.23N 21.49 E
Rujen 15 Fg 42.10N 22.31 E
Rūjiena/Ruiena 7 Fh 57.54N 25.17 E
Ruki 30 Ih 0.05N 18.17 E
Rukwa [3] 36 Fd 7.00S 31.20 E
Rukwa, Lake- 30 Ki 8.00S 32.15 E
Rūl Qadnah 24 Qk 25.33N 56.21 E
Rülzheim 12 Ke 49.10N 8.18 E
Ruma 15 Cd 45.01N 19.49 E
Rumaylah 35 Fc 12.57N 35.02 E
Rumbek 31 Jh 6.48N 29.41 E
Rumberpon, Pulau- 26 Jg 1.50S 134.15 E
Rum Cay 47 Jd 23.40N 74.53W
Rumes 12 Fd 50.33N 3.18 E
Rumford 44 Lc 44.33N 70.33W
Rumia 10 Ob 54.35N 18.25 E
Rumigny 12 Ge 49.48N 4.16 E
Rumija 15 Cg 42.06N 19.12 E
Rumilly 11 Li 45.52N 5.57 E
Rum Jungle 59 Gb 13.01S 131.00 E
Rummah, Wādī ar- 24 Ki 26.38N 44.18 E
Rumoi 27 Pc 43.56N 141.39 E
Rumphi 36 Fe 11.01S 33.52 E
Run 12 Hc 51.40N 5.20 E
Runan 28 Ci 33.00N 114.21 E
Runanga 62 De 42.24S 171.15 E
Runaway, Cape- 62 Gb 37.32S 177.59 E
Rundēni/Rundeni 8 Lh 56.14N 27.52 E
Rundeni/Rundēni 8 Lh 56.14N 27.52 E
Rundu 31 Ij 17.55S 19.45 E
Rungu 36 Eb 3.11N 27.52 E
Rungwa 31 Ki 6.57S 33.31 E
Rungwa 36 Fd 7.36S 31.50 E
Runmarö 8 He 59.15N 18.45 E
Runn 8 Fd 60.35N 15.40 E
Ruokolahti 7 Gf 61.17N 28.50 E
Ruoqiang/Qarkilik 22 Kf 39.02N 88.00 E
Ruo Shui 21 Le 40.20N 99.40 E
Ruotsalainen 8 Kc 61.15N 25.55 E
Ruotsinpyhtää/Strömfors 8 Ld 60.32N 26.27 E
Ruovesi 7 Ff 61.59N 24.05 E
Ruovesi 8 Kc 61.55N 24.10 E
Rupanco 56 Ff 40.46S 72.42W
Rupea 15 Ic 46.02N 25.13 E
Rupel 12 Gc 51.07N 4.19 E
Rupert 42 Jf 51.30N 78.48W
Rupert 46 Ie 42.37N 113.41W
Rupert, Baie de- 42 Jf 51.35N 79.00W
Ruppert Coast 66 Mf 75.45S 141.00W
Rur 10 Be 51.12N 5.59 E
Rurrenabaque 53 Jg 14.28S 67.34W
Rurstausee 12 Id 50.38N 6.24 E
Rurutu, Ile- 57 Lg 22.26S 151.20W
Rušan 19 Hh 37.57N 71.31 E
Rusape 37 Ec 18.32S 32.07 E
Ruşayriş, Khazzān ar- = Rusayris, Lake- (EN) 35 Ec 11.40N 34.20 E
Rusayris, Lake- (EN)= Ruşayriş, Khazzān ar- 35 Ec 11.40N 34.20 E
Ruse 6 Ig 43.50N 25.57 E
Ruse [2] 15 If 43.50N 25.57 E
Ruşeţu 15 Ke 44.57N 27.13 E
Rushan (Xiacun) 28 Ff 36.55N 121.30 E
Rushden 12 Bb 52.17N 0.35W
Rushville 45 Kf 40.07N 90.34W
Rusk 45 Ik 31.48N 95.09W

Index Symbols

[1] Independent Nation
[2] State, Region
[3] District, County
[4] Municipality
[5] Colony, Dependency
Continent
Physical Region
Historical or Cultural Region
Mount, Mountain
Volcano
Hill
Mountains, Mountain Range
Hills, Escarpment
Plateau, Upland
Pass, Gap
Plain, Lowland
Delta
Salt Flat
Valley, Canyon
Crater, Cave
Karst Features
Depression
Polder
Desert, Dunes
Forest, Woods
Heath, Steppe
Oasis
Cape, Point
Coast, Beach
Cliff
Peninsula
Isthmus
Sandbank
Island
Atoll
Rock, Reef
Islands, Archipelago
Rocks, Reefs
Coral Reef
Well, Spring
Geyser
River, Stream
Waterfall Rapids
River Mouth, Estuary
Lake
Salt Lake
Intermittent Lake
Reservoir
Swamp, Pond
Canal
Glacier
Ice Shelf, Pack Ice
Ocean
Sea
Gulf, Bay
Strait, Fjord
Lagoon
Bank
Seamount
Tablemount
Ridge
Shelf
Basin
Escarpment, Sea Scarp
Fracture
Trench, Abyss
National Park, Reserve
Point of Interest
Recreation Site
Cave, Cavern
Historic Site
Ruins
Wall, Walls
Church, Abbey
Temple
Scientific Station
Airport
Port
Lighthouse
Mine
Tunnel
Dam, Bridge

Rusken 8 Fg 57.17N 14.20 E
Rusne/Rusnė 8 Ii 55.19N 21.16 E
Rusnė/Rusne 8 Ii 55.19N 21.16 E
Russel 42 Hb 73.55N 98.35W
Russell [Man. Can.] 42 Hf 50.47N 101.15W
Russell [Ks.-U.S.] 45 Gg 38.54N 98.52W
Russell [N.Z.] 62 Fa 35.16S 174.08 E
Russell Islands 60 Fi 9.04S 159.12 E
Russellville [Al.-U.S.] 44 Dh 34.30N 87.44W
Russellville [Ar.-U.S.] 45 Ji 35.17N 93.08W
Russellville [Ky.-U.S.] 44 Dg 36.51N 86.53W
Russel Range 59 Ef 33.25S 123.30 E
Rüsselsheim 10 Eg 50.00N 8.25 E
Russian River 46 Dg 38.27N 123.08W
Russian SFSR (EN) = RSFSR [2] 19 Jc 60.00N 100.00 E
Rust 14 Kc 47.48N 16.40 E
Rustavi 19 Eg 41.33N 45.02 E
Rustenburg 37 De 25.37S 27.08 E
Ruston 43 Ie 32.32N 92.38W
Rutaki Passage 64p Bc 21.15S 159.48W
Rutana 36 Fc 3.55S 30.00 E
Rutanzige, Lac-=Edward, Lake- (EN) 30 Ji 0.25S 29.30 E
Rute 13 Hg 37.19N 4.22W
Ruteng 26 Hh 8.36S 120.27 E
Rutenga 37 Ed 21.15S 30.44 E
Rüthen 12 Kc 51.29N 8.27 E
Rutherfordton 44 Gh 35.22N 81.57W
Ruthin 9 Jh 53.07N 3.18W
Rutland 9 Mi 52.40N 0.40W
Rutland 44 Kd 43.37N 72.59W
Rutland 25 If 11.25N 92.10 E
Rutog 22 Jf 33.29N 79.42 E
Rutshuru 36 Ec 1.11S 29.27 E
Rutter 44 Gb 46.06N 80.40W
Rutul 16 Oi 41.33N 47.29 E
Ruutana 8 Kc 61.31N 24.02 E
Ruvo di Puglia 14 Ki 41.09N 16.29 E
Ruvu 36 Gd 6.48S 38.39 E
Ruvuma [3] 36 Ge 10.30S 35.50 E
Ruvuma 30 Lj 10.29S 40.28 E
Ruvuma (EN) = Rovuma 30 Lj 10.29S 40.28 E
Ruwayshid, Wādī 24 Hf 32.41N 38.04 E
Ruwer 12 Ie 49.47N 6.42 E
Ruya 37 Ec 16.34S 33.12 E
Ruyang 28 Bg 34.10N 112.28 E
Ru'yas, Wādī ar- 33 Cd 27.06N 19.24 E
Ruyigi 36 Fc 3.29S 30.15 E
Ruza 7 Ii 55.39N 36.18 E
Ruzajevka [Kaz.-U.S.S.R.] 17 Mj 52.49N 67.01 E
Ruzajevka [R.S.F.S.R.] 19 Ee 54.05N 44.54 E
Ružany 10 Ud 52.48N 24.58 E
Ružomberok 10 Pg 49.05N 19.18 E
Rwanda [1] 31 Ji 2.30S 30.00 E
Ry 8 Ch 56.05N 9.46 E
Ryan 45 Hi 34.01N 97.57W
Rybachi Peninsula (EN) = Rybači, Poluostrov- 5 Jb 69.45N 32.35 E
Rybači 8 Ii 55.09N 20.45 E
Rybači, Poluostrov- = Rybachi Peninsula (EN) 5 Jb 69.45N 32.35 E
Rybačje 19 Hg 42.28N 76.11 E
Rybinsk 6 Jd 58.03N 38.52 E
Rybinskoje Vodohranilišče = Rybinsk Reservoir (EN) 5 Jd 58.30N 38.25 E
Rybinsk Reservoir (EN) = Rybinskoje Vodohranilišče 5 Jd 58.30N 38.25 E
Rybnica 16 Ff 47.45N 29.01 E
Rybnik 10 Of 50.06N 18.32 E
Rybnoje 19 De 54.46N 39.33 E
Rybnovsk 20 Jf 53.15N 141.55 E
Rychnov nad Kněžnou 10 Mf 50.10N 16.17 E
Rychwał 10 Od 52.05N 18.09 E
Ryd 8 Fh 56.28N 14.41 E
Rydaholm 8 Fh 56.59N 14.16 E
Ryde 12 Ad 50.43N 1.10W
Rye 9 Mg 54.10N 0.45W
Rye 9 Nk 50.57N 0.44 E
Rye Bay 12 Cd 50.55N 0.48 E
Ryegate 46 Kc 46.18N 109.15W
Rye Patch Reservoir 46 Ff 40.38N 118.18W
Ryes 12 Be 49.19N 0.37W
Ryfylke 8 Be 59.30N 6.30 E
Ryki 10 Re 51.39N 21.56 E
Rylsk 19 De 51.36N 34.43 E
Rymanów 10 Rg 49.34N 21.53 E
Rymättylä/Rimito 8 Jd 60.25N 21.55 E
Ryn 10 Rc 53.56N 21.33 E
Ryńskie, Jezioro- 10 Rc 53.53N 21.30 E
Ryōhaku-Sanchi 29 Ec 36.05N 136.45 E
Ryōsō-Yosui 29 Gd 35.22N 140.25 E
Ryōtsu 28 Oe 38.05N 138.26 E
Ryōtsu-Wan 29 Fb 38.10N 138.30 E
Ryō-Zen 29 Gc 37.46N 140.41 E
Rypin 10 Pc 53.05N 19.25 E
Ryškany 16 Ef 47.57N 27.32 E
Ryssby 8 Fh 56.52N 14.10 E
Rytterknægten 8 Fi 55.06N 14.54 E
Ryūgasaki 29 Gd 35.54N 140.10 E
Ryukyu Islands (EN) = Nansei-Shotō 21 Og 26.30N 128.00 E
Ryūkyū-Shotō 27 Mf 25.30N 126.30 E
Ryukyu Trench (EN) 3 Ig 25.45N 128.00 E
Rzepin 10 Kd 52.22N 14.50 E
Rzeszów 6 Ie 50.03N 22.00 E
Rzeszów [2] 10 Rf 50.05N 22.00 E
Ržev 6 Jd 56.16N 34.20 E

S

Šaa, Gora- 16 Nh 42.39N 44.43 E
Sa'ādatābād [Iran] 24 Ph 28.02N 55.50 E
Sa'ādatābād [Iran] 24 Og 30.08N 52.38 E
Sa'ādatābād [Iran] 24 Og 30.06N 53.08 E
Sääksjarvi 8 Jc 61.24N 22.24 E
Saalbach 12 Ke 49.15N 8.27 E
Saale 10 He 51.57N 11.55 E
Saaler Bodden 10 Ib 54.20N 12.28 E
Saalfeld 10 Hf 50.39N 11.22 E
Saalfelden am Steinernen Meer 14 Gc 47.25N 12.51 E
Saaminki 8 Mc 61.52N 28.50 E
Saâne 12 Ce 49.54N 0.56 E
Saane 14 Bd 46.59N 7.16 E
Saanen 14 Bd 46.30N 7.15 E
Saar 10 Cg 49.42N 6.34 E
Saar-Bergland 12 Ie 49.27N 6.45 E
Saarbrücken 6 Gf 49.14N 7.00 E
Saarbrücken-Dudweiler 12 Je 49.17N 7.02 E
Saarburg 10 Cg 49.36N 6.33 E
Sääre/Sjare 8 Ig 57.57N 21.53 E
Saaremaa/Sarema 5 Id 58.25N 22.30 E
Saarijärvi 7 Fe 62.43N 25.16 E
Saaristomeri 8 Id 60.20N 21.10 E
Saarland [2] 10 Cg 49.20N 7.00 E
Saarlouis 10 Cg 49.19N 6.45 E
Šaartuz 19 Gh 37.16N 68.06 E
Saarwellingen 12 Ie 49.21N 6.49 E
Saas Fee 14 Bd 46.07N 7.55 E
Saatly 16 Pj 39.57N 48.26 E
Saavedra 55 Am 37.45S 62.22W
Sab, Tônlé- 25 Kf 11.34N 104.57 E
Saba 47 Le 17.38N 63.10W
Saba 8 Me 59.05N 29.10 E
Saba Bank (EN) 50 Ed 17.30N 63.30W
Šabac 15 Ce 44.45N 19.43 E
Sabadell 13 Oc 41.33N 2.06 E
Sabae 28 Ng 35.57N 136.11 E
Sabah [2] 26 Ge 5.30N 117.00 E
Sab'ah, Qārat as- 33 Cd 27.20N 17.10 E
Sabak Bernam 26 Df 3.46N 100.59 E
Sabalān, Kūhhā-ye- 21 Gf 38.15N 47.49 E
Sab'ān 24 Ii 27.04N 41.58 E
Sabana, Archipiélago de- 49 Hb 22.30N 79.00W
Sabana de la Mar 49 Md 19.04N 69.23W
Sabanagrande 49 Dg 13.50N 87.15W
Sabanalarga 54 Da 10.38N 74.56W
Sabancuy 48 Nh 18.58N 91.11W
Sabaneta 49 Ld 19.12N 70.58W
Sabaneta, Puntan- 64b Ba 15.17N 145.49 E
Sabang [Indon.] 26 Gf 0.11N 119.51 E
Sabang [Indon.] 26 Ce 5.55N 95.19 E
Şabanözü 24 Eb 40.29N 33.18 E
Săbăoani 15 Jb 47.01N 26.51 E
Sabarei 36 Gb 4.20N 36.55 E
Sab'Atayn, Ramlat as- 33 If 15.30N 46.10 E
Sabatini, Monti- 14 Gh 42.10N 12.15 E
Sabaudia 14 Hi 41.18N 13.01 E
Sabaudia, Lago di- 14 Hi 41.15N 13.05 E
Şabbāgh, Jabal- 24 Fh 28.12N 34.04 E
Sab 'Bi 'Ār 24 Gf 33.46N 37.41 E
Sabbioneta 14 Ee 45.00N 10.39 E
Sa Bec 25 Lf 10.18N 105.46 E
Sabhā [3] 33 Bd 26.00N 14.00 E
Sabhā 31 If 27.02N 14.26 E
Şabḥā 24 Gf 32.20N 36.30 E
Sabhā, Wāḥāt- = Sebha Oasis (EN) 30 If 27.00N 14.25 E
Sabi 30 Kk 21.00S 35.02 E
Sabidana, Jabal- 35 Fb 18.04N 36.50 E
Sabile 8 Jg 57.05N 22.29 E
Sabina 14 Gh 42.20N 12.45 E
Sabinal 48 Fb 30.57N 107.30W
Sabinal, Peninsula de- 49 Ic 21.40N 77.18W
Sabiñánigo 13 Lb 42.31N 0.22W
Sabinas 47 Dc 27.51N 101.07W
Sabinas, Rio- 48 Id 27.37N 100.42W
Sabinas Hidalgo 47 Dc 26.30N 100.10W
Sabine Lake 45 Jl 29.50N 93.50W
Sabine Pass 45 Jl 29.44N 93.52W
Sabine Peninsula 42 Ga 76.25N 109.50W
Sabine River 43 Ie 30.00N 93.45W
Sabini, Monti- 14 Gh 42.15N 12.50 E
Şabir, Jabal- 23 Fg 13.30N 44.03 E
Sabirabad 16 Pj 39.59N 48.29 E
Šabla 15 Lf 43.32N 28.32 E
Sable, Anse de- 51e b 16.07N 61.34W
Sable, Cape- [Can.] 38 Me 43.25N 65.35W
Sable, Cape- [U.S.] 38 Kg 25.12N 81.05W
Sable, Ile de- 57 Gf 19.15S 159.56 E
Sable Island 38 Ne 43.55N 59.55W
Sablé-sur-Sarthe 11 Fg 47.50N 0.20W
Sablūkah, Ash Shallāl as- = Sixth Cataract (EN) 30 Kg 16.20N 32.42 E
Sabonetau, Serra da- 55 Kb 15.20S 43.50W
Sabonkafi 34 Gc 14.38N 8.45 E
Sabor 13 Ec 41.10N 7.07W
Şabrātah 33 Bc 32.47N 12.29 E
Sabres 11 Fj 44.09N 0.44W
Sabrina Coast 66 He 67.00S 119.30 E
Sabtang 26 Hb 20.19N 121.52 E
Sabunči 16 Pi 40.27N 49.57 E
Şabyā 23 Ff 17.09N 42.37 E
Sabzevār 22 Hf 36.13N 57.42 E
Saca, Virful- 15 Ic 46.30N 25.15 E
Sacajawea Peak 43 Db 45.15N 117.17W
Sacalin, Insulă- 15 Me 44.50N 29.39 E
Sacandica 36 Cd 5.58S 15.56 E
Sacatepéquez [3] 49 Bf 14.35N 90.45W
Sacavém 13 Cf 38.46N 9.05W
Sac City 45 Ie 42.25N 95.00W
Sacco 14 Hi 41.31N 13.32 E
Sacedón 13 Jd 40.29N 2.43W
Săcel 15 Hb 47.38N 24.26 E
Săcele 15 Id 45.37N 25.41 E
Sachayoj 55 Bh 26.41S 61.50W
Sachere 16 Mh 42.20N 43.22 E
Sachigo 42 Ie 55.05N 89.00W
Sachsen = Saxony (EN) 10 Jf 51.00N 13.30 E
Sachsenhagen 12 Lb 52.24N 9.16 E
Sachs Harbour 42 Eb 72.00N 125.08W
Šack [R.S.F.S.R.] 7 Ji 54.04N 41.42 E
Šack [Ukr.-U.S.S.R.] 10 Je 51.30N 24.00 E
Sackets Harbor 44 Id 43.57N 76.07W
Saco [Me.-U.S.] 44 Ld 43.29N 70.28W
Saco [Mt.-U.S.] 46 Lb 48.28N 107.21W
Sacramento 38 Gf 38.03N 121.56W
Sacramento [Braz.] 54 Ig 19.53S 47.27W
Sacramento [Ca.-U.S.] 39 Gf 38.35N 121.30W
Sacramento, Pampa del- 54 Ce 8.00S 75.50W
Sacramento Mountains 38 If 33.10N 105.50W
Sacramento Valley 43 Cd 39.15N 122.00W
Sacre ou Timalacia, Rio- 55 Ca 13.55S 58.02W
Săcueni 15 Fb 47.21N 22.06 E
Sacuriuiná ou Ponte de Pedra, Rio- 55 Da 13.58S 57.18W
Sādaba 13 Kb 42.17N 1.16W
Sa'dābād 24 Nh 29.23N 51.07 E
Şa'dah 22 Gh 16.57N 43.44 E
Sada-Misaki 29b Ce 33.22N 132.01 E
Sada-Misaki-Hantō 29 Ce 33.25N 132.15 E
Sadani 36 Gd 6.03S 38.47 E
Sadao 25 Kg 6.39N 100.31 E
Sadd al 'Ālī 33 Fe 23.54N 32.52 E
Saddle Mountains 46 Fc 46.50N 119.55W
Saddle Peak [India] 25 If 13.09N 93.01 E
Saddle Peak [Mt.-U.S.] 46 Jd 45.57N 110.58W
Sad-e Eskandar 24 Pd 37.10N 55.00 E
Sadiya 25 Jc 27.50N 95.40 E
Sa'dīyah, Hawr as- 24 Lf 32.00N 46.45 E
Sad Kharv 24 Qd 36.19N 57.05 E
Sado 13 Df 38.29N 8.55W
Sado-Kaikyō 29 Fc 37.55N 138.40 E
Sado-Shima 21 Pf 38.00N 138.25 E
Sadowara 29 Be 32.04N 131.26 E
Şadrinsk 19 Gd 56.05N 63.38 E
Saeby 7 Ch 57.20N 10.32 E
Saeh, Teluk- 26 Gh 8.00S 117.30 E
Saengcheon 28 Ie 39.55N 126.34 E
Saerbeck 12 Jb 52.11N 7.38 E
Şafājah 24 Hi 26.30N 39.30 E
Şafājah, Jazīrat- 24 Ei 26.45N 33.59 E
Safané 34 Ec 12.08N 3.13W
Şafāqis = Sfax (EN) [3] 32 Jc 34.30N 10.30 E
Şafāqis = Sfax (EN) 31 Ie 34.44N 10.46 E
Safata Harbour 65c Bb 14.00S 171.50W
Saffāniyah, Ra's as- 23 Gd 27.59N 48.37 E
Säffle 7 Cg 59.08N 12.56 E
Safford 43 Fe 32.50N 109.43W
Saffron Walden 9 Ni 52.01N 0.15 E
Safi 31 Ge 32.18N 9.14W
Safi [3] 32 Fc 31.55N 9.00W
Safia, Hamâda- 34 Ea 23.10N 4.15W
Şafīābād 24 Qd 36.45N 57.58 E
Safid 23 Hb 37.23N 50.11 E
Safid, Kūh-e 24 Lf 33.55N 47.30 E
Safid Kūh, Salseleh-ye- 23 Jc 34.30N 63.30 E
Safonovo [R.S.F.S.R.] 19 Dd 55.06N 33.14 E
Safonovo [R.S.F.S.R.] 7 Ld 65.41N 47.43 E
Şafrā' al Asyāḥ 24 Ji 26.50N 43.57 E
Şafrā' as Sark 24 Kj 25.25N 44.20 E
Safranbolu 24 Eb 41.15N 32.42 E
Şafwān 24 Lg 30.07N 47.43 E
Saga [Jap.] 27 Ne 33.15N 130.18 E
Saga [Jap.] 29 Ce 33.05N 130.06 E
Saga [Kaz.-U.S.S.R.] 19 Fe 50.30N 64.14 E
Saga (Gya'gya) 27 Ef 29.22N 85.15 E
Sagae 29 Gb 38.22N 140.17 E
Sagaing [3] 25 Jd 23.30N 95.30 E
Sagaing 25 Jd 21.52N 95.59 E
Saga Ken [2] 28 Kh 33.15N 130.15 E
Sagamihara 29 Fd 35.34N 139.22 E
Sagami-Nada 29 Fd 35.00N 139.30 E
Sagami-Wan 29 Fd 35.15N 139.20 E
Sagan 35 Fd 5.17N 36.57 E
Şagan 19 He 50.37N 79.15 E
Saganaga Lake 45 Kb 48.14N 90.52W
Saganoseki 29 Be 33.15N 131.53 E
Şagany, Ozero- 15 Md 45.45N 29.55 E
Sāgar [India] 25 Ff 14.10N 75.02 E
Sāgar [India] 22 Jg 23.50N 78.42 E
Sagara 29 Fd 34.40N 138.12 E
Sagaredžo 16 Ni 41.43N 45.16 E
Sagavanirktok 40 Jb 70.20N 148.00W
Sagawa 29 Ce 33.29N 133.16 E
Sage 46 Jf 41.50N 110.56W
Saghād 24 Oq 31.12N 52.30 E
Saginaw 43 Kc 43.25N 83.58W
Saginaw Bay 43 Kc 43.50N 83.40W
Sagiz 19 Ff 47.32N 53.45 E
Sagiz [Kaz.-U.S.S.R.] 19 Ff 48.12N 54.56 E
Sagiz [Kaz.-U.S.S.R.] 16 Rf 47.32N 53.27 E
Saglek Bay 42 Le 58.30N 63.00W
Sagleouc → Salluit 39 Lc 62.12N 75.38W
Şagonar 20 Ef 51.32N 92.51 E
Sagone, Golfe de- 11a Aa 42.06N 8.41 E
Sagres 13 Dg 37.01N 8.56W
Sagres, Ponta de- 13 Dh 37.00N 8.57W
Sagter Ems 12 Ja 53.10N 7.40 E
Şagu 15 Ec 46.03N 21.17 E
Sagu/Sauvo 8 Jd 60.21N 22.42 E
Saguache 45 Cg 38.05N 106.08W
Sagua de Tánamo 49 Jc 20.35N 75.14W
Sagua la Grande 47 Hd 22.49N 80.05W
Saguenay 38 Me 48.10N 69.45W
Saguia el-Hamra 32 Ed 26.50N 12.00W
Sagunt/Sagunto 13 Le 39.41N 0.16W
Sagunto/Sagunt 13 Le 39.41N 0.16W
Sagunto-Grao de Sagunto 13 Le 39.40N 0.16W
Sa'gya 27 Ef 28.53N 88.10 E
Sahagún [Col.] 54 Cb 8.57N 75.27W
Sahagún [Sp.] 13 Gb 42.22N 5.02W
Sahalin, Ostrov- = Sakhalin (EN) 21 Qd 51.00N 143.00 E
Sahalinskaja Oblast [3] 20 Jf 50.00N 143.30 E
Sahalinski Zaliv 20 Jf 53.45N 141.30 E
Sahara 30 Hf 21.00N 6.00 E
Saharan Atlas (EN) = Atlas Saharien 30 He 34.00N 2.00 E
Sahāranpur 22 Jg 29.58N 77.23 E
Sahel [3] 34 Ec 14.10N 0.50W
Sahel 30 Gg 15.40N 8.30W
Şahin 15 Jh 41.01N 26.50 E
Sāhīwāl [Pak.] 25 Eb 30.41N 72.57 E
Sāhīwāl [Pak.] 25 Eb 31.58N 72.20 E
Sahlābād 23 Ic 32.10N 59.51 E
Sahneh 24 Le 34.29N 47.41 E
Sahnovščina 16 Ie 49.09N 35.57 E
Sahova Kosa, Mys- 16 Qi 40.13N 50.22 E
Sahrihan 18 Id 40.40N 72.03 E
Şahrisabz 19 Gh 39.03N 66.41 E
Šahristan, Pereval- 18 Ge 39.35N 68.38 E
Šahtersk [R.S.F.S.R.] 20 Jg 49.13N 142.09 E
Šahtersk [Ukr.-U.S.S.R.] 16 Ke 48.01N 38.32 E
Šahterski 20 Md 64.46N 177.47 E
Šahtinsk 19 Hf 49.40N 72.37 E
Šahty 19 Ef 47.42N 40.13 E
Sahuaripa 47 Cc 29.03N 109.14W
Sahuayo de Diaz 47 Dd 20.04N 102.43W
Šahunja 19 Ed 57.43N 46.35 E
Saḩūq, Wādī- 24 Jj 25.18N 42.20 E
Šahy 10 Oh 48.05N 18.58 E
Sahyadri/Western Ghats 21 Jh 14.00N 75.00 E
Sai Buri 25 Kg 6.42N 101.37 E
Saïda [3] 32 Hc 33.35N 0.30 E
Saïda 31 He 34.50N 0.09 E
Saïda, Monts de- 13 Mi 35.10N 0.30 E
Sa'īdābād 23 Id 29.28N 55.42 E
Saidaiji 29 Dd 34.39N 134.02 E
Said Bundas 35 Cd 8.35N 24.30 E
Saidia 13 Ji 35.04N 2.13W
Saidor 60 Di 5.37S 146.28 E
Saidu 25 Eb 34.45N 72.21 E
Saigō 29 Cc 36.13N 133.20 E
Saigon → Ho Chi Minh 22 Mh 10.45N 106.40 E
Saihan Tal → Sonid Youqi 27 Jc 42.45N 112.36 E
Saihan Toroi 27 Hc 41.54N 100.24 E
Saijō 29 Ce 33.55N 133.10 E
Saikai 29 Ae 33.03N 129.44 E
Sai-Kawa 29 Fc 36.37N 138.14 E
Saiki 28 Kh 32.57N 131.54 E
Saiki-Wan 29 Be 33.00N 131.55 E
Sail Rock 51n Bb 12.37N 61.16W
Saimaa 5 Ic 61.15N 28.15 E
Saimaa Canal (EN) = Sajmenski Kanal 8 Mc 61.05N 28.18 E
Sain Alto 48 Hf 23.35N 103.15W
Sā'in Dezh 24 Ld 36.40N 46.33 E
Sains-Richaumont 12 Fe 49.49N 3.42 E
Saint Abb's Head 9 Kf 55.54N 2.09W
Saint-Affrique 11 Ik 43.57N 2.53 E
Saint Agnes Head 9 Hk 50.23N 5.07W
Saint-Agrève 11 Ki 45.01N 4.24 E
Saint Albans [Eng.-U.K.] 9 Mj 51.46N 0.21W
Saint Albans [Vt.-U.S.] 44 Kc 44.49N 73.05W
Saint Albans [W.V.-U.S.] 44 Gf 38.24N 81.53W
Saint Alban's Head 9 Kk 50.34N 2.04W
Saint Albert 42 Gf 53.38N 113.38W
Saint-Amand-les-Eaux 11 Jd 50.26N 3.26 E
Saint-Amand-Mont-Rond 11 Ih 46.43N 2.31 E
Saint-André, Cap- 30 Lj 16.11S 44.27 E
Saint-André, Plaine de- 11 Hf 48.55N 1.10 E
Saint-André-de-Cubzac 11 Fi 45.00N 0.27W
Saint-André-de-l'Eure 12 Df 48.54N 1.17 E
Saint-André-sur-Cailly 12 De 49.33N 1.13 E
Saint Andrews [N.B.-Can.] 44 Nc 45.06N 67.02W
Saint Andrews [Scot.-U.K.] 9 Ke 56.20N 2.48W
Saint Anne 9 Kl 49.40N 2.10W
Saint Ann's Bay 49 Id 18.26N 77.16W
Saint Ann's Head 9 Hj 51.41N 5.10W
Saint Anthony [Id.-U.S.] 46 Je 43.58N 111.41W
Saint Anthony [Newf.-Can.] 42 Lf 51.22N 55.35W
Saint Arnaud 59 Ig 36.37S 143.15 E
Saint-Aubert 44 Lb 47.14N 70.15W
Saint-Aubin-sur-Mer 12 Be 49.20N 0.24W
Saint Augustine 43 Kf 29.51N 81.25W
Saint-Augustin-Saguenay 42 Lf 51.14N 58.39W
Saint Austell 9 Ik 50.20N 4.48W
Saint-Avold 11 Me 49.06N 6.42 E
Saint Barthélemy 47 Le 17.55N 62.50W
Saint-Barthélemy 11 Hl 42.49N 1.45 E
Saint Barthélemy, Canal de- 51b Bb 18.00N 63.00W
Saint Barthélemy, Kanaal Van- 51b Bb 18.00N 63.00W
Saint Bees Head 9 Jg 54.32N 3.38W
Saint-Benoit 37a b 21.02S 55.43 E
Saint-Benoît-sur-Loire 11 Ig 47.49N 2.18 E
Saint-Bonnet 11 Mj 44.41N 6.05 E
Saint-Brévin-les-Pins 11 Dg 47.15N 2.10W
Saint Brides Bay 9 Hj 51.48N 5.15W
Saint-Brieuc 11 Df 48.31N 2.47W
Saint-Brieuc, Baie de- 11 Df 48.38N 2.40W
Saint-Calais 11 Gg 47.55N 0.45 E
Saint-Camille 44 Lb 46.29N 70.12W
Saint Catharines 42 Jh 43.10N 79.15W
Saint Catherine, Monastery of- (EN) = Dayr Kātrīnā 33 Fd 28.31N 33.57 E
Saint Catherine, Mount- 51p Bb 12.10N 61.40W
Saint Catherines Island 44 Gj 31.38N 81.10W
Saint Catherine's Point 9 Lk 50.34N 1.15W
Saint-Céré 11 Hj 44.52N 1.54 E
Saint-Chamond 11 Ki 45.28N 4.30 E
Saint Charles 43 Id 38.47N 90.29W
Saint-Chély-d'Apcher 11 Jj 44.48N 3.17 E
Saint-Christol, Plateau de- 11 Lj 44.00N 5.50 E
Saint Christopher/Saint Kitts 38 Mh 17.21N 62.48W
Saint Christopher-Nevis [5] 39 Mh 17.21N 62.48W
Saint-Cirq-Lapopie 11 Hj 44.28N 1.40 E
Saint Clair, Lake- 38 Ke 42.25N 82.41W
Saint Clair River 44 Fd 42.37N 82.31W
Saint Clair Shores 44 Fd 42.30N 82.54W
Saint-Clair-sur-l'Elle 12 Ae 49.12N 1.02W
Saint-Claud 11 Gi 45.54N 0.28 E
Saint-Claude [Fr.] 11 Lh 46.23N 5.52 E
Saint Claude 45 Gb 49.40N 98.22W
Saint-Claude [Guad.] 51e Ab 16.02N 61.42W
Saint Cloud 39 Je 45.33N 94.10W
Saint Croix 47 Le 17.45N 64.45W
Saint Croix Falls 45 Jd 45.24N 92.38W
Saint Croix River 43 Ic 44.45N 92.49W
Saint-Cyr-l'Ecole 12 Ef 48.48N 2.04 E
Saint-Cyr-sur-Loire 11 Gg 47.24N 0.40 E
Saint David Bay 51g Bb 15.26N 61.15W
Saint David's [Gren.] 51p Bb 12.04N 61.39W
Saint David's [Wales-U.K.] 9 Hj 51.54N 5.16W
Saint David's Head 9 Hj 51.55N 5.19W
Saint David's Point 51p Bb 12.01N 61.40W
Saint-Denis [Fr.] 11 If 48.56N 2.22 E
Saint-Denis [May.] 31 Mk 20.52S 55.28 E
Saint-Dié 11 Mf 48.17N 6.57 E
Saint-Dizier 11 Kf 48.38N 4.57 E
Sainte-Adresse 12 Ce 49.30N 0.05 E
Sainte-Anne [Guad.] 51e Bb 16.14N 61.23W
Sainte-Anne [Mart.] 51h Bc 14.26N 60.53W
Sainte-Anne-des-Monts 44 Na 49.07N 66.29W
Sainte Baume, Chaîne de la- 11 Lk 43.20N 5.45 E
Sainte-Énimie 11 Jj 44.22N 3.25 E
Sainte Genevieve 45 Kh 37.59N 90.03W
Sainte-Geneviève 12 Ee 49.17N 2.12 E
Saint Elias, Mount- 38 Ec 60.18N 140.55W
Saint Elias Mountains 38 Fc 60.30N 139.30W
Saint-Elie 54 Hc 4.50N 53.17W
Sainte-Livrade-sur-Lot 11 Gj 44.24N 0.36 E
Saint-Eloy-les-Mines 11 Ih 46.09N 2.50 E
Sainte Luce 37 Hd 24.46S 47.12 E
Sainte-Luce 51h Bc 14.28N 60.56W
Sainte-Lucie, Canal de- = Saint Lucia Channel (EN) 50 Fe 14.09N 60.57W
Sainte-Marcellin 11 Li 45.09N 5.19 E
Sainte-Marie [Guad.] 51e Ab 16.06N 61.34W
Sainte-Marie [Mart.] 51h Ab 14.47N 61.00W
Sainte-Marie, Cap- = Sainte-Marie, Cape- (EN) 30 Lk 25.36S 45.08 E
Sainte-Marie, Cape- (EN) = Sainte-Marie, Cap- 30 Lk 25.36S 45.08 E
Sainte-Marie, Ile- 30 Lj 16.50S 49.55 E
Sainte-Marie-aux-Mines 11 Nf 48.15N 7.11 E
Sainte-Maure-de-Touraine 11 Gg 47.06N 0.37 E
Sainte-Maxime 11 Mk 43.18N 6.38 E
Sainte-Menehould 11 Ke 49.05N 4.54 E
Sainte-Rose 51e Ab 16.20N 61.42W
Sainte-Rose-du-Dégelé 44 Mb 47.33N 68.39W
Sainte Rose du Lac 45 Ga 51.03N 99.32W
Saintes 11 Fi 45.45N 0.38W
Saintes, Canal des- 51e Ac 15.55N 61.40W
Saintes, Iles des- 50 Fe 15.52N 61.37W
Sainte-Savine 11 Kf 48.18N 4.03 E
Saintes-Maries-de-la-Mer 11 Kk 43.27N 4.26 E
Sainte-Thérèse 44 Kc 45.22N 73.15W
Saint-Étienne 6 Gf 45.26N 4.24 E
Saint-Étienne-du-Rouvray 11 He 49.23N 1.06 E
Sainte Victoire, Montagne- 11 Lk 43.32N 5.39 E
Saint-Félicien 44 Ka 48.39N 72.28W
Saint-Florent 11a Ba 42.41N 9.18 E
Saint-Florent, Golfe de- 11a Ba 42.45N 9.16 E
Saint-Florentin 11 Jf 48.00N 3.44 E
Saint-Florent-sur-Cher 11 Ih 46.59N 2.15 E
Saint-Flour 11 Ji 45.02N 3.05 E
Saint Francis 45 Fg 39.46N 101.48W
Saint Francis River 45 Ki 34.38N 90.35W
Saint Francisville 45 Kk 30.47N 91.23W
Saint-François 51e Bb 16.15N 61.17W
Saint François Island 37b Bb 7.10S 52.44 E
Saint Francois Mountains 45 Kh 37.30N 90.35W
Saint-Gaudens 11 Gk 43.07N 0.44 E
Saint George 40 Fe 56.35N 169.35W
Saint George [Austl.] 59 Je 28.02S 148.35 E
Saint George [N.B.-Can.] 44 Nc 45.10N 66.48W
Saint George [Ut.-U.S.] 43 Ed 37.06N 113.35W
Saint George, Cape - [Newf.-Can.] 42 Lm 48.28N 59.16W
Saint George, Cape- [Pap.N.Gui.] 60 Eh 4.52S 152.52 E
Saint George, Point- 46 Cf 41.47N 124.15W
Saint George Harbour 44 Nd 43.15N 66.10W
Saint George Island 44 Ek 29.39N 84.55W
Saint George's 39 Mh 12.03N 61.45W
Saint-Georges 44 Lb 46.10N 70.38W
Saint George's Bay 42 Lg 48.20N 59.00W
Saint George's Channel 5 Fe 52.00N 6.00W
Saint George's Channel (EN) = Muir Bhreatan 5 Fe 52.00N 6.00W
Saint-Georges-du-Vièvre 12 Ce 49.15N 0.35 E
Saint-Germain-en-Laye 11 If 48.54N 2.05 E
Saint-Gervais-d'Auvergne 11 Ih 46.02N 2.49 E
Saint-Gervais-les-Bains 11 Mi 45.54N 6.43 E
Saint-Ghislain 12 Fd 50.27N 3.49 E
Saint-Ghislain-Baudour 12 Fd 50.29N 3.49 E
Saint-Gildas, Pointe de- 11 Dg 47.08N 2.15W
Saint-Gilles 11 Kk 43.41N 4.26 E
Saint-Gilles-Croix-de-Vie 11 Eh 46.41N 1.55W
Saint-Girons 11 Hl 42.59N 1.09 E
Saint-Gobain 12 Fe 49.36N 3.23 E
Saint Gotthard Pass (EN) = San Gottardo/Sankt Gotthard 5 Gf 46.30N 8.30 E
Saint Gotthard Pass (EN) = Sankt Gotthard/San Gottardo 5 Gf 46.30N 8.30 E
Saint Govan's Head 9 Ij 51.36N 4.55W
Saint Helena [5] 31 Gj 15.57S 5.42W
Saint Helena 30 Gj 15.57S 5.42W
Saint Helena Bay 30 Il 32.45S 18.05 E
Saint Helena Island 44 Gi 32.30N 80.30W

Index Symbols

[1] Independent Nation; [2] State, Region; [3] District, County; [4] Municipality; [5] Colony, Dependency; Continent; Physical Region
Historical or Cultural Region; Mount, Mountain; Volcano; Hill; Mountains, Mountain Range; Hills, Escarpment; Plateau, Upland
Pass, Gap; Plain, Lowland; Delta; Salt Flat; Valley, Canyon; Crater, Cave; Karst Features
Depression; Polder; Desert, Dunes; Forest, Woods; Heath, Steppe; Oasis; Cape, Point
Coast, Beach; Cliff; Peninsula; Isthmus; Sandbank; Island; Atoll
Rock, Reef; Islands, Archipelago; Rocks, Reefs; Coral Reef; Well, Spring; Geyser; River, Stream
Waterfall Rapids; River Mouth, Estuary; Lake; Salt Lake; Intermittent Lake; Reservoir; Swamp, Pond
Canal; Glacier; Ice Shelf, Pack Ice; Ocean; Sea; Gulf, Bay; Strait, Fjord
Lagoon; Bank; Seamount; Tablemount; Ridge; Shelf; Basin
Escarpment, Sea Scarp; Fracture; Trench, Abyss; National Park, Reserve; Point of Interest; Recreation Site; Cave, Cavern
Historic Site; Ruins; Wall, Walls; Church, Abbey; Temple; Scientific Station; Airport
Port; Lighthouse; Mine; Tunnel; Dam, Bridge

Saint Helena Sound 44 Gi 32.27N 80.25W
Saint Helens [Austl.] 59 Jh 41.20S 148.15 E
Saint Helens [Eng.-U.K.] 9 Kh 53.28N 2.44W
Saint Helens [Or.-U.S.] 46 Dd 45.52N 122.48W
Saint Helens, Mount- 46 Dc 46.12N 122.11W
Saint Helier 9 Kl 49.12N 2.07W
Saint-Hubert 12 Hd 50.03N 5.23 E
Saint-Hyacinthe 44 Kc 45.38N 72.57W
Saint Ignace Island 45 Mb 48.48N 87.55W
Saint Ignatius 46 Hc 47.19N 114.06W
Saint Ives [Eng.-U.K.] 9 Hk 50.12N 5.29W
Saint Ives [Eng.-U.K.] 12 Bb 52.18N 0.04W
Saint James 45 Ie 43.59N 94.38W
Saint James, Cape - 42 Ef 51.57N 131.01W
Saint-Jean 42 Kg 45.13N 73.15W
Saint-Jean, Baie de- 51b Bc 17.55N 62.51W
Saint-Jean, Lac- 38 Le 48.35N 72.00W
Saint-Jean-d'Angély 11 Fi 45.57N 0.31W
Saint-Jean-de-Luz 11 Ek 43.23N 1.40W
Saint-Jean-de-Maurienne 11 Mi 45.17N 6.21 E
Saint-Jean-de-Monts 11 Dh 46.47N 2.04W
Saint-Jean-du-Gard 11 Jj 44.06N 3.53 E
Saint-Jean-Pied-de-Port 11 Ek 43.10N 1.14W
Saint-Jérôme [Que.-Can.] 42 Kg 45.46N 74.00W
Saint-Jérôme [Que.-Can.] 44 La 48.26N 71.52W
Saint Joe River 46 Gc 47.21N 116.42W
Saint John 50 Dc 18.20N 64.42W
Saint John [Can.] 38 Me 45.15N 66.04W
Saint John [Ks.-U.S.] 45 Gh 38.00N 98.46W
Saint John [Lbr.] 34 Cd 5.55N 10.05W
Saint John [N.B.-Can.] 39 Me 45.16N 66.03W
Saint John's [Atg.] 47 Le 17.06N 61.51W
Saint Johns [Az.-U.S.] 46 Ki 34.30N 109.22W
Saint Johns [Mi.-U.S.] 44 Ed 43.00N 84.33W
Saint John's [Mont.] 51c Bc 16.48N 62.11W
Saint John's [Newf.-Can.] 39 Ne 47.34N 52.43W
Saint Johnsbury 44 Kc 44.25N 72.01W
Saint Johns River 44 Gj 30.24N 81.24W
Saint Joseph [Dom.] 51g Bb 15.24N 61.26W
Saint Joseph [La.-U.S.] 45 Kk 31.55N 91.14W
Saint-Joseph [Mart.] 51h Ab 14.40N 61.03W
Saint Joseph [Mi.-U.S.] 44 Dd 42.06N 86.29W
Saint Joseph [Mo.-U.S.] 43 Id 39.46N 94.51W
Saint-Joseph [New Caledonia] 63b Ce 20.27S 166.36 E
Saint-Joseph [Reu.] 37a Bb 21.22S 55.37 E
Saint Joseph, Lake- 42 If 51.06N 90.36W
Saint Joseph Island 44 Fb 46.13N 83.57W
Saint Joseph River 44 Dd 42.06N 86.29W
Saint-Junien 11 Gi 45.53N 0.54 E
Saint-Just-en-Chaussée 12 Ee 49.30N 2.26 E
Saint Kilda 9 Ed 57.49N 8.36W
Saint Kitts/Saint Christopher 38 Mh 17.21N 62.48W
Saint-Lary-Soulan 11 Gl 42.49N 0.19 E
Saint Laurent 53 Ke 5.30N 54.02W
Saint Laurent = Saint Lawrence (EN) 38 Me 49.15N 67.00W
Saint Lawrence 38 Bc 63.30N 170.30W
Saint Lawrence 38 Me 49.15N 67.00W
Saint Lawrence (EN) = Saint Laurent 38 Me 49.15N 67.00W
Saint Lawrence, Gulf of- 38 Me 48.00N 62.00W
Saint-Léger-en-Yvelines 12 Df 48.43N 1.46 E
Saint-Léonard 44 Nb 47.10N 67.56W
Saint-Léonard-de-Noblat 11 Hi 45.50N 1.29 E
Saint-Lewis 42 Lf 52.22N 55.58W
Saint-Lô 11 Ee 49.07N 1.05W
Saint Louis 39 Jf 38.38N 90.11W
Saint-Louis [Guad.] 51e Bc 15.57N 61.20W
Saint-Louis [Sen.] 31 Fg 16.02N 16.30W
Saint-Loup-sur-Semouse 11 Mg 47.53N 6.16 E
Saint Lucia 37 Ee 28.23S 32.25 E
Saint Lucia 39 Mh 13.53N 60.58W
Saint Lucia 38 Mh 13.53N 60.58W
Saint Lucia, Cape- 30 Kk 28.32S 32.24 E
Saint Lucia, Lake- 37 Ee 28.00S 32.30 E
Saint Lucia Channel 50 Fe 14.09N 60.57W
Saint Lucia Channel (EN) = Sainte-Lucie, Canal de- 50 Fe 14.09N 60.57W
Saint Magnus Bay 9 La 60.25N 1.35W
Saint-Maixent-l'Ecole 11 Fh 46.25N 0.12W
Saint-Malo 6 Ff 48.39N 2.01W
Saint-Malo, Golfe de- 5 Ff 48.45N 2.00W
Saint-Marc 47 Je 19.06N 72.43W
Saint-Marc, Canal de- 49 Kd 18.50N 72.45W
Saint Margaret's at Cliffe 12 Dc 51.09N 1.19 E
Saint Margaret's Hope 9 Kc 58.49N 2.57W
Saint Maries 46 Gc 47.19N 116.35W
Saint Martin 47 Le 18.04N 63.04W
Saint Martin, Cap- 51h Ab 14.52N 61.13W
Saint-Martin-Boulogne 12 Dd 50.43N 1.40 E
Saint-Martin-de-Ré 11 Eh 46.12N 1.22W
Saint-Martin-des-Besaces 12 Be 49.01N 0.51W
Saint Martins 44 Oc 45.21N 65.32W
Saint-Martin-Vésubie 11 Nj 44.04N 7.15 E
Saint Mary, Cape- 44 Nc 44.05N 66.13W
Saint Mary Peak [Austl.] 59 Hf 31.30S 138.35 E
Saint Mary Peak [U.S.] 46 Hc 46.40N 114.20W
Saint Mary's 9 Gl 49.55N 6.20W
Saint Marys [Austl.] 59 Jh 41.35S 148.10 E
Saint Marys [Oh.-U.S.] 44 Ee 40.32N 84.22W
Saint Marys [W.V.-U.S.] 44 Gf 39.24N 81.13W
Saint Mary's, Cape - 42 Mg 46.49N 54.12W
Saint Mary's Bay [N.S.-Can.] 44 Nc 44.25N 66.10W
Saint Mary's Bay [N.W.T.-Can.] 42 Mg 46.50N 53.47W
Saint Marys River 44 Gj 30.45N 81.30W
Saint-Mathieu, Pointe de- 5 Ff 48.20N 4.46W
Saint Matthew 38 Bb 60.30N 172.45W
Saint Matthias Group 57 Fe 1.30S 149.48 E
Saint-Maur-des-Fossés 11 If 48.48N 2.30 E
Saint-Maurice, Rivière- 42 Kg 46.21N 72.31W
Saint Michael 40 Gd 63.29N 162.02W
Saint Michaels 46 Ki 35.46N 109.04W
Saint-Michel 12 Ge 49.55N 4.08 E
Saint-Mihiel 11 Lf 48.54N 5.33 E
Saint-Nazaire 11 Dg 47.17N 2.12W
Saint Neots 12 Bb 52.13N 0.16W
Saint-Nicolas/Sint Niklaas 12 Gc 51.10N 4.08 E
Saint-Nicolas-d'Aliermont 12 De 49.53N 1.13 E
Saint-Nicolas-de-Port 11 Mf 48.38N 6.18 E
Saint-Omer 11 Id 50.45N 2.15 E
Saintonge 11 Fi 45.50N 0.30W
Saint Patrick's 51c Bc 16.41N 62.12W
Saint Paul 34 Cd 6.23N 10.48W
Saint-Paul 37a Bb 21.00S 55.16 E
Saint Paul 30 Ol 38.55S 77.41 E
Saint Paul [Ak.-U.S.] 40 Ee 57.07N 170.17W
Saint Paul [Alta.-Can.] 42 Gf 53.59N 111.17W
Saint Paul [Mn.-U.S.] 39 Je 44.58N 93.07W
Saint Paul [Nb.-U.S.] 45 Gf 41.13N 98.27W
Saint Paul, Cape- 34 Fd 5.49N 0.57 E
Saint-Paul-lès-Dax 11 Ek 43.44N 1.03W
Saint Paul's 51c Ab 17.24N 62.49W
Saint Paul's Point 64q Ab 25.04S 130.05W
Saint-Péray 11 Kj 44.57N 4.50 E
Saint Peter 45 Jd 44.17N 93.57W
Saint Peter Port 9 Kl 49.27N 2.32W
Saint Peter's 51c Bc 16.46N 62.12W
Saint Petersburg 39 Kg 27.46N 82.38W
Saint Petersburg Beach 44 Fl 27.45N 82.45W
Saint-Pierre [Mart.] 50 Fe 14.45N 61.11W
Saint-Pierre [May.] 31 Mk 21.19S 55.29 E
Saint-Pierre [St.P.M.] 42 Lg 46.46N 56.12W
Saint-Pierre, Lac- 44 Kb 46.10N 72.50W
Saint Pierre and Miquelon (EN) = Saint-Pierre et Miquelon 39 Ne 46.55N 56.10W
Saint-Pierre-en-Port 12 Ce 49.48N 0.29 E
Saint-Pierre et Miquelon 38 Ne 46.55N 56.10W
Saint-Pierre et Miquelon = Saint Pierre and Miquelon (EN) 39 Ne 46.55N 56.10W
Saint Pierre Island 37b Bb 9.19S 50.43 E
Saint-Pierre-sur-Dives 12 Be 49.01N 0.02W
Saint-Pol-de-Léon 11 Cf 48.41N 3.59W
Saint-Pol-sur-Mer 12 Ec 51.02N 2.21 E
Saint-Pol-sur-Ternoise 11 Id 50.23N 2.20 E
Saint-Pons 11 Ik 43.29N 2.46 E
Saint-Pourçain-sur-Sioule 11 Jh 46.18N 3.17 E
Saint-Quentin 11 Je 49.51N 3.17 E
Saint-Quentin, Canal de- 12 Fe 49.36N 3.11 E
Saint-Raphaël 11 Mk 43.25N 6.46 E
Saint-Rémy-de-Provence 11 Kk 43.47N 4.50 E
Saint-Rigaux, Mont- 11 Kh 46.12N 4.29 E
Saint-Riquier 12 Dd 50.08N 1.57 E
Saint Roch Basin 42 Ic 68.50N 95.00W
Saint Rogatien Bank (EN) 60 Mc 24.40N 167.10W
Saint-Romain-de-Colbosc 12 Ce 49.32N 0.22 E
Saint-Saëns 12 De 49.40N 1.17 E
Saint Sauflieu 12 Ee 49.47N 2.15 E
Saint-Savin 11 Gh 46.34N 0.52 E
Saint-Sébastien, Cap- 37 Hb 12.26S 48.44 E
Saint-Seine-l'Abbaye 11 Kg 47.26N 4.47 E
Saint-Servais, Namur- 12 Gd 50.28N 4.50 E
Saint Simon 12 Fe 49.45N 3.10 E
Saint Simons Island 44 Gj 31.14N 81.21W
Saint Stanislas Bay 64g Bb 1.53N 157.30W
Saint Stephen 42 Kg 45.12N 67.17W
Saint-Sylvain 12 Be 49.03N 0.13W
Saint Teresa Beach 44 Ek 29.58N 84.28W
Saint Thomas 44 Gd 42.47N 81.12W
Saint Thomas 47 Le 18.21N 64.55W
Saint-Trond/Sint-Truiden 11 Ld 50.49N 5.12 E
Saint-Tropez 11 Mk 43.16N 6.38 E
Saint-Tropez, Golfe de- 11 Mk 43.17N 6.38 E
Saint-Valéry-en-Caux 11 Ge 49.52N 0.44 E
Saint-Valery-sur-Somme 11 Hd 50.11N 1.38 E
Saint-Vallier 11 Ki 45.10N 4.49 E
Saint-Venant 12 Ed 50.37N 2.33 E
Saint Vincent 38 Be 45.45N 7.39 E
Saint Vincent 38 Mh 13.15N 61.12W
Saint-Vincent, Baie de- 63b Cf 22.00S 166.05 E
Saint Vincent, Cap- 30 Lk 21.57S 43.16 E
Saint Vincent, Gulf- 59 Hf 35.00S 138.05 E
Saint Vincent and the Grenadines 39 Mh 13.15N 61.12W
Saint-Vincent-de-Tyrosse 11 Ek 43.40N 1.18W
Saint Vincent Island 44 Ek 29.40N 85.07W
Saint Vincent Passage 50 Ff 13.30N 61.00W
Saint-Wandrille-Rançon 12 Ce 49.32N 0.46 E
Saint-Yrieix-la-Perche 11 Hi 45.31N 1.12 E
Saipan 64a Ad 6.54N 134.08 E
Saipan Channel 64b Ba 15.05N 145.41 E
Saipan Island 57 Fc 15.12N 145.45 E
Saira 55 Ak 32.24S 62.06W
Sairecabur, Cerro- 54 Eh 22.43S 67.54W
Saitama Ken 28 Of 36.00N 139.50 E
Saito 28 Kh 32.06N 131.24 E
Sajak 19 Hf 46.55N 77.22 E
Sajama 54 Eg 18.07S 69.00W
Sajama, Nevado de- 52 Jg 18.06S 68.54W
Sajānan 14 Dm 37.03N 9.14 E
Sajat 18 De 38.49N 63.51 E
Sajid 33 Hf 16.52N 41.55 E
Sajir, Ra's- 35 Ib 16.45N 53.35 E
Sajmenski Kanal = Saimaa Canal (EN) 8 Mc 61.05N 28.18 E
Sajn-Šand 22 Ne 44.55N 110.11 E
Sajó 10 Ri 47.56N 21.08 E
Sajószentpéter 10 Qh 48.13N 20.43 E
Sajram 18 Gc 42.18N 69.45 E
Sajzī 24 Of 32.41N 52.07 E
Saka 36 Gc 0.09S 39.20 E
Sakai 28 Mg 34.35N 135.28 E
Sakaide 29 Cd 34.19N 133.51 E
Sakaiminato 29 Cd 35.33N 133.15 E
Sakākah 23 Fd 29.59N 40.06 E
Sakakawea, Lake- 43 Gb 47.50N 102.20W
Sakala, Vozvyšennost-/Sakala Kõrgustik 8 Kf 58.00N 25.30 E
Sakala Kõrgustik/Sakala, Vozvyšennost- 8 Kf 58.00N 25.30 E
Sakami 42 Jf 53.18N 76.45W
Sakami, lac- 42 Jf 53.15N 76.45W
Sâkâne, 'Erg i-n- 34 Ea 20.40N 0.51W
Sakania 36 Ee 12.43S 28.33 E
Sakao 63b Cb 14.58S 167.07 E
Sakar 15 Jh 41.59N 26.16 E
Sakar 18 De 38.59N 63.45 E
Sakaraha 37 Gd 22.54S 44.32 E
Sakar-Čaga 18 Cf 37.39N 61.40 E
Sakārinah, Jabal as- 14 Do 35.45N 9.05 E
Sakartvelos Sabčata Socialisturi Respublica/Gruzinskaja SSR 19 Eg 42.00N 44.00 E
Sakarya 23 Da 41.07N 30.39 E
Sakata 27 Od 38.55N 139.50 E
Sakchu 28 Hd 40.23N 125.02 E
Sakhalin (EN) = Sahalin, Ostrov- 21 Qd 51.00N 143.00 E
Saki 16 Hg 45.07N 33.37 E
Šakiai/Šakjaj 7 Fi 54.57N 23.01 E
Sakishima Islands (EN) = Sakishima-Shotō 21 Og 24.30N 125.00 E
Sakishima-Shotō = Sakishima Islands (EN) 21 Og 24.30N 125.00 E
Sakito 29 Ae 33.02N 129.34 E
Sakiz Boğazı 15 Jk 38.20N 26.12 E
Šakjaj/Šakiai 7 Fi 54.57N 23.01 E
Sakmara 5 Le 51.46N 55.01 E
Sakon Nakhon 25 Ke 17.10N 104.01 E
Sakrivier 37 Cf 30.54S 20.28 E
Šakša 17 Hi 54.47N 56.15 E
Saksaulski 19 Gf 47.05N 61.13 E
Sakskøbing 8 Dj 54.48N 11.39 E
Saku 28 Of 36.09N 138.26 E
Sakuma 29 Ed 35.05N 137.47 E
Sakura 29 Gd 35.43N 140.13 E
Sakurai 29 Dd 34.31N 135.50 E
Sakura-Jima 29 Bf 31.35N 130.40 E
Säkylä 8 Jc 61.02N 22.20 E
Sal 30 Eg 16.45N 22.55W
Sal 19 Ef 47.31N 40.45 E
Sal, Cay- 49 Gb 23.42N 80.24W
Sal, Punta- 49 Df 15.53N 87.37W
Sala 35 Cb 17.00N 20.53 E
Šaľa 10 Nh 48.09N 17.53 E
Sala 7 Dg 59.55N 16.36 E
Salabangka, Kepulauan- 26 Hg 3.02S 122.25 E
Salaca 8 Kg 57.39N 24.15 E
Salacgriva/Salacgrīva 7 Fh 57.46N 24.27 E
Salacgrīva/Salacgriva 7 Fh 57.46N 24.27 E
Sala Consilina 14 Jj 40.23N 15.36 E
Salada 48 Hc 28.36N 103.28W
Salada, Laguna- 48 Ba 32.20N 115.40W
Saladas 56 Ic 28.15S 58.38W
Saladillo 56 Ie 35.38S 59.46W
Saladillo, Arroyo- 55 Bj 31.22S 60.30W
Saladillo Amargo, Arroyo- 55 Ci 31.01S 60.19W
Saladillo Dulce, Arroyo- 55 Bj 31.01S 60.19W
Salado, Arroyo- [Arg.] 55 Bm 36.27S 61.06W
Salado, Arroyo- [Mex.] 48 De 24.25N 111.30W
Salado, Riacho- 55 Ch 26.30S 58.18W
Salado, Rio- 55 Ci 34.16N 106.52W
Salado, Rio- 47 Ec 26.52N 99.19W
Salado, Rio- [Arg.] 52 Ji 31.42S 60.44W
Salado, Rio- [Arg.] 56 Ee 38.49S 64.57W
Salado, Rio- [Arg.] 52 Ki 35.44S 57.21W
Salado, Valle- 48 He 24.47N 102.50W
Salaga 34 Ed 8.33N 0.31W
Salagle 35 Ge 1.50N 42.18 E
Salāhuddīn 24 Je 34.40N 44.00 E
Salailua 65c Aa 13.41S 172.34W
Salairskij Krjaž 20 Df 54.00N 85.00 E
Šalaj 15 Fb 47.10N 23.00 E
Šalakuša 7 Je 62.15N 40.18 E
Salal 35 Bc 14.51N 17.13 E
Salālah [Oman] 22 Hh 17.05N 54.10 E
Salālah [Sud.] 35 Fa 21.19N 36.13 E
Salamá 49 Bf 15.06N 90.16W
Salamanca 13 Gd 40.50N 6.00W
Salamanca [Chile] 56 Fd 31.47S 70.58W
Salamanca [Mex.] 47 Dd 20.34N 101.12W
Salamanca [N.Y.-U.S.] 44 Hd 42.11N 78.43W
Salamanca [Sp.] 6 Fg 40.58N 5.39W
Salamat 35 Cc 11.00N 20.30 E
Salamat, Bahr- 35 Bd 9.27N 18.06 E
Salamina 49 Jh 10.30N 74.48W
Salamis 15 Gl 37.58N 23.29 E
Salamis 24 Ee 35.10N 33.54 E
Salamis 15 Gl 37.55N 23.30 E
Salang, Tünel-e- 23 Kb 35.19N 69.02 E
Salani 65c Bb 14.00S 171.34W
Salantai/Salantaj 8 Ih 56.05N 21.30 E
Salantaj/Salantai 8 Ih 56.05N 21.30 E
Salas 13 Fa 43.24N 6.16W
Salas de los Infant 13 Ib 42.01N 3.17W
Salat 64d Cb 7.14N 152.01 E
Salat 11 Gk 43.10N 0.58 E
Salatiga 26 Fh 7.19S 110.30 E
Salavat 6 Le 53.25N 55.58 E
Salawati, Pulau- 26 Jg 1.07S 130.52 E
Sala y Gómez 57 Qg 26.28S 105.28W
Sala y Gómez Ridge (EN) 3 Ml 25.00S 98.00W
Salazar 55 Am 36.18S 62.12W
Salbris 11 Ig 47.26N 2.03 E
Salcantay, Nevado de- 52 Ig 13.22S 72.34W
Šalčininkaj/Šalčininkai 8 Kj 54.18N 25.30 E
Šalčininkai/Šalčininkaj 8 Kj 54.18N 25.30 E
Salda Gölü 15 Ml 37.33N 29.42 E
Saldaña 13 Hb 42.31N 4.44W
Saldanha 31 Il 33.00S 17.56 E
Saldungaray 55 Bn 38.12S 61.47W
Saldus 19 Cd 56.40N 22.31 E
Sale 59 Jg 38.06S 147.04 E
Salé 32 Fc 34.04N 6.48W
Salebabu, Pulau- 26 If 3.55N 126.40 E
Šāleḥābād 24 Me 34.56N 48.20 E
Salehard 22 Ic 66.33N 66.40 E
Saleimoa 65c Ba 13.48S 171.52W
Salelologa 65c Aa 13.44S 172.10W
Salem [Fl.-U.S.] 44 Fk 29.58N 83.28W
Salem [Il.-U.S.] 45 Lg 38.38N 88.57W
Salem [India] 22 Jh 11.39N 78.10 E
Salem [In.-U.S.] 44 Df 38.36N 86.06W
Salem [Ma.-U.S.] 44 Ld 42.31N 70.55W
Salem [Mont.] 51c Bc 16.45N 62.13W
Salem [Mo.-U.S.] 45 Kh 37.39N 91.32W
Salem [N.J.-U.S.] 44 Jf 39.35N 75.28W
Salem [Oh.-U.S.] 44 Ge 40.54N 80.52W
Salem [Or.-U.S.] 39 Ge 44.57N 123.01W
Salem [S.D.-U.S.] 45 He 43.44N 97.23W
Salem [Va.-U.S.] 44 Gg 37.17N 80.03W
Salemi 14 Gm 37.49N 12.48 E
Sälen 8 Ec 61.10N 13.16 E
Salentine Peninsula (EN) = Penisola Salentina 5 Hg 40.30N 18.00 E
Sale Pit 9 Oh 53.40N 1.30 E
Salerno 6 Hg 40.41N 14.47 E
Salerno, Golfo di- 14 Ij 40.30N 14.40 E
Salers 11 Ii 45.08N 2.30 E
Salève, Mont- 11 Mh 46.07N 6.10 E
Salgir 16 Ig 45.38N 35.01 E
Salgótarján 10 Ph 48.07N 19.49 E
Salgueiro 54 Ke 8.04S 39.06W
Salher 25 Ed 20.41N 73.52 E
Salhus 7 Af 60.30N 5.16 E
Sali 14 Jg 43.56N 15.10 E
Šali 16 Nh 43.06N 45.56 E
Salice Terme 14 Df 44.55N 9.01 E
Salida 43 Fd 38.32N 106.00W
Salies-de-Béarn 11 Fk 43.29N 0.55W
Salihli 23 Cb 38.29N 28.09 E
Salima 36 Fe 13.47S 34.26 E
Salīma, Wāḥāt- = Salimah Oasis (EN) 31 Jf 21.22N 29.19 E
Salimah Oasis (EN) = Salīma, Wāḥāt- 31 Jf 21.22N 29.19 E
Salina 14 Il 38.35N 14.50 E
Salina [Ks.-U.S.] 39 Jf 38.50N 97.37W
Salina [Ut.-U.S.] 46 Jg 38.58N 111.51W
Salina Cruz 47 Ee 16.10N 95.12W
Salinas [Ca.-U.S.] 39 Gf 36.40N 121.38W
Salinas [Ec.] 54 Bd 2.13S 80.58W
Salinas [P.R.] 51a Bc 17.59N 66.17W
Salinas, Bahia de- 49 Eh 11.03N 85.43W
Salinas, Cabo de-/Ses Salines, Cap de- 13 Pe 39.16N 3.03 E
Salinas, Punta- [Dom.Rep.] 49 Ld 18.12N 70.34W
Salinas, Punta- [P.R.] 51a Bb 18.29N 66.10W
Salinas, Rio- 49 Be 16.28N 90.33W
Salinas de Hidalgo 48 If 22.38N 101.43W
Salinas Peak 45 Cj 33.18N 106.31W
Saline, Point- 50 Fg 12.00N 61.48W
Saline Island 51p Cb 12.26N 61.29W
Saline River [Ks.-U.S.] 45 Hg 38.51N 97.30W
Saline River [U.S.] 45 Jj 33.10N 92.08W
Salines, Pointe des- 51h Bc 14.24N 60.53W
Salinópolis 54 Id 0.37S 47.20W
Salins-les-Bains 11 Lh 46.57N 5.53 E
Salisbury 42 Jd 63.35N 77.00W
Salisbury [Dom.] 51g Bb 15.26N 61.27W
Salisbury [Eng.-U.K.] 9 Lj 51.05N 1.48W
Salisbury [Md.-U.S.] 43 Ld 38.22N 75.36W
Salisbury [N.C.-U.S.] 44 Gh 35.40N 80.29W
Salisbury Plain 9 Lj 51.15N 1.55W
Săliște 15 Gd 45.47N 23.53 E
Šalja 19 Fd 57.15N 58.43 E
Saljany 19 Eh 39.35N 48.59 E
Šalkar, Ozero- 16 Qd 50.35N 51.40 E
Šalkar-Jega-Kara, Ozero- 16 Vd 50.45N 60.55 E
Salkhad 24 Gf 32.29N 36.43 E
Salla 7 Gc 66.50N 28.40 E
Sallent de Gállego 13 Lb 42.46N 0.20W
Salling 8 Ch 56.40N 9.00 E
Salliqueló 56 He 36.45S 62.56W
Sallisaw 45 Ii 35.28N 94.47W
Salluit 39 Lc 62.12N 75.38W
Sallūm, Khalīj as- = Salum, Gulf of- (EN) 33 Ec 31.40N 25.20 E
Sallyana 25 Gc 28.22N 82.10 E
Salm 12 Ie 49.51N 6.51 E
Salmās 23 Fb 38.11N 44.47 E
Salmi 7 Hf 61.24N 31.54 E
Salmo 46 Gb 49.12N 117.17W
Salmon 43 Eb 45.11N 113.54W
Salmon Arm 42 Ff 50.42N 119.16W
Salmon Bank (EN) 60 Kb 26.56N 176.28W
Salmon Falls Creek Reservoir 46 He 42.05N 114.45W
Salmon Mountain 46 Hd 45.38N 114.50W
Salmon Mountains 46 Df 41.00N 123.00W
Salmon River 38 He 45.51N 116.46W
Salmon River Mountains 43 Dc 44.45N 115.30W
Salmtal 12 Ie 49.56N 6.48 E
Salmyš 16 Sc 52.01N 55.21 E
Salò 14 Ee 45.36N 10.31 E
Salo [C.A.R.] 35 Be 3.12N 16.07 E
Salo [Fin.] 7 Ff 60.23N 23.08 E
Salobra, Rio- 55 De 20.12S 56.29W
Salobreña 13 Ih 36.44N 3.35W
Salomon, Cape- 51h Ab 14.30N 61.06W
Salon-de-Provence 11 Lk 43.38N 5.06 E
Salonga 30 Ii 0.10S 19.50 E
Salonika (EN) = Thessaloniki 6 Ig 40.38N 22.56 E
Salonika, Gulf of- (EN) = Thermaikós Kólpos 5 Ig 40.20N 22.45 E
Salonta 15 Ec 46.48N 21.39 E
Salop 9 Ki 52.40N 2.50W
Salop 9 Ki 52.40N 2.50W
Salor 13 Ee 39.39N 7.03W
Salou 13 Nc 41.04N 1.08 E
Salouël 12 Ee 49.52N 2.15 E
Saloum 34 Bc 13.50N 16.45W
Salpausselkä 5 Ic 61.00N 26.30 E
Sal-Rei 32 Cf 16.11N 22.55W
Salsbruket 7 Cd 64.48N 11.52 E
Salseleh-ye Safīd Kūh/Paropamisus 21 If 34.30N 63.30 E
Salsipuedes, Canal de- 48 Cc 28.40N 113.00W
Salsipuedes, Punta- 49 Fi 8.28N 83.37W
Salsk 19 Ef 46.28N 41.29 E
Šalski 7 If 61.48N 36.03 E
Salso [It.] 14 Hm 37.06N 13.57 E
Salso [It.] 14 Im 37.39N 14.49 E
Salsola 14 Ji 41.37N 15.40 E
Salsomaggiore Terme 14 Df 44.49N 9.59 E
Salt 13 Oc 41.59N 2.47 E
Salta 56 Hb 25.00S 64.30W
Salta 53 Jh 24.47S 65.24W
Saltash 9 Ik 50.24N 4.12W
Salt Basin 45 Dk 31.50N 105.00W
Saltburn by the Sea 9 Mg 54.35N 0.58W
Salt Cay 49 Lc 21.20N 71.11W
Salt Creek 46 Gh 36.15N 116.49W
Salt Draw 45 Ek 31.19N 103.28W
Saltee Islands/Na Sailtí 9 Gi 52.07N 6.36W
Salten 7 Dc 67.45N 15.31 E
Salt Fork Arkansas River 45 Hh 36.36N 97.03W
Salt Fork Brazos 45 Gj 33.15N 100.00W
Salt Fork Red 45 Gi 34.30N 99.22W
Saltholm 8 Ei 55.40N 12.45 E
Saltillo 39 Ig 25.25N 101.01W
Salt Lake City 39 He 40.46N 111.53W
Salto 55 Dj 31.25S 57.00W
Salto 14 Gh 42.23N 12.54 E
Salto [Arg.] 56 Hd 34.17S 60.15W
Salto [Ur.] 53 Ki 31.23S 57.58W
Salto da Divisa 54 Kg 16.00S 39.57W
Salto Grande 55 Hf 22.54S 49.59W
Salton Sea 38 Hf 33.20N 115.50W
Salt River 43 Ee 33.23N 112.18W
Saltsjöbaden 8 He 59.17N 18.18 E
Saltvik 7 Ef 60.17N 20.03 E
Saluafata Harbour 65c Ba 13.55S 171.38W
Saluda 44 Ig 37.36N 76.36W
Salum, Gulf of- (EN) = Sallūm, Khalīj as- 33 Ec 31.40N 25.20 E
Saluzzo 14 Bf 44.39N 7.29 E
Salvación, Bahia- 56 Eh 50.55S 75.05W
Salvador [Braz.] 53 Mg 12.59S 38.31W
Salvador [Niger] 34 Ha 23.14N 12.05 E
Salvador, Lake- 45 Kl 29.45N 90.15W
Salvador Maza 56 Hb 22.10S 63.43W
Salvaterra de Magos 13 De 39.01N 8.48W
Salvatierra [Mex.] 48 Ig 20.13N 100.53W
Salvatierra [Sp.] 13 Jb 42.51N 2.23W
Salwa, Dawḥat as- 24 Nj 25.30N 50.40 E
Salwā Baḥrī 33 Fe 24.44N 32.56 E
Salween (EN) = Thanlwin 21 Lg 16.31N 97.37 E
Salyersville 44 Fg 37.45N 83.04W
Salza 14 Ic 47.40N 14.43 E
Salzach 10 Ih 48.12N 12.56 E
Salzburg 6 Hf 47.48N 13.02 E
Salzburg 14 Gc 47.20N 13.00 E
Salzburger Kalkalpen 14 Gc 47.35N 12.55 E
Salzgitter 10 Gd 52.05N 10.20 E
Salzkammergut 14 Hc 47.45N 13.30 E
Salzkotten 12 Kc 51.40N 8.36 E
Salzwedel 10 Hd 52.51N 11.09 E
Samadāy, Ra's- 24 Fj 25.00N 34.56 E
Samagaltaj 20 Ef 50.36N 95.03 E
Samaḥ [Lib.] 33 Cd 28.10N 19.10 E
Samaḥ [Sau.Ar.] 24 Kh 28.52N 45.30 E
Samaipata 54 Fg 18.09S 63.52W
Samalayuca 48 Fb 31.21N 106.28W
Samales Group 26 He 6.00N 121.45 E
Samalga Pass 40a Eb 52.48N 169.25W
Samālūṭ 33 Fd 28.18N 30.42 E
Samambaia, Rio- 55 Ff 22.45S 53.21W
Samaná 49 Md 19.13N 69.19W
Samaná, Bahia de- 47 Ke 19.10N 69.25W
Samaná, Cabo- 49 Md 19.18N 69.09W
Samana Cay 49 Kb 23.06N 73.42W
Samandaği 24 Fd 36.07N 35.56 E
Samangān 23 Kb 36.15N 67.40 E
Samani 27 Pc 42.07N 142.56 E
Samanli Dağlari 15 Mi 40.32N 29.10 E
Samar 21 Oh 12.00N 125.00 E
Samara [R.S.F.S.R.] 5 Le 53.10N 50.04 E
Samara [Ukr.-U.S.S.R.] 16 Ie 48.33N 35.12 E
Samarai 58 Gf 10.36S 150.39 E
Samarinda 22 Nj 0.30S 117.09 E
Samarkand 22 If 39.40N 66.58 E
Samarkandskaja Oblast 19 Gg 40.10N 66.20 E
Sāmarrā' 23 Fc 34.12N 43.52 E
Samar Sea 26 Hd 11.50N 124.32 E
Samaru 34 Gc 11.10N 7.38 E
Samatan 11 Gk 43.30N 0.56 E
Samate 26 Jg 0.58S 131.04 E
Samba [Zaire] 36 Ec 4.38S 26.22 E
Samba [Zaire] 36 Db 0.14N 21.19 E
Samba Caju 36 Cd 8.45S 15.25 E
Sambalpur 25 Gd 21.27N 83.58 E
Sambar, Tanjung- 26 Fg 2.59S 110.19 E
Sambas 26 Ef 1.20N 109.15 E
Sambava 37 Ib 14.15S 50.10 E
Sambor 11 Kd 50.28N 4.52 E
Sāmbhar 25 Fc 26.55N 75.12 E
Sambiase 14 Kl 38.58N 16.17 E
Samboja 26 Gg 1.02S 117.02 E
Sambor 19 Cf 49.32N 23.11 E
Samborombón, Bahia- 56 Ie 36.00S 57.12W
Samborombón, Rio- 55 Dl 35.43S 57.20W
Sambre 11 Kd 50.28N 4.52 E
Sambre à l'Oise, Canal de la- 11 Je 49.39N 3.20 E
Samburg 20 Cc 67.00N 78.25 E

Index Symbols

Independent Nation
State, Region
District, County
Municipality
Colony, Dependency
Continent
Physical Region
Historical or Cultural Region
Mount, Mountain
Volcano
Hill
Mountains, Mountain Range
Hills, Escarpment
Plateau, Upland
Pass, Gap
Plain, Lowland
Delta
Salt Flat
Valley, Canyon
Crater, Cave
Karst Features
Depression
Polder
Desert, Dunes
Forest, Woods
Heath, Steppe
Oasis
Cape, Point
Coast, Beach
Cliff
Peninsula
Isthmus
Sandbank
Island
Atoll
Rock, Reef
Islands, Archipelago
Rocks, Reefs
Coral Reef
Well, Spring
Geyser
River, Stream
Waterfall Rapids
River Mouth, Estuary
Lake
Salt Lake
Intermittent Lake
Reservoir
Swamp, Pond
Canal
Glacier
Ice Shelf, Pack Ice
Ocean
Sea
Gulf, Bay
Strait, Fjord
Lagoon
Bank
Seamount
Tablemount
Ridge
Shelf
Basin
Escarpment, Sea Scarp
Fracture
Trench, Abyss
National Park, Reserve
Point of Interest
Recreation Site
Cave, Cavern
Historic Site
Ruins
Wall, Walls
Temple
Scientific Station
Airport
Port
Lighthouse
Mine
Tunnel
Dam, Bridge

Samch'ŏk 27 Md 37.27N 129.10 E
Samch'ŏnp'o 27 Me 34.55N 128.04 E
Samdi Dağı 24 Kd 37.19N 44.15 E
Samdŏng-ni 28 Ie 39.21N 126.14 E
Samdŭng 28 Ie 38.59N 126.11 E
Same [Indon.] 26 Ih 8.59S 125.40 E
Same [Tan.] 36 Gc 4.04S 37.44 E
Samer 12 Dd 50.38N 1.45 E
Sam Ford Fiord 42 Kb 70.40N 70.35W
Samfya 36 Ee 11.20S 29.32 E
Šamhor 16 Oi 40.48N 46.01 E
Sāmi 15 Dk 38.15N 20.39 E
Sāmi Ghar 23 Kc 31.43N 67.01 E
Samīrah 24 Ji 26.18N 42.05 E
Samisu-Jima 27 Oe 31.40N 140.00 E
Şamli 15 Kj 39.48N 27.51 E
Samnah, Jabal- 24 Ei 26.26N 33.34 E
Samoa I Sisifo = Western Samoa (EN) [1] 58 Jf 13.40S 172.30W
Samoa Islands 57 Jf 14.00S 171.00W
Samobor 14 Je 45.48N 15.43 E
Samojlovka 16 Md 51.10N 43.43 E
Samokov 15 Gg 42.20N 23.33 E
Samolva 8 Lf 58.16N 27.45 E
Sámos 15 Jl 37.45N 26.58 E
Sámos 5 Ih 37.45N 26.48 E
Samosir, Pulau- 26 Cf 2.35N 98.50 E
Samothrace (EN) = Samothráki 15 Ii 40.27N 25.35 E
Samothráki 15 Ii 40.29N 25.31 E
Samothráki = Samothrace (EN) 15 Ii 40.27N 25.35 E
Sampacho 56 Hd 33.23S 64.43W
Sampaga 26 Gg 2.19S 119.07 E
Sampit 26 Fg 3.00S 113.03 E
Sampit 22 Nj 2.32S 112.57 E
Sampoku 29 Fb 38.30N 139.30 E
Sampwe 36 Ed 9.20S 27.23 E
Sam Rayburn Reservoir 45 Ik 31.27N 94.37W
Samro, Ozero- 8 Mf 58.55N 28.50 E
Samsjøen 8 Da 63.05N 10.40 E
Samsø 7 Ci 55.50N 10.35 E
Samsø Bælt 8 Di 55.50N 10.45 E
Sam Son 25 Ld 19.44N 105.54 E
Samsun 22 Fe 41.17N 36.20 E
Samsun Dağı 15 Kl 37.40N 27.15 E
Samtredia 16 Mh 42.11N 42.17 E
Samuel, Mount- 59 Gc 19.41S 134.09 E
Samuhú 55 Bh 27.31S 60.24W
Samui, Ko- 21 Li 9.30N 100.00 E
Samur 16 Pi 41.53N 48.32 E
Samur-Apšeronski Kanal 16 Pi 40.35N 49.35 E
Samus 20 De 56.46N 84.44 E
Samut Prakan 25 Kf 13.36N 100.36 E
Samut Sakhon 25 Kf 13.31N 100.15 E
San 31 Gg 13.08N 4.53W
San [Asia] 25 Lf 13.32N 105.57 E
San [Pol.] 10 Rf 50.45N 21.51 E
San'ā' 22 Gh 15.23N 44.12 E
Sana 14 Ke 45.03N 16.23 E
Sanaag [3] 35 Hc 10.10N 47.50 E
Şanabū 24 Di 27.30N 30.47 E
Sanae 66 Bf 70.18S 2.22W
Sanāfir 24 Fi 27.55N 34.42 E
Sanāg 35 Hd 7.45N 48.00 E
Sanaga 30 Hh 3.35N 9.38 E
San Agustin 55 Cn 38.01S 58.21W
San Agustín, Cabo- 48 Bc 28.05N 115.20W
San Agustin, Cape- 26 Ie 6.16N 126.11 E
Sanak Islands 40 Gf 54.25N 162.35W
Sanalona, Presa- 48 Fe 24.53N 107.00W
San Ambrosio, Isla- 56 Ec 26.21S 79.52W
Sanana 26 Ig 2.04S 125.08 E
Sanana, Pulau- 26 Ig 2.12S 125.55 E
Sanandaj 23 Gb 35.19N 47.00 E
San Andreas 46 Eg 38.12N 120.41W
San Andrés [3] 47 Hf 12.35N 81.42W
San Andres, Cerro- 48 Ih 19.48N 100.36W
San Andrés, Isla de- 52 Hd 12.32N 81.42W
San Andrés, Laguna de- 48 Kf 22.40N 97.50W
San Andrés de Giles 55 Cl 34.27S 59.27W
San Andrés del Rabanedo 13 Gb 42.37N 5.36W
San Andres Mountains 43 Fe 32.55N 106.45W
San Andres Peak 45 Cj 32.43N 106.30W
San Andrés Tuxtla 47 Ee 18.27N 95.13W
San Andrés y Providencia [2] 54 Ba 12.30N 81.45W
Sananduva 55 Gh 27.57S 51.48W
San Angelo 43 Ge 31.28N 100.26W
San Antonio [Blz.] 49 Ce 16.30N 89.02W
San Antonio [Chile] 56 Fd 33.35S 71.38W
San Antonio [Tx.-U.S.] 39 Jg 29.28N 98.31W
San Antonio [Ur.] 55 Dj 31.20S 57.45W
San Antonio, Cabo- [Arg.] 52 Ki 36.40S 56.42W
San Antonio, Cabo- [Cuba] 38 Kg 21.52N 84.57W
San Antonio, Cabo de-/Sant Antoni, Cap- 13 Mf 38.48N 0.12 E
San Antonio, Canal- 55 Aj 31.42S 62.15W
San Antonio, Punta- 48 Bc 29.45N 115.45W
San Antonio, Sierra de- 48 Db 30.00N 110.20W
San Antonio Abad 13 Nf 38.58N 1.18 E
San Antonio Bay 45 Hl 28.20N 96.45W
San Antonio de Caparo 49 Lj 7.35N 71.27W
San Antonio de Cortés 49 Cf 15.05N 88.04W
San Antonio de los Baños 49 Fb 22.53N 82.30W
San Antonio de los Cobres 56 Gb 24.11S 66.21W
San Antonio del Táchira 54 Db 7.50N 72.27W
San Antonio de Tamanaco 50 Ch 9.14N 66.03W
San Antonio Oeste 53 Jj 40.44S 64.57W
San Antonio River 43 Hf 28.30N 96.50W
Sanare 49 Mi 9.45N 69.39W
Sanary-sur-Mer 11 Lk 43.07N 5.48 E
San Augustin 53 Ie 1.53N 76.16W
San Augustine 45 Ik 31.32N 94.07W
Sanāw 35 Ib 17.50N 51.05 E
San Bartolomeo in Galdo 14 Ji 41.24N 15.01 E
San Baudilio de Llobregat/Sant Boi de Llobregat 13 Oc 41.21N 2.03 E
San Benedetto del Tronto 14 Hh 42.57N 13.53 E
San Benedetto Po 14 Ee 45.02N 10.55 E
San Benedicto, Isla- 47 Be 19.18N 110.49W
San Benito [Guat.] 49 Ce 16.55N 89.54W
San Benito [Tx.-U.S.] 45 Hm 26.08N 97.38W
San Benito, Islas- 48 Bc 28.20N 115.35W
San Benito Abad 49 Ji 8.56N 75.02W
San Benito Mountain 46 Eh 36.22N 120.38W
San Bernardino 39 Hf 34.06N 117.17W
San Bernardino, Passo del-/Sankt Bernardin Paß 14 Dd 46.30N 9.10 E
San Bernardino Mountains 46 Gi 34.10N 117.00W
San Bernardino Strait 26 Hd 12.32N 124.10 E
San Bernardo [Arg.] 55 Bh 27.17S 60.42W
San Bernardo [Chile] 56 Fd 33.36S 70.43W
San Bernardo [Mex.] 48 De 25.32N 111.45W
San Bernardo, Islas de- 49 Ji 9.45N 75.50W
San Bernardo, Punta de- 49 Ji 9.42N 75.42W
San Bernardo del Viento 54 Cb 9.22N 75.57W
San Blas [3] 49 Hi 7.50N 81.10W
San Blas [Mex.] 47 Cd 21.31N 105.16W
San Blas [Mex.] 47 Cc 26.05N 108.46W
San Blas [Mex.] 48 Id 27.25N 101.40W
San Blas, Archipiélago de- 49 Hi 9.30N 78.30W
San Blas, Cape- 43 Jf 29.40N 85.22W
San Blas, Cordillera de- 49 Hi 9.18N 79.00W
San Blas, Golfo de- 49 Hi 9.30N 79.00W
San Blas, Punta- 49 Hi 9.34N 78.58W
San Borja 54 Ef 14.49S 66.51W
San Borjas, Sierra de- 48 Cc 28.40N 113.45W
San Buenaventura 48 Id 27.05N 101.32W
Sancai 35 Fc 10.43N 35.40 E
San Carlos [Arg.] 55 Eh 27.45S 55.54W
San Carlos [Chile] 56 Fe 36.25S 71.58W
San Carlos [Mex.] 48 Je 24.35N 98.56W
San Carlos [Mex.] 48 Ic 29.01N 100.51W
San Carlos [Nic.] 49 Eh 11.07N 84.47W
San Carlos [Pan.] 49 Hi 8.29N 79.57W
San Carlos [Par.] 55 Df 22.16S 57.18W
San Carlos [Phil.] 26 Hd 10.30N 123.25 E
San Carlos [Phil.] 26 Hc 15.55N 120.20 E
San Carlos [Ur.] 56 Jd 34.48S 54.55W
San Carlos [Ven.] 54 Eb 9.40N 68.39W
San Carlos, Bahía- 48 Cd 27.55N 112.45W
San Carlos, Mesa de- 48 Bc 29.40N 115.25W
San Carlos, Punta- 48 Cc 28.00N 112.45W
San Carlos, Riacho- 55 Df 22.49S 57.53W
San Carlos, Rio- [C.R.] 49 Eh 10.47N 84.12W
San Carlos, Rio- [Ven.] 50 Bh 9.07N 68.25W
San Carlos de Bariloche 53 Ij 41.08S 71.15W
San Carlos de Bolívar 56 He 36.15S 61.06W
San Carlos de la Rápita/Sant Carles de la Ràpita 13 Md 40.37N 0.36 E
San Carlos del Zulia 54 Db 9.01N 71.55W
San Carlos de Rio Negro 54 Ec 1.55N 67.04W
San Carlos Reservoir 46 Jj 33.13N 110.24W
San Cataldo [It.] 14 Mj 40.23N 18.18 E
San Cataldo [It.] 14 Hm 37.29N 13.59 E
San Cayetano 55 Cn 38.20S 59.37W
Sancerre 11 Ig 47.20N 2.50 E
Sancerrois, Collines du- 11 Ig 47.20N 2.30 E
Sanchahe 28 Ib 44.59N 126.03 E
Sánchez 49 Md 19.14N 69.36W
Sánchez Magallanes 48 Mh 18.17N 93.59W
San Clemente [Ca.-U.S.] 43 De 33.26N 117.37W
San Clemente [Sp.] 13 Je 39.24N 2.26W
San Clemente del Tuyú 55 Dm 36.22S 56.43W
San Clemente Island 46 Fj 32.55N 118.30W
Sancois 11 Ih 46.50N 2.55 E
San Cosme 55 Ch 27.22S 58.31W
San Cristóbal [Arg.] 56 Hd 30.19S 61.14W
San Cristóbal [Bol.] 55 Ba 13.56S 61.50W
San Cristóbal [Cuba] 49 Fb 22.43N 83.03W
San Cristóbal [Dom.Rep.] 49 Ld 18.25N 70.06W
San Cristóbal [Mex.] 48 Li 17.49N 94.32W
San Cristóbal [Ven.] 53 Ie 7.46N 72.14W
San Cristobal, Baia de- 48 Bd 27.25N 114.40W
San Cristóbal, Isla- 52 Hf 0.50S 89.26W
San Cristóbal de las Casas 47 Fe 16.45N 92.38W
San Cristóbal Island 57 Hf 10.36S 161.45 E
San Cristóbal Verapaz 49 Bf 15.23N 90.24W
Sancti Spiritus 47 Id 21.56N 79.27W
Sancti Spiritus [3] 49 Hb 22.00N 79.30W
Sancy, Puy de- 11 Ii 45.32N 2.50 E
Sand 7 Bg 59.29N 6.15 E
Sand 37 Ed 22.25S 30.05 E
Sanda 29 Dd 34.53N 135.14 E
Sandai 26 Fg 1.15S 110.31 E
Sandakan 22 Ni 5.50N 118.07 E
Sandal, Baie de- 63b Ce 20.49S 167.10 E
Sandal, Ozero- 7 Ie 62.25N 34.10 E
Sandane 7 Bf 61.46N 6.13 E
Sandanski 15 Gh 41.34N 23.17 E
Sandaré 34 Cc 14.42N 10.18W
Sandared 8 Eg 57.43N 12.47 E
Sandarne 8 Gc 61.16N 17.10 E
Sanday 9 Kb 59.15N 2.30W
Sande 8 De 59.36N 10.12 E
Sandefjord 7 Cg 59.08N 10.14 E
Sandégué 34 Ed 7.59N 3.33W
Sandeid 7 Ag 59.33N 5.50 E
Sanders 46 Ki 35.13N 109.20W
Sanderson 43 Ge 30.09N 102.24W
Sandersville 44 Fi 32.59N 82.48W
Sandfontein 37 Bd 22.11S 19.58 E
Sandgate 12 Dc 51.04N 1.09 E
Sandhammaren 8 Fi 55.23N 14.12 E
Sandhamn 8 He 59.17N 18.55 E
Sand Hills 43 Gc 41.45N 102.00W
Sandia 54 Ef 14.17S 69.26W
Sandia Crest 45 Ci 35.13N 106.27W
San Diego [Bol.] 55 Bc 16.04S 60.28W
San Diego [Ca.-U.S.] 39 Hf 32.43N 117.09W
San Diego, Cabo- 52 Jk 54.38S 65.07W
Sandıklı 24 Dc 38.28N 30.17 E
San Dimitri Point 14 In 36.05N 14.05 E
Sand in Taufers / Campo Tures 14 Fd 46.55N 11.57 E
Sand Lake 45 Ia 50.05N 94.39W
Sand Mountain 44 Dh 34.20N 86.02W
Sandnes 7 Ag 58.51N 5.44 E
Sandnessjøen 7 Cc 66.01N 12.38 E
Sandoa 31 Ji 9.41S 22.52 E
Sandö bank 8 Hf 58.10N 19.15 E
Sandomierska, Kotlina- 10 Rf 50.30N 22.00 E
Sandomierz 10 Rf 50.41N 21.45 E
San Domino 14 Jh 42.05N 15.30 E
Sandoná 54 Cc 1.18N 77.28W
San Donà di Piave 14 Ge 45.38N 12.34 E
Sandoval, Boca de- 48 Ke 24.58N 97.32W
Sandover River 59 Hd 21.43S 136.32 E
Sandoway 25 Ie 18.28N 94.22 E
Sandown 9 Lk 50.39N 1.09W
Sand Point 40 Ge 55.20N 160.30W
Sandpoint 43 Db 48.16N 116.33W
Sandras Dağı 15 Ll 37.04N 28.51 E
Sandray 9 Fe 56.54N 7.25W
Sandspit 42 Ef 53.15N 131.50W
Sand Springs [Mt.-U.S.] 46 Lc 47.09N 107.27W
Sand Springs [Ok.-U.S.] 45 Hh 36.09N 96.07W
Sandstone [Austl.] 59 De 27.59S 119.17 E
Sandstone [Mn.-U.S.] 45 Jc 46.08N 92.52W
Sandu 27 Jf 26.08N 113.16 E
Sandusky [Mi.-U.S.] 44 Fd 43.25N 82.50W
Sandusky [Oh.-U.S.] 43 Kc 41.27N 82.42W
Sandveld 37 Cd 21.20S 20.10 E
Sandvig-Allinge 7 Di 55.15N 14.49 E
Sandvika 8 De 59.54N 10.31 E
Sandviken 7 Df 60.37N 16.46 E
Sandwich 9 Oj 51.17N 1.20 E
Sandwich Bay 42 Lf 53.35N 57.15W
Sandy 12 Bb 52.07N 0.17W
Sandy Cape [Austl.] 59 Ih 41.25S 144.45 E
Sandy Cape [Austl.] 57 Gg 24.40S 153.15 E
Sandy Desert 25 Cc 28.46N 62.30 E
Sandykači 19 Gh 36.32N 62.35 E
Sandy Lake 42 If 53.02N 92.55W
Sandy Lake 42 If 53.02N 93.14W
Sandy Point 44 Il 26.01N 77.24W
Sandy Point Town 50 Ed 17.22N 62.50W
Sandžak 15 Cf 43.10N 20.00 E
Sanem 12 He 49.33N 5.56 E
San Estanislao 56 Ib 24.39S 56.26W
San Esteban 49 Ef 15.17N 85.52W
San Esteban, Bahia de- 48 Ee 25.40N 109.15W
San Esteban, Isla- 48 Cc 28.42N 112.36W
San Esteban de Gormaz 13 Ic 41.35N 3.12W
San Felice Circeo 14 Hi 41.14N 13.05 E
San Felipe [Chile] 56 Fd 32.45S 70.44W
San Felipe [Col.] 54 Ec 1.55N 67.06W
San Felipe [Mex.] 47 Bb 31.00N 114.52W
San Felipe [Mex.] 48 Ig 21.29N 101.13W
San Felipe [Ven.] 54 Ea 10.20N 68.44W
San Felipe, Cayos de- 49 Fc 21.58N 83.30W
San Felipe, Cerro de- 13 Kd 40.24N 1.51W
San Felipe Creek 46 Hj 33.09N 115.46W
San Feliu de Guixols 13 Pc 41.47N 3.02 E
San Feliu de Llobregat/Sant Feliu de Llobregat 13 Oc 41.23N 2.03 E
San Felix, Isla- 56 Dc 26.17S 80.05W
San Fermin, Punta- 48 Bb 30.25N 114.40W
San Fernando [Chile] 56 Fd 34.35S 71.00W
San Fernando [Mex.] 48 Bb 29.59N 115.17W
San Fernando [Mex.] 47 Ed 24.51N 98.10W
San Fernando [Phil.] 26 Hc 16.37N 120.19 E
San Fernando [Phil.] 26 Hc 15.01N 120.41 E
San Fernando [Sp.] 13 Fh 36.28N 6.12W
San Fernando [Trin.] 54 Fa 10.17N 61.28W
San Fernando, Rio- [Bol.] 55 Cc 17.13S 58.23W
San Fernando, Rio- [Mex.] 48 Ke 24.55N 97.40W
San Fernando de Apure 53 Je 7.54N 67.28W
San Fernando de Atabapo 54 Ec 4.03N 67.42W
Sanford [Fl.-U.S.] 43 Kf 28.48N 81.16W
Sanford [Me.-U.S.] 44 Ld 43.26N 70.46W
Sanford [N.C.-U.S.] 44 Hh 35.29N 79.10W
Sanford, Mount- 40 Kd 62.13N 144.09W
San Francisco [Arg.] 56 Hd 31.26S 62.05W
San Francisco [Bol.] 55 Cc 17.42S 59.38W
San Francisco [Ca.-U.S.] 39 Gf 37.48N 122.24W
San Francisco [Pan.] 49 Gi 8.15N 80.58W
San Francisco, Isla- 48 De 24.50N 110.35W
San Francisco Bay 38 Gf 37.43N 122.17W
San Francisco Creek 45 El 29.53N 102.19W
San Francisco de Arriba 48 Hd 26.15N 102.50W
San Francisco de Bellocq 55 Bn 38.42S 60.01W
San Francisco de la Paz 49 Df 14.55N 86.14W
San Francisco del Laishi 55 Ch 26.14S 58.38W
San Francisco del Oro 47 Cc 26.52N 105.51W
San Francisco del Rincón 48 Ig 21.01N 101.51W
San Francisco de Macoris 47 Je 19.18N 70.15W
San Francisco Gotera 49 Cg 13.42N 88.06W
San Francisco Javier 13 Nf 38.42N 1.25 E
San Francisco Mountains 46 Kj 33.45N 109.00W
San Francisco River 46 Kj 32.59N 109.22W
San Fratello 14 Il 38.01N 14.36 E
San Gabriel 55 Di 28.58S 58.12W
San Gabriel, Punta- 48 Cc 28.25N 112.50W
San Gabriel Mountains 46 Gi 34.20N 117.45W
San Gallán, Isla- 54 Cf 13.50S 76.28W
Sangamon River 45 Kf 40.07N 90.20W
Sangar [Iran] 24 Md 37.08N 49.02 E
Sangar [R.S.F.S.R.] 22 Oc 63.55N 127.31 E
Sangatte 12 Dd 50.56N 1.45 E
San Gavino Monreale 14 Ck 39.33N 8.47 E
Sangay, Volcán- 52 If 2.00S 78.20W
Sange 36 Ed 7.02S 28.21 E
Sangeang, Pulau- 26 Gh 8.12S 119.04 E
San Gemini 14 Gh 42.37N 12.33 E
Sanger 46 Fh 36.42N 119.27W
Sangerhausen 10 He 51.28N 11.18 E
San Germán [Cuba] 49 Ic 20.36N 76.08W
San Germán [P.R.] 49 Nd 18.05N 67.03W
Sanggan He 28 Cd 40.24N 115.18 E
Sanggau 26 Ff 0.08N 110.36 E
Sangha 30 Ii 1.13S 16.49 E
Sangha [C.A.R.] [3] 35 Be 3.30N 16.00 E
Sangha [Con.] [3] 36 Cb 2.00N 15.00 E
Sangihe, Kepulauan- = Sangihe Islands (EN) 21 Oi 3.00N 125.30 E
Sangihe, Pulau- 26 If 3.35N 125.32 E
Sangihe Islands (EN) = Sangihe, Kepulauan- 21 Oi 3.00N 125.30 E
San Gil 54 Db 6.32N 73.08W
San Gimignano 14 Fg 43.28N 11.02 E
San Giovanni in Fiore 14 Kk 39.15N 16.42 E
San Giovanni in Persiceto 14 Ff 44.38N 11.11 E
San Giovanni Rotondo 14 Ji 41.42N 15.44 E
San Giovanni Valdarno 14 Fg 43.34N 11.32 E
Sangju 28 Jf 36.25N 128.10 E
Sāngli 22 Jh 16.52N 74.34 E
Sangmélima 34 He 2.56N 11.59 E
Sangoli 24 Pd 37.25N 54.35 E
San Gorgonio 38 Hf 34.05N 116.50W
San Gottardo/Sankt Gotthard = Saint Gotthard Pass (EN) 5 Gf 46.30N 8.30 E
Sangradouro Grande, Rio- 55 Dc 16.24S 57.10W
Sangre de Cristo Mountains 38 If 37.30N 105.15W
San Gregorio 55 Al 34.19S 62.02W
Sangre Grande 50 Fg 10.35N 61.07W
Sangri 27 Ff 29.20N 92.15 E
Sangro 14 Ih 42.14N 14.32 E
Sangue, Rio- 54 Gf 11.00S 58.40W
Sangüesa 13 Kb 42.35N 1.17W
Sanguinaires, Iles- 11 Ab 41.53N 8.35 E
San Gustavo 55 Cj 30.41S 59.23W
Sangyuan → Wuqiao 28 Df 37.38N 116.23 E
Sangzhi 27 Jf 29.23N 110.11 E
Sanhe [China] 28 Dd 40.00N 117.01 E
Sanhe [China] 27 La 50.30N 120.04 E
Sanhe-San 29 Cd 35.08N 132.37 E
Sanhezhen 28 Di 31.30N 117.15 E
San Hilario [Arg.] 55 Ch 26.02S 58.39W
San Hilario [Mex.] 48 De 24.22N 110.59W
San Hipolito, Bahia- 48 Cd 26.55N 113.55W
San Ignacio [Arg.] 55 Eh 27.16S 55.32W
San Ignacio [Blz.] 47 Ge 17.10N 89.04W
San Ignacio [Bol.] 54 Ef 14.53S 65.36W
San Ignacio [Bol.] 54 Fg 16.23S 60.59W
San Ignacio [Mex.] 48 Ff 25.55N 106.25W
San Ignacio [Mex.] 47 Bc 27.27N 112.51W
San Ignacio [Par.] 56 Ic 26.52S 57.03W
San Ignacio, Isla de- 48 Ee 25.25N 108.55W
San Ignacio, Laguna- 48 Cd 26.55N 113.15W
San Ildefonso, Cape- 26 Hc 16.02N 121.59 E
San Ildefonso, Cerro- 49 Cf 15.31N 88.17W
San Ildefonso o La Granja 13 Id 40.54N 4.00W
Saniquellie 34 Dd 7.22N 8.43W
San Isidro [Arg.] 56 Id 34.27S 58.30W
San Isidro [Phil.] 26 Hd 11.24N 124.21 E
San Isidro de El General 47 Hg 9.22N 83.42W
Sanīyah 24 If 33.49N 42.43 E
San Jacinto 49 Ji 9.50N 75.07W
San Jacinto Peak 46 Gj 33.49N 116.41W
San Jaime 55 Cj 30.20S 58.19W
San Javier [Arg.] 56 Id 30.35S 59.57W
San Javier [Chile] 56 Fe 35.36S 71.45W
San Javier [Sp.] 13 Lg 37.48N 0.51W
San Javier [Ur.] 55 Ck 32.41S 58.08W
San Javier, Rio- 55 Bj 31.30S 60.20W
San Jerónimo Taviche 48 Ki 16.44N 96.35W
Sanjiachang 27 Hg 24.45N 101.53 E
Sanjiaozhen → Haiyan 27 Hd 36.58N 100.50 E
Sanjō 28 Of 37.37N 138.57 E
San Joaquin 54 Ff 13.04S 64.49W
San Joaquin, Rio- 54 Ff 13.08S 63.41W
San Joaquin, Sierra de- 55 Eg 24.48S 56.00W
San Joaquin River 46 Eh 36.43N 121.50W
San Joaquin Valley 38 Gf 36.50N 120.10W
San Jon 45 Ei 35.06N 103.20W
San Jorge 56 Hd 31.54S 61.52W
San Jorge, Bahía de- 48 Cb 31.10N 113.15W
San Jorge, Golfe de-/Sant Jordi, Golf de- 13 Md 40.53N 1.00 E
San Jorge, Golfo- 52 Jj 46.00S 67.00W
San Jorge, Rio- 49 Ji 9.07N 74.44W
San Jorge, Serrania- 55 Be 20.21S 60.59W
San Jorge Island 63a Dc 8.27S 159.35 E
San José [2] 55 Dl 34.15S 56.45W
San José [3] 49 Ei 9.40N 84.00W
San José [Arg.] 55 Eh 27.46S 55.47W
San Jose [Ca.-U.S.] 39 Gf 37.20N 121.53W
San José [C.R.] 39 Ki 9.56N 84.05W
San José [Mex.] 48 Dd 27.32N 110.09W
San José [Par.] 55 Dg 25.33S 56.45W
San Jose [Phil.] 26 Hc 15.48N 121.00 E
San Jose [Phil.] 26 Hd 12.21N 121.04 E
San José, Isla- [Mex.] 47 Bc 25.00N 110.38W
San José, Isla- [Pan.] 49 Hi 8.15N 79.07W
San José, Salinas de- 55 Bd 19.07S 60.54W
San José, Serrania de- 55 Bc 17.52S 60.49W
San Jose de Buenavista 26 Hd 10.46N 122.30 E
San José de Chiquitos 54 Fg 17.51S 60.47W
San José de Feliciano 55 Cj 30.23S 58.45W
San José de Gracia 48 Fd 26.08N 107.58W
San José de Guanipa 54 Fb 8.54N 64.09W
San José de Jachal 56 Gd 30.14S 68.45W
San José de las Lajas 49 Fb 22.58N 82.09W
San José del Cabo 47 Cd 23.03N 109.41W
San José del Guaviare 53 Ie 2.35N 72.38W
San José del Rosario 55 Dg 24.12S 56.48W
San José de Mayo 56 Id 34.20S 56.42W
San José de Ocuné 54 Dc 4.15N 70.20W
San José de Tiznados 50 Ch 9.23N 67.33W
San Juan [2] 56 Gd 31.00S 69.00W
San Juan [Arg.] 53 Ji 31.30S 68.30W
San Juán [Bol.] 55 Cc 17.52S 59.59W
San Juán [Bol.] 55 Bd 18.08S 60.08W
San Juan [C.Amer.] 38 Kh 10.56N 83.42W
San Juan [Dom.Rep.] 47 Je 18.48N 71.14W
San Juan [P.R.] 39 Mh 18.28N 66.07W
San Juan [U.S.] 38 Hf 37.18N 110.28W
San Juan, Cabezas de- 51a Cb 18.23N 65.36W
San Juan, Cabo- 30 Hh 1.10N 9.21 E
San Juan, Muela de- 13 Kd 40.26N 1.44W
San Juan, Pico- 47 Hd 21.59N 80.09W
San Juan, Punta- 65d Ab 27.03S 109.22W
San Juan, Rio- [Arg.] 56 Gd 32.17S 67.22W
San Juan, Rio- [Mex.] 48 Jd 26.10N 99.00W
San Juan, Rio- [Mex.] 48 Lh 18.36N 95.40W
San Juan, Rio- [Ven.] 50 Eg 10.14N 62.39W
San Juan, Volcán- 48 Gg 21.30N 104.57W
San Juan Bautista [Par.] 56 Ic 26.38S 57.10W
San Juan Bautista [Sp.] 13 Ne 39.05N 1.30 E
San Juan Bautista Tuxtepec 48 Kh 18.06N 96.07W
San Juan de Colón 49 Ki 8.02N 72.16W
San Juan de Guadalupe 48 He 24.38N 102.44W
San Juan del César 49 Kh 10.46N 72.59W
San Juan de Lima, Punta- 48 Hh 18.36N 103.42W
San Juan del Norte 47 Hf 10.55N 83.42W
San Juan de los Cayos 54 Ea 11.10N 68.25W
San Juan de los Lagos 48 Hg 21.15N 102.14W
San Juan de los Morros 54 Ea 9.55N 67.21W
San Juan del Rio [Mex.] 48 Jg 20.29N 100.00W
San Juan del Rio [Mex.] 48 Ge 24.47N 104.27W
San Juan del Sur 47 Gf 11.15N 85.52W
San Juan de Payara 50 Ci 7.39N 67.36W
San Juanico, Isla- 48 Fg 21.55N 106.40W
San Juanico, Punta- 48 Cd 26.05N 112.15W
San Juan Island 46 Db 48.32N 123.05W
San Juan Mountains 43 Fd 37.35N 107.10W
San Juan Neembucú 55 Dh 26.39S 57.56W
San Juan Nepomuceno [Col.] 54 Cb 9.57N 75.05W
San Juan Nepomuceno [Par.] 55 Eh 26.06S 55.58W
San Juan y Martínez 49 Fb 22.16N 83.50W
San Julián 53 Jj 49.19S 67.40W
San Just, Sierra de- 13 Ld 40.46N 0.48W
San Justo 56 Hd 30.47S 60.35W
Sankarani 30 Gg 12.01N 8.19W
Sankt Anton am Arlberg 14 Ec 47.08N 10.16 E
Sankt Augustin 12 Jd 50.47N 7.11 E
Sankt Bernardin Paß/San Bernardino, Passo del- 14 Dd 46.30N 9.10 E
Sankt Gallen 14 Dc 47.25N 9.25 E
Sankt Gallen [2] 14 Dc 47.20N 9.10 E
Sankt Goar 10 Df 50.09N 7.43 E
Sankt Goarshausen 12 Jd 50.09N 7.44 E
Sankt Gotthard/San Gottardo = Saint Gotthard Pass (EN) 5 Gf 46.30N 8.30 E
Sankt Ingbert 10 Dg 49.17N 7.07 E
Sankt Johann im Pongau 14 Hc 47.21N 13.12 E
Sankt Michael im Lungau 14 Hc 47.06N 13.38 E
Sankt Michel/Mikkeli 6 If 61.41N 27.15 E
Sankt Moritz 14 Dd 46.30N 9.52 E
Sankt Peter-Ording 10 Eb 54.18N 8.38 E
Sankt Pölten 14 Jb 48.12N 15.38 E
Sankt Ulrich / Ortisei 14 Fd 46.34N 11.40 E
Sankt Veit an der Glan 14 Id 46.46N 14.22 E
Sankt-Vith 11 Md 50.17N 6.08 E
Sankt Wendel 10 Dg 49.28N 7.10 E
Sankt Wolfang im Salzkammergut 14 Hc 47.44N 13.27 E
Sankuru 30 Ji 4.17S 20.25 E
San Lázaro 56 Ib 22.10S 57.55W
San Lázaro, Cabo- 47 Bd 24.48N 112.19W
San Lazaro, Sierra de- 48 Df 23.25N 110.00W
San Leandro 46 Dh 37.43N 122.09W
San Lorenzo 47 Fe 17.44N 94.45W
San Lorenzo [Arg.] 55 Bk 32.45S 60.44W
San Lorenzo [Ec.] 53 Ie 1.17N 78.50W
San Lorenzo [Hond.] 49 Dg 13.25N 87.27W
San Lorenzo, Isla- [Mex.] 48 Cc 28.38N 112.51W
San Lorenzo, Isla- [Peru] 54 Cf 12.05S 77.15W
San Lorenzo, Rio- [Mex.] 48 Je 25.07N 98.32W
San Lorenzo, Rio- [Mex.] 48 Fe 24.15N 107.24W
San Lorenzo de El Escorial 13 Hd 40.35N 4.09W
San Louis Potosí [2] 47 Dd 22.30N 100.30W
Sanlúcar de Barrameda 13 Fh 36.47N 6.21W
Sanlúcar la Mayor 13 Fg 37.23N 6.12W
San Lucas [Mex.] 48 Gf 22.33N 104.24W
San Lucas [Mex.] 47 Cd 22.53N 109.54W
San Lucas, Cabo- 38 Ig 22.50N 109.55W
San Lucas, Serrania de- 54 Db 8.00N 74.20W
San Lucido 14 Kk 39.18N 16.03 E
San Luis [Arg.] 53 Ji 33.20S 66.20W
San Luis [2] 56 Gd 34.00S 66.00W
San Luis [Bol.] 55 Cc 17.39S 58.42W
San Luis [Cuba] 49 Jc 20.12N 75.51W
San Luis [Guat.] 49 Ce 16.14N 89.27W
San Luis [Mex.] 48 Dc 29.33N 111.05W
San Luis, Isla- 48 Bb 29.58N 114.26W
San Luis, Sierra de- 49 Mh 11.11N 69.42W
San Luis de la Paz 48 Ig 21.18N 100.31W
San Luis del Palmar 55 Ch 27.31S 58.34W
San Luis de Palenque 54 Db 5.25N 71.40W
San Luis Gonzaga, Bahia- 48 Bc 30.00N 114.25W
San Luis Obispo 39 Gf 35.17N 120.40W
San Luis Pass 45 Il 29.05N 95.08W
San Luis Peak 45 Ch 37.59N 106.56W
San Luis Potosí 39 Ig 22.09N 100.59W
San Luis Rio Colorado 47 Bb 32.29N 114.48W
San Luis Valley 43 Fd 37.25N 106.00W
Sanluri 14 Ck 39.34N 8.54 E
San Manuel [Arg.] 55 Cm 37.47S 58.50W
San Manuel [Az.-U.S.] 46 Jj 32.36N 110.38W

Index Symbols

[1] Independent Nation
[2] State, Region
[3] District, County
[4] Municipality
[5] Colony, Dependency
Continent
Physical Region
Historical or Cultural Region
Mount, Mountain
Volcano
Hill
Mountains, Mountain Range
Hills, Escarpment
Plateau, Upland
Pass, Gap
Plain, Lowland
Delta
Salt Flat
Valley, Canyon
Crater, Cave
Karst Features
Depression
Polder
Desert, Dunes
Forest, Woods
Heath, Steppe
Oasis
Cape, Point
Coast, Beach
Cliff
Peninsula
Isthmus
Sandbank
Island
Atoll
Rock, Reef
Islands, Archipelago
Rocks, Reefs
Coral Reef
Well, Spring
Geyser
River, Stream
Waterfall Rapids
River Mouth, Estuary
Lake
Salt Lake
Intermittent Lake
Reservoir
Swamp, Pond
Canal
Glacier
Ice Shelf, Pack Ice
Ocean
Sea
Gulf, Bay
Strait, Fjord
Lagoon
Bank
Seamount
Tablemount
Ridge
Shelf
Basin
Escarpment, Sea Scarp
Fracture
Trench, Abyss
National Park, Reserve
Point of Interest
Recreation Site
Cave, Cavern
Historic Site
Ruins
Wall, Walls
Church, Abbey
Temple
Scientific Station
Airport
Port
Lighthouse
Mine
Tunnel
Dam, Bridge

San Marcial, Punta- 48 De 25.30N 111.00W
San Marco, Capo- 14 Hm 37.30N 13.01 E
San Marcos [3] 49 Bf 15.00N 91.55W
San Marcos [Col.] 54 Cb 8.39N 75.08W
San Marcos [Guat.] 49 Bf 14.58N 91.48W
San Marcos [Hond.] 49 Cf 14.24N 88.56W
San Marcos [Mex.] 48 Gg 20.47N 104.11W
San Marcos [Mex.] 48 Ji 16.48N 99.21W
San Marcos [Nic.] 49 Dh 11.55N 86.12W
San Marcos [Tx.-U.S.] 43 Hf 29.53N 97.57W
San Marcos, Isla- 48 Cd 27.13N 112.06W
San Marcos, Sierra de- 48 Hd 26.30N 101.55W
San Marino 14 Gg 43.55N 12.28 E
San Marino [1] 6 Hg 43.55N 12.28 E
San Martin 56 Gd 33.04S 68.28W
San Martin 66 Qe 68.11S 67.00W
San Martin 48 Ab 30.30N 116.05W
San Martin [2] 54 Ce 7.00S 76.50W
San Martin, Cerro- 48 Lh 18.19N 94.48W
San Martin, Lago- 56 Fg 48.52S 72.40W
San Martin, Rio- 54 Ff 13.08S 63.43W
San Martin de los Andes 56 Ff 40.10S 71.21W
San Martin de Valdeiglesias 13 Hd 40.21N 4.24W
San Martino di Castrozza 14 Fd 46.16N 11.48 E
San Mateo [Ca.-U.S.] 46 Dh 37.35N 122.19W
San Mateo [Ven.] 50 Dh 9.45N 64.33W
San Mateo/Sant Mateu del Maestrat 13 Md 40.28N 0.11 E
San Mateo Ixtatán 49 Bf 15.50N 91.29W
San Mateo Mountains 45 Cj 33.10N 107.20W
San Matias 55 Cc 16.22S 58.24W
San Matías, Golfo- 52 Jj 41.30S 64.15W
Sanmen (Haiyou) 27 Lf 29.08N 121.22 E
Sanmen Wan 28 Fj 29.00N 121.45 E
Sanmenxia 27 Je 34.44N 111.19 E
San Miguel [Arg.] 55 Dh 27.59S 57.36W
San Miguel [Bol.] 55 Bc 16.42S 61.01W
San Miguel [Ca.-U.S.] 46 Ei 35.45N 120.42W
San Miguel [ElSal.] 39 Kh 13.29N 88.11W
San Miguel [Pan.] 49 Hi 8.27N 78.56W
San Miguel, Golfo de- 49 Hi 8.22N 78.17W
San Miguel, Río- [Bol.] 52 Jg 13.52S 63.56W
San Miguel, Río- [Mex.] 48 Dc 29.16N 110.53W
San Miguel, Río- [Mex.] 48 Fd 26.59N 107.58W
San Miguel, Río- [S.Amer.] 55 Cd 19.25S 58.20W
San Miguel, Salinas de- 55 Bd 19.12S 60.45W
San Miguel, Volcán de- 47 Gf 13.26N 88.16W
San Miguel Bay 26 Hd 13.50N 123.10 E
San Miguel de Allende 48 Ig 20.55N 100.45W
San Miguel de Horcasitas 48 Dc 29.29N 110.45W
San Miguel del Monte 55 Cl 35.27S 58.48W
San Miguel del Padrón 49 Fb 23.05N 82.19W
San Miguel de Tucumán 53 Jh 26.49S 65.13W
San Miguel Island 46 Ei 34.02N 120.22W
San Miguel Islands 26 Ge 7.45N 118.28 E
San Miguelito 55 Bc 17.20S 60.59W
San Miguel River 45 Bg 38.23N 108.48W
San Miguel Sola de Vega 48 Ki 16.31N 96.59W
San Millán 13 Ib 42.18N 3.12W
Sanming 27 Kf 26.11N 117.37 E
San Miniato 14 Eg 43.41N 10.51 E
Sannan 29 Dd 35.04N 135.03 E
Sannär 31 Kg 13.33N 33.38 E
Sannicandro Garganico 14 Ji 41.50N 15.34 E
San Nicolás, Río- [Bol.] 55 Bc 17.08S 61.17W
San Nicolás, Río- [Mex.] 48 Gh 19.40N 105.14W
San Nicolas de los Arroyos 56 Hd 33.20S 60.13W
San Nicolás de los Garzas 48 Ie 25.45N 100.18W
San Nicolas Island 46 Fj 33.15N 119.31W
Sannikova, Proliv- 20 Ib 74.30N 140.00 E
Sannio 14 Ii 41.20N 14.30 E
San'nohe 29 Ga 40.22N 141.15 E
San'nō-Tōge 29 Fc 37.06N 139.44 E
Sannūr, Wādī- 24 Dh 28.59N 31.03 E
Sanok 10 Sg 49.34N 22.13 E
Sanok-Zagórz 10 Sg 49.31N 22.17 E
San Onofre 54 Cb 9.45N 75.32W
San Pablo 22 Oh 14.04N 121.19 E
San Pablo, Punta- 48 Bd 27.15N 114.30W
San Pedro 56 Ib 24.07S 56.59W
San-Pédro 34 De 4.44N 6.37W
San Pedro [3] 55 Dg 24.15S 56.30W
San Pedro [Arg.] 56 Hb 24.14S 64.52W
San Pedro [Arg.] 55 Ck 33.40S 59.40W
San Pedro [Arg.] 56 Jc 26.38S 54.08W
San Pedro, Río- [Guat.] 49 Be 17.46N 91.26W
San Pedro, Río- [Mex.] 48 Gg 21.45N 105.30W
San Pedro, Sierra de- 13 Fe 39.20N 6.35W
San Pedro Carchá 49 Bf 15.29N 90.16W
San Pedro Channel 46 Fj 33.43N 118.23W
San Pedro de Alcántara 13 Hh 36.29N 5.00W
San Pedro de Atacama 56 Gb 22.55S 68.13W
San Pedro de Lloc 54 Ce 7.26S 79.31W
San Pedro de Macorís 49 Md 18.27N 69.18W
San Pedro Martir, Sierra de- 47 Ab 30.45N 115.13W
San Pedro Nolasco, Isla- 48 Dd 27.58N 111.25W
San Pedro Pochutla 48 Kj 15.44N 96.28W
San Pedros de las Colonias 47 De 25.45N 102.59W
San Pedro Sula 39 Kh 15.27N 88.02W
San Pedro Tapanatepec 48 Li 16.21N 94.12W
San Pedro Tututepec 48 Ki 16.09N 97.38W
San Pellegrino Terme 14 De 45.50N 9.40 E
San Pietro 14 Ck 39.10N 8.15 E
San Quentin, Bahía de- 48 Ab 30.20N 116.00W
San Quintin 47 Ab 30.29N 115.57W
San Rafael [Arg.] 53 Ji 34.40S 68.21W
San Rafael [Bol.] 55 Bc 16.45S 60.34W
San Rafael [Ca.-U.S.] 46 Dg 38.00N 122.31W
San Rafael [Mex.] 48 He 24.40N 102.01W
San Rafael [Mex.] 48 Ie 25.01N 100.33W
San Rafael [Ven.] 49 Lh 10.58N 71.44W
San Rafael, Cabo- 49 Md 19.01N 68.57W
San Rafael, Río- 55 Cd 18.26S 59.37W
San Rafael de Atamaica 50 Ci 7.32N 67.24W
San Rafael del Norte 49 Dg 13.12N 86.06W
San Rafael Knob 46 Jg 38.50N 110.48W
San Rafael Mountains 46 Fi 34.45N 119.50W
San Rafael River 46 Jg 38.47N 110.07W
San Ramón [Peru] 54 Cf 11.08S 75.20W
San Ramón [Ur.] 55 El 34.18S 55.58W
San Ramón, Río- 55 Bb 14.03S 61.35W
San Ramón de la Nueva Orán 56 Hb 23.08S 64.20W
San Raymundo, Arroyo- 48 Cd 26.21N 112.37W
San Remo 14 Bg 43.49N 7.46 E
Sanriku 29 Gb 39.08N 141.48 E
San Román, Cabo- 54 Ea 12.12N 70.00W
San Roque [Arg.] 55 Ci 28.34S 58.43W
San Roque [Sp.] 13 Gh 36.13N 5.24W
San Saba 45 Gk 31.12N 98.43W
Sansalé 34 Cc 11.07N 14.51W
San Salvador 13 Pe 39.27N 3.11 E
San Salvador [Arg.] 55 Di 29.16S 57.31W
San Salvador [Arg.] 56 Id 31.37S 58.30W
San Salvador [ElSal.] 39 Kh 13.42N 89.12W
San Salvador [Par.] 55 Dg 25.51S 56.28W
San Salvador (Watling) 47 Jd 24.02N 74.28W
San Salvador, Cuchilla- 55 Dk 33.56S 57.45W
San Salvador, Isla- 52 Gf 0.14S 90.45W
San Salvador, Río- 55 Ck 33.29S 58.23W
San Salvador de Jujuy 53 Jh 24.10S 65.20W
Sansanné-Mango 34 Fc 10.21N 0.28 E
San Sebastián [Col.] 49 Ji 9.13N 74.18W
San Sebastián [P.R.] 51a Bb 18.21N 67.00W
San Sebastián [Sp.] 6 Fg 43.19N 1.59W
San Sebastián, Bahía- 56 Gh 53.15S 68.23W
San Sebastián, Isla- 49 Cg 13.11N 88.26W
San Sebastián de la Gomera 32 Dd 28.06N 17.06W
Sansepolcro 14 Gg 43.34N 12.08 E
San Severo 14 Ji 41.41N 15.23 E
San Silvestre 49 Li 8.15N 70.02W
San Simeon 46 Ei 35.39N 121.11W
Sanski Most 14 Kf 44.46N 16.40 E
Santa Agueda 48 Cd 27.13N 112.20W
Santa Ana 63a Fd 10.50S 162.28 E
Santa Ana [Arg.] 55 Eh 27.22S 55.34W
Santa Ana [Bol.] 55 Bc 16.37S 60.43W
Santa Ana [Bol.] 54 Eg 15.31S 67.30W
Santa Ana [Bol.] 55 Cd 18.43S 58.44W
Santa Ana [Ca.-U.S.] 43 De 33.43N 117.54W
Santa Ana [ElSal.] 39 Kh 13.59N 89.34W
Santa Ana [Mex.] 47 Bb 30.33N 111.07W
Santa Ana [Ven.] 50 Dh 9.19N 64.39W
Santa Ana, Río- 49 Li 9.30N 71.57W
Santa Ana, Volcán de- 38 Kh 13.50N 89.39W
Santa Bárbara [3] 49 Cf 15.10N 88.20W
Santa Barbara 39 Hf 34.03N 118.15W
Santa Bárbara [Hond.] 49 Cf 14.53N 88.14W
Santa Bárbara [Mex.] 47 Cc 26.48N 105.49W
Santa Bárbara [Ven.] 49 Lj 7.47N 71.10W
Santa Bárbara, Puerto de- 13 Lb 42.30N 0.50W
Santa Bárbara, Serra de- 55 Fe 21.45S 53.23W
Santa Barbara Channel 46 Fi 34.15N 119.55W
Santa Catalina 63a Fd 10.54S 162.27 E
Santa Catalina [Col.] 49 Jh 10.37N 75.33W
Santa Catalina [Ven.] 50 Fh 8.33N 61.51W
Santa Catalina, Gulf of- 46 Gj 33.20N 117.45W
Santa Catalina, Isla- 48 De 25.40N 110.45W
Santa Catalina Island 46 Fj 33.23N 118.24W
Santa Catarina 48 Ie 25.41N 100.28W
Santa Catarina [2] 56 Kc 27.00S 50.00W
Santa Catarina, Ilha de- 52 Lh 27.36S 48.30W
Santa Catarina, Sierra- 48 Fc 29.40N 107.30W
Santa Cecilia 55 Gh 26.56S 50.27W
Santa Cesarea Terme 14 Mj 40.02N 18.28 E
Santa Clara [Ca.-U.S.] 46 Eh 37.21N 121.59W
Santa Clara [Cuba] 39 Lg 22.24N 79.58W
Santa Clara [Gabon] 36 Ab 0.34N 9.17 E
Santa Clara [Mex.] 48 Fc 29.17N 107.01W
Santa Clara [Ur.] 55 Ek 32.55S 54.58W
Santa Clara, Barragem do- 13 Dg 37.30N 8.20W
Santa Clara, Isla- 56 Ed 33.42S 79.00W
Santa Clara de Saguier 55 Bj 31.21S 61.50W
Santa Coloma de Farners/Santa Coloma de Farnés 13 Oc 41.52N 2.40 E
Santa Coloma de Farnés/Santa Coloma de Farners 13 Oc 41.52N 2.40 E
Santa Coloma de Gramanet 13 Oc 41.27N 2.13 E
Santa Coloma de Queralt 13 Nc 41.32N 1.23 E
Santa Comba 13 Da 43.02N 8.49W
Santa Croce Camerina 14 In 36.50N 14.31 E
Santa Cruz [Arg.] [2] 56 Gg 49.00S 70.00W
Santa Cruz [Azr.] 32 Bb 39.05N 28.01W
Santa Cruz [Azr.] 32 Ab 39.27N 31.07W
Santa Cruz [Bol.] 53 Jg 17.48S 63.10W
Santa Cruz [Bol.] [2] 54 Fg 17.30S 61.30W
Santa Cruz [Braz.] 54 Id 0.36S 49.11W
Santa Cruz [Braz.] 55 Dd 18.32S 57.12W
Santa Cruz [Ca.-U.S.] 43 Cd 36.58N 122.01W
Santa Cruz [Chile] 56 Fd 34.38S 71.22W
Santa Cruz [C.R.] 49 Eh 10.01N 84.02W
Santa Cruz [Phil.] 26 Hd 14.01N 121.21 E
Santa Cruz, Isla- 52 Gf 0.38S 90.23W
Santa Cruz, Isla de- 48 De 25.17N 110.43W
Santa Cruz, Río- 56 Gh 50.08S 68.20W
Santa Cruz, Serra da- 55 Jc 17.05S 45.17W
Santa Cruz Cabrália 54 Kg 16.17S 39.02W
Santa Cruz de la Palma 32 Dd 28.41N 17.45W
Santa Cruz de la Zarza 13 Ie 39.58N 3.10W
Santa Cruz del Quiché 49 Bf 15.02N 91.08W
Santa Cruz del Sur 47 Id 20.43N 78.00W
Santa Cruz de Mudela 13 If 38.38N 3.28W
Santa Cruz de Tenerife [3] 32 Dd 28.10N 17.20W
Santa Cruz de Tenerife 31 Ff 28.27N 16.14W
Santa Cruz do Rio Pardo 55 Hf 22.55S 49.37W
Santa Cruz do Sul 56 Jc 29.43S 52.26W
Santa Cruz Island 46 Fi 34.01N 119.45W
Santa Cruz Islands 57 Hf 10.45S 165.55 E
Santadi 14 Ck 39.05N 8.43 E
Santa Elena [Arg.] 55 Bm 37.21S 60.37W
Santa Elena [Arg.] 56 Id 30.57S 59.48W
Santa Elena [Ec.] 54 Bd 2.14S 80.52W
Santa Elena, Bahía de- [C.R.] 49 Eh 10.59N 85.50W
Santa Elena, Bahía de- [Ec.] 54 Bd 2.05S 80.55W
Santa Elena, Cabo- 47 Gf 10.55N 85.57W
Santa Elena de Uairén 54 Fc 4.37N 61.08W
Santa Eulalia 13 Kd 40.34N 1.19W
Santa Eulalia del Río 13 Nf 38.59N 1.31 E
Santa Fé 49 Fc 21.45N 82.45W
Santa Fe [2] 56 Hd 31.00S 61.00W
Santafé 13 Ig 37.11N 3.43W
Santa Fe [Arg.] 53 Ji 31.40S 60.40W
Santa Fe [N.M.-U.S.] 39 If 35.42N 106.57W
Santa Fé de Minas 55 Jc 16.41S 45.28W
Santa Fé do Sul 55 Ge 20.13S 50.56W
Sant'Agata di Militello 14 Il 38.04N 14.38 E
Santa Helena [Braz.] 55 Eg 24.56S 54.23W
Santa Helena [Braz.] 54 Id 2.14S 45.18W
Santa Helena de Goiás 54 Hg 17.43S 50.35W
Santa Inês 54 Id 3.39S 45.22W
Santa Inés 49 Mh 10.37N 69.18W
Santa Ines, Bahia- 48 Dd 27.00N 111.55W
Santa Inés, Isla- 52 Ik 53.45S 72.45W
Santa Isabel [Arg.] 55 Bk 33.54S 61.42W
Santa Isabel [Arg.] 56 Ge 36.15S 66.56W
Santa Isabel [Braz.] 55 Ba 13.40S 60.44W
Santa Isabel [P.R.] 51a Bc 17.58N 66.25W
Santa Isabel, Pico de- 34 Ge 3.35N 8.46 E
Santa Isabel Island 57 Ge 8.00S 159.00 E
Santa Izabel do Ivai 55 Ff 22.58S 53.14W
Santa Juliana 55 Id 19.19S 47.32W
Santa Lucia [Arg.] 56 Gd 31.32S 68.29W
Santa Lucia [Ur.] 55 Dl 34.27S 56.24W
Santa Lucia, Esteros del- 55 Ci 28.15S 58.20W
Santa Lucia, Río- [Arg.] 55 Ci 29.05S 59.13W
Santa Lucia, Río- [Ur.] 55 Dl 34.48S 56.22W
Santa Lucia Cotzumalguapa 49 Bf 14.20N 91.01W
Santa Lucia Range 43 Cd 36.00N 121.20W
Santa Luzia 32 Cf 16.46N 24.45W
Santa Luzia, Ribeirão- 55 Fe 21.31S 53.53W
Santa Margarita 55 Bi 28.18S 61.33W
Santa Margarita, Isla de- 47 Bd 24.27N 111.50W
Santa Margherita Ligure 14 Df 44.20N 9.12 E
Santa Maria [Braz.] 53 Kh 29.41S 53.48W
Santa Maria 30 Ee 36.58N 25.06W
Santa Maria [Ca.-U.S.] 43 Ce 34.57N 120.26W
Santa María 56 Gc 26.41S 66.02W
Santa Maria 47 Cb 31.00N 107.14W
Santa Maria 55 Bc 17.08S 61.01W
Santa María, Bahía de- 48 Ee 25.05N 108.10W
Santa Maria, Cabo de- [Ang.] 30 Ij 13.25S 12.32 E
Santa Maria, Cabo de- [Port.] 13 Eh 36.58N 7.54W
Santa Maria, Cape- 49 Jb 23.41N 75.19W
Santa María, Cayo- 49 Hb 22.40N 79.00W
Santa María, Isla- [Chile] 56 Fe 37.02S 73.33W
Santa María, Isla- [Ec.] 54a Ab 1.15S 90.25W
Santa María, Laguna de- 48 Fb 31.10N 107.15W
Santa María, Río- [Mex.] 48 Jg 21.37N 99.15W
Santa María, Río- [Pan.] 49 Gi 8.06N 80.29W
Santa Maria, Río- [Braz.] 55 Ee 21.50S 54.53W
Santa Maria, Río- [Braz.] 55 Ib 14.19S 46.49W
Santa María Asunción Tlaxiaco 48 Ki 17.16N 97.41W
Santa Maria Capua Vetere 14 Ii 41.05N 14.15 E
Santa Maria da Vitória 55 Ja 13.24S 44.12W
Santa Maria de Cuevas 48 Fd 27.55N 106.23W
Santa Maria de Ipire 50 Dh 8.49N 65.19W
Santa Maria del Oro 48 Ge 25.56N 105.22W
Santa Maria del Rio 48 Ig 21.48N 100.45W
Santa Maria di Leuca, Capo- 5 Hh 39.47N 18.22 E
Santa Maria la Real de Nieva 13 Hc 41.04N 4.24W
Santa Maria Zacatepec 48 Ki 16.46N 98.00W
Santa Marinella 14 Fh 42.02N 11.51 E
Santa Marta 53 Id 11.15N 74.13W
Santa Marta, Cabo de- 36 Be 13.52S 12.25 E
Santa Marta, Ria de- 13 Ea 43.42N 7.51W
Santa Marta Grande, Cabo de- 55 Hi 28.38S 48.45W
Santa Monica 43 De 34.01N 118.30W
Santan 26 Gg 0.03S 117.28 E
Santana 55 Ja 12.59S 44.03W
Santana, Coxilha de- 55 Ej 31.15S 55.15W
Santana, Rio- 55 Gd 19.43S 51.02W
Santana da Boa Vista 55 Fj 30.52S 53.07W
Santana do Livramento 56 Id 30.53S 55.31W
Santander [3] 13 Ia 43.10N 4.00W
Santander [2] 54 Db 6.35N 73.20W
Santander [Col.] 54 Cc 3.01N 76.29W
Santander [Phil.] 26 He 9.25N 123.20 E
Santander [Sp.] 6 Fg 43.28N 3.48W
Santander, Bahía de- 13 Ia 43.27N 3.48W
Santander Jiménez 47 Ed 24.13N 98.28W
Sant'Andrea 14 Lj 40.05N 17.55 E
Sant'Antioco 14 Ck 39.04N 8.27 E
Sant'Antioco 5 Gh 39.05N 8.25 E
Sant Antoni, Cap-/San Antonio, Cabo de- 13 Mf 38.48N 0.12 E
Santañy 13 Pe 39.22N 3.07 E
Santa Olalla 13 Hd 40.01N 4.26W
Santa Olalla del Cala 13 Fg 37.54N 6.13W
Santa Paula 46 Fi 34.21N 119.04W
Santa Pola 13 Lf 38.11N 0.33W
Sant'Arcangelo 14 Kj 40.15N 16.16 E
Santarcangelo di Romagna 14 Gf 44.04N 12.27 E
Santarém [2] 13 De 39.15N 8.35W
Santarém [Braz.] 53 Kf 2.26S 54.42W
Santarém [Port.] 13 De 39.14N 8.41W
Santaren Channel 47 Id 24.00N 79.30W
Santa Rita [Braz.] 55 Cc 16.15S 59.00W
Santa Rita [Col.] 54 Ec 4.55N 68.20W
Santa Rita [Guam] 64c Bb 13.23N 144.40 E
Santa Rita [Hond.] 49 Df 15.09N 87.53W
Santa Rita [Ven.] 50 Ch 8.08N 66.16W
Santa Rita [Ven.] 49 Lh 10.32N 71.32W
Santa Rita do Araguaia 55 Fc 17.20S 53.12W
Santa Rosa [3] 49 Bf 14.10N 90.18W
Santa Rosa [Arg.] 56 Gd 31.31S 65.04W
Santa Rosa [Arg.] 53 Ji 36.40S 64.15W
Santa Rosa [Braz.] 56 Jc 27.52S 54.29W
Santa Rosa [Ca.-U.S.] 43 Cd 38.26N 122.43W
Santa Rosa [Ec.] 54 Cd 3.27S 79.58W
Santa Rosa [N.M.-U.S.] 43 Ge 34.57N 104.41W
Santa Rosa [Par.] 55 Dh 26.52S 56.49W
Santa Rosa [Ven.] 49 Mi 8.26N 69.42W
Santa Rosa [Ven.] 50 Dh 9.38N 64.18W
Santa Rosa, Mount- 64c Ba 13.32N 144.55 E
Santa Rosa de Copán 49 Cf 14.47N 88.46W
Santa Rosa de la Roca 55 Bc 16.04S 61.32W
Santa Rosa Island 46 Ej 33.58N 120.06W
Santa Rosalia 39 Hg 27.19N 112.17W
Santa Rosalia 50 Bh 9.02N 69.01W
Santa Rosalia, Punta- 48 Bc 28.40N 114.20W
Santa Rosa Range 46 Gf 41.00N 117.40W
Santa Rosa Wash 46 Ij 33.10N 112.05W
Šantarskije Ostrova = Shantar Islands (EN) 21 Pd 55.00N 137.36 E
Santas Creus/Santes Creus 13 Nc 41.19N 1.18 E
Santa Sylvina 56 Hc 27.49S 61.09W
Santa Teresa [Arg.] 55 Bk 33.26S 60.47W
Santa Teresa [Mex.] 48 Ke 25.17N 97.51W
Santa Teresa [Peru] 54 Df 13.01S 72.39W
Santa Teresa, Rio- 55 Ha 12.40S 48.47W
Santa Teresa di Riva 14 Jm 37.57N 15.22 E
Santa Teresa Gallura 14 Di 41.14N 9.11 E
Santa Teresita 55 Dm 36.32S 56.41W
Santa Vitória do Palmar 56 Jd 33.31S 53.21W
Santa Vitória 55 Gd 18.50S 50.08W
Santa Barbara Island 46 Fj 33.23N 119.01W
Sant Boi de Llobregat/San Baudilio de Llobregat 13 Oc 41.21N 2.03 E
Sant Carles de la Ràpita/San Carlos de la Rápita 13 Md 40.37N 0.36 E
Santee River 43 Le 33.14N 79.28W
Santeh 24 Ld 36.10N 46.32 E
San Telmo 48 Ab 30.58N 116.06W
San Telmo, Bahía de- 48 Hh 18.45N 103.40W
San Telmo, Punta- 47 De 18.19N 103.30W
Santerno 14 Ff 44.34N 11.58 E
Santerre 11 Ie 49.55N 2.30 E
Santes Creus/Santas Creus 13 Nc 41.19N 1.18 E
Sant'Eufemia, Golfo di- 14 Kl 38.50N 16.05 E
Sant'Eufemia Lamezia 14 Kl 38.55N 16.15 E
Sant Feliu de Llobregat/San Feliu de Llobregat 13 Oc 41.23N 2.03 E
Santhià 14 Ce 45.22N 8.10 E
Santiago [2] 56 Fd 33.30S 70.50W
Santiago [Bol.] 54 Gg 18.19S 59.34W
Santiago [Bol.] 55 Bd 19.22S 60.51W
Santiago [Braz.] 56 Jc 29.11S 54.53W
Santiago [Chile] 53 Ii 33.27S 70.40W
Santiago [Dom.Rep.] 39 Lh 19.27N 70.42W
Santiago [Mex.] 48 Ie 25.25N 100.09W
Santiago [Mex.] 48 Cd 27.32N 112.49W
Santiago [Pan.] 39 Ki 8.05N 80.59W
Santiago [Par.] 55 Dh 27.09S 56.47W
Santiago, Cerro- 49 Gi 8.33N 81.44W
Santiago, Rio- 54 Cd 4.27S 77.36W
Santiago, Rio de- 48 Ge 25.11N 105.26W
Santiago, Serrania- 55 Cd 18.25S 59.25W
Santiago de Chuco 54 Ce 8.09S 78.11W
Santiago de Compostela 13 Db 42.53N 8.33W
Santiago de Cuba 39 Lg 20.01N 75.49W
Santiago de Cuba [3] 49 Ic 20.10N 76.10W
Santiago de la Ribera 13 Lg 37.48N 0.48W
Santiago del Estero 53 Jh 27.50S 64.15W
Santiago del Estero [2] 56 Hc 28.00S 63.30W
Santiago de Papasquiaro 48 Ge 25.03N 105.25W
Santiago do Cacém 13 Df 38.01N 8.42W
Santiago Ixcuintla 47 Cd 21.49N 105.13W
Santiago Mountains 45 El 29.40N 103.15W
Santiago Pinotepa Nacional 47 Ee 16.19N 98.01W
Santiaguillo, Isla- 48 Lh 19.05N 95.50W
Santiaguillo, Laguna de- 48 Ge 24.50N 104.50W
Santiam River 46 Dd 44.42N 123.55W
Santillana 13 Ha 43.23N 4.06W
San Timoteo 49 Li 9.48N 71.04W
Säntis 14 Dc 47.15N 9.20 E
Santisteban del Puerto 13 If 38.15N 3.12W
Sant Jordi, Golf de-/San Jorge, Golfe de- 13 Md 40.53N 1.00 E
Sant Mateu del Maestrat/San Mateo 13 Md 40.28N 0.11 E
Santo, Ile- 57 Hf 15.15S 166.50 E
Santo Anastácio 55 Ge 21.58S 51.39W
Santo André 55 If 23.40S 46.31W
Santo Ângelo 56 Jc 28.18S 54.16W
Santo Antão 30 Eg 17.05N 25.10W
Santo Antônio 56 Jc 26.03S 53.12W
Santo Antonio 34 Ge 1.39N 7.25 E
Santo Antônio de Jesus 54 Kf 12.58S 39.16W
Santo Antônio do Içá 54 Ed 3.05S 67.57W
Santo Antônio do Leverger 54 Gg 15.52S 56.05W
Santo Corazón 54 Gg 17.59S 58.51W
Santo Corazón, Rio- 55 Cc 17.23S 58.23W
Santo Domingo [Cuba] 49 Gb 22.35N 80.15W
Santo Domingo [Dom.Rep.] 39 Mh 18.28N 69.54W
Santo Domingo [Mex.] 48 Bb 30.43N 115.56W
Santo Domingo [Mex.] 48 Bc 28.12N 114.02W
Santo Domingo [Mex.] 48 If 23.20N 101.44W
Santo Domingo [Nic.] 49 Eg 12.16N 85.05W
Santo Domingo, Cay- 49 Jc 21.42N 75.46W
Santo Domingo, Punta- 48 Cd 26.20N 112.40W
Santo Domingo, Rio- [Mex.] 48 Kh 18.10N 96.08W
Santo Domingo, Rio- [Ven.] 49 Mi 8.01N 69.33W
Santo Domingo de la Calzada 13 Jb 42.26N 2.57W
Santo Domingo de los Colorados 54 Cd 0.15S 79.10W
Santo Domingo de Silos 13 Ic 41.58N 3.25W
Santo Domingo Pueblo 45 Ci 35.31N 106.22W
San Tomé 50 Dh 8.58N 64.08W
Santoña 13 Ia 43.27N 3.27W
Santos 53 Lh 23.57S 46.20W
Santos, Sierra de los- 13 Gf 38.15N 5.20W
Santos Dumont 55 Ke 21.28S 43.34W
Santos Unzué 55 Bl 35.45S 60.51W
Santo Tirso 13 Dc 41.21N 8.28W
Santo Tomás [Bol.] 55 Cc 17.46S 58.55W
Santo Tomás [Mex.] 48 Ab 31.33N 116.24W
Santo Tomás [Nic.] 49 Eg 12.04N 85.05W
Santo Tomás, Punta- 48 Ab 31.34N 116.42W
Santo Tomé 56 Ic 28.33S 56.03W
Santu Lussurgiu 14 Cj 40.08N 8.39 E
Santurce-Antiguo 13 Ia 43.20N 3.02W
Sanuki-Sanmyaku 29 Cd 34.05N 134.00 E
San Valentin, Cerro- 52 Ij 46.36S 73.20W
San Vicente [Arg.] 55 Cl 35.01S 58.25W
San Vicente [Mex.] 48 Ab 31.20N 116.15W
San Vicente [Phil.] 26 Hc 18.30N 122.09 E
San Vicente, Sierra de- 13 Hd 40.10N 4.45W
San Vicente de Cañete 54 Cf 13.05S 79.24W
San Vicente de la Barquera 13 Ha 43.26N 4.24W
San Vicente del Caguán 54 Dc 2.07N 74.46W
San Vicente de Raspeig 13 Lf 38.24N 0.31W
San Vincente 47 Gf 13.38N 88.48W
San Vincenzo 14 Eg 43.06N 10.32 E
San Vito [C.R.] 49 Fi 8.50N 82.58W
San Vito [It.] 14 Dk 39.26N 9.32 E
San Vito, Capo- 14 Gl 38.11N 12.44 E
Sanya→Yaxian 22 Mh 18.27N 109.28 E
Sanyati 37 Dc 16.49S 28.45 E
San'yō 29 Bd 34.03N 131.10 E
Sanza 14 Jj 40.15N 15.33 E
Sanza Pombo 36 Cd 7.20S 16.00 E
São Bartolomeu, Rio- 55 Ic 16.48S 47.55W
São Benedito 54 Jd 4.03S 40.53W
São Bento 54 Jd 2.42S 44.50W
São Bento do Sul 55 Hh 26.15S 49.23W
São Borja 56 Ic 28.39S 56.00W
São Brás de Alportel 13 Eg 37.09N 7.53W
São Caetano do Sul 56 Kb 23.36S 46.34W
São Carlos [Braz.] 56 Kb 22.01S 47.54W
São Carlos [Braz.] 55 Ej 33.47N 55.30W
São Domingos [Braz.] 55 Ia 13.24S 46.19W
São Domingos [Gui.Bis.] 34 Bc 12.24N 16.12W
São Domingos, Rio- [Braz.] 55 Fe 20.03S 53.13W
São Domingos, Rio- [Braz.] 55 Ia 13.24S 47.12W
São Domingos, Rio- [Braz.] 55 Gd 19.13S 50.44W
São Domingos, Rio- [Braz.] 55 Ib 15.37S 46.14W
São Felix 54 Hf 11.36S 50.39W
São Félix do Xingu 54 He 6.38S 51.59W
São Filipe 32 Cf 14.54N 24.31W
São Francisco [Braz.] 54 Jg 15.57S 44.52W
São Francisco [Braz.] 55 Dd 18.45S 56.55W
São Francisco, Ilha de- 52 Lh 26.18S 48.37W
São Francisco, Rio- 52 Mg 10.30S 36.24W
São Francisco de Assis 55 Ei 29.33S 55.08W
São Francisco de Paula 55 Gi 29.27S 50.35W
São Francisco de Sales 55 Hd 19.52S 49.46W
São Francisco do Sul 56 Kc 26.14S 48.39W
São Gabriel 56 Jd 30.20S 54.19W
São Gonçalo 54 Jh 22.51S 43.04W
São Gonçalo, Canal de- 55 Fk 32.10S 52.38W
São Gonçalo do Abaete 55 Jd 18.20S 45.49W
São Gonçalo do Sapucaí 55 Je 21.54S 45.36W
São Gotardo 55 Id 19.19S 46.03W
Sao Hill 36 Gd 8.20S 35.12 E
São Jerônimo, Serra de- 55 Ec 16.20S 54.55W
São João da Barra 54 Jh 21.38S 41.03W
São João da Boa Vista 55 Ie 21.58S 46.47W
São João d'Aliança 55 Ib 14.42S 47.31W
São João da Madeira 13 Dd 40.54N 8.30W
São João da Ponte 55 Kb 15.56S 44.01W
São João del Rei 54 Jh 21.09S 44.16W
São João de Meriti 55 Kf 22.48S 43.22W
São João do Araguaia 54 Ie 5.23S 48.46W
São João do Piauí 54 Je 8.21S 42.15W
São João dos Patos 54 Je 6.30S 43.42W
São João do Triunfo 55 Gg 25.41S 50.18W
São Joaquim 56 Kc 28.18S 49.56W
São Joaquim da Barra 55 Ie 20.35S 47.53W
São Jorge 30 Ee 38.38N 28.03W
São José da Serra 55 Eb 15.40S 55.18W
São José do Cerrito 55 Gh 27.40S 50.35W
São José do Norte 55 Fk 32.01S 52.03W
São José do Rio Pardo 56 Kb 21.36S 46.54W
São José do Rio Prêto 53 Lh 20.48S 49.23W
São José dos Campos 56 Kb 23.11S 45.53W
São José dos Dourados, Rio- 55 Ge 20.22S 51.21W
Saolat, Buku- 26 If 0.45N 127.59 E
São Leopoldo 56 Jc 29.46S 51.09W
São Lourenço 55 Ec 16.32S 55.02W
São Lourenço, Pantanal de- 54 Gg 17.45S 56.15W
São Lourenço, Rio- 54 Gg 17.53S 57.27W
São Lourenço, Serra de- 55 Ec 17.30S 54.50W
São Lourenço do Sul 56 Jd 31.22S 51.58W
São Luís 53 Lf 2.31S 44.16W
São Luís Gonzaga 56 Jc 28.24S 54.58W
São Mamede, Serra de- 13 Ee 39.19N 7.19W
São Manuel 55 Hf 22.44S 48.34W
São Marcos 55 Gi 28.58S 51.04W
São Marcos, Baía de- 52 Lf 2.30S 44.30W
São Marcos, Rio- 55 Id 18.15S 47.37W
São Mateus [Braz.] 54 Kg 18.44S 39.51W
São Mateus [Braz.] 55 Gg 25.52S 50.23W

Index Symbols

[1] Independent Nation
[2] State, Region
[3] District, County
[4] Municipality
[5] Colony, Dependency
Continent
Physical Region
Historical or Cultural Region
Mount, Mountain
Volcano
Hill
Mountains, Mountain Range
Hills, Escarpment
Plateau, Upland
Pass, Gap
Plain, Lowland
Delta
Salt Flat
Valley, Canyon
Crater, Cave
Karst Features
Depression
Polder
Desert, Dunes
Forest, Woods
Heath, Steppe
Oasis
Cape, Point
Coast, Beach
Cliff
Peninsula
Isthmus
Sandbank
Island
Atoll
Rock, Reef
Islands, Archipelago
Rocks, Reefs
Coral Reef
Well, Spring
Geyser
River, Stream
Waterfall Rapids
River Mouth, Estuary
Lake
Salt Lake
Intermittent Lake
Reservoir
Swamp, Pond
Canal
Glacier
Ice Shelf, Pack Ice
Ocean
Sea
Gulf, Bay
Strait, Fjord
Lagoon
Bank
Seamount
Tablemount
Ridge
Shelf
Basin
Escarpment, Sea Scarp
Fracture
Trench, Abyss
National Park, Reserve
Point of Interest
Recreation Site
Cave, Cavern
Historic Site
Ruins
Wall, Walls
Church, Abbey
Temple
Scientific Station
Airport
Port
Lighthouse
Mine
Tunnel
Dam, Bridge

Name	Page	Grid	Lat.	Long.
São Mateus, Rio-	55	Ia	13.48S	46.54W
São Miguel	30	Ee	37.47N	25.30W
São Miguel, Rio-	55	Ic	16.03S	46.07W
São Miguel do Araguaia	55	Ga	13.19S	50.13W
São Miguel d'Oeste	55	Fh	26.45S	53.34W
Saona, Isla-	49	Md	18.09N	68.40W
Saône	5	Gf	45.44N	4.50 E
Saône-et-Loire [3]	11	Kh	46.40N	4.30 E
Saonek	26	Jg	0.28S	130.47 E
São Nicolau	30	Eg	16.35N	24.15W
São Nicolau [Braz.]	55	Ei	28.11S	55.16W
São Patricio, Rio-	55	Hb	15.02S	49.15W
São Paulo	53	Lh	23.32S	46.37W
São Paulo [2]	56	Kb	22.00S	49.00W
São Paulo de Olivença	54	Ed	3.27S	68.48W
São Pedro, Ribeirão	55	Ic	16.54S	46.32W
São Pedro do Sul [Braz.]	55	Ei	29.37S	54.10W
São Pedro do Sul [Port.]	13	Dd	40.45N	8.04W
São Pedro e São Paulo, Penedos de-	52	Ne	0.56N	29.22W
São Raimundo Nonato	54	Je	9.01S	42.42W
São Romão [Braz.]	55	Ed	18.33S	54.27W
São Romão [Braz.]	54	Ig	16.22S	45.04W
São Roque	55	De	21.43S	57.46W
São Roque, Cabo de-	52	Mf	5.29S	35.16W
São Roque, Serra de-	55	Ib	14.40S	46.50W
São Sebastião	55	Jf	23.48S	45.25W
São Sebastião, Ilha de-	52	Lh	23.50S	45.18W
São Sebastião, Ponta-	30	Kk	22.05S	35.24 E
São Sebastião da Boa Vista	54	Id	1.42S	49.31W
São Sebastião do Paraiso	54	Ih	20.55S	47.00W
São Sepé	55	Fj	30.10S	53.34W
São Simão	54	Hg	18.56S	50.30W
São Tiago	30	Eg	15.05N	23.40W
São Tomé	30	Hh	0.12N	6.39 E
São Tomé	31	Hh	0.20N	6.44 E
São Tomé, Cabo de-	54	Jh	22.00S	40.59W
Sao Tome and Principe (EN) = São Tomé e Principe [1]	31	Hh	1.00N	7.00 E
São Tomé e Principe = Sao Tome and Principe (EN) [1]	31	Hh	1.00N	7.00 E
Saoura	32	Gd	27.50N	2.50W
Saoura	30	Gf	28.48N	0.50W
São Vicente	30	Eg	16.50N	25.00W
São Vicente [Braz.]	55	Ia	13.38S	46.31W
São Vicente [Braz.]	56	Kb	23.58S	46.23W
São Vicente, Cabo de-	5	Fh	37.01N	9.00W
São Xavier, Serra de-	55	Ei	29.15S	54.15W
Sápai	15	Ih	41.02N	25.42 E
Sapanca	15	Ni	40.41N	30.16 E
Sapanca Gölü	15	Ni	40.43N	30.15 E
Sape [Braz.]	54	Ke	7.06S	35.13W
Sape [Indon.]	26	Gh	8.34S	118.59 E
Sape, Selat-	26	Gh	8.39S	119.18 E
Sapele	34	Gd	5.55N	5.42 E
Sapelo Island	44	Gj	31.28N	81.15W
Şaphane	15	Mj	39.01N	29.14 E
Şaphane Dağı	15	Mj	39.03N	29.16 E
Sapiéntza	15	Em	36.45N	21.42 E
Šapkina	17	Fc	66.44N	52.25 E
Sapo, Serrania del-	49	Hi	7.50N	78.17W
Saponé	34	Ec	12.03N	1.36W
Sapopema	55	Gf	23.55S	50.35W
Saposoa	54	Ce	6.56S	76.48W
Sapphire Mountains	46	Ic	46.20N	113.45W
Sapporo	22	Qe	43.03N	141.21 E
Sapri	14	Jj	40.04N	15.38 E
Sapucaí, Rio-	55	He	20.08S	48.27W
Sapulpa	43	Hd	36.00N	96.06W
Sapulut	26	Gf	4.42N	116.29 E
Sāqiyat Sīdī Yūsuf	14	Cn	36.13N	8.21 E
Saqqez	23	Gb	36.14N	46.16 E
Sarāb	23	Gb	37.56N	47.32 E
Saraburi	25	Kf	14.30N	100.55 E
Saraf Doungous	35	Bc	12.33N	19.42 E
Sarafjagān	24	Ne	34.28N	50.28 E
Saragmatha = Everest, Mount- (EN)	21	Kg	27.59N	86.56 E
Saragossa (EN) = Zaragoza [Sp.]	6	Fg	41.38N	0.53W
Sarai	7	Jj	53.44N	41.03 E
Sarajevo	6	Hg	43.50N	18.25 E
Saraji Mine	59	Jd	22.30S	148.20 E
Sarakhs	23	Jb	36.32N	61.11 E
Sarakiná	15	Hk	38.40N	24.37 E
Šarakol	17	Kj	52.03N	62.47 E
Saraktaš	19	Fe	51.47N	56.18 E
Saraland	44	Cj	30.49N	88.02W
Saramati	25	Jc	25.44N	95.02 E
Saran	19	Hf	49.46N	72.52 E
Saran, Gunung-	26	Fg	0.25S	111.18 E
Saranac Lake	44	Jc	44.20N	74.08W
Saranci	15	Gg	42.43N	23.46 E
Saranda	15	Cj	39.52N	20.00 E
Sarandi	55	Fh	27.56S	52.55W
Sarandí, Arroyo-	55	Cj	30.13S	59.19W
Sarandí del Yí	55	Ek	33.21S	55.38W
Sarandí Grande	55	Dk	33.44S	56.20W
Šaranga	7	Lh	57.12N	46.34 E
Sarangani Bay	26	Ie	5.57N	125.11 E
Sarangani Islands	26	Ie	5.25N	125.26 E
Saranley	35	Ge	2.23N	42.16 E
Saransk	6	Ke	54.11N	45.11 E
Sarapul	6	Ld	56.28N	53.48 E
Sarapulskoje	20	Ig	48.50N	135.58 E
Sarare	49	Mi	9.47N	69.10W
Sararé, Rio-	55	Cb	14.51S	59.58W
Sarasota	43	Kf	27.20N	82.34W
Sarata	16	Ff	46.01N	29.41 E
Sărăţel	15	Kb	47.03N	27.25 E
Saratoga	46	Lf	41.27N	106.48W
Saratoga Springs	43	Mc	43.04N	73.47W
Saratok	26	Ff	1.24N	111.31 E
Saratov	6	Ke	51.34N	46.02 E
Saratov Reservoir (EN) = Saratovskoje Vodohranilišče	5	Ke	52.50N	47.50 E
Saratovskaja Oblast [3]	19	Ee	51.30N	47.00 E
Saratovskoje Vodohranilišče = Saratov Reservoir (EN)	5	Ke	52.50N	47.50 E
Saravan	25	Le	15.43N	106.25 E
Sarawak [2]	26	Ff	2.30N	113.30 E
Saray	24	Bb	41.26N	27.55 E
Saraya	34	Cc	12.50N	11.45W
Sarāyā	24	Fe	35.47N	35.58 E
Sarayköy	24	Cd	37.55N	28.56 E
Sarbāz	23	Jd	26.39N	61.15 E
Sárbogárd	10	Oj	46.53N	18.38 E
Sarca	14	Ee	45.52N	10.52 E
Sarcelle, Passe de la-	63b	Cf	22.28S	167.13 E
Sarcelles	12	Ef	49.00N	2.23 E
Sarcidano	14	Dk	39.40N	9.15 E
Sardara	14	Ck	39.37N	8.49 E
Sar Dasht [Iran]	24	Mf	32.32N	48.52 E
Sar Dasht [Iran]	24	Kd	36.09N	45.28 E
Sardegna [2]	14	Cj	40.00N	9.00 E
Sardegna = Sardinia (EN)	5	Gh	40.00N	9.00 E
Sardegna, Mar di-	14	Bk	40.00N	7.30 E
Sardes	15	Lk	38.29N	28.03 E
Sardinal	49	Eh	10.31N	85.39W
Sardinata	54	Db	8.07N	72.48W
Sardinia (EN) = Sardegna	5	Gh	40.00N	9.00 E
Sardis Lake	45	Li	34.27N	89.43W
Sarektjåkkå	7	Dc	67.25N	17.46 E
Sarema/Saaremaa	5	Id	58.25N	22.30 E
Sar-e Pol	23	Kb	36.14N	65.55 E
Sar Eskand Khān	24	Ld	37.29N	47.04 E
Sar-e Yazd	24	Pg	31.36N	54.35 E
Sargasso Sea	38	Mg	29.00N	65.00W
Sargatskoje	19	Hd	55.37N	73.30 E
Sargodha	25	Eb	32.05N	72.40 E
Šargun	18	Fe	38.31N	67.59 E
Sarh	31	Ih	9.09N	18.23 E
Sarhe	11	Fg	47.30N	0.32W
Sarhro, Jebel-	32	Fc	31.00N	6.00W
Sāri [Iran]	22	Hf	36.34N	53.04 E
Sāri [Iraq]	24	Je	34.42N	42.44 E
Sariá	15	Kn	35.50N	27.15 E
Sariçakaya	24	Db	40.02N	30.31 E
Sarigan Island	57	Fc	16.42N	145.47 E
Sarigöl	24	Cc	38.14N	28.43 E
Sarıkamış	24	Jb	40.15N	42.35 E
Sarıkaya	24	Fc	39.48N	35.24 E
Sarikei	26	Ff	2.07N	111.31 E
Sariköy	15	Ki	40.12N	27.36 E
Sarina	59	Jd	21.26S	149.13 E
Sarine	14	Bd	46.59N	7.16 E
Sariñena	13	Lc	41.48N	0.10W
Sarıoğlan	24	Fc	39.05N	35.59 E
Sarīr	33	Dd	27.30N	22.30 E
Sariwŏn	27	Md	38.30N	125.45 E
Sarıyer	24	Cb	41.10N	29.03 E
Sarj, Jabal as-	14	Do	35.56N	9.32 E
Šarja	6	Kd	58.24N	45.30 E
Sark	9	Kl	49.26N	2.21W
Sarkad	10	Rj	46.45N	21.23 E
Sarkand	19	Hf	45.25N	79.54 E
Şarkikaraağaç	24	Dc	38.04N	31.23 E
Sarkışla	24	Gc	39.21N	36.26 E
Šarkovščina	8	Li	55.22N	27.32 E
Sarköy	24	Bb	40.37N	27.06 E
Sarlat-la-Canéda	11	Hj	44.53N	1.13 E
Šarlyk	16	Sc	52.54N	54.42 E
Sarmi	58	Ee	1.51S	138.44 E
Sarmiento	53	Jj	45.35S	69.05W
Sarmizegetuza	15	Fd	45.31N	22.47 E
Särna	8	Ec	61.41N	13.08 E
Sarnen	14	Cd	46.54N	8.15 E
Sărnena Gora	15	Ig	42.35N	25.30 E
Sarnia	42	Jh	42.58N	82.23W
Sarny	19	Ce	51.21N	26.36 E
Saroako	26	Hg	2.31S	121.22 E
Sarolangun	26	Dg	2.18S	102.42 E
Saroma	29a	Ca	44.02N	143.45 E
Saroma-Ko	28	Qb	44.10N	143.40 E
Šaromy	20	Kf	54.23N	158.14 E
Saronic Gulf (EN) = Saronikós Kólpos	15	Gl	37.45N	23.30 E
Saronikós Kólpos = Saronic Gulf (EN)	15	Gl	37.45N	23.30 E
Saronno	14	De	45.38N	9.02 E
Saros, Gulf of- (EN) = Saros Körfezi	24	Bb	40.30N	26.20 E
Saros Körfezi = Saros, Gulf of- (EN)	24	Bb	40.30N	26.20 E
Sárospatak	10	Rh	48.19N	21.35 E
Sar Passage	64a	Ac	7.12N	134.23 E
Sarpinskije Ozera	16	Nf	47.45N	45.00 E
Šar Planina	15	Dg	42.05N	20.50 E
Sarpsborg	8	De	59.17N	11.07 E
Sarqaq	41	Gd	70.00N	51.39W
Sarrabus	14	Dk	39.20N	9.30 E
Sarralbe	11	Ne	49.00N	7.01 E
Sarrāt, Wādī-	14	Co	35.59N	8.23 E
Sarre	10	Cg	49.42N	6.34 E
Sarrebourg	11	Nf	48.44N	7.03 E
Sarreguemines	11	Ne	49.06N	7.03 E
Sarre-Union	12	Jf	48.56N	7.05 E
Sarria	13	Eb	42.47N	7.24W
Sarstún, Rio-	49	Cf	15.54N	88.54W
Sartang	20	Ic	67.30N	133.20 E
Sartène	11a	Ab	41.37N	8.59 E
Sarthe [3]	11	Gf	48.00N	0.05 E
Sartu → Anda	28	Ha	46.35N	125.00 E
Sarufutsu	29a	Ca	45.18N	142.13 E
Saru-Gawa	29a	Cb	42.30N	142.00 E
Saruhanlı	24	Bc	38.44N	27.34 E
Sarukaishi-Gawa	29	Gb	39.25N	141.08 E
Sārūq	24	Me	34.25N	49.30 E
Saruyama-Misaki	29	Ec	37.18N	136.43 E
Sárvár	10	Mi	47.15N	16.56 E
Sarvestān	24	Oh	29.16N	53.13 E
Sárvíz	10	Oj	46.22N	18.48 E
Saryagač	18	Gd	41.28N	69.11 E
Sarybarak	18	Hc	43.24N	71.29 E
Sary-Bulak	18	Jd	41.54N	75.47 E
Saryč, Mys-	5	Jg	44.23N	33.45 E
Saryg-Sep	20	Ef	51.30N	95.40 E
Sary-Išikotrau	18	Kb	45.15N	76.25 E
Sarykamys	19	Ff	46.00N	53.41 E
Sarykamyšskoje, Ozero-	19	Fg	41.58N	57.58 E
Sarykolski Hrebet	18	Je	38.30N	74.15 E
Šaryn-Gol	27	Ib	49.20N	106.30 E
Saryozek	19	Hg	44.22N	77.54 E
Saryšagan	19	Hf	46.05N	73.38 E
Saryšiganak, Zaliv-	18	Ca	46.35N	61.25 E
Sarysu	21	Ie	45.12N	66.36 E
Sary-Taš	19	Hh	39.44N	73.16 E
Saryžaz	18	Lc	42.54N	79.31 E
Sarzana	14	Df	44.07N	9.58 E
Sasabe	48	Db	31.27N	111.31W
Sasabeneh	35	Gd	8.00N	43.44 E
Sasa-ga-Mine	29	Ce	33.49N	133.17 E
Sasago-Tōge	29	Fd	35.37N	138.45 E
Sasamungga	63a	Cb	7.02S	156.47 E
Sasarām	25	Gd	24.57N	84.02 E
Sasari, Mount-	63a	Dc	8.11S	159.33 E
Sascut	15	Kc	46.11N	27.04 E
Sásd	10	Oj	46.15N	18.07 E
Sasebo	27	Me	33.12N	129.44 E
Saseginaga, Lac-	44	Hb	47.05N	78.34W
Saskatchewan [3]	42	Gf	54.00N	106.00W
Saskatchewan	38	Jd	53.12N	99.16W
Saskatoon	39	Id	52.07N	106.38W
Saskylah	20	Gb	72.00N	114.00 E
Saslaya, Cerro-	49	Eg	13.45N	85.03W
Sasovo	19	Ee	54.22N	41.54 E
Sassafras Mountain	44	Fh	35.03N	82.48W
Sassandra	30	Gh	4.58N	6.05W
Sassandra [3]	34	Dd	5.20N	6.10W
Sassandra	31	Gh	4.57N	6.05W
Sassari	6	Gg	40.43N	8.34 E
Sassenberg	12	Kc	51.59N	8.03 E
Sassenheim	12	Gb	52.14N	4.33 E
Sassetot-le-Mauconduit	12	Ce	49.48N	0.32 E
Saßnitz	10	Jb	54.31N	13.39 E
Sasso Marconi	14	Ff	44.24N	11.15 E
Sassuolo	14	Ef	44.33N	10.47 E
Sastobe	18	Hc	42.34N	70.03 E
Sastre	55	Bj	31.45S	61.50W
Sasyk, Ozero- (Kunduk)	16	Fg	45.45N	29.40 E
Sasykkol, Ozero-	19	If	46.40N	81.00 E
Sata	29	Bf	31.04N	130.42 E
Sata, Cape- (EN) = Sata Misaki	21	Pf	30.59N	130.37 E
Satakunta	8	Jc	61.30N	23.00 E
Sata-Misaki = Sata, Cape- (EN)	21	Pf	30.59N	130.37 E
Satan, Pointe de-	63b	Dd	19.00S	169.17 E
Sātāra	25	Ee	17.41N	73.59 E
Sataua	65c	Aa	13.28S	172.40W
Satawal Island	57	Fd	7.21N	147.02 E
Satawan Atoll	57	Gd	5.25N	153.35 E
Satellite Bay	42	Fa	77.25N	117.15W
Säter	7	Df	60.21N	15.45 E
Satihaure	7	Ec	67.30N	18.45 E
Satipo	54	Df	11.16S	74.37W
Satīt	35	Fc	14.20N	35.50 E
Satka	19	Fd	55.03N	59.01 E
Šatki	7	Ki	55.11N	44.08 E
Sātmāla Range	25	Fe	19.30N	78.45 E
Satna	25	Gd	24.35N	80.50 E
Šator	14	Kf	44.09N	16.37 E
Sátoraljaújhely	10	Rh	48.24N	21.40 E
Sātpura Range	21	Jg	21.25N	76.10 E
Satsuma-Hantō	29	Bf	31.25N	130.25 E
Satsunai-Gawa	29a	Cb	42.55N	143.15 E
Satsunan-Shotō	27	Mf	29.00N	130.00 E
Sattahip	25	Kf	12.39N	100.54 E
Satulung	15	Gb	47.34N	23.26 E
Satu Mare	15	Fb	47.48N	22.53 E
Satu Mare [2]	15	Fb	47.46N	22.56 E
Satun	25	Kg	6.39N	100.03 E
Saturniná ou Papagaio, Rio-	55	Ca	13.55S	58.18W
Saualpe	14	Id	46.50N	14.40 E
Sauce	56	Ic	30.00S	58.46W
Sauce Corto, Arroyo-	55	Bm	36.55S	61.48W
Sauceda Mountains	46	Ij	32.30N	112.30W
Sauce Grande, Río-	55	Bn	38.59S	61.07W
Saucillo	47	Cc	28.01N	105.17W
Sauda	8	Be	59.39N	6.20 E
Saudade, Serra da- [Braz.]	55	Jd	19.20S	45.50W
Saudade, Serra da- [Braz.]	55	Fc	16.20S	53.53W
Saudarkrókur	7a	Bb	65.45N	19.39W
Saudi Arabia (EN) = Al 'Arabīyah As-Su'ūdīyah [1]	22	Gg	25.00N	45.00 E
Sauer [Eur.]	10	Cg	49.44N	6.31 E
Sauer [Fr.]	12	Kf	48.55N	8.10 E
Sauerland	10	De	51.10N	8.00 E
Sauêruiná, Rio-	54	Gf	12.00S	58.40W
Sauga Jōgi	8	Kf	58.19N	24.25 E
Saugatuck	44	Dd	42.40N	86.12W
Saugues	11	Jj	44.58N	3.33 E
Sauk Centre	45	Id	45.44N	94.57W
Sauk Rapids	45	Id	45.34N	94.09W
Saül	54	Hc	3.37N	53.12W
Šaulder	18	Gc	42.47N	68.24 E
Sauldre	11	Hg	47.16N	1.30 E
Saulieu	11	Kg	47.16N	4.14 E
Saulkrasti/Saulkrasty	7	Fh	57.17N	24.29 E
Saulkrasty/Saulkrasti	7	Fh	57.17N	24.29 E
Saulnois	12	If	48.52N	6.30 E
Sault	11	Lj	44.05N	5.25 E
Sault Sainte Marie [Mi.-U.S.]	43	Kb	46.30N	84.21W
Sault Sainte Marie [Ont.-Can.]	39	Ke	46.31N	84.20W
Saumarez Reefs	57	Gg	21.50S	153.40 E
Saumâtre, Étang-	49	Kd	18.35N	72.00W
Saumlaki	26	Jh	7.57S	131.19 E
Saumur	11	Fg	47.16N	0.05W
Saunders	66	Ad	57.47S	26.27W
Saunders Coast	66	Mf	77.45S	150.00W
Saurimo	31	Ji	9.38S	20.24 E
Sauro	14	Kj	40.18N	16.21 E
Sautar	36	Ce	11.09S	18.25 E
Sauteurs	51p	Bb	12.14N	61.38W
Sauveterre, Causse de-	11	Jj	44.22N	3.17 E
Sauveterre-de-Guyenne	11	Fj	44.42N	0.05W
Sauvo/Sagu	8	Jd	60.21N	22.42 E
Sauwald	14	Hb	48.28N	13.40 E
Sava	5	Ig	44.50N	20.28 E
Savage River	59	Jh	41.33S	145.09 E
Savai'i Island	57	Jf	13.35S	172.25W
Savala	16	Ld	51.06N	41.29 E
Savalou	34	Fd	7.56N	1.58 E
Savanes [3]	34	Fc	10.30N	0.30 E
Savan Island	51n	Bb	12.48N	61.12W
Savanna	45	Ke	42.05N	90.08W
Savannah	38	Kf	32.02N	80.53W
Savannah [Ga.-U.S.]	39	Kf	32.04N	81.05W
Savannah [Tn.-U.S.]	44	Ch	35.14N	88.14W
Savannah Beach	44	Gi	32.01N	80.51W
Savannakhét	22	Mh	16.33N	104.45 E
Savanna-la-Mar	47	Ie	18.13N	78.08W
Savanne	45	Kb	48.59N	90.12W
Savannes Bay	51k	Bb	13.45N	60.56W
Savant Lake	42	If	50.15N	90.42W
Savant Lake	45	Ka	50.30N	90.20W
Savaştepe	24	Bc	39.22N	27.40 E
Savdirī	35	Dc	14.25N	29.05 E
Savé	31	Hh	8.02N	2.29 E
Save [Afr.]	30	Kk	21.00S	35.02 E
Save [Fr.]	11	Hk	43.47N	1.17 E
Saveån	8	Dg	57.43N	11.59 E
Sāveh	23	Hb	35.01N	50.20 E
Săveni	15	Jb	47.57N	26.52 E
Saverdun	11	Hk	43.14N	1.35 E
Saverne	11	Nf	48.44N	7.22 E
Savigliano	14	Bf	44.38N	7.40 E
Savigsivik	41	Fc	76.00N	64.45W
Săvineşti	15	Jc	46.51N	26.28 E
Savinjske Alpe	14	Id	46.20N	14.30 E
Savinski	19	Ec	62.57N	40.13 E
Savio	14	Gf	44.19N	12.20 E
Săvîrşin	15	Fc	46.01N	22.14 E
Savitaipale	7	Gf	61.12N	27.42 E
Šavnik	15	Cg	42.57N	19.06 E
Savo	63a	Dc	9.08S	159.48 E
Savo	8	Lb	62.30N	27.30 E
Savoie [3]	11	Mi	45.30N	6.25 E
Savoie = Savoy (EN)	11	Mi	45.24N	6.30 E
Savona	14	Cf	44.17N	8.30 E
Savonlinna/Nyslott	7	Gf	61.52N	28.53 E
Savonranta	7	Ge	62.11N	29.12 E
Savonselkä	8	Lb	62.05N	27.20 E
Savoonga	40	Ed	63.42N	170.27W
Savoy (EN) = Savoie	11	Mi	45.24N	6.30 E
Şavşat	24	Jb	41.15N	42.20 E
Savsjö	7	Dh	57.25N	14.40 E
Savudrija, Rt-	14	He	45.30N	13.31 E
Savukoski	7	Gc	67.17N	28.10 E
Savur	24	Id	37.33N	40.53 E
Savusavu	61	Ec	17.34S	178.15 E
Savusavu Bay	63d	Bb	16.45S	179.15 E
Savu Sea (EN) = Sawu, Laut-	21	Oj	9.40S	122.00 E
Savuto	14	Kk	39.02N	16.06 E
Sawahlunto	26	Dg	0.40S	100.47 E
Sawai Mādhopur	25	Fc	25.59N	76.22 E
Sawākin	31	Kg	19.07N	37.20 E
Sawākin, Jazā'ir- = Suakin Archipelago (EN)	30	Kg	19.07N	37.20 E
Sawankhalok	25	Je	17.19N	99.54 E
Sawara	29	Gd	35.53N	140.29 E
Sawasaki-Hana	28	Of	37.47N	138.12 E
Sawatch Range	45	Cg	39.10N	106.25W
Sawbā = Sobat (EN)	30	Kh	9.45N	31.45 E
Sawbridgeworth	12	Cc	51.49N	0.09 E
Sawdā', Jabal as-	33	Cd	28.40N	15.30 E
Sawfajjīn	33	Cc	31.54N	15.07 E
Sawhāj = Sohag (EN)	31	Kf	26.33N	31.42 E
Sawkanah	33	Cd	29.04N	15.47 E
Sawla	34	Ed	9.17N	2.25W
Sawqirah	23	If	18.10N	56.30 E
Şawqirah, Ghubbat-	23	If	18.35N	56.45 E
Sawtooth Mountains	46	He	44.00N	115.00W
Sawu, Kepulauan-	26	Hi	10.30S	121.50 E
Sawu, Laut- = Savu Sea (EN)	21	Oj	9.40S	122.00 E
Sawu, Pulau-	21	Ok	10.30S	121.54 E
Şawwān, Ard as-	24	Gg	31.00N	37.00 E
Sax	13	Lf	38.32N	0.49W
Saxby River	59	Ic	18.25S	140.53 E
Saxmundham	12	Db	52.13N	1.30 E
Saxony (EN) = Sachsen	10	Jf	51.00N	13.30 E
Say	34	Fc	13.07N	2.21 E
Sayabec	44	Na	48.36N	67.37W
Saya de Malha Bank (EN)	30	Nj	11.00S	61.00 E
Sayago	13	Fc	41.20N	6.10W
Sayan	54	Cf	11.08S	77.12W
Sayang, Pulau-	26	If	0.18N	129.54 E
Sayaxché	49	Be	16.31N	90.10W
Saydā	23	Ec	33.33N	35.22 E
Sayḩūt	22	Hh	15.12N	51.14 E
Saylorville Lake	45	Jf	41.48N	93.46W
Säynätsalo	8	Kb	62.08N	25.46 E
Sayō	29	Dd	35.01N	134.22 E
Sayram Hu	27	Dc	44.35N	81.10 E
Sayula	48	Hh	19.52N	103.37W
Saywūn	35	Hb	15.56N	48.47 E
Sazanit, Ishull i-	15	Ci	40.30N	19.16 E
Sázava	10	Kg	49.53N	14.24 E
Sázava	10	Kg	49.52N	14.54 E
Sbaa	32	Gd	28.13N	0.10W
Sbisseb	13	Pi	35.42N	3.51 E
Sbruč	16	Ee	48.32N	26.25 E
Scaër	11	Cf	48.02N	3.42W
Scafell Pike	9	Jg	54.27N	3.12W
Scalea	14	Jk	39.49N	15.47 E
Scalone, Passo dello-	14	Jk	39.38N	15.57 E
Scammon, Laguna-	48	Bd	27.45N	114.15W
Scammon Bay	40	Fd	61.53N	165.38W
Scandinavia (EN)	5	Hc	65.00N	16.00 E
Scanno	14	Hi	41.54N	13.53 E
Scansano	14	Fh	42.41N	11.20 E
Scapa Flow	9	Jc	58.54N	3.05W
Scapegoat Mountain	46	Ic	47.19N	112.50W
Ščapino	20	Ke	55.15N	159.25 E
Ščara	16	Dc	53.27N	24.44 E
Scaramia, Capo-	14	In	36.47N	14.29 E
Scarba	9	He	56.11N	5.42W
Scarborough [Eng.-U.K.]	9	Mg	54.17N	0.24W
Scarborough [Trin.]	54	Fa	11.11N	60.44W
Scarpe	11	Jd	50.30N	3.27 E
Sčastje	16	Ke	48.44N	39.14 E
Sceaux	12	Ef	48.47N	2.17 E
Ščekino	16	Jb	54.01N	37.29 E
Ščekurja	17	Jd	64.15N	60.52 E
Ščeljajur	19	Fb	65.21N	53.25 E
Scenic	45	Ee	43.47N	102.30W
Ščerbakty	19	He	52.29N	78.14 E
Schaalsee	10	Gc	53.35N	10.57 E
Schaarbeek/Schaerbeek	12	Gd	50.51N	4.23 E
Schaerbeek/Schaarbeek	12	Gd	50.51N	4.23 E
Schaffhausen [2]	14	Cc	47.45N	8.40 E
Schaffhausen	14	Cc	47.40N	8.40 E
Schagen	12	Gb	52.48N	4.48 E
Schärding	14	Hb	48.27N	13.26 E
Scharmützelsee	10	Kd	52.15N	14.03 E
Scharnhörn	10	Ec	53.57N	8.25 E
Scheeßel	12	La	53.10N	9.29 E
Schefferville	39	Md	54.47N	64.49W
Scheibbs	14	Jb	48.00N	15.10 E
Schela	15	Gd	45.10N	23.18 E
Schelde	11	Kc	51.22N	4.15 E
Schelde (EN) = Escaut	11	Kc	51.22N	4.15 E
Schell Creek Range	43	Ed	39.10N	114.40W
Schenectady	43	Mc	42.48N	73.57W
Scheno	35	Fd	9.35N	39.25 E
Scherfede, Warburg-	12	Lc	51.32N	9.02 E
Scherpenheuvel-Zichem	12	Gd	50.59N	4.59 E
Scheveningen, 's-Gravenhage-	11	Kb	52.06N	4.18 E
Schiedam	11	Kc	51.55N	4.24 E
Schiermonnikoog	11	Ma	53.28N	6.15 E
Schifferstadt	12	Ke	49.23N	8.22 E
Schiffgraben	10	Hd	52.02N	11.10 E
Schifflange	12	Ie	49.30N	6.01 E
Schijndel	12	Hc	51.37N	5.28 E
Schiltigheim	11	Nf	48.36N	7.45 E
Schio	14	Fe	45.43N	11.21 E
Schipbeek	12	Ib	52.15N	6.14 E
Schladming	14	Hc	47.23N	13.41 E
Schlei	10	Fb	54.35N	9.50 E
Schleiden	10	Cf	50.32N	6.28 E
Schleiz	10	Hf	50.35N	11.49 E
Schleswig	10	Fb	54.31N	9.33 E
Schleswig Holstein [2]	10	Gb	54.00N	10.30 E
Schlitz	10	Ff	50.40N	9.34 E
Schloß Holte-Stukenbrock	12	Kc	51.55N	8.38 E
Schloß Neuhaus, Paderborn-	12	Kc	51.44N	8.42 E
Schluchsee	10	Ei	47.49N	8.10 E
Schlüchtern	10	Ff	50.21N	9.31 E
Schmallenberg	12	Kc	51.09N	8.18 E
Schmallenberg-Bödefeld-Freiheit	12	Kc	51.15N	8.24 E
Schmallenberg-Oberkirchen	12	Kc	51.09N	8.18 E
Schmelz	12	Ie	49.26N	6.51 E
Schmida	14	Kb	48.20N	16.14 E
Schneeberg	10	If	50.36N	12.38 E
Schneeberg [Aus.]	14	Jc	47.46N	15.52 E
Schneeberg [Ger.]	10	Hf	50.00N	11.51 E
Schneifel	12	Id	50.16N	6.23 E
Schoberpaß	14	Ic	47.27N	14.40 E
Schoberspitze	14	Ic	47.17N	14.09 E
Schœlcher	51h	Ab	14.37N	61.06W
Schönebeck	10	Hd	52.01N	11.45 E
Schönecken	12	Id	50.10N	6.28 E
Schongau	10	Gi	47.49N	10.54 E
Schöningen	10	Gd	52.08N	10.57 E
Schoondijke	12	Fc	51.21N	3.33 E
Schoonebeek	12	Ib	52.40N	6.53 E
Schoonhoven	12	Gc	51.55N	4.51 E
Schorfheide	10	Jd	52.55N	13.35 E
Schoten	12	Gc	51.15N	4.30 E
Schotten	12	Ld	50.30N	9.08 E
Schouten Islands	57	Fe	3.30S	144.30 E
Schouwen	11	Jc	51.43N	3.50 E
Schramberg	10	Eh	48.14N	8.23 E
Schreiber	42	Ig	48.48N	87.15W
Schriesheim	12	Ke	49.29N	8.40 E
Schrobenhausen	10	Hh	48.33N	11.16 E
Schruns	14	Dc	47.04N	9.55 E
Schuls / Scuol	14	Ed	46.48N	10.17 E
Schultz Lake	42	Hd	64.45N	97.30W
Schurz	46	Fg	38.58N	118.46W
Schussen	10	Fi	47.37N	9.32 E
Schüttorf	12	Jb	52.19N	7.14 E
Schwabach	10	Hg	49.20N	11.02 E
Schwaben = Swabia (EN)	10	Gh	48.20N	10.30 E
Schwäbisch-Bayerisches Alpenvorland = Swabian-Bavarian Plateau (EN)	5	Hf	48.15N	10.30 E
Schwäbische Alb = Swabian Jura (EN)	5	Gf	48.25N	9.30 E

Index Symbols

- [1] Independent Nation
- [2] State, Region
- [3] District, County
- [4] Municipality
- [5] Colony, Dependency
- Continent
- Physical Region
- Historical or Cultural Region
- Mount, Mountain
- Volcano
- Hill
- Mountains, Mountain Range
- Hills, Escarpment
- Plateau, Upland
- Pass, Gap
- Plain, Lowland
- Delta
- Salt Flat
- Valley, Canyon
- Crater, Cave
- Karst Features
- Depression
- Polder
- Desert, Dunes
- Forest, Woods
- Heath, Steppe
- Oasis
- Cape, Point
- Coast, Beach
- Cliff
- Peninsula
- Isthmus
- Sandbank
- Island
- Atoll
- Rock, Reef
- Islands, Archipelago
- Rocks, Reefs
- Coral Reef
- Well, Spring
- Geyser
- River, Stream
- Waterfall Rapids
- River Mouth, Estuary
- Lake
- Salt Lake
- Intermittent Lake
- Reservoir
- Swamp, Pond
- Canal
- Glacier
- Ice Shelf, Pack Ice
- Ocean
- Sea
- Gulf, Bay
- Strait, Fjord
- Lagoon
- Bank
- Seamount
- Tablemount
- Ridge
- Shelf
- Basin
- Escarpment, Sea Scarp
- Fracture
- Trench, Abyss
- National Park, Reserve
- Point of Interest
- Recreation Site
- Cave, Cavern
- Historic Site
- Ruins
- Wall, Walls
- Church, Abbey
- Temple
- Scientific Station
- Airport
- Port
- Lighthouse
- Mine
- Tunnel
- Dam, Bridge

Schwäbisch Gmünd 10 Fh 48.48N 9.47 E
Schwäbisch Hall 10 Fg 49.06N 9.44 E
Schwalbach (Saar) 12 Ie 49.18N 6.49 E
Schwalm 12 Lc 51.07N 9.24 E
Schwalm 10 Ff 50.45N 9.25 E
Schwalmstadt 10 Ff 50.55N 9.12 E
Schwalmtal 12 Ic 51.15N 6.15 E
Schwandorf 10 Ig 49.20N 12.07 E
Schwaner, Pegunungan- 26 Fg 0.40S 112.40 E
Schwanewede 12 Ka 53.14N 8.36 E
Schwarzach 10 Ig 49.30N 12.10 E
Schwarzbach 12 Je 49.17N 7.40 E
Schwarze Elster 10 Ie 51.49N 12.51 E
Schwarzer Mann 12 Id 50.15N 6.22 E
Schwarzrand 37 Be 26.00S 17.10 E
Schwarzwald=Black Forest (EN) 5 Gf 48.00N 8.15 E
Schwarzwalder Hochwald 12 Ie 49.39N 6.55 E
Schwatka Mountains 40 Hc 67.25N 157.00W
Schwaz 14 Fc 47.20N 11.42 E
Schwechat 14 Kb 48.08N 16.28 E
Schwechat 14 Kb 48.08N 16.28 E
Schwedt 10 Kc 53.04N 14.18 E
Schweich 12 Ie 49.49N 6.45 E
Schweinfurt 10 Gf 50.03N 10.14 E
Schweiz / Suisse / Svizra / Svizzera = Switzerland (EN) 6 Gf 46.00N 8.30 E
Schweizer-Reneke 37 De 27.11S 25.18 E
Schwelm 12 Jc 51.17N 7.17 E
Schwerin 10 Hc 53.38N 11.23 E
Schweriner See 10 Hc 53.45N 11.28 E
Schwerte 12 Jc 51.27N 7.34 E
Schwetzingen 12 Ke 49.23N 8.34 E
Schwielochsee 10 Kd 52.03N 14.12 E
Schwyz (2) 14 Cc 47.10N 8.50 E
Schwyz 14 Cc 47.03N 8.40 E
Sciacca 14 Hm 37.31N 13.03 E
Scicli 14 In 36.47N 14.42 E
Ščigry 19 De 51.53N 36.55 E
Scilly, Isles of- 5 Ff 49.57N 6.15W
Scioto River 44 Ff 38.44N 83.01W
Ščirec 10 Tg 49.34N 23.54 E
Scobey 46 Mb 48.47N 105.25W
Scordia 14 Im 37.18N 14.51 E
Scoresby Land 41 Jd 71.45N 26.30W
Scoresbysund 67 Md 70.35N 21.40W
Scoresby Sund 67 Md 70.20N 23.30W
Scorff 11 Cg 47.46N 3.21W
Ščors 19 De 51.48N 31.59 E
Scotia Ridge (EN) 3 Co 57.00S 45.00W
Scotia Sea (EN) 52 Mk 57.00S 40.00W
Scotland (2) 9 Ie 56.30N 4.30W
Scotland 5 Fd 56.30N 4.30W
Scotlandville 45 Kk 30.31N 91.11W
Scotstown 44 Lc 45.31N 71.17W
Scott 42 Gf 52.27N 108.23W
Scott, Cape- [Austl.] 59 Fb 13.30S 129.50 E
Scott, Cape - [B.C.-Can.] 42 Ef 50.47N 128.25W
Scott, Mount- 46 De 42.56N 122.01W
Scott Base 66 Kf 77.51S 166.46 E
Scottburgh 37 Ef 30.19S 30.40 E
Scott Channel 46 Aa 50.45N 128.30W
Scott City 45 Fg 38.29N 100.54W
Scott Coast 66 Kf 76.30S 162.30 E
Scott Glacier [Ant.] 66 He 66.15S 100.05 E
Scott Glacier [Ant.] 66 Mg 85.45S 153.00W
Scott Inlet 42 Kb 71.05N 71.05W
Scott Island 66 Le 67.24S 179.55W
Scott Islands 46 Aa 50.48N 128.40W
Scott Peak 46 Id 44.21N 112.50W
Scott Reef 59 Eb 14.00S 121.50 E
Scottsbluff 39 Ie 41.52N 103.40W
Scottsboro 44 Dh 34.40N 86.01W
Scottsburg 44 Ef 38.41N 85.46W
Scottsdale [Austl.] 59 Jh 41.10S 147.31 E
Scottsdale [Az.-U.S.] 43 Ee 33.30N 111.56W
Scotts Head 51g Bb 15.13N 61.23W
Scottsville 44 Dg 36.45N 86.11W
Scottville 44 Dd 43.59N 86.17W
Scranton 39 Le 41.24N 75.40W
Scrivia 14 Ce 45.03N 8.54 E
Scrub Cays 49 Ia 24.07N 76.55W
Scrub Island 51b Bb 18.17N 62.57W
Ščučin 16 Dc 53.39N 24.48 E
Ščučinsk 19 He 53.00N 70.11 E
Ščučja 17 Nc 66.45N 68.20 E
Ščučje 19 Gd 55.15N 62.43 E
Scugog, Lake- 44 Hc 44.10N 78.51W
Ščugor 17 Hd 64.12N 57.32 E
Scunthorpe 9 Mh 53.36N 0.38W
Scuol / Schuls 14 Ed 46.48N 10.17 E
Scutari, Lake- (EN)= Shkodrës, Liqen i- 5 Hg 42.10N 19.20 E
Scutari, Lake- (EN)= Skadarsko Jezero 5 Hg 42.10N 19.20 E
Seaford 9 Nk 50.46N 0.06 E
Seahorse Point 42 Jd 63.47N 80.10W
Sea Islands 43 Ke 31.20N 81.20W
Seal 42 Ie 59.04N 94.47W
Seal Island 44 Nd 43.30N 66.01W
Sealpunt 30 Jl 34.06S 23.24 E
Searcy 45 Ki 35.15N 91.44W
Searles Lake 46 Gi 35.43N 117.20W
Seaside [Ca.-U.S.] 46 Eh 36.37N 121.50W
Seaside [Or.-U.S.] 46 Dc 46.01N 123.55W
Seattle 39 Ge 47.36N 122.20W
Seaward Kaikoura Range 62 Ee 42.15S 173.35 E
Seba 26 Hi 10.29S 121.50 E
Sébaco 49 Dg 12.51N 86.06W
Sebago Lake 44 Ld 43.50N 70.35W
Sebaiera 32 Ee 24.51N 13.02W
Sebaou 13 Ph 36.55N 3.51 E
Sebastian, Cape- 46 Ce 42.19N 124.26W
Sebastián Vizcaíno, Bahía- 38 Hg 28.00N 114.30W
Sebastopol 46 Dg 38.24N 122.49W
Sebatik, Pulau- 26 Gf 4.10N 117.45 E
Sebba 34 Fc 13.26N 0.32 E
Sebderat 35 Fb 15.27N 36.39 E
Sébé 36 Bc 1.02S 13.06 E
Šebekino 19 De 50.27N 37.00 E
Sébékoro 34 Dc 12.49N 8.50W
Seberi 55 Fh 27.29S 53.24W
Sebeş 15 Gd 45.58N 23.34 E
Sebeş 15 Gd 46.00N 23.34 E
Sebes-Körös 15 Dc 46.55N 20.59 E
Sebeşului, Munţii- 15 Gd 45.38N 23.27 E
Sebewaing 44 Fd 43.44N 83.27W
Sebež 19 Cd 56.19N 28.31 E
Sebha Oasis (EN)=Sabhā, Wāḥāt 30 If 27.00N 14.25 E
Şebinkarahisar 24 Hb 40.18N 38.26 E
Sebiş 15 Fc 46.22N 22.07 E
Sebou 30 Ge 34.16N 6.41W
Sebring 44 Gl 27.30N 81.26W
Sebugal 13 Ed 40.21N 7.05W
Sebuku, Pulau- 26 Gg 3.30S 116.22 E
Šebunino 20 Jg 46.24N 141.56 E
Secas, Islas- 49 Gi 7.58N 82.02W
Secchia 14 Ee 45.04N 11.00 E
Sechura 54 Be 5.33S 80.51W
Sechura, Bahia de- 54 Be 5.40S 81.00W
Sechura, Desierto de- 54 Be 6.00S 80.30W
Seckau 14 Ic 47.16N 14.47 E
Seclin 12 Fd 50.33N 3.02 E
Secondigny 11 Fh 46.37N 0.25W
Secos, Ilhéus- 32 Cf 14.58N 24.40W
Secretary Island 62 Bf 45.15S 166.55 E
Sécure, Rio- 54 Fg 15.10S 64.52W
Seda 8 Kg 57.38N 25.12 E
Sěda 13 Df 38.56N 8.03W
Seda [Lat.-U.S.S.R.] 8 Kg 57.32N 25.43 E
Seda [Lith.-U.S.S.R.] 8 Jh 56.10N 22.00 E
Sedalia 43 Id 38.42N 93.14W
Sedan 11 Ke 49.42N 4.57 E
Sedanka 40a Eb 53.50N 166.10W
Sedano 13 Ib 42.43N 3.45W
Sedbergh 9 Kg 54.20N 2.31W
Seddenga 35 Ea 20.33N 30.18 E
Seddon 62 Fd 41.40S 174.04 E
Seddon, Kap- 41 Gc 75.20N 58.45W
Seddonville 62 Dd 41.33S 171.59 E
Seddülbahir 15 Ji 40.03N 26.10 E
Sedelnikovo 19 Hd 56.57N 75.18 E
Séderon 11 Lj 44.12N 5.32 E
Sédhiou 34 Bc 12.44N 15.33W
Sedini 14 Ci 40.51N 8.49 E
Šedok 16 Lg 44.13N 40.52 E
Sedom 24 Fg 31.04N 35.24 E
Sedona 46 Ji 34.52N 111.46W
Sedrada 14 Bn 36.08N 7.32 E
Šedro 14 Kg 43.05N 16.42 E
Sedro Woolley 46 Db 48.30N 122.14W
Šeduva 7 Fi 55.48N 23.45 E
Sée 11 Ef 48.39N 1.26W
Seeheim [Ger.] 12 Ke 49.46N 8.40 E
Seeheim [Nam.] 37 Be 26.50S 17.45 E
Seeis 37 Bd 22.29S 17.39 E
Seeland 14 Bc 47.05N 7.05 E
Seeling, Mount- 66 Og 82.28S 103.00W
Seelow 10 Kd 52.31N 14.23 E
Sées 11 Gf 48.36N 0.10 E
Seesen 10 Ge 51.54N 10.11 E
Seewarte Seamounts (EN) 30 Ee 33.00N 28.30W
Şefaatli 24 Fc 39.31N 34.46 E
Sefadu 34 Cd 8.39N 10.59W
Seferihisar 24 Bc 38.11N 26.51 E
Séféto 34 Dc 14.08N 9.51W
Sefid Dasht 24 Nf 32.09N 51.10 E
Sefrou 32 Gc 33.50N 4.50W
Sefuri-San 29 Be 33.26N 130.22 E
Segaf, Kepulauan- 26 Jg 2.10S 130.28 E
Ségalas 11 Ij 44.09N 2.30 E
Segamat 26 Df 2.30N 102.49 E
Segangane 13 Ii 35.10N 3.01W
Şegarcea 15 Ge 44.06N 23.45 E
Şegarka 20 De 57.16N 84.02 E
Segbana 34 Fc 10.56N 3.42 E
Segeg 35 Gd 7.40N 42.50 E
Segesta 14 Gm 37.55N 12.50 E
Segeža 6 Jc 63.44N 34.19 E
Seghe 63a Cc 8.25S 157.51 E
Seglinge 8 Id 60.15N 20.40 E
Segmon 8 Ee 59.17N 13.01 E
Segorbe 13 Le 39.51N 0.29W
Ségou (3) 34 Dc 14.00N 6.20W
Ségou 31 Gg 13.27N 6.15W
Segovia 13 Hd 40.57N 4.07W
Segovia (3) 13 Ic 41.10N 4.00W
Segozero, Ozero- 5 Jc 63.18N 33.45 E
Segré 11 Fg 47.41N 0.52W
Segre 13 Mc 41.40N 0.43 E
Seguam 40a Db 52.17N 172.30W
Séguédine 34 Ha 20.12N 12.59 E
Séguéla 34 Dd 7.57N 6.40W
Séguéla (3) 34 Dd 8.05N 6.32W
Seguin 43 Hf 29.34N 97.58W
Segula 40a Bb 52.01N 178.07 E
Segura 13 Lf 38.06N 0.38W
Segura, Sierra de- 13 Jf 38.00N 2.45W
Segura de la Sierra 13 Jf 38.18N 2.39W
Sehithwa 37 Cd 20.27S 22.42 E
Seia 13 Ed 40.25N 7.42W
Seibal 49 Be 16.27N 90.05W
Seiche 11 Eg 48.00N 1.46W
Seiland 7 Fa 70.25N 23.15 E
Seiling 45 Gh 36.09N 98.56W
Seille [Fr.] 11 Me 49.07N 6.11 E
Seille [Fr.] 11 Kh 46.31N 4.56 E
Sein, Ile de- 11 Bf 48.02N 4.51W
Seinäjoki 7 Fe 62.47N 22.50 E
Seine 5 Gf 49.26N 0.26 E
Seine, Baie de la-=Seine, Bay of the- (EN) 5 Ff 49.30N 0.30W
Seine, Bay of the- (EN)= Seine, Baie de la- 5 Ff 49.30N 0.30W
Seine, Val de- 11 Jf 48.30N 3.20 E
Seine-et-Marne (3) 11 If 48.30N 3.00 E
Seine-Maritime (3) 11 Ge 49.45N 1.00 E
Seine-Saint-Denis (3) 11 If 48.55N 2.30 E
Seine Seamount (EN) 5 Ei 33.45N 14.25W
Seini 15 Gb 47.45N 23.17 E
Seistan (EN)=Sīstān 21 If 30.30N 62.00 E
Seixal 13 Cf 38.38N 9.06W
Séjaha 20 Cb 70.10N 72.30 E
Sejerø 8 Di 55.55N 11.10 E
Sejerø Bugt 8 Di 55.50N 11.15 E
Sejm 5 Je 51.27N 32.34 E
Sejmčan 20 Kd 62.52N 152.27 E
Sejny 10 Tb 54.07N 23.20 E
Sekakes 37 Df 30.04S 28.21 E
Sekenke 36 Fc 4.16S 34.10 E
Šeki 19 Eg 41.10N 47.11 E
Seki [Jap.] 29 Ed 35.28N 136.54 E
Seki [Tur.] 24 Cd 36.44N 29.33 E
Sekincau, Gunung- 26 Dh 5.05S 104.18 E
Seki-Zaki 29b Be 33.16N 131.54 E
Sekoma 37 Cd 24.36S 23.58 E
Sekondi-Takoradi 31 Gh 4.53N 1.45W
Sekota 35 Fc 12.37N 39.03 E
Šeksna 19 Dd 59.13N 38.32 E
Šelagskij, Mys- 20 Mb 70.10N 170.45 E
Selah 46 Ec 46.39N 120.32W
Selajar, Pulau- 26 Hh 6.05S 120.30 E
Selajar, Selat- 26 Hh 5.42S 120.28 E
Selaön 8 Ge 59.25N 17.10 E
Selaru, Pulau- 26 Jh 8.09S 131.00 E
Selatan, Cape- (EN)= Selatan, Tanjung- 21 Nj 4.10S 113.48 E
Selatan, Tanjung-=Selatan, Cape- (EN) 21 Nj 4.10S 113.48 E
Selawik 40 Gc 66.37N 160.03W
Selawik Lake 40 Hc 66.30N 160.40W
Selb 10 If 50.10N 12.08 E
Selbjørn 8 Ae 60.00N 5.10 E
Selbjørnsfjorden 8 Ae 59.55N 5.10 E
Selbu 8 Da 63.13N 11.02 E
Selbukta 66 Bf 71.40S 12.25W
Selbusjøen 8 Da 63.15N 10.55 E
Selby [Eng.-U.K.] 9 Lh 53.48N 1.04W
Selby [S.D.-U.S.] 45 Fd 45.31N 100.02W
Selco 16 Ic 53.23N 34.05 E
Selçuk 24 Bd 37.56N 27.22 E
Seldovia 40 Ie 59.27N 151.43W
Sele 14 Ij 40.29N 14.56 E
Sele, Piana del- 14 Ij 40.30N 14.55 E
Selebi-Pikwe 31 Jk 22.13S 27.58 E
Selečka Planina 15 Eh 41.05N 21.35 E
Šelehov 20 Ff 52.10N 104.01 E
Selemdža 20 Id 51.49N 128.53 E
Selencia 24 Kf 33.04N 44.33 E
Selendi 15 Lk 38.40N 28.41 E
Selendi 15 Lk 38.45N 28.53 E
Selenduma 20 Ff 50.55N 106.10 E
Selenga (Selenge) 21 Md 52.16N 106.16 E
Selenge [Mong.] 27 Hb 49.25N 103.59 E
Selenge [Zaire] 36 Cc 1.58S 18.11 E
Selenge→Selenga 21 Md 52.16N 106.16 E
Selenginsk 20 Ff 51.59N 106.57 E
Selenica 15 Ci 40.32N 19.38 E
Selennjah 20 Jc 67.55N 145.00 E
Sélestat 11 Nf 48.16N 7.27 E
Selety 19 He 53.06N 73.00 E
Seletyteniz, Ozero- 19 He 53.15N 73.15 E
Selevac 15 De 44.30N 20.53 E
Seleznevo 8 Md 60.44N 28.37 E
Selfoss 7a Bc 63.56N 21.00W
Seli 34 Cd 8.33N 12.48W
Sélibabi 32 Ef 15.10N 12.11W
Seliger, Ozero- 19 Dd 57.20N 33.05 E
Seligman 46 Ii 35.20N 112.53W
Šelihova, Zaliv-=Shelikhov Gulf (EN) 21 Rc 60.00N 158.00 E
Selimağa 15 Lj 39.35N 28.33 E
Selimiye 24 Bd 37.24N 27.40 E
Selingenstadt 12 Kd 50.03N 8.59 E
Selinunte 14 Gm 37.35N 12.48 E
Seližarovo 7 Hh 56.51N 33.29 E
Seljatin 15 Ib 47.52N 25.14 E
Selje 8 Ab 62.03N 5.22 E
Seljord 7 Bg 59.29N 8.37 E
Selkirk [Man.-Can.] 45 Ha 50.09N 96.52W
Selkirk [Scot.-U.K.] 9 Kf 55.33N 2.50W
Selkirk Mountains 42 Ff 50.00N 117.00W
Sella 13 Ga 43.28N 5.04W
Sellasia 15 Fl 37.10N 22.25 E
Selle 12 Fd 50.19N 3.23 E
Selles-sur-Cher 11 Hg 47.16N 1.33 E
Sells 46 Jk 31.55N 111.53W
Selm 12 Jc 51.42N 7.28 E
Selma [Al.-U.S.] 43 Je 32.25N 87.01W
Selma [Ca.-U.S.] 46 Fh 36.34N 119.37W
Selmer 44 Ch 35.11N 88.36W
Selmet Wielki, Jezioro- 10 Sc 53.50N 22.30 E
Šelon 7 Hg 58.14N 30.50 E
Selong 26 Gh 8.39S 116.32 E
Selsey 12 Bd 50.44N 0.47W
Selsey Bill 9 Mk 50.43N 0.48W
Seltz 12 Kf 48.53N 8.06 E
Selu, Pulau- 26 Jh 7.32S 130.54 E
Séluné 11 Ef 48.39N 1.51W
Selva 55 Ai 29.46S 62.03W
Selvagens, Ilhas- 30 Fe 30.05N 15.55W
Selvānā 24 Kd 37.25N 44.51 E
Selvas 52 Jf 5.00S 68.00W
Selway River 46 Hc 46.08N 115.36W
Selwyn, Détroit de- 63b Dc 16.04S 168.11 E
Selwyn Lake 42 He 60.00N 104.30W
Selwyn Mountains 38 Fc 63.10N 130.20W
Selwyn Range 57 Fg 21.35S 140.35 E
Selz 12 Ke 49.59N 8.02 E
Šemaha 16 Pi 40.39N 48.38 E
Semani 15 Ci 40.54N 19.26 E
Semara 31 Ff 26.44N 11.41W
Semarang 22 Nj 6.58S 110.25 E
Sematan 26 Ef 1.48N 109.46 E
Semau, Pulau- 26 Hi 10.13S 123.22 E
Sembakung 26 Gf 3.47N 117.30 E
Sembé 36 Bb 1.39N 14.36 E
Semberija 14 Nf 44.45N 19.10 E
Sembuan 26 Gg 0.19S 115.30 E
Semenicului, Munţii- 15 Fd 45.05N 22.05 E
Semenov 7 Kh 56.49N 44.29 E
Semenovka 16 Hc 52.11N 32.40 E
Semeru, Gunung- 21 Nj 7.58S 113.35 E
Semichi Islands 40a Db 52.42N 174.00 E
Semidi Islands 40 He 56.07N 156.44W
Semiluki 19 De 51.43N 39.02 E
Semily 10 Lf 50.36N 15.20 E
Seminoe Reservoir 46 Le 42.00N 106.50W
Seminole [Ok.-U.S.] 45 Hi 35.14N 96.14W
Seminole [Tx.-U.S.] 45 Ej 32.43N 102.39W
Seminole, Lake- 43 Ke 30.46N 84.50W
Semipalatinsk 22 Kd 50.28N 80.13 E
Semipalatinskaja Oblast (3) 19 If 48.30N 80.10 E
Semirara Islands 26 Hd 11.57N 121.27 E
Semirom 24 Ng 31.22N 51.47 E
Semisopochnoi 40a Cb 52.00N 179.35 E
Semitau 26 Ff 0.33N 111.58 E
Semiun, Pulau- 26 Ef 4.31N 107.44 E
Semizbugy 19 He 50.12N 74.48 E
Semliki 30 Kh 1.14N 30.28 E
Semmering 14 Jc 47.38N 15.49 E
Semnān (3) 23 Hb 35.00N 53.30 E
Semnān 22 Hf 35.33N 53.24 E
Semnon 11 Eg 47.54N 1.45W
Semois 11 Ke 49.53N 4.45 E
Šemonaiha 19 Ie 50.39N 81.54 E
Semporna 26 Gf 4.28N 118.36 E
Semuda 26 Fg 2.51S 112.58 E
Semur-en-Auxois 11 Kg 47.29N 4.20 E
Sén 25 Kf 12.32N 104.28 E
Senador Mourão 55 Kc 17.51S 43.22W
Senador Pompeu 54 Ke 5.35S 39.22W
Senaja 26 Ge 6.45N 117.03 E
Sena Madureira 54 Ee 9.04S 68.40W
Senanga 36 Df 16.07S 23.16 E
Senarpont 12 De 49.53N 1.43 E
Senatobia 45 Li 34.39N 89.58W
Sendai [Jap.] 28 Ki 31.49N 130.18 E
Sendai [Jap.] 22 Qf 38.15N 140.53 E
Sendai-Gawa [Jap.] 29 Bf 31.51N 130.12 E
Sendai-Gawa [Jap.] 29 Dd 35.34N 134.11 E
Sendai-Wan 28 Pe 38.10N 141.15 E
Senden 12 Jc 51.51N 7.30 E
Sendenhorst 12 Jc 51.50N 7.50 E
Senderg 22 Qi 26.52N 57.37 E
Seneca 45 Hg 39.50N 96.04W
Seneca Lake 44 Id 42.40N 76.57W
Sénégal=Senegal (EN) 30 Fg 15.48N 16.32W
Sénégal=Senegal (EN) (1) 31 Fg 14.00N 14.00W
Senegal (EN)=Sénégal (1) 31 Fg 14.00N 14.00W
Senegal (EN)=Sénégal 30 Fg 15.48N 16.32W
Sénégal Oriental (3) 34 Cc 13.30N 13.00W
Senekal 37 De 28.30S 27.32 E
Senetosa, Punta di- 11a Ab 41.33N 8.47 E
Seney 44 Eb 46.21N 85.56W
Senftenberg/Zły Komorow 10 Ke 51.31N 14.01 E
Sengata 22 Ni 0.28N 117.33 E
Sengilej 7 Lj 53.58N 48.46 E
Senguerr, Rio- 56 Gg 45.32S 68.54W
Sengwa 37 Dc 17.05S 28.03 E
Senhor do Bonfim 53 Lg 10.27S 40.11W
Senica 10 Nh 48.41N 17.23 E
Senigallia 14 Hg 43.43N 13.13 E
Senirkent 24 Dc 38.07N 30.33 E
Senj 14 If 45.00N 14.54 E
Senja 5 Hb 69.20N 17.30 E
Senjsko Bilo 14 Jf 44.55N 15.03 E
Senkaku-Shotō 27 Lf 25.45N 124.00 E
Şenkaya 24 Jb 40.35N 42.21 E
Senkevičevka 10 Vf 50.29N 25.05 E
Senkursk 19 Ec 62.08N 42.53 E
Senlin Shan 28 Kc 43.12N 130.38 E
Senlis 11 Ie 49.12N 2.35 E
Senmonorom 25 Lf 12.27N 107.12 E
Senn, Dahr Ou- 32 Ef 17.55N 11.00W
Sennestadt, Bielefeld- 12 Kc 51.57N 8.35 E
Senneterre 42 Jg 48.24N 77.14W
Senno 7 Gi 54.47N 29.41 E
Sennoj 16 Oc 52.07N 46.59 E
Senorbi 14 Dk 39.32N 9.08 E
Senqu 37 Be 28.38S 16.27 E
Sens 11 Jf 48.12N 3.17 E
Sensée 12 Fd 50.16N 3.06 E
Sensuntepeque 49 Cg 13.52N 88.38W
Senta 15 Dd 45.56N 20.05 E
Sentinel Peak 42 Ff 54.58N 122.00W
Sentinel Range 66 Pf 78.10S 85.30W
Senyavin Islands 57 Gd 6.55N 158.00 E
Şenyurt 24 Id 37.06N 40.40 E
Senzaki-Wan 29 Bd 34.25N 131.20 E
Senžarka 17 Mi 54.45N 67.50 E
Seo de Urgel/La Seu d'Urgell 13 Nb 42.21N 1.28 E
Seoni 25 Fd 22.05N 79.32 E
Seoul (EN)=Sŏul 22 Of 37.34N 127.00 E
Séoune 11 Gj 44.10N 0.41 E
Sepanjang, Pulau- 26 Gh 7.10S 115.50 E
Separation Point 62 Ed 40.47S 173.00 E
Sepetovka 19 Ce 50.12N 27.04 E
Sepik River 57 Fe 3.51S 144.34 E
Sępólno Krajeńskie 10 Nc 53.28N 17.32 E
Sepopol 10 Qb 54.15N 21.00 E
Sepopolska, Nizina- 10 Rb 54.15N 21.10 E
Septemvri 15 Hg 42.13N 24.06 E
Septentrional, Cordillera- 49 Ld 19.35N 70.45W
Septeuil 12 Df 48.54N 1.41 E
Sept-Iles 39 Md 50.12N 66.23W
Sepúlveda 13 Ic 41.18N 3.45W
Sequeros 13 Fd 40.31N 6.01W
Sequillo 13 Gc 41.45N 5.30W
Sera 29 Cd 34.36N 133.01 E
Sera, Pulau- 26 Jh 7.40S 131.05 E
Šerabad 19 Gh 37.43N 66.59 E
Šerabad 18 Ff 37.22N 67.03 E
Serafettin Dağları 24 Ic 39.05N 41.10 E
Serafimovič 16 Me 49.36N 42.47 E
Serahs 19 Gh 36.30N 61.13 E
Seraidi 14 Bn 36.55N 7.40 E
Seraing 11 Ld 50.36N 5.31 E
Seram 57 De 3.00S 129.00 E
Seram, Laut-=Ceram Sea (EN) 57 De 2.30S 128.00 E
Serang 26 Eh 6.07S 106.09 E
Serasan, Pulau- 26 Ef 2.30N 109.03 E
Serasan, Selat- 26 Ef 2.20S 109.00 E
Serbia (EN) = Srbija (2) 15 Df 44.00N 21.00 E
Serbia (EN) = Srbija 5 Ig 43.00N 21.00 E
Serbia (EN)=Srbija 15 Df 44.00N 21.00 E
Şercaia 15 Id 45.50N 25.08 E
Serchio 14 Eg 43.47N 10.16 E
Serdo 35 Gc 11.58N 41.18 E
Serdoba 16 Nc 52.34N 44.01 E
Serdobsk 19 Ee 52.29N 44.16 E
Sereba 35 Gc 13.12N 40.32 E
Serebrjansk 19 If 49.43N 83.20 E
Serebrjanski 7 Ib 68.52N 35.32 E
Sered' 10 Nh 48.17N 17.45 E
Seredka 8 Mf 58.10N 28.25 E
Şereflikoçhisar 24 Ec 38.56N 33.33 E
Serein 11 Jg 47.55N 3.31 E
Seremban 26 Df 2.43N 101.56 E
Serengeti Plain 36 Fc 2.50S 35.00 E
Serenje 36 Fe 13.14S 30.14 E
Šereševo 10 Ud 52.31N 24.19 E
Seret 16 De 48.38N 25.52 E
Serfopoúla 15 Hl 37.15N 24.36 E
Sergač 19 Ed 55.33N 45.28 E
Sergeievka 28 Lc 43.23N 133.22 E
Sergeja Kirova, Ostrova- 20 Da 77.10N 90.00 E
Sergejevka [Kaz.-U.S.S.R.] 19 Ge 53.51N 67.28 E
Sergejevka [R.S.F.S.R.] 28 Kb 44.20N 131.40 E
Sergino 22 Ic 62.30N 65.40 E
Sergipe (2) 54 Kf 10.30S 37.10W
Sergokala 16 Oh 42.30N 47.40 E
Sergozero, Ozero- 7 Ic 66.45N 36.50 E
Seria 26 Ff 4.37N 114.19 E
Serian 26 Ff 1.10N 110.34 E
Seriana, Val- 14 De 45.50N 9.50 E
Seribu, Kepulauan- 26 Eh 5.36S 106.33 E
Sérifontaine 12 De 49.21N 1.46 E
Sérifos 15 Hl 37.09N 24.30 E
Sérifos 15 Hl 37.10N 24.30 E
Serifou, Stenón- 15 Hl 37.15N 24.30 E
Serik 24 Dd 36.55N 31.06 E
Seringapatam Reef 59 Eb 13.40S 122.05 E
Serio 14 De 45.16N 9.45 E
Šerlovaja Gora 20 Gf 50.34N 116.18 E
Sermata, Kepulauan- 26 Ih 8.10S 128.40 E
Sermilik 41 Ie 66.00N 38.45W
Sernovodsk 7 Mj 53.54N 51.09 E
Sernur 7 Lh 56.57N 49.11 E
Sernyje Vody 7 Mj 53.53N 50.59 E
Sero 24 Kd 37.33N 44.40 E
Serock 10 Rd 52.31N 21.03 E
Serodino 55 Bk 32.37S 60.57W
Serov 22 Id 59.29N 60.31 E
Serowe 31 Jk 22.23S 26.43 E
Serpa 13 Eg 37.56N 7.36W
Serpent, Vallée du- 34 Dc 14.50N 8.00W
Serpentine Lakes 59 Fe 28.30S 129.10 E
Serpent's Mouth/Serpiente, Boca de la- 54 Fa 10.10N 61.58W
Serpiente, Boca de la-/ Serpent's Mouth 54 Fa 10.10N 61.58W
Serpis 13 Lf 38.59N 0.09W
Serpnevoje 15 Lc 46.23N 28.59 E
Serpuhov 6 Je 54.55N 37.25 E
Serra, Aparados da- 55 Hi 28.45S 49.45W
Serra Bonita 55 Ib 15.13S 46.49W
Serra das Araras 55 Jb 15.30S 45.21W
Serra do Navio 53 Ke 0.59N 52.03W
Serra do Salitre 55 Id 19.06S 46.41W
Serra Dourada 55 Ka 12.50S 43.56W
Sérrai 15 Gh 41.05N 23.33 E
Serralada Litoral Catalana/ Cadena Costero Catalana= Catalan Coastal Range (EN) 5 Gg 41.35N 1.40 E
Serralada Pirinenca= Pyrenees (EN) 5 Gg 42.40N 1.00 E
Serrana Bank 47 Hf 14.23N 80.12W
Serranilla Bank 47 Ie 15.50N 79.50W
Serranópolis 55 Fd 18.16S 52.00W
Serra San Bruno 14 Kl 38.35N 16.20 E
Serrat, Cap- 32 Ib 37.14N 9.13 E
Serra Talhada 54 Ke 7.59S 38.18W
Serre 11 Je 49.41N 3.23 E
Serre, Massif de la- 11 Lg 47.10N 5.35 E
Serre-Ponçon, Réservoir de- 11 Mj 44.27N 6.16 E
Serres 11 Lj 44.26N 5.43 E
Serrezuela 56 Gd 30.38S 65.23W
Serrinha 54 Kf 11.39S 39.00W
Serriola, Bocca- 14 Gg 43.31N 12.21 E
Serro 55 Kd 18.37S 43.23W
Serrota 13 Gd 40.30N 5.04W
Serrote, Rio- 55 Ee 21.27S 54.40W

Index Symbols

(1) Independent Nation
(2) State, Region
(3) District, County
(4) Municipality
(5) Colony, Dependency
Continent
Physical Region
Historical or Cultural Region
Mount, Mountain
Volcano
Hill
Mountains, Mountain Range
Hills, Escarpment
Plateau, Upland
Pass, Gap
Plain, Lowland
Delta
Salt Flat
Valley, Canyon
Crater, Cave
Karst Features
Depression
Polder
Desert, Dunes
Forest, Woods
Heath, Steppe
Oasis
Cape, Point
Coast, Beach
Cliff
Peninsula
Isthmus
Sandbank
Island
Atoll
Rock, Reef
Islands, Archipelago
Rocks, Reefs
Coral Reef
Well, Spring
Geyser
River, Stream
Waterfall Rapids
River Mouth, Estuary
Lake
Salt Lake
Intermittent Lake
Reservoir
Swamp, Pond
Canal
Glacier
Ice Shelf, Pack Ice
Ocean
Sea
Gulf, Bay
Strait, Fjord
Lagoon
Bank
Seamount
Tablemount
Ridge
Shelf
Basin
Escarpment, Sea Scarp
Fracture
Trench, Abyss
National Park, Reserve
Point of Interest
Recreation Site
Cave, Cavern
Historic Site
Ruins
Wall, Walls
Church, Abbey
Temple
Scientific Station
Airport
Port
Lighthouse
Mine
Tunnel
Dam, Bridge

Sersou, Plateau du- 13 Ni 35.30N 2.00 E
Sertã 13 De 39.48N 8.06W
Sertão 52 Lg 10.00S 41.00W
Sertãozinho 55 Ie 21.08S 47.59W
Sêrtar 27 He 32.20N 100.20 E
Serti 34 Hd 7.30N 11.22 E
Serua, Pulau- 26 Jh 6.18S 130.01 E
Serui 26 Kg 1.53S 136.14 E
Serule 37 Dd 21.55S 27.19 E
Sérvia 15 Ei 40.11N 22.00 E
Sêrxü 27 Ge 32.56N 98.02 E
Seryitsi 15 Ii 40.00N 25.10 E
Seryševo 20 Hf 51.02N 128.25 E
Sesayap 26 Gf 3.36N 117.15 E
Sese 36 Eb 2.11N 25.47 E
Seseganaga Lake 45 Ka 50.10N 90.15W
Sese Islands 36 Fc 0.20S 32.20 E
Sesfontein 37 Ac 19.07S 13.39 E
Sesheke 36 Df 17.29S 24.18 E
Sesia 14 Ce 45.05N 8.37 E
Sesibi 35 Ea 20.05N 30.31 E
Sesimbra 13 Cf 38.26N 9.06W
Šešma 7 Mi 55.20N 51.12 E
Sesnut 8 Be 59.42N 7.21 E
Sessa Aurunca 14 Hi 41.14N 13.56 E
Ses Salines, Cap de-/ Salinas, Cabo de- 13 Pe 39.16N 3.03 E
Sestao 13 Ja 43.18N 3.00W
Sesto Fiorentino 14 Fg 43.50N 11.12 E
Sesto San Giovanni 14 De 45.32N 9.14 E
Sestriere 14 Af 44.57N 6.53 E
Sestri Levante 14 Df 44.16N 9.24 E
Sestroreck 7 Gf 60.06N 29.59 E
Šešupė 7 Fi 55.00N 22.10 E
Šešuvis 8 Ji 55.12N 22.31 E
Sesvenna, Piz- 14 Ed 46.42N 10.25 E
Sesvete 14 Ke 45.50N 16.07 E
Šeta/Šēta 8 Ki 55.14N 24.18 E
Šēta/Šeta 8 Ki 55.14N 24.18 E
Setaka 29 Be 33.09N 130.28 E
Setana 28 Oc 42.26N 139.51 E
Sète 11 Jk 43.24N 3.41 E
Sete de Setembro, Rio- 55 Fa 12.56S 52.51W
Sete Lagoas 54 Jg 19.27S 44.14W
Setenil 13 Gh 36.51N 5.11W
Sete Quedas, Saltos das- = Guaíra Falls (EN) 56 Jb 24.02S 54.16W
Setermoen 7 Eb 68.52N 18.28 E
Setesdal 7 Bg 59.05N 7.35 E
Setesdalsheiane 8 Be 59.30N 7.10 E
Seti 25 Gc 28.58N 81.06 E
Sétif 32 Ib 36.05N 5.00 E
Sétif 31 He 36.12N 5.24 E
Seto 29 Ed 35.13N 137.05 E
Setonaikai = Inland Sea (EN) 21 Pf 34.10N 133.00 E
Setouchi 29b Ba 28.08N 129.20 E
Šetpe 19 Fg 44.06N 52.02 E
Settat 32 Fc 33.00N 7.37W
Settat 32 Fc 33.00N 7.30W
Setté Cama 36 Ac 2.32S 9.45 E
Sette-Daban, Hrebet- 20 Id 62.00N 138.00 E
Settle 9 Kg 54.04N 2.16W
Setúbal 13 Df 38.20N 8.30W
Setúbal 6 Fh 38.32N 8.54W
Setúbal, Baía de- 13 Df 38.27N 8.53W
Setúbal o de Guadalupe, Laguna- 55 Bj 31.33S 60.35W
Seudre 11 Ei 45.48N 1.09W
Seugne 11 Fi 45.42N 0.32W
Seui 14 Dk 39.50N 9.19 E
Seuil-d'Argonne 12 Hf 48.58N 5.03 E
Seul, Lac- 38 Jd 50.20N 92.30W
Seulles 12 Be 49.20N 0.27W
Seurre 11 Lg 47.00N 5.09 E
Sevan 19 Eg 40.32N 44.57 E
Sevan, Lake- (EN) = Sevan, Ozero- 5 Kg 40.20N 45.20 E
Sevan, Ozero- = Sevan, Lake- (EN) 5 Kg 40.20N 45.20 E
Sévaré 34 Ec 14.32N 4.06W
Sevastopol 6 Jg 44.36N 33.32 E
Ševčenko 16 He 43.35N 51.05 E
Ševčenko, Zaliv- 18 Ca 46.30N 60.15 E
Sevenoaks 9 Nj 51.16N 0.12 E
Sever 13 Ee 39.40N 7.32W
Sévérac-le-Château 11 Jj 44.19N 3.04 E
Severn 9 Kj 51.20N 3.10W
Severn [Can.] 38 Kd 56.02N 87.36W
Severn [U.K.] 9 Kj 51.35N 2.40W
Severnaja Dvina = Northern Dvina (EN) 5 Kc 64.32N 40.30 E
Severnaja Keltma 17 Ff 61.30N 54.00 E
Severnaja Pseašho, Gora- 16 Lh 43.47N 40.30 E
Severnaja Sosva 19 Gc 64.10N 65.28 E
Severnaja Zemlja = Severnaya Zemlya (EN) 21 Lb 79.30N 98.00 E
Severnaya Zemlya (EN) = Severnaja Zemlja 21 Lb 79.30N 98.00 E
Severn Lake 42 If 53.52N 90.58W
Severnoje [R.S.F.S.R.] 16 Rb 54.05N 52.32 E
Severnoje [R.S.F.S.R.] 20 Ce 56.21N 78.23 E
Severny 19 Gb 67.38N 64.06 E
Severnyje Uvaly = Northern Uvals (EN) 5 Kd 59.30N 49.00 E
Severny Kommunar 17 Gg 58.23N 54.02 E
Severny Ledovity Okean = Arctic Ocean (EN) 67 Be 85.00N 170.00 E
Severny Ural = Northern Urals (EN) 5 Lc 62.00N 59.00 E
Severobajkalsk 20 Fe 55.40N 109.25 E
Severočeský kraj 10 Kf 50.35N 14.15 E
Severodoneck 16 Ke 48.57N 38.31 E
Severodvinsk 6 Jc 64.34N 39.50 E
Severo-Jenisejski 20 Ed 60.28N 93.01 E
Severo-Kazahstanskaja Oblast 19 Ge 54.30N 68.00 E
Severo-Krymski Kanal 16 Ig 45.30N 34.35 E
Severo-Kurilsk 22 Rd 50.40N 156.08 E
Severomoravský kraj 10 Ng 49.45N 17.50 E
Severomorsk 19 Db 69.04N 33.24 E
Severo-Osetinskaja ASSR 19 Eg 43.00N 44.10 E
Severo-Sibirskaja Nizmennost = North Siberian Plain (EN) 21 Mb 72.00N 104.00 E
Severouralsk 19 Gc 60.09N 60.01 E
Sevier 46 Ig 38.35N 112.14W
Sevier Bridge Reservoir 46 Jg 39.21N 111.57W
Sevier Desert 46 Ig 39.25N 112.50W
Sevier Lake 43 Ed 38.55N 113.09W
Sevier River 43 Ed 39.04N 113.06W
Sevilla 13 Gg 37.30N 5.30W
Sevilla [Col.] 54 Cc 4.16N 75.53W
Sevilla [Sp.] = Seville (EN) 6 Fh 37.23N 5.59W
Sevilla, Isla- 49 Fi 8.14N 82.24W
Seville (EN) = Sevilla [Sp.] 6 Fh 37.23N 5.59W
Sevlijevo 15 If 43.01N 25.06 E
Sèvre Nantaise 11 Eg 47.12N 1.33W
Sèvre Niortaise 11 Eh 46.18N 1.08W
Sevron 11 Lh 46.32N 5.16 E
Sevsk 16 Ic 52.08N 34.30 E
Sewa 34 Cd 7.18N 12.08W
Seward [Ak.-U.S.] 39 Ec 60.06N 149.26W
Seward [Nb.-U.S.] 45 Hf 40.55N 97.06W
Seward Peninsula 38 Cc 65.00N 164.00W
Sewell 56 Fd 34.05S 70.21W
Seyāhkal 24 Md 37.09N 49.52 E
Seybaplaya 48 Nh 19.39N 90.40W
Seybaplaya, Punta- 48 Nh 19.45N 90.42W
Seybouse, Oued- 14 Bn 36.53N 7.46 E
Seychelles 31 Mi 8.00S 55.00 E
Seychelles Islands 30 Mi 4.35S 55.40 E
Seydān 24 Og 30.01N 53.01 E
Seydişehir 24 Dd 37.25N 31.51 E
Seyðisfjörður 6 Eb 65.16N 14.00W
Seyfe Gölü 24 Fc 39.13N 34.23 E
Seyf Ţāleh 24 Le 35.57N 46.19 E
Seyhan 23 Db 36.43N 34.53 E
Seyitgazi 24 Dc 39.27N 30.43 E
Seyitömer 15 Mj 39.34N 29.52 E
Seyla' 35 Gc 11.21N 43.30 E
Seymour [Austl.] 59 Jg 37.02S 145.08 E
Seymour [In.-U.S.] 44 Ef 38.58N 85.53W
Seymour [Mo.-U.S.] 45 Jh 37.09N 92.46W
Seymour [S.Afr.] 37 Df 32.33S 26.46 E
Seymour [Tx.-U.S.] 43 He 33.35N 99.16W
Sezana 14 He 45.42N 13.52 E
Sézanne 11 Jf 48.43N 3.43 E
Sfaktiria 15 Em 36.56N 21.40 E
Sfax (EN) = Şafāqis 32 Jc 34.30N 10.30 E
Sfax (EN) = Şafāqis 31 Ie 34.44N 10.46 E
Sferracavallo, Capo- 14 Dk 39.43N 9.40 E
Sfintu Gheorghe [Rom.] 15 Me 44.53N 29.26 E
Sfintu Gheorghe [Rom.] 15 Id 45.52N 25.47 E
Sfintu Gheorghe, Braţul- 15 Me 44.53N 29.36 E
Sfintu Gheorghe, Ostrovul- 15 Md 45.07N 29.22 E
Sfizef 13 Li 35.14N 0.15W
's-Gravenhage/Den Haag = The Hague (EN) 6 Ge 52.06N 4.18 E
's-Gravenhage-Scheveningen 11 Kb 52.06N 4.18 E
Shaan-hsi Sheng → Shaanxi Sheng = Shensi (EN) 27 Id 36.00N 109.00 E
Shaanxi Sheng (Shaan-hsi Sheng) = Shensi (EN) 27 Id 36.00N 109.00 E
Shaba 36 Ed 8.30S 25.00 E
Sha'bah, Wādī ash- 24 Ij 25.59N 41.55 E
Shabeellaha Dhexe 35 He 3.00N 46.00 E
Shabeellaha Hoose 35 Ge 2.00N 44.40 E
Shabēlle, Webi- = Shebeli Webi (EN) 30 Lh 0.12S 42.45 E
Shabestar 24 Kc 38.11N 45.42 E
Shabunda 36 Ec 2.42S 27.20 E
Shache/Yarkant 27 Cd 38.24N 77.15 E
Shacheng → Huailai 27 Kc 40.29N 115.30 E
Shackleton Coast 66 Kg 82.00S 162.00 E
Shackleton Glacier 66 Lg 84.35S 176.15W
Shackleton Ice Shelf 66 He 66.00S 101.00 E
Shackleton Range 66 Ag 80.40S 26.00W
Shaddādī 24 Id 36.02N 40.45 E
Shādegān 24 Mg 30.40N 48.38 E
Shadwān, Jazīrat- 33 Fd 27.30N 33.55 E
Shaftesbury 9 Kk 51.01N 2.12W
Shagedu → Jungar Qi 27 Jd 39.37N 110.58 E
Shāghir Bazar 24 Id 36.52N 40.53 E
Shag Rocks 66 Rd 54.26S 36.33W
Shāh 'Abbās 24 Oe 34.44N 52.10 E
Shah Alam 26 Df 3.05N 101.29 E
Shahdol 25 Gd 23.13N 81.18 E
Sha He [China] 28 Ch 33.39N 114.38 E
Sha He [China] 28 Cf 37.09N 114.46 E
Shahezhen → Linze 27 Hd 39.10N 100.21 E
Shah Jahān, Kūh-e- 24 Qd 37.02N 57.54 E
Shahjahānpur 25 Fc 27.53N 79.55 E
Shah Kūh 23 Hb 36.35N 54.31 E
Shahmīrzād 24 Oe 35.47N 53.20 E
Shāhpūr 24 Nh 32.50N 51.45 E
Shāhpūr 24 Nh 29.39N 51.03 E
Shahrak 24 Nd 36.14N 50.40 E
Shahr-e Bābak 24 Pg 30.10N 55.09 E
Shahr-e Khafr 24 Oh 28.56N 53.14 E
Shahr Kord 23 Hc 32.19N 50.50 E
Shāhrūd 24 Md 37.17N 48.43 E
Shahu, Kūh-e- 24 Le 34.45N 46.30 E
Shāh Zeyd 24 Od 36.13N 52.22 E
Sha'īb al Banāt, Jabal- 30 Kf 26.59N 33.29 E
Sha'īt, Wādī- 24 Ej 24.33N 33.01 E
Shakaga-Dake 29 Be 33.11N 130.53 E
Shakawe 31 Ji 18.23S 21.51 E
Shak Bay (Denham) 59 Ce 25.55S 113.32 E
Shaker Heights 44 Ge 41.29N 81.36W
Shaki 34 Fd 8.40N 3.23 E
Shakotan-Dake 29a Bb 43.16N 140.26 E
Shakotan-Hantō 29a Bb 43.15N 140.30 E
Shakotan-Misaki 29a Bb 43.23N 140.28 E
Shaktoolik 40 Gd 64.20N 161.09W
Shāl 24 Me 35.54N 49.46 E
Shala, Lake- 35 Fd 7.29N 38.32 E
Shalamzār 24 Nf 32.02N 50.49 E
Shalānbōd 35 Ge 1.40N 44.42 E
Shaler Mountains 42 Gb 71.45N 111.00W
Shaliuhe → Gangca 27 Hd 37.30N 100.14 E
Shaluli Shan 21 Lf 30.45N 99.45 E
Shām, Bādiyat ash- = Syrian Desert (EN) 21 Ff 32.00N 40.00 E
Shām, Jabal ash- 21 Hg 23.10N 57.20 E
Shamattawa 42 Ie 55.52N 92.05W
Shambe 35 Ed 7.07N 30.46 E
Shambu 35 Fd 9.33N 37.07 E
Shamil 24 Qi 27.30N 56.53 E
Shāmīyah 21 Ff 34.00N 39.59 E
Shammar, Jabal- 21 Gg 27.20N 41.45 E
Shamo, Lake- 35 Fd 5.50N 37.40 E
Shamokin 44 Ie 40.47N 76.34W
Shamrock 45 Fi 35.13N 100.15W
Shams 24 Pg 31.04N 55.02 E
Shamsī 35 Db 19.03N 29.54 E
Shamwa 37 Ec 17.18S 31.34 E
Shan 25 Jd 22.00N 98.00 E
Shandī 31 Kg 16.42N 33.26 E
Shandian He 28 Dc 42.20N 116.20 E
Shandong Bandao = Shantung Peninsula (EN) 21 Of 37.00N 121.00 E
Shandong Sheng (Shan-tung Sheng) = Shantung (EN) 27 Kd 36.00N 119.00 E
Shandūr Pass 25 Ea 36.04N 72.31 E
Shangani 37 Dc 19.42S 29.22 E
Shangani 37 Dc 18.30S 27.11 E
Shangbahe 28 Ci 30.39N 115.06 E
Shangcai 28 Ch 33.16N 114.15 E
Shangcheng 28 Ci 31.49N 115.24 E
Shangdu 27 Jc 41.31N 113.32 E
Shanggao 28 Cj 28.15N 114.55 E
Shanghai 22 Of 31.14N 121.28 E
Shanghai Shi (Shang-hai Shih) 27 Le 31.14N 121.28 E
Shang-hai Shih → Shanghai Shi 27 Le 31.14N 121.28 E
Shanghang 27 Kf 25.04N 116.21 E
Shanghe 28 Df 37.19N 117.09 E
Shanghekou 27 Lc 40.26N 124.51 E
Shangpaihe → Feixi 28 Di 31.42N 117.09 E
Shangqiu (Zhuji) 27 Ke 34.24N 115.37 E
Shangrao 27 Kf 28.29N 117.59 E
Shan Guan 27 Kf 27.28N 117.05 E
Shangxian 27 Ie 33.55N 109.57 E
Shangyi (Nanhaoqian) 28 Bd 41.06N 113.58 E
Shangyu (Baiguan) 28 Fi 30.01N 120.53 E
Shangzhi 27 Mb 45.13N 127.55 E
Shanhaiguan 28 Ed 40.01N 119.45 E
Shanhetun 28 Ib 44.43N 127.14 E
Shan-hsi Sheng → Shanxi Sheng = Shansi (EN) 27 Jd 37.00N 112.00 E
Shanklin 12 Ad 50.37N 1.11W
Shanmatang Ding 27 Jg 24.45N 111.50 E
Shannon 41 Kc 75.20N 18.10W
Shannon 62 Fd 40.33S 175.25 E
Shannon/Aerfort na Sionainne 9 Ei 52.42N 8.57W
Shannon/An tSionainn 5 Fe 52.36N 9.41W
Shannon, Mount- 59 Ie 29.58S 141.30 E
Shannon, Mouth of the- 9 Di 52.30N 9.53W
Shanshan (Piqan) 27 Fc 42.52N 90.10 E
Shansi (EN) = Shan-hsi Sheng → Shanxi Sheng 27 Jd 37.00N 112.00 E
Shansi (EN) = Shanxi Sheng (Shan-hsi Sheng) 27 Jd 37.00N 112.00 E
Shansonggang 28 Ic 42.30N 126.13 E
Shanţah, Ra's- 24 Qi 26.22N 56.26 E
Shantar Islands (EN) = Šantarskije Ostrova 21 Pd 55.00N 137.36 E
Shantou 22 Ng 23.26N 116.42 E
Shantung (EN) = Shandong Sheng (Shan-tung Sheng) 27 Kd 36.00N 119.00 E
Shantung (EN) = Shan-tung Sheng → Shandong Sheng 27 Kd 36.00N 119.00 E
Shantung Peninsula (EN) = Shandong Bandao 21 Of 37.00N 121.00 E
Shan-tung Sheng → Shandong Sheng = Shantung (EN) 27 Kd 36.00N 119.00 E
Shanxian 28 Dg 34.47N 116.05 E
Shanxi Sheng (Shan-hsi Sheng) = Shansi (EN) 27 Jd 37.00N 112.00 E
Shanyin (Daiyue) 28 Be 39.30N 112.48 E
Shanyincheng 28 Be 39.27N 112.56 E
Shaoguan 22 Ng 24.57N 113.34 E
Shaoshan 27 Jf 27.55N 112.32 E
Shaowu 27 Kf 27.21N 117.29 E
Shaoxing 22 Og 30.00N 120.30 E
Shaoyang 22 Ng 27.13N 111.31 E
Shapinsay 9 Kb 59.03N 2.51W
Shaqlāwah 24 Kd 36.23N 44.18 E
Shaqq al Ju'ayfir 35 Db 15.16N 26.00 E
Shaqrā' 23 Gg 13.21N 45.42 E
Shaqū 24 Qi 27.14N 56.22 E
Sharāf 24 Jg 30.37N 43.45 E
Sharafah 35 Dc 12.04N 27.07 E
Sharafkhāneh 24 Kc 38.11N 45.29 E
Sharāh, Jibāl ash- 24 Fg 30.10N 35.30 E
Sharā 'Iwah 24 Oj 25.02N 52.14 E
Shareh 24 Kd 37.38N 44.50 E
Shari 27 Pc 43.55N 144.40 E
Shārī, Buḩayrat- 24 Ke 34.23N 44.07 E
Shari-Dake 29a Db 43.46N 144.43 E
Sharifābād [Iran] 24 Nd 36.12N 50.08 E
Sharifābād [Iran] 24 Ne 35.25N 51.47 E
Shark Bay 57 Cg 25.30S 113.30 E
Sharm ash Shaykh 33 Fd 27.50N 34.16 E
Sharon 44 Ge 41.16N 80.30W
Sharon Springs 45 Fg 38.54N 101.45W
Sharp 9 Fc 58.05N 7.05W
Sharqīyah, Aş Şaḩrā' ash- = Arabian Desert (EN) 30 Kf 28.00N 32.00 E
Sharshar, Jabal- 24 Dk 23.52N 30.20 E
Shary 23 Fd 27.15N 43.27 E
Shashe 37 Dd 21.24S 27.27 E
Shashemene 35 Fd 7.13N 38.36 E
Shashi 22 Nf 30.22N 112.11 E
Shashi 30 Jk 22.12S 29.21 E
Shasta, Mount- 38 Ge 41.20N 122.20W
Shasta Lake 43 Cc 40.50N 122.25W
Shāţī', Wādī ash- 33 Bd 27.10N 13.25 E
Shattuck 45 Gh 36.16N 99.53W
Shaunavon 42 Gg 49.40N 108.25W
Shawan 27 Ec 44.21N 85.37 E
Shawano 45 Ld 44.47N 88.36W
Shawinigan 42 Kg 46.33N 72.45W
Shawnee 43 Hd 35.20N 96.55W
Shawneetown 45 Lh 37.42N 88.08W
Shaw River 59 Dd 20.20S 119.17 E
Shāwshāw, Jabal- 24 Ci 26.03N 28.56 E
Shayang 28 Bi 30.42N 112.34 E
Shaybārā 24 Gj 25.25N 36.51 E
Shaykh Aḥmad 24 Lf 32.53N 46.26 E
Shaykh Fāris 24 Lf 32.05N 47.36 E
Shaykh Sa'd 24 Lf 32.34N 46.17 E
Shaykh 'Uthmān 23 Fg 12.52N 44.59 E
Shebar, Kowtal-e- 23 Kc 34.54N 68.14 E
Shebele, Wabe- = Shebeli Webi (EN) 30 Lh 0.12S 42.45 E
Shebeli Webi (EN) = Shabēlle, Webi- 30 Lh 0.12S 42.45 E
Shebeli Webi (EN) = Shebele, Wabe- 30 Lh 0.12S 42.45 E
Sheberghān 22 If 36.41N 65.45 E
Sheboygan 45 Me 43.46N 87.44W
Shebshi Mountains 30 Ih 8.30N 11.45 E
Shediac 42 Ee 55.50N 127.00W
Sheelin, Lough-/Loch Sileann 9 Fh 53.48N 7.20W
Sheenjek 40 Kc 66.45N 144.33W
Sheep Haven/Cuan na gCaorach 9 Ff 55.10N 7.52W
Sheep Mountain 46 Hj 32.32N 114.14W
Sheep Range 46 Hh 36.45N 115.05W
s'Heerenberg, Bergh- 12 Ic 51.53N 6.16 E
Sheerness 9 Nj 51.27N 0.45 E
Sheffield [Al.-U.S.] 44 Dh 34.46N 87.40W
Sheffield [Eng.-U.K.] 6 Fe 53.23N 1.30W
Sheffield [Tx.-U.S.] 45 Fk 30.43N 101.50W
Shefford 12 Bb 52.02N 0.20W
Shek Hasan 35 Fc 12.04N 35.53 E
Shek Husen 35 Gd 7.45N 40.42 E
Shelburne [N.S.-Can.] 42 Kh 43.46N 65.19W
Shelburne [Ont.-Can.] 44 Gc 44.04N 80.12W
Shelby [Mt.-U.S.] 43 Eb 48.30N 111.51W
Shelby [N.C.-U.S.] 44 Gh 35.17N 81.32W
Shelbyville [Il.-U.S.] 45 Lg 39.24N 88.48W
Shelbyville [In.-U.S.] 44 Ef 39.31N 85.47W
Shelbyville [Tn.-U.S.] 44 Dh 35.29N 86.27W
Shelbyville, Lake- 45 Lg 39.30N 88.40W
Sheldon 45 Ie 43.11N 95.51W
Sheldon Point 40 Gd 63.32N 164.52W
Shelikhov Gulf (EN) = Šelihova, Zaliv- 21 Rc 60.00N 158.00 E
Shelikof Strait 40 Ie 57.30N 155.00W
Shell 46 Ld 44.33N 107.44W
Shellbrook 42 Gf 53.13N 106.24W
Shellharbour 58 Gh 34.35S 150.52 E
Shelter Point 62 Cg 47.06S 168.13 E
Shelton 46 Dc 47.13N 123.06W
Shenandoah 45 If 40.46N 95.22W
Shenandoah Mountain 44 Hf 38.58N 79.00W
Shenandoah Valley 44 Hf 38.45N 78.45W
Shenchi 28 Be 39.05N 112.11 E
Shendam 34 Gd 8.53N 9.32 E
Shending Shan 27 Nb 46.34N 133.27 E
Shenge 34 Cd 7.55N 12.57W
Shëngjini 15 Ch 41.49N 19.35 E
Shengsi (Caiyuanzhen) 28 Gi 30.42N 122.29 E
Shengsi Liedao 27 Le 30.45N 122.40 E
Shengxian 27 Lf 29.35N 120.45 E
Shengze 28 Fi 30.55N 120.39 E
Shenjiamen → Putuo 28 Gj 29.57N 122.18 E
Shenmu 27 Jd 38.52N 110.35 E
Shenqiu (Huaidian) 27 Ke 33.27N 115.05 E
Shensi (EN) = Shaan-hsi Sheng → Shaanxi Sheng 27 Id 36.00N 109.00 E
Shensi (EN) = Shaanxi Sheng (Shaan-hsi Sheng) 27 Id 36.00N 109.00 E
Shenton, Mount- 59 Ee 28.00S 123.22 E
Shenxian 28 Ce 38.01N 115.33 E
Shenyang (Mukden) 22 Oe 41.48N 123.24 E
Shenze 28 Ce 38.11N 115.11 E
Shepherd, Iles- = Shepherd Islands (EN) 63b Dc 16.55S 168.35 E
Shepherd Islands (EN) = Shepherd, Iles- 63b Dc 16.55S 168.35 E
Shepparton 58 Fh 36.23S 145.25 E
Sheppey 9 Nj 51.24N 0.50 E
Shepshed 12 Ab 52.45N 1.17W
Sheqi 28 Bh 33.04N 112.56 E
Sherard, Cape - 42 Jb 74.36N 80.10W
Sherard Osborn Fjord 41 Gb 82.10N 51.30W
Sherborne 9 Kk 50.57N 2.31W
Sherbro Island 30 Fh 7.33N 12.42W
Sherbrooke 39 Le 45.24N 71.54W
Sherda 35 Ba 20.08N 16.45 E
Shere Hill 34 Gd 9.57N 9.03 E
Sheridan [Mt.-U.S.] 46 Id 45.27N 112.12W
Sheridan [Wy.-U.S.] 39 Ie 44.48N 106.58W
Sheridan Lake 45 Eg 38.30N 102.15W
Sheringham 9 Oi 52.57N 1.12 E
Sherman 43 He 33.38N 96.36W
Sherman Station 44 Mc 45.54N 68.26W
Sherridon 42 He 55.07N 101.05W
's-Hertogenbosch/Den Bosch 11 Lc 51.41N 5.19 E
Sherwood Forest 9 Lh 53.10N 1.10W
She Shui 28 Ci 30.52N 114.22 E
Shetland 9 La 60.30N 1.30W
Shetland Islands (Zetland) 5 Fc 60.30N 1.30W
Shewa 35 Fd 9.20N 38.55 E
Shewa Gimira 35 Fd 7.00N 35.50 E
Shexian 28 Bf 36.33N 113.40 E
Shexian (Huicheng) 28 Ej 29.53N 118.27 E
Sheyang (Hede) 28 Fh 33.47N 120.15 E
Sheyenne River 43 Hb 47.05N 96.50W
Shiant Islands 9 Gd 57.54N 6.30W
Shibām 35 Hb 15.56N 48.38 E
Shibamīnah, Wādī- 23 Ie 22.12N 55.30 E
Shibata [Jap.] 28 Of 37.57N 139.20 E
Shibata [Jap.] 29 Gb 38.05N 140.50 E
Shibayama-Gata 29 Ec 36.21N 136.23 E
Shibazhan 27 Ma 42.28N 125.20 E
Shibecha 28 Rc 43.17N 144.36 E
Shibetsu [Jap.] 28 Rc 43.40N 145.08 E
Shibetsu [Jap.] 27 Pc 44.10N 142.23 E
Shibetsu-Gawa 29a Db 43.40N 145.06 E
Shibīn al Kawm 33 Fc 30.33N 31.01 E
Shibiutan 29a Ca 44.47N 142.35 E
Shibi-Zan 29 Bf 31.59N 130.22 E
Shib Kūh 23 Hd 27.20N 52.40 E
Shibukawa 28 Of 36.29N 139.00 E
Shibushi 29 Bf 31.28N 131.07 E
Shibushi-Wan 28 Ki 31.25N 131.12 E
Shichinohe 29 Ga 40.41N 141.10 E
Shichiyo Islands 64d Bb 7.23N 151.40 E
Shidao 27 Ld 36.51N 122.18 E
Shido 29 Dd 34.19N 134.10 E
Shidongsi → Gaolan 27 Hd 36.23N 103.55 E
Shiel, Loch- 9 He 56.50N 5.50W
Shiga Ken 28 Ng 35.15N 136.10 E
Shigu 27 Gf 26.54N 99.44 E
Shi He 28 Ch 32.32N 115.52 E
Shihezi 27 Ec 44.18N 86.02 E
Shiiba 29 Be 32.28N 131.09 E
Shijaku 15 Ch 41.20N 19.34 E
Shijiazhuang 22 Nf 38.00N 114.30 E
Shijiusuo 28 Eg 35.24N 119.32 E
Shika 29 Ec 37.01N 136.46 E
Shikabe 29a Bb 42.02N 140.47 E
Shikārpur 25 Dc 27.57N 68.38 E
Shiki Islands 64d Bb 7.24N 151.53 E
Shikine-Jima 29 Fd 34.19N 139.13 E
Shikoku 21 Pf 33.30N 133.30 E
Shikoku Basin (EN) 27 Oe 30.00N 135.30 E
Shikoku-Sanchi 29 Ce 33.45N 133.35 E
Shilabo 35 Gd 6.05N 44.45 E
Shiliguri 22 Kg 26.42N 88.26 E
Shilu → Changjiang 27 Ih 19.20N 109.03 E
Shilla 25 Fb 32.24N 78.12 E
Shillong 22 Lg 25.34N 91.53 E
Shimabara 28 Kh 32.47N 130.22 E
Shimabara-Hantō 29 Be 32.45N 130.15 E
Shimabara-Wan 29 Be 32.50N 130.30 E
Shimada 29 Fd 34.49N 138.09 E
Shima-Hantō 29 Ed 34.25N 136.45 E
Shimane-Hantō 29 Cd 35.30N 133.00 E
Shimane Ken 28 Lg 35.00N 132.20 E
Shimanto-Gawa 29 Ce 32.56N 133.00 E
Shimaura-Tō 29 Bd 34.50N 131.50 E
Shimian 27 Hf 29.10N 102.26 E
Shimizu [Jap.] 29a Cb 43.01N 142.51 E
Shimizu [Jap.] 28 Og 35.01N 138.29 E
Shimla 22 Jf 31.06N 77.10 E
Shimoda 28 Og 34.40N 138.57 E
Shimodate 29 Fc 36.19N 139.58 E
Shimoga 22 Jh 13.55N 75.34 E
Shimo-Jima 29 Be 32.25N 130.05 E
Shimokawa 29a Ca 44.18N 142.38 E
Shimokita-Hantō 29a Bc 41.15N 141.05 E
Shimo-Koshiki-Jima 29 Af 31.40N 129.40 E
Shimo la Tewa 36 Gc 3.57S 39.44 E
Shimoni 36 Gc 4.39S 39.23 E
Shimonoseki 27 Ne 33.57N 130.57 E
Shimono-Shima 29 Ad 34.15N 129.15 E
Shimotsu 29 Dd 34.07N 135.08 E
Shimotsuma 29 Fc 36.11N 139.58 E
Shin, Loch- 9 Ic 58.07N 4.32W
Shinano 29 Fc 36.47N 138.10 E
Shinano-Gawa 29 Fc 37.57N 139.04 E
Shināş 24 Qj 24.43N 56.27 E
Shindand 23 Jc 33.18N 62.08 E
Shinga 36 Dc 3.16S 24.38 E
Shingbwiyang 25 Jc 26.41N 96.13 E
Shingū 27 Oe 33.44N 135.59 E
Shingwidzi 37 Ed 23.01S 30.43 E
Shinji 29 Cd 35.24N 132.54 E
Shinji-Ko 28 Lg 35.27N 133.02 E
Shinjō 27 Pd 38.46N 140.18 E
Shinkafe 34 Gc 13.05N 6.31 E
Shinminato 29 Ec 36.47N 137.04 E
Shinnanyō 29 Bd 34.05N 131.45 E
Shinshiro 29 Ed 34.53N 137.30 E
Shintoku 28 Qc 43.12N 142.55 E
Shintotsugawa 29a Bb 43.32N 141.40 E
Shinyanga 31 Ki 3.40S 33.26 E
Shinyanga 36 Fc 3.30S 33.00 E
Shiogama 29 Gb 38.19N 141.01 E
Shiojiri 28 Nf 36.06N 137.58 E
Shiokubi-Misaki 29a Bc 41.43N 140.57 E
Shio-no-Misaki 27 Oe 33.25N 135.45 E
Shipai → Huaining 28 Di 30.25N 116.39 E

Index Symbols

Independent Nation
State, Region
District, County
Municipality
Colony, Dependency
Continent
Physical Region
Historical or Cultural Region
Mount, Mountain
Volcano
Hill
Mountains, Mountain Range
Hills, Escarpment
Plateau, Upland
Pass, Gap
Plain, Lowland
Delta
Salt Flat
Valley, Canyon
Crater, Cave
Karst Features
Depression
Polder
Desert, Dunes
Forest, Woods
Heath, Steppe
Oasis
Cape, Point
Coast, Beach
Cliff
Peninsula
Isthmus
Sandbank
Island
Atoll
Rock, Reef
Islands, Archipelago
Rocks, Reefs
Coral Reef
Well, Spring
Geyser
River, Stream
Waterfall Rapids
River Mouth, Estuary
Lake
Salt Lake
Intermittent Lake
Reservoir
Swamp, Pond
Canal
Glacier
Ice Shelf, Pack Ice
Ocean
Sea
Gulf, Bay
Strait, Fjord
Lagoon
Bank
Seamount
Tablemount
Ridge
Shelf
Basin
Escarpment, Sea Scarp
Fracture
Trench, Abyss
National Park, Reserve
Point of Interest
Recreation Site
Cave, Cavern
Historic Site
Ruins
Wall, Walls
Church, Abbey
Temple
Scientific Station
Airport
Port
Lighthouse
Mine
Tunnel
Dam, Bridge

Shiping 27 Hg 23.44N 102.28 E
Shipki La 27 Ce 31.49N 78.45 E
Shippegan 42 Lg 47.45N 64.42W
Shiprock 45 Bh 36.47N 108.41W
Shipshaw, Rivière- 44 La 48.30N 71.15W
Shipu 28 Fj 29.17N 121.57 E
Shipugi Shankou 27 Ce 31.49N 78.45 E
Shiquan 27 Ie 33.05N 108.15 E
Shiquanhe 22 Jf 32.24N 79.52 E
Shiquan He 27 Ce 32.28N 79.44 E
Shiragami Dake 29 Ga 40.30N 140.01 E
Shiragami-Misaki 28 Pd 41.25N 140.12 E
Shirahama 29 De 33.40N 135.20 E
Shirakawa [Jap.] 29 Ed 35.36N 137.12 E
Shirakawa [Jap.] 29 Ec 36.17N 136.53 E
Shirakawa [Jap.] 28 Pf 37.07N 140.13 E
Shirane-San [Jap.] 27 Od 36.48N 139.22 E
Shirane-San [Jap.] 29 Fd 35.40N 138.13 E
Shirane-San [Jap.] 29 Fc 36.38N 138.32 E
Shiranuka 28 Rc 42.57N 144.05 E
Shiraoi 28 Pc 42.31N 141.16 E
Shirase Coast 66 Mf 78.30S 156.00W
Shirataka 29 Gb 38.11N 140.06 E
Shirataki 29a Cb 43.53N 143.09 E
Shīrāz 22 Hg 29.36N 52.32 E
Shirbin 24 Dg 31.11N 31.32 E
Shire 30 Kj 17.42S 35.19 E
Shiren 28 Id 41.54N 126.34 E
Shiretoko-Dake 29a Da 44.15N 145.14 E
Shiretoko-Hantō 29a Da 44.00N 145.00 E
Shiretoko-Misaki 27 Qc 44.21N 145.20 E
Shirgāh 24 Od 36.17N 52.54 E
Shiribetsu-Gawa 29a Bb 42.52N 140.21 E
Shiriha-Misaki 29a Db 42.56N 144.45 E
Shirikishinai 29a Bc 41.48N 141.05 E
Shirin 24 Qi 27.10N 56.41 E
Shirin sū 24 Me 35.29N 48.27 E
Shiriya-Zaki 27 Pc 41.26N 141.28 E
Shīr Kūh 21 Hf 31.37N 54.04 E
Shirley Mountains 46 Le 42.15N 106.30W
Shiroishi 28 Pe 38.00N 140.37 E
Shirone 29 Fc 37.46N 139.00 E
Shirotori 29 Ed 35.53N 136.52 E
Shirouma-Dake 29 Ec 36.45N 137.46 E
Shirshov Ridge (EN) 20 Me 57.30N 171.00 E
Shirvān 24 Lf 33.33N 46.49 E
Shirwan Mazīn 24 Kd 37.03N 44.10 E
Shishaldin Volcano 38 Cd 54.45N 163.57W
Shishi-Jima 29 Be 32.17N 130.15 E
Shishmaref 40 Fc 66.14N 166.09W
Shishou 27 Jf 29.42N 112.23 E
Shitai (Qili) 28 Di 30.12N 117.28 E
Shitara 29 Ed 35.05N 137.34 E
Shitou Shan 27 Ma 51.02N 125.12 E
Shivwits Plateau 46 Ih 36.10N 113.40W
Shiwa 28 Pe 39.33N 141.35 E
Shiwan Dashan 27 Ig 21.45N 107.35 E
Shiwa Ngandu 36 Fe 11.12S 31.43 E
Shiwpuri 25 Fc 25.26N 77.39 E
Shixian 28 Jc 43.05N 129.46 E
Shiyan 27 Je 32.34N 110.48 E
Shiyang He 27 Hd 39.00N 103.25 E
Shizilu → Junan 28 Eg 35.10N 118.50 E
Shizugawa 29 Gb 38.40N 141.28 E
Shizui 28 Ic 43.03N 126.09 E
Shizuishan (Dawukou) 27 Id 39.03N 106.24 E
Shizukuishi 29 Gb 39.42N 140.59 E
Shizunai 28 Qc 42.20N 142.22 E
Shizunai-Gawa 29a Cb 42.20N 142.22 E
Shizuoka 22 Pf 34.58N 138.23 E
Shizuoka Ken [2] 28 Og 35.00N 138.25 E
Shkodra 6 Hg 42.05N 19.30 E
Shkodrës, Liqen i- = Scutari, Lake- (EN) 5 Hg 42.10N 19.20 E
Shkumbini 15 Ch 41.01N 19.26 E
Shoal Lake 45 Fa 50.26N 100.34W
Shoal Lake 45 Ib 49.32N 95.00W
Shoal Lakes 45 Ha 50.20N 97.40W
Shōbara 28 Lg 34.51N 133.01 E
Shodo-Shima 29 Dd 34.30N 134.15 E
Shō-Gawa 29 Ec 36.47N 137.04 E
Shokanbetsu-Dake 29a Bb 43.43N 141.31 E
Shokotsu-Gawa 29a Ca 44.23N 143.17 E
Sholāpur → Solāpur 22 Jh 17.41N 75.55 E
Shoqān 24 Qd 37.20N 56.58 E
Shoranūr 25 Ff 10.46N 76.17 E
Shoreham-by-Sea 9 Mk 50.49N 0.16W
Shortland Islands 60 Fi 6.55S 155.53 E
Shosambetsu 29a Ba 44.32N 141.46 E
Shoshone 46 He 42.56N 114.24W
Shoshone Mountains 43 Dd 39.15N 117.25W
Shoshone Peak 46 Gh 36.56N 116.16W
Shoshone River 46 Kd 44.52N 108.11W
Shoshong 37 Dd 23.02S 26.31 E
Shoshoni 46 Ke 43.14N 108.07W
Shotor Khūn 23 Jc 34.20N 64.55 E
Shouchang 28 Ej 29.23N 119.12 E
Shouguang 28 Ef 36.53N 118.44 E
Shouxian (Shouyang) 28 Dh 32.35N 116.47 E
Shouyang → Shouxian 28 Dh 32.35N 116.47 E
Shōwa 29 Gb 39.51N 140.03 E
Show Low 46 Ji 34.15N 110.02W
Shqiperia = Albania (EN) [1] 6 Hg 41.00N 20.00 E
Shreveport 39 Jf 32.30N 93.45W
Shrewsbury 9 Ki 52.43N 2.45W
Shuangcheng 27 Mb 45.21N 126.17 E
Shuangjiang 27 Gg 23.27N 99.50 E
Shuangjiang → Tongdao 27 If 26.14N 109.45 E
Shuangliao 27 Lc 43.30N 123.30 E
Shuangyang 27 Mc 43.31N 125.28 E
Shuangyashan 22 Pe 46.37N 131.10 E
Shucheng 28 Di 31.28N 116.57 E
Shufu 27 Cd 39.27N 75.52 E
Shuguri Falls 36 Gd 8.31S 37.23 E
Shu He 28 Eg 34.07N 118.30 E
Shuicheng 27 Hf 26.34N 104.52 E
Shuiding → Huocheng 27 Dc 44.03N 80.49 E
Shuiji → Laixi 28 Ff 36.52N 120.31 E
Shuijiahu → Changfeng 28 Dh 32.29N 117.10 E
Shuikou → Jianghua 27 Jg 24.58N 111.56 E
Shuiye 28 Cf 36.08N 114.06 E
Shuizhai → Xiangcheng 28 Ch 33.27N 114.53 E
Shūl 24 Ng 30.10N 51.38 E
Shulan 27 Mc 44.26N 126.55 E
Shule 27 Cd 39.25N 76.06 E
Shule He 21 Le 40.20N 92.50 E
Shulu (Xinji) 28 Cf 37.56N 115.14 E
Shumagin Islands 40 He 55.07N 159.45W
Shumarinai-Ko 29a Ca 44.20N 142.13 E
Shunayn, Sabkhat- 33 Dc 30.10N 21.00 E
Shungnak 40 Hc 66.53N 157.02W
Shunyi 28 Dd 40.09N 116.38 E
Shuolong 27 Ig 22.51N 106.55 E
Shuoxian 27 Jd 39.18N 112.25 E
Shūr [Iran] 24 Pi 26.59N 55.47 E
Shūr [Iran] 24 Oh 28.12N 52.09 E
Shūr [Iran] 24 Ne 35.09N 51.30 E
Shūr [Iran] 24 Oh 28.33N 53.12 E
Shūr Āb 24 Pg 31.45N 55.15 E
Shurāb 23 Ic 33.07N 55.18 E
Shūsf 23 Jc 31.48N 60.01 E
Shūsh 24 Mf 32.12N 48.17 E
Shushica 15 Ci 40.34N 19.34 E
Shūshtar 23 Gc 32.03N 48.51 E
Shuswap Lake 46 Fa 50.57N 119.15W
Shūt 24 Oe 34.44N 52.53 E
Shuwak 35 Fc 14.23N 35.52 E
Shuyang 27 Ke 34.01N 118.52 E
Shuzenji 29 Fd 34.58N 138.55 E
Shwebo 25 Jd 22.34N 95.42 E
Shwell 25 Jd 23.56N 96.17 E
Shyok 25 Fa 35.13N 75.53 E
Sia 26 Jh 6.49S 134.19 E
Siagne 11 Mk 43.32N 6.57 E
Siāh Band 23 Kc 33.25N 65.21 E
Siāh-Chashmeh 24 Kc 39.04N 44.23 E
Siāh-Kūh 24 Oe 34.38N 52.16 E
Siak 26 Df 1.13N 102.09 E
Sialkot [Pak.] 25 Ea 35.15N 73.17 E
Sialkot [Pak.] 22 Jf 32.30N 74.31 E
Sianów 10 Mb 54.15N 16.16 E
Siantan, Pulau- 26 Ef 3.10N 106.15 E
Siargao 26 Ie 9.53N 126.02 E
Šiaškotan, Ostrov- 21 Re 48.49N 154.06 E
Siátista 15 Ei 40.16N 21.33 E
Siau, Pulau- 26 If 2.42N 125.24 E
Šiauliai/Šjauljaj 6 Id 55.53N 23.19 E
Siavonga 36 Ef 16.32S 28.43 E
Siazan 19 Eg 41.04N 49.06 E
Sibā'i, Jabal as- 33 Fd 25.43N 34.09 E
Sibaj 19 Fe 52.42N 58.39 E
Sibasa 37 Ed 22.56S 30.29 E
Šibenik 14 Jg 43.44N 15.53 E
Siberimanua 26 Cg 2.09S 99.34 E
Siberut, Pulau- 21 Lj 1.20S 98.55 E
Siberut, Selat- 26 Cg 0.42S 98.35 E
Sibi 25 Dc 29.33N 67.53 E
Sibigo 26 Cf 2.51N 95.55 E
Sibillini, Monti- 14 Hh 42.55N 13.15 E
Sibircatajaha 17 Lb 69.05N 64.43 E
Sibircevo 20 Ih 44.16N 132.20 E
Sibirjakova, Ostrov- 20 Cb 72.50N 79.00 E
Sibiti 36 Bc 3.41S 13.21 E
Sibiu [2] 15 Hd 45.46N 24.12 E
Sibiu 6 If 45.48N 24.09 E
Sibolga 22 Li 1.45N 98.48 E
Sibsāgar 25 Ic 26.59N 94.38 E
Sibu 22 Ni 2.18N 111.49 E
Sibuguey Bay 26 He 7.30N 122.40 E
Sibut 31 Ih 5.44N 19.05 E
Sibutu Islands 26 Gf 4.45N 119.20 E
Sibutu Passage 26 Gf 4.56N 119.36 E
Sibuyan 26 Hd 12.25N 122.34 E
Sibuyan Sea 26 Hd 12.50N 122.40 E
Siby 34 Dc 12.22N 8.22W
Sibyllenstein 10 Ke 51.12N 14.05 E
Sicani, Monti- 14 Hm 37.40N 13.15 E
Sicasica 54 Eg 17.22S 67.45W
Si Chon 25 Jg 9.00N 99.56 E
Sichuan Pendi 21 Mf 30.01N 105.00 E
Sichuan Sheng (Ssu-ch'uan Sheng) = Szechwan (EN) [2] 27 He 30.00N 103.00 E
Sicilia [2] 14 Im 37.45N 14.15 E
Sicilia = Sicily (EN) 5 Hh 37.30N 14.00 E
Sicilia, Canale di- = Sicily, Strait of- (EN) 5 Hh 37.20N 11.20 E
Sicilia, Mar di- 14 Gn 36.30N 13.00 E
Sicily (EN) = Sicilia 5 Hh 37.30N 14.00 E
Sicily, Strait of- (EN) = Sicilia, Canale di- 5 Hh 37.20N 11.20 E
Sicily, Strait of- (EN) = Tūnis, Canal de- 5 Hh 37.20N 11.20 E
Sico Tinto, Rio- 49 Ef 15.58N 84.58W
Sicuani 53 Ig 14.15S 71.15W
Šid 15 Cd 45.08N 19.14 E
Sidamo [3] 35 Fd 5.48N 38.50 E
Siddipet 25 Fe 18.06N 78.51 E
Side 24 Dd 36.46N 31.22 E
Sidéradougou 34 Ec 10.40N 4.15W
Siderno 14 Kl 38.16N 16.18 E
Siders/Sierre 14 Bd 46.17N 7.32 E
Šiderty 19 He 52.32N 74.50 E
Šiderty 19 He 51.40N 74.50 E
Sidheros, Ákra- 15 Jn 35.19N 26.19 E
Sidhirókastron 15 Gh 41.14N 23.23 E
Sīdī 'Abd ar Raḩmān 24 Cg 30.58N 28.44 E
Sidi Aich 13 Qh 36.37N 4.41 E
Sidi-Akacha 13 Nh 36.28N 1.18 E
Sidi Ali 13 Mh 36.06N 0.25 E
Sīdī'Alī al Makkī, Ra's- 14 Em 37.11N 10.17 E
Sīdī Barrānī 33 Ec 31.36N 25.55 E
Sidi Bel Abbes [3] 32 Gc 34.45N 0.35W
Sidi Bel Abbes 32 Gb 35.12N 0.38W
Sidi Bennour 32 Fc 32.39N 8.26W
Sidi di Daoud 13 Ph 36.51N 3.52 E
Sidi Ifni 31 Ff 29.33N 10.10W
Sidi Kacem 32 Fc 34.13N 5.42W
Sidikalang 26 Cf 2.45N 98.19 E
Sidi Lakhdar 13 Mh 36.10N 0.27 E
Sīdī Zayd, Jabal- 14 En 36.29N 10.20 E
Sidlaw Hills 9 Ke 56.30N 3.00W
Sidmouth 9 Jk 50.41N 3.15W
Sidney [B.C.-Can.] 42 Fg 48.39N 123.24W
Sidney [Mt.-U.S.] 43 Gb 47.43N 104.09W
Sidney [Nb.-U.S.] 43 Gc 41.09N 102.59W
Sidney [Oh.-U.S.] 44 Ee 40.16N 84.10W
Sidney Lanier, Lake- 44 Fh 34.15N 83.57W
Sidobre 11 Ik 43.40N 2.30 E
Sidorovsk 20 Dc 66.35N 82.30 E
Sidra 10 Tc 53.33N 23.30 E
Sidra, Gulf of-(EN) = Surt, Khalīj- 30 Ie 31.30N 18.00 E
Sidrolândia 55 Ee 20.55S 54.58W
Siedlce [2] 10 Sd 52.10N 22.15 E
Siedlce 10 Sd 52.11N 22.16 E
Siedlecka, Wysoczyzna- 10 Sd 52.10N 22.15 E
Sieg [Ger.] 10 Df 50.45N 7.05 E
Sieg [Ger.] 12 Kd 50.55N 8.01 E
Siegburg 10 Df 50.48N 7.12 E
Siegen 10 Ef 50.52N 8.02 E
Siemiatycze 10 Sd 52.26N 22.53 E
Siĕmréab 25 Kf 13.22N 103.51 E
Siena 14 Fg 43.19N 11.21 E
Sieniawa 10 Sf 50.11N 22.36 E
Sienne 11 Ee 49.00N 1.34W
Sieradz 10 Oe 51.36N 18.45 E
Sieradz [2] 10 Oe 51.35N 18.45 E
Sieradzka, Niecka- 10 Oe 51.35N 18.50 E
Sierck-les-Bains 12 Ie 49.26N 6.21 E
Sierpc 10 Pd 52.52N 19.41 E
Sierra Blanca 45 Dk 31.11N 105.21W
Sierra Blanca Peak 43 Fe 33.23N 105.48W
Sierra Colorada 56 Gf 40.35S 67.48W
Sierra Leone [1] 31 Fh 8.30N 11.30W
Sierra Leone Basin (EN) 3 Di 5.00N 17.00W
Sierra Leone Rise (EN) 3 Di 5.30N 21.00W
Sierra Madre 21 Oh 16.20N 122.00 E
Sierra Mojada 47 Dc 27.17N 103.42W
Sierre/Siders 14 Bd 46.17N 7.32 E
Siete Palmas 55 Cg 25.13S 58.20W
Siete Puntas, Rio- 55 Df 23.34S 57.20W
Şieu 15 Hb 47.11N 24.13 E
Sifié 34 Dd 7.59N 6.55W
Sífnos 15 Hm 37.00N 24.40 E
Sig 32 Gb 35.32N 0.11W
Siğacik Körfezi 15 Jk 38.12N 26.45 E
Sigean 11 Ik 43.02N 2.59 E
Sighetu Marmaţiei 15 Gb 47.56N 23.53 E
Sighişoara 15 Hc 46.13N 24.48 E
Sigli 26 Ce 5.23N 95.57 E
Siglufjördur 7a Ba 66.09N 18.55W
Sigmaringen 10 Fh 48.05N 9.13 E
Signal Peak 46 Hj 33.22N 114.03W
Signy Island 66 Re 60.43S 45.38W
Signy-l'Abbaye 12 Ge 49.42N 4.25 E
Signy-le-Petit 12 Ge 49.54N 4.17 E
Sigtuna 7 Dg 59.37N 17.43 E
Siguanea, Ensenada de la- 49 Fc 21.38N 83.05W
Siguatepeque 49 Df 14.32N 87.49W
Sigüenza 13 Jc 41.04N 2.38W
Siguiri 31 Gg 11.25N 9.10W
Sigulda 7 Fh 57.09N 24.53 E
Si He 28 Dg 35.11N 116.42 E
Sihong 28 Eh 33.28N 118.13 E
Sihote-Alin 21 Pe 48.00N 138.00 E
Sihou → Changdao 28 Ff 37.56N 120.42 E
Sihuas 54 Ce 8.34S 77.37W
Siikainen 8 Ic 61.52N 21.50 E
Siilinjärvi 7 Ge 63.02N 27.40 E
Siirt 23 Fb 37.56N 41.57 E
Sijunjung 26 Dg 0.42S 100.58 E
Sikaiana 63a Fc 8.22S 162.45 E
Sikakap 26 Dg 2.46S 100.13 E
Sikanni Chief 42 Fe 58.17N 121.46W
Sīkar 25 Fc 27.37N 75.09 E
Sikasso 31 Gg 11.20N 5.40W
Sikasso [3] 34 Dc 10.55N 7.00W
Sikéa [Grc.] 15 Fm 36.46N 22.56 E
Sikéa [Grc.] 15 Gi 40.03N 23.58 E
Sikeston 43 Jd 36.53N 89.35W
Sikinos 15 Im 36.50N 25.05 E
Sikkim [3] 25 Hc 27.50N 88.30 E
Siklós 10 Ok 45.51N 18.18 E
Sikonge 36 Fd 5.38S 32.46 E
Šikotan, Ostrov/Tō, Shikotan- 20 Jh 43.47N 146.45 E
Siktjah 20 Hc 69.55N 125.10 E
Sil 13 Eb 42.27N 7.43W
Sila Grande 14 Kk 39.20N 16.30 E
Sila Greca 14 Kk 39.30N 16.30 E
Šilalė/Šilale 7 Fi 55.29N 22.12 E
Šilalé/Šilale 7 Fi 55.29N 22.12 E
Silao 48 Ig 20.56N 101.26W
Silaogou 28 Be 39.59N 113.03 E
Sila Piccola 14 Kk 39.05N 16.35 E
Silba 14 If 44.23N 14.42 E
Silchar 25 Id 24.49N 92.48 E
Šilda 16 Ud 51.47N 59.50 E
Sildagapet 8 Ab 62.05N 5.10 E
Sile 14 Ge 45.28N 12.35 E
Şile 24 Cb 41.05N 29.35 E
Silega 19 Ec 64.03N 44.02 E
Silesia (EN) = Śląsk 10 Me 51.00N 16.45 E
Silesia (EN) = Śląsk 5 He 51.00N 16.45 E
Silet 32 He 22.39N 4.35 E
Silhouette Island 37b Ca 4.29S 55.14 E
Silifke 23 Db 36.23N 33.56 E
Siligir 20 Gc 68.27N 114.50 E
Siling Co 21 Kf 31.50N 89.00 E
Siling Jiao 27 Ke 8.20N 115.27 E
Silisili, Mauga- 65c Aa 13.35S 172.27W
Silistra [2] 15 Kf 44.07N 27.16 E
Silistra 15 Ke 44.07N 27.16 E
Silivri 24 Cb 41.04N 28.15 E
Siljan 7 Df 60.50N 14.45 E
Šilka 20 Gf 51.51N 116.02 E
Šilka 21 Od 53.22N 121.32 E
Silkeborg 7 Bh 56.10N 9.34 E
Sillamäe/Sillamjae 7 Gg 59.24N 27.43 E
Sillamjae/Sillamäe 7 Gg 59.24N 27.43 E
Sillaro 14 Ff 44.34N 11.51 E
Silleiro, Cabo- 13 Db 42.07N 8.54W
Sillé-le-Guillaume 11 Ff 48.12N 0.08W
Sillian 14 Gd 46.45N 12.25 E
Silli 35 Gc 11.00N 43.26 E
Siloam Springs 45 Ih 36.11N 94.32W
Siloana Plains 36 Df 17.15S 23.10 E
Šilovo 19 Ee 54.24N 40.52 E
Silsbee 45 Ik 30.21N 94.11W
Siltou 35 Bb 16.52N 15.43 E
Šilutė/Šilute 19 Cd 55.21N 21.30 E
Šilute/Šilutė 19 Cd 55.21N 21.30 E
Silvan 24 Ic 38.08N 41.01 E
Silvassa 25 Ed 20.20N 73.05 E
Silver Bank (EN) 49 Mc 20.30N 69.45W
Silver Bay 43 Ib 47.17N 91.16W
Silver City 43 Fe 32.46N 108.17W
Silverdalen 8 Fg 57.32N 15.44 E
Silver Lake 46 Ee 43.06N 120.53W
Silver Spring 44 If 39.02N 77.03W
Silver Springs 46 Fg 39.25N 119.13W
Silverthrone Mountain 46 Ba 51.31N 126.06W
Silverton [Co.-U.S.] 45 Ch 37.49N 107.40W
Silverton [Tx.-U.S.] 45 Fi 34.28N 101.19W
Silves [Braz.] 54 Gd 2.54S 58.27W
Silves [Port.] 13 Dg 37.11N 8.26W
Silvi 14 Ih 42.34N 14.06 E
Silvia 54 Cc 2.37N 76.24W
Silviers River 46 Fe 43.22N 118.48W
Silvretta 14 Ed 46.50N 10.15 E
Silyānah [3] 32 Ib 36.00N 9.30 E
Silyānah 32 Ib 36.05N 9.22 E
Silyānah, Wādī- 14 Dn 36.33N 9.25 E
Sim 17 Hi 54.59N 57.41 E
Sim 17 Hi 54.32N 56.30 E
Sim, Cap- 32 Fc 31.23N 9.51W
Simanggang 26 Ff 1.15N 111.26 E
Šimanovsk 20 Hf 52.01N 127.36 E
Simao 27 Hg 22.40N 101.02 E
Simard, Lac- 44 Hb 47.38N 78.40W
Simareh 24 Mf 32.08N 48.03 E
Simav 23 Ca 40.23N 28.31 E
Simav 24 Cc 39.05N 28.59 E
Simav Dağ 15 Lj 39.04N 28.54 E
Simav Gölü 15 Lj 39.09N 28.55 E
Simayama-Jima 29 Ae 32.40N 128.38 E
Simba 36 Db 0.36N 22.55 E
Simbo 36 Fc 4.53S 29.44 E
Simbo 63a Cc 8.18S 156.34 E
Simbruini, Monti- 14 Hj 41.55N 13.15 E
Simcoe 44 Gd 42.50N 80.18W
Simcoe, Lake- 42 Jh 44.27N 79.20W
Simen 35 Fc 13.25N 38.00 E
Simenti 34 Cc 13.00N 13.25W
Simeria 15 Gd 45.51N 23.01 E
Simeto 14 Jm 37.24N 15.06 E
Simeulue, Pulau- 21 Li 2.35N 96.05 E
Simferopol 6 Jf 44.57N 34.06 E
Simhah, Jabal- 23 Hf 17.20N 54.50 E
Simi 15 Km 36.36N 27.50 E
Simi 15 Km 36.35N 27.50 E
Simiti 49 Kj 7.58N 73.58W
Simitli 15 Gh 41.53N 23.06 E
Şimleu Silvaniei 15 Fb 47.14N 22.48 E
Simmental 14 Bd 46.35N 7.25 E
Simmerath 12 Id 50.36N 6.18 E
Simmerbach 12 Je 49.48N 7.31 E
Simmern 10 Dg 49.59N 7.31 E
Simmertal 12 Je 49.48N 7.33 E
Simnas 8 Jj 54.20N 23.45 E
Simo 7 Fd 65.39N 24.55 E
Simojärvi 7 Gc 66.06N 27.03 E
Simojoki 7 Fd 65.37N 25.03 E
Simojovel de Allende 48 Mi 17.12N 92.38W
Simonstown 37 Bf 34.14S 18.26 E
Simpele 7 Gf 61.26N 29.22 E
Simpelejärvi 8 Mc 61.30N 29.25 E
Simplon 14 Cd 46.15N 8.00 E
Simpson Desert 57 Eg 25.00S 137.00 E
Simpson Hill 59 Fe 26.30S 126.30 E
Simpson Peninsula 42 Ic 68.45N 89.10W
Simrishamn 7 Di 55.33N 14.20 E
Simsonbaai 51b Ab 18.02N 63.08W
Simušir, Ostrov- 21 Re 46.58N 152.02 E
Sina 25 Fe 17.22N 75.54 E
Sīnā' = Sinai Peninsula (EN) 30 Kf 29.30N 34.00 E
Sinabang 26 Cf 2.29N 96.23 E
Sinadaqo 35 Hd 5.22N 46.22 E
Sinai, Mount- (EN) = Mūsa, Jabal- 24 Eh 28.32N 33.59 E
Sinaia 15 Id 45.21N 25.33 E
Sinai Peninsula (EN) = Sīnā' 30 Kf 29.30N 34.00 E
Sinajana 64c Bb 13.28N 144.45W
Sinaloa [2] 47 Cc 25.00N 107.30W
Sinaloa, Llanos de- 47 Cc 25.00N 107.30W
Sinaloa, Río- 48 Ee 25.18N 108.30W
Sinaloa de Leyva 48 Ee 25.50N 108.14W
Sinalunga 14 Fg 43.12N 11.44 E
Sinamaica 54 Da 11.05N 71.51W
Sinan 27 If 27.56N 108.11 E
Sinara 17 Kh 56.17N 62.23 E
Sināwin 33 Bc 31.02N 10.36 E
Sinazongwe 36 Ef 17.15S 27.28 E
Şincai 15 Hc 46.39N 24.23 E
Sincanli 24 Dc 38.45N 30.15 E
Sincé 49 Ji 9.14N 75.06W
Sincelejo 53 Ie 9.18N 75.24W
Sinch'am 28 Jc 42.07N 129.25 E
Sinch'ang 28 Jd 40.07N 128.28 E
Sinch'on 28 He 38.28N 125.27 E
Sinclair, Lake- 44 Fi 33.11N 83.16W
Sind [3] 25 Cc 25.30N 69.00 E
Sind 21 Ig 25.30N 69.00 E
Sindal 8 Dg 57.28N 10.13 E
Sindangbarang 26 Eh 7.27S 107.08 E
Sindara 36 Bc 1.02S 10.40 E
Sindelfingen-Böblingen 10 Fh 48.41N 9.01 E
Sindfeld 12 Kc 51.32N 8.48 E
Sindi 7 Fg 58.24N 24.42 E
Sındırgı 24 Cc 39.14N 28.10 E
Sındırgı Geçidi 15 Lj 39.10N 28.04 E
Sîndominic 15 Ic 46.35N 25.47 E
Sindri 25 Hd 23.42N 86.29 E
Sinegorje 20 Kd 62.03N 150.25 E
Sinegorski 16 Le 48.00N 40.53 E
Sine-Ider 27 Gb 48.56N 99.33 E
Sinekli 15 Lh 41.14N 28.12 E
Sinelnikovo 16 Ie 48.18N 35.31 E
Sines 13 Dg 37.57N 8.52W
Sines, Cabo de- 13 Dg 37.57N 8.53W
Sine-Saloum [3] 34 Bc 14.00N 15.50W
Singako 35 Bd 9.50N 19.29 E
Singapore / Singapura 22 Mi 1.17N 103.51 E
Singapore Strait (EN) = Singapura, Selat- 26 Df 1.15N 104.00 E
Singapura / Singapore 22 Mi 1.17N 103.51 E
Singapura, Selat- = Singapore Strait (EN) 26 Df 1.15N 104.00 E
Singaraja 26 Gh 8.07S 115.06 E
Singatoka 63d Ac 18.08S 177.30 E
Sing Buri 25 Kf 14.53N 100.25 E
Singen 10 Ei 47.46N 8.50 E
Singeroz Băi 15 Hb 47.22N 24.41 E
Singida [3] 36 Fd 5.30S 34.30 E
Singida 31 Ki 4.49S 34.45 E
Singitic Gulf (EN) = Singitikós Kólpos 15 Gi 40.10N 23.55 E
Singitikós Kólpos = Singitic Gulf (EN) 15 Gi 40.10N 23.55 E
Singkaling Hkamti 25 Jc 26.00N 95.42 E
Singkang 26 Hg 4.08S 120.01 E
Singkawang 26 Ef 0.54N 109.00 E
Singkep, Pulau- 26 Dg 0.30S 104.25 E
Singkil 26 Cf 2.17N 97.49 E
Singleton [Austl.] 59 Kf 32.34S 151.10 E
Singleton [Eng.-U.K.] 12 Bd 50.55N 0.44W
Singleton, Mount- 59 De 29.28S 117.18 E
Singö 8 Hd 60.10N 18.45 E
Siniscola 14 Dj 40.34N 9.41 E
Sini vrâh 15 Ih 41.51N 25.01 E
Sinj 14 Kg 43.42N 16.38 E
Sinjah 35 Ec 13.09N 33.56 E
Sinjai 26 Hh 5.07S 120.15 E
Sinjaja 8 Mg 57.05N 28.33 E
Sinjajevina 15 Cf 43.00N 19.18 E
Sinjār 24 Id 36.19N 41.52 E
Sinjār, Jabal- 24 Id 36.23N 41.52 E
Sinjuža 16 Ge 48.03N 30.50 E
Sinkiang (EN) = Hsin-chiang-wei-wu-erh Tzu-chih-ch'ü → Xinjiang Uygur Zizhiqu [2] 27 Ec 42.00N 86.00 E
Sinkiang (EN) = Xinjiang Uygur Zizhiqu (Hsin-chiang-wei-wu-erh Tzu-chih-ch'ü) [2] 27 Ec 42.00N 86.00 E
Sin-le-Noble 12 Fd 50.22N 3.07 E
Sinmi-Do 28 He 39.33N 124.53 E
Sinn 12 Kd 50.39N 8.20 E
Sinn al Kadhdhāb 23 Fe 23.30N 32.05 E
Sinnamary 54 Hb 5.23N 53.00W
Sinni 14 Kj 40.08N 16.41 E
Sînnicolau Mare 15 Dc 46.05N 20.38 E
Sinnūris 24 Dh 29.25N 30.52 E
Sinnyŏng 28 Jf 36.02N 128.47 E
Sinoe [3] 34 Dd 5.20N 8.40W
Sinoe, Lacul- 15 Le 44.38N 28.53 E
Sinop 23 Ea 41.59N 35.09 E
Sinop Burun 24 Fa 42.02N 35.12 E
Sinp'o 28 Jd 40.02N 128.12 E
Sinsang 28 Ie 39.39N 127.25 E
Sinsheim 12 Eg 49.15N 8.53 E
Sint-Amandsberg, Gent- 12 Fc 51.04N 3.45 E
Sîntana 15 Ec 46.21N 21.30 E
Sint-Andries, Brugge- 12 Fc 51.12N 3.10 E
Sintang 26 Ff 0.04N 111.30 E
Sint Eustatius 47 Le 17.30N 62.59W
Sint-Gillis-Waas 12 Gc 51.13N 4.08 E
Sint Kruis 50 Bf 12.18N 69.08W
Sint Laureins 12 Fc 51.15N 3.31 E
Sint Maarten 50 Ec 18.04N 63.04W
Sint Nicolaas 50 Bf 12.26N 69.55W
Sint Niklaas/Saint-Nicolas 11 Kc 51.10N 4.08 E
Sint-Oedenrode 12 Hc 51.34N 5.28 E
Sinton 45 Hl 28.02N 97.33W
Sint-Pieters-Leeuw 12 Gd 50.47N 4.14 E
Sintra 13 Cf 38.48N 9.23W
Sint-Truiden/Saint-Trond 11 Ld 50.49N 5.12 E
Sintu 35 Fd 8.12N 36.56 E
Sinú, Río- 49 Ji 9.24N 75.49W
Sinŭiju 22 Oe 40.06N 124.24 E
Sinujif 35 Hd 8.30N 48.59 E
Sinzig 12 Jd 50.33N 7.15 E
Sió 10 Oj 46.23N 18.40 E
Siocon 26 He 7.42N 122.08 E
Siófok 10 Oj 46.54N 18.03 E
Sioma 36 Df 16.40S 23.35 E

Index Symbols

[1] Independent Nation
[2] State, Region
[3] District, County
[4] Municipality
[5] Colony, Dependency
Continent
Physical Region
Historical or Cultural Region
Mount, Mountain
Volcano
Hill
Mountains, Mountain Range
Hills, Escarpment
Plateau, Upland
Pass, Gap
Plain, Lowland
Delta
Salt Flat
Valley, Canyon
Crater, Cave
Karst Features
Depression
Polder
Desert, Dunes
Forest, Woods
Heath, Steppe
Oasis
Cape, Point
Coast, Beach
Cliff
Peninsula
Isthmus
Sandbank
Island
Atoll
Rock, Reef
Islands, Archipelago
Rocks, Reefs
Coral Reef
Well, Spring
Geyser
River, Stream
Waterfall Rapids
River Mouth, Estuary
Lake
Salt Lake
Intermittent Lake
Reservoir
Swamp, Pond
Canal
Glacier
Ice Shelf, Pack Ice
Ocean
Sea
Gulf, Bay
Strait, Fjord
Lagoon
Bank
Seamount
Tablemount
Ridge
Shelf
Basin
Escarpment, Sea Scarp
Fracture
Trench, Abyss
National Park, Reserve
Point of Interest
Recreation Site
Cave, Cavern
Historic Site
Ruins
Wall, Walls
Church, Abbey
Temple
Scientific Station
Airport
Port
Lighthouse
Mine
Tunnel
Dam, Bridge

Sion/Sitten 14 Bd 46.15N 7.20 E
Siorapaluk 41 Ec 77.39N 71.00W
Sioule 11 Jh 46.22N 3.19 E
Sioux City 39 Je 42.30N 96.23W
Sioux Falls 39 Je 43.32N 96.44W
Sioux Lookout 42 If 50.06N 91.55W
Sipalay 26 He 9.45N 122.24 E
Šipan 14 Lh 42.43N 17.54 E
Siparia 50 Fg 10.08N 61.30W
Šipčenski prohod 15 Ig 42.46N 25.19 E
Siping 22 Oe 43.11N 124.24 E
Sipiwesk 42 He 55.27N 97.24W
Sipiwesk Lake 42 He 55.05N 97.35W
Siple, Mount- 66 Nf 73.15S 126.06W
Siple Coast 66 Mg 82.00S 153.00W
Siple Island 66 Nf 73.39S 125.00W
Siple Station 66 Pf 75.55S 83.55W
Sipora, Pulau- 26 Cg 2.12S 99.40 E
Sippola 8 Ld 60.44N 27.00 E
Siqueira Campos 55 Hf 23.42S 49.50W
Siquia, Río- 49 Eg 12.09N 84.13W
Siquijor 26 He 9.13N 123.31 E
Siquisique 54 Ea 10.34N 69.42W
Šira 20 Ef 54.29N 90.02 E
Sira 8 Be 58.17N 6.24 E
Sira 7 Bg 58.25N 6.38 E
Şir Abū Nu'Ayr 24 Pj 25.13N 54.13 E
Si Racha 25 Kf 13.10N 100.57 E
Siracusa=Syracuse (EN) 6 Hh 37.04N 15.18 E
Sir Alexander, Mount- 42 Ff 53.56N 120.23W
Sirasso 34 Dd 9.16N 6.06W
Şirāt, Jabal- 33 Hf 17.00N 43.50 E
Sirba 34 Fc 13.46N 1.40 E
Şir Banī Yās 24 Oj 24.19N 52.37 E
Sirdalen 8 Bf 58.50N 6.40 E
Sirdalsvatn 8 Bf 58.35N 6.40 E
Sire [Eth.] 35 Fd 8.58N 37.00 E
Sire [Eth.] 35 Fd 8.16N 39.30 E
Sir Edward Pellew Group 59 Hc 15.40S 136.50 E
Siret 5 If 45.24N 28.01 E
Siret 15 Jb 47.57N 26.04 E
Sirevåg 7 Ag 58.30N 5.47 E
Sīrīk 23 Id 26.29N 57.09 E
Sirik, Tanjong- 26 Ff 2.46N 111.19 E
Sirina 15 Jm 36.21N 26.41 E
Sirino 14 Jj 40.07N 15.50 E
Sirius Seamount (EN) 40 Gf 52.00N 160.50W
Sirjajevo 16 Gf 47.24N 30.13 E
Sir James Mac Brian, Mount- 42 Ed 62.08N 127.40W
Sirjān, Kavir-e- 24 Ph 29.30N 55.30 E
Sirmione 14 Ee 45.29N 10.36 E
Şırnak 24 Jd 37.32N 42.28 E
Širokaja Pad 20 Jf 50.15N 142.11 E
Široki 20 Jd 63.04N 148.01 E
Širokoje 16 Hf 47.38N 33.14 E
Sironcha 25 Fe 18.50N 79.58 E
Siros 15 Hl 37.26N 24.55 E
Sirpsindiği 15 Jh 41.50N 26.29 E
Sirr, Nafūd as- 24 Kj 25.15N 44.45 E
Sirrayn 33 Hf 19.38N 40.36 E
Sirretta Peak 46 Fi 35.59N 118.20W
Sirri, Jazīreh-ye- 24 Pj 25.55N 54.32 E
Sirsa 25 Fc 29.32N 75.01 E
Sir Sandford, Mount- 46 Ga 51.40N 117.52W
Sirte Desert (EN)=As Sidrah 30 Ie 30.30N 17.30 E
Sir Thomas, Mount- 59 Fe 27.11S 129.46 E
Širvintos 7 Fi 55.03N 25.01 E
Sir Wilfrid Laurier, Mount- 42 Ff 52.48N 119.45W
Sisak 14 Ke 45.29N 16.22 E
Si Sa Ket 25 Ke 15.07N 104.19 E
Sīsakht 24 Ng 30.47N 51.33 E
Sisal 48 Ng 21.10N 90.02W
Sisante 13 Je 39.25N 2.13W
Sisargas, Islas- 13 Da 43.22N 8.50W
Šišchid-Gol 27 Ga 51.30N 97.10 E
Sishen 37 Ce 27.55S 22.59 E
Sishui 28 Dg 35.40N 117.17 E
Sisian 16 Oj 39.31N 46.03 E
Sisili 34 Ec 10.16N 1.15W
Sisimiut/Holsteinsborg 67 Nc 67.05N 53.45W
Siskiyou Mountains 46 Df 41.55N 123.15W
Sisŏphŏn 25 Kf 13.35N 102.59 E
Sissano 60 Ch 3.00S 142.03 E
Sisseton 45 Hd 45.40N 97.03W
Sissonne 12 Fe 49.34N 3.54 E
Sīstān=Seistan (EN) 21 If 30.30N 62.00 E
Sistema Central 5 Fg 40.30N 5.00W
Sistema Ibérico=Iberian Mountains (EN) 5 Fg 41.30N 2.30W
Sistemas Béticos 5 Fh 37.35N 3.30W
Sisteron 11 Lj 44.12N 5.56 E
Sisters 46 Ed 44.17N 121.33W
Sistranda 7 Be 63.43N 8.50 E
Sitāpur 25 Gc 27.34N 80.41 E
Sitasjaure 7 Dc 68.00N 17.25 E
Siteki 37 Ee 26.27S 31.57 E
Sitges 13 Nc 41.14N 1.49 E
Sithonia 15 Gi 40.05N 23.55 E
Sitia 15 Jn 35.12N 26.07 E
Sitio d'Abadia 55 Ib 14.48S 46.16W
Sitio Nuevo 49 Jh 10.46N 74.43W
Sitka 39 Fd 57.03N 135.14W
Sitkalidak 40 Ie 57.10N 153.14W
Sitna 15 Kb 47.30N 27.10 E
Sitnica 15 Dg 42.53N 20.52 E
Sitona 35 Fc 14.23N 37.22 E
Sitrah [Bhr.] 24 Ni 26.10N 50.40 E
Sitrah [Eg.] 24 Bh 28.42N 26.54 E
Sittard 11 Ld 51.00N 5.53 E
Sittee Point 49 Ce 16.48N 88.15W
Sitten/Sion 14 Bd 46.15N 7.20 E
Sittingbourne 12 Cc 51.20N 0.45 E
Sittoung 25 Je 17.10N 96.58 E
Sittwe (Akyab) 22 Lg 20.09N 92.54 E
Siuna 49 Eg 13.44N 84.46W
Siuslaw River 46 Cd 44.01N 124.08W
Siva 7 Mh 56.49N 53.55 E
Sivac 15 Cd 45.42N 19.23 E
Sivaki 20 Hf 52.38N 126.45 E
Sivas 22 Ff 39.50N 37.03 E
Sivaš, Ozero- 16 Ig 45.50N 34.40 E
Sivasli 15 Mk 38.30N 29.42 E
Šiveluč, Vulkan- 20 Le 56.33N 161.25 E
Sivera, Ozero-/Sivera Ezers 8 Li 55.58N 27.25 E
Sivera Ezers/Sivera, Ozero- 8 Li 55.58N 27.25 E
Siverek 23 Eb 37.45N 39.19 E
Siverski 7 Hg 59.22N 30.02 E
Sivomaskinski 17 Kc 66.40N 62.31 E
Sivrice 24 Hc 38.27N 39.19 E
Sivrihisar 24 Dc 39.27N 31.34 E
Sivry-Rance 12 Gd 50.10N 4.16 E
Sivry Rance-Rance 12 Gd 50.09N 4.16 E
Sivry-sur-Meuse 12 He 49.19N 5.16 E
Siwah 31 Jf 29.12N 25.31 E
Siwah, Wāḥāt-=Siwa Oasis (EN) 30 Jf 29.10N 25.40 E
Siwalik Range 21 Jg 29.00N 80.00 E
Siwān 25 Gc 26.13N 84.22 E
Siwa Oasis (EN)=Siwah, Wāḥāt- 30 Jf 29.10N 25.40 E
Sixaola, Río- 49 Fi 9.35N 82.34W
Six Cross Road 51q Bb 13.07N 59.28W
Six-Fours-la-Plage 11 Lk 43.06N 5.51 E
Sixian 28 Dh 33.29N 117.53 E
Six Men's Bay 51q Ab 13.16N 59.38W
Sixth Cataract (EN)=Sablūkah, Ash Shallāl as- 30 Kg 16.20N 32.42 E
Siyah-Chaman 24 Ld 37.35N 47.10 E
Siyang (Zhongxing) 28 Eh 33.43N 118.40 E
Siziwang Qi (Ulan Hua) 28 Ad 41.31N 111.41 E
Sjaelland=Zealand (EN) 5 Hd 55.30N 11.45 E
Sjamozero, Ozero- 7 Hf 61.55N 33.15 E
Sjare/Sääre 8 Ig 57.57N 21.53 E
Sjas 7 Hf 60.10N 32.31 E
Sjasstroj 7 Hf 60.09N 32.36 E
Šjašupe 7 Fi 55.00N 22.10 E
Šjauljaj/Šiauliai 6 Id 55.53N 23.19 E
Sjenica 15 Cf 43.16N 20.00 E
Sjnjaja 20 Hd 61.00N 126.57 E
Sjoa 8 Cc 61.41N 9.33 E
Sjöbo 8 Ei 55.38N 13.42 E
Sjøholt 7 Be 62.29N 6.50 E
Sjujutlijka 15 Ig 42.17N 25.55 E
Sjun 17 Gi 55.43N 54.17 E
Sjuøyane 41 Ob 80.43N 20.45 E
Skadarsko Jezero=Scutari, Lake- (EN) 5 Hg 42.10N 19.20 E
Skadovsk 19 Df 46.07N 32.56 E
Skælskør 8 Di 55.15N 11.19 E
Skærbæk 8 Ci 55.09N 8.46 E
Skagatá 7a Ba 66.07N 20.06W
Skagen 7 Ch 57.44N 10.36 E
Skagern 8 Ff 59.00N 14.15 E
Skagerrak 5 Gd 57.45N 9.00 E
Skaget 8 Cc 61.17N 9.12 E
Skagit River 46 Db 48.20N 122.25W
Skagway 39 Fd 59.28N 135.19W
Skaidi 7 Fa 70.26N 24.30 E
Skaland 7 Db 69.27N 17.18 E
Skälderviken 8 Eh 56.20N 12.40 E
Skållevik 8 Bf 58.04N 8.00 E
Skalisty Golec, Gora- [R.S.F.S.R.] 20 Ge 56.20N 119.10 E
Skalisty Golec, Gora- [R.S.F.S.R.] 20 Ie 55.55N 130.35 E
Skanderborg 7 Bh 56.02N 9.56 E
Skåne 5 Hd 56.00N 13.30 E
Skånevik 8 Ae 59.44N 5.59 E
Skänninge 8 Ff 58.24N 15.05 E
Skanör 8 Ei 55.25N 12.52 E
Skántzoura 15 Hj 39.05N 24.07 E
Skara 7 Cg 58.22N 13.25 E
Skaraborg [2] 7 Cg 58.20N 13.30 E
Skärblacka 8 Ff 58.34N 15.54 E
Skärdu 25 Fa 35.18N 75.37 E
Skärhamn 8 Dg 57.59N 11.33 E
Skarnes 8 Dd 60.15N 11.41 E
Skarsstind 8 Cb 62.03N 8.35 E
Skarsvåg 7 Fa 71.06N 25.56 E
Skarszewy 10 Ob 54.05N 18.27 E
Skarvdalsegga 8 Cb 62.09N 8.03 E
Skaryszew 10 Re 51.19N 21.15 E
Skarżysko-Kamienna 10 Qe 51.08N 20.53 E
Skasøy 8 Ca 63.20N 8.35 E
Skåt 15 Gf 43.44N 23.51 E
Skattkärr 8 Ee 59.25N 13.41 E
Skattungbyn 8 Fc 61.12N 14.52 E
Skaudvile/Skaudvilė 7 Fi 55.27N 22.33 E
Skaudvilė/Skaudvile 7 Fi 55.27N 22.33 E
Skaulen 8 Be 59.38N 6.35 E
Skawa 10 Pf 50.02N 19.26 E
Skawina 10 Pg 49.59N 19.49 E
Skee 8 Df 58.56N 11.19 E
Skeena 38 Fd 54.09N 130.02W
Skeena Mountains 42 Ee 56.45N 128.40W
Skegness 9 Nh 53.10N 0.21 E
Skeidararsandur 7a Cc 63.54N 17.14W
Skeldon 54 Gb 5.53N 57.08W
Skeleton Coast 37 Ac 17.50S 12.45 E
Skellefteå 6 Ic 64.46N 20.57 E
Skellefteälven 5 Ic 64.42N 21.06 E
Skelleftehamn 7 Ed 64.41N 21.14 E
Skënderbeut, Mali i- 15 Ch 41.35N 19.50 E
Skene 8 Eg 57.29N 12.38 E
Skerki Bank (EN) 32 Jb 37.45N 10.50 E
Skerries/Na Sceiri 9 Gh 53.35N 6.07W
Skerryvore 9 Fe 56.20N 7.05W
Skhiza 15 Em 36.44N 21.46 E
Skhoinoúsa 15 Im 36.50N 25.30 E
Ski 7 Cg 59.43N 10.50 E
Skiathos 15 Gj 39.10N 23.28 E
Skiathos 15 Gj 39.10N 23.29 E
Skibbereen/An Sciobairin 9 Dj 51.33N 9.15W
Skibotn 7 Eb 69.24N 20.16 E
Skidel 16 Dc 53.38N 24.17 E
Skien 6 Gd 59.12N 9.36 E
Skierniewice 10 Qe 51.58N 20.08 E
Skierniewice [2] 10 Qe 52.00N 20.10 E
Skiftet/Kihti 8 Id 60.15N 21.05 E
Skikda 31 He 36.52N 6.54 E
Skikda [3] 32 Ib 36.45N 6.50 E
Skillet Fork 45 Lg 38.08N 88.07W
Skillingaryd 8 Fg 57.26N 14.05 E
Skinári, Ákra- 15 Dl 37.56N 20.42 E
Skinnskatteberg 8 Fe 59.50N 15.41 E
Skipton 9 Kh 53.58N 2.01W
Skiptvet 8 De 59.28N 11.11 E
Skiropoúla 15 Hk 38.50N 24.21 E
Skiros 15 Hk 38.54N 24.34 E
Skiros 15 Hk 38.53N 24.32 E
Skive 7 Bh 56.34N 9.02 E
Skive Å 8 Ch 56.34N 9.04 E
Skjærhalden 8 De 59.02N 11.02 E
Skjåk 8 Cc 61.52N 8.22 E
Skjálfandafljót 7a Cb 65.59N 17.38W
Skjeberg 8 De 59.14N 11.12 E
Skjern 7 Bi 55.57N 8.30 E
Skjern Å 7 Bi 55.55N 8.24 E
Skjervøy 7 Ea 70.02N 20.59 E
Skjoldungen 41 Hf 63.20N 41.20W
Sklad 20 Hb 71.52N 123.35 E
Šklov 16 Gb 54.14N 30.18 E
Skobeleva, Pik- 18 Ie 39.51N 72.47 E
Skœrfjorden 41 Kc 77.30N 19.10W
Škofja Loka 14 Id 46.10N 14.18 E
Skog 8 Gc 61.10N 16.55 E
Skógafoss 7a Bc 63.32N 19.31W
Skoghall 8 Ee 59.19N 13.26 E
Skogshorn 8 Cd 60.53N 8.42 E
Skokie 45 Me 42.02N 87.46W
Skole 10 Th 48.58N 23.32 E
Skópelos 15 Gj 39.07N 23.44 E
Skópelos 15 Gj 39.10N 23.40 E
Skopi 15 Jn 35.11N 26.02 E
Skopin 7 Jj 53.52N 39.37 E
Skopje 6 Ig 42.00N 21.29 E
Skórcz 10 Oc 53.48N 18.32 E
Skorovatn 7 Cd 64.39N 13.07 E
Skorpa 8 Ac 61.35N 4.50 E
Skørping 8 Ch 56.50N 9.53 E
Skorpiós 15 Dk 38.42N 20.45 E
Škotovo 28 Lc 43.20N 132.21 E
Skotselv 8 Ce 59.51N 9.53 E
Skoura 32 Fc 31.04N 6.43W
Skövde 7 Cg 58.24N 13.50 E
Skovorodino 22 Od 53.59N 123.55 E
Skowhegan 44 Mc 44.46N 69.43W
Skradin 14 Jg 43.49N 15.56 E
Skreia 8 Dd 60.34N 11.04 E
Skreia 8 Dd 60.39N 10.56 E
Skrekken 8 Bd 60.13N 7.49 E
Skridulaupen 8 Bc 61.55N 7.35 E
Skrimkolla 8 Cb 62.23N 9.04 E
Skriveri/Skriveri 8 Kh 56.37N 25.10 E
Skriveri/Skriveri 8 Kh 56.37N 25.10 E
Skrunda 7 Eh 56.41N 22.00 E
Skrwa 10 Pd 52.33N 19.32 E
Skudenesfjorden 8 Ae 59.05N 5.20 E
Skudeneshavn 7 Ag 59.09N 5.17 E
Skuodas 7 Eh 56.17N 21.31 E
Skurup 8 Ei 55.28N 13.30 E
Skutskär 8 Gd 60.38N 17.25 E
Skvira 16 Fe 49.44N 29.42 E
Skwierzyna 10 Ld 52.35N 15.30 E
Skye, Island of- 5 Fd 57.15N 6.10W
Slagelse 7 Ci 55.24N 11.22 E
Slagnäs 7 Ed 65.36N 18.10 E
Slamet, Gunung- 21 Mj 7.14S 109.12 E
Slaná 10 Ri 47.56N 21.08 E
Slancy 19 Cd 59.08N 28.02 E
Slaney/An tSláine 9 Gi 52.21N 6.30W
Slănic 15 Id 45.15N 25.56 E
Slănic Moldova 15 Jc 46.12N 26.26 E
Slannik 15 Jf 43.06N 26.13 E
Slano 14 Lh 42.47N 17.54 E
Slaný 10 Kf 50.14N 14.06 E
Śląsk=Silesia (EN) 10 Me 51.00N 16.45 E
Śląsk=Silesia (EN) 5 He 51.00N 16.45 E
Śląska, Wyżyna- 10 Of 50.28N 18.40 E
Slate Islands 45 Mb 48.34N 86.45W
Slatina 15 He 44.26N 24.22 E
Slatina 10 Ph 48.32N 19.10 E
Slaton 45 Fj 33.26N 101.39W
Slave Coast 30 Hh 6.00N 3.30 E
Slave Lake 42 Ge 55.17N 114.46W
Slave River 38 Hc 61.18N 113.39W
Slavgorod [Bye.-U.S.S.R.] 16 Gc 53.27N 31.01 E
Slavgorod [R.S.F.S.R.] 20 Cf 53.03N 78.48 E
Slavičín 10 Ng 49.06N 17.53 E
Slavjanka 20 Ih 42.55N 131.20 E
Slavjanka 15 Gh 41.23N 23.36 E
Slavjansk 6 Jf 48.52N 37.37 E
Slavjansk-na-Kubani 19 Df 45.15N 38.08 E
Slavkoje 10 Th 48.45N 23.31 E
Slavkoviči 8 Mg 57.37N 29.10 E
Slavonia (EN) = Slavonija 5 Hf 45.00N 18.00 E
Slavonia (EN)=Slavonija 14 Le 45.00N 18.00 E
Slavonija=Slavonia (EN) 14 Le 45.00N 18.00 E
Slavonija = Slavonia (EN) 5 Hf 45.00N 18.00 E
Slavonska Požega 14 Le 45.20N 17.41 E
Slavonski Brod 14 Me 45.09N 18.02 E
Slavsk 8 Ii 55.01N 21.37 E
Slavuta 19 Ce 50.18N 26.52 E
Sława 10 Me 51.53N 16.04 E
Sławatycze 10 Te 51.43N 23.30 E
Sławno 10 Mb 54.22N 16.40 E
Slayton 45 Id 44.01N 95.45W
Sleaford 9 Mh 53.00N 0.24W
Slea Head/Ceann Sléibhe 9 Ci 52.06N 10.27W
Sleat, Sound of- 9 Hd 57.10N 5.50W
Sleen 12 Ib 52.47N 6.49 E
Sleeper Islands 42 Je 57.25N 79.50W
Sléibhte Chill Mhantáin/Wicklow Mountains 9 Gh 53.02N 6.24W
Sleidinge, Evergem- 12 Fc 51.08N 3.41 E
Slesin 10 Od 52.23N 18.19 E
Slessor Glacier 66 Af 79.50S 28.30W
Slessor Peak 66 Qe 66.31S 64.58W
Slettefjell 8 Cc 61.13N 8.44 E
Sletterhage 8 Dh 56.06N 10.31 E
Ślęża 10 Me 51.10N 16.58 E
Ślęża 10 Mf 50.52N 16.45 E
Sliabh Bearnach/Slieve Bernagh 9 Ei 52.50N 8.35W
Sliabh Bladhma/Slieve Bloom 9 Fh 53.10N 7.35W
Sliabh Eachtai/Slieve Aughty 9 Eh 53.10N 8.30W
Sliabh Gamh/Ox or Slieve Gamph Mountains 9 Eg 54.10N 8.50W
Sliabh Mis/Slieve Mish 9 Di 52.10N 9.50W
Sliabh Speirin/Sperrin Mountains 9 Fg 54.50N 7.05W
Slidell 45 Lk 30.17N 89.47W
Slide Mountain 44 Jd 42.00N 74.23W
Slidre 8 Cc 61.10N 9.00 E
Sliedrecht 12 Gc 51.50N 4.46 E
Slieve Aughty/Sliabh Eachtai 9 Eh 53.10N 8.30W
Slieve Bernagh/Sliabh Bearnach 9 Ei 52.50N 8.35W
Slieve Bloom/Sliabh Bladhma 9 Fh 53.10N 7.35W
Slievefelim Mountains 9 Ei 52.45N 8.15W
Slieve Mish/Sliabh Mis 9 Di 52.10N 9.50W
Sligeach/Sligo [2] 9 Eg 54.10N 8.40W
Sligeach/Sligo 6 Fe 54.17N 8.28W
Sligo/Sligeach [2] 9 Eg 54.10N 8.40W
Sligo/Sligeach 6 Fe 54.17N 8.28W
Sligo Bay/Cuan Shligigh 9 Eg 54.20N 8.40W
Slinge 12 Ib 52.08N 6.31 E
Slingebeek 12 Ic 51.59N 6.18 E
Slite 8 Hg 57.43N 18.48 E
Sliven 15 Jg 42.40N 26.19 E
Sliven [2] 15 Jg 42.40N 26.19 E
Slivnica 15 Gg 42.51N 23.02 E
Sljudjanka 20 Ff 51.38N 103.40 E
Slobodka 15 Mb 47.54N 29.12 E
Slobodskoj 19 Fd 58.47N 50.12 E
Slobodzeja 16 Ff 46.43N 29.43 E
Slobozia [Rom.] 15 Ke 44.34N 27.22 E
Slobozia [Rom.] 15 Ie 44.30N 25.11 E
Slochteren 12 Ia 53.12N 6.50 E
Slocum Mountain 46 Gi 35.18N 117.13W
Slonim 19 Ce 53.05N 25.18 E
Sloten 12 Hb 52.54N 5.40 E
Slotermeer 12 Hb 52.55N 5.40 E
Slough 9 Mj 51.31N 0.36W
Slovakia (EN)=Slovensko 10 Ph 48.45N 19.30 E
Slovakia (EN)=Slovensko 5 Hf 48.45N 19.30 E
Slovečna 16 Fd 51.41N 29.42 E
Slovenia (EN) = Slovenija 5 Hf 46.00N 15.00 E
Slovenia (EN) = Slovenija 14 Id 46.00N 15.00 E
Slovenia (EN) = Slovenija [2] 14 Id 46.00N 15.00 E
Slovenija=Slovenia (EN) [2] 14 Id 46.00N 15.00 E
Slovenija = Slovenia (EN) 14 Id 46.00N 15.00 E
Slovenija = Slovenia (EN) 5 Hf 46.00N 15.00 E
Slovenska Bistrica 14 Jd 46.24N 15.34 E
Slovenske Gorice 14 Jd 46.35N 15.55 E
Slovenské rudohorie 10 Ph 48.45N 20.00 E
Slovensko [2] 10 Ph 48.45N 19.30 E
Slovensko=Slovakia (EN) 5 Hf 48.45N 19.30 E
Slovensko=Slovakia (EN) 10 Ph 48.45N 19.30 E
Slovenský kras 10 Qh 48.35N 20.40 E
Słubice 10 Kd 52.20N 14.35 E
Sluč [Bye.-U.S.S.R.] 16 Ec 52.08N 27.32 E
Sluč [Ukr.-U.S.S.R.] 16 Ed 51.37N 26.38 E
Sluck 19 Ce 53.02N 27.31 E
Slunj 14 Je 45.07N 15.35 E
Słupca 10 Nd 52.19N 17.52 E
Słupia 10 Mb 54.35N 16.50 E
Słupsk 10 Nb 54.28N 17.01 E
Słupsk [2] 10 Mb 54.30N 17.00 E
Slyne Head/Ceann Gólaim 9 Ch 53.24N 10.13W
Småland 7 Dh 57.20N 15.05 E
Smålandsfarvandet 8 Di 55.06N 11.20 E
Smålandsstenar 8 Eg 57.10N 13.24 E
Smalininkai/Smalininkaj 8 Ji 55.01N 22.32 E
Smalininkaj/Smalininkai 8 Ji 55.01N 22.32 E
Smallingerland-Drachten 11 Ma 53.06N 6.05 E
Smallwood Reservoir 38 Md 54.00N 64.30W
Smederevo 15 De 44.39N 20.56 E
Smederevska Palanka 15 De 44.22N 20.58 E
Smedjebacken 7 Df 60.08N 15.25 E
Smela 19 Df 49.13N 31.53 E
Smidovič 20 Ig 48.36N 133.50 E
Šmidta, Mys- 20 Nc 68.45N 178.40W
Šmidta, Ostrov- 21 La 81.08N 90.48 E
Šmidta, Poluostrov- 20 Jf 54.15N 142.40 E
Śmigiel 10 Md 52.01N 16.32 E
Smilde 12 Ib 52.56N 6.28 E
Smiltene 7 Fh 57.28N 25.56 E
Smirnovo 17 Ni 54.31N 69.28 E
Smirnyh 20 Jg 49.45N 142.53 E
Smith 55 Bl 35.30S 61.36W
Smith Arm 42 Fc 66.15N 124.00W
Smith Bay [Ak.-U.S.] 40 Ib 70.51N 154.25W
Smith Bay [Can.] 42 Ja 77.15N 79.00W
Smith Center 45 Gg 39.47N 98.47W
Smithers 42 Ef 54.47N 127.10W
Smithfield [S.Afr.] 37 Df 30.09S 26.30 E
Smithfield [Ut.-U.S.] 46 Jf 41.50N 111.50W
Smith Knoll 9 Pi 52.50N 2.10 E
Smith Mountain Lake 44 Hg 37.10N 79.40W
Smith Peak 46 Gb 48.50N 116.39W
Smith River 46 Jc 47.25N 111.29W
Smiths Falls 42 Jh 44.54N 76.01W
Smith Sound 46 Ba 51.18N 127.48W
Smithton 58 Fi 40.51S 145.07 E
Smjadovo 15 Kf 43.04N 27.01 E
Smjörfjoll 7a Cb 65.35N 14.46W
Smögen 8 Df 58.21N 11.13 E
Smoke Creek Desert 46 Ff 40.30N 119.40W
Smokey Dome 46 He 43.29N 114.56W
Smoky Bay 59 Gf 32.20S 133.45 E
Smoky Cape 59 Kf 30.56S 153.05 E
Smoky Falls 42 Jf 50.03N 82.10W
Smoky Hill 38 Jf 39.03N 96.48W
Smoky Hills 45 Gg 39.15N 99.00W
Smoky River 42 Fe 56.11N 117.19W
Smøla 8 Be 63.25N 8.00 E
Smolensk 6 Je 54.47N 32.03 E
Smolenskaja Oblast [3] 19 De 55.00N 33.00 E
Smolenskaja Vozvyšennost =Smolensk Upland (EN) 5 Je 54.40N 33.00 E
Smolensk Upland (EN)=Smolenskaja Vozvyšennost 5 Je 54.40N 33.00 E
Smoleviči 16 Fb 54.03N 28.02 E
Smolianica 10 Ud 52.40N 24.40 E
Smólikas Óros 5 Ig 40.06N 20.55 E
Smoljan 15 Hh 41.35N 24.41 E
Smoljan [2] 15 Hh 41.40N 24.40 E
Smooth Rock Falls 44 Ga 49.20N 81.39W
Smorgon 19 Ce 54.31N 26.23 E
Smørstabbren 8 Cc 61.32N 8.06 E
Smrdeš 15 Fh 41.34N 22.28 E
Smygehamn 8 Ei 55.21N 13.22 E
Smygehuk 8 Ei 55.21N 13.23 E
Smyley, Cape- 66 Qf 72.00S 78.50W
Smyrna 44 Ei 33.53N 84.31W
Smyrna (EN)=İzmir 22 Ef 38.25N 27.09 E
Smyšljaevka 7 Mj 53.17N 50.24 E
Smythe, Mount- 38 Gd 57.50N 124.59W
Snacke Point 51b Bb 18.17N 62.58W
Snæfell 7a Cb 64.48N 15.34W
Snaefell 9 Ig 54.16N 4.27W
Snæfellsjökull 7a Ab 64.49N 23.46W
Snag 42 Dd 62.23N 140.22W
Snake Bay Settlement 59 Gb 11.25S 130.40 E
Snake Range 46 Hg 39.00N 114.15W
Snake River [Can.] 42 Ec 65.57N 134.13W
Snake River [U.S.] 38 He 46.12N 119.02W
Snake River Plain 43 Ec 42.45N 114.30W
Snare 42 Fd 63.15N 116.08W
Snares Islands 61 Ci 48.00S 166.35 E
Snarumselva 8 Cc 59.57N 9.58 E
Snåsa 7 Cd 64.15N 12.22 E
Sneek 11 La 53.02N 5.40 E
Snekermeer 11 La 52.59N 5.40 E
Snežnaja, Gora- 20 Lc 65.18N 165.30 E
Sneżnik 14 Ie 45.26N 14.36 E
Snežnogorsk 20 Dc 68.15N 87.35 E
Šnežnoje 16 Kf 47.59N 38.50 E
Śniardwy, Jezioro- 10 Rc 53.45N 21.44 E
Śnieżka 5 He 50.45N 15.43 E
Śnieżnik 10 Mf 50.12N 16.50 E
Snigirevka 16 Hf 47.04N 32.45 E
Snillfjord 8 Ca 63.24N 9.30 E
Snina 10 Sh 48.59N 22.08 E
Snizort, Loch- 9 Gd 57.30N 6.25W
Snjatyn 16 De 48.29N 25.34 E
Snøhetta 5 Gc 62.20N 9.17 E
Snohomish 46 Dc 47.55N 122.06W
Snønuten 8 Be 59.31N 6.54 E
Snøonipa 8 Bc 61.42N 6.41 E
Snota 8 Cb 62.51N 9.06 E
Snov 16 Gd 51.32N 31.33 E
Snowbird Lake 42 Hd 60.40N 102.50W
Snowdon 5 Fe 53.04N 4.05W
Snowdonia 9 Jh 53.05N 3.55W
Snowdrift 42 Gd 62.23N 110.47W
Snowflake 46 Ji 34.30N 110.05W
Snow Hill 44 Jf 38.11N 75.24W
Snow Lake 42 Hf 54.53N 100.02W
Snow Mountain 43 Cd 39.23N 122.46W
Snowshoe Peak 46 Hb 48.13N 115.41W
Snowville 46 If 41.58N 112.43W
Snowy Mountain [B.C.-Can.] 46 Fb 49.02N 119.57W
Snowy Mountain [N.Y.-U.S.] 44 Jd 43.42N 74.23W
Snowy Mountains 59 Jg 36.30S 148.20 E
Snowy River 59 Jg 37.48S 148.32 E
Snudy, Ozero- 8 Li 55.40N 27.15 E
Snug Corner 49 Kb 22.32N 73.53W
Snuŏl 25 Lf 12.04N 106.26 E
Snyder 43 Ge 32.44N 100.55W
Soalala 37 Hc 16.07S 45.21 E
Soalara 37 Gd 23.35S 43.44 E
Soanierana-Ivongo 37 Hc 16.54S 49.34 E
Soar 12 Ab 52.52N 1.17W
Şoarş 15 Hd 45.56N 24.55 E
Soavinandriana 37 Hc 19.10S 46.43 E
Sob [R.S.F.S.R.] 17 Mc 66.20N 66.02 E

Index Symbols

[1] Independent Nation
[2] State, Region
[3] District, County
[4] Municipality
[5] Colony, Dependency
Continent
Physical Region

Historical or Cultural Region
Mount, Mountain
Volcano
Hill
Mountains, Mountain Range
Hills, Escarpment
Plateau, Upland

Pass, Gap
Plain, Lowland
Delta
Salt Flat
Valley, Canyon
Crater, Cave
Karst Features

Depression
Polder
Desert, Dunes
Forest, Woods
Heath, Steppe
Oasis
Cape, Point

Coast, Beach
Cliff
Peninsula
Isthmus
Sandbank
Island
Atoll

Rock, Reef
Islands, Archipelago
Rocks, Reefs
Coral Reef
Well, Spring
Geyser
River, Stream

Waterfall Rapids
River Mouth, Estuary
Lake
Salt Lake
Intermittent Lake
Reservoir
Swamp, Pond

Canal
Glacier
Ice Shelf, Pack Ice
Ocean
Sea
Gulf, Bay
Strait, Fjord

Lagoon
Bank
Seamount
Tablemount
Ridge
Shelf
Basin

Escarpment, Sea Scarp
Fracture
Trench, Abyss
National Park, Reserve
Point of Interest
Recreation Site
Cave, Cavern

Historic Site
Ruins
Wall, Walls
Church, Abbey
Temple
Scientific Station
Airport

Port
Lighthouse
Mine
Tunnel
Dam, Bridge

Sob [Ukr.-U.S.S.R.] 16 Fe 48.41N 29.17 E
Soba 34 Gc 10.59N 8.04 E
Sobaek-Sanmaek 28 Jf 36.00N 128.00 E
Sobat (EN)=Sawbā 30 Kh 9.45N 31.45 E
Sobernheim 12 Je 49.48N 7.39 E
Soběslav 10 Kg 49.16N 14.44 E
Sōbetsu 29a Bb 42.33N 140.51 E
Sobinka 7 Jh 56.01N 40.07 E
Sobolevo [R.S.F.S.R.] 16 Qd 51.59N 51.48 E
Sobolevo [R.S.F.S.R.] 20 Kf 54.17N 156.00 E
Sobolew 10 Re 51.41N 21.40 E
Sobo-San 29 Be 32.47N 131.21 E
Sobradinho 55 Fi 29.24S 53.03W
Sobral 53 Lf 3.42S 40.21W
Sobrarbe 13 Mb 42.20N 0.05 E
Soca 55 El 34.41S 55.41W
Soča=Isonzo (EN) 14 He 45.43N 13.33 E
Sochaczew 10 Qd 52.14N 20.14 E
Soči 6 Jg 43.35N 39.45 E
Société, Iles de la-=Society Islands (EN) 57 Lf 17.00S 150.00W
Society Islands (EN)= Société, Iles de la- 57 Lf 17.00S 150.00W
Socompa, Paso- 52 Jh 24.27S 68.18W
Socorro [Col.] 54 Db 6.27N 73.16W
Socorro [N.M.-U.S.] 43 Fe 34.04N 106.54W
Socotra (EN) = Suqutrā 21 Hh 12.30N 54.00 E
Soc Trang 25 Lg 9.36N 105.58 E
Socuéllamos 13 Je 39.17N 2.48W
Soda Lake 46 Gi 35.08N 116.04W
Sodankylä 7 Gc 67.25N 26.36 E
Soda Springs 46 Je 42.39N 111.36W
Söderåsen 8 Eh 56.04N 13.05 E
Söderfors 7 Df 60.23N 17.14 E
Söderhamn 7 Df 61.18N 17.03 E
Söderköping 8 Gf 58.29N 16.18 E
Södermanland 8 Ge 59.10N 16.50 E
Södermanland [2] 7 Dg 59.15N 16.40 E
Söderslätt 8 Ei 55.30N 13.15 E
Södertälje 7 Dg 59.12N 17.37 E
Södertörn 8 Ge 59.05N 18.00 E
Sodo 35 Fd 6.51N 37.45 E
Södra Dellen 8 Gc 61.50N 16.45 E
Södra Gloppet 8 Ia 63.05N 21.00 E
Södra Kvarken 8 Hd 60.20N 19.08 E
Södra-Midsjöbanken 8 Gi 55.40N 17.20 E
Södra Vi 8 Fg 57.45N 15.48 E
Soe 26 Hh 9.52S 124.17 E
Soekmekaar 37 Dd 23.28S 29.58 E
Soela, Proliv-/Soela Väin 8 Jf 58.40N 22.30 E
Soela Väin/Soela, Proliv- 8 Jf 58.40N 22.30 E
Soest [Ger.] 10 Ee 51.35N 8.07 E
Soest [Neth.] 12 Hb 52.10N 5.20 E
Soeste 12 Ja 53.10N 7.44 E
Soester Borde 12 Kc 51.38N 8.03 E
Soestwetering 12 Ib 51.30N 6.09 E
Sofádhes 15 Fj 39.20N 22.06 E
Sofala [3] 37 Ec 19.30S 34.40 E
Sofala, Baia de- 30 Kk 20.11S 34.45 E
Sofia 37 Hc 15.27S 47.23 E
Sofia [Bul.] [2] 15 Gg 42.43N 23.25 E
Sofia [Grc.] [2] 15 Gg 42.41N 23.19 E
Sofia (EN)=Sofija 6 Ig 42.41N 23.19 E
Sofija=Sofia (EN) 6 Ig 42.41N 23.19 E
Sofijsk 20 If 52.20N 134.01 E
Sofporog 19 Db 65.48N 31.28 E
Sofrána, Nisídhes- 15 Jm 36.04N 26.24 E
Sōfu-Gan 27 Pf 29.50N 140.20 E
Sogamoso 54 Db 5.43N 72.56W
Soganlı 24 Eb 41.11N 32.38 E
Sogara, Lake- 36 Fd 5.15S 31.00 E
Sogda 20 If 50.24N 132.18 E
Sögel 10 Dd 52.51N 7.31 E
Sogeri 60 Di 9.10S 147.32 E
Sogn 8 Ac 61.05N 5.55 E
Sogndalsfjøra 8 Bc 61.14N 7.06 E
Søgne 8 Bf 58.05N 7.49 E
Sognefjell 8 Bc 61.35N 7.55 E
Sognefjorden 5 Gc 61.05N 5.10 E
Sognesjøen 8 Ac 61.05N 5.00 E
Sogn og Fjordane [2] 7 Bf 61.30N 6.50 E
Sogod 26 Hd 10.23N 124.59 E
Sogo Nur 27 Hc 42.20N 101.20 E
Sogoža 7 Jg 58.30N 39.06 E
Söğüt 15 Nj 40.00N 30.11 E
Söğütalan 15 Li 40.03N 28.34 E
Söğüt Gölü 24 Cd 37.03N 29.53 E
Sog Xian 27 Fe 31.51N 93.42 E
Soh 18 He 39.57N 71.08 E
Sohag (EN)=Sawhāj 31 Kf 26.33N 31.42 E
Sohano 60 Ei 5.29S 154.41 E
Sohŭksan-Do 28 Hg 34.04N 125.07 E
Soignies/Zinnik 11 Kd 50.35N 4.04 E
Soini 8 Kb 62.52N 24.13 E
Soisalo 8 Mb 62.40N 28.10 E
Soissonnais, Plateau du- 11 Je 49.15N 3.10 E
Soissons 11 Je 49.22N 3.20 E
Sōja 29 Cd 34.40N 133.44 E
Sojana 7 Kd 65.53N 43.30 E
Sojma 17 Ec 67.00N 51.00 E
Šojna 17 Bc 67.52N 44.08 E
Sŏjosŏn-man=Korea Bay (EN) 21 Of 39.15N 125.00 E
Sojuznoje 16 Vd 50.50N 60.10 E
Sojuz Sovetskih Socialističeskih Respublik =USSR (EN) [1] 22 Jd 60.00N 80.00 E
Sojuz Sovetskih Socialističeskih Respublik (SSSR) [1] 22 Jd 60.00N 80.00 E
Sok 19 Fe 53.25N 50.10 E
Sokal 16 Dd 50.29N 24.17 E
Šokalskogo, Proliv- 20 Ea 79.00N 100.00 E
Sokch'o 27 Md 38.12N 128.36 E
Söke 23 Cb 37.45N 27.24 E
Sokele 36 Dd 9.55S 24.36 E
Sokirjany 16 Ee 48.28N 27.25 E
Sokna 7 Bf 60.14N 9.54 E
Soko Banja 15 Ef 43.39N 21.53 E
Sokodé 31 Hh 8.59N 1.08 E
Sokol 19 Ed 59.29N 40.13 E
Sokol 15 Ce 44.18N 19.25 E
Sokółka 10 Tc 53.25N 23.31 E
Sokolo 34 Dc 14.44N 6.07W
Sokolov 10 If 50.11N 12.38 E
Sokołów Podlaski 10 Sd 52.25N 22.15 E
Sokone 34 Bc 13.53N 16.22W
Sokosti 7 Gb 68.20N 28.01 E
Sokoto 30 Hg 11.24N 4.07 E
Sokoto [2] 34 Gc 12.20N 5.20 E
Sokoto 31 Hg 13.04N 5.15 E
Sokourala 34 Dd 9.13N 8.05W
Sòl 35 Hd 9.20N 49.25 E
Sòl 35 Hd 9.40N 48.30 E
Sol, Costa del- 13 Ih 36.46N 3.55W
Sol, Pico do- 55 Ke 20.07S 43.28W
Sola 10 Pf 50.04N 19.13 E
Sola 63b Ca 13.53S 167.33 E
Solai 36 Gb 0.02N 36.09 E
Solakrossen 8 Af 58.53N 5.36 E
Solander Island 61 Ci 46.35S 166.50 E
Solanet 55 Cm 36.51S 58.31W
Solāpur 22 Jh 17.41N 75.55 E
Solbad Hall in Tirol 14 Fc 47.17N 11.31 E
Solcy 19 Dd 58.09N 30.20 E
Sölden 14 Ed 46.58N 11.00 E
Soldier Point 51d Bb 17.02N 61.41W
Soldotna 40 Id 60.29N 151.04W
Solec Kujawski 10 Oc 53.06N 18.14 E
Soledad [Arg.] 55 Bj 30.37S 60.55W
Soledad [Ca.-U.S.] 46 Eh 36.26N 121.19W
Soledad [Col.] 54 Da 10.55N 74.46W
Soledad [Ven.] 54 Fb 8.10N 63.34W
Soledad, Boca de- 48 Ce 25.17N 112.09W
Soledad, Isla-/East Falkland 52 Kk 51.45S 58.50W
Soledade 56 Jc 28.50S 52.30W
Sølen 8 Dc 61.55N 11.30 E
Sølensjøen 8 Dc 61.55N 11.35 E
Solentiname, Archipiélago de- 49 Fh 11.10N 85.00W
Solenzara 11a Bb 41.51N 9.24 E
Solesmes 12 Fd 50.11N 3.30 E
Solferino 14 Ee 45.23N 10.34 E
Solgen 8 Fg 57.33N 15.07 E
Solgne 12 Ie 48.58N 6.18 E
Soligalič 7 Kg 59.07N 42.13 E
Soligorsk 19 Ce 52.49N 27.31 E
Solihull 9 Li 52.25N 1.45W
Solikamsk 19 Fd 59.39N 56.47 E
Sol-Ileck 6 Le 51.12N 55.03 E
Solimán, Punta- 48 Ph 19.50N 87.27W
Solimoes→Amazonas, Rio-=Amazon (EN) 52 Lf 0.10S 49.00W
Solingen 10 De 51.11N 7.05 E
Solińskie, Jezioro- 10 Sg 49.22N 22.30 E
Solis, Presa- 48 Ig 20.05N 100.36W
Sollebrunn 8 Ef 58.07N 12.32 E
Sollefteå 7 De 63.10N 17.16 E
Sollentuna 8 Ge 59.28N 17.54 E
Sóller 13 Oe 39.46N 2.42 E
Sollerön 8 Fd 60.55N 14.37 E
Solling 10 Fe 51.45N 9.35 E
Solms 12 Kd 50.46N 9.36 E
Solna 8 He 59.22N 18.01 E
Solnečnogorsk 7 Ih 56.10N 37.00 E
Solnečny 20 Id 60.10N 137.35 E
Sologne 11 Hg 47.50N 2.00 E
Sologne Bourbonnaise 11 Jh 46.40N 3.30 E
Solok 26 Dg 0.48S 100.39 E
Sololá [3] 49 Bf 14.40N 91.15W
Sololá 49 Bf 14.46N 91.11W
Solomon Islands [1] 58 Ge 8.00S 159.00 E
Solomon Islands 57 Ge 8.00S 159.00 E
Solomon Islands (British Solomon Islands) [1] 58 Ge 8.00S 159.00 E
Solomon River 43 Hd 38.54N 97.22W
Solomon Sea 57 Ge 8.00S 155.00 E
Solon Springs 45 Kc 46.22N 91.48W
Solør 8 Dd 60.30N 11.55 E
Solor, Kepulauan- 26 Hh 8.25S 123.30 E
Solothurn 14 Bc 47.15N 7.30 E
Solothurn [2] 14 Bc 47.20N 7.40 E
Solotvin 10 Uh 48.38N 24.31 E
Soloveckije Ostrova 7 Id 65.05N 35.45 E
Solovjevka 8 Nd 60.44N 30.20 E
Solovjevsk [R.S.F.S.R.] 20 Hf 54.15N 124.30 E
Solovjevsk [R.S.F.S.R.] 20 Gg 49.54N 115.43 E
Sölöz 15 Mi 40.23N 29.25 E
Solre-le-Château 12 Gd 50.10N 4.05 E
Solsona 13 Nc 41.59N 1.31 E
Solt 10 Oj 46.48N 19.00 E
Solta 14 Kg 43.23N 16.17 E
Soltānābād [Iran] 24 Mg 31.03N 49.42 E
Soltānābād [Iran] 24 Rd 36.23N 58.02 E
Soltānī, Khowr-e- 24 Nh 29.00N 50.50 E
Soltāniyeh 24 Md 36.26N 48.48 E
Soltau 10 Fd 52.59N 9.50 E
Soltvadkert 10 Pj 46.35N 19.23 E
Solvang 46 Ei 34.36N 120.08W
Sölvesborg 7 Dh 56.03N 14.33 E
Solvyčegodsk 7 Lf 61.21N 46.52 E
Solway Firth 9 Jg 54.50N 3.35W
Solwezi 31 Jj 12.11S 26.24 E
Sōma 28 Pf 37.48N 140.57 E
Soma 24 Bc 39.10N 27.36 E
Somain 12 Fd 50.22N 3.17 E
Somalia (EN)= Soomaaliya [1] 31 Lh 10.00N 49.00 E
Somali Basin (EN) 3 Fi 0.00 52.00 E
Sombo 36 Dd 8.42S 20.57 E
Sombor 15 Cd 45.46N 19.07 E
Sombrerete 47 Dd 23.38N 103.39W
Sombrero 47 Le 18.36N 63.26W
Sombrero Channel 25 Ig 7.41N 93.35 E
Sombrio 55 Hi 29.07S 49.40W
Sombrio, Lagoa do- 55 Hi 29.12S 49.42W
Somcuța Mare 15 Gb 47.31N 23.28 E
Someren 12 Hc 51.23N 5.43 E
Somero 8 Jd 60.37N 23.32 E
Somerset 38 Jb 73.30N 93.30W
Somerset [3] 9 Jk 51.10N 3.10W
Somerset 9 Kj 51.00N 3.00W
Somerset [Austl.] 59 Ib 10.35S 142.15 E
Somerset [Ky.-U.S.] 43 Kd 37.05N 84.36W
Somerset [Pa.-U.S.] 44 He 40.02N 79.05W
Somerset East 37 Df 32.42S 25.35 E
Somerton 46 Hj 32.36N 114.43W
Somerville Lake 45 Hk 30.18N 96.40W
Someș 15 Fa 48.07N 22.20 E
Someșu Mare 15 Gb 47.09N 23.55 E
Someșu Mic 15 Gb 47.09N 23.55 E
Somme [3] 11 Id 49.55N 2.30 E
Somme 11 Hd 50.11N 1.39 E
Somme, Baie de- 12 Dd 50.14N 1.33 E
Somme, Bassurelle de la- 12 Dd 50.15N 1.10 E
Somme, Canal de la- 11 He 50.11N 1.39 E
Somme-Leuze 12 Hd 50.20N 5.22 E
Somme-Leuze-Hogne 12 Hd 50.15N 5.17 E
Sommen 7 Dh 58.00N 15.15 E
Sommen 8 Ff 58.08N 14.58 E
Sommepy-Tahure 12 Ge 49.15N 4.33 E
Sömmerda 10 He 51.09N 11.06 E
Somogy [2] 10 Nj 46.25N 17.35 E
Somontano 13 Lc 42.02N 0.20W
Somosierra, Puerto ue- 13 Ic 41.09N 3.35W
Somosomo Strait 63d Bb 16.47S 179.58 E
Somotillo 49 Dg 13.02N 86.53W
Somoto 47 Gf 13.28N 86.35W
Somovo 16 Kd 51.45N 39.25 E
Sompolno 10 Od 52.24N 18.31 E
Somport, Puerto de- 13 Lb 42.48N 0.31W
Son 21 Kg 25.50N 84.55 E
Sona 10 Qd 52.33N 20.35 E
Soná 49 Gi 8.01N 81.19W
Sonaguera 49 Df 15.38N 86.20W
Sonári, Ákra 15 Lm 36.27N 28.13 E
Sönch'on 28 He 39.48N 124.55 E
Søndeled 7 Bg 58.46N 9.05 E
Sønderborg 7 Bi 54.55N 9.47 E
Sønder-Jylland [2] 8 Ci 55.00N 9.00 E
Sønder-Omme 8 Ci 55.50N 8.54 E
Sondershausen 10 Ge 51.22N 10.52 E
Søndre Strømfjord 67 Nc 66.59N 50.40W
Søndre Strømfjord 41 Ge 66.10N 53.10W
Søndre Upernavik 41 Gd 72.10N 55.38W
Sondrio 14 Dd 46.10N 9.52 E
Sonepat 25 Fc 28.59N 77.01 E
Song 34 Hd 9.50N 12.37 E
Songa 8 Be 59.47N 7.43 E
Songavatn 8 Be 59.50N 7.35 E
Song Cau 25 Lf 13.27N 109.13 E
Songe 8 Cf 58.41N 9.01 E
Songea 31 Kj 10.41S 35.39 E
Songeons 12 De 49.33N 1.52 E
Songhua Hu 28 Ic 43.30N 126.51 E
Songhua Jiang=Sungari (EN) 21 Pe 47.42N 132.30 E
Songjiang 27 Le 31.01N 121.14 E
Songjiang → Antu 28 Jc 42.33N 128.20 E
Songjianghe 28 Ic 42.10N 127.30 E
Söngjin → Kimch'aek 27 Mc 40.41N 129.12 E
Songjŏng 28 Ig 35.08N 126.48 E
Songkhla 22 Mi 7.13N 100.34 E
Songling 27 Lb 48.02N 121.08 E
Songnim 28 He 38.44N 125.38 E
Songo [Ang.] 36 Bd 7.21S 14.50 E
Songo [Moz.] 37 Ec 15.33S 32.48 E
Songololo 36 Bd 5.42S 14.02 E
Songpan (Sungqu) 27 He 32.37N 103.34 E
Songsa-dong 28 Hd 39.49N 124.49 E
Song Shan 27 Je 34.31N 113.00 E
Songshuzhen 28 Ic 42.01N 127.09 E
Songueur 13 Ni 35.11N 1.30 E
Songxian 28 Bg 34.12N 112.09 E
Songzi (Xinjiangkou) 28 Ai 30.10N 116.46 E
Sonid Youqi (Saihan Tal) 27 Jc 42.45N 112.36 E
Sonid Zuoqi (Mandalt) 27 Kc 43.50N 116.45 E
Sonkari 8 Lb 62.50N 26.35 E
Sonkël, Ozero- 18 Jd 41.50N 75.10 E
Sonkovo 7 Ih 57.47N 37.09 E
Son La 22 Mg 21.19N 103.54 E
Sonmiāni Bay 25 Dc 25.15N 66.30 E
Sonneberg 10 Hf 50.21N 11.10 E
Sono, Rio do- [Braz.] 55 Jc 17.02S 45.32W
Sono, Rio do- [Braz.] 54 Ie 9.00S 48.11W
Sonobe 29 Dd 35.07N 135.28 E
Sonoita 47 Bb 31.51N 112.50W
Sonoma Peak 46 Gf 40.52N 117.36W
Sonora [2] 47 Bc 29.20N 110.40W
Sonora 47 Bc 28.48N 111.49W
Sonora [Ca.-U.S.] 46 Eh 37.59N 120.23W
Sonora [Tx.-U.S.] 45 Fk 30.34N 100.39W
Sonqor 24 Le 34.47N 47.36 E
Sonsbeck 12 Ic 51.37N 6.22 E
Sonsonate 47 Gf 13.43N 89.44W
Sonsorol Islands 57 Ed 5.20N 132.13 E
Sonthofen 10 Gi 47.31N 10.17 E
Sontra 10 Fe 51.04N 9.56 E
Soomaaliya=Somalia (EN) [1] 31 Lh 10.00N 49.00 E
Soomenlaht=Finland, Gulf of- (EN) 5 Ic 60.00N 27.00 E
Soonwald 12 Je 49.56N 7.35 E
Sørværøy 7 Cc 67.38N 12.40 E
Sopi, Tanjung- 26 If 2.39N 128.34 E
Sopo 35 Dd 8.51N 26.11 E
Sopockin 10 Tc 53.50N 23.42 E
Sopot [Bul.] 15 Hg 42.39N 24.45 E
Sopot [Pol.] 10 Ob 54.28N 18.34 E
Sopron 10 Mi 47.41N 16.36 E
Sopur 25 Eb 34.18N 74.28 E
Sor 13 De 39.00N 8.17W
Sora 14 Hi 41.43N 13.37 E
Sorachi-Gawa 29a Bb 43.32N 141.52 E
Söråker 8 Gb 62.31N 17.30 E
Sorak-san 27 Md 38.07N 128.28 E
Sorano 14 Fh 42.41N 11.43 E
Soratteld 12 Kc 51.40N 8.53 E
Sorbas 13 Jg 37.07N 2.07W
Sorbe 13 Id 40.51N 3.08W
Sörberget 8 Gb 62.31N 17.22 E
Sore 11 Fj 44.19N 0.35W
Sorel 42 Kg 46.03N 73.07W
Sorell, Cape- 59 Jh 42.10S 145.10 E
Soresina 14 De 45.17N 9.51 E
Sorezaru Point 63a Cb 7.37S 156.38 E
Sørfjorden 8 Bd 60.25N 6.40 E
Sørfold 7 Dc 67.28N 15.28 E
Sorgues 11 Kj 44.00N 4.52 E
Sorgun 24 Fc 39.50N 35.19 E
Soria [3] 13 Jc 41.40N 2.40W
Soria 13 Jc 41.46N 2.28W
Soriano [2] 55 Dk 33.30S 57.45W
Sørkapp 67 Kd 76.28N 16.36 E
Sorkh, Godār-e- 24 Pf 33.05N 55.05 E
Sorkh, Kūh-e- 24 Pf 33.05N 55.05 E
Sorkheh 24 Oe 35.28N 53.12 E
Sorø 8 Di 55.26N 11.34 E
Sorocaba 53 Lh 23.29S 47.27W
Soroči Gory 7 Li 55.24N 49.55 E
Soročinsk 19 Fe 52.26N 53.10 E
Soroki 16 Fe 48.07N 28.16 E
Sorol Atoll 57 Fd 8.08N 140.23 E
Sorong 58 Ee 0.53S 131.15 E
Soroti 31 Kh 1.43N 33.37 E
Sørøya 5 Ia 70.36N 22.46 E
Sørøyane 8 Ab 62.20N 5.45 E
Sorraia 13 Df 38.56N 8.53W
Sørreisa 7 Eb 69.09N 18.10 E
Sorrentina, Penisola- 14 Ij 40.35N 14.30 E
Sorrento 14 Ij 40.37N 14.22 E
Sør Rondane 66 Df 72.00S 25.00 E
Sorsatunturi 7 Gc 67.24N 29.38 E
Sorsavesi 8 Lb 62.30N 27.35 E
Sorsele 7 Dd 65.32N 17.30 E
Sorsk 20 Ef 54.00N 90.20 E
Sorso 14 Cj 40.48N 8.34 E
Sorsogon 26 Hd 12.58N 124.00 E
Sort 13 Nb 42.24N 1.08 E
Sortandi 19 He 51.42N 71.05 E
Sortavala 19 Dc 61.44N 30.41 E
Sortland 7 Db 68.42N 15.24 E
Sør-Trøndelag [2] 7 Ce 63.00N 10.40 E
Sorum 17 Ne 63.50N 68.05 E
Sørumsand 8 De 59.58N 11.15 E
Šoša 7 Ih 56.33N 36.09 E
Sōsan 28 If 36.47N 126.27 E
Sösdala 8 Eh 56.02N 13.40 E
Sos del Rey Católico 13 Kb 42.30N 1.13W
Sosna 16 Kc 52.42N 38.55 E
Sosnogorsk 6 Lc 63.37N 53.51 E
Sosnovka [R.S.F.S.R.] 16 Lc 53.14N 41.22 E
Sosnovka [R.S.F.S.R.] 7 Mh 56.18N 51.17 E
Sosnovka [R.S.F.S.R.] 7 Jc 66.31N 40.33 E
Sosnovka [Ukr.-U.S.S.R.] 16 Dd 50.15N 24.13 E
Sosnovo 8 Nd 60.31N 30.29 E
Sosnovo-Ozerskoje 20 Gf 52.31N 111.35 E
Sosnovy Bor 8 Me 59.48N 29.10 E
Sosnowiec 10 Pf 50.18N 19.08 E
Sospel 11 Nk 43.53N 7.27 E
Šostka 19 De 51.52N 33.31 E
Sosumav 37 Hb 13.03S 48.54 E
Sosva 19 Gd 59.32N 62.20 E
Sosva [R.S.F.S.R.] 19 Gc 63.40N 62.02 E
Sosva [R.S.F.S.R.] 19 Gd 59.10N 61.50 E
Sotavento [3] 32 Cf 14.40N 23.25W
Sotavento, Islas de-= Windward Islands (EN) 52 Jd 11.10N 67.00W
Sotik 36 Gc 0.41S 35.07 E
Sotkamo 7 Gd 64.08N 28.25 E
Soto la Marina 48 Jf 23.48N 98.13W
Soto la Marina, Rio- 48 Kf 23.45N 97.45W
Sotonera, Embalse de la- 13 Lb 42.05N 0.48W
Sotouboua 34 Fd 8.34N 0.59 E
Sotra 8 Ad 60.20N 5.05 E
Sotsudaka-Zaki 29b Ba 28.15N 129.10 E
Sottern 8 Fe 59.05N 15.30 E
Sotteville-lès-Rouen 11 He 49.25N 1.06 E
Sottrum 12 La 53.07N 9.14 E
Sottunga 8 Id 60.10N 20.40 E
Sotuf, Adrar- 32 De 21.42N 15.36W
Sotuta 48 Og 20.36N 89.01W
Souanké 36 Bb 2.05N 14.03 E
Soubré 34 Dd 5.47N 6.36W
Soubré [3] 34 Dd 5.47N 6.38W
Soúdha 15 Hn 35.29N 24.04 E
Souf 30 He 33.25N 6.50 E
Soufflenheim 12 Jf 48.50N 7.58 E
Souflíon 15 Jh 41.12N 26.18 E
Soufrière 50 Ff 13.52N 61.04W
Soufrière [Guad.] 47 Le 16.03N 61.40W
Soufrière [St.Vin.] 47 Lf 13.21N 61.11W
Soufrière Bay 51g Bb 15.13N 61.22W
Soufrière Hills 51c Bc 16.43N 62.10W
Souillac 11 Hj 44.54N 1.29 E
Souilly 11 Le 49.01N 5.17 E
Souk Ahras 32 Ib 36.17N 7.57 E
Souk el Arba du Rharb 32 Fc 34.41N 5.59W
Sŏul=Seoul (EN) 22 Of 37.34N 127.00 E
Soulac-sur-Mer 11 Ei 45.30N 1.06W
Sŏul Si [2] 28 If 37.35N 127.00 E
Soultz-sous-Forêts 12 Jf 48.56N 7.53 E
Soumagne 12 Hd 50.37N 5.45 E
Soummam 13 Rh 36.44N 5.04 E
Sounding Creek 46 Ja 52.06N 110.28W
Soúnion 15 Hl 37.39N 24.02 E
Soúnion, Ákra- 15 Hl 37.39N 24.01 E
Sources, Mont aux- 30 Jk 28.46S 28.52 E
Soure [Braz.] 54 Id 0.44S 48.31W
Soure [Port.] 13 Dd 40.03N 8.38W
Sour el Ghozlane 32 Hb 36.09N 3.41 E
Souris 42 Hg 49.38N 100.15W
Souris 38 Je 49.39N 99.34W
Sous 32 Fc 30.22N 9.37W
Sous 32 Fc 30.25N 9.30W
Sousa 53 Mf 6.45S 38.14W
Sousel 13 Ef 38.57N 7.40W
Sous le Vent, Iles-= Leeward Islands (EN) 57 Lf 16.38S 151.30W
Sousse (EN)=Sūsah [3] 32 Jb 35.45N 10.30 E
Sousse (EN)=Sūsah [Tun.] 31 Ie 35.49N 10.38 E
Sout 37 Cf 33.03S 23.29 E
South Africa / Suid Africa [1] 31 Jl 30.00S 26.00 E
South Alligator River 59 Gb 12.15S 132.24 E
Southam 12 Ab 52.15N 1.23W
South America (EN) 52 Jg 15.00S 60.00W
Southampton 38 Kc 64.20N 84.40W
Southampton [Eng.-U.K.] 6 Fe 50.55N 1.25W
Southampton [N.Y.-U.S.] 44 Ke 40.54N 72.23W
Southampton, Cape- 42 Jd 62.08N 83.44W
Southampton Airport 12 Ad 50.55N 1.23W
Southampton Water 12 Ad 50.52N 1.20W
South Andaman 25 If 11.45N 92.45 E
Southard, Cape- 66 Ie 66.33S 122.04 E
South Auckland-Bay of Plenty [2] 62 Fb 38.00S 176.00 E
South Aulatsivik 42 Le 56.47N 61.30W
South Australia [2] 59 Ge 30.00S 135.00 E
South Australian Basin (EN) 3 Im 40.00S 128.00 E
Southaven 45 Li 35.00N 90.00W
South Baldy 45 Cj 33.59N 107.11W
South Bay 42 Jd 64.00N 83.25W
South Bend 43 Jc 41.41N 86.15W
South Benfleet 12 Cc 51.32N 0.33 E
Southborough 12 Cc 51.09N 0.15 E
South Boston 44 Hg 36.42N 78.58W
Southbridge 62 Ee 43.48S 172.15 E
South Buganda [3] 36 Fc 0.30S 32.00 E
South Caicos 49 Lc 21.31N 71.30W
South Carolina [2] 43 Ke 34.00N 81.00W
South China Basin (EN) 3 Hh 15.00N 115.00 E
South China Sea (EN)=Bien Dong 21 Ni 10.00N 113.00 E
South China Sea (EN)=Cina Selatan, Laut- 21 Ni 10.00N 113.00 E
South China Sea (EN)=Nan Hai 21 Ni 10.00N 113.00 E
South Dakota [2] 43 Gc 44.15N 100.00W
South Downs 9 Mk 50.55N 0.25W
South-East [3] 37 De 25.00S 25.45 E
South East Cape 57 Fi 43.39S 146.50 E
Southeast Indian Ridge (EN) 3 Ho 50.00S 110.00 E
Southeast Pacific Basin (EN) 3 Mp 60.00S 115.00W
South East Point [Austl.] 57 Fh 39.00S 146.20 E
South East Point [Kir.] 64g Bb 1.40N 157.10W
Southend 42 He 56.20N 103.14W
Southend-on-Sea 9 Nj 51.33N 0.43 E
Southern [Mwi.] [3] 36 Gf 15.30S 35.00 E
Southern [S.L.] [3] 34 Cd 7.40N 12.15W
Southern [Ug.] [3] 36 Fc 0.30S 30.30 E
Southern [Zam.] [3] 36 Ef 16.00S 27.00 E
Southern Alps 57 Ii 43.30S 170.35 E
Southern Cook Islands 57 Lg 20.00S 159.00W
Southern Cross 58 Ch 31.13S 119.19 E
Southern Desert (EN)= Janūbīyah, Aş Şahrā' al- 30 Jf 24.00N 30.00 E
Southern Ghats 25 Ff 10.00N 76.50 E
Southern Gilbert Islands 60 Jh 1.30S 175.30 E
Southern Indian Lake 38 Jd 57.10N 98.40W
Southern Pines 44 Hh 35.11N 79.24W
Southern Region (EN)= Iglim al Janūbīyah [2] 35 Dd 6.00N 30.00 E
Southern Sierra Madre (EN) =Madre del Sur, Sierra- 38 Jj 17.00N 100.00W
Southern Uplands 5 Fd 55.30N 3.30W
Southern Urals (EN)=Južny Ural 5 Le 54.00N 58.30 E
Southern Yemen (EN) → Yemen, People's Democratic Republic of- (EN) [1] 22 Gh 14.00N 46.00 E
South Esk 9 Ke 56.43N 2.28W
South Fiji Basin (EN) 3 Jl 26.00S 175.00 E
South Foreland 9 Oj 51.09N 1.23 E
South Fork 46 Ge 42.26N 116.53W
South Fork Flathead River 46 Ib 48.07N 113.45W
South Fork Grand River 45 Ed 45.43N 102.17W
South Fork Kern River 46 Fi 35.40N 118.27W
South Fork Moreau River 45 Ed 45.09N 102.50W
South Fork Powder River 46 Le 43.40N 106.30W
South Fork Republican River 45 Ff 40.03N 101.31W
South Georgia/Georgia del Sur, Islas- 66 Ad 54.15S 36.45W
South Glamorgan [3] 9 Jj 51.30N 3.15W
South Haven 44 Dd 42.24N 86.16W
South Honshu Ridge (EN) 3 Ig 24.00N 142.00 E
South Horr 36 Gb 2.06N 36.55 E
South Indian Basin (EN) 3 Ho 60.00S 120.00 E
South Island [F.S.M.] 64d Bc 6.55N 151.59 E
South Island [Kenya] 36 Gb 2.38N 36.36 E
South Island [N.Z.] 57 Ii 44.00S 171.00 E
South Island [Sey.] 37b Ab 9.25S 46.23 E
South Island [Sey.] 37b Bc 10.10S 51.10 E

Index Symbols

[1] Independent Nation
[2] State, Region
[3] District, County
[4] Municipality
[5] Colony, Dependency
Continent
Physical Region
Historical or Cultural Region
Mount, Mountain
Volcano
Hill
Mountains, Mountain Range
Hills, Escarpment
Plateau, Upland
Pass, Gap
Plain, Lowland
Delta
Salt Flat
Valley, Canyon
Crater, Cave
Karst Features
Depression
Polder
Desert, Dunes
Forest, Woods
Heath, Steppe
Oasis
Cape, Point
Coast, Beach
Cliff
Peninsula
Isthmus
Sandbank
Island
Atoll
Rock, Reef
Islands, Archipelago
Rocks, Reefs
Coral Reef
Well, Spring
Geyser
River, Stream
Waterfall Rapids
River Mouth, Estuary
Lake
Salt Lake
Intermittent Lake
Reservoir
Swamp, Pond
Canal
Glacier
Ice Shelf, Pack Ice
Ocean
Sea
Gulf, Bay
Strait, Fjord
Lagoon
Bank
Seamount
Tablemount
Ridge
Shelf
Basin
Escarpment, Sea Scarp
Fracture
Trench, Abyss
National Park, Reserve
Point of Interest
Recreation Site
Cave, Cavern
Historic Site
Ruins
Wall, Walls
Church, Abbey
Temple
Scientific Station
Airport
Port
Lighthouse
Mine
Tunnel
Dam, Bridge

Name	Page	Grid	Lat.	Long.
South Korea (EN)=Taehan-Min' guk	22	Of	38.00N	127.30 E
South Lake Tahoe	46	Eg	38.57N	120.01W
Southland	62	Bf	45.45S	168.00 E
South Loup River	45	Gf	41.04N	98.40W
South Lueti	36	Df	16.14S	23.12 E
South Magnetic Pole (1980)	66	Ie	65.08S	139.03 E
South Malosmadulu Atoll	25a	Ba	5.10N	72.58 E
South Mountain	46	Ge	42.44N	116.54W
South Nahanni	42	Fd	61.03N	123.22W
South Negril Point	47	Ie	18.16N	78.22W
South Orkney Islands	66	Re	60.35S	45.30W
South Pass	38	Ie	42.22N	108.55W
South Pass [F.S.M.]	64d	Bb	7.14N	151.48 E
South Pass [U.S.]	45	Ll	28.55N	89.20W
South Platte	38	Ie	41.07N	100.42W
South Point	51q	Ab	13.02N	59.31W
South Pole	66	Bg	90.00S	0.00
South Porcupine	44	Ga	48.28N	81.13W
Southport [Eng.-U.K.]	9	Jh	53.39N	3.01W
Southport [N.C.-U.S.]	44	Hi	33.55N	78.01W
South Reef	63a	Ee	13.00S	160.32 E
South Ronaldsay	9	Kc	58.46N	2.50W
South Rukuru	36	Fe	10.44S	34.14 E
South Saint Paul	45	Jd	44.52N	93.02W
South Sandwich Islands	66	Ad	56.00S	26.30W
South Sandwich Trench (EN)	3	Do	56.30S	25.00W
South Saskatchewan River	38	Id	53.15N	105.05W
South Shetland Islands	66	Re	62.00S	58.00W
South Shields	9	Lg	55.00N	1.25W
South Sioux City	45	He	42.28N	96.24W
South Sister	46	Ed	44.12N	121.45W
South Taranaki Bight	62	Fc	39.40S	174.15 E
South Trap	62	Bg	47.30S	167.55 E
South Tyne	9	Kg	54.59N	2.08W
South Uist	9	Fd	57.15N	7.24W
South Umpqua River	46	De	43.20N	123.25W
*Southwell	12	Ba	53.04N	0.57W
South Wellesley Islands	59	Hc	17.05S	139.25 E
South West Africa → Namibia	31	Ik	22.00S	17.00 E
Southwest Cape	57	Hi	47.17S	167.27 E
South West Cape	59	Jh	43.34S	146.02 E
Southwest Cape	51a	Dc	17.42N	64.53W
Southwest Indian Ridge (EN)	3	Fm	32.00S	55.00 E
Southwest Miramichi River	44	Ob	46.50N	65.45W
Southwest Pacific Basin (EN)	3	Km	40.00S	150.00W
Southwest Pass	45	Ll	29.00N	89.20W
Southwest Point	49	Jb	22.10N	74.10W
South West Point	64g	Ab	1.52N	157.33W
South West Point	51p	Cb	12.27N	61.30W
Southwold	9	Oi	52.20N	1.40 E
South Yorkshire	9	Lh	53.30N	1.25W
Soutpansberg	37	Dd	22.58S	29.50 E
Soverato	14	Kl	38.41N	16.33 E
Sovetabad	18	Gd	40.14N	69.42 E
Sovetsk [R.S.F.S.R.]	19	Ed	57.36N	48.58 E
Sovetsk [R.S.F.S.R.]	19	Cd	55.05N	21.52 E
Sovetskaja Gavan	22	Qe	48.58N	140.18 E
Sovetski [R.S.F.S.R.]	7	Lh	56.47N	48.30 E
Sovetski [R.S.F.S.R.]	8	Md	60.29N	28.40 E
Sovetski [R.S.F.S.R.]	19	Gc	61.20N	63.29 E
Sovetskoje	19	Ef	47.17N	44.30 E
Soviet Union (EN) → Union of Soviet Socialist Republics (EN)	22	Jd	60.00N	80.00 E
Şowghān	24	Qh	28.20N	56.54 E
Sowie, Góry-	10	Mf	50.38N	16.30 E
Sōya	29a	Ba	45.28N	141.53 E
Sōya-Kaikyō=La Perouse Strait (EN)	21	Qe	45.30N	142.00 E
Sōya-Misaki	27	Pb	45.31N	141.56 E
Soyatita	48	Fe	25.45N	107.22W
Soyo	36	Bd	6.05S	12.20 E
Sož	5	Je	51.57N	30.48 E
Sozopol	15	Kg	42.25N	27.42 E
Spa	11	Ld	50.29N	5.52 E
Spain (EN)=España	6	Fg	40.00N	4.00W
Špakovskoje	16	Lg	45.06N	42.00 E
Spalding	9	Mi	52.47N	0.10W
Spanish Fork	46	Jf	40.07N	111.39W
Spanish Peak	46	Fd	44.24N	119.46W
Spanish Point	51d	Ba	17.33N	61.44W
Spanish Sahara (EN) → Western Sahara (EN)	31	Ff	24.30N	13.00W
Spanish Town [B.V.I.]	51a	Db	18.27N	64.26W
Spanish Town [Jam.]	47	Ie	17.59N	76.57W
Sparbu	7	Ce	63.55N	11.28 E
Spargi, Isola-	14	Di	41.15N	9.20 E
Sparks	43	Dd	39.32N	119.45W
Sparreholm	8	Ge	59.04N	16.49 E
Sparta [Il.-U.S.]	45	Lg	38.07N	89.42W
Sparta [N.C.-U.S.]	44	Gg	36.30N	81.07W
Sparta [Tn.-U.S.]	44	Eh	35.56N	85.29W
Sparta [Wi.-U.S.]	45	Ke	43.57N	90.47W
Sparta (EN) = Spárti	15	Fl	37.05N	22.26 E
Spartanburg	43	Ke	34.57N	81.55W
Spartel, Cap-	30	Ge	35.48N	5.56W
Spárti = Sparta (EN)	15	Fl	37.05N	22.26 E
Spartivento, Capo- [It.]	14	Cl	38.53N	8.50 E
Spartivento, Capo- [It.]	5	Hh	37.55N	16.04 E
Spas-Demensk	16	Ib	54.24N	34.01 E
Spas-Klepiki	7	Ji	55.10N	40.13 E
Spassk-Rjazanski	7	Ji	54.27N	40.22 E
Spátha, Ákra- = Spatha, Cape- (EN)	15	Gn	35.42N	23.44 E
Spatha, Cape- (EN) = Spátha, Ákra-	15	Gn	35.42N	23.44 E
Spearfish	43	Gc	44.30N	103.52W
Spearman	45	Fh	36.12N	101.12W
Speedway	44	Df	39.47N	86.15W
Speicher	12	Ie	49.56N	6.38 E
Speightstown	50	Gf	13.15N	59.39W
Speke Gulf	36	Fc	2.20S	33.15 E
Spello	14	Gh	42.59N	12.40 E
Spenard	40	Jd	61.11N	149.55W
Spence Bay	39	Jc	69.32N	93.31W
Spencer [Ia.-U.S.]	43	Hc	43.09N	95.09W
Spencer [In.-U.S.]	44	Df	39.17N	86.46W
Spencer [Nb.-U.S.]	45	Ge	42.53N	98.42W
Spencer [W.V.-U.S.]	44	Gf	38.48N	81.22W
Spencer, Cape-	59	Hg	35.18S	136.53 E
Spencer Gulf	57	Eh	34.00S	137.00 E
Spenge	12	Kb	52.08N	8.29 E
Spenser Mountains	62	Ee	42.10S	172.35 E
Sperillen	8	Dd	60.30N	10.05 E
Sperkhiós	15	Fk	38.52N	22.34 E
Sperlonga	14	Hi	41.15N	13.26 E
Sperone, Capo-	14	Cl	38.55N	8.25 E
Sperrin Mountains/Sliabh Speirin	9	Fg	54.50N	7.05W
Spessart	10	Fg	49.55N	9.30 E
Spétsai	15	Gl	37.16N	23.09 E
Spétsai	15	Gl	37.16N	23.08 E
Spey	9	Jd	57.40N	3.06W
Spey Bay	9	Jd	57.40N	3.05W
Speyer	10	Eg	49.19N	8.26 E
Speyer-bach	12	Ke	49.19N	8.27 E
Speyside	50	Fg	11.18N	60.32W
Spezzano Albanese	14	Kk	39.40N	16.19 E
Spicer Islands	42	Jc	68.10N	79.00W
Spiekeroog	10	Dc	53.46N	7.42 E
Spiez	14	Bd	46.41N	7.42 E
Spijkenisse	12	Gc	51.51N	4.21 E
Spilimbergo	14	Gd	46.07N	12.54 E
Spilion	15	Hn	35.13N	24.32 E
Spilsby	12	Ca	53.11N	0.06 E
Spina	14	Gf	44.42N	12.08 E
Spinazzola	14	Kj	40.58N	16.05 E
Spincourt	12	He	49.20N	5.40 E
Spirit River	42	Fe	55.47N	118.50W
Spirovo	7	Ih	57.27N	35.01 E
Spiš	10	Qg	49.05N	20.30 E
Spišská Nová Ves	10	Qh	48.57N	20.34 E
Spitak	16	Ni	40.49N	44.14 E
Spitsbergen	67	Kd	78.00N	19.00 E
Spitsbergen	67	Kd	78.45N	16.00 E
Spittal an der Drau	14	Hd	46.48N	13.30 E
Spitzbergen Bank (EN)	41	Oc	76.00N	23.00 E
Spjelkavik	7	Be	62.28N	6.23 E
Split	6	Hg	43.31N	16.26 E
Split Lake	42	He	56.10N	96.10W
Spluga, Passo dello-	14	Dd	46.29N	9.20 E
Splügenpaß	14	Dd	46.29N	9.20 E
Spógi/Špogi	8	Lh	56.02N	26.52 E
Špogi/Spógi	8	Lh	56.02N	26.52 E
Spokane	39	He	47.40N	117.23W
Spokane, Mount-	46	Gc	47.55N	117.07W
Spokane River	46	Fc	47.44N	118.20W
Špola	19	Df	49.01N	31.24 E
Spoleto	14	Gh	42.44N	12.44 E
Spooner	45	Kd	45.50N	91.53W
Spoon River	45	Kf	40.18N	90.04W
Sporovo	10	Vd	52.25N	25.27 E
Spotsylvania	44	If	38.12N	77.35W
Sprague	46	Gc	47.18N	117.59W
Sprague River	46	Ee	42.34N	121.51W
Spray	46	Fd	44.50N	119.48W
Spreča	14	Mf	44.44N	18.06 E
Spree	10	Jd	52.32N	13.13 E
Spreewald	10	Je	51.55N	14.00 E
Spremberg/Grodk	10	Ke	51.33N	14.22 E
Sprengisandur	7a	Bb	64.40N	18.07W
Springbok	31	Ik	29.43S	17.15 E
Spring Creek	45	Fd	45.45N	100.18W
Springdale	45	Ih	36.11N	94.08W
Springe	10	Fd	52.13N	9.33 E
Springer	45	Dh	36.22N	104.36W
Springer, Mount-	44	Ja	49.48N	74.51W
Springerville	46	Ki	34.08N	109.17W
Springfield [Co.-U.S.]	45	Eh	37.24N	102.37W
Springfield [Il.-U.S.]	39	Kf	39.47N	89.40W
Springfield [Ma.-U.S.]	43	Mc	42.07N	72.36W
Springfield [Mn.-U.S.]	45	Id	44.14N	94.59W
Springfield [Mo.-U.S.]	39	Jf	37.14N	93.17W
Springfield [N.Z.]	62	De	43.20S	171.56 E
Springfield [Oh.-U.S.]	43	Kd	39.55N	83.48W
Springfield [Or.-U.S.]	43	Cc	44.03N	123.01W
Springfield [S.D.-U.S.]	45	He	42.49N	97.54W
Springfield [Tn.-U.S.]	44	Dg	36.31N	86.52W
Springfontein	37	Df	30.19S	25.36 E
Spring Garden	54	Gb	6.59N	58.31W
Spring Hall	51q	Ab	13.19N	59.36W
Springhill [La.-U.S.]	45	Jj	33.00N	93.28W
Springhill [N.S.-Can.]	42	Lg	45.39N	64.03W
Spring Mountains	46	Hh	36.10N	115.40W
Springs	37	De	26.13S	28.25 E
Springsure	59	Jd	24.07S	148.05 E
Spring Valley	46	Hg	39.10N	114.30W
Spring Valley	45	Je	43.41N	92.23W
Springville	46	Jf	40.10N	111.37W
Spruce Knob	38	Lf	38.42N	79.32W
Spruce Mountain [Az.-U.S.]	46	Ii	34.28N	112.24W
Spruce Mountain [Nv.-U.S.]	46	Hf	40.33N	114.49W
Spulico, Capo-	14	Kk	39.58N	16.38 E
Spurn Head	9	Nh	53.34N	0.07 E
Squamish	42	Fg	49.42N	123.09W
Squillace	14	Kl	38.47N	16.31 E
Squillace, Golfo di-	14	Kl	38.45N	16.50 E
Squinzano	14	Mj	40.26N	18.02 E
Srbica	15	Dg	42.45N	20.47 E
Srbija=Serbia (EN)	15	Df	44.00N	21.00 E
Srbija = Serbia (EN)	15	Df	44.00N	21.00 E
Srbija = Serbia (EN)	5	Ig	43.00N	21.00 E
Srbobran	15	Cd	45.33N	19.48 E
Srê Âmběl	25	Kf	11.07N	103.46 E
Sredinny Hrebet	21	Rd	56.00N	158.00 E
Sredna Gora	15	Hg	42.30N	25.00 E
Srednekolymsk	20	Kc	67.27N	153.41 E
Srednerusskaja Vozvyšennost=Central Russian Uplands (EN)	5	Je	52.00N	38.00 E
Srednesatyginski Tuman, Ozero-	17	Lg	59.45N	65.25 E
Srednesibirskoje Ploskogorje =Central Siberian Uplands (EN)	21	Mc	65.00N	105.00 E
Sredni Kujto, Ozero-	7	Hd	65.05N	31.30 E
Sredni Ural=Central Urals (EN)	5	Ld	58.00N	59.00 E
Sredni Urgal	20	If	51.13N	132.58 E
Sredni Verecki, Pereval-	16	Ce	48.49N	23.07 E
Srednjaja Ahtuba	16	Ne	48.43N	44.52 E
Srednjaja Olëkma	20	He	55.26N	120.40 E
Śrem	10	Nd	52.08N	17.01 E
Sremska Mitrovica	15	Ce	44.58N	19.37 E
Sremski Karlovci	15	Cd	45.12N	19.56 E
Sretensk	22	Nd	52.15N	117.43 E
Sri Gangānagar	25	Ec	29.55N	73.53 E
Sri Jayawardenepura	25	Gg	6.54N	80.02 E
Srijem	15	Cd	45.00N	19.40 E
Srīkākulam	25	Ge	18.18N	83.54 E
Sri Lanka (Ceylon)	22	Ki	7.40N	80.50 E
Srinagar	22	Jf	34.05N	74.49 E
Srivardhan	25	Ee	18.02N	73.01 E
Środa Śląska	10	Me	51.10N	16.36 E
Środa Wielkopolska	10	Nd	52.14N	17.17 E
Srpska Crnja	15	Dd	45.43N	20.42 E
Sruth na Maoile/North Channel	5	Fd	55.10N	5.40W
SSSR=Union of Soviet Socialist Republics (USSR) (EN)	22	Jd	60.00N	80.00 E
SSSR → Sojuz Sovetskih Socialističeskih Respublik	22	Jd	60.00N	80.00 E
Ssu-ch'uan Sheng → Sichuan Sheng = Szechwan (EN)	27	He	30.00N	103.00 E
Staaten River	59	Ic	16.24S	141.17 E
Stabroek	12	Gc	51.20N	4.22 E
Stack Skerry	9	Ib	59.02N	4.30W
Stade	10	Fc	53.36N	9.29 E
Staden	12	Fd	50.59N	3.01 E
Stadhavet	8	Ab	62.15N	5.05 E
Städjan	8	Ec	61.58N	12.52 E
Stadlandet	8	Ab	62.05N	5.20 E
Stadskanaal	11	Ma	53.00N	6.55 E
Stadskanaal-Musselkanaal	12	Jb	52.56N	7.02 E
Stadthagen	12	Lb	52.19N	9.12 E
Stadtkyll	12	Id	50.21N	6.32 E
Stadtlohn	12	Ic	51.59N	6.56 E
Stadtoldendorf	10	Fe	51.54N	9.38 E
Staffa	9	Ge	56.25N	6.10W
Staffanstorp	8	Ei	55.38N	13.13 E
Staffelsee	10	Hi	47.42N	11.10 E
Staffora	14	De	45.04N	9.01 E
Stafford	9	Li	52.50N	2.00W
Stafford	9	Ki	52.48N	2.07W
Staffordshire	9	Li	52.55N	2.00W
Staicele/Stajcele	8	Kg	57.44N	24.39 E
Stainach	14	Ic	47.32N	14.06 E
Staines	12	Bc	51.26N	0.31W
Stakčín	10	Sg	49.00N	22.13 E
Stalać	15	Ef	43.40N	21.25 E
Stalham	12	Db	52.46N	1.31 E
Stalingrad → Volgograd	6	Kf	48.44N	44.25 E
Ställdalen	8	Fe	59.56N	14.56 E
Stalowa Wola	10	Sf	50.35N	22.02 E
Starnberger See	10	Ii	47.55N	12.20 E
Stamford [Ct.-U.S.]	44	Ke	41.03N	73.32W
Stamford [Eng.-U.K.]	9	Mi	52.39N	0.29W
Stamford [Tx.-U.S.]	45	Gj	32.57N	99.48W
Stamford, Lake-	45	Gj	33.05N	99.35W
Stampriet	37	Bd	24.20S	18.28 E
Stamsund	7	Cb	68.08N	13.51 E
Stanberry	45	If	40.13N	94.35W
Stancija Jakkabag	18	Fe	38.59N	66.42 E
Stancija-Karakul	19	Gh	39.30N	63.50 E
Standerton	37	De	26.58S	29.07 E
Standish	44	Fd	44.00N	83.57W
Stanford	46	Jc	47.09N	110.13W
Stånga	8	Hg	57.17N	18.28 E
Stångån	8	Ff	58.27N	15.37 E
Stange	8	Dd	60.43N	11.11 E
Stanger	37	Ee	29.27S	31.14 E
Stanke Dimitrov	15	Gg	42.16N	23.07 E
Stanley [Austl.]	59	Jh	40.46S	145.18 E
Stanley [Falk. Is.]	53	Kk	51.42S	57.51W
Stanley [N.D.-U.S.]	45	Eb	48.19N	102.23W
Stanley Falls (EN)= Ngaliema, Chutes-	30	Jh	0.30N	25.30 E
Stann Creek	49	Ce	16.50N	88.30W
Stanovoje Nagorje= Stanovoy Upland (EN)	21	Nd	56.00N	114.00 E
Stanovoj Hrebet=Stanovoy Range (EN)	21	Od	56.20N	126.00 E
Stanovoy Upland (EN)= Stanovoje Nagorje	21	Nd	56.00N	114.00 E
Stans	14	Cd	46.58N	8.22 E
Stansted Airport	12	Cc	51.54N	0.13 E
Stansted Mountfitchet	12	Cc	51.54N	0.12 E
Stanthorpe	59	Ke	28.39S	151.57 E
Stanton Banks	9	Fe	56.15N	7.50W
Staphorst	12	Ib	52.38N	6.14 E
Staples	45	Ic	46.21N	94.48W
Stapleton	45	Ff	41.29N	100.31W
Stąporków	10	Qe	51.09N	20.34 E
Starachowice	10	Re	51.03N	21.04 E
Staraja Majna	7	Li	54.36N	48.59 E
Staraja Russa	19	Dd	57.59N	31.23 E
Staraja-Vyževka	10	Ue	51.27N	24.34 E
Stará L'ubovňa	10	Qg	49.18N	20.42 E
Stara Moravica	15	Cd	45.52N	19.28 E
Stara Pazova	15	De	44.59N	20.10 E
Stara Planina = Balkan Mountains (EN)	5	Ig	43.15N	25.00 E
Stara Zagora	15	Ig	42.25N	25.38 E
Stara Zagora	6	Ig	42.25N	25.38 E
Starbuck Island	57	Le	5.37S	155.53W
Staretina	14	Kf	44.02N	16.43 E
Stargard Szczeciński	10	Lc	53.20N	15.02 E
Stari Begejski kanal	15	Dd	45.29N	20.25 E
Starica	7	Ih	56.30N	34.56 E
Starigrad	14	Kg	43.11N	16.36 E
Stari Vlah	15	Df	43.23N	20.10 E
Starke	44	Fk	29.57N	82.07W
Starkville	45	Lj	33.28N	88.48W
Starnberg	10	Hh	48.00N	11.21 E
Starobelsk	19	Df	49.15N	38.58 E
Starodub	19	De	52.35N	32.46 E
Starogard Gdański	10	Oc	53.59N	18.33 E
Starokonstantinov	16	Ee	49.43N	27.13 E
Starominskaja	19	Df	46.31N	39.06 E
Staroščerbinovskaja	16	Kf	46.37N	38.42 E
Starosubhangulovo	17	Hj	53.06N	57.20 E
Starotimoškino	7	Lj	53.43N	47.32 E
Start Point	9	Jk	50.13N	3.38W
Staryje Dorógi	16	Fc	53.02N	28.17 E
Stary Krym	16	Ig	45.02N	35.05 E
Stary Oskol	19	De	51.18N	37.51 E
Stary Sambor	16	Ce	49.29N	23.01 E
Stary Terek	16	Og	44.01N	47.24 E
Staßfurt	10	He	51.52N	11.35 E
Staszów	10	Rf	50.34N	21.10 E
State College	44	Ie	40.48N	77.52W
Staten Island (EN)= Estados, Isla de los-	52	Jk	54.47S	64.15W
Statesboro	44	Gi	32.27N	81.47W
Statesville	44	Gh	35.47N	80.53W
Stathelle	8	Ce	59.03N	9.41 E
Stathmós Krioneríou	15	Ek	38.20N	21.35 E
Statland	7	Cd	64.30N	11.08 E
Staunton	43	Ld	38.10N	79.05W
Stavanger	6	Gd	58.58N	5.45 E
Stavelot	12	Hd	50.23N	5.56 E
Staveren	11	Lb	52.53N	5.22 E
Stavern	8	Df	59.00N	10.02 E
Stavnoje	10	Sh	48.59N	22.45 E
Stavropol	6	Kf	45.02N	41.59 E
Stavropolskaja Vozvyšennost	16	Mg	45.10N	43.00 E
Stavropolski Kraj	19	Eg	45.00N	43.15 E
Stavrós [Grc.]	15	Fj	39.19N	22.14 E
Stavrós [Grc.]	15	Gi	40.40N	23.42 E
Stavroúpolis	15	Hh	41.12N	24.42 E
Stawell	59	Ig	37.04S	142.46 E
Stawiski	10	Sc	53.23N	22.09 E
Stawiszyn	10	Oe	51.55N	18.07 E
Stayton	46	Dd	44.48N	122.48W
Steamboat Springs	43	Fc	40.29N	106.50W
Stebnik	10	Tg	49.14N	23.34 E
Stedingen	12	Ka	53.10N	8.30 E
Steele	45	Gc	46.51N	99.55W
Steelpoort	37	Ed	24.48S	30.12 E
Steenbergen	12	Gc	51.35N	4.19 E
Steen River	42	Fe	59.38N	117.06W
Steensby Inlet	42	Jb	70.10N	78.25W
Steenstrups Gletscher	41	Gc	75.15N	57.30W
Steenvoorde	12	Ed	50.48N	2.35 E
Steenwijk	11	Mb	52.47N	6.08 E
Ştefăneşti	15	Kb	47.48N	27.12 E
Stefanie, Lake- (EN)=Chew Bahir	30	Kh	4.38N	36.50 E
Stefansson	42	Gb	73.30N	105.30W
Ştefleşti, Virful-	15	Gd	45.32N	23.48 E
Stege	8	Ej	54.59N	12.18 E
Steiermark = Styria (EN)	14	Ic	47.15N	15.00 E
Steiermark = Styria (EN)	14	Ic	47.15N	15.00 E
Steigerwald	10	Gg	49.40N	10.20 E
Steilrandberge	37	Ac	17.53S	13.20 E
Steinach	14	Fc	47.05N	11.28 E
Steinbach	42	Hg	49.32N	96.41W
Steinen, Rio-	54	Hf	12.05S	53.46W
Steinfeld (Oldenburg)	12	Kb	52.36N	8.13 E
Steinfort/Steinfurt	12	He	49.40N	5.55 E
Steinfurt	10	Dd	52.09N	7.20 E
Steinfurt-Steinfort	12	He	49.40N	5.55 E
Steinfurt-Borghorst	12	Jb	52.08N	7.25 E
Steinhagen	12	Kb	52.01N	8.24 E
Steinhausen	37	Bd	21.49S	18.20 E
Steinheim	12	Lc	51.51N	9.06 E
Steinhuder Meer	10	Fd	52.28N	9.19 E
Steinkjer	7	Cd	64.01N	11.30 E
Steinkopf	37	Be	29.18S	17.43 E
Steinshamn	8	Bb	62.47N	6.29 E
Steinsøy	7	Ac	61.00N	4.30 E
Steirisch-Niederösterreichische Kalkalpen	14	Jc	47.45N	15.30 E
Stekene	12	Gc	51.12N	4.02 E
Stekolny	20	Ke	60.00N	150.50 E
Stella	37	Ce	26.33S	24.53 E
Stellenbosch	37	Bf	33.58S	18.50 E
Stello	11a	Ba	42.47N	9.25 E
Stelvio, Passo dello-/Stilfer Joch	14	Ed	46.32N	10.27 E
Stemwede	12	Kb	52.26N	8.26 E
Stenay	11	Le	49.29N	5.11 E
Stendal	10	Hd	52.36N	11.51 E
Stende	8	Jg	57.10N	22.28 E
Stende	8	Ig	57.40N	21.57 E
Stenhouse Bay	59	Hg	35.17S	136.56 E
Stenstorp	8	Ef	58.16N	13.43 E
Stenungsund	7	Cg	58.05N	11.49 E
Stepanakert	6	Kh	39.49N	46.44 E
Stepanavan	16	Ni	40.59N	44.20 E
Stephens, Cape-	62	Ed	40.42S	173.57 E
Stephens, Mount-	66	Rg	83.23S	51.27W
Stephens Passage	40	Me	57.50N	133.50W
Stephenville [Newf.-Can.]	42	Lg	48.33N	58.35W
Stephenville [Tx.-U.S.]	45	Gj	32.13N	98.12W
Steps Point	65c	Cb	14.22S	170.45W
Sterea Ellás kai Évvoia	15	Hk	38.20N	24.30 E
Sterkstroom	37	Df	31.32S	26.32 E
Sterlibaševo	17	Gj	53.28N	55.15 E
Sterling [Co.-U.S.]	43	Gc	40.37N	103.13W
Sterling [Il.-U.S.]	45	Lf	41.48N	89.42W
Sterling City	45	Fk	31.50N	100.59W
Sterlitamak	6	Le	53.37N	55.58 E
Šternberk	10	Ng	49.44N	17.19 E
Sterzing / Vipiteno	14	Fd	46.54N	11.26 E
Stettin (EN)=Szczecin	6	He	53.24N	14.32 E
Stettiner Haff	10	Kc	53.46N	14.14 E
Stettler	42	Gf	52.19N	112.43W
Steubenville	43	Kc	40.22N	80.39W
Stevenage	9	Mj	51.54N	0.11W
Stevenson Entrance	40	Ie	57.45N	152.20W
Stevens Point	43	Jc	44.31N	89.34W
Stewart	42	Dd	63.18N	139.24W
Stewart	42	Ee	55.56N	129.59W
Stewart Crossing	42	Dd	63.19N	136.33W
Stewart Island	57	Hi	47.00S	167.50 E
Stewart Islands	57	He	8.20S	162.40 E
Steyerberg	12	Lb	52.34N	9.02 E
Steyning	12	Bd	50.53N	0.20W
Steynsburg	37	Df	31.15S	25.49 E
Steyr	14	Ib	48.02N	14.25 E
Steyr	14	Ib	48.03N	14.25 E
Štiavnické vrchy	10	Oh	48.15N	18.50 E
Stidia	13	Li	35.50N	0.05W
Stiene	8	Kg	57.19N	24.28 E
Stiens, Leeuwarderadeel-	12	Ha	53.16N	5.46 E
Stigliano	14	Kj	40.24N	16.14 E
St. Ignace	43	Kb	45.52N	84.43W
Stigtomta	8	Gf	58.48N	16.47 E
Stikine	38	Fd	56.40N	132.30W
Stikine Ranges	42	Ee	57.35N	131.00W
Stilfer Joch/Stelvio, Passo dello-	14	Ed	46.32N	10.27 E
Stilfontein	37	De	26.50S	26.50 E
Stilis	15	Fk	38.55N	22.37 E
Stillwater [Mn.-U.S.]	45	Jd	45.04N	92.49W
Stillwater [Ok.-U.S.]	43	Hd	36.07N	97.04W
Stillwater Range	46	Fg	39.50N	118.15W
Stilo	14	Kl	38.29N	16.28 E
Stilo, Punta-	14	Kl	38.27N	16.35 E
Štimlje	15	Eg	42.26N	21.03 E
Stînişoarei, Munţii-	15	Ib	47.20N	26.00 E
Stinnett	45	Fi	35.50N	101.27W
Štip	15	Fh	41.44N	22.12 E
Stirling	9	Je	56.07N	3.57W
Stirling Range	59	Df	34.25S	117.50 E
Stjernøya	7	Fa	70.18N	22.45 E
Stjørdalshalsen	7	Ce	63.28N	10.44 E
Stobi	15	Eh	41.33N	21.59 E
Stobrawa	10	Nf	50.50N	17.32 E
Stocka	8	Gc	61.54N	17.20 E
Stockach	10	Fi	47.51N	9.01 E
Stockbridge	12	Ac	51.06N	1.29W
Stockerau	14	Kb	48.23N	16.13 E
Stockholm	7	Dg	59.20N	18.00 E
Stockholm	6	Hd	59.20N	18.03 E
Stockport	9	Kh	53.25N	2.10W
Stocks Seamount (EN)	52	Mg	12.15S	32.00W
Stockton [Ca.-U.S.]	39	Gf	37.57N	121.17W
Stockton [Mo.-U.S.]	45	Jh	37.42N	93.48W
Stockton Lake	45	Jh	37.40N	93.45W
Stockton-on-Tees	9	Lg	54.34N	1.19W
Stockton Plateau	43	Ge	30.30N	102.30W
Stoczek Łukowski	10	Re	51.58N	21.58 E
Stöde	7	De	62.25N	16.35 E
Stoĕng Trĕng	25	Lf	13.31N	105.58 E
Stoer, Point of-	9	Hc	58.20N	5.25W
Stogovo	15	Dh	41.29N	20.39 E
Stohod	10	Ve	51.52N	25.44 E
Stoholm	8	Ch	56.29N	9.10 E
Stoj, Gora-	16	Ce	48.39N	23.15 E
Stojba	22	Pd	52.49N	131.43 E
Stoke-on-Trent	9	Kh	53.00N	2.10W
Stokksnes	7a	Cb	64.14N	14.58W
Stokmarknes	7	Db	68.34N	14.55 E
Stol	15	Fe	44.11N	22.09 E
Stolac	14	Lg	43.05N	17.58 E
Stolbcy	16	Ec	53.31N	26.43 E
Stolberg	10	Cf	50.46N	6.14 E
Stolbovoj, Ostrov-	20	Ib	74.05N	136.00 E
Stolin	16	Ed	51.57N	26.52 E
Stolzenau	12	Lb	52.31N	9.04 E
Ston	14	Lh	42.50N	17.42 E
Stone	9	Ki	52.54N	2.10W
Stonehaven	9	Ke	56.58N	2.13W
Stonehenge	9	Lj	51.11N	1.49W
Stonehenge	59	Id	24.22S	143.17 E
Stoner	45	Bh	37.37N	108.18W
Stonewall	45	Ha	50.09N	97.21W
Stony	40	Hd	61.45N	156.35W
Stony Rapids	42	Ge	59.16N	105.50W
Stony River	40	Hd	61.47N	156.41W
Stony Stratford	12	Bb	52.03N	0.51W
Stony Tunguska (EN)= Podkamennaja Tunguska	21	Lc	61.36N	90.18 E
Stör	10	Fc	53.50N	9.25 E
Storå	8	Ch	56.19N	8.19 E
Storå	8	Fe	59.43N	15.08 E
Storå/Isojoki	7	Ee	62.07N	21.58 E
Stora Gla	8	Ee	59.30N	12.30 E
Stora Le	8	De	59.05N	11.55 E
Stora Lulevatten	7	Ec	67.08N	19.20 E
Storavan	7	Ed	65.42N	18.12 E
Storby	8	Hd	60.13N	19.34 E
Stord	7	Ag	59.55N	5.25 E
Storđa	7	Ee	62.07N	21.58 E
Stordal	8	Bb	62.23N	7.01 E

Index Symbols

Independent Nation · State, Region · District, County · Municipality · Colony, Dependency · Continent · Physical Region · Historical or Cultural Region · Mount, Mountain · Volcano · Hill · Mountains, Mountain Range · Hills, Escarpment · Plateau, Upland · Pass, Gap · Plain, Lowland · Delta · Salt Flat · Valley, Canyon · Crater, Cave · Karst Features · Depression · Polder · Desert, Dunes · Forest, Woods · Heath, Steppe · Oasis · Cape, Point · Coast, Beach · Cliff · Peninsula · Isthmus · Sandbank · Island · Atoll · Rock, Reef · Islands, Archipelago · Rocks, Reefs · Coral Reef · Well, Spring · Geyser · River, Stream · Waterfall Rapids · River Mouth, Estuary · Lake · Salt Lake · Intermittent Lake · Reservoir · Swamp, Pond · Canal · Glacier · Ice Shelf, Pack Ice · Ocean · Sea · Gulf, Bay · Strait, Fjord · Lagoon · Bank · Seamount · Tablemount · Ridge · Shelf · Basin · Escarpment, Sea Scarp · Fracture · Trench, Abyss · National Park, Reserve · Point of Interest · Recreation Site · Cave, Cavern · Historic Site · Ruins · Wall, Walls · Church, Abbey · Temple · Scientific Station · Airport · Port · Lighthouse · Mine · Tunnel · Dam, Bridge

Name	Page	Grid	Lat.	Long.
Store Bælt=Great Belt (EN)	5	Hd	55.30N	11.00 E
Storebro	8	Fg	57.35N	15.51 E
Storefiskbank	9	Oe	56.50N	4.00 E
Store Heddinge	8	Ei	55.19N	12.25 E
Store Hellefiske Bank (EN)	41	Ge	67.30N	55.00W
Store Koldewey	41	Kc	76.20N	18.30W
Store Kvien	8	Dc	61.34N	10.33 E
Støren	7	Ce	63.02N	10.18 E
Store Nupsfonn	8	Be	59.54N	7.08 E
Store Sølnkletten	8	Dc	61.59N	10.18 E
Storfjorden [Nor.]	8	Bb	62.25N	6.30 E
Storfjorden [Sval.]	41	Nc	77.30N	20.00 E
Storfors	8	Fe	59.32N	14.16 E
Storis Passage	42	Hc	67.40N	98.30W
Storkerson Bay	42	Fb	73.00N	124.00W
Storkerson Peninsula	42	Gb	73.00N	106.30W
Storlien	7	Ce	63.19N	12.06 E
Stormarn	10	Gc	53.45N	10.20 E
Storm Bay	59	Jh	43.10S	147.30 E
Storm Lake	43	Hc	42.39N	95.13W
Stornoway	9	Gc	58.12N	6.23W
Storøya	41	Ob	80.08N	27.50 E
Storožinec	16	De	48.10N	25.46 E
Storsjøen [Nor.]	8	Dd	60.25N	11.40 E
Storsjøen [Nor.]	8	Dd	61.35N	11.15 E
Storsjön [Swe.]	8	Gd	60.35N	16.45 E
Storsjön [Swe.]	5	Hc	63.15N	14.20 E
Storsteinfjellet	7	Db	68.14N	17.52 E
Storstrøm [2]	8	Dj	55.00N	11.50 E
Storstrømmen	41	Jc	77.20N	23.00W
Storsudret	8	Hh	57.00N	18.15 E
Storuman	7	Dd	65.14N	16.54 E
Storuman	6	Hb	65.06N	17.06 E
Storvätteshågna	8	Eb	62.07N	12.27 E
Storvigelen	8	Eb	62.32N	12.04 E
Storvik	8	Gd	60.35N	16.32 E
Storvreta	8	Ge	59.58N	17.42 E
Stöttingfjället	7	Dd	64.38N	17.44 E
Stoughton	46	Nb	49.41N	103.03W
Stour [Eng.-U.K.]	9	Lk	50.43N	1.46W
Stour [Eng.-U.K.]	9	Oj	51.52N	1.16 E
Stourbridge	9	Ki	52.27N	2.09W
Støvring	8	Ch	56.53N	9.51 E
Stowmarket	12	Cb	52.11N	0.59 E
Strabane/An Srath Bán	9	Fg	54.49N	7.27W
Stradella	14	De	45.05N	9.18 E
Straelen	12	Ic	51.27N	6.16 E
Strakonice	10	Jg	49.16N	13.55 E
Straldža	15	Jg	42.36N	26.41 E
Stralsund	10	Jb	54.18N	13.06 E
Strand	37	Bf	34.06S	18.50 E
Stranda	7	Be	62.19N	6.54 E
Strand Bay	42	Ia	79.00N	94.00W
Strangford Lough/Loch Cuan	9	Hg	54.26N	5.36W
Strängnäs	8	Ge	59.23N	17.02 E
Stranraer	9	Hg	54.54N	5.02W
Strasbourg [Fr.]	6	Gf	48.35N	7.45 E
Strasbourg [Sask.-Can.]	46	Ma	51.04N	104.57W
Strašeny	16	Ff	47.06N	28.34 E
Straßwalchen	14	Hc	47.59N	13.15 E
Stratford [N.Z.]	62	Fc	39.21S	174.17 E
Stratford [Ont.-Can.]	44	Gd	43.22N	80.57W
Stratford [Tx.-U.S.]	45	Eh	36.20N	102.04W
Stratford-upon-Avon	9	Li	52.12N	1.41W
Strathclyde [3]	9	If	55.50N	4.50W
Strathgordon	59	Jh	42.54S	146.10 E
Strathmore	9	Je	56.40N	3.05W
Strathmore	46	Ia	51.03N	113.23W
Strathroy	44	Gd	42.57N	81.38W
Strathy Point	9	Ic	58.35N	4.01W
Straubenhardt	12	Kf	48.50N	8.34 E
Straubing	10	Ih	48.53N	12.34 E
Straumnes	7a	Aa	66.26N	23.08W
Straumsjøen	7	Db	68.41N	14.30 E
Strausberg	10	Jd	52.35N	13.53 E
Strawberry Mountain	46	Fd	44.19N	118.43W
Strawberry River	46	Jf	40.10N	110.24W
Straža	15	Fg	42.15N	22.14 E
Stražica	15	If	43.14N	25.58 E
Strážiště	10	Kg	49.32N	14.58 E
Strażovské vrchy	10	Oh	48.55N	18.30 E
Streaky Bay	59	Gf	32.48S	134.13 E
Streaky Bay	59	Gf	32.35S	134.10 E
Streator	45	Lf	41.07N	88.50W
Středočeská pahorkatina	10	Kg	49.30N	14.15 E
Středočeský kraj [3]	10	Kg	49.55N	14.30 E
Středoslovenský kraj [3]	10	Ph	48.50N	19.10 E
Strehaia	15	Ge	44.37N	23.12 E
Strei	15	Gd	45.51N	23.03 E
Střela	10	Jg	49.54N	13.32 E
Strelasund	10	Jb	54.20N	13.05 E
Strelka	20	Ee	58.03N	93.05 E
Strelna	7	Jc	66.04N	38.39 E
Strenči	7	Fh	57.39N	25.38 E
Stresa	14	Ce	45.53N	8.32 E
Streževoj	20	Cd	60.42N	77.35 E
Stříbro	10	Ig	49.46N	13.00 E
Strickland River	59	Ia	6.00S	142.05 E
Strîmbeni	15	He	44.28N	24.58 E
Strimón	15	Gi	40.47N	23.51 E
Strimonikós Kólpos	15	Gi	40.40N	23.50 E
Strjama	15	Hg	42.10N	24.56 E
Strofádhes, Nisoi-	15	Dl	37.15N	21.00 E
Ströhen, Wagenfeld-	12	Kb	52.32N	8.39 E
Stromberg	12	Je	49.57N	7.46 E
Stromboli	14	Jl	38.45N	15.15 E
Strömfors/Ruotsinpyhtää	8	Ld	60.32N	26.27 E
Stromness	9	Jc	58.57N	3.18W
Strömsbro	8	Gd	60.42N	17.10 E
Strömsbruk	7	Dc	61.53N	17.19 E
Strömsnäsbruk	8	Eh	56.33N	13.43 E
Strömstad	7	Cf	58.56N	11.10 E
Strömsund	7	De	63.51N	15.35 E
Strongili	15	Hm	36.58N	24.55 E
Stròngoli	14	Lk	39.16N	17.03 E
Stronsay	9	Kb	59.08N	2.38W
Stropkov	10	Rg	49.12N	21.40 E
Stroud	9	Kj	51.45N	2.12W
Struer	7	Bh	56.29N	8.37 E
Struga	15	Dh	41.11N	20.41 E
Strugi-Krasnyje	7	Gg	58.17N	29.08 E
Strule	9	Fg	54.40N	7.20W
Struma	5	Ig	40.47N	23.51 E
Strumble Head	9	Hi	52.02N	5.04W
Strumica	15	Fh	41.26N	22.39 E
Stry	16	De	49.24N	24.13 E
Stry	19	Cf	49.14N	23.49 E
Strydenburg	37	Ce	29.58S	23.40 E
Stryn	7	Bf	61.55N	6.47 E
Strynsvatn	8	Bc	61.55N	7.05 E
Strzegom	10	Mf	50.57N	16.21 E
Strzegomka	10	Me	51.08N	16.50 E
Strzelce Krajeńskie	10	Ld	52.53N	15.32 E
Strzelce Opolskie	10	Of	50.31N	18.19 E
Strzelin	10	Nf	50.47N	17.03 E
Strzelno	10	Od	52.38N	18.11 E
Strzyżów	10	Rg	49.52N	21.47 E
Stuart	40	Gd	63.35N	162.30W
Stuart, Mount-	46	Ec	47.29N	120.54W
Stuart Bluff Range	59	Gd	22.45S	132.15 E
Stuart Lake	42	Ff	54.33N	124.35W
Stuart Range	59	Ge	29.10S	134.55 E
Stubaier Alpen	14	Fc	47.10N	11.05 E
Stubbekøbing	8	Ej	54.43N	12.03 E
Stubbenkammer	10	Jb	54.35N	13.40 E
Stubbs Bay	51n	Ba	13.08N	61.10W
Štubik	15	Fe	44.18N	22.21 E
Stucka	7	Fh	56.36N	25.17 E
Studenica, Manastir-	15	Df	43.28N	20.37 E
Studholme Junction	62	Df	44.44S	171.08 E
Stugun	7	De	63.10N	15.36 E
Stuhr	12	Ka	53.02N	8.45 E
Stupino	7	Ji	54.57N	38.03 E
Stura di Demonte	14	Bf	44.40N	7.53 E
Stura di Lanzo	14	Be	45.06N	7.44 E
Sturge Island	66	Ke	67.27S	164.18 E
Sturgeon Bay	45	Md	44.50N	87.23W
Sturgeon Falls	42	Jg	46.22N	79.55W
Sturgeon Lake	45	Kb	50.00N	90.45W
Sturgis [Mi.-U.S.]	44	Ee	41.48N	85.25W
Sturgis [S.D.-U.S.]	45	Ed	44.25N	103.31W
Sturkö	8	Fh	56.05N	15.40 E
Sturt Creek	59	Fd	20.08S	127.24 E
Sturt Desert	59	Ie	28.30S	141.00 E
Stutterheim	37	Df	32.33S	27.28 E
Stuttgart [Ar.-U.S.]	45	Ki	34.30N	91.33W
Stuttgart [Ger.]	6	Gf	48.46N	9.11 E
Stviga	16	Ec	52.04N	27.55 E
Stykkishólmur	7a	Ab	65.04N	22.44W
Styr	19	Ce	52.07N	26.35 E
Styria (EN) = Steiermark	14	Ic	47.15N	15.00 E
Styria (EN) = Steiermark [2]	14	Ic	47.15N	15.00 E
Styrsö	8	Dg	57.37N	11.46 E
Suafa Point	63a	Ec	8.19S	160.41 E
Suai	26	Ih	9.21S	125.17 E
Suakin Archipelago (EN)= Sawākin, Jazā'ir-	30	Kg	19.07N	37.20 E
Suao	27	Lg	24.36N	121.51 E
Suardi	55	Bj	30.32S	61.58W
Suavanao	60	Fi	7.34S	158.44 E
Subačius/Subačjus	8	Ki	55.44N	24.53 E
Subačjus/Subačius	8	Ki	55.44N	24.53 E
Subang	26	Eh	6.34S	107.45 E
Subansiri	25	Jc	26.48N	93.49 E
Subao Ding	27	Jf	27.10N	110.18 E
Šubarkuduk	19	Ff	49.09N	56.31 E
Šubarši	16	Te	48.38N	57.12 E
Subate	8	Lh	56.01N	26.04 E
Subay', 'Urūq-	33	He	22.15N	43.05 E
Subayṭilah	32	Ib	35.14N	9.08 E
Subbético, Sistema-	13	Jf	38.30N	2.30W
Subei (Dangchengwan)	27	Fd	39.36N	94.58 E
Subi, Pulau-	26	Ef	2.55N	108.50 E
Subiaco	14	Hi	41.55N	13.06 E
Sublette	45	Fh	37.29N	100.50W
Submeseta Norte	5	Fg	42.20N	4.50W
Submeseta Sur	5	Fh	39.30N	3.30W
Subotica	15	Cc	46.06N	19.40 E
Subpolar Urals (EN)= Pripoljarny Ural	5	Lb	65.00N	60.00 E
Subugo	36	Gc	1.40S	35.49 E
Suceava	15	Jb	47.32N	26.32 E
Suceava [2]	15	Ib	47.40N	25.45 E
Suceava	15	Jb	47.38N	26.15 E
Sucha Beskidzka	10	Pg	49.44N	19.36 E
Süchbaatar → Suhe-Bator	22	Md	50.15N	106.12 E
Suchedniów	10	Qe	51.03N	20.51 E
Suchiapa, Rio-	48	Mi	16.36N	93.01W
Suchitepéquez [3]	49	Bf	14.25N	91.20W
Sucia, Bahia-	51a	Ac	17.57N	67.10W
Sucio, Rio-	49	Ij	7.27N	77.07W
Suck/An tSuca	9	Eh	53.16N	8.03W
Suckling, Mount-	59	Ja	9.45S	148.55 E
Sucre [Bol.]	53	Jg	19.02S	65.17W
Sucre [Col.] [2]	54	Db	9.00N	75.00W
Sucre [Col.]	54	Db	8.50N	74.43W
Sucre [Ven.] [2]	54	Fa	10.25N	63.30W
Suçuarana, Serra da-	55	Jb	14.25S	45.00W
Sucunduri, Rio-	54	Ge	5.30S	59.40W
Sućuraj	14	Lg	43.08N	17.12 E
Sucuriú, Rio-	54	Hh	20.47S	51.38W
Sud, Canal du-	49	Kd	18.40N	73.05W
Sud, Massif du-	49	Kd	18.25N	73.55W
Suda	7	Ig	59.11N	37.33 E
Suda	7	Ig	59.12N	37.30 E
Sudak	19	Dg	44.50N	34.59 E
Sudan	30	Ig	11.30N	15.00 E
Sudan (EN)=As Sūdān [1]	31	Jg	15.00N	30.00 E
Sudbury [Eng.-U.K.]	9	Ni	52.02N	0.44 E
Sudbury [Ont.-Can.]	39	Ke	46.30N	81.00W
Suddie	50	Gi	7.07N	58.29W
Sude	10	Gc	53.22N	10.45 E
Sudeten (EN)	5	He	50.30N	16.00 E
Sudirman, Pegunungan-	26	Kg	4.12S	137.00 E
Sudočje, Ozero-	18	Bc	43.25N	58.30 E
Sudogda	7	Ji	55.59N	40.50 E
Sudost	16	Hc	52.19N	33.24 E
Sud-Ouest [Cam.] [3]	34	Gd	5.20N	9.20 E
Sud-Ouest [U.V.] [3]	34	Ec	10.30N	3.15W
Sudovaja Višnja	10	Tg	49.43N	23.26 E
Südradde	12	Jb	52.41N	7.34 E
Südtirol / Trentino-Alto Adige [2]	14	Fd	46.30N	11.20 E
Sudža	16	Id	51.13N	35.16 E
Sue	30	Jh	7.41N	28.03 E
Sueca	13	Le	39.12N	0.19W
Suess Land	41	Jd	72.45N	26.00W
Suez (EN)=As Suways	31	Kf	29.58N	32.33 E
Suez, Gulf of-(EN)= Suways, Khalīj as-	30	Kf	28.10N	33.27 E
Suez Canal (EN)=Suways, Qanāt as-	30	Ke	29.55N	32.33 E
Suffolk	9	Ni	52.25N	1.00 E
Suffolk	43	Ld	36.44N	76.37W
Suffolk [3]	9	Li	52.10N	1.05W
Sufiān	24	Kc	38.17N	45.59 E
Sugana, Val-	14	Fd	46.00N	11.40 E
Suga-no-Sen	29	Dd	35.22N	134.31 E
Sugar Island	44	Eb	46.25N	84.12W
Sugarloaf Mountain	44	Lc	45.01N	70.22W
Suğla Gölü	24	Ed	37.20N	32.02 E
Sugoj	20	Kd	64.15N	154.29 E
Suguta	36	Gb	2.03N	36.33 E
Suha	15	Ke	44.08N	27.36 E
Suhai Hu	27	Fd	38.55N	94.05 E
Şuḥār	23	Ie	24.22N	56.45 E
Suhe-Bator (Süchbaatar)	22	Md	50.15N	106.12 E
Suhiniči	16	Ib	54.06N	35.20 E
Suhl	10	Gf	50.36N	10.42 E
Suhodolskoje, Ozero-	8	Nd	60.35N	30.30 E
Suhoj Log	17	Kh	56.55N	62.01 E
Suhona	5	Kc	60.46N	46.24 E
Suhr	14	Cc	47.25N	8.04 E
Suhumi	6	Kg	43.01N	41.02 E
Suhurlui	15	Kd	45.25N	27.35 E
Suiá-Missu, Rio-	54	Hf	11.13S	53.15W
Suibara	29	Fc	37.50N	139.12 E
Suichang	27	Kf	28.34N	119.15 E
Suid Africa / South Africa [1]	31	Jl	30.00S	26.00 E
Suide	27	Jd	37.28N	110.15 E
Suifen He	28	Kc	43.20N	131.49 E
Suifenhe	27	Nc	44.25N	131.09 E
Sui He	28	Eh	33.29N	118.06 E
Suihua	27	Mb	46.38N	126.57 E
Suijiang	27	Hf	28.37N	104.00 E
Suileng	27	Mb	47.17N	127.08 E
Suining [China]	27	Ie	30.30N	105.34 E
Suining [China]	28	Dh	33.54N	117.56 E
Suipacha	55	Cl	34.45S	59.41W
Suiping	28	Bh	33.09N	113.59 E
Suippe	11	Je	49.25N	3.57 E
Suippes	11	Ke	49.08N	4.32 E
Suir/An tSiúir	9	Gi	52.15N	7.00W
Suisse / Svizra / Svizzera / Schweiz = Switzerland (EN) [1]	6	Gf	46.00N	8.30 E
Suisse Normande	12	Bf	48.53N	0.50W
Suita	29	Dd	34.45N	135.32 E
Suixi	28	Dh	33.55N	116.47 E
Suixian [China]	28	Cg	34.25N	115.04 E
Suixian [China]	27	Je	31.44N	113.25 E
Suiyang	28	Kb	44.26N	130.53 E
Suizhong	27	Lc	40.21N	120.20 E
Suj	27	Ic	42.12N	108.01 E
Šuja	7	If	61.54N	34.15 E
Šuja [R.S.F.S.R.]	7	If	61.59N	34.15 E
Šuja [R.S.F.S.R.]	19	Ed	56.52N	41.23 E
Sujer	17	Li	55.59N	65.47 E
Suji → Haixing	28	De	38.10N	117.29 E
Sujstamo	8	Nc	61.49N	31.05 E
Sukabumi	26	Eh	6.55S	106.56 E
Sukadana	26	Eg	1.15S	109.57 E
Sukagawa	28	Pf	37.17N	140.23 E
Sukaja	26	Fg	7.27S	108.12 E
Sukeva	7	Ge	63.54N	27.26 E
Sukhothai	25	Je	17.01N	99.49 E
Suki	35	Ec	13.23N	33.58 E
Sukkertoppen/Manitsoq	41	Ge	65.25N	53.00W
Sukkozero	19	Dc	63.09N	32.23 E
Sukkur	22	Ig	27.42N	68.52 E
Sukon	26	Hg	0.56S	123.10 E
Sukses	37	Bd	21.01S	16.52 E
Suksun	17	Hh	57.07N	57.24 E
Sukumo	27	Ne	32.56N	132.44 E
Sukumo-Wan	29	Ce	32.55N	132.40 E
Sul, Baia-	55	Hh	27.40S	48.35W
Sul, Canal do-	54	Id	0.10S	49.30W
Sula [Nor.]	7	Af	61.10N	4.55 E
Sula [Nor.]	8	Bb	62.25N	6.10 E
Sula [R.S.F.S.R.]	7	Ld	64.41N	47.46 E
Sula [R.S.F.S.R.]	17	Fc	67.16N	52.07 E
Sula [Ukr.-U.S.S.R.]	16	He	49.40N	32.43 E
Sula, Kepulauan-=Sulu Islands (EN)	57	De	1.52S	125.22 E
Sulaimāniya	23	Gb	35.33N	45.26 E
Sūlaimaniya [3]	24	Ke	35.40N	45.30 E
Sulaimān Range	21	Jf	30.30N	70.10 E
Sulak	16	Oh	43.17N	47.31 E
Sulak	19	Eg	43.17N	47.34 E
Sula Sgeir	9	Gb	59.05N	6.10W
Sulawesi/Celebes	21	Oj	2.00S	121.10 E
Sulawesi, Laut-=Celebes Sea (EN)	21	Oi	3.00N	122.00 E
Sulawesi Selatan [3]	26	Gg	4.00S	120.00 E
Sulawesi Tengah [3]	26	Hg	1.00S	121.00 E
Sulawesi Tenggara [3]	26	Hg	4.00S	122.30 E
Sulawesi Utara [3]	26	Hf	1.00N	123.00 E
Sulaymān	14	En	36.42N	10.30 E
Sulb	35	Ea	20.26N	30.20 E
Sulcis	14	Ck	39.05N	8.40 E
Suldalsvatn	8	Be	59.35N	6.45 E
Suldeh	24	Od	36.34N	52.01 E
Sulechów	10	Ld	52.06N	15.37 E
Sulęcin	10	Ld	52.26N	15.08 E
Suleja	17	Ii	55.11N	58.50 E
Sulejów	10	Pe	51.22N	19.53 E
Süleoğlu	15	Jh	41.46N	26.55 E
Sule Skerry	9	Ib	59.10N	4.10W
Sulima	34	Cd	6.58N	11.35W
Sulina	15	Md	45.09N	29.40 E
Sulina, Bratul-	15	Md	45.09N	29.41 E
Sulingen	10	Ed	52.41N	8.48 E
Sulitjelma	7	Dc	67.09N	16.03 E
Sulitjelma	7	Dc	67.08N	16.24 E
Suljukta	19	Gh	39.56N	69.37 E
Sulkava	7	Gf	61.47N	28.23 E
Sullana	53	Hf	4.53S	80.42W
Süller	15	Mk	38.09N	29.29 E
Sullivan [In.-U.S.]	44	Df	39.06N	87.24W
Sullivan [Mo.-U.S.]	45	Kg	38.13N	91.10W
Sullivan Lake	46	Ja	52.00N	112.00W
Sully-sur-Loire	11	Ig	47.46N	2.22 E
Sulmona	14	Hh	42.03N	13.55 E
Sulphur [La.-U.S.]	45	Jk	30.14N	93.23W
Sulphur [Ok.-U.S.]	45	Hi	34.31N	96.58W
Sulphur Creek	45	Ed	44.46N	102.25W
Sulphur River	45	Jj	33.07N	93.52W
Sulphur Springs	45	Ij	33.08N	95.36W
Sulphur Springs Draw	45	Fj	32.12N	101.36W
Sultandağı	24	Dc	38.32N	31.14 E
Sultan Dağları	24	Dc	38.20N	31.20 E
Sultanhanı	24	Ec	38.15N	33.33 E
Sultanhisar	15	Ll	37.53N	28.10 E
Sultānpur	25	Gc	26.16N	82.04 E
Sulu Archipelago	21	Oi	6.00N	121.00 E
Sulu Basin (EN)	26	Ge	8.00N	121.30 E
Sulu Islands (EN)=Sula, Kepulauan-	57	De	1.52S	125.22 E
Suluova	24	Fb	40.47N	35.42 E
Sulūq	33	Dc	31.40N	20.15 E
Sulu Sea	21	Ni	9.00N	120.00 E
Sulz am Neckar	10	Eh	48.21N	8.37 E
Sulzbach (Saar)	12	Je	49.18N	7.04 E
Sulzbach-Rosenberg	10	Hg	49.30N	11.45 E
Sulzberger Bay	66	Mf	77.00S	152.00W
Šumadija	15	De	44.20N	20.40 E
Sumalata	26	Hf	0.59N	122.30 E
Sumāmus	24	Nd	36.50N	50.30 E
Šumanaj	18	Bc	42.37N	58.55 E
Sumatera=Sumatra (EN)	21	Mj	0.01N	102.00 E
Sumatera Barat [3]	26	Dg	1.00S	100.30 E
Sumatera Selatan [3]	26	Dg	3.30S	104.00 E
Sumatera Utara [3]	26	Cf	2.00N	99.00 E
Sumatra (EN)= Sumatera	21	Mj	0.01N	102.00 E
Šumava=Bohemian Forest (EN)	5	Hf	49.00N	13.30 E
Sumayr	33	Hf	17.47N	41.26 E
Sumba, Pulau-	21	Nj	10.00S	120.00 E
Sumba, Selat-=Sumba Strait (EN)	26	Hh	9.05S	120.00 E
Sumbar	16	Jj	38.00N	55.15 E
Sumba Strait (EN)=Sumba, Selat-	26	Hh	9.05S	120.00 E
Sumbawa, Pulau-	21	Nj	8.40S	118.00 E
Sumbawa Besar	26	Gh	8.30S	117.26 E
Sumbawanga	36	Fd	7.58S	31.37 E
Sumber	27	Ib	46.21N	108.20 E
Sumbi Point	63a	Cb	7.19S	157.04 E
Sumbu	36	Fd	8.31S	30.29 E
Sumburgh Head	9	Lb	59.51N	1.16W
Sumedang	26	Eh	6.52S	107.55 E
Şüme'eh Sarā	24	Md	37.18N	49.19 E
Sümeg	10	Nj	46.59N	17.17 E
Šumen	15	Jf	43.16N	26.55 E
Šumen [2]	15	Jf	43.20N	27.00 E
Sumenep	26	Fh	7.01S	113.52 E
Sumerlja	6	Kd	55.30N	46.26 E
Sumgait	16	Pi	40.37N	49.37 E
Sumgait	6	Kg	40.33N	49.40 E
Sumidouro, Rio-	55	Da	13.28S	56.39W
Šumiha	19	Gd	55.14N	63.19 E
Sumkino	19	Gd	58.09N	68.21 E
Summer, Lake- [N.M.-U.S.]	45	Di	34.38N	104.26W
Summer, Lake- [N.Z.]	62	Ee	42.40S	172.15 E
Summer Lake	46	Ee	42.50N	120.45W
Summerland	46	Fb	49.39N	119.33W
Summerside	42	Lg	46.24N	63.47W
Summersville	44	Gf	38.17N	80.52W
Summerville	44	Eh	34.29N	85.21W
Summit Lake	42	Fe	54.17N	122.38W
Summit Mountain	46	Gg	39.23N	116.28W
Summit Peak	45	Ch	37.21N	106.42W
Sumoto	29	Dd	34.20N	134.54 E
Šumperk	10	Mg	49.58N	16.59 E
Sumprabum	25	Jc	26.33N	97.34 E
Sumsar	18	Hd	41.13N	71.23 E
Sumskaja Oblast [3]	19	De	51.00N	34.15 E
Šumšu, Ostrov-	20	Kf	50.45N	156.20 E
Sumter	43	Ke	33.55N	80.20W
Sumuşţā al Waqf	24	Dh	28.55N	30.51 E
Sumy	6	Je	50.54N	34.48 E
Suna	7	Mh	57.53N	50.07 E
Suna	7	Ie	62.08N	34.12 E
Sunagawa	28	Pc	43.29N	145.55 E
Šunak, Gora-	19	Hf	47.05N	72.35 E
Sunan	28	He	39.15N	125.40 E
Sunan (Hongwansi)	27	Gd	38.59N	99.25 E
Sunart, Loch-	9	He	56.45N	5.45W
Sunaysilah	24	Ie	35.35N	41.53 E
Sunburst	46	Jb	48.53N	111.55W
Sunbury	44	Ie	40.52N	76.47W
Sunchales	56	Hd	30.56S	61.34W
Suncho Corral	56	Hc	27.56S	63.27W
Sunch'ŏn [N. Kor.]	27	Me	34.57N	127.29 E
Sunch'ŏn [S. Kor.]	27	Md	39.25N	125.56 E
Sun City	46	Ij	33.36N	112.17W
Suncun → Xinwen	27	Kd	35.49N	117.38 E
Sunda, Selat-=Sunda Strait (EN)	21	Mj	6.00S	105.45 E
Sundance	46	Md	44.24N	104.23W
Sundarbans	25	Hd	22.00N	89.00 E
Sundargarh	25	Gd	22.07N	84.02 E
Sunda Strait (EN)=Sunda, Selat-	21	Mj	6.00S	105.45 E
Sunday Strait	59	Ec	16.20S	123.15 E
Sundborn	8	Fd	60.39N	15.46 E
Sundbron	8	Ha	63.01N	18.11 E
Sundbyberg	8	Ge	59.22N	17.58 E
Sunde	7	Ag	59.50N	5.43 E
Sunderland	9	Lg	54.55N	1.23W
Sundern (Sauerland)	12	Kc	51.20N	8.00 E
Sundgau	11	Ng	47.40N	7.15 E
Sündiken Dağları	24	Dc	39.55N	31.00 E
Sundridge	44	Hc	45.46N	79.24W
Sundsvall	6	Hc	62.23N	17.18 E
Sundsvallsbukten	8	Gb	62.20N	17.35 E
Sunflower, Mount-	45	Eg	39.04N	102.01W
Sungaidareh	26	Dg	0.58S	101.30 E
Sungaigerong	26	Dg	2.59S	104.52 E
Sungaiguntung	26	Df	0.18N	103.37 E
Sungai Kolok	25	Kg	6.02N	101.58 E
Sungai Lembing	26	Df	3.55N	103.02 E
Sungailiat	26	Eg	1.51S	106.08 E
Sungaipenuh	26	Dg	2.05S	101.23 E
Sungai Petani	26	De	5.39N	100.30 E
Sungai Siput	26	Df	4.49N	101.04 E
Sungari (EN)=Songhua Jiang	21	Pe	47.42N	132.30 E
Sungqu → Songpan	27	He	32.37N	103.34 E
Sungurlu	24	Fb	40.10N	34.23 E
Sunharon Roads	64b	Bb	14.57N	145.36 E
Suning	28	Ce	38.25N	115.50 E
Sunja	14	Ke	45.21N	16.33 E
Sunjiapuzi	28	Ic	42.02N	126.34 E
Sunkar, Gora-	18	Ib	44.12N	73.55 E
Sun Kosi	25	Hc	26.55N	87.09 E
Sunndalsøra	7	Be	62.40N	8.33 E
Sunnan	7	Cd	64.04N	11.38 E
Sunndalen	8	Cb	62.40N	8.45 E
Sunndalsfjorden	8	Cb	62.45N	8.25 E
Sunne	7	Cg	59.50N	13.09 E
Sunnerbo	8	Eh	56.45N	13.50 E
Sunnersta	8	Ge	59.48N	17.39 E
Sunnfjord	8	Ac	61.25N	5.20 E
Sunnhordland	8	Ae	59.55N	6.00 E
Sunnmøre	8	Bb	62.20N	6.40 E
Sunnyside	46	Fc	46.20N	120.00W
Sunnyvale	46	Dh	37.23N	122.01W
Su-no-Zaki	29	Fd	34.58N	139.45 E
Sun River	46	Jc	47.30N	111.25W
Sunsas, Serrania de-	55	Cc	17.57S	59.35W
Suntar	20	Gd	62.04N	117.40 E
Suntar-Hajata, Hrebet-= Suntar-Khayata Range (EN)	21	Qc	62.00N	143.00 E
Suntar-Khayata Range (EN) =Suntar-Hajata, Hrebet-	21	Qc	62.00N	143.00 E
Suntaži	8	Kh	56.49N	24.57 E
Sun Valley	43	Ec	43.42N	114.21W
Sunwu	27	Mb	49.27N	127.19 E
Sunyani	31	Gh	7.20N	2.20W
Sunža	16	Oh	43.26N	46.08 E
Suojarvi	19	Dc	62.04N	32.21 E
Suokonmäki	8	Kb	62.47N	24.30 E
Suolahti	7	Fe	62.34N	25.52 E
Suomenlahti=Finland, Gulf of- (EN)	5	Ic	60.00N	27.00 E
Suomenniemi	8	Lc	61.19N	27.27 E
Suomenselkä	5	Ic	62.50N	25.00 E
Suomi/Finland [1]	6	Ic	64.00N	26.00 E
Suomussalmi	7	Gd	64.54N	29.00 E
Suō-Nada	29	Be	33.50N	131.30 E
Suonenjoki	7	Ge	62.37N	27.08 E
Suontee	8	Lc	61.40N	26.35 E
Suordah	20	Ic	66.43N	132.04 E
Suozhen → Huantai	28	Ef	36.57N	118.05 E
Supamo, Rio-	50	Fi	6.48N	61.50W
Superior [Az.-U.S.]	46	Jj	33.18N	110.06W
Superior [Mt.-U.S.]	46	Hc	47.12N	114.53W
Superior [Nb.-U.S.]	45	Gf	40.01N	98.04W
Superior [Wi.-U.S.]	39	Je	46.44N	92.05W
Superior, Lake-	38	Ke	48.00N	88.00W
Suphan Buri	25	Kf	14.29N	100.10 E
Süphan Dağı	23	Fb	38.54N	42.48 E
Supiori, Pulau-	26	Kg	0.45S	135.30 E
Supoj	16	Ge	49.38N	31.50 E
Support Force Glacier	66	Rg	83.05S	47.30W
Suprasl	10	Tc	53.13N	23.20 E
Suprasl	10	Sc	53.12N	22.55 E
Sup'ung	27	Lc	40.27N	124.57 E
Sup'ung-chosuji	28	Hd	40.30N	125.05 E
Suq ash Shuyūkh	24	Lg	30.53N	46.28 E
Suqian	27	Ke	33.55N	118.13 E
Sūq Suwayq	24	Hj	24.23N	38.27 E
Suquṭrā=Socotra (EN)	21	Hh	12.30N	54.00 E
Sūr	22	Hg	22.31N	59.30 E
Şūr	23	Ec	33.16N	35.11 E
Sur, Cabo-	65d	Ac	27.12S	109.26W
Sur, Point-	46	Eh	36.18N	121.54W
Sura	16	Nc	53.53N	45.44 E
Sura	5	Kd	56.06N	46.00 E
Šurab	18	Hd	40.03N	70.33 E
Surabaya	22	Nj	7.15S	112.45 E

Index Symbols

[1] Independent Nation
[2] State, Region
[3] District, County
[4] Municipality
[5] Colony, Dependency
Continent
Physical Region
Historical or Cultural Region
Mount, Mountain
Volcano
Hill
Mountains, Mountain Range
Hills, Escarpment
Plateau, Upland
Pass, Gap
Plain, Lowland
Delta
Salt Flat
Valley, Canyon
Crater, Cave
Karst Features
Depression
Polder
Desert, Dunes
Forest, Woods
Heath, Steppe
Oasis
Cape, Point
Coast, Beach
Cliff
Peninsula
Isthmus
Sandbank
Island
Atoll
Rock, Reef
Islands, Archipelago
Rocks, Reefs
Coral Reef
Well, Spring
Geyser
River, Stream
Waterfall Rapids
River Mouth, Estuary
Lake
Salt Lake
Intermittent Lake
Reservoir
Swamp, Pond
Canal
Glacier
Ice Shelf, Pack Ice
Ocean
Sea
Gulf, Bay
Strait, Fjord
Lagoon
Bank
Seamount
Tablemount
Ridge
Shelf
Basin
Escarpment, Sea Scarp
Fracture
Trench, Abyss
National Park, Reserve
Point of Interest
Recreation Site
Cave, Cavern
Historic Site
Ruins
Wall, Walls
Church, Abbey
Temple
Scientific Station
Airport
Port
Lighthouse
Mine
Tunnel
Dam, Bridge

Name	Page	Grid	Lat.	Long.
Surahammar	8	Ge	59.43N	16.13 E
Sūrak	23	Id	25.43N	58.48 E
Surakarta	22	Nj	7.35S	110.50 E
Şūrān	24	Ge	35.17N	36.45 E
Šurany	10	Oh	48.06N	18.11 E
Surar	35	Gd	7.29N	40.54 E
Surat	22	Jg	21.10N	72.50 E
Surat Thani	22	Li	9.06N	99.20 E
Suraž [Bye.-U.S.S.R.]	7	Hi	55.26N	30.43 E
Suraž [R.S.F.S.R.]	19	De	53.02N	32.29 E
Surčin	15	De	44.47N	20.17 E
Sur del Cabo San Antonio, Punta-	56	Ie	36.52S	56.40W
Surduc	15	Gb	47.15N	23.21 E
Sûre	10	Cg	49.44N	6.31 E
Surendranagar	25	Ed	22.42N	71.41 E
Surgères	11	Fh	46.06N	0.45W
Surgut	22	Jc	61.14N	73.20 E
Surgutiha	20	Dd	63.47N	87.20 E
Surhandarinskaja Oblast [3]	19	Gh	38.00N	67.30 E
Surhandarja	18	Ff	37.14N	67.20 E
Surhob	19	Hh	38.54N	70.04 E
Surigao	26	Ie	9.45N	125.30 E
Surin	25	Kf	14.53N	103.30 E
Suriname [1]	53	Ke	4.00N	56.00W
Suripá, Río-	49	Mj	7.47N	69.53W
Sūrīyah=Syria (EN) [1]	22	Ff	35.00N	38.00 E
Sūrmaq	24	Og	31.03N	52.48 E
Surmelin	12	Fe	49.04N	3.31 E
Sürmene	24	Ib	40.55N	40.07 E
Surna	8	Cb	62.59N	8.40 E
Surnadalsøra	8	Cb	62.59N	8.39 E
Surovikino	19	Ef	48.36N	42.54 E
Surovo	20	Fe	55.39N	105.36 E
Sur-Pakri/Suur-Pakri	8	Je	59.50N	23.45 E
Surprise, Ile-	63b	Ad	18.32S	163.02 E
Surprise, Lac-	44	Ja	49.20N	74.57W
Surrey [3]	9	Mj	51.25N	0.30W
Surrey	9	Mj	51.20N	0.05W
Sursee	14	Cc	47.10N	8.07 E
Sursk	16	Nc	53.04N	45.42 E
Surskoje	7	Li	54.31N	46.44 E
Surt	31	Ie	31.13N	16.35 E
Surt, Khalīj-=Sidra, Gulf of-(EN)	30	Ie	31.30N	18.00 E
Surte	8	Eg	57.49N	12.01 E
Surtsey	7a	Bc	63.20N	20.38W
Sürüç	24	Hd	36.58N	38.24 E
Surud Ad	30	Lg	10.42N	47.09 E
Suruga-Wan	28	Og	34.55N	138.35 E
Surulangun	26	Dg	2.37S	102.45 E
Survey Pass	40	Ic	67.52N	154.10W
Sur-Vjajn/Suur Väin	8	Jf	58.30N	23.20 E
Surwold	12	Jb	52.57N	7.31 E
Suså	8	Di	55.11N	11.46 E
Šuša	16	Oj	39.43N	46.44 E
Susa [It.]	14	Be	45.08N	7.03 E
Susa [Jap.]	29	Bd	34.37N	131.36 E
Susa, Val di-	14	Be	45.10N	7.10 E
Sušac	14	Kh	42.46N	16.30 E
Sūsah [Lib.]	33	Dc	32.54N	21.58 E
Sūsah [Tun.] =Sousse (EN)	31	Ie	35.49N	10.38 E
Sūsah=Sousse (EN) [3]	32	Jb	35.45N	10.30 E
Susak	14	If	44.31N	14.18 E
Susaki	27	Ne	33.22N	133.17 E
Susami	29	De	33.33N	135.29 E
Susamyr	18	Ic	42.09N	73.59 E
Susanville	43	Cc	40.25N	120.39W
Suşehri	24	Hb	40.11N	38.06 E
Suseja	8	Kh	56.23N	25.00 E
Šušenskoje	20	Ef	53.19N	92.01 E
Sušice	10	Jg	49.14N	13.30 E
Susitna	40	Id	61.16N	150.30W
Suslonger	7	Lh	56.18N	48.12 E
Susoh	26	Cf	3.43N	96.50 E
Susong	28	Di	30.10N	116.06 E
Suspiro	55	Ej	30.38S	54.22W
Suspiro del Moro, Puerto del-	13	Ig	37.08N	3.40W
Susquehanna River	43	Ld	39.33N	76.05W
Susques	56	Gb	23.25S	66.29W
Sussex	9	Mk	50.55N	0.30W
Sussex	44	Oc	45.43N	65.31W
Sussex, Vale of-	9	Mk	51.00N	0.15W
Susubona	63a	Dc	8.19S	159.27 E
Susuman	22	Qc	62.47N	148.10 E
Susurluk	24	Cc	39.54N	28.10 E
Susuzmüsellim	15	Kh	41.06N	27.03 E
Šušvė	8	Ji	55.08N	23.53 E
Susz	10	Pc	53.44N	19.20 E
Suţeşti	15	Kd	45.13N	27.26 E
Sutherland	37	Cf	32.24S	20.40 E
Sutherland Falls	62	Bf	44.48S	167.44 E
Sutherlin	46	De	43.25N	123.19W
Sutla	14	Je	45.51N	15.41 E
Sutlej	21	Jg	29.23N	71.02 E
Sutton	44	Gf	38.41N	80.43W
Sutton, London-	12	Bc	51.21N	0.12W
Sutton Bridge	12	Cb	52.46N	0.11 E
Sutton in Ashfield	12	Aa	53.07N	1.16W
Sutton Scotney	12	Ac	51.09N	1.20W
Suttor River	59	Jd	21.25S	147.45 E
Suttsu	28	Pc	42.48N	140.14 E
Sütÿler	24	Dd	37.30N	30.59 E
Sutwik	40	He	56.34N	157.05W
Su'uholo	63a	Ec	9.46S	161.58 E
Suunduk	16	Ud	51.46N	58.46 E
Suure-Jaani	7	Fg	58.31N	25.29 E
Suur-Pakri/Sur-Pakri	8	Je	59.50N	23.45 E
Suur Väin/Sur-Vjajn	8	Jf	58.30N	23.20 E
Suva	58	If	18.08S	178.25 E
Suvadiva Atoll	21	Ji	0.30N	73.13 E
Suva Gora	15	Eh	41.51N	21.03 E
Suva Planina	15	Ff	43.08N	22.13 E
Suvasvesi	7	Ge	62.40N	28.10 E
Suvorov	16	Jb	54.08N	36.32 E
Suvorovo [Mold.-U.S.S.R.]	15	Mc	46.33N	29.35 E
Suvorovo [Ukr.-U.S.S.R.]	15	Ld	45.35N	29.00 E
Suvorovskaja	16	Mg	44.10N	42.38 E
Suwa	28	Of	36.02N	138.08 E
Suwa-Ko	29	Fc	36.03N	138.05 E
Suwałki	10	Sb	54.07N	22.56 E
Suwałki [2]	10	Sb	54.05N	22.55 E
Suwalskie, Pojezierze-	10	Sb	54.15N	23.00 E
Suwannee River	44	Fk	29.18N	83.09W
Suwanose-Jima	27	Mf	29.40N	129.45 E
Suwarrow Atoll	57	Kf	13.15S	163.05W
Suwayqīyah, Hawr as-	24	Lf	32.40N	46.03 E
Suways, Khalīj as-=Suez, Gulf of-(EN)	30	Kf	28.10N	33.27 E
Suways, Qanāt as-=Suez Canal (EN)	30	Ke	29.55N	32.33 E
Suwŏn	27	Md	37.16N	127.01 E
Suxian	27	Ke	33.36N	116.58 E
Suzaka	29	Fc	36.39N	138.18 E
Suzdal	7	Jh	56.28N	40.27 E
Suzhou	22	Of	31.16N	120.37 E
Suzhou/Jiuquan	22	Lf	39.46N	98.34 E
Suzi He	28	Hd	41.56N	124.20 E
Suzu	27	Od	37.25N	137.17 E
Suzuka	29	Ed	34.51N	136.35 E
Suzuka-Sanmyaku	29	Ed	35.10N	136.20 E
Suzu-Misaki	28	Nf	37.28N	137.20 E
Suzun	20	Df	53.47N	82.19 E
Suzzara	14	Ef	45.00N	10.45 E
Særholthalvøya	7	Ga	70.30N	26.05 E
Svågan	8	Gc	61.54N	16.33 E
Svalbard [5]	67	Kd	78.00N	20.00 E
Svaljava	16	Ce	48.32N	22.59 E
Svalöv	8	Ei	55.55N	13.06 E
Svaneholm	8	Ee	59.11N	12.33 E
Svaneke	7	Di	55.08N	15.09 E
Svängsta	8	Fh	56.16N	14.46 E
Svanøy	8	Ac	61.30N	5.05 E
Svapa	16	Id	51.44N	34.59 E
Svappavaara	7	Ec	67.39N	21.04 E
Svärdsjö	8	Fd	60.45N	15.55 E
Svartå	8	Fe	59.08N	14.31 E
Svartälven	8	Fe	59.20N	14.35 E
Svartån [Swe.]	8	Fe	59.17N	15.15 E
Svartån [Swe.]	8	Ff	58.28N	15.33 E
Svartån [Swe.]	8	Ge	59.37N	16.33 E
Svartenhuk Halvø= Svartenhuk Peninsula (EN)	41	Gd	71.30N	55.20W
Svartenhuk Peninsula (EN) =Svartenhuk, Halvø	41	Gd	71.30N	55.20W
Svartisen	7	Cc	66.38N	13.58 E
Svatoj Nos, Mys-	20	Jb	72.45N	140.45 E
Svatovo	19	Df	49.24N	38.13 E
Svay Riĕng	25	Lf	11.05N	105.48 E
Sveabreen	66	Cf	72.08S	1.53 E
Sveagruva	41	Nc	78.39N	16.25 E
Svealand	7	Dd	60.30N	15.30 E
Svealand	5	Hc	60.30N	15.30 E
Svedala	8	Ei	55.30N	13.14 E
Sveg	7	De	62.02N	14.21 E
Švėkšna	8	Ii	55.32N	21.30 E
Svelgen	7	Af	61.45N	5.18 E
Svelvik	8	De	59.37N	10.24 E
Švenčëneljaj/Švenčioneliai	7	Gi	55.09N	26.02 E
Švenčënis/Švenčionys	7	Gi	55.07N	26.12 E
Švenčioneliai/Švenčëneljaj	7	Gi	55.09N	26.02 E
Švenčionys/Švenčënis	7	Gi	55.07N	26.12 E
Svendborg	7	Ci	55.03N	10.37 E
Svendsen Peninsula	42	Ja	77.50N	84.00W
Svenljunga	7	Ch	57.30N	13.07 E
Svenska högarna	8	He	59.35N	19.35 E
Svenskøya	41	Oc	78.43N	26.30 E
Svenstavik	7	De	62.46N	14.27 E
Šventoj/Šventoji	8	Ih	56.04N	20.59 E
Šventoji	7	Fi	55.05N	24.24 E
Šventoji/Šventoj	8	Ih	56.04N	20.59 E
Sverdlovsk	22	Id	56.51N	60.36 E
Sverdlovskaja Oblast [3]	19	Gd	59.00N	62.00 E
Sverdrup, Ostrov-	20	Cb	74.30N	79.35 E
Sverdrup Channel	42	Ha	80.00N	96.30W
Sverdrup Islands	38	Jb	79.00N	98.00W
Sverige=Sweden (EN) [1]	6	Hc	62.00N	15.00 E
Svetac	14	Jg	43.02N	15.45 E
Svēte/Svete	8	Jh	56.40N	23.38 E
Svete/Svēte	8	Jh	56.40N	23.38 E
Sveti Naum	15	Di	40.55N	20.45 E
Sveti Nikola, Prohod-	15	Ff	43.27N	22.36 E
Sveti Nikole	15	Eh	41.52N	21.57 E
Sveti Stefan	15	Bg	42.16N	18.54 E
Svetlaja	20	Ig	46.31N	138.18 E
Svetli	20	Ge	58.34N	116.00 E
Svetlogorsk [Bye.-U.S.S.R.]	19	Ce	52.38N	29.42 E
Svetlogorsk [R.S.F.S.R.]	8	Ij	54.55N	20.08 E
Svetlograd	19	Ef	45.19N	42.40 E
Svetlovodsk	16	He	49.02N	33.15 E
Svetly [R.S.F.S.R.]	19	Ge	50.51N	60.53 E
Svetly [R.S.F.S.R.]	7	Ei	54.41N	20.08 E
Svetly Jar	16	Ne	48.29N	44.46 E
Svetogorsk	7	Gf	61.07N	28.58 E
Svetozarevo	15	Ef	43.59N	21.15 E
Sviča	10	Ug	49.04N	24.06 E
Svid	7	Jf	61.13N	38.45 E
Svidník	10	Rg	49.18N	21.35 E
Svidník	10	Kg	49.23N	14.58 E
Svijaga	19	Ed	55.39N	48.28 E
Svilaja	14	Kg	43.50N	16.26 E
Svilengrad	15	Jh	41.46N	26.12 E
Svincovy Rudnik	18	Ff	37.52N	66.28 E
Svinecea Mare, Vîrful-	15	Fe	44.48N	22.09 E
Svir	5	Jc	60.30N	32.48 E
Svir	8	Lj	54.50N	26.34 E
Svirica	7	Hf	60.30N	32.54 E
Svirsk	20	Ff	53.04N	103.18 E
Svisloč	16	Fc	53.27N	28.59 E
Svisloč	16	Dc	53.03N	24.07 E
Svištov	15	If	43.37N	25.20 E
Svit	10	Qg	49.03N	20.12 E
Svitava	10	Mg	49.11N	16.38 E
Svitavy	10	Mg	49.46N	16.27 E
Svizra / Svizzera / Schweiz / Suisse = Switzerland (EN) [1]	6	Gf	46.00N	8.30 E
Svizzera / Schweiz / Suisse / Svizra = Switzerland (EN) [1]	6	Gf	46.00N	8.30 E
Svjatoj Nos, Mys-	5	Jb	68.10N	39.43 E
Svobodny	22	Od	51.24N	128.07 E
Svoge	15	Gg	42.58N	23.21 E
Svolvær	7	Db	68.14N	14.34 E
Svratka	10	Mh	48.52N	16.38 E
Svrljig	15	Ff	43.25N	22.08 E
Svulrya	8	Ed	60.25N	12.24 E
Svytaya Anna Trough (EN)	67	He	80.00N	70.00 E
Swabia (EN)=Schwaben	10	Gh	48.20N	10.30 E
Swabian-Bavarian Plateau (EN)=Schwäbisch-Bayerisches Alpenvorland	5	Hf	48.15N	10.30 E
Swabian Jura (EN)= Schwäbische Alb	5	Gf	48.25N	9.30 E
Swaffham	12	Cb	52.39N	0.41 E
Swain Reefs	57	Gg	21.40S	152.15 E
Swains Atoll	57	Jf	11.03S	171.05W
Swainsboro	44	Fi	32.36N	82.20W
Swakop	37	Ad	22.41S	14.31 E
Swakopmund [3]	37	Ad	22.30S	15.00 E
Swakopmund	31	Ik	22.41S	14.34 E
Swale	9	Lg	54.06N	1.20W
Swalmen	12	Ic	51.14N	6.02 E
Swanage	9	Lk	50.37N	1.58W
Swan Hill	59	Ig	35.21S	143.34 E
Swan Range	46	Ic	47.50N	113.40W
Swan River	42	Hf	52.06N	101.16W
Swansboro	44	Ih	34.36N	77.07W
Swansea [Austl.]	59	Jh	42.08S	148.04 E
Swansea [Wales-U.K.]	6	Fe	51.38N	3.57W
Swansea Bay	9	Jj	51.35N	3.52W
Swans Island	44	Mc	44.10N	68.25W
Swanson Lake	45	Ff	40.09N	101.06W
Swan Valley	46	Je	43.28N	111.20W
Swartberge	30	Jl	33.23S	21.48 E
Swarzędz	10	Nd	52.26N	17.05 E
Swastika	44	Ga	48.07N	80.12W
Swaziland [1]	31	Kk	26.30S	31.10 E
Sweden (EN)=Sverige [1]	6	Hc	62.00N	15.00 E
Swedru	34	Ed	5.32N	0.42W
Sweet Grass Hills	46	Jb	48.55N	111.30W
Sweet Home	46	Dd	44.24N	122.44W
Sweetwater	43	Ge	32.28N	100.25W
Sweetwater River	43	Fc	42.31N	107.02W
Swellendam	37	Cf	34.02S	20.26 E
Świder	10	Rd	52.08N	21.12 E
Świdnica	10	Mf	50.51N	16.29 E
Świdnik	10	Se	51.14N	22.41 E
Świdwin	10	Lc	53.47N	15.47 E
Świebodzin	10	Ld	52.15N	15.32 E
Świecie	10	Oc	53.25N	18.28 E
Świętej Anny, Góra-	10	Of	50.28N	18.13 E
Świętokrzyskie, Góry-	10	Qf	50.55N	21.00 E
Swift Current	42	Gf	50.17N	107.50W
Swift Current Creek	46	La	50.40N	107.44W
Swift River	42	Ed	60.05N	131.11W
Swilly, Lough-/Loch Suilí	9	Ff	55.10N	7.38W
Swinburne, Cape -	42	Hb	71.14N	98.33W
Swindon	9	Lj	51.34N	1.47W
Swinford/Béal Átha na Muice	9	Eh	53.57N	8.57W
Świnoujście	10	Kc	53.53N	14.14 E
Swischenahner Meer	12	Ka	53.12N	8.01 E
Swisttal	12	Id	50.44N	6.54 E
Switzerland (EN) = Schweiz / Suisse / Svizra / Svizzera [1]	6	Gf	46.00N	8.30 E
Switzerland (EN) = Suisse / Svizra / Svizzera / Schweiz [1]	6	Gf	46.00N	8.30 E
Switzerland (EN) = Svizra / Svizzera / Schweiz / Suisse [1]	6	Gf	46.00N	8.30 E
Switzerland (EN) = Svizzera / Schweiz / Suisse / Svizra [1]	6	Gf	46.00N	8.30 E
Syčevka	16	Ib	55.51N	34.15 E
Syców	10	Ne	51.19N	17.43 E
Sydfalster-Gedser	7	Ci	54.35N	11.57 E
Sydkap Ice Cap	42	Ja	76.30N	85.00W
Sydney [Austl.]	58	Gh	33.52S	151.13 E
Sydney [N.S.-Can.]	39	Me	46.09N	60.11W
Sydney→Manra Atoll	57	Je	4.27S	171.15W
Sydney-Campbelltown	59	Kf	34.04S	150.49 E
Sydney Lake	45	Ia	50.40N	94.24W
Sydney Mines	42	Lg	46.14N	60.12W
Sydney-Penrith	59	Kf	33.45S	150.42 E
Syktyvkar	6	Lc	61.40N	50.46 E
Sylacauga	44	Di	33.10N	86.15W
Sylane	7	Ce	63.02N	12.13 E
Sylarna	7	Ce	63.02N	12.13 E
Sylhet	25	Id	24.54N	91.52 E
Sylling	8	De	59.54N	10.17 E
Sylt	10	Eb	54.55N	8.20 E
Sylva	17	Hh	57.40N	56.57 E
Sylvania	44	Gi	32.45N	81.38W
Sylvania Tablemount (EN)	60	Ge	11.58N	165.00 E
Sylvan Pass	43	Ec	44.28N	110.08W
Sylvester	44	Fj	31.32N	83.49W
Sylvester, Lake-	59	Hc	18.50S	135.50 E
Sym	20	Ed	60.15N	90.02 E
Syndassko	20	Fb	73.14N	108.05 E
Synja	17	Ld	65.12N	64.45 E
Synnfjell	8	Cc	61.05N	9.45 E
Syowa	66	De	69.00S	39.35 E
Syracuse [Ks.-U.S.]	45	Fh	37.59N	101.45W
Syracuse [N.Y.-U.S.]	39	Le	43.03N	76.09W
Syracuse (EN)=Siracusa	6	Hh	37.04N	15.18 E
Syrdarinskaja Oblast [3]	19	Gg	40.30N	68.40 E
Syrdarja	19	Gg	40.52N	68.38 E
Syrdarja=Syr Darya (EN)	21	Ie	46.03N	61.00 E
Syr Darya (EN)= Syrdarja	21	Ie	46.03N	61.00 E
Syria (EN)	21	Ff	35.00N	38.00 E
Syria (EN)=Sūrīyah [1]	22	Ff	35.00N	38.00 E
Syriam	25	Je	16.46N	96.15 E
Syrian Desert- (EN)=Shām, Bādiyat ash-	21	Ff	32.00N	40.00 E
Syrkovoje, Ozero-	17	Lf	60.40N	65.00 E
Syrski	16	Kc	52.36N	39.28 E
Sysert	17	Jh	56.31N	60.49 E
Sysmä	7	Ff	61.30N	25.41 E
Sysola	19	Fc	61.42N	50.58 E
Syssleback	8	Ed	60.44N	12.52 E
Sysulp, Gora-	15	Ha	48.29N	24.17 E
Syverma, Plato-	21	Lc	67.00N	99.00 E
Syzran	6	Ke	53.09N	48.27 E
Szabolcs-Szatmár [2]	10	Sh	48.00N	22.10 E
Szamocin	10	Nc	53.02N	17.08 E
Szamos	15	Fa	48.07N	22.20 E
Szamotuły	10	Md	52.37N	16.35 E
Szarvas	10	Qj	46.52N	20.33 E
Szczawnica Krościenko	10	Qg	49.26N	20.30 E
Szczebrzeszyn	10	Sf	50.42N	22.59 E
Szczecin [2]	10	Kc	52.35N	14.30 E
Szczecin=Stettin (EN)	6	He	53.24N	14.32 E
Szczecinek	10	Mc	53.43N	16.42 E
Szczeciński, Zalew-	10	Kc	53.46N	14.14 E
Szczekociny	10	Pf	50.38N	19.50 E
Szczerców	10	Pe	51.18N	19.09 E
Szczucin	10	Rf	50.18N	21.04 E
Szczuczyn	10	Sc	53.34N	22.18 E
Szczytno	10	Qc	53.34N	21.00 E
Szechwan (EN)=Sichuan Sheng (Ssu-ch'uan Sheng) [2]	27	He	30.00N	103.00 E
Szechwan (EN)=Ssu-ch'uan Sheng→Sichuan Sheng [2]	27	He	30.00N	103.00 E
Szécsény	10	Ph	48.05N	19.31 E
Szeged	6	If	46.15N	20.10 E
Szeged [2]	10	Qj	46.16N	20.08 E
Szeghalom	10	Ri	47.02N	21.10 E
Székesfehérvár	6	Hf	47.12N	18.25 E
Szekszárd	10	Oj	46.21N	18.43 E
Szendrő	10	Qh	48.24N	20.44 E
Szentendre	10	Pi	47.40N	19.05 E
Szentes	10	Qj	46.39N	20.16 E
Szentgotthárd	10	Mj	46.57N	16.17 E
Szérencs	10	Rh	48.10N	21.12 E
Szeskie Wzgórza	10	Sb	54.14N	22.22 E
Szigetvár	10	Nj	46.03N	17.48 E
Szkwa	10	Rc	53.10N	21.45 E
Szlichtyngowa	10	Me	51.43N	16.15 E
Szob	10	Oi	47.49N	18.52 E
Szolnok	10	Qi	47.11N	20.12 E
Szolnok [2]	10	Qi	47.15N	20.30 E
Szombathely	10	Mi	47.14N	16.37 E
Szprotawa	10	Le	51.34N	15.33 E
Szreniawa	10	Qf	50.10N	20.35 E
Sztum	10	Pc	53.56N	19.01 E
Szubin	10	Nc	53.00N	17.44 E
Szydłów	10	Rf	50.35N	21.01 E
Szydłowiec	10	Qe	51.14N	20.51 E
T				
Taakoka	64p	Cc	21.15S	159.43W
Taalintendas/Dalsbruk	8	Jd	60.02N	22.31 E
Taavetti	8	Ld	60.55N	27.34 E
Tab	10	Oj	46.44N	18.02 E
Tabacal	56	Hb	23.16S	64.15W
Ţābah	24	Ji	27.02N	42.08 E
Tabaqah	24	He	35.52N	38.34 E
Tabar Islands	57	Ge	2.50S	152.00 E
Ţabarqah	32	Ib	36.57N	8.45 E
Ţabas	24	Qf	33.36N	56.54 E
Tabasará, Serranía de-	49	Gi	8.33N	81.40W
Tabasco [2]	47	Fe	18.00N	92.40W
Tabasco y Campeche, Llanos de-	47	Fe	18.15N	91.00W
Tabašino	7	Lh	56.59N	47.43 E
Tābask, Kūh-e-	24	Nh	29.52N	51.49 E
Tabay	55	Ci	28.18S	58.17W
Tabelbala	32	Gd	29.24N	3.15W
Taber	42	Gg	49.47N	112.08W
Taberg	8	Fg	57.41N	14.05 E
Taberg	8	Fg	57.41N	14.05 E
Tabernacle	51c	Ab	17.23N	62.46W
Tabernas	13	Jg	37.03N	2.23W
Tabernes de Valldigna	13	Le	39.04N	0.16W
Tabiteuea Atoll	57	Ie	1.20S	174.50 E
Tabla	34	Fc	13.46N	3.01 E
Tablas	26	Hd	12.24N	122.02 E
Tablas Strait	26	Hd	12.40N	121.48 E
Tablat	13	Ph	36.25N	3.19 E
Tablazo, Bahía del-	49	Lh	10.52N	71.35W
Table Cape	62	Gc	39.06S	178.00 E
Table Rock Lake	45	Jh	36.35N	93.30W
Tabocas	55	Jb	14.39S	45.28W
Taboco, Rio-	55	Ed	19.53S	55.58W
Tabola	16	Pg	45.53N	48.20 E
Tábor	10	Kg	49.25N	14.41 E
Tabora	31	Ki	5.01S	32.48 E
Tabora [3]	36	Fd	5.20S	32.30 E
Tabory	17	Lg	58.31N	64.33 E
Tabou	31	Gh	4.25N	7.21W
Tabrīz	22	Gf	38.05N	46.18 E
Tábua	13	Dd	40.21N	8.02W
Tabuaeran Atoll (Fanning)	57	Ld	3.52N	159.20W
Tabūk	22	Fg	28.23N	36.35 E
Tabuk	26	Hc	17.24N	121.25 E
Ţaburbah	14	Dn	36.50N	9.50 E
Tabursuq	14	Dn	36.28N	9.15 E
Tabursuq, Monts de-	14	Dn	36.25N	9.05 E
Tabusintac	44	Ob	47.24N	65.02W
Tabwemasana	63b	Cb	15.22S	166.45 E
Täby	7	Eg	59.30N	18.03 E
Tacámbaro de Codallos	48	Ih	19.14N	101.28W
Tacarcuna, Cerro-	49	Ij	8.05N	77.17W
Tacarigua, Laguna de-	50	Dg	10.15N	65.50W
Tacheng/Qoqek	22	Ke	46.45N	82.57 E
Tachibana-Wan	29	Be	32.45N	130.05 E
Tachichilte, Isla de-	48	Ee	24.59N	108.04W
Tachikawa [Jap.]	29	Fd	35.42N	139.23 E
Tachikawa [Jap.]	29	Fb	38.48N	139.58 E
Táchira [2]	54	Db	7.50N	72.05W
Tachiumet	33	Bd	26.19N	10.03 E
Tachov	10	Ig	49.48N	12.40 E
Tachungnya	64b	Bb	14.58N	145.36 E
Tacinski	16	Le	48.13N	41.17 E
Tacir	15	Mi	40.32N	29.44 E
Tacloban	22	Oh	11.15N	125.00 E
Tacna	53	Ig	18.01S	70.15W
Tacna [2]	54	Dg	17.40S	70.20W
Tacoma	39	Ge	47.15N	122.27W
Tacotalpa, Río-	48	Mi	17.50N	92.52W
Tacuaral	55	Cd	18.59S	58.07W
Tacuarembó [2]	55	Ek	32.10S	55.30W
Tacuarembó, Río-	55	Ek	32.25S	55.29W
Tacuarí, Río-	55	Fk	32.46S	53.18W
Tacuati	55	Df	23.27S	56.35W
Tadamī	29	Fc	37.21N	139.17 E
Tadami-Gawa	29	Fc	37.38N	139.45 E
Tadarimana, Rio-	55	Ec	16.29S	54.31W
Tademaït, Plateau du-	30	Hf	28.30N	2.15 E
Tadine	63b	Ce	21.33S	167.53 E
Tadjeraout	32	He	21.17N	1.20 E
Tadjetaret	32	Ie	22.00N	7.30 E
Tadjourah	35	Gc	11.45N	42.54 E
Tadjourah, Golfe de-	35	Gc	11.45N	43.00 E
Tadoule Lake	42	He	58.35N	98.20W
Tadoussac	44	Ma	48.09N	69.43W
Tadžikskaja Sovetskaja Socialističeskaja Respublika [2]	19	Hh	39.00N	71.00 E
Tadžikskaja SSR/ Respublikai Soveth Socialisti Todžikiston	19	Hh	39.00N	71.00 E
Tadžikskaja SSR = Tajik SSR (EN) [2]	19	Hh	39.00N	71.00 E
T'aebaek-Sanmaek	21	Of	37.40N	128.50 E
Taechon	28	If	36.21N	126.36 E
T'aech'on	28	He	39.55N	125.30 E
Taedong-gang	28	He	38.42N	125.15 E
Taegu	22	Of	35.52N	128.36 E
Taeha-dong	28	Kf	37.31N	130.48 E
Taehan-Haehyŏp=Korea Strait (EN)	21	Of	34.40N	129.00 E
Taehan-Min' guk=South Korea (EN) [1]	22	Of	38.00N	127.30 E
Taehuksan-Do	28	Hg	34.40N	125.25 E
Taejŏn	22	Of	36.20N	127.26 E
Tafahi Island	57	Jf	15.52S	173.55W
Tafalla	13	Kb	42.31N	1.40W
Tafassasset	30	If	21.56N	10.12 E
Tafassasset, Ténéré du-	34	Ha	21.20N	11.00 E
Taff	9	Jj	51.27N	3.09W
Tafilalt	32	Gc	31.18N	4.18W
Tafiré	34	Dd	9.04N	5.10W
Tafí Viejo	56	Gc	26.44S	65.16W
Taflan	24	Gb	41.25N	36.09 E
Tafna	13	Ki	35.18N	1.28W
Tafraout	32	Fd	29.43N	9.00W
Tafresh	24	Ne	34.41N	50.01 E
Taft	24	Pg	31.45N	54.14 E
Taftān, Kuh-e-	21	Ig	28.36N	61.06 E
Taftanāz	24	Ge	35.59N	36.47 E
Taga	65c	Aa	13.46S	172.28W
Taga Dzong	25	Hc	27.04N	89.53 E
Tagajō	29	Gb	38.18N	140.58 E
Tagama	30	Hg	15.50N	8.12 E
Taganrog	6	Jf	47.12N	38.56 E
Taganrogski Zaliv	16	Kf	46.50N	38.25 E
Tagant [3]	32	Ef	18.30N	10.30W
Tagant	30	Fg	17.31N	12.07W
Tagarev, Gora-	18	Ae	38.19N	57.18 E
Tagawa	29	Be	33.39N	130.48 E
Tagbilaran	26	He	9.39N	123.51 E
Tageru, Jabal-	35	Db	16.25N	27.10 E
Taggia	14	Bg	43.52N	7.51 E
Taghit	32	Gc	30.55N	2.02W
Tagil	17	Kg	58.33N	62.30 E
Tagish Lake	42	Ed	60.00N	134.00W
Tagliamento	14	He	45.38N	13.06 E
Taglio di Po	14	Ge	45.00N	12.12 E
Tagomago, Isla de-	13	Ne	39.02N	1.39 E
Tagounit	32	Fd	29.58N	5.35W
Tagpochau, Ogso-	64b	Ba	15.11N	145.45 E
Tāgrīfat	33	Cd	29.12N	17.21 E
Taguatinga	54	If	12.25S	46.26W
Taguersimet	32	De	24.09N	15.07W
Tagula	63a	Ad	11.20S	153.00 E
Tagula Island	57	Gf	11.30S	153.30 E
Tagum	26	Ie	7.21N	125.50 E
Tagus (EN)=Tajo	5	Fh	38.40N	9.24W
Tagus (EN)=Tejo	5	Fh	38.40N	9.24W
Tah	32	Ed	27.37N	12.50W
Tahaa, Ile-	61	Kc	16.38S	151.30W
Tahakopa	62	Cg	46.31S	169.23 E
Tahan, Gunong-	21	Mi	4.39N	102.14 E
Tahanea Atoll	57	Mf	16.52S	144.45W

Index Symbols

[1] Independent Nation
[2] State, Region
[3] District, County
[4] Municipality
[5] Colony, Dependency
Continent
Physical Region
Historical or Cultural Region
Mount, Mountain
Volcano
Hill
Mountains, Mountain Range
Hills, Escarpment
Plateau, Upland
Pass, Gap
Plain, Lowland
Delta
Salt Flat
Valley, Canyon
Crater, Cave
Karst Features
Depression
Polder
Desert, Dunes
Forest, Woods
Heath, Steppe
Oasis
Cape, Point
Coast, Beach
Cliff
Peninsula
Isthmus
Sandbank
Island
Atoll
Rock, Reef
Islands, Archipelago
Rocks, Reefs
Coral Reef
Well, Spring
Geyser
River, Stream
Waterfall Rapids
River Mouth, Estuary
Lake
Salt Lake
Intermittent Lake
Reservoir
Swamp, Pond
Canal
Glacier
Ice Shelf, Pack Ice
Ocean
Sea
Gulf, Bay
Strait, Fjord
Lagoon
Bank
Seamount
Tablemount
Ridge
Shelf
Basin
Escarpment, Sea Scarp
Fracture
Trench, Abyss
National Park, Reserve
Point of Interest
Recreation Site
Cave, Cavern
Historic Site
Ruins
Wall, Walls
Church, Abbey
Temple
Scientific Station
Airport
Port
Lighthouse
Mine
Tunnel
Dam, Bridge

Tahat 30 Hf 23.18N 5.32 E
Tahe 27 La 52.22N 124.48 E
Ṭāherī 24 Oi 27.42N 52.21 E
Tahgong, Puntan- 64b Ba 15.06N 145.39 E
Tahiataş 18 Bc 42.20N 59.33 E
Tahifet 32 Ie 22.56N 5.59 E
Tahir Geçidi 24 Jc 39.52N 42.20 E
Tahiti, Ile- 57 Mf 17.37S 149.27W
Tahkuna Neem/Takuna, Mys- 8 Je 59.05N 22.30 E
Tahlequah 45 Ii 35.55N 94.58W
Tahoe, Lake- 46 Fg 38.54N 120.00W
Tahoua [2] 34 Gb 16.00N 5.30 E
Tahoua 31 Hg 14.54N 5.16 E
Ṭahṭā 33 Fd 26.46N 31.28 E
Tahta-Bazar 18 Dg 35.55N 62.55 E
Tahtabrod 19 Ge 52.40N 67.35 E
Tahtakaraça Pereval 18 Fe 39.17N 66.55 E
Tahtaköprü 15 Mj 39.57N 29.39 E
Tahtakupyr 19 Gg 43.01N 60.22 E
Tahtali Dağları 24 Gc 38.46N 36.47 E
Tahtamygda 20 Hf 54.09N 123.38 E
Tahuata, Ile- 57 Ne 9.57S 139.05W
Tahulandang, Pulau- 26 If 2.20N 125.25 E
Tahuna 26 If 3.37N 125.29 E
Tai 34 Dd 5.52N 7.27W
Tai'an [China] 28 Gd 41.24N 122.27 E
Tai'an [China] 27 Kd 36.09N 117.05 E
Taiarapu, Presqu'île de- 65e Fc 17.47S 149.14W
Taibai Shan 27 Ie 33.57N 107.40 E
Taibilla, Canal del- 13 Kg 37.43N 1.22W
Taibilla, Sierra de- 13 Jf 38.10N 2.10W
Taibus Qi (Baochang) 27 Kc 41.55N 115.22 E
Taicang 28 Fi 31.26N 121.06 E
Taichung 22 Og 24.09N 120.41 E
Taieri 62 Dg 46.03S 170.12 E
Taiga 20 De 56.04N 85.37 E
Taigonos Peninsula (EN) = Tajgonos, Poluostrov- 20 Ld 61.35N 161.00 E
Taigu 28 Bf 37.26N 112.33 E
Taihang Shan 21 Nf 37.00N 114.00 E
Taihape 62 Fc 39.41S 175.48 E
Taihe [China] 28 Ch 33.11N 115.38 E
Taihe [China] 27 Jf 26.50N 114.52 E
Taiheiyō = Pacific Ocean (EN) 3 Ki 5.00N 155.00W
Tai Hu 21 Of 31.15N 120.10 E
Taihu 27 Ke 30.26N 116.10 E
Taikang 27 Je 34.00N 114.56 E
Taiki 29a Cb 42.30N 143.16 E
Tailai 27 Lb 46.24N 123.26 E
Tailles, Plateau des- 12 Hd 50.15N 5.45 E
Taim 55 Fk 32.30S 52.35W
Tain 9 Id 57.48N 4.04W
Tainan 22 Og 23.00N 120.11 E
Tainaron, Ákra- = Matapan, Cape- (EN) 5 Ih 36.23N 22.29 E
Taiof 63a Ba 5.31S 154.39 E
Taipei 22 Og 25.03N 121.30 E
Taiping 26 Df 4.51N 100.44 E
Taiping (Gantang) 28 Ei 30.18N 118.07 E
Taipingchuan 28 Gb 44.24N 123.11 E
Taiping Dao 27 Jd 10.15N 113.42 E
Taiping Ling 27 Lb 47.36N 120.12 E
Tairadate 29a Bc 41.09N 140.38 E
Tairadate-Kaikyō 29a Bc 41.10N 140.40 E
Taisei 29a Ab 42.14N 139.49 E
Taisetsu-Zan 21 Qe 43.40N 142.48 E
Taisha 29 Cd 35.24N 132.40 E
Taishaku-San 29 Fc 36.58N 139.28 E
Tai Shan 21 Nf 36.30N 117.20 E
Taishō 29 Ce 33.12N 132.57 E
Taitao Peninsula (EN) = Taitao, Peninsula de- 52 Ij 46.30S 74.25W
Taitung 27 Lg 22.45N 121.09 E
Taiwa 29 Gb 38.26N 140.52 E
Taiwan [1] 22 Og 23.30N 121.00 E
Taiwan Haixia = Taiwan Strait (EN) 21 Ng 24.00N 119.00 E
Taixian 28 Fh 32.31N 120.08 E
Taixing 28 Fh 32.10N 120.00 E
Taiyang Shan 27 Ie 33.37N 106.26 E
Taiyetos Óros- 15 Fl 37.06N 22.18 E
Taiyuan 22 Nf 37.50N 112.37 E
Taiyue Shan 28 Bf 36.48N 112.00 E
Taizhou 28 Eh 32.29N 119.55 E
Taizhou → Linhai 27 Lf 28.52N 121.08 E
Taizhou Wan 28 Fj 28.40N 121.37 E
Taizi He 28 Gd 41.00N 122.23 E
Ta'izz 22 Gh 13.38N 44.02 E
Tājābād 24 Pg 30.02N 54.24 E
Tajarḥī 33 Be 24.21N 14.28 E
Tajgonos, Mys- 20 Ld 60.35N 160.10 E
Tajgonos, Poluostrov- = Taigonos Peninsula (EN) 20 Ld 61.35N 161.00 E
Tajik SSR (EN) = Tadžikskaja SSR 19 Hh 39.00N 71.00 E
Tajima 28 Of 37.12N 139.46 E
Tajimi 29 Ed 35.19N 137.08 E
Tājirwin 14 Co 35.54N 8.33 E
Tajito 48 Cb 30.58N 112.18W
Tajmba 20 Ed 60.22N 98.50 E
Tajmyr 20 Ea 76.05N 98.55 E
Tajmyr, Ozero- 21 Mb 74.30N 102.30 E
Tajmyr, Poluostrov- = Taymyr Peninsula (EN) 21 Mb 76.00N 104.00 E
Tajmyra 21 Lb 76.00N 99.40 E
Tajmyrlur 20 Hb 72.30N 121.39 E
Tajmyrski (Dolgano-Nenecki) Nacionalny okrug [3] 20 Eb 72.00N 95.00 E
Tajo = Tagus (EN) 5 Fh 38.40N 9.24W
Tajo-Segura, Canal de Trasvase- 13 Je 39.30N 2.05W
Tajrīsh 23 Hb 38.48N 51.25 E
Tajšet 22 Ld 55.57N 98.00 E
Tajumulco, Volcán- 38 Jh 15.02N 91.54W
Tajuña 13 Id 40.07N 3.35W
Tak 25 Je 16.52N 99.08 E
Taka Atoll 3 Ii 4.00N 146.45 E
Takāb 24 Ld 36.24N 47.07 E
Takaba 36 Hb 3.27N 40.14 E
Takahagi 28 Pf 36.42N 140.41 E
Takahama 29 Dd 35.29N 135.33 E
Takahara-Gawa 29 Ec 36.27N 137.15 E
Takaharu 29 Bf 31.55N 130.59 E
Takahashi 28 Lg 34.47N 133.37 E
Takahashi-Gawa 29 Cd 34.32N 133.42 E
Takahata 29 Gc 38.00N 140.12 E
Takahe, Mount- 66 Of 76.17S 112.05W
Takaka 62 Ed 40.51S 172.48 E
Takakuma-Yama 29 Bf 31.28N 130.49 E
Takalar 26 Gh 5.28S 119.24 E
Takalous 32 Ie 23.25N 7.02 E
Takamatsu 27 Ne 34.21N 134.03 E
Takamori 29 Be 32.48N 131.08 E
Takanabe 29 Be 32.08N 131.31 E
Takanawa-Hantō 29 Ce 34.00N 132.55 E
Takanawa-San 29 Ce 33.57N 132.50 E
Takanosu 29 Ga 40.14N 140.22 E
Takaoka [Jap.] 28 Nf 36.45N 137.01 E
Takaoka [Jap.] 29 Bf 31.57N 131.17 E
Takapoto Atoll 61 Lb 15.00S 148.10W
Takapuna 62 Fb 36.48S 174.47 E
Takara-Jima 27 Mf 29.10N 129.05 E
Takarazuka 29 Dd 34.49N 135.21 E
Takaroa Atoll 61 Mb 14.28S 144.58W
Takasaki 28 Of 36.20N 139.01 E
Taka-Shima [Jap.] 29 Be 32.40N 131.50 E
Taka-Shima [Jap.] 29 Af 31.26N 129.45 E
Takatshwane 37 Cd 22.36S 21.55 E
Takatsu-Gawa 29 Bd 34.42N 131.49 E
Takatsuki 28 Mg 34.51N 135.37 E
Takayama 28 Nf 36.08N 137.15 E
Takebe 29 Cd 34.53N 133.54 E
Takefu 28 Ng 35.54N 136.10 E
Takehara 29 Cd 34.21N 132.54 E
Takeo 29 Ae 33.12N 130.00 E
Tākern 8 Ff 58.20N 14.50 E
Take-Shima 28 Kf 37.22N 131.58 E
Tākestān 23 Gb 36.05N 49.14 E
Taketa 29 Be 32.58N 131.24 E
Takêv 25 Kf 10.59N 104.47 E
Takhādīd 24 Kh 29.59N 44.30 E
Takhār [3] 23 Kb 36.30N 69.30 E
Takhmaret 13 Mi 35.06N 0.41 E
Takht-e Soleimān 24 Nd 36.20N 51.00 E
Taki [Jap.] 29 Cd 35.16N 132.38 E
Taki [Pap.N.Gui.] 63a Bb 6.29S 155.50 E
Takijuq Lake 42 Gc 66.05N 113.00W
Takikawa 28 Pc 43.33N 141.54 E
Takingeun 26 Cf 4.38N 96.50 E
Takinoue 29a Ca 44.13N 143.03 E
Takko 29 Ga 40.20N 141.09 E
Takla Lake 42 Ee 55.30N 126.00W
Takla Landing 42 Ee 55.29N 125.58W
Takla Makan (EN) = Taklimakan Shamo 21 Kf 39.00N 83.00 E
Taklimakan Shamo = Takla Makan (EN) 21 Kf 39.00N 83.00 E
Takob 18 Ge 38.51N 69.00 E
Tako-Bana 29 Cd 35.35N 133.05 E
Takolokouzet, Massif de- 34 Gb 18.40N 9.30 E
Taku 29 Be 33.19N 130.06 E
Takuan, Mount- 63a Bb 6.27S 155.36 E
Takua Pa 25 Jg 8.52N 98.21 E
Takum 34 Gd 7.16N 9.59 E
Takuma 29 Cd 34.14N 133.40 E
Takume Atoll 57 Mf 15.49S 142.12W
Takuna, Mys-/Tahkuna Neem 8 Je 59.05N 22.30 E
Takutea Island 57 Lf 19.49S 158.18W
Tala 48 Hg 20.40N 103.42W
Tālah 32 Ib 35.35N 8.40 E
Talaimmannar 25 Fg 9.05N 79.44 E
Talāiyeh 24 Kd 37.50N 45.00 E
Talaja 20 Kd 61.03N 152.30 E
Talak 30 Hg 18.20N 6.00 E
Talamanca, Cordillera de- 49 Fi 9.30N 83.40W
Talara 53 Hf 4.35S 81.25W
Talas 19 Hg 42.29N 72.14 E
Talas 18 Ic 44.05N 70.20 E
Talasea 59 Ka 5.20S 150.05 E
Talasski Alatau, Hrebet- 18 Hc 42.10N 72.00 E
Talata Mafara 34 Gc 12.34N 6.04 E
Talaud, Kepulauan- = Talaud Islands (EN) 21 Oi 4.20N 126.50 E
Talaud Islands (EN) = Talaud, Kepulauan- 21 Oi 4.20N 126.50 E
Talavera, Isla- 55 Dh 27.32S 56.26W
Talavera de la Reina 13 He 39.57N 4.50W
Talawdī 35 Ec 10.38N 30.23 E
Talbot Inlet 42 Ja 77.55N 77.35W
Talca 53 Ii 35.26S 71.40W
Talcahuano 53 Ii 36.43S 73.07W
Tālcher 25 Hd 20.57N 85.13 E
Taldom 7 Ih 56.45N 37.32 E
Taldy-Kurgan 22 Je 44.59N 78.23 E
Taldy-Kurganskaja Oblast [3] 19 Hf 44.00N 78.00 E
Talēh 35 Hd 9.09N 48.26 E
Tal-e Khosravī 24 Ng 30.47N 51.29 E
Talence 11 Fj 44.49N 0.36W
Ṭalesh, Kūhhā-Ye- 24 Md 37.35N 48.38 E
Talgar 19 Hg 43.18N 77.13 E
Taliabu, Pulau- 26 Hg 1.48S 124.48 E
Talica 19 Gd 57.01N 63.43 E
Talimardžan 19 Gh 38.21N 65.31 E
Tali Post 35 Ed 5.54N 30.47 E
Talisajan 22 Ni 1.37N 118.11 E
Taliwang 26 Gh 8.44S 116.52 E
Talkeetna 40 Id 62.20N 150.07W
Talkeetna Mountains 40 Jd 62.10N 148.15W
Talkheh 24 Kd 37.40N 45.46 E
Talladega 44 Di 33.26N 86.06W
Tall 'Afar 23 Fb 36.22N 42.27 E
Tallah 24 Dh 28.05N 30.44 E
Tallahassee 39 Kf 30.25N 84.16W
Tallahatchie River 45 Kj 33.33N 90.10W
Tall al Abyaḍ 24 Hd 36.41N 38.57 E
Tallapoosa River 44 Di 32.30N 86.16W
Tallard 11 Mj 44.28N 6.03 E
Tällberg 8 Fd 60.49N 15.00 E
Tall Birāk at Taḥtānī 24 Id 36.38N 41.05 E
Tallinn 6 Id 59.25N 24.45 E
Tall Kayf 24 Jd 36.29N 43.08 E
Tall Kūshik 24 Jd 36.48N 42.04 E
Tallulah 45 Kj 32.25N 91.11W
Tălmaciu 15 Hd 45.39N 24.16 E
Talmenka 20 Df 53.51N 83.45 E
Talmest 32 Fc 31.09N 9.00W
Talnah 20 Dc 69.30N 88.15 E
Talnoje 16 Ge 48.53N 30.42 E
Talo 30 Kg 10.44N 37.55 E
Talofofo 64c Bb 13.20N 144.46 E
Talon 20 Je 59.48N 148.50 E
Tāloqān 23 Kb 36.44N 69.33 E
Talovaja 16 Ld 51.06N 40.48 E
Talpa de Allende 48 Gg 20.23N 104.51W
Talsi 7 Fh 57.17N 22.37 E
Taltal 53 Ih 25.24S 70.29W
Taltson 42 Gd 61.24N 112.45W
Taluk 26 Dg 0.32S 101.35 E
Talvik 7 Fa 70.03N 22.58 E
Talwār 24 Md 36.00N 48.00 E
Tama 35 Cc 14.45N 22.25 E
Tamaghzah 32 Ic 34.23N 7.57 E
Tamala 16 Mc 52.33N 43.18 E
Tamalameque 49 Ki 8.52N 73.38W
Tamale 31 Gh 9.24N 0.50W
Tamames 13 Fd 40.39N 6.06W
Tamana 29 Be 32.55N 130.33 E
Tamanaco, Río- 50 Dh 9.25N 65.23W
Tamana Island 57 Ie 2.29S 175.59 E
Tamano 28 Lg 34.30N 133.56 E
Tamanoura 29 Ae 32.38N 128.37 E
Tamanrasset 30 Hf 22.03N 0.10 E
Tamanrasset 31 Hf 22.47N 5.31 E
Tamanrasset [3] 32 Ie 23.00N 5.30 E
Tamar 9 Ik 50.22N 4.10W
Tamara 15 Cg 42.27N 19.33 E
Tamará 54 Db 5.50N 72.10W
Tamarit de Llitera/Tamarite de Litera 13 Mc 41.52N 0.26 E
Tamarite de Litera/Tamarit de Llitera 13 Mc 41.52N 0.26 E
Tamarro 14 Ii 41.09N 14.50 E
Tamarugal, Pampa del- 56 Gb 21.00S 69.25W
Tamási 10 Oj 46.38N 18.17 E
Tamassoumit 32 Ef 18.35N 12.39W
Tamaulipas [2] 47 Ed 24.00N 98.45W
Tamaulipas, Llanos de- 47 Ed 25.00N 98.25W
Tamaulipas, Sierra de- 48 Jf 23.30N 98.30W
Tamayama 29 Gb 39.50N 141.11 E
Tamazula de Gordiano 48 Hh 19.38N 103.15W
Tamazunchale 47 Ed 21.16N 98.47W
Tambach 36 Gb 0.36N 35.31 E
Tambacounda 31 Fg 13.12N 15.48W
Tambara 37 Ec 16.44S 34.15 E
Tambelan, Kepulauan- = Tambelan Islands (EN) 26 Ef 1.00N 107.30 E
Tambelan, Pulau- 26 Ef 0.58N 107.34 E
Tambelan Islands (EN) = Tambelan, Kepulauan- 26 Ef 1.00N 107.30 E
Tambo 59 Jd 24.53S 146.15 E
Tambohorano 37 Gc 17.29S 43.58 E
Tambora, Gunung- 26 Gh 8.14S 117.55 E
Tambores 55 Dj 31.52S 56.16W
Tambov 6 Ke 52.43N 41.27 E
Tambovskaja Oblast [3] 19 Ee 52.45N 41.40 E
Tambre 13 Db 42.49N 8.53W
Tambunan 26 Ge 5.40N 116.22 E
Tambura 31 Jh 5.36N 27.28 E
Tamchaket 32 Ef 17.20N 10.40W
Tame 54 Db 6.27N 71.45W
Tâmega 13 Dc 41.05N 8.21W
Tâmega 13 Dc 41.05N 8.21W
Tamel Aike 56 Fg 48.19S 70.58W
Tamesi 47 Ed 22.13N 97.52W
Tamesnar 30 Hg 18.25N 3.33 E
Tamgak, Monts- 30 Hg 19.11N 8.42 E
Tamgue, Massif du- 30 Fg 12.00N 12.18W
Tamiahua 48 Kg 21.16N 97.27W
Tamiahua, Laguna de- 47 Ed 21.35N 97.35W
Tamianglajang 26 Gg 2.07S 115.10 E
Tamil Nādu [3] 25 Ff 11.00N 78.00 E
Tamiš 15 De 44.51N 20.39 E
Tamise/Temse 12 Gc 51.08N 4.13 E
Tamitatoala, Río- 54 Hf 11.56S 53.36W
Ṭāmiyah 24 Dh 29.29N 30.58 E
Tam Ky 25 Le 15.34N 108.29 E
Tammela 8 Jd 60.48N 23.46 E
Tammerfors/Tampere 6 Ic 61.30N 23.45 E
Tammisaari/Ekenäs 7 Fg 59.58N 23.26 E
Tämnaren 8 Gd 60.10N 17.20 E
Tamnava 15 De 44.25N 20.05 E
Tamou 34 Fc 12.45N 2.11 E
Tampa 39 Kg 27.57N 82.27W
Tampa Bay 43 Kf 27.45N 82.35W
Tampake-Misaki 29a Bb 43.43N 141.20 E
Tampere/Tammerfors 6 Ic 61.30N 23.45 E
Tampico 39 Jg 22.13N 97.51W
Tampin 26 Df 2.28N 102.14 E
Tamri 32 Fc 30.43N 9.50 E
Tamsag-Bulak 27 Kb 47.14N 117.21 E
Tamsalu 7 Gg 59.10N 26.07 E
Tamsweg 14 Hc 47.08N 13.48 E
Tamu 25 Id 24.13N 94.19 E
Tamuin 48 Jg 21.59N 98.45W
Tamuin 47 Ed 22.00N 98.44W
Tamuín, Río- 48 Jg 21.47N 98.28W
Tamworth [Austl.] 58 Gh 31.05S 150.55 E
Tamworth [Eng.-U.K.] 9 Li 52.39N 1.40W
Tamyang 28 Ig 35.19N 126.59 E
Tana [Eur.] 5 Ia 70.28N 28.18 E
Tana [Kenya] 30 Li 2.32S 40.31 E
Tana, Lake- 30 Kg 12.00N 37.20 E
Tanabe 28 Mh 33.42N 135.44 E
Tana bru 7 Ga 70.16N 28.10 E
Tanacross 40 Kd 63.23N 143.21W
Tanafjorden 7 Ga 70.54N 28.40 E
Tanaga 40a Cb 51.50N 178.00W
Tanagro 14 Ij 40.38N 15.14 E
Tanagura 29 Gc 37.02N 140.23 E
Tanahbala, Pulau- 26 Cg 0.25S 98.25 E
Tanahgrogot 26 Gg 1.55S 116.12 E
Tanahjampea, Pulau- 26 Hh 7.05S 120.42 E
Tanahmasa, Pulau- 26 Cg 0.12S 98.27 E
Tanah Merah 26 De 5.48N 102.09 E
Tanahmerah 26 Lh 6.05S 140.17 E
Tanakpur 25 Gc 29.05N 80.07 E
Tanalyk 17 Ij 51.46N 58.45 E
Tanami 59 Fc 19.59S 129.43 E
Tanami Desert 57 Eg 20.00S 132.00 E
Tan An 25 Lf 10.32N 106.25 E
Tanana 40 Ic 65.10N 152.05W
Tanana 38 Dc 65.09N 151.55W
Tanapag 64b Ba 15.14N 145.45 E
Tanapag, Puetton- 64b Ba 15.14N 145.44 E
Tanāqib, Ra's at- 24 Mi 27.50N 48.53 E
Tanaro 14 Ce 45.01N 8.47 E
Tanba-Sanchi 29 Dd 35.15N 135.35 E
Tancheng 28 Eg 34.37N 118.20 E
Tanch'ŏn 27 Mc 40.25N 128.57 E
Tancitaro, Pico de- 47 De 19.26N 102.18W
Tanda 34 Ed 7.48N 3.10W
Tanda, Lac- 34 Eb 15.45N 4.42W
Tandag 26 Ie 9.04N 126.12 E
Tandaltī 35 Ec 13.01N 31.52 E
Tăndărei 15 Ke 44.39N 27.40 E
Tandjungbalai 26 Cf 2.58N 99.48 E
Tandil 53 Ki 37.20S 59.05W
Tandil, Sierras del- 55 Cm 37.24S 59.06W
Tandjilé [3] 35 Bd 9.30N 16.30 E
Tando Ādam 25 Dc 25.46N 68.40 E
Tandsjöborg 7 Df 61.42N 14.43 E
Tanḍūbāyah 35 Db 18.40N 28.37 E
Taneatua 62 Gc 38.04S 177.00 E
Tane-Ga-Shima 27 Ne 30.40N 131.00 E
Taneichi 29 Ga 40.24N 141.43 E
Tan Emmel 32 Id 27.28N 9.45 E
Tanew 10 Sf 50.27N 22.16 E
Tanezrouft 30 Gf 24.00N 0.45W
Tanezzuft 33 Bd 25.51N 10.19 E
Tanf, Jabal at- 24 Hf 33.30N 38.42 E
Tanga [3] 36 Gd 5.30S 38.00 E
Tanga 31 Ki 5.04S 39.06 E
Tangail 25 Hd 24.15N 89.55 E
Tanga Islands 57 Ge 3.30S 153.15 E
Tangalla 25 Gg 6.01N 80.48 E
Tanganyika [2] 36 Fd 6.00S 35.00 E
Tanganyika, Lac- = Tanganyika, Lake- (EN) 30 Ji 6.00S 29.30 E
Tanganyika, Lake- 30 Ji 6.00S 29.30 E
Tanganyika, Lake- (EN) = Tanganyika, Lac- 30 Ji 6.00S 29.30 E
Tangarā 54 Ke 6.11S 35.49W
Tangarare 63a Dc 9.35S 159.39 E
Tangdan → Dongchuan 27 Hf 26.07N 103.05 E
Tängehgol 24 Pd 37.25N 55.50 E
Tanger = Tangier (EN) [3] 32 Fb 35.45N 5.45W
Tanger = Tangier (EN) 31 Ge 35.48N 5.48W
Tangerang 26 Eh 6.11S 106.37 E
Tangermünde 10 Hd 52.33N 11.57 E
Tanggu 27 Kd 39.00N 117.36 E
Tanggula Shan (Dangla Shan) 21 Lf 33.00N 92.00 E
Tanggula Shankou 27 Fe 32.42N 92.27 E
Tanggulashanqu/Tuotuohe 22 Lf 34.15N 92.29 E
Tang He 28 Bh 32.10N 112.20 E
Tanghe 27 Je 32.37N 112.57 E
Tangier (EN) = Tanger 31 Ge 35.48N 5.48W
Tang La 21 Kg 28.00N 89.15 E
Tango 29 Dd 35.44N 135.05 E
Tangra Yumco 21 Kf 31.00N 86.25 E
Tangshan 22 Nf 39.35N 118.09 E
Tanguiéta 34 Fc 10.37N 1.16 E
Tanguro, Rio- 55 Fa 12.36S 52.56W
Tangxian 28 Ce 38.46N 114.58 E
Tangyin 28 Cg 35.54N 114.21 E
Tangyuan 27 Mb 46.45N 129.53 E
Tanhoj 20 Ff 51.33N 105.07 E
Tanhuijo, Arrecife- 48 Kg 21.07N 97.17W
Taniantaweng Shan 27 Ge 30.00N 98.00 E
Tanimbar, Kepulauan- = Tanimbar Islands (EN) 57 Ee 7.30S 131.30 E
Tanimbar Islands (EN) = Tanimbar, Kepulauan- 57 Ee 7.30S 131.30 E
Taninthayi 25 Jf 13.00N 99.00 E
Tanjung [Indon.] 26 Gg 2.11S 115.23 E
Tanjung [Indon.] 26 Dg 1.23S 103.58 E
Tanjungpandan 26 Eg 2.45S 107.39 E
Tanjungpinang 26 Df 0.55N 104.27 E
Tanjungredep 26 Gf 2.09N 117.29 E
Tanjungselor 26 Gf 2.51N 117.22 E
Tankenberg 12 Ib 52.21N 6.58 E
Tanna, Ile- 57 Hf 19.30S 169.20 E
Tännäs 7 Ce 62.27N 12.40 E
Tanner, Mount- 46 Fb 49.40N 118.34W
Tannis Bugt 8 Dg 57.40N 10.15 E
Tannu-Ola 21 Ld 51.00N 94.00 E
Tano 34 Ed 5.07N 2.56W
Tanout 31 Hg 14.58N 8.53 E
Ṭanṭā 31 Ke 30.47N 31.00 E
Tan Tan 32 Ed 28.30N 11.02W
Tan-Tan [3] 32 Ed 28.30N 11.00W
Tan Tan Plage 32 Ed 28.26N 11.15W
Tantoyuca 48 Jg 21.21N 98.14W
Tanum 7 Cg 58.43N 11.20 E
Tanzania [1] 31 Ki 6.00S 35.00 E
Tao, Ko- 25 Jf 10.05N 99.52 E
Tao'an (Taonan) 27 Lb 45.20N 122.46 E
Tao'er He 21 Oe 45.42N 124.05 E
Taoghe 37 Cd 20.37S 22.35 E
Tao He 27 Hd 35.50N 103.20 E
Taojiang 28 Bj 28.31N 112.05 E
Taonan → Tao'an 27 Lb 45.20N 122.46 E
Taongi Atoll 57 Hc 14.37N 168.58 E
Taormina 14 Jm 37.51N 15.17 E
Taos 43 Fd 36.24N 105.24W
Taoudenni 31 Gf 22.42N 3.56W
Taougrite 13 Mh 36.15N 0.55 E
Taounate 32 Gc 34.33N 4.39W
Taounate [3] 32 Gc 34.04N 4.06W
Taoura 14 Cn 36.10N 8.02 E
Taourirt 32 Gc 34.25N 2.54W
Taouz 32 Gc 31.00N 4.00W
Taoyuan 27 Lg 25.00N 121.18 E
Tapa 19 Cd 59.15N 25.59 E
Tapachula 39 Jh 14.54N 92.17W
Tapaga, Cape- 65c Bb 14.01S 171.23W
Tapah 26 Df 4.11N 101.16 E
Tapajera 55 Fi 28.09S 52.01W
Tapajós, Rio- 52 Kf 2.24S 54.41W
Tapaktuan 26 Cf 3.16N 97.11 E
Tapalqué 55 Bm 36.21S 60.01W
Tapan 26 Dg 2.10S 101.04 E
Tapanahoni Rivier 54 Hc 4.22N 54.27W
Tapanlieh 27 Lg 21.58N 120.47 E
Tapanui 62 Cf 45.57S 169.16 E
Tapauá 54 Fe 5.45S 64.23W
Tapauá, Rio- 52 Jf 5.40S 64.21W
Tapenagá, Rio- 55 Ci 28.04S 59.10W
Taperas 55 Bc 17.54S 60.23W
Tapes 56 Jd 30.40S 51.23W
Tapes, Serra do- 55 Fj 30.25S 51.55W
Tapeta 34 Dd 6.29N 8.51W
Taphan Hin 25 Ke 16.12N 100.26 E
Tapili 36 Eb 3.25N 27.40 E
Tapini 60 Di 8.19S 146.59 E
Tapiola, Espoo- 8 Kd 60.11N 24.49 E
Tapirai 55 Id 19.52S 46.01W
Tapirapuã 55 Db 14.51S 57.45W
Tapolca 10 Nj 46.53N 17.26 E
Tappahannock 44 Ig 37.55N 76.54W
Tappi-Zaki 28 Pd 41.18N 140.22 E
Tappu 29a Ba 44.04N 141.52 E
Tapsuj 19 Gc 62.20N 61.30 E
Tāpti 21 Jg 21.06N 72.41 E
Tapul Group 26 He 5.30N 121.00 E
Tapurucuara 54 Ed 0.24S 65.02W
Taputapu, Cape- 65c Cb 14.19S 170.50W
Tāqbostān 24 Le 34.30N 46.58 E
Ṭaqṭaq 24 Ke 35.53N 44.35 E
Taquara 56 Jc 29.39S 50.47W
Taquaral, Serra do- 55 Fb 15.42S 52.30W
Taquari 55 Fc 17.50S 53.17W
Taquari, Pantanal de- 54 Gg 18.10S 56.30W
Taquari, Rio- [Braz.] 55 Gi 29.56S 51.44W
Taquari, Rio- [Braz.] 55 Hf 23.16S 49.12W
Taquari, Rio- [Braz.] 52 Kg 19.15S 57.17W
Taquari, Serra do- 55 Fd 18.18S 53.49W
Taquaritinga 55 He 21.24S 48.30W
Taquarituba 55 Hf 23.31S 49.15W
Taquaruçu, Rio- 55 Fe 21.35S 52.08W
Tar 18 Id 40.38N 73.26 E
Tara 15 Cf 43.55N 19.25 E
Tara 9 Gh 53.34N 6.35W
Tara [Austl.] 59 Ke 27.17S 150.28 E
Tara [Jap.] 29 Be 33.02N 130.11 E
Tara [R.S.F.S.R.] 20 Ce 56.40N 74.50 E
Tara [R.S.F.S.R.] 19 Hd 56.54N 74.22 E
Tara [Yugo.] 15 Bf 43.21N 18.51 E
Taraba 34 Hd 8.34N 10.15 E
Tarabuco 54 Fg 19.10S 64.57W
Ṭarābulus = Tripoli (EN) [3] 33 Bc 32.40N 13.15 E
Ṭarābulus [Leb.] = Tripoli (EN) 23 Ec 34.26N 35.51 E
Ṭarābulus [Lib.] = Tripoli (EN) 31 Ie 32.54N 13.11 E
Ṭarābulus = Tripolitania (EN) 30 Ie 31.00N 14.00 E
Ṭarābulus = Tripolitania (EN) 33 Bc 30.00N 15.00 E
Taradale 62 Gc 39.32S 176.51 E
Tarāghin 33 Bd 25.59N 14.26 E
Tarahumara, Sierra- 47 Cc 28.26N 106.50W
Tarakan 22 Ni 3.18N 117.38 E
Tarakan, Pulau- 26 Gf 3.21N 117.36 E
Taraklija 16 Fg 45.57N 28.41 E
Tarama Jima 27 Lg 24.40N 124.40 E
Taran, Mys- 7 Ei 54.57N 19.59 E
Taranaki [2] 62 Fc 39.10S 174.20 E
Tarancón 13 Jd 40.01N 3.00W
Taranga Island 62 Fa 36.00S 174.45 E
Taransay 9 Fd 57.55N 7.10W
Taranto 6 Hg 40.28N 17.14 E
Taranto, Golfo di- = Taranto, Gulf of- (EN) 5 Hg 40.10N 17.20 E
Taranto, Gulf of- (EN) = Taranto, Golfo di- 5 Hg 40.10N 17.20 E
Tarapacá [2] 56 Ga 20.00S 69.20W
Tarapacá 56 Ga 19.55S 69.31W
Tarapaina 63a Ec 9.23S 161.24 E
Tarapoto 54 Ce 6.30S 76.25W
Taraquá 54 Ec 0.06N 68.28W
Tarara 63a Bb 6.02S 155.24 E
Tarare 11 Ki 45.54N 4.26 E
Tararua Range 62 Fd 40.45S 175.25 E
Tarašča 16 Ge 49.34N 30.31 E
Tarascon 11 Kk 43.48N 4.40 E
Tarascon-sur-Ariège 11 Hl 42.51N 1.36 E
Tarat 32 Id 26.08N 9.21 E
Tarata 54 Dg 17.27S 70.02W

Index Symbols

- [1] Independent Nation
- [2] State, Region
- [3] District, County
- [4] Municipality
- [5] Colony, Dependency
- Continent
- Physical Region
- Historical or Cultural Region
- Mount, Mountain
- Volcano
- Hill
- Mountains, Mountain Range
- Hills, Escarpment
- Plateau, Upland
- Pass, Gap
- Plain, Lowland
- Delta
- Salt Flat
- Valley, Canyon
- Crater, Cave
- Karst Features
- Depression
- Polder
- Desert, Dunes
- Forest, Woods
- Heath, Steppe
- Oasis
- Cape, Point
- Coast, Beach
- Cliff
- Peninsula
- Isthmus
- Sandbank
- Island
- Atoll
- Rock, Reef
- Islands, Archipelago
- Rocks, Reefs
- Coral Reef
- Well, Spring
- Geyser
- River, Stream
- Waterfall Rapids
- River Mouth, Estuary
- Lake
- Salt Lake
- Intermittent Lake
- Reservoir
- Swamp, Pond
- Canal
- Glacier
- Ice Shelf, Pack Ice
- Ocean
- Sea
- Gulf, Bay
- Strait, Fjord
- Lagoon
- Bank
- Seamount
- Tablemount
- Ridge
- Shelf
- Basin
- Escarpment, Sea Scarp
- Fracture
- Trench, Abyss
- National Park, Reserve
- Point of Interest
- Recreation Site
- Cave, Cavern
- Historic Site
- Ruins
- Wall, Walls
- Church, Abbey
- Temple
- Scientific Station
- Airport
- Port
- Lighthouse
- Mine
- Tunnel
- Dam, Bridge

Name	Page	Grid	Lat.	Long.
Tarauacá	54	De	8.10S	70.46W
Tarauacá, Rio	52	Jf	6.42S	69.48W
Taravao	65e	Fc	17.44S	149.19W
Taravao, Baie de-	65e	Fc	17.43S	149.17W
Taravo	11a	Ab	41.42N	8.48 E
Tarawa Atoll	57	Id	1.25N	173.00 E
Tarawera	62	Gc	39.02S	176.35 E
Tarazi	24	Mg	31.05N	48.18 E
Tarazona	13	Kc	41.54N	1.44W
Tarazona de la Mancha	13	Ke	39.15N	1.55W
Tarbagataj, Hrebet	21	Ke	47.10N	83.00 E
Tarbagatay Shan	27	Db	47.10N	83.00 E
Tarbat Ness	9	Jd	57.50N	3.40W
Tarbert [Scot.-U.K.]	9	Gd	57.54N	6.49W
Tarbert [Scot.-U.K.]	9	Hf	55.52N	5.26W
Tarbes	11	Gk	43.14N	0.05 E
Tarboro	44	Ih	35.54N	77.32W
Tarcăului, Munţii-	15	Jc	46.45N	26.20 E
Tarcoola	59	Gf	30.41S	134.33 E
Tardenois	12	Fe	49.12N	3.40 E
Tardienta	13	Lc	41.59N	0.32W
Tardoire	11	Gi	45.52N	0.14 E
Tardoki-Jani, Gora-	20	Ig	48.50N	137.55 E
Taree	58	Gh	31.54S	152.28 E
Taremert-n-Akli	32	Id	25.53N	5.18 E
Tarentaise	11	Mi	45.30N	6.30 E
Ţarfā', Ra's aţ-	33	Hf	17.02N	42.22 E
Ţarfā', Wādī aţ-	24	Dh	28.38N	30.43 E
Ţarfah, Jazīrat aţ-	33	Hg	14.37N	42.55 E
Tarfaya	31	Ff	27.57N	12.55W
Targa	13	Qi	35.41N	4.09 E
Târgoviški prohod	15	Jf	43.12N	26.30 E
Târgovište	15	Jf	43.15N	26.34 E
Târgovište [2]	15	Jf	43.15N	26.34 E
Tarhankut, Mys-	16	Hg	45.21N	32.30 E
Tarhăus, Vîrful-	15	Jc	46.38N	26.10 E
Tarhūnah	33	Bc	32.26N	13.38 E
Tarhūnī, Jabal at-	33	De	22.12N	22.25 E
Táriba	49	Kj	7.49N	72.13W
Tarīf	23	He	24.01N	53.45 E
Tarifa	13	Gh	36.01N	5.36W
Tarifa, Punta de-	13	Ih	36.00N	3.37W
Tarija	53	Jh	21.31S	64.45W
Tarija [2]	54	Fh	21.30S	64.00W
Tarik	64d	Bb	7.21N	151.47 E
Tariku	26	Kg	2.55S	138.26 E
Tarīm [Yem.]	23	Gf	16.03N	49.00 E
Tarīm [Sau.Ar.]	24	Fi	27.54N	35.24 E
Tarim Basin (EN) = Tarim Pendi	21	Ke	41.00N	84.00 E
Tarime	36	Fc	1.21S	34.22 E
Tarim He	21	Ke	41.05N	86.40 E
Tarim Pendi = Tarim Basin (EN)	21	Ke	41.00N	84.00 E
Tarin Kowt	23	Kc	32.52N	65.38 E
Taritatu	26	Kg	2.54S	138.27 E
Tarjalan	27	Hb	49.38N	101.59 E
Tarjannevesi	8	Kb	62.10N	24.05 E
Tarjat	27	Gb	48.10N	99.40 E
Tarka, Vallée de-	34	Gc	14.30N	6.30 E
Tarkastad	37	Df	32.00S	26.16 E
Tarkio	45	If	40.27N	95.23W
Tarko-Sale	20	Cd	64.55N	78.05 E
Tarkwa	34	Ed	5.18N	1.59W
Tarlac	22	Oh	15.29N	120.35 E
Tarm	8	Ci	55.55N	8.32 E
Tarma	54	Cf	11.25S	75.42W
Tarn	11	Hj	44.06N	1.02 E
Tarn [3]	11	Hk	43.50N	2.00 E
Tarna	10	Pi	47.31N	19.59 E
Tärnaby	7	Dd	65.43N	15.16 E
Tarn-et-Garonne [3]	11	Hj	44.00N	1.10 E
Tarnica	10	Sg	49.06N	22.47 E
Tarnobrzeg	10	Rf	50.35N	21.41 E
Tarnobrzeg [2]	10	Rf	50.35N	21.40 E
Tarnogród	10	Sf	50.23N	22.45 E
Tarnos	11	Ek	43.32N	1.28W
Tarnów	6	Ie	50.01N	21.00 E
Tarnów [2]	10	Qf	50.00N	21.00 E
Tarnowskie Góry	10	Of	50.27N	18.52 E
Tärnsjö	8	Gd	60.09N	16.56 E
Taro	14	Ef	45.00N	10.15 E
Taron	63a	Aa	4.28S	153.04 E
Taroom	58	Fg	25.39S	149.49 E
Taroudant	32	Fc	30.29N	8.52W
Tarpon Springs	44	Fk	28.09N	82.45W
Tarquinia	14	Fh	42.15N	11.45 E
Tarra, Río-	49	Ki	9.04N	72.27W
Tarrafal	32	Cf	15.17N	23.46W
Tarragona	6	Gg	41.07N	1.15 E
Tarragona [3]	13	Mc	41.10N	1.00 E
Tarraleah	59	Jh	42.10S	146.30 E
Tarrant	44	Di	33.38N	86.46W
Tarrasa	13	Oc	41.34N	2.01 E
Tárrega	13	Nc	41.39N	1.09 E
Tarsus	23	Db	36.55N	34.53 E
Tart	27	Fd	37.07N	92.57 E
Tartagal	56	Hb	22.32S	63.49W
Tartaro	14	Fe	45.02N	11.30 E
Tartas	11	Fk	43.50N	0.48W
Tartas	20	Ce	55.37N	76.44 E
Tartu	6	Id	58.23N	26.45 E
Tartūs	23	Ec	34.53N	35.53 E
Tarumae-Yama	29a	Bb	42.41N	141.23 E
Tarumizu	28	Ki	31.29N	130.42 E
Tarusa	16	Jb	54.43N	37.11 E
Tārūt	24	Ni	26.34N	50.04 E
Tarutau, Ko-	25	Jg	6.35N	99.40 E
Tarutino	16	Ff	46.12N	29.09 E
Tarutung	26	Cf	2.01N	98.58 E
Tarvisio	14	Hd	46.30N	13.35 E
Tarvo	55	Bb	15.06S	60.34W
Tarvo, Rio-	55	Bb	14.47S	61.03W
Tasajera, Sierra-	48	Gc	29.35N	105.35W
Tašanta	20	Dg	49.43N	89.11 E
Tasaral, Ostrov-	18	Ja	46.15N	74.05 E
Tašauz	19	Fg	41.52N	59.59 E
Tašauzskaja Oblast [3]	19	Fg	41.00N	58.40 E
Tasāwah	33	Bd	[illegible]5.59N	13.29 E
Tasbuget	19	Gg	44.[illegible]N	65.38 E
Tasejeva	20	Ee	58.06N	94.01 E
Taseko Lake	46	Da	51.15N	123.35W
Tasendjanet	32	Hd	25.40N	0.59 E
Tashk, Daryācheh-ye-	23	Hd	29.45N	53.35 E
Tasikmalaya	22	Mj	7.20S	108.12 E
Tåsinge	8	Di	55.00N	10.36 E
Tasiussaq	41	Gd	73.18N	56.00W
Taskan	20	Kd	62.58N	150.20 E
Taškent	22	Ie	41.20N	69.18 E
Taškentskaja Oblast [3]	19	Gg	41.20N	69.40 E
Taškepri	19	Gh	36.17N	62.38 E
Taškeprinskoje, Vodohranilišče-	18	Df	36.15N	62.40 E
Tasker	34	Hb	15.04N	10.42 E
Taşköprü	24	Fb	41.30N	34.14 E
Taš-Kumyr	19	Hg	41.20N	72.14 E
Taşlıçay	24	Jc	39.38N	43.23 E
Tasman, Mount-	62	De	43.34S	170.09 E
Tasman Basin (EN)	3	Jn	43.00S	158.00 E
Tasman Bay	61	Dh	41.10S	173.15 E
Tasmania	59	Jh	43.00S	147.00 E
Tasmania	57	Fi	43.00S	147.00 E
Tasman Peninsula	59	Jh	43.05S	147.50 E
Tasman Plateau (EN)	3	In	48.00S	148.00 E
Tasman Sea	57	Hh	40.00S	163.00 E
Tăşnad	15	Fb	47.29N	22.35 E
Taşova	24	Gb	40.46N	36.20 E
Tassah, Wādī-	24	Cn	36.35N	8.54 E
Tassara	34	Gb	16.01N	5.39 E
Taštagol	20	Df	52.47N	88.00 E
Tåstrup	8	Ei	55.39N	12.19 E
Tastūr	14	Dn	36.33N	9.27 E
Tasty-Taldy	19	Ge	50.47N	66.31 E
Ţaşūj	24	Kc	38.19N	45.21 E
Taşuou	24	Ed	36.19N	33.53 E
Tata [3]	32	Fd	29.40N	8.00W
Tata [Hun.]	10	Oi	47.39N	18.19 E
Tata [Mor.]	32	Fd	29.45N	7.59W
Tataba	26	Hg	1.18S	122.49 E
Tatabánya	10	Oi	47.34N	18.25 E
Tatakoto Atoll	57	Nf	17.20S	138.23W
Tata Mailau	26	Ih	8.55S	125.30 E
Tatarbunary	16	Fg	45.49N	29.35 E
Tatarsk	22	Jd	55.13N	75.58 E
Tatarskaja ASSR [3]	19	Fd	55.20N	50.50 E
Tatarski Proliv = Tatar Strait (EN)	21	Qd	50.00N	141.15 E
Tatar Strait (EN) = Tatarski Proliv	21	Qd	50.00N	141.15 E
Tatau	26	Ff	2.53N	112.51 E
Taţāwīn	32	Jc	32.56N	10.27 E
Tateyama	28	Og	34.59N	139.52 E
Tathlina Lake	42	Fd	60.30N	117.30W
Tathlīth	23	Ff	19.32N	43.30 E
Tatiščevo	16	Nd	51.40N	45.35 E
Tatla Lake	46	Ca	51.58N	124.25W
Tatla Lake	46	Ca	51.55N	124.36W
Tatlow, Mount-	46	Da	51.23N	123.52W
Tatnam, Cape -	42	Ie	57.16N	91.00W
Tatra Mountains (EN)	5	Hf	49.15N	20.00 E
Tatsuno [Jap.]	29	Dd	34.52N	134.33 E
Tatsuno [Jap.]	29	Ed	35.58N	137.58 E
Tatsuruhama	29	Ec	37.04N	136.53 E
Tatta	25	Dd	24.45N	67.55 E
Tatui	55	If	23.21S	47.51W
Tatum	45	Ej	33.16N	103.19W
Tatvan	23	Fb	38.30N	42.16 E
Tau	8	Ae	59.04N	5.54 E
Tau [Am.Sam.]	65c	Db	14.15S	169.30W
Tau [Ton.]	65b	Bc	21.01S	175.00W
Tauá	54	Je	6.01S	40.26W
Taubaté	53	Lh	23.02S	45.33W
Tauberbischofsheim	10	Fg	49.37N	9.40 E
Taučik	19	Fg	44.15N	51.20 E
Tauere Atoll	57	Mf	17.22S	141.30W
Tauern	5	Hf	47.15N	13.15 E
Taufstein	10	Ff	50.31N	9.14 E
Tauhunu	64n	Ac	10.25S	161.03W
Tauhunu	64n	Ac	10.25S	161.03W
Taujsk	20	Je	59.46N	149.20 E
Taujskaja Guba	20	Je	59.15N	150.00 E
Taukum	18	Jb	44.50N	75.30 E
Taumako	63c	Ba	9.57S	167.13 E
Taumarunui	62	Fc	38.52S	175.15 E
Taum Sauk Mountain	45	Kh	37.34N	90.44W
Taunay	55	De	20.18S	56.05W
Taung	37	Ce	27.33S	24.47 E
Taungdwingyi	25	Jd	20.01N	95.33 E
Taunggyi	25	Jd	20.47N	97.02 E
Taungthonlon	25	Jd	24.58N	95.48 E
Taungup	25	Ie	18.51N	94.14 E
Taunton [Eng.-U.K.]	9	Jj	51.01N	3.06W
Taunton [Ma.-U.S.]	44	Le	41.54N	71.06W
Taunus	10	Ef	50.10N	8.15 E
Taunusstein	12	Kd	50.08N	8.10 E
Taupo	61	Eg	38.41S	176.05 E
Taupo, Lake-	61	Eg	38.50S	175.55 E
Tauragė/Taurage	7	Fi	55.16N	22.19 E
Taurage/Tauragė	7	Fi	55.16N	22.19 E
Tauranga	58	Ih	37.42S	176.10 E
Taurianova	14	Kl	38.21N	16.01 E
Taurion	11	Hi	45.53N	1.24 E
Taurisano	14	Mk	39.57N	18.13 E
Tauroa Point	62	Ea	35.10S	173.04 E
Taurus Mountains (EN) = Toros Dağları	21	Ff	37.00N	33.00 E
Tauste	13	Kc	41.55N	1.15W
Tauu Islands	57	Ge	4.45S	157.00 E
Tauz	19	Eg	41.01N	45.35 E
Ţavālesh, Kūhhā-Ye-	24	Mc	38.42N	48.18 E
Tavas [Tur.]	24	Dd	39.54N	30.03 E
Tavas [Tur.]	24	Cd	37.34N	29.04 E
Tavas Ovasi	15	Ll	37.30N	28.55 E
Tavastehus/Hämeenlinna	7	Ff	61.00N	24.27 E
Tavau/Davos	14	Dd	46.47N	9.50 E
Tavda	19	Gd	58.03N	65.15 E
Tavda	21	Id	57.47N	67.16 E
Tavendroua	63b	Cc	16.21S	167.22 E
Taveta	36	Gc	3.24S	37.41 E
Taveuni Island	61	Fc	16.51S	179.58W
Taviano	14	Mk	39.59N	18.05 E
Tavignano	11a	Ba	42.06N	9.33 E
Tavira	13	Eg	37.07N	7.39W
Tavistock	9	Ik	50.33N	4.08W
Tavolara	14	Dj	40.55N	9.40 E
Tavoliere	14	Ji	41.35N	15.25 E
Tavolžan	19	He	52.44N	77.30 E
Tavoy → Dawei	22	Lh	14.05N	98.12 E
Tavričanka	28	Kc	43.20N	131.52 E
Tavropóu, Tekhniti Límni-	15	Ej	39.15N	21.40 E
Tavşan Adalari	15	Jj	39.55N	26.05 E
Tavşanlı	24	Cc	39.35N	29.30 E
Tavua	61	Ec	17.27S	177.51 E
Taw	9	Ij	51.04N	4.11W
Tawakoni, Lake-	45	Ij	32.55N	96.00W
Tawas City	43	Kc	44.16N	83.31W
Tawau	22	Ni	4.15N	117.54 E
Tawfīqiyah	35	Ed	9.26N	31.37 E
Ţawīlah, Juzur-	24	Ei	27.35N	33.46 E
Tawitawi Group	26	He	5.10N	120.15 E
Ţawkar	31	Kg	18.26N	37.44 E
Ţāwūq	24	Ke	35.08N	44.27 E
Tawūq Chāy	24	Ke	34.35N	44.31 E
Ţāwurghā', Sabkhat-	33	Cc	31.10N	15.15 E
Tawzar	32	Ic	33.55N	8.08 E
Taxco de Alarcón	48	Jh	18.33N	99.36W
Taxkorgan	27	Cd	37.47N	75.14 E
Tay	9	Je	56.30N	3.30W
Tay, Firth of-	9	Ke	56.28N	3.00W
Tay, Loch-	9	Ie	56.30N	4.10W
Tayandu, Kepulauan-	26	Jh	5.30S	132.15 E
Tayėgle	35	Ge	4.02N	44.36 E
Taylor [Nb.-U.S.]	45	Gf	41.46N	99.23W
Taylor [Tx.-U.S.]	43	He	30.34N	97.25W
Taylor, Mount-	43	Fd	35.14N	107.37W
Taylorville	45	Lg	39.33N	89.18W
Taymā'	23	Ed	27.38N	38.29 E
Taymyr Peninsula (EN) = Tajmyr, Poluostrov-	21	Mb	76.00N	104.00 E
Tay Ninh	25	Lf	11.18N	106.06 E
Tayside [3]	9	Je	56.30N	3.40W
Taytay	26	Gd	10.49N	119.31 E
Taza [3]	32	Gc	34.00N	4.00W
Taza [Mor.]	31	Ge	34.13N	4.01W
Taza [R.S.F.S.R.]	20	Gf	54.55N	111.05 E
Tāzah Khurmātū	24	Ke	35.18N	44.20 E
Tazawa-Ko	29	Gb	39.43N	140.40 E
Tazawako	29	Gb	39.42N	140.44 E
Tazenakht	32	Fc	30.35N	7.12W
Tazerbo Oasis (EN) = Tāzirbū, Wāḥāt al-	30	Jf	25.45N	21.00 E
Tazewell [Tn.-U.S.]	44	Fg	36.27N	83.34W
Tazewell [Va.-U.S.]	44	Gg	37.07N	81.34W
Tāzīāzet	32	De	20.55N	15.40W
Tazin Lake	42	Ge	59.48N	109.05W
Tāzirbū, Wāḥāt al- = Tazerbo Oasis (EN)	30	Jf	25.45N	21.00 E
Tazlău	15	Jc	46.16N	26.47 E
Tazmalt	13	Qh	36.43N	4.08 E
Tazouikert	34	Ea	21.46N	1.13W
Tazovskaja Guba	17	Qb	69.05N	76.00 E
Tazovski	20	Cc	67.28N	78.42 E
Tazrouk	32	Ie	23.27N	6.14 E
Tazumal	49	Cg	14.00N	89.40W
Tbilisi	6	Kg	41.43N	44.49 E
Tchad = Chad (EN) [1]	31	Ig	15.00N	19.00 E
Tchad, Lac- = Chad, Lake- (EN)	30	Ig	13.20N	14.00 E
Tchamba [Cam.]	34	Hd	8.37N	12.48 E
Tchamba [Togo]	34	Fd	9.02N	1.25 E
Tchibanga	36	Bc	2.51S	11.02 E
Tchien	34	Dd	6.04N	8.08W
Tchigai, Plateau du-	30	If	21.30N	14.50 E
Tchin Tabaraden	34	Gb	15.58N	5.50 E
Tcholliré	34	Hd	8.24N	14.10 E
Tczew	10	Ob	54.06N	18.47 E
Tea, Rio-	54	Ed	0.30S	65.09W
Teaca	15	Hc	46.55N	24.31 E
Teacapán	48	Gf	22.33N	105.45W
Teaiti Point	64p	Bb	21.11S	159.47W
Te Anau	62	Bf	45.25S	167.43 E
Te Anau, Lake-	61	Ci	45.15S	167.45 E
Teano	14	Ii	41.15N	14.04 E
Teapa	48	Mi	17.33N	92.57W
Te Araroa	61	Eg	37.38S	178.22 E
Te Aroha	62	Fb	37.32S	175.42 E
Tea Tree	59	Gd	22.11S	133.17 E
Te Atu Kura	64p	Bb	21.14S	159.45W
Te Awamutu	62	Fc	38.00S	175.19 E
Teberda	16	Lh	43.28N	41.43 E
Tébessa	31	He	35.24N	8.07 E
Tébessa [3]	32	Ic	35.00N	7.45 E
Tébessa, Oued-	14	Bo	35.48N	7.53 E
Tebicuary, Rio- [Par.]	55	Ch	26.36S	58.16W
Tebicuary, Rio- [Par.]	55	Dh	26.26S	56.51W
Tebingtinggi [Indon.]	26	Dg	3.36S	103.05 E
Tebingtinggi [Indon.]	26	Cf	3.20N	99.09 E
Tebulosmta, Gora-	16	Nh	42.33N	45.16 E
Teča	17	Kh	56.17N	62.59 E
Tecate	47	Ab	32.34N	116.38W
Tecer Dağları	24	Gc	39.27N	37.11 E
Techirghiol	15	Le	44.03N	28.36 E
Tecka	56	Ff	43.29S	70.48W
Tecklenburg	12	Jb	52.13N	7.50 E
Tecomán	47	De	18.55N	103.53W
Tecomate, Laguna-	48	Ji	16.45N	99.25W
Tecoripa	48	Ec	28.37N	109.57W
Tecpan de Galeana	47	De	17.15N	100.41W
Tecuala	47	Cd	22.23N	105.27W
Tecuci	15	Kd	45.52N	27.25 E
Tedegra	35	Ba	20.46N	19.34 E
Tedori-Gawa	29	Ec	36.29N	136.28 E
Tedžen	21	If	37.24N	60.38 E
Tedženstroj	19	Gh	36.54N	60.53 E
Teeli	20	Ef	50.57N	90.18 E
Teenuse Jõgi/Tenuze	7	Jf	58.44N	23.58 E
Tees	9	Lg	54.34N	1.16W
Tees Bay	9	Lg	54.35N	1.05W
Teesside → Middlesbrough	6	Fe	54.35N	1.14W
Tefé	53	Jf	3.22S	64.42W
Tefé, Rio-	54	Fd	3.35S	64.47W
Tefedest	32	Ie	24.40N	5.30 E
Tefenni	24	Cd	37.18N	29.47 E
Tegal	22	Mj	6.52S	109.08 E
Tegea (EN) = Teyéa	15	Fl	37.27N	22.25 E
Tegelen	12	Ic	51.20N	6.08 E
Tegernsee	10	Hi	47.43N	11.46 E
Tegina	34	Gc	10.04N	6.11 E
Tégoua	63b	Ca	13.15S	166.37 E
Tegucigalpa	39	Kh	14.06N	87.13W
Teguidda I-n-Tessoum	34	Gb	17.26N	6.39 E
Teguldet	20	De	57.20N	88.20 E
Tehachapi	46	Fi	35.08N	118.27W
Tehachapi Mountains	46	Fi	34.56N	118.40W
Tehamiyam	35	Fb	18.20N	36.32 E
Te Hapua	61	Df	34.30S	172.55 E
Tehaupoo	65e	Fc	17.49S	149.18W
Tehek Lake	42	Hd	64.55N	95.30W
Téhini	34	Ed	9.36N	3.40W
Tehi-n-Isser	32	Ie	24.48N	8.08 E
Tehoru	26	Ig	3.23S	129.30 E
Tehrān	22	Hf	35.40N	51.26 E
Tehrān → Markazi [3]	23	Hb	35.30N	51.30 E
Tehuacán	47	Ee	18.27N	97.23W
Tehuantepec	47	Ee	16.20N	95.14W
Tehuantepec, Golfo de- = Tehuantepec, Gulf of- (EN)	38	Jh	16.00N	94.50W
Tehuantepec, Gulf of- (EN) = Tehuantepec, Golfo de-	38	Jh	16.00N	94.50W
Tehuantepec, Isthmus of- (EN) = Tehuantepec, Istmo de-	38	Jh	17.00N	94.30W
Tehuantepec, Istmo de- = Tehuantepec, Isthmus of- (EN)	38	Jh	17.00N	94.30W
Tehuantepec Ridge (EN)	47	Ef	13.30N	98.00W
Tehuata Atoll	57	Mf	16.50S	141.55W
Teiga Plateau	35	Db	15.38N	25.40 E
Teignmouth	9	Jk	50.33N	3.30W
Teili/Delet	8	Id	60.15N	20.35 E
Teith	9	Ie	56.14N	4.20W
Teiuş	15	Gc	46.12N	23.41 E
Teixeira Pinto	34	Bc	12.04N	16.02W
Teja	20	Ed	60.27N	92.38 E
Tejkovo	19	Ed	56.50N	40.34 E
Tejo = Tagus (EN)	5	Fh	38.40N	9.24W
Teju	25	Jc	27.55N	96.10 E
Te Kaha	62	Gb	37.44S	177.41 E
Te Kao	62	Ea	34.39S	172.58 E
Tekapo, Lake-	62	De	43.50S	170.30 E
Te Karaka	62	Gc	38.28S	177.52 E
Tekax	48	Og	20.12N	89.17W
Teke	15	Mh	41.04N	29.39 E
Teke	15	Jh	41.21N	26.57 E
Teke Burun [Tur.]	15	Ji	40.02N	26.10 E
Teke Burun [Tur.]	15	Jk	38.05N	26.36 E
Tekeli	19	Hg	44.48N	78.57 E
Tekes	27	Dc	43.10N	81.43 E
Tekes He	27	Dc	43.35N	82.30 E
Tekeze	35	Fc	14.20N	35.50 E
Tekija	15	Fe	44.41N	22.25 E
Tekiliktag	27	Dd	36.35N	80.20 E
Tekirdağ	23	Ca	40.59N	27.31 E
Tekman	24	Ic	39.38N	41.31 E
Te Kopuru	62	Eb	36.02S	173.55 E
Te Kou	64p	Bb	21.14S	159.46W
Tekouiat	32	He	22.20N	2.31 E
Tekro	35	Cb	19.34N	20.57 E
Te Kuiti	62	Fc	38.20S	175.10 E
Tela	47	Ge	15.44N	87.27W
Telagh	32	Gc	34.47N	0.34W
Telataï	34	Fb	16.31N	1.30 E
Telavåg	7	Af	60.16N	4.49 E
Telavi	19	Eg	41.55N	45.29 E
Tel Aviv-Yafo	22	Ff	32.04N	34.46 E
Telč	10	Lg	49.11N	15.27 E
Telchac Puerto	48	Og	21.21N	89.16W
Telciu	15	Hb	47.26N	24.24 E
Tele	36	Db	2.48N	23.54 E
Teleac	15	Hc	46.41N	24.48 E
Telečkoje Ozero	20	Df	51.30N	87.45 E
Telefomin	60	Ci	5.08S	141.31 E
Telegraph Creek	42	Ee	57.54N	131.09W
Telekitonga	65b	Bb	20.24S	174.32W
Telekivavu'u	65b	Bb	20.19S	174.32W
Telêmaco Borba	55	Gg	24.23S	50.28W
Telemark [2]	7	Bg	59.30N	8.40 E
Telemark	8	Ce	59.30N	8.45 E
Telén	56	Ge	36.16S	65.30W
Telen	26	Gf	0.26N	116.42 E
Telenešty	15	Lb	47.30N	28.16 E
Teleno	13	Fb	42.21N	6.23W
Teleorman	15	If	43.52N	25.26 E
Teleorman [2]	15	If	44.10N	25.15 E
Telerhteba, Djebel-	32	Ie	24.10N	6.51 E
Telescope Peak	46	Gh	36.10N	117.05W
Telescope Point	51p	Bb	12.08N	61.36W
Telese	14	Ii	41.13N	14.32 E
Teles Pires, Rio- o São Manuel, Rio-	52	Kf	7.21S	58.03W
Telfän, Hadjer-	35	Bc	12.05N	18.57 E
Telford	9	Ki	52.40N	2.30W
Telgte	12	Jc	51.59N	7.47 E
Télimélé	34	Cc	10.54N	13.02W
Teljo, Jabal-	35	Dc	14.42N	25.56 E
Tell al Ubaid	24	Lg	30.59N	46.01 E
Tellaro	14	Jn	36.50N	15.06 E
Tell Atlas (EN) = Atlas Tellien	30	He	36.00N	2.00 E
Tell City	44	Dg	37.57N	86.46W
Teller	40	Fc	65.16N	166.22W
Telok Anson	26	Df	4.02N	101.01 E
Teloloapan	48	Jh	18.21N	99.51W
Telposiz, Gora-	5	Lc	63.54N	59.10 E
Telsen	56	Gf	42.24S	66.57W
Telšiai/Telšjaj	19	Cd	55.59N	22.17 E
Telšjaj/Telšiai	19	Cd	55.59N	22.17 E
Teltow	10	Jd	52.24N	13.16 E
Telukbetung	22	Mj	5.27S	105.16 E
Telukbutun	26	Ef	4.13N	108.12 E
Telukdalem	26	Cf	0.34N	97.49 E
Tema	31	Gh	5.37N	0.01W
Temacine	32	Ic	33.01N	6.01 E
Te Manga	64p	Bb	21.13S	159.45W
Tematangi Atoll	57	Mg	21.41S	140.40W
Tembenči	20	Ed	64.36N	99.58 E
Tembi	15	Fj	39.53N	22.35 E
Tembilahan	26	Dg	0.19S	103.09 E
Temblador	50	Eh	8.59N	62.44W
Tembleque	13	Ie	39.42N	3.30W
Temblor Range	46	Fi	35.30N	119.55W
Tembo	36	Cd	7.42S	17.17 E
Tembo, Chutes-	30	Ii	8.50S	15.20 E
Tembo, Mont-	36	Bb	1.50N	12.00 E
Tembué	37	Eb	14.51S	32.50 E
Teme	9	Ki	52.09N	2.18W
Temerin	15	Cd	45.25N	19.53 E
Temerloh	26	Df	3.27N	102.25 E
Teminabuan	26	Jg	1.26S	132.01 E
Temir	19	Ff	49.08N	57.09 E
Temir	16	Te	48.31N	57.29 E
Temirlanovka	18	Gc	42.36N	69.17 E
Temirtau	22	Jd	50.05N	72.56 E
Témiscaming	44	Hb	46.44N	79.06W
Témiscouata, Lac-	44	Mb	47.40N	68.50W
Temki	35	Bc	11.29N	18.13 E
Temnikov	7	Ki	54.40N	43.13 E
Temo	14	Cj	40.17N	8.28 E
Temoe, Ile-	57	Ng	23.20S	134.29W
Temores	48	Ed	27.16N	108.15W
Tempe	46	Jj	33.25N	111.56W
Tempio Pausania	14	Dj	40.54N	9.06 E
Temple	43	He	31.06N	97.21W
Templeman, Mount-	46	Ga	50.43N	117.14W
Templemore/An Teampall Mór	9	Fi	52.48N	7.50W
Templin	10	Jc	53.07N	13.30 E
Tempoal, Rio-	48	Jg	21.47N	98.27W
Tempué	36	Ce	13.27S	18.53 E
Temrjuk	16	Jg	45.15N	37.23 E
Temse/Tamise	12	Gc	51.08N	4.13 E
Temuco	53	Ii	38.44S	72.36W
Temuka	62	Df	44.15S	171.16 E
Tena	54	Cd	0.59S	77.48W
Tenacatita, Bahia de-	48	Gh	19.10N	104.50W
Tenala/Tenhola	8	Jd	60.04N	23.18 E
Tenāli	25	Ge	16.15N	80.35 E
Tenancingo de Degollado	48	Jh	18.58N	99.36W
Tenasserim	25	Jf	12.05N	99.01 E
Tenasserim	25	Jf	12.24N	98.37 E
Tenasserim	21	Lh	12.35N	97.52 E
Tenby	9	Ij	51.41N	4.43W
Tence	11	Ki	45.07N	4.17 E
Tench Island	60	Eh	1.38S	150.42 E
Tenda, Col di-	14	Bf	44.09N	7.34 E
Tendaho	35	Gc	11.38N	41.00 E
Tende	11	Nj	44.05N	7.36 E
Tende, Col de-	14	Bf	44.09N	7.34 E
Ten Degree Channel	21	Lh	10.00N	92.30 E
Tendō	29	Gb	38.22N	140.22 E
Tendrara	32	Gc	33.03N	2.00W
Tendre, Mont-	14	Ad	46.36N	6.19 E
Tendrovskaja Kosa	16	Gf	46.15N	31.45 E
Ténenkou	34	Ec	14.28N	4.55W
Tenente Lira, Rio-	55	Db	15.56S	57.39W
Ténéré	30	Ig	17.35N	10.55 E
Tenéré, 'Erg du-	34	Hb	17.35N	10.55 E
Tenerife	30	Ff	28.19N	16.34W
Ténès	32	Hb	36.31N	1.18 E
Ténès, Cap-	13	Nh	36.33N	1.21 E
Teng	25	Je	19.52N	97.45 E
Tengah, Kepulauan-	26	Gh	7.30S	117.30 E
Tengchong	27	Gg	24.59N	98.32 E
Te Nggano, Lake-	60	Gj	11.45S	160.25 E
Tenggarong	26	Gg	0.24S	116.58 E
Tengger Shamo	21	Mf	38.00N	104.10 E
Tengiz, Ozero-	21	Id	50.25N	69.00 E
Tengréla	34	Dc	10.29N	6.24W
Tengréla [3]	34	Dc	10.27N	6.25W
Tengxian [China]	27	Jg	23.18N	110.49 E
Tengxian [China]	28	Dg	35.07N	117.10 E
Tenhola/Tenala	8	Jd	60.04N	23.18 E
Teniente General Rosendo M. Fraga	55	Af	23.45S	62.09W
Tenkäsi	25	Fg	8.58N	77.18 E
Tenke	36	Ee	10.33S	26.08 E
Tenkeli	20	Jb	70.01N	140.55 E
Tenkodogo	34	Ec	11.47N	0.22W
Tenna	14	Hg	43.14N	13.47 E
Tennant Creek	58	Ef	19.40S	134.10 E
Tennessee	38	Kf	37.04N	88.33W
Tennessee [2]	43	Jd	35.50N	85.30W
Tenneville	12	Hd	50.06N	5.32 E
Tenioki	7	Ga	70.28N	28.18 E
Tenom	26	Ge	5.08N	115.57 E
Tenosique de Pino Suárez	47	Fe	17.29N	91.26W
Tenri	29	Dd	34.36N	135.49 E
Tenryū	29	Ed	34.52N	137.47 E
Tenryū-Gawa	28	Ng	34.35N	137.48 E
Tensift	32	Fc	32.02N	9.21W
Ten Sleep	46	Ld	44.02N	107.27W
Tenterden	12	Cc	51.03N	0.42 E

Index Symbols

[1] Independent Nation
[2] State, Region
[3] District, County
[4] Municipality
[5] Colony, Dependency
Continent
Physical Region

Historical or Cultural Region
Mount, Mountain
Volcano
Hill
Mountains, Mountain Range
Hills, Escarpment
Plateau, Upland

Pass, Gap
Plain, Lowland
Delta
Salt Flat
Valley, Canyon
Crater, Cave
Karst Features

Depression
Polder
Desert, Dunes
Forest, Woods
Heath, Steppe
Oasis
Cape, Point

Coast, Beach
Cliff
Peninsula
Isthmus
Sandbank
Island
Atoll

Rock, Reef
Islands, Archipelago
Rocks, Reefs
Coral Reef
Well, Spring
Geyser
River, Stream

Waterfall Rapids
River Mouth, Estuary
Lake
Salt Lake
Intermittent Lake
Reservoir
Swamp, Pond

Canal
Glacier
Ice Shelf, Pack Ice
Ocean
Sea
Gulf, Bay
Strait, Fjord

Lagoon
Bank
Seamount
Tablemount
Ridge
Shelf
Basin

Escarpment, Sea Scarp
Fracture
Trench, Abyss
National Park, Reserve
Point of Interest
Recreation Site
Cave, Cavern

Historic Site
Ruins
Wall, Walls
Church, Abbey
Temple
Scientific Station
Airport

Port
Lighthouse
Mine
Tunnel
Dam, Bridge

Tenterfield 59 Ke 29.03 S 152.01 E
Tenuku 25 Ge 81.40 N 16.45 E
Tenuze/Teenuse Jōgi 7 Jf 58.44 N 23.58 E
Ten-Zan 29 Be 33.20 N 130.08 E
Teocaltiche 48 Hg 21.26 N 102.35 W
Teodelina 55 Bl 34.11 S 61.32 W
Teodoro Sampaio 55 Ff 22.31 S 52.10 W
Teófilo Otoni 53 Lg 17.51 S 41.30 W
Teotepec, Cerro- 38 Ih 16.50 N 100.50 W
Teotihuacan 47 Ee 19.44 N 98.50 W
Teotilán del Camino 48 Kh 18.08 N 97.05 W
Tepa [Indon.] 26 Ih 7.52 S 129.31 E
Tepa [W.F.] 64h Bb 13.19 S 176.09 W
Te Pae Roa Ngake o Tuko 64n Bb 10.23 S 161.00 W
Tepako, Pointe- 64h Bb 13.16 S 176.08 W
Tepalcatepec, Río- 48 Ih 18.35 N 101.59 W
Tepa Point 64k Bb 19.07 S 169.56 W
Tepatitlán de Morelos 48 Hg 20.49 N 102.44 W
Tepehuanes 47 Cc 25.21 N 105.44 W
Tepehuanes, Río- 48 Ge 25.11 N 105.26 W
Tepehuanes, Sierra de- 47 Cc 25.00 N 105.40 W
Tepelena 15 Di 40.18 N 20.01 E
Tepi 35 Fd 7.03 N 35.30 E
Tepic 39 Ig 21.30 N 104.54 W
Teplá 10 Ig 49.59 N 12.52 E
Teplá 10 If 50.14 N 12.52 E
Teplice 10 Jf 50.39 N 13.50 E
Tepoca, Bahía de- 48 Cb 30.15 N 112.50 W
Tepopa, Cabo- 48 Cc 29.20 N 112.25 W
Te Puka 64n Ac 10.26 S 161.02 W
Te Puke 62 Gb 37.47 S 176.20 E
Tequepa, Bahía de- 48 Ii 17.17 N 101.05 W
Tequila 48 Hg 20.54 N 103.47 W
Tequisquiapan 48 Jg 20.31 N 99.52 W
Ter 13 Pb 42.01 N 3.12 E
Téra 31 Hg 14.01 N 0.45 E
Tera [Port.] 13 Df 38.56 N 8.03 W
Tera [Sp.] 13 Gc 41.54 N 5.44 W
Teradomari 29 Fc 37.38 N 138.45 E
Terai 21 Kg 26.30 N 85.15 E
Teraina Island (Washington) 57 Kd 4.43 N 160.24 W
Terakeka 35 Ed 5.26 N 31.45 E
Teramo 14 Hh 42.39 N 13.42 E
Terampa 26 Ef 3.14 N 106.14 E
Ter Apel, Vlagtwedde- 12 Jb 52.52 N 7.06 E
Terborg, Wisch- 12 Ic 51.55 N 6.22 E
Tercan 24 Ic 39.47 N 40.24 E
Terceira 30 Ee 38.43 N 27.13 W
Tercero, Río- 56 Hd 32.55 S 62.19 W
Terebovlja 16 De 49.18 N 25.42 E
Terehovka 28 Kc 43.38 N 131.55 E
Terek 16 Nh 43.29 N 44.08 E
Terek 5 Kg 43.44 N 47.30 E
Térékolé 34 Cb 15.07 N 10.53 W
Terek-Saj 18 Hd 41.29 N 71.13 E
Terenos 55 Ee 20.26 S 54.50 W
Teresa Cristina 55 Gg 24.48 S 51.07 W
Teresina 53 Lf 5.05 S 42.49 W
Teresinha 54 Hc 0.58 N 52.02 W
Tereška 16 Od 51.50 N 46.45 E
Terespol 10 Td 52.05 N 23.36 E
Teressa 25 Ig 8.15 N 93.10 E
Teresva 16 Cf 47.59 N 23.15 E
Terevaka, Cerro- 65d Ab 27.05 S 109.23 W
Tergnier 11 Je 49.39 N 3.18 E
Terhazza 34 Ea 23.36 N 4.56 W
Teriberka 7 Ib 69.10 N 35.10 E
Teriberka 7 Ib 69.09 N 35.08 E
Terlingua Creek 45 El 29.10 N 103.36 W
Termas de Río Hondo 56 Hc 27.29 S 64.52 W
Terme 24 Gb 41.12 N 36.59 E
Termez 22 If 37.14 N 67.16 E
Termini Imerese 14 Hm 37.59 N 13.42 E
Termini Imerese, Golfo di- 14 Hl 38.00 N 13.45 E
Terminillo 14 Hh 42.28 N 13.01 E
Términos, Laguna de- 47 Fe 18.37 N 91.33 W
Termit, Massif de- 34 Hb 16.15 N 11.17 E
Termit-Kaoboul 34 Hb 15.43 N 11.37 E
Termoli 14 Ii 42.00 N 15.00 E
Termonde/Dendermonde 12 Gc 51.02 N 4.07 E
Ternaard, Westdongeradeel- 12 Ha 53.23 N 5.58 E
Ternate 25 If 0.48 N 127.24 E
Ternej 20 Ig 45.05 N 136.35 E
Terneuzen 11 Jc 51.20 N 3.50 E
Terni 14 Gh 42.34 N 12.37 E
Ternitz 14 Kc 47.43 N 16.02 E
Ternois 12 Ed 50.25 N 2.19 E
Ternopol 6 If 49.34 N 25.38 E
Ternopolskaja Oblast [3] 19 Cf 49.20 N 25.35 E
Terpenija, Mys- 20 Jg 48.38 N 144.40 E
Terpenija, Zaliv- 21 Qe 49.00 N 143.30 E
Terrace 42 Ef 54.31 N 128.35 W
Terrace Bay 45 Mb 48.47 N 87.09 W
Terracina 14 Hi 41.17 N 13.15 E
Terra de Basto 13 Ec 41.25 N 8.00 W
Terra Firma 37 Ce 25.36 S 23.24 E
Terråk 7 Cd 65.05 N 12.25 E
Terralba 14 Ck 39.43 N 8.39 E
Terra Rica 55 Ff 22.43 S 52.38 W
Terrebonne Bay 45 Kl 29.09 N 90.35 W
Terre-de-Bas 51e Ac 15.51 N 61.39 W
Terre-de-Haut 51e Ac 15.58 N 61.35 W
Terre Froides 11 Li 45.30 N 5.30 E
Terre Haute 43 Jd 39.28 N 87.24 W
Terrell 45 Hj 32.44 N 96.17 W
Terre Plaine 11 Jg 47.25 N 4.00 E
Terril 13 Gh 37.00 N 5.11 W
Territoire de Belfort [3] 11 Mg 47.45 N 7.00 E
Terruca 13 Fc 41.45 N 6.25 W
Terry 46 Mc 46.47 N 105.19 W
Tersa 16 Nd 50.46 N 44.42 E
Terschelling 12 Ha 53.21 N 5.13 E
Terschelling 11 La 53.24 N 5.20 E
Terschelling-West-Terschelling 12 Ha 53.21 N 5.13 E
Tersef 35 Bc 12.55 N 16.49 E
Terskej-Alatau, Hrebet- 19 Hg 42.10 N 78.45 E
Terski Bereg 7 Jc 66.10 N 39.30 E
Tersko-Kumski Kanal 16 Ng 44.47 N 44.37 E
Terter 16 Oi 40.27 N 47.16 E
Teruel 13 Kd 40.21 N 1.06 W
Teruel [3] 13 Ld 40.40 N 0.40 W
Tervakoski 8 Kd 60.48 N 24.37 E
Tervel 15 Kf 43.45 N 27.24 E
Tervo 8 Lb 62.57 N 26.45 E
Tervola 7 Fc 66.05 N 24.48 E
Tes 27 Fa 50.27 N 93.30 E
Teša 7 Ki 55.38 N 42.10 E
Tesalia 54 Cc 2.29 N 75.44 W
Tesaret 32 Hd 25.40 N 2.43 E
Tesdrero, Cerro- 48 Hf 22.47 N 103.04 W
Teseney 35 Fb 15.07 N 36.40 E
Teshekpuk Lake 40 Ib 70.35 N 153.30 W
Teshikaga 28 Rc 43.29 N 144.28 E
Teshio 28 Pb 44.53 N 141.44 E
Teshio-Dake 28 Qc 43.58 N 142.50 E
Teshio-Gawa 28 Pb 44.53 N 141.44 E
Teshio-Sanchi 29a Ba 44.20 N 142.00 E
Tesijn → Tesijn Gol 21 Ld 50.28 N 93.04 E
Tesijn Gol (Tesijn) 21 Ld 50.28 N 93.04 E
Teslić 14 Lf 44.37 N 17.52 E
Teslin 42 Ed 61.34 N 134.50 W
Teslin 42 Ed 60.09 N 132.45 W
Teslin Lake 42 Ed 60.00 N 132.30 W
Teslui 15 He 44.09 N 24.29 E
Tesocoma 48 Ed 27.41 N 109.16 W
Tesouras, Rio- 55 Gb 14.36 S 50.51 W
Tesouro 55 Fc 16.04 S 53.34 W
Tessala, Monts du- 13 Li 35.15 N 0.45 W
Tessalit 31 Hf 20.14 N 0.59 E
Tessaoua 34 Gc 13.45 N 7.59 E
Tessenderlo 12 Hc 51.04 N 5.05 E
Test 9 Lk 50.55 N 1.29 W
Test, Tizi n'- 32 Fc 30.50 N 8.20 W
Testa, Capo- 14 Di 41.14 N 9.08 E
Têt 11 Jl 42.44 N 3.02 E
Tetari, Cerro- 49 Ki 9.59 N 72.55 W
Tetas, Punta- 56 Fc 23.31 S 70.38 W
Tete 31 Kj 16.10 S 33.36 E
Tete [3] 37 Ec 15.30 S 33.00 E
Te Teko 62 Gc 38.02 S 176.48 E
Tetepare Island 63a Cc 8.45 S 157.35 E
Téterchen 12 Ie 49.14 N 6.34 E
Tetere 63a Ec 9.25 S 160.15 E
Teterev 16 Gd 51.01 N 30.08 E
Teterow 10 Ic 53.47 N 12.34 E
Teteven 15 Hg 42.55 N 24.16 E
Tetiaroa Atoll 57 Mf 17.05 S 149.32 W
Tetijev 16 Fe 49.23 N 29.41 E
Tetjuši 7 Li 54.57 N 48.49 E
Teton Peak 46 Ic 47.55 N 112.48 W
Teton Range 46 Je 43.50 N 110.55 W
Teton River 46 Jc 47.56 N 110.31 W
Tétouan 31 Ge 35.34 N 5.22 W
Tétouan [3] 32 Fb 35.35 N 5.30 W
Tetovo 15 Dg 42.01 N 20.59 E
Tetri-Ckaro 16 Ni 41.33 N 44.27 E
Teuco, Río- 55 Bg 25.38 S 60.12 W
Teufelskopf 12 Ie 49.36 N 6.49 E
Teulada 14 Cl 38.58 N 8.46 E
Teulada, Capo- 5 Gh 38.52 N 8.38 E
Téul de Gonzales Ortega 48 Hg 21.28 N 103.29 W
Teun, Pulau- 26 Ih 6.59 S 129.08 E
Teupasenti 49 Df 14.13 N 86.42 W
Teuquito, Río- 55 Bg 24.22 S 61.09 W
Teuri-Tō 29a Ba 44.25 N 141.20 E
Teutoburger Wald 10 Ee 52.10 N 8.15 E
Teuva/Ostermark 7 Ee 62.29 N 21.44 E
Teuz 15 Ec 46.39 N 21.33 E
Tevai 63c Bb 11.37 S 166.55 E
Tevaïtoa 65e Db 16.46 S 151.28 W
Tevere = Tiber (EN) 5 Hg 41.44 N 12.14 E
Teverya 24 Ff 32.47 N 35.32 E
Teviot 9 Kf 55.36 N 2.26 W
Tevli 10 Ud 52.19 N 24.23 E
Tevriz 19 Hd 57.34 N 72.24 E
Tevšruleh 27 Hb 47.25 N 101.55 E
Te Waewae Bay 62 Bg 46.15 S 167.30 E
Tewkesbury 9 Kj 51.59 N 2.09 W
Têwo (Dêngkagoin) 27 He 34.03 N 103.21 E
Texada Island 46 Cb 49.40 N 124.24 W
Texarkana [Ar.-U.S.] 43 Ie 33.26 N 94.02 W
Texarkana [Tx.-U.S.] 39 Jf 33.26 N 94.03 W
Texas 59 Ke 28.51 S 151.11 E
Texas [2] 43 He 31.30 N 99.00 W
Texas City 43 If 29.23 N 94.54 W
Texcoco 48 Jh 19.31 N 98.53 W
Texel 12 Ga 53.03 N 4.47 E
Texel 11 Ka 53.05 N 4.45 E
Texel-De Koog 12 Ga 53.07 N 4.46 E
Texel-Den Burg 12 Ga 53.03 N 4.47 E
Texoma, Lake- 43 He 33.55 N 96.37 W
Teyéa = Tegea (EN) 15 Fl 37.27 N 22.25 E
Teza 7 Jh 56.32 N 41.57 E
Teze-Jel 19 Gh 37.55 N 60.22 E
Teziutlán 47 Ee 19.49 N 97.21 W
Tezpur 25 Ic 26.38 N 92.48 E
Tha-anne 42 Id 60.31 N 94.37 W
Thabana Ntlenyana 30 Jk 29.30 S 29.15 E
Thabazimbi 37 Dd 24.41 S 27.21 E
Thai, Ao- = Thailand, Gulf of- (EN) 21 Mh 10.00 N 102.00 E
Thai Binh 25 Ld 20.27 N 106.20 E
Thailand (EN) = Muang Thai [1] 22 Mh 15.00 N 100.00 E
Thailand, Gulf of- (EN) = Thai, Ao- 21 Mh 10.00 N 102.00 E
Thai Nguyen 25 Ld 21.36 N 105.50 E
Thal 25 Eb 31.30 N 71.40 E
Thālith, Ash Shallāl ath- = Third Cataract (EN) 30 Kg 19.49 N 30.19 E
Thamad Bū Ḩashīshah 33 Cd 25.50 N 18.05 E
Thamarīd 35 Ib 17.39 N 54.02 E
Thame 12 Bc 51.45 N 0.59 W
Thames 61 Eg 37.08 S 175.33 E
Thames 5 Ge 51.28 N 0.43 E
Thames River 44 Fd 42.19 N 82.28 W
Thamūd 23 Gf 17.15 N 49.54 E
Thāna 22 Jh 19.12 N 72.58 E
Thandaung 25 Je 19.04 N 96.41 E
Thanh Hoa 22 Mh 19.48 N 105.46 E
Thanh Pho Ho Chi Minh (Saigon) 22 Mh 10.45 N 106.40 E
Thanjāvūr 25 Ff 10.48 N 79.08 E
Thanlwin = Salween (EN) 21 Lg 16.31 N 97.37 E
Thann 11 Ng 47.49 N 7.05 E
Thaon-les-Vosges 11 Mf 48.15 N 6.25 E
Thap Sakae 25 Jf 11.14 N 99.31 E
Thar/Great Indian Desert 21 Ig 27.00 N 70.00 E
Thargomindah 59 Ie 28.00 S 143.49 E
Tharrawaddy 25 Je 17.39 N 95.48 E
Tharros 14 Ck 39.54 N 8.28 E
Tharthār, Baḩr ath- 23 Fc 33.59 N 43.12 E
Tharthār, Wādī ath- 23 Fc 33.59 N 43.12 E
Thasi Gang Dzong 25 Ic 27.19 N 91.34 E
Thásos 5 Ig 40.49 N 24.42 E
Thásos 15 Hi 40.47 N 24.43 E
Thásou, Dhiavlos- 15 Hi 40.49 N 24.42 E
Thathlīth, Wādī- 33 He 20.25 N 44.55 E
Thau, Bassin de- 11 Jk 43.23 N 3.36 E
Thaxted 12 Cc 51.57 N 0.22 E
Thaya 10 Mh 48.37 N 16.56 E
Thayetchaung 25 Jf 13.52 N 98.16 E
Thayetmyo 25 Je 19.19 N 95.11 E
Thaywthadangyi Kyun 25 Jf 12.20 N 98.00 E
The Alberga River 59 He 27.06 S 135.33 E
The Aldermen Islands 62 Gb 37.00 S 176.05 E
Thebai = Thebes (EN) 33 Fd 25.43 N 32.35 E
Thebes (EN) = Thebai 33 Fd 25.43 N 32.35 E
Thebes (EN) = Thívai 15 Gk 38.19 N 23.19 E
The Black Sugarloaf 59 Kf 31.20 S 151.33 E
The Borders 9 Kf 55.35 N 2.50 W
The Bottom 50 Ed 17.38 N 63.15 W
The Broads 9 Oi 52.40 N 1.30 E
The Cheviot 9 Kf 55.28 N 2.09 W
The Cheviot Hills 9 Kf 55.30 N 2.10 W
The Crane 51q Bb 13.06 N 59.26 W
The Dalles 43 Cb 45.36 N 121.10 W
Thedford 43 Gc 41.59 N 100.35 W
The Entrance 59 Kf 33.21 S 151.30 E
The Everglades 43 Kf 26.00 N 81.00 W
The Fens 9 Mi 5.24 N 0.02 W
The Gap 46 Jh 36.25 N 111.30 W
The Granites 59 Gd 20.35 S 130.21 E
The Hague (EN) = Den Haag/'s-Gravenhage 6 Ge 52.06 N 4.18 E
The Little Minch 9 Gd 57.35 N 6.55 W
Thelle 12 De 49.23 N 1.51 E
Thelon 38 Jc 64.16 N 96.05 W
The Macumba River 57 Eg 27.45 S 136.50 E
The Merse 9 Kf 55.50 N 2.10 W
The Naze 12 Dc 51.42 N 1.47 E
The Neales River 59 He 28.08 S 136.47 E
The Needles 9 Lk 50.39 N 1.34 W
Theniet el Had 13 Oi 35.32 N 2.01 E
Theodore 59 Kd 24.57 S 150.05 E
Theológos 15 Hi 40.40 N 24.42 E
The Pas 39 Id 53.50 N 101.15 W
The Pillories 51n Bb 12.54 N 61.12 W
Thérain 11 Ie 49.15 N 2.27 E
Thermaïkós Kólpos = Salonika, Gulf of- (EN) 5 Ig 40.20 N 22.45 E
Thermopílai = Thermopylae (EN) 15 Fk 38.48 N 22.32 E
Thermopolis 43 Fc 43.39 N 108.13 W
Thermopylae (EN) = Thermopílai 15 Fk 38.48 N 22.32 E
Thérouanne 12 Ed 50.38 N 2.15 E
The Round Mountain 59 Kf 30.27 S 152.16 E
The Sandlings 9 Oi 52.10 N 1.30 E
Thesiger Bay 42 Fb 71.30 N 124.00 W
The Slot → New Georgia Sound 60 Fi 8.00 S 158.10 E
The Solent Spithead 9 Lk 50.46 N 1.20 W
Thessalía [2] 15 Fj 39.30 N 22.10 E
Thessalía = Thessaly (EN) 5 Ih 39.30 N 22.10 E
Thessalía = Thessaly (EN) 15 Fj 39.30 N 22.10 E
Thessalon 44 Fb 46.15 N 83.34 W
Thessaloníki = Salonika (EN) 6 Ig 40.38 N 22.56 E
Thessaly (EN) = Thessalía 15 Fj 39.30 N 22.10 E
Thessaly (EN) = Thessalía 5 Ih 39.30 N 22.10 E
The Stevenson River 59 He 27.06 S 135.33 E
Thet 12 Cb 52.24 N 0.45 E
Thetford 9 Ni 52.25 N 0.45 E
Thetford Mines 44 Lb 46.05 N 71.18 W
The Twins 62 Ed 41.14 S 172.40 E
Theux 12 Hd 50.33 N 5.49 E
The Valley 47 Le 18.03 N 63.04 W
The Warburton River 59 He 27.55 S 137.28 E
The Wash 5 Ge 52.55 N 0.15 E
The Weald 9 Nj 51.05 N 0.05 E
The Witties 49 Ff 14.10 N 82.45 W
The Wolds 9 Mh 53.20 N 0.10 W
Thiaucourt-Regniéville 12 Hf 48.57 N 5.52 E
Thiberville 12 Ce 49.08 N 0.27 E
Thibodaux 45 Kl 29.48 N 90.49 W
Thief River Falls 43 Hb 48.07 N 96.10 W
Thiel Mountains 66 Pg 85.15 S 91.00 W
Thiene 14 Fe 45.42 N 11.29 E
Thiérache, Collines de la- 11 Je 49.48 N 3.55 E
Thiers 11 Ji 45.51 N 3.34 E
Thiès 31 Fg 14.48 N 16.56 W
Thiès [3] 34 Bc 14.45 N 16.50 W
Thiesi 14 Cj 40.31 N 8.43 E
Thika 36 Gc 1.03 S 37.05 E
Thikombia 61 Fc 15.44 S 179.55 W
Thimerais 11 Hf 48.40 N 1.20 E
Thimphu 22 Kg 27.28 N 89.39 E
Thio 61 Cd 21.37 S 166.14 E
Thionville 11 Me 49.22 N 6.10 E
Thiou 34 Ec 13.48 N 2.40 W
Thira 15 Im 36.25 N 25.26 E
Thíra = Thira (EN) 15 Im 36.24 N 25.26 E
Thira (EN) = Thíra 15 Im 36.24 N 25.26 E
Thirasia 15 Im 36.25 N 25.20 E
Third Cataract (EN) = Thālith, Ash Shallāl ath- 30 Kg 19.49 N 30.19 E
Thirsk 9 Lg 54.14 N 1.20 W
Thisted 7 Bh 56.57 N 8.42 E
Thithia 63d Cb 17.45 S 179.18 W
Thiu Khao Phetchabun 25 Ke 16.20 N 100.55 E
Thívai = Thebes (EN) 15 Gk 38.19 N 23.19 E
Thiviers 11 Gi 45.25 N 0.55 E
Thlewiaza 42 Id 60.28 N 94.42 W
Thoa 42 Gd 60.31 N 109.45 W
Tho Chu, Dao- 25 Kg 9.00 N 103.50 E
Thoen 25 Je 17.41 N 99.14 E
Tholen 12 Gc 51.32 N 4.13 E
Tholen 11 Kc 51.35 N 4.05 E
Tholey 12 Je 49.29 N 7.04 E
Thomasset, Rocher- 57 Nf 10.21 S 138.25 W
Thomaston 44 Ei 32.54 N 84.20 W
Thomasville [Al.-U.S.] 44 Dj 32.18 N 87.47 W
Thomasville [Ga.-U.S.] 43 Ke 30.50 N 83.59 W
Thomasville [N.C.-U.S.] 44 Gh 35.53 N 80.05 W
Thompson 42 He 55.45 N 97.45 W
Thompson Falls 46 Hc 47.36 N 115.21 W
Thompson River 45 Jg 39.45 N 93.36 W
Thompson Sound 62 Bf 45.10 S 167.00 E
Thomsen 42 Fb 73.40 N 119.30 W
Thomson 44 Fi 33.28 N 82.30 W
Thomson River 59 Ie 25.11 S 142.53 E
Thomson's Falls 36 Gb 0.02 N 36.22 E
Thon 12 Fe 49.53 N 3.55 E
Thon Buri 22 Mh 13.43 N 100.24 E
Thong Pha Phum 25 Jf 14.44 N 98.38 E
Thongwa 25 Je 16.46 N 96.32 E
Thonon-les-Bains 11 Mh 46.22 N 6.29 E
Thoreau 45 Bi 35.24 N 108.13 W
Thornaby-on-Tees 9 Lg 54.34 N 1.18 W
Thornbury 61 Ci 46.17 S 168.06 E
Thorney 12 Bb 52.37 N 0.06 W
Thornhill 9 Jf 55.18 N 3.40 W
Thorshavn 6 Fc 62.01 N 6.46 W
Thouars 11 Fh 46.58 N 0.13 W
Thouet 11 Fg 47.17 N 0.06 W
Thrace (EN) = Thráki 15 Jh 41.20 N 26.45 E
Thrace (EN) = Thráki 5 Ig 41.20 N 26.45 E
Thrace (EN) = Trakya 15 Jh 41.20 N 26.45 E
Thrace (EN) = Trakya 5 Ig 41.20 N 26.45 E
Thráki [2] 15 Ih 41.10 N 25.30 E
Thráki = Thrace (EN) 5 Ig 41.20 N 26.45 E
Thráki = Thrace (EN) 15 Jh 41.20 N 26.45 E
Thrakikón Pélagos 15 Hi 40.30 N 25.00 E
Thrapston 12 Bb 52.24 N 0.32 W
Three Forks 43 Eb 45.54 N 111.33 W
Three Kings Islands 57 Ih 34.10 S 172.10 E
Three Kings Trough (EN) 3 Jm 32.00 S 170.30 E
Three Points, Cape- 30 Gh 4.45 N 2.06 W
Three Rivers 44 Ee 41.57 N 85.38 W
Three Sisters Islands 63a Ed 10.10 S 161.57 E
Throckmorton 45 Gj 33.11 N 99.11 W
Throssel, Lake- 59 Ee 27.25 S 124.15 E
Thua 36 Gc 1.17 S 40.00 E
Thuin 11 Kd 50.20 N 4.17 E
Thule 66 Ad 59.27 S 27.19 W
Thule/Qânâq 67 Od 77.35 N 69.40 W
Thule, Mount - 42 Jb 73.00 N 78.27 W
Thun 14 Bd 46.45 N 7.40 E
Thunder Bay 39 Ke 48.23 N 89.15 W
Thunder Bay [Mi.-U.S.] 44 Fc 45.04 N 83.25 W
Thunder Bay [Ont.-Can.] 45 Lb 48.24 N 89.00 W
Thunder Butte 45 Fd 45.19 N 101.53 W
Thuner See 14 Bd 46.40 N 7.45 E
Thung Song 25 Jg 8.11 N 99.41 E
Thur 14 Cc 47.36 N 8.35 E
Thurgau [2] 14 Dc 47.40 N 9.10 E
Thüringen 10 Gf 50.40 N 11.00 E
Thüringer Wald = Thuringian Forest (EN) 5 He 50.30 N 11.00 E
Thuringian Forest (EN) = Thüringer Wald 5 He 50.30 N 11.00 E
Thurles/Durlas 9 Fi 52.41 N 7.49 W
Thurrock 9 Nj 51.28 N 0.20 E
Thursday Island 59 Ib 10.35 S 142.13 E
Thurso 6 Fd 58.35 N 3.32 W
Thurso 9 Jc 58.35 N 3.30 W
Thurston Island 66 Pf 72.06 S 99.00 W
Thury-Harcourt 12 Bf 48.59 N 0.29 W
Thusis/Tusaun 14 Dd 46.42 N 9.26 E
Thuwayrāt, Nafūd ath- 24 Kj 26.00 N 44.50 E
Thuy Phong 25 Lf 11.14 N 108.43 E
Thwaites Iceberg Tongue 66 Of 74.00 S 108.30 W
Thy 8 Ch 57.00 N 8.30 E
Thyborøn 8 Ch 56.42 N 8.13 E
Tianbaoshan 28 Jc 42.57 N 128.57 E
Tianchang 27 Ke 32.37 N 119.00 E
Tiandong (Pingma) 27 Ig 23.40 N 107.09 E
Tian'e (Liupai) 27 If 25.05 N 107.12 E
Tianguá 54 Jd 3.44 S 40.59 W
Tianjin = Tientsin (EN) 22 Nf 39.08 N 117.12 E
Tianjin Shi (T'ien-chin Shih) [4] 27 Kd 39.08 N 117.12 E
Tianjun (Xinyuan) 22 Lf 37.18 N 99.15 E
Tianlin (Leli) 27 Ig 24.22 N 106.11 E
Tian Ling 28 Kb 44.24 N 130.10 E
Tianmen 27 Je 30.40 N 113.10 E
Tianmu Shan 28 Ei 30.31 N 119.36 E
Tianmu Xi 28 Ej 29.59 N 119.24 E
Tianqiaoling 27 Mc 43.35 N 129.35 E
Tian Shan 21 Ke 42.00 N 80.01 E
Tianshan → Ar Horqin Qi 27 Lc 43.55 N 120.05 E
Tianshifu 27 Lc 41.15 N 124.20 E
Tianshui 22 Mf 34.35 N 105.43 E
Tiantal 28 Fj 29.08 N 121.00 E
Tianwangsi 28 Ei 31.45 N 119.12 E
Tianyi → Ningcheng 27 Kc 41.34 N 119.25 E
Tianzhen 28 Cd 40.24 N 114.05 E
Tianzhen → Gaoqing 28 Df 37.10 N 117.50 E
Tianzhuangtai 28 Gd 40.49 N 122.06 E
Tiaraju 55 Ej 30.15 S 54.23 W
Tiarei 65e Fc 17.32 S 149.20 W
Tiaret [3] 32 Hc 34.50 N 1.30 E
Tiaret 31 He 35.20 N 1.14 E
Tiaret, Monts de- 13 Ni 35.26 N 1.15 E
Tiassalé 34 Ed 5.54 N 4.50 W
Tiavea 65c Ba 13.57 S 171.24 W
Ţīb, Ra's Aţ- = Bon, Cape- (EN) 30 Ie 37.05 N 11.03 E
Tibaji 55 Gg 24.30 S 50.24 W
Tibaji, Rio- 55 Gf 22.47 S 51.01 W
Tibasti, Sarīr- 30 If 24.00 N 17.00 E
Tibati 31 Ih 6.28 N 12.38 E
Tiber (EN) = Tevere 5 Hg 41.44 N 12.14 E
Tiberina, Val- 14 Gg 43.30 N 12.10 E
Tibesti 30 If 21.30 N 17.30 E
Tibet (EN) = Xizang Zizhiqu (Hsi-tsang Tzu-chih-ch'ü) [2] 27 Ee 32.00 N 90.00 E
Tibet, Plateau of- (EN) = Qing Zang Gaoyuan 21 Kf 32.30 N 87.00 E
Tibidabo 13 Oc 41.25 N 2.07 E
Tibni 24 He 35.35 N 30.49 E
Tibro 8 Ff 58.26 N 14.10 E
Tibú 49 Ki 8.40 N 72.42 W
Tibugà, Golfo de- 54 Cb 5.45 N 77.20 W
Tiburón, Capo- 49 Ii 8.42 N 77.21 W
Tiburon, Isla- 47 Bc 29.00 N 112.25 W
Ticao 26 Hd 12.31 N 123.42 E
Tice 44 Gl 26.41 N 81.49 W
Tichá Orlice 10 Mf 50.09 N 16.05 E
Tîchît 31 Gg 18.26 N 9.31 W
Tîchît, Dahr- 32 Ff 18.30 N 9.25 W
Tichka, Tizı n'- 32 Fc 31.17 N 7.21 W
Tichla 32 Ee 21.36 N 14.58 W
Ticino [2] 14 Cd 46.20 N 9.00 E
Ticino 14 De 45.09 N 9.14 E
Ticul 47 Gd 20.24 N 89.32 W
Tidaholm 7 Cg 58.11 N 13.57 E
Tidan 8 Ef 58.42 N 13.48 E
Tiddim 25 Id 23.22 N 93.40 E
Tidikelt, Plaine du- 30 Hf 27.00 N 1.30 E
Tidirhine 32 Gc 34.51 N 4.31 W
Tidjikja 31 Fg 18.32 N 11.27 W
Tidore 26 If 0.40 N 127.26 E
Tidra, Ile- 30 Fg 19.44 N 16.24 W
Tiebissou 34 Dd 7.10 N 5.13 W
Tiechang 28 Id 41.40 N 126.12 E
Tiel 11 Lc 51.54 N 5.25 E
Tieli 27 Mb 47.04 N 128.02 E
Tieling 28 Gc 42.18 N 123.51 E
Tielt 11 Jc 51.00 N 3.20 E
Tienba 34 Dd 8.30 N 7.10 W
T'ien-chin Shih → Tianjin Shi [4] 27 Kd 39.08 N 117.12 E
Tienen/Tirlemont 12 Gd 50.48 N 4.57 E
Tiengemeten 12 Gc 51.45 N 5.20 E
Tientsin (EN) = Tianjin 22 Nf 39.08 N 117.12 E
Tieroko, Tarso- 35 Ba 20.45 N 17.52 E
Tierp 7 Df 60.20 N 17.30 E
Tierra Amarilla [Chile] 56 Fc 27.29 S 70.17 W
Tierra Amarilla [N.M.-U.S.] 45 Ch 36.42 N 106.33 W
Tierra Blanca 47 Ee 18.27 N 96.21 W
Tierra Colorada 48 Ji 17.10 N 99.35 W
Tierra del Fuego [2] 56 Gh 54.00 S 67.00 W
Tierra del Fuego (EN) = Tierra del Fuego, Isla Grande de- 52 Jk 54.00 S 69.00 W
Tierra del Fuego, Isla Grande de- = Tierra del Fuego (EN) 52 Jk 54.00 S 69.00 W
Tierralta 54 Cb 8.10 N 76.04 W
Tiétar 13 Fe 39.50 N 6.01 W
Tietê, Rio- 52 Kh 20.40 S 51.35 W
Tietjerksteradeel 12 Ia 53.12 N 6.00 E
Tietjerksteradeel-Bergum 12 Hb 52.17 N 5.58 E
Tifariti 32 Ed 26.09 N 10.33 W
Tiffany Mountain 46 Fb 48.40 N 119.56 W
Tiffin 44 Fe 41.07 N 83.11 W
Tifton 43 Ke 31.27 N 83.31 W
Tiga 63b Ce 21.08 S 167.49 E
Tigalda 40a Fb 54.05 N 165.05 W
Tigăneşti 15 If 43.54 N 25.22 E
Tighennif 13 Mi 35.25 N 0.15 E
Tigil 20 Ke 57.57 N 158.20 E
Tigil 20 Ke 57.48 N 158.40 E
Tignère 34 Hd 7.22 N 12.39 E
Tigray [3] 35 Fc 14.00 N 39.00 E
Tigre 48 Hh 19.53 N 102.59 W
Tigre, Cerro del- 48 Jf 23.03 N 99.16 W
Tigre, Río- [S.Amer.] 52 If 4.30 S 74.10 W
Tigre, Río- [Ven.] 50 Eh 9.20 N 62.30 W
Tigris (EN) = Dicle 21 Gf 31.00 N 47.25 E
Tigris (EN) = Dijlah 21 Gf 31.00 N 47.25 E
Tigrovy Hvost, Mys- 18 Bc 43.57 N 58.45 E
Tiguent 32 Df 17.15 N 16.00 W
Tiguentourine 32 Id 27.43 N 9.33 E
Tigui 35 Bb 18.38 N 18.47 E
Tigzirt 13 Qh 36.54 N 4.07 E
Tīh, Jabal at- 33 Fd 29.35 N 34.00 E
Tīh, Şaḩrā' at- = At Tīh Desert (EN) 33 Fc 30.05 N 34.00 E
Tihāmat 23 Ff 18.30 N 41.30 E
Tihāmat Ash Shām 33 Hf 19.15 N 41.10 E

Index Symbols

[1] Independent Nation
[2] State, Region
[3] District, County
[4] Municipality
[5] Colony, Dependency
Continent
Physical Region
Historical or Cultural Region
Mount, Mountain
Volcano
Hill
Mountains, Mountain Range
Hills, Escarpment
Plateau, Upland
Pass, Gap
Plain, Lowland
Delta
Salt Flat
Valley, Canyon
Crater, Cave
Karst Features
Depression
Polder
Desert, Dunes
Forest, Woods
Heath, Steppe
Oasis
Cape, Point
Coast, Beach
Cliff
Peninsula
Isthmus
Sandbank
Island
Atoll
Rock, Reef
Islands, Archipelago
Rocks, Reefs
Coral Reef
Well, Spring
Geyser
River, Stream
Waterfall Rapids
River Mouth, Estuary
Lake
Salt Lake
Intermittent Lake
Reservoir
Swamp, Pond
Canal
Glacier
Ice Shelf, Pack Ice
Ocean
Sea
Gulf, Bay
Strait, Fjord
Lagoon
Bank
Seamount
Tablemount
Ridge
Shelf
Basin
Escarpment, Sea Scarp
Fracture
Trench, Abyss
National Park, Reserve
Point of Interest
Recreation Site
Cave, Cavern
Historic Site
Ruins
Wall, Walls
Church, Abbey
Temple
Scientific Station
Airport
Port
Lighthouse
Mine
Tunnel
Dam, Bridge

Name	Page	Grid	Lat.	Long.
Tihāmat 'Asīr	33	Hf	17.30N	42.20 E
Tihi Okean=Pacific Ocean (EN)	3	Ki	5.00N	155.00W
Tihoreck	6	Kf	45.51N	40.09 E
Tihuța, Pasul-	15	Hb	47.15N	25.00 E
Tihvin	19	Dd	59.38N	33.31 E
Tiirismaa	8	Kc	61.01N	25.31 E
Tiji	33	Bc	32.01N	11.22 E
Tijirît	32	Ee	20.30N	15.00W
Tijuana	39	Hf	32.32N	117.01W
Tijucas	55	Hh	27.14S	48.38W
Tijucas, Baía do-	55	Hh	27.15S	48.31W
Tijucas, Rio-	55	Hh	27.15S	48.38W
Tijucas, Serra do-	55	Hh	27.16S	49.10W
Tijucas do Sul	55	Hg	25.56S	49.10W
Tijuco, Rio-	55	Gd	18.40S	50.05W
Tikal	39	Kh	17.20N	89.39W
Tikanlik	27	Ec	40.42N	87.38 E
Tikchik Lakes	40	Hd	60.07N	158.35W
Tikehau Atoll	61	Lb	15.00S	148.10W
Tikei, Ile-	61	Mb	14.58S	144.32W
Tikitiki	62	Hb	37.47S	178.25 E
Tikkakoski	8	Kb	62.24N	25.38 E
Tikkurila	8	Kd	60.18N	25.03 E
Tiko	34	Ge	4.05N	9.22 E
Tikopia Island	57	Hf	12.19S	168.49 E
Tikrit	23	Fc	34.36N	43.42 E
Tikšeozero, Ozero-	7	Hc	66.15N	31.45 E
Tiksi	22	Ob	71.36N	128.48 E
Tiladummati Atoll	25a	Ba	6.50N	73.05 E
Tilamuta	26	Hf	0.30N	122.20 E
Tilburg	11	Lc	51.34N	5.05 E
Tilbury, Gravesend-	9	Nj	51.28N	0.23 E
Tilcara	56	Gb	23.34S	65.22W
Til-Châtel	11	Lg	47.31N	5.10 E
Tileagd	15	Fb	47.04N	22.12 E
Tilemsès	34	Fb	15.37N	4.44 E
Tilemsi, Vallée du-	30	Hg	19.00N	0.02 E
Tilia	32	Gd	27.22N	0.02W
Tiličiki	20	Ld	60.20N	166.03 E
Tiligul	16	Gf	47.07N	30.57 E
Tiligulski Liman	16	Gf	46.50N	31.10 E
Till	9	Kf	55.41N	2.12W
Tillabéry	34	Fc	14.13N	1.27 E
Tillamook	46	Dd	45.27N	123.51W
Tillamook Bay	46	Dd	45.30N	123.53W
Tillanchong	25	Ig	8.30N	93.37 E
Tillberga	8	Ge	59.41N	16.37 E
Tille	11	Lg	47.07N	5.21 E
Tillia	34	Fb	16.08N	4.47 E
Tillières-sur-Avre	12	Df	48.46N	1.04 E
Tillingham	12	Cd	50.58N	0.44 E
Tillsonburg	44	Gd	42.51N	80.44W
Tilly-sur-Seulles	12	Be	49.11N	0.37W
Tiloa	34	Fb	15.04N	2.03 E
Tilos	15	Km	36.25N	27.25 E
Tilpa	59	If	30.57S	144.24 E
Tim	16	Jd	51.37N	37.11 E
Tim	16	Jc	52.15N	37.22 E
Ţimā	33	Fd	26.54N	31.26 E
Timagami	44	Gb	47.00N	80.05W
Timagami, Lake-	42	Jg	46.57N	80.05W
Timane, Rio-	55	Be	20.16S	60.08W
Timan Ridge (EN)= Timanski Krjaž	5	Lc	65.00N	51.00 E
Timanski Bereg	17	Eb	68.20N	51.45 E
Timanski Krjaž=Timan Ridge (EN)	5	Lc	65.00N	51.00 E
Timaru	58	Ii	44.24S	171.15 E
Timaševsk	16	Jf	45.35N	38.58 E
Timbalier Bay	45	Kl	29.10N	90.20W
Timbalier Island	45	Kl	29.04N	90.28W
Timbaúba	54	Ke	7.31S	35.19W
Timbédra	32	Ff	16.14N	8.10W
Timbó	55	Hh	26.50S	49.18W
Timbuktu (EN)= Tombouctou	31	Gg	16.46N	2.59W
Timedouine, Ras-	13	Qh	36.28N	4.09 E
Timétrine	34	Eb	19.20N	0.42W
Timétrine	34	Eb	19.27N	0.26W
Timfi Óros	15	Dj	39.57N	20.50 E
Timfristós	15	Ek	38.57N	21.49 E
Timia	34	Gb	18.04N	8.40 E
Timimoun	31	Hf	29.15N	0.15 E
Timimoun, Sebkha de-	32	Hd	29.00N	0.05 E
Timiris, Cap—	32	Df	19.23N	16.32W
Timirjazevo	19	Ge	53.45N	66.33 E
Timiş	15	De	44.51N	20.39 E
Timiş [2]	15	Ed	45.38N	21.13 E
Timiskaming, Lake-	44	Hb	47.35N	79.35W
Timişoara	6	If	45.45N	21.13 E
Ti-m-Merhsoi	34	Gb	18.00N	5.40 E
Timmins	39	Ke	48.28N	81.20W
Timmoudi	32	Gd	29.19N	1.08W
Timms Hill	45	Kd	45.27N	90.11W
Timok	15	Fe	44.13N	22.40 E
Timon	54	Je	5.06S	42.49W
Timor, Laut-=Timor Sea (EN)	57	Df	11.00S	128.00 E
Timor, Pulau-	21	Oj	8.50S	126.00 E
Timor Sea (EN)=Timor, Laut-	57	Df	11.00S	128.00 E
Timor Timur [3]	26	Ih	8.35S	126.00 E
Timor Trough (EN)	3	Ij	9.50S	126.00 E
Timote	56	He	35.21S	62.14W
Timotes	54	Db	8.59N	70.44W
Timpton	20	He	58.43N	127.12 E
Timrå	7	De	62.29N	17.18 E
Tims Ford Lake	44	Dh	35.15N	86.10W
Tin, Ra's at-	33	Dc	32.37N	23.08 E
Tinaca Point	21	Oi	5.33N	125.20 E
Tinaco	50	Bh	9.42N	68.26W
Tinakula	63c	Ab	10.24S	165.47 E
Ti-n-Alkoum	32	Je	24.34N	10.11 E
Ti-n-Amzi [Alg.]	32	He	20.32N	4.37 E
Ti-n-Amzi [Niger]	34	Fb	17.54N	4.32 E
Tinaquillo	50	Bh	9.55N	68.18W
Tinchebray	12	Bf	48.46N	0.44W
Tindalo	35	Ed	5.39N	31.03 E
Tindari	14	Jl	38.10N	15.04 E
Tindila	34	Dc	10.16N	8.15W
Tindouf	31	Gf	27.42N	8.09W
Tindouf, Hamada de-	32	Fd	27.45N	8.25W
Tindouf, Sebkha de-	32	Fd	27.45N	7.35W
Tinée	11	Nk	43.55N	7.11 E
Tineo	13	Fa	43.20N	6.25W
Ti-n-Essako	34	Fb	18.27N	2.29 E
Tin Fouye	32	Id	28.15N	7.45 E
Tinghert, Ḩamādat-	30	Hf	28.50N	10.00 E
Tinglev	8	Cj	54.56N	9.15 E
Tingmiarmiut	41	Hf	62.25N	42.15W
Tingo María	54	Ce	9.10S	76.00W
Tingri (Xêgar)	27	Ef	28.41N	87.00 E
Tingsryd	7	Dh	56.32N	14.59 E
Tingstäde	8	Hg	57.44N	18.36 E
Tingvoll	7	Be	62.54N	8.12 E
Tinian Channel	64b	Bb	14.54N	145.37 E
Tinian Island	57	Fc	15.00N	145.38 E
Tini Wells	35	Cb	15.02N	22.48 E
Tinkisso	34	Dc	11.21N	9.10W
Tinnelva	8	Ce	59.34N	9.15 E
Tinniswood, Mount-	46	Da	50.19N	123.50W
Tinnoset	8	Ce	59.43N	9.02 E
Tinnsjo	8	Ce	59.54N	8.55 E
Tinogasta	56	Gc	28.04S	67.34W
Tinos	15	Il	37.35N	25.10 E
Tinos	15	Il	37.32N	25.10 E
Tinou, Stenón-	15	Il	37.38N	25.10 E
Tinrhert, Hamada de-	30	Hf	28.50N	10.00 E
Tinrhir	32	Fc	31.31N	5.32W
Tinsukia	25	Jc	27.30N	95.22 E
Tintagel Head	9	Ik	50.41N	4.46W
Tintamarre, Ile-	51b	Bb	18.07N	63.00W
Ti-n-Tarabine	32	Ie	21.16N	7.24 E
Tîntăreni	15	Ge	44.36N	23.29 E
Tintina	56	Hc	27.02S	62.43W
Tinto	13	Fg	37.12N	6.55W
Ti-n-toumma	30	Ig	16.04N	12.40 E
Tinwald	62	De	43.55S	171.43 E
Ti-n-Zaouâtene	31	Hg	19.56N	2.55 E
Tiobraid Árann/Tipperary	9	Ei	52.29N	8.10W
Tiobraid Árann/Tipperary [2]	9	Ei	52.40N	8.20W
Tioga	45	Eb	48.24N	102.56W
Tioman, Pulau-	26	Df	2.48N	104.11 E
Tione di Trento	14	Ed	46.02N	10.43 E
Tioro, Selat-=Tioro, Strait (EN)	26	Hg	4.40S	122.20 E
Tioro Strait (EN)=Tioro, Selat-	26	Hg	4.40S	122.20 E
Tiøtta	7	Cd	65.50N	12.24 E
Tiouilit	32	Df	18.52N	16.10W
Tipasa	13	Oh	36.35N	2.27 E
Tipitapa	47	Gf	12.12N	86.06W
Tipperary/Tiobraid Árann	9	Ei	52.29N	8.10W
Tipperary/Tiobraid Árann [2]	9	Ei	52.40N	8.20W
Tipton, Mount-	46	Hi	35.32N	114.12W
Tip Top Mountain	45	Nb	48.16N	85.59W
Tiptree	12	Cc	51.49N	0.45 E
Tiracambu, Serra do-	54	Id	3.15S	46.30W
Tirahart	32	He	23.45N	2.30 E
Tirān	24	Nf	32.42N	51.09 E
Tirān, Maḑīq-	24	Fi	27.55N	34.28 E
Tirana	6	Hg	41.20N	19.50 E
Tirania	32	Ie	23.08N	9.01 E
Tirano	14	Ed	46.13N	10.10 E
Tiraspol	19	Cf	46.50N	29.37 E
Tirat Karmel	24	Ff	32.46N	34.58 E
Tire	23	Cb	38.04N	27.45 E
Tirebolu	24	Hb	41.00N	38.50 E
Tiree	9	Ge	56.31N	6.49W
Tiree, Passage of-	9	Ge	56.30N	6.30W
Tîrgovişte	15	Ie	44.56N	25.27 E
Tîrgu Bujor	15	Kd	45.52N	27.54 E
Tîrgu Cărbuneşti	15	Ge	44.57N	23.31 E
Tîrgu Frumos	15	Jb	47.12N	27.00 E
Tîrgu Jiu	15	Gd	45.03N	23.17 E
Tîrgu Lăpuş	15	Gb	47.27N	23.52 E
Tîrgu Mureş	6	If	46.33N	24.34 E
Tîrgu Neamț	15	Jb	47.12N	26.22 E
Tîrgu Ocna	15	Jc	46.17N	26.37 E
Tîrgu Secuiesc	15	Jd	46.00N	26.08 E
Tîrguşor	15	Le	44.27N	28.25 E
Tirich Mir	21	Jf	36.15N	71.50 E
Tirins	15	Fl	37.36N	22.48 E
Tiririca, Serra da-	55	Ic	17.06S	47.06W
Tiris	30	Ff	23.10N	13.30W
Tiris Zemmour [3]	32	Fe	24.00N	10.00W
Tirlemont/Tienen	12	Gd	50.48N	4.57 E
Tirljanski	17	Ii	54.12N	58.33 E
Tîrnava Mare	15	Gc	46.09N	23.42 E
Tîrnava Mică	15	Gc	46.11N	23.55 E
Tîrnăveni	15	Hc	46.20N	24.17 E
Tirnavos	15	Fj	39.45N	22.17 E
Tiro	34	Cd	9.45N	10.39W
Tirol/Tirolo=Tyrol (EN)	14	Fd	47.00N	11.20 E
Tirol=Tyrol (EN) [2]	14	Fc	47.10N	11.25 E
Tirolo/Tirol=Tyrol (EN)	14	Fd	47.00N	11.20 E
Tiros	55	Jd	19.00S	45.58W
Tirreno, Mar-=Tyrrhenian Sea (EN)	5	Hh	40.00N	12.00 E
Tirschenreuth	10	Ig	49.53N	12.21 E
Tirso	14	Ck	39.53N	8.32 E
Tirstrup	8	Dh	56.18N	10.42 E
Tirua Point	62	Fc	38.23S	174.38 E
Tiruchchirappalli	22	Jh	10.49N	78.41 E
Tiruliai/Tiruliaj	8	Ji	55.44N	23.18 E
Tiruliaj/Tiruliai	8	Ji	55.44N	23.18 E
Tirunelveli	22	Ji	8.44N	77.42 E
Tirupati	25	Ff	13.39N	79.25 E
Tirza	8	Lg	57.09N	26.37 E
Tisa=Tisza (EN)	5	If	45.15N	20.17 E
Tis Abay	35	Fc	11.20N	37.40 E
Tisdale	42	Hf	52.51N	104.04W
Tisnaren	8	Ff	58.55N	15.55 E
Tisovec	10	Ph	48.42N	19.57 E
Tissemsilt	32	Hb	35.36N	1.49 E
Tissø	8	Di	55.35N	11.20 E
Tisza	5	If	45.15N	20.17 E
Tisza (EN)=Tisa	5	If	45.15N	20.17 E
Tiszaföldvár	10	Qj	46.59N	20.15 E
Tiszafüred	10	Qi	47.37N	20.46 E
Tiszakécske	10	Qj	46.56N	20.06 E
Tiszántúl	10	Qj	47.00N	21.00 E
Tiszavasvári	10	Ri	47.58N	21.21 E
Titao	34	Ec	13.46N	2.04W
Titarisios	15	Fj	39.47N	22.23 E
Tit-Ary	20	Hb	71.55N	127.01 E
Titicaca, Lago-	52	Jg	15.50S	69.20W
Titikaveka	64p	Bc	21.15S	159.45W
Titlagarh	25	Gd	20.18N	83.09 E
Titlis	14	Cd	46.47N	8.26 E
Titograd	6	Hg	42.26N	19.16 E
Titova Korenica	14	Jf	44.45N	15.42 E
Titovo Užice	15	Cf	43.52N	19.51 E
Titov Veles	15	Eh	41.42N	21.48 E
Titov vrh	15	Dh	41.58N	20.50 E
Titran	7	Be	63.40N	8.18 E
Titteri	13	Pi	35.59N	3.15 E
Titule	36	Eb	3.17N	25.32 E
Titusville [Fl.-U.S.]	43	Kf	28.37N	80.49W
Titusville [Pa.-U.S.]	44	He	41.37N	79.42W
Tituvenaj/Tytuvėnai	8	Ji	55.33N	23.09 E
Tiva	36	Gc	2.20S	39.55 E
Tivaouane	34	Bc	14.57N	16.49W
Tiveden	8	Ff	58.45N	14.40 E
Tiverton	9	Jk	50.55N	3.29W
Tivoli [Gren.]	51p	Bb	12.10N	61.37W
Tivoli [It.]	14	Gi	41.58N	12.48 E
Ţiwāl	35	Cc	10.22N	22.43 E
Tiwi	36	Gc	4.14S	39.35 E
Tiyo	35	Gc	14.41N	40.57 E
Tizatlán	48	Jh	19.21N	98.15W
Tizimín	47	Gd	21.09N	88.09W
Tizi Ouzou [3]	32	Hb	36.35N	4.05 E
Tizi Ouzou	32	Hb	36.42N	4.03 E
Tiznados, Rio-	50	Ch	8.16N	67.47W
Tiznit	32	Fd	29.43N	9.43W
Tiznit [3]	32	Fd	29.07N	9.04W
Tjačev	10	Th	48.02N	23.36 E
Tjanšan	27	Dc	42.00N	80.01 E
Tjasmin	16	He	49.03N	32.50 E
Tjeggelvas	7	Dc	66.35N	17.40 E
Tjeukemeer	11	Lb	52.54N	5.50 E
Tjøme	8	De	59.10N	10.25 E
Tjørn	8	Df	58.00N	11.38 E
Tjub-Karagan, Mys-	16	Qg	44.38N	50.20 E
Tjubuk	17	Jh	56.03N	60.58 E
Tjuhtet	20	De	56.32N	89.29 E
Tjukalinsk	19	Hd	55.52N	72.12 E
Tjuleni, Ostrov-	16	Og	44.30N	47.30 E
Tjuleni, Ostrova-	16	Qg	44.55N	50.10 E
Tjulgan	16	Fe	52.22N	56.12 E
Tjumen	22	Id	57.09N	65.32 E
Tjumenskaja Oblast [3]	19	Gd	57.00N	69.00 E
Tjung	20	Hd	63.42N	121.30 E
Tjup	18	Lc	42.44N	78.20 E
Tjuri/Türi	7	Fg	58.50N	25.27 E
Tjust	8	Gg	57.50N	16.15 E
Tjuters Maly, Ostrov-	8	Le	59.45N	26.53 E
Tjuzašu, Pereval-	18	Ic	42.19N	73.50 E
Tkibuli	16	Mh	42.19N	42.59 E
Tkvarčeli	19	Eg	42.52N	41.40 E
Tlacolula	48	Ki	16.57N	96.29W
Tlacotalpan	48	Lh	18.37N	95.40W
Tlahualilo, Sierra del-	48	Hd	26.30N	103.20W
Tlalnepantla	48	Jh	19.33N	99.12W
Tlapa de Comonfort	48	Ji	17.33N	98.33W
Tlapaneco, Rio-	48	Jh	18.00N	98.48W
Tlaquepaque	48	Hg	20.39N	103.19W
Tlaxcala [2]	47	Ee	19.25N	98.10W
Tlaxcala	47	Ee	19.19N	98.14W
Tlemcen	32	Gc	34.52N	1.19W
Tlemcen [3]	32	Gc	34.45N	1.30W
Tleń	10	Oc	53.38N	18.20 E
Tleta Rissana	13	Gi	35.14N	5.59W
Tletat ed Douair	13	Oi	35.59N	2.55 E
Tljarata	16	Oh	42.06N	46.22 E
Tlumač	10	Vh	48.46N	25.06 E
Tłuszcz	10	Rd	52.26N	21.26 E
Tmassah	33	Cd	26.22N	15.48 E
Tō, Shikotan-/Šikotan, Ostrov-	20	Jh	43.47N	146.45 E
Toaca, Vîrful-	15	Ic	46.55N	25.59 E
Toagel Mlungui	64a	Ab	7.32N	134.28 E
Toamasina	31	Lj	18.10S	49.24 E
Toamasina [3]	37	Hc	18.00S	48.40 E
Toau Atoll	61	Lc	15.55S	146.00W
Toay	56	He	36.40S	64.21W
Toba	28	Ng	34.29N	136.51 E
Toba, Danau-=Toba, Lake- (EN)	26	Li	2.35N	98.50 E
Toba, Lake- (EN)=Toba, Danau-	26	Li	2.35N	98.50 E
Tobago	52	Jd	11.15N	60.40W
Tobago Basin (EN)	50	Ff	12.30N	60.30W
Tobago Cays	51n	Bb	12.39N	61.22W
Toba Kākar Range	25	Db	31.15N	68.00 E
Tobarra	13	Kf	38.35N	1.41W
Tobe	29	Ce	33.44N	132.47 E
Tobejuba, Isla-	50	Fh	9.20N	60.52W
Tobelo	26	If	1.25N	127.31 E
Tobermory [Ont.-Can.]	44	Gc	45.15N	81.40W
Tobermory [Scot.-U.K.]	9	Ge	56.37N	6.05W
Tōbetsu	29a	Bb	43.14N	141.29 E
Tobi Island	57	Ed	3.00N	131.10 E
Tobin, Kap-	41	Jd	70.30N	21.30W
Tobin, Mount-	46	Gf	40.22N	117.32W
Tobin Lake [Austl.]	59	Fd	21.45S	125.50 E
Tobin Lake [Sask.-Can.]	42	Hf	53.40N	103.20W
Tobi-Shima	29	Fb	39.12N	139.32 E
Toblach / Dobbiaco	14	Gd	46.44N	12.14 E
Toboali	26	Eg	3.00S	106.30 E
Tobol	19	Ge	52.40N	62.39 E
Tobol	21	Id	58.10N	68.12 E
Tobolsk	22	Id	58.12N	68.16 E
Tobruk (EN)=Ţubruq	31	Je	32.05N	23.59 E
Tobseda	19	Fb	68.36N	52.18 E
Tobyš	17	Ed	65.30N	51.00 E
Tocantinópolis	53	Lf	6.20S	47.25W
Tocantins, Rio-	52	Lf	1.45S	49.10W
Tocantinzinho, Rio-	55	Ha	13.57S	48.20W
Toccoa	44	Fh	34.35N	83.19W
Toce	14	Ce	45.56N	8.29 E
Tochigi	29	Fc	36.23N	139.44 E
Tochigi Ken [2]	28	Of	36.50N	139.50 E
Tochio	29	Fc	37.29N	138.58 E
Töcksfors	8	De	59.31N	11.50 E
Toco	50	Fg	10.50N	60.57W
Tocoa	49	Df	15.41N	86.03W
Toconao	56	Gb	23.11S	68.01W
Tocopilla	53	Ih	22.05S	70.12W
Tocumen	49	Hi	9.05N	79.23W
Tocuyo, Rio-	49	Mh	11.03N	68.20W
Todd Mountain	44	Nb	46.32N	66.43W
Todi	14	Gh	42.47N	12.24 E
Tōdi	14	Cd	46.49N	8.55 E
Todo-ga-Saki	27	Pd	39.33N	142.05 E
Todos os Santos, Baía de-	52	Mg	12.48S	38.38W
Todos Santos	47	Bd	23.27N	110.13W
Todos Santos, Bahía-	48	Ab	31.48N	116.42W
Tofino	42	Eg	49.09N	125.54W
Tofte	8	De	59.33N	10.34 E
Toftlund	8	Ci	55.11N	9.04 E
Tofua Island	61	Fc	19.45S	175.05W
Toga	63b	Ca	13.26S	166.41 E
Tōgane	29	Gd	35.33N	140.21 E
Tog Ḑarōr	35	Hc	10.25N	50.00 E
Togdere	35	Hd	9.01N	47.07 E
Tog-Dheer [3]	35	Hd	9.50N	45.50 E
Togi	29	Ec	37.08N	136.43 E
Togiak	40	Ge	59.04N	160.24W
Togian, Kepulauan-=Togian Islands (EN)	26	Hg	0.20S	122.00 E
Togian Islands (EN)= Togian, Kepulauan-	26	Hg	0.20S	122.00 E
Togliatti	6	Ke	53.31N	49.26 E
Togni	35	Fb	18.05N	35.10 E
Togo [1]	31	Hh	8.00N	1.10 E
Togrog Ul → Qahar Youyi Qianqi	28	Bd	40.46N	113.13 E
Togtoh	27	Jc	40.17N	111.15 E
Togučin	20	De	55.16N	84.33 E
Toguzak	17	Ki	54.05N	62.48 E
Toğwotee Pass	43	Ec	43.45N	110.04W
Tohen	35	Ic	11.44N	51.15 E
Tohma	24	Hc	38.31N	38.25 E
Tohmajärvi	7	He	62.11N	30.23 E
Tohopekaliga, Lake-	44	Gk	28.12N	81.23W
Toi	29	Fd	34.54N	138.47 E
Toijala	7	Ff	61.10N	23.52 E
Toi-Misaki	28	Ki	31.26N	131.19 E
Toisvesi	8	Jb	62.20N	23.45 E
Tōjō	29	Cd	34.53N	133.16 E
Tojtepa	18	Gd	41.03N	69.22 E
Tok	10	Jg	49.43N	13.50 E
Tok	16	Rc	52.46N	52.22 E
Tok	40	Kd	63.20N	142.59W
Tokachi-Dake	29a	Cb	43.25N	142.41 E
Tokachi-Gawa	29a	Cb	42.41N	143.37 E
Tokachi-Heiya	29a	Cb	43.00N	143.20 E
Tokachimitsumata	29a	Cb	43.31N	143.07 E
Tōkai [Jap.]	29	Gc	36.27N	140.34 E
Tōkai [Jap.]	29	Ed	35.01N	136.51 E
Tokaj	16	Ld	51.18N	41.04 E
Tokaj	10	Rh	48.07N	21.25 E
Tōkamachi	28	Of	37.08N	138.46 E
Tokanui	62	Cg	46.34S	168.57 E
Tokara Islands (EN)= Tokara-Rettō	21	Og	29.35N	129.45 E
Tokara-Kaikyō	28	Ki	30.10N	130.15 E
Tokara-Rettō=Tokara Islands (EN)	21	Og	29.35N	129.45 E
Tokashiki-Jima	29b	Ab	26.13N	127.21 E
Tokat	23	Ea	40.19N	36.34 E
Tŏkch'ŏn	28	Ie	39.45N	126.15 E
Tok-Do	28	Kf	37.15N	131.52 E
Tokelau [5]	58	Je	9.00S	171.46W
Tokelau/Union Islands	57	Je	9.00S	171.45W
Toki	29	Ed	35.22N	137.11 E
Tokke	8	Ce	59.00N	9.15 E
Tokke	8	Be	59.27N	7.58 E
Tokkuztara/Gongliu	27	Dc	43.30N	82.15 E
Tokmak [Kirg.-U.S.S.R.]	19	Hg	42.49N	75.19 E
Tokmak [Ukr.-U.S.S.R.]	19	Df	47.13N	35.43 E
Tokomaru Bay	61	Eg	38.08S	178.20 E
Tokoname	29	Ed	34.53N	136.49 E
Tokoro	29a	Da	44.08N	144.03 E
Tokoroa	61	Eg	38.13S	175.52 E
Tokoro-Gawa	29a	Da	44.08N	144.04 E
Toksovo	8	Nd	60.10N	30.42 E
Toksu/Xinhe	27	Dc	41.34N	82.38 E
Toksun	27	Ec	42.47N	88.38 E
Toktogul	19	Hg	41.50N	73.01 E
Toktogulskoje Vodohranilišče	18	Id	41.45N	73.00 E
Tokuji	29	Bd	34.11N	131.39 E
Tokulu	65b	Bb	20.06S	174.48W
Toku-no-Shima	27	Mf	27.45N	128.50 E
Tokunoshima	29b	Bb	27.45N	129.00 E
Tokur	20	If	53.09N	132.50 E
Tokushima	27	Ne	34.04N	134.34 E
Tokushima Ken [2]	28	Mh	33.50N	134.10 E
Tokuyama [Jap.]	29	Ed	35.43N	136.27 E
Tokuyama [Jap.]	28	Kg	34.03N	131.49 E
Tokwe	37	Ed	20.09S	31.54 E
Tōkyō	22	Pf	35.40N	139.46 E
Tokyo Bay (EN)=Tōkyō-Wan	28	Og	35.38N	139.57 E
Tōkyō To [2]	28	Og	35.40N	139.20 E
Tōkyō-Wan=Tokyo Bay (EN)	28	Og	35.38N	139.57 E
Tola	21	Me	48.57N	104.48 E
Tolaga Bay	62	Hc	38.22S	178.18 E
Tolbazy	17	Gi	54.02N	55.59 E
Tolbuhin [2]	15	Kf	43.34N	27.50 E
Tolbuhin	15	Kf	43.34N	27.50 E
Toledo [3]	13	Ie	39.50N	4.00W
Toledo [Blz.]	47	Ge	16.25N	88.50W
Toledo [Braz.]	56	Jb	24.44S	53.45W
Toledo [Oh.-U.S.]	39	Ke	41.39N	83.32W
Toledo [Phil.]	26	Hd	10.23N	123.38 E
Toledo [Sp.]	6	Fh	39.52N	4.01W
Toledo, Montes de-	13	He	39.35N	4.20W
Toledo Bend Reservoir	43	Ie	31.30N	93.45W
Tolentino	14	Hg	43.12N	13.17 E
Tolfa	14	Fh	42.09N	11.56 E
Tolfa, Monti della-	14	Fh	42.10N	11.55 E
Tolga	7	Ce	62.25N	11.00 E
Toli	27	Db	45.57N	83.37 E
Toliara	37	Gd	22.00S	44.00 E
Toliara	31	Lk	23.21S	43.39 E
Tolima [2]	54	Cc	3.45N	75.15W
Tolima, Nevado del-	52	Ie	4.40N	75.19W
Toling→Zanda	27	Ce	31.28N	79.50 E
Tolitoli	26	Hf	1.02N	120.49 E
Toll	64d	Bb	7.22N	151.37 E
Tollarp	8	Ei	55.56N	13.59 E
Tollja, Zaliv-	20	Ea	76.40N	100.00 E
Tolmačevo	8	Nf	58.48N	30.01 E
Tolmezzo	14	Hd	46.24N	13.01 E
Tolmin	14	Hd	46.11N	13.44 E
Tolna	10	Oj	46.26N	18.47 E
Tolna [2]	10	Oj	46.30N	18.35 E
Tolo	36	Cc	2.56S	18.34 E
Tolo, Gulf of- (EN)=Tolo, Teluk-	21	Oj	2.00S	122.30 E
Tolo, Teluk-=Tolo, Gulf of- (EN)	21	Oj	2.00S	122.30 E
Toločin	7	Gi	54.25N	29.41 E
Tolosa	13	Ja	43.08N	2.04W
Tolstoj, Mys-	5	Rd	59.10N	155.05 E
Toltén	56	Fe	39.13S	73.14W
Tolú	54	Cb	9.32N	75.34W
Toluca, Nevado de-	38	Jh	19.08N	99.44W
Toluca de Lerdo	39	Jh	19.17N	99.40W
Tom	21	Kd	56.50N	84.27 E
Toma	34	Ec	12.46N	2.53W
Tomah	45	Ke	43.59N	90.30W
Tomakomai	27	Pc	42.38N	141.36 E
Tomamae	29a	Ba	44.18N	141.39 E
Tomanivi	63d	Bb	17.37S	178.01 E
Tomar	13	De	39.36N	8.25W
Tómaros	15	Dj	39.32N	20.45 E
Tomaševka	16	Cd	51.33N	23.40 E
Tomás Young	55	Ai	28.36S	62.11W
Tomaszów Lubelski	10	Tf	50.28N	23.25 E
Tomaszów Mazowiecki	10	Qe	51.32N	20.01 E
Tomatlán	48	Gh	19.56N	105.15W
Tombador, Serra dos-	54	Gf	12.00S	57.40W
Tombigbee River	43	Je	31.04N	87.58W
Tomboco	36	Bd	6.45S	13.18 E
Tombouctou=Timbuktu (EN)	31	Gg	16.46N	2.59W
Tombstone	46	Jk	31.43N	110.04W
Tombua	31	Ij	15.48S	11.52 E
Tomé	56	Fe	36.37S	72.57W
Tomé-Açu	54	Id	2.25S	48.09W
Tomelilla	7	Ci	55.33N	13.57 E
Tomelloso	13	Ie	39.10N	3.01W
Tomichi Creek	45	Cg	38.31N	106.58W
Tomie	29	Ae	32.37N	128.46 E
Tomini, Gulf of- (EN)= Tomini, Teluk-	21	Oj	0.20S	121.00 E
Tomini, Teluk-=Tomini, Gulf of- (EN)	21	Oj	0.20S	121.00 E
Tominian	34	Ec	13.17N	4.35W
Tomioka [Jap.]	29	Gc	37.20N	140.59 E
Tomioka [Jap.]	29	Fc	36.15N	138.52 E
Tomkinson Ranges	59	Fe	26.10S	129.05 E
Tomma	7	Cc	66.15N	12.48 E
Tomo, Rio-	54	Eb	5.20N	67.48W
Tomochic	48	Fc	28.20N	107.51W
Tomorit, Mali i-	15	Di	40.40N	20.09 E
Tomotu Neo	63c	Ab	10.41S	165.47 E
Tomotu Noi	63c	Bb	10.50S	166.02 E
Tompa	10	Pj	46.12N	19.33 E
Tompe	26	Gg	0.12S	119.48 E
Tompo	20	Id	62.50N	134.47 E
Tompo	20	Id	64.00N	136.00 E
Tom Price	59	Dd	22.40S	117.55 E
Tomsk	22	Kd	56.30N	84.58 E
Tomskaja Oblast [3]	20	De	58.20N	81.30 E
Tomtabacken	8	Fg	57.30N	14.28 E
Tomur Feng	21	Ke	42.02N	80.05 E
Tom White, Mount-	40	Kd	60.40N	143.40W
Tonaki-Shima	29b	Ab	26.21N	127.09 E
Tonalá	47	Fe	16.04N	93.45W
Tonale, Passo del-	14	Ed	46.16N	10.35 E
Tonami	29	Ec	36.38N	136.57 E
Tonara	14	Dj	40.02N	9.10 E
Tonasket	46	Fb	48.42N	119.26W
Tonb-e Bozorg	24	Pi	26.15N	55.03 E
Tonbetsu-Gawa	29a	Ca	45.08N	142.23 E
Tonbridge	9	Nj	51.12N	0.16 E
Tondano	26	Hf	1.19N	124.54 E
Tondela	13	Dd	40.31N	8.05W
Tønder	7	Bi	54.56N	8.54 E
Tone-Gawa	29	Gd	35.44N	140.51 E
Tonekābon	23	Hb	36.53N	50.56 E
Toney	66	Of	75.48S	115.48W
Tonga [1]	58	Jf	20.00S	175.00W
Tonga	35	Ed	9.28N	31.03 E

Index Symbols

- [1] Independent Nation
- [2] State, Region
- [3] District, County
- [4] Municipality
- [5] Colony, Dependency
- Continent
- Physical Region
- Historical or Cultural Region
- Mount, Mountain
- Volcano
- Hill
- Mountains, Mountain Range
- Hills, Escarpment
- Plateau, Upland
- Pass, Gap
- Plain, Lowland
- Delta
- Salt Flat
- Valley, Canyon
- Crater, Cave
- Karst Features
- Depression
- Polder
- Desert, Dunes
- Forest, Woods
- Heath, Steppe
- Oasis
- Cape, Point
- Coast, Beach
- Cliff
- Peninsula
- Isthmus
- Sandbank
- Island
- Atoll
- Rock, Reef
- Islands, Archipelago
- Rocks, Reefs
- Coral Reef
- Well, Spring
- Geyser
- River, Stream
- Waterfall Rapids
- River Mouth, Estuary
- Lake
- Salt Lake
- Intermittent Lake
- Reservoir
- Swamp, Pond
- Canal
- Glacier
- Ice Shelf, Pack Ice
- Ocean
- Sea
- Gulf, Bay
- Strait, Fjord
- Lagoon
- Bank
- Seamount
- Tablemount
- Ridge
- Shelf
- Basin
- Escarpment, Sea Scarp
- Fracture
- Trench, Abyss
- National Park, Reserve
- Point of Interest
- Recreation Site
- Cave, Cavern
- Historic Site
- Ruins
- Wall, Walls
- Church, Abbey
- Temple
- Scientific Station
- Airport
- Port
- Lighthouse
- Mine
- Tunnel
- Dam, Bridge

Tongaat 37 Ee 29.37S 31.03 E
Tonga Islands 57 Jf 20.00S 175.00W
Tonga Ridge (EN) 57 Jg 21.00S 175.00W
Tongariki 63b Dc 17.01S 168.37 E
Tongatapu Group 57 Jg 21.10S 175.10W
Tongatapu Island 61 Fd 21.10S 175.10W
Tonga Trench (EN) 3 Kl 20.00S 173.00W
Tongbai 28 Bh 32.21N 113.24 E
Tongbai Shan 27 Je 32.20N 113.14 E
Tongcheng [China] 28 Bj 29.15N 113.49 E
Tongcheng [China] 28 Di 31.04N 116.56 E
Tongcheng → Dong'e 28 Df 36.19N 116.14 E
Tongchuan 27 Id 35.10N 109.03 E
Tongdao (Shuangjiang) 27 If 26.14N 109.45 E
Tongde 27 Hd 35.29N 100.32 E
Tongeren/Tongres 11 Ld 50.47N 5.28 E
Tonggu 28 Cj 28.33N 114.21 E
Tongguzbasti 27 Dd 38.23N 82.00 E
Tonggu Zhang 27 Kg 24.12N 116.22 E
Tong-Hae = Japan, Sea of- (EN) 21 Pf 40.00N 134.00 E
Tonghai 22 Mg 24.15N 102.45 E
Tonghe 27 Mb 46.01N 128.42 E
Tonghua 22 Oe 41.43N 125.55 E
Tongjiang 27 Nb 47.39N 132.30 E
Tongjosŏn-man 21 Of 39.30N 128.00 E
Tongliao 22 Oe 43.37N 122.15 E
Tongling 27 Ke 30.49N 117.47 E
Tonglu 28 Ej 29.48N 119.39 E
Tongmun'gŏ-ri 27 Mc 40.58N 127.08 E
Tongoa 63b Dc 16.54S 168.33 E
Tongoy 56 Fd 30.15S 71.30W
Tongren [China] 27 If 27.45N 109.09 E
Tongren [China] 27 Hd 35.40N 102.07 E
Tongres/Tongeren 11 Ld 50.47N 5.28 E
Tongsa Dzong 25 Ic 27.31N 90.30 E
Tongshan 28 Cj 29.36N 114.30 E
Tongta 25 Jd 21.20N 99.16 E
Tongtian He/Zhi Qu 21 Lf 33.26N 96.36 E
Tongue 9 Ic 58.28N 4.25W
Tongue of the Ocean 49 Ia 24.12N 77.10W
Tongue River 43 Fb 46.24N 105.52W
Tongxian 27 Kd 39.52N 116.38 E
Tongxin 27 Id 36.59N 105.50 E
Tongxu 28 Cg 34.29N 114.27 E
Tongyu (Kaitong) 27 Lc 44.47N 123.05 E
Tongyu Yunhe 28 Eg 34.46N 119.51 E
Tongzi 27 If 28.09N 106.50 E
Tonichi 48 Ec 28.35N 109.34W
Tönisvorst 12 Ic 51.19N 6.28 E
Tonj 35 Dd 7.17N 28.45 E
Tonj 30 Jh 7.31N 29.25 E
Tonk 25 Fc 26.10N 75.47 E
Tonkin (EN) = Bac-Phan 21 Mg 22.00N 105.00 E
Tonkin, Gulf of- (EN) = Beibu Wan 21 Mh 20.00N 108.00 E
Tonkin, Gulf of- (EN) = Vinh Bac Phan 21 Mh 20.00N 108.00 E
Tônlé Sab, Bœng- = Tonle Sap (EN) 21 Mh 13.00N 104.00 E
Tonle Sap (EN) = Tônlé Sab, Bœng- 21 Mh 13.00N 104.00 E
Tonnay-Charente 11 Fi 45.57N 0.54W
Tonneins 11 Gj 44.23N 0.19 E
Tönning 10 Eb 54.19N 8.57 E
Tōno 28 Pe 39.19N 141.32 E
Tonopah 43 Dd 38.04N 117.14W
Tonoshō 29 Dd 34.29N 134.11 E
Tonosí 49 Gj 7.24N 80.27W
Tønsberg 7 Cg 59.17N 10.25 E
Tonstad 7 Bg 58.40N 6.43 E
Tonumeia 65b Bb 20.28S 174.46W
Tonya 24 Hb 40.53N 39.16 E
Tooele 43 Ec 40.32N 112.18W
Toora-Hem 20 Ef 52.28N 96.22 E
Tootsi 8 Kf 58.34N 24.43 E
Toowoomba 58 Gg 27.33S 151.57 E
Topalu 15 Le 44.33N 28.03 E
Topa Taung 25 Jd 21.08N 95.12 E
Topeka 39 Jf 39.03N 95.41W
Topki 20 De 55.18N 85.40 E
Topko, Gora- 20 Ie 57.00N 137.23 E
Topl'a 10 Rh 48.45N 21.45 E
Toplet 15 Fe 44.48N 22.24 E
Toplica 15 Ef 43.13N 21.51 E
Toplița 15 Ic 46.55N 25.20 E
Topola 15 De 44.16N 20.42 E
Topoľčany 10 Oh 48.34N 18.10 E
Topolnica 15 Hg 42.11N 24.18 E
Topolobampo 47 Cc 25.36N 109.03W
Topolobampo, Bahía de- 48 Ee 25.30N 109.05W
Topolog 15 Hd 44.56N 24.16 E
Topolovgrad 15 Jg 42.05N 26.20 E
Topozero, Ozero- 5 Jb 65.40N 32.00 E
Toppenish 46 Ec 46.23N 120.19W
Toprakkale 24 Gd 37.06N 36.07 E
Top Springs 59 Gc 16.38S 131.50 E
Toquepala 54 Eg 17.38S 69.56W
Tor 35 Ed 7.51N 33.36 E
Tora 64d Ba 7.39N 151.53 E
Toraigh/Tory Island 9 Ef 55.16N 8.13W
Tora Island Pass 64d Ba 7.39N 151.53 E
Toråker 8 Gd 60.31N 16.29 E
Torbalı 24 Bc 38.10N 27.21 E
Torbat-e Heydariyeh 22 Hf 35.16N 59.13 E
Torbat-e Jam 23 Jb 35.14N 60.36 E
Torbay 9 Jk 50.28N 3.30W
Torbert, Mount- 40 Id 61.25N 152.24W
Torch Lake 44 Ec 45.00N 85.19W
Torčin 10 Vf 50.44N 25.05 E
Tordesillas 13 Hc 41.30N 5.00W
Tordino 14 Hh 42.44N 13.59 E
Töre 7 Fd 65.54N 22.39 E
Töreboda 7 Dg 58.43N 14.08 E
Torekov 8 Eh 56.26N 12.37 E
Torenberg 11 Lb 52.15N 5.55 E
Torez 16 Kf 47.59N 38.41 E
Torgau 10 Ie 51.34N 13.00 E
Torgelow 10 Kc 53.38N 14.01 E
Torgun 16 Od 50.10N 46.20 E
Torhamn 8 Fh 56.05N 15.50 E
Torhout 11 Jc 51.04N 3.06 E
Toribulu 26 Hg 0.19S 120.01 E
Torigni-sur-Vire 12 Be 49.05N 0.59W
Torii-Tōge 29 Ed 35.59N 137.49 E
Tori-Jima 29b Ab 26.35N 126.50 E
Torino = Turin (EN) 6 Gf 45.03N 7.40 E
Toriparu 55 Fc 16.20S 53.55W
Tori-Shima [Jap.] 27 Pe 30.25N 140.15 E
Tori-Shima [Jap.] 29b Bb 27.52N 128.14 E
Torit 35 Ee 4.24N 32.34 E
Torixoreu 54 Hg 16.15S 52.26W
Torkoviči 7 Hg 58.53N 30.20 E
Törmänen 7 Gb 68.36N 27.29 E
Tormes 13 Fc 41.18N 6.29W
Tornado Mountain 46 Hb 49.58N 114.39W
Tornavacas, Puerto de- 13 Gd 40.16N 5.37W
Torneå/Tornio 7 Fd 65.51N 24.08 E
Torneälven 5 Ib 65.48N 24.08 E
Torneträsk 7 Eb 68.22N 19.06 E
Torngat Mountains 38 Md 59.00N 64.00W
Tornio/Torneå 7 Fd 65.51N 24.08 E
Tornionjoki 5 Ib 65.48N 24.08 E
Tornquist 55 An 38.06S 62.14W
Toro 13 Gc 41.31N 5.24W
Toro 8 Gf 58.50N 17.50 E
Toro, Cerro del- 52 Jh 29.08S 69.48W
Toro, Isla del- 48 Kg 21.35N 97.32W
Toro, Monte- 13 Qe 39.59N 4.07 E
Toroiaga, Vîrful- 15 Hb 47.44N 24.43 E
Torokina 63a Bb 6.14S 155.03 E
Tōro-Ko 29a Db 43.08N 144.30 E
Törökszentmiklós 10 Qi 47.11N 20.25 E
Torola, Río- 49 Cg 13.52N 88.30W
Toronto 39 Le 43.39N 79.23W
Toropec 19 Dd 56.31N 31.39 E
Tororo 36 Fb 0.41N 34.11 E
Toros Dağları = Taurus Mountains (EN) 21 Ff 37.00N 33.00 E
Torquato Severo 55 Ej 31.02S 54.11W
Torquay 9 Jk 50.29N 3.29W
Torrà, Cerro- 52 Ie 4.38N 76.15W
Torrance 46 Fj 33.50N 118.19W
Torre Annunziata 14 Ij 40.45N 14.27 E
Torreblanca 13 Md 40.13N 0.12 E
Torrecilla 13 Hh 36.41N 5.00W
Torrecilla en Cameros 13 Jb 42.16N 2.37W
Torre del Greco 14 Ij 40.47N 14.22 E
Torre del Mar 13 Hh 36.44N 4.06W
Torredembarra 13 Nc 41.09N 1.24 E
Torre de Moncorvo 13 Ec 41.10N 7.03W
Torre de' Passeri 14 Hh 42.14N 13.56 E
Torredonjimeno 13 Ig 37.46N 3.57W
Torrejón de Ardoz 13 Id 40.27N 3.29W
Torrelaguna 13 Id 40.50N 3.32W
Torrelavega 13 Ha 43.21N 4.03W
Torre Miró, Puerto de- 13 Ld 40.42N 0.05W
Torremolinos 13 Hh 36.37N 4.30W
Torrens, Lake- 57 Eh 31.00S 137.50 E
Torrens Creek 59 Jd 20.46S 145.02 E
Torrent de l'Horta/Torrente 13 Le 39.26N 0.28W
Torrente/Torrent de l'Horta 13 Le 39.26N 0.28W
Torrenueva 13 If 38.38N 3.22W
Torreón 39 Ig 25.33N 103.26W
Torre-Pacheco 13 Lg 37.44N 0.57W
Torre Pellice 14 Bf 44.49N 7.13 E
Torres 64d Ab 7.19N 151.27 E
Tôrres 56 Kc 29.21S 49.44W
Torrès, Iles- = Torres Islands (EN) 57 Hf 13.15S 166.37 E
Torres Islands (EN) = Torrès, Iles- 57 Hf 13.15S 166.37 E
Torres Novas 13 De 39.29N 8.32W
Torres Strait 57 Ff 10.25S 142.10 E
Torres Vedras 13 Ce 39.06N 9.16W
Torrevieja 13 Lg 37.59N 0.41W
Torridon, Loch- 9 Hd 57.35N 5.50W
Torriglia 14 Df 44.31N 9.10 E
Torrijos 13 He 39.59N 4.17W
Torrington [Ct.-U.S.] 44 Ke 41.48N 73.08W
Torrington [Wy.-U.S.] 43 Gc 42.04N 104.11W
Torroella de Montgri 13 Pb 42.02N 3.08 E
Torröjen 7 Cf 63.55N 12.56 E
Torrox 13 Ih 36.46N 3.58W
Torsås 7 Dh 56.24N 16.00 E
Torsby 7 Cf 60.08N 13.00 E
Torshälla 8 Ge 59.25N 16.28 E
Torsken 7 Db 69.20N 17.06 E
Torsö 7 Cg 58.50N 13.50 E
Torto 14 Hm 37.58N 13.46 E
Tortola 47 Le 18.27N 64.36W
Tortoli 14 Dk 39.55N 9.39 E
Tortona 14 Cf 44.54N 8.52 E
Tortorici 14 Il 38.02N 14.49 E
Tortosa 13 Md 40.48N 0.31 E
Tortosa, Cabo de-/Tortosa, Cap de- 13 Md 40.43N 0.55 E
Tortosa, Cap de-/Tortosa, Cabo de- 13 Md 40.43N 0.55 E
Tortue, Ile de la- 47 Jd 20.04N 72.49W
Tortuga, Isla- 48 Dd 27.26N 111.55W
Tortum 24 Ib 40.19N 41.35 E
Torud 24 Pe 35.26N 55.07 E
Torugart, Pereval- 21 Je 40.32N 75.24 E
Torul 24 Hb 40.35N 39.18 E
Toruń (2) 10 Oc 53.00N 18.35 E
Toruń 10 Oc 53.02N 18.35 E
Torunos 49 Li 8.30N 70.04W
Toruńska, Kotlina- 10 Oc 53.00N 18.30 E
Torup 7 Ch 56.58N 13.05 E
Tõrva/Tyrva 7 Fg 58.01N 25.59 E
Tory Island/Toraigh 9 Ef 55.16N 8.13W
Torysa 10 Rh 48.39N 21.21 E
Toržok 19 Dd 57.03N 35.01 E
Tosa 28 Lh 33.29N 133.25 E
Tosas, Puerto de-/Toses, Port de- 13 Ob 42.20N 2.01 E
Tosashimizu 28 Lh 32.46N 132.57 E
Tosa-Wan 28 Lh 33.25N 133.35 E
Tosa-yamada 29 Ce 33.36N 133.40 E
Toscana = Tuscany (EN) (2) 14 Eg 43.25N 11.00 E
Toses, Port de-/Tosas, Puerto de- 13 Ob 42.20N 2.01 E
Toshibetsu-Gawa [Jap.] 29a Cb 42.54N 143.25 E
Toshibetsu-Gawa [Jap.] 29a Ab 42.25N 139.48 E
Tōshi-Jima 29 Ed 34.31N 136.52 E
To-Shima 29 Fd 34.31N 139.17 E
Tosno 7 Hg 59.34N 30.50 E
Toson-Cengel 27 Gb 48.47N 98.15 E
Toson Hu 27 Gd 37.08N 96.52 E
Töss 14 Cc 47.33N 8.33 E
Tossa de Mar 13 Oc 41.43N 2.56 E
Tostado 56 Hc 29.14S 61.46W
Tõstamaa/Tystama 8 Jf 58.17N 23.52 E
Tosu 29 Be 33.22N 130.30 E
Tosya 24 Fb 41.01N 34.02 E
Totak 8 Be 59.40N 7.55 E
Totana 13 Kg 37.46N 1.30W
Toten 8 Dd 60.40N 10.50 E
Toteng 37 Cd 20.23S 22.59 E
Tôtes 11 He 49.41N 1.03 E
Totes Gebirge 14 Hc 47.42N 13.55 E
Tôtias 35 Ge 3.57N 43.58 E
Totland 12 Ad 50.40N 1.32W
Totma 19 Ed 60.00N 42.45 E
Totness 54 Gb 5.53N 56.19W
Toto 36 Bd 7.10S 14.25 E
Totonicapán (3) 49 Bf 15.00N 91.20W
Totonicapán 47 Ff 14.55N 91.22W
Totora 54 Eg 17.42S 65.09W
Totoras 55 Bk 32.35S 61.11W
Totota 34 Dd 6.49N 9.56W
Totoya 63d Cc 18.57S 179.50W
Totten Glacier 66 He 66.45S 116.10 E
Totton 12 Ad 50.55N 1.29W
Tottori 27 Nd 35.30N 134.14 E
Tottori Ken (2) 28 Lg 35.25N 133.50 E
Tou, Motu- 64p Bb 21.11S 159.48W
Touâjil 32 Ee 21.45N 12.35W
Touat 30 Gf 27.40N 0.01W
Touba (3) 34 Dd 8.15N 7.45W
Touba 34 Dd 8.17N 7.41W
Toubkal, Jebel- 30 Ge 31.03N 7.55W
Touch 11 Hk 43.38N 1.24 E
Toucy 11 Jg 47.44N 3.18 E
Tougan 34 Ec 13.04N 3.04W
Touggourt 31 He 33.06N 6.04 E
Tougué 34 Cc 11.27N 11.41W
Touho 63b Be 20.47S 165.14 E
Touil 32 Hb 35.33N 2.36 E
Toûil 13 Oi 35.33N 2.36 E
Toukoto 34 Dc 13.28N 9.52W
Toul 11 Lf 48.41N 5.54 E
Toulépleu 34 Dd 6.35N 8.25W
Toulon 6 Gg 43.07N 5.56 E
Toulouse 6 Gg 43.36N 1.26 E
Toulumne River 46 Eh 37.36N 121.10W
Toumodi 34 Dd 6.33N 5.01W
Tounassine, Hamada- 32 Fd 28.36N 5.10W
Toungo 34 Hd 8.07N 12.03 E
Toungoo 22 Lh 18.56N 96.26 E
Touques 11 Ge 49.22N 0.06 E
Toura 35 Bc 10.30N 15.19 E
Touraine 11 Hg 47.12N 1.30 E
Touraine, Val de- 11 Hg 47.20N 1.30 E
Tourcoing 11 Jd 50.43N 3.09 E
Touriñan, Cabo de- 13 Ca 43.03N 9.18W
Tourine 32 Ee 22.00N 12.15W
Tournai/Doornik 11 Jd 50.36N 3.23 E
Tournai-Kain 12 Fd 50.38N 3.22 E
Tournon 11 Ki 45.04N 4.50 E
Tournus 11 Kh 46.34N 4.54 E
Touros 54 Ke 5.12S 35.28W
Tours 6 Gf 47.23N 0.41 E
Tourteron 12 Ge 49.32N 4.39 E
Toury 11 Hf 48.12N 1.56 E
Touside, Pic- 35 Ba 21.02N 16.25 E
Toussoro 35 Cd 9.02N 23.55 E
Toutouba 63b Cb 15.34S 167.16 E
Touwsrivier 37 Cf 33.20S 20.00 E
Toužim 10 If 50.04N 12.59 E
Tovar 49 Li 8.20N 71.46W
Tovarkovski 16 Kc 53.43N 38.13 E
Tovdalselva 8 Cf 58.12N 8.06 E
Tove 12 Bb 52.04N 0.50W
Tōwa 29 Gb 39.23N 141.15 E
Towada 28 Pd 40.35N 141.13 E
Towada-Kō 29 Ga 40.28N 140.55 E
Towanda 44 Ie 41.46N 76.27W
Tower 45 Jc 47.48N 92.17W
Towner 45 Fb 48.21N 100.25W
Townsend 46 Jc 46.19N 111.31W
Townshend, Cape- 59 Kd 22.15S 150.30 E
Townsville 58 Ff 19.16S 146.48 E
Towot 35 Ed 6.12N 34.25 E
Towson 44 If 39.24N 76.36W
Towuti, Danau- 26 Hg 2.45S 121.32 E
Toxkan He 27 Dc 41.08N 80.11 E
Tōya 29a Bb 42.39N 140.48 E
Toyah Creek 45 Ek 31.18N 103.27W
Tōya-Ko 28 Pc 42.33N 140.50 E
Toyama 22 Pf 36.41N 137.13 E
Toyama Ken (2) 28 Nf 30.40N 137.10 E
Toyama Trench (EN) 29 Ec 38.00N 138.00 E
Toyama-Wan 28 Nf 37.00N 137.15 E
Tōyō 28 Mh 33.22N 134.18 E
Toyohashi 27 Oe 34.46N 137.23 E
Toyokoro 29a Cb 42.48N 143.28 E
Toyonaka 29 Dd 34.47N 135.28 E
Toyo'oka 27 Od 35.33N 137.54 E
Toyosaka 29 Fc 37.55N 139.12 E
Toyota 28 Ng 35.05N 137.09 E
Toyotama 29 Ad 34.27N 129.19 E
Toyotomi 29a Ba 45.08N 141.47 E
Toyoura 29 Bd 34.10N 130.55 E
Trabancos 13 Gc 41.27N 5.11W
Traben Trabach 12 Je 49.57N 7.07 E
Trabzon 22 Fe 40.59N 39.43 E
Traer 45 Je 42.12N 92.28W
Trafalgar, Cabo- 13 Fh 36.11N 6.02W
Tragacete 13 Kd 40.21N 1.51W
Traiguén 56 Fe 38.15S 72.41W
Trail 39 He 49.06N 117.43W
Traill 41 Jd 72.45N 24.00W
Trairas, Rio- 55 Hb 14.07S 48.31W
Trairi 54 Kd 3.17S 39.15W
Traisen 14 Jb 48.22N 15.46 E
Trakai/Trakaj 7 Fi 54.38N 24.57 E
Trakaj/Trakai 7 Fi 54.38N 24.57 E
Trakt 17 Ee 62.44N 51.11 E
Trakya = Thrace (EN) 15 Jh 41.20N 26.45 E
Trakya = Thrace (EN) 5 Ig 41.20N 26.45 E
Tralee/Trá Lí 9 Di 52.16N 9.42W
Tralee Bay/Bá Thrá Lí 9 Di 52.15N 9.59W
Trá Lí/Tralee 9 Di 52.16N 9.42W
Trá Mhór/Tramore 9 Fi 52.10N 7.10W
Tramore/Trá Mhór 9 Fi 52.10N 7.10W
Tramping Lake 46 Ka 52.10N 108.48W
Trân 15 Fg 42.50N 22.39 E
Tranås 7 Dg 58.03N 14.59 E
Trancoso 13 Ed 40.47N 7.21W
Tranebjerg 8 Di 55.50N 10.36 E
Tranemo 8 Eg 57.29N 13.21 E
Trang 22 Li 7.33N 99.36 E
Trani 14 Ki 41.17N 16.25 E
Transantarctic Mountains (EN) 66 Jg 85.00S 175.00W
Transcaucasia (EN) 5 Kg 41.00N 45.00 E
Transilvania (EN) = Transylvania (EN) 15 Hc 46.30N 25.00 E
Transilvania (EN) = Transylvania (EN) 5 If 46.30N 25.00 E
Transkei 30 Jl 31.30S 29.00 E
Transkei 37 Df 32.45S 28.30 E
Transtrand 8 Ec 61.05N 13.19 E
Transtrandsfjällen 8 Ec 61.15N 12.58 E
Transvaal (2) 37 Dd 25.00S 30.00 E
Transylvania (EN) = Transilvania 15 Hc 46.30N 25.00 E
Transylvania (EN) = Transilvania 5 If 46.30N 25.00 E
Transylvanian Alps (EN) = Carpații Meridionali 5 If 45.30N 24.15 E
Trants Bay 51c Bc 16.46N 62.09W
Trapani 6 Hh 38.01N 12.29 E
Trapper Peak 46 Hd 45.54N 114.18W
Trappes 12 Ef 48.47N 2.01 E
Traralgon 59 Jg 38.12S 146.32 E
Trarza (3) 32 Ef 18.00N 15.00W
Trarza 30 Fg 17.20N 14.40W
Trașcăului, Munții- 15 Gc 46.23N 23.33 E
Trasimeno, Lago- 14 Gg 43.10N 12.05 E
Traslövsläge 8 Eg 57.04N 12.16 E
Trás os Montes e Alto Douro 13 Ec 41.30N 7.15W
Trat 25 Kf 12.13N 102.16 E
Traun 14 Ib 48.13N 14.14 E
Traun 14 Ib 48.16N 14.22 E
Traunsee 14 Hc 47.52N 13.48 E
Traunstein 10 Ii 47.53N 12.39 E
Trave 10 Gc 53.54N 10.50 E
Travemünde, Lübeck- 10 Gc 53.57N 10.52 E
Travers, Mount- 61 Dh 42.01S 172.44 E
Traverse, Lake- 45 Hd 45.43N 96.40W
Traverse City 43 Jc 44.46N 85.37W
Traverse Islands 66 Ad 56.36S 27.43W
Travers Reservoir 46 Ia 50.14N 112.51W
Tra Vinh 25 Lg 9.56N 106.20 E
Travis, Lake- 45 Hk 30.27N 98.00W
Travnik 23 Ff 44.14N 17.40 E
Travo 11a Bb 41.54N 9.24 E
Trbovlje 14 Jd 46.10N 15.03 E
Treasurers 63c Ba 9.53S 167.09 E
Treasury Islands 63a Bb 7.22S 155.37 E
Trebbia 14 De 45.04N 9.41 E
Třebíč 10 Lg 49.13N 15.53 E
Trebinje 14 Mh 42.43N 18.21 E
Trebisacce 14 Kk 39.52N 16.32 E
Trebišnjica 14 Lg 43.01N 17.47 E
Trebišov 10 Rh 48.40N 21.43 E
Treblinka 10 Sd 52.40N 22.03 E
Trebnje 14 Je 45.54N 15.01 E
Třeboň 10 Kg 49.01N 14.48 E
Třeboňská pánev 10 Kg 49.00N 14.50 E
Trégorrois 11 Cf 48.45N 3.15W
Tregrosse Islets 57 Gf 17.40S 150.45 E
Tréguier 11 Cf 48.47N 3.14W
Treherne 45 Gb 49.38N 98.41W
Treignac 11 Hi 45.32N 1.48 E
Treinta y Tres (2) 55 Ek 33.00S 54.15W
Treinta y Tres 56 Jd 33.14S 54.23W
Treis-Karden 12 Jd 50.11N 7.17 E
Trélazé 11 Fg 47.27N 0.28W
Trelew 56 Gf 43.15S 65.18W
Trelleborg 6 Hd 55.22N 13.10 E
Trélon 12 Gd 50.04N 4.06 E
Tremadoc Bay 9 Ii 52.40N 4.10W
Tremblant, Mount- 38 Le 46.15N 74.34W
Tremiti, Isole- = Tremiti Islands (EN) 5 Hg 42.10N 15.30 E
Tremiti Islands (EN) = Tremiti, Isole- 5 Hg 42.10N 15.30 E
Tremonton 46 If 41.43N 112.10W
Tremp 13 Mb 42.10N 0.54 E
Třemšín 10 Jg 49.33N 13.48 E
Trenche, Rivière- 44 Kb 47.35N 72.58W
Trenčín 10 Oh 48.54N 18.04 E
Trenque Lauquen 56 He 35.58S 62.42W
Trent 9 Mh 53.42N 0.41W
Trent, Vale of- 9 Li 52.45N 1.50W
Trentino-Alto Adige/Südtirol (2) 14 Fd 46.30N 11.20 E
Trento 14 Fd 46.04N 11.08 E
Trenton [Mo.-U.S.] 45 Jf 40.05N 93.37W
Trenton [N.J.-U.S.] 39 Le 40.13N 74.45W
Trenton [Ont.-Can.] 44 Ic 44.06N 77.35W
Tréon 12 Df 48.41N 1.20 E
Trepassey 42 Mg 46.44N 53.22W
Tres Arboles [Ur.] 56 Id 32.24S 56.43W
Tres Arroyos 53 Ji 38.22S 60.15W
Tres Bocas 55 Ck 32.44S 59.45W
Tres Caraçoes 54 Ih 21.42S 45.16W
Tres Cruces, Cerro- 48 Mj 15.28N 92.24W
Três de Maio 55 Eh 27.47S 54.14W
Tres Esquinas 54 Cc 0.43N 75.15W
Tres Isletas 55 Bh 26.21S 60.26W
Treska 15 Eh 41.59N 21.19 E
Treskavica 14 Mg 43.35N 18.24 E
Três Lagoas 53 Kh 20.48S 51.43W
Três Marias, Represa- 54 Ig 18.15S 45.15W
Tres Montes, Peninsula- 56 Eg 46.50S 75.30W
Três Passos 56 Jc 27.27S 53.56W
Tres Picos, Cerro- [Arg.] 52 Ji 38.09S 61.57W
Tres Picos, Cerro- [Mex.] 48 Li 16.36N 94.13W
Três Pontas 55 Je 21.22S 45.31W
Tres Puntas, Cabo- [Arg.] 52 Jj 47.06S 65.53W
Tres Puntas, Cabo- [Guat.] 49 Cf 15.58N 88.37W
Três Ranchos 55 Id 18.22S 47.47W
Tres Rios 55 Kf 22.07S 43.12W
Třešť 10 Lg 49.18N 15.28 E
Tres Valles 48 Kh 18.15N 96.08W
Tres Zapotes 47 Ee 18.28N 95.24W
Tretten 7 Cf 61.19N 10.19 E
Treuer Range 59 Gd 22.15S 130.50 E
Treungen 8 Ce 59.02N 8.33 E
Trêve, Lac la- 44 Ja 49.58N 75.31W
Trevi 14 Gh 42.52N 12.45 E
Trévières 12 Be 49.19N 0.54W
Treviglio 14 De 45.31N 9.35 E
Trevinca, Peña- 13 Fb 42.15N 6.46W
Treviño 13 Jb 42.44N 2.45W
Treviso 14 Ge 45.40N 12.15 E
Trevose Head 9 Hk 50.33N 5.01W
Trgovište 15 Fg 42.21N 22.06 E
Triánda 15 Lm 36.24N 28.10 E
Triangle 37 Ed 21.02S 31.28 E
Triángulos, Arrecifes- 48 Mg 20.57N 92.16W
Trianísia 15 Jm 36.18N 26.45 E
Tribeč 10 Oh 48.27N 18.15 E
Tribune 45 Fg 38.28N 101.45W
Tricarico 14 Kj 40.37N 16.09 E
Tricase 14 Mk 39.56N 18.22 E
Trichūr 25 Ff 10.31N 76.13 E
Tri City 46 De 43.02N 123.15W
Trie-Château 12 De 49.17N 1.50 E
Triel-sur-Seine 12 Ef 48.59N 2.01 E
Trier 10 Cg 49.45N 6.38 E
Trier-Ehrang 12 Ie 49.49N 6.41 E
Trier-Pfalzel 12 Ie 49.46N 6.41 E
Trieste 6 Hf 45.40N 13.46 E
Trieste, Golfo di- 14 He 45.40N 13.30 E
Trieux 11 Cf 48.50N 3.03W
Trifels 12 Je 49.11N 7.59 E
Triglav 5 Hf 46.23N 13.50 E
Trigno 14 Ih 42.04N 14.48 E
Trikala 15 Ej 39.33N 21.46 E
Trikhonis, Limni- 15 Ek 38.34N 21.30 E
Trikomo → Yeniboğaziçi 24 Ee 35.17N 33.52 E
Trikomon → Yeniboğaziçi 24 Ee 35.17N 33.52 E
Trikora, Puncak- 26 Kg 4.15S 138.45 E
Trilport 12 Ef 48.57N 2.57 E
Trim/Baile Átha Troim 9 Gh 53.34N 6.47W
Trincheras 48 Gc 28.55N 104.18W
Trincomalee 22 Ki 8.34N 81.14 E
Trindade 54 Ig 16.40S 49.30W
Trindade, Ilha da- 52 Nh 20.31S 29.19W
Třinec 10 Og 49.41N 18.42 E
Tring 12 Bc 51.47N 0.39W
Tringia 15 Ej 39.38N 21.25 E
Trinidad 52 Jd 10.30N 61.15W
Trinidad [Bol.] 53 Jg 14.47S 64.47W
Trinidad [Ca.-U.S.] 46 Cf 41.07N 124.07W
Trinidad [Co.-U.S.] 39 If 37.10N 104.31W
Trinidad [Cuba] 47 Id 21.48N 79.59W
Trinidad [Mex.] 48 Ec 28.25N 109.06W
Trinidad [Ur.] 56 Id 33.32S 56.54W
Trinidad, Golfo- 56 Eg 49.55S 75.25W
Trinidad, Isla- 55 Bn 39.08S 61.58W
Trinidad, Laguna- 55 Be 20.21S 61.35W
Trinidad and Tobago 53 Jd 11.00N 61.00W
Trinidade Spur (EN) 3 Cl 21.00S 35.00W
Trinitapoli 14 Ki 41.21N 16.05 E
Trinity 45 Ik 30.57N 95.22W
Trinity 38 Jg 29.47N 94.42W
Trinity Bay [Austl.] 59 Jc 16.25S 145.35 E
Trinity Bay [Can.] 42 Mg 48.15N 53.10W
Trinity Islands 40 Ie 56.33N 154.25W
Trinity Range 46 Ff 40.20N 118.45W
Trinity River 46 Df 41.11N 123.42W
Trinkitat 35 Fb 18.41N 37.43 E
Trino 14 Ce 45.12N 8.18 E
Trionto 14 Kk 39.37N 16.45 E
Trionto, Capo- 14 Kk 39.37N 16.45 E
Triora 14 Bf 43.59N 7.46 E
Tripoli (EN) = Ţarābulus (3) 33 Bc 32.40N 13.15 E
Tripoli (EN) = Ţarābulus [Leb.] 23 Ec 34.26N 35.51 E
Tripoli (EN) = Ţarābulus [Lib.] 31 Ie 32.54N 13.11 E
Tripolis 15 Fl 37.31N 22.22 E
Tripolitania (EN) = Tarābulus 30 Ie 31.00N 14.00 E
Tripolitania (EN) = Ţarābulus 33 Bc 30.00N 15.00 E

Index Symbols

(1) Independent Nation
(2) State, Region
(3) District, County
(4) Municipality
(5) Colony, Dependency
Continent
Physical Region
Historical or Cultural Region
Mount, Mountain
Volcano
Hill
Mountains, Mountain Range
Hills, Escarpment
Plateau, Upland
Pass, Gap
Plain, Lowland
Delta
Salt Flat
Valley, Canyon
Crater, Cave
Karst Features
Depression
Polder
Desert, Dunes
Forest, Woods
Heath, Steppe
Oasis
Cape, Point
Coast, Beach
Cliff
Peninsula
Isthmus
Sandbank
Island
Atoll
Rock, Reef
Islands, Archipelago
Rocks, Reefs
Coral Reef
Well, Spring
Geyser
River, Stream
Waterfall Rapids
River Mouth, Estuary
Lake
Salt Lake
Intermittent Lake
Reservoir
Swamp, Pond
Canal
Glacier
Ice Shelf, Pack Ice
Ocean
Sea
Gulf, Bay
Strait, Fjord
Lagoon
Bank
Seamount
Tablemount
Ridge
Shelf
Basin
Escarpment, Sea Scarp
Fracture
Trench, Abyss
National Park, Reserve
Point of Interest
Recreation Site
Cave, Cavern
Historic Site
Ruins
Wall, Walls
Church, Abbey
Temple
Scientific Station
Airport
Port
Lighthouse
Mine
Tunnel
Dam, Bridge

Tripura [3] 25 Id 24.00N 92.00 E
Trisanna 14 Ec 47.07N 10.30 E
Tristan da Cunha 30 Fi 37.05S 12.17W
Tristan da Cunha Group 30 Fi 37.15S 12.30W
Triste, Golfo- 50 Bg 10.40N 68.10W
Triunfo 55 Ee 20.46S 55.47W
Trivandrum 22 Ji 8.29N 76.55 E
Trivento 14 Ii 41.47N 14.33 E
Trjavna 15 Ig 42.52N 25.30 E
Trnava 10 Nh 48.22N 17.35 E
Troarn 12 Be 49.11N 0.11W
Trobriand Islands 57 Ge 8.30S 151.05 E
Trödje 8 Gd 60.49N 17.12 E
Trofors 7 Cd 65.34N 13.25 E
Trögd 8 Ge 59.30N 17.15 E
Trogir 14 Kg 43.32N 16.15 E
Troglav [Yugo.] 14 Kg 43.58N 16.36 E
Troglav [Yugo.] 14 Mg 43.02N 18.33 E
Trøgstad 8 De 59.38N 11.18 E
Troia 14 Ji 41.22N 15.18 E
Troick [R.S.F.S.R.] 22 Id 54.06N 61.35 E
Troick [R.S.F.S.R.] 20 Ee 57.23N 94.55 E
Troickoje [R.S.F.S.R.] 20 Df 52.58N 84.45 E
Troickoje [R.S.F.S.R.] 20 Ig 49.30N 136.32 E
Troickoje [Ukr.-U.S.S.R.] 15 Nb 47.38N 30.12 E
Troicko Pečorsk 19 Fc 62.44N 56.06 E
Troina 14 Im 37.47N 14.36 E
Troisdorf 12 Jd 50.49N 7.10 E
Trois Fourches, Cap des- 32 Gb 35.26N 2.58W
Trois-Pistoles 44 Ma 48.07N 69.10W
Trois Pitons, Morne- 51g Bb 15.22N 61.20W
Trois-Ponts 12 Hd 50.22N 5.52 E
Trois-Rivières [Guad.] 51e Ac 15.59N 61.39W
Trois-Rivières [Que.-Can.] 39 Le 46.21N 72.33W
Troissereux 12 Ee 49.29N 2.03 E
Troisvierges/Ulflingen 12 Hd 50.07N 6.00 E
Trojah 15 Hg 42.53N 24.43 E
Trojanovka 10 Ve 51.21N 25.25 E
Trojanski Manastir 15 Hg 42.53N 24.48 E
Trojanski prohod 15 Hg 42.48N 24.40 E
Trojebratski 19 Ge 54.25N 66.03 E
Trollhättan 7 Cg 58.16N 12.18 E
Trollheimen 7 Be 62.50N 9.05 E
Trollhetta 8 Cb 62.51N 9.19 E
Trolltindane 8 Bd 62.29N 7.43 E
Tromba 55 Ha 13.28S 48.45W
Trombetas, Rio- 52 Kf 1.55S 55.35W
Tromelin 30 Mj 15.52S 54.25 E
Tromøya 8 Cf 58.30N 8.50 E
Troms [3] 7 Eb 69.07N 19.15 E
Tromsø 6 Hb 69.40N 19.00 E
Tron 8 Db 62.10N 10.43 E
Tronador, Monte- 52 Ij 41.10S 71.54W
Trondheim 6 Hc 63.25N 10.25 E
Trondheimsfjorden 5 Hc 63.40N 10.50 E
Tronto 14 Hh 42.54N 13.55 E
Tropea 14 Jl 38.41N 15.54 E
Tropeiros, Serra dos- 55 Jb 14.43S 44.33W
Tropoja 15 Dg 42.24N 20.10 E
Trosa 7 Dg 58.54N 17.33 E
Troškūnai/Troškunaj 8 Ki 55.32N 24.59 E
Troškunaj/Troškūnai 8 Ki 55.32N 24.59 E
Trostberg 10 Ih 48.02N 12.33 E
Trostjanec 12 Id 50.29N 34.59 E
Trotuş 15 Kc 46.03N 27.14 E
Trou Gras Point 51k Bb 13.52N 60.53W
Troumasse 51k Bb 13.49N 60.54W
Trout Lake [Mi.-U.S.] 44 Eb 46.12N 85.01W
Trout Lake [N.W.T.-Can.] 42 Fd 60.35N 121.10W
Trout Lake [Ont.-Can.] 42 If 51.12N 93.19W
Trout Lake [Ont.-Can.] 42 If 53.54N 89.56W
Trout Peak 46 Kd 44.36N 109.32W
Trout River 42 Lg 49.29N 58.08W
Trouville-sur-Mer 11 Ge 49.22N 0.05 E
Trowbridge 9 Kj 51.20N 2.13W
Troy [Al.-U.S.] 43 Je 31.48N 85.58W
Troy [Mo.-U.S.] 45 Kg 38.59N 90.59W
Troy [Mt.-U.S.] 46 Hb 48.28N 115.53W
Troy [N.Y.-U.S.] 43 Mc 42.43N 73.40W
Troy [Oh.-U.S.] 44 Ee 40.02N 84.12W
Troy (EN)=Truva 24 Bc 39.57N 26.15 E
Troyes 6 Gf 48.18N 4.05 E
Troy Peak 43 Dd 38.19N 115.30W
Trstenik 15 Df 43.37N 21.00 E
Trubčevsk 19 De 52.36N 33.46 E
Truc Giang 25 Lf 10.14N 106.23 E
Truchas Peak 45 Di 35.58N 105.39W
Trucial Coast (EN) 21 Hg 24.00N 53.00 E
Trucial States (EN) → United Arab Emirates (EN) [1] 22 Hg 24.00N 54.00 E
Truckee 46 Eg 39.20N 120.11W
Trudfront 16 Og 45.56N 47.41 E
Trudovoje 20 Ih 43.18N 132.05 E
Trufanova 7 Kd 64.29N 44.05 E
Trujillo [2] 54 Db 9.25N 70.30W
Trujillo [Hond.] 47 Ge 15.55N 86.00W
Trujillo [Peru] 53 If 8.10S 79.02W
Trujillo [Sp.] 13 Ge 39.28N 5.53W
Trujillo [Ven.] 54 Db 9.22N 70.26W
Trujillo, Rio- 48 Hf 23.39N 103.08W
Truk Islands 57 Gd 7.25N 151.47 E
Trumann 45 Ki 35.41N 90.31W
Trumbull, Mount- 43 Ed 36.25N 113.10W
Trun 12 Gf 48.51N 0.02 E
Trung Phan=Annam (EN) 21 Me 15.00N 108.00 E
Truro [Eng.-U.K.] 9 Hk 50.16N 5.03W
Truro [N.S.-Can.] 39 Me 45.22N 63.16W
Truskavec 16 Ce 49.17N 23.34 E
Truth or Consequences (Hot Springs) 43 Fe 33.08N 107.15W
Trutnov 10 Lf 50.34N 15.54 E
Truva=Troy (EN) 24 Bc 39.57N 26.15 E
Truyère 11 Ij 44.38N 2.34 E
Trysil 8 Ec 61.25N 12.25 E
Trysil 7 Cf 61.18N 12.16 E
Trysilelva 5 Hd 59.23N 13.32 E
Trysilfjellet 8 Ec 61.18N 12.11 E
Trzcianka 10 Mc 53.03N 16.28 E
Trzcińsko Zdrój 10 Kd 52.58N 14.35 E
Trzebiatów 10 Lb 54.04N 15.14 E
Trzebież 10 Kc 53.42N 14.31 E
Trzebinia-Siersza 10 Pf 50.11N 19.25 E
Trzebnica 10 Ne 51.19N 17.03 E
Trzebnicki, Wał- 10 Me 51.30N 16.20 E
Trzebnickie, Wzgórza- 10 Me 51.15N 17.00 E
Trzemeszno 10 Nd 52.35N 17.50 E
Tsaidam Basin (EN)= Qaidam Pendi 27 Fd 37.00N 95.00 E
Tsamandá, Óri- 15 Dj 39.48N 20.21 E
Tsarap 25 Fb 33.31N 76.56 E
Tsaratanana 37 Hc 16.46S 47.38 E
Tsaratanana (EN)= Tsaratanana, Massif du- 30 Lj 14.00S 49.00 E
Tsaratanana, Massif du-= Tsaratanana (EN) 30 Lj 14.00S 49.00 E
Tsau 37 Cd 20.10S 22.27 E
Tsavo 36 Gc 2.59S 38.28 E
Tses 37 Be 25.58S 18.08 E
Tsévié 34 Fd 6.25N 1.13 E
Tshabong 31 Jk 26.02S 22.06 E
Tshane 31 Jk 24.01S 21.43 E
Tshangalele, Lac- 36 Ee 10.55S 27.03 E
Tshela 31 Ii 4.59S 12.56 E
Tshesebe 37 Dd 20.43S 27.37 E
Tshibala 36 Dd 6.56S 21.28 E
Tshibamba 36 Dd 9.06S 22.34 E
Tshikapa 31 Ji 6.25S 20.48 E
Tshilenge 36 Dd 6.15S 23.46 E
Tshimbalanga 36 Dd 9.43S 23.06 E
Tshimbulu 36 Dd 6.29S 22.51 E
Tshinsenda 36 Ee 12.16S 27.55 E
Tshofa 36 Ed 5.14S 25.15 E
Tshopo 36 Eb 0.33N 25.07 E
Tshuapa 30 Ji 0.14S 20.42 E
Tshwane 37 Cd 22.38S 22.05 E
Tsiafajavona 37 Hc 19.21S 47.15 E
Tsihombe 37 He 25.17S 45.30 E
Tsimlyansk Reservoir (EN)= Cimljanskoje Vodohranilišče 5 Kf 48.00N 43.00 E
Tsinan (EN)=Jinan 22 Nf 36.35N 117.00 E
Tsinghai (EN)=Ch'ing-hai Sheng → Qinghai Sheng [2] 27 Gd 36.00N 96.00 E
Tsinghai (EN)=Qinghai Sheng (Ch'ing-hai Sheng) [2] 27 Gd 36.00N 96.00 E
Tsingtao (EN)=Qingdao 22 Of 36.05N 120.21 E
Tsiribihina 37 Gc 19.42S 44.31 E
Tsiroanomandidy 37 Hc 18.50S 46.00 E
Tsis 64d Bb 7.18N 151.50 E
Tsjokkarassa 7 Fb 69.59N 24.32 E
Tsodilo Hill 37 Cc 18.50S 21.45 E
Tsu 27 Oe 34.43N 136.31 E
Tsubame 29 Fc 37.39N 138.56 E
Tsubata 28 Nf 36.40N 136.44 E
Tsubetsu 29a Db 43.43N 144.01 E
Tsuchiura 28 Pf 36.05N 140.12 E
Tsugaru-Hantō 29a Bc 41.00N 140.30 E
Tsugaru-Kaikyō=Tsugaru Strait (EN) 21 Qe 41.40N 140.55 E
Tsugaru Strait (EN)= Tsugaru-Kaikyō 21 Qe 41.40N 140.55 E
Tsuken-Jima 29b Ab 26.15N 127.57 E
Tsukidate 29 Gb 38.44N 141.01 E
Tsukigata 29a Bb 43.20N 141.39 E
Tsukuba-San 29 Gc 36.13N 140.06 E
Tsukumi 29 Be 33.04N 131.52 E
Tsukura-Se 29 Af 31.18N 129.47 E
Tsukushi-Sanchi 29 Be 33.25N 130.30 E
Tsumeb 31 Ij 19.13S 17.42 E
Tsumeb [3] 37 Bc 19.00S 17.30 E
Tsumkwe 37 Cc 19.32S 20.30 E
Tsuna 29 Dd 34.26N 134.54 E
Tsuno-Shima 29 Bd 34.22N 130.52 E
Tsuru 29 Fd 35.35N 138.50 E
Tsuruga 27 Od 35.39N 136.04 E
Tsuruga-Wan 29 Ed 35.45N 136.05 E
Tsurugi 29 Ec 36.26N 136.37 E
Tsurugi-San 29 De 33.51N 134.03 E
Tsurui 29a Db 43.14N 144.21 E
Tsurumi-Dake 29 Be 33.18N 131.27 E
Tsurumi-Saki 29 Ce 32.56N 132.05 E
Tsuruoka 28 Oe 38.44N 139.50 E
Tsuruta 29 Ga 40.44N 140.26 E
Tsushima 21 Of 34.30N 129.20 E
Tsushima [Jap.] 29 Ce 33.07N 132.30 E
Tsushima [Jap.] 29 Ed 35.10N 136.43 E
Tsushima-Kaikyō=Korea, Strait (EN) 21 Of 34.40N 129.00 E
Tsuwano 29 Bd 34.28N 131.46 E
Tsuyama 28 Lg 35.03N 134.00 E
Tua 13 Ec 41.13N 7.26W
Tuai 62 Gc 38.49S 177.08 E
Tuaim/Tuam 9 Eh 53.31N 8.50W
Tuakau 62 Fb 37.15S 174.57 E
Tual 26 Jh 5.40S 132.45 E
Tuam/Tuaim 9 Eh 53.31N 8.50W
Tuamotu, Iles-=Tuamotu Archipelago (EN) 57 Mf 19.00S 142.00W
Tuamotu Archipelago (EN) =Tuamotu, Iles- 57 Mf 19.00S 142.00W
Tuamotu Ridge (EN) 3 Ll 20.00S 145.00W
Tuapa 64k Ba 18.57S 169.54W
Tuapse 6 Jg 44.07N 39.05 E
Tuaran 26 Ge 6.11N 116.14 E
Tuasivi 65c Aa 13.40S 172.07W
Tuasivi, Cape- 65c Aa 13.40S 172.07W
Tuatapere 61 Ci 46.08S 167.41 E
Tuba 20 Ef 54.00N 91.40 E
Tuba City 46 Jh 36.08N 111.14W
Tubai, Ile- 57 Mg 23.18S 149.30W
Tubai-Manu → Maiao, Ile- 57 Lf 17.34S 150.35W
Tubal, Wādī at- 24 Jf 32.19N 42.13 E
Tuban 26 Fh 6.54S 112.03 E
Tubarão 56 Kc 28.30S 49.01W
Ţubayq, Jabal at- 24 Gh 29.32N 37.30 E
Tubbataha Reefs 26 Ge 8.51N 119.56 E
Tubeke/Tubize 12 Gd 50.41N 4.12 E
Tübingen 10 Fh 48.32N 9.03 E
Tubize/Tubeke 12 Gd 50.41N 4.12 E
Tubruq=Tobruk (EN) 31 Je 32.05N 23.59 E
Tubuai, Iles-/Australes, Iles- =Tubuai Islands (EN) 57 Lg 23.00S 150.00W
Tubuai Islands (EN)= Australes, Iles-/Tubuai, Iles- 57 Lg 23.00S 150.00W
Tubuai Islands (EN)= Tubuai, Iles-/Australes, Iles- 57 Lg 23.00S 150.00W
Tubutama 48 Db 30.53N 111.29W
Tucacas 54 Ea 10.48N 68.19W
Tucacas, Punta- 49 Mh 10.52N 68.13W
Tucavaca 55 Cd 18.36S 58.55W
Tucavaca, Rio- 55 Cd 18.37S 58.59W
Tuchola 10 Nc 53.35N 17.50 E
Tucholska, Równina- 10 Oc 53.40N 18.00 E
Tuchów 10 Rg 49.54N 21.03 E
Tucker Glacier 66 Kf 72.35S 169.20 E
Tucson 39 Hf 32.13N 110.58W
Tucuarembó 56 Id 31.44S 55.59W
Tucumán [2] 56 Gc 27.00S 65.30W
Tucumcari 43 Gd 35.10N 103.44W
Tucunuí 54 Id 3.42S 49.27W
Tucupido 54 Eb 9.17N 65.47W
Tucupita 54 Fb 9.04N 62.03W
Tudela 13 Kb 42.05N 1.36W
Tudia, Sierra de- 13 Ff 38.05N 6.20W
Tudmur 23 Ec 34.33N 38.17 E
Tudora 15 Jb 47.31N 26.38 E
Tuela 13 Ec 41.30N 7.12W
Tuensang 25 Ic 26.17N 94.40 E
Tuerto 13 Gb 42.18N 5.53W
Tufanbeyli 24 Gc 38.18N 36.11 E
Tufi 58 Fe 9.08S 149.20 E
Tugela 30 Kk 29.14S 31.30 E
Tug Fork 44 Ff 38.25N 82.35W
Tuguegarao 26 Hc 17.37N 121.44 E
Tugulym 17 Lh 57.04N 64.39 E
Tugur 20 If 53.51N 136.52 E
Tuhai He 28 Ee 38.05N 118.13 E
Tujiabu → Yongxiu 27 Kf 29.05N 115.49 E
Tujmazy 19 Fe 54.36N 53.42 E
Tukan 17 Hj 53.50N 57.31 E
Tukangbesi, Kepulauan-= Tukangbesi Islands (EN) 26 Hh 5.40S 123.50 E
Tukangbesi Islands (EN)= Tukangbesi, Kepulauan- 26 Hh 5.40S 123.50 E
Tukayel 35 Hd 8.05N 45.20 E
Tukayyid 24 Kh 29.47N 45.36 E
Tukituki 62 Gc 39.36S 176.56 E
Tuko Village 64n Ab 10.22S 161.02W
Tūkrah 33 Dc 32.32N 20.34 E
Tuktoyaktuk 39 Fc 69.27N 133.02W
Tukums 7 Fh 56.59N 23.10 E
Tukuringra, Hrebet- 20 Hf 54.30N 126.00 E
Tukuyu 36 Fd 9.15S 33.39 E
Tula 47 Ed 20.06N 99.19W
Tula 36 Gc 0.50S 39.51 E
Tula [Mex.] 48 Jf 23.00N 99.43W
Tula [R.S.F.S.R.] 6 Je 54.12N 37.37 E
Tula de Allende 48 Jg 20.03N 99.21W
Tula Mountains 66 Ee 66.54S 51.06 E
Tulancingo 47 Ed 20.05N 98.22W
Tulare 46 Fh 36.13N 119.21W
Tulare Lake Bed 46 Fh 36.03N 119.49W
Tularosa 45 Cj 33.04N 106.01W
Tularosa Valley 45 Cj 32.45N 106.10W
Tulcán 54 Cc 0.48N 77.43W
Tulcea [2] 15 Md 45.12N 29.10 E
Tulcea 15 Ld 45.10N 28.48 E
Tulčin 16 Fe 48.39N 28.52 E
Tulelake 46 Ef 41.57N 121.29W
Tulemalu Lake 42 Hd 62.55N 99.25W
Tulgheş 15 Ic 46.57N 25.46 E
Tuli 37 Dd 21.55S 29.12 E
Tuli 37 Dd 21.48S 29.04 E
Tulia 45 Fi 34.32N 101.46W
Tulihe 27 La 50.30N 121.51 E
Tullahoma 44 Dh 35.22N 86.11W
Tullamore/An Tulach Mhór 9 Fh 53.16N 7.30W
Tulle 11 Hi 45.16N 1.46 E
Tulln 14 Kb 48.22N 16.03 E
Tulln 14 Kb 48.20N 16.03 E
Tullner Becken 14 Jb 48.25N 15.55 E
Tullow/An Tulach 9 Gi 52.48N 6.44W
Tullus 35 Cc 11.03N 24.33 E
Tully 59 Jc 17.56S 145.56 E
Ţulmaythah 33 Dc 32.43N 20.57 E
Tuloma 5 Jb 68.52N 32.49 E
Tulos, Ozero- 7 He 63.35N 30.35 E
Tulsa 39 Jf 36.09N 95.58W
Tulskaja Oblast [3] 19 De 54.00N 37.30 E
Tuluá 54 Cc 4.05N 76.12W
Tuluksak 40 Gd 61.06N 160.58W
Tulum 47 Gd 20.13N 87.27W
Tulum 48 Pg 20.13N 87.28W
Tulun 22 Md 54.35N 100.33 E
Tulungagung 26 Fh 8.04S 111.54 E
Tuma 7 Ji 55.10N 40.36 E
Tuma, Rio- 49 Eg 13.03N 84.44W
Tumaco 53 Ie 1.49N 78.46W
Tumaco, Rada de- 54 Cc 1.50N 78.40W
Tumacuarí, Pico- 54 Fc 1.15N 64.40W
Tuman-gang 28 Kc 42.18N 130.41 E
Tumba 8 Ge 59.12N 17.49 E
Tumbarumba 59 Jg 35.47S 148.01 E
Tumbes [2] 54 Bd 3.50S 80.30W
Tumbes 53 Hf 4.05S 80.35W
Tumča 7 Hc 66.35N 31.45 E
Tumd Youqi 27 Jc 40.33N 110.32 E
Tumd Zuoqi 27 Jc 40.43N 111.06 E
Tumen 22 Oe 42.58N 129.49 E
Tumen Jiang 28 Kc 42.18N 130.41 E
Tumeremo 54 Fb 7.18N 61.30W
Tumkur 25 Ff 13.21N 77.05 E
Tummel 9 Je 56.43N 3.44W
Tummo 33 Be 23.00N 14.10 E
Tumon Bay 64c Ba 13.31N 144.48 E
Tumpat 26 De 6.12N 102.10 E
Tumu 34 Ec 10.52N 1.59W
Tumucumaque, Serra- 52 Ke 2.20N 55.00W
Tumwater 46 Dc 47.01N 122.54W
Tuna, Punta- 51a Cc 18.00N 65.52W
Tunapuna 50 Fg 10.38N 61.23W
Tunas 55 Hg 24.58S 49.06W
Tunas, Sierra de las- 48 Fc 29.40N 107.15W
Tunas Chicas, Laguna- 55 Am 36.01S 62.20W
Tunaydah 24 Cj 25.31N 29.21 E
Tunçbilek 15 Mj 39.37N 29.29 E
Tunduma 36 Fd 9.18S 32.46 E
Tunduru 36 Ge 11.07S 37.21 E
Tundža 15 Jh 41.40N 26.34 E
Tunga 34 Gd 8.07N 9.12 E
Tungabhadra 25 Fe 15.57N 78.15 E
Tungaru 35 Ec 10.14N 30.42 E
Tungnaá 7a Bb 64.10N 19.34W
Tungokočen 20 Gf 53.33N 115.34 E
Tungsten 42 Ed 62.05N 127.42W
Tungua 65b Bb 20.01S 174.46W
Tuni 25 Ge 17.21N 82.33 E
Tūnis=Tunis (EN) [3] 32 Jb 36.30N 10.00 E
Tūnis=Tunis (EN) 31 Ie 36.48N 10.11 E
Tūnis=Tunisia (EN) [1] 31 He 34.00N 9.00 E
Tunis (EN)=Tūnis 31 Ie 36.48N 10.11 E
Tunis (EN)=Tūnis [3] 32 Jb 36.30N 10.00 E
Tūnis, Canal de-=Sicily, Strait of- (EN) 5 Hh 37.20N 11.20 E
Tūnis, Khalīj- 32 Jb 37.00N 10.30 E
Tunisia (EN)=Tūnis [1] 31 He 34.00N 9.00 E
Tunja 53 Ie 5.31N 73.22W
Tunkhannock 44 Je 41.32N 75.57W
Tunliu 28 Bf 36.18N 112.53 E
Tunnhovdfjorden 8 Cd 60.25N 8.55 E
Tunø 8 Di 55.55N 10.25 E
Tunumuk 42 Ec 69.00N 134.57W
Tununak 40 Fd 60.35N 165.16W
Tunungayualok 42 Le 56.05N 61.05W
Tunxi 27 Kf 29.45N 118.15 E
Tuo He 28 Dh 33.16N 117.45 E
Tuo Jiang 27 If 28.55N 105.26 E
Tuostah 20 Ic 67.50N 135.40 E
Tuotuo He 27 Fe 34.03N 92.46 E
Tuotuohe/Tanggulashanqu 22 Lf 34.15N 92.29 E
Tupă 56 Jb 21.56S 50.30W
Tupaciguara 55 Hd 18.35S 48.42W
Tupai Atoll (Motu-Iti) 61 Kc 16.17S 151.50W
Tupanciretã 56 Jc 29.05S 53.51W
Tupelo 43 Je 34.16N 88.43W
Tupik 20 Gf 54.28N 119.57 E
Tupinambarana, Ilha- 54 Gd 3.00S 58.00W
Tupiraçaba 55 Hb 14.29S 48.34W
Tupper Lake 44 Jc 44.13N 74.29W
Tupungato, Cerro- 56 Gd 33.22S 69.47W
Tuquan 27 Lb 45.22N 121.33 E
Túquerres 54 Cc 1.06N 77.37W
Tur 15 Fa 48.04N 22.33 E
Tura 19 Gd 57.12N 66.56 E
Tura [India] 25 Ic 25.31N 90.13 E
Tura [R.S.F.S.R.] 22 Mc 64.17N 100.15 E
Turabah [Sau.Ar.] 23 Fe 21.13N 41.39 E
Turabah [Sau.Ar.] 23 Fd 28.13N 42.59 E
Turagua, Serranías- 50 Di 7.20N 64.35W
Turakina 62 Fd 40.02S 175.13 E
Turán 24 Qe 35.40N 56.50 E
Turan 20 Ef 52.08N 93.55 E
Turana, Hrebet- 20 If 51.30N 132.00 E
Turangi 62 Fc 38.59S 175.48 E
Turano 14 Gh 42.26N 12.47 E
Turanskaja Nizmennost 21 Ie 44.30N 63.00 E
Turawa 10 Of 50.45N 18.05 E
Turawskie, Jezioro- 10 Of 50.43N 18.10 E
Turbaco 49 Jh 10.19N 75.25W
Turbat 25 Cc 25.59N 63.04 E
Turbo 53 Ie 8.06N 76.43W
Turcoaia 15 Ld 45.07N 28.11 E
Turda 15 Gc 46.34N 23.47 E
Tūreh 24 Me 34.02N 49.17 E
Tureia Atoll 57 Ng 20.50S 138.32W
Turek 10 Od 52.02N 18.30 E
Turenki 8 Kd 60.55N 24.38 E
Turfan Depression (EN)= Turpan Pendi 21 Ke 42.30N 89.30 E
Turgai Gates (EN)= Turgajskaja Ložbina 21 Id 51.00N 64.30 E
Turgai Upland (EN)= Turgajskoje Plato 21 Id 51.00N 64.00 E
Turgaj [Kaz.-U.S.S.R.] 19 Gf 49.38N 63.28 E
Turgaj [U.S.S.R.] 21 Ie 48.01N 62.45 E
Turgajskaja Ložbina=Turgai Gates (EN) 21 Id 51.00N 64.30 E
Turgajskaja Oblast [3] 19 Ge 50.30N 66.00 E
Turgajskoje Plato=Turgai Upland (EN) 21 Id 51.00N 64.00 E
Turgeon, Rivière- 44 Ha 50.00N 78.55W
Turgutlu 24 Bc 38.30N 27.50 E
Turhal 24 Gb 40.24N 36.06 E
Türi/Tjuri 7 Fg 58.50N 25.27 E
Turia 13 Le 39.27N 0.19W
Turiaçu, Baia de- 54 Id 1.30S 45.15W
Turiec 10 Og 49.06N 18.52 E
Turijsk 10 Ue 51.10N 24.37 E
Turimiquire, Cerro- 54 Fa 10.03N 64.00W
Turin (EN) = Torino 6 Gf 45.03N 7.40 E
Turinsk 19 Gd 58.03N 63.42 E
Turja 16 Dd 51.48N 24.52 E
Turka [R.S.F.S.R.] 20 Ff 52.57N 108.13 E
Turka [Ukr.-U.S.S.R.] 10 Tg 49.07N 23.01 E
Turkana 36 Gb 4.00N 35.30 E
Turkana, Lake-/Rudolf, Lake- 30 Kh 3.30N 36.00 E
Türkeli 24 Fb 41.57N 34.21 E
Turkenstanski Hrebet 19 Gh 39.35N 69.00 E
Turkestan 22 Ie 43.18N 68.15 E
Türkeve 10 Qi 47.06N 20.45 E
Turkey (EN)=Türkiye [1] 22 Fg 39.00N 35.00 E
Turkey Creek 59 Fc 17.02S 128.12 E
Turki 16 Mc 52.01N 43.16 E
Türkiye=Turkey (EN) [1] 22 Fg 39.00N 35.00 E
Turkmenistan Sovet Socialistik Respublikasy/ Turkmenskaja SSR [2] 19 Fh 40.00N 60.00 E
Turkmen-Kala 18 Df 37.26N 62.19 E
Turkmenskaja Sovetskaja Socialističeskaja Respublika [2] 19 Fh 40.00N 60.00 E
Turkmenskaja SSR/ Turkmenistan Sovet Socialistik Respublikasy [2] 19 Fh 40.00N 60.00 E
Turkmenskaja SSR= Turkmen SSR (EN) [2] 19 Fh 40.00N 60.00 E
Turkmenski Zaliv 16 Ff 39.00N 53.30 E
Turkmen SSR (EN)= Turkmenskaja SSR [2] 19 Fh 40.00N 60.00 E
Türkoğlu 24 Gd 37.31N 36.49 E
Turks and Caicos Islands [5] 39 Ff 21.45N 71.35W
Turks Island Passage 49 Lc 21.25N 71.19W
Turks Islands 47 Jd 21.24N 71.07W
Turku/Åbo 6 Ic 60.27N 22.17 E
Turku-Pori [2] 7 Ff 61.00N 22.30 E
Turkwel 36 Gb 3.06N 36.06 E
Turlock 46 Eh 37.30N 120.51W
Turmantas 8 Li 55.42N 26.34 E
Turnagain, Cape- 62 Gd 40.30S 176.37 E
Turneffe Islands 47 Ge 17.22N 87.51W
Turnhout 11 Kc 51.19N 4.57 E
Turnov 10 Lf 50.35N 15.09 E
Turnu Roşu, Pasul- 15 Hd 45.33N 24.16 E
Turnu Măgurele 15 Hf 43.45N 24.52 E
Turočak 20 Df 52.16N 87.05 E
Turó de l'Home 13 Oc 41.45N 2.25 E
Turopolje 14 Ke 45.38N 16.07 E
Turpan 22 Ke 42.56N 89.10 E
Turpan Pendi=Turfan Depression 21 Ke 42.30N 89.30 E
Turquino, Pico- 47 Ie 19.59N 76.51W
Turrialba 49 Fi 9.54N 83.41W
Tursuntski Tuman, Ozero- 17 Kf 60.35N 63.55 E
Turtas 17 Ng 58.57N 69.10 E
Turtas 17 Ng 59.06N 68.50 E
Turtkul 19 Gg 41.35N 61.00 E
Turtle Mountain 45 Fb 49.05N 100.15W
Turugart Shankou 21 Je 40.32N 75.24 E
Turuhan 20 Dc 65.56N 87.42 E
Turuhansk 20 Dc 65.49N 87.59 E
Turvânia 55 Gc 16.39S 50.09W
Turvo 55 Hi 28.56S 49.41W
Turvo, Rio- [Braz.] 55 Hd 19.56S 49.55W
Turvo, Rio- [Braz.] 55 Gc 17.46S 50.12W
Tusaun/Thusis 14 Dd 46.42N 9.26 E
Tuscaloosa 43 Je 33.13N 87.33W
Tuscan Archipelago (EN)= Arcipelago Toscano 5 Hg 42.45N 10.20 E
Tuscania 14 Fh 42.25N 11.52 E
Tuscany (EN) = Toscana [2] 14 Eg 43.25N 11.00 E
Tuscarora Mountain 44 Ie 40.10N 77.45W
Tuscarora Mountains 46 Gf 41.00N 116.20W
Tuščibas, Zaliv- 18 Ba 46.10N 59.45 E
Tuscola 45 Lg 39.48N 88.17W
Tusenøyane 41 Oc 77.05N 22.00 E
Tuskar 16 Jd 51.40N 36.15 E
Tuskegee 44 Ei 32.26N 85.42W
Tuşnad Băi 15 Ic 46.09N 25.51 E
Tustna 8 Ca 63.10N 8.05 E
Tuszymka 10 Rf 50.09N 21.30 E
Tuszyn 10 Pe 51.37N 19.34 E
Tutajev 19 Dd 57.52N 39.32 E
Tutak 24 Jc 39.32N 42.46 E
Tuticorin 25 Fg 8.47N 78.08 E
Tutira 62 Gc 39.12S 176.53 E
Tutóia 54 Jd 2.45S 42.16W
Tutoko Peak 62 Bf 44.36S 167.58 E
Tutončana 20 Ed 64.05N 93.50 E
Tutova 15 Kc 46.06N 27.32 E
Tutrakan 15 Je 44.03N 26.37 E
Tuttle Creek Lake 45 Hg 39.22N 96.40W
Tuttlingen 10 Ei 47.59N 8.49 E
Tutuala 26 Ih 8.24S 127.15 E
Tutuila Island 57 Jf 14.18S 170.42W
Tutupaca, Volcán- 54 Dg 17.01S 70.22W
Tuupovaara 8 Nb 62.29N 30.36 E
Tuusniemi 7 Ge 62.49N 28.30 E
Tuvalu (Ellice Islands) [1] 58 Ie 8.00S 178.00 E
Tuvalu Islands 57 Ie 8.00S 178.00 E
Tuvana-i-Ra Island 61 Fd 21.00S 178.43W
Tuvana-i-Tholo Island 57 Ig 21.02S 178.49W
Tuvinskaja ASSR [3] 20 Ef 51.30N 94.00 E
Tuvutha 63d Cb 17.40S 178.48W
Tuwayq, Jabal- 21 Gg 25.30N 46.20 E
Tuxer Alpen 14 Fc 47.10N 11.45 E
Tuxford 12 Ba 53.13N 0.53W
Tuxpan 48 Hh 19.33N 103.24W
Tuxpán 47 Cd 21.57N 105.18W
Tuxpan, Arrecife- 48 Kg 21.02N 97.13W
Tuxpan, Rio- 48 Kg 20.53N 97.18W
Tuxpán de Rodríguez Cano 47 Ed 20.57N 97.24W
Tuxtla Gutiérrez 39 Jh 16.45N 93.07W
Túy 13 Db 42.03N 8.38W
Tuy, Rio- 50 Dg 10.24N 65.59W
Tuy An 25 Lf 13.17N 109.16 E

Index Symbols

[1] Independent Nation
[2] State, Region
[3] District, County
[4] Municipality
[5] Colony, Dependency
Continent
Physical Region
Historical or Cultural Region
Mount, Mountain
Volcano
Hill
Mountains, Mountain Range
Hills, Escarpment
Plateau, Upland
Pass, Gap
Plain, Lowland
Delta
Salt Flat
Valley, Canyon
Crater, Cave
Karst Features
Depression
Polder
Desert, Dunes
Forest, Woods
Heath, Steppe
Oasis
Cape, Point
Coast, Beach
Cliff
Peninsula
Isthmus
Sandbank
Island
Atoll
Rock, Reef
Islands, Archipelago
Rocks, Reefs
Coral Reef
Well, Spring
Geyser
River, Stream
Waterfall Rapids
River Mouth, Estuary
Lake
Salt Lake
Intermittent Lake
Reservoir
Swamp, Pond
Canal
Glacier
Ice Shelf, Pack Ice
Ocean
Sea
Gulf, Bay
Strait, Fjord
Lagoon
Bank
Seamount
Tablemount
Ridge
Shelf
Basin
Escarpment, Sea Scarp
Fracture
Trench, Abyss
National Park, Reserve
Point of Interest
Recreation Site
Cave, Cavern
Historic Site
Ruins
Wall, Walls
Church, Abbey
Temple
Scientific Station
Airport
Port
Lighthouse
Mine
Tunnel
Dam, Bridge

Tuy Hoa 25 Lf 13.05N 109.18 E
Tüyserkān 24 Me 34.33N 48.27 E
Tuz, Lake- (EN) = Tuz Gölü 21 Ff 38.45N 33.25 E
Tuz Gölü = Tuz, Lake- (EN) 21 Ff 38.45N 33.25 E
Tuzkan, Ozero- 18 Fd 40.35N 67.30 E
Tūz Khurmātū 23 Fc 34.53N 44.38 E
Tuzla 14 Mf 44.33N 18.41 E
Tuzlov 16 Lf 47.23N 40.08 E
Tuzluca 24 Jb 40.03N 43.39 E
Tuzly 15 Nd 45.56N 30.05 E
Tvååker 8 Eg 57.03N 12.24 E
Tvărdica 15 Ig 42.42N 25.54 E
Tvedestrand 7 Bg 58.37N 8.55 E
Tver' = Kalinin 6 Jd 56.52N 35.55 E
Tweed 9 Lf 55.46N 2.00W
Tweedsmuir Hills 9 Jf 55.30N 3.22W
Tweerivier 37 Be 25.35S 19.37 E
Twello, Voorst- 12 Ib 52.14N 6.07 E
Twente 11 Mb 52.17N 6.40 E
Twentekanaal 12 Ib 52.13N 6.53 E
Twilight Cove 59 Ff 32.20S 126.00 E
Twin Buttes Reservoir 45 Fk 31.20N 100.35W
Twin Falls 39 He 42.34N 114.28W
Twin Islands 42 Jf 53.50N 80.00W
Twin Peaks 46 Hd 44.35N 114.29W
Twisp 46 Eb 48.22N 120.07W
Twiste 12 Lc 51.29N 9.09 E
Twistringen 10 Ed 52.48N 8.39 E
Two Butte Creek 45 Eg 38.02N 102.08W
Two Harbors 45 Kc 47.01N 91.40W
Two Rivers 45 Md 44.09N 87.34W
Two Thumb Range 62 De 43.45S 170.40 E
Tychy 10 Of 50.09N 18.59 E
Tyczyn 10 Sg 49.58N 22.02 E
Tydal 7 Ce 63.04N 11.34 E
Tygda 20 Hf 53.07N 126.20 E
Tyin 8 Cc 61.15N 8.15 E
Tyin 8 Cc 61.14N 8.14 E
Tyler 43 He 32.21N 95.18W
Tylertown 45 Kk 31.07N 90.09W
Tylösand 8 Eh 56.39N 12.44 E
Tylöskog 8 Ff 58.40N 15.10 E
Tym 20 De 59.30N 80.07 E
Tymovskoje 20 Jf 50.50N 142.41 E
Tympákion 15 Hn 35.06N 24.45 E
Tynda 22 Od 53.07N 126.20 E
Tyne 9 Lf 55.01N 1.26W
Tyne and Wear [3] 9 Lg 55.00N 1.35W
Tynemouth 9 Lf 55.01N 1.24W
Týn nad Vltavou 10 Kg 49.14N 14.26 E
Tynset 7 Ce 62.17N 10.47 E
Tyra, Cayos- 49 Fg 12.50N 83.20W
Tyrifjorden 8 De 60.05N 10.10 E
Tyringe 8 Eh 56.10N 13.35 E
Tyrma 20 If 50.01N 132.10 E
Tyrnyauz 16 Mh 43.23N 42.56 E
Tyrol (EN) = Tirol [2] 14 Fc 47.10N 11.25 E
Tyrol (EN) = Tirol/Tirolo 14 Fd 47.00N 11.20 E
Tyrol (EN) = Tirolo/Tirol 14 Fd 47.00N 11.20 E
Tyrone 44 He 40.41N 78.15W
Tyrrell, Lake- 59 Ig 35.20S 142.50 E
Tyrrel Lake 42 Gd 63.05N 105.30W
Tyrrhenian Basin (EN) 5 Hh 40.00N 13.00 E
Tyrrhenian Sea (EN) = Tirreno, Mar- 5 Hh 40.00N 12.00 E
Tyrva/Tõrva 7 Fg 58.01N 25.59 E
Tyrvää 8 Jc 61.21N 22.53 E
Tysmenica 10 Uh 48.49N 24.56 E
Tyšmienica 10 Se 51.33N 22.30 E
Tysnesøy 7 Af 60.00N 5.35 E
Tysse 8 Ad 60.22N 5.45 E
Tyssedal 8 Bd 60.07N 6.34 E
Tystama/Tõstamaa 8 Jf 58.17N 23.52 E
Tystberga 8 Gf 58.52N 17.15 E
Tyszowce 10 Tf 50.36N 23.41 E
Tytuvénai/Tituvenaj 8 Ji 55.33N 23.09 E
Tywyn 9 Ii 52.35N 4.05W
Tzanconeja, Río- 48 Ni 16.51N 91.47W
Tzaneen 37 Ed 23.50S 30.09 E
Tzintzuntzan 48 Ih 19.38N 101.34W
Tzucacab 48 Og 20.04N 89.05W

U

Uaboe 64e Ab 0.31S 166.54 E
Uacurizal, Ilha do- 55 Dc 16.25S 56.05W
Ua Huka, Ile- 57 Ne 8.54S 139.33W
Uanukuhahaki 65b Ba 19.58S 174.29W
Ua Pou, Ile- 57 Me 9.23S 140.03W
Uaroo 59 Dd 23.00S 115.10 E
Uatumã, Rio- 52 Kf 2.26S 57.37W
Uaupés 53 Jf 0.08S 67.05W
Uaupés, Rio- 52 Je 0.02N 67.16W
Uaxactún 47 Ge 17.25N 89.29W
Ub 15 De 44.27N 20.05 E
Ubá 54 Jh 21.07S 42.56W
Übach-Palenberg [F.R.G.] 12 Cd 50.56N 6.05 E
Ubagan 19 Ge 54.23N 64.40 E
Ubaila 24 If 33.06N 40.15 E
Ubaitaba 54 Kf 14.18S 39.20W
Ubajay 55 Cj 31.47S 58.18W
Ubangi 30 Ii 0.30S 17.42 E
Ubatuba 55 Jf 23.26S 45.04W
Ubay 26 Hd 10.03N 124.28 E
Ubaye 11 Mj 44.28N 6.18 E
Ubayyiḑ, Wādī al- 23 Fc 32.34N 43.48 E
Ube 28 Kh 33.56N 131.15 E
Ubeda 13 If 38.01N 3.22W
Ubekendt Ejland 41 Gd 71.10N 53.45W
Uberaba 53 Lg 19.45S 47.55W
Uberaba, Lagoa- 55 Dc 17.30S 57.45W
Uberlândia 53 Lg 18.56S 48.18W
Überlingen 10 Fi 47.46N 9.10 E
Ubiaja 34 Gd 6.39N 6.23 E
Ubiña, Peña- 13 Ga 43.01N 5.57W
Ubiratã 55 Fg 24.32S 52.56W
Ubon Ratchathani 22 Mh 15.15N 104.54 E
Ubort 16 Fc 52.06N 28.30 E
Ubrique 13 Gh 36.41N 5.27W
Ubsu-Nur (Uvs nuur) 21 Ld 50.20N 92.45 E
Ubundu 31 Ji 0.21S 25.29 E
Učaly 19 Fe 54.20N 59.31 E
Učami 20 Ed 63.50N 96.39 E
Učaral 19 If 46.08N 80.52 E
Ucayali, Río- 52 If 4.30S 73.30W
Uccle/Ukkel 12 Gd 50.48N 4.19 E
Üçdoruk Tepe 24 Ib 40.45N 41.05 E
Ucero 13 Ic 41.31N 3.04W
Uchiko 29 Ce 33.34N 132.38 E
Uchi Lake 45 Ja 51.05N 92.35W
Uchinomi 29 Dd 34.30N 134.19 E
Uchinoura 29 Bf 31.16N 131.05 E
Uchiura-Wan 28 Pc 42.18N 140.35 E
Uchte 12 Ed 52.30N 8.55 E
Učka 14 Ie 45.17N 14.12 E
Uckange 12 Ie 49.18N 6.09 E
Uckermark 10 Jc 53.10N 13.35 E
Uckfield 12 Cd 50.58N 0.06 E
Učkuduk 19 Gg 42.10N 63.30 E
Učkurgan 18 Id 41.01N 72.04 E
Ucrainskaja Sovetskaja Socialističeskaja Respublika [2] 19 Df 49.00N 32.00 E
Ucross 46 Ld 44.33N 106.31W
Ucua 36 Bd 8.40S 14.12 E
Učur 21 Pd 58.48N 130.35 E
Uda [R.S.F.S.R.] 21 Pd 54.42N 135.14 E
Uda [R.S.F.S.R.] 20 Ff 51.45N 107.25 E
Uda [R.S.F.S.R.] 20 Ee 56.05N 99.34 E
Udačny 20 Gc 66.25N 112.20 E
Udaipur 22 Jg 24.35N 73.41 E
Udaj 16 Hd 50.05N 33.07 E
Udaquiola 55 Cm 36.34S 58.31W
Udbina 14 Jf 44.32N 15.46 E
Uddevalla 7 Cg 58.21N 11.55 E
Uddjaure 5 Hb 65.58N 17.50 E
Uden 12 Hc 51.40N 5.37 E
Udgīr 25 Fe 18.23N 77.07 E
Udhampur 25 Fb 32.56N 75.08 E
Udimski 7 Kf 61.09N 45.52 E
Udine 14 Hd 46.03N 13.14 E
Udipi 25 Ef 13.21N 74.45 E
Udmurtskaja ASSR [3] 19 Fd 57.20N 52.50 E
Udoha 8 Mg 57.58N 29.50 E
Udomlja 7 Ih 57.56N 35.02 E
Udone-Jima 29 Fd 34.28N 139.17 E
Udon Thani 25 Ke 17.25N 102.48 E
Udot 64d Bb 7.23N 151.43 E
Udskaja Guba 21 Pd 55.00N 136.00 E
Udskoje 20 If 54.36N 134.30 E
Udy 16 Je 49.47N 36.35 E
Udžary 16 Oi 40.31N 47.40 E
Udzungwa Range 36 Gd 8.05S 35.50 E
Uebonti 26 Hg 0.55S 121.38 E
Uecker 10 Kc 53.45N 14.04 E
Ueckermünde 10 Kc 53.44N 14.03 E
Ueda 28 Of 36.24N 138.16 E
Uele 30 Jh 4.09N 22.26 E
Uelen 20 Oc 66.13N 169.48W
Uelzen 10 Gd 52.58N 10.34 E
Ueno 29 Ed 34.46N 136.06 E
Uere 30 Jh 3.42N 25.24 E
Ufa 5 Le 54.40N 56.00 E
Ufa 6 Le 54.44N 55.56 E
Uftjuga 7 Lf 61.28N 46.12 E
Ugab 30 Ik 21.12S 13.38 E
Ugale/Ugăle 8 Ig 57.19N 21.52 E
Ugăle/Ugale 8 Ig 57.19N 21.52 E
Ugalla 36 Fd 5.08S 30.42 E
Uganda [1] 31 Kh 1.00N 32.00 E
Ugărčin 15 Hf 43.06N 24.25 E
Ugashik 40 He 57.32N 157.25W
Ughelli 34 Gd 5.30N 5.59 E
Ugijar 13 Ih 36.57N 3.03W
Uglegorsk 20 Jg 49.05N 142.06 E
Uglekamensk 20 Ih 43.18N 133.08 E
Ugleuralski 17 Hg 58.59N 57.38 E
Uglič 19 Dd 57.33N 38.23 E
Ugljan 14 Jf 44.05N 15.10 E
Uglovoje 28 Lc 43.20N 132.06 E
Ugnev 10 Tf 50.20N 23.45 E
Ugo 29 Gb 39.13N 140.23 E
Ugolnyje Kopi 20 Md 64.42N 177.50 E
Ugoma 36 Ec 4.55S 26.50 E
Ugra 19 De 54.30N 36.07 E
Ugtal-Cajdam 27 Ib 48.25N 105.30 E
Uh 10 Rh 48.33N 22.00 E
Uherské Hradiště 10 Ng 49.04N 17.27 E
Úhlava 10 Jg 49.45N 13.23 E
Uhlenhorst 37 Bd 23.45S 17.55 E
Uhta 6 Lc 63.33N 53.40 E
Uibh Fhaili/Offaly [2] 9 Fh 53.20N 7.30W
Uig 9 Gd 57.30N 6.20W
Uige 31 Ii 7.35S 15.04 E
Uige [3] 36 Cd 7.00S 15.30 E
'Uiha 65b Ba 19.54S 174.25W
Uijec 64d Bb 7.10N 151.57 E
Ŭijŏngbu 28 If 37.44N 127.02 E
Uiju 28 Hd 40.12N 124.32 E
Uil 19 Ff 48.36N 52.30 E
Uil 19 Ff 49.04N 54.42 E
Uilpata, Gora- 16 Mh 42.47N 43.44 E
Uinta Mountains 43 Ec 40.45N 110.05W
Uinta River 46 Kf 40.14N 109.51W
Uis 37 Ad 21.08S 14.49 E
Ŭisŏng 28 Jf 36.21N 128.42 E
Uitenhage 31 Jl 33.40S 25.28 E
Uithoorn 12 Gb 52.14N 4.52 E
Uithuizen 12 Ia 53.25N 6.42 E
Uithuizerwad 12 Ia 53.30N 6.40 E
Ujae Atoll 57 Hd 9.05N 165.40 E
Ujān 24 Og 30.45N 52.05 E
Ujandina 20 Jc 68.23N 145.50 E
Ujar 20 Ee 55.48N 94.20 E
Ujarrás 49 Fi 9.50N 83.40W
Ujedinenija, Ostrov- 20 Da 77.30N 82.30 E
Ujelang Atoll 57 Hd 9.49N 160.55 E
Újfehértó 10 Ri 47.48N 21.41 E
Uji 29 Dd 34.53N 135.47 E
Uji 19 Ge 54.20N 63.58 E
Uji-Guntō 28 Ji 31.10N 129.28 E
Ujiie 29 Fc 36.41N 139.57 E
Ujiji 31 Ji 4.55S 29.41 E
Ujjain 22 Jg 23.11N 75.46 E
Ujunglamuru 26 Gg 4.40S 119.58 E
Ujung Pandang (Makasar) 22 Nj 5.07S 119.24 E
Uk 20 Ee 55.04N 98.52 E
Ukata 34 Gc 10.50N 5.50 E
Ukeng, Bukit- 26 Gf 1.45N 115.08 E
Ukerewe Island 36 Fc 2.03S 33.00 E
Uke-Shima 29b Ba 28.02N 129.15 E
Ukhaydir 24 Jf 32.26N 43.36 E
Ukiah [Ca.-U.S.] 43 Cd 39.09N 123.13W
Ukiah [Or.-U.S.] 46 Fd 45.08N 118.56W
Uki Ni Masi 63a Ed 10.15S 161.44 E
Ukkel/Uccle 12 Gd 50.48N 4.19 E
Ukmerge/Ukmergė 7 Fi 55.14N 24.47 E
Ukmergė/Ukmerge 7 Fi 55.14N 24.47 E
Ukraine (EN) [2] 5 Jf 49.00N 32.00 E
Ukrainian SSR (EN) = Ukrainskaja SSR [2] 19 Df 49.00N 32.00 E
Ukrainskaja SSR/Ukrainska Radyanska Socialističná Respublika [2] 19 Df 49.00N 32.00 E
Ukrainskaja SSR = Ukrainian SSR (EN) [2] 19 Df 49.00N 32.00 E
Ukrainska Radyanska Socialističná Respublika/Ukrainskaja SSR [2] 19 Df 49.00N 32.00 E
Ukrina 14 Le 45.05N 17.56 E
Uku-Jima 29 Ae 33.16N 129.07 E
Ula 24 Cd 37.05N 28.26 E
Ulah Lake 45 Hh 36.58N 96.10W
Ulaidh/Ulster 9 Gg 54.30N 7.00W
Ulalu 64d Bb 7.25N 151.40 E
Ulan (Xiligou) 27 Gd 36.55N 98.16 E
Ulan → Otog Qi 27 Id 39.07N 108.00 E
Ulanbaatar → Ulan-Bator 22 Me 47.55N 106.53 E
Ulan-Badrah 28 Ac 43.58N 110.37 E
Ulan-Bator (Ulaanbaatar) 22 Me 47.55N 106.53 E
Ulanbel 19 Hg 44.49N 71.10 E
Ulan-Burgasy, Hrebet- 20 Ff 52.30N 108.30 E
Ulangom 22 Le 49.58N 92.02 E
Ulanhad/Chifeng 27 Kc 42.16N 118.57 E
Ulan Hol 19 Ef 45.27N 46.46 E
Ulan Hot/Horqin Youyi Qianqi 22 Oe 46.04N 122.00 E
Ulan Hua → Siziwang Qi 28 Ad 41.31N 111.41 E
Ulan-Hus 27 Eb 49.02N 89.23 E
Ulanów 10 Sf 50.30N 22.16 E
Ulansuhai Nur 27 Ic 40.56N 108.49 E
Ulan-Tajga 27 Ga 50.45N 98.30 E
Ulan-Ude 22 Md 51.50N 107.37 E
Ulan Ul Hu 27 Fe 34.45N 90.25 E
Ulas 24 Gc 39.27N 37.03 E
Ulawa Island 60 Gi 9.46S 161.57 E
Ulbeja 20 Je 59.20N 144.25 E
Ulchin 28 Jf 36.59N 129.24 E
Ulcinj 15 Ch 41.56N 19.13 E
Uleåborg/Oulu 6 Ib 65.01N 25.30 E
Ulefoss 7 Bg 59.17N 9.16 E
Ulegej 22 Ke 48.56N 89.57 E
Ulety 20 Gf 51.22N 112.30 E
Uleza 15 Ch 41.40N 19.53 E
Ulfborg 8 Ch 56.16N 8.20 E
Ulflingen/Troisvierges 12 Hd 50.07N 6.00 E
Ulft, Gendringen- 12 Ic 51.54N 6.24 E
Ulgain Gol 27 Kb 45.31N 117.50 E
Ulhāsnagar 25 Ee 19.10N 73.07 E
Uliastai → Dong Ujimqin Qi 27 Kc 45.31N 116.58 E
Uliga 58 Id 7.09N 171.13 E
Ulindi 30 Ji 1.40S 25.52 E
Ulithi Atoll 57 Ed 9.58N 139.40 E
Ulja 20 Je 58.48N 141.40 E
Uljanovka [R.S.F.S.R.] 8 Ne 59.37N 30.55 E
Uljanovka [Ukr.-U.S.S.R.] 16 Ge 48.20N 30.13 E
Uljanovsk 6 Ke 54.20N 48.24 E
Uljanovskaja Oblast [3] 19 Ee 54.00N 48.00 E
Uljanovski 19 He 50.05N 73.45 E
Uljasutaj 22 Le 47.45N 96.49 E
Ulkan 20 Fe 55.55N 107.55 E
Ulla 13 Db 42.39N 8.44W
Ullapool 9 Hd 57.54N 5.10W
Ullared 7 Ch 57.08N 12.43 E
Ulldecona 13 Md 40.36N 0.27 E
Ullsfjorden 7 Eb 69.58N 20.00 E
Ullswater 9 Kg 54.34N 2.54W
Ullŭng-Do 28 Kf 37.29N 130.52 E
Ullvettern 8 Fe 59.25N 14.15 E
Ulm 10 Fh 48.25N 10.00 E
Ulmen 12 Id 50.13N 6.59 E
Ulmeni 15 Jd 45.04N 26.39 E
Ulmu 15 Je 44.16N 26.55 E
Ulongwé 37 Eb 14.43S 34.21 E
Ulricehamn 7 Ch 57.47N 13.25 E
Ulrichstein 12 Ld 50.35N 9.12 E
Ulrum 12 Ia 53.22N 6.20 E
Ulrum-Zoutkamp 12 Ia 53.20N 6.18 E
Ulsan 27 Md 35.33N 129.19 E
Ulsteinvik 7 Ae 62.20N 5.53 E
Ulster 10 Ff 50.51N 9.59 E
Ulster/Ulaidh 9 Gg 54.30N 7.00W
Ulster Canal 9 Gg 54.27N 6.40W
Ulu 35 Ec 10.43N 33.29 E
Ulu/Uulu 8 Kf 58.13N 24.29 E
Ulúa, Río- 47 Ge 15.56N 87.43W
Ulubat Gölü 24 Cb 40.10N 28.35 E
Ulubey 24 Cc 38.09N 29.33 E
Uludağ 23 Ca 40.04N 29.13 E
Uludere 24 Jd 37.27N 42.51 E
Ulugqat/Wuqia 27 Cd 39.40N 75.07 E
Ulukışla 24 Fd 37.33N 34.30 E
Ulungur He 21 Ke 46.58N 87.28 E
Ulungur Hu 27 Eb 47.20N 87.10 E
Ulus 24 Eb 41.35N 32.39 E
Ulus Dağ 15 Lj 39.18N 28.24 E
Ulva 9 Ge 56.28N 6.12W
Ulverston 9 Jg 54.12N 3.06W
Ulverstone 59 Jh 41.09S 146.10 E
Ulvik 8 Bd 60.34N 6.54 E
Ulvön 8 Ha 63.05N 18.40 E
Ulysses 45 Fh 37.35N 101.22W
Ulytau 19 Gf 48.35N 67.05 E
Ulytau, Gora- 19 Gf 48.45N 67.00 E
Uly-Žilanšik 19 Gf 48.51N 63.47 E
Uma 27 La 52.36N 120.38 E
Umag 14 He 45.25N 13.32 E
Umala 54 Eg 17.24S 67.58W
Umán 48 Og 20.53N 89.45W
Uman 64d Bb 7.18N 151.53 E
Uman 19 Df 48.47N 30.09 E
'Umān 21 Hg 22.10N 58.00 E
'Umān = Oman (EN) [1] 22 Hg 21.00N 57.00 E
'Umān, Khalīj- = Oman, Gulf of- (EN) 21 Hg 25.00N 58.00 E
Umanak 41 Gd 70.36N 52.15W
Ũmánarssuaq/Farvel, Kap- 67 Nb 59.50N 43.50W
Umatac 64c Bb 13.18N 144.40 E
Umba 19 Db 66.41N 34.17 E
Umbelasha 35 Cd 9.51N 24.50 E
Umbertide 14 Gg 43.18N 12.20 E
Umberto de Campos 54 Jd 2.37S 43.27W
Umboi Island 57 Fe 5.36S 148.00 E
Umbozero, Ozero- 7 Ic 67.45N 34.20 E
Umbria [2] 14 Gh 43.00N 12.30 E
Ume 37 Dc 17.15S 28.20 E
Umeå 6 Ic 63.50N 20.15 E
Umeälven 5 Ic 63.47N 20.16 E
Umm al Arānib 33 Bd 26.08N 14.45 E
Umm al Hayf, Wādī- 23 Hf 18.37N 53.59 E
Umm al Jamāājim 24 Ki 26.59N 45.19 E
Umm al Qaywayn 23 Id 25.35N 55.34 E
Ummanz 10 Jb 54.30N 13.10 E
Umm ar Rizam 33 Dc 32.32N 23.00 E
Umm as Samīm 23 Ie 21.30N 56.45 E
Umm Bāb 24 Nj 25.12N 50.48 E
Umm Bel 35 Dc 13.32N 28.04 E
Umm Buru 35 Cb 15.01N 23.36 E
Umm Dhibbān 35 Dc 14.14N 29.37 E
Umm Durmān = Omdurman (EN) 31 Kg 15.38N 32.30 E
Umm Inderaba 35 Eb 15.12N 31.54 E
Umm Kaddādah 35 Dc 13.36N 26.42 E
Umm Lajj 23 Ed 25.04N 37.13 E
Umm Naqqāt, Jabal- 24 Fj 25.30N 34.14 E
Umm Qam'ul 24 Pj 24.47N 54.42 E
Umm Ruwābah 31 Kg 12.54N 31.13 E
Umm Sayyālah 35 Ec 14.25N 31.00 E
Umm Urūmah 24 Gj 25.46N 36.33 E
Umnak 38 Cd 58.25N 168.10W
Umne-Gobi 27 Fb 49.06N 91.43 E
Umpqua River 46 Ce 43.42N 124.03W
Umpulu 36 Ce 12.42S 17.40 E
Umsini, Gunung- 26 Jg 1.35S 133.30 E
Umtata 31 Jl 31.35S 28.47 E
Umuarama 56 Jb 23.45S 53.20W
Umurbey 15 Ji 40.14N 26.36 E
Umvukwes 37 Ec 17.01S 30.52 E
Umvuma 37 Ec 19.15S 30.35 E
Umzingwani 37 Dd 22.12S 29.56 E
Una 14 Ke 45.16N 16.55 E
Unabetsu-Dake 29a Db 43.52N 144.51 E
Unac 14 Kf 44.29N 16.08 E
Unai 54 Ig 16.23S 46.53W
Unalakleet 40 Gd 63.53N 160.47W
Unalaska 38 Cd 53.45N 166.45W
Unare, Río- 50 Dg 10.06N 65.12W
Unauna, Pulau- 26 Hg 0.10S 121.35 E
'Unayzah [Jor.] 24 Fg 30.29N 35.48 E
'Unayzah [Sau. Ar.] 22 Gg 26.06N 43.56 E
Uncia 54 Eg 18.27S 66.37W
Uncompahgre Peak 43 Fd 38.04N 107.28W
Uncompahgre Plateau 45 Bg 38.30N 108.25W
Unden 8 Ff 58.45N 14.25 E
Underberg 37 De 29.50S 29.22 E
Under-Han 22 Ne 47.19N 110.39 E
Undjulung 20 Hc 66.20N 124.40 E
Undu Point 63d Cb 16.08S 179.57W
Undva Neem/Kiprarenukk, Mys- 8 If 58.25N 21.45 E
Uneča 16 Hc 52.50N 32.44 E
'Ung, Jabal al- 14 Dn 36.45N 9.35 E
Unga 40 Ge 55.15N 160.45W
Ungava, Péninsule d'- = Ungava Peninsula (EN) 38 Lc 60.00N 74.00W
Ungava Bay 38 Md 59.30N 67.30W
Ungava Peninsula (EN) = Ungava, Péninsule d'- 38 Lc 60.00N 74.00W
Ungeny 16 Ef 47.13N 27.50 E
Unggi 28 Kc 42.21N 130.23 E
Ungureni 15 Jb 47.53N 26.47 E
Ungwatiri 35 Fb 16.55N 36.05 E
União 54 Jd 4.35S 42.52W
União da Vitória 56 Jc 26.13S 51.05W
União dos Palmares 54 Ke 9.10S 36.02W
Uničov 10 Ng 49.49N 17.07 E
Uniejów 10 Oe 51.58N 18.49 E
Unije 14 If 44.38N 14.15 E
Unimak 38 Cd 54.50N 164.00W
Unimak Pass 40 Gf 54.35N 164.43W
Unini, Rio- 54 Fd 1.41S 61.30W
Union [Mo.-U.S.] 45 Kg 38.27N 91.00W
Union [S.C.-U.S.] 44 Gh 34.42N 81.37W
Union City 44 Cg 36.26N 89.03W
Uniondale 37 Cf 33.40S 23.08 E
Unión de Reyes 49 Gb 22.48N 81.32W
Unión de Tula 48 Gh 19.58N 104.16W
Union Island 50 Ff 12.36N 61.26W
Union Islands/Tokelau 57 Je 9.00S 171.45W
Union of Soviet Socialist Republics (USSR) (EN) = SSSR [1] 22 Jd 60.00N 80.00 E
Union Seamount (EN) 42 Eg 49.35N 132.45W
Union Springs 44 Ei 32.09N 85.49W
Uniontown 44 Hf 39.54N 79.44W
Unionville 45 Jf 40.29N 93.01W
United Arab Emirates (EN) = Al Imārāt al 'Arabīyah al Muttaḩidah [1] 22 Hg 24.00N 54.00 E
United Arab Republic (EN) → Egypt (EN) [1] 31 Jf 27.00N 30.00 E
United Kingdom [1] 6 Fe 54.00N 2.00W
United Kingdom of Great Britain and Northern Ireland [1] 6 Fe 54.00N 2.00W
United States [1] 39 Jf 38.00N 97.00W
United States of America [1] 39 Jf 38.00N 97.00W
Unity [Or.-U.S.] 46 Fd 44.29N 118.13W
Unity [Sask.-Can.] 42 Gf 52.27N 109.10W
Universales, Montes- 13 Kd 40.18N 1.33W
University City 45 Kg 38.39N 90.19W
Unna 10 De 51.32N 7.41 E
Unnāb, Wādī al- 24 Gg 30.11N 36.39 E
Unnukka 8 Lb 62.25N 27.55 E
Unst 5 Fc 60.45N 0.55W
Unstrut 10 He 51.10N 11.48 E
Unterfranken 10 Fg 50.00N 10.00 E
Unterwalden-Nidwalden [2] 14 Cd 46.55N 8.30 E
Unterwalden-Obwalden [2] 14 Cd 46.50N 8.20 E
Unuli Horog 27 Fd 35.12N 91.58 E
Ünye 23 Ea 41.08N 37.17 E
Unža 5 Kd 57.20N 43.08 E
Unzen-Dake 29 Be 32.45N 130.17 E
Uoleva 65b Ba 19.51S 174.24W
Uozu 28 Nf 36.48N 137.24 E
Úpa 10 Lf 50.22N 15.54 E
Upata 54 Fb 8.01N 62.24W
Upemba, Lac- 36 Ed 8.36S 26.26 E
Upernavik 41 Gd 72.20N 56.00W
Upin 26 Ig 2.56S 129.11 E
Upington 31 Jk 28.25S 21.15 E
Upland 12 Kc 51.18N 8.42 E
Upolu Island 57 Jf 13.55S 171.45W
Upolu Point 60 Oc 20.16N 155.52W
Upper [3] 34 Ec 10.30N 1.30W
Upper Arlington 44 Fe 40.01N 83.03W
Upper Arrow Lake 46 Ga 50.30N 117.55W
Upper Austria (EN) = Oberösterreich [2] 14 Hb 48.15N 14.00 E
Upper Hutt 62 Fd 41.07S 175.04 E
Upper Klamath Lake 43 Cc 42.23N 122.00W
Upper Lake 46 Ef 41.44N 120.08W
Upper Lough Erne/Loch Éirne Uachtair 9 Fg 54.20N 7.30W
Upper Red Lake 45 Ib 48.10N 94.40W
Upper Sandusky 44 Fe 40.48N 83.17W
Upper Sheik 35 Hd 9.57N 45.09 E
Upper Thames Valley 9 Lj 51.40N 1.40W
Upper Trajan's Wall (EN) = Verhni Traijanov Val 15 Lc 46.40N 29.00 E
Upper Volta → Burkina Faso [1] 31 Gg 13.00N 2.00W
Uppingham 12 Bb 52.35N 0.43W
Uppland 8 Gd 60.00N 17.50 E
Upplands Väsby 8 Ge 59.31N 17.54 E
Uppsala [2] 7 Df 60.00N 17.45 E
Uppsala 6 Hd 59.52N 17.38 E
Upsala 45 Kb 49.02N 90.29W
Upshi 25 Fb 33.50N 77.49 E
Upton 46 Md 44.06N 104.38W
Uqbān 33 Hf 15.30N 42.23 E
'Uqlat aş Şuqūr 24 Jj 25.53N 42.15 E
Uqturpan/Wushi 27 Cc 41.10N 79.16 E
Ur 23 Gc 30.58N 46.06 E
Urabá, Golfo de- 54 Cb 8.25N 77.00W
Uracoa 50 Eh 9.00N 62.21W
Uracoa, Río- 50 Eh 9.08N 62.20W
Uradarja 18 Fe 38.51N 66.02 E
Urad Qianqi 27 Ic 40.49N 108.37 E
Urad Zhonghou Lianheqi (Haliut) 27 Ic 41.34N 108.32 E
Uraga-Suido 29 Fd 35.15N 139.45 E
Ura-Guba 7 Hb 69.18N 32.48 E
Urahoro 29a Cb 42.48N 143.38 E
Urahoro-Gawa 29a Cb 42.44N 143.40 E
Uraj 19 Gc 60.08N 64.40 E
Urakawa 28 Qc 42.09N 142.47 E
Ural 5 Lf 47.00N 51.48 E
Ural Mountains (EN) = Uralskije Gory 5 Ld 57.00N 60.00 E
Uralsk 6 Le 51.14N 51.22 E
Uralskaja Oblast [3] 19 Ff 49.45N 51.00 E
Uralskije Gory = Ural Mountains (EN) 5 Ld 57.00N 60.00 E
Urambo 36 Fd 5.04S 32.03 E
Uranium City 39 Id 59.34N 108.36W
Uraricoera 54 Fc 3.27N 60.59W
Uraricoera, Rio- 52 Je 3.02N 60.30W
Ura-Tjube 19 Gh 39.53N 69.01 E
Urawa 28 Og 35.51N 139.39 E
'Uray'irah 24 Mj 25.57N 48.53 E
Urayq, Nafūd al- 24 Jj 25.17N 42.25 E
Urbana [Il.-U.S.] 45 Lf 40.07N 88.12W
Urbana [Oh.-U.S.] 44 Fe 40.06N 83.45W
Urbandale 45 Jf 41.38N 93.48W
Urbania 14 Gg 43.40N 12.31 E

Index Symbols

[1] Independent Nation
[2] State, Region
[3] District, County
[4] Municipality
[5] Colony, Dependency
Continent
Physical Region
Historical or Cultural Region
Mount, Mountain
Volcano
Hill
Mountains, Mountain Range
Hills, Escarpment
Plateau, Upland
Pass, Gap
Plain, Lowland
Delta
Salt Flat
Valley, Canyon
Crater, Cave
Karst Features
Depression
Polder
Desert, Dunes
Forest, Woods
Heath, Steppe
Oasis
Cape, Point
Coast, Beach
Cliff
Peninsula
Isthmus
Sandbank
Island
Atoll
Rock, Reef
Islands, Archipelago
Rocks, Reefs
Coral Reef
Well, Spring
Geyser
River, Stream
Waterfall Rapids
River Mouth, Estuary
Lake
Salt Lake
Intermittent Lake
Reservoir
Swamp, Pond
Canal
Glacier
Ice Shelf, Pack Ice
Ocean
Sea
Gulf, Bay
Strait, Fjord
Lagoon
Bank
Seamount
Tablemount
Ridge
Shelf
Basin
Escarpment, Sea Scarp
Fracture
Trench, Abyss
National Park, Reserve
Point of Interest
Recreation Site
Cave, Cavern
Historic Site
Ruins
Wall, Walls
Church, Abbey
Temple
Scientific Station
Airport
Port
Lighthouse
Mine
Tunnel
Dam, Bridge

Name	Page	Grid	Lat.	Long.
Urbano Santos	54	Jd	3.12S	43.23W
Urbino	14	Gg	43.43N	12.38 E
Urbino, Étang d'-	11a	Ba	42.02N	9.28 E
Urbión, Picos de-	13	Jb	42.01N	2.52W
Urcel	12	Fe	49.30N	3.33 E
Urcos	54	Df	13.42S	71.38W
Urdinarrain	55	Ck	32.41S	58.53W
Urdoma	7	Lf	61.47N	48.29 E
Urdžar	19	If	47.05N	81.37 E
Ure	9	Lg	54.01N	1.12W
Uré	49	Jj	7.46N	75.31W
Uren	19	Ed	57.29N	45.48 E
Urenui	62	Fc	39.00S	174.23 E
Ures	47	Bc	29.26N	110.24W
Ureshino	29	Ab	33.06N	129.59 E
'Urf, Jabal al-	24	Ei	27.49N	32.55 E
Urfa	23	Eb	37.08N	38.46 E
Urfa Platosu	24	Hd	37.10N	38.50 E
Urgal	20	If	51.00N	132.50 E
Urgel, Llanos de-	13	Lc	41.25N	0.36W
Urgel, Llanos de-/Urgell, Pla d'-	13	Lc	41.25N	0.36W
Urgell, Pla d'-	13	Lc	41.25N	0.36W
Urgell, Pla d'-/Urgel, Llanos de-	13	Lc	41.25N	0.36W
Urgen	28	Ab	44.45N	110.40 E
Urgenč	22	Ie	41.33N	60.38 E
Ürgüp	24	Fc	38.38N	35.56 E
Urgut	19	Gh	39.23N	67.14 E
Uri	25	Eb	34.05N	74.02 E
Uri [2]	14	Cd	46.40N	8.30 E
Uribia	54	Da	11.42N	72.17W
Uricki	19	Ge	53.19N	65.34 E
Urique, Río-	48	Fd	26.29N	107.58W
Urjala	8	Jc	61.05N	23.32 E
Urjupinsk	19	Ee	50.48N	42.02 E
Urk	11	Lb	52.39N	5.36 E
Urkan	20	Hf	53.27N	126.56 E
Urla	24	Bc	38.18N	26.46 E
Urlaţi	15	Je	44.59N	26.14 E
Urluk	20	Ff	50.03N	107.55 E
Urmi	20	Ig	48.43N	134.16 E
Urmia, Lake- (EN)= Orumıyeh, Daryācheh-ye	21	Gf	37.40N	45.30 E
Uromi	34	Gd	6.42N	6.20 E
Uroševac	15	Eg	42.22N	21.10 E
Urshult	8	Fh	56.32N	14.47 E
Ursus	10	Qd	52.12N	20.53 E
Urtazym	17	Ij	52.15N	58.50 E
Urtigueira, Serra da-	55	Gg	24.15S	51.00W
Uru, Rio-	55	Hb	15.24S	49.36W
Uruaçu	54	If	14.30S	49.10W
Uruana	55	Hb	15.30S	49.41W
Uruapan del Progreso	47	De	19.25N	101.58W
Uruará, Rio-	54	Hd	2.00S	53.38W
Urubamba, Río-	52	Ig	10.43S	73.48W
Urubici	55	Hi	28.02S	49.37W
Urubú, Cachoeira do-	55	Ha	12.52S	48.13W
Urucará	54	Gd	2.32S	57.45W
Uruçui	54	Je	7.14S	44.33W
Urucuia, Rio- [Braz.]	55	Ib	15.38S	46.10W
Urucuia, Rio- [Braz.]	55	Jc	16.08S	45.05W
Urucum, Serra do-	55	Dd	19.13S	57.33W
Urucurituba	54	Gd	2.41S	57.40W
Uruguai, Rio-	52	Ki	34.12S	58.18W
Uruguaiana	53	Kh	29.45S	57.05W
Uruguay [1]	53	Ki	33.00S	56.00W
Uruguay, Río-	52	Ki	34.12S	58.18W
Urukthapel	64a	Ac	7.15N	134.24 E
Urumbaba Dağı	15	Lj	38.25N	28.49 E
Ürümqi	22	Ke	43.48N	87.35 E
Urup	16	Lg	44.59N	41.10 E
Urup, Ostrov-	21	Qe	46.00N	150.00 E
Uruša	20	Hf	54.03N	122.55 E
Urussu	7	Mi	54.38N	53.24 E
Uruwira	36	Fd	6.27S	31.21 E
Urville, Cape D'- (EN)= Perkam, Tanjung-	26	Kg	1.28S	137.54 E
Uryū	29a	Bb	43.39N	141.51 E
Uryū-Gawa	29a	Bb	43.40N	141.54 E
Urziceni	15	Je	44.43N	26.38 E
Uržum	19	Fd	57.10N	50.01 E
Usa	29	Be	33.31N	131.22 E
Usa [R.S.F.S.R.]	16	Nc	53.02N	45.18 E
Usa [R.S.F.S.R.]	5	Lb	65.57N	56.55 E
Uşak	23	Cb	38.41N	29.25 E
Usakos	37	Bd	22.01S	15.32 E
Ušakovo	20	Hf	51.54N	126.35 E
Ušakovskoje	20	Nb	71.00N	178.35W
Usambara Mountains	30	Ki	4.45S	38.30 E
Usarp Mountains	66	Jf	71.10S	160.00 E
Usas Escarpment	66	Nf	76.00S	125.00W
Ušba, Gora-	16	Mh	43.06N	42.40 E
Usborne, Mount-	56	Ih	51.42S	58.50W
Ušće	15	Df	43.29N	20.38 E
Usedom	10	Jb	54.00N	14.00 E
Useldange	12	He	49.46N	5.59 E
'Ushayrah [Sau. Ar.]	33	He	21.46N	40.38 E
'Ushayrah [Sau. Ar.]	24	Kj	25.35N	45.46 E
Ushibuka	29	Be	32.13N	130.01 E
Ushikubi-Misaki	29a	Bc	41.08N	140.48 E
Ushimado	29	Dd	34.37N	134.09 E
'Ushsh, Wādī al-	24	Fd	27.18N	42.15 E
Ushuaia	53	Jk	54.47S	68.20W
Usingen	12	Kd	50.20N	8.32 E
Usinsk	19	Fb	65.57N	57.29 E
Usküdar	24	Cb	41.01N	29.03 E
Üsküp	15	Kh	41.44N	27.24 E
Uslar	10	Fe	51.40N	9.39 E
Úslava	10	Jg	49.54N	13.32 E
Usman	16	Kd	51.54N	39.20 E
Usman	19	De	52.00N	39.43 E
Usmas, Ozero-/Usmas Ezers	8	Ig	57.13N	22.00 E
Usmas Ezers/Usmas, Ozero-	8	Ig	57.13N	22.00 E
Usogorsk	19	Ec	63.28N	48.35 E
Usoke	36	Fd	5.06S	32.20 E
Usolje	19	Fd	59.25N	56.41 E
Usolje-Sibirskoje	20	Ff	52.47N	103.38 E
Usora	14	Mf	44.43N	18.04 E
Ussel	11	Ii	45.33N	2.19 E
USSR (EN)=Sojuz Sovetskih Socialističeskih Respublik [1]	22	Jd	60.00N	80.00 E
Ussuri	21	Pe	48.28N	135.02 E
Ussurijsk	22	Pe	43.48N	131.59 E
Usta	7	Kh	56.53N	45.28 E
Ust-Barguzin	20	Ff	53.27N	108.59 E
Ust-Bolšereck	20	Kf	52.40N	156.18 E
Ust-Cilma	19	Fb	65.27N	52.06 E
Ust-Čorna	10	Uh	48.17N	24.02 E
Ust-Donecki	16	Lf	47.39N	40.55 E
Ust-Džeguta	16	Mg	44.05N	42.01 E
Uster	14	Cc	47.20N	8.43 E
Ustevatn	8	Bd	60.30N	8.00 E
Ust-Hajrjuzovo	20	Ke	57.04N	156.50 E
Ustica	5	Hh	38.40N	13.10 E
Ustica	14	Hl	38.42N	13.11 E
Ust-Ilimsk	22	Md	58.03N	102.43 E
Ustilug	10	Uf	50.50N	24.09 E
Ústí nad Labem	10	Kf	50.40N	14.02 E
Ústí nad Orlicí	10	Mg	49.58N	16.24 E
Ustinov → Iževsk	6	Ld	56.51N	53.14 E
Ust-Išim	19	Hd	57.44N	71.10 E
Ust-Judoma	20	Ie	59.10N	135.02 E
Ustjurt, Plato	21	He	43.00N	56.00 E
'Ustjužna	7	Ig	58.53N	36.28 E
Ustka	10	Mb	54.35N	16.50 E
Ust-Kamčatsk	22	Sd	56.15N	162.30 E
Ust-Kamenogorsk	22	Ke	49.58N	82.38 E
Ust-Kan	20	Df	50.57N	84.55 E
Ust-Kara	19	Gb	69.15N	64.59 E
Ust-Karsk	20	Gf	52.41N	118.45 E
Ust-Katav	17	Ii	54.56N	58.10 E
Ust-Kujga	22	Pc	70.00N	135.36 E
Ust-Kut	22	Md	56.46N	105.40 E
Ust-Labinsk	19	Df	45.13N	39.40 E
Ust-Luga	7	Gg	59.39N	28.15 E
Ust-Maya	22	Pc	60.25N	134.32 E
Ust-Muja	20	Ge	56.28N	115.30 E
Ust-Nera	22	Qc	64.34N	143.12 E
Ust-Njukža	20	He	56.30N	121.48 E
Uštobe	19	Hf	45.13N	77.59 E
Ust-Olenëk	20	Gb	72.58N	119.42 E
Ust-Omčug	20	Jd	61.05N	149.30 E
Ust-Ordynski	20	Ff	52.48N	104.45 E
Ust-Ordynski Burjatski Nacionalny okrug [3]	20	Ff	53.30N	104.00 E
Ustovo	15	Hh	41.34N	24.47 E
Ust-Pinega	7	Jd	64.10N	41.58 E
Ust-Pit	20	Ee	58.59N	92.00 E
Ust-Port	20	Dc	69.45N	84.25 E
Ust-Požva	17	Hg	59.05N	56.05 E
Ustrzyki Dolne	10	Sg	49.26N	22.37 E
Ust-Sobolevka	20	Ig	46.10N	137.59 E
Ust-Šonoša	7	Jf	61.11N	41.20 E
Ust-Uda	20	Ff	54.10N	103.03 E
Ust-Ujskoje	17	Ki	54.15N	63.57 E
Ust-Umalta	20	If	51.42N	133.18 E
Ustupo	49	Ii	9.08N	77.56W
Usú	22	Ke	44.27N	84.37 E
Usui-Tōge	29	Fc	36.22N	138.38 E
Usuki	28	Kh	33.08N	131.49 E
Usuki-Wan	29	Be	33.10N	131.50 E
Usulután	49	Cg	13.21N	88.27W
Usumacinta	38	Jh	18.22N	92.40W
Ušumun	20	Hf	52.46N	126.37 E
Usu-San	29a	Bb	42.32N	140.49 E
Usva	17	Hg	58.40N	57.35 E
Usva	17	Hg	58.17N	57.47 E
Utah [2]	43	Ed	39.30N	111.30W
Utah Lake	43	Ec	40.13N	111.49W
Utajärvi	7	Gd	64.45N	26.23 E
Utashinai	29a	Cb	43.31N	142.03 E
Utata	20	Ff	50.51N	102.45 E
Ute Creek	45	Ei	35.21N	103.50W
Utembo	30	Jj	17.06S	22.01 E
Utena	7	Fi	55.29N	25.40 E
Ute Reservoir	45	Ei	35.21N	103.31W
Utete	36	Gd	7.59S	38.47 E
Uthai Thani	25	Ke	15.20N	100.02 E
Utiariti	55	Ca	13.02S	58.17W
Utica	43	Lc	43.06N	75.15W
Utiel	13	Ke	39.34N	1.12W
Utiel, Sierra de-	13	Ke	39.36N	1.08W
Utila	49	De	16.06N	86.54W
Utila, Isla de-	49	De	16.06N	86.56W
Utique	14	Em	37.04N	10.04 E
Utirik Atoll	57	Hc	11.15N	169.48 E
Utlängan	8	Fh	56.00N	15.45 E
Utljukski Liman	16	If	46.20N	35.15 E
Uto	28	Kh	32.40N	130.41 E
Utö [Fin.]	8	Ie	59.45N	21.25 E
Utö [Swe.]	7	Eg	58.55N	18.15 E
Utoro	29a	Da	44.06N	144.58 E
Utrata	10	Qd	52.13N	20.15 E
Utrecht [3]	12	Hb	52.05N	5.08 E
Utrecht [Neth.]	6	Ge	52.05N	5.08 E
Utrecht [S.Afr.]	37	Ee	27.28S	30.20 E
Utrera	13	Gg	37.11N	5.47W
Utsira	8	Ae	59.20N	4.55 E
Utsjoki	7	Gb	69.53N	27.00 E
Utsunomiya	22	Pf	36.33N	139.52 E
Uttaradit	25	Ke	17.38N	100.06 E
Uttar Pradesh [3]	25	Fc	28.00N	80.00 E
Utuado	49	Nd	18.16N	66.42W
Utukok	40	Gb	70.04N	162.18W
Utuloa	64h	Ab	13.16S	176.11W
Utupua Island	57	Hf	11.20S	166.36 E
Uturoa	65e	Db	16.44S	151.26W
Utva	16	Rd	51.29N	52.40 E
Uudenmaa [2]	7	Ff	60.30N	25.00 E
Uukuniemi	8	Nc	61.47N	30.01 E
Uulu/Ulu	8	Kf	58.13N	24.29 E
Uusikaupunki/Nystad	7	Ef	60.48N	21.25 E
Uusimaa	8	Kd	60.30N	25.00 E
Uva	19	Fd	56.58N	52.14 E
Uvac	15	Cf	43.36N	19.30 E
Uvalde	43	Hf	29.13N	99.47W
Uvarovo	19	Ee	52.00N	42.15 E
Uvdal	8	Cd	60.20N	8.30 E
Uvéa, Ile-	57	Jf	13.18S	176.10W
Uvelka	17	Ji	54.05N	61.35 E
Uvelski	17	Ji	54.26N	61.27 E
Uvildy, Ozero-	17	Ji	55.35N	60.30 E
Uvinza	36	Fd	5.06S	30.22 E
Uvira	31	Ji	3.24S	29.08 E
Uvs nuur → Ubsu-Nur	21	Ld	50.20N	92.45 E
Uwa	29	Ce	33.21N	132.30 E
Uwajima	27	Ne	33.13N	132.34 E
Uwajima-Wan	29	Ce	33.15N	132.30 E
Uwa-Kai	29	Ce	33.20N	132.15 E
Uwayl	35	Dd	8.46N	27.24 E
'Uwaynāt, Jabal al-= Uweinat, Gebel- (EN)	30	Jf	21.54N	24.58 E
'Uwaynat Wannīn	33	Bd	28.05N	12.59 E
Uweinat, Gebel- (EN)= 'Uwaynāt, Jabal al-	30	Jf	21.54N	24.58 E
Uwekuli	26	Hg	1.25S	121.06 E
Uwi, Pulau-	26	Ef	1.05N	107.24 E
Uxin Qi (Dabqig)	27	Id	38.27N	109.08 E
Uxmal	39	Kg	20.20N	89.46W
Uyo	34	Gd	5.07N	7.57 E
Uyuni	53	Jh	20.28S	66.50W
Uyuni, Salar de-	52	Jh	20.20S	67.42W
Už [Eur.]	10	Rh	48.33N	22.00 E
Už [Ukr.-U.S.S.R.]	16	Gd	51.15N	30.12 E
Uza	8	Mg	57.47N	29.38 E
Uzbekiston Sovet Socialistik Respublikasy/Uzbekskaja SSR [2]	19	Gg	41.00N	64.00 E
Uzbekskaja Sovetskaja Socialističeskaja Respublika [2]	19	Gg	41.00N	64.00 E
Uzbekskaja SSR/Uzbekiston Sovet Socialistik Respublikasy [2]	19	Gg	41.00N	64.00 E
Uzbekskaja SSR=Uzbek SSR (EN) [2]	19	Gg	41.00N	64.00 E
Uzbek SSR (EN)= Uzbekskaja SSR [2]	19	Gg	41.00N	64.00 E
Uzbel Shankou	27	Bd	38.42N	73.48 E
Uzen	19	Fg	43.22N	52.50 E
Uzerche	11	Hi	45.25N	1.34 E
Uzès	11	Kj	44.01N	4.25 E
Uzgen	18	Id	40.44N	73.21 E
Užgorod	19	Cf	48.37N	22.22 E
Uzin	16	Ge	49.52N	30.27 E
Uzlovaja	16	Kb	54.01N	38.12 E
Uzlovoje	10	Sh	48.23N	22.27 E
Užokski, pereval-	16	Ce	49.02N	22.58 E
Uzümlü	15	Mm	36.44N	29.14 E
Uzun Ada	15	Jk	38.28N	26.42 E
Uzunagač [Kaz.-U.S.S.R.]	18	Kc	43.08N	76.20 E
Uzunagač [Kaz.-U.S.S.R.]	18	Kc	43.36N	76.19 E
Uzunköprü	24	Bb	41.16N	26.41 E
Užur	20	De	55.20N	90.00 E
Užventis	8	Ji	55.44N	22.37 E
Uzynkair, Mys-	18	Bb	45.47N	59.20 E

V

Name	Page	Grid	Lat.	Long.
Vääksy	8	Kc	61.11N	25.33 E
Vaal	30	Jk	29.24S	23.38 E
Vaala	7	Gd	64.34N	26.50 E
Vaals	12	Id	50.46N	6.01 E
Vaalwater	37	Dd	24.20S	28.03 E
Vaasa [2]	7	Fe	63.12N	23.00 E
Vaasa/Vasa	6	Ic	63.06N	21.36 E
Vaassen, Epe-	12	Hb	52.17N	5.58 E
Vabalninkas	8	Ki	55.58N	24.49 E
Vác	10	Pi	47.47N	19.08 E
Vacacai, Rio-	55	Fi	29.55S	53.06W
Vacaria	56	Jc	28.30S	50.56W
Vacaria, Rio-	55	Fe	21.55S	53.59W
Vacaville	46	Eg	38.21N	121.59W
Vaccarès, Étang de-	11	Kk	43.32N	4.34 E
Vache, Ile à-	49	Kd	18.04N	73.38W
Väddö	8	Hd	60.00N	18.50 E
Vadehavet	8	Ci	55.15N	8.40 E
Vădeni	15	Kd	45.22N	27.56 E
Vadheim	8	Ac	61.13N	5.49 E
Vadodara	22	Jg	22.18N	73.12 E
Vado Ligure	14	Cf	44.17N	8.27 E
Vadsø	6	Ia	70.05N	29.46 E
Vadstena	7	Dg	58.27N	14.54 E
Vaduz	6	Gf	47.08N	9.30 E
Værlandet	8	Ac	61.20N	4.45 E
Vaga	5	Kc	62.48N	42.56 E
Vagaj	17	Mh	56.28N	67.18 E
Vagaj	17	Nh	57.55N	69.01 E
Vågåmo	7	Bf	61.53N	9.06 E
Vaganjski vrh	14	Jf	44.21N	15.30 E
Vågåvatn	8	Cc	61.50N	8.50 E
Vaggeryd	7	Dh	57.30N	14.07 E
Vaghena	63a	Cb	7.25S	157.43 E
Vagil	17	Kg	59.45N	62.40 E
Vagis, Gora-	20	Jf	52.20N	142.15 E
Vagnhärad	8	Gf	58.57N	17.31 E
Vågsøy	8	Ac	62.00N	5.05 E
Váh	10	Ni	47.55N	18.00 E
Vah	21	Jc	60.45N	76.45 E
Vahitahi Atoll	57	Nf	18.44S	138.52W
Vahruši	7	Mg	58.43N	50.02 E
Vahš	18	Gf	37.43N	68.49 E
Vahsel Bay → Herzog-Ernst-Bucht	66	Af	77.48S	34.39W
Vahtan	7	Lh	57.59N	46.42 E
Vaïaau	65e	Db	16.52S	151.28W
Vaigat	41	Gd	70.30N	54.00W
Vaihingen an der Enz	12	Kf	48.56N	8.58 E
Vaihú	65d	Ab	27.10S	109.23W
Väike-Maarja/Vjaike-Maarja	8	Le	59.04N	26.12 E
Väike-Pakri/Vjajke-Pakri	8	Je	59.50N	23.50 E
Väike Väin/Vjajke-Vjajn	8	Jf	58.30N	23.10 E
Vailala	64h	Bb	13.13S	176.09W
Vailala, Pointe-	64h	Ab	13.13S	176.10W
Vaileka	63d	Bb	17.23S	178.09 E
Vailheu, Récif-	37	Gb	11.48S	43.04 E
Vailly-sur-Aisne	12	Fe	49.25N	3.31 E
Vainikkala	8	Md	60.52N	28.18 E
Vainode/Vajnëde	8	Ih	56.26N	21.45 E
Vairaatea Atoll	57	Nf	19.19S	139.20W
Vaison-la-Romaine	11	Lj	44.14N	5.04 E
Vaïtape	65e	Db	16.31S	151.45W
Vaïtoare	65e	Db	16.41S	151.28W
Vaitupu Island	57	Ie	7.28S	178.41 E
Vajgač, Ostrov-	5	La	70.00N	59.30 E
Vajnëde/Vainode	8	Ih	56.26N	21.45 E
Vakaga [3]	35	Cd	10.00N	23.30 E
Vakfıkebir	24	Hb	41.03N	39.20 E
Vaksdal	8	Ad	60.29N	5.44 E
Val	20	Jf	52.19N	143.09 E
Vala	7	Mh	56.59N	51.16 E
Valaam	7	Hf	61.24N	30.59 E
Valaam, Ostrov-	8	Nc	61.20N	31.05 E
Valahia = Walachia (EN)	15	He	44.00N	25.00 E
Valahia = Walachia (EN)	5	Ig	44.00N	25.00 E
Valais [2]	14	Bd	46.15N	7.30 E
Valamares, Mali i-	15	Di	40.47N	20.28 E
Valamaz	7	Mh	57.36N	52.14 E
Valandovo	15	Fh	41.19N	22.34 E
Valašské Meziříčí	10	Ng	49.29N	17.58 E
Valáxa	15	Hk	38.49N	24.29 E
Vålberg	8	Ee	59.24N	13.12 E
Valburg	12	Hc	51.55N	5.49 E
Valcabra	13	Jg	37.30N	2.43W
Vălčedrăm	15	Gf	43.42N	23.27 E
Valcheta	56	Gf	40.42S	66.09W
Valdagno	14	Fe	45.39N	11.18 E
Valdahon	11	Mg	47.09N	6.21 E
Valdai Hills (EN)= Valdajskaja Vozvyšennost	5	Jd	57.00N	33.30 E
Valdaj	19	Dd	57.59N	33.14 E
Valdajskaja Vozvyšennost= Valdai Hills (EN)	5	Jd	57.00N	33.30 E
Valdarno	14	Fg	43.45N	11.15 E
Valdavia	13	Hb	42.24N	4.16W
Valdecañas, Embalse de-	13	Ge	39.45N	5.30W
Valdeganga	13	Ke	39.09N	1.40W
Val-de-Marne [3]	11	If	48.47N	2.29 E
Valdemārpils/Valdemarpils	7	Fh	57.24N	22.39 E
Valdemarpils/Valdemārpils	7	Fh	57.24N	22.39 E
Valdemarsvik	7	Dg	58.12N	16.32 E
Valdepeñas	13	If	38.46N	3.23W
Valderaduey	13	Gc	41.31N	5.42W
Valderas	13	Gb	42.05N	5.27W
Valderrama, Cienaga de-	49	Ki	8.56N	72.10W
Valderrobres/Vall-de-roures	13	Ld	40.53N	0.09W
Valdés, Península-	52	Jj	42.30S	64.00W
Valdez	39	Ec	61.07N	146.16W
Val d'Isère	11	Mi	45.27N	6.59 E
Valdivia	53	Ii	39.48S	73.14W
Valdivia Seamount (EN)	30	Hk	25.20S	6.15 E
Valdobbiadene	14	Fe	45.54N	12.00 E
Val-d'Oise [3]	11	Ie	49.10N	2.10 E
Val-d'Or	39	Le	48.07N	77.47W
Valdosta	39	Kf	30.50N	83.17W
Valdres	8	Cc	60.55N	9.10 E
Vale [Geo.-U.S.S.R.]	16	Mi	41.36N	42.51 E
Vale [Or.-U.S.]	46	Gd	44.01N	117.15W
Valea Ierii	15	Gc	46.39N	23.21 E
Valea lui Mihai	15	Fb	47.31N	22.09 E
Valea Vişeului	15	Hb	47.51N	24.10 E
Valença [Braz.]	55	Kf	22.15S	43.43W
Valença [Braz.]	54	Kf	13.22S	39.05W
Valença do Minho	13	Db	42.02N	8.38W
Valença do Piaui	54	Je	6.24S	41.45W
Valençay	11	Hg	47.09N	1.34 E
Valence [Fr.]	11	Gj	44.06N	0.55 E
Valence [Fr.]	11	Kj	44.56N	4.54 E
Valencia	6	Fh	39.28N	0.22W
Valencia [3]	13	Le	39.20N	0.50W
Valencia	13	Le	39.30N	0.40W
València/Valencia	6	Fh	39.28N	0.22W
Valencia/València	6	Fh	39.28N	0.22W
València, Golf de-/Valencia, Golfo de-	5	Fh	39.30N	0.00
Valencia, Golfo de-/ València, Golf de-	5	Fh	39.30N	0.00
Valencia, Lago de-	50	Cg	10.11N	67.45W
Valencia de Alcántara	13	Ee	39.25N	7.14W
Valencia de Don Juan	13	Gb	42.18N	5.31W
Valencia-El Grao	13	Le	39.27N	0.20W
Valenciennes	11	Jd	50.21N	3.32 E
Vălenii de Munte	15	Jd	45.11N	26.02 E
Valentia/Dairbhre	9	Cj	51.55N	10.20W
Valentin	28	Mc	43.07N	134.19 E
Valentine	43	Gc	42.52N	100.33W
Valenza	14	Ce	45.01N	8.38 E
Våler	7	Cf	60.40N	11.50 E
Valera	54	Db	9.19N	70.37W
Valerie Seamount (EN)	57	Ki	42.00S	163.30W
Valga	19	Cd	57.49N	26.05 E
Valge Jõgi	8	Ke	59.32N	25.36 E
Valhalla Mountains	46	Gb	49.45N	117.48W
Valiente, Península-	49	Gi	9.05N	81.51W
Valier	46	Ib	48.18N	112.15W
Valinco, Golfe de-	11a	Ab	41.40N	8.49 E
Valjevo	15	Ce	44.16N	19.53 E
Valka	7	Gh	57.47N	26.01 E
Valkeakoski	7	Ff	61.16N	24.02 E
Valkeala	8	Ld	60.57N	26.48 E
Valkenswaard	12	Hc	51.21N	5.28 E
Valkininkai/Valkininkaj	8	Kj	54.18N	25.55 E
Valkininkaj/Valkininkai	8	Kj	54.18N	25.55 E
Valko/Valkom	8	Ld	60.25N	26.15 E
Valkom/Valko	8	Ld	60.25N	26.15 E
Valkumej	20	Mc	69.41N	170.30 E
Valladolid [3]	13	Hc	41.35N	4.40W
Valladolid [Mex.]	47	Gd	20.41N	88.12W
Valladolid [Sp.]	6	Fg	41.39N	4.43W
Valldal	8	Bb	62.20N	7.21 E
Vall-de-Roures/Valderrobres	13	Ld	40.53N	0.09W
Vall de Uxó	13	Le	39.49N	0.14W
Valle [2]	54	Cc	3.40N	76.30W
Valle [3]	49	Dg	13.30N	87.35W
Valle	7	Bg	59.12N	7.32 E
Vallecas, Madrid-	13	Id	40.23N	3.37W
Valle d'Aosta / Vallée d'Aoste [2]	14	Be	45.45N	7.15 E
Valle de Cabuerniga	13	Ha	43.14N	4.18W
Valle de Guanape	50	Dh	9.54N	65.41W
Valle dei Templi	14	Hm	37.18N	13.35 E
Valle de la Pascua	54	Eb	9.13N	66.00W
Valle de Santiago	48	Ig	20.23N	101.12W
Valle de Topia	48	Fe	25.13N	106.25W
Valle de Zaragoza	48	Gd	27.28N	105.49W
Valledupar	54	Da	10.28N	73.15W
Vallée d'Aoste / Valle d'Aosta [2]	14	Be	45.45N	7.15 E
Vallée Jonction	44	Lb	46.23N	70.55W
Valle Hermoso	48	Ke	25.39N	97.52W
Vallejera, Puerto de-	13	Gd	40.30N	5.42W
Vallejo	43	Cd	38.07N	122.14W
Vallejo, Sierra de-	48	Gg	20.55N	105.20W
Valle Nacional	48	Ki	17.47N	96.19W
Vallenar	53	Ih	28.35S	70.46W
Vallentuna	8	He	59.32N	18.05 E
Valles/El Valles	13	Oc	41.35N	2.15 E
Valles de los Daidos	13	Hd	40.39N	4.09W
Valletta	6	Hh	35.54N	14.31 E
Valley City	43	Hb	46.55N	97.59W
Valley Falls	46	Ee	42.31N	120.15W
Valleyfield	42	Kg	45.15N	74.08W
Valley Station	44	Ef	38.06N	85.52W
Valleyview	42	Fe	55.02N	117.08W
Vallgrund	7	Ee	63.12N	21.14 E
Vallhagar	8	Hg	57.20N	18.10 E
Vallimanca	55	Bm	36.21S	61.02W
Vallimanca, Arroyo-	55	Bl	35.40S	60.02W
Vallo della Lucania	14	Jj	40.14N	15.16 E
Valloires, Abbaye de-	12	Dd	50.20N	1.47 E
Vallorbe	14	Ad	46.43N	6.23 E
Valls	13	Nc	41.17N	1.15 E
Valls d'Andorra → Andorra [1]	6	Gg	42.30N	1.30 E
Vallsta	8	Gc	61.32N	16.22 E
Vallvik	8	Gc	61.11N	17.11 E
Valmaseda	13	Ia	43.12N	3.12W
Valmiera	19	Cd	57.32N	25.29 E
Valmont	12	Ce	49.44N	0.31 E
Valnera	13	Ia	43.10N	3.45W
Valognes	11	Ee	49.31N	1.28W
Valois, Plaine du-	11	Ie	49.10N	2.45 E
Valoria la Buena	13	Hc	41.48N	4.32W
Valpaços	13	Ec	41.36N	7.19W
Valparaiso	44	De	41.28N	87.03W
Valparaiso [Braz.]	55	Ge	21.13S	50.51W
Valparaiso [Chile]	53	Ii	33.02S	71.38W
Valparaiso [Mex.]	48	Hf	22.46N	103.34W
Valpovo	14	Me	45.39N	18.25 E
Valréas	11	Kj	44.23N	4.59 E
Vals	30	Jk	27.23S	26.31 E
Vals, Tanjung-	26	Kh	8.26S	137.38 E
Valsjöbyn	7	Dd	64.04N	14.08 E
Valtellina	14	Dd	46.10N	9.55 E
Valtimo	7	Ge	63.40N	28.48 E
Váltou, Óri-	15	Ej	39.10N	21.20 E
Valujki	19	De	50.12N	38.08 E
Valul-Lui Traian	15	Le	44.15N	28.30 E
Valverde	32	Dd	27.48N	17.55W
Valverde de Júcar	13	Je	39.43N	2.12W
Valverde del Camino	13	Fg	37.34N	6.45W
Valverde del Fresno	13	Ff	40.13N	6.52W
Vamdrup	8	Ci	55.25N	9.17 E
Våmhus	7	Df	61.08N	14.28 E
Vamizi, Ilha-	37	Gb	11.02S	40.40 E
Vammala	7	Ff	61.20N	22.54 E
Vámos	15	Hn	35.25N	24.12 E
Van	23	Fb	38.28N	43.20 E
Van, Lake- (EN)=Van Gölü	21	Gf	38.33N	42.46 E
Vanajanselkä	7	Ff	61.09N	24.15 E
Vanak	24	Ng	31.41N	50.52 E
Vanak	24	Ng	31.32N	51.19 E
Vanån	8	Fd	60.31N	14.14 E
Vanault-les-Dames	12	Gf	48.51N	4.46 E
Vanavana Atoll	57	Ng	20.47S	139.09W
Vanavara	20	Fd	60.22N	102.16 E
Van Buren [Ar.-U.S.]	45	Ii	35.26N	94.21W
Van Buren [Me.-U.S.]	44	Nb	47.09N	67.56W
Vanč	18	He	38.23N	71.29 E
Vanceburg	44	Ff	38.36N	83.19W
Vancouver [B.C.-Can.]	39	Ge	49.16N	123.07W
Vancouver [Wa.-U.S.]	43	Cb	45.39N	122.40W
Vancouver Island	38	Ge	49.45N	126.00W
Vandalia [Il.-U.S.]	45	Lg	38.58N	89.06W
Vandalia [Oh.-U.S.]	44	Ef	39.53N	84.12W
Vanderbijl Park	37	De	26.42S	27.54 E
Vanderhoof	42	Ff	54.01N	124.01W
Vanderlin Island	59	Hc	15.45S	137.00 E
Van Diemen, Cape-	59	Gb	11.10S	130.25 E
Van Diemen Gulf	59	Gb	11.50S	132.00 E
Vandmtor, Ozero-	17	Le	62.15N	65.45 E
Vändra/Vjandra	7	Fg	58.40N	25.01 E
Vänern	5	Hd	58.55N	13.30 E
Vänersborg	7	Cg	58.22N	12.19 E

Index Symbols

[1] Independent Nation
[2] State, Region
[3] District, County
[4] Municipality
[5] Colony, Dependency
Continent
Physical Region
Historical or Cultural Region
Mount, Mountain
Volcano
Hill
Mountains, Mountain Range
Hills, Escarpment
Plateau, Upland
Pass, Gap
Plain, Lowland
Delta
Salt Flat
Valley, Canyon
Crater, Cave
Karst Features
Depression
Polder
Desert, Dunes
Forest, Woods
Heath, Steppe
Oasis
Cape, Point
Coast, Beach
Cliff
Peninsula
Isthmus
Sandbank
Island
Atoll
Rock, Reef
Islands, Archipelago
Rocks, Reefs
Coral Reef
Well, Spring
Geyser
River, Stream
Waterfall Rapids
River Mouth, Estuary
Lake
Salt Lake
Intermittent Lake
Reservoir
Swamp, Pond
Canal
Glacier
Ice Shelf, Pack Ice
Ocean
Sea
Gulf, Bay
Strait, Fjord
Lagoon
Bank
Seamount
Tablemount
Ridge
Shelf
Basin
Escarpment, Sea Scarp
Fracture
Trench, Abyss
National Park, Reserve
Point of Interest
Recreation Site
Cave, Cavern
Historic Site
Ruins
Wall, Walls
Church, Abbey
Temple
Scientific Station
Airport
Port
Lighthouse
Mine
Tunnel
Dam, Bridge

Vang 8 Cc 61.08N 8.35 E
Vangaindrano 37 Hd 23.23S 47.33 E
Van Gölü=Van, Lake- (EN) 21 Gf 38.33N 42.46 E
Vangunu Island 57 Ge 8.40S 158.05 E
Van Horn 43 Ge 31.03N 104.50W
Vanick, Rio- 55 Fa 13.06S 52.52W
Vanier 42 Ha 76.00N 103.50W
Vanikolo 63c Bb 11.37S 166.58 E
Vanikolo Islands 57 Hf 11.37S 167.03 E
Vanimo 60 Ch 2.40S 141.18 E
Vanino 20 Jg 49.11N 140.19 E
Vankavesi 8 Jc 61.50N 23.50 E
Vanna 7 Ea 70.09N 19.51 E
Vännäs 7 Ee 63.55N 19.45 E
Vanne 11 Jf 48.12N 3.16 E
Vannes 11 Dg 47.40N 2.45W
Van Ninh 25 Lf 12.42N 109.14 E
Vannsjø 8 De 59.25N 10.50 E
Vanoise, Massif de la- 11 Mi 45.20N 6.40 E
Vanona Lava, Ile- 57 Hf 14.00S 167.30 E
Van Phong, Vung- 25 Lf 12.33N 109.18 E
Van Rees, Pegunungan- 26 Kg 2.35S 138.15 E
Vanrhynsdorp 37 Bf 31.36S 18.44 E
Vansbro 7 Df 60.31N 14.13 E
Vanse 8 Bf 58.07N 6.42 E
Vansittart 42 Jc 65.50N 84.00W
Vantaa 8 Kd 60.13N 24.59 E
Vänte Litets grund 8 Hb 62.35N 18.12 E
Vanua Levu 57 If 17.28S 177.03 E
Vanua Mbalavu 61 Fc 17.14S 178.57W
Vanuatu [1] 58 Hf 16.00S 167.00 E
Vanua Vatu 63d Cc 18.22S 179.16W
Van Wert 44 Ee 40.53N 84.36W
Van Wyksviei 37 Cf 30.18S 21.49 E
Vanzylsrus 37 Ce 26.52S 22.04 E
Vao 63b Cf 22.40S 167.29 E
Vao, Nosy- 37 Gc 17.30S 43.45 E
Vão das Almas 55 Ia 13.42S 47.27W
Vapnjarka 16 Fe 48.32N 28.46 E
Var [3] 11 Mk 43.30N 6.20 E
Var 11 Nk 43.39N 7.12 E
Vara 14 Df 44.09N 9.53 E
Vara 8 Ef 58.16N 12.57 E
Varaita 14 Bf 44.49N 7.36 E
Varakļāni/Varakljany 7 Gh 56.36N 26.48 E
Varakljany/Varakļāni 7 Gh 56.36N 26.48 E
Varaldsøy 8 Ad 60.10N 6.00 E
Varalé 34 Ed 9.40N 3.17W
Varallo 14 Ce 45.49N 8.15 E
Varāmīn 24 Ne 35.20N 51.39 E
Vārānasi (Benares) 22 Kg 25.20N 83.00 E
Varangerfjorden 5 Ia 70.00N 30.00 E
Varangerhalvøya=Varanger Peninsula (EN) 5 Ia 70.25N 29.30 E
Varanger Peninsula (EN)= Varangerhalvøya 5 Ia 70.25N 29.30 E
Varano, Lago di- 14 Ji 41.53N 15.45 E
Varāvī 24 Oi 27.25N 53.06 E
Varaždin 14 Kd 46.18N 16.20 E
Varazze 14 Cf 44.22N 8.34 E
Varberg 7 Ch 57.06N 12.15 E
Vardak [3] 23 Kc 34.15N 68.00 E
Vardar 5 Ig 40.35N 22.50 E
Varde 7 Bi 55.38N 8.29 E
Varde Å 8 Ci 55.35N 8.20 E
Vardhoúsia Óri 15 Fk 38.40N 22.10 E
Vårdo 8 Id 60.15N 20.20 E
Vardø 7 Ha 70.22N 31.06 E
Varel 10 Ec 53.24N 8.08 E
Varėna/Varena 7 Fi 54.15N 24.39 E
Varena/Varėna 7 Fi 54.15N 24.39 E
Värend 8 Fh 56.45N 14.55 E
Varengeville-sur-Mer 12 Ce 49.55N 0.59 E
Varenikovskaja 16 Jg 45.06N 37.37 E
Varenne 11 Ff 48.24N 0.39W
Varennes-en-Argonne 12 He 49.14N 5.02 E
Varennes-sur-Allier 11 Jh 46.19N 3.24 E
Vareš 14 Mf 44.10N 18.20 E
Varese 14 Ce 45.48N 8.50 E
Varese, Lago di- 14 Ce 45.50N 8.45 E
Vårgårda 8 Ef 58.02N 12.48 E
Vargaši 19 Gd 55.23N 65.48 E
Vargem Grande 54 Jd 3.33S 43.56W
Varginha 54 Ih 21.33S 45.26W
Vargön 8 Ef 58.21N 12.22 E
Varhaug 8 Af 58.37N 5.39 E
Varjão 55 Hc 17.03S 49.37W
Varkaus 6 Ic 62.19N 27.55 E
Värmdö 8 He 59.20N 18.35 E
Värmeln 8 Ee 59.30N 12.55 E
Värmland 8 Ee 59.50N 13.05 E
Värmland [2] 7 Cg 59.45N 13.15 E
Värmlandsnäs 8 Ee 59.00N 13.10 E
Varna [2] 15 Kf 43.10N 27.35 E
Varna [Bul.] 6 Ig 43.13N 27.55 E
Varna [R.S.F.S.R.] 17 Jj 53.24N 60.58 E
Värnamo 7 Dh 57.11N 14.02 E
Varnenski Zaliv 15 Kf 43.11N 27.56 E
Varniai/Varnjaj 8 Ji 55.44N 22.17 E
Varnjaj/Varniai 8 Ji 55.44N 22.17 E
Varnsdorf 10 Kf 50.54N 14.38 E
Várpalota 10 Oi 47.12N 18.08 E
Văršec 15 Gf 43.12N 23.17 E
Varsinais-Suomi/Egentliga Finland 8 Jd 60.40N 22.30 E
Värska 8 Lg 57.58N 27.38 E
Vartašen 16 Oi 41.05N 47.29 E
Varto 24 Ic 39.10N 41.28 E
Vartofta 8 Ef 58.06N 13.38 E
Värtsilä 8 Nb 62.15N 30.40 E
Varzaneh 24 Of 32.25N 52.39 E
Varzaqān 24 Lc 38.31N 46.39 E
Varzarīn, Kūh-e- 23 Gc 33.24N 46.48 E
Várzea, Rio da- 55 Fh 27.13S 53.19W
Várzea da Palma 55 Jc 17.36S 44.44W
Varzea Grande 54 Gg 15.39S 56.08W
Varzelândia 55 Jb 15.42S 44.02W
Varzi 14 Df 44.49N 9.12 E
Varzuga 7 Ic 66.17N 36.50 E
Varzy 11 Jg 47.22N 3.23 E
Vas [2] 10 Mi 47.10N 16.45 E
Vasa/Vaasa 6 Ic 63.06N 21.36 E
Vasai (Bassein) 25 Ee 19.21N 72.48 E
Vasalemma/Vazalemma 8 Ke 59.15N 24.11 E
Vásárosnamény 10 Sh 48.08N 22.19 E
Vascão 13 Eg 37.31N 7.31W
Vaşcău 15 Fc 46.28N 22.28 E
Vascoeuil 12 De 49.27N 1.23 E
Vascongadas/Euzkadi= Basque Provinces (EN) 13 Ja 43.00N 2.30W
Vascos, Montes- 13 Jb 42.50N 2.10W
Vasgūn 24 Qe 34.55N 56.30 E
Vasilevići 16 Fc 52.14N 29.47 E
Vasiliká 15 Gi 40.28N 23.08 E
Vasiljevka 16 If 47.23N 35.18 E
Vasilkov 19 De 50.12N 30.22 E
Vasilkovka 16 Je 48.13N 36.03 E
Vasiss 19 Hd 57.30N 74.55 E
Vasjugan 20 De 59.10N 80.50 E
Vasjuganje 21 Jd 58.00N 77.00 E
Vaška 19 Ec 64.53N 45.47 E
Vaškovcy 15 Ia 48.16N 25.34 E
Vaslui 15 Kc 46.38N 27.44 E
Vaslui 15 Kc 46.37N 27.44 E
Vaslui [2] 15 Kc 46.41N 27.43 E
Väsman 8 Fd 60.11N 15.04 E
Vassako 35 Bd 8.36N 19.07 E
Vassdalsegga 7 Bg 59.46N 7.07 E
Vassy 12 Bf 48.51N 0.40W
Västeras 6 Hd 59.37N 16.33 E
Västerbotten [2] 7 Dd 64.58N 17.28 E
Västerdalälven 7 Df 60.33N 15.08 E
Västergötland 8 Eg 58.00N 13.05 E
Västerhaninge 8 He 59.07N 18.06 E
Västernorrland [2] 7 De 63.00N 17.30 E
Västervik 7 Dh 57.45N 16.38 E
Västmanland 8 Fe 59.40N 15.15 E
Västmanland [2] 7 Dg 59.45N 16.20 E
Vasto 14 Ih 42.07N 14.42 E
Västra Silen 8 Ee 59.15N 12.10 E
Vasvár 10 Mi 47.03N 16.48 E
Vatan 11 Hg 47.04N 1.49 E
Vatersay 9 Fe 56.53N 7.28W
Vatican City (EN) = Città del Vaticano [1] 6 Hg 41.54N 12.27 E
Vaticano, Capo- 14 Jl 38.37N 15.50 E
Vatilau 63a Ec 8.53S 160.01 E
Vatnajökull 5 Ec 64.24N 16.48W
Vatneyri 7a Ab 65.35N 24.00W
Vatoa Island 57 Jf 19.50S 178.13W
Vatomandry 37 Hc 19.20S 48.59 E
Vatra Dornei 15 Ib 47.21N 25.22 E
Vättern 5 Hd 58.25N 14.35 E
Vatu-i-Ra Channel 63d Bb 17.24S 178.29 E
Vatulele 63d Ac 18.33S 177.38 E
Vatutino 16 Ge 49.02N 31.09 E
Vatu Vara 61 Fc 17.26S 179.32W
Vaubecourt 12 Hf 48.56N 5.07 E
Vauclin, Pointe du- 51h Bb 14.34N 60.50W
Vaucluse [3] 11 Lj 44.00N 5.10 E
Vaucluse, Montagne du- 11 Lk 44.32N 5.11 E
Vaucouleurs 11 Lf 48.36N 5.40 E
Vaud [2] 14 Ad 46.35N 6.30 E
Vaudemont, Butte de- 11 Lf 48.25N 6.00 E
Vaughn 43 Fe 34.36N 105.13W
Vaupés [2] 54 Dc 1.00N 71.00W
Vaupés, Rio- 52 Je 0.02N 67.16W
Vauvilliers 63b Ce 21.09S 167.35 E
Vaux 12 Ge 49.31N 4.17 E
Vaux-le-Vicomte 11 If 48.34N 2.43 E
Vavatenina 37 Hc 17.26S 49.22 E
Vava'u Group 57 Jf 18.40S 174.00W
Vava'u Island 61 Gc 18.36S 174.00W
Vavoua 34 Dd 7.23N 6.29W
Vavuniya 25 Gg 8.45N 80.30 E
Vaxholm 8 He 59.24N 18.20 E
Växjö 6 Hd 56.53N 14.49 E
Vaza-Barris, Rio- 54 Kf 11.10S 37.10W
Vazalemma/Vasalemma 8 Ke 59.15N 24.11 E
Vazante 54 Ig 18.00S 46.54W
Vazuza 16 Ia 56.10N 34.35 E
Vding Skovhøj 8 Ch 56.01N 9.48 E
Veadeiros, Chapada dos- 54 If 14.05S 47.28W
Vecht 10 Cd 52.35N 6.05 E
Vechta 10 Ed 52.43N 8.17 E
Vechte 10 Cd 52.35N 6.05 E
Vecpiebalga 8 Kh 56.57N 25.50 E
Vecsés 10 Pi 47.24N 19.17 E
Vedavågen 8 Ae 59.19N 5.12 E
Veddige 8 Eg 57.16N 12.19 E
Vedea 15 He 44.47N 24.37 E
Vedea 15 Ie 43.59N 25.59 E
Vedeno 16 Oh 42.57N 46.05 E
Vedia 55 Bl 34.30S 61.32W
Vedrá Isla- 13 Nf 38.52N 1.12 E
Veendam 11 Ma 53.06N 6.58 E
Veenendaal 12 Hb 52.02N 5.35 E
Veere 12 Fc 51.33N 3.40 E
Vega 7 Cd 65.39N 11.50 E
Vega 45 Ei 35.15N 102.26W
Vega Baja 51a Bb 18.25N 66.23W
Veganj 14 Kg 43.50N 16.45 E
Vegår 8 Cf 58.48N 8.47 E
Vegårshei 8 Cf 58.46N 8.48 E
Veghel 12 Hc 51.37N 5.32 E
Veglie 14 Lj 40.20N 17.58 E
Vegorrítis, Límni- 15 Ei 40.45N 21.48 E
Vègre 11 Fg 47.51N 0.14W
Vegreville 42 Gf 53.30N 112.03W
Vehmersalmi 8 Mb 62.46N 28.02 E
Vehnemoor 12 Ka 53.04N 8.02 E
Veinge 8 Eh 56.34N 13.05 E
Veinticinco de Mayo [Arg.] 56 He 35.26S 60.10W
Veinticinco de Mayo [Ur.] 55 Dl 34.12S 56.22W
Veio 14 Gh 42.02N 12.23 E
Veisiejai/Vejsejaj 8 Jj 54.03N 23.46 E
Vejen 7 Bi 55.29N 9.09 E
Vejer de la Frontera 13 Gh 36.15N 5.58W
Vejle [2] 8 Ci 55.45N 9.20 E
Vejle 7 Bi 55.42N 9.32 E
Vejsejaj/Veisiejai 8 Jj 54.03N 23.46 E
Vel 7 Kf 61.06N 42.10 E
Vela, Cabo de la- 49 Kg 12.13N 72.11W
Vela Luka 14 Kh 42.58N 16.44 E
Velas 32 Bb 38.41N 28.13W
Velas, Cabo- 49 Eh 10.22N 85.53W
Velásquez 55 El 34.02S 54.17W
Velay, Plateaux du- 11 Ji 45.10N 3.50 E
Velaz 55 Ch 26.42S 58.40W
Velbăždski prohod 15 Fg 42.14N 22.28 E
Velbert 10 De 51.20N 7.02 E
Velddrif 37 Bf 32.47S 18.10 E
Velden am Wörthersee 14 Id 46.37N 14.03 E
Veldhoven 12 Hc 51.24N 5.24 E
Velebit 5 Hg 44.17N 15.12 E
Velebitski kanal 14 If 44.45N 14.50 E
Veleka 15 Kg 42.04N 27.58 E
Velencei-tó 10 Oi 47.13N 18.36 E
Velenje 14 Jd 46.22N 15.07 E
Velestinon 15 Fj 39.23N 22.45 E
Veleta 13 Ig 37.04N 3.22W
Velež 14 Lg 43.20N 18.00 E
Vélez Blanco 13 Jg 37.41N 2.05W
Vélez de La Gomera, Peñón de- 13 Hi 35.11N 4.54W
Vélez-Málaga 13 Hh 36.47N 4.06W
Vélez Rubio 13 Jg 37.39N 2.04W
Velhas, Rio das- 52 Lg 17.13S 44.49W
Velika Gorica 14 Ke 45.44N 16.04 E
Velikaja 20 Md 64.35N 176.03 E
Velikaja-Gluša 10 Ve 51.49N 25.11 E
Velikaja Guba 7 Ie 62.17N 35.06 E
Velikaja Kema 20 Ig 45.29N 137.08 E
Velikaja Lepetiha 16 Hf 47.09N 33.59 E
Velikaja Mihajlovka 16 Ff 47.04N 29.52 E
Velika Kapela 14 Je 45.13N 15.02 E
Velika Kladuša 14 Je 45.11N 15.49 E
Velika Morava 15 Ee 44.43N 21.03 E
Velika Plana 15 Ee 44.20N 21.05 E
Veliki Berezny 10 Sh 48.54N 22.30 E
Veliki Byčkov 10 Ui 47.58N 24.04 E
Veliki Drvenik 14 Kg 43.27N 16.09 E
Veliki Jastrebac 15 Ef 43.24N 21.26 E
Velikije Luki 6 Jd 56.20N 30.32 E
Velikije Mosty 10 Uf 50.10N 24.12 E
Veliki kanal 15 Bd 45.52N 18.52 E
Veliki Ljuben 10 Tg 49.37N 23.45 E
Veliki Trnovac 15 Eg 42.29N 21.45 E
Veliki Ustjug 6 Kc 60.46N 46.20 E
Velikodolinskoje 15 Nc 46.20N 30.29 E
Veliko Gradište 15 Ee 44.46N 21.32 E
Veliko Tărnovo [2] 15 If 43.04N 25.39 E
Veliko Tărnovo 6 Ig 43.04N 25.39 E
Velikovisočnoje 19 Fb 67.16N 52.01 E
Veli Lošinj 14 If 44.31N 14.31 E
Vélingara 34 Cc 13.09N 14.07W
Velingrad 15 Gg 42.01N 24.00 E
Velino 14 Hh 42.09N 13.23 E
Velino 14 Gh 42.33N 12.43 E
Veliž 16 Gb 55.36N 31.12 E
Vel'ká Fatra 10 Ph 49.00N 19.05 E
Velké Meziříčí 10 Lg 49.21N 16.00 E
Vel'ký Krtíš 10 Ph 48.13N 19.20 E
Vella Lavella Island 57 Ge 7.45S 156.40 E
Velletri 14 Gi 41.41N 12.47 E
Vellinge 8 Ei 55.28N 13.01 E
Vellore 22 Jh 14.26N 79.58 E
Velmerstot 10 Ee 51.50N 9.00 E
Velmo 20 Ed 61.43N 92.25 E
Velopoúla 15 Gm 36.55N 23.28 E
Vels 17 If 60.45N 58.45 E
Velsen-IJmuiden [Neth.] 11 Kb 52.27N 4.39 E
Velsen-IJmuiden [Neth.] 12 Gb 52.28N 4.35 E
Velsk 19 Ec 61.05N 42.05 E
Veluwe 11 Lb 52.20N 5.50 E
Veluwemeer 12 Hb 52.23N 5.40 E
Velva 45 Fb 48.04N 100.56W
Velvendós 15 Fi 40.15N 22.04 E
Veman 8 Fb 62.02N 14.16 E
Vema Seamount (EN) 30 Hl 31.38S 8.19 E
Vemdalen 8 Eb 62.27N 13.52 E
Ven 8 Ei 55.55N 12.40 E
Venable Ice Shelf 66 Pf 73.03S 87.20W
Venado 48 If 22.56N 101.05W
Venado, Cerro- 50 Ei 6.17N 62.45W
Venado Tuerto 56 Hd 33.45S 61.58W
Venafro 14 Ii 41.29N 14.02 E
Venamo, Río- 50 Fi 6.43N 61.07W
Vence 11 Nk 43.43N 7.07 E
Venceslau Brás 55 Hf 23.51S 49.48W
Venda 37 Ed 22.35S 30.45 E
Venda Nova 54 Jg 19.45S 43.50W
Vendas Novas 13 Df 38.41N 8.27W
Vendée [3] 11 Eh 46.40N 1.20W
Vendée 11 Hh 46.40N 1.10 E
Vendée 11 Fh 46.19N 0.58W
Vendéen, Bocage- 11 Eh 46.50N 1.20W
Vendéenne, Plaine- 11 Eh 46.40N 1.20W
Vendel 8 Gd 60.10N 17.36 E
Vendeuvre-sur-Barse 11 Kf 48.14N 4.29 E
Vendôme 11 Hg 47.48N 1.04 E
Vendrell/El Vendrell 13 Nc 41.13N 1.32 E
Vendsyssel 8 Cg 57.20N 10.00 E
Venetia (EN) = Veneto [2] 14 Fe 45.30N 12.00 E
Venétiko [Grc.] 15 Jk 38.08N 26.01 E
Venétiko [Grc.] 15 Em 36.42N 21.53 E
Veneto = Venetia (EN) [2] 14 Fe 45.30N 12.00 E
Venev 16 Kb 54.22N 38.18 E
Venezia = Venice (EN) 6 Hf 45.27N 12.21 E
Venezia, Golfo di- = Venice, Gulf of- (EN) 5 Hf 45.15N 13.00 E
Venezia-Lido 14 Ge 45.25N 12.22 E
Venezia-Marghera 14 Ge 45.28N 12.44 E
Venezia-Mestre 14 Ge 45.29N 12.14 E
Venezuela [2] 53 Je 8.00N 65.00W
Venezuela, Golfo de- = Venezuela, Gulf of- (EN) 52 Id 11.30N 71.00W
Venezuela, Gulf of- (EN) = Venezuela, Golfo de- 52 Id 11.30N 71.00W
Venezuelan Basin (EN) 38 Mh 15.00N 68.00W
Vengerovo 20 Ce 55.41N 76.55 E
Veniaminof, Mount- 40 He 56.13N 159.18W
Venice 44 Fl 27.06N 82.27W
Venice (EN) = Venezia 6 Hf 45.27N 12.21 E
Venice, Gulf of- (EN) = Venezia, Golfo di- 5 Hf 45.15N 13.00 E
Vénissieux 11 Ki 45.41N 4.53 E
Venjan 8 Ed 60.57N 13.55 E
Venjansjön 8 Ed 60.55N 14.00 E
Venlo 11 Mc 51.24N 6.10 E
Venlock River 59 Ib 12.15S 142.00 E
Vennesla 7 Bg 58.17N 7.59 E
Venosa 14 Jj 40.58N 15.49 E
Venosta, Val-/ Vintschgau 14 Ed 46.40N 10.35 E
Venraij 11 Lc 51.32N 5.59 E
Vent, Canal du-=Windward Passage (EN) 49 Lh 20.00N 73.50W
Vent, Iles du-=Windward Islands (EN) 57 Mf 17.30S 149.30W
Venta 7 Eh 57.23N 21.32 E
Venta de Baños 13 Hc 41.55N 4.30W
Ventana, Cerro- 48 Fe 24.15N 106.20W
Ventersdorp 37 De 26.17S 26.48 E
Venterstad 37 Df 30.47S 25.48 E
Venticinco de Diciembre 55 Dg 24.42S 56.33W
Ventimiglia 14 Bg 43.47N 7.36 E
Ventnor 12 Ad 50.36N 1.11W
Ventotene 14 Hj 40.45N 13.25 E
Ventoux, Mont- 11 Lj 44.10N 5.17 E
Ventspils 19 Cd 57.24N 21.33 E
Ventuari, Rio- 52 Je 3.58N 67.02W
Ventura 43 De 34.17N 119.18W
Vénus, Pointe- 65e Fc 17.29S 149.29W
Venus Bay 59 Jg 38.40S 145.45 E
Venustiano Carranza 48 Mi 16.21N 92.33W
Venustiano Carranza, Presa- 48 Id 27.30N 100.40W
Ver 12 Bc 51.31N 0.27W
Vera [Arg.] 56 Hc 29.28S 60.13W
Vera [Sp.] 13 Kg 37.15N 1.52W
Verá, Laguna- 55 Dh 26.05S 57.39W
Veracruz [2] 47 Ee 19.20N 96.40W
Veracruz Llave 39 Jh 19.12N 96.08W
Veraguas [3] 49 Gj 8.30N 81.00W
Verāval 25 Ed 20.54N 70.22 E
Vera y Pintado 55 Bj 30.09S 60.21W
Verbania 14 Ce 45.56N 8.33 E
Verbovski 7 Ji 55.29N 41.59 E
Vercelli 14 Ce 45.19N 8.25 E
Vercors 11 Lj 44.57N 5.25 E
Verdalsøra 7 Ce 63.48N 11.29 E
Verde, Cape- 49 Jb 22.50N 74.52W
Verde, Cay- 49 Jb 22.02N 75.12W
Verde, Costa- 13 Ga 43.40N 5.40W
Verde, Rio- 52 Kh 23.09S 57.37W
Verde, Rio- [Braz.] 54 Hh 21.12S 51.53W
Verde, Rio- [Braz.] 55 Hb 15.07S 48.40W
Verde, Rio- [Braz.] 55 Hd 19.50S 49.45W
Verde, Rio- [Braz.] 55 Ge 21.12S 51.53W
Verde, Rio- [Braz.] 55 Gd 18.01S 50.14W
Verde, Rio- [Braz.] 55 Je 21.27S 45.40W
Verde, Rio- [Braz.] 55 Ca 13.33S 58.01W
Verde, Rio- [Braz.] 54 Gf 11.54S 55.50W
Verde, Rio- [Braz.] 54 Hg 19.11S 50.44W
Verde, Río- [Mex.] 48 Jg 21.37N 99.15W
Verde, Río- [Mex.] 48 Hg 20.42N 103.14W
Verde, Rio- [S.Amer.] 55 Ba 13.59S 60.20W
Verde Grande, Rio- 55 Kb 14.35S 43.53W
Verden (Aller) 10 Fd 52.55N 9.14 E
Verde River 43 Ee 33.33N 111.40W
Verdigris River 45 Ii 35.48N 95.18W
Verdinho, Rio- 55 Gc 17.29S 50.27W
Verdon 11 Lk 43.43N 5.46 E
Verdun [Fr.] 11 Le 49.10N 5.23 E
Verdun [Que.-Can.] 44 Kc 45.28N 73.34W
Verdura 14 Hm 37.28N 13.12 E
Vereeniging 37 De 26.38S 27.57 E
Vereščagino 19 Fd 58.05N 54.40 E
Verga, Cap- 34 Cc 10.12N 14.27W
Vergara [Arg.] 55 Dl 35.23S 57.48W
Vergara [Sp.] 13 Ja 43.07N 2.25W
Vergara [Ur.] 55 Fk 32.56S 53.57W
Vergato 14 Ff 44.17N 11.07 E
Verhnedneprovsk 16 Ie 48.39N 34.21 E
Verhnedneprovski 16 Hb 55.01N 33.21 E
Verhnedvinsk 7 Gi 55.46N 27.59 E
Verhneimbatsk 20 Dd 63.02N 88.00 E
Verhne-Karabahski Kanal 16 Oj 39.44N 47.57 E
Verhnespasskoje 7 Kg 58.45N 45.28 E
Verhnetulomski 7 Hb 68.38N 31.48 E
Verhnetulomskoje Vodohranilišče 7 Hb 68.35N 31.00 E
Verhneuralsk 17 Ij 53.53N 59.13 E
Verhneviljujsk 20 Hd 63.20N 120.25 E
Verhni At-Urjah 20 Kd 62.38N 150.03 E
Verhni Avzjan 17 Hj 53.32N 57.33 E
Verhni Kujto, Ozero- 7 Hd 65.00N 30.40 E
Verhni Most 8 Mg 57.29N 29.00 E
Verhni Tagil 17 Jh 57.22N 60.01 E
Verhni Trajanov Val=Upper Trajan's Wall (EN) 15 Lc 46.40N 29.00 E
Verhni Ufalej 19 Gd 56.04N 60.14 E
Verhnjaja Inta 17 Jd 65.59N 60.29 E
Verhnjaja Pyšma 17 Jh 56.59N 60.37 E
Verhnjaja Salda 17 Jg 58.02N 60.33 E
Verhnjaja Tojma 19 Ec 62.13N 45.01 E
Verhnjaja Tura 17 Ig 58.22N 59.49 E
Verhnj Uslon 7 Li 55.47N 48.58 E
Verhnoje Sinevidnoje 10 Tg 49.02N 23.36 E
Verhojansk 22 Pc 67.35N 133.27 E
Verhojanski Hrebet= Verhoyansk Mountains (EN) 21 Oc 67.00N 129.00 E
Verhoturje 17 Jg 58.52N 60.48 E
Verhovcevo 16 Ie 48.31N 34.12 E
Verhovina 15 Ha 48.08N 24.48 E
Verhovje 16 Jc 52.49N 37.14 E
Verhoyansk Mountains (EN)= Verhojanski Hrebet 21 Oc 67.00N 129.00 E
Verin 13 Ec 41.56N 7.26W
Veriora 8 Lg 58.00N 27.21 E
Veríssimo, Rio- 55 Hd 18.23S 48.20W
Verissimo, Serra do- 55 Hd 19.33S 48.25W
Verl 12 Kc 51.53N 8.31 E
Vermand 12 Fe 49.52N 3.09 E
Vermeille, Côte- 11 Jl 42.30N 3.20 E
Vermelho, Rio- [Braz.] 55 Ib 14.26S 46.26W
Vermelho, Rio- [Braz.] 55 Ed 19.36S 55.58W
Vermelho, Rio- [Braz.] 55 Gb 14.54S 51.06W
Vermenton 11 Jg 47.40N 3.44 E
Vermilion Bay 42 Ig 49.51N 93.24W
Vermilion Cliffs 46 Ih 37.10N 112.35W
Vermilion Lake 45 Jc 47.53N 92.25W
Vermilion River 44 Gb 46.16N 81.41W
Vermillion 45 He 42.47N 96.56W
Vermillion River 45 He 42.44N 96.53W
Vermillon, Rivière- 44 Kb 47.38N 72.59W
Vérmion Óros 15 Ei 40.30N 22.00 E
Vermont [2] 43 Mc 43.50N 72.45W
Vernal 43 Fc 40.27N 109.32W
Verneuil-sur-Avre 11 Gf 48.44N 0.56 E
Vernhi Barskunčak 16 Oe 48.14N 46.42 E
Vernon [B.C.-Can.] 42 Ff 50.16N 119.16W
Vernon [Fr.] 11 He 49.05N 1.29 E
Vernon [Tx.-U.S.] 43 He 34.09N 99.17W
Vérnon Óros 15 Ei 40.39N 21.22 E
Vernou 51e Ab 16.11N 61.39W
Verny 12 Ie 49.01N 6.12 E
Vero 13 Mb 42.00N 0.10 E
Vero Beach 43 Kf 27.38N 80.24W
Véroia 15 Fi 40.31N 22.12 E
Verona 6 Hf 45.27N 11.00 E
Verónica 56 Ie 35.22S 57.20W
Versailles [Fr.] 11 If 48.48N 2.08 E
Versailles [In.-U.S.] 44 Ef 39.04N 85.15W
Versilia 14 Eg 43.55N 10.15 E
Veršino-Darasunski 20 Gf 52.18N 115.32 E
Veršino-Šahtaminski 20 Gf 51.16N 117.55 E
Versmold 12 Kb 52.03N 8.09 E
Verson 12 Be 49.09N 0.27W
Vert, Cap-=Vert, Cape- (EN) 30 Fg 14.43N 17.30W
Vert, Cape- (EN)=Vert, Cap- 30 Fg 14.43N 17.30W
Vertentes, Serra das- 55 Je 20.56S 44.00W
Vértes 10 Oi 47.25N 18.20 E
Vertientes 49 Hc 21.16N 78.09W
Vertiskos Óros 15 Gi 40.50N 23.19 E
Verviers 11 Ld 50.36N 5.52 E
Vervins 12 Fe 49.50N 3.54 E
Vesanto 8 Lb 62.56N 26.25 E
Vescovato 11a Ba 42.29N 9.26 E
Vesder/Vesdre 12 Hd 50.37N 5.37 E
Vesdre/Vesder 12 Hd 50.37N 5.37 E
Veselí nad Lužnici 10 Kg 49.11N 14.43 E
Veselovskoje Vodohranilišče 16 Lf 47.00N 41.15 E
Vešenskaja 19 Ef 49.38N 41.46 E
Vesgre 12 Df 48.53N 1.28 E
Vesijarvi 8 Kc 61.05N 25.30 E
Vesjegonsk 7 Ig 58.41N 37.16 E
Veškajma 7 Li 54.03N 47.08 E
Vesle 11 Je 49.23N 3.28 E
Vesljana 17 Gf 60.20N 54.03 E
Vesoul 11 Mg 47.38N 6.10 E
Vessigebro 8 Eh 56.59N 12.39 E
Vest-Agder [2] 7 Bg 58.30N 7.10 E
Vestbygd 7 Bg 58.06N 6.35 E
Vesterålen 5 Hb 68.45N 15.00 E
Vesterøhavn 8 Dg 57.18N 10.56 E
Vestfjorden 5 Hb 68.35N 14.30 E
Vestfold [2] 7 Cg 59.15N 10.10 E
Vestfonna 41 Oc 79.58N 20.15 E
Vestgrønland = West Greenland (EN) [2] 41 He 69.00N 49.30W
Véstia 55 Ge 20.23S 51.25W
Vestmannæyjar 7a Bc 63.26N 20.16W
Vestnes 8 Bb 62.38N 7.06 E
Vestre Jakobselv 7 Ga 70.07N 29.25 E
Vestsjælland [2] 8 Di 55.30N 11.30 E
Vestvågøy 7 Cb 68.15N 13.50 E
Vésubie 11 Nk 43.52N 7.12 E
Vesuvio = Vesuvius (EN) 5 Hg 40.49N 14.26 E
Vesuvius (EN) = Vesuvio 5 Hg 40.49N 14.26 E
Veszprém [2] 10 Ni 47.10N 17.40 E
Veszprém 10 Ni 47.06N 17.55 E
Vésztő 10 Rj 46.55N 21.16 E
Vétaoundé, Ile- 57 Hf 13.15S 167.38 E
Vetauua 63d Ca 15.57S 179.24W
Vétê, Pointe- 63b Ca 13.27S 166.41 E
Vetka 16 Gc 52.34N 31.13 E
Vetlanda 7 Dh 57.26N 15.04 E
Vetljanka 7 Mj 52.52N 51.09 E
Vetluga 5 Kd 56.18N 46.24 E
Vetluga 7 Kh 57.52N 45.46 E

Index Symbols

[1] Independent Nation
[2] State, Region
[3] District, County
[4] Municipality
[5] Colony, Dependency
Continent
Physical Region
Historical or Cultural Region
Mount, Mountain
Volcano
Hill
Mountains, Mountain Range
Hills, Escarpment
Plateau, Upland
Pass, Gap
Plain, Lowland
Delta
Salt Flat
Valley, Canyon
Crater, Cave
Karst Features
Depression
Polder
Desert, Dunes
Forest, Woods
Heath, Steppe
Oasis
Cape, Point
Coast, Beach
Cliff
Peninsula
Isthmus
Sandbank
Island
Atoll
Rock, Reef
Islands, Archipelago
Rocks, Reefs
Coral Reef
Well, Spring
Geyser
River, Stream
Waterfall Rapids
River Mouth, Estuary
Lake
Salt Lake
Intermittent Lake
Reservoir
Swamp, Pond
Canal
Glacier
Ice Shelf, Pack Ice
Ocean
Sea
Gulf, Bay
Strait, Fjord
Lagoon
Bank
Seamount
Tablemount
Ridge
Shelf
Basin
Escarpment, Sea Scarp
Fracture
Trench, Abyss
National Park, Reserve
Point of Interest
Recreation Site
Cave, Cavern
Historic Site
Ruins
Wall, Walls
Church, Abbey
Temple
Scientific Station
Airport
Port
Lighthouse
Mine
Tunnel
Dam, Bridge

Vetlužski [R.S.F.S.R.] 7 Kh 57.11N 45.07 E
Vetlužski [R.S.F.S.R.] 7 Kg 58.26N 45.28 E
Vetreny 20 Jd 61.43N 149.40 E
Vetreny Pojas, Krjaž- 7 Ie 63.20N 37.30 E
Vetrino 8 Mi 55.25N 28.31 E
Vetschau/Wětošow 10 Ke 51.47N 14.04 E
Vettore 14 Hh 42.49N 13.16 E
Vetzstein 10 Hf 50.25N 11.25 E
Veules-les-Roses 12 Ce 49.52N 0.48 E
Veulettes-sur-Mer 12 Ce 49.51N 0.36 E
Veurne/Furnes 11 Ic 51.04N 2.40 E
Vevey 14 Ad 46.28N 6.50 E
Vevis/Vievis 8 Kj 54.45N 24.58 E
Vexin 11 He 49.10N 1.40 E
Veynes 11 Lj 44.32N 5.49 E
Vézelay 11 Jg 47.28N 3.44 E
Vežen 15 Hg 42.45N 24.24 E
Vézère 11 Gj 44.53N 0.53 E
Vezirköprü 24 Fb 41.09N 35.28 E
Viadana 14 Ef 44.56N 10.31 E
Viale 55 Bj 31.53S 60.01W
Viana 54 Jd 3.13S 45.00W
Viana del Bollo 13 Eb 42.11N 7.06W
Viana do Alentejo 13 Ef 38.20N 8.00W
Viana do Castelo 13 Dc 41.42N 8.50W
Viana do Castelo [2] 13 Dc 41.55N 8.25W
Vianden 12 Ie 49.55N 6.16 E
Viangchan (Vientiane) 22 Mh 17.58N 102.36 E
Vianópolis 55 Hc 16.45S 48.32W
Viar 13 Gg 37.36N 5.50W
Viareggio 14 Eg 43.52N 10.14 E
Viarmes 12 Ee 49.08N 2.22 E
Viaur 11 Hj 44.08N 1.58 E
Viborg [2] 8 Ch 56.30N 9.30 E
Viborg 7 Bh 56.26N 9.24 E
Vibo Valentia 14 Kl 38.40N 16.06 E
Vic 13 Oc 41.56N 2.15 E
Vicari 14 Hm 37.49N 13.34 E
Vicecomodoro Marambio 66 Re 64.16S 56.44W
Vicente Guerrero 47 Dd 23.45N 103.59W
Vicenza 14 Fe 45.33N 11.33 E
Vichada [2] 54 Ec 5.00N 69.30W
Vichada, Río- 52 Je 4.55N 67.50W
Vichadero 55 Ej 31.48S 54.43W
Vichy 11 Jh 46.07N 3.25 E
Vicksburg 43 Ie 32.14N 90.56W
Vico, Lago di- 14 Gh 42.19N 12.10 E
Vic-sur-Aisne 12 Fe 49.24N 3.07 E
Vic-sur-Cère 11 Ij 44.59N 2.37 E
Victor Bay 66 Ie 66.20S 136.30 E
Victor Harbour 59 Hg 35.34S 138.37 E
Victoria 38 Hb 71.00N 114.00W
Victoria [Arg.] 56 Hd 32.37S 60.10W
Victoria [Austl.] 59 Ig 38.00S 145.00 E
Victoria [B.C.-Can.] 39 Ge 48.25N 123.22W
Victoria [Cam.] 34 Ge 4.01N 9.12 E
Victoria [Chile] 56 Fe 38.13S 72.20W
Victoria [Gren.] 50 Ff 12.12N 61.42W
Victoria [Mala.] 26 Ge 5.17N 115.15 E
Victoria [Malta] 14 In 36.02N 14.14 E
Victoria [Rom.] 15 Hd 45.44N 24.41 E
Victoria [Sey.] 31 Mi 4.38S 55.27 E
Victoria [Tx.-U.S.] 39 Jg 28.48N 97.00W
Victoria/Ying zhan 22 Ng 22.17N 114.09 E
Victoria, Lake- [Afr.] 30 Ki 1.00S 33.00 E
Victoria, Lake- [Austl.] 59 If 34.00S 141.15 E
Victoria, Mount- [Bur.] 21 Lg 21.14N 93.55 E
Victoria, Mount- [Pap.N.Gui.] 57 Fe 8.53S 147.33 E
Victoria, Sierra de la- 55 Fg 25.55S 54.00W
Victoria and Albert Mountains 42 Ka 79.00N 75.00W
Victoria de Durango 39 Ig 24.02N 104.40W
Victoria de las Tunas 47 Id 20.58N 76.57W
Victoria Falls 31 Jj 17.56S 25.50 E
Victoria Falls 30 Jj 17.55S 25.21 E
Victoria Fjord 41 Hb 82.20N 48.00W
Victoria Land (EN) 66 Jf 75.00S 159.00 E
Victoria Nile 30 Kh 2.14N 31.26 E
Victoria Peak [B.C.-Can.] 46 Ba 50.03N 126.06W
Victoria Peak [Blz.] 49 Ce 16.48N 88.37W
Victoria River 57 Df 15.12S 129.43 E
Victoria River Downs 59 Gc 16.24S 131.00 E
Victoria Strait 42 Hc 69.30N 100.00W
Victoriaville 42 Kg 46.03N 71.58W
Victoria West 37 Cf 31.25S 23.04 E
Victorija 41 Pb 80.10N 36.45 E
Victorville 46 Gi 34.32N 117.18W
Victory, Mount- 59 Ja 9.10S 149.05 E
Vičuga 19 Ed 57.15N 42.00 E
Vicuña 56 Fc 29.59S 70.44W
Vicuña Mackenna 56 Hd 33.54S 64.23W
Vidå 8 Cj 54.58N 8.41 E
Vidal 46 Hi 34.11N 114.34W
Vidalia 45 Kk 31.34N 91.26W
Videbæk 8 Ch 56.05N 8.38 E
Videira 56 Jc 27.00S 51.08W
Videla 55 Bj 30.56S 60.39W
Videle 15 Ie 44.17N 25.31 E
Vidigueira 13 Ef 38.13N 7.48W
Vidin [2] 15 Ff 43.59N 22.52 E
Vidin 15 Ff 43.59N 22.52 E
Vidisha 25 Fd 23.42N 77.47 E
Vidlič 15 Ff 43.08N 22.47 E
Vidojevica 15 Ef 43.10N 21.32 E
Vidöstern 8 Fg 57.04N 14.01 E
Vidourle 11 Kk 43.32N 4.08 E
Vidra [Rom.] 15 Jd 45.55N 26.54 E
Vidra [Rom.] 15 Je 44.16N 26.09 E
Vidsel 7 Ed 65.49N 20.31 E
Viduša 14 Mh 42.54N 18.18 E
Vidzeme 8 Kg 57.10N 26.00 E
Vidzemes Augstiene/Vidzemskaja Vozvyšennost 8 Kh 56.45N 26.00 E
Vidzemskaja Vozvyšennost/Vidzemes Augstiene 8 Kh 56.45N 26.00 E
Vidzy 8 Li 55.23N 26.47 E
Vie 12 Be 49.09N 0.04W
Viechtach 10 Ig 49.05N 12.53 E
Viedma 53 Jj 40.50S 63.00W
Viedma, Lago- 52 Ij 49.35S 72.35W
Vieille Case 51g Ba 15.36N 61.24W
Vieja, Sierra- 45 Dk 30.30N 104.40W
Viejo, Cerro- 47 Bb 30.20N 112.15W
Viekšniai/Viekšnjai 8 Jh 56.14N 22.28 E
Viekšnjai/Viekšniai 8 Jh 56.14N 22.28 E
Viella 13 Mb 42.42N 0.48 E
Vielsalm 12 Hd 50.17N 5.55 E
Viels-Maisons 12 Ff 48.54N 3.24 E
Vienna [Mo.-U.S.] 45 Kg 38.11N 91.57W
Vienna [W.V.-U.S.] 44 Gf 39.20N 81.33W
Vienna (EN) = Wien 6 Hf 48.12N 16.22 E
Vienna Woods (EN)=Wienerwald 14 Jb 48.10N 16.00 E
Vienne 11 Ki 45.31N 4.52 E
Vienne [3] 11 Gh 46.30N 0.30 E
Vienne 5 Gf 47.13N 0.05 E
Vientiane→Viangchan 22 Mh 17.58N 102.36 E
Vientos, Paso de los-=Windward Passage (EN) 38 Lh 20.00N 73.50W
Vieques, Isla de- 47 Ke 18.08N 65.25W
Vieques, Pasaje de- 51a Cb 18.08N 65.40W
Vieques, Sonda de- 51a Cb 18.17N 65.25W
Vierge Point 51k Bb 13.49N 60.53W
Viersen 10 Ce 51.15N 6.23 E
Vierville-sur-Mer 12 Be 49.22N 0.54W
Vierwaldstätter-See = Lucerne, Lake- (EN) 14 Cc 47.00N 8.30 E
Vierzon 11 Ig 47.13N 2.05 E
Viesca 48 He 25.21N 102.48W
Viesīte/Viesite 8 Kh 56.20N 25.38 E
Viesite/Viesīte 8 Kh 56.20N 25.38 E
Vieste 14 Ki 41.53N 16.10 E
Viet Nam [1] 22 Mh 13.00N 108.00 E
Viet Tri 25 Ld 21.18N 105.26 E
Vieux Fort 50 Ff 13.44N 60.57W
Vieux-Fort, Pointe du- 51e Ac 15.57N 61.43W
Vieux Fort Bay 51k Bb 13.44N 60.58W
Vieux-Habitants 51e Ab 16.04N 61.46W
Vievis/Vevis 8 Kj 54.45N 24.58 E
Viga 7 Kg 59.15N 43.42 E
Vigala 8 Kf 58.43N 24.22 E
Vigan 26 Hc 17.34N 120.23 E
Vigeland 8 Bf 58.05N 7.18 E
Vigevano 14 Ce 45.19N 8.51 E
Vigia 54 Id 0.48S 48.08W
Vigia Chico 48 Ph 19.46N 87.35W
Vignacourt 12 Ed 50.01N 2.12 E
Vignemale 13 Lb 42.46N 0.08W
Vigneulles-lès-Hattonchâtel 12 Hf 48.59N 5.43 E
Vignoble 11 Lh 46.50N 5.30 E
Vignola 14 Ef 44.29N 11.00 E
Vigny 12 De 49.05N 1.56 E
Vigo 6 Fg 42.14N 8.43W
Vigo, Ría de- 13 Db 42.15N 8.45W
Vigra 8 Bb 62.30N 6.05 E
Vigrestad 8 Af 58.34N 5.42 E
Vihanti 7 Fd 64.30N 25.00 E
Vihiers 11 Fg 47.09N 0.32W
Vihorevka 20 Fe 56.12N 101.09 E
Vihorlat 10 Sh 48.55N 22.10 E
Vihren 15 Gh 41.46N 23.24 E
Vihti 7 Ff 60.25N 24.20 E
Viiala 8 Jc 61.13N 23.47 E
Viinijärvi 8 Mb 62.45N 29.15 E
Viinijärvi 8 Mb 62.39N 29.14 E
Viitasaari 7 Fe 63.04N 25.52 E
Viivikonna/Vijvikonna 8 Le 59.14N 27.41 E
Vijayawāda 22 Kh 16.31N 80.37 E
Vijvikonna/Viivikonna 8 Le 59.14N 27.41 E
Vik 7a Bc 63.25N 19.01W
Vika 8 Fd 60.57N 14.27 E
Vikarbyn 8 Fd 60.55N 15.01 E
Vikbolandet 8 Gf 58.30N 16.40 E
Viken 8 Eh 56.09N 12.34 E
Viken 8 Ff 58.40N 14.20 E
Vikenara Point 63a Dc 8.34S 159.53 E
Vikersund 8 De 59.59N 10.02 E
Vikingbanken 9 Pa 60.20N 2.30 E
Vikmanshyttan 8 Fd 60.17N 15.49 E
Vikna 7 Cd 64.53N 10.58 E
Vikna 7 Cd 64.54N 11.00 E
Viksoyri 7 Bf 61.05N 6.34 E
Vila da Bispo 13 Dg 37.05N 8.55W
Vila da Maganja 37 Fc 17.18S 37.31 E
Vila de Rei 13 De 39.40N 8.09W
Vila do Conde 13 Dc 41.21N 8.45W
Vila do Porto 32 Bb 36.56N 25.09W
Vila Flor 13 Ec 41.18N 7.09W
Vilafranca del Penedès/Villafranca del Panadés 13 Nc 41.21N 1.42 E
Vila Franca de Xira 13 Df 38.57N 8.59W
Vila Franca do Campo 32 Bb 37.43N 25.26W
Vila Franca do Save 37 Ed 21.09S 34.32 E
Vila Gamito 37 Eb 14.10S 32.59 E
Vila Gouveia 37 Ec 18.03S 33.11 E
Vilaine 11 Dg 49.23N 2.27W
Viļaka/Viljaka 7 Gh 57.14N 27.46 E
Vila Machado 37 Ec 19.17S 34.12 E
Vilanculos 31 Kk 22.00S 35.19 E
Viļani/Viljani 7 Gh 56.33N 26.59 E
Vila Nova da Cerveira 13 Dc 41.56N 8.45W
Vila Nova de Famalicao 13 Dc 41.25N 8.32W
Vila Nova de Foz Côa 13 Ec 41.05N 7.12W
Vila Nova de Gaia 13 Dc 41.08N 8.37W
Vilanova i la Geltrú/Villanueva y Geltrú 13 Nc 41.14N 1.44 E
Vila Paiva de Andrada 37 Ec 18.41S 34.04 E
Vila Pouca de Aguiar 13 Ec 41.30N 7.39W
Vila Real [2] 13 Ec 41.35N 7.35W
Vila Real 13 Ec 41.18N 7.45W
Vila-Real de los Infantes/Villarreal de los Infantes 13 Le 39.56N 0.06W
Vila Real de Santo António 13 Eg 37.12N 7.25W
Vilar Formoso 13 Fd 40.37N 6.50W
Vila Velha 54 Jh 20.20S 40.17W
Vila Velha de Ródão 13 Ee 39.40N 7.42W
Vila Viçosa 13 Ef 38.47N 7.25W
Vilcea [2] 15 He 45.10N 24.10 E
Vilches 13 If 38.12N 3.30W
Vildbjerg 8 Ch 56.12N 8.46 E
Viled 7 Lf 61.22N 47.15 E
Vilejka 19 Ce 54.30N 26.53 E
Vilhelmina 7 Dd 64.37N 16.39 E
Vilhena 53 Jg 12.43S 60.07W
Vilija 16 Db 54.55N 25.40 E
Viljaka/Viļaka 7 Gh 57.14N 27.46 E
Viljandi 19 Cd 58.22N 25.35 E
Viljany/Viļani 7 Gh 56.33N 26.59 E
Viljuj 21 Oc 64.24N 126.26 E
Viljujsk 20 Hd 63.40N 121.33 E
Viljujskoje Plato=Vilyui Range (EN) 21 Mc 66.00N 108.00 E
Viljujskoje Vodohranilišče 20 Gd 62.30N 111.00 E
Vilkaviškis 7 Fi 54.43N 23.02 E
Vilkickogo, Ostrov- [R.S.F.S.R.] 20 Cb 73.30N 76.00 E
Vilkickogo, Ostrov- [R.S.F.S.R.] 20 Ka 75.40N 152.30 E
Vilkickogo, Proliv-=Vilkitski Strait (EN) 21 Mb 77.55N 103.00 E
Vilkija 7 Fi 55.03N 23.35 E
Vilkitski Strait (EN)=Vilkickogo, Proliv- 21 Mb 77.55N 103.00 E
Vilkovo 16 Fg 45.23N 29.35 E
Villa Aberastain 56 Gd 31.39S 68.35W
Villa Ahumada 47 Cb 30.37N 106.31W
Villa Altagracia 49 Ld 18.40N 70.10W
Villa Ana 55 Ci 28.29S 59.37W
Villa Angela 56 Hc 27.35S 60.43W
Villa Atuel 56 Gd 34.50S 67.54W
Villa Berthet 55 Bh 27.17S 60.25W
Villablino 13 Fb 42.56N 6.19W
Villa Bruzual 54 Eb 9.20N 69.06W
Villa Cañás 55 Bk 34.00S 61.36W
Villacañas 13 Ie 39.38N 3.20W
Villacarrillo 13 If 38.07N 3.05W
Villacastín 13 Hd 40.47N 4.25W
Villach 14 Hd 46.36N 13.50 E
Villacidro 14 Ck 39.27N 8.44 E
Villa Clara 55 Cj 31.50S 58.49W
Villaclara [3] 49 Hb 22.30N 80.00W
Villa Constitución [Arg.] 56 Hd 33.14S 60.20W
Villa Constitución [Mex.] 47 Bc 25.09N 111.43W
Villa Coronado 48 Gd 26.45N 105.10W
Villada 13 Hb 42.15N 4.58W
Villa de Arriaga 48 Ig 21.54N 101.23W
Villa de Cos 48 Hf 23.17N 102.21W
Villa de Cura 50 Cg 10.02N 67.29W
Villa de Maria 56 Hc 29.54S 63.43W
Villa de Reyes 48 Ig 21.48N 100.56W
Villa de San Antonio 49 Df 14.16N 87.36W
Villadiego 13 Ib 42.31N 4.00W
Villa Dolores 56 Gd 31.56S 65.12W
Villa Elisa 55 Ck 32.10S 58.24W
Villa Flores 48 Mi 16.14N 93.14W
Villa Florida 55 Dh 26.23S 57.09W
Villafranca del Bierzo 13 Fb 42.36N 6.48W
Villafranca del Cid 13 Ld 40.25N 0.15W
Villafranca de los Barros 13 Ff 38.34N 6.20W
Villafranca del Panadés/Vilafranca del Penedès 13 Nc 41.21N 1.42 E
Villafranca di Verona 14 Ee 45.21N 10.50 E
Villa Frontera 47 Dc 26.56N 101.27W
Villagarcia de Arosa 13 Db 42.36N 8.45W
Villa General Roca 56 Gd 32.39S 66.28W
Villa Gesell 55 Dm 37.15S 56.55W
Villagrán 48 Je 24.29N 99.29W
Villaguay 56 Id 31.51S 59.01W
Villa Guillermina 55 Ci 28.14S 59.28W
Villa Hayes 56 Ic 25.06S 57.34W
Villa Hermandarias 55 Cj 31.13S 59.59W
Villahermosa 39 Jh 17.59N 92.55W
Villa Hidalgo 48 Gd 26.16N 104.54W
Villa Huidobro 56 Hd 34.50S 64.35W
Villajoyosa/La Vila Jojosa 13 Lf 38.30N 0.14W
Villalba 13 Ea 43.18N 7.41W
Villaldama 48 Id 26.30N 100.26W
Villalón de Campos 13 Gb 42.06N 5.02W
Villalpando 13 Gc 41.52N 5.24W
Villamalea 13 Ke 39.22N 1.35W
Villamanrique 13 Jf 38.33N 3.00W
Villa María 53 Ji 32.25S 63.15W
Villamartín 13 Gh 36.52N 5.38W
Villa Matamoros 48 Gd 26.50N 105.35W
Villa Media Agua 56 Gd 31.59S 68.25W
Villamil 54a Ab 0.56S 91.01W
Villa Minetti 55 Bi 28.37S 61.39W
Villa Montes 53 Jh 21.15S 63.30W
Villandraut 11 Fj 44.28N 0.22W
Villa Nueva 56 Gd 32.54S 68.47W
Villanueva 49 Kh 10.37N 72.59W
Villanueva [Mex.] 48 Hf 22.21N 102.53W
Villanueva [N.M.-U.S.] 45 Di 35.17N 105.23W
Villanueva de Córdoba 13 Hf 38.20N 4.37W
Villanueva del Arzobispo 13 Jf 38.10N 3.00W
Villanueva de la Serena 13 Gf 38.58N 5.48W
Villanueva del Fresno 13 Ef 38.23N 7.10W
Villanueva de los Infantes 13 If 38.44N 3.01W
Villanueva del Rio y Minas 13 Gg 37.39N 5.42W
Villanueva y Geltrú/Vilanova i la Geltrú 13 Nc 41.14N 1.44 E
Villa Ocampo [Arg.] 56 Ic 28.28S 59.22W
Villa Ocampo [Mex.] 47 Cc 26.27N 105.31W
Villa Ojo de Agua 56 Hc 29.31S 63.42W
Villa Oliva 55 Dh 26.01S 57.53W
Villa Pesqueira 48 Ec 29.08N 109.58W
Villaputzu 14 Dk 39.26N 9.34 E
Villa Ramírez 55 Bk 32.11S 60.12W
Villarcayo 13 Ib 42.56N 3.34W
Villar del Arzobispo 13 Le 39.44N 0.49W
Villa Regina 56 Ge 39.06S 67.04W
Villarica (Chile) 56 Fe 39.16S 72.16W
Villarica [Par.] 53 Kh 25.45S 56.26W
Villa Rosario 54 Db 7.50N 72.29W
Villarreal de los Infantes/Vila-Real de los Infantes 13 Le 39.56N 0.06W
Villarrobledo 13 Je 39.16N 2.36W
Villasalto 14 Dk 39.29N 9.23 E
Villa San Giovanni 14 Jl 38.13N 15.38 E
Villa San Martín 56 Hc 28.18S 64.12W
Villasimius 14 Dk 39.08N 9.31 E
Villatoro, Puerto de- 13 Gd 40.33N 5.10W
Villa Unión [Mex.] 47 Cd 23.12N 106.16W
Villa Unión [Mex.] 48 Ic 28.15N 100.43W
Villaverde, Madrid- 13 Id 40.21N 3.42W
Villavicencio 53 Ie 4.09N 73.37W
Villaviciosa 13 Ga 43.29N 5.26W
Villazón 54 Eh 22.06S 65.36W
Ville-de-Laval 42 Kc 45.33N 73.44W
Ville de Paris [3] 11 If 48.52N 2.20 E
Ville de Toulouse Bank (EN) 38 Hh 11.30N 117.00W
Villedieu-les-Poêles 11 Ef 48.50N 1.13W
Ville-en-Tardenois 12 Fe 49.11N 3.48 E
Villefranche-de-Lauragais 11 Hk 43.24N 1.44 E
Villefranche-de-Rouergue 11 Ij 44.21N 2.03 E
Villefranche-sur-Saône 11 Ki 45.59N 4.43 E
Ville-Marie 44 Hb 47.20N 79.26W
Villemur-sur-Tarn 11 Hk 43.52N 1.31 E
Villena 13 Lf 38.38N 0.51W
Villeneuve d'Ascq 12 Fd 50.38N 3.09 E
Villeneuve-Saint-Georges 12 Ef 48.44N 2.27 E
Villeneuve-sur-Lot 11 Gj 44.24N 0.43 E
Villeneuve-sur-Yonne 11 Jf 48.05N 3.18 E
Ville Platte 45 Jk 30.42N 92.16W
Villers-Bocage [Fr.] 12 Be 49.05N 0.39W
Villers-Bocage [Fr.] 12 Ee 50.00N 2.20 E
Villers-Bretonneux 12 Ee 49.52N 2.31 E
Villers-Carbonnel 12 Ee 49.52N 2.54 E
Villers-Cotterêts 12 Fe 49.15N 3.05 E
Villers-la-Ville 12 Gd 50.35N 4.32 E
Villers-sur-Mer 12 Be 49.19N 0.01W
Villerupt 12 He 49.28N 5.56 E
Villerville 12 Ce 49.24N 0.08 E
Ville-sur-Tourbe 12 Ge 49.11N 4.47 E
Villeurbanne 11 Ki 45.59N 4.43 E
Villiersdorp 37 Bf 33.59S 19.17 E
Villingen-Schwenningen 10 Eh 48.04N 8.28 E
Villmanstrand/Lappeenranta 6 Ic 61.04N 28.11 E
Villmar 12 Kd 50.23N 8.12 E
Vilnius/Vilnjus 6 Ie 54.41N 25.19 E
Vilnjus/Vilnius 6 Ie 54.41N 25.19 E
Vilok 10 Sh 48.08N 22.50 E
Vilppula 8 Kb 62.01N 24.31 E
Vils [Ger.] 10 Hg 49.10N 11.59 E
Vils [Ger.] 10 Jh 48.35N 13.10 E
Vilsandi 8 If 58.20N 21.45 E
Vilsbiburg 10 Ih 48.27N 12.21 E
Vilshofen 10 Jh 48.38N 13.11 E
Vilusi 15 Bg 42.44N 18.36 E
Vilvoorde/Vilvorde 11 Kd 50.56N 4.26 E
Vilvorde/Vilvoorde 11 Kd 50.56N 4.26 E
Vilyui Range (EN)=Viljujskoje Plato 21 Mc 66.00N 108.00 E
Vimeu 12 Dd 50.05N 1.35 E
Vimianzo 13 Ca 43.07N 9.02W
Vimmerby 7 Dh 57.40N 15.51 E
Vimoutiers 11 Gf 48.55N 0.12 E
Vimperk 10 Jg 49.03N 13.47 E
Vimy 12 Ed 50.22N 2.49 E
Vina 34 Id 7.45N 15.36 E
Viña del Mar 53 Ii 33.02S 71.34W
Vinalhaven Island 44 Mc 44.05N 68.52W
Vinalopó 13 Lf 38.11N 0.36W
Vinaròs/Vinaroz 13 Md 40.28N 0.29 E
Vinaroz/Vinaròs 13 Md 40.28N 0.29 E
Vinātori 15 Hc 46.14N 24.56 E
Vincennes 43 Jd 38.41N 87.32W
Vincennes Bay 66 He 66.30S 109.30 E
Vincente, Puntan- 64b Bb 14.56N 145.40 E
Vinci 14 Eg 43.47N 10.55 E
Vindafjorden 8 Ae 59.20N 5.55 E
Vindelälven 7 Ee 63.54N 19.52 E
Vindeln 7 Ed 64.12N 19.44 E
Vinderup 8 Ch 56.29N 8.47 E
Vindhya Range 21 Kg 24.37N 82.00 E
Vindö 8 He 59.20N 18.40 E
Vineland 44 Jf 39.29N 75.02W
Vingåker 7 Dg 59.02N 15.52 E
Vingeanne 12 Lg 47.45N 5.18 E
Vinh 22 Mh 18.40N 105.40 E
Vinhais 13 Fc 41.50N 7.00W
Vinh Bac Phan=Tonkin, Gulf of- (EN) 21 Mh 20.00N 108.00 E
Vinh Linh 25 Le 17.04N 107.02 E
Vinica [Yugo.] 14 Jg 45.28N 77.00 E
Vinica [Yugo.] 15 Fh 41.53N 22.30 E
Vinita 45 Ih 36.39N 95.09W
Vinju Mare 15 Fe 44.25N 22.52 E
Vinkovci 14 Me 45.17N 18.49 E
Vinnica 6 If 49.14N 28.29 E
Vinnickaja Oblast [3] 19 Cf 49.00N 28.50 E
Vinniki 16 De 49.48N 24.11 E
Vino, Tierra del- 13 Gc 41.30N 5.30W
Vinogradov 16 Ce 48.09N 23.02 E
Vinslöv 8 Eh 56.06N 13.55 E
Vinson Massif 66 Pf 78.35S 85.25W
Vinstervatn 8 Cc 61.20N 9.00 E
Vinstra 7 Bf 61.36N 9.45 E
Vinstra 8 Cc 61.36N 9.45 E
Vintilă Vodă 15 Jd 45.28N 26.43 E
Vintjärn 8 Gd 60.50N 16.03 E
Vinton 45 Ke 42.10N 92.00W
Vintschgau/Venosta, Val- 14 Ed 46.40N 10.35 E
Vipiteno / Sterzing 14 Fd 46.54N 11.26 E
Vipya Plateau 36 Fe 11.09S 34.00 E
Viqueque 26 Ih 8.52S 126.22 E
Vir 14 Jf 44.18N 15.03 E
Virac 26 Hd 13.35N 124.15 E
Viramgām 25 Ed 23.07N 72.02 E
Virandozero 7 Id 64.01N 36.03 E
Viranşehir 24 Hd 37.13N 39.45 E
Virbalis 8 Jj 54.37N 22.49 E
Vircava 8 Jh 56.35N 23.43 E
Virden 42 Hg 49.51N 100.55W
Virdois/Virrat 7 Fe 62.14N 23.47 E
Vire 11 Ff 48.50N 0.53W
Vire 11 Ee 49.20N 1.07W
Virei 36 Bf 15.43S 12.54 E
Vireux-Wallerand 12 Gd 50.05N 4.44 E
Virgenes, Cabo- 52 Jk 52.19S 68.21W
Virgin Gorda 50 Dc 18.30N 64.25W
Virginia [2] 43 Ld 37.30N 78.45W
Virginia [Mn.-U.S.] 43 Ib 47.31N 92.32W
Virginia [S.Afr.] 37 De 28.12S 26.49 E
Virginia Beach 43 Ld 36.51N 75.59W
Virginia City 46 Fg 39.19N 119.39W
Virgin Islands 38 Mg 18.20N 66.45W
Virgin Islands of the United States [5] 39 Mh 18.20N 64.52W
Virgin Mountains 46 Ih 36.40N 113.50W
Virgin Passage 51a Cb 18.20N 65.10W
Virgin River 46 Hh 36.35N 114.18W
Virihaure 7 Dc 67.22N 16.33 E
Virkby/Virkkala 8 Kd 60.13N 24.01 E
Virkkala/Virkby 8 Kd 60.13N 24.01 E
Virmasvesi 8 Lb 62.50N 26.55 E
Virôchey 25 Lf 13.59N 106.49 E
Viroin 12 Kd 50.05N 4.43 E
Viroinval 12 Gd 50.05N 4.33 E
Viroinval-Nismes 12 Gd 50.05N 4.33 E
Virojoki 7 Gf 60.35N 27.42 E
Viroqua 45 Ke 43.34N 90.53W
Virovitica 14 Le 45.50N 17.23 E
Virpazar 15 Cg 42.15N 19.06 E
Virrat/Virdois 7 Fe 62.14N 23.47 E
Virserum 7 Dh 57.19N 15.35 E
Virsko More 14 If 44.20N 15.00 E
Virton 11 Le 49.34N 5.32 E
Virton-Ethe 12 He 49.35N 5.35 E
Virtsu 7 Fg 58.37N 23.31 E
Virudunagar 25 Fg 9.36N 77.58 E
Virvičia/Virvyčia 8 Jh 56.14N 22.30 E
Virvyčia/Virvičia 8 Jh 56.14N 22.30 E
Vis 14 Kg 43.02N 16.10 E
Vis 14 Kg 43.03N 16.12 E
Visalia 43 Dd 36.20N 119.18W
Visayan Sea 26 Hd 11.35N 123.51 E
Visby 7 Eh 57.38N 18.18 E
Viscount Melville Sound 38 Hb 74.10N 113.00W
Visé/Wezet 12 Hd 50.44N 5.42 E
Višegrad 15 Jh 41.59N 26.20 E
Višegrad 14 Ng 43.48N 19.17 E
Višera [R.S.F.S.R.] 19 Fc 61.57N 52.25 E
Višera [R.S.F.S.R.] 5 Ld 59.55N 56.50 E
Viseu [2] 13 Ed 40.45N 7.50W
Viseu [Braz.] 54 Id 1.12S 46.07W
Viseu [Port.] 13 Ed 40.39N 7.55W
Vişeu de Sus 15 Hb 47.43N 24.26 E
Vishākhapatnam 22 Kh 17.42N 83.18 E
Visingsö 8 Ff 58.03N 14.20 E
Viskafors 8 Eg 57.38N 12.50 E
Viskan 7 Cg 57.14N 12.12 E
Viški Kanal 14 Kg 43.07N 16.17 E
Vislanda 7 Dh 56.47N 14.27 E
Vislinski Zaliv 10 Pb 54.27N 19.40 E
Visnes 8 Ae 59.21N 5.14 E
Višnevka 15 Lc 46.22N 28.27 E
Visoki Dečani 15 Dg 42.33N 20.16 E
Visoko 14 Mg 43.59N 18.11 E
Visokoi 66 Ad 56.42S 27.12W
Visonggo 63d Bb 16.13S 179.40 E
Visp 14 Bd 46.17N 7.53 E
Vissefjärda 8 Fh 56.32N 15.35 E
Vista 46 Gj 33.12N 117.15W
Visten 8 Ee 59.40N 13.20 E
Vistonias, Órmos- 15 Ii 40.58N 25.05 E
Vistonis, Limni- 15 Ih 41.03N 25.07 E
Vistula (EN)=Wisła 5 He 54.22N 18.55 E
Vištytis 8 Jj 54.27N 22.44 E
Visuvisu Point 63a Cb 7.57S 157.31 E
Vit 15 Hf 43.41N 24.45 E
Vitebsk 6 Jd 55.12N 30.11 E
Vitebskaja Oblast [3] 19 Cd 55.20N 29.00 E
Viterbo 14 Gh 42.25N 12.06 E
Vithkuqi 15 Di 40.31N 20.35 E
Vitichi 54 Eh 20.13S 65.29W
Vitigudino 13 Fc 41.01N 6.26W
Viti Levu 57 If 18.00S 178.00 E
Vitim 20 Ge 59.33N 112.28 E
Vitim 21 Nd 59.26N 112.34 E
Vitimski 20 Ge 58.18N 113.18 E
Vitimskoje Ploskogorje 20 Gf 54.00N 114.00 E
Vitinja 15 Gg 42.47N 23.45 E
Vitjaz Strait 60 Di 5.35S 147.00 E
Vitološte 15 Eh 41.11N 21.50 E
Vitória 13 Jb 42.51N 2.40W
Vitória 53 Lh 20.19S 40.21W
Vitória da Conquista 53 Lg 14.51S 40.51W
Vitória de Santo Antão 54 Ke 8.07S 35.18W
Vitorog 14 Lf 44.08N 17.03 E
Vitosa 15 Gg 42.33N 23.15 E
Vitré 11 Ef 48.08N 1.12W
Vitry-en-Artois 12 Ed 50.20N 2.59 E
Vitry-le-François 11 Kf 48.44N 4.35 E
Vitsi 15 Ei 40.39N 21.23 E

Index Symbols

[1] Independent Nation
[2] State, Region
[3] District, County
[4] Municipality
[5] Colony, Dependency
Continent
Physical Region
Historical or Cultural Region
Mount, Mountain
Volcano
Hill
Mountains, Mountain Range
Hills, Escarpment
Plateau, Upland
Pass, Gap
Plain, Lowland
Delta
Salt Flat
Valley, Canyon
Crater, Cave
Karst Features
Depression
Polder
Desert, Dunes
Forest, Woods
Heath, Steppe
Oasis
Cape, Point
Coast, Beach
Cliff
Peninsula
Isthmus
Sandbank
Island
Atoll
Rock, Reef
Islands, Archipelago
Rocks, Reefs
Coral Reef
Well, Spring
Geyser
River, Stream
Waterfall Rapids
River Mouth, Estuary
Lake
Salt Lake
Intermittent Lake
Reservoir
Swamp, Pond
Canal
Glacier
Ice Shelf, Pack Ice
Ocean
Sea
Gulf, Bay
Strait, Fjord
Lagoon
Bank
Seamount
Tablemount
Ridge
Shelf
Basin
Escarpment, Sea Scarp
Fracture
Trench, Abyss
National Park, Reserve
Point of Interest
Recreation Site
Cave, Cavern
Historic Site
Ruins
Wall, Walls
Church, Abbey
Temple
Scientific Station
Airport
Port
Lighthouse
Mine
Tunnel
Dam, Bridge

Vittangi 7 Ec 67.41N 21.39 E
Vitteaux 11 Kg 47.24N 4.32 E
Vittel 11 Lf 48.12N 5.57 E
Vittinge 8 Ge 59.54N 17.04 E
Vittoria 14 In 36.57N 14.32 E
Vittorio Veneto 14 Ge 45.59N 12.18 E
Vityaz Depth (EN) 3 Je 44.00N 151.00 E
Vityaz I Depth (EN) 3 Ih 11.20N 141.30 E
Vityaz II Depth (EN) 3 Kl 23.27S 175.00W
Vityaz III Depth (EN) 3 Km 32.00S 178.00W
Vityaz Seamount (EN) 57 Jc 13.30N 173.15W
Vityaz Trench (EN) 3 Jj 10.00S 170.00 E
Vivarais, Monts du- 11 Ki 44.55N 4.15 E
Vivarais, Plateaux du- 11 Kj 44.50N 4.45 E
Viver 13 Le 39.55N 0.36W
Vivero 13 Ea 43.40N 7.35W
Viverone, Lago di- 14 Ce 45.25N 8.05 E
Vivi 20 Ed 63.52N 97.50 E
Vivian 45 Jj 32.53N 93.59W
Viviers 11 Kj 44.29N 4.41 E
Vivo 37 Dd 23.03S 29.17 E
Vivoratá 55 Dm 37.40S 57.39W
Vivorillo, Cayos- 49 Ff 15.50N 83.18W
Viwa 63d Ab 17.08S 176.56 E
Vizcaíno, Desierto de- 47 Bc 27.40N 114.40W
Vizcaíno, Sierra- 48 Bd 27.20N 114.00W
Vizcaya 13 Ja 43.15N 2.55W
Vizcaya, Golfo de- 5 Fg 44.00N 4.00W
Vize 15 Kh 41.34N 27.45 E
Vize, Ostrov 21 Jb 79.30N 77.00 E
Vizianagaram 25 Ge 18.07N 83.25 E
Vizille 11 Li 45.05N 5.46 E
Vizinga 19 Fc 61.05N 50.10 E
Viziru 15 Kd 45.00N 27.42 E
Vižnica 16 De 48.14N 25.12 E
Vizzini 14 Im 37.10N 14.45 E
Vjaike-Maarja/Väike-Maarja 8 Le 59.04N 26.12 E
Vjajke-Pakri/Väike-Pakri 8 Je 59.50N 23.50 E
Vjajke-Vjajn/Väik Vain 8 Jf 58.30N 23.10 E
Vjalje, Ozero- 8 Ne 59.00N 30.20 E
Vjalozero, Ozero- 7 Ic 66.50N 35.10 E
Vjandra/Vändra 7 Fg 58.40N 25.01 E
Vjartsilja 7 He 62.10N 30.48 E
Vjatka 5 Ld 55.36N 51.30 E
Vjatskije Poljany 19 Fd 56.14N 51.04 E
Vjatski Uval 7 Lg 58.00N 49.45 E
Vjazemski 20 Ig 47.31N 134.45 E
Vjazma 6 Jd 55.13N 34.18 E
Vjazniki 7 Kh 56.15N 42.12 E
Vjeio, Rio- 49 Dg 12.17N 86.54W
Vjosa 15 Ci 40.37N 19.20 E
Vlaamse Banken 12 Ec 51.15N 2.30 E
Vlaanderen/Flandres=Flanders (EN) 5 Ge 51.00N 3.20 E
Vlaanderen/Flandres=Flanders (EN) 11 Jc 51.00N 3.20 E
Vlaardingen 11 Kc 51.54N 4.21 E
Vlădeasa, Vîrful- 15 Fc 46.45N 22.48 E
Vlădeni 15 Kb 47.25N 27.20 E
Vladičin Han 15 Fg 42.43N 22.04 E
Vladimir 6 Kd 56.10N 40.25 E
Vladimirskaja Oblast 19 Ed 56.00N 40.40 E
Vladimirskij Tupik 16 Hb 55.42N 33.18 E
Vladimir-Volynski 19 Ce 50.51N 24.22 E
Vladivostok 22 Pe 43.10N 131.56 E
Vlad Ţepeş 15 Ke 44.21N 27.05 E
Vlagtwedde 12 Ja 53.02N 7.08 E
Vlagtwedde-Ter Apel 12 Jb 52.52N 7.06 E
Vlahina 15 Fi 41.54N 22.52 E
Vlăhiţa 15 Ic 46.21N 25.31 E
Vlamse Vlakte=Flanders Plain (EN) 11 Id 50.40N 2.50 E
Vlasenica 14 Mf 44.11N 18.57 E
Vlašic [Yugo.] 14 Lf 44.19N 17.40 E
Vlašim 10 Kg 49.42N 14.54 E
Vlasotince 15 Fg 42.58N 22.08 E
Vlasovo 20 Ib 70.40N 134.35 E
Vlieland 11 Ka 53.15N 5.00 E
Vlieland 12 Ha 53.17N 5.06 E
Vlieland-Oost Vlieland 12 Ha 53.17N 5.06 E
Vliestroom 12 Ha 53.17N 5.10 E
Vlissingen 11 Jc 51.26N 3.35 E
Vlissingen-Oost-Souburg 12 Fc 51.28N 3.36 E
Vloesberg/Flobecq 12 Fd 50.44N 3.44 E
Vlora 6 Hg 40.27N 19.30 E
Vlorës, Gjiri i- 15 Ci 40.25N 19.25 E
Vlotho 12 Kb 52.10N 8.51 E
Vltava=Moldau (EN) 5 He 50.21N 14.30 E
Vöcklabruck 14 Hb 48.01N 13.39 E
Vodice 14 Jg 43.46N 15.47 E
Vodla 7 If 61.49N 36.00 E
Vodlozero, Ozero- 7 Ie 62.20N 37.00 E
Vodňany 10 Kg 49.09N 14.11 E
Vodnjan 14 Hf 44.57N 13.51 E
Vodny 17 Fe 63.32N 53.20 E
Voerde (Niederrhein) 12 Ce 51.35N 6.41 E
Voeren/Fouron 12 Hd 50.45N 5.48 E
Vogel Peak 34 Hd 8.24N 11.47 E
Vogelsberg 10 Ff 50.30N 9.15 E
Voghera 14 Df 44.59N 9.01 E
Vogtland 10 If 50.30N 12.05 E
Voh 63b Be 20.58S 164.42 E
Võhandu Jõgi/Vyhandu 8 Lf 58.03N 27.40 E
Vohémar 37 Ib 13.22S 50.00 E
Vohipeno 37 Hd 22.20S 47.52 E
Vöhl 12 Kc 51.12N 8.56 E
Vohma 7 Lg 58.45N 46.36 E
Vohma 19 Ed 58.58N 46.45 E
Voi 31 Ki 3.23S 38.34 E
Voikoski 8 Lc 61.16N 26.48 E
Voinjama 31 Gh 8.25N 9.45W
Voïon Óros 15 Ei 40.15N 21.03 E
Voire 11 Kf 48.27N 4.25 E
Voiron 11 Li 45.22N 5.35 E
Voitsberg 14 Jc 47.02N 15.09 E
Voiviis, Limni- 15 Fj 39.32N 22.45 E
Vojens 8 Ci 55.15N 9.19 E
Vojkar 17 Ld 65.38N 64.40 E
Vojmsjön 7 Dd 65.00N 16.24 E
Vojnić 14 Je 45.19N 15.42 E
Vojnilov 10 Ug 49.04N 24.33 E
Vojvodina 15 Cd 45.00N 20.00 E
Voj-Vož 19 Fc 62.56N 54.59 E
Voknavolok 7 Hd 64.57N 30.31 E
Vokré, Hoséré- 30 Ih 8.21N 13.15 E
Volary 10 Jh 48.55N 13.54 E
Volcán 49 Fi 8.46N 82.38W
Volcánica, Cordillera- 38 Ih 18.00N 101.00W
Volcano 65a Fd 19.26N 155.20W
Volcano Islands (EN)=Iō/Kazan-Rettō 21 Qg 25.00N 141.00 E
Volcano Islands (EN)=Kazan-Rettō/Iō 21 Qg 25.00N 141.00 E
Volcán Rana Roi 65d Ab 27.05S 109.23W
Volčansk [R.S.F.S.R.] 17 Jg 59.59N 60.04 E
Volčansk [Ukr.-U.S.S.R.] 16 Jd 50.16N 37.01 E
Volčiha 20 Df 52.02N 80.23 E
Volda 7 Be 62.09N 6.06 E
Voldafjorden 8 Ab 62.10N 6.00 E
Volga 5 Kf 45.55N 47.52 E
Volga 7 Jh 57.57N 38.25 E
Volga-Baltic Canal (EN)=Volgo-Baltijski vodny put imeni V. I. Lenina 5 Jd 59.58N 37.10 E
Volga Delta (EN) 5 Kf 46.30N 47.00 E
Volga Hills (EN)=Privolžkaja Vozvyšennost 5 Ke 52.00N 46.00 E
Volgo-Baltijski vodny put imeni V.I. Lenina=Volga-Baltic Canal (EN) 5 Jd 59.58N 37.10 E
Volgodonsk 19 Ef 47.33N 42.08 E
Volgo-Donskoj sudohodny kanal imeni V. I. Lenina=Lenin Canal (EN) 5 Kf 48.40N 43.37 E
Volgograd (Stalingrad) 6 Kf 48.44N 44.25 E
Volgograd Reservoir (EN)=Volgogradskoje Vodohranilišče 5 Kf 49.20N 45.00 E
Volgogradskaja Oblast 19 Ef 49.30N 44.30 E
Volgogradskoje Vodohranilišče=Volgograd Reservoir (EN) 5 Kf 49.20N 45.00 E
Volhov 5 Jc 60.08N 32.20 E
Volhov 6 Jd 59.55N 32.20 E
Volhynia 5 Ie 51.00N 25.00 E
Volissós 15 Ik 38.29N 25.55 E
Volja 17 Je 63.11N 61.16 E
Volka 10 Vd 52.43N 25.43 E
Völkermarkt 14 Id 46.39N 14.38 E
Völklingen 10 Cg 49.15N 6.51 E
Volkmarsen 12 Lc 51.24N 9.07 E
Volkovysk 16 Dc 53.10N 24.31 E
Volkovysskaja Vozvyšennost 10 Kc 53.10N 24.30 E
Volksrust 37 De 27.24S 29.53 E
Vollenhove 12 Hb 52.40N 5.57 E
Vollsjö 8 Ei 55.42N 13.46 E
Volme 12 Jc 51.24N 7.27 E
Volmunster 12 Je 49.07N 7.21 E
Volna, Gora- 20 Kd 63.30N 154.57 E
Volnjansk 16 If 47.54N 35.29 E
Volnovaha 16 Jf 47.37N 37.36 E
Voločajevka 2-ja 20 Ig 48.36N 134.36 E
Voločisk 16 Ee 49.31N 26.13 E
Volodarsk 7 Kh 56.14N 43.13 E
Volodarski 16 Pf 46.26N 48.31 E
Volodarskoje 19 Ge 53.18N 68.08 E
Vologda 6 Jd 59.12N 39.55 E
Vologodskaja Oblast 19 Ed 60.00N 41.00 E
Volokolamsk 7 Ih 56.03N 35.58 E
Volokonovka 16 Jd 50.29N 37.52 E
Vólos 6 Ih 39.22N 22.57 E
Vološka 7 Jf 61.42N 39.15 E
Vološka 7 Jf 61.21N 40.03 E
Volosovo 7 Gg 59.28N 29.31 E
Volovec 10 Jh 48.42N 23.17 E
Volovo 16 Kc 53.35N 38.01 E
Voložin 16 Eb 54.06N 26.32 E
Volquart Boons Kyst 41 Jd 70.20N 24.20W
Volsini, Monti- 14 Fh 42.40N 11.55 E
Volsk 19 Ee 52.02N 47.23 E
Volta 30 Hh 5.46N 0.41 E
Volta 34 Fd 7.00N 0.30 E
Volta Blanche=White Volta (EN) 30 Gh 8.38N 0.59W
Volta Lake 30 Hh 7.30N 0.15 E
Volta Noire=Black Volta (EN) 30 Gh 8.38N 1.30W
Volta Noire=Black Volta (EN) 34 Ec 12.30N 4.00W
Volta Redonda 53 Lh 22.32S 44.07W
Volta Rouge=Red Volta (EN) 30 Gh 10.34N 0.30W
Volterra 14 Eg 43.24N 10.51 E
Voltoya 13 Hc 41.13N 4.31W
Voltri, Genova- 14 Cf 44.26N 8.45 E
Volturino 14 Jj 40.25N 15.48 E
Volturno 14 Hi 41.01N 13.55 E
Volubilis 32 Fc 34.04N 5.33W
Völvi, Limni- 15 Gi 40.41N 23.28 E
Volynskaja Grjada 10 Ue 51.05N 25.00 E
Volynskaja Oblast 19 Ce 51.10N 25.00 E
Volynskaja Vozvyšennost 16 Dd 50.30N 25.00 E
Volžsk 19 Ed 55.55N 48.19 E
Volžski [R.S.F.S.R.] 6 Kf 48.48N 44.44 E
Volžski [R.S.F.S.R.] 7 Mj 53.28N 50.08 E
Voma 63d Bc 18.00S 178.08 E
Vomano 14 Ih 42.39N 14.02 E
Vonavona 63a Cc 8.12S 157.05 E
Vondrozo 37 Hd 22.47S 47.17 E
Von Frank Mountain 40 Id 63.33N 154.20W
Vónitsa 15 Dk 38.55N 20.53 E
Vonne 11 Gh 46.25N 0.15 E
Võnnu/Vynnu 8 Lf 58.15N 27.10 E
Voorne 12 Gc 51.52N 4.05 E
Voorschoten 12 Gb 52.08N 4.28 E
Voorst 12 Ib 52.10N 6.09 E
Voorst-Twello 12 Ib 52.14N 6.07 E
Vop 16 Hb 54.56N 32.44 E
Vopnafjördur 7a Cb 65.45N 14.50W
Vora 15 Ch 41.23N 19.40 E
Vörå/Vöyri 8 Ja 63.09N 22.15 E
Vorarlberg 14 Dc 47.15N 9.50 E
Vóras Óros 15 Ei 41.00N 21.50 E
Vorau 14 Jc 47.24N 15.53 E
Vorden 12 Ib 52.06N 6.20 E
Vorderrhein 14 Dd 46.49N 9.26 E
Vordingborg 7 Ci 55.01N 11.55 E
Voreifel 12 Jd 50.10N 7.00 E
Vorga Šor 17 Kc 67.35N 63.40 E
Voria Pindhos 15 Dj 40.20N 20.55 E
Vórioi Sporádhes, Nisoi-=Northern Sporades (EN) 5 Ih 39.15N 23.55 E
Vórios Evvoïkós Kólpos=Évvoia, Gulf of- (EN) 15 Gk 38.45N 23.10 E
Vorkuta 6 Mb 67.27N 63.58 E
Vorma 7 Cf 60.09N 11.27 E
Vormsi 8 Je 59.02N 23.05 E
Vormsi 7 Fg 59.00N 23.15 E
Vorniceni 15 Jb 47.59N 26.40 E
Vorogovo 20 Dd 60.58N 89.28 E
Vorona 16 Md 51.22N 42.03 E
Voroncovo [R.S.F.S.R.] 20 Db 71.40N 83.40 E
Voroncovo [R.S.F.S.R.] 8 Mg 57.15N 28.49 E
Voronež 6 Je 51.40N 39.10 E
Voronež 16 Kd 51.31N 39.05 E
Voronežskaja Oblast 19 Ee 51.00N 40.15 E
Voronin Trough (EN) 67 Ge 80.00N 85.00 E
Voronja 7 Ib 69.09N 35.47 E
Voronovo 8 Kj 54.09N 25.19 E
Voropajevo 8 Li 55.07N 27.19 E
Vorošilovgrad → Lugansk 6 Jf 48.34N 39.20 E
Vorošilovgradskaja Oblast 19 Df 49.00N 39.10 E
Vorotan 16 Oj 39.15N 46.43 E
Vorotynec 7 Kh 56.02N 45.52 E
Vorožba 16 Id 51.10N 34.11 E
Vorskla 16 Ie 48.52N 34.05 E
Vorsma 7 Ki 55.58N 43.17 E
Vörts Järv/Vyrtsjarv, Ozero- 7 Gg 58.15N 26.05 E
Võru/Vyru 19 Cd 57.52N 27.05 E
Voruh 18 He 39.52N 70.35 E
Vosges 5 Gf 48.30N 7.10 E
Vosges 11 Mf 48.10N 6.20 E
Voskresensk 7 Ji 55.22N 38.42 E
Voskresenskoje 7 Kh 56.51N 45.27 E
Voss 8 Bd 60.40N 6.30 E
Vossa 8 Ad 60.39N 5.42 E
Vossevangen 7 Bd 60.39N 6.26 E
Vostočno-Kazahstanskaja Oblast 19 If 49.00N 84.00 E
Vostočno-Kounradski 19 Hf 46.58N 75.07 E
Vostočno Sibirskoje More=East Siberian Sea (EN) 67 Cd 74.00N 166.00 E
Vostočny [R.S.F.S.R.] 20 Jg 48.19N 142.40 E
Vostočny [R.S.F.S.R.] 17 Jg 58.48N 61.52 E
Vostočny, Hrebet- 20 Lf 55.00N 160.30 E
Vostočny Sajan=Eastern Sayans (EN) 21 Ld 53.00N 97.00 E
Vostok 66 Hf 78.28S 106.48 E
Vostok Island 57 Lf 10.06S 152.23W
Vostrecovo 20 Ig 45.56N 134.59 E
Vošu/Vyzu 8 Ke 59.30N 25.50 E
Votkinsk 19 Fd 57.05N 53.59 E
Votkinskoje Vodohranilišče=Votkinsk Reservoir (EN) 5 Ld 57.30N 55.10 E
Votkinsk Reservoir (EN)=Votkinskoje Vodohranilišče 5 Ld 57.30N 55.10 E
Votuporanga 55 He 20.24S 49.59W
Vouga 13 Dd 40.41N 8.40W
Vouillé 11 Gh 46.38N 0.10 E
Voulgára 15 Ej 39.06N 21.54 E
Vouliagméni 15 Gl 37.49N 23.47 E
Voúrinos Óros 15 Ei 40.11N 21.40 E
Voúxa, Ákra- 15 Gn 35.38N 23.36 E
Vouziers 11 Ke 49.24N 4.42 E
Voves 11 Hf 48.16N 1.38 E
Vovodo 35 Cd 5.40N 24.21 E
Voxna 8 Fc 61.21N 15.34 E
Voxnan 8 Gc 61.17N 16.26 E
Voyeykov Ice Shelf 66 Ie 66.20S 124.38 E
Vöyri/Vörå 8 Ja 63.09N 22.15 E
Vože, Ozero- 7 Jf 60.35N 39.05 E
Vožega 7 Jf 60.33N 39.13 E
Vožega 7 Jf 60.30N 40.12 E
Voznesenje 7 If 61.01N 35.27 E
Voznesensk 19 Df 47.35N 31.20 E
Vozroždenija, Ostrov- 18 Bb 45.05N 59.15 E
Vraca 15 Gf 43.12N 23.33 E
Vraca 15 Dh 41.54N 20.45 E
Vraca 15 Gf 43.12N 23.33 E
Vradijevka 16 Gf 47.51N 30.34 E
Vrakhiónas 15 Dl 37.48N 20.45 E
Vran 14 Lg 43.39N 17.27 E
Vrancea 15 Jd 45.50N 26.42 E
Vranica 14 Lg 43.57N 17.44 E
Vranje 15 Eg 42.33N 21.54 E
Vranov nad Topľou 10 Rh 48.54N 21.41 E
Vráška čuka, Prohod- 15 Ff 43.50N 22.23 E
Vratnica 15 Eg 42.08N 21.07 E
Vratnik, prohod- 15 Jg 42.49N 26.10 E
Vrbas 14 Le 45.07N 17.31 E
Vrbas 15 Cd 45.34N 19.39 E
Vrbno pod Pradědem 10 Nf 50.08N 17.23 E
Vrbovsko 14 Je 45.22N 15.05 E
Vrchlabí 10 Lf 50.38N 15.37 E
Vrede 37 De 27.30S 29.06 E
Vreden 12 Ib 52.02N 6.50 E
Vredenburg 37 Bf 32.54S 17.59 E
Vredendal 37 Bf 31.41S 18.35 E
Vresse, Vresse-sur-Semois- 12 Ge 49.52N 4.56 E
Vresse-sur-Semois 12 Ge 49.52N 4.56 E
Vresse-sur-Semois-Vresse 12 Ge 49.52N 4.56 E
Vretstorp 8 Fe 59.02N 14.52 E
Vrhnika 14 Ie 45.58N 14.18 E
Vries 12 Ia 53.05N 6.36 E
Vriezenveen 12 Ib 52.26N 6.36 E
Vrigstad 8 Fg 57.21N 14.28 E
Vron 12 Dd 50.19N 1.45 E
Vršac 15 Ed 45.07N 21.18 E
Vryburg 31 Jk 26.55S 24.45 E
Vryheid 37 Ee 27.52S 30.38 E
Vsetín 10 Ng 49.21N 18.00 E
Vsevidof, Mount- 40a Eb 53.07N 168.43W
Vsevoložsk 7 Hf 60.04N 30.41 E
Vstrečny 20 Lc 68.00N 165.58 E
Vtačnik 10 Oh 48.42N 18.37 E
Vuanggava 63d Cc 18.52S 178.54W
Vučitrn 15 Dg 42.49N 20.58 E
Vučjak 15 Fh 41.28N 22.20 E
Vuka 14 Me 45.21N 19.00 E
Vukovar 14 Me 45.21N 19.00 E
Vuktyl 19 Fc 63.50N 57.25 E
Vulavu 63a Dc 8.31S 159.48 E
Vulcan 15 Gd 45.23N 23.16 E
Vulcan, Vîrful- 15 Fc 46.14N 22.58 E
Vulcano 14 Il 38.25N 15.00 E
Vulkanešty 16 Fg 45.38N 28.27 E
Vulture 14 Jj 40.57N 15.38 E
Vung Tau 25 Lf 10.21N 107.04 E
Vunindawa 63d Bb 17.49S 178.19 E
Vunisea Station 61 Ec 19.03S 178.09 E
Vuohijarvi 8 Lc 61.10N 26.40 E
Vuoksa 8 Nd 60.35N 30.42 E
Vuoksa, Ozero- [R.S.F.S.R.] 8 Mc 61.00N 30.00 E
Vuoksa, Ozero- [R.S.F.S.R.] 8 Md 60.38N 29.55 E
Vuollerim 7 Ec 66.25N 20.36 E
Vuosjärvi 8 Ka 63.00N 25.30 E
Vuotso 7 Gb 68.06N 27.08 E
Vuranimala 63a Ec 9.05S 160.51 E
Vyborg 6 Ic 60.42N 28.45 E
Vyčegda 5 Kc 61.18N 46.36 E
Vyčegodski 7 Lf 61.17N 46.48 E
Vychodočeský kraj 10 Lf 50.10N 16.00 E
Východoslovenska nížina 10 Rh 48.35N 21.50 E
Východoslovenský kraj 10 Rg 49.00N 21.15 E
Vyg 7 Ie 63.17N 35.17 E
Vygoda [Ukr.-U.S.S.R.] 15 Nc 46.38N 30.24 E
Vygoda [Ukr.-U.S.S.R.] 10 Uh 48.52N 24.01 E
Vygozero, Ozero- 5 Jc 63.35N 34.45 E
Vyhandu/Võhandu Jõgi 8 Lf 58.03N 27.40 E
Vyja 7 Le 62.57N 46.42 E
Vyksa 19 Ed 55.20N 42.12 E
Vym 19 Fc 62.13N 50.25 E
Vynnu/Võnnu 8 Lf 58.15N 27.10 E
Vyrica 19 Dd 59.24N 30.19 E
Vyrnwy 9 Ki 52.45N 2.50W
Vyrtsjarv, Ozero-/Vörts Järv 7 Gg 58.15N 26.05 E
Vyru/Võru 19 Cd 57.52N 27.05 E
Vyša 16 Mb 54.03N 42.06 E
Vyšgorod 16 Gd 50.38N 30.29 E
Vyšgorodok 8 Mh 56.55N 28.05 E
Vyškov 10 Mg 49.17N 17.00 E
Vyškovsk, pereval 10 Th 48.38N 23.45 E
Vyšni Voloček 19 Dd 57.37N 34.32 E
Vysock 7 Gf 60.36N 28.36 E
Vysoké Tatry=High Tatra (EN) 10 Pg 49.10N 20.00 E
Vysokogorny 20 If 50.07N 139.10 E
Vysokogorsk 28 Mb 44.23N 135.23 E
Vysokoje 10 Td 52.22N 23.26 E
Vysokovsk 7 Ih 56.21N 36.29 E
Vyšši Brod 10 Kh 48.37N 14.18 E
Vytebet 16 Ic 53.53N 35.38 E
Vytegra 19 Dc 61.01N 36.28 E
Vyvenka 20 Ld 60.10N 165.20 E
Vyzu/Vošu 8 Ke 59.30N 25.50 E
Vzmorje 20 Jg 47.45N 142.30 E

W

Wa 34 Ec 10.03N 2.29W
Waal 11 Kc 51.55N 4.30 E
Waalre 12 Hc 51.23N 5.27 E
Waalwijk 12 Hc 51.41N 5.04 E
Waar, Meos- 26 Jg 2.05S 134.23 E
Waardgronden 12 Ha 53.12N 5.05 E
Waarschoot 12 Fc 51.09N 3.36 E
Wabana 42 Mg 47.38N 52.57W
Wabao, Cap- 63b Ce 21.36S 167.51 E
Wabasca 42 Ge 56.00N 113.53W
Wabasca 42 Fe 58.21N 115.20W
Wabash 38 Kf 37.46N 88.02W
Wabash 44 Ee 40.48N 85.49W
Wabasha 45 Jd 44.23N 92.02W
Wabash River 45 Lh 37.46N 88.02W
Wabowden 42 Hf 54.55N 98.38W
Wąbrzeźno 10 Oc 53.17N 18.57 E
Wabu Hu 27 Ke 32.20N 116.55 E
Wachau 14 Jb 48.20N 15.25 E
Wachile 35 Fe 4.33N 39.03 E
Wachusett Seamount (EN) 57 Lh 32.00S 151.20W
Waco 39 Jf 31.55N 97.08W
Waconda Lake 45 Gg 39.30N 98.30W
Wadayama 29 Dd 35.20N 134.51 E
Wad Bandah 35 Dc 13.06N 27.57 E
Waddān 33 Cd 29.10N 16.08 E
Waddān, Jabal- 33 Cd 29.20N 16.20 E
Waddeneilanden=West Frisian Islands (EN) 11 Ka 53.30N 5.00 E
Waddenzee 12 Ha 53.20N 5.30 E
Waddington, Mount- 38 Gd 51.23N 125.15W
Wadena 45 Ic 46.26N 95.08W
Wadern 12 Ie 49.32N 6.53 E
Wadern-Nunkirchen 12 Ie 49.32N 6.53 E
Wadersloh 12 Kc 51.44N 8.15 E
Wadersloh-Liesborn 12 Kc 51.43N 8.16 E
Wadesboro 44 Gh 34.58N 80.04W
Wadhams 46 Ba 51.30N 127.31W
Wādī Bishah 23 Fe 21.24N 43.26 E
Wādī Fajr 23 Ec 30.17N 38.18 E
Wādī Ḥalfā' 31 Kf 21.56N 31.20 E
Wādī Jimāl, Jazīrat- 24 Fj 24.40N 35.10 E
Wādī Mūsā 24 Fg 30.19N 35.29 E
Wādī Shiḥan 35 Ib 18.10N 52.57 E
Wad Madanī 31 Kg 14.24N 33.32 E
Wad Nimr 35 Ec 14.32N 32.08 E
Wadowice 10 Pg 49.53N 19.30 E
Wadsworth 46 Fg 39.38N 119.17W
Wafangdian → Fuxian 27 Ld 39.38N 121.59 E
Wafrah 23 Gd 28.25N 47.56 E
Waga-Gawa 29 Gb 39.18N 141.07 E
Wagenfeld 12 Kb 52.33N 8.35 E
Wagenfeld-Ströhen 12 Kb 52.32N 8.39 E
Wageningen 12 Hc 51.57N 5.41 E
Wagēr, Qar- 35 Hc 10.01N 45.30 E
Wager Bay 38 Kc 65.26N 88.40W
Wagga Wagga 58 Fh 35.07S 147.22 E
Waghäusel 12 Ke 49.15N 8.30 E
Wagin 58 Ch 33.18S 117.21 E
Waginger See 10 Ii 47.58N 12.50 E
Wagoner 45 Ii 35.58N 95.22W
Wagon Mound 45 Dh 36.01N 104.42W
Wagontire Mountain 46 Fe 43.21N 119.53W
Wagrien 10 Gb 54.15N 10.45 E
Wągrowiec 10 Nd 52.49N 17.11 E
Wah 25 Eb 33.48N 72.42 E
Waha 31 If 28.10N 19.57 E
Wahai 26 Ig 2.48S 129.30 E
Wahiawa 60 Oc 21.30N 158.02W
Wahoo 45 Hf 41.13N 96.37W
Wahpeton 43 Hb 46.16N 96.36W
Waialeale, Mount- 65a Ba 22.04N 159.30W
Waialua 65a Cb 21.35N 158.08W
Waianae 65a Cb 21.27N 158.12W
Waiau 62 Ee 42.47S 173.22 E
Waiau 61 Dh 42.39S 173.03 E
Waiblingen 10 Fh 48.50N 9.18 E
Waibstadt 12 Ke 49.18N 8.56 E
Waidhofen an der Thaya 14 Jb 48.49N 15.17 E
Waidhofen an der Ybbs 14 Ic 47.58N 14.46 E
Waigame 26 Ig 1.50S 129.49 E
Waigeo, Pulau- 57 Ee 0.14S 130.45 E
Waihi 62 Fb 37.24S 175.50 E
Waihou 62 Fb 37.10S 175.33 E
Waikabubak 26 Gh 9.38S 119.25 E
Waikare, Lake- 62 Fb 37.25S 175.10 E
Waikaremoana, Lake- 61 Eg 38.45S 177.05 E
Waikato 62 Fb 37.23S 174.43 E
Waikawa 62 Cg 46.38S 169.08 E
Waikouaiti 62 Df 45.36S 170.41 E
Wailangilala 63d Cb 16.45S 179.06W
Wailua 65a Ba 22.03N 159.20W
Wailuku 60 Oc 20.53N 156.30W
Waimamaku 62 Ea 35.34S 173.29 E
Waimanalo Beach 65a Db 21.20N 157.42W
Waimangaroa 62 Dd 41.43S 171.46 E
Waimate 62 Df 44.45S 171.03 E
Waimea 65a Fc 20.02N 155.40W
Waimes 12 Id 50.25N 6.07 E
Wainfleet All Saints 12 Ca 53.06N 0.15 E
Wainganga 21 Jh 19.36N 79.48 E
Waingapu 26 Hh 9.39S 120.16 E
Waini Point 50 Gh 8.24N 59.49W
Waini River 50 Gh 8.24N 59.51W
Wainwright [Ak.-U.S.] 40 Gb 70.38N 160.01W
Wainwright [Alta.-Can.] 42 Gf 52.49N 110.52W
Waiouru 61 Eg 39.29S 175.40 E
Waipahu 65a Cb 21.23N 158.01W
Waipara 62 Ee 43.03S 172.45 E
Waipawa 62 Gc 39.56S 176.35 E
Waipiro 62 Hc 38.02S 178.20 E
Waipu 62 Fa 35.59S 174.26 E
Waipukurau 62 Gd 40.00S 176.33 E
Wairakei 62 Gc 38.37S 176.05 E
Wairarapa, Lake- 62 Fd 41.15S 175.15 E
Wairau 62 Fd 41.31S 174.03 E
Wairoa 61 Eg 39.03S 177.26 E
Wairoa 62 Fb 36.11S 174.02 E
Waitaki 62 Df 44.56S 171.09 E
Waitangi 61 Fh 43.56S 176.34W
Waitara 61 Dg 39.00S 174.14 E
Waitati 62 Df 45.45S 170.34 E
Waitemata 62 Fb 36.50S 174.40 E
Waitotara 62 Fc 39.48S 174.44 E
Waiuku 62 Fb 37.15S 174.44 E
Waiwerang 26 Hh 8.23S 123.09 E
Waiyevo 61 Fc 16.48S 179.59W
Wājid 35 Ge 3.50N 43.14 E
Wajima 28 Nf 37.24N 136.54 E
Wajir 31 Ih 1.42N 40.04 E
Waka [Eth.] 35 Fd 7.09N 37.19 E
Waka [Zaire] 36 Db 1.01N 20.13 E
Wakamatsu-Shima 29 Ae 32.54N 129.00 E
Wakasa-Wan 27 Od 35.45N 135.40 E
Wakatipu, Lake- 61 Ci 45.05S 168.35 E
Wakaya 63d Bb 17.37S 179.00 E
Wakayama 22 Pf 34.13N 135.11 E
Wakayama Ken 28 Mh 33.55N 135.20 E
Wake 29 Dd 34.48N 134.08 E
Wa Keeney 45 Gg 39.01N 99.53W
Wakefield [Eng.-U.K.] 9 Lh 53.42N 1.29W
Wakefield [N.Z.] 62 Ed 41.24S 173.03 E

Index Symbols

- [1] Independent Nation
- [2] State, Region
- [3] District, County
- [4] Municipality
- [5] Colony, Dependency
- Continent
- Physical Region
- Historical or Cultural Region
- Mount, Mountain
- Volcano
- Hill
- Mountains, Mountain Range
- Hills, Escarpment
- Plateau, Upland
- Pass, Gap
- Plain, Lowland
- Delta
- Salt Flat
- Valley, Canyon
- Crater, Cave
- Karst Features
- Depression
- Polder
- Desert, Dunes
- Forest, Woods
- Heath, Steppe
- Oasis
- Cape, Point
- Coast, Beach
- Cliff
- Peninsula
- Isthmus
- Sandbank
- Island
- Atoll
- Rock, Reef
- Islands, Archipelago
- Rocks, Reefs
- Coral Reef
- Well, Spring
- Geyser
- River, Stream
- Waterfall Rapids
- River Mouth, Estuary
- Lake
- Salt Lake
- Intermittent Lake
- Reservoir
- Swamp, Pond
- Canal
- Glacier
- Ice Shelf, Pack Ice
- Ocean
- Sea
- Gulf, Bay
- Strait, Fjord
- Lagoon
- Bank
- Seamount
- Tablemount
- Ridge
- Shelf
- Basin
- Escarpment, Sea Scarp
- Fracture
- Trench, Abyss
- National Park, Reserve
- Point of Interest
- Recreation Site
- Cave, Cavern
- Historic Site
- Ruins
- Wall, Walls
- Church, Abbey
- Temple
- Scientific Station
- Airport
- Port
- Lighthouse
- Mine
- Tunnel
- Dam, Bridge

Wake Island [5] 58 Jd 19.18N 166.36W
Wake Island 57 Hc 19.18N 166.36W
Wakkanai 22 Qe 45.25N 141.40 E
Wakunai 63a Ba 5.52S 155.13 E
Wakuya 29 Gb 38.33N 141.05 E
Wala 36 Fd 5.46S 32.04 E
Walachia (EN) = Valahia 5 Ig 44.00N 25.00 E
Walachia (EN) = Valahia 15 He 44.00N 25.00 E
Wałbrzych [2] 10 Mf 50.45N 16.15 E
Wałbrzych 6 He 50.46N 16.17 E
Walchensee 10 Hi 47.35N 11.20 E
Walcheren 11 Jc 51.33N 3.35 E
Walcott, Lake- 46 Ie 42.40N 113.23W
Walcourt 12 Gd 50.15N 4.25 E
Walcourt-Fraire 12 Gd 50.16N 4.30 E
Wałcz 10 Mc 53.17N 16.28 E
Waldböckelheim 12 Je 49.49N 7.43 E
Waldbröl 10 Df 50.53N 7.37 E
Waldeck 12 Kc 51.17N 8.50 E
Waldeck 12 Lc 51.12N 9.05 E
Waldems 12 Kd 50.15N 8.18 E
Walden 45 Cf 40.44N 106.17W
Waldfischbach-Burgalben 12 Je 49.17N 7.40 E
Waldkirchen 10 Jh 48.44N 13.36 E
Waldkraiburg 10 Ih 48.12N 12.25 E
Wald-Michelbach 12 Ke 49.34N 8.49 E
Waldnaab 10 Ig 49.35N 12.07 E
Waldorf 44 If 38.37N 76.54W
Waldrach 12 Ie 49.45N 6.45 E
Waldron 45 Ii 34.54N 94.05W
Waldshut 10 Ei 47.37N 8.13 E
Waldviertel 14 Jb 48.30N 15.30 E
Waleabahi, Pulau- 26 Hg 0.15S 122.20 E
Wales 40 Fc 65.36N 168.05W
Wales 42 Ic 67.50N 86.40W
Wales 5 Fe 52.30N 3.30W
Wales [2] 9 Ji 52.30N 3.30W
Walewale 34 Ec 10.21N 0.48W
Walferdange 12 Ie 49.39N 6.08 E
Walgett 58 Fh 30.01S 148.07 E
Walgreen Coast 66 Of 75.15S 105.00W
Walhalla 45 Hb 48.55N 97.55W
Walikale 36 Ec 1.25S 28.03 E
Walker 45 Ic 47.06N 94.35W
Walker Lake 43 Dd 38.40N 118.43W
Walkerston 59 Jd 21.10S 149.10 E
Wall 45 Ed 44.01N 102.14W
Wallace 46 Hc 47.28N 115.56W
Wallaceburg 44 Fd 42.36N 82.23W
Wallangarra 59 Ke 28.56S 151.56 E
Wallaroo 59 Hf 33.56S 137.38 E
Wallary Island 59 Ic 15.05S 141.50 E
Wallasey 9 Jh 53.26N 3.03W
Walla Walla 43 Db 46.08N 118.20W
Walldorf 12 Ke 49.20N 8.39 E
Wallenhorst 12 Kb 52.21N 8.01 E
Wallibu 51n Ba 13.19N 61.15W
Wallingford 12 Ac 51.36N 1.08W
Wallis, Iles-=Wallis Islands (EN) 57 Jf 13.18S 176.10W
Wallis and Futuna (EN)= Wallis-et-Futuna, Iles- [5] 58 Jf 14.00S 177.00W
Walliser Alpen/Alpes Valaisannes 14 Bd 46.10N 7.30 E
Wallis-et-Futuna, Iles-= Wallis and Futuna (EN) [5] 58 Jf 14.00S 177.00W
Wallis Islands (EN)=Wallis, Iles- 57 Jf 13.18S 176.10W
Wallowa 46 Gd 45.34N 117.32W
Wallowa Mountains 46 Gd 45.10N 117.30W
Walmer 12 Dc 51.12N 1.24 E
Walney, Isle of- 9 Jg 54.07N 3.15W
Walnut Ridge 43 Id 36.04N 90.57W
Walpole, Ile- 57 Hg 22.37S 168.57 E
Walrus Islands 40 Ge 58.45N 160.20W
Walsall 9 Li 52.35N 1.58W
Walsenburg 43 Gd 37.37N 104.47W
Walsrode 10 Fd 52.52N 9.35 E
Walterboro 44 Gi 32.54N 80.39W
Walter F. George Lake 44 Ej 31.49N 85.08W
Walter Lake 43 Dd 38.44N 118.43W
Walters 45 Gi 34.22N 98.19W
Waltershausen 10 Gf 50.54N 10.34 E
Waltham 44 Ic 45.58N 76.57W
Walton-on-the-Naze 12 Dc 51.51N 1.17 E
Waltrop 12 Jc 51.38N 7.24 E
Walvisbaai/Walvis Bay [3] 37 Ad 23.00S 14.30 E
Walvisbaai=Walvis Bay (EN) 31 Ik 22.59S 14.31 E
Walvisbaai=Walvis Bay (EN) [5] 31 Ik 22.59S 14.31 E
Walvisbaai=Walvis Bay (EN) 30 Ik 22.57S 14.30 E
Walvis Bay/Walvisbaai [3] 37 Ad 23.00S 14.30 E
Walvis Bay (EN)= Walvisbaai 30 Ik 22.57S 14.30 E
Walvis Bay (EN)= Walvisbaai [5] 31 Ik 22.59S 14.31 E
Walvis Bay (EN)= Walvisbaai 31 Ik 22.59S 14.31 E
Walvis Ridge (EN) 3 El 28.00S 3.00 E
Wamba 30 Ii 3.56S 17.12 E
Wamba [Kenya] 36 Gb 0.59N 37.19 E
Wamba [Nig.] 34 Gd 8.56N 8.36 E
Wamba [Zaire] 36 Eb 2.09N 28.00 E
Wamena 26 Kg 4.00S 138.57 E
Wami 30 Ki 6.08S 38.49 E
Wampusirpi 49 Ef 15.15N 84.37W
Wamsutter 46 Lf 41.40N 107.58W
Wan 26 Kh 8.23S 137.56 E
Wana 25 Db 32.17N 69.35 E
Wanaka 58 Hi 44.42S 169.08 E
Wanaka, Lake- 62 Cf 44.30S 169.10 E
Wan'an 27 Jf 26.32N 114.48 E
Wanapiri 26 Kg 4.33S 135.59 E
Wanapitei Lake 44 Gb 46.45N 80.45W
Wandel Hav=Wandel Sea (EN) 41 Gb 83.00N 15.00W
Wandel Sea (EN)=Wandel Hav 41 Gb 83.00N 15.00W
Wandsworth, London- 12 Bc 51.27N 0.12W
Wanganui 62 Fc 39.58S 175.00 E
Wanganui 61 Eg 39.56S 175.02 E
Wangaratta 59 Jg 36.22S 146.20 E
Wangcun [China] 28 Df 36.41N 117.42 E
Wangcun [China] 27 Jd 39.58N 112.53 E
Wangda/Zogang 27 Gf 29.37N 97.58 E
Wangdu 28 Ce 38.43N 115.09 E
Wangen im Allgäu 10 Fi 47.41N 9.50 E
Wangerooge 10 Dc 53.46N 7.55 E
Wanggameti, Gunung- 26 Hi 10.07S 120.14 E
Wanggezhuang → Jiaonan 28 Eg 35.53N 119.58 E
Wangiwangi, Pulau- 26 Hh 5.20S 123.35 E
Wangjiang 28 Di 30.08N 116.41 E
Wangkui 27 Mb 46.50N 126.29 E
Wangpan Yang 21 Of 30.33N 121.26 E
Wangping 27 Mc 43.18N 129.46 E
Wangying → Huaiyin 28 Eh 33.35N 119.02 E
Wani, Laguna- 49 Ff 14.50N 83.25W
Wanie-Rukula 36 Eb 0.14N 25.34 E
Wanitsuka-Yama 29 Bf 31.45N 131.17 E
Wanlewēyn 35 Ge 2.35N 44.55 E
Wan Namton 25 Jd 22.03N 99.33 E
Wannian (Chenying) 28 Dj 28.42N 117.04 E
Wanning 27 Jh 18.59N 110.24 E
Wanquan 28 Cd 40.52N 114.44 E
Wansbeck 9 Lf 55.10N 1.34W
Wan Shui 28 Di 30.30N 117.01 E
Wanxian 22 Mf 30.48N 108.21 E
Wanyuan 27 Ie 32.03N 108.04 E
Wanzai 28 Cj 28.06N 114.27 E
Wanzhi → Wuhu 28 Ei 31.21N 118.23 E
Wapato 46 Ec 46.27N 120.25W
Wapiti 46 Kd 44.28N 109.28W
Wapiti 42 Fe 55.08N 118.19W
Wapsipinicon River 45 Kf 41.44N 90.20W
Waqooyi Galbeed [3] 35 Gc 10.00N 44.00 E
Warangal 22 Jh 18.18N 79.35 E
Waratah Bay 59 Jg 38.50S 146.05 E
Warburg 10 Fe 51.30N 9.10 E
Warburger Borde 12 Lc 51.35N 9.12 E
Warburg-Scherfede 12 Lc 51.32N 9.02 E
Warburton Bay 42 Gd 63.50N 111.30W
Warburton Mission 59 Fe 26.10S 126.35 E
Warburton Range 59 Fe 26.10S 126.40 E
Ward 62 Fd 41.50S 174.08 E
Warden 37 De 27.56S 29.00 E
Wardenburg 12 Ka 53.04N 8.12 E
Wardha 25 Fd 20.45N 78.37 E
Ward Hunt Strait 59 Ja 9.25S 149.55 E
Ware [B.C.-Can.] 42 Ee 57.27N 125.38W
Ware [Eng.-U.K.] 12 Bc 51.49N 0.01W
Waregem 12 Fd 50.53N 3.25 E
Waremme/Borgworm 12 Hd 50.42N 5.15 E
Waren [Ger.] 10 Ic 53.31N 12.41 E
Waren [Indon.] 58 Ee 2.16S 136.20 E
Warendorf 10 De 51.57N 7.59 E
Warin Chamrap 25 Ke 15.14N 104.52 E
Warka 10 Re 51.47N 21.10 E
Warkworth 62 Fb 36.24S 174.40 E
Warmbad [3] 37 Be 28.00S 18.30 E
Warmbad [Nam.] 37 Be 28.29S 18.41 E
Warmbad [S.Afr.] 37 Dd 24.53S 28.17 E
Warming Land 41 Gb 81.50N 52.45W
Warmington 12 Ab 52.08N 1.24W
Warminster 9 Kj 51.13N 2.12W
Warm Springs [Nv.-U.S.] 46 Gg 38.13N 116.20W
Warm Springs [Or.-U.S.] 46 Ed 44.46N 121.16W
Warnemünde, Rostock- 10 Ib 54.10N 12.05 E
Warner, Mount- 46 Da 51.03N 123.12W
Warner Mountains 43 Cc 41.40N 120.20W
Warner Peak 46 Fe 42.27N 119.44W
Warner Robins 43 Ke 32.37N 83.36W
Warner Valley 46 Fe 42.30N 119.55W
Warnes 54 Fg 17.30S 63.10W
Warnow 10 Ib 54.06N 12.09 E
Waroona 59 Df 32.50S 115.55 E
Warragul 59 Jg 38.10S 145.56 E
Warrego Range 59 Je 25.00S 145.45 E
Warrego River 57 Fh 30.24S 145.21 E
Warren [Ar.-U.S.] 45 Jj 33.38N 92.05W
Warren [Mi.-U.S.] 44 Fd 42.28N 83.01W
Warren [Mn.-U.S.] 45 Hb 48.12N 96.46W
Warren [Oh.-U.S.] 43 Kc 41.15N 80.49W
Warren [Pa.-U.S.] 44 He 41.52N 79.09W
Warrenpoint/An Pointe 9 Gg 54.06N 6.15W
Warrensburg 45 Jg 38.46N 93.44W
Warrenton 37 Ce 28.09S 24.47 E
Warri 34 Gd 5.31N 5.45 E
Warrington [Eng.-U.K.] 9 Kh 53.24N 2.37W
Warrington [Fl.-U.S.] 44 Dj 30.23N 87.16W
Warrior Reefs 59 Ia 9.35S 143.10 E
Warrnambool 58 Fh 38.23S 142.29 E
Warroad 43 Hb 48.54N 95.19W
Warrumbungle Range 59 Jf 31.30S 149.40 E
Warsaw [In.-U.S.] 44 Ee 41.14N 85.51W
Warsaw [Mo.-U.S.] 45 Jg 38.15N 93.23W
Warsaw [N.Y.-U.S.] 44 Hd 42.45N 78.07W
Warsaw (EN)=Warszawa 6 Ie 52.15N 21.00 E
Warshīkh 35 He 2.18N 45.48 E
Warstein 12 Kc 51.27N 8.22 E
Warstein-Belecke 12 Kc 51.29N 8.20 E
Warszawa [2] 10 Qd 52.15N 21.00 E
Warszawa=Warsaw (EN) 6 Ie 52.15N 21.00 E
Warta 5 He 52.35N 14.39 E
Waru 26 Jg 3.24S 130.40 E
Warwich 59 Ke 28.13S 152.02 E
Warwick 9 Li 52.15N 1.30W
Warwick [Eng.-U.K.] 9 Li 52.17N 1.34W
Warwick [R.I.-U.S.] 44 Le 41.42N 71.23W
Warwickshire [3] 9 Li 52.10N 1.35W
Wasagu 34 Gc 11.22N 5.48 E
Wasatch Range 38 He 41.15N 111.30W
Wascana Creek 46 Ma 50.40N 104.55W
Wasco 46 Fi 35.36N 119.20W
Waseca 45 Jd 44.05N 93.30W
Washburn 45 Fc 47.17N 101.02W
Washess Bay 64g Ab 1.49N 157.31W
Wāshim 25 Fd 20.10N 76.58 E
Washington [2] 43 Cb 47.30N 120.30W
Washington [D.C.-U.S.] 39 Lf 38.54N 77.01W
Washington [Eng.-U.K.] 9 Lg 54.54N 1.31W
Washington [Ga.-U.S.] 44 Fi 33.44N 82.44W
Washington [Ia.-U.S.] 45 Kf 41.18N 91.42W
Washington [In.-U.S.] 44 Df 38.40N 87.10W
Washington [N.C.-U.S.] 44 Ih 35.33N 77.03W
Washington [Pa.-U.S.] 44 Ge 40.11N 80.16W
Washington → Teraina Island 57 Kd 4.43N 160.24W
Washington, Mount- 38 Le 44.15N 71.15W
Washington Court House 44 Ff 39.32N 83.29W
Washington Island 45 Md 45.23N 86.55W
Washington Land 41 Fb 80.15N 65.00W
Washita River 45 Hi 34.12N 96.50W
Washtucna 46 Fc 46.45N 118.19W
Wasile 26 If 1.04N 127.59 E
Wasilków 10 Tc 53.12N 23.12 E
Wasior 26 Jg 2.43S 134.30 E
Wāsiţ [3] 24 Lf 32.35N 46.00 E
Waskaganish 39 Ld 51.25N 78.45W
Wąsosz 10 Me 51.34N 16.42 E
Waspán 47 Hf 14.44N 83.58W
Wassamu 29a Ca 44.02N 142.24 E
Wassenaar 12 Gb 52.09N 4.24 E
Wassenberg 12 Ic 51.06N 6.09 E
Wasserburg am Inn 10 Ih 48.04N 12.14 E
Wasserkuppe 10 Ff 50.30N 9.56 E
Wassigny 12 Fd 50.01N 3.36 E
Wassuk Range 46 Fg 38.40N 118.50W
Wassy 11 Kf 48.30N 4.57 E
Waswanipi, Lac- 44 Ia 49.32N 76.29W
Watampone 22 Oj 4.32S 120.20 E
Watansoppeng 26 Gg 4.21S 119.53 E
Watari 29 Gb 38.02N 140.51 E
Waterbeach 12 Cb 52.16N 0.12 E
Waterberg 37 Bd 20.25S 17.15 E
Waterbury 43 Mc 41.33N 73.02W
Water Cays 49 Ib 23.40N 77.45W
Wateree Pond 44 Gh 34.25N 80.50W
Waterford/Port Láirge 6 Fe 52.15N 7.06W
Waterford/Port Láirge [2] 9 Fi 52.10N 7.40W
Waterford Harbour/Cuan Phort Láirge 9 Gi 52.10N 6.57W
Wateringues 11 Ic 51.00N 2.30 E
Waterloo [Bel.] 11 Kd 50.43N 4.24 E
Waterloo [Ia.-U.S.] 43 Ic 42.30N 92.20W
Waterloo [Il.-U.S.] 45 Kg 38.20N 90.09W
Waterlooville 12 Ad 50.52N 1.01W
Watersmeet 44 Cb 46.18N 89.11W
Watertown [N.Y.-U.S.] 43 Lc 43.57N 75.56W
Watertown [S.D.-U.S.] 43 Hc 44.54N 97.07W
Watertown [Wi.-U.S.] 45 Le 43.12N 88.43W
Waterville 43 Nc 44.33N 69.38W
Watford 9 Mj 51.40N 0.25W
Watford City 45 Ec 47.48N 103.17W
Wa'th 35 Ed 8.10N 32.07 E
Watheroo 59 Df 30.17S 116.04 E
Watīr, Wādī- 24 Fh 29.01N 34.40 E
Watkins Glen 44 Id 42.23N 76.53W
Watling → San Salvador 47 Jd 24.02N 74.28W
Watlington 12 Ac 51.38N 1.00W
Watonga 45 Gi 35.51N 98.25W
Watou, Poperinge- 12 Ed 50.51N 2.37 E
Watrous 42 Gf 51.40N 105.28W
Watsa 31 Jh 3.03N 29.32 E
Watseka 45 Mf 40.47N 87.44W
Watsi [C.R.] 49 Fi 9.37N 82.52W
Watsi [Zaire] 36 Dc 0.19S 21.04 E
Watsi Kengo 36 Dc 0.48S 20.33 E
Watson Lake 39 Gc 60.07N 128.48W
Watsonville 46 Eh 36.55N 121.45W
Watt, Morne- 51g Bb 15.19N 61.19W
Watton 12 Cb 52.34N 0.50 E
Watts Bar Lake 44 Eh 35.48N 84.39W
Wattwil 14 Dc 47.18N 9.05 E
Watubela, Kepulauan- 26 Jg 4.35S 131.40 E
Wau 59 Ja 7.20S 146.45 E
Waubay Lake 45 Hd 45.25N 97.25W
Wauchope 59 Kf 31.27S 152.44 E
Wauchula 44 Gl 27.33N 81.49W
Waucoba Mountain 46 Fh 37.00N 118.01W
Waukara, Gunung- 26 Gg 1.15S 119.42 E
Waukarlycarly, Lake- 59 Ed 21.25S 121.50 E
Waukegan 43 Jc 42.22N 87.50W
Waukesha 45 Le 43.01N 88.14W
Waupaca 45 Ld 44.21N 89.05W
Wausau 43 Jc 44.59N 89.39W
Wauseon 44 Ee 41.33N 84.09W
Wauwatosa 45 Me 43.03N 88.00W
Wave Hill 59 Gc 17.29S 130.57 E
Waveney 9 Oi 52.28N 1.45 E
Waver/Wavre 11 Kd 50.43N 4.37 E
Waverly [Ia.-U.S.] 45 Je 42.44N 92.29W
Waverly [Oh.-U.S.] 44 Ff 39.07N 82.59W
Waverly [Tn.-U.S.] 44 Dg 36.05N 87.48W
Waves 44 Jh 35.37N 75.29W
Wavre/Waver 11 Kd 50.43N 4.37 E
Wāw 31 Jh 7.42N 28.00 E
Wawa [Nig.] 34 Fd 9.55N 4.27 E
Wawa [Ont.-Can.] 42 Jg 47.59N 84.47W
Wawa, Rio- 49 Fg 13.53N 83.28W
Wāw al Kabir 31 If 25.20N 16.43 E
Wāw an Nāmūs 33 Ce 24.55N 19.45 E
Wāw Nahr 35 Dd 7.03N 27.13 E
Wawo 26 Hg 3.41S 121.02 E
Wawotobi 26 Hg 3.51S 122.06 E
Waxahachie 45 Hj 32.24N 96.51W
Waxweiler 12 Id 50.06N 6.22 E
Waxxari 27 Ed 38.37N 87.22 E
Way, Lake- 59 Ee 26.50S 120.20 E
Waya 63d Ab 17.18S 177.08 E
Wayabula 26 If 2.17N 128.12 E
Wayan 46 Je 43.00N 111.22W
Waycross 43 Ke 31.13N 82.21W
Wayne [Nb.-U.S.] 45 He 42.14N 97.01W
Wayne [W.V.-U.S.] 44 Ff 38.14N 82.27W
Waynesboro [Ga.-U.S.] 44 Fi 33.06N 82.01W
Waynesboro [Ms.-U.S.] 45 Lk 31.40N 88.39W
Waynesboro [Pa.-U.S.] 44 If 39.45N 77.36W
Waynesboro [Va.-U.S.] 44 Hf 38.04N 78.54W
Waynesville [Mo.-U.S.] 45 Jh 37.50N 92.12W
Waynesville [N.C.-U.S.] 44 Fh 35.29N 83.00W
Waynoka 45 Gh 36.35N 98.53W
Waziers 12 Fd 50.23N 3.07 E
Wda 10 Oc 53.25N 18.29 E
Wdzydze, Jezioro- 10 Nc 54.00N 17.50 E
Wé 61 Cd 20.55S 167.16 E
We, Pulau- 26 Ce 5.51N 95.18 E
Wear 9 Lg 54.55N 1.22W
Weatherford [Ok.-U.S.] 45 Gi 35.32N 98.42W
Weatherford [Tx.-U.S.] 43 He 32.46N 97.48W
Weaverville 46 Df 40.44N 122.56W
Weber 62 Gd 40.24S 176.20 E
Webster 45 Hd 45.20N 97.31W
Webster City 45 Je 42.28N 93.49W
Webster Springs 44 Gf 38.29N 80.25W
Weda 26 If 0.21N 127.52 E
Weda, Teluk- 26 If 0.20N 128.00 E
Weddell Island 56 Hh 51.50S 61.00W
Weddel Sea (EN) 66 Rf 72.00S 45.00W
Wedel 10 Fc 53.35N 9.41 E
Wedgeport 44 Od 43.44N 65.59W
Wedza 37 Ec 18.35S 31.35 E
Weed 46 Df 41.25N 122.27W
Weener 10 Dc 53.10N 7.21 E
Weerdinge, Emmen- 12 Ib 52.49N 6.57 E
Weert 11 Lc 51.15N 5.43 E
Weesp 12 Hb 52.18N 5.02 E
Wegberg 12 Ic 51.09N 6.16 E
Węgliniec 10 Le 51.17N 15.13 E
Węgorzewo 10 Rb 54.14N 21.44 E
Wegrów 10 Sd 52.25N 22.01 E
Wehni 35 Fc 12.40N 36.42 E
Weichang (Zhuizishan) 28 Kc 41.55N 117.45 E
Weida 10 If 50.46N 12.04 E
Weiden in der Oberpfalz 10 Ig 49.41N 12.10 E
Weifang 22 Nf 36.43N 119.06 E
Weihai 27 Ld 37.27N 122.02 E
Weihe 28 Jb 44.55N 128.23 E
Wei He 21 Nf 34.36N 110.10 E
Weilburg 10 Ef 50.29N 8.15 E
Weilerbach 12 Je 49.29N 7.38 E
Weilerswist 12 Id 50.46N 6.50 E
Weilheim in Oberbayern 10 Hi 47.50N 11.09 E
Weilmünster 12 Kd 50.26N 8.21 E
Weimar [Ger.] 12 Kd 50.46N 8.43 E
Weimar [Ger.] 10 Hf 50.59N 11.19 E
Weinan 27 Ie 34.30N 109.34 E
Weingarten 10 Fi 47.48N 9.38 E
Weinheim 10 Eg 49.33N 8.40 E
Weining 27 Hf 26.46N 104.18 E
Weinsberger Wald 14 Ib 48.25N 15.00 E
Weinstraße 12 Ke 49.20N 8.05 E
Weinviertel 14 Kb 48.35N 16.30 E
Weipa 58 Ff 12.41S 141.52 E
Weirton 44 Ge 40.24N 80.37W
Weiser 46 Gd 44.15N 116.58W
Weiser River 46 Gd 44.15N 116.59W
Weishan Hu 27 Ke 34.35N 117.15 E
Weishi 28 Cg 34.25N 114.10 E
Weishui → Jingxing 28 Ce 38.03N 114.09 E
Weiße Elster 10 Hf 51.26N 11.57 E
Weißenberg 12 Je 49.15N 7.49 E
Weißenburg in Bayern 10 Gg 49.02N 10.59 E
Weißenfels 10 He 51.12N 11.58 E
Weißer Main 10 Hf 50.05N 11.24 E
Weißerstein 12 Id 50.24N 6.22 E
Weißkugel/Palla Bianca 14 Ed 46.48N 10.44 E
Weiss Lake 44 Eh 34.15N 85.35W
Weißwasser/Běła Woda 10 Ke 51.31N 14.38 E
Weitra 14 Ib 48.42N 14.53 E
Weixi 27 Gf 27.13N 99.19 E
Weixian 28 Cf 36.59N 115.15 E
Weixin (Zhaxi) 27 If 27.46N 105.04 E
Weiz 14 Jc 47.13N 15.37 E
Wejherowo 10 Ob 54.37N 18.15 E
Welbourn Hill 58 Eg 27.21S 134.06 E
Welch 44 Gg 37.26N 81.36W
Weldiya 35 Fc 11.48N 39.35 E
Weld Range 59 De 26.55S 117.25 E
Welega [3] 35 Fd 8.38N 35.40 E
Welel 35 Ed 8.56N 34.52 E
Weligama 25 Gg 5.58N 80.25 E
Welkenraedt 12 Hd 50.39N 5.58 E
Welker Seamount (EN) 40 Ke 55.07N 140.20W
Welkite 35 Fd 8.17N 37.49 E
Welkom 31 Jk 27.59S 26.45 E
Welland 42 Jh 42.59N 79.15W
Welland 9 Ni 52.53N 0.02 E
Welland Canal 44 Hd 43.14N 79.13W
Wellesley Islands 57 Ef 16.45S 139.30 E
Wellin 12 Hd 50.05N 5.07 E
Wellingborough 9 Mi 52.19N 0.42W
Wellington [2] 62 Fd 40.10S 175.30 E
Wellington [Austl.] 59 Jf 32.33S 148.57 E
Wellington [Eng.-U.K.] 9 Jk 50.59N 3.14W
Wellington [Ks.-U.S.] 45 Hh 37.16N 97.24W
Wellington [Nv.-U.S.] 46 Fg 38.45N 119.22W
Wellington [N.Z.] 58 Ii 41.17S 174.46 E
Wellington, Isla- 52 Ij 49.20S 74.40W
Wellington, Lake- 59 Jg 38.10S 147.15 E
Wellington Channel 42 Ia 75.10N 93.00W
Wells [Eng.-U.K.] 9 Kj 51.13N 2.39W
Wells [Nv.-U.S.] 43 Dc 41.07N 115.01W
Wells, Lake- 59 Ee 26.45S 123.15 E
Wells, Mount- 59 Fc 17.26S 127.14 E
Wellsboro 44 Ie 41.45N 77.18W
Wellsford 62 Fb 36.18S 174.31 E
Wells-next-the-Sea 9 Ni 52.58N 0.51 E
Wellton 46 Hj 32.40N 114.08W
Welmel 35 Gd 5.35N 40.55 E
Wełna 10 Md 52.36N 16.50 E
Welo [3] 35 Fc 12.00N 40.00 E
Wels 14 Ib 48.10N 14.02 E
Welshpool 9 Ji 52.40N 3.09W
Welver 12 Jc 51.37N 7.58 E
Welwitschia 37 Ad 20.21S 14.57 E
Welwyn Garden City 9 Mj 51.48N 0.13W
Wema 36 Dc 0.26S 21.38 E
Wemding 10 Gh 48.52N 10.43 E
Wen'an 28 De 38.52N 116.30 E
Wenatchee 43 Cb 47.25N 120.19W
Wenatchee Mountains 46 Ec 47.20N 120.45W
Wenchang 27 Jh 19.43N 110.44 E
Wenchi 34 Ed 7.44N 2.06W
Wenchit 35 Fc 10.03N 38.35 E
Wenden 12 Jd 50.58N 7.52 E
Wendeng 27 Ld 37.10N 122.01 E
Wendland 10 Gc 53.10N 11.00 E
Wendo 35 Fd 6.37N 38.25 E
Wengyuan (Longxian) 27 Jg 24.21N 114.13 E
Wen He 28 Ef 37.06N 119.29 E
Wenling 27 Lf 28.23N 121.22 E
Wenquan 27 Fe 33.15N 91.55 E
Wenquan/Arixang 27 Dc 44.59N 81.04 E
Wenshan 27 Hg 23.22N 104.23 E
Wenshui 28 Bf 37.26N 112.01 E
Wensu 27 Dc 41.15N 80.14 E
Wensum 12 Db 52.37N 1.22 E
Wentworth 59 If 34.07S 141.55 E
Wenxian 27 He 32.52N 104.40 E
Wenzhou 22 Og 27.57N 120.38 E
Wenzhu 27 Jf 27.00N 114.00 E
Wepener 37 De 29.46S 27.00 E
Wépion, Namur- 12 Gd 50.25N 4.52 E
Werda 37 Ce 25.16S 23.17 E
Werder 31 Lh 7.00N 45.21 E
Werder 10 Jc 53.40N 13.25 E
Werdohl 12 Jc 51.16N 7.46 E
Were Ilu 35 Fc 10.38N 39.23 E
Werkendam 12 Gc 51.49N 4.55 E
Werl 12 Jc 51.33N 7.55 E
Werlte 12 Jb 52.51N 7.41 E
Wermelskirchen 12 Jc 51.09N 7.13 E
Werne 12 Jc 51.40N 7.38 E
Wernigerode 10 Ge 51.50N 10.47 E
Werra 5 Ge 51.26N 9.39 E
Werribee 59 Ig 37.54S 144.40 E
Werris Creek 59 Kf 31.21S 150.39 E
Werse 12 Jb 52.02N 7.41 E
Wertach 10 Gh 48.24N 10.53 E
Wertheim 10 Fg 49.45N 9.31 E
Wesel 10 Ce 51.40N 6.37 E
Weser 5 Ge 53.32N 8.34 E
Weserbergland 10 Fe 51.55N 9.30 E
Wesergebirge 10 Fd 52.15N 9.10 E
Weslaco 45 Gm 26.09N 98.01W
Wesley 51g Ba 15.34N 61.19W
Wesleyville 42 Mg 49.09N 53.34W
Wessel, Cape- 59 Hb 11.00S 136.45 E
Wesseling 12 Id 50.50N 6.59 E
Wessel Islands 57 Ef 12.00S 136.45 E
Wessington Springs 45 Gd 44.05N 98.34W
West Allis 45 Me 43.01N 88.00W
West Baines River 59 Gc 15.26S 130.08 E
West Bay 45 Ll 29.00N 89.30W
West Bend 45 Le 43.25N 88.11W
West Bengal [3] 25 Hd 24.00N 88.00 E
West Berlin (EN) = Berlin 6 He 52.31N 13.24 E
West Branch 44 Ec 44.17N 84.14W
West Bridgford 12 Ab 52.55N 1.07W
West Bromwich 9 Li 52.31N 1.59W
Westbrook 44 Ld 43.41N 70.21W
West Burra 9 La 60.05N 1.10W
West Caicos 49 Kc 21.47N 72.17W
West Cape 57 Hi 45.55S 166.26 E
West Caroline Basin (EN) 3 Ii 4.00N 138.00 E
West Carpathians (EN)= Západné Karpaty 10 Og 49.30N 19.00 E
West Des Moines 45 Jf 41.35N 93.43W
Westdongeradeel 12 Ha 53.23N 5.58 E
Westdongeradeel-Holwerd 12 Ha 53.22N 5.54 E
Westdongeradeel-Ternaard 12 Ha 53.23N 5.58 E
Westeinderplassen 12 Gb 52.15N 4.30 E
West Elk Mountains 45 Cg 38.40N 107.15W
West End 44 Hl 26.41N 78.58W
Westende, Middelkerke- 12 Ec 51.10N 2.46 E
West End Village 51b Ab 18.11N 63.09W
West Entrance 64a Bb 7.57N 134.30 E
Westerbork 12 Ib 52.51N 6.36 E
Westerburg 12 Jd 50.34N 7.59 E
Westerland 10 Eb 54.54N 8.18 E
Westerlo 12 Gc 51.05N 4.55 E
Western [Ghana] [3] 34 Ed 5.30N 2.30W
Western [Kenya] [3] 36 Fb 0.30N 34.35 E
Western [S.L.] [3] 34 Cd 8.20N 13.00W
Western [Ug.] [3] 36 Fb 1.00N 31.00 E
Western [Zam.] [3] 36 Df 15.00S 24.00 E
Western Australia [2] 59 Ed 25.00S 122.00 E
Western Desert (EN)= Gharbīyah, Aş Şaḩrā' Al- 30 Jf 27.30N 28.00 E
Western Dvina (EN)= Zapadnaja Dvina 5 Id 57.04N 24.03 E
Western Entrance 63a Bb 6.55S 155.40 E
Western Ghats/Sahyadri 21 Jh 14.00N 75.00 E
Western Isles [3] 9 Fd 57.40N 7.10W
Western Port 59 Jg 38.25S 145.10 E
Western River 42 Gc 66.22N 107.15W
Western Sahara (EN) [5] 31 Ff 24.30N 13.00W

Index Symbols

[1] Independent Nation
[2] State, Region
[3] District, County
[4] Municipality
[5] Colony, Dependency
Continent
Physical Region
Historical or Cultural Region
Mount, Mountain
Volcano
Hill
Mountains, Mountain Range
Hills, Escarpment
Plateau, Upland
Pass, Gap
Plain, Lowland
Delta
Salt Flat
Valley, Canyon
Crater, Cave
Karst Features
Depression
Polder
Desert, Dunes
Forest, Woods
Heath, Steppe
Oasis
Cape, Point
Coast, Beach
Cliff
Peninsula
Isthmus
Sandbank
Island
Atoll
Rock, Reef
Islands, Archipelago
Rocks, Reefs
Coral Reef
Well, Spring
Geyser
River, Stream
Waterfall Rapids
River Mouth, Estuary
Lake
Salt Lake
Intermittent Lake
Reservoir
Swamp, Pond
Canal
Glacier
Ice Shelf, Pack Ice
Ocean
Sea
Gulf, Bay
Strait, Fjord
Lagoon
Bank
Seamount
Tablemount
Ridge
Shelf
Basin
Escarpment, Sea Scarp
Fracture
Trench, Abyss
National Park, Reserve
Point of Interest
Recreation Site
Cave, Cavern
Historic Site
Ruins
Wall, Walls
Church, Abbey
Temple
Scientific Station
Airport
Port
Lighthouse
Mine
Tunnel
Dam, Bridge

Western Samoa (EN)= Samoa I Sisifo 58 Jf 13.40S 172.30W
Western Sayans (EN)= Zapadny Sajan 21 Ld 53.00N 94.00 E
Western Sierra Madre (EN) =Madre Occidental, Sierra- 38 Ig 25.00N 105.00W
Western Turkistan (EN) 21 He 41.00N 60.00 E
Westerschelde=West Schelde (EN) 11 Jc 51.25N 3.45 E
Westerschouwen 12 Fc 51.41N 3.43 E
Westerschouwen-Haamstede 12 Fc 51.42N 3.45 E
Westerstede 10 Dc 53.15N 7.56 E
Westerwald 10 Df 50.40N 7.55 E
Westerwoldse A 12 Ja 53.10N 7.10 E
West European Basin (EN) 3 De 47.00N 15.00W
West Falkland 52 Kk 51.40S 60.00W
West Falkland/Gran Malvina, Isla- 52 Kk 51.40S 60.00W
West Fayu Island 57 Fd 8.05N 146.44 E
West Fork Big Blue River 45 Hf 40.42N 96.59W
Westfriesland=West Friesland (EN) 11 Kb 52.45N 4.50 E
West Friesland (EN)= Westfriesland 11 Kb 52.45N 4.50 E
West Frisian Islands (EN)= Waddeneilanden 11 Ka 53.30N 5.00 E
Westgate-on-Sea 12 Dc 51.22N 1.21 E
West Glacier 46 Ib 48.30N 113.59W
West Glamorgan (3) 9 Jj 51.40N 3.55W
West Grand Lake 44 Nc 45.15N 67.52W
West Greenland (EN) = Vestgrønland (2) 41 He 69.00N 49.30W
West Helena 45 Ki 34.33N 90.39W
West Hollywood 44 Gm 25.59N 80.11W
Westhope 45 Fb 48.55N 101.01W
West Ice Shelf 66 Ge 67.00S 85.00 E
West Indies 47 Je 19.00N 70.00W
West Indies (EN)=Indias Occidentales 47 Je 19.00N 70.00W
West Island 37b Ab 9.22S 46.13 E
Westkapelle 12 Fc 51.31N 3.26 E
Westkapelle, Knokke- 12 Fc 51.19N 3.18 E
West Lafayette 44 De 40.27N 86.55W
Westland (2) 62 De 43.10S 170.30 E
West Liberty 44 Fg 37.55N 83.16W
Westlock 42 Gf 54.09N 113.52W
West Lunga 36 De 13.06S 24.39 E
Westmalle 12 Gc 51.18N 4.41 E
West Mariana Basin (EN) 3 Ih 15.00N 137.00 E
Westmeath/An Iarmhí (2) 9 Fh 53.30N 7.30W
West Melanesian Trench (EN) 60 Dh 1.00S 150.00 E
West Memphis 43 Id 35.08N 90.11W
West Mersea 12 Cc 51.46N 0.54 E
West Midlands (3) 9 Li 52.30N 2.00W
Westminster 44 If 39.35N 76.59W
Westminster, London- 12 Bc 51.30N 0.07W
West Monroe 45 Jj 32.31N 92.09W
Westmorland 9 Kg 54.30N 2.40W
West Nicholson 31 Jk 21.03S 29.22 E
West Nueces River 45 Gl 29.16N 99.56W
Weston [Mala.] 26 Ge 5.13N 115.36 E
Weston [W.V.-U.S.] 44 Gf 39.03N 80.28W
Weston [Wy.-U.S.] 46 Md 44.42N 105.18W
Weston-super-Mare 9 Kj 51.21N 2.59W
Westoverledingen 12 Ja 53.10N 7.27 E
Westoverledingen - Ihrhove 12 Ja 53.10N 7.27 E
West Palm Beach 39 Kg 26.43N 80.04W
West Pensacola 44 Dj 30.27N 87.15W
West Plains 43 Id 36.44N 91.51W
West Point [Ms.-U.S.] 45 Lj 33.36N 88.39W
West Point [Nb.-U.S.] 45 Hf 41.51N 96.43W
Westport 58 Ii 41.45S 171.36 E
Westport/Cathair na Mart 9 Dh 53.48N 9.32W
Westray 9 Kb 59.20N 3.00W
Westree 44 Gb 47.27N 81.32W
Westrich 12 Je 49.20N 7.25 E
West Road 12 Cd 50.52N 0.50 E
West Schelde (EN)= Westerschelde 11 Jc 51.25N 3.45 E
West Scotia Basin (EN) 52 Kk 57.00S 53.00W
West Siberian Plain (EN)= Zapadno Sibirskaja Ravnina 21 Jc 60.00N 75.00 E
Weststellingwerf 12 Ib 52.53N 6.00 E
Weststellingwerf-Wolvega 12 Ib 52.53N 6.00 E
West Sussex (3) 9 Mk 51.00N 0.40W
West Tavaputs Plateau 46 Jf 40.00N 110.25W
West-Terschelling, Terschelling- 12 Ha 53.21N 5.13 E
West Union [Ia.-U.S.] 45 Ke 42.57N 91.49W
West Union [Oh.-U.S.] 44 Ff 38.48N 83.33W
West Virginia (2) 43 Kd 38.45N 80.30W
West-Vlaanderen (3) 12 Ec 51.00N 3.00 E
Westwood 46 Ef 40.18N 121.00W
West Wyalong 59 Jf 33.55S 147.13 E
West Yellowstone 43 Eb 44.30N 111.05W
West Yorkshire (3) 9 Lh 53.40N 1.30W
Wetar, Pulau- 57 De 7.48S 126.18 E
Wetaskiwin 42 Gf 52.58N 113.22W
Wete 36 Gd 5.04S 39.43 E
Wětošow/Vetschau 10 Ke 51.47N 14.04 E
Wetter 12 Kd 50.18N 8.49 E
Wetter (Hessen) 12 Kd 50.54N 8.43 E
Wetter (Ruhr) 12 Jc 51.23N 7.24 E
Wetterau 10 Ef 50.15N 8.50 E
Wetteren 11 Jc 51.00N 3.53 E
Wetzlar 10 Ef 50.33N 8.30 E
Wevelgem 12 Fd 50.48N 3.10 E
Wewahitchka 44 Ej 30.07N 85.12W
Wewak 58 Fe 3.34S 143.38 E
Wexford/Loch Garman (2) 9 Gi 52.20N 6.40W
Wexford/Loch Garman 6 Fe 52.20N 6.27W
Wexford Harbour/Cuan Loch Garman 9 Gi 52.20N 6.25W
Wey 9 Mj 51.23N 0.28W
Weyburn 42 Hg 49.41N 103.52W
Weyhe 12 Kb 52.59N 8.52 E
Weyhe-Leeste 12 Kb 52.59N 8.50 E
Weymouth 9 Kk 50.36N 2.28W
Wezet/Visé 12 Hd 50.44N 5.42 E
Whakatane 61 Eg 37.58S 177.00 E
Whale Cove 42 Id 62.14N 92.10W
Whalsay 9 Ma 60.22N 0.59W
Whangarei 58 Ih 35.43S 174.19 E
Wharfe 9 Lh 53.51N 1.07W
Wharton 45 Hl 29.19N 96.06W
Wharton Basin (EN) 3 Hk 19.00S 100.00 E
Wharton Lake 42 Hd 64.00N 99.55W
Whataroa 62 De 43.16S 170.22 E
Wheatland 46 Me 42.03N 104.57W
Wheat Ridge 45 Dg 39.46N 105.07W
Wheeler 42 Ke 57.02N 67.14W
Wheeler 46 Dd 45.42N 123.52W
Wheeler Lake 44 Dh 34.40N 87.05W
Wheeler Peak [N.M.-U.S.] 43 Fd 36.34N 105.25W
Wheeler Peak [U.S.] 38 Hf 38.59N 114.19W
Wheeling 43 Kc 40.05N 80.43W
Whidbey Island 46 Db 48.15N 122.40W
Whitby 9 Mg 54.29N 0.37W
Whitchurch [Eng.-U.K.] 9 Ki 52.58N 2.41W
Whitchurch [Eng.-U.K.] 12 Bc 51.53N 0.50W
Whitchurch [Eng.-U.K.] 12 Ac 51.13N 1.20W
White 42 Jc 65.50N 85.00W
White, Lake- 59 Fd 21.05S 129.00 E
White Bay 38 Nd 50.00N 56.30W
White Bear Lake 45 Jd 45.04N 93.01W
White Butte 45 Ec 46.23N 103.19W
White Carpathians (EN) = Bílé Karpaty 10 Nh 48.55N 17.50 E
White Cliffs 59 If 30.51S 143.05 E
White Cloud 44 Ed 43.33N 85.46W
Whitecourt 42 Ff 54.09N 115.41W
Whitefish 43 Eb 48.25N 114.20W
Whitefish Bay 44 Eb 46.40N 84.50W
Whitefish Point 44 Eb 46.45N 85.00W
Whitefish Range 46 Hb 48.40N 114.26W
Whitehall [Mi.-U.S.] 44 Dd 43.24N 86.21W
Whitehall [Mt.-U.S.] 46 Id 45.52N 112.06W
Whitehall [Oh.-U.S.] 44 Ff 39.58N 82.54W
Whitehall [Wi.-U.S.] 45 Kd 44.22N 91.19W
Whitehaven 9 Jg 54.33N 3.35W
Whitehorse 39 Fc 60.43N 135.03W
White Island [Ant.] 66 Ee 66.44S 48.35 E
White Island [N.Z.] 62 Gb 37.30S 177.10 E
White Lake 45 Jl 29.45N 92.30W
White Lake (EN)=Beloje Ozero 5 Jc 60.11N 37.35 E
Whiteman Range 59 Ja 5.50S 149.55 E
Whitemark 59 Jh 40.07S 148.01 E
White Mountain 40 Db 64.35N 163.04W
White Mountain Peak 43 Dd 37.38N 118.15W
White Mountains [Ak.-U.S.] 40 Jc 65.30N 147.00W
White Mountains [U.S.] 46 Fh 37.30N 118.15W
White Mountains [U.S.] 43 Mc 44.10N 71.35W
Whitemouth Lake 45 Ib 49.14N 95.40W
Whitemouth River 45 Ha 50.07N 96.02W
White Nile (EN)=Abyaḍ, Al Baḥr al- 30 Kg 15.38N 32.31 E
White Nile (EN)=Abyaḍ, Al Baḥr al- (3) 35 Ec 12.40N 32.30 E
White Pass [N.Amer.] 40 Le 59.37N 135.08W
White Pass [Wa.-U.S.] 46 Ec 46.38N 121.24W
Whiteriver 46 Kj 33.50N 109.58W
White River [In.-U.S.] 44 Df 38.25N 87.44W
White River [Nv.-U.S.] 46 Hh 37.18N 115.08W
White River [Ont.-Can.] 42 Ig 48.35N 85.17W
White River [S.D.-U.S.] 45 Fe 43.34N 100.45W
White River [Tx.-U.S.] 45 Fj 33.14N 100.56W
White River [U.S.] 46 Kf 40.04N 109.41W
White River [U.S.] 43 Hc 43.45N 99.30W
White River [U.S.] 38 Jf 33.53N 91.03W
White River [Yuk.-Can.] 42 Dd 63.10N 139.32W
White Salmon 46 Ed 45.44N 121.29W
Whitesand Bay 9 Ik 50.20N 4.35W
White Sea (EN)=Beloje More 5 Kb 66.00N 44.00 E
White sea-Baltic Canal (EN) =Belomorsko-Baltijski Kanal 5 Jc 63.30N 34.48 E
White Settlement 45 Hj 32.45N 97.27W
White Sulphur Springs 46 Jc 46.33N 110.54W
Whiteville 44 Hh 34.20N 78.42W
White Volta 30 Gh 8.38N 0.59W
White Volta (EN)=Volta Blanche 30 Gh 8.38N 0.59W
Whitewater 45 Bg 38.59N 108.27W
Whitewater Baldy 45 Bj 33.20N 108.39W
Whitewater Bay 44 Gm 25.16N 81.00W
Whitewater Lake 45 La 50.50N 89.10W
Whitewood 45 Ea 50.20N 102.15W
Whitianga 62 Fb 36.50S 175.42 E
Whitmore Mountains 66 Og 82.35S 104.30W
Whitney 44 Hc 45.30N 78.14W
Whitney, Lake- 45 Hk 31.55N 97.23W
Whitney, Mount- 38 Hf 36.35N 118.18W
Whitstable 12 Dc 51.21N 1.06 E
Whitsunday Island 59 Jd 20.15S 149.00 E
Whittier 40 Jd 60.46N 148.41W
Whittlesea 59 Jg 37.31S 145.07 E
Whittlesey 12 Bb 52.33N 0.08W
Wholdaia Lake 42 Hd 60.45N 104.10W
Whyalla 59 Hf 33.02S 137.35 E
Wiarton 44 Gc 44.45N 81.09W
Wiawso 34 Ed 6.12N 2.29W
Wibaux 46 Mc 46.59N 104.11W
Wichita 39 Jf 37.41N 97.20W
Wichita Falls 39 Jf 33.54N 98.30W
Wichita Mountains 45 Gi 34.45N 98.40W
Wichita River 45 Gi 34.07N 98.10W
Wick 9 Jc 58.26N 3.06W
Wick 9 Jc 58.25N 3.05W
Wickenburg 46 Ij 33.58N 112.44W
Wickepin 59 Df 32.46S 117.30 E
Wickham 12 Ad 50.54N 1.10W
Wickham Market 12 Db 52.09N 1.22 E
Wickiup Reservoir 46 Ee 43.40N 121.43W
Wickliffe 44 Cg 36.58N 89.05W
Wicklow/Cill Mhantáin (2) 9 Gi 53.00N 6.30W
Wicklow/Cill Mhantáin 9 Gi 52.59N 6.03W
Wicklow Head/Ceann Chill Mhantáin 9 Hi 52.58N 6.00W
Wicklow Mountains/ Sléibhte Chill Mhantáin 9 Gh 53.02N 6.24W
Wicko, Jezioro- 10 Mb 54.33N 16.35 E
Wickrath, Mönchengladbach- 12 Ic 51.08N 6.25 E
Widawa 10 Me 51.13N 16.55 E
Wide Bay 59 Ka 5.05S 152.05 E
Widefield 45 Dg 38.42N 104.40W
Widgiemooltha 59 Ef 31.30S 121.34 E
Wi-Do 28 Ig 35.38N 126.17 E
Więcbork 10 Nc 53.22N 17.30 E
Wied 12 Jd 50.27N 7.28 E
Wiedenbrück 12 Kc 51.50N 8.19 E
Wiehengebirge 10 Ed 52.20N 8.40 E
Wiehl 12 Jd 50.57N 7.32 E
Wieliczka 10 Qg 49.59N 20.04 E
Wielimie, Jezioro- 10 Mc 53.47N 16.50 E
Wielki Dział 10 Tf 50.18N 23.25 E
Wielkopolska 10 Ne 51.50N 17.20 E
Wielkopolskie-Kujawskie, Pojezierze- 10 Md 52.25N 16.30 E
Wieluń 10 Oe 51.14N 18.34 E
Wien (2) 14 Kb 48.15N 16.25 E
Wien = Vienna (EN) 6 Hf 48.12N 16.22 E
Wiener Becken 14 Kc 48.00N 16.28 E
Wiener Neustadt 14 Kc 47.48N 16.15 E
Wienerwald=Vienna Woods (EN) 14 Jb 48.10N 16.00 E
Wieprz 10 Re 51.32N 21.49 E
Wieprza 10 Mb 54.26N 16.22 E
Wieprz-Krzna, Kanał- 10 Se 51.56N 22.56 E
Wierden 12 Ib 52.22N 6.36 E
Wieringen 12 Hb 52.56N 5.02 E
Wieringen-Den Oever 12 Hb 52.56N 5.02 E
Wieringen-Hippolytushoef 12 Gb 52.54N 4.59 E
Wieringermeer 12 Hb 52.51N 5.01 E
Wieringermeer Polder 12 Gb 52.50N 5.00 E
Wieringermeer-Wieringerwerf 12 Hb 52.51N 5.01 E
Wieringerwerf, Wieringermeer- 12 Hb 52.51N 5.01 E
Wieruszów 10 Oe 51.18N 18.08 E
Wierzchowo, Jezioro- 10 Mc 53.50N 16.45 E
Wierzyca 10 Oc 53.51N 18.50 E
Wiesbaden 6 Ge 50.05N 8.15 E
Wiese 10 Di 47.35N 7.35 E
Wieslautern 12 Je 49.05N 7.49 E
Wiesloch 10 Eg 49.18N 8.42 E
Wietingsmoor 12 Kb 52.39N 8.39 E
Wietmarschen 12 Jb 52.32N 7.08 E
Wieżyca 10 Ob 54.17N 18.10 E
Wigan 9 Kh 53.32N 2.35W
Wigger 14 Bc 47.15N 7.55 E
Wiggins 45 Lk 30.51N 89.08W
Wight, Isle of- 5 Fe 50.40N 1.20W
Wigry, Jezioro- 10 Tb 54.05N 23.07 E
Wigston 12 Ab 52.35N 1.06W
Wigtown 9 Ig 54.52N 4.26W
Wigtown Bay 9 Ig 54.46N 4.15W
Wijchen 12 Hc 51.48N 5.44 E
Wijdefjorden 41 Nc 79.50N 15.30 E
Wijk bij Duurstede 12 Hc 51.59N 5.22 E
Wil 14 Dc 47.27N 9.05 E
Wilbur 46 Fc 47.46N 118.42W
Wilburton 45 Ii 34.55N 95.19W
Wilcannia 58 Fh 31.34S 143.23 E
Wild Coast 30 Jl 32.00S 29.50 E
Wilder Seamount (EN) 57 Jd 9.00N 173.00W
Wildeshausen 10 Ed 52.54N 8.26 E
Wild Horse 46 Jb 49.01N 110.12W
Wildspitze 14 Ed 46.53N 10.52 E
Wilga 10 Re 51.50N 21.20 E
Wilhelm-II-Land 66 Ge 69.00S 90.00 E
Wilhelminakanaal 12 Gc 51.43N 4.53 E
Wilhelm-Pieck-Stadt-Guben 10 Ke 51.57N 14.43 E
Wilhelmshaven 10 Ec 53.31N 8.08 E
Wilhelmstal 37 Bd 21.54S 16.20 E
Wilkes-Barre 43 Lc 41.15N 75.50W
Wilkesboro 44 Gg 36.09N 81.09W
Wilkes Land (EN) 66 Hf 71.00S 120.00 E
Wilkins Coast 66 Qe 69.40S 63.00W
Wilkins Sound 66 Qf 70.15S 73.00W
Willamette River 46 Dd 45.39N 122.46W
Willandra Billabong Creek 59 If 33.08S 144.06 E
Willapa Bay 46 Dc 46.37N 124.00W
Willard 45 Ci 34.36N 106.02W
Willards, Punta- 48 Cc 28.50N 112.35W
Willcox 46 Kj 32.15N 109.50W
Willebadessen 12 Lc 51.38N 9.02 E
Willebadessen-Peckelsheim 12 Lc 51.36N 9.08 E
Willebroek 12 Gc 51.04N 4.22 E
Willemstad [Neth.] 12 Gc 51.41N 4.26 E
Willemstad [Neth.Ant.] 53 Jd 12.06N 68.56W
Willeroo 59 Gc 15.17S 131.35 E
William Bill Dannelly Reservoir 44 Di 32.15N 86.45W
Williams 43 Ed 35.15N 112.11W
Williamsburg [Ky.-U.S.] 44 Eg 36.44N 84.10W
Williamsburg [Va.-U.S.] 44 Ig 37.17N 76.43W
Williams Lake 42 Ff 52.08N 122.09W
Williamson Glacier 66 He 66.30S 114.30 E
Williamsport 43 Lc 41.16N 77.03W
Williamston 44 Ih 35.50N 77.06W
Williamstown 44 Ef 38.38N 84.34W
Willich 12 Ic 51.16N 6.33 E
Willikie's 51d Bb 17.03N 61.42W
Willingdon, Mount- 46 Ga 51.48N 116.17W
Willis Group 57 Gf 16.20S 150.00 E
Williston [N.D.-U.S.] 43 Gb 48.09N 103.37W
Williston [S.Afr.] 37 Cf 31.20S 20.53 E
Williston Lake 38 Gd 50.57N 122.23W
Willits 46 Dg 39.25N 123.21W
Willmar 43 Hb 45.07N 95.03W
Willoughby Bay 51d Bb 17.02N 61.44W
Willow Bunch Lake 46 Mb 49.27N 105.28W
Willowlake 42 Fd 62.42N 123.08W
Willowmore 37 Cf 33.17S 23.29 E
Willows 46 Dg 39.31N 122.12W
Willow Springs 45 Kh 36.59N 91.58W
Wills, Lake- 59 Fd 21.20S 128.40 E
Wills Point 45 Ij 32.43N 95.57W
Wilma Glacier 66 Ee 67.12S 56.00 E
Wilmington [De.-U.S.] 43 Ld 39.44N 75.33W
Wilmington [N.C.-U.S.] 39 Lf 34.13N 77.55W
Wilmington [Oh.-U.S.] 44 Ff 39.28N 83.50W
Wilnsdorf 12 Kd 50.49N 8.06 E
Wilseder Berg 10 Fc 53.10N 9.56 E
Wilson 43 Ld 35.44N 77.55W
Wilson, Cape - 42 Jc 66.59N 81.27W
Wilson, Mount- 45 Ch 37.51N 107.59W
Wilson Bluff 66 Ff 74.20S 66.47 E
Wilson Lake [Al.-U.S.] 44 Dh 34.49N 87.30W
Wilson Lake [Ks.-U.S.] 45 Gg 38.57N 98.40W
Wilsons Promontory 59 Jg 38.55S 146.20 E
Wilton River 59 Gb 14.45S 134.33 E
Wilts (3) 9 Lj 51.20N 2.00W
Wiltshire (3) 9 Lj 51.30N 2.00W
Wiltz 11 Le 49.58N 5.55 E
Wiluna 59 Ee 26.36S 120.13 E
Wimereux 12 Dd 50.46N 1.37 E
Winamac 44 De 41.03N 86.36W
Winburg 37 De 28.37S 27.00 E
Winchelsea 12 Cd 50.55N 0.43 E
Winchester [Eng.-U.K.] 9 Lj 51.04N 1.19W
Winchester [In.-U.S.] 44 Ee 40.10N 84.59W
Winchester [Ky.-U.S.] 44 Ef 38.01N 84.11W
Winchester [Va.-U.S.] 43 Ld 39.11N 78.12W
Windeck 12 Jd 50.49N 7.34 E
Windemin, Pointe- 63b Cc 16.34S 167.27 E
Winder 44 Fi 34.00N 83.47W
Windermere 9 Kg 54.22N 2.56W
Windermere [B.C.-Can.] 46 Ha 50.30N 115.58W
Windermere [Eng.-U.K.] 9 Kg 54.23N 2.54W
Windhoek 31 Ik 22.34S 17.06 E
Windhoek (3) 37 Bd 22.30S 17.00 E
Windischgarsten 14 Ic 47.43N 14.20 E
Wind Mountain 45 Dj 32.02N 105.34W
Windom 45 Ie 43.52N 95.07W
Windom Mountain 45 Ch 37.37N 107.35W
Windorah 59 Ie 25.26S 142.39 E
Window Rock 46 Ki 35.41N 109.03W
Wind River 46 Ke 43.08N 108.12W
Wind River Peak 46 Ke 42.42N 109.07W
Wind River Range 43 Fc 43.05N 109.25W
Windrush 9 Lj 51.42N 1.25W
Windsor [Eng.-U.K.] 9 Mj 51.29N 0.38W
Windsor [N.S.-Can.] 42 Lh 44.59N 64.09W
Windsor [Ont.-Can.] 42 Jh 42.18N 83.01W
Windsor Forest 44 Gj 31.58N 81.10W
Windward Islands 47 Lf 13.00N 61.00W
Windward Islands (EN)= Barlovento, Islas de- 38 Mh 15.00N 61.00W
Windward Islands (EN) = Sotavento, Islas de- 52 Jd 11.10N 67.00W
Windward Islands (EN)= Vent, Iles du- 57 Mf 17.30S 149.30W
Windward Passage (EN)= Vent, Canal du- 49 Lh 20.00N 73.50W
Windward Passage (EN)= Vientos, Paso de los- 38 Lh 20.00N 73.50W
Winfield [Al.-U.S.] 44 Di 33.56N 87.49W
Winfield [Ks.-U.S.] 43 Hd 37.15N 96.59W
Wingene 12 Fc 51.04N 3.16 E
Wingen-sur-Moder 12 Jf 48.55N 7.22 E
Winisk 38 Kd 55.17N 85.05W
Winisk 39 Kd 55.15N 85.12W
Winisk Lake 42 If 52.55N 87.20W
Winkler 45 Hb 49.11N 97.56W
Winklern 14 Gd 46.52N 12.52 E
Winneba 34 Ed 5.20N 0.37W
Winnebago, Lake- 43 Jc 44.00N 88.25W
Winnemucca 43 Dc 40.58N 117.44W
Winnemucca Lake 46 Ff 40.10N 119.20W
Winner 43 Hc 43.22N 99.51W
Winnett 46 Kc 47.00N 108.21W
Winnfield 45 Jk 31.55N 92.38W
Winnibigoshish, Lake- 45 Ic 47.27N 94.12W
Winnipeg 39 Je 49.53N 97.09W
Winnipeg 38 Jd 50.38N 96.19W
Winnipeg, Lake- 38 Jd 52.00N 97.00W
Winnipeg Beach 45 Ha 50.31N 96.58W
Winnipegosis 42 Hf 51.39N 99.56W
Winnipegosis, Lake- 38 Jd 52.30N 100.00W
Winnipesaukee, Lake- 44 Ld 43.35N 71.20W
Winnsboro 45 Kj 32.10N 91.43W
Winnweiler 12 Je 49.34N 7.51 E
Winona [Mn.-U.S.] 43 Ic 44.03N 91.39W
Winona [Mo.-U.S.] 45 Kh 37.06N 91.19W
Winona [Ms.-U.S.] 45 Lj 33.29N 89.44W
Winschoten 11 Na 53.08N 7.02 E
Winsen 10 Gc 53.22N 10.13 E
Winslow [Az.-U.S.] 43 Ed 35.01N 110.42W
Winslow [Eng.-U.K.] 12 Bc 51.57N 0.52W
Winslow Reef 57 Je 1.36S 174.57W
Winston-Salem 43 Kd 36.06N 80.15W
Winterberg 10 Ee 51.12N 8.32 E
Winter Harbour 42 Gb 74.46N 110.40W
Winter Haven 43 Kf 28.01N 81.44W
Winter Park [Co.-U.S.] 45 Dg 39.47N 105.45W
Winter Park [Fl.-U.S.] 44 Gk 28.36N 81.20W
Winters 45 Gk 31.57N 99.58W
Winterset 45 If 41.20N 94.01W
Winterswijk 11 Mc 51.58N 6.44 E
Winterthur 14 Cc 47.30N 8.45 E
Winton [Austl.] 58 Fg 22.23S 143.02 E
Winton [N.C.-U.S.] 44 Ig 36.24N 76.56W
Winton [N.Z.] 62 Cg 46.09S 168.20 E
Wipper [Ger.] 10 He 51.20N 11.10 E
Wipper [Ger.] 10 He 51.47N 11.42 E
Wisbech 9 Ni 52.40N 0.10 E
Wiscasset 44 Mc 44.00N 69.40W
Wisch 12 Ic 51.55N 6.22 E
Wisch-Terborg 12 Ic 51.55N 6.22 E
Wisconsin (2) 43 Jc 44.45N 89.30W
Wisconsin 38 Je 43.00N 91.15W
Wisconsin Range 66 Ng 85.45S 125.00W
Wisconsin Rapids 43 Jc 44.23N 89.49W
Wiseman 40 Ic 67.25N 150.06W
Wisła 10 Og 49.39N 18.50 E
Wisła=Vistula (EN) 5 He 54.22N 18.55 E
Wiślana, Mierzeja- 10 Pb 54.25N 19.30 E
Wiślane, Żuławy- 10 Ob 54.10N 19.00 E
Wiślany, Zalew- 10 Pb 54.27N 19.40 E
Wisłok 10 Sf 50.13N 22.32 E
Wisłoka 10 Rf 50.27N 21.23 E
Wismar 10 Hc 53.54N 11.28 E
Wismarbucht 10 Hc 53.57N 11.25 E
Wissant 12 Dd 50.53N 1.40 E
Wissembourg 11 Ne 49.02N 7.57 E
Wissen 10 Df 50.47N 7.45 E
Wissenkerke 12 Fc 51.35N 3.45 E
Wissey 12 Cb 52.34N 0.21 E
Witbank 31 Jk 25.56S 29.07 E
Witchekar Lake 45 Fb 49.15N 100.16W
Witdraai 37 Ce 26.58S 20.41 E
Witham 12 Cc 51.47N 0.38 E
Witham 9 Ni 52.56N 0.04 E
Withernsea 9 Nh 53.44N 0.02 E
Witkowo 10 Nd 52.27N 17.47 E
Witmarsum, Wonseradeel- 12 Ha 53.06N 5.28 E
Witney 9 Lj 51.48N 1.29W
Witnica 10 Kd 52.40N 14.55 E
Witputz 37 Be 27.37S 16.42 E
Witten 10 De 51.26N 7.20 E
Wittenberg [Ger.] 10 Ie 51.52N 12.39 E
Wittenberg [Wi.-U.S.] 45 Ld 44.49N 89.10W
Wittenberge 10 Hc 53.00N 11.45 E
Wittenoom 59 Dd 22.17S 118.19 E
Wittingen 10 Gd 52.44N 10.43 E
Wittlich 10 Cg 49.59N 6.53 E
Wittmund 10 Dc 53.34N 7.47 E
Wittow 10 Jb 54.38N 13.19 E
Wittstock 10 Ic 53.09N 12.30 E
Witu 36 Hc 2.23S 40.26 E
Witu Islands 60 Dh 4.40S 149.18 E
Witvlei 37 Bd 22.23S 18.32 E
Witzenhausen 10 Fe 51.20N 9.52 E
Wivenhoe 12 Cc 51.51N 0.58 E
Wizard Reef 30 Mi 8.57S 51.01 E
Wizna 10 Sc 53.13N 22.26 E
Widawka 10 Oe 51.32N 18.52 E
W. J. Van Blommestein Meer 54 Hc 4.45N 55.00W
Wkra 10 Qd 52.27N 20.44 E
Władysławowo 10 Ob 54.49N 18.25 E
Włocławek 10 Pd 52.39N 19.02 E
Włocławek (2) 10 Od 52.40N 19.00 E
Włodawa 10 Te 51.34N 23.32 E
Włoszczowa 10 Pf 50.25N 19.59 E
Wodonga 59 Jg 36.17S 146.54 E
Wodzisław Śląski 10 Of 50.00N 18.28 E
Woensdrecht 12 Gc 51.25N 4.18 E
Woerden 12 Gb 52.05N 4.52 E
Woerth 12 Jf 48.56N 7.45 E
Woëvre, Plaine de la- 11 Le 49.15N 5.50 E
Wohlthat-Massif 66 Cf 71.35S 12.20 E
Woippy 12 Ie 49.09N 6.09 E
Wojerecy/Hoyerswerda 10 Ke 51.26N 14.15 E
Wokam, Pulau- 26 Jh 5.37S 134.30 E
Woken He 28 Ja 46.19N 129.34 E
Woking 9 Mj 51.20N 0.34W
Wokingham 12 Bc 51.25N 0.50W
Wolbrom 10 Pf 50.24N 19.46 E
Wolcott 44 Id 43.13N 76.42W
Wołczyn 10 Oe 51.01N 18.03 E
Woldberg 12 Hb 52.25N 5.55 E
Woleai Atoll 57 Fd 7.21N 143.52 E
Woleu-Ntem (3) 36 Bb 2.00N 12.00 E
Wolf, Isla- 54a Aa 1.23N 91.49W
Wolf, Volcán- 54a Ab 0.01S 91.20W
Wolfach 10 Eh 48.18N 8.13 E
Wolf Creek 45 Gh 36.35N 99.30W
Wolf Creek 46 Ic 47.00N 112.04W
Wolfen 10 Ie 51.40N 12.17 E
Wolfenbüttel 10 Gd 52.10N 10.33 E
Wolfhagen 10 Fe 51.19N 9.10 E
Wolf Point 43 Fb 48.05N 105.39W
Wolfratshausen 10 Hi 47.54N 11.25 E
Wolf River 45 Ld 44.11N 88.48W
Wolfsberg 14 Id 46.50N 14.50 E
Wolfsburg 10 Gd 52.26N 10.48 E
Wolfstein 12 Je 49.35N 7.36 E
Wolgast 10 Jb 54.03N 13.46 E
Wolica 10 Tf 50.54N 23.12 E
Wolin 10 Kc 53.51N 14.38 E
Wolin 10 Kc 53.50N 14.35 E
Wollaston 12 Bb 52.15N 0.40W
Wollaston, Islas- 56 Gi 55.40S 67.30W
Wollaston Forland 41 Jd 74.35N 20.15W
Wollaston Lake 38 Id 58.15N 103.20W
Wollaston Lake 42 He 58.05N 103.38W
Wollaston Peninsula 38 Hc 70.00N 115.00W
Wollongong 58 Gh 34.25S 150.54 E
Wöllstein 12 Je 49.49N 7.58 E
Wolmaransstad 37 De 27.12S 26.13 E
Wołomin 10 Rd 52.21N 21.14 E
Wołów 10 Me 51.29N 16.55 E

Index Symbols

Independent Nation · State, Region · District, County · Municipality · Colony, Dependency · Continent · Physical Region · Historical or Cultural Region · Mount, Mountain · Volcano · Hill · Mountains, Mountain Range · Hills, Escarpment · Plateau, Upland · Pass, Gap · Plain, Lowland · Delta · Salt Flat · Valley, Canyon · Crater, Cave · Karst Features · Depression · Polder · Desert, Dunes · Forest, Woods · Heath, Steppe · Oasis · Cape, Point · Coast, Beach · Cliff · Peninsula · Isthmus · Sandbank · Island · Atoll · Rock, Reef · Islands, Archipelago · Rocks, Reefs · Coral Reef · Well, Spring · Geyser · River, Stream · Waterfall Rapids · River Mouth, Estuary · Lake · Salt Lake · Intermittent Lake · Reservoir · Swamp, Pond · Canal · Glacier · Ice Shelf, Pack Ice · Ocean · Sea · Gulf, Bay · Strait, Fjord · Lagoon · Bank · Seamount · Tablemount · Ridge · Shelf · Basin · Escarpment, Sea Scarp · Fracture · Trench, Abyss · National Park, Reserve · Point of Interest · Recreation Site · Cave, Cavern · Historic Site · Ruins · Wall, Walls · Church, Abbey · Temple · Scientific Station · Airport · Port · Lighthouse · Mine · Tunnel · Dam, Bridge

Wolseley 42 Hf 50.25N 103.19W
Wolstenholme, Cap - 42 Jd 62.34N 77.30W
Wolstenholme Fjord 41 Ec 76.40N 69.45W
Wolsztyn 10 Md 52.08N 16.06 E
Wolvega, Weststellingwerf- 12 Ib 52.53N 6.00 E
Wolverhampton 9 Ki 52.36N 2.08W
Wolverton 9 Mi 52.04N 0.50W
Wŏnju 27 Md 37.21N 127.58 E
Wŏnsan 22 Of 39.10N 127.26 E
Wonseradeel 12 Ha 53.06N 5.28 E
Wonseradeel-Witmarsum 12 Ha 53.06N 5.28 E
Wonthaggi 59 Jg 38.36S 145.35 E
Woodall Mountain 45 Li 34.45N 88.11W
Woodbridge 9 Oi 52.06N 1.19 E
Woodbridge Bay 51g Bb 15.19N 61.25W
Woodhall Spa 12 Ba 53.09N 0.13W
Woodland [Ca.-U.S.] 46 Eg 38.41N 121.46W
Woodland [Wa.-U.S.] 46 Dd 45.54N 122.45W
Woodlark Island 57 Ge 9.05S 152.50 E
Wood Mountain 46 Lb 49.14N 106.20W
Woodridge 45 Hb 49.17N 96.09W
Wood River 46 Lb 50.08N 106.10W
Wood River Lakes 46 He 59.30N 158.45W
Woodroffe, Mount- 59 Ge 26.20S 131.45 E
Woods, Lake- 59 Gc 17.50S 133.30 E
Woods, Lake of the- 38 Je 49.15N 94.45W
Woods Hole 44 Le 41.31N 70.40W
Woodside 46 Jg 39.21N 110.18W
Woodstock [Eng.-U.K.] 9 Lj 51.52N 1.21W
Woodstock [N.B.-Can.] 42 Kg 46.09N 67.34W
Woodstock [Ont.-Can.] 44 Gd 43.08N 80.45W
Woodstock [Vt.-U.S.] 44 Kd 43.37N 72.31W
Woodville [Ms.-U.S.] 45 Kk 31.01N 91.18W
Woodville [N.Z.] 62 Fd 40.20S 175.52 E
Woodville [Tx.-U.S.] 45 Ik 30.46N 94.25W
Woodward 43 Hd 36.26N 99.24W
Wooler 9 Kf 55.33N 2.01W
Woomera 59 Hf 31.11S 137.10 E
Wooramel River 59 Ce 25.47S 114.10 E
Wooster 44 Ge 40.46N 81.57W
Worcester 9 Ki 52.15N 2.10W
Worcester [Eng.-U.K.] 9 Ki 52.11N 2.13W
Worcester [Ma.-U.S.] 43 Mc 42.16N 71.48W
Worcester [S.Afr.] 31 Il 33.39S 19.27 E
Worcester Range 66 Jf 78.50S 161.00 E
Wörgl 14 Gc 47.29N 12.04 E
Workai, Pulau- 26 Jh 6.40S 134.40 E
Workington 9 Jg 54.39N 3.33W
Worksop 9 Lh 53.18N 1.07W
Workum 12 Hb 52.59N 5.27 E
Worland 43 Fc 44.01N 107.57W
Wormer 12 Gb 52.30N 4.52 E
Wormhout 12 Ed 50.53N 2.28 E
Worms 10 Eg 49.38N 8.21 E
Worms Head 9 Ij 51.34N 4.20W
Wörrstadt 12 Ke 49.50N 8.06 E
Wörth am Rhein 12 Ke 49.03N 8.16 E
Wörther-See 14 Id 46.37N 14.10 E
Worthing 9 Mk 50.48N 0.23W
Worthington 43 Hc 43.37N 95.36W
Wosi 26 Ig 0.11S 127.58 E
Wotho Atoll 57 Hc 10.06N 165.59 E
Wotje Atoll 57 Id 9.27N 170.02 E
Woudenberg 12 Hb 52.05N 5.25 E
Wounnioné, Pointe- 63b Db 14.54S 168.02 E
Wounta, Laguna de- 49 Fg 13.38N 83.34W
Wour 35 Ba 21.21N 15.57 E
Wousi 63b Cb 15.22S 166.39 E
Wowoni, Pulau- 26 Hg 4.08S 123.06 E
Woy Woy 59 Kf 33.30S 151.20 E
Wrangel, Ostrov-=Wrangel Island (EN) 21 Tb 71.00N 179.30 E
Wrangel Island (EN)=Wrangel, Ostrov- 21 Tb 71.00N 179.30 E
Wrangell 39 Fd 56.28N 132.23W
Wrangell, Cape- 40a Ab 52.50N 172.26 E
Wrangell Mountains 38 Ec 62.00N 143.00W
Wrath, Cape- 9 Fd 58.37N 5.01W
Wray 43 Gc 40.05N 102.13W
Wreake 12 Ab 52.41N 1.05W
Wreck Reef 57 Gg 22.15S 155.10 E
Wrecks, Bay of- 64g Bb 1.52N 157.17W
Wrexham 9 Kh 53.03N 3.00W
Wright Island 66 Of 74.03S 116.45W
Wright Patman Lake 45 Ij 33.16N 94.14W
Wrightson, Mount- 46 Jk 31.42N 110.50W
Wrigley 42 Fd 63.19N 123.38W
Wrigley Gulf 66 Nf 74.00S 129.00W
Wrocław 10 Me 51.05N 17.00 E
Wrocław=Breslau (EN) 6 He 51.06N 17.00 E
Wronki 10 Md 52.43N 16.23 E
Wrotham 12 Cc 51.18N 0.19 E
Wroxham 12 Db 52.42N 1.24 E
Września 10 Nd 52.20N 17.34 E
Wschowa 10 Me 51.48N 16.19 E
Wu'an 28 Cf 36.42N 114.12 E
Wuchale 35 Fc 11.31N 39.37 E
Wuchang 28 Ib 44.55N 127.11 E
Wuchang, Wuhan- 28 Ci 30.32N 114.18 E
Wucheng (Jiucheng) 28 Df 37.12N 116.04 E
Wuchiu Hsu 27 Kg 25.00N 119.27 E
Wuchuan 28 Ad 41.08N 111.25 E
Wuchuan (Duru) 27 If 28.28N 107.57 E
Wuchuan (Meilü) 27 Jg 21.28N 110.44 E
Wuda 27 Id 39.30N 106.33 E
Wudan → Ongniud Qi 27 Kc 42.58N 119.01 E
Wudao 27 Ld 39.28N 121.30 E
Wudaoliang 27 Fd 35.15N 93.14 E
Wudi 28 Df 37.44N 117.36 E
Wudil 34 Gc 11.49N 8.51 E
Wuding 27 Hf 25.36N 102.27 E
Wudu 27 He 33.24N 105.00 E
Wugang 27 Jf 26.48N 110.32 E
Wugong (Puji) 27 Ie 34.15N 108.14 E
Wuhai 27 Id 39.32N 106.55 E
Wuhan 22 Nf 30.30N 114.20 E
Wuhan-Hankou 28 Ci 30.35N 114.16 E
Wuhan-Hanyang 28 Ci 30.33N 114.16 E
Wuhan- Wuchang 28 Ci 30.32N 114.18 E
Wuhe 27 Ke 33.08N 117.51 E
Wuhu 22 Nf 31.18N 118.27 E
Wuhu (Wanzhi) 28 Ei 31.21N 118.23 E
Wujia He 27 Ic 40.56N 108.52 E
Wu Jiang 21 Mg 29.43N 107.24 E
Wujiang 28 Fi 31.09N 120.38 E
Wukari 31 Hh 7.51N 9.47 E
Wukro 35 Fc 13.48N 39.37 E
Wular 25 Eb 34.30N 74.30 E
Wulff Land 41 Hb 82.19N 50.00W
Wulian (Hongning) 28 Eg 35.45N 119.13 E
Wuliang Shan 27 Hg 24.00N 101.00 E
Wuliaru, Pulau- 26 Jh 7.27S 131.04 E
Wuling Shan 21 Mg 28.20N 110.00 E
Wulongbei 28 Hd 40.15N 124.16 E
Wulongji → Huaibin 28 Ci 32.27N 115.23 E
Wulur 26 Ih 7.09S 128.39 E
Wum 34 Hd 6.23N 10.04 E
Wumei Shan 28 Cj 28.47N 114.50 E
Wümme 12 Ka 53.10N 8.40 E
Wuning 28 Cj 29.17N 115.05 E
Wünnenberg 12 Kc 51.31N 8.42 E
Wünnenberg-Haaren 12 Kc 51.34N 8.44 E
Wunnummin Lake 42 If 52.55N 89.10W
Wun Rog 35 Dd 9.00N 28.21 E
Wunstrof 10 Fd 52.26N 9.25 E
Wuntho 25 Jd 23.54N 95.41 E
Wupper 10 Ce 51.05N 7.00 E
Wuppertal 10 De 51.16N 7.11 E
Wuqi 27 Id 36.57N 108.15 E
Wuqia/Ulugqat 27 Cd 39.40N 75.07 E
Wuqiao (Sangyuan) 28 Df 37.38N 116.23 E
Wuqing (Yangcun) 28 De 39.23N 117.04 E
Würm 12 Kf 48.53N 8.42 E
Wurno 34 Gc 13.18N 5.26 E
Würselen 12 Id 50.49N 6.08 E
Würzburg 6 Gf 49.48N 9.56 E
Wurzen 10 Ie 51.22N 12.44 E
Wu Shan 27 Ie 31.00N 110.00 E
Wushaoling 27 Hd 37.15N 102.50 E
Wuski/Uqturpan 27 Cc 41.10N 79.16 E
Wusong 28 Fi 31.23N 121.29 E
Wüst Seamount (EN) 30 Gl 34.00S 3.40W
Wusuli Jiang 27 Ob 48.28N 135.02 E
Wutach 10 Ei 47.37N 8.15 E
Wutai [China] 28 Be 38.43N 113.14 E
Wutai [China] 27 Dc 44.38N 82.06 E
Wutai Shan 27 Jd 39.04N 113.28 E
Wuustwezel 12 Gc 51.23N 4.36 E
Wuvulu Island 57 Fe 1.43S 142.50 E
Wuwei 28 Di 31.17N 117.54 E
Wuwei (Liangzhou) 22 Mf 37.58N 102.48 E
Wuxi [China] 22 Of 31.32N 120.18 E
Wuxi [China] 27 Ie 31.27N 109.34 E
Wu Xia 27 Je 31.02N 110.10 E
Wuxiang (Duancun) 28 Bf 36.50N 112.51 E
Wuxing (Huzhou) 27 Le 30.47N 120.07 E
Wuxue→Guangji 27 Kf 29.58N 115.32 E
Wuyang [China] 28 Bh 33.26N 113.35 E
Wuyang [China] 27 Jd 36.29N 113.07 E
Wuyang → Zhenyuan 27 If 27.05N 108.26 E
Wuyi [China] 28 Cf 37.49N 115.54 E
Wuyi [China] 28 Ej 28.54N 119.50 E
Wuyiling 27 Mb 48.37N 129.20 E
Wuyi Shan 21 Ng 27.00N 117.00 E
Wuyuan [China] 22 Me 41.08N 108.17 E
Wuyuan [China] 28 Dj 29.15N 117.52 E
Wuyuanzhen→Haiyan 28 Fi 30.31N 120.56 E
Wuzhai 28 Ae 38.54N 111.49 E
Wuzhen 28 Ai 31.42N 112.00 E
Wuzhi Shan [China] 28 Ed 40.31N 118.02 E
Wuzhi Shan [China] 27 Ih 18.54N 109.40 E
Wuzhong 27 Id 38.00N 106.10 E
Wuzhou 22 Ng 23.32N 111.21 E
Wyalkatchem 59 Df 31.10S 117.22 E
Wyandotte 44 Fd 42.12N 83.10W
Wyandra 59 Je 27.15S 145.59 E
Wye 9 Kj 51.37N 2.39W
Wye 12 Cc 51.11N 0.56 E
Wyemandoo, Mount- 59 De 28.31S 118.32 E
Wyk auf Föhr 10 Eb 54.42N 8.34 E
Wylie, Lake- 44 Gh 35.07N 81.02W
Wymondham 9 Oi 52.34N 1.07 E
Wyndham [Austl.] 58 Df 15.28S 128.06 E
Wyndham [N.Z.] 62 Cg 46.20S 168.51 E
Wyndmere 45 Hc 46.16N 97.08W
Wynne 45 Ki 35.14N 90.47W
Wynniatt Bay 42 Gb 72.50N 111.00W
Wynyard [Austl.] 59 Jh 40.59S 145.41 E
Wynyard [Sask.-Can.] 42 Hf 51.47N 104.10W
Wyoming 44 Ed 42.54N 85.42W
Wyoming 43 Fc 43.00N 107.30W
Wyoming Peak 43 Ec 42.36N 110.37W
Wyśmierzyce 10 Qe 51.38N 20.49 E
Wysoka 10 Nc 53.11N 17.05 E
Wysokie Mazowieckie 10 Sd 52.56N 22.32 E
Wyszków 10 Rd 52.36N 21.28 E
Wyszogród 10 Qd 52.23N 20.11 E
Wytheville 44 Gg 36.57N 81.07W
Wyville Thomson Ridge (EN) 9 Fa 60.10N 8.00W
Wyvis, Ben- 9 Id 57.42N 4.30W

X

Xaintrie 11 Ii 45.00N 2.10 E
Xainza 27 Ee 30.50N 88.37 E
Xaitongmoin 27 Ef 29.26N 88.08 E
Xai-Xai 31 Kk 25.04S 33.39 E
Xamba→Hanggin Houqi 27 Ic 40.59N 107.07 E
Xam Nua 25 Kd 20.25N 104.02 E
Xangongo 31 Ij 16.46S 14.59 E
Xang Qu 27 Ef 29.22N 89.09 E
Xanten 10 Ce 51.40N 6.27 E
Xánthi 15 Hh 41.08N 24.53 E
Xanthos 24 Cd 36.20N 29.20 E
Xanxerê 56 Jc 26.53S 52.23W
Xapuri 54 Ef 10.39S 68.31W
Xar Hudag 27 Jb 45.06N 114.30 E
Xar Moron 28 Ac 42.37N 111.02 E
Xar Moron He 27 Lc 43.24N 120.39 E
Xarrama 13 Df 38.14N 8.20W
Xàtiva/Játiva 13 Lf 38.59N 0.31W
Xau, Lake- 37 Cd 21.15S 24.44 E
Xavantes, Represa de- 55 Hf 23.20S 49.35W
Xavantina 55 Fe 21.15S 52.48W
Xayar 27 Dc 41.15N 82.50 E
Xebert 28 Fc 44.00N 122.00 E
Xêgar → Tingri 27 Ef 28.41N 87.00 E
Xenia 44 Ff 39.41N 83.56W
Xiabin Ansha 27 Ke 9.48N 116.38 E
Xiachengzi 28 Kb 44.41N 130.26 E
Xiacun → Rushan 28 Ff 36.55N 121.30 E
Xiaguan 27 Hf 25.32N 100.12 E
Xiahe (Labrang) 27 Hd 35.18N 102.30 E
Xiajin 28 Cf 36.57N 116.00 E
Xiamen 22 Ng 24.32N 118.06 E
Xi'an 22 Mf 34.15N 108.50 E
Xianfeng 27 If 29.41N 109.09 E
Xiangcheng 28 Bh 33.51N 113.29 E
Xiangcheng/Qagchêng 27 Gf 28.56N 99.46 E
Xiangcheng (Shuizhai) 28 Ch 33.27N 114.53 E
Xiangfan 22 Nf 32.03N 112.05 E
Xianggang/Hong Kong 22 Ng 22.15N 114.10 E
Xianghua Ling 27 Jf 25.26N 112.32 E
Xianghuang Qi (Xin Bulag) 27 Jc 42.12N 113.59 E
Xiang Jiang 21 Ng 29.26N 113.08 E
Xiangkhoang 25 Ke 19.20N 103.22 E
Xiangkhoang, Plateau de- 25 Ke 19.30N 103.10 E
Xiangquan He 27 Ce 32.05N 79.20 E
Xiangshan (Dancheng) 27 Lf 29.29N 121.52 E
Xiangshan Gang 28 Fj 29.35N 121.38 E
Xiangtan 22 Ng 27.54N 112.55 E
Xiangtang 28 Cj 28.26N 115.59 E
Xiangyin 28 Bj 28.41N 112.53 E
Xiangyuan 28 Bf 36.32N 113.02 E
Xianju 27 Lf 28.50N 120.42 E
Xianning 28 Cj 29.52N 114.17 E
Xiannümiao→Jiangdu 28 Eh 32.30N 119.33 E
Xiantaozhen → Mianyang 28 Bi 30.22N 113.27 E
Xianxia Ling 28 Ej 28.24N 118.40 E
Xianxian 28 De 38.12N 116.07 E
Xianyang 27 Ie 34.26N 108.40 E
Xiaobole Shan 27 La 51.46N 124.09 E
Xiao'ergou 27 Lb 49.10N 123.43 E
Xiaogan 27 Je 30.52N 113.58 E
Xiao He 28 Bf 37.38N 112.24 E
Xiao Hinggan Ling=Lesser Khingan Range (EN) 21 Oe 48.45N 127.00 E
Xiaoling He 28 Fd 40.55N 121.12 E
Xiaoluan He 28 Dd 41.36N 117.05 E
Xiaoqing He 28 Ef 37.19N 118.59 E
Xiaowutai Shan 28 Ce 39.57N 114.59 E
Xiaoxian 28 Dg 34.11N 116.56 E
Xiaoyi 28 Af 37.07N 111.48 E
Xiaoyi → Gongxian 28 Bg 34.46N 112.57 E
Xiapu 27 Kf 26.57N 119.59 E
Xiawa 27 Kc 42.36N 120.33 E
Xiayi 28 Dg 34.14N 116.07 E
Xiazhuang → Linshu 28 Eg 34.56N 118.38 E
Xicalango, Punta- 48 Nh 19.41N 92.00W
Xichang 22 Mg 27.52N 102.15 E
Xicheng → Yangyuan 28 Cd 40.08N 114.10 E
Xicoténcatl 48 Jf 23.00N 98.56W
Xicotepec de Juárez 48 Kg 20.17N 97.57W
Xiejiaji → Qingyun 28 Df 37.46N 117.22 E
Xifei He 28 Dh 32.38N 116.39 E
Xifeng 28 Hc 42.45N 124.44 E
Xifengzhen 27 Id 35.40N 107.42 E
Xigazê 22 Kg 29.15N 88.52 E
Xi He [China] 27 Hc 42.23N 101.03 E
Xi He [China] 28 Dj 29.38N 116.53 E
Xiheying 28 Ce 39.53N 114.42 E
Xihua 28 Ch 33.48N 114.31 E
Xi Jiang 22 Ng 23.05N 114.23 E
Xiji [China] 27 Id 35.52N 105.35 E
Xiji [China] 28 Ia 46.09N 127.08 E
Xi Jiang 27 Jg 23.05N 114.23 E
Xijir Ulan Hu 27 Fd 35.12N 90.18 E
Xikouzi 27 La 42.58N 120.29 E
Xiligou → Ulan 27 Gd 36.55N 98.16 E
Xilin 27 Ig 24.30N 105.05 E
Xilin Gol 28 Dc 43.55N 116.05 E
Xilin Hot→Abagnar Qi 22 Ne 43.58N 116.08 E
Xilitla 48 Jg 21.20N 98.58W
Xilókastron 15 Fk 38.05N 22.38 E
Ximiao 27 Hc 41.04N 100.14 E
Xin'an 28 Bg 34.43N 112.09 E
Xin'anjiang 28 Ei 29.27N 119.15 E
Xin'anjiang Shuiku 27 Kf 29.25N 119.05 E
Xin'anzhen → Guannan 28 Eg 34.04N 119.21 E
Xin'anzhen → Xinyi 27 Ke 34.17N 118.14 E
Xin Barag Youqi (Altan-Emel) 27 Kb 48.41N 116.47 E
Xin Barag Zuoqi (Amgalang) 27 Kb 48.13N 118.14 E
Xinbin 28 Hd 41.44N 125.02 E
Xin Bulag→Xianghuang Qi 27 Jc 42.12N 113.59 E
Xincai 27 Je 32.40N 114.57 E
Xinchang 28 Fj 29.30N 120.54 E
Xincheng [China] 28 Bf 37.57N 112.33 E
Xincheng [China] 27 Ig 24.04N 108.39 E
Xincheng [China] 27 Id 38.33N 106.10 E
Xincheng (Gaobeidian) 28 Ce 39.20N 115.50 E
Xindi → Honghu 28 Bj 29.50N 113.28 E
Xing'an→Ankang 22 Mf 32.37N 109.03 E
Xingcheng 28 Fd 40.38N 120.43 E
Xingguo 27 Kf 26.22N 115.21 E
Xinghai 27 Gd 35.45N 99.59 E
Xinghe 27 Jc 40.52N 113.56 E
Xinghua 28 Eh 32.56N 119.49 E
Xingkai Hu=Khanka Lake (EN) 21 Pe 45.00N 132.24 E
Xinglong 28 Dd 40.25N 117.31 E
Xinglongzhen 28 Ia 46.26N 127.03 E
Xingren 27 If 25.26N 105.08 E
Xingtai 22 Nf 37.00N 114.30 E
Xingtang 28 Ce 38.26N 114.33 E
Xingu, Rio- 52 Kf 1.30S 51.53W
Xingxingxia 27 Gc 41.47N 95.07 E
Xingyang 28 Bg 34.47N 113.21 E
Xinryi (Huangcaoba) 27 Hf 25.03N 104.55 E
Xingzi 28 Dj 29.28N 116.03 E
Xinhe 28 Cf 37.32N 115.14 E
Xinhe/Toksu 27 Dc 41.34N 82.38 E
Xin Hot→Abag Qi 27 Jc 44.01N 114.59 E
Xinhuai He 28 Fg 34.23N 120.05 E
Xinhui → Aohan Qi 28 Ec 42.18N 119.53 E
Xining 22 Mf 36.37N 101.46 E
Xinji → Shulu 28 Cf 37.56N 115.14 E
Xinjian 28 Cj 28.41N 115.50 E
Xin Jiang 28 Dj 28.37N 116.40 E
Xinjiangkou → Songzi 28 Ai 30.10N 116.46 E
Xinjiang Uygur Zizhiqu (Hsin-chiang-wei-wu-erh Tzu-chih-ch'ü)=Sinkiang (EN) 27 Ec 42.00N 86.00 E
Xinjin 27 He 30.25N 103.46 E
Xinjin (Pulandian) 27 Ld 39.24N 121.59 E
Xinkai He 28 Gc 43.36N 122.31 E
Xinle 28 Ce 38.15N 114.40 E
Xinlin 28 Ec 43.58N 118.03 E
Xinlitun [China] 27 Ma 50.58N 126.39 E
Xinlitun [China] 28 Gc 42.01N 122.11 E
Xinlong/Nyagrong 27 He 30.57N 100.12 E
Xinmin 28 Gc 42.00N 122.50 E
Xinpu→Lianyungang 22 Nf 34.34N 119.15 E
Xinqing 27 Mb 48.15N 129.31 E
Xintai 28 Dg 35.54N 117.44 E
Xinwen (Suncun) 27 Kd 35.49N 117.38 E
Xinxian [China] 27 Jd 38.24N 112.43 E
Xinxian [China] 28 Ci 31.42N 114.50 E
Xinxiang 22 Nf 35.17N 113.50 E
Xinyang 27 Je 32.05N 114.07 E
Xinye 28 Bh 32.30N 112.22 E
Xinyi (Xin'anzhen) 27 Ke 34.17N 118.14 E
Xinyi He 28 Eg 34.29N 119.49 E
Xinyuan/Künes 27 Dc 43.24N 83.18 E
Xinyuan → Tianjun 22 Lf 37.18N 99.15 E
Xinzhan 28 Ic 43.52N 127.20 E
Xin Zhen→Hanggin Qi 27 Id 39.54N 108.55 E
Xinzheng 28 Bg 34.25N 113.46 E
Xinzhou 28 Ci 30.51N 114.49 E
Xioashan 28 Fi 30.10N 120.16 E
Xiong Xian 28 De 38.59N 116.06 E
Xionyuecheng 28 Gd 40.12N 122.08 E
Xiping [China] 28 Ej 28.27N 119.29 E
Xiping [China] 28 Bh 33.22N 114.00 E
Xisha Qundao=Paracel Islands (EN) 21 Nh 16.30N 112.15 E
Xishuangbanna 27 Gg 22.15N 100.00 E
Xishuanghe → Kenli 28 Ef 37.35N 118.30 E
Xishui 28 Ci 30.28N 115.15 E
Xitianmu Shan 27 Ke 30.21N 119.25 E
Xiuanzi → Chongli 28 Cd 40.57N 115.12 E
Xi Ujimqin Qi (Bayan Ul Hot) 27 Kc 44.31N 117.33 E
Xiuning 28 Ej 29.47N 118.11 E
Xiushan 27 If 28.29N 108.58 E
Xiu Shui 28 Cj 29.13N 116.00 E
Xiushui 27 Jf 29.02N 114.33 E
Xiuwu 28 Bg 35.13N 113.27 E
Xiuyan 27 Lc 40.18N 123.10 E
Xiwanzi→Chongli 28 Cf 36.50N 115.10 E
Xixabangma Feng 27 Ef 28.21N 85.47 E
Xixian 28 Ch 32.21N 114.43 E
Xixiang 27 Ie 32.58N 107.45 E
Xiyang 28 Bf 37.38N 113.41 E
Xizang Zizhiqu (Hsi-tsang Tzu-chih-ch'ü)=Tibet (EN) 27 Ee 32.00N 90.00 E
Xizhong Dao 28 Fe 39.25N 121.18 E
Xi Taijnar Hu 27 Fd 37.15N 93.30 E
Xochicalco 48 Jh 18.45N 99.20W
Xochimilco 48 Jh 19.16N 99.06W
Xorkol 27 Fd 39.04N 91.05 E
Xpujil 48 Oh 18.35N 89.25W
Xuancheng 28 Ei 30.56N 118.44 E
Xuande Qundao 26 Fc 17.08N 111.30 E
Xuan'en 27 Ie 30.02N 109.30 E
Xuanhan 27 Ie 31.23N 107.39 E
Xuanhua 27 Kc 40.39N 115.05 E
Xuanwei 27 Hf 26.19N 104.05 E
Xuchang 22 Nf 34.00N 113.58 E
Xuecheng (Lincheng) 28 Dg 34.38N 117.14 E
Xuefeng Shan 27 Jf 27.35N 110.50 E
Xue Shan 27 Gf 27.30N 99.55 E
Xugezhuang → Fengnan 28 Ee 39.34N 118.05 E
Xugou 28 Eg 34.37N 119.08 E
Xugui 27 Gd 35.45N 96.08 E
Xuguit Qi (Yakeshi) 27 Lb 49.16N 120.41 E
Xümatang 27 Ge 33.57N 97.00 E
Xun Jiang 23 Hf 23.28N 111.18 E
Xunke (Qike) 27 Mb 49.34N 128.28 E
Xunwu 27 Kg 24.59N 115.33 E
Xunxian 28 Cg 35.40N 114.33 E
Xupu 27 Jf 27.54N 110.35 E
Xúquer/Júcar 5 Fh 39.09N 0.14W
Xushui 28 Ce 39.02N 115.40 E
Xuwen 27 Jg 20.22N 110.10 E
Xuyi 27 Ke 32.58N 118.33 E
Xuyong (Yongning) 27 If 28.13N 105.26 E
Xuzhou 22 Nf 34.12N 117.13 E

Y

Ya'an 22 Mg 30.00N 102.57 E
Yabassi 34 Ge 4.28N 9.58 E
Yabe 29 Be 32.42N 130.59 E
Yabebyry 55 Dh 27.24S 57.11W
Yabelo 35 Fe 4.53N 38.07 E
Yablonovy Range (EN)=Jablonovy Hrebet 21 Nd 53.30N 115.00 E
Yabrai Shan 27 Hc 40.00N 103.10 E
Yabrīn 35 Ha 23.15N 48.59 E
Yabrūd 24 Gf 33.58N 36.40 E
Yabucoa 51a Cb 18.03N 65.53W
Yabuli 27 Mc 44.56N 128.37 E
Yabulu 59 Jc 19.00S 146.40 E
Yacaré Cururú, Cuchilla- 55 Dj 30.30S 56.33W
Yacaré Norte, Riacho- 55 Cf 22.43S 58.14W
Yacaré Sur, Riacho- 55 Cf 22.43S 58.14W
Yachats 46 Cd 44.20N 124.03W
Yacuma, Rio- 54 Ef 13.38S 65.23W
Yacyretá, Isla- 55 Dh 27.25S 56.30W
Yadé, Massif du- 35 Bd 7.00N 15.30 E
Yādgīr 25 Fe 16.46N 77.08 E
Yadong/Chomo 27 Ef 27.38N 89.03 E
Yae-Dake 29b Ab 26.38N 127.56 E
Yaeyama-Rettō 27 Lg 24.20N 124.00 E
Yafran 33 Bc 32.04N 12.31 E
Yağcilar 15 Lj 39.25N 28.23 E
Yagishiri-Tō 29a Ba 44.26N 141.25 E
Yagoua 34 Ic 10.20N 15.14 E
Yagradagzê Shan 27 Gd 35.09N 95.39 E
Yaguajay 49 Hb 22.19N 79.14W
Yaguari 55 Ej 31.31S 54.58W
Yaguari, Arroyo- 55 Di 29.44S 57.37W
Yahalica de Gonzáles Gallo 48 Hg 21.08N 102.51W
Yahuma 36 Db 1.06N 23.10 E
Yaita 29 Fc 36.50N 139.55 E
Yaizu 29 Fd 34.51N 138.19 E
Yajiang/Nyagquka 27 He 30.07N 100.58 E
Yakacik 24 Ed 36.05N 32.45 E
Yake-Dake 29 Ec 36.14N 137.35 E
Yakeishi-Dake 29 Gb 39.10N 140.50 E
Yakeshi → Xuguit Qi 27 Lb 49.16N 120.41 E
Yake-Yama 29 Gb 39.58N 140.48 E
Yakima 39 Ge 46.36N 120.31W
Yakima River 46 Fc 46.15N 119.02W
Yako 34 Ec 12.58N 2.16W
Yakumo 27 Pc 42.15N 140.16 E
Yaku-Shima 27 Ne 30.20N 130.30 E
Yakutat 40 Le 59.33N 139.44W
Yakutat Bay 40 Ke 59.45N 140.45W
Yala 25 Kg 6.32N 101.19 E
Yalahán, Laguna de- 48 Pg 21.30N 87.15W
Yalcubul, Punta- 48 Og 21.35N 88.35W
Yale Point 46 Kh 36.25N 109.48W
Yalewa Kalou 63d Ab 16.40S 177.46 E
Yalgoo 59 De 28.20S 116.41 E
Yalikavak 15 Kl 37.06N 27.18 E
Yaliköy 15 Lh 41.29N 28.17 E
Yalinga 35 Cd 6.31N 23.13 E
Yaloké 35 Bd 5.19N 17.05 E
Yalong Jiang 21 Mg 26.37N 101.48 E
Yalova 24 Cb 40.39N 29.15 E
Yalu Jiang 21 Of 39.55N 124.20 E
Yalvaç 24 Dc 38.17N 31.11 E
Yām, Ramlat- 33 If 17.42N 45.09 E
Yamada [Jap.] 28 Pe 39.28N 141.57 E
Yamada [Jap.] 29 Be 33.33N 130.45 E
Yamada-Wan 29 Hb 39.30N 142.00 E
Yamaga 29 Be 33.01N 130.41 E
Yamagata 27 Pd 38.15N 140.15 E
Yamagata Ken 28 Pe 38.30N 140.00 E
Yamagawa 29 Bf 31.12N 130.39 E
Yamaguchi 27 Ne 34.10N 131.29 E
Yamaguchi Ken 28 Kh 34.10N 131.30 E
Yamakuni 29 Be 33.24N 131.02 E
Yamal Peninsula (EN)=Jamal, Poluostrov- 21 Ib 70.00N 70.00 E
Yamamoto 29 Ga 40.06N 140.03 E
Yamanaka 29 Ec 36.15N 136.22 E
Yamanashi Ken 28 Og 35.30N 138.45 E
Yamashiro 29 Ce 33.57N 133.43 E
Yamato Rise (EN) 28 Me 39.30N 134.30 E
Yamatsuri 29 Gc 36.53N 140.25 E
Yamazaki 29 Dd 35.00N 134.33 E
Yambi, Mesa de- 54 Dc 1.30N 71.20W
Yambio 31 Jh 4.34N 28.23 E
Yambo 35 Fd 8.25N 36.00 E
Yambu Head 51n Ba 13.09N 61.09W
Yambuya 36 Db 1.16N 24.33 E
Yame 29 Be 33.13N 130.34 E
Yamethin 25 Jd 20.26N 96.09 E
Yamma Yamma, Lake- 59 Ie 26.20S 141.25 E
Yamoto 29 Gb 38.25N 141.13 E
Yamoussoukro 34 Dd 6.49N 5.17W
Yampa River 43 Fc 40.32N 108.59W
Yampi Sound 59 Ec 16.11S 123.40 E
Yamuna 21 Kg 25.30N 81.53 E
Yamunanagar 25 Fb 30.08N 76.59 E
Yamzho Yumco 27 Ff 29.00N 90.40 E
Yanagawa 29 Be 33.10N 130.24 E
Yanahara 29 Dd 34.57N 134.05 E
Yanahuanca 54 Cf 10.30S 76.30W
Yanai 29 Ce 33.58N 132.07 E
Yanam 25 Ge 16.51N 82.15 E
Yan'an 22 Mf 36.36N 109.30 E
Yanaoca 54 Df 14.13S 71.26W
Yanbian 27 Hf 26.51N 101.32 E
Yanbu' 23 Ee 24.05N 38.03 E
Yanchang 27 Jd 36.39N 110.03 E
Yancheng [China] 28 Bh 33.35N 114.00 E
Yancheng [China] 27 Le 33.16N 120.10 E
Yanchi 27 Id 37.47N 107.24 E
Yandé 63b Ae 20.03S 163.48 E
Yandina 63a Dc 9.07S 159.13 E
Yandja 36 Cc 1.41S 17.43 E

Index Symbols

Independent Nation; State, Region; District, County; Municipality; Colony, Dependency; Continent; Physical Region; Historical or Cultural Region; Mount, Mountain; Volcano; Hill; Mountains, Mountain Range; Hills, Escarpment; Plateau, Upland; Pass, Gap; Plain, Lowland; Delta; Salt Flat; Valley, Canyon; Crater, Cave; Karst Features; Depression; Polder; Desert, Dunes; Forest, Woods; Heath, Steppe; Oasis; Cape, Point; Coast, Beach; Cliff; Peninsula; Isthmus; Sandbank; Island; Atoll; Rock, Reef; Islands, Archipelago; Rocks, Reefs; Coral Reef; Well, Spring; Geyser; River, Stream; Waterfall Rapids; River Mouth, Estuary; Lake; Salt Lake; Intermittent Lake; Reservoir; Swamp, Pond; Canal; Glacier; Ice Shelf, Pack Ice; Ocean; Sea; Gulf, Bay; Strait, Fjord; Lagoon; Bank; Seamount; Tablemount; Ridge; Shelf; Basin; Escarpment, Sea Scarp; Fracture; Trench, Abyss; National Park, Reserve; Point of Interest; Recreation Site; Cave, Cavern; Historic Site; Ruins; Wall, Walls; Church, Abbey; Temple; Scientific Station; Airport; Port; Lighthouse; Mine; Tunnel; Dam, Bridge

Yandua 63d Bb 16.49S 178.18 E
Yanfolila 34 Dc 11.11N 8.08W
Yangalia 35 Cd 6.58N 21.01 E
Yangambi 31 Jh 0.47N 24.28 E
Yangcheng 28 Bg 35.32N 112.36 E
Yangchun 27 Jg 22.11N 111.48 E
Yangcun → Wuqing 28 De 39.23N 117.04 E
Yangdŏg-ŭp 28 Ie 39.13N 126.39 E
Yangganga 63d Bb 16.35S 178.35 E
Yanggang-Do [2] 28 Jd 41.15N 128.00 E
Yanggao 27 Jc 40.21N 113.47 E
Yanggeta 63d Ab 17.01S 177.20 E
Yanggu 28 Cf 36.08N 115.48 E
Yang He 28 Cd 40.24N 115.18 E
Yangi 15 Mm 36.55N 29.01 E
Yangjiang 27 Jg 21.59N 111.59 E
Yangjiazhangzi 28 Fd 40.48N 120.30 E
Yangon = Rangoon (EN) 22 Lh 16.47N 96.10 E
Yangor 64e Ab 0.32S 166.54 E
Yangqu (Huangzhai) 28 Be 38.05N 112.37 E
Yangquan 27 Jd 37.49N 113.34 E
Yangquanqu 27 Jd 37.04N 111.30 E
Yangshuo 27 Jg 24.46N 110.28 E
Yang Sin, Chu- 25 Lf 12.24N 108.26 E
Yangtze Kiang → Chang Jiang 21 Of 31.48N 121.10 E
Yangxian 27 Ie 33.20N 107.35 E
Yangxin [China] 28 Df 37.39N 117.34 E
Yangxin [China] 27 Kf 29.50N 115.11 E
Yangyuan (Xicheng) 28 Cd 40.08N 114.10 E
Yangzhou 27 Ke 32.20N 119.25 E
Yanhe (Heping) 27 If 28.31N 108.28 E
Yanji 27 Mc 42.56N 129.30 E
Yanjin 28 Cg 35.09N 114.11 E
Yankton 43 Hc 42.53N 97.23W
Yanling 28 Cg 34.07N 114.11 E
Yanqi 22 Ke 42.04N 86.34 E
Yanqing 28 Cd 40.28N 115.57 E
Yan Shan 21 Ne 40.18N 117.36 E
Yanshan [China] 28 De 38.03N 117.12 E
Yanshan [China] 27 Hg 23.38N 104.24 E
Yanshan (Hekou) 28 Dj 28.18N 117.41 E
Yanshi 28 Bg 34.44N 112.47 E
Yanshou 28 Jb 45.28N 128.19 E
Yantai 22 Of 37.28N 121.24 E
Yanutha 63d Ac 16.14S 178.00 E
Yanweigang 28 Eg 34.28N 119.46 E
Yanyuan 27 Hf 27.26N 101.32 E
Yanzhou 27 Kd 35.33N 116.49 E
Yao [Chad] 35 Bc 12.51N 17.34 E
Yao [Jap.] 29 Dd 34.38N 135.36 E
Yaodu → Dongzhi 28 Di 30.06N 117.01 E
Yaoundé 31 Ih 3.52N 11.31 E
Yapei 34 Ed 9.10N 1.10W
Yapen, Pulau- 57 Ee 1.45S 136.15 E
Yapen, Selat- 26 Kg 1.30S 136.10 E
Yapeyú 55 Di 29.28S 56.49W
Yap Islands 57 Ed 9.32N 138.08 E
Yapraklı 24 Eb 40.46N 33.47 E
Yapu 25 Jf 14.51N 98.03 E
Yaqian → Yuexi 28 Di 30.51N 116.22 E
Yaque del Norte, Rio- 49 Ld 19.51N 71.41W
Yaque del Sur, Rio- 49 Ld 18.17N 71.06W
Yaqueling 28 Ai 30.40N 111.36 E
Yaqui 38 Hg 27.37N 110.39W
Yaracuy [2] 54 Ea 10.20N 68.45W
Yaraka 58 Fg 24.53S 144.04 E
Yaralıgöz 24 Fb 41.45N 34.10 E
Yare 9 Oi 52.35N 1.44 E
Yaren 64e Ab 0.33S 166.54 E
Yari, Rio- 52 If 0.23S 72.16W
Yariga-Take 29 Ec 36.20N 137.39 E
Yarim 23 Fg 14.21N 44.22 E
Yaritagua 54 Ea 10.05N 69.08W
Yarkant/Shache 27 Cd 38.24N 77.15 E
Yarkant He 21 Ke 40.28N 80.52 E
Yarlung Zangbo Jiang 21 Lg 24.02N 90.59 E
Yarmouth [Eng.-U.K.] 12 Ad 50.41N 1.30W
Yarmouth [N.S.-Can.] 39 Me 43.50N 66.07W
Yarram 59 Jg 38.33S 146.41 E
Yarumal 54 Cb 6.58N 75.25W
Yasawa 63d Ab 16.47S 177.31 E
Yasawa Group 57 If 17.00S 177.23 E
Yashi 34 Gc 12.22N 7.55 E
Ya-Shima 29 Ce 33.45N 132.10 E
Yashima 29 Gb 39.09N 140.10 E
Yashiro-Jima 29 Ce 33.55N 132.15 E
Yasothon 25 Ke 15.46N 104.12 E
Yass 59 Jf 34.50S 148.55 E
Yassıören 15 Lh 41.18N 28.35 E
Yasugi 29 Cd 35.26N 133.15 E
Yāsūj 23 Hc 30.45N 51.33 E
Yasun Burnu 24 Gb 41.09N 37.41 E
Yatağan 24 Cd 37.20N 28.09 E
Yatate Tōge 29 Ga 40.26N 140.37 E
Yatate-Yama 29 Ad 34.12N 129.14 E
Yatenga 34 Ec 13.48N 2.10W
Yaté-Village 61 Cd 22.09S 166.57 E
Yathata 63d Cb 17.15S 179.32W
Yathkyed Lake 42 Hd 62.40N 98.00W
Yatolema 36 Db 0.21N 24.33 E
Yatou → Rongcheng 28 Gf 37.10N 122.25 E
Yatsu-ga-Take 29 Fd 35.59N 138.23 E
Yatsushiro 27 Ne 32.30N 130.36 E
Yatsushiro-Kai 29 Be 32.20N 130.25 E
Yatta Plateau 36 Gc 2.00S 38.00 E
Yauco 49 Nd 18.02N 66.51W
Yauri 54 Df 14.47S 71.29W
Yauyos 54 Cf 12.24S 75.57W
Yavari, Rio- 54 Dd 4.21S 70.02W
Yavi, Cerro- 54 Eb 5.32N 65.59W
Yaviza 49 Ii 8.11N 77.41W
Yawatahama 28 Lh 33.27N 132.24 E
Yaxchilán 47 Fe 16.54N 90.58W
Yaxian (Sanya) 22 Mh 18.27N 109.28 E
Yayalı 24 Fc 38.05N 35.25 E
Yayladağı 24 Ge 35.56N 36.01 E
Yazd 22 Hf 31.53N 54.25 E
Yazd [3] 23 Hc 31.30N 54.30 E
Yazoo City 45 Kj 32.51N 90.28W
Yazoo River 45 Kj 32.22N 91.00W
Ybbs 14 Jb 48.10N 15.06 E
Ybbs an der Donau 14 Jc 48.10N 15.05 E
Ydre 8 Fg 57.52N 15.15 E
Ydstebøhamn 8 Ae 59.03N 5.25 E
Ye 22 Lh 15.15N 97.51 E
Yebaishou → Jianping 27 Kc 41.55N 119.37 E
Yebbi Bou 35 Ba 20.58N 18.04 E
Yébigé 35 Ba 22.04N 17.49 E
Yecheng/Kargilik 22 Jf 37.54N 77.26 E
Yech'ŏn 28 Jf 36.39N 128.27 E
Yecla 13 Kf 38.37N 1.07W
Yécora 47 Cc 28.20N 108.58W
Yëd 35 Ge 4.48N 43.02 E
Yedi Burun 15 Mm 36.23N 29.05 E
Yedseram 34 Hc 12.16N 14.09 E
Yegros 55 Dh 26.24S 56.25W
Yeguas 13 Hf 38.02N 4.15W
Yeha 35 Fc 14.21N 39.05 E
Yei 35 Ee 4.05N 30.40 E
Yei 35 Ee 4.40N 30.30 E
Yeji [China] 28 Ci 31.51N 115.55 E
Yeji [Ghana] 34 Ed 8.13N 0.39W
Yekepa 34 Dd 7.35N 8.32W
Yelgu 35 Ec 10.01N 32.31 E
Yélimané 34 Cb 15.07N 10.36W
Yell 5 Fc 60.35N 1.05W
Yellice Dağı 15 Mj 39.23N 29.57 E
Yellowhead Pass 42 Ff 52.50N 117.55W
Yellowknife 42 Gd 62.23N 114.20W
Yellowknife 39 Hc 62.27N 114.21W
Yellow River (EN) = Huang He 21 Nf 37.32N 118.19 E
Yellow Sea (EN) = Huang-Hai 21 Of 36.00N 124.00 E
Yellow Sea (EN) = Hwang-Hae 21 Of 36.00N 124.00 E
Yellowstone 38 Ie 47.58N 103.59W
Yellowstone Lake 38 He 44.25N 110.22W
Yellowstone National Park 46 Jd 44.58N 110.42W
Yell Sound 9 La 60.33N 1.15W
Yeltes 13 Fd 40.56N 6.31W
Yelwa [Nig.] 34 Gd 8.51N 9.37 E
Yelwa [Nig.] 34 Fc 10.50N 4.44 E
Yemen (EN) = Al Yaman 22 Gh 15.00N 44.00 E
Yemen, People's Democratic Republic of- (EN) → Al Yaman 22 Gh 15.00N 44.00 E
Yenagoa 34 Ge 4.55N 6.16 E
Yenangyaung 25 Id 20.28N 94.53 E
Yen Bay 25 Kd 21.42N 104.52 E
Yendi 34 Ed 9.26N 0.01W
Yenge 36 Dc 0.55S 20.40 E
Yengisar 27 Cd 38.56N 76.09 E
Yengo 36 Cb 0.22N 15.29 E
Yeniboğaziçi 24 Ee 35.17N 33.52 E
Yenice [Tur.] 15 Kj 39.55N 27.18 E
Yenice [Tur.] 24 Fd 36.59N 35.03 E
Yeni Erenkoy 24 Fe 35.35N 34.15 E
Yenifoça 15 Jk 38.44N 26.51 E
Yenihisar 15 Kl 37.22N 27.15 E
Yenimahalle 24 Ec 39.56N 32.52 E
Yenipazar 15 Ll 37.48N 28.12 E
Yenişehir 24 Cb 40.16N 29.39 E
Yenisey (EN) = Jenisej 21 Kb 71.50N 82.40 E
Yenisey Bay (EN) = Jenisejski Zaliv 20 Db 72.00N 81.00 E
Yenisey Ridge (EN) = Jenisejski Krjaž 21 Ld 59.00N 92.30 E
Yennádhion 15 Km 36.01N 27.56 E
Yeo, Lake- 59 Ee 28.05S 124.25 E
Yeovil 9 Kk 50.57N 2.39W
Yepes 13 Ie 39.54N 3.38W
Yeppoon 59 Kd 23.08S 150.45 E
Yerákion 15 Fm 37.00N 22.42 E
Yerbabuena 48 Hf 23.00N 103.30W
Yerer 35 Gd 7.32N 42.05 E
Yerington 46 Fg 38.59N 119.10W
Yerkesik 15 Ll 37.07N 28.17 E
Yerköy 24 Fc 39.38N 34.29 E
Yerlisu 15 Ji 40.46N 26.39 E
Yermak Plateau (EN) 41 Mb 82.00N 6.00 E
Yeroham 24 Fg 31.00N 34.55 E
Yerres 11 If 48.43N 2.27 E
Yerupaja, Nevado- 52 Ig 10.16S 76.54W
Yerushalayim = Jerusalem (EN) 22 Ff 31.46N 35.14 E
Yerville 12 Ce 49.40N 0.54 E
Yerwa 34 Hc 11.13N 12.53 E
Yesa, Embalse de- 13 Kb 42.36N 1.09W
Yesan 28 If 36.41N 126.51 E
Yeşilhisar 24 Fc 38.21N 35.06 E
Yeşilırmak 23 Ea 41.24N 36.35 E
Yeşilköy 24 Cb 40.57N 29.49 E
Yeşilova 15 Ml 37.30N 29.46 E
Yeşilyurt 15 Ll 37.11N 28.17 E
Yeso 55 Cj 30.56S 59.28W
Yeste 13 Jf 38.22N 2.18W
Yetti 30 Gf 26.10N 7.50W
Ye-u 25 Jd 22.46N 95.26 E
Yeu, Ile d'- 11 Dh 46.43N 2.20W
Yexian [China] 28 Ef 37.11N 119.58 E
Yexian [China] 28 Bh 33.38N 113.21 E
Yguazú, Rio- 55 Eg 25.20S 55.00W
Yhú 55 Eg 24.59S 55.59W
Yi, Rio- 55 Dk 33.07S 57.08W
Yiali 15 Km 36.40N 27.05 E
Yi'an 27 Mb 47.53N 125.17 E
Yiannitsá 15 Fi 40.48N 22.25 E
Yiaros 15 Hl 37.37N 24.43 E
Yibin 22 Mg 28.47N 104.35 E
Yibug Caka 27 Ee 33.55N 87.05 E
Yichang 22 Nf 30.42N 111.22 E
Yicheng [China] 28 Ag 35.44N 111.43 E
Yicheng [China] 28 Bi 31.42N 112.16 E
Yichuan 27 Jd 36.00N 110.06 E
Yichun [China] 27 Jf 27.47N 114.25 E
Yichun [China] 27 Mb 47.41N 128.55 E
Yıdızeli 24 Gc 39.52N 36.38 E
Yidu [China] 27 Je 30.23N 111.28 E
Yidu [China] 27 Kd 36.41N 118.29 E
Yidun (Dagxoi) 27 Ge 30.25N 99.28 E
Yifag 35 Fc 12.02N 37.41 E
Yifeng 28 Cj 28.25N 114.47 E
Yığılca 24 Db 40.58N 31.27 E
Yigo 64c Ba 13.32N 144.53W
Yi He [China] 28 Eg 34.07N 118.15 E
Yi He [China] 28 Bg 34.41N 112.33 E
Yilan 27 Mb 46.18N 129.33 E
Yıldız Dağı 23 Ea 40.08N 36.56 E
Yıldız Dağları 24 Bb 41.50N 27.10 E
Yiliang 27 Hg 24.59N 103.08 E
Yimianpo 28 Jb 45.04N 128.03 E
Yimin He 27 Kb 49.15N 119.42 E
Yinan (Jiehu) 28 Eg 35.33N 118.27 E
Yinchuan 22 Mf 38.28N 106.19 E
Yindarlgooda, Lake- 59 Ef 30.45S 121.55 E
Yingcheng [China] 28 Hb 44.08N 125.54 E
Yingcheng [China] 28 Bi 30.57N 113.33 E
Yingde 27 Jg 24.13N 113.24 E
Ying He 27 Ke 32.30N 116.31 E
Yingjiang 27 Gg 24.45N 97.58 E
Yingjin He 28 Ec 42.20N 119.19 E
Yingkou 22 Oe 40.40N 122.12 E
Yingkou (Dashiqiao) 28 Gd 40.39N 122.31 E
Yingshan 28 Ci 30.45N 115.40 E
Yingshang 28 Dh 32.38N 116.16 E
Yingshouyingzi 28 Dd 40.33N 117.37 E
Yingtan 28 Dj 28.13N 117.00 E
Yingxian 28 Be 39.33N 113.10 E
Ying zhan/Victoria 22 Ng 22.17N 114.09 E
Yining/Gulja 27 Dc 43.54N 81.21 E
Yinma He 28 Hb 44.50N 125.45 E
Yinqing Qunjiao 26 Fe 8.55N 112.35 E
Yin Shan 21 Me 41.30N 109.00 E
Yi'ong Zangbo 27 Gf 29.56N 95.10 E
Yioúra 15 Hj 39.24N 24.10 E
Yipinglang 27 Hf 25.13N 101.55 E
Yiquan → Meitan 27 If 27.48N 107.32 E
Yirga Alem 35 Fd 6.44N 38.24 E
Yirol 35 Ed 6.33N 30.30 E
Yirshi 27 Kb 47.17N 119.55 E
Yishui 28 Eg 35.47N 118.38 E
Yisra'el = Israel (EN) [1] 22 Ff 31.30N 35.00 E
Yithion 15 Fm 36.45N 22.34 E
Yitong 28 Hc 43.20N 125.17 E
Yitong He 28 Hb 44.45N 125.40 E
Yitulihe 27 La 50.41N 121.33 E
Yiwu 28 Fj 29.19N 120.04 E
Yiwu/Aratürük 27 Fc 43.15N 94.35 E
Yixian [China] 28 Ce 39.21N 115.30 E
Yixian [China] 28 Dj 29.56N 117.56 E
Yixian [China] 28 Fd 41.33N 121.14 E
Yixing 28 Ei 31.21N 119.48 E
Yixun He 28 Dd 41.00N 117.41 E
Yiyang [China] 27 Jf 28.41N 112.20 E
Yiyang [China] 28 Dj 28.24N 117.24 E
Yiyang [China] 28 Bg 34.30N 112.10 E
Yiyuan (Nanma) 28 Ef 36.11N 118.10 E
Yizheng 28 Eh 32.16N 119.10 E
Yläne 8 Jd 60.53N 22.25 E
Ylikitka 7 Gc 66.08N 28.30 E
Yli-Li 7 Fd 65.22N 25.50 E
Ylimarkku/Övermark 8 Ib 62.37N 21.28 E
Ylistaro 7 Fe 62.57N 22.31 E
Ylitornio 7 Fc 66.18N 23.40 E
Ylivieska 7 Fd 64.05N 24.33 E
Ylöjärvi 8 Jc 61.33N 23.36 E
Ymers 41 Jd 73.20N 25.00W
Yngaren 8 Gf 58.50N 16.35 E
Yngen 8 Fe 59.45N 14.20 E
Ynykčanski 20 Id 60.08N 137.47 E
Yoboki 35 Gc 11.28N 42.06 E
Yobuko 29 Ae 33.33N 129.54 E
Yodo-Gawa 29 Dd 34.41N 135.25 E
Yogan, Cerro- 52 Jk 54.38S 69.29W
Yogoum 35 Bb 17.27N 19.31 E
Yoğuntaş 15 Kh 41.50N 27.04 E
Yogyakarta 22 Nj 7.48S 110.22 E
Yoichi 28 Pc 43.12N 140.41 E
Yojoa, Lago de- 49 Df 14.50N 88.00W
Yōju 28 If 37.18N 127.38 E
Yokadouma 31 Ih 3.31N 15.03 E
Yōkaichi 29 Ed 35.07N 136.11 E
Yōkaichiba 29 Gd 35.40N 140.28 E
Yokkaichi 28 Ng 34.58N 136.37 E
Yoko 34 Hd 5.32N 12.19 E
Yokoate-Jima 27 Mf 28.50N 129.00 E
Yokohama 22 Pf 35.27N 139.39 E
Yokosuka 28 Og 35.18N 139.40 E
Yokote 27 Pd 39.18N 140.34 E
Yola 31 Ih 9.12N 12.29 E
Yolania, Serranías de- 49 Fh 11.40N 84.20W
Yolombo 36 Dc 1.32S 23.15 E
Yom 25 Ke 15.52N 100.16 E
Yŏmju 28 He 39.50N 124.33 E
Yomou 34 Dd 7.34N 9.16W
Yomra 24 Hb 40.58N 39.54 E
Yon 11 Eh 46.30N 1.18W
Yona 64c Bb 13.25N 144.47 E
Yonago 28 Lg 35.26N 133.20 E
Yonaguni-Jima 27 Lg 24.25N 123.00 E
Yonaha-Dake 29b Ab 26.43N 128.13 E
Yonan 28 If 37.55N 126.05 E
Yoneshiro-Gawa 29 Ga 40.13N 140.00 E
Yonezawa 27 Pd 37.55N 140.07 E
Yong 34 He 4.54N 13.12 E
Yŏngan 27 Mc 41.15N 129.30 E
Yong'an 27 Kf 25.58N 117.29 E
Yongchang 27 Hd 38.17N 102.07 E
Yongcheng 28 Dh 33.56N 116.21 E
Yongch'on 28 Jg 35.59N 127.59 E
Yongchuan 27 If 29.22N 105.59 E
Yongch'u-gap 28 Jf 37.03N 129.26 E
Yongdeng 27 Hd 36.44N 103.24 E
Yongding He 27 Kd 39.20N 117.04 E
Yŏngdŏk 28 Jf 36.24N 129.22 E
Yŏngdong 28 If 36.10N 127.47 E
Yonghung 28 Ie 39.33N 127.14 E
Yongji (Kouqian) 28 Ic 43.40N 126.30 E
Yongjing 27 Hd 36.00N 103.17 E
Yŏngju 27 Md 36.49N 128.37 E
Yongkang 27 Lf 28.51N 120.05 E
Yongle Qundao 26 Fc 16.35N 111.40 E
Yongnian (Linmingguan) 28 Cf 36.47N 114.30 E
Yongning → Xuyong 27 If 28.13N 105.26 E
Yongqing 28 De 39.19N 116.29 E
Yŏngsanp'o 28 Ig 35.00N 126.43 E
Yongsheng 27 Hf 26.41N 100.45 E
Yongshu Jiao 26 Fe 9.35N 112.50 E
Yŏngwŏl 28 Jf 37.11N 128.28 E
Yongxiu (Tujiabu) 27 Kf 29.05N 115.49 E
Yonibana 34 Cd 8.26N 12.14W
Yonkers 44 Ke 40.56N 73.54W
Yonne [3] 11 Jg 47.55N 3.45 E
Yonne 11 If 48.23N 2.58 E
Yopal 54 Db 5.21N 72.23W
Yopurga 27 Cd 39.15N 76.45 E
York 9 Lg 54.10N 1.30W
York [Al.-U.S.] 44 Ci 32.29N 88.18W
York [Austl.] 59 Df 31.53S 116.46 E
York [Eng.-U.K.] 9 Lh 53.58N 1.05W
York [Nb.-U.S.] 45 Hf 40.52N 97.36W
York [Pa.-U.S.] 43 Ld 39.57N 76.44W
York, Cape- 57 Ff 10.40S 142.30 E
York, Kap- 67 Od 76.05N 67.05W
York, Vale of- 9 Lg 54.10N 1.20W
Yorke Peninsula 59 Hf 35.00S 137.30 E
Yorkshire Dales 9 Kg 54.15N 2.10W
Yorkshire Wolds 9 Mh 54.00N 0.40W
York Sound 59 Fb 14.50S 125.05 E
Yorkton 39 Id 51.13N 102.28W
Yorktown 44 Ig 37.14N 76.32W
Yoro [3] 49 Df 15.15N 87.15W
Yoro 49 Df 15.09N 87.07W
Yoron-Jima 29b Bb 27.03N 128.26 E
Yoro-Shima 29b Ba 28.02N 129.10 E
Yorosso 34 Ec 12.21N 4.47W
Yorubaland Plateau 34 Fd 8.00N 4.30 E
Yörük 15 Ki 40.56N 27.04 E
Yosemite National Park 43 Dd 35.28N 119.33W
Yosemite Rock 52 Hi 31.58S 83.15W
Yoshida [Jap.] 29 Ce 33.16N 132.32 E
Yoshida [Jap.] 29 Cd 34.40N 132.42 E
Yoshii 29 Ae 33.18N 129.40 E
Yoshii-Gawa 29 Dd 34.36N 134.02 E
Yoshino-Gawa 29 Dd 34.05N 134.36 E
Yŏsu 27 Me 34.44N 127.44 E
Yotaú 54 Fg 16.03S 63.03W
Yōtei-Zan 29a Bb 42.49N 140.47 E
Yotvata 24 Fh 29.53N 35.03 E
Youghal/Eochaill 9 Fj 51.57N 7.50W
Youghal Harbour/Cuan Eochaille 9 Fj 51.52N 7.50W
You Jiang 21 Mg 22.50N 108.06 E
Youllemmedene 30 Hg 16.00N 1.00 E
Young [Austl.] 59 Jf 34.19S 148.18 E
Young [Ur.] 55 Dk 32.41S 57.38W
Young, Cape- 62 Je 43.42S 176.37W
Younghusband Peninsula 59 Hg 36.00S 139.30 E
Young Island 66 Ke 66.25S 162.30 E
Young's Island 51n Ba 13.08N 61.13W
Youngs Rock 64q Ab 25.03S 130.06W
Youngstown 43 Kc 41.05N 80.40W
Youshashan 27 Fd 38.04N 90.53 E
Youssoufia 32 Fc 32.15N 8.32W
Youyang 27 If 28.49N 108.45 E
Yozgat 23 Db 39.50N 34.48 E
Ypacarai 56 Ic 25.23S 57.16W
Ypacarai, Laguna- 55 Dg 25.17S 57.20W
Ypané, Rio- 55 Df 23.29S 57.19W
Ypé Jhú 55 Ef 23.54S 55.20W
Ypoá, Lago- 55 Dg 25.48S 57.28W
Yport 12 Ce 49.44N 0.19 E
Ypres/Ieper 11 Id 50.51N 2.53 E
Yreka 43 Cc 41.44N 122.43W
Yser 11 Ic 51.09N 2.43 E
Yssingeaux 11 Ki 45.08N 4.07 E
Ystad 7 Ci 55.25N 13.49 E
Ytambey, Rio- 55 Eg 24.46S 54.24W
Ythan 9 Ld 57.25N 2.00W
Ytre Arna 8 Ad 60.28N 5.26 E
Ytre Sula 8 Ac 61.05N 4.40 E
Ytterhogdal 8 Fb 62.11N 14.56 E
Ytterlännäs 7 De 63.01N 17.41 E
Yttermalung 8 Ed 60.35N 13.50 E
Ytyk-Kjuël 20 Id 62.28N 133.25 E
Yu 'Alliq, Jabal- 24 Eg 30.22N 33.31 E
Yuan'an 28 Ai 31.04N 111.39 E
Yuanbaoshan 28 Ec 42.19N 119.19 E
Yuanbao Shan 27 If 25.24N 109.11 E
Yuan Jiang [Asia] = Red River (EN) 21 Mg 20.17N 106.34 E
Yuanjiang [China] 28 Bj 28.50N 112.23 E
Yuanjiang [China] 27 Hg 23.22N 102.26 E
Yuan Jiang [China] 21 Ng 28.58N 111.49 E
Yuanling 27 Jf 28.30N 110.25 E
Yuanmou 27 Hf 25.45N 101.54 E
Yuanping 27 Jd 38.43N 112.42 E
Yuanqu (Liuzhangzhen)) 27 Jd 35.19N 111.44 E
Yuanshi 28 Cf 37.45N 114.30 E
Yuba City 43 Cd 39.08N 121.37W
Yūbari 27 Pc 43.04N 141.59 E
Yūbari-Dake 29a Cb 43.06N 142.15 E
Yūbari-Gawa 29a Bb 43.08N 141.35 E
Yūbari-Sanchi 29a Cb 43.10N 142.15 E
Yuba River 46 Eg 39.07N 121.36W
Yubdo 35 Fd 8.58N 35.27 E
Yūbetsu 28 Qb 43.13N 144.05 E
Yūbetsu-Gawa 29a Ca 44.14N 143.37 E
Yucatán [2] 47 Gd 20.50N 89.00W
Yucatán, Canal de- = Yucatan Channel (EN) 38 Kg 21.45N 85.45W
Yucatán, Peninsula de- = Yucatan Peninsula (EN) 38 Kh 19.30N 89.00W
Yucatan Basin (EN) 47 Ge 20.00N 84.00W
Yucatan Channel (EN) = Yucatán, Canal de- 38 Kg 21.45N 85.45W
Yucatan Peninsula (EN) = Yucatán, Peninsula de- 38 Kh 19.30N 89.00W
Yucheng 28 Df 36.56N 116.39 E
Yuci 27 Jd 37.41N 112.49 E
Yucuyácua, Cerro- 47 Ee 17.07N 97.40W
Yuda 29 Gb 39.19N 140.48 E
Yudi Shan 27 Lb 52.17N 121.52 E
Yueliang Pao 28 Gb 45.44N 123.55 E
Yueqing 27 Lf 28.08N 120.58 E
Yuexi 27 Hf 28.37N 102.36 E
Yuexi (Yaqian) 28 Di 30.51N 116.22 E
Yueyang 27 Jf 29.18N 113.12 E
Yufu-Dake 29 Be 33.17N 131.23 E
Yugan 27 Kf 28.42N 116.39 E
Yugoslavia (EN) = Jugoslavija [1] 6 Hg 44.00N 19.00 E
Yu He 28 Be 39.51N 113.26 E
Yuhuang Ding 28 Df 36.20N 117.01 E
Yuki [Jap.] 29 Cd 34.29N 132.16 E
Yuki [Zaire] 36 Cc 3.55S 19.25 E
Yukon 45 Hi 35.31N 97.44W
Yukon 38 Cc 62.33N 163.59W
Yukon Flats 40 Jc 66.35N 146.00W
Yukon Plateau 38 Fc 61.30N 135.40W
Yukon Territory [3] 42 Dd 63.00N 136.00W
Yüksekova 24 Kd 37.19N 44.10 E
Yukuhashi 29 Be 33.44N 130.58 E
Yule River 59 Dd 20.41S 118.17 E
Yuli/lopnur 27 Ec 41.22N 86.09 E
Yulin [China] 22 Ng 22.39N 110.08 E
Yulin [China] 22 Mf 38.14N 109.48 E
Yuling Guan 27 Ke 30.04N 118.53 E
Yulin Jiao 21 Mh 17.50N 109.30 E
Yulongxue Shan 27 Hf 27.09N 100.12 E
Yuma [Az.-U.S.] 39 Hf 32.43N 114.37W
Yuma [Co.-U.S.] 45 Ef 40.08N 102.43W
Yuma, Bahia de- 49 Md 18.21N 68.35W
Yumare 50 Bg 10.37N 68.41W
Yumari, Cerro- 54 Ec 4.27N 66.50W
Yumbe 36 Fb 3.28N 31.15 E
Yumbi [Zaire] 36 Ec 1.14S 26.14 E
Yumbi [Zaire] 36 Cc 1.53S 16.32 E
Yumen (Laojunmiao) 22 Lf 39.50N 97.44 E
Yumenkou 27 Jd 35.42N 110.37 E
Yumenzhen 27 Gc 40.17N 97.12 E
Yumin 27 Db 45.59N 82.28 E
Yumurtalik 24 Fd 36.49N 35.45 E
Yuna, Rio- 49 Md 19.12N 69.37W
Yunak 24 Dc 38.49N 31.45 E
Yunaska 40a Db 52.40N 170.50W
Yuncheng [China] 27 Jd 35.02N 111.00 E
Yuncheng [China] 28 Cg 35.35N 115.56 E
Yungas 52 Jg 16.20S 66.45W
Yungay 56 Fe 37.07S 72.01W
Yungui Gaoyuan 21 Mg 26.00N 105.00 E
Yunhe → Peixian 28 Dg 34.44N 116.56 E
Yuni 29a Bb 42.59N 141.46 E
Yunjinghong → Jinghong 27 Hg 21.59N 100.48 E
Yunkai Dashan 27 Jg 22.30N 111.00 E
Yunlin 27 Lg 23.43N 120.33 E
Yun Ling 27 Gf 27.00N 99.30 E
Yunmeng 28 Bi 31.01N 113.45 E
Yunnan Sheng (Yün-nan Sheng) [2] 27 Hg 25.00N 102.00 E
Yün-nan Sheng → Yunnan Sheng [2] 27 Hg 25.00N 102.00 E
Yunomae 29 Be 32.15N 130.57 E
Yunotsu 29 Cd 35.05N 132.21 E
Yun Shui 28 Bi 30.43N 113.57 E
Yunxian 27 Je 32.50N 110.50 E
Yunxiao 27 Kg 24.05N 117.18 E
Yunyang 27 Ie 31.00N 108.55 E
Yunzhong Shan 27 Jd 38.50N 112.27 E
Yuquan 28 Ib 45.27N 127.08 E
Yuqueri 55 Ci 28.53S 58.02W
Yura 54 Dg 16.12S 71.42W
Yura-Gawa 29 Dd 35.31N 135.17 E
Yurimaguas 53 If 5.54S 76.05W
Yuriria 48 Ig 20.12N 101.09W
Yuruari, Rio- 50 Fi 6.44N 61.40W
Yurungkax He 27 Dd 38.05N 80.20 E
Yuscarán 49 Dg 13.55N 86.51W
Yushan 21 Og 23.30N 121.00 E
Yu Shan 27 Kf 27.00N 116.00 E
Yushan 28 Ej 28.41N 118.15 E
Yushe 28 Bf 37.04N 112.58 E
Yushu 28 Ib 44.50N 126.33 E
Yushutun 27 Lb 47.06N 123.41 E
Yūsuf, Bahr- 24 Dh 29.19N 30.50 E
Yusufeli 24 Ib 40.50N 41.33 E
Yutai (Guting) 28 Dg 35.00N 116.40 E
Yutian 28 De 39.53N 117.45 E
Yutian/Keriya 22 Kf 36.52N 81.42 E
Yuty 56 Ic 26.32S 56.18W
Yutz 12 Ie 49.21N 6.11 E
Yuwan-Dake 29b Ba 28.18N 129.19 E
Yuxi 27 Hg 24.27N 102.34 E
Yuxian [China] 27 Jd 39.49N 114.35 E
Yuxian [China] 27 Jd 38.03N 113.28 E
Yuxian [China] 28 Bg 34.09N 113.29 E
Yuxikou 28 Ei 31.26N 118.18 E
Yuyao 28 Fi 30.04N 121.10 E
Yuya-Wan 29 Bd 34.20N 130.55 E
Yuza 29 Fb 39.01N 139.53 E
Yuzawa [Jap.] 28 Pe 39.10N 140.30 E

Index Symbols

[1] Independent Nation
[2] State, Region
[3] District, County
Municipality
Colony, Dependency
Continent
Physical Region
Historical or Cultural Region
Mount, Mountain
Volcano
Hill
Mountains, Mountain Range
Hills, Escarpment
Plateau, Upland
Pass, Gap
Plain, Lowland
Delta
Salt Flat
Valley, Canyon
Crater, Cave
Karst Features
Depression
Polder
Desert, Dunes
Forest, Woods
Heath, Steppe
Oasis
Cape, Point
Coast, Beach
Cliff
Peninsula
Isthmus
Sandbank
Island
Atoll
Rock, Reef
Islands, Archipelago
Rocks, Reefs
Coral Reef
Well, Spring
Geyser
River, Stream
Waterfall Rapids
River Mouth, Estuary
Lake
Salt Lake
Intermittent Lake
Reservoir
Swamp, Pond
Canal
Glacier
Ice Shelf, Pack Ice
Ocean
Sea
Gulf, Bay
Strait, Fjord
Lagoon
Bank
Seamount
Tablemount
Ridge
Shelf
Basin
Escarpment, Sea Scarp
Fracture
Trench, Abyss
National Park, Reserve
Point of Interest
Recreation Site
Cave, Cavern
Historic Site
Ruins
Wall, Walls
Church, Abbey
Temple
Scientific Station
Airport
Port
Lighthouse
Mine
Tunnel
Dam, Bridge

Yuzawa [Jap.] 29 Fc 36.56N 138.47 E
Yuzhou → Chongqing = Chungking (EN) 22 Mg 29.34N 106.27 E
Yvel 11 Dg 47.59N 2.23W
Yvelines [3] 11 Hf 48.50N 1.50 E
Yverdon 14 Ad 46.46N 6.40 E
Yvetot 11 Ge 49.37N 0.46 E
Yvette 12 Ef 48.40N 2.20 E
Yxlan 8 He 59.40N 18.50 E
Yxningen 8 Gf 58.15N 16.20 E

Z

Zaajatskaja 17 Jj 52.53N 61.35 E
Zaalajski Hrebet 18 Ie 39.25N 72.50 E
Zaanstad 11 Kb 52.26N 4.49 E
Žabaj 17 Nj 51.42N 68.22 E
Zabajkalsk 20 Gg 49.40N 117.21 E
Zabarjad 33 Ge 23.37N 36.12 E
Zāb-e Kūchek 24 Ke 36.00N 45.15 E
Zabīb, Ra's az- 14 Em 37.16N 10.04 E
Zabīd 23 Fg 14.12N 43.18 E
Zabīd, Wādī- 23 Fg 14.07N 43.06 E
Žabinka 16 Dc 52.13N 24.01 E
Ząbkowice Śląskie 10 Mf 50.36N 16.53 E
Žabljak 15 Cf 43.09N 19.08 E
Zabłudów 10 Tc 53.01N 23.20 E
Zabok 14 Jd 46.02N 15.55 E
Zābol [3] 23 Kc 32.00N 67.15 E
Zabolotje [Bye.-U.S.S.R.] 8 Kk 53.56N 24.46 E
Zabolotje [Ukr.-U.S.S.R.] 10 Ue 51.37N 24.26 E
Zabolotov 15 Ia 48.25N 25.23 E
Zabré 34 Ec 11.10N 0.38W
Zábřeh 10 Mg 49.53N 16.52 E
Zabrze 10 Of 50.18N 18.46 E
Zacapa [3] 49 Cf 15.00N 89.30W
Zacapa 47 Gf 14.58N 89.32W
Zacapu 48 Ih 19.50N 101.43W
Zacatecas 39 Ig 22.47N 102.35W
Zacatecas [2] 47 Dd 23.00N 103.00W
Zacatecoluca 49 Cg 13.30N 88.52W
Zacatepec 48 Jh 18.39N 99.12W
Zacatlán 48 Kh 19.56N 97.58W
Zaccar, Djebel- 13 Oh 36.20N 2.13 E
Zacoalco de Torres 48 Hg 20.14N 103.35W
Zacualtipán 48 Jg 20.39N 98.36W
Zaculeu 49 Bf 15.21N 91.29W
Zadar 6 Hg 44.07N 15.15 E
Zadarski Kanal 14 Jf 44.10N 15.10 E
Zadetkyi Kyun 25 Jg 9.58N 98.13 E
Zadi 36 Bc 4.46S 14.52 E
Zadoi 27 Fe 33.10N 94.58 E
Zadonsk 16 Kc 52.23N 38.58 E
Za'farānah 33 Fd 29.07N 32.33 E
Zafferano, Capo- 14 Hl 38.07N 13.32 E
Ẓafir 23 He 23.07N 53.46 E
Zafra 13 Ff 38.25N 6.25W
Żagań 10 Le 51.37N 15.19 E
Zagare/Žagarė 8 Jh 56.19N 23.14 E
Žagarė/Zagare 8 Jh 56.19N 23.14 E
Zāgheh 24 Mf 33.30N 48.42 E
Zāgh Marz 24 Od 36.47N 53.17 E
Zaghrah, Wādī- 24 Fh 28.40N 34.20 E
Zaghwān 32 Jb 36.24N 10.09 E
Zaghwān [3] 32 Jb 36.25N 10.10 E
Zaghwān, Jabal- 14 En 36.21N 10.07 E
Zagora 31 Ge 30.19N 5.50W
Zagora 14 Kg 43.40N 16.15 E
Zagória 15 Dj 39.45N 20.50 E
Zagorje 14 Jd 46.05N 16.00 E
Zagorodje 10 Vd 52.15N 25.30 E
Zagórów 10 Nd 52.11N 17.55 E
Zagorsk 6 Jd 56.18N 38.08 E
Zagórz, Sanok- 10 Sg 49.31N 22.17 E
Zagreb 6 Hf 45.48N 16.00 E
Zāgros, Kūhhā-ye- = Zagros Mountains (EN) 21 Gf 33.40N 47.00 E
Zagros Mountains (EN) = Zāgros, Kūhhā-ye- 21 Gf 33.40N 47.00 E
Žagubica 15 Ee 44.12N 21.48 E
Za'gya Zangbo 27 Ee 31.55N 88.58 E
Zagyva 10 Qi 47.10N 20.12 E
Zāhedān 22 Ig 29.30N 60.52 E
Zahlah 24 Ff 33.51N 35.53 E
Zahmet 19 Gh 37.48N 62.29 E
Ẓahrān 33 Hf 17.40N 43.30 E
Zahrez Chergui 13 Pi 35.14N 3.32 E
Zailijski Alatau, Hrebet- 18 Kc 43.00N 77.00 E
Žailma 19 Ge 51.32N 61.40 E
Zaire 30 Ii 6.04S 12.24 E
Zaire 30 Ii 6.04S 12.24 E
Zaire [3] 36 Bd 6.30S 13.30 E
Zaire (Congo, Dem. Rep. of the-) [1] 31 Ji 1.00S 25.00 E
Zaisan, Lake- (EN) = Zajsan, Ozero- 21 Ke 48.10N 83.50 E
Zaj 7 Mi 55.36N 51.40 E
Zaječar 15 Ff 43.54N 22.17 E
Zajsan 22 Ke 47.30N 84.55 E
Zajsan, Ozero- = Zaisan, Lake- (EN) 21 Ke 48.10N 83.50 E
Zak 30 Jk 29.39S 21.11 E
Zaka 37 Ed 20.20S 31.29 E
Zakamensk 20 Ff 50.23N 103.20 E
Zakarpatskaja Oblast [3] 19 Cf 48.20N 23.20 E
Zakataly 19 Eg 41.38N 46.37 E
Zakháro 15 El 37.29N 21.39 E
Zākhū 23 Fb 37.08N 42.41 E
Zákinthos 15 Dl 37.47N 20.54 E
Zákinthos = Zante (EN) 5 Ih 37.47N 20.47 E
Zákinthou Dhíavlos- 15 Dl 37.50N 21.00 E
Zakopane 10 Pg 49.19N 19.57 E
Zakouma 35 Bc 10.54N 19.49 E
Žaksy 19 Ge 51.53N 67.20 E
Zala [2] 10 Mj 46.40N 16.50 E
Zala 10 Nj 46.43N 17.16 E
Zālābiyah 24 He 35.39N 39.51 E
Zalaegerszeg 10 Mj 46.50N 16.51 E
Zalāf 24 Gf 32.55N 37.20 E
Zalalövő 10 Mj 46.51N 16.36 E
Zalamea de la Serena 13 Gf 38.39N 5.39W
Zalamea la Real 13 Fg 37.41N 6.39W
Zalantum → Butha Qi 27 Lb 48.02N 122.42 E
Zalari 20 Ff 53.36N 102.32 E
Zalaszentgrót 10 Nj 46.57N 17.05 E
Zalău 15 Gb 47.12N 23.03 E
Zaleščiki 16 De 48.39N 25.44 E
Ẓalim 23 Fe 22.43N 42.10 E
Zalingei 35 Cc 12.54N 23.29 E
Zalṭan 33 Cd 28.55N 19.50 E
Zaltbommel 12 Hc 51.49N 5.17 E
Žaltidjal 15 Ih 41.30N 25.05 E
Žaltyr 19 Ge 51.35N 69.58 E
Žaltyr, Ozero- 16 Qf 47.25N 51.05 E
Zamakh 23 Gf 16.28N 47.35 E
Zamami-Shima 29b Ab 26.15N 127.18 E
Zamarkh 33 If 16.30N 47.18 E
Zambeze = Zambezi (EN) 30 Kj 18.50N 36 17 E
Zambezi (EN) = Zambeze 30 Kj 18.50N 36.17 E
Zambézia [3] 37 Fc 17.00S 37.00 E
Zambezi Escarpment 37 Ec 16.15S 30.10 E
Zambia [1] 31 Jj 15.00S 30.00 E
Zamboanga 22 Oi 6.54N 122.04 E
Zamboanga Peninsula 26 He 7.32N 122.16 E
Zambrah, Jazīrat- 32 Jb 37.08N 10.48 E
Zambrano 49 Ji 9.45N 74.49W
Zambrów 10 Sd 53.00N 22.15 E
Zambué 37 Ec 15.07S 30.49 E
Zamfara 34 Fc 12.02N 4.03 E
Zamkova, Gora- 10 Vc 53.34N 25.53 E
Zamkowa, Góra- 10 Qb 54.25N 20.25 E
Zammar 24 Jd 36.47N 42.40 E
Zamora [3] 13 Gc 41.45N 6.00W
Zamora [Ec.] 54 Cd 4.04S 78.52W
Zamora [Sp.] 13 Gc 41.30N 5.45W
Zamora, Río- 54 Cd 2.59S 78.15W
Zamora de Hidalgo 47 De 19.59N 102.16W
Zamość [2] 10 Tf 50.44N 23.15 E
Zamość 10 Tf 50.44N 23.15 E
Zampa-Misaki 29b Ab 26.26N 127.43 E
Zamtang (Gamda) 27 He 32.23N 101.05 E
Zamuro, Punta- 49 Mh 11.26N 68.50W
Zamzam 33 Cc 31.24N 15.17 E
Zanaga 36 Bc 2.51S 13.50 E
Žanatas 19 Gg 43.36N 69.43 E
Zancara 13 Je 39.18N 3.18W
Zanda (Toling) 27 Ce 31.28N 79.50 E
Zandvoort 11 Kb 52.22N 4.32 E
Zanesville 43 Kd 39.55N 82.02W
Zangelan 16 Oj 39.05N 46.38 E
Zanhuang 28 Cf 37.38N 114.26 E
Zanjān [3] 23 Gb 36.35N 48.15 E
Zanjān 23 Gb 36.40N 48.29 E
Zanjānrūd 24 Ld 37.08N 47.47 E
Zannone 14 Hj 40.55N 13.05 E
Zante (EN) = Zákinthos 5 Ih 37.47N 20.47 E
Zanthus 59 Ef 31.02S 123.34 E
Zanzibar 31 Ki 6.10S 39.11 E
Zanzibar [3] 36 Gd 6.00S 39.50 E
Zanzibar [2] 36 Gd 6.10S 39.20 E
Zanzibar Channel 36 Gd 6.00S 39.00 E
Zanzibar Island 30 Ki 6.10S 39.20 E
Zaolin 27 Jd 39.09N 113.03 E
Zaō-San 29 Gb 38.08N 140.28 E
Zaouatallaz 32 Ie 24.52N 8.26 E
Zaousfana 32 Gc 30.30N 2.18W
Zaoyang 27 Je 32.08N 112.45 E
Zaozerny 20 Ee 55.57N 94.42 E
Zaozhuang 27 Ke 34.58N 117.34 E
Zapacos Norte, Río- 55 Ac 17.03S 62.23W
Zapacos Sur, Río- 55 Ac 17.03S 62.23W
Zapadnaja Dvina 7 Hh 56.17N 32.03 E
Zapadnaja Dvina = Western Dvina (EN) 5 Id 57.04N 24.03 E
Zapadna Morava 15 Ef 43.41N 21.24 E
Západné Karpaty = West Carpathians (EN) 10 Og 49.30N 19.00 E
Zapadni Rodopi 15 Hh 41.45N 24.05 E
Zapadno-Karelskaja Vozvyšennost 7 He 63.40N 31.40 E
Zapadno Sibirskaja Ravnina = West Siberian Plain (EN) 21 Jc 60.00N 75.00 E
Zapadny Sajan = Western Sayans (EN) 21 Ld 53.00N 94.00 E
Západočeský kraj [3] 10 Ig 49.45N 13.00 E
Západoslovenský kraj [3] 10 Nh 48.20N 18.00 E
Zapala 53 Ii 38.55S 70.05W
Zapardiel 13 Gc 41.29N 5.02W
Zapata 45 Gm 26.52N 99.19W
Zapata, Peninsula de- 49 Gb 22.20N 81.35W
Zapatera, Isla- 49 Eh 11.45N 85.50W
Zapatosa, Cienaga de- 49 Ki 9.05N 73.50W
Zapljusje 8 Mf 58.24N 29.56 E
Zapoljarny 19 Db 69.26N 30.48 E
Zapopan 48 Hg 20.43N 103.24W
Zaporožje 6 Jf 47.50N 35.10 E
Zaporožskaja Oblast [3] 19 Df 47.15N 35.50 E
Zapotitlán, Punta- 48 Lh 18.33N 94.49W
Zapovednik Belovežskaja Pušča 10 Kd 52.45N 24.15 E
Za Qu 27 Ge 32.00N 96.55 E
Zara 24 Gc 39.55N 37.48 E
Zarāf, Baḥr az- 35 Ed 9.25N 31.10 E
Zarafšan 19 Gg 41.39N 64.10 E
Zaragoza [3] 13 Lc 41.35N 1.00W
Zaragoza [Col.] 54 Db 7.30N 74.52W
Zaragoza [Mex.] 48 Jf 23.58N 99.46W
Zaragoza [Mex.] 48 Ic 28.29N 100.55W
Zaragoza [Mex.] 48 If 22.02N 100.44W
Zaragoza [Sp.] = Saragossa (EN) 6 Fg 41.38N 0.53W
Zarajsk 7 Ji 54.47N 38.53 E
Zarand [Iran] 24 Qg 30.48N 56.53 E
Zarand [Iran] 24 Me 35.08N 49.00 E
Zarand-e-Kohneh 24 Ne 35.17N 50.30 E
Zărandului, Munții- 15 Fc 46.10N 22.15 E
Zaranj 22 If 31.06N 61.53 E
Zarasai/Zarasaj 7 Gi 55.43N 26.19 E
Zarasaj/Zarasai 7 Gi 55.43N 26.19 E
Zárate 53 Ki 34.05S 59.02W
Zarauz 13 Ja 43.17N 2.10W
Zaraza 54 Eb 9.21N 65.19W
Žarcovski 7 Hi 55.53N 32.16 E
Zard Kūh 21 Hf 32.22N 50.04 E
Zardob 16 Oi 40.14N 47.42 E
Zarečensk 7 Hc 66.40N 31.23 E
Zarghaṭ 24 Ii 26.32N 40.29 E
Zarghun 25 Db 30.31N 68.50 E
Zarghūn Shahr 23 Kc 32.51N 68.25 E
Zaria 31 Hg 11.04N 7.42 E
Žarkamys 19 Ff 47.59N 56.29 E
Žarma 19 If 48.48N 80.55 E
Zărneşti 15 Id 45.33N 25.18 E
Zarqān 24 Oh 29.46N 52.43 E
Zarrineh 24 Kd 37.05N 45.40 E
Zarrīnshahr 24 Nf 32.30N 51.25 E
Zaruma 54 Cd 3.42S 79.38W
Zarumilla 54 Bd 3.30S 80.16W
Žary 10 Le 51.38N 15.09 E
Žaryk 19 Hf 48.52N 72.54 E
Zarzaïtine 32 Id 28.05N 9.45 E
Zasa 8 Lh 56.15N 26.01 E
Zāskar 25 Fb 34.10N 77.20 E
Zaškov 16 Ge 49.15N 30.09 E
Zaslavl 8 Lj 54.00N 27.22 E
Zaslavskoje Vodohranilišče 8 Lj 54.00N 27.30 E
Zastavna 15 Ia 48.25N 25.49 E
Zastron 37 Df 30.18S 27.07 E
Žatec 10 Jf 50.20N 13.33 E
Zatišje 15 Mb 47.47N 29.48 E
Zatobolsk 17 Kj 53.12N 63.43 E
Zatoka 15 Nc 46.07N 30.25 E
Zauche 10 Id 52.15N 12.35 E
Zavadovskogo Island 66 Ge 66.30S 86.00 E
Zavāreh 24 Of 33.30N 52.29 E
Zaventem 12 Gd 50.53N 4.28 E
Zavety Iliča 20 Jg 49.02N 140.19 E
Zavidovići 14 Mf 44.27N 18.09 E
Zavitinsk 20 Hg 50.01N 129.26 E
Zavodoukovsk 19 Gd 56.33N 66.32 E
Zavodovski 66 Ad 56.20S 27.35W
Zavolžje 7 Kh 56.38N 43.21 E
Zavolžsk 7 Kh 57.32N 42.10 E
Zawidów 10 Le 51.01N 15.02 E
Zawiercie 10 Pf 50.30N 19.25 E
Zawīlah 33 Cd 26.10N 15.07 E
Zāwiyat al Mukhaylá 33 Dc 32.10N 22.17 E
Zāwiyat Masūs 33 Dc 31.35N 21.01 E
Zāwiyat Qirzah 33 Bc 31.00N 14.20 E
Zāwiyat Shammās 24 Bg 31.31N 26.24 E
Zawr, Ra's az- 24 Mi 27.26N 49.19 E
Zaya 14 Kb 48.31N 16.55 E
Zāyandeh 24 Of 32.20N 52.50 E
Zaydūn, Wādī- 24 Ej 25.53N 33.04 E
Zayü (Gyigang) 27 Gf 28.43N 97.25 E
Zaza, Río- 49 Hc 21.37N 79.32W
Zazir 32 If 19.50N 5.13 E
Zbaraž 16 De 49.42N 25.47 E
Zbąszyń 10 Ld 52.16N 15.55 E
Zborov 10 Vg 49.37N 25.09 E
Ždanichý les 10 Mg 49.05N 16.50 E
Ždanov → Mariupol' 6 Jf 47.00N 37.33 E
Ždanovsk 16 Oj 39.45N 47.33 E
Žďárské vrchy 10 Mg 49.35N 16.03 E
Ždiar 10 Qg 49.16N 20.15 E
Zdolbunov 16 Ed 50.33N 26.15 E
Zduńska Wola 10 Oe 51.36N 18.57 E
Zealand (EN) = Sjælland 5 Hd 55.30N 11.45 E
Zebediela 37 Dd 24.19S 29.16 E
Zebes, Mali i- 15 Dh 41.55N 20.14 E
Zebil 15 Le 44.57N 28.46 E
Zeča 14 If 44.46N 14.19 E
Zeddine 13 Nh 36.12N 1.50 E
Zedelgem 12 Fc 51.09N 3.08 E
Zeehan 58 Fi 41.53S 145.20 E
Zeeland 11 Jc 51.27N 3.45 E
Zeeland [3] 12 Fc 51.27N 3.45 E
Zeerust 37 De 25.33S 26.06 E
Zefat 24 Ff 32.58N 35.30 E
Zegrzyńskie, Jezioro- 10 Rd 52.30N 21.05 E
Zehdenick 10 Jd 52.59N 13.20 E
Zeil, Mount- 59 Gd 23.25S 132.25 E
Žeimelis/Zeimjalis 8 Jh 56.14N 23.58 E
Žeimena/Žejmena 7 Fi 54.54N 23.53 E
Zeimjalis/Žeimelis 8 Jh 56.14N 23.58 E
Zeist 11 Lb 52.05N 5.15 E
Zeitz 10 Ie 51.03N 12.09 E
Zeja 21 Od 50.13N 127.35 E
Zeja 22 Od 53.45N 127.15 E
Žejmena/Žeimena 7 Fi 54.54N 23.53 E
Zejskoje Vodohranilišče 20 Hf 54.40N 127.30 E
Zékog 27 Hd 35.00N 101.35 E
Želanija, Mys- 21 Ib 76.57N 68.35 E
Zelaya [3] 49 Eg 13.00N 84.00W
Želča 8 Lf 58.18N 27.50 E
Zele 12 Gc 51.04N 4.02 E
Żelechów 10 Re 51.49N 21.54 E
Zelee, Cape- 63a Ec 9.44S 161.34 E
Zelenaja Rošča 8 Md 60.08N 29.14 E
Zelenčukskaja 16 Lh 43.51N 41.34 E
Zelengora 14 Mg 43.22N 18.35 E
Zelenoborsk 19 Gc 61.29N 63.59 E
Zelenoborski 19 Db 66.50N 32.18 E
Zelenodolsk 19 Ed 55.53N 48.31 E
Zelenogorsk 19 Cc 60.12N 29.42 E
Zelenograd 7 Ih 56.01N 37.12 E
Zelenogradsk 8 Ij 54.57N 20.27 E
Zelenokumsk 19 Eg 44.23N 43.53 E
Zeletin 15 Kc 46.03N 27.23 E
Železné hory 10 Lg 49.50N 15.45 E
Zeleznik 15 De 44.43N 20.23 E
Železnodorožny [R.S.F.S.R.] 20 Fe 57.55N 102.50 E
Železnodorožny [R.S.F.S.R.] 7 Ei 54.23N 21.19 E
Železnodorožny [R.S.F.S.R.] 19 Fc 62.37N 50.55 E
Železnogorsk 19 De 52.21N 35.23 E
Železnogorsk-Ilimski 20 Fe 56.40N 104.05 E
Železnovodsk 16 Mg 44.08N 43.00 E
Zelfana 32 Hc 32.24N 4.14 E
Želiezovce 10 Oh 48.03N 18.40 E
Zelivka 10 Lg 49.43N 15.06 E
Zeljin 15 Df 43.29N 20.48 E
Zell am See 14 Gc 47.19N 12.47 E
Zell am Ziller 14 Fc 47.14N 11.53 E
Zelów 10 Pe 51.28N 19.13 E
Želtau Ajtau 18 Ib 44.30N 74.00 E
Želtyje Vody 16 He 48.23N 33.31 E
Zeludok 10 Vc 53.33N 25.07 E
Želva 8 Ki 55.13N 25.13 E
Zelva 10 Uc 53.04N 24.54 E
Zelzate 11 Jc 51.12N 3.49 E
Žemaičiu Aukštuma/Žemajtskaja Vozvyšennost 8 Ji 55.45N 22.30 E
Žemaiciy-Naumiestis/Žemajčju-Naumiestis 8 Ii 55.21N 21.37 E
Žemaitija 8 Ji 55.55N 22.30 E
Žemajčju-Naumiestis/Žemaiciy-Naumiestis 8 Ii 55.21N 21.37 E
Zemajtskaja Vozvyšennost/Žemaičiu Aukštuma 8 Ji 55.45N 22.30 E
Zembin 8 Mj 54.24N 28.19 E
Zembretta, Ile- 14 Em 37.07N 10.53 E
Zemetčino 16 Mc 53.31N 42.38 E
Zemgale 8 Kh 56.30N 25.00 E
Zémio 35 Dd 5.19N 25.08 E
Zemmora 13 Mi 35.43N 0.45 E
Zemmour 30 Ff 25.30N 12.00W
Zemplinska Sirava, údolná nádrž- 10 Sh 48.50N 22.02 E
Zempoala 47 Ee 19.27N 96.23W
Zempoaltepec 38 Jh 17.00N 96.50W
Zemra, Djebel- 13 Pi 35.14N 3.54 E
Zemst 12 Gd 50.59N 4.28 E
Zemun, Beograd- 15 De 44.53N 20.25 E
Zengfeng Shan 28 Jc 42.25N 128.44 E
Zenica 23 Ff 44.13N 17.55 E
Zenkov 16 Id 50.13N 34.22 E
Zenne 12 Gc 51.04N 4.26 E
Zenobia Peak 45 Bf 40.40N 108.48W
Zentsūji 29 Cd 34.14N 133.47 E
Zenzach 13 Pi 35.21N 3.22 E
Zenza do Itombe 36 Bd 9.16S 14.13 E
Žepče 14 Mf 44.26N 18.03 E
Zepu/Poskam 27 Cd 38.12N 77.18 E
Zéralda 13 Oh 36.43N 2.50 E
Zeravšan 21 If 39.22N 63.45 E
Zeravšan 18 Ge 39.10N 68.40 E
Zeravšanski Hrebet 19 Gh 39.15N 68.30 E
Zerbst 10 Ie 51.58N 12.05 E
Žerdevka 19 Ee 51.53N 41.28 E
Zerind 15 Ec 46.37N 21.31 E
Zermatt 14 Bd 46.02N 7.44 E
Zernez 14 Ed 46.42N 10.07 E
Zernograd 19 Ef 46.48N 40.19 E
Zeroua 13 Ph 36.22N 3.21 E
Žešart 17 De 62.05N 49.31 E
Zestafoni 16 Mh 42.07N 43.02 E
Zeta 15 Cg 42.28N 19.16 E
Zetland → Shetland Islands 5 Fc 60.30N 1.30W
Žetybaj 19 Fg 43.34N 52.04 E
Žetykol Ozero- 16 Vd 51.05N 60.55 E
Zeune Islands 63a Bb 6.18S 155.50 E
Zeven 10 Fc 53.18N 9.17 E
Zevenaar 12 Ic 51.55N 6.05 E
Zevenbergen 12 Gc 51.38N 4.36 E
Zeydābād 24 Ph 29.37N 55.33 E
Zeydār 24 Pd 36.20N 55.53 E
Zeytinbağı 15 Li 40.23N 28.47 E
Zeytindağ 15 Kk 38.58N 27.04 E
Zêzere 13 Dd 39.28N 8.20W
Žežmarjaj/Žiežmariai 8 Kj 54.47N 24.36 E
Zghartā 24 Fe 34.24N 35.54 E
Zgierz 10 Pe 51.52N 19.25 E
Zgorzelec 10 Le 51.12N 15.01 E
Zhabdün → Zhongba 22 Kg 29.41N 84.10 E
Zhag'yab 27 Ge 30.40N 97.40 E
Zhangbei 27 Jc 41.13N 114.43 E
Zhangde → Anyang 22 Nf 36.01N 114.25 E
Zhangdian → Zibo 27 Kd 36.48N 118.04 E
Zhangguangcai 28 Jb 45.00N 129.00 E
Zhang He 28 Cf 36.27N 114.42 E
Zhangjiakou 22 Ne 40.49N 114.57 E
Zhangjiapan → Jingbian 27 Id 37.32N 108.45 E
Zhangling 27 La 52.39N 123.31 E
Zhanglou 28 Dh 32.40N 116.47 E
Zhangping 27 Kf 25.25N 117.27 E
Zhangqiu (Mingshui) 28 Df 36.44N 117.33 E
Zhangshuzhen → Qingjiang 27 Kf 28.02N 115.31 E
Zhangwei Xinhe 28 Dg 38.13N 117.48 E
Zhangwu 27 Lc 42.23N 122.33 E
Zhangye 22 Mf 38.57N 100.28 E
Zhangzhou 22 Ng 24.38N 117.39 E
Zhangzi 27 Jd 36.04N 112.53 E
Zhan He 27 Mb 49.21N 128.07 E
Zhanhua (Fuguo) 28 Ef 37.42N 118.08 E
Zhanjiang 22 Ng 21.13N 110.23 E
Zhanyi 27 Hf 25.40N 103.46 E
Zhao'an 27 Kg 23.49N 117.10 E
Zhaodong 27 Mb 46.04N 125.56 E
Zhaoge → Qixian 28 Cg 35.35N 114.12 E
Zhaojue 27 Hf 28.02N 102.50 E
Zhaoqing 27 Jg 23.04N 112.28 E
Zhaosu/Monggolküre 27 Dc 43.10N 81.07 E
Zhaosutai He 28 Gc 42.42N 123.35 E
Zhaotong 22 Mg 27.20N 103.46 E
Zhaoxian 28 Cf 37.46N 114.46 E
Zhaoyang Hu 28 Dg 35.00N 116.48 E
Zhaoyuan [China] 28 Ff 37.22N 120.23 E
Zhaoyuan [China] 28 Hb 45.30N 125.06 E
Zhaozhou 28 Hb 45.42N 125.15 E
Zhari Namco 27 Ee 31.05N 85.35 E
Zhaxi → Weixin 27 If 27.46N 105.04 E
Zhaxi Co 27 Ee 32.12N 85.10 E
Zhecheng 28 Cg 34.05N 115.17 E
Zheduo Shankou 27 He 30.06N 101.48 E
Zhejiang Sheng (Che-Chiang Sheng) [2] 27 Kf 29.00N 120.00 E
Zhen'an 27 Ie 33.27N 109.10 E
Zhenba 27 Ie 32.37N 107.50 E
Zhenghe 27 Kf 27.20N 118.58 E
Zhenghe Qunjiao 26 Fd 10.20N 114.20 E
Zhenglan Qi (Dund Hot) 28 Cc 42.14N 115.59 E
Zhengxiangbai Qi (Qagan Nur) 27 Jc 42.16N 114.59 E
Zhengyang 28 Ci 32.36N 114.23 E
Zhengzhou 22 Nf 34.42N 113.41 E
Zhenhai 28 Fj 29.57N 121.43 E
Zhenjiang 27 Ke 32.03N 119.26 E
Zhenkang (Fengweiba) 27 Gg 23.54N 99.00 E
Zhenlai 27 Lb 45.50N 123.14 E
Zhenning 27 If 26.05N 105.46 E
Zhenping 28 Bh 33.02N 112.14 E
Zhenxiong 27 Hf 27.28N 104.52 E
Zhenyuan 27 Hg 23.52N 100.53 E
Zhenyuan (Wuyang) 27 If 27.05N 108.26 E
Zhicheng 27 Je 30.17N 111.29 E
Zhidan (Bao'an) 27 Id 36.48N 108.46 E
Zhidoi 27 Ge 34.46N 95.46 E
Zhijiang 27 If 27.32N 109.42 E
Zhi Qu/Tongtian He 21 Lf 33.26N 96.36 E
Zhiziluo → Bijiang 27 Gf 26.39N 99.00 E
Zhob 25 Db 32.04N 69.50 E
Zhongba (Zhabdun) 22 Kg 29.41N 84.10 E
Zhongba → Jiangyou 27 He 31.48N 104.39 E
Zhongdian 27 Gf 27.42N 99.41 E
Zhōngguó 21 Mg 35.00N 105.00 E
Zhonghua Renmin Gongheguo = China (EN) [1] 22 Mf 35.00N 105.00 E
Zhongjian Dao 26 Fc 15.52N 111.13 E
Zhongmou 28 Cg 34.45N 114.01 E
Zhongning 27 Id 37.28N 105.41 E
Zhongshan 27 Jg 22.31N 113.23 E
Zhongwei 22 Mf 37.30N 105.09 E
Zhongxian 27 Ie 30.20N 108.02 E
Zhongxiang 27 Je 31.10N 112.38 E
Zhongxing → Siyang 28 Eh 33.43N 118.40 E
Zhongyaozhan 27 Ma 50.46N 125.53 E
Zhongye Qundao 26 Fd 11.20N 114.30 E
Zhoukoudianzhen 28 Ce 39.41N 115.55 E
Zhoukouzhen 27 Je 33.32N 114.40 E
Zhoushan Dao 28 Gi 30.00N 122.00 E
Zhoushan Qundao 21 Of 30.00N 122.00 E
Zhuanghe 27 Ld 39.42N 122.58 E
Zhucheng 27 Kd 35.58N 119.28 E
Zhu Dao 28 Fe 39.05N 121.10 E
Zhugqu 27 He 33.46N 104.18 E
Zhuhe 28 Bj 29.44N 113.07 E
Zhuizishan → Weichang 27 Kc 41.55N 117.39 E
Zhuji 28 Fj 29.43N 120.13 E
Zhuji → Shangqiu 27 Ke 34.24N 115.37 E
Zhujiang Kou 27 Jg 22.20N 113.45 E
Zhumadian 27 Je 32.54N 114.03 E
Zhuolu 28 Cd 40.23N 115.13 E
Zhuoxian 27 Kd 39.26N 116.00 E
Zhuozhang He 28 Bf 36.36N 113.10 E
Zhuozi 28 Bd 40.52N 112.33 E
Zhuozi Shan 27 Id 39.36N 107.00 E
Zhushan 27 Je 32.16N 110.12 E
Zhuzhou 22 Ng 27.52N 113.12 E
Ziama Mansouria 32 Ib 36.40N 5.29 E
Ziar nad Hronom 10 Oh 48.36N 18.52 E
Ẓibā' 23 Ed 27.21N 35.40 E
Zibo (Zhangdian) 27 Kd 36.48N 118.04 E
Zicavo 11a Bb 41.54N 9.08 E
Židačov 10 Ug 49.17N 24.12 E
Zielona Góra 10 Le 51.56N 15.31 E
Zielona Góra [2] 10 Le 51.55N 15.30 E
Zierikzee 11 Jc 51.38N 3.55 E
Žiežmariai/Žežmarjaj 8 Kj 54.47N 24.36 E
Ziftá 24 Dg 30.43N 31.15 E
Žigalovo 20 Ff 54.48N 105.08 E
Zigana Geçidi 24 Hb 40.38N 39.25 E
Žigansk 20 Hc 66.45N 123.30 E
Zigey 35 Bc 14.43N 15.47 E
Zighan, Wāḥāt- 33 Dd 25.35N 22.06 E
Zigong 22 Mg 29.20N 104.48 E
Zigui 27 Je 31.01N 110.42 E
Ziguinchor 31 Fg 12.35N 16.16W
Žigulevsk 19 Ee 53.27N 49.29 E
Zihuatanejo 47 De 17.38N 101.33W
Zijing Shan 27 Jd 37.12N 112.50 E
Zijpenberg 12 Hb 52.04N 6.00 E
Zilālet 34 Gb 18.28N 7.48 E
Zile 23 Ea 40.18N 35.54 E
Žilina 6 Hf 49.14N 18.45 E
Žilino 8 Ij 54.55N 21.48 E
Zillah 31 If 28.33N 17.35 E
Ziller 14 Fc 47.24N 11.50 E
Zillertaler Alpen 10 Hi 47.00N 11.55 E
Žiloj 16 Qi 40.19N 50.33 E
Zilupe 7 Gh 56.25N 28.07 E
Zima 22 Md 53.55N 102.04 E
Zimapán 48 Jg 20.45N 99.21W
Zimatlán de Alvarez 48 Ki 16.52N 96.47W
Zimba 36 Ef 17.02S 26.30 E
Zimbabwe 37 Ed 20.16S 30.55 E
Zimbabwe (Rhodesia) [1] 31 Jj 20.00S 30.00 E

Index Symbols

[1] Independent Nation
[2] State, Region
[3] District, County
[4] Municipality
[5] Colony, Dependency
Continent
Physical Region
Historical or Cultural Region
Mount, Mountain
Volcano
Hill
Mountains, Mountain Range
Hills, Escarpment
Plateau, Upland
Pass, Gap
Plain, Lowland
Delta
Salt Flat
Valley, Canyon
Crater, Cave
Karst Features
Depression
Polder
Desert, Dunes
Forest, Woods
Heath, Steppe
Oasis
Cape, Point
Coast, Beach
Cliff
Peninsula
Isthmus
Sandbank
Island
Atoll
Rock, Reef
Islands, Archipelago
Rocks, Reefs
Coral Reef
Well, Spring
Geyser
River, Stream
Waterfall Rapids
River Mouth, Estuary
Lake
Salt Lake
Intermittent Lake
Reservoir
Swamp, Pond
Canal
Glacier
Ice Shelf, Pack Ice
Ocean
Sea
Gulf, Bay
Strait, Fjord
Lagoon
Bank
Seamount
Tablemount
Ridge
Shelf
Basin
Escarpment, Sea Scarp
Fracture
Trench, Abyss
National Park, Reserve
Point of Interest
Recreation Site
Cave, Cavern
Historic Site
Ruins
Wall, Walls
Church, Abbey
Temple
Scientific Station
Airport
Port
Lighthouse
Mine
Tunnel
Dam, Bridge

Name	Page	Grid	Lat.	Long.
Zimbor	15	Gc	47.00N	23.16 E
Zimi	34	Cd	7.19N	11.18W
Zimni Bereg	7	Jd	66.00N	40.45 E
Zimnicea	15	If	43.40N	25.22 E
Zimovniki	16	Mf	47.08N	42.29 E
Zina	34	Hc	11.16N	14.58 E
Zincirli	24	Gd	37.00N	36.41 E
Zinder	31	Hg	13.48N	8.59 E
Zinder [2]	34	Hb	15.00N	10.00 E
Zinga	35	Be	3.43N	18.35 E
Zingst	10	Ib	54.25N	12.50 E
Zinjibār	33	Ig	13.08N	45.23 E
Zinnik/Soignies	11	Kd	50.35N	4.04 E
Zinsel du Nord	12	Jf	48.49N	7.44 E
Zion [Il.-U.S.]	45	Me	42.27N	87.50W
Zion [St.C.N.]	51c	Ab	17.09N	62.32W
Zipaquirá	54	Db	5.02N	74.01W
Zirc	10	Ni	47.16N	17.52 E
Žirje	14	Jg	43.39N	15.40 E
Zirkel, Mount-	45	Cf	40.52N	106.36W
Žirnovsk	19	Ee	51.01N	44.48 E
Ziro	25	Ic	27.32N	93.32 E
Zi Shui	27	Jf	28.41N	112.43 E
Žitava	10	Oi	47.53N	18.11 E
Žitkoviči	16	Fc	52.16N	28.02 E
Zitkovo	7	Gf	60.42N	29.23 E
Žitomir	6	Ie	50.16N	28.40 E
Žitomirskaja Oblast [3]	19	Ce	50.40N	28.30 E
Zittau	10	Kf	50.54N	14.50 E
Zitterwald	12	Id	50.27N	6.25 E
Zitundo	37	Ee	26.44S	32.49 E
Živinice	14	Mf	44.27N	18.39 E
Ziwa Magharibi [3]	36	Fc	2.00S	31.30 E
Ziway, Lake-	35	Fd	8.00N	38.48 E
Ziyamet	24	Fe	35.22N	34.00 E
Ziyang	27	Ie	32.34N	108.37 E
Ziz	32	Gc	30.29N	4.26W
Žizdra	16	Ic	53.45N	34.43 E
Žizdra	16	Jb	54.14N	36.12 E
Zlatar	15	Cf	43.23N	19.51 E
Zlaté Moravce	10	Oh	48.23N	18.24 E
Zlatibor	15	Cf	43.40N	19.43 E
Zlatica	15	Hg	42.43N	24.08 E
Zlatica	15	Dd	45.49N	20.10 E
Zlatijata	15	Gf	43.40N	23.36 E
Zlatiški prohod	15	Hg	42.45N	24.05 E
Zlatna	15	Gc	46.07N	23.13 E
Zlatograd	15	Ih	41.23N	25.06 E
Zlatoust	6	Ld	55.10N	59.40 E
Zlatoustovsk	20	If	52.59N	133.41 E
Zletovo	15	Fh	41.59N	22.15 E
Zlīţan	33	Bc	32.28N	14.34 E
Žlobin	19	De	52.59N	30.03 E
Złocieniec	10	Mc	53.33N	16.01 E
Złoczew	10	Oe	51.25N	18.36 E
Zlot	15	Ee	44.01N	21.59 E
Złotoryja	10	Le	51.08N	15.55 E
Złotów	10	Nc	53.22N	17.02 E
Žły Komorow/Senftenberg	10	Ke	51.31N	14.01 E
Zlynka	16	Gc	52.27N	31.44 E
Zmeinogorsk	20	Df	51.10N	82.13 E
Žmerinka	19	Cf	49.02N	28.05 E
Żmigród	10	Me	51.29N	16.55 E
Zmijev	16	Je	49.41N	36.20 E
Zmijevka	16	Jc	52.40N	36.24 E
Zna	7	Ih	57.33N	34.25 E
Znamenka [R.S.F.S.R.]	16	Lc	52.24N	41.28 E
Znamenka [Ukr.-U.S.S.R.]	16	He	48.41N	32.40 E
Znamensk	8	Ij	54.39N	21.15 E
Znamenskoje	19	Hd	57.08N	73.55 E
Żnin	10	Nd	52.52N	17.43 E
Znojmo	10	Mh	48.51N	16.03 E
Zobia	36	Eb	2.53N	26.02 E
Zóbuè	37	Ec	15.36S	34.26 E
Žodino	16	Fb	54.07N	28.19 E
Žodiški	8	Lj	54.40N	26.33 E
Zoetermeer	12	Gb	52.04N	4.30 E
Zogang/Wangda	27	Gf	29.37N	97.58 E
Žohova, Ostrov-	20	Ka	76.10N	153.05 E
Zohreh	24	Mg	30.04N	49.34 E
Zolgê	27	He	33.38N	103.00 E
Zoločev [Ukr.-U.S.S.R.]	16	Id	50.18N	35.59 E
Zoločev [Ukr.-U.S.S.R.]	19	Cf	49.49N	24.58 E
Zolotaja Gora	20	Hf	54.21N	126.41 E
Zolotoje	16	Ke	48.40N	38.30 E
Zolotonoša	16	He	49.40N	32.02 E
Zolotuhino	16	Jc	52.07N	36.25 E
Žolymbet	19	He	51.45N	71.44 E
Zomba	31	Kj	15.23S	35.20 E
Zongga → Gyirong	27	Ef	28.57N	85.12 E
Zongo	36	Cb	4.21N	18.36 E
Zonguldak	23	Da	41.27N	31.49 E
Zongyang	28	Di	30.42N	117.12 E
Zonkwa	34	Gd	9.47N	8.17 E
Zonnebeke	12	Ed	50.52N	2.59 E
Zontehuitz, Cerro-	48	Mi	16.50N	92.38W
Zonūz	24	Kc	38.35N	45.50 E
Zonza	11a	Bb	41.44N	9.10 E
Zorita	13	Ge	39.17N	5.42W
Zorkassa, Gora-	18	Ge	38.01N	68.10 E
Zorleni	15	Kc	46.16N	27.43 E
Zorritos	54	Bd	3.40S	80.40W
Zorzor	34	Dd	7.47N	9.26W
Zottegem	12	Fd	50.52N	3.48 E
Zou [3]	34	Fd	8.00N	2.15 E
Zouar	31	If	20.27N	16.32 E
Zouîrât	31	Ff	22.46N	12.27W
Zoutkamp, Ulrum-	12	Ia	53.20N	6.18 E
Zouxian	28	Dg	35.24N	116.59 E
Žovten	15	Nb	47.14N	30.14 E
Žovtnevoje	16	Hf	46.52N	32.02 E
Zpouping	28	Df	36.53N	117.44 E
Zrenjanin	15	Dd	45.23N	20.23 E
Zrinska Gora	14	Ke	45.10N	16.15 E
Zrmanja	14	Jf	44.12N	15.35 E
Zruč nad Sázavou	10	Lg	49.45N	15.07 E
Zschopau	10	Je	51.08N	13.03 E
Žuantobe	19	Gg	44.47N	68.52 E
Zuata, Río-	50	Di	7.52N	65.22W
Zubayr, Jazā'ir az-	33	Hf	15.05N	42.08 E
Zubcov	7	Ih	56.10N	34.31 E
Zubova Poljana	7	Ki	54.05N	42.50 E
Zudañez	54	Fg	19.06S	64.44W
Zuénoula	34	Dd	7.26N	6.03W
Zuénoula [3]	34	Dd	7.22N	6.12W
Zuera	13	Lc	41.52N	0.47W
Zufāf	33	Hf	16.43N	41.46 E
Zufallspitze/Cevedale	14	Ed	46.27N	10.37 E
Zufār	21	Hh	17.30N	54.00 E
Zug [2]	14	Cc	47.10N	8.40 E
Zug [Switz.]	14	Cc	47.10N	8.30 E
Zug [W.Sah.]	32	Ee	21.36N	14.09W
Zugdidi	19	Eg	42.29N	41.48 E
Zugersee	14	Cc	47.10N	8.30 E
Zugspitze	10	Gi	47.25N	10.59 E
Zuid Beveland	12	Fc	51.25N	3.45 E
Zuidelijke Flevoland	12	Hb	52.25N	5.20 E
Zuid-Holland [3]	12	Gc	52.00N	4.30 E
Zuid-Ijselmeerpolders [3]	12	Hb	52.20N	5.20 E
Zuidlaren	12	Ia	53.06N	6.42 E
Zuid-Willemsvaart	12	Hd	50.50N	5.41 E
Zuidwolde	12	Ib	52.40N	6.25 E
Zújar	13	Ge	39.01N	5.47W
Zújar, Embalse del-	13	Gf	38.50N	5.20W
Zujevka	19	Fd	58.26N	51.12 E
Žukovka	19	De	53.33N	33.47 E
Žukovski	7	Ji	55.37N	38.12 E
Zula	35	Fb	15.14N	39.40 E
Zulia [2]	54	Db	10.00N	72.10W
Zulia, Río-	49	Ki	9.04N	72.18W
Zülpich	12	Id	50.42N	6.39 E
Zumbo	37	Ec	15.36S	30.25 E
Zundert	12	Gc	51.29N	4.40 E
Zungeru	34	Gd	9.48N	6.09 E
Zunhua	28	Dd	40.12N	117.58 E
Zuni	45	Bi	35.04N	108.51W
Zuni River	46	Ki	34.39N	109.40W
Zunyi	22	Mg	27.40N	106.56 E
Zuoquan	28	Bf	37.05N	113.22 E
Zuoyun	28	Be	39.58N	112.40 E
Županja	14	Me	45.04N	18.42 E
Zuqāq	33	Hf	18.04N	40.48 E
Zurak	34	Hd	9.14N	10.34 E
Zürich [2]	14	Cc	47.30N	8.30 E
Zürich	6	Gf	47.20N	8.35 E
Zurich, Lake- (EN) = Zürichsee	14	Cc	47.15N	8.45 E
Zürichsee = Zurich, Lake- (EN)	14	Cc	47.15N	8.45 E
Zurmi	34	Gc	12.47N	6.47 E
Żuromin	10	Pc	53.04N	19.55 E
Zuru	34	Gc	11.26N	5.14 E
Zuša	16	Jc	53.27N	36.25 E
Zusam	10	Gh	48.42N	10.45 E
Žut	14	Jg	43.52N	15.19 E
Zutiua, Rio-	54	Id	3.43S	45.30W
Zutphen	11	Mb	52.08N	6.12 E
Zuwārah	33	Bc	32.56N	12.06 E
Zvenigorodka	16	Ge	49.04N	30.59 E
Zverinogolovskoje	17	Li	54.28N	64.50 E
Zvezdny	20	Fe	56.40N	106.30 E
Zvičina	10	Lf	50.25N	15.41 E
Žvirca	10	Uf	50.24N	24.16 E
Zvolen	10	Ph	48.35N	19.08 E
Zvornik	14	Nf	44.23N	19.07 E
Zwardoń	10	Og	49.30N	18.59 E
Zwarte Bank = Black Bank (EN)	12	Fa	53.15N	3.55 E
Zweibrücken	10	Dg	49.15N	7.22 E
Zweisimmen	14	Bd	46.34N	7.25 E
Zwesten	12	Lc	51.03N	9.11 E
Zwettl in Niederösterreich	14	Jb	48.37N	15.10 E
Zwickau	10	If	50.44N	12.30 E
Zwickauer Mulde	10	Ie	51.10N	12.48 E
Zwierzyniec	10	Sf	50.37N	22.58 E
Zwiesel	10	Jg	49.01N	13.14 E
Zwijndrecht	12	Gc	51.50N	4.41 E
Zwischenahn	10	Dc	53.11N	8.00 E
Zwoleń	10	Re	51.22N	21.35 E
Zwolle	11	Mb	52.30N	6.05 E
Żychlin	10	Pd	52.15N	19.39 E
Żyrardów	10	Qd	52.04N	20.25 E
Zyrjanka	20	Kc	65.45N	105.51 E
Zyrjanovsk	19	If	49.45N	84.16 E
Żywiec	10	Pg	49.41N	19.12 E

Index Symbols

[1] Independent Nation
[2] State, Region
[3] District, County
[4] Municipality
[5] Colony, Dependency
Continent
Physical Region
Historical or Cultural Region
Mount, Mountain
Volcano
Hill
Mountains, Mountain Range
Hills, Escarpment
Plateau, Upland
Pass, Gap
Plain, Lowland
Delta
Salt Flat
Valley, Canyon
Crater, Cave
Karst Features
Depression
Polder
Desert, Dunes
Forest, Woods
Heath, Steppe
Oasis
Cape, Point
Coast, Beach
Cliff
Peninsula
Isthmus
Sandbank
Island
Atoll
Rock, Reef
Islands, Archipelago
Rocks, Reefs
Coral Reef
Well, Spring
Geyser
River, Stream
Waterfall Rapids
River Mouth, Estuary
Lake
Salt Lake
Intermittent Lake
Reservoir
Swamp, Pond
Canal
Glacier
Ice Shelf, Pack Ice
Ocean
Sea
Gulf, Bay
Strait, Fjord
Lagoon
Bank
Seamount
Tablemount
Ridge
Shelf
Basin
Escarpment, Sea Scarp
Fracture
Trench, Abyss
National Park, Reserve
Point of Interest
Recreation Site
Cave, Cavern
Historic Site
Ruins
Wall, Walls
Church, Abbey
Temple
Scientific Station
Airport
Port
Lighthouse
Mine
Tunnel
Dam, Bridge